W9-AZI-516

TEACHER'S EDITION

PRENTICE HALL LITERATURE

Timeless Voices, Timeless Themes

WORLD MASTERPIECES

VOLUME II

Upper Saddle River, New Jersey
Boston, Massachusetts

ISBN 0-13-180234-8
4 5 6 7 8 9 10 09 08 07 06

PRENTICE HALL LITERATURE

WORLD MASTERPIECES

Upper Saddle River, New Jersey
Boston, Massachusetts

ISBN 0-13-180235-6
4 5 6 7 8 9 10 07 06 05 04 03

Acknowledgments

Grateful acknowledgment is made to the following for copyrighted material:

The American University in Cairo Press
"Half a Day," extract from "The Time and Place" by Naguib Mahfouz, first published in Arabic in 1962 as "Nisf Yawm, in al-fajn al Kadhib (The False Dawn)." Copyright © 1991 by The American University in Cairo Press. Reprinted by permission of The American University in Cairo Press.

The Asia Society and Dr. Nguyen Ngoc Bich
"Thoughts of Hanoi" by Nguyen Thi Vinh, from *A Thousand Years of Vietnamese Poetry*, edited by Nguyen Ngoc Bich. Copyright © 1962, 1967, 1968, 1969, 1970, 1971, 1974 by The Asia Society and Nguyen Ngoc Bich. Reprinted by permission.

Georges Borchardt, Inc.
"The Metamorphosis" by Franz Kafka, edited and translated by Stanley Corngold. Copyright © 1972 by Stanley Corngold. Reprinted by permission of Georges Borchardt, Inc.

The Citadel Press/Kensington Publishing Corp.
"The Lorelei" by Heinrich Heine, translated by Aaron Kramer, from *The Poetry of Heinrich Heine*. Copyright © 1969 by Citadel Press, Inc. All rights reserved. Reprinted by permission of Citadel Press/Kensington Publishing Corp. **www.kensingtonbooks.com**

(Continued on page R45, which is hereby considered an extension of this copyright page.)

PRENTICE HALL LITERATURE

COPPER

BRONZE

SILVER

GOLD

PLATINUM

THE AMERICAN EXPERIENCE

THE BRITISH TRADITION

WORLD MASTERPIECES

Contributing Authors

The contributing authors guided the direction and philosophy of *Prentice Hall Literature: Timeless Voices, Timeless Themes.* Working with the development team, they helped to build the pedagogical integrity of the program and to ensure its relevance for today's teachers and students.

Kate Kinsella

Kate Kinsella, Ed.D., is a faculty member in the Department of Secondary Education at San Francisco State University. A specialist in second-language acquisition and adolescent reading and writing, she teaches coursework addressing language and literacy development across the secondary curricula. She has taught high-school ESL, and directed SFSU's *Intensive English Program* for first-generation bilingual college students. She maintains secondary classroom involvement by teaching an academic literacy class for second-language learners through the University's *Step to College* partnership program. A former Fulbright lecturer and perennial institute leader for TESOL, the California Reading Association, and the California League of Middle Schools, Dr. Kinsella provides professional development nationally, on topics ranging from learning-style enhancement to second-language reading. Her scholarship has been published in journals such as the *TESOL Journal*, the *CATESOL Journal*, and the *Social Studies Review.*

Kevin Feldman

Kevin Feldman, Ed.D., is the Director of Reading and Early Intervention with the Sonoma County Office of Education (SCOE). His career in education spans thirty-three years. As the Director of Reading and Early Intervention for SCOE, he develops, organizes, and monitors programs related to K–12 literacy and prevention of reading difficulties. He also serves as a Leadership Team Consultant to the California Reading and Literature Project and assists in the development and implementation of K–12 programs throughout California. Dr. Feldman earned his undergraduate degree in Psychology from Washington State University and has a Master's degree in Special Education, Learning Disabilities, and Instructional Design from U.C. Riverside. He earned his Ed.D. in Curriculum and Instruction from the University of San Francisco.

Colleen Shea Stump

Colleen Shea Stump, Ph.D., is a Special Education supervisor in the area of Resource and Inclusion for Seattle Public Schools. She served as a professor and chairperson for the Department of Special Education at San Francisco State University. She continues as a lead consultant in the area of collaboration for the California State Improvement Grant and travels the state of California providing professional development training in the areas of collaboration, content literacy instruction, and inclusive instruction. Dr. Stump earned her doctorate at the University of Washington, her M.A. in Special Education from the University of New Mexico, and her B.S. in Elementary Education from the University of Wisconsin–Eau Claire.

Joyce Armstrong Carroll

In her forty-two-year career, Joyce Armstrong Carroll, Ed.D., has taught on every grade level from primary to graduate school. In the past twenty years, she has trained teachers in the teaching of writing. A nationally known consultant, she has served as president of TCTE and on NCTE's Commission on Composition. More than fifty of her articles have appeared in journals such as *Curriculum Review, English Journal, Media & Methods, Southwest Philosophical Studies, English in Texas,* and the *Florida English Journal.* With Edward E. Wilson, Dr. Carroll co-authored *Acts of Teaching: How to Teach Writing* and co-edited *Poetry After Lunch: Poetry to Read Aloud.* She co-directs the New Jersey Writing Project in Texas.

Edward E. Wilson

A former editor of *English in Texas,* Edward E. Wilson has served as a high-school English teacher and a writing consultant in school districts nationwide. Wilson has served on both the Texas Teacher Professional Practices Commission and NCTE's Commission on Composition. Wilson's poetry appears in Paul Janeczko's anthology *The Music of What Happens.* With Dr. Carroll, he co-wrote *Acts of Teaching: How to Teach Writing* and co-edited *Poetry After Lunch: Poetry to Read Aloud.* Wilson co-directs the New Jersey Writing Project in Texas.

PROGRAM ADVISORS

The program advisors provided ongoing input throughout the development of *Prentice Hall Literature: Timeless Voices, Timeless Themes.* Their valuable insights ensure that the perspectives of teachers throughout the country are represented within this literature series.

Leslie Ballard
Teacher of English
South Vigo High School
Terre Haute, Indiana

Lee Bromberger
English Department Chairperson
Mukwonago High School
Mukwonago, Wisconsin

Denise Campbell
Student Achievement Resource Center
CCSD Literacy Content Coordinator
Centennial, Colorado

Holly Carr
Teacher of English
Central Crossing High School
Grove City, Ohio

Melody Chalmers
Teacher of English
E. E. Smith High School
Fayetteville, North Carolina

Karen Gibson, Ph.D.
Communication Arts Program Leader
Appleton Area School District
Appleton, Wisconsin

Gail Hacker
Teacher of English
North Charleston High School
North Charleston, South Carolina

Kim Hartman
English Department Chairperson
Franklin Heights High School
Columbus, Ohio

Helen Hudson, Ph.D.
Teacher of English
Crawfordsville High School
Crawfordsville, Indiana

Carrie Lichtenberg
Teacher of English
Highlands High School
Fort Thomas, Kentucky

Agathaniki Locklear
Teacher of English
Simon Kenton High School
Independence, Kentucky

John Ludy
Teacher of English
Fremont High School
Fremont, Indiana

Sherrie McDowell
English Department Chairperson
Central High School
Cheyenne, Wyoming

Nancy Monroe
Teacher of English
Bolton High School
Alexandria, Louisiana

Cathy Robbs
English Department Chairperson
Chattanooga Central High School
Harrison, Tennessee

Matthew Scanlon
Teacher of English
West Morris Central High School
Chester, New Jersey

John Scott
Teacher of English, Retired
Hampton High School
Hampton, Virginia

Helen Spaith
English Department Chair, Retired
Franklin Heights High School
Columbus, Ohio

Barbra Thompson
Teacher of English
Westover High School
Fayetteville, North Carolina

Sandra Van Belois
English Department Chairperson
Jack Britt High School
Fayetteville, North Carolina

Cheryl Wong-Lee
Teacher of English
Douglas Byrd High School
Fayetteville, North Carolina

Charles Youngs
Teacher of English
Bethel Park High School
Bethel Park, Pennsylvania

Key

10TH GRADE Selections indicated with this icon are particularly suitable for a tenth-grade course, providing students with a balanced program that presents the richness of world literature. See the table of contents on pp. T46–T48 for the complete tenth-grade suggested syllabus.

RC Selections indicated with this icon are supported by the *Reader's Companion* ancillaries, including the *Adapted Reader's Companion* and the *English-Language Learner's Companion*. The *Companions* feature interactive reading support and practice, as well as alternative reading strategies.

Ancient Worlds (3000 B.C.–A.D. 1400)

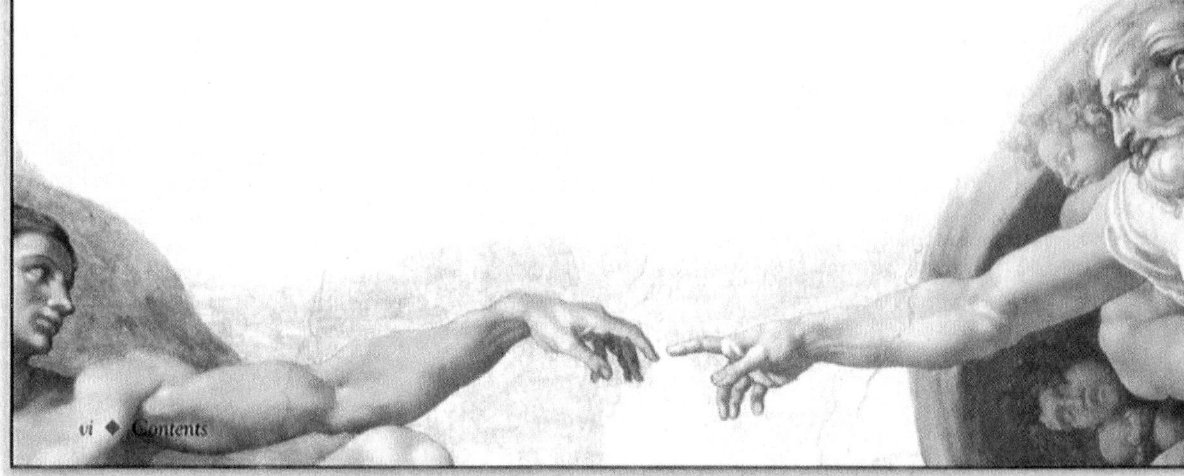

TEACHING FROM THE TABLE OF CONTENTS

Guide to Using the Table of Contents as a Teaching Tool

Before students have read a single selection, you can use the table of contents and the following TE notes to prepare them for the course:

- activating prior knowledge and anticipating (page vii)
- the scope of the course (page viii)
- transliterating and romanizing Chinese characters (pages ix–x)
- translators and translation (pages xi–xii)
- pronunciation of foreign names (page xiii)
- systems of dating events and geography (pages xiv–xv)
- art and world literature (pages xvi–xvii)
- genres in world literature (pages xviii–xix)
- reasons for studying world literature (pages xx–xxi)

For more information on these and other Penguin Group (USA) titles, see pages R1–R6. You may want to consult your teacher before choosing one of these books.

TEACHING FROM THE TABLE OF CONTENTS

Activating Prior Knowledge and Anticipating

You can use the table of contents to activate students' prior knowledge, elicit questions to be answered later, and create anticipation. Following is an example of an approach that you can apply to any of the units:

Call students' attention to *The Epic of Gilgamesh* on the table of contents, page vi. Remind them that a quest is an adventurous journey in search of something, and tell them that this work is about a hero's quest for immortality. Ask them whether today's heroes go on quests. Then, have them review the listed episodes and speculate about each one. For example, ask them who Humbaba might be and what the battle with him might involve. Encourage them to make their descriptions vivid. Point out that they can also read about battles in the selection from the *Ramayana* (Unit 2) and Book 22 of the *Iliad* (Unit 4)

Finally, have students formulate questions to answer about Unit 1 selections and have them search the entire table of contents for selections that seem to be about heroes.

Indian Literature (c. 1400 B.C. – A.D. 500)

Skills Workshops

Suggestions for Sustained Reading *from Penguin Group (USA)*

Related World Literature: R. K. Narayan, *A Tiger for Malgudi*
Mohandas K. Gandhi, *The Penguin Gandhi Reader*

Related British Literature: Rudyard Kipling, *Kim*

Related American Literature: Martin Luther King, Jr., *Why We Can't Wait*

Other Suggestion: R. K. Narayan, *The Ramayana*

For more information on these and other Penguin Group (USA) titles, see pages R1–R6. You may want to consult your teacher before choosing one of these books.

TEACHING FROM THE TABLE OF CONTENTS

The Organization of the Book	Previewing the Scope of the Course
This book is divided into nine units. Each of Units 1–3 focuses on one or more ancient cultures—Mesopotamian, Hebrew, Egyptian, Arabic, Persian, African, Indian, Chinese, and Japanese—with selections appearing chronologically within a culture. Units 4–7 have a European focus, progressing from the classical world through the Middle Ages, Renaissance, and Age of Rationalism. Units 8 and 9 cover the nineteenth century to the present and contain literature from around the world.	Have students thumb through the table of contents and note the different cultures, nationalities, and languages that are included. Write their responses on the chalkboard so that the scope of the book begins to take on meaning. Then ask them to review the table of contents again and figure out how it is organized. Lead them to see how the book is organized by culture and chronology. Finally, explain which units or portions of units you will be covering in your course, but encourage them to explore other selections as well.

Chinese and Japanese Literature (1000 B.C. – A.D. 1890)

ENRICHMENT: Language Connection

The Wade-Giles and Pinyin Systems for Romanizing Chinese Characters

The Wade-Giles and Pinyin systems offer different ways to romanize, or transliterate, Chinese characters. The Wade-Giles system, devised by Sir Thomas Francis Wade and refined by Herbert Allen Giles, was standard for almost seventy years. Chinese names in this book are written according to this system, which uses many hyphens and apostrophes and sometimes represents the same sound with different characters.

In 1979, China endorsed the Pinyin system, which derives from a Peking dialect of Mandarin Chinese. Pinyin uses fewer hyphens and apostrophes than Wade-Giles and establishes a clearer link between sounds and symbols. For example, it replaces the Wade-Giles *ts* and *tz,* which represent the same sound, with *z.* Most social studies texts and newspapers use the Pinyin system, spelling the name of China's first communist leader *Mao Zedong,* not *Mao Tse-tung.* In the Student Edition of this book, Pinyin versions of names appear in parentheses in the Unit 3 Introduction. In the Teacher's Edition, Pinyin versions of authors' names appear with the relevant selections.

Japanese Literature

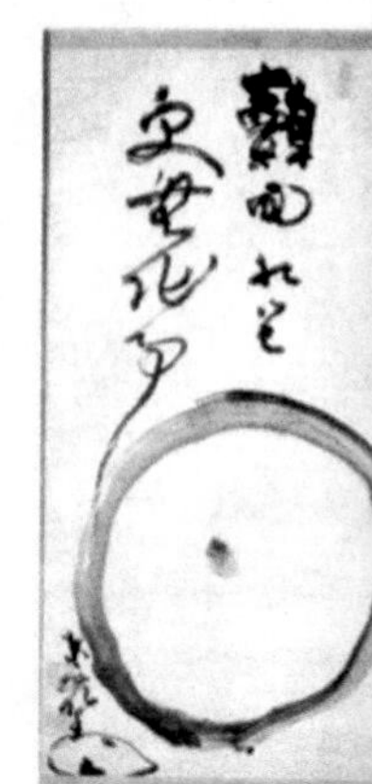

Skills Workshops

Suggestions for Sustained Reading *from Penguin Group (USA)*

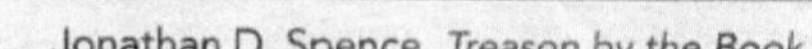

Related World Literature: Jonathan D. Spence, *Treason by the Book*
Matsuo Bashō, *The Narrow Road to the Deep North*
Related British Literature: Lian Hearn, *Across the Nightingale Floor*
Related American Literature: Amy Tan, *The Joy Luck Club*
Other Suggestion: Confucius, *The Analects*

For more information on these and other Penguin Group (USA) titles, see pages R1–R6. You may want to consult your teacher before choosing one of these books.

TEACHING FROM THE TABLE OF CONTENTS

The Wade-Giles and Pinyin Transliterations of Chinese

Explain to students the concept of *transliteration*, "writing words or letters from one alphabet in those of another." Tell them that, in English, there are two ways of transliterating Chinese characters: the Wade-Giles system and the Pinyin system.

Have them look at and pronounce the names of Chinese authors in the table of contents. Explain that these names are written according to the Wade-Giles system, which uses more hyphens, apostrophes, and different spellings of the same sound than the Pinyin system does. On a chalkboard, write the Wade-Giles and Pinyin versions of several names): Li Po (Wade-Giles)/Li Bo (Pinyin); Mao Tse-tung (Wade-Giles)/Mao Zedong (Pinyin); T'ao Ch'ien (Wade-Giles)/Tao Qian (Pinyin). Have students look for the differences you mentioned. Point out that the author's name sounds basically the same in each version.

Point out that most social studies texts and newspapers use the Pinyin system. Explain that this book uses Wade-Giles because many people are familiar with it but that it provides Pinyin versions of names in parentheses in the Unit 3 Introduction.

Ancient Greece and Rome (c. 800 B.C. – A.D. 500)

Greek Literature

Roman Literature

ENRICHMENT: Language Connection

Translators, the Unsung Heroes

The roll call of great writers associated with world literature includes names like Homer, Sappho, Virgil, Dante, and Tolstoy. Much less prominent, and often forgotten, are the names of the translators who make it possible for us to read these and many other authors.

At first glance, it may seem that translation requires nothing more than the knowledge of a foreign language. Yet in reality, translation requires several talents. Translators must have a thorough appreciation of two languages, the original language of the work they are translating and the language into which they are translating it. Such knowledge enables them to move beyond literal, word-for-word translation to find an equivalent in the second language for the nuances, idioms, and phrasing in the original.

Translators must also understand the literary forms and techniques used in the original work so that they can adapt them to a second language. Because of the literary abilities required, translators are often themselves successful writers.

Skills Workshops

Suggestions for Sustained Reading *from Penguin Group (USA)*

Related World Literature: Sophocles, *The Three Theban Plays*
Plutarch, *The Fall of the Roman Republic (Six Lives)*

Related British Literature: Barry Cunliffe, *The Extraordinary Voyage of Pytheas the Greek*

Related American Literature: Alexander Hamilton et al., *The Federalist Papers*

Other Suggestions: Homer, *The Iliad*
Virgil, *The Aeneid*

For more information on these and other Penguin Group (USA) titles, see pages R1–R6. You may want to consult your teacher before choosing one of these books.

TEACHING FROM THE TABLE OF CONTENTS

Appreciating the Role That Translators Play

Have students look at the table of contents for Unit 4 and identify authors and selections. Lead them to see that the selections from ancient Greece were first written in ancient Greek and the selections from Rome were written in Latin.

Ask them how it is that selections originally written in another language now appear in English. Students will probably refer to *translators* and the act of *translation*. Tell them that these words come from a Latin word root meaning"to transfer," and that *translation* means "rendering something written or spoken from one language to another."

Point out that many of the works in this book are translated and that translation is not a mechanical, one-for-one transferring of individual words. Instead, it involves finding equivalents in one language for idioms and word connotations in another. Help them distinguish among *translation, interpreting* ("translation of spoken words"), and *transliteration* ("respelling in one language the words from a language with a different alphabet").

UNIT 5 The Middle Ages (A.D. 450–1300)

SUGGESTIONS FOR SUSTAINED READING *from Penguin Group (USA)*

Related World Literature: Dante Alighieri, *The Divine Comedy: Paradiso*
Snorri Sturluson, *Egil's Saga*

Related British Literature: Geoffrey Chaucer, *The Canterbury Tales*

Related American Literature: Mark Twain, *A Connecticut Yankee in King Arthur's Court*

Other Suggestions: A. T. Hatto, *The Nibelungenlied*
Glyn S. Burgess, *The Song of Roland*

For more information on these and other Penguin Group (USA) titles, see pages R1–R6. You may want to consult your teacher before choosing one of these books.

TEACHING FROM THE TABLE OF CONTENTS

Pronunciation of Foreign Names	Teaching the Pronunciation of Foreign Names
When reading about a different culture, students may have difficulty in pronouncing the names of people, places, and cultural products. This textbook provides parenthetical pronunciations—using dictionary symbols—for hard-to-pronounce author, place, and title names. You will find these pronunciations in unit introductions, on the Prepare to Read pages that introduce selections, and in footnotes within selections.	Ask students to pronounce the names in the Unit 5 table of contents (above). If they have trouble, tell them that it is natural to stumble over names that come from foreign languages. Explain to them that in this textbook, hard-to-pronounce names are followed by pronunciation symbols that explain how to pronounce the name. Have them turn to the Pronunciation Key in a dictionary, and go over the sounds with them. Then, have them apply what they have learned to the pronunciation symbols on pages 18, 155, 163, 325, and 1121.

UNIT 6 The Renaissance and Rationalism (1300–1800)

TEACHING FROM THE TABLE OF CONTENTS

Systems for Dating Events	Teaching About Systems for Dating Events
The most common system of dating events—and the one used in this book—designates them as either *B.C.* ("Before Christ") or *A.D.* (from the Latin *Anno Domini*, "in the year of the Lord," or "After Christ.") This system uses the life of Jesus Christ and the coming of Christianity as a central marker. Jews and Muslims, however, use the designations *B.C.E.* (Before the Christian, or Common, Era) and *C.E.* (Christian, or Common, Era). Depending on the system you use, the Middle Ages roughly began at A.D. 450 or 450 C.E.	Ask students what "A.D." indicates in the date for Unit 5 (p. xiii). Lead them to see that it stands for *Anno Domini,* Latin for "in the year of the Lord" meaning that a date occurred after the birth of Jesus Christ. Then, explain the meaning of *B.C.* Also explain that Jews and Muslims use the abbreviations *B.C.E.* ("Before the Christian, or Common, Era") for *B.C.* and *C.E.* ("Christian, or Common, Era") for *A.D.* Ask them why others might use an alternate system. Then, have them give the dates for the Middle Ages using this system.

The Age of Rationalism

Skills Workshops

Suggestions for Sustained Reading *from Penguin Group (USA)*

Related World Literature: Niccolò Machiavelli, *The Prince*
Jean-Baptiste Molière, *Tartuffe and Other Plays*
Related British Literature: William Shakespeare, *The Tempest*
Related American Literature: John Tanner, *The Falcon*
Dava Sobel, *Galileo's Daughter*
Other Suggestions: Voltaire, *Candide*
Miguel de Cervantes, *Don Quixote*

For more information on these and other Penguin Group (USA) titles, see pages R1–R6. You may want to consult your teacher before choosing one of these books.

TEACHING FROM THE TABLE OF CONTENTS

Why Teach the Geography of World Literature?

In reading world literature, students encounter foreign-sounding names, a wide range of texts from a variety of eras and cultures, and belief systems and assumptions that may seem very different from their own. Teaching students the geography of world literature can help orient them and give them the confidence to create meaning from texts. You can reinforce this geography lesson by using the maps in many of the unit introductions and the locator globes that appear with every selection.

Using the Table of Contents to Teach Geography

Divide the class into groups, and give each group a world map or globe. As you point to the map or globe, tell them that they are going to dramatize the global nature of world literature by using the table of contents to take a "world tour." Have one member of each group read each region or culture mentioned on the table of contents, while other group members find it on the globe. Check to see that each group has accurately located the region. Finally, point out the locator globes on Prepare to Read pages (see, for example, pages 12 and 1192) and ask if these are helpful.

Romanticism and Realism (1800–1890)

ENRICHMENT: Art Connection

Art and World Literature

The art that appears above, a detail from *The Three Graces,* 1482, by Alessandro Botticelli, is representative of the many works of fine art in this text. You can use these works to elicit responses to literary selections, identify qualities of a culture or historical era that also appear in the literature, and teach the history of fine art.

Caspar David Friedrich's *The Wanderer Over the Sea of Clouds,* 1818, for example, on page 762, illustrates aspects of Romanticism. In this striking picture, the beauty and grandeur of nature inspire feelings of awe and reverence associated with the sublime. Also, the picture seems to stress the subjective response of the individual, rather than the values of society.

By eliciting students' responses to the art throughout the book, you can teach them about different cultures and eras while encouraging them to speculate on and anticipate the literature they will read. (See page xvii for a sample lesson.)

For more information on these and other Penguin Group (USA) titles, see pages R1–R6. You may want to consult your teacher before choosing one of these books.

TEACHING FROM THE TABLE OF CONTENTS

Using Fine Art to Anticipate Literature

Direct students' attention to Caspar-David Friedrich's painting *The Wanderer Over the Sea of Clouds* on page 762. Have the class contribute to two lists that you write on the chalkboard: details from the painting and their responses to these details.

Students should point out that there is a single figure, whose back is to us, and that he seems to be standing atop a mountain. At an appropriate moment, mention the title of the painting and have students respond to it. Lead them to see how their descriptions and responses reveal the assumptions of Romanticism, one of the two movements discussed in Unit 7.

Finally, have students read the titles of the selections in Unit 7 (above) and, based on what they have learned from the painting, decide which of these works could be called Romantic. For example, *A Doll House* seems to refer to the smallness of life rather than its grandeur, but "Invitation to the Voyage" has a sense of adventure like that in the painting.

UNIT 8 The Modern World (1890–1945)

ENRICHMENT: Literary History Connection

Genres in World Literature

In the table of contents, the literary genre of a selection appears immediately before the page number. This textbook contains examples of many genres, including epic poetry, lyric poetry, scripture, folk tale, proverb, fable, philosophical text, parable, historical account, tragedy, poetic drama, realistic drama, novel, short story, and essay.

The scope of this book makes it possible to follow the historical development of a genre or to compare and contrast its use by different authors during the same historical period. For example, you can trace the development of the epic from *The Epic of Gilgamesh,* through the *Iliad* and the *Aeneid,* up to the *Song of Roland* and the *Divine Comedy.* You can also study the nineteenth-century short story by comparing and contrasting de Maupassant's "Two Friends" and Tolstoy's "How Much Land Does a Man Need?" or twentieth-century nonfiction by comparing and contrasting Primo Levi's *Survival in Auschwitz* and Alexander Solzhenitsyn's Nobel Lecture.

For more information on these and other Penguin Group (USA) titles, see pages R1–R6. You may want to consult your teacher before choosing one of these books.

TEACHING FROM THE TABLE OF CONTENTS

Exploring Genres in World Literature

Review with students the concept of *literary genre*, "the type or category into which literary works are grouped." Ask them to name some genres, and write them on the chalkboard as they speak. Briefly discuss some of the ways in which these genres differ from one another. Then, point out that in the table of contents, the genre of a selection is indicated immediately before the page number. Have them find examples of genre designations in the Unit 8 table of contents.

Divide the class into groups, and have these groups compete with one another to find the greatest number of different genres in the table of contents. Then, have the groups compete to find the earliest example of an epic (*The Epic of Gilgamesh*, Unit 1), the earliest example of a lyric poem (one of the ancient Egyptian poems, Unit 1), and six short stories written between 1890 and 1945 ("The Metamorphosis," "The Bracelet," "War" "The Glass of Milk," "Under Reconstruction," or "My Old Home").

The Contemporary World (1946 – Present)

ENRICHMENT: Philosophical Connection

Why Study World Literature?

It is natural for students to wonder about the reasons for studying world literature. Following are a variety of answers to this question:

- to satisfy our curiosity about the thoughts, emotions, values, and goals of people who lived in different places, cultures, and times
- to find universal human values in the literature of different places and times
- to appreciate the artistry of writers from different cultures and times
- to be entertained by exciting narratives
- to learn more about the history of genres like epic poetry, the novel, the short story, the lyric poem, and the essay
- to discover how today's writers have been influenced by writers of different cultures and times
- to discover how world literature is related to art, music, dance, technology, and science

Skills Workshops

Suggestions for Sustained Reading *from Penguin Group (USA)*

Related World Literature: Chinua Achebe, *Things Fall Apart*
Alexander Solzhenitsyn, *One Day in the Life of Ivan Denisovich*

Related British Literature: William Golding, *Lord of the Flies*

Related American Literature: Julia Alvarez, *Something to Declare*

Other Suggestion: Elie Wiesel, *Night*

For more information on these and other Penguin Group (USA) titles, see pages R1–R6. You may want to consult your teacher before choosing one of these books.

TEACHING FROM THE TABLE OF CONTENTS

Why Study World Literature?

Have students scan the table of contents for Unit 9, The Contemporary World. Ask: "Can you get the news from these authors?" Allow students to struggle with this question. Then, tell them Ezra Pound's definition of literature as "news that stays news." Lead them to see that Pound meant literature never gets stale because it is never mere information. World literature represents what writers of different times and places *made* of the information available to them. It is information transformed into delight and wisdom.

Finally, have them keep this definition of "news" in mind as they offer reasons for studying world literature. Lead them to see that such reasons might include discovering universal human values in the literature of different times and places; satisfying one's curiosity about different cultures and eras; being entertained by exciting narratives; appreciating the artistry of writers; learning more about the history of various genres; and discovering connections between world literature and art, music, and science.

Resources

Comparing Literary Works

Reading Informational Materials

Connections

A Closer Look

WRITING WORKSHOPS

LISTENING AND SPEAKING WORKSHOPS

ASSESSMENT WORKSHOPS

Unit Objectives

1. To read selections from world literature written during the period of 1300 to 1800
2. To apply a variety of reading strategies, particularly those appropiate for reading fiction and poetry
3. To analyze literary elements
4. To use a variety of strategies to read unfamiliar words and to build vocabulary
5. To learn elements of grammar, usage, and style
6. To use recursive writing processes to write in a variety of forms
7. To develop listening and speaking skills
8. To express and support responses to various types of texts
9. To prepare, organize, and present literary interpretations

Meeting the Objectives

With each selection, you will find instructional materials through which students can meet these objectives. Further, you will find additional practice pages for reading strategies, literary analysis, vocabulary, and grammar in the **Selection Support: Skills Development Workbook** in your **Teaching Resources.**

Background

Art

The School of Athens, by Raphael Sanzio

Raphael (1483–1520) painted *The School of Athens* for Pope Julius II in the early 1500s. It depicts philosophers and scholars such as Plato, Aristotle, Socrates, Pythagoras, Euclid, Ptolemy, and Zoroaster and a portrait of Raphael himself. The pope was so pleased with the work that he asked Raphael to continue painting for him.

Use the following question for discussion:

Why do you think Raphael included these men of wisdom?

Possible response: The men were all contributors to Western culture.

UNIT 6 The Renaissance and Rationalism

The School of Athens, Raphael Sanzio

UNIT FEATURES

Connections	Reading Informational Material
Every unit contains a feature that connects literature to a related topic, such as art, science, or history. In this unit students will read: **William Shakespeare: Sonnets 29 and 116** on pp. 684–685. Use the information and questions on the Connections page to enrich students' understanding of the selections presented within the unit.	These selections will help students learn to analyze and evaluate informational texts, such as workplace documents, technical directions, and consumer materials. They will expose students to the organization and features unique to nonnarrative texts. In this unit, the focus is on Feature Articles. **Leonardo: The Eye, the Hand, the Mind** is on p. 741.

(1300–1800)

“Of course Sacred Scripture is the basic authority in everything; yet I sometimes run across ancient sayings or pagan writings— even the poets’—so purely and reverently expressed, and so inspired, that I can’t help believing their authors’ hearts were moved by some divine power.”

— from “The Godly Feast,” by Erasmus

ASSESSMENT RESOURCES

The following resources can be used to assess students' knowledge and skills.

Selection Assessment

- **Selection Support:** Skills Development Workbook
- **Formal Assessment**
- **Open-Book Tests**
- **Performance Assess. and Portfolio Mgmt.**
- **Extension Activities**

Assessing Student Progress

Listed below are the tools that are available to measure the degree to which students meet the unit objectives.

Informal Assessment

The questions in the Review and Assess sections are a first level of response to the concepts and skills presented within the selections. Students' responses are a brief, informal measure of their grasp of the material. These responses can indicate where further instruction and practice are needed. Then, follow up with the practice pages in the **Selection Support: Skills Development Workbook.**

Formal Assessment

The **Formal Assessment** booklet contains Selection Tests and Unit Tests.

- Selection Tests measure comprehension and skills acquisition for each selection or group of selections.
- Each Unit Test provides students with thirty multiple-choice questions and five essay questions designed to assess students' knowledge of the literature and skills taught in the unit.

The **Open-Book Tests** ask students to demonstrate their ability to synthesize and communicate information from selections or groups of selections.

To assess student writing, you will find rubrics and scoring models in the **Performance Assessment and Portfolio Management** booklet. In this booklet, you will also find scoring rubrics for listening and speaking activities.

Alternative Assessment

The **Extension Activities** booklet contains writing activities, listening and speaking activities, and research and technology activities that are appropriate for students with different ability levels. You may also use these activities as an alternative measurement of students' growth.

Using the Timeline

The Timeline can serve a number of instructional purposes, as follows:

Getting an Overview

Use the Timeline to help students get a quick overview of themes and events of the period. This approach will benefit all students but may be especially helpful for Visual/Spatial Learners, English Learners, and Less Proficient Readers. (For strategies in using the Timeline as an overview, see the bottom of this page.)

Thinking Critically

Questions are provided on the facing page. Use these questions to have students review the events, discuss their significance, and examine the "so what" behind the "what happened."

Connecting to Selections

Have students refer to the Timeline when they begin to read individual selections. By consulting the Timeline regularly, they will gain a better sense of the period's chronology. In addition, they will appreciate world events that gave rise to these works of literature.

Projects

Students can use the Timeline as a launching pad for projects like these:

- **Literary Timeline** Have students create a literary timeline of the Renaissance in England and Italy. Have them begin with the birth of Petrarch and finish with the end of the Renaissance in England in 1625.
- **Reflections of a Life** Have students choose either the Renaissance period or the Age of Reason and play the role of an imaginary person who has lived through that period. Have students review the Timeline of that period and present an oral reflection of what took place during that person's life.

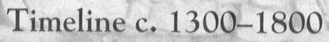

Timeline c. 1300–1800

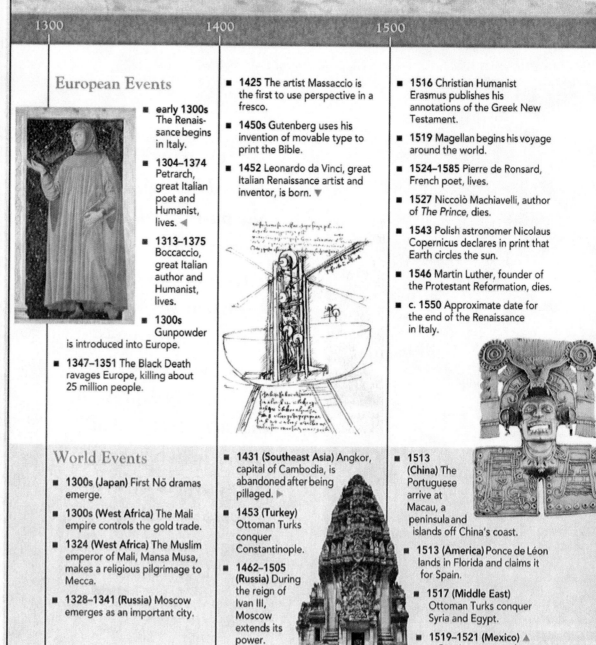

1300 | 1400 | 1500

European Events

- **early 1300s** The Renaissance begins in Italy.
- **1304–1374** Petrarch, great Italian poet and Humanist, lives. ◄
- **1313–1375** Boccaccio, great Italian author and Humanist, lives.
- **1300s** Gunpowder is introduced into Europe.
- **1347–1351** The Black Death ravages Europe, killing about 25 million people.
- **1425** The artist Massaccio is the first to use perspective in a fresco.
- **1450s** Gutenberg uses his invention of movable type to print the Bible.
- **1452** Leonardo da Vinci, great Italian Renaissance artist and inventor, is born. ▼

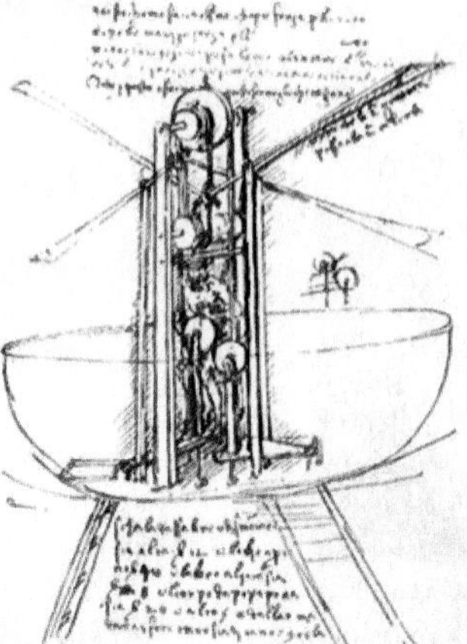

- **1516** Christian Humanist Erasmus publishes his annotations of the Greek New Testament.
- **1519** Magellan begins his voyage around the world.
- **1524–1585** Pierre de Ronsard, French poet, lives.
- **1527** Niccolò Machiavelli, author of *The Prince*, dies.
- **1543** Polish astronomer Nicolaus Copernicus declares in print that Earth circles the sun.
- **1546** Martin Luther, founder of the Protestant Reformation, dies.
- **c. 1550** Approximate date for the end of the Renaissance in Italy.

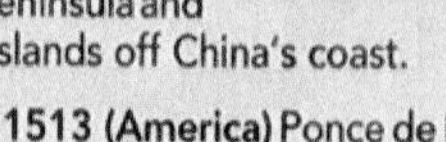

World Events

- **1300s (Japan)** First Nō dramas emerge.
- **1300s (West Africa)** The Mali empire controls the gold trade.
- **1324 (West Africa)** The Muslim emperor of Mali, Mansa Musa, makes a religious pilgrimage to Mecca.
- **1328–1341 (Russia)** Moscow emerges as an important city.
- **1431 (Southeast Asia)** Angkor, capital of Cambodia, is abandoned after being pillaged. ►
- **1453 (Turkey)** Ottoman Turks conquer Constantinople.
- **1462–1505 (Russia)** During the reign of Ivan III, Moscow extends its power.

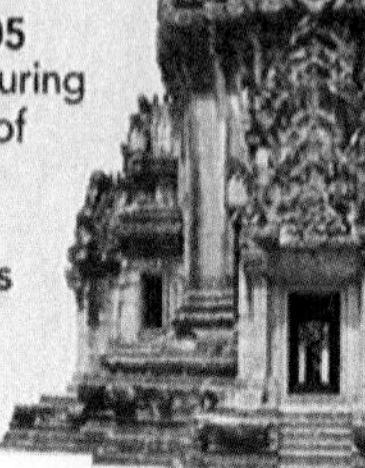

- **1513 (China)** The Portuguese arrive at Macau, a peninsula and islands off China's coast.
- **1513 (America)** Ponce de Léon lands in Florida and claims it for Spain.
- **1517 (Middle East)** Ottoman Turks conquer Syria and Egypt.
- **1519–1521 (Mexico)** ▲ Cortés conquers the Aztec empire.

ENRICHMENT: Getting an Overview of the Period

Introduction	Key Events
To give students an overview of the period, indicate the span of dates in the title of the Timeline. Next, point out that the Timeline is divided into European Events (on the top) and World Events (on the bottom). Have students scan the Timeline, looking at both the European Events and the World Events. Finally, point out that the events in the Timeline often represent beginnings, turning points, and endings. (For example, Magellan began his voyage around the world in 1519.)	Ask students to identify key events related to the Renaissance and to Rationalism. Possible response: Gutenberg used his printing press to print the Bible (1450s), and Copernicus declared in print that the Earth circles the sun (1543). Ask students which events indicate progress in science. Possible response: Galileo improved the telescope; the Royal Society was formed to promote science; and Newton published his work on the laws of gravity and motion (1609) / (1660) / (1687).

European and World Events

1600 | 1700 | 1800

- **1605** Cervantes publishes the first part of *Don Quixote.*
- **1608–1674** English poet John Milton lives.
- **1609** Galileo improves the telescope and begins observing the solar system with telescopes that magnify up to 20x.
- **1610** Galileo observes four moons orbiting around Jupiter. ▼

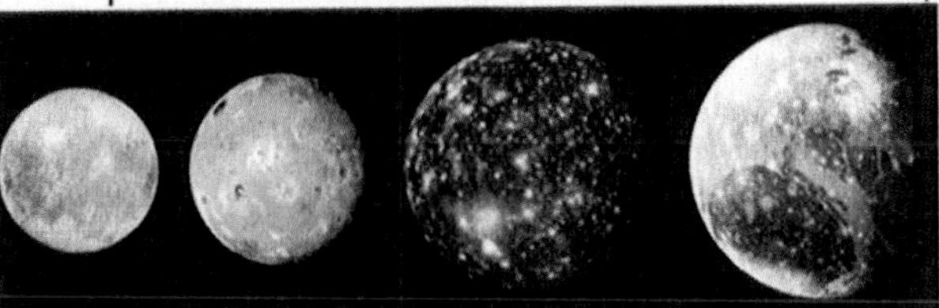

- **1625** The Renaissance in England ends.
- **1657** Pascal begins writing his *Pensées.*
- **1660** The Royal Society, a group formed to promote science, is founded in London, England.
- **1664–1666** There is an outbreak of plague in London, England.
- **1687** Sir Isaac Newton publishes a book describing the laws of gravity and motion.

Night of August 4, 1789, or "Patriotic Delirium," Bibliothèque Nationale, Paris, Giraudon

- **1702** First daily English newspaper appears.
- **early 1700s** Addison and Steele publish periodicals.
- **1744** English poet Alexander Pope dies.
- **1765** James Watt helps launch the Industrial Revolution by improving the steam engine.
- **1772** Diderot completes the *Encyclopedia,* a major achievement of the Enlightenment.
- **1778** Voltaire, author of *Candide,* dies.
- **1787–1799** The French Revolution is fought. ▲
- **1799** Napoleon Bonaparte assumes control in France.

- **1613 (Russia)** The Time of Troubles, a fifteen-year period of political crisis, ends.
- **1633 (Japan)** The Tokugawas close Japan to the rest of the world. ◄
- **1644 (China)** The Ming dynasty is overthrown by armies from Manchuria.
- **1644–1694 (Japan)** Haiku poet Matsuo Bashō lives.
- **1669 (Greece)** The Ottoman empire seizes Crete.

- **1703 (Russia)** Czar Peter the Great begins the construction of St. Petersburg. ▼
- **1776–1781 (America)** The colonies defeat Great Britain in the American Revolution.

Analyzing the Timeline

1. **(a)** When did Gutenberg first print the Bible using movable type? **(b)** What effect did the availability of movable type have on the accessibility of ideas? **[Analyze Cause and Effect]**
   Answer: **(a)** Gutenberg first used movable type to print the Bible in the 1450s. **(b)** Movable type provided printed materials so that more people could learn and share their ideas.
2. **(a)** What kinds of events were taking place in the world during the Italian Renaissance? **(b)** Compare and contrast the events in Europe with world events. **[Compare and Contrast]**
   Possible response: **(a)** There were many wars and conquests. **(b)** This was a time of intellectual and cultural growth for Europe. The rest of the world showed some intellectual and cultural growth, but growth seemed impeded by war and conquest.
3. **(a)** When was gunpowder introduced into Europe? **(b)** What effects might the availability of gunpowder have had on European explorers? **[Analyze Cause and Effect]**
   Answer: **(a)** Gunpowder was introduced in the 1300s. **(b)** The introduction of gunpowder made it easier for European explorers to conquer the areas they explored.
4. **(a)** When did the Renaissance end in Italy? **(b)** Why do you think it ended later in England? **[Speculate]**
   Answer: **(a)** The Renaissance ended in Italy around 1550. **(b)** The Renaissance began in Italy and then spread to England. Because the Renaissance came to England later, it may have ended later. Ideas traveled slowly, and England was not a part of the European continent.
5. **(a)** When was the Royal Society founded in London? **(b)** What events might have prompted the founding of the society? **[Analyze Cause and Effect]**
   Answer: **(a)** The Royal Society was founded in 1660. **(b)** The advances in science made scientific discovery a new priority for Europe.

continued

continued from right column

▶Critical Viewing

1. On the basis of the painting of Petrarch (1304–1374), how would you describe the poet's demeanor? **[Analyze]**
   Possible response: Petrarch appears serious but kind; his gesture indicates an openness and a desire to share his knowledge.
2. What does the drawing of the ornithopter in the center of the page (1452) indicate about Leonardo da Vinci? **[Infer]**
   Possible response: It shows da Vinci's interest in science, invention, and detail as well as his ability as an artist.
3. What does the picture from the French Revolution (1787–1799) indicate about that particular war? **[Generalize]**
   Possible response: It indicates that the middle class rose up against the monarchy of King Louis XIV.

Literature of the Period

- In "Federigo's Falcon," found on p. 688, students will find Boccaccio's tale of a man who parts with something of great value to him.
- In *Don Quixote,* by Miguel de Cervantes Saavedra, on p. 700, students will find one of the strangest and funniest characters in literature.

➔➔ *POINT/COUNTERPOINT*

Point out that the Renaissance was a time for great change. Invention, exploration, and rediscovery marked the time period, and many previous beliefs were altered. How the Renaissance affected the people of the time has been and still is a subject of debate among scholars.

Ask students the following questions:

1. What do these two viewpoints have in common?
   Possible response: Both viewpoints imply that great changes took place during the Renaissance and that these changes affected the individual.
2. In what ways do these viewpoints differ?
   Possible response: They differ in the degree of rebirth of human consciousness evident in the Renaissance. Rice believes that the age saw as much continuity and tradition as it did change and innovation. Burckhardt believes that during the Renaissance, man became a spiritual *individual.*
3. What are some current controversies about the effect of an intellectual movement on the people who experienced it?
   Possible response: People may debate the effects of the protests of the 1960s or the civil rights movement.

The Renaissance and Rationalism

(c. 1300–1800)

Historical Background

The Renaissance in Western Europe The Renaissance, which means "rebirth," is a period that saw many changes and innovations. Among them were the rediscovery of classical art and literature; the exploration of regions of the globe that were previously unknown in Europe; the discovery that Earth revolves around the sun; and an upsurge in trade and invention. This rebirth, which lasted in Italy from the early 1300s until 1550, gradually extended its influence northward. In England, it lasted from 1485 to 1625.

Status and Insecurity The Renaissance was a period during which rank and status mattered a great deal. For every social class, however, this era was a time of insecurity. The Black Death (see page 666) devastated Europe in the late 1340s, toward the beginning of the Italian Renaissance.

Point/Counterpoint

Was the Renaissance a Rebirth of Consciousness?

Did the Renaissance mark a complete rebirth of human consciousness? Two scholars—writing about a hundred years apart—disagree on this question.

Yes! In the Middle Ages both sides of human consciousness—that which was turned within as that which was turned without—lay dreaming or half awake beneath a common veil. The veil was woven of faith, illusion, and childish prepossession, through which the world and history were seen clad in strange hues. Man was conscious of himself only as a member of a race, people, party, family, or corporation—only through some general category. In Italy this veil first melted into air . . . man became a spiritual *individual*, . . .

—**Jacob Burckhardt, from *The Civilization of the Renaissance in Italy* (1860)**

No! Certainly the hundred years before and after 1450 were enormously fertile in innovation. But the great discoveries and historical mutations of the age were not confined to Italy; while even in Italy continuity and tradition mark the age as deeply as change and innovation. The history of discovery and novelty must be balanced by the equally interesting and important story of the survival and adaptation of traditional institutions, social distinctions, professional disciplines, and modes of thought.

—**Eugene F. Rice, Jr., from *The Columbia History of the World* (1972)**

ENRICHMENT: Culture Connection

The Role of Women

For the most part, women's lives changed little during the Renaissance. Many women still devoted themselves to raising a family. Some also worked outside their homes as servants or spinners and weavers. Others ran small businesses, selling their handiwork or the produce of their gardens.

A few women gained national or international prominence. Isabella d'Este (born 1474), for instance, was a brilliant woman and skillful diplomat. Her family ruled the wealthy Italian city-state of Ferrara. Isabella married the ruler of Mantua, established herself as a patron of the arts, and helped her husband govern.

In addition to sickness, other disasters contributed to the insecurity of the times. With the exception of castles and churches, most buildings were built of wood, and fire in cities was a constant hazard.

Kings Up, Nobles Down Against this backdrop of general insecurity, the power of kings tended to increase during the Renaissance. This centralization of power helped create the nations that are familiar to us today. Meanwhile, the great nobility were losing their importance. Their mighty castles, for instance, were threatened by the introduction of gunpowder into Europe in the 1300s. Castle walls became vulnerable to cannon shot, and even well-armored knights could be toppled by a well-placed bullet.

Humanism: Out of the "Dark" Ages The most important cultural movement of the Renaissance was Humanism, which advocated a return to classical studies and ideals. This movement began in fourteenth-century Italy, where the first Humanists were the famous writers Petrarch (pē´ trärk´) and Boccaccio (bō kä´ chô). For the first time in about a thousand years, the intellectual life of Western Europe was directly influenced by the works of classical writers known before only through inaccurate summaries or quotations. The Humanists viewed the classics as sources of moral and practical wisdom. Humanist ideals also influenced Italian Renaissance artists like Michelangelo (mī´ kel an´ jə lō´) and Leonardo da Vinci (də vin´ chē), who followed classical artists in portraying the beauty of the human form.

According to the Humanists, the Middle Ages were "dark" because the Germanic tribes that had invaded Rome, the Goths, had destroyed classical civilization. Humanists believed that with the rediscovery of classical learning, these "dark" times had given way to an age of "enlightenment." Today, scholars no longer accept this belief, which might be called the Humanist Myth, without qualifications. (See Point/Counterpoint on page 664.)

Humanism started in Italy, yet as it moved northward it changed somewhat in character. The enthusiasm for classical antiquity remained, but it was influenced by a Christian fervor. This slightly different movement, called Christian Humanism, tended to look back to early Christian as well as classical sources. Unlike medieval thinkers, Christian Humanists stressed the importance of the active life. They also ridiculed the performing of mechanical acts in the place of inner worship. In this way, Christian Humanism prepared for the more radical protests of the Reformation.

Mona Lisa, Leonardo da Vinci, Louvre, Dep. des Peintures, Paris, France

▲ **Critical Viewing** The *Mona Lisa* by Leonardo da Vinci is one of the most famous paintings of all time. Many critics and viewers have remarked on the "mystery" of the subject's smile. What, if anything, do you think is mysterious about her expression? Explain. **[Interpret]**

Background

Art

Mona Lisa, by Leonardo da Vinci

In the early 1500s, Leonardo da Vinci (1452–1519) painted this portrait of Francesco del Giocondo's wife. The expression on her face has created curiosity among her viewers for centuries. The *Mona Lisa*, also known as *La Gioconda*, is displayed in Paris at the Louvre.

Use the following question for discusion.

How is this painting an outstanding representation of the Renaissance?

Possible response: Da Vinci's painting captures the beauty of the human form; the painting also reflects Renaissance artists' interest in nature and perspective.

▶Critical Viewing

Possible response: It is difficult to tell whether the subject's expression is a true smile or if it is her response to another emotion.

Background

Leonardo da Vinci

Although he is best known as a painter, Leonardo da Vinci was also an engineer and scientist. Because of his insatiable curiosity about the physical world, Leonardo experimented in geology, botany, hydraulics, and mechanics. His resulting drawings, rendered with scientific precision and artistry, range from flying machines to anatomical studies of people, animals, and plants.

Background Art

Show students Art Transparency 6: *Mona Lisa* by Leonardo da Vinci in the **Fine Art Transparencies** booklet. Have them discuss ways in which Leonardo's painting demonstrates an interest in classical forms.

CUSTOMIZE INSTRUCTION FOR UNIVERSAL ACCESS

For Less Proficient Readers	For English Learners	For Advanced Readers
Students may have difficulty pronouncing some of the words in this section. List difficult words such as *Renaissance, Humanism, Rationalism*, and *Reformation* on the board. Review these words with students, pronouncing them clearly. Have students list and define the words as they encounter them in their reading.	Point out to students the words *Renaissance, Humanism, Rationalism*, and *Reformation*. As students read, have them write down the definitions of these words from the text. Then, have students work with an English-speaking partner to explain the terms in their own words, asking for clarification as needed.	Have students select one of the following terms and research the effect the movement had on society: *Renaissance, Humanism, Rationalism*, or *Reformation*. Have students create a poster explaining the movement and listing representative writings. Remind students to list their sources.

Background

Martin Luther

German peasants greeted Luther's ideas enthusiastically. They resented the fact that they had to pay so much tax money to the Church. They also began to voice other long-suppressed complaints they had against the Church and the noble landlords. In 1524, their resentment flamed into a full-scale rebellion, known as the Peasants' Revolt. Peasants demanded not only the right to read the Bible and choose their own ministers but also an end to serfdom. At first, Luther supported this revolt. He withdrew his support, however, when he heard accounts of peasants looting and destroying property. Moreover, he sided with the nobles who stamped out the revolt, and he rejected political revolution once and for all.

▶Critical Viewing

Possible response: The skeleton's expansive gestures may indicate the wide-reaching effects of the plague. In addition, the skeleton—astride coffins and with arrows in hand—appears almost victorious, suggesting the triumph of death over life.

The Reformation: From Debate to Bloodshed In the early 1500s, an obscure German professor of theology, Martin Luther, protested against the corruption of the church. His key ideas—that salvation depends on one's faith, rather than one's actions, and that the priesthood and church ritual are less important than the truths of the Bible—launched the movement called the Reformation. This movement gave birth to new Protestant denominations, whose name comes from the term *to protest*. Protestants dominated in Switzerland, northern Germany, parts of France, and eventually in England and Scotland. The Catholic Church, on the other hand, was strong in Spain, Italy, most of France, and southern Germany. Religious debates soon escalated into war, and in France the civil conflict led to years of bloodshed.

The Globe Explored, the Earth Displaced Not only were religious truths being questioned, but the face of the globe was changing with each new voyage of discovery. (See the map on page 667.) In 1492, for instance, Columbus sailed to the West Indies; and in 1519, Magellan began a voyage around the world.

The image of the universe itself was changing. According to older views, Earth was the center of the universe. The astronomer Copernicus (1473–1543), however, argued that Earth revolved around the sun.

Close-up on History

The Black Death

Between 1347 and 1351, a disease people called the Black Death, and which we know as the plague, ravaged Europe. It killed about one fourth of the population, perhaps 25 million people. Those afflicted with the disease developed fever and other symptoms, either swellings that turned into black spots or infected lungs together with weakness and loss of memory. Few recovered.

The plague was usually spread by fleas that lived on rodents—the rats that in fourteenth-century Europe were everywhere in the overcrowded and dirty cities and in the countryside as well. When a rat died, its fleas often migrated to a nearby person. To people of the time, however, it seemed a terrible mystery why some were spared and some perished.

Faced with this horrible and mysterious disease, people looked for someone to blame. Usually, outsiders of some kind—Arabs, lepers, or Jews—were chosen as scapegoats. Massacres of these groups only added to the sum of suffering.

Among the longer-lasting effects of the plague were a decrease in farmed land, an increase in wages for surviving workers, and—in northern Europe—a new obsession with death. Thomas Nashe, writing about a later outbreak of plague in England, expressed such a mood in his poem "Litany in Time of Plague": "Physic [the doctor] himself must fade, / all things to end are made."

▼ **Critical Viewing** This image is a detail from a picture depicting the effects of the Great Plague of London in 1665. What do the gestures of the skeleton indicate about the outbreak of the plague? Why? **[Infer]**

ENRICHMENT: Science

Humors

Medieval and Renaissance medical science had no way of understanding the bacilli that caused the plague. The best medical opinion held that the body was dominated by four different fluid "humors"—blood, phlegm, yellow bile, and black bile—and that each of these humors had a different physical and psychological effect.

In the healthy individual, these humors were all in balance, each of them canceling out the bad effects of the others. Sickness consisted of an excess of one humor over another. The primary cure for such an excess was bleeding the patient to get rid of the excessive humor. Tragically, this bleeding weakened patients, making them more likely to die.

Renaissance Europe and the World

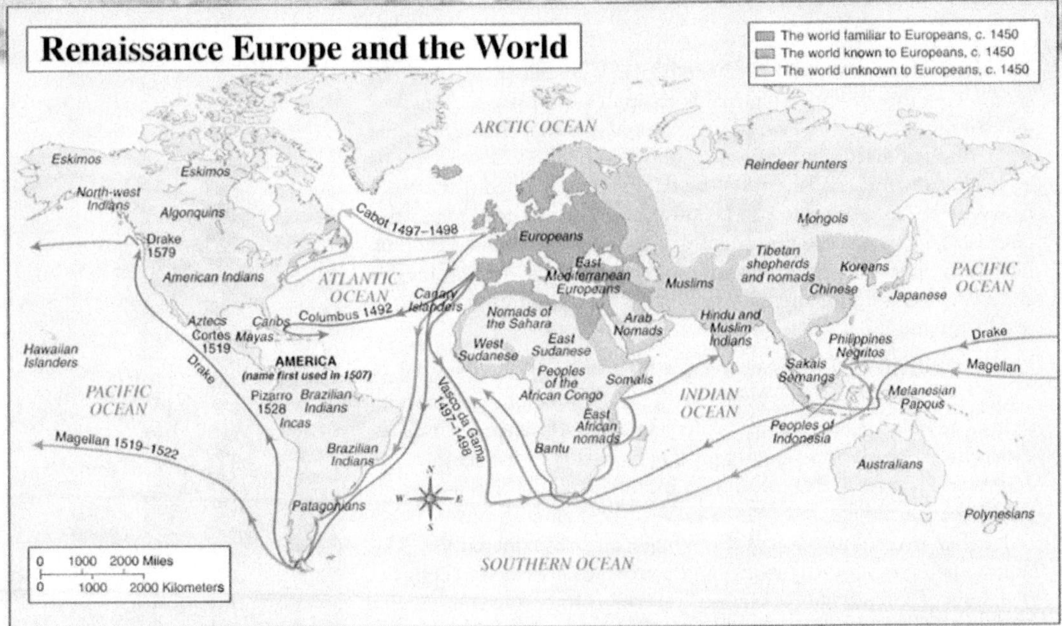

▲ **Critical Viewing** Compare and contrast the world familiar or known to Europeans in 1450 with the world unknown to them. **[Read a Map]**

The Age of Rationalism: From Lore to Law The Renaissance ushered in the Age of Rationalism, or the Enlightenment, an era that spanned the seventeenth and eighteenth centuries. During this time, reason was accepted as the greatest authority in art, thought, and politics. Philosophers challenged folk wisdom, attempting to replace traditional lore with formal laws based on the analysis of natural phenomena.

Rationalism and Nature: Mud Baths and Artful Foliage The application of reason to natural phenomena coincided with a renewed focus on nature throughout society. Notable painters, such as the French artist Jean-Antoine Watteau (wä tō´), for example, captured the beauty of outdoor scenes. In addition, people who could afford to do so made pilgrimages to spas and hot springs. There, nature could exert its healing influence as sufferers bathed in the waters and coated their limbs with medicinal mud. Nature could also delight the eye in formal gardens, whose symmetrical rows of plants showed that even foliage followed reason's laws.

The new interest in nature included human nature as well. The English Enlightenment philosopher John Locke described the human mind as a blank slate on which impressions are recorded. By denying the existence of prenatal, and therefore unlearned, ideas, Locke placed a stronger emphasis on experience and the satisfaction of natural curiosity.

Rationalism and Science: Falling Apples and Orbiting Planets In science, the delights of curiosity led to intellectual triumphs. Sir Isaac Newton, the greatest scientist of the age, discovered the laws of motion, the

Background
The New World

Renaissance Europeans did not discover the New World: they rediscovered it. Centuries before, the greatest sailors of their time, the Vikings, had ventured as far as North America. It is even misleading to assert that the Vikings discovered our continent, however. A prior claim belongs to the peoples who migrated to the Americas over land bridges from Asia thousands of years earlier. These were the ancestors of Native Americans.

▶Critical Viewing

Possible response: The world known to Europeans in 1450 was much smaller than the world unknown to them. The unknown world included all of the Western Hemisphere, much of Africa, and much of Asia.

Background
Sir Isaac Newton

Sir Isaac Newton (1642–1727) is considered one of the greatest scientists of all time. During the period between 1664 and 1666, this English scientist and mathematician discovered not only the law of gravity and the properties of white light, but he also developed calculus. (German mathematician Gottfried Leibniz is also credited with developing calculus.) For a short time, Newton worked at England's mint. He was warden of the mint in 1696 and master in 1699. In 1705, Queen Anne knighted Newton in recognition of his services in the mint and for his scientific accomplishments. He died in 1727 and is buried in Westminster Abbey, where England's most notable kings, queens, and subjects are buried.

ENRICHMENT: History Connection
Magellan's Expedition

On September 20, 1519, Portuguese navigator Ferdinand Magellan set sail on the first expedition around the world. On October 18, 1520, Magellan discovered a passage off the southern tip of South America that led from the Atlantic Ocean to another ocean. This passage was later named the Strait of Magellan.

Magellan named the new ocean the Pacific, which means "peaceful" because, in comparison with the stormy Atlantic Ocean, the Pacific appeared calm. Magellan's voyage proved that the world is round, not flat as many had previously believed. The voyage also led to further European expeditions to the Pacific.

▶ Critical Viewing

Possible response: This telescope shows that Galileo and his Renaissance colleagues took scientific observation seriously. The telescope's graceful, detailed construction suggests that scientific observation—including the tools employed for that observation—was viewed as an art.

Historical Background

Comprehension Check

1. In what ways was the Renaissance a time of insecurity?
   Answer: The Black Death immediately preceded this era. Fires were also common because most buildings were made of wood.
2. How did the power of kings change during this period?
   Answer: Kings became more powerful because of the general insecurity of the times.
3. What is Humanism?
   Answer: Humanism is the most important cultural movement of the Renaissance. It encourages a return to the study of the classics and the ideals they embodied.
4. What beliefs held by Martin Luther led to the Reformation?
   Answer: Martin Luther believed in salvation by faith and in the importance of following the truths of the Bible rather than the priesthood and church ritual.
5. How did the ideas of Rationalism affect politics?
   Answer: John Locke declared that all people have a right to life, liberty, and property, and that government is a contract between the government and the governed. These ideas undermined the idea of the divine right of kings.

law of gravitation, and the mathematical system called calculus. By showing that gravity governed both apples and planets, Newton seemed to prove that the world was rational and that the mind could make sense of matter.

While Newton was revealing the laws that controlled distant heavenly bodies, Antonie van Leeuwenhoek (lā′ vən ho͝ok′) used the microscope to study the miniature worlds that swarmed in a drop of rainwater. Also, Robert Boyle earned a reputation as the "father of chemistry," and Edward Jenner discovered a vaccination for the deadly disease smallpox.

The Industrial Revolution: Steam Flexes Its Muscles Across a wide span of human activities, people were employing reason not only to advance theory but also to regulate and enhance their daily existence. James Watt's significant improvements to the steam engine in 1765 helped revolutionize industrial production and paved the way for steam-powered railroad engines and ships.

Further, inventions such as the syringe, air pump, mercury thermometer, mainspring clock, and cotton gin provided effective new ways of solving old problems. The establishment of the Greenwich Observatory in England (1675) led to the systematic use of astronomy for such practical purposes as navigation and timekeeping.

Rationalism and Politics: Experiment and Explosion Like a chemistry experiment, the application of reason to political discontent led to an explosion called revolution. John Locke declared that government was a contract between ruler and ruled and that all people had natural rights to life, liberty, and property. These two "rational" ideas undermined the notion that kings had a divine right to rule. In America, these ideas added to the dissatisfaction of colonists with British repression, a dissatisfaction that erupted into the American Revolution (1776–1781). After the colonists won, the ideas of Locke and other Enlightenment thinkers influenced the framers of the American Constitution.

The French Revolution (1787–1799) was also inspired by Enlightenment ideas, especially those of Jean-Jacques Rousseau (zhän zhäk ro͞o sō′). This philosopher wrote in *The Social Contract* (1762), "Man was born free, but he is everywhere in chains." In France, however, sharper differences between the rich and the poor made the conflict more of a war between classes than the American Revolution had been. The result was a Reign of Terror in the early 1790s during which the king and many aristocrats were executed. By 1799, the revolution yielded to the dictatorial rule of Napoleon Bonaparte.

These two "experiments" in revolution indicated two different ways in which the Age of Rationalism would influence politics in the following centuries: on the one hand, the "reasonableness" of democratic institutions; on the other, the use of "reason" to justify revolt or even repression.

▲ Critical Viewing
This telescope belonged to Galileo, the Italian Renaissance scientist who pioneered astronomical studies. Galileo's observations helped dispel the belief that, in contrast to Earth, the heavens were a perfect, unchanging realm. What, if anything, does this telescope reveal about the attitudes of Galileo and his Renaissance colleagues toward scientific observation? Why? **[Infer]**

Critical Thinking

1. Compare the Renaissance and Rationalism. **[Compare and Contrast]**
   Possible response: The Renaissance was a period of great creativity and the rediscovery of classical art and literature. It also focused on exploration of the world and a new view of the relationship between the Earth and the sun. Rationalism emphasized

continued

continued from left column

reason as the greatest authority in art, thought, and politics.

2. How did the Renaissance and Humanism help lead to the Reformation? **[Support]**
   Possible response: The spread of literacy and the return to the classics in Italy led to the spread of Christian Humanism. This movement encouraged its followers to study early Christian sources, which led to an emphasis on the Bible as the most important source of information for believers.
3. Evaluate the impact Rationalism had on science. **[Evaluate]**
   Possible response: People began to analyze what happened in the natural world, eliminating superstitions and traditional beliefs. Science provided an avenue for that analysis and for organizing the information gathered from that analysis.

Literature

Renaissance Literature: A Branch of Rhetoric During the years of the Renaissance, literature was classified as a branch of rhetoric—the art of using spoken language to teach, give pleasure, and persuade. Literature was therefore closely related to the art of speechmaking, and it is not surprising that Renaissance writing is full of elaborate speeches. As a branch of rhetoric, literature also had the function of persuading readers to do good. Its purpose was to train the will by increasing our horror of evil and by strengthening our resolve to act well.

Machiavelli: Do Well, Not Good One major exception to literature in the service of the good is *The Prince*, a book of political philosophy by Niccolò Machiavelli (nē kô lô′ mak′ ē ə vel′ ē). While other theorists said that public deeds should reflect private morality, Machiavelli insisted that personal morality has no place in politics. Rulers are saved not by their goodness but by their strength, cunning, and ability. Because he took this approach, the adjective *Machiavellian* has come to mean "crafty and deceitful."

Literature and the Vernacular In the Middle Ages, literature in native languages, or the vernacular, had already begun to emerge. The Renaissance, however, saw a new emphasis on Italian, French, Spanish, German, Dutch, and English. In this period of linguistic patriotism, many of the great works of the period were written in the vernacular: in Italian, the sonnets of Petrarch, Boccaccio's prose tales in the *Decameron*, and Machiavelli's *The Prince*; in French, the poetry of Pierre de Ronsard (pē er′ də rōn sär′); and in Spanish, the novel *Don Quixote* by Miguel de Cervantes (mē gel′ *the ther* vän′ tes).

Latin, however, still served an important function. The Dutch scholar Erasmus, who translated the New Testament into Latin, Sir Thomas More, and many of the great Humanists wrote primarily in Latin.

Originality Through Imitation: "as the bees make honey" Rather than inventing new stories or forms, Renaissance authors often altered old

▼ Critical Viewing
Which details in this portrait of Lorenzo de' Medici, an Italian Renaissance merchant prince, suggest that he had the leadership qualities recommended by Machiavelli? Explain. **[Connect]**

Lorenzo il Magnifico, G. Vasari, Scala

CUSTOMIZE INSTRUCTION FOR UNIVERSAL ACCESS

For Special Needs Students	For Gifted/Talented Students
To help students keep information organized regarding important figures of this time period, have them make a chart. The chart should include several of the names mentioned in the Timeline and information about how each person contributed to the time period. Students can draw pictures or write their information, or they can cut and paste information from sources they may find on the Internet.	Have small groups do further research on some of the important figures from this time period, such as Antonie van Leeuwenhoek, Robert Boyle, James Watt, Niccolò Machiavelli, Galileo Galilei, or Sir Thomas More. Groups can present their findings as dramatic readings, interviews, skits, or videos.

Background

Art

Lorenzo il Magnifico (Lorenzo the Magnificent),
by Giorgio Vasari

Vasari (1511–1574) was an Italian painter and architect and the author of an important study of Italian Renaissance art. He received the patronage of the Medicis, an influential Florentine banking family.

Lorenzo the Magnificent (1449–1492) was one of the most prominent members of this family, which played a dominant role in Florence for more than three centuries. As a patron of the arts, Lorenzo supported such famous painters as Leonardo da Vinci, Michelangelo, and Botticelli.

Vasari has posed Lorenzo in profile so that his features adjoin those of a mask seen head-on. Another mask lies on a shelf. Perhaps these masks suggest the different roles Lorenzo was able to play in his astute mastery of politics.

Use the following items for discussion:

1. Vasari posed Lorenzo in profile, with a mask right next to his face. What is the effect of this positioning of face and mask?
   Answer: It appears that someone is looking over Lorenzo's shoulder.
2. Choose an important leader of our time, and describe how you would pose him or her for a portrait.
   Possible response: Hillary Clinton, dressed as a warrior, might be posed peeking through a curtain at the male-dominated Senate with a toy-filled children's nursery in the background.

▶Critical Viewing

Possible response: The subject's intense gaze indicates his strength and cunning. His relaxed posture suggests that he is confident and capable.

▶Critical Viewing

Possible response: The lines converge in the space behind the cross. This space appears to be the "deepest" point in the picture.

Background

Humanism

As the Humanist movement developed in Italy, its followers made an effort to master once more the Greek language and to recover Greek texts, from Homer and Sophocles to Plato and Thucydides. For the first time in a thousand years, the intellectual life of Western Europe was directly influenced by the works of Greek writers known before only by inaccurate summaries or inadequate quotations.

Listening to Music

Play for students European Renaissance Music: "Fa una canzone," Orazio Vecchi. Track 9, on **Prentice Hall Listening to Music: World Masterpieces,** as an example of the music from this time period.

Background

The Lute

The lute is a pear-shaped eleven-stringed instrument that was popular during the late Middle Ages and the Renaissance. During this period, the lute, as a symbol of harmony, was written about extensively and was featured in much literature.

Art in the Historical Context

The Invention of Perspective

You may assume that viewing a painting should always give you the illusion of looking into three-dimensional space. Yet it was Renaissance artists who invented perspective, the method for conveying this illusion. In the Middle Ages, paintings did not convey an accurate sense of depth. The Renaissance architect Brunelleschi (bro͞o′ nel les′ kē) devised the system by which lines of sight, perpendicular to the vertical plane of the picture, seem to converge at a vanishing point on the horizon within the picture.

In 1425, Masaccio (mä säch′ ē ō) became the first artist to use perspective in a fresco, or wall painting. His work *The Holy Trinity with the Virgin and St. John* shows Jesus being crucified in a space that is truly three-dimensional. (See this painting to the right.) From this time on, flat surfaces could open into imaginary but realistic worlds. The scholar Eugene F. Rice, Jr., compares the invention of perspective in art to the newly acquired historical perspective by which Renaissance thinkers viewed classical antiquity as a separate period in history. Medieval scholars, says Rice, could not make such a distinction.

The Trinity (detail), Masaccio, Nicolo Orsi Battaglini

▲ Critical Viewing Masaccio painted this picture on a church wall so that the platform supporting the cross is about at eye level. Where is the point at which all sight-lines going "into" the picture seem to converge? Explain. **[Analyze]**

forms to give them new meanings. Many authors, for example, wrote epics modeled in part on Virgil's *Aeneid*, odes modeled on the odes of Horace, and histories modeled on the work of Pliny and Tacitus. Yet just as the Romans copied and changed the forms of Greek literature to fit their own culture, so the writers of Renaissance Europe changed classical forms. Petrarch, for instance, asserted that "we must write just as the bees make honey, not keeping the flowers [works of other writers] but turning them into a sweetness all our own, blending many different flavors into one, which shall be unlike them all, and better."

The Classics in the Age of Reason Like Renaissance Humanists, Enlightenment writers admired ancient Greek and Roman literature. The English poet John Milton (1608–1674), for example, mastered Greek, Latin, and Hebrew, as well as several modern European languages. Not only was he widely read in the classics, but he used Homer's *Iliad* and *Odyssey* and Virgil's *Aeneid* as models for his own Christian epic, *Paradise Lost*.

The Classics Pay Alexander Pope (1688–1744), an English Neoclassical (or "new classical") poet, translated Homer's *Iliad* and *Odyssey* into elegant eighteenth-century verse. His efforts earned him the princely sum of £10,000 and assured his financial independence.

In France, Jean de La Fontaine (zhän′ də lä fōn ten′) based many of his fables in verse on the prose fables of the Greek author Aesop (ē′ səp). In addition, the grace and restraint of La Fontaine's style are qualities that mark his writing as classical in spirit.

ENRICHMENT: Literature Connection

The *Encyclopedia*

Denis Diderot, a French philosopher and scholar, helped create the first encyclopedia. Originally the *Encyclopedia* was meant to be only a translation of Ephraim Chambers's *Cyclopaedia,* but Diderot and his coeditor, Jean Le Rond d'Alembert, decided to use the *Encyclopedia* for more drastic purposes. Their focus was to spread knowledge and further the minds of humans, going against the limitations imposed by government and the church.

The project, begun in 1745 and completed in 1772, provided a rational look at all the arts and sciences. Because the editors believed in man's ability to reason, Rationalism drove their task. In spite of much interference, including Diderot's imprisonment for some of his views as well as the censorship of the French government, the work continued. The first volume was published in 1751. Despite opposition, Diderot published more than seventeen volumes by the time the work was completed in 1772.

Reason Rolls Up Its Sleeves Invention, the use of reason to solve life's problems, affected reading habits as well as navigation and industry. The creation of movable type by Johannes Gutenberg in the mid-1400s had made possible the printing and widespread distribution of the Bible for the first time, paving the way for the Protestants' emphasis on biblical authority. Then, in the 1600s, the new methods of printing helped foster the growth of newspapers. The first English daily newspaper appeared in 1702, and a few years later, the English authors Addison and Steele founded *The Tatler* and *The Spectator*. These periodicals served up humorous essays and witty commentaries on current topics. The growth of newspapers and periodicals created a new entity called Public Opinion.

The Encyclopedia Is Born In France, Denis Diderot (dē′ də rō′) brought to a public hungry for knowledge the world's first *encyclopedia*—a word based on the Greek for "instruction in the circle of arts and sciences." Because its commentary often clashed with accepted principles, this multivolume work suffered repeated censorship. Yet upon its completion in 1772 after long years of toil, the *Encyclopedia* became a major achievement of the Enlightenment.

Pascal and Voltaire: Reason's Differing Children Finally, it is worth remembering that in an age of reason, not every thinker reasoned in the same way. Blaise Pascal (blēz′ päs kal′), for example, was a French mathematician and physicist whose credentials as a rationalist were as good as anyone's. Yet in his book *Pensées* ("Thoughts"), he emphasizes human frailty and urges readers to approach God through feelings, not thought. His fellow Frenchman Voltaire (1694–1778), author of the novel *Candide*, disapproved of Pascal's concern with finding happiness in heaven. Voltaire stressed the use of reason to foster progress and happiness on Earth.

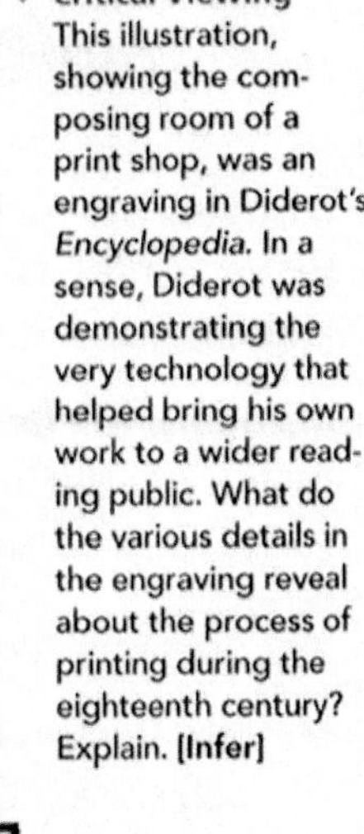

▼ **Critical Viewing** This illustration, showing the composing room of a print shop, was an engraving in Diderot's *Encyclopedia*. In a sense, Diderot was demonstrating the very technology that helped bring his own work to a wider reading public. What do the various details in the engraving reveal about the process of printing during the eighteenth century? Explain. **[Infer]**

▶**Critical Viewing**

Possible response: The work looks very labor intensive and time consuming, as the typesetting was done by hand and the printed sheets had to be hung to dry.

Literature of the Period

Comprehension Check

1. How was literature classified during the Renaissance?
   Answer: Literature was classified as a branch of rhetoric, the art of using spoken language to teach, give pleasure, and persuade.
2. What effect did the Renaissance have on the language of writing?
   Answer: As a result of the Renaissance, people placed new emphasis on writing in the vernacular.
3. On what was much Renaissance writing based?
   Answer: Much Renaissance writing was based on the classics, as writers modeled their works on Greek and Roman forms.
4. How did the printing press affect people during the Renaissance and the Age of Reason?
   Answer: The printing press made books and newspapers available to many more people, and people used the information from these sources to become better informed.
5. Who created the first encyclopedia?
   Answer: Denis Diderot created the first encyclopedia.

Critical Thinking

1. Why would Alexander Pope's translation of the *Iliad* and *Odyssey* be so valuable during the Age of Reason? **[Draw Conclusions]**
   Possible response: The focus on the classics demanded that they be accessible to the public. Translating them into elegant verse provided a high quality version in English.
2. Speculate about why the French government would be so opposed to an encyclopedia. **[Speculate]**
   Possible response: The control the church had over the people and the government on the basis of the divine right of kings made people who used reason

continued

continued from right column

to evaluate and solve problems seem dangerous. Consequently, the government and the church did not want the encyclopedia published.

3. Evaluate the impact that the printing press had on European and English literacy. **[Evaluate]**
   Possible response: The availability of printed material increased the level of literacy among the population. As more people became literate, they created more demand for information; consequently, newspapers and magazines became popular.

Laura • The White Doe • Spring • To Hélène • Roses

Lesson Objectives

1. **To analyze and respond to literary elements**
   - Literary Analysis: The Sonnet
   - Comparing Literary Works: Imagery
2. **To read, comprehend, analyze, and critique a sonnet**
   - Reading Strategy: Reading in Sentences
   - Reading Check Questions
   - Review and Assess Questions
   - Assessment Practice (ATE)
3. **To develop word analysis skills, fluency, and systematic vocabulary**
   - Vocabulary Development Lesson: Related Words: *languish*
4. **To understand and apply written and oral language conventions**
   - Spelling Strategy
   - Grammar and Style Lesson: Predicate Adjective
5. **To understand and apply appropriate writing and research strategies**
   - Writing Lesson: Journal Passage
   - Extension Activity: Informative Essay
6. **To understand and apply listening and speaking strategies**
   - Extension Activity: Dramatic Reading

10TH GRADE TEACHING A TENTH-GRADE COURSE

The literature in this section can be taught as part of a rich, balanced world literature course for tenth-grade students. For a full outline of such a course, see pp. T46–T48 in Volume 1 of this Teacher's Edition.

STEP-BY-STEP TEACHING GUIDE	PACING GUIDE
PRETEACH	
Motivate Students and Provide Background	
Use the Motivation activity (ATE p. 672)	5 min.
Read and discuss author and background features (SE pp. 672, 674, 678; ATE p. 672) A	5 min.
Introduce the Concepts	
Introduce the Literary Analysis and Reading Strategy (SE/ATE p. 673) A	15 min.
Pronounce the vocabulary words and read their definitions (SE p. 673)	5 min.
TEACH	
Monitor Comprehension	
Informally monitor comprehension by circulating while students read independently or in groups A	30 min.
Monitor students' comprehension with the Reading Check notes (SE/ATE p. 675)	as students read
Develop vocabulary with Vocabulary notes (SE pp. 676, 677, 678; ATE p. 680)	as students read
Develop Understanding	
Develop students' understanding of the sonnet with the Literary Analysis annotations (SE/ATE pp. 676, 678, 680; ATE pp. 675, 679) A	5 min.
Develop students' ability to read in sentences with the Reading Strategy annotations (SE/ATE pp. 675, 677)	5 min.
ASSESS	
Assess Mastery	
Assess students' mastery of the Reading Strategy and Literary Analysis concepts by having them answer the Review and Assess questions (SE/ATE p. 681)	15 min.
Use one or more of the print, software, or transparency Assessment Resources (ATE p. 683) A	up to 45 min.
EXTEND	
Apply Understanding	
Have students complete the Vocabulary Development Lesson and the Grammar and Style Lesson (SE p. 682) A	20 min.
Apply students' ability to incorporate details, using the Writing Lesson (SE/ATE p. 683) A	45 min.
Apply students' understanding of the selection, using one or more of the Extension Activities (SE p. 683)	20–90 min.

A ACCELERATED INSTRUCTION: Use the strategies and activities identified with an A.

10TH GRADE TEACHING TENTH-GRADE STUDENTS For support in teaching the selection(s) to tenth-grade students, see the Step-by-Step Teaching notes identified with the icon shown here.

UNIVERSAL ACCESS
- ● = Below-Level Students
- ▲ = On-Level Students
- ■ = Above-Level Students

Time and Resource Manager

Reading Level: Average, Challenging, Challenging, Challenging, Challenging
Average Number of Instructional Days: 3

RESOURCES		
PRINT	**TRANSPARENCIES**	**TECHNOLOGY**
• **Beyond Literature,** Cross-Curricular Connection: Music, p. 32 ▲ ■		• **Interest Grabber Video,** Tape 1, Unit 6, Segment 12 ● ■ ▲
• **Selection Support Workbook:** ● ▲ ■ Literary Analysis, p. 128 Reading Strategy, p. 127 Build Vocabulary, p. 125	• **Literary Analysis and Reading Transparencies,** pp. 63 and 64 ● ▲ ■	
		• **Listening to Literature** ● ▲ ■ Audiocassettes Audio CDs • **World Masterpieces iText CD-ROM**
• **Literary Analysis for Enrichment,** p. 32 ■	• **Fine Art Transparencies,** Art Transparency 6	
• **Formal Assessment:** Selection Test, pp. 114–116 ● ▲ ■ • **Open-Book Tests,** pp. 94–96 ● ▲ ■ • **Performance Assessment and Portfolio Management,** pp. 9, 28 • PRENTICE HALL ASSESSMENT SYSTEM ● ▲ ■	• PRENTICE HALL ASSESSMENT SYSTEM ● ▲ ■ **Skills Practice Answers and Explanations on Transparencies**	• **Test Bank Software** ● ▲ ■
• **Selection Support Workbook:** ● ▲ ■ Grammar and Style, p. 126 • **Writing and Grammar,** Diamond Level ● ▲ ■ • **Extension Activities,** p. 32 ● ▲ ■	• **Daily Language Practice Transparencies** ● ■ • **Writing Models and Graphic Organizers on Transparencies,** pp. 75–77 ● ▲ ■	• **Writing and Grammar iText CD-ROM** ● ▲ ■ ***Take It to the Net*** PHSchool.com

BLOCK SCHEDULING: Use one 90-minute class period to preteach the selections and have students read them. Use a second 90-minute class period to assess students' mastery of skills and have them complete one of the Extension Activities.

PRETEACH

Step-by-Step Teaching Guide for pp. 672–673

Motivation

Tell students that they will read several love poems from the fourteenth and sixteenth centuries. Ask them to use what they know about contemporary love poems and songs to predict the kinds of statements and images they might encounter in these poems. Discuss students' responses, and suggest that they keep their predictions in mind as they read each poem.

Interest Grabber Video

As an alternative, play "The Renaissance: Humanism" on Tape 1 to engage student interest.

❶ Background

More About the Authors

As an adolescent, Petrarch had already developed what he later described as "an unquenchable thirst for literature." His father, however, wanted him to be a lawyer and was afraid that literature would distract him from more profitable legal studies. According to a famous anecdote, Petrarch's father once hurled the boy's literary books into a fire. Petrarch pleaded with his father and finally persuaded him to retrieve copies of Cicero and Virgil from the flames.

During his long life, Pierre de Ronsard wrote sonnets to many different women. Of them, Helen was the last. Ronsard was already over fifty when he met her and wooed her, and while she seems to have enjoyed talking with him, she was not interested in his advances.

Geography Note

Draw students' attention to the map on this page. Point out Italy and France, the respective homes of Petrarch and Ronsard. Although Petrarch was from Italy and wrote much of his poetry in Italian, he first saw Laura, the subject of his love poetry, in the French city of Avignon.

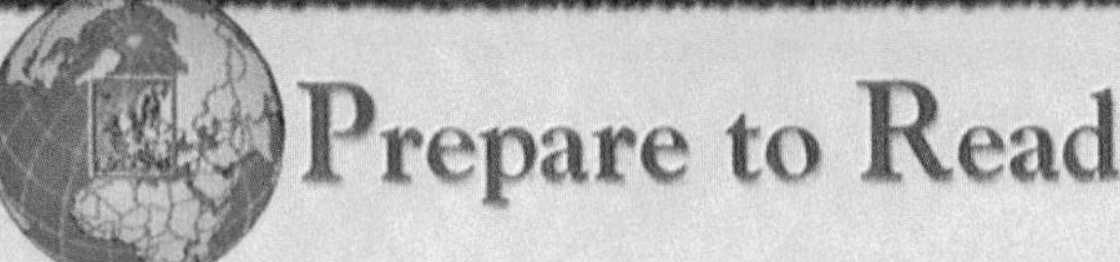

Prepare to Read

Laura ◆ The White Doe ◆ Spring ◆ To Hélène ◆ Roses ❶

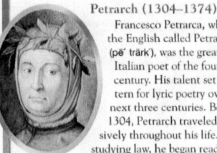

Petrarch (1304–1374)

Francesco Petrarca, whom the English called Petrarch (pē′ trärk′), was the greatest Italian poet of the fourteenth century. His talent set a pattern for lyric poetry over the next three centuries. Born in 1304, Petrarch traveled extensively throughout his life. While studying law, he began reading classical works and writing poetry. In 1327, in Avignon, France, he first saw the Laura whom he celebrates in his love poetry.

Literary Inspiration Little is known about the Laura who inspired Petrarch to write some of the world's greatest love poetry. She may have been Laura de Noyes, the wife of Hugues de Sade. Petrarch himself creates a picture of her as golden-haired, beautiful, and rich. Whoever she was, Petrarch loved her hopelessly for twenty years, and her beauty inspired the *Canzoniere* (kän tsô nyer′ ē), a vast collection of hundreds of love lyrics that Petrarch wrote and revised until the end of his life.

After his first trip to Rome in 1337, Petrarch composed two ambitious projects in Latin, leading a new Latin cultural flowering and prompting the city of Rome to crown him poet laureate. After years of travel through France and Italy, he finally completed his two major Italian works: the *Triumphs* and the *Canzoniere*.

Petrarch's prose—Latin letters, dialogues, and treatises—centers on himself, examining his own thoughts and emotions with extraordinary subtlety and depth, while his poetry exhaustively analyzes his uncertainties about love. It is this self-analysis and self-proclamation that made him a model for subsequent Renaissance writers.

Pierre de Ronsard (1524–1585)

Pierre de Ronsard (pē er′ də rōn sär′) was called the "Prince of Poets" by his contemporaries, and the title suited his range and ambition. He wrote verse of many different kinds—epics, satires, political commentaries, and the odes and sonnets for which he is famous.

A Poet's Career Ronsard was the youngest son of a noble French family. When illness ended his chances for a life of diplomatic service, he turned to writing. He was slow to publish his work, but in 1550 he released his first four books of odes, modeled on the works of the classical poets Pindar and Horace. The following year, he published a book of love poetry addressed largely to a woman named Cassandre. From then on, he worked prolifically, writing books of odes, hymns, and love poetry alike. Ronsard saw poetry as a kind of inspired discipline, with the poet acting as a receiver and transmitter of divine energies. At times, this vision could lead to self-importance and heavy-handedness, but it often resulted in exciting and vibrant work. His verse is marked by intensity, energy, and deep feelings for the natural world.

In 1572, he published the first four books of his *Franciade*, a patriotic epic about France that he never completed. His last major sequence of love poems, the *Sonnets pour Hélène*, appeared in 1578. Ronsard's devotion to his calling made him an untiring reviser of his poetry. During his later years, he revised his collected works over and over, preparing a seventh and final edition just before his death in 1585.

TEACHING RESOURCES

The following resources can be used to enrich or extend the instruction for pp. 672–673.

Motivation

Interest Grabber Video, Tape 1

Background

Beyond Literature, p. 32

Take It to the Net

Visit PHSchool.com for background on the authors.

Literary Analysis

Literary Analysis and Reading Transparencies, The Sonnet, p. 63

Reading

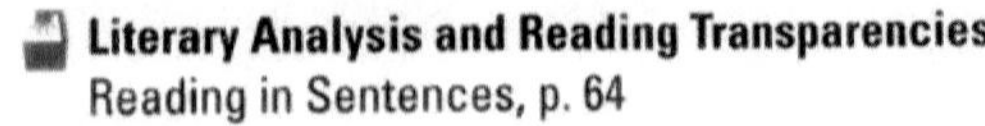

Literary Analysis and Reading Transparencies, Reading in Sentences, p. 64

Selection Support: Reading Strategy, p. 127

BLOCK SCHEDULING: Resources marked with this symbol provide varied instruction during 90-minute blocks.

Preview

Connecting to the Literature

Today, love is the subject of all genres of popular music, from country to rap to heavy metal. Despite the passage of centuries, the similarities you find between your favorite love songs and these poems may be striking.

❷ Literary Analysis

The Sonnet

Petrarch established the **sonnet** as the dominant form of lyric poetry during the Italian Renaissance. A sonnet is a fourteen-line poem focused on a single theme. The following characteristics are typical of the highly structured Petrarchan sonnet:

- It is divided into an eight-line *octave* followed by a six-line *sestet*.
- The octave usually has a rhyme scheme of *abba abba*.
- The sestet usually has one of three rhyme patterns: *cdecde*, *cdcdcd*, or *cdedce*.
- The octave often poses a question or makes a statement that is then brought to closure in the sestet.

Look for these characteristics as you read the poems in this grouping.

Comparing Literary Works

All five poems in this grouping are Petrarchan sonnets, and all share the subject of love, but the poets use a variety of images to describe their beloved. **Imagery** is descriptive language that re-creates sensory experiences. For example, Ronsard uses the image of a rose to describe his young beloved. Use a chart like the one shown to compare imagery in the five poems and to determine the overall effect the imagery produces.

Senses	Image
Touch	
Sight	
Hearing	
Smell	
Taste	
Overall Effect of the Images	

❸ Reading Strategy

Reading in Sentences

Reading in sentences will help you understand the meaning of a poem. Although these poems are written in sentences, the end of each sentence does not always coincide with the end of the poetic line. A sentence may extend for several lines or end in the middle of a line. To read in sentences, notice the punctuation. Do not pause or make a full stop at the end of a line unless there is a period, comma, colon, semicolon, or dash.

Vocabulary Development

sated (sāt′ ed) *v.* completely satisfied (p. 676)

exults (eg zults′) *v.* rejoices greatly (p. 677)

sojourn (sō′ jərn) *n.* visit (p. 677)

crone (krōn) *n.* very old woman (p. 678)

languishing (laŋ′ gwish iŋ) *v.* becoming weak (p. 680)

reposes (ri pōz′ əz) *v.* puts to rest (p. 680)

CUSTOMIZE INSTRUCTION FOR UNIVERSAL ACCESS

For Less Proficient Readers	For English Learners	For Advanced Readers
Before students read, have them skim the poems to find the punctuation marks that indicate the end of a thought. This process will help them look for closure beyond the end of each line. Then, have them read each stanza, paying close attention to all the punctuation marks.	Model reading the poems in lines and then reading the poems in sentences. Discuss with students how reading in sentences helps them understand the poem's meaning. Encourage them to use the Reading in Sentences transparency in **Literary Analysis and Reading Transparencies,** p. 64, as they read.	Tell students that poets sometimes use inverted word order for effect or to maintain the rhythm and rhyme of the lines. Point out line 12 in "The White Doe" as an example. Ask students why the translator might have chosen the word order in the line. Have students locate and discuss examples of inverted word order.

❷ Literary Analysis

The Sonnet

- Read aloud the Petrarchan sonnet characteristics listed on p. 673. Discuss and define each element.
- Tell students that the rhyme schemes of Petrarchan sonnets may vary slightly. Direct students to the poem "The White Doe" on p. 676. Have them read the last word of each line and write the rhyme scheme used in the poem. Then, have students discuss how the rhyme scheme varies from the usual rhyme scheme of a Petrarchan sonnet.
  Answer: The rhyme scheme is *abab, cddc, efe, fef.*
- Discuss the Comparing Literary Works graphic organizer on p. 673. Have students give an example of imagery that reflects each of the senses.
- Ask students to consider how imagery can create an overall effect in a work of literature. For example, ask what overall effect might be created by the image of an elderly woman sitting alone by a fire and reading old love letters. Discuss ways in which this image could appeal to the senses.
- Point out that in each of the following poems, the poet uses vivid imagery to create an overall effect regarding his beloved.

❸ Reading Strategy

Reading in Sentences

- Read aloud the Reading Strategy instruction on p. 673. Point out that sometimes the entire stanza of a poem can be a single sentence.
- Explain that different stops, such as commas or periods, indicate longer or shorter pauses.
- Demonstrate the appropriate pauses by reading one or more lines from one of the poems.

Vocabulary Development

- Pronounce each vocabulary word for students, and read the definitions as a class. Have students identify any words with which they are already familiar.

 **e-Teach**

Visit e-Teach at PHSchool.com for teachers' essays on how to teach, with questions and answers.

TEACH

Step-by-Step Teaching Guide for pp. 674–680

Teaching Tenth-Grade Students

10TH GRADE To help tenth-grade students understand "The White Doe," review the meaning of *allegory*. Have students explain how the speaker's experience with a doe could be an allegory for Petrarch and Laura.

❶ About the Selection

The earliest lyrics in Petrarch's *Canzoniere* were written in the 1320s. Although most of the collection concerns the poet's unrequited love for Laura, it also includes many sonnets on political and religious matters not directly related to Laura.

❷ Background

Art

detail from *Three Graces*, by Sandro Botticelli

The three Graces were ancient Greek goddesses representing beauty, charm, and grace. They were associated with the Muses, the goddesses of art, and with Venus.

In *Primavera*, the painting from which *Three Graces* is taken, the Graces dance beside Venus, who is decorously clothed and wears the cap of a married Florentine woman. The scene is set in an orange grove, and the oranges in the trees could symbolize the coat of arms of the Medicis.

Botticelli is famous for the linear rhythms of his paintings. The vertical lines of the background make an excellent backdrop for the rhythmic curves of the dancers.

Use the following question for discussion:

How does Botticelli convey the feeling of a dance?

Possible response: The graceful positions of the women's arms suggest movement.

❸ ▶ Critical Viewing

Possible response: The golden hair and the "angelic progress" in which the three goddesses move recall the imagery in "Laura."

from CANZONIERE ❶

Petrarch

Background

Petrarch's *Canzoniere* features 366 poems dedicated to his beloved Laura. Although Petrarch gives no clue about her real identity, many scholars agree that Laura was a married woman whom he supposedly first saw on April 6, 1327. Even though she apparently gave his affection no encouragement, at least so far as he describes in his poetry, Petrarch loved Laura all his life—even after her death in 1348.

The *Canzoniere* is divided into two parts—those poems to Laura "in life" and those to her "in death." Her importance in the sequence of poems lies in her effect on the poet, whose desire for her is never fulfilled. This "Petrarchan" scenario, in which the lovers' relationship is never fully realized, would become a standard model for generations to come.

❷

Three Graces (detail), Botticelli, Giraudon

◀ **Critical Viewing** ❸ Compare the visual details in this painting with the imagery in "Laura." **[Compare]**

TEACHING RESOURCES

The following resources can be used to enrich or extend the instruction for pp. 674–680.

Literary Analysis

Selection Support: Literary Analysis, p. 128

Reading

Selection Support Reading Strategy, p. 127; build Vocabulary, p. 125

Listening to Literature Audiocassettes ■

Listening to Literature Audio CDs ■

Extension

Fine Art Transparencies, Art Transparency 6 (Have students discuss ways in which both Leonardo's painting and Petrarch's poetry exemplify the celebration of the individual in the Renaissance.)

■ **BLOCK SCHEDULING:** Resources marked with this symbol provide varied instruction during 90-minute blocks.

Laura ❹

Petrarch

translated by Morris Bishop

She used to let her golden hair fly free
  For the wind to toy and tangle and molest;
  Her eyes were brighter than the radiant west.
  (Seldom they shine so now.) I used to see
Pity look out of those deep eyes on me.
  ("It was false pity," you would now protest.)
  I had love's tinder[1] heaped within my breast;
  What wonder that the flame burned furiously?
She did not walk in any mortal way,
  But with angelic progress; when she spoke,
  Unearthly voices sang in unison.
She seemed divine among the dreary folk
  Of earth. You say she is not so today?
  Well, though the bow's unbent,[2] the wound bleeds on.

❺ ❻

Reading Strategy
Reading in Sentences
In the octave, which lines require you to read on to the next line without stopping? Why?

❼ **✓Reading Check**
What emotion did Laura once feel for the speaker?

1. **tinder** (tin′ dər) *n.* dry, easily flammable material used for starting a fire.
2. **though the bow's unbent** though she is older and does not have her original beauty; the bow is Cupid's.

CUSTOMIZE INSTRUCTION FOR UNIVERSAL ACCESS

For Special Needs Students	For Advanced Readers
Because students tend to stop at the end of each line, model reading the poem aloud. Tell students to pay attention to how you read the lines according to punctuation. Remind them that poets often structure lines in a way that preserves the rhythm or rhyme of the poem; however, the poem must be read in sentences so thats its meaning is clear. Before students read, have them listen to the recordings on the **Listening to Literature Audiocassettes** or **Audio CDs.**	Point out that the translator of this poem is Morris Bishop. Encourage students to locate another translation of the poem in the school library, the local public library, or online. Have students read aloud the other translation in class, pointing out the differences between the translations they have located and Bishop's translation. Have them pay special attention to the way in which the sentences are structured and the places in each line where the punctuation falls.

❹ About the Selection

In "Laura," Petrarch reverently describes his idealized beloved, noting that although time has passed and she may not be as beautiful or kind as he has always imagined—and although she has never loved him—he loves her still.

❺ Reading Strategy

Reading in Sentences

- Review with students the Reading Strategy information on p. 673. Remind them that reading in sentences will help them understand a poem's meaning.
- Have a student read aloud the bracketed passage and carefully follow the punctuation. Then, ask the Reading Strategy question on p. 675: In the octave, which lines require you to read on to the next line without stopping? Why?
  Answer: Line 1 and the last four words of line 4 require readers to go on to the next line without stopping; because those lines have no end punctuation.
- Point out the midline stops in lines 10 and 13. Note that the stops force the reader to emphasize the balance of the lines.

❻ Literary Analysis

The Sonnet

- Review with students the characteristics on p. 673 of the Petrarchan sonnet. Have them clarify the difference between an *octave* and a *sestet.*
- After students have finished reading the poem, have them contrast the speaker's description of Laura in the octave with the description of her in the sestet.
  Possible response: In the octave, Laura is presented as a beautiful young woman; in the sestet, she is described as having been a divine creature who is now changed.
- Ask students: Do you think Petrarch presents a realistic portrait of Laura? Why or why not?
  Possible response: The picture is not realistic because Petrarch is blinded by love.

❼ ✓Reading Check

Answer: Laura used to pity the speaker.

8 About the Selection

"The White Doe" again explores the pain of Petrarch's love for Laura. The poem's speaker (Petrarch) finds the doe (Laura) so beautiful that he feels compelled to pursue her, though she wears a sign warning that she is not to be touched (she is unattainable). Focused on her, he falls into the stream (of love), and she vanishes.

9 Background

Allegory

One of the greatest allegories in literature is *The Divine Comedy* by Dante Alighieri (1265–1321). The allegory is divided into three sections: *Inferno, Purgatorio,* and *Paradiso*. The poem describes the allegorical journey of the poet Dante from darkness and ignorance—the *Inferno*—to the light of the divine vision of God—*Paradiso*.

10 Literary Analysis

The Sonnet and Imagery

- Remind students that imagery is descriptive language that appeals to the senses.
- Have students independently read the poem. Then, discuss how the impression of the speaker's beloved changes in the sestet.
- Have students respond to the Literary Analysis item on p. 676: Identify two visual images in the octave.
- Possible response: Two visual images are the white doe with golden antlers and a green grove of trees.

Monitor Progress Have students identify the characteristics of a Petrachan sonnet that are found in "The White Doe." Answer: "The White Doe" is divided into an eight-line octave and a six-line sestet; it presents the appearance of a deer and then brings it to closure by having the deer disappear.

Reteach As students read, have them use The Sonnet transparency in **Literary Analysis and Reading Transparencies,** p. 63.

8

The White Doe

Petrarch

translated by Anna Maria Armi

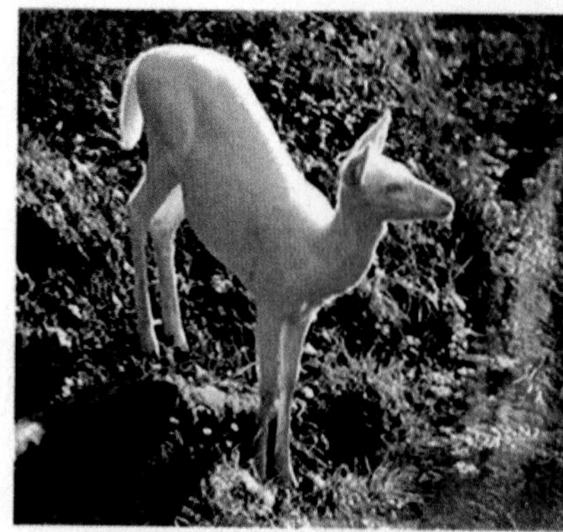

10

A pure-white doe in an emerald glade
Appeared to me, with two antlers of gold,
Between two streams, under a laurel's shade,
At sunrise, in the season's bitter cold.

Her sight was so suavely[1] merciless
That I left work to follow her at leisure,
Like the miser who looking for his treasure
Sweetens with that delight his bitterness.

Around her lovely neck "Do not touch me"
Was written with topaz[2] and diamond stone,
"My Caesar's will has been to make me free."

Already toward noon had climbed the sun,
My weary eyes were not sated to see,
When I fell in the stream and she was gone.
Zephyr[1] returns, and scatters everywhere

1. **suavely** (swäv′ lē) in a smoothly gracious manner.
2. **topaz** (tō′ paz) yellow gem.

Themes in

9 ***Allegory***

An **allegory** is an extended metaphor or a story line with both a literal and a symbolic level. The poem "The White Doe," for example, is an allegory in which the speaker sees his beloved in the form of "a pure-white doe in an emerald glade." Like his beloved Laura, Petrarch's doe is beautiful, pure, and untouchable. In the end, the doe disappears from sight, just as the real Laura disappears in death.

Italian poet Dante Alighieri wrote one of the most famous allegories, the *Divine Comedy,* in the early 1300s. In *Moby-Dick* (1851), American novelist Herman Melville incorporated allegorical elements concerning the human struggle against evil and fate. Although the message in Petrarch's "The White Doe" seems lighter in comparison with these other allegories, the fleeting nature of love remains a powerful theme despite the passage of centuries.

Literary Analysis
The Sonnet and Imagery Identify two visual images in the octave.

sated (sāt′ ed) *v.* completely satisfied

ENRICHMENT: Culture Connection

Greek and Roman Mythology

The poem "Spring" on p. 677 makes repeated references to Greek and Roman mythology. The ancient Greeks developed a mythology in which most gods represented a moral principle or an aspect of nature. For example, Aphrodite was the Greek goddess of love; Ares was the god of war. These early Greek gods—and the human heroes with whom they interacted—were interestingly flawed, much as humans are. For example, sometimes they tripped themselves on their own jealousy and self-involvement.

The Romans based their mythology on that of the Greeks. Thus, Jove, the chief god in Roman mythology, had the same characteristics as Zeus, the chief god in Greek mythology. Most of the other major Greek gods had mirror images in Roman mythology. Have interested students create "family trees" of the major Greek and Roman gods.

11

12

Spring

Petrarch

translated by Morris Bishop

13

New flowers and grass, and company does bring,
Procne and Philomel[2] in sweet despair,
And all the tender colors of the Spring.
Never were fields so glad, nor skies so fair;
And Jove exults in Venus'[3] prospering.
Love is in all the water, earth, and air,
And love possesses every living thing.
But to me only heavy sighs return
For her who carried in her little hand
My heart's key to her heavenly sojourn.
The birds sing loud above the flowering land;
Ladies are gracious now.—Where deserts burn
The beasts still prowl on the ungreening sand.

Reading Strategy
Reading in Sentences
In what way does the third sentence relate to the entire octave?

exults (eg zults′) *v.* rejoices greatly

sojourn (sō′ jʉrn) *n.* visit

1. **Zephyr** (zef′ ər) the west wind.
2. **Procne** (präk′ nē) **and Philomel** (fil′ ō mel′) In Greek mythology, Philomel was a princess of Athens who was raped by Tereus, husband of her sister Procne. The gods changed Philomel into a nightingale, Procne into a swallow, and Tereus into a hawk.
3. **Jove . . . Venus'** Jove was the chief god in Roman mythology, and Venus was the goddess of love.

Review and Assess

Thinking About the Selections

1. **Respond:** What do you imagine Petrarch's Laura was like?
2. **(a) Recall:** List four details about Laura that the speaker recalls in "Laura." **(b) Analyze:** What are the common qualities of the details that he remembers about her?
3. **(a) Recall:** In "The White Doe," which details of time does the speaker mention? **(b) Interpret:** What do you think these references to time mean? Explain.
4. **Interpret:** In "Spring," in what ways are the speaker's "heart keys" responsible for these contrasting images he sees?
5. **Relate:** Do you think the feelings or situations Petrarch describes in his poems are still relevant today? Why or why not?

CUSTOMIZE INSTRUCTION FOR UNIVERSAL ACCESS

For English Learners	For Gifted/Talented Students	For Advanced Readers
Ask volunteers to tell the class about traditions of love poetry in their cultures. Have students describe any common elements that the love poems from their culture have with Petrarch's love poems. For example, how is the beloved usually described? Is there a tradition of poems about lost love or unrequited love?	Encourage students to write their own modern love poems, using some of the elements found in Petrarch's sonnets. Students might choose to use a symbol to stand for the beloved, such as in "The White Doe"; they might describe their feelings of loss, such as in "Spring." Invite volunteers to read their poems to the class.	Point out that love poetry from around the world often has much in common. Have students use the library to locate other love poetry. You might suggest the work of American poet Edna St. Vincent Millay or British poets Sir Edmund Spenser or Elizabeth Barrett Browning. Invite students to read their poems to the class.

11 About the Selection

In "Spring," the speaker acknowledges the beauty and joy of spring, observing that love "possesses" every living thing. However, he notes that his own possession by love is a source of suffering.

12 Critical Thinking

Predict

- Have students consider how and why people often associate romantic love with the season of spring.
- Then, ask students to make predictions about the content of the poem "Spring."
  Possible response: "Spring" will compare spring's beauty with love's joy.

13 Reading Strategy

Reading in Sentences

- Have a volunteer read aloud the octave. Point out that except for line 8, each line ends with a pause or a stop.
- Have a volunteer read aloud the sestet. Note how the last three lines differ in structure and rhythm from the rest of the poem.
- Ask students the Reading Strategy question on p. 677: In what way does the third sentence relate to the entire octave?
  Answer: The sentence sums up the imagery and idea of the entire octave, which is that love is everywhere.

Answers for p. 677

Review and Assess

1. Possible response: Laura was a beautiful, elegant young woman.
2. **(a)** Laura had golden hair; deep, bright eyes; an angelic walk; and a beautiful voice. **(b)** The details portray her as beautiful.
3. **(a)** Time references include "at sunrise" and "toward noon." **(b)** Possible response: The time references symbolize stages in the speaker's love for Laura.
4. Possible response: The speaker sees that spring has returned love to the world; however, because his love is gone, he sees desolation.
5. Possible response: Petrarch's poems are still relevant because people still fall in love and suffer without it.

14 About the Translation

Help students understand the difference between a translation, such as Norman Shapiro's translation of "To Hélène," and an adaptation, such as that by William Butler Yeats, which follows:

"When You Are Old"

When you are old and gray and full of sleep,

And nodding by the fire, take down this book,

And slowly read, and dream of the soft look

Your eyes had once, and of their shadows deep;

How many loved your moments of glad grace,

And loved your beauty with love false or true,

But one man loved the pilgrim soul in you,

And loved the sorrows of your changing face;

And bending down beside the glowing bars,

Murmur, a little sadly, how Love fled

And paced upon the mountains overhead

And hid his face amid a crowd of stars.

Here are the elements that make Yeats's poem an adaptation rather than a translation:

- Unlike the original, it has twelve lines and is not a sonnet.
- It omits the "servant."
- It contains "eye" imagery that is not in the original.
- Unlike the original, it contrasts love of the soul with love of the body.
- It ends with the image of Love hiding "his face amid a crowd of stars," rather than with the injunction to "Gather life's roses. . . ."

14

To Hélène

Pierre de Ronsard

translated by Norman Shapiro

Background

The Latin phrase *carpe diem* means "seize the day"—in other words, make use of the present time and enjoy life while you can. This popular theme acknowledges the brevity and uncertainties of life and provides encouragement to grasp the good that the world has to offer. In "To Hélène," for example, the speaker urges his beloved to "Gather life's roses while still fresh they grow."

15

When you are very old, by candle's flame,
Spinning beside the fire, at end of day,
Singing my verse, admiring, you will say:
"When I was fair, Ronsard's muse I became."

Your servant then, some weary old beldame[1]—
Whoever she may be—nodding away,
Hearing "Ronsard," will shake off sleep, and pray
Your name be blessed, to live in deathless fame.

Buried, I shall a fleshless phantom be,
Hovering by the shadowed myrtle tree;
You, by the hearth, a pining crone, bent low,

Whose pride once scorned my love, much to your sorrow.
Heed me, live for today, wait not the morrow:
Gather life's roses while still fresh they grow.

Literary Analysis
The Sonnet What is the rhyme scheme of the octave?

crone (krōn) *n.* very old woman

1. **beldame** (bel´ dam) old woman.

ENRICHMENT: Literature Connection

Critical Evaluation of Ronsard

Literary critic Annette Elizabeth Armstrong has called Ronsard "The most eminent and prolific poet of the French Renaissance. . . . To the twentieth-century reader he is perhaps most appealing when celebrating his native countryside, reflecting on the brevity of youth and beauty, or voicing the various states of unrequited love. . . . He was a master of lyric themes and forms, and his poetry remains attractive to composers; some of his odes, such as 'Mignonne allons voir si la rose . . .' ["Mignonne, let us go to see if the rose . . ."], were set to music half a dozen times in the sixteenth century alone and have become as familiar to the general public in France as folk songs."

17 ▲ Critical Viewing Look closely at the expression on this woman's face. Compare and contrast her attitude with your perception of Hélène. **[Compare and Contrast]**

CUSTOMIZE INSTRUCTION FOR UNIVERSAL ACCESS

For Special Needs Students	For Less Proficient Readers	For Gifted/Talented Students
As students read Ronsard's poetry, have them study the word choices he makes to create a mood and explore a theme. Organize students in groups, and have each group identify specific words in "To Hélène" and "Roses" that are particularly effective at evoking each poem's mood and theme.	Point out that in "To Hélène," the speaker describes to the young woman what will happen if she does not accept and return his love. In "Roses," the speaker describes how his love dies when she is young and lovely. Discuss with students how this reflects the brevity and uncertainty of life.	Challenge students to write essays comparing and contrasting the treatment of the *carpe diem* theme in "To Hélène" and "Roses." Suggest that they consider the theme in terms of the particular effects of time on each of the women being addressed by the poems' speakers.

15 Literary Analysis

The Sonnet

- Tell students that "To Hélène," like the previous poems in this grouping, is a Petrarchan sonnet.
- Have students read the poem in its entirety. Then, ask them the Literary Analysis question on p. 678: What is the rhyme scheme of the octave?
  Answer: The rhyme scheme is *abba, abba*.
- Discuss with students how the poet uses images to appeal to the senses. Ask: What overall effect does the imagery in this poem produce?
  Possible responses: The imagery gives readers a sense of sadness, regret, loneliness, or anger.

16 Background

Art

***The Nurse Resigning to Ursula's Decision* (detail),** by Vittore Carpaccio

Born in Venice, Italy, Vittore Carpaccio (1460–1526) is best known for his cycles of narrative paintings. This detail, taken from *Arrival of the English Ambassadors at the Court of Maurus, King of Brittany,* is part of *The Legend of Saint Ursula* cycle. The cycle consists of nine large paintings that tell the story of St. Ursula, a fourth-century British princess who was martyred by the Huns, nomadic invaders of southeastern Europe. It was completed between 1490 and 1495.

Use the following question for discussion:

- What mood does the artist create?
  Possible response: The painting conveys a gloomy, serious mood.

17 ▶ Critical Viewing

Possible response: The woman appears to be solemn, sad, and deep in thought, which is how Hélène is perceived.

ASSESS

⓲ About the Selection

In "Roses," the speaker compares his young beloved and her early death to the image of a May rose that is just beginning to flower.

⓳ Literary Analysis

The Sonnet and Imagery

- Discuss the contrasting description of the sun's impact on the rose in lines 3 and 7. Note that in line 3, the sun at dawn is seen as gentle and benevolent; in line 7 it is "oppressive." Explain that the contrast anticipates the sestet in which the fair woman withers in her early death.
- Ask students the Literary Analysis question on p. 680: What image does the speaker use to describe his love?
  Answer: The speaker describes a rose just beginning to bloom.

⓴ Vocabulary Development

Related Words: *languish*

- Call students' attention to the word *languishing,* its definition, and its use in the poem.
- Write on the board the words *languish, languor,* and *languid.*
- Have students use dictionaries to define these words.

Answers for p. 680

Review and Assess

1. Possible response: Hélène might have been insulted by the poem.
2. **(a)** The speaker describes an old woman spinning by the fire while her servant dozes beside her. **(b)** Possible response: The speaker may have been hurt by the woman's rejection.
3. **(a)** Phrases include "the rose in her beautiful youth"; "dawn of her flower"; "softens her life with the shower"; "grace lingers in her leaf"; and "enchanting with fragrance the trees of her bower." **(b)** Nature has brought rain and an "oppressive" sun. **(c)** The speaker's beloved is delicate and becoming ill.
4. Possible response: Ronsard might write about a movie star or singer because these people are usually young and attractive.

Roses ⓲

Pierre de Ronsard

translated by Vernon Watkins

As one sees on the branch in the month of May the rose
In her beautiful youth, in the dawn of her flower,
When the break of day softens her life with the shower,
Make jealous the sky of the damask[1] bloom she shows: ⓳
Grace lingers in her leaf and love sleeping glows
Enchanting with fragrance the trees of her bower,
But, broken by the rain or the sun's oppressive power,
⓴ Languishing she dies, and all her petals throws.
Thus in thy first youth, in thy awakening fair
When thy beauty was honored by lips of Earth and Air,
Atropos[2] has killed thee and dust thy form reposes.
O take, take for obsequies[3] my tears, these poor showers,
This vase filled with milk, this basket strewn with flowers,
That in death as in life thy body may be roses.

Literary Analysis
The Sonnet and Imagery What image does the speaker use to describe his love?

languishing (laŋ´ gwish iŋ) *v.* becoming weak

reposes (ri pōz´ əz) *v.* puts to rest

1. **damask** (dam´ əsk) deep pink or rose.
2. **Atropos** (a´ trə päs) in Greek and Roman mythology, the goddess who cuts the thread of life.
3. **obsequies** (äb´ si kwēz) funeral rites or ceremonies.

Review and Assess

Thinking About the Selections

1. **Respond:** How do you think Hélène might have responded to the poem about her? Explain.
2. **(a) Recall:** Describe the scene that the speaker presents in the octave of "To Hélène." **(b) Speculate:** What feelings might have prompted the speaker's emotions in this poem? Explain.
3. **(a) Recall:** Which phrases in the first six lines of "Roses" describe the gentleness of nature? **(b) Interpret:** What change has nature brought in line seven? **(c) Draw Conclusions:** What does this suggest about the well-being of the speaker's beloved?
4. **Hypothesize:** If Ronsard were alive today, what famous person might the poet immortalize in verse? Why?

ASSESSMENT PRACTICE: Reading Comprehension

Evaluate and Make Judgments (For more practice, see Test Preparation Workshop, p. 32.)

The reading comprehension and vocabulary sections of standardized tests often require students to evaluate and make judgments about an author's word choice. Write the following lines of "Roses" on the board, along with the sample test item.

As one sees on the branch in the month of May the rose
In her beautiful youth, in the dawn of her flower . . .

In the poem, the word *dawn* means—

A the time of first daylight
B to begin to be understood
C first appearance
D the beginning of history

B is incorrect because it defines the use of the word as a verb. *A* and *D* do not fit with the rest of the phrase, "in her flower." Therefore, *C* is the best answer.

Review and Assess

Literary Analysis

The Sonnet

1. In what way does the two-part structure of the **sonnet** "Laura" reflect the speaker's recollections of Laura?
2. (a) What is the rhyme scheme of "The White Doe"? (b) In what ways does the pattern vary from that of a typical sonnet?
3. How do the poems "The White Doe" and "Roses" reflect the popular Petrarchan scenario in which the lovers' relationship will never be fully realized?

Comparing Literary Works

4. (a) List three **images** describing the doe in "The White Doe" that relate to images of Laura in "Laura." (b) Why might the speaker choose to associate Laura with a white doe?
5. (a) What is the condition of the speaker in "To Hélène"? (b) In what ways do the speaker and the object of his desire differ from those in the other poems in this grouping?
6. Which of Ronsard's two sonnets is most like Petrarch's three sonnets in imagery and feeling? Explain.

Reading Strategy

Reading in Sentences

7. (a) To analyze how **reading in sentences** affects the meaning in a poem, choose sentences from the poem "Spring" to complete the chart below. (b) Then, explain the meaning of each sentence and relate its meaning to the poem.

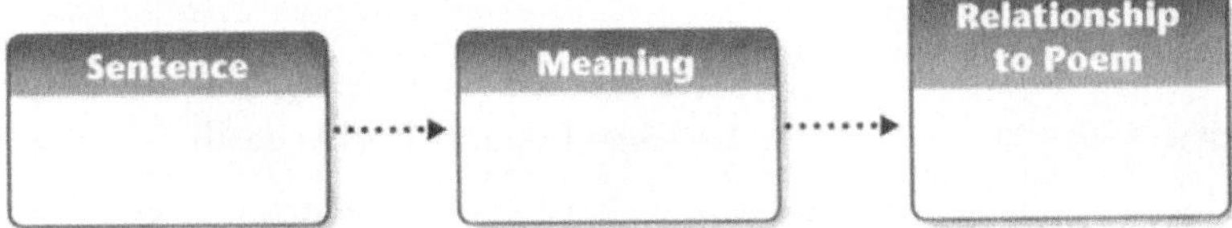

8. (a) How many complete sentences are in "The White Doe"? (b) How does the arrangement of complete sentences in the poem reflect the imagery?

Extend Understanding

9. **Psychology Connection:** Do you think that writing these poems comforted the poets or caused them more suffering? Explain.

Quick Review

A **sonnet** is a fourteen-line poem focused on a single theme. A sonnet has two parts and a structured rhyme scheme.

Imagery is descriptive language that re-creates sensory experiences.

To **read in sentences,** note the punctuation in a poem, and stop at the end of a line only if there is a period, comma, semicolon, colon, or dash.

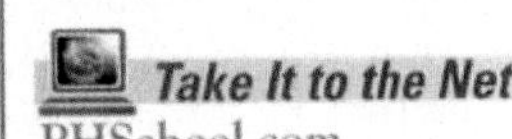

PHSchool.com

Take the interactive test online to check your understanding of these poems.

ENRICHMENT: Further Reading

Other Works by the Authors:

We strongly encourage you to review any selection before assigning or recommending it to students.

Works by Petrarch

Canzoniere

My Secret Book

Triumphs

Works by Pierre de Ronsard

Folies

Poems of Pierre de Ronsard, translated and edited by Nicholas Kilmer

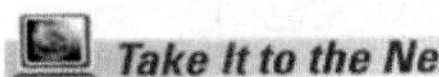

Visit PHSchool.com for more information on the authors.

Review and Assess

1. In the first section, the speaker remembers Laura the way she was when she was young and beautiful; in the second section, he is remembering her as older.
2. **(a)** The rhyme scheme is *abab, cddc, efe, fef.* **(b)** A typical sonnet has a rhyme scheme of *abba, abba, cde, cde.*
3. In "The White Doe," the woman is unattainable and unreachable; in "Roses," the woman dies in her youth.
4. **(a)** Three images are the woman's ethereal appearance as a white doe with golden antlers; her "suavely merciless" look of disdain; and the sign "Do not touch me" around her neck. **(b)** Possible response: The white doe is beautiful, pure, and rare.
5. **(a)** The speaker is scornful. **(b)** The speaker is frustrated and irritated with the woman; she is not distant and unattainable; she simply rejects him.
6. "Roses" is similar to Petrarch's sonnets; it describes a beautiful young woman who dies young, like Laura, especially in "Spring," and it describes how the speaker will continue to mourn, as does the speaker in "Laura."
7. Possible response: **Sentence:** "But to me only heavy sighs return / For her who carried in her little hand / My heart's key to her heavenly sojourn." **Meaning:** The sentence means that when spring returns, the speaker feels only sadness and sighs as he mourns for his beloved who has died and taken his heart with her. **Relationship to Poem:** The sentence is in contrast to the first part of the poem in which the speaker describes the beauty and love that returns with the season of spring.
8. **(a)** Four complete sentences are in "The White Doe." **(b)** Each sentence reflects a different image: the doe; the speaker leaving his work to follow her; the sign around her neck; and the speaker following her until her disappearance.
9. Possible response: Writing these poems might have comforted the poets because it helped them express their pain.

EXTEND

Answers for p. 682

❶ Vocabulary Development

Related Words: *languish*

1. languid
2. languor
3. languishing

Fluency: Sentence Completion

1. sated
2. reposes
3. crone
4. exults
5. languishing
6. sojourn

Spelling Strategy

1. *wi*
2. *oo*
3. *i*

❷ Grammar and Style

Practice

1. Her eyes were *brighter* than the sun. (modifies eyes)
2. She seemed *divine* among the dreary folk of earth. (modifies She)
3. I was *fair,* [and] Ronsard's muse I became. (modifies I)
4. Her sight was so . . . *merciless* that I left work to follow her at leisure. (modifies sight)
5. He seems *languid* since her death. (modifies He)

Writing Application

Possible response:

1. Her hair is *golden.* (modifies hair)
2. Her eyes seem *brighter* than the stars. (modifies eyes)
3. Her voice sounds *musical,* like angels singing. (modifies voice)
4. She is *lovelier* than an angel. (modifies She)

10TH GRADE For support in teaching the Grammar and Style Lesson to tenth graders, use **Writing and Grammar,** Platinum Level, Chapter 19, Section 4.

Integrate Language Skills

❶ Vocabulary Development Lesson

Related Words: *languish*

The word *languish* means "to become weak," or "to fail in vitality and health." Other words related to *languish* include the following:

languishing (participle and verb form): "becoming weak"

languor (noun): "the feeling of being weak"

languid (adjective): "weak; without energy or vitality"

Complete each of the following sentences with one of the related words listed above.

1. The deep sadness he felt at her death left him feeling _____.
2. His _____ prevents him from working on his poetry.
3. She is _____ and very near death.

Fluency: Sentence Completion

Fill in the blanks below with the correct word from the vocabulary list on page 673.

1. He felt _____ after the great feast.
2. She _____ upon the satin pillows.
3. The old _____ sat knitting by the fire.
4. He _____ in knowing that she loves him.
5. He is _____ still, though the worst of his illness has passed.
6. A short _____ restored his spirits.

Spelling Strategy

The letters *ui* can represent several sounds: long *i* as in *guide;* short *i* as in *biscuit; oo* as in *fruit;* and *wi* as in *languish.* Indicate which sound is found in each of these words.

1. distinguish 2. suit 3. circuit

❷ Grammar and Style Lesson

Predicate Adjective

A **predicate adjective** appears only with a linking verb and describes the subject of a sentence. Common linking verbs include *is, am, are, was, were, sound, taste, appear, feel, look,* and *seem.*

Ladies are *gracious* now. (modifies Ladies)

Practice Underline the subject in each item below, and draw an arrow from the predicate adjective to the word it modifies.

1. Her eyes were brighter than the sun.
2. She seemed divine among the dreary folk of earth.
3. I was fair, [and] Ronsard's muse I became.
4. Her sight was so . . . merciless that I left work to follow her at leisure.
5. He seems languid since her death.

Writing Application Write four sentences describing a great beauty. In each sentence, underline the subject and draw an arrow from the predicate adjective to the word it modifies. Note that action verbs do not take predicate adjectives.

WG Prentice Hall Writing and Grammar Connection: Diamond Level, Chapter 18, Section 3

TEACHING RESOURCES

The following resources can be used to enrich or extend the instruction for pp. 682–683.

Vocabulary

- **Selection Support:** Build Vocabulary, p. 125
- **Vocabulary and Spelling Practice Book** (Use this booklet for skills instruction.)

Grammar

- **Selection Support:** Grammar and Style, p. 126
- **Writing and Grammar,** Diamond Level, p. 426
- **Daily Language Practice Transparencies**

Writing

- **Performance Assess. and Portfolio Mgmt.,** p. 9
- **Writing and Grammar,** Diamond Level, p. 58
- **Writing and Grammar iText CD-ROM**
- **Writing Models and Graphic Organizers on Transparencies,** pp. 75–77

Listening and Speaking

- **Performance Assess. and Portfolio Mgmt.,** p. 28

BLOCK SCHEDULING: Resources marked with this symbol provide varied instruction during 90-minute blocks.

❸ Writing Lesson

Journal Passage

For Petrarch and Ronsard, writing poems was much like keeping a journal—the poetry preserved the thoughts and feelings each poet experienced. Write a journal passage responding to any of these poems, using the voice of the love object in the poem. Use details from the poem to establish the personality of the beloved.

Prewriting Begin by choosing one of the poems. Then, list details that reveal both the relationship the speaker shared with his beloved and how the love object might respond to the poem.

Drafting In the voice of the beloved, state your feelings about the poem and the poet. Add details from your list along with fictitious but logical encounters or conversations between the love object and the speaker.

Model: Incorporating Details

When I was young, I inspired every great poet I knew. Even now, *though I am old,* I am considered a great beauty.

Adding details makes writing more interesting and provides a more complete picture.

Revising Check your finished draft against the details in your list. Replace any vague words or phrases with concrete details that reflect the voice of the beloved.

WG Prentice Hall Writing and Grammar Connection: Diamond Level, Chapter 4, Section 3

❹ Extension Activities

Listening and Speaking Working with a partner, perform a **dramatic reading** of "Laura" and "To Hélène." As you rehearse, consider these tips:

- Adjust your voice to reflect the speaker of each poem.
- Consider the emotions expressed in the poem, and try to reflect them in your voice.
- Remember to read in complete sentences.

Perform your reading for your class, and invite questions from the audience. **[Group Activity]**

Research and Technology Compose an **informative essay** on William Butler Yeats's poem "When You Are Old" using your library's Internet or electronic sources. Address the relationship between this poem and Ronsard's. Be sure to cite your sources and include Yeats's poem.

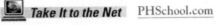

Take It to the Net PHSchool.com

Go online for an additional research activity using the Internet.

❸ Writing Lesson

- Read aloud the Writing Lesson instruction on p. 683. Have students work in small groups to reread each of the poems and discuss the relationship between the speaker and his beloved.
- Encourage students to visualize the love object of the poem they select and to imagine themselves as that person.
- Have students use the Herringbone Organizer in **Writing Models and Graphic Organizers on Transparencies,** pp. 75–77, to organize their passage details.
- Use the Narration: Autobiographical Narrative rubric in **Performance Assessment and Portfolio Management,** p. 9, to evaluate students' journal passages.

10TH GRADE For support in working through the Writing Lesson with tenth graders, use **Writing and Grammar,** Platinum Level, Chapter 4, Section 3.

❹ Listening and Speaking

- Have students independently read the Listening and Speaking instruction on p. 683. Explain that a dramatic reading will help them understand and interpret a poem's meaning.
- Students may wish to record their readings and listen to their own performances before presenting the readings to the class.
- Use the Speaking: Delivering a Narrative Presentation rubric in **Performance Assessment and Portfolio Management,** p. 28, to evaluate students' speeches.

CUSTOMIZE INSTRUCTION For Universal Access

To address different learning styles, use the following activities suggested in the **Extension Activities** booklet, p. 32:

- For Verbal/Linguistic and Interpersonal Learners, use Activity 5.
- For Visual/Spatial Learners, use Activity 6.
- For Musical/Rhythmic Learners, use Activity 7.

ASSESSMENT RESOURCES

The following resources can be used to assess students' knowledge and skills.

Selection Assessment

Formal Assessment, pp. 114–116

Open-Book Tests, pp. 94–96

Test Bank Software

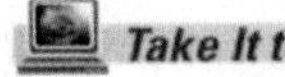

Take It to the Net

Visit PHSchool.com for self-tests on the selections.

Writing Rubric

Performance Assess. and Portfolio Mgmt., p. 9

Listening and Speaking Rubric

Performance Assess. and Portfolio Mgmt., p. 28

For additional diagnostics and remediation for skills covered in this grouping, use materials from the Prentice Hall Assessment System.

Lesson Objectives

1. To understand the connection between Petrarchan sonnets and Shakespearean sonnets
2. To understand how form affects meaning

Connections

Although the Petrarchan sonnet is slightly different from the Shakespearean sonnet in form and style, both types of sonnets address the emotions that are experienced by a speaker who is in love. Have students reread the Petrarchan sonnets on pp. 675–677 after they have read the Shakespearean sonnets. What similarities and differences do students notice between the two types of sonnets?

Love and the Sonnet

- Explain to students that the first sonnets were written, scholars believe, in the thirteenth century in Italy. About a hundred years later, Petrarch wrote so many beautiful sonnets that the Italian form (an octave followed by a sestet) was named after him.
- Explain the unique rhyme scheme of Petrarchan sonnets. Often the octave rhymes *abbaabba,* and the sestet rhymes *cdecde* or uses some combination of *cd* rhymes.
- Then, explain the rhyme scheme of the Shakespearean sonnet. Each of the three quatrains has a rhyme pattern of its own, followed by a rhymed couplet. A typical rhyme scheme would be *abab cdcd efef gg.*
- Point out that in a Shakespearean sonnet, each of the three quatrains usually explores a different variation of the main theme. The sonnet is usually not printed with the stanzas divided, but a reader can see distinct ideas in each.

CONNECTIONS
Literature Past and Present
Love and the Sonnet

The fourteen-line poem called the *sonnet* has traditionally been a poem of love. Petrarch, whose sonnets to Laura set the thematic course of the genre, uses an octave (eight lines) and a sestet (six lines) to give his poems a kind of statement/response structure: The octave often takes a position that the sestet contradicts or modifies. The Petrarchan sonnets in this unit, selected from a sonnet sequence charting the pangs of a speaker's unfulfilled love for an idealized lady, provide an interesting take on the ups and downs of someone in love.

Elizabethan Variations Shakespeare's sonnets 29 and 116, presented here, have also been selected from a sonnet sequence. Shakespeare uses a variation of Petrarch's sonnet form: three quatrains (four lines each) and a couplet (two lines), with the couplet often a dramatic statement that resolves, restates, or redefines the central problem of the sonnet. Like Petrarch, Shakespeare creates a speaker who addresses his beloved. Both speaker and beloved, however, are less ideal and more real than the lovers in Petrarch's sonnets.

Though Petrarch wrote in fourteenth-century Italy and Shakespeare in sixteenth- and seventeenth-century England, the pain and exultation, longing and joy, despair and hope in their poetry will be familiar to anyone who has ever been in love.

Sonnet 29
William Shakespeare

When in disgrace with fortune and men's eyes,
I all alone beweep my outcast state,
And trouble deaf heaven with my bootless[1] cries,
And look upon myself and curse my fate,
Wishing me like to one more rich in hope,
Featured like him, like him with friends possessed,
Desiring this man's art, and that man's scope,
With what I most enjoy contented least.
Yet in these thoughts myself almost despising,
Haply[2] I think on thee, and then my state,
Like to the lark at break of day arising
From sullen earth, sings hymns at heaven's gate;
    For thy sweet love remembered such wealth brings
    That then I scorn to change my state with kings.

scope *n.* range of perception or understanding

sullen *adj.* gloomy; dismal

1. **bootless** *adj.* futile.
2. **haply** *adv.* by chance.

ENRICHMENT: History Connection
The Beloved in Shakespeare's Sonnets

Debate has long raged over the identity of the beloved in Shakespeare's sonnets. Whereas the traditional sonnet sequence is addressed to a single love object, some of Shakespeare's sonnets are clearly addressed to a Young Man and others are addressed to the famous "Dark Lady." Still other sonnets seem to be addressed to neither the Young Man nor the Lady, but to time, love itself, or the speaker's own soul. Various scholars have suggested that the Young Man was either the Earl of Pembroke or the Earl of Southampton, and the Dark Lady was one of the queen's maids of honor.

Sonnet 116

William Shakespeare

The Storm at Sea, Pieter Bruegel the Elder

Let me not to the marriage of true minds
Admit impediments. Love is not love
Which alters when it alteration finds,
Or bends with the remover to remove.
O, no! It is an ever-fixèd mark
That looks on tempests and is never shaken;
It is the star to every wandering bark,[1]
Whose worth's unknown, although his height be taken.[2]
Love's not Time's fool, though rosy lips and cheeks
Within his bending sickle's compass[3] come;
Love alters not with his brief hours and weeks,
But bears it out even to the edge of doom.[4]
If this be error, and upon me proved,
I never writ, nor no man ever loved.

▲ **Critical Viewing**
What connections do you see between this painting and "Sonnet 116"? **[Connect]**

impediments *n.* obstacles

alters *v.* changes

1. **star . . . bark** the star that guides every wandering ship: the North Star.
2. **Whose . . . be taken** whose value is unmeasurable, although navigators measure its height in the sky.
3. **compass** *n.* range; scope.
4. **doom** Judgment Day.

William Shakespeare

(1564–1616)

William Shakespeare was born in the country town of Stratford-on-Avon, England, and probably attended the town's free grammar school. Well known as an actor and a playwright, Shakespeare was part owner of a London theater, the Globe, where many of his plays were performed. From 1592 to 1594, London's theaters were closed because of the plague—this period may have provided an opportunity for Shakespeare to write some of his 154 sonnets.

Connecting Literature Past and Present

1. Compare the speaker's attitude toward his beloved in "Laura" with the speaker's attitude in "Sonnet 29." (a) Which speaker is more optimistic? (b) Is the central figure in each poem the speaker or the beloved? (c) Indicate the specific lines that provide that information.
2. (a) In what way is the speaker's perspective on the inevitable changes of time in "Sonnet 116" similar to the perspective of the speaker in "Laura"? (b) In what way are the perspectives different?
3. Of the three poems by Petrarch and the two by Shakespeare, which one is your favorite? Explain.

Background

Art

The Storm at Sea, by Pieter Bruegel the Elder

Bruegel (c. 1525–1569) is generally considered the greatest of the sixteenth-century Flemish painters. Known for his narrative style, Bruegel used vivid landscapes and charming figures to depict myths, biblical episodes, religious allegories, proverbs, and peasant life.

His later works, such as the one shown here, are marked by a simplification of figures and an exploration of mood through landscapes. The unfinished painting *The Storm at Sea* may have been Bruegel's final work.

Use the following questions to stimulate discussion.

What is the mood of this painting? What details in the painting create this mood?
Possible response: The roiling clouds and wind-tossed sea, as well as the dark, opaque colors and heavy brush strokes, create a foreboding and frightening tone. The sky and sea, a unified force, threaten to envelop the small ships in its path.

▶ Critical Viewing

Possible response: With its depiction of ships attempting to hold steady against the turmoil of a storm, this painting correlates to lines 5–6 of the sonnet, in which love is compared to an "ever-fixèd mark / That looks on tempests and is never shaken."

Answers

Connecting Literature Past and Present

1. **(a)** The speaker in "Sonnet 29" seems more optimistic than the speaker in "Laura." Despite his suffering and jealousy, he realizes that love brings him "such wealth." However, in "Laura," the speaker feels great pain at the thought of his unrequited love. **(b)** In "Sonnet 29," the central figure is the speaker. In "Laura," the central figure is the beloved. **(c)** In "Sonnet 29," the speaker refers to himself and his suffering in lines 1–9 and in line 14. In "Laura," the speaker refers to the beloved in lines 1–5 and 9–13.

continued

continued from right column

2. **(a)** Like the speaker in "Sonnet 116," the speaker in "Laura" acknowledges the inevitable ravages of time. The beloved in "Laura" is not as beautiful, kind, or divine as she once was—as Shakespeare would say, her rosy lips and cheeks have come "within [time's] bending sickle's compass." **(b)** Both speakers regard love as steadfast despite the inevitable changes of time, but the speaker in "Laura" sees this permanence as a source of pain; the speaker in "Sonnet 116" sees this permanence as a source of comfort.
3. Possible response: Shakespeare's "Sonnet 116" eloquently defines true love in contrast to the many emotions that often masquerade as love in one's life.

from the Decameron

Lesson Objectives

1. **To analyze and respond to literary elements**
   - Literary Analysis: Novella
   - Connecting Literary Elements: Frame
2. **To read, comprehend, analyze, and critique a novella**
   - Reading Strategy: Identifying With Characters
   - Reading Check Questions
   - Review and Assess Questions
   - Assessment Practice (ATE)
3. **To develop word analysis skills, fluency, and systematic vocabulary**
   - Vocabulary Development Lesson: Latin Suffix *-ence*
4. **To understand and apply written and oral language conventions**
   - Spelling Strategy
   - Grammar and Style Lesson: Varying Sentence Beginnings
5. **To understand and apply appropriate writing and research strategies**
   - Writing Lesson: Literary Analysis
   - Extension Activity: Classroom Display
6. **To understand and apply listening and speaking strategies**
   - Extension Activity: Storytelling Circle

10TH GRADE TEACHING TENTH-GRADE COURSE

The literature in this section can be taught as part of a rich, balanced world literature course for tenth-grade students. For a full outline of such a course, see pp. T46–T48 in Volume 1 of this Teacher's Edition.

STEP-BY-STEP TEACHING GUIDE	PACING GUIDE
PRETEACH	
Motivate Students and Provide Background	
Use the Motivation activity (ATE p. 686)	5 min.
Read and discuss author and background features (SE pp. 686, 688; ATE p. 686) [A]	5 min.
Introduce the Concepts	
Introduce the Literary Analysis and Reading Strategy concepts (SE/ATE p. 687) [A]	15 min.
Pronounce the vocabulary words and read their definitions (SE p. 687)	5 min.
TEACH	
Monitor Comprehension	
Informally monitor comprehension by circulating while students read [A]	35 min.
Monitor students' comprehension with the Reading Check notes (SE/ATE pp. 689, 691, 693)	as students read
Develop vocabulary with Vocabulary notes (SE pp. 689, 692, 693; ATE p. 692)	as students read
Develop Understanding	
Develop students' understanding of the novella with the Literary Analysis annotations (SE/ATE pp. 688, 689, 691, 692, 693) [A]	5 min.
Develop students' ability to restate for understanding, using the Reading Strategy annotations (SE p. 690; ATE pp. 689, 690, 691)	5 min.
ASSESS	
Assess Mastery	
Assess students' mastery of the Reading Strategy and Literary Analysis concepts by having them answer the Review and Assess questions (SE/ATE p. 695)	15 min.
Use one or more of the print, software, or transparency Assessment Resources (ATE p. 697) [A]	up to 45 min.
EXTEND	
Apply Understanding	
Have students complete the Vocabulary Development Lesson and the Grammar and Style Lesson (SE p. 696) [A]	20 min.
Apply students' ability to use relevant citations, using the Writing Lesson (SE/ATE p. 697) [A]	45 min.
Apply students' understanding of the selection, using one or more of the Extension Activities (SE p. 697)	20–90 min.

[A] ACCELERATED INSTRUCTION: Use the strategies and activities identified with an [A].

10TH GRADE TEACHING TENTH-GRADE STUDENTS For support in teaching tenth graders, see the Step-By-Step Teaching notes identified with this icon.

UNIVERSAL ACCESS

- ● = Below-Level Students
- ▲ = On-Level Students
- ■ = Above-Level Students

Time and Resource Manager

Reading Level: Challenging
Average Number of Instructional Days: 3

RESOURCES		
PRINT	**TRANSPARENCIES**	**TECHNOLOGY**
• **Beyond Literature,** Community Connection: Preventing Epidemics, p. 33 ▲ ■		• **Interest Grabber Video,** Tape 1, Unit 6, Segment 13 ● ▲ ■
• **Selection Support Workbook:** ● ▲ ■ Literary Analysis, p. 132 Reading Strategy, p. 131 Build Vocabulary, p. 129	• **Literary Analysis and Reading Transparencies,** pp. 65 and 66 ● ▲ ■	
• **Reader's Companion** ● • **Adapted Reader's Companion** ●		• **Listening to Literature** ● ▲ ■ Audiocassettes Audio CDs • **Reader's Companion Audio Program** ● • **Reader's Companion Adapted and English Learner's Version Audio Program** ● ▲
• **English Learner's Companion** ● ▲ • **Literary Analysis for Enrichment,** p. 33 ■		• **World Masterpieces iText CD-ROM**
• **Formal Assessment:** Selection Test, pp. 117–119 ● ▲ ■ • **Open-Book Tests,** pp. 97–99 ● ▲ ■ • **Performance Assessment and Portfolio Management,** pp. 13, 16 ● ▲ ■ • PRENTICE HALL ASSESSMENT SYSTEM ● ▲ ■	• PRENTICE HALL ASSESSMENT SYSTEM ● ▲ ■ **Skills Practice Answers and Explanations on Transparencies**	• **Test Bank Software** ● ▲ ■
• **Selection Support Workbook:** ● ▲ ■ Grammar and Style, p. 130 • **Writing and Grammar,** Diamond Level ● ▲ ■ • **Extension Activities,** p. 33 ● ▲ ■	• **Daily Language Practice Transparencies** ● ■ • **Writing Models and Graphic Organizers on Transparencies,** pp. 53–59, 75–77 ● ▲ ■	• **Writing and Grammar iText CD-ROM** ● ▲ ■ ***Take It to the Net*** PHSchool.com

BLOCK SCHEDULING: Use one 90-minute class period to preteach the selections and have students read them. Use a second 90-minute class period to assess students' mastery of skills and have them complete one of the Extension Activities.

PRETEACH

Step-by-Step Teaching Guide for pp. 686–687

Motivation

Ask students whether they own a particular object or pet that has great value to them. Have them consider under what circumstances, if any, they might part with it. Use the phrase "not for love or money" in the discussion to underscore the attachment people sometimes have for an object or animal. Tell students that they are about to read a story that deals with such a strong attachment.

Interest Grabber Video

As an alternative, play "'Federigo's Falcon': Working with Falcons" on Tape 1 to engage student interest.

❶ Background

More About the Author

The whole direction of Boccaccio's career changed as a result of his meeting with Petrarch. Boccaccio no longer wrote in Italian, with the exception of one late work, and he rejected imaginative writing in favor of humanist scholarship. Until the final years of his life, Petrarch was not even aware that his younger friend had once written in Italian a work called the *Decameron.*

Geography Note

Draw students' attention to the map on this page. Point out that although Boccaccio lived most of his life in Italy, he also spent about eight years living in Paris. During this time, he first became acquainted with Petrarch's poetry, which would strongly influence his work for the rest of his life.

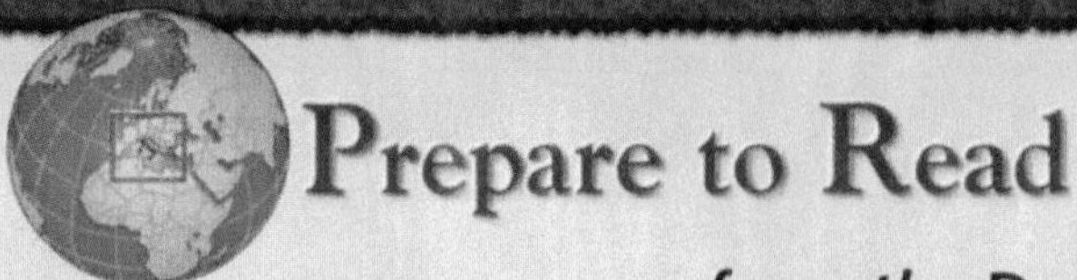

Prepare to Read

from the Decameron ❶

Giovanni Boccaccio (1313–1375)

Born in 1313, Giovanni Boccaccio [bô kä′ chō] was the illegitimate son of a Florentine merchant, an associate of a well-known banking family. His father sent him at the age of ten to work in one of his firm's banks in Naples. This southern Italian city was ruled by the Frenchman Robert of Anjou, whose court was known for its splendor and sophistication. As a member of the banking firm that lent this ruler money, Boccaccio was able to attend court functions, and he later remembered this period of his life as a time of happiness and pleasure.

Boccaccio's father encouraged his son to become a businessman and, later, a lawyer specializing in church law; Boccaccio showed little interest in either field. He did, however, begin to write while at the Neapolitan court, and he continued to write prolifically for the rest of his life. His early works, written mostly in Italian, include several long narratives. One of them, *Filocolo*, demonstrates Boccaccio's deep insights into human motives and behaviors.

A Wider Worldview In 1340, financial problems caused Boccaccio's family to recall him to Florence, and he had to leave behind the cultivated court that he loved. His letters suggest that the return to what seemed at first a petty, middle-class, money-grubbing environment was difficult. However, this change provided essential experience for the future author of the *Decameron*, a book dealing with all kinds and classes of people. As time passed, Boccaccio became more sympathetic to Florence and its citizens—he actively engaged in Florentine politics, serving as an ambassador to other countries.

Scholar and Poet In 1350, Boccaccio met the celebrated Italian poet Francesco Petrarch, the only contemporary whose gifts matched his own. This meeting was the start of a lifelong friendship. Boccaccio admired Petrarch greatly, and Petrarch's example encouraged Boccaccio in his own writings. Boccaccio produced a series of scholarly Latin works arising out of his vast reading in classical literature. In addition, with the help of a Greek collaborator, he produced the first European translation of Homer's works into Latin. He also wrote a biography of poet Dante Alighieri. In Boccaccio's last year, he began an important commentary on Dante's great work, the *Divine Comedy*.

Greatest Achievements Although Boccaccio was famous for his Latin works—and he would have regarded them as his greatest achievement—the *Decameron* is a collection of amusing and artful stories that reveal Boccaccio's impressive literary versatility. Far from being a musty old classic, the *Decameron* has delighted readers and inspired writers for half a millennium. Like many best-selling novels of our own time, it has been the inspiration for numerous full-length film adaptations.

The men and women who narrate the tales within the *Decameron* share the harrowing experience of escaping an outbreak of bubonic plague, similar to the 1348 epidemic that killed Boccaccio's parents as well as more than half of Florence's population. Framed by their medieval setting, the narratives in the *Decameron* feature a multitude of characters representing an array of social classes. Boccaccio explores deeply human themes of love, loss, deception, fortune, and more, creating a work of universality and timelessness.

TEACHING RESOURCES

The following resources can be used to enrich or extend the instruction for pp. 686–687.

Motivation

Interest Grabber Video, Tape 1

Background

Beyond Literature, p. 33

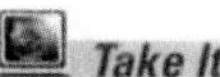

Take It to the Net

Visit PHSchool.com for background on the author.

Literary Analysis

Literary Analysis and Reading Transparencies, Novella, p. 65

Reading

Literary Analysis and Reading Transparencies, Identifying With Characters, p. 66

Selection Support: Reading Strategy, p.131

BLOCK SCHEDULING: Resources marked with this symbol provide varied instruction during 90-minute blocks.

Preview

Connecting to the Literature

Cherished items are keepsakes, objects you might not willingly give away. In Boccaccio's story, the main character's generous sacrifice of such an item may seem noble to some readers but very foolish to others.

2 Literary Analysis

Novella

A **novella** is a short prose tale. First written as early as the fourteenth century, the novella influenced the later development of the novel and the modern short story. Boccaccio's *Decameron* is a group of one hundred novellas, including "Federigo's Falcon." Like other short prose stories, these novellas share the following elements:

- a setting
- well-developed characters
- a theme, or a message about life
- a plot that includes the main events, conflicts, a climax or turning point in the story, and a final resolution

Use a chart like the one shown to identify details of these elements in "Federigo's Falcon."

Novella "Federigo's Falcon"
Setting:
Characters:
Plot:
Theme:

Connecting Literary Elements

Rather than tell his stories directly, Boccaccio creates a fictional background, or **frame,** surrounding the novellas of the *Decameron*. In the frame, ten young people leave Florence to escape the bubonic plague. To pass the time, they tell each other stories—including "Federigo's Falcon"—that fit within the shared frame. As you read, look for characters and dialogue from the frame and watch for the transition into the novella itself.

3 Reading Strategy

Identifying With Characters

Identifying with characters helps you connect to your reading. To identify with characters, put yourself into a character's place and relate his or her thoughts, feelings, and experiences to your own life. Note each character's situations and choices and consider the ways you might act in similar circumstances.

Vocabulary Development

courtly (kôrt´ lē) *adj.* dignified; polite; elegant (p. 689)

sumptuous (sump´ cho͞o əs) *adj.* costly; lavish (p. 689)

frugally (fro͞o´ gə lē) *adv.* thriftily; economically (p. 689)

deference (def´ ər əns) *n.* courteous regard or respect (p. 692)

affably (af´ ə blē) *adv.* in a friendly manner (p. 692)

impertinence (im purt´ 'n əns) *n.* insolence; impudence (p. 692)

despondent (di spän´ dənt) *adj.* dejected; hopeless (p. 693)

2 Literary Analysis

Novella

- Read aloud the characteristics of a novella on p. 687. Explain that the novella was a precursor to the short story and the novel.
- Encourage students to complete the graphic organizer on p. 687 as they read "Federigo's Falcon."
- Read aloud the Connecting Literary Elements text on p. 687. Ask students to describe what they know about the collection of tales *The Thousand and One Nights*. Tell students that these tales are part of a larger frame story. In it, a young woman named Scheherazade postpones her execution by entertaining the king with her clever tales every night for a thousand and one nights.
- Then, point out that the story of the ten young people is the frame for the *Decameron*.

3 Reading Strategy

Identifying With Characters

- Explain to students that identifying with characters means understanding and sympathizing with how the characters act and feel. Identifying with characters helps readers better understand a story.
- Point out that the main character in this story goes to extremes to impress the woman he loves. Ask students to put themselves in his place as they read. Encourage them to imagine what it feels like to try very hard to impress a loved one.
- Review with students the Identifying With Characters transparency in **Literary Analysis and Reading Transparencies,** p. 66.

Vocabulary Development

- Pronounce each vocabulary word for students, and read the definitions as a class. Have students identify any words with which they are already familiar.

CUSTOMIZE INSTRUCTION FOR UNIVERSAL ACCESS

For Special Needs Students	For Less Proficient Readers	For English Learners
Have students read "Federigo's Falcon" from the *Decameron* in the **Adapted Reader's Companion.** This version provides basic-level instruction in an interactive format with questions and write-on lines. Completing the adapted version will prepare students to read the selection in the Student Edition.	Have students read the adapted version of the selection in the **Reader's Companion.** This version provides basic-level instruction in an interactive format with questions and write-on lines. After students finish the selection in the **Reader's Companion,** have them complete the questions and activities in the Student Edition.	Have students read the adapted version of the selection in the **English Learner's Companion.** This version provides basic-level instruction in an interactive format with questions and write-on lines. Completing the adapted version will prepare students to read the selection in the Student Edition.

 ***e-Teach***

Visit e-Teach at PHSchool.com for teachers' essays on how to teach, with questions and answers.

TEACH

Step-by-Step Teaching Guide for pp. 688–694

Teaching Tenth-Grade Students

10TH GRADE Tenth-grade students should not have much difficulty with this story. In order to motivate their interest, however, you might ask them to do further research on falconry.

1 About the Selection

In "Federigo's Falcon," Federigo is an aristocratic young man known for his deeds of chivalry. From the beginning, he is willing to give up all his wealth in an attempt to win his beloved, Monna Giovanna. When all of his money is spent, Federigo shows no sign of bitterness, and his final act of generosity epitomizes his unhesitating devotion to his love.

2 Critical Viewing

Possible response: A sharp beak and powerful claws enable falcons to capture quarry.

3 Literary Analysis

Novella and Frame

- Read aloud the Background information on p. 688. Emphasize that the "king" or "queen" presides over the storytelling.
- Then, have students independently read the bracketed passage. Ask them to identify the characters mentioned in the first paragraph of the story.
  Answer: Three characters are mentioned: Filomena, the queen, and Dioneo.
- Ask students the Literary Analysis question on p. 688: Which character from the frame is the narrator of the novella?
  Answer: The queen is the narrator.
- Ask students what might be an advantage of having a frame story.
  Possible response: A frame story allows a writer to weave a number of different stories into one long grouping.

from the

Decameron 1

Giovanni Boccaccio

translated by G. H. McWilliam

Background

In the *Decameron*, a group of ten young aristocrats—seven women and three men—take up residence at a country estate to wait out an outbreak of the plague. To entertain themselves, each of them tells one story a day for ten days—hence, the name *Decameron*, which means "ten days." Each day, they elect a "king" or "queen" from among their number to preside over the day's storytelling. "Federigo's Falcon" is told on the fifth day.

2 ▲ **Critical Viewing** What physical attributes enable falcons, like this one, to find and capture quarry such as rabbits and game birds? **[Analyze]**

Federigo's Falcon

Once Filomena had finished, the queen, finding that there was no one left to speak apart from herself (Dioneo being excluded from the reckoning because of his privilege), smiled cheerfully and said:

3 It is now my own turn to address you, and I shall gladly do so, dearest ladies, with a story similar in some respects to the one we have just heard. This I have chosen, not only to acquaint you with the power of your beauty over men of noble spirit, but so that you may learn to choose for yourselves, whenever necessary, the persons on whom to bestow your largesse,[1] instead of always leaving these matters to be decided for you by Fortune, who, as it happens, nearly always scatters her gifts with more abundance than discretion.

Literary Analysis
Novella and Frame Which character from the frame is the narrator of the novella?

You are to know, then, that Coppo di Borghese Domenichi, who once used to live in our city and possibly lives there still, one of the most highly respected men of our century, a person worthy of eternal fame, who achieved his position of pre-eminence by dint of his character and

1. **largesse** (lär jes′) *n.* generous gifts.

TEACHING RESOURCES

The following resources can be used to enrich or extend the instruction for pp. 688–694.

Literary Analysis

- **Selection Support:** Literary Analysis, p. 132
- **Literary Analysis and Reading Transparencies,** Novella, p. 65

Reading

- **Reader's Companion**
- **Selection Support:** ReadingStrategy, p. 131; Build Vocabulary, p. 129
- **Adapted Reader's Companion**
- **English Learner's Companion**
- **Listening to Literature Audiocassettes** ■
- **Listening to Literature Audio CDs** ■

■ **BLOCK SCHEDULING:** Resources marked with this symbol provide varied instruction during 90-minute blocks.

abilities rather than by his noble lineage, frequently took pleasure during his declining years in discussing incidents from the past with his neighbors and other folk. In this pastime he excelled all others, for he was more coherent, possessed a superior memory, and spoke with greater eloquence. He had a fine repertoire, including a tale he frequently told concerning a young Florentine called Federigo, the son of Messer Filippo Alberighi, who for his deeds of chivalry and courtly manners was more highly spoken of than any other squire in Tuscany. In the manner of most young men of gentle breeding, Federigo lost his heart to a noble lady, whose name was Monna[2] Giovanna, and who in her time was considered one of the loveliest and most adorable women to be found in Florence. And with the object of winning her love, he rode at the ring, tilted, gave sumptuous banquets, and distributed a large number of gifts, spending money without any restraint whatsoever. But since she was no less chaste than she was fair, the lady took no notice, either of the things that were done in her honor, or of the
4 person who did them.

In this way, spending far more than he could afford and deriving no
5 profit in return, Federigo lost his entire fortune (as can easily happen) and reduced himself to poverty, being left with nothing other than a tiny little farm, which produced an income just sufficient for him to live very frugally, and one falcon of the finest breed in the whole world. Since he was as deeply in love as ever, and felt unable to go on living the sort of life in Florence to which he aspired, he moved out to Campi, where his little farm happened to be situated. Having settled in the country, he went hunting as often as possible with his falcon, and, without seeking assistance from anyone, he patiently resigned himself to a life of poverty.

Now one day, while Federigo was living in these straitened circumstances, the husband of Monna Giovanna happened to fall ill, and, realizing that he was about to die, he drew up his will. He was a very rich man, and in his will he left everything to his son, who was just growing up, further stipulating that, if his son should die without legitimate issue, his estate should go to Monna Giovanna, to whom he had always been deeply devoted.

Shortly afterward he died, leaving Monna Giovanna a widow, and every summer, in accordance with Florentine custom, she went away with her son to a country estate of theirs, which was very near Federigo's farm. Consequently this young lad of hers happened to become friendly with Federigo, acquiring a

Literary Analysis
Novella Identify the setting of the novella.

courtly (kôrt′ lē) *adj.* dignified; polite; elegant

sumptuous (sump′ cho͞o əs) *adj.* costly; lavish

frugally (fro͞o′ gə lē) *adv.* thriftily; economically

6 ✔**Reading Check**
What remains of Federigo's fortune after pursuing Monna Giovanna's affection?

7 

Robert Cheseman, Hans Holbein the Younger, Scala

2. **Monna** Lady.

8 **Critical Viewing** ▶ In what ways might this portrait be an accurate representation of Federigo? **[Analyze]**

CUSTOMIZE INSTRUCTION FOR UNIVERSAL ACCESS

For Gifted/Talented Students

In this story, Federigo starts out wealthy and gradually depletes his fortune. Ask students to read p. 689, which describes how Federigo spent his money and sank into poverty.

Have students work together to create a mural showing Federigo's attempts to win Monna Giovanna's love. Encourage them to research images of medieval and Italian Renaissance costumes, banquets, and architecture, as well as tournaments and other activities. Remind students that Federigo is a native of Florence.

Students may use watercolors, pastels, colored pencils, or any medium they wish to create the mural. They might include images of a jousting tournament, a hunt, or a banquet. Encourage students to illustrate as accurately as possible details such as dress, furnishings, buildings, or landscapes. Have them include images of Federigo and Monna Giovanna. Display the finished mural in the classroom.

4 Literary Analysis

Novella

- Review with students the characteristics of the novella on p. 687.
- Ask a volunteer to read aloud the bracketed passage. Then, ask students to respond to the Literary Analysis item on p. 689: Identify the setting of the novella.
  Answer: The story is set in Florence and in Campi, where Federigo's farm is located.

5 Reading Strategy

Identifying With Characters

- Ask students how Federigo expresses his feelings about Monna Giovanna.
  Answer: Federigo expresses his love by participating in tournaments, giving lavish banquets, spending money, and giving out gifts.
- Ask students: Can you identify with Federigo's futile efforts to win Monna Giovanna's heart? Why or why not?
  Possible response: Some readers may identify with Federigo because they have tried to win someone's attention; others may not identify with Federigo, saying that he is foolish.

6 ✔Reading Check

Answer: Federigo is left with a small farm and a falcon.

7 Background

Art

Robert Cheseman, by Hans Holbein the Younger

Holbein (c. 1498–1543) is considered one of the finest portrait painters of all time. At the age of twenty-eight, he became the court artist of King Henry VIII. Holbein's portraits of the royalty and nobility of England convey the flavor of court life.

Use the following question for discussion:

What does this portrait suggest about Cheseman?
Possible response: Cheseman appears to be a serious aristocrat with a passion for falconry.

8 ▶Critical Viewing

Possible response: Like Cheseman, Federigo cherishes his falcon.

9 Reading Strategy

Identifying With Characters

- Have students independently read the bracketed passage. Then, ask whether any students have ever been seriously ill. Ask what their parents or caretakers did—or were willing to do—to help them feel better.
- Remind students that to identify with a character, they should relate the character's thoughts and feelings to their own experiences.
- Ask the Reading Strategy question on p. 690: What might you be willing to do if you were in Monna Giovanna's place?
  Possible response: Most students will say that they would do anything to save the life of their child.

Reteach Have students review the Identifying With Characters transparency in **Literary Analysis and Reading Transparencies,** p. 66.

10 Background

Art

Departure for the Hunt

Tapestry is a decorative fabric made by creating a design or picture through the process of weaving. Traditionally, tapestries were hung, often in sets, as decorative items on interior walls of homes or churches.

The art of tapestry flourished in Europe in the Middle Ages. During the sixteenth century, tapestries—such as the one shown here—changed to reflect the influence of Italian Renaissance art.

Use the following questions for discussion:

- Where are the events in this tapestry taking place?
  Answer: The events are taking place just outside the city.
- What are some of the small details in the foreground of this tapestry?
  Answer: Some small details of the tapestry include the birds, the dog, and the small flowers and plants.

11 Critical Viewing

Possible response: The tapestry depicts a story about young noblemen preparing to go on a hunt.

passion for birds and dogs; and, having often seen Federigo's falcon in flight, he became fascinated by it and longed to own it, but since he could see that Federigo was deeply attached to the bird, he never ventured to ask him for it.

9 And there the matter rested, when, to the consternation of his mother, the boy happened to be taken ill. Being her only child, he was the apple of his mother's eye, and she sat beside his bed the whole day long, never ceasing to comfort him. Every so often she asked him whether there was anything he wanted, imploring him to tell her what it was, because if it was possible to acquire it, she would move heaven and earth to obtain it for him.

After hearing this offer repeated for the umpteenth time, the boy said:

"Mother, if you could arrange for me to have Federigo's falcon, I believe I should soon get better."

On hearing this request, the lady was somewhat taken aback, and began to consider what she could do about it. Knowing that Federigo had been in love with her for a long time, and that she had never deigned to cast so much as a single glance in his direction, she said to herself: "How can I possibly go to him, or even send anyone, to ask him for this falcon, which to judge from all I have heard is the finest that ever flew, as well as being the only thing that keeps him alive? And how can I be so heartless as to deprive so noble a man of his one remaining pleasure?"

Reading Strategy
Identifying With Characters What might you be willing to do if you were in Monna Giovanna's place?

10

Departure for the Hunt, 16th century, Réunion des Musées Nationaux, Paris

11 **Critical Viewing** Medieval and Renaissance tapestries, like the one shown, often tell stories or depict specific events. What detailed story might this tapestry narrate? **[Speculate]**

ENRICHMENT: History Connection

The Black Plague

The frame story of the *Decameron* is centered on young people who are fleeing the plague. In the introduction to the *Decameron,* Boccaccio describes the terrible plague, which probably killed a third of the population of Western Europe. In 1348, says Boccaccio, "the deadly plague broke out in the great city of Florence, . . ." The disease was called the Black Plague or Black Death, but we know it as the bubonic plague. Those afflicted with the disease were covered with swellings that grew to "the size of a common apple or egg."

Soon, those swellings gave way to "black or livid spots appearing on the arms, thighs, and the whole person." Few of the sick recovered; most died after the third day. The plague caused severe social breakdown. According to Boccaccio, "The calamity had instilled such horror into the hearts of men and women that . . . parents avoided visiting or nursing their very children, as though these were not their own flesh. . . ."

Her mind filled with reflections of this sort, she remained silent, not knowing what answer to make to her son's request, even though she was quite certain that the falcon was hers for the asking.

12 At length, however, her maternal instincts gained the upper hand, and she resolved, come what may, to satisfy the child by going in person to Federigo to collect the bird, and bring it back to him. And so she replied:

"Bear up, my son, and see whether you can start feeling any better. I give you my word that I shall go and fetch it for you first thing tomorrow morning."

Next morning, taking another lady with her for company,[3] his mother left the house as though intending to go for a walk, made her way to Federigo's little cottage, and asked to see him. For several days, the weather had been unsuitable for hawking, so Federigo was attending to one or two little jobs in his garden, and when he heard, to his utter astonishment, that Monna Giovanna was at the front door and wished to speak to him, he happily rushed there to greet her.

When she saw him coming, she advanced with womanly grace to meet him. Federigo received her with a deep bow, whereupon she said:

"Greetings, Federigo!" Then she continued: "I have come to make amends for the harm you have suffered on my account, by loving me more than you ought to have done. As a token of my esteem, I should like to take breakfast with you this morning, together with my companion here, but you must not put yourself to any trouble."

"My lady," replied Federigo in all humility, "I cannot recall ever having suffered any harm on your account. On the contrary I have gained so much that if ever I attained any kind of excellence, it was entirely because of your own great worth and the love I bore you. Moreover I can assure you that this visit which you have been generous enough to
13 pay me is worth more to me than all the money I ever possessed, though I fear that my hospitality will not amount to very much."

14 So saying, he led her unassumingly into the house, and thence into his garden, where, since there was no one else he could call upon to chaperon her, he said:

"My lady, as there is nobody else available, this good woman, who is the wife of the farmer here, will keep you company whilst I go and see about setting the table."

Though his poverty was acute, the extent to which he had squandered his wealth had not yet been fully borne home to Federigo; but on this particular morning, finding that he had nothing to set before the lady for whose love he had entertained so lavishly in the past, his eyes were well and truly opened to the fact. Distressed beyond all measure, he silently cursed his bad luck and rushed all over the house like one possessed, but could find no trace of either money or valuables. By now the morning was well advanced, he was still determined to entertain

Literary Analysis
Novella What fear motivates Monna Giovanna to ask Federigo for the falcon?

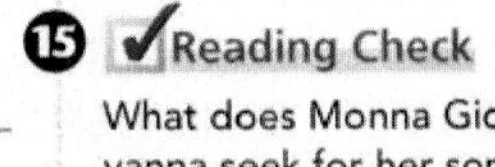

15 **Reading Check**
What does Monna Giovanna seek for her son?

3. **taking . . . company** A young woman of the upper classes would not go out by herself.

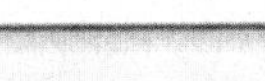

12 Literary Analysis
Novella

- Have a volunteer read aloud the last paragraph on p. 690. Ask students to summarize the conflict that Monna Giovanna is experiencing.
  Answer: Monna Giovanna knows that Federigo will give her the falcon, but she fears that it will cause him great suffering to do so. She knows that she has no right to make the request but also believes that the health of her son hinges on whether he gets the falcon.
- Have a volunteer read aloud the rest of the bracketed passage. Then, ask the Literary Analysis question on p. 691: What fear motivates Monna Giovanna to ask Federigo for the falcon?
  Answer: Monna Giovanna is motivated by the fear of losing her son.

13 Reading Strategy
Identifying With Characters

- Discuss with students Federigo's attitude toward Monna Giovanna revealed in the bracketed passage.
- Ask students: Can you identify with Federigo's feelings here? Why or why not?
  Possible response: Some readers may say that they can identify with Federigo and his pleasure at having the woman he loves finally take notice of him; others may say that they cannot identify with his feelings because they would probably feel angry or resentful toward her.

14 Background
Federigo's Generosity

This story is very much concerned with the aristocratic virtue of generosity. From the beginning, Federigo, known for his deeds of chivalry, is willing to give up all his wealth for Monna Giovanna. His lavishness has a positive side because it is part of a larger kind of generosity. Federigo is someone who holds back nothing. He "loses his heart" to the lady, and his subsequent actions simply elaborate this openness of spirit.

15 Reading Check

Answer: Monna Giovanna seeks Federigo's falcon for her son.

CUSTOMIZE INSTRUCTION FOR UNIVERSAL ACCESS

For Advanced Readers

Tell students that Boccaccio lived at the beginning of the Italian Renaissance, a historical period of cultural rebirth and flowering that spanned from about 1340 to about 1550. During the Italian Renaissance, literature, art, and architecture flourished. The city of Florence, where the character of Federigo originally lived, was the center of the Renaissance during this period.

Have students research and prepare a multimedia report on the Italian Renaissance. Encourage them to focus on one element, such as art or architecture, or on one individual, such as Leonardo da Vinci, Michelangelo, or the architect Filippo Brunelleschi. You may wish to have students use the Herringbone Organizer in **Writing Models and Graphic Organizers on Transparencies,** pp. 75–77, to guide their research.

Have students present their reports to the class, displaying photocopies or sketches of paintings, sculpture, or architecture.

16 Literary Analysis

Novella

- Read aloud the bracketed passage.
- Then, ask students the Literary Analysis question on p. 692: What does the phrase "without thinking twice" reveal about Federigo's character?
  Answer: The phrase reveals that Federigo is very generous.

Monitor Progress Review with students the elements of a novella listed on p. 687. Have them give an example from "Federigo's Falcon" of each of the elements (with the exception of the theme).

17 Vocabulary Development

Latin Suffix *-ence*

- Call students' attention to the word *deference,* its definition, and its use in the story. Explain that the Latin suffix *-ence* means "quality of" or "state of being."
- Tell students that they can change an adjective that ends in *-ent* to a noun by changing the word's suffix to *-ence*. Have students brainstorm examples of these words.
  Answer: *Absence* and *silence* are possible suggestions.

18 Background

Art

Girl at the Window, by Nicolaes Maes

Nicolaes Maes (1634–1693) studied under Rembrandt, the great Dutch master. After Maes established his own studio, he turned to painting domestic scenes, primarily of women spinning or cooking.

Use the following question for discussion:

What is the effect of Maes's emphasis on the young woman's face and hands?
Possible response: The emphasis draws the viewer's attention to the thoughtful look on the woman's face.

19 Critical Viewing

Possible response: The woman's pensive expression illustrates Monna Giovanna's dilemma.

---

the gentlewoman to some sort of meal, and, not wishing to beg assistance from his own farmer (or from anyone else, for that matter),
16 his gaze alighted on his precious falcon, which was sitting on its perch in the little room where it was kept. And having discovered, on picking it up, that it was nice and plump, he decided that since he had nowhere else to turn, it would make a worthy dish for such a lady as this. So without thinking twice about it he wrung the bird's neck and promptly handed it over to his housekeeper to be plucked, dressed, and roasted carefully on a spit. Then he covered the table with spotless linen, of which he still had a certain amount in his possession, and returned in high spirits to the garden, where he announced to his lady that the meal, such as he had been able to prepare, was now ready.

The lady and her companion rose from where they were sitting and
17 made their way to the table. And together with Federigo, who waited on them with the utmost deference, they made a meal of the prize falcon without knowing what they were eating.

On leaving the table they engaged their host in pleasant conversation for a while, and when the lady thought it time to broach the subject she had gone there to discuss, she turned to Federigo and addressed him affably as follows:

"I do not doubt for a moment, Federigo, that you will be astonished at my impertinence when you discover my principal reason for coming here, especially when you recall your former mode of living and my virtue, which you possibly mistook for harshness and cruelty. But if you had ever had any children to make you appreciate the power of parental love, I should think it certain that you would to some extent forgive me.

"However, the fact that you have no children of your own does not exempt me, a mother, from the laws common to all other mothers. And being bound to obey those laws, I am forced, contrary to my own wishes and to all the rules of decorum and propriety, to ask you for something to which I know you are very deeply attached—which is only natural, seeing that it is the only consolation, the only pleasure, the only recreation remaining to you in your present extremity of fortune. The gift I am seeking is your falcon, to which my son has taken so powerful a liking, that if I fail to take it to him I fear he will succumb to the illness from which he is suffering, and consequently I shall lose him. In imploring you to give me this falcon, I appeal, not to your love, for you are under no obligation to me on that account, but rather to your noble heart, whereby you have proved yourself superior to all others in the practice of courtesy. Do me this favor, then, so that I may claim that through your generosity I have saved my son's life, thus placing him forever in your debt."

Literary Analysis
Novella What does the phrase "without thinking twice" reveal about Federigo's character?

deference (def′ ər əns) *n.* courteous regard or respect

affably (af′ ə blē) *adv.* in a friendly manner

impertinence (im purt′ 'n əns) *adj.* insolence; impudence

19 **Critical Viewing**
Which details from "Federigo's Falcon" are aptly represented in this painting? Explain. **[Interpret]**

18
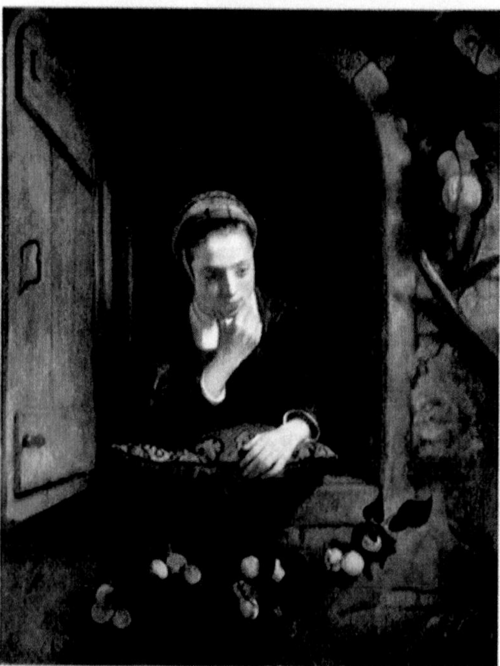

ENRICHMENT: Sports Connection

Falconry

In Boccaccio's story, Federigo is extremely attached to his pet falcon. The sport of falconry was popular among the nobility in medieval and Renaissance Europe. (Actually, it was developed in ancient China, Persia, and Egypt and came to Western Europe by way of Eastern Europe.) This sport used falcons to hunt small birds. Peregrine falcons were taken from the nest when quite young and subjected to a rigorous course of training so that they would respond to the falconer's calls and perch quietly on the falconer's wrist when they were hooded. They were also trained to leave their prey untouched after it was killed.

Although falconry was often associated with the aristocracy, people in the lower classes also engaged in the sport for purposes of feeding their families. By the seventeenth century, people had developed faster and more efficient ways of obtaining food, and, as a result, falconry declined in popularity.

When he heard what it was that she wanted, and realized that he could not oblige her because he had given her the falcon to eat, Federigo burst into tears in her presence before being able to utter a single word in reply. At first the lady thought his tears stemmed more from his grief at having to part with his fine falcon than from any other motive, and was on the point of telling him that she would prefer not to have it. But on second thoughts she said nothing, and waited for Federigo to stop crying and give her his answer, which eventually he did.

20 "My lady," he said, "ever since God decreed that you should become the object of my love, I have repeatedly had cause to complain of Fortune's hostility towards me. But all her previous blows were slight by comparison with the one she has dealt me now. Nor shall I ever be able to forgive her, when I reflect that you have come to my poor dwelling, which you never deigned to visit when it was rich, and that you desire from me a trifling favor which she has made it impossible for me to concede. The reason is simple, and I shall explain it in few words.

"When you did me the kindness of telling me that you wished to breakfast with me, I considered it right and proper, having regard to your excellence and merit, to do everything within my power to prepare a more sumptuous dish than those I would offer to my ordinary guests. My thoughts therefore turned to the falcon you have asked me for and, knowing its quality, I reputed it a worthy dish to set before you. So I had it roasted and served to you on the trencher this morning, and I could not have wished for a better way of disposing of it. But now that I discover that you wanted it in a different form, I am so distressed by my inability to grant your request that I shall never forgive myself for as long as I live."

In confirmation of his words, Federigo caused the feathers, talons and beak to be cast on the table before her. On seeing and hearing all this, the lady reproached him at first for killing so fine a falcon, and serving it up for a woman to eat; but then she became lost in admiration for his magnanimity[4] of spirit, which no amount of poverty had managed to diminish, nor ever would. But now that her hopes of obtaining the falcon had vanished she began to feel seriously concerned for the health of her son, and after thanking Federigo for his hospitality and good intentions, she took her leave of him, looking all despondent, and returned to the child. And to his mother's indescribable sorrow, within the space of a few days, whether through his disappointment in not being able to have the falcon, or because he was in any case suffering from a mortal illness, the child passed from this life.

4. **magnanimity** (mag′ nə nim′ ə tē) *n.* noble generosity.

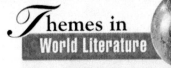

Themes in World Literature

21 *Boccaccio's Influence on Geoffrey Chaucer*

Boccaccio's *Decameron* became a model for many subsequent writers. The English poet Geoffrey Chaucer (1340?–1400) made use of this narrative model to write *The Canterbury Tales.*

Chaucer's frame features twenty-nine pilgrims who embark on a pilgrimage to the cathedral at Canterbury, England. To pass the time, the pilgrims agree to a storytelling contest in which each traveler tells two tales along the way to Canterbury and two more tales on the return journey. The winner will receive a free dinner at the Tabard Inn upon return. Like Boccaccio's *Decameron, The Canterbury Tales* features richly developed characters whose flaws and strengths make them very human.

Literary Analysis
Novella In what way is Monna Giovanna's visit a deeply bittersweet occasion for Federigo?

despondent (di spän′ dənt) *adj.* dejected; hopeless

22  **Reading Check**
What emotional response does Federigo have to Monna Giovanna's request?

CUSTOMIZE INSTRUCTION FOR UNIVERSAL ACCESS

For Special Needs Students	For Gifted/Talented Students	For Advanced Readers
Have students work in pairs to develop lists of simple acts of generosity. Have them discuss what makes these simple acts possible. Use these lists and discussions as a springboard for helping students identify and describe the acts of generosity in "Federigo's Falcon."	Point out that belief in the role of Fortune was strong during this time period. Fortune, usually personified as a woman, was a combination of fate (that which happens because it is meant to) and luck (that which happens by chance). Have students draw Fortune as a medieval person might have imagined her.	Organize students in small groups. Have each group discuss the actions of the main characters in the selection. Each group should use its discussion to write a code of behavior appropriate for a Renaissance lady and gentleman in love. Have students research the topic of courtly love to confirm or add to their codes.

20 Literary Analysis

Novella

- Allow time for students to read the bracketed passage.
- Discuss with them the irony of the situation in which Federigo finds himself: He freely sacrifices his falcon to serve Monna Giovanna, only to learn that it is the one thing that she asks of him.
- Ask students the Literary Analysis question on p. 693: In what way is Monna Giovanna's visit a deeply bittersweet occasion for Federigo?
Answer: Federigo still loves Monna Giovanna, so her visit brings him great happiness; however, this feeling is tempered by the knowledge that he has sacrificed the falcon that she wanted for her son.

21 Background

Boccaccio's Influence on Geoffrey Chaucer

Like Boccaccio, Geoffrey Chaucer borrows from other sources for his *Canterbury Tales.* In fact, one of his stories in the collection, the "Knight's Tale," is adapted from Boccaccio's epic story of the Greek hero Theseus.

Chaucer develops his frame story more fully than does Boccaccio. Chaucer describes the pilgrims gathering at the Tabard Inn and agreeing to tell the stories. Most of the framework stories reflect the characters who tell them. For example, one of the pilgrims is a nun who tells a story about a saint.

Chaucer's frame characters—the pilgrims who narrate the tales—are developed in far more detail than Boccaccio develops his narrators. Chaucer introduces the characters in the General Prologue, giving details about their appearance, personalities, and private lives. More details are revealed in the prologues to individual tales. Some of the characters in the frame are more memorable than the characters in the framework stories themselves. In fact, one of the frame characters—the Wife of Bath—is one of the most interesting and vibrant characters in all of English literature.

22 ✓Reading Check

Answer: Federigo bursts into tears.

ASSESS

23 Critical Thinking

Infer

- Have students read the bracketed passage and note the comments that Monna Giovanna makes about marrying Federigo.
- Ask students: Do you think that Monna Giovanna loves Federigo? Explain.
  Possible response: Although Monna Giovanna admires Federigo, she does not love him because she says that she would rather remain a widow.

Answers for p. 694

Review and Assess

1. Possible responses: Federigo was noble in so generously giving up all that he had without a thought for material goods; on the other hand he was foolish to impoverish himself without receiving any benefit from his generosity.
2. **(a)** Federigo spends all of his money on lavish banquets and expensive gifts, and he participates in tournaments. **(b)** Because of the customs of the time, it was considered unladylike to be influenced by such displays of affection.
3. **(a)** Federigo bows graciously; he makes sure that Monna Giovanna is comfortably seated, and he arranges for someone to be with her while he prepares the meal; he sacrifices his most precious possession for her meal. **(b)** Federigo is generous, thoughtful, and courteous.
   (c) Possible response: Monna Giovanna may have expected Federigo to be angry or hostile because he was impoverished by trying to win her love.
4. **(a)** At first, Monna Giovanna scolds Federigo for serving a fine bird as food, but then she admires his generosity. **(b)** She is kind, gracious, and noble.
5. Possible response: Young women are not compelled to ignore suitors today; young men usually do not expend so much effort to win the favor of a woman. Love is based on nobility of character, not current notions of romantic love.

After a period of bitter mourning and continued weeping, the lady was repeatedly urged by her brothers to remarry, since not only had she been left a vast fortune but she was still a young woman. And though she would have preferred to remain a widow, they gave her so little peace that in the end, recalling Federigo's high merits and his latest act of generosity, namely to have killed such a fine falcon in her honor, she said to her brothers:

23 "If only it were pleasing to you, I should willingly remain as I am; but since you are so eager for me to take a husband, you may be certain that I shall never marry any other man except Federigo degli Alberighi."

Her brothers made fun of her, saying:

"Silly girl, don't talk such nonsense! How can you marry a man who hasn't a penny with which to bless himself?"

"My brothers," she replied, "I am well aware of that. But I would sooner have a gentleman without riches, than riches without a gentleman."

Seeing that her mind was made up, and knowing Federigo to be a gentleman of great merit even though he was poor, her brothers fell in with her wishes and handed her over to him, along with her immense fortune. Thenceforth, finding himself married to this great lady with whom he was so deeply in love, and very rich into the bargain, Federigo managed his affairs more prudently, and lived with her in happiness to the end of his days.

Review and Assess

Thinking About the Selection

1. **Respond:** Do you think Federigo was noble or misguided in serving up the falcon? Explain.
2. **(a) Recall:** What early efforts does Federigo make to win Monna Giovanna's love? **(b) Infer:** What does the narrator mean when she says Monna Giovanna's chastity compelled her to take no notice of Federigo?
3. **(a) Recall:** What gestures of hospitality does Federigo make when Monna Giovanna visits? **(b) Connect:** In what ways do his efforts reflect his former life as a wealthy gentleman? **(c) Speculate:** Do you think Monna Giovanna expected such behavior from him? Why or why not?
4. **(a) Recall:** How does Monna Giovanna respond to the news of the falcon's death? **(b) Infer:** What does her response indicate about her character?
5. **Apply:** In what ways do the ideals of love expressed in this story differ from current notions of romantic love?

ASSESSMENT PRACTICE: Reading Comprehension

Evaluate and Make Judgments (For more practice, see Test Preparation Workbook, p. 33.)

Standardized tests often require students to evaluate and make judgments about texts. Use the following sample test item to help students practice this skill.

Knowing that Federigo had been in love with her for a long time, and that she had never deigned to cast so much as a single glance in his direction, she said to herself: "How can I possibly . . . ask him for this falcon, which to judge from all I have heard is the finest that ever flew, as well as being the only thing that keeps him alive?"

Which of the following is the best description of the speaker in this passage?

A She is arrogant.
B She is cruel and heartless.
C She is kind and thoughtful.
D She is indifferent.

A, B, and *D* are incorrect because the speaker expresses concern about Federigo. *C* is the best answer.

Review and Assess

Literary Analysis

Novella

1. Do you think "Federigo's Falcon" contains all the elements of a **novella**? Why or why not?
2. How does the setting reflect Federigo's change of fortune?
3. What lesson about loss and restoration does this story teach? Use details from the tale to support your answer.

Connecting Literary Elements

4. (a) In the *Decameron's* **frame,** what does the queen claim her story teaches? (b) Which details in the novella might her listening audience relate to their own lives? Explain.
5. (a) Who is Coppo di Borghese Domenichi? (b) What credibility does he add to the novella and its narrator?

Reading Strategy

Identifying With Characters

6. Using a chart like the one shown, choose two events involving Federigo and two involving Monna Giovanna. Then, **identifying with each character,** explain what your reaction might be if you experienced similar events.

	Their Experiences	My Reactions
Federigo	1.	1.
	2.	2.
Monna Giovanna	1.	1.
	2.	2.

7. (a) For which character do you feel the most sympathy? (b) In what way does identifying with the character influence your ability to sympathize? Explain.

Extend Understanding

8. **Cultural Connection:** What can you infer from the characters' behavior about love, marriage, and the status of women during this period? Explain.

Quick Review

A **novella** is a short prose tale.

A **frame** is a unifying background that links together a series of stories.

When you **identify with characters,** you relate to their thoughts and feelings and connect them to your own experiences.

Take It to the Net

PHSchool.com

Take the interactive self-test online to check your understanding of this selection.

ENRICHMENT: Further Reading

Other Works by Giovanni Boccaccio

We strongly encourage you to review any selection before assigning or recommending it to students.

Decameron

Famous Women

Take It to the Net

Visit PHSchool.com for more information on Boccaccio.

Answers for p. 695

Review and Assess

1. The story contains all the elements of a novella. The setting is Florence and the countryside; the characters are well developed; the theme is nobility of spirit; the plot includes Federigo's loss of fortune, the climax of giving up his falcon, and the final resolution of his marriage to Monna Giovanna.
2. The story begins in lavish Florence and changes to Federigo's farm, just as Federigo is wealthy at the beginning and spirals into poverty.
3. The lesson taught is that even when everything seems lost, good things can be restored in unexpected ways. Monna Giovanna loses her husband and son; Federigo loses his heart and his wealth. Their marriage returns wealth and love to Federigo and a noble husband to Monna Giovanna.
4. **(a)** The queen claims that the story will teach the ladies the power of their beauty, and it will teach people to bestow their wealth carefully. **(b)** Possible response: The queen's listeners might relate to Monna Giovanna's ignoring Federigo's attentions, as was the custom there.
5. **(a)** Coppo di Borghese Domenichi originally told the story to the narrator. **(b)** Coppo di Borghese Domenichi adds credibility because he is a respected man with a good memory.
6. Possible response: **Federigo's Experiences:** 1. Federigo attempts to win Monna Giovanna's love by spending his fortune. 2. Federigo is surprised by a visit from Monna Giovanna. **Reactions:** 1. Readers may say that they would feel depressed at their inability to win her love. 2. Readers may say that they would be excited by her visit. **Monna Giovanna's Experiences:** 1. Monna Giovanna's child is ill. 2. Monna Giovanna's brothers want her to remarry. **Reactions:** 1. Readers may say that they would do anything to help the child recover. 2. Readers may say that they would not be ready or willing to remarry.

continued

continued from right column

7. **(a)** Possible response: Some readers will sympathize most with Federigo. **(b)** Identifying with the character increases a person's ability to sympathize because he or she imagines how it would feel to be that character.
8. Possible response: Men idolized women, and they went to great lengths to prove their love. Women were expected to marry.

EXTEND

Answers for p. 696

❶ Vocabulary Development

Word Analysis: Latin Suffix *-ence*

1. turbulence
2. insistence
3. munificence

Spelling Strategy

1. affably
2. gently
3. sparkly

Concept Development: Synonym or Antonym

1. A
2. S
3. A
4. S
5. A
6. S
7. A

❷ Grammar and Style

Practice

1. On hearing his request, she was shocked. (prepositional phrase)
2. Shortly afterward, he died, leaving Monna Giovanna a widow. (transition)
3. When she saw him coming, she advanced with womanly grace to meet him. (dependent clause)
4. As a token of his esteem, he took breakfast with her. (prepositional phrase)
5. After leaving the table, they had a pleasant conversation. (prepositional phrase)

Writing Application

Possible response: Because we have become friends, I would like to issue an invitation. (dependent clause) Although I seldom celebrate my birthday, I am having a party this year. (dependent clause) In spite of the weather, I am planning a picnic. (prepositional phrase) Of course I know that you don't usually like picnics, but I think you'll enjoy this one. (transition)

10TH GRADE For support in teaching the Grammar and Style Lesson to tenth graders, use **Writing and Grammar,** Platinum Level, Chapter 21, Section 3.

Integrate Language Skills

❶ Vocabulary Development Lesson

Word Analysis: Latin Suffix *-ence*

The Latin suffix *-ence* means "quality of" or "state of being." To change an adjective ending in *-ent* to a noun, replace the *-ent* suffix with *-ence*. For example, the adjective *impertinent*, meaning "insolent or impudent," becomes *impertinence*, meaning "the quality of being impertinent."

Change the following adjectives to nouns by replacing the suffix *-ent* with *-ence*.

1. turbulent 2. insistent 3. munificent

Spelling Strategy

Many words end in an unstressed syllable spelled with a consonant + *-le*, as in *remarkable*. To add *-ly*, drop the *-le*: *remarkable* becomes *remarkably*. Rewrite these words, adding *-ly*.

1. affable 2. gentle 3. sparkle

Concept Development: Synonym or Antonym?

Review the vocabulary words on page 687 and notice the use of the words in context in the selections. Then, for each pair of words below, write *S* for *synonym* if the words have similar meanings or A for *antonym* if they have opposite meanings.

1. courtly, impolite
2. sumptuous, expensive
3. frugally, lavishly
4. deference, respect
5. affably, nastily
6. impertinence, rudeness
7. despondent, cheerful

❷ Grammar and Style Lesson

Varying Sentence Beginnings

By **varying sentence beginnings,** an author adds interest to the text and helps avoid repetition. In addition to starting sentences with a subject, writers can vary sentence beginnings by using prepositional phrases, transitions, or dependent clauses.

Prepositional Phrase: *In due time*, Federigo lost his heart to a noble lady.

Transition: *Now one day* . . . the husband of Monna Giovanna happened to fall ill.

Dependent Clause: *Though his poverty was acute*, the extent of it was yet unknown.

Practice Revise the following sentences so they begin with a prepositional phrase, a transition, or a dependent clause. Underline your new sentence beginnings and identify each by type.

1. She was shocked on hearing his request.
2. He died leaving Monna Giovanna a widow shortly afterward.
3. She advanced with womanly grace to meet him when she saw him coming.
4. He took breakfast with her as a token of his esteem.
5. They had a pleasant conversation after leaving the table.

Writing Application Write a short letter of invitation. Use a variety of sentence beginnings, underlining each and identifying its type.

WG *Prentice Hall Writing and Grammar Connection: Diamond Level, Chapter 20, Section 3*

TEACHING RESOURCES

The following resources can be used to enrich or extend the instruction for pp. 696–697.

Vocabulary
- **Selection Support:** Build Vocabulary, p. 129
- **Vocabulary and Spelling Practice Book** (Use this booklet for skills instruction.) ■

Grammar
- **Selection Support:** Grammar and Style, p. 130
- **Writing and Grammar,** Diamond Level, p. 488
- **Daily Language Practice Transparencies**

Writing
- **Performance Assess. and Portfolio Mgmt.,** p. 16
- **Writing and Grammar,** Diamond Level, p. 315
- **Writing and Grammar iText CD-ROM** ■
- **Writing Models and Graphic Organizers on Transparencies,** pp. 53–59

Research and Technology
- **Performance Assess. and Portfolio Mgmt.,** p. 13

■ **BLOCK SCHEDULING:** Resources marked with this symbol provide varied instruction during 90-minute blocks.

❸ Writing Lesson

Literary Analysis

One theme, or universal message, in "Federigo's Falcon" is that people should preserve their nobility of spirit at all costs. Write an essay supporting this theme, or choose a different one and defend its presence in the novella.

Prewriting Begin by explaining the theme you have chosen and the ways in which it relates to readers today. Reread the story, listing points and specific quotations that support your idea.

Drafting In your introduction, include a statement of the theme and its meaning. Then, in the body of your essay, identify specific details from the novella and explain how each example supports your point.

Revising Revise your draft to include enough evidence to defend your main point. Consider strengthening your point by adding relevant citations.

Model: Using Relevant Citations

Federigo shows remarkable nobility of spirit as he faces his dwindling wealth. He never complains about sacrificing his fortune in vain. ^*As the narrator describes, "he patiently resigned himself to a life of poverty."*

One effective way to cite details from a literary work is to use a direct quotation.

WG Prentice Hall Writing and Grammar Connection: Diamond Level, Chapter 14, Section 3

❹ Extension Activities

Listening and Speaking With a small group, organize a **storytelling circle.** Choose a central idea, such as generosity, love, or trickery. Have each group member create a story exemplifying this idea. Use the following tips as you prepare:

- Choose events that illustrate the theme.
- Add details to the story to make it vivid.
- Consider exaggerating the details to make your point more strongly.

Take turns telling your stories to the class. Then, invite the class to identify the central theme. [Group Activity]

Research and Technology Use library and Internet resources to research falconry. Find images from both Boccaccio's time and the present that show how falcons are handled and how they are used to hunt. Create a **classroom display** that compares or contrasts the use of falconry through the centuries, including captions that explain each image. Share your display with the class.

 ***Take It to the Net*** PHSchool.com

Go online for an additional research activity using the Internet.

ASSESSMENT RESOURCES

The following resources can be used to assess students' knowledge and skills.

Selection Assessment

- **Formal Assessment,** pp. 117–119
- **Open-Book Tests,** pp. 97–99
- **Test Bank Software**

 ***Take It to the Net***

Visit PHSchool.com for self-tests on the selection.

Writing Rubric

- **Performance Assess. and Portfolio Mgmt.,** p. 16

Research and Technology Rubric

- **Performance Assess. and Portfolio Mgmt.,** p. 13

For additional diagnostics and remediation for skills covered in this grouping, use materials from the Prentice Hall Assessment System.

❸ Writing Lesson

- Read aloud the Writing Lesson instruction on p. 697. Remind students that a literary analysis closely examines and evaluates something specific in a literary work.
- Explain that a story can have more than one theme. Encourage students to think about a lesson or message from the story of Federigo.
- Use the Interpreting a Work of Literature writing model in **Writing Models and Graphic Organizers on Transparencies,** pp. 53–59, to help students develop their essays.
- Use the Response to Literature rubric in **Performance Assessment and Portfolio Management,** p. 16, to evaluate students' essays.

10TH GRADE For support in working through the Writing Lesson with tenth graders, use **Writing and Grammar,** Platinum Level, Chapter 13, Section 3.

❹ Research and Technology

- Ask a volunteer to read aloud the Research and Technology instruction on p. 697.
- Encourage students to brainstorm topics they want to cover in their classroom display. Then, organize students into small groups. Assign each group a particular topic to research.
- After the classroom display is completed, have each group present a report on their particular topic.
- Use the Research Writing rubric in **Performance Assessment and Portfolio Management,** p. 13, to evaluate students' reports.

CUSTOMIZE INSTRUCTION For Universal Access

To address different learning styles, use the following activities suggested in the **Extension Activities** booklet, p. 33:

- For Verbal/Linguistic and Intrapersonal Learners, use Activity 5.
- For Bodily/Kinesthetic and Interpersonal Learners, use Activity 6.
- For Visual/Spatial Learners, use Activity 7.

from Don Quixote

Lesson Objectives

1. **To analyze and respond to literary elements**
   - Literary Analysis: Parody
   - Connecting Literary Elements: Theme
2. **To read, comprehend, analyze, and critique fiction**
   - Reading Strategy: Comparing and Contrasting
   - Reading Check Questions
   - Review and Assess Questions
   - Assessment Practice (ATE)
3. **To develop word analysis skills, fluency, and systematic vocabulary**
   - Vocabulary Development Lesson: Latin Root *-ject-*
4. **To understand and apply written and oral language conventions**
   - Spelling Strategy
   - Grammar and Style Lesson: Gerunds
   - Assessment Practice
5. **To understand and apply appropriate writing and research strategies**
   - Writing Lesson: Profile of a Comic Hero
   - Extension Activity: Visual Essay
6. **To understand and apply listening and speaking strategies**
   - Extension Activity: Role-play a Scene

10TH GRADE TEACHING A TENTH-GRADE COURSE

The literature in this section can be taught as part of a rich, balanced world literature course for tenth-grade students. For a full outline of such a course, see pp. T46–T48 in Volume 1 of this Teacher's Edition.

STEP-BY-STEP TEACHING GUIDE	PACING GUIDE
PRETEACH	
Motivate Students and Provide Background	
Use the Motivation activity (ATE p. 698)	5 min.
Read and discuss author and background features (SE pp. 698, 700; ATE p. 698) [A]	5 min.
Introduce the Concepts	
Introduce the Literary Analysis and Reading Strategy concepts (SE/ATE p. 699) [A]	15 min.
Pronounce the vocabulary words and read their definitions (SE p. 699)	5 min.
TEACH	
Monitor Comprehension	
Informally monitor comprehension by circulating while students read independently or in groups [A]	35 min.
Monitor students' comprehension with the Reading Check notes (SE/ATE pp. 703, 705, 709, 711, 713)	as students read
Develop vocabulary with the Vocabulary notes (SE pp. 700, 702, 704, 707, 708, 710; ATE p. 700)	as students read
Develop Understanding	
Develop students' understanding of parody with the Literary Analysis annotations (SE pp. 700, 707, 708, 712; ATE pp. 700, 702, 706, 707, 708, 712) [A]	5 min.
Develop students' ability to compare and contrast by using the Reading Strategy annotations (SE/ATE pp. 703, 704, 710, 711, 713) [A]	5 min.
ASSESS	
Assess Mastery	
Assess students' mastery of the Reading Strategy and Literary Analysis concepts by having them answer the Review and Assess questions (SE/ATE p. 714)	15 min.
Use one or more of the print, software, or transparency Assessment Resources (ATE p. 717) [A]	up to 45 min.
EXTEND	
Apply Understanding	
Have students complete the Vocabulary Development Lesson and the Grammar and Style Lesson (SE/ATE p. 716) [A]	20 min.
Apply students' ability to gather details, using the Writing Lesson (SE/ATE p. 717) [A]	45 min.
Apply students' understanding, using one or more of the Extension Activities (SE p. 717)	20–90 min.

ACCELERATED INSTRUCTION:
Use the strategies and activities identified with an [A].

10TH GRADE TEACHING TENTH-GRADE STUDENTS
For support in teaching the selection(s) to tenth-grade students, see the Step-By-Step Teaching notes identified with the icon shown here.

UNIVERSAL ACCESS
● = Below-Level Students
▲ = On-Level Students
■ = Above-Level Students

Time and Resource Manager

Reading Level: Average
Average Number of Instructional Days: 4

RESOURCES		
PRINT	**TRANSPARENCIES**	**TECHNOLOGY**
• **Beyond Literature,** Cultural Connection: Spain's Golden Age, p. 34 ▲ ■		• **Interest Grabber Video,** Tape 1, Unit 6, Segment 14 ● ▲ ■
• **Selection Support Workbook:** ● ▲ ■ Literary Analysis, p. 136 Reading Strategy, p. 135 Build Vocabulary, p. 133	• **Literary Analysis and Reading Transparencies,** pp. 67 and 68 ● ▲ ■	
• **Reader's Companion** ● • **Adapted Reader's Companion** ●		• **Listening to Literature** ● ▲ ■ Audiocassettes Audio CDs • **Reader's Companion Audio Program** ● • **Reader's Companion Adapted and English Learner's Version Audio Program** ● ▲
• **English Learner's Companion** ● ■ • **Literary Analysis for Enrichment,** p. 34 ▲		• **World Masterpieces iText CD-ROM**
• **Formal Assessment:** Selection Test, pp. 120–122 ● ▲ ■ • **Open-Book Tests,** pp. 100–102 ● ▲ ■ • **Performance Assessment and Portfolio Management,** p. 19 ● ▲ ■ • Prentice Hall Assessment System ● ▲ ■	• Prentice Hall Assessment System ● ▲ ■ **Skills Practice Answers and Explanations on Transparencies**	• **Test Bank Software** ● ▲ ■
• **Selection Support Workbook:** ● ▲ ■ Grammar and Style, p. 134 • **Writing and Grammar,** Diamond Level ● ▲ ■ • **Extension Activities,** p. 34 ● ▲ ■	• **Daily Language Practice Transparencies** ● ▲ • **Writing Models and Graphic Organizers on Transparencies,** pp. 79–81 ● ▲ ■	• **Writing and Grammar iText CD-ROM** ● ▲ ■ *Take It to the Net* PHSchool.com

BLOCK SCHEDULING: Use one 90-minute class period to preteach the selection(s) and have students read them. Use a second 90-minute class period to assess students' mastery of skills and have them complete one of the Extension Activities.

PRETEACH

Step-by-Step Teaching Guide for pp. 698–699

Motivation

Ask students to describe some superheroes they have seen in films. Then, invite them to brainstorm ideas for scenes in a new film they would create that makes fun of superheroes. Encourage them to use exaggeration and distortion to heighten the humor of their invented scenes. Finally, point out that these techniques are similar to those Cervantes uses in his parody of knights and chivalry.

Interest Grabber Video

As an alternative, play *"Don Quixote:* Miguel de Cervantes" on Tape 1 to engage student interest.

❶ Background

More About the Author

In his personal life, Cervantes often exhibited the gallant traits and the adventuresome spirit of a knight-errant embodied in his character Don Quixote. Besides fighting in the Battle of Lepanto, Cervantes fought with the Spanish army in Italy. His travels took him to Italian cities such as Naples and Genoa. There he learned a great deal about Italian culture, no doubt familiarizing himself with Italian literature.

Cervantes made a name for himself as well when he was enslaved by the Algerians. He led several escape attempts with his fellow slaves, and when they were recaptured, he always took the blame upon himself. His bravery is mentioned in records written by other captives in Algiers.

Geography Note

Use the map on this page to identify Spain, the highlighted area. Point out central Spain, where Madrid is located and where Cervantes spent much of his life. Tell students that Madrid is known for its many impressive public squares, one of which is Plaza Mayor, adjacent to Calle Cervantes, the street named for the beloved author of *Don Quixote.*

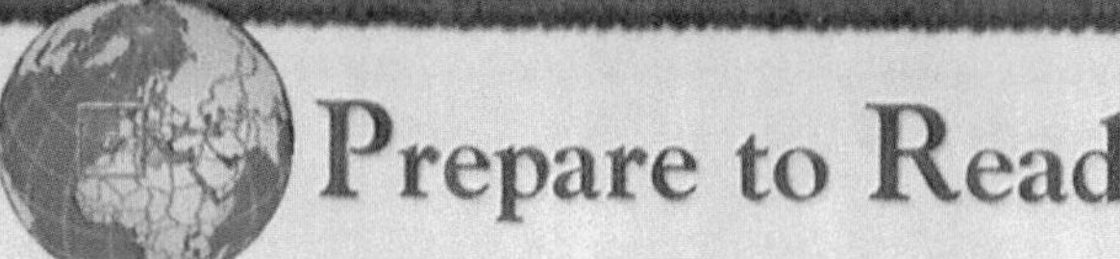

Prepare to Read

❶ *from* Don Quixote

Miguel de Cervantes Saavedra (1547–1616)

Miguel de Cervantes Saavedra (sər van′ tēz sä′ ə vä′ drə) led a life that was every bit as exciting as that of his famous character, knight-errant Don Quixote (dän′ kē hōt′ ē). Cervantes also displayed, on occasion, the almost foolhardy bravery that was so characteristic of his absurd knight.

Military Career Born into a poor family, Cervantes received little education. At the age of twenty, he joined the Spanish army and shortly afterward fought in the battle of Lepanto against the Turks. This naval battle saw the destruction of the Turkish fleet by the combined forces of Spain and Italy. Cervantes was among the 30,000 soldiers transported by the Spanish and Italian galleys. Although he was ill when the battle began, he plunged into the fighting and was wounded twice in the chest and once in the left arm. For the rest of his life, he regarded his maimed left arm as a badge of honor.

Cervantes went on to fight in a number of other battles, but he was captured by Barbary pirates while sailing home from the wars. Sold into slavery in Algiers, he repeatedly tried to escape. Although he was always recaptured, his bravery so impressed the Algerians that they did not put him to death. Believing that Cervantes was a citizen of great importance, his captors demanded a considerable ransom for his release. After he had been a prisoner for five years, the ransom was finally paid, and Cervantes was free to return to Madrid.

Difficult Times Back in Spain, Cervantes pursued an ambitious goal: to become Spain's most successful dramatist. Although he wrote prolifically, his significant collection of theatrical works was largely overlooked. Cervantes braved difficult economic circumstances during his years as a playwright and eventually found a bookkeeping job with the government to support his large household. Problems with his account books, however, led to his imprisonment on two occasions. According to legend, Cervantes began writing *Don Quixote* during one of these spells in prison.

A Wealth of Imagination When the first part of the novel appeared in 1605, it was a great success. Within only a few years, the novel had been translated into English, French, and a number of other European languages. When a false, or unauthorized, sequel to *Don Quixote* appeared on the market, Cervantes quickly embarked upon the continuation of his story—*Don Quixote, Part II*—which was published in 1615. Despite his appreciable success, Cervantes received only a small sum from his publisher for the works. At the time of his death in 1616, he was still a poor man.

It is clear that Cervantes invested his true wealth—his keen observation, playfulness, and imagination—in the creation of his novel. That is why it remains, as one translator called it, "one of the best adventure stories in the world." To date, Cervantes's masterpiece has been published in more than sixty languages, and the novel continues to be studied, critiqued, and debated by scholars around the world.

TEACHING RESOURCES

The following resources can be used to enrich or extend the instruction for pp. 698–699.

Motivation

Interest Grabber Video, Tape 1

Background

Beyond Literature, p. 34

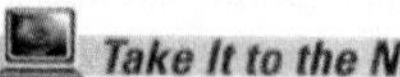

Take It to the Net

Visit PHschool.com for background on the author.

Literary Analysis

Literary Analysis and Reading Transparencies, Parody, p. 67

Selection Support: Literary Analysis, p. 136

Reading

Literary Analysis and Reading Transparencies, Comparing and Contrasting, p. 68

BLOCK SCHEDULING: Resources marked with this symbol provide varied instruction during 90-minute blocks.

Preview

Connecting to the Literature

Literature is filled with dreamers—people who hook their wagons to a star or try to lasso the moon. Perhaps the best-known dreamer of all is Don Quixote de la Mancha, an unlikely hero who gets swept away by the stories he reads and the dreams they inspire.

2 Literary Analysis

Parody

A **parody** is a humorous imitation of another, usually serious, work. Most often, a parody uses exaggeration or distortion to ridicule the work, its style, or its author. *Don Quixote* affectionately parodies the literature of chivalry—elaborate stories about knights; their code of honor, courage, and chastity; and their adventures. The central character, for example, makes swords out of oak branches and helmets of cardboard, yet he considers himself a well-dressed knight. As you read, look for details that parody chivalric romances.

Connecting Literary Elements

Parodies lend themselves to discussions of **theme,** the central message or idea revealed through a literary work. *Don Quixote* uses parody to explore the idea of reality versus fantasy, prompting readers to ask:

- At what point do flights of fancy interfere with reality?
- Is a life of hard-nosed realism more rewarding than a life filled with fantastic adventures?

Note thematic questions like these as you read.

3 Reading Strategy

Comparing and Contrasting

Comparing and contrasting an ideal knight and Don Quixote's version means looking for similarities and differences between the two. Before you read, use a chart like the one shown to list the details you know about an ideal knight, such as his armor, squire, horse, and adventures. Then, as you read, record the details from Don Quixote's world. Identify any conclusions you can draw from comparing and contrasting those details.

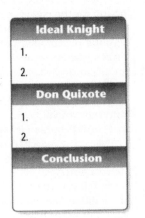

Ideal Knight
1.
2.
Don Quixote
1.
2.
Conclusion

Vocabulary Development

constitution (kän′ stə to͞o′ shən) *n.* structure or makeup of a person or thing (p. 700)

conjectures (kən jek′ chərz) *n.* guesses (p. 700)

infatuation (in fach′ o͞o ā′ shən) *n.* foolish or shallow feelings of affection (p. 702)

ingenuity (in′ jə no͞o′ ə tē) *n.* cleverness; inventiveness (p. 704)

incongruous (in käŋ′ gro͞o əs) *adj.* inconsistent; lacking in harmony (p. 707)

appropriate (ə prō′ prē āt′) *v.* take for one's own use (p. 708)

illustrious (i lus′ trē əs) *adj.* distinguished or outstanding (p. 710)

2 Literary Analysis

Parody

- Tell students that a parody works best when the object of its ridicule is something that is taken seriously. Don Quixote entertains readers because his behavior exaggerates that of the traditional "knight in shining armor."
- Point out that characters in a parody take their actions seriously. View with students a clip from *Saturday Night Live* in which an actor portrays the President or another well-known figure.
- Ask students to observe the actor's attempt to present the character seriously, even though his or her behavior may be quite funny. Be sure to preview the clip before showing it, and limit viewing to that particular scene only.
- Tell students that Don Quixote likewise believes he is part of the world of knights and chivalry. Remind them that the reader, not the characters, determines what is being ridiculed.

3 Reading Strategy

Comparing and Contrasting

- Point out that much of the humor in *Don Quixote* comes from the sharp difference between the ideal knight and Don Quixote's version. Compare and contrast the two to highlight the humor of *Don Quixote.*
- Review with students the chart on p. 699. Have them brainstorm details about an ideal knight. Encourage them to be precise.
- Have each student copy these notes. As students read, ask them to look for Don Quixote's version of each detail and add it to the chart.

Vocabulary Development

- Pronounce each vocabulary word for students, and read the definitions as a class. Have students identify any words with which they are already familiar.

CUSTOMIZE INSTRUCTION FOR UNIVERSAL ACCESS

For Special Needs Students	For Less Proficient Readers	For English Learners
Have students read *Don Quixote* in the **Adapted Reader's Companion.** This version provides basic-level instruction in an interactive format with questions and write-on lines. Completing the adapted version will prepare students to read the selection in the Student Edition.	Have students read the adapted version of *Don Quixote* in the **Reader's Companion.** This version provides basic-level instruction in an interactive format with questions and write-on lines. After students finish the selection in the **Reader's Companion,** have them complete the questions and activities in the Student Edition.	Have students read the adapted version of *Don Quixote* in the **English Learner's Companion.** This version provides basic-level instruction in an interactive format with questions and write-on lines. Completing the adapted version will prepare students to read the selection in the Student Edition.

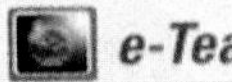 **e-Teach**

Visit e-Teach at PHSchool.com for teachers' essays on how to teach, with questions and answers.

TEACH

Step-by-Step Teaching Guide for pp. 700–714

Teaching Tenth-Grade Students

10TH GRADE Ask a tenth-grade student to look up the word *quixotic* in the dictionary. After he or she reads the definition aloud, tell students that this word was coined with Don Quixote in mind.

1 About the Selection

The list of 'enchantments, quarrels, battles, challenges, woundes," tales of love, and its torments summerizes the "impossible things" in the stories of knights that Cervantes parodies.

2 Literary Analysis

Parody

- Remind students that parodies assume that the audience has knowledge of the topic being mocked. Ask students to offer ideas about the average knight's financial situation.
  Possible response: Knights were able to provide well for themselves.
- Ask how Don Quixote's life parodies knighthood.
  Answer: Don Quixote barely manages to feed and clothe himself.
- Ask students the Literary Analysis question on p. 700: In what way do Don Quixote's age and physical appearance parody the typical heroic knight?
  Answer: Don Quixote is older than the average knight and skinny.

3 Vocabulary Development

Latin Root *-ject-*

- Refer students to the word *conjectures* in the bracketed passage.
- Tell students that this word has the Latin root *-ject-*, which means "to throw."
- Ask students to offer ideas about the connection between "to throw" and *guesses*, the word's definition.
  Answer: Someone "throws in" a guess when he or she does not have an exact answer.

1

from
Don Quixote
Miguel de Cervantes
translated by Samuel Putnam

Background

In traditional courtly romances, a knight-errant is a great fighter who has earned renown in jousting and tournaments. He spends his life wandering the land, performing deeds of bravery in the name of a noble woman who can never return his affection. This impossible love and its accompanying code of honor justify the knight's death-defying adventures. Don Quixote sees himself as such a knight, and no reality can resist his fabulous imagination.

Chapter I

Which treats of the station in life and the pursuits of the famous gentleman, Don Quixote de la Mancha.

2 In a village of La Mancha[1] the name of which I have no desire to recall, there lived not so long ago one of those gentlemen who always have a lance in the rack, an ancient buckler, a skinny nag, and a greyhound for the chase. A stew with more beef than mutton in it, chopped meat for his evening meal, scraps for a Saturday, lentils on Friday, and a young pigeon as a special delicacy for Sunday, went to account for three-quarters of his income. The rest of it he laid out on a broadcloth greatcoat and velvet stockings for feast days, with slippers to match, while the other days of the week he cut a figure in a suit of the finest homespun. Living with him were a housekeeper in her forties, a niece who was not yet twenty, and a lad of the field and market place who saddled his horse for him and wielded the pruning knife.

This gentleman of ours was close on to fifty, of a robust constitution but with little flesh on his bones and a face that was lean and gaunt. 3 He was noted for his early rising, being very fond of the hunt. They will try to tell you that his surname was Quijada or Quesada—there is some difference of opinion among those who have written on the subject—but according to the most likely conjectures we are to understand

Literary Analysis
Parody In what way do Don Quixote's age and physical appearance parody the typical heroic knight?

constitution (kän′ stə to͞o′ shən) *n.* structure or makeup of a person or thing

conjectures (kən jek′ chərz) *n.* guesses

1. **La Mancha** province in south central Spain.

TEACHING RESOURCES

The following resources can be used to enrich or extend the instruction for pp. 700–714.

Literary Analysis
- **Selection Support:** Literary Analysis, p. 136

Reading
- **Selection Support:** Reading Strategy, p. 135; Build Vocabulary, p. 133

- **Reader's Companion**
- **Adapted Reader's Companion**
- **English Learner's Companion**
- **Listening to Literature Audiocassettes** ■
- **Listening to Literature CDs** ■

■ **BLOCK SCHEDULING:** Resources marked with this symbol provide varied instruction during 90-minute blocks.

4

5 ▲ **Critical Viewing** Which details from this painting match the description in Chapter I of Don Quixote and his horse? **[Analyze]**

4 Background

Art

Don Quixote on Horseback,
by Honoré Daumier

Caricaturist, painter, and sculptor Honoré Daumier (1808–1879) is best known for his cartoons satirizing the politics and society of nineteenth-century France. He found a wide audience for his cartoons attacking certain public figures and aspects of society. After 1850, Daumier produced a series of works based on *Don Quixote.* This image of Don Quixote on his horse is very loosely rendered and appears incomplete when compared to earlier, more detailed versions of the painting. Nevertheless, his lively use of line and texture captures the essence of the gentleman of La Mancha.

Use the following questions for discussion:

- Why do you think Daumier painted Don Quixote as a faceless figure? Possible response: Don Quixote masquerades as a knight. By painting him as faceless, Daumier suggests that the "real" Don Quixote is unknown, despite his being a highly recognizable literary figure.
- Ask students to identify details from the painting that show Daumier's respect for Don Quixote. Possible response: Don Quixote's good posture suggests confidence, as does the casual way he holds his shield. His lance looks serviceable.

5 ▶Critical Viewing

Possible response: The man appears skinny; his horse is bony; he carries a lance; and he wears a helmet.

CUSTOMIZE INSTRUCTION FOR UNIVERSAL ACCESS

For Gifted/Talented Students

Point out to students the relation between parodies, such as this story of Don Quixote, and caricatures, or pictures of people that exaggerate certain physical attributes. Tell students that parodies and caricatures are both meant to create a humorous effect.

Most students will know caricature from political cartoons. Have them find examples of caricatures by classic or contemporary artists. Invite interested students to write short essays that explain the parody in the caricatures.

Other students may be interested in creating their own caricatures. Have each student choose a well-known figure, such as a movie or rock star, and draw a caricature of that person, exaggerating some physical attribute in a humorous way.

Have students read their parodies and display their caricatures to the class.

6 Critical Thinking

Draw Conclusions

- Remind students that although conclusions are based on information provided by the text, prior knowledge is often needed.
- Have students discuss Don Quixote's interest described in the bracketed passage.
- Ask students what conclusions they can draw about Don Quixote's interest in books of chivalry.
Answer: Because reading is taking over his life, Don Quixote may lose a great deal if he does not resume meeting his responsibilities.

7 Literary Analysis

Parody

- Have a student volunteer read aloud the bracketed passage.
- Ask students to name details in the quoted passages that suggest a parody for literary works.
Answer: The mock loftiness of the passage and the absurd repetitions within it suggest parody.
- Ask students why they think Cervantes included this passage.
Possible response: Cervantes wanted to show the artificiality and banality of the typical heroic novel.

8 ▶Critical Viewing

Possible response: Don Quixote would be fascinated with the bravery conveyed in the knight's confident stance; the knight's armor, flag, and sword; and his standing in water—unusual since knights are often seen on horseback.

that it was really Quejana. But all this means very little so far as our story is concerned, providing that in the telling of it we do not depart one iota from the truth.

6 You may know, then, that the aforesaid gentleman, on those occasions when he was at leisure, which was most of the year around, was in the habit of reading books of chivalry with such pleasure and devotion as to lead him almost wholly to forget the life of a hunter and even the administration of his estate. So great was his curiosity and infatuation in this regard that he even sold many acres of tillable land in order to be able to buy and read the books that he loved, and he would carry home with him as many of them as he could obtain.

Of all those that he thus devoured none pleased him so well as the ones that had been composed by the famous Feliciano de Silva, whose lucid prose style and involved conceits[2] were as precious to him as pearls; especially when he came to read those tales of love and amorous challenges that are to be met with in many places, such a passage as the following, 7 for example: "The reason of the unreason that afflicts my reason, in such a manner weakens my reason that I with reason lament me of your comeliness." And he was similarly affected when his eyes fell upon such lines as these: ". . . the high Heaven of your divinity divinely fortifies you with the stars and renders you deserving of that desert your greatness doth deserve."

The poor fellow used to lie awake nights in an effort to disentangle the meaning and make sense out of passages such as these, although Aristotle himself would not have been able to understand them, even if he had been resurrected for that sole purpose. He was not at ease in his mind over those wounds that Don Belianís gave and received; for no matter how great the surgeons who treated him, the poor fellow must have been left with his face and his entire body covered with marks and scars. Nevertheless, he was grateful to the author for closing the book with the promise of an interminable adventure to come; many a time he was tempted to take up his pen and literally finish the tale as had been promised, and he undoubtedly would have done so, and would have succeeded at it very well, if his thoughts had not been constantly occupied with other things of greater moment.

8 ▲ Critical Viewing Which details in this picture might Don Quixote find fascinating? Explain. **[Speculate]**

infatuation (in fach´ o͞o ā´ shən) *n.* foolish or shallow feelings of affection

2. **conceits** elaborate comparisons or metaphors.

ENRICHMENT: Literature Connection

Amadis of Gaul

Among the stories that Don Quixote reads voraciously is the chivalric romance *Amadis of Gaul.* The story dates to the late thirteenth century, but it was first published in Spain in 1508.

The story was so popular that its hero, Amadis, became the model for the perfect knight: brave, romantic, and chaste. Influenced by the Arthurian legends, it is the tale of the battles Amadis must fight to win the love of Oriana, an English princess.

Because *Amadis of Gaul* was so well known, the romance spawned many sequels and poor imitations. Cervantes was familiar with both the original and its derivatives, and he drew from them both in writing his parody, *Don Quixote.* This is particularly apparent in the quotation from "the famous Feliciano de Silva" on p. 702.

The 1605 publication of *Don Quixote* ended the popularity of the more serious chivalric romances.

He often talked it over with the village curate,[3] who was a learned man, a graduate of Sigüenza,[4] and they would hold long discussions as to who had been the better knight, Palmerin of England or Amadis of Gaul; but Master Nicholas, the barber of the same village, was in the
9 habit of saying that no one could come up to the Knight of Phoebus, and that if anyone *could* compare with him it was Don Galaor, brother of Amadis of Gaul, for Galaor was ready for anything—he was none of your finical[5] knights, who went around whimpering as his brother did, and in point of valor he did not lag behind him.

In short, our gentleman became so immersed in his reading that he spent whole nights from sundown to sunup and his days from dawn to dusk in poring over his books, until, finally, from so little sleeping and so much reading, his brain dried up and he went completely out of his mind. He had filled his imagination with everything that he had read, with enchantments, knightly encounters, battles, challenges, wounds, with tales of love and its torments, and all sorts of impossible things,
10 and as a result had come to believe that all these fictitious happenings were true; they were more real to him than anything else in the world. He would remark that the Cid Ruy Díaz[6] had been a very good knight, but there was no comparison between him and the Knight of the Flaming Sword, who with a single backward stroke had cut in half two fierce and monstrous giants. He preferred Bernardo del Carpio, who at Roncesvalles had slain Roland despite the charm the latter bore, availing himself of the stratagem which Hercules employed when he strangled Antaeus, the son of Earth, in his arms.

He had much good to say for Morgante who, though he belonged to the haughty, overbearing race of giants, was of an affable disposition and well brought up. But, above all, he cherished an admiration for Rinaldo of Montalbán, especially as he beheld him sallying forth from his castle to rob all those that crossed his path, or when he thought of him overseas stealing the image of Mohammed which, so the story has it, was all of gold. And he would have liked very well to have had his fill of kicking that traitor Galalón, a privilege for which he would have given his housekeeper with his niece thrown into the bargain.

At last, when his wits were gone beyond repair, he came to conceive the strangest idea that ever occurred to any madman in this world. It now appeared to him fitting and necessary, in order to win a greater amount of honor for himself and serve his country at the same time, to become a knight-errant and roam the world on horseback, in a suit of armor; he would go in quest of adventures, by way of putting into practice all that he had read in his books; he would right every manner of wrong, placing himself in situations of the greatest peril such as would

3. **curate** clergyman in charge of a parish.
4. **Sigüenza** (se gwän′ sä) one of a group of "minor universities" granting degrees that were often laughed at by Spanish humorists.
5. **finical** (fin′i kəl) finicky.
6. **Cid Ruy Díaz** (cēd ro͞o′ ē dē′ äs) famous Spanish soldier Ruy Diaz de Vivar: called the Cid, a derivation of the Arabic word for *lord*.

Reading Strategy
Comparing and Contrasting Compare and contrast Don Quixote's current lifestyle with that of the knights described in this passage.

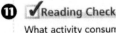

11 **✓Reading Check**
What activity consumes Don Quixote's time from dawn to dusk each day?

9 Critical Thinking

Relate

- Point out that in the bracketed passage, Cervantes is poking fun at certain aspects of the culture of the day. Ask students to identify what these might be.
  Answer: People invest much time and energy in thinking about stories that simply are meant to entertain them.
- Ask students to identify aspects of our culture that compare to the ones Cervantes mocks in this passage.
  Answer: This passage relates to contemporary people's tendency to talk hypothetically about characters from action and horror movies, telling what those characters could do in the "real" world, or to each other, if they should meet.

10 Reading Strategy

Comparing and Contrasting

- Remind students that Don Quixote's interest in books about knights was not unique: many people enjoyed the same works. Ask students to compare his approach to his reading with that of other readers.
  Possible response: Most readers do not confuse stories with reality, no matter how much they enjoy reading them.
- Have students respond to the Reading Strategy item on p. 703: Compare and contrast Don Quixote's current lifestyle with that of the knights described in this passage.
  Answer: Don Quixote is a poor and sedentary gentleman who spends his time reading, whereas the knights described in this passage pursue adventure and perform feats of valor.

11 ✓Reading Check

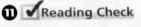

Answer: Reading books about the adventures of knights consumes Don Quixote's time.

CUSTOMIZE INSTRUCTION FOR UNIVERSAL ACCESS

For Special Needs Students	For Gifted/Talented Students	For Advanced Readers
Tell students that *Don Quixote* inspired a film and a Broadway musical, both entitled *Man of La Mancha*. Obtain a copy of the film, and show segments to students. Ask students to talk about what they learned about Don Quixote from watching the segments.	Tell students that *Don Quixote* inspired a film and a Broadway musical, both entitled *Man of La Mancha*. Obtain a copy of the film, and show segments. Ask students who play musical instruments to find the sheet music for one of the songs and play it for the class.	Obtain a copy of the film *Man of La Mancha* and show segments to students. Ask students to obtain a copy of the novel *Don Quixote*, and assign parts of it for them to read independently. Ask students to write a report about the film's degree of faithfulness to these parts of the novel.

12 Reading Strategy

Comparing and Contrasting

- Have students read and discuss the bracketed passage. Ask students why they think Don Quixote refrains from testing the latest version of his helmet.
  Answer: Don Quixote wants to believe that this version, unlike his earlier attempts, will not fall apart.
- Ask students the Reading Strategy item on p. 704: Compare and contrast Don Quixote's armor with that of a traditional knight.
  Answer: A traditional knight's helmet is polished, impressive-looking, fully closed, and able to withstand cuts and blows. Don Quixote's helmet is a crude and improvised piece of old armor with a cardboard visor.

13 Critical Thinking

Connect

- Refer students to the bracketed passage, and have them discuss the appearance of the horse. Ask students to draw conclusions about the condition of the animal.
  Answer: Cracks in its hoof, the old nag, blemishes, and the reference to skin and bones indicate that the horse is in poor condition.
- Ask students in what ways Don Quixote's approach to naming his horse is similar to his approach to outfitting himself with armor.
  Answer: In both cases, he uses his imagination to transform something shabby into something heroic; he does all he can to model himself on the famous knights whom he admires.

redound to the eternal glory of his name. As a reward for his valor and the might of his arm, the poor fellow could already see himself crowned Emperor of Trebizond[7] at the very least; and so, carried away by the strange pleasure that he found in such thoughts as these, he at once set about putting his plan into effect.

12 The first thing he did was to burnish up some old pieces of armor, left him by his great-grandfather, which for ages had lain in a corner, moldering and forgotten. He polished and adjusted them as best he could, and then he noticed that one very important thing was lacking: there was no closed helmet, but only a morion, or visorless headpiece, with turned up brim of the kind foot soldiers wore. His ingenuity, however, enabled him to remedy this, and he proceeded to fashion out of cardboard a kind of half-helmet, which, when attached to the morion, gave the appearance of a whole one. True, when he went to see if it was strong enough to withstand a good slashing blow, he was somewhat disappointed; for when he drew his sword and gave it a couple of thrusts, he succeeded only in undoing a whole week's labor. The ease with which he had hewed it to bits disturbed him no little, and he decided to make it over. This time he placed a few strips of iron on the inside, and then, convinced that it was strong enough, refrained from putting it to any further test; instead, he adopted it then and there as the finest helmet ever made.

ingenuity (in′je no͞o′ ə tē) *n.* cleverness; inventiveness

Reading Strategy
Comparing and Contrasting Compare and contrast Don Quixote's armor with that of a traditional knight.

13 After this, he went out to have a look at his nag; and although the animal had more *cuartos*, or cracks, in its hoof than there are quarters in a real, [8] and more blemishes than Gonela's steed which *tantum pellis et ossa fuit*,[9] it nonetheless looked to its master like a far better horse than Alexander's Bucephalus or the Babieca of the Cid.[10] He spent all of four days in trying to think up a name for his mount; for—so he told himself—seeing that it belonged to so famous and worthy a knight, there was no reason why it should not have a name of equal renown. The kind of name he wanted was one that would at once indicate what the nag had been before it came to belong to a knight-errant and what its present status was; for it stood to reason that, when the master's worldly condition changed, his horse also ought to have a famous, high-sounding appellation, one suited to the new order of things and the new profession that it was to follow.

After he in his memory and imagination had made up, struck out, and discarded many names, now adding to and now subtracting from the list, he finally hit upon "Rocinante," a name that impressed him as being sonorous and at the same time indicative of what the steed had

7. **Trebizond** (treb′ i zänd) in medieval times, a Greek empire off the southeast coast of the Black Sea.
8. **real** (rā äl′) former coin of Spain. In a real, there were eight *cuartos*, which means both "quarters" and "cracks."
9. ***tantum pellis et ossa fuit*** (tän′ tum pel′ is et äs′ə fo͞o′ it) Latin: "It was nothing but skin and bones."
10. **Alexander's Bucephalus** (byo͞o sef′ ə les) **or the Babieca** (bäb ē ä′kä) **of the Cid** Bucephalus was Alexander the Great's war horse; Babieca was the Cid's war horse.

ENRICHMENT: History Connection

History of Armor

The first thing that Don Quixote does after deciding to become a knight-errant is to clean up some old and rusty armor that had belonged to his ancestors. The outfit that he restores would have dated from the period in which the manufacturing and use of armor reached its peak in Europe—the 1300s to the mid-1500s. After this time, gunpowder was increasingly used in battle and the production of armor, useful in hand-to-hand combat, declined.

Don Quixote Preparing His Armor; scene from the novel by Cervantes, Zacarias Velazquez Gonzalez, Caylus Anticuario, Madrid, Spain

◀ **Critical Viewing** 15
In most cases, only the wealthy could afford the costly armor, horse, and training necessary to become a knight. Which details in this painting suggest that Don Quixote did not possess such wealth? **[Interpret]**

↑ been when it was but a hack,[11] whereas now it was nothing other than the first and foremost of all the hacks in the world.

Having found a name for his horse that pleased his fancy, he then desired to do as much for himself, and this required another week, and by the end of that period he had made up his mind that he was henceforth to be known as Don Quixote, which, as has been stated, has led the authors of this veracious history to assume that his real name 16

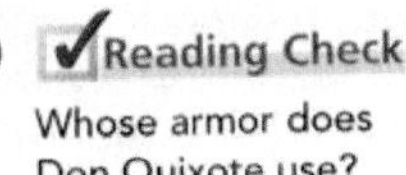

Reading Check
Whose armor does Don Quixote use?

11. **hack** horse used in all kinds of work and usually well worn out in service.

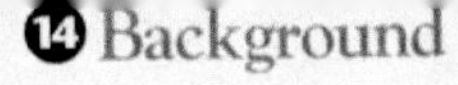

14 Background

Art

Don Quixote Preparing His Armour,
by Zacarías González Velázquez

Zacarías González Velázquez (1763–1834) belonged to the González Velázquez family of Spanish artists. His grandfather, father, uncles, and brothers were all artists.

In this painting, Velázquez portrays Don Quixote getting his armor ready for his great adventure. The plainness of the room, with its drab walls and sparse furnishings, contrasts with Don Quixote's dreams of becoming a magnificent knight-errant.

Use these questions for discussion:

- What items in the room show Don Quixote's interest in knighthood?
  Answer: The pieces of armor, the sword, and the scroll on the wall all show interest in knighthood.
- What crucial part of his interest in knighthood is missing from the painting?
  Answer: None of Quixote's many books of chivalry appear in the painting.
- How would you describe the attitude or pose of Don Quixote in this painting?
  Answer: He appears to be full of energy, purposeful, and impatient to complete his work.

15 ▶ Critical Viewing

Answer: The rough, unfinished look of his door, window, and floor; his nearly unadorned walls; and his rustic furniture show that Don Quixote is not a wealthy man.

16 ✓ Reading Check

Answer: Don Quixote uses his great-grandfather's armor.

CUSTOMIZE INSTRUCTION FOR UNIVERSAL ACCESS

For Less Proficient Readers	For English Learners	For Advanced Readers
Ask students to explain the events of the story so far. Have them offer details about Don Quixote that make him unique. Then, work with them to complete **Selection Support: Literary Analysis,** p. 136.	Discuss with students the events of the story so far. Have them describe the character of Don Quixote. Make sure they understand that Don Quixote is a parody of a real knight. Review qualities of a real knight, if needed. Then, work with them to complete **Selection Support: Literary Analysis,** p. 136.	Have students discuss their impressions of Don Quixote so far. Ask them why they think he is a character remembered by many readers. Then, challenge them to complete **Literary Analysis for Enrichment,** p. 34.

17 Background

Art

Dulcinea del Toboso, by Charles Robert Leslie

Charles Robert Leslie (1794–1856) was born in London to American parents. Although he was raised and educated for the most part in the United States, he studied art in England.

Much of his work focused on scenes from literary works, such as this painting depicting Don Quixote's ladylove, Dulcinea.

Use these questions for discussion:

- According to this painting, what kind of person does Dulcinea appear to be?
  Possible response: Some students will note that she appears to be innocent and have a sweet disposition; however, others may find her expression coy.
- How would you describe the expression on her face?
  Answer: She appears thoughtful and not self-conscious, perhaps unaware that she is being observed.

18 ▶Critical Viewing

Possible response: Although the young woman is pretty, her dress does not look like one worn by a princess or a great lady, nor is her casual gesture or facial expression commonly found in portraits of such women.

19 Literary Analysis

Parody

- Point out that the knight Amadis chose to take the name of Gaul, the ancient Roman province that was his "kingdom and fatherland."
- Have students note what name Don Quixote has chosen for himself. Ask them what makes this a humorous parody of the character Amadis of Gaul.
  Answer: Don Quixote de la Mancha means Don Quixote of La Mancha, which is an undistinguished province of south central Spain, not a "kingdom and fatherland."

17

Dulcinea del Toboso from *Don Quixote* by Cervantes, 1839, Charles Robert Leslie

◀ **Critical Viewing 18** Do you think the woman in this painting conveys "the suggestion of a princess or a great lady" worthy of being Don Quixote's ladylove? Why or why not? **[Make a Judgment]**

must undoubtedly have been Quijada, and not Quesada as others would have it. But remembering that the valiant Amadis was not content to call himself that and nothing more, but added the name of his kingdom and fatherland that he might make it famous also, and thus
19 came to take the name Amadis of Gaul, so our good knight chose to add his place of origin and become "Don Quixote de la Mancha"; for by this means, as he saw it, he was making very plain his lineage and was conferring honor upon his country by taking its name as his own.

And so, having polished up his armor and made the morion over into a closed helmet, and having given himself and his horse a name, he naturally found but one thing lacking still: he must seek out a lady of

CUSTOMIZE INSTRUCTION FOR UNIVERSAL ACCESS

For English Learners

Have students discuss the conversation in which Sancho Panza urges Don Quixote to talk about the pain he is in. Ask students to discuss the main points each character makes and why he makes those points. Remind students that Sancho Panza, as a parent and a farmer, is accustomed to taking care of people and things that need his help, whereas Don Quixote wants to emulate a brave knight by keeping his pain a secret.

Have students work in pairs to role-play the parts of both characters. Encourage them also to use both facial expressions and gestures to help them communicate the personality traits of the characters.

Let students evaluate their own and their classmates' work. After each performance you might ask the following; Did the scene bring out the contrasts between the characters? How did it show these contrasts?

whom he could become enamored; for a knight-errant without a ladylove was like a tree without leaves or fruit, a body without a soul.

20 "If," he said to himself, "as a punishment for my sins or by a stroke of fortune I should come upon some giant hereabouts, a thing that very commonly happens to knights-errant, and if I should slay him in a hand-to-hand encounter or perhaps cut him in two, or, finally, if I should vanquish and subdue him, would it not be well to have someone to whom I may send him as a present, in order that he, if he is living, may come in, fall upon his knees in front of my sweet lady, and say in a humble and submissive tone of voice, 'I, lady, am the giant Caraculiambro, lord of the island Malindrania, who has been overcome in single combat by that knight who never can be praised enough, Don Quixote de la Mancha, the same who sent me to present myself before your Grace that your Highness may dispose of me as you see fit'?"

Oh, how our good knight reveled in this speech, and more than ever when he came to think of the name that he should give his lady! As the story goes, there was a very good-looking farm girl who lived near by, with whom he had once been smitten, although it is generally believed that she never knew or suspected it. Her name was Aldonza Lorenzo, and it seemed to him that she was the one upon whom he should bestow the title of mistress of his thoughts. For her he wished a name that should not be incongruous with his own and that would convey the suggestion of a princess or a great lady; and, accordingly, he resolved to call her "Dulcinea del Toboso," she being a native of that place. A musical name to his ears, out of the ordinary and significant, like the others he had chosen for himself and his appurtenances.

Literary Analysis
Parody List three details from chivalric romances that are parodied in this paragraph.

incongruous (in kän' groo̅ əs) *adj.* inconsistent; lacking in harmony

Review and Assess

Thinking About the Selection

1. **Respond:** What do you find most humorous about Don Quixote's behavior? Why?
2. **(a) Recall:** What name does Don Quixote choose for his horse? **(b) Infer:** Identify two considerations Don Quixote makes as he chooses names. **(c) Speculate:** In what way might a simple change of name affect Don Quixote's entire world?
3. **(a) Recall:** Who is Aldonza Loreno? **(b) Analyze:** What role will she play in Don Quixote's adventures? **(c) Compare:** In what way does she fulfill the stereotype of a knight's ladylove?
4. **(a) Make a Judgment:** What theme do you think Don Quixote embodies? **(b) Support:** Which details in Chapter I reflect that theme?
5. **Evaluate:** Do you consider Don Quixote insane or the noble victim of an overactive imagination? Explain.

CUSTOMIZE INSTRUCTION FOR UNIVERSAL ACCESS

For Special Needs Students	For Less Proficient Readers	For English Learners
Review with students the elements of the life of a "knight-errant" that Don Quixote has created so far. Help students review the story thus far by having them read along with the **Listening to Literature** audiotape or CD for this selection.	Ask students to describe the elements of the life of a "knight-errant" that Don Quixote has created so far. Have students review the story thus far by using the **Listening to Literature** audiotape or CD for this selection.	Review with students some of the difficult vocabulary words on p. 707. Ask students to describe the elements of a "knight-errant" that Don Quixote has created so far. Review the story thus far by using the **Listening to Literature** audiotape or CD for this selection.

20 Literary Analysis

Parody

- Ask students to whom Don Quixote is speaking in the bracketed passage.
  Answer: He is speaking to himself.
- Have students respond to the Literary Analysis item on p. 707: List three details from chivalric romances that are parodied in this paragraph.
  Possible response: Don Quixote refers to encounters with giants as "common occurrences" within such tales; he imitates the absurdly flowery style of speech in these tales when he imagines the dying words of the giant Caraculiambro, and he finds a pretext to refer to himself immodestly and ridiculously as "that knight who never can be praised enough."

Answers for p. 707

Review and Assess

1. Possible response: Repairing his helmet by adding a cardboard visor is humorous; it shows Don Quixote's foolishness because the helmet could not withstand a real blow.
2. **(a)** Don Quixote names his horse Rocinante. **(b)** Don Quixote wants the name to sound musical, pleasing, and noble. **(c)** Changing a name transforms Don Quixote's everyday world into a world of fantasy.
3. **(a)** Aldonza Lorenzo is Don Quixote's chosen ladylove, whom he renames Dulcinea. **(b)** Aldonza will be the lady to whom he dedicates his deeds of valor. **(c)** Aldonza is young and attractive.
4. **(a)** Possible response: Don Quixote embodies the theme that fantasy, or imagination, enriches a person's life. **(b)** Don Quixote takes ordinary things such as old, rusty armor; a broken-down nag; and a farm girl and places them in a fantasy world of knights and chivalry.
5. Don Quixote may be insane because he is completely out of touch with reality. He may simply have an overactive imagination, because he very carefully constructs the details of his fantasy world.

21 Critical Thinking

Analyze

- Have students explain the subject of the conversations described in the bracketed passage.
  Answer: Don Quixote argues that the world needs a revival of chivalry, complete with knights-errant.
- Ask students to explain the curate's "artifice" and why he needs to use it in talking with Don Quixote.
  Answer: The curate pretends that Don Quixote has persuaded him to agree with the need for knights and chivalry. The "artifice" stops Quixote from arguing and may even help the curate change the subject.

22 Literary Analysis

Parody

- Ask a volunteer to read the bracketed passage aloud. Ask students to describe the character of Sancho Panza.
  Answer: Sancho Panza is a poor farmer, good hearted but not very bright; he is gullible and believes Don Quixote's promises about winning an island.
- Tell students that squires were usually young men who were expected to help the knights they served in order to prove themselves worthy of becoming knights themselves.
- Ask students the Literary Analysis question on p. 708: In what ways is Sancho Panza a parody of an ideal knight's squire?
  Answer: Sancho Panza is not young; he already has responsibilities to his family and the farm he tends; because he freely admits to not walking very much, he wants to bring along a donkey.

Chapter VII

Of the second sally of our good knight, Don Quixote de la Mancha.

. . . He remained at home very tranquilly for a couple of weeks, without giving sign of any desire to repeat his former madness. During that time he had the most pleasant conversations with his two old friends, the curate and the barber, on the point he had raised to the effect that what the world needed most was knights-errant and a revival of chivalry. The curate would occasionally contradict him and again would give in, for it was only by means of this artifice that he could carry on a conversation with him at all. **21**

In the meanwhile Don Quixote was bringing his powers of persuasion to bear upon a farmer who lived near by, a good man—if this title may be applied to one who is poor—but with very few wits in his head. The short of it is, by pleas and promises, he got the hapless rustic to agree to ride forth with him and serve him as his squire.[1] Among other things, Don Quixote told him that he ought to be more than willing to go, because no telling what adventure might occur which would win them an island, and then he (the farmer) would be left to be the governor of it. As a result of these and other similar assurances, Sancho Panza forsook his wife and children and consented to take upon himself the duties of squire to his neighbor. **22**

Next, Don Quixote set out to raise some money, and by selling this thing and pawning that and getting the worst of the bargain always, he finally scraped together a reasonable amount. He also asked a friend of his for the loan of a buckler and patched up his broken helmet as well as he could. He advised his squire, Sancho, of the day and hour when they were to take the road and told him to see to laying in a supply of those things that were most necessary, and, above all, not to forget the saddlebags. Sancho replied that he would see to all this and added that he was also thinking of taking along with him a very good ass that he had, as he was not much used to going on foot.

With regard to the ass, Don Quixote had to do a little thinking, trying to recall if any knight-errant had ever had a squire thus asininely mounted. He could not think of any but nevertheless he decided to take Sancho with the intention of providing him with a nobler steed as soon as occasion offered; he had but to appropriate the horse of the first discourteous knight he met. Having furnished himself with shirts and all

Literary Analysis
Parody In what ways is Sancho Panza a parody of an ideal knight's squire?

appropriate (ə prō′ prē āt′) *v.* take for one's own use

1. **squire** (skwir) knight's attendant.

ENRICHMENT: History Connection

Sign of the Times

Cervantes was born at the peak of Spain's Golden Age, a time when Spanish power and influence in Europe and the Western Hemisphere were greater than ever before or since. By the time Cervantes wrote *Don Quixote*, however, Spain's fortunes were fast declining because of a series of disastrous wars, bad economic policies, and the stunning defeat of the Spanish Armada by the British navy in 1588. This last event signaled the end of Spain's rule of the seas and the beginning of England's rule.

To some extent, Spain's fall from great confidence to deep despair is echoed in the novel, as Don Quixote takes refuge in chivalry from the realities of an unfriendly world.

23 the other things that the innkeeper had recommended, he and Panza rode forth one night unseen by anyone and without taking leave of wife and children, housekeeper or niece. They went so far that by the time morning came they were safe from discovery had a hunt been started for them.

24  **Reading Check**

What service does Don Quixote persuade Sancho Panza to provide?

25

Don Quixote and Sancho Panza Riding Clavileno, Zacarias Velazquez Gonzalez, Caylus Antiquario, Madrid, Spain

26 ▲ **Critical Viewing** Compare and contrast the preparations for knighthood that Don Quixote makes to the training depicted in this painting. **[Compare and Contrast]**

CUSTOMIZE INSTRUCTION FOR UNIVERSAL ACCESS

For Advanced Readers

Have students conduct research to find out what knights did when there were no wars to wage. Ask them to find information about tournaments, jousts, melees, and the special armor made for these activities.

Tell students that in the twelfth century, the Catholic Church was so alarmed at the number of deaths that occurred during these "peaceful" events, that it banned all tournaments. Ask students to research this topic as well.

Arrange a debate between a knight who wants the tournaments to continue and a church official who is steadfast in upholding the ban. Arrange students into two groups to prepare the speakers' remarks and rebuttals by reviewing their research. As the debate unfolds, other students should listen carefully, evaluate both arguments, and reach a consensus on whether the tournaments should continue.

23 Critical Thinking

Infer

- Have students read the bracketed passage.
- Ask students why they think Sancho Panza and Don Quixote set out on their adventure in the night, without telling anyone. **Answer:** Don Quixote and Sancho Panza do not want anyone to know they are leaving because they are afraid people might try to stop them.

24 Reading Check

Answer: Don Quixote persuades Sancho Panza to become his squire.

25 Background

Art

Don Quixote and Sancho Panza Riding Clavileno, by Zacarías González Velázquez

This painting illustrates an episode from Part II of *Don Quixote* in which Don Quixote and Sancho Panza ride the wooden horse, Clavileno. Don Quixote believes that the wooden horse is magical and was originally constructed by the magician Merlin.

In this painting, Don Quixote and Sancho Panza believe they are about to fly away on Clavileno to rescue the Princess Antonomasia.

Use this question for discussion: What details of the painting capture the humor of the situation? **Answer:** Don Quixote and Sancho Panza do not look like valiant knights as they perch awkwardly on the rough, wooden horse, which seems to lack magical potential.

26 ▶ Critical Viewing

Possible response: Real knights probably practice jousting with each other and use reliable armor, weapons, and horses as they learn battle maneuvers.

27 Background

Chivalric Romances

Although little is know about the twelfth-century French writer, Chrétien de Troyes, the influence of his writings has lasted for more than eight centuries. Indeed, stories like the ones he wrote enchanted Don Quixote, a character invented four centuries later. Chrétien de Troyes did more than any other writer to introduce tales of King Arthur's knights to literature.

The author's three major works, *Yvain, Lancelot,* and *Perceval,* are all tales of knights of King Arthur's Round Table. *Yvain* and *Lancelot* explore the conflict between love and the knight's chivalric duty to seek out new adventures to bring greater glory to himself or to his lord. Lancelot sacrifices his honor for love. Yvain abandons the woman he loves in favor of a quest for knightly glory, only to learn of the foolishness of his choice. *Perceval,* on the other hand, focuses on a knight's spiritual quest.

28 Reading Strategy

Comparing and Contrasting

- Point out that in the bracketed passage, Sancho Panza claims that he could govern any island that Don Quixote might give him. Ask students to compare Sancho Panza's confidence in himself with what they know about his abilities and his previous work experience.
  Possible response: Because Sancho Panza impulsively leaves his family and farm to be Don Quixote's squire, he seems to be more of a follower than a leader; he is dim-witted, gullible, and has no political experience, all of which further contradict his belief that he can successfully govern an island.
- Ask students to respond to the Reading Strategy item on p. 710: Compare and contrast the promises Don Quixote makes with the actual abilities of a knight to grant such favors.
  Answer: Knights are usually in the service of great lords or of the

Mounted on his ass, Sancho Panza rode along like a patriarch, with saddlebags and flask, his mind set upon becoming governor of that island that his master had promised him. Don Quixote determined to take the same route and road over the Campo de Montiel[2] that he had followed on his first journey; but he was not so uncomfortable this time, for it was early morning and the sun's rays fell upon them slantingly and accordingly did not tire them too much.

"Look, Sir Knight-errant," said Sancho, "your Grace should not forget that island you promised me; for no matter how big it is, I'll be able to govern it right enough."

28 "I would have you know, friend Sancho Panza," replied Don Quixote, "that among the knights-errant of old it was a very common custom to make their squires governors of the islands or the kingdoms that they won, and I am resolved that in my case so pleasing a usage shall not fall into desuetude.[3] I even mean to go them one better; for they very often, perhaps most of the time, waited until their squires were old men who had had their fill of serving their masters during bad days and worse nights, whereupon they would give them the title of count, or marquis at most, of some valley or province more or less. But if you live and I live, it well may be that within a week I shall win some kingdom with others dependent upon it, and it will be the easiest thing in the world to crown you king of one of them. You need not marvel at this, for all sorts of unforeseen things happen to knights like me, and I may readily be able to give you even more than I have promised."

"In that case," said Sancho Panza, "if by one of those miracles of which your Grace was speaking I should become king, I would certainly send for Juana Gutiérrez, my old lady, to come and be my queen, and the young ones could be infantes."[4]

"There is no doubt about it," Don Quixote assured him.

"Well, I doubt it," said Sancho, "for I think that even if God were to rain kingdoms upon the earth, no crown would sit well on the head of Mari Gutiérrez,[5] for I am telling you, sir, as a queen she is not worth two maravedis.[6] She would do better as a countess, God help her."

"Leave everything to God, Sancho," said Don Quixote, "and he will give you whatever is most fitting; but I trust you will not be so pusillanimous[7] as to be content with anything less than the title of viceroy."

"That I will not," said Sancho Panza, "especially seeing that I have in your Grace so illustrious a master who can give me all that is suitable to me and all that I can manage."

Themes in World Literature

27 *Chivalric Romances*

Stories of the legendary deeds of King Arthur's knights make up a genre called medieval romances. These romances typically feature idealized knights who are gentlemanly, courteous, and honorable—men whose oaths bind them in fidelity to God, the king, and their lady-loves and whose journeys take them to distant holy lands.

Chivalric romances can be found throughout world literature. The *Song of Roland* recounts heroic deeds in the seventh-century court of Charlemagne. *Perceval*, by Chrétien de Troyes, features a quest for the Grail, or holy cup. Although *Don Quixote* parodies medieval romances like these, the novel nonetheless retains a strong connection to this rich literary heritage.

Reading Strategy
Comparing and Contrasting Compare and contrast the promises that Don Quixote makes with the actual abilities of a knight to grant such favors.

illustrious (i lus´ trē əs) *adj.* distinguished or outstanding

2. **Campo de Montiel** (käm´ pо dā mōn tyĕl´) site of a major battle in Spain in 1369.
3. **desuetude** (des´ wi to͞od) *n.* disuse.
4. **infantes** (in fan´ tāz) sons of Spanish or Portuguese monarchs.
5. **Mari Gutiérrez** Sancho Panza's wife (also called Juana Gutiérrez).
6. **maravedis** (mar´ ə vā dēz) former Spanish coin of trivial monetary value.
7. **pusillanimous** (pyo͞o´ si lan´ ə məs) *adj.* cowardly.

ENRICHMENT: Literature Connection

Cervantes's Dream

Cervantes understood Don Quixote's desire to be something that he could not be. All through his life, Cervantes wanted to be a great poet. He wrote twenty to thirty plays in verse in the years immediately following 1585, but he was not pleased with them. By the time he wrote *Don Quixote,* he knew that he lacked poetic gifts. The absurdity and appeal of this great character at the center of a masterpiece derive not only from Cervantes's graceful style but also from his identification with his hero.

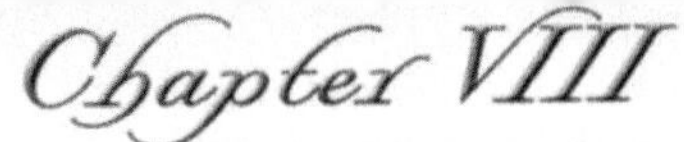

Of the good fortune which the valorous Don Quixote had in the terrifying and never-before-imagined adventure of the windmills, along with other events that deserve to be suitably recorded.

At this point they caught sight of thirty or forty windmills which were standing on the plain there, and no sooner had Don Quixote laid eyes upon them than he turned to his squire and said, "Fortune is guiding our affairs better than we could have wished; for you see there before you, friend Sancho Panza, some thirty or more lawless giants with whom I mean to do battle. I shall deprive them of their lives, and with the spoils from this encounter we shall begin to enrich ourselves; for this is righteous warfare, and it is a great service to God to remove so accursed a breed from the face of the earth."

"What giants?" said Sancho Panza.

"Those that you see there," replied his master, "those with the long arms some of which are as much as two leagues[8] in length."

"But look, your Grace, those are not giants but windmills, and what appear to be arms are their wings which, when whirled in the breeze, cause the millstone to go."

29 "It is plain to be seen," said Don Quixote, "that you have had little experience in this matter of adventures. If you are afraid, go off to one side and say your prayers while I am engaging them in fierce, unequal combat."

Saying this, he gave spurs to his steed Rocinante, without paying any heed to Sancho's warning that these were truly windmills and not giants that he was riding forth to attack. Nor even when he was close upon them did he perceive what they really were, but shouted at the top of his lungs, "Do not seek to flee, cowards and vile creatures that you are, for it is but a single knight with whom you have to deal!"

At that moment a little wind came up and the big wings began turning.

"Though you flourish as many arms as did the giant Briareus," said Don Quixote when he perceived this, "you still shall have to answer to me."

He thereupon commended himself with all his heart to his lady Dulcinea, beseeching her to succor him in this peril; and, being well covered with his shield and with his lance at rest, he bore down upon them at a full gallop and fell upon the first mill that stood in his way,
30 giving a thrust at the wing, which was whirling at such a speed that his lance was broken into bits and both horse and horseman went rolling over the plain, very much battered indeed. Sancho upon his donkey came hurrying to his master's assistance as fast as he could, but when he reached the spot, the knight was unable to move, so great was the shock with which he and Rocinante had hit the ground. 31

8. **league** unit of distance measuring approximately 3.5 miles.

Reading Strategy
Comparing and Contrasting Do you think that, as a knight, Don Quixote is an effective role model for his squire? Why or why not?

Reading Strategy
Comparing and Contrasting Do you think the outcome of Don Quixote's battle is different from that which a real knight would experience? Explain.

31 **✓Reading Check**
What are the giants that Don Quixote intends to fight?

king; they do not have the power to give away kingdoms.

29 Reading Strategy
Comparing and Contrasting

- Ask a volunteer to read the bracketed passage aloud. Ask students what Don Quixote means when he says that he is going to engage the "giants" in "unequal combat."
  Answer: He means that the contest is unequal because he is only one knight and there are many "giants."
- Ask students the first Reading Strategy question on p. 711: Do you think that, as a knight, Don Quixote is an effective role model for his squire? Why or why not?
  Answer: Yes; Don Quixote is an effective role model because he is independent, fearless, and willing to confront what he perceives as evil, even when he is outnumbered. On the other hand, he is not an effective role model, because he behaves foolishly.

Monitor Progress Ask students to point out the differences between the character of Don Quixote and the character of Sancho Panza.
Answer: Don Quixote is a dreamer who does not comprehend reality; Sancho Panza is practical and sees the world for what it is.

30 Reading Strategy
Comparing and Contrasting

- Tell students that the "tilting at windmills" scene is the most famous episode of the novel.
- Ask students the second Reading Strategy question on p. 711: Do you think the outcome of Don Quixote's battle is different from that which a real knight would experience? Explain.
  Possible response: Don Quixote's encounter with the windmill is not a real battle because the windmill is an inanimate object; however, a real knight might also find himself unhorsed and injured after a defeat.

31 ✓Reading Check
Answer: The giants are actually windmills.

CUSTOMIZE INSTRUCTION FOR UNIVERSAL ACCESS

For Gifted/Talented Students

Tell students that the scene described on p. 711—tilting at windmills—is not only the most famous from this novel, it is one of the most famous scenes in all of Western literature. The phrase itself—"tilting at windmills"—has entered the English language and refers to an act that is courageous but foolish or is based on an incomplete understanding of the situation.

Ask students to draw or paint an image of this scene, showing Don Quixote on Rocinante, "tilting at windmills." Refer students to the image on p. 713, which depicts the end of Quixote's "battle."

Suggest that students capture Don Quixote's earnest pursuit of defeating "giants" or the humor of the situation in their artwork. Have students display their completed work in the classroom.

32 Critical Thinking

Infer

- Point out that the magician Frestón, to whom Don Quixote refers in the bracketed passage, was introduced in a chapter that precedes this episode.
- Ask students who they think Frestón might be.
  Possible response: Frestón might be an evil magician whom Don Quixote has invented, or he may be a real person who has taken Quixote's possessions because he has failed to fulfill his "real world" responsibilities.

33 Literary Analysis

Parody

- Read and discuss with students the bracketed passage.
- Ask students what aspects of knights' conduct is parodied in this passage.
  Possible response: Don Quixote's refusal to admit that he is injured makes him feel like a brave knight, but Sancho Panza cannot perform his duty as squire if he does not know his knight needs help.
- Have students respond to the Literary Analysis item on p. 712: List three "things that are almost beyond belief" that Don Quixote has already experienced.
  Possible response: Don Quixote's renaming of the horse and Aldonza Lorenzo to make them appear to be figures of chivalry; the assembly of a suit of armor from old pieces or armor, cardboard, and scrap metal; and the battle with the windmills are almost beyond belief.

"God help us!" exclaimed Sancho, "did I not tell your Grace to look well, that those were nothing but windmills, a fact which no one could fail to see unless he had other mills of the same sort in his head?"

"Be quiet, friend Sancho," said Don Quixote. "Such are the fortunes of war, which more than any other are subject to constant change. What is more, when I come to think of it, I am sure that this must be the work of that magician Frestón, the one who robbed me of my study and my books, and who has thus changed the giants into windmills in order to deprive me of the glory of overcoming them, so great is the enmity that he bears me; but in the end his evil arts shall not prevail against this trusty sword of mine."

"May God's will be done," was Sancho Panza's response. And with the aid of his squire the knight was once more mounted on Rocinante, who stood there with one shoulder half out of joint. And so, speaking of the adventure that had just befallen them, they continued along the Puerto Lápice highway; for there, Don Quixote said, they could not fail to find many and varied adventures, this being a much traveled thoroughfare. The only thing was, the knight was exceedingly downcast over the loss of his lance.

"I remember," he said to his squire, "having read of a Spanish knight by the name of Diego Pérez de Vargas, who, having broken his sword in battle, tore from an oak a heavy bough or branch and with it did such feats of valor that day, and pounded so many Moors, that he came to be known as Machuca, and he and his descendants from that day forth have been called Vargas y Machuca. I tell you this because I too intend to provide myself with just such a bough as the one he wielded, and with it I propose to do such exploits that you shall deem yourself fortunate to have been found worthy to come with me and behold and witness things that are almost beyond belief."

Literary Analysis
Parody List three "things that are almost beyond belief" that Don Quixote has already experienced.

"God's will be done," said Sancho. "I believe everything that your Grace says; but straighten yourself up in the saddle a little, for you seem to be slipping down on one side, owing, no doubt, to the shaking-up that you received in your fall."

"Ah, that is the truth," replied Don Quixote, "and if I do not speak of my sufferings, it is for the reason that it is not permitted knights-errant to complain of any wound whatsoever, even though their bowels may be dropping out."

"If that is the way it is," said Sancho, "I have nothing more to say; but, God knows, it would suit me better if your Grace did complain when something hurts him. I can assure you that I mean to do so, over the least little thing that ails me—that is, unless the same rule applies to squires as well."

Don Quixote laughed long and heartily over Sancho's simplicity, telling him that he might complain as much as he liked and where and when he liked, whether he had good cause or not; for he had read nothing to the contrary in the ordinances of chivalry.[9] Sancho then called

9. **ordinances of chivalry** codes, or rules, of knighthood.

34 

Don Quixote and the Windmill, Francisco J. Torrome, Bonhams, London

35 ◀ **Critical Viewing** Which details from the story has the artist incorporated to make this work humorous? **[Analyze]**

his master's attention to the fact that it was time to eat. The knight replied that he himself had no need of food at the moment, but his squire might eat whenever he chose. Having been granted this permission, Sancho seated himself as best he could upon his beast, and, taking out from his saddlebags the provisions that he had stored there, he rode along leisurely behind his master, munching his victuals and taking a good, hearty swig now and then at the leather flask in a manner that might well have caused the biggest-bellied tavernkeeper of Málaga to envy him. Between drafts he gave not so much as a thought to any promise that his master might have made him, nor did he look upon it as any hardship, but rather as good sport, to go in quest of adventures
36 however hazardous they might be.

The short of the matter is, they spent the night under some trees, from one of which Don Quixote tore off a withered bough to serve him as a lance, placing it in the lance head from which he had removed the broken one. He did not sleep all night long for thinking of his lady Dulcinea; for this was in accordance with what he had read in his books, of men of arms in the forest or desert places who kept a wakeful vigil, sustained by the memory of their ladies fair. Not so with Sancho, whose stomach was full, and not with chicory water. He fell into a dreamless slumber, and had not his master called him, he would not have been awakened either by the rays of the sun in his face or by the many birds who greeted the coming of the new day with their merry song.

Upon arising, he had another go at the flask, finding it somewhat more flaccid than it had been the night before, a circumstance which grieved his heart, for he could not see that they were on the way to remedying the deficiency within any very short space of time. Don Quixote did not wish any breakfast; for, as has been said, he was in the habit of nourishing himself on savorous memories. They then set out once more

Reading Strategy
Comparing and Contrasting In what ways do Don Quixote and Sancho Panza accurately imitate the lifestyle of a knight and his squire?

37 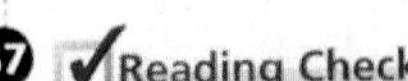
Reading Check
Where did Don Quixote spend the night?

CUSTOMIZE INSTRUCTION FOR UNIVERSAL ACCESS

For Less Proficient Readers	For Gifted/Talented Students
Tell students that the selections they have read here are only a very small portion of the complete novel. Have students work in pairs to obtain a copy of the novel and to select and read another episode together. Point out that most translations contain a brief summary at the beginning of each chapter. Encourage students to read the summaries to help them choose the chapter they wish to read.	Tell students that the selections they have read here are only a very small portion of the complete novel. Have students obtain copies of the novel and select another episode to read. Encourage students to read the summaries to help them choose the chapter that they wish to read. Then, have them write updated versions of the account they read, set in the present day. Have students read their episodes aloud to the class.

34 Background

Art

Don Quixote and the Windmill, by Francisco J. Torrome

This image by Francisco J. Torrome captures the decisive moment in the "Terrible and Undreamed-of Adventure of the Windmills." Don Quixote loses his battle with the windmill and is dashed to the ground as a dismayed Sancho Panza clutches his head in the distance. The idyllic landscape behind Sancho Panza contrasts with the chaotic scene in the foreground.

Use this question for discussion:

How does this illustration contrast Don Quixote and Sancho Panza?
Answer: Don Quixote perceives the windmills as monsters, where as Sancho Panza—a realist—sees them for what they are.

35 ▶ Critical Viewing

Answer: The artist has painted the windmills very clearly and shows Don Quixote as he falls. Sancho Panza clutches his head, waiting for the scene to end.

36 Reading Strategy

Comparing and Contrasting

- Discuss with students the adventures that Don Quixote has had to this point. Then, ask students to read the bracketed passage.
- Ask students the Reading Strategy question on p. 713: In what ways do Don Quixote and Sancho Panza accurately imitate the lifestyle of a knight and his squire?
  Answer: Like a real knight and squire, the two travel together searching out adventures; they sleep out of doors; Don Quixote focuses on destroying "giants" and other evil doers, and he spends time thinking about his lady; Sancho Panza follows Don Quixote's lead and acts as his servant.

37 ✔ Reading Check

Answer: Don Quixote spends the night under some trees.

ASSESS

38 Critical Thinking

Infer

- Ask two volunteers to read aloud the bracketed passage, with one reading the part of Don Quixote and the other reading the part of Sancho Panza.
- Point out how readily Sancho Panza agrees with Don Quixote's request. Ask students why they think Sancho Panza complies so quickly.
  Possible response: Sancho Panza is happy to avoid putting himself at risk of physical harm.

Answers for p. 714

Review and Assess

1. Possible response: Don Quixote's endearing qualities are his optimism, his courage in facing his imaginary foes, and his devotion to upholding the "rules" he has read about in books, even though those books are fictional.
2. **(a)** Don Quixote promises to make him governor of an island. **(b)** Possible response: No; Don Quixote is irrational and will never conquer anything.
3. **(a)** Don Quixote believes that the windmills are "lawless giants" and that he must take their riches. **(b)** The wings of the windmill appear to be long arms that remind him of a giant he has read about in tales of knighthood. **(c)** Sancho Panza means that Don Quixote is unrealistic, or lives in a dream world, and is out of touch with reality.
4. **(a)** Seeing things as they are, Sancho Panza keeps his master from even greater danger, but he is mild-mannered enough neither to quit nor to stand in Don Quixote's way. **(b)** Possible response: Sancho Panza likes Don Quixote; he feels sorry for him and wants to protect him; he enjoys the game of playing "squire" to Don Quixote's "knight-errant."
5. Possible response: Don Quixote might make a good writer or movie director.

along the road to Puerto Lápice, and around three in the afternoon they came in sight of the pass that bears that name.

"There," said Don Quixote as his eyes fell upon it, "we may plunge our arms up to the elbow in what are known as adventures. But I must warn you that even though you see me in the greatest peril in the world, you are not to lay hand upon your sword to defend me, unless it be that those who attack me are rabble and men of low degree, in which case you may very well come to my aid; but if they be gentlemen, it is in no wise permitted by the laws of chivalry that you should assist me until you yourself shall have been dubbed a knight."

38 "Most certainly, sir," replied Sancho, "your Grace shall be very well obeyed in this; all the more so for the reason that I myself am of a peaceful disposition and not fond of meddling in the quarrels and feuds of others. However, when it comes to protecting my own person, I shall not take account of those laws of which you speak, seeing that all laws, human and divine, permit each one to defend himself whenever he is attacked."

"I am willing to grant you that," assented Don Quixote, "but in this matter of defending me against gentlemen you must restrain your natural impulses."

"I promise you I shall do so," said Sancho. "I will observe this precept as I would the Sabbath day."

Review and Assess

Thinking About the Selection

1. **Respond:** Which aspects of Don Quixote's appearance or behavior—if any—do you find endearing? Explain.
2. **(a) Recall:** What promise does Don Quixote make to convince Sancho Panza to be his squire? **(b) Speculate:** Do you think this promise will be fulfilled? Why or why not?
3. **(a) Recall:** What reasons does Don Quixote give for fighting the windmills? **(b) Infer:** What characteristics of the windmills convince him that they are worthy foes? **(c) Interpret:** What does Sancho Panza mean when he says Don Quixote has "other mills of the same sort in his head"?
4. **(a) Infer:** Why is Sancho Panza a particularly helpful squire to Don Quixote? **(b) Draw Conclusions:** Why do you think Sancho Panza stays with Don Quixote even after realizing that Don Quixote has lost touch with reality?
5. **Speculate:** For which careers might it be considered an asset to have a vivid imagination like that of Don Quixote?

ASSESSMENT PRACTICE: Reading Comprehension

Evaluate and Make Judgments (For more practice, see **Test Preparation Workbook**, p. 34.)

Standardized tests require students to make judgments about an author's meaning. Use this item, which features a passage from Jorge Luis Borges's poem about Cervantes.

"Defeated by reality, by Spain, Don Quixote died in his native village around 1614."

Which best expresses Borges's view of Spanish culture in the early 1600's?

A Spanish people should have traveled more.
B Spanish people wanted to stay in their native village.
C Spain was a place that did not value imagination.
D Spain was a place where older people felt defeated.

Answer *C* is correct because it is the only one that makes a connection between Spain and its focus on reality instead of the imagination.

Review and Assess

Literary Analysis

Parody

1. (a) List three characteristics of a medieval romance that *Don Quixote* **parodies.** (b) What details indicate that the parody is affectionate or gentle? (c) In what way does Cervantes suggest his admiration for chivalric tales? Explain.
2. Using the chart shown below, identify details from the selection that parody elements of a real knight's life. Indicate how Don Quixote's personality or circumstances influence the parody.

Real Knight	Details	Don Quixote's Influence
Training		
Weapons		
Ladylove		

Connecting Literary Elements

3. (a) Identify three events that suggest a struggle between reality and fantasy. (b) What **theme** or insight into life do these events reveal?
4. (a) In what ways does Don Quixote embody the theme that a vivid imagination makes a life richer? (b) Do you agree with this theme? Why or why not?
5. (a) List two ways in which Sancho Panza is a realist—someone who sees the world as it is. (b) What theme does he embody?

Reading Strategy

Comparing and Contrasting

6. (a) **Compare and contrast** the appearance, attitude, and motives of Don Quixote and Sancho Panza as they embark on their quest. (b) Do you think their personalities complement each other, or are their differences obstacles to be overcome? Explain.
7. In what ways is Don Quixote, at least in his own mind, similar to the knights of old?

Extend Understanding

8. **Career Connection:** What careers require the kind of determination Don Quixote needed to become a knight? Explain.

Quick Review

A **parody** is an imitation of another work of literature for amusement or for instruction.

A **theme** is a central message or idea revealed through a literary work.

To **compare and contrast,** note the similarities and differences between two things.

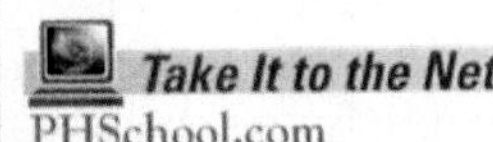

PHSchool.com

Take the interactive self-test online to check your understanding of this selection.

ENRICHMENT: Further Reading

Other Works by Cervantes

We strongly encourage you to review any selection before assigning or recommending it to students.

La Galatea

Exemplary Novels

Eight Comedies and Eight Entremeses

Take It to the Net

Visit PHSchool.com for more information on Cervantes.

Answers for p. 715

Review and Assess

1. **(a)** Some characteristics include his armor, his horse, and his squire. **(b)** Cervantes portrays Don Quixote as courageous, idealistic, and committed to behaving honorably at all times. **(c)** Cervantes mentions many of the knights who were the heroes of these tales and includes details of their adventures; it is clear that he knows much about these writings.
2. Possible response: **Training: Details:** Don Quixote reads about the knight's code of honor in order to prepare. **Influence:** He takes his reading to extremes. **Weapons: Details:** He uses old, rusted armor; he repairs a helmet with cardboard; **Influence:** Don Quixote's imagination allows him to use things like cardboard and oak branches to create his equipment. **Ladylove: Details:** Don Quixote knows that knights have noble women they idealize. **Influence:** His ladylove is a farm girl.
3. **(a)** Possible response: Don Quixote chooses a broken-down nag for his horse; he chooses a farmer as his squire; he tilts at windmills. **(b)** These events reveal that a vivid imagination enriches life.
4. **(a)** He shows that he can take the mundane and create fantasy. **(b)** Possible response: Yes; it is better to live a richer life through imagination. No; it is more important to be practical.
5. **(a)** He recognizes that Don Quixote can get hurt acting out his fantasies; he believes in tending to the needs of the body, such as food and sleep. **(b)** Possible response: One must be a realist to survive.
6. **(a)** Both Don Quixote and Sancho Panza are dressed poorly but are optimistic and have high expectations. Don Quixote lives in a fantasy world and is motivated by idealism; Sancho Panza lives in the real world and is motivated by the hope of material rewards. **(b)** Possible response: Don Quixote brings excitement to Sancho Panza who, in turn, helps protect Don Quixote.

continued

continued from right column

7. Possible response: Don Quixote is well bred, honorable, and adventurous.
8. Possible response: Bring a professional athlete or member of the armed forces requires determination.

EXTEND

Answers for p. 716

❶ Vocabulary Development

Word Analysis: Latin Root *-ject-*

1. b
2. d
3. a
4. c

Concept Development: Synonyms

1. conjectures
2. appropriate
3. infatuation
4. constitution
5. ingenuity
6. illustrious
7. incongruous

Spelling Strategy

1. irreverent
2. irrefutable

❷ Grammar and Style

Practice

1. Smashing; subject
2. ending; object of preposition *of*
3. attacking; direct object
4. Eating; subject
5. supporting; predicate nominative

Writing Application

Possible response: Righting wrongs is the usual practice of knights. (subject)

A knight leaves the task of cleaning the equipment to his squire. (object of preposition)

A chivalrous knight holds serving his lady uppermost in his mind. (direct object)

A knight's most important task is defending the weak. (predicate nominative)

Fighting dragons and giants can win fame for a knight. (subject)

10TH GRADE For support in teaching the Grammar and Style Lesson to tenth graders, use **Writing and Grammar**, Platinum Level, Chapter 20, Section 1.

Integrate Language Skills

❶ Vocabulary Development Lesson

Word Analysis: Latin Root *-ject-*

The Latin root *-ject-* means "to throw." If you make a *conjecture*, you "throw in," or offer, a thought or a guess. Each numbered word below contains the root *-ject-*. Match each word with the letter of the correct definition.

1. rejection (*re-* = back)
2. inject (*in-* = to bring in)
3. project (*pro-* = before, or forward)
4. trajectory (*tra-* = across)

a. to throw forward
b. the condition of being thrown back
c. the path of something thrown through space
d. to throw or put into

Concept Development: Synonyms

Review the vocabulary list on page 699. Then, for each item below, identify the vocabulary word with the closest meaning.

1. theories
2. confiscate
3. shallow affection
4. composition
5. imagination
6. famous
7. unsuitable

Spelling Strategy

The prefix *im-* or *in-*, meaning "not," changes to *ir-* when it is added to words beginning with *r*: *irreparable* = not able to be repaired; *irregular* = not regular. Use the prefix *ir-* to write the words for each definition below.

1. not reverent
2. not refutable

❷ Grammar and Style Lesson

Gerunds

A **gerund** is a verb form ending in *-ing* that acts as a noun. Gerunds can perform all the roles of a noun in a sentence: subject, direct or indirect object, object of a preposition, and predicate nominative.

Subject: *Jousting* becomes a challenge, for he owns no lance.

Direct Object: Sancho Panza wants *fighting* the windmills to end peacefully.

Object of a Preposition: Don Quixote is an early riser and fond of *hunting*.

Predicate Nominative: Don Quixote's favorite pastime is *reading*.

Practice Identify each gerund below, and name its function in the sentence.

1. Smashing the makeshift armor with his sword gave Don Quixote no pleasure.
2. He commends the author's way of ending his books.
3. On his journey, Don Quixote tries attacking windmills.
4. Eating is one of Sancho's greatest pleasures.
5. The foremost goal of a squire is supporting his knight.

Writing Application Write four sentences describing the activities of a knight-errant. Use a gerund in each sentence, underlining the gerund and identifying its use in the sentence.

WG *Prentice Hall Writing and Grammar Connection: Diamond Level, Chapter 19, Section 2*

716 ◆ The Renaissance and Rationalism

TEACHING RESOURCES

The following resources can be used to enrich or extend the instruction for pp. 716–717.

Vocabulary

- **Selection Support:** Build Vocabulary, p. 133
- **Vocabulary and Spelling Practice Book** (Use this booklet for skills instruction.)

Grammar

- **Selection Support:** Grammar and Style, p. 134
- **Writing and Grammar,** Diamond Level, p. 446
- **Daily Language Practice Transparencies**

Writing

- **Performance Assess. and Portfolio Mgmt.,** p. 19
- **Writing and Grammar,** Diamond Level, p. 108
- **Writing and Grammar iText CD-ROM**
- **Writing Models and Graphic Organizers on Transparencies,** pp. 79–81

BLOCK SCHEDULING: Resources marked with this symbol provide varied instruction during 90-minute blocks.

❸ Writing Lesson

Profile of a Comic Hero

A hero in literature is often a very serious character on an important quest. In *Don Quixote,* however, Cervantes reinvented this character by creating a comic hero. In the spirit of *Don Quixote,* create your own comic hero and write a profile of his or her idiosyncrasies and achievements.

Prewriting Start by creating a chart like the one shown to categorize the traits of your comic hero. Then, give an example of each trait in action.

Model: Gathering Details

Trait	Trait in Action

Drafting Begin your profile with a catchy introduction, such as a quotation or an anecdote that illustrates a humorous quality of your hero. Then, present the traits of your hero and specific examples of each.

Revising Compare the details you gathered in your chart against your draft. Keep Cervantes's model in mind, and make sure that you have provided enough information to convey your hero's comic qualities. If necessary, add further details to develop those traits.

WG *Prentice Hall Writing and Grammar Connection: Diamond Level, Chapter 6, Section 4*

❹ Extension Activities

Listening and Speaking Work with a partner to **role-play** the scene in which Sancho Panza tries to talk Don Quixote out of attacking the windmills. Use the following tips to prepare your scene:

- Make a few notes to capture the personality of the character you will role-play.
- Adjust your voice to reflect the emotions being expressed.
- Decide how, if at all, you will refer to his transformation.
- Speak directly to your partner as if you are having a conversation.

Present the scene for the class. **[Group Activity]**

Research and Technology Create a **visual essay** on the subject of heroes. Use computer programs such as music or imaging software to enhance your essay. Include scanned or downloaded images, and write captions that illustrate how your examples relate to the central message about heroes. Display your essay for the class.

 ***Take It to the Net*** PHSchool.com

Go online for an additional research activity using the Internet.

ASSESSMENT RESOURCES

The following resources can be used to assess students' knowledge and skills.

Selection Assessment

- **Formal Assessment,** pp. 120–122
- **Open-Book Tests,** pp. 100–102
- **Test Bank Software**

 ***Take It to the Net***

Visit PHSchool.com for self-tests on the selection.

Writing Rubric

- **Performance Assess. and Portfolio Mgmt.,** p. 19

For additional diagnostics and remediation for skills covered in this grouping, use materials from the Prentice Hall Assessment System.

❸ Writing Lesson

- Explain that a profile, unlike a biography, does not tell the full story of a person's life but focuses on specific aspects of an individual. Tell students that they will write a profile that focuses on elements that make a character humorous and heroic.
- Tell students to choose traits that illustrate the humorous or heroic side of their characters.
- Encourage students to use the Grid Organizer, pp. 79–81, in **Writing Models and Graphic Organizers on Transparencies,** to help them develop details for their profiles.
- Use the Description rubric in **Performance Assessment and Portfolio Management,** p. 19, to evaluate students' profiles.

10TH GRADE For support in working through the Writing Lesson with tenth graders, use **Writing and Grammar,** Platinum Level, p. 206.

❹ Research and Technology

- Point out to students that as they begin to research the subject of heroes, they will encounter various types of heroes: knights, superheroes, and everyday heroes.
- Have students meet in small groups to brainstorm the heroes or types of heroes they would like to include in their essays.

CUSTOMIZE INSTRUCTION For Universal Access

To address different learning styles, use the following activities suggested in the **Extension Activities** booklet, p. 34:

- For Bodily/Kinesthetic and Interpersonal Learners, use Activity 5.
- For Musical/Rhythmic and Interpersonal Learners, use Activity 6.
- For Mathematical/Logical Learners, use Activity 7.

The Fox and the Crow • The Oak and the Reed

Lesson Objectives

1. **To analyze and respond to literary elements**
   - Literary Analysis: Fables
   - Comparing Literary Works: Personification
2. **To read, comprehend, analyze, and critique a fable**
   - Reading Strategy: Drawing Conclusions
   - Reading Check Questions
   - Review and Assess Questions
   - Assessment Practice (ATE)
3. **To develop word analysis skills, fluency, and systematic vocabulary**
   - Vocabulary Development Lesson: Latin Prefix *im-*
4. **To understand and apply written and oral language conventions**
   - Spelling Strategy
   - Grammar and Style Lesson: Adjective Clauses
5. **To understand and apply appropriate writing and research strategies**
   - Writing Lesson: Children's Story
   - Extension Activity: Research Report on Fables
6. **To understand and apply listening and speaking strategies**
   - Extension Activity: Dramatic Reading

10TH GRADE TEACHING A TENTH-GRADE COURSE

The literature in this section can be taught as part of a rich, balanced world literature course for tenth-grade students. For a full outline of such a course, see pp. T46–T48 in Volume 1 of this Teacher's Edition.

STEP-BY-STEP TEACHING GUIDE	PACING GUIDE
PRETEACH	
Motivate Students and Provide Background	
Use the Motivation activity (ATE p. 718)	5 min.
Read and discuss author and background features (SE pp. 718, 720; ATE p. 718) A	5 min.
Introduce the Concepts	
Introduce the Literary Analysis and Reading Strategy concepts (SE/ATE p. 719) A	15 min.
Pronounce the vocabulary words and read their definitions (SE p. 719)	5 min.
TEACH	
Monitor Comprehension	
Informally monitor comprehension by circulating while students read independently or in groups A	15 min.
Monitor students' comprehension with the Reading Check note (SE/ATE p. 723)	as students read
Develop vocabulary with the Vocabulary notes (SE pp. 723, 724; ATE p. 724)	as students read
Develop Understanding	
Develop students' understanding of fables with the Literary Analysis annotations (SE/ATE pp. 720, 723) A	5 min.
Develop students' ability to draw conclusions, using the Reading Strategy annotations (SE/ATE p. 720) A	5 min.
ASSESS	
Assess Mastery	
Assess students' mastery of the Reading Strategy and Literary Analysis by having them answer the Review and Assess questions (SE/ATE p. 725)	15 min.
Use one or more of the print, software, or transparency Assessment Resources (ATE p. 727) A	up to 45 min.
EXTEND	
Apply Understanding	
Have students complete the Vocabulary Development Lesson and the Grammar and Style Lesson (SE p. 726) A	20 min.
Apply students' ability to punctuate for dialogue, using the Writing Lesson (SE/ATE p. 727) A	45 min.
Apply students' understanding of the selections, using one or more of the Extension Activities (SE p. 727)	20–90 min.

A ACCELERATED INSTRUCTION: Use the strategies and activities identified with an A.

10TH GRADE TEACHING TENTH-GRADE STUDENTS For support in teaching the selection(s) to tenth-grade students, see the Step-By-Step Teaching notes identified with the icon shown here.

UNIVERSAL ACCESS
- ● = Below-Level Students
- ▲ = On-Level Students
- ■ = Above-Level Students

Time and Resource Manager

Reading Level: Average
Average Number of Instructional Days: 2

RESOURCES		
PRINT	**TRANSPARENCIES**	**TECHNOLOGY**
• **Beyond Literature,** Humanities Connection: Tricksters, p. 35 ▲ ■		
• **Selection Support Workbook:** ● ▲ ■ Literary Analysis, p. 140 Reading Strategy, p. 139 Build Vocabulary, p. 137	• **Literary Analysis and Reading Transparencies,** pp. 69 and 70 ● ▲ ■	
		• **Listening to Literature** ● ▲ ■ Audiocassettes Audio CDs
• **Literary Analysis for Enrichment,** p. 35 ■		
• **Formal Assessment:** Selection Test, pp. 123–125 ● ▲ ■ • **Open-Book Tests,** pp. 103–105 ● ▲ ■ • **Performance Assessment and Portfolio Management,** pp. 14, 28 ● ▲ ■ • PRENTICE HALL ASSESSMENT SYSTEM ● ▲ ■	• PRENTICE HALL ASSESSMENT SYSTEM ● ▲ ■ **Skills Practice Answers and Explanations on Transparencies**	• **Test Bank Software** ● ▲ ■
• **Selection Support Workbook:** ● ▲ ■ Grammar and Style, p. 138 • **Writing and Grammar,** Diamond Level ● ▲ ■ • **Extension Activities,** p. 35 ● ▲ ■	• **Daily Language Practice Transparencies** ● ▲ • **Writing Models and Graphic Organizers on Transparencies,** pp. 83–85 ● ▲ ■	• **Writing and Grammar iText CD-ROM** ● ▲ ■ ***Take It to the Net*** PHSchool.com

BLOCK SCHEDULING: Use one 90-minute class period to preteach the selection(s) and have students read them. Use a second 90-minute class period to assess students' mastery of skills and have them complete one of the Extension Activities.

Step-by-Step Teaching Guide for pp. 718–719

Motivation

Remind students that clichés are expressions that have become worn because of constant use. Moral clichés address issues of right and wrong or good character. Ask students to brainstorm a list of moral clichés. Record the clichés on the board, and add these to the list: *"A bird in the hand is worth two in the bush," "Haste makes waste," "The early bird catches the worm,"* and *"A stitch in time saves nine."* Then, lead students in a discussion about how moral clichés have become an important part of our culture. Use these questions to stimulate discussion: What role do moral clichés play in American culture? Why do they remain popular? Whose morality do they reflect? Are there such things as common moral values?

❶ Background

More About the Author

Relatively little is known about Jean de La Fontaine: He left no memoirs and few letters. The few documents that do survive provide tantalizing hints about his life, however. From a marriage contract, we know that twenty-six-year-old Jean married fourteen-year-old Marie Hericart on November 19, 1647. The couple lived together on and off for another fifteen years, but the marriage did not endure. They parted ways permanently in 1671.

It appears that La Fontaine went to Limoges in 1663, voluntarily or by force, to prevent himself from becoming embroiled in his patron's disgrace. In 1664, he applied for a license in Paris to publish a book, indicating that his exile was relatively brief.

Geography Note

Use the map on this page to identify France. Tell students that La Fontaine spent much of his time in Paris in north central France but that later he was exiled to the city of Limoges in the west central part of the country.

Prepare to Read

❶ The Fox and the Crow ◆ The Oak and the Reed

Jean de La Fontaine (1621–1695)

An early French example of the somewhat absent-minded professor, Jean de La Fontaine (zhän də lä fōn ten') delighted his seventeenth-century audience, as well as later generations, with his outpouring of short stories, poems, and fables. While learning to compose verses, La Fontaine dabbled with the possibilities of studying law, entering the priesthood, or following his father's profession of forest ranger before he finally settled on a literary career. An admirer of ancient poets and playwrights, La Fontaine began publishing his own stories in his early thirties and continued to write for nearly forty years.

Patrons of the Arts Like many creative people of the era, La Fontaine depended upon patrons for his room and board. He enjoyed the semipermanent patronage of various hosts and hostesses, choosing to remain in the stimulating circles of Paris rather than with his wife and son in his quiet hometown of Château Thierry. During his long residency in the French capital, he met and befriended some of the greatest minds of the age, including Racine, Molière, and Boileau. In 1683, after many years of failed attempts, the poet was finally elected to the French Academy, the inner circle to which French writers aspired.

La Fontaine wrote in a variety of genres and styles, including prose tales, religious poetry, letters, and even an epitaph for his friend Molière. It is his vast collections of verse fables, however, for which La Fontaine is best remembered.

Words of Wisdom La Fontaine was a voracious reader of histories and literature. In fact, his own writings reflect the influences of Homer, Plato, and Boccaccio, among others. Many of La Fontaine's poems are adaptations of other works. Most contain quirky statements of ethics and philosophy, often in the form of homilies, or wise sayings.

One of the major sources of his stories is Aesop, a sixth-century B.C. Greek storyteller of beast fables. A much-loved work by both authors, "The Ant and the Grasshopper," is a moralistic yet entertaining tale that contrasts the frolicsome grasshopper with the frugal, hard-working ant who collects stores of food to carry him through the winter.

Virtues and Vices La Fontaine's succinct, homespun animal stories address human idiosyncrasies, such as cowardice, curiosity, greed, and laziness. Stopping short of heavy-handed preaching, the stories contain common-sense reminders that delight as they instruct. La Fontaine used a wide range of nonhuman characters in his fables: ants, cats, wolves, trees, and mice are just a few. By putting animals in the place of humans, La Fontaine creates droll restatements of themes that continue to capture the imagination of his readers.

La Fontaine's 238 fables are so popular that French schoolchildren memorize them in their entirety and dramatize them as recital pieces. The French language is heavily salted with La Fontaine's witty aphorisms, such as "The sign brings customers," "A hungry stomach cannot hear," and "On the wings of Time grief flies away."

TEACHING RESOURCES

The following resources can be used to enrich or extend the instruction for pp. 718–719.

Background

Beyond Literature, p. 35

Take It to the Net

Visit PHSchool.com for background on the author.

Literary Analysis

Literary Analysis and Reading Transparencies, Fables, p. 69

Reading

Literary Analysis and Reading Transparencies, Drawing Conclusions, p. 70

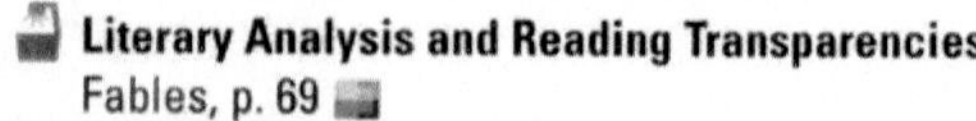

Selection Support: Reading Strategy, p. 139; Build Vocabulary, p. 137

BLOCK SCHEDULING: Resources marked with this symbol provide varied instruction during 90-minute blocks.

Preview

Connecting to the Literature

Winnie the Pooh, Snoopy, Garfield, Roadrunner, Wile E. Coyote, and the animal characters of Dr. Seuss—all figures from children's literature and cartoons—pass along useful bits of wisdom wrapped in laughter and entertainment. The seventeenth-century poetry of La Fontaine presents advice in a similar format.

2 Literary Analysis

Fables

Whether in the form of a poem or a short story, a **fable** dramatizes a simple lesson or principle of behavior. Most fables share the following elements:

- creatures—animals or inanimate objects—who speak and interact as though they were human
- a clearly worded moral at either the beginning or the end
- a single compressed episode
- an implied frailty or fault of character that is often the object of satire

Look for these characteristics in the fables of La Fontaine.

Comparing Literary Works

Because many fables include creatures as main characters, these works often employ **personification,** a type of figurative language in which a nonhuman subject is given human characteristics. For example, in "The Oak and the Reed," the oak tree has a conversation with his neighbor, the reed. By giving human qualities to nonhumans, La Fontaine subtly charms his readers, teaching them valuable life lessons from the experiences of imaginary beings. As you read the poems in this grouping, note the variety and degree of human responses the creatures possess.

3 Reading Strategy

Drawing Conclusions

La Fontaine does not directly state a moral or lesson to be learned from his fables. Instead, he allows readers to **draw conclusions** about the meaning of his works. To draw conclusions, consider the details of the fable, and use them to infer a larger message or meaning. Use a chart like the one shown to determine the moral, or general truth, that La Fontaine's fable teaches.

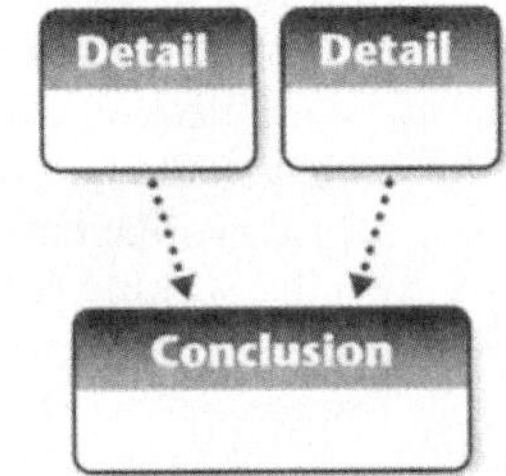

Vocabulary Development

buffeted (buf′ it id) *v.* struck sharply (p. 723)

hazards (haz′ ərdz) *n.* dangers (p. 723)

impervious (im pur′ vē əs) *adj.* not affected by, or unable to be damaged (p. 724)

prone (prōn) *adj.* lying face downward (p. 724)

2 Literary Analysis

Fables

- Tell students that Aesop, an ancient Greek, is credited with some of the most famous fables. Remind students of the fable about the tortoise and the hare: The hare challenges the tortoise to a race. Because the tortoise is slow, the hare believes that he will win easily. The hare, feeling secure about victory, stops to take a nap during the race, while the tortoise plods ahead and wins.
- Help students see the elements of fable found in "The Tortoise and the Hare": a fault of character, a clear moral, animals who act human, and a compressed episode.
- Point out that the two characters, the tortoise and the hare, are examples of personification.

3 Reading Strategy

Drawing Conclusions

- Remind students that fables teach moral lessons.
- Refer students to the graphic organizer on p. 719. Tell them to use the organizer to identify the moral of "The Tortoise and the Hare." Possible response: **Detail:** The tortoise walks slowly but keeps moving. **Detail:** The hare stops to take a nap and awakens to find that the tortoise has won the race. **Conclusion:** The moral of the fable is "Slow but steady wins the race."
- Encourage students to use a graphic organizer like the one on p. 719 to determine the moral of each of La Fontaine's fables.

Vocabulary Development

- Pronounce each vocabulary word for students, and read the definitions as a class. Have students identify any words with which they are already familiar.

CUSTOMIZE INSTRUCTION FOR UNIVERSAL ACCESS

For Less Proficient Readers	For English Learners	For Advanced Readers
To help students read La Fontaine's poems, obtain a prose version of these fables. Ask students to discuss similarities and differences between the prose fables and La Fontaine's poems. Suggest that students use a Venn diagram to help with the comparison.	To help students read La Fontaine's poems, obtain a prose version of these fables. Read them aloud along with students. Later, ask students to discuss comparisons between the prose fables and La Fontaine's poems. Suggest that students use a Venn diagram to help them discover and list the similarities and differences.	Tell students that many American writers have been influenced by La Fontaine's fables. Help students locate *Archy and Mehitabel* by Don Marquis. Suggest that students use a Venn diagram to compare and contrast *Archy and Mehitabel* with La Fontaine's fables. Invite students to share their observations with the class.

***e*-Teach**

Visit e-Teach at PHSchool.com for teachers' essays on how to teach, with questions and answers.

TEACH

Step-by-Step Teaching Guide for pp. 720–724

Teaching Tenth-Grade Students

10TH GRADE Encourage tenth-grade students to brainstorm a list of characteristics that they associate with the fox and the crow. Record the associations on the board. After students have read "The Fox and the Crow," refer to the list on the board, and discuss why La Fontaine's choice of animals is suitable or unsuitable for the fable.

❶ About the Selection

In this fable, the cunning fox tricks the vain crow into giving up his cheese.

❷ Literary Analysis

Fables and Personification

- Remind students that personification is a type of figurative language that ascribes human characteristics to nonhuman beings and objects.
- Ask students the Literary Analysis question on p. 720: What human traits does the fox possess?
  Answer: The fox possesses cunning and speech.

❸ Reading Strategy

Drawing Conclusions

- Remind students that fables express morals, or universal truths about correct behavior.
- Ask students the Reading Strategy question on p. 720: What general truth does the crow learn about pride?
  Answer: The crow learns that the "flatterer lives at the flattered listener's cost."

▶ **Monitor Progress** Ask students to paraphrase the fox's message to the crow.
Possible response: A person who praises another insincerely does so to win favor at the listener's expense.

▶ **Reteach** If students are having difficulty drawing conclusions, suggest that they use the Drawing Conclusions transparency on p. 70 in **Literary Analysis and Reading Transparencies** for help.

❶

The Fox and the Crow

Jean de La Fontaine ***translated by* Marianne Moore**

Background

La Fontaine's fables were well suited to the Age of Reason. In them, he instructs the reader in prudent living, basing his aphorisms on the mind-over-emotions philosophy of seventeenth-century moralists. A key feature of these fables is the logical and carefully worded statement of advice—or moral—on such ethical issues as integrity, diligence, compromise, and pride. Although his poems seem simple and light, La Fontaine characteristically dwells on the dangers that lurk in seemingly innocent surroundings.

On his airy perch among the branches
Master Crow was holding cheese in his beak.
❷ Master Fox, whose pose suggested fragrances,[1]
Said in language which of course I cannot speak,
"Aha, superb Sir Ebony, well met.
How black! who else boasts your metallic jet!
If your warbling[2] were unique,
Rest assured, as you are sleek,
One would say that our wood had hatched nightingales."
All aglow, Master Crow tried to run a few scales,
Risking trills and intervals,
Dropping the prize as his huge beak sang false.
❸ The fox pounced on the cheese and remarked, "My dear sir,
Learn that every flatterer
Lives at the flattered listener's cost:
A lesson worth more than the cheese that you lost."
The tardy learner, smarting under ridicule,
Swore he'd learned his last lesson as somebody's fool.

Literary Analysis
Fables and Personification What human traits does the fox possess?

Reading Strategy
Drawing Conclusions What general truth does the crow learn about pride?

1. **fragrances** false and devious charm.
2. **warbling** melodious singing.

TEACHING RESOURCES

The following resources can be used to enrich or extend the instruction for pp. 720–724.

Literary Analysis

- **Selection Support:** Literary Analysis, p. 140
- **Literary Analysis and Reading Transparencies,** Fable, p. 69

Reading

- **Literary Analysis and Reading Transparencies,** Drawing Conclusions, p. 70 ▪
- **Selection Support:** Reading Strategy, p. 139; Build Vocabulary, p. 137 ▪
- **Listening to Literature Audiocassettes** ▪
- **Listening to Literature Audio CDs**

▪ **BLOCK SCHEDULING:** Resources marked with this symbol provide varied instruction during 90-minute blocks.

4 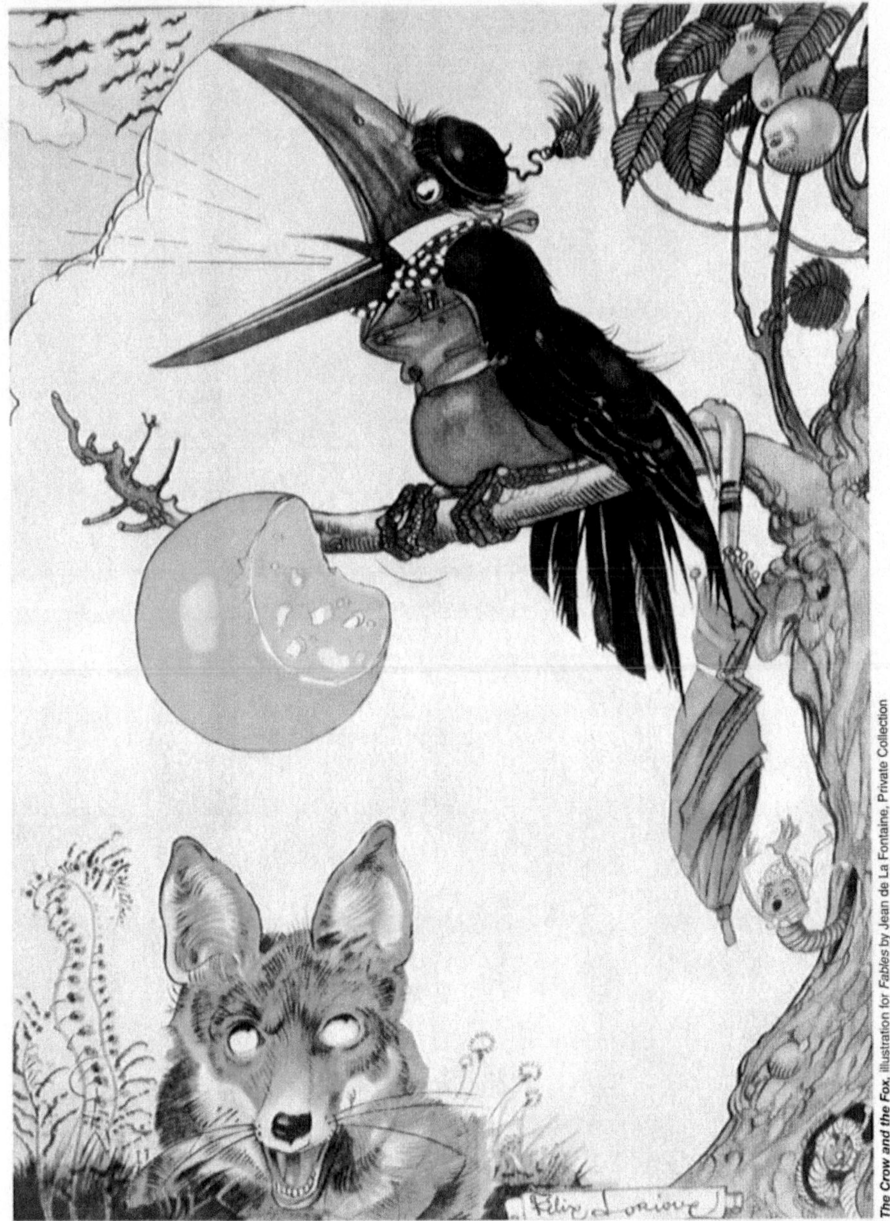

The Crow and the Fox, illustration for *Fables* by Jean de La Fontaine, Private Collection

5 ▲ **Critical Viewing** Identify details in this illustration that might interest young readers of La Fontaine's poems. **[Analyze]**

4 Background

Art

The Crow and the Fox, by Félix Lorioux

This twentieth-century color engraving by French publicity and fashion designer Félix Lorioux (1872–1964) is characteristic of the artist's children's illustrations. Lorioux favors joyful images, mischievous animals and plants, and brilliant colors.

Use the following question for discussion:

What characteristics of the fox and the crow does this illustration capture?

Possible response: The illustration captures the expression of greed in the fox, with his upturned eyes and open mouth, and the foolishness of the crow, with his exuberant singing.

5 ▶Critical Viewing

Possible response: The umbrella hanging on the limb, the crow's necktie, the whimsical worms, the personified tree, and the falling cheese might interest young readers.

CUSTOMIZE INSTRUCTION FOR UNIVERSAL ACCESS

For Special Needs Students	For Gifted/Talented Students
Help students locate examples of visual art forms, like cartoons or video games, that use personified animals for amusing effect. Make sure that each student has an example to analyze. Ask each student to respond to the following items in writing: Describe one animal in this example. What human traits does this animal have? How does the artist convey these human traits to the viewer? How does the artist achieve a comic effect?	Tell students that the critic David Lee Rubins laments that "La Fontaine's work runs a grave risk of being taken for granted, underread, misread, and finally misjudged" because many readers imagine his work is aimed primarily at children. Direct students to research the illustrative work that Jean-Baptiste Oudry did for the 1755 publication of "La Fontaine." Tell students to analyze Oudry's work in essay form. Suggest that students bring copies of Oudry's work to class and share their analyses with classmates.

6 Background

Art

The oak tree is an important symbol in world literature. Generally, it represents strength and protection. The acorn, the seed of the oak tree, is recognized as a symbol of life.

The oak has traditionally played a part in different cultures. It is often associated with thunder gods and thunder. In Graeco-Roman culture, Zeus, the sky god, and Hera, his wife, are also the oak gods. Worshippers of Zeus and Hera wore oak leaf crowns. Christians see the oak tree as a symbol of Christ's strength in difficult times. The tree is sometimes thought to be the tree of the cross. In Judaism, the oak tree is a symbol of divine presence. On the other hand, the Chinese associate the oak tree with physical weakness because it does not bend with the wind.

Use the following questions for discussion:

- Why might the acorn have become a symbol of life?
  Possible response: In addition to their role in the propagation of oak trees, acorns provide food for animals and people.
- Why might not bending with the wind be a sign of weakness rather than strength?
  Possible response: Not bending with the wind might indicate stubborness, inflexibility, and lack of awareness.

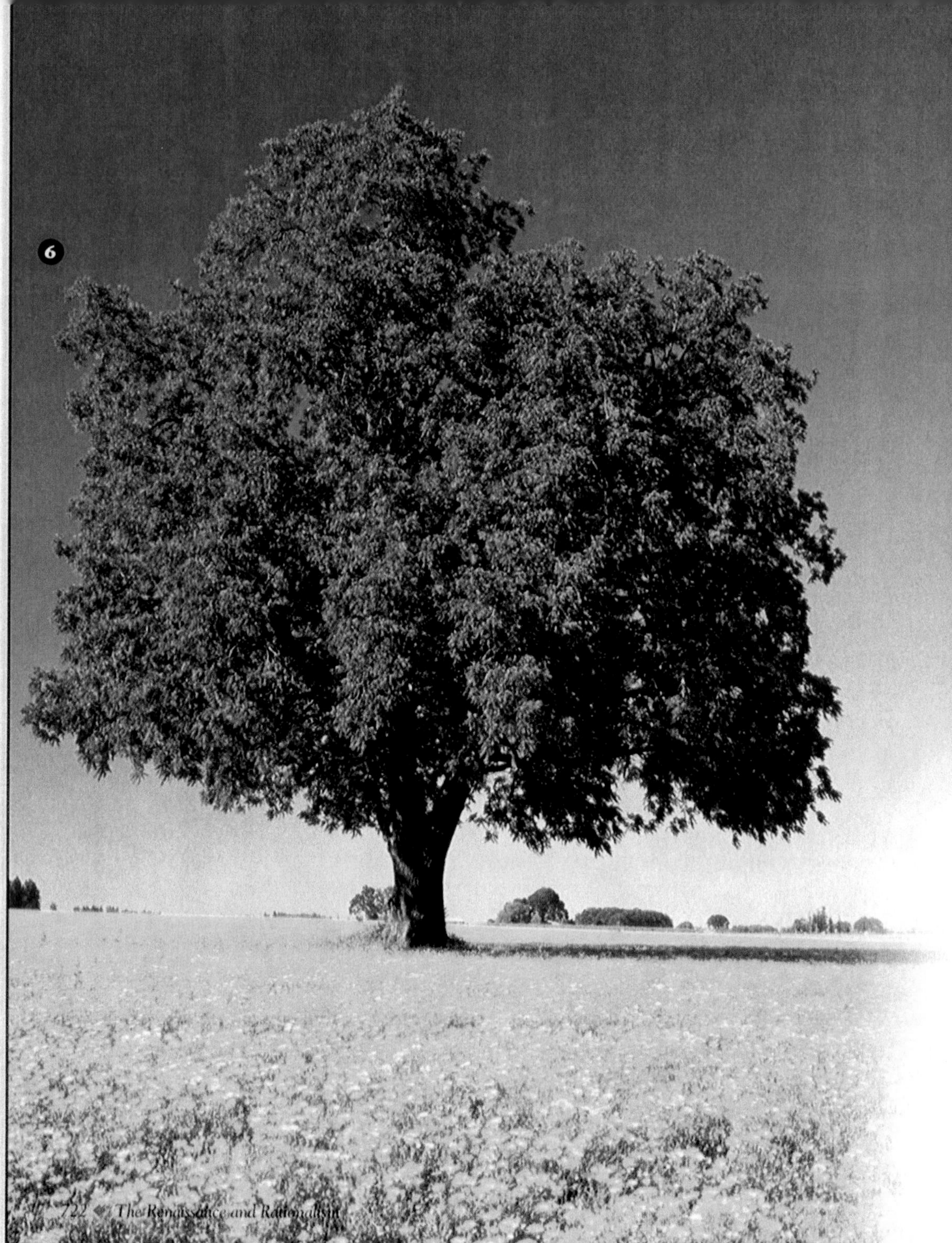

ENRICHMENT: Culture Connection

Fable in the Western World

The fable is a popular mainstay of literature. Permeating all levels of writing, it has influenced Western society through the works of Aesop and his Roman collector, Phaedrus, before being retold in the writings of La Fontaine. Other important fabulists include Horace, the Roman poet who relates the story of the city mouse and the country mouse; Chaucer, who incorporates the tale of Chanticleer and the fox in his *Canterbury Tales;* Rudyard Kipling, the author of *The Jungle Book* and *Just So Stories;* and Julius Lester who reclaimed Joel Chandler Harris's Uncle Remus stories. These stories, which originated with African slaves, emphasize the wisdom of weaker animals who must use their wits to survive the attacks of stronger, more ferocious beasts.

The Oak and the Reed

7

Jean de La Fontaine
***translated by* Marianne Moore**

8
The oak said to the reed, "You grow
Too unprotectedly. Nature has been unfair;
A tiny wren[1] alights, and you are bending low;
If a fitful breath of air
Should freshen till ripples show,
You heed her and lower your head;
My form not only makes shade where the sun would play
But like the Caucasus[2] it does not sway.
However it is buffeted.
9
Your so-called hurricanes are too faint to fear.
Would that you'd been born beneath this towering tent I've made,
Which could afford you ample shade;
Your hazards would not be severe:
I'd shield you when the lightning played;
But grow you will, time and again,
On the misty fringe of the wind's domain.
I perceive that you are grievously oppressed."

buffeted (buf′ it id) *v.* struck sharply

hazards (haz′ ərdz) *n.* dangers

Literary Analysis
Fables What human foible, or weakness, does the oak possess?

10 **✓Reading Check**
From what would the oak shield the reed?

1. **wren** (ren) small, sparrowlike songbird.
2. **Caucasus** (kô′ kə səs) mountain range between southeastern Europe and western Asia.

◄ **Critical Viewing** Which images in the poem match details visible in the photograph? Explain. **[Connect]**

7 About the Selection

In this fable, an oak tree brags about its superior size and strength and expresses pity for the reed, who the oak believes is oppressed. However, the oak quickly discovers which of the two is better able to survive.

8 Critical Thinking

Make an Inference

- Ask a volunteer to read aloud the first three lines of "The oak and the Reed."
- Invite students to make an inference about the oak tree on the basis of the opening three lines.
  Possible response: The oak begins by criticizing the reed. Criticism often stems from one's feelings of superiority over another. Therefore, the oak probably feels superior.

9 Literary Analysis

Fables

- Remind students that fables satirize human weakness. Then, read aloud the bracketed passage.
- Ask students whether they believe that the oak tree is genuinely concerned about the reed's welfare. Why or why not?
  Possible response: The oak tree is not really concerned about the reed; it is simply bragging about its own perceived superiority.
- Ask students the Literary Analysis question on p. 723: What human foible, or weakness, does the oak possess?
  Answer: The oak tree is proud and believes itself superior to the reed.

10 ✓Reading Check

Answer: The oak tree would shield the reed from the sun and from lightning.

CUSTOMIZE INSTRUCTION FOR UNIVERSAL ACCESS

For Less Proficient Readers	For English Learners	For Gifted/Talented Students
Students may have difficulty with the vocabulary and the sentence structure of the fables. Have them read the fables aloud, reminding them to read according to sentence punctuation. Then, have students reenact the exchange between the fox and the crow or the oak and the reed, using the language of everyday conversation.	Students may have difficulty with the vocabulary and the sentence structure of the fables. Read the fables along with them, modeling how to read according to sentence punctuation. Explain difficult vocabulary or phrases. Then, have students reenact the exchange between the fox and the crow or the oak and the reed.	Encourage students to create original fables. Remind students that their fables must personify creatures, illustrate a moral, and revolve around a human weakness. Students should also compress their fables into a single episode. Encourage students to illustrate their fables as well.

ASSESS

11 Vocabulary Development

Latin Prefix *im-*

- Call students' attention to the word *impervious* and its definition. Tell students that the prefix *im-* means "no, not, without."
- Have students suggest and define words that contain this prefix, and list them on the board.
  Possible response: *Immature, immortal, impossible* and *imprudent* are possible suggestions.

Answers for p. 724

Review and Assess

1. Possible response: "The Fox and the Crow" has the more useful moral. Although the crow's vanity makes him the victim of another character, he can control the situation in the future. The oak's sense of superiority, however, makes it the victim of the wind, over which he has no control.
2. **(a)** The crow has a piece of cheese that the fox wants. **(b)** The fox flatters the crow's appearance but questions his voice. **(c)** Possible response: Although he vows to relinquish his role as the fool, the crow, smarting from ridicule, does not learn the lesson of humility.
3. **(a)** The fox's pose, or body language, suggests that he has false and devious charm. **(b)** The fox uses his intelligence to take advantage of the crow's vanity. **(c)** Possible response: The fox is known as a symbol of cunning.
4. **(a)** The oak speaks more than the reed. **(b)** Possible response: The oak's sense of superiority is emphasized by its verbosity.
5. **(a)** The reed is better able to withstand the storm. **(b)** The reed can bend with the wind. **(c)** Possible response: Adaptability is essential for survival.
6. Possible response: The fables address human weaknesses of vanity and feelings of superiority.

The rush[3] said, "Bless you for fearing that I might be distressed;
It is you alone whom the winds should alarm.
I bend and do not break. You've seemed consistently
Impervious to harm—
Erect when blasts rushed to and fro;
As for the end, who can foresee how things will go?"
Relentless wind was on them instantly—
A fury of destruction
Which the North had nursed in some haunt known to none.
The bulrush bent, but not the tree.
Confusion rose to a roar,
Until the hurricane threw prone
That thing of kingly height whose head had all but touched God's throne—
Who had shot his root to the threshold of Death's door.

impervious (im pur' vē əs) *adj.* not affected by, or unable to be damaged

prone (prōn) *adj.* lying face downward

3. **rush** *n.* reed.

Review and Assess

Thinking About the Selections

1. **Respond:** Which of these fables do you think has the more important or useful moral? Why?
2. (a) **Recall:** What is the situation in "The Fox and the Crow"? (b) **Interpret:** What is the fox's strategy for getting what he wants? (c) **Draw Conclusions:** Do you think the crow learned the value of humility from his experience? Why or why not?
3. (a) **Recall:** Which of the fox's physical traits does the fable reveal? (b) **Interpret:** Why is the fox's intelligence a featured characteristic? (c) **Speculate:** Why do you think the speaker uses a fox in this fable?
4. (a) **Recall:** Which of the two characters in "The Oak and the Reed" speaks more? (b) **Infer:** What does this suggest about the character of the oak tree?
5. (a) **Recall:** Is the oak or the reed better able to withstand the storm? (b) **Analyze:** What physical trait does the reed possess that the oak does not? (c) **Speculate:** What does this fable suggest about the traits necessary for survival in a harsh world?
6. **Connect:** In what ways do the morals of these two fables apply to life today?

ASSESSMENT PRACTICE: Reading Comprehension

Distinguish Between Fact and Nonfact (For more practice, see Test Preparation Workbook, p. 35.)

On standardized tests, students are often asked to distinguish between fact and nonfact. Use this sample test item with students: "I perceive that you are grievously oppressed."

> The rush said, "Bless you for fearing that I might be distressed;
> I bend and do not break. You've seemed consistently impervious to harm—
> As for the end, who can foresee how things will go?"

Which is an OPINION expressed in the passage?

A The reed bends but does not break.
B The reed is uncertain about the future.
C The reed blesses the oak.
D The reed is grievously oppressed.

The oppression of the reed is a perception of the oak, so ***D*** is the correct answer.

Review and Assess

Literary Analysis

Fables

1. (a) Compare the elements of a **fable** found in each of the poems using a Venn diagram like the one shown below. (b) In what ways do the poems differ?

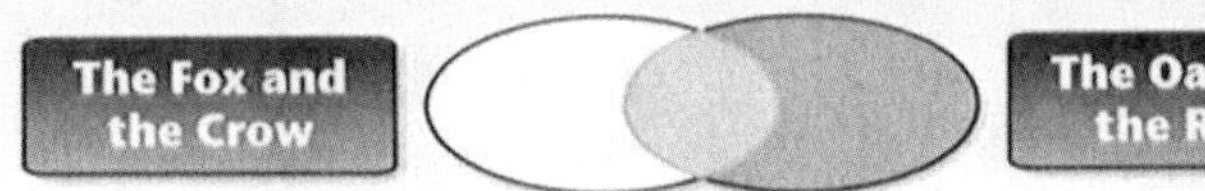

2. Which lines in "The Fox and the Crow" make it clear that the poem is a fable?
3. (a) Besides the oak and the reed, what nonhuman contributes to the moral in "The Oak and the Reed"? (b) What moral does this character teach?

Comparing Literary Works

4. (a) List three examples of **personification** in "The Fox and the Crow." (b) In what typically human way does the crow respond to the fox's flattery? (b) What type of person might the fox represent?
5. (a) Besides physical traits, what other methods of personification are used in "The Oak and the Reed"? (b) In what way is the sun personified?
6. In what ways does the use of personification help these fables teach ethical issues?

Reading Strategy

Drawing Conclusions

7. (a) Why does the crow consider himself "somebody's fool"? (b) What **conclusions** can you draw from his experience?
8. (a) What role does extreme weather play in the lesson the oak learns? (b) What conclusions can you draw from the fable about man's ability to withstand the forces of nature?

Extend Understanding

9. **Science Connection:** Like the reed, which plants possess highly specialized abilities to survive in difficult circumstances?

Quick Review

A **fable** is a brief work that dramatizes a simple lesson or principle of behavior.

Personification is the literary technique of applying human characteristics to nonhuman or inanimate objects.

To **draw conclusions,** note details in a work and infer a larger message or meaning from them.

PHSchool.com

Take the interactive self-test online to check your understanding of these selections.

ENRICHMENT: Further Reading

Other Works by Jean de La Fontaine:

We strongly encourage you to review any selection before assigning or recommending it to students.

Fifty Fables of La Fontaine

Once Again, La Fontaine: 60 More Fables

Take It to the Net

Visit PHSchool.com for more information on Jean de La Fontaine.

Answers for p. 725

Review and Assess

1. **(a) The Fox and the Crow:** animal characters; loss of possession; **Overlap:** personification of nonhuman characters; compressed episode; human weakness; moral; **The Oak and the Reed:** plant characters; loss of life. **(b)** "The Fox and the Crow" features animal characters in conflict over a possession. "The Oak and the Reed" features plant characters, one of whom does not survive.
2. The last two lines state the moral, thus indicating that the poem is a fable.
3. **(a)** The wind contributes to the moral in "The Oak and the Reed." **(b)** Possible response: The wind teaches the oak that the inability to adapt to change will cause destruction.
4. **(a)** Possible response: Examples of personification include the following: the fox talks; the fox's pose suggests false and devious charm; and the crow sings musical scales. **(b)** The crow tries to elicit more flattery. **(c)** The fox might represent a con artist.
5. **(a)** Possible response: Other methods include the following: the reed lowers its head, and the North nurses the wind. **(b)** The sun plays.
6. Possible response: The use of personification distances the animal and plant characters from the reader so that the reader appreciates the lesson without feeling directly attacked for his or her own weaknesses.
7. **(a)** The crow allows the fox to manipulate him; as a result, he loses his cheese and is subjected to ridicule. **(b)** Possible response: Flattery should cause suspicion.
8. **(a)** The strong wind fells the oak. **(b)** Possible response: To withstand the forces of nature, humans must be adaptable.
9. Possible response: The cactus survives with very little water.

EXTEND

Answers for p. 726

❶ Vocabulary Development

Word Analysis: Latin Prefix *im-*

1. not mature or well developed
2. not subject to death
3. not prudent or wise
4. not keeping within normal bounds

Spelling Strategy

1. subterraneous
2. delicious
3. prodigious

Fluency: Sentence Completions

1. hazards
2. impervious
3. buffeted
4. prone

❷ Grammar and Style

Practice

1. who was as black as ebony; modifies *crow*
2. whom the crow never suspected of being sly and deceitful; modifies *fox*
3. whose slender form bent to the earth; modifies *reed*
4. whose fury blasted the tree and the tender reeds; modifies *gale*
5. who was once again standing straight; modifies *reed*

Writing Application

Possible response:

- The fox, whose stomach was growling with hunger, had a plan to steal the cheese. [modifies *fox*]
- The crow, who was especially vain, listened with pleasure to the flattery. [modifies *crow*]
- The tortoise, who refused to give up, won the race. [modifies *tortoise*]
- The grasshopper laughed at the hard-working ant, who was preparing for winter. [modifies *ant*]

10TH GRADE For support in teaching the Grammar and Style Lesson to tenth graders, use **Writing and Grammar,** Platinum Level, Chapter 20, Section 2.

Integrate Language Skills

❶ Vocabulary Development Lesson

Word Analysis: Latin Prefix *im-*

The word *impervious* contains the prefix *im-*, meaning "no, not, without." *Impervious*, therefore, means "not affected by." Use the meaning of this prefix to define the words below.

1. immature
2. immortal
3. imprudent
4. immoderate

Spelling Strategy

The ending *-ious* is used to form an adjective, like the word *impervious*. Although the spelling *ious* is more common, some adjectives are spelled with *eous*. Add *-ious* or *-eous* to each item below. Use a dictionary to check your work.

1. subterran- 2. delic- 3. prodig-

Fluency: Sentence Completions

Review the words from the vocabulary list on page 719. Then, copy each sentence below, filling in the blanks with the appropriate vocabulary word.

1. The old tree had faced many _____, yet it remained strong.
2. The tree seemed _____ to the forces of nature.
3. Despite being _____ by the wind and rain, the oak stood straight and tall.
4. The delicate reeds, however, were often laid _____ by the gales, but their resilient stems soon straightened again.

❷ Grammar and Style Lesson

Adjective Clauses Using *who, whom,* and *whose*

Subordinate clauses contain a subject and a verb, and they act as a single part of speech. **Adjective clauses** are subordinate clauses that modify nouns or pronouns. They are often introduced by the relative pronouns *who*, *whom*, and *whose*.

Example: Master Fox, whose *pose suggested fragrances*, said in language which of course I cannot speak . . . (modifies "Master Fox")

Practice Identify the adjective clause and the word it modifies in each of the following sentences.

1. The crow, who was as black as ebony, sat holding cheese in his beak.
2. The crow was flattered by the fox, whom the crow never suspected of being sly and deceitful.
3. The reed, whose slender form bent to the earth, waited for the storm to pass.
4. The mighty gale, whose fury blasted the tree and the tender reeds, finally destroyed the great oak.
5. After the storm passed, the reed, who was once again standing straight, saw that the tree had fallen.

Writing Application Write four sentences about animals. Include an adjective clause in each sentence, and identify both the clause and the noun it modifies.

WG Prentice Hall Writing and Grammar Connection: Diamond Level, Chapter 19, Section 3

TEACHING RESOURCES

The following resources can be used to enrich or extend the instruction for pp. 726–727.

Vocabulary

- **Selection Support:** Build Vocabulary, p. 137 ▪
- **Vocabulary and Spelling Practice Book** (Use this booklet for skills instruction.)

Grammar

- **Selection Support:** Grammar and Style, p. 138
- **Writing and Grammar,** Diamond Level, p. 458
- **Daily Language Practice Transparencies**

Writing

- **Performance Assess. and Portfolio Mgmt.,** p. 14
- **Writing and Grammar,** Diamond Level, p. 722
- **Writing and Grammar iText CD-ROM**
- **Writing Models and Graphic Organizers on Transparencies,** pp. 83–85 ▪

Listening and Speaking

- **Performance Assess. and Portfolio Mgmt.,** p. 28

▪ **BLOCK SCHEDULING:** Resources marked with this symbol provide varied instruction during 90-minute blocks.

❸ Writing Lesson

A Children's Story

Fables and stories with animal characters have always been popular with children. Use one of La Fontaine's poems as a basis for a fully developed children's story that teaches the same lesson as the original poem. Use additional characters if you wish.

Prewriting Start by writing an outline of the plot, or main events, of La Fontaine's fable. Then, jot down notes about his characters, adding your own ideas to describe how they sound, look, and move.

Drafting As you draft, use vivid details and dialogue to make your story entertaining. Include descriptions of each character.

Revising Compare your draft with the original poem to be sure the moral of the story is clear. Make certain that all the dialogue is set in quotation marks and that other punctuation in your fable is used correctly.

Writing Model: Punctuating for Dialogue

"I see you have a lovely piece of cheese," said the fox in a greasy voice. "It must surely be delicious!"

"Grt hgach tuk," garbled the crow, whose beak was full of cheddar.

"Tell me, Sir Ebony," said the fox, "was that your beautiful warbling I heard this morning?"

To make dialogue clear, all punctuation that is part of the dialogue is set inside the quotation marks.

Prentice Hall Writing and Grammar Connection: Diamond Level, Chapter 27, Section 4

❹ Extension Activities

Listening and Speaking Work with a partner to prepare a **dramatic reading** of one of La Fontaine's poems. Use these storytelling strategies to enliven your reading:

- Sit at eye level with your audience.
- Adjust your voice and your facial expressions to reflect the characters.
- Use props, such as plants or stuffed animals, to add interest.

Present the reading to the kindergarten class at a local school. **[Group Activity]**

Research and Technology Use the Internet or library resources to compose a **research report** on fables. Describe the types of animals that the stories feature and the lessons that they teach. Compare your findings with La Fontaine's pieces.

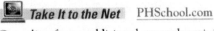

 ***Take It to the Net*** PHSchool.com

Go online for an additional research activity using the Internet.

❸ Writing Lesson

- Remind students that stories for children should focus on simple plots with a great deal of action.
- Encourage students to use the Story Map, pp. 83–85, in **Writing Models and Graphic Organizers on Transparencies,** to help them develop their stories.
- Tell students to use effective methods of characterization when describing characters: what the narrator says about a character; what a character says about himself or herself; what a character does; and what other characters say about a character.
- Remind each student to verify that the moral of the story is directly stated or clearly implied.
- Use the Narration: Short Story rubric in **Performance Assessment and Portfolio Management,** p. 14, to evaluate students' stories.

10TH GRADE For support in working through the Writing Lesson with tenth graders, use **Writing and Grammar,** Platinum Level, Chapter 5, Section 3.

❹ Listening and Speaking

- Instruct students to practice eye contact by rehearsing their performances in front of a mirror.
- Encourage students to develop different voices for each of the characters.
- Help students locate or design props for their performances.
- Use the Speaking: Delivering a Narrative Presentation rubric in **Performance Assessment and Portfolio Management,** p. 28, to evaluate students' performances.

CUSTOMIZE INSTRUCTION For Universal Access

To address different learning styles, use the following activities suggested in the **Extension Activities** booklet, p. 35:

- For Visual/Spatial Learners, use Activity 5.
- For Musical/Rhythmic and Interpersonal Learners, use Activity 6.
- For Verbal/Linguistic and Intrapersonal Learners, use Activity 7.

ASSESSMENT RESOURCES

The following resources can be used to assess students' knowledge and skills.

Selection Assessment

- **Formal Assessment,** pp. 123–125
- **Open-Book Tests,** pp. 103–105
- **Test Bank Software**

 ***Take It to the Net***

Visit PHSchool.com for self-tests on the selections.

Writing Rubric

- **Performance Assess. and Portfolio Mgmt.,** p. 14

Listening and Speaking Rubric

- **Performance Assess. and Portfolio Mgmt.,** p. 28

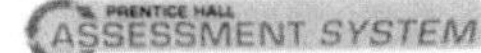

For additional diagnostics and remediation for skills covered in this grouping, use materials from the Prentice Hall Assessment System.

Background

Niccolò Machiavelli

Niccolò Machiavelli has often been characterized as cool, skeptical, and cautious. He was, however, passionate and patriotic on behalf of his native city of Florence. When Florence went to war with Pisa, for example, Machiavelli was asked to remain at headquarters and not take part in the fighting. However, he insisted on commanding the troops he had trained and declared that if he were kept out of the battle, he would die of sadness.

Background

Pascal's Calculator

In 1642, when Blaise Pascal was nineteen, he built a calculator to help his father in his work as a customs officer. Pascal's calculator—a wooden box with six wheels—allowed the user to deal with numbers up to 999,999. In order to add numbers, the user would dial digits into the device and view the resulting sum in the machine's six windows. Later, Pascal developed a calculator made of brass with eight dials. This version, however, was a commercial failure because it was so expensive.

A Closer Look

Great Minds Do Not Think Alike

The power of the mind itself fascinated the greatest thinkers of the Age of Rationalism.

Toward the end of the sixteenth century, the French essayist Michel de Montaigne created a medallion with a motto encapsulating his life and work: *Que scay-je?* or "What do I know?"

If Montaigne had lived during the Middle Ages, he might have asked, "What do I *believe?*" If he had lived during the Romantic Age, he might have asked, "What do I *feel?*" His question "What do I *know?*" is the central theme of his time—the Age of Rationalism.

During the Renaissance, artists and thinkers celebrated human potential. The creative explosion of the fourteenth, fifteenth, and sixteenth centuries reflected a new confidence in human nature. By the seventeenth and eighteenth centuries, Europeans recognized the vast power of the mind itself. The power of thought forced tradition and complacency deeper into the shadows.

Niccolò Machiavelli—The Mind as Weapon The idea of the mind as a political tool found practical expression in the writings of Niccolò Machiavelli (1469–1527). As a diplomat for the Florentine republic, Machiavelli observed firsthand how governments should, and should not, be run. After enduring prison and exile, he settled down on a small farm, where he wrote one of the world's most influential books of political theory—*The Prince*.

In Machiavelli's fiercely realistic view, a ruler maintains control not with goodness but with strength and mental agility. A Machiavellian ruler must possess both force and cunning and use them without sentiment. For Renaissance humanists, a good king had been an ideal Christian who loved his subjects and cherished peace. By contrast, Machiavelli's prince seeks first and foremost to retain and extend his power by any means that will work. He is wily, aggressive, and ruthless, and his greatest weapon is his mind.

Blaise Pascal—The Dialogue of Reason and Religion Blaise Pascal (1623–1662), French mathematician, physicist, and religious philosopher, pondered problems both earthly and heavenly. He manifested his mathematical genius at the age of twelve by independently rediscovering Euclid's first thirty-two propositions of geometry. He also engineered the world's first calculator.

Pascal sought harmony between mathematical certainty and moral truth. In 1657, he began writing his *Pensées*, short philosophical "thoughts" that integrate science and spirituality. Some of Pascal's *pensées* reveal his logical mind, while others reveal his more poetic side. All argue his

ENRICHMENT: Philosophy Connection

The Age of Rationalism

The late seventeenth and eighteenth centuries were a time of concern for truth as revealed through reason. Philosophers of the Age of Rationalism challenged traditions, folk wisdom, and other unscientific beliefs and attempted to replace them with laws derived from contemplation and analysis of natural phenomena. During this time of enlightenment, reason was accepted as the greatest authority in matters of art and the intellect.

Leaning on the structure of arithmetic, algebra, geometry, and the newly evolved study of calculus, the application of rationalism required considerable training. As Galileo, a forerunner of the rationalist movement, pointed out, "Truth is written in the great book of Nature, but only he can read it who can decipher the letters in which it is written." Rationalism soon came to be connected with great depth of thought, maturity, and scholarly training.

fundamental idea that the true nature of humanity is a paradox—a logical contradiction.

Pascal's paradox is that the mind has vast power but is virtually powerless in comparison with the infinite. Human beings are, therefore, "incapable of absolute ignorance and of certain knowledge." As if to answer Montaigne's "What do I know?" Pascal believed that we do know many things, and yet we do not really know much at all. The *pensées* are a rational and beautifully articulated balance of humility and pride: "Man is but a reed, the weakest in nature, but he is a thinking reed."

John Locke—Reason and Revolution To the English philosopher John Locke (1632–1704), the human mind is a *tabula rasa*, or blank slate, and people are not born with innate ideas or moral precepts. Locke believed that everything we experience makes impressions on that blank slate. We then develop ideas by reflecting on those experiences. In this approach, called empiricism, the consciousness of every human being develops independently, based on personal experience, reflections, and decisions.

Locke was also a highly influential political philosopher. In his *Two Treatises of Government* (1690), Locke argued that people are free to choose their own government. Locke reasoned that government is not based on "myth, mysticism, and mystery"; rather, it has a rational purpose—to protect life, liberty, and property. If it fails, it may be overthrown. Thomas Jefferson and other founders of the American Republic were deeply influenced by Locke's ideas.

Jean-Jacques Rousseau—The Social Contract The most extraordinarily multifaceted mind to emerge during the Age of Rationalism was that of Jean-Jacques Rousseau (1712–1778). Orphan, footman, music teacher, tutor, encyclopedia writer, political philosopher, social critic, novelist, autobiographer, wanderer, radical, free spirit—Rousseau was all of these and more.

For Rousseau, civilization corrupted humanity's natural goodness. He believed that people are fundamentally noble and virtuous, but society has made it impossible for the best in human nature to flourish; therefore, a new social order needs to be created. In *The Social Contract* (1762), Rousseau outlined what that society ought to be—a state in which a ruler leads at the will of the people, who can revoke their support if they wish. This social contract achieved its most complete embodiment in American democracy.

Rousseau's belief in reason and his efforts to formulate the idea of a democratic society place him at the pinnacle of Enlightenment thought. His devotion to nature and his belief in the unique and passionate individual make him the intellectual bridge to the Age of the Romantics.

▼Critical Viewing

In what way does this portrait of Rousseau reflect the philosopher's ideas? **[Connect]**

Background

John Locke

John Locke was a lifelong scholar. From his early years at Oxford, where he studied rhetoric, grammar, philosophy, geometry, and Greek, to his later years, when he met with learned friends to discuss philosophical and scientific issues, he pursued individual studies across disciplines. Locke's scholarship encompassed theology, politics, physics, and even medicine.

▶Critical Viewing

Possible response: Rousseau is enjoying nature, away from the corruption of civilization.

Critical Thinking

1. What would Jean-Jacques Rousseau have to say about Machiavelli's description of a ruler's primary purpose? **[Connect]**
   Possible response: Rousseau would declare that people should overthrow such a ruler if he or she takes away their liberties.
2. Would Rousseau be pleased with the governmental processes in place within the United States today? Explain. **[Apply]**
   Possible response: Rousseau might pleased with the democratic nature of the United States government that allows the people to change leaders by voting.

from Candide

Lesson Objectives

1. **To analyze and respond to literary elements**
   - Literary Analysis: Satire
   - Connecting Literary Elements: Satirical Tools
2. **To read, comprehend, analyze, and critique a satire**
   - Reading Strategy: Connecting to Historical Context
   - Reading Check Questions
   - Review and Assess Questions
   - Assessment Practice (ATE)
3. **To develop word analysis skills, fluency, and systematic vocabulary**
   - Vocabulary Development Lesson: Latin Suffix *-ity*
4. **To understand and apply written and oral language conventions**
   - Spelling Strategy
   - Grammar and Style Lesson: Parallel Structure
5. **To understand and apply appropriate writing and research strategies**
   - Writing Lesson: Satirical Short Story
   - Extension Activity: Visual Report on Satirical Cartoons
6. **To understand and apply listening and speaking strategies**
   - Extension Activity: Group Discussion of Musical Version of *Candide*

STEP-BY-STEP TEACHING GUIDE	PACING GUIDE
PRETEACH	
Motivate Students and Provide Background	
Use the Motivation activity (ATE p. 730)	5 min.
Read and discuss author and background features (SE pp. 730, 732; ATE p. 730) [A]	5 min.
Introduce the Concepts	
Introduce the Literary Analysis and Reading Strategy concepts (SE/ATE p. 731) [A]	15 min.
Pronounce the vocabulary words and read their definitions (SE p. 731)	5 min.
TEACH	
Monitor Comprehension	
Informally monitor comprehension by circulating while students read independently or in groups [A]	40 min.
Monitor students' comprehension with the Reading Check notes (SE/ATE pp. 733, 735)	as students read
Develop vocabulary with the Vocabulary notes (SE pp. 732, 734, 735, 736; ATE p. 734)	as students read
Develop Understanding	
Develop students' understanding of satire with the Literary Analysis annotations (SE pp. 732, 734; ATE pp. 732, 733, 734) [A]	10 min.
Develop students' ability to connect to historical context, using the Reading Strategy annotations (SE/ATE p. 735) [A]	10 min.
ASSESS	
Assess Mastery	
Assess students' mastery of the Reading Strategy and Literary Analysis concepts by having them answer the Review and Assess questions (SE/ATE p. 737)	15 min.
Use one or more of the print, software, or transparency Assessment Resources (ATE p. 739) [A]	up to 45 min.
EXTEND	
Apply Understanding	
Have students complete the Vocabulary Development Lesson and the Grammar and Style Lesson (SE/ATE p. 738) [A]	20 min.
Apply students' ability to organize details, using the Writing Lesson (SE/ATE p. 739) [A]	45 min.
Apply students' understanding of the selections, using one or more of the Extension Activities (SE p. 739)	20–90 min.

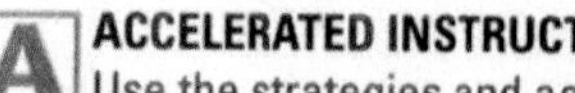

ACCELERATED INSTRUCTION: Use the strategies and activities identified with an [A].

UNIVERSAL ACCESS
● = Below-Level Students
▲ = On-Level Students
■ = Above-Level Students

10TH GRADE **TEACHING TENTH-GRADE STUDENTS**
For support in teaching the selection(s) to tenth-grade students, see the Step-by-Step Teaching notes identified with the icon shown here.

Time and Resource Manager

Reading Level: Average
Average Number of Instructional Days: 4

RESOURCES		
PRINT	**TRANSPARENCIES**	**TECHNOLOGY**
• **Beyond Literature,** Historical Connection: Frederick the Great, p. 36 ▲ ■		
• **Selection Support Workbook:** ● ▲ ■ Literary Analysis, p. 144 Reading Strategy, p. 143 Build Vocabulary, p. 141	• **Literary Analysis and Reading Transparencies,** pp. 71 and 72 ● ▲ ■	
		• **Listening to Literature** ● ▲ ■ Audiocassettes Audio CDs
• **Literary Analysis for Enrichment,** p. 36 ■	• **Fine Art Transparencies,** Art Transparency 10 ● ▲ ■	
• **Formal Assessment:** Selection Test, pp. 126–128 ● ▲ ■ • **Open-Book Tests,** pp. 106–108 ● ▲ ■ • **Performance Assessment and Portfolio Management,** p. 14 ● ▲ ■ • PRENTICE HALL ASSESSMENT SYSTEM ● ▲ ■	• PRENTICE HALL ASSESSMENT SYSTEM ● ▲ ■ **Skills Practice Answers and Explanations on Transparencies**	• **Test Bank Software** ● ▲ ■
• **Selection Support Workbook:** ● ▲ ■ Grammar and Style, p. 142 • **Writing and Grammar,** Diamond Level ● ▲ ■ • **Extension Activities,** p. 36 ● ▲ ■	• **Daily Language Practice Transparencies** ● ▲ • **Writing Models and Graphic Organizers on Transparencies,** pp. 75–77 ● ▲ ■	• **Writing and Grammar iText CD-ROM** ● ▲ ■ *Take It to the Net* PHSchool.com

BLOCK SCHEDULING: Use one 90-minute class period to preteach the selection(s) and have students read them. Use a second 90-minute class period to assess students' mastery of skills and have them complete one of the Extension Activities.

PRETEACH

Step-by-Step Teaching Guide for pp. 730–731

Motivation

Tell students that stories about the adventures of young people in search of some special dream are plentiful in world literature and film. If possible, show students excerpts from such films as *The Adventures of Huckleberry Finn* or *Great Expectations*. Lead students in a discussion about the popularity of this plot.

Use the following questions to stimulate discussion:

- Why is this plot appealing to readers and viewers?
- Why does this plot remain popular across time and cultures?
- Can you name other stories or films that make use of this plot?

1 Background

More About the Author

During Voltaire's exile in England, he learned to speak the English language. He met such important English writers and thinkers as Alexander Pope, Jonathan Swift, William Congreve, and the philosopher George Berkeley. Voltaire was particularly impressed by the freedom of the English to discuss openly religion and philosophy. He believed that this freedom was responsible for the advances in thought exemplified by English scientists such as Sir Isaac Newton and John Locke.

Geography Note

Draw students' attention to the map of France on this page. Point out that Voltaire's estate in Ferney, France, is near the Swiss border.

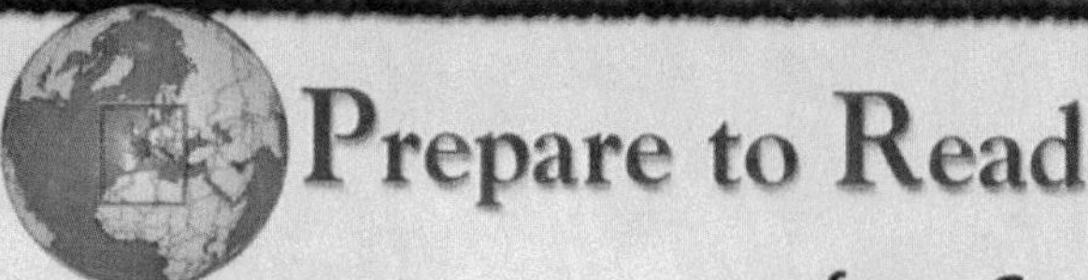

Prepare to Read

from Candide

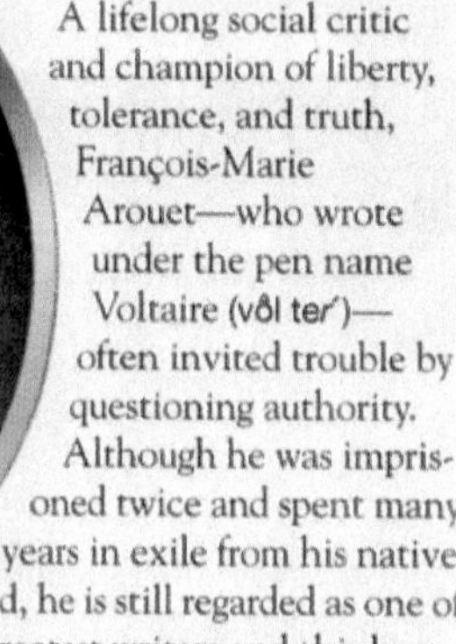

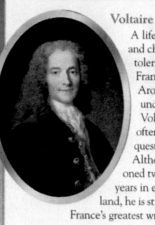

Voltaire (1694–1778)

A lifelong social critic and champion of liberty, tolerance, and truth, François-Marie Arouet—who wrote under the pen name Voltaire (vōl ter′)—often invited trouble by questioning authority. Although he was imprisoned twice and spent many years in exile from his native land, he is still regarded as one of France's greatest writers and thinkers.

Man-About-Paris Voltaire grew up in the French capital of Paris in the waning years of King Louis XIV's reign. Although his family expected him to study law, he was more interested in literature and the theater. Clever and witty, he was an immediate success when his godfather introduced him to the best of Paris society after he left school. He attended all the trendy gatherings, and his short satirical poems were much quoted by fashionable Parisians.

Fame—and Prison In 1715, Louis XIV died, and his five-year-old great-grandson came to the French throne as Louis XV. Two years later, Voltaire was accused of penning satirical barbs criticizing the late king and the Duc d'Orléans, who was serving as regent, or acting ruler, for young Louis XV. As punishment, Voltaire was at first exiled, and then he was sent to the Bastille, the notorious Paris prison, for nearly a year.

He made the most of his prison stay by completing *Oedipe*, the first of his many tragic dramas, and beginning work on the *Henriade*, his epic poem in tribute to Henry IV. After Voltaire's release from prison, *Oedipe* was staged in Paris to much acclaim. It was also around this time that Voltaire adopted his famous pen name.

Voltaire's favor in Paris was short-lived, however. In 1725, never one to hold his tongue, he made the mistake of quarreling with the powerful Chevalier de Rohan. When Voltaire challenged Rohan to a duel, Voltaire was sent briefly to the Bastille again and then into exile from his homeland.

The English Influence Voltaire spent his exile in England, a nation he found more tolerant and open-minded than the France of his day. He especially admired the achievements of English scientist Sir Isaac Newton and the ideas of English philosopher John Locke, whose principles of liberty had helped justify England's Glorious Revolution of 1688. Voltaire concluded that the freedom of thought he found in England encouraged scientific advancement and thus helped the nation prosper. When he was allowed to return home, he produced his *Lettres philosophiques*, in which he compared England favorably to France. With its emphasis on reason, religious tolerance, and freedom of thought, the work is considered a landmark of the eighteenth-century Age of Enlightenment.

Later Years Voltaire considered himself an enemy of injustice; his determination to help others, his strong opinions, and his argumentative disposition caused him trouble throughout his life. In 1750, he was invited to Berlin by the Prussian leader Frederick the Great, but three years later he angered Frederick by mocking one of Prussia's leading scientists. In Geneva, Switzerland, the Calvinist religious leaders who at first welcomed him as a champion of religious tolerance were disturbed by some of his more radical ideas.

In 1758, just after publishing his best-known work, the satirical novel *Candide*, Voltaire retired to Ferney, a property he had bought near Geneva. There, he lived in semiretirement for the last two decades of his life—writing, running the estate, instituting agricultural reforms, and, of course, getting into arguments with the locals.

TEACHING RESOURCES

The following resources can be used to enrich or extend the instruction for pp. 730–731.

Background

Beyond Literature, p. 36

Take It to the Net

Visit PHSchool.com for background on the author.

Literary Analysis

Literary Analysis and Reading Transparencies, Satire, p. 71

Reading

Literary Analysis and Reading Transparencies, Connecting to Historical Context, p. 72

Selection Support: Reading Strategy, p. 143
Building Vocabulary, p. 141

BLOCK SCHEDULING: Resources marked with this symbol provide varied instruction during 90-minute blocks.

Preview

Connecting to the Literature

Moviemakers and authors entertain the public with wildly comedic characters. *Candide* features such personalities, yet they serve a higher purpose: to expose social inequities and to suggest a means of escaping them.

Literary Analysis

Satire

Satire is writing that uses humor to expose and ridicule human foolishness. Although satirists take aim at individuals, institutions, types of behavior, or humanity in general, the ultimate goal of a satirical piece is to inspire positive change. *Candide* prompts readers to question the conditions of their lives by calling attention to social injustices such as corrupt political systems. As you read this selection, note cases of injustice or inhumanity just under the humorous surface of this work.

Connecting Literary Elements

Satirists ridicule their subjects by using tools such as **exaggeration, understatement,** and **faulty logic.** Consider these examples from the selection:

- *Exaggeration:* ". . . The Baron's castle was the best of castles. . . ."
- *Understatement:* ". . . the next day he drilled not so badly and received only twenty strokes [of the lash]."
- *Faulty logic:* "Observe that noses were made to wear spectacles: and so we have spectacles."

As you read, notice how the repeated use of these tools contributes to the humor and persuades a reader toward the speaker's point of view.

Reading Strategy

Connecting to Historical Context

When you **connect a work to its historical context,** you identify the ideas and events in a piece that may be responses to its era. To make the connection, use a chart like the one shown to list details from the story that reflect the time period. Then, consider the way the details connect to history.

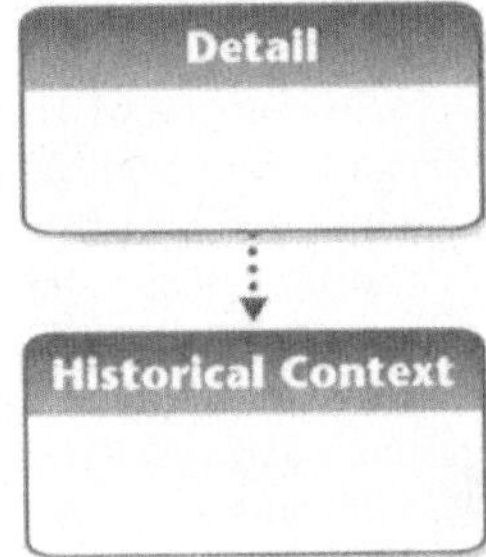

Vocabulary Development

endowed (en dou̇d′) *v.* given, or provided with (p. 732)

candor (kan′ dər) *n.* open honesty and frankness (p. 732)

vivacity (vī vas′ ə tē) *n.* liveliness or animation (p. 734)

prodigy (präd′ ə jē) *n.* person of very great ability (p. 735)

clemency (klem′ ən sē) *n.* mercy toward an enemy or offender (p. 736)

❷ Literary Analysis

Satire

- Read aloud the Literary Analysis instruction on p. 731. Tell students that satire pokes fun at situations, ideas, or people, through the use of exaggeration, understatement, and faulty logic.
- Review with students the examples on p. 731. Then, encourage student pairs to construct an original example of each satiric strategy. Invite students to share their examples with the class.
- Instruct students to note examples of each satiric strategy as they read the excerpt from *Candide*.

❸ Reading Strategy

Connecting to Historical Context

- Tell students that many works of literature bear a direct relation to the time and place in which they were written. For example, Voltaire was shocked by the terrible earthquake that struck Lisbon, Portugal, in 1755, claiming nearly 25,000 lives. Voltaire uses this event in satirizing the philosophic idea that this is "the best of all possible worlds."
- Direct students to use a graphic organizer like the one on p. 731 to record details regarding political situations, wars, or other events in *Candide*. Help students research Voltaire's time period to locate the historical context for these details.
- If students need more practice with this strategy, use the Connecting to Historical Context transparency in **Literary Analysis and Reading Transparencies,** p. 72.

Vocabulary Development

- Pronounce each vocabulary word for students, and read the definitions as a class. Have students identify any words with which they are already familiar.

CUSTOMIZE INSTRUCTION FOR UNIVERSAL ACCESS

For Less Proficient Readers	For English Learners	For Advanced Readers
Students may have difficulty connecting literature to a historical context. Help students construct a timeline of French and European social and political history that reflects Voltaire's lifetime (1694–1778). Make sure that students include an entry for the 1755 Lisbon earthquake.	Help students construct a timeline of French and European social and political history that reflects Voltaire's lifetime (1694–1778). Make sure that students include an entry for the 1755 Lisbon earthquake. It may help students to add visual icons for each entry on the timeline.	Help students locate and read "The Myth of Sisyphus" by Albert Camus. Ask them to respond to the following question in essay form: "The Myth of Sisyphus" was written during World War II. Why do you think this particular myth had a powerful appeal for people who experienced the terrible events of that time?

 ***e-Teach***

Visit e-Teach at PHSchool.com for teachers' essays on how to teach, with questions and answers.

TEACH

Step-by-Step Teaching Guide for pp. 732–736

Teaching Tenth-Grade Students

10TH GRADE Tenth-grade students are likely to have recently studied William Shakespeare's *Romeo and Juliet* and possibly *West Side Story*. Students should therefore identify with the young Candide and his girlfriend Cunegonde and the problems they have with her father. After students have read Chapter 1, encourage them to state what seems realistic about the Baron's reaction to the young lovers and what is purely satirical.

❶ About the Selection

In this story, the adolescent Candide and his girlfriend Cunegonde have been taught to believe in the innocence and goodness of all things by the famous Doctor Pangloss. But misfortune soon arrives when Cunegonde's father catches her kissing Candide and throws him off the estate. So begins an intercontinental whirlwind that will take Candide around the world, surviving disasters, tortures, mayhem, and massacres in an attempt to become reunited with Cunegonde.

❷ Literary Analysis

Satire

- Remind students that satirists make use of tools such as faulty logic and exaggeration. To help students recognize instances of faulty logic, instruct them to look for stated or implied thinking verbs *(think, reason, contemplate, ponder, deliberate, mediate, mull over, ruminate,* or *cogitate)* that serve as clue words to a character's thought process.
- Read aloud the bracketed passage. Then, ask students to respond to the Literary Analysis item on p. 732: Identify two tools of satire in the first paragraph.
  Possible response: Voltaire uses faulty logic ("His judgment was quite honest and he was extremely simple-minded; and this was the reason, I think, that he was named Candide.") and exaggeration ("this young lady would never marry because he could only prove seventy-one quarterings").

❶ from Candide

Voltaire ***translated by*** **Richard Aldington**

Background

Subtitled "Optimism," *Candide* is deeply rooted in historical events and ideas close to Voltaire's heart. For example, his work alludes to a devastating earthquake in Lisbon in 1755 and to a popular philosophy claiming that this world is the best of all possible worlds.

Candide is an innocent youth who suffers severe hardships as he searches for his beloved, Cunegonde. Along the way, Candide learns firsthand that life is often shaped by incomprehensible forces and by the cruelty and frivolity of the ruling classes.

CHAPTER I

How Candide was brought up in a noble castle and how he was expelled from the same

❷ In the castle of Baron Thunder-ten-tronckh in Westphalia[1] there lived a youth, endowed by Nature with the most gentle character. His face was the expression of his soul. His judgment was quite honest and he was extremely simple-minded; and this was the reason, I think, that he was named Candide. Old servants in the house suspected that he was the son of the Baron's sister and a decent honest gentleman of the neighborhood, whom this young lady would never marry because he could only prove seventy-one quarterings[2] and the rest of his genealogical tree was lost, owing to the injuries of time.

endowed (en doud′) *v.* given, or provided with

Literary Analysis
Satire Identify two tools of satire in the first paragraph.

The Baron was one of the most powerful lords in Westphalia, for his castle possessed a door and windows. His Great Hall was even decorated with a piece of tapestry. The dogs in his stable-yards formed a pack of hounds when necessary; his grooms were his huntsmen; the village curate was his Grand Almoner. They all called him "My Lord," and laughed heartily at his stories.

The Baroness weighed about three hundred and fifty pounds, was therefore greatly respected, and did the honors of the house with a dignity which rendered her still more respectable. Her daughter Cunegonde, aged seventeen, was rosy-cheeked, fresh, plump and tempting. The Baron's son appeared in every respect worthy of his father. The tutor Pangloss was the oracle of the house, and little Candide followed his lessons with all the candor of his age and character.

candor (kan′ dər) *n.* open honesty and frankness

1. **Baron . . . Westphalia** The Baron is a lesser member of nobility in a historic region of northwestern Germany.
2. **quarterings** divisions on a coat-of-arms indicating generations of noble or distinguished ancestry.

TEACHING RESOURCES

The following resources can be used to enrich or extend the instruction for pp. 732–736.

Literary Analysis
Selection Support: Literary Analysis, p. 144

Reading
Selection Support: Reading Strategy, p. 143; Build Vocabulary, p. 141
Listening to Literature Audiocassettes
Listening to Literature Audio CDs

Extension
Fine Art Transparencies, Art Transparency 10 (Have students analyze the attitudes being satirized in Hogarth's painting and then discuss ways in which *Candide* shares a similar good-natured skepticism about human folly.)

BLOCK SCHEDULING: Resources marked with this symbol provide varied instruction during 90-minute blocks.

Pangloss taught metaphysico-theologo-cosmolonigology.[3] He proved admirably that there is no effect without a cause and that in this best of all possible worlds, My Lord the Baron's castle was the best of castles and his wife the best of all possible Baronesses.

4

3 "'Tis demonstrated," said he, "that things cannot be otherwise; for, since everything is made for an end, everything is necessarily for the best end. Observe that noses were made to wear spectacles; and so we have spectacles. Legs were visibly instituted to be breeched, and we have breeches. Stones were formed to be quarried and to build castles; and My Lord has a very noble castle; the greatest Baron in the province should have the best house; and as pigs were made to be eaten, we eat pork all the year round; consequently, those who have asserted that all is well talk nonsense; they ought to have said that all is for the best."

Candide listened attentively and believed innocently; for he thought Mademoiselle Cunegonde extremely beautiful, although he was never bold enough to tell her so. He decided that after the happiness of being born Baron of Thunder-ten-tronckh, the second degree of happiness was to be Mademoiselle Cunegonde; the third, to see her every day; and the fourth to listen to Doctor Pangloss, the greatest philosopher of the province and therefore of the whole world.

One day when Cunegonde was walking near the castle, in a little wood which was called The Park, she observed Doctor Pangloss in the bushes, giving a lesson in experimental physics to her mother's waiting-maid, a very pretty and docile brunette. Mademoiselle Cunegonde had a great inclination for science and watched breathlessly the reiterated experiments she witnessed; she observed clearly the Doctor's sufficient reason, the effects and the causes, and returned home very much excited, pensive, filled with the desire of learning, reflecting that she might be the sufficient reason of young Candide and that he might be hers.

On her way back to the castle she met Candide and blushed; Candide also blushed. She bade him good-morning in a hesitating voice; Candide replied without knowing what he was saying. Next day, when they left the table after dinner, Cunegonde and Candide found themselves behind a

5 **▲ Critical Viewing** Which details in this engraving illustrate action from the story? **[Connect]**

6 **✓Reading Check** What service does Pangloss provide to Candide and the Baron's family?

3. **metaphysico-theologo-cosmolonigology** Voltaire satirizes philosophical studies by inventing an entirely fake school of thought.

CUSTOMIZE INSTRUCTION FOR UNIVERSAL ACCESS

For Gifted/Talented Students	For Advanced Readers
Direct students to continue the list of philosophical inquiries noted in the Advanced Readers box. Then, instruct students to create a book with a question on the left-hand page and multiple responses to the question on the right-hand page. Require that students include a response to the question from a film, a historical text, and a religious text in addition to both a literary and philosophical text. Students may also want to include a visual response to the question, such as a painting or sculpture.	Voltaire's *Candide* leaves important questions unanswered: What place has fortune in life? Why do the innocent suffer unfairly? Are people never constant enough to be reliable? Is it possible to find some escape from a fate that seems haphazard? Direct students to continue this list of inquiries. Then, instruct students to create a book with a question on the left-hand page and a response from a poet, writer, or philosopher on the right-hand page.

3 Literary Analysis

Satire

- Ask a student to read aloud the bracketed passage.
- Ask students to identify the satirical tool illustrated in the passage.
  Answer: Faulty logic is illustrated in Pangloss's "proofs."

4 Background

Art

Illustration from *Candide*, by Jean-Michel Moreau le Jeune

Jean-Michel Moreau le Jeune (1741–1814) was an illustrator, painter, and engraver. He was known as Moreau le Jeune to distinguish him from his brother who was also an artist.

The son of a wigmaker, Moreau made a name for himself as the illustrator of a costume book. The book remains today one of the finest records of the manners and tastes of the French nobility.

Although Moreau studied painting and engraving, he eventually concentrated on illustrating. He illustrated a number of literary works, including the collected works of Voltaire, from which this image is taken.

Moreau was known for his talent for capturing fine details of gesture, pose, and light.

Use the following questions for discussion:

- Which characters are portrayed in this illustration?
  Answer: This illustration portrays Candide, the Baron, Cunegonde, and the Baroness.
- What emotions does the artist portray in the characters in this illustration?
  Possible response: The illustration captures the emotions of anger from the Baron, excitement from the Baroness, and despair from Cunegonde.

5 ▶Critical Viewing

Answer: Candide and Cunegonde are behind a screen, where the Baron discovers them. The Baron kicks Candide, while Cunegonde faints.

6 

Answer: Pangloss is a tutor.

7 Vocabulary Development

Latin Suffix *-ity*

- Draw students' attention to the word *vivacity,* and read its definition. Tell students that the word combines the Latin suffix *-ity,* which means "quality or state of," with the root *-viv-* which means "life."
- Encourage students to brainstorm other words that use the suffix *-ity.* Write students' suggestions on the board.
  Possible response: *Veracity, opacity,* and *prosperity* are possible suggestions.
- Then, tell students to write a short satire of a current issue in popular culture using some of the suggested words.

8 Literary Analysis

Satire and Exaggeration

- Read aloud the bracketed passage. Have students discuss what they find humorous in the scene.
- Ask students the Literary Analysis question on p. 734: Which details in the paragraph might be exaggerations? Why?
  Possible response: The Baron's castle is referred to as an earthly paradise, but it clearly is not perfect; The noble castles are associated with Heaven, but they are built by humans; Candide calls Cundegonde the most beautiful of baronesses, but this is an opinion; The town is called Waldberghoff-trarbk-dikdorff, a ridiculously long name that is difficult to pronounce.

Monitor Progress Ask students to cite one example of each of the tools of satire they have seen in Chapter 1.
Possible response: **Exaggeration:** "The Baroness weighed about three hundred and fifty pounds" (p. 732). **Understatement:** The Great Hall was "even decorated with a piece of tapestry" (p. 732). **Faulty Logic:** "As pigs were made to be eaten, we eat pork" (p. 733).

Reteach If students continue to have difficulty with the tools of satire, help them use the Satire transparency on p. 71 of **Literary Analysis and Reading Transparencies** to clarify the strategy.

---

screen; Cunegonde dropped her handkerchief, Candide picked it up; she 7 innocently held his hand; the young man innocently kissed the young lady's hand with remarkable vivacity, tenderness and grace; their lips met, their eyes sparkled, their knees trembled, their hands wandered. Baron Thunder-ten-tronckh passed near the screen, and, observing this cause and effect, expelled Candide from the castle by kicking him in the backside frequently and hard. Cunegonde swooned; when she recovered her senses, the Baroness slapped her in the face; and all was in consternation in the noblest and most agreeable of all possible castles.

vivacity (vivas′ ə tē) *n.* liveliness or animation

CHAPTER II

What happened to Candide among the Bulgarians

Candide, expelled from the earthly paradise, wandered for a long time without knowing where he was going, turning up his eyes to Heaven, gazing back frequently at the noblest of castles which held the most beautiful of young Baronesses; he lay down to sleep supperless 8 between two furrows in the open fields: it snowed heavily in large flakes. The next morning the shivering Candide, penniless, dying of cold and exhaustion, dragged himself towards the neighboring town, which was called Waldberghoff-trarbk-dikdorff. He halted sadly at the door of an inn. Two men dressed in blue noticed him.

Literary Analysis
Satire and Exaggeration Which details in the paragraph might be exaggerations? Why?

"Comrade," said one, "there's a well-built young man of the right height." They went up to Candide and very civilly invited him to dinner.

"Gentlemen," said Candide with charming modesty, "you do me a great honor, but I have no money to pay my share."

"Ah, sir," said one of the men in blue, "persons of your figure and merit never pay anything; are you not five feet five tall?"

"Yes, gentlemen," said he, bowing, "that is my height."

"Ah, sir, come to table; we will not only pay your expenses, we will never allow a man like you to be short of money; men were only made to help each other."

"You are in the right," said Candide, "that is what Doctor Pangloss was always telling me, and I see that everything is for the best."

They begged him to accept a few crowns,[4] he took them and wished to give them an IOU, they refused to take it and all sat down to table.

"Do you not love tenderly . . ."

"Oh, yes," said he. "I love Mademoiselle Cunegonde tenderly."

"No," said one of the gentlemen." "We were asking if you do not tenderly love the King of the Bulgarians."

"Not a bit," said he, "for I have never seen him."

"What! He is the most charming of Kings, and you must drink his health."

"Oh, gladly, gentlemen."

And he drank.

4. **crowns** monetary units.

ENRICHMENT: Philosophy Connection

Gottfried Wilhelm Leibniz

Author Gottfried Wilhelm Leibniz (1646–1716) was one of the great philosophers of the Age of Rationalism. He was a brilliant mathematician (he invented infinitesimal calculus), as well as a diplomat, historian, and court librarian. His primary contribution was in the field of logic. To him, logic was a kind of mathematics. In his words, "True reasoning depends upon necessary or eternal truths, such as those of logic, numbers, [and] geometry, which establish an indubitable connection of ideas and unfailing consequences."

For Leibniz, this world is the "best" even though it has evil, because God had a "sufficient reason" to choose to create this world above all others. Other worlds would have evils even greater than this one. Therefore, God created this "best of all possible worlds."

It is this idea that Voltaire satirizes in *Candide.*

9 "That is sufficient," he was told. "You are now the support, the aid, the defender, the hero of the Bulgarians, your fortune is made and your glory assured."

They immediately put irons on his legs and took him to a regiment. He was made to turn to the right and left, to raise the ramrod[5] and return the ramrod, to take aim, to fire, to march double time, and he was given thirty strokes with a stick; the next day he drilled not quite so badly, and received only twenty strokes; the day after, he only had ten and was looked on as a prodigy by his comrades.

Candide was completely mystified and could not make out how he was a hero. One fine spring day he thought he would take a walk, going straight ahead, in the belief that to use his legs as he pleased was a

5. **ramrod** long rod used to tamp the charge of a muzzle-loading firearm.

Reading Strategy
Connecting to Historical Context In what way is bitterness toward Prussia reflected in this characterization of Prussia's military training?

prodigy (präd´ ə jē) *n.* person of very great ability

10 **✓Reading Check**
Which army does Candide join?

12 **▼ Critical Viewing**
Why might Candide consider it the best of all worlds to live in a castle such as this one? **[Speculate]**

11

CUSTOMIZE INSTRUCTION FOR UNIVERSAL ACCESS

For Special Needs Students	Less Proficient Readers
Help students research and add the Seven Years' War (1756–1763) and Frederick the Great to their timelines. If possible, show the action from Chapter 2 to the students in the film version of Leonard Bernstein's *Candide* (1991). Guide students to use a Venn diagram to compare and contrast Voltaire's treatment of the Prussians with Bernstein's. Use the Venn diagrams as the basis for a discussion about the historical context and satirical message for this part of the novel. Students might benefit from watching the action from both Chapters 1 and 2 before reading or rereading the text.	If they have not already done so, direct students to research and add the Seven Years' War (1756–1763) and Frederick the Great to their timelines. If possible show students the action from Chapter2 in the film version of Leonard Bernstein's *Candide* (1991). Ask students to use a Venn diagram to compare and contrast Voltaire's treatment of the Prussians with Bernstein's. Use the Venn diagrams as the basis for a discussion about the historical context and satirical message for this part of the novel.

9 Reading Strategy
Connecting to Historical Context

- Have students read the bracketed passage independently. Tell students that the Bulgarians that Voltaire refers to in this passage represent the Prussians. France fought against Prussia during the Seven Years' War (1756–1763).
- Ask students the Reading Strategy question on p. 735: In what way is bitterness toward Prussia reflected in this characterization of Prussia's military training?
  Answer: The Bulgarians call Candide a hero, but they put him in leg irons and force him to stay in the army against his will. Voltaire portrays the Prussians as brutal and authoritarian.

10 ✓Reading Check

Answer: Candide joins the Bulgarian army.

11 Background
Art

Neu-schwanstein Castle
Neu-schwanstein Castle in the Bavarian Alps was begun in 1869 by Bavaria's King Louis II (sometimes called "Mad Ludwig") and was meant to imitate the "old German Knightly fortresses." This magnificent building—of the sort that Candide might refer to as "the best of all possible castles"—gives the appearance of a romantic medieval castle, built in the Romanesque style of the early thirteenth century, with spires, towers, and a walled courtyard. It sits on a rock ledge overlooking the Pöllat Gorge, offering a spectacular view of the Bavarian Alps.

The castle was left unfinished upon the death of King Louis in 1886, and it has since become a popular tourist attraction. It may seem familiar to American viewers, because it served as the model for Sleeping Beauty's castle in Disneyland.

12 ▶Critical Viewing

Possible response: This castle is magical and picturesque.

Use the following question for discussion:

Which of the castles' architechtural details do you find most striking?
Possible response: the tremendous spires are quite striking.

ASSESS

13 Critical Thinking

Connect

- Read the bracketed passage aloud. Draw students' attention to the footnoted definition of the word *metaphysician*.
- Ask students to name writers whose works they have read who would fit the definition of a metaphysician.
  Possible response: Lao Tzu and Confucius both fit the definition of a metaphysician.

Answers for p. 736

Review and Assess

1. Possible response: Candide's world is not "the best of all possible worlds" because of the injustices and suffering Candide encounters.
2. **(a)** Details include the Baron who is the "most powerful lord in Westphalia" because his castle has a door and window; the Baroness, who weighs three hundred and fifty pounds and is therefore "greatly respected"; the Baron's son, who is "in every respect worthy of his father." **(b)** Possible response: Pangloss is the perfect tutor for the Baron's family because his logic supports their superiority.
3. **(a)** The men are recruiters for the Bulgarian army. **(b)** Possible response: Candide believes that they are just being nice to him when they buy him food and give him money, and he attempts to give them an IOU. **(c)** Possible response: Candide accepts without question the teachings of people who outrank him socially and educationally. His role as a simpleton emphasizes for the reader the ridiculousness of this blind acceptance of authority.
4. Possible response: Contemporary authors use essays, editorials, and novels to illustrate injustices.

privilege of the human species as well as of animals. He had not gone two leagues when four other heroes, each six feet tall, fell upon him, bound him and dragged him back to a cell. He was asked by his judges whether he would rather be thrashed thirty-six times by the whole regiment or receive a dozen lead bullets at once in his brain. Although he protested that men's wills are free and that he wanted neither one nor the other, he had to make a choice; by virtue of that gift of God which is called *liberty*, he determined to run the gauntlet[6] thirty-six times and actually did so twice. There were two thousand men in the regiment. That made four thousand strokes which laid bare the muscles and nerves from his neck to his backside. As they were about to proceed to a third turn, Candide, utterly exhausted, begged as a favor that they would be so kind as to smash his head; he obtained this favor; they bound his eyes and he was made to kneel down. At that moment the King of the Bulgarians came by and inquired the victim's crime, and as this King was possessed of a vast genius, he perceived from what he learned about Candide that he was a young metaphysician[7] very ignorant in worldly matters, and therefore pardoned him with a clemency which will be praised in all newspapers and all ages. An honest surgeon healed Candide in three weeks with the ointments recommended by Dioscorides.[8] He had already regained a little skin and could walk when the King of the Bulgarians went to war with the King of the Abares.[9]

clemency (klem′ ən sē) *n.* mercy toward an enemy or offender

6. **gauntlet** (gônt′ lit) double row of soldiers armed with clubs or weapons used to strike an individual who ran between them.
7. **metaphysician** one who studies worldly matters, such as the order and nature of the universe.
8. **Dioscorides** (dī′ əs kor′ ə dēz′) Greek physician (c. 40–c. 90) and author of *De materia medica*, the definitive text about botany and pharmacology for more than 1500 years.
9. **Bulgarians . . . Abares** (ab ar äs′) In *Candide*, the Bulgarians are Frederic the Great's Prussian army, and the Abares are the French.

Review and Assess

Thinking About the Selection

1. **Respond:** Do you think that Candide's world is "the best of all possible worlds"? Why or why not?
2. **(a) Recall:** What details concerning the Baron and his family have earned them great respect? **(b) Analyze:** In what ways is Pangloss the perfect tutor for this family?
3. **(a) Recall:** Who are the "men dressed in blue" whom Candide meets at the inn? **(b) Analyze:** In what ways does Candide reveal his innocence as he speaks with them? **(c) Evaluate:** Why do you think Candide is made to look like such a simpleton?
4. **Apply:** What kinds of writing do authors use today to address social injustices like those satirized in *Candide*?

ASSESSMENT PRACTICE: Reading Comprehension

Distinguish Between Fact and Nonfact (For more practice, see Test Preparation Workbook, p. 36.)

Standardized tests often require students to distinguish between fact and nonfact. Use the following sample test item to demonstrate.

Candide, expelled from the earthly paradise, wandered for a long time . . . gazing back frequently at the noblest of castles which held the most beautiful of young Baronesses; he lay down to sleep supperless between two furrows in the open fields: it snowed heavily in large flakes.

Which of the following is an OPINION expressed in the passage?

A Candide . . . wandered for a long time . . .
B it snowed heavily in large flakes.
C the most beautiful of young Baronesses . . .
D He lay down to sleep supperless . . .

Responses *A, B, and D* are facts expressed in the passage. Beauty is subjective. Therefore, the correct answer is ***C***.

iterary Analysis

tire

1. (a) Identify two kinds of social injustices that are **satirized** in *Candide*. (b) What types of social reform do you think the work attempts to inspire? Explain.
2. What attitude is satirized in the statement, "... Doctor Pangloss, the greatest philosopher of the province and therefore of the whole world"?
3. What satirical message about political freedom does Candide reveal by choosing to run the gauntlet rather than be shot for deserting the Bulgarian army?

onnecting Literary Elements

4. (a) Use a chart like the one shown to identify at least one example of each of the tools of satire—**exaggeration, understatement,** and **faulty logic**—used in *Candide*.

Detail From *Candide*	Tool of Satire Used

(b) What conclusions can you draw about the use of satirical tools in this work?

5. (a) Describe the ways in which humor is used as a tool of satire in this selection. (b) What risks do you think satirists take when using this tool to address serious issues? Explain.

eading Strategy

onnecting to Historical Context

6. Connect two details about the Baron's family to the **historical context** of Voltaire's era.
7. (a) What philosophy of the day does Pangloss teach? (b) What effect might this philosophy have on a society that practices it over time? Explain.
8. Why do you think the Bulgarian army is represented in a critical light?

xtend Understanding

9. **Social Studies Connection:** In what ways is a satire such as *Candide* similar to political cartoons you might find in today's newspapers and magazines?

Quick Review

Satire uses humor to ridicule or criticize a specific subject and to inspire change.

To create satire, authors use various tools, such as **exaggeration, understatement,** and **faulty logic.**

To **connect works to their historical contexts,** note ideas, assumptions, and events that are specific to the selection's era.

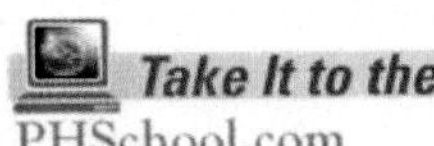

PHSchool.com

Take the interactive self-test online to check your understanding of this selection.

Answers for p. 737

Review and Assess

1. **(a)** Possible response: Two injustices are the inability of a young woman to choose to marry a man who is not a nobleman and the forced conscription of young men into the army. **(b)** The work attempts to inspire the values of equality and liberty.
2. Possible response: The attitude satirized is the belief that one's own province is the most important in the world.
3. Possible response: Candide reveals the message that a so-called free choice amounts to nothing but a choice between two evils.
4. **(a)** Possible responses: **Exaggeration:** "the greatest philosopher of the province and therefore of the whole world." **Understatement:** "One fine spring day he thought he would take a walk" **Faulty Logic:** "Legs were visibly instituted to be breeched, and we have breeches." **(b)** Voltaire makes heavy use of satirical tools to convey his messages.
5. **(a)** Possible response: Voltaire uses Dr. Pangloss's humorous "proofs" to satirize philosophers; he uses the humorous exaggeration of Candide's punishment by the army to satirize the Prussian army. **(b)** Satirists risk making the subject seem light or frivolous by using humor.
6. Possible response: The Baron is a nobleman, and his family lives in a castle. During Voltaire's time, most countries in Europe were ruled by an aristocracy, whose members frequently lived in castles.
7. **(a)** Pangloss teaches the philosophy of Leibniz, which states that this is the best of all possible worlds. **(b)** Possible response: A society that practices this philosophy may ignore the sufferings of people, reasoning that because this is the best of all possible worlds, suffering does not need to be addressed.

continued

continued from right column

8. Possible response: Voltaire presents the Bulgarian army, which represents the Prussian army, in a critical light because the Prussians were at war with France.
9. Possible response: *Candide* uses humor to address serious social and political issues and injustices, just as political cartoons do, in the hope that people will think about the issues and attempt to change the situations.

ENRICHMENT: Further Reading

Other Works by Voltaire

We strongly encourage you to review any selection before assigning or recommending it to students.

The Portable Voltaire

Candide, Zadig, and Other Stories

Voltaire: Treatise on Tolerance

Take It to the Net

Visit PHSchool.com for more information on Voltaire.

EXTEND

Answers for p. 738

❶ Vocabulary Development

Word Analysis: Latin Suffix *-ity*

1. the quality of being unknown
2. the quality of inventiveness
3. the quality acquired by length of service
4. the quality of being genuine

Spelling Strategy

1. exhibitor
2. traitor
3. chamber
4. manner

Fluency: Sentence Completion

1. vivacity
2. candor
3. clemency
4. prodigy
5. endowed

❷ Grammar and Style

Practice

1. the best of castles; the best of Baronesses
2. noses were made to wear glasses; legs were made to wear breeches
3. to take aim; to fire; and to double up
4. the support; the aid; the defender; the hero
5. Your fortune is made; your glory is assured

Writing Application

Possible response: Candide is the most innocent, the most naïve, and the most simple-minded of characters. Candide believes that the castle is the best of all castles and that Cunegonde is the best of all Baronesses. The father is a powerful lord, and the mother is a respected Baroness. Cunegonde is rosy-cheeked, fresh, and lovely.

10TH GRADE For support in teaching the Grammar and Style Lesson to tenth graders, use **Writing and Grammar,** Platinum Level, Chapter 7, Section 4.

Integrate Language Skills

❶ Vocabulary Development Lesson

Word Analysis: Latin Suffix *-ity*

The Latin suffix *-ity* means "quality or state of." For example, the word *vivacity* means "a quality or state of liveliness." Use your understanding of this suffix to define the following words:

1. anonymity
2. ingenuity
3. seniority
4. authenticity

Spelling Strategy

Although the word ending *-er* is more common, words that name a quality or a role, such as *candor* and *juror,* usually end in *-or.* Add the correct word ending to each item below. Use a dictionary to check your answers.

1. exhibit-
2. trait-
3. chamb-
4. mann-

Fluency: Sentence Completion

Review the words from the vocabulary list on page 731. Then, complete each sentence below with the correct word from the vocabulary list.

1. The volunteers' enthusiasm and ______ make difficult work more enjoyable for everyone.
2. She spoke with _____ about her hurt feelings.
3. The judge granted _____ to the remorseful offender.
4. The piano, flute, and violin were a few of the instruments mastered by the child _____.
5. Little money remained in the trust fund _____ by her parents.

❷ Grammar and Style Lesson

Parallel Structure

Parallel structure, or parallelism, is the repetition of equal ideas in a similar grammatical form. Parallelism can involve the repeated use of words, phrases, clauses, or sentences.

> *Their* lips met, *their* eyes sparkled, *their* knees trembled. . . .
>
> Candide *listened attentively* and *believed innocently*. . . .

Practice Identify the parallel structures in the following sentences.

1. The Baron's castle was the best of castles and his wife, the best of Baronesses.
2. According to Dr. Pangloss, noses were made to wear glasses and legs were made to wear breeches.
3. While he was in the army, he learned to take aim, to fire, and to double up.
4. You are now the support, the aid, the defender, the hero of Bulgarians.
5. Your fortune is made and your glory is assured.

Writing Application Write four sentences describing your impression of Candide and Cunegonde, using parallel structures in each one. Then, identify the parallelism in your sentences.

Prentice Hall Writing and Grammar Connection: Diamond Level, Chapter 20, Section 6

TEACHING RESOURCES

The following resources can be used to enrich or extend the instruction for pp. 738–739.

Vocabulary

- **Selection Support:** Build Vocabulary, p. 141
- **Vocabulary and Spelling Practice Book** (Use this booklet for skills instruction.)

Grammar

- **Selection Support:** Grammar and Style, p. 142
- **Writing and Grammar,** Diamond Level, p. 505
- **Daily Language Practice Transparencies**

Writing

- **Performance Assess. and Portfolio Mgmt.,** p. 14
- **Writing and Grammar,** Diamond Level, p. 78
- **Writing and Grammar iText CD-ROM**
- **Writing Models and Graphic Organizers on Transparencies,** pp. 75–77

BLOCK SCHEDULING: Resources marked with this symbol provide varied instruction during 90-minute blocks.

❸ Writing Lesson

Short Satirical Story

Satirists write about something they would like to change in the world. Choose a foolish behavior, a social injustice, or an institution you believe worthy of reform, and write a **short satirical story** that encourages people to bring about change.

Prewriting Use a chart like the one shown to organize your story. Start by identifying a subject. Then, list specific details that you want to satirize. Finally, state the suggested reform you hope your satire will inspire.

Writing Model: Organizing Details

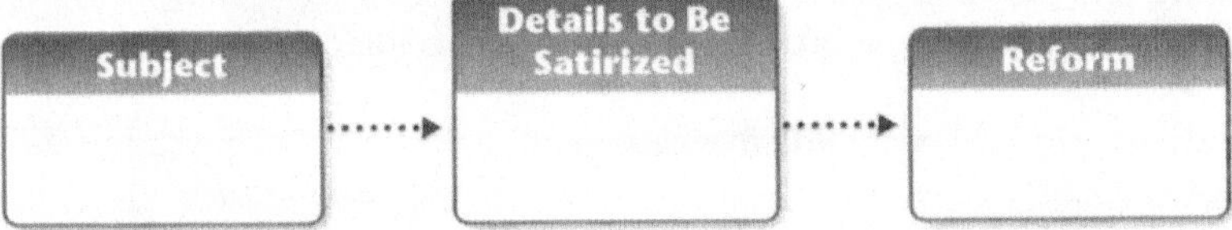

Drafting As you draft your satire, use a variety of tools, such as exaggeration, faulty logic, and understatement. Remember that to be effective, the satire should be humorous.

Revising Check your finished draft against your prewriting chart, noting any details you may have omitted. Be sure that your story ends in a way that supports the purpose of your satire. Add more details or alter the ending if necessary.

WG Prentice Hall Writing and Grammar Connection: Diamond Level, Chapter 5, Section 2

❹ Extension Activities

Listening and Speaking Listen to selections from a musical version of *Candide*. Then, participate in a **group discussion** to determine the ways in which the music reflects Voltaire's written work. Be sure to address these questions:

- Does the music add to or detract from the story?
- Do the lyrics accurately represent the characters and events?

Compare your group's reactions to other groups' opinions. **[Group Activity]**

Research and Technology Find three political cartoons that use satire to make a point. You might check the editorial pages of major newspapers or some online magazines that cover politics and world events. Use the cartoons to create a **visual report** that explains what satire is and what is satirized in the cartoons.

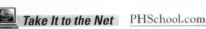

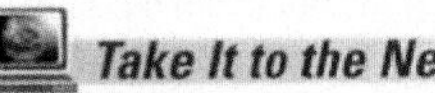

PHSchool.com

Go online for an additional research activity using the Internet.

❸ Writing Lesson

- Suggest that students meet in small groups to brainstorm topics for their satires. Ask group members to continue to work together to help one another develop humorous details.
- Encourage students to use the Herringbone Organizer, pp. 75–77, in **Writing Models and Graphic Organizers on Transparencies,** to help them develop their stories. Students can treat the center line as a plot line and use the extended lines to make notes about details, characters, and satirical tools.
- Use the Narration: Short Story rubric in **Performance Assessment and Portfolio Management,** p. 14, to evaluate students' stories.

10TH GRADE For support in working through the Writing Lesson with tenth graders, use **Writing and Grammar,** Platinum Level, Chapter 5, Section 2.

❹ Research and Technology

- Tell students that most major newspapers can be found online. Students may find not only current issues but archives as well.
- Suggest that students write a caption for each cartoon, explaining what is being satirized and what satirical tool is being used.
- Suggest that students share their reports with the class.

CUSTOMIZE INSTRUCTION For Universal Access

To address different learning styles, use the following activities suggested in the **Extension Activities** booklet, p. 36:

- For Bodily/Kinesthetic Learners, use Activity 5.
- For Verbal/Linguistic Learners, use Activities 6 and 7.

ASSESSMENT RESOURCES

The following resources can be used to assess students' knowledge and skills.

Selection Assessment

- **Formal Assessment,** pp. 126–128
- **Open-Book Tests,** pp. 106–108
- **Test Bank Software**

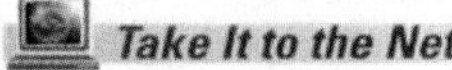

Visit PHSchool.com for self-tests on the selection.

Writing Rubric

- **Performance Assess. and Portfolio Mgmt.,** p. 14

For additional diagnostics and remediation for skills covered in this grouping, use materials from the Prentice Hall Assessment System.

Lesson Objectives

1. To evaluate support in feature articles
2. To learn the difference between news articles and feature articles
3. To identify opinions in a feature article

About Feature Articles

- Have students read "About Feature Articles" on p. 740. Then, ask them to name types of feature articles that they have read in newspapers.
Possible responses: Movie reviews, restaurant reviews, interviews with sports figures, and profiles of interesting people are types of feature articles.
- If possible, bring several newspapers to class and have students look through them for feature articles. Then, lead a discussion about how these feature articles differ from news articles.
- Ask why it is important to know the difference between a news article and a feature article.
Possible response: Knowing the difference between the two is important because feature articles are not objective; they contain a mix of facts and opinions.

Reading Strategy

Evaluating Support

- Have students read the information about the Reading Strategy.
- Explain that students evaluate support for opinions in everyday life, such as when they hear advertisements, political speeches, and their friends' and families' views.
- Ask students why it is important to evaluate support for an opinion in a feature article.
Answer: By evaluating the support for an opinion, the reader can tell whether the support is reliable and sufficient.
- Point out the chart at the bottom of p. 740. Have students copy the chart and list as they read the article each opinion, its support, and their evaluation of the support.
- Explain to students that feature articles are often written in a relaxed, informal style that is more conversational than the language used in news articles.

READING INFORMATIONAL MATERIALS

Feature Articles

About Feature Articles

Most people turn to newspapers for current information about recent events. Daily papers include news articles on local and world events, but they also include a variety of other types of information. For example, **feature articles** showcase various topics of interest and are written to inform and entertain the public. Unlike news articles that present information formally and objectively, features can be written in a more informal style. In addition, feature articles often include the opinion of the writer.

Because they are meant to entertain, feature articles usually present the lighter side of life, and they address topics that are less time-sensitive than those found in straightforward news articles. Here are some common topics for feature writers:

- The Arts
- Fashion
- Health
- Entertainment
- Unusual occurrences
- Family
- Leisure
- People

"Leonardo: The Eye, The Hand, The Mind" is a feature on an exhibit of the works of Leonardo da Vinci, one of the great masters of art in Renaissance Italy.

Reading Strategy

Evaluating Support

In addition to the information they showcase, feature articles often present a writer's opinion or evaluation of a topic. These opinions must be supported with evidence such as facts, statistics, observations, and examples. To determine whether you agree with the writer's opinions, **evaluate the support,** deciding whether or not the evidence is persuasive and valid. Use a chart like the one shown to list each opinion in the following feature. For each one, identify the details that support that opinion. Then, evaluate the support to decide whether the writer's opinion is valid.

Opinion	Support	Evaluation of Support
Cotter says Leonardo's strengths lie in art, science, engineering, and aesthetic theory.	Cotter lists Leonardo's accomplishments in hydrodynamics, anatomy, physics, astronomy, invention, and art.	The list of accomplishments supports Cotter's opinion that Leonardo's strengths lie in many areas.

The New York Times January 24, 2003

Leonardo: The Eye, the Hand, the Mind

By Holland Cotter

In the opening sentence, the writer expresses an opinion, an element that is often found in a feature article.

LEONARDO DA VINCI (1452–1519) is the Great Oz of European art. At least that's the way he sometimes seems, glimpsed through the fogs and fumes of history: a cultural force more than a man, a colossal brain and a sovereign hand at the controls of a multidisciplinary universe.

This paragraph introduces an opinion about Leonardo da Vinci's accomplishments and supports it with examples.

Where did his supreme gift lie? In art? Science? Engineering? Aesthetic theory? All of the above. We all have our strengths; I have mastered MetroCard dispensers and a home computer. Yet Leonardo understood, described and illustrated the principles of hydrodynamics, gross anatomy, physics and astronomy. He invented the helicopter, the armored tank and the submarine. He painted like an angel and despite being phobic about deadlines, wrote often and well. In addition, according to Vasari, he was drop-dead gorgeous.

And, perhaps most confounding, he generated all this near-magical accomplishment from behind a curtain of personal discretion so dense and insulating that no historian or psychologist—and dozens, maybe hundreds, have tried—has been able to pull it aside to reveal the person behind the personage.

"Leonardo da Vinci, Master Draftsman" at the Metropolitan Museum of Art also tries, and manages to part the curtain just a crack. We may not learn exactly what made this artist tick, but we can see him ticking away, at length and in some depth.

Naturally, the show had blockbuster written all over it from the word go. With 118 Leonardo drawings, it is the largest gathering of his work in America. The lending institutions are a superstarry lot: the Uffizi, the Louvre,

Leonardo: The Eye, the Hand, the Mind

- Tell students that this feature article about Leonardo da Vinci is the type of article that might appear as an arts feature in a newspaper.
- Ask students to share their background knowledge about Leonardo da Vinci. Point out that he is known not only as an artist but also as a scientist and an inventor.
- Have students read "Leonardo: The Eye, the Hand, the Mind" and the notes that identify the elements of this article.
- Direct students' attention to the first paragraph. Have them summarize the author's opinion about Leonardo da Vinci.
  Possible response: The author sees Leonardo da Vinci as an intellectual and artistic giant who could do almost anything.
- Call students' attention to the second paragraph. Ask: What support does Cotter provide to show that Leonardo da Vinci is not like most normal people?
  Answer: Cotter is proud to have mastered MetroCard dispensers and a home computer; Leonardo da Vinci, on the other hand, invented the helicopter, the armored tank, and the submarine; explained and illustrated complicated scientific topics; and painted and wrote prolifically and beautifully.

CUSTOMIZE INSTRUCTION FOR UNIVERSAL ACCESS

For Less Proficient Readers	For English Learners	For Advanced Readers
As students read, have them independently fill out the first two columns of the chart on p. 740. In addition, tell them to record the page on which they found the information. After students have finished reading the article, have them work in pairs to evaluate the support for each opinion that they identified.	You may wish to show students pictures of some of Leonardo da Vinci's creations to give students an idea of his genius. If possible, obtain copies of the drawings specifically mentioned in the article. Then, as students read, have them compare the author's descriptions of Leonardo's work with the images.	To demonstrate the difference between a feature article and a news article, have students read an encyclopedia article on Leonardo da Vinci. Tell students to list the similarities and differences between the two articles and then report their findings to the class.

Leonardo: The Eye, the Hand, the Mind

- Point out the first full paragraph on this page. Ask students to identify which phrases in the paragraph make the article both informative and entertaining.
Possible response: Informal language—"a few are just weird, so weird you find yourself wondering: what planet was this guy from?" —is followed by descriptive information about drawing.
- If students have trouble identifying informal language, point out the second call-out note on p. 742. Read aloud the examples such as "hit parade" and "they've created something like." Then, ask students how this informal language affects the article.
Possible response: The informal language makes the article interesting and easy to read.
- Draw students' attention to the evaluation of Leonardo's work pattern. Ask: How does the author lead up to this evaluation?
Answer: The author provides information on Leonardo's training, background, and first important job.

the Vatican, the Royal Library at Windsor Castle. And the Met has given it the imperial treatment: crimson walls, acres of space, a catalog as thick as *The Physician's Desk Reference*.

The language the writer uses makes this article both informative and entertaining.

Are the drawings worth the fuss? In a word, totally. Individually, many are glorious; some are workmanlike; a few are just weird, so weird you find yourself wondering: what planet was this guy from? As a package, though, as the datastream output of a single sensibility, they're huge. They are also very alive. People always say that you can't know painting from a book, that you have to experience it. This is at least as true of drawing, a profoundly physical medium, where a smudge or erasure can be a heart-catching event, and a pen stroke can leap like a solar flare.

The informal language in this paragraph is characteristic of feature articles.

The show comes with some fresh scholarship, not blindingly revealing, but solid and worthwhile. The curators Carmen C. Bambach and George R. Goldner, both of the Met's department of drawings and prints, have avoided a hit parade approach in their selection, opting instead for some less familiar material. They've also brought related drawings—10 studies for the Florentine mural "The Battle of Anghiari" alone—together, in some cases for the first time. Finally, by arranging the work chronologically, they've created something like an organic picture of the history of one man's polymathic life.

Leonardo was born in 1452 and started life with certain disadvantages. He was a small-town kid, . . . indifferently educated and—a liability for an artist, you would think—left-handed. But he also had luck. His supportive father took him to Florence, by then a major node on the information highway of Renaissance Europe. There he was apprenticed to Andrea del Verrocchio, a leading sculptor but also a painter (five gorgeous drawings of his open the show) from whom Leonardo learned much.

For one thing, he learned to draw sculpturally. This meant drawing with a command of volume, as several early drapery studies demonstrate. It also meant executing fleet, notational sketches to capture the look of real things viewed from many angles in actual space, as seen in Leonardo's serial depictions of squirming babies and wide-awake cats. From Verrocchio he also learned to carry a notebook with him at all times and to use it, so that whatever went in through the eye came out through his hand.

In 1481, he landed a substantial job, an altarpiece painting of "The Adoration of the Magi." And at that point, he seemed to have settled on a work pattern that, for better or worse, he would follow thereafter. Basically, it entailed conceiving pictorial designs so complex and technically demanding that he would never complete them.

Here the writer offers an evaluation of da Vinci's work pattern.

For "The Adoration," for example, he planned to place more than 60 figures in an elaborate perspectival setting. He drew and drew; several well-known studies, one of them madly

Leonardo: The Eye, the Hand, the Mind

- Read aloud the call-out note on p. 743. Then, have students read independently the bracketed passage and the following paragraph.
- Have students discuss the support the writer provides to justify the opinion on p. 742 that Leonardo conceived "pictorial designs so complex and technically demanding that he would never complete them."
  Answer: Details concerning the equestrian monument and the unfinished painting *St. Jerome in the Wilderness* serve as support.

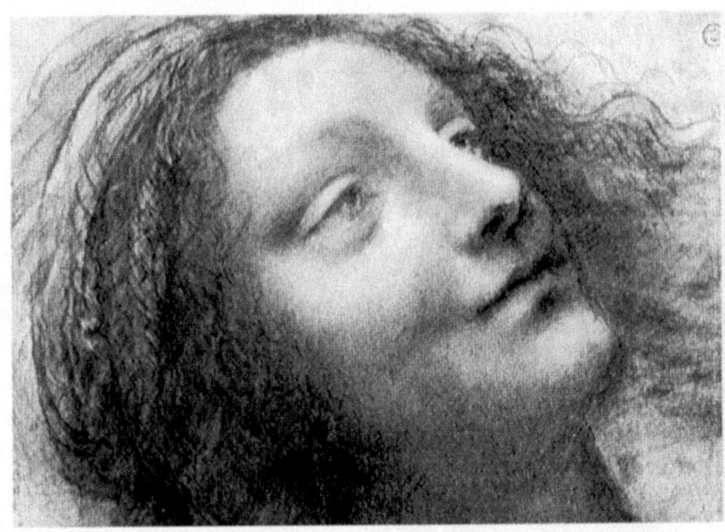

complicated, are in the show. But the ideas never really gelled, and he eventually headed to Milan in search of different work, leaving an unfinished painting behind.

In this paragraph, the writer provides support for his evaluation of da Vinci's work pattern.

He stayed in Milan, employed by the city's ruler, Ludovico Sforza, for 15 years, which were among the most productive of his life. His first commission—he proposed it himself—was an outsize equestrian monument to Ludovico's father. Again, he produced studies galore, dashed off and spirited, fastidious and polished. But the monument never materialized, and the plans were abandoned.

In any case, Leonardo was, as usual, working on several other things. One was the unfinished painting, now owned by the Vatican, titled "St. Jerome in the Wilderness." It's at the Met and gives a stark, almost agonizing sense of how he carried his obsessive, draftsmanlike self-correction right into what should have been the final stages of a painting.

And there was "The Last Supper," painted from 1493 to 1498 in the refectory of Santa Maria della Grazie. One renowned sheet from Windsor carries what could be a preliminary sketch of that painting's composition, mixed in with geometric and architectural designs. And from the Albertina in Vienna comes a powerfully resolved drawing on blue paper of an old man who is sometimes identified as St. Peter. Whatever his identity, he is animated by the tense, urgent gravitas of the painting itself.

When French troops invaded Milan in 1499, Leonardo made his way back to Florence. There he whipped up a large-scale drawing titled "Virgin and Child With Saint Anne" and gave himself a one-man show. The drawing—now lost, though later versions on the same theme exist—was rapturously received

CUSTOMIZE INSTRUCTION FOR UNIVERSAL ACCESS

For Special Needs Students	For Gifted/Talented Students
Students may have difficulty sorting out the order of events in Leonardo da Vinci's life discussed in the article. As they read, have students create timelines to help track the main events of Leonardo's life and his major works. Then, have students work in pairs to compare their timelines.	Encourage students to create collages to represent Leonardo da Vinci's impact on art or science. Have students begin by researching Leonardo's achievements; as they learn more, students may wish to narrow their focus (his major achievements, for example, or his contributions to future generations). Ask volunteers to discuss the elements of their collages and explain to the class what those elements represent.

Leonardo: The Eye, the Hand, the Mind

- Allow students to review the writer's evaluation of Leonardo da Vinci's work pattern on p. 742.
- Then, have a student read aloud the first full paragraph on p. 744. Ask students whether the writer has provided enough support for this evaluation.
  Possible response: Yes; the writer has supported his evaluation. Drawing conclusions from established facts is adequate support for the opinion.
- Have students reread the last paragraph of the article. Draw their attention to the informal wording in this paragraph. Ask: How does this language add to the article?
  Possible response: Informal language such as "for me" and the last sentence of the paragraph makes the article more personal and appealing.

and resulted in a commission from the city government for the Battle of Anghiari mural, to be painted in the Palazzo della Signoria. Its subject was a Florentine military victory.

Details in this paragraph continue to support the writer's evaluation of da Vinci's work pattern.

The assignment was a very big, very public deal; Michelangelo, the local reigning prince of art, was to paint the opposite wall. Once more, Leonardo feverishly poured out ideas on paper, and the studies in the show are fantastic, from an explosive drawing of a horse in motion (several legs, many heads) to a hyperrealistic depiction of a screaming soldier. As for the mural, Leonardo designed a cartoon and expensive scaffolding, then left town, heading back to Milan.

Once there, he did what he had always done: many things simultaneously. He painted; he taught; he studied anatomy and geometry. He designed maps, architectural plans and stage sets. He conducted scientific experiments and recorded his findings in notebooks, writing from right to left and in mirror image, which, as a lefty, he had always done.

And he sketched. Small drawings of grotesque human heads flowed from his hand like telephone pad doodles. His famous "Deluge" pictures date to this time. Imaginary scenes of tidal waves overwhelming minute towns, they are both aquatic studies and apocalyptic visions. In 1516, the French king Francis I, who collected trophy artists as well as art, invited him to live at his court. Leonardo, old at 64, moved to France and died there three years later.

He left behind a godlike reputation, worshipful disciples, a scant handful of paintings—about 15 survive—and the 4,000 works on paper that are his primary visual legacy. Some of his drawings are art historical icons; the face of Mary in a study for the painting of "The Virgin and Child With St. Anne," now in the Louvre, is one. He invented this expressive type, with its interior smile and apparitional draftsmanship, and with it a Western ideal of human perfection.

My favorite drawings, though, are of a different kind. They're ones where everything is happening, nonlinearly, all at once, and anything goes: double-sided sheets filled with animals, armaments, allegorical scenes, geometrical diagrams, exploding buildings, . . . dissected muscles, wheels and bridges, flowing water, reminder notes, sums, scratches, spots and stains.

In these, for me, the curtain parts that little bit, to reveal an artist who always preferred to dream and draw rather than to do, who remained at some level a venturesome child controlling his world by taking it apart, piece by piece, to see how the whole thing worked. By thinking big, Leonardo became big; illusions sometimes work that way. And the neat thing is that in his company, we get to think big, too.

The language of this conclusion reflects the informal style of a feature article.

Check Your Comprehension

1. According to Cotter, what are Leonardo da Vinci's supreme gifts?
2. What three things did Leonardo invent?

Applying the Reading Strategy

Evaluating Support

3. (a) What support does Cotter give to prove that da Vinci did not always finish a commission? (b) Is the support convincing? Explain.
4. (a) What is Cotter's overall message in this article? (b) Evaluate two examples of details that support the overall message.
5. Does Cotter offer enough support to persuade you to accept his perspective on Leonardo da Vinci? Explain.

Activity

Conducting a Survey on Newspaper Reading

With a group, design and conduct a survey to find out how people get their news. Use a format like the one shown here. Tally the answers and share them with the class.

Model Questionnaire

Name: ____________

Choose the category that describes you and answer the question that follows.

☐ Student: What grade are you in? ________
☐ Adult: What is your occupation? ________

1. How often do you read a newspaper? Check one:

☐ Less than once a week ☐ 1 or 2 times a week
☐ 3–5 times a week ☐ Every day

2. When you read a newspaper, which sections do you regularly read? Check all that apply:

☐ Front page ☐ Local news ☐ National news
☐ Sports ☐ Business ☐ Editorials/Opinion
☐ Classified section ☐ Lifestyle ☐ Entertainment
☐ Other, please indicate ____________

Contrasting Informational Materials

News Articles and Feature Articles

Review a current newspaper to identify both a news report and a feature article. Compare the two, using questions like these to focus your analysis:

- What bias, or writer's opinions, do you detect in each article? Explain.
- Which one contains more facts? Explain.
- From the lead, or opening, paragraph, are you able to identify the most important idea of each article? Explain.
- What details does each provide to support its claims?
- Which article might become outdated first? Why?

Share your findings with the class.

Answers for p. 745

Check Your Comprehension

1. Leonardo da Vinci's supreme gifts are an extraordinary intellect and an ability to comprehend and master several disciplines.
2. Leonardo da Vinci invented the helicopter, the armored tank, and the submarine.

Applying the Reading Strategy

3. **(a)** Support includes the altarpiece painting *The Adoration of the Magi,* which Leonardo drew extensively but never finished painting; the unfinished equestrian monument in Milan; the unfinished painting *St. Jerome in the Wilderness*; and the unfinished Battle of Anghiari mural. **(b)** Yes; the support is convincing because it provides a pattern of grand plans and unfinished works.
4. **(a)** Cotter's overall message is that Leonardo was a brilliant yet intensely private genius who people can begin to know and appreciate through the Metropolitan Museum of Art exhibit. **(b)** Possible response: The author provides details about Leonardo da Vinci's inventions and contributions to art and science. The author talks about the drawings to be exhibited, stating that a person can learn much from a drawing.
5. Yes; Cotter does offer enough support to persuade readers to accept his perspective on Leonardo da Vinci. He describes and analyzes multiple works by Leonardo as well as provides information about the artist and the times.

Activity

Encourage students to expand on the Model Questionnaire on p. 745. Then, have them decide whom their surveys will target and how each group will administer the survey. Point out that a long survey will discourage people from responding. Have students create the surveys on a word-processing program, and then distribute them and compile the answers. Ask students to draw conclusions from the information they gather.

continued

continued from right column

Contrasting Informational Materials

Students may find it helpful to create two-column charts to answer the questions. Students' comparisons should show an understanding of the content and purpose of both news and feature articles.

Lesson Objectives

1. To write an essay analyzing literary periods
2. To synthesize analyses of different literary themes to discuss the influence of humanism on Renaissance and Rationalist works
3. To use writing strategies to generate ideas, plan, organize, evaluate, and revise writing

Prewriting

- Have students work independently to review the Unit Opener. Then, ask them to define the terms *humanism, Renaissance,* and *Rationalism.*
- After students have identified the authors and selections about which they will write, encourage them to review the selections to renew their familiarity with them. Then, have students answer the bulleted questions on p. 746.
- Explain the use of the model chart on p. 746, and guide students as they begin their own charts for the selections they have chosen.
- Have students use the details they have gathered to draft their working theses. Point out that when drafting their thesis statements, students should focus on one or two characteristics of humanism—its return to classical texts, for example, or its emphasis on education and human perfectibility.

Writing About Literature

Analyze Literary Periods

The literature of the Renaissance and the Age of Rationalism was influenced by the cultural movement known as humanism. During the Renaissance, humanists celebrated the rediscovered ideals of classical antiquity. Scholars studied the classics in their original languages: Greek, Latin, and Hebrew. The humanist belief in the value of an active life of involvement with the world overtook the medieval ideal of a contemplative life devoted to God. Humanity's achievements and faculties—knowledge, love, and reason—took center stage. The arts and sciences took on new life, while traditional religious authority was questioned.

To explore the influences of humanism on the selections in this unit, complete the assignment described in the box at right.

Assignment: Humanism in the Literature of the Renaissance and the Age of Rationalism

Write an analytical essay that traces the influence of humanism on the writings of the Renaissance authors—Petrarch, Boccaccio, Ronsard, and Cervantes—or the Rationalist authors—La Fontaine and Voltaire—whose works are excerpted in this unit.

Criteria:

- Include a thesis statement that defines humanism and explains its influence on the works you discuss.
- Support your thesis with detailed analyses of the works.
- Cite examples from each work you explore.
- Approximate length: 1,500 words

Prewriting

Find a focus. Begin by reviewing the discussion of humanism and rationalism in the Unit Introduction on pages 662–671. Then, review the literature in this unit and relate it to humanism. Fill out a chart similar to the one shown below, using these questions as a guide:

- What is the theme of the selection?
- How do the characters and plot reveal the theme?
- How does the theme relate to humanism?

Model: Charting Humanism in Renaissance and Rationalist Literature

Selection	Characteristic of Humanism	Example/Quote
"The White Doe"	speaker's ideals are expressed in a vision of his human beloved, not in a religious vision	"A pure-white doe in an emerald glade/Appeared to me . . ."

Gather evidence. After you have filled in the chart, review the chart carefully. Choose those examples you have listed that most strongly express characteristics of humanism. Then, look for other examples illustrating the same characteristics.

Write a working thesis. After you have decided which characteristics of humanism will be the focus of your paper, write a working thesis. Introduce the characteristics you will discuss, and explain why they were central to the selections.

Read to Write

As you reread the texts, keep in mind that the writer may be reacting *against* the values of humanism. Look for both positive and negative influences of humanism in the selections.

TEACHING RESOURCES

The following resources can be used to enrich or extend the instruction for pp. 746–747.

Writing and Grammar, Diamond Level, Chapter 14, pp. 306–324

Performance Assess. and Portfolio Mgmt., p. 16

Writing Models and Graphic Organizers on Transparencies, pp. 71–73

Writing and Grammar iText CD-ROM

Students can use the following tools as they complete their analysis of literary periods:

- Topic Web
- Transition Word Bin
- Unity and Coherence Revising Tool

Drafting

Clarify your thesis statement. As you write your first draft, make sure that your thesis statement explains clearly the characteristics of humanism that you are discussing in your paper.

Model: Focusing a Thesis Statement

Literature of the Renaissance and the Age of Rationalism ~~was influenced by humanism, so it was different from medieval literature, which was written before this point of view was popular.~~ *reflected a major shift from the medieval ideal of the contemplative life to the humanist notion of taking action in the world.*

Choose examples for maximum effect. Illustrate the characteristics of humanism that you discuss with specific quotations from the selections. For each example, ask yourself whether it clearly supports the point you are making. Use only examples that give strong support.

Write to Learn
If you have difficulty writing a thesis statement, you may need to do some additional research on the values and characteristics of humanism. The more you know about this cultural movement, the easier it will be to write your thesis statement.

Revising and Editing

Review content: Check connections. Underline each example you use, and draw an arrow to the general point it illustrates. For any example that does not clearly support a general point, either replace it with a stronger example or add a sentence clarifying the connection.

Review style: Combine sentences and use transition words. Review your draft for choppy passages made up of short sentences. Revise these passages by combining sentences and adding transitions.

Original: Petrarch's "Spring" shows the influence of humanism. Humanism looks for inspiration in classical antiquity. This poem includes several references to Greek and Roman mythology. It mentions Zephyr, Procne, Philomel, Jove, and Venus.

Revised: Petrarch's "Spring" shows the influence of humanism, which looks for inspiration in classical antiquity. Petrarch emphasizes this inspiration with references to characters of Greek and Roman myths: Zephyr, Procne, Philomel, Jove, and Venus.

Write to Explain
To make every example and quotation in your paper count, directly connect these details to the point you are trying to make about humanism. Don't expect your readers to infer connections that you don't explain clearly.

Publishing and Presenting

Present an informal summary. List the main points of your paper, and explain each in an informal talk to your classmates. Encourage the audience to ask questions.

WG *Writing and Grammar Connection: Diamond Level, Chapter 14*

Drafting

- Tell students to underline the characteristics of humanism identified in their thesis statements. If students have difficulty completing this step, the thesis statements should be clarified. In the model, the humanist characteristic is the "notion of taking action in the world."
- Remind students that a list of examples does not constitute an argument. Within each paragraph, examples should be connected to one another with transition words, phrases, sentences, and explanations.
- Remind students that each example in an essay should work to advance the thesis statement.

Revising and Editing

- If students find it difficult to find examples that support the general point they are making, suggest that they revise their thesis statements.
- As they combine sentences, encourage students to experiment with punctuation marks such as semicolons, colons, and dashes.

Publishing and Presenting

- In their talks, have students focus on a single characteristic of humanism and several strong, clear examples.
- Have students who wrote about Renaissance authors give their talks first, followed by those who wrote about Rationalist authors.

CUSTOMIZE INSTRUCTION FOR UNIVERSAL ACCESS

For Less Proficient Writers	For English Learners	For Advanced Writers
Work with students to identify characteristics of humanism, and list these on the board. Then, have each student select a single characteristic about which to write. Help students identify selections that reflect the chosen characteristics, and then instruct them to locate other selections on their own.	Before students begin prewriting, write the word *humanism* on the board. Circle the root *human,* and ask students to discuss what this word means. Point out that humanism is a way of thinking that emphasizes the accomplishments and abilities of human beings.	Have students trace the evolution of one humanist idea over the course of the Renaissance and the Age of Rationalism. (To achieve balance, students may want to discuss two selections from each period.) Does the idea strengthen or weaken over time? What historical events may have influenced each writer's thinking?

Lesson Objectives

1. To write a comparison-and-contrast essay
2. To use writing strategies to generate ideas, plan, organize, evaluate, and revise writing

Model from Literature

In *Don Quixote*, Miguel de Cervantes compares the qualities of the comic hero Don Quixote to those of an ideal knight.

Prewriting

- Have students suggest general areas of interest, and list these on the board. Students can then brainstorm independently within one of these areas.
- Within a given area, encourage students to choose two or more items that have a strong commonality. For example, if comparing and contrasting movies, students should choose films of the same genre—not, for example, an adventure film and a romantic comedy.
- Explain that a *rationale* is a reason. Ask students to identify some reasons for writing a comparison-and-contrast essay.
  Possible response: Reasons for writing a comparison-and-contrast essay might be to examine similarities and differences or to evaluate the quality of similar items.
- Emphasize the importance of researching and gathering details. The more details students gather now, the easier their drafting process will be.
- Before students begin their drafts, have them review the Rubric for Self-Assessment, p. 751, so that they know what is expected of their essays.

Writing WORKSHOP

Exposition: Comparison-and-Contrast Essay

A **comparison-and-contrast essay** is an expository piece that describes similarities and differences between two or more items. In this workshop, you will plan, draft, and revise a comparison-and-contrast essay about a topic of your choice.

Assignment Criteria Your comparison-and-contrast essay should feature the following elements:

- A purpose for comparing and contrasting two or more items
- A thesis statement
- Evidence to support the thesis, consisting of descriptions of similarities and differences among the items
- A logical organizational plan suited to the topic
- Focused paragraphs that employ effective transitions

To preview the criteria on which your comparison-and-contrast essay may be assessed, refer to the Rubric on page 751.

Prewriting

Choose a topic. One way to choose a topic for a comparison-and-contrast essay is to make a **list**. First, choose a general subject area of interest, such as music, sports, presidents, or novels. Next, brainstorm for issues within this broad area that intrigue you. Choose a topic for your essay from your list.

Evaluate the topic. To decide whether your subjects have sufficient points of comparison for an effective comparison-and-contrast essay, use a Venn diagram similar to the one shown. If your diagram suggests too few connections, consider choosing a richer topic.

Write a thesis statement. Write a thesis statement that identifies your topic and sets out a clear rationale for your essay. Include this statement in the introductory paragraph of your essay.

Gather details. Make notes about similarities and differences between your subjects. Conduct any research necessary to provide a detailed comparison.

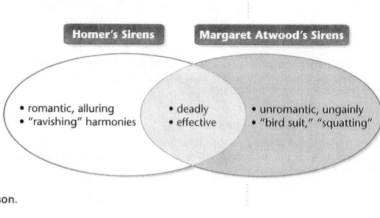

Homer's Sirens
Margaret Atwood's Sirens
• romantic, alluring
• "ravishing" harmonies
• deadly
• effective
• unromantic, ungainly
• "bird suit," "squatting"

TEACHING RESOURCES

The following resources can be used to enrich or extend the instruction for pp. 748–751.

 **Writing and Grammar,** Diamond Level, Chapter 14, pp. 306–324

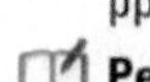 **Performance Assess. and Portfolio Mgmt.,** p. 15

 **Writing Models and Graphic Organizers on Transparencies,** pp. 95–97

 **Writing and Grammar iText CD-ROM**

Students can use the following tools as they complete their comparison-and-contrast essays:

- Topic Bank
- Venn Diagram
- Transition Words

Student Model

Before you begin drafting, read this student model and review the characteristics of a successful comparison-and-contrast essay.

Anna Lvovsky
Rockville, MD

Sirens: His and Hers

Femininity in classical myth has been treated differently by men and women. Men tend to romanticize mythic females, while women tend to reject such fictionalization. These divergent viewpoints are exemplified by Homer's and Margaret Atwood's portrayals of the legendary Sirens. Homer's *Odyssey* relays an idealized vision of alluring, powerful females, whereas Atwood's "Siren Song" bluntly depicts the Sirens as miserable victims of their own condition.

> In her introduction, Anna identifies the subjects she will compare.

The *Odyssey* is narrated from a masculine perspective and presents a romantic but superficial impression of the Sirens. The speaker remarks on the "ravishing" quality of their harmonies, suggesting their power to overcome. His reference to "honeyed" voices evokes sweetness and appeal. The creatures' very song is stirring; the speaker refers to the music as "thrilling." As a man, the speaker of the poem responds in the expected fashion to these stimuli: He is seduced. His reaction completes an image of the Sirens as powerful, enthralling creatures, capable of manipulating all men. Homer's creatures compel a reader's awed respect.

> Anna uses a subject-by-subject organization and begins by discussing Homer.

Immune to the Sirens' feminine allure, Atwood takes a tersely unromantic approach. By adopting the perspective of a Siren, she portrays the creatures, not as deadly beauties, but as helpless victims. Atwood's narrator presents herself as trapped in a "bird suit" and "squatting" on an island, depictions that strip away dignity and beauty. "Beached skulls" convey the destructiveness and barrenness of her occupation. Whereas Homer's narrator finds the song exciting, she herself dismisses it as "boring."

> The essay offers equivalent depth and detail in discussing the second subject.

Exciting or boring, the song's lethal efficiency does provide one point of agreement between Homer and Atwood: The song induces men to leap to their deaths and, as Atwood writes, "it works every time." Ultimately, though, Atwood conjures an image diametrically opposed to Homer's idealized suggestion of alluring women. Her Sirens are dejected creatures who merit not our awe or respect but our pity.

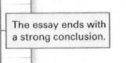

> Anna acknowledges a similarity between her subjects; then, she sharpens the contrast between them.

It is unsurprising that men of traditional literature judge women entirely by external attributes. Homer's *Odyssey* epitomizes this tendency, representing the Sirens as powerful, desirable creatures on the basis of a brief impression. It is up to Margaret Atwood in "Siren Song" to rebut such a shallow interpretation and portray the true vulnerability of these idealized figures.

> The essay ends with a strong conclusion.

CUSTOMIZE INSTRUCTION FOR UNIVERSAL ACCESS

For Less Proficient Writers	For English Learners	For Advanced Writers
As students develop their thesis statements, have them use the following sentence patterns: Both item A and item B ________. However, item A ________, whereas item B ________. Students can use these sentences as a drafting guide and revise them for clarity and interest later.	Encourage students to choose concrete objects rather than abstract ideas to compare and contrast. Before students begin writing, tell them to use a Venn diagram to brainstorm describing words that apply to each object.	Point out that the writer of the model essay takes a particular critical approach to her subjects—a *feminist* approach. Have students identify some other critical vantage points, such as socioeconomic, historical, and cultural views. Encourage students to adopt one of these approaches in their own writing.

Student Model

- Explain that the Student Model is a sample and that students' own essays may be longer.
- Ask a volunteer to read aloud the first paragraph. Ask another student to identify the two subjects that will be compared and contrasted in the essay.
  Answer: The two subjects to be compared and contrasted are Homer's portrayal of the Sirens and Atwood's portrayal of the Sirens.
- After students read the second paragraph silently, point out that it addresses *only* Homer's representation of the Sirens.
- Read aloud the third paragraph. Then, ask how it is similar to and different from the second paragraph.
  Possible response: Each paragraph focuses mainly on a single writer. However, the third paragraph, which addresses Atwood's viewpoint, briefly refers to the discussion of Homer in the preceding paragraph.
- Have students finish reading the essay. Then, ask them at what point in the essay the writer identifies a similarity between the two subjects.
  Answer: The fourth paragraph shows a similarity between the two subjects.
- Point out that the differences between two subjects are usually more interesting than the similarities, and so may warrant more attention.
- Have students offer personal responses to the essay's conclusion. Explain that strong, even debatable, language piques the reader's interest and creates a lasting impression.

Real-World Connection

Comparison-and-contrast essays in the workplace: Business professionals are often required to perform comparative analyses on competitors' products or services. Such analyses can help a company develop new products or services or improve the quality of existing ones.

Drafting

- To help students distinguish between the two types of organization, write the following values on the board: Subject A = Pizza World pizza; Subject B = Pizza Time pizza; Point 1 = crust; Point 2 = sauce; Point 3 = toppings. Have students plug these values into the model outlines on this page. Then, have students write two more outlines, this time using subjects and points of their choice. Finally, have them decide which outline better suits their needs.
- Challenge students to use each kind of evidence (examples, facts, and quotations) at least once.

Revising

- Explain that topic sentences within an essay are like road signs for the reader: They tell what is being left behind and what is coming up. Have students underline—or, if missing, supply—a topic sentence for each paragraph in the essay. Then, have them verify that each topic sentence clearly identifies the subject or point being discussed.
- Point out that evidence should be balanced not only in quantity but in kind. To make sure that they have provided similar kinds of support for each major point, have students label each highlighted piece of evidence *E* (example), *F* (fact), or *Q* (quotation), and then check for overall balance.

(continued on page 751)

Drafting

Organize your essay. Comparison-and-contrast essays are generally organized in one of two ways: subject by subject or point by point. In subject-by-subject organization, you first discuss all the features of one item and then discuss all the features of the second, the third, and so on. Using point-by-point organization, in contrast, you begin by discussing the same point about all of the items and then move on to the second, third, and subsequent points. The outlines to the right illustrate these two kinds of organization.

Organizational Plans

Point by Point
Point 1
- Subject A
- Subject B

Point 2
- Subject A
- Subject B

Point 3
- Subject A
- Subject B

Subject by Subject
Subject A
- Point 1
- Point 2
- Point 3

Subject B
- Point 1
- Point 2
- Point 3

Elaborate. Provide evidence to support all of the important points you make in your essay. Supporting evidence may take any or all of the following forms:

- **Examples:** Use examples that illustrate the similarities and differences between the items.
- **Facts:** Whenever possible, use detailed, factual evidence that will help readers gain a clear understanding of each item.
- **Quotations:** Quotations from experts on your topic lend authority to your arguments.

Revising

Revise for clarity. Because the essay compares two or more items, clear organization is essential. The reader must know which item is under discussion in each part of the essay, so be sure to revise the essay to achieve this clarity. Reorder details, grouping related points, or add transitions as needed.

Revise for balance. As you reread your draft, highlight your supporting evidence, using a different color for each item you compare and contrast. Determine whether you have included approximately the same amount of detail about every item. If not, add or delete examples, facts, quotations, and other supporting details.

Model: Revising to Balance Comparisons

The speaker remarks on the "ravishing" quality of their harmonies, suggesting their power to overcome. His reference to "honeyed" voices evokes sweetness and appeal. *The creatures' very song is stirring; the speaker refers to the music as "thrilling."*

Anna matches Atwood's reference to the Sirens' "boring song" with a contrasting reference in Homer.

USING TECHNOLOGY IN WRITING

Have students put their drafts into a word processing software program. As they revise, encourage them to use the program's Font Color function to check for balanced evidence. (See the second bullet under Revising above.) Have students apply different colors to different pieces of evidence. Next, using the Find function, students can search for and count pieces of evidence they have formatted in different colors. As an alternative, students can insert a letter code (such as [EV-SUBJ 1]) after each piece of evidence, and then use the Find function to count the number of times the code appears.

Students can also use the organizing tools and revision checkers on the **Writing and Grammar iText CD-ROM.**

Revise for effective transitions. Review your draft to make sure that you have used effective transitions between sentences and paragraphs. Use words and phrases that signal and clarify transitions, such as *by contrast* and *on the other hand.*

No transition: The theme of the first story emphasizes acceptance of one's lot in life. The theme of the second focuses on struggling against one's fate.

Transition: The theme of the first story emphasizes acceptance of one's lot in life. **By contrast,** the theme of the second focuses on struggling against one's fate.

Compare the model and the nonmodel.

Nonmodel	Model
. . . the song induces men to leap to their deaths and, as Atwood writes, "it works every time." Atwood conjures an image diametrically opposed to Homer's idealized suggestion of alluring women.	. . . the song induces men to leap to their deaths and, as Atwood writes, "it works every time." Ultimately, though, Atwood conjures an image diametrically opposed to Homer's idealized suggestion of alluring women.

Publishing and Presenting

Choose one of the following ways to share your writing.

Give an oral presentation. Outline your essay and present the main points orally to the class. Use charts, diagrams, or other visual aids to help clarify your message.

Publish your essay electronically. Post your essay on a Web site or upload it onto a classroom computer.

WG *Writing and Grammar Connection: Diamond Level, Chapter 14*

Rubric for Self-Assessment

Evaluate your comparison-and-contrast essay using the following criteria and rating scale:

Criteria	Rating Scale Not very				Very
Does the essay include a thesis statement in the introductory paragraph?	1	2	3	4	5
Is the thesis supported by adequate evidence?	1	2	3	4	5
Do all the items have the same amount of support?	1	2	3	4	5
Is the organization logical and consistent?	1	2	3	4	5
Does the essay use transitions effectively?	1	2	3	4	5

Revising (continued)

- On the board, write the following sentences: *Pizza Time's pizza sauce is rich and robust. Pizza World's toppings are the freshest in town.*
- Ask students to establish a relationship between the two sentences by using as many different transition words or phrases as they can. Write their responses on the board.
  Possible responses: Pizza Time's pizza sauce is rich and robust, *but* Pizza World's . . . ; *Although* Pizza Time's . . . , Pizza World's . . . ; Pizza Time's pizza sauce . . . *By contrast,* Pizza World's . . . ; Pizza Time's pizza sauce . . . *On the other hand,* Pizza World's . . . .

Publishing and Presenting

- Suggest that students model their charts and diagrams after the outlines that appear on p. 750.
- If groups of students have written on similar topics, have them post their essays on the same Web site. Encourage them to compose an introduction welcoming visitors to the site, giving an overview of its content, and introducing its authors.

Assessment

- Before students begin revising, review the assessment criteria in class. Encourage students to use these criteria as a revision guide.
- To make sure students understand the rubric, have them use it to score the Student Model on p. 749. After students do this independently, discuss the scoring process as a class. Have students justify their scores by citing particular passages from the model.
- An alternative rubric can be found on p. 15 of **Performance Assessment and Portfolio Management.**

TEST-TAKING TIP

Explain to students that comparison-and-contrast writing prompts often appear on standardized tests. Point out that it is tempting to read the prompt and begin writing immediately. Remind students, though, that about one-quarter of the total time allotted (or, if open-ended, about 15 minutes) should be used to plan and organize the essay. In most comparison-and-contrast prompts, the objects or ideas to be compared will be provided. Therefore, students can use their planning time for these purposes:

- to decide their position in regard to each object or idea (1–2 minutes)
- to decide on the type of organization they will use—point-by-point or subject-by-subject (1–2 minutes)
- to brainstorm possible details and pieces of evidence, and then select the strongest and most relevant (5 minutes)
- to write a rough outline (5 minutes)

Lesson Objectives

1. To develop and deliver a literary interpretation
2. To choose an interesting, thought-provoking topic
3. To gather sufficient supporting details from the work itself and from other sources
4. To use speaking techniques to deliver an effective presentation

Plan Your Content

- Ask students to tell about some "Wow!" moments they have had while reading specific passages of stories, novels, or poems. Encourage them to pinpoint what inspired their awe: Was it the innovative way in which the writer used language? Was it an empathetic connection with a character, a place, or a situation? Then, use a favorite piece of literature to model a "Wow!" moment of your own.
- Next, have each student consider how the passage that he or she identified relates to the work as a whole: Does it capture a character's essence? Does it express a central theme? Does it exemplify the writer's style? Then, ask each student to draft a thesis statement stating why the selected passage is important.
- Finally, have each student look for other passages in the work—or in other sources—that support his or her thesis statement. Remind students to use only the most interesting or relevant evidence in their drafts.

Prepare Your Presentation

- During a first practice session with partners or groups, have students devise hand signals to use while listening; for example, a lowered hand might mean *slow down.* Speakers can then adjust their volume and pace according to their classmates' signals.
- During a second practice session, have partners or group members fill out Feedback Forms for speakers to use as they make final revisions to their presentations.

Listening and Speaking WORKSHOP

Presenting a Literary Interpretation

In a **literary interpretation,** a speaker analyzes an element of a work of literature such as theme, characterization, language, or plot, persuading an audience to accept his or her views. Use the strategies on this page to develop and deliver an effective literary interpretation.

Plan Your Content

Analyze literature that intrigues you and about which you have strong feelings or ideas. An interpretation that shows a work in a dramatically new light is sure to pique your audience's interest.

Choose a topic. Ask yourself: What have I read recently that made my mind race? Which selections raised the most questions in my mind? Which ones generated the liveliest discussions? Choose your topic from among those works that come to mind.

Formulate a thesis statement. Your presentation should focus on a strong thesis, or a central point. Start by reviewing the features—or the questions—that led you to select the work. Formulate your main point about the work in a clear sentence, and build your talk around this thesis statement.

Gather ammunition. As with all persuasive presentations, rely on supporting details to make your case. For most literary presentations, you will rely on the work under discussion, though you may want to cite other works or biographical information about the author. Select quotes and specific references. Be accurate!

Feedback Form for Literary Interpretation

Rating System
+ = Excellent ✓ = Average – = Weak

Content
Organization ________
Appeal to reason ________
Appeal to emotion ________
Addresses counterarguments ________

Evaluate the quality of the supporting evidence:
____

Delivery
Volume ________
Pacing ________
Eye contact ________
Body language ________

Suggestions for improvement: ________
____

Prepare Your Presentation

Use these speaking techniques to make sure your presentation is a success.

- **Control volume and pace.** Your most important responsibility for any oral presentation is to speak clearly and slowly enough so that everyone can hear you and understand what you say. Vary your volume and pace to emphasize key points.
- **Practice your presentation.** You can't practice too often! Experiment with tone of voice, pacing, gestures, and eye contact. Memorize your talk, or use notes for the main points and improvise.

Activity: Presentation and Feedback Select one or more works of literature to interpret that most of your audience has read, and prepare a three-minute presentation. Practice with a partner or in a small group, videotaping the practice sessions if possible. Have your partners fill out a Feedback Form like the one above to use as a basis for discussing your content and delivery.

CUSTOMIZE INSTRUCTION FOR UNIVERSAL ACCESS

For Less Proficient Readers	For English Learners
Have students practice their presentations, using sticky notes to identify any difficult or confusing passages. Students can then revisit these passages and rephrase lines they find long-winded or unclear.	Encourage students who are intimidated by speaking in front of a group of peers to read their presentations several times before delivering them. Tell them that by practicing repeatedly in front of friends, family members, and even a mirror, and repeating any words that give them difficulty, students will build confidence.

Critical Reasoning

In the reading sections of many tests, you may be required to use critical reasoning skills. Use the following strategies to help you answer questions testing these skills:

- Identify a writer's implicit assumptions: Ask yourself what else must be true for the writer's claims to be true.
- Read actively, making inferences based on the passage and testing those inferences against your own knowledge.

Test-Taking Strategies

- Read the test questions before you read the passage.
- After you have read the passage, jot down a sentence summarizing the main idea.

Sample Test Item

Directions: Read "The White Doe" by Petrarch, below, and then answer the question.

A pure-white doe in an emerald glade
Appeared to me, with two antlers of gold,
Between two streams, under a laurel's
  shade,
At sunrise, in the season's bitter cold.

Her sight was so suavely merciless
That I left work to follow her at leisure,
Like the miser who looking for his treasure
Sweetens with that delight his bitterness.

Around her lovely neck "Do not touch me"
Was written with topaz and diamond
  stone,
"My Caesar's will has been to make me free."

Already toward noon had climbed the sun,
My weary eyes were not sated to see,
When I fell in the stream and she was gone.

1. The poet assumes that the reader will
   - **A** recognize the poem as an allegory.
   - **B** have seen all the things the speaker mentions.
   - **C** know about the behavior of deer.
   - **D** all of the above

Answer and Explanation

The correct answer is *A*. Answers ***B, C,*** and ***D*** are incorrect because the reader will be able to understand the poem even without direct experience of what it describes.

Practice

Directions: Read "Spring" by Petrarch, below, and then answer the question.

Zephyr returns, and scatters everywhere
  New flowers and grass, and company
    does bring,
  Procne and Philomel, in sweet despair,
  And all the tender colors of the Spring.
Never were fields so glad, nor skies so fair;
  And Jove exults in Venus' prospering.
  Love is in all the water, earth, and air,
  And love possesses every living thing.
But to me only heavy sighs return
  For her who carried in her little hand
  My heart's key to her heavenly sojourn.
The birds sing loud above the flowering
    land;
  Ladies are gracious now.—Where
    deserts burn
  The beasts still prowl on the ungreening
    sand.

1. Which adjective best describes the speaker's feelings about spring?
   - **A** delighted
   - **B** indifferent
   - **C** curious
   - **D** bitter

2. The "ungreening sand" refers to
   - **A** spring.
   - **B** summer.
   - **C** the speaker's unrequited love.
   - **D** the speaker's beloved.

Lesson Objective

To use critical reasoning skills when answering standardized test questions

Applying Reading Strategies

Explain that when students think critically, they identify what the writer is trying to say and make educated guesses about the writer's motives, feelings, or beliefs.

Test-Taking Skills

- Have students read and reread the Sample Test Item passage until its meaning is clear. Then, ask them to paraphrase the passage.
  Possible response: The speaker sees a white doe with a "Do Not Touch" sign around her neck. Enchanted, the speaker follows her for an entire morning. But when the speaker falls in a stream and re-emerges, the doe has disappeared.
- Have students read the Answer and Explanation for the Sample Test Item. Guide them to recognize that A is the correct answer because it identifies the writer's desire to create a powerful allegory.
- Have students read and respond to the Practice items.

Answer

1. The correct answer is D. After describing nature's joyous response to spring in lines 1–8, the speaker reveals in line 9 his own despair. These feelings of rejection and frustration are elaborated in lines 13–14. Answers *A, B,* and *C* are incorrect because a person who breathes "heavy sighs" and who likens his own emotional landscape to burning deserts could not be said to feel delighted, indifferent, or curious. Guide students to see that the clues provided in lines 9 and 13–14 cannot be used to support the inferences offered by answers *A, B,* or *C*.
2. The correct answer is C. Spring is described in the lines 1–8, so the answer is not *A*. Summer is not mentioned in the poem, so *B* is not the correct answer. The speaker discusses unrequited

continued

continued from right column

love in lines 10–15. The final image of beasts prowling on ungreening sand is a metaphor for the speaker's love for the beloved rather than a reference to the beloved herself, so *C* is the best answer.

TEACHING RESOURCES

The following resources can be used to enrich or extend the instruction for p. 753.

For additional diagnostics and remediation for skills covered in this grouping, use materials from the Prentice Hall Assessment System.

Unit Objectives

1. To read selections from the periods of Romanticism and Realism (1800–1890)
2. To apply a variety of reading strategies, particularly those appropriate for reading fiction
3. To analyze literary elements
4. To use a variety of strategies to read unfamiliar words and build vocabulary
5. To learn elements of grammar, usage, and style
6. To use recursive writing processes to write in a variety of forms
7. To develop listening and speaking skills
8. To express and support responses to various types of texts
9. To prepare, organize, and present literary interpretations

Meeting the Objectives

With each selection, you will find instructional materials through which students can meet these objectives. Further, you will find additional practice pages for reading strategies, literary analysis, vocabulary, and grammar in the **Selection Support: Skills Development Workbook** in your **Teaching Resources.**

Background

Art

Terrace at Sainte-Adresse, by Claude Monet

As a young man, Monet (1840–1926), along with other French painters, formed the movement known as Impressionism. These painters focused on capturing the transient colors of nature as they appeared at any given moment and as affected by weather, distance, and surrounding objects.

Use the following question for discussion:
What impression does the painting convey of the scene it depicts?
Possible response: The impression is one of a stylish terrace in a busy seaside town. The flowers suggest the lush abundance and fertility of spring or summer.

Terrace at Sainte-Adresse, Claude Monet, The Metropolitan Museum of Art

UNIT FEATURES

Connections	Reading Informational Materials
Every unit contains a feature that connects literature to a related topic, such as art, science, or history. In this unit, students will read **Christopher Marlowe: from *Dr. Faustus*** on p. 788. Use the information and questions on the Connections page to help students enrich their understanding of the selections presented in the unit.	These selections will help students learn to analyze and evaluate informational texts, such as workplace documents, technical directions, and consumer materials. They will expose students to the organization and features unique to nonnarrative texts. In this unit, the focus is on Critical Reviews. ***CurtainUp* Review: A Doll's House** in on p. 950.

(1800–1890)

"Would you realize what Revolution is, call it Progress; and would you realize what Progress is, call it Tomorrow."

— Victor Hugo

ASSESSMENT RESOURCES

The following resources can be used to assess students' knowledge and skills.

Selection Assessment

- **Selection Support:** Skills Development Workbook
- **Formal Assessment**
- **Open-Book Tests**
- **Performance Assessment and Portfolio Management**
- **Extension Activities**

Assessing Student Progress

Listed below are the tools that are available to measure the degree to which students meet the unit objectives.

Informal Assessment

The questions in the Review and Assess sections are a first level of response to the concepts and skills presented within the selections. Students' responses are a brief, informal measure of their grasp of the material. These responses can indicate where further instruction and practice are needed. Then follow up with the practice pages in the **Selection Support: Skills Development Workbook.**

Formal Assessment

The **Formal Assessment** booklet contains Selection Tests and Unit Tests.

- Selection Tests measure comprehension and skills acquisition for each selection or group of selections.
- Each Unit Test provides students with thirty multiple-choice questions and five essay questions designed to assess students' knowledge of the literature and skills taught in the unit.

The **Open-Book Tests** ask students to demonstrate their ability to synthesize and communicate information from selections or groups of selections.

To assess students' writing, you will find rubrics and scoring models in the **Performance Assessment and Portfolio Management** booklet. In this booklet you will also find scoring rubrics for listening and speaking activities.

Alternative Assessment

The **Extension Activities** booklet contains writing activities, listening and speaking activities, and research and technology activities that are appropriate for students with different ability levels. You may also use these activities as an alternative measurement of students' growth.

Using the Timeline

The Timeline can serve a number of instructional purposes, as follows:

Getting an Overview

Use the Timeline to help students get a quick overview of themes and events of the period. This approach will benefit all students but may be especially helpful for Visual/Spatial Learners, English Learners, and Less Proficient Readers. (For strategies in using the Timeline as an overview, see the bottom of this page.)

Thinking Critically

Questions are provided on the facing page. Use these questions to have students review the events, discuss their significance, and examine the "so what" behind the "what happened."

Connecting to Selections

Have students refer to the Timeline when they begin to read individual selections. By consulting the Timeline regularly, they will gain a better sense of the period's chronology. In addition, they will appreciate world events that gave rise to these works of literature.

Projects

Students can use the Timeline as a launching pad for projects like these:

- **Focused Timeline** Have students research the events leading up to an item on the Timeline and create a smaller, more focused timeline on which to record them. For example, students can use a biography of Johann Wolfgang von Goethe on p. 766, as well as other sources, to show the events leading to the publication of Part I of *Faust* in 1808.
- **Additional Illustrations** Have students search for additional illustrations for items in the Timeline. They can find such illustrations in biographies of the figures mentioned in the Timeline, encyclopedias, books on world history, and books on the history of technology. Students should be prepared to justify each new illustration they suggest.

Timeline 1800–1890

1800 | 1820 | 1840

European Events

- **1800** Wordsworth and Coleridge publish *Lyrical Ballads*, 2nd edition.
- **1804** Napoleon declares himself emperor. ◄
- **1804** Beethoven completes Symphony No. 3, the first Romantic symphony.
- **1808** Goethe publishes Part I of *Faust*.
- **1812** Napoleon invades Russia.
- **1825** In Russia, the forces of the czar crush an uprising by army officers.
- **1829** In England, George Stephenson creates a better steam locomotive.
- **1827** Heinrich Heine publishes *The Book of Songs*.
- **1831** Victor Hugo publishes his novel *Notre-Dame de Paris*. ▼

- **1848** Insurrections break out across Europe; the Second French Republic is declared.
- **1849** Gustave Courbet paints *The Stone Breakers*, a Realist work. ▼

- **1852** Second French Republic ends; the Second Empire begins.
- **1856** In England, Robert Bessemer develops process for mass-producing steel.
- **1857** Flaubert publishes *Madame Bovary*, a masterpiece of Realist fiction.

World Events

- **1803 (United States)** The Louisiana Purchase doubles the size of the country. ▼

- **1808 (Sierra Leone)** Britain acquires Sierra Leone as a colony; goes on to acquire Gambia (1816) and Gold Coast (1821).
- **1818 (India)** British control most of India.
- **1820–1821 (Egypt)** Muhammad Ali, ruler of Egypt, begins creating an African empire.
- **1825 (United States)** Erie Canal opens.
- **1825 (United States)** An organized baseball club exists in upstate New York.
- **1828 (Japan)** Poet Kobayashi Issa dies.
- **1842 (China)** China loses to Western powers in the Opium War.

- **1842 (United States)** Dr. Crawford Long begins using ether as an anesthetic.
- **1853–1854 (Japan)** Commander Matthew Perry forces Japan to trade with the West. ◄

ENRICHMENT: Getting an Overview of the Period

Introduction	Key Events
To give students an overview of the period, have them indicate the span of dates in the title of the Timeline. Next, point out that the Timeline is divided into European Events (on the top) and World Events (on the bottom). Have students scan the Timeline, looking at both the European Events and the World Events. Finally, point out that the events in the Timeline often represent beginnings, turning points, and endings (for example, Napoleon declared himself emperor in 1804).	Have students identify key events related to political and industrial change. **Possible response:** In the United States, the Civil War begins (1861); in England, Robert Bessemer develops process for mass-producing steel (1856). What events indicate the growing dominance of Europe and the United States? **Possible response:** The Louisiana Purchase doubles the size of the United States (1803); British control most of India (1818).

European and World Events

1860 — 1880 — 1900

- **1861** In Russia, the serfs are freed.
- **1861** A united Italy is established.
- **1864** Fyodor Dostoyevsky publishes *Notes from the Underground*.
- **1867** Karl Marx publishes the first volume of *Das Kapital*, a criticism of capitalism.
- **1869** Leo Tolstoy completes his novel *War and Peace*.
- **1870** The Franco-Prussian War begins.
- **1871** The Franco-Prussian War ends with France's defeat; the Third French Republic is established.
- **1871** The German empire begins.
- **1873** Arthur Rimbaud stops writing poetry, at the age of 19.
- **1880s** Swedish chemist Alfred Nobel builds dynamite factories.
- **1881** In Russia, Czar Alexander II is assassinated.
- **1885** Émile Zola publishes the novel *Germinal*, which depicts life in a mining town. ◄
- **1896** Alfred Nobel's will endows the Nobel Prizes.

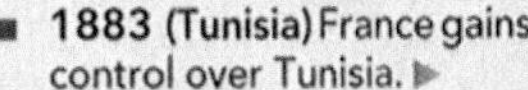

- **1861 (United States)** The American Civil War begins.
- **1864 (China)** A destructive civil war ends.
- **1865 (United States)** The Civil War ends; President Lincoln is assassinated.
- **1869 (Egypt)** Suez Canal opens.
- **1876 (United States)** Alexander Graham Bell invents the telephone. ◄

- **1883 (Tunisia)** France gains control over Tunisia. ►
- **c. 1884 (United States)** Hiram Stevens Maxim uses smokeless powder in a new type of machine gun.
- **1886 (United States)** John Pemberton invents Coca-Cola.
- **1890 (United States)** In the West, fenced pasture has largely replaced range land.
- **1898 (Palestine)** Theodor Herzl visits Palestine to look into setting up a Jewish state.

Analyzing the Timeline

1. **(a)** Which two entries in European events mention Napoleon? **(b)** What do these entries reveal about Napoleon's attitudes? **[Infer]**
   Answer: **(a)** In 1804, Napoleon declares himself emperor; in 1812, Napoleon invades Russia. **(b)** He believed that he had a right to assert his rule over France and Russia.
2. **(a)** According to the Timeline, What happened in France in 1848 and 1871? **(b)** What do these events suggest about the political climate in France during this time? **[Connect]**
   Answer: **(a)** In 1848, the Second French Republic is declared; in 1871, the Franco-Prussian War ends with France's defeat, and the Third French Republic is established. **(b)** These events suggest that the political climate in France was turbulent.
3. **(a)** What events occurred in Russia and in the United States in 1861? **(b)** What do these events suggest about changing world attitudes toward the individual? **[Generalize]**
   Answer: **(a)** In Russia, the serfs are freed, and in the United States, the Civil War begins. **(b)** These events suggest awareness of the importance of individual freedom.
4. **(a)** How are the facts about the United States in 1825 and Egypt in 1869 related? **(b)** What do these facts indicate about trade and transportation? **[Synthesize]**
   Answer: **(a)** In these years, both countries opened canals. **(b)** These facts indicate a growing worldwide interest in trade and transportation.
5. **(a)** Which events in the 1880s relate to the development of weapons? **(b)** How did these events change the face of war? **[Deduce]**
   Answer: **(a)** In the 1880s, Alfred Nobel built dynamite factories, and c. 1884, Hiram Stevens Maxim used smokeless powder in a new type of machine gun. **(b)** Dynamite and machine guns increased the efficiency of weapons.

continued

continued from right column

►Critical Viewing

1. What does the portrait of Napoleon (1804) suggest about the emperor's character? Explain. **[Analyze]**
   Possible response: Napoleon appears confident and proud in the portrait.
2. What attitude about exploration does the sign for the Lewis and Clark Trail (1803) suggest? **[Infer]**
   Possible response: The United States is ready to be explored by ambitious people.
3. What mood does the picture of Alexander Graham Bell with the first telephone (1876) convey? **[Analyze]**
   Possible response: The crowd conveys a mood of excitement, expectation, and an awareness of the significance of the invention.

Literature of the Period

- In the excerpt from *The Expiation* by Victor Hugo, p. 806, students will read about a low point in Napoleon's career, when his army suffered a devastating defeat in Russia.
- For a view of life in Paris during the Franco-Prussian War, students can read the story "Two Friends" by Guy de Maupassant, p. 828.
- To get a greater understanding of Realism in literature, students can read Leo Tolstoy's story "How Much Land Does a Man Need?" on p. 835.
- For a taste of realistic prose drama, students can read Henrik Ibsen's *A Doll House*, p. 864.

→← *POINT/COUNTERPOINT*

Emphasize to students that the rights we take for granted in the United States were not always so well accepted. In the aristocratic societies of England and France in the late eighteenth century, the idea that people could self-govern was widely debated.

1. What right does Burke deny people?
   Answer: Burke denies the right to share in the power and authority of the state.
2. How does Paine's view differ from Burke's?
   Answer: Paine says that no group in any country is entitled to control the state to the "end of time."
3. Identify and explain ways in which the United States today reflects the ideas of both Burke and Paine.
   Possible response: People in the United States today have the right to inherit property, and all children are entitled to an education, as Burke argues. In keeping with Paine's ideas, the United States has no formal aristocracy with the power to rule the country politically.

Romanticism and Realism

(1800–1890)

Historical Background

Throughout Europe, the nineteenth century was marked by political and industrial revolutions, progress, and hope for the future. Yet it was also an era characterized by unfulfilled expectations and by the emergence of new problems.

The Seeds of Revolution Inspired by the ideas of political and social philosophers such as John Locke (1632–1704) and Jean-Jacques Rousseau (zhän zhäk′ rōō sō′) (1712–1778), the American colonists revolted against British rule and declared their independence in 1776. The success of the American Revolution helped stir up political unrest throughout Europe, especially in France. There, revolutionary activities that had begun in 1787 reached their first high point in 1789 when a Paris mob attacked and destroyed the prison known as the Bastille. In the years that followed, the monarchy was abolished, and France was declared a republic. On January 21, 1793, the leaders of the newly established French republican government

Point/Counterpoint

Do people have a right to revolt against their rulers?
Stirred by the French Revolution (1787–1799), two important thinkers of the time expressed opposing views on this question.

No! Men have a right . . . to justice. . . . They have a right to the fruits of their industry; . . . They have a right to the acquisitions of their parents; to the nourishment and improvement of their offspring; to instruction in life, and to consolation in death. . . . [A]nd as to the share of power, authority, and direction which each individual ought to have in the management of the state, that I must deny to be amongst the direct original rights of man in civil society. . . .

—from ***Reflections on the Revolution in France*** by Edmund Burke

Yes! There never did, there never will, and there never can exist a parliament, or any description of men, or any generation of men, in any country, possessed of the right or the power of binding and controlling posterity to the "end of time," or of commanding for ever how the world shall be governed, or who shall govern it; and therefore, all such clauses, . . . are . . . null and void. . . . Man has no property in man. . . .

—from ***Rights of Man: Being an Answer to Mr. Burke's Attack on the French Revolution*** by Thomas Paine

ENRICHMENT: History Connection

Europe at War

In 1814, the allied armies of Britain, Austria, Russia, and Prussia captured Paris. Forced to abdicate the throne, Napoleon went into exile on the island of Elba, off the coast of Italy. He returned to Paris a year later and again proclaimed himself emperor, but his second reign was short-lived.

One hundred days after his reemergence, he was easily defeated at Waterloo by the allied forces commanded by the Duke of Wellington. Napoleon was forced back into exile on the island of St. Helena, where he died in 1821.

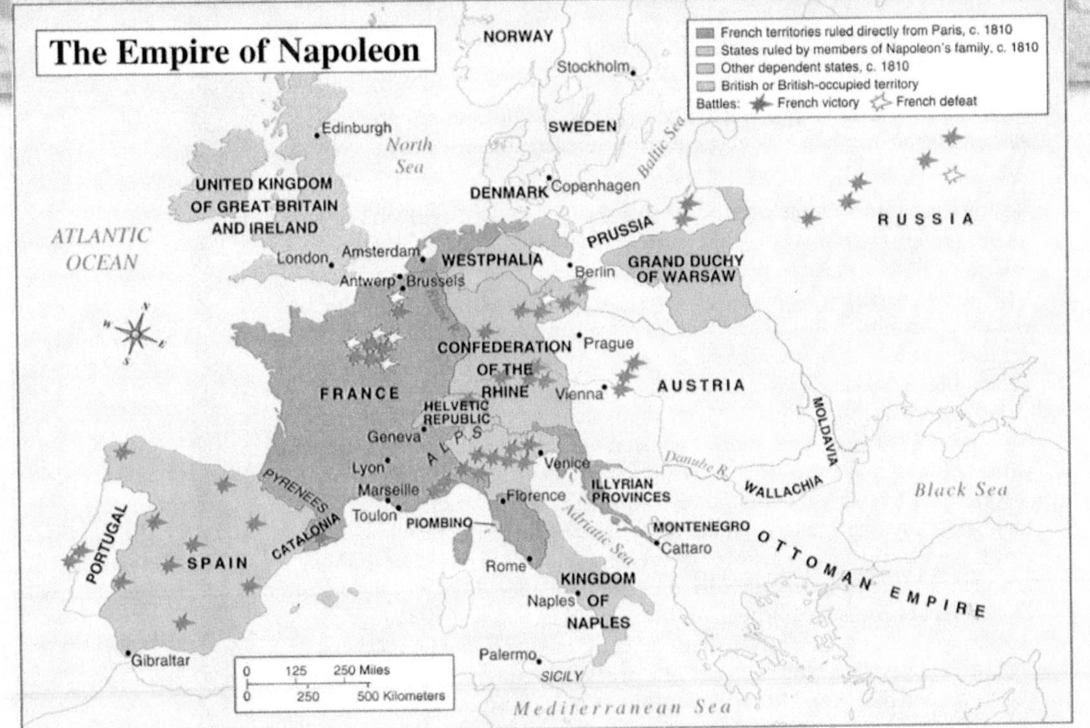

executed the king. Then, from September 5, 1793, to July 27, 1794, there was a period in France known as the Reign of Terror, during which the revolutionary government executed 17,000 people.

Napoleon In 1799, a successful and popular young general, Napoleon Bonaparte (nə pō′ lē ən bō′ nə pärt′), assumed political power in France. Five years later, he made himself emperor. Although in many respects Napoleon ruled as a military dictator, he did accomplish many domestic reforms. In addition, he aroused a strong sense of nationalism among the French people.

Europe at War Between 1792 and 1815, France was almost constantly at war with other nations. At first, France defended itself against monarchies that were frightened by the Revolution and hoped to destroy it. Later, as Napoleon came to power, France embarked on a series of military conquests in which it seized control of nearly all of Europe as far east as the Russian border (see map above).

In 1812, however, Napoleon overextended himself by invading Russia. There, his army suffered a disastrous defeat. Napoleon's final defeat came in 1815 at the Battle of Waterloo, when his forces were overpowered by an allied army led by Great Britain.

Although Napoleon dominated Europe for only a brief period, his conquests had lasting effects. His armies spread many of the achievements of the French Revolution throughout Europe.

▲ **Critical Viewing** In 1810, which countries or territories were part of the French empire, dependent on it, or ruled by members of Napoleon's family? Explain. **[Read a Map]**

▶ Critical Viewing

The countries or territories that were part of the French empire, dependent on it, or ruled by members of Napoleon's family in 1810 were as Spain, Catalonia, France, Piombino, the Kingdom of Naples, the Helvetic Republic, the Confederation of the Rhine, Westphalia, the Illyrian Provinces, and the Grand Duchy of Warsaw.

Background

Napoleon Bonaparte

Napoleon Bonaparte—Napoleon I—crowned himself emperor of France in 1804. During his ten-year reign, "the Little Corporal" created an empire that spanned most of central and western Europe. Napoleon's downfall resulted in part from his pride and stubbornness and from his betrayal of many people.

Toward the end of his rule, people around him began to desert him. Finally, his commanders insisted he give up the throne. The French crowned Louis XVIII king and exiled Napoleon to Elba in 1814.

The following year Napoleon escaped and returned to France. During the Hundred Days—the period from his escape to his final defeat at Waterloo—Napoleon ruled once again. After Waterloo, Napoleon was once again exiled, this time to the barren island of St. Helena, off the coast of west Africa, where he died of cancer in 1821.

CUSTOMIZE INSTRUCTION FOR UNIVERSAL ACCESS

For Less Proficient Readers	For English Learners	For Advanced Readers
Ask each student to become an expert on a particular section of "Romanticism and Realism" by reading it several times and writing a paragraph summarizing it.	Have students use the art and illustrations on these pages to speculate about the era. Have them read the bold-faced headings and formulate questions based on them. Then, have students read the text to find the answers.	Instruct students to read pp. 758–765 independently, noting key ways in which the national identities of many European countries changed during those years. Then, have students discuss ways they might expect to find those changes expressed in the literature of the period.

Background
France

The Vienna conference reduced France to its 1790 boundaries and strengthened the countries on the borders of France.

Background
Poland

Poland was among the countries in revolt during this time. The revolt in Poland was led by nationalists seeking to win their independence from Russia. The revolt was crushed by the Russian army, however, and its leaders were executed.

Background
Russia

Although the serfs in Russia gained their freedom in 1861, Russia remained a repressive society characterized by major social and political inequalities.

▶Critical Viewing

Details of Bismarck's portrait indicating that his government was authoritarian and militaristic include his military dress and stern facial expression.

Background
Art

Show students *The Burghers of Calais* by Auguste Rodin, Art Transparency 17 in the **Fine Art Transparencies** booklet. Lead a discussion about the ways in which Rodin uses anatomical realism and emotion to create a sense of dynamism.

While such reforms were welcomed by many, public opinion turned against Napoleon when his occupying forces began assessing high taxes and conscripting local men into his armies.

Revolutions and Reactions Following the collapse of Napoleon's empire, a large group of national delegates gathered in Vienna to reestablish the traditions that had existed before the French Revolution. Although they were able to restore royal authority throughout Europe, they were unable to erase the desire for political and social justice. As a result, the rest of the century was marked by an ongoing conflict between traditional political beliefs and democratic ideals.

Nowhere was this conflict more apparent than in France. In the aftermath of Napoleon's downfall, royal rule had been reestablished. In 1830, however, when the king took measures to restrict the people's freedom, the people revolted and forced him out of power. Although this revolt brought about a number of important reforms, it did not bring an end to the monarchy. The new king, however, was a member of the upper middle class rather than the aristocracy. When another revolution occurred in 1848, however, a second French republic was established. Yet the Second Republic lasted only four years, and it was not until 1871 that the Third French Republic was born.

The French uprising of 1848 was one of several armed rebellions breaking out in Europe that year. Others took place in Italy, Austria, and Germany, but unlike the rebellion in France, they did not lead to the abolition of absolute monarchy. Meanwhile, in Denmark, Belgium, and the Netherlands, the spirit of the age manifested itself in reform rather than armed revolt.

▼ **Critical Viewing** Does this portrait of Bismarck offer any evidence that his government was authoritarian and militaristic? Why or why not? **[Interpret]**

Prince Otto von Bismarck in uniform with Prussian helmet, Franz von Lenbach

The Unification of Germany Also in 1848, a movement arose among the German people that was aimed at unifying the many German states into a single nation controlled by a democratic government. Like the revolts in the other European nations, this movement was thwarted. In 1871, however, after Prussia defeated France in the Franco-Prussian War, the Prussian prime minister, Otto von Bismarck (biz′ märk′), did succeed in unifying the German states. While the newly established German empire was a source of pride for nationalists, it was a major disappointment for reformers.

Similarly, Russian reformers had little success in bringing about political and social changes. Russia remained a repressive, autocratic state throughout the nineteenth century.

The Industrial Revolution Like the French Revolution, the Industrial Revolution took shape in the 1700s. In the British textile industry, inventors produced new machines that reduced the time needed to spin and weave cloth. The new machines led to the growth of the factory system, which brought workers and machinery together in one place to manufacture goods.

ENRICHMENT: History Connection
Nineteenth-Century European Factory Town

In his novel *Hard Times,* Charles Dickens offers a description of a typical nineteenth-century European factory town. He refers to it as "a town of machinery and tall chimneys, out of which interminable serpents of smoke trailed themselves forever and ever, and never got uncoiled."

Dickens describes the mundane lives of the people who lived in the town: They were "equally like one another ... all went in and out at the same hours, with the same sound on the pavement, to do the same work and to whom every day was the same as yesterday and tomorrow, and every year the counterpart of the last and the next."

Conditions for workers improved somewhat as the century progressed. In fact, in France and Britain wages nearly doubled during the last half of the nineteenth century.

Industry got a further boost with the invention of the steam engine. By the 1850s, steam was the main source of power, not only in factories but also in new means of transportation such as the railroad and the steamship.

By the end of the century, the Industrial Revolution had transformed Europe's entire way of life. Scientists and inventors had developed countless new products, including the first automobiles. Electricity became an important new source of power.

Gare Saint-Lazare, Claude Oscar Monet

▲ Critical Viewing Which details in this picture reveal the influence of the Industrial Revolution? Explain. **[Infer]**

Industrial Hardships The Industrial Revolution brought many benefits. It created millions of new jobs and produced a variety of goods more cheaply than ever before. At the same time, the rise of industry brought new problems. Early industrial workers often faced great hardships. Pay was low, hours were long, and working conditions were often dangerous. As people moved from the countryside to the growing industrial cities, they crowded into unhealthy urban slums.

By the end of the century, reformers were at work to raise wages, outlaw child labor, and win better conditions in factories and slums. Gradually, the standard of living for workers and their families improved.

The Middle Class and Women's Rights Industry and the growth of cities sparked the rise of a new middle class. The values of this new class—values that influenced all of society—included duty, thrift, honesty, hard work, and, above all, respectability.

By the middle of the century, some reformers had begun to protest restrictions on women. Even in the most democratic nations, such as Britain, women could not vote. They were banned from most schools, and married women could not legally control their own property.

A Controversial New Idea In the mid-nineteenth century, the theories of British biologist Charles Darwin created a tremendous uproar that shook the entire Western world. According to Darwin, all forms of life evolve, or change, over a long period of time. Simpler forms of life evolve into more complex forms, and new forms evolve out of older ones. Some people attacked Darwin's theories, believing that they contradicted the Bible. Today, however, evolution is (according to the *Encyclopedia Britannica*) "one of the fundamental keystones of modern biological theory."

▶Critical Viewing

Possible response: The details that reveal the influence of the Industrial Revolution include the train, the train tracks, smoke, steam, and the factory.

Historical Background

Comprehension Check

1. Between 1792 and 1815, which country was almost continually at war with the other European nations?
   Answer: France was almost continually at war.
2. **(a)** Which European country became a unified nation in 1871? **(b)** Under whose leadership did this happen?
   Answer: **(a)** Germany became a unified nation. **(b)** Germany was unified under Bismark.
3. What were some of the benefits of the Industrial Revolution?
   Answer: The Industrial Revolution created millions of new jobs and allowed a variety of goods to be produced more cheaply than ever before.
4. What were some of the problems caused by the Industrial Revolution?
   Answer: Workers faced great hardships, such as low pay, long hours, and dangerous working conditions. They also crowded into unhealthy urban slums.
5. How did the Industrial Revolution change the structure of European society?
   Answer: The Industrial Revolution resulted in the emergence of a new middle class whose values included duty, thrift, honesty, hard work, and respectability.

Critical Thinking

1. Ralph Waldo Emerson referred to the opening shot of the Revolutionary War as "the shot heard round the world." In what way do the events in Europe following the American Revolution reflect this view? **[Connect]**
   Possible response: The success of the American revolutionaries inspired Europeans, especially the French, to rebel against monarchic rule.

continued

continued from right column

2. In what ways did the Industrial Revolution encourage the growth of cities? **[Analyze Causes and Effects]**
   Possible response: New machines led to the growth of the factory system, which relied on the need for a large number of workers. These workers tended to live near the factory, resulting in the growth of cities around the factories.
3. Do you think the Industrial Revolution was more of a benefit or a detriment to humanity? Explain your answer. **[Make a Judgment]**
   Possible response: Some students may say that it was a benefit because as more goods were cheaply produced, many jobs were created and cities grew. Others may say that it was a detriment because of the tedium of factory work, the decline of the craftsman's role in the production of goods, and the polluting effects of big cities and industry on the environment.

Background

Art

The Wanderer Over the Sea of Clouds, by Caspar David Friedrich

Primarily self-taught, Friedrich (1774–1840) was one of a group of artists in the early nineteenth-century German Romantic movement. The works of this circle of writers and artists are characterized by their studies of nature and their symbolic and mysterious representations of the natural world. Friedrich's early drawings gained the notice and approval of the poet Goethe and were awarded a prize from the Weimar Art Society in 1805. Friedrich painted *Wanderer Over the Sea of Clouds* in 1818.

Use the following question for discussion:

What is the most unusual aspect of the painting that is representative of the Romantic period? Possible response: The man appears to be walking in the clouds and is at the same height as the mountains. This composition suggests that the relationship between the individual and nature has a magical quality.

Background

The French Revolution

The French people overthrew their ancient monarchy. The slogan, *Liberté, Égalité, Fraternité*—Liberty, Equality, Fraternity—was important to the revolutionaries. They wanted to stop the inequality they saw in their government, including exclusion of the nobility and clergy from paying taxes. The revolutionaries wanted everyone treated equally before the law. In Paris on July 14, 1789, a group of revolutionaries stormed the Bastille prison and freed the prisoners; then, the revolutionaries established a committee of middle-class citizens to govern Paris. Other provinces joined in the revolution and elevated average citizens to government posts throughout France.

▶ Critical Viewing

Romantic elements include the individual at the center of the painting and the wild, untamed scene over which he is looking. These details illustrate the Romantic elevation of the individual and love of wild nature.

Literature

Shaped by the major events and developments of the time, four major artistic movements dominated nineteenth-century literature: Romanticism, Realism, Naturalism, and Symbolism.

Romanticism: The French Revolution on a Page The first of these movements, Romanticism, rejected the objectivity, rationality, and harmony that many eighteenth-century writers admired in ancient Greek and Roman artists. Romantic writers, painters, and musicians responded not to an idealized image of ancient civilization but to the real unrest of their own times: the fervor of political revolution and the squalor of the Industrial Revolution. Rebelling against Neoclassical values, they prized subjectivity, the imagination, and the wildness associated with untamed nature.

Although there were many differences in the concerns and approaches of the various writers associated with this movement, they generally shared a desire to discard the dominant forms and approaches of the eighteenth century and to forge a new type of literature. In this sense, Romanticism might be called the French Revolution carried over to the literary page. The English poet William Wordsworth, a pioneer of literary Romanticism, was at first inspired by the French Revolution and its emphasis on the worth of the ordinary person. Later, when he became disillusioned with the violence in France, he began plotting the literary revolution known as Romanticism. He would uphold the dignity of ordinary people by writing about them with imagination and respect.

In his preface to *Lyrical Ballads* (1798), a collection of poetry he co-authored with his friend Samuel Taylor Coleridge, Wordsworth outlined the dominant principles of Romanticism. He stressed the need to employ "language really used by men" in describing "situations from common life," emphasized the role of nature as a source of inspiration, and asserted that poetry should be a "spontaneous overflow of powerful feelings." These principles contrasted with the practice of eighteenth-century Neoclassical writers, who used witty language to portray upper-class people in social rather than natural settings.

The Lure of the Exotic and the Supernatural Among the other important characteristics of the Romantics were their fascination with folklife in general and the folklore of the Middle Ages specifically, their attraction to exotic cultures and the supernatural, their sense of optimism, their emphasis on individualism, their refusal to accept human limitations, and their desire for social change. Again, most of these characteristics contrast with those of Neoclassical writers.

▼ **Critical Viewing** Which details in this painting suggest that it is a Romantic work? Explain. **[Connect]**

The Wanderer Over the Sea of Clouds, 1818, Caspar David Friedrich, Kunsthalle, Hamburg

ENRICHMENT: Science Connection

Charles Darwin

From 1831 to 1836, Charles Darwin (1809–1882) served as a naturalist with a British scientific expedition aboard the H.M.S. *Beagle*. Scientists on the expedition studied plants and animals throughout the world. Darwin's studies aboard the *Beagle* convinced him that through millions of years all species of plants and animals evolved, or developed gradually, from a few common ancestors. He documented his theories and presented them at a meeting of scientists in 1858. Although Darwin's theories of evolution and natural selection are widely accepted by scientists today, they also created a wave of controversy because of the perception that they challenge the biblical account of the Creation.

Music in the Historical Context

Beethoven Writes the First Romantic Symphony

It is 1802 and the virtuoso pianist and promising composer Ludwig von Beethoven (lōōt′ viH vän bā′ tō′ vən) can no longer deny that he is growing deaf. He retreats to a country village to write a confession of his deepest fears: ". . . reflect now that for six years I have been in a hopeless case, made worse by ignorant doctors, yearly betrayed in the hope of getting better, finally forced to face the prospect of a permanent malady. . . ." He will soon have to end his career as a pianist, focusing more and more on composing.

It is 1802 and Napoleon, commanding the armies of the French Revolution, has recently defeated the Austrians and forced a peace treaty with the British. At home, a grateful populace votes him consul, or ruler, for life.

Soon, Beethoven begins working on his Symphony No. 3, which will inaugurate a musical revolution. It will be the first Romantic symphony, an expression of thought and feeling on a more ambitious scale than can be found in symphonies of the previous century. Unlike these classical works, it will have an audience wider than a small circle of aristocrats. Beethoven labors on this composition in his sketchbooks, leaving empty spaces where he will fill in melodies later. Heroic in defiance of his "malady," the composer will dedicate his work to the hero who is bringing freedom to all of Europe: Napoleon.

It is 1804 and Napoleon's agents have just discovered an assassination plot against him. An influential adviser whispers that by making himself emperor, Napoleon will discourage future conspiracies. The consul agrees. The empire begins.

It is 1804 and Symphony No. 3 is complete. When he learns that Napoleon has declared himself emperor, Beethoven angrily strikes the leader's name from the dedication. This will be the *Eroica* ("Heroic") Symphony, dedicated not to a great man but, in disillusionment and defiance, to "the memory of a great man."

Ludwig von Beethoven, Joseph Karl Stieler, 1820, Beethoven-Haus, Bonn

▲ Critical Viewing Which details in this portrait of Beethoven suggest aspects of the new Romantic music—for example, the powerful expression of emotion and the heroic stature of the composer? Explain. **[Interpret]**

In addition to Wordsworth and Coleridge, the Romantic movement included the German poet and dramatist Johann Wolfgang von Goethe (yō′ hän vôlf gäŋ fôn gö′ tə), the Russian poet Alexander Pushkin, the German poet Heinrich Heine (hīn′ riH hī′ nə), and the French author Victor Hugo (hyōō′ gō).

Realism: The Discovery of Contemporary Life During the middle of the nineteenth century in France, a new literary movement known as Realism emerged, partly as a reaction against Romanticism and partly as a result of the industrial and scientific developments that were transforming society. Just as the Romantics had focused on humble people ignored by the Neoclassicists, Realists sought to portray previously ignored figures in contemporary life, such as middle- and working-class city dwellers.

▶Critical Viewing

Beethoven's wild and unkempt hair suggests the Romantic love of wild, untamed nature. His facial expression suggests powerful emotions.

Background

Ludwig von Beethoven

In 1812, Beethoven met Johann Wolfgang von Goethe, whose poetry and drama Beethoven greatly admired. They were introduced by Bettina Brentano, who was a friend of Goethe's. Beethoven's famous letter of July 1812 to the "Immortal Beloved" may have been addressed to Brentano's sister-in-law Antonia. Apparently, Beethoven wanted to marry Antonia, but when his hopes were dashed, his musical output declined dramatically for more than a year. The 1994 film *Immortal Beloved,* based on Beethoven's life, gets its title from the 1812 letter.

Listening to Music

Point out that in addition to literature and visual art, the ideas of Romanticism also affected the music of this period. Play for students "European Romantic Music: from *Piano Sonata no. 14,* Ludwig von Beethoven," Track 11, on **Prentice Hall Listening to Music: World Masterpieces.**

Background

Art

Show students *The Tiger Hunt* by Eugène Delacroix, Art Transparency 12 in the **Fine Art Transparencies** booklet. Lead students in a discussion about how Delacroix uses line, color, and theme to stir an emotional response in the viewer. Have students contrast these works with works from other periods with which they may be familiar.

ENRICHMENT: Literature Connection

Realism in America

The harsh reality of American frontier life, coupled with reaction to the Civil War gave rise to a new movement in American literature called Realism. Realism in literature began after the Civil War. Although the outcome of the war had given the nation a hard-won sense of unity, the enormous cost of human life had shattered the nation's idealism. Young writers turned away from the Romanticism that was popular before the war. Instead, writers began to focus on portraying "real life" as ordinary people lived it, and attempted to show characters and events in an honest, objective, almost factual way. Willa Cather, for example, was a Realist noted for her unflinching portrayal of the loneliness and cultural isolation of life on the prairie. Edith Wharton wrote fiction in the Realist vein about the Eastern high society into which she had been born.

Background

Ralph Ellison

Ralph Ellison developed a new type of black protagonist in reaction to the characters of Richard Wright, a popular African American writer of the mid-1900s. Wright's characters, victims of societal oppression, typically were enraged and lacked education. In contrast, Ellison's Invisible Man was schooled and introspective. Ellison did not believe that blacks were victims of white America but rather participants in cultural creation. Ellison saw the affirmation of black culture—its songs, folktales, and rituals—as a path to freedom. Raised in Oklahoma, a state without a history of slavery, Ellison navigated the borders between white and black America. *Invisible Man* is a novel that asserts black identity but also offers guidance to a person of any color or gender who feels "invisible." Ellison said that it is the job of the writer to "tell us about the unity of American experience beyond all considerations of class, of race, of religion." Ellison saw America as a place where anyone could forge an identity. He viewed the racial divide in America as a microcosm of the larger human struggle to find individual meaning in a world of chaos.

The French writer Honoré de Balzac (ô nô rā′ dae bál zák′) (1799–1850) anticipated Realism in scores of novels that give a vast and detailed picture of nineteenth-century French society, from criminals and lowlifes to upper-class women. Balzac's compatriot Gustave Flaubert (güs táv′ flō ber′) (1821–1880) wrote the classic Realist novel, *Madame Bovary*, which dissects the life of an unhappy middle-class woman. Other Realists were the English novelist Charles Dickens (1812–1870) and the Russian novelists Feodor Dostoyevsky (fyô′ dôr dôs′ tô yef′ skē) (see below) and Leo Tolstoy. In the latter part of the century, Henrik Ibsen wrote the first realistic prose dramas.

Naturalism and Greek Tragedy Realism eventually gave birth to the literary movement known as Naturalism. One of the leaders of this movement was the French writer Émile Zola (ā mēl′ zō′ lä′) (1840–1902). Like realists, Naturalists attempted to depict life accurately, but Naturalists were even more pessimistic than their forebears. They were reacting to the worst excesses of the Industrial Revolution and to misinterpretations of Darwinian theory that viewed society as a jungle in which only the fittest survived. As a result, they believed that the scientific laws governing heredity and society, like the Fates in ancient Greek mythology, determined the course of a person's life. Characters in naturalistic novels are therefore shaped

A Living Tradition

Feodor Dostoyevsky and Ralph Ellison

One nineteenth-century work with many literary descendants is *Notes from the Underground* (1864) by Russian author Feodor Dostoyevsky. In this novel, a nameless first-person narrator begins by announcing, "I am a sick man. . . . I am a spiteful man." This narrator is an angry stepchild of the Industrial Revolution, a nasty disbeliever in the progress of science and reason.

A literary descendant of this character is the narrator of Ralph Ellison's novel *Invisible Man*, written nearly 100 years after *Notes*. Ellison, who had been studying Dostoyevsky's work, created an African American protagonist who feels "invisible" in white society and therefore does not share that society's belief in progress:

> I am an invisible man. No, I am not a spook like those who haunted Edgar Allan Poe; nor am I one of your Hollywood-movie ectoplasms. I am a man of substance, of flesh and bone, fiber and liquids—and I might even be said to possess a mind. I am invisible, understand, simply because people refuse to see me. Like the bodiless heads you see sometimes in circus sideshows, it is as though I have been surrounded by mirrors of hard, distorting glass. When they approach me they see only my surroundings, themselves, or figments of their imagination—indeed, everything and anything except me.

ENRICHMENT: Literature Connection

Naturalism Around the World

Naturalism flourished in Europe during the late nineteenth and early twentieth centuries. In fact, scholars point to France as the birthplace of the movement. The writer Émile Zola was its leading practitioner. His approach to literature was similar to a scientist's approach to an experiment. Characters should be subjected to tests, Zola suggested, and the author should record their reactions objectively.

Overall, Naturalism drew on advances in the world of science. Scientific principles were imported into literature, and writers created characters whose lives were shaped and whose actions were dictated by powerful forces—heredity and nature, but also social and economic pressure—entirely beyond their control. Major American Naturalist authors include Jack London, Stephen Crane, Frank Norris, and Theodore Dreiser.

by forces they can neither understand nor control. In a sense, these novels are like Greek tragedies rendered in prose, with characters who live in slums, not palaces, and with scientific laws replacing the decrees of the gods.

On the Bank of the Seine, Bennecourt, 1868, Claude Monet, The Art Institute of Chicago

▲ **Critical Viewing** In what ways might this Impressionist painting by Monet differ from a photograph of the same scene? Explain. **[Compare and Contrast]**

The Symbolist Movement Throughout the nineteenth century, literary movements reacted to previous movements as well as to social conditions: Realism was a response to Romanticism, and Naturalism grew out of Realism. The Symbolist movement, proclaimed in an 1886 manifesto in France but based on the work of earlier writers, followed this same pattern. It rejected the fate-driven world of the Naturalist novel and the Realist drama. In a sense, it was a rebellion of poets against novelists and dramatists.

Led by Stéphane Mallarmé (stā fän′ mȧ lȧr mā′) (1842–1898), these poets were looking for an exit from the materialistic nineteenth century. Dismayed by the drabness of everyday life and the vulgar taste of the rising middle class, they searched for an otherworldly spiritual reality. Taking the earlier French poet Charles Baudelaire (shȧrl bōd ler′) as their guide, Symbolist poets sought to suggest this reality through musical phrasing and unusual figurative language.

In addition to Baudelaire, poets who anticipated this movement were Paul Verlaine (pôl ver len′) and Arthur Rimbaud (ȧr tür′ ram bō′). Verlaine, famous for the musicality of his verse, expressed a Symbolist credo when he wrote in "The Art of Poetry," "Let there be music, again and forever!" Rimbaud, a visionary poet who believed he could create a new world and a new language in his verse, stopped writing poetry when he was still a teenager!

The Visual Arts: From Splendor to Strangeness Some of the same movements influencing literature affected the visual arts, as well. Romantic painters like Caspar David Friedrich (frē′ driH) (page 762) depicted mysterious, lonely views of natural splendor. Then, as in literature, Realists rebelled against Romantics. Gustave Courbet (güs tȧv′ ko͞or be′), for example, painted such gritty subjects as laborers breaking stones (page 756). He declared, "I cannot paint an angel because I have never seen one." In their turn, Impressionists rebelled against Realists. Trying to capture fleeting impressions of shimmering light and color, they treated their paintings less like windows onto reality and more like colorful flat surfaces. Still later, Symbolists like Odilon Redon (ō dē lōn′ rə dōn′) painted such strange and unreal subjects as a drifting balloon in the form of a gigantic eyeball.

Literature of the Period

Comprehension Check

1. What was the dominant literary movement during the first half of the nineteenth century in Europe?
Answer: Romanticism was the dominant literary movement at this time.
2. What are some characteristics of Romanticism?
Answer: Characteristics include an emphasis on subjectivity, the imagination, and the wildness of untamed nature.
3. **(a)** During the middle of the nineteenth century, what literary movement emerged in Europe? **(b)** What type of characters were portrayed in this literature?
Answer: **(a)** Realism emerged at this time. **(b)** Middle- and working-class city dwellers were portrayed.
4. **(a)** What literary movement followed Realism in Europe? **(b)** What are its characteristics?
Answer: **(a)** Naturalism followed Realism. **(b)** It is characterized by a portrayal of individuals who are shaped by forces they can neither understand nor control.
5. **(a)** What literary movement was a reaction to Naturalism and Realism in Europe? **(b)** What was the goal of this literary movement?
Answer: **(a)** Symbolism was a reaction to these movements. **(b)** The goal was to escape from the drabness of everyday life and the vulgarity of the middle class and to find an otherworldly spiritual reality.

Critical Thinking

1. Why do you think the nineteenth century saw the emergence of four distinct literary styles, whereas the previous 150 years—the Age of Rationalism—saw only one? **[Analyze]**
Possible response: Rapid political, social, and economic changes in the nineteenth century had a great effect on people's lives and attitudes. These changes were reflected in the literature of the time.
2. How does the Symbolist credo expressed by Paul Verlaine's declaration "Let there be music, again and forever!" reflect the ideas of the Romantics? **[Compare and Contrast]**

continued

continued from right column

Possible response: Paul Verlaine's declaration is an emotional outburst. Both the Romantics and the Symbolists thought emotion was important, but they sought different means of expressing that emotion. The Romantics used the language of everyday life, whereas the Symbolists used musical phrasing and unusual figurative language.

3. In what way is the literature of the Realists and the Naturalists a reflection of the world at the time? **[Generalize]**
Possible response: The Realists and Naturalists wrote about conditions during the Industrial Revolution.

▶ Critical Viewing

Possible response: The painting shows the artist's impression of the shimmering light and color; a photograph might be more realistic.

from Faust

Lesson Objectives

1. **To analyze and respond to literary elements**
   - Literary Analysis: Romanticism
   - Connecting Literary Elements: Legends
2. **To read, comprehend, analyze, and critique drama**
   - Reading Strategy: Drawing Inferences
   - Reading Check Questions
   - Review and Assess Questions
   - Assessment Practice (ATE)
3. **To develop word analysis skills, fluency, and systematic vocabulary**
   - Vocabulary Development Lesson: Related Words: *prime*
4. **To understand and apply written and oral language conventions**
   - Spelling Strategy
   - Grammar and Style Lesson: Usage: *who* and *whom*
5. **To understand and apply appropriate writing and research strategies**
   - Writing Lesson: Writing a Film Script
   - Extension Activity: Film Version of a Scene
6. **To understand and apply listening and speaking strategies**
   - Extension Activity: Dialogue Based on the Play

10TH GRADE TEACHING A TENTH-GRADE COURSE

The literature in this section can be taught as part of a rich, balanced world literature course for tenth-grade students. For a full outline of such a course, see pp. T46–T48 in Volume I of this Teacher's Edition.

STEP-BY-STEP TEACHING GUIDE	PACING GUIDE
PRETEACH	
Motivate Students and Provide Background	
Use the Motivation activity (ATE p. 766)	5 min.
Read and discuss author and background features (SE pp. 766, 768, 773; ATE p. 766) [A]	5 min.
Introduce the Concepts	
Introduce the Literary Analysis and Reading Strategy concepts (SE/ATE p. 767) [A]	15 min.
Pronounce the vocabulary words and read their definitions (SE p. 767)	5 min.
TEACH	
Monitor Comprehension	
Informally monitor comprehension by circulating while students read independently or in groups [A]	45 min.
Monitor students' comprehension with the Reading Check notes (SE/ATE pp. 769, 771, 773, 775, 777, 779, 781, 783)	as students read
Develop vocabulary with Vocabulary notes (SE pp. 769, 770, 771, 775, 780, 783, 784; ATE p. 771)	as students read
Develop Understanding	
Develop students' understanding of Romanticism with the Literary Analysis annotations (SE pp. 769, 770, 774, 776, 778, 782, 783; ATE pp. 768, 769, 770, 774, 776, 778, 782, 783) [A]	10 min.
Develop students' ability to draw inferences, using the Reading Strategy annotations (SE/ATE pp. 770, 772, 775, 777, 778, 780, 783, 784)	10 min.
ASSESS	
Assess Mastery	
Assess students' mastery of the Reading Strategy and Literary Analysis concepts by having them answer the Review and Assess questions (SE/ATE p. 785)	20 min.
Use one or more of the print, software, or transparency Assessment Resources (ATE p. 787) [A]	up to 45 min.
EXTEND	
Apply Understanding	
Have students complete the Vocabulary Development Lesson and the Grammar and Style Lesson (SE p. 786) [A]	20 min.
Apply students' ability to write stage directions by using the Writing Lesson (SE/ATE p. 787) [A]	45 min.
Apply students' understanding of the selection, using one or more of the Extension Activities (SE p. 787)	20–90 min.

[A] ACCELERATED INSTRUCTION:
Use the strategies and activities identified with an [A].

10TH GRADE TEACHING TENTH-GRADE STUDENTS
For support teaching tenth-graders, see the Step-by-Step Teaching notes identified with this icon.

UNIVERSAL ACCESS
● = Below-Level Students
▲ = On-Level Students
■ = Above-Level Students

Time and Resource Manager

Reading Level: Challenging
Average Number of Instructional Days: 4

RESOURCES		
PRINT	**TRANSPARENCIES**	**TECHNOLOGY**
• **Beyond Literature,** Humanities Connection: Names for the Personification of Evil, p. 37 ▲ ■		
• **Selection Support Workbook:** ● ▲ ■ Literary Analysis, p. 148 Reading Strategy, p. 147 Build Vocabulary, p. 145	• **Literary Analysis and Reading Transparencies,** pp. 73 and 74 ● ▲ ■	
• **Reader's Companion** ● • **Adapted Reader's Companion** ●	• **Fine Art Transparencies,** Art Transparency 12 ● ▲ ■	• **Liste ning to Literature** ● ▲ ■ Audiocassettes Audio CDs • **Reader's Companion Audio Program** ● • **Reader's Companion Adapted and English Learner's Version Audio Program** ● ▲
• **English Learner's Companion** ● ▲ • **Literary Analysis for Enrichment,** p. 37 ■		• **World Masterpieces iText CD-ROM**
• **Formal Assessment:** Selection Test, pp. 133–135 ● ▲ ■ • **Open-Book Tests,** pp. 109–111 ● ▲ ■ • **Performance Assess. and Portfolio Mgmt,.** pp. 32, 28 ● ▲ ■ • PRENTICE HALL ASSESSMENT SYSTEM ● ▲ ■	• PRENTICE HALL ASSESSMENT SYSTEM ● ▲ ■ **Skills Practice Answers and Explanations on Transparencies**	• **Test Bank Software** ● ▲ ■
• **Selection Support Workbook:** ● ▲ ■ Grammar and Style, p. 146 • **Writing and Grammar,** Diamond Level ● ▲ ■ • **Extension Activities,** p. 37 ● ▲ ■	• **Daily Language Practice Transparencies** ● ▲	• **Writing and Grammar iText CD-ROM** ● ▲ ■ ***Take It to the Net*** PHSchool.com

BLOCK SCHEDULING: Use one 90-minute class period to preteach the selection(s), and have students read them. Use a second 90-minute class period to assess students' mastery of skills and have them complete one of the Extension Activities.

PRETEACH

Step-by-Step Teaching Guide for pp. 766–767

Motivation

Have students discuss stories, tales, or poems they have read in which a character makes a bargain with the Devil. Then, have students explore reasons that such stories recur throughout world literature. Ask: Why are people so fascinated by the idea of a person making a pact with the Devil?

❶ Background

More About the Author

Goethe was greatly influenced by two of his friends, Johann von Herder and Friedrich von Schiller. Goethe was still a young man when he met the older Herder, whom he came to regard as the most brilliant person he had known. "If I am destined to be your satellite," wrote Goethe, "then I will be, gladly and faithfully." To some degree, Goethe was Herder's satellite, becoming part of Herder's *Sturm und Drang* movement and embracing Herder's appreciation for Shakespeare. Many years later, when Goethe was middle-aged and losing the poetic drive, he met the young Schiller, whose enthusiasm for Goethe's work revitalized the older author. Yet their friendship did not always go smoothly. Although Goethe insisted on deference, Schiller was not about to become Goethe's satellite.

Geography Note

Draw students' attention to the map on this page and identify Germany. Remind students that Goethe spent most of his life in Weimar, in central Germany. Tell students that Goethe and Friedrich von Schiller are buried together in Weimar, in a mausoleum in the ducal cemetery.

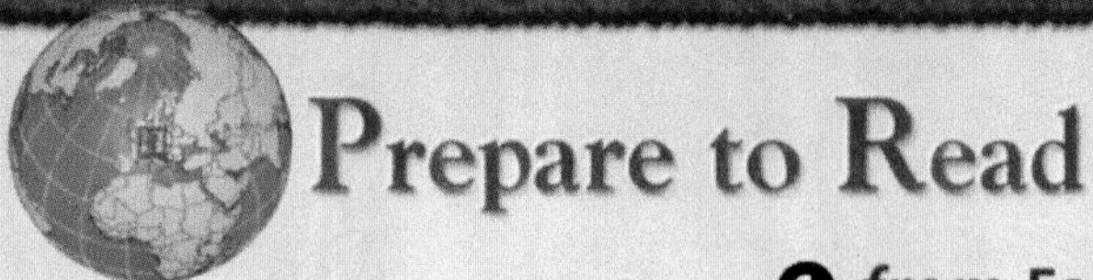

Prepare to Read

❶ *from* Faust

Johann Wolfgang von Goethe (1749–1832)

Because of the tremendous diversity of his talents and interests, Johann (yō hän′) Wolfgang von Goethe (gö′ tə) is best described as a true Renaissance man. He was not only a gifted writer but also a scientist, painter, statesman, philosopher, and educator.

The son of a wealthy lawyer, Goethe was born in the German town of Frankfurt am Main. After receiving a thorough education from private tutors, he was sent to the University of Leipzig to study law. More interested in the arts than in law, Goethe spent most of his free time writing poetry, studying art, and attending concerts. Nonetheless, he finished his legal studies in 1771.

A Developing Novelist Goethe practiced law for a brief period, during which he wrote *The Sorrows of Young Werther* (1774), an autobiographical novel inspired by an unhappy love affair and the suicide of one of his friends. One of the most important novels of the eighteenth century, *The Sorrows of Young Werther* earned Goethe international fame.

A year after the novel's publication, Goethe accepted an invitation to the court of the reigning duke of Weimar, Charles Augustus. Developing a close friendship with the duke, Goethe lived in Weimar for the rest of his life, and for ten years he served as the duke's chief minister. In 1786, he traveled to Italy in an effort to dedicate time and energy to his writing. He remained there for two years, writing, traveling, painting, and studying classical culture.

Shortly after returning to Weimar, Goethe fell in love with Christiane Vulpus, whom he later married. He also became the director of the court theater and began devoting much of his energy to scientific studies. Through a close friendship with the noted German writer Friedrich von Schiller (1759–1805), Goethe gained valuable guidance and advice concerning his writing and assistance in revising a number of his important works.

A Legendary Figure Probably the most notable of these works was *Faust.* With Schiller's advice and direction, Goethe revised an early draft of the play, adding a prologue. Unfortunately, Schiller died three years before *Faust, Part I* (1808) was published.

The final and greatest achievement of Goethe's literary career was the completion of *Faust, Part II.* The poet's vision of the legendary Faust transformed the traditional character into a newer, more sympathetic one that has fascinated readers and scholars for centuries. Goethe had begun his work on *Part II* while still a young man; because he contributed to the piece throughout his life, *Faust, Part II* ultimately reflects the deep philosophy of life and wry wisdom of the poet's mature years. Goethe never knew of the success of *Faust, Part II*, as it was published in 1833, one year after his death.

Faust was by no means the only literary work that Goethe completed. Among his other notable works are his novels *Wilhelm Meister's Apprenticeship* (1795), *Elective Affinities* (1809), and *Wilhelm Meister's Travels* (1821–1829), and his autobiographical work *Poetry and Truth* (1811–1833). By the time of his death, Goethe had become a legendary figure throughout the Western world.

TEACHING RESOURCES

The following resources can be used to enrich or extend the instruction for pp. 766–767.

Background

Beyond Literature, p. 37

 ***Take It to the Net***

Visit PHSchool.com for background on the author.

Literary Analysis

Literary Analysis and Reading Transparencies, Romanticism, p. 73

Reading

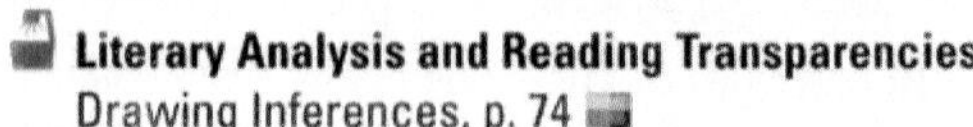

Literary Analysis and Reading Transparencies, Drawing Inferences, p. 74

Selection Support: Reading Strategy, p. 147; Build Vocabulary, p. 145

BLOCK SCHEDULING: Resources marked with this symbol provide varied instruction during 90-minute blocks.

Preview

Connecting to the Literature

The Devil lurks in many forms in literature across time and cultures, often trying to convince victims to sell their souls in exchange for their heart's desire. Compare Faust's dilemma to the situation of other characters from books or movies who were tempted by the Devil.

2 Literary Analysis

Romanticism

Romanticism is a literary and artistic movement that is characterized by the following elements:

- The Romantics favored emotion over reason, intuition over intellect, the subjective over the objective.
- They celebrated creativity, individuality, and imagination.
- Their writings reflect nature, self-knowledge, folklore, and the mysterious and exotic.

Look for these characteristics of Romanticism in *Faust*.

Connecting Literary Elements

A **legend** is a traditional story, handed down through many generations. It usually deals with a hero, a saint, or a national leader. Often, legends reflect a people's cultural values. Notice how Goethe uses facts from the real Faust's life to develop his story.

3 Reading Strategy

Drawing Inferences

Drawing inferences means making educated guesses based on specific details the author provides.

- Read between the lines to look for any implied meaning.
- Explore passages for clues about characters, setting, plot, and mood.
- Examine significant word choices, patterns of events, and other clues to help you understand the writer's implied message.

Use an organizer like the one shown as you read.

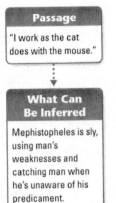

Passage

"I work as the cat does with the mouse."

What Can Be Inferred

Mephistopheles is sly, using man's weaknesses and catching man when he's unaware of his predicament.

Vocabulary Development

envoys (än′ voiz′) *n.* messengers (p. 769)

fervent (fur′ vənt) *adj.* intensely devoted or earnest (p. 770)

primal (prī′ məl) *adj.* original; fundamental (p. 771)

obstinate (äb′ stə nət) *adj.* determined to have one's way; stubborn (p. 775)

fetters (fet′ ərz) *n.* shackles, chains (p. 780)

tenacity (tə nas′ ə tē) *n.* persistence; stubbornness (p. 783)

insatiableness (in sā′ shə bəl nəs) *n.* the quality of being impossible to fill (p. 784)

CUSTOMIZE INSTRUCTION FOR UNIVERSAL ACCESS

For Special Needs Students	For Less Proficient Readers	For English Learners
Have students read "Prologue in Heaven" in the **Adapted Reader's Companion.** This version provides basic-level instruction in an interactive format with questions and write-on lines. Completing the adapted version will prepare students to read the selection in the Student Edition.	Have students read the adapted version of the selection in the **Reader's Companion.** This version provides basic-level instruction in an interactive format with questions and write-on lines. After students finish the selection in **Reader's Companion,** have them complete the questions and activities in the Student Edition.	Have students read the adapted version of the selection in the **English Learner's Companion.** This version provides basic-level instruction in an interactive format with questions and write-on lines. Completing the adapted version will prepare students to read the selection in the Student Edition.

2 Literary Analysis

Romanticism

- Explain to students that they will focus on the elements of Romanticism that are exhibited in each selection.
- As a class, read the list of characteristics of Romanticism on p. 767. Point out that although elements of Romanticism appear in the literature of many ages, including ours, Romanticism as a prevailing movement began in the eighteenth century and flourished during the nineteenth.
- Tell students that Goethe's *Faust* is an excellent example of Romanticism. Because Romanticism was later replaced by two contrasting literary movements—Realism and Naturalism—Goethe's work is in many ways different from the literary works of the later part of the century.
- Use the Romanticism transparency in **Literary Analysis and Reading Transparencies,** p. 73, to demonstrate for students how they can recognize Romanticism in a literary work.

3 Reading Strategy

Drawing Inferences

- Ask students to describe the mood you are projecting when you fold your arms across your chest and frown. When students say that you look angry, tell them that they have just drawn an inference on the basis of your body language. Remind them that they can use the same skill to draw inferences as they read, using clues in the text to infer the writer's meaning.
- Explain the use of the graphic organizer on p. 767. Have students use the graphic organizer as they read the selections.

Vocabulary Development

- Pronounce each vocabulary word for students, and read the definitions as a class. Have students identify any words with which they are already familiar.

 ***E-Teach***

Visit e-Teach at PHSchool.com for teachers' essays on how to teach, with questions and answers.

TEACH

Step-by-Step Teaching Guide for pp. 768–784

Teaching Tenth-Grade Students

10TH GRADE Have tenth-grade students silently read "Prologue in Heaven" and the excerpt from "The First Part of the Tragedy." Then, have students summarize the events that Goethe dramatizes in the selections.

❶ About the Selection

"Prologue in Heaven" opens with the angels praising God's creation. This dialogue is followed by a scene in which God (the Lord) and the Devil (Mephistopheles) have a discussion about humanity in general and Faust in particular. Mephistopheles asks for permission to try to steer Faust down the path of evil, and God grants it, saying that he never hated the Devil.

❷ Literary Analysis

Romanticism

- Point out to students that the Romantics had a deep love and appreciation for nature and were most concerned with the thoughts and emotions that nature aroused in them.
- Have a volunteer read aloud the bracketed passage.
- Then, ask students how these lines reflect elements of Romanticism. Answer: This description of nature creates a mysterious and awe-inspiring portrait of the universe. Goethe even has the angels acknowledge the beauty of the sun and "his brother spheres" (the stars) as they move through the universe.

❶ *from* **Faust**

JOHANN WOLFGANG VON GOETHE
translated by Louis MacNeice

Background

Few historical figures have fueled the imagination of the Western world as much as the German scholar and traveling magician Georg Faust (or Faustus), who lived from about 1480 to 1540. According to legend, Faust sold his soul to the Devil in exchange for youth, knowledge, and magical powers. At the time of its origin, the Faust legend was widely thought to be true. In contrast, when Goethe's *Faust* was published, few people believed that the type of events it depicted could actually happen.

Many versions of the Faust legend portray Faust as a man with an unquenchable thirst for knowledge. In Faust's time, only the very wealthy could afford to dedicate their lives to learning. Faust's quest, though noble in theory, drives him into a contract with the Devil. Goethe's version transforms Faust into something of a Romantic hero, embodying the ideal of limitless spiritual aspirations.

Prologue in Heaven

The LORD. *The* HEAVENLY HOSTS. MEPHISTOPHELES[1] *following.*
The THREE ARCHANGELS[2] *step forward.*

❷

RAPHAEL: The chanting sun, as ever, rivals
The chanting of his brother spheres
And marches round his destined circuit—
A march that thunders in our ears.
His aspect cheers the Hosts of Heaven
Though what his essence none can say;
These inconceivable creations

1. **Mephistopheles** (mef´ ə stäf´ ə lēz´) the Devil.
2. **three archangels** the three chief angels—Raphael, Gabriel, and Michael.

TEACHING RESOURCES

The following resources can be used to enrich or extend the instruction for pp. 768–784.

Literary Analysis

Selection Support: Literary Analysis, p. 148

Reading

Reader's Companion

Adapted Reader's Companion

English Learner's Companion

Listening to Literature Audiocassettes,

Listening to Literature Audio CDs,

Extension

Fine Art Transparencies, Art Transparency 12 (Use the transparency of Eugène Delacroix's *The Tiger Hunt* to discuss the Romantics' focus on emotion.)

BLOCK SCHEDULING: Resources marked with this symbol provide varied instruction during 90-minute blocks.

Keep the high state of their first day.

GABRIEL: And swift, with inconceivable swiftness,
The earth's full splendor rolls around,
Celestial radiance alternating
With a dread night too deep to sound;
The sea against the rocks' deep bases
Comes foaming up in far-flung force,
And rock and sea go whirling onward
In the swift spheres' eternal course.

4 **MICHAEL:** And storms in rivalry are raging
From sea to land, from land to sea,
In frenzy forge the world a girdle
From which no inmost part is free.
The blight of lightning flaming yonder
Marks where the thunder-bolt will play;
And yet Thine envoys, Lord, revere
The gentle movement of Thy day.

CHOIR OF ANGELS: Thine aspect cheers the Hosts of Heaven
Though what Thine essence none can say,
And all Thy loftiest creations
Keep the high state of their first day.

[*Enter* MEPHISTOPHELES.]

MEPHISTOPHELES: Since you, O Lord, once more approach and ask
If business down with us be light or heavy—
And in the past you've usually welcomed me—
That's why you see me also at your levee.[3]

3 **Critical Viewing** Which of the archangels' words could describe the scene in this photograph? **[Connect]**

Literary Analysis
Romanticism Which words in Michael's dialogue are charged with emotional intensity?

envoys (än′ voiz′) *n.* messengers

5 **Reading Check**
According to Michael, what girdles, or imprisons, the earth?

3. **levee** (lev′ ē) *n.* morning reception held by a person of high rank.

3 **Critical Viewing**

Answer: In lines 21–22 of the play, Michael says: "The blight of lightning flaming yonder / Marks where the thunder-bolt will play."

4 Literary Analysis

Romanticism

- Review with students the defining characteristics of Romanticism listed on p. 767. Emphasize that the expression of heightened emotion is one of these defining characteristics.
- Have students review lines 1–28, and then ask them to comment on the emotions the angels are expressing here.
  Answer: The angels are expressing wonder at the beauty, excitement, and wildness of nature; they are also expressing reverence at the gentleness of the day.
- Ask students the Literary Analysis question on p. 769: Which words in Michael's dialogue are charged with emotional intensity?
  Answer: Words such as *storms, rivalry, raging, frenzy, forge, blight, lightning* and *flaming* are charged with emotional intensity.

5 **Reading Check**

Answer: According to Michael, storms girdle the earth.

CUSTOMIZE INSTRUCTION FOR UNIVERSAL ACCESS

For Advanced Readers

Other known writers who have offered versions of the Faust legend include the nineteenth-century poets Heinrich Heine (1797–1856) and Paul Valéry (1871–1945) as well as the modern novelist Thomas Mann (1875–1955). Mann's *Doktor Faustus* (1947) is probably the most famous literary work connected to the Faust legend. Suggest that students read *Doktor Faustus* and form study groups to compare Mann's version with *Faust.* Encourage each study group to prepare a presentation for the class in which students discuss how Mann links the downfall of a demonic composer to the tragic events that occurred in Germany during the first half of the twentieth century.

6 Reading Strategy

Drawing Inferences

- Ask students to summarize how readers can determine an author's intended meaning when the message is conveyed indirectly.
  Answer: The reader must draw inferences after taking note of textual details, especially the writer's use of description and dialogue. In a play, description is often included in the dialogue.
- Ask a volunteer to read aloud lines 38–50. Then, ask students the Reading Strategy question on p. 770: What does Mephistopheles imply that Faust is unable to accomplish with his ability to reason?
  Possible response: Mephistopheles implies that Faust, like all other men, has been unable to rise above the level of the beasts. Even with the ability to reason, he makes no progress.

7 Literary Analysis

Romanticism

- Have students read and then paraphrase the bracketed lines. Make sure that they understand the meaning of such phrases as "the ferment in him" and "the deep-sea swell of his breast."
  Possible response: By "the ferment in him," Mephistopheles means that Faust is agitated by the quest for knowledge; by "the deep-sea swell of his breast," Mephistopheles means that Faust's desire is so vast that it will never be satisfied.
- Then, ask students the Literary Analysis question on p. 770: Explain how these lines reflect the Romantics' attitude toward the importance of the individual and the value of unbounded spiritual aspirations.
  Possible response: These lines describe Faust's own passionate quest for knowledge and experience. They suggest that this quest is for spiritual rather than physical fulfillment, because he "has no earthly habits in meat and drink." The line "He serves you oddly enough, I think" indicates that this quest is unusual or "odd," thus defining Faust as an individual.

Excuse me, I can't manage lofty words—
Not though your whole court jeer and find me low;
My pathos[4] certainly would make you laugh
Had you not left off laughing long ago.
Your suns and worlds mean nothing much to me;
How men torment themselves, that's all I see.
The little god of the world, one can't reshape, reshade him;
He is as strange to-day as that first day you made him.
His life would be not so bad, not quite,
Had you not granted him a gleam of Heaven's light;
He calls it Reason, uses it not the least
Except to be more beastly than any beast.
He seems to me—if your Honor does not mind—
Like a grasshopper—the long-legged kind—
That's always in flight and leaps as it flies along
And then in the grass strikes up its same old song.
I could only wish he confined himself to the grass!
He thrusts his nose into every filth, alas.

LORD: Mephistopheles, have you no other news?
Do you always come here to accuse?
Is nothing ever right in your eyes on earth?

MEPHISTOPHELES: No, Lord! I find things there as downright bad as ever.
I am sorry for men's days of dread and dearth;
Poor things, *my* wish to plague 'em isn't fervent.

LORD: Do you know Faust?

MEPHISTOPHELES: The Doctor?[5]

LORD: Aye, my servant.

MEPHISTOPHELES: Indeed! He serves you oddly enough, I think.
The fool has no earthly habits in meat and drink.
The ferment in him drives him wide and far,
That he is mad he too has almost guessed;
He demands of heaven each fairest star
And of earth each highest joy and best,
And all that is new and all that is far
Can bring no calm to the deep-sea swell of his breast.

LORD: Now he may serve me only gropingly,
Soon I shall lead him into the light.
The gardener knows when the sapling first turns green
That flowers and fruit will make the future bright.

Reading Strategy
Drawing Inferences What does Mephistopheles imply that Faust is unable to accomplish with his ability to reason?

fervent (fur′ vənt) *adj.* intensely devoted or earnest

Literary Analysis
Romanticism Explain how these lines reflect the Romantics' attitude toward the importance of the individual and the value of unbounded spiritual aspirations.

4. **pathos** (pā′ thäs) *n.* suffering.
5. **Doctor** Doctor of Philosophy.

ENRICHMENT: History Connection

Georg Faust

In the Middle Ages, the story of Georg Faust, the man who was the historical basis for the literary character Faust, spread far and wide and became part of folk legend. In 1587, Faustbuch—a crude, loosely organized narrative about the life of Faust—was published in Germany. Written by an anonymous author, the book not only drew upon the existing tales about Faust, but it also attributed to Faust numerous stories about other legendary magicians, such as Merlin. Concluding with Faust's death and descent into Hell, the book had a major impact on readers throughout Europe. The book was the first translated into English in 1592 under the title *The History of the Damnable Life and Deserved Death of Doctor John Faustus.*

Mephistopheles, 1863, Eugène Delacroix, Giraudon

MEPHISTOPHELES: What do you wager?
You will lose him yet,
Provided *you* give *me* permission
To steer him gently the course I set.

LORD: So long as he walks the earth alive,
So long you may try what enters your head;
Men make mistakes as long as they strive.

MEPHISTOPHELES: I thank you for that; as regards the dead,
The dead have never taken my fancy.
I favor cheeks that are full and rosy-red;
No corpse is welcome to my house;
I work as the cat does with the mouse.

LORD: Very well; you have my full permission.
Divert this soul from its primal source
And carry it, if you can seize it,
Down with you upon your course—
And stand ashamed when you must needs admit:
A good man with his groping intuitions
Still knows the path that is true and fit.

MEPHISTOPHELES: All right—but it won't last for long.
I'm not afraid my bet will turn out wrong.
And, if my aim prove true and strong,
Allow me to triumph wholeheartedly.
Dust shall he eat—and greedily—
Like my cousin the Snake[6] renowned in tale and song.

6. **my cousin the Snake** In Genesis, the devil assumes the form of a serpent in order to tempt Eve to eat from the Tree of Knowledge.

9 Critical Viewing What impression of Mephistopheles does the artist convey? **[Explain]**

primal (prī′ məl) *adj.* original; fundamental

11 Reading Check What wager has Mephistopheles made with the Lord?

8 Background

Art

Mephistopheles, by Eugène Delacroix.

Eugène Delacroix (1798–1863) is widely regarded as the greatest of the French Romantic painters. Three of his main sources of inspiration were literature, music, and history. In fact, many of his works were interpretations of scenes from history or literature. This depiction of Mephistopheles is one of seventeen bizarre and intriguing lithographs that Delacroix produced for a French edition of Goethe's *Faust*.

Use the following question for discussion:

Would this lithograph be more or less effective if it were in color? Explain.

Answer: This lithograph would be less effective in color because the use of only white and black suggests the seriousness of the struggle between good and evil.

9 Critical Viewing

Possible response: The artist conveys the impression that Mephistopheles is a fallen angel. The weight of his body seems to pull him down. The darkness and shading of the art suggest evil.

10 Vocabulary Development

Related Words: *prime*

- Draw students' attention to the word *primal* and its definition.
- Tell students that *primal* is related to the word *prime*, which comes from a Latin root meaning "first."
- Invite students to suggest words related to *prime*, and list the words on the board.
  Possible responses: Students may suggest *primate, primarily,* and *primordial.*
- Then, have students use dictionaries to find the meanings of these words and write a short paragraph for each word, describing how the meaning "first" contributes to the word's definition.

11 Reading Check

Answer: The Lord has wagered that Mephistopheles will not be able to win Faust over to the side of evil, and Mephistopheles has wagered that he will.

CUSTOMIZE INSTRUCTION FOR UNIVERSAL ACCESS

For Advanced Readers

The illustration on page 771 is a lithograph by Eugène Delacroix (1798–1863). Explain to students that the process of lithography was invented in 1796 by the playwright Aloys Senefelder. To create a lithograph, an artist produces a drawing, which is then etched onto a smooth stone. The stone is then inked with a roller and used to make prints. Have students use reference materials or the Internet to research other nineteenth-century artists who created lithographs, such as Goya, Manet, Degas, and Whistler.

Students who want to read more about lithography can visit the Tamarind Institute's Web page at http://www.unm.edu/~tamarind/process.html. Encourage students to create presentations to share their research with the class.

⓬ Reading Strategy

Drawing Inferences

- Have students discuss their impressions of the relationships between the Lord and Mephistopheles, between the Lord and humanity, and between Mephistopheles and humanity.
- Read aloud the bracketed passage. Then, ask students the Reading Strategy question on p. 772: What can you infer about the purpose of the Devil from the Lord's words?
  Possible response: One might infer that the Devil's purpose is to keep man from relaxing too much.

Answers for p. 772

Review and Assess

1. Possible response: Some students might imagine that Mephistopheles will win the wager because he knows how to tempt Faust in a way that Faust will find difficult to resist. Others might imagine that the Lord will win the wager because it has already been established that Faust is basically a good man.
2. **(a)** Mephistopheles is shrewd and cynical and has a surprising sense of humor. **(b)** Mephistopheles has little respect for or faith in humanity.
3. **(a)** Mephistopheles says that Faust has an insatiable quest for knowledge that cannot be satisfied. As a result, Faust is extremely agitated and nearly mad. **(b)** Possible response: Faust is a restless seeker of knowledge and experience and does not indulge in earthly pleasures.
4. **(a)** The Lord is tolerant of Mephistopheles and understands Mephistopheles's role in the cosmos. **(b)** The Lord says that he has never hated Mephistopheles and allows him to compete for Faust's soul.
5. Possible response: Yes; making mistakes is part of being human. No; humans should strive to be perfect.

LORD: That too you are free to give a trial;
I have never hated the likes of you.
⓬ Of all the spirits of denial
The joker is the last that I eschew.
Man finds relaxation too attractive—
Too fond too soon of unconditional rest;
Which is why I am pleased to give him a companion
Who lures and thrusts and must, as devil, be active.
But ye, true sons of Heaven, it is your duty
To take your joy in the living wealth of beauty.
The changing Essence which ever works and lives
Wall you around with love, serene, secure!
And that which floats in flickering appearance
Fix ye it firm in thoughts that must endure.

CHOIR OF ANGELS: Thine aspect cheers the Hosts of Heaven
Though what Thine essence none can say,
And all Thy loftiest creations
Keep the high state of their first day.

[*Heaven closes.*]

MEPHISTOPHELES [*alone*]: I like to see the Old One now and then
And try to keep relations on the level.
It's really decent of so great a person
To talk so humanely even to the Devil.

Reading Strategy
Drawing Inferences
What can you infer about the purpose of the Devil from the Lord's words?

Review and Assess

Thinking About the Selection

1. **Respond:** What do you imagine will be the outcome of Mephistopheles's wager with the Lord? Explain your answer.
2. **(a) Recall:** How would you characterize Mephistopheles as he appears in "Prologue in Heaven"? **(b) Infer:** What is his attitude toward humanity?
3. **(a) Recall:** How does Mephistopheles describe Faust?
   (b) Deduce: Based on Mephistopheles's description, what type of person do you imagine Faust to be?
4. **(a) Recall:** What is the Lord's attitude toward Mephistopheles?
   (b) Support: How is this attitude conveyed?
5. **Take a Position:** Do you agree with the Lord's statement that "Men make mistakes as long as they strive" (line 75)? Explain.

from Faust ⓭

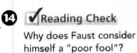

Background

In "Prologue in Heaven," Mephistopheles and the Lord disagree about Faust's true soul, and the Lord gives Mephistopheles permission to compete for Faust's soul. Only a great test will determine whether Faust recognizes the value of the life he currently lives or whether greed and irrationality will drive him to sell his soul to the Devil. Mephistopheles knows Faust's weakness—an unquenchable desire for knowledge—and seeks to use it as his means of luring Faust into a high-stakes bargain. Will Faust be tempted? Will Mephistopheles be forced to admit that Faust is like other good men who know "the path that is true and fit"? Look for the answers to these questions in "The First Part of the Tragedy."

from The First Part of the Tragedy

NIGHT

In a high-vaulted narrow Gothic[1] *room* FAUST, *restless, in a chair at his desk.*

FAUST: Here stand I, ach, Philosophy
Behind me and Law and Medicine too
And, to my cost, Theology—
All these I have sweated through and through
And now you see me a poor fool
As wise as when I entered school!
They call me Master, they call me Doctor,
Ten years now I have dragged my college
Along by the nose through zig and zag

⓮  Reading Check

Why does Faust consider himself a "poor fool"?

1. **Gothic** (gäth′ ik) *adj.* of a style of architecture characterized by the use of ribbed vaulting, flying buttresses, pointed arches, and steep, high roofs.

Teaching Tenth-Grade Students

10TH GRADE After reading "Prologue in Heaven," tenth-grade students will know that Mephistopheles is after Faust's soul. They also will have some sense of Faust's character. Review with students this prior knowledge, emphasizing the Romantic characteristics of the story.

⓭ About the Selection

This excerpt from "The First Part of the Tragedy" continues the story begun in "Prologue in Heaven." In this section, Mephistopheles, in the form of a traveling scholar, appears to Faust. As Faust becomes aware of who the scholar really is, Mephistopheles offers a bargain: He will satisfy Faust's thirst for knowledge and experience in exchange for his soul. Faust accepts this bargain and agrees that on the day he is satisfied, his soul will belong to Mephistopheles.

⓮ Reading Check

Answer: Faust considers himself a "poor fool" because after all his years of study, he is no wiser than when he entered school.

CUSTOMIZE INSTRUCTION FOR UNIVERSAL ACCESS

For Less Proficient Readers	For Gifted/Talented Students
To help students visualize the scene, point out the word *Gothic* in the stage directions at the beginning of the selection, and read aloud the footnote at the bottom of page 773. Display images of Gothic architectural elements, such as ribbed vaulting, flying buttresses, pointed arches, and steep, high roofs. Have students preview the selection and point out Gothic elements in the artwork. Then, ask students to discuss why Goethe chose a Gothic setting for *Faust*.	Direct students' attention to the footnote at the bottom of page 773. Then, have students research Gothic architecture and create a drawing of Faust's room. Students can reference a diagram of Gothic architectural elements, a glossary of terms, and images of Gothic structures on the Charlotte-Mecklenburg Historic Landmarks Commission Web page at http://www.cmhpf.org/kids/Guideboox/GothicArchitecture.html.

15 Literary Analysis

Romanticism and Legends

- Have a volunteer read aloud Faust's opening monologue beginning on p. 773.
- Ask students the Literary Analysis question on p. 774: How does Faust's speech reflect what you know about the real Faust from the Background on p. 768?
  Answer: According to Faust's speech, he, like the real Faust, is a scholar who is also very interested in magic.

16 Background

Art

Martin Luther at Erfurt, 1861
by Sir Joseph Noel Paton

Although Scottish painter Paton (1821–1901) was never a member of the Pre-Raphaelites, many of his works, with their attention to detail and concern with Romantic themes, clearly reflect the movement's influence.

Use the following question to initiate a discussion:

Do you think that this piece of art is a good or poor choice for an illustration of this selection? Explain.
Possible reponses: It is a good choice because the man in the painting is consumed with his studies, just as Faust is consumed with his quest for knowledge. The painting's Gothic setting is similar to the setting of Faust's room. However, the man in the painting is too devout to consider bargaining with the Devil.

17 ▶ Critical Viewing

Answer: Faust might sympathize with the man in the painting because it appears that the man shares many of Faust's interests. He is obviously interested in learning and spends a great deal of time pursuing knowledge.

Through up and down and round and round
And this is all that I have found—
The impossibility of knowledge!
It is this that burns away my heart;
Of course I am cleverer than the quacks,
Than master and doctor, than clerk and priest,
I suffer no scruple or doubt in the least,
I have no qualms about devil or burning,
Which is just why all joy is torn from me,
I cannot presume to make use of my learning,
I cannot presume I could open my mind
To proselytize[2] and improve mankind.

Besides, I have neither goods nor gold,
Neither reputation nor rank in the world;
No dog would choose to continue so!
Which is why I have given myself to Magic
To see if the Spirit may grant me to know
Through its force and its voice full many a secret,
May spare the sour sweat that I used to pour out
In talking of what I know nothing about,
May grant me to learn what it is that girds
The world together in its inmost being,
That the seeing its whole germination, the seeing
Its workings, may end my traffic in words.

Literary Analysis
Romanticism and Legends How does Faust's speech reflect what you know about the real Faust from the Background on page 768?

After summoning the Earth Spirit and finding it unwilling to assist him in his quest for knowledge, Faust lapses into a state of despair. He decides to end his life by drinking a cup of poison but abruptly changes his mind when he hears the tolling of church bells and the singing of choruses, celebrating the arrival of Easter. Setting out on a walk through the countryside with Wagner, his assistant, Faust is inspired by the beauty of spring and soothed by the peasants' expressions of admiration and affection for him. When he returns to his study, however, his sense of contentment quickly dissipates. Alerted by the growling of his dog, Faust becomes aware of another presence in the room. When Faust threatens to use magic to defend himself against the unseen intruder, Mephistopheles comes forward from behind the stove, disguised as a traveling scholar. Faust soon becomes aware of Mephistopheles's true identity, and he is intrigued by the possibility of establishing a contract with the devil. However, Faust falls asleep before the two can reach an agreement. In the following scene, Mephistopheles returns to the study to resume his discussion with Faust.

17 ▼ Critical Viewing
Why might Faust sympathize with the man in this painting? **[Hypothesize]**

2. **proselytize** (präs´ ə li tīz´) *v.* to try to convert.

ENRICHMENT: Culture Connection

Myths, Folk Tales, and Legends

Because the story of Faust is based on a historical figure, it is classified as a legend. To clarify the distinctions among myths, folk tales, and legends, offer students an American example of each. Some Native American tribes still have living myths. The kachinas of the Pueblo Indians, for example, are mythical figures whose purposes include bringing rain for the spring crops. Examples of American folk tales include the stories of Paul Bunyan. Explain that although there were undoubtedly some tall, brawny lumberjacks in the upper Midwest, Paul Bunyan is not based on any actual historical figure. Johnny Appleseed, on the other hand, is an example of a legendary figure, because the stories about him are derived from the exploits of an actual person named John Chapman, who devoted his life to planting apple trees.

[*The same room. Later.*]

FAUST: Who's knocking? Come in! *Now* who wants to annoy me?

MEPHISTOPHELES [*outside door*]: It's I.

FAUST: Come in!

MEPHISTOPHELES [*outside door*]:
You must say "Come in" three times.

FAUST: Come in then!

18 **MEPHISTOPHELES** [*entering*]:
Thank you; you overjoy me.
We two, I hope, we shall be good friends;
To chase those megrims[3] of yours away
I am here like a fine young squire to-day,
In a suit of scarlet trimmed with gold
And a little cape of stiff brocade,
With a cock's feather in my hat
And at my side a long sharp blade,
And the most succinct advice I can give
Is that you dress up just like me,
So that uninhibited and free
You may find out what it means to live.

FAUST: The pain of earth's constricted life, I fancy,
Will pierce me still, whatever my attire;
I am too old for mere amusement,
Too young to be without desire.
How can the world dispel my doubt?
You must do without, you must do without!
That is the everlasting song
Which rings in every ear, which rings,
And which to us our whole life long
Every hour hoarsely sings.
I wake in the morning only to feel appalled,
My eyes with bitter tears could run
To see the day which in its course
Will not fulfil a wish for me, not one;
The day which whittles away with obstinate carping
All pleasures—even those of anticipation,
Which makes a thousand grimaces to obstruct
My heart when it is stirring in creation.
And again, when night comes down, in anguish
I must stretch out upon my bed

3. **megrims** (mē′ grəmz) *n.* low spirits.

Reading Strategy
Drawing Inferences Why has Mephistopheles changed his costume from that of a traveling scholar to "a suit of scarlet trimmed with gold"?

obstinate (äb′ stə nət) *adj.* determined to have one's way; stubborn.

19 ✔ **Reading Check**
What torments Faust every day?

18 Reading Strategy
Drawing Inferences

- Have a pair of students read aloud the opening exchange between Faust and Mephistopheles, acting it out with appropriate expression.
- Then, ask students the Reading Strategy question on p. 775: Why has Mephistopheles changed his costume from that of a traveling scholar to "a suit of scarlet trimmed with gold"?
  Answer: Mephistopheles has changed his costume in order to demonstrate to Faust that dressing in a certain way can help change one's attitude.

Reteach If students have difficulty answering the Reading Strategy question, use the Drawing Inferences transparency in **Literary Analysis and Reading Transparencies, p. 74,** to provide more support in using this strategy.

19 ✔ Reading Check
Answer: Faust is tormented by "the pain of earth's constricted life." He believes he is "too old for mere amusement" yet "Too young to be without desire." He is tired of having to "do without" and defeated in knowing that none of his wishes will be fulfilled.

CUSTOMIZE INSTRUCTION FOR UNIVERSAL ACCESS

For Less Proficient Readers	For English Learners	For Advanced Readers
Have pairs of students read aloud the opening dialogue between Faust and Mephistopheles, as suggested in the Reading Strategy note. Students may find it difficult to capture a natural rhythm when reading the dialogue. To model appropriate rhythm and tone, read aloud one or two sections of dialogue.	Have pairs of students read aloud the opening dialogue between Faust and Mephistopheles, as suggested in the Reading Strategy note. Pair students with more proficient partners, and have those partners model the pronunciation of unfamiliar words. Students can keep track of new words by keeping a vocabulary journal.	Before students perform the opening dialogue, have them analyze the language in Faust's opening speech, noting the rhyme scheme and looking for examples of alliteration, parallel structure, repetition, and other poetic devices. Challenge students to write a similar statement about themselves, in which they imitate Goethe's style.

20 Critical Thinking

Connect

- After students have read the bracketed sentence, refer them to the italicized material on page 774.
- Then, ask students to explain Mephistopheles's remark on p. 776. Ask: To whom is he referring? What is the "brown juice" that this person failed to drink?
  Answer: Mephistopheles is referring to Faust. The "brown juice" is the poison Faust was preparing to drink before he changed his mind upon hearing the bells on Easter morning.

21 Literary Analysis

Romanticism

- Have students read the bracketed passage independently. Then, work with students to make a list of the things that Faust curses in this passage.
  Answer: Faust curses all things that lure the soul, such as high opinion, appearance, dreams of glory and fame, personal belongings, servants, ploughs, children, wives, greed, luxurious living, wine, love, hope, faith, and patience.
- Ask students the Literary Analysis question on p. 776: In what way does this passage exhibit the Romantics' interest in emotion and the individual?
  Answer: This passage is an outpouring of Faust's emotions, showing his innermost feelings concerning his own past and human attachments to worldly pleasures and goals.

And again no rest is granted me,
For wild dreams fill my mind with dread.
The God who dwells within my bosom
Can make my inmost soul react;
The God who sways my every power
Is powerless with external fact.
And so existence weighs upon my breast
And I long for death and life—life I detest.

MEPHISTOPHELES: Yet death is never a wholly welcome guest.

FAUST: O happy is he whom death in the dazzle of victory
Crowns with the bloody laurel in the battling swirl!
Or he whom after the mad and breakneck dance
He comes upon in the arms of a girl!
O to have sunk away, delighted, deleted,
Before the Spirit of the Earth, before his might!

20

MEPHISTOPHELES: Yet I know someone who failed to drink
A brown juice on a certain night.

FAUST: Your hobby is espionage—is it not?

MEPHISTOPHELES: Oh I'm not omniscient[4]—but I know a lot.

21

FAUST: Whereas that tumult in my soul
Was stilled by sweet familiar chimes
Which cozened the child that yet was in me
With echoes of more happy times,
I now curse all things that encompass
The soul with lures and jugglery
And bind it in this dungeon of grief
With trickery and flattery.
Cursed in advance be the high opinion
That serves our spirit for a cloak!
Cursed be the dazzle of appearance
Which bows our senses to its yoke!
Cursed be the lying dreams of glory,
The illusion that our name survives!
Cursed be the flattering things we own,
Servants and ploughs, children and wives!
Cursed be Mammon[5] when with his treasures
He makes us play the adventurous man
Or when for our luxurious pleasures
He duly spreads the soft divan![6]

Literary Analysis
Romanticism In what way does this passage exhibit the Romantics' interest in emotion and the individual?

4. **omniscient** (äm nish' ənt) *adj.* knowing all things.
5. **Mammon** (mam' ən) Generally, Mammon refers to riches regarded as an object of worship and greedy pursuit; here, the word is used to refer to the Devil, as an embodiment of greed.
6. **divan** (di van') *n.* large, low couch or sofa, usually without armrests or a back.

ENRICHMENT: Linguistics Connection

Translations of *Faust*

Share with students Walter Kaufmann's translation of lines 76–77: "And thus existence is for me a weight, / Death is desirable, and life I hate." Some readers may prefer this translation to MacNeice's because the words *weight* and *hate* seem more direct and powerful than *breast* and *detest.* Other readers may prefer MacNeice's translation because it sounds more intellectual and "lofty." The sound device used in both translations is rhyme.

22

◀ Critical Viewing 23
How does the study portrayed here fit Faust's personality? **[Connect]**

A curse on the balsam of the grape!
A curse on the love that rides for a fall!
A curse on hope! A curse on faith!
And a curse on patience most of all!

[*The* INVISIBLE SPIRITS *sing again.*]

SPIRITS: Woe! Woe!
You have destroyed it,
The beautiful world;
By your violent hand
'Tis downward hurled!
A half-god has dashed it asunder!
From under
We bear off the rubble to nowhere
And ponder
Sadly the beauty departed.
Magnipotent
One among men,

24

Reading Strategy
Drawing Inferences
Which details help you determine whether these invisible spirits are on the side of good or evil?

25 
What has Faust destroyed?

CUSTOMIZE INSTRUCTION FOR UNIVERSAL ACCESS

For Special Needs Students	For English Learners
Remind students that a contraction is a word made up of two words with an apostrophe taking the place of the missing letters. Explain to students that the word *'Tis* (line 117) on page 777 is a contraction meaning "it is." Then, call students' attention to the contraction *it's* (line 35) on page 775. Tell students that this contraction also means "it is." On the board, show students how each contraction is formed, demonstrating which letter the apostrophe replaces in each case.	Call students' attention to the use of the word *'Tis* in line 117. Explain that this word is a contraction meaning "it is." Ask students to read the entire sentence in which the word appears, and then point out that the *it* in *'Tis* refers to "the beautiful world." A more common way to express the thought would be: "By your violent hand, the beautiful world is hurled downward."

22 Background

Art

Faust and Mephistopheles, by Alfred Louis Vigny Jacomin
Jacomin created this gravure reproduction in 1869 after an oil on canvas.

Use the following question for discussion:

- Do you think this image accurately captures the relationship between Mephistopheles and Faust? Explain.
  Possible response: Yes; the art shows Faust as weary, but intrigued by Mephistopheles. Mephistopheles is shown as a suave, yet imposing figure.

23 ▶ Critical Viewing

Answer: The study portrayed here fits Faust's personality because the room seems to be littered with the kinds of objects he would use in his studies and perhaps in his magic.

24 Reading Strategy

Drawing Inferences

- Remind students that the theme of a literary work is often implied rather than stated directly. To determine the theme, students must draw inferences from details in the text.
- Ask a small group to read aloud the bracketed passage. Make sure they understand that the Spirits are talking to Faust, responding to his speech in which he curses so many things that most people find enjoyable and valuable.
- Ask students the Reading Strategy question on p. 777: Which details help you determine whether these invisible spirits are on the side of good or evil?
  Answer: The fact that the spirits are sad about Faust's negativism and mourn the loss of beauty puts them in a positive light.

25 ✓Reading Check

Answer: Faust has destroyed "the beautiful world"; that is, his rejection of the world causes its beauty to vanish for him.

26 Literary Analysis

Romanticism

- Have students read the bracketed passage independently. Ask them how they would characterize the method Mephistopheles is using to get Faust to accept Mephistopheles's offer.
  Answer: First, Mephistopheles minimizes the importance of the invisible spirits. Then, he flatters Faust by saying that he doesn't really belong with the common men. Finally, he offers his services to help Faust in his "career through life."
- Ask students the Literary Analysis question on p. 778: In what ways does Mephistopheles's speech reflect the Romantics' interest in emotions?
  Answer: Mephistopheles's speech plays on Faust's emotions. He mentions Faust's grief and tells him that it acts like a vulture on his life and mind. He also appeals to Faust's desire to have a partner through life who can help him achieve his goals of acquiring knowledge and experience.

27 Reading Strategy

Drawing Inferences

- Direct students' attention to the bracketed line on p. 778.
- Ask students the Reading Strategy question on p. 778: What does Faust mean when he refers to Mephistopheles as "a servant like you"?
  Answer: Faust means that he recognizes Mephistopheles's "servitude" as potentially dangerous.

Magnificent
Build it again,
Build it again in your breast!
Let a new course of life
Begin
With vision abounding
And new songs resounding
To welcome it in!

MEPHISTOPHELES: These are the juniors
Of my faction.
Hear how precociously[7] they counsel
Pleasure and action.
Out and away
From your lonely day
Which dries your senses and your juices
Their melody seduces.

Stop playing with your grief which battens
Like a vulture on your life, your mind!
26 The worst of company would make you feel
That you are a man among mankind.
Not that it's really my proposition
To shove you among the common men;
Though I'm not one of the Upper Ten,
If you would like a coalition
With me for your career through life,
I am quite ready to fit in,
I'm yours before you can say knife.
I am your comrade;
If you so crave,
I am your servant, I am your slave.

FAUST: And what have I to undertake in return?

MEPHISTOPHELES: Oh it's early days to discuss what that is.

FAUST: No, no, the devil is an egoist
And ready to do nothing gratis
Which is to benefit a stranger.
Tell me your terms and don't prevaricate![8]
27 A servant like you in the house is a danger.

MEPHISTOPHELES: I will bind myself to your service in this world,
To be at your beck and never rest nor slack;

Literary Analysis
Romanticism In what ways does Mephistopheles's speech reflect the Romantics' interest in emotions?

Reading Strategy
Drawing Inferences What does Faust mean when he refers to Mephistopheles as "a servant like you"?

7. **precociously** (pri kō′ shəs lē) *adv.* exhibiting maturity to a point beyond that which is normal for the age.
8. **prevaricate** (pri var′ i kāt) *v.* to tell an untruth.

ENRICHMENT: Philosophy Connection

Rousseau and Kant

The French Revolution and the Industrial Revolution, along with the ideas of eighteenth-century philosophers Jean-Jacques Rousseau (1712–1778) and Immanuel Kant (1724–1804), gave rise to a variety of new European cultural attitudes and beliefs, including those Romantic attitudes expressed in *Faust.* Influenced by the French revolutionary spirit and by the writings of Rousseau, who argued that society must respect but typically infringes on personal liberty, many writers and thinkers of the early nineteenth century stressed the need for freedom and equality. These beliefs were accompanied by an emphasis on individuality and the fundamental power of the imagination, which reflected the teachings of Kant. The early nineteenth-century writers and thinkers were also influenced by industrialization, which prompted them to emphasize the importance of nature and the need to return to a simpler way of life.

When we meet again on the other side,
In the same coin you shall pay me back.

FAUST: The other side gives me little trouble;
First batter this present world to rubble,
Then the other may rise—if that's the plan.
This earth is where my springs of joy have started,
And this sun shines on me when broken-hearted;
If I can first from them be parted,
Then let happen what will and can!
I wish to hear no more about it—
Whether there too men hate and love
Or whether in those spheres too, in the future,
There is a Below or an Above.

MEPHISTOPHELES: With such an outlook you can
risk it.
Sign on the line! In these next days you will get
Ravishing samples of my arts;
I am giving you what never man saw yet.

FAUST: Poor devil, can *you* give anything ever?
Was a human spirit in its high endeavor
Even once understood by one of your breed?
Have you got food which fails to feed?
Or red gold which, never at rest,
Like mercury runs away through the hand?
A game at which one never wins?
A girl who, even when on my breast,
Pledges herself to my neighbor with her eyes?
The divine and lovely delight of honor
Which falls like a falling star and dies?
Show me the fruits which, before they are plucked,
decay
And the trees which day after day renew their green!

MEPHISTOPHELES: Such a commission doesn't
alarm me,
I have such treasures to purvey.
But, my good friend, the time draws on when we
Should be glad to feast at our ease on something good.

FAUST: If ever I stretch myself on a bed of ease,
Then I am finished! Is that understood?
If ever your flatteries can coax me
To be pleased with myself, if ever you cast
A spell of pleasure that can hoax me—
Then let *that* day be my last!
That's my wager!

28 

Themes in World Literature

The Terrible Bargain

Over the years, the Faust legend has appeared in many variations and adaptations. Each retelling involves a person who trades his soul for experience, knowledge, or treasure. "The Devil and Tom Walker" by Washington Irving is just one of these variations. Set in colonial Massachusetts, the short story features the miser Tom Walker and his overbearing wife. Wishing for untold wealth, Tom makes a pact with the Devil, whom he encounters in a swampy forest. Like other fictional characters who sell their souls, he obtains his heart's desire in exchange.

Adaptations do not share the same ending—in some, such as "The Devil and Tom Walker," the protagonist is doomed; in others, such as "The Devil and Daniel Webster" by Stephen Vincent Benét, he is redeemed. Variations of the legend appear across genres and generations as well. In Oscar Wilde's novel *A Picture of Dorian Gray* (1891), Gray trades his soul for perpetual youth. In *Bedazzled,* a Hollywood film released in 2000, the terrible bargain is reinvented when a man trades his soul to the Devil—who appears in the form of a beautiful woman—in exchange for seven wishes. Look for variations of the Faust legend in art, movies, music, and, of course, literature.

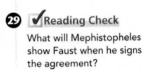

29  **Reading Check**

What will Mephistopheles show Faust when he signs the agreement?

28 Background

The Terrible Bargain

Washington Irving traveled extensively and learned about European customs, traditions, and folklore. Inspired by the European folk heritage, Irving created two of his most famous stories, "The Legend of Sleepy Hollow" and "Rip Van Winkle." Both stories transform traditional German tales into distinctly American narratives set in the Hudson Valley. While living in Europe, Irving completed *Tales of a Traveler,* which contains "The Devil and Tom Walker." Irving's adaptation of the Faust legend is set in New England during the 1720s, a time when the Puritan belief in devoting one's life to God was being replaced by materialism and the desire for personal gain.

29 Reading Check

Answer: Mephistopheles will show Faust "ravishing samples" of his arts, things that no other man has ever seen.

CUSTOMIZE INSTRUCTION FOR UNIVERSAL ACCESS

For Special Needs Students	For Less Proficient Readers	For English Learners
Draw students' attention to lines 197–202. To check comprehension, discuss with students what will happen to Faust if he loses his bet and whether Mephistopheles will lose his bet with the Lord even if he wins his bet with Faust.	Check students' comprehension by asking them what Faust means in lines 156–160. Make sure they understand that Faust is fully aware that the devil is not his friend and does not intend to reward him without exacting a heavy price.	Draw students' attention to the phrase "at your beck" in line 162. Tell them that this is a shortened version of the idiom "at your beck and call," which means "ready and willing to do whatever you ask."

30 Reading Strategy

Drawing Inferences

- Have students reread lines 197–212. Ask students to describe the terms of the agreement between Faust and Mephistopheles. **Answer:** Mephistopheles will help Faust get whatever he wants from life. Faust will experience life until the day he is so pleased with himself that he stretches "on a bed of ease." If that day ever comes, it will be Faust's last day on Earth. From then on, Faust will serve Mephistopheles.
- Read aloud the bracketed passage. Ask students the Reading Strategy question on p. 780: Why does Mephistopheles want the agreement recorded in writing? **Answer:** Mephistopheles wants the agreement recorded in writing in case Faust tries to back out of it later.

31 ▶ Critical Viewing

Answer: The painting shows the power of a storm at sea. The raging of the winds and the surging of the waves suggest the emotional turmoil that Faust has felt in his quest for knowledge.

MEPHISTOPHELES: Done!

FAUST: Let's shake!
If ever I say to the passing moment
"Linger a while! Thou art so fair!"
Then you may cast me into fetters,
I will gladly perish then and there!
Then you may set the death-bell tolling,
Then from my service you are free,
The clock may stop, its hand may fall,
And that be the end of time for me!

fetters (fet′ ərz) *n.* shackles, chains

MEPHISTOPHELES: Think what you're saying, we shall not
forget it.

FAUST: And you are fully within your rights;
I have made no mad or outrageous claim.
If I stay as I am, I am a slave—
Whether yours or another's, it's all the same.

30

MEPHISTOPHELES: I shall this very day at the College Banquet[9]
Enter your service with no more ado,
But just one point—As a life-and-death insurance
I must trouble you for a line or two.

FAUST: So you, you pedant, you too like things in writing?
Have you never known a man? Or a man's word? Never?
Is it not enough that my word of mouth
Puts all my days in bond for ever?
Does not the world rage on in all its streams
And shall a promise hamper *me*?
Yet this illusion reigns within our hearts
And from it who would be gladly free?
Happy the man who can inwardly keep his word;
Whatever the cost, he will not be loath to pay!
But a parchment, duly inscribed and sealed,
Is a bogey[10] from which all wince away.
The word dies on the tip of the pen
And wax and leather lord it then.
What do you, evil spirit, require?
Bronze, marble, parchment, paper?
Quill or chisel or pencil of slate?
You may choose whichever you desire.

Reading Strategy
Drawing Inferences
Why does Mephistopheles want the agreement recorded in writing?

MEPHISTOPHELES: How can you so exaggerate
With such a hectic rhetoric?

31 **Critical Viewing ▶**
How does this painting convey the powers of nature that Faust has experienced? **[Analyze]**

9. **the College Banquet** the *Doctorschmaus,* a dinner given by a successful candidate for a Ph.D. degree.
10. **bogey** (bō′ gē) *n.* anything one especially, and often needlessly, fears.

ENRICHMENT: Literature Connection

The Romantic "Love of Life"

In an essay written in 1910, George Santayana, an American philosopher and poet, discussed the qualities that make Faust a work of Romantic literature. He wrote that Faust is the drama of a philosophical adventure; a rebellion against convention; a flight to nature, to tenderness, to beauty; and then a return to convention again, with a feeling that nature, tenderness, and beauty, unless found there, will not be found at all. Goethe never depicts, as Dante does, the object his hero is pursuing; he is satisfied with depicting the pursuit. . . . [When Goethe wrote *Faust*] the love of life, primal and adventurous, was gathering head in many an individual. In the Romantic movement and in the French Revolution, this love of life freed itself from the politic compromises and conventions that had been stifling it for two hundred years. Goethe's hero embodies this. . . romantic emancipation of the mind. . . . He cries for air, for nature, and for experience.

Any little snippet is quite good—
And you sign it with one little drop of blood.

FAUST: If that is enough and is some use,
One may as well pander to your fad.

MEPHISTOPHELES: Blood is a very special juice.

FAUST: Only do not fear that I shall break this contract.
What I promise is nothing more
Than what all my powers are striving for.
I have puffed myself up too much, it is only
Your sort that really fits my case.
The great Earth Spirit has despised me
And Nature shuts the door in my face.
The thread of thought is snapped asunder,
I have long loathed knowledge in all its fashions.
In the depths of sensuality

32 ✔Reading Check
Why does Mephistopheles want Faust to sign the agreement in blood?

33

Dunstanburgh Castle in a Thunderstorm, Thomas Girtin, Ashmolean Museum, Oxford, UK

CUSTOMIZE INSTRUCTION FOR UNIVERSAL ACCESS

For Less Proficient Readers	For English Learners	For Advanced Readers
Have students use dictionaries to find the meaning of the word *loathed* (line 255). Then, have students list on the board synonyms for *loathed.* Ask volunteers to read line 255, substituting a different synonym for *loathed* with each reading. Lead students in a discussion about which word choice is the most powerful and why.	Draw students' attention to line 254: "The thread of thought is snapped asunder." Explain to students that this line contains a metaphor, or a figure of speech. In this example, thought is compared to a thread, which can be broken or "snapped." Have students skim the selection for examples of metaphor, and help them understand the comparisons.	Draw students' attention to the word *fad* in line 245. Ask them to research its etymology and meaning. Then, have them find words with meanings similar to that of *fad* but with positive or neutral, rather than negative, connotations.

32 ✔Reading Check

Answer: Mephistopheles wants Faust to sign the agreement in blood because "Blood is a very special juice," a vital life force with symbolic overtones, and Faust will presumably be unable to escape any agreement signed in blood.

33 Background

Art

Dunstanburgh Castle in a Thunderstorm, by Thomas Girtin

By creating dramatic depictions of light effects and natural phenomena, watercolorist Thomas Girtin (1775–1802) presented an alternative to the standard tinted drawing, revolutionizing the watercolor genre in the process.

Use the following questions to stimulate discussion:

- Imagine that a person lives in the castle shown in this painting. How do you think that person would feel upon seeing this scene?
  Possible response: The person would feel frightened because of the castle's isolated location and the severity of the raging storm. Because the person would be sheltered within the castle's wall, he or she would feel safe from the elements.
- Describe the mood of this painting. What details and elements contribute to the mood?
  Answer: The mood of this painting is tumultuous and ominous. Details that contribute to the mood include the crashing waves; the lightning; the looming, rocky cliffs; and the dark, billowing clouds.

34 Literary Analysis

Romanticism

- Review with students the characteristics of Romanticism listed on p. 767. Then, have students read aloud the bracketed passage on pp. 781–782.
- Ask students to respond to the Literary Analysis item on p. 782: Identify two characteristics of Romanticism in lines 256–265.
  Answer: Faust emphasizes the Romantic concern with emotion in the lines, "In the depths of sensuality/Let us now quench our glowing passions." The reference to "unpenetrated sorcery" reveals the Romantic interest in the mysterious and the exotic.

35 Background

Art

Vanitas by Edwaert Collier

Vanitas still-life paintings depict objects that function symbolically to represent fleeting earthly pleasures.

Use the following questions for discussion:

- Why is this painting an appropriate choice to accompany this selection?
  Answer: The painting depicts the vanity of knowledge, represented by the various books and the globe.
- The Latin word *vanitas* refers to the vanity of indulging in these pleasures, such as music, knowledge, and riches. How does Faust exhibit vanity in his own search for knowledge and in his dealings with Mephistopheles?
  Answer: Faust is vain in thinking he's worthy of knowing all there is to know. He also exhibits vanity by underestimating Mephistopheles and the pact they have made.

36 ▶ Critical Viewing

Answer: Because Faust is on a quest for knowledge in general, he would find all the arts and sciences—including geography (represented by the globe), music (represented by the recorder), and literature (represented by the books)—interesting.

Let us now quench our glowing passions!
And at once make ready every wonder
Of unpenetrated sorcery!
Let us cast ourselves into the torrent of time,
Into the whirl of eventfulness,
Where disappointment and success,
Pleasure and pain may chop and change
As chop and change they will and can;
It is restless action makes the man.

MEPHISTOPHELES: No limit is fixed for you, no bound;
If you'd like to nibble at everything
Or to seize upon something flying round—
Well, may you have a run for your money!
But seize your chance and don't be funny!

FAUST: I've told you, it is no question of happiness.
The most painful joy, enamored hate, enlivening
Disgust—I devote myself to all excess.
My breast, now cured of its appetite for knowledge,
From now is open to all and every smart,
And what is allotted to the whole of mankind
That will I sample in my inmost heart,
Grasping the highest and lowest with my spirit,
Piling men's weal and woe upon my neck,
To extend myself to embrace all human selves
And to founder in the end, like them, a wreck.

MEPHISTOPHELES: O believe *me*, who have been
chewing
These iron rations many a thousand year,
No human being can digest
This stuff, from the cradle to the bier[11]
This universe—believe a devil—
Was made for no one but a god!
He exists in eternal light
But *us* he has brought into the darkness
While *your* sole portion is day and night.

FAUST: I will all the same!

MEPHISTOPHELES: That's very nice.
There's only one thing I find wrong;
Time is short, art is long.
You could do with a little artistic advice.
Confederate with one of the poets
And let him flog his imagination

11. **bier** (bir) *n.* coffin and its supporting platform.

Literary Analysis
Romanticism Indentify two characteristics of Romanticism in lines 256–265.

36 ▼ Critical Viewing
What arts and sciences represented in this still life would Faust find interesting? **[Speculate]**

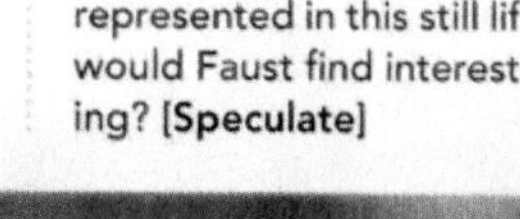
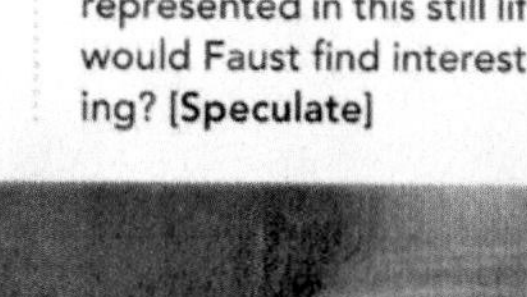

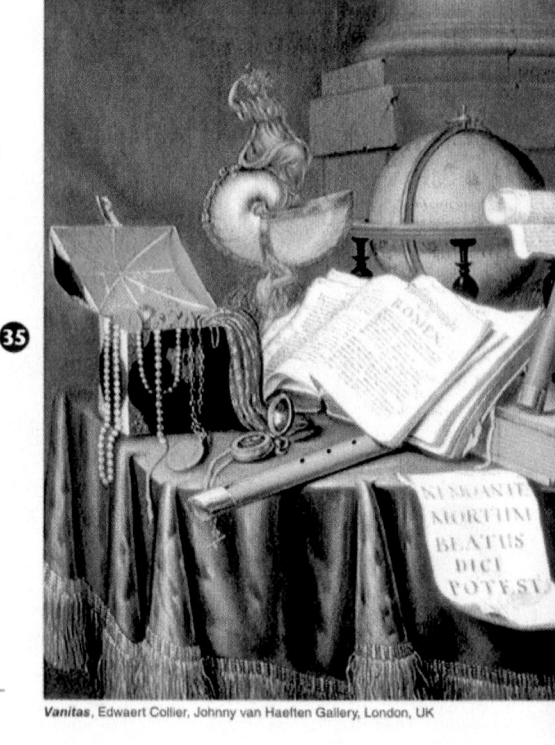

Vanitas, Edwaert Collier, Johnny van Haeften Gallery, London, UK

ENRICHMENT: Literature Connection

Common Quotations

Tell students that certain quotations recur throughout the literary works of different cultures and eras. The line "Time is short, art is long" (line 293) is an example of such a quotation. Four hundred years before Christ, Hippocrates wrote, "Art is long, life is short" (quoted in Latin as "Ars longa, vita brevis"). In the fourteenth century, Geoffrey Chaucer wrote, "The lyf so short, the craft so long to lerne." During the nineteenth century, Robert Browning wrote, "Art's long, though time is short," and Henry Wadsworth Longfellow wrote, "Art is long, and Time is fleeting."

To heap all virtues on your head,
A head with such a reputation:
Lion's bravery,
Stag's velocity,
Fire of Italy,
Northern tenacity.
Let *him* find out the secret art
Of combining craft with a noble heart
And of being in love like a young man,
Hotly, but working to a plan.
Such a person—*I'd* like to meet him;
"Mr. Microcosm"[12] is how I'd greet him.

FAUST: What am I then if fate must bar
My efforts to reach that crown of humanity
After which all my senses strive?

37 **MEPHISTOPHELES:** You are in the end . . . what you are.
You can put on full-bottomed wigs with a million locks,
You can put on stilts instead of your stocks,
You remain for ever what you are.

38 **FAUST:** I feel my endeavors have not been worth a pin
When I raked together the treasures of the human mind,
If at the end I but sit down to find
No new force welling up within.
I have not a hair's breadth more of height,
I am no nearer the Infinite.

MEPHISTOPHELES: My very good sir, you look at things
Just in the way that people do;
We must be cleverer than that
Or the joys of life will escape from you.
Hell! You have surely hands and feet,
Also a head and you-know-what;
The pleasures I gather on the wing,
Are they less mine? Of course they're not!
Suppose I can afford six stallions,
I can add that horse-power to my score
And dash along and be a proper man
As if my legs were twenty-four.
So good-bye to thinking! On your toes!
The world's before us. Quick! Here goes!
I tell you, a chap who's intellectual
Is like a beast on a blasted heath
Driven in circles by a demon
While a fine green meadow lies round beneath.

12. **Mr. Microcosm** man regarded as the epitome of the world.

tenacity (tə nas´ ə tē) *n.* persistence; stubbornness

Reading Strategy
Drawing Inferences What can you infer about Faust from line 312?

Literary Analysis
Romanticism and Legends Do you think Faust hopes to become a legendary figure? Explain.

39 **✓ Reading Check**

After all Faust's efforts to gain knowledge, what will he become in the end?

37 Reading Strategy

Drawing Inferences

- Read aloud the bracketed line. Ask students the Reading Strategy question on p. 783: What can you infer about Faust from line 312?
  Answer: Mephistopheles implies that Faust has been trying to disguise or escape his true nature and that Faust perhaps has been aiming for a goal that is higher than he is capable of attaining.

Monitor Progress Ask students what wigs and stilts have in common.
Answer: They both change a person's appearance. Guide students to see that Mephistopheles is implying that for all of Faust's striving, Faust will be unable to change himself.

- Then, ask students to explain Mephistopheles's attitude toward Faust.
  Possible response: As described in the *Prologue*, Mephistopheles believes that men are "always in flight." Mephistopheles believes that Faust is no different from other men because Faust cannot be content with his station in life.

38 Literary Analysis

Romanticism and Legends

- Read aloud the bracketed line. Have students answer the Literary Analysis question on p. 783: Do you think Faust hopes to become a legendary figure? Explain.
  Answer: Faust's yearning for a "new force welling up within," more "height," and closeness to "the infinite" indicate that he hopes to achieve more than the ordinary person and hopes to be remembered after his death.

39 ✓ Reading Check

Answer: According to Mephistopheles, Faust will become simply what he is: "You are in the end… what you are."

CUSTOMIZE INSTRUCTION FOR UNIVERSAL ACCESS

For Special Needs Students	For English Learners	For Gifted/Talented Students
Encourage students to read pages 782–783 without stopping to analyze dialogue. Then, have them reread the text more slowly, asking themselves what each character's lines reveal about his attitudes. Students may read along with the recordings on **Listening to Literature: Audiocassettes, or Audio CDs.**	Suggest that students share some of their cultural tales about the Devil or other evil figures. Students may draw pictures to illustrate characters or plot points of their tales. Encourage the rest of the class to ask questions about the tales that are shared.	Have students write a dialogue between God and Mephistopheles modeled after the interchange in the *Prologue*. Tell students to begin by deciding how they want to portray Mephistopheles. Encourage students to focus on conveying their intended impression of Mephistopheles as they write their dialogues.

ASSESS

40 Reading Strategy

Drawing Inferences

- Read aloud the bracketed passage.
- Then ask students the Reading Strategy question on p. 784: What does Mephistopheles mean by "meat and drink"?
Answer: Mephistopheles is referring not to the physical meat and drink that would nourish Faust's body, but to the "meat and drink" for Faust's spirit. This "meat and drink" would include joy, satisfaction, a feeling of accomplishment, and the things that Faust has been unable to achieve.

Answers for p. 784

Review and Assess

1. Possible response: Faust's feelings of accomplishing so little despite being an honored and respected scholar might have surprised some students.
2. **(a)** Faust is in a state of deep despair. **(b)** Possible response: Despite his learning, Faust believes he knows nothing of real value.
3. **(a)** Mephistopheles will serve Faust until the day on which Faust becomes pleased with himself. On that day, Faust will die and be given over to Mephistopheles. **(b)** Possible response: Mephistopheles has the better bargain because he will serve Faust only until Faust dies, but Faust will serve Mephistopheles for eternity.
4. **(a)** Faust uses his own blood to sign the agreement. **(b)** Faust may not believe in an afterlife or he would not sign such an agreement.
5. Possible response: Faust would be no happier in today's world because he would still be unable to answer life's ultimate questions.

FAUST: How do we start?

MEPHISTOPHELES: We just say go—and skip.
But please get ready for this pleasure trip.

[*Exit* FAUST.]

Only look down on knowledge and reason,
The highest gifts that men can prize,
Only allow the spirit of lies
To confirm you in magic and illusion,
And then I have you body and soul.
Fate has given this man a spirit
Which is always pressing onward, beyond control,
And whose mad striving overleaps
All joys of the earth between pole and pole.
Him shall I drag through the wilds of life
And through the flats of meaninglessness,
I shall make him flounder and gape and stick
And to tease his insatiableness
Hang meat and drink in the air before his watering lips;
In vain he will pray to slake his inner thirst,
And even had he not sold himself to the devil
He would be equally accursed.

40

Reading Strategy
Drawing Inferences
What does Mephistopheles mean by "meat and drink"?

insatiableness (in sā' she b'el nes) *n.* the quality of being impossible to fill

Review and Assess

Thinking About the Selection

1. **Respond:** Which of Faust's feelings in the selection, if any, surprised you? Explain.
2. **(a) Recall:** What is Faust's state of mind in the opening scene? **(b) Deduce:** What does Faust mean when he says that he has discovered "the impossibility of knowledge"?
3. **(a) Recall:** What are the terms of the agreement between Faust and Mephistopheles? **(b) Evaluate:** Which character has the better part of the bargain?
4. **(a) Recall:** What does Faust use to sign his agreement with Mephistopheles? **(b) Infer:** What can you infer about Faust's attitude regarding the afterlife from his willingness to sign the agreement?
5. **Hypothesize:** Would Faust be a more satisfied person if he were living in today's world? Explain.

ASSESSMENT PRACTICE: Reading Comprehension

Distinguish Between Fact and Nonfact (For more practice, see Test Preparation Workbook, p. 37.)

Use the sample test item to show students how to distinguish between fact and nonfact.

I am here like a fine young squire to-day, / In a suit of scarlet trimmed with gold / And a little cape of stiff brocade, / With a cock's feather in my hat / And at my side a long sharp blade, / And the most succinct advice I can give / Is that you dress up just like me, / So that uninhibited and free / You may find out what it means to live.

Which of the following is an OPINION?

A Mephistopheles is carrying a sword.
B Mephistopheles is a better dresser than Faust.
C Mephistopheles offers Faust advice.
D Mephistopheles is wearing a cape.

Choices *A, C,* and *D* are facts from the passage. Only choice *B* is a personal belief that cannot be proved. The correct answer is *B*.

Review and Assess

Literary Analysis

Romanticism

1. Use a chart like the one shown to cite passages from *Faust* that demonstrate key features of **Romanticism.**

Features of Romanticism	Passage from *Faust*
favoring emotion over reason	
favoring intuition over intellect	
favoring the subjective over the objective	
celebrating the individual	

2. (a) Identify three details from *Faust* that express the Romantics' love of the mysterious and exotic. (b) Why is this characteristic of Romantic writing particularly suitable for *Faust*?
3. In what way does the treatment of Mephistopheles reflect the idealism and optimism of the Romantics? Explain.

Connecting Literary Elements

4. Which details in *Faust* point to the fact that Goethe embellishes the truth about the real Faust and adds to the **legend** about him?
5. What does this version of *Faust* tell you about the values and beliefs of Goethe's society?

Reading Strategy

Drawing Inferences

6. By **drawing inferences** from lines 10–24 of "The First Part of the Tragedy," explain why Faust makes a pact with the Devil.
7. In lines 180–192, what crucial knowledge does Faust imply is missing in Mephistopheles?
8. What can you infer about Mephistopheles's true character from lines 343–359, lines that are spoken after Faust has exited?

Extend Understanding

9. **Cultural Connection:** In Goethe's *Faust*, the Devil offers the temptation of knowledge. (a) Do you think this offer would be valuable in all cultures? (b) What other prizes might tempt people?

Quick Review

Romanticism is a literary and artistic movement characterized by imagination, emotion, nature, individuality, and the exotic.

A **legend** is a traditional story, usually based on a hero, a saint, or a national leader.

To **draw inferences,** use a variety of clues to interpret the author's message.

Take It to the Net

PHSchool.com

Take the interactive self-test online to check your understanding of this selection.

ENRICHMENT: Further Reading

Other Works by Johann Wolfgang von Goethe

We strongly encourage you to review any selection before assigning or recommending it to students.

The Sorrows of Young Werther

Italian Journey

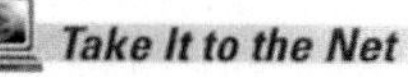

Take It to the Net

Visit PHSchool.com for more information on Johann Wolfgang von Goethe.

Answers for p. 785

Review and Assess

1. Possible response: **favoring emotion over reason:** "And this is all that I have found— / The impossibility of knowledge! / It is this that burns away my heart. ..." ("First Part of the Tragedy," lines 11–13); **favoring intuition over intellect:** "A good man with his groping intuitions / Still knows the path that is true and fit." ("Prologue in Heaven," lines 86–87); **favoring the subjective over the objective:** "How can the world dispel my doubt?" ("First Part of the Tragedy," line 54); **celebrating the individual:** "You are in the end ... what you are." ("Prologue in Heaven," line 312)
2. **(a)** References to magic, conversations in Heaven, and bargains with the devil all add to the mystery and exoticism of *Faust*. **(b)** Faust's quest is for something beyond the ordinary human experience.
3. Romantics believed that the Devil could be dealt with, bargained with, and maybe even thwarted.
4. Goethe has embellished the truth about the real Faust with details of his conversations and his bargain with the Devil.
5. Goethe's society believed in the struggle between good and evil, believed that people deserved fulfillment, and believed in the value of knowledge.
6. Faust is so weary of his present life that he is willing to wager everything.
7. Faust believes that the Devil has no appreciation for human yearning and striving.
8. Lines 343–359 reveal that Mephistopheles is cunning and evil. Despite their agreement, he plans to torment Faust for the rest of his life.
9. **(a)** Possible response: Yes; this offer would be valuable in all cultures. No; some cultures might value wealth or fame over knowledge. **(b)** Other prizes that might tempt people include material wealth, beauty,

continued

continued from right column

strength, power, family, love, admiration, and athletic ability.

Integrate Language Skills

❶ Vocabulary Development Lesson

Related Words: *prime*

The word *prime*, from a Latin root meaning "first," is the basis for many related words.

From the following list, choose the related word that best completes each sentence below. Use a dictionary to check your responses.

a. primal b. primitive c. primary d. primeval

1. She is held back by the ___ nature of the technology she uses.
2. One of our ___ instincts is the need to protect our young.
3. He lives on one hundred acres of ___ forest, untouched by an ax.
4. The doctor's ___ concern is for the health of his patients.

Concept Development: Synonyms

Match each vocabulary word on the left to the word on the right that has a similar meaning.

1. envoys	a. shackles
2. fervent	b. basic
3. primal	c. greediness
4. obstinate	d. eager
5. fetters	e. messengers
6. tenacity	f. stubborn
7. insatiableness	g. persistence

Spelling Strategy

In English, the suffix *-ity*, as used in the word *laity*, is more common than the suffix *-ety*. For each of the following words, write its noun form ending in *-ity*.

1. tenacious 2. scarce 3. possible

❷ Grammar and Style Lesson

Usage: *who* and *whom*

The words *who* and *whom* are often used incorrectly. *Who*, like *he* or *she*, is used as a subject or subject complement. *Whom*, like *him* or *her*, is used as a direct object or as an object of a preposition. Study these examples:

> "The God who dwells within my bosom . . ."
>
> "Happy is he whom death . . . Crowns with the bloody laurel . . ."

Practice Copy each item below, adding *who* or *whom* as needed. Then, identify the word's function in the phrase or sentence.

1. "*Now* ___ wants to annoy me?"
2. "The God ___ sways my every power /Is powerless with external fact."
3. "O happy is he . . . ___ after the mad and breakneck dance / He comes upon . . ."
4. "Yet I know someone ___ failed to drink / A brown juice on a certain night."
5. It is the Devil ___ Faust meets in the study.

Writing Application Write a paragraph in which you predict how this play might end. Include two sentences in which you use *who* and *whom* correctly.

WG Prentice Hall Writing and Grammar Connection: Diamond Level, Chapter 22, Section 2

EXTEND

Answers for p. 786

❶ Vocabulary Development

Related Words: *prime*

1. b
2. a
3. d
4. c

Concept Development: Synonyms

1. e
2. d
3. b
4. f
5. a
6. g
7. c

Spelling Strategy

1. tenacity
2. scarcity
3. possibility

❷ Grammar and Style

Practice

1. who
2. who
3. whom
4. who
5. whom

Writing Application

Sample sentences: I predict that Mephistopheles, with whom Faust has made a wager, will torment the scholar. As to who will win the wager, I believe Faust will keep his soul.

10TH GRADE For support in teaching the Grammar and Style Lesson to tenth graders, use **Writing and Grammar**, Platinum Level, Chapter 23, Section 2.

TEACHING RESOURCES

The following resources can be used to enrich or extend the instruction for pp. 786–787.

Vocabulary

- **Selection Support:** Build Vocabulary, p. 145
- **Vocabulary and Spelling Practice Book** (Use this booklet for skills instruction.)

Grammar

- **Selection Support:** Grammar and Style, p. 146
- **Writing and Grammar,** Diamond Level, p. 574
- **Daily Language Practice Transparencies** ■

Writing

- **Performance Assess. and Portfolio Mgmt.**, p. 32
- **Writing and Grammar,** Diamond Level, p. 21
- **Writing and Grammar iText CD-ROM** ■

Listening and Speaking

- **Performance Assess. and Portfolio Mgmt.**, p. 28

■ **BLOCK SCHEDULING:** Resources marked with this symbol provide varied instruction during 90-minute blocks.

3 Writing Lesson

Writing a Film Script

Imagine that you are a screenwriter who has been hired to create a film adaptation of Goethe's *Faust*. Think about the ways in which the original text should be expanded in preparation for filming. Your script should focus only on the parts of Goethe's poetic drama that you have read.

Prewriting Begin by imagining what the scene would look like on a movie screen. List any special effects that you would expect to see, such as lighting, sound effects, and camera angles.

Drafting Once you have a good idea of the adaptations that should be made, begin writing your screenplay. Format the script like the model below.

> **Model: Writing Stage Directions**
>
> [*Camera on Faust, deep in study. Candlelight on him and his books. Sound of knocking on door.*]
>
> **Faust:** Who's knocking? [*Camera close-up on Faust's face as he looks up.*] Come in! *Now* who wants to annoy me?
>
> **Mephistopheles:** [*Camera shot of Mephistopheles.*] It's I.
>
> Stage directions describe actions, camera angles, sound effects, lighting, and special effects.

Revising Ask a classmate to read your finished screenplay to see if your stage directions are clear. Finally, keeping your classmate's comments in mind, revise your screenplay, and prepare a final copy.

WG Prentice Hall Writing and Grammar Connection: Diamond Level, Chapter 2, Section 2

4 Extension Activities

Listening and Speaking With a partner, rehearse and present a **brief dialogue** based on the play. As you rehearse, keep the following elements consistent:

- the tone and mood of the work
- the character development
- the culture in which the dialogue is set

As you prepare your presentation, be sure to use your voice and facial expressions effectively. [Group Activity]

Research and Technology Using a video camera, make a **film** version of a segment from the play. Your short film might include unusual camera angles, sound effects, planned lighting, and other special effects.

Take It to the Net PHSchool.com

Go online for an additional research activity using the Internet.

ASSESSMENT RESOURCES

The following resources can be used to assess students' knowledge and skills.

Selection Assessment

- **Formal Assessment,** pp. 133–135
- **Open-Book Tests,** pp. 109–111
- **Test Bank Software**

Take It to the Net

Visit PHSchool.com for self-tests on selection.

Writing Rubric

- **Performance Assess. and Portfolio Mgmt.,** p. 32

Listening and Speaking Rubric

- **Performance Assess. and Portfolio Mgmt.,** p. 28

For additional diagnostics and remediation for skills covered in this grouping, use materials from the Prentice Hall Assessment System.

Lesson Support for p. 787

3 Writing Lesson

- Tell students that a film script is the written version of a film that the directors, actors, and other personnel follow as they make a film.
- Remind students that an effective film script has detailed stage directions. These directions guide the people involved in the film in how to act and deliver lines, hold the camera, and arrange and execute the lighting, sound, and other special effects.
- Adapt the Speaking: Multimedia Presentation rubric in **Performance Assessment and Portfolio Management,** p. 32, to evaluate students' work.

10TH GRADE For support in working through the Writing Lesson with tenth graders, use **Writing and Grammar**, Platinum Level, Chapter 2, Section 2.

4 Listening and Speaking

- Have partners discuss the scene or scenes from the play on which they will base their dialogue. Students should understand the scene thoroughly before they develop the dialogue.
- Remind students to pay attention to the listed elements as they rehearse.
- Allow enough time for students to rehearse with partners before their presentations.
- Adapt the Speaking: Delivering a Narrative Presentation rubric in **Performance Assessment and Portfolio Management**, p. 28, to evaluate students' work.

CUSTOMIZE INSTRUCTION
For Universal Access

To address different learning styles, use the following activities suggested in the **Extension Activities** booklet, p. 37:

- For Visual/Spatial and Verbal/Linguistic Learners, use Activity 5.
- For Logical/Mathematical Learners, use Activity 6.
- For Musical/Rhythmic and Verbal/Linguistic Learners, use Activity 7.

Lesson Objectives

1. To understand the connection between various legends about the devil
2. To compare and contrast two plays about the Faust legend

Connections

The Faust legend, in which a learned scholar sells his soul to the devil in exchange for worldly gain, is but one of the many legends of the devil that have appeared in literature. Have students reread the excerpts from Goethe's *Faust*, pp. 768–784, after they have read the excerpt from Marlowe's *The Tragical History of Doctor Faustus.* Ask students what similarities and differences they notice between the two plays.

Legends of the Devil

- Ask students to discuss whether they have ever read a story or seen a movie in which a character makes a bargain with the devil to get something he or she wants very much, such as "The Devil and Daniel Webster" by Stephen Vincent Benét. Then, guide a discussion in which students consider the similarities between these stories or movies.
- Point out to students that Marlowe's Doctor Faustus is a brilliant man with a gift for powerful and challenging speech. When he invokes the devil, however, he is out of his depth. He believes that giving up his soul will give him a godlike power to satisfy all of his wishes.
- Ask students to use what they already know about Goethe's Faust and Marlowe's Doctor Faustus to comment on the character of these two men. Are these men admirable? Are they ignorant? Are they arrogant? Possible response: The determination and chutzpah of both men are admirable. However, both men are ultimately arrogant and foolish.

CONNECTIONS
Literature Past and Present
Legends of the Devil

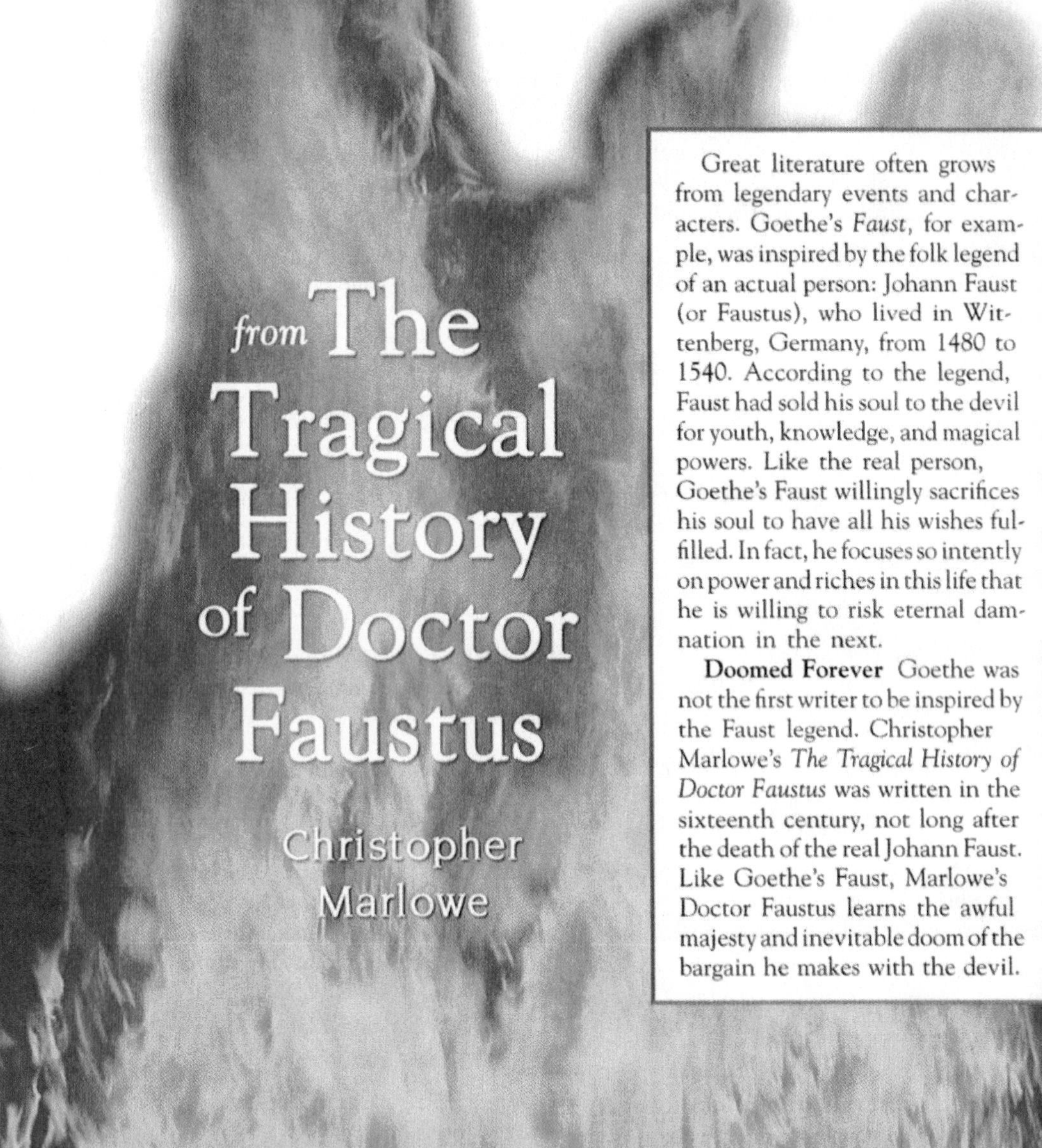

from The Tragical History of Doctor Faustus
Christopher Marlowe

Great literature often grows from legendary events and characters. Goethe's *Faust*, for example, was inspired by the folk legend of an actual person: Johann Faust (or Faustus), who lived in Wittenberg, Germany, from 1480 to 1540. According to the legend, Faust had sold his soul to the devil for youth, knowledge, and magical powers. Like the real person, Goethe's Faust willingly sacrifices his soul to have all his wishes fulfilled. In fact, he focuses so intently on power and riches in this life that he is willing to risk eternal damnation in the next.

Doomed Forever Goethe was not the first writer to be inspired by the Faust legend. Christopher Marlowe's *The Tragical History of Doctor Faustus* was written in the sixteenth century, not long after the death of the real Johann Faust. Like Goethe's Faust, Marlowe's Doctor Faustus learns the awful majesty and inevitable doom of the bargain he makes with the devil.

ENRICHMENT: Literature Connection

Marlowe's Dramas

Clifford Leech declared that Marlowe "is historically important for his achievement in stimulating the astonishingly rapid growth of drama in Elizabethan England. Before him, dramatic blank verse had been wooden: he made it triumphantly flexible. His *Tamburlaine* and his *Doctor Faustus* were the first truly tragic plays in English."

ACT I. SCENE III. IN A GROVE.

Enter FAUSTUS.

FAUSTUS: Now that the gloomy shadow of the earth,
Longing to view Orion's drizzling look,
Leaps from th' antarctic world unto the sky,
And dims the welkin[1] with her pitchy breath,
Faustus, begin thine incantations,
And try if devils will obey thy hest,
Seeing thou hast pray'd and sacrific'd to them.
Within this circle is Jehovah's name,
Forward and backward anagrammatiz'd,[2]
The breviated names of holy saints,
Figures of every adjunct to the heavens,
And characters of signs and erring stars,
By which the spirits are enforc'd to rise:
Then fear not, Faustus, but be resolute,
And try the uttermost magic can perform.—
Sint mihi dei Acherontis propitii! Valeat numen
triplex Jehovœ! Ignei, aërii, aquatani spiritus, salvete!
Orientis princeps Belzebub, inferni ardentis monarcha, et
Demogorgon, propitiamus vos, ut appareat et surgat
Mephistophilis: quid tu moraris? Per Jehovam, Gehennam,
et consecratam aquam quam nunc spargo, signumque
crucis quod nunc facio, et per vota nostra, ipse nunc surgat
nobis dicatus Mephistophilis![3]

Enter MEPHISTOPHILIS.

I charge thee to return, and change thy shape;
Thou art too ugly to attend on me:
Go, and return an old Franciscan friar;
That holy shape becomes a devil best.

Exit MEPHISTOPHILIS.

I see there's virtue[4] in my heavenly words:
Who would not be proficient in this art?
How pliant is this Mephistophilis,

Thematic Connection
Why do you think the physical appearance of Mephistophilis is important to Faustus?

1. **welkin** sky or vault of heaven.
2. **Jehovah's name . . . anagrammatiz'd** (an′ ə gram′ ə tizd) Jehovah, the holy name of God in the Old Testament, has been spelled backward and forward in a magical rite.
3. ***Sint . . . Mephistophilis*** May the gods of the underworld (Acheron) be kind to me! May the triple deity of Jehovah be gone! To the spirits of fire, air, and water, greetings. Prince of the east, Beelzebub, monarch of the fires below, and Demogorgon, we appeal to you, so that Mephistophilis may appear and rise: why do you delay? By Jehovah, hell, and the hallowed water which I now sprinkle, and the sign of the cross which I now make, and by our vows, let Mephistophilis himself now arise to serve us!
4. **virtue** power, as well as goodness.

Background

Latin

Tell students that the language used in lines 16–22 is Latin. Point out that Latin was a spoken language during the time of the Holy Roman Empire. After the fall of that empire, Latin slowly became a "dead" language, used only in certain academic and religious applications. As a medieval scholar, Faust would have been familiar with the language. His use of Latin as he addresses the gods of the underworld follows the tradition of magicians and sorcerers using mysterious-sounding words in their incantations. Such language seems to add to the solemnity of the moment.

Thematic Connection

Possible response: Doctor Faustus is concerned with all that is sensory, therefore, he wants to look upon something pleasing, or at least bearable.

CUSTOMIZE INSTRUCTION FOR UNIVERSAL ACCESS

For Special Needs Students	For Gifted/Talented Students
Students may have difficulty with Marlowe's style of language. Have partners reread the selection, helping each other decode difficult words. If necessary, partners should read the play aloud. To increase student comprehension, have students stop frequently to paraphrase sections of the play. If possible, students can also listen to a prerecorded version of the selection, stopping as necessary to paraphrase and clarify the language with a partner.	Have students create visual interpretations of this excerpt from Marlowe's play. Students should include in their artwork some kind of interpretation of both Mephistophilis and Faustus and something that indicates the setting of the play. Encourage students to think about how they will portray the characters' facial expressions and body language, as well as the theme of the selection. When students have finished their visual interpretations, ask volunteers to present and explain their work to the class.

Thematic Connection

Answer: Mephistophilis says that he cannot obey Faustus without first getting permission from Lucifer.

Legends of the Devil

- Remind students that dramatic irony results when the audience knows more than the characters and sees more in their words and actions than they do.
- Ask a volunteer to read aloud lines 35–64. Then, ask: What is ironic about this scene?
  Answer: It is ironic that Faustus believes he will gain power to do whatever he wants, when in fact, he is able to do only what the devil will allow him to do. Faustus fantasizes that he will command Mephistophilis, when really he agrees to obey Lucifer. In giving up his soul, he loses himself, becoming Lucifer's servant.

▶ Critical Viewing

Possible response: The more flamboyant and colorful clothing of Mephistophilis suggests a confident and dramatic personality, whereas the dark, somber clothing of Faustus suggests a scholarly, conservative personality. Mephistophilis's posture and visage suggest that he is composed and in control of the situation. Faustus's upraised hand and furrowed brow make him appear harried.

Full of obedience and humility!
Such is the force of magic and my spells:
Now, Faustus, thou art conjuror laureat,[5]
That canst command great Mephistophilis:
Quin regis Mephistophilis fratris imagine.[6]

Enter MEPHISTOPHILIS (*like a Franciscan friar*).

MEPHISTOPHILIS: Now, Faustus, what wouldst thou have me do?

FAUSTUS: I charge thee wait upon me whilst I live,
To do whatever Faustus shall command,
Be it to make the moon drop from her sphere,
Or the ocean to overwhelm the world.

MEPHISTOPHILIS: I am a servant to great Lucifer,
And may not follow thee without his leave:
No more than he commands must we perform.

FAUSTUS: Did not he charge thee to appear to me?

MEPHISTOPHILIS: No, I came hither of mine own accord.

FAUSTUS: Did not my conjuring speeches raise thee? speak.

MEPHISTOPHILIS: That was the cause, but yet *per accidens:*[7]
For, when we hear one rack the name of God,
Abjure[8] the Scriptures and his Savior Christ,
We fly, in hope to get his glorious soul;
Nor will we come, unless he use such means
Whereby he is in danger to be damn'd.
Therefore the shortest cut for conjuring
Is stoutly to abjure the Trinity,
And pray devoutly to the prince of Hell.

FAUSTUS: So Faustus hath
Already done; and holds this principle,
There is no chief but only Belzebub;[9]
To whom Faustus doth dedicate himself.
This word "damnation" terrifies not him,
For he confounds hell in Elysium:
His ghost be with the old philosophers![10]
But, leaving these vain trifles of men's souls,
Tell me what is that Lucifer, thy Lord?

5. **conjuror laureat** the greatest magician.
6. ***Quin . . . imagine*** Why do you not return, Mephistophilis, in the appearance of a friar?
7. ***per accidens*** by the immediate, not the ultimate, cause.
8. **abjure** (ab joor′) *v.* give up; renounce.
9. **Belzebub,** variant spelling of **Beelzebub** (bē el′ zə bub′) the chief devil, whose name means "god of flies" in Hebrew.
10. **For he . . . philosophers** He thinks that hell is really Elysium. In Greek mythology, Elysium was the dwelling place of the virtuous after death. In Dante's *Inferno,* it is a pleasant abode for righteous pagans in a special part of hell.

Thematic Connection
What reason does Mephistophilis give Faustus for not immediately obeying Faustus's commands?

Critical Viewing ▶
What can you infer about the different personalities of Faustus and Mephistophilis from their clothing and their attitudes in this painting?

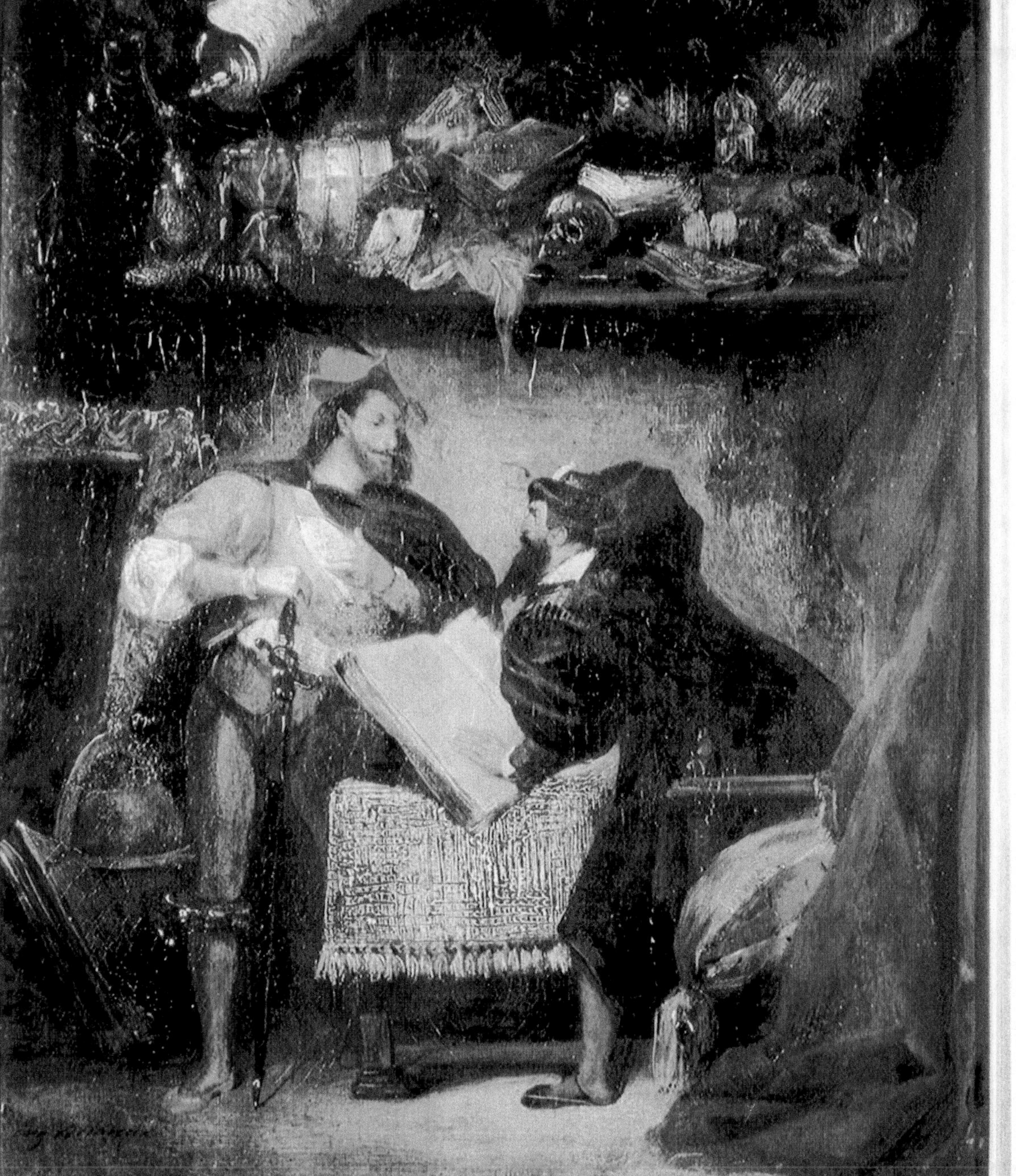

Mephistopheles Appears Before Faust, Eugène Delacroix, The Wallace Collection

Background

Art

Mephistopheles Appears Before Faust, by Eugène Delacroix

A great French Romantic painter, Delacroix (1798–1863) was inspired by literature, art, and music. This lithograph is one of seventeen he made to illustrate a French edition of Goethe's *Faust*. In making a lithograph, an artist carves an image on a flat surface such as a smooth stone or a metal plate. The surface is then inked (the image absorbs the ink and the blank area repels it) and used to print paper.

Use the following questions for discussion:

- Which elements in this scene are dramatic?
  Possible response: Faust's uplifted right hand and Mephistopheles's hand poised on his sword create drama. In addition, Delacroix's use of dark reds creates a feeling of tension and drama.
- This picture was painted more than two hundred years after Marlowe lived, and it was meant to illustrate Goethe's *Faust*. Does it go well with Marlowe's play? Explain.
  Possible response: The general mood of the painting goes with Marlowe's play, but the depiction of Mephistopheles does not. In Marlowe's play, Mephistophilis appears as a friar.

CUSTOMIZE INSTRUCTION FOR UNIVERSAL ACCESS

For Less Proficient Readers	For English Learners	For Advanced Readers
Students may have difficulty with words such as *thou, art,* and *hither.* Have students find synonyms for these words and replace the words with the synonyms. For example, students can replace *thou* with *you, art* with *are,* and *hither* with *here.*	Students may find the language in this selection difficult, especially because much of it is obsolete. Help them by defining unfamiliar or difficult words and phrases. Have students write down unfamiliar words and their definitions to create a glossary of terms to use as a reference as they read.	Have students create word webs or synonym lists based on words in this selection. For example, the word *abjure* might inspire a word web with the following words: *renounce, disown, disavow, deny, forswear, recant, retract.* Encourage students to note the connotations of each synonym.

Thematic Connection

Answer: Mephistophilis says that hell is the mental torment he feels because he is deprived of God's presence.

Legends of the Devil

- Ask students to read and paraphrase lines 83–86.
  Possible response: Mephistophilis, do you have such strong feelings because you're not in heaven? Watch me, and you'll learn to be stronger and more manly and be able to turn your back on those joys you can never have.
- Ask students to consider how these lines are similar to Faustus's speeches in lines 27–33 and in lines 36–39.
  Answer: In each speech, Faustus asserts his strength and importance.

MEPHISTOPHILIS: Arch-regent and commander of all spirits.

FAUSTUS: Was not that Lucifer an angel once?

MEPHISTOPHILIS: Yes, Faustus, and most dearly lov'd of God.

FAUSTUS: How comes it, then, that he is prince of devils?

MEPHISTOPHILIS: O, by aspiring pride and insolence;
For which God threw him from the face of heaven.

FAUSTUS: And what are you that live with Lucifer?

MEPHISTOPHILIS: Unhappy spirits that fell with Lucifer,
Conspir'd against our God with Lucifer,
And are for ever damn'd with Lucifer.

FAUSTUS: Where are you damn'd?

MEPHISTOPHILIS: In hell.

FAUSTUS: How comes it, then, that thou art out of hell?

MEPHISTOPHILIS: Why this is hell, nor am I out of it;
Think'st thou that I, who saw the face of God,
And tasted the eternal joys of heaven,
Am not tormented with ten thousand hells,
In being depriv'd of everlasting bliss?
O Faustus, leave these frivolous[11] demands,
Which strike a terror to my fainting soul!

FAUSTUS: What, is great Mephistophilis so passionate
For being deprivèd of the joys of heaven?
Learn thou of Faustus manly fortitude,
And scorn those joys thou never shalt possess.
Go bear these tidings to great Lucifer:
Seeing Faustus hath incurr'd eternal death
By desperate thoughts against Jove's deity,
Say, he surrenders up to him his soul,
So he will spare him four and twenty years,
Letting him live in all voluptuousness;[12]
Having thee ever to attend on me,
To give me whatsoever I shall ask,
To tell me whatsoever I demand,
To slay mine enemies, and aid my friends,
And always be obedient to my will.
Go and return to mighty Lucifer,
And meet me in my study at midnight,
And then resolve me of thy master's mind.

MEPHISTOPHILIS: I will, Faustus.

Thematic Connection
What is Mephistophilis's definition of hell?

11. **frivolous** (friv′ ə ləs) *adj.* of little value, trifling.
12. **voluptuousness** (və lup′ cho͞o əs nis) *n.* indulgence in sensual delights and pleasures.

ENRICHMENT: Literature Connection

Where Is Hell?

Faustus wishes to think of hell as a particular place, but the truth is worse. Marlowe portrays hell as a state of mind; it exists in the terrible absence of God's love.

In the first book of John Milton's *Paradise Lost,* Satan is portrayed as haunted by the same incompleteness that bedevils Marlowe's Faustus. Satan, adopting something like Faustus's position, boasts that the hell that surrounds him is not going to destroy his inner fortitude:

> The mind is its own place, and in itself
> Can make a heav'n of hell, a hell of heav'n.
> What matter where, if still I be the same. . . .

Later, when Satan flies to Paradise and realizes that he cannot enjoy it, he sees that what he said is true in a way he never meant. If the mind is its own "place," then there is no escape from oneself: "Which way I fly is hell; myself am hell."

Exit MEPHISTOPHILIS.

FAUSTUS: Had I as many souls as there be stars,
I'd give them all for Mephistophilis.
By him I'll be great emperor of the world,
And make a bridge thorough the moving air,
To pass the ocean with a band of men;
I'll join the hills that bind the Afric[13] shore,
And make that country continent to Spain,
And both contributory to my crown:
The Emperor shall not live but by my leave,
Nor any potentate of Germany.
Now that I have obtain'd what I desire,
I'll live in speculation of this art,[14]
Till Mephistophilis return again.

Exit FAUSTUS.

13. **Afric** African.
14. **speculation of this art** deep study of this art.

Christopher Marlowe

(1564–1593)

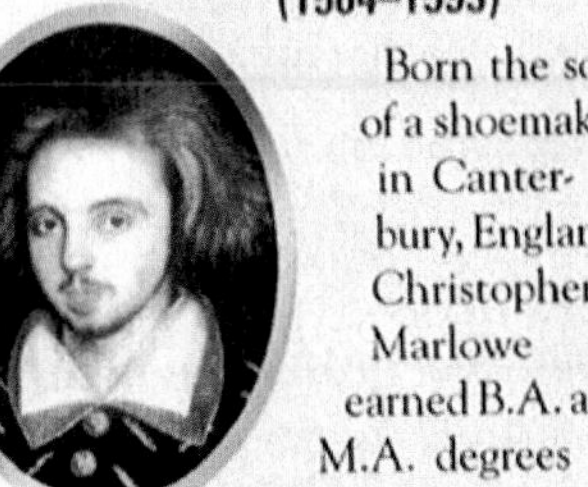

Born the son of a shoemaker in Canterbury, England, Christopher Marlowe earned B.A. and M.A. degrees from Cambridge University and later moved to London, where he wrote a series of plays. Marlowe was unorthodox in his opinions and his life. His plays treat controversial topics, and he had a reputation for heretical opinions. In 1593, he was brought before a government council on charges of speaking against the doctrines of the Church of England. Before the case was resolved, however, he was killed in a tavern brawl.

Connecting Literature Past and Present

1. What universal human temptations are at the heart of both *Faust* and *The Tragical History of Doctor Faustus*?
2. (a) In what ways is Faustus in *The Tragical History of Doctor Faustus* like Faust in Goethe's *Faust*? (b) In what ways are these two characters different?
3. Which of these two characters do you find more sympathetic? Explain.

Background

Christopher Marlowe

Marlowe's murder in a tavern brawl is still a disturbing case, more than three hundred years later. Marlowe had just been arrested by the Privy Council (a government body) and then, somewhat suspiciously, released. On the day he was killed, May 30, 1593, he had been drinking in a tavern with three dubious characters. Two of these companions were known spies and plotters. The third man claimed that he killed Marlowe in self-defense when Marlowe drew a knife.

Was Marlowe killed by agents of the Privy Council? This august body may have believed that as a former spy, Marlowe knew too much about them. Or was he killed by friends who feared that, under torture, he would implicate them in seditious plots? This fear was not unrealistic. The dramatist Thomas Kyd had just been tortured and had accused his friend Marlowe of treason.

Answers

Connecting Literature Past and Present

1. The universal human temptations that are at the heart of both *Faust* and *The Tragical History of Doctor Faustus* include the desire to be powerful, respected, and wealthy; and the opportunity and ability to live according to one's deepest wishes.
2. **(a)** Faustus in *The Tragical History of Doctor Faustus* is like Faust in Goethe's *Faust* in that he is willing to give up his soul in exchange for temporal rewards. **(b)** The two characters are different in that Doctor Faustus is interested in power and sensual pleasure, whereas Faust is obsessed with his quest for knowledge.
3. Possible response: Faust is more sympathetic because his desire for knowledge is more admirable than Doctor Faustus's desire for sensual pleasures.

I Have Visited Again • The Lorelei • The Lotus Flower

Lesson Objectives

1. **To analyze and respond to literary elements**
   - Literary Analysis: Lyric Poetry
   - Comparing Literary Works: Symbols
2. **To read, comprehend, analyze, and critique poetry**
   - Reading Strategy: Reading Between the Lines
   - Reading Check Questions
   - Review and Assess Questions
   - Assessment Practice (ATE)
3. **To develop word analysis skills, fluency, and systematic vocabulary**
   - Vocabulary Development Lesson: Anglo-Saxon Suffix *-less*
4. **To understand and apply written and oral language conventions**
   - Spelling Strategy
   - Grammar and Style Lesson: Pronouns and Antecedents
5. **To understand and apply appropriate writing and research strategies**
   - Writing Lesson: Analytical Essay
   - Extension Activity: Museum Exhibit on Sirens
6. **To understand and apply listening and speaking strategies**
   - Extension Activity: Oral Interpretive Reading

STEP-BY-STEP TEACHING GUIDE	PACING GUIDE
PRETEACH	
Motivate Students and Provide Background	
Use the Motivation activity (ATE p. 794)	5 min.
Read and discuss author and background features (SE p. 794, 796, 799; ATE p. 794) [A]	5 min.
Introduce the Concepts	
Introduce the Literary Analysis and Reading Strategy concepts (SE/ATE p. 795) [A]	15 min.
Pronounce the vocabulary words and read their definitions (SE p. 795)	5 min.
TEACH	
Monitor Comprehension	
Informally monitor comprehension by circulating while students read independently or in groups [A]	20 min.
Monitor students' comprehension with the Reading Check note (SE/ATE p. 797)	as students read
Develop vocabulary with the Vocabulary notes (SE pp. 796, 797, 798, 800; ATE p. 797)	as students read
Develop Understanding	
Develop students' understanding of lyric poetry with the Literary Analysis annotations (SE/ATE pp. 796, 799) [A]	5 min.
Develop students' ability to read between the lines, using the Reading Strategy annotations (SE/ATE pp. 797, 800)	5 min.
ASSESS	
Assess Mastery	
Assess students' mastery of the Reading Strategy and Literary Analysis concepts by having them answer the Review and Assess questions (SE/ATE p. 801)	15 min.
Use one or more of the print, software, or transparency Assessment Resources (ATE p. 803) [A]	up to 45 min.
EXTEND	
Apply Understanding	
Have students complete the Vocabulary Development Lesson and the Grammar and Style Lesson (SE p. 802) [A]	20 min.
Apply students' ability to clarify meaning, using the Writing Lesson (SE/ATE p. 803) [A]	45 min.
Apply students' understanding of the selections, using one or more of the Extension Activities (SE p. 803)	20–90 min.

[A] ACCELERATED INSTRUCTION: Use the strategies and activities identified with an [A].

10TH GRADE TEACHING TENTH-GRADE STUDENTS
For support in teaching the selection(s) to tenth-grade students, see the Step-by-Step Teaching notes identified with the icon shown here.

UNIVERSAL ACCESS
● = Below-Level Students
▲ = On-Level Students
■ = Above-Level Students

Time and Resource Manager

Reading Level: Average, Average, Average
Average Number of Instructional Days: 3

RESOURCES		
PRINT	**TRANSPARENCIES**	**TECHNOLOGY**
• **Beyond Literature,** Cross Curricular Connection: Music, p. 38 ▲ ■		
• **Selection Support Workbook:** ● ▲ ■ Literary Analysis, p. 152 Reading Strategy, p. 151 Build Vocabulary, p. 149	• **Literary Analysis and Reading Transparencies,** pp. 75 and 76 ● ▲ ■	
		• **Listening to Literature** ● ▲ ■ Audiocassettes Audio CDs
• **Literary Analysis for Enrichment,** p. 38 ■		
• **Formal Assessment:** Selection Test, pp. 136–138 ● ▲ ■ • **Open-Book Tests,** pp. 112–114 ● ▲ ■ • **Performance Assessment and Portfolio Management,** pp. 16, 32 ● ▲ ■ • Prentice Hall Assessment System ● ▲ ■	• Prentice Hall Assessment System ● ▲ ■ **Skills Practice Answers and Explanations on Transparencies**	• **Test Bank Software** ● ▲ ■
• **Selection Support Workbook:** ● ▲ ■ Grammar and Style, p. 150 • **Writing and Grammar,** Diamond Level ● ▲ ■ • **Extension Activities,** p. 38 ● ▲ ■	• **Daily Language Practice Transparencies** ● ▲	• **Writing and Grammar iText CD-ROM** ● ▲ ■ *Take It to the Net* PHSchool.com

BLOCK SCHEDULING: Use one 90-minute class period to preteach the selection(s) and have students read them. Use a second 90-minute class period to assess students' mastery of skills and have them complete one of the Extension Activities.

PRETEACH

Step-by-Step Teaching Guide for pp. 794–795

Motivation

Tell students that today's pop songs have their roots in lyric poetry, and enumerate the fundamental similarities between pop songs and early lyric poems: Both are verbal expressions of personal thoughts and feelings, and both are accompanied by music. Pop songs are often written out of romantic love for another person or as a tribute to a person or a place. Similarly, these poems by Pushkin and Heine express emotions directed toward people and places.

❶ Background

More About the Authors

Alexander Pushkin's experiences in exile may seem curious to modern students. For three years, he lived in the city of Kishinev, near the Romanian border, under the supervision of a kindly general. When he was transferred to a post in Odessa, he paid too much attention to his new superior's wife. He was then exiled to his own home, the family estate near Pskov. Pushkin's father was supposed to act as his supervisor this time, but the two quarreled so much that his father moved away, taking the rest of the family with him.

Throughout his life, Heinrich Heine felt like an outsider. According to the critic S. S. Prawer, Heine considered himself "a Jew among Germans, a German among Frenchmen, a Hellene [one loyal to classical Greek ideals] among Jews, a rebel among the bourgeois, and a conservative among revolutionaries."

Geography Note

Draw students' attention to the map on this page. Remind them that geography helped define Pushkin and Heine as outsiders. Born in the urban center of Moscow, Russia, Pushkin was exiled to the provinces. Heine, born in Düsseldorf, Germany, was also banished for political reasons and lived as a German exile in Paris, France.

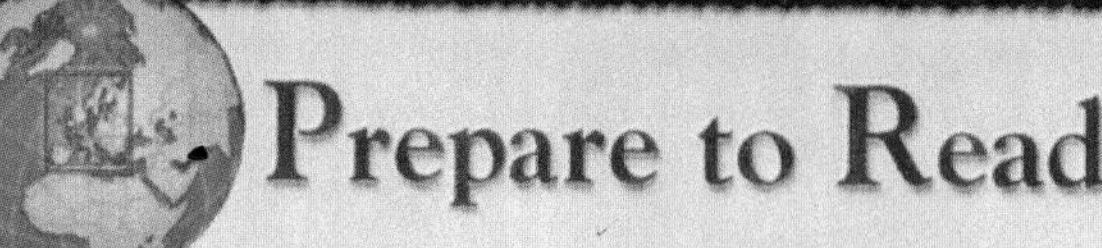

Prepare to Read

❶ I Have Visited Again ◆ The Lorelei ◆ The Lotus Flower

Alexander Pushkin (1799–1837)

Russian author Alexander Pushkin was born in Moscow into an aristocratic family. As a youth, he led a life of relative privilege and wrote with a skill that would hint at his eventual fame. While working in government service in St. Petersburg, he aroused suspicion by associating with political rebels and writing poems advocating government changes. In 1820, the government acted upon its suspicions by reappointing Pushkin to a post in a remote province in southern Russia. During the five years Pushkin spent there, he enhanced his reputation as a writer and began working on his masterpiece, the verse novel *Yevgeny Onegin* (1833). Unfortunately, his unrestrained and sometimes violent behavior resulted in his dismissal from civil service in 1824 and banishment to his family's estate.

Though isolated and unhappy on the estate, Pushkin channeled most of his energy into his writing. He spent much of his time interacting with the peasants who lived on the estate, learning about their lifestyles and incorporating their legends and folklore into a number of his finest poems.

Acts of Rebellion Pushkin was allowed to return to Moscow in 1826. Yet again, he became the object of political distrust and was eventually put under police surveillance. Despite limited freedoms, Pushkin produced some of his finest works during this time, including his collection of prose tales *Tales of the Late I.P. Belkin* (1830).

After marrying Natalya Goncharova in 1831, Pushkin grudgingly returned to government service. In a final act of rebellion, Pushkin entered into a duel that cost him his life. Despite the pointless ending of his brief life, Pushkin is now regarded as the finest poet Russia has ever produced.

Heinrich Heine (1797–1856)

German poet Heinrich Heine [hin′ rik hī′ nə] wrote brilliant love poems that have been set to music by various composers. Yet he was also a gifted satirist and political writer, and his fierce attacks on repression and prejudice made him a highly controversial figure.

Born and raised in Düsseldorf, Heine earned a law degree in 1825 but abandoned it to pursue a career as a writer. In 1827, he gained prominence as a poet with *The Book of Songs* (1827), a collection regarded by many as his finest work. Influenced by the Romantic poets, these love poems were inspired by Heine's unrequited attachment to his cousin, Amalie.

A Controversial Poet Heine moved to Paris in 1831, and from this vantage point he wrote scathing criticisms of the political and social situation in Germany. After publishing his views in *The Romantic School* (1833–1835) and "On the History of Religion and Philosophy in Germany" (1834–1835), his popularity was soon overshadowed by outrage. The German government banned all his books and made it clear that he was no longer welcome in his homeland.

Even after his death in 1856, Heine remained controversial. Riots broke out in several German cities when attempts were made to erect monuments in his honor, and when the Nazis assumed power in the 1930s, many of his works were suppressed. After World War II, Heine became a controversial figure in other countries, including the United States, because his political beliefs resembled Marxism. Despite such controversy, Heine is still generally regarded as one of the finest writers of the nineteenth century.

TEACHING RESOURCES

The following resources can be used to enrich or extend the instruction for pp. 794–795.

Background

Beyond Literature, p. 38

Take It to the Net

Visit PHSchool.com for background on the authors.

Literary Analysis

Literary Analysis and Reading Transparencies, Lyric Poetry, p. 75

Reading

Literary Analysis and Reading Transparencies, Reading Between the Lines, p. 76

Selection Support: Reading Strategy, p. 151; Build Vocabulary, p. 149

BLOCK SCHEDULING: Resources marked with this symbol provide varied instruction during 90-minute blocks.

Preview

Connecting to the Literature

Elements of nature, such as trees, rivers, flowers, and the night sky, often have an emotional effect on us. As you read, think about how you would feel if you were standing with the speaker, looking at the same sights.

2 Literary Analysis

Lyric Poetry

Lyric poetry, or lyrics, are brief poems that express a speaker's personal thoughts and feelings. Many early lyrics were written to be sung to the accompaniment of a lyre, which looks much like a small, modern-day harp. Most of these poems still tend to be melodic, like songs, and generally focus on producing a single, unified effect. In these lines from "The Lotus Flower," notice the melancholy effect of the words.

> With sunken head and sadly
> She dreamily waits for the night.

As you read these poems, use a chart like the one shown to record the words and phrases that contribute to a single unifying effect.

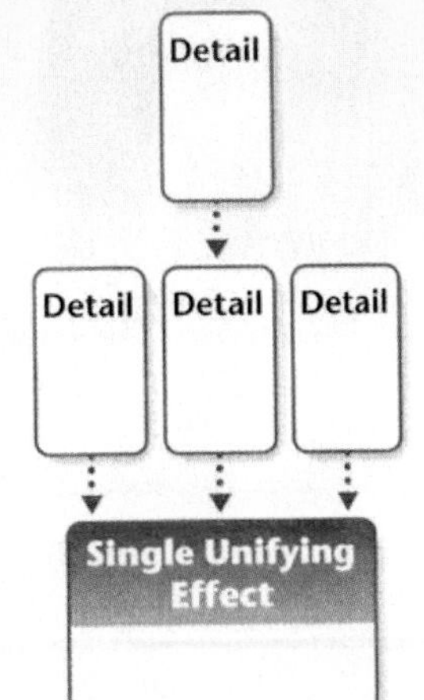

Comparing Literary Works

Each of these poems uses **symbols** to achieve a desired effect. A symbol is a person, place, or object that has its own meaning but also suggests a larger or secondary meaning. For example, in "I Have Visited Again," the growing trees symbolize the passing of time and inspire the speaker to reflect on his mortality. As you read, compare the way each speaker uses symbols to express observations and emotions.

3 Reading Strategy

Reading Between the Lines

Reading between the lines reveals different or deeper meanings in poems, meanings that clarify a speaker's words, a character's actions, and even a poem's relevance to readers of all backgrounds. To read between the lines:

- Make inferences, or educated guesses, about the meanings of whole lines or passages.
- Find clues about the characters, setting, mood, and symbolism.
- Examine specific word choices, including words in the title.

Vocabulary Development

painstakingly (pānz′ tāk iŋ lē) *adv.* using great diligence or care (p. 796)

fathomless (fath′ əm les) *adj.* immeasurably deep (p. 797)

ancestral (an ses′ trəl) *adj.* inherited, as from an ancestor (p. 797)

morose (mə rōs′) *adj.* gloomy; in a bad or sullen mood (p. 798)

resplendent (ri splen′ dənt) *adj.* brightly shining; dazzling (p. 800)

mutely (myoot′ lē) *adv.* silently; without the capacity to speak (p. 800)

2 Literary Analysis

Lyric Poetry

- Read the definition of lyric poetry together with the class. If students have difficulty with the definition, point out that the term as it is used today is very broad. Almost any poem that is fairly short and is not a narrative or an exercise in wit, such as a limerick, can be classified as a lyric. Have students keep this broad definition in mind as they name lyric poems they have read in previous literature courses.
- After discussing the Literary Analysis instruction, have students preview the selections for words that evoke emotion, such as *embrace*, *scarred*, and *trembles*. Then, explain the use of the graphic organizer on p. 795. As students read the poems, have them use the graphic organizer to identify words and phrases that create a single, unifying effect.
- Use the Lyric Poetry transparency in **Literary Analysis and Reading Transparencies,** p. 75, to demonstrate for students how they can recognize the elements of lyric poetry.

3 Reading Strategy

Reading Between the Lines

- Tell students that reading a poem can be like solving a mystery. Few poets simply state outright what they want the reader to know. Instead, they give the reader details about characters, setting, and mood. When a reader puts these details together, he or she is able to read between the lines and discover the poem's deeper meaning.
- Tell students to focus on specific words, lines, and passages that reveal the poems' deeper meanings.

Vocabulary Development

- Pronounce each vocabulary word for students, and read the definitions as a class. Have students identify any words with which they are already familiar.

CUSTOMIZE INSTRUCTION FOR UNIVERSAL ACCESS

For Less Proficient Readers	For English Learners	For Advanced Readers
Make the language and style of Pushkin and Heine more accessible and less intimidating by previewing with students the vocabulary and footnotes. This activity will allow students to concentrate on the tone and imagery of the selections as they read.	As students read, encourage them to mark unfamiliar or challenging passages with self-sticking notes. They may want to meet with partners after each page to discuss these passages or meet after finishing the poems to share their strategies for determining the meaning of these passages.	Invite students to serve as classroom role models, reading the poems aloud with expression. Have them comment on the differences between reading rhymed and unrhymed verse. Allow time for students to read the poetry aloud on their own before reading for the class.

E-Teach

Visit e-Teach at PHSchool.com for teachers' essays on how to teach, with questions and answers.

TEACH

Step-by-Step Teaching Guide for pp. 796–800

Teaching Tenth-Grade Students

10TH GRADE Invite tenth-grade students to share their experiences of leaving a familiar place, such as moving to a new city or changing schools. Ask them to imagine how it would feel to revisit a place where they had spent some time in the past. How might the place have changed? How might they react to the changes?

❶ About the Selection

In "I Have Visited Again," the speaker recounts his return to his family home after being away for ten years. As he remembers people and events from the past, he compares his memories to the current appearance of the land.

❷ Background

Russian Writers

Critic Edmund Wilson called Pushkin the "great fountainhead of Russian literature," the writer from whom Turgenev, Chekhov, Tolstoy, Dostoevsky "in more or less degree derive."

❸ Literary Analysis

Lyric Poetry

- As students read the bracketed passage, have them consider what the speaker is saying about the passage of time.
  Answer: The speaker is saying that the changes that occurred during the last ten years seem immaterial now that he has returned home.
- Ask students to respond to the Literary Analysis item on p. 796: Explain how Pushkin achieves a single, unifying effect in this stanza.
  Answer: Pushkin refers to the passage of time repeatedly in such phrases as "two / Unnoticed, exiled years," "Ten years have passed," and "only yesterday."

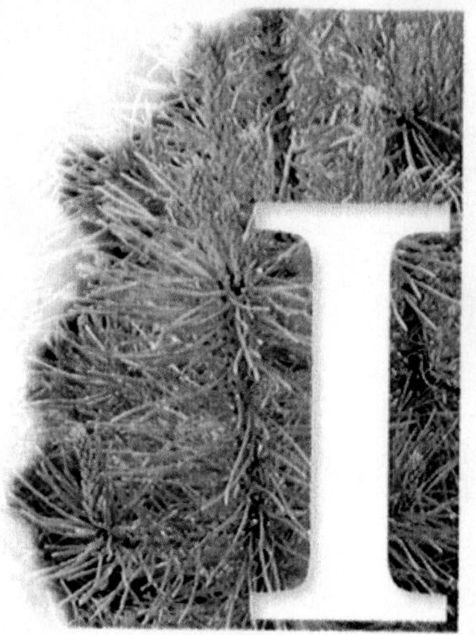

I Have Visited Again

Alexander Pushkin
***translated by* D.M. Thomas**

Background

Initially, Alexander Pushkin found the inspiration to write in the politics of his homeland. His rebellious writings, as well as his unruly behavior, resulted in banishment to his family estate. Such a personality seems distantly related to the speaker of the gentle words and images in "I Have Visited Again." In this poem, the speaker revisits the estate to find that time and nature have hardly stood still in the intervening years.

❸

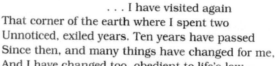

. . . I have visited again
That corner of the earth where I spent two
Unnoticed, exiled years. Ten years have passed
Since then, and many things have changed for me,
And I have changed too, obedient to life's law—
But now that I am here again, the past
Has flown out eagerly to embrace me, claim me,
And it seems that only yesterday I wandered
Within these groves.

Here is the cottage, sadly
Declined now, where I lived with my poor old nurse.
She is no more. No more behind the wall
Do I hear her heavy footsteps as she moved
Slowly, painstakingly about her tasks.

Literary Analysis
Lyric Poetry Explain how Pushkin achieves a single, unifying effect in this stanza.

painstakingly (pānz′ tāk iŋ lē) *adv.* using great diligence or care

TEACHING RESOURCES

The following resources can be used to enrich or extend the instruction for pages 796–800.

Literary Analysis

- **Selection Support:** Literary Analysis, p. 152
- **Literary Analysis and Reading Transparencies,** Lyric Poetry, p. 75 ■

Reading

- **Selection Support:** Reading Strategy, p. 151; Build Vocabulary, p. 149

- **Listening to Literature Audiocassettes**
- **Listening to Literature Audio CDs** ■

■ **BLOCK SCHEDULING:** Resources marked with this symbol provide varied instruction during 90-minute blocks.

Here are the wooded slopes where often I
Sat motionless, and looked down at the lake,
Recalling other shores and other waves . . .
4 It gleams between golden cornfields and green meadows,
A wide expanse; across its fathomless waters
A fisherman passes, dragging an ancient net.
Along the shelving banks, hamlets are scattered
—Behind them the mill, so crooked it can scarcely
5 Make its sails turn in the wind . . .
On the bounds
Of my ancestral acres, at the spot
Where a road, scarred by many rainfalls, climbs
The hill, three pine-trees stand—one by itself,
The others close together. When I rode
On horseback past them in the moonlit night,
The friendly rustling murmur of their crowns
Would welcome me. Now, I have ridden out
Upon that road, and seen those trees again.

fathomless (fath′ əm les) *adj.* immeasurably deep

ancestral (an ses′ trəl) *adj.* inherited, as from an ancestor

Reading Strategy Reading Between the Lines By using words like *ancient, ancestral,* and *many rainfalls* in lines 19–24, what does the speaker suggest about the land and the people who live there?

6 **✓Reading Check**

In what ways has the estate changed since the speaker last visited it?

8 **▼Critical Viewing** Which details in this landscape could serve to illustrate Pushkin's poem? **[Support]**

Lake Scene in France, Josephine Bowes, The Bowes Museum, Barnard Castle, County Durham, UK

7

CUSTOMIZE INSTRUCTION FOR UNIVERSAL ACCESS

For Special Needs Students	For Gifted/Talented Students
Tell students that in "I Have Visited Again," Pushkin uses *personification,* a type of figurative language in which a nonhuman subject is given human characteristics. Work with students to identify examples of personification in the poem, such as "the past has flown out eagerly to embrace me" (lines 6–7) and "friendly rustling murmur" (line 28).	Challenge students to identify examples of personification in Pushkin's poem and discuss the purpose or effect of this figurative language. Then, have students write their own examples of figurative language in which they personify a landscape and incorporate them into original poems. Have a poetry reading in which students present their poems to the class.

4 Vocabulary Development

Anglo-Saxon Suffix *-less*

- Draw students' attention to the word *fathomless* and its definition on p. 797.
- Tell students that the suffix *-less* means "without," "not able to," or "not able to be."
- Ask students to suggest and define words containing this suffix. Possible response: *Restless, friendless,* or *needless* are possible suggestions.

5 Reading Strategy

Reading Between the Lines

- Read aloud the bracketed passage.
- Ask students the Reading Strategy question on p. 797: By using words like *ancient, ancestral,* and *many rainfalls* in lines 19–24, what does the speaker suggest about the land and the people who live there? Answer: The speaker suggests that the land is weather-beaten and that people have occupied and depended on it for a long time.

6 ✓Reading Check

Answer: The cottage has become dilapidated; the nurse is no longer alive.

7 Background

Art

Lake Scene in France, by Josephine Bowes

Josephine Bowes (1825–1874) was a French painter and actress. She and her husband, businessman John Bowes, created the Bowes Museum—a public gallery featuring European fine and decorative arts.

Use the following question for discussion:
Would this painting cause the speaker to feel nostalgic for his family's estate? Why or why not?
Possible response: The details captured in the painting, such as the cottage, might cause the speaker to feel nostalgic.

8 ▶Critical Viewing

Answer: The cottage, the wooded hillsides, the view of the lake, and the trees in the foreground illustrate the poem.

Critical Thinking

Apply

- Read aloud the bracketed line.
- Ask: To what universal human desire does the poem's final line appeal?
  Possible response: The poem's final line appeals to the desire to be remembered after death.

Answers for p. 798

Review and Assess

1. Possible response: The poem conveys feelings of melancholy with its use of words such as *declined, painstakingly, crooked, scarred, solitary,* and *morose.* Or the poem may create a feeling of hope with words such as *eagerly, embrace, golden, green, friendly, welcome, children, lively, gay,* and *pleasant.*
2. **(a)** Four familiar landmarks that have changed are the cottage, the mill, the road, and the old trees. **(b)** The speaker, like these landmarks, has aged.
3. **(a)** The speaker would sit on the slopes and think of "other shores and other waves." **(b)** By "other shores," the speaker means other places he has visited. **(c)** Possible response: The speaker might have yearned to be in another place because the estate, as the location of his exile, was a place of isolation.
4. **(a)** The "unknown tribe of pine-trees" grows around the aging roots of the older pine trees. **(b)** In the future, the new pines will shield the older trees "from the gaze / Of passers-by." These young trees may also provide someone comfort, as the older trees have provided the speaker comfort. **(c)** The new pines symbolize the continuity of life.
5. Possible response: Most readers will probably agree with Thomas Wolfe's comment. Often when people do return home, they are made instantly aware of how both they and the environments have changed.

They have remained the same, make the same murmur—
But round their ageing roots, where all before
Was barren, naked, a thicket of young pines
Has sprouted; like green children round the shadows
Of the two neighbouring pines. But in the distance
Their solitary comrade stands, morose,
Like some old bachelor, and round its roots
All is barren as before.

I greet you, young
And unknown tribe of pine-trees! I'll not see
Your mighty upward thrust of years to come
When you will overtop these friends of mine
And shield their ancient summits from the gaze
Of passers-by. But may my grandson hear
Your welcome murmur when, returning home
From lively company, and filled with gay
And pleasant thoughts, he passes you in the night,

And thinks perhaps of me . . .

morose (mə rōs′) *adj.* gloomy; in a bad or sullen mood

Review and Assess

Thinking About the Selection

1. **Respond:** What single effect does the entire poem convey to you? Identify words that Pushkin used to evoke this feeling.
2. (a) **Recall:** Identify four familiar landmarks in the poem that have changed over the years. **(b) Infer:** How has the speaker changed in a similar fashion?
3. (a) **Recall:** In stanza three, what thoughts occupied the speaker while he looked down at the lake? **(b) Infer:** What does the speaker mean by "other shores"? **(c) Hypothesize:** Why might the speaker have yearned to be in another place?
4. (a) **Recall:** Where does the "unknown tribe of pine-trees" grow? (b) **Speculate:** What role will those pines play in the future? (c) **Interpret:** What do those pines symbolize?
5. **Apply:** Novelist Thomas Wolfe commented on how our lives change by saying that we "can't go home again," a theme shared by "I Have Visited Again." Do you agree or disagree with such a claim? Explain your answer.

ENRICHMENT: Music Connection

Pushkin and Mozart

The distinguished American critic Edmund Wilson wrote: "The Russians are in the habit of comparing Pushkin with Mozart, and this is perhaps the nearest one can come to a simple comparison. Pushkin does, through both his career and his qualities, somewhat recall Mozart: He is able to express through an art that is felicitous and formal a feeling that is passionate and exquisite; he has a wide range of moods and emotions, yet he handles them all with precision...."

The Lorelei
Heinrich Heine
translated by Aaron Kramer
10

Background

The lorelei is a legendary sea nymph whose irresistible singing from the rocks in the Rhine River lured unsuspecting sailors to shipwrecks. Both this poem and "The Lotus Flower" seem to be inspired by Heine's deep attachment to his cousin Amalie. Fearing her father's reaction, Amalie did not return Heine's affection. While lyric poetry often explores the joys of love, "The Lorelei" and "The Lotus Flower" focus on love's difficulties.

I cannot explain the sadness
That's fallen on my breast.
An old, old fable haunts me,
And will not let me rest.

The air grows cool in the twilight,
And softly the Rhine[1] flows on;
The peak of a mountain sparkles
Beneath the setting sun.

More lovely than a vision,
A girl sits high up there;
Her golden jewelry glistens,
She combs her golden hair.

11

With a comb of gold she combs it,
And sings an evensong;
The wonderful melody reaches
A boat, as it sails along.

The boatman hears, with an anguish
More wild than was ever known;
He's blind to the rocks around him;
His eyes are for her alone.

—At last the waves devoured
The boat, and the boatman's cry;
And this she did with her singing,
The golden Lorelei.

Literary Analysis
Lyric Poetry Which words convey strong emotions in the poem?

1. **Rhine** (rīn) river in western Europe.

10 About the Selection

The speaker in "The Lorelei" is sad and haunted by the old fable of the lorelei. In the fable, the lorelei, a lovely girl sitting high up on a mountain over the Rhine River, combs her golden hair and sings. A boat sails by, and the boatman hears her song. Filled with wild anguish, he does not see the rocks around him. His boat, overcome by the waves, sinks, and the boatman drowns.

11 Literary Analysis

Lyric Poetry

- Have a volunteer read the poem to the class. Then, ask students to comment on the emotions this poem evokes from them.
  Possible response: The second stanza evokes a sense of contentment with the beauty of the scene, and the third and fourth stanzas evoke the emotions of joy and wonder at the beauty of the lorelei. Finally, the poem as a whole evokes emotions of anguish and sadness at the fate of the boatman.
- Ask students the Literary Analysis question on p. 799: Which words convey strong emotions in the poem?
  Possible response: The words *sadness, haunts, lovely, wonderful, anguish, wild, blind,* and *cry* convey strong emotions.

Monitor Progress Have students complete for this poem a graphic organizer like the one on p. 795.

Reteach If students are having difficulty with lyric poetry, have them use the Lyric Poetry transparency in **Literary Analysis and Reading Transparencies,** p. 75.

CUSTOMIZE INSTRUCTION FOR UNIVERSAL ACCESS

For Special Needs Students	For English Learners	For Advanced Readers
To emphasize the reason the boatman is unable to resist the lorelei, have students identify the images in the poem that convey her physical appeal. Then, have students use this description to draw their own pictures of the lorelei. Students can share their drawings with the class.	The lorelei character may be similar to characters in stories from students' own cultures. Ask students to share myths or fables from their cultures that feature such characters. Then, organize students into pairs. Ask each pair to illustrate one of the fable's settings, characters, or events on a storyboard.	After students have read Heine's poem, have them research other mythical characters who are similar to the lorelei, such as the three sirens from Greek mythology. Then, challenge each student to create his or her own myth, depicting a character or creature who lures someone to a tragic end.

ASSESS

12 About the Selection

The lotus flower is bothered by the light of the sun, so she waits for the night. When the "moon appears as her wooer," the lotus flower wakes and opens up to him. As the lotus flower gazes at the moon, she cries and "trembles with love and the sorrows of love."

13 Reading Strategy

Reading Between the Lines

- Read aloud the first stanza.
- Ask the Reading Strategy question on p. 800: What kind of person does Heine describe as "the sun"?
  Answer: The sun has "resplendent light," so the sun may represent an outgoing, joyous personality.

Answers for p. 800

Review and Assess

1. Possible response: The lorelei is beautiful, with golden jewelry, golden hair, a golden comb, and a lovely singing voice. The lorelei's beauty, voice, and unattainable quality are alluring and haunting.
2. **(a)** The boatman is drawn to the lorelei so strongly that he becomes agitated. **(b)** Heine believed that his uncle's daughter lured him as the lorelei lured sailors; like the lorelei, she was unattainable.
3. **(a)** The words *troubled, sunken head, sadly, dreamily waits, wakes, kindly uncovers, sweetly flowering face, mutely, gazes, weeps, exhales,* and *trembles* give human traits to the lotus flower; the words *wooer* and *fond embrace* give human traits to the moon. **(b)** The moon might symbolize a secret lover. **(c)** Possible response: On a symbolic level, the lotus flower sees her wooer only at night because the moon might represent a forbidden love.
4. **(a)** The speaker links the ideas of love and sorrow. **(b)** The speaker is referring to the pain of unrequited or forbidden love.
5. Possible response: The legend could apply to any situation in which a person feels a strong desire that turns out to be his or her ruin.

12

The Lotus Flower

Heinrich Heine

translated by Edgar Alfred Bowring

13

The lotus flower is troubled
At the sun's resplendent light;
With sunken head and sadly
She dreamily waits for the night.

The moon appears as her wooer,
She wakes at his fond embrace;
For him she kindly uncovers
Her sweetly flowering face.

She blooms and glows and glistens,
And mutely gazes above;
She weeps and exhales and trembles
With love and the sorrows of love.

resplendent (ri splen′ dənt) *adj.* brightly shining; dazzling

Reading Strategy
Reading Between the Lines What kind of person does Heine describe as "the sun"?

mutely (myoot′ lē) *adv.* silently; without capacity to speak

Review and Assess

Thinking About the Selections

1. **Respond:** How do you envision the lorelei in Heine's "The Lorelei"? Explain. What is it about this vision that would seem so alluring and haunting to the boatman?
2. **(a) Recall:** What effect does the lorelei have on the boatman? **(b) Interpret:** What similarities do you see between the legend of the lorelei and Heine's situation with his uncle's daughter?
3. **(a) Recall:** What words does the speaker use in "The Lotus Flower" to give human traits to both the lotus flower and the moon? **(b) Interpret:** Whom might the moon symbolize? **(c) Apply:** Why does the lotus flower see her wooer only at night?
4. **(a) Recall:** In "The Lotus Flower," what two ideas does the speaker link in the last line? **(b) Infer:** What does the speaker mean when he refers to the "sorrows of love"?
5. **Apply:** To what types of situations in real life could you relate the legend of the lorelei? Explain your answer.

ASSESSMENT PRACTICE: Reading Comprehension

Distinguish Between Fact and Nonfact (For more practice, see Test Preparation Workbook, p. 38.)

Many tests require students to distinguish between fact and nonfact. Use the following sample item.

In the aftermath of World War II, Heinrich Heine became a controversial figure in Europe and in the United States, because of the similarities of his political beliefs to Marxism. Yet, despite all the controversy that has surrounded him, he is still generally regarded as one of the finest writers of the nineteenth century.

Which is an OPINION from this passage?

A Heine is considered one of the finest writers of the nineteenth century.
B Heine became a controversial figure.
C Heine wrote during the nineteenth century.
D Heine's work became known throughout Europe and the United States.

A is an opinion, or nonfact, because it cannot be proved. Choices *B*, *C*, and *D* are facts that can be proved.

Review and Assess

Literary Analysis

Lyric Poetry

1. Which specific emotions expressed in "I Have Visited Again" qualify it as a **lyric poem**?
2. (a) What words in "The Lorelei" refer to sounds? (b) How do these words reflect the original purpose of many lyric poems?
3. What is the single effect produced in "The Lotus Flower"?

Comparing Literary Works

4. (a) Complete a chart like the one shown to analyze the **symbols** in "I Have Visited Again." Begin by listing persons, places, or objects and the words the speaker uses to describe them. (b) In the last column, use the speaker's description to determine what the symbols mean.

Person, Place, or Object	Words Describing the Image	Symbolic Meaning of the Image

5. In "The Lorelei," the girl is wearing golden jewelry, and she combs her "golden hair" with a "comb of gold." (a) What does the girl have in common with gold? (b) What does this suggest about what the girl symbolizes?

Reading Strategy

Reading Between the Lines

6. By **reading between the lines**, what deeper understanding of the speaker can you discover in the fifth stanza of "I Have Visited Again"?
7. (a) According to the first stanza of "The Lorelei," what haunts the speaker? (b) What connection might exist between the sadness he feels and the lorelei?

Extend Understanding

8. **Science Connection:** In what ways are modern ships equipped to prevent the kinds of shipwrecks described in "The Lorelei"?

Quick Review

Lyric poems are brief poems that express a speaker's personal thoughts and feelings and create a unified effect.

A **symbol** is a person, place, or object that stands for or represents something else.

When you **read between the lines,** you use clues in the text to discover deeper meaning in literature.

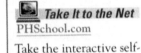

PHSchool.com

Take the interactive self-test online to check your understanding of these selections.

Answers for p. 801

Review and Assess

1. The emotions expressed in "I Have Visited Again" that qualify it as a lyric poem include sorrow, nostalgia, and hope.
2. **(a)** The words in "The Lorelei" that refer to sounds are *sings, evensong, melody, hears, cry,* and *singing.* **(b)** Because ancient lyric poems were devised to be sung to the accompaniment of a lyre, the musicality of these words would lend themselves to singing.
3. The single effect produced in "The Lotus Flower" is a feeling of dreamy, sorrowful romance.
4. Possible response: **Person, Place, or Object:** cottage; **Words Describing the Image:** "sadly / Declined"; **Symbolic Meaning of the Image:** the toll time takes; **Person, Place, or Object:** nurse; **Words Describing the Image:** "poor," "old," "moved slowly," "painstakingly"; **Symbolic Meaning of the Image:** the toll time takes; **Person, Place, or Object:** mill; **Words Describing the Image:** "so crooked it can scarcely / Make its sails turn"; **Symbolic Meaning of the Image:** the toll time takes; **Person, Place, or Object:** young pines; **Words Describing the Image:** "like green children"; **Symbolic Meaning of the Image:** the continuity of life.
5. **(a)** Like gold, the girl is beautiful and costly. **(b)** These similarities suggest that the girl symbolizes anything in life that is alluring, costly, and out of reach.
6. The predictions about the trees and grandchild suggest that the speaker thinks being part of a family is a happier, friendlier, and productive way of life than remaining solitary, like the lone pine tree.
7. **(a)** An old fable haunts the speaker in "The Lorelei." **(b)** The sadness the speaker feels and the legend of the lorelei might be connected in that the speaker's sadness, like that of the boatman, may be caused by a longing for something unattainable.

continued

continued from right column

8. Modern ships have the means to track weather and avoid bad storms; they have sonar to detect underwater hazards; they have global positioning technology to stay precisely on course; and their modern communication equipment allows sailors to summon help in emergencies.

ENRICHMENT: Further Reading

Other Works by the Authors

We strongly encourage you to review any selection before assigning or recommending it to students.

Pushkin: *Eugene Onegin* — *Boris Godunov*

Heine: *Deutschland: A Winter's Tale* — *Journey to Italy*

Take It to the Net

Visit PHSchool.com for more information on the authors.

EXTEND

Answers for p. 802

1 Vocabulary Development

Word Analysis: Anglo-Saxon Suffix *-less*

1. fathomless
2. guileless
3. pitiless
4. sunless

Spelling Strategy

1. scarcely
2. lovely
3. tuneful

Fluency: Clarify Word Meaning

1. mutely
2. ancestral
3. painstakingly
4. fathomless
5. morose
6. resplendent

2 Grammar and Style

Practice

1. They (trees)
2. its (pine)
3. They (bracelet, necklace)
4. him (boatman)
5. It (boat)

Writing Application

Possible response: The mountains rise to the west; they are dusted with white. At the foot of the mountains runs a fence, and around it grow yellow asters.

The yellow asters sway in the breeze; they dance left and then right. The barbed wire of the fence squeaks in the wind; its sound keeps a beat for the dancing asters. The horses in the pasture at the base of the mountain stomp on the ground; they keep time with nature's song, too.

10TH GRADE For support in teaching the Grammar and Style Lesson to tenth graders, use **Writing and Grammar,** Platinum Level, Chapter 16, Section 2.

Integrate Language Skills

1 Vocabulary Development Lesson

Word Analysis: Anglo-Saxon Suffix *-less*

The suffix *-less*, which means "without," "not able to," or "not able to be," can be added to many nouns to form an adjective. Use your understanding of *-less* to write the word that means the same as each of the following phrases.

1. not able to be fathomed
2. without guile
3. without pity
4. without sun

Spelling Strategy

When adding a suffix that begins with a consonant to a word that ends with a silent *e*, retain the silent *e*. On a separate piece of paper, add *-ly* or *-ful* to each of the following words.

1. scarce 2. love 3. tune

Fluency: Clarify Word Meaning

Select the word from the vocabulary list on page 795 that matches or best relates to each description below.

1. How you might respond to a surprise that left you speechless
2. The land from which your great-grandparents came
3. The way you might walk across a rocky field in the dark
4. The deepest lake ever discovered
5. A very sad child
6. A dazzling display of gold

2 Grammar and Style Lesson

Pronouns and Antecedents

A **pronoun** must agree with its **antecedent**—the word to which it refers—in the following ways:

- in number—singular or plural
- in gender—masculine or feminine

ANTECEDENT PRONOUN
. . . my poor old *nurse*. *She* is no more.
(feminine, singular)

Practice For each item that follows, choose the correct pronoun. Then, identify its antecedent.

1. I saw those trees again. (It, They) remained the same.
2. The solitary pine stands alone, and around (its, their) roots are no young pines.
3. A lovely girl wore a gold bracelet and necklace. (It, They) sparkled in the twilight.
4. The boatman hears the lorelei singing. The song lures (him, her) to the rocks.
5. At last the waves devoured the boat. (It, They) sank beneath the surface of the river.

Writing Application Write five sentences describing scenes in nature. In each, use a pronoun that correctly matches its antecedent.

WG *Prentice Hall Writing and Grammar Connection: Diamond Level, Chapter 23, Section 2*

TEACHING RESOURCES

The following resources can be used to enrich or extend the instruction for pp. 802–803.

Vocabulary

- **Selection Support:** Build Vocabulary, p. 149
- **Vocabulary and Spelling Practice Book** (Use this booklet for skills instruction.)

Grammar

- **Selection Support:** Grammar and Style, p. 150
- **Writing and Grammar,** Diamond Level, p. 600
- **Daily Language Practice Transparencies** ■

Writing

- **Performance Assess. and Portfolio Mgmt.,** p. 16
- **Writing and Grammar,** Diamond Level, p. 289
- **Writing and Grammar iText CD-ROM** ■

Listening and Speaking

- **Performance Assess. and Portfolio Mgmt.,** p. 32

■ **BLOCK SCHEDULING:** Resources marked with this symbol provide varied instruction during 90-minute blocks.

❸ Writing Lesson

Analytical Essay

Pushkin reflects on the passing of time in "I Have Visited Again." In the poem, the speaker relies on images from nature to mark the passing stages of his life. Write an essay in which you analyze the treatment of time in this poem.

Prewriting Begin by rereading the poem and taking notes about how time progresses. You might make an informal outline with headings such as "past," "present," and "future." Under each heading, write phrases used in the poem.

Drafting Use your informal outline or your notes as you begin writing your analytical essay.

Revising After completing the first draft of your essay, trade papers with a partner and read each other's essay. Circle any points that lack support or seem vague, and suggest clarifying details that will strengthen each point in your partner's essay.

Model: Clarifying Meaning

The speaker sees the effects of time in the old cottage, which has "sadly / Declined" and deteriorated, *in the ten years since his exile there.*

Specific examples or illustrations can clarify the writer's points.

WG Prentice Hall Writing and Grammar Connection: Diamond Level, Chapter 13, Section 4

❹ Extension Activities

Listening and Speaking Lyric poems have often been set to music. With a partner, find appropriate background music for either "The Lorelei" or "The Lotus Flower." As you choose the music, keep these questions in mind:

- Does the music express the same mood as the poem?
- Does the music enhance the poem's meaning?

Then, prepare and perform an **oral interpretive reading** of the poem for your classmates, using the music to enrich the performance. **[Group Activity]**

Research and Technology The term *siren* has a special meaning in literature. Use the Internet and electronic encyclopedias to research this term, and prepare a **museum exhibit** of images and artifacts related to literary sirens. Write placards that connect your findings to "The Lorelei."

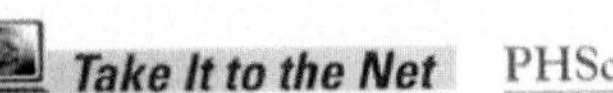

PHSchool.com

Go online for an additional research activity using the Internet.

❸ Writing Lesson

- Tell students that in an analytical essay, a writer interprets various smaller elements of a topic. By examining smaller parts, a writer can develop conclusions about the whole.
- Tell students that a good analytical essay begins with a strong thesis statement that establishes the purpose and parameters of the analysis.
- Use the Writing Lesson to guide students in developing their essays.
- Use the Response to Literature rubric in **Performance Assessment and Portfolio Management,** p. 16, to evaluate students' work.

10TH GRADE For support in working through the Writing Lesson with tenth graders, use **Writing and Grammar,** Platinum Level, Chapter 13, Section 4.

❹ Listening and Speaking

- Have partners choose a poem and determine the mood that is expressed in the poem.
- Remind students that the mood, or atmosphere, of a literary work is the feeling created in the reader. Elements that can influence mood include setting, tone, and events.
- Once students have selected their music and prepared their interpretive readings, allow time for presentations.
- Adapt the Speaking: Multimedia Presentation rubric in **Performance Assessment and Portfolio Management,** p. 32, to evaluate students' work.

CUSTOMIZE INSTRUCTION For Universal Access

To address different learning styles, use the following activities suggested in the **Extension Activities** booklet, p. 38.

- For Bodily/Kinesthetic Learners, use Activity 5.
- For Verbal/Linguistic and Interpersonal Learners, use Activity 6.
- For Visual/Spatial and Verbal Linguistic Learners, use Activity 7.

ASSESSMENT RESOURCES

The following resources can be used to assess students' knowledge and skills.

Selection Assessment

- **Formal Assessment,** pp. 136–138
- **Open-Book Tests,** pp. 112–114
- **Test Bank Software**

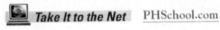

Take It to the Net

Visit PHSchool.com for self-tests on the selections.

Writing Rubric

- **Performance Assess. and Portfolio Mgmt.,** p. 16

Listening and Speaking Rubric

- **Performance Assess. and Portfolio Mgmt.,** p. 32

For additional diagnositics and remediation for skills covered in this grouping, use materials from the Prentice Hall Assessment System.

from The Expiation

Lesson Objectives

1. **To analyze and respond to literary elements**
   - Literary Analysis: Mood
   - Connecting Literary Elements: Tone
2. **To read, comprehend, analyze, and critique a poem**
   - Reading Strategy: Responding to Imagery
   - Reading Check Questions
   - Review and Assess Questions
   - Assessment Practice (ATE)
3. **To develop word analysis skills, fluency, and systematic vocabulary**
   - Vocabulary Development Lesson: Latin Prefix *sub-*
4. **To understand and apply written and oral language conventions**
   - Spelling Strategy
   - Grammar and Style Lesson: Participial Phrases
5. **To understand and apply appropriate writing and research strategies**
   - Writing Lesson: Writing a War Poem
   - Extension Activity: Illustrated Timeline
6. **To understand and apply listening and speaking strategies**
   - Extension Activity: Brief Speech

STEP-BY-STEP TEACHING GUIDE	PACING GUIDE
PRETEACH	
Motivate Students and Provide Background	
Use the Motivation activity (ATE p. 804)	5 min.
Read and discuss author and background features (SE pp. 804, 806; ATE p. 804) [A]	5 min.
Introduce the Concepts	
Introduce the Literary Analysis and Reading Strategy concepts (SE/ATE p. 805) [A]	15 min.
Pronounce the vocabulary words and read their definitions (SE p. 805)	5 min.
TEACH	
Monitor Comprehension	
Informally monitor comprehension by circulating while students read independently or in groups [A]	20 min.
Monitor students' comprehension with the Reading Check notes (SE/ATE p. 807)	as students read
Develop vocabulary with Vocabulary notes (SE pp. 806, 807, 808; ATE p. 806)	as students read
Develop Understanding	
Develop students' understanding of mood with the Literary Analysis annotations (SE/ATE pp. 806, 808) [A]	10 min.
Develop students' ability to respond to imagery, using the Reading Strategy annotations (SE/ATE p. 807)	10 min.
ASSESS	
Assess Mastery	
Assess students' mastery of the Reading Strategy and Literary Analysis concepts by having them answer the Review and Assess questions (SE/ATE p. 809)	20 min.
Use one or more of the print, software, or transparency Assessment Resources (ATE p. 811) [A]	up to 45 min.
EXTEND	
Apply Understanding	
Have students complete the Vocabulary Lesson and the Grammar and Style Lesson (SE/ATE p. 810)	20 min.
Apply students' ability to develop imagery by using the Writing Lesson (SE/ATE p. 811) [A]	45 min.
Apply students' understanding of the selection using one or more of the Extension Activities (SE p. 811)	20–90 min.

[A] **ACCELERATED INSTRUCTION:** Use the strategies and activities identified with an [A].

10TH GRADE **TEACHING TENTH-GRADE STUDENTS** For support in teaching the selection(s) to tenth-grade students, see the Step-By-Step Teaching notes identified with the icon shown here.

UNIVERSAL ACCESS
- ● = Below-Level Students
- ▲ = On-Level Students
- ■ = Above-Level Students

Time and Resource Manager

Reading Level: Challenging
Average Number of Instructional Days: 3

RESOURCES		
PRINT	**TRANSPARENCIES**	**TECHNOLOGY**
• **Beyond Literature,** Cross-Curricular Connection: Social Studies, p. 39 ▲ ■		
• **Selection Support Workbook:** ● ▲ ■ Literary Analysis, p. 156 Reading Strategy, p. 155 Build Vocabulary, p. 153	• **Literary Analysis and Reading Transparencies,** pp. 77 and 78 ● ▲ ■	
		• **Listening to Literature** ● ▲ ■ Audiocassettes Audio CDs
• **Literary Analysis for Enrichment,** p. 39 ■		
• **Formal Assessment:** Selection Test, pp. 139–141 ● ▲ ■ • **Open-Book Tests,** pp. 115–117 ● ▲ ■ • **Performance Assess. and Portfolio Mgmt.,** p. 19 ● ▲ ■ • PRENTICE HALL ASSESSMENT SYSTEM ● ▲ ■	• PRENTICE HALL ASSESSMENT SYSTEM ● ▲ ■ **Skills Practice Answers and Explanations on Transparencies**	• **Test Bank Software** ● ▲ ■
• **Selection Support Workbook:** ● ▲ ■ Grammar and Style, p. 154 • **Writing and Grammar,** Diamond Level ● ▲ ■ • **Extension Activities,** p. 39 ● ▲ ■	• **Daily Language Practice Transparencies** ● ▲	• **Writing and Grammar iText CD-ROM** ● ▲ ■ ***Take It to the Net*** PHSchool.com

BLOCK SCHEDULING: Use one 90-minute class period to preteach the selection(s) and have students read them. Use a second 90-minute class period to assess students' mastery of skills and have them complete one of the Extension Activities.

PRETEACH

Step-by-Step Teaching Guide for pp. 804–805

Motivation

Ask students whether they have read or seen film or theater adaptations of any of Victor Hugo's prose works, such as *The Hunchback of Notre-Dame* or *Les Misérables*. Then, introduce the excerpt from *The Expiation* by explaining that Hugo was famous for his poetry as well as for his prose.

❶ Background

More About the Author

Victor Hugo's lifelong interest in architecture is especially evident in his novel *The Hunchback of Notre-Dame*, which includes vivid descriptions of France's most famous Gothic cathedral. Consequently, the novel had a remarkable effect on French architecture. Prior to the novel's publication, medieval buildings could be redecorated, sold, or destroyed at will. When the novel was published, however, buildings that for generations had been considered ugly and expendable became overnight, in the words of the French writer André Maurois, "Bibles in stone."

Geography Note

Use the map on this page to identify France. Remind students that Hugo was born in Besançon, France, a city about twenty-five miles from the Swiss border. Then, point out the location of Russia in relation to France, and tell students that *The Expiation* describes the French army's retreat from Moscow. Tell students that there were devastating consequences from the long winter journey for the French, who were stranded far from fresh supplies.

Prepare to Read

❶ *from* The Expiation

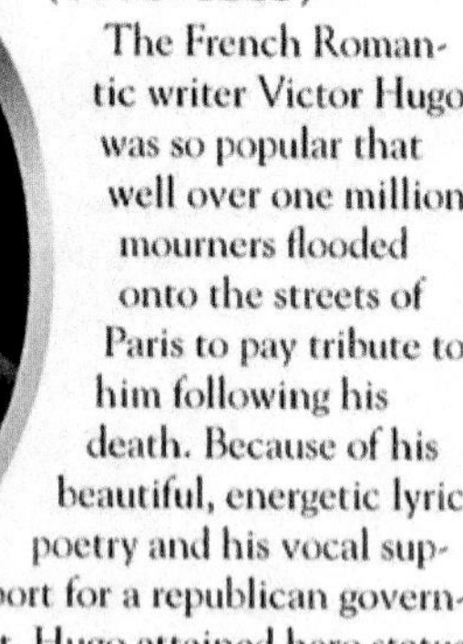

Victor Hugo (1802–1885)

The French Romantic writer Victor Hugo was so popular that well over one million mourners flooded onto the streets of Paris to pay tribute to him following his death. Because of his beautiful, energetic lyric poetry and his vocal support for a republican government, Hugo attained hero status among the French people. In fact, their admiration for Hugo was exceeded only by Hugo's tremendous admiration for himself—a trait reflected in his suggestion that Paris be renamed *Hugo* in his honor.

A Career Blossoms Hugo was born in Besançon in 1802, the son of a high-ranking officer in Napoleon's army. Hugo's talents as a writer were first recognized during his teens, when he won a poetry contest sponsored by the French Academy. Encouraged by his success, he began focusing all of his energy on writing and studying poetry. By 1822, he had founded a literary magazine, married his childhood sweetheart, and published his first collection of poetry, *Odes et poésies diverses*.

Hugo's career as a writer continued to blossom with the publication of his first novel, *Han d'Islande* (1823), as well as two more collections of verse. Continuing to write at a prolific pace, Hugo produced three plays, *Cromwell* (1827), *Marion de Lorme* (1829), and *Hernani* (1830), which earned him public recognition and established him as the leading French Romantic writer. His fame as a writer continued to grow with the publication of one of his most popular novels, *The Hunchback of Notre-Dame* (1831).

Literature of Politics After 1831, much of Hugo's writing expressed his political and social beliefs. Overwhelming grief over the drowning of his daughter Léopoldine and a love affair with the actress Juliette Drouet drove him further from his literary career.

Following the revolution of 1848, Hugo was elected to a government position in which he acted as a champion of workers and educational reforms. However, when Napoleon III seized power and appointed himself emperor, Hugo was forced to flee to Brussels. Hugo spent nineteen years in exile, continuing his involvement in politics and producing his most stirring piece of social commentary, the novel *Les Misérables*. Published in 1862, the novel was a tremendous success, and in 1870, the year in which Napoleon III fell from power, Hugo returned to his homeland in triumph.

Following his return to France, Hugo once again became active in the French government. Although deeply shaken by the deaths of his two sons in 1871 and 1873, and suffering from serious illness by age seventy-six, he managed to continue writing until his death.

"Russia 1812" is an excerpt from Hugo's lengthy poem *The Expiation*. The piece depicts the long, tragic retreat of Napoleon's Grand Army following their unsuccessful invasion of Russia in 1812. As Napoleon's army advanced upon Moscow, the Russian forces withdrew from the city, thus avoiding major clashes with the French while luring Napoleon's army farther and farther away from its supply sources. When the French army finally reached the city in September of 1812, they found it abandoned, completely stripped of supplies, and set on fire. Realizing that it would be pointless to continue his advance, Napoleon ordered his broken troops to retreat. Hugo's poem describes the event in vivid but painful detail and with the grandeur of vision that marked the poet's career.

TEACHING RESOURCES

The following resources can be used to enrich or extend the instruction for pp. 804–805.

Background

Beyond Literature, p. 39

Take It to the Net

Visit PHSchool.com for background on the author.

Literary Analysis

Literary Analysis and Reading Transparencies, Mood, p. 77

Reading

Literary Analysis and Reading Transparencies, Responding to Imagery, p. 78

Selection Support: Reading Strategy, p. 155; Build Vocabulary, p. 153

BLOCK SCHEDULING: Resources marked with this symbol provide varied instruction during 90-minute blocks.

Preview

Connecting to the Literature

Since the dawn of the written word, authors have penned their impressions and experiences of war: triumph, defeat, upheaval, and peace. Look for timeless messages like these in this excerpt from *The Expiation*.

2 Literary Analysis

Mood

Mood, or atmosphere, is the feeling a literary work or passage creates in a reader through the use of descriptive details. Notice how the following lines create a mood of misery and cold despair:

> ". . . one saw the picket dying at his post, / still standing in his saddle, white with frost, / the stone lips frozen to the bugle's mouth!"

As you read, be aware of the details that create a specific mood.

Connecting Literary Elements

The **tone** of a literary work is the speaker's attitude toward the audience or subject. Tone can be formal or informal, friendly or distant. The speaker uses simple but very powerful words in *The Expiation*, allowing the horrific events to speak for themselves. Look for words that create the tone and mood as you read this excerpt.

3 Reading Strategy

Responding to Imagery

When you **respond to imagery,** you notice details in the writing that appeal to your senses, and you take special note of how those details make you feel. These strategies will help you respond to imagery as you read:

- Focus on details that create vivid pictures in your mind.
- Call on your own sense memories to see, hear, taste, smell, and touch what the words are describing.
- Picture yourself in the same situation that is being described, and imagine how you would feel.

Use a chart like the one shown as you respond to the imagery in the poem.

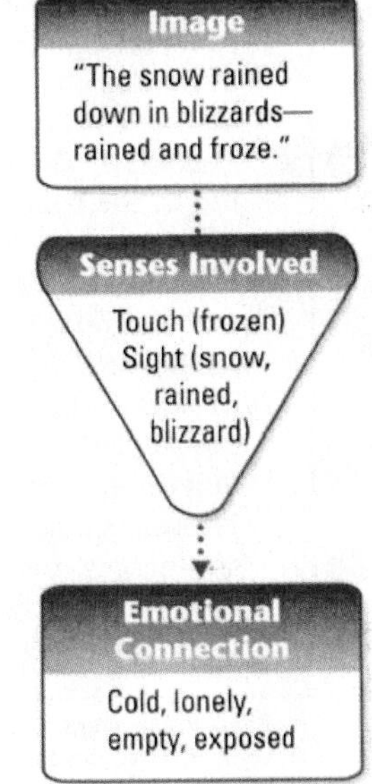

Vocabulary Development

dregs (dregz) *n.* last, most undesirable parts (p. 806)

submerges (səb murj´ əz) *v.* covers over (p. 806)

solitude (säl´ ə to͞od´) *n.* seclusion, isolation, or remoteness (p. 807)

avenger (ə venj´ ər) *n.* one who exacts punishment for wrongdoing (p. 807)

shroud (shroud) *n.* cloth sometimes used to wrap a corpse for burial (p. 807)

obsessed (əb sest´) *adj.* greatly preoccupied (p. 807)

leaden (led´ 'n) *adj.* depressed; dispirited (p. 808)

CUSTOMIZE INSTRUCTION FOR UNIVERSAL ACCESS

For Less Proficient Readers	For English Learners	For Advanced Readers
Read the poem aloud to students, stopping to define any difficult words. Then, ask students to summarize the poem in their own words. Correct any misinterpretations students have made.	Have students note one or two unfamiliar or difficult words in the selection. Then, have them use dictionaries to look up each word's definition and origin. Ask students to exchange word lists with partners and then work together until both have learned all the new words.	Ask students to use dictionaries to define the word *expiation.* After they have defined the word, ask them to write a paragraph or two in which they predict what the poem's title might indicate about the topic of this work.

2 Literary Analysis

Mood

- Tell students that descriptive details about setting, events, and characters can help create the mood of a literary work. Help students understand that a literary work may evoke a mood that is much different from that expressed by its characters. Just as a painter may use grays and blues to suggest sorrow in a painting, a poet may choose details that suggest dreariness to create a similar mood.
- Review with students the definition of tone, using the Connecting Literary Elements instruction. Make sure students understand the difference between mood and tone.
- Use the Mood transparency in **Literary Analysis and Reading Transparencies,** p. 77, to demonstrate for students how they can determine mood as they read.

3 Reading Strategy

Responding to Imagery

- Review with students the Reading Strategy instruction on p. 805. Tell students that engaging their senses will help them fully experience and appreciate the richness of characters and settings.
- Encourage students to describe in a sentence or two some of the sights, smells, textures, sounds, or tastes of holiday celebrations or of specific places. Remind students that many images appeal to more than one sense.
- Explain the use of the graphic organizer on p. 805. Have students use the graphic organizer as they read the excerpt from *The Expiation.*

Vocabulary Development

- Pronounce each vocabulary word for students, and read the definitions as a class. Have students identify any words with which they are already familiar.

E-Teach

Visit e-Teach at PHSchool.com for teachers' essays on how to teach, with questions and answers.

TEACH

Step-by-Step Teaching Guide for pp. 806–808

Teaching Tenth-Grade Students

10TH GRADE Ask tenth-grade students to share any prior knowledge they have of Napoleon and the Napoleonic Wars. Discuss Napoleon's invasion of Russia, making sure that students grasp the devastating impact that the retreat from Moscow had on the French army.

❶ About the Selection

Hugo describes the horrible suffering endured by French forces as they retreated across Russia in the winter of 1812. As men die of exposure and starvation, Napoleon suddenly feels terrified. He asks God whether this is the end. From the shadows, someone calls out to him and says, "No, Napoleon."

❷ Literary Analysis

Mood

- As students read the bracketed passage, ask them how many times "the snow" appears.
  Answer: The phrase appears five times.
- Ask students the Literary Analysis question on p. 806: How does the repetition of the words "the snow" affect the mood of the poem?
  Possible response: The repetition shows the relentlessness of winter, reinforcing the moods of hopelessness, misery, and horror.

❸ Vocabulary Development

Latin Prefix *sub-*

- Draw students' attention to the word *submerges*, and then read its definition.
- Tell students that the prefix *sub-* means "under" or "below."
- Organize students into small groups, to brainstorm a list of words that use the prefix *sub-*.
  Possible responses: *Subterranean, subdivision,* and *subculture* are possible suggestions.

from The Expiation
Russia 1812

Victor Hugo ❶

translated by Robert Lowell

Background

The speaker of "Russia 1812" describes the agonized retreat of Napoleon's Grand Army from Moscow in 1812. During their march across the frigid, barren Russian plains, countless French soldiers died from frostbite, starvation, and constant attacks by Russian snipers. By the time the retreat had ended, two thirds of France's Grand Army had died. The unsuccessful invasion of Russia signaled the beginning of the end for Napoleon and his empire.

The snow fell, and its power was multiplied.
For the first time the Eagle[1] bowed its head—
dark days! Slowly the Emperor returned—
behind him Moscow! Its onion domes still burned.
The snow rained down in blizzards—rained and froze.
Past each white waste a further white waste rose.
None recognized the captains or the flags.
Yesterday the Grand Army, today its dregs!
No one could tell the vanguard[2] from the flanks.
❷ The snow! The hurt men struggled from the ranks,
hid in the bellies of dead horses, in stacks
of shattered caissons.[3] By the bivouacs,[4]
one saw the picket[5] dying at his post,
still standing in his saddle, white with frost,
the stone lips frozen to the bugle's mouth!
Bullets and grapeshot[6] mingled with the snow,
that hailed . . . The Guard, surprised at shivering, march
in a dream now; ice rimes the gray mustache.
The snow falls, always snow! The driving mire
❸ submerges; men, trapped in that white empire,
have no more bread and march on barefoot—gaps!
They were no longer living men and troops,

Literary Analysis
Mood How does the repetition of the words "the snow" affect the mood of the poem?

dregs (dregz) *n.* last, most undesirable parts

submerges (səb murj´ əz) *v.* covers over

Campaign of France, 1814, Ernest Meissonier, Giraudon

1. **Eagle** the standard of Napoleon's military forces.
2. **vanguard** (van´ gärd´) *n.* the part of an army that goes ahead of the main body in an advance.
3. **caissons** (kā´ sänz) *n.* two-wheeled wagons used for transporting ammunition.
4. **bivouacs** (biv´ waks) *n.* temporary encampments.
5. **picket** (pik´ it) *n.* soldier responsible for guarding a body of troops from surprise attack.
6. **grapeshot** (grāp´ shät´) *n.* cluster of small iron balls fired from a cannon.

TEACHING RESOURCES

The following resources can be used to enrich or extend the instruction for pp. 806–808.

Literary Analysis

- **Selection Support:** Literary Analysis, p. 156 ■
- **Literary Analysis and Reading Transparencies,** Mood, p. 77 ■

Reading

- **Selection Support:** Reading Strategy, p. 155; Build Vocabulary, p. 153
- **Listening to Literature Audiocassettes**
- **Listening to Literature Audio CDs** ■

■ **BLOCK SCHEDULING:** Resources marked with this symbol provide varied instruction during 90-minute blocks.

but a dream drifting in a fog, a mystery,
mourners parading under the black sky.
The solitude, vast, terrible to the eye,
was like a mute avenger everywhere,
as snowfall, floating through the quiet air,
buried the huge army in a huge shroud.
Could anyone leave this kingdom? A crowd—
each man, obsessed with dying, was alone.
Men slept—and died! The beaten mob sludged on,
ditching the guns to burn their carriages.
Two foes. The North, the Czar.[7] The North was worse.
In hollows where the snow was piling up,
one saw whole regiments fallen asleep.
Attila's dawn, Cannaes of Hannibal![8]
The army marching to its funeral!
Litters, wounded, the dead, deserters—swarms,
crushing the bridges down to cross a stream.
They went to sleep ten thousand, woke up four.
Ney,[9] bringing up the former army's rear,
hacked his horse loose from three disputing Cossacks[10] . . .
All night, the *qui vive?*[11] The alert! Attacks; retreats!
White ghosts would wrench away our guns,
or we would see dim, terrible squadrons,
circles of steel, whirlpools of savages,

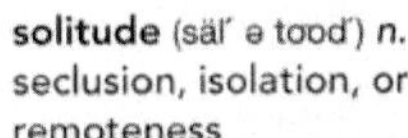

solitude (säl′ ə tōōd′) *n.* seclusion, isolation, or remoteness

avenger (ə venj′ ər) *n.* one who exacts punishment for wrongdoing

shroud (shroud) *n.* cloth sometimes used to wrap a corpse for burial

obsessed (əb sest′) *adj.* greatly preoccupied

Reading Strategy
Responding to Imagery What is the strongest word among the images in lines 37–40?

7. **the Czar** (zär) the Russian emperor.
8. **Attila's . . . Hannibal** references to the defeat of Attila, the leader of the Huns, at Gaul in A.D. 451, and to the final victory of Hannibal, the Carthaginian general who invaded Rome in 218 B.C.
9. **Ney** (nā) the French officer in charge of defending the rear in the retreat from Moscow.
10. **Cossacks** (käs′ aks′) people of southern Russia, famous as horsemen and cavalrymen.
11. ***qui vive?*** (kē vēv′) French: "Who goes there?" (literally, "(long) live who?" meaning "whose side are you on?")

Reading Check
What conditions make it impossible for Napoleon's army to wage a successful fight?

Critical Viewing
Which details in the painting suggest that Napoleon's army is in retreat? **[Analyze]**

4 Reading Strategy

Responding to Imagery

- Have a volunteer read aloud the bracketed passage and then identify the main idea of this passage.
  Answer: Most of the men on the march do not survive.
- Ask students the Reading Strategy question on p. 807: What is the strongest word among the images in lines 37–40?
  Possible response: *Funeral* is the strongest word in these lines because it evokes highly emotional images and feelings. Other possibilities include *wounded, dead, swarms,* and *crushing.*

Reteach To establish links between images and emotions, have students use the graphic organizer on p. 805.

5 Reading Check

Answer: The conditions that make it impossible for Napoleon's army to wage a successful fight are the weather and the army's lack of preparation for the cold. The men are also hungry and exhausted, and some are barefoot.

6 Background

Art

Campagne de France, by Ernest Meissonier

Meissonier (1815–1891) was a renowned French painter, sculptor, etcher, and lithographer. He often painted military subjects, producing numerous depictions of Napoleon's various campaigns. This painting, which depicts the French army in retreat near the end of Napoleon's reign, is considered one of Meissonier's greatest works.

Use the following question for discussion:

- How is the mood of the poem similar to the mood of the painting?
  Answer: Both have moods that are dark, bleak, and depressing.

7 Critical Viewing

Answer: Details that suggest retreat include the posture of Napoleon and of the men following him. Their facial expressions do not look proud and aggressive, as an advancing army might; rather, they look defeated, dejected, and depressed.

CUSTOMIZE INSTRUCTION FOR UNIVERSAL ACCESS

For Special Needs Students	For Gifted/Talented Students
Have students work in small groups, reading along with a recording of the selection at least twice. During the first reading, have them pause frequently (after each ten lines or so) to summarize what they have just read. During the second reading, have them read the entire selection straight through. Because this is a difficult selection, consider having students read it a third or even a fourth time to ensure comprehension.	After students have read the excerpt from *The Expiation,* have them create their own poems or paintings that describe defeat. Students' works should reflect the theme, mood, and tone—but not necessarily the subject—of Hugo's poem. Have students present their work to the rest of the class.

ASSESS

❽ Literary Analysis

Mood and Tone

- Ask several volunteers to take turns reading aloud the bracketed passage on pp. 807–808 as the rest of the class reads along. Have students notice how each reader emphasizes different words.
- Ask students the Literary Analysis question on p. 808: Which words and phrases reveal a horrified tone, the tone of someone who is shocked at the waste of war?
Answer: The words and phrases that reveal a horrified tone are *"terrible squadrons, circles of steel, whirlpools of savages, sabering ... like dervishes."*

Answers for p. 808

Review and Assess

1. Possible response: Hugo's descriptions are convincing because of the vivid imagery and the emotional tone it creates.
2. **(a)** The snow falls harder and harder. **(b)** Possible response: The coldness and barrenness of the landscape are emphasized by *white waste* (line 6) and *white empire* (line 20).
3. **(a)** Napoleon and his troops are compared to an oak tree about to fall. **(b)** Possible response: This comparison is appropriate because oak trees are known for their strength and toughness, qualities for which Napoleon and his troops were famous. Also, because it is impossible to stop a tree from falling, the image suggests the certainty of a French defeat.
4. **(a)** Possible response: The speaker seems ambivalent toward Napoleon. **(b)** Possible response: The "god of armies" forgives Napoleon, but the speaker seems unconvinced that the soldiers' continuing faith in their leader is justified.
5. Possible response: Works such as Hugo's support a negative attitude toward war. The vivid images of the dying soldiers emphasize the waste and tragedy of war.

rush sabering through the camp like dervishes.[12]
And in this way, whole armies died at night.

The Emperor was there, standing—he saw.
This oak already trembling from the axe,
watched his glories drop from him branch by branch:
chiefs, soldiers. Each one had his turn and chance—
they died! Some lived. These still believed his star,
and kept their watch. They loved the man of war,
this small man with his hands behind his back,
whose shadow, moving to and fro, was black
behind the lighted tent. Still believing, they
accused their destiny of *lèse-majesté*.[13]
His misfortune had mounted on their back.
The man of glory shook. Cold stupefied[14]
him, then suddenly he felt terrified.
Being without belief, he turned to God:
"God of armies, is this the end?" he cried.
And then at last the expiation[15] came,
as he heard some one call him by his name,
someone half-lost in shadow, who said, "No,
Napoleon." Napoleon understood,
restless, bareheaded, leaden, as he stood
before his butchered legions in the snow.

Literary Analysis
Mood and Tone Which words and phrases reveal a horrified tone, the tone of someone who is shocked at the waste of war?

leaden (led′'n) *adj.* depressed; dispirited

12. **dervishes** (dur′ vish ez) *n.* Muslims dedicated to lives of poverty and chastity.
13. ***lèse-majesté*** (lez′ ma′ zhes tā′) French: treason; crime against one's sovereign (literally, "injured majesty").
14. **stupefied** (stōō′ pe fīd′) *v.* stunned; made dull or lethargic.
15. **expiation** (eks′ pē ā′ shen) *n.* reparation; atonement.

Review and Assess

Thinking About the Selection

1. **Respond:** Do you find the descriptions of the suffering of the French forces convincing? Why or why not?
2. **(a) Recall:** What does the speaker mean when he says in line 1 that the snow's "power was multiplied"? **(b) Analyze:** Which words emphasize the coldness and barrenness of the landscape?
3. **(a) Recall:** In lines 50–52, what comparison does the speaker make to describe the downfall of the French army? **(b) Infer:** Why is this comparison appropriate?
4. **(a) Recall:** What seems to be the speaker's attitude toward Napoleon? **(b) Support:** Which details reveal the speaker's attitude?
5. **Apply:** What impact, if any, do literary works such as Hugo's have on your attitude toward war?

ASSESSMENT PRACTICE: Reading Comprehension

Distinguish Between Fact and Nonfact (For more practice, see Test Preparation Workbook, p. 39.)

Standardized tests require students to distinguish between fact and nonfact. Use this sample test item to give students practice with this skill.

The great prose classic of the Napoleonic wars is Leo Tolstoy's novel *War and Peace*. Napoleon appears in person only a few times in the novel, but he is never far from the thoughts of most of the characters.

Which is a NONFACT from this passage?

A. *War and Peace* is a work of prose.

B. *War and Peace* is a great classic.

C. Napoleon is featured in *War and Peace*.

D. Leo Tolstoy is the author of *War and Peace*.

Students should recognize that choices *A, C,* and *D* can all be proven. The words *great* and *classic* signal that choice *B* is an opinion. *B* is the correct choice.

Review and Assess

Literary Analysis

Mood

1. (a) Use an organizer like the one shown to jot down details in the poem. (b) Use those details to determine the **mood**.

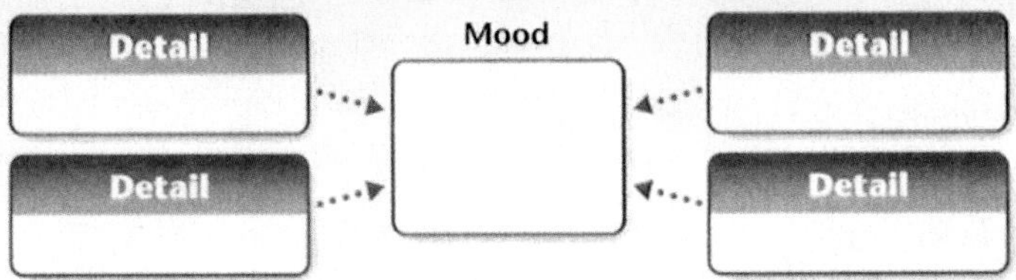

2. (a) What does the French retreat from Russia reveal about the role of nature in determining the course of human history? (b) How does this revelation contribute to the mood of the poem?

Connecting Literary Elements

3. (a) Choose one word that might describe the **tone** of the first stanza. (b) List three details that support this idea.
4. (a) What is the speaker's tone toward Napoleon in lines 49–69? (b) Support your response with two details from the poem.

Reading Strategy

Responding to Imagery

5. (a) In lines 1–24, what are the dominant colors in the speaker's descriptions? (b) How do these colors contribute to your **response to the imagery** in these lines? Explain.
6. (a) Identify one strong image in lines 1–37. (b) Which of your senses responds to the imagery?
7. How does the imagery in *The Expiation* affect your understanding of what the troops had to endure?

Extend Understanding

8. **Psychology Connection:** (a) Explain how it is possible that the French soldiers still love and believe in Napoleon despite the disastrous outcome of the Russian campaign. (b) Why is this phenomenon common in other wars, with other leaders and soldiers?

Quick Review

Mood, or atmosphere, is the feeling a literary work or passage creates in a reader through the use of descriptive details.

The **tone** of a literary work is the narrator's or speaker's attitude toward his or her audience or subject as revealed through word choice.

To **respond to imagery,** notice details in the writing that appeal to your senses, and take special note of how those details make you feel.

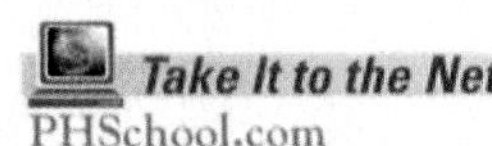

PHSchool.com

Take the interactive self-test online to check your understanding of this selection.

ENRICHMENT: Further Reading

Other Works by Victor Hugo

We strongly encourage you to review any selection before assigning or recommending it to students.

The Hunchback of Notre-Dame

Les Misérables

The Toilers of the Sea

Take It to the Net

Visit PHSchool.com for more information on Victor Hugo.

Answers for p. 809

Review and Assess

1. **(a) Details:** description of snow, men hiding in "the bellies of dead horses," man dying in the saddle with "stone lips frozen to the bugle's mouth," words like *shroud* and *funeral*. **(b)** These details contribute to the mood of horror and hopelessness.
2. **(a)** The retreat reveals that nature often plays a major role in shaping human history. **(b)** This suggests that humans are often helpless against the power of nature, thus adding to the mood of defeat and sorrow.
3. **(a)** Possible response: One word that might describe the tone of the first stanza is *astonishment*.
   (b) Possible response: Astonishment is reflected in "the Eagle bowed its head" (line 2), "Yesterday the Grand Army, today its dregs!" (line 8), and the image of the picket, dead but still at his post with bugle raised (lines 13–15).
4. **(a)** Possible response: The speaker's tone toward Napoleon in lines 49–69 is ambivalent. **(b)** At first, the speaker seems to sympathize with Napoleon comparing him to an oak tree "already trembling from the ax." Later, however, the speaker refers to Napoleon's "butchered legions in the snow." The speaker seems to imply that Napoleon does not deserve the loyalty of his troops.
5. **(a)** The dominant colors are white, gray, and black.
   (b) Possible response: These colors emphasize the somber nature of what is being described.
6. **(a)** Possible response: One strong image in lines 1–37 is the snowfall "floating through the quiet air" and burying "the huge army in a huge shroud" (lines 27–28). **(b)** The senses of sight, hearing, and touch respond to this imagery.
7. Possible response: The vivid imagery makes the reader more aware of the troops' hardship.
8. **(a)** Possible response: The soldiers have been trained to trust, respect, and obey their commanders, who have led them to

continued

continued from right column

victory in the past. **(b)** This phenomenon is common because military success depends upon loyalty and trust. A belief in one's country, shared ideals, and charismatic leaders inspire troops to fight on, despite hardships.

EXTEND

Answers for p. 810

❶ Vocabulary Development

Word Analysis: Latin prefix *sub-*

1. submarine: vessel that goes under the surface of the water
2. subpar: below the usual standard
3. subordinate: person who is under the direction of another
4. submerge: go under or put under the surface

Spelling Strategy

1. b
2. a
3. a

Word Fluency: Sentence Completions

1. obsessed
2. shroud
3. solitude
4. dregs
5. submerges
6. avenger
7. leaden

❷ Grammar and Style

Practice

1. "men, ***trapped*** *in that white empire* / have no more bread ..." (describes *men*)
2. "a dream ***drifting*** *in a fog*, a mystery ..." (describes *dream*)
3. "mourners ***parading*** *under the black sky*." (describes *mourners*)
4. "the Guard, ***surprised*** *by the shivering* ..." (describes *Guard*)
5. "each man, ***obsessed*** *with dying*, was alone." (describes *man*)

Writing Application

Sample Sentences: (Swirling) off the highest peaks of the mountains, the cold wind cut through our jackets and numbed our fingers (describes *wind*). The children, (bundled) from head to toe, trudged on through the knee-deep snow (describes *children*).

For support in teaching the 10TH GRADE Grammar and Style Lesson to tenth graders, use **Writing and Grammar,** Platinum Level, Chapter 20, Section 1.

Integrate Language Skills

❶ Vocabulary Development Lesson

Word Analysis: Latin Prefix *sub-*

The Latin prefix *sub-* means "under" or "below." Use this meaning as you define the words below.

1. submarine
2. subpar
3. subordinate
4. submerge

Spelling Strategy

Words whose final syllable includes a long vowel sound followed by a single consonant often end in a silent *e*. Identify the letter of the correct spelling of each word below.

1. (a) solitud (b) solitude
2. (a) inspire (b) inspir
3. (a) squadron (b) squadrone

Word Fluency: Sentence Completion

Review the vocabulary list on page 805. Then, complete each sentence below with the best word from the list.

1. Napoleon seemed __?__ with power.
2. The only __?__ the dead soldier had was his own uniform.
3. Their feeling of __?__ was intensified by the darkness of night.
4. Only the __?__ remained of the once-great army.
5. The doctor __?__ the soldier's cold feet in warm water.
6. Each sniper considered himself a great __?__ for Russia.
7. The soldier, __?__, hungry, and cold, thought of home.

❷ Grammar and Style Lesson

Participial Phrases

A participle is a form of a verb that can act as an adjective. A **participial phrase** is made up of a participle and its modifiers and complements. The whole phrase acts as an adjective. In this example, the participle is in boldface and the participial phrase is underlined:

> the stone lips **frozen** to the bugle's mouth . . . (describes lips)
>
> the snowfall, **floating** through the quiet air . . . (describes *snowfall*)

Practice Identify the participles and participial phrases in the numbered items below. Then, identify the word that each participial phrase describes.

1. "men, trapped in that white empire, / have no more bread . . ."
2. "a dream drifting in a fog, a mystery . . ."
3. "mourners parading under the black sky."
4. "the Guard, surprised by the shivering . . ."
5. "each man, obsessed with dying, was alone."

Writing Application Write two sentences about an extreme weather condition using participial phrases. In each sentence, circle the participle, underline the participial phrase, and identify the word it describes.

WG Prentice Hall Writing and Grammar Connection: Diamond Level, Chapter 19, Section 2

TEACHING RESOURCES

The following resources can be used to enrich or extend the instruction for pp. 810–811.

Vocabulary

- **Selection Support:** Build Vocabulary, p. 153
- **Vocabulary and Spelling Practice Book** (Use this booklet for skills instruction.)

Grammar

- **Selection Support:** Grammar and Style, p. 154
- **Writing and Grammar,** Diamond Level, p. 446
- **Daily Language Practice Transparencies** ▪

Writing

- **Performance Assess. and Portfolio Mgmt.**, p. 19
- **Writing and Grammar,** Diamond Level, p. 102
- **Writing and Grammar iText CD-ROM** ▪

▪ **BLOCK SCHEDULING:** Resources marked with this symbol provide varied instruction during 90-minute blocks.

❸ Writing Lesson

Writing a War Poem

The powerful events of war have inspired writers throughout history. Write a poem describing a battle or another scene from a war.

Prewriting Brainstorm about the depiction of war in books and movies or on television, noting accounts of battles by soldiers who participated in them. Develop a list of words and details that could contribute to the mood of your poem.

Model: Developing a List of Words and Details

Sound Images	Visual Images	Tactile Images	Emotions

Drafting Using these words and details, begin writing your poem. Choose vivid, precise images that will evoke an emotional response from the reader.

Revising To revise your poem, circle the words that create mood. Change repetitive words or images that do not create the mood you want.

WG Prentice Hall Writing and Grammar Connection: Diamond Level, Chapter 6, Section 2

❹ Extension Activities

Listening and Speaking Learn more about Napoleon and the war with Russia by conducting an interview with your history teacher or by doing research on the topic. Prepare a **brief speech** to share some of the results of your research. As you prepare, keep these guidelines in mind:

- Make sure that you understand everything said in the interview well enough to explain it to others.
- Choose details to help your audience understand more about Napoleon.
- Choose language that has vivid imagery to make it more interesting to your audience.

Write your brief speech, and then share it with the class.

Research and Technology With a partner, prepare an **illustrated timeline** of the major events in Napoleon's life, both personal and political. You may illustrate it yourself or use software, photocopies, or printouts of appropriate art. Present your timeline by posting it on a bulletin board in your classroom. [Group Activity]

Take It to the Net PHSchool.com

Go online for an additional research activity using the Internet.

ASSESSMENT RESOURCES

The following resources can be used to assess students' knowledge and skills.

Selection Assessment

 **Formal Assessment,** pp. 139–141

 **Open-Book Tests,** pp.115–117

Test Bank Software

Take It to the Net

isit PHSchool.com for self-tests on the selection.

Writing Rubric

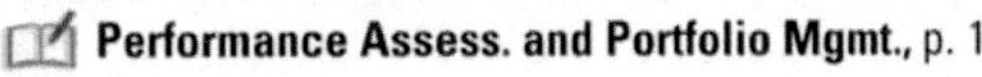

Performance Assess. and Portfolio Mgmt., p. 19

For additional diagnostics and remediation for skills covered in this grouping, use materials from the Prentice Hall Assessment System.

❸ Writing Lesson

- Review with students the characteristics of poetry: In poetry, form and content are closely connected. Poems are often divided into lines and stanzas and can employ regular rhythmical patterns, or meters.
- Tell students that powerful poetry uses concise, musical, and emotionally charged language; many poems also feature vivid imagery, figurative language, and special devices such as rhyme.
- Suggest one or two books or movies depicting war, and then have students suggest others.
- Use the Writing Lesson to guide students in developing their poems.
- Use the Description rubric in **Performance Assessment and Portfolio Management,** p. 19, to evaluate students' work.

10TH GRADE For support in working through the Writing Lesson with tenth graders, use **Writing and Grammar, Platinum** Level, Chapter 6, Section 2.

❹ Research and Technology

- Have students find a variety of resources such as historical Internet sites, historical atlases, and other books.
- Then, provide a sample timeline of the complexity level you expect to see from students' timelines.
- Direct students to sketch their timelines before they create their finalized version.

CUSTOMIZE INSTRUCTION
For Universal Access

To address different learning styles, use the following activities suggested in the **Extension Activities** booklet, p. 39:

- For Visual/Spatial and Interpersonal Learners, use Activity 5.
- For Verbal/Linguistic Learners, use Activity 6.
- For Musical/Rhythmic and Verbal/Linguistic Learners, use Activity 7.

Invitation to the Voyage • The Albatross • The Sleeper in the Valley • Ophelia • Autumn Song

Lesson Objectives

1. **To analyze and respond to literary elements**
   - Literary Analysis: Romantic Poetry
   - Comparing Literary Works: Nature as a Subject
2. **To read, comprehend, analyze, and critique poetry**
   - Reading Strategy: Judging a Poet's Message
   - Reading Check Questions
   - Review and Assess Questions
   - Assessment Practice (ATE)
3. **To develop word analysis skills, fluency, and systematic vocabulary**
   - Vocabulary Development Lesson: Greek Prefix *mono-*
4. **To understand and apply written and oral language conventions**
   - Spelling Strategy
   - Grammar and Style Lesson: Adjectival Modifiers
5. **To understand and apply appropriate writing and research strategies**
   - Writing Lesson: Comparison-and-Contrast Essay
   - Extension Activity: Multimedia Travelogue
6. **To understand and apply listening and speaking strategies**
   - Extension Activity: Discussion About Ophelia

STEP-BY-STEP TEACHING GUIDE	PACING GUIDE
PRETEACH	
Motivate Students and Provide Background	
Use the Motivation activity (ATE p. 812)	5 min.
Read and discuss author and background features (SE pp. 812, 814, 819; ATE p. 812) [A]	5 min.
Introduce the Concepts	
Introduce the Literary Analysis and Reading Strategy concepts (SE/ATE p. 813) [A]	15 min.
Pronounce the vocabulary words and read their definitions (SE p. 813)	5 min.
TEACH	
Monitor Comprehension	
Informally monitor comprehension by circulating while students read independently or in groups [A]	25 min.
Monitor students' comprehension with the Reading Check notes (SE/ATE p. 819)	as students read
Develop vocabulary with the Vocabulary notes (SE pp. 815, 816, 819, 820, 822; ATE p. 822)	as students read
Develop Understanding	
Develop students' understanding of Romantic poetry with the Literary Analysis annotations (SE/ATE pp. 814, 815, 817, 819, 822) [A]	5 min.
Develop students' ability to judge a poet's message, using the Reading Strategy annotations (SE/ATE pp. 815, 816, 817, 821) [A]	5 min.
ASSESS	
Assess Mastery	
Assess students' mastery of the Reading Strategy and Literary Analysis concepts by having them answer the Review and Assess questions (SE/ATE p. 823)	15 min.
Use one or more of the print, software, or transparency Assessment Resources (ATE p. 825) [A]	up to 45 min.
EXTEND	
Apply Understanding	
Have students complete the Vocabulary Development Lesson and the Grammar and Style Lesson (SE p. 824) [A]	20 min.
Apply students' ability to outline an essay, using the Writing Lesson (SE/ATE p. 825) [A]	45 min.
Apply students' understanding of the selections, using one or more of the Extension Activities (SE p. 825)	20–90 min.

ACCELERATED INSTRUCTION:
Use the strategies and activities identified with an [A].

10TH GRADE **TEACHING TENTH-GRADE STUDENTS**
For support in teaching the selection(s) to tenth-grade students, see the Step-By-Step Teaching notes identified with the icon shown here.

UNIVERSAL ACCESS
● = Below-Level Students
▲ = On-Level Students
■ = Above-Level Students

Time and Resource Manager

Reading Level: Challenging, Challenging, Challenging, Challenging, Challenging
Average Number of Instructional Days: 3

RESOURCES		
PRINT	**TRANSPARENCIES**	**TECHNOLOGY**
• **Beyond Literature,** Cross-Curricular Connection: Science, p. 40 ▲ ■		
• **Selection Support Workbook:** ● ▲ ■ Literary Analysis, p. 160 Reading Strategy, p. 159 Build Vocabulary, p. 157	• **Literary Analysis and Reading Transparencies,** pp. 79 and 80 ● ▲ ■	
		• **Listening to Literature** ● ▲ ■ Audiocassettes Audio CDs
• **Literary Analysis for Enrichment,** p. 40 ■		
• **Formal Assessment:** Selection Test, pp. 142–144 ● ▲ ■ • **Open-Book Tests,** pp. 118–120 ● ▲ ■ • **Performance Assessment and Portfolio Management,** pp. 15, 32 ● ▲ ■ • PRENTICE HALL ASSESSMENT SYSTEM ● ▲ ■	• PRENTICE HALL ASSESSMENT SYSTEM ● ▲ ■ **Skills Practice Answers and Explanations on Transparencies**	• **Test Bank Software** ● ▲ ■
• **Selection Support Workbook:** ● ▲ ■ Grammar and Style, p. 158 • **Writing and Grammar,** Diamond Level ● ▲ ■ • **Extension Activities,** p. 40 ● ▲ ■	• **Daily Language Practice Transparencies** ● ▲ • **Writing Models and Graphic Organizers on Transparencies,** pp. 103–106 ● ▲ ■	• **Writing and Grammar iText CD-ROM** ● ▲ ■ *Take It to the Net* PHSchool.com

BLOCK SCHEDULING: Use one 90-minute class period to preteach the selection(s) and have students read them. Use a second 90-minute class period to assess students' mastery of skills and have them complete one of the Extension Activities.

Step-by-Step Teaching Guide for pp. 812–813

Motivation

Have students discuss their perceptions of poets. Do students believe that poets are somehow different from other people? If so, why? Explain that a number of nineteenth-century poets—including Baudelaire, Rimbaud, and Verlaine—felt alienated from the rest of society. Ask students to discuss how a poet might express this sense of alienation.

❶ Background

More About the Authors

Charles Baudelaire was one of the most inventive poets of his time. A Romantic in his taste for what was remote and mysterious, he went beyond Romanticism in his accurate portrayal of the modern city. He pioneered a new type of writing called Symbolism—viewing things in the visible world as symbols of a greater spiritual reality.

When Arthur Rimbaud was sixteen, he wrote a letter to his friend Paul Demeny in which he spoke of the poet as a visionary who "searches his soul, inspects it, tries it, learns it," and who virtually creates a new language.

While in prison for attempting to murder Arthur Rimbaud, Paul Verlaine returned to Roman Catholicism. His renewed religious faith, at first, seemed to change his life. However, his failure to reconcile with his wife and Rimbaud and the deaths of both Verlaine's mother and his star pupil finally caused him to return to his former life of debauchery.

Geography Note

Draw students' attention to the map on this page, and tell them that France was home to Baudelaire, Rimbaud, and Verlaine. It was here that the poets participated in the bohemian lifestyle of the Parisian artistic community.

Prepare to Read

Invitation to the Voyage ◆ The Albatross ◆ ❶ The Sleeper in the Valley ◆ Ophelia ◆ Autumn Song

Charles Baudelaire (1821–1867)

Charles Baudelaire (shärl bōd ler′) was one of the most colorful, startling, and innovative poets of the nineteenth century. Attempting to break away from the Romantic tradition, Baudelaire created poems that are objective rather than sentimental. His works celebrate the city and the artificial rather than nature.

As a youth, Baudelaire rebelled against his family to pursue a career as a writer. To dissuade him from such a dissolute life, they sent him on an ocean voyage to India. Instead of completing the voyage, he returned to France to claim his share of his late father's fortune. Soon, extravagant living drove him into debt, a problem that would plague him for the rest of his life.

Baudelaire published short stories, translated works by Edgar Allan Poe into French, and both wrote and collected poems for *Flowers of Evil* (1857), which would become his signature work. Although his talents were not widely recognized during his lifetime, Baudelaire's reputation blossomed posthumously, and he came to be considered one of the finest nineteenth-century poets.

Arthur Rimbaud (1854–1891)

Arthur Rimbaud (är tür′ ran bō′) earned recognition for his poetry at the age of eight, was first published at age fifteen, and stopped writing altogether at nineteen. Renowned French poet Paul Verlaine introduced Rimbaud to many of the most prominent poets of the day and encouraged Rimbaud as he wrote some of his finest poetry.

Unfortunately, Verlaine and Rimbaud quarreled frequently; ultimately, Verlaine attempted to murder his young friend. After serving a two-year prison sentence for his crime, Verlaine published Rimbaud's collection of poetry, *Illuminations* (1876). The collection earned widespread acclaim among critics and writers and was applauded as the work of a mature and remarkably talented poet. By the time of his death in 1891, Rimbaud's poetry had already begun to influence other writers; during the twentieth century, his lifestyle became a model for such vagabond writers, artists, and musicians as Jack Kerouac and Bob Dylan.

Paul Verlaine (1844–1896)

Like many of his fellow poets, Paul Verlaine (ver lān′) was an accomplished writer at a very young age; his body of work includes exquisitely musical lyrics, religious verse, and sonnets. Verlaine benefited from associations with renowned authors such as Baudelaire, Rimbaud, and novelist Victor Hugo. In particular, Verlaine shared a tumultuous friendship with Rimbaud that ended badly—Verlaine shot his friend in a murder attempt that landed him in prison for two years.

Through the success of his poems, Verlaine brought early attention to the Symbolists, an emerging group of writers whose works relied on complex patterns of symbols to convey deeply personal themes.

Like so many of his fellow poets, Verlaine craved a bohemian lifestyle. Though the last years of his life were spent in poverty and dissolution, Verlaine was honored as Prince of Poets in 1894 and given a public funeral in Paris upon his death in 1896.

TEACHING RESOURCES

The following resources can be used to enrich or extend the instruction for pp. 812–813.

Background

Beyond Literature, p. 40

Take It to the Net

Visit PHSchool.com for background on the authors.

Literary Analysis

Literary Analysis and Reading Transparencies, Romantic Poetry, p. 79

Reading

Literary analysis and Reading Transparencies, Judging a Poet's Message, p. 80

Selection Support: Reading Strategy, p. 159; Build Vocabulary, p. 157

BLOCK SCHEDULING: Resources marked with this symbol provide varied instruction during 90-minute blocks.

Preview

Connecting to the Literature

Baudelaire, Rimbaud, and Verlaine believed that personal, immediate, and emotional responses were valid subjects for poetry. Pay attention to the emotion in these poems, and notice the part nature plays in those feelings.

2 Literary Analysis

Romantic Poetry

Romantic poetry is part of a literary and artistic movement called Romanticism. While earlier poems often relied on wit and stylish pretense, Romantic works placed a premium on elements closer to the heart:

- imagination
- emotion
- nature
- individuality
- the exotic

As you read, notice how these elements guide a reader's imagination toward an emotional response, and identify the emotions you feel.

Comparing Literary Works

All the poems in this grouping use nature as a subject or as a way to communicate a message. Consider these questions as you read:

- Is nature something to interact with, wonder at, fear, or appreciate?
- Is nature indifferent to human suffering or sympathetic toward it?
- Is nature—especially its colors and seasons—used symbolically?

Look for the poets' attitudes toward nature and contrast the messages these poems communicate.

3 Reading Strategy

Judging a Poet's Message

As a reader, your job is not only to discover the point a poet is making but also to weigh what the poet says against your own experiences and past readings. When you **judge a poet's message,** you assess the validity of the poet's ideas and decide whether you agree or disagree with them.

As you read these poems, use a chart like the one shown to identify and judge the message each poet expresses.

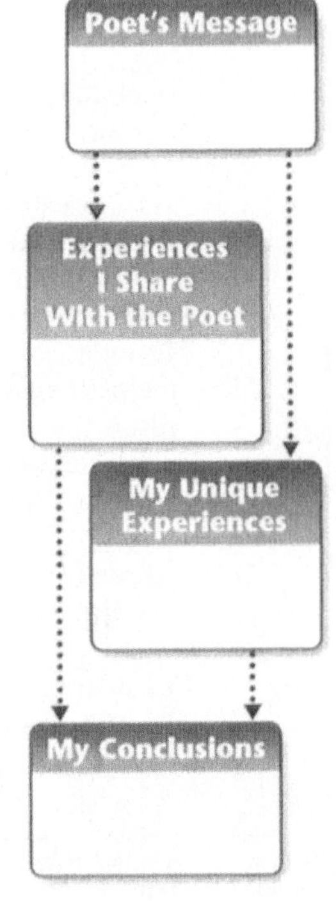

Vocabulary Development

proffering (präf′ ər iŋ) *v.* offering (p. 815)

nonchalantly (nän′ shə länt′ lē) *adv.* in a casually indifferent manner (p. 816)

sovereign (säv′ rən) *n.* monarch or ruler (p. 816)

adroit (ə droit′) *adj.* skillful in a physical or mental way (p. 816)

flourish (flur′ ish) *n.* fanfare, as of trumpets (p. 819)

strains (stränz) *n.* passages of music; tunes; airs (p. 820)

monotone (män′ ə tōn′) *n.* sound or song that repeats a single note (p. 822)

CUSTOMIZE INSTRUCTION FOR UNIVERSAL ACCESS

For Less Proficient Readers	For English Learners	For Advanced Readers
Make the language and style of these poems more accessible and less intimidating by previewing with students the vocabulary and footnotes. This will help students concentrate on the tone and rhythm of the selections as they read.	As students read, have them mark difficult or challenging passages with self-sticking notes. They may want to stop after each page and discuss these passages with partners, or meet after finishing each poem to share their strategies for assessing the meaning of these passages.	As students read, have them list each poem's primary message, along with the ways each poet conveys it. Students should note imagery, figurative language, rhyme scheme, and other elements that may directly or indirectly convey the message.

2 Literary Analysis

Romantic Poetry

- Read aloud the list of elements found in Romantic poetry. Discuss and define each element.
- Then, ask students to give an example of how each element might be conveyed poetically. For example, imagination and nature might be conveyed through a description of a beautiful, idyllic landscape.
- Read with the class the questions in the Comparing Literary Works instruction on p. 813. Point out that each of the poems in this grouping contains a reference to nature, one of the elements of Romantic poetry.
- Encourage students to identify other elements of Romantic poetry as they read the poems.
- Use the Romantic Poetry transparency in **Literary Analysis and Reading Transparencies,** p. 79, to help students identify the elements of Romantic poetry.

3 Reading Strategy

Judging a Poet's Message

- Point out that identifying imagery and using the questions in the Comparing Literary Works instruction can help students understand a poem's message.
- Guide students to understand how to judge a poet's message by using the graphic organizer on p. 813. Suggest the following poetic message: Modern society has lost touch with the power and mystery of nature. Ask students to suggest some of their experiences that either support or contradict this message. Then, have students draw a conclusion about, or judge, the validity of the message.
- Encourage students to use a graphic organizer like the one on p. 813 as they read the poems in this grouping.

Vocabulary Development

- Pronounce each vocabulary word for students, and read the definitions as a class. Have students identify any words with which they are familiar.

 ***E-Teach***

Visit e-Teach at PHSchool.com for teachers' essays on how to teach, with questions and answers.

TEACH

Step-by-Step Teaching Guide for pp. 814–822

Teaching Tenth-Grade Students

10TH GRADE Explain to tenth-grade students that the albatross is a bird found mainly in the South Pacific. With a wingspan that extends up to nine feet, it excels at flying and gliding. During the 1800s, albatrosses were often slaughtered for their feathers and wings.

❶ About the Translation

Richard Wilbur, the translator of Baudelaire's "Invitation to the Voyage," is an important poet and a superb translator of French poetry. In this translation, Wilbur is faithful to the original while moving beyond a literal translation. To appreciate his achievement, consider the refrain. This is the literal translation of the couplet: "There, all is only order and beauty, / Luxury, calm, and voluptuousness." Wilbur has rendered this "There, there is nothing else but grace and measure, / Richness, quietness, and pleasure."

❷ Literary Analysis

Romantic Poetry

- Direct students' attention to the Literary Analysis instruction on p. 813, and read aloud the elements of Romantic poetry.
- Then, ask students to respond to the Literary Analysis item on p. 814: List three characteristics of Romantic poetry in lines 8–11.
  Possible response: The poem shows a concern with nature with its description of the "cloud-disheveled air." The exotic and the imaginative are reflected in the "mystery" of "those other skies." The description of "treacherous eyes" evokes the Romantic interest in emotion.

❸ ▶Critical Viewing

Possible response: The stormy sky, the rough waves, and the beauty and grace of the ship's sails might inspire poets.

❶ Invitation to the Voyage

Charles Baudelaire
translated by Richard Wilbur

Background

There is little doubt that Charles Baudelaire's ocean voyage to India was a significant event in his life. Although the journey was cut short—lasting only eight months instead of eighteen—the experience clearly inspired him as a poet. The voyage, his desire for a life of ease and luxury, and his yearning to escape reality all find expression in his poems "Invitation to the Voyage" and "The Albatross."

My child, my sister, dream
How sweet all things would seem
Were we in that kind land to live together
And there love slow and long,
There love and die among
Those scenes that image you, that sumptuous[1] weather.
Drowned suns that glimmer there
Through cloud-disheveled[2] air
❷ Move me with such a mystery as appears
Within those other skies
Of your treacherous eyes
When I behold them shining through their tears.

There, there is nothing else but grace and measure,
Richness, quietness, and pleasure.

Furniture that wears
The luster of the years
Softly would glow within our glowing chamber,

Literary Analysis
Romantic Poetry List three characteristics of Romantic poetry in lines 8–11.

❸ **Critical Viewing ▶** Which details in this seascape might inspire a poet? **[Interpret]**

1. **sumptuous** (sump' cho͞o əs) *adj.* magnificent or splendid.
2. **disheveled** (di shev' əld) *adj.* disarranged and untidy.

TEACHING RESOURCES

The following resources can be used to enrich or extend the instruction for pp. 814–822.

Literary Analysis

- **Selection Support:** Literary Analysis, p. 160
- **Literary Analysis and Reading Transparencies:** Romantic Poetry, p. 79

Reading

- **Selection Support,** Reading Strategy, p. 159; Build Vocabulary, p. 157
- **Listening to Literature Audiocassettes** ■
- **Listening to Literature Audio CDs** ■

■ **BLOCK SCHEDULING:** Resources marked with this symbol provide varied instruction during 90-minute blocks.

Flowers of rarest bloom
Proffering their perfume
Mixed with the vague fragrances of amber;
Gold ceilings would there be,
Mirrors deep as the sea,
The walls all in an Eastern splendor hung—
Nothing but should address
The soul's loneliness,
Speaking her sweet and secret native tongue.

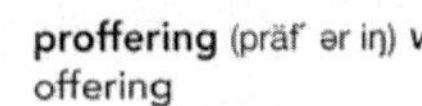

proffering (präf' ər iŋ) *v.* offering

4
There, there is nothing else but grace and measure,
Richness, quietness, and pleasure.

Reading Strategy
Judging a Poet's Message What message is the speaker determined to communicate through these repeated lines?

See, sheltered from the swells
There in the still canals
Those drowsy ships that dream of sailing forth;
5
It is to satisfy
Your least desire, they ply
Hither through all the waters of the earth.
The sun at close of day
Clothes the fields of hay,
Then the canals, at last the town entire
In hyacinth and gold:
Slowly the land is rolled
Sleepward under a sea of gentle fire.

Literary Analysis
Romantic Poetry Explain how individuality is presented in lines 32–34.

There, there is nothing else but grace and measure,
Richness, quietness, and pleasure.

6

Erminia in the Rough Sea, 1869, National Trust Photographic Library

4 Reading Strategy
Judging a Poet's Message

- Remind students that a reader cannot judge a poet's message until he or she identifies the message.
- Have a volunteer read aloud the bracketed passage. Then, ask students the Reading Strategy question on p. 815: What message is the speaker determined to communicate through these repeated lines?
Possible response: Through repetition, the speaker is trying to reinforce the pleasurable qualities of the voyage. He may also be trying to convince his beloved to join him on the voyage or trying to reassure himself that the voyage does indeed have these qualities.

5 Literary Analysis
Romantic Poetry

- Remind students that individuality is often a theme of Romantic poetry. Then, have a volunteer read aloud the bracketed passage.
- Ask students to respond to the Literary Analysis item on p. 815: Explain how individuality is presented in lines 32–34.
Possible response: Lines 32–34 describe the ships as sailing to fulfill an individual's personal desire.

6 Background
Art

Erminia in the Rough Sea, **1869**

The artist created this nineteenth-century English painting using gouache, which is a type of thick and opaque watercolor paint.

Use the following question for discussion:

What details in this painting illustrate ideas similar to the poet's message?
Possible response: The vibrant colors and darkening sky reflect the exotic and mysterious qualities of the poem.

CUSTOMIZE INSTRUCTION FOR UNIVERSAL ACCESS

For Special Needs Students	For Gifted/Talented Students
Students may have difficulty with words such as *treacherous, luster, proffering, splendor,* and *ply.* On the board, list these words. Then, organize students into small groups, and have them use dictionaries to find synonyms for the listed words. After students have found synonyms, have students read "Invitation to the Voyage," replacing the difficult words with the synonyms. Encourage students to use this strategy as they read the other poems in this grouping.	If any students are currently studying French, ask them to obtain the text of "Invitation to the Voyage" in French. Then, have students read the poem in French to their classmates. This should help give students a sense of how the poem sounds in its original language, and it will remind students that this poem, as well as the other poems in the grouping, were translated from French.

❼ About the Selection

"The Albatross" may have been inspired by an incident that Baudelaire actually witnessed during an ocean voyage in 1841. The poem describes the cruel treatment of a captured albatross by a ship's crew.

❽ Reading Strategy

Judging a Poet's Message

- Read aloud the bracketed passage. Then, ask students the Reading Strategy question on p. 816: What message does the speaker convey about the albatross in its natural setting?
  Possible response: In its natural setting, the albatross is a regal creature, impervious to various threats such as a storm and a marksman.
- Ask students: What is Baudelaire suggesting about society's treatment of poets?
  Possible response: Baudelaire is suggesting that, like the albatross, a poet has special gifts but is a victim of misunderstanding and cruelty.

❾ ▶Critical Viewing

Possible response: Rimbaud describes a silvery river, a valley, a cloud, and abundant green.

Answers for p. 816

Review and Assess

1. Possible responses: Some readers may say that they would enjoy the voyage because of its exotic and dreamlike feeling; others may say that they would not like the unrealistic or mysterious nature of such a trip.
2. **(a)** The land's "kind" attributes are its "sumptuous weather," rich furnishings, fragrant flowers, ships that will bring anything desired, and beautiful scenes of fields and canals. **(b)** The details give the impression of an exotic, dreamlike land that offers its occupants varied luxuries.
3. **(a)** The speaker describes a poet living a life that is underappreciated and ridiculed by the masses. The poet's ability to "soar" is limited by the realities of everyday life. **(b)** Possible response: Most readers will say that contemporary poets are revered, as evidenced by the existence of the title "Poet Laureate."
4. **(a)** Possible responses: Some readers may find the luxurious world described enticing because of its ease and pleasure; others may find that it is too comfortable and thus boring. **(b)** Possible responses: Some readers may suggest that this world reflects their ideal of peace and comfort; others may say that they would prefer a different world, one that presents challenges and opportunities for action.

continued

Continued from left column

The Albatross ❼

Charles Baudelaire *translated by* **Richard Howard**

Often, to pass the time on board, the crew
will catch an albatross, one of those big birds
which <u>nonchalantly</u> chaperone a ship
across the bitter fathoms of the sea.

Tied to the deck, this <u>sovereign</u> of space,
as if embarrassed by its clumsiness,
pitiably lets its great white wings
drag at its sides like a pair of unshipped oars.

How weak and awkward, even comical
this traveler but lately so <u>adroit</u>—
one deckhand sticks a pipestem in its beak,
another mocks the cripple that once flew!

❽ The Poet is like this monarch of the clouds
riding the storm above the marksman's range;
exiled on the ground, hooted and jeered,
he cannot walk because of his great wings.

nonchalantly (nän′shə länt′ lē) *adv.* in a casually indifferent manner

sovereign (säv′ rən) *n.* monarch or ruler

adroit (ə droit′) *adj.* skillful in a physical or mental way

Reading Strategy
Judging a Poet's Message What message does the speaker convey about the albatross in its natural setting?

Review and Assess

Thinking About the Selections

1. **Respond:** Would you like to experience the type of voyage that the speaker describes in "Invitation to the Voyage"? Why or why not?
2. **(a) Recall:** Which details describe the "kind land" in "Invitation to the Voyage"? **(b) Interpret:** What impression of the land do these details convey?
3. **(a) Interpret:** What message about the life of a poet does the speaker convey in "The Albatross"? **(b) Evaluate:** Do you think this message can be applied to contemporary poets? Why or why not?
4. **(a) Connect:** Explain whether the world described in "Invitation to the Voyage" is enticing to you. **(b) Compare:** How does this place compare to your ideal world?

❾ **Critical Viewing ▶** Which images in Rimbaud's poem describe the scene in this landscape? **[Connect]**

10 # The Sleeper in the Valley

Arthur Rimbaud *translated by* William Jay Smith

This is the green wherein a river chants
Whose waters on the grasses wildly toss
Its silver tatters, where proud sunlight slants
Within a valley thick with beams like moss.

A youthful soldier, mouth agape, head bare,
And nape where fresh blue water cresses drain
Sleeps stretched in grass, beneath the cloud, where
On abundant green the light descends like rain.

12 His feet on iris roots, smiling perhaps
As would some tiny sickly child, he naps.
O nature, he is cold: make warm his bed.

This quiver of perfume will not break his rest;
In the sun he sleeps, his hand on quiet breast.
Upon one side there are two spots of red.

Literary Analysis
Romantic Poetry
List four visual images of nature in the first stanza.

Reading Strategy
Judging a Poet's Message
What philosophy about death does the speaker imply by referring to the soldier as being in a bed?

13

CUSTOMIZE INSTRUCTION FOR UNIVERSAL ACCESS

For English Learners	For Gifted/Talented Students
Students may have difficulty decoding the first stanza of "The Sleeper in the Valley." Point out to students that rearranging the order of words and paraphrasing may help them understand what is being said. Guide students to rewrite the first two sentences of the first stanza by rearranging or paraphrasing the lines (This is the green valley where a river chants / the river's waters toss wildly as they flow over the grasses).	Have students create illustrations of the scene Rimbaud describes in "The Sleeper in the Valley." Before students begin their illustrations, have them list those visual elements in the poem they intend to depict. Students should note details concerning the use of color and the placement of the soldier's body. Have students share their illustrations with the class and discuss how their depictions parallel Rimbaud's imagery.

10 About the Selection

In this poem, Rimbaud uses intense sensory detail to describe a dead soldier "sleeping" on the bed of nature. The soothing imagery transforms what would usually be a disturbing scene into one of quiet repose.

11 Literary Analysis

Romantic Poetry

- Remind students that the Romantic poets often use descriptions of nature as a vehicle for their larger poetic messages.
- Then, have students respond to the Literary Analysis item on p. 817: List four visual images of nature in the first stanza.

Possible response: Four visual images of nature are the green of the valley, the turbulent water of the river, the river in "silver tatters," and the slant of the sunlight.

12 Reading Strategy

Judging a Poet's Message

- Draw students' attention to line 11, and read the line aloud. Then, ask students whom the speaker is addressing in this line.
  Answer: The speaker is addressing nature.
- Ask students the Reading Strategy question on p. 817: What philosophy about death does the speaker imply by referring to the soldier as being in a bed?
  Answer: The speaker is implying that death is merely a long sleep, not an end of being.

13 Background

Art

The Seine Near Rouen, by Jean-Baptiste-Camille Corot

Widely known for his landscape paintings, French artist Corot (1796–1875) sought to capture the effects of sunlight on the natural form of the land. His work drew the attention of Baudelaire, who wrote in an 1845 review that "Corot stands at the head of the modern school of landscape."

Use the following question for discussion.

How would you describe the mood of this painting?
Possible response: The mood is one of serenity.

14 About the Selection

In "Ophelia," Rimbaud shifts the focus from Hamlet's painful internal struggle revealed in Shakespeare's play to Ophelia and the suffering that she experienced. Rimbaud builds on Shakespeare's characterization of Ophelia and probes into possible explanations for her death.

15 Background

Art

Ophelia, by John Everett Millais

Millais (1829–1896) was a highly regarded nineteenth-century English artist. For a brief period, he was a member of the Pre-Raphaelite Brotherhood, a group of painters dedicated to revitalizing craftsmanship, design, and decorative naturalism in an increasingly machine-dominated society. Throughout his career, Millais was known for his detailed, realistic paintings and illustrations. Because of his attention to detail, his works were often used to illustrate the writings of major British writers.

Use the following questions for discussion:

- What impression of Ophelia does this painting convey?
  Possible response: Ophelia's posture and expression convey her submission and oneness with nature.
- How does the artist's depiction compare with Rimbaud's depiction?
  Possible response: The painting does not give a sense of Ophelia as a "great lily" as Rimbaud suggests; the painting does, however, give a sense of nature mourning Ophelia as the plants and trees are shown sheltering and enveloping her.

16 ▶ Critical Viewing

Possible response: The colors and images evoke a sense of melancholy.

14 Ophelia

Arthur Rimbaud

translated by Daisy Aldan

15

16 ▲ Critical Viewing What emotions do the colors and images in this painting evoke in you? **[Respond]**

Ophelia, John Everett Millais, Tate Gallery, London

ENRICHMENT: Literature Connection

Characters from Previous Literary Works

Rimbaud borrows a character from Shakespeare's *Hamlet* in this poem "Ophelia." One of the many ways in which writers draw on the accomplishments of earlier writers is by borrowing, reusing, or redefining characters from previous literary works. In fact, in many cases, a writer will borrow not only the characters but also the plot from an earlier literary work, reshaping and recasting it to create a new and original work of literature. For example, both sixteenth-century playwright Christopher Marlowe's *Dr. Faustus* and Johann Wolfgang von Goethe's *Faust* are based on the Faust legend from German folklore. Yet, the numerous differences between the two works reveal that each writer transformed the legend into his own distinctive literary work.

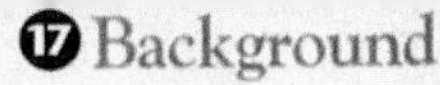

17 Background

Arthur Rimbaud's rare talent for poetry came at an early age. He wrote "Ophelia," for example, at age fifteen. Many critics consider it a remarkable piece—not only because of the author's youth but also because of the poem's quality as a literary piece. By the time Rimbaud's brief career ended at nineteen, novice poets were crafting their own poems in imitation of his widely recognized lyrical style.

In his poem "Ophelia," Rimbaud borrows a character from *Hamlet*. In Shakespeare's play, Ophelia is a beautiful, innocent, impressionable young maiden who is in love with Hamlet, the play's protagonist. Confused by Hamlet's sudden rejection of her, and grief-stricken by her father's death, Ophelia spirals into depression and insanity. The poem "Ophelia" presents one interpretation of Ophelia's life, the troubled relationship she endures with Hamlet, and the way in which her life ends.

I

On the calm black wave where the stars sleep
Floats white Ophelia like a great lily,
Floats very slowly, lying in her long veils . . .
—From the distant woods, the flourish of the kill.

For more than a thousand years sad Ophelia
White phantom, passes, on the long black river.
For more than a thousand years her sweet obsession
Whispers her love to the evening breeze.

18 The wind embraces her breasts and unfolds her great veils
In a corolla[1] gently rocked by the waters;
Trembling willows weep on her shoulder,
Reeds lean on her lofty pensive[2] brow.

flourish (flʉr′ ish) *n.* fanfare, as of trumpets

Literary Analysis
Romantic Poetry
What comparison is the speaker making through the use of phrases such as "the wind embraces" and "willows weep"?

19  **Reading Check**
How long has the spirit of Ophelia passed on the dark river?

1. **corolla** (kə räl′ ə) *n.* the petals, or inner floral leaves, of a flower.
2. **pensive** (pen′ siv) *adj.* thinking deeply or seriously, often of sad or melancholy things.

CUSTOMIZE INSTRUCTION FOR UNIVERSAL ACCESS

For Gifted/Talented Students	For Advanced Readers
Have students select one of their favorite characters from a literary work or a movie. Then, ask students to write journal entries in which they describe their impressions of the characters' personality. At the end of their entries, students should explore the ways in which they would further develop the characters if students were to create new literary works or movies involving the characters.	Remind students that Rimbaud was fifteen when he wrote "Ophelia." Then, have them discuss some other precocious writers whose works they have read. If they have studied English literature, remind them that Alexander Pope wrote "Ode on Solitude" when he was only twelve. Also, point out that John Keats wrote all of his poems while still in his early twenties. The American writer Stephen Crane wrote *The Red Badge of Courage* when he was just twenty-one.

17 Background

Drama

Hamlet is considered one of William Shakespeare's greatest tragedies. In it, Ophelia is a beautiful, innocent, modest maiden who is in love with Hamlet, the play's protagonist. Tortured by his inability to avenge his father's death, Hamlet, who had previously courted Ophelia, casts her away and claims that he never actually loved her. Hamlet then mistakenly kills Ophelia's father, Polonius, while attempting to stab his father's murderer. Unable to cope with her father's death, coupled with Hamlet's rejection, Ophelia loses her sanity and becomes completely absorbed with singing and gathering flowers, which she laces in her hair. Eventually, she is found drowned in a river, and her death prompts a strong emotional reaction from Hamlet.

18 Literary Analysis

Romantic Poetry

- Tell students that, when reading Romantic poetry, they should consider the poet's attitude toward nature.
- Ask a volunteer to read aloud the bracketed passage. Then, ask: What literary technique does Rimbaud use in the third stanza of the poem?
  Answer: Rimbaud is using personification to give natural elements human qualities.
- Ask students the Literary Analysis question on p. 819: What comparison is the speaker making through the use of phrases such as "the wind embraces" and "willows weep"?
  Answer: The speaker is comparing the wind and the willows to human beings who mourn for Ophelia.

19 Reading Check

Answer: The spirit of Ophelia has passed on the dark river for more than a thousand years.

20 Background

Art

Ophelia Among the Flowers, by Odilon Redon

Odilon Redon (1840–1916) was a French painter and graphic artist associated with the art movement known as Symbolism. Redon began his career making black and white charcoal drawings and lithographs, which were heavily influenced by the words of poet and author Edgar Allan Poe. Later in his career, Redon turned to painting and color drawing, creating imaginative, sensitive works of radiant color, featuring mythological scenes and delicate flowers, such as those shown in this painting.

Use the following question for discussion:

Which painting of Ophelia—John Everett Millais's or Odilon Redon's—do you think more accurately portrays the scene in Rimbaud's poem?
Possible response: Millais's painting is the more accurate because it is detailed and realistic; however, Redon's impressionistic depiction more accurately evokes the eerie, ethereal quality of Rimbaud's poem.

21 ▶ Critical Viewing

Possible response: The details of the painting show Ophelia floating in the water surrounded by flowers, as described in the poem. However, the water of the river is blue, not black as in the poem; the painting does not show Ophelia's veils; nor does it capture nature mourning her death.

22 Critical Thinking

Infer

- Read aloud the bracketed passage. Ask students to focus on the natural images.
- Ask: On the basis of these images, what can you infer about Ophelia's relationship with nature?
Possible response: The images suggest that Ophelia, while alive, was especially attuned to nature and that it had a haunting effect on her. Rimbaud depicts nature as speaking or appealing to Ophelia's very soul.

20

Ophelia Among the Flowers, Odilon Redon

21 ▲ **Critical Viewing**
How do details in this painting compare and contrast with images in the poem? **[Compare and Contrast]**

Bruised water lilies sigh about her;
Sometimes in a sleeping alder tree she awakens
A nest; a tiny wing-flutter escapes;
Mysterious sounds fall from the golden stars.

II

22

O pale Ophelia! fair as snow!
You died, child, yes, carried off by a river!
Because the winds falling from the great cliffs of Norway
Spoke low to you of fierce freedom;

Because a wind, tearing your long hair,
Bore strange shouts to your dreaming spirit;
Because your heart listened to the strains of Nature
In the wails of the tree and the sighs of the nights.

strains (stränz) *n.* passages of music; tunes; airs

ENRICHMENT: Science Connection

Water Lilies

In "Ophelia," Rimbaud uses images of water lilies to create a vivid picture of the fragility of Shakespeare's character. Water lilies, however, are aggressive, sturdy plants that grow in thick patches on lakes, ponds, and other natural bodies of water. These patches make it difficult to fish, swim, or even boat on colonized water. New plants develop from seeds and from the large root networks that extend underwater.

The plant's beauty and its fragrant blossoms may have inspired Rimbaud's choice of image. Or, perhaps the poet knew that the water lily—with its circular leaves and large, bold flower—would be an easily recognizable and everlasting symbol.

Because the voice of mad seas, immense rattle,
Bruised your child's heart, too sweet and too human;
Because on an April morning, a handsome pale courtier,
A sorry fool, sat mutely at your feet!

Heaven! Love! Freedom! What a dream, O Foolish girl!
You melted toward him as snow near flame:
Your words were strangled by your great visions
—And the terrible Infinite frightened your blue eyes!

Reading Strategy
Judging a Poet's Message What does the speaker seem to say about people who seek nature, love, and freedom?

III

And the Poet says you come at night
To gather flowers in the rays of the stars;
And he has seen on the water, lying in her long veils,
White Ophelia floating, like a great lily.

Review and Assess

Thinking About the Selections

1. **Respond:** What are your impressions of Ophelia after reading Rimbaud's poem? How do you feel about the choices she made? Explain.
2. **(a) Recall:** In "The Sleeper in the Valley," who appears to be sleeping? **(b) Draw Conclusions:** What evidence in the poem suggests that the sleeper is not really asleep?
3. **(a) Recall:** Identify three words or phrases the speaker uses to describe the gentle qualities of nature in "The Sleeper in the Valley." **(b) Compare and Contrast:** How does the speaker's depiction of nature contrast with the actual events that took place there? Refer to specific lines and details to support your answers.
4. **(a) Recall:** In "Ophelia," what colors are mentioned in the first four lines? **(b) Analyze:** How are these colors used to establish Ophelia's purity and innocence?
5. **(a) Apply:** In what way is nature indifferent to human affairs? **(b) Speculate:** How does nature affect people emotionally?

23 Reading Strategy

Judging a Poet's Message

- Have a volunteer read aloud the bracketed passage.
- Ask students the Reading Strategy question on p. 821: What does the speaker seem to say about people who seek nature, love, and freedom? Possible response: The speaker seems to say that those who seek nature, love, and freedom are foolish for thinking that these things are attainable.

Monitor Progress If students have difficulty judging the speaker's message, encourage them to weigh this message against their own experiences.

Reteach Help students judge the speaker's message by guiding them as they complete a graphic organizer like the one shown on p. 813.

Answers for p. 821

Review and Assess

1. Possible response: Ophelia is gentle, sensitive, and vulnerable. Possible response: Ophelia made a foolish choice.
2. **(a)** A young soldier appears to be sleeping. **(b)** The descriptions of the sleeper as a "sickly child," as cold, and as having two spots of red on his side are evidence that he is not really asleep.
3. **(a)** The gentle qualities of nature are suggested by "abundant green," "the light descends like rain," and "this quiver of perfume." **(b)** The descriptions of the beautiful, scenic valley contrast with the sleeper's apparent violent encounter with death.
4. **(a)** The colors mentioned in the first four lines are black and white. **(b)** Ophelia's whiteness—like a lily or a phantom—contrasts with the black water on which she floats, emphasizing her purity.
5. **(a)** Nature, as an entity, takes no notice of human suffering or vulnerability. **(b)** Possible response: Weather has the power to make people melancholy or happy. The beauty and vastness of nature can also awe and inspire people.

CUSTOMIZE INSTRUCTION FOR UNIVERSAL ACCESS

For Special Needs Students	For Less Proficient Readers
Students may have difficulty understanding Rimbaud's poem if they are unfamiliar with Ophelia's role in *Hamlet.* Spend extra time going over the information about Ophelia in the Background note on p. 819. Encourage students to ask questions about the play, and clarify any plot points or characterization elements to foster students' understanding.	Write on the board the following words: *beautiful, innocent, modest, impressionable,* and *frail.* Remind students that these are the main characteristics of Ophelia's personality as she is portrayed in *Hamlet.* Have a student read aloud Rimbaud's poem. Then, guide students to identify additional characteristics of Ophelia's personality that are conveyed in the poem. Discuss what message the speaker is attempting to convey about Ophelia.

ASSESS

24 About the Selection

In Verlaine's brief poem, the speaker expresses the feelings of melancholy brought on by autumn.

25 Literary Analysis

Romantic Poetry

- Remind students of the importance of emotion in poetry.
- Then, ask students the Literary Analysis question on p. 822: What comparison in the first stanza helps the reader understand the intense emotion the speaker feels?
  Answer: The comparison is between the sound of violins that "sob and moan" with sadness and the sound of the speaker's heartstrings.

26 Vocabulary Development

Greek Prefix *mono-*

- Read aloud the word *monotone* and its definition.
- Tell students that *monotone* contains the Greek prefix *mono-*, which means "alone," "one," or "single." Have students list and define other words that contain this prefix.
  Possible response: *Monolith, monochromatic,* and *monorail* are possible suggestions.

Answers for p. 822

Review and Assess

1. Possible response: Sorrow, like the seasons, is fleeting. Therefore, sorrow is bearable.
2. **(a)** Possible response: Choices include *complain, sob, moan, ache,* or *make.* **(b)** The verbs create a feeling of sadness or pain.
3. **(a)** The speaker is mourning the passing of time and the change of seasons that mark this passage. **(b)** Possible response: The speaker might mourn a lost love or childhood innocence.
4. **(a)** Possible response: The poem would not be as mournful; it would contain images of sunshine and warm winds. **(b)** Possible response: Flutes sing of summer again. They giggle with glee. And my heartstrings soar.

24

Paul Verlaine *translated by* Louis Simpson

25

Violins complain
Of autumn again,
They sob and moan.
And my heartstrings ache
Like the song they make,
A monotone. 26

Suffocating, drowned,
And hollowly, sound
The midnight chimes.
Then the days return
I knew, and I mourn
For bygone times.

And I fall and drift
With the winds that lift
My heavy grief.
Here and there they blow,
And I rise and go
Like a dead leaf.

Literary Analysis
Romantic Poetry
What comparison in the first stanza helps the reader understand the intense emotion the speaker feels?

monotone (män′ ə tōn′) *n.* sound or song that repeats a single note

Review and Assess

Thinking About the Selection

1. **Respond:** What advice would you give to the speaker in "Autumn Song"? Why?
2. **(a) Recall:** Identify four verbs in lines 1–12. **(b) Analyze:** What overall feeling is created by these verbs?
3. **(a) Recall:** What is the speaker mourning? **(b) Speculate:** What events or conditions in the speaker's past might be worth mourning?
4. **(a) Make a Judgment:** In what ways would this poem be different if it were called "Summer Song"? **(b) Extend:** Compose three lines of this new poem.

ASSESSMENT PRACTICE: Critical Thinking

Distinguish Between Fact and Nonfact (For more practice, see Test Preparation Workbook, p. 40.)

Many tests require students to distinguish between fact and nonfact. Use the following sample test item to demonstrate how students can use this skill when reading.

Charles Baudelaire was the most inventive poet of his time. He was born in France in 1821. A rebellious young man, Baudelaire was expelled from school in 1839. He then moved to Paris. A Romantic in taste, he went beyond Romanticism to accurately portray the modern city. He died in 1867.

Which of the following is an opinion from the passage?

A Baudelaire was born in France in 1821.
B Baudelaire was expelled from school.
C Baudelaire was the most inventive poet of his time.
D Baudelaire died in 1867.

Lead students to recognize that the correct answer is C; choices *A, B,* and *D* can be proved, and *C* cannot.

Review and Assess

Literary Analysis

Romantic Poetry

1. For each poem in this grouping, complete an organizer like the one below, noting details that are typical of **Romantic poetry.**

Imagination	Emotion	Nature	Individuality	The Exotic

2. In "Invitation to the Voyage," how do the images of the "kind land" in line 3 relate to the ideas expressed in the poem's refrain?
3. (a) In line 26 of "Ophelia," what does the speaker mean when he says that Ophelia was "too human"? (b) What element of Romantic poetry does this sentiment evoke?

Comparing Literary Works

4. (a) Compare the ways in which "Invitation to the Voyage" and "Autumn Song" express the emotion of longing. (b) Which poem do you think is more effective in expressing longing? Why?
5. (a) Which sensory details are used to describe Ophelia in "Ophelia" and the soldier in "The Sleeper in the Valley"? (b) Identify three factors contributing to the perception that these characters deserve sympathy.

Reading Strategy

Judging a Poet's Message

6. (a) Explain how the desire to escape to an ideal or imaginary world is a message in "Invitation to the Voyage." (b) **Judge the poet's message** by explaining the possible benefits of escapism. (c) What negative consequences result from escapist behavior?
7. (a) Which details in "The Albatross" best communicate the speaker's attitude toward the crew? (b) Do you agree with this attitude? Explain.

Extend Understanding

8. **Science Connection:** How might a naturalist react to the treatment of the bird in "The Albatross"?

Quick Review

Romantic poetry focuses on imagination, emotion, nature, individuality, and the exotic.

To **judge a poet's message,** test the message against your own experiences, assess the validity of the message, and decide whether you agree or disagree with it.

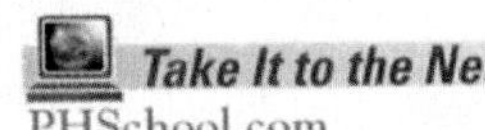

Take It to the Net

PHSchool.com

Take the interactive self-test online to check your understanding of these selections.

Review and Assess

1. Possible response: **Imagination:** the simile of the poet and the albatross; **Emotion:** "embarrassed . . ."; **Nature:** the albatross; **Individuality:** "The Poet is like this monarch . . ."; **The Exotic:** the albatross.
2. The refrain serves to reinforce and summarize the details provided about the "kind land."
3. **(a)** By saying that Ophelia was "too human," the speaker means that she was too sensitive. **(b)** This sentiment evokes the element of emotion.
4. **(a)** "Invitation to the Voyage" expresses longing for a place of ease and comfort; "Autumn Song" expresses longing for "bygone times." **(b)** Possible response: "Invitation to the Voyage" is more effective because it gives more details and reasons for the longing.
5. **(a)** Possible response: **"Ophelia": touch details**—wind embracing, wind "tearing" Ophelia's hair; **sound details**—sweet obsession whispering, wing-flutter, mysterious sounds, wind speaking low. **"The Sleeper in the Valley": smell details**—"this quiver of perfume"; **sound details**—river chanting. **(b)** The speaker refers to Ophelia's "bruised" child's heart; the speaker of "The Sleeper in the Valley" compares the soldier with a "tiny sickly child." By comparing these characters with children, the speaker suggests that these characters were not mature and thus did not deserve the fates that befell them.
6. **(a)** The refrain demonstrates the speaker's desire for the ideal world described in the poem. **(b)** The benefits of escapism include peace and freedom from stress and responsibility. **(c)** Negative consequences of escapism include an inability to accept reality and the responsibilities of life.
7. **(a)** Details such as "another mocks the cripple" and the hoots and jeers of the crew communicate the speaker's attitude of disapproval. **(b)** Possible response: It is cruel to torment the bird.

continued

continued from the right column

8. Possible response: A naturalist probably would be horrified at the abuse of such a magnificent and harmless creature.

ENRICHMENT: Further Reading

Other Works by the Authors

We strongly encourage you to review any selection before assigning or recommending it to students.

Complete Poems, Baudelaire

Collected Poems, Rimbaud

Selected Poems, Verlaine

Take It to the Net

Visit PHSchool.com for more information about the authors.

EXTEND

Answers for p. 824

1 Vocabulary Development

Word Analysis: Greek Prefix *mono-*

1. monotone: repetition of the same sound
2. monologue: a long speech by a single speaker
3. monopoly: the control of something by a single person or company

Spelling Strategy

1. one sound
2. two sounds
3. one sound
4. one sound

Concept Development: Analogies

1. proffering
2. flourish
3. strains
4. monotone
5. nonchalantly
6. sovereign
7. adroit

2 Grammar and Style

Practice

1. "Drowned suns that glimmer there . . ."; modifies *suns*
2. "The Poet is like this monarch . . ."; modifies *Poet*
3. "Because a wind, tearing your long hair, . . ."; modifies *wind*
4. "This is the green wherein a river chants . . ."; modifies *green*
5. "With the winds that lift / My heavy grief . . ."; modifies *winds*

Writing Application

Possible response: We'll sail on waves of golden water (modifies *waves*); We'll visit lands that are fragrant with spices and flowers (modifies *lands*).

10TH GRADE For support in teaching the Grammar and Style Lesson to tenth graders, use **Writing and Grammar,** Platinum Level, Chapter 20, Section 1.

Integrate Language Skills

1 Vocabulary Development Lesson

Word Analysis: Greek Prefix *mono-*

The Greek prefix *mono-* means "alone," "one," or "single." Add the prefix *mono-* to each of the roots given below. Use your understanding of the prefix and the clues provided to define the new word.

1. ______tone (sound)
2. ______logue (speaking)
3. ______poly (commerce)

Spelling Strategy

In words like *indignant*, the *g* and the *n* each stand for a separate sound. Sometimes, *gn* stands for only the *n* sound, as in *sign*. In these cases, it usually follows the letters *ai*, *ei*, or *i*. For each word below, identify whether *gn* stands for two separate sounds or just one sound.

1. sovereign
2. malignant
3. arraign
4. sovereignty

Concept Development: Analogies

An *analogy* compares the relationship between word meanings. For example, in analogies, word pairs often represent these common relationships:

synonym: *talk* is to *chat*
antonym: *noise* is to *silence*
degree: *cold* is to *freezing*
part to whole: *clarinet* is to *orchestra*

Review the vocabulary list on page 813. Then, choose the word from that list that best completes each analogy below.

1. *Wanting* is to *desiring* as *offering* is to ___.
2. *Noisy* is to *loud* as *fanfare* is to ___.
3. *Fiddle* is to *violin* as *tunes* is to ___.
4. *Felicitous* is to *felicity* as *monotonous* is to ___.
5. *Elegant* is to *refined* as *casually* is to ___.
6. *Student* is to *teacher* as *subject* is to ___.
7. *Plain* is to *beautiful* as *incapable* is to ___.

2 Grammar and Style Lesson

Adjectival Modifiers

An **adjectival modifier** is a phrase or clause that describes a noun or pronoun. Adjectival modifiers can come in many different forms. Study the examples provided below.

Prepositional Phrase: "Flowers *of rarest bloom* . . ." (modifies *Flowers*)

Participial Phrase: ". . . When I behold them *shining through their tears*." (modifies *them*)

Adjective Clause: ". . . drowsy ships *that dream of sailing forth* . . ." (modifies *ships*)

Practice For each item below, underline the adjectival modifier. Then, circle the word that the adjectival modifier describes.

1. "Drowned suns that glimmer there . . ."
2. "The Poet is like this monarch . . ."
3. "Because a wind, tearing your long hair, . . ."
4. "This is the green wherein a river chants . . ."
5. "With the winds that lift / My heavy grief . . ."

Writing Application Write two sentences about a journey, using adjectival modifiers. In each sentence, underline the adjectival modifier and circle the word it describes.

WG *Prentice Hall Writing and Grammar Connection: Diamond Level, Chapter 19, Section 1*

TEACHING RESOURCES

The following resources can be used to enrich or extend the instruction for pp. 824–825.

Vocabulary

Selection Support: Build Vocabulary, p. 157

Vocabulary and Spelling Practice Book (Use this booklet for skills instruction.)

Grammar

Selection Support: Grammar and Style, p. 158

Writing and Grammar, Diamond Level, p. 440

Daily Language Practice Transparencies

Writing

Performance Assess. and Portfolio Mgmt., p. 15

Writing and Grammar, Diamond Level, p. 178

Writing and Grammar iText CD-ROM

Writing Models and Graphic Organizers on Transparencies, pp. 103–106

Research and Technology

Performance Assess. and Portfolio Mgmt., p. 32

BLOCK SCHEDULING: Resources marked with this symbol provide varied instruction during 90-minute blocks.

❸ Writing Lesson

Comparison-and-Contrast Essay

In all of the poems within this grouping, nature significantly affects both the speakers and the events in the poems. Write an essay in which you compare and contrast the treatment of nature in three of the poems you have read.

Prewriting Choose three poems and take note of how nature is depicted in each one. Make an outline of the similarities and differences, organizing your observations into points you want to make.

Model: Making an Outline

I. Comparisons between "Invitation to the Voyage" and "The Albatross"
  A. Nature is presented positively in both.
  B. Examples: "Flowers of rarest bloom," albatross as "monarch of the clouds"

An outline for your own use can be formal, with numerals and letters as shown here, or informal, using bullets.

Drafting Using the words and details in your outline, write your essay. Address each of the points you have outlined.

Revising Compare your finished draft to your outline. Revise your essay to add any details that were missed.

WG Prentice Hall Writing and Grammar Connection: Diamond Level, Chapter 9, Section 3

❹ Extension Activities

Listening and Speaking Read Queen Gertrude's monologue in *Hamlet* at the end of Act IV, Scene vii. Then, read section II of Rimbaud's "Ophelia." In a **discussion** with a partner:

1. Consider each speaker and each audience.
2. Note the passage of time in each.
3. Evaluate how each speaker feels about Ophelia's death.

Draw conclusions about the differences you find. **[Group Activity]**

Research and Technology Build a **multimedia travelogue** illustrating Baudelaire's sea voyage to India. Select images and music or sounds that connect to his poem. You may also be able to include scents and items to touch. Present your travelogue to the class.

Take It to the Net PHSchool.com

Go online for an additional research activity using the Internet.

ASSESSMENT RESOURCES

The following resources can be used to assess students' knowledge and skills.

Selection Assessment

- **Formal Assessment,** pp. 142–144
- **Open-Book Tests,** pp. 118–120
- **Test Bank Software**

Take It to the Net

Visit PHSchool.com for self-tests on the selections.

Writing Rubric

- **Performance Assess. and Portfolio Mgmt.,** p. 15

Research and Technology Rubric

- **Performance Assess. and Portfolio Mgmt.,** p. 32

PRENTICE HALL ASSESSMENT SYSTEM

For additional diagnostics and remediation for skills covered in this grouping, use materials from the Prentice Hall Assessment System.

❸ Writing Lesson

- Before students create their outlines, have them refer to the graphic organizer that they completed for question 1 on p. 823.
- Students can use the Outline in **Writing Models and Graphic Organizers,** pp. 103–106, to help them complete their outlines.
- After students have finished their essays, use the Exposition: Comparison-and-Contrast Composition rubric in **Performance Assessment and Portfolio Management,** p. 15, to evaluate students' work.

10TH GRADE For support in working through the Writing Lesson with tenth-graders, use **Writing and Grammar,** Platinum Level, Chapter 9, Section 3.

❹ Research and Technology

- Encourage students to consult maps or a globe to find the sea route from France to India.
- Suggest that students use travel brochures from cruise lines, Internet resources, and print resources to locate images.
- Have students consult their local library's music collection for suitable music or sound effects to accompany their presentations.
- Use the Speaking: Multimedia Presentation rubric in **Performance Assessment and Portfolio Management,** p. 32, to assess students' presentations.

CUSTOMIZE INSTRUCTION
For Universal Access

To address different learning styles, use the following activities suggested in the **Extension Activities** booklet, p. 40:

- For Verbal/Linguistic Learners, use Activities 5, 6, and 7.
- For Visual/Spatial Learners, use Activities 5 and 7.
- For Musical/Rhythmic Learners, use Activity 6.

Two Friends • How Much Land Does a Man Need? • A Problem

Lesson Objectives

1. **To analyze and respond to literary elements**
   - Literary Analysis: Dynamic and Static Characters
   - Comparing Literary Works: Characters' Decisions
2. **To read, comprehend, analyze, and critique short stories**
   - Reading Strategy: Evaluating Characters' Decisions
   - Reading Check Questions
   - Review and Assess Questions
   - Assessment Practice (ATE)
3. **To develop word analysis skills, fluency, and systematic vocabulary**
   - Vocabulary Development Lesson: Latin Prefix *dis-*
4. **To understand and apply written and oral language conventions**
   - Spelling Strategy
   - Grammar and Style Lesson: Restrictive and Nonrestrictive Adjective Clauses
5. **To understand and apply appropriate writing and research strategies**
   - Writing Lesson: Analyzing a Character's Decision
   - Extension Activity: Coat of Arms
6. **To understand and apply listening and speaking strategies**
   - Extension Activity: Monologue

10TH GRADE TEACHING A TENTH-GRADE COURSE

The literature in this section can be taught as part of a rich, balanced world literature course for tenth-grade students. For a full outline of such a course, see pp. T46–T48 in Volume I of this Teacher's Edition.

STEP-BY-STEP TEACHING GUIDE	PACING GUIDE
PRETEACH	
Motivate Students and Provide Background	
Use the Motivation activity (ATE p. 826)	5 min.
Read and discuss author and background features (SE pp. 826, 828, 835, 851; ATE p. 826) A	5 min.
Introduce the Concepts	
Introduce the Literary Analysis and Reading Strategy concepts (SE/ATE p. 827) A	15 min.
Pronounce the vocabulary words and read their definitions (SE p. 827)	5 min.
TEACH	
Monitor Comprehension	
Informally monitor comprehension by circulating while students read A	25 min.
Monitor students' comprehension with the Reading Check notes (SE/ATE pp. 829, 831, 833, 835, 837, 839, 841, 843, 845, 847, 851, 853, 855, 857)	as students read
Develop vocabulary with the Vocabulary notes (SE pp. 830, 833, 837, 845, 852; ATE p. 837)	as students read
Develop Understanding	
Develop students' understanding of imagery with the Literary Analysis annotations (SE/ATE pp. 829, 830, 832, 836, 843, 846, 848, 851, 854, 856; ATE pp. 839, 841, 852, 855) A	5 min.
Develop students' ability to restate for understanding, using the Reading Strategy annotations (SE/ATE pp. 830, 833, 838, 841, 844, 847, 848, 852, 855, 857; ATE pp. 831, 851)	5 min.
ASSESS	
Assess Mastery	
Assess students' mastery of the Reading Strategy and Literary Analysis concepts by having them answer the Review and Assess questions (SE/ATE p. 859)	15 min.
Use one or more of the print, software, or transparency Assessment Resources (ATE p. 861) A	up to 45 min.
EXTEND	
Apply Understanding	
Have students complete the Vocabulary Development Lesson and the Grammar and Style Lesson (SE p. 860) A	20 min.
Apply students' ability to use transitions for coherence, using the Writing Lesson (SE/ATE p. 861) A	45 min.
Apply students' understanding of the selections, using one or more of the Extension Activities (SE p. 861)	20–90 min.

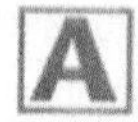

ACCELERATED INSTRUCTION:
Use the strategies and activities identified with an A.

10TH GRADE TEACHING TENTH-GRADE STUDENTS
For support in teaching tenth-graders, see the Step-by-Step Teaching notes identified with the icon.

UNIVERSAL ACCESS
- ● = Below-Level Students
- ▲ = On-Level Students
- ■ = Above-Level Students

Time and Resource Manager

Reading Level: Easy, Average, Average
Average Number of Instructional Days: 3

RESOURCES		
PRINT	**TRANSPARENCIES**	**TECHNOLOGY**
• **Beyond Literature,** Cross-Curricular Connection: Social Studies, p. 41 ▲ ■		• **Interest Grabber Video,** Tape 2, Unit 7, Segments 1 and 2 ● ▲ ■
• **Selection Support Workbook:** ● ▲ ■ Literary Analysis, p. 164 Reading Strategy, p. 163 Build Vocabulary, p. 161	• **Literary Analysis and Reading Transparencies,** pp. 81 and 82 ● ▲ ■	
• **Reader's Companion** ● • **Adapted Reader's Companion** ●		• **Listening to Literature** ● ▲ ■ Audiocassettes Audio CDs • **Reader's Companion Audio Program** ●
• **English Learner's Companion** ● ▲ ■ • **Literary Analysis for Enrichment,** p. 41 ■	• **Fine Art Transparencies,** Art Transparency 17	• **World Masterpieces iText CD-ROM** • Reader's Companion Adapted and English Learner's Version Audio Program ● ▲
• **Formal Assessment:** Selection Test, pp. 145–147 ● ▲ ■ • **Open-Book Tests,** pp. 121–123 ● ▲ ■ • **Performance Assessment and Portfolio Management,** pp. 14, 28 ● ▲ ■ • PRENTICE HALL ASSESSMENT SYSTEM ● ▲ ■	• PRENTICE HALL ASSESSMENT SYSTEM ● ▲ ■ **Skills Practice Answers and Explanations on Transparencies**	• **Test Bank Software** ● ▲ ■
• **Selection Support Workbook:** ● ▲ ■ Grammar and Style, p. 162 • **Writing and Grammar,** Diamond Level ● ▲ ■ • **Extension Activities,** p. 41 ● ▲ ■	• **Daily Language Practice Transparencies** ● ▲ • **Writing Models and Graphic Organizers on Transparencies,** pp. 83–85 ● ▲ ■	• **Writing and Grammar iText CD-ROM** ● ▲ ■ *Take It to the Net* PHSchool.com

BLOCK SCHEDULING: Use one 90-minute class period to preteach the selection(s) and have students read them. Use a second 90-minute class period to assess students' mastery of skills and have them complete one of the Extension Activities.

Step-by-Step Teaching Guide for pp. 826–827

Motivation

Have students discuss some of the potential dangers of making foolish, spur-of-the-moment decisions. Ask whether they have ever made a decision that was foolish or too hasty. If so, what were the consequences?

Interest Grabber Video

As an alternative, play "'Two Friends': On Friendship" and "'How Much Land Does a Man Need?': Czars and Peasants" on Tape 2 to engage student interest.

❶ Background

More About the Authors

Maupassant's first short story, "Ball of Fat," won praise from the great French realist Gustave Flaubert, who wrote in a letter to Maupassant: "I consider 'Ball of Fat' a *masterpiece.*"

During Tolstoy's childhood, 800 serfs lived on the Tolstoy estate of Yasnaya Polyana ("Clear Glade"). When he inherited the estate at the age of nineteen, he tried to make a better life for them.

When Chekhov was an adolescent, his parents moved to Moscow, leaving him to finish school in his hometown of Taganrog. Living essentially on his own for three years, Chekhov completed high school, attended the theater, read widely, and began writing.

Geography Note

Use the map on this page to identify Russia, the native country of both Tolstoy and Chekhov. Explain that during the authors' lifetimes, millions of peasants were required to work the land for wealthy, often brutal, landowners. The peasants, or serfs, were freed in 1861 but were still subject to restrictions.

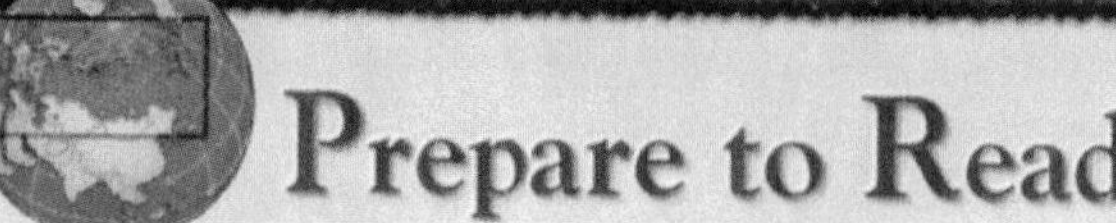

Prepare to Read

❶ Two Friends ◆ How Much Land Does a Man Need? ◆ A Problem

Guy de Maupassant (1850–1893)

Guy de Maupassant (gē də mō′ pä sän) first wrote under the guidance of famous French writers Gustave Flaubert and Émile Zola. Encouraged by Zola, Maupassant published his first short story in 1880. The story earned him immediate fame, establishing his career as a prolific and extremely popular writer. The royalties from his first volume of short stories, *Madame Tellier's Establishment* (1881), and his novels *A Woman's Life* (1883) and *Bel-Ami* (1884) enabled him to live a life of luxury. He traveled extensively, incorporating his recollections into his early works. Maupassant's later stories, however, reflect his growing inner turmoil, often presenting an uncomplimentary but realistic portrait of the world. In "Two Friends," for example, Maupassant presents a graphic depiction of the violence and destruction of war.

Health problems and bouts of depression plagued Maupassant. Finally, Maupassant was committed to an asylum, where he died in 1893.

Leo Tolstoy (1828–1910)

Leo Tolstoy (tōl′ stōi) was born at his family's estate near Moscow. The tragic loss of his parents and a beloved aunt affected him profoundly, leading to a lifelong obsession with the inevitability of death.

Tolstoy's first novel was published in 1852, followed by a collection of stories in 1856. *War and Peace* (1869), a novel about Napoleon's invasion of Russia in 1812, was immediately regarded as a masterpiece for its graphic depiction of war, its insights into Russian culture, and its exploration into the meaning of life. The deeply tragic novel (1874–1876) confirmed Tolstoy's already lofty reputation as a writer.

Struggling through a spiritual crisis, Tolstoy created his own religious faith that emphasized a natural existence, universal love, equality, and nonviolence. In accordance with his beliefs, Tolstoy renounced the rights to his works published after 1881 and gave his property to his family. In 1910, shortly after leaving his wife and family, Tolstoy died in an obscure railroad station.

Anton Chekhov (1860–1904)

Anton Chekhov (chek′ôf) is one of only a few major writers who also studied and practiced medicine. Despite the demands of a medical career, Chekhov published a substantial body of work, including both scientific pieces and great literary works. One of his finest plays, *The Seagull* (1896), focuses on intergenerational conflict.

Toward the end of the nineteenth century, declining health forced Chekhov to move to the warmer climate of Yalta. Illness did not impair his literary output, however, and in his last years he produced two critically acclaimed plays, *The Sisters* (1901) and *The Cherry Orchard* (1904). When Chekhov finally succumbed to tuberculosis in 1904, his literary reputation had not yet extended beyond Russia. Since World War I, however, he has come to be regarded as one of the finest short-story writers the world has ever produced.

TEACHING RESOURCES

The following resources can be used to enrich or extend the instruction for pp. 826–827.

Motivation

Interest Grabber Video, Tape 2

Background

Beyond Literature, p. 41

Take It to the Net

Visit PHSchool.com for background on the authors.

Literary Analysis

Literary Analysis and Reading Transparencies, Dynamic and Static Characters, p. 81

Reading

Literary Analysis and Reading Transparencies, Evaluating Characters' Decisions, p. 82

Selection Support: Reading Strategy, p. 163
Build Vocabulary, p. 161

BLOCK SCHEDULING: Resources marked with this symbol provide varied instruction during 90-minute blocks.

Preview

Connecting to the Literature

Sometimes, even the smallest decision can be difficult to make. The protagonists in these stories are forced to make important choices that have disastrous consequences. Look for the challenges the characters face as they make their decisions, and imagine what you might have done in their place.

❷ Literary Analysis

Dynamic and Static Characters

Like people in life, characters in literature can change as a story progresses. A **dynamic character** experiences a change or shift in attitude and behavior during the course of a literary work. However, a **static character's** attitudes and behavior remain essentially stable throughout.

As you become acquainted with the characters in these stories, create a chart like the one shown to identify each of the characters as either dynamic or static. Consider how the contrasts between these character types add tension within each story.

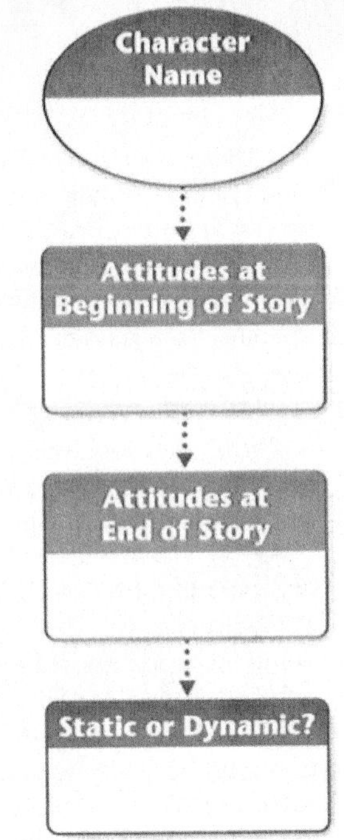

Comparing Literary Works

These short stories feature characters making decisions that direct the outcomes of their lives. Every decision brings consequences—some good, some bad. These anticipated consequences often drive the choices characters make. Look at the way each character approaches his or her choices, and compare the factors each one considers before he or she acts.

❸ Reading Strategy

Evaluating Characters' Decisions

Evaluate characters' decisions just as you would assess your own. Follow these steps to critically consider a choice and its effect on future actions:

- Consider whether the character benefits from the decision the way he or she imagined.
- Analyze the effect each decision has on other characters.
- Finally, judge whether the decision turns out to be good or bad.

Use this process to evaluate characters' decisions in each story you read.

Vocabulary Development

pillaging (pil' ij iŋ) *v.* plundering; looting (p. 830)

superimposed (so͞o' pər im pōzd') *v.* placed on top of something else (p. 830)

placidly (plas' id lē) *adv.* calmly (p. 833)

discord (dis' kôrd) *n.* dissension; conflict (p. 837)

prostrate (präs' trāt) *adj.* lying with one's face down (p. 845)

taciturn (tas' ə tʉrn) *adj.* almost always silent (p. 852)

benevolent (bə nev' ə lənt) *adj.* doing or inclined to do good; kindly; charitable (p. 852)

❷ Literary Analysis

Dynamic and Static Characters

- Point out that dynamic characters usually learn something as a result of the events of a story. Static characters remain the same no matter what happens to them. Tell students that the interaction of dynamic and static characters often creates conflict in a story.
- Review with students the chart on p. 827. Model the use of the chart with a character familiar to students. Suggest that students use the chart to examine each of the characters they encounter in the following stories.

❸ Reading Strategy

Evaluating Characters' Decisions

- Tell students that the decisions characters make move the plot of a story forward.
- Discuss with students what might constitute a good or bad decision. Give the example of a character who, under pressure from his family, decides to cheat on a college entrance exam. Explain that in order to evaluate the decision, students must consider how the decision affects the character and others around him.
- Remind students that sometimes the consequences of a decision are not explicitly stated in the story; they must be inferred.
- Encourage students to use the Evaluating Characters' Decisions transparency in **Literary Analysis and Reading Transparencies,** p. 82, as they read the selections.

Vocabulary Development

- Pronounce each vocabulary word for students, and read the definitions as a class. Have students identify any words with which they are already familiar.

CUSTOMIZE INSTRUCTION FOR UNIVERSAL ACCESS

For Special Needs Students	For Less Proficient Readers	For English Learners
Have students read "Two Friends" in the **Adapted Reader's Companion.** This version provides basic-level instruction in an interactive format, with questions and write-on lines. Completing the adapted version will prepare students to read the selection.	Have students read the adapted version of the selection in the **Reader's Companion.** This version provides basic-level instruction in an interactive format, with questions and write-on lines. After students finish the selection in the **Reader's Companion,** have them complete the questions and activities in the Student Edition.	Have students read the adapted version of the selection in the **English Learner's Companion.** This version provides basic-level instruction in an interactive format, with questions and write-on lines. Completing the adapted version will prepare students to read the selection in the Student Edition.

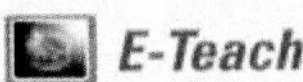

E-Teach

Visit e-Teach at PHSchool.com for teachers' essays on how to teach, with questions and answers.

TEACH

Step-by-Step Teaching Guide for pp. 828–858

Teaching Tenth-Grade Students

10TH GRADE Make sure that tenth-grade students understand the historical context of "Two Friends." Explain that the French were badly defeated in the Franco-Prussian War. At the time of the story, the Germans had surrounded the city of Paris, cutting off access to supplies and preventing people from leaving or going into the city. Have students briefly discuss what life might have been like for a civilian in Paris during the siege. Explain that students are about to find out how two fictional Frenchmen respond to this situation.

1 About the Selection

In this story, Morissot (mô' rē sō) and Sauvage (sō' vazh) try to conduct their friendship in a business-as-usual manner against the backdrop of the Franco-Prussian War. War perplexes and disgusts these two characters, and they wish only to recapture the simple pleasures they shared before war changed their lives. When they are captured by the enemy, they must choose between honor and survival.

2 ▶ Critical Viewing

Possible response: Sauvage and Morissot might find the river and the rural location enticing.

1 

Two Friends

Guy de Maupassant *translated by* Gordon R. Silber

Background

The backdrop for "Two Friends" is the Franco-Prussian War, also called the Franco-German War. In this ten-month conflict, a coalition of German states known as Prussia fought to defeat France and capture its emperor, Napoleon III. In one military strategy, the German army blockaded Paris, starving the city's inhabitants into compliance. As Maupassant's story begins, Paris is on the verge of surrender.

Paris was blockaded, starved, in its death agony. Sparrows were becoming scarcer and scarcer on the rooftops and the sewers were being depopulated. One ate whatever one could get.

As he was strolling sadly along the outer boulevard one bright January morning, his hands in his trousers pockets and his stomach empty, M.[1] Morissot, watchmaker by trade but local militiaman for the time being, stopped short before a fellow militiaman whom he recognized as a friend. It was M. Sauvage, a riverside acquaintance.

Every Sunday, before the war, Morissot left at dawn, a bamboo pole in his hand, a tin box on his back. He would take the Argenteuil railroad, get off at Colombes, and walk to Marante Island. As soon as he arrived at this ideal spot he would start to fish; he fished until nightfall.

Every Sunday he would meet a stout, jovial little man, M. Sauvage, a haberdasher[2] in Rue Notre-Dame-de-Lorette, another ardent fisherman. Often they spent half a day side by side, line in hand and feet dangling above the current. Inevitably they had struck up a friendship.

Some days they did not speak. Sometimes they did; but they understood one another admirably without saying anything because they had similar tastes and responded to their surroundings in exactly the same way.

2 **Critical Viewing ▶** What might Sauvage and Morissot find enticing about the setting of this landscape? **[Speculate]**

1. **M.** abbreviation for French title *Monsieur* (mə syö'), equivalent to *Mister* or *Sir.*
2. **haberdasher** (hab' ər dash' ər) *n.* person who is in the business of selling men's clothing.

TEACHING RESOURCES

The following resources can be used to enrich or extend the instruction for pp. 828–858.

Literary Analysis

Selection Support: Literary Analysis, p. 164 ■

Reading

Selection Support: Reading Strategy, p. 163; Build Vocabulary, p. 16 ■

Reader's Companion

Adapted Reader's Companion

English Learner's Companion

Listening to Literature Audiocassettes

Listening to Literature Audio CDs

Extension

Fine Art Transparencies, Art Transparency 17 (Have students discuss ways in which lower- or middle-class people and realistic details are prominently featured both in the selections and in Rodin's sculpture.)

■ **BLOCK SCHEDULING:** Resources marked with this symbol provide varied instruction during 90-minute blocks.

3 On a spring morning, toward ten o'clock, when the young sun was drawing up from the tranquil stream wisps of haze which floated off in the direction of the current and was pouring down its vernal warmth on the backs of the two fanatical anglers,[3] Morissot would sometimes say to his neighbor, "Nice, isn't it?" and M. Sauvage would answer, "There's nothing like it." And that was enough for them to understand and appreciate each other.

On an autumn afternoon, when the sky, reddened by the setting sun, cast reflections of its scarlet clouds on the water, made the whole river crimson, lighted up the horizon, made the two friends look as ruddy as fire, and gilded the trees which were already brown and beginning to tremble with a wintery shiver, M. Sauvage would look at Morissot with a smile and say, "Fine sight!" And Morissot, awed, would answer, "It's better than the city, isn't it?" without taking his eyes from his float.

As soon as they recognized one another they shook hands energetically, touched at meeting under such changed circumstances. M. Sauvage, with a sigh, grumbled, "What goings-on!" Morissot groaned dismally, "And what weather! This is the first fine day of the year."

The sky was, in fact, blue and brilliant.

Literary Analysis
Dynamic and Static Characters In what way do these opening paragraphs prepare you for changes that may occur in the main characters?

4 ✓ **Reading Check**
What hobby do Sauvage and Morissot have in common?

3. **anglers** (aŋ′ glərz) *n.* people who fish.

5 

Les Maisons Cabassud à la Ville d'Avray, Camille Corot, The Louvre, Paris

CUSTOMIZE INSTRUCTION FOR UNIVERSAL ACCESS

For Less Proficient Readers	For English Learners	For Gifted/Talented Students
The early part of the narrative of "Two Friends" moves back and forth in time. Help students identify the flashbacks by calling their attention to such signal phrases as "some days," "On a spring morning," and "On an autumn afternoon." Students may wish to mark the flashbacks with sticky notes.	To help clarify challenging vocabulary, especially in Maupassant's descriptions of nature, pair students with native English speakers. Have partners work together to use context clues to determine the meanings of such words as *scarlet, ruddy,* and *gilded.*	Tell students that friendship is a universal theme in literature around the world. Have them brainstorm words and images that call to mind the friendship between Sauvage and Morissot. Suggest that students use magazines to make collages illustrating the characters' relationship.

3 Literary Analysis
Dynamic and Static Characters

- Ask students to describe what they have learned about the characters of Morissot and Sauvage from reading pp. 828–829.
  Answer: The characters are both pleasant, friendly men who enjoy fishing, the country and each other's company.
- Call students' attention to the bracketed passage. Ask them to describe the friendship between the two characters.
  Possible response: The characters understand each other and appreciate each other's company.
- Ask students the Literary Analysis question on p. 829: In what way do these opening paragraphs prepare you for changes that may occur in the main characters?
  Possible response: The two friends have not been fishing since before the war began. The men may try to find a way to fish because the hobby brings them so much pleasure.

4 ✓ Reading Check

Answer: Sauvage and Morissot have fishing in common.

5 Background
Art

Les Maisons Cabassud à la Ville d'Avray (The Cabassud Houses in the Town of Avray), by Jean-Baptiste-Camille Corot

A predecessor of the Impressionists, Jean-Baptiste-Camille Corot (1796–1875) was one of the first French painters devoted to capturing the vitality and freshness of nature. One of Corot's favorite painting sites was northern France, especially the town of Avray, which is the subject of this painting.

Use the following question for discussion:

What elements in the painting convey a sense of harmony and peacefulness?
Possible response: The small, unhurried human figures convey a sense of harmony. The rural buildings and open countryside convey a sense of peace.

6 Literary Analysis

Dynamic and Static Characters

- Review with students the definitions of dynamic and static characters on p. 827.
- Read aloud the bracketed passage. Then, discuss with students the characters' behavior. Ask: Why do the men stop at the cafe? How do they feel after they stop?
  Answer: The men stop at the cafe to have a drink. Afterward, they feel giddy and do not appear to be thinking clearly.
- Ask students the Literary Analysis question on p. 830: What is changing in the relationship between the characters?
  Answer: The characters discover that they like to spend time with each other outside of fishing.

7 Reading Strategy

Evaluating Characters' Decisions

- Remind students that evaluating characters' decisions leads to a deeper understanding of a story. Review the steps on p. 827 for making an evaluation.
- Ask a volunteer to read aloud the bracketed passage. Then, ask students what influences the characters' decision to go fishing.
  Answer: The alcohol and warm weather influence the characters' decision.
- Ask students the Reading Strategy question on p. 830: Which details prove that the decision to go to the island is a dangerous one?
  Possible response: The existence of an outpost, the emptiness and silence of the towns and countryside, the nearby presence of Prussians, the description of the Prussians' pillaging and massacring, and the two men's fear that they may meet the Prussians all indicate that the decision to go to the island is a dangerous one.

They started to walk side by side, absent-minded and sad. Morissot went on, "And fishing! Ah! Nothing but a pleasant memory."

"When'll we get back to it?" asked M. Sauvage.

6 They went into a little café and had an absinthe,[4] then resumed their stroll along the sidewalks.

Morissot stopped suddenly. "How about another, eh?" M. Sauvage agreed, "If you want." And they entered another wine shop.

On leaving they felt giddy, muddled, as one does after drinking on an empty stomach. It was mild. A caressing breeze touched their faces.

The warm air completed what the absinthe had begun. M. Sauvage stopped. "Suppose we went?"

"Went where?"

"Fishing, of course."

"But where?"

"Why, on our island. The French outposts are near Colombes. I know Colonel Dumoulin; they'll let us pass without any trouble."

Morissot trembled with eagerness: "Done! I'm with you." And they went off to get their tackle.

An hour later they were walking side by side on the highway. They reached the villa which the Colonel occupied. He smiled at their request and gave his consent to their whim. They started off again, armed with a pass.

Soon they passed the outposts, went through the abandoned village of Colombes, and reached the edge of the little vineyards which slope toward the Seine. It was about eleven.

7 Opposite, the village of Argenteuil seemed dead. The heights of Orgemont and Sannois dominated the whole countryside. The broad plain which stretches as far as Nanterre was empty, absolutely empty, with its bare cherry trees and its colorless fields.

Pointing up to the heights, M. Sauvage murmured, "The Prussians are up there!" And a feeling of uneasiness paralyzed the two friends as they faced this deserted region.

"The Prussians!" They had never seen any, but for months they had felt their presence—around Paris, ruining France, pillaging, massacring, starving the country, invisible and all-powerful. And a kind of superstitious terror was superimposed on the hatred which they felt for this unknown and victorious people.

Morissot stammered, "Say, suppose we met some of them?"

His Parisian jauntiness coming to the surface in spite of everything, M. Sauvage answered, "We'll offer them some fish."

But they hesitated to venture into the country, frightened by the silence all about them.

Literary Analysis
Dynamic and Static Characters What is changing in the relationship between the characters?

Reading Strategy
Evaluating Characters' Decisions Which details prove that the decision to go to the island is a dangerous one?

pillaging (pil' ij iŋ) *v.* plundering; looting

superimposed (so͞o' pər im pōzd') *v.* placed on top of something else

4. **absinthe** (ab' sinth) *n.* bitter, anise-flavored liqueur.

ENRICHMENT: Geography Connection

A Closer Look at the City of Paris

"Two Friends" is set in Paris, France, in the 1870s. Many important water and land routes in Europe cross Paris. Under the ancient Romans, the city was the capital of the Parisii tribe, from which the city took its name. In the late 900s, the city became the focal point for what was becoming modern France. The historical city of Paris is situated on the river Seine and is divided into three main parts: the Île de la Cité (the word *île* means "island," and *cité* refers to the center of the ancient city); the left bank, which has been considered the artistic and intellectual center of Paris; and the right bank, which is the city's economic center.

The early city was circular in shape; it has generally retained that shape as it has grown over the centuries. From its early beginnings on an island in the Seine, the city has grown to include neighboring towns.

Finally M. Sauvage pulled himself together: "Come on! On our way! But let's go carefully." And they climbed over into a vineyard, bent double, crawling, taking advantage of the vines to conceal themselves, watching, listening.

8 A stretch of bare ground had to be crossed to reach the edge of the river. They began to run, and when they reached the bank they plunged down among the dry reeds.

Morissot glued his ear to the ground and listened for sounds of anyone walking in the vicinity. He heard nothing. They were indeed alone, all alone.

Reassured, they started to fish.

Opposite them Marante Island, deserted, hid them from the other bank. The little building which had housed a restaurant was shut up and looked as if it had been abandoned for years.

M. Sauvage caught the first gudgeon,[5] Morissot got the second, and from then on they pulled in their lines every minute or two with a silvery little fish squirming on the end, a truly miraculous draught.

9 Skillfully they slipped the fish into a sack made of fine net which they had hung in the water at their feet. And happiness pervaded their whole being, the happiness which seizes upon you when you regain a cherished pleasure of which you have long been deprived.

The good sun was pouring down its warmth on their backs. They heard nothing more; they no longer thought about anything at all; they forgot about the rest of the world—they were fishing!

But suddenly a dull sound which seemed to come from under ground made the earth tremble. The cannon were beginning.

Morissot turned and saw, over the bank to the left, the great silhouette of Mount Valérien wearing a white plume on its brow, powder-smoke which it had just spit out.

And almost at once a second puff of smoke rolled from the summit, and a few seconds after the roar still another explosion was heard.

Then more followed, and time after time the mountain belched forth death-dealing breath, breathed out milky-white vapor which rose slowly in the calm sky and formed a cloud above the summit.

M. Sauvage shrugged his shoulders. "There they go again," he said.

As he sat anxiously watching his float bob up and down, Morissot was suddenly seized by the wrath which a peace-loving man will feel toward madmen who fight, and grumbled, "Folks sure are stupid to kill one another like that."

M. Sauvage answered, "They're worse than animals."

And Morissot, who had just pulled in a bleak, went on, "And to think that it will always be like this as long as there are governments."

M. Sauvage stopped him: "The Republic[6] wouldn't have declared war—"

10 ✓Reading Check

Why are Sauvage and Morissot anxious while approaching their favorite spot?

5. **gudgeon** (guj′ ən) *n.* small European freshwater fish.

6. **The Republic** the provisional republican government that assumed control when Napoleon III was captured by the Prussians.

8 Reading Strategy

Evaluating Characters' Decisions

- Review the bracketed passage with students. Ask students: Which of the men's actions suggests that their decision to go fishing is a foolhardy one?
  Answer: Morissot's attempt to listen for sounds of someone approaching by pressing his ear to the ground suggests that the men's decision to go fishing is foolhardy.
- Ask: Do you think the men believe at this point that their decision is foolhardy? Why or why not?
  Possible response: The men probably realize that their decision is foolhardy, but they quickly forget their nervousness as they begin to fish.

9 Critical Thinking

Analyze

- Have a volunteer read aloud the bracketed passage. Invite students to comment on the description of the two men fishing.
  Answer: The description shows fishing as a delightful and peaceful pleasure of life.
- Ask: How does this passage help readers understand why the men decide to go fishing?
  Possible response: To the men, fishing represents one of the simple and precious pleasures of life. They are unwilling to give up that pleasure despite the risks.

10 ✓Reading Check

Answer: Sauvage and Morissot are afraid of being seen by the Prussians.

CUSTOMIZE INSTRUCTION FOR UNIVERSAL ACCESS

For Special Needs Students	For Advanced Readers
Some readers tend to skip passages of description. Tell students that because Maupassant's stories tend to be very spare, it is important for them to read his descriptions carefully. Point out that the descriptions on pp. 830 and 831 highlight the lifelessness of the countryside. Lead a discussion about how the lifelessness of the countryside shows that the men are in a dangerous area.	Encourage students to read the descriptions on pp. 830 and 831 carefully. Have them contrast the lifeless countryside with the "truly miraculous draught" of fishes that the men catch. Ask them to speculate on the symbolism behind the juxtaposition of lifelessness and abundant life. What message is Maupassant trying to convey through this juxtaposition? Have volunteers share their speculations with the class.

11 Literary Analysis

Dynamic and Static Characters

- Direct students to the bracketed passage that begins on p. 831. Ask one student to read Sauvage's lines and another student to read Morissot's lines.
- Have students summarize the men's conversation.
  Answer: The men oppose killing people in war, but they decide that war seems an inevitable part of human affairs.
- Ask students the Literary Analysis question on p. 832: In what way does the characters' conversation show that the men have changed?
  Possible response: Their conversation shows that the men have grown closer as friends because they are comfortable talking about their political beliefs.

12 ►Critical Viewing

Possible response: The grand and imposing details of the uniforms—such as the epaulets and tall hats—as well as the soldiers' weapons might intimidate citizens like the two friends.

Morissot interrupted: "Under kings you have war abroad; under the Republic you have war at home."

11 And they started a leisurely discussion, unraveling great political problems with the sane reasonableness of easy-going, limited individuals, and found themselves in agreement on the point that men would never be free. And Mount Valérien thundered unceasingly, demolishing French homes with its cannon, crushing out lives, putting an end to the dreams which many had dreamt, the joys which many had been waiting for, the happiness which many had hoped for, planting in wives' hearts, in maidens' hearts, in mothers' hearts, over there, in other lands, sufferings which would never end.

"That's life for you," opined M. Sauvage.

"You'd better say 'That's death for you,'" laughed Morissot.

But they shuddered in terror when they realized that someone had just come up behind them, and looking around they saw four men standing almost at their elbows, four tall men, armed and bearded, dressed like liveried[7] servants, with flat caps on their heads, pointing rifles at them.

The two fish lines dropped from their hands and floated off down stream.

In a few seconds they were seized, trussed up, carried off, thrown into a rowboat and taken over to the island.

And behind the building which they had thought deserted they saw a score of German soldiers.

A kind of hairy giant who was seated astride a chair smoking a porcelain pipe asked them in excellent French: "Well, gentlemen, have you had good fishing?"

Then a soldier put down at the officer's feet the sack full of fish which he had carefully brought along. The Prussian smiled: "Aha! I see that it didn't go badly. But we have to talk about another little matter. Listen to me and don't get excited.

"As far as I am concerned, you are two spies sent to keep an eye on me. I catch you and I shoot you. You were pretending to fish in order to conceal your business. You have fallen into my hands, so much the worse for you. War is like that.

Literary Analysis
Dynamic and Static Characters In what way does the characters' conversation show that the men have changed?

12 ▼**Critical Viewing**
Which details of these Prussian officers' uniforms might intimidate citizens like the two friends? **[Analyze]**

7. **liveried** (liv′ ər ēd) *adj.* uniformed.

ENRICHMENT: History Connection

The Prussian Army

The Prussian forces in "Two Friends" are portrayed as heartless and cruel. The Prussian army, under the leadership of General Helmuth von Moltke (1800–1891), was arguably the most formidable army of the nineteenth century. Many military historians consider von Moltke a master of military strategy.

Under his leadership, the Prussian army defeated the French in the Franco-Prussian War, the period in which "Two Friends" is set. Von Moltke was a brilliant leader and molded the army into a well-disciplined fighting machine. He was one of the first generals to use the telegraph and train to communicate and move troops. This gave his forces an enormous advantage.

"But—since you came out past the outposts you have, of course, the password to return. Tell me that password and I will pardon you."

The two friends, side by side, pale, kept silent. A slight nervous trembling shook their hands.

The officer went on: "No one will ever know. You will go back placidly. The secret will disappear with you. If you refuse, it is immediate death. Choose."

placidly (plas′ id lē) *adv.* calmly

They stood motionless, mouths shut.

The Prussian quietly went on, stretching out his hand toward the stream: "Remember that within five minutes you will be at the bottom of that river. Within five minutes! You have relatives, of course?"

13 Mount Valérien kept thundering.

The two fishermen stood silent. The German gave orders in his own language. Then he moved his chair so as not to be near the prisoners and twelve men took their places, twenty paces distant, rifles grounded.

Reading Strategy
Evaluating Characters' Decisions What will be the consequences for Paris if the two men reveal the password?

The officer went on: "I give you one minute, not two seconds more."

Then he rose suddenly, approached the two Frenchmen, took Morissot by the arm, dragged him aside, whispered to him, "Quick, the password? Your friend won't know. I'll pretend to relent."

Morissot answered not a word.

The Prussian drew M. Sauvage aside and put the same question.

M. Sauvage did not answer.

They stood side by side again.

And the officer began to give commands. The soldiers raised their rifles.

Then Morissot's glance happened to fall on the sack full of gudgeons which was lying on the grass a few steps away.

A ray of sunshine made the little heap of still squirming fish gleam. And he almost weakened. In spite of his efforts his eyes filled with tears.

He stammered, "Farewell, Monsieur Sauvage."

M. Sauvage answered, "Farewell, Monsieur Morissot."

14 They shook hands, trembling from head to foot with a shudder which they could not control.

The officer shouted, "Fire!"

The twelve shots rang out together.

M. Sauvage fell straight forward, like a log. Morissot, who was taller, tottered, half turned, and fell crosswise on top of his comrade, face up, as the blood spurted from his torn shirt.

Reading Strategy
Evaluating Characters' Decisions Do you think the fate of the two friends would have been different if they had revealed the password? Explain.

The German gave more orders.

His men scattered, then returned with rope and stones which they tied to the dead men's feet. Then they carried them to the bank.

Mount Valérien continued to roar, its summit hidden now in a mountainous cloud of smoke.

Two soldiers took Morissot by the head and the feet, two others seized M. Sauvage. They swung the bodies for a moment then let go.

15 **✓ Reading Check**
What does the Prussian officer demand of Sauvage and Morissot?

CUSTOMIZE INSTRUCTION FOR UNIVERSAL ACCESS

For Gifted/Talented Students	For Advanced Readers
Have a small group of students act out the scene in which the two men confront the Prussian officer. Suggest that they use the dialogue from the story. Point out that, in much of the scene, the two men remain silent. Encourage students to use body language and facial expressions to convey the emotions the men are feeling at the time. Allow students time to practice, and then have them present the scene to the class.	Tell students that one of the recurring criticisms of Maupassant is that he has no compassion for his characters. He puts them into difficult situations and lets them suffer. To some readers and critics, it seems that Maupassant does not care about his characters' sufferings. Have students form a small discussion group to review this criticism of Maupassant. Have them identify examples within the story that either prove or disprove the criticism. Then, have students present the results of their discussion to the class.

13 Reading Strategy
Evaluating Characters' Decisions

- Remind students that when they evaluate a character's decision, they should consider the effects the decision has on the character and others around him or her.
- Read aloud the bracketed passage. Then, ask the first Reading Strategy question on p. 833: What will be the consequences for Paris if the two men reveal the password?
  Possible response: With the password, soldiers in disguise could enter Paris and sabotage its defenses, causing the city to fall to its enemies.

Monitor Progress Encourage students to speculate about the final decision these two men have to make. Lead a discussion about what students might do in such circumstances and how difficult it would be to face this decision.

Reteach If students have difficulty mastering the Reading Strategy, have them examine the men's decision using the Evaluating Characters' Decisions transparency in **Literary Analysis and Reading Transparencies,** p. 82.

14 Reading Strategy
Evaluating Characters' Decisions

- Read aloud the bracketed passage. Discuss what might have motivated the two men's decision.
  Possible response: The men felt a sense of honor and duty to their city.
- Ask the second Reading Strategy question on p. 833: Do you think the fate of the two friends would have been different if they had revealed the password? Explain.
  Possible response: Revealing the password would have made no difference because the Prussians would probably have executed the friends anyway.

15 ✓ Reading Check

Answer: The officer wants the men to reveal a password to pass through the French outpost.

Answers for p. 834

Review and Assess

1. Possible response: The execution of the two men and the disposal of their bodies were especially disturbing because the friends are stripped of their humanity by the Prussians. Their deaths as well as their "catch" simply feed the machine that is war.
2. **(a)** The men's similar way of thinking, their mutual enjoyment of fishing, and their loyalty to Paris are characteristics of their friendship. **(b)** Giddiness from the absinthe and the warm weather motivate them to try fishing again.
3. **(a)** The villages and surrounding areas are deserted because the Prussians have seized control of the region. **(b)** The emptiness reflects the fact that the Prussians are in control of the region, and the Prussians pose a great danger to the two friends.
4. **(a)** The men think war is ignorant but inevitable, regardless of whether a country is republic or a monarchy. **(b)** Their comments reveal that the men dislike war but have accepted it as a harsh reality of life. **(c)** These attitudes affect the outcome because although the men see war as inevitable, they do what they can to lessen its effects on others.
5. **(a)** The soldiers are tall, bearded, wearing flat caps, and carrying weapons; the two men are "seized, trussed up, carried off, and thrown into" a boat. **(b)** The forces are described as cold-blooded and callous; they act "worse than animals," as the two men had observed earlier.
6. **(a)** The officer threatens the friends' lives; he separates the men and offers each one freedom for the information. **(b)** Possible responses: Trying to get the men to turn on each other is unethical. Or, a soldier's duty is to get the information, by duplicity, if necessary.

continued

They described an arc and plunged into the river feet first, for the weights made them seem to be standing upright.

There was a splash, the water trembled, then grew calm, while tiny wavelets spread to both shores.

A little blood remained on the surface.

The officer, still calm, said in a low voice: "Now the fish will have their turn."

And he went back to the house.

And all at once he caught sight of the sack of gudgeons in the grass. He picked it up, looked at it, smiled, shouted, "Wilhelm!"

A soldier in a white apron ran out. And the Prussian threw him the catch of the two and said: "Fry these little animals right away while they are still alive. They will be delicious."

Then he lighted his pipe again.

Review and Assess

Thinking About the Selection

1. **Respond:** What did you find especially shocking or disturbing about this story? Explain.
2. **(a) Recall:** List three characteristics of the friendship between M. Morissot and M. Sauvage. **(b) Infer:** What motivates the two men to go fishing?
3. **(a) Recall:** Why are the villages of Colombes and Argenteuil and the surrounding areas deserted? **(b) Connect:** How does the emptiness of the landscape foreshadow, or hint at, the events that occur later in the story?
4. **(a) Recall:** What do the two men say about war in relation to republics and monarchies? **(b) Draw Conclusions:** What do their comments reveal about their own attitudes? **(c) Connect:** In what way do these attitudes affect the outcome of the story?
5. **(a) Recall:** Which words describe the physical appearance and actions of the Prussian soldiers? **(b) Support:** How does this description support the two men's earlier impressions of the Prussian forces?
6. **(a) Recall:** What strategies does the Prussian officer use to force the password from the two friends? **(b) Judge:** Would you describe the Prussian officer as an ethical soldier? Explain.
7. **(a) Relate:** If you were in the place of one of the two friends in Maupassant's story, would you have gone fishing? Why or why not? **(b) Take a Position:** Should the two friends be blamed for their own deaths? Why or why not?

continued from left column

7. **(a)** Possible responses: Some readers may say that they would not have gone because of the danger of war; others may say they would have gone to prove that they could have some kind of a normal life in the midst of war. **(b)** Possible responses: The men should be blamed, because it was silly for them to leave the safety of Paris just to fish. Or, the men should not be blamed for the brutality of the Prussian soldiers.

16 # HOW MUCH LAND DOES A MAN NEED?

Leo Tolstoy

translated by Louise and Aylmer Maude

Background

From the sixteenth century to the mid-nineteenth century, Russian peasants were bound by law to work land they could rent but not own. They grew food meant to feed others, cultivated crops that others would sell, and worked to exhaustion to make a profit for the landowner. Peasants could even be bought and sold with the land they worked. This story takes place after the laws were changed to allow ordinary people to purchase land. To those who had never owned it, land represented the ability to control one's destiny. Tolstoy uses land, an image close to the heart of every Russian, to explore the age-old question, "How much is enough?"

I

17 An elder sister came to visit her younger sister in the country. The elder was married to a tradesman in town, the younger to a peasant in the village. As the sisters sat over their tea talking, the elder began to boast of the advantages of town life: saying how comfortably they lived there, how well they dressed, what fine clothes her children wore, what good things they ate and drank, and how she went to the theater, promenades,[1] and entertainments.

The younger sister was piqued, and in turn disparaged the life of a tradesman, and stood up for that of a peasant.

"I would not change my way of life for yours," said she. "We may live roughly, but at least we are free from anxiety. You live in better style than we do, but though you often earn more than you need, you are very likely to lose all you have. You know the proverb, 'Loss and gain are brothers twain.'[2] It often happens that people who are wealthy one day are begging their bread the next. Our way is safer. Though a peasant's life is not a fat one, it is a long one. We shall never grow rich, but we shall always have enough to eat."

1. **promenades** (präm′ ə nädz) *n.* balls or formal dances.
2. **twain** (twān) *n.* two.

18 

Which sister lives the life of a country peasant?

16 About the Selection

"How Much Land Does a Man Need?" is a parable that illuminates Tolstoy's sentiments about the perils of private ownership. A peasant named Pakhom seeks to acquire more and more land. He rejects the advantages of cooperative ownership and finds fault with each new land acquisition until, far from his home, he dies in a final, desperate grasp for even more land.

Tolstoy would have approved of the peasants' owning the land jointly. It is owning private property, this story tells us, that encourages individual greed.

17 Background

History

The disparity between town and country living was far greater in Tolstoy's day than it is today. A tradesman's wife, although not rich, was in an entirely different class from a peasant's wife and had access to many more luxuries.

18 ✔Reading Check

Answer: The younger sister lives the life of a country peasant.

CUSTOMIZE INSTRUCTION FOR UNIVERSAL ACCESS

For Special Needs Students	For Less Proficient Readers	For Advanced Readers
To help students better understand the story, have them follow along in their books as they listen to the recorded version on **Listening to Literature Audiocassettes** or **Audio CDs.** Pause the recording after each numbered section, and ask students to summarize the main idea.	Have students pause after they read each numbered section of the story and summarize its main idea before continuing. You may wish to have them organize the main ideas using an outline. transparency in **Writing Models and Graphic Organizers on Transparencies,** pp. 103–105.	Remind students that a parable is a simple, brief narrative that teaches a lesson by using characters and events to represent abstract ideas or moral principles. Have students brainstorm and discuss other parables they have read.

19 Literary Analysis

Dynamic and Static Characters

- Remind students that this story is a parable, which teaches a lesson by using characters or events to represent abstract ideas or moral principles. Explain that the character of the Devil will help convey the lesson Tolstoy wishes to teach.
- Have students read the bracketed passage independently. Then, ask: Do you think the Devil will be a static or dynamic character? Explain.
  Possible response: The Devil will be a static character because he is an archetypal figure and never changes; his sole intent is evil.
- Ask students the Literary Analysis question on p. 836: In what ways does Pakhom think his life would change if he had enough land?
  Answer: Pakhom believes that his life will be free from worry and fear.

20 Background

Art

The Village of Andreikovo, by Vladimir Stozharov

Stozharov (1926–1973) strongly admired and was inspired by traditional Russian ways of life. This admiration is reflected in many of his works. In this painting, for example, Stozharov offers a lyrical portrait of life in a rural village. The painting vividly captures the simplicity and tranquility of the villagers' lives, while at the same time offering a glimpse of their dignity and strength.

Use the following questions for discussion:

- What impression does the artist convey of life in a rural Russian village?
  Possible response: The artist conveys an impression of a poverty-stricken yet peaceful life.
- Why is this painting an appropriate illustration for the story?
  Possible response: The painting shows what life might have been like for Pakhom.

21 ▶ Critical Viewing

Possible response: The painting shows farm animals, a lack of elegance, and the lack of "temptations"; it also shows what appears to be a friendly community, which is not mentioned by either sister.

The elder sister said sneeringly:

"Enough? Yes, if you like to share with the pigs and the calves! What do you know of elegance or manners! However much your goodman may slave, you will die as you are living—on a dung heap—and your children the same."

"Well, what of that?" replied the younger. "Of course our work is rough and coarse. But, on the other hand, it is sure, and we need not bow to any one. But you, in your towns, are surrounded by temptations; today all may be right, but tomorrow the Evil One may tempt your husband with cards, wine, or women, and all will go to ruin. Don't such things happen often enough?"

Pakhom, the master of the house, was lying on the top of the stove and he listened to the women's chatter.

19 "It is perfectly true," thought he. "Busy as we are from childhood tilling mother earth, we peasants have no time to let any nonsense settle in our heads. Our only trouble is that we haven't land enough. If I had plenty of land, I shouldn't fear the Devil himself!"

The women finished their tea, chatted a while about dress, and then cleared away the tea-things and lay down to sleep.

But the Devil had been sitting behind the stove, and had heard all that was said. He was pleased that the peasant's wife had led her husband into boasting, and that he had said that if he had plenty of land he would not fear the Devil himself.

Literary Analysis
Dynamic and Static Characters In what ways does Pakhom think his life would change if he had enough land?

20

The Village of Andreikovo (detail), 1958, Vladimir Stozharov, The Tretyakov Gallery, Moscow

21 ▲ **Critical Viewing** Compare and contrast the details in this painting with the sisters' description of peasant life. **[Compare and Contrast]**

ENRICHMENT: History Connection

The Demise of Serfdom

Tolstoy uses land to explore the question "How much is enough?" This image would have been close to the heart of every Russian, particularly the serfs who could rent but not own land.

In 1861, Czar Alexander II freed the Russian serfs. Although most of the wealthy landowning class objected, Alexander believed that it was too dangerous to continue serfdom. In his words, "It is better to abolish serfdom from above than to wait until the serfs begin to liberate themselves from below."

Under the system instituted by Alexander, peasants were able to buy their own land; however, they rarely saw any actual benefit from owning land. In some parts of the country, the plots of land the peasants were allotted were even smaller than the plots they had used as serfs.

"All right," thought the Devil. "We will have a tussle. I'll give you land enough; and by means of that land I will get you into my power."

II

Close to the village there lived a lady, a small landowner who had an estate of about three hundred acres. She had always lived on good terms with the peasants until she engaged as her steward an old soldier, who took to burdening the people with fines. However careful Pakhom tried to be, it happened again and again that now a horse of his got among the lady's oats, now a cow strayed into her garden, now his calves found
22 their way into her meadows—and he always had to pay a fine.

Pakhom paid up, but grumbled, and, going home in a temper, was rough with his family. All through that summer, Pakhom had much trouble because of this steward, and he was even glad when winter came and the cattle had to be stabled. Though he grudged the fodder when they could no longer graze on the pasture-land, at least he was free from anxiety about them.

In the winter the news got about that the lady was going to sell her land and that the keeper of the inn on the high road was bargaining for it. When the peasants heard this they were very much alarmed.

"Well," thought they, "if the innkeeper gets the land, he will worry us with fines worse than the lady's steward. We all depend on that estate."

So the peasants went on behalf of their commune, and asked the lady not to sell the land to the innkeeper, offering her a better price for it themselves. The lady agreed to let them have it. Then the peasants tried to arrange for the commune to buy the whole estate, so that it might be held by them all in common. They met twice to discuss it, but
23 could not settle the matter; the Evil One sowed discord among them and they could not agree. So they decided to buy the land individually, each according to his means; and the lady agreed to this plan as she had to the other.

discord (dis′ kôrd) *n.* dissension; conflict

Presently Pakhom heard that a neighbor of his was buying fifty acres, and that the lady had consented to accept one half in cash and to wait a year for the other half. Pakhom felt envious.

"Look at that," thought he, "the land is all being sold, and I shall get none of it." So he spoke to his wife.

"Other people are buying," said he, "and we must also buy twenty acres or so. Life is becoming impossible. That manager is simply crushing us with his fines."

So they put their heads together and considered how they could manage to buy it. They had one hundred rubles[3] laid by. They sold a colt and one half of their bees, hired out one of their sons as a laborer and took his wages in advance, borrowed the rest from a brother-in-law, and so scraped together half the purchase money.

24  **Reading Check**

What motivates Pakhom and the villagers to buy land?

3. **rubles** (ro͞o′ bəlz) *n.* Russian money.

22 Critical Thinking

Speculate

- Read aloud the bracketed passage with students. Point out how the landowner's actions affect Pakhom and his family.
- Ask students to speculate about how this experience with the landowner will affect Pakhom if he acquires more land.
  Possible response: Pakhom will be a more understanding landowner because he remembers the anxiety he felt as a peasant paying rent.

23 Vocabulary Development

Latin Prefix *dis-*

- Direct students' attention to the word *discord,* its definition, and its use in the story. Explain that the prefix *dis-* can mean "apart" or "not." It often changes the meaning of a word to its opposite.
- Ask students to name words that use this prefix. Write their suggestions on the board.
  Possible response: *Disobey, disuse,* and *disarray* all use the prefix *dis-*.
- Have students suggest definitions for the words on the board and then use dictionaries to check those definitions.
- Encourage students to write a short summary of "Two Friends" using at least these words with the prefix *dis-*.

24 Reading Check

Answer: Pakhom and the villagers are afraid that the new landowner of the estate will burden them with heavy fines.

CUSTOMIZE INSTRUCTION FOR UNIVERSAL ACCESS

For English Learners	For Advanced Readers
Some of the longer sentences in this story may be confusing for students. Choose some of the longer sentences, and model the process of breaking a sentence into its main subject and action to determine its basic meaning. Have students answer these questions: Who or what is this sentence about? What is happening to the subject of the sentence?	Suggest that students meet in a group to compare and contrast Tolstoy's style in this parable with the writing style of other works they have recently read. Encourage them to discover the relationship between an author's style and the central message of the story. Of the works they analyze, students should select a story style that fits its message and then explain their choice.

25 Reading Strategy

Evaluating Characters' Decisions

- Remind students that the Devil has a hand in Pakhom's decision to buy the land by sowing discord among the commune members who want to buy it.
- Ask students what financial arrangement makes it easier for Pakhom to buy the land.
  Answer: Although Pakhom initially has to pay half the money for the land, he has two years to pay the remainder.
- Read aloud the bracketed passage. Then, ask students the first Reading Strategy question on p. 838: Considering the costs of purchasing the land, do you think Pakhom made the right decision? Explain.
  Possible responses: On the one hand, Pakhom made the right decision because he needed the land and had time to pay it off. On the other hand, it was too risky to go so heavily in debt for the land.

26 Reading Strategy

Evaluating Characters' Decisions

- Tell students to read the first paragraph in the bracketed passage independently.
- Ask the second Reading Strategy question on p. 838: Which of Pakhom's past experiences may have influenced his decision to overlook his neighbors' behavior?
  Answer: Pakhom's experience of being fined by the landowner may have influenced his decision to overlook his neighbors' behavior.
- Have students read the rest of the bracketed passage. Then, discuss as a class whether Pakhom is being reasonable in teaching a lesson to the peasants.

25 Having done this, Pakhom chose a farm of forty acres, some of it wooded, and went to the lady to bargain for it. They came to an agreement, and he shook hands with her upon it and paid her a deposit in advance. Then they went to town and signed the deeds; he paying half the price down, and undertaking to pay the remainder within two years.

So now Pakhom had land of his own. He borrowed seed, and sowed it on the land he had bought. The harvest was a good one, and within a year he had managed to pay off his debts both to the lady and to his brother-in-law. So he became a landowner, plowing and sowing his own land, making hay on his own land, cutting his own trees, and feeding his cattle on his own pasture. When he went out to plow his fields, or to look at his growing corn, or at his grass-meadows, his heart would fill with joy. The grass that grew and the flowers that bloomed there seemed to him unlike any that grew elsewhere. Formerly, when he had passed by that land, it had appeared the same as any other land, but now it seemed quite different.

Reading Strategy
Evaluating Characters' Decisions Considering the costs of purchasing the land, do you think Pakhom made the right decision? Explain.

III

So Pakhom was well-contented, and everything would have been right if the neighboring peasants would only not have trespassed on his corn-fields and meadows. He appealed to them most civilly, but they still went on: now the communal herdsmen would let the village cows stray into his meadows, then horses from the night pasture would get among his corn. Pakhom turned them out again and again, and forgave their owners, and for a long time he forbore to prosecute anyone. But at
26 last he lost patience and complained to the district court. He knew it was the peasants' want of land, and no evil intent on their part, that caused the trouble, but he thought:

"I cannot go on overlooking it or they will destroy all I have. They must be taught a lesson."

So he had them up, gave them one lesson, and then another, and two or three of the peasants were fined. After a time Pakhom's neighbors began to bear him a grudge for this, and would now and then let their cattle on to his land on purpose. One peasant even got into Pakhom's wood at night and cut down five young lime trees for their bark. Pakhom, passing through the wood one day, noticed something white. He came nearer and saw the stripped trunks lying on the ground, and close by stood the stumps where the trees had been. Pakhom was furious.

"If he had only cut one here and there it would have been bad enough," thought Pakhom, "but the rascal has actually cut down a whole clump. If I could only find out who did this, I would pay him out."

He racked his brains as to who it could be. Finally he decided: "It must be Simon—no one else could have done it." So he went to Simon's homestead to have a look round, but he found nothing, and only had an angry scene. However, he now felt more certain than ever that Simon had done it, and he lodged a complaint. Simon was summoned. The case was tried, and retried, and at the end of it all Simon was

Reading Strategy
Evaluating Characters' Decisions Which of Pakhom's past experiences may have influenced his decision to overlook his neighbors' behavior?

ENRICHMENT: Mathematics Connection

Mortgages

Pakhom buys his forty-acre farm by scraping together half the purchase price and agreeing to pay the remainder within two years. Today, most home buyers apply to a local bank for a mortgage. The buyer pays a certain amount of the total asking price up front—for example, ten or fifteen percent—and the bank lends the buyer the money for the rest of the payment. The buyer repays the remainder to the bank with interest over a period of years (usually longer than Pakhom's two-year period).

Have students inquire at local banks or lending agencies about current interest rates for loans to purchase real estate. Have them find out the total cost of a specified mortgage—say, $50,000 or $100,000—over several time periods, including twenty-five, thirty, and forty years. Students may be interested in finding out how amortization rates are calculated, discovering the incremental benefits of repaying a loan in a shorter period of time.

acquitted, there being no evidence against him. Pakhom felt still more aggrieved, and let his anger loose upon the elder and the judges.

"You let thieves grease your palms," said he. "If you were honest folk yourselves you would not let a thief go free."

So Pakhom quarreled with the judges and with his neighbors.
27 Threats to burn his building began to be uttered. So though Pakhom had more land, his place in the commune was much worse than before.

About this time a rumor got about that many people were moving to new parts.

"There's no need for me to leave my land," thought Pakhom. "But some of the others may leave our village and then there would be more room for us. I would take over their land myself and make my estate a bit bigger. I could then live more at ease. As it is, I am still too cramped to be comfortable."

One day Pakhom was sitting at home when a peasant, passing through the village, happened to call in. He was allowed to stay the night, and supper was given him. Pakhom had a talk with this peasant and asked him where he came from. The stranger answered that he came from beyond the Volga,[4] where he had been working. One word led to another, and the man went on to say that many people were settling in those parts. He told how some people from his village had settled there. They had joined the commune, and had had twenty-five acres per man granted them. The land was so good, he said, that the rye sown on it
28 grew as high as a horse, and so thick that five cuts of a sickle made a sheaf. One peasant, he said, had brought nothing with him but his bare hands, and now he had six horses and two cows of his own.

Pakhom's heart kindled with desire. He thought:

"Why should I suffer in this narrow hole, if one can live so well elsewhere? I will sell my land and my homestead here, and with the money I will start afresh over there and get everything new. In this crowded place one is always having trouble. But I must first go and find out all about it myself."

Toward summer he got ready and started. He went down the Volga
29 on a steamer to Samara,[5] then walked another three hundred miles on foot, and at last reached the place. It was just as the stranger had said. The peasants had plenty of land: every man had twenty-five acres of communal land given him for his use, and any one who had money could buy, besides, at two shillings an acre as much good freehold land[6] as he wanted.

Having found out all he wished to know, Pakhom returned home as autumn came on, and began selling off his belongings. He sold his land at a profit, sold his homestead and all his cattle, and withdrew from

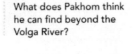

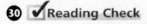

4. **Volga** (väl′ gə) the major river in western Russia.
5. **Samara** (Sə ma′ rə) city in eastern Russia.
6. **freehold land** privately owned land that the owner can lease to others for a fee.

 **✔Reading Check**

What does Pakhom think he can find beyond the Volga River?

CUSTOMIZE INSTRUCTION FOR UNIVERSAL ACCESS

For Special Needs Students	For Less Proficient Readers	For English Learners
Tell students that the use of communal land, like that mentioned in the passage on p. 839, is typical of many agrarian societies. Usually, a section of land is set aside on which everyone in a village may graze cattle or plant a garden. Discuss with students the pros and cons of the communal land system.	Organize students into small groups. Have them discuss the decisions that Pakhom has made so far. Urge students to offer their opinions about whether these decisions have been good for Pakhom and his family. Explain that this information will help them evaluate Pakhom's decisions throughout the story.	As students read, have them list land-related words that they encounter, such as *fallow, sheaf,* and *arable.* Tell students to work in pairs to discuss the meanings of these words. Allow them to use dictionaries to find definitions and pronunciations.

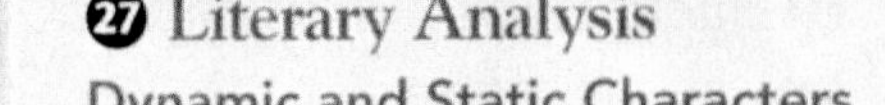

27 Literary Analysis

Dynamic and Static Characters

- Discuss with students whether at this point in the story they think Pakhom is changing or the people around him are changing.
- Remind them that a character who changes is a dynamic character; a character who remains the same is a static character.
- Then, read aloud the bracketed passage. Ask students: What new challenges plague Pakhom now that he is a landowner?
  Answer: Pakhom quarrels with his neighbors and the judges, and he receives threats against his property.

28 Critical Thinking

Infer

- Have students read aloud the bracketed passage. Discuss the description the peasant gives about the land beyond the Volga.
- Guide students to see that the Devil may be playing a role in this passage. Ask: Do you think the description about the land is truthful? If not, why is the man telling Pakhom about the land?
  Possible response: The man, who may be the Devil in disguise, is exaggerating, trying to tempt Pakhom to buy more land.

29 Background

Geography

Samara is a river that rises in the Ural Mountains and flows northeast into the Volga. At the time of the story, Samara was also the name of a city at the junction of the Volga and Samara Rivers.

30 ✔Reading Check

Answer: Pakhom thinks he can get more and better land as well as freedom from the problems he is having with the peasants in his village.

31 **Background**

Art

Cornfield at Ewell, by William Holman Hunt

This landscape depicts a large field of grain similar to those Pakhom would have cultivated in Russia. The artist, William Holman Hunt, was a member of the Pre-Raphaelite Brotherhood in England, a group of artists and poets who held to pre- and early Renaissance standards and ideals in art. They strove to portray nature in a way that demonstrated both its detail and its simplicity.

Use the following questions for discussion:

- What quality does this field have that might appeal to Pakhom? Possible response: The field is vast and potentially productive.
- Do you think this is an appropriate illustration for this story? Explain. Possible response: The image of a lone man in a vast expanse of land suits the story well. It illustrates Pakhom's desire for more and more land.

32 **Critical Viewing**

Possible response: The vast expanse in the painting is a large amount of land for one man to manage. Should Pakhom be hurt or sick, he stands to lose a great deal.

membership of the commune. He only waited till the spring, and then started with his family for the new settlement.

IV

As soon as Pakhom and his family reached their new abode, he applied for admission into the commune of a large village. He stood treat to the elders and obtained the necessary documents. Five shares of communal land were given him for his own and his sons' use: that is to say—125 acres (not all together, but in different fields) besides the use of the communal pasture. Pakhom put up the buildings he needed, and bought cattle. Of the communal land alone he had three times as

32 **Critical Viewing** In what ways does this painting convey the challenges Pakhom might face as an independent landowner? **[Analyze]**

31

Cornfield at Ewell, William Holman Hunt

ENRICHMENT: Science Connection

Crop Rotation

On p. 841, Pakhom mentions the practices of rotating crops and of sowing wheat for one or two years and then allowing the field to lie fallow until it is covered with grass. This process has a scientific justification. Certain crops, such as wheat and corn, leach nutrients from the soil. Other crops, such as alfalfa or soybeans, can reconstitute the soil, making it ready for planting grain again. By rotating crops from year to year, farmers can increase the productivity of their cropland. Sometimes, farmers let the land "rest": They do not plant it but let it lie fallow.

Students might like to speculate on how greed might make a farmer sacrifice productivity over time. If a farmer were shortsighted and planted grain year after year in hopes of making the best profit, eventually the grain crop would fail because the soil would be barren.

much as at his former home, and the land was good corn-land. He was ten times better off than he had been. He had plenty of arable land and pasturage, and could keep as many head of cattle as he liked.

At first, in the bustle of building and settling down, Pakhom was pleased with it all, but when he got used to it he began to think that even here he had not enough land. The first year, he sowed wheat on his share of the communal land and had a good crop. He wanted to go on sowing wheat, but had not enough communal land for the purpose, and what he had already used was not available; for in those parts wheat is only sown on virgin soil or on fallow land. It is sown for one or two years, and then the land lies fallow till it is again overgrown with prairie grass. There were many who wanted such land and there was not enough for all; so that people quarreled about it. Those who were better off wanted it for growing wheat, and those who were poor wanted it to let to dealers, so that they might raise money to pay their taxes. Pakhom wanted to sow more wheat, so he rented land from a dealer for a year. He sowed much wheat and had a fine crop, but the land was too far from the village—the wheat had to be carted more than ten miles. After a time Pakhom noticed that some peasant-dealers were living on separate farms and were growing wealthy; and he thought:

"If I were to buy some freehold land and have a homestead on it, it would be a different thing altogether. Then it would all be nice and compact."

The question of buying freehold land recurred to him again and again.

He went on in the same way for three years, renting land and sowing wheat. The seasons turned out well and the crops were good, so that he began to lay money by. He might have gone on living contentedly, but he grew tired of having to rent other people's land every year, and having to scramble for it. Wherever there was good land to be had, the peasants would rush for it and it was taken up at once, so that unless you were sharp about it you got none. It happened in the third year that he and a dealer together rented a piece of pasture land from some peasants; and they had already plowed it up, when there was some dispute and the peasants went to law about it (35) and things fell out so that the labor was all lost.

Reading Strategy
Evaluating Characters' Decisions What happiness have Pakhom's decisions brought him?

✓Reading Check
What thought continues to bother Pakhom?

(33) Reading Strategy
Evaluating Characters' Decisions

- Ask a volunteer to read aloud the bracketed passage.
- Then, ask students the Reading Strategy question on p. 841: What happiness have Pakhom's decisions brought him?
  Possible response: Pakhom seems happy at first after he gets additional land. Then, he gradually becomes dissatisfied and wants more land.

Monitor Progress Review with students the decisions that Pakhom has made so far: the decision to go into debt to buy land in his home village; the decision to penalize some peasants who encroached on his land; the decision to move to a new area; the decision to rent additional land. Ask students to explain the consequences of each decision.

(34) Literary Analysis
Dynamic and Static Characters

- Read aloud the bracketed passage. Discuss with students whether Pakhom will be content if he buys freehold land and has a homestead on it.
- Ask students how Pakhom has changed since he was first introduced in the story.
  Answer: Pakhom has grown more and more greedy for land.
- Have students discuss what role the Devil may be playing in Pakhom's discontent.

(35) ✓Reading Check

Answer: The thought of buying freehold land continues to bother Pakhom.

CUSTOMIZE INSTRUCTION FOR UNIVERSAL ACCESS

For Less Proficient Readers	For Gifted/Talented Students
Students may not recognize that a number of years have passed since the beginning of the story. To help students understand the passage of time, have them create timelines. Divide the timelines into one-year increments, beginning with Pakhom's first land acquisition. Show how long he held the land, when he acquired the next parcel, and so on. Encourage students to display their completed timelines in class.	Refer students to the picture of the sickle on p. 842. Tell them that this was one of the hand tools that nineteenth-century Russian peasants used in farming. Have students locate pictures and information about other nineteenth-century tools and create a sketchbook of farm implements that Pakhom might have used. Under each sketch, have students write a brief caption describing the tool's use.

36 Background

Pakhom's Travels

The Bashkirs live "far away" from Pakhom's present home, but their land is still in Europe, not Asia. Pakhom is moving eastward (somewhat like America's westward-moving pioneers) in search of cheaper and more abundant land.

37 Critical Thinking

Analyze

- Have a volunteer read aloud the bracketed passage. Point out Pakhom's interest in obtaining thousands of acres of land.
- Remind students that Pakhom once told his wife that he needed only twenty acres of land. Ask why he now chooses to pass up acquiring "only thirteen hundred acres" to try to acquire even more land?
Answer: Pakhom is becoming increasingly greedy for land.

38 ▶ Critical Viewing

Possible response: Pakhom's desire for more land seems foolish because it would be extremely difficult to tend such a large amount of land with hand tools.

"If it were my own land," thought Pakhom, "I should be independent, and there would not be all this unpleasantness."

So Pakhom began looking out for land which he could buy; and he came across a peasant who had bought thirteen hundred acres, but having got into difficulties was willing to sell again cheap. Pakhom bargained and haggled with him, and at last they settled the price at 1,500 rubles, part in cash and part to be paid later. They had all but clinched the matter when a passing dealer happened to stop at Pakhom's one day to get a feed for his horses. He drank tea with Pakhom and they had a talk. The dealer said that he was just returning from the land of the Bashkirs,[7] far away, where he had bought thirteen thousand acres of land, all for 1,000 rubles. Pakhom questioned him further, and the tradesman said:

"All one need do is to make friends with the chiefs. I gave away about one hundred rubles' worth of silk robes and carpets, besides a case of tea, and I gave wine to those who would drink it; and I got the land for less than a penny[8] an acre." And he showed Pakhom the title-deeds, saying:

"The land lies near a river, and the whole prairie is virgin soil."

Pakhom plied him with questions, and the tradesman said:

"There is more land there than you could cover if you walked a year, and it all belongs to the Bashkirs. They are as simple as sheep, and land can be got almost for nothing."

"There, now," thought Pakhom, "with my 1,000 rubles, why should I get only thirteen hundred acres, and saddle myself with a debt besides? If I take it out there, I can get more than ten times as much for the money."

38 ▲ Critical Viewing
An iron sickle such as this might be used to clear fields of tall weeds and grasses. With this information in mind, does Pakhom's desire for more land seem foolish? Explain. **[Criticize]**

V

Pakhom inquired how to get to the place, and as soon as the tradesman had left him, he prepared to go there himself. He left his wife to look after the homestead, and started on his journey taking his man with him. They stopped at a town on their way and bought a case of tea, some wine, and other presents, as the trademan had advised. On and on they went until they had gone more than three hundred miles, and on the seventh day they came to a place where the Bashkirs had pitched their tents. It was all just as the tradesman had said. The people lived on the steppes,[9] by a river, in felt-covered tents. They neither tilled the ground, nor ate bread. Their cattle and horses grazed in herds on the steppe. The colts were tethered behind the tents, and the mares were driven to them twice a day. The mares were milked, and from the milk kumiss[10] was made. It was the women who prepared kumiss, and they also made cheese. As far as the men were concerned,

7. **Bashkirs** (bash kirz') nomadic people who live in the plains of southwestern Russia.
8. **penny** here, one hundredth of a ruble.
9. **steppe** (step) *n.* high grassland of central Asia.
10. **kumiss** (ko͞o' mis) *n.* mare's milk that has been fermented and is used as a drink.

39 drinking kumiss and tea, eating mutton, and playing on their pipes, was all they cared about. They were all stout and merry, and all the summer long they never thought of doing any work. They were quite ignorant, and knew no Russian, but were good-natured enough.

As soon as they saw Pakhom, they came out of their tents and gathered round their visitor. An interpreter was found, and Pakhom told them he had come about some land. The Bashkirs seemed very glad; they took Pakhom and led him into one of the best tents, where they made him sit on some down cushions placed on a carpet, while they sat round him. They gave him some tea and kumiss, and had a sheep killed, and gave him mutton to eat. Pakhom took presents out of his cart and distributed them among the Bashkirs, and divided the tea amongst them. The Bashkirs were delighted. They talked a great deal among themselves, and then told the interpreter to translate.

"They wish to tell you," said the interpreter, "that they like you, and that it is our custom to do all we can to please a guest and to repay him for his gifts. You have given us presents, now tell us which of the things we possess please you best, that we may present them to you."

"What pleases me best here," answered Pakhom, "is your land. Our land is crowded and the soil is exhausted; but you have plenty of land and it is good land. I never saw the like of it."

The interpreter translated. The Bashkirs talked among themselves for a while. Pakhom could not understand what they were saying, but saw that they were much amused and that they shouted and laughed. Then they were silent and looked at Pakhom while the interpreter said:

"They wish me to tell you that in return for your presents they will gladly give you as much land as you want. You have only to point it out with your hand and it is yours."

The Bashkirs talked again for a while and began to dispute. Pakhom asked what they were disputing about, and the interpreter told him that some of them thought they ought to ask their chief about the land and not act in his absence, while others thought there was no need to wait for his return.

VI

While the Bashkirs were disputing, a man in a large fox-fur cap appeared on the scene. They all became silent and rose to their feet. The interpreter said, "This is our chief himself."

Pakhom immediately fetched the best dressing-gown and five pounds of tea, and offered these to the chief. The chief accepted them, and seated himself in the place of honor. The Bashkirs at once began telling him something. The chief listened for a while, then made a sign with his head for them to be silent, and addressing himself to Pakhom, said in Russian:

"Well, let it be so. Choose whatever piece of land you like; we have plenty of it."

Literary Analysis
Dynamic and Static Characters Which elements of the Bashkirs' lifestyle has Pakhom sought for himself since his days as a peasant farmer?

40 **✓Reading Check**
What generosities do the Bashkirs show Pakhom?

39 Literary Analysis

Dynamic and Static Characters

- Have students read the bracketed passage beginning on p. 842 describing the lifestyle of the Bashkirs.
- Then, have them discuss how the Bashkir way of life differs from Pakhom's way of life.
- Ask students the Literary Analysis question on p. 843: Which elements of the Bashkirs' lifestyle has Pakhom sought for himself since his days as a peasant farmer?
  Possible response: Pakhom has sought to have an easy, comfortable life and not have to work very hard. Similarly, the Bashkirs spend their days eating, drinking, and playing music, instead of working.

40 ✓Reading Check

Answer: The Bashkirs treat Pakhom as an honored guest, give him food and drink, and offer to give him land.

CUSTOMIZE INSTRUCTION FOR UNIVERSAL ACCESS

For Special Needs Students	For Less Proficient Readers
Students may enjoy looking at a topographical map of Russia to get a sense of the vast distances Pakhom covers in his quest for land. Ask them to find some of the points of reference in the story: the Volga, the Samara, and the steppes or plains of southwestern Russia.	The conversation between Pakhom and the Bashkirs on pp. 843–844 demonstrates Pakhom's obsessive nature. Point out specific context clues in this section that show Pakhom's obsession with acquiring land. Discuss with students how Pakhom's tense feelings contrast with the carefree attitude of the Bashkirs.

41 Reading Strategy

Evaluating Characters' Decisions

- Have a volunteer read aloud the bracketed passage in which Pakhom asks for a deed. Remind students that the Bashkirs are nomadic herders. Discuss how the Bashkirs might view the land differently than farmers such as Pakhom view it.
- Ask students the Reading Strategy question on p. 844: What past experiences might have influenced Pakhom's decision to obtain a deed from the Bashkirs?
Answer: Pakhom's previous experience of buying land and obtaining a deed, as well as his experience of renting land and not having a deed, might have influenced his decision to request a deed from the Bashkirs.

42 Critical Thinking

Speculate

- Have students read aloud the bracketed passage. Then, have them discuss what might be going through Pakhom's mind when he hears that, for one price, he can get as much land as he can walk around in a day.
- Ask students to speculate about how this chance of getting land might be Pakhom's downfall and the fulfillment of the Devil's plan.
Possible response: In his greed, Pakhom will try to take too much land and something bad will happen as a result.

"How can I take as much as I like?" thought Pakhom. "I must get a deed to make it secure, or else they may say, 'It is yours,' and afterward may take it away again."

"Thank you for your kind words," he said aloud. "You have much land, and I only want a little. But I should like to be sure which bit is mine. Could it not be measured and made over to me? Life and death are in God's hands. You good people give it to me, but your children
41 might wish to take it away again."

"You are quite right," said the chief. "We will make it over to you."

"I heard that a dealer had been here," continued Pakhom, "and that you gave him a little land, too, and signed title-deeds to that effect. I should like to have it done in the same way."

The chief understood.

"Yes," replied he, "that can be done quite easily. We have a scribe, and we will go to town with you and have the deed properly sealed."

"And what will be the price?" asked Pakhom.

"Our price is always the same: one thousand rubles a day."

Pakhom did not understand.

"A day? What measure is that? How many acres would that be?"

"We do not know how to reckon it out," said the chief. "We sell it by
42 the day. As much as you can go around on your feet in a day is yours, and the price is one thousand rubles a day."

Pakhom was surprised.

"But in a day you can get around a large tract of land," he said.

The chief laughed.

"It will all be yours!" said he. "But there is one condition: If you don't return on the same day to the spot whence you started, your money is lost."

"But how am I to mark the way that I have gone?"

"Why, we shall go to any spot you like, and stay there. You must start from that spot and make your round, taking a spade with you. Wherever you think necessary, make a mark. At every turning, dig a hole and pile up the turf; then afterward we will go round with a plow from hole to hole. You may make as large a circuit as you please, but before the sun sets you must return to the place you started from. All the land you cover will be yours."

Pakhom was delighted. It was decided to start early next morning. They talked a while, and after drinking some more kumiss and eating some more mutton, they had tea again, and then the night came on. They gave Pakhom a feather-bed to sleep on, and the Bashkirs dispersed for the night, promising to assemble the next morning at daybreak and ride out before sunrise to the appointed spot.

Reading Strategy
Evaluating Characters' Decisions What past experiences might have influenced Pakhom's decision to obtain a deed from the Bashkirs?

VII

Pakhom lay on the feather-bed, but could not sleep. He kept thinking about the land.

"What a large tract I will mark off!" thought he. "I can easily do thirty-five miles in a day. The days are long now, and within a circuit of thirty-

ENRICHMENT: Culture Connection

The Bashkirs

The Bashkirs that Pakhom deals with have lived in what is now the eastern part of European Russia since the thirteenth century. Their lands came under Russian control in the sixteenth century, and the Russians began colonizing the land, gradually pushing the Bashkirs out. Angry and resentful of the colonists, the Bashkirs staged many uprisings, but they were harshly repressed by the Russian government.

Originally, the Bashkirs were nomadic herders who raised horses, sheep, goats, cattle, and at one time, camels. By the end of the nineteenth century, pressure from colonization forced the Bashkirs to give up their nomadic way of life and become farmers living in settled villages.

five miles what a lot of land there will be! I will sell the poorer land, or let it to peasants, but I'll pick out the best and farm it. I will buy two ox-teams, and hire two more laborers. About a hundred and fifty acres shall be plowland, and I will pasture cattle on the rest."

Pakhom lay awake all night, and dozed off only just before dawn. Hardly were his eyes closed when he had a dream. He thought he was lying in that same tent and heard somebody chuckling outside. He wondered who it could be, and rose and went out, and he saw the Bashkir chief sitting in front of the tent holding his sides and rolling about with laughter. Going nearer to the chief, Pakhom asked: "What are you laughing at?" But he saw that it was no longer the chief, but the dealer who had recently stopped at his house and had told him about the land. Just as Pakhom was going to ask, "Have you been
44 here long?" he saw that it was not the dealer, but the peasant who had come up from the Volga, long ago, to Pakhom's old home. Then he saw that it was not the peasant either, but the Devil himself with hoofs and horns, sitting there and chuckling, and before him lay a man barefoot, prostrate on the ground, with only trousers and a shirt on. And Pakhom dreamt that he looked more attentively to see what sort of a man it was that was lying there, and he saw that the man was dead, and that it was himself! He awoke horror-struck.

"What things one does dream," thought he.

Looking round he saw through the open door that the dawn was breaking.

"It's time to wake them up," thought he. "We ought to be starting."

He got up, roused his man (who was sleeping in his cart), bade him harness; and went to call the Bashkirs.

"It's time to go to the steppe to measure the land," he said.

The Bashkirs rose and assembled, and the chief came too. Then they began drinking kumiss again, and offered Pakhom some tea, but he would not wait.

"If we are to go, let us go. It is high time," said he.

VIII

The Bashkirs got ready and they all started; some mounted on horses, and some in carts. Pakhom drove in his own small cart with his servant and took a spade with him. When they reached the steppe, the morning red was beginning to kindle. They ascended a hillock (called by the Bashkirs a *shikhan*) and, dismounting from their carts and their horses, gathered in one spot. The chief came up to Pakhom and stretching out his arm toward the plain;

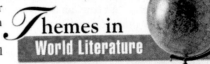

Themes in World Literature

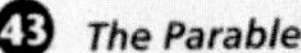

43 *The Parable*

A **parable** is a story used to teach a lesson. Generally, parables focus on one or two characters and deal with a specific circumstance that motivates their actions. In addition, the outcome of a parable seems inevitable. The lessons taught by the main characters reflect moral choices motivated by ambition, greed, or wisdom. Since the aim of most parables is to reach as many people as possible, the stories tend to be extremely simple and brief.

Many cultures use parables to teach values that are specific to their culture, but the similarities in stories from all over the world is often striking. For example, the Lenape, a Native American people, use the story "The Greedy Maiden" to answer the same question posed by Russian Leo Tolstoy: How much is enough?

Critics have noted that Tolstoy's story echoes the biblical parable of the rich fool (Luke 12:16–20), the story of a wealthy farmer who incurs the wrath of God by tearing down his barns and building larger ones.

prostrate (präs´ trāt) *adj.* lying with one's face down

45 ✓Reading Check

How many miles does Pakhom plan to walk?

43 Background

The Parable

The following biblical parable of the rich fool (Luke 12: 16–20, King James Version) is similar to Pakhom's tale:

16 And he spake a parable unto them, saying, The ground of a certain rich man brought forth plentifully:
17 And he thought within himself, saying, What shall I do, because I have no room where to bestow my fruits?
18 And he said, This will I do: I will pull down my barns, and build greater; and there will I bestow all my fruits and my goods.
19 And I will say to my soul, Soul, thou have much goods laid up for many years; take thine ease, eat, drink, and be merry.
20 But God said unto him, Thou fool, this night thy soul shall be required of thee: then whose shall those things be, which thou has provided?

44 Critical Thinking

Speculate

- Have students read the bracketed passage independently. Discuss what the dream says about the Devil's role in Pakhom's life.
- Ask students to speculate about the outcome of the story on the basis of Pakhom's dream. Possible response: Pakhom will die in the end.

45 ✓Reading Check

Answer: Pakhom plans to walk thirty-five miles.

CUSTOMIZE INSTRUCTION FOR UNIVERSAL ACCESS

For Advanced Readers

Tell students that thirty-five miles is a very long distance to walk in one day. Ask students to calculate how many square miles of land Pakhom would acquire if he walked that far, forming a square. Help students begin by suggesting that they divide 35 by 4 ($35 \div 4 =$ 8.75 miles per side; $8.75 \times 8.75 = 76.5$ square miles). After students complete their calculations, tell them that 76.5 square miles equals 48,960 acres.

Then, have students calculate how fast Pakhom would have to walk to cover thirty-five miles in one day.

Suggest that they assume a fourteen-hour day from sunrise to sunset (2.5 miles per hour). Discuss with students how difficult it would be to maintain a pace of two and a half miles per hour for fourteen hours in the summer heat without a single moment of rest.

46 Literary Analysis

Dynamic and Static Characters

- Direct students' attention to the bracketed passage.
- Remind students that years have passed since Pakhom first set out to increase his land holdings. Have them note how much land Pakhom is now considering.
- Then, ask students the Literary Analysis question on p. 846: In what ways has ambition changed Pakhom? Answer: Pakhom has become greedy for land. He is no longer striving to have a life of ease; he wants only to acquire as much land as possible, even though one man could not work it all.

47 Background

Photography

Field, Moscow, Idaho, by David Brookover

This photograph illustrates the principle of *linear perspective*. Objects appear smaller as they recede into the distance, and lines that seem parallel actually converge at a vanishing point on the horizon. This vision of land as far as the eye can see would have tempted Pakhom.

Use the following questions for discussion:

- How do you think this scene would have made Pakhom feel? Possible response: Pakhom would have become excited at the prospect of buying this land, or he would have felt envy because he did not own it.
- How would you react to owning such a vast tract of land? Possible response: Some viewers may think they would enjoy the experience of ownership; others may think life would be lonely.

48 ▶ Critical Viewing

Possible response: Pakhom might imagine all the land planted with his own grain.

"See," said he, "all this, as far as your eye can reach, is ours. You may have any part of it you like."

46 Pakhom's eyes glistened: it was all virgin soil, as flat as the palm of your hand, as black as the seed of a poppy, and in the hollows different kinds of grasses grew breast high.

The chief took off his fox-fur cap, placed it on the ground and said:

"This will be the mark. Start from here, and return here again. All the land you go round shall be yours."

Pakhom took out his money and put it on the cap. Then he took off his outer coat, remaining in his sleeveless under-coat. He unfastened his girdle[11] and tied it tight below his stomach, put a little bag of bread into the breast of his coat, and tying a flask of water to his girdle, he drew up the tops of his boots, took the spade from his man, and stood ready to start. He considered for some moments which way he had better go—it was tempting everywhere.

"No matter," he concluded, "I will go toward the rising sun."

He turned his face to the east, stretched himself, and waited for the sun to appear above the rim.

"I must lose no time," he thought, "and it is easier walking while it is still cool."

The sun's rays had hardly flashed above the horizon, before Pakhom, carrying the spade over his shoulder, went down into the steppe.

Pakhom started walking neither slowly nor quickly. After having gone a thousand yards he stopped, dug a hole, and placed pieces of turf one on another to make it more visible. Then he went on; and now that he had walked off his stiffness he quickened his pace. After a while he dug another hole.

Pakhom looked back. The hillock could be distinctly seen in the sunlight, with the people on it, and the glittering tires of the cartwheels. At a rough guess Pakhom concluded that he had walked three miles. It was growing warmer; he took off his under-coat, flung it across his

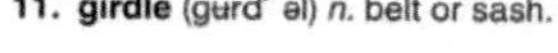

11. **girdle** (gurd′ əl) *n.* belt or sash.

Literary Analysis
Dynamic and Static Characters In what ways has ambition changed Pakhom?

48 ▼ **Critical Viewing** What might Pakhom imagine for himself while looking at land such as this?

47

shoulder, and went on again. It had grown quite warm now; he looked at the sun, it was time to think of breakfast.

49 "The first shift is done, but there are four in a day, and it is too soon yet to turn. But I will just take off my boots," said he to himself.

He sat down, took off his boots, stuck them into his girdle, and went on. It was easy walking now.

"I will go on for another three miles," thought he, "and then turn to the left. This spot is so fine, that it would be a pity to lose it. The further one goes, the better the land seems."

He went straight on for a while, and when he looked round, the hillock was scarcely visible and the people on it looked like black ants, and he could just see something glistening there in the sun.

"Ah," thought Pakhom, "I have gone far enough in this direction, it is time to turn. Besides I am in a regular sweat, and very thirsty."

He stopped, dug a large hole, and heaped up pieces of turf. Next he untied his flask, had a drink, and then turned sharply to the left. He went on and on; the grass was high, and it was very hot.

Pakhom began to grow tired: he looked at the sun and saw that it was noon.

"Well," he thought, "I must have a rest."

He sat down, and ate some bread and drank some water; but he did not lie down, thinking that if he did he might fall asleep. After sitting a little while, he went on again. At first he walked easily: the food had strengthened him; but it had become terribly hot and he felt sleepy. Still he went on, thinking: "An hour to suffer, a lifetime to live."

He went a long way in this direction also, and was about to turn to the left again, when he perceived a damp hollow: "It would be a pity to leave that out," he thought. "Flax would do well there." So he went on past the hollow and dug a hole on the other side of it before he turned the corner. Pakhom looked toward the hillock. The heat made the air hazy: it seemed to be quivering, and through the haze the people on the hillock could scarcely be seen.

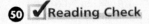

Reading Strategy
Evaluating Characters' Decisions What are the possible implications of Pakhom's decision to "go on for another three miles"?

50 **Reading Check**

What obstacles does Pakhom encounter as he walks?

49 Reading Strategy

Evaluating Characters' Decisions

- Have a student read aloud the bracketed passage. Ask: What does Pakhom mean when he says "The first shift is done, but there are four in a day"?
  Answer: Pakhom means that he has gone one quarter of the square, or one side of the square, he plans to walk.
- Ask students the Reading Strategy question on p. 847: What are the possible implications of Pakhom's decision to "go on for another three miles"?
  Possible response: By going that far, Pakhom may not be able to get back to the starting point before sunset.

Monitor Progress Review with students the decisions Pakhom has made up to this point. Have students discuss at what point they think Pakhom began to make bad decisions.

Reteach To clarify the Reading Strategy for students, have them evaluate Pakhom's decisions using the Evaluating Characters' Decisions transparency in **Literary Analysis and Reading Transparencies,** p. 82.

50 Reading Check

Answer: Pakhom encounters extreme heat, thirst, hunger, and fatigue.

CUSTOMIZE INSTRUCTION FOR UNIVERSAL ACCESS

For Less Proficient Readers	For English Learners	For Gifted/Talented Students
As students read pp. 846–848, tell them to note when Pakhom turns the three corners to form the sides of his new property. This will help them keep track of his progress and give clues about what will happen in the story.	Make sure that students understand that the words in quotation marks on p. 847 are words that Pakhom is thinking. Point out that Pakhom is alone and is not having a conversation with anyone. Have students review the selection and identify other examples of this technique.	Remind students that as Pakhom walks, the Bashkirs are watching him from where they are waiting on a hill. Suggest that students write a brief dialogue between the Bashkir chief and the other tribesmen as they watch Pakhom walk the land. Have students share their dialogues with the class.

51 Literary Analysis

Dynamic and Static Characters

- Remind students of Pakhom's growing ambition and his eventual discontent each time he acquires additional land. Then, read aloud the bracketed section.
- Ask the Literary Analysis question on p. 848: Do you think Pakhom will be satisfied with his new tract of land? Explain.
  Answer: Pakhom is never satisfied with his acquisitions, and he will eventually become dissatisfied with this amount of land as well.
- At this point, you may want to discuss how Pakhom's changing character affects his decisions. Have students explain how Pakhom's greed has influenced the decisions he has made so far.

52 Reading Strategy

Evaluating Characters' Decisions

- Discuss the image of Pakhom described in the opening of Section IX. Point out that he is on the last leg of his walk but still far from the end.
- Ask the Reading Strategy question on p. 848: Why do you think Pakhom did not prepare for his exhaustion as the day progressed?
  Possible response: In Pakhom's greed, he did not want to slow down or shorten the distance that he walked, and so he became exhausted.

"Ah!" thought Pakhom, "I have made the sides too long; I must make this one shorter." And he went along the third side, stepping faster. He looked at the sun: it was nearly half-way to the horizon, and he had not yet done two miles of the third side of the square. He was still ten miles
51 from the goal.

"No," he thought, "though it will make my land lop-sided, I must hurry back in a straight line now. I might go too far, and as it is I have a great deal of land."

So Pakhom hurriedly dug a hole, and turned straight toward the hillock.

Literary Analysis
Dynamic and Static Characters Do you think Pakhom will be satisfied with his new tract of land? Explain.

IX

Pakhom went straight toward the hillock, but he now walked with difficulty. He was exhausted from the heat, his bare feet were cut and bruised, and his legs began to fail. He longed to rest, but it was impossible if he meant to get back before sunset. The sun waits for no man, and it was sinking lower and lower.

"Oh, dear," he thought, "if only I have not blundered trying for too
52 much! What if I am too late?"

He looked toward the hillock and at the sun. He was still far from his goal, and the sun was already near the rim.

Pakhom walked on and on; it was very hard walking but he went quicker and quicker. He pressed on, but was still far from the place. He began running, threw away his coat, his boots, his flask, and his cap, and kept only the spade which he used as a support.

"What shall I do?" he thought again. "I have grasped too much and ruined the whole affair. I can't get there before the sun sets."

And this fear made him still more breathless. Pakhom went on running, his soaking shirt and trousers stuck to him and his mouth was parched. His breast was working like a blacksmith's bellows, his heart was beating like a hammer, and his legs were giving way as if they did not belong to him. Pakhom was seized with terror lest he should die of the strain.

Though afraid of death, he could not stop. "After having run all that way they will call me a fool if I stop now," thought he. And he ran on and on, and drew near and heard the Bashkirs yelling and shouting to him, and their cries inflamed his heart still more. He gathered his last strength and ran on.

The sun was close to the rim, and cloaked in mist looked large, and red as blood. Now, yes now, it was about to set! The sun was quite low, but he was also quite near his aim. Pakhom could already see the people on the hillock waving their arms to hurry him up. He could see the fox-fur cap on the ground and the money on it, and the chief sitting on the ground holding his sides. And Pakhom remembered his dream.

"There's plenty of land," thought he, "but will God let me live on it? I have lost my life, I have lost my life! I shall never reach that spot!"

Pakhom looked at the sun, which had reached the earth: one side of it had already disappeared. With all his remaining strength he rushed on, bending his body forward so that his legs could hardly follow fast

Reading Strategy
Evaluating Characters' Decisions Why do you think Pakhom did not prepare for his exhaustion as the day progressed?

ENRICHMENT: Literature Connection

The Image of the Sun

In his critical biography of Tolstoy, William W. Rowe applauds the effectiveness of the ending of Tolstoy's story:

> The image of the sun (which "will not wait") is particularly successful, as it races in its arching journey across the sky against the wide curve of Pakhom's greed upon the ground. The fact that Pakhom's heart pounds like a hammer while the sun turns blood-red is a grimly apt anticipation of the blood that will issue from his mouth when he dies. . . .

At the end, both Pakhom and the sun disappear beneath the ground after tracing their curving courses above the earth—a focus that appropriately reinforces the deadly playfulness of the story's title.

enough to keep him from falling. Just as he reached the hillock it suddenly grew dark. He looked up—the sun had already set! He gave a cry: "All my labor has been in vain," thought he, and was about to stop, but he heard the Bashkirs still shouting, and remembered that though to him, from below, the sun seemed to have set, they on the hillock could still see it. He took a long breath and ran up the hillock. It was still light there. He reached the top and saw the cap. Before it sat the chief laughing and holding his sides. Again Pakhom remembered his dream, and he uttered a cry: his legs gave way beneath him, he fell forward and reached the cap with his hands.

"Ah, that's a fine fellow!" exclaimed the chief. "He has gained much land!"

Pakhom's servant came running up and tried to raise him, but he saw that blood was flowing from his mouth. Pakhom was dead!

The Bashkirs clicked their tongues to show their pity.

His servant picked up the spade and dug a grave long enough for Pakhom to lie in, and buried him in it. Six feet from his head to his heels was all he needed.

Review and Assess

Thinking About the Selection

1. **Respond:** If you were in Pakhom's place, at what point might you be satisfied with your property? Explain.
2. (a) **Recall:** What does the younger sister say about peasant life and city life? (b) **Connect:** Considering the outcome of the story, what is ironic, or surprising, about the younger sister's comments?
3. (a) **Recall:** What changes Pakhom's attitude toward his first plot of land? (b) **Speculate:** Explain whether you think that Pakhom's attitude would have remained the same if he had not had difficulties with his neighbors.
4. (a) **Recall:** Besides Pakhom, who is featured in his dream? (b) **Infer:** What does the dream suggest about the Devil's role in the story?
5. (a) **Recall:** In the end, how much land did Pakhom need? (b) **Analyze:** What is ironic about the final line? (c) **Criticize:** Did you find the ending satisfying? Why or why not?
6. (a) **Apply:** Greek playwright Socrates wrote, "He is richest who is content with the least. He who has little and wants less is richer than he that has much and wants more." Apply this sentiment to the story. (b) **Take a Stand:** Do you agree with Socrates? Why or why not?

CUSTOMIZE INSTRUCTION FOR UNIVERSAL ACCESS

For Gifted/Talented Students	For Advanced Readers
Invite students to choose scenes from the story to role-play. For example, they might choose the conversation between the two sisters, Pakhom's quarrel with the judges, or Pakhom's interaction with the Bashkirs. Allow students time to practice, and then have them present their scenes to the class. Have students explain how the scenes they chose reveal how the characters involved changed or stayed the same throughout the story.	Encourage students to write parables of their own modeled after Tolstoy's story. Tell them to start by deciding what they want the parables to teach. Then, have them choose a setting and develop one or two characters. Emphasize to students that when writing their parables, they should make their messages clear. Explain that setting aside their stories for a day or two will help students evaluate them more objectively. If students wish, have them share their completed parables with the class.

Answers for p. 849

Review and Assess

1. Possible responses: Some readers may suggest that they would be happy with twenty acres because they could live at ease on that land; others may say that they would need more so that they could have some luxury.
2. **(a)** The sister says that city people are wealthy but their lives are unstable, and city people may succumb to the temptation of the Devil. In contrast, she says that peasants are poor, but they are content and their lives are long. **(b)** Her husband is the one who succumbs to temptation by the Devil and, despite becoming wealthy, ends up dying an early death as a result of his greed.
3. **(a)** The peasants trespass on Pakhom's fields, and he argues with his neighbors. **(b)** Possible response: He would have grown dissatisfied with his land anyway because he kept wanting more of it.
4. **(a)** Pakhom sees the Bashkir chief, the grain dealer, the wandering peasant, and the Devil. **(b)** The Devil plays a crucial recurring role.
5. **(a)** Pakhom needed only six feet of land for his grave. **(b)** The final line is ironic because Pakhom believes that he needs more and more land throughout the story, but in the end he needs only six feet.
   (c) Possible response: The end is satisfying because Pakhom would never have stopped trying to acquire more and more land.
6. **(a)** Tolstoy's story shows what can happen to someone who "has much and wants more." **(b)** Possible responses: Some students may agree with Socrates, because wanting more always makes one dissatisfied; others may say that it is natural for people to want more and that having more increases one's comfort.

53 About the Selection

In "A Problem," three uncles grapple with the question of what to do about their errant nephew, Sasha. Instead of welcoming their decision to be lenient as an opportunity to mend his ways, Sasha seizes it as an opportunity to continue his irresponsible habits, with just one difference—he has gained self-knowledge. He now sees how he can manipulate his relatives and avoid facing the consequences he deserves. The story raises important questions about forgiveness and responsibility.

54 Background

Art

The Library at Windsor Castle, by Joseph Nash

Joseph Nash (1808–1878) was an English wood engraver and lithographer known for his fine-art lithography, such as this color lithograph of the library in Windsor Castle. In lithography, the artist draws a picture directly on stone using grease-based paints or crayons. The image is then imprinted on paper. Great detail and luminous color can be achieved with this process, as the image on this page shows. The great advantage of fine-art lithography over oil painting on canvas is that many copies of the pieces can be reproduced. This detailed lithograph represents the wealth and dignity surrounding nineteenth-century aristocratic families such as the Uskovs.

Use the following questions for discussion:

- Which details in this image reflect an opulent and luxurious lifestyle?
  Possible response: The high and ornate ceiling, the elegant furniture, and the many books reflect a luxurious lifestyle.
- Do you think this is an appropriate illustration for this story? Why or why not?
  Possible response: The painting is appropriate because it resembles the study where the uncles meet to discuss Sasha's fate.

55 ▶ Critical Viewing

Possible response: The elegance of the room —its structure and its decorations— reflects family honor and pride.

53 A Problem

Anton Chekhov *translated by* **Constance Garnett**

54

The Library at Windsor Castle, Joseph Nash, National Trust Photographic Library

55 ▲ **Critical Viewing** In what ways is family honor reflected in a formal study like this one? **[Analyze]**

ENRICHMENT: History Connection

Russia in the Twentieth Century

The lifestyle of Russian aristocrats such as those described in "A Problem" ended in the early twentieth century. The Russian Revolution took place in 1917, and the establishment of a communist state soon followed. Under communism, all land and means of production is owned by the state. Private ownership is banned, and all workers theoretically have an equal share in the wealth of the nation. After the revolution, many aristocratic families like the Uskovs lost their land and wealth, and many fled to other countries.

In 1922, Russia became part of the newly established Union of Soviet Socialist Republics (USSR), better known as the Soviet Union. The Soviet Union initially consisted of four republics, the strongest and most influential being the Russian Republic. The Soviet Union gained further territory after World War II, under Joseph Stalin's rule. Increasing disillusionment with communism and demands for greater freedoms led to the eventual defeat of Communist party rule and the dissolution of the Soviet Union in 1991.

Background

In the nineteenth century, members of the Russian aristocracy lived on wealth that had been accumulated generations earlier. For this class, honor meant more than displays of good behavior. Honor required preserving the reputation and heritage of a long-standing family name. When good fortunes changed and money became unavailable, a family name and its history of prosperity suggested the promise of stability to come. Such a promise was often all the aristocrats could rely on to save them from imminent financial disaster.

The strictest measures were taken that the Uskovs' family secret might not leak out and become generally known. Half of the servants were sent off to the theater or the circus; the other half were sitting in the kitchen and not allowed to leave it. Orders were given that no one was to be admitted. The wife of the Colonel, her sister, and the governess, though they had been initiated into the secret, kept up a pretense of knowing nothing; they sat in the dining-room and did not show themselves in the drawing-room or the hall.

Sasha Uskov, the young man of twenty-five who was the cause of all the commotion, had arrived some time before, and by the advice of kind-hearted Ivan Markovitch, his uncle, who was taking his part, he sat meekly in the hall by the door leading to the study, and prepared himself to make an open, candid explanation.

The other side of the door, in the study, a family council was being held. The subject under discussion was an exceedingly disagreeable and delicate one. Sasha Uskov had cashed at one of the banks a false promissory note[1] and it had become due for payment three days before, and now his two paternal uncles and Ivan Markovitch, the brother of his dead mother, were deciding the question whether they should pay the money and save the family honor, or wash their hands of it and leave the case to go to trial.

Literary Analysis
Dynamic and Static Characters Which clues about the character of Sasha Uskov does this paragraph present?

✓Reading Check
Who is at the center of the Uskov family's secret?

1. **promissory note** written promise to pay a certain sum of money on demand; an IOU.

56 Literary Analysis

Dynamic and Static Characters

- Read aloud the second paragraph in the bracketed passage. Then, ask the Literary Analysis question on p. 851: Which clues about the character of Sasha Uskov does this paragraph present?
  Answer: Sasha seems ashamed but willing to tell the truth about what happened.
- Direct students' attention to the third paragraph in the bracketed passage. Explain that cashing a false promissory note is equivalent today to writing a bad check. Ask what further clues this paragraph offers about Sasha.
  Answer: Sasha is irresponsible and dishonest.

57 Reading Strategy

Evaluating Characters' Decisions

- Further explain that the bracketed passage describes a family council. Point to clues on the page that show that the family is deciding a serious matter.
- Tell students that two of the uncles are the brothers of Sasha's father; the other uncle, Ivan Markovitch, is the brother of Sasha's mother. Ask students to speculate about how this fact might affect the men's decision.
  Possible response: Because the uncles are from both sides of the family, they may have different interests and may reach different decisions.

58 

✓Reading Check

Answer: Sasha Uskov is at the center of the family's secret.

CUSTOMIZE INSTRUCTION FOR UNIVERSAL ACCESS

For English Learners	For Gifted/Talented Students
This story contains many difficult vocabulary words with which students may be unfamiliar. Have them work in pairs to review these words before beginning to read. Suggest that students use dictionaries when necessary to help with the definitions. Encourage each pair of students to write sentences using each of the words.	Suggest to students that this story presents enough information for the eventual trial of Sasha. Ask one group of students to create an opening statement for the prosecution of Sasha, detailing the reasons he should be found guilty. Another group can create the opening statement for Sasha's defense. You may wish to allot time for students to present the statements to the class.

59 Literary Analysis

Dynamic and Static Characters

- Have several volunteers take turns reading aloud the bracketed passage.
- Have students note that the author is giving clues about the characters of the three uncles. Point out that the first paternal uncle was a colonel in the army. Ask students how this fact affects his attitude and character.
  Possible response: The Colonel is firm and believes that being honorable means being honest.
- Have students discuss the differences in temperament of each uncle.

60 Reading Strategy

Evaluating Characters' Decisions

- Call students' attention to the bracketed passage.
- Remind students that each of the three uncles has his own reason for urging his solution to the problem. Furthermore, each uncle's opinion is grounded in his own character and personality.
- Have students explain how the two paternal uncles disagree about the solution.
  Answer: The Colonel believes that Sasha should be forced to accept the punishment for his behavior. The other paternal uncle simply wants the affair kept out of the papers, presumably by paying the money.
- Ask students the Reading Strategy question on p. 852: With which paternal uncle do you agree? Explain.
  Possible responses: Some readers may agree with the Colonel, saying that Sasha should accept responsibility for his behavior; others may agree with the other paternal uncle, saying that it is important to keep family secrets private.

To outsiders who have no personal interest in the matter such questions seem simple; for those who are so unfortunate as to have to decide them in earnest they are extremely difficult. The uncles had been talking for a long time, but the problem seemed no nearer decision.

"My friends!" said the uncle who was a colonel, and there was a note of exhaustion and bitterness in his voice. "Who says that family honor is a mere convention? I don't say that at all. I am only warning you against a false view; I am pointing out the possibility of an unpardonable mistake. How can you fail to see it? I am not speaking Chinese; I am speaking Russian!"

"My dear fellow, we do understand," Ivan Markovitch protested mildly.

"How can you understand if you say that I don't believe in family honor? I repeat once more; fa-mil-y ho-nor false-ly un-der-stood is a prejudice! Falsely understood! That's what I say: whatever may be the motives for screening a scoundrel, whoever he may be, and helping him to escape punishment, it is contrary to law and unworthy of a gentleman. It's not saving the family honor; it's civic cowardice! Take the army, for instance. . . . The honor of the army is more precious to us than any other honor, yet we don't screen our guilty members, but condemn them. And does the honor of the army suffer in consequence?
59 Quite the opposite!"

60 The other paternal uncle, an official in the Treasury, a taciturn, dull-witted, and rheumatic man, sat silent, or spoke only of the fact that the Uskovs' name would get into the newspapers if the case went for trial. His opinion was that the case ought to be hushed up from the first and not become public property; but, apart from publicity in the newspapers, he advanced no other argument in support of this opinion.

taciturn (tas´ə turn) *adj.* almost always silent

Reading Strategy
Evaluating Characters' Decisions With which paternal uncle do you agree? Explain.

The maternal uncle, kind-hearted Ivan Markovitch, spoke smoothly, softly, and with a tremor in his voice. He began with saying that youth has its rights and its peculiar temptations. Which of us has not been young, and who has not been led astray? To say nothing of ordinary mortals, even great men have not escaped errors and mistakes in their youth. Take, for instance, the biography of great writers. Did not every one of them gamble, drink, and draw down upon himself the anger of right-thinking people in his young days? If Sasha's error bordered upon crime, they must remember that Sasha had received practically no education; he had been expelled from the high school in the fifth class; he had lost his parents in early childhood, and so had been left at the tenderest age without guidance and good, benevolent influences. He was nervous, excitable, had no firm ground under his feet, and, above all, he had been unlucky. Even if he were guilty, anyway he deserved indulgence and the sympathy of all compassionate souls. He ought, of course, to be punished, but he was punished as it was by his conscience and the agonies he was enduring now while awaiting the sentence of his relations. The comparison with the army made by the Colonel was

benevolent (bə nev´ ə lənt) *adj.* doing or inclined to do good; kindly; charitable

ENRICHMENT: Literature Connection

A Critic's View of Chekhov's Style

"When I write," Chekhov once noted, "I rely fully on the reader, presuming that he himself will add the subjective elements missing in my story."

In *The Russian Short Story: 1880–1917,* the critic Julian W. Connolly adds:

> Chekhov's observation points to a fundamental principle of his narrative art: by declining to mold his reader's attitudes through traditional methods of authorial omniscience, he requires the reader to work at extracting meaning from his stories.

Structurally, Chekhov eliminated much of the expository material that earlier writers used to establish a background for their characters and plots. Paring descriptions of people and settings to a minimum, Chekhov relied on the use of a few details chosen for their suggestive potential. In many stories an internal conflict engenders expectations that are never met. Chekhov's plots have been compared to gradual curves that start out in one direction and gently arc to end up in an entirely unexpected place.

delightful, and did credit to his lofty intelligence; his appeal to their feeling of public duty spoke for the chivalry of his soul, but they must not forget that in each individual the citizen is closely linked with the Christian. . . .

"Shall we be false to civic duty," Ivan Markovitch exclaimed passionately, "if instead of punishing an erring boy we hold out to him a helping hand?"

Ivan Markovitch talked further of family honor. He had not the honor to belong to the Uskov family himself, but he knew their distinguished family went back to the thirteenth century; he did not forget for a minute, either, that his precious, beloved sister had been the wife of one of the representatives of that name. In short, the family was dear to him for many reasons, and he refused to admit the idea that, for the sake of a paltry fifteen hundred rubles[2] a blot should be cast on the escutcheon[3] that was beyond all price. If all the motives he had brought forward were not sufficiently convincing, he, Ivan Markovitch, in conclusion, begged his listeners to ask themselves what was meant by

61  **Reading Check**

Which uncle defends the mistakes made by all men in their youth?

2. **rubles** (ro͞o´ bəlz) *n.* Russian unit of currency.
3. **escutcheon** (e skuch´ ən) *n.* shield on which a coat of arms is displayed.

62

Ball at the Moulin de la Galette, 1876, Pierre Auguste Renoir

63 ▲ **Critical Viewing** What do you think Sasha might find attractive about the lifestyle captured in this painting? **[Speculate]**

61 ✔ **Reading Check**

Answer: Ivan Markovitch defends the mistakes made by all men in their youth.

62 **Background**

Art

Ball at the Moulin de la Galette, **by Pierre Auguste Renoir**

Sasha Uskov might well have enjoyed a gathering such as depicted in this painting by Renoir (1841–1919). *Ball at the Moulin de la Galette* is one of the most important and popular examples of the school of painting known as Impressionism, and Renoir was one of the most famous Impressionist painters. Impressionism is noted for the use of light and color to portray life accurately. This work, for example, captures the dramatic play of light on the dancers as they move to the music. The Moulin de la Galette was a place where workers, young women, and artists gathered to dance and enjoy themselves in the garden. Renoir's biographer, Georges Rivière, claims that Renoir probably painted the entire work on the spot, rather than finishing it in the studio, as was the common practice.

Use the following questions for discussion:

- How would you describe this scene?
  Possible response: The scene is lively and shows people enjoying themselves.
- How does this painting differ from the painting on p. 850? Which setting do you think Sasha would find more appealing?
  Possible response: This painting is more energetic and dynamic than the painting on p. 850. The action here takes place outdoors, and people are enjoying themselves. The library scene is static and austere. Sasha would probably find Renoir's setting more appealing than the library.

63 ▶ **Critical Viewing**

Possible response: Sasha would be drawn to the carefree, lively, and fun-loving lifestyle that this painting captures.

CUSTOMIZE INSTRUCTION FOR UNIVERSAL ACCESS

For Special Needs Students

Draw a web diagram on the board, and use it to help students understand the problem and the decision that has to be made in the story. Explain that the web will illustrate the problem and the reasons for the possible solutions. In the center, write *Problem: Sasha has written a bad note. The bank demands the money.* Draw two circles from the center for the two solutions: *Pay the money; Let Sasha go to jail.* From each solution circle, draw circles showing the consequences: (1) *Pay the money: The family honor is preserved; Sasha does not get his just punishment and shirks responsibility.* (2) *Let Sasha go to jail: The family is humiliated; Sasha is punished for what could be considered a youthful mistake.*

64 Literary Analysis

Dynamic and Static Characters

- Remind students that Sasha is waiting outside the study while the three uncles argue. Have a student read aloud the bracketed passage on pp. 854–855.
- Ask students the Literary Analysis question on p. 854: What is Sasha's attitude toward his misdeed at this point?
  Answer: Sasha feels neither ashamed nor guilty about cashing the false promissory note.

Monitor Progress Remind students that a static character does not change during the course of a story. Ask students to name the qualities that Sasha demonstrates so far (obedience to his uncle's summons, patiently and "meekly" waiting outside the study, willingness to accept whatever happens).

65 Background

Art

E. Duranty, by Edgar Degas

Along with artists such as Monet and Renoir, Edgar Degas (1834–1917) was one of the Impressionist painters in France during the latter half of the nineteenth century. Degas's work focused on the complexity of human expression as found in daily life.

Use the following question for discussion:

What do you think the man in this portrait is thinking?
Possible response: The man is puzzling over a problem presented in the papers on his desk; he may be worrying about family or financial problems.

66 ▶Critical Viewing

Possible response: The man's earnest and serious expression matches what Ivan Markovitch might be feeling.

crime? Crime is an immoral act founded upon ill-will. But is the will of man free? Philosophy has not yet given a positive answer to that question. Different views were held by the learned. The latest school of Lombroso,[4] for instance, denies the freedom of the will, and considers every crime as the product of the purely anatomical peculiarities of the individual.

"Ivan Markovitch," said the Colonel, in a voice of entreaty, "we are talking seriously about an important matter, and you bring in Lombroso, you clever fellow. Think a little, what are you saying all this for? Can you imagine that all your thunderings and rhetoric will furnish an answer to the question?"

64 Sasha Uskov sat at the door and listened. He felt neither terror, shame, nor depression, but only weariness and inward emptiness. It seemed to him that it made absolutely no difference to him whether they forgave him or not; he had come here to hear his sentence and to explain himself simply because kind-hearted Ivan Markovitch had

Literary Analysis
Dynamic and Static Characters What is Sasha's attitude toward his misdeed at this point?

4. **Lombroso** Cesare Lombroso (1836–1909), an Italian physician and criminologist who believed that a criminal was a distinct human type, with specific physical and mental deviations, and that a criminal tendency was the result of hereditary factors.

65

E. Duranty, 1879, Edgar Degas, Glasgow Museums

66 ◀ **Critical Viewing**
In what way does the expression on this man's face match what Ivan Markovitch might be feeling? **[Connect]**

ENRICHMENT: Career Connection

Criminology

While arguing for leniency for Sasha, Ivan Markovitch brings up the latest theories of *criminology*—the scientific study of crime and criminal behavior. Although the particular ideas that this Chekhov character cites have long been out of fashion, criminology remains an important field of social science.

Among the questions that modern criminologists study are the causes of crime, the nature of criminal organizations, the prevention of crime, and the rehabilitation of convicted criminals. Criminologists may work within the criminal justice system, or they may teach and conduct studies within a college or university setting.

begged him to do so. He was not afraid of the future. It made no difference to him where he was: here in the hall, in prison, or in Siberia.

"If Siberia, then let it be Siberia, damn it all!"

He was sick of life and found it insufferably hard. He was inextricably involved in debt; he had not a farthing[5] in his pocket; his family had become detestable to him; he would have to part from his friends and his women sooner or later, as they had begun to be too contemptuous of his sponging on them. The future looked black.

Sasha was indifferent, and was only disturbed by one circumstance; the other side of the door they were calling him a scoundrel and a criminal. Every minute he was on the point of jumping up, bursting into the study and shouting in answer to the detestable metallic voice of the Colonel:

"You are lying!"

"Criminal" is a dreadful word—that is what murderers, thieves, robbers are; in fact, wicked and morally hopeless people. And Sasha was very far from being all that. . . . It was true he owed a great deal and did not pay his debts. But debt is not a crime, and it is unusual for a man not to be in debt. The Colonel and Ivan Markovitch were both in debt. . . .

"What have I done wrong besides?" Sasha wondered.

He had discounted a forged note. But all the young men he knew did the same. Handrikov and Von Burst always forged IOU's from their par-
67 ents or friends when their allowances were not paid at the regular time,
68 and then when they got their money from home they redeemed them before they became due. Sasha had done the same, but had not redeemed the IOU because he had not got the money which Handrikov had promised to lend him. He was not to blame; it was the fault of circumstances. It was true that the use of another person's signature was considered reprehensible; but, still, it was not a crime but a generally accepted dodge, an ugly formality which injured no one and was quite harmless, for in forging the Colonel's signature Sasha had had no intention of causing anybody damage or loss.

"No, it doesn't mean that I am a criminal . . . " thought Sasha. "And it's not in my character to bring myself to commit a crime. I am soft, emotional. . . . When I have the money I help the poor. . . . "

Sasha was musing after this fashion while they went on talking the other side of the door.

"But, my friends, this is endless," the Colonel declared, getting excited. "Suppose we were to forgive him and pay the money. You know he would not give up leading a dissipated life, squandering money, making debts, going to our tailors and ordering suits in our names! Can you guarantee that this will be his last prank? As far as I am concerned, I have no faith whatever in his reforming!"

The official of the Treasury muttered something in reply; after him Ivan Markovitch began talking blandly and suavely again. The Colonel moved his chair impatiently and drowned the other's words with his

5. **farthing** (fär′ *th*iŋ) *n.* coin of little value.

Reading Strategy
Evaluating Characters' Decisions Do you think that Sasha's line of reasoning adequately excuses the decision he made to discount the note? Explain.

69 ✔**Reading Check**
What terrible wrong has Sasha committed?

67 Reading Strategy
Evaluating Characters' Decisions

- Remind students that to evaluate characters' decisions, they should consider how the outcome of the decision affects the characters and others around them.
- Read aloud the bracketed passage. Discuss each reason Sasha gives to show he has done nothing wrong.
- Ask students the Reading Strategy question on p. 855: Do you think that Sasha's line of reasoning adequately excuses the decision he made to discount the note? Explain.
Possible response: Sasha's reasons are not adequate: He says everyone does it; he blames others or blames circumstances; he says that he did not mean any harm.

68 Literary Analysis
Dynamic and Static Characters

- Call students' attention to the bracketed passage. Ask what character traits Sasha exhibits in explaining his reasons for cashing the note. Have students give examples to support their claims.
Possible response: Sasha shows irresponsibility (he was deeply in debt; it was not his fault) and a lack of concern for others (he forged the Colonel's signature).
- Ask students whether they believe Sasha when he says that he gives money to the poor. Why or why not?
Possible response: Sasha's story is hard to believe; it seems that Sasha usually does not have money, and he is too self-absorbed to care about the poor.

69 
Reading Check

Answer: Sasha has forged his uncle's signature on an IOU and cashed it.

CUSTOMIZE INSTRUCTION FOR UNIVERSAL ACCESS

For Special Needs Students	For English Learners
To help students understand the characters and their decisions, have students use **Selection Support:** Literary Analysis, p. 164 and **Selection Support:** Reading Strategy, p. 163. Work with students to help them understand what decision Sasha has made and what decision the uncles will make. Have them identify the characters' traits and understand how these traits influence characters' decisions.	Point out that the consequences of actions can vary according to the rules of a person's culture. In "A Problem," Sasha's uncles have gathered to determine how to deal with the decision Sasha made to cash an IOU dishonestly. Ask students to share their own knowledge of the consequences that would come from such actions in their own and other cultures.

70 Literary Analysis

Dynamic and Static Characters

- Read aloud the bracketed passage on pp. 855–856. Point out the stance and attitude of each uncle.
- Remind students that the family council has been going on for several hours and still no decision has been reached—the uncles are holding their positions.
- Ask students the first Literary Analysis question on p. 856: Which details suggest that the Colonel and Ivan Markovitch are static characters?
  Answer: Ivan Markovitch and the Colonel do not show changes in personality traits, attitudes, or beliefs. Therefore, they are static characters.

71 Literary Analysis

Dynamic and Static Characters

- Refer students to the bracketed passage.
- Ask students the second Literary Analysis question on p. 856: Do you think Sasha's unemotional response to his aunt is consistent with his character? Why or why not?
  Possible response: Sasha's unemotional response is consistent with his character, as earlier in the story he is described as being "indifferent" and "sick of life."

70 detestable metallic voice. At last the door opened and Ivan Markovitch came out of the study; there were patches of red on his lean shaven face.

"Come along," he said, taking Sasha by the hand. "Come and speak frankly from your heart. Without pride, my dear boy, humbly and from your heart."

Sasha went into the study. The official of the Treasury was sitting down; the Colonel was standing before the table with one hand in his pocket and one knee on a chair. It was smoky and stifling in the study. Sasha did not look at the official or the Colonel; he felt suddenly ashamed and uncomfortable. He looked uneasily at Ivan Markovitch and muttered:

Literary Analysis
Dynamic and Static Characters Which details suggest that the Colonel and Ivan Markovitch are static characters?

"I'll pay it . . . I'll give it back. . . ."

"What did you expect when you discounted the IOU?" he heard a metallic voice.

"I . . . Handrikov promised to lend me the money before now."

Sasha could say no more. He went out of the study and sat down again on the chair near the door. He would have been glad to go away altogether at once, but he was choking with hatred and he awfully wanted to remain, to tear the Colonel to pieces, to say something rude to him. He sat trying to think of something violent and effective to say to his hated uncle, and at that moment a woman's figure, shrouded in the twilight, appeared at the drawing-room door. It was the Colonel's wife. She beckoned Sasha to her, and, wringing her hands, said, weeping:

"*Alexandre*, I know you don't like me, but . . . listen to me; listen, I beg you. . . . But, my dear, how can this have happened? Why, it's awful, awful! For goodness' sake, beg them, defend yourself, entreat them."

71 Sasha looked at her quivering shoulders, at the big tears that were rolling down her cheeks, heard behind his back the hollow, nervous voices of worried and exhausted people, and shrugged his shoulders. He had not in the least expected that his aristocratic relations would raise such a tempest over a paltry fifteen hundred rubles! He could not understand her tears nor the quiver of their voices.

Literary Analysis
Dynamic and Static Characters Do you think Sasha's unemotional response to his aunt is consistent with his character? Why or why not?

An hour later he heard that the Colonel was getting the best of it; the uncles were finally inclining to let the case go for trial.

"The matter's settled," said the Colonel, sighing. "Enough."

After this decision all the uncles, even the emphatic Colonel, became noticeably depressed. A silence followed.

"Merciful Heavens!" sighed Ivan Markovitch. "My poor sister!"

And he began saying in a subdued voice that most likely his sister, Sasha's mother, was present unseen in the study at that moment. He felt in his soul how the unhappy, saintly woman was weeping, grieving, and begging for her boy. For the sake of her peace beyond the grave, they ought to spare Sasha.

The sound of a muffled sob was heard. Ivan Markovitch was weeping and muttering something which it was impossible to catch through the door. The Colonel got up and paced from corner to corner. The long conversation began over again.

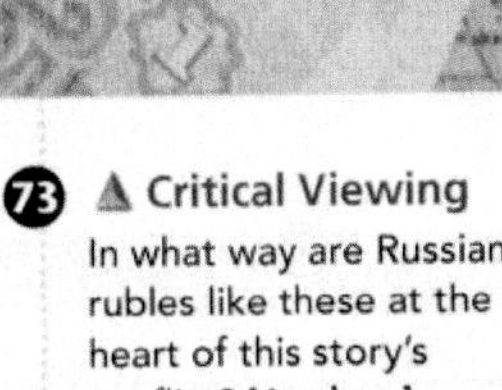

72 But then the clock in the drawing-room struck two. The family council was over. To avoid seeing the person who had moved him to such wrath, the Colonel went from the study, not into the hall, but into the vestibule. . . . Ivan Markovitch came out into the hall. . . . He was agitated and rubbing his hands joyfully. His tear-stained eyes looked good-humored and his mouth was twisted into a smile.

"Capital," he said to Sasha. "Thank God! You can go home, my dear, and sleep tranquilly. We have decided to pay the sum, but on condition that you repent and come with me tomorrow into the country and set to work."

A minute later Ivan Markovitch and Sasha in their great coats and caps were going down the stairs. The uncle was muttering something edifying. Sasha did not listen, but felt as though some uneasy weight were gradually slipping off his shoulders. They had forgiven him; he was free! A gust of joy sprang up within him and sent a sweet chill to his heart. He longed to breathe, to move swiftly, to live! Glancing at the street lamps and the black sky, he remembered that Von Burst was celebrating his name-day[6] that evening at the "Bear," and again a rush of joy flooded his soul. . . .

"I am going!" he decided.

But then he remembered he had not a farthing, that the companions he was going to would despise him at once for his empty pockets. He must get hold of some money, come what may!

"Uncle, lend me a hundred rubles," he said to Ivan Markovitch.

74 His uncle, surprised, looked into his face and backed against a lamp-post.

"Give it to me," said Sasha, shifting impatiently from one foot to the other and beginning to pant. "Uncle, I entreat you, give me a hundred rubles."

His face worked; he trembled, and seemed on the point of attacking his uncle. . . .

"Won't you?" he kept asking, seeing that his uncle was still amazed and did not understand. "Listen. If you don't, I'll give myself up tomorrow! I won't let you pay the IOU! I'll present another false note tomorrow!"

6. **name-day** feast day of the saint after whom a person is named.

73 ▲ **Critical Viewing**

In what way are Russian rubles like these at the heart of this story's conflict? **[Analyze]**

Reading Strategy

Evaluating Characters' Decisions What consequences might occur if Ivan Markovitch gives the hundred rubles to Sasha?

75 

Who agrees to pay Sasha's debt?

72 Critical Thinking

Infer

- Have students read the bracketed passage, focusing on the different attitudes of the two men. Discuss why the Colonel walks through the vestibule to avoid seeing Sasha and why Ivan Markovitch seems joyful.
- Then, ask students how they think each of the men expects Sasha to behave.
  Answer: The Colonel expects Sasha to continue in his irresponsible ways; Ivan Markovitch expects Sasha to reform and not repeat his bad behavior.

73 ▶ Critical Viewing

Answer: Sasha cashed the IOU to get money to pursue his carefree and idle lifestyle.

74 Reading Strategy

Evaluating Characters' Decisions

- Read aloud the bracketed passage. Tell students to pay special attention to the uncle's horror and to Sasha's attitude.
- Then, ask the Reading Strategy question on p. 857: What consequences might occur if Ivan Markovitch gives the hundred rubles to Sasha?
  Answer: Sasha will probably spend it all and possibly forge another IOU, realizing that his uncle will once again get him out of trouble.

Reteach If students have difficulty evaluating characters' decisions, suggest that students use the **Selection Support** booklet, p. 163, for help.

75 ✓ Reading Check

Answer: Sasha's uncles agree to pay Sasha's debt.

CUSTOMIZE INSTRUCTION FOR UNIVERSAL ACCESS

For Less Proficient Readers

To help students summarize the events in the story and relate it to their lives, help them conduct a round-table discussion to address the following questions:

- What choices does Sasha make in the story? What are the possible consequences of these choices?
- What choices do his family members make?
- What kind of person would be the modern equivalent of Sasha?

Point out that students need to provide specific examples to support the answers to the discussion questions. Have students explore these questions and present a summary of their discussion to the class.

ASSESS

Answers for p. 858

Review and Assess

1. Possible response: Some readers may sympathize with Ivan Markovitch because his trust and kindness are betrayed by his nephew. Others may think that Sasha is deeply troubled and needs help.
2. **(a)** Sasha has forged an IOU and cashed it. **(b)** Possible response: Sasha takes his offense lightly because his friends forge and cash IOUs.
3. **(a)** The relatives want Sasha to face the consequences. **(b)** Sasha has been irresponsible before, and they have grown tired of it.
4. **(a)** Ivan Markovitch wants to forgive Sasha and pay the money. **(b)** Possible response: His attitude is harmful because Sasha will not have to reform his dishonest ways.
5. **(a)** Ivan Markovitch argues that they should spare Sasha to give peace to his dead mother. **(b)** Ivan Markovitch is clever, kind, tolerant, and forgiving. **(c)** Possible response: The Colonel, who has previously appeared unyielding, is surprisingly affected by Ivan Markovitch's emotional plea. His willingness to reopen negotiations adds depth to his character and forces readers to reevaluate their assessments of him.
6. **(a)** Ivan Markovitch is horrified. **(b)** He realizes that Sasha really is a criminal with no morals or conscience.
7. Possible response: Letting Sasha go to trial would have done him the most good because he would have faced the consequences of his behavior.

Petrified, muttering something incoherent in his horror, Ivan Markovitch took a hundred-ruble note out of his pocket-book and gave it to Sasha. The young man took it and walked rapidly away from him. . . .

Taking a sledge,[7] Sasha grew calmer, and felt a rush of joy within him again. The "rights of youth" of which kind-hearted Ivan Markovitch had spoken at the family council woke up and asserted themselves. Sasha pictured the drinking party before him, and, among the bottles, the women, and his friends, the thought flashed through his mind:

"Now I see that I am a criminal; yes, I am a criminal."

7. **sledge** (slej) *n.* strong, heavy sled.

Review and Assess

Thinking About the Selection

1. **Respond:** With which character in "A Problem" do you sympathize most? Why?
2. **(a) Recall:** What has Sasha done that has so upset the family? **(b) Infer:** Why do you think Sasha takes his offense so lightly?
3. **(a) Recall:** What do most of the relatives want to do about Sasha and the problem he has created? **(b) Speculate:** How has Sasha's past behavior influenced his relatives' attitude toward his current situation?
4. **(a) Recall:** What does Ivan Markovitch want to do about the problem? **(b) Make a Judgment:** Do you think Uncle Ivan's attitude helps or harms Sasha?
5. **(a) Recall:** What is Ivan Markovitch's most important, and ultimately most convincing, point in his defense of Sasha? **(b) Infer:** What inferences can you make about Ivan Markovitch's character based on his tearful speech to the uncles? **(c) Analyze Cause and Effect:** Does the Colonel's reaction to the speech change your impression of him? Why or why not?
6. **(a) Recall:** What is Ivan Markovitch's emotional reaction to Sasha's final request? **(b) Interpret:** Why does Ivan Markovitch react this way?
7. **Evaluate:** Of the two choices facing the family—to let the case go to trial or to pay Sasha's debt—which would have done Sasha the most good? Why?

ASSESSMENT PRACTICE: Reading Comprehension

Analyzing Literary Language (For more practice, see Test Preparation Workbook, p. 41.)

Many standardized tests require students to analyze the literary language of texts. Use the following sample test item to give students practice with the skill.

> Opposite, the village of Argenteuil seemed dead. The heights of Orgemont and Sannois dominated the whole countryside. The broad plain which stretches as far as Nanterre was empty, absolutely empty, with its bare cherry trees and its colorless fields.
>
> —"Two Friends" by Guy de Maupassant

What kind of mood is set by this passage?

A danger
B joy
C romance
D humor

Students should recognize that words such as "dead," "empty," "bare," and "colorless" lend a mood of danger to the passage; therefore, *A* is the correct answer.

Review and Assess

Literary Analysis

Dynamic and Static Characters

1. Are the main characters in "Two Friends" **dynamic or static characters?** Use details from the story to support your response.
2. In "How Much Land Does a Man Need?" which details suggest that Pakhom is a static character in spite of the changes he experiences?
3. Which details in "A Problem" suggest that the character of Sasha Uskov will never change?

Comparing Literary Works

4. (a) How much consideration did Pakhom give to his family each time he decided to buy more land? (b) In what way does Pakhom's attitude compare with Sasha's in "A Problem"?
5. Do the main characters in "Two Friends" and "A Problem" pass a point of no return? Explain.

Reading Strategy

Evaluating Characters' Decisions

6. **Evaluate the characters' decisions** in the three stories by completing a chart like the one shown. Criteria for evaluating their choices are provided.

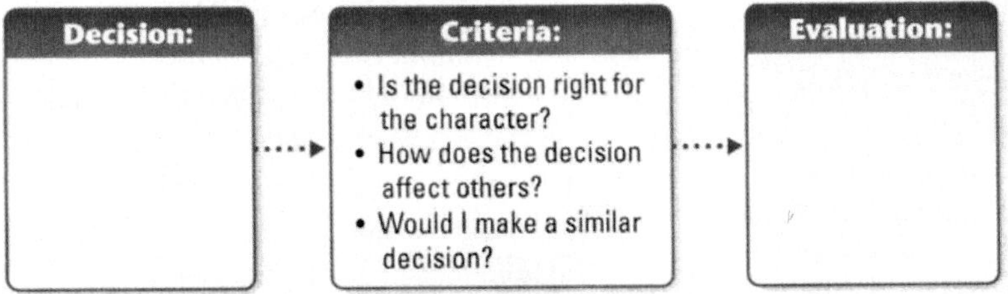

Decision:
Criteria:
• Is the decision right for the character?
• How does the decision affect others?
• Would I make a similar decision?
Evaluation:

7. Choose one character who, in your opinion, makes a bad decision. (a) What good or harmless intentions might have been at the heart of the decision? (b) Does having such good intentions make the character's behavior forgivable? Explain.

Extend Understanding

8. **Psychology Connection:** In Pakhom's culture, land is a status symbol indicating wealth, power, and social rank. What kinds of status symbols do people crave today? Explain.

Quick Review

A **dynamic character** experiences changes in behavior and attitude throughout a story.

A **static character** stays the same.

To **evaluate characters' decisions,** make judgments as to whether their decisions are good or bad.

PHSchool.com

Take the interactive self-test online to check your understanding of these selections.

ENRICHMENT: Further Reading

Other Works by the Authors

Works by Guy de Maupassant

Madame Tellier's Establishment

A Woman's Life

Works by Leo Tolstoy

War and Peace

Anna Karenina

Works by Anton Chekhov

The Seagull

The Sisters

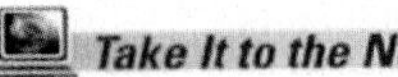

Visit PHSchool.com for more information about the authors.

Answers for p. 859

Review and Assess

1. The two friends are dynamic; they evolve from being acquaintances to being friends; they begin the story meek and accepting of war, and they end the story with a heroic decision that protects their city.
2. Pakhom maintains his desire for more and more land, even when he sees that his greed is killing him.
3. Sasha never accepts responsibility for his acts; instead, he blames others. When he is finally forgiven, he demands more money to continue his dissolute lifestyle.
4. **(a)** Pakhom never consulted his family and assumed that they would pick up and move whenever he wanted. **(b)** Possible response: Both men are self-centered.
5. Possible response: The two friends pass a point of no return when they are accosted by the Prussian soldiers. In "A Problem," Sasha passes a point of no return when he threatens Ivan Markovitch.
6. Possible response: **Decision:** The two friends refuse to give the password; **Evaluation:** The decision costs the friends their lives; but heroically, they save the lives of other Parisians. **Decision:** Pakhom buys a forty-acre farm; **Evaluation:** Pakhom becomes a landowner, but, in so doing, greed becomes the primary focus of his life. **Decision:** Sasha forges an IOU; **Evaluation:** The decision benefits Sasha but hurts Sasha's credibility with his family.
7. **(a)** Possible response: When Sasha forges the IOU, he probably wants to have fun with his friends and does not think about the consequences of his actions. **(b)** Possible response: Sasha's family should forgive him; however, they should make him learn from his mistakes instead of cover for him.
8. Possible response: Expensive cars, homes, and clothing as well as high-tech gadgets, such as cell phones, DVD players, and HDTVs are status symbols. Acquiring them is proof of wealth, power, or social rank.

EXTEND

Answers for p. 860

❶ Vocabulary Development

Word Analysis: Latin Prefix *dis-*

1. disgrace: to lose respect
2. disclaim: to renounce
3. disorient: to confuse

Spelling Strategy

1. violent, violently
2. absent, absently
3. prudent, prudently

Concept Development: Synonyms

1. b
2. g
3. a
4. e
5. d
6. c
7. f

❷ Grammar and Style

Practice

1. restrictive; *anyone*
2. restrictive; *escutcheon*
3. restrictive; *land*
4. nonrestrictive; *sun*
5. nonrestrictive; *soldier*

Writing Application

Possible response:

Nonrestrictive: My (friend), *who is on the team*, is going to the movies with us.

Restrictive: We're going to see the new action (movie) *that opened today.*

10TH GRADE For support in teaching the Grammar and Style Lesson to tenth graders, use **Writing and Grammar**, Platinum Level, Chapter 20, Section 2.

Integrate Language Skills

❶ Vocabulary Development Lesson

Word Analysis: Latin Prefix *dis-*

The Latin prefix *dis-* can mean "apart" or "not," changing the meaning of a word to its opposite. Add the prefix *dis- to* each word below, and define the new words you create.

1. grace 2. claim 3. orient

Spelling Strategy

Nouns ending in *-ence* usually end in *-ent* and *-ently* in their adjective and adverb forms. Write the adjective and adverb forms of each of the following nouns.

1. violence 2. absence 3. prudence

Concept Development: Synonyms

Choose the word from the list on the right that is closest in meaning to each vocabulary word below.

1. benevolent	a. looting
2. discord	b. charitable
3. pillaging	c. over
4. placidly	d. face down
5. prostrate	e. calmly
6. superimposed	f. silent
7. taciturn	g. conflict

❷ Grammar and Style Lesson

Restrictive and Nonrestrictive Adjective Clauses

Restrictive—essential—**adjective clauses** limit, or restrict, the meaning of the nouns they modify. They identify and define, and they are necessary to the meaning.

Restrictive: "[He] sowed it on the land *he had bought*." (modifies *land)*

Nonrestrictive—nonessential—**adjective clauses** give additional information about nouns. They describe, but they are not necessary to the noun's meaning. Use commas to set off these clauses.

Nonrestrictive: Sasha Uskov, *who was the cause of all the trouble* . . . (modifies *Sasha Uskov)*

Practice Identify each italicized clause that follows as restrictive or nonrestrictive. Then, circle the word it modifies.

1. Anyone *who had money* could buy . . . as much freehold land as he wanted.
2. . . . a blot should be cast on the escutcheon *that was beyond all price*.
3. He borrowed seed and sowed it on the land *he had bought*.
4. Pakhom looked at the sun, *which had reached the earth*.
5. She engaged . . . an old soldier, *who took to burdening the people with fines*.

Writing Application Write two sentences about a friend. Use a restrictive clause in one sentence and a nonrestrictive clause in the other. Identify each clause and circle the word it modifies.

WG *Prentice Hall Writing and Grammar Connection: Diamond Level, Chapter 19, Section 3*

TEACHING RESOURCES

The following resources can be used to enrich or extend the instruction for pp. 860–861.

Vocabulary

- **Selection Support:** Build Vocabulary, p. 161 ■
- **Vocabulary and Spelling Practice Book** (Use this booklet for skills instruction.)

Grammar

- **Selection Support:** Grammar and Style, p. 162
- WG **Writing and Grammar,** Diamond Level, p. 458
- **Daily Language Practice Transparencies** ■

Writing

- **Performance Assess. and Portfolio Mgmt.,** p. 14
- **Writing and Grammar,** Diamond Level, p. 37
- **Writing and Grammar iText CD-ROM**
- **Writing Models and Graphic Organizers on Transparencies,** pp. 83–85

Listening and Speaking

- **Performance Assess. and Portfolio Mgmt.,** p. 28

■ **BLOCK SCHEDULING:** Resources marked with this symbol provide varied instruction during 90-minute blocks.

❸ Writing Lesson

Analyzing a Character's Decision

For many of the characters in these stories, changing one critical decision would create an entirely new ending to the story. Write an essay analyzing a character's decision at such a major turning point.

Prewriting Choose a character from one of the stories you have read, and identify a key decision. Then, brainstorm for a plausible alternative decision and a new, logical ending to the story.

Drafting As you write, refer to specific moments in the text to support your new ending, and address any other characters in the story who might be affected by your character's decision.

Revising Review your essay, identifying sentences that do not connect logically. Use transitions to build a flowing, coherent paragraph.

Model: Using Transitions for Coherence

Ivan Markovitch forgot that Sasha had never worked for anything in life. ^*For his nephew's own good,* Ivan Markovitch should force Sasha to recognize his errors.

Transitional words and phrases build paragraph coherence and establish a clear line of reasoning.

WG Prentice Hall Writing and Grammar Connection: Diamond Level, Chapter 3, Section 2

❹ Extension Activities

Listening and Speaking Create a **monologue** in which Sasha speaks to Uncle Ivan five years after the events in "The Problem." In your monologue, address the following topics:

- how Sasha's life progressed after the events of the story
- what Sasha has learned about himself since taking the hundred rubles from Uncle Ivan
- what kind of relationship Sasha would like to have with Uncle Ivan and the family

Perform your monologue for your class.

Research and Technology With a partner, use library or Internet sources to research the topic of heraldry. Build a **coat of arms** for a character in the story based on the examples you find. Include a brief report explaining how the parts of the heraldic shield apply to the character. **[Group Activity]**

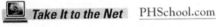

Take It to the Net PHSchool.com

Go online for an additional research activity using the Internet.

❸ Writing Lesson

- Suggest that after students choose a story, they work in pairs or small groups to brainstorm plausible new decisions and new endings.
- Use the Writing Lesson to guide students in developing their analyses. Have students use the Story Map organizer in **Writing Models and Graphic Organizers on Transparencies,** pp. 83–85, to organize details for the story ending.
- Use the Narration: Short Story rubric in **Performance Assessment and Portfolio Management,** p. 14, to evaluate students' story endings.

10TH GRADE For support in working through the Writing Lesson with tenth graders, use **Writing and Grammar**, Platinum Level, Chapter 3, Section 2.

❹ Listening and Speaking

- Encourage students to review the ending of the story and to keep in mind Sasha's character traits as described in the story.
- Suggest that students brainstorm with a partner what might have happened after the events in the story.
- Use the Speaking: Delivering a Narrative Presentation rubric in **Performance Assessment and Portfolio Management,** p. 28, to evaluate students' monologues.

CUSTOMIZE INSTRUCTION For Universal Access

To address different learning styles, use the following activities suggested in the **Extension Activities** booklet, p. 41:

- For Visual/Spatial Learners, use Activity 5.
- For Musical/Rhythmic and Verbal/Linguistic Learners, use Activity 6.
- For Verbal/Linguistic and Bodily/Kinesthetic Learners, use Activity 7.

ASSESSMENT RESOURCES

The following resources can be used to assess students' knowledge and skills.

Selection Assessment

- **Formal Assessment,** pp. 145–147
- **Open-Book Tests,** pp. 121–123
- **Test Bank Software**

Take It to the Net

Visit PHSchool.com for self-tests on the selections.

Writing Rubric

- **Performance Assess. and Portfolio Mgmt.,** p. 14

Listening and Speaking Rubric

- **Performance Assess. and Portfolio Mgmt.,** p. 28

For additional diagnostics and remediation for skills covered in this grouping, use materials from the Prentice Hall Assessment System.

A Doll House

Lesson Objectives

1. **To analyze and respond to literary elements**
   - Literary Analysis: Modern Realistic Drama
   - Connecting Literary Elements: Internal and External Conflict
2. **To read, comprehend, analyze, and critique drama**
   - Reading Strategy: Reading Drama
   - Reading Check Questions
   - Review and Assess Questions
   - Assessment Practice (ATE)
3. **To develop word analysis skills, fluency, and systematic vocabulary**
   - Vocabulary Development Lesson: Coined Words
4. **To understand and apply written and oral language conventions**
   - Spelling Strategy
   - Grammar and Style Lesson: Compound Predicates
5. **To understand and apply appropriate writing and research strategies**
   - Writing Lesson: Persuasive Essay (after Act Three)
   - Extension Activity: Monologue
6. **To understand and apply listening and speaking strategies**
   - Extension Activity: Radio Play (after Act Two)

10TH GRADE **TEACHING A TENTH-GRADE COURSE**

The literature in this section can be taught as part of a rich, balanced world literature course for tenth-grade students. For a full outline of such a course, see pp. T46–T48 in Volume 1 of this Teacher's Edition.

STEP-BY-STEP TEACHING GUIDE	PACING GUIDE
PRETEACH	
Motivate Students and Provide Background	
Use the Motivation activity (ATE p. 862)	5 min.
Read and discuss author and background features (SE pp. 862, 864; ATE p. 862) A	5 min.
Introduce the Concepts	
Introduce the Literary Analysis and Reading Strategy concepts (SE/ATE p. 863) A	15 min.
Pronounce the vocabulary words and read their definitions (SE p. 863)	5 min.
TEACH	
Monitor Comprehension	
Informally monitor comprehension by circulating while students read independently or in groups A	50 min.
Monitor students' comprehension with the Reading Check notes (SE/ATE pp. 865, 867, 869, 871, 873, 875, 877, 879, 881, 885, 887, 889, 891)	as students read
Develop vocabulary with the Vocabulary notes (SE pp. 865, 867, 875, 880, 885; ATE p. 865)	as students read
Develop Understanding	
Develop students' understanding of imagery with the Literary Analysis annotations (SE/ATE pp. 866, 867, 871, 872, 876, 878, 879, 880, 882, 885, 886, 887, 888, 891, 892) A	10 min.
Develop students' ability to read drama by using the Reading Strategy annotations (SE pp. 865, 868, 869, 870, 872, 874, 877, 881, 882, 884, 887, 889, 892; ATE pp. 865, 868, 869, 870, 872, 874, 877, 879, 881, 882, 884, 885, 887, 889, 892) A	10 min.
ASSESS	
Assess Mastery	
Assess students' mastery of the Reading Strategy and Literary Analysis concepts by having them answer the Review and Assess questions (SE/ATE p. 894)	20 min.
Use one or more of the print, software, or transparency Assessment Resources (ATE p. 895) A	up to 45 min.
EXTEND	
Apply Understanding	
Have students complete the Vocabulary Development Lesson and the Grammar and Style Lesson (SE p. 895) A	20 min.
Apply students' understanding of the selection, using one or more of the Extension Activities (SE p. 895)	20–90 min.

ACCELERATED INSTRUCTION: Use the strategies and activities identified with an A.

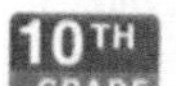

TEACHING TENTH-GRADE STUDENTS

For support in teaching the selection(s) to tenth-grade students, see the Step-by-Step Teaching notes identified with the icon shown here.

UNIVERSAL ACCESS

● = Below-Level Students
▲ = On-Level Students
■ = Above-Level Students

Time and Resource Manager

Reading Level: Average
Average Number of Instructional Days: 5

RESOURCES		
PRINT	**TRANSPARENCIES**	**TECHNOLOGY**
• **Beyond Literature,** Media Connection: Realism in Modern TV, Film, and Drama, p. 42 ▲ ■		• **Interest Grabber Video,** Tape 2, Unit 7, Segment 3 ● ▲ ■
• **Selection Support Workbook:** ● ▲ ■ Literary Analysis, p. 168 Reading Strategy, p. 167 Build Vocabulary, p. 165	• **Literary Analysis and Reading Transparencies,** pp. 83 and 84 ● ▲ ■	
		• **Listening to Literature** ● ▲ ■ Audiocassettes Audio CDs
• **Literary Analysis for Enrichment,** p. 42 ■		
• **Formal Assessment:** Selection Test, pp. 148–150 ● ▲ ■ • **Open-Book Tests,** pp. 124–126 ● ▲ ■ • Prentice Hall Assessment System ● ▲ ■	• Prentice Hall Assessment System ● ▲ ■ **Skills Practice Answers and Explanations on Transparencies**	• **Test Bank Software** ● ▲ ■
• **Selection Support Workbook:** ● ▲ ■ Grammar and Style, p. 166 • **Writing and Grammar,** Diamond Level ● ▲ ■ • **Extension Activities,** p. 42 ● ▲ ■	• **Daily Language Practice Transparencies** ● ▲ • **Writing Models and Graphic Organizers on Transparencies,** pp. 75–77; 83–85; 87–89 ● ▲ ■	• **Writing and Grammar iText CD-ROM** ● ▲ ■ *Take It to the Net* PHSchool.com

BLOCK SCHEDULING: Use one 90-minute class period to preteach the selection(s) and have students read them. Use a second 90-minute class period to assess students' mastery of skills and have them complete one of the Extension Activities.

PRETEACH

Step-by-Step Teaching Guide for pp. 862–863

Motivation

Refer students to the title of this play, and ask them what associations they have with the idea of a dollhouse. Students may suggest that a dollhouse is a toy, a miniature house where children like to play. Then, ask them to make inferences about the play on the basis of its title. Have students keep their inferences in mind as they read the play to see how accurate they are.

Interest Grabber Video

As an alternative, play *"A Doll House*: Women's Rights" on Tape 2 to engage student interest.

❶ Background

More About the Author

Visitors to Ibsen's tomb in Oslo, Norway, will find the image of an arm holding a hammer. Ibsen had this image placed on his tomb to symbolize the way in which his plays shattered illusions about life. In later years, Ibsen turned the focus away from the world and onto himself. His last play, *When We Dead Awaken*, written in 1899, is the most autobiographical play Ibsen wrote. It is a monologue (a speech by one character) by an aging playwright who questions the path he took during his life as a writer and as a human being.

Geography Note

Have students look at the map on this page. Students should understand that Norway is so far north that nearly half of the country is situated above the Arctic Circle. Ibsen describes his native land and its people as follows: "The magnificent, but severe, natural environment surrounding people up there in the north ... forces them to ... become introspective and serious .... At home every other person is a philosopher!"

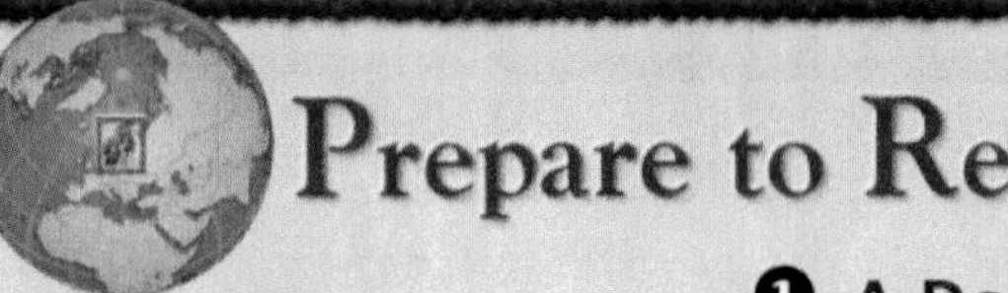

Prepare to Read

❶ A Doll House

Henrik Ibsen (1828–1906)

When the drama *Ghosts* by Henrik Ibsen (hen′ rik ib′ sən) was first performed in 1881, one critic attacked the play, calling it "an open drain, a loathsome sore, an abominable piece, a repulsive and degrading work." Critics and even audiences of his day sometimes responded negatively to Ibsen's works because he was a literary pioneer. He was not only the creator of the modern realistic prose drama but also one of the first modern writers to make drama a vehicle for social commentary by exploring issues considered socially unacceptable. Because of his bold innovation and his extraordinary talent, Ibsen is widely regarded as the greatest and most influential dramatist of the nineteenth century.

Difficult Beginnings Ibsen was born in Skein, Norway. Although his father had once been a successful merchant, bankruptcy reduced his family to poverty and social rejection. When he was fifteen, Ibsen became a druggist's apprentice. He hated the work and chose to live in virtual isolation, writing poetry in his spare time. After failing a university entrance examination, he became determined to forge a living as a writer. With two finished plays to his credit—*Catiline* (1850) and *The Burial Mound* (1850)—Ibsen was hired as a playwright by the National Theater in the city of Bergen, where he remained for six years.

A Career in Theater In 1857, Ibsen accepted an opportunity to manage a new theater. The theater went bankrupt in 1862, however, leaving Ibsen deeply in debt and in a state of despair. Two years later, he left Norway for Italy, where he wrote most of his finest plays. With the completion of *Brand* (1866), the tragedy of a misunderstood idealist, and *Peer Gynt* (1867), a dramatic fantasy based on Norwegian folklore, he established himself as a popular playwright among both critics and theatergoers.

Controversial Art Ibsen's talent blossomed, though his plays were not always greeted enthusiastically by the public. *A Doll House* (1879), for example, aroused controversy because it portrayed a woman whose actions were unacceptable for that time. In response to the public's hostile reception of *Ghosts* (1881), Ibsen wrote *An Enemy of the People* (1882), which portrays a man who comes into conflict with the inhabitants of a village.

The Problem Plays Ibsen's later work defied the prevailing tastes in theater of the day. The typical dramatic style was modeled after the Romantic movement, with plot-heavy, idealized storylines whose endings were unfailingly happy. Ibsen eventually departed completely from such a style to create psychological dramas in which the conflict is internal and the plot's action is limited. Although Ibsen's later works often earned scathing reviews from critics and even from his audiences, emerging and notable playwrights like George Bernard Shaw embraced Ibsen's talent and defended his work. Ibsen's innovative pieces, often called "Problem Plays," constitute serious drama in which the problems of human life caused by society and its accepted practices are presented as such and are not masked by unrelated details.

Ibsen wrote prolifically through the nineteenth century, completing such well-known plays as *The Wild Duck* (1884) and *Hedda Gabler* (1890). When Ibsen died in 1906, it was already clear that his controversial work challenged the traditional expectations of theater. Only later in the twentieth century did it become obvious that Isben's contributions to dialogue, plot, set design, and acting style forged an entirely new form of modern theater.

TEACHING RESOURCES

The following resources can be used to enrich or extend the instruction for pp. 862–863.

Motivation

Interest Grabber Video, Tape 2

Background

Beyond Literature, p. 42

Take It to the Net

Visit PHSchool.com for background on the authors.

Literary Analysis

Literary Analysis and Reading Transparencies, Modern Realistic Drama, p. 83

Selection Support: Literary Analysis, p. 168

Reading

Literary Analysis and Reading Transparencies, Reading Drama, p. 84

BLOCK SCHEDULING: Resources marked with this symbol provide varied instruction during 90-minute blocks.

Preview

Connecting to the Literature

A nickname meant to express affection can sometimes offend or create a false impression. In Act One of *A Doll House*, Torvald has pet names for his wife, Nora, that reflect his impression of her personality and behavior.

2 Literary Analysis

Modern Realistic Drama

Ibsen developed the **modern realistic drama**—a type of play unlike anything audiences had seen before—which included these characteristics:

- To reflect ordinary language, it is written in prose, not verse.
- It depicts characters and situations as they really are.
- It addresses controversial issues and society's assumptions.

A Doll House (1879) focuses on the role and status of women in the late nineteenth century. As you read Act One, notice Nora's subordinate role.

Connecting Literary Elements

Like real life, modern realistic dramas include **conflict,** the struggle between two opposing forces. Conflict can be either **internal,** occurring within the mind of a character, or **external,** occurring between a character and society, nature, another person, God, or fate.

In *A Doll House*, Nora faces both internal and external conflicts as she struggles to live life by her own rules.

3 Reading Strategy

Reading Drama

A drama is written to be performed by actors. When **reading drama,** imagine how the scenes would look on stage, how the dialogue would sound, and how the characters would move. To get the most out of your reading:

- Picture the setting described in the stage directions.
- Imagine voice and tone as you read dialogue.
- Picture characters' gestures and movements.

Look for details in *A Doll House* that will help you envision the drama. Then, use a chart like the one shown to help you form mental images.

Detail From the Play

Torvald's nicknames for Nora: *squirrel, skylark*

Mental Image

Nora should move as though she were a small animal, with quick, skipping steps.

Vocabulary Development

spendthrift (spend′ thrift′) *n.* person who spends money carelessly (p. 865)

squandering (skwän′ dər iŋ) *v.* spending money wastefully (p. 865)

prodigal (präd′ i gəl) *n.* person who spends money wastefully (p. 867)

indiscreet (in′ di skrēt′) *adj.* unwise or not careful (p. 875)

frivolous (friv′ ə ləs) *adj.* silly and light-minded; not sensible (p. 875)

contraband (kän′ trə band′) *n.* unlawful or forbidden goods (p. 880)

subordinate (sə bôr′ də nit) *adj.* inferior; ranking under or below (p. 885)

2 Literary Analysis

Modern Realistic Drama

- Tell students that Ibsen was one of the first playwrights to use ordinary people as characters and to allow them to speak in everyday language. For many years, in Norway and Europe, plays were based on myth or highly romanticized stories about kings and queens. The language was usually poetic, and the themes of the plays had little to do with ordinary life.
- On p. 863, read the three changes that Ibsen brought to drama. Point out that theatergoers of Ibsen's time might have been insulted by the changes. Many thought he had demeaned the theater. Point out that rather than ruining theater, Ibsen revitalized it.
- Use the Modern Realistic Drama transparency in **Literary Analysis and Reading Transparencies,** p. 83, to identify the ways in which Ibsen's plays use ordinary characters and language to address social assumptions.

3 Reading Strategy

Reading Drama

- Remind students that dramas are meant to be heard and seen, not just read. Ask students to compare their experiences of reading and seeing plays.
- Explain the use of the graphic organizer on p. 863. Remind students that in both the dialogue and the stage directions, playwrights often include clues about their characters' actions, tone of voice, and appearance.

Vocabulary Development

- Pronounce each vocabulary word for students, and read the definition as a class. Have students identify any words with which they are already familiar.

CUSTOMIZE INSTRUCTION FOR UNIVERSAL ACCESS

For Less Proficient Readers	For English Learners	For Advanced Readers
Students may need some visual context before they read the play to help them picture the characters, their surroundings, and costumes. Before students begin reading the play, allow them to skim pp. 864–893, looking at the images and photographs. Lead students in a discussion of their observations.	Allow students to meet with a partner and to look at the illustrations that appear on pp. 864–893. Ask students to make a list of words that come to mind as they look at the illustrations. Challenge students to write nouns that identify objects and adjectives that identify mood or atmosphere.	Lead students in a discussion about what they know about life in nineteenth-century Europe. Ask students to share knowledge of historical events, inventions, traditions, and social conventions. If students are uncertain about a particular fact or event, challenge them to research it and to share their findings with the class.

 **E-Teach**

Visit e-Teach at PHSchool.com for teacher's essays on how to teach, with questions and answers.

Step-by-Step Teaching Guide for pp. 864–893

Teaching Tenth-Grade Students

10TH GRADE Start a discussion with tenth-grade students about how a society shapes the people who live in it. Ask students to identify and evaluate some ways that American society has shaped them. For example, American society values education, so many students probably will go to college.

❶ About the Translation

A Doll's House or *A Doll House*

An important issue in translation is the rendering of a literary work's title. The translated title will be the name of the work in the second language, and it will generate expectations about how the work is read and understood.

In English, the title has been traditionally rendered *A Doll's House*. Rolf Fjelde, the translator of this version of the play and the founder of the Ibsen Society of America, takes issue with the title. In the Foreword to his translation, he comments:

"There is certainly no sound justification for perpetuating the awkward and blindly traditional misnomer of *A Doll's House*: the house is not Nora's, as the possessive implies; the familiar children's toy is called a doll house; and one can make a reasonable supposition that Ibsen ... at least partially includes Torvald with Nora in the original title ... for the two of them at the play's opening are still posing like the little marzipan bride and groom atop the wedding cake."

❷ Background

Art

Have students notice the doll pictured here. Its costume is from the period in which the play is set, and its face, hands, and feet are probably made of porcelain.

Use the following question for discussion:

What words would you use to describe this doll?
Possible response: The doll is delicate, breakable, lovely, and fragile.

A Doll House

Henrik Ibsen
translated by **Rolf Fjelde**

Background

Critics regard Nora Helmer, one of the main characters in *A Doll House*, as among the most remarkable women characters in drama, primarily because of the personal journey she experiences in the play. As the drama opens, she appears to be a picture-perfect nineteenth-century wife to her husband, Torvald. The Helmers belonged to the upper middle class, and the elaborately decorated set would represent a typical wealthy home in the Victorian period. Like most other married women of her day, Nora would have made certain that every aspect of her home reflected the Helmers' social class and supported the comfortable, almost lavish lifestyle they enjoyed.

The Characters

Torvald Helmer, a lawyer
Nora, his wife
Dr. Rank
Mrs. Linde
Nils Krogstad, a bank clerk
The Helmers' Three Small Children
Anne-Marie, their nurse
Helene, a maid
A Delivery Boy

The action takes place in HELMER'S *residence.*

TEACHING RESOURCES

The following resources can be used to enrich or extend the instruction for pp. 864–893.

Literary Analysis

- **Selection Support:** Literary Analysis, p. 168
- **Literary Analysis and Reading Transparencies,** Modern Realistic Drama, p. 83

Reading

- **Selection Support:** Reading Strategy, p. 167; Building Vocabulary, p. 165 ■
- **Listening to Literature Audiocassettes**
- **Listening to Literature Audio CDs** ■

■ **BLOCK SCHEDULING:** Resources marked with this symbol provide varied instruction during 90-minute blocks.

ACT ONE

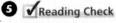

3 *A comfortable room, tastefully but not expensively furnished. A door to the right in the back wall leads to the entryway; another to the left leads to* HELMER'S *study. Between these doors, a piano. Midway in the left-hand wall a door, and farther back a window. Near the window a round table with an armchair and a small sofa. In the right-hand wall, toward the rear, a door, and nearer the foreground a porcelain stove with two armchairs and a rocking chair beside it. Between the stove and the side door, a small table. Engravings on the walls. An étagère*[1] *with china figures and other small art objects; a small bookcase with richly bound books; the floor carpeted; a fire burning in the stove. It is a winter day.*

A bell rings in the entryway; shortly after we hear the door being unlocked. NORA *comes into the room humming happily to herself; she is wearing street clothes and carries an armload of packages, which she puts down on the table to the right. She has left the hall door open; and through it a* DELIVERY BOY *is seen, holding a Christmas tree and a basket, which he gives to the* MAID *who let them in.*

Reading Strategy
Reading Drama List four details in the stage directions that indicate the Helmers' social standing.

NORA: Hide the tree well, Helene. The children mustn't get a glimpse of it till this evening, after it's trimmed. [*To the* DELIVERY BOY, *taking out her purse*:] How much?

DELIVERY BOY: Fifty, ma'am.

NORA: There's a crown.[2] No, keep the change. [*The* BOY *thanks her and leaves.* NORA *shuts the door. She laughs softly to herself while taking off her street things. Drawing a bag of macaroons from her pocket, she eats a couple, then steals over and listens at her husband's study door.*] Yes, he's home. [*Hums again as she moves to the table right.*]

HELMER [*from the study*]: Is that my little lark twittering out there?

NORA [*busy opening some packages*]: Yes, it is.

HELMER: Is that my squirrel rummaging around?

NORA: Yes!

HELMER: When did my squirrel get in?

NORA: Just now. [*Putting the macaroon bag in her pocket and wiping her mouth.*] Do come in, Torvald, and see what I've bought.

HELMER: Can't be disturbed. [*After a moment he opens the door and peers in, pen in hand.*] Bought, you say? All that there? Has the little
4 spendthrift been out throwing money around again?

NORA: Oh, but Torvald, this year we really should let ourselves go a bit. It's the first Christmas we haven't had to economize.

HELMER: But you know we can't go squandering.

NORA: Oh yes, Torvald, we can squander a little now. Can't we?

spendthrift (spend' thrift') *n.* person who spends money carelessly

squandering (skwän' dər iŋ) *v.* spending money wastefully

5 **Reading Check**
What surprise is Nora preparing for her children?

1. **étagère** (ā tà zher') *n.* stand with open shelves for displaying small art objects and ornaments.
2. **crown** basic monetary unit of Norway; *krone* (krō' nə) in Norwegian.

3 Reading Strategy
Reading Drama

- Have students read the first bracketed passage on p. 865.
- Make sure students notice that stage directions do two things: They describe the set and the wordless actions of the characters as the play begins.
- Ask students to identify what they learn about the play even before a character has spoken.

  Possible response: The play is set in a well-appointed home, in a cold climate, at Christmas time.
- Have students respond to the Reading Strategy item on p. 865: List four details in the stage directions that indicate the Helmers' social standing.
  Possible response: A piano, engravings on the walls, small art objects, books, a thick carpet, and a roaring fire all suggest that the Helmers are educated and have money to spend on comfort and decorative objects.

4 Vocabulary Development
Word Analysis: Coined Words

- Read aloud the sentence that includes the word *spendthrift*, and have students read the definition of the word that appears in the margin of p. 865.
- Point out to students that *spendthrift* is a compound word—two or more words joined together. Ask students to identify the two words (*spend* and *thrift*) that make up this compound.
- Invite students to think of other compound words and to watch for others in the play.

5 Reading Check
Answer: The surprise is a Christmas tree with all the trimmings.

CUSTOMIZE INSTRUCTION FOR UNIVERSAL ACCESS

For Special Needs Students	For English Learners	For Gifted/Talented Students
The Norwegian names of the characters may be difficult for some students to pronounce and remember. Take time to introduce the cast, character information, and pronunciations of the various names. Suggest that students make a list of the names. Then, as they read the play, they can add notes to help them identify the characters.	Some students may be unfamiliar with stage directions. Have them work together with a native English speaker to examine the description of the set on p. 865. Direct students to create sketches of the set based upon the description. Post students' sketches in the classroom.	Suggest that students meet in a group after reading each act to interpret the behavior of each of the major characters. Each group member may choose a different character, such as Nora, Torvald, Mrs. Linde, or Krogstad, to role-play or defend during the group meeting.

6 Literary Analysis

Modern Realistic Drama

- Have students read the first bracketed passage.
- Ask students to respond to the Literary Analysis item on p. 866: Identify two of Nora's words that reflect everyday, informal speech.
  Answer: Two words that reflect informal speech are "wee" and "pooh."
- Then, tell students that Nora will prove herself to be much more complex than she appears here.

7 Critical Thinking

Analyze

- Have a volunteer read aloud the second bracketed passage. Ask students to list the nicknames Torvald calls Nora.
  Answer: Torvald calls Nora "little lark" and "squirrel."
- Have students explain what initial impression of Torvald the use of these names suggests about him and his relationship with Nora.
  Possible response: Torvald's use of the names gives a negative impression of him and makes Nora appear stupid and childlike. The balance of power in Nora and Torvald's relationship is unequal, Torvald the dominant figure.

8 ▶Critical Viewing

Answer: This illustration suggests that the characters are happy because they are holding hands and smiling. They seem close to and interested in each other.

Just a tiny, wee bit. Now that you've got a big salary and are going to make piles and piles of money.

6 **HELMER:** Yes—starting New Year's. But then it's a full three months till the raise comes through.

NORA: Pooh! We can borrow that long.

HELMER: Nora! [*Goes over and playfully takes her by the ear.*] Are your scatterbrains off again? What if today I borrowed a thousand crowns, and you squandered them over Christmas week, and then on New Year's Eve a roof tile fell on my head, and I lay there—

NORA [*putting her hand on his mouth*]: Oh! Don't say such things!

HELMER: Yes, but what if it happened—then what?

NORA: If anything so awful happened, then it just wouldn't matter if I had debts or not.

HELMER: Well, but the people I'd borrowed from?

NORA: Them? Who cared about them! They're strangers.

HELMER: Nora, Nora, how like a woman! No, but seriously, Nora, you know what I think about that. No debts! Never borrow! Something of freedom's lost—and something of beauty, too—from a home that's founded on borrowing and debt. We've made a brave stand up to now, the two of us; and we'll go right on like that the little while we have to.

NORA [*going toward the stove*]: Yes, whatever you say, Torvald.

7 **HELMER** [*following her*]: Now, now, the little lark's wings mustn't droop. Come on, don't be a sulky squirrel. [*Taking out his wallet.*] Nora, guess what I have here.

NORA [*turning quickly*]: Money!

HELMER: There, see. [*Hands her some notes.*] Good grief, I know how costs go up in a house at Christmastime.

NORA: Ten—twenty—thirty—forty. Oh, thank you, Torvald; I can manage no end on this.

HELMER: You really will have to.

NORA: Oh yes, I promise I will! But come here so I can show you everything I bought. And so cheap! Look, new clothes for Ivar here—and a sword. Here a horse and a trumpet for Bob. And a doll and a doll's bed here for Emmy; they're nothing much, but she'll tear them to bits in no time anyway. And here I have

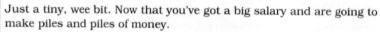

Literary Analysis
Modern Realistic Drama Identify two of Nora's words that reflect everyday, informal speech.

8 **▼ Critical Viewing** Can you tell that Nora and Torvald share a troubled relationship? Why or why not? **[Interpret]**

ENRICHMENT: Career Connection

Banking Then and Now

Banking now is different from the way it was in Torvald Helmer's day. Banks were subject to far fewer laws and regulations in the nineteenth and early twentieth centuries than they are today. Also, bankers did not go to business school or study finance before starting their jobs. As you learn in the play, Torvald was a lawyer before going into banking.

In spite of the portrayal of Torvald Helmer in *A Doll House,* bankers do much more than read newspapers and order people around. Bankers play a very important role in modern society, whether at the international or local level. The kind of bank with which most students will be familiar is the commercial bank. These are the local banks that offer savings and checking accounts; make loans for cars, homes, college educations, and other purposes; and provide many other services.

dress material and handkerchiefs for the maids. Old Anne-Marie really deserves something more.

HELMER: And what's in that package there?

NORA [*with a cry*]: Torvald, no! You can't see that till tonight!

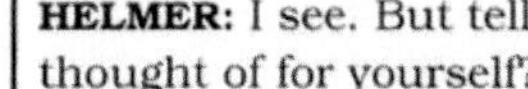

9 **HELMER:** I see. But tell me now, you little prodigal, what have you thought of for yourself?

NORA: For myself? Oh, I don't want anything at all.

HELMER: Of course you do. Tell me just what—within reason—you'd most like to have.

NORA: I honestly don't know. Oh, listen, Torvald—

HELMER: Well?

NORA [*fumbling at his coat buttons, without looking at him*]: If you want to give me something, then maybe you could—you could—

HELMER: Come on, out with it.

NORA [*hurriedly*]: You could give me money, Torvald. No more than you think you can spare; then one of these days I'll buy something with it.

HELMER: But Nora—

NORA: Oh, please, Torvald darling, do that! I beg you, please. Then I could hang the bills in pretty gilt paper on the Christmas tree. Wouldn't that be fun?

HELMER: What are those little birds called that always fly through their fortunes?

NORA: Oh yes, spendthrifts; I know all that. But let's do as I say, Torvald; then I'll have time to decide what I really need most. That's very sensible, isn't it?

HELMER [*smiling*]: Yes, very—that is, if you actually hung onto the money I give you, and you actually used it to buy yourself something.

10 But it goes for the house and for all sorts of foolish things, and then I only have to lay out some more.

NORA: Oh, but Torvald—

HELMER: Don't deny it, my dear little Nora. [*Putting his arm around her waist.*] Spendthrifts are sweet, but they use up a frightful amount of money. It's incredible what it costs a man to feed such birds.

NORA: Oh, how can you say that! Really, I save everything I can.

HELMER [*laughing*]: Yes, that's the truth. Everything you can. But that's nothing at all.

11 **NORA** [*humming, with a smile of quiet satisfaction*]: Hm, if you only knew what expenses we larks and squirrels have, Torvald.

HELMER: You're an odd little one. Exactly the way your father was. You're never at a loss for scaring up money; but the moment you have it, it runs right out through your fingers; you never know what you've

prodigal (präd′ i gəl) *n.* person who spends money wastefully

Literary Analysis
Modern Realistic Drama Explain how Torvald and Nora manage the family's money.

12 ✔**Reading Check**

What is Torvald's attitude toward borrowing money?

CUSTOMIZE INSTRUCTION FOR UNIVERSAL ACCESS

For Less Proficient Readers	For English Learners
By this point in the play, students should begin to appreciate the differences between the two main characters. Students may benefit from creating a two-column chart, with one column labeled *Nora* and one labeled *Torvald*. Have students jot down the identifying characteristics of each character. Then, challenge students to identify the points on which Torvald and Nora disagree, such as their ideas about money and about sweets. Tell students that more points of disagreement will appear later in the play.	The whole class may be interested to know that there is no single English word for "little birds … that always fly through their fortunes." The translator chose the word *spendthrift* to convey the meaning of one Norwegian word. Have English learners tell how they translate English ideas and phrases into their native languages and vice versa. Ask volunteers to share examples of difficult translations with the class. As a class, talk about how ideas are lost or enhanced when translated into another language.

9 Critical Thinking

Connect

- Have a volunteer read aloud the bracketed sentence, and point out the word *prodigal*.
- Students may be familiar with the parable of the prodigal son told by Jesus in Luke 15:11–32. Have students review the definition of the term.
- Then, ask them to explain the parable and how its meaning relates to Nora in *A Doll House*.
  Possible response: The prodigal son in the Bible squanders all his possessions. Signs in the play indicate that Nora may be a spendthrift; Torvald already considers her one.

10 Literary Analysis

Modern Realistic Drama

- Remind students that Ibsen's play was one of the first to focus on an ordinary marriage, with its strengths and its flaws.
- Ask students to identify the strengths and flaws of the marriage as they see them now.
  Possible response: The marriage gets its strength from the man and the woman playing clear roles. However, Torvald talks down to Nora and does not trust her with money.
- Have students respond to the Literary Analysis item on p. 867: Explain how Torvald and Nora manage the family's money.
  Answer: Nora spends the money that Torvald gives her in small amounts.

11 Background

Foreshadowing

This remark of Nora's is an example of foreshadowing, the literary technique by which authors use clues to suggest events that have yet to occur in the story. By using foreshadowing, Ibsen is creating suspense. Other examples of foreshadowing appear throughout the act.

12 ✔Reading Check

Answer: Torvald disapproves of borrowing money because it eliminates the borrower's sense of freedom.

13 Reading Strategy

Reading Drama

- Remind students that stage directions tell actors how to say their lines and which gestures to use.
- Call students' attention to the bracketed passage, and ask two volunteers to read it aloud, one volunteer assuming the role of Torvald and the other that of Nora.
- Ask the Reading Strategy question on p. 868: What do the stage directions suggest about Torvald's attitude toward Nora?
  Answer: By shaking his finger at Nora, Torvald is acting like a parent who is scolding a child.

Monitor Progress Ask students what other exchange between Nora and Torvald indicates the imbalance of their relationship, such as the recent discussion about money.

Reteach Have students reread the dialogue on pp. 866–867. Lead them to understand that Torvald considers Nora extravagant and distrusts her with money.

14 Critical Thinking

Analyze

- Read aloud the bracketed passage. Ask students how Torvald might have known that Nora has eaten some macaroons.
  Possible response: He might have seen crumbs on her face or clothing or heard her crumpling the bag earlier when he entered the room.
- Next, ask students what this exchange tells them about Nora, Torvald, and their relationship.
  Possible response: Nora is willing to lie to her husband, and Torvald thinks he has the right to forbid Nora to do certain things. Their relationship is based on unequal power and deceit.

15 Critical Viewing

Possible response: The bird is delicate and sings beautifully. Torvald sees these traits in Nora.

done with it. Well, one takes you as you are. It's deep in your blood. Yes, these things are hereditary, Nora.

NORA: Ah, I could wish I'd inherited many of Papa's qualities.

HELMER: And I couldn't wish you anything but just what you are, my sweet little lark. But wait; it seems to me you have a very—what should I call it?—a very suspicious look today—

NORA: I do?

HELMER: You certainly do. Look me straight in the eye.

NORA [*looking at him*]: Well?

HELMER [*shaking an admonitory[3] finger*]: Surely my sweet tooth hasn't been running riot in town today, has she?

13 **NORA:** No. Why do you imagine that?

HELMER: My sweet tooth really didn't make a little detour through the confectioner's?

NORA: No, I assure you, Torvald—

HELMER: Hasn't nibbled some pastry?

14 **NORA:** No, not at all.

HELMER: Not even munched a macaroon or two?

NORA: No, Torvald, I assure you, really—

Reading Strategy
Reading Drama What do the stage directions suggest about Torvald's attitude toward Nora?

3. **admonitory** (ad män' i tôr' ē) *adj.* warning.

A Lark, Archibald Thorburn, John Spike Fine Watercolours, London, UK

15 **Critical Viewing** Which characteristics of a lark, like the one shown, does Torvald see in Nora? **[Connect]**

ENRICHMENT: Biography Connection

The Real Nora

Like many writers, Henrik Ibsen based some of his characters on real people. The real-life model for Nora Helmer in *A Doll House* was a friend of the writer, a woman named Laura Kieler. She was extremely displeased at the way she was portrayed in the play. One biographer of Ibsen wrote, "It is ironical that the play which established Ibsen as the champion of women should have been so deeply resented by the woman who had inspired it."

Ask students to discuss which aspects of the portrayal might have upset Laura Kieler, as well as situations in which a living person might resent being used as the model for a fictional character.

HELMER: There, there now. Of course I'm only joking.

NORA [*going to the table, right*]: You know I could never think of going against you.

HELMER: No, I understand that; and you *have* given me your word. [*Going over to her.*] Well, you keep your little Christmas secrets to yourself, Nora darling. I expect they'll come to light this evening, when the tree is lit.

NORA: Did you remember to ask Dr. Rank?

HELMER: No. But there's no need for that; it's assumed he'll be dining with us. All the same, I'll ask him when he stops by here this morning. I've ordered some fine wine. Nora, you can't imagine how I'm looking forward to this evening.

NORA: So am I. And what fun for the children, Torvald!

HELMER: Ah, it's so gratifying to know that one's gotten a safe, secure job, and with a comfortable salary. It's a great satisfaction, isn't it?

NORA: Oh, it's wonderful!

HELMER: Remember last Christmas? Three whole weeks before, you shut yourself in every evening till long after midnight, making flowers for the Christmas tree, and all the other decorations to surprise us. Ugh, that was the dullest time I've ever lived through.

NORA: It wasn't at all dull for me.

HELMER [*smiling*]: But the outcome *was* pretty sorry, Nora.

NORA: Oh, don't tease me with that again. How could I help it that the cat came in and tore everything to shreds.

16 **HELMER:** No, poor thing, you certainly couldn't. You wanted so much to please us all, and that's what counts. But it's just as well that the hard times are past.

NORA: Yes, it's really wonderful.

HELMER: Now I don't have to sit here alone, boring myself, and you don't have to tire your precious eyes and your fair little delicate hands—

NORA [*clapping her hands*]: No, is it really true, Torvald, I don't have to? Oh, how wonderfully lovely to hear! [*Taking his arm.*] Now I'll tell you just how I've thought we should plan things. Right after Christmas— [*The doorbell rings.*] Oh, the bell. [*Straightening the room up a bit.*] Somebody would have to come. What a bore!

HELMER: I'm not at home to visitors, don't forget.

MAID [*from the hall doorway*]: Ma'am, a lady to see you—

NORA: All right, let her come in.

MAID [*to* HELMER]: And the doctor's just come too.

HELMER: Did he go right to my study?

MAID: Yes, he did.

Reading Strategy
Reading Drama What mental image do you have of the Helmers as Torvald makes this speech? Explain.

17  **Reading Check**
Who will join the Helmers for dinner in the evening?

16 Reading Strategy

Reading Drama

- Have two students read the bracketed passage on p. 869.
- Ask students to track the moods Nora exhibits here.
  Possible response: Nora is unhappy or even peeved as Torvald teases her; then, she becomes happy, as she claps her hands and realizes her troubles are over; then, she becomes irritated again when the doorbell rings.
- Ask students to read the Reading Strategy question on p. 869: What mental image do you have of the Helmers as Torvald makes this speech? Explain.
  Possible response: Torvald is talking down to his wife as she sits in a child-like way. Nora's eyes might be averted as Torvald paints an image of Nora slaving away in a dark room.
- Remind students to return to this moment in the play after Nora admits to Mrs. Linde what she was really working on last Christmas.

17  Reading Check

Answer: Dr. Rank is expected to join the Helmers for dinner.

CUSTOMIZE INSTRUCTION FOR UNIVERSAL ACCESS

For Less Proficient Readers	For Advanced Readers
Help students track Ibsen's foreshadowing by creating a two-column chart. Have students label one column *Before Mrs. Linde* and the other column *After Mrs. Linde.* In the first column, students should jot down all the information they know about Nora. Make sure that they mention Nora's thoughts about money and last Christmas. Then, after they read pp. 870–882, have them jot down what they have learned about Nora in her conversation with Mrs. Linde. Students should realize that Nora has secrets.	Advanced readers already will probably be suspicious of Nora, thinking that she is not what she seems. Invite students to make a list of predictions about Nora—what will happen to her and what her secrets might be. Students should be able to support their predictions with lines of dialogue from the play. Allow students to compare predictions and notes and to update and change them as they continue to read the play.

18 Reading Strategy

Reading Drama

- Remind students that one of the features of modern realistic drama is dialogue that reflects natural speech.
- Have students analyze this passage and identify aspects of it that reflect natural speech.
  Answer: Nora and Mrs. Linde talk in incomplete sentences, express incomplete thoughts, interrupt each other, change their train of thought in mid-sentence, and use contractions.
- Ask a volunteer to read aloud the first Reading Strategy question on p. 870: What gestures might the actors use during these lines? Why?
  Possible response: The actors might extend their arms to greet each other but pull back because they do not recognize each other or are embarrassed.

19 Reading Strategy

Reading Drama

- Ask a volunteer to read aloud the second bracketed passage on p. 870.
- Then, ask the second Reading Strategy question on p. 870: What do you imagine Nora's movements might be during these lines? Explain.
  Possible response: Nora might be fluttering around Mrs. Linde, helping her with her coat, taking her by the hand, and leading her to a comfortable chair by the fire.
- Ask students whether they think that Nora's words and actions convey a sense of concern for her friend.
  Answer: Nora's words and actions convey nervous discomfort rather than genuine concern.

[HELMER *goes into his room. The* MAID *shows in* MRS. LINDE, *dressed in traveling clothes, and shuts the door after her.*]

18

MRS. LINDE [*in a dispirited and somewhat hesitant voice*]: Hello, Nora.

NORA [*uncertain*]: Hello—

MRS. LINDE: You don't recognize me.

NORA: No, I don't know—but wait, I think— [*Exclaiming.*] What! Kristine! Is it really you?

MRS. LINDE: Yes, it's me.

NORA: Kristine! To think I didn't recognize you. But then, how could I? [*More quietly.*] How you've changed, Kristine!

Reading Strategy
Reading Drama What gestures might the actors use during these lines? Why?

MRS. LINDE: Yes, no doubt I have. In nine—ten long years.

NORA: Is it so long since we met! Yes, it's all of that. Oh, these last eight years have been a happy time, believe me. And so now you've come in to town, too. Made the long trip in the winter. That took courage.

MRS. LINDE: I just got here by ship this morning.

19

NORA: To enjoy yourself over Christmas, of course. Oh, how lovely! Yes, enjoy ourselves, we'll do that. But take your coat off. You're not still cold? [*Helping her.*] There now, let's get cozy here by the stove. No, the easy chair there! I'll take the rocker here. [*Seizing her hands.*] Yes, now you have your old look again; it was only in that first moment. You're a bit more pale, Kristine—and maybe a bit thinner.

Reading Strategy
Reading Drama What do you imagine Nora's movements might be during these lines? Explain.

MRS. LINDE: And much, much older, Nora.

NORA: Yes, perhaps a bit older; a tiny, tiny bit; not much at all. [*Stopping short; suddenly serious.*] Oh, but thoughtless me, to sit here, chattering away. Sweet, good Kristine, can you forgive me?

MRS. LINDE: What do you mean, Nora?

NORA [*softly*]: Poor Kristine, you've become a widow.

MRS. LINDE: Yes, three years ago.

NORA: Oh, I knew it, of course; I read it in the papers. Oh, Kristine, you must believe me; I often thought of writing you then, but I kept postponing it, and something always interfered.

MRS. LINDE: Nora dear, I understand completely.

NORA: No, it was awful of me, Kristine. You poor thing, how much you must have gone through. And he left you nothing?

MRS. LINDE: No.

NORA: And no children?

MRS. LINDE: No.

NORA: Nothing at all, then?

MRS. LINDE: Not even a sense of loss to feed on.

NORA [*looking incredulously at her*]: But Kristine, how could that be?

ENRICHMENT: Geography Connection

Norway

Henrik Ibsen's homeland, Norway, is one of the northernmost countries in the world. It lies on the western half of the Scandinavian peninsula, which it shares with its neighbor, Sweden. Norway is about the size of New Mexico and is home to about 4.5 million people. In spite of its northern location, warm ocean currents give most of the country a relatively mild climate, although winters are long and cold and summers are short. About two thirds of the country is covered by mountains. Norway's most famous geographic features are the many *fjords,* or long narrow inlets of sea water surrounded by steep, rocky cliffs. The coastline is also dotted by around 50,000 islands of all sizes. Norway's important natural resources include wood and paper products, oil and natural gas, and fish. Because of its many waterfalls and dammable rivers, Norway is a world leader in the production of hydroelectric power.

MRS. LINDE [*smiling wearily and smoothing her hair*]: Oh, sometimes it happens, Nora.

NORA: So completely alone. How terribly hard that must be for you. I have three lovely children. You can't see them now; they're out with the maid. But now you must tell me everything—

MRS. LINDE: No, no, no, tell me about yourself.

NORA: No, you begin. Today I don't want to be selfish. I want to think only of you today. But there *is* something I must tell you. Did you hear of the wonderful luck we had recently?

20 **MRS. LINDE:** No, what's that?

NORA: My husband's been made manager in the bank, just think!

MRS. LINDE: Your husband? How marvelous!

NORA: Isn't it? Being a lawyer is such an uncertain living, you know, especially if one won't touch any cases that aren't clean and decent. And of course Torvald would never do that, and I'm with him completely there. Oh, we're simply delighted, believe me! He'll join the bank right after New Year's and start getting a huge salary and lots of commissions. From now on we can live quite differently—just as we want. Oh, Kristine, I feel so light and happy! Won't it be lovely to have stacks of money and not a care in the world?

MRS. LINDE: Well, anyway, it would be lovely to have enough for necessities.

NORA: No, not just for necessities, but stacks and stacks of money!

MRS. LINDE [*smiling*]: Nora, Nora, aren't you sensible yet? Back in school you were such a free spender.

NORA [*with a quiet laugh*]: Yes, that's what Torvald still says. [*Shaking her finger.*] But "Nora, Nora" isn't as silly as you all think. Really, we've been in no position for me to go squandering. We've had to work, both of us.

MRS. LINDE: You too?

NORA: Yes, at odd jobs—needlework, crocheting, embroidery, and such—[*Casually.*] and other things too. You remember that Torvald left the department when we were married? There was no chance of promotion in his office, and of course he needed to earn more money. But that first year he drove himself terribly. He took on all kinds of extra work that kept him going morning and night. It wore him down, and then he fell deathly ill. The doctors said it was essential for him to travel south.

21 **MRS. LINDE:** Yes, didn't you spend a whole year in Italy?

NORA: That's right. It wasn't easy to get away, you know. Ivar had just been born. But of course we had to go. Oh, that was a beautiful trip, and it saved Torvald's life. But it cost a frightful sum, Kristine.

MRS. LINDE: I can well imagine.

Literary Analysis
Modern Realistic Drama
Identify three ways that Nora's and Mrs. Linde's social situations differ.

22 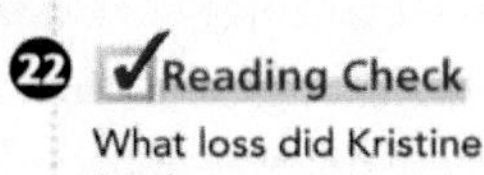
Reading Check
What loss did Kristine suffer three years ago?

20 Literary Analysis

Modern Realistic Drama

- Remind students that Torvald and Nora are living a little beyond their means but still have a comfortable home. Explain that Mrs. Linde represents a different economic bracket here. She is a poor working widow.
- Ask students to respond to the Literary Analysis item on p. 871: Identify three ways that Nora's and Mrs. Linde's social situations differ. Possible response: Mrs. Linde is widowed and childless; her thin and haggard appearance suggests that she has seen hard times. Nora, on the other hand, is married, has children, and lives in a comfortable home.

21 Background

Heakth

Make sure that students understand that Nora and her husband traveled to Italy because Torvald's illness made it necessary for him to recuperate in a warmer climate.

22 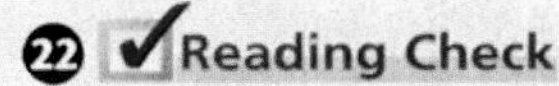 Reading Check

Answer: Kristine's husband died three years ago.

CUSTOMIZE INSTRUCTION FOR UNIVERSAL ACCESS

For Special Needs Students	For Less Proficient Readers
When Mrs. Linde appears, the play's plot begins to unfold. Students may benefit from creating a story timeline using the Story Map transparency found on pp. 83–85 in **Writing Models and Graphic Organizers on Transparencies.** Students should use the story map to plot the events that actually happen during the course of the play as well as the important events that took place before the play began, such as Nora's father's death.	Students may be interested in comparing Ibsen's dialogue with a real conversation. Ask students to work in pairs to tape-record themselves having a short conversation (a minute or two in length). Then, have students listen to the recorded conversation and develop it as a script. Students should notice the similarities between their scripts and the dialogue between Nora and Kristine. Both will have interruptions, changes of thought, modern language, and awkward pauses.

㉓ Literary Analysis

Modern Realistic Drama

- Ask students what turning point in her life Mrs. Linde is describing in the first bracketed passage on p. 872 and whether they think she made the right decision.
  Answer: Mrs. Linde is describing how she decided to marry her husband. She seems to think it was the right decision but not a happy one.
- Next, have students answer the Literary Analysis question on p. 872: What factors motivated Mrs. Linde to marry someone she did not love?
  Answer: Mrs. Linde had a sick mother and two brothers who needed support. She probably needed the husband's financial support to help her family.

㉔ Reading Strategy

Reading Drama

- Point out that Mrs. Linde has financial and family problems that many people face every day. Remind students that a character with ordinary problems was an innovation in theater when Ibsen was writing.
- Ask students to answer the Reading Strategy question on p. 872: What might Mrs. Linde's voice sound like in these lines?
  Answer: Her voice might sound tired, flat, shaky, or distant.

NORA: Four thousand, eight hundred crowns it cost. That's really a lot of money.

MRS. LINDE: But it's lucky you had it when you needed it.

NORA: Well, as it was, we got it from Papa.

MRS. LINDE: I see. It was just about the time your father died.

NORA: Yes, just about then. And, you know, I couldn't make that trip out to nurse him. I had to stay here, expecting Ivar any moment, and with my poor sick Torvald to care for. Dearest Papa, I never saw him again, Kristine. Oh, that was the worst time I've known in all my marriage.

MRS. LINDE: I know how you loved him. And then you went off to Italy?

NORA: Yes. We had the means now, and the doctors urged us. So we left a month after.

MRS. LINDE: And your husband came back completely cured?

NORA: Sound as a drum!

MRS. LINDE: But—the doctor?

NORA: Who?

MRS. LINDE: I thought the maid said he was a doctor, the man who came in with me.

NORA: Yes, that was Dr. Rank—but he's not making a sick call. He's our closest friend, and he stops by at least once a day. No, Torvald hasn't had a sick moment since, and the children are fit and strong, and I am, too. [*Jumping up and clapping her hands.*] Oh, dear God, Kristine, what a lovely thing to live and be happy! But how disgusting of me—I'm talking of nothing but my own affairs. [*Sits on a stool close by* KRISTINE, *arms resting across her knees.*] Oh, don't be angry with me! Tell me, is it really true that you weren't in love with your husband? Why did you marry him, then?

MRS. LINDE: My mother was still alive, but bedridden and helpless—and I had my two younger brothers to look after. In all conscience, I didn't think I could turn him down.

㉓ **NORA:** No, you were right there. But was he rich at the time?

MRS. LINDE: He was very well off, I'd say. But the business was shaky, Nora. When he died, it all fell apart, and nothing was left.

NORA: And then—?

MRS. LINDE: Yes, so I had to scrape up a living with a little shop and a little teaching and whatever else I could find. The last three years have been like one endless workday without a rest for me. Now it's over,
㉔ Nora. My poor mother doesn't need me, for she's passed on. Nor the boys, either; they're working now and can take care of themselves.

NORA: How free you must feel—

MRS. LINDE: No—only unspeakably empty. Nothing to live for now. [*Standing up anxiously.*] That's why I couldn't take it any longer out in

Literary Analysis
Modern Realistic Drama What factors motivated Mrs. Linde to marry someone she did not love?

Reading Strategy
Reading Drama What might Mrs. Linde's voice sound like in these lines?

ENRICHMENT: Science Connection

Progress in Nineteenth-Century Medicine

The nineteenth century was a time of great innovation and progress, particularly in the field of medicine. For hundreds of years, European medicine was largely a matter of superstition and luck. It was not until the mid-1800s that scientists agreed that health was not dictated by a balance of mysterious forces in the body called humors.

By the early 1800s, doctors had developed a more accurate physiology of the body (the major organs, muscles, and bones and where they are located). More importantly, doctors began to accept the idea that microscopic organisms, such as viruses and germs, were responsible for illnesses and infections.

The nature of Torvald's illness is not made clear in the play. Patients with illnesses such as tuberculosis, which would not have reliable treatment or prevention until the next century, were often sent to milder climates to recover.

that desolate hole. Maybe here it'll be easier to find something to do and keep my mind occupied. If I could only be lucky enough to get a steady job, some office work—

NORA: Oh, but Kristine, that's so dreadfully tiring, and you already look so tired. It would be much better for you if you could go off to a bathing resort.

MRS. LINDE [*going toward the window*]: I have no father to give me travel money, Nora.

NORA [*rising*]: Oh, don't be angry with me.

MRS. LINDE [*going to her*]: Nora dear, don't you be angry with me. The worst of my kind of situation is all the bitterness that's stored away. No one to work for, and yet you're always having to snap up your opportunities. You have to live; and so you grow selfish. When you told me the happy change in your lot, do you know I was delighted less for your sakes than for mine?

25 **NORA:** How so? Oh, I see. You think maybe Torvald could do something for you.

MRS. LINDE: Yes, that's what I thought.

NORA: And he will, Kristine! Just leave it to me; I'll bring it up so delicately—find something attractive to humor him with. Oh, I'm so eager to help you.

MRS. LINDE: How very kind of you, Nora, to be so concerned over me—double kind, considering you really know so little of life's burdens yourself.

NORA: I—? I know so little—?

MRS. LINDE [*smiling*]: Well, my heavens—a little needlework and such—Nora, you're just a child.

NORA [*tossing her head and pacing the floor*]: You don't have to act so superior.

MRS. LINDE: Oh?

NORA: You're just like the others. You all think I'm incapable of anything serious.

MRS. LINDE: Come now—

NORA: That I've never had to face the raw world.

MRS. LINDE: Nora dear, you've just been telling me all your troubles.

NORA: Hm! Trivia! [*Quietly.*] I haven't told you the big thing.

MRS. LINDE: Big thing? What do you mean?

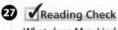

26 ▲ Critical Viewing
What type of household might pay Nora to complete needlework like that on the chair in this photograph? **[Connect]**

27 ✓Reading Check
What does Mrs. Linde hope to gain by visiting the Helmers?

25 Critical Thinking

Speculate

- Have students read the bracketed passage on p. 873.
- Then, have students speculate about whether Torvald will give Mrs. Linde a job. On what do they base their speculations?
  Possible response: Torvald will give Mrs. Linde a job because Nora seems able to make her husband do what she wants him to do.
- Later, when students reach the end of p. 873, ask them to speculate about what Nora's secret is.
  Possible response: The secret probably has to do with money.
- Indicate to students that this point in the play is crucial to the plot and to Nora's development as a character.

26 ▶Critical Viewing

Possible response: A wealthy household would probably pay Nora for such needlework. The needlework itself is elaborate and detailed. It would take much time and effort to complete and would be worth a great deal of money.

27 ✓Reading Check

Answer: Mrs. Linde hopes to gain a job.

CUSTOMIZE INSTRUCTION FOR UNIVERSAL ACCESS

For Special Needs Students	For English Learners
To help students follow the development of the characters, suggest that they create a sunburst diagram. Have students draw circles with lines radiating from them. Have students write the name of a character inside each circle. As they read the play, they should write down lines of dialogue or descriptive words that reveal information about the character's personality. These quotations and words should be written on the radiating lines.	Ask students to draw circles with lines radiating from them. Next, they should write the name of a character inside each circle. As they read, they should write down words or bits of dialogue that reveal something about each character's personality. These words or lines of dialogue should be written on the radiating lines. Encourage students to translate or use words from their native languages to help them get a better sense of the characters. Allow students to work in pairs.

28 Reading Strategy

Reading Drama

- Have two volunteers read aloud the dialogue between Nora and Mrs. Linde. Ask the first Reading Strategy question on p. 874: Why do you think the stage direction specifies that Nora draw Mrs. Linde down onto the sofa?
  Answer: By drawing Mrs. Linde onto the sofa, Nora builds suspense and gives both Mrs. Linde and the audience a sense that she is going to say something important.
- As students read this passage, have them identify the different moods or tones of voice that Nora is suggesting by her actions and gestures.
  Answer: Nora shifts from plainly smiling to speaking disdainfully to humming and smiling mysteriously.

29 Background

Law

Students should understand the importance of Mrs. Linde's comment here. According to Norwegian law at the time, Nora had no legal right to borrow money without her husband's approval. Students should suspect that Nora has done something wrong.

30 Reading Strategy

Reading Drama

- Ask students to read the bracketed passage independently and then describe Nora's actions.
  Answer: She tosses her head and throws herself on the sofa.
- Next, ask students the second Reading Strategy question on p. 874: What do the stage directions suggest about Nora's attitude toward her money scheme?
  Possible response: Nora is proud and pleased, in a childlike way, by the success of her scheme.
- Lead students in a discussion about whether a person has the right to be proud of making sacrifices for others. If appropriate, have students describe how they, or someone they know, felt after making a sacrifice for someone else.

NORA: You look down on me so, Kristine, but you shouldn't. You're proud that you worked so long and hard for your mother.

MRS. LINDE: I don't look down on a soul. But it *is* true: I'm proud—and happy, too—to think it was given to me to make my mother's last days almost free of care.

NORA: And you're also proud thinking of what you've done for your brothers.

MRS. LINDE: I feel I've a right to be.

NORA: I agree. But listen to this, Kristine—I've also got something to be proud and happy for.

MRS. LINDE: I don't doubt it. But whatever do you mean?

NORA: Not so loud. What if Torvald heard! He mustn't, not for anything in the world. Nobody must know, Kristine. No one but you.

MRS. LINDE: But what is it, then?

NORA: Come here. [*Drawing her down beside her on the sofa.*] It's true—I've also got something to be proud and happy for. I'm the one who saved Torvald's life.

MRS. LINDE: Saved—? Saved how?

NORA: I told you about the trip to Italy. Torvald never would have lived if he hadn't gone south—

MRS. LINDE: Of course; your father gave you the means—

NORA [*smiling*]: That's what Torvald and all the rest think, but—

28 **MRS. LINDE:** But—?

NORA: Papa didn't give us a pin. I was the one who raised the money.

MRS. LINDE: You? That whole amount?

NORA: Four thousand, eight hundred crowns. What do you say to that?

MRS. LINDE: But Nora, how was it possible? Did you win the lottery?

NORA [*disdainfully*]: The lottery? Pooh! No art to that.

MRS. LINDE: But where did you get it from then?

NORA [*humming, with a mysterious smile*]: Hmm, tra-la-la-la.

MRS. LINDE: Because you couldn't have borrowed it.

29 **NORA:** No? Why not?

MRS. LINDE: A wife can't borrow without her husband's consent.

NORA [*tossing her head*]: Oh, but a wife with a little business sense, a wife who knows how to manage—

MRS. LINDE: Nora, I simply don't understand—

30 **NORA:** You don't have to. Whoever said I *borrowed* the money? I could have gotten it other ways. [*Throwing herself back on the sofa.*] I could have gotten it from some admirer or other. After all, a girl with my ravishing appeal—

Reading Strategy
Reading Drama Why do you think the stage direction specifies that Nora draws Mrs. Linde down onto the sofa?

Reading Strategy
Reading Drama What do the stage directions suggest about Nora's attitude toward her money scheme?

ENRICHMENT: History Connection

Women's Rights

A Doll House explores the theme of women's rights through the story of one particular family in one country. In Europe and the United States, women lobbied for their economic and political rights for many decades. Women in Norway received the right to vote in 1913, thirty-five years after Ibsen wrote his play. Norwegian women received the right to vote five years before women (aged 30 and older) in Great Britain and seven years before women in the United States. Women's struggle to obtain rights equal to those of men has been occurring throughout the world for more than a century.

Have students research and prepare a presentation on the status of women in a particular country today. Countries of particular interest that students may wish to study include Iran, India, Afghanistan, China, Russia, Mexico, Ireland, South Africa, Sweden, Denmark, and the Netherlands.

31 ◀ **Critical Viewing**
Which details in this photo suggest that Kristine and Nora enjoy each other's company? **[Interpret]**

MRS. LINDE: You lunatic.

NORA: I'll bet you're eaten up with curiosity, Kristine.

MRS. LINDE: Now listen here, Nora—you haven't done something indiscreet?

indiscreet (in' di skrēt') *adj.* unwise or not careful

NORA [*sitting up again*]: Is it indiscreet to save your husband's life?

MRS. LINDE: I think it's indiscreet that without his knowledge you—

32 **NORA:** But that's the point: he mustn't know! My Lord, can't you understand? He mustn't ever know the close call he had. It was to *me* the doctors came to say his life was in danger—that nothing could save him but a stay in the south. Didn't I try strategy then! I began talking about how lovely it would be for me to travel abroad like other young wives; I begged and I cried; I told him please to remember my condition, to be kind and indulge me; and then I dropped a hint that he could easily take out a loan. But at that Kristine, he nearly exploded. He said I was frivolous, and it was his duty as man of the house not to indulge me in whims and fancies—as I think he called them. Aha, I thought, now you'll just have to be saved—and that's when I saw my chance.

frivolous (friv' ə ləs) *adj.* silly and light-minded; not sensible

MRS. LINDE: And your father never told Torvald the money wasn't from him?

NORA: No, never. Papa died right about then. I'd considered bringing him into my secret and begging him never to tell. But he was too sick at the time—and then, sadly, it didn't matter.

MRS. LINDE: And you've never confided in your husband since?

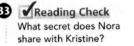

33 ✔ **Reading Check**
What secret does Nora share with Kristine?

31 ▶ **Critical Viewing**

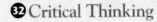

Possible response: Nora appears excited or happy to talk to Kristine; Kristine, although serious, seems eager to know what Nora has to tell her.

32 Critical Thinking

Evaluate

- Ask students to summarize Nora's strategies for getting Torvald to go to Italy.
  Answer: Nora tried reasoning, begging and crying, and finally scheming.
- Next, ask students whether Nora should have told Torvald that his life was in danger, and have them explain their answers.
  Possible response: Those who think she should have told him may say that honesty is an absolute necessity in a relationship. Those who that say she should not have told him may claim that Nora withheld the truth out of love and concern for Torvald's well-being.

33 

Answer: Nora tells Kristine that she did not get the money she needed from her father, as everyone believes.

CUSTOMIZE INSTRUCTION FOR UNIVERSAL ACCESS

For Advanced Readers

In the more than 120 years since *A Doll House* was written, the lives of women have changed in many important ways. Students can understand these changes in a more personal way by arranging to interview older women in their community about the changes they have seen in their own lifetimes. Students may wish to interview older relatives, friends, residents of retirement homes, or people active in senior centers or other activities. Have students arrange interviews, prepare interview questions, conduct the interviews, organize their information, and present their findings to the class. If appropriate, students may record their interviews on audiotape or videotape.

Encourage students to prepare questions about different types of change that have occurred in the status and condition of women, including economic, social, political, and psychological factors. It is recommended that you preview students' questions before the interviews.

34 Literary Analysis

Modern Realistic Drama

- Read aloud the first bracketed passage on p. 876
- Then, ask the first Literary Analysis question on p. 876: Do you think the Helmers' "beautiful, happy home" is built on the foundation of a lie? Why or why not?
  Possible response: Yes; the Helmers' finances and marriage are secure only because of Nora's debt. No; *lie* is too harsh a word for Nora's self-sacrifice, which she made out of love.

Monitor Progress After students read Nora's words here, ask them to review how her character fits the mold of the modern realistic drama.
Possible response: Nora is an ordinary person; she has flaws and can be, in turn, silly, loving, arrogant, and patronizing. She has ordinary problems; she does not understand money; and she lies to her husband. The character is a lens through which readers and theatergoers can see the life of an ordinary nineteenth-century wife and mother.

Reteach If necessary, have students revisit the characteristics of modern realistic drama on p. 863. Ask students for examples of each of the characteristics found in the play so far.

35 Literary Analysis

Modern Realistic Drama and Conflict

- Ask students to comment on Nora's idea that it will be safe to tell Torvald her secret when she is older and unattractive. What does it say about her?
  Possible response: Nora has a shallow idea of marriage. She expects her husband to lose interest in her when she is older and will not be so angry or disappointed in her.
- Ask students the second Literary Analysis question on p. 876: What type of conflict motivates Nora to maintain her house allowance? Explain.
  Answer: Nora must maintain her house allowance so that no one is uncomfortable or suspects that the family is in financial trouble.

34 **NORA:** For heaven's sake, no! Are you serious? He's so strict on that subject. Besides—Torvald, with all his masculine pride—how painfully humiliating for him if he ever found out he was in debt to me. That would just ruin our relationship. Our beautiful, happy home would never be the same.

MRS. LINDE: Won't you ever tell him?

35 **NORA** [*thoughtfully, half smiling*]: Yes—maybe sometime, years from now, when I'm no longer so attractive. Don't laugh! I only mean when Torvald loves me less than now, when he stops enjoying my dancing and dressing up and reciting for him. Then it might be wise to have something in reserve—[*Breaking off.*] How ridiculous! That'll never happen—Well, Kristine, what do you think of my big secret? I'm capable of something too, hm? You can imagine, of course, how this thing hangs over me. It really hasn't been easy meeting the payments on time. In the business world there's what they call quarterly interest and what they call amortization,[4] and these are always so terribly hard to manage. I've had to skimp a little here and there, wherever I could, you know. I could hardly spare anything from my house allowance, because Torvald has to live well. I couldn't let the children go poorly dressed; whatever I got for them, I felt I had to use up completely—the darlings!

MRS. LINDE: Poor Nora, so it had to come out of your own budget, then?

NORA: Yes, of course. But I was the one most responsible, too. Every time Torvald gave me money for new clothes and such, I never used more than half; always bought the simplest, cheapest outfits. It was a godsend that everything looks so well on me that Torvald never noticed. But it did weigh me down at times, Kristine. It *is* such a joy to wear fine things. You understand.

MRS. LINDE: Oh, of course.

NORA: And then I found other ways of making money. Last winter I was lucky enough to get a lot of copying to do. I locked myself in and sat writing every evening till late in the night. Ah, I was tired so often, dead tired. But still it was wonderful fun, sitting and working like that, earning money. It was almost like being a man.

MRS. LINDE: But how much have you paid off this way so far?

NORA: That's hard to say, exactly. These accounts, you know, aren't easy to figure. I only know that I've paid out all I could scrape together. Time and again I haven't known where to turn. [*Smiling.*] Then I'd sit here dreaming of a rich old gentleman who had fallen in love with me—

MRS. LINDE: What! Who is he?

NORA: Oh, really! And that he'd died, and when his will was opened, there in big letters it said, "All my fortune shall be paid over in cash, immediately, to that enchanting Mrs. Nora Helmer."

4. **amortization** (am′ ər ti zā′ shən) *n.* putting aside money at intervals for gradual payment of a debt.

Literary Analysis
Modern Realistic Drama Do you think the Helmers' "beautiful, happy home" is built on the foundation of a lie? Why or why not?

Literary Analysis
Modern Realistic Drama and Conflict What type of conflict motivates Nora to maintain her house allowance? Explain.

MRS. LINDE: But Nora dear—who *was* this gentleman?

NORA: Good grief, can't you understand? The old man never existed; that was only something I'd dream up time and again whenever I was at my wits' end for money. But it makes no difference now; the old fossil can go where he pleases for all I care; I don't need him or his will—because now I'm free. [*Jumping up.*] Oh, how lovely to think of that, Kristine! Carefree! To know you're carefree, utterly carefree; to be able to romp and play with the children, and to keep up a beautiful, charming home—everything just the way Torvald likes it! And think, spring is coming, with big blue skies. Maybe we can travel a little then. Maybe I'll see the ocean again. Oh yes, it *is* so marvelous to live and be happy!

[*The front doorbell rings.*]

MRS. LINDE [*rising*]: There's the bell. It's probably best that I go.

NORA: No, stay. No one's expected. It must be for Torvald.

MAID [*from the hall doorway*]: Excuse me, ma'am—there's a gentleman here to see Mr. Helmer, but I didn't know—since the doctor's with him—

NORA: Who is the gentleman?

KROGSTAD [*from the doorway*]: It's me, Mrs. Helmer.

[MRS. LINDE *starts and turns away toward the window.*]

NORA [*stepping toward him, tense, her voice a whisper*]: You? What is it? Why do you want to speak to my husband?

KROGSTAD: Bank business—after a fashion. I have a small job in the investment bank, and I hear now your husband is going to be our chief—

37 **NORA:** In other words, it's—

KROGSTAD: Just dry business, Mrs. Helmer. Nothing but that.

NORA: Yes, then please be good enough to step into the study. [*She nods indifferently as she sees him out by the hall door, then returns and begins stirring up the stove.*]

MRS. LINDE: Nora—who was that man?

NORA: That was a Mr. Krogstad—a lawyer.

MRS. LINDE: Then it really was him.

NORA: Do you know that person?

MRS. LINDE: I did once—many years ago. For a time he was a law clerk in our town.

NORA: Yes, he's been that.

Literature in context Cultural Connection

36 ***The Norwegian Krone***

The krone, or crown, is a unit of Norwegian currency. Today, the forty kroner [plural form] Torvald gives Nora would be worth only about five dollars and fifty cents, less than half the price of a typical compact disc. In 1879, however, the year *A Doll House* was first produced, those forty kroner would have bought considerably more. At that time, a pound of bacon cost about eight cents in the United States; a skilled laborer brought home about ten dollars a week. So, while forty kroner does not sound like a significant sum, Torvald was being rather generous. On a larger scale, Nora would need to devote considerable time and effort to paying back four thousand eight hundred crowns. Its current equivalent is more than six hundred American dollars.

Reading Strategy

Reading Drama How does the atmosphere onstage change when Krogstad enters?

38  **Reading Check**

What kind of work did Nora perform to pay off her debt?

36 Background

The Norwegian Krone

Unlike many European nations, Norway still uses its traditional kroner as money. Many European countries, in joining the European Union (EU), have given up their individual currencies and use the euro instead. In 1992, the Norwegian government applied for a place in the EU, but two years later, in 1994, the voters of Norway rejected the idea of joining. Norway is one of the few developed European nations that has refused to join.

37 Reading Strategy

Reading Drama

- Make sure that students notice the emotional ebb and flow in the play.
- Ask volunteers to read the bracketed dialogue among Nora, Krogstad, and Mrs. Linde.
- Ask students the Reading Strategy question on p. 877: How does the atmosphere onstage change when Krogstad enters?
  Answer: Nora appears uneasy around him. Mrs. Linde seems surprised to see him. The atmosphere becomes tense and awkward.
- Challenge students to predict why the two women react as they do upon seeing Krogstad. Explain that his relationship with Nora will become clearer later in the act.

38 Reading Check

Answer: Nora copied documents by hand to make money to pay off her debt.

CUSTOMIZE INSTRUCTION FOR UNIVERSAL ACCESS

For Gifted/Talented Students	For Advanced Readers
Have students identify a favorite protagonist from another work of literature or from a movie, television, or video. Invite students to work in groups to role-play a panel discussion featuring Nora and at least two other protagonists. In character, students should discuss their characters' goals, as well as their problems and how they solved them. Have students perform their panel discussion for the class. Ask another student to serve as moderator to lead the discussion and take questions from the students in the audience.	Have students consider leading female protagonists they have encountered and admired in other works of literature or in film, video, or television. Ask them to write a brief comparison of one of those protagonists and Nora. Students should identify the two characters' conflicts, flaws, and goals. If students read ahead, they can also compare the two characters' solutions to their problems. Invite students to share their comparisons with the class, without revealing the ending of the play.

39 Literary Analysis

Modern Realistic Drama and Conflict

- Point out how, once again, the background of a character is presented in a natural, conversational way. Ask students to compare Krogstad's entrance with Dr. Rank's. Possible response: Unlike Dr. Rank, Krogstad appears onstage and provokes unexpected reactions in Nora and Kristine.
- Ask students the Literary Analysis question on p. 878: What conflict motivates Nora to change the topic of the conversation so abruptly?
  Answer: Nora is clearly uncomfortable talking to or about Krogstad, so she changes the subject.

40 ▶Critical Viewing

Possible response: The rich-looking tablecloth, the objects in the cabinet behind Nora, the furniture, and Nora's clothes suggest that the Helmers are well off.

MRS. LINDE: How he's changed.

NORA: I understand he had a very unhappy marriage.

MRS. LINDE: He's a widower now.

39 **NORA:** With a number of children. There now, it's burning. [*She closes the stove door and moves the rocker a bit to one side.*]

MRS. LINDE: They say he has a hand in all kinds of business.

NORA: Oh? That may be true; I wouldn't know. But let's not think about business. It's so dull.

[DR. RANK *enters from* HELMER'S *study.*]

RANK [*still in the doorway*]: No, no, really—I don't want to intrude, I'd just as soon talk a little while with your wife. [*Shuts the door, then notices* MRS. LINDE.] Oh, beg pardon. I'm intruding here too.

NORA: No, not at all. [*Introducing him.*] Dr. Rank, Mrs. Linde.

RANK: Well now, that's a name much heard in this house. I believe I passed the lady on the stairs as I came.

MRS. LINDE: Yes, I take the stairs very slowly. They're rather hard on me.

RANK: Uh-hm, some touch of internal weakness?

MRS. LINDE: More overexertion, I'd say.

RANK: Nothing else? Then you're probably here in town to rest up in a round of parties?

MRS. LINDE: I'm here to look for work.

RANK: Is that the best cure for overexertion?

MRS. LINDE: One has to live, Doctor.

RANK: Yes, there's a common prejudice to that effect.

NORA: Oh, come on, Dr. Rank—you really do want to live yourself.

RANK. Yes, I really do. Wretched as I am, I'll gladly prolong my torment indefinitely. All my patients feel like that. And it's quite the same, too, with the morally sick. Right at this moment there's one of those moral invalids in there with Helmer—

MRS. LINDE [*softly*]: Ah!

NORA: Who do you mean?

RANK: Oh, it's a lawyer, Krogstad, a type you wouldn't know. His character is rotten to the root—but even he began chattering all-importantly about how he had to *live.*

NORA: Oh? What did he want to talk to Torvald about?

Literary Analysis
Modern Realistic Drama and Conflict What conflict motivates Nora to change the topic of conversation so abruptly?

40 **▼Critical Viewing**
Which details in this photo reveal the economic status of the Helmers? **[Interpret]**

ENRICHMENT: Art Connection

Ibsen: Painter Turned Plotter

As a young man, Henrik Ibsen wanted to be a painter. Many critics have seen in the plots of his plays evidence of his strong sense of composition. Composition is the way images are arranged in an artwork. It helps viewers make sense of the images by guiding their eyes around the artwork. Similarly, all the pieces of *A Doll House* are carefully arranged, as if woven together into a seamless structure. In fact, a friend of Ibsen's compared the playwright's editing process with that of a sculptor: "the Master has for the last two or three years been chiseling away everything unnecessary" from the plot. The tightness of the plot led another critic to call *A Doll House* "a structural miracle."

In Ibsen's plays, the audience is offered a series of striking ideas and images communicated through the dialogue. The story gradually unfolds in a natural and believable way, and each event or exchange of dialogue seems to build on and grow from the one before it. In addition, all actions and words serve a purpose.

RANK: I really don't know. I only heard something about the bank.

41 **NORA:** I didn't know that Krog—that this man Krogstad had anything to do with the bank.

42 **RANK:** Yes, he's gotten some kind of berth down there. [*To* MRS. LINDE.] I don't know if you also have, in your neck of the woods, a type of person who scuttles about breathlessly, sniffing out hints of moral corruption, and then maneuvers his victim into some sort of key position where he can keep an eye on him. It's the healthy these days that are out in the cold.

MRS. LINDE: All the same, it's the sick who most need to be taken in.

RANK [*with a shrug*]: Yes, there we have it. That's the concept that's turning society into a sanatorium.

[NORA, *lost in her thoughts, breaks out into quiet laughter and claps her hands.*]

RANK: Why do you laugh at that? Do you have any real idea of what society is?

Literary Analysis
Modern Realistic Drama
In what ways do Dr. Rank's words reflect characteristics of modern realistic drama?

43 **Reading Check**
What does Dr. Rank know of Krogstad's personality?

41 Reading Strategy
Reading Drama

- Read aloud the first bracketed passage on p. 879.
- Point out how Nora corrects herself here in the middle of saying Krogstad's name. Ask students why she does this.
  Answer: In calling Krogstad by his last name only, Nora is showing that she is familiar with him. By saying "this man Krogstad" instead, she suggests that he is a stranger to her, which is what she wants people to think.

42 Literary Analysis
Modern Realistic Drama

- This is one of the first speeches by Dr. Rank. Ask students to name adjectives that describe him.
  Possible response: Adjectives such as *down-to-earth, bitter, straightforward*, or *cynical* describe Dr. Rank.
- Ask students the Literary Analysis question on p. 879: In what ways do Dr. Rank's words reflect characteristics of modern realistic drama?
  Answer: Dr. Rank uses informal language and figures of speech, such as "your neck of the woods." He sounds like a real person.

43 Reading Check

Answer: Dr. Rank characterizes Krogstad as "rotten to the root."

CUSTOMIZE INSTRUCTION FOR UNIVERSAL ACCESS

For Special Needs Students	For Less Proficient Readers
Because the characters in this play are complex, students may have trouble keeping track of their characteristics. Provide students with a Herringbone organizer like the one that appears on pp. 75–77 of **Writing Models and Graphic Organizers on Transparencies.** Have students write the name of one of the characters in the middle bar of the diagram. Then, have them identify and write positive character traits on the diagonal lines at the top of the diagram and negative traits on the diagonal lines at the bottom of the diagram.	Dr. Rank is a character whose language is full of figures of speech and higher-level vocabulary, and his words may not be clear to students. Help students by reading aloud Dr. Rank's first few lines of dialogue. Ask students to jot down their impressions of him and the overall idea of what he is saying. Students should understand that Rank has a low opinion of lawyers in general and Krogstad in particular. If time allows, let students use a dictionary to help them write a paraphrase of one of Dr. Rank's speeches.

44 Literary Analysis

Modern Realistic Drama

- Have students read the first bracketed passage and examine it for signs that Nora has reached some kind of turning point.
  Answer: Nora laughs, smiles, hums, and pulls out the bag of macaroons.
- Then, ask students what the information might be that has made her so happy.
  Possible response: The idea that the bank employees, including Krogstad, are now under Torvald's control makes her happy.
- Ask students the first Literary Analysis question on p. 880: What social benefits might Nora gain from Torvald's "power now over all those people"?
  Possible response: Nora may gain prestige and respect in the community. Also, the Helmers will have enough money, and Nora will be able to pay off her debt.

45 Literary Analysis

Modern Realistic Drama

- Have three volunteers read aloud the second bracketed passage.
- Then, ask students the second Literary Analysis question on p. 880: Why are Mrs. Linde and Dr. Rank so shocked by Nora's words?
  Possible response: Nora's words are not something a proper middle-class woman would say. Mrs. Linde and Dr. Rank are shocked only in the way parents are shocked when a child says something inappropriate.
- Finally, point out to students that despite Nora's daring vocabulary, she does not say the words to Torvald and in fact hides her forbidden bag of macaroons when he enters the room.

NORA: What do I care about dreary old society? I was laughing at something quite different—something terribly funny. Tell me, Doctor—is everyone who works in the bank dependent now on Torvald?

44 **RANK:** Is that what you find so terribly funny?

NORA [*smiling and humming*]: Never mind, never mind! [*Pacing the floor.*] Yes, that's really immensely amusing: that we—that Torvald has so much power now over all those people. [*Taking the bag out of her pocket.*] Dr. Rank, a little macaroon on that?

RANK: See here, macaroons! I thought they were contraband here.

contraband (kän′ trə band′) *n.* unlawful or forbidden goods

NORA: Yes, but these are some that Kristine gave me.

MRS. LINDE: What? I—?

NORA: Now, now, don't be afraid. You couldn't possibly know that Torvald had forbidden them. You see, he's worried they'll ruin my teeth. But hmp! Just this once! Isn't that so, Dr. Rank? Help yourself. [*Puts a macaroon in his mouth.*] And you too, Kristine. And I'll also have one, only a little one—or two, at the most. [*Walking about again.*] Now I'm really tremendously happy. Now there's just one last thing in the world that I have an enormous desire to do.

Literary Analysis
Modern Realistic Drama
What social benefits might Nora gain from Torvald's "power now over all those people"?

RANK: Well! And what's that?

NORA: It's something I have such a consuming desire to say so Torvald could hear.

RANK: And why can't you say it?

NORA: I don't dare. It's quite shocking.

MRS. LINDE: Shocking?

45 **RANK:** Well, then it isn't advisable. But in front of us you certainly can. What do you have such a desire to say so Torvald could hear?

NORA: I have such a huge desire to say—to hell and be damned!

RANK: Are you crazy?

MRS. LINDE: My goodness, Nora!

RANK: Go on, say it. Here he is.

NORA [*hiding the macaroon bag*]: Shh, shh, shh!

[HELMER *comes in from his study, hat in hand, overcoat over his arm.*]

Literary Analysis
Modern Realistic Drama
Why are Mrs. Linde and Dr. Rank so shocked by Nora's words?

ENRICHMENT: Culture Connection

Norwegian Food for Thought

A macaroon is a small chewy cookie made of a few simple ingredients, including flour, sugar, egg white, almond paste, and coconut. Macaroons are often flavored with vanilla or liqueurs and decorated with whole nuts or dried fruit. They are not a traditional Norwegian food, however, and Nora's fondness for them suggests that she is being extravagant in buying them.

Norwegians eat a wide array of sweets at Christmastime, including gingersnap cookies, doughnuts, and cakes. People in different regions may eat fish, lamb, or pork for their Christmas meals. Some eat a special rice porridge for their Christmas lunch and then have rice cream and red fruit sauce as their Christmas dinner dessert.

NORA [*going toward him*]: Well, Torvald dear, are you through with him?

HELMER: Yes, he just left.

NORA: Let me introduce you—this is Kristine, who's arrived here in town.

HELMER: Kristine—? I'm sorry, but I don't know—

NORA: Mrs. Linde, Torvald dear. Mrs. Kristine Linde.

HELMER: Of course. A childhood friend of my wife's, no doubt?

MRS. LINDE: Yes, we knew each other in those days.

NORA: And just think, she made the long trip down here in order to talk with you.

46 **HELMER:** What's this?

MRS. LINDE: Well, not exactly—

NORA: You see, Kristine is remarkably clever in office work, and so she's terribly eager to come under a capable man's supervision and add more to what she already knows—

HELMER: Very wise, Mrs. Linde.

NORA: And then when she heard that you'd become a bank manager—the story was wired out to the papers—then she came in as fast as she could and—Really, Torvald, for my sake you can do a little something for Kristine, can't you?

HELMER: Yes, it's not at all impossible. Mrs. Linde, I suppose you're a widow?

MRS. LINDE: Yes.

HELMER: Any experience in office work?

MRS. LINDE: Yes, a good deal.

HELMER: Well, it's quite likely that I can make an opening for you—

NORA [*clapping her hands*]: You see, you see!

HELMER: You've come at a lucky moment, Mrs. Linde.

47 **MRS. LINDE:** Oh, how can I thank you?

HELMER: Not necessary. [*Putting his overcoat on.*] But today you'll have to excuse me—

RANK: Wait, I'll go with you. [*He fetches his coat from the hall and warms it at the stove.*]

NORA: Don't stay out long, dear.

HELMER: An hour; no more.

NORA: Are you going too, Kristine?

MRS. LINDE [*putting on her winter garments*]: Yes, I have to see about a room now.

HELMER: Then perhaps we can all walk together.

Reading Strategy
Reading Drama In what ways might Nora's determination to help Mrs. Linde be apparent in Nora's body language? Explain.

48 **✔Reading Check**
What contraband does Nora hide from Torvald?

46 Reading Strategy

Reading Drama

- Tell students that Torvald is a little confused by the appearance of Mrs. Linde, someone he does not know.
- Ask students the Reading Strategy question on p. 881: In what ways might Nora's determination to help Mrs. Linde be apparent in Nora's body language? Explain.
  Possible response: Nora may put her hand on Torvald's arm and draw Mrs. Linde closer to him.

47 Critical Thinking

Infer

- Read aloud the bracketed passage. Have students discuss how Torvald's openness to the idea of Mrs. Linde's working for him might relate to the conversation he just had with Krogstad.
- Then, ask them why Torvald tells Mrs. Linde that she has "come at a lucky moment."
  Possible response: Torvald has just finished telling Krogstad that he will lose his job; that is why there is suddenly an opening for Mrs. Linde.

48 

Answer: Nora hides the bag of macaroons.

CUSTOMIZE INSTRUCTION FOR UNIVERSAL ACCESS

For Less Proficient Readers	For Gifted/Talented Students
Students may benefit from a quick review of the characters and how they know one another. Work as a class to create a graphic organizer that shows the different relationships. Draw five circles on the board and label them *Nora, Torvald, Mrs. Linde, Dr. Rank,* and *Krogstad.* Ask students to guide you as you draw lines to connect the circles to show which characters know one another. Then, challenge students to think of words that characterize these relationships.	Randomly assign students the name of a character from the play. Then, randomly place the students in pairs. Challenge them to have an unscripted conversation in the roles of their characters. Allow students to talk for three minutes. Afterward, ask students to talk about the experience. Were they able to capture the essence of their characters or master the way the characters talk? What did they learn about the characters from the exercise?

49 Literary Analysis

Modern Realistic Drama

- Tell students to pay attention to the small talk in the hallway as the adults are leaving and the children enter. Ask students what each character's contribution to the small talk says about him or her.
  Possible response: Each character is true to himself or herself here. Nora sounds like an enthusiastic and proud young mother; Dr. Rank is worried about standing in a draft; Torvald is eager to leave the scene and let the children be with their mother.
- Ask students the Literary Analysis question on p. 882: Judging by Torvald's comment, what role did men of that time seem to have in raising children?
  Answer: Men seem to have had little interest or involvement in raising children. Torvald seems eager to leave Nora with the children.

50 Reading Strategy

Reading Drama

- Point out that the children do not have any written dialogue in this scene with Nora, and the actors who play the children must think of things to say that mesh with Nora's dialogue.
- Next, ask students the Reading Strategy question on p. 882: How do the stage directions help clarify the relationship Nora has with her children?
  Answer: The stage directions show that Nora is actively playing with the children by hiding under furniture and crawling around on the floor with them. These directions clarify Nora's own childishness.

NORA [*helping her*]: What a shame we're so cramped here, but it's quite impossible for us to—

MRS. LINDE: Oh, don't even think of it! Good-bye, Nora dear, and thanks for everything.

NORA: Good-bye for now. Of course you'll be back this evening. And you too, Dr. Rank. What? If you're well enough? Oh, you've got to be! Wrap up tight now.

[*In a ripple of small talk the company moves out into the hall; children's voices are heard outside on the steps.*]

NORA: There they are! There they are! [*She runs to open the door. The children come in with their nurse,* ANNE-MARIE.] Come in, come in! [*Bends down and kisses them.*] Oh, you darlings—! Look at them, Kristine. Aren't they lovely!

49 **RANK:** No loitering in the draft here.

HELMER: Come, Mrs. Linde—this place is unbearable now for anyone but mothers.

[DR. RANK, HELMER, *and* MRS. LINDE *go down the stairs.* ANNE-MARIE *goes into the living room with the children.* NORA *follows, after closing the hall door.*]

NORA: How fresh and strong you look. Oh, such red cheeks you have! Like apples and roses. [*The children interrupt her throughout the following.*] And it was so much fun? That's wonderful. Really? You pulled both Emmy and Bob on the sled? Imagine, all together! Yes, you're a clever boy, Ivar. Oh, let me hold her a bit, Anne-Marie. My sweet little doll baby! [*Takes the smallest from the nurse and dances with her.*] Yes, yes, Mama will dance with Bob as well. What? Did you throw snowballs? Oh, if I'd only been there! No, don't bother, Anne-Marie—I'll undress them myself. Oh yes, let me. It's such fun. Go in and rest; you look half frozen. There's hot coffee waiting for you on the stove. [*The nurse goes into the room to the left.* NORA *takes the children's winter things off, throwing them about, while the children talk to her all at once.*] Is that so? A big dog chased you? But it didn't bite? No, dogs never bite little, lovely doll babies. Don't peek in the packages, Ivar! What is it? Yes, wouldn't you like to know. No, no, it's an ugly something. Well? Shall we play? What shall we play? Hide-and-seek? Yes, let's play hide-and-seek. Bob must hide first. I must? Yes, let me hide first.

50 [*Laughing and shouting, she and the children play in and out of the living room and the adjoining room to the right. At last* NORA *hides under the table. The children come storming in, search, but cannot find her, then hear her muffled laughter, dash over to the table, lift the cloth up and find her. Wild shouting. She creeps forward as if to scare them. More shouts. Meanwhile, a knock at the hall door; no one has noticed it. Now the door half opens, and* KROGSTAD *appears. He waits a moment; the game goes on.*]

KROGSTAD: Beg pardon, Mrs. Helmer—

NORA [*with a strangled cry, turning and scrambling to her knees*]: Oh! What do you want?

Literary Analysis
Modern Realistic Drama Judging by Torvald's comment, what role did men of that time seem to have in raising children?

Reading Strategy
Reading Drama How do the stage directions help clarify the relationship Nora has with her children?

ENRICHMENT: Literature Connection

Contemporary Criticism: Shaw Looks at Ibsen

In his book *The Quintessence of Ibsenism,* Irish playwright George Bernard Shaw, a great follower of Ibsen, describes the Helmer household.

> In the famous *Doll's House,* the pillar of the society who owns the doll is a model husband. In his little household, with the three darling children and the affectionate little wife, all on the most loving terms with one another, we have the sweet home, the womanly woman, the happy family life of the idealist's dream. Mrs. Nora Helmer is happy in the belief that she has attained a valid realization of all these illusions that she is an ideal wife and mother; and that Helmer is an ideal husband who would, if the necessity arose, give his life to save her reputation.

Challenge students to explain why Shaw uses such a dark tone. They may suggest that his tone helps convey the dark side of the play and the characters.

51 ▶ Critical Viewing

Possible response: The children appear warmly and fashionably dressed. They have on warm coats, hats, and gloves. They appear happy and comfortable.

51 ▲ **Critical Viewing** Which details in this photograph support Nora's assertions that her children did not "go poorly dressed" as she paid her debt to Krogstad? **[Connect]**

CUSTOMIZE INSTRUCTION FOR UNIVERSAL ACCESS

For Less Proficient Readers	For English Learners
Allow students to work in pairs to select a line or two of dialogue from the play to accompany the photograph on p. 883. Have students write the dialogue on a sticky note and place the note on the corner of the page. As a class, discuss students' choices. Students should be able to explain the connections they made among the image, the characters' expressions and body language, and the dialogue they selected. Discuss why their choices work.	Have students work in pairs to write a description of the photograph on p. 883. Ask students to use complete sentences to identify the objects and people they see in the photograph and to write a sentence or two explaining what is happening in the photograph and what the characters may be saying. Discuss students' descriptions as a group. If time allows, repeat this activity with the photographs that appear on pp. 866, 875, and 878–879.

52 Reading Strategy

Reading Drama

- Have students notice that Nora speaks both to her children and to Krogstad here. What different tones of voice do they think she would use?
  Possible response: Nora switches from a guarded or flat tone with Krogstad to a soft, calming tone with the children.
- Point out that the children suspect Nora is afraid of Krogstad because one of them prompts her to say "No, the strange man won't hurt Mama."
- Ask students to read the first Reading Strategy question on p. 884: What gestures might Nora use to convey her "tense and nervous" emotions?
  Possible response: Nora might clench or wring her hands or hold her arms tightly across her body.

53 Reading Strategy

Reading Drama

- Have students notice how Nora's answers to Krogstad's questions are short and to the point. Ask students what Nora's short answers suggest about her relationship with Krogstad.
  Possible response: Nora is keeping her answers short because she does not want to talk to him.
- Ask a volunteer to read aloud the second Reading Strategy question on p. 884: What tone of voice do you think Nora uses in these lines? Explain.
  Answer: Nora probably uses a haughty or arrogant tone of voice here. She is suggesting to Krogstad that she is above him, one of her husband's employees.
- Ask students to explain the irony in Nora's warning to Krogstad about being in a subordinate position.
  Possible response: Although she is referring to Krogstad's inferior position at the bank, she herself is in a subordinate position in her marriage.

KROGSTAD: Excuse me. The outer door was ajar; it must be someone forgot to shut it—

NORA [*rising*]: My husband isn't home, Mr. Krogstad.

KROGSTAD: I know that.

52 **NORA:** Yes—then what do you want here?

KROGSTAD: A word with you.

NORA: With—? [*To the children, quietly.*] Go in to Anne-Marie. What? No, the strange man won't hurt Mama. When he's gone, we'll play some more. [*She leads the children into the room to the left and shuts the door after them. Then, tense and nervous:*] You want to speak to me?

Reading Strategy
Reading Drama What gestures might Nora use to convey her "tense and nervous" emotions?

KROGSTAD: Yes, I want to.

NORA: Today? But it's not yet the first of the month—

KROGSTAD: No, it's Christmas Eve. It's going to be up to you how merry a Christmas you have.

NORA: What is it you want? Today I absolutely can't—

KROGSTAD: We won't talk about that till later. This is something else. You do have a moment to spare, I suppose?

NORA: Oh, yes, of course—I do, except—

KROGSTAD: Good. I was sitting over at Olsen's Restaurant when I saw your husband go down the street—

NORA: Yes?

KROGSTAD: With a lady.

NORA: Yes. So?

KROGSTAD: If you'll pardon my asking: wasn't that lady a Mrs. Linde?

NORA: Yes.

KROGSTAD: Just now come into town?

NORA: Yes, today.

53 **KROGSTAD:** She's a good friend of yours?

NORA: Yes, she is. But I don't see—

KROGSTAD: I also knew her once.

NORA: I'm aware of that.

KROGSTAD: Oh? You know all about it. I thought so. Well, then let me ask you short and sweet: is Mrs. Linde getting a job in the bank?

NORA: What makes you think you can cross-examine me, Mr. Krogstad—you, one of my husband's employees? But since you ask, you might as well know—yes, Mrs. Linde's going to be taken on at the bank. And I'm the one who spoke for her, Mr. Krogstad. Now you know.

Reading Strategy
Reading Drama What tone of voice do you think Nora uses in these lines? Explain.

KROGSTAD: So I guessed right.

NORA [*pacing up and down*]: Oh, one does have a tiny bit of influence, I should hope. Just because I am a woman, don't think it means that— When one has a subordinate position, Mr. Krogstad, one really ought to be careful about pushing somebody who—hm—

subordinate (sə bôr′ də nit) *adj.* inferior; ranking under or below

KROGSTAD: Who has influence?

NORA: That's right.

KROGSTAD [*in a different tone*]: Mrs. Helmer, would you be good enough to use your influence on my behalf?

54 **NORA:** What? What do you mean?

KROGSTAD: Would you please make sure that I keep my subordinate position in the bank?

NORA: What does that mean? Who's thinking of taking away your position?

KROGSTAD: Oh, don't play the innocent with me. I'm quite aware that your friend would hardly relish the chance of running into me again; and I'm also aware now whom I can thank for being turned out.

NORA: But I promise you—

KROGSTAD: Yes, yes, yes, to the point: there's still time, and I'm advising you to use your influence to prevent it.

NORA: But Mr. Krogstad, I have absolutely no influence.

KROGSTAD: You haven't? I thought you were just saying—

NORA: You shouldn't take me so literally. I! How can you believe that I have any such influence over my husband?

KROGSTAD: Oh, I've known your husband from our student days. I don't think the great bank manager's more steadfast than any other married man.

NORA: You speak insolently about my husband, and I'll show you the door.

KROGSTAD: The lady has spirit.

NORA: I'm not afraid of you any longer. After New Year's, I'll soon be done with the whole business.

KROGSTAD [*restraining himself*]: Now listen to me, Mrs. Helmer. If necessary, I'll fight for my little job in the bank as if it were life itself.

NORA: Yes, so it seems.

KROGSTAD: It's not just a matter of income; that's the least of it. It's something else—All right, out with it! Look, this is the thing. You know, just like all the others, of course, that once, a good many years ago, I
55 did something rather rash.

NORA: I've heard rumors to that effect.

KROGSTAD: The case never got into court; but all the same, every door was closed in my face from then on. So I took up those various

Literary Analysis
Modern Realistic Drama and Conflict What conflicts have troubled Krogstad for many years?

56  **Reading Check**

What favor does Krogstad ask of Nora?

54 Reading Strategy

Reading Drama

- Have a volunteer read the first bracketed passage on p. 885.
- Point out that the stage directions here say that Krogstad speaks "in a different tone." Ask students to identify the tone he has been speaking in and the tone he switches to. Then, ask students to explain their answers.
  Possible response: Krogstad was asking Nora many questions and probably had a more commanding tone. Now, he switches, probably to a pleading tone, because he is essentially asking Nora to save his job at the bank.

55 Literary Analysis

Modern Realistic Drama and Conflict

- Have two volunteers read aloud the bracketed passage.
- Tell students that some critics have thought that Krogstad is not a believable or realistic character. With this criticism in mind, have students make notes on his character in order to agree or disagree with the critics' evaluations.
- Ask students the Literary Analysis question on p. 885: What conflicts have troubled Krogstad for many years?
  Answer: Krogstad's conflicts involve the loss of his reputation over a legal matter. He also seems to have a conflict with Mrs. Linde.

56 ✓Reading Check

Answer: Krogstad asks Nora to use her influence with Torvald to let him keep his job at the bank.

CUSTOMIZE INSTRUCTION FOR UNIVERSAL ACCESS

For Special Needs Students	For Advanced Readers
Students may benefit from a short writing exercise based on a cubing organizer. Give students a copy of the Cubing organizer found on pp. 87–89 of **Writing Models and Graphic Organizers on Transparencies.** Adapt the first four questions as follows: *Describe Nora:* What is Nora like? *Compare Nora:* What person or character is she like? *Associate Nora:* Of whom or what does Nora remind you? *Apply Nora:* What can you learn from Nora? Allow students a minute or two to jot down responses.	Challenge students to "translate" a section of Act One from play form to prose. In their prose versions, students should include descriptions of the setting and the characters as well as dialogue with tag lines. They should also reveal the characters' inner thoughts. Students may experiment with different types of narrators. For example, they might write a version of the play from Nora's point of view. Or they might rely on a third-person narrator. Ask students to share their prose with the class.

57 Critical Thinking

Analyze

- Point out to students that Nora calls her secret "her pride and joy." Ask them what she means by this. Possible response: Nora sees her secret (obtaining money for a trip to Italy) as an accomplishment; she credits herself with saving her family.
- Next, make sure students are aware that Nora believes that should Krogstad tell Torvald about the loan, Torvald would save her.
- Hint that Nora is misguided on both of these points by asking students to predict what will happen.

58 Literary Analysis

Modern Realistic Drama

- Tell students to be aware that the play is leading up to another turning point and that they will learn that Nora has not been as clever as she thinks.
- Read aloud the second bracketed passage on p. 886.
- Ask students the Literary Analysis question on p. 886: In what way does this passage indicate that women in nineteenth-century Norway could not legally get loans on their own? Possible response: Krogstad had to leave lines for Nora's father's signature. Even though she was a married woman, Nora needed the signature of a man to whom she was related in order to get the loan.

activities you know about. I had to grab hold somewhere; and I dare say I haven't been among the worst. But now I want to drop all that. My boys are growing up. For their sakes, I'll have to win back as much respect as possible here in town. That job in the bank was like the first rung in my ladder. And now your husband wants to kick me right back down in the mud again.

NORA: But for heaven's sake, Mr. Krogstad, it's simply not in my power to help you.

KROGSTAD: That's because you haven't the will to—but I have the means to make you.

NORA: You certainly won't tell my husband that I owe you money?

KROGSTAD: Hm—what if I told him that?

NORA: That would be shameful of you. [*Nearly in tears.*] This secret—my joy and my pride—that he should learn it in such a crude and disgusting way—learn it from you. You'd expose me to the most horrible unpleasantness—

KROGSTAD: Only unpleasantness?

57 **NORA** [*vehemently*]: But go on and try. It'll turn out the worse for you, because then my husband will really see what a crook you are, and then you'll never be able to hold your job.

KROGSTAD: I asked if it was just domestic unpleasantness you were afraid of?

NORA: If my husband finds out, then of course he'll pay what I owe at once, and then we'd be through with you for good.

KROGSTAD [*a step closer*]: Listen, Mrs. Helmer—you've either got a very bad memory, or else no head at all for business. I'd better put you a little more in touch with the facts.

NORA: What do you mean?

KROGSTAD: When your husband was sick, you came to me for a loan of four thousand, eight hundred crowns.

NORA: Where else could I go?

KROGSTAD: I promised to get you that sum—

NORA: And you got it.

KROGSTAD: I promised to get you that sum, on certain conditions. You were so involved in your husband's illness, and so eager to finance your trip, that I guess you didn't think out all the details. It might just be a good idea to remind you. I promised you the money on the strength of a note I drew up.

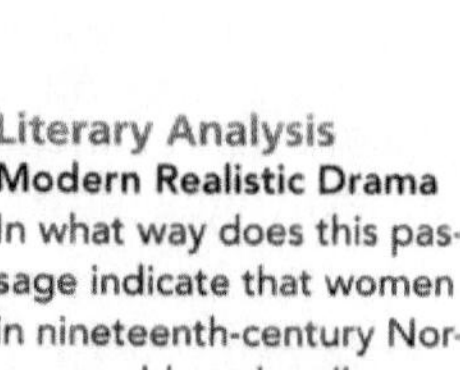

NORA: Yes, and that I signed.

58 **KROGSTAD:** Right. But at the bottom I added some lines for your father to guarantee the loan. He was supposed to sign down there.

Literary Analysis
Modern Realistic Drama In what way does this passage indicate that women in nineteenth-century Norway could not legally get loans on their own?

ENRICHMENT: Law Connection

Forgery and Counterfeiting

Forgery is the use of false writing in a document that is used to mislead or defraud others. Nora's form of forgery was to falsify her father's signature in order to secure a loan, but there are other kinds of forgery.

Entering false information on a form or document and then signing it is one form of forgery. Another is creating a document, such as a letter of recommendation, and signing another person's name without his or her knowledge. Forgery also covers altering or falsifying information on documents of personal identification, such as passports, driver's licenses, and birth certificates.

Artworks such as paintings, etchings, and drawings can also be forged; some artists train themselves to copy valuable artworks and then sell them as if they were the originals. Another form of forgery is counterfeiting, the making and using of fake money.

NORA: Supposed to? He did sign.

KROGSTAD: I left the date blank. In other words, your father would have dated his signature himself. Do you remember that?

NORA: Yes, I think—

KROGSTAD: Then I gave you the note for you to mail to your father. Isn't that so?

NORA: Yes.

KROGSTAD: And naturally you sent it at once—because only some five, six days later you brought me the note, properly signed. And with that, the money was yours.

NORA: Well, then; I've made my payments regularly, haven't I?

KROGSTAD: More or less. But—getting back to the point—those were hard times for you then, Mrs. Helmer.

NORA: Yes, they were.

KROGSTAD: Your father was very ill, I believe.

NORA: He was near the end.

KROGSTAD: He died soon after?

59 **NORA:** Yes.

KROGSTAD: Tell me, Mrs. Helmer, do you happen to recall the date of your father's death? The day of the month, I mean.

NORA: Papa died the twenty-ninth of September.

KROGSTAD: That's quite correct; I've already looked into that. And now we come to a curious thing— [*Taking out a paper.*] which I simply cannot comprehend.

NORA: Curious thing? I don't know—

KROGSTAD: This is the curious thing: that your father co-signed the note for your loan three days after his death.

NORA: How—? I don't understand.

KROGSTAD: Your father died the twenty-ninth of September. But look. Here your father dated his signature October second. Isn't that curious, Mrs. Helmer? [NORA *is silent.*] Can you explain it to me? [NORA *remains silent.*] It's also remarkable that the words "October second" and the year aren't written in your father's hand, but rather in one that I think I know. Well, it's easy to understand. Your father forgot perhaps
60 to date his signature, and then someone or other added it, a bit sloppily, before anyone knew of his death. There's nothing wrong in that. It all comes down to the signature. And there's no question about that, Mrs. Helmer. It really *was* your father who signed his own name here, wasn't it?

NORA [*after a short silence, throwing her head back and looking squarely at him*]: No, it wasn't. *I* signed Papa's name.

Reading Strategy
Reading Drama In what ways might stage directions indicating movements or gestures add tension to this dialogue?

Literary Analysis
Modern Realistic Drama and Conflict Identify three sources of external conflict against which Nora is struggling.

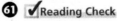

61  **Reading Check**
For whose sake does Krogstad wish to build a better life?

CUSTOMIZE INSTRUCTION FOR UNIVERSAL ACCESS

For Less Proficient Readers	For Gifted/Talented Students
Encourage students to use their artistic skills to draw or create a collage that represents the play up to this point. Students may draw, cut and paste images from magazines, or download images from appropriate Internet sources. Their work should include key images from the play as well as words that convey the play's plot and Nora's conflicts. Ask volunteers to present their work to the class with a brief explanation of their choices and arrangement of images.	Challenge students to find one or more reproductions of works of art that represent or symbolize key images or moments in the play's first act. Students may look at traditional, abstract, or popular art. The art may represent literal aspects of the play, but encourage students to find art that also suggests the play's tone or social importance. Ask students to write short essays that explain their choices. Invite them to show the art and read their essays to the class.

59 Reading Strategy

Reading Drama

- Have two volunteers read aloud the first bracketed passage.
- Ask students of what the short question-answer format of this passage reminds them. Remind students that Krogstad was trained as a lawyer.
  Answer: The dialogue is similar to the cross-examination stage of a legal trial, familiar from television shows and movies.
- Next, ask students the Reading Strategy question on p. 887: In what ways might stage directions indicating movements or gestures add tension to this dialogue?
  Answer: Stage direction might help readers picture how the characters interact. For example, stage directions might have Nora move away from or toward Krogstad, or they might identify how Krogstad changes his tone.

60 Literary Analysis

Modern Realistic Drama and Conflict

- Have the same volunteers continue reading the second bracketed passage.
- Ask students to explain why Nora's forgery was a turning point in her life.
  Possible response: By committing a crime, Nora placed herself in the power of an unethical person. The action will affect the rest of the play.
- Ask a student to respond to the Literary Analysis item on p. 887: Identify three sources of external conflict against which Nora is struggling.
  Answer: Nora is struggling against Krogstad's attempts to get her to save his job, Krogstad's threat to reveal her secret to Torvald, and the law she has broken in order to get the loan.

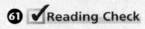

61 Reading Check

Answer: Krogstad wishes to build a better life for his sons.

62 Literary Analysis

Modern Realistic Drama and Conflict

- Have two volunteers read aloud the bracketed dialogue between Nora and Krogstad.
- Ask students to describe Nora's feelings about Krogstad.
  Possible response: She believes that he is cold-hearted and dislikes him.
- Have students respond to the first Literary Analysis item on p. 888: List three points of conflict for Nora in this scene.
  Answer: The scene touches on conflicts Nora has had involving Krogstad, her husband, and her father.

63 Literary Analysis

Modern Realistic Drama

- Make sure that students understand the distinction between Krogstad's common language and his gentlemanly gesture of bowing before leaving the room.
- Read the second bracketed passage aloud.
- Next, ask the second Literary Analysis question on p. 888: In what two ways are Krogstad's words characteristic of modern realistic drama?
  Answer: Krogstad speaks in incomplete sentences, uses common language, and interrupts himself.

KROGSTAD: Wait, now—are you fully aware that this is a dangerous confession?

NORA: Why? You'll soon get your money.

KROGSTAD: Let me ask you a question—why didn't you send the paper to your father?

NORA: That was impossible. Papa was so sick. If I'd asked him for his signature, I also would have had to tell him what the money was for. But I couldn't tell him, sick as he was, that my husband's life was in danger. That was just impossible.

KROGSTAD: Then it would have been better if you'd given up the trip abroad.

62 **NORA:** I couldn't possibly. The trip was to save my husband's life. I couldn't give that up.

KROGSTAD: But didn't you ever consider that this was a fraud against me?

NORA: I couldn't let myself be bothered by that. You weren't any concern of mine. I couldn't stand you, with all those cold complications you made, even though you knew how badly off my husband was.

KROGSTAD: Mrs. Helmer, obviously you haven't the vaguest idea of what you've involved yourself in. But I can tell you this: it was nothing more and nothing worse that I once did—and it wrecked my whole reputation.

NORA: You? Do you expect me to believe that you ever acted bravely to save your wife's life?

KROGSTAD: Laws don't inquire into motives.

NORA: Then they must be very poor laws.

KROGSTAD: Poor or not—if I introduce this paper in court, you'll be judged according to law.

NORA: This I refuse to believe. A daughter hasn't a right to protect her dying father from anxiety and care? A wife hasn't a right to save her husband's life? I don't know much about laws, but I'm sure that somewhere in the books these things are allowed. And you don't know anything about it—you who practice the law? You must be an awful lawyer, Mr. Krogstad.

63 **KROGSTAD:** Could be. But business—the kind of business we two are mixed up in—don't you think I know about that? All right. Do what you want now. But I'm telling you *this:* if I get shoved down a second time, you're going to keep me company. [*He bows and goes out through the hall.*]

NORA [*pensive*[5] *for a moment, then tossing her head*]: Oh, really! Trying to frighten me! I'm not so silly as all that. [*Begins gathering up the*

Literary Analysis
Modern Realistic Drama and Conflict List three points of conflict for Nora in this scene.

Literary Analysis
Modern Realistic Drama In what two ways are Krogstad's words characteristic of modern realistic drama?

5. **pensive** (pen' siv) *adj.* thinking deeply or seriously, often of sad or melancholy things.

64 *children's clothes, but soon stops.*] But—? No, but that's impossible! I did it out of love.

THE CHILDREN [*In the doorway, left*]: Mama, that strange man's gone out the door.

NORA: Yes, yes, I know it. But don't tell anyone about the strange man. Do you hear? Not even Papa!

THE CHILDREN. No, Mama. But now will you play again?

NORA: No, not now.

THE CHILDREN. Oh, but Mama, you promised.

NORA: Yes, but I can't now. Go inside; I have too much to do. Go in, go in, my sweet darlings. [*She herds them gently back in the room and shuts the door after them. Settling on the sofa, she takes up a piece of embroidery and makes some stitches, but soon stops abruptly.*] No! [*Throws the work aside, rises, goes to the hall door and calls out.*] Helene! Let me have the tree in here. [*Goes to the table, left, opens the table drawer, and stops again.*] No, but that's utterly impossible!

MAID [*with the Christmas tree*]: Where should I put it, ma'am?

NORA: There. The middle of the floor.

MAID: Should I bring anything else?

NORA: No, thanks. I have what I need.

[*The* MAID, *who has set the tree down, goes out.*]

65 **NORA** [*absorbed in trimming the tree*]: Candles here—and flowers here. That terrible creature! Talk, talk, talk! There's nothing to it at all. The tree's going to be lovely. I'll do anything to please you, Torvald. I'll sing for you, dance for you—

[HELMER *comes in from the hall, with a sheaf of papers under his arm.*]

NORA: Oh! You're back so soon?

HELMER: Yes. Has anyone been here?

NORA: Here? No.

HELMER: That's odd. I saw Krogstad leaving the front door.

NORA: So? Oh yes, that's true. Krogstad was here a moment.

HELMER: Nora, I can see by your face that he's been here, begging you to put in a good word for him.

NORA: Yes.

HELMER: And it was supposed to seem like your own idea? You were to hide it from me that he'd been here. He asked you that, too, didn't he?

NORA: Yes, Torvald, but—

HELMER: Nora, Nora, and you could fall for that? Talk with that sort of person and promise him anything? And then in the bargain, tell me an untruth.

Reading Strategy
Reading Drama What tone of voice do you think Nora uses here? Explain.

66 **✓Reading Check**
What kind of lawyer does Nora believe Krogstad to be?

64 Critical Thinking

Make a Judgment

- Review with students the scene between Nora and Krogstad. Make sure students understand that Nora has committed forgery.
- Call students' attention to the first bracketed passage on p. 889.
- Discuss whether the fact that Nora committed forgery "out of love" for her husband in any way excuses her actions.
  Possible response: Some readers might think that nothing excuses breaking the law and that Nora should have found another, legal way to help Torvald. Others will be more charitable toward Nora, saying that little harm was done compared with the good that resulted.

65 Reading Strategy

Reading Drama

- Remind students that stream of consciousness is a literary technique that imitates the way our minds work by offering a continual and often jumbled flow of thoughts, feelings, ideas, images, memories, and other mental elements.
- Ask students how this passage reflects the stream-of-consciousness technique and also characterizes modern realistic drama.
  Possible response: Nora is talking to herself here, so she can let her true thoughts come out. As in stream of consciousness, her thoughts are jumbled and confused.
- Ask students the Reading Strategy question on p. 889: What tone of voice do you think Nora uses here? Explain.
  Possible response: Nora is confused and anxious, so her tone may be rushed or worried.

66 ✓Reading Check

Answer: Nora believes that Krogstad must be an awful lawyer.

CUSTOMIZE INSTRUCTION FOR UNIVERSAL ACCESS

For Less Proficient Readers	For English Learners
It may help students to review the characters in the play and the choices they have made so far. Ask students to create a five-column chart and to label each column with one of the main character's names. In each column, students should identify at least one choice the character has made. Discuss students' answers as a class. Nora should, of course, be the character with the most choices so far. Talk with students about consequences of the characters' choices.	Challenge students to participate in a round-robin review of the plot. Have students sit in a circle. Then, begin by saying, "The first thing that happened in the play was ..." and ask one student to identify the first plot event. Each student in the circle should add one element of plot development. If students get their events out of order, ask them to use prepositions to help reestablish the order. For example, they might say, "Before that happened, ... and then ..."

67 ▶ **Critical Viewing**

Possible response: The room is crowded with a large, ornately decorated tree, and many presents. The children are happily playing with toys; the mother is holding the baby. Both parents are present with their children. The picture represents a happy nineteenth-century family enjoying Christmas gifts.

▲ **Critical Viewing** Which details in this illustration depict the perfect Christmas that Nora hopes to provide for her family? **[Speculate]**

ENRICHMENT: Film Connection

Ibsen on Film

Several of Henrik Ibsen's plays have been made into films, including at least three versions of *A Doll House*. Here is a list of some of them:

A Doll's House (1973), a filmed stage presentation featuring a star-studded cast, with Claire Bloom, Anthony Hopkins, Ralph Richardson, and Denholm Elliot. (This is the film that provided the photographs used in this textbook.)

A Doll's House (1973), a more cinematic version with Jane Fonda, David Warner, and Trevor Howard.

Nora Helmer (1973), German director Rainer Werner Fassbinder's eccentric, hard-hitting version of *A Doll House*.

You should preview these films before recommending them to your students.

NORA: An untruth—?

HELMER: Didn't you say that no one had been here? [*Wagging his finger.*] My little songbird must never do that again. A songbird needs a clean beak to warble with. No false notes. [*Putting his arm about her waist.*] That's the way it should be, isn't it? Yes, I'm sure of it. [*Releasing her.*] And so, enough of that. [*Sitting by the stove.*] Ah, how snug and cozy it is here. [*Leafing among his papers.*]

NORA [*busy with the tree, after a short pause*]: Torvald!

HELMER: Yes.

NORA: I'm so much looking forward to the Stenborgs' costume party, day after tomorrow.

HELMER: And I can't wait to see what you'll surprise me with.

68 **NORA:** Oh, that stupid business!

HELMER: What?

NORA: I can't find anything that's right. Everything seems so ridiculous, so inane.[6]

HELMER: So my little Nora's come to *that* recognition?

NORA [*going behind his chair, her arms resting on his back*]: Are you very busy, Torvald?

HELMER: Oh—

NORA: What papers are those?

HELMER: Bank matters.

NORA: Already?

HELMER: I've gotten full authority from the retiring management to make all necessary changes in personnel and procedure. I'll need Christmas week for that. I want to have everything in order by New Year's.

NORA: So that was the reason this poor Krogstad—

HELMER: Hm.

NORA [*still leaning on the chair and slowly stroking the nape of his neck*]: If you weren't so very busy, I would have asked you an enormous favor, Torvald.

HELMER: Let's hear. What is it?

69 **NORA:** You know, there isn't anyone who has your good taste—and I want so much to look well at the costume party. Torvald, couldn't you take over and decide what I should be and plan my costume?

HELMER: Ah, is my stubborn little creature calling for a lifeguard?

NORA: Yes, Torvald, I can't get anywhere without your help.

HELMER: All right—I'll think it over. We'll hit on something.

6. **inane** (in ān') *adj.* foolish; silly.

Literary Analysis
Modern Realistic Drama and Conflict What conflict makes everything else in Nora's life seem unimportant to her?

70  **Reading Check**

What changes at the bank is Torvald planning to make during Christmas week?

68 Literary Analysis

Modern Realistic Drama and Conflict

- Have two students read aloud the first bracketed passage on p. 891.
- Point out that this section of dialogue begins with a pair of seemingly happy observations by Nora and Torvald, but the reality of Nora's conflict soon intrudes.
- Ask the Literary Analysis question on p. 891: What conflict makes everything else in Nora's life seem unimportant to her?
  Answer: Nora's conflict with Krogstad over the forgery makes everything else seem unimportant.

69 Critical Thinking

Interpret

- Ask two students to read aloud the second bracketed passage. Suggest that the student reading Nora's lines exaggerate them.
- Ask students what Nora may be doing by showing affection toward Torvald and praising him.
  Possible response: Nora may be trying to flatter her husband in order to get him to do what she wants later.
- Ask students to predict what Nora might want Torvald to do for her.

70 ✓Reading Check

Answer: Torvald is going to fire people during Christmas week.

CUSTOMIZE INSTRUCTION FOR UNIVERSAL ACCESS

For Special Needs Students	For Gifted/Talented Students
Pair students and assign each pair half a page of dialogue. Ask students to reread the assigned dialogue and then work together to write a two- or three-sentence summary of what happened. If students need help, ask them to identify which characters were speaking and what, in general, they discussed. Ask pairs to share their summaries. Students should feel free to make corrections to their summaries.	Challenge students to create a soundtrack for Act 1 of *A Doll House*. Students may work alone or with a partner to find appropriate recordings that suit the mood, characters, and plot developments of the first act. Students should find at least three songs to match three points in the act. Also, challenge students to find a theme song for Nora. Allow students to play their selections in class and explain their choices.

71 Reading Strategy

Reading Drama

- Ask two students to read aloud the first bracketed passage.
- Have students explain why Torvald's comments about children might hit Nora especially hard. Possible response: Nora considers herself a good mother and does not want to believe that her illegal actions, done out of love, could create an "atmosphere of lies" that could infect her home.
- Ask students the Reading Strategy question on p. 892: What emotions is Torvald experiencing as he says these lines? Explain. Possible response: Torvald is probably experiencing feelings of moral outrage. He is offended and disgusted by Krogstad's deceit.
- Encourage students to predict how Torvald will react if he learns that Nora, too, has committed forgery. Possible response: He will not be forgiving of Nora.

72 Literary Analysis

Modern Realistic Drama and Conflict

- Ask students to read the second bracketed passage on p. 892.
- Have students answer the Literary Analysis question on p. 892: In what ways might Torvald's words cause Nora more inner conflict? Possible response: His comments about poisoning children with lies are particularly difficult for Nora because she loves her children and would never wish for her actions to harm them. His comments about feeling physically revolted by Krogstad make Nora suspect that he would feel the same about her if he knew her secret.

NORA: Oh, how sweet of you. [*Goes to the tree again. Pause.*] Aren't the red flowers pretty—? But tell me, was it really such a crime that this Krogstad committed?

HELMER: Forgery. Do you have any idea what that means?

NORA: Couldn't he have done it out of need?

HELMER: Yes, or thoughtlessness, like so many others. I'm not so heartless that I'd condemn a man categorically for just one mistake.

NORA: No, of course not, Torvald!

HELMER: Plenty of men have redeemed themselves by openly confessing their crimes and taking their punishment.

NORA: Punishment—?

HELMER: But now Krogstad didn't go that way. He got himself out by sharp practices, and that's the real cause of his moral breakdown.

NORA: Do you really think that would—?

71 **HELMER:** Just imagine how a man with that sort of guilt in him has to lie and cheat and deceive on all sides, has to wear a mask even with the nearest and dearest he has, even with his own wife and children. And with the children, Nora—that's where it's most horrible.

NORA: Why?

HELMER: Because that kind of atmosphere of lies infects the whole life of a home. Every breath the children take in is filled with the germs of something degenerate.

NORA [*coming closer behind him*]: Are you sure of that?

HELMER: Oh, I've seen it often enough as a lawyer. Almost everyone who goes bad early in life has a mother who's a chronic liar.

NORA: Why just—the mother?

72 **HELMER:** It's usually the mother's influence that's dominant, but the father's works in the same way, of course. Every lawyer is quite familiar with it. And still this Krogstad's been going home year in, year out, poisoning his own children with lies and pretense; that's why I call him morally lost. [*Reaching his hands out toward her.*] So my sweet little Nora must promise me never to plead his cause. Your hand on it. Come, come, what's this? Give me your hand. There, now. All settled. I can tell you it'd be impossible for me to work alongside of him. I literally feel physically revolted when I'm anywhere near such a person.

NORA [*withdraws her hand and goes to the other side of the Christmas tree*]: How hot it is here! And I've got so much to do.

HELMER [*getting up and gathering his papers*]: Yes, and I have to think about getting some of these read through before dinner. I'll think about your costume, too. And something to hang on the tree in gilt paper, I may even see about that. [*Putting his hand on her head.*] Oh you, my darling little songbird. [*He goes into his study and closes the door after him.*]

Reading Strategy
Reading Drama What emotions is Torvald experiencing as he says these lines? Explain.

Literary Analysis
Modern Realistic Drama and Conflict In what ways might Torvald's words cause Nora more inner conflict?

ASSESSMENT PRACTICE: Reading Comprehension

Comparing and Contrasting Texts (For more practice, see Test Preparation Workbook, p. 42.)

Some tests require students to compare and contrast two or more texts. Read the following excerpts from Ibsen. One is from a speech. The other is from *A Doll House.*

> I am not afraid of these so-called unpractical women; women have something in common with the true artist, just as young people have. Helmer: Nora! Are your scatterbrains off again? What if today I borrowed a thousand crowns, and you squandered them ... Nora, Nora, how like a woman!

From the texts, one can tell that men in the nineteenth century often viewed women as—

A heroic.
B childlike.
C generous.
D irresponsible.

Lead students to recognize that both Ibsen and Helmer recognize that women had a reputation for being impractical, or irresponsible. The answer is *D.*

NORA [*softly, after a silence*]: Oh, really! It isn't so. It's impossible. It must be impossible.

ANNE-MARIE [*in the doorway, left*]: The children are begging so hard to come in to Mama.

NORA: No, no, no, don't let them in to me! You stay with them, Anne-Marie.

ANNE-MARIE: Of course, ma'am. [*Closes the door.*]

NORA [*pale with terror*]: Hurt my children—? Poison my home? [*A moment's pause; then she tosses her head.*] That's not true. Never in all the world.

Review and Assess

Thinking About Act One

1. **Respond:** Considering the Helmers' current situation, do you feel more sympathy for Torvald or for Nora? Explain.
2. **(a) Recall:** What are some of the pet names Torvald uses for Nora? **(b) Infer:** What does Torvald's use of these pet names suggest about his attitude toward his wife? **(c) Assess:** Do you think these nicknames represent Nora's entire personality? Explain.
3. **(a) Recall:** What lie concerning the macaroons does Nora tell Torvald? **(b) Interpret:** How would you describe Torvald's treatment of Nora as he questions her about the macaroons? **(c) Draw Conclusions:** What does Torvald's attitude reveal about the relationship he has with his wife?
4. **(a) Recall:** How does Nora behave toward her husband? **(b) Compare and Contrast:** How is Nora's behavior different when she is around Krogstad? **(c) Make a Judgment:** Do you think Nora is "just a child" and "incapable of anything serious," as others seem to believe? Explain.
5. **(a) Recall:** Which details in the first act indicate that Nora and her husband do not know each other very well? **(b) Interpret:** What is ironic about Nora's comment that if Torvald found out her secret, it "would just ruin [their] relationship"?
6. **Draw Conclusions:** What developments in Act One suggest that Nora is in trouble? Explain.
7. **Relate:** Based on the behavior of the characters during Act One, what differences can you see between our society and the one depicted in the play?

ASSESS

Answers for p. 893

Review and Assess

1. Possible response: Nora is a good-hearted person who has made a mistake that may have terrible consequences. However, the morally upright Torvald has been deceived by his wife.
2. **(a)** Torvald's pet names include *squirrel, little prodigal, my sweet tooth, skylark, little songbird,* and *my stubborn little creature.* **(b)** The nicknames suggest that he thinks Nora is childlike and serves as a plaything. **(c)** The nicknames reflect the part of Nora that Torvald wants to see, but they do not represent her entire personality.
3. **(a)** Nora tells Torvald that she has not eaten or bought macaroons. **(b)** Torvald seems parental when he questions Nora. **(c)** Torvald's attitude suggests that he feels superior toward his wife.
4. **(a)** Nora is playful and flirtatious with her husband. **(b)** Nora is more adult with Krogstad; she acts superior and cold. **(c)** Nora is a good mother and has taken care of her husband and father; but she is shallow, naive, and ignorant.
5. **(a)** Nora assumes that Torvald would defend her and pay off her debt if Krogstad were to tell him her secret. Torvald treats Nora like a child, particularly around money issues. He does not know how she has handled the household affairs. **(b)** The irony is that some would say that their relationship is already ruined because it is based on lies.
6. Nora lies on several occasions; she is insincere toward Torvald and haughty toward Mrs. Linde; she is worried by what Krogstad knows about her; and she will not see her children after Krogstad leaves.
7. In modern society, marriages tend to be between equals. Women today can control their own money and work outside the home.

ENRICHMENT: Further Reading

Other Works by Henrik Ibsen

We strongly encourage you to review any selection before assigning or recommending it to students.

Six Plays (A Doll's House, Ghosts, An Enemy of the People, Rosmersholm, Hedda Gabler, and *The Master Builder),* translated by Eva Le Gallienne

Take It to the Net

Visit PHSchool.com for more information on Henrik Ibsen.

Review and Assess

1. Possible response: **Ordinary language:** informal language such as "pooh" and "wee"; characters changing train of thought in mid-sentence or letting ideas trail off **Realistic characters:** the bitter Dr. Rank, the hard-working Mrs. Linde **Controversial issues:** women taking financial matters into their own hands; marital relationships
2. **(a)** Nora is frustrated by having so few ways to make the money she needs. **(b)** She pretends to be doing housework when she is earning money doing copying; she flatters her husband into giving her money. **(c)** Her strategies seem realistic, especially for the time period.
3. **(a)** Nora has owed Krogstad money for several years. **(b)** Krogstad threatens to tell Torvald about the debt and Nora's forgery if she does not help him keep his job at Torvald's bank.
4. **(a)** Torvald believes that an "atmosphere of lies" will poison a family and harm the children. **(b)** Nora would lose Torvald's love, respect, financial support, and probably her children as well.
5. **(a)** Stage directions help a reader understand the physical relationships between the characters onstage. They also give hints about how certain lines are said. **(b)** For example, when Nora pulls Mrs. Linde down onto the sofa next to her, the reader can tell something important is going to be said.
6. On p. 888, when Nora says "I refuse to believe ...," she might be standing with her hands on her hips and speaking angrily. She might point at Krogstad when she calls him "an awful lawyer."
7. Possible response: A counselor might suggest that they be honest with each other, express feelings, and avoid falling into parent and child roles.

Review and Assess

Literary Analysis

Modern Realistic Drama

1. Use an organizer like this one to record details that establish *A Doll House* as a **modern realistic drama.**

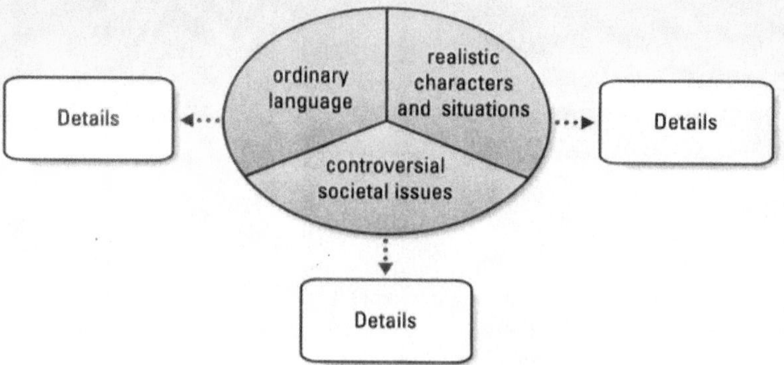

2. (a) What limitations on women does Nora find especially frustrating? (b) What strategies does she use to break through these restrictions? (c) Do you find her methods realistic? Explain.

Connecting Literary Elements

3. (a) What **conflict** has existed between Krogstad and Nora for the past few years? (b) What new circumstances does Krogstad introduce that intensify this conflict?
4. (a) What is Torvald's attitude about an "atmosphere of lies" in the home? (b) What would Nora lose if he discovered her secrets?

Reading Strategy

Reading Drama

5. (a) Explain how stage directions help clarify the relationships between characters when **reading a drama.** (b) Identify one example from the play that supports your response.
6. Select a passage in Act One that has no stage directions, and then add directions that make the passage easier to visualize.

Extend Understanding

7. **Psychology Connection:** What advice might a relationship expert offer Nora and Torvald?

Quick Review

Modern realistic drama reflects the way people actually talk and depicts characters and situations as they really are. It often addresses controversial issues and questions society's assumptions.

Conflict, which can be internal or external, is the struggle between two opposing forces.

When you **read drama,** use stage directions to help you picture the play as it would be performed on stage.

 ***Take It to the Net***

PHSchool.com

Take the interactive self-test online to check your understanding of this selection.

TEACHING RESOURCES

The following resources can be used to enrich or extend the instruction for pp. 894–895.

Vocabulary

- **Selection Support:** Build Vocabulary, p. 165
- **Vocabulary and Spelling Practice Book** (Use this booklet for skills instruction.)

Grammar

- **Selection Support:** Grammar and Style, p. 166
- **Writing and Grammar,** Diamond Level, p. 412
- **Daily Language Practice Transparencies**

Writing

- **Performance Assess. and Portfolio Mgmt.,** p. 16
- **Writing and Grammar iText CD-ROM**

BLOCK SCHEDULING: Resources marked with this symbol provide varied instruction during 90-minute blocks.

Integrate Language Skills

❶ Vocabulary Development Lesson

Word Analysis: Coined Words

Coined words are manufactured, often by combining existing words. *Spendthrift* combines *spend* and *thrift* in a new word meaning "one who spends money carelessly." Replace each phrase with a lively coined word.

1. snow-covered trees 2. someone who gossips

Spelling Strategy

Adding a prefix to a word never changes the spelling of the base word. For each item, combine the prefix and the root to form an existing word.

1. *mis-* + understand 2. *dis-* + honest

Concept Development: Antonyms

Choose the letter of the word in each item below that is opposite in meaning to the first word.

1. spendthrift: (a) miser, (b) shopper
2. squandering: (a) spending, (b) saving
3. prodigal: (a) penny-pincher, (b) party-giver
4. indiscreet: (a) shocking, (b) prudent
5. frivolous: (a) wise, (b) foolish
6. contraband: (a) loot, (b) purchases
7. subordinate: (a) superior, (b) inferior

❷ Grammar and Style Lesson

Compound Predicates

A predicate states the action or condition of the subject. A **compound predicate** has two or more verbs or verb phrases that relate to the same subject. Compound predicates are usually connected by a conjunction, such as *and* or *or*.

S V V
"The *cat* **came** in and **tore** everything to shreds. . . ."

Practice Copy the examples below. In each one, circle the subject and underline the verbs or verb phrases in each compound predicate.

1. *The maid shows in Mrs. Linde . . . and shuts the door after her.*
2. "He'll join the bank right after New Year's and start getting a huge salary. . . ."
3. ". . . [he] scuttles about breathlessly . . . and then maneuvers his victims into some sort of key position. . . ."
4. *. . . she takes up a piece of embroidery and makes some stitches, but soon stops abruptly.*
5. *Nora . . . breaks out into quiet laughter and claps her hands.*

Writing Application Write two sentences about Nora's situation in *A Doll House*. Use compound predicates in each sentence, circling the subject and underlining the verbs or verb phrases.

❸ Extension Activities

Writing Write a **monologue** in which Nora confesses her secrets to Torvald. Use details that reflect her personality and experiences. Rehearse your piece and present it to your class.

Research and Technology With a partner, make a **rendering of the set** from Act One using art supplies or computer software. Display your work for the class. **[Group Activity]**

WG *Prentice Hall Writing and Grammar Connection: Diamond Level, Chapter 18, Section 1*

ASSESSMENT RESOURCES

The following resources can be used to assess students' knowledge and skills.

Selection Assessment

- **Formal Assessment,** pp. 148–150
- **Open-Book Tests,** pp. 124–126
- **Test Bank Software**

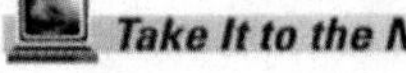

Take It to the Net

Visit PHSchool.com for self-tests on the selections.

Writing Rubric

- **Performance Assess. and Portfolio Mgmt.,** p. 16

For additional diagnostics and remediation for skills covered in this grouping, use materials from the Prentice Hall Assessment System.

EXTEND

Answers for p. 895

❶ Vocabulary Development

Word Analysis: Coined Words

1. snowshoulders 2. yakspreader

Spelling Strategy

1. misunderstand 2. dishonest

Concept Development: Antonyms

1. a 2. b 3. a 4. b 5. a 6. b 7. a

❷ Grammar and Style

Practice

1. (maid) shows in, shuts
2. (He) will join, will start
3. (he) scuttles, maneuvers
4. (she) takes, makes, stops
5. (Nora) breaks out, claps

Writing Application

Possible response:
(Nora) takes sewing and copying jobs and pays her debt. (Torvald) works in his study and has no idea of Nora's problems.

10TH GRADE For support in teaching the Grammar and Style Lesson to tenth graders, use **Writing and Grammar,** Platinum Level, Chapter 19, Section 1.

❸ Extension Activities

Writing

- Encourage students to reread Nora's speeches.
- Have students attempt to capture Nora's rhythm, vocabulary, and style, and urge them to rehearse.
- Use the rubric in **Performance Assessment and Portfolio Management,** p. 16, to evaluate students' work.

CUSTOMIZE INSTRUCTION For Universal Access

To address different learning styles, use the following activities in the **Extension Activities** booklet, p. 42.

- For Interpersonal and Bodily/Kinesthetic Learners, use Activity 5.
- For Logical/Mathematical and Verbal/Linguistic Learners, use Activity 6.
- For Verbal/Linguistic Learners, use Activity 7.

A Doll House, Act Two

Lesson Objectives

1. **To analyze and respond to literary elements**
   - Literary Analysis: Characterization in Drama
   - Connecting Literary Elements: Protagonist and Antagonist
2. **To read, comprehend, analyze, and critique drama**
   - Reading Strategy: Inferring Beliefs of the Period
   - Reading Check Questions
   - Review and Assess Questions
   - Assessment Practice (ATE)
3. **To develop word analysis skills, fluency, and systematic vocabulary**
   - Vocabulary Development Lesson: Latin Prefix *re-*
4. **To understand and apply written and oral language conventions**
   - Spelling Strategy
   - Writing Lesson: Persuasive Essay (after Act III)
   - Grammar and Style Lesson: Commas After Introductory Words
5. **To understand and apply appropriate writing and research strategies**
   - Extension Activity: Letter
6. **To understand and apply listening and speaking strategies**
   - Extension Activity: Radio Play

10TH GRADE TEACHING A TENTH-GRADE COURSE

The literature in this section can be taught as part of a rich, balanced world literature course for tenth-grade students. For a full outline of such a course, see pp. T46–T48 in Volume I of this Teacher's Edition.

STEP-BY-STEP TEACHING GUIDE	PACING GUIDE
PRETEACH	
Motivate Students and Provide Background	
Use the Motivation activity (ATE p. 896)	5 min.
Introduce the Concepts	
Introduce the Literary Analysis and Reading Strategy concepts (SE/ATE p. 896) A	15 min.
Pronounce the vocabulary words and read their definitions (SE p. 896)	5 min.
TEACH	
Monitor Comprehension	
Informally monitor comprehension by circulating while students read independently or in groups A	50 min.
Monitor students' comprehension with the Reading Check notes (SE/ATE pp. 897, 901, 903, 905, 907, 909, 911, 913, 915, 917)	as students read
Develop vocabulary with the Vocabulary notes (SE pp. 900, 901, 904, 907, 914; ATE p. 907)	as students read
Develop Understanding	
Develop students' understanding of characterization in drama with the Literary Analysis annotations (SE/ATE pp. 897, 898, 904, 905, 906, 909, 911, 914, 916, 918; ATE pp. 902, 913, 917) A	10 min.
Develop students' ability to infer beliefs of the period by using the Reading Strategy annotations (SE/ATE pp. 898, 900, 901, 903, 907, 910, 915; ATE p. 908)	10 min.
ASSESS	
Assess Mastery	
Assess students' mastery of the Reading Strategy and Literary Analysis concepts by having them answer the Review and Assess questions (SE/ATE p. 920)	20 min.
Use one or more of the print, software, or transparency Assessment Resources* (ATE p. 921) A	up to 45 min.
EXTEND	
Apply Understanding	
Have students complete the Vocabulary Development Lesson and the Grammar and Style Lesson (SE p. 921) A	20 min.
Apply students' understanding of the selection, using one or more of the Extension Activities (SE p. 921)	20–90 min.

ACCELERATED INSTRUCTION: Use the strategies and activities identified with an A.

10TH GRADE TEACHING TENTH-GRADE STUDENTS For support in teaching tenth graders, see the Step-by-Step Teaching notes identified with this icon.

UNIVERSAL ACCESS

- ● = Below-Level Students
- ▲ = On-Level Students
- ■ = Above-Level Students

Time and Resource Manager

Reading Level: Average
Average Number of Instructional Days: 5

RESOURCES		
PRINT	**TRANSPARENCIES**	**TECHNOLOGY**
• **Beyond Literature,** Career Connection: Theatrical Set Designer, p. 43 ▲ ■		
• **Selection Support Workbook:** ● ▲ ■ Literary Analysis, p. 172 Reading Strategy, p. 171 Build Vocabulary, p. 169	• **Literary Analysis and Reading Transparencies,** pp. 85 and 86 ● ▲ ■	
		• **Listening to Literature** ● ▲ ■ Audiocassettes Audio CDs
• **Literary Analysis for Enrichment,** p. 43 ■		
• **Formal Assessment:** Selection Test, pp. 151–153 ● ▲ ■ • **Open-Book Tests,** pp. 127–129 ● ▲ ■ • **Performance Assessment and Portfolio Management,** p. 28 ● ▲ ■ • PRENTICE HALL ASSESSMENT SYSTEM ● ▲ ■	• PRENTICE HALL ASSESSMENT SYSTEM ● ▲ ■ **Skills Practice Answers and Explanations on Transparencies**	• **Test Bank Software** ● ▲ ■
• **Selection Support Workbook:** ● ▲ ■ Grammar and Style, p. 170 • **Writing and Grammar,** Diamond Level ● ▲ ■ • **Extension Activities,** p. 43 ● ▲ ■	• **Daily Language Practice Transparencies** ● ▲	• **Writing and Grammar iText CD-ROM** ● ▲ ■ ***Take It to the Net*** PHSchool.com

BLOCK SCHEDULING: Use one 90-minute class period to preteach the selection(s) and have students read them. Use a second 90-minute class period to assess students' mastery of skills and have them complete one of the Extension Activities.

Step-by-Step Teaching Guide for p. 896

Motivation

Act One ends with Nora afraid to see her children in case she "poisons" them or her home. Have students brainstorm a list of Nora's priorities, and write their suggestions on the board (for example, healthy children, happy husband, festive Christmas). Discuss conflicts of interest that Nora faces in Act One to secure these priorities.

❶ Literary Analysis

Characterization in Drama

- To illustrate the role stage directions can play in characterization, have students reread the scene on p. 882 in which Nora plays hide-and-seek with her children. Discuss how the stage directions show Nora's vigor and vitality.
- Use the Characterization in Drama transparency in **Literary Analysis and Reading Transparencies,** p. 85, to enhance students' understanding of characterization.

❷ Reading Strategy

Inferring Beliefs of the Period

- Explain that to infer beliefs of nineteenth-century Europeans, readers must focus on the clues in the play. Tell students that in this play, characters' ideas about money, women's roles, respectability, and love affect their actions.
- Call attention to the graphic organizer on p. 896. Explain that using the organizer as they read will help students focus on details that reveal characters' values.

Vocabulary Development

- Pronounce each vocabulary word for students, and read the definitions as a class. Have students identify any words with which they are already familiar.

 ***E-Teach***

Visit e-Teach at PHSchool.com for teachers' essays on how to teach, with questions and answers.

Prepare to Read

A Doll House, Act Two

❶ Literary Analysis

Characterization in Drama

Characterization is the means by which a writer reveals a character's personality. In most fiction, characterization is developed through one or more of the following methods:

- direct statements about a character
- a character's actions, thoughts, or comments
- comments about a character made by other characters

Along with these methods, **characterization in drama** uses the additional elements of stage directions and dialogue. Look for these methods as you read Act Two of *A Doll House.*

Connecting Literary Elements

In a literary work, the main character, called the **protagonist,** is central to the action and often the one with whom the audience sympathizes. The **antagonist** is the character or force in conflict with the protagonist.

In *A Doll House,* Nora Helmer is the protagonist. Instead of a single antagonist, however, Nora encounters various adversaries. Note Nora's many antagonists as you read.

❷ Reading Strategy

Inferring Beliefs of the Period

Inferring beliefs of the period means observing how social, religious, and cultural practices of a time period affect the characters and their choices. To infer the beliefs of the period as you read:

- Notice how husbands and wives relate to each other.
- Pay attention to the role of women in society.
- Look for clues to social, religious, or cultural practices.

Use an organizer like the one shown to infer the beliefs of a period.

What a Character Says or Does

Anne-Marie had given her daughter up for adoption.

↕

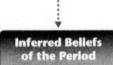

Inferred Beliefs of the Period

Society provided little or no assistance to young, unmarried mothers.

Vocabulary Development

proclaiming (prō klām′ iŋ) *v.* announcing publicly and loudly (p. 900)

intolerable (in täl′ ər ə bəl) *adj.* unbearable; painful; cruel (p. 901)

impulsive (im pul′ siv) *adj.* sudden and unthinking (p. 904)

tactless (takt′ lis) *adj.* unskilled in dealing with people (p. 904)

excruciating (eks kro͞o′ shē āt′ iŋ) *adj.* causing intense mental or bodily pain (p. 904)

retribution (re′ trə byo͞o′ shən) *n.* punishment; revenge (p. 907)

disreputable (dis rep′ yo͞o tə bəl) *adj.* not fit to be seen or approved (p. 914)

TEACHING RESOURCES

The following resources can be used to enrich or extend the instruction for p. 896.

Background

Beyond Literature, p. 43 ■

 ***Take It to the Net***

Visit PHSchool.com for background on the author.

Literary Analysis

Literary Analysis and Reading Transparencies, Characterization in Drama, p. 85

Selection Support: Literary Analysis, p. 172 ■

Reading

Literary Analysis and Reading Transparencies, Inferring Beliefs of the Period, p. 86

■ **BLOCK SCHEDULING:** Resources marked with this symbol provide varied instruction during 90-minute blocks.

❶ Review and Anticipate

Years ago, Nora secretly borrowed money from Krogstad to help her husband Torvald recover from a serious illness. Desperate for a signature to guarantee the loan but reluctant to disturb her dying father, she forged her father's name on the document. In Act One, Nora shares her secret with Mrs. Linde, her childhood friend who hopes to get a position at Torvald's bank. Nora persuades Torvald to hire Mrs. Linde, but he can do so only by firing Krogstad. Now Krogstad threatens to expose Nora's secret if she does not urge Torvald to keep him employed at the bank. Will Krogstad expose Nora's secrets to Torvald? Will Nora buy herself enough time to solve her dilemma without involving Torvald? Find the answers to these questions in Act Two.

ACT TWO

Same room. Beside the piano the Christmas tree now stands stripped of ornament, burned-down candle stubs on its ragged branches. NORA's *street clothes lie on the sofa.* NORA, *alone in the room, moves restlessly about; at last she stops at the sofa and picks up her coat.*

❷ **NORA** [*dropping the coat again*]: Someone's coming! [*Goes toward the door, listens.*] No—there's no one. Of course—nobody's coming today, Christmas Day—or tomorrow, either. But maybe—[*Opens the door and looks out.*] No, nothing in the mailbox. Quite empty. [*Coming forward.*] What nonsense! He won't do anything serious. Nothing terrible could happen. It's impossible. Why, I have three small children.

[ANNE-MARIE, *with a large carton, comes in from the room to the left.*]

ANNE-MARIE: Well, at last I found the box with the masquerade clothes.

NORA: Thanks. Put it on the table.

ANNE-MARIE [*does so*]: But they're all pretty much of a mess.

NORA: Ahh! I'd love to rip them in a million pieces!

ANNE-MARIE: Oh, mercy, they can be fixed right up. Just a little patience.

NORA: Yes, I'll go get Mrs. Linde to help me.

ANNE-MARIE: Out again now? In this nasty weather? Miss Nora will catch cold—get sick.

NORA: Oh, worse things could happen— How are the children?

Literary Analysis
Characterization in Drama What does Nora's comment to herself reveal about her character?

❸ **✔Reading Check**
What is in the box Anne-Marie brings to Nora?

TEACHING RESOURCES

The following resources can be used to enrich or extend the instruction for pp. 897–919.

Literary Analysis

- **Selection Support:** Literary Analysis, p.172
- **Literary Analysis and Reading Transparencies,** Characterization in Drama, p. 85 ■

Reading

- **Selection Support:** Reading Strategy, p. 171; Build Vocabulary, p. 169 ■
- **Listening to Literature Audiocassettes**
- **Listening to Literature Audio CDs**

■ **BLOCK SCHEDULING:** Resources marked with this symbol provide varied instruction during 90-minute blocks.

TEACH

Step-by-Step Teaching Guide for pp. 897–919

Teaching Tenth-Grade Students

10TH GRADE Write each character's name on the board. Have students list comments and actions from the first act that reveal each character's personality. Students can use these lists to help predict events in Act Two.

❶ About the Selection

Act Two focuses on Nora's increasing burden, the realization that her family life can be destroyed by the knowledge that Krogstad possesses. The act also contains two surprise announcements that promise to influence the outcome of the play. Perhaps most important, readers begin to sense a subtle yet critical shift in Nora's attitude toward her marriage.

❷ Literary Analysis

Characterization in Drama

- Ask a student to read aloud the bracketed passage on p. 897. Remind students that "he" is Krogstad, and ask: On the basis of what you already know about Krogstad, will Nora's having three young children deter him from revealing her crime?
  Possible response: Krogstad seems desperate, so he will probably reveal Nora's crime.
- Have students respond to the Literary Analysis question on p. 897: What does Nora's comment to herself reveal about her character?
  Possible response: Nora reveals that she is naive.

❸ ✔Reading Check

Answer: The masquerade clothes are in the box.

❹ Reading Strategy

Inferring Beliefs of the Period

- Review with students the Reading Strategy instruction on p. 896.
- Then, read aloud the bracketed passage.
- Explain that this kind of frank talk between two female characters would have scandalized the audiences of Ibsen's time, as would Anne-Marie's matter-of-factness about having had a child outside of marriage and keeping in touch with her.
- Ask students the Reading Strategy question on p. 898: In what ways does Anne-Marie imply that religion and marriage were significant social concerns at this time?
Answer: Although Anne-Marie gave up her child in order to keep her job, she is proud that her daughter has been confirmed and has married.

❺ Literary Analysis

Characterization in Drama

- Point out to students that Nora's speeches will sound a bit more erratic than in the previous act. She talks at length to herself and interrupts herself.
- Have students silently read the bracketed passage. Then, ask students to respond to the Literary Analysis item on p. 898: Identify three of Nora's thoughts that reveal her anxiety over her situation.
Possible response: Nora is full of nervous wishing ("Oh, if only ..."); she calls her thoughts "craziness" because she wants to deny the possibility that her worries may come true; she tells herself to "let it go" in an attempt to relax.

ANNE-MARIE: The poor mites are playing with their Christmas presents, but—

NORA: Do they ask for me much?

ANNE-MARIE: They're so used to having Mama around, you know.

NORA: Yes, but Anne-Marie, I *can't* be together with them as much as I was.

ANNE-MARIE: Well, small children get used to anything.

NORA: You think so? Do you think they'd forget their mother if she was gone for good?

ANNE-MARIE: Oh, mercy—gone for good!

NORA: Wait, tell me, Anne-Marie—I've wondered so often—how could you ever have the heart to give your child over to strangers?

ANNE-MARIE: But I had to, you know, to become little Nora's nurse.

NORA: Yes, but how could you *do* it?

ANNE-MARIE: When I could get such a good place? A girl who's poor and who's gotten in trouble is glad enough for that. Because that slippery fish, he didn't do a thing for me, you know.

❹ **NORA:** But your daughter's surely forgotten you.

ANNE-MARIE: Oh, she certainly has not. She's written to me, both when she was confirmed and when she was married.

NORA [*clasping her about the neck*]: You old Anne-Marie, you were a good mother for me when I was little.

ANNE-MARIE: Poor little Nora, with no other mother but me.

NORA: And if the babies didn't have one, then I know that you'd— What silly talk! [*Opening the carton.*] Go in to them. Now I'll have to— Tomorrow you can see how lovely I'll look.

ANNE-MARIE: Oh, there won't be anyone at the party as lovely as Miss Nora. [*She goes off into the room, left.*]

❺ **NORA** [*begins unpacking the box, but soon throws it aside*]: Oh, if I dared to go out. If only nobody would come. If only nothing would happen here while I'm out. What craziness—nobody's coming. Just don't think. This muff—needs a brushing. Beautiful gloves, beautiful gloves. Let it go. Let it go! One, two, three, four, five, six— [*With a cry.*] Oh, there they are! [*Poises to move toward the door, but remains irresolutely standing.* MRS. LINDE *enters from the hall, where she has removed her street clothes.*]

NORA: Oh, it's you, Kristine. There's no one else out there? How good that you've come.

MRS. LINDE: I hear you were up asking for me.

NORA: Yes, I just stopped by. There's something you really can help me with. Let's get settled on the sofa. Look, there's going to be a costume party tomorrow evening at the Stenborgs' right above us, and now

Reading Strategy
Inferring Beliefs of the Period In what way does Anne-Marie imply that religion and marriage were significant social concerns at this time?

Literary Analysis
Characterization in Drama Identify three of Nora's thoughts that reveal her anxiety over her situation.

ENRICHMENT: Literature Connection

Ibsen's Method

Ibsen once offered the following explanation of how he developed characters for his plays:

> Before I write down one word, I have to have the character in mind through and through. I must penetrate into the last wrinkle of his soul. I always proceed from the individual; the stage setting, the dramatic ensemble, all that comes naturally and does not cause me any worry, as soon as I am certain of the individual in every aspect of his humanity. But I have to have his exterior in mind also, down to the last button, how he stands and walks, how he conducts himself, what his voice sounds like. Then I do not let him go until his fate is fulfilled.

Tell students to keep this method of creating characters in mind as they read the second act. Have them evaluate how successful Ibsen has been in capturing his characters "down to the last button."

6

Lady with a Fur Muff, Theodore Bruckner, Whitford & Hughes, London, UK

7 **Critical Viewing** ▶ In what ways might Nora dress like the woman in this painting? **[Interpret]**

6 Background

Art

Lady with a Fur Muff, by Theodore Bruckner

A painter of frescoes, portraits, and genre subjects, Theodore Bruckner (1870–1921) lived most of his life in his native Vienna. His best works were his portraits of ordinary people, but he was also well known for the theatrical stage sets he designed and painted. Bruckner's works were popular enough in his day to be displayed in exhibits in Europe's capital cities.

Use the following questions for discussion:

- How would you characterize the mood of this painting?
  Possible response: The mood of the painting is dark and somber.
- Why is this painting an appropriate illustration for Act Two of *A Doll House?*
  Possible responses: The subject of the painting—a richly dressed woman—appears serious, as if contemplating something important. The painting itself is dark, which is appropriate because the play takes a darker turn in Act Two.

7 ▶Critical Viewing

Possible response: Nora lives in a cold climate, so she probably wears warm clothes similar to those shown in the painting. Nora also likes herself and her family to be well dressed, so her clothing might look similar to the elegant attire of the woman in the painting.

CUSTOMIZE INSTRUCTION FOR UNIVERSAL ACCESS

For Less Proficient Readers	For English Learners	For Advanced Readers
Read aloud the vocabulary words on p. 896 to demonstrate correct pronunciation. Ask volunteers to read aloud the definitions. Guide students toward understanding that the words refer to punishment, pain, and sudden action. Challenge students to predict how Act Two will unfold, given the vocabulary words.	Review with students the list of vocabulary words on p. 896. Read aloud the words and their definitions. Point out that all the words have suffixes and all but *tactless* have prefixes. Allow students time to use a dictionary to identify the meanings of the prefixes, roots, and suffixes of the words.	Have students review the vocabulary words on p. 896. Challenge them to use all the words to write short vignettes or scenes. The scene may take place anywhere and may be in narrative play form. Tell students to notice how the vocabulary words affect their scenes' settings, characterizations, and moods.

8 Critical Thinking

Infer

- Have two students read aloud the bracketed passage beginning on p. 898; one student should read Nora's lines, and one student should read Mrs. Linde's lines.
- Then, ask why Nora relies on Mrs. Linde to sew her costume. Answer: Mrs. Linde has had to work at such jobs as sewing, so she is probably quite good at it.
- Ask: What do these circumstances reveal about the women's respective abilities and lifestyles? Answer: Nora and Mrs. Linde are in different social positions. Nora, as a woman of the upper-middle class, has not needed to earn a living. Mrs. Linde has had to work to survive.

9 Reading Strategy

Inferring Beliefs of the Period

- Ask students to review the bracketed passage.
- Then, have them respond to the Reading Strategy item on p. 900: Identify two talents or accomplishments that upper-class society of that time expected of women like Nora. Possible response: Upper-class women were expected to have at least one musical talent, such as singing or dancing, and they were expected to run their households efficiently and tastefully. Women were also expected to have children.
- Discuss with students whether Nora has met these expectations, and encourage them to predict what may change as the story progresses.

10 Background

Careful Language

Women, and many men, in the 1800s used careful, roundabout language when talking about sexual matters. According to Nora, Dr. Rank's condition was inherited from his loose-living father.

8

Torvald wants me to go as a Neapolitan[1] peasant girl and dance the tarantella that I learned in Capri.[2]

MRS. LINDE: Really, are you giving a whole performance?

NORA: Torvald says yes, I should. See, here's the dress. Torvald had it made for me down there; but now it's all so tattered that I just don't know—

MRS. LINDE: Oh, we'll fix that up in no time. It's nothing more than the trimmings—they're a bit loose here and there. Needle and thread? Good, now we have what we need.

NORA: Oh, how sweet of you!

9

MRS. LINDE [*sewing*]: So you'll be in disguise tomorrow, Nora. You know what? I'll stop by then for a moment and have a look at you all dressed up. But listen, I've absolutely forgotten to thank you for that pleasant evening yesterday.

NORA [*getting up and walking about*]: I don't think it was as pleasant as usual yesterday. You should have come to town a bit sooner, Kristine— Yes, Torvald really knows how to give a home elegance and charm.

MRS. LINDE: And you do, too, if you ask me. You're not your father's daughter for nothing. But tell me, is Dr. Rank always so down in the mouth as yesterday?

10

NORA: No, that was quite an exception. But he goes around critically ill all the time—tuberculosis of the spine, poor man. You know, his father was a disgusting thing who kept mistresses and so on—and that's why the son's been sickly from birth.

MRS. LINDE [*lets her sewing fall to her lap*]: But my dearest Nora, how do you know about such things?

NORA [*walking more jauntily*]: Hmp! When you've had three children, then you've had a few visits from—from women who know something of medicine, and they tell you this and that.

MRS. LINDE [*resumes sewing; a short pause*]: Does Dr. Rank come here every day?

NORA: Every blessed day. He's Torvald's best friend from childhood, and *my* good friend, too. Dr. Rank almost belongs to this house.

MRS. LINDE: But tell me—is he quite sincere? I mean, doesn't he rather enjoy flattering people?

NORA: Just the opposite. Why do you think that?

MRS. LINDE: When you introduced us yesterday, he was proclaiming that he'd often heard my name in this house; but later I noticed that your husband hadn't the slightest idea who I really was. So how could Dr. Rank—?

Reading Strategy
Inferring Beliefs of the Period Identify two talents or accomplishments that upper-class society of that time expected of women like Nora.

proclaiming (prō klām′ iŋ) *v.* announcing publicly and loudly

1. **Neapolitan** (nē ə päl′ ət ′n) of Naples, a seaport in southern Italy.
2. **Capri** (kä prē′) island near the entrance to the Bay of Naples.

ENRICHMENT: Science Connection

Dr. Rank's Illness: Real or Symbolic?

Ibsen has given the character of Dr. Rank a fatal disease, which he and the characters call spinal tuberculosis. Spinal tuberculosis is a condition caused by tubercular bacteria. It is also called Pott's disease after the English doctor who studied it. Spinal tuberculosis affects a person's spine by attacking the vertebrae; it causes great pain and, in some cases, a deforming hunchbacked condition in the patient. The disease can also cause paralysis. Today, chemotherapy is used to treat spinal tuberculosis, but no effective treatments existed in the nineteenth century.

Dr. Rank's disease, however, is probably not tuberculosis. Both he and Nora talk about how he might have gotten the disease from his father, but tuberculosis is not inherited; it is caused by bacteria. Students should understand that the true nature of Dr. Rank's illness is not very important. The illness is really a symbol. It is another example of what Torvald was talking about in Act One—how the errors of the parents cause misfortune and pain for the children.

11 **NORA:** But it's all true, Kristine. You see, Torvald loves me beyond words, and, as he puts it, he'd like to keep me all to himself. For a long time he'd almost be jealous if I even mentioned any of my old friends back home. So of course I dropped that. But with Dr. Rank I talk a lot about such things, because he likes hearing about them.

Reading Strategy
Inferring Beliefs of the Period What does Nora suggest about Torvald's personality?

MRS. LINDE: Now listen, Nora; in many ways you're still like a child. I'm a good deal older than you, with a little more experience. I'll tell you something: you ought to put an end to all this with Dr. Rank.

NORA: What should I put an end to?

MRS. LINDE: Both parts of it, I think. Yesterday you said something about a rich admirer who'd provide you with money—

NORA: Yes, one who doesn't exist—worse luck. So?

MRS. LINDE: Is Dr. Rank well off?

NORA: Yes, he is.

MRS. LINDE: With no dependents?

NORA: No, no one. But—?

MRS. LINDE: And he's over here every day?

NORA: Yes, I told you that.

MRS. LINDE: How can a man of such refinement be so grasping?

NORA: I don't follow you at all.

12 **MRS. LINDE:** Now don't try to hide it, Nora. You think I can't guess who loaned you the forty-eight hundred crowns?

NORA: Are you out of your mind? How could you think such a thing! A friend of ours, who comes here every single day. What an intolerable situation that would have been!

intolerable (in täl′ ər ə bəl) *adj.* unbearable; painful; cruel

MRS. LINDE: Then it really wasn't him.

NORA: No, absolutely not. It never even crossed my mind for a moment— And he had nothing to lend in those days; his inheritance came later.

MRS. LINDE: Well, I think that was a stroke of luck for you, Nora dear.

NORA: No, it never would have occurred to me to ask Dr. Rank— Still, I'm quite sure that if I had asked him—

MRS. LINDE: Which you won't, of course.

NORA: No, of course not. I can't see that I'd ever need to. But I'm quite positive that if I talked to Dr. Rank—

MRS. LINDE: Behind your husband's back?

NORA: I've got to clear up this other thing; *that's* also behind his back. I've got to clear it all up.

MRS. LINDE: Yes, I was saying that yesterday, but—

NORA [*pacing up and down*]: A man handles these problems so much better than a woman—

13 ✓**Reading Check**
From what illness is Dr. Rank suffering?

CUSTOMIZE INSTRUCTION FOR UNIVERSAL ACCESS

For Special Needs Students	For English Learners
Ask each student to keep an informal journal in which to respond to the play. Encourage students to respond on a personal level, rather than on a literary level. To help them begin, ask students to address what they hope or fear will happen. Allow students time throughout the act to write their responses to the events. After students finish the play, have volunteers summarize their reactions over the course of the play.	Point out to students that they already know a good deal about Nora, Torvald, Mrs. Linde, and Krogstad from the first act. Have them suggest adjectives that describe each of these characters. List the suggestions on the board under each name, and have students give reasons for assigning each adjective, on the basis of what they learned in Act One.

11 Reading Strategy

Inferring Beliefs of the Period

- Have a volunteer read aloud Nora's lines at the top of p. 901.
- As a class, summarize the situation that Nora describes to Mrs. Linde. Ask students what Nora lost when she stopped mentioning her friends to her husband.
  Possible response: By talking less about her old friends, Nora lost the chance to remember her past and who she was before becoming Torvald's wife.
- Ask students the Reading Strategy question on p. 901: What does Nora suggest about Torvald's personality?
  Answer: Torvald is jealous and controlling.
- Ask students whether they think such behavior from husbands is outdated or whether it still happens.
  Possible response: Husbands, and wives, still get jealous. However, most people do not get so jealous that they force their spouses not to mention people from their past, as Torvald expects from Nora.

12 Reading Strategy

Inferring Beliefs of the Period

- Have two volunteers read aloud the bracketed passage as the other students follow along in their textbooks.
- Make sure students realize that Mrs. Linde is more concerned than curious about the possibility of Nora's talking to Dr. Rank behind Torvald's back.
- Ask students what Mrs. Linde's questions reveal about relationships between unmarried men and women in the nineteenth century.
  Possible response: It was probably considered improper for men and women who were not related or married to one another to spend time alone together talking.
- Help students understand that even Nora's ease with Dr. Rank in public could be seen as improper behavior because it suggests familiarity.

13 ✓Reading Check

Answer: Dr. Rank is suffering from tuberculosis of the spine.

14 **Critical Viewing**

Possible response: The adoring expression on the actress's face conveys Nora's great pride in and admiration for Torvald. The way she stands so close to Torvald and rests her hand on his shoulder shows how much Nora cares for him and trusts in him.

15 Literary Analysis

Characterization in Drama

- Remind students that stage directions can help reveal a character's thoughts and feelings.
- Read aloud the bracketed passage, and then point out the stage directions for Mrs. Linde. Ask students why Mrs. Linde looks "hard" at Nora.
  Answer: Mrs. Linde suspects that Nora's debt is not her only problem.
- Ask students what this reveals about Mrs. Linde's character.
  Possible response: Mrs. Linde is observant, sharp, and concerned about Nora's situation.

Monitor Progress Ask students: In addition to stage directions, how else can character be revealed in a drama?
Answer: Character can be revealed through direct statements or physical descriptions of a character; a character's actions, thoughts, or comments; or comments that other characters make about a character.

Reteach Help students find an example from the text for each method of characterization. Encourage them to refer to these examples as they explore the concept of characterization throughout the play.

MRS. LINDE: One's husband does, yes.

NORA: Nonsense. [*Stopping.*] When you pay everything you owe, then you get your note back, right?

MRS. LINDE: Yes, naturally.

NORA: And can rip it into a million pieces and burn it up—that filthy scrap of paper!

15 **MRS. LINDE** [*looking hard at her, laying her sewing aside, and rising slowly*]: Nora, you're hiding something from me.

NORA: You can see it in my face?

MRS. LINDE: Something's happened to you since yesterday morning. Nora, what is it?

NORA [*hurrying toward her*]: Kristine! [*Listening.*] Shh! Torvald's home. Look, go in with the children a while. Torvald can't bear all this snipping and stitching. Let Anne-Marie help you.

14 ▲ **Critical Viewing** In what ways does the actress portraying Nora show the faith Nora has in her husband? **[Analyze]**

ENRICHMENT: Literature Connection

Ibsen's Contemporary: Anton Chekhov

Ibsen was not the only European playwright to transform drama; the Russian master Anton Chekhov (1860–1904) also shares this accomplishment. Born in a small town, Chekhov moved to Moscow in 1879—the year *A Doll House* was written—to study medicine. He first gained literary fame for his short stories, many of which are now considered masterpieces.

Chekhov's career as a dramatist began in the late 1880s with some minor plays, one of which he revised later into the great *Uncle Vanya* (1897). At about the same time, he wrote *Ivanov* (1887). Other masterpieces soon followed: *The Seagull* (1896), *Three Sisters* (1901), and *The Cherry Orchard* (1904). These five plays have established Chekhov as one of the most influential dramatists of all time. His plays are built on a calm and methodical examination of the secret lives of characters who seem dull and inactive on the surface but who actually feel and love strongly.

MRS. LINDE [*gathering up some of the things*]: All right, but I'm not leaving here until we've talked this out. [*She disappears into the room, left, as* TORVALD *enters from the hall.*]

NORA: Oh, how I've been waiting for you, Torvald dear.

HELMER: Was that the dressmaker?

NORA: No, that was Kristine. She's helping me fix up my costume. You know, it's going to be quite attractive.

HELMER: Yes, wasn't that a bright idea I had?

16 **NORA:** Brilliant! But then wasn't I good as well to give in to you?

HELMER: Good—because you give in to your husband's judgment? All right, you little goose, I know you didn't mean it like that. But I won't disturb you. You'll want to have a fitting, I suppose.

NORA: And you'll be working?

HELMER: Yes. [*Indicating a bundle of papers.*] See. I've been down to the bank. [*Starts toward his study.*]

NORA: Torvald.

HELMER [*stops*]: Yes.

NORA: If your little squirrel begged you, with all her heart and soul, for something—?

HELMER: What's that?

NORA: Then would you do it?

HELMER: First, naturally, I'd have to know what it was.

17 **NORA:** Your squirrel would scamper about and do tricks, if you'd only be sweet and give in.

HELMER: Out with it.

NORA: Your lark would be singing high and low in every room—

HELMER: Come on, she does that anyway.

NORA: I'd be a wood nymph and dance for you in the moonlight.

HELMER: Nora—don't tell me it's that same business from this morning?

NORA [*coming closer*]: Yes, Torvald, I beg you, please!

HELMER: And you actually have the nerve to drag that up again?

NORA: Yes, yes, you've got to give in to me; you *have* to let Krogstad keep his job in the bank.

HELMER: My dear Nora, I've slated his job for Mrs. Linde.

NORA: That's awfully kind of you. But you could just fire another clerk instead of Krogstad.

HELMER: This is the most incredible stubbornness! Because you go

Reading Strategy
Inferring Beliefs of the Period What common social beliefs about men and women can you infer from Nora's comment? Explain.

Reading Strategy
Inferring Beliefs of the Period Why does Nora compare herself to a squirrel as she pleads with Torvald?

18 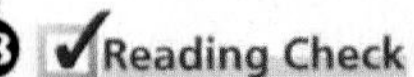

What does Nora call "that filthy scrap of paper"?

CUSTOMIZE INSTRUCTION FOR UNIVERSAL ACCESS

For Less Proficient Readers	For Advanced Readers
In the play, there are no formal scene breaks, but scenes change tone whenever one character leaves the stage and another enters. Show students how to organize the events of the play by helping them identify Act Two "scene" changes on the basis of character entrances and exits. As a class, complete a summary for one of these scenes. Then, allow students to work in pairs to continue summarizing each scene or section in the act.	Remind students that a theme is not merely a statement of fact but a universal idea supported by the words and ideas in a text. The theme of a literary work is usually inferred from the characters' actions and words. Discuss the themes of other works of literature that students have read, such as *Great Expectations* and the theme of dreams versus reality. Then, have students work in small groups to identify a major theme being built in the first two acts of *A Doll House*.

16 Reading Strategy

Inferring Beliefs of the Period

- As a class, list the stresses Nora must address at this point in the play (for example, making her husband's money last through the Christmas season and performing well at the masquerade). Ask students why Nora wants to meet these challenges.
  Answer: Nora wants to do these things to please her husband and to keep him from being suspicious about her spending.
- Read aloud the bracketed line. Then, ask the first Reading Strategy question on p. 903: What common social beliefs about men and women can you infer from Nora's comment? Explain.
  Possible response: Nora suggests that she had a right to reject her husband's "bright idea." Torvald's response, however, indicates that this rejection is unacceptable.
- Encourage students to look for clues that indicate Nora's changing attitude toward her husband. Tell students that they will begin to see increasing signs that Nora is actually disenchanted with her dollhouse marriage.

17 Reading Strategy

Inferring Beliefs of the Period

- Have two volunteers read aloud the bracketed passage. Then, ask the second Reading Strategy question on p. 903: Why does Nora compare herself to a squirrel as she pleads with Torvald?
  Answer: Nora's childish flirtations with Torvald cater to his idea of her as helpless. By portraying herself as such, she hopes to manipulate his decisions and actions.
- Explain that Nora is playing her familiar game of flirting with Torvald to get him to do what she wants. Ask students whether they believe that such behavior would be successful today. Why or why not?
  Possible response: Nora is being too obvious; few probably would be fooled by her flattery and flirting today.

18 ✔Reading Check

Answer: The scrap of paper is the loan agreement on which Nora's forged signature appears.

19 Critical Thinking

Make a Judgment

- Read aloud the first bracketed passage on p. 904. Remind students that in the first act, Torvald speaks almost fondly of Nora's father's inability to handle money. Here, though, Torvald is clearly judgmental.
- Ask students: Do you find it surprising that Nora does not seem bothered by Torvald's attitude about her father? Why or why not? Possible response: It is not suprising; Nora is used to accepting Torvald's opinions without question. She is also preoccupied with Krogstad's threat.
- Guide students to recognize that Torvald's comments support the recurring idea that parents' immoral behavior affects their children. Torvald believes that Nora has inherited her father's immoral approach to business.

20 Literary Analysis

Characterization in Drama

- Point out that until now, Torvald has come across as proud, stubborn, and self-righteous. Ask students to explain what seems to bother Torvald most about Krogstad. Answer: Torvald is annoyed that his old friend calls him by his first name at the office.
- Discuss with students what this attitude reveals about Torvald's character. Point out that Torvald apparently has never bothered to ask Krogstad not to address him familiarly. Instead, he has decided that the only solution is to fire Krogstad.
- Read aloud the Literary Analysis question on p. 904: What do Torvald's real reasons for firing Krogstad reveal about Torvald's personality? Possible response: Torvald is petty, small-minded, insecure, and preoccupied with how his coworkers perceive him.

and give an impulsive promise to speak up for him, I'm expected to—

NORA: That's not the reason, Torvald. It's for your own sake. That man does writing for the worst papers; you said it yourself. He could do you any amount of harm. I'm scared to death of him—

HELMER: Ah, I understand. It's the old memories haunting you.

NORA: What do you mean by that?

HELMER: Of course, you're thinking about your father.

NORA: Yes, all right. Just remember how those nasty gossips wrote in the papers about Papa and slandered him so cruelly. I think they'd have had him dismissed if the department hadn't sent you up to investigate, and if you hadn't been so kind and open-minded toward him.

19 **HELMER:** My dear Nora, there's a notable difference between your father and me. Your father's official career was hardly above reproach. But mine is; and I hope it'll stay that way as long as I hold my position.

NORA: Oh, who can ever tell what vicious minds can invent? We could be so snug and happy in our quiet, carefree home—you and I and the children, Torvald! That's why I'm pleading with you so—

HELMER: And just by pleading for him you make it impossible for me to keep him on. It's already known at the bank that I'm firing Krogstad. What if it's rumored around now that the new bank manager was vetoed by his wife—

NORA: Yes, what then—?

HELMER: Oh yes—as long as our little bundle of stubbornness gets her way—! I should go and make myself ridiculous in front of the whole office—give people the idea I can be swayed by all kinds of outside pressure. Oh, you can bet I'd feel the effects of that soon enough! Besides—there's something that rules Krogstad right out at the bank as long as I'm the manager.

NORA: What's that?

HELMER: His moral failings I could maybe overlook if I had to—

NORA: Yes, Torvald, why not?

20 **HELMER:** And I hear he's quite efficient on the job. But he was a crony of mine back in my teens—one of those rash friendships that crop up again and again to embarrass you later in life. Well, I might as well say it straight out: we're on a first-name basis. And that tactless fool makes no effort at all to hide it in front of others. Quite the contrary—he thinks that entitles him to take a familiar air around me, and so every other second he comes booming out with his "Yes, Torvald!" and "Sure thing, Torvald!" I tell you, it's been excruciating for me. He's out to make my place in the bank unbearable.

NORA: Torvald, you can't be serious about all this.

HELMER: Oh no? Why not?

NORA: Because these are such petty considerations.

impulsive (im pul′ siv) *adj.* sudden and unthinking

Literary Analysis
Characterization in Drama What do Torvald's real reasons for firing Krogstad reveal about Torvald's personality?

tactless (takt′ lis) *adj.* unskilled in dealing with people

excruciating (eks kro͞o′ shē āt′ iŋ) *adj.* causing intense mental or bodily pain

ENRICHMENT: Literature Connection

Ibsen's Politics

Shortly before he finished writing *A Doll House*, Ibsen received a letter from an old friend, Bjornstjerne Bjornson. The letter urged Ibsen to join the fight to free Norway from Swedish influence. Ibsen had no sympathy for this cause. He responded:

> I have not much sympathy for symbols.... I regard it as a sin against our people to make an issue burningly important when it is not.... We have only one thing which I think worth fighting for, and that is the introduction of up-to-date education for our children.... It is quite immaterial whether our politicians bring about isolated reforms if they do not achieve liberty for the individual.... [T]ake away the mark of prejudice and narrow-mindedness and short-sightedness and subservience and unthinking trust in authority, so that every individual can sail under his own flag....

HELMER: What are you saying? Petty? You think I'm petty!

NORA: No, just the opposite, Torvald dear. That's exactly why—

HELMER: Never mind. You call my motives petty; then I might as well be just that. Petty! All right! We'll put a stop to this for good. [*Goes to the hall door and calls.*] Helene!

NORA: What do you want?

HELMER [*searching among his papers*]: A decision. [*The* MAID *comes in.*] Look here; take this letter; go out with it at once. Get hold of a messenger and have him

21 deliver it. Quick now. It's already addressed. Wait, here's some money.

22 **MAID:** Yes, sir. [*She leaves with the letter.*]

HELMER [*straightening his papers*]: There, now, little Miss Willful.

NORA [*breathlessly*]: Torvald, what was that letter?

HELMER: Krogstad's notice.

NORA: Call it back, Torvald! There's still time. Oh, Torvald, call it back! Do it for my sake—for your sake, for the children's sake! Do you hear, Torvald; do it! You don't know how this can harm us.

HELMER: Too late.

NORA: Yes, too late.

HELMER: Nora dear, I can forgive you this panic, even though basically you're insulting me. Yes, you are! Or isn't it an insult to think that *I* should be afraid of a courtroom hack's revenge? But I forgive you anyway, because this shows so beautifully how much you love me. [*Takes her in his arms.*] This is the way it should be, my darling Nora. Whatever comes, you'll see: when it really counts, I have strength and courage enough as a man to take on the whole weight myself.

NORA [*terrified*]: What do you mean by that?

HELMER: The whole weight, I said.

NORA [*resolutely*]: No, never in all the world.

HELMER: Good. So we'll share it, Nora, as man and wife. That's as it should be. [*Fondling her.*] Are you happy now? There, there, there—not these frightened dove's eyes. It's nothing at all but empty fantasies—Now you should run through your tarantella and practice your tambourine. I'll go to the inner office and shut both doors, so I won't hear a thing; you can make all the noise you like. [*Turning in the doorway.*] And when Rank comes, just tell him where he can find me. [*He nods to her and goes with his papers into the study, closing the door.*]

Literary Analysis
Characterization in Drama Does Torvald's decision to send the maid with Krogstad's notice reveal a cowardly personality? Explain.

23 **✓Reading Check**
Why does Torvald fire Krogstad?

21 Literary Analysis

Characterization in Drama

- Choose three volunteers to read aloud the bracketed lines for Torvald, the maid, and Nora.
- Help students understand that Torvald has sent the letter in part because he is insulted by Nora's suggestion that he is being petty.
- Ask students the Literary Analysis question on p. 905: Does Torvald's decision to send the maid with Krogstad's notice reveal a cowardly personality? Explain.
  Possible response: It is cowardly to send a letter rather than tell Krogstad the news in person. Torvald does this to avoid an unpleasant situation.
- Point out the irony in Torvald's claiming to have "strength and courage"; Torvald says this just after he sends the letter, which allows him to avoid a possible confrontation with Krogstad.

22 Critical Thinking

Predict

- Discuss with students how Torvald's decision to send the letter firing Krogstad is a turning point in the play that reaffirms gender roles and seals Nora's fate.
- Challenge students to predict what will happen now that Torvald has sent the letter.
  Possible response: Krogstad may ruin Nora's reputation, which will end her marriage and destroy her family. Nora may find a way to intercept Krogstad's letter. Nora may finally convince her husband to change his mind about firing Krogstad.

23 ✓Reading Check

Answer: Torvald fires Krogstad because Krogstad calls him by his first name at the office.

CUSTOMIZE INSTRUCTION FOR UNIVERSAL ACCESS

For Special Needs Students

Have students imagine that they are employees in Torvald's bank. Ask them to work in pairs to examine Act Two of the play for evidence that Torvald is a difficult or unfair supervisor. For example, have students consider how Torvald fires Krogstad by writing him a letter instead of speaking to him in person.

Have each pair use the Problem/Solution Organizer transparency in **Writing Models and Graphic Organizers on Transparencies**, pp. 91–93, to identify half a dozen or so instances of Torvald's poor methods of management. Then, have students brainstorm more positive ways that Torvald could act in each instance, such as asking Krogstad not to call him by his first name at the office rather than just firing him.

Ask students to share with the class their problems and solutions. Discuss how Torvald's personality would have to change in order for him to carry out some of the solutions that students present.

24 Critical Thinking

Interpret

- Point out the last sentence of the stage directions: "During the following scene, it begins getting dark."
- Ask students to interpret the significance of this stage direction.
  Answer: As it grows dark outside, the atmosphere in the apartment is getting darker. The plot is closing in on Nora, and more dark news is about to be announced.
- Brainstorm as a class how the set might reflect this stage direction.
  Possible response: The windows in the set could turn dark as if the sun were setting, or the stage lights could dim slightly every time a significant line is spoken.

25 Literary Analysis

Characterization in Drama

- Ask students to read the bracketed passage silently, focusing on the stage directions for Nora. Then, ask why Nora breathes easier when she learns that Dr. Rank is dying.
  Answer: Nora is relieved that Dr. Rank is not referring to Nora's situation with Krogstad.
- Next, ask the Literary Analysis question on p. 906: What do the stage directions reveal about Nora's concern for Dr. Rank?
  Possible response: Nora is more concerned about her own problems than she is about the health of Dr. Rank.
- Ask students what this passage reveals about Nora's friendship with Dr. Rank.
  Possible response: Nora apparently does not value Dr. Rank's friendship as much as she claims she does. On the other hand, her problem with Krogstad is so overwhelming that she cannot spare thoughts for another person's problems.

NORA [*standing as though rooted, dazed with fright, in a whisper*]: He really could do it. He will do it. He'll do it in spite of everything. No, not that, never, never! Anything but that! Escape! A way out— [*The doorbell rings.*] Dr. Rank! Anything but that! *Anything*, whatever it is! [*Her hands pass over her face, smoothing it; she pulls herself together, goes over and opens the hall door.* DR. RANK *stands outside, hanging his fur*
24 *coat up. During the following scene, it begins getting dark.*]

NORA: Hello, Dr. Rank. I recognized your ring. But you mustn't go in to Torvald yet; I believe he's working.

RANK: And you?

NORA: For you, I always have an hour to spare—you know that. [*He has entered, and she shuts the door after him.*]

RANK: Many thanks. I'll make use of these hours while I can.

NORA: What do you mean by that? While you can?

RANK: Does that disturb you?

NORA: Well, it's such an odd phrase. Is anything going to happen?

RANK: What's going to happen is what I've been expecting so long—but I honestly didn't think it would come so soon.

NORA [*gripping his arm*]: What is it you've found out? Dr. Rank, you have to tell me!

RANK [*sitting by the stove*]: It's all over with me. There's nothing to be done about it.

NORA [*breathing easier*]: Is it you—then—?

25 **RANK:** Who else? There's no point in lying to one's self. I'm the most miserable of all my patients, Mrs. Helmer. These past few days I've been auditing my internal accounts. Bankrupt! Within a month I'll probably be laid out and rotting in the churchyard.

Literary Analysis
Characterization in Drama What do the stage directions reveal about Nora's concern for Dr. Rank?

NORA: Oh, what a horrible thing to say.

RANK: The thing itself is horrible. But the worst of it is all the other horror before it's over. There's only one final examination left; when I'm finished with that, I'll know about when my disintegration will begin. There's something I want to say. Helmer with his sensitivity has such a sharp distaste for anything ugly. I don't want him near my sickroom.

NORA: Oh, but Dr. Rank—

RANK: I won't have him in there. Under no condition. I'll lock my door to him— As soon as I'm completely sure of the worst, I'll send you my calling card marked with a black cross, and you'll know then the wreck has started to come apart.

NORA: No, today you're completely unreasonable. And I wanted you so much to be in a really good humor.

RANK: With death up my sleeve? And then to suffer this way for somebody else's sins. Is there any justice in that? And in every single family,

ENRICHMENT: Literature Connection

Symbolism and Figurative Language in Ibsen's Writing

Ibsen first gained recognition as a poet. In fact, he was once considered Norway's leading poet. He wrote his early plays in verse, and after his "realistic period" (which included *A Doll House*), he wrote a number of plays that some critics think contain an excess of symbolism.

During the period in which Ibsen concentrated on prose realism, he tried to portray his characters precisely—their words, actions, attitudes, and beliefs. His literary technique at the time prevented him from using much figurative language or overt symbolism because they would have detracted from the realism. Consequently, the figures of speech in the dialogue of *A Doll House* are mostly clichéd metaphors from everyday life.

For example, Torvald calls Nora a "lark," a "goose," a "squirrel," and so on. These are the words of a narrow-minded lawyer, not of a poet. Similarly, the play's realistic quality prevents Ibsen from including many symbols, aside from Nora's beloved macaroons.

26 in some way or another, this inevitable retribution of nature goes on—

NORA [*her hands pressed over her ears*]: Oh, stuff! Cheer up! Please—be gay!

RANK: Yes, I'd just as soon laugh at it all. My poor, innocent spine, serving time for my father's gay army days.

NORA [*by the table, left*]: He was so infatuated with asparagus tips and *pâté de foie gras*,[3] wasn't that it?

27 **RANK:** Yes—and with truffles.

NORA: Truffles, yes. And then with oysters, I suppose?

RANK: Yes, tons of oysters, naturally.

NORA: And then the port and champagne to go with it. It's so sad that all these delectable things have to strike at our bones.

RANK: Especially when they strike at the unhappy bones that never shared in the fun.

NORA: Ah, that's the saddest of all.

RANK [*looks searchingly at her*]: Hm.

NORA [*after a moment*]: Why did you smile?

RANK: No, it was you who laughed.

NORA: No, it was you who smiled, Dr. Rank!

RANK [*getting up*]: You're even a bigger tease than I'd thought.

NORA: I'm full of wild ideas today.

RANK: That's obvious.

NORA [*putting both hands on his shoulders*]: Dear, dear Dr. Rank, you'll never die for Torvald and me.

RANK: Oh, that loss you'll easily get over. Those who go away are soon forgotten.

NORA [*looks fearfully at him*]: You believe that?

RANK: One makes new connections, and then—

NORA: Who makes new connections?

RANK: Both you and Torvald will when I'm gone. I'd say you're well under way already. What was that Mrs. Linde doing here last evening?

NORA: Oh, come—you can't be jealous of poor Kristine?

RANK: Oh yes, I am. She'll be my successor here in the house. When I'm down under, that woman will probably—

NORA: Shh! Not so loud. She's right in there.

RANK: Today as well. So you see.

3. ***pâté de foie gras*** (pä tā´ də fwä´ grä´) paste or spread made of the livers of fattened geese.

retribution (re´ trə byo͞o´ shən) *n.* punishment; revenge

Reading Strategy
Inferring Beliefs of the Period What modern knowledge of health and heredity does Rank imply when he refers to his father's lavish lifestyle?

28 **✓Reading Check**

What will Dr. Rank send the Helmers when his death becomes imminent?

CUSTOMIZE INSTRUCTION FOR UNIVERSAL ACCESS

For Less Proficient Readers	For Gifted/Talented Students
Help students connect the characters, their problems, and corresponding symbols. Write the names of the characters on the board, and ask students to identify each character's problem. Then, ask students to identify objects that symbolize each character's problem or personality. For example, Nora is trapped like a bird or a doll. Hardworking Mrs. Linde is shown using a needle and thread. Krogstad has power over Nora on paper—the original loan contract and the letter he writes to Torvald. Discuss students' choices.	The dialogue between Dr. Rank and Nora on pp. 906–907 is rooted in the nineteenth century, with its limited ideas about how illnesses are transmitted and its quaint traditions, such as leaving calling cards. Challenge students to rewrite this scene with modern characters and a modern setting. Allow students to work alone or with partners to write updated versions of the scene. Have volunteers perform their scenes for the class.

26 Vocabulary Development

Latin Prefix *re-*

- Point out the word *retribution*, its definition, and its use in the play. Tell students that the prefix *re-* means "again" or "back." The Latin word *tribuere* means "to pay"; *retribution* means "payback for evil done."
- Have students work in pairs to compile a list of words containing the Latin prefix *re-* and their definitions.
  Possible response: *Recoil, recreate, recapitulate,* and *recite* all contain the Latin prefix *re-*.
- When students finish their lists, have them double-check their definitions in a dictionary.
- Ask students to use words with *re-* to write a paragraph or two about a scene or theme in the play.

27 Reading Strategy

Inferring Beliefs of the Period

- Ask two students to read aloud the lines for Dr. Rank and Nora in the bracketed passage.
- Explain that Dr. Rank is repeating an important theme of the play: The sins or mistakes of parents filter down to affect the next generation.
- Ask students: How does this idea, as expressed here by the doctor about himself, relate to Torvald's expression of the same idea in Act One?
  Answer: Torvald believes that a life of lies infects one's home and turns children into chronic liars. Dr. Rank claims that his father's immoral behavior and rich diet caused the son's illness.
- Have students respond to the Reading Strategy question on p. 907: What modern knowledge of health and heredity does Rank imply when he refers to his father's lavish lifestyle?
  Answer: Today, we know that many health problems are passed down genetically from parent to child.

28 ✓Reading Check

Answer: Dr. Rank will send his calling card with a black cross marked on it.

29 Reading Strategy

Inferring Beliefs of the Period

- Review with students the Reading Strategy instruction on p. 896.
- Have students independently read the bracketed passage on p. 908. Then, explain that Nora's showing her stockings to Dr. Rank might have been scandalous to audiences of Ibsen's time. In the nineteenth century, most European cultures considered it improper for a married woman to show her legs or stockings to any man other than her husband. Once again, Nora behaves improperly by her society's standards.
- Ask students what is ironic when Nora says "Shame on you" to Dr. Rank.
  Answer: Nora has initiated this flirtation by showing Dr. Rank the stockings, so she is the one who should feel ashamed according to the dictates of society.

30 ▶Critical Viewing

Possible response: The sewing kit would be valued because part of a woman's reputation in nineteenth-century society was based on her ability to sew. In addition, some women earned a living by sewing.

31 Critical Thinking

Speculate

- Have students read the bracketed passage independently. Then, ask them to identify the "exceptionally big favor" that Nora is about to ask of Dr. Rank.
  Possible response: Nora probably will ask Dr. Rank for the money to pay off her debt.
- Remind students that on p. 901 Nora tells Mrs. Linde that it never occurred to her originally to ask Dr. Rank for the forty-eight hundred crowns.
- Have students speculate on why Nora may be about to ask him for money.
  Possible response: Nora is growing increasingly desperate. She hopes that Dr. Rank will pay off her debt for the sake of her and her family.

NORA: Only to sew on my dress. Good gracious, how unreasonable you are. [*Sitting on the sofa.*] Be nice now, Dr. Rank. Tomorrow you'll see how beautifully I'll dance; and you can imagine then that I'm dancing only for you—yes, and of course for Torvald, too—that's understood. [*Takes various items out of the carton.*] Dr. Rank, sit over here and I'll show you something.

RANK [*sitting*]: What's that?

NORA: Look here. Look.

RANK: Silk stockings.

29 **NORA:** Flesh-colored. Aren't they lovely? Now it's so dark here, but tomorrow— No, no, no, just look at the feet. Oh well, you might as well look at the rest.

RANK: Hm—

NORA: Why do you look so critical? Don't you believe they'll fit?

RANK: I've never had any chance to form an opinion on that.

NORA [*glancing at him a moment*]: Shame on you. [*Hits him lightly on the ear with the stockings.*] That's for you. [*Puts them away again.*]

RANK: And what other splendors am I going to see now?

NORA: Not the least bit more, because you've been naughty. [*She hums a little and rummages among her things.*]

RANK [*after a short silence*]: When I sit here together with you like this, completely easy and open, then I don't know—I simply can't imagine—whatever would have become of me if I'd never come into this house.

NORA [*smiling*]: Yes, I really think you feel completely at ease with us.

RANK [*more quietly, staring straight ahead*]: And then to have to go away from it all—

NORA: Nonsense, you're not going away.

RANK [*his voice unchanged*]: —and not even be able to leave some poor show of gratitude behind, scarcely a fleeting regret—no more than a vacant place that anyone can fill.

NORA: And if I asked you now for—? No—

31 **RANK:** For what?

NORA: For a great proof of your friendship—

RANK: Yes, yes?

NORA: No, I mean—for an exceptionally big favor—

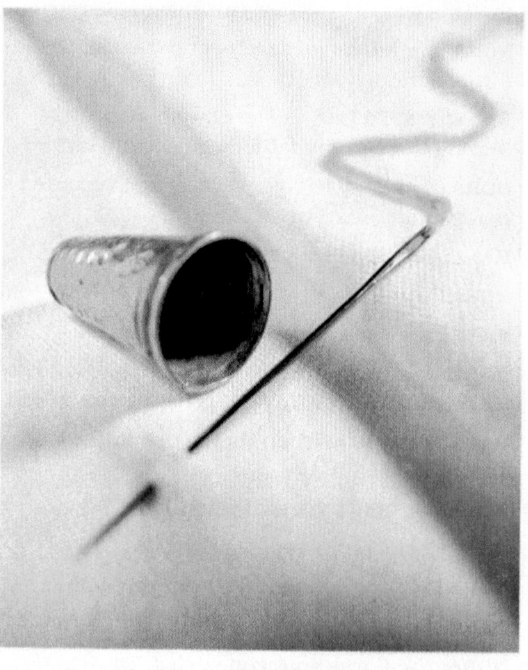

30 ▲ Critical Viewing

Why might a lady's sewing kit be a valued piece of property for women like Nora and Mrs. Linde? **[Hypothesize]**

ENRICHMENT: Literature Connection

More About the Real Nora

In his biography of Ibsen, Halvdan Koht offers some information about Laura Kieler, the young and vivacious woman who served as Ibsen's model for Nora Helmer (see ATE, p. 868).

> Mrs. Kieler had a tendency to color facts with imagination. It was this very quality that made her so valuable to Ibsen. She had a warm heart and a desire to help all that suffered. And although she had a sense of the beautiful and a genuine sense of justice, she had no comprehension of the letter of the law and no consideration for the simple facts. In copies of Ibsen's letters that she sent to the author of this book [Koht] there appeared statements that did not correspond to the given dates. When he inquired about this, she answered in all innocence that she had simply exchanged something in one letter with a passage in another letter that she thought was better expressed. She did not understand that it could make any difference.

RANK: Would you really, for once, make me so happy?

NORA: Oh, you haven't the vaguest idea what it is.

32 **RANK:** All right, then tell me.

NORA: No, but I can't, Dr. Rank—it's all out of reason. It's advice and help, too—and a favor—

RANK: So much the better. I can't fathom what you're hinting at. Just speak out. Don't you trust me?

NORA: Of course. More than anyone else. You're my best and truest friend, I'm sure. That's why I want to talk to you. All right, then, Dr. Rank: there's something you can help me prevent. You know how deeply, how inexpressibly dearly Torvald loves me; he'd never hesitate a second to give up his life for me.

RANK [*leaning close to her*]: Nora—do you think he's the only one—

NORA [*with a slight start*]: Who—?

RANK: Who'd gladly give up his life for you.

NORA [*heavily*]: I see.

RANK: I swore to myself you should know this before I'm gone. I'll never find a better chance. Yes, Nora, now you know. And also you know now that you can trust me beyond anyone else.

NORA [*rising, natural and calm*]: Let me by.

RANK [*making room for her, but still sitting*]: Nora—

NORA [*in the hall doorway*]: Helene, bring the lamp in. [*Goes over to the stove.*] Ah, dear Dr. Rank, that was really mean of you.

RANK [*getting up*]: That I've loved you just as deeply as somebody else? Was *that* mean?

NORA: No, but that you came out and told me. That was quite unnecessary—

RANK: What do you mean? Have you known—?

[*The* MAID *comes in with the lamp, sets it on the table, and goes out again.*]

RANK: Nora—Mrs. Helmer—I'm asking you: have you known about it?

NORA: Oh, how can I tell what I know or don't know? Really, I don't know what to say— Why did you have to be so clumsy, Dr. Rank!
33 Everything was so good.

RANK: Well, in any case, you now have the knowledge that my body and soul are at your command. So won't you speak out?

NORA [*looking at him*]: After that?

RANK: Please, just let me know what it is.

NORA: You can't know anything now.

RANK: I have to. You mustn't punish me like this. Give me the chance to do whatever is humanly possible for you.

Literary Analysis
Characterization in Drama Why do you think Nora is willing to ask Dr. Rank for money in spite of his impending bankruptcy?

Literary Analysis
Characterization in Drama What does Nora's refusal to ask Dr. Rank for money suggest about her personality?

34  **Reading Check**

What does Dr. Rank claim he would give up for Nora?

CUSTOMIZE INSTRUCTION FOR UNIVERSAL ACCESS

For Special Needs Students	For Advanced Readers
To help students see the connections between characters' actions and the consequences of those actions, have them use the Cause-and-Effect organizer in **Writing Models and Graphic Organizers on Transparencies**, pp. 99–101. Work with students to identify key events and their consequences so far. For example, the effect of Dr. Rank's declaration of love is that Nora refuses to ask him for a favor. Challenge students to predict the next consequence of this refusal.	Ask students to compare the scene between Nora and Dr. Rank with scenes from other books, plays, stories, or poems. For example, how are Dr. Rank and Nora similar to Shakespeare's Romeo and Juliet? Allow students to meet in small groups to discuss love in literature and to make generalizations about the topic from their comparisons. List each group's generalizations on the board, and discuss how literature reflects society's changing ideologies.

32 Literary Analysis

Characterization in Drama

- Have two students read aloud the lines for Dr. Rank and Nora in the bracketed passage. Ask students why Dr. Rank has decided to declare his love for Nora.
  Possible response: Dr. Rank knows he will die soon. He may want Nora to know how he feels before she asks a favor.
- Ask students the first Literary Analysis question on p. 909: Why do you think Nora is willing to ask Dr. Rank for money in spite of his impending bankruptcy?
  Answer: Nora is concerned only with obtaining the money to pay her debt.
- Ask students whether they are surprised by Nora's actions. Have them consider how she has been characterized thus far in the play.
  Possible response: Nora has grown increasingly unstable and distraught.

33 Literary Analysis

Characterization in Drama

- With a volunteer, read aloud the lines for Dr. Rank and Nora.
- Then, ask students the second Literary Analysis question on p. 909: What does Nora's refusal to ask Dr. Rank for money suggest about her personality?
  Possible response: Now that Nora knows Dr. Rank loves her, she does not think it would be right to take advantage of him, especially because the money would save her marriage to Torvald; or, Nora is offended by Dr. Rank's proclamation of love and is punishing them both.
- Review with students the Connecting Literary Elements instruction on p. 896. Ask: After this exchange, would you consider Dr. Rank an antagonist? Why or why not?
  Answer: Dr. Rank is an antagonist because his declaration of love prevents Nora from solving her problem.

34 ✔Reading Check

Answer: Dr. Rank claims that he would give up his life for Nora.

35 Critical Thinking

Interpret

- Have two volunteers read aloud the bracketed passage, and then lead a discussion about Nora's hazy concept of love. Note that Nora seems to be saying that although she likes Dr. Rank and the maids in her father's house, she cannot love them.
- Ask students why society might dictate Nora's emotions regarding these people.
  Possible response: Nora feels bound by duty to love the people society thinks she is supposed to love, first her father and then her husband. These men take care of her and are responsible for her social status. Society, however, frowns upon a woman loving another man or people of a lower class; thus, Nora is discouraged from loving Dr. Rank and the maids with whom she has lived.

36 Reading Strategy

Inferring the Beliefs of the Period

- Ask students to explain how stage directions might enhance a play's real-life quality.
  Possible response: Stage directions tell actors and actresses how to react to dialogue and how to move on stage. Such actions can enhance a play's real-life quality.
- Have students read the bracketed passage, paying special attention to the stage directions. Then, ask students the Reading Strategy question on p. 910: What common cultural practices are revealed in the stage directions?
  Answer: Visitors did not just enter a house. They waited while a maid took their calling cards to the person they wanted to see.
- To help students realize the impact realistic stage directions have on a scene, list modern-day equivalents for "She whispers to Nora and hands her a calling card." For example, "He heard the doorbell ring, looked through the peephole, and then opened the front door."

NORA: Now there's nothing you can do for me. Besides, actually, I don't need any help. You'll see—it's only my fantasies. That's what it is. Of course! [*Sits in the rocker, looks at him, and smiles.*] What a nice one you are, Dr. Rank. Aren't you a little bit ashamed, now that the lamp is here?

RANK: No, not exactly. But perhaps I'd better go—for good?

NORA: No, you certainly can't do that. You must come here just as you always have. You know Torvald can't do without you.

RANK: Yes, but *you?*

NORA: You know how much I enjoy it when you're here.

RANK: That's precisely what threw me off. You're a mystery to me. So many times I've felt you'd almost rather be with me
35 than with Helmer.

NORA: Yes—you see, there are some people that one loves most and other people that one would almost prefer being with.

RANK: Yes, there's something to that.

NORA: When I was back home, of course I loved Papa most. But I always thought it was so much fun when I could sneak down to the maids' quarters, because they never tried to improve me, and it was always so amusing, the way they talked to each other.

RANK: Aha, so it's *their* place that I've filled.

NORA [*jumping up and going to him*]: Oh, dear, sweet Dr. Rank, that's not what I meant at all. But you can understand that with Torvald it's just the same as with Papa—

[*The* MAID *enters from the hall.*]

36 **MAID:** Ma'am—please! [*She whispers to* NORA *and hands her a calling card.*]

NORA [*glancing at the card.*]: Ah! [*Slips it into her pocket.*]

RANK: Anything wrong?

NORA: No, no, not at all. It's only some—it's my new dress—

RANK: Really? But—there's your dress.

NORA: Oh, that. But this is another one—I ordered it—Torvald mustn't know—

RANK: Ah, now we have the big secret.

NORA: That's right. Just go in with him—he's back in the inner study. Keep him there as long as—

RANK: Don't worry. He won't get away. [*Goes into the study.*]

NORA [*to the* MAID]: And he's standing waiting in the kitchen?

Reading Strategy
Inferring the Beliefs of the Period What common cultural practices are revealed in the stage directions?

ENRICHMENT: Linguistics Connection

The Norwegian Language

Henrik Ibsen's native Norwegian is one of the North Germanic family of languages, along with Danish, Swedish, and Icelandic. This makes it a close relative of the English language, which, along with Dutch, is a member of the West Germanic family. Norwegian is descended from Old Norse, the language of the Vikings. Because Denmark controlled Norway from 1380 until 1814, Danish heavily influences one version of Norwegian.

Another, newer, version of Norwegian was created in the mid-1800s as an expression of nationalism. Both versions are characterized by a pleasant, singsong quality.

Show students a map of northern Europe, and point out the proximity of the countries whose people speak North and West Germanic languages. If possible, find a recording of Norwegian being spoken, and play it for students.

MAID: Yes, he came up by the back stairs.

NORA: But didn't you tell him somebody was here?

MAID: Yes, but that didn't do any good.

37 **NORA:** He won't leave?

MAID: No, he won't go till he's talked with you, ma'am.

NORA: Let him come in, then—but quietly. Helene, don't breathe a word about this. It's a surprise for my husband.

MAID: Yes, yes, I understand— [*Goes out.*]

NORA: This horror—it's going to happen. No, no, no, it can't happen, it mustn't. [*She goes and bolts* HELMER*'s door. The* MAID *opens the hall door for* KROGSTAD *and shuts it behind him. He is dressed for travel in a fur coat, boots, and a fur cap.*]

NORA [*going toward him*]: Talk softly. My husband's home.

KROGSTAD: Well, good for him.

NORA: What do you want?

KROGSTAD: Some information.

NORA: Hurry up, then. What is it?

KROGSTAD: You know, of course, that I got my notice.

38 **NORA:** I couldn't prevent it, Mr. Krogstad. I fought for you to the bitter end, but nothing worked.

KROGSTAD: Does your husband's love for you run so thin? He knows everything I can expose you to, and all the same he dares to—

NORA: How can you imagine he knows anything about this?

KROGSTAD: Ah, no—I can't imagine it either, now. It's not at all like my fine Torvald Helmer to have so much guts—

NORA: Mr. Krogstad, I demand respect for my husband!

KROGSTAD: Why, of course—all due respect. But since the lady's keeping it so carefully hidden, may I presume to ask if you're also a bit better informed than yesterday about what you've actually done?

NORA: More than you ever could teach me.

KROGSTAD: Yes, I *am* such an awful lawyer.

NORA: What is it you want from me?

KROGSTAD: Just a glimpse of how you are, Mrs. Helmer. I've been thinking about you all day long. A cashier, a night-court scribbler, a—well, a type like me also has a little of what they call a heart, you know.

NORA: Then show it. Think of my children.

KROGSTAD: Did you or your husband ever think of mine? But never mind. I simply wanted to tell you that you don't need to take this thing too seriously. For the present, I'm not proceeding with any action.

Literary Analysis
Characterization in Drama What do Nora's instructions to Helene suggest about Nora's desperation?

39 **✓Reading Check**

Who waits for Nora in the kitchen?

CUSTOMIZE INSTRUCTION FOR UNIVERSAL ACCESS

For Special Needs Students	For Gifted/Talented Students
Remind students that Torvald believes that he has strength and courage, and Nora believes that Torvald will act nobly when he learns of the forgery. On p. 911, Krogstad expresses a lower opinion of Torvald. Have students work in pairs to complete three-column charts, with the headings *Torvald, Nora,* and *Krogstad.* Under the character's name, students should write the person's opinion of Torvald (including Torvald's of himself). Have students revise their charts as they read.	Ask each student to write a short monologue from the point of view of Dr. Rank at the moment he goes into the study to see Torvald. Have students consider how Dr. Rank must feel about his approaching death and his declaration of love for Nora. Also, challenge students to use language that sounds like Dr. Rank's speech. Ask volunteers to share their monologues with the class.

37 Literary Analysis

Characterization in Drama

- Have two volunteers read aloud the bracketed passage. Ask what this exchange makes clear about Krogstad's character.
  Answer: Even though Krogstad appears proper, he is improper because he enters the house by the back stairs and refuses to leave without seeing Nora.
- Have students answer the Literary Analysis question on p. 911: What do Nora's instructions to Helene suggest about Nora's desperation?
  Answer: Nora must be desperate if she talks to a man who behaves rudely.

Monitor Progress Have students identify the main method of characterization employed in the bracketed passage.
Answer: Comments by Nora and the maid help reveal Krogstad's character.

Reteach If students have difficulty understanding methods of characterization, review the Characterization in Drama transparency in **Literary Analysis and Reading Transparencies,** p. 85.

38 Critical Thinking

Analyze

- Tell students to read the bracketed passage independently. Point out that Krogstad initially believes Nora has told her husband about the loan. He apparently reasoned that when Torvald was faced with the possible revelation of Nora's crime, Torvald would keep Krogstad at the bank to avoid scandal.
- Ask students what assumption Krogstad must have made when he received his notice.
  Answer: Krogstad must have assumed that Torvald did not care what happened to Nora.
- Invite students to explain how Ibsen develops Torvald's character in this conversation.
  Possible response: Krogstad's perception of Torvald as a man who would sacrifice his wife's reputation suggests that Torvald is not the devoted husband that he and Nora portray him to be.

39 ✓Reading Check

Answer: Krogstad waits for Nora.

40 Critical Thinking

Interpret

- Ask two students to read aloud the lines for Nora and Krogstad in the bracketed passage. Make sure students understand that the "something worse" being discussed is suicide.
- Have students discuss whether they think Nora will choose suicide as the way out of her dilemma. Would this choice be consistent with her character? Why or why not?
Possible response: Nora loves her children too much to commit suicide. On the other hand, Nora is impetuous and misguided enough to commit suicide.

41 Background

Playwriting

People often use sentence fragments, or incomplete sentences, in their everyday conversations. Consequently, the dialogue in a realistic prose drama is likely to be filled with sentence fragments. For example, notice the sentence fragments in the bracketed passages on pp. 912 and 913.

If Ibsen had written this dialogue without sentence fragments, characters would not interrupt each other, and the language would have sounded formal and contrived.

42 ▶Critical Viewing

Possible response: The two characters are standing far apart and not facing each other. Both seem very serious.

NORA: Oh no, really! Well—I knew that.

KROGSTAD: Everything can be settled in a friendly spirit. It doesn't have to get around town at all; it can stay just among us three.

NORA: My husband must never know anything of this.

KROGSTAD: How can you manage that? Perhaps you can pay me the balance?

NORA: No, not right now.

KROGSTAD: Or you know some way of raising the money in a day or two?

NORA: No way that I'm willing to use.

KROGSTAD: Well, it wouldn't have done you any good, anyway. If you stood in front of me with a fistful of bills, you still couldn't buy your signature back.

NORA: Then tell me what you're going to do with it.

KROGSTAD: I'll just hold onto it—keep it on file. There's no outsider who'll even get wind of it. So if you've been thinking of taking some desperate step—

NORA: I have.

KROGSTAD: Been thinking of running away from home—

NORA: I have!

40

KROGSTAD: Or even of something worse—

NORA: How could you guess that?

KROGSTAD: You can drop those thoughts.

NORA: How could you guess I was thinking of *that*?

KROGSTAD: Most of us think about *that* at first. I thought about it too, but I discovered I hadn't the courage—

NORA [*lifelessly*]: I don't either.

KROGSTAD [*relieved*]: That's true, you haven't the courage? You too?

NORA: I don't have it—I don't have it.

41

KROGSTAD: It would be terribly stupid, anyway. After that first storm at home blows out, why, then— I have here in my pocket a letter for your husband—

NORA: Telling everything?

42 ▲ **Critical Viewing** In what ways do the actors in this photograph capture the tension between Nora and Krogstad? **[Interpret]**

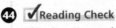

KROGSTAD: As charitably as possible.

NORA [*quickly*]: He mustn't ever get that letter. Tear it up. I'll find some way to get money.

KROGSTAD: Beg pardon, Mrs. Helmer, but I think I just told you—

NORA: Oh, I don't mean the money I owe you. Let me know how much you want from my husband, and I'll manage it.

KROGSTAD: I don't want any money from your husband.

NORA: What do you want, then?

43 **KROGSTAD:** I'll tell you what. I want to recoup, Mrs. Helmer; I want to get on in the world—and there's where your husband can help me. For

44 **✓Reading Check**

What does Krogstad plan to do with the signature Nora forged?

43 Literary Analysis

Characterization in Drama

- Read aloud the bracketed passage on pp. 913–914. Ask students to make a general statement about what the passage reveals about Krogstad's character.
  Possible response: The passage indicates that Krogstad is not the one-dimensional character he at first appears to be.
- Encourage students to discuss how their feelings about Krogstad have changed, if at all, after reading this passage.
  Possible response: Krogstad may inspire sympathy after readers learn that he has feelings, goals, and fears as any other person does.

44 ✓Reading Check

Answer: Krogstad plans to keep Nora's forged signature so that he can use it to blackmail Torvald.

CUSTOMIZE INSTRUCTION FOR UNIVERSAL ACCESS

For Less Proficient Readers	For English Learners
In scenes where key plot developments take place, students will benefit from hearing a recording of the play. Have them follow along in their textbooks as they listen to the **Listening to Literature Audiocassettes** or **Audio CDs.** Then, have students work in pairs or small groups to summarize key scenes throughout the play.	Tell students that Ibsen uses many sentence fragments, or incomplete sentences, to make his dialogue more realistic. Remind students that a sentence fragment is a sentence that lacks a subject, a verb, or both. Challenge each student to find at least two examples of sentence fragments in the dialogue in Act Two. Then, have students work alone or in pairs to rewrite the fragments as complete sentences. Ask students to share their work in small groups.

45 Literary Analysis

Characterization in Drama

- Remind students that Krogstad recently revealed his desire for a better position at the bank, not money from Nora.
- Have a volunteer read aloud the bracketed passage. Point out that, at this point, readers know Torvald almost as well as Krogstad does. Ask students whether they agree with Krogstad's assessment that Torvald will not protest Krogstad's appointment at the bank.
Possible response: Torvald may protest because he dislikes Krogstad and wants to maintain control at the bank; however, Torvald is probably not brave enough to stand up to a blackmailer and may agree to Krogstad's demands.
- Have students respond to the Literary Analysis question on p. 914: Does knowing Krogstad's past and his plans for the future make him seem more or less villainous? Explain.
Possible response: Krogstad's troubled past makes him more sympathetic, but his future plans, which involve blackmailing Torvald and Nora, make him more villainous.

46 Critical Thinking

Evaluate

- Remind students that in order to evaluate a statement or an action, a reader must judge whether the statement or action is valid—that is, whether it makes sense and is well supported.
- Have students independently read the bracketed passage. Then, ask: Do you agree that Torvald has forced Krogstad "back to [his] own ways"? Why or why not?
Possible response: Krogstad is free to make his own choices in life. However, Krogstad would not be doing this if Torvald had not fired him.

a year and a half I've kept myself clean of anything disreputable—all that time struggling with the worst conditions; but I was satisfied, working my way up step by step. Now I've been written right off, and I'm just not in the mood to come crawling back. I tell you, I want to move on. I want to get back in the bank—in a better position. Your husband can set up a job for me—

NORA: He'll never do that!

45 **KROGSTAD:** He'll do it. I know him. He won't dare breathe a word of protest. And once I'm in there together with him, you just wait and see! Inside of a year, I'll be the manager's right-hand man. It'll be Nils Krogstad, not Torvald Helmer, who runs the bank.

NORA: You'll never see the day!

KROGSTAD: Maybe you think you can—

NORA: I have the courage now—for *that.*

KROGSTAD: Oh, you don't scare me. A smart, spoiled lady like you—

NORA: You'll see; you'll see!

KROGSTAD: Under the ice, maybe? Down in the freezing, coal-black water? There, till you float up in the spring, ugly, unrecognizable, with your hair falling out—

NORA: You don't frighten me.

KROGSTAD: Nor do you frighten me. One doesn't do these things, Mrs. Helmer. Besides, what good would it be? I'd still have him safe in my pocket.

NORA: Afterwards? When I'm no longer—?

46 **KROGSTAD:** Are you forgetting that *I'll* be in control then over your final reputation? [NORA *stands speechless, staring at him.*] Good; now I've warned you. Don't do anything stupid. When Helmer's read my letter, I'll be waiting for his reply. And bear in mind that it's your husband himself who's forced me back to my old ways. I'll never forgive him for that. Good-bye, Mrs. Helmer. [*He goes out through the hall.*]

NORA [*goes to the hall door, opens it a crack, and listens*]: He's gone. Didn't leave the letter. Oh no, no, that's impossible too! [*Opening the door more and more.*] What's that? He's standing outside—not going downstairs. He's thinking it over? Maybe he'll—? [*A letter falls in the mailbox; then* KROGSTAD'*s footsteps are heard, dying away down a flight of stairs.* NORA *gives a muffled cry and runs over toward the sofa table. A short pause.*] In the mailbox. [*Slips warily over to the hall door.*] It's lying there. Torvald, Torvald—now we're lost!

MRS. LINDE [*entering with the costume from the room, left*]: There now, I can't see anything else to mend. Perhaps you'd like to try—

NORA [*in a hoarse whisper*]: Kristine, come here.

MRS. LINDE [*tossing the dress on the sofa*]: What's wrong? You look upset.

disreputable (dis rep' yoo tə bəl) *adj.* not fit to be seen or approved

Literary Analysis
Characterization in Drama Does knowing Krogstad's past and his plans for the future make him seem more or less villainous? Explain.

ENRICHMENT: Culture Connection

"National" Writers and Poets

To many Norwegians, the plays of Henrik Ibsen are a source of great national pride. He is one of the authors who are considered "national" writers because, in the opinion of many of his fellow Norwegians, he expressed the hopes, fears, and characters of his fellow citizens better than anyone else.

Other countries also have national writers. Perhaps some of the best known are William Shakespeare and Charles Dickens in England, James Joyce and William Butler Yeats in Ireland, Rabindranath Tagore in India, Honoré de Balzac and Victor Hugo in France, Dante in Italy, Nazlm Hikmet in Turkey, Johann Wolfgang von Goethe in Germany, Pablo Neruda in Chile, and Leo Tolstoy and Anton Chekhov in Russia.

Ask students which writers might best be called national writers in the United States. Have them give reasons for their choices. Students may suggest Emily Dickinson, Mark Twain, Walt Whitman, Toni Morrison, or William Faulkner.

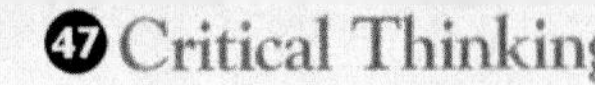

NORA: Come here. See that letter? *There!* Look—through the glass in the mailbox.

MRS. LINDE: Yes, yes, I see it.

NORA: That letter's from Krogstad—

MRS. LINDE: Nora—it's Krogstad who loaned you the money!

NORA: Yes, and now Torvald will find out everything.

MRS. LINDE: Believe me, Nora, it's best for both of you.

NORA: There's more you don't know. I forged a name.

MRS. LINDE: But for heaven's sake—?

NORA: I only want to tell you that, Kristine, so that you can be my witness.

MRS. LINDE: Witness? Why should I—?

NORA: If I should go out of my mind—it could easily happen—

MRS. LINDE: Nora!

NORA: Or anything else occurred—so I couldn't be present here—

MRS. LINDE: Nora, Nora, you aren't yourself at all!

47 **NORA:** And someone should try to take on the whole weight, all of the guilt, you follow me—

MRS. LINDE: Yes, of course, but why do you think—?

NORA: Then you're the witness that it isn't true, Kristine. I'm very much myself; my mind right now is perfectly clear; and I'm telling you: nobody else has known about this; I alone did everything. Remember that.

MRS. LINDE: I will. But I don't understand all this.

NORA: Oh, how could you ever understand it? It's the miracle now that's going to take place.

MRS. LINDE: The miracle?

NORA: Yes, the miracle. But it's so awful, Kristine. It mustn't take place, not for anything in the world.

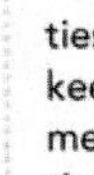

MRS. LINDE: I'm going right over and talk with Krogstad.

48 **NORA:** Don't go near him; he'll do you some terrible harm!

MRS. LINDE: There was a time once when he'd gladly have done anything for me.

NORA: He?

MRS. LINDE: Where does he live?

NORA: Oh, how do I know? Yes. [*Searches in her pocket.*] Here's his card. But the letter, the letter—!

HELMER [*from the study, knocking on the door*]: Nora!

NORA [*with a cry of fear*]: Oh! What is it? What do you want?

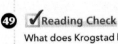

Reading Strategy
Inferring Beliefs of the Period What social realities of the time would keep Mrs. Linde from mentioning her prior relationship with Krogstad?

49 **Reading Check**

What does Krogstad leave for Torvald?

47 Critical Thinking

Infer

- Have a volunteer read aloud the bracketed passage.
- Point out that Nora seems incoherent here. She is talking mostly about possibilities—that she might leave or commit suicide or that Torvald might "take on the whole weight."
- Ask students to consider why Nora insists "nobody else has known about this." Have them make inferences about whom she might be trying to protect.
  Possible response: Nora is trying to protect Torvald, who might claim responsibility for her mistake. Or, she might be trying to protect Dr. Rank, whom Nora has just attempted to ask for help.

48 Reading Strategy

Inferring Beliefs of the Period

- Read aloud the bracketed passage. Make sure students understand that Mrs. Linde's final statement reveals a romantic relationship between her and Krogstad.
- Ask students the Reading Strategy question on p. 915: What social realities of the time would keep Mrs. Linde from mentioning her prior relationship with Krogstad?
  Answer: It was not appropriate for women to discuss relationships with men who were not or did not become their husbands.

Monitor Progress Ask students to discuss what this conclusion suggests about nineteenth-century society.
Possible response: Nineteenth-century society was conservative and placed great importance on maintaining proper, appearances.

49 Reading Check

Answer: Krogstad leaves a letter for Torvald that explains Nora's crime.

CUSTOMIZE INSTRUCTION FOR UNIVERSAL ACCESS

For Less Proficient Readers	For Advanced Readers
To help students analyze character development in Act Two, ask each student to select a character and write a two-paragraph journal entry from the character's point of view. In the first paragraph, have students identify the character's problems and concerns. In the second, ask students to speculate on how their characters will solve their problems. Invite volunteers to read their entries to the class.	Point out that many stories involve letters—sent, unread, misplaced, or misdelivered—as plot devices. Challenge students to think of letters in other works of literature, such as Jane Austen's *Pride and Prejudice* or Thomas Hardy's *Tess of the d'Urbervilles*. Ask students to compare the roles of letters in their examples with that of the letter in *A Doll House*. Guide students to understand that the letters are a way for characters to communicate or miscommunicate and a way to build suspense.

50 Literary Analysis

Characterization in Drama

- Have students read the bracketed passage. Explain that mailboxes at the time of the play often had locks on them, even though the mailboxes were not in public spaces.
- Ask students the Literary Analysis question on p. 916: Why might Torvald carry the mailbox key instead of Nora?
  Answer: Torvald is responsible for household business and financial matters, so the mail would be most relevant to him.
- Ask students whether they think that had Nora wanted a key for the mailbox, she might have been able to get one. Guide students to see that Ibsen probably gave the only key to Torvald to show his role as the controlling adult in the household.

51 Critical Thinking

Analyze

- Read aloud the bracketed passage. Guide students to realize that Nora is once again flattering Torvald—this time in order to keep him away from the mailbox.
- Ask students to discuss why Nora is so easily able to convince Torvald that she is nervous about the party.
  Possible response: Nora is a good actress, as well as desperate, and the physical symptoms of fear and nervousness look the same; Torvald is so self-absorbed and confident in his own observations that he is willing to believe her when what she says matches his own beliefs.

HELMER: Now, now, don't be so frightened. We're not coming in. You locked the door—are you trying on the dress?

NORA: Yes, I'm trying it. I'll look just beautiful, Torvald.

MRS. LINDE [*who has read the card*]: He's living right around the corner.

NORA: Yes, but what's the use? We're lost. The letter's in the box.

50 **MRS. LINDE:** And your husband has the key?

NORA: Yes, always.

MRS. LINDE: Krogstad can ask for his letter back unread; he can find some excuse—

NORA: But it's just this time that Torvald usually—

MRS. LINDE: Stall him. Keep him in there. I'll be back as quick as I can. [*She hurries out through the hall entrance.*]

NORA [*goes to* HELMER's *door, opens it, and peers in*]: Torvald!

HELMER [*from the inner study*]: Well—does one dare set foot in one's own living room at last? Come on, Rank, now we'll get a look— [*In the doorway.*] But what's this?

NORA: What, Torvald dear?

HELMER: Rank had me expecting some grand masquerade.

RANK [*in the doorway*]: That was my impression, but I must have been wrong.

NORA: No one can admire me in my splendor—not till tomorrow.

HELMER: But Nora, dear, you look so exhausted. Have you practiced too hard?

NORA: No, I haven't practiced at all yet.

HELMER: You know, it's necessary—

NORA: Oh, it's absolutely necessary, Torvald. But I can't get anywhere without your help. I've forgotten the whole thing completely.

HELMER: Ah, we'll soon take care of that.

51 **NORA:** Yes, take care of me, Torvald, please! Promise me that? Oh, I'm so nervous. That big party— You must give up everything this evening for me. No business—don't even touch your pen. Yes? Dear Torvald, promise?

HELMER: It's a promise. Tonight I'm totally at your service—you little helpless thing. Hm—but first there's one thing I want to— [*Goes toward the hall door.*]

NORA: What are you looking for?

HELMER: Just to see if there's any mail.

NORA: No, no, don't do that, Torvald!

Literary Analysis
Characterization in Drama Why might Torvald carry the mailbox key instead of Nora?

ENRICHMENT: Literature Connection

Ibsen's Influence on James Joyce

James Joyce had great admiration for Ibsen's plays. In fact, Joyce's play *Exiles* (1918) reflects the influence of Ibsen. In *Joyce and Ibsen,* critic B. J. Tysdahl writes:

> In appearance *Exiles* is like one of Ibsen's realistic dramas from beginning to end. Joyce's stage directions begin, as if copied from *A Doll's House* . . ., with a minute description of the drawing room; then follows, in a new paragraph, a sketch of the persons we see on stage.
>
> Throughout the play, stage directions are frequent, often in the form of an adverb to indicate the tone of speech. Behind these outer resemblances lies the fact that, like Ibsen, Joyce deliberately chose the present time and the ordinary parlor as a setting. . . . Joyce had praised the Norwegian dramatist for his courage to put life—real life—on the stage, without the conventions or embellishments that had often served to veil reality.

HELMER: Now what?

NORA: Torvald, please. There isn't any.

HELMER: Let me look, though. [*Starts out.* NORA, *at the piano, strikes the first notes of the tarantella.* HELMER, *at the door, stops.*] Aha!

NORA: I can't dance tomorrow if I don't practice with you.

HELMER [*going over to her*]: Nora dear, are you really so frightened?

NORA: Yes, so terribly frightened. Let me practice right now; there's still time before dinner. Oh, sit down and play for me, Torvald. Direct me. Teach me, the way you always have.

HELMER: Gladly, if it's what you want. [*Sits at the piano.*]

NORA [*snatches the tambourine up from the box, then a long, varicolored shawl, which she throws around herself, whereupon she springs forward and cries out*]: Play for me now! Now I'll dance! [HELMER *plays and* NORA *dances.* RANK *stands behind* HELMER *at the piano and looks on.*]

53 **HELMER** [*as he plays*]: Slower. Slow down.

NORA: Can't change it.

HELMER: Not so violent, Nora!

NORA: Has to be just like this.

HELMER [*stopping*]: No, no, that won't do at all.

NORA [*laughing and swinging her tambourine*]: Isn't that what I told you?

RANK: Let me play for her.

HELMER [*getting up*]: Yes, go on. I can teach her more easily then. [RANK *sits at the piano and plays;* NORA *dances more and more wildly.* HELMER *has stationed himself by the stove and repeatedly gives her directions; she seems not to hear them; her hair loosens and falls over her shoulders; she does not notice, but goes on dancing.* MRS. LINDE *enters.*]

54 **MRS. LINDE** [*standing dumbfounded at the door*]: Ah—!

NORA [*still dancing*]: See what fun, Kristine!

HELMER: But Nora darling, you dance as if your life were at stake.

NORA: And it is.

HELMER: Rank, stop! This is pure madness. Stop it, I say!

[RANK *breaks off playing, and* NORA *halts abruptly.*]

HELMER [*going over to her*]: I never would have believed it. You've forgotten everything I taught you.

NORA [*throwing away the tambourine*]: You see for yourself.

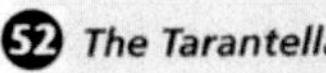

Literature in context — History Connection

52 *The Tarantella*

Henrik Ibsen had important dramatic reasons for choosing this specific dance for Nora to perform. Both the dance and the tarantula spider were named for the southern Italian city of Taranto. In the 1400s, it was believed that the bite of the tarantula was deadly, and the only way to counteract its fatal bite was to dance wildly to distribute the poison throughout the body and sweat it out. The folk dance itself features quick steps, teasing behavior, and a tambourine.

Associated with the tarantella was tarantism, a form of mass hysteria in which the victims, thought to be bitten by the tarantula, danced themselves into a frenzy. Two other forms of this hysteria were the St. Vitus dance, a bizarre twitching of seemingly possessed people, and the dance of death, in which a skeleton led a line of dancers across the countryside. Historians believe all three dances may have been a response to the horrors of the Black Death, the plague that killed a third of all people in Europe in the 1300s. For Nora, the frenetic dancing of the tarantella releases the fear and desperation that torture her as Torvald comes closer to discovering her secrets.

55 ✔Reading Check

What key does Torvald always carry?

CUSTOMIZE INSTRUCTION FOR UNIVERSAL ACCESS

For Special Needs Students	For Gifted/Talented Students
Students will benefit from seeing as well as reading the tarantella scene from *A Doll House*. Find a videotape of a filmed version of *A Doll House*, and show the tarantella scene to students. Ask students to pay attention to Nora's desperate movements and Torvald's reaction to her. Have students suggest adjectives that describe both Nora's movements and the scene itself. Then, discuss with students why Ibsen chose the tarantella as Nora's dance.	Challenge students to learn more about the tarantella. Have them find videos that demonstrate the dance and recordings of music used with the dance. If possible, invite volunteers to learn the steps and perform the dance for the class or teach the dance to classmates. Ask students to write brief statements explaining how learning about the dance helped them understand Nora's actions in particular and the play in general.

52 Background

The Tarantella

Norwegians in Ibsen's time would have considered the tarantella exotic. The dance's quick mood changes and suggestive movements would have signaled to audiences that it was from a warmer climate and a more volatile culture. Such an erratic dance was very different from traditional Scandinavian folk dances. In traditional Scandinavian folk dances, the women wore long, heavy skirts for warmth, so their dance steps were restricted. They danced mostly in place, using facial expressions and gestures to add drama.

53 Critical Thinking

Analyze

- Have students read the bracketed passage independently.
- Tell students that Nora's dance is one of the most highly charged moments in the play. Point out that, until now, there has been little physical action in the play. Now, the play bursts into violent motion.
- Ask students what Nora's initial purpose is for dancing and whether she succeeds.
  Answer: Nora dances to keep Torvald from opening the mailbox. Her dancing is so uncontrolled that Torvald decides to stop what he is doing and teach her all over again.

54 Literary Analysis

Characterization in Drama

- Read aloud the bracketed passage. Then, discuss with students the reasons that Nora responds "And it is" to Torvald's comment that she is dancing as if her "life were at stake."
- Ask students to describe how Torvald reacts to her response. Does he comprehend her meaning?
  Answer: Torvald is so self-involved that he either ignores or does not understand Nora's remark. Instead of following up on her dramatic statement, his only observation is that she has "forgotten everything [he] taught [her]."

55 ✔Reading Check

Answer: Torvald always carries the key to the mailbox.

56 Literary Analysis

Characterization in Drama

- Have two volunteers read aloud the lines for Nora and Torvald in the bracketed passage.
- Then, ask students to respond to the Literary Analysis item on p. 918: Explain how Nora's urgent pleading reflects her attitude toward her present situation.
  Answer: Nora believes that she is losing control of her life, so her behavior is becoming increasingly desperate.
- Point out that Dr. Rank is the one who finally persuades Torvald to leave the letter in the mailbox until tomorrow when he says, "You shouldn't deny her."
- Ask students what Dr. Rank's comment says about him and his feelings for Nora.
  Possible response: Dr. Rank wants to indulge Nora because he loves her. Also, he may be concerned, as a doctor, about Nora's frantic state.

57 Critical Thinking

Interpret

- Have a volunteer read aloud the bracketed passage.
- Have students respond to the sudden change in Nora's disposition. Ask: What does this change reveal about Nora's emotional state?
  Possible response: The sudden change reveals the instability and fragility of Nora's emotional state.

HELMER: Well, there's certainly room for instruction here.

NORA: Yes, you see how important it is. You've got to teach me to the very last minute. Promise me that, Torvald?

HELMER: You can bet on it.

NORA: You mustn't, either today or tomorrow, think about anything else but me; you mustn't open any letters—or the mailbox—

HELMER: Ah, it's still the fear of that man—

56 **NORA:** Oh yes, yes, that too.

HELMER: Nora, it's written all over you—there's already a letter from him out there.

NORA: I don't know. I guess so. But you mustn't read such things now; there mustn't be anything ugly between us before it's all over.

RANK [*quietly to* HELMER]: You shouldn't deny her.

HELMER [*putting his arm around her*]: The child can have her way. But tomorrow night, after you've danced—

NORA: Then you'll be free.

MAID [*in the doorway, right*]: Ma'am, dinner is served.

NORA: We'll be wanting champagne, Helene.

MAID: Very good, ma'am. [*Goes out.*]

HELMER: So—a regular banquet, hm?

NORA: Yes, a banquet—champagne till daybreak! [*Calling out.*] And some macaroons, Helene. Heaps of them—just this once.

HELMER [*taking her hands*]: Now, now, now—no hysterics. Be my own little lark again.

NORA: Oh, I will soon enough. But go on in—and you, Dr. Rank. Kristine, help me put up my hair.

RANK [*whispering, as they go*]: There's nothing wrong—really wrong, is there?

HELMER: Oh, of course not. It's nothing more than this childish anxiety I was telling you about. [*They go out, right.*]

NORA: Well?

MRS. LINDE: Left town.

NORA: I could see by your face.

MRS. LINDE: He'll be home tomorrow evening. I wrote him a note.

57 **NORA:** You shouldn't have. Don't try to stop anything now. After all, it's a wonderful joy, this waiting here for the miracle.

Literary Analysis
Characterization in Drama Explain how Nora's urgent pleading reflects her attitude toward her present situation.

ASSESSMENT PRACTICE: Reading Comprehension

Analyzing Literary Language (For more practice, see Test Preparation Workbook, p. 43.)

Many standardized tests require students to analyze the literary language of a text. To help students practice this skill, use the following sample test item.

Poor little Nora, with no other mother but me.

The word little reveals the speaker's desire to—

A make fun of Nora's height.
B make Nora unhappy.
C comfort Nora.
D insult Nora's real mother.

The correct response is *C*. The person who speaks this sentence describes herself as Nora's mother, so she is probably not trying to make fun of Nora, make her unhappy, or insult her real mother. Also, because *poor* precedes *little*, the word *little* probably refers to Nora's emotional state, not her height.

MRS. LINDE: What is it you're waiting for?

NORA: Oh, you can't understand that. Go in to them; I'll be along in a moment. [MRS. LINDE *goes into the dining room.* NORA *stands a short while as if composing herself; then she looks at her watch.*]

NORA: Five. Seven hours to midnight. Twenty-four hours to the midnight after, and then the tarantella's done. Seven and twenty-four? Thirty-one hours to live.

HELMER [*in the doorway, right*]: What's become of the little lark?

NORA [*going toward him with open arms*]: Here's your lark!

Review and Assess

Thinking About Act Two

1. **Respond:** What would you advise Nora to do about her dilemma? Why?
2. **(a) Recall:** How does Nora describe her relationship with Dr. Rank? **(b) Recall:** What role did Anne-Marie fulfill for Nora in the past? **(c) Analyze:** What do Dr. Rank and Anne-Marie offer Nora that Torvald does not?
3. **(a) Recall:** What does Dr. Rank confess to Nora? **(b) Speculate:** What favor do you think Nora might have asked of Dr. Rank? **(c) Analyze:** Why do you think she changes her mind? **(d) Take a Stand:** Do you think Nora made the right decision? Why or why not?
4. **(a) Recall:** What does Krogstad say about Torvald? **(b) Infer:** What opinion of Torvald does Krogstad seem to have?
5. **(a) Interpret:** What does Nora mean when she says she has thirty-one hours left to live? **(b) Speculate:** What "miracle" do you think Nora hopes for at the end of the act? Explain.
6. **(a) Compare and Contrast:** Compare and contrast the situations of Dr. Rank, Krogstad, Torvald, and Nora as Act Two ends. **(b) Assess:** Of these four characters, which one seems most likely to experience an improved situation in the near future? **(c) Support:** Identify details in Act Two that help explain your answer.
7. **(a) Make a Judgment:** Is Mrs. Linde a loyal friend to Nora? **(b) Support:** Support your answer with evidence from the play.
8. **Extend:** What lessons can be learned about personal relationships from the problems facing Nora and Torvald?

ASSESS

Answers for p. 919

Review and Assess

1. Possible response: Nora should be honest and hope for the best.
2. **(a)** Nora describes Dr. Rank as "*my* good friend." **(b)** Anne-Marie was Nora's nanny. **(c)** Dr. Rank and Anne-Marie accept Nora as she is.
3. **(a)** Dr. Rank confesses his love. **(b)** Nora might have asked for the money to pay her debt. **(c)** She is upset by Dr. Rank's feelings for her. She believes that to ask him would be wrong because she is married. **(d)** Possible response: Nora was wrong not to ask for help. He would have helped her.
4. **(a)** Krogstad says that Torvald is the reason Krogstad is sliding back into disrepute. **(b)** Krogstad thinks that Torvald is weak.
5. **(a)** Possible response: Nora has only a short time to live normally before her secret becomes known and her life changes. **(b)** Possible response: The miracle is that Torvald will help Nora deal with the situation. Nora fears he will be too angry to help her, so she describes his mercy as a miracle.
6. **(a)** Dr. Rank is dying and has confessed his love to Nora; Krogstad believes his power over Nora will lead to a better job; Torvald is unaware of the emotions and events taking place in his house; Nora is under intense stress. **(b)** Krogstad might gain an improved situation in the near future. **(c)** Krogstad has lost his job but might be rehired because he knows Nora's secret.
7. **(a)** Possible response: Mrs. Linde may not be so loyal as she appears. **(b)** Possible response: Although she arrives when Nora needs her, her motive is not clear, nor is her attachment to Krogstad. She has used Nora to get a job; she may use her again.
8. Possible response: It is important to be honest in relationships.

ENRICHMENT: Further Reading

Criticism of Henrik Ibsen's Works

We strongly encourage you to review any selection before assigning or recommending it to students.

Ibsen's Drama: Right Action and Tragic Joy by Theoharis Constantine Theoharis

The Quintessence of Ibsenism: Now Completed to the Death of Ibsen by Bernard Shaw

Stella Adler on Ibsen, Strindberg, and Chekhov by Stella Adler (edited by Barry Paris)

Take It to the Net

Visit PHSchool.com for more information on Henrik Ibsen.

Answers for p. 920

Review and Assess

1. **(a)** Possible response: **Behavior:** flirts and lies; talks to herself; **Comments She Makes:** "I loved Papa most. But I always thought it was so much fun when I could sneak down to the maids' quarters, because they never tried to improve me." **Comments by Others: Dr. Rank:** "You're even a bigger tease than I'd thought"; **Mrs. Linde:** "in many ways you're still like a child"; **Torvald:** "It's nothing more than this childish anxiety." **(b)** Possible response: Nora retains childlike qualities as an adult.
2. Dr. Rank does not see himself as memorable and shows himself as a realist.
3. Krogstad once loved Mrs. Linde; he is relieved that Nora will not attempt suicide; he has been working to redeem himself.
4. Nora interacts with all the characters; the audience sympathizes with her situation. She has internal and external conflicts.
5. **(a)** As the protagonist, Nora works for familial security and stability. She acts as her own antagonist in that the unveiling of her secret threatens to undermine her goal. **(b)** Nora's dual nature makes her character realistic because the complexity of human motivation and behavior often breeds cross purposes.
6. **(a)** Krogstad wants a better position at the bank and treatment as Torvald's equal. **(b)** Krogstad is a physical, mental, and emotional threat to Nora. The revelation of Nora's secret threatens her physical well-being because she may go to jail or lose her family. Krogstad also inspires mental anguish in Nora that leads to emotional instability.
7. Possible response: The women's duties are household-related. Women's education was considered unimportant or home-centered.
8. **(a)** Nora considers her role as a mother her most important job. **(b)** Women were expected to serve their husbands and raise children.
9. Many would punish Krogstad; he has broken the law more than once and his motives are selfish and hurtful.

Review and Assess

Literary Analysis

Characterization in Drama

1. (a) Using a chart like the one below, track the **characterization** of Nora through descriptions of her behavior, the comments she makes, and comments made about her by other characters.

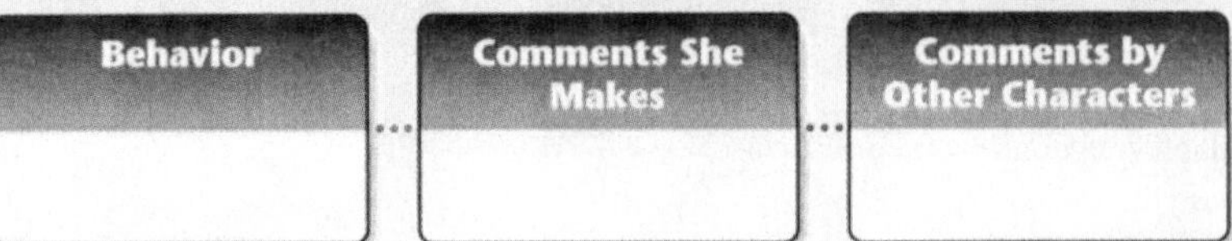

   (b) Based on your findings, what conclusions can you draw about Nora?
2. When Dr. Rank says, "Those who go away are soon forgotten," what do we learn about his character?
3. Identify three details in Act Two that suggest that Krogstad was once a decent man.

Connecting Literary Elements

4. Which details in the play—or in your response to it—confirm that Nora is the **protagonist** of this work?
5. (a) In what way does Nora act as an **antagonist** to herself? (b) Does this dual nature make her character more or less realistic? Explain.
6. (a) Besides money, what does Krogstad want from the Helmers? (b) Is Krogstad a threat to Nora physically, mentally, or emotionally? Explain.

Reading Strategy

Inferring Beliefs of the Period

7. Based on the type of work that Mrs. Linde, Anne-Marie, and Nora are qualified to do, what can you **infer about beliefs of the period** regarding the importance of educating women?
8. (a) What does Nora see as her most important role in life? (b) How does this reflect the attitudes of her time?

Extend Understanding

9. **Career Connection:** If you were a judge, whom would you punish more severely—Nora, for forging her father's signature, or Krogstad, for blackmailing the Helmers? Why?

Quick Review

Characterization is the means by which a writer reveals a character's personality. In drama, stage directions and dialogue are key elements of characterization.

The **protagonist** is the main character, the one at the center of the action with whom the audience sympathizes most. The **antagonist** is the character or force in conflict with the protagonist.

To **infer the beliefs of the period,** observe how social, religious, and cultural practices affect a character's behavior.

PHSchool.com

Take the interactive self-test online to check your understanding of this selection.

TEACHING RESOURCES

The following resources can be used to enrich or extend the instruction for p. 920.

Vocabulary

- **Selection Support:** Build Vocabulary, p. 169
- **Vocabulary and Spelling Practice Book** (Use this booklet for skills instruction.)

Grammar

- **Selection Support:** Grammar and Style, p. 170
- **Writing and Grammar,** Diamond Level, p. 699
- **Daily Language Practice Transparencies**

Listening and Speaking

- **Performance Assessment and Portfolio Management,** p. 28

BLOCK SCHEDULING: Resources marked with this symbol provide varied instruction during 90-minute blocks.

Integrate Language Skills

Vocabulary Development Lesson

Word Analysis: Latin Prefix *re-*

The prefix *re-*, which means "again" or "back," can help you define many words. For example, the Latin word *tribuere* means "to pay," and *retribution* can be defined as "payback for evil done." Match each word in the left column with its definition in the right column.

1. reproach	**a.** to restore
2. reinstate	**b.** to accuse

Spelling Strategy

The long *a* sound can be spelled in several different ways—for example, *ei* (*deign*), *ai* (*train*), *ey* (*they*), *a* (*apron*), and *ay* (*essay*). Complete the spelling of each word below.

1. ob___ **2.** del___ **3.** b___by

Fluency: Words in Context

Explain why each statement is true or false.

1. An *impulsive* shopper buys without first considering his or her budget.
2. An employee seeks *retribution* when awarded a day off from work.
3. A library is a place for *proclaiming* your thoughts to all of the patrons.
4. For their *disreputable* behavior, criminals are sent to prison.
5. A sleepy child finds a warm bed *intolerable*.
6. Many consider it *tactless* to compliment a friend on her new clothes.
7. *Excruciating* pain in a tooth would need a dentist's immediate care.

Grammar and Style Lesson

Commas After Introductory Words

Use commas to set off a mild interjection or another interrupter that introduces a sentence.

Examples: "Oh, of course not. . . ."

"Now, now, don't be frightened. . . ."

Practice Add commas to set off introductory words. If a sentence is correct as is, write *Correct*.

1. Hey did you ever see *A Doll House*?
2. Yes I saw a film version of the stage play.
3. Well which actors played the major roles?
4. I must say that I found the play very disturbing.
5. Perhaps but you could learn a great deal from the play.

Writing Application Using dialogue, write a brief scene that involves two or more characters. Use commas to set off at least three introductory words.

Extension Activities

Writing Put yourself in Krogstad's place and write the **letter** that he mailed to Torvald. Proofread your letter, prepare a final copy, and share it with your classmates.

Listening and Speaking With a group, prepare a **radio play** based on a scene from Act Two. Use language that is appropriate to each character. **[Group Activity]**

WG *Prentice Hall Writing and Grammar Connection: Diamond Level, Chapter 27, Section 2*

ASSESSMENT RESOURCES

The following resources can be used to assess students' knowledge and skills.

Selection Assessment

Formal Assessment, pp. 151–153

Open-Book Tests, pp. 127–129

Test Bank Software

Take It to the Net

Visit PHSchool.com for self-tests on the selections.

Listening and Speaking Rubric

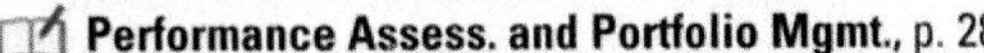

Performance Assess. and Portfolio Mgmt., p. 28

For additional diagnostics and remediation for skills covered in this grouping, use materials from the Prentice Hall Assessment System.

EXTEND

Answers for p. 921

❶ Vocabulary Development

Word Analysis: Latin Prefix *re-*

1. b **2.** a

Spelling Strategy

1. obey **2.** delay **3.** baby

Fluency: Words in Context

1. True. Impulsive shoppers act suddenly without thinking.
2. False. An employee seeks retribution when treated badly.
3. False. One is quiet in a library.
4. True. Such behavior is punished.
5. False. A warm bed is cozy.
6. False. Complimenting is polite.
7. True. Severe pain needs attention.

❷ Grammar and Style

Practice

1. Hey, did you ever see . . . ?
2. Yes, I saw a film version. . . .
3. Well, which actors . . . ?
4. Correct
5. Perhaps, but you could learn. . . .

Writing Application

Possible response:

Mrs. Linde: Oh, Nora. You look lovely.

Nora: Really, you're so kind. Well, let's go.

10TH GRADE For support in teaching the Grammar and Style Lesson to tenth graders, use **Writing and Grammar,** Platinum Level, Chapter 28, Section 2.

❸ Listening and Speaking

- Tell students that radio plays include many sound effects.
- Use the Speaking: Delivering a Narrative Presentation rubric in **Performance Assessment and Portfolio Management,** p. 28, to evaluate students' work.

CUSTOMIZE INSTRUCTION For Universal Access

To address different learning styles, use these activities in the **Extension Activities** booklet, p. 43:

- For Musical/Rhythmic Learners, use Activity 5.
- For Visual/Spatial and Verbal/Linguistic Learners, use Activity 6.
- For Logical/Mathematical Learners, use Activity 7.

A Doll House, Act Three

Lesson Objectives

1. **To analyze and respond to literary elements**
   - Literary Analysis: Theme
   - Connecting Literary Elements: Foreshadowing
2. **To read, comprehend, analyze, and critique drama**
   - Reading Strategy: Recognizing Dramatic Tension
   - Reading Check Questions
   - Review and Assess Questions
   - Assessment Practice (ATE)
3. **To develop word analysis skills, fluency, and systematic vocabulary**
   - Vocabulary Development Lesson: Greek Prefix *hypo-*
4. **To understand and apply written and oral language conventions**
   - Spelling Strategy
   - Grammar and Style Lesson: Infinitives and Infinitive Phrases
5. **To understand and apply appropriate writing and research strategies**
   - Writing Lesson: Persuasive Essay
   - Extension Activity: Costume Design Display
6. **To understand and apply listening and speaking strategies**
   - Extension Activity: Round-table Discussion

10TH GRADE **TEACHING A TENTH-GRADE COURSE**

The literature in this section can be taught as part of a rich, balanced world literature course for tenth-grade students. For a full outline of such a course, see pp. T46–T48 in Volume 1 of this Teacher's Edition.

STEP-BY-STEP TEACHING GUIDE	PACING GUIDE
PRETEACH	
Motivate Students and Provide Background	
Use the Motivation activity (ATE p. 922)	5 min.
Read and discuss author and background features (SE/ATE p. 923) A	5 min.
Introduce the Concepts	
Introduce the Literary Analysis and Reading Strategy concepts (SE/ATE p. 922)	15 min.
Pronounce the vocabulary words and read their definitions (SE p. 922)	5 min.
TEACH	
Monitor Comprehension	
Informally monitor comprehension by circulating while students read independently or in groups A	50 min.
Monitor students' comprehension with the Reading Check notes (SE/ATE pp. 923, 925, 927, 929, 931, 933, 935, 937, 939, 941, 943)	as students read
Develop vocabulary with the Vocabulary notes (SE pp. 924, 926, 928, 935, 937; ATE p. 935)	as students read
Develop Understanding	
Develop students' understanding of theme with the Literary Analysis annotations (SE/ATE pp. 924, 926, 929, 930, 932, 933, 935, 936, 937, 938, 939, 940, 943) A	10 min.
Develop students' ability to recognize dramatic tension by using the Reading Strategy annotations (SE/ATE pp. 923, 925, 926, 928, 930, 932, 936, 938, 940, 941, 943) A	10 min.
ASSESS	
Assess Mastery	
Assess students' mastery of the Reading Strategy and Literary Analysis concepts by having them answer the Review and Assess questions (SE/ATE p. 945)	20 min.
Use one or more of the print, software, or transparency Assessment Resources (ATE p. 947) A	up to 45 min.
EXTEND	
Apply Understanding	
Have students complete the Vocabulary Development Lesson and the Grammar and Style Lesson (SE p. 946) A	20 min.
Apply students' ability to revise to remove unnecessary words and phrases, using the Writing Lesson (SE/ATE p. 947) A	45 min.
Apply students' understanding of the selection, using one or more of the Extension Activities (SE p. 947)	20–90 min.

ACCELERATED INSTRUCTION:
Use the strategies and activities identified with an A.

10TH GRADE **TEACHING TENTH-GRADE STUDENTS**
For support in teaching tenth graders, see the Step-by-Step Teaching notes identified with this icon.

UNIVERSAL ACCESS
● = Below-Level Students
▲ = On-Level Students
■ = Above-Level Students

Time and Resource Manager

Reading Level: Average
Average Number of Instructional Days: 5

RESOURCES		
PRINT	**TRANSPARENCIES**	**TECHNOLOGY**
• **Beyond Literature,** Cross-Curricular Connection: History, p. 44 ▲ ■		• **Interest Grabber Video,** Tape 2, Unit 7, Segment 3 ● ▲ ■
• **Selection Support Workbook:** ● ▲ ■ Literary Analysis, p. 176 Reading Strategy, p. 175 Build Vocabulary, p. 173	• **Literary Analysis and Reading Transparencies,** pp. 87 and 88 ● ▲ ■	
		• **Listening to Literature** ● ▲ ■ Audiocassettes Audio CDs
• **Literary Analysis for Enrichment,** p. 44 ■		
• **Formal Assessment:** Selection Test, pp. 154–156 ● ▲ ■ • **Open-Book Tests,** pp. 130–132 ● ▲ ■ • **Performance Assessment. and Portfolio Management,** pp. 11, 23 ● ▲ ■ • PRENTICE HALL ASSESSMENT SYSTEM ● ▲ ■	• PRENTICE HALL ASSESSMENT SYSTEM ● ▲ ■ **Skills Practice Answers and Explanations on Transparencies**	• **Test Bank Software** ● ▲ ■
• **Selection Support Workbook:** ● ▲ ■ Grammar and Style, p. 174 • **Writing and Grammar,** Diamond Level ● ▲ ■ • **Extension Activities,** p. 44 ● ▲ ■	• **Daily Language Practice Transparencies** ● ▲	• **Writing and Grammar iText CD-ROM** ● ▲ ■ *Take It to the Net* PHSchool.com

BLOCK SCHEDULING: Use one 90-minute class period to preteach the selection(s) and have students read them. Use a second 90-minute class period to assess students' mastery of skills and have them complete one of the Extension Activities.

PRETEACH

Step-by-Step Teaching Guide for p. 922

❶ Literary Analysis

Theme

- Ask students to discuss the plots of their favorite books or movies. Tell them to explain what lessons or insights the work tries to get readers or viewers to consider in their own lives or apply to the world in general.
- Tell students that these universal ideas are called themes and that themes help readers think and talk about works. Give them the example of *A Doll House,* and ask them to identify general points the play raises about families and marriage.
  Possible response: Themes include the following: parents' sins and mistakes affect children; honesty is important in relationships; good intentions have limits.
- Tell students that foreshadowing can often help them identify themes; a suggested event or condition may emerge as a theme.
- Use the Theme transparency in **Literary Analysis and Reading Transparencies** on p. 87 to help students identify themes.

❷ Reading Strategy

Recognizing Dramatic Tension

- Explain the difference between suspense and dramatic tension: readers feel suspense when something frightening or damaging is about to happen. They feel dramatic tension as concern about what may eventually happen.
- Review with students the graphic organizer on p. 922. Remind them to record moments of conflict or mystery as they read Act Three.

Vocabulary Development

- Pronounce each vocabulary word for students, and read the definition as a class. Have students identify any words with which they are already familiar.

 ***E-Teach***

Visit e-Teach at PHSchool.com for teachers' essays on how to teach, with questions and answers.

Prepare to Read

A Doll House, Act Three

❶ Literary Analysis

Theme

A **theme** is a central message, idea, or insight into life that is revealed by a literary work. In a drama, a theme may be stated directly or suggested through dialogue and actions. A complex play like *A Doll House* may have several themes:

- Real love has little to do with physical beauty or social status.
- A successful relationship is based on trust, equality, individuality.
- Every person has the right to individuality.

As you read Act Three, pay close attention to how the characters' actions or dialogue convey the theme.

Connecting Literary Elements

To prepare readers to recognize key themes, Ibsen uses **foreshadowing,** a technique of incorporating details that suggest events or conditions to come. In Act Two, for example, Nora tells Torvald that he will soon be free, but she does not indicate from what he will be free. The outcome is revealed in Act Three. Note how foreshadowing keeps you guessing.

❷ Reading Strategy

Recognizing Dramatic Tension

Dramatic tension is the sense of suspense that an audience feels while watching a drama unfold. To **recognize dramatic tension,** monitor the anticipation you feel while reading each scene. Ask questions such as these:

- Why are these characters in conflict with one another?
- In what way are the stakes being raised, making it clear that the protagonist stands to lose more and more as the play progresses?

Record moments of conflict or mystery in a chart like the one shown. For each one, write a question to reflect the suspense you experience in that moment.

Moment of Conflict or Mystery
Mrs. Linde asks Krogstad to speak with her about Nora's debt.

Question
Will Mrs. Linde reveal Nora's desperation?

Vocabulary Development

calculating (kal′ kyōō lāt′ iŋ) *adj.* shrewd or cunning (p. 924)

evasions (ē vā′ zhənz) *n.* attempts to avoid duties or questions (p. 926)

naturalistic (nach′ ər əl is′ tik) *adj.* faithful to nature (p. 928)

proprieties (prō prī′ ə tēz) *n.* conformities with what is considered fitting, suitable, or proper (p. 928)

hypocrite (hip′ ə krit′) *n.* someone who merely pretends to be virtuous (p. 935)

grafter (graft′ ər) *n.* someone who takes advantage of his or her position to gain money or property dishonestly (p. 935)

bewildered (bē wil′ dərd) *adj.* puzzled; confused (p. 937)

TEACHING RESOURCES

The following resources can be used to enrich or extend the instruction for p. 922.

Motivation

Interest Grabber Video, Tape 2

Background

Beyond Literature, p. 44

 ***Take It to the Net***

Visit PHSchool.com for background on the author.

Literary Analysis

Literary Analysis and Reading Transparencies, Theme, p. 87

Selection Support: Literary Analysis, p. 176

Reading

Literary Analysis and Reading Transparencies, Recognizing Dramatic Tension, p. 88

BLOCK SCHEDULING: Resources marked with this symbol provide varied instruction during 90-minute blocks.

Review and Anticipate

In Act Two, Torvald's misgivings prompt him to fire Krogstad in spite of Nora's pleas to retain him. Not to be bested, Krogstad arrives with a letter for Torvald that reveals Nora's deception. Krogstad plans to blackmail Torvald into giving him back his job at the bank and leaves the letter in the Helmers' locked mailbox.

Desperate to protect her home and marriage, Nora exhausts every available tactic to change Krogstad's mind and to prevent Torvald from reading the letter. Will Nora salvage Torvald's good name or allow him to take the blame for her actions? What, if anything, will she learn from her mistakes? As you read, look for answers to these questions in the conclusion to Ibsen's *A Doll House*.

❶ ACT THREE

Same scene. The table, with chairs around it, has been moved to the center of the room. A lamp on the table is lit. The hall door stands open. Dance music drifts down from the floor above. MRS. LINDE *sits at the table, absently paging through a book, trying to read, but apparently unable to focus her thoughts. Once or twice she pauses, tensely listening for a sound at the outer entrance.*

❷ **MRS. LINDE** [*glancing at her watch*]: Not yet—and there's hardly any time left. If only he's not—[*Listening again.*] Ah, there he is. [*She goes out in the hall and cautiously opens the outer door. Quiet footsteps are heard on the stairs. She whispers.*] Come in. Nobody's here.

KROGSTAD [*in the doorway*]: I found a note from you at home. What's back of all this?

MRS. LINDE: I just *had* to talk to you.

KROGSTAD: Oh? And it just *had* to be here in this house?

MRS. LINDE: At my place it was impossible; my room hasn't a private entrance. Come in; we're all alone. The maid's asleep, and the Helmers are at the dance upstairs.

KROGSTAD [*entering the room*]: Well, well, the Helmers are dancing tonight? Really?

MRS. LINDE: Why not?

KROGSTAD: How true—why not?

MRS. LINDE: All right, Krogstad, let's talk.

Reading Strategy
Recognizing Dramatic Tension What effect does time have on the dramatic tension in this scene?

❸ ✓**Reading Check**

Who left a note for Krogstad at his home?

TEACHING RESOURCES

The following resources can be used to enrich or extend the instruction for pp. 923–944.

Literary Analysis

- **Selection Support:** Literary Analysis, p. 176
- **Literary Analysis and Reading Transparencies,** Theme, p. 87 ■

Reading

- **Selection Support:** Reading Strategy, p. 175; Build Vocabulary, p. 173 ■
- **Listening to Literature Audiocassettes**
- **Listening to Literature Audio CDs**

■ **BLOCK SCHEDULING:** Resources marked with this symbol provide varied instruction during 90-minute blocks.

TEACH

Step-by-Step Teaching Guide for pp. 923–944

Teaching Tenth-Grade Students

10TH GRADE To help tenth-grade students understand and appreciate the play, highlight the difference between the status of women today and their status at the time the play was written. Tell students that the women of Nora's time had fewer opportunities than women have today. Women like Nora were expected to devote their lives to their husbands and families. After you have provided students with a sense of the changes in the status of women, have the class discuss how the play might be different had it been written today.

❶ About the Selection

As the events of the final act unfold, the approaching catastrophe comes nearer. Torvald's reaction to Nora's crime, long hinted at, is revealed; and Nora's response will surprise many readers.

❷ Reading Strategy

Recognizing Dramatic Tension

- Tell students that several clues in the stage directions suggest Mrs. Linde's anxiety. Challenge students to identify them.
  Possible response: Mrs. Linde is distracted from her reading; she listens for someone at the door; when Krogstad arrives, she speaks in a whisper.
- Ask students the Reading Strategy question on p. 923: What effect does time have on the dramatic tension in this scene?
  Answer: Because Mrs. Linde and Krogstad have only a few minutes to talk, their conversation seems urgent.

❸ ✓Reading Check

Answer: Mrs. Linde left a note at Krogstad's home.

❹ Critical Thinking

Make a Judgment

- Read aloud the bracketed passage.
- Make sure that students understand the meaning of the vocabulary word *calculating.* Have them read the definition in the margin of p. 924.
- Then, ask: Do you think Mrs. Linde's behavior can be characterized as calculating?
  Possible response: Some students may think that Mrs. Linde has been calculating in the way she appeared at the Helmers' house and obtained a job, but others might claim that she is simply trying to provide for herself.

❺ Literary Analysis

Theme and Foreshadowing

- Have two volunteers read aloud the bracketed passage.
- Challenge students to see that Mrs. Linde's story reinforces one of the themes Ibsen has revealed in early acts: that women must make sacrifices for their families, often at the expense of their own happiness.
- Ask students to explain what Mrs. Linde sacrificed to save her family.
  Possible response: She gave up her attachment to Krogstad to marry a man who could support her family.
- Point out that Mrs. Linde's past feelings for Krogstad may affect or foreshadow her actions now.
- Then, ask the Literary Analysis question on p. 924: What action on Mrs. Linde's part might these words foreshadow?
  Possible response: Mrs. Linde's statement that "help may be near" may foreshadow an arrangement with Krogstad.

KROGSTAD: Do we two have anything more to talk about?

MRS. LINDE: We have a great deal to talk about.

KROGSTAD: I wouldn't have thought so.

MRS. LINDE: No, because you've never understood me, really.

❹ **KROGSTAD:** Was there anything more to understand—except what's all too common in life? A calculating woman throws over a man the moment a better catch comes by.

calculating (kal′ kyōō lāt′ iŋ) *adj.* shrewd or cunning

MRS. LINDE: You think I'm so thoroughly calculating? You think I broke it off lightly?

KROGSTAD: Didn't you?

MRS. LINDE: Nils—is that what you really thought?

KROGSTAD: If you cared, then why did you write me the way you did?

MRS. LINDE: What else could I do? If I had to break off with you, then it was my job as well to root out everything you felt for me.

KROGSTAD [*wringing his hands*]: So that was it. And this—all this, simply for money!

MRS. LINDE: Don't forget I had a helpless mother and two small brothers. We couldn't wait for you, Nils; you had such a long road ahead of you then.

KROGSTAD: That may be; but you still hadn't the right to abandon me for somebody else's sake.

❺ **MRS. LINDE:** Yes—I don't know. So many, many times I've asked myself if I did have that right.

KROGSTAD [*more softly*]: When I lost you, it was as if all the solid ground dissolved from under my feet. Look at me; I'm a half-drowned man now, hanging onto a wreck.

MRS. LINDE: Help may be near.

Literary Analysis
Theme and Foreshadowing What action on Mrs. Linde's part might these words foreshadow?

KROGSTAD: It was near—but then you came and blocked it off.

MRS. LINDE: Without my knowing it, Nils. Today for the first time I learned that it's you I'm replacing at the bank.

KROGSTAD: All right—I believe you. But now that you know, will you step aside?

MRS. LINDE: No, because that wouldn't benefit you in the slightest.

KROGSTAD: Not "benefit" me, hm! I'd step aside anyway.

MRS. LINDE: I've learned to be realistic. Life and hard, bitter necessity have taught me that.

KROGSTAD: And life's taught me never to trust fine phrases.

MRS. LINDE: Then life's taught you a very sound thing. But you do have to trust in actions, don't you?

KROGSTAD: What does that mean?

ENRICHMENT: Literature Connection

Spotlight on Two Characters

Ibsen scholar Keith M. May wrote this about the significance of Krogstad and Mrs. Linde:

> Krogstad's role is plainly necessary, for by sending his letter to Torvald … he precipitates the final disclosures and Nora's metamorphosis. But apart from that Krogstad is an interesting and indeed necessary figure of frustration and embitterment, the perfect though surprising partner for Mrs. Linde. In addition to aiding the mechanics of the plot these two enrich the theme, for they have both suffered in humiliating ways, as the relatively comfortable Helmers have not. At the end there is an appropriate kind of ripening for them both.
>
> There is a touch of seediness about both of them: the self-sacrificing, mildly represented Mrs. Linde, plain as well as spirited; Krogstad hitherto steeped in malice. And they come together tragically, which is to say with no higher hopes for a happy future than their pasts will allow.

MRS. LINDE: You said you were hanging on like a half-drowned man to a wreck.

KROGSTAD: I've good reason to say that.

MRS. LINDE: I'm also like a half-drowned woman on a wreck. No one to suffer with; no one to care for.

KROGSTAD: You made your choice.

MRS. LINDE: There wasn't any choice then.

6 **KROGSTAD:** So—what of it?

MRS. LINDE: Nils, if only we two shipwrecked people could reach across to each other.

KROGSTAD: What are you saying?

MRS. LINDE: Two on one wreck are at least better off than each on his own.

KROGSTAD: Kristine!

MRS. LINDE: Why do you think I came into town?

KROGSTAD: Did you really have some thought of me?

7 **MRS. LINDE:** I have to work to go on living. All my born days, as long as I can remember, I've worked, and it's been my best and my only joy. But now I'm completely alone in the world; it frightens me to be so empty and lost. To work for yourself—there's no joy in that. Nils, give me something—someone to work for.

KROGSTAD: I don't believe all this. It's just some hysterical feminine urge to go out and make a noble sacrifice.

MRS. LINDE: Have you ever found me to be hysterical?

KROGSTAD: Can you honestly mean this? Tell me—do you know everything about my past?

MRS. LINDE: Yes.

KROGSTAD: And you know what they think I'm worth around here.

MRS. LINDE: From what you were saying before, it would seem that with me you could have been another person.

KROGSTAD: I'm positive of that.

MRS. LINDE: Couldn't it happen still?

KROGSTAD: Kristine—you're saying this in all seriousness? Yes, you are! I can see it in you. And do you really have the courage, then—?

MRS. LINDE: I need to have someone to care for; and your children need a mother. We both need each other. Nils, I have faith that you're good at heart—I'll risk everything together with you.

KROGSTAD [*gripping her hands*]: Kristine, thank you, thank you— Now I know I can win back a place in their eyes. Yes—but I forgot—

MRS. LINDE [*listening*]: Shh! The tarantella. Go now! Go on!

Reading Strategy
Recognizing Dramatic Tension If Krogstad rejects Mrs. Linde, will it raise the dramatic tension in this scene? Why or why not?

8  **Reading Check**

What information has Mrs. Linde learned about her position at the bank?

CUSTOMIZE INSTRUCTION FOR UNIVERSAL ACCESS

For Less Proficient Readers	For Advanced Readers
Point out to students that by having only a handful of characters in his play, Ibsen can create some vivid contrasts among them. Call students' attention to the contrast between the renewed relationship of Krogstad and Mrs. Linde and the possible destruction of Nora and Torvald's marriage. Ask students to draw a simple graphic representation of what this contrast might look like. Students might draw two intersecting arrows, one going up (Krogstad and Mrs. Linde's relationship) and one going down (Nora and Torvald's).	Suggest that students assume the role of theater critics, identifying the best and worst parts they have read in the play so far. Remind them to consider all the different components of the play—character, plot, theme, setting, and so on. Ask students to write short explanations of their choices. Students can exchange their ideas with classmates in small groups.

6 Critical Thinking

Interpret

- Ask two volunteers to read aloud the bracketed passage. Ask students why Mrs. Linde picks up on Krogstad's metaphor of being shipwrecked as she explains why she rejected his marriage proposal.
  Possible response: She feels shipwrecked now that she is alone and unneeded.
- Ask students what Mrs. Linde suggests and whether this suggestion surprises them.
  Possible response: Mrs. Linde's suggestion that she and Krogstad marry may surprise students who think Krogstad may still harbor bitter feelings toward Mrs. Linde. Others may not find this suggestion surprising, citing the romantic history the two share.

7 Reading Strategy

Recognizing Dramatic Tension

- Remind students that dramatic tension arises when readers feel the pressure characters put on one another to make certain decisions.
- Ask students to consider what motivation Mrs. Linde and Krogstad have for marrying each other.
  Possible response: Mrs. Linde is lonely, and because she is used to working for others, her life is empty without someone to work and care for. Krogstad needs someone to help raise his children.
- Have students read the bracketed passage independently. Ask students the Reading Strategy question on p. 925: If Krogstad rejects Mrs. Linde, will it raise the dramatic tension in this scene? Why or why not?
  Answer: The dramatic tension will increase if Krogstad rejects Mrs. Linde because it will lead to more questions, such as "What will happen to Mrs. Linde?" and "If she is angered by the rejection, what will she do?"

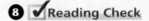

8 Reading Check

Answer: Mrs. Linde has learned that Krogstad will lose his position at the bank so that she can work there.

9 Reading Strategy

Recognizing Dramatic Tension

- Before a pair of students read the passage, tell students that dramatic tension can be created by elements in the setting as well as by the actors onstage.
- Draw students' attention to the bracketed passage, and then ask students the Reading Strategy question on p. 926: In what way does the music of the tarantella affect the dramatic tension in this scene?
  Possible response: The tarantella reminds the characters and the audience that time is running out.

10 Literary Analysis

Theme

- Have two students read aloud the bracketed passage. Make sure students realize that this is an important turning point in the play: Mrs. Linde declines Krogstad's offer to retrieve his letter so that Nora and Torvald learn from the experience.
- Ask students the Literary Analysis question on p. 926: What general theme about people or life does Mrs. Linde express?
  Possible response: Mrs. Linde's actions reflect the theme that although truth can sometimes be difficult to take, it can be a powerful teaching tool.

11 Background

Krogstad's Character

This is Krogstad's last appearance onstage. During this scene he has undergone an amazingly rapid transformation from a miserable man whose life is about to collapse to someone who has "never been so happy." Many critics have objected to this transformation. One calls Krogstad "the only exonerated blackmailer [he] can think of in fiction."

KROGSTAD: Why? What is it?

MRS. LINDE: Hear the dance up there? When that's over, they'll be coming down.

9 **KROGSTAD:** Oh, then I'll go. But—it's all pointless. Of course, you don't know the move I made against the Helmers.

MRS. LINDE: Yes, Nils, I know.

KROGSTAD: And all the same, you have the courage to—?

MRS. LINDE: I know how far despair can drive a man like you.

KROGSTAD: Oh, if I only could take it all back.

MRS. LINDE: You easily could—your letter's still lying in the mailbox.

KROGSTAD: Are you sure of that?

MRS. LINDE: Positive. But—

KROGSTAD [*looks at her searchingly*]: Is that the meaning of it, then? You'll save your friend at any price. Tell me straight out. Is that it?

MRS. LINDE: Nils—anyone who's sold herself for somebody else once isn't going to do it again.

KROGSTAD: I'll demand my letter back.

MRS. LINDE: No, no.

KROGSTAD: Yes, of course. I'll stay here till Helmer comes down; I'll tell him to give me my letter again—that it only involves my dismissal—that he shouldn't read it—

MRS. LINDE: No, Nils, don't call the letter back.

KROGSTAD: But wasn't that exactly why you wrote me to come here?

10 **MRS. LINDE:** Yes, in that first panic. But it's been a whole day and night since then, and in that time I've seen such incredible things in this house. Helmer's got to learn everything; this dreadful secret has to be aired; those two have to come to a full understanding; all these lies and evasions can't go on.

KROGSTAD: Well, then, if you want to chance it. But at least there's one thing I can do, and do right away—

MRS. LINDE [*listening*]: Go now, go quick! The dance is over. We're not safe another second.

KROGSTAD: I'll wait for you downstairs.

MRS. LINDE: Yes, please do; take me home.

11 **KROGSTAD:** I can't believe it; I've never been so happy. [*He leaves by way of the outer door; the door between the room and the hall stays open.*]

MRS. LINDE [*straightening up a bit and getting together her street clothes*]: How different now! How different! Someone to work for, to live for—a home to build. Well, it is worth the try! Oh, if they'd only come! [*Listening.*] Ah, there they are. Bundle up. [*She picks up her hat and coat.* NORA*'s and* HELMER*'s voices can be heard outside; a key turns in*

Reading Strategy
Recognizing Dramatic Tension In what way does the music of the tarantella affect the dramatic tension in this scene?

Literary Analysis
Theme What general theme about people or life does Mrs. Linde express?

evasions (ē vā′ zhənz) *n.* attempts to avoid duties or questions

---

ENRICHMENT: Literature Connection

August Strindberg

Another great author who helped create modern drama was the Swedish playwright August Strindberg (1849–1912), who was born in Stockholm. Strindberg joined the realistic style of Ibsen to the intense examination of inner psychological realities and sometimes disordered imaginations. From this style developed the Expressionist drama, focused more on characters' inner states than on external reality.

Strindberg's childhood was unhappy. After trying several different careers, he settled on journalism and began to publish novels and short stories. His first play, strongly influenced by Ibsen's *Brand,* was *Master Olaf* (1881). Its rejection was deeply wounding. His intense but unhappy marriage led him to the subject he is most identified with—the conflict between men and women.

His best-known works are *The Father* (1887), *Miss Julie* (1888), *Creditors* (1890), *A Dream Play* (1902), and *The Ghost Sonata* (1907). Most of Strindberg's plays present dark views of humanity.

the lock, and HELMER *brings* NORA *into the hall almost by force. She is wearing the Italian costume with a large black shawl about her; he has on evening dress, with a black domino*[1] *open over it.*]

NORA [*struggling in the doorway*]: No, no, no, not inside! I'm going up again. I don't want to leave so soon.

HELMER: But Nora dear—

NORA: Oh, I beg you, please, Torvald. From the bottom of my heart, *please*—only an hour more!

HELMER: Not a single minute, Nora darling. You know our agreement. Come on, in we go; you'll catch cold out here. [*In spite of her resistance, he gently draws her into the room.*]

MRS. LINDE: Good evening.

NORA: Kristine!

HELMER: Why, Mrs. Linde—are you here so late?

MRS. LINDE: Yes, I'm sorry, but I did want to see Nora in costume.

NORA: Have you been sitting here, waiting for me?

MRS. LINDE: Yes. I didn't come early enough; you were all upstairs; and then I thought I really couldn't leave without seeing you.

HELMER [*removing* NORA's *shawl*]: Yes, take a good look. She's worth looking at, I can tell you that, Mrs. Linde. Isn't she lovely?

MRS. LINDE: Yes, I should say—

HELMER: A dream of loveliness, isn't she? That's what everyone thought at the party, too. But she's horribly stubborn—this sweet little
13 thing. What's to be done with her? Can you imagine, I almost had to use force to pry her away.

NORA: Oh, Torvald, you're going to regret you didn't indulge me, even for just a half hour more.

HELMER: There, you see. She danced her tarantella and got a tumultuous[2] hand—which was well earned, although the performance may have

12 **Critical Viewing**
In what way does Nora's attitude in Act Three match the expression of the actress in this picture? **[Connect]**

14 **Reading Check**
What does Mrs. Linde want Krogstad to do with the letter to Torvald?

1. **domino** (däm′ ə nō′) *n.* loose cloak or robe with wide sleeves and hood, worn with a mask at masquerades.
2. **tumultuous** (to͞o mul′ cho͞o əs) *adj.* wild and noisy.

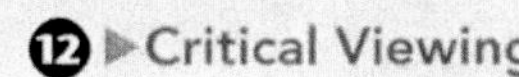
12 ▶ **Critical Viewing**

Possible response: In Act Three, Nora realizes that her life is about to fall apart. She is full of apprehension. Similarly, the actress looks thoughtful and apprehensive. Nora is contemplating the changes she faces as she waits for her secret to be discovered.

13 Critical Thinking

Analyze Causes and Effects

- Have a volunteer read aloud the bracketed passage. Ask students why Nora does not want to leave the party.
  Answer: She knows that Torvald will read Krogstad's letter and that her life will change forever.
- Then, ask students what Torvald must be thinking about Nora's refusal to leave.
  Answer: Torvald thinks that Nora is being stubborn and unreasonable, like a child who does not want to go home, although he may also be secretly pleased that his wife is "the life of the party" because it brings more attention to him.

14 **Reading Check**

Answer: Mrs. Linde wants Krogstad to leave the letter so that Nora and Torvald can deal with Nora's secret.

CUSTOMIZE INSTRUCTION FOR UNIVERSAL ACCESS

For English Learners	For Gifted/Talented Students
Point out the first stage direction on p. 926 and the use of the word *searchingly*. Explain that this is one of many adverbs formed by adding the suffix *-ly* to an adjective to give more specific meaning to the verb it modifies. Have students supply a definition for *searchingly* (in a searching manner) and list other adverbs formed in the same way. Some examples include *angrily, proudly, happily, sadly, willingly,* and *cheerfully.*	Remind students that the play revolves around a lack of communication among its characters. Have students work in pairs or groups to identify at least one passage in the play in which Nora could have confessed her crime to Torvald. Then, have them work together to write additional dialogue for that scene in which Nora confesses and Torvald reacts. Have students read or act out their dialogues in class.

⓯ Critical Thinking

Make an Inference

- Ask a volunteer to read aloud the bracketed passage on pp. 927–928. Tell students that Torvald's tendency to offer his unsolicited opinion is obvious in this passage.
- Challenge students to make an inference about Torvald's character on the basis of his conversational style. Possible response: Torvald is very concerned about what other people think, finding himself more interested in the impression Nora made on the audience than on her actual dancing.

⓰ Reading Strategy

Recognizing Dramatic Tension

- Read aloud the second bracketed passage on p. 928. Remind students that the letter holds the potential of elevating the play's dramatic tension.
- Ask students the Reading Strategy question on p. 928: If Krogstad is no longer a threat to Nora, why does the letter continue to be a cause of dramatic tension? Answer: The letter is still a threat because Torvald will find out that his wife has deceived him.

⓯ been a bit too naturalistic—I mean it rather overstepped the proprieties of art. But never mind—what's important is, she made a success, an overwhelming success. You think I could let her stay on after that and spoil the effect? Oh no; I took my lovely little Capri girl—my capricious[3] little Capri girl, I should say—took her under my arm; one quick tour of the ballroom, a curtsy to every side, and then—as they say in novels—the beautiful vision disappeared. An exit should always be effective, Mrs. Linde, but that's what I can't get Nora to grasp. Phew, its hot in here. [*Flings the domino on a chair and opens the door to his room.*] Why's it dark in here? Oh, yes, of course. Excuse me. [*He goes in and lights a couple of candles.*]

naturalistic (nach' ər əl is' tik) *adj.* faithful to nature

proprieties (prō prī' ə tēz) *n.* conformities with what is considered fitting, suitable, or proper

NORA [*in a sharp, breathless whisper*]: So?

MRS. LINDE [*quietly*]: I talked with him.

NORA: And—?

MRS. LINDE: Nora—you must tell your husband everything.

NORA [*dully*]: I knew it.

⓰ **MRS. LINDE:** You've got nothing to fear from Krogstad, but you have to speak out.

NORA: I won't tell.

MRS. LINDE: Then the letter will.

NORA: Thanks, Kristine. I know now what's to be done. Shh!

Reading Strategy Recognizing Dramatic Tension If Krogstad is no longer a threat to Nora, why does the letter continue to be a cause of dramatic tension?

HELMER [*reentering*]: Well, then, Mrs. Linde—have you admired her?

MRS. LINDE: Yes, and now I'll say good night.

HELMER: Oh, come, so soon? Is this yours, this knitting?

MRS. LINDE: Yes, thanks. I nearly forgot it.

HELMER: Do you knit, then?

MRS. LINDE: Oh yes.

HELMER: You know what? You should embroider instead.

MRS. LINDE: Really? Why?

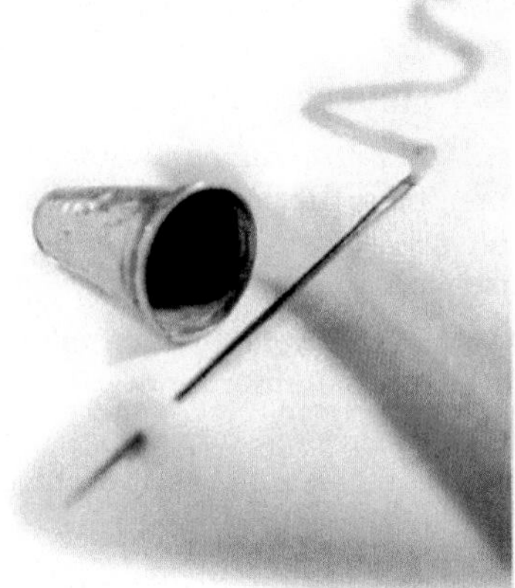

HELMER: Yes, because it's a lot prettier. See here, one holds the embroidery so, in the left hand, and then one guides the needle with the right—so—in an easy, sweeping curve—right?

MRS. LINDE: Yes, I guess that's—

HELMER: But, on the other hand, knitting—it can never be anything but ugly. Look, see here, the arms tucked in, the knitting needles going up and down, there's something Chinese about it. Ah, that was really a glorious champagne they served.

3. **capricious** (kə prish' əs) *adj.* erratic; flighty.

CUSTOMIZE INSTRUCTION FOR UNIVERSAL ACCESS

For Less Proficient Readers	For Advanced Readers
Tell students that like a short story, a play is a narrative made up of basic elements—plot, characters, setting, and theme. Have students treat each act as a short story. Help them identify the setting and the main characters, summarize the plot, and determine the overall theme or themes. As a follow-up, have students discuss which of these four elements seems to contribute most to the play as a whole.	Ask students to review all of what they have read so far and then write these notes: a plot outline, a short description of the setting, and brief character sketches of Nora, Torvald, Mrs. Linde, Dr. Rank, and Krogstad. Have students write a short story based on the play and their notes. Because students have not yet finished reading the play, ask them to write an ending of their own without reading ahead.

17 **MRS. LINDE:** Yes, good night, Nora, and don't be stubborn anymore.

HELMER: Well put, Mrs. Linde!

MRS. LINDE: Good night, Mr. Helmer.

HELMER [*accompanying her to the door*]: Good night, good night. I hope you get home all right. I'd be very happy to—but you don't have far to go. Good night, good night. [*She leaves. He shuts the door after her and returns.*] There, now, at last we got her out the door. She's a deadly bore, that creature.

NORA: Aren't you pretty tired, Torvald?

HELMER: No, not a bit.

NORA: You're not sleepy?

HELMER: Not at all. On the contrary, I'm feeling quite exhilarated. But you? Yes, you really look tired and sleepy.

NORA: Yes, I'm very tired. Soon now I'll sleep.

HELMER: See! You see! I was right all along that we shouldn't stay longer.

NORA: Whatever you do is always right.

18 **HELMER** [*kissing her brow*]: Now my little lark talks sense. Say, did you notice what a time Rank was having tonight?

NORA: Oh, was he? I didn't get to speak with him.

HELMER: I scarcely did either, but it's a long time since I've seen him in such high spirits. [*Gazes at her a moment, then comes nearer her.*] Hm—it's marvelous, though, to be back home again—to be completely alone with you. Oh, you bewitchingly lovely young woman!

NORA: Torvald, don't look at me like that!

HELMER: Can't I look at my richest treasure? At all that beauty that's mine, mine alone—completely and utterly.

NORA [*moving around to the other side of the table*]: You mustn't talk to me that way tonight.

HELMER [*following her*]: The tarantella is still in your blood, I can see—and it makes you even more enticing. Listen. The guests are beginning to go. [*Dropping his voice.*] Nora—it'll soon be quiet through this whole house.

19 **NORA:** Yes, I hope so.

HELMER: You do, don't you, my love? Do you realize—when I'm out at a party like this with you—do you know why I talk to you so little, and keep such a distance away; just send you a stolen look now and then—you know why I do it? It's because I'm imagining then that you're my secret darling, my secret young bride-to-be, and that no one suspects there's anything between us.

NORA: Yes, yes; oh, yes, I know you're always thinking of me.

Literary Analysis
Theme What does Mrs. Linde suggest about everyone's right to become an individual when she tells Nora not to be stubborn?

Literary Analysis
Theme In what way is Torvald preventing Nora from finding happiness in their marriage?

20  **Reading Check**
What advice does Mrs. Linde give Nora regarding Torvald?

17 Literary Analysis

Theme

- Read aloud the bracketed line. Point out Mrs. Linde's echoing Torvald in calling Nora "stubborn." Ask students to explain what Mrs. Linde means by this characterization of Nora.
  Possible response: Mrs. Linde is reminding Nora to tell Torvald her secret and stop being stubborn about withholding it.
- Ask the first Literary Analysis question on p. 929: What does Mrs. Linde suggest about everyone's right to become an individual when she tells Nora not to be stubborn?
  Possible response: Mrs. Linde suggests that people cannot be independent if they are dishonest.

18 Background

Torvald as Caricature

Some critics have observed that Torvald can be viewed almost as a caricature. Throughout the play, he lacks even a hint of self-awareness. In his own eyes he is the perfect husband, which means that in regard to his wife, he is infallible. Most husbands would immediately detect the sarcasm in the line, "Whatever you do is always right." Torvald, on the other hand, replies, "Now my little lark talks sense."

19 Literary Analysis

Theme

- Have two volunteers read the bracketed passage aloud. Make sure that students understand the nature of Torvald's advances and Nora's negative response.
- Ask students the second Literary Analysis question on p. 929: In what way is Torvald preventing Nora from finding happiness in their marriage?
  Possible response: Torvald does not recognize Nora's need to find fulfillment in life beyond receiving compliments from other people.

20 Reading Check

Answer: Mrs. Linde tells Nora to be honest with Torvald.

CUSTOMIZE INSTRUCTION FOR UNIVERSAL ACCESS

For Less Proficient Readers	For Advanced Readers
Ask students to choose two characters and make a word web for each that includes both good qualities and faults. As students read further, encourage them to note on the web additional personality traits and brief quotations that support them. Then, use these graphic organizers to generate a discussion about the characters. As a follow-up, have students discuss what this mix of good and bad in each character suggests about the play's major themes.	Ask students to classify the play's characters as major (those who take a prominent part in the action) and minor (those who have relatively few lines and play a small part in the action). Remind students that even characters with relatively few lines can have a profound impact on the play. Have students work in small groups to decide how important each character is and why. Challenge students to create a pie chart that shows the percentages of each character's importance to the play.

21 Literary Analysis

Theme and Foreshadowing

- Point out to students that this line contains Nora's first open expression of irritation with Torvald. Ask students to connect her reaction to the theme that self-expression is a basic human right.
  Possible response: Faced with real problems, Nora finally objects to Torvald's seeing her as a character he has created.
- Ask students the Literary Analysis question on p. 930: What personality change in Nora might be foreshadowed when she speaks up to Torvald?
  Possible response: This utterance may be Nora's first step toward honesty, especially in defining herself as an individual.

22 Reading Strategy

Recognizing Dramatic Tension

- Read aloud the bracketed passage. Then, point out to students how Dr. Rank's knock at the door immediately changes the mood onstage. Ask students to explain why a knock at the door has this power.
  Possible response: The reader knows that Nora is distressed; the knock at the door means her distress will be prolonged or even made worse, depending on the visitor and the purpose for the visit.
- Ask students the Reading Strategy question on p. 930: What effect does Torvald's irritation have on the dramatic tension in this scene?
  Possible response: Torvald's annoyance with Nora may reveal itself as annoyance with Dr. Rank, a mistake that may lead to more problems.

HELMER: And then when we leave and I place the shawl over those fine young rounded shoulders—over that wonderful curving neck—then I pretend that you're my young bride, that we're just coming from the wedding, that for the first time I'm bringing you into my house—that for the first time I'm alone with you—completely alone with you, your trembling young beauty! All this evening I've longed for nothing but you. When I saw you turn and sway in the tarantella—my blood was pounding till I couldn't stand it—that's why I brought you down here so early—

21 **NORA:** Go away, Torvald! Leave me alone. I don't want all this.

HELMER: What do you mean? Nora, you're teasing me. You will, won't you? Aren't I your husband—?

[*A knock at the outside door.*]

NORA [*startled*]: What's that?

HELMER [*going toward the hall*]: Who is it?

22 **RANK** [*outside*]: It's me. May I come in a moment?

HELMER [*with quiet irritation*]: Oh, what does he want now? [*Aloud.*] Hold on. [*Goes and opens the door.*] Oh, how nice that you didn't just pass us by!

RANK: I thought I heard your voice, and then I wanted so badly to have a look in. [*Lightly glancing about.*] Ah, me, these old familiar haunts. You have it snug and cozy in here, you two.

HELMER: You seemed to be having it pretty cozy upstairs, too.

RANK: Absolutely. Why shouldn't I? Why not take in everything in life? As much as you can, anyway, and as long as you can. The wine was superb—

HELMER: The champagne especially.

RANK: You noticed that too? It's amazing how much I could guzzle down.

NORA: Torvald also drank a lot of champagne this evening.

RANK: Oh?

NORA: Yes, and that always makes him so entertaining.

RANK: Well, why shouldn't one have a pleasant evening after a well-spent day?

HELMER: Well spent? I'm afraid I can't claim that.

RANK [*slapping him on the back*]: But I can, you see!

NORA: Dr. Rank, you must have done some scientific research today.

RANK: Quite so.

HELMER: Come now—little Nora talking about scientific research!

NORA: And can I congratulate you on the results?

RANK: Indeed you may.

Literary Analysis
Theme and Foreshadowing What personality change in Nora might be foreshadowed when she speaks up to Torvald?

Reading Strategy
Recognizing Dramatic Tension What effect does Torvald's irritation have on the dramatic tension in this scene?

ENRICHMENT: Literature Connection

A Moral Disease?

The critic John Northam has explored the parallels between Nora's "moral disease" and Dr. Rank's physical illness:

> Ibsen also emphasizes the climax of the disease and death theme by bringing on Rank. Nora has danced her tarantella at the party upstairs—her last fling. At the same party, Rank has been enjoying his last fling—at the champagne—before retiring to his deathbed. The last link which Ibsen forges between the two victims of the poison and corruption is that their death warrants share the same letterbox. Rank leaves behind him a visiting card marked with a black cross, a sign that he has crawled away to die; the card lies beside Krogstad's letter to Torvald, and when Torvald reads that, Nora must die so as not to inflict her moral disease on others; physical and moral corruption burn themselves out together.

NORA: Then they were good?

RANK: The best possible for both doctor and patient—certainty.

NORA [*quickly and searchingly*]: Certainty?

RANK: Complete certainty. So don't I owe myself a gay evening afterwards?

NORA: Yes, you're right, Dr. Rank.

HELMER: I'm with you—just so long as you don't have to suffer for it in the morning.

RANK: Well, one never gets something for nothing in life.

NORA: Dr. Rank—are you very fond of masquerade parties?

RANK: Yes, if there's a good array of odd disguises—

NORA: Tell me, what should we two go as at the next masquerade?

HELMER: You little featherhead—already thinking of the next!

RANK: We two? I'll tell you what: you must go as Charmed Life—

HELMER: Yes, but find a costume for *that*!

24 **RANK:** Your wife can appear just as she looks every day.

HELMER: That was nicely put. But don't you know what you're going to be?

RANK: Yes, Helmer, I've made up my mind.

HELMER: Well?

RANK: At the next masquerade I'm going to be invisible.

HELMER: That's a funny idea.

RANK: They say there's a hat—black, huge—have you never heard of the hat that makes you invisible? You put it on, and then no one on earth can see you.

HELMER [*suppressing a smile*]: Ah, of course.

23  **Reading Check**

What does Dr. Rank tell Nora regarding the results of his scientific research?

25 **Critical Viewing ▶**

What information has Dr. Rank learned that might explain the serious demeanor of the actor in this picture? **[Connect]**

23 **Reading Check**

Answer: Dr. Rank tells Nora that the scientific results were the best possible because they offered certainty.

24 **Critical Thinking**

Analyze

- Tell students that as they read this passage they should assume Nora understands that Dr. Rank will not be alive for the next masquerade and that she herself may not be around either.
- Challenge students to explain why Nora asks, "Tell me, what should we two go as at the next masquerade?"
  Possible response: Nora plays on the idea that masquerades are events for which people assume different forms: by the next masquerade, Nora knows that Dr. Rank will be transformed by death, and that she will be transformed by dishonor and scandal.

25 ▶ **Critical Viewing**

Dr. Rank has learned that he will die very soon and has come to say his final goodbye to Nora.

CUSTOMIZE INSTRUCTION FOR UNIVERSAL ACCESS

For Special Needs Students	For Less Proficient Readers
Ask students to identify the characters pictured in the photographs that accompany *A Doll House*. Ask them to identify each character of the play. Help students understand how they have used context clues to help them identify the characters. Ask them to discuss the actors' costumes, props, or facial expressions in determining which characters are depicted in the photographs.	Have students discuss the photographs used to illustrate the play. Challenge students to explain what the illustrations add to their understanding of the play. Then, have students explain how the photographs illustrate nineteenth-century Europe. Ask students to write brief paragraphs about life in the nineteenth century from looking at the illustrations.

26 Reading Strategy

Recognizing Dramatic Tension

- Have volunteers read aloud the bracketed passage. Tell students that there is nothing particularly dramatic about Dr. Rank's request for a cigar, but that he asks for a specific type of cigar and then bids his friends farewell suggests that this is his last request, a revelation that adds tension to this scene.
- Ask students the Reading Strategy question on p. 932: Do you think Dr. Rank's secrecy about his illness creates dramatic tension in this scene? Why or why not?
  Possible response: Because this is Dr. Rank's last chance to share his secret, his silence creates dramatic tension. Nora knows the secret, so there is also suspense about whether she will reveal it.

27 Literary Analysis

Theme and Foreshadowing

- Point out that in this passage Nora seems to have forgotten that her own troubles will begin once Torvald goes to the mailbox.
- Then, ask students the Literary Analysis question on p. 932: What possible confrontation might be foreshadowed when Torvald goes to the mailbox?
  Answer: The final confrontation between Nora and Torvald is foreshadowed.

RANK: But I'm quite forgetting what I came for. Helmer, give me a cigar, one of the dark Havanas.

HELMER: With the greatest pleasure. [*Holds out his case.*]

RANK: Thanks. [*Takes one and cuts off the tip.*]

NORA [*striking a match*]: Let me give you a light.

26 **RANK:** Thank you. [*She holds the match for him; he lights the cigar.*] And now good-bye.

HELMER: Good-bye, good-bye, old friend.

NORA: Sleep well, Doctor.

RANK: Thanks for that wish.

NORA: Wish me the same.

RANK: You? All right, if you like— Sleep well. And thanks for the light. [*He nods to them both and leaves.*]

HELMER [*his voice subdued*]: He's been drinking heavily.

27 **NORA** [*absently*]: Could be. [HELMER *takes his keys from his pocket and goes out in the hall.*] Torvald—what are you after?

HELMER: Got to empty the mailbox; it's nearly full. There won't be room for the morning papers.

NORA: Are you working tonight?

HELMER: You know I'm not. Why—what's this? Someone's been at the lock.

NORA: At the lock—?

HELMER: Yes, I'm positive. What do you suppose—? I can't imagine one of the maids—? Here's a broken hairpin. Nora, it's yours—

NORA [*quickly*]: Then it must be the children—

HELMER: You'd better break them of that. Hm, hm—well, opened it after all. [*Takes the contents out and calls into the kitchen.*] Helene! Helene, would you put out the lamp in the hall. [*He returns to the room, shutting the hall door, then displays the handful of mail.*] Look how it's piled up. [*Sorting through them.*] Now what's this?

NORA [*at the window*]: The letter! Oh, Torvald, no!

HELMER: Two calling cards—from Rank.

NORA: From Dr. Rank?

HELMER [*examining them*]: "Dr. Rank, Consulting Physician." They were on top. He must have dropped them in as he left.

NORA: Is there anything on them?

HELMER: There's a black cross over the name. See? That's a gruesome notion. He could almost be announcing his own death.

NORA: That's just what he's doing.

Reading Strategy
Recognizing Dramatic Tension Do you think Dr. Rank's secrecy about his illness creates dramatic tension in this scene? Why or why not?

Literary Analysis
Theme and Foreshadowing What possible confrontation might be foreshadowed when Torvald goes to the mailbox?

CUSTOMIZE INSTRUCTION FOR UNIVERSAL ACCESS

For English Learners	For Gifted/Talented Students
Check comprehension and help maintain interest by asking students to draft a list of questions they would like to ask the characters at this point in the play. Have students work in pairs to answer each other's questions. If students have trouble preparing questions, offer them the following question and answer to get them started: **Question:** Mrs. Linde, why did you want Torvald to read Krogstad's letter? Don't you care about Nora? **Possible answer:** I wanted Torvald to know the truth.	Ask students to list questions they would like to ask the characters at this point in the play. After students have generated lists for Nora, Torvald, Mrs. Linde, Krogstad, and Dr. Rank, assign these "parts" to students who will appear in character, and perhaps in costume, during mock interviews conducted by other students.

HELMER: What! You've heard something? Something he's told you?

NORA: Yes. That when those cards came, he'd be taking his leave of us. He'll shut himself in now and die.

HELMER: Ah, my poor friend! Of course I knew he wouldn't be here much longer. But so soon— And then to hide himself away like a wounded animal.

NORA: If it has to happen, then it's best it happens in silence—don't you think so, Torvald?

28 **HELMER** [*pacing up and down*]: He'd grown right into our lives. I simply can't imagine him gone. He with his suffering and loneliness—like a dark cloud setting off our sunlit happiness. Well, maybe it's best this way. For him, at least. [*Standing still.*] And maybe for us too, Nora. Now we're thrown back on each other, completely. [*Embracing her.*] Oh you, my darling wife, how can I hold you close enough? You know what, Nora—time and again I've wished you were in some terrible danger, just so I could stake my life and soul and everything, for your sake.

NORA [*tearing herself away, her voice firm and decisive*]: Now you must read your mail, Torvald.

HELMER: No, no, not tonight. I want to stay with you, dearest.

NORA: With a dying friend on your mind?

HELMER: You're right. We've both had a shock. There's ugliness between us—these thoughts of death and corruption. We'll have to get free of them first. Until then—we'll stay apart.

NORA [*clinging about his neck*]: Torvald—good night! Good night!

HELMER [*kissing her on the cheek*]: Good night, little songbird. Sleep well, Nora. I'll be reading my mail now. [*He takes the letters into his room and shuts the door after him.*]

NORA [*with bewildered glances, groping about, seizing* HELMER'S *domino, throwing it around her, and speaking in short, hoarse, broken whispers*]: Never see him again. Never, never. [*Putting her shawl over her head.*] Never see the children either—them, too. Never, never. Oh, the freezing black water! The depths—down—Oh, I wish it were over—He has it now; he's reading it—now. Oh no, no, not yet. Torvald, good-bye, you and the children—[*She starts for the hall; as she does,* HELMER *throws*
29 *open his door and stands with an open letter in his hand.*]

HELMER: Nora!

NORA [*screams*]: Oh—!

HELMER: What is this? You know what's in this letter?

NORA: Yes, I know. Let me go! Let me out!

HELMER [*holding her back*]: Where are you going?

NORA [*struggling to break loose*]: You can't save me, Torvald!

Literary Analysis
Theme and Foreshadowing Do you think Torvald's lines foreshadow that he will take the blame for Nora? Explain.

30  **Reading Check**

What discovery does Torvald make when he empties the mailbox?

28 Literary Analysis

Theme and Foreshadowing

- After reading the bracketed passage aloud, remind students that earlier in the play (p. 905), Torvald told Nora that he had the "strength and courage enough as a man to take on the whole weight" of Krogstad's threats.
- Then, ask students the Literary Analysis question on p. 933: Do you think Torvald's lines foreshadow that he will take the blame for Nora? Explain.
  Possible response: Torvald has said a great deal about courage, but he may not rise to the challenge of defending Nora: he prizes his respectability too much. On the other hand, Torvald may see this as his chance to start over with Nora, so it is likely that he will defend her.

29 Critical Thinking

Speculate

- Ask students to read the bracketed passage independently.
- Ask students what Nora's plan is.
  Answer: Nora's plan is to commit suicide by drowning herself.
- Ask students to discuss the possibility that Torvald prevents Nora from killing herself because he loves her, not just because he wants her to explain the letter.

30 Reading Check

Answer: Torvald discovers the letter from Krogstad and two of Dr. Rank's calling cards that have small black crosses over the name.

CUSTOMIZE INSTRUCTION FOR UNIVERSAL ACCESS

For Special Needs Students	For Less Proficient Readers
Help students prepare for the play's climax by reviewing the rise of the play's action to p. 933. Have students compile lists of the main events of the play. On the board, create a line graph that charts the rise and fall of the plot. As students continue to read, have them add to the chart additional elements that contribute to the resolution of the plot.	Make sure students understand that p. 933 is the start of a powerful exchange between Torvald and Nora that leads toward the play's climax and conclusion. Help students understand the conflicts Nora and Torvald face. On the board, draw a two-column chart with these headings: *What is important to Nora?* and *What is important to Torvald?* In each column, list an example such as "forgiveness" or "freedom" in Nora's column and "public approval" in Torvald's.

31 ▶ Critical Viewing

Possible response: Nora now looks away from Torvald even though he stands close to her; her expression suggests a new resolve.

32 Critical Thinking

Interpret

- Read aloud the stage directions in the bracketed passage. Guide students to understand that the word *hardening* suggests that Nora has become serious and purposeful.
- Tell students that this is a turning point in the play. Ask students to express in their own words why Nora now wears this hardened expression.
  Possible response: Nora understands that Torvald is not noble, he does not love her, and he thinks only of how her crime will affect his reputation. The miracle she has been hoping for and dreading will not happen. Torvald will not rescue her, and her marriage will not be saved.

HELMER [*slumping back*]: True! Then it's true what he writes? How horrible! No, no it's impossible—it can't be true.

NORA: It *is* true. I've loved you more than all this world.

HELMER: Ah, none of your slippery tricks.

NORA [*taking one step toward him*]: Torvald—!

HELMER: What is this you've blundered into!

NORA: Just let me loose. You're not going to suffer for my sake. You're not going to take on my guilt.

HELMER: No more playacting. [*Locks the hall door.*] You stay right here and give me a reckoning. You understand what you've done? Answer! You understand?

32 **NORA** [*looking squarely at him, her face hardening*]: Yes. I'm beginning to understand everything now.

31 ▲ Critical Viewing

In what ways does this photograph capture the change in the relationship between Torvald and Nora? **[Interpret]**

33 **HELMER** [*striding about*]: Oh, what an awful awakening! In all these eight years—she who was my pride and joy—a hypocrite, a liar—worse, worse—a criminal! How infinitely disgusting it all is! The shame! [NORA *says nothing and goes on looking straight at him. He stops in front of her.*] I should have suspected something of the kind. I should have known. All your father's flimsy values— Be still! All your father's flimsy values have come out in you. No religion, no morals, no sense of duty— Oh, how I'm punished for letting him off! I did it for your sake, and you repay me like this.

NORA: Yes, like this.

HELMER: Now you've wrecked all my happiness—ruined my whole future. Oh, it's awful to think of. I'm in a cheap little grafter's hands; he can do anything he wants with me, ask for anything, play with me like a puppet—and I can't breathe a word. I'll be swept down miserably into the depths on account of a featherbrained woman.

NORA: When I'm gone from this world, you'll be free.

HELMER: Oh, quit posing. Your father had a mess of those speeches too. What good would that ever do me if you were gone from this world, as you say? Not the slightest. He can still make the whole thing known; and if he does, I could be falsely suspected as your accomplice. They might even think that I was behind it—that I put you up to it. And all that I can thank you for—you that I've coddled the whole of our marriage. 34 Can you see now what you've done to me?

NORA [*icily calm*]: Yes.

HELMER: It's so incredible, I just can't grasp it. But we'll have to patch up whatever we can. Take off the shawl. I said, take it off! I've got to appease him somehow or other. The thing has to be hushed up at any cost. And as for you and me, it's got to seem like everything between us is just as it was—to the outside world, that is. You'll go right on living in this house, of course. But you can't be allowed to bring up the children; I don't dare trust you with them— Oh, to have to say this to someone I've loved so much! Well, that's done with. From now on happiness doesn't matter; all that matters is saving the bits and pieces, the appearance— [*The doorbell rings.* HELMER *starts.*] What's that? And so late. Maybe the worst—? You think he'd—? Hide, Nora! Say you're sick. [NORA *remains standing motionless.* HELMER *goes and opens the door.*]

MAID [*half dressed, in the hall*]: A letter for Mrs. Helmer.

HELMER: I'll take it. [*Snatches the letter and shuts the door.*] Yes, it's from him. You don't get it; I'm reading it myself.

NORA: Then read it.

HELMER [*by the lamp*]: I hardly dare. We may be ruined, you and I. But—I've got to know. [*Rips open the letter, skims through a few lines,* 35 *glances at an enclosure, then cries out joyfully.*] Nora! [NORA *looks inquiringly at him.*] Nora! Wait!—better check it again— Yes, yes, it's true. I'm saved. Nora, I'm saved!

hypocrite (hip′ə krit′) *n.* someone who merely pretends to be virtuous

grafter (graft′ər) *n.* someone who takes advantage of his or her position to gain money or property dishonestly

Literary Analysis
Theme and Foreshadowing In what way might Nora's "icily calm" reaction foreshadow her behavior from this point on?

36 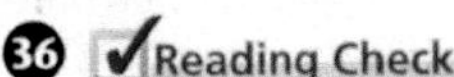 **Reading Check**

Other than Krogstad, whom does Torvald now consider a criminal and a grafter?

CUSTOMIZE INSTRUCTION FOR UNIVERSAL ACCESS

For Less Proficient Readers	For Gifted/Talented Students
It may help students to track the sides of the final arguments between Nora and Torvald. Ask students to draw a two-column chart on a sheet of paper, labeling one column *Nora's Reasons* and the other *Torvald's Reasons*. In the first column, students should write all of the reasons Nora has given for her crime. In the second column, students should write all of Torvald's reasons for being angry with Nora. Ask students to work with a partner to create a generalized statement about the two characters.	Organize students into small groups. Assign one student in each group the role of either Torvald or Nora. Tell the other group members to portray the character's friends. Have students carry on a conversation in these roles to share insight about the argument Torvald and Nora have just had. Invite groups to reenact their conversations for the whole class.

33 Vocabulary Development

Greek Prefix *hypo-*

- Draw students' attention to the word *hypocrite* and its definition, "someone who merely pretends to be virtuous."
- Explain that the prefix *hypo-* means "under," "less than," or "slightly." The word *hypocrite* comes from the ancient Greek word *hypokrites,* which means "actor or pretender"; this is particularly appropriate for Nora.
- Have students list other words that contain the prefix *hypo-*.
  Possible response: The words *hypochondriac* and *hypothesis* contain *hypo-*.

34 Literary Analysis

Theme and Foreshadowing

- Have two volunteers read aloud the bracketed passage. Make sure that students notice Torvald's long remarks in contrast to Nora's short ones. Ask students to discuss the significance of the unequal number of lines.
  Possible response: Torvald is so busy ranting that he fails to "hear" his wife imply that she meant to hurt him and that she is thinking about death. These lines reinforce Torvald's character.
- Ask students the Literary Analysis question on p. 935: In what way might Nora's "icily calm" reaction foreshadow her behavior from this point on?
  Possible response: Nora's reaction signals a significant change: there will be no more theatrics, distractions, or false flattery on Nora's part because she is no longer afraid of Torvald's learning her secret.

35 Background

Revision

Tell students that in an earlier draft of the play, the last lines in the bracketed passage read, "We're saved! Nora, we're saved." In revising his play, Ibsen changed the line to "I'm saved. Nora, I'm saved!"

36 Reading Check

Answer: Torvald considers Nora a criminal and a grafter.

37 Reading Strategy

Recognizing Dramatic Tension

- Read aloud the bracketed passage. Point out that in burning these papers, Torvald seems to think he has also erased the things he has said to Nora. Ask students to identify the dramatic tension in this passage.
  Possible response: As Torvald speaks at length, the audience must wait to learn Nora's reaction, wondering whether she will back down from the assertive stance she took earlier.
- Ask students the Reading Strategy question on p. 936: In what ways does Torvald change when the dramatic tension breaks?
  Possible response: Torvald realizes that he can control the situation again and becomes his old self again, acting like Nora's protector.

38 Literary Analysis

Theme and Foreshadowing

- Have a volunteer read aloud the bracketed passage. Ask students to discuss how Nora may feel as Torvald attempts to comfort her.
  Possible response: Nora likely doubts Torvald's sincerity because just a moment earlier, he told her that she was unfit to care for their children.
- Ask students the Literary Analysis question on p. 936: Do you think Torvald recognizes his wife's individuality? Explain.
  Possible response: No; Torvald sees Nora as little more than a part of his public image.

39 Background

Sign of the Times

Modern audiences often think that Torvald is impossibly ignorant and insensitive at this point in the play. However, Torvald's behavior was completely realistic to Ibsen's audiences. In fact, Laura Kieler, the model for Nora, was committed to an insane asylum by her husband after a series of events similar to those in the play.

NORA: And I?

37 **HELMER:** You too, of course. We're both saved, both of us. Look. He's sent back your note. He says he's sorry and ashamed—that a happy development in his life—oh, who cares what he says! Nora, we're saved! No one can hurt you. Oh, Nora, Nora—but first, this ugliness all has to go. Let me see— [*Takes a look at the note.*] No, I don't want to see it; I want the whole thing to fade like a dream. [*Tears the note and both letters to pieces, throws them into the stove and watches them burn.*] There—now there's nothing left— He wrote that since Christmas Eve you— Oh, they must have been three terrible days for you, Nora.

NORA: I fought a hard fight.

HELMER: And suffered pain and saw no escape but— No, we're not going to dwell on anything unpleasant. We'll just be grateful and keep on repeating: it's over now, it's over! You hear me, Nora? You don't seem to realize—it's over. What's it mean—that frozen look? Oh, poor little Nora, I understand. You can't believe I've forgiven you. But I have Nora; I swear I have. I know that what you did, you did out of love for me.

38 **NORA:** That's true.

39 **HELMER:** You loved me the way a wife ought to love her husband. It's simply the means that you couldn't judge. But you think I love you any the less for not knowing how to handle your affairs? No, no—just lean on me; I'll guide you and teach you. I wouldn't be a man if this feminine helplessness didn't make you twice as attractive to me. You mustn't mind those sharp words I said—that was all in the first confusion of thinking my world had collapsed. I've forgiven you, Nora; I swear I've forgiven you.

NORA: My thanks for your forgiveness. [*She goes out through the door, right.*]

HELMER: No, wait— [*Peers in.*] What are you doing in there?

NORA [*inside*]: Getting out of my costume.

HELMER [*by the open door*]: Yes, do that. Try to calm yourself and collect your thoughts again, my frightened little songbird. You can rest easy now; I've got wide wings to shelter you with. [*Walking about close by the door.*] How snug and nice our home is, Nora. You're safe here; I'll keep you like a hunted dove I've rescued out of a hawk's claws. I'll bring peace to your poor, shuddering heart. Gradually it'll happen, Nora; you'll see. Tomorrow all this will look different to you; then everything will be as it was. I won't have to go on repeating I forgive you; you'll feel it for yourself. How can you imagine I'd ever conceivably want to disown you—or even blame you in any way? Ah, you don't know a man's heart, Nora. For a man there's something indescribably sweet and satisfying in knowing he's forgiven his wife—and forgiven her out of a full and open heart. It's as if she belongs to him in two ways now: in a sense he's given her fresh into the world again, and she's become his wife and his child as well. From now on that's what you'll be to me—you little,

Reading Strategy
Recognizing Dramatic Tension In what ways does Torvald change when the dramatic tension breaks?

Literary Analysis
Theme and Foreshadowing Do you think Torvald recognizes his wife's individuality? Explain.

bewildered, helpless thing. Don't be afraid of anything, Nora; just open your heart to me, and I'll be conscience and will to you both—[NORA *enters in her regular clothes.*] What's this? Not in bed? You've changed your dress?

NORA: Yes, Torvald, I've changed my dress.

40 **HELMER:** But why now, so late?

NORA: Tonight I'm not sleeping.

HELMER: But Nora dear—

NORA [*looking at her watch*]: It's still not so very late. Sit down, Torvald; we have a lot to talk over. [*She sits at one side of the table.*]

HELMER: Nora—what is this? That hard expression—

NORA: Sit down. This'll take some time. I have a lot to say.

HELMER [*sitting at the table directly opposite her*]: You worry me, Nora. And I don't understand you.

NORA: No, that's exactly it. You don't understand me. And I've never understood you either—until tonight. No, don't interrupt. You can just listen to what I say. We're closing out accounts, Torvald.

HELMER: How do you mean that?

NORA [*after a short pause*]: Doesn't anything strike you about our
41 sitting here like this?

HELMER: What's that?

NORA: We've been married now eight years. Doesn't it occur to you that this is the first time we two, you and I, man and wife, have ever talked seriously together?

HELMER: What do you mean—seriously?

NORA: In eight whole years—longer even—right from our first acquaintance, we've never exchanged a serious word on any serious thing.

HELMER: You mean I should constantly go and involve you in problems you couldn't possibly help me with?

NORA: I'm not talking of problems. I'm saying that we've never sat down seriously together and tried to get to the bottom of anything.

HELMER: But dearest, what good would that ever do you?

NORA: That's the point right there: you've never understood me. I've been wronged greatly, Torvald—first by Papa, and then by you.

HELMER: What! By us—the two people who've loved you more than anyone else?

NORA [*shaking her head*]: You never loved me. You've thought it fun to be in love with me, that's all.

HELMER: Nora, what a thing to say!

bewildered (bē wil′ dərd) *adj.* puzzled, confused

Literary Analysis
Theme and Foreshadowing What do you think Nora's change of dress foreshadows? Explain.

Literary Analysis
Theme In what way do these lines reflect the theme that a successful relationship is based on equality and partnership?

✓Reading Check

According to Torvald, what motivated Nora to get involved with Krogstad?

CUSTOMIZE INSTRUCTION FOR UNIVERSAL ACCESS

For English Learners	For Gifted/Talented Students
Explain to students that beginning on p. 937, Nora's character changes dramatically and what she has to say is the message of the play. Allow students to work in pairs or small groups, stopping after every half-page or so to review and summarize what Nora and Torvald have said. Allow students to use dictionaries and ask questions to clarify the characters' meanings. If possible, ask a student who is proficient in English to participate in order to help with questions students might have.	Invite students to write a song from Nora or Torvald's point of view or to write a duet that incorporates both. Tell students to make their songs entertaining, but to make sure that the lyrics remain true to the characters as revealed in the play. Have students write their own music or use the tune of a popular song and then perform their songs for the class.

40 Literary Analysis

Theme and Foreshadowing

- Read aloud the bracketed passage. Remind students that Nora's costume has also served as a symbol of her playacting. Ask students to offer ideas about the costume's symbolic meaning.
  Possible response: By changing out of the costume, Nora sheds the role she has been playacting—that of Torvald's dutiful wife.
- Ask students the first Literary Analysis question on p. 937: What do you think Nora's change of dress foreshadows? Explain.
  Possible response: Nora does not plan to stay. She is getting dressed so that she can leave.

41 Literary Analysis

Theme

- Have two volunteers read aloud the bracketed passage. Point out Nora's use of banking language in this passage when she says, "We're closing out accounts." Help students understand that Nora chooses language that Torvald will understand easily and quickly because the points she is about to raise are important to her.
- Ask students with what Torvald equates serious conversation and how this attitude fits one of the play's themes.
  Possible response: Torvald believes that serious conversations have to do with solving problems, not discussing ideas.
- Ask students the second Literary Analysis question on p. 937: In what ways do these lines reflect the theme that a successful relationship is based on equality and partnership?
  Possible response: Torvald's belief that Nora cannot help him with his problems indicates that he does not view their marriage as a partnership between equals; that Nora has never spoken about this rift between them also confirms that she does not share power with Torvald in their relationship.

42 ✓Reading Check

Answer: Torvald believes that Nora got involved with Krogstad because she did not know any better.

43 Literary Analysis

Theme

- Have students read the bracketed passage independently. Point out to students how Torvald responds to Nora's realization that she has been treated like a doll, not an equal.
- Ask students the Literary Analysis question on p. 938: Which of the play's themes is Nora stating in these lines? Explain.
  Possible response: Nora furthers the theme that a successful relationship is based on trust, equality, and individuality; she realizes that she has not been an equal in her marriage, and she is no longer willing to participate in a marriage that is not a partnership.

44 Reading Strategy

Recognizing Dramatic Tension

- Read the bracketed passage aloud. Before asking students the Reading Strategy question, ask them to review what Nora has meant to Torvald.
  Answer: Nora has been a comfort, a source of entertainment, a prize, and a sign of respectability.
- Ask students the Reading Strategy question on p. 938: What does Torvald stand to lose if Nora leaves him?
  Possible response: Torvald loses not only his wife but also his respectability in the community. He loses the comfort of his home and his self-esteem.

NORA: Yes, it's true now, Torvald. When I lived at home with Papa, he told me all his opinions, so I had the same ones too; or if they were different I hid them, since he wouldn't have cared for that. He used to call me his doll-child, and he played with me the way I played with my dolls. Then I came into your house—

HELMER: How can you speak of our marriage like that?

NORA [*unperturbed*]: I mean, then I went from Papa's hands into yours. You arranged everything to your own taste, and so I got the same taste as you—or I pretended to; I can't remember. I guess a little of both, first one, then the other. Now when I look back, it seems as if I'd lived here like a beggar—just from hand to mouth. I've lived by doing tricks for you, Torvald. But that's the way you wanted it. It's a great sin what you and Papa did to me. You're to blame that nothing's become of me.

HELMER: Nora, how unfair and ungrateful you are! Haven't you been happy here?

NORA: No, never. I thought so—but I never have.

43 **HELMER:** Not—not happy!

NORA: No, only lighthearted. And you've always been so kind to me. But our home's been nothing but a playpen. I've been your doll-wife here, just as at home I was Papa's doll-child. And in turn the children have been my dolls. I thought it was fun when you played with me, just as they thought it fun when I played with them. That's been our marriage, Torvald.

Literary Analysis
Theme Which of the play's themes is Nora stating in these lines? Explain.

HELMER: There's some truth in what you're saying—under all the raving exaggeration. But it'll all be different after this. Playtime's over; now for the schooling.

NORA: Whose schooling—mine or the children's?

HELMER: Both yours and the children's, dearest.

NORA: Oh, Torvald, you're not the man to teach me to be a good wife to you.

HELMER: And you can say that?

NORA: And I—how am I equipped to bring up children?

HELMER: Nora!

NORA: Didn't you say a moment ago that that was no job to trust me with?

44 **HELMER:** In a flare of temper! Why fasten on that?

NORA: Yes, but you were so very right. I'm not up to the job. There's another job I have to do first. I have to try to educate myself. You can't help me with that. I've got to do it alone. And that's why I'm leaving you now.

Reading Strategy
Recognizing Dramatic Tension What does Torvald stand to lose if Nora leaves him?

HELMER [*jumping up*]: What's that?

CUSTOMIZE INSTRUCTION FOR UNIVERSAL ACCESS

For Gifted/Talented Students	For Advanced Readers
Ask students to create a daytime talk-show skit that features visits from characters in *A Doll House*. Students can pattern the show after sit-down formats or choose the audience-participation style. Encourage them to make their skits entertaining, but remind them that the guests must remain true to their characters as revealed in the play. Have groups present their skits to the class. Discuss issues that arise during the presentations.	Have students research the evolution of laws protecting and providing for women in Norway in 1879, the time in which the play was written. Ask students to present short reports to the class and then speculate on what Nora's life will be like if she leaves Torvald. Make sure that they mention how she will earn income, who will likely have custody of the children, and so on.

NORA: I have to stand completely alone, if I'm ever going to discover myself and the world out there. So I can't go on living with you.

HELMER: Nora, Nora!

NORA: I want to leave right away. Kristine should put me up for the night—

HELMER: You're insane! You've no right! I forbid you!

NORA: From here on, there's no use forbidding me anything. I'll take with me whatever is mine. I don't want a thing from you, either now or later.

HELMER: What kind of madness is this?

NORA: Tomorrow I'm going home—I mean, home where I came from. It'll be easier up there to find something to do.

HELMER: Oh, you blind, incompetent child!

NORA: I must learn to be competent, Torvald.

HELMER: Abandon your home, your husband, your children! And you're not even thinking what people will say.

NORA: I can't be concerned about that. I only know how essential this is.

HELMER: Oh, it's outrageous. So you'll run out like this on your most sacred vows.

NORA: What do you think are my most sacred vows?

HELMER: And I have to tell you that! Aren't they your duties to your husband and children?

NORA: I have other duties equally sacred.

HELMER: That isn't true. What duties are they?

NORA: Duties to myself.

HELMER: Before all else, you're a wife and a mother.

46 **NORA:** I don't believe in that anymore. I believe that, before all else, I'm a human being, no less than you—or anyway, I ought to try to become one. I know the majority thinks you're right, Torvald, and plenty of books agree with you, too. But I can't go on believing what the majority says, or what's written in books. I have to think over these things myself and try to understand them.

HELMER: Why can't you understand your place in your own home? On a point like that, isn't there one everlasting guide you can turn to? Where's your religion?

NORA: Oh, Torvald, I'm really not sure what religion is.

HELMER: What—?

NORA: I only know what the minister said when I was confirmed. He told me religion was this thing and that. When I get clear and away by

Literature in context History Connection

45 ***Independent Women, 1879***

A Doll House shocked its original audience because it addressed a controversial issue: the status of women. In 1879, when the play was written, it was virtually unthinkable in Europe and America that a middle-class wife could be a wholly independent person. Few women were highly educated or had careers of their own. Women in Norway could not vote until 1913—in the United States and Britain, women did not win full voting rights until 1920 and 1928, respectively.

When Nora tells Torvald she is leaving him and her children, they both recognize the difficulties she will face on her own. Torvald—and Isben's audience—would find Nora's choice shocking, and perhaps even foolhardy.

Literary Analysis

Theme Who or what is the "majority" whose opinion Nora questions?

47 **✓Reading Check**

What decision has Nora made about her life with Torvald?

45 Background

Independent Women, 1879

At the time Ibsen was writing *A Doll House*, women activists in the United States had already been lobbying for the right to vote for more than thirty years. The first women's rights convention had been held in Seneca Falls, New York, in 1848. At the convention, leading women's rights proponents presented their own version of the Declaration of Independence, called the Declaration of Sentiments. Using the language that appeared in the original declaration, the writers, who included Elizabeth Cady Stanton and Lucretia Mott, pointed out the inequalities women historically had faced. The most striking line in the Declaration of Sentiments was the simple addition of the two words "and women" to the most important sentence in the original Declaration of Independence: "We hold these truths to be self-evident: that all men and women are created equal." The Seneca Falls convention was the first organized attempt to call for the right of women to vote in the United States.

46 Literary Analysis

Theme

- Remind students of the theme "Every person has a right to individuality." Point out that society is a strong force that sometimes tries to coerce individuals to act or think a certain way.
- Ask students the Literary Analysis question on p. 939: Who or what is the "majority" whose opinion Nora questions?
  Answer: The majority is probably society.

Reteach Have students recall the ways a playwright develops a theme. If students need help, have them review the Literary Analysis instruction on p. 922.

47 ✓Reading Check

Answer: Nora has decided that she must leave Torvald.

CUSTOMIZE INSTRUCTION FOR UNIVERSAL ACCESS

For Special Needs Students	For Less Proficient Readers
Help students review events in the last act using cause-and-effect questions. Offer students the questions below to get them started. Make sure students answer with *because*. Then, challenge students to ask and answer their own cause-and-effect questions. • Why is Torvald angry with Nora? He is angry because he thinks she has put him at the mercy of Krogstad. • Why does Torvald forgive Nora? He forgives her because Krogstad has dropped his claims against Torvald.	Help students understand the problems that Nora and Torvald discuss before she leaves. Work with students to identify the problems Nora raises, Torvald's objections, and Nora's solutions. For example, Nora says that Torvald has treated her like a doll. Torvald responds by telling her that he will teach her. Nora's solution is to leave him. The Problem/Solution organizer on pp. 91–93 of **Writing Models and Graphic Organizers on Transparencies** may help students complete this exercise.

48 Literary Analysis

Theme and Foreshadowing

- Help students understand that this deeper side of Nora shows her development as a character, and it foreshadows even more changes ahead for her.
- Have students read the Literary Analysis question on p. 940: What future conflicts might Nora's lines foreshadow?
  Possible response: Nora will have to learn to make her own way in the world.

49 Reading Strategy

Recognizing Dramatic Tension

- Point out that Nora has clearly thought about the consequences of leaving and that her certainty creates concern that Torvald may prevent her from leaving.
- Have students identify what each character stands to lose if Nora leaves.
  Possible response: Nora stands to lose her children, her financial security, and her respectability; Torvald stands to lose his comfort and standing in the community.
- Read aloud the Reading Strategy question on p. 940: In what ways does Nora raise the stakes, making it clear that she and Torvald may lose more than Torvald imagined?
  Possible response: Nora suggests that Torvald lost her belief in him when he automatically turned against her; witnessing his behavior may have taken away Nora's belief in love.

myself, I'll go into that problem too. I'll see if what the minister said was right, or, in any case, if it's right for me.

HELMER: A young woman your age shouldn't talk like that. If religion can't move you, I can try to rouse your conscience. You do have some moral feeling? Or, tell me—has that gone too?

48 **NORA:** It's not easy to answer that, Torvald. I simply don't know. I'm all confused about these things. I just know I see them so differently from you. I find out, for one thing, that the law's not at all what I'd thought—but I can't get it through my head that the law is fair. A woman hasn't a right to protect her dying father or save her husband's life! I can't believe that.

HELMER: You talk like a child. You don't know anything of the world you live in.

NORA: No, I don't. But now I'll begin to learn for myself. I'll try to discover who's right, the world or I.

HELMER: Nora, you're sick; you've got a fever. I almost think you're out of your head.

NORA: I've never felt more clearheaded and sure in my life.

HELMER: And—clearheaded and sure—you're leaving your husband and children?

NORA: Yes.

HELMER: Then there's only one possible reason.

NORA: What?

HELMER: You no longer love me.

NORA: No. That's exactly it.

HELMER: Nora! You can't be serious!

NORA: Oh, this is so hard, Torvald—you've been so kind to me always. But I can't help it. I don't love you anymore.

HELMER [*struggling for composure*]: Are you also clearheaded and sure about that?

49 **NORA:** Yes, completely. That's why I can't go on staying here.

HELMER: Can you tell me what I did to lose your love?

NORA: Yes, I can tell you. It was this evening when the miraculous thing didn't come—then I knew you weren't the man I'd imagined.

HELMER: Be more explicit; I don't follow you.

NORA: I've waited now so patiently eight long years—for, my Lord, I know miracles don't come every day. Then this crisis broke over me, and such a certainty filled me: *now* the miraculous event would occur. While Krogstad's letter was lying out there, I never for an instant dreamed that you could give in to his terms. I was so utterly sure you'd

Literary Analysis
Theme and Foreshadowing What future conflicts might Nora's lines foreshadow?

Reading Strategy
Recognizing Dramatic Tension In what way does Nora raise the stakes, making it clear that she and Torvald may lose more than Torvald imagined?

ENRICHMENT: Culture Connection

Norway's Modern Social Welfare System

If Nora Helmer were living in Norway today, chances are that she would be much better prepared for a life on her own than she was in the 1870s. In fact, she would be among the most fortunate women in the world.

Today's Norway is one of the world's richest countries, with 100 percent literacy (compared with 97 percent in the United States) and almost universal free education and health care. Norwegians live, on the average, several years longer than Americans. Fewer Norwegian babies die at birth than do those in the United States.

Also, Norwegians receive a variety of social benefits unknown in the United States. These include, in addition to free medical care and college education, cash benefits during pregnancy, free dental care for children, a generous pension, state-financed home loans for most people, and a minimum of four weeks of paid vacation for every worker. In return for these benefits, Norwegians pay very high taxes.

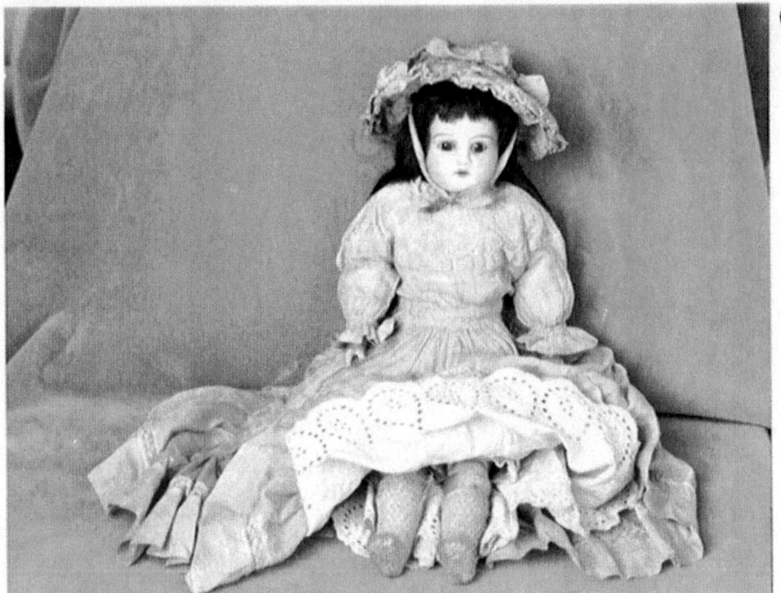

50 ◀ **Critical Viewing** What characteristics does Nora share with this china doll? In what ways is Nora very different? **[Compare and Contrast]**

say to him: go on, tell your tale to the whole wide world. And when he'd done that—

HELMER: Yes, what then? When I'd delivered my own wife into shame and disgrace—!

NORA: When he'd done that, I was so utterly sure that you'd step forward, take the blame on yourself and say: I am the guilty one.

HELMER: Nora—!

51 **NORA:** You're thinking I'd never accept such a sacrifice from you? No, of course not. But what good would my protests be against you? That was the miracle I was waiting for, in terror and hope. And to stave that off, I would have taken my life.

52 **HELMER:** I'd gladly work for you day and night, Nora—and take on pain and deprivation. But there's no one who gives up honor for love.

NORA: Millions of women have done just that.

HELMER: Oh, you think and talk like a silly child.

NORA: Perhaps. But you neither think nor talk like the man I could join myself to. When your big fright was over—and it wasn't from any threat against me, only for what might damage you—when all the danger was past, for you it was just as if nothing had happened. I was exactly the same, your little lark, your doll, that you'd have to handle with double care now that I'd turned out so brittle and frail. [*Gets up.*] Torvald—in that instant it dawned on me that for eight years I've been living here with a stranger, and that I'd even conceived three children—oh, I can't stand the thought of it! I could tear myself to bits.

Reading Strategy
Recognizing Dramatic Tension In what ways does Nora's speech explain the increasing dramatic tension throughout the play?

53 
Reading Check
How long has Nora waited for some "miraculous" change to occur in her life?

50 ▶ **Critical Viewing**

Possible response: Like the doll, Nora is pretty, well dressed, and subject to other's wishes. Unlike the doll, Nora is a real person who comes to realize that she has made mistakes and can take steps to improve herself and her life.

51 Reading Strategy

Recognizing Dramatic Tension

- Point out to students that Nora's expectation that Torvald would act nobly has been a source of dramatic tension throughout the play.
- Have students answer the Reading Strategy question on p. 941: In what ways does Nora's speech explain the increasing dramatic tension throughout the play?
  Possible response: Nora's response clarifies that she has been waiting throughout the play for Torvald to act nobly.

52 Critical Thinking

Relate

- Have students read the bracketed passage.
- Ask students: Do you agree with Nora that millions of women have sacrificed honor for love?
  Possible response: Marriages or relationships require some sacrifice, although it is possible to have both honor and love.
- Is this sacrifice more or less common today than in the 1870s?
  Possible response: Because women have many more rights today, such a sacrifice is less common.

53 Reading Check

Answer: Nora has waited eight years.

CUSTOMIZE INSTRUCTION FOR UNIVERSAL ACCESS

For Gifted/Talented Students	For Advanced Readers
Invite students to write an alternative ending to *A Doll House*. Ask students either to maintain Ibsen's realism and keep to the characters' personalities or to take the play and characters in a different direction. Ask volunteers to read aloud or act out their alternative endings for the class. Ask the listeners for their reactions.	Ask students to write a paragraph or two predicting what will happen to the characters after the ending of the play. Encourage students to base their predictions on their understanding of the characters and of the nineteenth-century world. Ask students to share their predictions with the class for discussion. Talk about why students think the way they do about the characters' chances after the play.

54 Background

Art

The Customs, by Antonio Mancini

Italian painter Antonio Mancini (1852–1930) began his formal training as an artist at age twelve. After graduating from the Institute of Fine Art in Naples, he joined artists such as Vincenzo Gemito in creating a style of painting called Verismo (Italian for *Realism*). The paintings of the Verismo style depicted real people, particularly working-class people, in their own environment without idealizing them. Mancini's subjects included street people and artists, and his paintings of them tended to be dark and somber.

In 1875, Mancini traveled to Paris, where he met the leading painters of the day, Manet and Degas, who influenced his style. *The Customs* (1877) reflects a change. Although the painting has shadows and is dark overall, the gold of the walls adds a lightness and richness to the scene and sets off the woman's dark figure.

Use the following question for discussion:

What does the painting tell you about life for women in the nineteenth century?

Possible response: The woman may be waiting for something or someone to help her. She seems hemmed in by her clothes and the luggage at her feet. One can infer that women in the nineteenth-century were restricted in many ways beyond what appears here in this painting.

55 ▶ Critical Viewing

Possible response: Like the woman in the painting, Nora is about to embark on a journey. Unlike the woman in the painting, however, Nora tries to free herself rather than remain trapped by her status and belongings.

54

55 ▲ **Critical Viewing** Which details in this painting suit this final scene of *A Doll House*? **[Interpret]**

ENRICHMENT: Linguistics Connection

Translations Are Not All the Same

This translation of *A Doll House* by Rolf Fjelde is so clear and informal in tone that a reader might easily forget that it is a translation from the Norwegian. Not every translation is as good as Fjelde's. Here are some excerpts from an English translation made by a Danish teacher.

Helmer: Don't utter such stupid shuffles.... From this moment it depends no longer on felicity; it depends on saving the rests, remnants, and the appearance.

(Compare with text on p. 935.)

Nora: As I am now, I am no wife to you.
Helmer: I have the power to grow another.

(Compare with text on p. 943.)

Helmer: Change yourself in such a manner that—
Nora: —cohabitation between you and me might become a matrimony. Good-bye.

(Compare with text on p. 944.)

HELMER [*heavily*]: I see. There's a gulf that's opened between us—that's clear. Oh, but Nora, can't we bridge it somehow?

NORA: The way I am now, I'm no wife for you.

HELMER: I have the strength to make myself over.

NORA: Maybe—if your doll gets taken away.

HELMER: But to part! To part from you! No, Nora, no—I can't imagine it.

NORA [*going out, right*]: All the more reason why it has to be. [*She reenters with her coat and a small overnight bag, which she puts on a chair by the table.*]

HELMER: Nora, Nora, not now! Wait till tomorrow.

NORA: I can't spend the night in a strange man's room.

HELMER: But couldn't we live here like brother and sister—

56 **NORA:** You know very well how long that would last. [*Throws her shawl about her.*] Good-bye, Torvald. I won't look in on the children. I know they're in better hands than mine. The way I am now, I'm no use to them.

HELMER: But someday, Nora—someday—?

NORA: How can I tell? I haven't the least idea what'll become of me.

HELMER: But you're my wife, now and wherever you go.

NORA: Listen, Torvald—I've heard that when a wife deserts her husband's house just as I'm doing, then the law frees him from all responsibility. In any case, I'm freeing you from being responsible. Don't feel yourself bound, any more than I will. There has to be absolute freedom for us both. Here, take your ring back. Give me mine.

HELMER: That too?

NORA: That too.

HELMER: There it is.

57 **NORA:** Good. Well, now it's all over. I'm putting the keys here. The maids know all about keeping up the house—better than I do. Tomorrow, after I've left town, Kristine will stop by to pack up everything that's mine from home. I'd like those things shipped up to me.

HELMER: Over! All over! Nora, won't you ever think about me?

NORA: I'm sure I'll think of you often, and about the children and the house here.

HELMER: May I write you?

NORA: No—never. You're not to do that.

HELMER: Oh, but let me send you—

NORA: Nothing. Nothing.

HELMER: Or help you if you need it.

Reading Strategy
Recognizing Dramatic Tension Which of Nora's words in this line best reveals the dramatic tension in the scene?

Literary Analysis
Theme and Foreshadowing Identify three details in Acts One and Two that foreshadow Nora's realization that she knows very little about her own home.

✓Reading Check

From what is Nora freeing Torvald?

CUSTOMIZE INSTRUCTION FOR UNIVERSAL ACCESS

For Less Proficient Readers	For Advanced Readers
Ask students to write a short review of *A Doll House*. Remind them that a review should include their opinions about the plot, characters, or themes in the play and support for those opinions with words or ideas from the play. Finally, students should recommend or not recommend the play and give a reason why. If students need help getting started, allow them to look at reviews of movies, plays, or musical performances that have appeared in local newspapers. Encourage students to share their reviews with the class.	Ask students to write a review of *A Doll House* from the viewpoint of a nineteenth-century audience member. Students should give their opinions about the plot, characters, and themes from the perspective (and, if possible, in the language) of a nineteenth-century person. If students wish, they may research how early audiences responded to the play. Invite students to share their reviews with the class.

56 Reading Strategy

Recognizing Dramatic Tension

- Students should notice that Torvald is increasing the dramatic tension by refusing to let Nora go and offering her options that she does not want.
- Point out that Torvald's suggestions show that he no longer knows his wife.
- Have students read the Reading Strategy question on p. 943: Which of Nora's words in this line best reveals the dramatic tension in the scene?
  Answer: The word *strange* reveals the tension; Nora realizes that she barely knows her husband.

57 Literary Analysis

Theme and Foreshadowing

- Remind students that throughout the play, Nora has appeared helpless. Review the areas in her life where she has needed help.
  Possible response: Nora has needed help raising her children, maintaining the house, dealing with money, and even selecting a costume.
- Ask students to respond to the Literary Analysis item on p. 943: Identify three details in Acts One and Two that foreshadow Nora's realization that she knows very little about her own home.
  Possible responses: In both acts it is clear that Nora is ignorant of situations within her home. On a literal level, Nora has little involvement with household activities; she has a nursemaid to care for her children and a maid to accept deliveries and admit visitors. More significant, however, is her ignorance of the people who are part of her home. Thinking that Krogstad's revelation of her secret to Torvald will cause mere "unpleasantness," assuming Torvald capable of change, and obliviousness to Dr. Rank's love for her, despite his daily visits, might foreshadow Nora's realization that she knows very little about her home and the nature of those who are part of it.

58 ✓Reading Check

Answer: Nora is freeing Torvald from responsibility for her or her actions.

ASSESS

Answers for p. 944

Review and Assess

1. Many students will be sympathetic with Nora's decision because they believe that she deserves a better life. Others may fear that she does not realize what she is getting into or may find her selfish.
2. **(a)** Mrs. Linde proposes that she and Krogstad marry. **(b)** Mrs. Linde is no longer lonely. Krogstad is so happy that he drops his plans to blackmail the Helmers. **(c)** Possible response: Unlike Nora and Torvald, Mrs. Linde and Krogstad are honest in their relationship and understand each other's flaws.
3. **(a)** Torvald is furious with Nora when he reads the first letter. He fears for his reputation. **(b)** Possible response: His behavior proves that he is not noble and that he is more concerned about the appearance of his honor than his love for Nora.
4. **(a)** Nora agrees to accept nothing from Torvald in the future. **(b)** Possible response: Nora has grown up and wants to be responsible for herself alone; she does not want help from anyone. **(c)** Possible response: Torvald does not understand. Even as Nora leaves him, he talks about transforming himself and has a sudden hope for "the greatest miracle."
5. **(a)** Nora's marriage to Torvald has been like living in a doll house. She has been like a toy or a source of amusement for him, not his equal. His love for her has been like a child's for a doll. When Nora realizes this situation, she decides that she must leave in order to become an individual. **(b)** Possible response: It may be possible for Nora to find happiness later, in an equal partnership, after she has discovered more about herself.
6. Possible response: Nora's desire to be in an honest and equal relationship is relevant today, as is her awareness that people can change their lives when necessary.

NORA: No. I accept nothing from strangers.

HELMER: Nora—can I never be more than a stranger to you?

NORA [*picking up the overnight bag*]: Ah, Torvald—it would take the greatest miracle of all—

HELMER: Tell me the greatest miracle!

NORA: You and I both would have to transform ourselves to the point that— Oh, Torvald, I've stopped believing in miracles.

HELMER: But I'll believe. Tell me! Transform ourselves to the point that?

NORA: That our living together could be a true marriage. [*She goes out down the hall.*]

HELMER [*sinks down on a chair by the door, face buried in his hands*]: Nora! Nora! [*Looking about and rising.*] Empty. She's gone. [*A sudden hope leaps in him.*] The greatest miracle—?

[*From below, the sound of a door slamming shut.*]

Review and Assess

Thinking About Act Three

1. **Respond:** What is your response to Nora's decision to leave her husband and children? Explain.
2. **(a) Recall:** What plan does Mrs. Linde propose for herself and Krogstad? **(b) Analyze:** How does Mrs. Linde manage to solve several problems at once with this plan? **(c) Compare and Contrast:** What advantages do Mrs. Linde and Krogstad have over Torvald and Nora?
3. **(a) Recall:** What is Torvald's reaction when he reads the first letter from Krogstad? **(b) Draw Conclusions:** What does Torvald's reaction indicate to Nora about her husband's personality?
4. **(a) Recall:** What help does Nora agree to accept from Torvald in the future? **(b) Speculate:** Why do you think Nora refuses his help? **(c) Make a Judgment:** Do you think Torvald truly understands Nora's reasons for leaving? Why or why not?
5. **(a) Synthesize:** In what way does the play's title relate to Nora's discoveries about Torvald and to her decision to leave him? **(b) Speculate:** Do you think Nora might find happiness in another relationship in the future? Explain.
6. **Relate:** Which of Nora's experiences are still relevant today? Explain.

ASSESSMENT PRACTICE: Reading Comprehension

Analyzing Literary Language (For more practice, see Test Preparation Workbook, p. 44.)

Students must analyze the literary language of texts, including what the author's word choice reveals about a character. Use this sample test item.

> I have to work to go on living. All my born days, as long as I can remember, I've worked, and it's been my best and only joy. But now I'm completely alone in the world; it frightens me to be so empty and lost. To work for yourself—there's no joy in that. Nils, give me something—someone to work for.

The series of sentences about work emphasizes that for Mrs. Linde working for others represents —

A an intolerable burden.
B a way to pass the time.
C a way to establish independence.
D an unselfish purpose for living.

Help students see that Mrs. Linde begins with a few general statements about working and then moves to her specific desire. The correct response is *D*.

Review and Assess

Literary Analysis

Theme

1. (a) One **theme** of *A Doll House* relates to discovering the keys to a successful relationship. Use a chart like the one shown to cite three examples of dialogue from Act Three that relate to this theme.

Character	Dialogue	Keys to a Successful Relationship

(b) What conclusions about a successful relationship can you draw from the dialogue you noted?

2. Identify three details supporting the theme that society and authority hinder the development of the individual.
3. Which characters embody the theme that all people must live their lives according to their convictions? Explain.

Connecting Literary Elements

4. Mrs. Linde says to Krogstad, "Anyone who's sold herself for somebody else once isn't going to do it again." In what way does this comment **foreshadow** Nora's decision to leave Torvald?
5. (a) What events are foreshadowed when Torvald remarks that "an exit should always be effective, Mrs. Linde, but that's what I can't get Nora to grasp"? (b) What is ironic or unexpected about Torvald's statement?

Reading Strategy

Recognizing Dramatic Tension

6. (a) Which moment in Act Three marks the height of **dramatic tension**? (b) Which conflicts are resolved when the dramatic tension breaks? (c) Which conflicts remain unresolved?
7. (a) What is at stake for Nora if she remains with Torvald? (b) List three lines in Act Three that show the extent to which Torvald fails to understand what Nora stands to lose. (c) Explain the way in which those lines increase the dramatic tension.

Extend Understanding

8. **Career Connection:** Consider the résumé Nora might build. What marketable skills has Nora acquired during her years with Torvald that will allow her to support herself without his help?

Quick Review

A drama's **theme** is its central message, idea, or insight.

Foreshadowing is the use of details or clues that hint at events or conditions to come.

To **recognize dramatic tension,** look for moments of conflict and mystery that build suspense and anticipation.

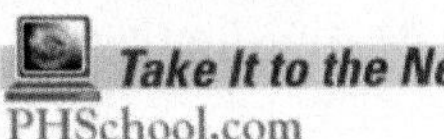

Take It to the Net

PHSchool.com

Take the interactive self-test online to check your understanding of *A Doll House*.

Answers for p. 945

Review and Assess

1. Possible response:
(a) **Character:** Mrs. Linde **Dialogue:** "We both need each other. Nils, I have faith that you're good at heart—I'll risk everything together with you." **Key:** Partners should have faith in each other. **Character:** Nora **Dialogue:** "I'm saying that we've never sat down seriously together and tried to get to the bottom of anything." **Key:** Communication is important to a relationship. **Character:** Nora **Dialogue:** "You never loved me. You've thought it fun to be in love with me, that's all." **Key:** A good relationship should be based on authentic love.
(b) A good relationship is based on faith, open communication, honesty, respect, and love.
2. Possible response: Mrs. Linde married unhappily to save her family; now she is able to make a choice as an individual. Torvald is so afraid of losing his respectability that he shows himself to be a coward. Nora has been kept like a doll in a doll house, so she must leave her marriage to become an individual.
3. Dr. Rank lives in the moment because he knows that he will die soon. Mrs. Linde accepts Krogstad despite his flaws. Nora learns that she must leave her home and family to develop.
4. Like Mrs. Linde, Nora has "sold herself" in marriage, and she is not going to compromise herself by staying with Torvald.
5. **(a)** His remark foreshadows Nora's exit at the end of the play. **(b)** The irony is that Nora will make an exit that is far more effective than any Torvald could imagine.
6. **(a)** Torvald reads Krogstad's letter. **(b)** The conflicts between Torvald and Nora, Krogstad and the Helmers, and within Nora are resolved. **(c)** The conflict between Nora and society is unresolved.
7. **(a)** Nora's ability to become an individual is at stake. **(b)** "But someday, Nora—someday—?"; "Over! All over! Nora, won't you ever think about me?"; "The greatest miracle—?" **(c)** The lines

continued

continued from right column

increase the dramatic tension by confirming Torvald's inability to understand Nora's feelings and thus prolonging the conflict so that viewers will realize that the Helmers' marriage is finished. They are left to wonder whether Nora will indeed walk out.

8. Nora can sew and copy manuscript. She knows something about raising children and running a house.

ENRICHMENT: Further Reading

Other Works by Henrik Ibsen

We strongly encourage you to review any selection before assigning or recommending it to students.

Hedda Gabler | *The Master Builder*
Ghosts | *An Enemy of the People*
The Wild Duck | *Peer Gynt*

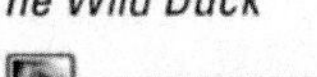

Take It to the Net

Visit PHSchool.com for more information on Henrik Ibsen.

EXTEND

Answers for p. 946

❶ Vocabulary Development

Word Analysis: Greek Prefix *hypo-*

1. b
2. a

Spelling Strategy

1. hypocrite
2. mystery
3. trilogy
4. vicarious

Fluency: Context

1. grafter
2. calculating
3. proprieties
4. bewildered
5. evasions
6. hypocrite
7. naturalistic

❷ Grammar and Style

Practice

1. to talk about; adjective (modifies *anything*)
2. to abandon me; adjective (modifies *right*)
3. to be realistic; noun (direct object of *learned*)
4. to see Nora in costume; noun (direct object of *did want*)
5. to sit with me; adverb (modifies *brought*)

Writing Application

When she sees Torvald open the mailbox, Nora plans to drown herself. (noun; direct object of *plans*) Torvald needs someone to blame. (adjective; modifies *someone*) Nora feels ready to become an individual. (adverb; modifies *ready*)

10TH GRADE For support in teaching the Grammar and Style Lesson to tenth graders, use **Writing and Grammar,** Platinum Level, Chapter 20, Section 1.

Integrate Language Skills

❶ Vocabulary Development Lesson

Word Analysis: Greek Prefix *hypo-*

The Greek prefix *hypo-* means "under," "less than," or "slightly." Use your understanding of the meaning of *hypo-* to identify the word that best completes each sentence below.

a. hypocrite   b. hypothermia

1. After being rescued from the cold river, she suffered from ___.
2. The ___ pretended to be someone that he was not.

Spelling Strategy

Both the letter *i* and the letter y can represent either the short or long *i* sound in words. Complete each word below with either the letter *i* or the letter y.

1. h___pocrite
2. m___stery
3. tr___logy
4. v___carious

Fluency: Context

Review the vocabulary words on page 922. Then, complete each of the following sentences.

1. The ____ looted a local business.
2. She used her___ ways to convince her brother to finish her chores.
3. By paying attention to social ___, he earned a spotless reputation.
4. The child seemed ___ by the unjust punishment.
5. The suspect responded with ___ to all questions.
6. The lawyer was branded a ___ when he committed perjury on the witness stand.
7. The audience was shocked by the ___ appearance of the robot.

❷ Grammar and Style Lesson

Infinitives and Infinitive Phrases

An **infinitive** is a verb form consisting of the base form of a verb, usually with the word *to*. An **infinitive phrase** combines an infinitive plus its complements or modifiers to act as a single part of speech. Infinitive phrases function as nouns, adjectives, or adverbs.

As a Noun: "Life's taught me never to trust fine phrases. . . ." (direct object of the verb *taught*)

As an Adjective: "Someone to work for, to live for. . . ." (modifying the pronoun *someone*)

As an Adverb: "How am I equipped to bring up children?" (modifying the verb *equipped*)

Practice Copy each item below, underlining the infinitive phrase and identifying its function in the sentence.

1. "Do we two have anything more to talk about?"
2. ". . . you hadn't the right to abandon me for somebody else's sake."
3. "I've learned to be realistic."
4. ". . . I did want to see Nora in costume."
5. "That is why I brought you down to sit with me."

Writing Application Write a paragraph about Nora in which you use three infinitive phrases. Underline each phrase, and identify its function.

Prentice Hall Writing and Grammar Connection: Diamond Level, Chapter 19, Section 2

TEACHING RESOURCES

The following resources can be used to enrich or extend the instruction for pp. 946–947

Vocabulary

- **Selection Support:** Build Vocabulary, p. 173
- **Vocabulary and Spelling Practice Book** (Use this booklet for skills instruction.)

Grammar

- **Selection Support:** Grammar and Style, p. 174
- **Writing and Grammar,** Diamond Level, p. 446
- **Daily Language Practice Transparencies**

Writing

- **Writing and Grammar,** Diamond Level, p. 137
- **Performance Assess. and Portfolio Mgmt.,** p. 11
- **Writing and Grammar iText CD-ROM**

Listening and Speaking

- **Performance Assess. and Portfolio Mgmt.,** p. 23

BLOCK SCHEDULING: Resources marked with this symbol provide varied instruction during 90-minute blocks.

❸ Writing Lesson

Writing a Persuasive Essay

When one is faced with a difficult choice, it can be extremely hard to make the right decision. Write a persuasive essay in which you argue for or against Nora's decision to leave Torvald, basing your arguments on events or lines from the play.

Prewriting Review the play and decide whether or not you agree with Nora's decision. Create an outline, listing points that confirm your opinion and including references to the play that support each point.

Drafting As you write, anticipate your readers' objections to the position you are taking. For example, if you think Nora's decision is the right one, you might consider who will take care of Nora's children or how she might support herself. Answer each objection, and write your counterarguments clearly and effectively.

Revising Review your draft, removing any empty or unnecessary words or phrases that do not add to your argument.

Model: Removing Unnecessary Words or Phrases

~~It seems to me that~~ Nora could never be happy if her marriage continued in the same pattern. Her husband's weaknesses and her own shortcomings force her to seek ~~a sense of~~ independence.

Removing unnecessary words and phrases focuses your sentences and makes them more effective.

WG Prentice Hall Writing and Grammar Connection: Diamond Level, Chapter 7, Section 4

❹ Extension Activities

Listening and Speaking In a small group, participate in a **round-table discussion** of the themes in *A Doll House*. Follow these rules of courtesy:

1. Pay attention as others speak.
2. Do not interrupt.
3. Speak clearly.

Compare the opinions shared in the discussion with those of other groups in your class. [Group Activity]

Research and Technology Choose one character and scene from *A Doll House* and develop a **costume design display.** Begin by researching the dress of the time. Make a sketch of the character wearing a costume appropriate for the scene. Choose fabric swatches and include them in a display that you share with your class.

Take It to the Net PHSchool.com

Go online for an additional research activity using the Internet.

ASSESSMENT RESOURCES

The following resources can be used to assess students' knowledge and skills.

Selection Assessment

- **Formal Assessment,** pp. 154–156
- **Open-Book Tests,** pp. 130–132
- **Test Bank Software**

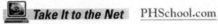

Take It to the Net

Visit PHSchool.com for self-tests and additional questions on the selections.

Writing Rubric

- **Performance Assess. and Portfolio Mgmt.,** p. 11

Speaking and Listening Rubric

- **Performance Assess. and Portfolio Mgmt.,** p. 23

PRENTICE HALL ASSESSMENT SYSTEM

For additional diagnostics and remediation for skills covered in this grouping, use materials from the Prentice Hall Assessment System.

❸ Writing

- Tell students that a persuasive essay is a written statement that presents a position and tries to persuade readers to accept or support that position.
- Remind students that a good essay has an introduction with a strong opinion statement, a body that presents evidence, and a conclusion that sums up the argument. Tell students to use transition words to help readers follow the flow of their ideas.
- Use the Persuasive Composition rubric in **Performance Assessment and Portfolio Management,** p. 11, to evaluate students' work.

10TH GRADE For support in working through the Writing Lesson with tenth graders, use **Writing and Grammar,** Platinum Level, Chapter 7, Section 4.

❹ Listening and Speaking

- Have students use the themes listed on p. 922 to begin their discussion. Students should use their discussion time to review the details of the play that support the different themes.
- Challenge students to identify the theme that they consider the most dominant or important in the play.
- Ask one student to take notes during the discussion and one to moderate and make sure that each student in the group contributes to the discussion.
- Use the Effective Listening rubric in **Performance Assessment and Portfolio Management,** p. 23, to evaluate students' work.

CUSTOMIZE INSTRUCTION For Universal Access

To address different learning styles, use the following activities in the **Extension Activities** booklet, p. 44.

- For Logical/Mathematical and Visual/Spatial Learners, use Activity 5.
- For Verbal/Linguistic Learners, use Activity 6.
- For Bodily/Kinesthetic and Visual/Spatial Learners, use Activity 7.

Background

George Bernard Shaw and Henrik Ibsen

Many later playwrights, including the great Irish playwright George Bernard Shaw, were influenced by Henrik Ibsen. Commenting on Ibsen's impact on the theater, Shaw wrote: "When Ibsen began to make plays, the art of the dramatist had shrunk into the art of contriving a situation. And it was held that the stranger the situation, the better the play. Ibsen saw that, on the contrary, the more familiar the situation, the more interesting the play."

Shaw greatly admired Ibsen's interest in social reform but acknowledged that after the reforms addressed in a play had taken place, the play might become outdated. Shaw wrote: "*A Doll House* will be as flat as ditchwater when *A Midsummer Night's Dream* will still be as fresh as paint; but it will have done more work in the world, and that is enough for the highest genius, which is always intensely utilitarian."

Background

The Nineteenth Amendment

In most American states, women did not gain the right to vote until the early 1900s. In fact, no state allowed women to vote until Wyoming entered the Union in 1890. Three decades later, however, the nineteenth Amendment to the United States Constitution was ratified, giving all American women the right to vote. The amendment reads: "The right of citizens of the United States to vote shall not be denied or abridged by the United States or by any state on account of sex."

A Closer Look

The Slamming of the Door

The slamming of the door at the end of *A Doll House* was a sound heard round the world.

The last words of Henrik Ibsen's play *A Doll House* are not spoken by any of the characters. Rather, they are a single stage direction: "From below, the sound of a door slamming shut."

In 1879, when the play was first performed, that sound—a symbol of Nora's escape from her constrictive marriage—represented a direct challenge to the existing beliefs concerning the roles of men and women. In the decades after the publication of the play, the status of women in Western society began undergoing a dramatic transformation. Today, many scholars view Nora's slamming of the door as a pivotal point in the evolution of the modern feminist movement. In fact, as the great British playwright George Bernard Shaw wrote, the slamming of the door can be regarded as "the end of a chapter in human history."

Women in the Nineteenth Century At the time Ibsen wrote *A Doll House*, the idea that a woman might choose to leave her husband and children in order to live independently was not merely unacceptable—it was inconceivable for the vast majority of people. Common belief suggested that women were inferior to men, a notion that was supported by the laws of that time. As a result, women did not enjoy the same rights and privileges as men. Few women were educated. They could not own property. They could not vote. They had severely limited career opportunities. Women were expected to marry and to devote their lives to serving their husbands and raising their children. They were expected to obey their husbands without question.

Nora's Rebellion When Nora leaves Torvald and her children in order to educate herself and seek her own fulfillment, she rebels not only against Torvald's authority but also against the expectations of society as a whole. She first tells Torvald that she is leaving him, and he forbids her to go. Then, he warns her that she is "not even thinking about what people will say." Nora responds that she is not concerned with other people's opinions, adding that her duty to herself is more important than her duties as a wife and mother. She declares, "I'm a human being, no less than you—or anyway, I ought to try to become one. I know the majority thinks you're right, Torvald, and plenty of books agree with you, too. But I can't go on believing what the majority says, or what's written in books."

The Impact of Nora's Rebellion When Nora finally leaves and she slams the door shut behind her, Torvald remains in a state of shock and dismay. Similarly, Ibsen's first audiences were shocked and dismayed by what they saw

ENRICHMENT: Drama Connection

Ibsen's Modern Dramas

Prior to Henrik Ibsen's time, dramas, known as "well-made plays," were meant to entertain audiences by appealing to people's imaginations. Consequently, dramatists generally did not depict events in an accurate manner but instead wove together intricate plots filled with coincidences that would be unlikely to occur in real life and offered tidy resolutions to "unravel" these plots. In addition, characters often revealed their inner thoughts directly to the audience.

In contrast, Ibsen sought to depict life accurately and realistically in his plays, while delving into the types of conflicts and dilemmas that he viewed as characteristic of his time. He focused on situations that could easily occur in real life, and he patterned his dialogue after real-life conversations. Just as in a typical discussion between friends or family, emotions and inner thoughts unfold between Ibsen's characters. According to critic John Gassner, it was with this dramatic technique—the discussion—"that the distinctly modern drama was born."

and heard. Yet, this sense of shock forced many people to reevaluate their ideas about men and women; in the years that followed the play's first performances, women began to gain some of the rights and privileges that they had previously been denied. For example, one historian points out that "within five years of the publication of *A Doll House*, women were being admitted to the private Liberal Club in the tradition-bound city of Oslo" in Ibsen's native land of Norway.

During the course of the twentieth century, the status of women in most countries of the world continued to improve. Women gained the right to vote and to own property. In addition, the educational and professional opportunities available to women expanded tremendously. Many women became involved in politics; in a number of countries, including Great Britain, Pakistan, and the Philippines, women were elected to the highest government posts.

Ibsen and Feminism Because of the stories he tells in *A Doll House* and other works, Ibsen is often regarded as one of the pioneering spirits in the feminist movement. Although Ibsen himself might have argued that he did not deserve this label, it cannot be denied that he was one of the first men to openly express concern about the status of women. Ibsen's notes to *A Doll House* clearly indicate that he wanted the play to capture the ways in which society restricted women's freedom and growth. He wrote, "There are two kinds of spiritual law, two kinds of conscience, one in man and another, altogether different, in women. They do not understand each other; but in practical life the woman is judged by man's law, as though she were not a woman but a man. . . . A woman cannot be herself in the society of the present day, which is exclusively a masculine society. . . . "

Today, many questions about gender remain unanswered. For example, are the psyches of men and women fundamentally different, as Ibsen suggests? Yet, even without answers to these questions, common attitudes and laws no longer support the notion that women are inferior. Nora's slamming of the door may no longer shock, but the echoes it created continue to resonate.

▲ Critical Viewing

In what ways can doors, like those shown above, serve as symbols for ideas or emotions? **[Generalize]**

Ibsen and Women's "Instinctive Genius"

At the time Henrik Ibsen was writing *A Doll House,* he delivered a speech to the Scandinavian Club at its annual meeting in which he proposed that women should be allowed to vote. He remarked: "I am not afraid of these so-called impractical women; women have something in common with the true artist, just as young people in general have—something that is a good substitute for worldly understanding. Look at our student societies in Norway! Matters are decided there which are ten times more complicated than ours; yet do they not manage well, although youth, untried, unpracticed and unpractical youth there enjoys an overwhelming majority? And why? Because youth has an instinctive genius which unconsciously hits upon the right answer. And it is precisely this instinct which women share with youth, and with the true artist."

▶ Critical Viewing

Possible response: Doors, like ideas and emotions, can be open or closed, large or small, colorful or dull. An open door can be seen as an invitation to enter, explore, and see what exists on the other side. A closed door can be seen as an obstacle, a barrier, and a challenge to the adventurous spirit.

Critical Thinking

1. Explain why Nora's actions at the end of *A Doll House* would or would not be considered acceptable in contemporary American society. **[Make a Judgment]**
   Possible response: Nora's actions would not be considered surprising in contemporary American society but would generally be considered unacceptable because she essentially is abandoning her children.
2. Do you agree with Ibsen that the psyches of men and women are fundamentally different? Why or why not? **[Defend]**
   Possible responses: Men may be more aggressive and less nurturing than women. However, their apparent differences may also

continued

continued from right column

be merely the result of training and society's gender expectations.

Lesson Objectives

1. To learn the essential elements of critical reviews
2. To compare and contrast critical reviews
3. To understand the significance of differing views among several reviewers

About Critical Reviews

- After students read "About Critical Reviews" on p. 950, ask them to name products, performances, or other items about which they have read critical reviews.
  Possible responses: Television shows, films, plays, musical groups, comedy acts, and restaurants are all reviewed.
- Ask students what they expect to learn when reading a critical review.
  Possible response: Students may say that they expect to learn opinions about various aspects of the item being reviewed. Critical reviews often make recommendations to the reader.
- Discuss with students the terms *argumentative presentations* and *powerful language.* Make sure that students understand that effective critical reviews use assertive words—rather than noncommittal language such as *sort of* and *kind of*—to convince the reader.

Reading Strategy

Comparing and Contrasting Critical Reviews

- Have a volunteer read aloud the information about the Reading Strategy. Make sure that students understand that a good critical review is a judgment based on established criteria. A reviewer must carefully select criteria against which to measure the subject of the review.
- Point out that reviewers may use different criteria in their reviews. However, in reviews of a certain genre—in this case, theatrical performance—reviewers often consider the same criteria. Draw students' attention to the Critical Reviews chart on p. 950, and explain that the labels down the left side list criteria addressed in all three reviews.

Critical Reviews

About Critical Reviews

A critical review analyzes and evaluates a product, an artistic performance, or even the behavior of a person or group. As the name suggests, critical reviews usually contain strong opinions. In this context, however, the word *critical* can mean either a positive or a negative judgment. Most critical reviews will contain the following:

- a brief summary of the subject matter
- a carefully thought out and stated opinion
- supporting evidence

Because the purpose of a critical review is often to persuade, expect to find argumentative presentations and powerful language.

Reading Strategy

Comparing and Contrasting Critical Reviews

Opinions can vary greatly from person to person. For objectivity, you should read multiple critical reviews on a single subject to arrive at the "big picture" of what is being reviewed. Compare the reviews to determine where critics share the same point of view. Then, note the contrasts—points where the critics differ. Making these comparisons and contrasts will help you evaluate both the critical reviews and their subject matter.

As critics, the writers of the following critical reviews saw the same performance of Ibsen's *A Doll's House*. Yet their impressions of the show—particularly the performance of the leading actress—range from glowing praise to lukewarm acceptance. To determine an overall impression of the show, complete the following chart by filling in the critics' names and opinions as you read the reviews.

Critical Reviews			
Critic			
Lead Actress's Performance			
Director and/or Script			
Overall Evaluation (+ or -)			

CurtainUp Review: A Doll's House

by Judd Hollander & Sue Feinberg

From the moment she steps onto the stage of the Belasco Theater, Janet McTeer delivers a riveting performance as Nora Helmer, the heroine of Henrik Ibsen's *A Doll's House*, currently playing at the Belasco Theatre.

Set in a small Norwegian town during Christmas 1879 (and inspired by actual events), the play tells the story of a young wife (McTeer) and mother who's still pretty much a child herself. This time out, however, the 118-year-old work has been given a 1990s feel. McTeer's Nora is a whirling dervish, full of life and laughter, a woman who would be more at home on the stage of an English Music Hall than with her husband Torvald (Owen Teale) and three children. (Her idea of a perfect life is having "pots and pots and pots of money.")

After years of struggle, the couple has finally achieved a measure of financial security, thanks to Torvald's new job as a bank manager. But then a ghost from Nora's past appears in the form of Nils Krogstad (Peter Gowen). Several years earlier, Nora secretly borrowed money for a trip to a warmer climate to allow her desperately ill husband to recover. In order to guarantee the loan, she forged a signature on a contract. Krogstad wants his money back and Nora, not able to give it, is terrified that Torvald will learn the truth.

As events unfold, Nora slowly comes to realize that the "perfect" life she has led is nothing but a fairy tale. Her life has been that of a *doll* to be pampered and protected, first by her father and then by her husband. But even as she's forced to face reality, she tries to do the *right* thing, only to realize that what she loves the most is the biggest lie of all.

Ibsen's work caused quite a shock when it first premiered in 1879 and was heralded as one of the first modern, post-Shakespeare "women's plays." McTeer takes the role of Ibsen's

This critical review begins with a brief summary of the subject matter.

* CurtainUp.com is an online theater magazine. URL: www.curtainup.com

CurtainUp Review: A Doll's House

- Explain to students that critical reviews appear in a variety of publications, including newspapers and magazines.
- Ask students to identify the reviewers and the publication that features this review.
  Answer: Judd Hollander and Sue Feinberg are the reviewers. The review appeared in CurtainUp.com, an online theater magazine.
- Call students' attention to the first call-out note. Point out that the brief summary of the subject matter helps readers immediately identify the reviewer's position. Ask students: Will this review of Janet McTeer's performance be positive or negative? Explain.
  Answer: The use of the word *riveting* reveals that this will be a positive review of the performance.

CUSTOMIZE INSTRUCTION FOR UNIVERSAL ACCESS

For Less Proficient Readers	For English Learners
Students may have difficulty with the following words and phrases: *riveting, whirling dervish, forged,* and *heralded.* Have students work in pairs to use dictionaries to find the definitions for these words and phrases. Encourage students to use dictionaries to define other troublesome words or phrases encountered in the critical reviews and to begin a vocabulary journal in which they record these words and phrases.	Students may have difficulty with the description of Nora as a "whirling dervish," the reference to "a ghost from Nora's past," and the assertion that Nora's life has been a "fairy tale." Help students understand the figurative nature of these phrases by explaining that they are not meant to be taken literally. Then, guide a discussion in which students consider the meanings of these phrases and what the author wants to express through their use.

CurtainUp Review: A Doll's House

- Direct students' attention to the first call-out note on p. 952. Remind them that a reviewer must establish the criteria he or she will consider in the review. In a review of a stage performance, the director, the actors, the producers, and the script are the criteria evaluated.
- Ask students to list other criteria a reviewer might consider when evaluating a stage performance. Possible response: Costumes, lighting, set design, and musical accompaniment are other criteria a reviewer might consider.
- Read aloud the second call-out note on p. 952 and the paragraph to which it refers. Remind students that this paragraph functions as a conclusion, summing up the opinions presented in the review.
- Ask students to identify those words and phrases in the last paragraph that support a positive recommendation. Answer: The words *intense* and *compelling* and the phrase *well worth the trip* indicate that the recommendation is positive.

doll wife and brilliantly makes it her own. Her Nora runs the gamut of emotions from fear to rage to loathing to desperation. Even her demeanor and manner alter and she seems to age before our eyes, gaining not experience or wisdom, but the understanding that these are the qualities she must find. Just before the show ends, there's a scene where she mocks her former "sing-song" persona. That Nora is light-years removed from the one we first met only three hours or, according to the play's time frame, three days before.

While McTeer is the play's linchpin, she does not have the toughest role in the piece. That honor goes to Owen Teale. His Torvald at first glance seems the stereotypical nineteenth-century husband, a man with a keen sense of propriety who *knows* that a man is ruler of his home. He unquestionably loves Nora, and Teale lets us see and feel the passion beneath the propriety of the character—as well as a mean streak that makes him dangerous if crossed.

Many of Teale's lines, which would not have raised an eyebrow in 1879 Norway, drew roars of contemptuous laughter from the 1997 audience. Yet when his whole world comes crashing down and he's forced (after much prodding) to confront the lie his life has become, he makes a subtle, almost unnoticed, transformation. Slowly he begins to understand his wife's pain and the role he has played in letting it continue. When he says to Nora "I have the strength in me to become another man," we're seeing a soul laid bare in a way that's totally convincing.

Director Anthony Page keeps the pace moving during the more active scenes, and he and the actors managed to hold the audience's interest even during the slow sections, which consist of lengthy, two-person conversations with very little action (though they do provide vital plot information).

The script, taken from a literal translation of the work, could probably have been cut by a half-hour. However, the cast and producers seemed more interested in presenting a definitive version of the Ibsen work rather than adapting it to suit a 90s audience. And in this, they have succeeded admirably. Despite its wordiness, the play gradually draws you into its emotional web and delivers a knockout punch of a payoff.

A thorough critical review covers all the parts of what is being reviewed. Here, the critics discuss the director, the actors, the producers, and the script.

Quibbles about slow-pacing aside, *A Doll's House* is an intense and compelling journey through the human spirit and well worth the trip.

The review ends with a positive recommendation to potential theatergoers.

Sunday, April 20, 1997

A Lot of Baggage for Nora to Carry

A subhead gives readers a preview of the opinion to follow.

After a History of Misinterpretation, Ibsen's Leave-Taking Heroine Finally Gets Her Due

By Lloyd Rose
Washington Post Staff Writer

As Nora in the London-produced *A Doll's House* now playing on Broadway, the tall, rangy Janet McTeer is as gawkily graceful as a young swan. This Nora is a six-foot bundle of adorability—and she knows it. Everything in her movement and manner—especially her hoarse, self-conscious giggle—says to the men in her life, "Aren't I silly, aren't I scatterbrained, aren't I helpless, don't you adore me?" And they do.

A Doll's House, the story of a pampered bourgeois wife who rebelliously leaves her domineering husband, has a problematic reputation. . . . At least one reviewer felt constrained to point out that the New York production is more than "a feminist screed." Henrik Ibsen . . . has been getting bopped with accusations of feminism since the play's debut in 1880. When Nora realized her life was a lie and walked out on her husband and children, nineteenth-century audiences were scandalized.

Rose states his opinion and then supports his point of view with evidence from the performance.

McTeer and director Anthony Page bring this production very close to what I've always thought is the essential truth of *A Doll's House*. . . . McTeer's Nora doesn't realize so much that Torvald is a cad (Owen Teale's honorable, grounded performance makes that impossible anyway) as that she has constructed a fantasy about his being a hero. The mistake is hers, for being a grown woman who believes in a fairy tale. This discovery doesn't put Nora in a lecturing mood. She's staggered, a little dazed, as if she'd been punched in the head by reality.

As McTeer plays it, the last speech isn't superior and scolding; she doesn't even don her coat until toward the end. Her Nora is tentative, feeling her way through the revelations that have been forced upon her, realizing what she has done. As a result, the character is fascinating, surprising, disturbing, instead of being all dreary and moral and right.

This production doesn't go quite as far as it could—Nora still scores some too-easy points over Torvald—but it goes a long, brave way. In London McTeer won an Olivier Award for her performance, beating out such powerhouse talents as Diana Rigg and Vanessa Redgrave, and you certainly see why. She's not as luminous as Redgrave. She's not as witty and fierce as Rigg. But she is certainly, as Ralph Richardson used to say of Laurence Olivier, "bold . . . very, very bold."

A Lot of Baggage for Nora to Carry

- Draw students' attention to the first call-out note on p. 953. Ask students to predict what the reviewer's opinion will be, on the basis of the headline and subhead. Possible response: The headline, with its mention of "baggage," indicates that this performance is burdened by past interpretations and by social commentary on the play as a whole. The subhead, however, indicates that despite this burden, the performance is a successful one.
- Point out to students that in his review, Rose acknowledges other dramatic interpretations as well as other critical discussions of *A Doll House*. These interpretations and discussions become part of the criteria against which Rose weighs this particular performance.
- Read aloud the third paragraph of the review. Make sure that students understand that Rose is considering the intentions of Ibsen's play itself.
- Draw students' attention to the second call-out note on p. 953. Ask students to restate Rose's opinion. Answer: Rose believes that this performance captures the essence of Ibsen's play: McTeer's Nora understands that her life is an illusion and that she is at fault for creating such an illusion.
- Then, have students read the remainder of the text independently. Ask: What evidence does Rose use to support his opinion? Answer: Rose says that McTeer's Nora is not "superior and scolding," but "tentative." This characterization supports Rose's interpretation of Nora as feeling foolish when her fantasies crumble.

CUSTOMIZE INSTRUCTION FOR UNIVERSAL ACCESS

For Special Needs Students	For Gifted/Talented Students
Students may have difficulty with words such as *gawkily, adorability, bourgeois, domineering,* and *cad.* Have students use thesauruses to find synonyms for these words. Then, encourage students to reread the selection, replacing the difficult words with the synonyms. For example, students might replace *gawkily* with *awkwardly, adorability* with *cuteness, bourgeois* with *middle-class, domineering* with *controlling,* and *cad* with *rascal.*	Pair students, and have them perform the final scene of *A Doll House,* first portraying Nora as "superior and scolding ... dreary and moral and right" and then as "tentative." When students have finished their performances, ask them how these two dramatic interpretations change the meaning of the play. Which characterization of Nora do students think Ibsen intended? Which characterization do students prefer?

A Doll's House

- Read the review's title and subtitle for students. Then, discuss with students what the subtitle "A New Version by Frank McGuiness" might mean. Tell students that plays, especially those written in earlier times, are often reinterpreted or rewritten for modern audiences.
- Ask a volunteer to read aloud the first two sentences of the selection. Then, ask: On the basis of these sentences, how would you characterize David Spencer's attitude toward this "new" version of Ibsen's play? Explain.
  Answer: Spencer seems wary of this version, made evident by the fact that he begins the review with an explanation of the performance's "newness." He wants the reader to realize that his review considers the performance in relation to other, more traditional interpretations of the play.
- Draw students' attention to the first call-out note on p. 954. Remind students that reviewers use powerful language to convince the audience that their opinions are valid. The tone of a review should be confident. If a reviewer questions his or her own assessments, the reader will, too.
- Then, draw students' attention to the last call-out note on p. 954. Explain that this last paragraph offers an overall assessment of McTeer's performance and McGuiness's version of the play. Ask students to summarize this assessment.
  Answer: Overall, Spencer expresses a positive opinion of McTeer's performance, calling her a "magnificent actress." However, in Spencer's opinion, McGuiness's version as a whole leaves much to be desired.

A Doll's House

By Henrik Ibsen
A New Version by Frank McGuiness

Reviewed by David Spencer

The first thing you have to understand about this so-called revival of *A Doll's House*—which comes to Broadway by way of London—is that it's not a revival at all. It follows the general outline of Ibsen's famous drama about a woman's coming of age—it contains the same characters and the same events—but it's essentially a new play by Frank ("Someone Who'll Watch over Me") McGuiness. Note his credit: not "translation by" but "a new version by." It's a credit I note with particular emphasis because I have one such on my own resumé. . . . So as you read all the pæans to Janet McTeer's performance as a devastating "new" Nora, keep in mind that a new Nora is precisely, *literally*, what's on offer. And it starts not with the actress, but with the script—whose spin on Ibsen is both compelling and subversive.

That [Janet McTeer] is vivacious, sensual, charismatic, explosive—everything you want a "star" to be—is undeniable. Her Nora trembles with suppressed giggles, bursts with surprise, teases mercilessly, touches, hugs, whispers conspiratorially, revels in her own outrageousness. In the play's first act, this electrifies the audience—palpably. At first, it all but overwhelms Owen Teale's performance as her husband Torvald (a portrayal of a vigorously insecure martinet wannabe) . . . but it creates a buzz of excitement and discovery.

Notice the powerful words Spencer uses to communicate his opinion of the performance.

It's not a buzz that sustains, though. Because after intermission, with Acts Two and Three (performed in one stretch), the vivacity turns to a jittery desperation and finally to out-and-out hysteria. It seems like a perfectly logical progression: once the tight rein on Nora's sense of stability is released by the threat of blackmail and ruination, her energy *would* fly out of control, she *would* find herself without moorings. But in the playing, it is merely relentless.

Happily, in Acts Two and Three, with the shock of the new Nora no longer a novelty, we do get to concentrate on the others in the ensemble—and they are fine within the parameters of the script.

They don't, however, bring the audience closer to the play. Yes, with this *Doll's House* being so different, so modern of intent, it is endlessly fascinating—but it's a fascination experienced from a distance. You are always *aware* of the revisionist take on things, always pausing to *note* the controversial new choices, to *compare* them to Ibsen's original . . . rather than just experiencing them on a visceral level.

I don't mean to condemn this production—or, for that matter, Ms. McTeer. McGuiness' revisionist take is a fine and noble experiment,and his Nora is clearly a magnificent actress. I just feel as if—in the final analysis, in the grand karmic sweep of the universe—this *A Doll's House* is *not* the be-all, end-all revelation the hype would have you believe, but rather an intermediary step.

The writer id[entifies] both pos[itive] and negative aspects of th[e] production.

954 ◆ *Romanticism and Realism*

CUSTOMIZE INSTRUCTION FOR UNIVERSAL ACCESS

For Special Needs Students	For Less Proficient Readers	For Advanced Readers
Revisit the Critical Reviews charts, making sure that students have completed each column. If students have difficulty assessing the reviews, guide them with the following questions: Would you see this performance? Why or why not? Which reviews would help you make your decision?	Have students use an outline organizer to find the main idea of each paragraph on p. 954 and then identify supporting details. Because Spencer uses a high level of diction, students may benefit from working with more proficient partners who read easily and fluently.	Lead a panel discussion in which students consider the advantages and disadvantages of revising classic works. Begin the discussion by brainstorming a list of revised works. Include movie revisions of literary works, such as Baz Luhrmann's modern take on Shakespeare's *Romeo and Juliet.*

Check Your Comprehension

1. According to critic David Spencer, why is the 1997 production of *A Doll's House* "not the be-all, end-all" version of the play?
2. What evidence do the *CurtainUp* critics use to prove that the role of Torvald is the toughest one to portray in *A Doll's House*? Explain.

Applying the Reading Strategy

Comparing and Contrasting Critical Reviews

3. The *CurtainUp* review describes the show as having a "1990s feel" to it. Which critic would most likely agree with this assessment?
4. This 1997 production of *A Doll's House* won the Tony Award for Best Revival of a Play. (a) Which review supports this choice? (b) Which critic would probably disagree with this choice? Explain.
5. Complete a chart like the one shown to identify the points on which the reviewers agree and disagree.

Shared Opinions	Differing Opinions

Activity

Writing a Critical Review

Write a critical review of a movie or television show. Before you write, watch the movie or show and take notes on the following elements:

- acting
- costumes
- script
- overall quality

Address each element in your critical review, supporting your opinions with evidence.

Contrasting Informational Materials

Critical Reviews and Advertisements

Critical reviews share several elements with advertisements. In fact, it is a common practice in the theater to incorporate statements from critical reviews into a play's advertisements. Using the information in the three critical reviews, create a print advertisement for this production of *A Doll's House*. Then, answer these questions:

1. What elements do reviews and ads share?
2. What information from a critical review would *not* be present in an ad?
3. What words or phrases from a review would be effective in your ad?

Answers for p. 955

Check Your Comprehension

1. David Spencer believes that this production of *A Doll's House* is not the "be-all, end-all" version of the play because it differs from the original script and is essentially an "experiment."
2. The *CurtainUp* critics indicate that Torvald is the most difficult character to portray because he may seem the most dated to modern audiences.

Applying the Reading Strategy

3. David Spencer would most likely agree with the assessment of the show as having a "1990s feel" to it, especially in light of his objections to McGuiness's version.
4. **(a)** The *CurtainUp* review most strongly supports the play's Tony Award. **(b)** David Spencer would disagree with this choice. He found the performance inaccessible and distracting.
5. **Shared Opinions:** The reviewers agree that Janet McTeer gives a strong performance, that Owen Teale gives a strong performance, and that the production could have done a better job updating Ibsen's story. **Differing Opinions:** The reviewers disagree on the strength of the script and the overall impact the play has on the audience.

Activity

Emphasize that students' reviews should express more than their personal likes and dislikes. Students should focus on their criteria (the bulleted items listed on p. 955) and measure the movie or television show against those criteria. Have students present their reviews to the class, and invite other class members to weigh in on the validity of each review.

continued

continued from right column

Contrasting Informational Materials

Students' advertisements should contain the basic facts about the production, such as the title, cast, director, and playwright, along with review quotations that encourage attendance. All quotations should be attributed to a reviewer and publication.

1. Both reviews and ads contain persuasive language and opinions about a product or performance.
2. An ad would not include negative opinions about a performance or a product.
3. Powerful, positive language would be effective in an ad.

Lesson Objectives

1. To write an analytical essay comparing and contrasting literary periods
2. To identify and understand the influence of a literary movement on a literary work
3. To gather evidence to support an idea
4. To utilize writing strategies to generate ideas, plan, organize, evaluate and revise writing

Prewriting

- Have students list a few selections they have particularly enjoyed from previous units. Then, have them review the introductions to those units.
- Point out the chart on p. 956. Instruct students to copy the chart onto their papers or to devise a similar chart to help them select their works.
- Remind students as they gather details to provide sufficient evidence to support their essays. If students cannot find sufficient support, ask them to select different works.
- Have students meet in peer groups to review their thesis statements. If their statements are not clear or are too long, ask students to revise them. If necessary, explain the difference between a topic sentence and a thesis statement.

Writing About Literature

Compare and Contrast Literary Periods

Two movements, Romanticism and Realism, define the literature of the nineteenth century. Romantic writers—often inspired by nature—turned inward to tap spontaneous emotions. At the same time, they turned outward to celebrate the lives, language, and folklore of ordinary people. Realism, which emerged later, continued the Romantics' interest in ordinary life, but the Realists' pessimistic view of the suffering of the working class contrasted sharply with the Romantic vision of simple, contented folk.

Write an essay comparing Romantic and Realist literature with the literature of another literary period of your choice. See the box at the right for details of the assignment.

Assignment: Different Times, Different Literature

Write an analytical essay that compares and contrasts Romantic and Realist works of the nineteenth century with works of another literary period. Suggest how events of the period and reactions to other literary works influenced the works you analyze.

Criteria:

- Include a thesis statement drawn from your analysis of the works of two different literary eras.
- Support your thesis with detailed analyses of at least two works from each era.
- Highlight likenesses and differences among the works of different periods.
- Approximate length: 1,500 words

Prewriting

Find a focus. Review the literature both in this unit and in the unit against which you will compare these selections. For an overview of the periods, read the Unit Introduction for each unit as well. Use a chart similar to the one below to take notes. As you review selections, consider these questions to narrow your focus:

- Which aspects of a literary movement does this work reflect?
- Which parts of the work illustrate these aspects?
- What historical developments influenced this work?
- Which other works or literary trends influenced this work?

Model: Focus to Compare and Contrast Literary Periods

Selection	Literary Period	Evidence
"The Lorelei"	Romantic	Influence of folklore; irrational power of desire
"The Fox and the Crow"	Age of Reason	Rational analysis of motives; teaches a lesson

Review your chart, and select two works from each period on which you will focus. In making your choice, consider interesting contrasts as well as similarities between works.

Gather details. Go back to each work you have chosen and gather specific details of plot, setting, and characterization for comparison.

Write a working thesis. Write a single sentence summing up the main points of comparison and contrast between the work of the 1800s that you will discuss and the ones you have chosen from another literary era.

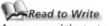

Read to Write
As you reread the texts, identify the themes and decide how these themes reflect the interests and values of the era in which the works were written.

TEACHING RESOURCES

The following resources can be used to enrich or extend the instruction for pp. 956–957.

Writing and Grammar, Diamond Level, Chapter 9, pp. 168–188

Performance Assess. and Portfolio Mgmt., p. 15

Writing Models and Graphic Organizers on Transparencies, pp. 95–97

Writing and Grammar iText CD-ROM

Students can use the following tools as they complete their comparison and contrast of literary periods:

- Venn Diagram
- Transition Word Bin
- Comparitives Revising Tool

Drafting

Write an outline. Preparing a detailed outline will help you organize your thoughts and guide you as you draft. Each main heading of the outline indicated by a capital letter will become a paragraph. Numbered subheadings indented under each heading will be supporting sentences.

Model: Making a Detailed Outline

B. Elements of realism in Tolstoy story
- **1.** simple language
- **2.** main character is a peasant
- **3.** realistic details about Russia
  - **a.** kumiss (fermented mare's milk)

C. Comparison to elements in Renaissance story
- **1.** courtly language
- **2.** main characters are aristocrats
- **3.** some realistic details
  - **a.** details of Federigo's search for a suitable breakfast

Write to Learn
Each time you reread the selections that you are analyzing in your paper, you will find additional nuances of meaning. Don't hesitate to add more information to your essay as your understanding of the works deepens.

Write to Explain
Make sure that you have a good reason for including the details and quotations that you use in your essay. Explain those reasons clearly to your readers.

Revising and Editing

Review content: Eliminate unnecessary details. Identify the main idea in each paragraph. No matter how "interesting" they might be, eliminate details in a paragraph that do not support the main idea.

Review style: Strengthen word choice. Alter dull sentences to make them more interesting, replacing vague words with ones that are more expressive and words you use repeatedly with synonyms.

Original: Pakhom's enemy is his greed. He doesn't get greedy all at once—he becomes greedy little by little. When he has some land, he wants more. When he gets more land, he wants even more. His greed makes the devil happy.

Revised: Pakhom's enemy is his greed. His avarice doesn't sweep over him all at once—it creeps up on him little by little. When he has a modest amount of land, he craves more. His dissatisfaction delights the devil.

Publishing and Presenting

Submit your essay to a literary magazine. Revise your essay, adding necessary background to help a general audience who may be unfamiliar with your topic. Then, submit your essay to the school literary magazine.

WG *Writing and Grammar Connection: Diamond Level, Chapter 9*

Drafting

- Explain to students that a detailed outline will show them whether they have sufficient support for their thesis statements before they begin writing.
- Point out the outline format. Tell students that each main heading listed should support their thesis statements and that they need sufficient support for each heading.
- Have students work from their notes to develop a detailed outline. If they think they lack sufficient support or information, have them return to the texts to find more information or revise their thesis statements.
- As students draft their essays, remind them that this is a working outline. They may make changes as necessary, but they must always be careful that their points advance their thesis statements.

Revising and Editing

- Have students highlight or underline the main idea in each of their paragraphs. Then, have them evaluate whether the main ideas support their thesis statements.
- Next, have students number the details that support their thesis statements. If the details do not provide support, tell students tore-place or eliminate them.
- Review the style models on p. 957. Then, have students work in peer groups to look at word choice and point out for one another overused words and expressions that weaken the essay.

Publishing and Presenting

- Have students check the submission guidelines for the literary magazine.
- Then, ask students to use a word processing program to create their submission copies. Remind them to follow all of the requirements, to proofread carefully, and to save their work on disks. Then, have students submit their work.

CUSTOMIZE INSTRUCTION FOR UNIVERSAL ACCESS

For Less Proficient Writers	For English Learners	For Advanced Writers
Work with students to help them select suitable works, or assign selections instead. Then, guide students to help them find details, develop their thesis statements, and create their outlines. If students lack sufficient support for their thesis statements, help them search for details or allow them to work in pairs.	Review the terms *literary movement, analysis, formal outline,* and *literary trends.* Review thesis statements, including their purpose, structure, and content. Have students work with a partner to draft clear thesis statements. Partners should also help to make sure that thesis statements have enough support.	Encourage students to select challenging works for their essays. Point out that challenging works provide better preparation for future writing assignments and are likely to provide more points of comparison for the essay. Have students work with partners to identify selections that will challenge them.

Lesson Objectives

1. To write a response to literature
2. To use writing strategies to generate ideas, plan, organize, evaluate, and revise writing

Model from Literature

In "Reading for Information" on p. 951, three reviewers of *A Doll House* respond to the drama.

Prewriting

- Tell students that they will write a response to literature. Have them look at the Assignment Criteria on p. 958.
- As a class, have students brainstorm a list of works that they have recently read. Then, have students select those works that they found most enjoyable or most engaging.
- Ask each student to select one work. Point out the hexagonal diagram on p. 958, and model its use with one aspect of a work. Then, have students copy the diagram onto their papers and complete the hexagon for their own topics.
- Point out that their audience may affect their choice of a selection. If they use a selection covered in class, they can assume that the audience is familiar with the work. If they choose another piece of literature, they will need to adjust their papers to the background of the audience.
- Before students draft their essays, have them review the Rubric for Self-Assessment on p. 961, so that they know what is expected of their essays.

Writing WORKSHOP

Response to Literature

A **response to literature** presents an individual's reaction to one aspect of a work of literature, such as its theme, plot, characterization, or use of language. Responses to literature may range from formal and academic to informal and personal. In this workshop, you will write a formal response to a favorite literary work.

Assignment Criteria Your response to literature should display the following characteristics:

- A discussion of the themes or significant ideas of a piece of literature
- Accurate references to the text, including examples, quotations, and allusions
- A personal response drawn from your ideas and experiences
- A logical organizational plan
- A thesis statement, introduction, and conclusion

To preview the criteria on which your response to literature may be assessed, refer to the Rubric on page 961.

Prewriting

Choose a topic. **Brainstorm** to generate ideas. List works of literature you have read lately that most fully engaged your attention or related most strongly to your own life. Consider also works that raised many questions for you. Choose the piece from your list that sparks the most ideas, one that you would like to explore in depth.

Gather evidence. Make sure you have enough ideas about the work you chose to construct an interesting essay with sufficient supporting details. To generate ideas, consider using the technique of **hexagonal writing,** in which you explore six aspects of a piece of literature. Make a hexagonal chart similar to the one shown here, and follow the directions in the example to complete a hexagon based on your topic.

Consider your audience. Identify the interests and level of sophistication of your audience. To help you choose supporting evidence and decide how much explanation to provide, decide how familiar your audience is with the literature you intend to discuss. Then, shape your material in order to convince your audience that the work and its theme are relevant to them.

Plot
Summarize the plot briefly.
Personal Connection
Relate the work to your life.
Theme
State the overall message about life that the work conveys.
Analysis
Cite evidence to support your idea of the theme.
Literary Elements
Cite how other elements from the work support the theme.
Evaluation
State your reaction to the work and its theme.

TEACHING RESOURCES

The following resources can be used to enrich or extend the instruction for pp. 958–961.

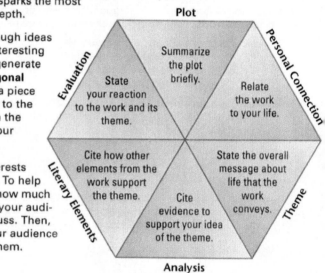
Writing and Grammar, Diamond Level, Chapter 14, pp. 306–m324

Performance Assess. and Portfolio Mgmt., p. 16

Writing Models and Graphic Organizers on Transparencies, pp. 53–59

Writing and Grammar iText CD-ROM

Students can use the following tools as they complete their responses to literature:

- Hexagonal Organizer
- Audience Profile Organizer
- Character Trait Word Bin
- Editing Revising Tool

Student Model

Before you begin your first draft, read this student model and review the characteristics of a response to literature.

Nick Groesch
Decatur, Illinois

The Tarantella in Ibsen's *A Doll House*

Many great playwrights have used performing arts as a way to exemplify themes in their works. Shakespeare, for example, uses a play within *Hamlet* to reveal the guilt of Claudius and to deplore the evil of regicide. In *A Doll House,* Ibsen makes use of the tarantella, an Italian folk dance, in several dramatic ways. In Act Two, Ibsen uses the tarantella to increase suspense, to reveal a deeply flawed marriage, and to symbolize Nora's utter desperation.

> Nick's thesis statement clearly defines the scope of his response essay.

On a practical level, Nora's dancing serves as a distraction. By deliberately dancing badly, Nora draws Helmer's attention away from the arrival of Krogstad's letter, which will shatter her world. "Yes, you see how important [the tarantella] is. You've got to teach me to the very last minute" (Act Two). Nora successfully delays the reading of the letter, increasing the play's suspense.

On another level, Ibsen uses the tarantella rehearsal to reveal problems in the Helmers' marriage. As he instructs Nora, Helmer shows that he views his wife as a "doll," a performing toy to be played with and shown off to his friends. Among his significant remarks: "you little helpless thing"; "Be my own little lark again"; "It's nothing more than this childish anxiety I was telling you about." By showing Helmer's patronizing attitude in this scene, Ibsen prepares the viewer for Nora's explosion of resentment and rebellion.

> Nick accurately quotes lines of dialogue from the play to support his points.

Finally, Nora's wild dancing is a symbol of her desperation. The tarantella was believed to cure its dancer from the poison of a tarantula. Krogstad's threats and letter are poison to Nora's happiness and marriage. Nora takes it upon herself to practice the tarantella because she wishes to rid herself of this "poison." Unfortunately, the tarantella does not cure poison, nor does Nora's dance solve her problems. She realizes this and, at the end of Act Two, she says, "Seven hours to midnight. Twenty-four hours to the midnight after, and then the tarantella's done. Seven and twenty-four? Thirty-one hours to live."

> Nick gives essential background information in order to explore the tarantella as a symbol.

Ibsen uses the tarantella for plot reasons, as a ruse that distracts Helmer; to develop character, as a picture of a troubled marriage; and finally as a symbol of Nora's life spinning out of control. Though it does not "cure" anything, the tarantella sets up and intensifies the final showdown between Helmer and Nora, an epic climax that defines *A Doll House* as Ibsen's most influential play.

> Nick concludes his response with a summary and a forceful statement on the importance of the scene to Ibsen's play.

CUSTOMIZE INSTRUCTION FOR UNIVERSAL ACCESS

For Less Proficient Writers	For English Learners	For Advanced Writers
Using a copy of the student model on an overhead transparency, help students see the organization of the essay by using different colored markers to mark the main points and the support for each.	Review the terms on each side of the hexagon on p. 958. Have students write the terms in their notebooks for future use. Then, guide them through the use of the hexagon with the selections they have chosen for their essays.	Have students use the Internet to find responses to literature. Have them select two examples of effective introductions and effective conclusions. Then, have them print the essays, citing their sources and highlighting the introductions and conclusions. Have students explain why these introductions and conclusions are effective.

Student Model

- Explain that the Student Model is a sample and that student essays may be longer.
- Ask students to identify the thesis statement in Nick's essay.
  Answer: The thesis statement is, "In Act Two, Ibsen uses the tarantella to increase suspense, to reveal a deeply flawed marriage, and to symbolize Nora's utter desperation."
- Discuss the importance of using direct quotations to support a point. Call attention to the fact that Nick cites the act from which he draws the quotations.
- Ask students how Nick's discussion of the essential background information about the tarantella supports his thesis.
  Possible response: The background information about the tarantella helps Nick prove that Ibsen utilizes the dance as a symbol of Nora's plight.
- Direct students' attention to the final paragraph. Have students evaluate the paragraph as a conclusion and explain how it supports the thesis statement.
  Possible response: It is an effective conclusion because it restates Nick's main points and ties together the support he has provided for his thesis statement.

Real-World Connection

Response to literature in the workplace: Tell students that a response to literature or any other art is a type of writing that journalists might use. Explain that teachers and librarians may use this type of writing as well. Other people may also need to write responses, however. These may be required in the workplace when workers are asked to respond to a new policy or procedure. Workers may also be asked to respond to workplace design or to a new assignment. Although this is not responding to literature, any type of written response requires a thesis statement with main points and support for those points.

Drafting

- Remind students that their thesis statements can be revised if they lack support.
- As students begin to organize their essays, point out the chart "Organization of a Response to Literature" on p. 960. Tell students that this chart indicates the basic information that they should include in each part of their essays. Students may wish to use an informal outline based on the points included in the organizational chart.
- Remind students that they must provide relevant and sufficient evidence to support their thesis statements. Point out that information from other sources must be cited.

Revising

- Direct students' attention to the revised conclusion in the Model. Ask students how this revision improves the essay.
  Possible response: In the revision, Nick addresses all three points of his thesis statement and provides examples of each.

(continued on page 961)

Drafting

Draft a thesis statement. Review your notes, and decide which critical point you want to make about the piece of literature. Then, write a thesis statement that introduces your ideas. Include the thesis statement as the main idea of your introductory paragraph.

Organize your essay. Follow a logical plan of organization to write your first draft. Consider a basic three-part organization, as shown at the right.

Elaborate. Give reasons for your analysis of the themes and for your response to them. Cite evidence from the work, from other pieces of literature, and from your life experience.

Organization of a Response to Literature

Introduction
- State thesis.
- Introduce work of literature, theme, and response.

Body
- Elaborate on thesis statement.
- Provide evidence: examples, quotations, personal reactions.

Conclusion
- Summarize main ideas and provide final insight.

Revising

Revise the introduction and conclusion. Read through the introduction and conclusion of your essay. Revise so that the conclusion restates or further explains the main points of the introduction in an interesting way.

Model: Revise Introduction and Conclusion

Introduction

In Act Two, Ibsen uses the tarantella to increase suspense, to reveal a deeply flawed marriage, and to symbolize Nora's utter desperation.

Conclusion

~~Ibsen uses the tarantella both practically as a ruse to distract Helmer and as a symbol of Nora's life spinning out of control.~~ ^ *Ibsen uses the tarantella for plot reasons, as a ruse that distracts Helmer; to develop character, as a picture of a troubled marriage; and finally as a symbol of Nora's life spinning out of control. Though it does not "cure" anything, the tarantella sets up and intensifies the final showdown between Helmer and Nora, an epic climax that defines* A Doll House *as Ibsen's most influential play.*

Nick revised his conclusion to better match his introduction and to add a final insight.

USING TECHNOLOGY IN WRITING

Explain to students using word processing software that although programs that check spelling can be helpful, they do not take the place of proofreading. These programs check only for correct spelling, not correct usage. The only way that students can be sure that their papers are correct is to read them carefully.

Students can also use the organizing tools and revision checkers on the **Writing and Grammar iText CD-ROM.**

Revise for clarity. Remember that your readers are most likely not as familiar as you are with the work of literature that is the subject of your essay. Provide enough background information to help all your readers follow your essay.

Compare the model and the nonmodel below to evaluate the clarity of each one.

Nonmodel	Model
On a practical level, Nora's dancing serves as a distraction. By dancing badly, Nora draws Helmer's attention away from the arrival of Krogstad's letter.	On a practical level, Nora's dancing serves as a distraction. By deliberately dancing badly, Nora draws Helmer's attention away from the arrival of Krogstad's letter, which will shatter her world.

Publishing and Presenting

Choose one of the following ways to share your writing with classmates or a wider audience.

Present to a book group. Invite a group of classmates or friends to read the work of literature that is the topic of your essay. After everyone has read the piece, get the group together and present a summary of your essay. Afterwards, have a discussion in which group members compare their own reactions to the work.

Publish an online review of the work. Post your response to the work on a student or bookstore Web site. Be sure to follow the submission requirements for the site to make sure your submission is accepted and posted.

WG *Writing and Grammar Connection: Diamond Level, Chapter 14*

Rubric for Self-Assessment

Evaluate your response to literature using the following criteria and rating scale:

Criteria	Rating Scale: Not very				Very
How clear and accurate is my thesis statement?	1	2	3	4	5
How well have I explained the significant ideas of the piece?	1	2	3	4	5
How well have I supported my personal reactions with evidence from the text?	1	2	3	4	5
How logical is the organization of my essay?	1	2	3	4	5
How accurately does the conclusion summarize my ideas?	1	2	3	4	5
How well does my conclusion reflect and extend my introduction?	1	2	3	4	5

Revising (continued)

- Point out the Nonmodel and Model on p. 961. After reviewing these examples, tell students to ask partners to read their papers, looking for sentences and ideas that may be unclear. Then, have students revise their papers, clarifying any confusing sections.

Publishing and Presenting

- If some students have written about the same selection, have them form a group and discuss their reactions to the literature. Students can use their essays as a basis for discussion.
- Point out that many online bookstores have a place for comments about literary selections. Remind students that when they enter their essays on the Web site, correct grammar and punctuation are still important because these help give credibility to their opinions.

Assessment

- Review the assessment criteria in class.
- Encourage students to use the assessment rubric to evaluate the Student Model. Then, have them use the rubric to assess their own essays.
- An alternative rubric can be found on p. 16 of **Performance Assessment and Portfolio Management.**

TEST-TAKING TIP

When taking a test that requires a response to literature, students should read the question before reading the literature. Then, when they read the literature, they can identify and underline specific information that relates to the question. When students begin to write, they will have already labeled supporting information for their papers. This strategy will save time.

Lesson Objectives

1. To respond orally to literature
2. To prepare content for an oral presentation
3. To choose a logical structure for an oral presentation
4. To develop an effective opening and conclusion for an oral presentation

Prepare Your Content

- Remind students that it will be difficult for them to sound enthusiastic about a topic that does not interest them. Point out that when a speaker is enthusiastic about a topic, it is likely that his or her audience will share that enthusiasm.
- Point out to students that if their focus is too broad, they will lose the interest of their audience. Also, remind them that a focused idea is far more effective and easy to support than one that is too broad.
- Remind students that their audience may determine the level of support required in their presentations. If an audience is likely to disagree with their ideas, students must provide more convincing support.

Prepare Your Delivery

- Have students look at the content of their responses. Discuss what types of content work best with which organizational strategies. For example, if students are responding to changes in a character, guide them to understand that chronological order may be the best way to organize the response.
- Have students discuss ways to create effective openings and conclusions. Point out that action, dialogue, or reactions are ways to create effective openings. Remind students to avoid the "I am going to tell you..." opening.
- Have students complete the Activity on the student page. Allow students time to rehearse their presentations. Have students work with partners who will complete the feedback forms. Then, have students revise their work and present their responses to the class.

Listening and Speaking WORKSHOP

Delivering an Oral Response to Literature

An **oral response to literature** might be an offhand comment to a friend about a bestseller you read, a panel discussion about the relevance of literature to the critical issues of the day, or a formal presentation on a theme in the work of a great author. The following strategies will help you prepare and present an effective formal oral response to a work.

Prepare Your Content

Choose a topic that excites you. What have you read recently that made you angry, puzzled, or elated? That piece would make an excellent subject for your presentation.

Narrow your focus. What will be the main idea or theme of your talk? Keep that most important idea in mind as you prepare your presentation. Assume that you must persuade your audience to accept your viewpoint. Anticipate and address potential objections.

Support your ideas. Your ideas will be most convincing if they are supported with quotations from and references to the text under discussion and other relevant works. Read over the work several times. Then, carefully choose the evidence that supports your viewpoint.

Prepare Your Delivery

Use the following techniques to prepare your presentation of a response to literature:

- **Choose a logical structure.** Which structure will work most effectively for your presentation: chronological order, order of importance, part to whole, comparison and contrast? Select a specific pattern and use it consistently throughout your talk.
- **Develop an effective opening and conclusion.** The impact of your talk as a whole is only as strong as its introduction and conclusion. An intriguing beginning snares the attention of the audience, and a dramatic conclusion leaves your main point etched in the audience's memory. Revise the opening and conclusion of your presentation until they are effective.
- **Rehearse your presentation.** Practice to make your delivery conversational and comfortable. Try to avoid reading an essay word for word. Instead, use your notes as a guide.

Feedback Form for an Oral Response to Literature

Rating System
+ = Excellent ✓ = Average – = Weak

Content
Clarity of main idea ______
Persuasiveness of viewpoint ______
Supporting evidence ______

Suggestions for improvement: ______

Delivery
Organization ______
Opening ______
Conclusion ______

Other comments on delivery: ______

Activity: Presentation and Feedback Choose a short story or a short piece of nonfiction. Prepare a three-minute oral response to the work. Have a partner use the Feedback Form to evaluate your preparation, and revise your work based on your partner's observations. Present your response to your class.

CUSTOMIZE INSTRUCTION FOR UNIVERSAL ACCESS

For Less Proficient Readers	For English Learners	For Advanced Readers
Remind students that they must indicate to the reader when they are using a direct quotation. Have students provide the writer or character's name and tell the listener that the material is a direct quotation. Students may also say, "This passage can be found on page 94," for example.	Show students how to support their ideas with direct quotations and references to the text. Point out that only a short quotation may be needed for support. Ask students to have their partners give them feedback on their use of quotations and help them revise as necessary.	Encourage students to find other resources for support as well as their own in response to the selection. Ask students to use library resources or the Internet to find additional responses. Students should include at least one of these additional resources in their presentations. They must be sure to cite this material correctly.

Strategy, Organization, and Style

On some tests, you may be asked to read a passage with numbered sentences or paragraphs and to answer questions about its organization and use of language. Use these strategies to help you answer such questions:

- Summarize, in logical order, the events or ideas in the passage. Next to each event or idea, write the number of the sentence or paragraph in which it appears. Use your outline to help you answer questions about reordering parts of the passage.
- Note the purpose of the passage—to persuade readers to hold an opinion, to inform them about a topic, or to entertain them. Recall this purpose when answering questions about main ideas, supporting details, and irrelevant sentences.

Test-Taking Strategies

- Read the entire passage before answering the questions.
- Eliminate any answers that are obviously incorrect.

Sample Test Item

Directions: Read the passage, and then choose the letter of the best answer to the question.

(1) In five years the plague, which had no cure, caused a gruesome death for 25 million people—one third of Europe's population. (2) The fleas on rodents soon carried the plague from China throughout Europe. (3) Smaller outbreaks of the plague continued until the 1600s. (4) In the 1330s, China was stricken by the bubonic plague, which got its name from buboes, the swellings of the lymph glands.

1. Which sentence sequence makes the most sense?

A 4, 2, 1, 3
B 2, 4, 3, 1
C 3, 1, 2, 4
D 1, 2, 3, 4

Answer and Explanation

The correct answer is *A* because it arranges the sentences describing the outbreak and spread of the plague in sequential order. Each of the other choices presents events out of sequence.

Practice

Directions: Read the passage, and then choose the letter of the best answer to the question.

(1) Beginning in the late ninth century, Viking raids from the north, Magyar raids from the east, and Muslim raids from the south endangered Europe. (2) After Charlemagne's death in 814, Europe once again faced the threat of invasion. (3) As a result of these attacks, the feudal system was born: a system of mutual defense pacts between lords and vassals. (4) The Holy Roman Empire, ruled by Charlemagne, returned some semblance of security to Europe. (5) The Roman Empire was overrun by Germanic tribes in the fifth century A.D., and its fall left Europe vulnerable to more invaders.

1. Which sentence sequence makes the most sense?

A 1, 3, 2, 5, 4
B 5, 4, 2, 1, 3
C 4, 1, 3, 2, 5
D 2, 1, 3, 5, 4

Lesson Objective

To identify strategy, organization, and style in a standardized test situation

Applying Reading Strategies

Explain to students that summarizing can help them organize a passage. When reading the sample test question, tell students to summarize each sentence. Then, they will be able to organize the ideas in logical order.

Test-Taking Skills

- Have students read the Sample Test Item. As they read, have them summarize what is happening in each sentence. Then, have students organize the items in sequential order and select the correct answer.
- Then, have students read the Answer and Explanation on p. 963. Make sure that students understand the answer and how it was reached.
- Have students read and respond to the Practice question.

Answer

The correct answer is *B*. The passage mentions the fifth century A.D., and that is followed by Charlemagne's rule. Charlemagne's death in 814 is followed by invasions, and the feudal pacts follow the raids. Answer *A* is incorrect because the ninth century follows the fifth century. Answer *C* is incorrect because it ends with the fifth century. Answer *D* is incorrect because this answer indicates that Charlemagne died before he ruled.

TEACHING RESOURCES

The following resources can be used to enrich or extend the instruction for p. 963.

For additional diagnostics and remediation for skills covered in this grouping, use materials from the Prentice Hall Assessment System.

Unit Objectives

1. To read selections from world literature written during the period of 1890 to 1945
2. To apply a variety of reading strategies, particularly those that are appropriate for reading fiction
3. To analyze literary elements
4. To use a variety of strategies to read unfamiliar words and to build vocabulary
5. To learn elements of grammar, usage, and style
6. To use recursive writing processes to write in a variety of forms
7. To develop listening and speaking skills
8. To express and support responses to various types of texts
9. To prepare, organize, and present literary interpretations

Meeting the Objectives

With each selection, you will find instructional materials through which students can meet these objectives. Further, you will find additional practice pages for reading strategies, literary analysis, vocabulary, and grammar in the **Selection Support: Skills Development Workbook** in your **Teaching Resources.**

Background

Art

Guernica, by Pablo Picasso

Probably the most famous twentieth-century painter, Picasso (1881–1973) opposed the Nationalist cause during the Spanish Civil War. In 1937, the Nationalist forces destroyed the small Basque town of Guernica. Within days, Picasso began sketches for what would become a haunting and immense (11′ 6″ × 25′ 8″) work entitled *Guernica.*

Use the following questions for discussion:

1. What message does Picasso convey about the Spanish Civil War?
   Possible response: Picasso shows the destruction and grief causedby war.
2. What emotions does this painting evoke?
   Possible response: It may evoke sadness, horror, or confusion.

UNIT 8 The Modern World

Guernica, 1937, Pablo Picasso, © 2004 Estate of Pablo Picasso

UNIT FEATURES

Connections	Reading Informational Materials
Every unit contains a feature that connects literature to a related topic, such as art, science, or history. In this unit, students will read **Sherwood Anderson: The Corn Planting** on p. 1064. Use the information and questions on the Connections pages to help students enrich their understanding of the selections presented within the unit.	These selections will help students learn to analyze and evaluate informational texts, such as workplace documents, technical directions, and consumer materials. They will expose students to the organization and features unique to nonnarrative texts. In this unit, the focus is on Scientific Texts. **What Is an Insect** is on p. 1024.

"Almost all of the affairs of men remain a terrible uncertainty. We think of what has disappeared, and we are almost destroyed by what has been destroyed; we do not know what will be born, and we fear the future, not without reason. . . ."

— Paul Valéry

ASSESSMENT RESOURCES

The following resources can be used to assess students' knowledge and skills.

- **Selection Support:** Skills Development Workbook
- **Formal Assessment**
- **Open-Book Tests**
- **Performance Assessment and Portfolio Management**
- **Extension Activities**

Assessing Student Progress

Listed below are the tools that are available to measure the degree to which students meet the unit objectives.

Informal Assessment

The questions in the Review and Assess sections are a first level of response to the concepts and skills presented within the selections. Students' responses are a brief, informal measure of their grasp of the material. These responses can indicate where further instruction and practice are needed. Then, follow up with the practice pages in the **Selection Support: Skills Development Workbook.**

Formal Assessment

The **Formal Assessment** booklet contains Selection Tests and Unit Tests.

- Selection Tests measure comprehension and skills acquisition for each selection or group of selections.
- Each Unit Test provides students with thirty multiple-choice questions and five essay questions designed to assess students' knowledge of the literature and skills taught in the unit.

The **Open-Book Tests** ask students to demonstrate their ability to synthesize and communicate information from selections or groups of selections.

To assess students' writing, you will find rubrics and scoring models in the **Performance Assessment and Portfolio Management** booklet. In this booklet, you will also find scoring rubrics for listening and speaking activities.

Alternative Assessment

The **Extension Activities** booklet contains writing activities, listening and speaking activities, and research and technology activities that are appropriate for students with different ability levels. You may also use these activities as an alternative measurement of students' growth.

Using the Timeline

The Timeline can serve a number of instructional purposes, as follows:

Getting an Overview

Use the Timeline to help students get a quick overview of themes and events of the period. This approach will benefit all students but may be especially helpful for Visual/Spatial Learners, English Learners, and Less Proficient Readers. (For strategies in using the Timeline as an overview, see the bottom of this page.)

Thinking Critically

Questions are provided on the facing page. Use these questions to have students review the events, discuss their significance, and examine the "so what" behind the "what happened".

Connecting to Selections

Have students refer to the Timeline when they begin to read individual selections. By consulting the Timeline regularly, they will gain a better sense of the period's chronology. In addition, they will appreciate world events that gave rise to these works of literature.

Projects

Students can use the Timeline as a launching pad for projects like these:

- **Letter to the Editor** Have students study the Timeline events leading up to World War II. Then, have students write a letter to the editor attempting to persuade readers that the entry of the United States into the war was inevitable. Students should use Timeline events for support.
- **Technology Timeline** Have students study the Timeline and select events that show technological advancements. Then, have students create a poster-sized timeline, showing the technological advances that took place from 1890 to 1945. Ask students to illustrate their timelines and display them in the classroom.

Timeline 1890–1945

1890 | 1900 | 1910

Historical and Cultural Events

- **1890** Ohio inventor builds first internal combustion automobile in the United States.
- **1899** Sigmund Freud publishes *The Interpretation of Dreams.* ▼

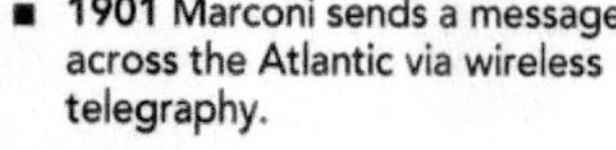

- **1901** Marconi sends a message across the Atlantic via wireless telegraphy.
- **1903** Orville Wright makes the first successful flight in an airplane. ▼

- **1903** Henri Becquerel and Pierre and Marie Curie win a Nobel Prize for work on radioactivity.
- **1905** Einstein proposes his theory of special relativity.
- **1907** Pablo Picasso completes *The Young Women of Avignon.*
- **1907** Tungsten filament lamps first used in the United States.
- **1908** Henry Ford starts producing standardized Model T automobiles.
- **1911** Marie Curie wins second Nobel Prize, for isolating pure radium.
- **1914–1918** World War I is fought, killing millions. ▼
- **1917** Communists seize power in Russia.
- **1919** U. S. Senate rejects League of Nations.

Literary Events

- **1890** Japanese author Mori Ōgai publishes his story "The Dancing Girl."
- **1893** Nicaraguan poet Rubén Darío becomes Colombian consul in Buenos Aires, Argentina.
- **1896** Alfred Nobel dies; his will endows the Nobel Prize in Literature.
- **1896** French author Paul Valéry publishes *An Evening With Monsieur Teste.*
- **1900** French novelist Colette publishes *Claudine at School.*
- **1900** Spanish poet Juan Ramón Jiménez comes to Madrid at the invitation of Rubén Darío.
- **1907–1908** Austro-German poet Rainer Maria Rilke publishes *New Poems.*
- **1911–1913** Mori Ōgai publishes his novel *The Wild Goose.*
- **c. 1912** Ezra Pound and others create the Imagist movement. ◀
- **1913** Rabindranath Tagore receives the Nobel Prize in Literature.
- **1913** Marcel Proust publishes the first volume of *Remembrance of Things Past.*
- **1913** French poet Guillaume Apollinaire publishes *Alcools.*

ENRICHMENT: Getting an Overview of the Period

Introduction	Key Events
To give students an overview of the period, have them indicate the span of dates in the title of the Timeline. Next, point out that the Timeline is divided into Historical and Cultural Events (on the top) and Literary Events (on the bottom). Have students scan the Timeline, looking at both the Historical and Cultural Events and the Literary Events. Finally, point out that the events in the Timeline often represent beginnings, turning points, and endings (for example, the start of World War II in 1939).	Have students identify key events of the Modern World. **Possible response:** Key events are the first successful airplane flight and the use of the atomic bomb. Ask students to describe the impact of these key events. **Possible response:** Flight essentially reduced the size of the world, and the atomic bomb increased the destructive power of human beings.

World Events

1920 | 1930 | 1940 | 1950

- **1927** Charles Lindbergh makes a successful solo flight across the Atlantic.
- **1928** Stalin begins forcing peasants onto collective farms, killing those who resist.
- **1929** Great Depression begins, lasting until about 1939. ▼

- **1931** Japan seizes Manchuria from China.
- **1932** Franklin Roosevelt elected President of the U. S. (serves 1932–1945). ▼
- **1933** Hitler becomes chancellor of Germany.
- **1934** Stalin begins a campaign of terror against those who are "disloyal."
- **1937** Japan launches a full-scale war against China.
- **1939** Hitler invades Poland, starting World War II.

- **1940** Churchill becomes Prime Minister of Great Britain.
- **1940** Japanese enter the war on the side of the Axis Powers.
- **1941** Germany invades the Soviet Union.
- **1941** The United States enters the war on the side of the Allies.
- **1945** America drops two atom bombs on Japan. ▶
- **1945** The Allies defeat the Axis Powers, ending World War II.

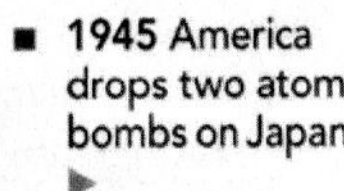

- **1921** André Breton meets Sigmund Freud.
- **1921** Italian author Luigi Pirandello publishes the play *Six Characters in Search of an Author.*
- **1922** James Joyce publishes *Ulysses.*
- **1922** Russian poet Boris Pasternak publishes *My Sister—Life.*
- **1923** Rainer Maria Rilke publishes *Duino Elegies* and *Sonnets to Orpheus.*
- **1924** Franz Kafka dies of tuberculosis.

- **1935–1940** Anna Akhmatova composes *Requiem.*
- **1936** Federico García Lorca (portrayed here by actor Andy Garcia) is assassinated by fascists. ▼

- **1942** Albert Camus publishes his novel *The Stranger.*
- **1944** Colette publishes her novel *Gigi.*
- **1945** Gabriela Mistral becomes the first Latin American to win the Nobel Prize in Literature.

continued from right column

▶Critical Viewing

1. On the basis of the illustration of Orville Wright's first airplane (1903), what can you deduce about his first flight? **[Deduce]**
   Possible response: The plane does not look sturdy enough to fly for very long. Therefore, the flight was probably dangerous and short.
2. What does the cover of the *Literary Digest* (1914–1918) imply about the fighting in World War I? **[Infer]**
   Possible response: The cover suggests that the fighting was difficult and primarily hand-to-hand.
3. What does the illustration of the atomic bomb blast (1945) suggest about its power? **[Analyze]**
   Possible response: The illustration suggests that the blast was extremely powerful, destructive, and could be seen from a great distance.

Analyzing the Timeline

1. **(a)** When did Marconi send a message across the Atlantic via wireless telegraphy? **(b)** How might this action eventually have affected the entry of the United States into World War I? **[Analyze Causes and Effects]**
   Answer: **(a)** Marconi sent the message in 1901. **(b)** Communication between the United States and Europe became faster. Consequently, people became more aware of what was happening in Europe.
2. **(a)** When did Charles Lindbergh make his successful solo flight across the Atlantic? **(b)** What advances in aviation must have taken place between Lindbergh's flight and World War II? **[Synthesize]**
   Answer: **(a)** Charles Lindbergh made his flight in 1927. **(b)** In the years between Lindbergh's flight and World War II, aviation improved significantly.
3. **(a)** When did Henri Becquerel and Pierre and Marie Curie win a Nobel Prize for their work on radioactivity? **(b)** What later event was an eventual outgrowth of their work? **[Deduce]**
   Answer: **(a)** Becquerel and the Curies won the Nobel Prize in 1903. **(b)** Their discovery led to the development and use of the atomic bomb in 1945.
4. **(a)** When did the United States enter World War II? **(b)** Why did the United States enter the war two years after it had begun in Europe? **[Infer]**
   Answer: **(a)** The United States entered World War II in 1941. **(b)** The late entry of the United States into the war demonstrates an isolationist policy.
5. **(a)** When did Japan seize Manchuria from China? **(b)** How might this action influence Japan's future relationship with China? **[Speculate]**
   Answer: **(a)** Japan seized Manchuria in 1931. **(b)** It would lead to poor relations between the countries. In fact, Japan invaded China in 1937.

continued

Literature of the Period

- In Franz Kafka's "The Metamorphosis," p. 978, students will meet a character who wakes up to find that he has been transformed into a giant insect. This selection exemplifies the Modernist theme of alienation.
- As they read "The Bracelet" by Colette, p. 1046, students will find a Modernist nontraditional plot structure that deals with memories of a lost childhood gift, one as inexpensive as it was priceless.
- During the twentieth century, many writers examined how rapid change affects longstanding customs and traditions. In Mori Ōgai's "Under Reconstruction," p. 1116, students will find a character who must deal with the fusion of eastern and western traditions.

Background

Marie Curie

Marie Curie was born in Poland in 1867. As a child, Curie had an exceptional memory. She completed her secondary education at the age of sixteen but was forced to find work because her father's poor investing left the family with little money. Marie took jobs as a teacher and a governess to pay for her sister's education. Curie left for Paris in 1891, where she studied physics. She married Pierre Curie in 1895. The Curies became known throughout the world because of their work with radium and radioactivity. Marie Curie received the 1911 Nobel Prize in Chemistry for her work with radium, which she discovered in 1898. She died from leukemia in 1934.

▶Critical Viewing

Possible response: Nuclear power, radiation treatments for cancer, and other scientific advances have been positive results; nuclear weapons and nuclear accidents have been negative results.

The Modern World

(1890–1945)

Historical Background

Breakthroughs in Technology and Science Sparked by the efforts of brilliant scientists and inventors, major technological advances began occurring in the late nineteenth and early twentieth centuries that would permanently alter the ways in which people lived. Within a period of just a few decades, the airplane, the automobile, the radio, and the telephone were introduced, making travel and communication faster and easier than ever before. At the same time, other discoveries and inventions, such as electricity, central heating, movies, and new medical remedies, were improving the quality of people's lives. Still other advances, such as the development of the machine gun and the tank, made it easier for people to destroy one another.

Scientific breakthroughs rivaled these technological advances. The husband and wife team of Marie and Pierre Curie, for example, pioneered in studying radioactivity. Then, in 1905, German-born physicist Albert Einstein proposed his special theory of relativity, showing that calculations of time and motion depend on an observer's relative position. Einstein also proved that energy and matter can be converted into each other, as expressed by the famous formula $E = mc^2$.

Understanding Human Behavior Austrian psychiatrist Sigmund Freud (froid) proposed an equally radical theory of human behavior. Using a method of gathering information about mental processes known as psychoanalysis, Freud concluded that people's behavior is largely shaped by unconscious influences stemming from experiences during infancy and early childhood. Because Freud's theories challenged the belief that human activity sprang from rational thought, they initially sparked controversy. Yet as time passed, his ideas gained increasing acceptance. World War I itself seemed the greatest proof that humans were basically irrational!

World War I Encouraged by advances in science and technology, many people became increasingly optimistic about the future of humanity. To some, it even seemed possible that people could ultimately solve all their problems and establish lasting peace. This sense of optimism was utterly shattered, however, by the horrifying realities of World War I.

▼ Critical Viewing This photograph shows Marie Curie in her laboratory, where she studied radioactivity. What positive and negative results have come from the study of radioactivity? Explain. **[Draw Conclusions]**

ENRICHMENT: Science Connection

Albert Einstein and the Theory of Relativity

Albert Einstein (1879–1955), who was born in Germany, is known as the greatest physicist of all time. He is best known for his theory of relativity.

Einstein argued that because all matter is in constant motion, there is no fixed point from which to measure motion. The motion of one object can be measured only by comparing it with the motion of another. All measurements are therefore relative. This theory is called the theory of relativity.

In 1921, Einstein won the Nobel Prize in Physics for his work on photoelectric effect. He became an American citizen in 1940.

Art in the Historical Context

The Art of Colonized Lands Conquers the West

In the late nineteenth and early twentieth centuries, Western colonizers sought new markets and mineral wealth in Africa, the Pacific Islands, and other so-called primitive places. Western artists sought a different kind of wealth in these same lands. They realized how much they could learn from the art of tribal peoples, from sculptures and masks that broke up the human figure and face in startling ways. Instead of imitating nature as Western works did, tribal art used abstractions—geometric shapes and fantastic forms—to convey spiritual realities.

In 1906–7, Pablo Picasso incorporated the abstractions of tribal art in a painting that made people gasp, *Les Demoiselles d'Avignon* ("The Young Women of Avignon"). Picasso himself was so uncertain about the canvas that he put it aside for a while. Today, it is recognized as the work that revolutionized Western art. With his slashing lines, Picasso attacked ideals of beauty and techniques of perspective that dated back to the Renaissance.

Les Demoiselles d'Avignon (detail), 1907, Pablo Picasso, The Museum of Modern Art, New York, NY

▲ **Critical Viewing** Compare and contrast this mask from the South Pacific island of New Britain (top) with the head of a young woman in Picasso's painting (bottom). Use details from each work to support your points. **[Compare and Contrast]**

Beginning late in the summer of 1914, the war was a conflict between the Allies (France, Russia, Great Britain, Italy, and Japan, joined later by the United States) and the Central Powers (Germany, Austria-Hungary, and Turkey). This war eventually involved much of the world.

Throughout most of the conflict, neither side was able to make any significant advances. Having reached a stalemate early in the war, the opposing armies settled into trenches protected by mines and barbed wire. For the next few years, the two sides took turns rushing the opposing trenches. With each of these charges, hundreds of soldiers would be mowed down by machine-gun fire. By the time the war ended in 1918 with the Allies victorious, about eight and a half million soldiers had died of wounds or disease and about thirteen million civilians had lost their lives from a variety of war-related causes.

The Rise of Nazism In the aftermath of the war, the Allies drafted a treaty that required Germany to accept full blame and pay reparations for the total cost of the war. Germany signed the treaty, but its harsh terms created strong feelings of resentment among the German people. These feelings, coupled with the inflation caused by war reparations that Germany had to pay, generated unrest that plagued the nation throughout the 1920s.

The Great Depression In 1929, a severe economic slump hit the United States and, soon afterward, other industrialized nations such as Germany. Known as the Great Depression, it lasted through the 1930s and contributed to the rise of Hitler and other political extremists. In the early 1930s, the Nazis exploited the turmoil resulting from political unrest and economic decline to seize control of Germany.

Background

World War I Artists

During World War I, governments hired artists to record the major events of the war. In addition to capturing major battles, these artists depicted soldiers at rest, long convoys of vehicles and marching men, and troops preparing for battle. One of the leading combat artists of World War I was William J. Aylward, whose paintings are now part of the collection at the Smithsonian Institution.

Background

Art

Les Demoiselles d'Avignon, by Pablo Picasso

This famous painting by Picasso (1881–1973) exemplifies an extreme change in the type of art being produced in the early 1900s. Picasso uses asymmetrical shapes; sharp, uneven lines; and African masks to portray a group of women. Picasso uses the masks in the painting to show magical protection from dangerous spirits.

Use the follwing question for discussion:

1. How does Picasso's painting indicate a new direction in art?
   Possible response: Unlike most nineteenth-century artists, Picasso is not concerned here with imitating reality.

▶Critical Viewing

Possible response: The mask and the young woman share some features such as almond-shaped eyes and a sharp nose, but the mask from New Britain is recognizably shaped like a human head; whereas in Picasso's painting, the young woman's head is fragmented.

Background

Art

Show students *Le Tourangeau (The Man from Tours)* by Juan Gris, on Transparency 20 in **Fine Art Transparencies.** Use the image to help students understand the importance of multiple perspectives in both modern art and literature.

CUSTOMIZE INSTRUCTION FOR UNIVERSAL ACCESS

For Less Proficient Readers	For English Learners	For Advanced Readers
Help students understand the Historical Background by focusing on the key events of World War I and the Great Depression. Ask students to consider the historical causes and effects associated with these two events. Students may wish to record their observations in a cause-and-effect chart.	Have students discuss the events that occurred in their native cultures during this period. Ask students to interview older friends or family members about the impact of these events both on individuals and on the culture as a whole and present their findings to the class.	Have students research one improvement in science and technology during this time that affected daily life. Students should focus their research on one category of improvement–for example, medical remedies. Ask volunteers to present their findings to the class.

Background

The Attack on Pearl Harbor

On December 7, 1941, Japanese carrier planes swept in over Pearl Harbor without warning. The raid on the United States Pacific Fleet damaged or destroyed eight American battleships, including the *U.S.S. Tennessee*, the *U.S.S. West Virginia*, and the *U.S.S. Arizona*. On December 8, 1941, the United States declared war on Japan.

Background

Hitler's Power

When Hitler's power was at its height, the Axis nations controlled much of Europe, Sweden, and Spain. Switzerland remained neutral and never fought the Axis powers. In the east, Germany held Austria, Czechoslovakia, western Poland, Hungary, Romania, and Bulgaria.

Background

Japan

During this period, Japan was also undergoing a period of rapid change. After reestablishing ties with the Western world during the mid-1800s, Japan had begun a program of modernization and militarization. Japan's newly acquired military strength first became evident in 1904, when it easily defeated the Russian navy in the Russo-Japanese War.

▶ Critical Viewing

Possible response: The people standing at attention as Hitler passes and the swastika-emblazoned flags held at attention show Hitler's charismatic power.

▲ **Critical Viewing** Which details in these pictures suggest the charismatic power that Hitler exercised over the German people? Explain. **[Interpret]**

Persecution of Jews Hitler quickly molded the nation into a totalitarian state, brutally suppressing all dissent. The word *totalitarian* refers to "a state in which one party or group retains total authority under a dictator." The Nazis assumed control of every aspect of German life, including religion, schools, and the press. They burned books and destroyed works of art they judged to be "un-German," and they forced radio stations to play military music and Nazi speeches. At the same time, they began ruthlessly persecuting German Jews, stripping them of their citizenship and expelling them from government posts and teaching positions.

Other Totalitarian Regimes Hitler's government was only one of a number of totalitarian regimes to emerge during the first half of the twentieth century. In Russia, where communists had seized power in the November Revolution of 1917, a totalitarian state was established after Joseph Stalin rose to power in the early 1920s. Like Hitler, Stalin brutally suppressed all dissent, executing millions of people who resisted his policies. Another totalitarian ruler, Benito Mussolini, gained control of Italy and later became one of Hitler's chief allies. In Spain, Francisco Franco established a fascist regime after winning a bloody civil war.

The German Invasion of Poland During the Spanish Civil War (1936–1939), both the Germans and the Italians provided Franco with military support. Pablo Picasso's painting *Guernica* (see pages 964–965) is a reaction to news of a German bombing raid on the Spanish city of Guernica in 1937. Because the democratic powers did little to discourage German and Italian involvement in Spain, Hitler and Mussolini did not hesitate to engage in further acts of military aggression. On September 1, 1939, German forces invaded Poland, subduing the country in little over a month. Britain and France responded by declaring war on Germany. Another world conflict had begun.

World War II pitted the Axis Powers (led by Germany, Italy, and Japan) against the Allies (led by Britain, France, the Soviet Union, and the United States). It is important to remember, however, that France was under German Occupation from 1940 to 1944, the Soviet Union was originally on Germany's side, Japan did not join the Axis immediately, and the United States did not enter the war until late in 1941.

The Russian Campaign Only weeks before the German invasion of Poland, Hitler had signed a Nonaggression Pact with the Soviet Union. On June 22, 1941, this famous "friendship" of dictators ended as German forces staged a surprise invasion of the Soviet Union.

ENRICHMENT: History Connection

The Soviet Union

Although the Soviet Union eventually fought with the Allies, it was not a free country. In the 1920s, under Joseph Stalin, the Soviet Union underwent a rapid process of industrialization. In addition, Stalin took extreme measures designed to improve the productivity of the Soviet agricultural system. He ordered all peasants to give up their land and farm animals. The seized lands were combined into large collective farms that were run by the government. Millions of peasants resisted forced collectivization and were either executed or sent to labor camps in Siberia. In fact, it has been estimated that over ten million people lost their lives during the process of collectivization.

German forces advanced rapidly at first but could not achieve victory by the winter of 1941. Like Napoleon, Hitler would pay dearly for hurling his armies eastward. The German dictator would not be able to contend with the huge reserves of Soviet manpower or with the icy assaults of "General Winter," as historians have sometimes called the Russian winter.

The Attack on Pearl Harbor On July 27, 1940, the Japanese aligned themselves with the Germans and the Italians. At the time the Japanese officially entered the war, the United States had not become directly involved in the conflict. On December 7, 1941, however, the Japanese drew the United States into the war by launching a surprise air attack on the American naval base at Pearl Harbor in Hawaii.

The End of the War and the Beginning of the Atomic Age In May of 1945, after years of savage fighting, the Nazis surrendered to the Allies. About three months later, Japan also surrendered, after the United States had dropped atomic bombs on the Japanese cities of Hiroshima and Nagasaki. With the defeat of Japan, peace had finally arrived. Yet so had the atomic age.

The destruction caused by World War II was staggering. It is estimated that some 50 million people lost their lives as a result of the war. In addition, bombing raids reduced much of Europe and Japan to rubble, and millions of people were uprooted from their homes.

The Holocaust One of the most shocking aspects of the war was not fully discovered until the Allied forces marched into Germany. In response to Hitler's diabolical plan to exterminate the Jewish people, the Nazis had imprisoned and executed about six million Jews in concentration camps. They had also executed millions of others, including people of Slavic descent and Gypsies. This systematic slaughter of Jews and others is one of the most tragic events in human history. It has come to be known as the Holocaust, from the Greek *holokauston*, a translation of the Hebrew *'olah*, meaning "burnt sacrifice offered to God." Jews also refer to this event as the Shoah, a Hebrew word meaning "catastrophe."

▼ **Critical Viewing** This view of the Nazis' Terezin concentration camp was painted by an inmate who suffered its horrors. Does anything in the painting reveal the harsh realities of the camp? Why or why not? **[Interpret]**

View of Terezin, Hanus Weinberg, State Jewish Museum, Prague

▶Critical Viewing

Possible response: The sharp lines of the image exemplify the harshness of the camp. That no humans are depicted could symbolize the deaths that took place there.

Historical Background

Comprehension Check

1. According to Sigmund Freud, what shapes human behavior?
   Answer: Freud believed that unconscious influences coming from experiences in infancy and early childhood—not from rational thought—shape human behavior.
2. What generated unrest in Germany throughout the 1920s?
   Answer: The harsh terms of the treaty after World War I and the costly reparations caused resentment among the German people.
3. Why did Britain and France declare war on Germany in 1939?
   Answer: Britain and France declared war on Germany because Germany invaded Poland.
4. What ended the "friendship" between Germany and the Soviet Union?
   Answer: In 1941, German forces invaded the Soviet Union in spite of Germany's signing of a Nonaggression Pact with the Soviets.
5. What did the Allied forces find when they marched into Germany?
   Answer: The Allied forces found that Hitler had carried out a plan to exterminate the Jewish population and had executed over six million Jews as well as millions of others.

Critical Thinking

1. Compare and contrast an optimistic view of humanity's future with the realities of World War I. **[Compare and Contrast]**
   Possible response: The rapid advances in technology led people to believe that technological advances could solve humankind's problems and lead to a bright future. When World War I broke out, people saw eight and a half million soldiers and about thirteen million civilians killed.

continued

Continued from right column

The optimistic view of humanity's future faded quickly in light of the war.

2. How did the Great Depression help lead to the rise of Hitler? **[Analyze Causes and Effects]**
   Possible response: Difficult economic conditions in Germany added to the resentment the Germans felt after World War I. Because of this dissatisfaction, the Germans were more willing to elect political extremists to try to alleviate their problems.
3. In what ways can the conclusion that World War II might have lasted much longer if Hitler had not sent his troops to attack the Soviet Union be supported? **[Support]**
   Possible response: Hitler's troops were trapped by winter weather. Supplying those troops, took extensive manpower and transportation. Had Hitler maintained his friendship with the Soviet Union, he could have concentrated his forces against the rest of the European countries, and the war probably would have lasted much longer.

Background

Gabriela Mistral

As Gabriela Mistral stated in her Nobel address, she devoted her life to improving the position of, and education for, women and children. As a young poet and schoolteacher, Mistral wrote poems to help children learn to read. As her reputation as a poet grew, so did her status and reputation as an educator. During her career, Mistral initiated what were then progressive methods of education, which included visual aids, extracts from literature, and games in place of textbooks.

Mistral's efforts to help children extended beyond her own country. In 1938, Mistral published *Tala*, her third collection of poetry, in Buenos Aires. At the time of this publication, Spain was in civil war. Mistral donated the proceeds from her book to the orphans living in children's camps in Catalonia and in France.

When the news reached her homeland that Mistral had died, Chilean president Ibañez decreed three days of national mourning.

Literature

The modern age was one of the most turbulent and violent periods of human history. Yet it was also an era of tremendous artistic and literary achievement. Responding to the events and developments of their time and experimenting with new literary forms and approaches, modern writers from across the world created a fresh and remarkably diverse body of literature.

Worldwide Literary Connections With the advances in travel and communication, the various regions of the world became increasingly intertwined during the modern age. Consequently, the literary world became more interconnected than ever before, as writers from all countries were exposed to the literary movements and traditions of other cultures.

For the first time, writers from non-Western and less developed countries began to receive worldwide attention. The modern Indian writer Rabindranath Tagore (rə bēn′ drə nät′ tə gôr′), for example, earned a Nobel Prize in Literature. The Chilean poet Gabriela Mistral (gä brē ä′ lä mēs träl′) also won a Nobel Prize in Literature, after the Nicaraguan poet Rubén Darío (ro͞o ben′ dä rē′ ō) had drawn the attention of the literary world to Latin America. Darío not only received worldwide acclaim but also influenced a number of important European poets.

The Birth of Modernism The term *Modernism* refers to a movement or group of movements in all the arts that occurred in the late nineteenth and early twentieth centuries. Modernist writers, painters, and composers sensed

Close-up on Culture

Nobel Launches "World Literature" With a Bang!

Alfred Nobel (1833–1896), the Swedish inventor of dynamite, was also the founder of the famous Nobel Prizes. One of these, the Nobel Prize in Literature, helped launch the modern idea of "World Literature." This world-class prize confirmed that writers were part of an international fellowship of the imagination, whether they worked in Chile or Nigeria, France or Australia.

Nobel had invented dynamite to serve peaceful uses, but it was later used to kill people in wars. Not wanting to be associated with death and destruction, the Swedish inventor set up a fund in his will to endow five Nobel Prizes (more were added later). One of the original five, the Nobel Prize in Literature is awarded by the Swedish Academy. Each winner receives a gold medal, a diploma, and a sum of money—by 1996, it was more than one million dollars! Not only has the prize established a standard by which all writers can be judged equally, but it has also helped publicize individual authors and groups of authors. For example, the 2002 prize awarded to Hungarian author Imre Kertész brought renewed attention to Holocaust literature.

ENRICHMENT: Art Connection

Pablo Picasso

Pablo Picasso (1881–1973), one of the greatest painters of the twentieth century, had a long career that can be divided into several stages. Born in Malaga, Spain, Picasso demonstrated his artistic gift at an early age. After abandoning realism as a young man, he entered a phase of his career known as the Blue Period. During this period, he produced works that featured many shades of blue and evoked feelings of loneliness and despair. When this stage of his career came to an end, he began creating paintings that contained startling combinations of jagged and often distorted images. These paintings gave birth to a major artistic movement known as Cubism. The next stage of his career was marked by his use of colorful, dreamlike images. In the 1920s and 1930s, he focused on expressing his reactions to current events in his works. Finally, as his career drew to a close, he produced paintings and sculptures with a more relaxed, gentle feeling.

that dramatic changes in society—advances in transportation and communication, the growth of cities, devastating new modes of warfare—were calling into question the values and traditions of the past. In response, these artists began to question artistic traditions as well. They wanted to create works of art that expressed the radically different *modern* world in which they lived.

The first flowering of Modernism was in pre-World War I Paris and London. Paris especially was a laboratory for artistic experimentation. There, in 1906, the young Spanish painter Pablo Picasso looked to primitive art as a means of challenging Western traditions (see page 969).

▲ Critical Viewing This illustration for the bound sheet music of Stravinsky's ballet *Pétrouchka* contains Russian words because the dance was performed by the Russian Ballet. Which visual details suggest that the dance will be new and boldly imaginative? Explain. **[Interpret]**

Art That Provoked Riots If Picasso's work caused astonishment, the music of Russian-born composer Igor Stravinsky provoked riots. In 1913, the performance of his ballet piece *The Rite of Spring* at a Paris theater caused an uproar in the audience that drowned out the music. The audience was reacting to the changing rhythms and the lack of traditional harmony in a work that, like Picasso's, drew on primitive sources for inspiration.

In the field of literature, two great experimenters were the poet Guillaume Apollinaire (gē yōm′ ȧ pô lē ner′) (1880–1918) and the novelist Marcel Proust (mär sel′ pro͞ost′) (1871–1922). Apollinaire astonished readers with unexpected associations, and Proust explored the meaning of time and memory in his multivolume novel *Remembrance of Things Past* (1913–1927).

An Imagist's Marching Orders Meanwhile, across the Channel in London, a group of poets that included the American Ezra Pound were struggling to make poetry in English more colloquial and concrete. In a literary manifesto expressing the beliefs of this new Imagist movement, Pound gave twentieth-century poets their marching orders: In presenting images or clear pictures, he commanded, "Use no superfluous word, . . . Go in fear of abstractions. . . . Don't make each line stop dead at the end . . . "

The War and a Second Flowering of Modernism The unprecedented destruction during World War I finally proved—to anyone who still doubted—that a new historical age had arrived. The war forever divided what came to seem like an innocent time from a modern era whose innocence was another battlefield casualty.

Background

Igor Stravinsky

Igor Stravinsky, born June 17, 1882, near St. Petersburg, Russia, wrote in the Modernist, or Neoclassic, style. He came from a musical and theatrical family and was tutored by composer Nikolay Rimsky-Korsakov. His works were revolutionary, and his ballet *The Firebird,* which opened in Paris in 1910, made him an overnight success. His work *The Rite of Spring* was far different from the types of music and dance to which audiences were accustomed. Stravinsky was considered a major force in Modernism.

▶Critical Viewing

Possible response: The juxtaposition of the sword, the jester, and the rose indicate a theme that may be nontraditional.

Listening to Music

Play for students "European Ballet Music: from *The Rite of Spring,* Igor Stravinsky," Track 12, on **Prentice Hall Listening to Music: World Masterpieces** as an example of Stravinsky's work.

ENRICHMENT: Literature Connection

Thomas Mann

The German writer Thomas Mann (1875–1955) tried to warn people of the dangers posed by Fascism and Nazism. By doing so, he incurred the wrath of the Nazis; and when they seized control of Germany in 1933, he was forced into exile in Switzerland. After living there for five years, he moved to the United States.

Throughout the war, he continued to use his talents as both a writer and a speaker to attack the Nazi regime. Two years after the war ended, he published his despairing novel, *Doctor Faustus,* an allegorical tale that symbolically depicts the rise of Nazism. Mann moved back to Switzerland in 1952 and remained there for the last years of his life.

Background

André Breton

André Breton was born in 1896 in France. During medical school, Breton studied the writing of Sigmund Freud because of his interest in mental illness. In the early 1900s, Breton started the Surrealist movement with Philippe Soupault in their work titled *"Les Champs Magnétiques"* ("Magnetic Fields"). Breton was able to escape from France during German occupation, and in 1942 continued his Surrealist work at Yale University. He eventually returned to France and continued to write. André Breton died in Paris in 1966.

To many artists who participated in the second flowering of Modernism during the 1920s, the war was the ultimate proof of human irrationality. It seemed to verify Freud's theories about the irrational motivations of human behavior, and these theories gained in influence during the postwar period. For example, they were the basis for the literary and artistic movement called Surrealism, which viewed the unconscious as a source of inspiration. The French poet André Breton (än drā´ brə tôn´) (1896–1966), who led the movement, advocated writing quickly and without thinking. This technique would enable authors to bypass the rational mind and write directly from the unconscious.

Eliminating the Traditional Links Other great Modernists of the 1920s, while not Surrealists themselves, shared the Surrealists' tendency to remove connecting language and structures from their work—all the expositions, transitions, resolutions, and explanations that readers had come to expect. To reflect the disjointedness and irrationality of the modern world, they often

A Living Tradition

James Joyce's *Ulysses* and Homer's *Odyssey*

In searching for new techniques to record modern realities, twentieth-century writers often returned to age-old sources. Irishman James Joyce, for example, went as far back as ancient Greece. In his novel *Ulysses*, besides pioneering a stream-of-consciousness narrative that reveals characters' thoughts directly, Joyce organizes events according to the episodes of Homer's ancient epic the *Odyssey*. (Ulysses is the Roman name of that epic's hero, Odysseus.) The epic describes the ten-year homeward journey of Odysseus from the Trojan War and his reunion with his son, Telemachus, and his faithful wife, Penelope.

Joyce's book follows two characters—young Irishman Stephen Dedalus and middle-aged Jew Leopold Bloom—as they traverse Dublin on June 16, 1904. Following in Odysseus' footsteps, Bloom goes on a one-day journey to meet his spiritual son, Stephen, and reunite with his wife, Molly. His thoughts and adventures humorously parallel the Greek hero's encounters with mythological characters. The result is a detailed realistic narrative with mythological dimensions.

For example, Bloom's casual thoughts as he passes a tea-merchant's window recall the lotus-eaters, who tempt Odysseus' men to taste the sleep-inducing lotus plant and forget their homeward journey:

> . . . The far east. Lovely spot it must be: the garden of the world, big lazy leaves to float about on, cactuses, flowery meads, snaky lianas they call them. Wonder is it like that. Those Cinghalese [people of Sri Lanka] lobbing around in the sun, in *dolce far niente* [Italian for "sweet doing nothing"]. Not doing a hand's turn all day. Sleep six months out of twelve. . . .

ENRICHMENT: Psychology Connection

The Human Mind

Austrian psychiatrist Sigmund Freud (1856–1939) is the founder of psychoanalysis. Psychoanalysis, one type of psychotherapy used in psychiatry, has had great influence on child rearing, education, the cultural and social sciences, medicine, and the arts. Freud's theories of a dynamic unconscious and dreams as key to the unconscious were instrumental in influencing André Breton's Surrealism Manifesto and the subsequent Surrealist movement in literature.

Sigmund Freud believed that the human mind could be divided into three parts: the id, the ego, and the superego. The id includes the most basic human drives, such as the drive to satisfy thirst and hunger. The ego, on the other hand, connects the internal mind to the outside environment. Finally, the superego is the part of the mind that governs moral behavior.

built their work from fragments. James Joyce, for example, used a stream-of-consciousness narration to immerse readers in the flow of a character's fragmentary thoughts. Yet even as he did so, he created a new type of structure (see page 974).

Implied Themes, Elusive Realities In keeping with the uncertainties of modern life, Modernist writers tended to imply, rather than directly state, the themes of their works. This approach forced readers to draw their own conclusions. For example, at the beginning of Franz Kafka's novel *The Trial*, a man named Joseph K. (his last name is never more than an initial) wakes up one morning to find that he has been accused of a crime. Neither he nor the reader ever discovers the reason for the accusation. What is even stranger, this Austrian novelist describes the most bizarre events using prose suitable for a bland business report.

As Kafka's novel suggests, Modernists questioned the nature of reality itself. They no longer assumed that it was comprehensible, let alone comforting. In Luigi Pirandello's drama *Six Characters in Search of an Author*, for example, fictional characters that the author has discarded take over the stage.

La condition humaine (The Human Condition), 1933, René Magritte. National Gallery of Art, Washington, D.C.

▲ **Critical Viewing** Belgian artist René Magritte often painted scenes as strange as those evoked by authors like Kafka and Pirandello. Which details in this painting are strangely unreal? Why? **[Interpret]**

"'Can you describe this?'...'I can.'" The turbulent events of the first half of the twentieth century directly affected the lives of many writers. It made them both victims and witnesses, falling prey to wars and the persecutions of tyrants but also nobly recording injustices. The Spanish poet Federico García Lorca (fe dе rē′ kô gär sē′ ə lôr′ kə) was murdered by supporters of Franco during the early stages of the Spanish Civil War. The Russian poet Anna Akhmatova (ukh mät′ ə və), like many of her compatriots, suffered grievously at the hands of Stalin. In the poem *Requiem*, she laments the dictator's imprisonment of her son but also bears witness to the pain of all oppressed Russians. Likewise, her introduction to the poem could serve as a testament for all modern writers who battled injustice with their pens. In it, she describes how another woman waiting to see an imprisoned relative asks her, "Can you describe this?" She answers, "I can."

Beyond the Modern Age Although the end of World War II marks the official close of the modern age, the literary innovations and accomplishments of this era did not end in 1945. Many modern writers, including Albert Camus (ka mōō′), Gabriela Mistral, Boris Pasternak (pas′ tər nak′), and Anna Akhmatova remained productive long after the end of the war. At the same time, a new generation of talented writers arose across the globe, bringing with them fresh ideas and approaches.

▶**Critical Viewing**

Possible response: The unreal elements include the objects floating in the sky and the placement of the painting as resting on an easel. By giving viewers the impression that they are seeing a picture within a picture, Magritte hints at another world beyond the viewer's sight.

Literature of the Period

Comprehension Check

1. What caused attention to be given to authors from non-Western and less-developed countries in the early twentieth century?
Answer: Advances in transportation and travel caused the world to be more interconnected.
2. How did changes in society cause the emergence of Modernism?
Answer: Changes in society made artists question everything, including artistic tradition.
3. What did the Imagist poet Ezra Pound command others do to make poetry more concrete and colloquial?
Answer: Pound told poets to use no unnecessary words, to fear abstractions, and not to stop dead at the end of each line.
4. From what did Surrealism draw inspiration, and on whose ideas was it based?
Answer: Surrealism, influenced by Freud, drew inspiration from the unconscious.
5. Why did Modernist writers imply the themes of their works rather than state?
Answer: By implying the themes of their works, Modernist writers forced readers to draw their own conclusions.

Critical Thinking

1. Support the idea that literature from non-Western and less-developed countries was being recognized and was influencing other writers. **[Support]**
Possible response: The Indian writer Rabindranath Tagore and the Chilean poet Gabriela Mistral both won the Nobel Prize in Literature. Nicaraguan poet Rubén Darío helped draw attention to Latin America with his writing.

continued

continued from right column

2. Speculate on why Modernism took root in Europe first rather than in other parts of the world. **[Speculate]**
Possible response: The first-hand experience of Europeans with the destructiveness of war solidified the death of innocence and spawned the artistic questioning of values and traditions that became known as Modernism.
3. How did the Modernists' implied themes reflect their view of the world? **[Infer]**
Possible response: The Modernists saw the world as changing and unpredictable. By implying their themes and forcing readers to draw their own conclusions, the writers reflected the idea that there were no longer any certainties.

The Metamorphosis

Lesson Objectives

1. **To analyze and respond to literary elements**
   - Literary Analysis: Modernism
   - Connecting Literary Elements: Literature of the Fantastic
2. **To read, comprehend, analyze, and critique a short story**
   - Reading Strategy: Applying the Author's Biography
   - Reading Check Questions
   - Review and Assess Questions
   - Assessment Practice (ATE)
3. **To develop word analysis skills, fluency, and systematic vocabulary**
   - Vocabulary Development Lesson: Latin Prefix *im-*
4. **To understand and apply written and oral language conventions**
   - Spelling Strategy
   - Grammar and Style Lesson: Adverb Clauses
5. **To understand and apply appropriate writing and research strategies**
   - Writing Lesson: Essay Responding to a Critical Perspective
   - Extension Activity: Multimedia Classroom Presentation on Modernism
6. **To understand and apply listening and speaking strategies**
   - Extension Activity: Eulogy

10TH GRADE TEACHING TENTH-GRADE STUDENTS

For support in teaching tenth graders, see the Step-By-Step Teaching notes identified with this icon.

STEP-BY-STEP TEACHING GUIDE	PACING GUIDE
PRETEACH	
Motivate Students and Provide Background	
Use the Motivation activity (ATE p. 976)	5 min.
Read and discuss author and background features (SE p. 976, 978; ATE p. 976) [A]	5 min.
Introduce the Concepts	
Introduce the Literary Analysis and Reading Strategy concepts (SE/ATE p. 977) [A]	15 min.
Pronounce the vocabulary words and read their definitions (SE p. 977)	5 min.
TEACH	
Monitor Comprehension	
Informally monitor comprehension by circulating while students read [A]	50 min.
Monitor students' comprehension with the Reading Check notes (SE/ATE pp. 979, 981, 983, 985, 987, 989, 993, 995, 997, 999, 1001, 1003, 1005, 1007, 1009, 1011, 1013, 1015, 1017, 1019)	as students read
Develop vocabulary with Vocabulary notes (SE pp. 978, 985, 986, 988, 989, 990, 992, 1015; ATE p. 989)	as students read
Develop Understanding	
Develop students' understanding of Modernism with the Literary Analysis annotations (SE pp. 978, 980, 981, 982, 984, 985, 986, 987, 988, 992, 994, 995, 998, 999, 1001, 1002, 1004, 1007, 1008, 1009, 1011, 1012, 1013, 1014, 1015, 1016, 1018; ATE pp. 995) [A]	10 min.
Develop students' ability to apply the author's biography, using the Reading Strategy annotations (SE/ATE pp. 979, 983, 989, 990, 997, 998, 1005)	10 min.
ASSESS	
Assess Mastery	
Assess students' mastery of the Reading Strategy and Literary Analysis concepts by having them answer the Review and Assess questions (SE/ATE p. 1021)	20 min.
Use one or more of the print, software, or transparency Assessment Resources (ATE p. 1023) [A]	up to 45 min.
EXTEND	
Apply Understanding	
Have students complete the Vocabulary Development Lesson and the Grammar and Style Lesson (SE p. 1022) [A]	20 min.
Apply students' ability to use quotations to support a position, using the Writing Lesson (SE/ATE p. 1023) [A]	45 min.
Apply students' understanding of the selection, using one or more of the Extension Activities (SE p. 1023)	20–90 min.

[A] **ACCELERATED INSTRUCTION:** Use the strategies and activities identified with an [A].

UNIVERSAL ACCESS
- ● = Below-Level Students
- ▲ = On-Level Students
- ■ = Above-Level Students

Time and Resource Manager

Reading Level: Challenging
Average Number of Instructional Days: 5

RESOURCES		
PRINT	**TRANSPARENCIES**	**TECHNOLOGY**
• **Beyond Literature,** Media Connection: Film Adaptation, p. 45 ▲ ■		• **Interest Grabber Video,** Tape 2, Unit 8, Segment 4 ● ▲ ■
• **Selection Support Workbook:** ● ▲ ■ Literary Analysis, p. 180 Reading Strategy, p. 179 Build Vocabulary, p. 177	• **Literary Analysis and Reading Transparencies,** pp. 89 and 90 ● ▲ ■	
		• **Listening to Literature** ● ▲ ■ Audiocassettes Audio CDs
• **Literary Analysis for Enrichment,** p. 45 ■	• **Fine Art Transparencies,** Art Transparency 21 ● ▲ ■	
• **Formal Assessment:** Selection Test, pp. 161–163 ● ▲ ■ • **Open-Book Tests,** pp. 133–135 ● ▲ ■ • **Performance Assessment and Portfolio Management,** pp. 16, 29 ● ▲ ■ • PRENTICE HALL ASSESSMENT SYSTEM ● ▲ ■	• PRENTICE HALL ASSESSMENT SYSTEM ● ▲ ■ **Skills Practice Answers and Explanations on Transparencies**	• **Test Bank Software** ● ▲ ■
• **Selection Support Workbook:** ● ▲ ■ Grammar and Style, p. 178 • **Writing and Grammar,** Diamond Level ● ▲ ■ • **Extension Activities,** p. 45 ● ▲ ■	• **Daily Language Practice Transparencies** ● ▲ • **Writing Models and Graphic Organizers on Transparencies,** pp. 53–59 ● ▲ ■	• **Writing and Grammar iText CD-ROM** ● ▲ ■ *Take It to the Net* PHSchool.com

BLOCK SCHEDULING: Use one 90-minute class period to preteach the selection(s) and have students read them. Use a second 90-minute class period to assess students' mastery of skills and have them complete one of the Extension Activities.

PRETEACH

Step-by-Step Teaching Guide for pp. 976–977

Motivation

Point out to students that myths, legends, and science fiction are filled with stories of metamorphosis, or transformation. An amorous god becomes a swan; a resentful girl becomes a spider; a vain man becomes a flower. Sailors become pigs; a scientist becomes a fly. Have students describe their favorite transformation from literature or film. Point out that modern movies often use elaborate computer-generated effects to create dramatic transformations. Tell them that in the story they are about to read, Franz Kafka accomplishes a shocking transformation in his first twenty-one words.

Interest Grabber Video

As an alternative, play "'The Metamorphosis': Student Response" on Tape 2 to engage student interest.

❶ Background

About the Author

To his co-workers in the insurance business, Franz Kafka must have seemed like a thoroughly modern man. They might have described him as bright, hard-working, and ambitious. Personally, he was a humorous and charming companion. Because of the demands of his work, writing could not be given his full or even primary attention; it was something he did in the evenings after work. Nonetheless, Kafka produced a large volume of work during his short life. He published only a few pieces while still living—"The Metamorphosis" was one of them—and those only because certain avant-garde publishers actively sought him out.

Geography Note

Draw students' attention to the map on this page, and help them identify the Czech Republic. Explain that at the time of Kafka's birth, Prague was part of the Austro-Hungarian Empire, not the capital of Czechoslovakia.

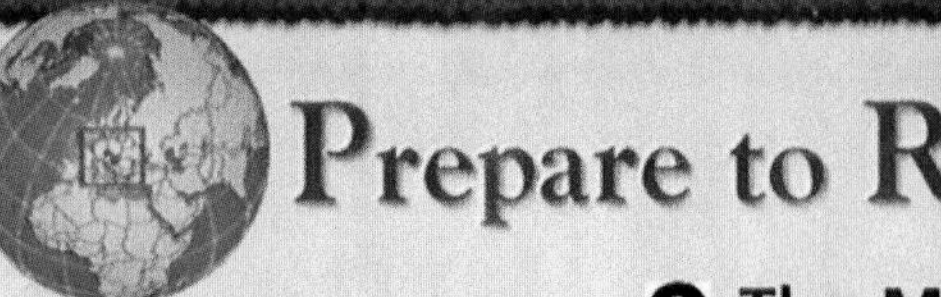

Prepare to Read

❶ The Metamorphosis

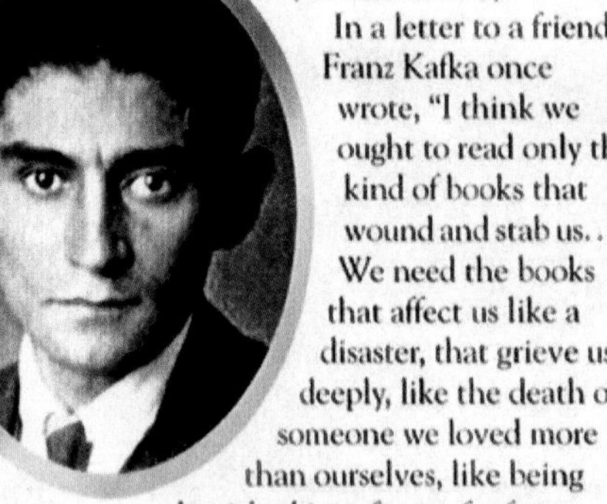

Franz Kafka (1883–1924)

In a letter to a friend, Franz Kafka once wrote, "I think we ought to read only the kind of books that wound and stab us. . . . We need the books that affect us like a disaster, that grieve us deeply, like the death of someone we loved more than ourselves, like being banished into forests far from everyone. . . . A book must be the axe for the frozen sea inside us." Although he was not discussing his own writing at the time, Kafka's description of a book's potential power probably fits his own fiction better than that of any other writer. In fact, few writers have created literary works more tragic, disturbing, and unsettling than Kafka's.

The Writer's Beginnings Born in Prague, which is now the capital of the Czech Republic, Kafka was one of four children and the only son. His father was a successful and domineering businessman, and Kafka spent a good part of his life alternately longing for his father's approval and resenting his strictness. Kafka lived with his family until he was thirty-two, and his relationship with his father, along with his feelings of familial obligation, guilt, and duty, are reflected in much of his writing. In *Letter to My Father* (1919) Kafka wrote: "My writing was all about you; all I did there, after all, was to bemoan what I could not bemoan upon your breast. It was an intentionally long-drawn-out leave-taking from you."

Kafka began writing short stories and plays at a very young age. Despite his interest in writing, however, he chose to study law at the University of Prague. After serving a legal internship, he took a job as a lawyer with an Italian insurance company. A year later, he was offered a position with the state Worker's Accident Insurance Institute, where he remained employed until 1922. Kafka's career never hindered his writing. In fact, the bureaucratic chaos that he observed in the business world actually served as an inspiration for his fiction.

Being an Outsider As a German-speaking Jew in a country inhabited mainly by Czech-speaking gentiles, Kafka knew what it meant to be an outsider. His sense of alienation is apparent in nearly all his fiction. In his early works, including "The Metamorphosis" (1915), he explored the awful consequences of ignoring one's true desires and aspirations and living according to the expectations of others. During the later stages of his career, Kafka depicted the conflict of the individual who rejects society yet truly longs for its acclaim. In his story "A Hunger Artist" (1924), for example, the protagonist attracts the attention of the public by sitting in a cage and refusing to eat. Eventually, however, people lose interest in him, and he starves to death in obscurity and despair.

Posthumous Acclaim In 1917, Kafka was diagnosed with tuberculosis. Shortly before his death in 1924, he told his friend Max Brod to destroy all his papers and personal documents, as well as his unfinished and unpublished works. Brod did not believe that Kafka had truly wanted his work destroyed, so he ignored the request. Instead, he arranged for the publication of Kafka's unfinished novels, *The Trial*, *The Castle*, and *America*, along with his personal diaries, *Letter to My Father*, and a number of unpublished short stories. The publication of these works earned Kafka critical acclaim and public acceptance, neither of which he had known during his lifetime. Kafka's reputation continued to grow, and he is now widely recognized as one of the finest and most influential writers of the twentieth century.

TEACHING RESOURCES

The following resources can be used to enrich or extend the instruction for pp. 976–977.

Motivation

Interest Grabber Videotape, Tape 2

Background

Beyond Literature, p. 45

Take It to the Net

Visit PHSchool.com for background on the author.

Literary Analysis

Literary Analysis and Reading Transparencies, Modernism, p. 89

Reading

Literary Analysis and Reading Transparencies, Applying the Author's Biography, p. 90

Selection Support: Reading Strategy, p. 179; Build Vocabulary, p. 177

BLOCK SCHEDULING: Resources marked with this symbol provide varied instruction during 90-minute blocks.

Preview

Connecting to the Literature

Imagine that when you woke up one day, your friends did not recognize you, found you repulsive, and could not understand you when you spoke. In this story, the main character experiences just such a terrible transformation.

❷ Literary Analysis

Modernism

In the late nineteenth and early twentieth centuries, many writers began turning away from the style, form, and content of nineteenth-century literature in favor of new themes and techniques. While this movement, known as **Modernism,** encompassed a vast number of smaller literary movements, most Modernist works share certain characteristics:

- They attempt to capture the realities of modern life.
- They express a sense of uncertainty and alienation.
- They leave readers to draw their own conclusions.

Consider how these and other Modernist views and techniques are at work in Kafka's story.

Connecting Literary Elements

The first paragraph of this story drops you into a world in which something impossible has happened. The presence of this imaginative element in an otherwise realistic story makes "The Metamorphosis" an example of **literature of the fantastic,** a genre that mixes imagination and reality to entertain and challenge readers. As you read, note the presence of both imaginative and realistic details, and think about the effects they create.

❸ Reading Strategy

Applying the Author's Biography

"The Metamorphosis" is not an autobiography, but **applying the author's biography**—making connections to Kafka's life—can shed light on its meaning. For example, Kafka's troubled relationship with his father probably helped him write realistically about the father and son in this story. Use a diagram like the one shown to record facts from Kafka's life that you think shed light on "The Metamorphosis."

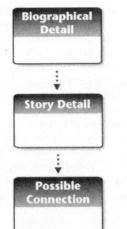

Biographical Detail → Story Detail → Possible Connection

Vocabulary Development

impracticable (im prak´ ti kə bəl) *adj.* not capable of being put into practice (p. 978)

obstinacy (äb´ stə nə sē) *n.* stubbornness (p. 985)

exuded (ig zo͞od´ id) *v.* discharged a liquid through the skin (p. 986)

rectify (rek´ tə fī) *v.* to set things right or restore balance (p. 988)

imminent (im´ ə nənt) *adj.* ready to happen at any moment (p. 989)

gyration (jī rā´ shən) *n.* circular or spiral motion (p. 990)

pallid (pal´ id) *adj.* pale (p. 992)

debacle (di bäk´ əl) *n.* overwhelming failure or defeat (p. 1015)

CUSTOMIZE INSTRUCTION FOR UNIVERSAL ACCESS

For Less Proficient Readers	For English Learners	For Advanced Readers
Because of unexpected twists in this story, students may have difficulty following the plot. Suggest that they create drawings of significant scenes in order to visualize what is happening. Later, students can assemble their sketches into a storyboard to use for review.	Organize students into pairs, and have each member of the pair take turns reading portions of the story aloud. Help clarify the meanings of any words with which they are unfamiliar.	Point out to students that this story, with its odd mixture of the ordinary and the fantastic, functions as a metaphor for life in the modern world. Have students look for details in the text that support this claim.

❷ Literary Analysis

Modernism

- Tell students that Modernism was an extremely broad and diverse movement. Although there were significant differences in their interests and approaches, all Modernists shared the desire to create literature that was new and different.
- With the class, read the three characteristics of Modernism listed. Explain that Modernists often set their characters free in a fragmented, confusing, and unpredictable world and gave them the task of making sense of it. For example, in "The Metamorphosis," a man lives in a seemingly ordinary modern world until he wakes one morning to discover that he has been transformed into an insect.
- Use the Modernism transparency in **Literary Analysis and Reading Transparencies,** p. 89, to demonstrate for students how they can recognize the elements of Modernism within a literary work.

❸ Reading Strategy

Applying the Author's Biography

- Remind students that most authors draw upon personal experiences when creating fictional worlds. Kafka was no different. Therefore, clues to the meaning of "The Metamorphosis" may be found in his biography. Emphasize that, as discussed in the biography on page 976, Kafka's relationship with his own father left him yearning for his father's approval. Ask students to take note of the relationship between father and son in the story as they read.
- Explain the use of the diagram on page 977. Encourage students to use the organizer as they read the story.

Vocabulary Development

- Pronounce each vocabulary word for students, and read the definitions as a class. Have students identify any words with which they are already familiar.

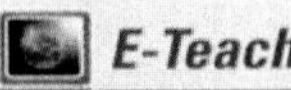

E-Teach

Visit e-Teach at PHSchool.com for teachers' essays on how to teach, with questions and answers.

TEACH

Step-by-Step Teaching Guide for pp. 978–1020

Teaching Tenth-Grade Students

10TH GRADE Remind tenth-grade students that a metamorphosis is a transformation, or change, from one form of existence to another. Have students discuss metamorphoses they have studied in science class. Then, ask students to consider the type of metamorphosis that might occur in a modern story.

❶ About the Selection

In this haunting Modernist tale, Gregor Samsa, a traveling salesman, wakes up one morning to find that he has metamorphosed into a giant insect. Both Gregor and his family struggle as they try to cope with the horror of the situation. As students read, they will realize that this story describes not only a physical transformation but also several psychological ones.

❷ Literary Analysis

Modernism

- Remind students that the Modernists wanted to discard traditional forms of literature and adopt new ways of looking at the world.
- Ask students the Literary Analysis question on p. 978: From the very first paragraph, what seems new or different about Kafka's approach to telling this story?
  Answer: Kafka challenges the logic of modern life. Clearly, a man cannot turn into an insect, yet Gregor Samsa does.

❶

THE Metamorphosis

FRANZ KAFKA *translated by* Stanley Corngold

Background

Many authors produce great writing that moves, challenges, and inspires readers. Only a few, however, make such distinctive contributions that their names become synonymous with specific literary qualities. Such is the case with Kafka. The term *kafkaesque* describes a nightmarish mood—specifically, the feeling that one is trapped in an intense, distorted world and that danger or doom is close at hand. As you read "The Metamorphosis," decide how well the adjective *kafkaesque* describes this tale, which many scholars consider one of the greatest stories of the twentieth century.

Part I

❷ When Gregor Samsa woke up one morning from unsettling dreams, he found himself changed in his bed into a monstrous vermin. He was lying on his back as hard as armor plate, and when he lifted his head a little, he saw his vaulted brown belly, sectioned by arch-shaped ribs, to whose dome the cover, about to slide off completely, could barely cling. His many legs, pitifully thin compared with the size of the rest of him, were waving helplessly before his eyes.

"What's happened to me?" he thought. It was no dream. His room, a regular human room, only a little on the small side, lay quiet between the four familiar walls. Over the table, on which an unpacked line of fabric samples was all spread out—Samsa was a traveling salesman—hung the picture which he had recently cut out of a glossy magazine and lodged in a pretty gilt frame. It showed a lady done up in a fur hat and a fur boa, sitting upright and raising up against the viewer a heavy fur muff in which her whole forearm had disappeared.

Gregor's eyes then turned to the window, and the overcast weather—he could hear raindrops hitting against the metal window ledge—completely depressed him. "How about going back to sleep for a few minutes and forgetting all this nonsense," he thought, but that was completely impracticable, since he was used to sleeping on his right side and in his present state could not get into that position. No matter

Literary Analysis
Modernism From the very first paragraph, what seems new or different about Kafka's approach to telling this story?

impracticable (im prak' ti ke bel) *adj.* not capable of being put into practice

TEACHING RESOURCES

The following resources can be used to enrich or extend the instruction for pp. 978–1020.

Literary Analysis

- **Selection Support:** Literary Analysis, p. 180
- **Literary Analysis and Reading Transparencies,** Modernism, p. 89

Reading

- **Listening to Literature Audiocassettes** ■
- **Listening to Literature Audio CDs**

Extension

- **Fine Art Transparencies,** Art Transparency 21 (Discuss with students ways in which both de Chirico's painting and Kafka's story "make strange" the familiar world. Ask students to consider the role that such "making strange" might have in a culture that no longer believes in faraway magical lands.) ■

■ **BLOCK SCHEDULING:** Resources marked with this symbol provide varied instruction during 90-minute blocks.

how hard he threw himself onto his right side, he always rocked onto his back again. He must have tried it a hundred times, closing his eyes so as not to have to see his squirming legs, and stopped only when he began to feel a slight, dull pain in his side, which he had never felt before.

"Oh God," he thought, "what a grueling job I've picked. Day in, day out—on the road. The upset of doing business is much worse than the actual business in the home office, and besides, I've got the torture of traveling, worrying about changing trains, eating miserable food at all hours, constantly seeing new faces, no relationships that last or get more intimate. To the devil with it all!" He felt a slight itching up on top of his belly; shoved himself slowly on his back closer to the bedpost, so as to be able to lift his head better; found the itchy spot, studded with small white dots which he had no idea what to make of; and wanted to touch the spot with one of his legs but immediately pulled it back, for the contact sent a cold shiver through him.

He slid back again into his original position. "This getting up so early," he thought, "makes anyone a complete idiot. Human beings
3 have to have their sleep. Other traveling salesmen live like harem women. For instance, when I go back to the hotel before lunch to write up the business I've done, these gentlemen are just having breakfast. That's all I'd have to try with my boss; I'd be fired on the spot. Anyway, who knows if that wouldn't be a very good thing for me. If I didn't hold back for my parents' sake, I would have quit long ago, I would have marched up to the boss and spoken my piece from the bottom of my heart. He would have fallen off the desk! It is funny, too, the way he sits on the desk and talks down from the heights to the employees, especially when they have to come right up close on account of the boss's being hard of hearing. Well, I haven't given up hope completely; once I've gotten the money together to pay off my parents' debt to him—that will probably take another five or six years—I'm going to do it without fail. Then I'm going to make the big break. But for the time being I'd better get up, since my train leaves at five."

And he looked over at the alarm clock, which was ticking on the chest of drawers. "God Almighty!" he thought. It was six-thirty, the hands were

Reading Strategy
Applying the Author's Biography In what ways might Kafka's career as an accident-insurance lawyer have helped him to write this scene?

4 **✓Reading Check**

Into what kind of creature has Gregor Samsa been transformed?

3 Reading Strategy

Applying the Author's Biography

- Have a volunteer read the bracketed passage on p. 979. Then, have the class discuss the frustrations of a job like Gregor's.
- Ask students to name aspects of Kafka's own job that might have involved the need to "hold back" experienced by Gregor.
  Possible response: Kafka would have been accountable to managers and clients, with whom he could not always share his true feelings.
- Ask students the Reading Strategy question on p. 979: In what ways might Kafka's career as an accident-insurance lawyer have helped him to write this scene?
  Possible response: As a lawyer dealing with workers, Kafka would have been familiar with complaints such as Gregor's. As a worker answerable to a manager, Kafka might have experienced similar frustrations himself. He probably drew on such experiences to describe Gregor's dissatisfaction.

4 ✓Reading Check

Answer: Gregor has become an insect of some sort, possibly a beetle.

CUSTOMIZE INSTRUCTION FOR UNIVERSAL ACCESS

For Special Needs Students	For Less Proficient Readers
Organize the class into reading groups of three or four students. Have them read aloud pp. 978–979, taking each paragraph in turn, as you monitor their progress. Stop the reading at the end of each paragraph to ask a comprehension question and to help students clarify any points of confusion. In particular, help students define words that might be unfamiliar, such as *vermin, gilt, boa,* and *studded.*	To help students visualize Gregor's perception of his boss's attitude toward his employees, have students pantomime the scene on p. 979. Read the description aloud, starting with the line, "It is funny, too, the way he sits on the desk…." Then, assign two students the roles of the boss and the employee, and guide them as they assume the postures described. Ask students to discuss what these postures indicate about the employer-employee relationship in Gregor's office.

5 Critical Thinking

Apply

- Read the bracketed passage aloud. Then, tell students that as an accident-insurance lawyer in an organization for workers, Kafka was sympathetic to his clients and worked hard to win claims for injured workers.
- Ask students how knowing this information about Kafka changes the way they understand this passage.
  Answer: Knowing this information reveals Kafka's tongue-in-cheek attitude. He is poking fun at himself and people in his business.

6 ▶Critical Viewing

Answer: The image of the jangling alarm clock reflects the frantic atmosphere in which Gregor is immersed. He cannot get up, and he is late for work. People are going to be checking on him, and he does not know what to do or what to tell them.

7 Literary Analysis

Modernism

- Review with students the characteristics of Modernist works listed on p. 977. Emphasize that alienation is a key Modernist theme.
- Read aloud the bracketed passage. Then, ask students the Literary Analysis question on p. 980: In what ways does the change in Gregor's voice suggest the Modernist theme of alienation?
  Answer: Gregor can no longer communicate with his family because his voice has become unintelligible. Gregor can still understand what his family is saying, however.
- Have students identify other details in the conversation that suggest alienation or isolation.
  Answer: Gregor is surprised by his mother's soft voice; he is surprised by his own voice; he speaks briefly because he cannot explain in detail; Gregor's failure to respond incites his father's anger.

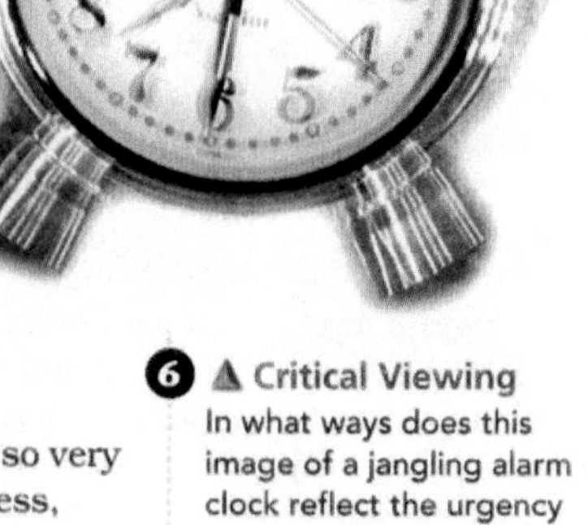

quietly moving forward, it was actually past the half-hour, it was already nearly a quarter to. Could it be that the alarm hadn't gone off? You could see from the bed that it was set correctly for four o'clock; it certainly had gone off, too. Yes, but was it possible to sleep quietly through a ringing that made the furniture shake? Well, he certainly hadn't slept quietly, but probably all the more soundly for that. But what should he do now? The next train left at seven o'clock; to make it, he would have to hurry like a madman, and the line of samples wasn't packed yet, and he himself didn't feel especially fresh and ready to march around. And even if he did make the train, he could not avoid getting it from the boss, because the messenger boy had been waiting at the five-o'clock train and would have long ago reported his not showing up. He was a tool of the boss, without brains or backbone. What if he were to say he was sick? But that would be extremely embarrassing and suspicious because during his five years with the firm Gregor had not been sick even once. The boss would be sure to come with the health-insurance doctor, blame his parents for their lazy
5 son, and cut off all excuses by quoting the health-insurance doctor, for whom the world consisted of people who were completely healthy but afraid to work. And, besides, in this case would he be so very wrong? In fact, Gregor felt fine, with the exception of his drowsiness, which was really unnecessary after sleeping so late, and he even had a ravenous appetite.

Just as he was thinking all this over at top speed, without being able to decide to get out of bed—the alarm clock had just struck a quarter to seven—he heard a cautious knocking at the door next to the head of his bed. "Gregor," someone called—it was his mother—"it's a quarter to seven. Didn't you want to catch the train?" What a soft voice! Gregor was shocked to hear his own voice answering, unmistakably his own voice, true, but in which, as if from below, an insistent distressed chirping intruded, which left the clarity of his words intact only for a moment really, before so badly garbling them as they carried that no one could be sure if he had heard right. Gregor had wanted to answer in detail and to explain everything, but, given the circumstances, con-
7 fined himself to saying, "Yes, yes, thanks, Mother, I'm just getting up." The wooden door must have prevented the change in Gregor's voice from being noticed outside, because his mother was satisfied with this explanation and shuffled off. But their little exchange had made the rest of the family aware that, contrary to expectations, Gregor was still in the house, and already his father was knocking on one of the side doors, feebly but with his fist. "Gregor, Gregor," he called, "what's going on?" And after a little while he called again in a deeper, warning voice, "Gregor! Gregor!" At the other side door, however, his sister moaned gently, "Gregor? Is something the matter with you? Do you want anything?" Toward both sides Gregor answered: "I'm all ready," and made

6 ▲ Critical Viewing In what ways does this image of a jangling alarm clock reflect the urgency of Gregor's situation? **[Connect]**

Literary Analysis
Modernism In what ways does the change in Gregor's voice suggest the Modernist theme of alienation?

ENRICHMENT: Biography Connection

Kafka's Familial Relationships

The Samsas' complicated familial relationships reflect the complexity of Kafka's own family life. Kafka himself could never really resolve his ambivalent feelings about his own family. In many of his stories, a son is destroyed by his rebellion against his family's wishes; in others, a son lovingly sacrifices himself for the family's good. In discussing how Kafka's relationship with his family influenced his writing, the critic Michael Carrouges wrote: "His art flows out of the conflict with his father, it manifests that conflict and re-creates it all over again.... If Kafka's short stories and novels are reread in the light of this perspective, one will see that apart from any other significant aspects, they conceal with them first of all a significant familial and, more especially, a paternal orientation that is central to them...."

an effort, by meticulous pronunciation and by inserting long pauses between individual words, to eliminate everything from his voice that might betray him. His father went back to his breakfast, but his sister whispered, "Gregor, open up, I'm pleading with you." But Gregor had absolutely no intention of opening the door and complimented himself instead on the precaution he had adopted from his business trips, of locking all the doors during the night even at home.

First of all he wanted to get up quietly, without any excitement; get dressed; and the main thing, have breakfast, and only then think about what to do next, for he saw clearly that in bed he would never think things through to a rational conclusion. He remembered how even in the past he had often felt some kind of slight pain, possibly caused by lying in an uncomfortable position, which, when he got up, turned out to be purely imaginary, and he was eager to see how today's fantasy would gradually fade away. That the change in his voice was nothing more than the first sign of a bad cold, an occupational ailment of the traveling salesman, he had no doubt in the least.

8 It was very easy to throw off the cover; all he had to do was puff himself up a little, and it fell off by itself. But after this, things got difficult, especially since he was so unusually broad. He would have needed hands and arms to lift himself up, but instead of that he had only his numerous little legs, which were in every different kind of perpetual motion and which, besides, he could not control. If he wanted to bend one, the first thing that happened was that it stretched itself out; and if he finally succeeded in getting this leg to do what he wanted, all the others in the meantime, as if set free, began to work in the most intensely painful agitation. "Just don't stay in bed being useless," Gregor said to himself.

First he tried to get out of bed with the lower part of his body, but this lower part—which by the way he had not seen yet and which he could not form a clear picture of—proved too difficult to budge; it was taking so long; and when finally, almost out of his mind, he lunged forward with all his force, without caring, he had picked the wrong direction and slammed himself violently against the lower bedpost, and the searing pain he felt taught him that exactly the lower part of his body was, for the moment anyway, the most sensitive.

He therefore tried to get the upper part of his body out of bed first and warily turned his head toward the edge of the bed. This worked easily, and in spite of its width and weight, the mass of his body finally followed, slowly, the movement of his head. But when at last he stuck his head over the edge of the bed into the air, he got too scared to continue any further, since if he finally let himself fall in this position, it would be a miracle if he didn't injure his head. And just now he had better not for the life of him lose consciousness; he would rather stay in bed.

9 But when, once again, after the same exertion, he lay in his original position, sighing, and again watched his little legs struggling, if possible more fiercely, with each other and saw no way of bringing peace and

Literary Analysis
Modernism and Literature of the Fantastic In what ways does this scene combine realistic details with fantastic ones in order to express a Modernist sense of alienation?

10  **Reading Check**

What does each member of Gregor's family urge him to do?

CUSTOMIZE INSTRUCTION FOR UNIVERSAL ACCESS

For Less Proficient Readers	For Advanced Readers
Read the passage on p. 980 that describes the scene between Gregor's mother, father, and sister as they talk to Gregor through different doors. Tell students that while the situation is shocking and disturbing, it also has a comic quality that Kafka fully intended. To help students visualize what is happening, have volunteers act out the scene.	Tell students that many other literary works feature incredible transformations. One of the most famous examples is *The Strange Case of Dr. Jekyll and Mr. Hyde* by Robert Louis Stevenson. Ask students to read Stevenson's work and compare it with "The Metamorphosis." Then, ask students to create presentations in which they discuss the similarities and differences between the characters and between their strange transformations.

8 Literary Analysis

Modernism and Literature of the Fantastic

- Tell students that Gregor, despite knowing that he has turned into an insect, is determined to go to work. Ask students why Gregor is in denial of his situation.
  Answer: Gregor is in denial because he probably believes that carrying on his daily routine will restore normalcy.
- Ask students the Literary Analysis question on p. 981: In what ways does this scene combine realistic details with fantastic ones in order to express a Modernist sense of alienation?
  Answer: Despite his transformation into an insect, Gregor remains somewhat calm, continues to have rational thoughts, and attempts to complete "normal" activities. This disconnection between Gregor's physical and mental reality creates alienation: He still has human thoughts and feelings, yet he is unwelcome in the human realm.

9 Critical Thinking

Deduce

- Read aloud the bracketed passage on pp. 981–982. Ask: Why can't Gregor control his legs?
  Answer: Gregor's insect body is still unfamiliar to him. The legs work differently from his human legs, so he will have to learn how to use them.
- Ask: How long do you think it will take Gregor to master his new legs?
  Possible response: He will learn to walk quickly once he is on his feet, the usual position for an insect, rather than lying on his back.

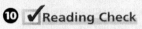

10 ✓Reading Check

Answer: Gregor's mother urges him to get up and go to work; his father demands an explanation; his sister urges him to open the door.

⓫ Literary Analysis

Modernism

- Review with students the second bulleted characteristic of Modernist works listed on p. 977. Emphasize the Modernist themes of uncertainty and alienation.
- Read aloud the bracketed passage. Then, ask students the Literary Analysis question on p. 982: In what ways does the view from Gregor's window reflect a Modernist perception of twentieth-century life?
  Answer: The fog reflects a Modernist view by concealing the other side of the street, creating, for Gregor, a sense of isolation and disallowing a feeling of well-being.
- Ask students to discuss how Gregor's comment about the fog and the time of day reflects a Modernist view.
  Answer: Gregor notes a discrepancy between what is and what should be. In his mind, the fog should have burned off, yet it remains. This disparity indicates Gregor's alienation from reality and reflects the Modernist concern with uncertainty.

⓬ Background

Art

Walking Man, by Rick Amor

Born in Frankston, Victoria, Australia, a suburb of Melbourne, Rick Amor (b. 1948) is an award-winning painter, printmaker, and sculptor. In 1999, the Australia War Memorial appointed Amor Official War Artist to document Australia's involvement in East Timor.

Use the following activity to stimulate discussion:

- Have students list adjectives they would use to describe the feelings and movement conveyed by this figure.
  Possible response: Adjectives such as *defeated* and *sad* describe the feelings conveyed, and adjectives such as *trudging* and *slouching* describe the movement.
- Then, ask students to use the adjectives they have listed in brief stories about the man depicted.

continued

order into this mindless motion, he again told himself that it was impossible for him to stay in bed and that the most rational thing was to make any sacrifice for even the smallest hope of freeing himself from the bed. But at the same time he did not forget to remind himself occasionally that thinking things over calmly—indeed, as calmly as possible—was much better than jumping to desperate decisions. At such moments he fixed his eyes as sharply as possible on the window, but unfortunately there was little confidence and cheer to be gotten from the view of the morning fog, which shrouded even the other side of ⓫ the narrow street. "Seven o'clock already," he said to himself as the alarm clock struck again, "seven o'clock already and still such a fog." And for a little while he lay quietly, breathing shallowly, as if expecting, perhaps, from the complete silence the return of things to the way they really and naturally were.

But then he said to himself, "Before it strikes a quarter past seven, I must be completely out of bed without fail. Anyway, by that time someone from the firm will be here to find out where I am, since the office opens before seven." And now he started rocking the complete length of his body out of the bed with a smooth rhythm. If he let himself topple out of bed in this way, his head, which on falling he planned to lift up sharply, would presumably remain unharmed. His back seemed to be hard; nothing was likely to happen to it when it fell onto the carpet. His biggest misgiving came from his concern about the loud crash that was bound to occur and would probably create, if not terror, at least anxiety behind all the doors. But that would have to be risked.

When Gregor's body already projected halfway out of bed—the new method was more of a game than a struggle, he only had to keep on rocking and jerking himself along—he thought how simple everything would be if he could get some help. Two strong persons—he thought of his father and the maid—would have been completely sufficient; they would only have had to shove their arms under his arched back, in this way scoop him off the bed, bend down with their burden, and then just be careful and patient while he managed to swing himself down onto the floor, where his little legs would hopefully acquire some purpose. Well, leaving out the fact that the doors were locked, should he really call for help? In spite of all his miseries, he could not repress a smile at this thought.

He was already so far along that when he rocked more strongly he could hardly keep his balance, and very soon he would have to commit himself, because in five minutes it would be a quarter past seven—

Literary Analysis
Modernism In what ways does the view from Gregor's window reflect a Modernist perception of twentieth-century life?

⓭ ▼ **Critical Viewing**
Which elements of this sculpture of a businessman seem to express an attitude toward work that is similar to Gregor's? Explain. **[Analyze]**

⓬

Walking Man, bronze statue 150 x 60 x 133 cm, Rick Amor, Niagara Galleries

continued from left column

⓭ ▶ Critical Viewing

Possible response: The man's shoulders are slouched, his head is bent, and he walks with resignation but determination. As a salesman, Gregor shared these feelings, knowing he had to work, but dreading every day of it.

when the doorbell rang. "It's someone from the firm," he said to himself and almost froze, while his little legs only danced more quickly. For a moment everything remained quiet. "They're not going to answer," Gregor said to himself, captivated by some senseless hope. But then, of course, the maid went to the door as usual with her firm stride and opened up. Gregor only had to hear the visitor's first word of greeting to know who it was—the office manager himself. Why was only Gregor condemned to work for a firm where at the slightest omission they immediately suspected the worst? Were all employees louts without exception, wasn't there a single loyal, dedicated worker among them who, when he had not fully utilized a few hours of the morning for the firm, was driven
14 half-mad by pangs of conscience and was actually unable to get out of bed? Really, wouldn't it have been enough to send one of the apprentices to find out—if this prying were absolutely necessary—did the manager himself have to come, and did the whole innocent family have to be shown in this way that the investigation of this suspicious affair could be entrusted only to the intellect of the manager? And more as a result of the excitement produced in Gregor by these thoughts than as a result of any real decision, he swung himself out of bed with all his might. There was a loud thump, but it was not a real crash. The fall was broken a little by the carpet, and Gregor's back was more elastic than he had thought, which explained the not very noticeable muffled sound. Only he had not held his head carefully enough and hit it; he turned it and rubbed it on the carpet in anger and pain.

"Something fell in there," said the manager in the room on the left. Gregor tried to imagine whether something like what had happened to him today could one day happen even to the manager; you really had to grant the possibility. But, as if in rude reply to this question, the manager took a few decisive steps in the next room and made his patent leather boots creak. From the room on the right his sister whispered, to inform Gregor, "Gregor, the manager is here." "I know," Gregor said to himself; but he did not dare raise his voice enough for his sister to hear.

"Gregor," his father now said from the room on the left, "the manager has come and wants to be informed why you didn't catch the early train. We don't know what we should say to him. Besides, he wants to speak to you personally. So please open the door. He will certainly be so kind as to excuse the disorder of the room." "Good morning, Mr. Samsa," the manager called in a friendly voice. "There's something the matter with him," his mother said to the manager while his father was still at the door, talking. "Believe me, sir, there's something the matter with him. Otherwise how would Gregor have missed a train? That boy has nothing on his mind but the business. It's almost begun to rile me that he never goes out nights. He's been back in the city for eight days now, but every night he's been home. He sits there with us at the table, quietly reading the paper or studying timetables. It's already a distraction for him when he's busy working with his fretsaw.[1] For instance, in

1. **fretsaw** (fret' sô) *n.* saw with a long, narrow, fine-toothed blade.

Reading Strategy
Applying the Author's Biography Do you think Gregor's anger toward his employers may reflect Kafka's work experiences? Explain?

 **Reading Check**

Who arrives to speak with Gregor?

14 Reading Strategy

Applying the Author's Biography

- Have a volunteer read the bracketed passage aloud.
- Then, ask students the Reading Strategy question on p. 983: Do you think Gregor's anger toward his employers may reflect Kafka's work experiences? Explain.
  Answer: Gregor's anger may reflect Kafka's experiences. The description of Gregor's anger is realistic and detailed, indicating that it may have been based on personal experience or on attitudes Kafka encountered among workers in his job as an accident-insurance lawyer.

Monitor Progress Display the diagram from p. 977, and have students complete it with information from pp. 982–983.

Reteach You may wish to use the Applying the Author's Biography transparency in **Literary Analysis and Reading Transparencies,** p. 90, to review the strategy.

15 

Reading Check

Answer: The office manager arrives to speak with Gregor.

CUSTOMIZE INSTRUCTION FOR UNIVERSAL ACCESS

For Special Needs Students	For Less Proficient Readers
Kafka sometimes uses long sentence structures with multiple punctuation marks. The bracketed passage on p. 983 contains several examples. Work with students to break apart these complex sentences by identifying the main subjects and verbs. Then, have students explain how the other groups of words in the sentences relate to the main subjects and verbs.	Read aloud the first full paragraph on p. 983. Ask students to consider what they know about the manager from the details Kafka provides. For example, have students discuss what can they tell about the manager's personality from the fact that he walks with "decisive steps." Have students look for other details about the manager and discuss what they can tell about him from these clues.

16 Literary Analysis

Modernism

- Read aloud the bracketed passage on pp. 983–984. Ask students to compare Gregor's attitude toward his manager with Mr. and Mrs. Samsa's attitude toward the manager.
  Answer: Gregor and his parents seem to share the same attitude of distrust and fear.
- Then, ask students the Literary Analysis question on p. 984: Why do Gregor's parents try to impress the office manager with a sense of Gregor's individuality?
  Answer: Gregor's parents want the manager to know Gregor personally and not judge him as if he were like every other employee. They are attempting to appeal to the manager's "human" side so he will not reprimand or fire Gregor.

Monitor Progress Point out that Gregor and his family have been allies. They live together and help one another. Ask: In what sense does the manager's arrival express the Modernist theme of alienation?
Answer: The manager is part of the world outside the family. He is an alien and antagonistic presence.

17 Critical Viewing

Possible response: The image of this isolated figure conveys a mood of loneliness.

16 the span of two or three evenings he carved a little frame. You'll be amazed how pretty it is; it's hanging inside his room. You'll see it right away when Gregor opens the door. You know, I'm glad that you've come, sir. We would never have gotten Gregor to open the door by ourselves; he's so stubborn. And there's certainly something wrong with him, even though he said this morning there wasn't." "I'm coming right away," said Gregor slowly and deliberately, not moving in order not to miss a word of the conversation. "I haven't any other explanation myself," said the manager. "I hope it's nothing serious. On the other hand, I must say that we businessmen—fortunately or unfortunately, whichever you prefer—very often simply have to overcome a slight indisposition[2] for business reasons." "So can the manager come in now?" asked his father, impatient, and knocked on the door again. "No," said Gregor. In the room on the left there was an embarrassing silence; in the room on the right his sister began to sob.

Literary Analysis
Modernism Why do Gregor's parents try to impress the office manager with a sense of Gregor's individuality?

Why didn't his sister go in to the others? She had probably just got out of bed and not even started to get dressed. Then what was she crying about? Because he didn't get up and didn't let the manager in, because he was in danger of losing his job, and because then the boss would start hounding his parents about the old debts? For the time being, certainly, her worries were unnecessary. Gregor was still here and hadn't the slightest intention of letting the family down. True, at the moment he was lying on the carpet, and no one knowing his condition could seriously have expected him to let the manager in. But just because of this slight discourtesy, for which an appropriate excuse would easily be found later on, Gregor could not simply be dismissed. And to Gregor it seemed much more sensible to leave him alone now than to bother him with crying and persuasion. But it was just the uncertainty that was tormenting the others and excused their behavior.

"Mr. Samsa," the manager now called, raising his voice, "what's the matter? You barricade yourself in your room, answer only 'yes' and 'no,' cause your parents serious, unnecessary worry, and you neglect—I mention this only in passing—your duties to the firm in a really shocking manner. I am speaking here in the name of your par-

17 **Critical Viewing** What mood do you think this image of a traveling salesman conveys? Explain. **[Interpret]**

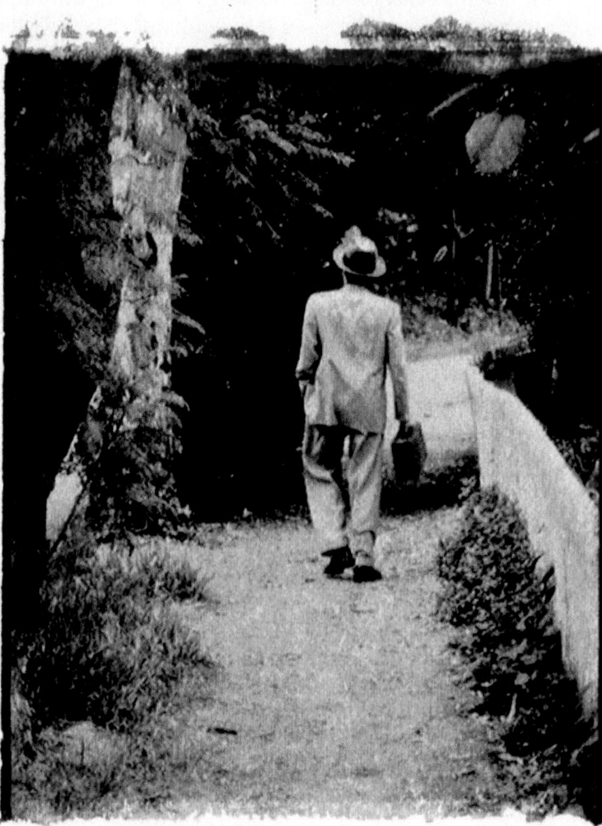

2. **indisposition** (in' dis pə zish' ən) *n.* slight illness.

ENRICHMENT: Literature Connection

Kafka's Influence in America

In discussing Kafka's influence on twentieth-century American writers, the critic Leo Hamalian notes:

> Kafka became something of a vogue among intellectuals and the avant-garde in America shortly after the end of World War II, but those special states of mind conveyed in his writing did not attract a wider audience until the 1950s, that age of anxiety in which the events of the McCarthy era overtook fiction. As Americans began to discover that mass society had neuroses of its own, they consumed in paperback and anthology the man who prophesied the ailments of our age....

ents and of your employer and ask you in all seriousness for an immediate, clear explanation. I'm amazed, amazed. I thought I knew you to be a quiet, reasonable person, and now you suddenly seem to want to start strutting about, flaunting strange whims. The head of the firm did suggest to me this morning a possible explanation for your tardiness—it concerned the cash payments recently entrusted to you—but really, I practically gave my word of honor that this explanation could not be right. But now, seeing your incomprehensible obstinacy, I am about to lose even the slightest desire to stick up for you in any way at all. And your job is not the most secure. Originally I intended to tell you all this in private, but since you make me waste my time here for nothing, I don't see why your parents shouldn't hear too. Your performance of late has been very unsatisfactory; I know it is not the best season for doing business, we all recognize that; but a season for not doing any business, there is no such thing, Mr. Samsa, such a thing cannot be tolerated."

18

"But sir," cried Gregor, beside himself, in his excitement forgetting everything else, "I'm just opening up, in a minute. A slight indisposition, a dizzy spell, prevented me from getting up. I'm still in bed. But I already feel fine again. I'm just getting out of bed. Just be patient for a minute! I'm not as well as I thought yet. But really I'm fine. How something like this could just take a person by surprise! Only last night I was fine, my parents can tell you, or wait, last night I already had a slight premonition.[3] They must have been able to tell by looking at me. Why didn't I report it to the office! But you always think that you'll get over a sickness without staying home. Sir! Spare my parents! There's no basis for any of the accusations that you're making against me now; no one has ever said a word to me about them. Perhaps you haven't seen the last orders I sent in. Anyway, I'm still going on the road with the eight o'clock train; these few hours of rest have done me good. Don't let me keep you, sir. I'll be at the office myself right away, and be so kind as to tell them this, and give my respects to the head of the firm."

And while Gregor hastily blurted all this out, hardly knowing what he was saying, he had easily approached the chest of drawers, probably as a result of the practice he had already gotten in bed, and now he tried to raise himself up against it. He actually intended to open the door, actually present himself and speak to the manager; he was eager to find out what the others, who were now so anxious to see him, would say at the sight of him. If they were shocked, then Gregor had no further responsibility and could be calm. But if they took everything calmly, then he, too, had no reason to get excited and could, if he hurried, actually be at the station by eight o'clock. At first he slid off the polished chest of drawers a few times, but at last, giving himself a final push, he stood upright; he no longer paid any attention to the pains in his abdomen, no matter how much they were burning. Now he let himself fall against the back of a nearby chair, clinging to its slats with his

19

obstinacy (äb′ stə nə sē) *n.* stubbornness

Literary Analysis
Modernism According to the office manager, how is Gregor's odd behavior alienating him from daily life?

Literary Analysis
Modernism In opening the door and showing himself, what does Gregor hope to learn about his own state of mind?

20 **✓Reading Check**
What is the warning the office manager gives Gregor about his job?

3. **premonition** (prēm′ ə nish′ ən) *n.* a warning in advance of an event.

CUSTOMIZE INSTRUCTION FOR UNIVERSAL ACCESS

For English Learners	For Advanced Readers
Point out the word *obstinacy* on p. 985, and have students read aloud the definition in the margin. Then, ask a volunteer to read the following sentence aloud, substituting the word *stubbornness* for the word *obstinacy*: "But now, seeing your incomprehensible obstinacy, I am about to lose even the slightest desire to stick up for you in any way at all." Tell students that they can use this substitution strategy to help them remember the meanings of unfamiliar words.	Tell students that the German writer Thomas Mann observed the following of those who read Kafka: "They all swear by the name of the great invalid, thanks to whose madness they no longer need to be mad." Organize students into groups, and have them analyze the quote, discussing Mann's use of the words *invalid* and *madness*. Then, have each group present and defend their analysis in a panel discussion.

18 Literary Analysis
Modernism

- Remind students that Modernist characters are usually isolated, alienated figures. Discuss the office manager's behavior. Ask: Does he seem to be an appropriate character for a Modernist story? Why or why not?
  Answer: The manager is both alienated and alienating. Because he represents the outside world, the manager is alienated from the Samsa family. His lack of concern for Gregor's condition and his unreasonable response alienate Gregor and Mr. and Mrs. Samsa.
- Read aloud the bracketed passage. Ask students the first Literary Analysis question on p. 985: According to the office manager, how is Gregor's odd behavior alienating him from daily life?
  Answer: According to the manager, Gregor is becoming proud and stubborn, which prevents him from functioning as a member of modern society.

19 Literary Analysis
Modernism

- Read the bracketed passage aloud. Point out that Gregor is now eager to let the others see him. Ask students: How does this attitude demonstrate Gregor's struggle against feelings of alienation?
  Answer: Gregor's eagerness to be seen demonstrates his desire to make contact and be accepted by his family.
- Then, ask students the second Literary Analysis question on p. 985: In opening the door and showing himself, what does Gregor hope to learn about his own state of mind?
  Answer: Gregor wants to know whether he really has turned into an insect or is imagining it. If the others are shocked, Gregor will know that the transformation is real but that he is not responsible for it. If the others are calm, Gregor will know that the transformation is not real, and he will resume normal activities.

20 ✓Reading Check

Answer: The office manager warns Gregor to get up, get to work, stop being stubborn, and improve his sales performance.

21 ▶Critical Viewing

Possible response: Yes; the performer playing Gregor has assumed an awkward physical posture to suggest a physical transformation. The walls are extremely close to Gregor, emphasizing his isolation, and the family and the manager listening in on him with confused expressions reveal their uncertainty.

22 Literary Analysis

Modernism

- Ask students to identify a phrase in the bracketed passage on p. 986 that indicates that Gregor's confidence in the doctor and the locksmith is based on an emotional need to believe in authority and expertise.
  Possible response: The phrase "felt integrated into human society once again" reveals Gregor's confidence in authority and expertise.
- Ask students the Literary Analysis question on p. 986: In what ways might Gregor's confidence in the locksmith and the doctor reflect society's misplaced faith in both technology and medicine?
  Answer: Gregor does not focus on his dire situation, but instead assumes that the "experts" will be able to solve all problems. This attitude reflects society's reliance on medicine and technology for quick and easy solutions.

little legs. But by doing this he had gotten control of himself and fell silent, since he could now listen to what the manager was saying.

"Did you understand a word?" the manager was asking his parents. "He isn't trying to make fools of us, is he?" "My God," cried his mother, already in tears, "maybe he's seriously ill, and here we are, torturing him. Grete! Grete!" she then cried. "Mother?" called his sister from the other side. They communicated by way of Gregor's room. "Go to the doctor's immediately. Gregor is sick. Hurry, get the doctor. Did you just hear Gregor talking?" "That was the voice of an animal," said the manager, in a tone conspicuously soft compared with the mother's yelling. "Anna!" "Anna!" the father called through the foyer into the kitchen, clapping his hands, "get a locksmith right away!" And already the two girls were running with rustling skirts through the foyer—how could his sister have gotten dressed so quickly?—and tearing open the door to the apartment. The door could not be heard slamming; they had probably left it open, as is the custom in homes where a great misfortune has occurred.

But Gregor had become much calmer. It was true that they no longer understood his words, though they had seemed clear enough to him, clearer than before, probably because his ear had grown accustomed to them. But still, the others now believed that there was something the matter with him and were ready to help him. The assurance and confidence with which the first measures had been taken did him good. He
22 felt integrated into human society once again and hoped for marvelous, amazing feats from both the doctor and the locksmith, without really distinguishing sharply between them. In order to make his voice as clear as possible for the crucial discussions that were approaching, he cleared his throat a little—taking pains, of course, to do so in a very muffled manner, since this noise, too, might sound different from human coughing, a thing he no longer trusted himself to decide. In the next room, meanwhile, everything had become completely still. Perhaps his parents were sitting at the table with the manager, whispering; perhaps they were all leaning against the door listening.

Gregor slowly lugged himself toward the door, pushing the chair in front of him, then let go of it, threw himself against the door, held himself upright against it—the pads on the bottom of his little legs exuded a little sticky substance—and for a moment rested there from the exertion. But then he got started turning the key in the lock with his mouth. Unfortunately it seemed that he had no real teeth—what was he supposed to grip the key with?—but in compensation his jaws, of course, were very strong; with their help he actually got the key moving and paid no attention to the fact that he was undoubtedly hurting himself in some way, for a brown liquid came out of his mouth, flowed over the key, and dripped onto the floor. "Listen," said the manager in the next room, "he's turning the key." This was great encouragement to Gregor; but everyone should have cheered him on, his father and mother too. "Go, Gregor," they should have called, "keep going, at that lock, harder, harder!" And in the delusion that they were all following his efforts with suspense, he clamped his jaws madly on the key with all the strength he could muster.

21 Critical Viewing ▶ Does this image from a dramatic adaptation of "The Metamorphosis" effectively capture both Gregor's physical transformation and his social alienation? Explain. **[Evaluate]**

Literary Analysis
Modernism In what ways might Gregor's confidence in the locksmith and the doctor reflect society's misplaced faith in both technology and medicine?

exuded (ig zood′ id) *v.* discharged a liquid through the skin

ENRICHMENT: Linguistics Connection

Kafkaesque

When a person has exhibited and achieved notoriety for special characteristics, his or her name is sometimes associated with and used as an adjective for those characteristics. The adjective might end with *-esque,* a suffix meaning "in the style of" or "like." For example, the word *Jordanesque* might be used to describe special skills or achievements related to the basketball star Michael Jordan. Franz Kafka is so well known for his novels and stories about fantastic, surreal dreams and looming danger that the term *Kafkaesque* is often used to describe works or situations with the same qualities.

23

Depending on the progress of the key, he danced around the lock; holding himself upright only by his mouth, he clung to the key, as the situation demanded, or pressed it down again with the whole weight of his body. The clearer click of the lock as it finally snapped back literally woke Gregor up. With a sigh of relief he said to himself, "So I didn't need the locksmith after all," and laid his head down on the handle in order to open wide one wing of the double doors.

Since he had to use this method of opening the door, it was really opened very wide while he himself was still invisible. He first had to edge slowly around the one wing of the door, and do so very carefully if he was not to fall flat on his back just before entering. He was still busy with this difficult maneuver and had no time to pay attention to anything else when he heard the manager burst out with a loud "Oh!"—it sounded like a rush of wind—and now he could see him, standing closest to the door, his hand pressed over his open mouth, slowly backing away, as if repulsed by an invisible, unrelenting force. His mother—in spite of the manager's presence she stood with her hair still unbraided from the night, sticking out in all directions—first looked at his father with her hands clasped, then took two steps toward Gregor, and sank
24 down in the midst of her skirts spreading out around her, her face completely hidden on her breast. With a hostile expression his father clenched his fist, as if to drive Gregor back into his room, then looked

Literary Analysis
Modernism How do his parents' reactions to seeing Gregor underscore key Modernist ideas?

25 ✓**Reading Check**
What does Gregor finally succeed in doing after great effort?

23 Background

Metamorphosis

Steven Berkoff's dramatic adaptation of Kafka's story was first produced in 1969 in London. This scene from *Metamorphosis* is from the 1989 Broadway production starring Mikhail Baryshnikov. Baryshnikov earned a Tony nomination and a Drama Critics Award for his performance as Gregor.

24 Literary Analysis

Modernism

- Ask students to imagine for a moment that they have been transformed into monstrous creatures. Ask them how they might feel if friends and family failed to recognize them and even recoiled in shock.
  Possible response: Students may say that they would react with hurt, confusion, or anger.
- Explain to students that these reactions are central to the idea of alienation, a condition in which one fails to recognize others or to be acknowledged by them, precisely when one expects or relies on mutual acknowledgement.
- Read aloud the bracketed passage on pp. 986–987.
- Ask students the Literary Analysis question on p. 987: How do his parents' reactions to seeing Gregor underscore key Modernist ideas?
  Answer: Gregor's parents' reactions reflect uncertainty and alienation. Mrs. Samsa collapses in despair. Mr. Samsa is angry and then begins to sob.

25 

Answer: Gregor gets the door open.

CUSTOMIZE INSTRUCTION FOR UNIVERSAL ACCESS

For English Learners	For Gifted/Talented Students
Have students look at the photograph on this page and note key details that help them understand the story. Students might point out the narrow room that closes in on Gregor, the family and the manager listening at both sides, the confused look on Gregor's face, and the overall gloomy mood. Tell students that the other images that accompany the story can provide information about characters, plot, mood, and tone. Have students preview the images in the selection, and ask volunteers to discuss their observations with the class.	Help students locate a copy of Steven Berkoff's stage play *Metamorphosis*. Encourage them to read the play and to note the similarities and differences between the play and Kafka's short story. Direct students to write literary analysis essays in which they discuss how the transformation from narrative to stage changes the original story. Students should consider whether Berkoff's transformation of Kafka's work helps reinforce the Modernist characteristics of the original or mutates the story in subtle or obvious ways.

26 Literary Analysis

Modernism and Literature of the Fantastic

- Review with students the Connecting Literary Elements instruction on p. 977.
- Read the bracketed passage aloud. Ask: How does the photograph of Gregor compare with his current situation?
  Answer: The photo shows Gregor as a "carefree" lieutenant, "demanding respect" for his status. In contrast, Gregor as an insect is confined to an alien body and receives no respect.
- Ask students the Literary Analysis question on p. 988: In what ways does the realistic description of Gregor in uniform emphasize the horror of his transformation?
  Answer: The description of the photograph humanizes Gregor and makes the reader realize how drastic Gregor's transformation is. The reader sees Gregor's "human" past, not just the insect that he has become.

Monitor Progress Ask students how the realistic description of the photograph compares and contrasts with the Modernist themes in the story and Gregor's current transformation.
Answer: In the photograph, Gregor demands respect for his bearing and rank as a member of a highly regimented group. There is an acute contrast between the Gregor in the photograph and the Gregor who is now alienated from participation in any human group. In his current state as an insect, Gregor belongs to a group that is almost uniformly disrespected by the human community.

uncertainly around the living room, shielded his eyes with his hands, and sobbed with heaves of his powerful chest.

Now Gregor did not enter the room after all but leaned against the inside of the firmly bolted wing of the door, so that only half his body was visible and his head above it, cocked to one side and peeping out at the others. In the meantime it had grown much lighter; across the street one could see clearly a section of the endless, grayish-black building opposite—it was a hospital—with its regular windows starkly piercing the façade; the rain was still coming down, but only in large, separately visible drops that were also pelting the ground literally one at a time. The breakfast dishes were laid out lavishly on the table; since for his father breakfast was the most important meal of the day, which he would prolong for hours while reading various newspapers. On the wall directly opposite hung a photograph of Gregor from his army days, in a lieutenant's uniform, his hand on his sword, a carefree smile on his lips, demanding respect for his bearing and his rank. The door to the foyer was open, and since the front door was open too, it was possible to see out onto the landing and the top of the stairs going down.

Literary Analysis
Modernism and Literature of the Fantastic In what ways does the realistic description of Gregor in uniform emphasize the horror of his transformation?

"Well," said Gregor—and he was thoroughly aware of being the only one who had kept calm—"I'll get dressed right away, pack up my samples, and go. Will you, will you please let me go? Now, sir, you see, I'm not stubborn and I'm willing to work; traveling is a hardship, but without it I couldn't live. Where are you going, sir? To the office? Yes? Will you give an honest report of everything? A man might find for a moment that he was unable to work, but that's exactly the right time to remember his past accomplishments and to consider that later on, when the obstacle has been removed, he's bound to work all the harder and more efficiently. I'm under so many obligations to the head of the firm, as you know very well. Besides, I also have my parents and my sister to worry about. I'm in a tight spot, but I'll also work my way out again. Don't make things harder for me than they already are. Stick up for me in the office, please. Traveling salesmen aren't well liked there, I know. People think they make a fortune leading the gay life. No one has any particular reason to rectify this prejudice. But you, sir, you have a better perspective on things than the rest of the office, an even better perspective, just between the two of us, than the head of the firm himself, who in his capacity as owner easily lets his judgment be swayed against an employee. And you also know very well that the traveling salesman, who is out of the office practically the whole year round, can so easily become the victim of gossip, coincidences, and unfounded accusations, against which he's completely unable to defend himself, since in most cases he knows nothing at all about them except

rectify (rek′ tə fī′) *v.* to set things right or restore balance

ENRICHMENT: Psychology Connection

Freud

Explain that Sigmund Freud was doing his work on human psychology in the early 1900s, during the time when Kafka was writing. At the foundation of many of Freud's theories is his claim that there are no accidents, only events resulting from unconscious motives. This theory may explain Gregor's transformation in "The Metamorphosis." Gregor felt trapped in a job he hated. He could not quit or get fired because his family depended upon him. He could not even pretend to be sick; he would simply be fired. However, he *could* turn into an insect. Hence, Gregor's transformation is not "random," but rather a manifestation of his unconscious desire to escape the confinements of modern life.

when he returns exhausted from a trip, and back home gets to suffer on his own person the grim consequences, which can no longer be traced back to their causes. Sir, don't go away without a word to tell me you think I'm at least partly right!"

But at Gregor's first words the manager had already turned away and with curled lips looked back at Gregor only over his twitching shoulder. And during Gregor's speech he did not stand still for a minute but, without letting Gregor out of his sight, backed toward the door, yet very gradually, as if there were some secret prohibition against leaving the room. He was already in the foyer, and from the sudden movement with which he took his last step from the living room, one might have thought he had just burned the sole of his foot. In the foyer, however, he stretched his right hand far out toward the staircase, as if nothing less than an unearthly deliverance were awaiting him there.

Gregor realized that he must on no account let the manager go away in this mood if his position in the firm were not to be jeopardized in the extreme. His parents did not understand this too well; in the course of the years they had formed the conviction that Gregor was set for life in this firm; and furthermore, they were so preoccupied with their imme-
27 diate troubles that they had lost all consideration for the future. But Gregor had this forethought. The manager must be detained, calmed down, convinced, and finally won over; Gregor's and the family's future depended on it! If only his sister had been there! She was perceptive; she had already begun to cry when Gregor was still lying calmly on his back. And certainly the manager, this ladies' man, would have listened to her; she would have shut the front door and in the foyer talked him out of his scare. But his sister was not there, Gregor had to handle the situation himself. And without stopping to realize that he had no idea what his new faculties of movement were, and without stopping to realize either that his speech had possibly—indeed, probably—not been understood again, he let go of the wing of the door; he shoved himself through the opening, intending to go to the manager, who was already on the landing, ridiculously holding onto the banisters with both hands; but groping for support, Gregor immediately fell down with a little cry onto his numerous little legs. This had hardly happened when for the first time that morning he had a feeling of physical well-being; his little legs were on firm ground; they obeyed him completely, as he noted to his joy; they even strained to carry him away wherever he wanted to go; and he already believed that final recovery from all his
28 sufferings was imminent. But at that very moment, as he lay on the floor rocking with repressed motion, not far from his mother and just opposite her, she, who had seemed so completely self-absorbed, all at once jumped up, her arms stretched wide, her fingers spread, and cried, "Help, for God's sake, help!" held her head bent as if to see Gregor better, but inconsistently darted madly backward instead; had forgotten that the table laden with the breakfast dishes stood behind her; sat down on it hastily, as if her thoughts were elsewhere, when she

Reading Strategy
Applying the Author's Biography How might Gregor's reactions reflect Kafka's feelings about his financial responsibilities for his family?

imminent (im' ə nənt) *adj.* ready to happen at any moment

29 ✔**Reading Check**
Once his door is open, what does Gregor insist he be permitted to do?

27 Reading Strategy

Applying the Author's Biography

- Ask a volunteer to read aloud the bracketed passage.
- Ask students the Reading Strategy question on p. 989: How might Gregor's reactions reflect Kafka's feelings about his financial responsibilities for his family?
  Answer: As Gregor witnesses the manager's reaction to his new insect form, Gregor is struck with a sense of panic about the security of his job. Like Kafka, Gregor is responsible for his family's financial security, so Gregor wants to secure his position with his employer.

28 Vocabulary Development

Latin Prefix *im-*

- Draw students' attention to the word *imminent*, and read its definition.
- Tell students that the prefix *im-* means "not," "into," or "toward."
- Have students suggest other words that contain the prefix *im-*.
  Possible response: *Immigrant, immediate, immense, immerse, important, impossible,* and *impression* all contain the prefix *im-*.
- Ask students to use dictionaries to research each suggested word's etymology and explain how the prefix *im-*. contributes to each word's meaning.

29 ✔Reading Check

Answer: Gregor insists on talking to the manager to prevent him from leaving the house.

CUSTOMIZE INSTRUCTION FOR UNIVERSAL ACCESS

For Less Proficient Readers	For Gifted/Talented Students
Read aloud the passage near the bottom of p. 989 that describes how Gregor feels when he discovers the use of his legs. Call students' attention to the line "he already believed that final recovery from all his sufferings was imminent." Initiate a discussion about what Gregor has been through, both before and since his metamorphosis. Then, help students recognize that Gregor is feeling a sense of liberty that he has not felt all morning.	Ask students to imagine that they have arrived at school one morning and no one recognizes them or understands a thing they say. Ask students to write journal entries in which they describe how it might feel to suddenly find themselves in this situation. Encourage students to provide details about how they might be treated and their responses to this treatment.

30 Reading Strategy

Applying the Author's Biography

- Read the bracketed passage aloud. Ask: What details bring this portrait of a powerful, dominating, yet subtly ridiculous, father alive?
  Answer: Kafka provides several sensory details to help the reader picture the father as an authority figure. We see Mr. Samsa wielding a cane and newspaper, and we hear him stamping his feet and "hissing like a wild man."
- Remind students that Kafka's father was a strict, domineering figure, and emphasize that Kafka incorporated these qualities into his characterization of Mr. Samsa.
- Then, ask students the Reading Strategy question on p. 990: In what ways does this description of Gregor's father reflect your knowledge about Kafka's father?
  Answer: The description of Mr. Samsa as an intimidator reflects what we know about Kafka's own domineering father. If faced with the same situation, Kafka's father, like Mr. Samsa, might have tried to regain control of his household.

31 Critical Thinking

Analyze

- Discuss Mrs. Samsa's actions while this wild scene is taking place. Ask students what they think she is feeling.
  Possible response: She is probably feeling despair, panic, and confusion.
- Ask: Why has Mrs. Samsa thrown open the window?
  Possible response: She may feel unable to breathe as a result of anxiety caused by the realization of what has happened to her son and may be trying to get more air. She may have put her head out the window to escape the scene taking place in the apartment.

reached it; and did not seem to notice at all that near her the big coffeepot had been knocked over and coffee was pouring in a steady stream onto the rug.

"Mother, Mother," said Gregor softly and looked up at her. For a minute the manager had completely slipped his mind; on the other hand at the sight of the spilling coffee he could not resist snapping his jaws several times in the air. At this his mother screamed once more, fled from the table, and fell into the arms of his father, who came rushing up to her. But Gregor had no time now for his parents; the manager was already on the stairs; with his chin on the banister, he was taking a last look back. Gregor was off to a running start, to be as sure as possible of catching up with him; the manager must have suspected something like this, for he leaped down several steps and disappeared; but still he shouted "Agh," and the sound carried through the whole staircase. Unfortunately the manager's flight now seemed to confuse his father completely, who had been relatively calm until now, for instead of running after the manager himself, or at least not hindering Gregor in his pursuit, he seized in his right hand the manager's cane, which had been left behind on a chair with his hat and overcoat, picked up in his left hand a heavy newspaper from the table, and stamping his feet, started brandishing the cane and the newspaper to drive Gregor back
30 into his room. No plea of Gregor's helped, no plea was even understood; however humbly he might turn his head, his father merely stamped his feet more forcefully. Across the room his mother had thrown open a window in spite of the cool weather, and leaning out, she buried her 31
face, far outside the window, in her hands. Between the alley and the staircase a strong draft was created, the window curtains blew in, the newspapers on the table rustled, single sheets fluttered across the floor. Pitilessly his father came on, hissing like a wild man. Now Gregor had not had any practice at all walking in reverse, it was really very slow going. If Gregor had only been allowed to turn around, he could have gotten into his room right away, but he was afraid to make his father impatient by this time-consuming gyration, and at any minute the cane in his father's hand threatened to come down on his back or his head with a deadly blow. Finally, however, Gregor had no choice, for he noticed with horror that in reverse he could not even keep going in one direction; and so, incessantly throwing uneasy side-glances at his father, he began to turn around as quickly as possible, in reality turning only very slowly. Perhaps his father realized his good intentions, for he did not interfere with him; instead, he even now and then directed the maneuver from afar with the tip of his cane. If only his father did not keep making this intolerable hissing sound! It made Gregor lose his head completely. He had almost finished the turn when— his mind continually on this hissing—he made a mistake and even started turning back around to his original position. But when he had at last successfully managed to get his head in front of the opened door, it turned out that his body was too broad to get through as it was. Of course in his father's present state of mind it did not even remotely occur to him

Reading Strategy
Applying the Author's Biography In what ways does this description of Gregor's father reflect your knowledge about Kafka's father?

gyration (jī rā' shən) *n.* circular or spiral motion

to open the other wing of the door in order to give Gregor enough room to pass through. He had only the fixed idea that Gregor must return to his room as quickly as possible. He would never have allowed the complicated preliminaries Gregor needed to go through in order to stand up on one end and perhaps in this way fit through the door. Instead he drove Gregor on, as if there were no obstacle, with exceptional loudness; the voice behind Gregor did not sound like that of only a single father; now this was really no joke anymore, and Gregor forced himself—come what may—into the doorway. One side of his body rose up, he lay lop-sided in the opening, one of his flanks was scraped raw, ugly blotches marred the white door, soon he got stuck and could not have budged anymore by himself, his little legs on one side dangled tremblingly in midair, those on the other were painfully crushed against the floor—when from behind his father gave him a hard shove, which was truly his salvation, and bleeding profusely, he flew far into his room. The door was slammed shut with the cane, then at last everything was quiet.

Review and Assess

Thinking About Part I

1. **Respond:** In what ways, if any, did the characters in this story remind you of people whom you have met?
2. **(a) Recall:** What is Gregor's first reaction to his transformation? **(b) Generalize:** How does Gregor's family react to his transformation? **(c) Analyze:** In what ways do the differences in their reactions set up a challenge for this family?
3. **(a) Recall:** Who visits Gregor on the first morning of his transformation? **(b) Generalize:** How would you describe Gregor's relationship to this person? Explain. **(c) Analyze:** Was Gregor happy in his life before his transformation? Explain.
4. **(a) Recall:** In what ways are Gregor's parents indebted to Gregor's boss? **(b) Analyze Cause and Effect:** What does Gregor seem to fear will happen to his family if he loses his job?
5. **(a) Speculate:** Why do you think neither his family nor the office manager ever questions whether the creature before them is actually Gregor? **(b) Support:** Which details, if any, in Part I suggest that Gregor's physical transformation is an outward expression of an alienation he has already experienced both at home and at work? Explain.
6. **Analyze:** Do you think Gregor's inner sense of self has changed as a result of his physical transformation? Explain.

CUSTOMIZE INSTRUCTION FOR UNIVERSAL ACCESS

For Less Proficient Readers	For Advanced Readers
Remind students that only moments after ferociously driving Gregor back into his room, Mr. Samsa uses the tip of his cane to help guide Gregor as he attempts to turn around. Students may be confused by this incongruous behavior. Lead a discussion in which students consider the motivations behind Mr. Samsa's reactions.	Tell students that "The Metamorphosis" is an odd story because it blends the tragic and incomprehensible with humor. Ask students to identify some of the humorous scenes in Part I and discuss why these scenes are humorous and how the humor affects their understanding and appreciation of the story. Volunteers can share their ideas with the class.

Answers for p. 991

Review and Assess

1. Possible response: Gregor's dread of work, dislike of his employers, and feeling of being trapped in his job may remind students of people they know. The overbearing father, the mild-mannered mother, and the helpful sister may recall to students other people they know.
2. **(a)** Gregor is calm and thinks he may return to his normal state if he goes back to sleep. **(b)** Gregor's family is shocked and confused. His mother collapses in despair. His father becomes angry and then cries. Then, they become repulsed and fearful. His sister, however, shows compassion. **(c)** The family must adjust to a new situation. They must each sort out the conflicts among the father's anger, the mother's protective love, and the sister's compassion.
3. **(a)** The office manager visits Gregor. **(b)** Gregor has a tense relationship with the manager. Gregor dislikes and fears him, but he must work for him in order to pay off the family's debts. **(c)** Gregor was not happy before his transformation. He disliked his job but felt obligated to keep working to support his family.
4. **(a)** Mr. Samsa owes Gregor's boss money. **(b)** If Gregor loses his job, the family will not be able to repay the debt.
5. **(a)** Possible response: Kafka does not want his readers to question the plausibility of the transformation, so he does not allow the characters to question it. **(b)** As a salesman, Gregor lives among strangers. He has a strained relationship with his employer. He describes himself as a pawn, whom the boss abuses. At home he is the money-earner, while his family lives a somewhat leisurely life. Gregor's transformation into an insect (which lacks a backbone) and his inability to communicate make his alienation physically apparent.
6. No; Gregor still thinks, worries, and responds as a human. He has felt isolated for a long time; now the isolation has manifested itself in an extreme physical form.

32 About the Selection

In Part II, the tragedy intensifies as Gregor continues to think and feel as a human being while his transformation into an insect becomes more grotesque. The Samsa family, meanwhile, is trying to adapt to the monster in their midst.

33 Literary Analysis

Modernism

- Ask students to read the bracketed passage on p. 992.
- Then, ask them the Literary Analysis question on p. 992: In what ways does Gregor's rejection of the food brought by Grete symbolize his growing alienation?
  Answer: Gregor's taste in food has changed. What was once his favorite drink no longer interests him. Gregor's inability to eat a former favorite food reflects his alienation from his human identity.
- Point out that Gregor was attracted to the smell of the food but rejected it when he tasted it. Ask students what this might indicate about the progress of his metamorphosis.
  Answer: Gregor's transformation is not yet complete. He is both drawn to his old attitudes and unable to continue in them.

Review and Anticipate

Part I of "The Metamorphosis" ends with Gregor being driven back into his room by his cane-wielding father. The office manager has fled in horror, the family is in shock, and Gregor himself is wounded and bloody. Do you think Gregor will be able to overcome his family's revulsion? Do you think he will become normal and human again, or will he grow increasingly alienated and different? Read Part II to see what happens as the first day of Gregor's strange transformation continues.

32

Part II

It was already dusk when Gregor awoke from his deep, comalike sleep. Even if he had not been disturbed, he would certainly not have woken up much later, for he felt that he had rested and slept long enough, but it seemed to him that a hurried step and a cautious shutting of the door leading to the foyer had awakened him. The light of the electric street-lamps lay in pallid streaks on the ceiling and on the upper parts of the furniture, but underneath, where Gregor was, it was dark. Groping clumsily with his antennae, which he was only now beginning to appreciate, he slowly dragged himself toward the door to see what had been happening there. His left side felt like one single long, unpleasantly tautening scar, and he actually had to limp on his two rows of legs. Besides, one little leg had been seriously injured in the course of the morning's events—it was almost a miracle that only one had been injured—and dragged along lifelessly.

pallid (pal' id) *adj.* pale

Only after he got to the door did he notice what had really attracted him—the smell of something to eat. For there stood a bowl filled with fresh milk, in which small slices of white bread were floating. He could almost have laughed for joy, since he was even hungrier than he had been in the morning, and he immediately dipped his head into the milk, almost to over his eyes. But he soon drew it back again in disappointment; not only because he had difficulty eating on account of the soreness in his left side—and he could eat only if his whole panting body cooperated—but because he didn't like the milk at all, although it used to be his favorite drink, and that was certainly why his sister had put it in the room; in fact, he turned away from the bowl almost with repulsion and crawled back to the middle of the room. 33

Literary Analysis
Modernism In what ways does Gregor's rejection of the food brought by Grete symbolize his growing alienation?

In the living room, as Gregor saw through the crack in the door, the gas had been lit, but while at this hour of the day his father was in the habit of reading the afternoon newspaper in a loud voice to his mother and sometimes to his sister too, now there wasn't a sound. Well, perhaps this custom of reading aloud, which his sister was always telling

ENRICHMENT: Science Connection

Entomology

Entomology is the scientific study of insects. The term *entomologist* comes from the Greek word *entomon*, meaning insect. Aristotle (384–322 B.C.), the great Greek philosopher, coined the name for this profession, and the ancient Greeks were its first serious practitioners. Some entomologists specialize in specific insects, including those that undergo complete metamorphosis, such as *Lepidoptera* (butterflies and moths) and *Coleoptera* (beetles).

Students interested in this profession might contact a biology teacher, a college or vocational program, a natural history museum, or a zoo to find out specifically what is required to train for and become successful in a career in entomology.

him and writing him about, had recently been discontinued altogether. But in all the other rooms too it was just as still, although the apartment certainly was not empty. "What a quiet life the family has been leading," Gregor said to himself, and while he stared rigidly in front of him into the darkness, he felt very proud that he had been able to provide such a life in so nice an apartment for his parents and his sister. But what now if all the peace, the comfort, the contentment were to come to a horrible end? In order not to get involved in such thoughts, Gregor decided to keep moving, and he crawled up and down the room.

During the long evening first one of the side doors and then the other was opened a small crack and quickly shut again; someone had probably had the urge to come in and then had had second thoughts. Gregor now settled into position right by the living-room door, determined somehow to get the hesitating visitor to come in, or at least to find out who it might be; but the door was not opened again, and Gregor waited in vain. In the morning, when the doors had been locked, everyone had wanted to come in; now that he had opened one of the doors and the others had evidently been opened during the day, no one came in, and now the keys were even inserted on the outside.

34

It was late at night when the light finally went out in the living room, and now it was easy for Gregor to tell that his parents and his sister had stayed up so long, since, as he could distinctly hear, all three were now retiring on tiptoe. Certainly no one would come in to Gregor until the morning; and so he had ample time to consider undisturbed how best to rearrange his life. But the empty high-ceilinged room in which he was forced to lie flat on the floor made him nervous, without his being able to tell why—since it was, after all, the room in which he had lived for the past five years—and turning half unconsciously and not without a slight feeling of shame, he scuttled under the couch where, although his back was a little crushed and he could not raise his head anymore, he immediately felt very comfortable and was only sorry that his body was too wide to go completely under the couch.

There he stayed the whole night, which he spent partly in a sleepy trance, from which hunger pangs kept waking him with a start, partly in worries and vague hopes, all of which, however, led to the conclusion that for the time being he would have to lie low and, by being patient and showing his family every possible consideration, help them bear

35 ▲ **Critical Viewing**

Why do you think Kafka insisted that the illustration for the cover of the first edition of "The Metamorphosis," shown above, not depict the insect itself? **[Speculate]**

36 ✓**Reading Check**

Where have the keys to Gregor's room been moved?

34 **Background**

Art

Front Cover of *Die Verwandlung*, by Ottomar Sturke

When "The Metamorphosis" (called *Die Verwandlung* in German) was to be published as a book in 1915, Kafka, fearful that the cover illustrator "might want to draw the insect itself," wrote the publisher, "Not that, please not that! ... The insect itself cannot be depicted. It cannot even be shown from a distance." He suggested instead an illustration with "the parents and the chief clerk in front of the closed door or, even better, the parents and the sister in the illuminated room while the door to the entirely dark adjoining room stands open."

Use the following questions for discussion:

- What is the effect of leaving the door ajar?
  Possible response: The open door hints at a mysterious presence in the darkened room that may emerge at any moment.
- What emotions does the man's posture evoke?
  Possible response: The man holding his head in his hands evokes a range of emotions, including terror, disgust, and sorrow.

35 ▶**Critical Viewing**

Possible response Kafka may have thought that the image of Gregor would be more powerful if readers were forced to imagine him; he may have wished to emphasize the symbolic, not literal, meaning of the transformation.

36 ✓**Reading Check**

Answer: The keys have been moved to the outside of the doors so Gregor can be locked inside.

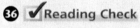

CUSTOMIZE INSTRUCTION FOR UNIVERSAL ACCESS

For English Learners	For Gifted/Talented Students
In a long selection, students may have an especially difficult time resolving questions about content. Suggest that students use self-sticking notes to mark passages, sentences, idioms, or other elements that are confusing. Encourage students to refer to these notes and ask their questions during class discussions.	Have students work independently to create their own illustrations for the cover of "The Metamorphosis." Encourage students to consider the Modernist notions of mystery and uncertainty as well as Kafka's wish that Gregor not be depicted. Ask volunteers to present their book covers to the class and discuss their creative process, detailing the mood they hoped to evoke and citing specific inspirational portions of the text. Students may display their book covers on a class bulletin board.

37 Literary Analysis

Modernism

- Read aloud the bracketed passage on pp. 993–994. Tell students that Gregor's shame amplifies his feelings of alienation. Then, ask: What are the sources of Gregor's shame?
  Answer: Gregor is ashamed of his insect body; he is embarrassed because he is uneasy in his own room; he is ashamed that he feels comfortable only when hiding under the couch.
- Ask students the first Literary Analysis question on p. 994: Do Gregor's thoughts reflect a realistic viewpoint on his life and prospects? Explain.
  Possible response: Yes; by planning how to adapt to his new condition, Gregor shows that he has begun to accept his life as an insect and no longer expects that he will be able to change back into a human. He recognizes that he must become almost invisible in order to survive.

Monitor Progress Tell students that Gregor seems to be guessing how to behave. Ask: In what way does Gregor's lack of clear guidelines reflect a Modernist point of view?
Answer: Modernists expect life to be filled with uncertainty.

38 Literary Analysis

Modernism

- Read aloud the bracketed passage on p. 994.
- Ask students: Why has Gregor's sister given him a selection of foods? What might she learn from his decisions?
  Answer: Grete does not know what foods Gregor will eat now that he is an insect. She will learn what to bring him to eat in the future.
- Ask students the second Literary Analysis question on p. 994: What evidence does this passage describing his meal provide for the view that Gregor is more alienated from the world of humans than he realizes?
  Answer: Even though Gregor thinks like a human, his needs and instincts are becoming more and more insectlike.

37 the inconvenience which he simply had to cause them in his present condition.

Early in the morning—it was still almost night—Gregor had the opportunity of testing the strength of the resolutions he had just made, for his sister, almost fully dressed, opened the door from the foyer and looked in eagerly. She did not see him right away, but when she caught sight of him under the couch—God, he had to be somewhere, he couldn't just fly away—she became so frightened that she lost control of herself and slammed the door shut again. But, as if she felt sorry for her behavior, she immediately opened the door again and came in on tiptoe, as if she were visiting someone seriously ill or perhaps even a stranger. Gregor had pushed his head forward just to the edge of the couch and was watching her. Would she notice that he had left the milk standing, and not because he hadn't been hungry, and would she bring in a dish of something he'd like better? If she were not going to do it of her own free will, he would rather starve than call it to her attention, although, really, he felt an enormous urge to shoot out from under the couch, throw himself at his sister's feet, and beg her for something good to eat. But his sister noticed at once, to her astonishment, that the bowl was still full, only a little milk was spilled around it; she picked it up immediately—not with her bare hands, of course, but with a rag—and carried it out. Gregor was extremely curious to know what she would bring him instead, and he racked his brains on the subject. But he would never have been able to guess what his sister, in the goodness of her heart, actually did. To find out his likes and dislikes, she brought him a wide assortment of things, all spread out on an old newspaper: old, half-rotten vegetables; bones left over from the evening meal, caked with congealed white sauce; some raisins and almonds; a piece of cheese, which two days before Gregor had declared inedible; a plain slice of bread, a slice of bread and butter, and one with butter and salt. In addition to all this she put down some water in the bowl apparently permanently earmarked for Gregor's use. And out of a sense of delicacy, since she knew that Gregor would not eat in front of her, she left hurriedly and even turned the key, just so that Gregor should know that he might make himself as comfortable as he wanted. Gregor's legs began whirring now that he was going to eat. Besides, his bruises must have completely healed, since he no longer felt any handicap, and marveling at this he thought how, over a month ago he had cut his finger very slightly with a knife and how this wound was still hurting him only
38 the day before yesterday. "Have I become less sensitive?" he thought, already sucking greedily at the cheese, which had immediately and forcibly attracted him ahead of all the other dishes. One right after the other, and with eyes streaming with tears of contentment, he devoured the cheese, the vegetables, and the sauce; the fresh foods, on the other hand, he did not care for; he couldn't even stand their smell and even dragged the things he wanted to eat a bit further away. He had finished with everything long since and was just lying lazily at the same spot when his sister slowly turned the key as a sign for him to withdraw.

Literary Analysis
Modernism Do Gregor's thoughts reflect a realistic viewpoint on his life and prospects? Explain.

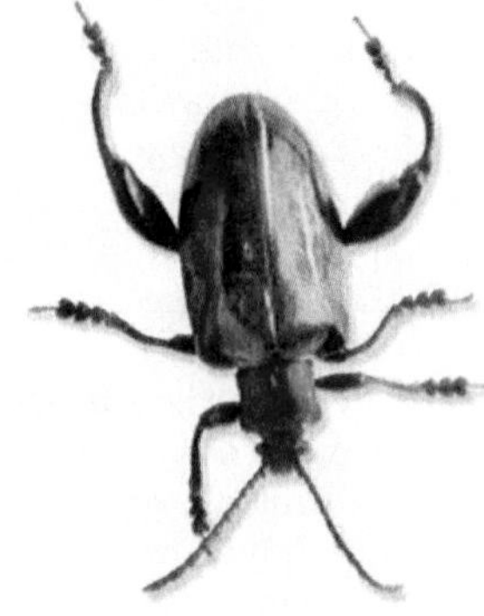

Literary Analysis
Modernism What evidence does this passage describing his meal provide for the view that Gregor is more alienated from the world of humans than he realizes?

ENRICHMENT: Biography Connection

Kafka's Metamorphosis

A year before Kafka wrote "The Metamorphosis," he watched an artist grimacing and mimicking what he was drawing. That day, Kafka wrote this prophetic comment in his diary:

> [The artist] reminds me that I too have a pronounced talent for metamorphosing myself, which no one notices.... Yesterday evening, on the way home, if I had observed myself from the outside I should have taken myself for Tucholsky [a German writer]. The alien being must be in me, then, as distinctly and invisibly as the hidden object in a picture-puzzle, where too, one would never find anything if one did not know that it is there. When these metamorphoses take place, I should especially like to believe in a dimming of my own eyes.

That immediately startled him although he was almost asleep, and he scuttled under the couch again. But it took great self-control for him to stay under the couch even for the short time his sister was in the room, since his body had become a little bloated from the heavy meal, and in his cramped position he could hardly breathe. In between slight attacks of suffocation he watched with bulging eyes as his unsuspecting sister took a broom and swept up, not only his leavings, but even the
40 foods which Gregor had left completely untouched—as if they too were no longer usable—and dumping everything hastily into a pail, which she covered with a wooden lid, she carried everything out. She had hardly turned her back when Gregor came out from under the couch, stretching and puffing himself up.

This, then, was the way Gregor was fed each day, once in the morning, when his parents and the maid were still asleep, and a second time in the afternoon after everyone had had dinner, for then his parents took a short nap again, and the maid could be sent out by his sister on some errand. Certainly they did not want him to starve either, but perhaps they would not have been able to stand knowing any more about his meals than from hearsay, or perhaps his sister wanted to spare them even what was possibly only a minor torment, for really, they were suffering enough as it was.

Gregor could not find out what excuses had been made to get rid of the doctor and the locksmith on that first morning, for since the others could not understand what he said, it did not occur to any of them, not even to his sister, that he could understand what they said, and so he had to be satisfied, when his sister was in the room, with only occasionally hearing her sighs and appeals to the saints. It was only later, when she had begun to get used to everything—there could never, of course, be any question of a complete adjustment—that Gregor sometimes caught a remark which was meant to be friendly or could be interpreted as such. "Oh, he liked what he had today," she would say when Gregor had tucked away a good helping, and in the opposite case, which gradually occurred more and more frequently, she used to say, almost sadly, "He's left everything again."

But if Gregor could not get any news directly, he overheard a great deal from the neighboring rooms, and as soon as he heard voices, he would immediately run to the door concerned and press his whole body against it. Especially in the early days, there was no conversation that was not somehow about him, if only implicitly. For two whole days there were family consultations at every mealtime about how they should cope; this was also the topic of discussion between meals, for at least two members of the family were always at home, since no one probably wanted to stay home alone and it was

Themes in World Literature

39 *The Modernist Revolution*

During the late nineteenth and early twentieth centuries, major scientific, technological, and industrial developments occurred that dramatically altered the way people lived. Not only did this period witness such breakthroughs as the invention of the automobile, the airplane, the telephone, and the machine gun, but it also saw the emergence of brilliant thinkers and scientists, including Sigmund Freud, Albert Einstein, and Friedrich Nietzsche, whose ideas reshaped people's understanding of themselves and the world around them. This period of rapid change culminated in World War I, a bloody conflict that wiped out almost an entire generation of European men. As a result of these events and developments, many people felt the need to discard the ideas and values of the past and to find new ideas that more appropriately reflected twentieth-century life. Franz Kafka's disturbing fictional world is one of the best literary examples of this new vision, but the Modernist movement affected every creative discipline. The Modernists' vibrant, unsettling, and profound artistic experiments continue to resonate in our culture to this day.

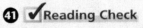

41 **Reading Check**

What kinds of food does Gregor now prefer?

39 Background

The Modernist Revolution

Generally, the themes of Modernist writers were subtly implied rather than directly stated in order to force readers to draw their own conclusions. Likewise, writers began abandoning traditional plot structure, omitting the expositions and resolutions that clarified the work. As a result, the Modernist story seems to begin arbitrarily and to end without resolution, leaving the reader with possibilities, not solutions. This technique reflected the uncertainties and questions about life provoked by the intellectual revolutions—and mass destruction—of the time.

40 Literary Analysis

Modernism

- Read aloud the bracketed passage.
- Ask students how this scene indicates that another degree of alienation has occurred.
  Answer: Grete treats the food as tainted, showing that she now feels that Gregor is dirty, like any other vermin.
- How does Gregor seem to feel about the way his sister cleans up after him? Explain.
  Answer: Gregor seems surprised and hurt, because he does not think of himself as dirty.
- Ask students why food is an especially apt symbol for the Modernist theme of alienation.
  Possible response: The need for food is a basic individual need, and traditions in the choice and sharing of food help define an individual's membership in a family or culture. Not eating the same food as others or not eating with others are basic signs of not belonging.

41 Reading Check

Answer: Gregor prefers half-rotten, smelly foods to fresh foods.

CUSTOMIZE INSTRUCTION FOR UNIVERSAL ACCESS

For English Learners	For Advanced Readers
Ask students to list new or unfamiliar words from Part II of the selection. Have students use dictionaries to look up each word's definition and origin. Then, have students exchange word lists with partners and work together until both have learned all the new words. Encourage students to create word journals in which they record newly learned words.	Call students' attention to the word *earmarked* in the following passage from p. 994: "In addition to all this she put down some water in the bowl apparently permanently *earmarked* for Gregor's use." Have students work with partners to research the etymology of this word. Each pair can prepare a presentation about the origins and meaning of the word and how Kafka uses it in the selection.

42 Critical Thinking

Analyze

- Read aloud the bracketed passage.
- Ask students: Why does the maid promise, without being asked, to tell no one about the family's situation?

  Possible response: The maid may want to protect the Samsas or put them at ease. She understands the shameful and horrifying nature of their predicament and recognizes the uproar Gregor could cause in the community. Or perhaps she fears retribution by the monstrous Gregor. The Samsas do not ask the maid to make this promise because they know that if she were to tell, no one would believe her.

43 ▶Critical Viewing

Possible response: Gregor might be overhearing the conversation about the family finances and be considering his father's deceit in not telling him he had money left from his business.

42 impossible to leave the apartment completely empty. Besides, on the very first day the maid—it was not completely clear what and how much she knew of what had happened—had begged his mother on bended knees to dismiss her immediately; and when she said goodbye a quarter of an hour later, she thanked them in tears for the dismissal, as if for the greatest favor that had ever been done to her in this house, and made a solemn vow, without anyone asking her for it, not to give anything away to anyone.

Now his sister, working with her mother, had to do the cooking too; of course that did not cause her much trouble, since they hardly ate anything. Gregor was always hearing one of them pleading in vain with one of the others to eat and getting no answer except, "Thanks, I've had enough," or something similar. They did not seem to drink anything either. His sister often asked her father if he wanted any beer and gladly offered to go out for it herself; and when he did not answer, she said, in order to remove any hesitation on his part, that she could also send the janitor's wife to get it, but then his father finally answered with a definite "No," and that was the end of that.

In the course of the very first day his father explained the family's financial situation and prospects to both the mother and the sister. From time to time he got up from the table to get some kind of receipt or notebook out of the little strongbox he had rescued from the collapse of his business five years before. Gregor heard him open the complicated lock and secure it again after taking out what he had been looking for. These explanations by his father were to some extent the first pleasant news Gregor had heard since his imprisonment. He had always believed that his father had not been able to save a penny from the business, at least his father had never told him anything to the con-

43 ▼ Critical Viewing In this photograph of Mikhail Baryshnikov as Gregor Samsa, what information do you think Gregor might be overhearing? Explain. **[Hypothesize]**

ENRICHMENT: Cultural Connection

Ottla Kafka

Kafka's father had very definite ideas about everything. Among them were his ideas about his children's futures. He never approved of Franz's literary interests; he wanted him to study something more useful and profitable, which led Franz to study law. Franz's sister Ottla wished to study agricultural economy. Franz encouraged her and even wrote to some colleges to inquire about courses. He urged Ottla not to talk about the cost of the education with their father. "I'll very gladly pay for it," Kafka wrote. "Money has less and less value anyway, and if I invest in you it will be the first mortgage on your future economy." He even volunteered to go with Ottla as she looked at schools.

trary, and Gregor, for his part, had never asked him any questions. In those days Gregor's sole concern had been to do everything in his power to make the family forget as quickly as possible the business disaster which had plunged everyone into a state of total despair. And so he had begun to work with special ardor[4] and had risen almost overnight from stock clerk to traveling salesman, which of course had opened up very different money-making possibilities, and in no time his successes on the job were transformed, by means of commissions, into hard cash that could be plunked down on the table at home in front of his astonished and delighted family. Those had been wonderful times, and they had never returned, at least not with the same glory, although later on Gregor earned enough money to meet the expenses of the entire family and actually did so. They had just gotten used to it, the family as well as Gregor, the money was received with thanks and given with pleasure, but no special feeling of warmth went with it any more. Only his sister had remained close to Gregor, and it was his secret plan that she who, unlike him, loved music and could play the violin movingly, should be sent next year to the Conservatory, regardless of the great expense involved, which could surely be made up for in

44 some other way. Often during Gregor's short stays in the city, the Conservatory would come up in his conversations with his sister, but always merely as a beautiful dream which was not supposed to come true, and his parents were not happy to hear even these innocent allusions; but Gregor had very concrete ideas on the subject and he intended solemnly to announce his plan on Christmas Eve.

Thoughts like these, completely useless in his present state, went through his head as he stood glued to the door, listening. Sometimes out of general exhaustion he could not listen anymore and let his head bump carelessly against the door, but immediately pulled it back again, for even the slight noise he made by doing this had been heard in the next room and made them all lapse into silence. "What's he carrying on about in there now?" said his father after a while, obviously turning toward the door, and only then would the interrupted conversation gradually be resumed.

Gregor now learned in a thorough way—for his father was in the habit of often repeating himself in his explanations, partly because he himself had not dealt with these matters for a long time, partly, too, because his mother did not understand everything the first time around—that in spite of all their misfortunes a bit of capital, a very little bit, certainly, was still intact from the old days, which in the meantime had increased a little through the untouched interest. But besides that, the money Gregor had brought home every month—he had kept only a few dollars for himself—had never been completely used up and had accumulated into a tidy principal. Behind his door Gregor nodded emphatically, delighted at this unexpected foresight and thrift. Of course he actually could have paid off more of his father's debt to the

4. **ardor** (är′ dər) *n.* emotional warmth.

Reading Strategy
Applying the Author's Biography Kafka's father did not support his son's literary aspirations. How does that information add meaning to this discussion about the Conservatory?

45 

Reading Check
What event, five years before, had plunged the family into financial distress?

44 **Reading Strategy**

Applying the Author's Biography

- Have a volunteer read aloud the bracketed passage on p. 997. Then, have the class discuss the value some members of society place on practical skills or academic subjects versus the arts.
- Ask students the Reading Strategy question on p. 997: Kafka's father did not support his son's literary aspirations. How does that information add meaning to this discussion about the Conservatory?
  Answer: Kafka identifies with the sister and her love of art, so he symbolically nurtures his own aspirations by having Gregor wish to support Grete despite Mr. and Mrs. Samsa's objections.
- In light of the biographical nature of this passage, invite students to speculate on how Kafka felt about his parents' lack of support for his literary aspirations.
  Possible response: Kafka may have resented his parents' lack of support.

45 

Reading Check

Answer: Mr. Samsa's business collapsed, and he lost nearly everything.

CUSTOMIZE INSTRUCTION FOR UNIVERSAL ACCESS

For Less Proficient Readers	For English Learners
Organize students into three groups. Assign each group one of the following characters: father, mother, Grete. Have each group list personality and character traits of its assigned character along with details from the story that illustrate those traits. Have each group share and discuss its list with the class.	Students may have been in situations in which they were capable of understanding those around them but were not understood by others. Encourage students to discuss their experiences and compare their feelings with Gregor's feelings. Ask students what advice they would give Gregor to help alleviate the stress of his being unable to communicate. On the board, write students' suggestions, and have students use your notes to write a letter of advice or comfort to Gregor.

46 Literary Analysis

Modernism

- Read aloud the bracketed passage. Then, ask students the Literary Analysis question on p. 998: In what ways does this information about their finances and work skills emphasize the entire family's alienation from the world at large?
  Answer: Neither Gregor's parents nor his sister are used to working or contributing to life outside the apartment.
- Ask students: Does the Samsa family seem unhappy about, or even aware of, its alienation? Explain.
  Possible response: No; the family seems content with the way things have been. They have established a life of complacency, with Gregor providing for them while they remain sheltered from the world.

47 Reading Strategy

Applying the Author's Biography

- Ask a volunteer to read aloud the bracketed passage.
- Then, ask students why being able to look out the window is important to Gregor.
  Answer: Gregor wants to recapture the feeling of freedom he once experienced while looking out the window.
- Ask students the Reading Strategy question on p. 998: How would living in a city have helped Kafka write this description?
  Answer: As a city-dweller, Kafka understood how limited the views are and how a person can get tired of seeing the same thing every day. He also understood the importance of windows when so much time is spent indoors.

boss with this extra money, and the day on which he could have gotten rid of his job would have been much closer, but now things were undoubtedly better the way his father had arranged them.

46 Now this money was by no means enough to let the family live off the interest; the principal was perhaps enough to support the family for one year, or at the most two, but that was all there was. So it was just a sum that really should not be touched and that had to be put away for a rainy day; but the money to live on would have to be earned. Now his father was still healthy, certainly, but he was an old man who had not worked for the past five years and who in any case could not be expected to undertake too much; during these five years, which were the first vacation of his hard-working yet unsuccessful life, he had gained a lot of weight and as a result had become fairly sluggish. And was his old mother now supposed to go out and earn money, when she suffered from asthma, when a walk through the apartment was already an ordeal for her, and when she spent every other day lying on the sofa under the open window, gasping for breath? And was his sister now supposed to work—who for all her seventeen years was still a child and whom it would be such a pity to deprive of the life she had led until now, which had consisted of wearing pretty clothes, sleeping late, helping in the house, enjoying a few modest amusements, and above all playing the violin? At first, whenever the conversation turned to the necessity of earning money, Gregor would let go of the door and throw himself down on the cool leather sofa which stood beside it, for he felt hot with shame and grief.

47 Often he lay there the whole long night through, not sleeping a wink and only scrabbling on the leather for hours on end. Or, not balking at the huge effort of pushing an armchair to the window, he would crawl up to the window sill and, propped up in the chair, lean against the window, evidently in some sort of remembrance of the feeling of freedom he used to have from looking out the window. For, in fact, from day to day he saw things even a short distance away less and less distinctly; the hospital opposite, which he used to curse because he saw so much of it, was now completely beyond his range of vision, and if he had not been positive that he was living in Charlotte Street—a quiet but still very much a city street—he might have believed that he was looking out of his window into a desert where the gray sky and the gray earth were indistinguishably fused. It took his observant sister only twice to notice that his armchair was standing by the window for her to push the chair back to the same place by the window each time she had finished cleaning the room, and from then on she even left the inside casement of the window open.

If Gregor had only been able to speak to his sister and thank her for everything she had to do for him, he could have accepted her services more easily; as it was, they caused him pain. Of course his sister tried to ease the embarrassment of the whole situation as much as possible, and as time went on, she naturally managed it better and better, but in time Gregor, too, saw things much more clearly. Even the way she came

Literary Analysis
Modernism In what ways does this information about their finances and work skills emphasize the entire family's alienation from the world at large?

Reading Strategy
Applying the Author's Biography How would living in a city have helped Kafka write this description?

in was terrible for him. Hardly had she entered the room than she would run straight to the window without taking time to close the door—though she was usually so careful to spare everyone the sight of Gregor's room— then tear open the casements with eager hands, almost as if she were suffocating, and remain for a little while at the window even in the coldest weather, breathing deeply. With this racing and crashing she frightened Gregor twice a day; the whole time he cowered under the couch, and yet he knew very well that she would certainly have spared him this if only she had found it possible to stand being in a room with him with the window closed.

One time—it must have been a month since Gregor's metamorphosis, and there was certainly no particular reason any more for his sister to be astonished at Gregor's appearance—she came a little earlier than usual and caught Gregor still looking out the window, immobile and so in an excellent position to be terrifying. It would not have surprised Gregor if she had not come in, because his position prevented her from immediately opening the window, but not only did she not come in, she even sprang back and locked the door; a stranger might easily have thought that Gregor had been lying in wait for her, wanting to bite her. Of course Gregor immediately hid under the couch, but he had to wait until noon before his sister came again, and she seemed much more uneasy than usual. He realized from this that the sight of him was still repulsive to her and was bound to remain repulsive to her in the future, and that she probably had to overcome a lot of resistance not to run away at the sight of even the small part of his body that jutted out from under the couch. So, to spare her even this sight, one day he carried the sheet on his back to the couch—the job took four hours—and
48 arranged it in such a way that he was now completely covered up and his sister could not see him even when she stooped. If she had considered this sheet unnecessary, then of course she could have removed it, for it was clear enough that it could not be for his own pleasure that Gregor shut himself off altogether, but she left the sheet the way it was, and Gregor thought that he had even caught a grateful look when one time he cautiously lifted the sheet a little with his head in order to see how his sister was taking the new arrangement.

During the first two weeks, his parents could not bring themselves to come in to him, and often he heard them say how much they appreciated his sister's work, whereas until now they had frequently been annoyed with her because she had struck them as being a little useless. But now both of them, his father and his mother, often waited outside Gregor's room while his sister straightened it up, and as soon as she came out she had to tell them in great detail how the room looked, what Gregor had eaten, how he had behaved this time, and whether he had perhaps shown a little improvement. His mother, incidentally, began relatively soon to want to visit Gregor, but his father and his sister at first held her back with reasonable arguments to which Gregor listened very attentively and of which he wholeheartedly approved. But later she had to be restrained by force, and then when she cried out,

Literary Analysis
Modernism What does Gregor now do, deliberately, to alienate himself? Why does he do this?

49 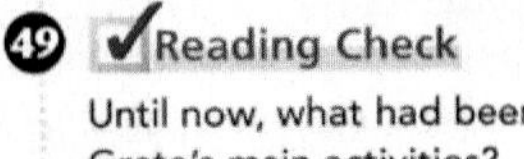

Until now, what had been Grete's main activities?

48 Literary Analysis

Modernism

- Read aloud the bracketed passage. Then have students discuss why Gregor's sister has been unable to accept and trust him.
  Answer: Grete has trouble adjusting to Gregor because she sees him as "alien." Grete's discomfort is intensified by Gregor's size and by her repulsion of his insect ways and odor.
- Ask students the Literary Analysis question on p. 999: What does Gregor now do, deliberately, to alienate himself? Why does he do this?
  Answer: Gregor puts a sheet over the couch to hide himself completely from view. He wants to spare his sister the sight of him.

49 

Answer: Grete's usual activities had been wearing pretty clothes, sleeping late, helping around the apartment, enjoying a few amusements, and playing her violin.

CUSTOMIZE INSTRUCTION FOR UNIVERSAL ACCESS

For Less Proficient Readers	For Gifted/Talented Students
Draw students' attention to the passage on p. 998: "For, in fact, from day to day he saw things even a short distance away less and less distinctly. . . ." Help students understand that Gregor's diminishing sight is another indication that his metamorphosis is continuing. Organize students into pairs, and assign each pair a portion of the text that they have read so far. Tell each pair to list the progression of Gregor's metamorphosis.	Have students list the progression of Gregor's metamorphosis in the text they have read so far. Organize students into groups, and assign each group a state of metamorphosis: for example, 1) Gregor awakes with an insect's body; 2) Gregor tries to speak; 3) Gregor unlocks the door; 4) Gregor's tastes in food changes; 5) Gregor's vision changes; 6) Gregor hides from Grete, and so on. Ask each group to illustrate a scene for and describe the stage of transformation.

50 Background

What Kind of Insect Is Gregor Samsa?

In his lectures on "The Metamorphosis" at Cornell University, Vladimir Nabokov made several observations that raise questions about Gregor's insect identity. First, he observed that Gregor, when trying to get out of bed, is "closing his eyes." Nabokov pointed out that, "a regular beetle has no eyelids and cannot close its eyes." Nabokov also noted that in Part III, the cleaning woman calls Gregor a "dung beetle." Nabokov dismissed this identification as an endearing epithet used "only to be friendly."

Nabokov believed Gregor to be a kind of beetle, but one whose "metamorphosis is not quite complete as yet."

These speculations only confirm what is suggested by Kafka's insistence that his publisher not provide illustrations for Gregor the "insect"—Gregor's new identity is not a scientifically classifiable one but is rather a condition in which personal identity flounders, revealing its unpleasant obverse side.

51 Critical Thinking

Speculate

- Explain to students that in the bracketed passage on p. 1000, Grete intends to remove the furniture as an act of kindness.
- Ask students to speculate about what will happen once the furniture is removed.
  Possible response: The removal of the furniture will further alienate Gregor from his sister and from the human world. Gregor will want to keep his things but will struggle to communicate this message.

"Let me go to Gregor, he is my unfortunate boy! Don't you understand that I have to go to him?" Gregor thought that it might be a good idea after all if his mother did come in, not every day of course, but perhaps once a week; she could still do everything much better than his sister, who, for all her courage, was still only a child and in the final analysis had perhaps taken on such a difficult assignment only out of childish flightiness.

Gregor's desire to see his mother was soon fulfilled. During the day Gregor did not want to show himself at the window, if only out of consideration for his parents, but he couldn't crawl very far on his few square yards of floor space, either; he could hardly put up with just lying still even at night; eating soon stopped giving him the slightest pleasure, so, as a distraction, he adopted the habit of crawling crisscross over the walls and the ceiling. He especially liked hanging from the ceiling; it was completely different from lying on the floor; one could breathe more freely; a faint swinging sensation went through the body; and in the almost happy absent-mindedness which Gregor felt up there, it could happen to his own surprise that he let go and plopped onto the floor. But now, of course, he had much better control of his body than before and did not hurt himself even from such a big drop. His sister immediately noticed the new entertainment Gregor had discovered for
51 himself—after all, he left behind traces of his sticky substance wherever he crawled—and so she got it into her head to make it possible for Gregor to crawl on an altogether wider scale by taking out the furniture which stood in his way—mainly the chest of drawers and the desk. But she was not able to do this by herself; she did not dare ask her father for help; the maid would certainly not have helped her, for although this girl, who was about sixteen, was bravely sticking it out after the previous cook had left, she had asked for the favor of locking herself in the kitchen at all times and of only opening the door on special request. So there was nothing left for his sister to do except to get her mother one day when her father was out. And his mother did come, with exclamations of excited joy, but she grew silent at the door of Gregor's room. First his sister looked to see, of course, that everything in the room was in order; only then did she let her mother come in. Hurrying as fast as he could, Gregor had pulled the sheet down lower still and pleated it more tightly—it really looked just like a sheet accidentally thrown over the couch. This time Gregor also refrained from spying from under the sheet; he renounced seeing

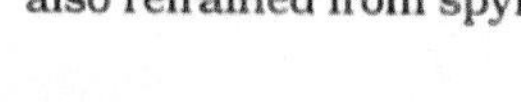

Literature in context Science Connection

50 What Kind of Insect Is Gregor Samsa?

Readers of "The Metamorphosis" have long debated what kind of "vermin" Gregor has become. American novelist John Updike writes: "Popular belief has him a cockroach. . . . But, as Vladimir Nabokov, who knew his entomology, pointed out . . . , Gregor is too broad and convex to be a cockroach. . . . Gregor Samsa, awaking, sees 'numerous legs, which were pitifully thin compared to the rest of his bulk.' If 'numerous' is more than six, then he must be a centipede—not an insect at all. From evidence in the story he is brown in color and about as long as the distance between a doorknob and the floor. He has a kind of voice at first . . . which disappears as the story progresses. His jaws don't work as ours do but he has eyelids, nostrils, and a neck. He is, in short, impossible to picture except when the author wants to evoke his appearance, to bump the reader up against some astounding, poignant new aspect of Gregor's embodiment. . . ."

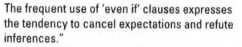

ENRICHMENT: Linguistics Connection

Kafka's Language

Critic Walter H. Sokel observed that Kafka's characters are almost universally uncertain about their condition. This uncertainty is reflected in Kafka's language, which creates a mood that affects the reader's response: "Kafka's vocabulary is one of inference and conjecture.... Kafka prefers 'it seems' to 'it is.' His sentences often consist of two clauses: the first states a fact or a guess; the second qualifies, questions, negates it. The conjunction 'but' is, therefore, most characteristic of Kafka's thought structure. The frequent use of 'even if' clauses expresses the tendency to cancel expectations and refute inferences."

One example of this structure is the sentence at the top of p. 1000 that begins, "Gregor thought that it might be a good idea ..."

his mother for the time being and was simply happy that she had come after all. "Come on, you can't see him," his sister said, evidently leading her mother in by the hand. Now Gregor could hear the two frail women moving the old chest of drawers—heavy for anyone—from its place and his sister insisting on doing the harder part of the job herself, ignoring the warnings of her mother, who was afraid that she would overexert herself. It went on for a long time. After struggling for a good quarter of an hour, his mother said that they had better leave the chest where it was, because, in the first place, it was too heavy, they would not finish before his father came, and with the chest in the middle of the room, Gregor would be completely barricaded; and, in the second place, it was not at all certain they were doing Gregor a favor by removing his furniture. To her the opposite seemed to be the case; the sight of the bare
52 wall was heart-breaking; and why shouldn't Gregor also have the same feeling, since he had been used to his furniture for so long and would feel abandoned in the empty room. "And doesn't it look," his mother concluded very softly—in fact she had been almost whispering the whole time, as if she wanted to avoid letting Gregor, whose exact whereabouts she did not know, hear even the sound of her voice, for she was convinced that he did not understand the words—"and doesn't it look as if by removing his furniture we were showing him that we have given up all hope of his getting better and are leaving him to his own devices without any consideration? I think the best thing would be to try to keep the room exactly the way it was before, so that when Gregor comes back to us again, he'll find everything unchanged and can forget all the more easily what's happened in the meantime."

When he heard his mother's words, Gregor realized that the monotony of family life, combined with the fact that not a soul had addressed a word directly to him, must have addled[5] his brain in the course of the past two months, for he could not explain to himself in any other way how in all seriousness he could have been anxious to have his room cleared out. Had he really wanted to have his warm room, comfortably fitted with furniture that had always been in the family, changed into a cave, in which, of course, he would be able to crawl around unhampered in all directions but at the cost of simultaneously, rapidly, and totally forgetting his human past? Even now he had been on the verge of forgetting, and only his mother's voice, which he had not heard for so long, had shaken him up. Nothing should be removed; everything had to stay; he could not do without the beneficial influence of the furniture on his state of mind; and if the furniture prevented him from carrying on this senseless crawling around, then that was no loss but rather a great advantage.

But his sister unfortunately had a different opinion; she had become accustomed, certainly not entirely without justification, to adopt with her parents the role of the particularly well-qualified expert whenever Gregor's affairs were being discussed; and so her mother's advice was now

5. **addled** (ad' 'ld) *v.* muddled or confused.

Literary Analysis
Modernism What does the removal of the furniture suggest to Gregor's mother about the permanence of her son's alienation from the family?

53 **✔Reading Check**
What change to Gregor's room does Grete decide to make?

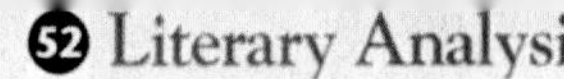

52 Literary Analysis
Modernism

- Have several volunteers take turns reading the bracketed passage aloud.
- Then, ask students why Mrs. Samsa is reluctant to let Gregor hear her voice.
  Answer: Mrs. Samsa seems to want to spare Gregor the pain of hearing, and not being able to comprehend, her voice. At the same time, she might be fearful or repulsed by the thought of sharing anything, even the sound of her voice, with this insect.
- Ask students the Literary Analysis question on p. 1001: What does the removal of the furniture suggest to Gregor's mother about the permanence of her son's alienation from the family?
  Answer: The removal of the furniture suggests to Mrs. Samsa that Gregor will not return to his human form and that his alienation is permanent.

Monitor Progress Ask: On the basis of what you know about Modernism, do you think Gregor will return to his human form? Explain.
Possible response: Gregor will remain an insect. If Gregor were to return to his human form, it would provide a resolution, which is uncharacteristic of Modernist work.

53 ✔Reading Check

Answer: Grete decides to remove the furniture so Gregor can move around more easily.

CUSTOMIZE INSTRUCTION FOR UNIVERSAL ACCESS

For Less Proficient Readers	For Gifted/Talented Students
Remind students that point of view is the perspective from which a story is told. Tell students that if the knowledge of the storyteller is limited to the internal states of one character, then the point of view is *limited.* Ask students the following questions about "The Metamorphosis": Who is telling the story? Is he or she outside the story? Does the narrator know about the feelings and thoughts of all the characters?	"The Metamorphosis" is a fantastic tale, yet the reader is willing to accept it without an unusual sense of awe partly because the narrator tells it from the third-person limited point of view. The narrator presents only the thoughts and feelings of Gregor, who remains calm and matter-of-fact throughout. Ask students to consider how readers might respond to this story if it were told from another character's perspective. Challenge them to select a scene and rewrite it from Mr. Samsa's, Mrs. Samsa's, or Grete's perspective.

54 Literary Analysis

Modernism

- Explain to students that in the bracketed passage, the narrator supposes that the removal of the furniture will terrify Gregor. Ask students to consider whether this supposition is correct.
  Answer: Yes; this supposition is correct. Gregor is already alienated within a strange body, which is very unsettling and frightening. Removing more evidence of his human life will only enhance these feelings of alienation and cause terror.
- Ask students the Literary Analysis question on p. 1002: Do you think this explanation for Grete's desire to intensify Gregor's alienation is valid? Explain.
  Possible response: Yes; people like to have a sense of purpose and want to feel needed. No; Grete has shown no sign that she would do anything to hurt, or terrify, Gregor up to this point. It seems unlikely that she would start now.

sufficient reason for her to insist, not only on the removal of the chest of drawers and the desk, which was all she had been planning at first, but also on the removal of all the furniture with the exception of the indispensable couch. Of course it was not only childish defiance and the self-confidence she had recently acquired so unexpectedly and at such a cost that led her to make this demand; she had in fact noticed that Gregor needed plenty of room to crawl around in; and on the other hand, as best as she could tell, he never used the furniture at all. Perhaps, however, the romantic enthusiasm of girls her age, which seeks to indulge itself at every opportunity, played a part, by tempting her to make Gregor's situation even more terrifying in order that she might do even more for him. Into a room in which Gregor ruled the bare walls all alone, no human being besides Grete was ever likely to set foot.

Literary Analysis
Modernism Do you think this explanation for Grete's desire to intensify Gregor's alienation is valid? Explain.

And so she did not let herself be swerved from her decision by her mother, who, besides, from the sheer anxiety of being in Gregor's room, seemed unsure of herself, soon grew silent, and helped her daughter as best she could to get the chest of drawers out of the room. Well, in a pinch Gregor could do without the chest, but the desk had to stay. And hardly had the women left the room with the chest, squeezing against it and groaning, than Gregor stuck his head out from under the couch to see how he could feel his way into the situation as considerately as possible. But unfortunately it had to be his mother who came back first, while in the next room Grete was clasping the chest and rocking it back and forth by herself, without of course budging it from the spot. His mother, however, was not used to the sight of Gregor, he could have made her ill, and so Gregor, frightened, scuttled in reverse to the far end of the couch but could not stop the sheet from shifting a little at the front. That was enough to put his mother on the alert. She stopped, stood still for a moment, and then went back to Grete.

Although Gregor told himself over and over again that nothing special was happening, only a few pieces of furniture were being moved, he soon had to admit that this coming and going of the women, their little calls to each other, the scraping of the furniture along the floor had the effect on him of a great turmoil swelling on all sides, and as much as he tucked in his head and his legs and shrank until his belly touched the floor, he was forced to admit that he would not be able to stand it much longer. They were clearing out his room; depriving him of everything that he loved; they had already carried away the chest of drawers, in which he kept the fretsaw and other tools; were now budging the desk firmly embedded in the floor, the desk he had done his homework on when he was a student at business college, in high school, yes, even in public school—now he really had no more time to examine the good intentions of the two women, whose existence, besides, he had almost forgotten, for they were so exhausted that they were working in silence, and one could hear only the heavy shuffling of their feet.

And so he broke out—the women were just leaning against the desk in the next room to catch their breath for a minute—changed his course four times, he really didn't know what to salvage first, then he saw hang-

ENRICHMENT: Literature Connection

Gregor's Picture

In his essay "Gregor Samsa and Modern Spirituality," the critic Martin Greenberg grants that Gregor has been treated badly by his parents but sees his metamorphosis as a fitting punishment for his own shallowness:

> He pretends that he will get up and resume his old life.... But the human self whose claims he always postponed and continues to postpone, is past being put off, having declared itself negatively by changing him from a human into an insect. His metamorphosis is a judgment on himself by his defeated humanity....
>
> His mother succinctly describes its deathly aridity as she pleads with the chief clerk: "The only amusement he gets is doing fretwork. For instance, he spent two or three evenings cutting out a little picture frame." That is about what Gregor's "human past" amounts to: a pin-up.

55 ing conspicuously on the wall, 56 which was otherwise bare already, the picture of the lady all dressed in furs, hurriedly crawled up on it and pressed himself against the glass, which gave a good surface to stick to and soothed his hot belly. At least no one would take away this picture, while Gregor completely covered it up. He turned his head toward the living-room door to watch the women when they returned.

They had not given themselves much of a rest and were already coming back; Grete had put her arm around her mother and was practically carrying her. "So what should we take now?" said Grete and looked around. At that her eyes met Gregor's as he clung to the wall. Probably only because of her mother's presence she kept her self-control, bent her head down to her mother to keep her from looking around, and said, though in a quavering and thoughtless voice: "Come, we'd better go back into the living room for a minute." Grete's intent was clear to Gregor, she wanted to bring his mother into safety and then chase him down from the wall. Well, just let her try! He squatted on his picture and would not give it up. He would rather fly in Grete's face.

But Grete's words had now made her mother really anxious; she stepped to one side, caught sight of the gigantic brown blotch on the flowered wallpaper, and before it really dawned on her that what she saw was Gregor, cried in a hoarse, bawling voice: "Oh, God, Oh, God!"; and as if giving up completely, she fell with outstretched arms across the couch and did not stir. "You, Gregor!" cried his sister with raised fist and piercing eyes. These were the first words she had addressed directly to him since his metamorphosis. She ran into the next room to get some kind of spirits to revive her mother; Gregor wanted to help

Lady in Yellow (Eleanor Reeves), ca. 1905, Susan Watkins, Chrysler Museum of Art, Norfolk, VA

57 **Critical Viewing**

In what ways do you think this portrait is both similar to and different from Gregor's picture of a lady "all dressed in furs"? **[Compare and Contrast]**

58 **Reading Check**

What does Gregor do in reaction to the removal of his furniture?

CUSTOMIZE INSTRUCTION FOR UNIVERSAL ACCESS

For Less Proficient Readers

Help students design a chart to record the feelings of each of the characters during the scene described on pp. 1002–1003. Have students compare Grete's feelings with those of her mother. Then, have students discuss whether Gregor has ever before placed his own feelings before those of his family.

55 Critical Thinking

Analyze

- Ask a volunteer to read aloud the bracketed passage, which begins on p. 1002. Then, read Kafka's earlier description of this picture, which appears in the second paragraph on p. 978. Ask students what this picture might symbolize for Gregor.
  Possible response: The picture symbolizes the personal human relationship Gregor has always wanted and now wants more than ever.
- Ask: What might the glass symbolize? Explain.
  Possible response: The glass might symbolize alienation. It separates Gregor from the woman in the picture and represents his inability to achieve human contact.

56 Background

Art

Lady in Yellow (Eleanor Reeves), by Susan Watkins

Watkins (1875–1913), a California native, trained at the Art Students League in New York City before traveling to Paris to continue her studies. Her skillful portraits and landscape paintings garnered praise in both American and European art circles.

Use the following prompt to stimulate discussion:

Contrast the scene depicted in this painting with Gregor's reality.
Answer: The woman in the painting looks serene and comfortable. She is seated in a plush setting, surrounded by pillows. Gregor, in contrast, is agitated and uncomfortable in his insect body. His room is being stripped of all its comforts. Unlike the woman shown in this painting, Gregor's reality is fantastical and horrifying.

57 Critical Viewing

Answer: Like the woman in Gregor's picture, the lady in the portrait is dressed opulently, but the woman in the portrait does not have fur as a significant part of her clothing.

58 Reading Check

Answer: Gregor crawls up the wall and presses himself against a picture that he is determined to keep.

59 Literary Analysis

Modernism

- After reading aloud the bracketed passage on pp. 1003–1004, help students envision this scene by asking: Why does Gregor think he can help his sister get what she needs?
  Possible response: Gregor again forgets that he is an insect and, at first, doesn't realize that he cannot help in this situation.
- Ask students the first Literary Analysis question on p. 1004: How does this scene capture key Modernist themes, especially those of helplessness and alienation?
  Answer: Gregor can do nothing to help his mother or his sister. Even the sight of him interferes with his sister's efforts to help his mother, which emphasizes his alienation.

60 Literary Analysis

Modernism and Literature of the Fantastic

- Review with students the description of "literature of the fantastic" on p. 977. Remind them that this story documents both fantastical transformations and realistic transformations. Then, ask students what metamorphosis the bracketed passage on pp. 1004–1005 describes.
  Answer: The passage describes the metamorphosis of Gregor's father from a tired, weak old man to a robust and energetic man in his prime.
- Ask students the second Literary Analysis question on p. 1004: In what ways does Gregor's surprise about his father's changed appearance reflect the fantastic nature of this story?
  Answer: The story is fantastic because it mixes a plausible, realistic metamorphosis (the father's) with a fantastical one (Gregor's). The combination is emphasized by the fact that Gregor never seems surprised by his own fantastical metamorphosis—but is shocked by his father's.

too—there was time to rescue the picture—but he was stuck to the glass and had to tear himself loose by force; then he too ran into the next room, as if he could give his sister some sort of advice, as in the old days; but then had to stand behind her doing nothing while she
59 rummaged among various little bottles; moreover, when she turned around she was startled, a bottle fell on the floor and broke, a splinter of glass wounded Gregor in the face, some kind of corrosive medicine flowed around him; now without waiting any longer, Grete grabbed as many little bottles as she could carry and ran with them inside to her mother; she slammed the door behind her with her foot. Now Gregor was cut off from his mother, who was perhaps near death through his fault; he could not dare open the door if he did not want to chase away his sister, who had to stay with his mother; now there was nothing for him to do except wait; and tormented by self-reproaches and worry, he began to crawl, crawled over everything, walls, furniture and ceiling, and finally in desperation, as the whole room was beginning to spin, fell down onto the middle of the big table.

Literary Analysis
Modernism How does this scene capture key Modernist themes, especially those of helplessness and alienation?

A short time passed; Gregor lay there prostrate; all around, things were quiet, perhaps that was a good sign. Then the doorbell rang. The maid, of course, was locked up in her kitchen and so Grete had to answer the door. His father had come home. "What's happened?" were his first words; Grete's appearance must have told him everything. Grete answered in a muffled voice, her face was obviously pressed against her father's chest; "Mother fainted, but she's better now. Gregor's broken out." "I knew it," his father said. "I kept telling you, but you women don't want to listen." It was clear to Gregor that his father had put the worst interpretation on Grete's all-too-brief announcement and assumed that Gregor was guilty of some outrage. Therefore Gregor now had to try to calm his father down, since he had neither the time nor the ability to enlighten him. And so he fled to the door of his room and pressed himself against it for his father to see, as soon as he came into the foyer, that Gregor had the best intentions of returning to his room immediately and that it was not necessary to drive him back; if only the door were opened for him, he would disappear at once.

But his father was in no mood to notice such subtleties; "Ah!" he cried as he entered, in a tone that sounded as if he were at once furious and glad. Gregor turned his head away from the door and lifted it toward his father. He had not really imagined his father looking like this, as he stood in front of him now; admittedly Gregor had been too absorbed recently in his newfangled crawling to bother as much as before about events in the rest of the house and should really have been prepared to find some changes. And yet, and yet—was this still his father? Was this the same man who in the old days used to lie wearily buried in bed when Gregor left on a business trip; who greeted him
60 on his return in the evening, sitting in his bathrobe in the armchair, who actually had difficulty getting to his feet but as a sign of joy only lifted up his arms; and who, on the rare occasions when the whole family went out for a walk, on a few Sundays in June and on the major hol-

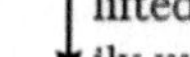

Literary Analysis
Modernism and Literature of the Fantastic In what ways does Gregor's surprise about his father's changed appearance reflect the fantastic nature of this story?

ENRICHMENT: Biography Connection

Herman Kafka

In 1919, Kafka wrote "Letter to His Father"—an actual letter, but one that he never mailed. In the letter, he writes:

> There is only one episode in the early years of which I have a direct memory.... One night I kept on whimpering for water.... After several vigorous threats had failed to have any effect, you took me out of bed, carried me out onto the *pavlatche* [balcony on the inner courtyard], and left me there alone for a while in my nightshirt, outside the shut door. I am not going to say that this was wrong—perhaps there was really no other way of getting peace and quiet that night—but I mention it as typical of your methods of bringing up a child and their effect on me.... Years afterward, I suffered from the tormenting fancy that the huge man, my father, ... would come almost for no reason at all and take me out of bed in the night and carry me out onto the *pavlatche,* and that consequently I meant absolutely nothing as far as he was concerned.

idays, used to shuffle along with great effort between Gregor and his mother, who were slow walkers themselves, always a little more slowly than they, wrapped in his old overcoat, always carefully planting down his crutch-handled cane, and, when he wanted to say something, nearly always stood still and assembled his escort around him? Now, however, he was holding himself very erect, dressed in a tight-fitting blue uniform with gold buttons, the kind worn by messengers at banking concerns; above the high stiff collar of the jacket his heavy chin protruded; under his bushy eyebrows his black eyes darted bright, piercing glances; his usually rumpled white hair was combed flat, with a scrupulously exact, gleaming part. He threw his cap—which was adorned with a gold monogram, probably that of a bank—in an arc across the entire room onto the couch, and with the tails of his long uniform jacket slapped back, his hands in his pants pockets, went for Gregor with a sullen look on his face. He probably did not know himself what he had in mind; still he lifted his feet unusually high off the floor, and Gregor staggered at the gigantic size of the soles of his boots. But he did not linger over this, he had known right from the first day of his new life that his father considered only the strictest treatment called for in dealing with him. And so he ran ahead of his father, stopped when his father stood still, and scooted ahead again when his father made even the slightest movement. In this way they made more than one tour of the room, without anything decisive happening; in fact the whole
61 movement did not even have the appearance of a chase because of its slow tempo. So Gregor kept to the floor for the time being, especially since he was afraid that his father might interpret a flight onto the walls or the ceiling as a piece of particular nastiness. Of course Gregor had to admit that he would not be able to keep up even this running for long, for whenever his father took one step, Gregor had to execute countless movements. He was already beginning to feel winded, just as in the old days he had not had very reliable lungs. As he now staggered around, hardly keeping his eyes open in order to gather all his strength for the running; in his obtuseness[6] not thinking of any escape other than by running; and having almost forgotten that the walls were at his disposal, though here of course they were blocked up with elaborately carved furniture full of notches and points—at that moment a lightly flung object hit the floor right near him and rolled in front of him. It was an apple; a second one came flying right after it; Gregor stopped dead with fear; further running was useless, for his father was determined to bombard him. He had filled his pockets from the fruit bowl on the buffet and was now pitching one apple after another, for the time being without taking good aim. These little red apples rolled around on the floor as if electrified, clicking into each other. One apple, thrown weakly, grazed Gregor's back and slid off harmlessly. But the very next one that came flying after it literally forced its way into Gregor's back;

Reading Strategy
Applying the Author's Biography How might Kafka have drawn on personal experience to describe this encounter between Gregor and his father?

62 **Reading Check**

What objects does Mr. Samsa throw at Gregor?

6. **obtuseness** (äb to͞os′ nes) *n.* slowness to understand or perceive.

61 Reading Strategy

Applying the Author's Biography

- Explain to students that Franz Kafka was thin and short. His father and the other men in his family were generally tall, strong men with loud voices. Ask students how Kafka's attitude toward his father's physical presence is reflected in this passage.
  Answer: Kafka's intimidation by his father's presence might be reflected in the description of Gregor "stagger[ing] at the gigantic size of the soles of [his father's] boots," and the description of Gregor's need to "gather all his strength for the running."
- Ask students the Reading Strategy question on p. 1005: How might Kafka have drawn on personal experience to describe this encounter between Gregor and his father?
  Answer: As a child, Kafka might have been frightened by his father, especially if Kafka believed he had done something wrong. We see this anxiety as Gregor attempts to escape his father's anger.

62 Reading Check

Answer: Mr. Samsa throws apples at Gregor.

CUSTOMIZE INSTRUCTION FOR UNIVERSAL ACCESS

For Special Needs Students	For Less Proficient Readers
Organize students into pairs, and assign each pair a portion of Part II. Have each pair review their assigned pages and identify one or two important events that occur on each page. Then, have students meet as a group to discuss their events and create a timeline on the board.	Have students meet in groups to review events that have occurred thus far in the story. Then, ask students to discuss what they think will happen in Part III, the final section of the story. Have students work individually to write their own predictions, and encourage them to refer to and revise these predictions as they read Part III.

Answers for p. 1006

Review and Assess

1. Possible responses: Some students will feel sympathy for Gregor because he has become isolated through no fault of his own. He longs for human contact, but it is forever out of his reach. Others will feel disgust for Gregor because he is a filthy and grotesquely huge insect.
2. **(a)** Gregor learns that his family has money to live on. **(b)** Gregor is relieved that the family is not destitute but realizes that the day that he could have left his job would have been much closer. **(c)** The news shows that Gregor was already alienated from his family: The family did not confide in Gregor but kept information secret that would have lessened his burden.
3. **(a)** Grete hurries straight to the window, opens it, and stands breathing in the fresh air. **(b)** The room must have a bad odor because of Gregor. **(c)** Gregor is becoming more insectlike and repulsive; he is intolerable even to his own sister.
4. **(a)** Gregor is determined to keep the magazine picture of the woman in the fur hat and boa. **(b)** Possible response: The picture might symbolize a relationship with a woman, Gregor's human life, or humanity in general.
5. **(a)** Grete did little but dress in pretty clothes, sleep late, help around the apartment, enjoy a few amusements, and play her violin. **(b)** Possible response: Grete has become more responsible while caring for Gregor. She has shown courage in entering his room every day. She has shown good judgment and empathy in providing what he needs. **(c)** Possible response: These changes are positive: They demonstrate strength of character and Grete's willingness to care for her isolated and helpless brother.

Gregor tried to drag himself away, as if the startling, unbelievable pain might disappear with a change of place; but he felt nailed to the spot and stretched out his body in a complete confusion of all his senses. With his last glance he saw the door of his room burst open, as his mother rushed out ahead of his screaming sister, in her chemise, for his sister had partly undressed her while she was unconscious in order to let her breathe more freely; saw his mother run up to his father and on the way her unfastened petticoats slide to the floor one by one; and saw as, stumbling over the skirts, she forced herself onto his father, and embracing him, in complete union with him—but now Gregor's sight went dim—her hands clasping his father's neck, begged for Gregor's life.

Review and Assess

Thinking About Part II

1. **Respond:** Do you primarily feel sympathy or disgust for Gregor? Explain your answer.
2. **(a) Recall:** What surprising news about the family's finances does Gregor learn? **(b) Interpret:** With what mixed feelings does Gregor react to this news? **(c) Analyze:** What does this news suggest about Gregor's alienation from his family even before his metamorphosis?
3. **(a) Interpret:** Each time Grete enters Gregor's room, how does she react? **(b) Draw Conclusions:** What does her reaction suggest about the condition and smell of the room? **(c) Analyze:** In what ways does this situation emphasize Gregor's isolation from humanity?
4. **(a) Recall:** Which item in his room is Gregor determined to keep? **(b) Interpret:** What emotions, relationships, or desires might this item symbolize to him? Explain.
5. **(a) Generalize:** Why might Grete's parents have seen her as "useless" prior to Gregor's transformation? **(b) Compare and Contrast:** In what ways has Grete changed as a result of Gregor's transformation? **(c) Evaluate:** Are these changes positive or negative? Explain.

ENRICHMENT: Philosophy Connection

The Apple

The apple is an important symbol in Western literature. The "forbidden fruit" in the Garden of Eden is traditionally depicted as an apple. When Adam and Eve disobediently eat the fruit, they gain wisdom, but they suffer guilt and are driven from the Garden. Writers often use the apple to symbolize the attainment of wisdom and a subsequent fall from grace. In "The Metamorphosis," the apple functions similarly. The apple that lodges in Gregor's exoskeleton represents his knowledge that his role in the family has changed. He no longer occupies the role of breadwinner, nor does the family consider him a son and brother.

Now his only role is that of pest. Gregor carries this knowledge—figuratively and literally—with him to his death.

Review and Anticipate

By the end of Part II, Gregor's situation has reached a crisis. His enraged father has attacked Gregor, causing a severe injury. His furious sister has tried both to care for Gregor and to protect her parents. Although the sight of him sickens her, Gregor's mother now pleads for his life. Do you think Gregor can survive in this environment? Do you think the family can tolerate the strain? If not, what does their future hold? Read Part III, in which the story concludes, to find out.

63

Part III

Gregor's serious wound, from which he suffered for over a month—the apple remained imbedded in his flesh as a visible souvenir since no one dared to remove it—seemed to have reminded even his father that Gregor was a member of the family, in spite of his present pathetic and repulsive shape, who could not be treated as an enemy; that, on the contrary, it was the commandment of family duty to swallow their disgust and endure him, endure him and nothing more.

And now, although Gregor had lost some of his mobility probably for good because of his wound, and although for the time being he needed long, long minutes to get across his room, like an old war veteran—crawling above ground was out of the question—for this deterioration of his situation he was granted compensation which in his view was entirely satisfactory: every day around dusk the living-room door—which he was in the habit of watching closely for an hour or two beforehand—was opened, so that, lying in the darkness of his room, invisible from the living room, he could see the whole family sitting at the table under the lamp and could listen to their conversation, as it were with general permission; and so it was completely different from before.

64 Of course these were no longer the animated conversations of the old days, which Gregor used to remember with a certain nostalgia in small hotel rooms when he'd had to throw himself wearily into the damp bedding. Now things were mostly very quiet. Soon after supper his father would fall asleep in his armchair; his mother and sister would caution each other to be quiet; his mother, bent low under the light, sewed delicate lingerie for a clothing store; his sister, who had taken a job as a salesgirl, was learning shorthand and French in the evenings in order to attain a better position some time in the future. Sometimes his father woke up, and as if he had absolutely no idea that he had been asleep, said to his mother, "Look how long you're sewing again today!" and went right back to sleep, while mother and sister smiled wearily at each other.

Literary Analysis
Modernism Would you consider this after-supper scene a slice of real modern life? Why or why not?

65 **Reading Check**
What does the family now allow Gregor to do every day around dusk?

63 About the Selection

Gregor remains in the Samsa family's midst, but as the family falls into a routine, they think less and less about him. While Gregor's metamorphosis continues, Mr. Samsa, Mrs. Samsa, and Grete are undergoing transformations of their own.

64 Literary Analysis

Modernism

- Ask students to read the bracketed passage on p. 1007.
- Point out that Gregor is now more a part of the family. Gregor was treated as an outcast at first, locked in and isolated from the family at all times. Now, the family opens Gregor's door so he can observe and listen to them. Ask students to share some verbal descriptions of their own families after a meal.
- Ask students the Literary Analysis question on p. 1007: Would you consider this after-supper scene a slice of real modern life? Why or why not?
  Possible response: This scene includes some typical patterns of traditional family life: a man resting from his work, a woman working for a second income, a daughter studying to improve her job prospects. This simulation of "real family life," however, orbits around the absurdity of Gregor's predicament. Gregor's current state as it relates to his family may be viewed simply as an exaggeration of the breakdown in modern familial relationships.

65 Reading Check

Answer: The family allows Gregor to sit and watch them and listen to their conversations.

CUSTOMIZE INSTRUCTION FOR UNIVERSAL ACCESS

For Special Needs Students	For Less Proficient Readers
Discuss with students Gregor's injuries and general health. Then, ask students to work in groups to list the events that have led to his current condition. To help clarify the events in the story and Gregor's condition, refer students back to the last page of Part I (p. 991), the first page of Part II (p. 992), the last page of Part II (p. 1006), and the first page of Part III (p. 1007). Have students consider other factors that have contributed to Gregor's ill health, such as the foods he consumes and his environment.	Discuss with students Gregor's injuries and have them summarize his general health. Remind students that Gregor has suffered two injuries—one at the end of Part I, when Mr. Samsa pushes him through the door, and another at the end of Part II, when Mr. Samsa throws an apple at him. Explain to students that Gregor continues to grow weaker and weaker. Have students discuss whether they think Gregor's condition will worsen or improve, and ask them to support their responses with details from the text.

66 Literary Analysis

Modernism and Literature of the Fantastic

- Ask a volunteer to read aloud the bracketed passage on pp. 1008–1009. Ask: Could a modern American family face similar worries as those of the Samsas?
  Possible response: Yes; a modern American family could face the same financial concerns as those of the Samsa family. The Samsa family's concern about moving a giant bug out of the apartment without detection is not one any other family is likely to experience, however.
- Ask students the Literary Analysis question on p. 1008: In what ways does this discussion of the family's struggles mix reality and fantasy?
  Answer: The discussion involves ordinary things that might happen in modern life, except for the issue of how to relocate Gregor. This topic acts as a reminder of Gregor's fantastic transformation from human to insect.

With a kind of perverse obstinacy his father refused to take off his official uniform even in the house; and while his robe hung uselessly on the clothes hook, his father dozed, completely dressed, in his chair, as if he were always ready for duty and were waiting even here for the voice of his superior. As a result his uniform, which had not been new to start with, began to get dirty in spite of all the mother's and sister's care, and Gregor would often stare all evening long at this garment, covered with stains and gleaming with its constantly polished gold buttons, in which the old man slept most uncomfortably and yet peacefully.

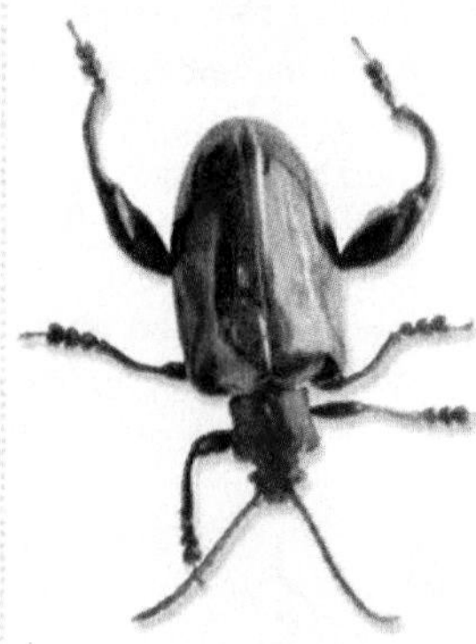

As soon as the clock struck ten, his mother tried to awaken his father with soft encouraging words and then persuade him to go to bed, for this was no place to sleep properly, and his father badly needed his sleep, since he had to be at work at six o'clock. But with the obstinacy that had possessed him ever since he had become a messenger, he always insisted on staying at the table a little longer, although he invariably fell asleep and then could be persuaded only with the greatest effort to exchange his armchair for bed. However much mother and sister might pounce on him with little admonitions,[7] he would slowly shake his head for a quarter of an hour at a time, keeping his eyes closed, and would not get up. Gregor's mother plucked him by the sleeves, whispered blandishments into his ear, his sister dropped her homework in order to help her mother, but all this was of no use. He only sank deeper into his armchair. Not until the women lifted him up under his arms did he open his eyes, look alternately at mother and sister, and usually say, "What a life. So this is the peace of my old age." And leaning on the two women, he would get up laboriously, as if he were the greatest weight on himself, and let the women lead him to the door, where, shrugging them off, he would proceed independently, while Gregor's mother threw down her sewing and his sister her pen as quickly as possible so as to run after his father and be of further assistance.

Who in this overworked and exhausted family had time to worry about Gregor any more than was absolutely necessary? The household was stinted more and more; now the maid was let go after all; a gigantic bony cleaning woman with white hair fluttering about her head came mornings and evenings to do the heaviest work; his mother took care of everything else, along with all her sewing. It even happened that various pieces of family jewelry, which in the old days his mother and sister had been overjoyed to wear at parties and celebrations, were sold, as Gregor found out one evening from the general discussion of the prices they had fetched. But the biggest complaint was always that they could not give up the apartment, which was much too big for their present needs, since no one could figure out how Gregor was supposed to be moved. But Gregor understood easily that it was not only consideration for him which prevented their moving, for he could easily have been transported in a suitable crate with a few air holes; what mainly

Literary Analysis
Modernism and Literature of the Fantastic
In what ways does this discussion of the family's struggles mix reality and fantasy?

7. **admonitions** (ad′ mə nish′ ənz) *n.* mild rebukes; reprimands.

prevented the family from moving was their complete hopelessness and the thought that they had been struck by a misfortune as none of their relatives and acquaintances had ever been hit. What the world demands of poor people they did to the utmost of their ability; his father brought breakfast for the minor officials at the bank, his mother sacrificed herself to the underwear of strangers, his sister ran back and forth behind the counter at the request of the customers; but for anything more than this they did not have the strength. And the wound in Gregor's back began to hurt anew when mother and sister, after getting his father to bed, now came back, dropped their work, pulled their chairs close to each other and sat cheek to cheek; when his mother, pointing to Gregor's room, said, "Close that door, Grete"; and when Gregor was back in darkness, while in the other room the women mingled their tears or stared dry-eyed at the table.

Gregor spent the days and nights almost entirely without sleep. Sometimes he thought that the next time the door opened he would take charge of the family's affairs again, just as he had done in the old days; after this long while there again appeared in his thoughts the boss and the manager, the salesmen and the trainees, the handyman who was so dense, two or three friends from other firms, a chambermaid in a provincial hotel—a happy fleeting memory—a cashier in a millinery store,[8] whom he had courted earnestly but too slowly—they all appeared, intermingled with strangers or people he had already forgotten; but instead of helping him and his family, they were all inaccessible, and he was glad when they faded away. At other times he was in no mood to worry about his family, he was completely filled with rage at his miserable treatment, and although he could not imagine anything that would pique his appetite, he still made plans for getting into the pantry to take what was coming to him, even if he wasn't hungry. No longer considering what she could do to give Gregor a special treat, his sister, before running to busi-
67 ness every morning and afternoon, hurriedly shoved any old food into Gregor's room with her foot; and in the evening, regardless of whether the food had only been toyed with or—the most usual case—had been left completely untouched, she swept it out with a swish of the broom. The cleaning up of Gregor's room, which she now always did in the evenings, could not be done more hastily. Streaks of dirt ran along the walls, fluffs of dust and filth lay here and there on the floor. At first, whenever his sister came in, Gregor would place himself in those corners which were particularly offending, meaning by his position in a sense to reproach her. But he could probably have stayed there for weeks without his sister's showing any improvement; she must have seen the dirt as clearly as he did, but she had just decided to leave it. At the same time she made sure—with an irritableness that was completely new to her and which had in fact infected the whole family—that the cleaning of Gregor's room remain her province. One time his mother had submitted Gregor's room to a major housecleaning, which she managed

Literary Analysis
Modernism How do the conditions in which Gregor is now living suggest that his alienation from his family and his former life has reached a new low?

Reading Check
For what reason does the family say they cannot move from their current apartment?

8. **millinery** (mil' ə ner' ē) **store** one that sells women's hats.

67 Literary Analysis

Modernism

- Read the first line of the bracketed passage aloud. Ask students to discuss how Gregor's rage is a symptom of his alienation.
  Answer: Gregor's rage is uncharacteristic and thus demonstrates how alienated from his old self Gregor has become.
- Then, ask students the Literary Analysis question on p. 1009: How do the conditions in which Gregor is now living suggest that his alienation from his family and his former life has reached a new low?
  Answer: Gregor's sister no longer gives him the attention that she gave him in the past. Gregor has been abandoned, and, as a result, he has ceased at times to worry about his family.

68  Reading Check

Answer: The family says they do not know how to move Gregor.

CUSTOMIZE INSTRUCTION FOR UNIVERSAL ACCESS

For Less Proficient Readers	For Advanced Readers
Explain to students that on p. 1009, Gregor is described as alternately angry and sad. Have students identify the occasions when he is angry and when he is sad, and discuss what Gregor is thinking about and why he is experiencing these intense feelings.	Have students discuss the dramatic fluctuations in Gregor's thoughts that occur on p. 1009. Then, have students discuss the significance of the images that come to Gregor's mind when he imagines that he is about to take charge of the family's affairs again. Ask students to consider whether Gregor is glad when these images fade away.

69 Critical Thinking

Analyze

- Have students describe what is happening in the bracketed passage on pp. 1009–1010. Then, ask: What motivated Gregor's mother to clean Gregor's room when it had been Grete's job?
  Answer: Mrs. Samsa saw the filthy conditions in which Gregor was living and could not allow him to live that way. Even though he has been transformed into something so alien, he is still her son.
- Ask students why Grete breaks into tears.
  Answer: Grete has endured the difficult task of taking care of Gregor all this time. When her mother cleans the room, she probably regards it as a criticism. She feels sorry for herself and is overwhelmed.
- Ask students why the family gets into such an uproar over Mrs. Samsa's good deed.
  Answer: The stress of the situation has pushed the family to its limits. The family's emotions are brought to the surface with little provocation.

70 ▶Critical Viewing

Answer: The dancer's "antennae" and her buglike facemask emphasize Gregor's physical transformation. The dancer's posture emphasizes the freedom Gregor experienced upon first using his insect legs.

only after employing a couple of pails of water—all this dampness, of course, irritated Gregor too and he lay prostrate, sour and immobile, on the couch—but his mother's punishment was not long in coming. For hardly had his sister noticed the difference in Gregor's room that evening than, deeply insulted, she ran into the living room and, in spite of her mother's imploringly uplifted hands, burst out in a fit of crying, which his parents—his father had naturally been startled out of his armchair—at first watched in helpless amazement; until they too got going; turning to the right, his father blamed his mother for not letting his sister clean Gregor's room; but turning to the left, he screamed at his sister that she would never again be allowed to clean Gregor's room; while his mother tried to drag his father, who was out of his mind with excitement, into the bedroom, his sister, shaken with sobs, hammered the table with her small fists; and Gregor hissed loudly with rage because it did not occur to any of them to close the door and spare him such a scene and a row. 69

But even if his sister, exhausted from her work at the store, had gotten fed up with taking care of Gregor as she used to, it was not necessary at all for his mother to take her place and still Gregor did not have to be neglected. For now the cleaning woman was there. This old widow, who thanks to her strong bony frame had probably survived the worst in a long life, was not really repelled by Gregor. Without being in the least inquisitive, she had once accidentally opened the door of Gregor's room, and at the sight of Gregor—who, completely taken by surprise, began to race back and forth although no one was chasing him—she had remained standing, with her hands folded on her stomach, marveling. From that time on she never failed to open the door a crack every morning and every evening and peek in hurriedly at Gregor. In the beginning she also used to call him over to her with words she probably considered friendly, like, "Come over here for a minute, you old dung beetle!" or "Look at that old dung beetle!" To forms of address like these Gregor would not respond but remained immobile where he was, as if the door had not been opened. If only they had given this cleaning woman orders to clean up his room every day, instead of letting her disturb him uselessly whenever the mood took her. Once, early in the morning—heavy rain, perhaps already a sign of approaching spring,

70 ▲ Critical Viewing
Which aspects of Gregor's transformation does this ballet adaptation emphasize? Explain. **[Interpret]**

ENRICHMENT: Literature Connection

Irony

Irony is a contrast between what is stated and what is meant or between what is expected to happen and what actually happens. In *irony of situation,* an event occurs that contradicts the expectations of the characters, of the reader, or of the audience. Point out to students that Gregor's family has often mistakenly viewed his actions as menacing. When Gregor does try to frighten the cleaning woman, he fails miserably, creating a humorous and tragic irony of situation.

was beating on the window panes—Gregor was so exasperated when the cleaning woman started in again with her phrases that he turned on her, of course slowly and decrepitly, as if to attack. But the cleaning woman, instead of getting frightened, simply lifted up high a chair near the door, and as she stood there with her mouth wide open, her intention was clearly to shut her mouth only when the chair in her hand came crashing down on Gregor's back. "So, is that all there is?" she asked when Gregor turned around again, and she quietly put the chair back in the corner.

Gregor now hardly ate anything anymore. Only when he accidentally passed the food laid out for him would he take a bite into his mouth just for fun, hold it in for hours, and then mostly spit it out again. At first he thought that his grief at the state of his room kept him off food, but it was the very changes in his room to which he quickly became adjusted. His family had gotten into the habit of putting in this room things for which they could not find any other place, and now there were plenty of these, since one of the rooms in the apartment had been rented to three boarders. These serious gentlemen—all three had long beards, as Gregor was able to register once through a crack in the door—were obsessed with neatness, not only in their room, but since they had, after all, moved in here, throughout the entire household and especially in the kitchen. They could not stand useless, let alone dirty junk. Besides, they had brought along most of their own household goods. For this reason many things had become superfluous, and though they certainly weren't salable, on the other hand they could not just be thrown out. All these things migrated into Gregor's room. Likewise the ash can and the garbage can from the kitchen. Whatever was not being used at the moment was just flung into Gregor's room by the cleaning woman, who was always in a big hurry; fortunately Gregor generally saw only the object involved and the hand that held it. Maybe the cleaning woman intended to reclaim the things as soon as she had
71 a chance or else to throw out everything together in one fell swoop, but in fact they would have remained lying wherever they had been thrown in the first place if Gregor had not squeezed through the junk and set it in motion, at first from necessity, because otherwise there would have been no room to crawl in, but later with growing pleasure, although after such excursions, tired to death and sad, he did not budge again for hours.

Since the roomers sometimes also had their supper at home in the common living room, the living-room door remained closed on certain evenings, but Gregor found it very easy to give up the open door, for on many evenings when it was opened he had not taken advantage of it, but instead, without the family's noticing, had lain in the darkest corner of his room. But once the cleaning woman had left the living-room door slightly open, and it also remained opened a little when the roomers came in in the evening and the lamp was lit. They sat down at the head of the table where in the old days his father, his mother, and Gregor had eaten, unfolded their napkins, and picked up their knives

Literary Analysis

Modernism Which details in this discussion of the state of his room suggest that Gregor has become useless or disposable? Explain.

72 

Reading Check

To whom has a room in the Samsa apartment been rented?

71 Literary Analysis

Modernism

- Ask students to read the bracketed passage on p. 1011. Then, ask students to discuss the purpose and connotations of a "junk room."
- Ask students the Literary Analysis question on p. 1011: Which details in this discussion of the state of his room suggest that Gregor has become useless or disposable? Explain.
  Answer: Gregor's family and the cleaning woman have begun placing junk and even trashcans in his room. These details suggest that the room is a place for useless, disposable things and imply that Gregor, too, is useless.
- Call students' attention to the line that describes Gregor's "growing pleasure" with crawling through the trash. Ask students how Gregor's response reveals his passage into another stage of alienation from human society.
  Answer: Insects are often found crawling through trash. Gregor's adoption and enjoyment of this habit indicates that his metamorphosis is nearly complete.

Monitor Progress Ask students how the presence of the three roomers emphasizes Gregor's alienation from society.
Answer: The roomers come from the outside world and want everything very clean and neat. Gregor is confined to his filthy room and has even begun to enjoy roaming through the accumulating trash, which exists because of the roomers.

72 Reading Check

Answer: A room has been rented to three gentlemen with long beards.

CUSTOMIZE INSTRUCTION FOR UNIVERSAL ACCESS

For Special Needs Students	For English Learners
Call students' attention to the ways Grete's behavior toward Gregor has changed in the course of the story. Students should cite specific examples from the text concerning how Grete feeds, cares for, and protects Gregor. Help students create a comparison and contrast chart to record their observations.	The term *boarder* may present a challenge for students because of the multiple meanings of the word *board*. Tell students that the word *board* can mean "daily meals supplied in exchange for pay." Ask students to work in pairs to find the definition for the word *boarder* and to discuss how it relates to the definition for *board* provided above. Then, have each student pair write two sentences using the word *boarder*.

73 Literary Analysis

Modernsim

- Tell students that many Modernists depict the individual as powerless. Read aloud the bracketed passage, and call students' attention to the roomers' behavior toward the Samsa family and remind them of the way Gregor's manager treated Gregor when he came into the home. Ask students how these parallel incidents reflect a Modernist view of the individual.
  Answer: Both examples of behavior show how the outside world looks down on the individual and assumes the right to control and belittle a person who lacks power.
- Ask students the Literary Analysis question on p. 1012: In what ways does the family's behavior toward the boarders reveal changes in their sense of identity?
  Answer: The family is no longer independent; they have become subservient to these three roomers, who are representatives of the outside world.

and forks. At once his mother appeared in the doorway with a platter of meat, and just behind her came his sister with a platter piled high with potatoes. A thick vapor steamed up from the food. The roomers bent over the platters set in front of them as if to examine them before eating, and in fact the one who sat in the middle, and who seemed to be 73 regarded by the other two as an authority, cut into a piece of meat while it was still on the platter, evidently to find out whether it was tender enough or whether it should perhaps be sent back to the kitchen. He was satisfied, and mother and sister, who had been watching anxiously, sighed with relief and began to smile.

The family itself ate in the kitchen. Nevertheless, before going into the kitchen, his father came into this room and, bowing once, cap in hand, made a turn around the table. The roomers rose as one man and mumbled something into their beards. When they were alone again, they ate in almost complete silence. It seemed strange to Gregor that among all the different noises of eating he kept picking up the sound of their chewing teeth, as if this were a sign to Gregor that you needed teeth to eat with and that even with the best make of toothless jaws you couldn't do a thing. "I'm hungry enough," Gregor said to himself, full of grief, "but not for these things. Look how these roomers are gorging themselves, and I'm dying!"

On this same evening—Gregor could not remember having heard the violin during the whole time—the sound of violin playing came from the kitchen. The roomers had already finished their evening meal, the one in the middle had taken out a newspaper, given each of the two others a page, and now, leaning back, they read and smoked. When the violin began to play, they became attentive, got up, and went on tiptoe to the door leading to the foyer, where they stood in a huddle. They must have been heard in the kitchen, for his father called, "Perhaps the playing bothers you, gentlemen? It can be stopped right away." "On the contrary," said the middle roomer. "Wouldn't the young lady like to come in to us and play in here where it's much roomier and more comfortable?" "Oh, certainly," called Gregor's father, as if he were the violinist. The boarders went back into the room and waited. Soon Gregor's father came in with the music stand, his mother with the sheet music, and his sister with the violin. Calmly his sister got everything ready for playing; his parents—who had never rented out rooms before and therefore behaved toward the roomers with excessive politeness—did not even dare sit down on their own chairs; his father leaned against the door, his right hand inserted between two buttons of his uniform coat, which he kept closed; but his mother was offered a chair by one of the roomers, and since she left the chair where the roomer just happened to put it, she sat in a corner to one side.

His sister began to play. Father and mother, from either side, attentively followed the movements of her hands. Attracted by the playing, Gregor had dared to come out a little further and already had his head in the living room. It hardly surprised him that lately he was showing so little consideration for the others; once such consideration had been

Literary Analysis
Modernism In what ways does the family's behavior toward the boarders reveal changes in their sense of identity?

ENRICHMENT: Music Connection

Kafka's Response to Music

Many people feel that the climax of "The Metamorphosis" is the scene in which Gregor is drawn out of his room by his sister's violin playing. Given the importance of this scene, it seems logical to conclude that Kafka himself had a deep love for music. Yet, in reality, Kafka failed in his attempts to learn to play the violin and the piano as a young man, and he felt unresponsive to music for the rest of his life. In his diary he wrote, "The essence of my unmusicalness consists in my inability to enjoy music connectedly; it only now and then has an effect on me, and how seldom it is a musical one. The natural effect of music on me is to circumscribe me with a wall, and its only constant influence on me is that, confined in this way, I am different from what I am when free.... There is, among the public, no such reverence for literature as there is for music."

his greatest pride. And yet he would never have had better reason to keep hidden; for now, because of the dust which lay all over his room and blew around at the slightest movement, he too was completely covered with dust; he dragged around with him on his back and along his sides fluff and hairs and scraps of food; his indifference to everything was much too deep for him to have gotten on his back and scrubbed himself clean against the carpet, as once he had done several times a day. And in spite of his state, he was not ashamed to inch out a little farther on the immaculate living-room floor.

Admittedly no one paid any attention to him. The family was completely absorbed by the violin-playing; the roomers, on the other hand, who at first had stationed themselves, hands in pockets, much too close behind his sister's music stand, so that they could all have followed the score, which certainly must have upset his sister, soon withdrew to the window, talking to each other in an undertone, their heads lowered, where they remained, anxiously watched by his father. It now seemed only too obvious that they were disappointed in their expectation of hearing beautiful or entertaining violin-playing, had had enough of the whole performance, and continued to let their peace be disturbed only out of politeness. Especially the way they all blew the cigar smoke out of their nose and mouth toward the ceiling suggested great nervousness. And yet his sister was playing so beautifully. Her face was inclined to one side, sadly and probingly her eyes followed the lines of music. Gregor crawled forward a little farther, holding his head close to the floor, so that it might be possible to catch her eye. Was he an animal, that music could move him so? He felt as if the way to the unknown nourishment he longed for were coming to light. He was determined to force himself on until he reached his sister, to pluck at her skirt, and to let her know in this way that she should bring her violin into his room, for no one here appreciated her playing the way he would appreciate it. He would never again let her out of his
75 room—at least not for as long as he lived; for once, his nightmarish looks would be of use to him; he would be at all the doors of his room at the same time and hiss and spit at the aggressors; his sister, however, should not be forced to stay with him, but would do so of her own free will; she should sit next to him on the couch, bending her ear down to him, and then he would confide to her that he had had the firm intention of sending her to the Conservatory, and that, if the catastrophe had not intervened, he would have announced this to everyone last Christmas—certainly Christmas had come and gone?—without taking notice of any objections. After this declaration his sister would burst into tears of emotion, and Gregor would raise himself up to her shoulder and kiss her on the neck which, ever since she started going out to work, she kept bare, without a ribbon or collar.

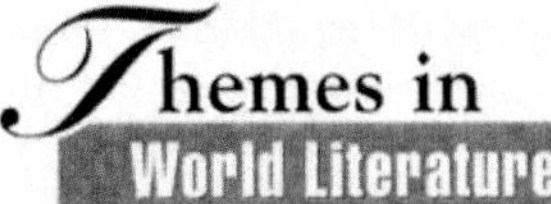

Themes in World Literature

74 *Magical Realism*

Franz Kafka tells Gregor Samsa's tale by mixing reality and fantasy. Many critics consider Kafka's approach a forerunner of **magical realism,** a literary movement that has gained popularity in the past few decades. Magical realism is especially strong in Latin America, where its best-known authors include Jorge Luis Borges, Julio Cortázar, Gabriel García Márquez, and Isabel Allende.

Magical realists create worlds that are based in reality and describe everyday settings. However, reality is often punctuated by "magical" elements—fantastic characters, events, or both. For example, in the García Márquez story "A Very Old Man With Enormous Wings," a couple takes captive an elderly, shabby-looking angel. Such magical elements can help readers gain deeper, more vivid insights into the nature of the world and human relationships.

Literary Analysis
Modernism The music appears to move Gregor to reach out for some meaning to his situation. Do you think that he will find that meaning? Explain.

76  **Reading Check**

What does Gregor's sister do to entertain the boarders?

74 Background

Magical Realism

For Gabriel García Márquez, the work of Franz Kafka was the key that opened the door to his own writing. It was the strange combination of fantastic and realistic details in "The Metamorphosis" that most impressed García Márquez: "The first line almost knocked me off the bed.... When I read the line I thought to myself that I didn't know anyone was allowed to write things like that. If I had known, I would have started writing a long time ago. So I immediately started writing short stories."

75 Literary Analysis

Modernism

- Read the bracketed passage aloud.
- Ask students the Literary Analysis question on p. 1013: The music appears to move Gregor to reach out for some meaning to his situation. Do you think that he will find that meaning? Explain.
  Possible response: No, because in Gregor's imagination he sees himself talking to Grete, keeping her with him, and kissing her on the neck. Gregor can't talk, and Grete would never submit to such close contact with him now.

76 ✓Reading Check

Answer: Grete plays her violin for the boarders.

CUSTOMIZE INSTRUCTION FOR UNIVERSAL ACCESS

For Less Proficient Readers	For English Learners	For Advanced Readers
On the board, write the words *score, performance,* and *Conservatory.* Explain to students that these words, which appear on p. 1013, refer to music. Guide students in using context clues to develop definitions for these terms. Then, have students use dictionaries to check their definitions.	Work with students to use simpler language to paraphrase difficult passages. Use the sentence on p. 1013 as a model: "He felt as if the way to the unknown nourishment he longed for were coming to light." Explain to students that in this sentence, the phrase "coming to light" is a figure of speech meaning "being revealed."	Some readers view "The Metamorphosis" as writing in reverse. The story begins with the climax. After this point everything can be considered falling action. Others claim that the climax occurs when Grete plays the violin. Have students offer their interpretations.

77 Literary Analysis

Modernism

- After students read the bracketed passage independently, point out that two of the roomers look to the third one for leadership and initiative. Have students discuss why some people need or rely on authorities and trendsetters to tell them what to think and what to do.
- Ask students the Literary Analysis question on p. 1014: How do the boarders' words and actions create new uncertainty for the Samsas?
Answer: The Samsas were relying on the boarders' rent to help the family financially. Now, the rent will not be paid, and the Samsas may face a lawsuit, which will cost them money as well. The Samsas must be wondering what they will do now.

78 Critical Thinking

Analyze

- Have a volunteer read aloud the bracketed passage.
- Call students' attention to the words *groping, staggered,* and *collapsed,* and list the words on the board.
- Remind students that a connotation is an association that a word calls to mind in addition to its dictionary meanings. Words can have positive and negative connotations. Ask: Do the listed words have positive or negative connotations?
Answer: The listed words have negative connotations.
- Ask: How does Kafka's word choice in this passage lend to the characterization of Mr. Samsa?
Possible response: The words *groping, staggered,* and *collapsed*—with their negative connotations—reinforce the physical and mental toll Gregor's transformation has taken on Mr. Samsa. These words suggest physical struggle, one which has left Mr. Samsa drained.

"Mr. Samsa!" the middle roomer called to Gregor's father and without wasting another word pointed his index finger at Gregor, who was slowly moving forward. The violin stopped, the middle roomer smiled first at his friends, shaking his head, and then looked at Gregor again. Rather than driving Gregor out, his father seemed to consider it more urgent to start by soothing the roomers although they were not at all upset, and Gregor seemed to be entertaining them more than the violin-playing. He rushed over to them and tried with outstretched arms to drive them into their room and at the same time with his body to block their view of Gregor. Now they actually did get a little angry—it was not clear whether because of his father's behavior or because of their dawning realization of having had without knowing it such a next door neighbor as Gregor. They demanded explanations from his father; in their turn they raised their arms, plucked excitedly at their beards, and, dragging their feet, backed off toward their room. In the meantime his sister had overcome the abstracted mood into which she had fallen after her playing had been so suddenly interrupted; and all at once, after holding violin and bow for a while in her slackly hanging hands and continuing to follow the score as if she were still playing, she pulled herself together, laid the instrument on the lap of her mother—who was still sitting in her chair, fighting for breath, her lungs violently heaving—and ran into the next room, which the roomers, under pressure from her father, were nearing more quickly than before. One could see the covers and bolsters on the beds, obeying his sister's practiced hands, fly up and arrange themselves. Before the boarders had reached the room, she had finished turning down the beds and had slipped out. Her father seemed once again to be gripped by his perverse obstinacy to such a degree that he completely forgot any respect still due his tenants. He drove them on and kept on driving until, already at the bedroom door, the middle boarder stamped his foot thunderingly and thus brought him to a standstill. "I herewith declare," he said, raising his hand and casting his eyes around for Gregor's mother and sister too, "that in view of the disgusting conditions prevailing in this apartment and family"—here he spat curtly and decisively on the floor—"I give notice as of now. Of course I won't pay a cent for the days I have been 77 living here, either; on the contrary, I shall consider taking some sort of action against you with claims that—believe me—will be easy to substantiate." He stopped and looked straight in front of him, as if he were expecting something. And in fact his two friends at once chimed in with the words, "We too give notice as of now." Thereupon he grabbed the door knob and slammed the door with a bang.

Gregor's father, his hands groping, staggered to his armchair and collapsed into it; it looked as if he were stretching himself out for his 78 usual evening nap, but the heavy drooping of his head, as if it had lost all support, showed that he was certainly not asleep. All this time Gregor had lain quietly at the spot where the roomers had surprised him. His disappointment at the failure of his plan—but perhaps also the weakness caused by so much fasting—made it impossible for him to

Literary Analysis
Modernism How do the boarders' words and actions create new uncertainty for the Samsas?

move. He was afraid with some certainty that in the very next moment a general <u>debacle</u> would burst over him, and he waited. He was not even startled by the violin as it slipped from under his mother's trembling fingers and fell off her lap with a reverberating clang.

"My dear parents," said his sister and by way of an introduction pounded her hand on the table, "things can't go on like this. Maybe you don't realize it, but I do. I won't pronounce the name of my brother in front of this monster, and so all I say is: we have to try to get rid of it. We've done everything humanly possible to take care of it and to put up with it; I don't think anyone can blame us in the least."

"She's absolutely right," said his father to himself. His mother, who still could not catch her breath, began to cough dully behind her hand, a wild look in her eyes.

His sister rushed over to his mother and held her forehead. His father seemed to have been led by Grete's words to more definite thoughts, had sat up, was playing with the cap of his uniform among the plates which were still lying on the table from the roomers' supper, and from time to time looked at Gregor's motionless form.

"We must try to get rid of it," his sister now said exclusively to her father, since her mother was coughing too hard to hear anything. "It will be the death of you two, I can see it coming. People who already have to work as hard as we do can't put up with this constant torture at home, too. I can't stand it anymore either." And she broke out crying so bitterly that her tears poured down onto her mother's face, which she wiped off with mechanical movements of her hand.

"Child," said her father kindly and with unusual understanding, "but what can we do?"

Gregor's sister only shrugged her shoulders as a sign of the bewildered mood that had now gripped her as she cried, in contrast with her earlier confidence.

"If he could understand us," said her father, half questioning; in the midst of her crying Gregor's sister waved her hand violently as a sign that that was out of the question.

"If he could understand us," his father repeated and by closing his eyes, absorbed his daughter's conviction of the impossibility of the idea, "then maybe we could come to an agreement with him. But the way things are——"

79 "It has to go," cried his sister. "That's the only answer, Father. You just have to try to get rid of the idea that it's Gregor. Believing it for so long, that is our real misfortune. But how can it be Gregor? If it were Gregor, he would have realized long ago that it isn't possible for human beings to live with such a creature, and he would have gone away of his own free will. Then we wouldn't have a brother, but we'd be able to go on living and honor his memory. But as things are, this animal persecutes us, drives the roomers away, obviously wants to occupy the whole apartment and for us to sleep in the gutter. Look, Father," she suddenly shrieked, "he's starting in again!" And in a fit of terror that was completely incomprehensible to Gregor, his sister abandoned even her

debacle (di bäk′ əl) *n.* overwhelming failure or defeat

Literary Analysis
Modernism Do you agree with Grete that Gregor could have gone away of his own free will? Why or why not?

80 
Reading Check
What action against Gregor does Grete insist the family take?

79 Literary Analysis

Modernism

- Read aloud the bracketed passage.
- Discuss the plan that Grete and Mr. Samsa are formulating.
  Ask: What can you infer from Mr. Samsa's "half questioning" whether or not Gregor can understand them? Is this questioning consistent with Mr. Samsa's previous behavior?
  Answer: Mr. Samsa half questions his own assumption that Gregor is unable to communicate with the family. This questioning is somewhat inconsistent with Mr. Samsa's behavior because he has previously acted as though Gregor could understand nothing. However, it is Mr. Samsa's own selfish interests that now cause this questioning of his prior assumptions. Mr. Samsa's longing for communication with Gregor is not based on any desire to repair the relationship with his son but rather to rid the family of Gregor altogether.
- Then, ask students the Literary Analysis question on p. 1015: Do you agree with Grete that Gregor could have gone away of his own free will? Why or why not?
  Possible responses: Yes; no one would have stopped Gregor, and he could have survived like any other insect. No; Gregor is so huge and helpless that someone surely would have killed him. Besides, Gregor was injured and probably could not have fed himself.

80  Reading Check

Answer: Grete insists that they get rid of Gregor.

CUSTOMIZE INSTRUCTION FOR UNIVERSAL ACCESS

For English Learners	For Gifted/Talented Students
Read aloud to students the first full paragraph on p. 1015. Call students' attention to Grete's use of the pronoun *it* when referring to Gregor. Explain that *it* is a gender-neutral pronoun that indicates that the object to which it refers is neither male nor female. Help students understand that Grete's use of the pronoun *it* depersonalizes Gregor, making it easier for the family to take action against him. Guide them to the conclusion that the Samsas see Gregor's metamorphosis as complete. He is no longer human; he is a thing.	The scene describing Gregor's slow movement toward the violin, his discovery by the roomers, Mr. Samsa's response, and Grete's tears and rejection of Gregor is especially vivid and intense. Organize students into groups, and have them study the scene. Then, ask students to assign roles and perform this scene for the class.

81 Literary Analysis

Modernism

- Remind students that Modernists attempt to capture the realities of modern life. Emphasize that these realities often are conveyed through descriptions.
- Have students read the bracketed passage.
- Then, ask students the Literary Analysis question on p. 1016: How does this description of Gregor's struggles reveal that his family no longer regards him as even remotely human? Explain.
  Answer: Gregor struggles greatly to turn around and walk the few feet back to his room. He is in pain, and yet no one makes an effort to help him.

mother, literally shoved herself off from her chair, as if she would rather sacrifice her mother than stay near Gregor, and rushed behind her father, who, upset only by her behavior, also stood up and half-lifted his arms in front of her as if to protect her.

But Gregor had absolutely no intention of frightening anyone, let alone his sister. He had only begun to turn around in order to trek back to his room; certainly his movements did look peculiar, since his ailing condition made him help the complicated turning maneuver along with his head, which he lifted up many times and knocked against the floor. He stopped and looked around. His good intention seemed to have been recognized; it had only been a momentary scare. Now they all watched him, silent and sad. His mother lay in her armchair, her legs stretched out and pressed together, her eyes almost closing from exhaustion; his father and his sister sat side by side, his sister had put her arm around her father's neck.

81 Now maybe they'll let me turn around, Gregor thought and began his labors again. He could not repress his panting from the exertion, and from time to time he had to rest. Otherwise no one harassed him, he was left completely on his own. When he had completed the turn, he immediately began to crawl back in a straight line. He was astonished at the great distance separating him from his room and could not understand at all how, given his weakness, he had covered the same distance a little while ago almost without realizing it. Constantly intent only on rapid crawling, he hardly noticed that not a word, not an exclamation from his family interrupted him. Only when he was already in the doorway did he turn his head—not completely, for he felt his neck stiffening; nevertheless he still saw that behind him nothing had changed except that his sister had gotten up. His last glance ranged over his mother, who was now fast asleep.

Literary Analysis
Modernism How does this description of Gregor's struggles reveal that his family no longer regards him as even remotely human? Explain.

He was hardly inside his room when the door was hurriedly slammed shut, firmly bolted, and locked. Gregor was so frightened at the sudden noise behind him that his little legs gave way under him. It was his sister who had been in such a hurry. She had been standing up straight, ready and waiting, then she had leaped forward nimbly. Gregor had not even heard her coming, and she cried "Finally!" to her parents as she turned the key in the lock.

"And now?" Gregor asked himself, looking around in the darkness. He soon made the discovery that he could no longer move at all. It did not surprise him; rather, it seemed unnatural that until now he had actually been able to propel himself on these thin little legs. Otherwise he felt relatively comfortable. He had pains, of course, throughout his whole body, but it seemed to him that they were gradually getting fainter and fainter and would finally go away altogether. The rotten apple in his back and the inflamed area around it, which were completely covered with fluffy dust, already hardly bothered him. He thought back on his family with deep emotion and love. His conviction that he would have to disappear was, if possible, even firmer than his sister's. He remained in this state of empty and peaceful reflection until

ENRICHMENT: Biography Connection

Grete Samsa

In a letter to a woman named Grete Bloch, Kafka discussed the role of Gregor's sister in "The Metamorphosis." He wrote, "Whether you should be looking forward to the 'story' ['The Metamorphosis'], I don't know.... Incidentally, the heroine's name is Grete and she doesn't discredit you, at least not in the first section. Later on, though, when the agony becomes too great, she withdraws, embarks on a life of her own, and leaves the one who needs her."

the tower clock struck three in the morning. He still saw that outside the window everything was beginning to grow light. Then, without his consent, his head sank down to the floor, and from his nostrils streamed his last weak breath.

82

When early in the morning the cleaning woman came—in sheer energy and impatience she would slam all the doors so hard although she had often been asked not to, that once she had arrived, quiet sleep was no longer possible anywhere in the apartment—she did not at first find anything out of the ordinary on paying Gregor her usual short visit. She thought that he was deliberately lying motionless, pretending that his feelings were hurt; she credited him with unlimited intelligence. Because she happened to be holding the long broom, she tried from the doorway to tickle Gregor with it. When this too produced no results, she became annoyed and jabbed Gregor a little, and only when she had shoved him without any resistance to another spot did she begin to take notice. When she quickly became aware of the true state of things, she opened her eyes wide, whistled softly, but did not dawdle; instead, she tore open the door of the bedroom and shouted at the top of her voice into the darkness: "Come and have a look, it's croaked; it's lying there, dead as a doornail!"

The couple Mr. and Mrs. Samsa sat up in their marriage bed and had a struggle overcoming their shock at the cleaning woman before they could finally grasp her message. But then Mr. and Mrs. Samsa hastily scrambled out of bed, each on his side, Mr. Samsa threw the blanket around his shoulders, Mrs. Samsa came out in nothing but her nightgown; dressed this way, they entered Gregor's room. In the meantime the door of the living room had also opened, where Grete had been sleeping since the roomers had moved in; she was fully dressed, as if she had not been asleep at all; and her pale face seemed to confirm this. "Dead?" said Mrs. Samsa and looked inquiringly at the cleaning woman, although she could scrutinize everything for herself and could recognize the truth even without scrutiny. "I'll say," said the cleaning
84 woman, and to prove it she pushed Gregor's corpse with her broom a good distance sideways. Mrs. Samsa made a movement as if to hold the broom back but did not do it. "Well," said Mr. Samsa, "now we can thank God!" He crossed himself, and the three women followed his example. Grete, who never took her eyes off the corpse, said, "Just look how thin he was. Of course he didn't eat anything for such a long time. The food came out again just the way it went in." As a matter of fact, Gregor's body was completely flat and dry; this was obvious now for the first time, really, since the body was no longer raised up by his little legs and nothing else distracted the eye.

83 **▲ Critical Viewing**
Compare and contrast this depiction of the scene in which the cleaning woman discovers Gregor's body with Kafka's description of the event. **[Compare and Contrast]**

85 **✔ Reading Check**
Before he dies, what final thoughts about his family does Gregor have?

82 Background

Art

Promena, by Otto Coester

Coester's illustration juxtaposes bold lines, grotesque figures, and distorted perspectives with realistic elements to capture the bizarre and horrifying nature of Gregor's transformation.

Use the following questions for discussion:

- What images from the story does the artist evoke?
  Answer: The artist evokes the cleaning woman's shocked reaction, the family's conflicted attitude, and the cramped living conditions.
- What is the mood of this illustration?
  Possible responses: The illustration is comical because of the exaggerated figures and whimsical details, such as the cleaning woman's patterned clothing. The illustration is nightmarish because of Gregor's gruesome position and the family's disturbed expressions.

83 ▶ Critical Viewing

Answer: The description and illustration are similar. The picture depicts the moment when the cleaning woman is standing over Gregor's body with her broom, apparently explaining his death to Mr. and Mrs. Samsa and Grete, who stand in the doorways.

84 Critical Thinking

Infer

- Call students' attention to Mr. Samsa's words "'now we can thank God!'" Ask: Is he relieved to be rid of Gregor, or is he grateful that Gregor is now free of pain and misery? Explain.
  Possible response: Mr. Samsa is relieved to be rid of Gregor.
- When the cleaning woman reaches out with her broom to push Gregor, Mrs. Samsa starts to hold back the broom, but then does not. Ask students what they can infer about Mrs. Samsa from this scene.
  Possible response: Mrs. Samsa wants to protect her son in his death, but she is alienated by his insect form.

85 ✔ Reading Check

Answer: Gregor thinks about his family with "deep emotion and love."

CUSTOMIZE INSTRUCTION FOR UNIVERSAL ACCESS

For Less Proficient Readers	For Advanced Readers
Tell students that Kafka often introduces variations in sentence length to emphasize sudden shifts in mood or in the pace at which events occur. For instance, he often uses long sentences to suggest a long, drawn-out struggle and then introduces short, dramatic sentences that signal an abrupt end to the struggle or to announce a drastic turn of events. Guide students as they find passages that feature this technique, and help them recognize the effect produced by the sentence variation in each passage.	Tell students that Kafka often introduces variations in sentence length to emphasize sudden shifts in mood or in the pace at which events occur. Challenge students to write a paragraph in which they vary the length of their sentences to emphasize an abrupt shift in mood or an unexpected turn of events. Students may want to describe a slowly developing sequence of events, such as a long-distance race. Invite students to share their paragraphs with the class.

86 Literary Analysis

Modernism and Literature of the Fantastic

- After reading aloud the bracketed passage, point out to students that Kafka presents an image of Gregor's "corpse" in the same paragraph as descriptions of spring, the "mildness," the "fresh air," and the "already very bright room." Ask: What does the description of this bright room imply has happened now that Gregor is dead? Explain.
  Answer: This description implies renewal. Now that Gregor is gone, the world is bright again.
- Review with students the important combination of imaginative and realistic details in "literature of the fantastic." Then, ask students the first Literary Analysis question on p. 1018: Does this scene following Gregor's death strike you as realistic? Explain.
  Possible response: The family's shock at the unexpected death is realistic. They are quiet and polite and want to spend a few moments alone together to comfort one another. Families in mourning often act like this—and yet they are mourning the death of a giant insect who burdened their lives, a fantastic aspect of the scene.

87 Literary Analysis

Modernism

- Call students' attention to the description of the Samsas marching arm-in-arm toward the roomer. Ask students what Kafka, as a Modernist writer, might have intended with this image.
  Answer: Kafka wanted to present these three characters as united against the outside world, which the roomers represent.
- Ask students the second Literary Analysis question on p. 1018: What is surprising about the effects of Gregor's death on the family?
  Answer: The family seems stronger. The Samsas are no longer willing to act servile toward the roomers or even to have them in their home.

"Come in with us for a little while, Grete," said Mrs. Samsa with a melancholy smile, and Grete, not without looking back at the corpse, followed her parents into their bedroom. The cleaning woman shut the door and opened the window wide. Although it was early in the morning, there was already some mildness mixed in with the fresh air. After all, it was already the end of March.

86 The three boarders came out of their room and looked around in astonishment for their breakfast; they had been forgotten. "Where's breakfast?" the middle roomer grumpily asked the cleaning woman. But she put her finger to her lips and then hastily and silently beckoned the boarders to follow her into Gregor's room. They came willingly and then stood, their hands in the pockets of their somewhat shabby jackets, in the now already very bright room, surrounding Gregor's corpse.

At that point the bedroom door opened, and Mr. Samsa appeared in his uniform, his wife on one arm, his daughter on the other. They all looked as if they had been crying; from time to time Grete pressed her face against her father's sleeve.

87 "Leave my house immediately," said Mr. Samsa and pointed to the door, without letting go of the women. "What do you mean by that?" said the middle roomer, somewhat nonplussed, and smiled with a sugary smile. The two others held their hands behind their back and incessantly rubbed them together, as if in joyful anticipation of a big argument, which could only turn out in their favor. "I mean just what I say," answered Mr. Samsa and with his two companions marched in a straight line toward the roomer. At first the roomer stood still and looked at the floor, as if the thoughts inside his head were fitting themselves together in a new order. "So, we'll go, then," he said and looked up at Mr. Samsa as if, suddenly overcome by a fit of humility, he were asking for further permission even for this decision. Mr. Samsa merely nodded briefly several times, his eyes wide open. Thereupon the roomer actually went immediately into the foyer, taking long strides; his two friends had already been listening for a while, their hands completely still, and now they went hopping right after him, as if afraid that Mr. Samsa might get into the foyer ahead of them and interrupt the contact with their leader. In the foyer all three took their hats from the coatrack, pulled their canes from the umbrella stand, bowed silently, and left the apartment. In a suspicious mood which proved completely unfounded, Mr. Samsa led the two women out onto the landing; leaning over the banister, they watched the three roomers slowly but steadily going down the long flight of stairs, disappearing on each landing at a particular turn of the stairway and a few moments later emerging again; the farther down they got, the more the Samsa family's interest in them wore off, and when a butcher's boy with a carrier on his head came climbing up the stairs with a proud bearing, toward them and then up on past them, Mr. Samsa and the women quickly left the banister and all went back, as if relieved, into their apartment.

Literary Analysis
Modernism and Literature of the Fantastic Does this scene following Gregor's death strike you as realistic? Explain.

Literary Analysis
Modernism What is surprising about the effects of Gregor's death on the family?

They decided to spend this day resting and going for a walk; they not only deserved a break in their work, they absolutely needed one. And so they sat down at the table and wrote three letters of excuse, Mr. Samsa to the management of the bank, Mrs. Samsa to her employer, and Grete to the store owner. While they were writing, the cleaning woman came in to say that she was going, since her morning's work was done. The three letter writers at first simply nodded without looking up, but as the cleaning woman still kept lingering, they looked up, annoyed. "Well?" asked Mr. Samsa. The cleaning woman stood smiling in the doorway, as if she had some great good news to announce to the family but would do so only if she were thoroughly questioned. The little ostrich feather which stood almost upright on her hat and which had irritated Mr. Samsa the whole time she had been with them swayed 88 lightly in all directions. "What do you want?" asked Mrs. Samsa, who inspired the most respect in the cleaning woman. "Well," the cleaning woman answered, and for good-natured laughter could not immediately go on, "look, you don't have to worry about getting rid of 89 the stuff next door. It's already been taken care of." Mrs. Samsa and Grete bent down over their letters, as if to continue writing; Mr. Samsa, who noticed that the cleaning woman was now about to start describing everything in detail, stopped her with a firmly outstretched hand. But since she was not going to be permitted to tell her story, she remembered that she was in a great hurry, cried, obviously insulted, "So long, everyone," whirled around wildly, and left the apartment with a terrible slamming of doors.

"We'll fire her tonight," said Mr. Samsa, but did not get an answer from either his wife or his daughter, for the cleaning woman seemed to have ruined their barely regained peace of mind. They got up, went to the window, and stayed there, holding each other tight. Mr. Samsa turned around in his chair toward them and watched them quietly for a while. Then he called, "Come on now, come over here. Stop brooding over the past. And have a little consideration for me, too." The women obeyed him at once, hurried over to him, fondled him, and quickly finished their letters.

Then all three of them left the apartment together, something they had not done in months, and took the trolley into the open country on the outskirts of the city. The car, in which they were the only

90 ▼ Critical Viewing
Which aspects of this photograph of Prague, Kafka's home, reflect the mood of this story? Explain. **[Connect]**

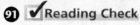

91 ✓Reading Check
After Gregor's death, what does Mr. Samsa tell the boarders?

88 Critical Thinking

Draw Conclusions

- Read the bracketed passage aloud. Then, ask: Why is the cleaning woman in such a good humor?
  Answer: The cleaning woman has evidently disposed of Gregor in a manner that might be particularly gruesome but which she finds satisfying and humorous.
- Ask: Why are the Samsas uninterested in hearing about how the cleaning woman disposed of Gregor's body?
  Answer: It would be an awful story for the family to hear.

89 Background

Art

Model of Prague, by Antonín Langweil

Langweil (1791–1837) created this 20-square-foot model of Prague between 1826 and 1837. It is currently on exhibit in The City of Prague Museum.

Use the following questions for discussion:

- What does this model indicate about living conditions in Prague?
  Possible response: Residents of Prague had to live in very close quarters. There appear to be no parks, yards, or gardens; only buildings, streets, and squares.
- On the basis of this model, does Prague look like a place you would like to live? Why or why not?
  Possible response: With its red roofs and intricate architecture, Prague looks like a very charming place to live. However, the cramped arrangement of the buildings and lack of natural, open spaces is unappealing.

90 ▶Critical Viewing

Answer: Like Kafka's story, the photograph suggests a feeling of isolation and detachment. The buildings of the city seem to loom over the empty city square.

91 ✓Reading Check

Answer: Mr. Samsa tells the boarders to leave his home.

CUSTOMIZE INSTRUCTION FOR UNIVERSAL ACCESS

For Advanced Readers

Emphasize to students that every member of the Samsa family undergoes some kind of metamorphosis in this story. Have students create a chart to track the changes that each character experiences. Then, have students write essays in which they discuss which character changes the most. Students can share their essays with the class or post their work on a classroom bulletin board.

ASSESS

Answers for p. 1020

Review and Assess

1. Possible responses: Some students will say that Gregor's family treated him very badly. They should have supported and cared for him. After all, he supported them for a long time. Other students will have more sympathy for the family, recognizing the stress the metamorphosis put on them.
2. **(a)** Gregor inches closer to be near Grete. **(b)** When he emerges from his room, Gregor explains to himself that he is indifferent to everything, including the feelings of others. As he moves closer, roused by the music, he feels that the music is the nourishment he craves. **(c)** Gregor's sudden passion for his sister's music, which was once so important to him, and his desire to seize and protect her while warding off his enemies, show an intense desire for human companionship and a will to assert himself.
3. **(a)** The family talks about their future and their prospects. **(b)** Possible response: The family is better off without Gregor. His death removes stress and worry from their lives, permits them more flexibility in where and how they live, and results in their taking responsibility for themselves.
4. **(a)** Gregor's body is thin and wasted away from lack of food. **(b)** Possible response: Gregor was neglected both physically and emotionally. Grete no longer tried to find food that Gregor would eat. He toyed with his food or left it entirely untouched. Gregor's room was scarcely cleaned. He was not welcomed when he tried to listen to his sister's music.
5. The Samsas' uplifted mood is a direct result of Gregor's death. Their happiness is at the expense of Gregor's happiness.
6. Possible response: The author might simply portray Gregor as a deeply depressed man who has emotionally and physically separated himself from his family.

passengers, was completely filled with warm sunshine. Leaning back comfortably in their seats, they discussed their prospects for the time to come, and it seemed on closer examination that these weren't bad at all, for all three positions—about which they had never really asked one another in any detail—were exceedingly advantageous and especially promising for the future. The greatest immediate improvement in their situation would come easily, of course, from a change in apartments; they would now take a smaller and cheaper apartment, but one better situated and in every way simpler to manage than the old one, which Gregor had picked for them. While they were talking in this vein, it occurred almost simultaneously to Mr. and Mrs. Samsa, as they watched their daughter getting livelier and livelier, that lately, in spite of all the troubles which had turned her cheeks pale, she had blossomed into a good-looking, shapely girl. Growing quieter and communicating almost unconsciously through glances, they thought that it would soon be time, too, to find her a good husband. And it was like a confirmation of their new dreams and good intentions when at the end of the ride their daughter got up first and stretched her young body.

Review and Assess

Thinking About Part III

1. **Respond:** How do you feel about the Samsa family's treatment of Gregor? Explain.
2. **(a) Recall:** What does Gregor do when he hears Grete playing the violin? **(b) Interpret:** How does he explain his own actions to himself? **(c) Analyze:** In what ways might this scene represent Gregor's desire to hold onto his humanity?
3. **(a) Recall:** What do Gregor's parents and sister discuss when they leave the apartment at the end of the story? **(b) Make a Judgment:** Is the family better off without Gregor? Explain.
4. **(a) Describe:** At the story's end, what is the state of Gregor's body? **(b) Support:** Which details in the story support the statement that Gregor suffers from a profound lack of nourishment, both physically and emotionally?
5. **Analyze:** The early spring setting and the Samsas' uplifted mood seem to set up a traditional happy ending. What makes this ending neither traditional nor happy?
6. **Modify:** How might an author portray similar relationship problems in a fictional family without the use of fantastic or supernatural details?

ASSESSMENT PRACTICE: Reading Comprehension

Comparing and Contrasting Texts (For more practice, see Test Preparation Workbook, p. 45.)

Have students read the following passage and the first sentence on p. 978.

> Seated on the bucket, my hands on the handle, the simplest kind of bridle, I propel myself with difficulty down the stairs; but once downstairs my bucket ascends, superbly, superbly …
> —"The Bucket Rider" by Franz Kafka

Both passages feature—

A allusions.
B sensory details.
C fantastical scenarios.
D figurative language.

The correct answer is C. Both passages feature fantastical scenarios.

Review and Assess

Literary Analysis

Modernism

1. Before the rise of **Modernism,** works of fiction often began with expositions, or background information. Why would an exposition make this story less effective?
2. Using a chart like the one shown, discuss two details from Part I of "The Metamorphosis" that show the realities of modern life.

Detail	What It Reveals About Modern Life
1.	
2.	

3. In a typical Modernist work, the narrator neither judges characters nor interprets events. Is this true of "The Metamorphosis"? Explain.
4. (a) How do Gregor's perceptions shape the portrayal of other characters? (b) Is Gregor's point of view reliable? Why or why not?

Connecting Literary Elements

5. (a) Which details in the opening scene, in which Gregor's parents and the office manager speak through the closed door, are realistic? (b) Which details are fantastic? (c) In what ways is this scene an example of **literature of the fantastic**?
6. (a) How does Gregor feel about his job? (b) Might his transformation be something he unconsciously wanted? Explain.

Reading Strategy

Applying the Author's Biography

7. Kafka's father was a domineering man who instilled in his son a sense of duty, as well as feelings of fear and guilt. (a) **Apply the author's biography** by stating whether Kafka's father served as a model for Mr. Samsa. (b) Which details support your point of view?
8. Kafka's father took a dim view of his son's literary aspirations. Does this story symbolically express this conflict? Explain.

Extend Understanding

9. **Cultural Connection:** Stories in which humans are changed into animals abound in mythology, literature, and popular culture. Select one such story, and discuss the emotions and personality traits that are associated with the transformation.

Quick Review

Modernism was a literary movement that expressed the uncertainties of modern life. Modernists used experimental techniques, avoided traditional plot structures, and drew no final conclusions or meaning.

Literature of the fantastic mixes imaginative and realistic elements to entertain and challenge readers.

When you **apply the author's biography** to his or her work, you think about the writing as an expression of the author's life and times.

Take It to the Net

PHSchool.com

Take the interactive self-test online to check your understanding of this selection.

Answers for p. 1021

Review and Assess

1. Possible response: The first sentence in the story is extremely startling. To precede this sentence with exposition would destroy its impact.
2. Possible response: Detail One: grueling job; people must make compromises. Detail Two: boss would come with the health-insurance doctor; employers do not trust their employees.
3. Yes; the narrator makes few direct statements about the characters and allows the events to unfold without drawing conclusions about their meaning.
4. **(a)** Possible response: Because the story uses the third-person limited point of view, Gregor's thoughts shape the portrayals of the other characters. For example, Gregor's affection for Grete results in an appealing portrayal of her. **(b)** Possible response: The point of view is not reliable because it is influenced by Gregor's personal biases, although the reader can generally see beyond these biases.
5. **(a)** Possible response: Realistic details include the plea with Gregor to get up, the boss's threats, and his mother's excuses and her concerns for his health. **(b)** Possible response: Fantastic details include the transformation of Gregor into an insect and his inability to talk and stand up. **(c)** Some of the details given are imaginative, while others are realistic. Fantastic literature mixes the two, as is done here.
6. **(a)** Gregor hates his job and wants to quit. **(b)** Gregor may have wanted a metamorphosis to occur because it provides him with an escape from a situation that he abhors. He can do nothing about this change, so he is free and absolved of guilt.
7. **(a)** It seems likely that Kafka's father served as a model for Mr. Samsa. **(b)** Like Kafka's father, Mr. Samsa is strict and domineering. He has instilled in Gregor a sense of duty and a feeling of guilt.
8. The story addresses the conflict through Grete's love of music. Despite his father's disapproval,

continued

continued from right column

Gregor encourages and supports Grete's interest and wants to send her to the Conservatory.

9. Possible response: During Odysseus' wanderings, he visits the island of the witch Circe, who turns his men into pigs. The men retain their human intelligence and suffer more because they know they are pigs.

ENRICHMENT: Further Reading

Other Works by Franz Kafka

We strongly encourage you to review any selection before assigning or recommending it to students.

The Castle

The Trial

Take It to the Net

Visit PHSchool.com for more information on Franz Kafka.

EXTEND

Answers for p. 1022

❶ Vocabulary Development

Word Analysis: Latin Prefix *im-*

1. not patient
2. a migrating, or moving, into a new place
3. bearing the mark of something pressed into the mind; strongly affected in mind or feelings
4. a state of not being balanced

Spelling Strategy

1. correct
2. correct
3. mackerel

Concept Development: Analogies

1. obstinacy
2. pallid
3. imminent
4. exuded
5. gyration
6. rectify
7. debacle
8. impracticable

❷ Grammar and Style

Practice

1. If I didn't hold back for my parents' sake; under what circumstances
2. since my train leaves at five; why
3. When he reached the edge; when
4. as you know; under what circumstances
5. wherever he wanted to go; where

Writing Application

Sample sentences: *When Gregor woke up*, he realized he was an insect. As soon as he struggled out of bed, Gregor looked through the door into the living room. He was hurting *because the apple had begun to rot*. *If he did not get food*, he would go hungry.

10TH GRADE For support in teaching the Grammar and Style Lesson to tenth graders, use **Writing and Grammar**, Platinum Level, Chapter 20, Section 2.

Integrate Language Skills

❶ Vocabulary Development Lesson

Word Analysis: Latin Prefix *im-*

The Latin prefix *im-* means "not," as in *immature*, or "into" or "toward," as in *impact*. Use your knowledge of this prefix to define each of the following words.

1. impatient
2. immigration
3. impressed
4. imbalance

Spelling Strategy

When words end in *-le* or *-el*, their ending sound is the same. When a *k* sound precedes the ending, as in *debacle*, *-le* usually is the correct spelling. For each word below, write the correct spelling. If the spelling is correct, write *correct*.

1. tickle
2. excel
3. mackerle

Concept Development: Analogies

In each item below, match the relationship between the first two words by selecting a word from the vocabulary list on page 977.

1. *Wisdom* is to *owl* as __?__ is to *donkey*.
2. *Dull* is to *sparkling* as __?__ is to *colorful*.
3. *Near* is to *place* as __?__ is to *time*.
4. *Exhaled* is to *breath* as __?__ is to *sweat*.
5. *Spiral* is to *shape* as __?__ is to *movement*.
6. *Offend* is to *insult* as __?__ is to *apology*.
7. *Achievement* is to *success* as __?__ is to *failure*.
8. *Improbable* is to *true* as __?__ is to *possible*.

❷ Grammar and Style Lesson

Adverb Clauses

Adverb clauses are subordinate clauses—groups of words containing a subject and a verb that cannot stand by themselves as sentences—that modify verbs, adjectives, or adverbs. Adverb clauses often begin with conjunctions such as *when*, *where*, *if*, *as if*, *as*, *because*, or *since* and explain *how*, *where*, *when*, *why*, *to what extent*, or *under what circumstances*.

CONJ. S V

Example: *When Gregor Samsa awoke one morning from unsettling dreams*, he found himself changed into a monstrous vermin. **[Tells when]**

Practice Identify the adverb clause in each item below. Indicate whether it tells *how*, *where*, *when*, *why*, *to what extent*, or *under what circumstances*.

1. If I didn't hold back for my parents' sake, I would have quit long ago.
2. I'd better go, since my train leaves at five.
3. When he reached the edge, he stopped.
4. I'm obligated to the firm, as you know.
5. His little legs strained to carry him away wherever he wanted to go.

Writing Application Write four sentences about Gregor Samsa. Use an adverb clause in each one.

WG *Prentice Hall Writing and Grammar Connection: Diamond Level, Chapter 19, Section 3*

TEACHING RESOURCES

The following resources can be used to enrich or extend the instruction for pp. 1022–1023.

Vocabulary

- **Selection Support:** Build Vocabulary, p. 177
- **Vocabulary and Spelling Practice Book** (Use this booklet for skills instruction.) ▪

Grammar

- **Selection Support:** Grammar and Style, p. 178
- **Writing and Grammar,** Diamond Level, p. 458
- **Daily Language Practice Transparencies** ▪

Writing

- **Performance Assess. and Portfolio Mgmt.,** p. 16
- **Writing and Grammar,** Diamond Level, p. 315
- **Writing and Grammar iText CD-ROM**
- **Writing Models and Graphic Organizers on Transparencies,** pp. 53–59

Listening and Speaking

- **Performance Assess. and Portfolio Mgmt.,** p. 29

▪ **BLOCK SCHEDULING:** Resources marked with this symbol provide varied instruction during 90-minute blocks.

❸ Writing Lesson

Essay Responding to a Critical Perspective

In an essay about "The Metamorphosis," Vladimir Nabokov wrote: "Kafka's art consists in accumulating on the one hand, Gregor's insect features, all the sad detail of his insect disguise, and on the other hand, in keeping vivid and limpid before the reader's eyes Gregor's sweet and subtle human nature." Write an essay in response to this statement. Agree or disagree with Nabokov, but defend your view.

Prewriting Review the story. Make one list of details that describe Gregor's insectlike traits. Make a second list that suggests Gregor's human qualities. Decide whether you agree or disagree with Nabokov.

Drafting Express and defend your opinion. Include details from the text that support your view.

Model: Elaborating to Add Support

Gregor Samsa looks like an insect, but he still has human compassion. For example, when the office manager criticizes Gregor's work, Gregor fears for his parents. He calls out, "Sir! Spare my parents!"

Using quotations from the story can strengthen your ideas.

Revising As you reread your essay, make sure that your supporting details are accurate and easy to follow. Remove any ideas or details that stray from the main purpose of each paragraph.

WG Prentice Hall Writing and Grammar Connection: Diamond Level, Chapter 14, Section 3

❹ Extension Activities

Listening and Speaking Memorial services often include a **eulogy,** or speech of praise, about the deceased. Use these tips to write a eulogy about Gregor Samsa:

- Skim the story and make notes about any traits in Gregor that you find praiseworthy.
- Decide how, if at all, you will refer to his transformation.

Present the eulogy for the class.

Research and Technology In a small group, research Modernism in the visual arts, music, drama, and architecture. Prepare a **multimedia classroom presentation** that identifies similarities among various expressions of Modernism. **[Group Activity]**

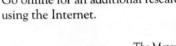

 ***Take It to the Net*** PHSchool.com

Go online for an additional research activity using the Internet.

ASSESSMENT RESOURCES

The following resources can be used to assess students' knowledge and skills.

Selection Assessment

- **Formal Assessment,** pp. 161–163
- **Open-Book Tests,** pp. 133–135
- **Test Bank Software**

 ***Take It to the Net***

Visit PHSchool.com for self-tests on the selection.

Writing Rubric

- **Performance Assess. and Portfolio Mgmt.,** p. 16

Listening and Speaking Rubric

- **Performance Assess. and Portfolio Mgmt.,** p. 29

For additional diagnostics and remediation for skills covered in this grouping, use materials from the Prentice Hall Assessment System.

❸ Writing Lesson

- Explain to students that an essay responding to a critical perspective is a response to literature that is focused on showing whether a given opinion of the work is well founded.
- Model an effective critical essay using Writing Process Model 8: Interpreting a Work of Literature in **Writing Models and Graphic Organizers on Transparencies,** pp. 53–59.
- Use the Writing Lesson to guide students in developing their essays. Have each student begin by writing a thesis sentence that states his or her opinion.
- Use the Response to Literature rubric in **Performance Assessment and Portfolio Management,** p. 16, to evaluate students' essays.

10TH GRADE For support in working through the Writing Lesson with tenth graders, use **Writing and Grammar,** Platinum Level, Chapter 13, Section 3.

❹ Listening and Speaking

- Explain that a eulogy usually describes the deceased's best qualities. Tell students to think about Gregor's intentions as well as his actions, considering what he did not do as well as what he did do.
- Remind students that their audience consists of Gregor's relatives, friends, and co-workers. Have students practice their speeches with partners.
- Use the Speaking: Delivering a Descriptive Presentation rubric in **Performance Assessment and Portfolio Management,** p. 29, to evaluate students' work.

CUSTOMIZE INSTRUCTION
For Universal Access

To address different learning styles, use the following activities suggested in the **Extension Activity** booklet, p. 45.

- For Visual/Spatial Learners, use Activity 5.
- For Bodily/Kinesthetic and Interpersonal Learners, use Activity 6.
- For Verbal/Linguistic and Interpersonal Learners, use Activity 7.

Lesson Objectives

1. To analyze the features of scientific texts
2. To use text features to understand and recall scientific material

About Scientific Texts

- Point out to students that scientific texts describe experiments, hypotheses, and theories. These texts often include diagrams or illustrations that support the text.
- Ask why students might want to analyze scientific texts.
  Possible response: Students can use scientific reports in school for classes and reports.
- Have students read "About Scientific Texts."
- Ask students why each type of listed information is important.
  Answer: Each type of factual information about theories, hypotheses, and experiments explains how scientists reach conclusions.
- Explain to students that reading about experiments allows them to follow the steps of a scientific process through to a hypothesis. Diagrams allow students to picture scientific details without reading lengthy descriptions.

Reading Strategy

Analyzing Text Features

- Have students read "Analyzing Text Features."
- Ask how students can use this information to read scientific texts more efficiently.
  Answer: Students can preview specific material, such as introductions and summaries, diagrams, and study questions, and use text styles to know what information is most important.
- Point out the graphic organizer at the bottom of the page. Have students copy the organizer on a sheet of paper to use later.

READING INFORMATIONAL MATERIALS

Scientific Texts

About Scientific Texts

Science is systematic knowledge, acquired through observation and experimentation, of the structure and behavior of our physical world. **Scientific texts** contain detailed information about science for those who wish to study it. The typical scientific text contains the following:

- Facts about a variety of science topics
- *Hypotheses*, or theories, to explain scientific facts
- Descriptions of experiments conducted to verify these hypotheses
- Opportunities to duplicate these experiments in other environments
- Diagrams of relevant scientific details

In the section of a scientific text that you are about to read, you can expect to learn facts and details about insects and the process of metamorphosis.

Reading Strategy

Analyzing Text Features

Textbook reading is a complex process. Because your goal as you read a textbook is to understand, to learn, and to remember what you have read, you should read more carefully and more thoughtfully than when you are reading for other purposes.

Analyzing text features will help you meet your goal. Here are some tips to help you analyze text features:

- Find and preview the major headings, charts, diagrams, and pictures.
- Read the introductory and summary paragraphs.
- Study the review questions.
- Note any text that is printed in bold or italics.

As you read this excerpt from a biology textbook, use a chart like the one shown to help you record each text feature, describe its use, and determine how it helps you learn.

Text Feature	How It Is Used	How It Helps Me Learn
Checkpoint	Asks questions about the content	Checks to see that I remember and have understood what I have read

What Is an Insect?

Like all arthropods, insects have a segmented body, an exoskeleton, and jointed appendages. They also have several features that are specific to insects. **Insects have a body divided into three parts—head, thorax, and abdomen. Three pairs of legs are attached to the thorax.** The beetle in **Figure 28–15** exhibits these characteristics. In many insects such as ants, the body parts are clearly separated from each other by narrow connections. In other insects, such as grasshoppers, the divisions between the three body parts are not as sharply defined. A typical insect also has a pair of antennae and a pair of compound eyes on the head, two pairs of wings on the thorax, and tracheal tubes that are used for respiration.

The essential life functions in insects are carried out in basically the same ways as they are in other arthropods. However, insects have a variety of interesting adaptations that deserve a closer look.

CHECKPOINT *What are the names of the three parts of an insect's body?*

Responses to Stimuli Insects use a multitude of sense organs to respond to stimuli. Compound eyes are made of many lenses that detect minute changes in color and movement. The brain assembles this information into a single, detailed image. Compound eyes produce an image that is less detailed than what we see. However, eyes with multiple lenses are far better at detecting movement—one reason it is so hard to swat a fly!

Insects have chemical receptors for taste and smell on their mouthparts, as might be expected, and also on their antennae and legs. When a fly steps in a drop of water, it knows immediately whether the water contains salt or sugar. Insects also have sensory hairs that detect slight movements in the surrounding air or water. As objects move toward insects, the insects can feel the movement of the displaced air or water and respond appropriately. Many insects also have well-developed ears that hear sounds far above the human range. These organs are located in what we would consider odd places—behind the legs in grasshoppers, for example.

Guide for Reading

Key Concepts
- What are the distinguishing features of insects?
- What two types of development can insects undergo?
- What types of insects form societies?

Vocabulary
incomplete metamorphosis
nymph
complete metamorphosis
pupa

An italicized question helps readers check their understanding of what they have read.

This diagram shows the three divisions of an insect's body.

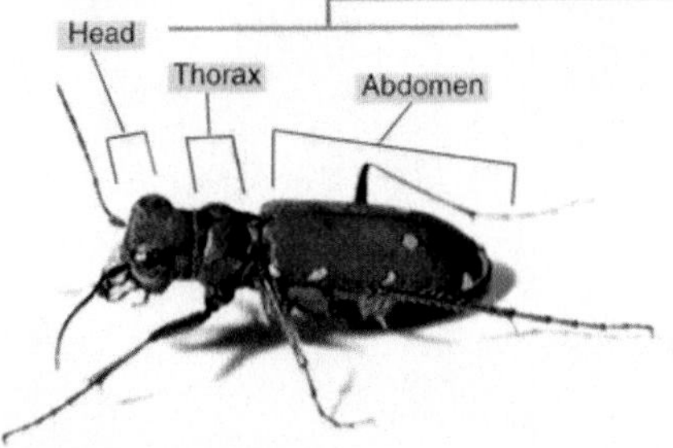

◀ **Figure 28–15** **Insects have a body divided into three parts—head, thorax, and abdomen. Three pairs of legs are attached to the thorax.** In addition to these features, this green tiger beetle has other characteristics of a typical insect—wings, antennae, compound eyes, and tracheal tubes for respiration.

Reading Informational Materials: Scientific Texts ◆ 1025

What Is an Insect?

- Point out to students that they may find this type of material in a scientific text.
- Direct students' attention to the Guide for Reading at the top of the page. Point out that this guide provides information that readers should gain from the chapter. By reading the guide first, students will know what information to look for as they read the text.
- Point out the Vocabulary text feature. Tell students that they will read these terms in the context of the chapter.
- Have students read the first call-out note that corresponds to the Checkpoint feature. Tell students that these questions allow them to test their comprehension. If they cannot answer a question, they need to reread the material. Point out that the answer to a question appears in bold print in the passage and is noted with a key icon, showing that it is a key concept.
- Point out that the second call-out note corresponds to a diagram of the three divisions of an insect's body. Remind students that important concepts are often accompanied by diagrams or other graphics.

CUSTOMIZE INSTRUCTION FOR UNIVERSAL ACCESS

For Special Needs Students	For Less Proficient Readers	For English Learners
Have students create a two-column chart on a poster. In the first column, have them copy each Key Concept question. In the second column, ask them to answer the questions using complete sentences.	Have students work in groups, using the chart on p. 1024 to identify several text features as they reread "What Is an Insect?" Remind students to use headings, key icons, boldface text, and diagrams as starting points in their charts. Ask groups to present their findings to the class.	Provide students with a copy of the chart on p. 1024 and colored markers. Ask students to identify several text features in "What Is an Insect?" by writing each feature in a different color. Then, have students complete the "How It Is Used" columns for these text features.

What Is an Insect?

- Point out to students that reading the headings and the material in boldface type will help them scan a page for the most important information. Have students use the boldface type to find the definition for *complete metamorphosis*.
  Answer: A complete metamorphosis is defined as a process during which many insects undergo a dramatic change in body form.
- Have students look at Figure 28–18. Ask students to explain the purpose of this diagram.
  Answer: The diagram shows the difference between complete metamorphosis and incomplete metamorphosis.

Metamorphosis **The growth and development of insects usually involve metamorphosis, which is a process of changing shape and form. Insects undergo either incomplete metamorphosis or complete metamorphosis.** Both complete and incomplete metamorphosis are shown in **Figure 28–18.** The immature forms of insects that undergo gradual or **incomplete metamorphosis,** such as the chinch bug, look very much like the adults. These immature forms are called **nymphs** (NIMFS). Nymphs lack functional sexual organs and other adult structures, such as wings. As they molt several times and grow, the nymphs gradually acquire adult structures. This type of development is characterized by a similar appearance throughout all stages of the life cycle.

Many insects, such as bees, moths, and beetles, undergo a more dramatic change in body form during a process called **complete metamorphosis.** These animals hatch into larvae that look and act nothing like their parents. They also feed in completely different ways from adult insects. The larvae typically feed voraciously and grow rapidly. They molt a few times and grow larger but change little in appearance. Then they undergo a final molt and change into a **pupa** (PYOO-puh; plural: pupae)—the stage in which an insect changes from larva to adult. During the pupal stage, the body is completely remodeled inside and out. The adult that emerges seems like a completely different animal. Unlike the larva, the adult typically can fly and is specialized for reproduction. **Figure 28–18** shows the complete metamorphosis of a ladybug beetle.

A heading and the definition in boldface type provide basic information about what readers will learn on this page.

CHECKPOINT *What is a pupa?*

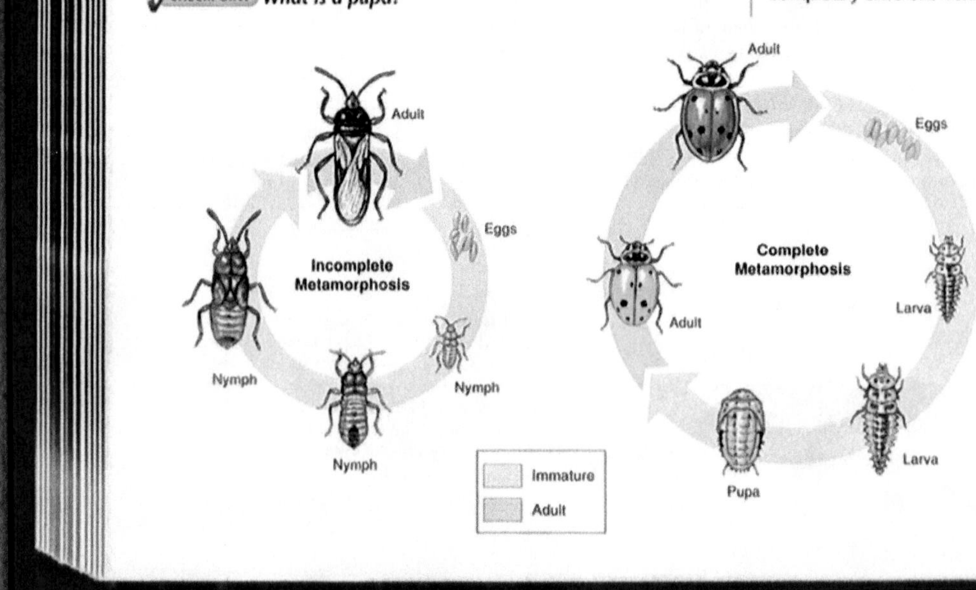

Figure 28–18 **The growth and development of insects usually involve metamorphosis, which is a process of changing shape and form. Insects undergo incomplete metamorphosis or complete metamorphosis.** The chinch bug (left) undergoes incomplete metamorphosis, and the developing nymphs look similar to the adult. The ladybug (right) undergoes complete metamorphosis, and during the early stages the developing larva and pupa look completely different from the adult.

CUSTOMIZE INSTRUCTION FOR UNIVERSAL ACCESS

For Less Proficient Readers	For English Learners	For Gifted Talented Students
Have students work in groups to compare and contrast the two diagrams in Figure 28–18. Ask groups to summarize their findings and present brief oral reports to the class using the diagrams.	Review with students the pronunciations and definitions of the vocabulary words in this selection. Encourage students to identify and list other unfamiliar words and phrases, and guide them to use dictionaries to clarify these terms.	Instruct each student to draw a diagram that shows a familiar scientific process, such as the seasonal cycles of leaf growth on a tree. Then, have students give brief oral presentations about their diagrams to the class.

Check Your Comprehension

1. Into how many parts is an insect's body divided?
2. What types of changes can compound eyes detect?
3. What is the definition of *metamorphosis*?

Applying the Reading Strategy

Analyzing Text Features

4. **(a)** How many sections does this selection have? **(b)** Why is this organization particularly well suited to this subject matter?
5. Why are some of the sentences printed in boldface type?
6. What information did you learn from Figure 28–18 on page 1026?

Activity

Generating Questions for Research

1. **(a)** To find out more about insects, prepare a chart like the one below to focus your research. In the first column, record the details you already know about insects. In the second column, list questions that you still have about insects.

What I Know	Questions for Research
The life cycle of an insect usually involves metamorphosis.	What types of insects do not go through metamorphosis?

(b) Next, choose two of the questions that interest you the most. Consult reliable Internet sources, library reference books, and other nonfiction materials to find the answers to your questions. Record the answers and identify where you found them.

Contrasting Informational Materials

Fact or Fiction?

Sometimes, works of fiction such as short stories or novels present scientific, historical, or other information that seems accurate and true—but is not. For example, in Franz Kafka's short story *The Metamorphosis*, Gregor Samsa transforms into a gigantic, hideous vermin. Kafka's detailed description of Samsa's metamorphosis is vivid and convincing—but scientifically impossible.

1. Why are you more likely to trust the accuracy of the scientific information in the biology textbook pages?
2. Do you think an author writing fiction should be scientifically accurate? Why or why not?

Answers for p. 1027

Check Your Comprehension

1. An insect's body is divided into three parts: a head, a thorax, and an abdomen.
2. Compound eyes can detect minute changes in color and movement.
3. Metamorphosis is a process of changing shape and form.

Applying the Reading Strategy

4. **(a)** This selection has three sections. **(b)** This organization is well suited to this subject matter because it covers three main topics relating to insects.
5. Some of the sentences are printed in boldface type because they are key concepts, headings, or vocabulary words.
6. Possible response: A complete metamorphosis has six steps and an incomplete metamorphosis has five steps.

Activity

Before students begin their research, review their charts. Have students look over their guidelines for reliable Internet sources and other references. Then, ask students to record the answers to their questions clearly, using complete sentences and paragraphs. Make sure that students cite the sources for their answers.

Contrasting Informational Materials

1. The purpose of the information in a biology textbook is to teach science, not to entertain. It is written by people who have studied the information. Therefore, it should be scientifically accurate, whereas Kafka's story may not be.
2. Possible response: If all fiction were scientifically accurate, we would have no science fiction or fantasy genre. If all fiction had to be scientifically accurate, fiction would be less interesting and less thought-provoking. On the other hand, fiction that is not scientifically accurate misleads the reader and promotes ideas that are improbable or impossible.

Poems by Anna Akhmatova, Boris Pasternak, Rainer Maria Rilke, and Paul Valéry

Lesson Objectives

1. **To analyze and respond to literary elements**
   - Literary Analysis: Speaker in a Poem
   - Comparing Literary Works: Poet's Vision
2. **To read, comprehend, analyze, and critique a poem**
   - Reading Strategy: Analyzing Images
   - Reading Check Questions
   - Review and Assess Questions
   - Assessment Practice (ATE)
3. **To develop word analysis skills, fluency, and systematic vocabulary**
   - Vocabulary Development Lesson: Latin Word Part *omni-*
4. **To understand and apply written and oral language conventions**
   - Spelling Strategy
   - Grammar and Style Lesson: Concrete Nouns and Abstract Nouns
5. **To understand and apply appropriate writing and research strategies**
   - Writing Lesson: Reflective Essay
   - Extension Activity: Comparison-and-Contrast Report
6. **To understand and apply listening and speaking strategies**
   - Extension Activity: Poem in Response to Art

10TH GRADE TEACHING TENTH-GRADE STUDENTS

For support in teaching the selection(s) to tenth-grade students, see the Step-by-Step Teaching notes, identified with the icon shown here.

STEP-BY-STEP TEACHING GUIDE	PACING GUIDE
PRETEACH	
Motivate Students and Provide Background	
Use the Motivation activity (ATE p. 1028)	5 min.
Read and discuss author and background features (SE pp. 1028, 1030, 1032, 1034, 1037; ATE p. 1028) [A]	5 min.
Introduce the Concepts	
Introduce the Literary Analysis and Reading Strategy concepts (SE/ATE p. 1029) [A]	15 min.
Pronounce the vocabulary words and read their definitions (SE p. 1029)	5 min.
TEACH	
Monitor Comprehension	
Informally monitor comprehension by circulating while students read [A]	40 min.
Monitor students' comprehension with the Reading Check note (SE/ATE p. 1037)	as students read
Develop vocabulary with the Vocabulary notes (SE pp. 1030, 1034, 1035, 1037, 1038, 1040; ATE p. 1040)	as students read
Develop Understanding	
Develop students' understanding of the speaker in a poem with the Literary Analysis annotations (SE/ATE pp. 1032, 1035, 1036, 1038, 1039; ATE p. 1034) [A]	10 min.
Develop students' ability to analyze images, using the Reading Strategy annotations (SE/ATE pp. 1038; ATE pp. 1037, 1040)	10 min.
ASSESS	
Assess Mastery	
Assess students' mastery of the Reading Strategy and Literary Analysis concepts by having them answer the Review and Assess questions (SE/ATE p. 1041)	20 min.
Use one or more of the print, software, or transparency Assessment Resource (ATE p. 1043) [A]	up to 45 min.
EXTEND	
Apply Understanding	
Have students complete the Vocabulary Development Lesson and the Grammar and Style Lesson (SE p. 1042) [A]	20 min.
Apply students' ability to strengthen connections between life and literature, using the Writing Lesson (SE/ATE p. 1043) [A]	45 min.
Apply students' understanding of the selections, using one or more of the Extension Activities (SE p. 1043)	20–90 min.

ACCELERATED INSTRUCTION: Use the strategies and activities identified with an [A].

UNIVERSAL ACCESS
● = Below-Level Students
▲ = On-Level Students
■ = Above-Level Students

Time and Resource Manager

Reading Level: Average, Average, Challenging, Challenging, Challenging, Challenging, Challenging, Challenging, Challenging, Challenging
Average Number of Instructional Days: 4

RESOURCES		
PRINT	**TRANSPARENCIES**	**TECHNOLOGY**
• **Beyond Literature,** Cross-Curricular Connection: Science, p. 46 ▲ ■		• **Interest Grabber Video,** Tape 2, Unit 8, Segment 5
• **Selection Support Workbook:** ● ▲ ■ Literary Analysis, p. 184 Reading Strategy, p. 183 Build Vocabulary, p. 181	• **Literary Analysis and Reading Transparencies,** pp. 91 and 92 ● ▲ ■	
	• **Fine Art Tranparencies,** Art Transparency 20 ● ▲ ■	• **Listening to Literature** ● ▲ ■ Audiocassettes Audio CDs
• **Literary Analysis for Enrichment,** p. 46 ■		
• **Formal Assessment:** Selection Test, pp. 164–166 ● ▲ ■ • **Open-Book Tests,** pp. 136–138 ● ▲ ■ • **Performance Assess. and Portfolio Mgmt.,** pp. 12, 15 ● ▲ ■ • Prentice Hall Assessment System ● ▲ ■	• Prentice Hall Assessment System ● ▲ ■ **Skills Practice Answers and Explanations on Transparencies**	• **Test Bank Software** ● ▲ ■
• **Selection Support Workbook:** ● ▲ ■ Grammar and Style, p. 182 • **Writing and Grammar,** Diamond Level ● ▲ ■ • **Extension Activities,** p. 46 ● ▲ ■	• **Daily Language Practice Transparencies** ● ▲ • **Writing Models and Graphic Organizers on Transparencies,** pp. 95–97; 103–105	• **Writing and Grammar iText CD-ROM** ● ▲ ■ ***Take It to the Net*** PHSchool.com

BLOCK SCHEDULING: Use one 90-minute class period to preteach the selection(s) and have students read them. Use a second 90-minute class period to assess students' mastery of skills and have them complete one of the Extension Activities.

PRETEACH

Step-by-Step Teaching Guide for pp. 1028–1029

Motivation

Ask students to name and discuss some common symbols, such as the American flag. Point out that a symbol may have a specific meaning, multiple meanings, or a meaning that varies from reader to reader. Tell students that the poems in this section rely heavily on symbols.

Interest Grabber Video

As an alternative, play "The Poetry of Anna Akhmatova: The Russian Revolution" on Tape 2 to engage student interest.

❶ Background

More About the Authors

Like Anna Akhmatova, Boris Pasternak experienced the horrors of war. In the 1940s, Pasternak turned away from poetry to concentrate on writing a novel about the Russian revolution, *Doctor Zhivago*.

Although Rainer Maria Rilke's family wanted him to pursue a career in business or law, Rilke had his sights set on writing. While still a student, he wrote poetry, plays, and short stories. In 1895, he published his first collection of poems, *Sacrifice to the Lares;* a year later, he published his second collection, *Crowned by Dream*.

By nineteen, Paul Valéry had written almost two hundred poems. With the publication of "The Young Fate" in 1897, Valéry won critical acclaim that brought public notoriety and a greater demand for his poetry and commentary.

Geography Note

Direct students' attention to the map on this page. Explain that during the period when these authors were writing, European countries were being redefined by war and revolution.

Prepare to Read

❶ Poems by Anna Akhmatova, Boris Pasternak, Rainer Maria Rilke, and Paul Valéry

Anna Akhmatova (1889–1966)

Anna Akhmatova (äk mä′ tō və) was born on June 11, 1889, in Odessa, a small town on the coast of the Black Sea. Throughout her career, she wrote about the people she knew and the events she witnessed. The Russo-Japanese War, the two World Wars, and Stalin's totalitarianism greatly affected her. During Stalin's purge of writers and intellectuals in the late 1930s, Akhmatova's work was banned and her life was threatened. Despite these pressures, she continued to write. In 1940, when the ban was lifted, she published the collections *Anno Domini MCMXXI* and *From Six Books*.

Rainer Maria Rilke (1875–1926)

Rainer Maria Rilke (rī′ nər mä rē′ ä ril′ kə) is considered one of the most important poets of the twentieth century. He spent his childhood in Prague and later lived in Russia, France, and Switzerland. An air of solitude, along with a sense of the urgency and intensity of the inner life, fills his poetry. Rilke published many poetry collections, including *Sonnets to Orpheus* (1923) and *Duino Elegies* (1923). He also published a short-story collection, *Stories of God* (1904), and a novel, *The Tale of the Love and Death of Cornet Christopher Rilke* (1906), which earned him both critical and popular success.

Boris Pasternak (1890–1960)

One of Russia's greatest writers, Boris Pasternak (pas′ tər nak′) was born in Moscow on February 10, 1890. During the two World Wars and the years of Stalinist oppression, most Russian writers emigrated, were exiled, or suffered in prison camps, but Pasternak led a fairly calm life. He did not, however, avoid persecution entirely. In 1956, when he completed his great novel *Doctor Zhivago*, Soviet authorities forbade its publication. (The novel was published throughout the world to great acclaim, but it was not published in Russia until 1988.) When Pasternak received the Nobel Prize in Literature in 1958, Soviet authorities forced him to decline the honor. The writer spent the remaining two years of his life in near exile in an artists' community outside Moscow.

Paul Valéry (1871–1945)

Paul Valéry (pôl vá lā rē′) was born on October 30, 1871, in Sète, a small Mediterranean coastal town in France. He attended law school in Montpellier, where he met the Symbolist poet Stéphane Mallarmé (stā fan′ mä lär mā′), who would greatly influence him. Valéry was also inspired by the work of American writer Edgar Allan Poe, whose work taught him about the melodious verbal combinations that are possible in poetry.

From 1892 to 1917, Valéry faded into reclusive investigations of creativity, mathematics, and psychology. When he emerged from this "silent period," he received numerous awards, appointments, and honorary degrees.

TEACHING RESOURCES

The following resources can be used to enrich or extend the instruction for pp. 1028–1029.

Motivation

Interest Grabber Video, Tape 2

Background

Beyond Literature, p. 46

Take It to the Net

Visit PHSchool.com for background on the authors.

Literary Analysis

Literary Analysis and Reading Transparencies, Speaker in a Poem, p. 91

Selection Support: Literary Analysis, p. 184

Reading

Literary Analysis and Reading Transparencies, Analyzing Images, p. 92

BLOCK SCHEDULING: Resources marked with this symbol provide varied instruction during 90-minute blocks.

Preview

Connecting to the Literature

Many poets who wrote during the first half of the twentieth century lived through turbulent times that forced them to question everything—people's relationships to society, the divine, nature, nation, and their own inner lives. These poems ask the important questions about what it means to be human.

❷ Literary Analysis

Speaker in a Poem

Like a narrator in a story, the **speaker in a poem** is the one who "says" its words. There are several kinds of poetic speakers:

- The speaker may be the voice of the poet him- or herself.
- The speaker may be a fictional character.
- The speaker may be a human being, a nonhuman entity, or even an inanimate object.

In order to fully understand a poem, it is important to identify the speaker. To do so, answer these questions as you read: Who is the speaker? Whom is the speaker addressing? Why does the speaker want to share his or her thoughts?

Comparing Literary Works

Every poem expresses some aspect of the **poet's vision**—the writer's view of the world. As you read these poems, identify the ideas each poet finds important, as well as his or her feelings about people, society, and nature. Together, these elements suggest a vision or worldview that is distinctive to each poet. After you have grasped each poet's vision, compare the ways in which they are similar and the ways in which they are different.

❸ Reading Strategy

Analyzing Images

Poets often use imagery—language that appeals to one or more of the five senses—to express ideas. **Analyzing images,** therefore, is a key to interpreting poems. As you read, rephrase each image in the most literal, or plain, way you can. The literal meanings can lead you to a better understanding of deeper meanings. Use a chart like the one shown to state the literal meanings of the images you find.

Image

"... the gloomy eyes/ Pregnant with eagles and battles of foreseen fall"

↓

Literal Meaning

Even though he looks ahead to victory in battle, he is sad or troubled.

Vocabulary Development

plundered (plun′ dərd) *adj.* stripped of possessions (p. 1030)

opaque (ō pāk′) *adj.* not shining or lustrous; dull (p. 1034)

tremulous (trem′ yo͞o ləs) *adj.* trembling; quivering (p. 1035)

accolade (ak′ ə lād′) *n.* anything done as a sign of praise or respect (p. 1037)

profusion (prō fyo͞o′ zhən) *n.* abundance; rich or lavish supply (p. 1037)

imperishable (im per′ ish ə bəl) *adj.* indestructible (p. 1038)

despond (di spänd′) *v.* to lose courage or hope (p. 1038)

omnipotent (äm nip′ ə tənt) *adj.* having unlimited power or authority (p. 1040)

CUSTOMIZE INSTRUCTION FOR UNIVERSAL ACCESS

For Less Proficient Readers	For English Learners	For Advanced Readers
All the following poems contain challenging vocabulary. To increase comprehension, encourage students to read the poems with a dictionary at hand. Each time students encounter a difficult or unfamiliar word whose meaning they cannot determine from context, they should look up the word.	Organize students into groups, and have them preview each poem to identify difficult imagery and vocabulary. Then, ask students to create a group list of unfamiliar items. Encourage students to discuss the list and to use dictionaries or thesauruses to clarify meanings.	Have students preview each poem to identify words or phrases that have religious connotations. Then, ask students to create a group list of these items. Ask students to discuss and note how these items underscore a poetic attempt by Akhmatova to reach God through an understanding of life.

❷ Literary Analysis

Speaker in a Poem

- Explain to students that the speaker in a poem is similar to the narrator of a short story.
- Emphasize that although a poem may be written in the first-person singular, the speaker may not be the poet.
- Use the Speaker in a Poem transparency in **Literary Analysis and Reading Transparencies,** p. 91, to demonstrate to students how to identify the speaker in a poem.

❸ Reading Strategy

Analyzing Images

- Explain that imagery is often called "sensory detail," because it evokes sights, sounds, tastes, textures, and smells in the reader's imagination.
- Read aloud the following example from Akhmatova's "Everything Is Plundered": "Death's great black wing scrapes the air, / Misery gnaws to the bone."
- Then, ask students: To what senses does this imagery appeal? Possible response: The phrase "black wing" appeals to the sense of sight; the words "scrapes" and "gnaws" appeal to the senses of touch and hearing.
- Lead students in a discussion about why Akhmatova might have used these images to describe death.
- Explain the use of the graphic organizer on p. 1029. Have students use an organizer like this one as they read the poems.

Vocabulary Development

- Pronounce each vocabulary word for students, and read the definitions as a class. Have students identify any words with which they are already familiar.

 **E-Teach**

Visit e-Teach at PHSchool.com for teachers' essays on how to teach, with questions and answers.

TEACH

Step-by-Step Teaching Guide for pp. 1030–1040

Teaching Tenth-Grade Students

10TH GRADE Tell tenth-grade students that the following poems all use vivid imagery and symbolism to convey meaning and emotion. Lead a discussion about the purpose of these literary techniques. Then, have students preview each poem, noting the images and symbols in each.

❶ About the Selections

In "Everything Is Plundered," Akhmatova addresses the despair and destruction of war, yet offers a celebratory, hopeful vision of life.

Akhmatova's poem "I Am Not One of Those Who Left the Land" suggests that in times of trouble, securing personal safety is not worth sacrificing national identity. She suggests that those who stay and face the dangers will emerge on the other side of the tragedy with fewer regrets and more pride than those who leave.

❷ Background

Art

Starry Night, by Edvard Munch

Norwegian artist Munch (1863–1944) is considered a forerunner of the German Expressionist movement. He is best known for his paintings of people in emotional distress, such as his most famous work, *The Scream* (1893). He painted a series of night scenes entitled *Starry Night* (1923–1924), including this late version.

Use the following question for discussion:

What elements of this painting capture the images in the poem? Possible response: The shades of blue capture the melancholy expressed in the poem's first stanza. The yellow suggests the hope Akhmatova expresses in the second and third stanzas.

❸ ▶ Critical Viewing

Possible response: The stars suggest the miraculous, and the people seem ordinary.

❶ Everything Is Plundered

Anna Akhmatova

translated by *Stanley Kunitz*

Background

Anna Akhmatova was part of a group of poets known as the Acmeists. Unlike the Symbolists, who used poetry to transcend reality, the Acmeists used poetry to understand and embrace the present moment. As Amanda Haight writes of the Acmeists in *Anna Akhmatova: A Poetic Pilgrimage,* ". . . there was to be no escape for them from the world's realities as these grew harsher. It was necessary for them to try to reach God and to understand His purposes through understanding, living, and loving life." In the following two poems, consider Akhmatova's responses to the tragically harsh reality of war.

Everything is plundered, betrayed, sold,
Death's great black wing scrapes the air,
Misery gnaws to the bone.
Why then do we not despair?

By day, from the surrounding woods,
cherries blow summer into town;
at night the deep transparent skies
glitter with new galaxies.

And the miraculous comes so close
to the ruined, dirty houses—
something not known to anyone at all,
but wild in our breast for centuries.

plundered (plun′ dərd) *adj.* stripped of possessions

❷

Starry Night, 1923–1924, Edvard Munch, The Munch Museum/The Munch-Ellingsen Group

❸ **Critical Viewing ▶** In what ways might this painting suggest a meeting of the miraculous and the ordinary? Explain. **[Interpret]**

TEACHING RESOURCES

The following resources can be used to enrich or extend the instruction for pp. 1030–1040.

Literary Analysis

- **Selection Support:** Literary Analysis, p. 184
- **Literary Analysis and Reading Transparencies,** Speaker in a Poem, p. 91

Reading

- **Selection Support:** Reading Strategy, p. 183; Build Vocabulary, p. 181 ■
- **Listening to Literature Audiocassettes**
- **Listening to Literature Audio CDs**

Extension

- **Fine Art Transparencies,** Art Transparency 20 (Discuss with students Cubist attempts to represent multiple perspectives on an object. Have them compare the multiple perspectives in Juan Gris's painting with Pasternak's, Rilke's, and Valéry's poetic perspectives on people, scenes, and objects.) ■

■ **BLOCK SCHEDULING:** Resources marked with this symbol provide varied instruction during 90-minute blocks.

1 # I Am Not One of Those Who Left the Land

Anna Akhmatova
translated by Stanley Kunitz

I am not one of those who left the land
to the mercy of its enemies.
Their flattery leaves me cold,
my songs are not for them to praise.

But I pity the exile's lot.
Like a felon, like a man half-dead,
dark is your path, wanderer;
wormwood[1] infects your foreign bread.

But here, in the murk of conflagration,[2]
where scarcely a friend is left to know,
we, the survivors, do not flinch
from anything, not from a single blow.

Surely the reckoning will be made
after the passing of this cloud.
We are the people without tears,
straighter than you . . . more proud . . .

1. **wormwood** (wurm' wood') *n.* bitter herb that often symbolizes grief.
2. **conflagration** (kän' flə grā' shən) *n.* destructive fire.

4 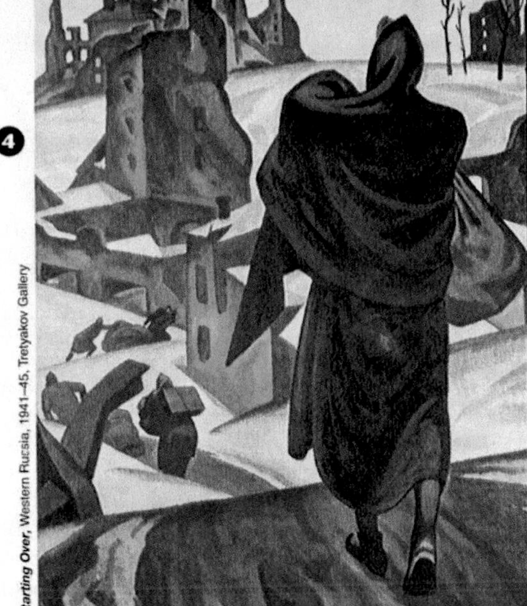

Starting Over, Western Russia, 1941–45, Tretyakov Gallery

5 ▲ **Critical Viewing**
Does this image portray those who left the land or those who remained? Explain. **[Distinguish]**

Review and Assess

Thinking About the Selections

1. **Respond:** Did you feel optimistic or pessimistic after reading these poems? Explain.
2. **(a) Recall:** In stanza 1 of "Everything Is Plundered," what abstract idea has a "great black wing"? **(b) Analyze:** What is the effect of the poet's describing this idea as a living creature?
3. **(a) Interpret:** In stanza 3, what is "wild in our breast"? **(b) Analyze:** How do stanzas 2 and 3 answer the question posed in line 4?
4. **(a) Define:** In line 3 of "I Am Not One of Those Who Left the Land," to whom does the pronoun "their" refer? **(b) Analyze:** Why might the speaker not enjoy their flattery?
5. **Extend:** What do you think Akhmatova would say to refugees of recent or current wars?

CUSTOMIZE INSTRUCTION FOR UNIVERSAL ACCESS

For Special Needs Students	For Advanced Readers
Help students understand that the first two lines of "I Am Not One of Those Who Left the Land" refer to the fact that many of the upper classes in Russia became exiles in countries such as England and France to avoid execution by the revolutionary forces during the Russian Revolution of 1917. Then, guide students to understand Akhmatova's attitude toward these exiles by citing portions of the text, and challenge students to paraphrase these sections.	Organize students into small groups, and have them discuss the diction of each poem. Ask students to identify particularly powerful words and to consider their connotations and denotations. Encourage students to analyze each word choice by asking themselves the following questions: What feelings does the word evoke? Why? What tone and mood does the word create? Then, have students share their analyses and discuss how the meaning or effect of each poem might change if the diction were altered.

4 Background

Art

Starting Over,
by Petr Ossorsky

Ossorsky's painting, which comes from a series titled *Lifelines of the Motherland* (1941–1945), depicts Russian villagers returning home after the suspension of the German advance during World War II.

Use the following question for discussion:

What effect do the painting's sharp angles have on its mood?
Possible response: The painting's angularity and bold figures emphasize the stark landscape and suggest the difficulty of the times.

5 ▶ Critical Viewing

Possible response: The painting may portray those who left. The people walk through the war-torn land, carrying their few possessions. They move toward a city in the distance.

Answers for p. 1031

Review and Assess

1. Possible response: Even though each poem tells of war and despair, the main idea of each poem is optimistic. The final words give hope.
2. **(a)** The abstract idea is death. **(b)** Possible response: This description makes the abstract idea of death concrete.
3. **(a)** The miraculous wonders of life and the human spirit are "wild in our breast." **(b)** Stanzas 2 and 3 explain that nature continues and restores the physical world. The nearness of the miraculous restores the will to live and alleviates despair.
4. **(a)** "Their" refers to those who have left the land. **(b)** Possible response: The speaker views the exiles as enemies of Russia.
5. Possible response: Akhmatova might say that the refugees should return to rebuild their countries or should never have left.

6 About the Selections

In the poem "The Weeping Orchard," Boris Pasternak uses the image of a rain-soaked orchard as a metaphor for the speaker's sadness.

The poem "The Drowsy Garden" presents a tranquil image of a garden at night. Pasternak layers the physical descriptions of the garden with images of sacred mystery to create a scene of wonder.

7 Literary Analysis

Speaker in a Poem

- Have a volunteer read the bracketed passage aloud. Then, ask: What is the speaker describing?
  Possible response: The speaker is describing an orchard in the rain.
- Remind students that identifying the speaker in a poem can help them determine the poem's meaning.
- Ask students the first Literary Analysis question on p. 1032: In the first stanza, where do you think the speaker is and what is the speaker doing? Explain.
  Answer: The speaker is standing at a window looking out at the orchard, wondering whether anyone else is witnessing the same sight.

8 Literary Analysis

Speaker in a Poem

- Point out that in the first stanza, the speaker asks whether the orchard is "the only one in the world." In stanza 4, the speaker asks, "am I the only one in the world… ?"
- Ask students why the speaker wonders about the presence of other orchards and other people.
  Possible response: The speaker feels isolated and alone.
- Then, ask students the second Literary Analysis question on p. 1032: In the fourth stanza, how do the reader's impressions of the speaker become more precise?
  Answer: The stanza reveals that the speaker is on the brink of tears, thus providing the reader with more information about the speaker's emotional state.

6 *The Weeping Orchard*

Boris Pasternak

translated by Mark Rudman with Bohdan Boychuk

Background

Both of these poems by Boris Pasternak are thick with imagery and metaphorical meaning that reaches beyond their immediate subject matter. This density of images reflects Pasternak's involvement with a literary movement in Russia known as Imagism. As their name suggests, the Imagists stressed the use of imagery and believed that the true basis of poetry was the metaphor—language that reveals similarities between dissimilar things. Imagist poems, like the two here, offer little explanation, instead focusing the reader's attention on a single, sharply defined moment in time.

7

It's eerie—how the orchard drips and listens:
is it the only one in the world
to crumple a branch on this window like lace,
or is there a witness?

The spongy, bruised earth heaves
and chokes under the burden.
In the distances you can hear, as in August,
midnight ripen in the fields.

Not a sound. No one looks on.
Assured there's no one there
it reverts to old tricks—rolls down roof
to gutter, and spills over.

8

I will bring it to my lips and listen:
am I the only one in the world,
ready to weep on the slightest occasion,
or is there a witness?

Silence. No breath of leaf, nothing
in the dark but this weird
gulping, and flapping of slippers,
and sighs, broken by tears.

Literary Analysis
Speaker in a Poem In the first stanza, where do you think the speaker is and what is the speaker doing? Explain.

Literary Analysis
Speaker in a Poem In the fourth stanza, how do the reader's impressions of the speaker become more precise?

ENRICHMENT: Literature Connection

Pasternak's Poems

In *The Three Worlds of Boris Pasternak,* Robert Payne writes the following about Pasternak's work:

> From the beginning … [Pasternak] was concerned with the tangible earth, with nature in all her moods, with the human condition in all its amazing variety. He remains a difficult poet because his vision is intricate and conveyed with an extraordinary density of imagery. He defies translation; and no one has yet succeeded in conveying in English the richness of his vocabulary, the leaping brilliance of his rhythms, the way he gives the impression of writing in a language he has invented this morning. Yet no one could be more tradition-bound. His verse patterns are the simplest imaginable….

6 # The Drowsy Garden

Boris Pasternak

translated by Babette Deutsch

The drowsy garden scatters insects
Bronze as the ash from braziers[1] blown.
Level with me and with my candle,
Hang flowering worlds, their leaves full-grown.

As into some unheard-of dogma[2]
I move across into this night,
9 Where a worn poplar age has grizzled
Screens the moon's strip of fallow[3] light,

Where the pond lies, an open secret,
Where apple bloom is surf and sigh,
And where the garden, a lake dwelling,
Holds out in front of it the sky.

---

1. **braziers** (brā′ zhərz) *n.* metal pans or bowls used to hold burning coals or charcoal.
2. **dogma** (dôg′ mə) *n.* doctrine or belief, or a set of doctrines and beliefs.
3. **fallow** (fal′ ō) *adj.* pale-yellow; brownish-yellow.

Review and Assess

Thinking About the Selections

1. **Respond:** Which images in these poems were the most vivid for you? Explain.
2. (a) **Recall:** In stanza 2 of "The Weeping Orchard," what words does the speaker use to describe the earth? **(b) Interpret:** Which emotions do these words suggest the speaker feels?
3. (a) **Recall:** What objects and sounds are described in the final stanza? **(b) Analyze:** How does this stanza suggest that the speaker has projected his own emotions onto nature? Explain.
4. (a) **Recall:** In lines 5–6 of "The Drowsy Garden," to what abstract idea does the speaker compare his entrance into the garden? **(b) Analyze:** What might this garden symbolize for the speaker?
5. (a) **Interpret:** In what sense does the final image move the reader from the garden into the larger world? **(b) Summarize:** Summarize the philosophy that the poem expresses.

9 Critical Thinking

Modify

- Tell students that it is sometimes necessary to rephrase a passage in order to determine its meaning.
- Ask students to offer alternative readings of the bracketed passage by rephrasing.
  Possible response: A worn and age-grizzled poplar screens the fallow light of the moon.

Answers for p. 1033

Review and Assess

1. Possible response: The image of "the moon's strip of fallow light" is vivid because it creates a familiar, yet haunting, picture.
2. **(a)** The speaker uses the words *spongy* and *bruised* to describe the earth. **(b)** These words suggest that the speaker feels vulnerable.
3. **(a)** Objects and sounds described include "silence," "breath of leaf," "the dark," "weird gulping," "flapping of slippers," "sighs," and "tears." **(b)** The personification of the rain-soaked orchard as gulping and the parallel between the rain and tears indicate that nature may be a symbol for the speaker's own sadness.
4. **(a)** The speaker compares his entrance into the garden to entering a realm of unheard-of doctrines. **(b)** Possible response: The garden might symbolize a place of mystery and contemplation.
5. **(a)** The final image suggests that because of its important role, the garden is at the crux of the universe. **(b)** Possible response: The world and its wonders are encompassed in small circles of existence.

CUSTOMIZE INSTRUCTION FOR UNIVERSAL ACCESS

For Less Proficient Readers	For English Learners
Some students may have difficulty reading poetry with a rhythmic, natural pace. Tell students to follow along in their books and listen as you read "The Drowsy Garden" aloud. After you have finished reading, explain to students that reading poetry is much like reading prose. A reader should pause briefly to indicate a comma and come to a full stop to indicate a period. Encourage students to preview the poems for punctuation and to read each poem aloud according to its punctuation.	Explain to students that like the Russian originals, the English versions of these two poems use syntax, or word order, that is often condensed and elliptical. Read aloud each poem to the class before looking at it more closely so that students can experience the flow of the language. Then, have volunteers read each poem individually, making sure that students understand what is being said.

10 About the Selection

Rilke's poem "The Grownup" describes the passage from the wonder and ignorance of childhood to the knowledge of adulthood.

11 Literary Analysis

Speaker in a Poem

- Remind students that identifying the speaker is essential to understanding the poem's meaning.

  After students have read the poem, ask: How does the speaker feel about this transition?
  Possible response: The speaker regards growing up as inevitable but sorrowful.
- Ask students: Does the speaker seem sympathetic toward the person described in this poem? Explain.
  Answer: Yes; the speaker understands the significance of the transition and the loss it inflicts.

12 Background

Art

Inger on the Beach, by Edvard Munch

Munch (1863–1944) was a Norwegian artist whose work is famous for its ability to express powerful emotions, such as fear, loneliness, and jealousy.

Use the following question for discussion:

Why do you think Munch put his model on shore looking out at sea?
Possible response: The sea is sometimes used as a symbol for the unknown, so it may emphasize the subject's feelings of uncertainty.

13 ▶ Critical Viewing

Possible response: *Solemn*, *unmoved*, and *serene* describe the woman.

10 

The Grownup

Rainer Maria Rilke
translated by **Randall Jarrell**

Background

In 1899, Rainer Maria Rilke traveled to Russia, where he met the great writer and religious mystic Leo Tolstoy. As a result of this encounter, Rilke came to see all things as saturated with a mystical, divine energy. His association with French sculptor Auguste Rodin, who believed that the work of an artist held religious meaning, reinforced that philosophy. Rilke applied this view not only to elements of nature but even to inanimate objects. Look for signs of Rilke's philosophy in the three poems that follow.

All this stood on her and was the world
And stood on her with all things, pain and grace,
As trees stand, growing and erect, all image
And imageless as the ark of the Lord God,[1]
And solemn, as if set upon a state.

And she bore it, bore, somehow, the weight
Of the flying, fleeting, faraway,
The monstrous and the still unmastered,
Unmoved, serene, as the water bearer
Stands under a full jar. Till in the midst
of play,
Transfiguring,[2] preparing for the other,
The first white veil fell smoothly, softly,

Over her opened face, almost opaque,
Never to raise itself again, and giving
somehow
To all her questions one vague answer:
In thee, thou once a child, in thee.

opaque (ō pāk′) *adj.* not shining or lustrous; dull

1. **all image . . . the Lord God** The Ark of the Covenant, the sacred chest of the Hebrews that contained the Tablets of the Law, represented God. Because the Jews had been commanded by God not to reproduce His image, the chest was not adorned with the image of God.
2. **transfiguring** (trans fig′ yer iŋ) *v.* changing in form or appearance.

12 

Inger on the Beach, Edvard Munch, Rasmus Meyers Samlinger

13 **▲ Critical Viewing**
Which words and phrases from "The Grownup" might be used to describe the woman in this painting? **[Connect]**

ENRICHMENT: Literature Connection

Critical View of Rilke

About Rainer Maria Rilke, the literary scholar Robert Hass has written,

> Looking at things, [Rilke] saw nothing—or, to paraphrase Wallace Stevens, "the nothing"—that arose from his hunger for a more vivid and permanent world. He had a wonderful eye for almost anything he really looked at, dogs, children, qualities of light, works of art [,] but in the end he looked at them in order to take them inside himself and transform them: to soak them in his homelessness and spiritual hunger so that when he returned them to the world, they were no longer more at home in it than he was, and gave off unearthly light. . . .

INTERIOR OF THE Rose

(14)

Rainer Maria Rilke *translated by* **Kate Flores**

Where, for this within,
Is there a without? And upon what wound
Lies a weft[1] so thin?
What heavens are reflected
In the inward seas
Of these opening roses
Thus reposing?[2] See
How loosely in looseness
They lie, as though never
(15) A tremulous hand could spill them.
They cannot hold themselves still;
Many are filling
Up unto their brim and flowing
Over with interior space
Into days, which seem ever
Grown fuller and fuller,
Until all of summer a room
Has become, a room enclosed in a dream.

Literary Analysis
Speaker in a Poem What do you think the speaker in this poem is doing?

tremulous (trem′ yo͞o ləs) *adj.* trembling; quivering

1. **weft** (weft) *n.* something woven.
2. **reposing** (ri pōz′ iŋ) *v.* resting.

Review and Assess

Thinking About the Selections

1. **Respond:** Do you find either of these poems surprising? Explain.
2. **(a) Recall:** In "The Grownup," what happens to the person at "play"? **(b) Interpret:** What change does this event symbolize?
3. **(a) Recall:** In stanza 2, which words describe the nature of the weight "she" bears? **(b) Classify:** Which two adjectives and one image describe how she bears the weight? **(c) Contrast:** How does her attitude toward the weight differ from the weight itself?
4. **(a) Define:** In lines 1–2 of "Interior of the Rose," note two words that have opposite meanings. **(b) Distinguish:** In lines 2–7, what other words or phrases suggest a similar opposition? **(c) Support:** Using these details, support the idea that the roses symbolize both the physical and the spiritual worlds.

CUSTOMIZE INSTRUCTION FOR UNIVERSAL ACCESS

For English Learners	For Gifted/Talented Students	For Advanced Readers
Point out the word *wound* in line 2 of "Interior of the Rose." Pronounced another way, it is a homograph, or a word that has two different pronunciations and/or meanings. Have students offer other examples of homographs.	Have students write a monologue from the perspective of the subject of "The Grownup." Students should have the woman respond to the speaker's assertions and offer her own observations about her transformation into adulthood. Ask volunteers to perform their monologues for the class.	In his poem "Ode: Intimations of Immortality from Recollections of Early Childhood," British Romantic poet William Wordsworth captures how common experiences lose their freshness as people grow older. Have students research and read other works that address the passage from childhood into adulthood.

(14) About the Selection

The speaker in "Interior of the Rose" observes the fragility and endurance of a rose as it blooms.

(15) Literary Analysis

Speaker in a Poem

- Remind students to consider whom the speaker addresses and why the speaker wants to share his or her thoughts.
- Ask the Literary Analysis question on p. 1035: What do you think the speaker in this poem is doing?
  Answer: The speaker is observing a rose very closely and marveling at its fragility and endurance.

Answers for p. 1035

Review and Assess

1. Possible response: "The Grownup" is surprising because the transition from childhood to adulthood is more difficult than many adults remember or realize. "Interior of the Rose" is surprising because the speaker discovers so much by looking into the petals of a flower.
2. **(a)** The person experiences the first stage of her transformation. **(b)** This event symbolizes growth into adulthood.
3. **(a)** The words *flying, fleeting, faraway, monstrous,* and *unmastered* describe the weight the child bears. **(b)** The adjectives are *unmoved* and *serene*. The image is that of a water bearer carrying a full jar on her head. **(c)** The weight seems overwhelming, "monstrous" even, yet the child remains poised as though she scarcely notices it.
4. **(a)** The words are *within* and *without*. **(b)** Other words are *heavens* and *inward seas* and roses *opening* and *reposing*. **(c)** Possible response: The exterior of the rose can be seen as the tangible world and the interior, the spiritual world.

16 About the Translation

Compare this literal translation of lines 1–4 of "Archaic Torso of Apollo" with Stephen Mitchell's version (see SE page):

We knew not his unheard-of head, in which the eye-apples ripened. But his torso glows still like a candelabrum, in which his look, only wound down....

The literal translation sounds strange because it follows the German word order and is a word-for-word translation rather than a rendering of the meaning. Also, it contains the translated phrase "eye-apples," for which Mitchell has substituted the simile "eyes like ripening fruit." Finally, the literal translation hobbles along on lines of unequal length, while Mitchell re-creates Rilke's iambic pentameter.

17 Literary Analysis

Speaker and Poet's Vision

- After students have read the poem, ask: Why does the speaker describe the torso as brilliant?
  Answer: The torso still contains all the power that the artist gave it.
- Ask students the Literary Analysis question on p. 1036: How closely do you think the speaker's words reflect Rilke's personal worldview? Explain.
  Answer: The boldness and intensity of the imagery, the stirring direct address of the reader in the last line, and the use of *we*, all suggest that the speaker is expressing Rilke's views.

Answers for p. 1036

Review and Assess

1. Possible response: It is easy to visualize the statue because Rilke provides specific details.
2. **(a)** The head is missing. **(b)** The word *gaze* suggests sight.
   (c) The contrast suggests that the torso, even without eyes, can still see.
3. **(a)** The words *suffused, brilliance, lamp, gleams, dazzle, dark, flared, translucent, glisten,* and *star* relate to light.
   (b) Apollo was associated with the sun.

continued

16 Archaic Torso of *Apollo*[1]

Rainer Maria Rilke
translated by *Stephen Mitchell*

We cannot know his legendary head
with eyes like ripening fruit. And yet his torso
is still suffused[2] with brilliance from inside,
like a lamp, in which his gaze, now turned to low,

gleams in all its power. Otherwise
the curved breast could not dazzle you so, nor could
a smile run through the placid hips and thighs
17 to that dark center where procreation[3] flared.

Otherwise this stone would seem defaced
beneath the translucent cascade of the shoulders
and would not glisten like a wild beast's fur:

would not, from all the borders of itself,
burst like a star: for here there is no place
that does not see you. You must change your life.

Literary Analysis
Speaker and Poet's Vision How closely do you think the speaker's words reflect Rilke's personal worldview? Explain.

1. **Archaic . . . Apollo:** The Archaic period of Greek art lasted from the late seventh century to about 480 B.C. Apollo was the Greek god of music, poetry, prophecy, and medicine. He was associated with the sun and portrayed as a handsome, athletic young man.
2. **suffused** (sə fyo͞ozd′) *v.* filled with a glow, color, or liquid.
3. **procreation** (prō′ krē ā′ shən) *n.* the process of producing or bringing into existence.

Review and Assess

Thinking About the Selection

1. **Respond:** Do you find it easy to picture the statue? Explain.
2. **(a) Recall:** In line 1, which part of the statue does the speaker say is missing? **(b) Identify:** In line 4, which word suggests sight? **(c) Analyze:** How does this surprising contrast relate to the idea expressed in the poem's final two lines?
3. **(a) Classify:** Which words in the poem relate to light? **(b) Analyze:** How might the energy of the statue relate to the god that it depicts?
4. **Take a Position:** Do you think works of art have the power to transform individual lives in a permanent way? Why or why not?

continued from left column

4. Possible response: Yes, but a transformation occurs only if the viewer is willing and able to accept the insights the art offers.

ENRICHMENT: Mythology Connection

Apollo

Explain to students that Apollo, who is depicted in Rilke's poem "The Archaic Torso of Apollo," is one of the most important Greek gods. He is associated with beauty, medicine, law, the fine arts, courage, and wisdom. Two Greek maxims, "Know Thyself" and "Nothing in Excess," were inscribed on the walls of his temple at Delphi. Depictions of Apollo often show him wearing a laurel wreath.

18

Palm

Paul Valéry

translated by **Barbara Gibbs**

Background

Paul Valéry was influenced by the literary movement known as Symbolism. The Symbolists rebelled against the Realist writers' goal of representing life factually and accurately. Instead, the Symbolists used symbols (images that represent abstract ideas and thus express deeper meanings) to suggest key ideas and to manipulate reality. The purpose of poetry, according to the Symbolists, is to take the reader beyond the poem itself to another level of meaning or experience. See if you can detect that purpose at work in the following three poems.

An angel sets at my place
—Barely screening the accolade
Of his formidable grace—
Fresh milk, new-baked bread;
With his lids he makes a sign
That is like a petition
That says to my vision:
19 Calm, calm, be calm,
Know the heaviness of a palm
Bearing its profusion!

Even as it bends
Under abundant good things
The shape perfectly rounds,
The heavy fruits are strings.
Wonder how it sheds
Vibrancy, how a slow thread
That parcels out the moment
Adjudicates[1] without mystery
The heaviness of the sky
And the earth's enticement!

accolade (ak΄ ə lād΄) *n.* anything done as a sign of praise or respect

profusion (prō fyo͞o΄ zhən) *n.* abundance; rich or lavish supply

✓Reading Check

What gifts does the angel set at the speaker's place?

1. **adjudicates** (ə jo͞o΄ də kātz) *v.* serves as a judge.

18 About the Selection

Paul Valéry wrote "Palm" in 1917. Originally part of a longer piece, "Palm" describes a palm as a microcosm of the natural world.

19 Reading Strategy

Analyzing Images

- Remind students that imagery appeals to one of the five senses.

  Read aloud the bracketed passage to students, and ask: What senses are evoked by the images?
  Answer: The senses of sight, smell, and taste are evoked.
- Draw students' attention to lines 11–14, and ask them to rephrase the description in the most literal way possible.
  Possible response: A palm tree bends under the weight of the fruit it bears.

Monitor Progress Have students discuss what they envision when they think of palm trees.
Possible response: The large mass of leaves perched on a palm's long thin trunk is a familiar image.

- Then, ask what the line "The shape perfectly rounds" means.
  Possible response: The palm tree's trunk curves under the weight of its fruit and leaves.

Reteach To help students determine the literal meaning of the image of the palm tree, have them use a graphic organizer like the one shown on p. 1029.

CUSTOMIZE INSTRUCTION FOR UNIVERSAL ACCESS

For English Learners	For Gifted/Talented Students
The imagery in these poems may present special difficulties for students who are still trying to master the literal meanings of words. Organize students into pairs, and ask each pair to identify and list any confusing words or images they encounter. Then, have each pair write three questions about the images they have identified. Have pairs take turns asking their questions, and use each question to initiate a class discussion.	Have students create visual representations—such as drawings, paintings, or sculptures—of the image in "Archaic Torso of Apollo." Encourage students to use their representations to go beyond the literal descriptions of the image and to suggest the ideas and feelings associated with it. Have students present their representations and discuss how the representations reflect Rilke's poetic intent and their own artistic intent.

20 Background

Poe's Influence on Valéry

The French poets, beginning with Baudelaire and including Valéry, were very interested in Poe's theory of literature. Poe argued that poetry is not merely a result of divine inspiration, as the Romantics insisted. It is the result of conscious effort and craft. The art of poetry, Poe would say, is more science than inspiration. Valéry would agree.

21 Reading Strategy

Analyzing Images

- Remind students that poets often use imagery to express ideas.
- Then, read aloud the bracketed passage. Initiate a discussion about how the images in this passage draw the reader into the scene by evoking personal experiences of gentleness.
- Ask students the Reading Strategy question on p. 1038: To what senses do the images in lines 45–50 appeal? Explain.
  Answer: The images appeal to the senses of sight ("gold"), taste ("juice"), and smell ("love's perfume").

22 Literary Analysis

Speaker and Poet's Vision

- After students have read "Palm," ask them whether they think the speaker and the poet have the same vision.
  Possible response: The speaker and the poet have the same vision because Valéry has not created a narrator with a distinctive voice or personality. The poem's purpose, especially in this final stanza, seems to be to express a view of life. It seems likely that Valéry himself is the speaker.
- Ask students the Literary Analysis question on p. 1038: Based on the final stanza, how would you describe the poet's view of the human condition?
  Possible response: The poet seems to view life as filled with hope.

This fair mobile arbitress
Between shadow and sunlight
Wears the sibyl's[2] dress,
Wisdom of day, sleep of night.
All round the one spot
The wide palm wearies not
Of welcomes and farewells . . .
How noble and soft it is
And worthy to dispose
The comforts of immortals!

The faint gold it sighs
Rings like a mere finger of air
Burdening the desert skies
With a silken signature.
An imperishable sound
Which it gives to the sandy wind
That waters it with its grains
Serves it as oracle[3]
And foretells the miracle
Of the chanting pain.

Between sand and sky,
Ignorant of its own nature,
Each brightening day
Adds honey to its store.
This gentleness is ordered by
The divine continuity
Which does not mark passing time (21)
But rather hides it
In a juice wherein secretes
All of love's perfume.

If you sometimes despond—
If the ardored[4] rigor
In spite of tears responds
Under a shadow of languor[5]—
Never blame of avarice[6] (22)
A Wisdom that is nurse
To so much gold and authority:
An everlasting hope
Rises through the dark sap
To maturity! . . .

Themes in World Literature

20 *Poe's Influence on Valéry*

The French Symbolists greatly admired American author Edgar Allan Poe, whose works Charles Baudelaire had translated into French between 1848 and 1857. Much of Valéry's literary philosophy reflects Poe's theories and beliefs about literature. In addition, Valéry's style often shows Poe's influence. In "Palm," for example, Valéry's focus on the musicality of words is strongly reminiscent of the creative use of sound in Poe's poetry.

imperishable (im per′ ish ə bəl) *adj.* indestructible

Reading Strategy
Analyzing Images To what senses do the images in lines 45–50 appeal? Explain.

despond (di spänd′) *v.* to lose courage or hope

Literary Analysis
Speaker and Poet's Vision Based on the final stanza, how would you describe the poet's view of the human condition?

2. **sibyl's** (sib′ əlz) In ancient Greece and Rome, sibyls were female prophets.
3. **oracle** (ôr′ ə kəl) *n.* person of great knowledge or wisdom, especially in revealing mysteries.
4. **ardored** (är′ dərd) *adj.* passionate.
5. **languor** (laŋ′ gər) *n.* lack of interest or spirit.
6. **avarice** (av′ ə ris) *n.* greed for riches.

ENRICHMENT: Literature Connection

Valéry's Creative Process

Paul Valéry was intensely curious about the creative process and the role of poetry and poets. In his book *Paul Valéry,* H.A.L. Fisher describes Valéry's curiosity in the following way:

> The things that interest [Valéry] are the theory of the arts and processes of his own thinking. . . . As he conceives the business of the poet, it is not to paint the outward face of nature or the visible spectacle of human events, but to dive into the processes of the personal consciousness and to extract whatever pearls the deep may yield. . . . It is only by the dragnets of the mind sunk to the uttermost depths of human nature that the most precious secrets of the spirit are revealed.

㉓ 

The Friendly Wood

Paul Valéry *translated by* Vernon Watkins

Meditations pure were ours
Side by side, along the ways;
We held each other's hand without
Speaking, among the hidden flowers.

Alone we walked as if betrothed,
Lost in the green night of the fields;
We shared this fruit of fairy reels,
㉔ The moon, to madmen well disposed.

And then, we were dead upon the moss,
Far, quite alone, among the soft
Shades of this intimate, murmuring wood;

And there, in the vast light aloft,
We found ourselves with many a tear,
O my companion of silence dear!

Literary Analysis
Speaker in a Poem
Whom is the speaker addressing?

Review and Assess

Thinking About the Selections

1. **Respond:** "Palm" was part of a collection entitled *Charmes*, or "songs." In what ways is "Palm" like a song?
2. **(a) Recall:** According to the first line of "Palm," with which being is the speaker in contact? **(b) Interpret:** What message does the being bring in stanza 1?
3. **(a) Recall:** In lines 21–22, what does the palm stand "between"? **(b) Classify:** What other words in stanza 3 suggest a similar balance? **(c) Analyze:** What does the speaker admire about the palm?
4. **(a) Deduce:** In "The Friendly Wood," note three activities that the speaker does with a companion. **(b) Interpret:** How would you describe the relationship between the speaker and the companion?
5. **Generalize:** Why do you think the natural world moves some people more than others?

㉓ About the Selections

"The Friendly Wood" describes the speaker's companionship with nature.

In the poem "Caesar," on p. 1040, Valéry expresses his view on the power and influence of a typical dictator he calls "Caesar."

㉔ Literary Analysis

Speaker in a Poem

- Remind students that the speaker in a poem is the one who "says" its words. Then, read the poem aloud, asking students to look for clues to the identity of the speaker's companion.
- Ask students the Literary Analysis question on p. 1039: Whom is the speaker addressing?
  Possible answer: The speaker is addressing a lover.
- Ask students why the two companions find themselves with "many a tear."
  Possible response: The companions may be weeping for the beauty of nature.

Answers for p. 1039

Review and Assess

1. Possible response: In many places, the sound and rhythm of the words seem almost as important as the meaning.
2. **(a)** The speaker is in contact with an angel. **(b)** The being tells the speaker to be calm.
3. **(a)** The palm stands between shadow and sunlight. **(b)** Other phrases that suggest balance include "Wisdom of day, sleep of night" and "welcomes and farewells." **(c)** The palm does not weary and offers comfort and hope.
4. **(a)** Possible response: The companions meditate, walk, hold hands, rest, and cry together. **(b)** The relationship is an intimate one; the companions can be together in both silence and tears.
5. Possible response: Some people regard nature in a personal way, as though it were a lover or close relative, and they revel in that closeness.

CUSTOMIZE INSTRUCTION FOR UNIVERSAL ACCESS

For Special Needs Students	For Gifted/Talented Students	For Advanced Readers
Draw students' attention to the word *betrothed* in the first line of the second stanza. Tell students that this word can be a verb or a noun. Then, ask students to write two sentences using *betrothed*—once as a verb and once as a noun.	Have students write a journal entry in which they describe a time that they felt a connection with nature. Have students address the following question in their entries: What lesson did you learn from your connection with nature?	Point out to students that a common characteristic of Symbolist poetry is the blurring of the senses; for example, smells become sounds and sights become tastes, and so on. Have students discuss how Valéry blurs the senses in "The Friendly Wood."

25 Vocabulary Development

Latin Word Part *omni-*

- Read aloud the word *omnipotent* and its definition. Explain that *omni-* means "all," "unlimited," or "universally."
- Ask students to offer examples of other words that use *omni-*, and list them on the board. Possible response: *Omnipresent, omniscient,* or *omnivorous* are possible suggestions.

26 Reading Strategy

Analyzing Images

- Tell students that understanding the literal meaning of an image will give them a better understanding of its deeper meaning.
- Ask: Which images in the first stanza suggest Caesar's military power and skill? Explain. Answer: Some images include "The hard fists," and "eagles and battles." The images imply the physical dominance and power associated with battle.

Answers for p. 1040

Review and Assess

1. Possible response: Readers may realize that a decision for a war that will affect many depends on the will of one or a few military leaders.
2. **(a)** Caesar's eyes are pregnant with visions of eagles and battles. **(b)** If Caesar acts on these, nothing will escape the consequences of war.
3. **(a)** Caesar is depicted as an all-powerful leader; the images of the lake and wheat depict a vulnerable natural world. **(b)** Nature will not stop Caesar.
4. **(a)** The fisherman may become a victim of war. **(b)** The poem would not be as effective; the final stanza suggests how Caesar's decisions affect an average citizen.
5. Possible response: Caesar seems violent and disruptive rather than admirable.

23 CAESAR[1]

Paul Valéry
***translated by* C. F. MacIntyre**

25 Caesar, serene Caesar, your foot on all,
The hard fists in the beard, and the gloomy eyes
26 Pregnant with eagles and battles of foreseen fall,
Your heart swells, feeling itself omnipotent cause.

In vain the lake trembles, licking its rosy bed,
Vainly glistens the gold of the young wheat straws.
You harden in the knots of your gathered body
The word which must finally rive[2] your tight-clenched jaws.

The spacious world, beyond the immense horizon,
The Empire awaits the torch, the order, the lightning
Which will turn the evening to a furious dawn.

Happily there on the waves, and cradled in hazard,
A lazy fisherman is drifting and singing,
Not knowing what thunder collects in the center of Caesar.

omnipotent (äm nip′ ə tent) *adj.* having unlimited power or authority

1. **Caesar** (sē′ zər) here, any emperor or dictator.
2. **rive** (rīv) *v.* tear apart; rend.

Review and Assess

Thinking About the Selection

1. **Respond:** Did this poem suggest a new way of thinking about war or military leadership? Why or why not?
2. **(a) Recall:** In line 3, with which visions are Caesar's eyes "pregnant"? **(b) Analyze Cause and Effect:** How will these private visions alter the world?
3. **(a) Compare and Contrast:** In what ways do the images in lines 4–5 differ from those that describe Caesar? **(b) Deduce:** Why are the efforts of these items made "in vain"?
4. **(a) Speculate:** How might the fisherman's life change because of Caesar? **(b) Modify:** If "Caesar" ended with the third stanza, would the poem lose its effectiveness? Explain.
5. **Make a Judgment:** Is leadership of the kind Caesar displays admirable? Explain.

ASSESSMENT PRACTICE: Reading Comprehension

Comparing and Contrasting Texts (For more practice, see the Test Preparation Workbook, p. 46.)

Some tests require students to compare and contrast aspects of two texts. Use the following sample item to give students practice using this skill.

at night the deep transparent skies / glitter with new galaxies.

I move across into this night, / Where a worn poplar age has grizzled / Screens the moon's strip of fallow light,

How are these passages similar?

A Both have humorous tones.
B Both describe scenes at night.
C Both are written to persuade.
D Both use personification.

The passages are not humorous, persuasive, or personified, so answers *A, C,* and *D* are not correct. Each passage describes a scene at night, so the correct answer is *B*.

Review and Assess

Literary Analysis

Speaker in a Poem

1. (a) What information about the **speaker's** identity do the details in "Everything Is Plundered" suggest? (b) Do you think the speaker in this poem is Akhmatova herself? Why or why not?
2. In "Archaic Torso of Apollo," what do we learn about the speaker through the description of the statue? Explain.
3. Use a chart like the one shown to examine how the sensory details used in "The Weeping Orchard" reveal the speaker's thoughts and feelings.

Sensory Detail	Speaker's Feelings/Thoughts

Comparing Literary Works

4. Both "Everything Is Plundered" and "Caesar" could be described as war poems. How are the two **poets' visions** of war both similar and different?
5. (a) Compare and contrast the lessons each speaker learns through close observation of an object in "Archaic Torso of Apollo" and "Palm." (b) What worldviews do these lessons express?

Reading Strategy

Analyzing Images

6. (a) Begin to **analyze images** by noting one example of a pleasant image and one example of a disturbing image in "Caesar."
(b) What does the use of both types of images suggest about the meaning of the poem?
7. (a) Identify images of water and the feelings or moods they create in each of the poems by Pasternak. (b) Explain a possible symbolic meaning for the images of water in each poem.

Extend Understanding

8. **Career Connection:** From this grouping, choose one poem whose topic might interest a journalist. Explain how the journalist's approach would differ from the poet's.

Quick Review

The **speaker** in a poem is the poem's "voice," the one who "tells" the poem to the reader.

The speaker's words might suggest the **poet's vision** — the poet's view of life.

To **analyze images,** think carefully about the purpose and meaning of sensory language in literary works.

Take It to the Net

PHSchool.com

Take the interactive self-test online to check your understanding of these selections.

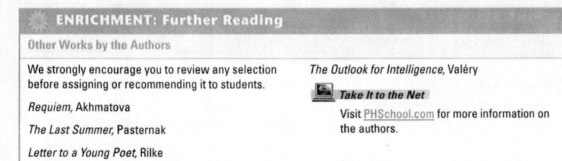

ENRICHMENT: Further Reading

Other Works by the Authors

We strongly encourage you to review any selection before assigning or recommending it to students.

Requiem, Akhmatova

The Last Summer, Pasternak

Letter to a Young Poet, Rilke

The Selected Poetry of Rainer Maria Rilke, Rilke

The Outlook for Intelligence, Valéry

Take It to the Net

Visit PHSchool.com for more information on the authors.

Answers for p. 1041

Review and Assess

1. **(a)** Possible response: The details suggest that the speaker has experienced war and is looking for hope. **(b)** Possible response: The speaker is probably Akhmatova because she lived through war and knew details of the poem from experience.
2. The reader learns that the speaker reveres ancient art and believes that it can affect people's lives.
3. Possible response: **Sample: Detail:** "orchard drips and listens"; **Feelings:** The speaker is pensive and observant.
4. Both poets view war as violent and destructive. Akhmatova sees its misery and destruction, but she believes that the human spirit can prevail. Valéry's vision is of the power and glory of war and its ability to affect all things. He emphasizes the negative effects of war on everyday life.
5. **(a)** The speaker in "Archaic Torso of Apollo" learns that ancient art can affect a viewer's life. In contrast, the speaker in "Palm" learns that people can be like palms, with hope surging from within. **(b)** Both express a belief that people can grow and change by applying insights they have gained to their own lives.
6. **(a)** A pleasant image is that of the fisherman drifting and singing. A disturbing image is that of the Empire awaiting "the torch, the order, the lightning." **(b)** They suggest a violent conflict that will disrupt daily life.
7. Possible response: **(a)** In "The Weeping Orchard," water drips from the trees and "rolls down roof/ to gutter," creating a pensive, sorrowful mood. In "The Drowsy Garden," a "pond lies, an open secret," and a lake reflects the sky. The mood is quiet. **(b)** Water symbolizes life. In "The Weeping Orchard" it symbolizes life's sorrow. In "The Drowsy Garden," water symbolizes how life connects all things—it reflects the sky.
8. Possible response: A journalist might give facts about the torso of Apollo. The poet looks into the statue to find its meaning or purpose.

EXTEND

Answers for p. 1042

❶ Vocabulary Development

Word Analysis: Latin Word Part *omni-*

1. c
2. b
3. a

Spelling Strategy

1. accept
2. accompany
3. acquaint
4. acclaim
5. accord
6. acquiesce

Fluency: Sentence Completions

1. imperishable
2. opaque
3. despond
4. plundered
5. omnipotent
6. tremulous
7. profusion
8. accolade

❷ Grammar and Style

Practice

1. abstract
2. concrete
3. abstract
4. concrete
5. abstract
6. abstract
7. concrete
8. concrete

Writing Application

Possible response: I marveled at the beauty [abstract] of the desert [concrete]. The majesty [abstract] of its vastness [abstract] touched my heart [concrete]. A dry wind [concrete] swept away all my thoughts [abstract]. I stared out across the sands [concrete], considering the mystery [abstract] of wild places [concrete].

10TH GRADE For support in teaching the Grammar and Style Lesson to tenth graders, use **Writing and Grammar,** Platinum Level, Chapter 16, Section 1.

Integrate Language Skills

❶ Vocabulary Development Lesson

Word Analysis: Latin Word Part *omni-*

The word part *omni-* means "all," "unlimited," or "universally," as in *omnipotent*, which means "all-powerful." Match each numbered word below with its definition.

1. omnipresent
2. omniscient
3. omnivore

a. creature that eats everything
b. having unlimited knowledge
c. existing in all places at all times

Spelling Strategy

Words beginning with an *ak* sound often contain the Latin prefix *ad-*, which means "to," "toward," or "akin to." That prefix is spelled *ac* before the letter *c* or *q* (as in *accident* and *acquire*).

Each of the following words is misspelled. In your notebook, write the correct spelling.

1. acept
2. acompany
3. aquaint
4. aclaim
5. acqord
6. aquiesce

Fluency: Sentence Completions

Review the vocabulary list on page 1029. Then, using the context clues in the following passage, fill in each blank in the paragraph below with a word from the vocabulary list.

It was a battle royal: our Centerburg Panthers against the Jackson Tigers. The ancient, __?__ rivalry between our schools was alive and well—and we were losing. No ray of cheer was passing through the __?__ cloud of doom above my head. "I must not __?__," I said. "Those Tigers will be __?__ of their trophy. Our __?__ Panthers will win!" Just then a __?__ cry ran through the crowd: We had the ball! One basket and then another scored as the buzzer sounded. There were cries of jubilation. Cheers rang out in __?__, for we had won! The Panthers waved to acknowledge the crowd's __?__, while the defeated Tigers straggled off the court.

❷ Grammar and Style Lesson

Concrete Nouns and Abstract Nouns

Concrete nouns name things that people can physically see, touch, taste, hear, or smell. **Abstract nouns** name things that cannot be perceived through the physical senses.

Examples:
Concrete: *trees, child, lace, lightning, perfume*
Abstract: *questions, life, vibrancy, miracle*

Practice Identify whether each noun below is concrete or abstract.

1. gentleness
2. fisherman
3. wisdom
4. garden
5. flattery
6. dogma
7. eagles
8. tears

Writing Application Write four sentences about a natural scene. In each sentence, use at least one concrete noun and one abstract noun.

WG *Prentice Hall Writing and Grammar Connection: Diamond Level, Chapter 17, Section 1*

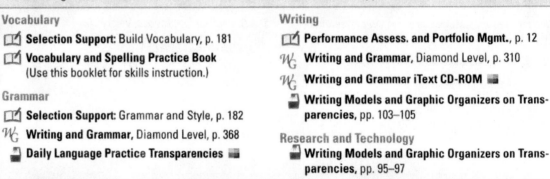

TEACHING RESOURCES

The following resources can be used to enrich or extend the instruction for pp. 1042–1043.

Vocabulary
- **Selection Support:** Build Vocabulary, p. 181
- **Vocabulary and Spelling Practice Book** (Use this booklet for skills instruction.)

Grammar
- **Selection Support:** Grammar and Style, p. 182
- **Writing and Grammar,** Diamond Level, p. 368
- **Daily Language Practice Transparencies** ■

Writing
- **Performance Assess. and Portfolio Mgmt.**, p. 12
- **Writing and Grammar,** Diamond Level, p. 310
- **Writing and Grammar iText CD-ROM** ■
- **Writing Models and Graphic Organizers on Transparencies,** pp. 103–105

Research and Technology
- **Writing Models and Graphic Organizers on Transparencies,** pp. 95–97

■ **BLOCK SCHEDULING:** Resources marked with this symbol provide varied instruction during 90-minute blocks.

❸ Writing Lesson

Reflective Essay

In a reflective essay, a writer relates ideas about a subject to his or her personal experience. Write a reflective essay in which you discuss Rilke's poem "The Grownup" and offer your interpretation of its meaning. Then, discuss your perspective on the process of maturing from a child into an adult.

Prewriting As you reread "The Grownup," take notes about its meaning and any personal experience it brings to mind.

Drafting Begin by summarizing "The Grownup." Then, write at least one paragraph on its meaning and at least another paragraph on your perspective. Tie your ideas together in your conclusion.

Revising As you review your draft, underline your main ideas. Then, make sure that the personal experiences you describe clearly relate to and support those ideas.

Model: Revising to Connect Literature to Life

Rilke's speaker says that growing up happens "in the midst of play." *That comment reminds me of the first time that I felt childish while playing "house." The game suddenly seemed foolish.* Clearly, maturity can come as a shock.

A reflective essay uses personal experience to support ideas.

WG Prentice Hall Writing and Grammar Connection: Diamond Level, Chapter 14, Section 2

❹ Extension Activities

Listening and Speaking Rilke wrote "Archaic Torso of Apollo" in response to a sculpture. Following his example, write and present a **poem** in response to a work of art. Consider these suggestions:

- Skim through art books or electronic art resources to find a work you like.
- Note details about the work and the thoughts and feelings that it inspires in you.
- Write a poem that will inspire similar thoughts and feelings in others.

Present both the poem and the art to the class.

Research and Technology During the 1920s, the Russian art world gave rise to many literary movements, including Futurism, Acmeism, and Constructivism. In a small group, research two such movements. Then, choose one poem that best represents each movement, and create a **comparison-and-contrast report** for the class. [Group Activity]

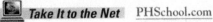

 ***Take It to the Net*** PHSchool.com

Go online for an additional research activity using the Internet.

ASSESSMENT RESOURCES

The following resources can be used to assess students' knowledge and skills.

Selection Assessment

- **Formal Assessment,** pp. 164–166
- **Open-Book Tests,** pp. 136–138
- **Test Bank Software**

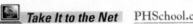

 ***Take It to the Net***

Visit PHSchool.com for self-tests on the selections.

Writing Rubric

- **Performance Assess. and Portfolio Mgmt.,** p. 12

Research and Technology Rubric

- **Performance Assess. and Portfolio Mgmt.,** p. 15

For additional diagnostics and remediation for skills covered in this grouping, use materials from the Prentice Hall Assessment System.

❸ Writing Lesson

- Explain to students that a reflective essay is autobiographical writing that provides insight into a personal experience.
- Encourage students to use the Outline organizer in **Writing Models and Graphic Organizers,** pp. 103–105, to help them organize their essays.
- Use the Writing Lesson to guide students in developing their reflective essays.
- Use the Reflective Essay rubric in **Performance Assessment and Portfolio Management,** p. 12, to evaluate students' work.

10TH GRADE For support in working through the Writing Lesson with tenth graders, use **Writing and Grammar,** Platinum Level, Chapter 13, Section 2.

❹ Research and Technology

- Remind students that their comparison-and-contrast reports should tell how the two movements are both alike and different. Students should cite specific examples to support their discussion.
- Encourage students to use the Comparison-and-Contrast Organizer in **Writing Models and Graphic Organizers on Transparencies,** pp. 95–97, to help them clarify their ideas.
- Use the Exposition: Comparison-and-Contrast Composition rubric in **Performance Assessment and Portfolio Management,** p. 15, to evaluate students' reports.

CUSTOMIZE INSTRUCTION For Universal Access

To address different learning styles, use the following activities suggested in the **Extension Activities** booklet, p. 46:

- For Intrapersonal Learners, use Activity 5.
- For Verbal/Linguistic Learners, use Activities 5 and 6.
- For Visual/Spatial Learners, use Activity 6.

The Bracelet

Lesson Objectives

1. **To analyze and respond to literary elements**
   - Literary Analysis: Epiphany
   - Connecting Literary Elements: Descriptive Details
2. **To read, comprehend, analyze, and critique a short story**
   - Reading Strategy: Drawing Conclusions
   - Reading Check Questions
   - Review and Assess Questions
   - Assessment Practice (ATE)
3. **To develop word analysis skills, fluency, and systematic vocabulary**
   - Vocabulary Development Lesson: Latin Prefix *en-*
4. **To understand and apply written and oral language conventions**
   - Spelling Strategy
   - Grammar and Style Lesson: Correct Use of *Sit* and *Set*
5. **To understand and apply appropriate writing and research strategies**
   - Writing Lesson: Analytical Essay
   - Extension Activity: Set and Costume Design
6. **To understand and apply listening and speaking strategies**
   - Extension Activity: Monologue

10TH GRADE **TEACHING A TENTH-GRADE COURSE**

The literature in this section can be taught as part of a rich, balanced world literature course for tenth-grade students. For a full outline of such a course, see pp. T46–T48 in Volume 1 of this Teacher's Edition.

STEP-BY-STEP TEACHING GUIDE	PACING GUIDE
PRETEACH	
Motivate Students and Provide Background	
Use the Motivation activity (ATE p. 1044)	5 min.
Read and discuss author and background features (SE pp. 1044, 1046; ATE p. 1044) [A]	5 min.
Introduce the Concepts	
Introduce the Literary Analysis and Reading Strategy concepts (SE/ATE p. 1045) [A]	15 min.
Pronounce the vocabulary words and read their definitions (SE p. 1045)	5 min.
TEACH	
Monitor Comprehension	
Informally monitor comprehension by circulating while students read independently or in groups [A]	20 min.
Monitor students' comprehension with the Reading Check notes (SE/ATE pp. 1046, 1049)	as students read
Develop vocabulary with Vocabulary notes (SE pp. 1046, 1049; ATE p. 1049)	as students read
Develop Understanding	
Develop students' understanding of epiphany with the Literary Analysis annotation (ATE p. 1050) [A]	5 min.
Develop students' ability to draw conclusions, using the Reading Strategy annotations (SE/ATE pp. 1046, 1048)	5 min.
ASSESS	
Assess Mastery	
Assess students' mastery of the Reading Strategy and Literary Analysis concepts by having them answer the Review and Assess questions (SE/ATE p. 1051)	15 min.
Use one or more of the print, software, or transparency Assessment Resources (ATE p. 1053) [A]	up to 45 min.
EXTEND	
Apply Understanding	
Have students complete the Vocabulary Development Lesson and the Grammar and Style Lesson (SE p. 1052) [A]	20 min.
Apply students' ability to analyze an image, using the Writing Lesson (SE/ATE p. 1053) [A]	45 min.
Apply students' understanding of the story, using one or more of the Extension Activities (SE p. 1053)	20–90 min.

[A] **ACCELERATED INSTRUCTION:** Use the strategies and activities identified with an [A].

10TH GRADE **TEACHING TENTH-GRADE STUDENTS:** For support in teaching the selection(s) to tenth-grade students, see the Step-by-Step Teaching notes identified wih the icon shown here.

UNIVERSAL ACCESS

● = Below-Level Students
▲ = On-Level Students
■ = Above-Level Students

Time and Resource Manager

Reading Level: Challenging, Average
Average Number of Instructional Days: 3

RESOURCES		
PRINT	**TRANSPARENCIES**	**TECHNOLOGY**
• **Beyond Literature,** Cross-Curricular Connection: Science, p. 47 ▲ ■		
• **Selection Support Workbook:** ● ▲ ■ Literary Analysis, p. 188 Reading Strategy, p. 187 Build Vocabulary, p. 185	• **Literary Analysis and Reading Transparencies,** pp. 93 and 94 ● ▲ ■	
• **Reader's Companion** ● • **Adapted Reader's Companion** ●		• **Listening to Literature** ● ▲ ■ Audiocassettes Audio CDs • **Reader's Companion Audio Program** ● • **Reader's Companion Adapted and English Learner's Version Audio Program** ● ▲
• **English Learner's Companion** ● ▲ • **Literary Analysis for Enrichment,** p. 47 ■		• **World Masterpieces iText CD-ROM**
• **Formal Assessment:** Selection Test, pp. 167–169 ● ▲ ■ • **Open-Book Tests,** pp. 139–141 ● ▲ ■ • **Performance Assessment and Portfolio Management,** pp. 16, 33 ● ▲ ■ • PRENTICE HALL ASSESSMENT SYSTEM ● ▲ ■	• PRENTICE HALL ASSESSMENT SYSTEM ● ▲ ■ **Skills Practice Answers and Explanations on Transparencies**	• **Test Bank Software** ● ▲ ■
• **Selection Support Workbook:** ● ▲ ■ Grammar and Style, p. 186 • **Writing and Grammar,** Diamond Level ● ▲ ■ • **Extension Activities,** p. 47 ● ▲ ■	• **Daily Language Practice Transparencies** ● ▲ ■ • **Writing Models and Graphic Organizers on Transparencies,** pp. 71–73	• **Writing and Grammar iText CD-ROM** ● ▲ ■ ***Take It to the Net*** PHSchool.com

BLOCK SCHEDULING: Use one 90-minute class period to preteach the selection(s) and have students read them. Use a second 90-minute class period to assess students' mastery of skills and have them complete one of the Extension Activities.

PRETEACH

Step-by-Step Teaching Guide for pp. 1044–1045

Motivation

On the board, write this quotation, the first line from English writer L. P. Hartley's novel *The Go-Between*: "The past is a foreign country: they do things differently there." Discuss with students what Hartley might mean by this statement and whether they agree with it, based on their own experiences. Conclude by explaining that the story they are about to read concerns one woman's encounter with this "foreign country."

❶ Background

More About the Author

Sidonie-Gabrielle Colette (the author's full name) was the first woman president of the Goncourt Academy, an institute established to recognize literary talent. She was also the second woman to become a grand officer of the French Legion of Honor.

Geography Note

Draw students' attention to the map at the top of the page. Remind students that Colette was born in the French province of Burgundy. One of twenty-two provincial regions, Burgundy is located in the east-central part of the country and provides both agricultural and industrial resources.

Prepare to Read

❶ The Bracelet

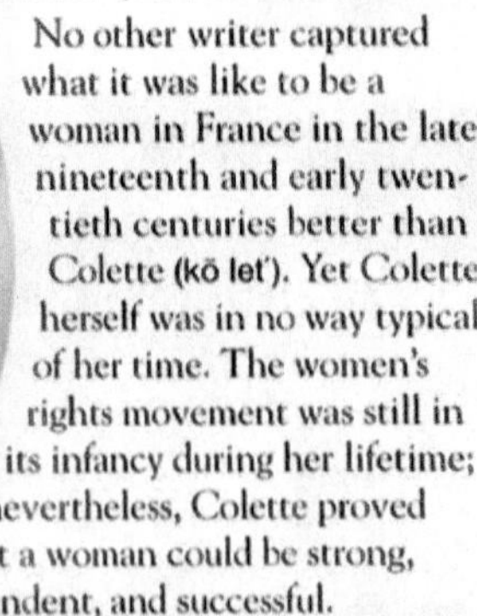

Colette (1873–1954)

No other writer captured what it was like to be a woman in France in the late nineteenth and early twentieth centuries better than Colette (kō let'). Yet Colette herself was in no way typical of her time. The women's rights movement was still in its infancy during her lifetime; nevertheless, Colette proved that a woman could be strong, independent, and successful.

First Marriage Colette was born in the small village of St. Sauveur-en-Puisaye (san' sō vėr' än püē zā) in the French province of Burgundy. As a child, she was taught by her mother to savor the sights, sounds, and textures of country life, an appreciation that her fiction would later reflect. Before her twentieth birthday, she married Henri Gauthier-Villars (än rē' gō tyā' vē lär'), a mediocre writer fourteen years her senior. By providing her with encouragement and support and by introducing her to many of the most prominent French writers of the time, Gauthier-Villars played a vital role in launching Colette's literary career. In fact, her husband published her first series of books, known as the "Claudine" novels, under the pseudonym Willy. The "Claudine" novels centered on the misadventures of a teenage girl and became a huge popular success. They inspired numerous related projects and products, including a musical, Claudine clothing, and Claudine soap, perfume, and cigars.

After her marriage ended in 1906, Colette lived alone for several years. During this period, she continued to develop her literary skills while also indulging in a number of other creative endeavors, including singing, dancing, and hairdressing. Colette's experiences during this period of her life inspired two successful books, *The Vagabond* (1911) and *Recaptured* (1913).

Her Star Rises In 1912, Colette married Henri de Jouvenel (də zhōō və nel'), a prominent journalist. The marriage ended in divorce in 1924. As her second marriage failed, however, Colette's fame grew. She published such highly regarded works as *Chéri* (1920), *My Mother's House* (1922), *The Ripening* (1923), *The Last of Chéri* (1926), and *Sido* (1929). Two of these works—*Chéri* and *The Last of Chéri*—focus on a tragic love affair between a young man and an older woman, while the other works deal with the experiences of childhood and adolescence.

Colette married her third husband, Maurice Goudeket (mō rēs' gōō də kā'), another writer, in 1935. Unlike her first two marriages, her marriage to Goudeket brought her great contentment and lasted for the remainder of her life. Unfortunately, her happiness was tainted by the onset of crippling arthritis and by her husband's arrest and imprisonment by the Nazis during World War II. These setbacks did not affect her productivity as a writer, however, and in the 1930s and 1940s she wrote many successful books, including *The Cat* (1933), *Duo* (1934), *Gigi* (1944), and *The Blue Light* (1949).

A Literary Legend By the time of her death in 1954, Colette had written more than fifty novels or novellas and an even greater number of short stories. Among the French public, she had established herself as a literary legend, and she had received a number of distinguished honors, including her induction into both the Royal Belgian Academy and the French Goncourt Academy. During the years since her death, her reputation has continued to grow, and she is now regarded by many as the outstanding French fiction writer of her time.

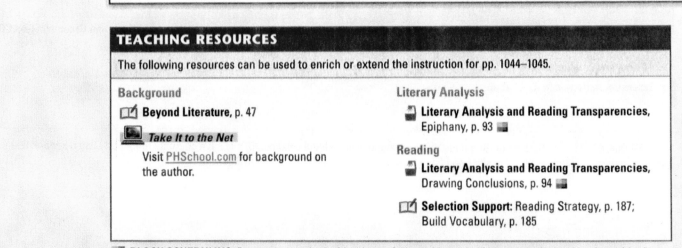

TEACHING RESOURCES

The following resources can be used to enrich or extend the instruction for pp. 1044–1045.

Background

Beyond Literature, p. 47

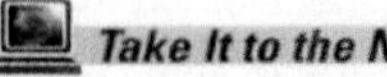

Take It to the Net

Visit PHSchool.com for background on the author.

Literary Analysis

Literary Analysis and Reading Transparencies, Epiphany, p. 93

Reading

Literary Analysis and Reading Transparencies, Drawing Conclusions, p. 94

Selection Support: Reading Strategy, p. 187; Build Vocabulary, p. 185

BLOCK SCHEDULING: Resources marked with this symbol provide varied instruction during 90-minute blocks.

Preview

Connecting to the Literature

If we are unhappy, we sometimes think back with fondness to a better time in our lives. Such is the case of the wealthy but dissatisfied Madame Augelier, whose childhood memory becomes a driving force in her life.

2 Literary Analysis

Epiphany

An **epiphany** is a sudden flash of insight that a person has about himself or herself, another person, a situation, or life itself. That revelation may be positive, but it may also be negative. In traditional plots, a series of events leads to the resolution of a conflict. However, in many modern stories, the series of events leads to an epiphany that may alter the conflict without resolving it. As you read, use a chart like the one shown to identify details that suggest the nature of the epiphany Madame Augelier experiences. Then, decide whether the conflict is resolved or merely changed.

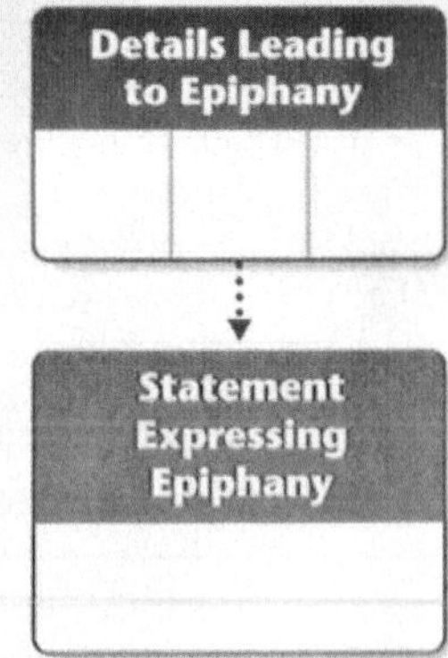

Connecting Literary Elements

An author's choice of the best words to convey meaning contributes to the power and beauty of a work of writing. Colette's use of precise **descriptive details**—words and phrases that appeal to the senses—is one reason her story is so vivid and clear. Compare these two phrases:

Apples in a bowl   Calville apples in a silver bowl

While their meaning is essentially the same, the second phrase creates an image, or word picture, that is both more informative and more suggestive of emotion. As you read, notice the many descriptive details Colette employs.

3 Reading Strategy

Drawing Conclusions

When you **draw conclusions,** you use your reasoning to reach logical decisions on the basis of evidence. For example, if someone comes inside shaking out a wet umbrella, you might draw the conclusion that it is raining. When reading, you draw conclusions by applying your knowledge and experiences to details from the work. As you read "The Bracelet," draw conclusions about Madame Augelier's life and character.

Vocabulary Development

supple (sup′ əl) *adj.* easily bent; flexible (p. 1046)

connoisseur (kän′ ə sur′) *n.* person with expert judgment and taste (p. 1046)

convalescent (kän′ və les′ ənt) *n.* person who is recovering health after illness (p. 1049)

enraptured (en rap′ chərd) *adj.* filled with great pleasure (p. 1049)

iridescent (ir′ i des′ ənt) *adj.* showing rainbowlike shifts in color (p. 1049)

serpentine (sur′ pən tēn′) *adj.* resembling a snake (p. 1049)

congealed (kən jēld′) *v.* thickened; solidified (p. 1049)

2 Literary Analysis

Epiphany

- Read aloud the Literary Analysis instruction on p. 1045. Tell students that both a character and a reader can experience an epiphany.
- Have volunteers share with the class their experiences with epiphanies. Have students discuss what they learned as a result of their epiphanies.
- Then, point out the graphic organizer on p. 1045. Tell students that recognizing significant details or events will help them identify an epiphany in a literary work. Have students use the organizer as they read the story.

3 Reading Strategy

Drawing Conclusions

- Have a volunteer read aloud the Reading Strategy instruction on p. 1045.
- Tell students that many literary works are built of layers of meaning. To uncover deeper meanings, a reader must draw conclusions.
- As students read "The Bracelet," have them use details from the selection and their own experiences to draw conclusions about the story's deeper meanings.
- Use the Drawing Conclusions transparency in **Literary Analysis and Reading Transparencies,** p. 94, to demonstrate for students how to draw conclusions.

Vocabulary Development

- Pronounce each vocabulary word for students, and read the definitions as a class. Have students identify any words with which they are already familiar.

CUSTOMIZE INSTRUCTION FOR UNIVERSAL ACCESS

For Special Needs Students	For Less Proficient Readers	For English Learners
Have students read "The Bracelet" in the **Adapted Reader's Companion.** This version provides basic-level instruction in an interactive format with questions and write-on lines. Completing the adapted version will prepare students to read the selection in the Student Edition.	Have students read the adapted version of the selection in the **Reader's Companion.** This version provides basic-level instruction in an interactive format with questions and write-on lines. After students finish the selection in the **Reader's Companion,** have them complete the questions and activities in the Student Edition.	Have students read the adapted version of the selection in the **English Learner's Companion.** This version provides basic-level instruction in an interactive format with questions and write-on lines. Completing the adapted version will prepare students to read the selection in the Student Edition.

E-Teach

Visit e-Teach at PHSchool.com for teachers' essays on how to teach, with questions and answers.

TEACH

Step-by-Step Teaching Guide for pp. 1046–1050

Teaching Tenth-Grade Students

10TH GRADE Ask tenth-grade students to recall a special gift they cherished in younger years. Have them explain why they think that no new present could ever take its place.

1 About the Selection

In Colette's story "The Bracelet," a woman of fifty looks back on her life of wealth and privilege to discover a disturbing but unavoidable truth about life, possessions, and the passage of time.

2 Reading Strategy

Drawing Conclusions

- Remind students that when a reader draws a conclusion, he or she makes a general statement that can be explained or supported with details from the selection.
- Read aloud the bracketed passage. Then, ask: What conclusions can you draw about Madame Augelier?
  Answer: She is wealthy, and she must be concerned about aging because she notices the wrinkles around her wrist.
- Then, ask students the Reading Strategy question on p. 1046: What conclusions might you draw about the Augeliers' relationship, based on Madame's comment about her husband?
  Possible response: François faithfully buys Madame Augelier an anniversary gift every year, but despite this gesture, or perhaps because of it, Madame Augelier pities her husband.

3 Reading Check

Answer: She has received a diamond bracelet for her twenty-ninth wedding anniversary.

1 

The Bracelet

Colette

translated by Matthew Ward

Background

At the turn of the twentieth century, the women's rights movement was very new. Women in the West were just beginning to enjoy educational and employment opportunities, and marriage generally was the best guarantee of economic security. Like most of Colette's fiction, "The Bracelet" touches on the changing role of women in France in the early twentieth century. The main character, Madame Augelier, is married to a wealthy business executive. In a subtle fashion, the story asks whether the security and predictability of such a marriage is enough for happiness.

". . . Twenty-seven, twenty-eight, twenty-nine . . . There really are twenty-nine . . ."

2 Madame Augelier mechanically counted and recounted the little *pavé*[1] diamonds. Twenty-nine square brilliants, set in a bracelet, which slithered between her fingers like a cold and supple snake. Very white, not too big, admirably matched to each other—the pretty bijou[2] of a connoisseur. She fastened it on her wrist, and shook it, throwing off blue sparks under the electric candles; a hundred tiny rainbows, blazing with color, danced on the white tablecloth. But Madame Augelier was looking more closely instead at the other bracelet, the three finely engraved creases encircling her wrist above the glittering snake.

"Poor François . . . what will he give me next year, if we're both still here?"

François Augelier, industrialist, was traveling in Algeria at the time, but, present or absent, his gift marked both the year's end and their wedding anniversary. Twenty-eight jade bowls, last year; twenty-seven old enamel plaques mounted on a belt, the year before . . .

"And the twenty-six little Royal Dresden[3] plates . . . And the twenty-four meters of antique Alençon lace[4] . . ." With a slight effort of memory

supple (sup´ əl) *adj.* easily bent; flexible

connoisseur (kän´ ə sʉr´) *n.* person with expert judgment and taste

Reading Strategy
Drawing Conclusions What conclusions might you draw about the Augeliers' relationship, based on Madame's comment about her husband?

3 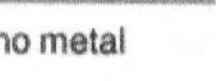
Reading Check
For what occasion has Madame Augelier received a diamond bracelet from her husband?

1. ***pavé*** (pa vā´) jewelry setting in which the gems are placed close together so that no metal shows.
2. **bijou** (bē zhōō´) *n.* jewel.
3. **Royal Dresden** (drez´ dən) fine, decorated porcelain or chinaware made near Dresden, a city in southeast-central Germany.
4. **Alençon** (ə len´ sän´) **lace** needlepoint lace with a solid design on a net background.

TEACHING RESOURCES

The following resources can be used to enrich or extend the instruction for pp. 1046–1050.

Literary Analysis

- **Selection Support:** Literary Analysis, p. 188
- **Literary Analysis and Reading Transparencies,** p. 93 ■

Reading

- **Selection Support:** Reading Strategy, p. 187; Build Vocabulary, p. 185
- **Adapted Reader's Companion**

- **Reader's Companion**
- **English Learner's Companion**
- **Listening to Literature Audiocassettes** ■
- **Listening to Literature Audio CDs**

■ **BLOCK SCHEDULING:** Resources marked with this symbol provide varied instruction during 90-minute blocks.

4

5 ▲ **Critical Viewing** In what ways is this portrait similar to and different from your image of Madame Augelier? Explain. **[Compare and Contrast]**

CUSTOMIZE INSTRUCTION FOR UNIVERSAL ACCESS

For Special Needs Students	For Gifted/Talented Students
Explain to students that "The Bracelet" is rich in sensory details. For example, in the second paragraph on p. 1046, the description of the bracelet as "like a cold and supple snake" appeals to the sense of touch. Tell students that Colette uses vivid imagery. Have students preview the selection to identify and list other sensory details. Then, discuss images and their intended effects on the reader.	Many students may be struck by the mood of this story. Have them choose or compose a piece of background music to match the mood of gentle melancholy and resignation in "The Bracelet." Ask students to play the music for the class and explain their choices or compositions. Then, initiate a discussion about the suitability and effectiveness of each musical selection, and have students suggest other music that would be appropriate.

4 Background

Art

Madame Mayden,
by Amedeo Modigliani

The Italian painter Amedeo Modigliani (1884–1920) spent most of his artistic life in Paris. He was strongly influenced not only by Picasso and French painters Cézanne and Rousseau but also by the great painters of the Italian Renaissance, especially Sandro Botticelli. Modigliani is best known for his portraits and nudes. The portraits, including the one of Madame Mayden, feature elongated oval shapes. Many of his subjects seem to have melancholy expressions. Modigliani was also a sculptor; his three-dimensional works have many of the characteristics of West African art and masks he had seen displayed in Paris.

Use the following questions for discussion:

- How would you describe the subject's mood?
  Answer: The woman appears resigned and weary.
- What is most striking about the woman's pose?
  Possible response: Students may mention the woman's tilted head and uncomfortable neck position or her long, entwined fingers.

5 ▶ Critical Viewing

Answer: Like Madame Augelier, the woman in the portrait seems melancholy, as if she were assessing her life and the changes that have overtaken her. However, she looks younger than Madame Augelier is described.

6 Critical Thinking

Take a Position

- Draw students' attention to the last sentence in the first paragraph on p. 1048.
- Ask: On the basis of this sentence, what can you conclude about the narrator's view of marriage?
  Answer: In the absence of love, affection and fidelity can be the basis of a good marriage.

7 Reading Strategy

Drawing Conclusions

- Have a volunteer read the bracketed passage.
- Then, ask students the Reading Strategy question on p. 1048: Based on her comments about her husband and her feelings about his gifts, what conclusions can you draw about Madame Augelier's happiness with her life? Explain.
  Answer: Madame Augelier is dissatisfied with her life. She acknowledges that her husband is good to her, but she believes that she does not love him enough and knows that the gifts will not satisfy her.

Monitor Progress Ask students: What details from the story did you use to draw your conclusion about Madame Augelier's feelings about her life?
Answer: Students may include the description of her husband as "poor François," her guilt at not loving him enough, and her boredom with the bracelet.

Reteach Direct students' attention to the Reading Strategy instruction on p. 1045. Remind students that when drawing conclusions, a reader must supply textual evidence as support.

8 Critical Viewing

Possible response: François would have given jewels like these later in the marriage; early in their marriage, he could not have afforded such gifts.

Madame Augelier could have gone back as far as four modest silver place settings, as far as three pairs of silk stockings . . .

"We weren't rich back then. Poor François, he's always spoiled me so . . ." To herself, secretly, she called him "poor François," because she believed herself guilty of not loving him enough, underestimating the
6 strength of affectionate habits and abiding fidelity.

Madame Augelier raised her hand, tucked her little finger under,
7 extended her wrist to erase the bracelet of wrinkles, and repeated intently, "It's so pretty . . . the diamonds are so white . . . I'm so pleased . . ." Then she let her hand fall back down and admitted to herself that she was already tired of her new bracelet.

"But I'm not ungrateful," she said naïvely with a sigh. Her weary eyes wandered from the flowered tablecloth to the gleaming window. The smell of some Calville apples in a silver bowl made her feel slightly sick and she left the dining room.

In her boudoir[5] she opened the steel case which held her jewels, and adorned her left hand in honor of the new bracelet. Her ring had on it a black onyx band and a blue-tinted brilliant; onto her delicate, pale, and

5. **boudoir** (bōō´ dwär´) *n.* woman's bedroom, dressing room, or private sitting room.

Reading Strategy
Drawing Conclusions Based on her comments about her husband and her feelings about his gifts, what conclusions can you draw about Madame Augelier's happiness with her life? Explain.

8 **▼ Critical Viewing** Do you think Monsieur Augelier would have given jewels like these to his wife earlier or later in their marriage? Explain. **[Connect]**

ENRICHMENT: Science Connection

Glass

Madame Augelier longs to reclaim her glass bangle for its symbolic value, but the beauty and functionality of glass has been treasured for thousands of years.

Glass beads dating from around 2500 B.C. have been found in Egypt and Mesopotamia. Early glass items were made by pouring molten glass over a sand core. The core was removed after the glass hardened, leaving the hollow container behind. The glassblowing technique most likely developed in Syria during the final years of the first century B.C.

At the end of the thirteenth century, Venice, Italy, became a major European center for glassmaking. Venetians might have learned glassmaking from the Near Eastern people they encountered during the Crusades.

Silica, in the form of sand, is the primary ingredient for making glass. Adding various metallic compounds to a mixture of silica and its modifiers and stabilizers produces colored glass. For example, gold, cadmium, or cuprous oxide added to the mixture makes red glass.

somewhat wrinkled little finger, Madame Augelier slipped a circle of dark sapphires. Her prematurely white hair, which she did not dye, appeared even whiter as she adjusted amid slightly frizzy curls a narrow fillet sprinkled with a dusting of diamonds, which she immediately untied and took off again.

"I don't know what's wrong with me. I'm not feeling all that well. Being fifty is a bore, basically . . ."

She felt restless, both terribly hungry and sick to her stomach, like a convalescent whose appetite the fresh air has yet to restore.

"Really now, is a diamond actually as pretty as all that?"

Madame Augelier craved a visual pleasure which would involve the sense of taste as well; the unexpected sight of a lemon, the unbearable squeaking of the knife cutting it in half, makes the mouth water with desire . . .

"But I don't want a lemon. Yet this nameless pleasure which escapes me does exist, I know it does, I remember it! Yes, the blue glass bracelet . . ."

10 A shudder made Madame Augelier's slack cheeks tighten. A vision, the duration of which she could not measure, granted her, for a second time, a moment lived forty years earlier, that incomparable moment as she looked, enraptured, at the color of the day, the iridescent, distorted image of objects seen through a blue glass bangle, moved around in a circle, which she had just been given. That piece of perhaps Oriental glass, broken a few hours later, had held in it a new universe, shapes not the inventions of dreams, slow, serpentine animals moving in pairs, lamps, rays of light congealed in an atmosphere of indescribable blue . . .

The vision ended and Madame Augelier fell back, bruised, into the present, into reality.

But the next day she began searching, from antique shops to flea markets, from flea markets to crystal shops, for a glass bracelet, a certain color of blue. She put the passion of a collector, the precaution, the dissimulation[6] of a lunatic into her search. She ventured into what she called "impossible districts," left her car at the corner of strange streets, and in the end, for a few centimes, she found a circle of blue glass which she recognized in the darkness, stammered as she paid for it, and carried it away.

6. **dissimulation** (di sim' yo͞o lā' shən) *n.* hiding of one's feelings or motives by pretense.

Literature in context World Events Connection

9 ***Algeria and France***

At the time of this story, France governed much of western and west-central Africa. Algeria, a French colony since 1834, played an important role in France's economy, partly through its production and export of citrus fruit and wine. Yet the relationship between Algeria and France was never an easy one. Cultural and economic conflicts between the country's poor Muslim majority and wealthy Europeans erupted into armed conflict in 1954, the year of Colette's death. After eight years of struggle, Algeria finally secured its independence from France in July of 1962. In this story, Colette subtly places Madame Augelier's life within a broader cultural context by mentioning the absent Monsieur Augelier's travels in Algeria.

convalescent (kän' və les' ənt) *n.* person who is recovering health after illness

enraptured (en rap' chərd) *adj.* filled with great pleasure

iridescent (ir' i des' ənt) *adj.* showing rainbowlike shifts in color

serpentine (sur' pən tēn') *adj.* resembling a snake

congealed (kən jēld') *adj.* thickened; solidified

11 ✔**Reading Check**

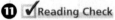

What object does Madame Augelier long to find?

9 Background

Algeria and France

French influences remain in Algeria. Although Arabic was made the only official language in 1996, newspapers and television shows are still produced in both languages. Three radio networks exist; one of them broadcasts in Arabic, one in Berber, and one in French.

France is still overwhelmingly the major source of imports to Algeria and the third-largest receiver of exports from Algeria. The French also make up Algeria's largest foreign tourist population.

10 Vocabulary Development

Latin Prefix *en-*

- Draw students' attention to the word *enraptured* on p. 1049, and read its definition.
- Tell students that this word includes the prefix *en-*, which has several meanings, including "to put into or cover," "to cause to be," and "to provide with."
- Ask students to list common words that contain the prefix *en-*, and discuss how the prefix helps create the meaning of the word. Possible responses: Students may suggest *encapsulate, enable, encrypt, encourage, enclose, endear, enjoy, enlarge,* and *enlighten*.

11 ✔Reading Check

Answer: She wants to find a blue glass bracelet like one she had in her youth.

CUSTOMIZE INSTRUCTION FOR UNIVERSAL ACCESS

For Less Proficient Readers	For Advanced Readers
Organize students into small groups, and have them discuss whether adults view childhood nostalgically. Tell each group to make a list of five or six interview questions they could ask adults about their views of childhood. Then, have each group interview a parent, grandparent, neighbor, or other adult and record the responses. Have groups present their findings to the class and discuss the results. Then, lead students in a discussion about whether Madame Augelier's feelings about her childhood are realistic.	Tell students that in *As You Like It* (II, vii, 139), Shakespeare describes the stages of life. Ask students to read the "All the world's a stage" speech and to discuss it with classmates. Then, have students consider Madame Augelier's changes and speculate on what she must have been like at age ten. Finally, have students explain what stage of life they think Madame Augelier has reached by the end of the story.

ASSESS

12 Literary Analysis

Epiphany

- Have a volunteer read aloud the bracketed passage.
- Then, ask: Who is the "stranger"? Answer: The stranger is Madame Augelier at ten years old.
- Ask: What insight into herself does Madame Augelier experience at the story's end? Answer: She learns that she has aged and cannot recapture her youthful feelings.

Answers for p. 1050

Review and Assess

1. Possible response: Some readers will feel sorry for her loss of childhood innocence; others may think her spoiled and naïve.
2. **(a)** Madame Augelier is bored. **(b)** Madame Augelier's boredom reveals that she is jaded both toward the gift and toward her husband's affections. **(c)** It is safe and secure. Surrounded by wealth, she feels no passion or love.
3. **(a)** In the third year, Madame Augelier received three pairs of silk stockings; in the fourth, she received four modest silver place settings. **(b)** The Augeliers have become financially secure and can afford expensive gifts, but their relationship has lost its passion.
4. **(a)** Madame Augelier remembers a blue glass bracelet. **(b)** She goes shopping for a bracelet like the one from her youth. **(c)** She is hoping to recapture the feelings of youth.
5. **(a)** It is now a trinket worthy of only a "child or savage." **(b)** Madame Augelier has seen and experienced much since childhood but has lost her passion for life.
6. The title refers to both bracelets. The diamond bracelet is the impetus for Madame Augelier's search for the blue glass bracelet. The blue glass bracelet is the object that leads to her epiphany.

In the discreet light of her favorite lamp she set the bracelet on the dark field of an old piece of velvet, leaned forward, and waited for the shock . . . But all she saw was a round piece of bluish glass, the trinket of a child or a savage, hastily made and blistered with bubbles; an object whose color and material her memory and reason recognized; but the powerful and sensual genius who creates and nourishes the marvels of childhood, who gradually weakens, then dies mysteriously within us, did not even stir.

12 Resigned, Madame Augelier thus came to know how old she really was and measured the infinite plain over which there wandered, beyond her reach, a being detached from her forever, a stranger, turned away from her, rebellious and free even from the bidding of memory: a little ten-year-old girl wearing on her wrist a bracelet of blue glass.

Review and Assess

Thinking About the Selection

1. **Respond:** Do you sympathize with Madame Augelier? Why or why not?
2. **(a) Recall:** As the story begins, with what attitude does Madame Augelier count the diamonds in her bracelet? **(b) Analyze:** How does this description show that the bracelet was given and received with little true feeling? **(c) Define:** What does the beginning of the story tell you about the nature of Madame Augelier's world?
3. **(a) Recall:** What gifts did Madame Augelier receive from her husband in their third and fourth years of marriage? **(b) Generalize:** How has the couple's relationship and lifestyle changed since then? Explain.
4. **(a) Recall:** What object does Madame Augelier suddenly remember from her childhood? **(b) Infer:** Why does she go shopping? **(c) Deduce:** What is Madame Augelier truly hoping to find when she goes shopping?
5. **(a) Compare and Contrast:** When Madame Augelier examines the glass bracelet at home, how does it compare with the vision from her childhood? **(b) Interpret:** What has changed since her childhood?
6. **Make a Judgment:** Do you think the title of this story refers to the diamond bracelet or to the blue bracelet? Support your answer.

ASSESSMENT PRACTICE: Reading Comprehension

Comparing and Contrasting Texts (For more practice, see Test Preparation Workbook, p. 47)

Many tests require students to compare and contrast texts. Use the following sample test item to give students practice at this skill.

> Twenty-nine square brilliants, set in a bracelet, which slithered between her fingers like a cold and supple snake. ("The Bracelet" by Colette)
>
> She had started to turn the knob when a hoarse growl, like that of a wild beast surprised in his lair, quickly stopped her. ("A Breath of Air" by Luigi Pirandello)

These passages are similar in that they both use—

A onomatopoeia
B repetition
C simile
D metaphor

Choice *C* is correct. Both passages feature a simile, or a figure of speech that makes a direct comparison between two subjects, using *like* or *as*. No examples of onomatopoeia, repetition, or metaphor appear in either passage.

Review and Assess

Literary Analysis

Epiphany

1. Colette provides an **epiphany** instead of a resolution to the conflict in this story. (a) What is the main conflict in "The Bracelet"? (b) At the end of the story, Madame Augelier is "resigned." Why is that an important term in understanding Madame Augelier and the conflict?
2. (a) What sudden realization does Madame Augelier experience in "The Bracelet"? (b) How does she react to that epiphany?
3. Early in the story, how do Madame Augelier's memories of past anniversary presents help prepare readers for her epiphany?
4. Does Madame Augelier's epiphany seem believable? Explain.

Connecting Literary Elements

5. What **descriptive details** about anniversary gifts of the past help draw the reader into the story?
6. (a) What details about the blue glass bracelet does Madame Augelier remember? (b) In what ways do these details lead to the story's epiphany?

Reading Strategy

Drawing Conclusions

7. Use a chart like the one shown to identify details that allow you to **draw the conclusion** that Madame Augelier is unhappy.

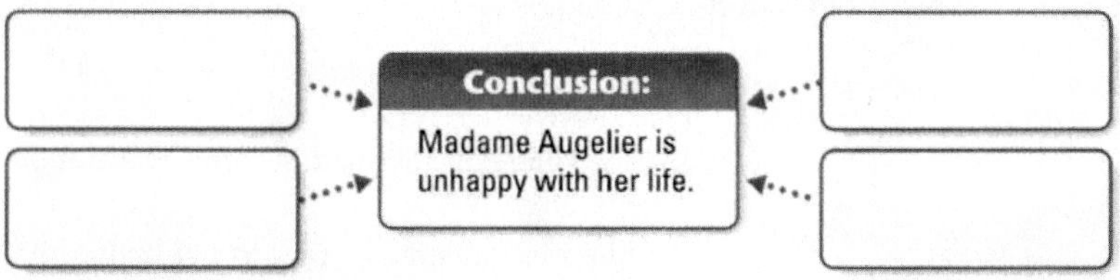
Conclusion:
Madame Augelier is unhappy with her life.

8. (a) At the beginning of the story, how does Madame Augelier feel about getting older? (b) Do her feelings change at the end of the story? (c) Which details led you to draw each of these conclusions?

Extend Understanding

9. **Social Studies Connection:** What does this story reveal about upper-class life in France in the early twentieth century? Explain.

Quick Review

An **epiphany** is a sudden, profound thought or insight that a character experiences.

Descriptive details are words and phrases that appeal to the senses and create vivid word pictures.

To **draw conclusions** as you read, make decisions about characters and situations by applying your knowledge and experiences to details from the work.

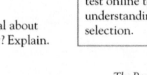

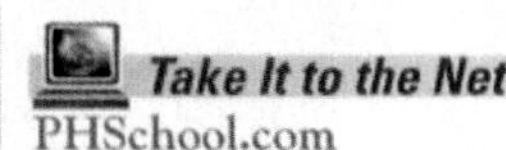
Take It to the Net
PHSchool.com

Take the interactive self-test online to check your understanding of this selection.

Review and Assess

1. **(a)** The aging Madame Augelier wants to recapture the freshness and passion of her youth. **(b)** The term implies that Madame Augelier has accepted her age and situation.
2. **(a)** She senses how old she has become and how little is left of the child she was. **(b)** She resigns herself to this realization.
3. She recalls each gift without passion or nostalgia, implying her boredom with life and emphasizing her age.
4. Possible response: The epiphany seems believable because a mature, jaded woman would have difficulty rediscovering passion and enthusiasm.
5. The descriptions of the progressively valuable gifts that represent the number of anniversary years provide a history that draws the reader into the story. The reader wants to learn more about this woman who is indifferent to such gifts.
6. **(a)** She remembers the color and iridescence of the bracelet, the distorted image of objects seen through its blue glass, and that it broke within a few hours. **(b)** Madame Augelier's epiphany about her youth mirrors those details provided about the bracelet. Her youth, like the bracelet, is "broken" and gone forever. The distorted image Madame Augelier once saw through the glass parallels the distorted image she now sees of her childhood.
7. Details include her wondering whether she and her husband will still be around in a year; her boredom with the diamond bracelet; her guilt at not loving her husband; her "weary eyes"; her restlessness; and her craving for sensory stimulation.
8. **(a)** She feels that getting older is a bore. **(b)** Her boredom changes to helplessness and resignation. **(c)** At the beginning of the story, Madame Augelier's boredom is revealed by her jaded attitude toward her possessions. At the end of the story, her helplessness and resignation are supported by her recognition

continued

answers continued from right column

of herself as a child—a "stranger," "detached" and unattainable.

9. Upper-class people lived lives of comfort and leisure. Women almost never worked outside the home.

ENRICHMENT: Further Reading

Other Works by Colette

We strongly encourage you to review any selection before assigning or recommending it to students.

Chéri	*My Mother's House*
Claudine at School	*Sido*

Take It to the Net

Visit PHSchool.com for more information on Colette.

EXTEND

Answers for p. 1052

❶ Vocabulary Development

Word Analysis: Latin Prefix *en-*

1. to put courage into
2. to put in danger
3. to cause to be larger
4. covered with a robe
5. to provide with light
6. to cause to be cumbered or burdened

Spelling Strategy

1. absent
2. impatient
3. opulent
4. eloquent

Fluency: Sentence Completion

1. convalescent
2. enraptured
3. iridescent
4. connoisseur
5. congealed
6. serpentine
7. supple

❷ Grammar and Style

Practice

1. sat
2. set
3. sitting
4. set
5. sat

Writing Application

Possible response: Yesterday I *sat* in a beautiful iridescent blue sports car. The owner let me *sit* behind the wheel. He was *sitting* beside me so that I wouldn't drive off. Someday, I hope to own one like it. I can just see it *sitting* in my driveway. I even *set* a picture of it on my dresser.

10TH GRADE For support in teaching the Grammar and Style Lesson to tenth graders, use **Writing and Grammar**, Platinum Level, Chapter 16, Section 3.

Integrate Language Skills

❶ Vocabulary Development Lesson

Word Analysis: Latin Prefix *en-*

The prefix *en-* has several related meanings, including "to put into or cover," "to cause to be," or "to provide with." The vocabulary word *enraptured* literally means "put into a state of rapture." Use the meanings of *en-* to define each of the following words.

1. encourage
2. endanger
3. enlarge
4. enrobed
5. enlighten
6. encumbered

Spelling Strategy

If a noun ends in *-ence*, the adjective form of the word ends in *-ent*. For example, the noun *iridescence* becomes the adjective *iridescent*. Write the adjective form of each of the following nouns.

1. absence
2. impatience
3. opulence
4. eloquence

Fluency: Sentence Completions

Complete each sentence below with a word from the vocabulary list on page 1045.

1. The __?__ struggled to his feet and, with some assistance, took a few steps.
2. He gave a(n) __?__ grin at finally being able to walk again.
3. She admired the sparkling, __?__ beads that decorated the gown.
4. At the five-star restaurant, the __?__ examined his dessert with a scowl.
5. "This __?__ chocolate sauce is inedible!" he complained to the waiter.
6. The lioness took a __?__ path as she followed the herd.
7. Her __?__ body glided through the grass with ease.

❷ Grammar and Style Lesson

Commonly Confused Words: *sit* and *set*

Be careful to distinguish between **sit** and **set,** two easily confused verbs. *Sit* means "to be seated or resting in a particular spot." *Set* means "to put (something) in a certain place."

> . . . He asked her to *sit* down.
>
> . . . she *set* the bracelet on an old piece of velvet . . .

The main forms of *sit* are *sit*, *sitting*, *sat*, and *(have) sat*. The main forms of *set* are *set*, *setting*, *set*, and *(have) set*.

Practice Identify the correct verb in each of the following sentences.

1. Twenty-nine square stones (sat, set) in the bracelet.
2. Madame Augelier (sat, set) the bracelet in the box.
3. She was (sitting, setting) in her bedroom.
4. She had (sat, set) the box on the dresser.
5. She paced around the room and then (sat, set) down again.

Writing Application Write a paragraph about things you think you might own someday. Five times in the paragraph, use a form of the verb *sit* or *set* correctly.

WG Prentice Hall Writing and Grammar Connection: Diamond Level, Chapter 21, Section 1

1052 ◆ The Modern World

TEACHING RESOURCES

The following resources can be used to enrich or extend the instruction for pp. 1052–1053.

Vocabulary

- **Selection Support:** Build Vocabulary, p. 185
- **Vocabulary and Spelling Practice Book** (Use this booklet for skills instruction.)

Grammar

- **Selection Support:** Grammar and Style, p. 186
- **Writing and Grammar,** Diamond Level, p. 520
- **Daily Language Practice Transparencies** ■

Writing

- **Performance Assess. and Portfolio Mgmt.**, p. 16
- **Writing and Grammar,** Diamond Level, p. 310
- **Writing Models and Graphic Organizers on Transparencies,** pp. 71-73 ■

Listening and Speaking

- **Performance Assess. and Portfolio Mgmt.**, p. 33

■ **BLOCK SCHEDULING:** Resources marked with this symbol provide varied instruction during 90-minute blocks.

❸ Writing Lesson

Analytical Essay

Write an essay in which you analyze how Colette's use of images—words or phrases that appeal to the senses and create word pictures—helps convey the theme, or message about life, in "The Bracelet."

Prewriting In one sentence, state the story's theme or message. Then, reread the story, listing images that you associate with that theme. Use a chart like the one shown to explore each image.

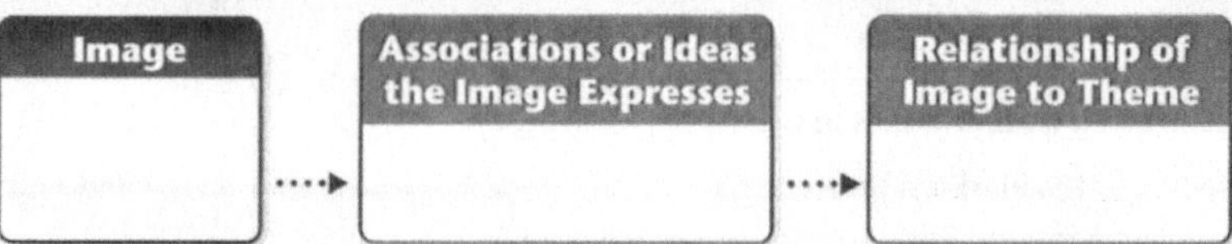

Drafting Begin with a general statement about the theme, or main idea, of "The Bracelet." Then, cite specific examples of images in the story that suggest or develop that theme or main idea.

Revising As you review your draft, underline your main ideas and check that each one is clearly stated and well supported. Add examples of images as needed to illustrate your points.

WG *Prentice Hall Writing and Grammar Connection: Diamond Level, Chapter 14, Section 2*

❹ Extension Activities

Listening and Speaking Adapt "The Bracelet" as a **monologue** given by Madame Augelier. Use these tips to prepare:

- Decide whether Madame Augelier will address the audience or will speak as if she is alone and thinking aloud.
- Determine what confessions Madame Augelier might make.
- Include her epiphany in some way.

Deliver the monologue to a small group or to the class.

Research and Technology "The Bracelet" takes place in France at the turn of the twentieth century. With a partner, research the clothing and decorating styles of that era. Then, prepare a **set and costume design** that accurately reflect Madame Augelier's clothing and home and that could be used for a dramatic performance of the story. **[Group Activity]**

 ***Take It to the Net*** PHSchool.com

Go online for an additional research activity using the Internet.

ASSESSMENT RESOURCES

The following resources can be used to assess students' knowledge and skills.

Selection Assessment

- **Formal Assessment,** pp. 167–169
- **Open-Book Tests,** pp. 139–141
- **Test Bank Software**

 ***Take It to the Net***

Visit PHSchool.com for self-tests on the selection.

Writing Rubric

- **Performance Assess. and Portfolio Mgmt.,** p. 16

Listening and Speaking Rubric

- **Performance Assess. and Portfolio Mgmt.,** p. 33

For additional diagnostics and remediation for skills covered in this grouping, use materials from the Prentice Hall Assessment System.

Lesson Support for p. 1053

❸ Writing Lesson

- Read aloud the Writing Lesson instruction on p. 1053. Tell students that in an analytical essay, the writer looks critically at various important elements in a work of literature. Explain how the author has used those elements.
- Suggest to students that they use the Analysis Map in **Writing Models and Graphic Organizers on Transparencies,** pp. 71–73, to organize their essays.
- Use the Response to Literature rubric in **Performance Assessment and Portfolio Management,** p. 16, to evaluate students' work.

10TH GRADE For support in working through the Writing Lesson with tenth graders, use **Writing and Grammar,** Platinum Level, Chapter 13, Section 2.

❹ Listening and Speaking

- Explain to students that a monologue is a speech or performance given entirely by one person.
- Have students follow the tips as they prepare their monologues. Encourage students to use an appropriate tone of voice and gestures to emphasize important thoughts or feelings.
- Use the Listening and Speaking Progress Chart in **Performance Assessment and Portfolio Management,** p. 33, to evaluate students' monologues.

CUSTOMIZE INSTRUCTION For Universal Access

To address different learning styles, use the following activities suggested in the **Extension Activities** booklet, p. 47:

- For Visual/Spatial Learners, use Activity 5.
- For Verbal/Linguistic Learners and Interpersonal Learners, use Activity 6.
- For Logical/Mathematical Learners, use Activity 7.

War

Lesson Objectives

1. **To analyze and respond to literary elements**
   - Literary Analysis: Setting
   - Connecting Literary Elements: Characterization
2. **To read, comprehend, analyze, and critique a short story**
   - Reading Strategy: Comparing and Contrasting Characters
   - Reading Check Questions
   - Review and Assess Questions
   - Assessment Practice (ATE)
3. **To develop word analysis skills, fluency, and systematic vocabulary**
   - Vocabulary Development Lesson: Latin Root *-patr-*
4. **To understand and apply written and oral language conventions**
   - Spelling Strategy
   - Grammar and Style Lesson: Adjective Clauses
5. **To understand and apply appropriate writing and research strategies**
   - Writing Lesson: Newspaper Article
   - Extension Activity: Multimedia Report
6. **To understand and apply listening and speaking strategies**
   - Extension Activity: Dramatic Reading

10TH GRADE TEACHING A TENTH-GRADE COURSE

The literature in this section can be taught as part of a rich, balanced world literature course for tenth-grade students. For a full outline of such a course, see pp. T46–T48 in Volume 1 of this Teacher's Edition.

STEP-BY-STEP TEACHING GUIDE	PACING GUIDE
PRETEACH	
Motivate Students and Provide Background	
Use the Motivation activity (ATE p. 1054)	5 min.
Read and discuss author and background features (SE pp. 1054, 1056; ATE p. 1054) A	5 min.
Introduce the Concepts	
Introduce the Literary Analysis and Reading Strategy concepts (SE/ATE p. 1055) A	15 min.
Pronounce the vocabulary words and read their definitions (SE p. 1055)	5 min.
TEACH	
Monitor Comprehension	
Informally monitor comprehension by circulating while students read independently or in groups A	25 min.
Monitor students' comprehension with the Reading Check notes (SE/ATE pp. 1057, 1059)	as students read
Develop vocabulary with Vocabulary notes (SE pp. 1057, 1058, 1059, 1060; ATE p. 1057)	as students read
Develop Understanding	
Develop students' understanding of setting with the Literary Analysis annotation (SE/ATE p. 1056) A	5 min.
Develop students' ability to compare and contrast, using the Reading Strategy annotation (SE/ATE p. 1059)	5 min.
ASSESS	
Assess Mastery	
Assess students' mastery of the Reading Strategy and Literary Analysis concepts by having them answer the Review and Assess questions (SE/ATE p. 1061)	15 min.
Use one or more of the print, software, or transparency Assessment Resources (ATE p. 1063) A	up to 45 min.
EXTEND	
Apply Understanding	
Have students complete the Vocabulary Development Lesson and the Grammar and Style Lesson (SE p. 1062) A	20 min.
Apply students' ability to maintain journalistic objectivity, using the Writing Lesson (SE/ATE p. 1063) A	45 min.
Apply students' understanding of the story, using one or more of the Extension Activities (SE p. 1063)	20–90 min.

A ACCELERATED INSTRUCTION: Use the strategies and activities identified with an A.

10TH GRADE TEACHING TENTH-GRADE STUDENTS For support in teaching the selection(s) to tenth-grade students, see the Step-by-Step Teaching notes identified with the icon shown here.

UNIVERSAL ACCESS
● = Below-Level Students
▲ = On-Level Students
■ = Above-Level Students

Time and Resource Manager

Reading Level: Average
Average Number of Instructional Days: 3

	RESOURCES		
	PRINT	**TRANSPARENCIES**	**TECHNOLOGY**
	• **Beyond Literature,** Humanities Connection: Consolation, p. 48 ▲ ■		• **Interest Grabber Video,** Tape 2, Unit 8, Segment 6 ● ▲ ■
	• **Selection Support Workbook:** ● ▲ ■ Literary Analysis, p. 192 Reading Strategy, p. 191 Build Vocabulary, p. 189	• **Literary Analysis and Reading Transparencies,** pp. 95 and 96 ● ▲ ■	
	• **Reader's Companion** ● • **Adapted Reader's Companion** ●		• **Listening to Literature** ● ▲ ■ Audiocassettes Audio CDs • **Reader's Companion Audio Program** ● • **Reader's Companion Adapted and English Learner's Version Audio Program** ● ▲
	• **English Learner's Companion** ● ▲ • **Literary Analysis for Enrichment,** p. 48 ■		• **World Masterpieces iText CD-ROM**
	• **Formal Assessment:** Selection Test, pp. 170–172 ● ▲ ■ • **Open-Book Tests,** pp. 142–144 ● ▲ ■ • **Performance Assessment. and Portfolio Management.,** p. 33 ● ▲ ■ • PRENTICE HALL ASSESSMENT SYSTEM ● ▲ ■	• PRENTICE HALL ASSESSMENT SYSTEM ● ▲ ■ **Skills Practice Answers and Explanations on Transparencies**	• **Test Bank Software** ● ▲ ■
	• **Selection Support Workbook:** ● ▲ ■ Grammar and Style, p. 190 • **Writing and Grammar,** Diamond Level ● ▲ ■ • **Extension Activities,** p. 48 ● ▲ ■	• **Daily Language Practice Transparencies** ● ▲ • **Writing Models and Graphic Organizers on Transparencies,** pp. 103–105 ● ▲ ■	• **Writing and Grammar iText CD-ROM** ● ▲ ■ ***Take It to the Net*** PHSchool.com

BLOCK SCHEDULING: Use one 90-minute class period to preteach the selection(s) and have students read them. Use a second 90-minute class period to assess students' mastery of skills and have them complete one of the Extension Activities.

PRETEACH

Step-by-Step Teaching Guide for pp. 1054–1055

Motivation

Explain to students that the characters of Pirandello's story "War" share intimate and painful details about their lives. Discuss with students situations in which perfect strangers might begin talking about their most private matters. Then, invite students to share any experiences they may have had with "sudden familiarity."

Interest Grabber Video

As an alternative, play "War: World War I" on Tape 2 to engage student interest.

❶ Background

More About the Author

The collapse of the sulfur mines in 1903 became a major turning point in Pirandello's life. The resulting financial disaster triggered the onset of his wife's paranoid schizophrenia. Soon after the collapse of the mines, she began having suspicions about her husband's fidelity, which intensified into a frantic jealousy that caused both of them great suffering. In 1919, she was committed to a sanatorium, where she remained until her death in 1959. This dreadful experience caused Pirandello to develop a strong fascination with the complex, hidden world of the human personality—a fascination that is clearly reflected in his later works.

Geography Note

Draw students' attention to the map on this page. Remind students that Pirandello was born in Sicily, the largest island in the Mediterranean Sea. A center for seismic and volcanic activity, the island of Sicily is home to Mount Etna, Europe's highest active volcano.

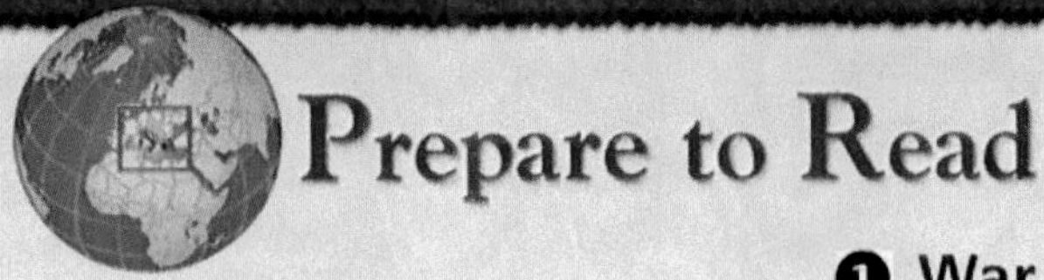

Prepare to Read

❶ War

Luigi Pirandello (1867–1936)

With the completion of his masterpiece, *Six Characters in Search of an Author* (1921)—a play about a group of characters who, in their quest to find an author to tell their story, interrupt a group of actors rehearsing another play—Luigi Pirandello (lōō ē´ jē pir´ ən del´ ō) established himself as one of the most innovative dramatists of his time. Unfortunately, however, Pirandello's success as a playwright has overshadowed his numerous accomplishments as a fiction writer. Today, many people are unaware that in Italy, his native land, Luigi Pirandello is widely recognized as the master of the short story.

Early Trials The son of a successful sulfur merchant, Pirandello was born on the island of Sicily, off the southern tip of Italy. After high school, he attended the University of Rome and later received a doctorate from the University of Bonn in Germany. In 1894, he married the daughter of another sulfur merchant, and with the financial support of both his parents and his in-laws, he devoted the next ten years entirely to writing. When the sulfur mines collapsed in 1903, however, the fortunes of both families were wiped out, and Pirandello became a teacher in order to earn a living. At about the same time, his wife showed symptoms of the mental illness for which she would later be institutionalized.

First Triumphs Despite these setbacks, Pirandello continued to write. Having already established himself as a gifted short-story writer, Pirandello published his best-known novel, *The Late Mattia Pascal*, in 1904. Like many of his early stories, the novel explored the complexities of personal identity and questioned the distinction between appearance and reality. These themes were also the focus of *It Is So (If You Think So)* (1917), Pirandello's first successful play, and were fully developed in his greatest dramatic works, *Six Characters in Search of an Author* and *Henry IV* (1922).

An International Star Having established a worldwide reputation as a playwright, Pirandello was able to open his own theater company in 1924. At the same time, he continued to write and publish prolifically. Although his later works did not achieve the popularity of his early successful plays, Pirandello received the ultimate recognition for his achievements in 1934 when he was awarded the Nobel Prize in Literature. He died two years later in Rome.

A Great Legacy At the time of his death, it was already clear that Luigi Pirandello's artistic vision had exerted a great influence on the theater, as well as on the literary world in general. However, the full force of his influence did not become clear until the emergence of new generations of playwrights, who found in his work an ideal reflection of modern uncertainties. Perhaps Pirandello summed up his work best when he wrote, "Life is full of infinite absurdities, which, strangely enough, do not even need to appear plausible, since they are true." Because of his originality and his influence on other writers, Luigi Pirandello will be remembered as one of the most important writers of the twentieth century.

TEACHING RESOURCES

The following resources can be used to enrich or extend the instruction for pp. 1054–1055.

Motivation

Interest Grabber Video, Tape 2

Background

Beyond Literature, p. 48

Take It to the Net

Visit PHSchool.com for background on the author.

Literary Analysis

Literary Analysis and Reading Transparencies, Setting, p. 95

Selection Support: Literary Analysis, p. 192

Reading

Literary Analysis and Reading Transparencies, Comparing and Contrasting characters, p. 96

BLOCK SCHEDULING: Resources marked with this symbol provide varied instruction during 90-minute blocks.

Preview

Connecting to the Literature

While war can have a powerful effect upon the soldiers who see combat, it also affects the families who worry about their loved ones on the front lines. This story focuses on those whom the soldiers leave behind.

❷ Literary Analysis

Setting

The **setting** of a literary work is the time and place in which it occurs. Some settings provide a mere backdrop for the action, while others present a force, such as a winter storm or a cultural bias, that affects the characters. In "War," Pirandello establishes the setting with these words:

> At dawn, in a stuffy and smoky second-class carriage . . .

As you read "War," think about the role the setting itself plays in driving the story.

Connecting Literary Elements

Characterization is the art of creating and developing characters. There are two types of characterization:

- **Direct characterization:** The writer simply states what a character is like.
- **Indirect characterization:** The writer reveals what a character is like by describing his or her appearance, words, and actions and by noting what other characters say about him or her.

As you meet the characters in "War," consider not only *what* you learn about them but *how* you learn it.

❸ Reading Strategy

Comparing and Contrasting Characters

"War" is populated by characters who share similar concerns but react in very different ways. Clarify their similarities and differences by **comparing and contrasting the characters.** To do so, use a chart like the one shown.

Character	1	2
Appearance		
Behavior		
Words		
Emotions		
Beliefs		

Vocabulary Development

plight (plīt) *n.* sad or difficult situation (p. 1057)

paternal (pə tʉr´ nəl) *adj.* like a father (p. 1057)

discrimination (di skrim´ i nā´ shən) *n.* show of partiality or prejudice (p. 1057)

vitality (vī tal´ ə tē) *n.* energy; life force (p. 1058)

retorted (ri tôrt´ id) *v.* replied, especially in a sharp or challenging way (p. 1058)

stoically (stō´ i klē) *adv.* done with indifference to pain or pleasure (p. 1059)

incongruous (in käŋ´ grōō əs) *adj.* not fitting a situation; inappropriate (p. 1060)

harrowing (har´ ō iŋ) *adj.* disturbing; frightening (p. 1060)

CUSTOMIZE INSTRUCTION FOR UNIVERSAL ACCESS

For Special Needs Students	For Less Proficient Readers	For English Learners
Have students read "War" in the **Adapted Reader's Companion.** This version provides basic-level instruction in an interactive format with questions and write-on lines. Completing the adapted version will prepare students to read the selection in the Student Edition.	Have students read the adapted version of the selection in the **Reader's Companion.** This version provides basic-level instruction in an interactive format with questions and write-on lines. After students finish the selection in the **Reader's Companion,** have them complete the questions and activities in the Student Edition.	Have students read the adapted version of the selection in the **English Learner's Companion.** This version provides basic-level instruction in an interactive format with questions and write-on lines. Completing the adapted version will prepare students to read the selection in the Student Edition.

❷ Literary Analysis

Setting

- Read aloud the Literary Analysis instruction on p. 1055. Emphasize to students that setting includes time as well as place.
- Have students imagine that they are writing a story about their class. Then, have them describe the setting of their classroom. Remind them that the setting of a story helps establish its mood and tone and gives characters context.
- Then, tell students that the setting of "War"—a passenger train during World War I—is crucial to the story. Have students look for the details Pirandello provides to establish this setting.
- Use the Setting transparency in **Literary Analysis and Reading Transparencies,** p. 95, to help students identify the setting of Pirandello's story.

❸ Reading Strategy

Comparing and Contrasting Characters

- After students have read the Reading Strategy instruction, remind them that the characters are the actors of a story. Some characters do not change in the course of a story. They are known as *static characters.* Others, known as *dynamic characters,* change and learn something from their experiences.
- Encourage students to look for static and dynamic characters as they read "War."
- Explain the use of the chart on p. 1055. Have students use a chart like this one as they read to record details that help distinguish each character.

Vocabulary Development

- Pronounce each vocabulary word for students, and read the definitions as a class. Have students identify any words with which they are already familiar.

E-Teach

Visit e-Teach at PHSchool.com for teachers' essays on how to teach, with questions and answers.

TEACH

Step-by-Step Teaching Instruction for pp. 1056–1060

Teaching Tenth-Grade Students

10TH GRADE Discuss with tenth graders the fact that during a tragedy, people do not always think clearly or react normally. Some may rise above the disaster. Others may crumple under the weight of their grief or terror. Still others may put on a mask and deny the tragic circumstance. Have students read "War" to learn how the people on the train deal with their tragedies.

1 About the Selection

World War I devastated both the landscape and people of Europe. In countries such as Italy, many families had one or more sons who had fought or died in the war. In this story, Pirandello examines the toll such sacrifice took on families.

2 Literary Analysis

Setting

- Draw students' attention to the Literary Analysis instruction on p. 1055, and emphasize that the setting of a story is sometimes as important as the characters.
- Read the bracketed passage aloud, and point out that it contains the first descriptions of the setting. Ask: How does Pirandello create a believable setting?
  Possible response: In the first paragraph, Pirandello provides realistic details about the train, including its destination and the reason for the passengers' wait at the station. Sensory details, such as the description of the carriage as "stuffy" and "smoky," appeal to the reader's senses and thus make the scene familiar.
- Ask students the Literary Analysis question on p. 1056: Which details in this description of the setting suggest closeness and discomfort? Explain.
  Answer: Details that suggest closeness and discomfort include the adjectives "stuffy," "smoky," "bulky;" the verbs "hoisted," "puffing," and "moaning;" and the image of the carriage in which five adults have spent the night.

1 

War

Luigi Pirandello *translated by* Samuel Putnam

Background

In the late nineteenth and early twentieth centuries, political tensions in Europe led to alliances among several major powers. Germany, Austria-Hungary, and Italy formed the Triple Alliance; Great Britain, France, and Russia formed the Triple Entente. When World War I broke out in 1914, however, Italy did not join in on the side of its allies. Instead, Italian officials made a secret treaty with the Triple Entente, promising Italy's military help in return for land gains at the war's end. Italy then declared war on its former allies. In the years of fighting that followed, approximately 650,000 Italians died—nearly 2 percent of the country's population—and almost 950,000 more were wounded. It is against this bitter cultural landscape that Pirandello's story unfolds.

The passengers who had left Rome by the night express had had to stop until dawn at the small station of Fabriano[1] in order to continue their journey by the small old-fashioned "local" joining the main line with Sulmona.[2]

2 At dawn, in a stuffy and smoky second-class carriage in which five people had already spent the night, a bulky woman in deep mourning, was hoisted in—almost like a shapeless bundle. Behind her—puffing and moaning, followed her husband—a tiny man, thin and weakly, his face death-white, his eyes small and bright and looking shy and uneasy.

Literary Analysis
Setting Which details in this description of the setting suggest closeness and discomfort? Explain.

Having at last taken a seat he politely thanked the passengers who had helped his wife and who had made room for her; then he turned round to the woman trying to pull down the collar of her coat and politely enquired:

"Are you all right, dear?"

The wife, instead of answering, pulled up her collar again to her eyes, so as to hide her face.

"Nasty world," muttered the husband with a sad smile.

And he felt it his duty to explain to his travelling companions that the poor woman was to be pitied for the war was taking away from her her only son, a boy of twenty to whom both had devoted their entire life,

1. **Fabriano** (fa' brē a' nō) city in eastern Italy, approximately 100 miles from Rome.
2. **Sulmona** (sōōl mō' na) city in eastern Italy, approximately 75 miles from Rome.

TEACHING RESOURCES

The following resources can be used to enrich or extend the instruction for pp. 1056–1060.

Literary Analysis
- **Selection Support:** Literary Analysis, p. 192
- **Literary Analysis and Reading Transparencies,** Setting, p. 95

Reading
- **Selection Support:** Reading Strategy, p. 191; Build Vocabulary, p. 189 ■
- **Reader's Companion**

- **Adapted Reader's Companion**
- **English Learner's Companion**
- **Listening to Literature Audiocassettes**
- **Listening to Literature Audio CDs** ■

■ **BLOCK SCHEDULING:** Resources marked with this symbol provide varied instruction during 90-minute blocks.

even breaking up their home at Sulmona to follow him to Rome where he had to go as a student, then allowing him to volunteer for war with an assurance, however, that at least for six months he would not be sent to the front and now, all of a sudden, receiving a wire saying that he was due to leave in three days' time and asking them to go and see him off.

The woman under the big coat was twisting and wriggling, at times growling like a wild animal, feeling certain that all those explanations would not have aroused even a shadow of sympathy from those people who—most likely—were in the same plight as herself. One of them, who had been listening with particular attention, said:

"You should thank God that your son is only leaving now for the front. Mine has been sent there the first day of the war. He has already come back twice wounded and been sent back again to the front." 3

"What about me? I have two sons and three nephews at the front," said another passenger.

"Maybe, but in our case it is our *only* son," ventured the husband.

"What difference can it make? You may spoil your only son with excessive attentions, but you cannot love him more than you would all your other children if you had any. Paternal love is not like bread that can be broken into pieces and spilt amongst the children in equal shares. A father gives all his love to each one of his children without discrimination, whether it be one or ten, and if I am suffering now for my two sons, I am not suffering half for each of them but double. . . ." 4

"True . . . true . . . " sighed the embarrassed husband, "but suppose (of course we all hope it will never be your case) a father has two sons at the front and he loses one of them, there is still one left to console him . . . while . . . "

"Yes," answered the other, getting cross, "a son left to console him but also a son left for whom he must survive, while in the case of

plight (plīt) *n.* sad or difficult situation

paternal (pə tʉr′ nəl) *adj.* like a father

discrimination (di skrim′ i nā′ shən) *n.* show of partiality or prejudice

3 **Reading Check**

According to her husband, why is the woman in the big coat to be pitied?

5

A Star Shell, exh. 1916, Christopher R.W. Nevinson, Tate Gallery, London

6 **Critical Viewing** ▶

Do you think this painting of a World War I battlefield suggests hope or terror? Explain.

CUSTOMIZE INSTRUCTION FOR UNIVERSAL ACCESS

For Less Proficient Readers	For Advanced Readers
Explain to students that the first two paragraphs of the story introduce the setting and the characters. Organize students into pairs, and have them read the paragraphs aloud. Then, discuss the details of the description, and make sure that students understand where the characters are and what is happening. To clarify the situation, have students draw pictures of the railroad carriage and the people who occupy it. Students can share and discuss their drawings with the class.	In his journal, Pirandello wrote, "There is somebody who is living my life and I know nothing about him." In this statement, the author expresses a theme that he revisits in his plays and fiction. People, he contends, wear social "masks," or facades, and may not be aware of doing so. Ask students to write an essay examining the "masks" they find in "War." Encourage students to answer the following questions as they write: Who in this story is wearing a "mask"? Are these characters aware that they are wearing "masks"?

3 Reading Check

Answer: The woman should be pitied because her only son has been sent to the front.

4 Vocabulary Development

Latin Root *-patr-*

- Draw students' attention to the word *paternal*, and ask a volunteer to read its definition.
- On the board, write the following list of words that share the root *-patr-: patrician, patriotic, patriarch.*
- Then, have students use dictionaries to find the definitions of the listed words. Ask students to infer, on the basis of these definitions, what the Latin root *-patr-* means.
  Answer: The root *-patr-* comes from the Latin word *pater*, meaning "father."

5 Background

Art

A Star Shell, by Christopher R.W. Nevinson

British artist Christopher R.W. Nevinson (1889–1946) experienced the horrors of World War I firsthand as a Red Cross ambulance driver in France. Because of illness, he left active service in 1916, but in 1917, he became an Official War Artist and returned to the front. Like Nevinson's other depictions of war, *A Star Shell* captures the stark and disturbing realities of battle.

Use the following question for discussion.

Nevinson chose not to show a human presence in this painting. What is the effect of this choice?
Answer: The absence of humans not only emphasizes the destruction of the land but also suggests the larger human toll.

6 ▶ Critical Viewing

Possible response: The painting suggests terror. The land, which has been dug up for the trenches, has been decimated. A fiery shell, not a star, provides light. The scene provides little reason for hope.

7 Critical Thinking

Infer

- Have a volunteer read aloud the bracketed passage. Then, point out that Pirandello describes the "fat, red-faced man" as having "inner violence of an uncontrolled vitality."
- Ask students what they think Pirandello is trying to suggest about this character.
  Answer: There is something unhealthy, feverish, or unbalanced about this character.

8 Background

Art

Italian Soldiers by Karl Fahringer

This drawing appears in the Heeresgeschichtliches Museum of Military History in Vienna, Austria. The museum is the oldest museum in Vienna and houses a collection of historical artillery as well as an exhibit of World War I uniforms, guns, mortars, and other equipment.

Use the following questions for discussion:

- How does the style of this drawing reflect the realities of war?
  Possible response: The jumbled and vigorous lines reflect the chaos and tension of battle. The lines almost appear to tie the soldiers together, illustrating their comraderie.
- Is this drawing an appropriate illustration for Pirandello's story? Explain.
  Possible responses: Yes; The drawing is appropriate because it depicts the realities of war about which the families are concerned. No; The drawing is not appropriate because it does not depict the present action of Pirandello's story, and is thus distracting.

9 ▶ Critical Viewing

Possible response: The drawing, with its energetic lines, emphasizes the violence and chaos of combat.

---

the father of an only son if the son dies the father can die too and put an end to his distress. Which of the two positions is the worse? Don't you see how my case would be worse than yours?"

"Nonsense," interrupted another traveller, a fat, red-faced man with bloodshot eyes of the palest grey.

He was panting. From his bulging eyes seemed to spurt inner violence of an uncontrolled vitality which his weakened body could hardly contain. 8

7 "Nonsense," he repeated, trying to cover his mouth with his hand so as to hide the two missing front teeth. "Nonsense. Do we give life to our children for our own benefit?"

The other travellers stared at him in distress. The one who had had his son at the front since the first day of the war sighed: "You are right. Our children do not belong to us, they belong to the Country. . . ."

"Bosh," retorted the fat traveller. "Do we think of the Country when we give life to our children? Our sons are born because . . . well, because they must be born and when they come to life they take our own life with them. This is the truth. We belong to them but they never belong to us. And when they reach twenty they are exactly what we were at their age. We too had a father and mother, but there were so many other things as well . . . girls, cigarettes, illusions, new ties . . . and the Country, of course, whose call we would have answered—when we were twenty—even if father and mother had said no. Now, at our age, the love of our Country is still great, of course, but stronger than it is the love for our children. Is there any one of us here who wouldn't gladly take his son's place at the front if he could?"

There was a silence all round, everybody nodding as to approve.

"Why then," continued the fat man, "shouldn't we consider the feelings of our children when they are twenty? Isn't it natural that at their age they should consider the love for their Country (I am speaking of decent boys, of course) even greater than the love for us? Isn't it natural that it should be so, as after all they must look upon us as upon old boys who cannot move any more and must stay at home? If Country exists, if Country is a natural necessity like bread, of which each of us must eat in order not to die of hunger, somebody must go to defend it. And our sons go, when they are twenty, and they don't want tears, because if they die, they die inflamed and happy (I am speaking, of

Italian Soldiers, Karl Fahringer, Heeresgeschichtliches Museum, Vienna, Austria

9 ▲ **Critical Viewing**
Which aspects of war does this drawing emphasize? **[Interpret]**

vitality (vī tal′ ə tē) *n.* energy; life force

retorted (ri tôrt′ id) *v.* replied, especially in a sharp or challenging way

ENRICHMENT: History Connection

The Nobel Prize

In 1934, Luigi Pirandello won the Nobel Prize for Literature, which is awarded to recognize the most distinguished body of literary work. This prize has been beneficial in bringing otherwise little-known writers and their countries into the public light as contributors to world literature.

At the same time, however, the Nobel Prize for Literature has had its share of controversy. The Nobel committee for literature is made up of four to five members, primarily from Sweden. Some critics suspect a small bias, citing the fact that Scandinavian countries have received the Nobel Prize for Literature most often, monopolizing 17.4 percent of the prizes. France is the runner-up, taking home 15.1 percent of the prizes. Most recently, however, the awards have spanned the globe, introducing writers from Guatemala, Czechoslovakia, and Iceland.

10 course, of decent boys). Now, if one dies young and happy, without having the ugly sides of life, the boredom of it, the pettiness, the bitterness of disillusion . . . what more can we ask for him? Everyone should stop crying: everyone should laugh, as I do . . . or at least thank God—as I do—because my son, before dying, sent me a message saying that he was dying satisfied at having ended his life in the best way he could have wished. That is why, as you see, I do not even wear mourning. . . ."

He shook his light fawn[3] coat as to show it; his livid[4] lip over his missing teeth was trembling, his eyes were watery and motionless and soon after he ended with a shrill laugh which might well have been a sob.

"Quite so . . . quite so . . . " agreed the others.

The woman who, bundled in a corner under her coat, had been sitting and listening had—for the last three months—tried to find in the words of her husband and her friends something to console her in her deep sorrow, something that might show her how a mother should resign herself to send her son not even to death but to a probable danger of life. Yet not a word had she found amongst the many which had been said . . . and her grief had been greater in seeing that nobody—as she thought—could share her feelings.

But now the words of the traveller amazed and almost stunned her. She suddenly realized that it wasn't the others who were wrong and could not understand her but herself who could not rise up to the same height of those fathers and mothers willing to resign themselves, without crying, not only to the departure of their sons but even to their death. 12

She lifted her head, she bent over from her corner trying to listen with great attention to the details which the fat man was giving to his companions about the way his son had fallen as a hero, for his King and his Country, happy and without regrets. It seemed to her that she had stumbled into a world she had never dreamt of, a world so far unknown to her and she was so pleased to hear everyone joining in congratulating that brave father who could so stoically speak of his child's death.

Reading Strategy
Comparing and Contrasting Characters In what ways does the fat man seem different from the other passengers?

stoically (stō´ i klē) *adv.* done with indifference to pain or pleasure

11 **✓Reading Check**
What message did the fat man's son send to him?

3. **fawn** (fôn) pale, yellowish brown.
4. **livid** (liv´ id) discolored, as from a bruise; black-and-blue.

13 **Critical Viewing** ▶ In what ways do you think the couple in this drawing are similar to and different from the couple in this story? **[Compare and Contrast]**

10 Reading Strategy
Comparing and Contrasting Characters

- Ask: What do the characters in the story have in common?
  Answer: They are saddened by the war and worried about their sons who are fighting.
- Read aloud the bracketed passage on pp. 1058–1059. Ask students the Reading Strategy question on p. 1059: In what ways does the fat man seem different from the other passengers?
  Answer: Instead of feeling sad and sorry for himself, the fat man energetically justifies the participation of their children in the war.

Monitor Progress Ask students to discuss whether they learned about the character of the fat man directly or indirectly.
Answer: The fat man's character is revealed indirectly through Pirandello's descriptions of his appearance and speech.

Reteach Draw a Venn diagram on the board, and guide students as they compare and contrast characters.

11 ✓Reading Check
Answer: The message was that the fat man's son was proud and satisfied to die in battle.

12 Background
Art
Old Couple, by Käthe Kollwitz

Born in Königsberg, Prussia, Käthe Kollwitz (1867–1945) was known for her dramatic etchings, woodcuts, lithographs, and sculptures.

Use the following question for discussion.

How does lack of color contribute to the mood of this piece?
Possible response: Because the piece and the emotions exhibited by its subjects are not "colored" by connotation, both remain raw and pure.

13 ▶Critical Viewing
Possible response: The man appears small, and the woman appears shapeless as Pirandello describes. However, the woman in the story is described as bulky, while this woman appears small.

CUSTOMIZE INSTRUCTION FOR UNIVERSAL ACCESS

For English Learners	For Gifted/Talented Students
Draw students' attention to the word *livid* on p. 1059, and read the corresponding footnote. Tell students that people sometimes use the word *livid* to mean "enraged." Have students discuss how this particular use of the word relates to the definition provided in the footnote.	In "War," Pirandello offers several physical descriptions of the fat man, including those on pp. 1058 and 1059. Ask students to use these descriptions to create an illustration of the character. Then, have students consider how these physical, external descriptions contrast with the man's emotions. Ask students to create another illustration—this time depicting the man's internal state. Have students share their illustrations and discuss how the conflict between the external and the internal add meaning to Pirandello's story.

ASSESS

Answers for p. 1060

Review and Assess

1. Possible response: The man inspires pity because he is at last acknowledging his grief.
2. **(a)** The bulky woman wears a big coat and is dressed for mourning. **(b)** The woman's clothing reflects her sorrow and her wish to hide and protect herself from the outside world.
3. **(a)** The son sent a message telling his parents that he was being sent to the front and asking them to see him off. **(b)** The son assured his parents that he would not go to the front for at least six months. **(c)** War is unpredictable and takes no heed of promises.
4. **(a)** The husband claims that his suffering is worse because if he loses his son, he will have no one to console him. **(b)** The other passengers do not agree because they all believe that their own circumstances are worse. **(c)** Possible response: The argument cannot be won because no external standard exists by which to measure grief.
5. **(a)** Parents' love for their children is greater than love of their country. **(b)** Children place their love of country before the love of their parents. **(c)** The fat man reasons that his son died young and happy, never experiencing the boredom of life and the bitterness of disillusionment.
6. **(a)** The woman asks whether the fat man's son is really dead. **(b)** He stares at the woman for a long time and then breaks into uncontrollable sobs. **(c)** The question shatters the fat man's collected façade and makes him realize for the first time that his son is really dead.
7. Possible response: The story helps readers understand manifestations of grief and will cause them to be sympathetic.

Then suddenly, just as if she had heard nothing of what had been said and almost as if waking up from a dream, she turned to the old man, asking him:

"Then . . . is your son really dead?"

Everybody stared at her. The old man, too, turned to look at her, fixing his great, bulging, horribly watery light grey eyes, deep in her face. For some little time he tried to answer, but words failed him. He looked and looked at her, almost as if only then—at that silly, incongruous question—he had suddenly realized at last that his son was really dead . . . gone for ever . . . for ever. His face contracted, became horribly distorted, then he snatched in haste a handkerchief from his pocket and, to the amazement of everyone, broke into harrowing, heart-rending, uncontrollable sobs.

incongruous (in käŋʹ gro͞o əs) *adv.* not fitting a situation; inappropriate

harrowing (harʹ ō iŋ) *adj.* disturbing; frightening

Review and Assess

Thinking About the Selection

1. **Respond:** How did you feel about the fat man's emotional breakdown at the end of the story? Explain.
2. **(a) Recall:** What is the "bulky" woman wearing? **(b) Connect:** In what way does her clothing reflect her mental and emotional state?
3. **(a) Recall:** What message did the son send by "wire" to his parents? **(b) Recall:** What assurance had the parents received when their son joined the military? **(c) Draw Conclusions:** What is suggested about the nature of war when this promise is not kept?
4. **(a) Recall:** According to the husband, why is his suffering worse than the suffering of those with more than one child? **(b) Infer:** Do the other passengers agree with him? Explain. **(c) Assess:** Is this an argument that can be won? Why or why not?
5. **(a) Recall:** According to the fat man, what love is greater than the love of country? **(b) Compare and Contrast:** How do the feelings of young people toward their country differ from the feelings of their parents? **(c) Analyze:** How does the fat man use reason to explain away his own personal tragedy? Explain.
6. **(a) Recall:** What question does the mother ask the fat man? **(b) Analyze Cause and Effect:** How does he react to her question? **(c) Draw Conclusions:** Why does he react as he does? Explain.
7. **Synthesize:** In what ways might this story help you react toward people who have suffered a personal loss?

ASSESSMENT PRACTICE: Reading Comprehension

Identify Patterns of Organization (For more practice, see the Test Preparation Workbook, p. 48.)

Many tests require students to identify patterns of organization. Use the following sample test item to help students practice this skill.

In the late nineteenth and early twentieth centuries, political tensions in Europe led to alliances among several major powers. Germany, Austria-Hungary, and Italy formed the Triple Alliance; Great Britain, France, and Russia formed the Triple Entente. When war broke out in 1914, however, Italy did not join on the side of its allies.

Which of the following patterns of organization is **NOT** used in the passage?

A cause and effect
B specific to general
C general to specific
D chronological

The passage uses cause-and-effect, general-to-specific, and chronological patterns of organization. It does not provide information in a specific-to-general pattern. Choice *B* is correct.

Review and Assess

Literary Analysis

Setting

1. Using a chart like the one shown below, clarify the **setting** of "War" by naming two details about the time, two details about the place, and two details about the passengers' cultural attitudes.

Time	Place	Attitudes
1.	1.	1.
2.	2.	2.

2. (a) How does the historical context—Italy during World War I—affect the characters in this story? (b) In what ways does that context help suggest the theme, or message, of the story? Explain.
3. (a) In what ways might the setting of this story be similar to a combat zone? (b) In what ways might such a setting motivate characters to interact with one another?

Connecting Literary Elements

4. (a) Cite two examples of **indirect characterization** that Pirandello uses to present the husband and wife. (b) What information about the characters does each of these examples provide? Explain.
5. Write one sentence of **direct characterization** for each of the three main characters—the mother, the father, and the fat traveler.

Reading Strategy

Comparing and Contrasting Characters

6. (a) **Compare and contrast the characters** by examining Pirandello's descriptions of the eyes and the clothes of both the mother and the fat man. (b) How do those descriptions suggest similarities and differences between the two characters?
7. (a) For which character do you feel the most sympathy? (b) What do you think sets him or her apart from the others?

Extend Understanding

8. **Cultural Connection:** (a) According to the fat man, why is the attention of young people "fragmented"? (b) Do you see that kind of fragmentation in today's youth culture? Explain.

Quick Review

The **setting** of a literary work is the time and place of the action.

Characterization is the art of creating and developing characters. In **direct characterization,** the author simply states what a character is like. In **indirect characterization,** the author implies what a character is like through details.

When you **compare and contrast characters,** you look for similarities and differences among them.

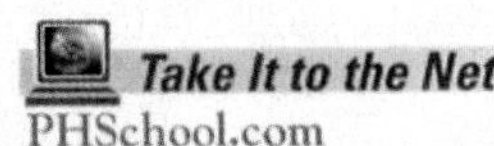
Take It to the Net
PHSchool.com

Take the interactive self-test online to check your understanding of this selection.

ENRICHMENT: Further Reading

Other Works by Luigi Pirandello

We strongly encourage you to review any selection before assigning or recommending it to students.

As You Desire Me

The Late Mattia Pascal

Six Characters in Search of an Author

Take It to the Net

Visit PHSchool.com for more information about Luigi Pirandello.

Answers for p. 1061

Review and Assess

1. Possible response: **Time:** dawn, during World War I; **Place:** carriage of a train, Italy; **Attitudes:** love of country, sadness about the effects of war
2. **(a)** The characters' grown sons serve in the army. **(b)** The historical context suggests that the theme will address the consequences of war.
3. **(a)** All of the characters are placed in immediate contact for a confrontation. **(b)** Because they have spent a long time together in a confined space, the characters talk out of politeness, boredom, or grief.
4. **(a)** Possible response: The wife is described as bulky and her husband as thin and weak. **(b)** Possible response: The first detail suggests that the wife is trying to conceal herself; the second, that the husband's sorrow has caused him to waste away physically.
5. Possible response: The mother has begun mourning for her son, even though he is still alive. The father needs to explain his wife's behavior to other travelers. The fat traveler has not fully accepted the reality of his son's death.
6. **(a)** The mother is dressed for mourning and in a big coat, and she looks like a shapeless bundle. She pulls the coat up to her eyes, attempting to hide. In contrast, the fat man's eyes are bulging and bloodshot and openly reflect his distress. **(b)** The woman, although attempting to hide, grieves openly. The fat man is physically exposed but keeps his sorrow and rage hidden.
7. **(a)** Possible response: The fat man inspires sympathy because he has trouble accepting his son's death. **(b)** Possible response: The fat man feels actual loss while the others feel only the possibility of death.
8. **(a)** The attention of young people is fragmented because they have so many interests. **(b)** Possible response: Many

continued

answers continued from right column

young people are pressured to do well in school, to be involved in sports or creative activities, and to participate in community service projects.

EXTEND

Answers for p. 1062

❶ Vocabulary Development

Word Analysis: Latin Root *-patr-*

1. patriarch
2. Patriotic
3. patrician

Spelling Strategy

1. delight
2. foresight

Concept Development: Synonyms

1. h	5. d
2. e	6. b
3. g	7. f
4. a	8. c

❷ Grammar and Style

Practice

1. who had helped; restrictive; modifies *men*
2. whom everyone was watching; nonrestrictive; modifies *woman*
3. that grieved her; restrictive; modifies *topic*
4. which had claimed many lives; nonrestrictive, modifies *war*
5. whose children are in the military; restrictive; modifies *parents*

Writing Application

Possible response: The mother, *who needed help getting on the train,* was wrapped in a big coat. She sat down among the other passengers *who had sons in the war.* The sacrifice *that parents make* was the main topic of discussion. The fat traveler, *who had never shed a tear,* suddenly burst into uncontrollable sobs.

10TH GRADE For support in teaching the Grammar and Style Lesson to tenth graders, use **Writing and Grammar**, Platinum Level, Chapter 20, Section 2.

Integrate Language Skills

❶ Vocabulary Development Lesson

Word Analysis: Latin Root *-patr-*

The root *-patr-*, found in the word *paternal*, comes from the Latin word *pater*, which means "father." Complete each sentence below by filling in the blank with one of the words listed.

patrician patriotic patriarch

1. Grandfather is the family's __?__.
2. __?__ people love their homeland.
3. A person of high birth is a __?__.

Spelling Strategy

Words that contain a long *i* sound followed by a *t* are often, but not always, spelled with the letter combination *ight*. In each pair of words below, select the word that is spelled correctly.

1. delight/delite 2. foresight/foresyte

Concept Development: Synonyms

Review the vocabulary list on page 1055. Then, select the word in the right column that is similar in meaning to the vocabulary word in the left column.

1. plight	a. vigor
2. paternal	b. impassively
3. discrimination	c. distressing
4. vitality	d. retaliated
5. retorted	e. fatherly
6. stoically	f. absurd
7. incongruous	g. favoritism
8. harrowing	h. difficulty

❷ Grammar and Style Lesson

Adjective Clauses

Adjective clauses are subordinate clauses that modify nouns or pronouns and often begin with the word *that*, *which*, *who*, *whom*, or *whose*. Restrictive adjective clauses are essential to the meaning of the sentence and are not set off by commas. Nonrestrictive adjective clauses are not essential to the meaning and are set off by commas.

Examples:

Restrictive: The passengers who had left Rome on the night express had had to stop . . . [modifies *passengers*]

Nonrestrictive: One of them, who had been listening with particular attention, said . . . [modifies *one*]

Practice Identify the adjective clause in each sentence below. Then, indicate whether it is restrictive or nonrestrictive, and name the word it modifies.

1. He thanked the men who had helped.
2. The unhappy woman, whom everyone was watching, listened to the conversation.
3. They discussed a topic that grieved her.
4. The war, which had claimed many lives, soon might claim her son.
5. Combat brings grief to many parents whose children are in the military.

Writing Application Write a paragraph about the characters in "War." Include at least two restrictive and two nonrestrictive adjective clauses.

WG Prentice Hall Writing and Grammar Connection: Diamond Level, Chapter 19, Section 3

TEACHING RESOURCES

The following resources can be used to enrich or extend the instruction for pp. 1062–1063.

Vocabulary

- **Selection Support:** Build Vocabulary, p. 189
- **Vocabulary and Spelling Practice Book** (Use this booklet for skills instruction.)

Grammar

- **Selection Support:** Grammar and Style, p. 190
- **Writing and Grammar,** Diamond Level, p. 458
- **Daily Language Practice Transparencies** ■

Writing

- **Writing and Grammar,** Diamond Level, p. 831
- **Writing and Grammar iText CD-ROM**
- **Writing Models and Graphic Organizers on Transparencies,** pp. 103–105 ■

Listening and Speaking

- **Performance Assess. and Portfolio Mgmt.**, p. 33

■ **BLOCK SCHEDULING:** Resources marked with this symbol provide varied instruction during 90-minute blocks.

❸ Writing Lesson

Newspaper Article

Imagine yourself in the setting of "War." As a journalist on the train, you have witnessed the exchange among the passengers. Write a newspaper article reporting what you observed. Include a general statement about the impact of the war on ordinary people.

Prewriting Write a rough outline of the events described in the story and the statements the characters make. Review the outline, circling the items that you want to include in the article.

Drafting Begin with a lead, a strong first paragraph that introduces the subject in an interesting way. Follow with a logically ordered report of the events that you witnessed.

Revising Review your draft. To maintain objectivity, remove material that is not factual and replace language that suggests a personal bias.

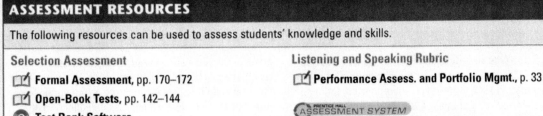

Model: Revising to Maintain Objectivity

Then ~~a foolish old~~ *an older* man interrupted. With great animation, he ~~babbled~~ *said* that young men naturally love their country and want to fight. ~~It was crazy talk.~~

A newspaper article sticks to the facts and does not express bias.

WG Prentice Hall Writing and Grammar Connection: Diamond Level, Chapter 30, Section 2

❹ Extension Activities

Listening and Speaking In a small group, prepare a **dramatic reading** of this story. Use these tips to help your planning:

- Select readers for the narrator, the husband, the wife, the fat man, and the two passengers who speak.
- Vary the volume and tone of your voice to capture the characters' emotions.
- Use eye contact and appropriate gestures.

Deliver the dramatic reading in class. **[Group Activity]**

Research and Technology Using print and electronic sources, prepare a **multimedia report** about a typical soldier's experience in battle during World War I. Include information about military technology, trench warfare, standard-issue equipment, and attitudes toward the war. Present the report to the class, using appropriate handouts to clarify information.

Go online for an additional research activity using the Internet.

❸ Writing Lesson

- Read the Writing Lesson instruction aloud. Then, explain to students that a newspaper article should present information in a factual, objective manner. Information is usually ordered from most important to least important.
- Remind students to answer in their article the questions *who? what? when? where? why?* and *how?*
- Use the Writing Lesson to guide students in developing their articles.
- Students can use the Outline organizer in **Writing Models and Graphic Organizers on Transparencies,** pp. 103–105, to organize their articles.

10TH GRADE For support in working through the Writing Lesson with tenth graders, use **Writing and Grammar,** Platinum Level, Chapter 31, Section 2.

❹ Listening and Speaking

- Tell students that a dramatic reading is an oral presentation that conveys the feelings and mood of a literary work.
- Encourage students to rehearse their presentations individually or with partners several times. Have them experiment with various ways of reading the story. Students might try stressing certain words or passages; changing the tone, volume, and rate at which they speak; and inserting pauses to emphasize meaningful sections.
- Use the Listening and Speaking Progress Chart in **Performance Assessment and Portfolio Management,** p. 33, to evaluate students' readings.

CUSTOMIZE INSTRUCTION For Universal Access

To address different learning styles, use the following activities suggested in the **Extension Activities** booklet, p. 48.

- For Visual/Spatial Learners, use Activity 5.
- For Musical/Rhythmic and Verbal/Linguistic Learners, use Activity 6.

ASSESSMENT RESOURCES

The following resources can be used to assess students' knowledge and skills.

Selection Assessment

- **Formal Assessment,** pp. 170–172
- **Open-Book Tests,** pp. 142–144
- **Test Bank Software**

Take It to the Net

Visit PHSchool.com for self-tests on the selection.

Listening and Speaking Rubric

- **Performance Assess. and Portfolio Mgmt.,** p. 33

For additional diagnostics and remediation for skills covered in this grouping, use materials from the Prentice Hall Assessment System.

Lesson Objectives

1. To understand the connection between the treatment of grief in Luigi Pirandello's story "War" and Sherwood Anderson's story "The Corn Planting"
2. To compare and contrast how various people deal with grief and loss

Connections

War, whether justified or not, always has the same result: people—especially young people—are killed, and their families are left to grieve for them. Have students reread Pirandello's story "War" on pp. 1056–1060 after they have read "The Corn Planting." What similarities and differences do students notice between the two stories and the ways in which the characters deal with grief?

Journeys of Grief

- Ask students to list some ways that people react to grief. Prompt them to consider various reactions to grief that they may have observed in movies, read about in books, observed in person, or experienced personally.
 Possible response: Various reactions to grief include denial, shock, withdrawal, crying, depression, and anger.
- Tell students that the selection they are about to read describes a unique reaction to the news of an only child's death.

CONNECTIONS
Literature Past and Present
Journeys of Grief

The mother in Pirandello's short story "War," in this unit, feels desperate and distraught when she thinks of her only son in battle. Human responses to anxiety and grief, however, are individual and unique. On the train with the mother are other travelers who also have sons in combat. These parents have come up with various ways to calm their fears and worries—and even to deal with the ultimate tragedy of losing a child.

Love and Grief The parents of Will Hutchenson in "The Corn Planting" are, like the mother and father in "War," parents of an only son. Their lives revolve around Will, and when they suffer a crushing loss, they have their own special way of dealing with their sorrow. You may notice these parents' similarities to the parents in Pirandello's story, but take note of their differences as well.

The Corn Planting

Sherwood Anderson

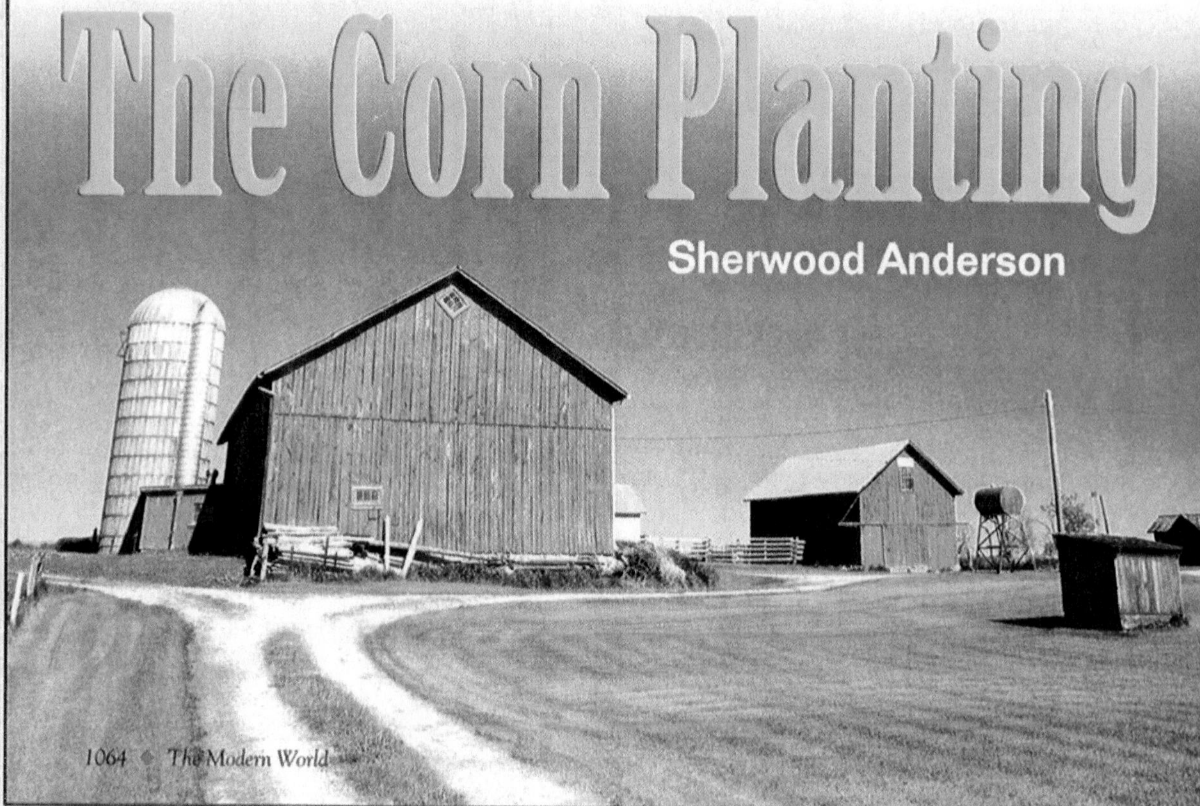

ENRICHMENT: History Connection

Chicago

Chicago was already a major city in the Midwest when Will Hutchenson went there to study at the Art Institute. In 1847, when it was incorporated, Chicago had a population of about 4,200. By the time of the Great Fire in 1871, the population had soared to 300,000. By 1893, the city had sufficiently recovered to host the World Columbian Exposition commemorating the four hundredth anniversary of the European discovery of America. With unlimited opportunities to rebuild after the Great Fire, Chicago provided America's finest architects with an unprecedented boost; as a result, the city became filled with decorative and monumental buildings. The Art Institute is one such structure that today houses an impressive collection of artwork.

The farmers who come to our town to trade are a part of the town life. Saturday is the big day. Often the children come to the high school in town.

It is so with Hatch Hutchenson. Although his farm, some three miles from town, is small, it is known to be one of the best-kept and best-worked places in all our section. Hatch is a little gnarled old figure of a man. His place is on the Scratch Gravel Road and there are plenty of poorly kept places out that way.

Hatch's place stands out. The little frame house is always kept painted, the trees in his orchard are whitened with lime halfway up the trunks, and the barn and sheds are in repair, and his fields are always clean-looking.

Hatch is nearly seventy. He got a rather late start in life. His father, who owned the same farm, was a Civil War man and came home badly wounded, so that, although he lived a long time after the war, he couldn't work much. Hatch was the only son and stayed at home, working the place until his father died. Then, when he was nearing fifty, he married a schoolteacher of forty, and they had a son. The schoolteacher was a small one like Hatch. After they married, they both stuck close to the land. They seemed to fit into their farm life as certain people fit into the clothes they wear. I have noticed something about people who make a go of marriage. They grow more and more alike. Then even grow to look alike.

Their one son, Will Hutchenson, was a small but remarkably strong boy. He came to our high school in town and pitched on our town baseball team. He was a fellow always cheerful, bright and alert, and a great favorite with all of us.

For one thing, he began as a young boy to make amusing little drawings. It was a talent. He made drawings of fish and pigs and cows, and they looked like people you knew. I never did know, before, that people could look so much like cows and horses and pigs and fish.

When he had finished in the town high school, Will went to Chicago, where his mother had a cousin living, and he became a student in the Art Institute out there. Another young fellow from our town was also in Chicago. He really went two years before Will did. His name was Hal Weyman, and he was a student at the University of Chicago. After he graduated, he came home and got a job as principal of our high school.

Hal and Will Hutchenson hadn't been close friends before, Hal being several years older than Will, but in Chicago they got together, went together to see plays, and, as Hal later told me, they had a good many long talks.

I got it from Hal that, in Chicago, as at home here when he was a young boy, Will was immediately popular. He was good-looking, so the girls in the art school liked him, and he had a straightforwardness that made him popular with all the young fellows.

Hal told me that Will was out to some party nearly every night, and

Thematic Connection
Why do you think the description of Will is so positive?

◀ Critical Viewing
In what ways does the farm setting impact the characters in this story? **[Connect]**

Journeys of Grief

- Have a volunteer read aloud the third paragraph of the story. Then, ask students to paraphrase the paragraph.
  Possible response: Hatch's place is unusual in that it is always kept in good condition, including the house, the trees, the barn, the sheds, and the fields.
- Ask students what this description of the farm tells the reader about Hatch's personality.
  Answer: Hatch is a hard worker who takes pride in caring for his farm.

Thematic Connection

Possible response: The description of Will is positive because it is setting the stage for the terrible grief the parents will feel when they hear of their son's death.

▶Critical Viewing

Possible response: The isolation of the farm setting has allowed the characters to develop not only a strong connection to the land, but to each other.

Thematic Connection

Answer: The Hutchensons' anticipation of and excitement about Will's correspondence shows the pride these parents have in their son's accomplishments. In addition, the voracity with which they consume the letters demonstrates the Hutchensons' curiosity and desire to live vicariously through Will.

right away he began to sell some of his amusing little drawings and to make money. The drawings were used in advertisements, and he was well paid.

He even began to send some money home. You see, after Hal came back here, he used to go quite often out to the Hutchenson place to see Will's father and mother. He would walk or drive out there in the afternoon or on summer evenings and sit with them. The talk was always of Will.

Hal said it was touching how much the father and mother depended on their one son, how much they talked about him and dreamed of his future. They had never been people who went about much with the town folks or even with their neighbors. They were of the sort who work all the time, from early morning till late in the evenings, and on moonlight nights, Hal said, and after the little old wife had got the supper, they often went out into the fields and worked again.

You see, by this time old Hatch was nearing seventy and his wife would have been ten years younger. Hal said that whenever he went out to the farm they quit work and came to sit with him. They might be in one of the fields, working together, but when they saw him in the road, they came running. They had got a letter from Will. He wrote every week.

The little old mother would come running following the father. "We got another letter, Mr. Weyman," Hatch would cry, and then his wife, quite breathless, would say the same thing, "Mr. Weyman, we got a letter."

The letter would be brought out at once and read aloud. Hal said the letters were always delicious. Will larded them with little sketches. There were humorous drawings of people he had seen or been with, rivers of automobiles on Michigan Avenue in Chicago, a policeman at a street crossing, young stenographers hurrying into office buildings. Neither of the old people had ever been to the city and they were curious and eager. They wanted the drawings explained, and Hal said they were like two children wanting to know every little detail Hal could remember about their son's life in the big city. He was always at them to come there on a visit and they would spend hours talking of that.

Thematic Connection
In what way does Will's parents' reaction to his letters indicate his importance in their lives?

"Of course," Hatch said, "we couldn't go."

"How could we?" he said. He had been on that one little farm since he was a boy. When he was a young fellow, his father was an invalid and so Hatch had to run things. A farm, if you run it right, is very exacting. You have to fight weeds all the time. There are the farm animals to take care of. "Who would milk our cows?" Hatch said. The idea of anyone but him or his wife touching one of the Hutchenson cows seemed to hurt him. While he was alive, he didn't want anyone else plowing one of his fields, tending his corn, looking after things about the barn. He felt that way about his farm. It was a thing you couldn't explain, Hal said. He seemed to understand the two old people.

ENRICHMENT: Psychology Connection

Stages of Grief

In her book *On Death and Dying,* Dr. Elisabeth Kübler-Ross, a Swiss-born psychiatrist, details the five stages of grief. Briefly, these stages are as follows:

Stage 1, Denial: The person reacts with a shocked, "No. It's not possible."

Stage 2, Anger: The person wants to blame someone else or even God for what has happened.

Stage 3, Bargaining: The person tries to bargain with God or with another person, as in, "Give me some more time, and I'll ..."

Stage 4, Depression: The person begins to face what is happening and feels depressed about it.

Stage 5, Acceptance: The person realizes that he or she must accept what cannot be changed.

The Hailstorm, Thomas Hart Benton, Joslyn Art Museum, Omaha, Nebraska

It was a spring night, past midnight, when Hal came to my house and told me the news. In our town we have a night telegraph operator at the railroad station and Hal got a wire. It was really addressed to Hatch Hutchenson, but the operator brought it to Hal. Will Hutchenson was dead, had been killed. It turned out later that he was at a party with some other young fellows and there might have been some drinking. Anyway, the car was wrecked, and Will Hutchenson was killed. The operator wanted Hal to go out and take the message to Hatch and his wife, and Hal wanted me to go along.

I offered to take my car, but Hal said no, "Let's walk out," he said. He wanted to put off the moment, I could see that. So we did walk. It was early spring, and I remember every moment of the silent walk we took, the little leaves just coming on the trees, the little streams we crossed, how the moonlight made the water seem alive. We loitered and loitered, not talking, hating to go on.

▲ Critical Viewing

In what ways does the storm in this painting reflect the blow that the Hutchensons are about to receive? **[Connect]**

Background

Art

The Hailstorm, by Thomas Hart Benton

Like Will Hutchenson in "The Corn Planting," Thomas Hart Benton (1889–1975) left his small, rural home to attend the Art Institute of Chicago. After a year of study, he traveled to Paris, where he became interested in modern art movements. Benton then returned to the United States and lived in New York City, becoming part of the cutting-edge art scene and experimenting with painting styles. Benton soon abandoned modernism, however, and returned to a more realistic style, painting people and landscapes of the Midwest.

Use the following questions for discussion.

Which details in this painting reflect a realistic style? Which details are unrealistic?
Possible response: The shading and detail of the tree's trunk and leaves are very realistic, as is the shelter shown in the right side of the painting. The stylized, distorted figures and flat, cartoonlike colors are unrealistic.

▶Critical Viewing

Possible response: The storm—like the news of Will's death—is sudden and violent. The figures depicted in the painting are struggling against the wind, much like the Hutchensons will have to struggle with the reality of their son's death.

Background

Telegraph

"The Corn Planting" is set during the early 1900s, a time when most people did not have telephones. Therefore, the news of Will's death is sent by telegraph. The telegraph was an important means of communication. Morse code, which uses a series of dots and dashes to represent letters of the alphabet, was transmitted over the telegraph wires. After the telegraph operator translated a message, it had to be delivered to the intended recipient.

CUSTOMIZE INSTRUCTION FOR UNIVERSAL ACCESS

For Less Proficient Readers	For English Learners	For Advanced Readers
Ask students why the Hutchensons do not visit their son in Chicago. Propose that the Hutchensons' reluctance stems from either a sense of responsibility to their land or from a fear of modern life. Have students discuss each of the two possibilities.	Draw students' attention to the fourth full paragraph on p. 1066. Then, point out that it is unconventional to present in one paragraph what two different speakers say. Explain that Anderson puts Hatch and his wife's dialogue in one paragraph to suggest a lack of individual identity. Ask students to identify another place this technique could be used in this story.	Have students contrast Will's life in Chicago with his parents' lives. Explain that Will and his parents are separated by a period of enormous change. Have students research the differences between Will's generation and that of his parents and present a short essay on their findings.

- Read aloud the second paragraph on p. 1068. Then, ask students: How will the Hutchensons react to Hal's news?
  Possible responses: The Hutchensons will react with extreme sorrow. They will not fully absorb the news.
- Have students read the sixth paragraph on the page. Ask students to predict what the Hutchensons are going to do after they emerge from the house.
  Possible responses: The Hutchensons will begin digging a grave; they will sit somewhere in the field and pray or meditate; or they will bury Will's letters.

▶Critical Viewing

Possible response: The couple in the picture appears to be similar to the Hutchensons in that they are looking upon the land with great pride. The picture has a contemplative feel, so this couple may be thinking of a child.

Then we got out there, and Hal went to the front door of the farmhouse while I stayed in the road. I heard a dog bark, away off somewhere. I heard a child crying in some distant house. I think that Hal, after he got to the front door of the house, must have stood there for ten minutes, hating to knock.

Then he did knock, and the sound his fist made on the door seemed terrible. It seemed like guns going off. Old Hatch came to the door, and I heard Hal tell him. I know what happened. Hal had been trying, all the way out from town, to think up words to tell the old couple in some gentle way, but when it came to the scratch, he couldn't. He blurted everything right out, right into old Hatch's face.

That was all. Old Hatch didn't say a word. The door was opened, he stood there in the moonlight, wearing a funny long white nightgown, Hal told him, and the door went shut again with a bang, and Hal was left standing there.

He stood for a time, and then came back out into the road to me. "Well," he said, and "Well," I said. We stood in the road looking and listening. There wasn't a sound from the house.

And then—it might have been ten minutes or it might have been a half-hour—we stood silently, listening and watching, not knowing what to do—we couldn't go away—"I guess they are trying to get so they can believe it," Hal whispered to me. I got his notion all right. The two old people must have thought of their son Will always only in terms of life, never of death.

We stood watching and listening, and then, suddenly, after a long time, Hal touched me on the arm. "Look," he whispered. There were two white-clad figures going from the house to the barn. It turned out, you see, that old Hatch had been plowing that day. He had finished plowing and harrowing a field near the barn.

The two figures went into the barn and presently came out. They went into the field, and Hal and I crept across the farmyard to the barn and got to where we could see what was going on without being seen.

It was an incredible thing. The old man had got a hand corn-planter

▲ Critical Viewing
In what way might this couple be similar to the Hutchensons? [Compare]

ENRICHMENT: Culture Connection

Corn

Corn, a member of the grass family, was first cultivated in Central America. In the history of the domestication of plants, corn is actually a latecomer, trailing by a thousand years the cultivation of beans and squash. The original wild corn is small. The much larger size and shape of the modern corncob is a result of centuries of selective breeding.

Corn has long been a staple of Native American societies throughout North America, and different groups have celebrated its cultivation in one way or another. For example, the Pueblo people have traditionally honored their Corn Mothers by providing all newborn children with corn fetishes. Mississippi groups like the Muskogee, Chickasaw, Choctaw, and Cherokee have held Green Corn Dances after each summer's harvest.

out of the barn and his wife had got a bag of seed corn, and there, in the moonlight, that night, after they got that news, they were planting corn.

It was a thing to curl your hair—it was so ghostly. They were both in their nightgowns. They would do a row across the field, coming quite close to us as we stood in the shadow of the barn, and then, at the end of each row, they would kneel side by side by the fence and stay silent for a time. The whole thing went on in silence. It was the first time in my life I ever understood something, and I am far from sure now that I can put down what I understood and felt that night—I mean something about the connection between certain people and the earth—a kind of silent cry, down into the earth, of these two old people, putting corn down into the earth. It was as though they were putting death down into the ground that life might grow again—something like that.

They must have been asking something of the earth, too. But what's the use? What they were up to in connection with the life in their field and the lost life in their son is something you can't very well make clear in words. All I know is that Hal and I stood the sight as long as we could, and then we crept away and went back to town, but Hatch Hutchenson and his wife must have got what they were after that night, because Hal told me that when he went out in the morning to see them and to make the arrangements for bringing their dead son home, they were both curiously quiet and Hal thought in command of themselves. Hal said he thought they had got something. "They have their farm and they have still got Will's letters to read," Hal said.

Sherwood Anderson

(1876–1941)

Born the third of seven children, Sherwood Anderson grew up in a small town in Ohio. His father, a harness maker and house painter, was not always able to earn enough to support the family. Anderson dropped out of school at fourteen to work but finished high school in his twenties, after a year in the army. Much of Anderson's writing, which uses everyday speech to capture the essence of characters, features small-town life in the rural Midwest.

Connecting Literature Past and Present

1. (a) What do Hatch Hutchenson and his wife have in common with the man and woman who enter the train at Fabriano in Pirandello's "War"? (b) In what ways are the two couples' lives different?
2. In what way does nature help Hatch and his wife cope with their devastating loss?
3. (a) What do you think the parents in "War" would say to Hatch Hutchenson and his wife? (b) What do you think Hatch Hutchenson and his wife would say to the parents in "War"?

Journeys of Grief

- Ask a volunteer to read aloud the first full paragraph on p. 1069. Then, have students describe the scene in their own words.
  Possible response: The Hutchensons—dressed only in their nightgowns—plant row upon row of corn, stopping at the end of each row to kneel in silence.
- Ask students to discuss activities that might be comforting to an individual who had just received terrible news.

Answers

Connecting Literature Past and Present

1. **(a)** For both the Hutchensons and the couple on the train, their only child, a son, has left home at an early age to study in a faraway city. **(b)** The two couples' lives are different in that the unnamed couple have left their home in Sulmona to follow their son to Rome, whereas the Hutchensons remain on their farm when Will goes to Chicago. Another more profound difference is that the Hutchensons have lost their son in a car accident, whereas the unnamed couple's son is still alive.
2. The Hutchensons take comfort in working the land. Unlike death, this work is something they have some experience with and control over. The act of planting corn not only serves as an example of the solace the land provides but also works symbolically to suggest that the Hutchensons are burying Will's death so that "life might grow again."
3. **(a)** Possible response: The parents in "War" would sympathize with the Hutchensons, offering their condolences. **(b)** Possible response: The Hutchensons might sympathize with the parents in "War," understanding the anguish they must feel as their son goes to the war front. The Hutchensons might advise the couple to focus on another meaningful aspect of their lives as a method of coping with their anxiety and sorrow.

The Guitar • *from* Lament for Ignacio Sánchez Mejías: Absent Soul • Ithaka • The Soul With Boundaries

Lesson Objectives

1. **To analyze and respond to literary elements**
   - Literary Analysis: Lyric Poetry and Epiphany
   - Comparing Literary Works: Metaphor and Extended Metaphor
2. **To read, comprehend, analyze, and critique a poem**
   - Reading Strategy: Reading Stanzas as Units of Meaning
   - Reading Check Questions
   - Review and Assess Questions
   - Assessment Practice (ATE)
3. **To develop word analysis skills, fluency, and systematic vocabulary**
   - Vocabulary Development Lesson: Latin Prefix *dis-*
4. **To understand and apply written and oral language conventions**
   - Spelling Strategy
   - Grammar and Style Lesson: The Understood *You* in Imperative Sentences
5. **To understand and apply appropriate writing and research strategies**
   - Writing Lesson: Sentence Outline and Summary
   - Extension Activity: Allusion Chart
6. **To understand and apply listening and speaking strategies**
   - Extension Activity: Reading to Music

STEP-BY-STEP TEACHING GUIDE	PACING GUIDE
PRETEACH	
Motivate Students and Provide Background	
Use the Motivation activity (ATE p. 1070)	5 min.
Read and discuss author and background features (SE pp. 1070, 1072, 1076, 1079; ATE p. 1070) [A]	5 min.
Introduce the Concepts	
Introduce the Literary Analysis and Reading Strategy concepts (SE/ATE p. 1071) [A]	15 min.
Pronounce the vocabulary words and read their definitions (SE p. 1071)	5 min.
TEACH	
Monitor Comprehension	
Informally monitor comprehension by circulating while students read independently or in groups [A]	25 min.
Monitor students' comprehension with the Reading Check note (SE/ATE p. 1079)	as students read
Develop vocabulary with the Vocabulary notes (SE pp. 1073, 1074, 1076, 1077, 1079, 1080; ATE p. 1079)	as students read
Develop Understanding	
Develop students' understanding of lyric poetry and epiphany with the Literary Analysis annotations (SE/ATE pp. 1073, 1077, 1079) [A]	5 min.
Develop students' ability to read stanzas as units of meaning, using the Reading Strategy annotations (SE/ATE pp. 1074, 1076, 1080)	5 min.
ASSESS	
Assess Mastery	
Assess students' mastery of the Reading Strategy and Literary Analysis concepts by having them answer the Review and Assess questions (SE/ATE p. 1081)	15 min.
Use one or more of the print, software, or tranparency Assessment Resources (ATE p. 1083) [A]	up to 45 min.
EXTEND	
Apply Understanding	
Have students complete the Vocabulary Development Lesson and the Grammar and Style Lesson (SE p. 1082) [A]	20 min.
Apply students' ability to clarify key ideas, using the Writing Lesson (SE/ATE p. 1083) [A]	45 min.
Apply students' understanding of the selections, using one or more of the Extension Activities (SE p. 1083)	20–90 min.

A ACCELERATED INSTRUCTION:
Use the strategies and activities identified with an [A].

10TH GRADE TEACHING TENTH-GRADE STUDENTS:
For support in teaching the selection(s) to tenth-grade students, see the Step-by-Step Teaching notes identified wih the icon shown here.

UNIVERSAL ACCESS
● = Below-Level Students
▲ = On-Level Students
■ = Above-Level Students

Time and Resource Manager

Reading Level: Challenging, Challenging, Average, Challenging
Average Number of Instructional Days: 3

RESOURCES		
PRINT	**TRANSPARENCIES**	**TECHNOLOGY**
• **Beyond Literature,** Community Connection: Eulogy, p. 49 ▲ ■		
• **Selection Support Workbook:** ● ▲ ■ Literary Analysis, p. 196 Reading Strategy, p. 195 Build Vocabulary, p. 193	• **Literary Analysis and Reading Transparencies,** pp. 97 and 98 ● ▲ ■	
		• **Listening to Literature** ● ▲ ■ Audiocassettes Audio CDs
• **Literary Analysis for Enrichment,** p. 49 ■		
• **Formal Assessment:** Selection Test, pp. 173–175 ● ▲ ■ • **Open-Book Tests,** pp. 145–147 ● ▲ ■ • **Performance Assessment and Portfolio Management,** p. 32 ● ▲ ■ • PRENTICE HALL ASSESSMENT SYSTEM ● ▲ ■	• PRENTICE HALL ASSESSMENT SYSTEM ● ▲ ■ **Skills Practice Answers and Explanations on Transparencies**	• **Test Bank Software** ● ▲ ■
• **Selection Support Workbook:** ● ▲ ■ Grammar and Style, p. 194 • **Writing and Grammar,** Diamond Level ● ▲ ■ • **Extension Activities,** p. 49 ● ▲ ■	• **Daily Language Practice Transparencies** ● ▲ • **Writing Models and Graphic Organizers on Transparencies,** pp. 79–81; 103–105	• **Writing and Grammar iText CD-ROM** ● ▲ ■ *Take It to the Net* PHSchool.com

BLOCK SCHEDULING: Use one 90-minute class period to preteach the selection(s) and have students read them. Use a second 90-minute class period to assess students' mastery of skills and have them complete one of the Extension Activities.

PRETEACH

Step-by-Step Teaching Guide for pp. 1070–1071

Motivation

On the board, write the word *Poetry* in the center of a cluster diagram; around it, write *Music, Death, Life*, and *The Self*. Tell students that this diagram shows some of the major themes of lyric poetry. Emphasize that a lyric poem can express anything a person feels or observes. Tell students that they are going to read four lyric poems. Each is like a snapshot of the poet's feelings.

❶ Background

More About the Authors

Federico García Lorca was especially influenced by the music of the gypsies—*cante jondo* (kan′ ta hon′ do), which expresses the pain and the happiness of the Andalusian gypsies. The deeply reflective lyrics of these songs influenced García Lorca's tragic and comic vision of life and crystallized the themes that run through his work.

As a boy, Constantine Cavafy helped his father with the family export business. As a young man, however, Cavafy lost interest in the business and became a government clerk.

Fernando Pessoa earned his living as a translator. Although Pessoa wrote a large number of poems, very few were published during his lifetime. He lived in a furnished room in Lisbon, avoiding social contact, and was virtually unknown at the time of his death.

Geography Note

Draw students' attention to the map on this page. Explain that García Lorca, Cavafy, and Pessoa represent a range of cultures. García Lorca was born in Spain and wrote in Spanish. Cavafy was born in Egypt, but became a Greek citizen and wrote in Greek. Pessoa was born in Portugal, but grew up in South Africa. He returned to Portugal, where he wrote in English and Portuguese.

Comparing Literary Works

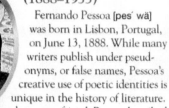

Prepare to Read

❶ The Guitar ◆ *from* Lament for Ignacio Sánchez Mejías: Absent Soul ◆ Ithaka ◆ The Soul With Boundaries

Federico García Lorca (1898–1936)

In August 1936, one month after the start of the Spanish Civil War, the Spanish newspaper *El Diario de Albacete* broke the shocking story that Federico García Lorca had been assassinated. Subsequent reports confirmed that he had been murdered by right-wing Nationalists, who deemed his writings politically offensive.

Ironically, García Lorca did not write explicitly political poetry. His inspiration came from the people and culture of rural Andalusia, where the poet was born. Andalusia is the homeland of the gypsies, or flamencos. With the exception of the poems collected in *Poet in New York*, all of García Lorca's work reflects the dark beauty of Andalusian culture.

García Lorca also wrote several major plays, including *Blood Wedding* (1933) and *The House of Bernarda Alba* (1934). Although his writing career was tragically cut short, García Lorca is considered one of Spain's greatest poets and playwrights.

Constantine Cavafy (1863–1933)

Constantine Cavafy [kə vä′ fē] was born in 1863 in Alexandria, Egypt. Although he never lived in Greece, he became a Greek citizen as soon as he was of age. Today, he is considered the most original and influential Greek poet of the twentieth century.

In his poems, Cavafy combines two distinct kinds of Greek: demotic Greek, the language of the common people, and purist Greek, the official language of the church and state. Although the distinctions between the two do not translate into English, Cavafy's use of both forms of Greek can be seen as a political statement.

During his lifetime, Cavafy never published a single book of poems. However, when *The Poems of Constantine P. Cavafy* was published posthumously in 1935, Cavafy began to draw the attention of the world. Ever since then, his reputation—both in Greece and abroad—has continued to grow.

Fernando Pessoa (1888–1935)

Fernando Pessoa [pes′ wä] was born in Lisbon, Portugal, on June 13, 1888. While many writers publish under pseudonyms, or false names, Pessoa's creative use of poetic identities is unique in the history of literature.

In a letter to a friend, Pessoa described the birth of his first literary alter ego: ". . . I wrote thirty-odd poems straight off, in a kind of ecstasy whose nature I cannot define. . . . I started with a title—'The Keeper of Sheep.' And what followed was the apparition of somebody in me, to whom I at once gave the name of Alberto Caeiro."

Alberto Caeiro was one of four personas, whom Pessoa called *heteronyms*, who wrote and published poems. The others were Ricardo Reis, Alvaro de Campos, and Fernando Pessoa himself. For each of these heteronyms, Pessoa invented a biography, personality, beliefs, physical appearance, and literary style. One critic wrote, "Pessoa was a poet who wrote poets as well as poems."

Over the course of his life, Pessoa created at least seventy distinct identities who wrote thousands of literary works. His many books of poetry and prose include *Antinous* (1918), *Sonnets* (1918), and *English Poems* (1921).

TEACHING RESOURCES

The following resources can be used to enrich or extend the instruction for pp. 1070–1071.

Background

Beyond Literature, p. 49

Take It to the Net

Visit PHSchool.com for background on the poets.

Literary Analysis

Literary Analysis and Reading Transparencies, Lyric Poetry and Epiphany, p. 97

Reading

Literary Analysis and Reading Transparencies, Reading Stanzas as Units of Meaning, p. 98

Selection Support: Reading Strategy, p. 195

BLOCK SCHEDULING: Resources marked with this symbol provide varied instruction during 90-minute blocks.

❷ Preview

Connecting to the Literature

When traveling, you can journey by car or by plane; you might walk, take a bus, or even ride a horse. If life itself is a journey, how should one travel? These poems look at the long journey of life and express ideas about the best ways to make the trip.

Literary Analysis

Lyric Poetry and Epiphany

Lyric poetry is melodic verse that expresses the observations of a single speaker. Unlike narrative poems, lyric poems do not tell complete stories. Instead, they build to express a moment of insight—an **epiphany,** or revelation. The poet Dante Gabriel Rossetti called the sonnet, which is a type of lyric poem, a "moment's monument." Because of this emphasis on the moment, lyric poems exclude details that a narrative would supply. As you read, look for the moment of insight captured by each poem.

Comparing Literary Works

A **metaphor** is an implied comparison between two seemingly different things. In the example below, García Lorca likens the sound of a guitar to a woeful utterance, and he then characterizes the sky as a kind of building:

Now begins the cry / Of the guitar, / Breaking the vaults / Of dawn.

While most metaphors are brief, an **extended metaphor** flows throughout a literary work. Several comparisons may be made along the way, combining to create a larger meaning. All of the poems in this grouping contain metaphors, some of which are extended. As you read, compare the use of metaphor in each poem.

❸ Reading Strategy

Reading Stanzas as Units of Meaning

Many poems take the form of stanzas, or formal groupings of lines. Like a paragraph in a work of prose, a stanza usually expresses one main idea. To aid your understanding of poetry, **read stanzas as units of meaning** in the same way that you read paragraphs. You might pause after each stanza and consider its main thought. Use a chart like the one shown to record statements expressing these ideas.

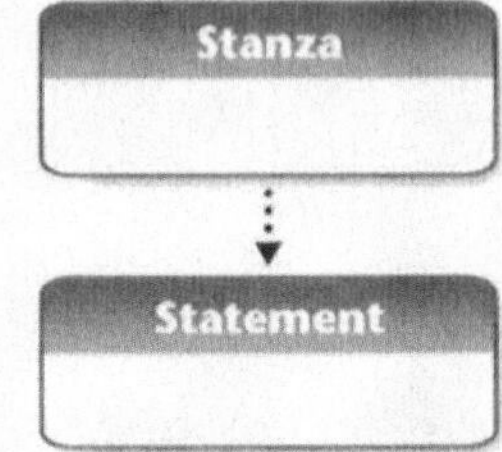

Vocabulary Development

monotonously (mə nätʹ'n əs lē) *adv.* done in a way that goes on and on without variation (p. 1073)

posterity (päs terʹ ə tē) *n.* future generations of people (p. 1074)

exalted (eg zôltʹ id) *adj.* lifted high because of dignity or honor (p. 1076)

sensual (senʹ sho͞o əl) *adj.* pleasing to the senses (p. 1077)

summit (sumʹ it) *n.* highest point (p. 1079)

dispersed (di spurstʹ) *adj.* broken up and scattered (p. 1079)

divergent (di vurʹ jənt) *adj.* differing from each other (p. 1080)

CUSTOMIZE INSTRUCTION FOR UNIVERSAL ACCESS

For Less Proficient Readers	For English Learners	For Advanced Readers
The sentence length, complicated syntax, and complex language of these poems may prove difficult for students. To increase comprehension, have students read a line or two and then paraphrase the feelings and observations conveyed. Then, discuss the differences in students' paraphrasing.	Tell students that in poetry, a sentence may extend over several lines, or it may end in the middle of a line. Encourage students to read each poem according to its sentences, not its lines. Remind students to follow punctuation.	Organize students into pairs, and have them identify and analyze the figurative language in these poems. Then, have students share their analyses, supporting their interpretations with evidence from the text.

❷ Literary Analysis

Lyric Poetry and Epiphany

- Read the Literary Analysis instruction on p. 1071. Then, remind students that lyric poetry was originally accompanied by music; therefore, musicality is a distinctive feature of this poetry.
- Draw students' attention to the word *epiphany.* Remind them that an epiphany is a sudden flash of recognition or insight that may take the form of disillusionment.
- Encourage students to look for the musical qualities in the poems that follow and to note the details or images that lead to each poem's moment of insight.
- Use the Lyric Poetry and Epiphany transparency in **Literary Analysis and Reading Transparencies,** p. 97, to help students recognize elements of lyric poetry and identify a poem's epiphany.

❸ Reading Strategy

Reading Stanzas as Units of Meaning

- Point out to students that a stanza, like a paragraph, can be of any length. In many traditional poems, stanzas are unified by a set number of lines in each stanza.
- Preview with students García Lorca's poem "Absent Soul" and Cavafy's poem "Ithaka." Point out that "Absent Soul," with one exception, has four-line stanzas. "Ithaka" combines stanzas of varying lengths, but each stanza is unified primarily by a main idea.
- Explain the use of the graphic organizer on p. 1071. Tell students that noting the main thought of each stanza may help them understand the meaning of a poem as a whole. Have students use the organizer as they read the poems.

Vocabulary Development

- Pronounce each vocabulary word for students, and read the definitions as a class. Have students identify any words with which they are already familiar.

E-Teach

Visit e-Teach at PHSchool.com for teachers' essays on how to teach, with questions and answers.

TEACH

Step-by-Step Teaching Guide for pp. 1072–1080

Teaching Tenth-Grade Students

10TH GRADE Tell tenth-grade students that a lyric poem, unlike a narrative poem, never tells a full story. Rather, it emphasizes an experience or creates and explores a single effect.

1 About the Selection

In "The Guitar," the speaker compares the mourning notes of a guitar to a wounded heart.

2 Background

Art

The Old Guitarist, **by Pablo Picasso**

Spanish-born Pablo Picasso (1881–1973) is considered one of the most important visual artists of the twentieth century. During his long career, Picasso went through numerous periods in which he painted in distinctly different styles. In his Blue Period (c. 1901–1904), his work projects a dark, somber, melancholy mood. *The Old Guitarist* is from this period.

Use the following question for discussion:

How does Picasso suggest sadness?
Possible response: The angle at which the guitarist is bent suggests that he is defeated or in mourning. The guitarist's gauntness and torn shirt suggest poverty. The colors are dark and opaque.

3 ▶ Critical Viewing

Possible Response: The mood of this painting fits the mood of the poem as both evoke melancholy. The painting does so with its blue-green coloring and the man's anguished face and posture. The poem establishes the same mood with words such as "cry," "weeps," "mourns," and "dead."

1 The Guitar

Federico García Lorca
translated by
Elizabeth du Gué Trapier

2

The Old Guitarist, 1903, Pablo Picasso, The Art Institute of Chicago

Background

García Lorca did not accept the label of "Gypsy Poet." Instead, he insisted, "I could just as well be a poet of sewing needles and hydraulic landscapes. . . ." Nevertheless, Gypsy culture pervades García Lorca's work, providing him with images that transcend the local and become universal.

"The Guitar" captures the flamenco music of the Gitanos, the Gypsy population of Andalusia. Some flamenco music is festive, but García Lorca admired the *cante jondo* (kan′ tā hōn′ dō), a deeper and more somber tradition. "Absent Soul" is the final section of "Lament for Ignacio Sánchez Mejías," an elegy to a famous bullfighter who was a friend of García Lorca's. Sánchez Mejías died in 1934 after having been gored during a bullfight.

3 ◀ Critical Viewing
Does the mood of this painting fit the mood of the poem? Explain. **[Interpret]**

TEACHING RESOURCES

The following resources can be used to enrich or extend the instruction for pp. 1072–1080.

Literary Analysis

- **Selection Support:** Literary Analysis, p. 196
- **Literary Analysis and Reading Transparencies,** Lyric Poetry and Epiphany, p. 97

Reading

- **Selection Support:** Reading Strategy, p. 195; Build Vocabulary, p. 193 ■
- **Listening to Literature Audiocassettes**
- **Listening to Literature Audio CDs** ■

■ **BLOCK SCHEDULING:** Resources marked with this symbol provide varied instruction during 90-minute blocks.

Now begins the cry
Of the guitar,
Breaking the vaults
Of dawn.
Now begins the cry
Of the guitar.
Useless
To still it.
Impossible
To still it.
❹ It weeps monotonously
As weeps the water,
As weeps the wind
Over snow.
Impossible
To still it.
It weeps
For distant things,
Warm southern sands
Desiring white camellias[1]
It mourns the arrow without a target,
The evening without morning,
And the first bird dead
Upon a branch.
O guitar!
A wounded heart,
Wounded by five swords.

Literary Analysis
Lyric Poetry and Epiphany Which words and individual sounds help give lines 7–16 a musical feeling?

monotonously (mə nät′'n əs lē) *adv.* done in a way that goes on and on without variation

1. **camellias** (kə mēl′ yəz) showy, roselike flowers of an ornamental evergreen shrub native to eastern Asia.

Review and Assess

Thinking About the Selection

1. **Respond:** Which image in this poem do you find most striking?
2. **(a) Recall:** In lines 3–4, what effect does the guitar's cry have upon the "vaults / Of dawn"? **(b) Interpret:** What does this image suggest about the intensity of emotion expressed by the guitar?
3. **(a) Recall:** In lines 21–24, for what three things does the speaker say the guitar mourns? **(b) Analyze:** How does each of these things capture a sense of unfulfilled promise? Explain.
4. **(a) Recall:** In lines 25–27, which objects wound the guitar? **(b) Interpret:** What is your interpretation of this image? Explain.
5. **Extend:** What musical instrument seems most like a person to you? Explain.

❹ Literary Analysis

Lyric Poetry and Epiphany

- Have a volunteer read the poem aloud.• Then, ask the Literary Analysis question on p. 1073: Which words and individual sounds help give lines 7–16 a musical feeling?
  Possible response: The repetition of "Of the guitar," "To still it," and "As weeps" and the repetition of individual sounds, like /s/ in "Impossible" and "still" and /g/ in "begins" and "guitar" create a musical feeling.
- Tell students that elements of a lyric poem build to an epiphany for the speaker, the reader, or both.
- Ask: Where does the epiphany of this poem occur?
  Answer: It occurs in the final two lines.
- Ask: What elements of the poem point to this revelation?
  Answer: The personification of the guitar, the emphasis on its mournful tune, and the descriptions equating it with a force of nature point to this revelation.

Answers for p. 1073

Review and Assess

1. Possible response: The most striking image is that of the guitar as a heart, wounded by five swords.
2. **(a)** It breaks open the vaults of dawn. **(b)** This image suggests that the emotions are extremely powerful.
3. **(a)** The guitar mourns for "the arrow without a target, the evening without morning, and the first bird dead upon a branch." **(b)** All represent incomplete events.
4. **(a)** Five swords wound the guitar. **(b)** Possible response: The five swords are the five senses, which bring pain and experience to the heart.
5. Possible response: The violin may seem most like a person because its tone and expression resemble the human voice.

CUSTOMIZE INSTRUCTION FOR UNIVERSAL ACCESS

For English Learners	For Gifted/Talented Students
If you have Spanish-speaking students who are literate in Spanish, provide them with the original Spanish version of "The Guitar." Have students discuss the difference in sound, tempo, and tone between the English and Spanish versions. Ask students to consider which version more effectively captures the musicality characteristic of lyric poetry.	Call students' attention to the parallel mood and theme expressed in García Lorca's poem and Picasso's painting. Challenge students to create or locate another piece of art to accompany these two pieces. They may write or find a poem, a piece of music, or a short story. Or students may find or create a painting, drawing, or sculpture. Have each student present his or her piece and discuss how it relates to the works of García Lorca and Picasso.

❺ About the Selection

In "Absent Soul," García Lorca uses vivid descriptions of the Andalusian landscape and powerful metaphors to honor and preserve the memory of a friend.

❻ Reading Strategy

Stanzas as Units of Meaning

- Have students take turns reading the poem by stanzas. Point out that all but one of the stanzas have four lines. Then, ask students how many main ideas each stanza has.
  Answer: Each stanza has one main idea.
- Ask students the Reading Strategy question on p. 1074: What is the main idea expressed in the fourth stanza?
  Answer: The main idea is that Mejías has died and will be forgotten as dead dogs are forgotten.

Monitor Progress Ask students: How is this stanza like a paragraph?
Answer: This stanza is about one main idea, and all the details support that main idea.

Reteach Draw students' attention to the graphic organizer on p. 1071. Tell students that they can use the organizer to record the main idea of each stanza.

❼ Critical Thinking

Infer

- Direct students' attention to the fifth stanza.
- Ask: With what power does the poet endow himself?
  Possible response: The poet endows himself with the power to defy death by immortalizing the memory of his friend with his poem.

from "Lament for Ignacio Sánchez Mejías"

❺ Absent Soul

Federico García Lorca

translated by Stephen Spender and J. L. Gili

The bull does not know you, nor the fig tree,
nor the horses, nor the ants in your own house.
The child and the afternoon do not know you
because you have died for ever.

The back of the stone does not know you,
nor the black satin in which you crumble.
Your silent memory does not know you
because you have died for ever.

The autumn will come with small white snails,
misty grapes and with clustered hills,
but no one will look into your eyes
because you have died for ever.

❻ Because you have died for ever,
like all the dead of the Earth,
like all the dead who are forgotten
in a heap of lifeless dogs.

❼ Nobody knows you. No. But I sing of you.
For posterity I sing of your profile and grace.
Of the signal[1] maturity of your understanding.
Of your appetite for death and the taste of its mouth.
Of the sadness of your once valiant gaiety.

It will be a long time, if ever, before there is born
an Andalusian[2] so true, so rich in adventure.
I sing of his elegance with words that groan,
and I remember a sad breeze through the olive trees.

Reading Strategy
Stanzas as Units of Meaning What is the main idea expressed in the fourth stanza?

posterity (päs ter´ ə tē) *n.* future generations of people

1. **signal** (sig´ nel) *adj.* extraordinary; distinguished.
2. **Andalusian** inhabitant of Andalusia, a region of Spain bordering both the Atlantic Ocean and the Mediterranean Sea.

ENRICHMENT: Literature Connection

Poetic Immortality

With his poem "Absent Soul," García Lorca adds his voice to a long history of poetic concern over the power of time to destroy beauty and memory. García Lorca follows writers such as Shakespeare, some of whose poetry defied death by granting immortality to loved ones through the written word. The body may die, but the poet's words allow the beloved's spirit and memory to live on throughout the ages. Shakespeare's final couplet in "Sonnet XVIII" claims, "So long as men can breathe, or eyes can see, / So long lives this, and this gives life to thee." In essence, the sonnet immortalizes both Shakespeare's beloved and the poet himself. García Lorca also suggests that without his poem, the memory of his friend would die forever: "Your silent memory does not know you / because you have died for ever. . . . But I sing of you. For posterity I sing of your profile and grace."

Suggest that students use a Venn diagram to compare and contrast further Shakespeare's "Sonnet XVIII" and García Lorca's "Absent Soul."

❽ ▲ **Critical Viewing** Based on this photograph of an olive grove, why might olive trees be an appropriate image in a poem of lament? **[Analyze]**

Review and Assess

Thinking About the Selection

1. **Respond:** After reading this poem, do you feel that you know Sánchez Mejías? Explain.
2. **(a) Recall:** In the first stanza, what six things do not know Sánchez Mejías? **(b) Generalize:** In what ways might each of these things reflect some aspect of Sánchez Mejías's life?
3. **(a) Infer:** Whom does the speaker address in the first five stanzas? **(b) Interpret:** How does that address change in the last stanza? **(c) Analyze:** What emotional shift might this change reflect? Explain.
4. **(a) Distinguish:** In line 20, what trait of Sánchez Mejías does the speaker celebrate? **(b) Interpret:** What do you think García Lorca is saying about how to live life to the fullest? Explain.

❽ ▸Critical Viewing

Answer: The olive trees in the photograph have dark, ominous shapes that produce a haunting and lonely feeling.

Answers for p. 1075

Review and Assess

1. Possible answer: Sánchez Mejías is presented in fragments; the speaker describes only some of his qualities, such as his profile, grace, valiant gaiety, and elegance. There is much more about Mejías that the reader could know.
2. **(a)** These things do not know Sánchez Mejías: the bull, the fig tree, the horses, the ants, the child, and the afternoon. **(b)** Sánchez Mejías fought the bull; he lived in a land where fig trees are common; he probably rode horses; he had ants in his house; he probably had a child; and he had lived through many afternoons, but would not survive this one.
3. **(a)** The speaker addresses Sánchez Mejías. **(b)** In the last stanza, the speaker talks of Sánchez Mejías in the third person. **(c)** This change might reflect the speaker's acknowledgment that Sánchez Mejías is dead. Sánchez Mejías can no longer be spoken to, only spoken about.
4. **(a)** The speaker celebrates Sánchez Mejías's love for risking his life. **(b)** García Lorca is endorsing the way Sánchez Mejías lived his life. By staring death in the face, Sánchez Mejías was able to savor life, and García Lorca admires him.

CUSTOMIZE INSTRUCTION FOR UNIVERSAL ACCESS

For Special Needs Students	For Advanced Readers
Students may have difficulty with some of the subtle references in "Absent Soul." For example, students may not understand that "back of the stone" in line 5 refers to the headstone on Sánchez Mejías's grave, or that "black satin" in line 6 refers to the satin lining of a casket. Clarify these references for students, and encourage them to identify other references or images with which they are unfamiliar. Provide time for students to ask questions, and discuss the answers with the class.	Tell students that the landscape of Andalusia plays an important role in this poem. Have students skim the poem to find references to this landscape, and list these references on the board. Then, ask students to consider the meaning or importance of each reference and discuss why García Lorca chose these particular descriptions to convey the message of the poem. Suggest that students do research on the landscape and people of Andalusia and present their findings to the class.

9 About the Selection

This poem, in which Cavafy compares the long journey of life to the journey of Odysseus, invites the reader on a spiritual adventure.

10 Reading Strategy

Reading Stanzas as Units of Meaning

- Remind students that it may be helpful for them to read the stanzas of a poem as they would read paragraphs.
- Read aloud the first stanza. Then, ask: What is the main idea of this stanza?
  Answer: The main idea is that one's journey through life will be long and without obstacles if one remains dignified and does not bring on inner strife.
- Ask students the Reading Strategy question on p. 1076: In the first stanza, what attitude toward their journey does the speaker advise travelers to take?
  Answer: The speaker advises travelers to focus on life as a journey rather than a destination, to be excited by what life has to offer, and to live life with dignity. The speaker encourages travelers to be wary of the figurative monsters that travelers may encounter within themselves.

9 

Constantine Cavafy

translated by
Edmund Keeley
and Philip Sherrard

Background

Constantine Cavafy found special inspiration in the Homeric epics—the *Iliad* and the *Odyssey*—and paid tribute to them in at least nine poems and an essay. "Ithaka," published in 1911, is the last of these tributes.

In Homer's *Odyssey*, the hero Odysseus spends twenty years struggling to return to his home, the city of Ithaka. Along the way, he meets monsters and goddesses, suffers losses, and experiences rapture. In this poem, Cavafy uses Odysseus' legendary tale to describe a way to live one's life.

When you set out for Ithaka[1]
Pray that your road's a long one,
full of adventure, full of discovery.
Laistrygonians, Cyclops,
angry Poseidon[2]—don't be scared of them:
you won't find things like that on your way
10 as long as your thoughts are exalted,
as long as a rare excitement
stirs your spirit and your body.
Laistrygonians, Cyclops,
wild Poseidon—you won't encounter them
unless you bring them along inside you,
unless your soul raises them up in front of you.

Pray that your road's a long one.
May there be many a summer morning when—
full of gratitude, full of joy—
you come into harbors seen for the first time;
may you stop at Phoenician[3] trading centers
and buy fine things,
mother of pearl and coral, amber and ebony,

Reading Strategy
Reading Stanzas as Units of Meaning In the first stanza, what attitude toward their journey does the speaker advise travelers to take?

exalted (eg zôlt′ id) *adj.* lifted high because of dignity or honor

1. **Ithaka** often spelled Ithaca; one of a group of islands off the west coast of Greece; the legendary home of Odysseus.
2. **Laistrygonians** (les trə gōn′ ē ənz), **Cyclops, angry Poseidon** In Homer's *Odyssey*, the Laistrygonians are a race of giants, the Cyclops is a one-eyed monster, and Poseidon is the sea god. All of these characters pose varying threats to Odysseus and his crew.
3. **Phoenician** of or relating to Phoenicia, the ancient name for a narrow strip of land, now largely modern Lebanon, on the eastern coast of the Mediterranean Sea. The Phoenicians were famous as traders and sailors.

ENRICHMENT: History Connection

Phoenician Trade

The ancient Phoenician trading centers, to which Cavafy's poem refers, were bustling centers of economy. Phoenicia carried on trade by land and sea routes with its colonies and with other trade partners. Most colonies were established to expedite trade by taking advantage of a particular commodity available at that location. For example, Cyprus was colonized as a source of copper and timber. Sardinia and Spain supplied various metals. Phoenicia, in turn, provided the colonies with manufactured goods such as fabrics, pottery, and glass.

Phoenician ships traveled the Mediterranean, Red, and Black Seas; the North Atlantic; the Indian Ocean; and around the west coast of Africa. Some historians believe that Phoenician traders traveled as far as the Americas.

11 sensual perfumes of every kind,
as many sensual perfumes as you can;
may you visit numerous Egyptian cities
to fill yourself with learning from the wise.

Keep Ithaka always in mind.
Arriving there is what you're destined for.
But don't hurry the journey at all.
Better if it goes on for years
so you're old by the time you reach the island,
wealthy with all you've gained on the way,
not expecting Ithaka to make you rich.

Ithaka gave you the marvelous journey.
Without her you wouldn't have set out.
She hasn't anything else to give.

And if you find her poor, Ithaka won't have fooled you.
Wise as you'll have become, and so experienced,
you'll have understood by then what an Ithaka means.

sensual (sen′ shōō əl) *adj.* pleasing to the senses

Literary Analysis
Lyric Poetry and Epiphany In what ways do the details in lines 20–22 help convey the excitement of the journey?

Review and Assess

Thinking About the Selection

1. **Respond:** How do you feel about the journey that this poem describes? Explain your answer.
2. **(a) Recall:** In the first stanza, what three characters from the *Odyssey* does the speaker say the traveler need not fear? **(b) Infer:** According to the speaker in lines 12–13, under what circumstances might such characters appear? **(c) Analyze:** What real-life experiences might these characters represent? Explain.
3. **(a) Infer:** In the second stanza, identify two places that the speaker urges travelers to visit. **(b) Interpret:** What values do these places represent to the speaker? **(c) Evaluate:** Do you think these values are critical to happiness in life? Explain your answer.
4. **(a) Recall:** In line 31, what expectation does the speaker say one should not have of Ithaka? **(b) Draw Conclusions:** What, then, is the value of Ithaka?
5. **Analyze:** In the poem's final line, the poet refers to "an Ithaka," rather than to "Ithaka." In what way does this change suggest that Ithaka has taken on new meaning?
6. **Evaluate:** "Ithaka" was a favorite poem of Jacqueline Kennedy Onassis, the widow of President John F. Kennedy, and it was read at her funeral. In your opinion, is "Ithaka" a good memorial poem? Why or why not?

11 Literary Analysis

Lyric Poetry and Epiphany

- Read aloud the second stanza. Then, reread the bracketed passage. Ask students the Literary Analysis question on p. 1077: In what ways do the details in lines 20–22 help convey the excitement of the journey?
  Answer: The sensory details about the exotic and rewarding nature of the journey create excitement.
- Ask: What kinds of treasures might the items listed in lines 20–22 represent in the journey of life? Explain.
  Possible response: The items may represent experience and personal accomplishments. Or they may represent rewarding relationships with friends and family.

Answers for p. 1077

Review and Assess

1. Possible response: The journey sounds exciting and rewarding.
2. **(a)** The speaker tells the traveler not to fear the Laistrygonians, Cyclops, and Poseidon. **(b)** Such characters might appear if the traveler brings them along in his or her mind or soul. **(c)** These characters represent negative emotions and evil actions that, like these creatures, can impede or endanger an individual.
3. **(a)** The speaker urges travelers to visit Phoenician trading centers and Egyptian cities.
   (b) Phoenicia may represent beauty and sensory experience. Egypt may stand for wisdom.
   (c) Possible response: People can be happy without these values if they have love and personal relationships.
4. **(a)** One should not expect Ithaka to provide riches. **(b)** Ithaka provides a reason for the journey.
5. The change suggests that Ithaka is not a single place but a state of mind. It suggests that each person's Ithaka is different.
6. Possible response: "Ithaka" is a good memorial poem because it recalls the joy of life's journey.

CUSTOMIZE INSTRUCTION FOR UNIVERSAL ACCESS

For Less Proficient Readers	For Advanced Readers
Tell students to imagine that they have embarked on the journey to Ithaka that Cavafy describes in his poem. Ask students to use the following questions to write a travel description of their journey: • What adventures did you have? • Did you see the Laistrygonians, Cyclops, or Poseidon? Explain. • What piece of wisdom did you acquire in Egypt? • Have you enjoyed the journey so far? Why or why not?	English novelist E. M. Forster wrote: History, too, is full of courage, cowardice, lust, and is to that extent domestic. But it is something more. It is an external inspiration. And [Cavafy] found in the expanses and recesses of the past...something that transcended his local life and freshened and strengthened his art. Ask students to write a short essay discussing this quotation in relation to Cavafy's poem "Ithaka."

⓬ Background

Art

Tombstone Mountain, by Stephen Krasemann

Tombstone Mountain rises majestically within Canada's Tombstone Territorial Park. This black granite peak is the best known landform in the park. At 2,193 meters, it serves as a stunning example of the beauty of the Yukon wilderness.

Use the following question for discussion:

What emotions does this photograph evoke?
Possible response: This photograph evokes feelings of awe and causes the viewer to wonder at the beauty and vastness of nature.

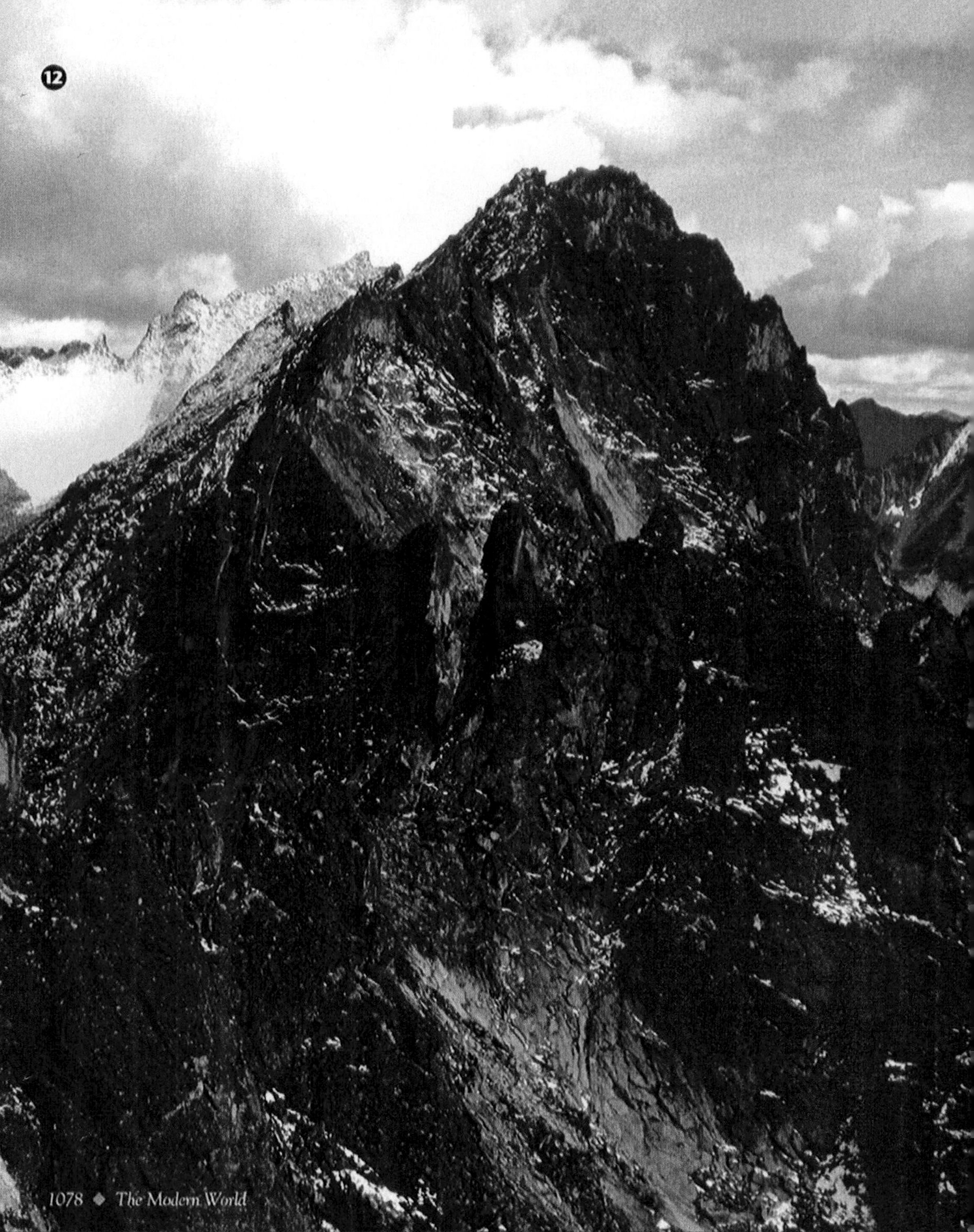

ENRICHMENT: Literature Connection

Pessoa's Pen Names

Fernando Pessoa used several pen names—or *heteronyms,* as he called them—when writing poetry. He was certainly not the only writer to use multiple pen names. For centuries, writers have used pseudonyms to escape gender or ethnic biases. In some cultures, pseudonyms are a way to escape political or religious persecution. Some writers may wish to attempt a new genre or style of writing without having their reputations damaged if they should fail. Some very prolific writers use multiple pseudonyms to disguise their total literary output. Pessoa assumed multiple names to explore the nature of identity.

13

The Soul With Boundaries

Fernando Pessoa

translated by Richard Zenith

Background

Fernando Pessoa believed that the human self is fundamentally divided. It is no surprise, therefore, that many of his poems ponder one or both of two questions that are basic to modern literature: *Who am I? What is real?* This poem considers both questions.

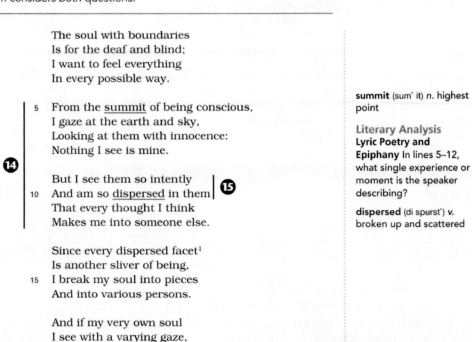

The soul with boundaries
Is for the deaf and blind;
I want to feel everything
In every possible way.

14

From the summit of being conscious,
I gaze at the earth and sky,
Looking at them with innocence:
Nothing I see is mine.

But I see them so intently
And am so dispersed in them 15
That every thought I think
Makes me into someone else.

Since every dispersed facet[1]
Is another sliver of being,
I break my soul into pieces
And into various persons.

And if my very own soul
I see with a varying gaze,
How can I have anything
Definite to say?

1. **facet** (fas′ it) any of a number of sides or aspects of a whole.

summit (sum′ it) *n.* highest point

Literary Analysis
Lyric Poetry and Epiphany In lines 5–12, what single experience or moment is the speaker describing?

dispersed (di spurst′) *v.* broken up and scattered

16 

According to the first stanza, what does the speaker want?

17 

In what ways does this photograph suggest the idea of the "summit of being conscious"? **[Analyze]**

13 About the Selection

In Fernando Pessoa's poem "The Soul With Boundaries," the speaker examines questions of identity.

14 Literary Analysis

Lyric Poetry and Epiphany

- Remind students that lyric poetry emphasizes a moment in time.
- Have a volunteer read aloud the bracketed passage. Then, ask: What does the speaker mean by the phrase, "summit of being conscious"?
  Answer: The speaker uses this phrase to describe a moment of being entirely aware—not distracted by other activities or under the influence of other ideas.
- Ask students the Literary Analysis question on p. 1079: In lines 5–12, what single experience or moment is the speaker describing?
  Answer: The speaker is recognizing the soul or identity as part of everything.

15 Vocabulary Development

The Latin Prefix *dis-*

- Draw students' attention to the word *dispersed,* and read its definition.
- Explain that *dis-* is a Latin prefix that can mean "away or apart," "cause to be the opposite of," "fail to," and "not."
- Discuss the meaning of *dispersed,* and help students build a definition from the two word parts.
- Cite additional examples, such as *dispense* and *disappoint*. Ask students to use their understanding of *dis-* to define these words as well.

16 ✓Reading Check

Answer: The speaker wants to feel everything there is to feel and to experience these feelings in every possible way.

17 ▶Critical Viewing

Answer: The summit of a mountain is the highest one can climb. The "summit of being conscious" is the point of ultimate awareness.

CUSTOMIZE INSTRUCTION FOR UNIVERSAL ACCESS

For Gifted/Talented Students	For Advanced Readers
Challenge students to create a representation of this poem by assembling a collage. Each student should create a drawing, sketch, painting, or other work to represent the dominant image or meaning of each stanza. Then, ask students to assemble their collages, adding the title "The Soul With Boundaries." Encourage students to share their collages with the class.	Have each student write a detailed analysis and interpretation of this poem's meaning. Students can try paraphrasing lines and stanzas in their search for what the poem means. Encourage students to do some background reading on Pessoa and to examine other works by the poet as they plan and write their interpretations. Have students present their interpretations in the form of a panel discussion.

ASSESS

18 Reading Strategy

Reading Stanzas as Units of Meaning

- Read aloud the bracketed passage. Ask: How are the sky and sea diverse?
  Answer: The sky, for example, is cloudy and clear, dark and light, filled with stars and sunlight. The sea can be choppy and calm, warm and cold.
- Ask students to respond to the Reading Strategy question on p. 1080: Restate the idea expressed in this stanza— lines 21–24— in your own words.
  Possible response: I am deceiving myself if I think that I am a separate being. Like the sky and sea, I am ever-changing and a part of the larger universe.

19 Critical Thinking

Analyze

- Read aloud the bracketed passage, and point out the question that appears in the last two lines.
- Ask students: What is the purpose of this question?
  Possible response: It reveals the speaker's struggle in determining the origins of the soul. This is the crucial question.

Answers for p. 1080

Review and Assess

1. Possible response: This friend would provide one with valuable insight about life.
2. **(a)** It belongs to the deaf and blind. **(b)** The speaker wants to use all five senses to feel everything in every way.
3. **(a)** The speaker is transformed into someone else. **(b)** The speaker questions whether in this fractured state, anything definite can be said.
4. **(a)** All things are slivers of the "universal intelligence." **(b)** Like the speaker, God is in all things.
5. Possible response: The poem has a practical application. By suggesting the interconnectedness of all things, the poem causes the reader to assess his or her life.

If I think I belong to me,
I'm merely self-deceived.
I'm diverse and not my own,
Like sky and land and sea.

If all things are but slivers
Of the universal intelligence,
Then let me be my parts,
Scattered and divergent.

If from myself I'm absent
And whatever I feel is distant,
How did my soul come to have
An individual existence?

I've learned to adapt my self
To the world God has made.
His mode of being is different;
My being has different modes.

Thus I imitate God,
Who, when he made what is,
Took from it the infinite
And even its unity.

Reading Strategy
Reading Stanzas as Units of Meaning Restate the idea expressed in this stanza—lines 21–24—in your own words.

divergent (dī vur′ jənt) *adj.* differing from each other

Review and Assess

Thinking About the Selection

1. **Respond:** Would you like to have the speaker of this poem as a friend? Why or why not?
2. **(a) Recall:** In the first stanza, to whom does the speaker say a "soul with boundaries" belongs? **(b) Compare and Contrast:** By contrast, what does the speaker want to experience?
3. **(a) Recall:** According to the speaker in lines 11–12, what happens in the process of thinking different thoughts? **(b) Analyze Cause and Effect:** How does the question asked in lines 19–20 directly relate to this process?
4. **(a) Interpret:** According to the speaker in lines 25–26, all things might be "slivers" of what entity? **(b) Interpret:** Based on lines 33–36, how does the speaker's sense of self mirror his view of God?
5. **Evaluate:** Is "The Soul With Boundaries" a poem that can instruct readers in a practical way, or is it intended primarily as a mental exercise? Explain your answer.

ASSESSMENT PRACTICE: Reading Comprehension

Notice Word Choice (For more practice, see Test Preparation Workbook, p. 49.)

Many tests require students to notice word choice in a reading passage. Use the following sample test item to give students practice at this skill.

> It will be a long time, if ever, before there is born
> an Andalusian so true, so rich in adventure.
> I sing of his elegance with words that groan,
> and I remember a sad breeze through the olive trees.
>
> —from "Lament for Ignacio Sánchez Mejías: Absent Soul"

Which of the following best describes the mood created by the phrases "words that groan" and "sad breeze"?

A comforting **C** mournful
B religious **D** relieved

The correct answer is *C*. The phrases "words that groan" and "sad breeze" create a mournful mood.

Review and Assess

Literary Analysis

Lyric Poetry and Epiphany

1. (a) What is the **epiphany,** or moment of perception, that García Lorca explores in his **lyric poem** "The Guitar"? (b) What perception does Cavafy share in "Ithaka"?
2. (a) In lines 9–10 of "Absent Soul," what letter sounds are repeated? (b) How do these sounds create a musical feeling?
3. In what sense do the observations in "The Soul With Boundaries" celebrate the poet's vision of life?

Comparing Literary Works

4. (a) Use a chart like the one shown below to examine the meaning of one **metaphor** from each of the poems in this grouping.

Poem	Metaphor	Two Things Compared	Meaning

(b) How does each metaphor express or clarify an abstract, or intangible, idea?

5. (a) What is the **extended metaphor** in "Ithaka"? (b) What brief comparisons build to create the extended metaphor? (c) What does Ithaka itself represent?

Reading Strategy

Reading Stanzas as Units of Meaning

6. Begin to **read stanzas as units of meaning** by writing a one-sentence statement expressing the main idea for each stanza of "Absent Soul."
7. Would you recommend this reading strategy to a friend who was struggling with poetry? Why or why not?

Extend Understanding

8. **Geography Connection:** If you were to update "Ithaka," omitting the Homeric references, what modern locations might you use? Why?

Quick Review

Lyric poetry is melodic poetry that expresses the observations and feelings of a single speaker and often contains an **epiphany,** or a sudden moment of insight.

A **metaphor** is an implied comparison between two seemingly dissimilar things.

An **extended metaphor** is a metaphor that is developed throughout a literary work.

To better understand a poem, **read stanzas as units of meaning** by pausing after each stanza to state the main idea.

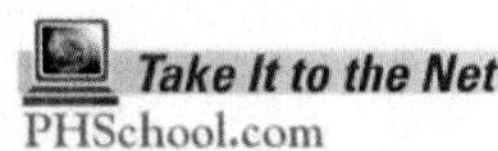

PHSchool.com

Take the interactive self-test online to check your understanding of these selections.

ENRICHMENT: Further Reading

Other Works by the Authors

We strongly encourage you to review any selection before assigning or recommending it to students.

Other Works by Federico García Lorca

Blood Wedding, Poet in New York

The House of Bernarda Alba

Other Works by Constantine Cavafy

The Poems of Constantine P. Cavafy

Other Works by Fernando Pessoa

Antinous, Sonnets, English Poems

Visit PHSchool.com for more information about the authors.

Answers for p. 1081

Review and Assess

1. **(a)** The guitar is like a wounded heart. **(b)** Life is a journey that should be long and exciting.
2. **(a)** *Um, s,* and *l* are repeated. **(b)** The repetiton of these sounds creates a rhythm.
3. The observations of the soul's breaking into pieces echo Pessoa's selection of heteronyms.
4. **(a)** Possible response: **"The Guitar"** "O guitar! / A wounded heart"; a guitar is compared to a wounded heart; Sound is the best expression of human emotion. **"Absent Soul"** "a heap of lifeless dogs"; the dead are compared to dead dogs; the dead often are forgotten like dead dogs. **"Ithaka"** "Laistrygonians, Cyclops, / angry Poseidon— don't be scared of them"; the creatures from the *Odyssey* are compared to life's trials; readers should not fear difficulties they may face. **"The Soul With Boundaries"** "From the summit of being conscious, / I gaze at the earth and sky"; a state of awareness is compared to standing on a mountaintop; one can see farther and clearer in a state of heightened awareness, just as one can see farther and clearer on a mountain summit. **(b)** It compares an abstract to something concrete.
5. **(a)** The extended metaphor is the comparison of Odysseus' journey home to Ithaka to an individual's journey through life. **(b)** The comparison of Laistrygonians, Cyclops, and Poseidon to life's dangers; the comparison of harbors to pleasant life events; and the comparison of sensual perfumes to life's experiences and pleasures build the metaphor. **(c)** Possible response: Ithaka is a philosophy for living one's life, or life itself.
6. Sample response: **Stanza One:** The things of life do not know you after you die.
7. Possible response: The skill may help a reader analyze the poem in small parts.
8. Possible response: The Lewis and Clark Expedition or the moon landing might replace Ithaka.

EXTEND

Answers for p. 1082

❶ Vocabulary Development

Word Analysis: Latin Prefix *dis-*

1. digress
2. disbelieve
3. disagreeable
4. disable

Spelling Strategy

1. electrician
2. visual
3. patiently
4. expulsion

Concept Development: Synonyms or Antonyms?

1. synonyms
2. antonyms
3. synonyms
4. antonyms
5. synonyms
6. antonyms
7. antonyms

❷ Grammar and Style

Practice

1. Listen to the sound of the guitar.
2. Don't be afraid of its sad melody.
3. While the music plays, hear its grief.
4. Ask the guitarist about the song, but don't be surprised at his answer.
5. Don't hurry the journey at all.

Writing Application

Possible response: Live life to the fullest. Be kind to those around you. Do not be afraid to try new things. Never give up on those you love.

10TH GRADE For support in teaching the Grammar and Style Lesson to tenth graders, use Writing and Grammar, Platinum Level, Chapter 19, Section 2.

Integrate Language Skills

❶ Vocabulary Development Lesson

Word Analysis: Latin Prefix *dis-*

The prefix *dis-* can mean "away or apart," "cause to be the opposite of," "fail to," and "not." Complete the definitions below with the correct word from the following list.

disable | disbelieve
disagreeable | digress

1. You _____ when you stray from a topic.
2. You _____ when you do not have faith.
3. You are _____ when you quarrel.
4. You _____ something when you break it.

Spelling Strategy

The *sh* sound can be spelled with *su (sensual)*, *ti (caution)*, *si (session)*, or *ci (delicious)*. For each of the words below, spell the *sh* sound correctly.

1. electri__an
2. vi__al
3. pa__ently
4. expul__on

Concept Development: Synonyms or Antonyms?

Review the vocabulary list on page 1071. Then, classify each of the following pairs of words as either synonyms (words with similar meanings) or antonyms (words with opposite meanings).

1. monotonously, tediously
2. posterity, ancestry
3. exalted, uplifted
4. sensual, repugnant
5. summit, apex
6. dispersed, gathered
7. divergent, similar

❷ Grammar and Style Lesson

The Understood *You* in Imperative Sentences

Imperative sentences are sentences that give orders or directions. Often in such sentences, the subject is not stated explicitly but is understood to be *you*, or the person being addressed.

Examples:

Pray that your road's a long one. *[You pray that . . .]*

Keep Ithaka always in mind. *[You keep Ithaka always in mind.]*

Practice Rewrite each sentence below so that it contains the understood *you* as its subject.

1. You listen to the sound of the guitar.
2. Don't you be afraid of its sad melody.
3. While the music plays, you hear its grief.
4. You ask the guitarist about the song, but don't you be surprised at his answer.
5. Don't you hurry the journey at all.

Writing Application Write four imperative sentences of advice. Use the understood *you* as the subject in each sentence.

WG *Prentice Hall Writing and Grammar Connection: Diamond Level, Chapter 18, Section 2*

TEACHING RESOURCES

The following resources can be used to enrich or extend the instruction for pp. 1082–1083.

Vocabulary

- **Selection Support:** Build Vocabulary, p. 193
- **Vocabulary and Spelling Practice Book** (Use this booklet for skills instruction.)

Grammar

- **Selection Support:** Grammar and Style, p. 194
- **Writing and Grammar,** Diamond Level, p. 420
- **Daily Language Practice Transparencies**

Writing

- **Writing and Grammar,** Diamond Level, p. 847
- **Writing and Grammar iText CD-ROM**
- **Writing Models and Graphic Organizers on Transparencies,** pp. 103–105

Research and Technology

- **Writing Models and Graphic Organizers on Transparencies,** pp. 79–81.

BLOCK SCHEDULING: Resources marked with this symbol provide varied instruction during 90-minute blocks.

❸ Writing Lesson

Sentence Outline and Summary

In "The Soul With Boundaries," Fernando Pessoa constructs a carefully reasoned train of thought that explains his ideas about the nature of the self. Clarify Pessoa's ideas by writing a sentence outline—an outline that states ideas in complete sentences—of the poem. Then, write a one-paragraph summary of the poem.

Prewriting Reread "The Soul With Boundaries," stanza by stanza. After each stanza, write a sentence that expresses its main idea.

Drafting Review the sentences that you wrote. Then, look for points in the poem in which Pessoa's focus shifts slightly, and add a sentence that clarifies that shift. Finally, write a paragraph that summarizes the main points of the poem.

Revising As you review your work, highlight any vague words and phrases. Consider replacing them with more precise choices.

Model: Revising to Clarify Key Ideas

wonders / *with authority*
The speaker ~~asks~~ how he can speak if he has such
fragmented / *The question*
a ~~strange~~ view of existence and of himself. ~~He really~~
bother him.
does not ~~care~~. Indeed, being "scattered and divergent"
is a quality that he celebrates
~~makes him happy~~. . .

Precise words and phrases clarify the writer's ideas.

WG *Prentice Hall Writing and Grammar Connection: Diamond Level, Chapter 31, Section 1*

❹ Extension Activities

Listening and Speaking Lyric poems were originally sung to music. Using García Lorca's "The Guitar," connect to that tradition by delivering a **reading to music.** Follow these tips to prepare:

- Find examples of classical Spanish or Gypsy guitar music.
- Choose one piece that matches the mood of the poem.
- Play the music for the class—once by itself and once as you read "The Guitar" aloud.

After the reading, explain to listeners why you chose the music you did.

Research and Technology Cavafy's poem includes allusions, or references, to Homer's epic poem the *Odyssey*. With a partner, research three of these allusions—the Laistrygonians, Cyclops, and Poseidon—and create an **allusion chart.** Identify the characters' qualities, the challenges that they created for Odysseus, and specific meanings that they add to Cavafy's poem "Ithaka." **[Group Activity]**

Take It to the Net PHSchool.com

Go online for an additional research activity using the Internet.

ASSESSMENT RESOURCES

The following resources can be used to assess students' knowledge and skills.

Selection Assessment

Formal Assessment, pp. 173–175

Open-Book Tests, pp. 145–147

Test Bank Software

Take It to the Net

Visit PHSchool.com for self-tests on the selection.

Research and Technology Rubric

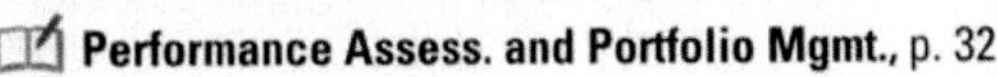
Performance Assess. and Portfolio Mgmt., p. 32

For additional diagnostics and remediation for skills covered in this grouping, use materials from the Prentice Hall Assessment System.

❸ Writing Lesson

- After reading aloud the Writing Lesson instruction, tell students that each stanza of a poem is about one main idea. These main ideas will correspond to the main ideas in their outlines.
- Guide students to use the Outline organizer in **Writing Models and Graphic Organizers on Transparencies,** pp. 103–105, to write their outlines.
- Explain to students that their summary paragraphs should show how the main ideas and details fit together.

10TH GRADE For support in working through the Writing Lesson with tenth graders, use **Writing and Grammar,** Platinum Level, Chapter 32, Section 1.

❹ Research and Technology

- Discuss with students potential research resources, such as mythology books or Web sites.
- Encourage students to use the Grid organizer in **Writing Models and Graphic Organizers on Transparencies,** pp. 79–81, as a basis for their charts.
- Invite students to present their allusion charts to the class. Then, use the Multimedia Presentation rubric in **Performance Assessment and Portfolio Management,** p. 32, to assess students' presentations.

CUSTOMIZE INSTRUCTION
For Universal Access

To address different learning styles, use the following activities suggested in the **Extension Activities** booklet, p. 49.

- For Bodily/Kinesthetic Learners, use Activity 5.
- For Logical/Mathematical Learners, use Activity 6.
- For Visual/Spatial Learners, use Activity 7.

Background

The Nobel Legacy

Alfred Nobel's dynamite legacy originated in part with his father, Immanuel Nobel. The elder Nobel, an engineer and inventor in his own right, built bridges and buildings in Stockholm and experimented with different methods of blasting rock. Later, in St. Petersburg, Russia, he advised the Russian army to block enemy ships by planting naval mines. He created these devices by filling wooden casks with gunpowder and anchoring the casks on the ocean floor, where they deterred British navy ships during the Crimean War of 1853–1856. Later, Immanuel Nobel worked closely with his son to develop a usable form of nitroglycerine.

Background

Science

Although dynamite can be used in warfare and for other violent purposes, it has an impressive range of industrial applications. It has been used to blast out canal beds, mines, dam sites, and quarries. It also has been used to create or level building sites and passages for roads and railways.

▶ **Critical Viewing**

Possible response: The photograph of V. S. Naipaul projects a mood of pride and joviality. The photograph of José Saramago, on the other hand, projects a solemn, dignified mood. Both photographs convey the deep significance of the event in the lives of two Nobel laureates.

A Closer Look

The Nobel Prize: A Dynamite Idea

Alfred Nobel, the inventor of dynamite, was—surprisingly—a pacifist who sought to honor hope, creativity, and the pursuit of peace.

"If I have a thousand ideas a year, and only one turns out to be good, I'm satisfied," Alfred Bernhard Nobel once said. Nobel exceeded his goal many times. The Swedish scientist who invented dynamite and the blasting cap is also the founder of the most distinguished of all international honors—the Nobel Prize.

A Scientist With the Soul of a Poet Alfred Nobel was born in Stockholm on October 21, 1833. Although he had a deep interest in literature, he was trained as a chemist and physicist and pursued a career that successfully combined science with business. In the 1850s, Nobel became interested in the problems presented by nitroglycerine, an invention of the Italian chemist Ascanio Sobrero. Nitroglycerine is an extremely volatile liquid that can explode unpredictably under heat or pressure. Nobel wanted to find a way to tame nitroglycerine and put it to practical use in construction work.

Nobel's experiments with nitroglycerine were often unsuccessful and deadly. In one accident, Nobel's brother Emil and several other people were killed. Yet, Nobel remained undeterred in his quest. In 1866, he finally found a successful formula that stabilized nitroglycerine and allowed it to be shaped into rods. He patented the material under the name of dynamite. In order to detonate the dynamite, he also invented a detonator, or blasting cap, which could be ignited by lighting a fuse. These inventions helped dramatically reduce the costs of construction work, especially where large-scale excavations were required.

▲ ▼ **Critical Viewing**

While these photographs of Nobel laureates V. S. Naipaul, above, and José Saramago, below, show similar moments in the lives of these two men, they capture very different emotions. Compare and contrast the moods these pictures convey. **[Compare and Contrast]**

A Man of Peace The invention of dynamite was a huge success. It made Nobel wealthy, and it transformed the construction industry, but Nobel was not happy. A man who valued literature, wrote his own poetry, and held pacifist views, Nobel was deeply disturbed that dynamite was being used in the making of weapons. Nobel held himself responsible for the deaths his invention had caused and would cause. To redeem his legacy, he established a fund of $9 million; after his death, the interest from this fund was to be used to generate an annual prize honoring actions promoting peace, as well as achievements in literature, physics, chemistry, medicine, and economics. Nobel died in 1896, and the first prizes were awarded in 1901.

ENRICHMENT: Science Connection

Nitroglycerine and Dynamite

To create nitroglycerine, Ascanio Sobrero added glycerol, an alcohol, to nitric and sulfuric acids. When these substances are mixed, a chemical reaction occurs. This reaction is highly exothermic—that is, it generates large amounts of heat. If the mixture cools to below 78° Fahrenheit, it will freeze and form needle-like crystals. If the crystals are heated or broken, they will explode.

Alfred Nobel stabilized nitroglycerine by mixing the thick, oily liquid with a crystalline compound known as silica. The paste that resulted—dynamite—could be kneaded and shaped into explosive rods. The explosive liquid nitroglycerine is mixed with other materials and packed into cylinders. These cylinders, or cartridges, are fitted with a detonating cap and placed into a hole that has been bored in the material to be blasted. The explosion is then set off from a distance by a fuse or an electrical current.

▶ **Critical Viewing**

Possible response: The attendees are wearing formal attire and appear to be in the Concert Hall in Stockholm, Sweden, one of the two locations in which the prize is awarded to the laureate. The venue itself is grand and rich with tradition and history, imparting the sense of a prestigious celebration.

The Literature Prize The Nobel Prize in Literature, which recognizes the most distinguished body of literary work created by a single author, is one of the most highly publicized of all the prizes. The prize represents an international literary standard, and it has helped bring both individual authors and entire countries to the world's attention. For example, Nobel Prizes awarded to Chilean poet Pablo Neruda (1971) and Colombian author Gabriel García Márquez (1982) placed Latin American literature at the forefront of public awareness; Wole Soyinka's prize (1986) created new appreciation of African literature, and Naguib Mahfouz's prize (1988) placed Egyptian literature in the public spotlight. The same has happened for Japanese literature, with awards to Yasunari Kawabata (1968) and Kenzaburo Oe (1994).

Controversies and Criticism At the same time, however, the Nobel Prize in Literature has had its share of controversy. The Nobel committee is made up of four to five members, most of whom are Swedish citizens. Scandinavian countries have received the Nobel Prize in Literature most often, gaining 17.4 percent of the prizes. France is runner-up, taking home 15.1 percent of the prizes. In the past two decades, however, the awards have honored writers from countries around the globe, including Guatemala, the Czech Republic, Poland, Italy, China, and Iceland.

Some critics claim that the decisions of the Nobel committee are politically motivated, honoring the most acceptable rather than the best. These critics cite the omission of some of the greatest and most influential writers of the twentieth century, such as Marcel Proust, Franz Kafka, and James Joyce, from the list of prize winners. Yet, the good that Alfred Nobel achieved in the establishment of the prize that bears his name far outweighs any controversies or criticisms. Imperfect as it may be, the Nobel Prize in Literature positions literature in the forefront of human experience and accomplishment. When the prize is announced, the news makes headlines, stirs debate, and causes celebrations. For a brief moment every year, Nobel achieves his dream of bringing the world together, not for purposes of war or commerce but simply to honor human goodness, creativity, and achievement.

▲ **Critical Viewing**

Which elements in this photograph of the ceremony for the Nobel laureates of 2001 indicate the importance of the occasion? Explain. **[Deduce]**

Background

The Nobel Prize Selection Process

In his will, Alfred Nobel assigned the responsibility of selecting each prizewinner to a different Swedish or Norwegian institution; for example, the chemistry and physics prizewinners are selected by the Swedish Academy of Sciences. Although the specific prize-awarding procedures vary from institute to institute, most of them follow a similar process. First, a committee of institution members sends invitations to university professors and other members of academic institutions around the world. These experts are invited to nominate Nobel Prize candidates for the following year. After the nominations are in, the committee members review them and select a single nominee. This nominee is presented to all the members of the institution for a vote. If approved, the prize recipient, or "laureate," is announced. Each year on December 10—the anniversary of Alfred Nobel's death—the awards are given in Stockholm, Sweden, and Oslo, Norway. Each laureate receives a medal, a diploma, and approximately one million U.S. dollars.

Critical Thinking

1. Why might the life and legacy of Alfred Nobel be considered paradoxical? **[Generalize]**
   Possible response: Nobel's life and legacy are paradoxical because Nobel was a pacifist, but his most significant invention, dynamite, is often used for violent purposes.
2. Have students imagine that they have earned a great sum of money from an invention that was used for a purpose other than that for which it was

continued

continued from right column

intended and of which they disapproved. Ask students what kind of legacy they might establish with the money. Explain. **[Hypothesize]**
Possible response: Students might use the money to counteract the misuse of their inventions or to promote alternative uses.

The Glass of Milk

Lesson Objectives

1. **To analyze and respond to literary elements**
   - Literary Analysis: Autobiographical Fiction
   - Connecting Literary Elements: Point of View
2. **To read, comprehend, analyze, and critique a short story**
   - Reading Strategy: Judging Characters' Actions
   - Reading Check Questions
   - Review and Assess Questions
   - Assessment Practice (ATE)
3. **To develop word analysis skills, fluency, and systematic vocabulary**
   - Vocabulary Development Lesson: Word Analysis: Latin Suffix *-ity*
4. **To understand and apply written and oral language conventions**
   - Spelling Strategy
   - Grammar and Style Lesson: Conjunctive Adverbs
5. **To understand and apply appropriate writing and research strategies**
   - Writing Lesson: Character Analysis
   - Extension Activity: Human Hunger Chart
6. **To understand and apply listening and speaking strategies**
   - Extension Activity: Retelling of the Story

STEP-BY-STEP TEACHING GUIDE	PACING GUIDE
PRETEACH	
Motivate Students and Provide Background	
Use the Motivation activity (ATE p. 1086)	5 min.
Read and discuss author and background features (SE pp. 1086, 1088; ATE p. 1086) A	5 min.
Introduce the Concepts	
Introduce the Literary Analysis and Reading Strategy concepts (SE/ATE p. 1087) A	15 min.
Pronounce the vocabulary words and read their definitions (SE p. 1087)	5 min.
TEACH	
Monitor Comprehension	
Informally monitor comprehension by circulating while students read independently or in groups A	35 min.
Monitor students' comprehension with the Reading Check notes (SE/ATE pp. 1091, 1093, 1095)	as students read
Develop vocabulary with Vocabulary notes (SE pp. 1090, 1093; ATE p. 1090)	as students read
Develop Understanding	
Develop students' understanding of autobiographical fiction with the Literary Analysis annotations (SE/ATE pp. 1093, 1095) A	10 min.
Develop students' ability to judge characters' actions, using the Reading Strategy annotations (SE p. 1090; ATE pp. 1090, 1093, 1094)	10 min.
ASSESS	
Assess Mastery	
Assess students' mastery of the Reading Strategy and Literary Analysis concepts by having them answer the Review and Assess questions (SE/ATE p. 1097)	20 min.
Use one or more of the print, software, or transparency Assessment Resources (ATE p. 1099) A	up to 45 min.
EXTEND	
Apply Understanding	
Have students complete the Vocabulary Development Lesson and the Grammar and Style Lesson (SE p. 1098)	20 min.
Apply students' ability to create unity, using the Writing Lesson (SE/ATE p. 1099) A	45 min.
Apply students' understanding of the selection, using one or more of the Extension Activities (SE p. 1099)	20–90 min.

A **ACCELERATED INSTRUCTION:**
Use the strategies and activities identified with an A.

TEACHING TENTH-GRADE STUDENTS
For support in teaching the selection(s) to tenth-grade students, see the Step-by-Step Teaching notes identified with the icon shown here.

UNIVERSAL ACCESS
● = Below-Level Students
▲ = On-Level Students
■ = Above-Level Students

Time and Resource Manager

Reading Level: Average
Average Number of Instructional Days: 3

RESOURCES		
PRINT	**TRANSPARENCIES**	**TECHNOLOGY**
• **Beyond Literature,** Cross-Curricular Connection: Social Studies, p. 50 ▲ ■		• **Interest Grabber Video,** Tape 2, Unit 8, Segment 7 ● ▲ ■
• **Selection Support Workbook:** ● ▲ ■ Literary Analysis, p. 200 Reading Strategy, p. 199 Build Vocabulary, p. 197	• **Literary Analysis and Reading Transparencies,** pp. 99 and 100 ● ▲ ■	
		• **Listening to Literature** ● ▲ ■ Audiocassettes Audio CDs
• **Literary Analysis for Enrichment,** p. 50 ■		
• **Formal Assessment:** Selection Test, pp. 176–178 ● ▲ ■ • **Open-Book Tests,** pp. 148–150 ● ▲ ■ • **Performance Assessment and Portfolio Management,** pp. 16, 28 ● ▲ ■ • Prentice Hall Assessment System ● ▲ ■	• Prentice Hall Assessment System ● ▲ ■ **Skills Practice Answers and Explanations on Transparencies**	• **Test Bank Software** ● ▲ ■
• **Selection Support Workbook:** ● ▲ ■ Grammar and Style, p. 198 • **Writing and Grammar,** Diamond Level ● ▲ ■ • **Extension Activities,** p. 50 ● ▲ ■	• **Daily Language Practice Transparencies** ● ▲ • **Writing Models and Graphic Organizers on Transparencies,** pp. 103–106 ● ▲ ■	• **Writing and Grammar iText CD-ROM** ● ▲ ■ ***Take It to the Net*** PHSchool.com

BLOCK SCHEDULING: Use one 90-minute class period to preteach the selection(s) and have students read them. Use a second 90-minute class period to assess students' mastery of skills and have them complete one of the Extension Activities.

PREteach

Step-by-Step Teaching Guide for pp. 1086–1087

Motivation

Bring in photographs of a South American city such as Buenos Aires, the capital of Argentina. Tell students that "The Glass of Milk" is about a character who is stranded with no money in a city similar to the one in the photographs. Have students speculate about what might happen to this character. How will he feed himself? Where will he sleep? Will other people help him? Will he survive?

Interest Grabber Video

As an alternative, play "'The Glass of Milk': Student Response" on Tape 2 to engage student interest.

❶ Background

More About the Author

Manuel Rojas's experiences as a laborer during his youth provided him with a sensitivity to the problems of the lower and middle classes. This sensitivity is evident throughout his largely autobiographical fiction. However, Rojas did not always portray the hardships of the working class in a purely realistic manner. His first novel, for example, satirizes the ills of Chilean society, and his finest work, *Son of a Thief,* reflects his interest in existential philosophy.

Geography Note

Direct students' attention to the map on this page, and identify Chile. Explain that poverty and unemployment are rampant in Chilean cities such as Santiago, where Rojas spent much of his life. Poor Chileans from the countryside flood the cities in search of work. Remind students that Rojas's firsthand experience with poverty and hunger strongly influenced his work.

Prepare to Read

❶ The Glass of Milk

Manuel Rojas (1896–1973)

A man of great strength and vigor, Manuel Rojas (män wel' rō' häs) is known for his forceful and moving prose. Not only is he regarded as the master of the modern Chilean short story, but he is also considered to be one of the finest of all the modern Latin American fiction writers.

Years of Hard Labor Although he was of Chilean descent, Manuel Rojas was born and reared in Argentina. His father died when Rojas was not yet five years old, leaving the child in poverty. When he reached his early teens, Rojas began working as a laborer in order to support himself. At the age of sixteen, he moved to Chile, where he worked as a sailor, housepainter, bargeman, night watchman, typographer, and railroad worker. Then, in 1924, he settled permanently in Santiago, the Chilean capital, and his life changed. He began devoting his energies to journalism and creative writing. Two years later, he published his first collection of short stories, *Men of the South* (1926).

Rojas's early stories, and many that he wrote later, mined his own life experiences for inspiration. The stories in *Men of the South* described characters, like Rojas himself, who worked as laborers in both Argentina and Chile. The book immediately established Rojas as one of the most promising Latin American writers of his generation.

Laborer Turned Writer In 1931, Rojas was named the director of the University of Chile Press. This appointment, along with the publication of his novel *Launches in the Bay* (1932), contributed to his growing stature in the Latin American literary community. Throughout the next three decades, his reputation among critics, writers, and the general public continued to grow. The works he produced during this period include *The Biretta From Maule* (1943), *Son of a Thief* (1951), and *Better Than Wine* (1958).

His Greatest Novel Regarded as Rojas's finest work, the novel *Son of a Thief* is an account of the sufferings of a young Argentine boy. Following his father's arrest and imprisonment for burglary, the boy spends his childhood in poverty. Like Rojas himself, the boy later works as a laborer to support himself and makes a lone journey to Chile in search of a better life. There, he accidentally becomes involved in a street riot and is unjustly imprisoned. Rojas describes the boy's experiences in a graphically realistic manner. More than any other quality, however, it is Rojas's penetrating insights into the inner workings of the boy's mind that have established this novel as one of the best ever produced in Latin America. The book was translated into the major European languages and established Rojas as an international literary figure. In 1964, Rojas's novel *Shadows Against the Wall,* which features many of the characters from *Son of a Thief,* was published to international acclaim.

A Major Influence Rojas's contributions to Latin American fiction in the twentieth century cannot be overestimated. Influenced by the American writer William Faulkner, Rojas incorporated some of the experimental devices—interior monologues, flashbacks, and stream-of-consciousness techniques—that Faulkner used in his novels and short stories. Rojas did not use these techniques simply because they were different or dazzling but rather to intensify the portrayals of his characters. These techniques later caught the interest of a new generation of Latin American writers, including Gabriel García Márquez, who used them to great effect. Rojas's fiction displays a simplicity, restraint, and deep humanity that is as affecting today as when it was first written.

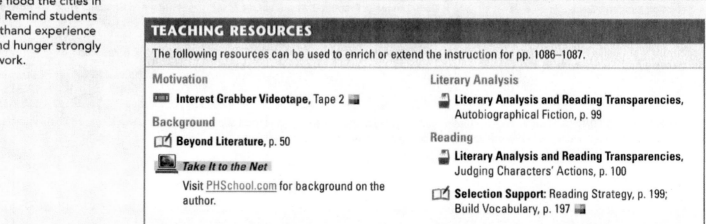

TEACHING RESOURCES

The following resources can be used to enrich or extend the instruction for pp. 1086–1087.

Motivation

Interest Grabber Videotape, Tape 2

Background

Beyond Literature, p. 50

Take It to the Net

Visit PHSchool.com for background on the author.

Literary Analysis

Literary Analysis and Reading Transparencies, Autobiographical Fiction, p. 99

Reading

Literary Analysis and Reading Transparencies, Judging Characters' Actions, p. 100

Selection Support: Reading Strategy, p. 199; Build Vocabulary, p. 197

BLOCK SCHEDULING: Resources marked with this symbol provide varied instruction during 90-minute blocks.

Preview

Connecting to the Literature

Imagine being alone in a strange city, with no money, friends, or food. The boy in this story faces precisely this predicament and must figure out a way to survive.

❷ Literary Analysis

Autobiographical Fiction

Autobiographical fiction is storytelling that is based on the writer's life. Unlike autobiography or memoir, autobiographical fiction does not try to relate events exactly as they happened. Instead, it may

- exaggerate, minimize, or omit events.
- change names, omit characters, or add fictional characters.
- change the setting.

Regardless of such changes, the essence of the story remains rooted in the author's experience. Manuel Rojas was known for his autobiographical fiction. As you read, note details that seem to emerge from Rojas's own life.

Connecting Literary Elements

Point of view refers to the perspective assumed by the narrator in a story. Three commonly used types of point of view are first person, third-person omniscient, and third-person limited.

- *First person:* The narrator is a character in the story who uses the pronouns "I," "me," "we," and "us."
- *Third person:* The narrator uses the pronouns "he," "she," "it," or "them." The *omniscient* narrator relates the thoughts of all the characters; the *limited* narrator relates those of a single character.

This story uses the third-person limited point of view. As you read, notice the kinds of information this perspective both reveals and conceals.

❸ Reading Strategy

Judging Characters' Actions

When you judge characters' actions, you evaluate their behavior in light of specific criteria, such as your values, experience, and sense of what is reasonable. As you read, use a chart like the one shown to analyze characters' behavior and decide whether you find their actions defensible.

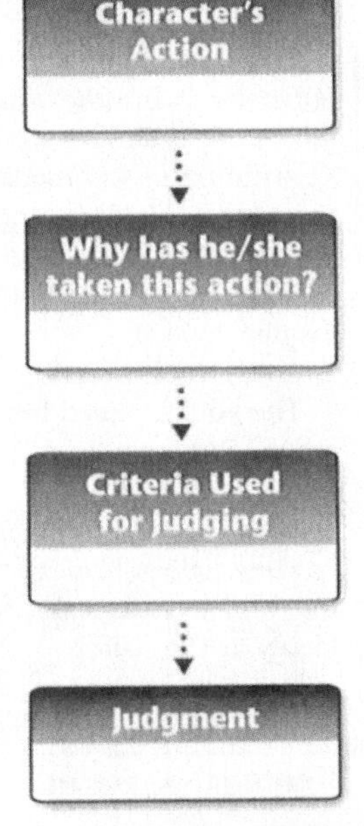

Vocabulary Development

gaudy (gôd' ē) *adj.* cheaply bright and showy (p. 1090)

timidity (tə mid' ə tē) *n.* quality of being shy and easily frightened (p. 1090)

drudgery (druj' ər ē) *n.* hard, tiresome work (p. 1090)

anguished (aŋ' gwisht) *adj.* showing worry, grief, or pain (p. 1093)

acute (ə kyo͞ot') *adj.* very serious; sharp; intense (p. 1093)

entrails (en' trālz) *n.* intestines; guts (p. 1093)

CUSTOMIZE INSTRUCTION FOR UNIVERSAL ACCESS

For Less Proficient Readers	For English Learners	For Advanced Readers
Have students read the story once, marking difficult words. Help them pronounce and define these words. Then, have students read along with **Listening to Literature Audiocassettes** or **Audio CDs.**	To give students practice with the reading strategy, use the Judging Characters' Actions transparency in **Literacy Analysis and Reading Transparencies,** p. 100. Students also may find it helpful to discuss and list values and experiences that a reading can use as criteria.	Tell readers to pay special attention to point of view as they read "The Glass of Milk." Explain that the story would likely reveal more information if it had a first-person or a third-person omniscient point of view. After students read the story, have them rewrite key scenes from a different point of view.

❷ Literary Analysis

Autobiographical Fiction

- Read the Literary Analysis instruction on p. 1087, and then explain to students that autobiographical fiction uses characters, settings, or events from the author's experiences but also has elements that are purely fictional.
- Make sure that students understand that autobiographical fiction does not carry the burden of accuracy as autobiography does; writers of autobiographical fiction can fill in gaps in their memory with invented details or make other changes as they see fit.
- Have students review the biographical information about Manuel Rojas on p. 1086. Encourage them to look for elements in "The Glass of Milk" that could be drawn from Rojas's life.
- Use the Autobiographical Fiction transparency in **Literary Analysis and Reading Transparencies,** p. 99, to demonstrate how students can connect the story to Rojas's life.

❸ Reading Strategy

Judging Characters' Actions

- Explain to students that they need criteria—rules or standards—to judge a character's actions. Criteria can be cultural customs, laws, a student's own values, or another moral code.
- Use the graphic organizer on p. 1087 to model the strategy. Offer students the example of a starving person stealing a loaf of bread. Make sure that students define their criteria before making judgments.

Vocabulary Development

- Pronounce each vocabulary word for students, and read the definitions as a class. Have students identify any words with which they are already familiar.

 ***e-Teach***

Visit E-Teach at PHSchool.com for teachers' essays on how to teach, with questions and answers.

TEACH

Step-by-Step Teaching Guide for pp. 1088–1096

Teaching Tenth-Grade Students

10TH GRADE Have tenth-grade students write questions that come to mind as they read the story. Then, have a class discussion in which students ask the questions they have written.

❶ About the Selection

After stowing away on a ship, a young boy is stranded in a South American port city without money, shelter, work, or food. He is desperately hungry but refuses to take handouts. He wonders whether he is morally capable of stealing. He considers begging. Finally, the boy orders food in a café but breaks down sobbing when it arrives. A kindly waitress allows him to cry—and to eat.

❷ Critical Thinking

Speculate

- Have students read the bracketed passage independently. Then, ask them to describe the setting and characters introduced in these first two paragraphs.
  Answer: The setting is a ship docked at a port. The characters are a sailor smoking a pipe and holding a greasy white package, and a thin boy walking near the ship.
- Then, ask students to speculate about which of the two characters mentioned in these paragraphs will be the central character of the story. On what do students base their speculations?
  Possible response: The sailor may be the central character because he is the first person mentioned. However, the youth may be the central character because he has more in common with Rojas's experiences.

❶ The Glass of Milk

Manuel Rojas
translated by Zoila Nelken

Background

The setting for this story is an unnamed port city north of Punta Arenas in southern Chile. Chile is a long, narrow country on the Pacific coast of South America. With 2,700 miles of coastline, Chile relies on shipping as one of its main industries. Although the Chilean economy has enjoyed periods of prosperity, the country has always had a sizable population of poor, unskilled laborers like the main character in this story.

❷ Propped on the starboard[1] rail, the sailor seemed to be waiting for someone. A bundle wrapped in white paper, grease-spotted, was in his left hand; his right tended his pipe.

From behind some freight-cars, a thin youth appeared; he paused a moment, looked out to sea, and then walked on along the edge of the wharf with his hands in his pockets, idling or thinking.

When he passed in front of the ship, the sailor called out to him in English:

"I say, look here!"

The youth raised his head, and without stopping, answered in the same language:

"Hello! What?"

"Are you hungry?"

There was a brief silence during which the youth seemed to be thinking, and took one shorter step as if to stop, but then replied, smiling feebly at the sailor:

"No. I'm not hungry. Thanks, sailor."

1. **starboard** (stär' bərd) *adj.* on the right-hand side of a ship.

TEACHING RESOURCES

The following resources can be used to enrich or extend the instruction for pp. 1088–1096.

Literary Analysis

Selection Support: Literary Analysis, p. 200 ■

Reading

Selection Support: Reading Strategy, p. 199; Build Vocabulary, p. 197

Listening to Literature Audiocassettes ■

Listening to Literature Audio CDs ■

■ **BLOCK SCHEDULING:** Resources marked with this symbol provide varied instruction during 90-minute blocks.

Puerto de Villefranche, Joaquim Torres-Garcia, Christie's, New York

4 ▲ **Critical Viewing** Which details in this painting of a South American port city help convey a mood similar to that of the opening scene of the story? Explain. **[Analyze]**

3 Background

Art

Puerto de Villefranche, by Joaquín Torres-García

Torres-García (1874–1949) was one of the leading Uruguayan painters of the early twentieth century. While traveling in Spain as a young man, he collaborated with another artist to produce the stained-glass windows for a cathedral in Majorca. Later, he painted murals for both churches and secular buildings. In 1934, Torres-García returned to Uruguay where he continued his career as a mural artist.

Torres-García's early works combine neoclassical and modern forms. His later works are more avant-garde. In this painting, Torres-García offers an impressionistic view of a seemingly tranquil fishing port.

Use the following questions for discussion:

- What do the details in this painting suggest about the tone of the story?
  Possible response: The gray skies, dark colors, and absence of people suggest that the story will have a sad, melancholy tone.
- Does the fishing port depicted in this painting seem like a good place to visit? Why or why not?
  Possible responses: No; the port seems dirty and lonely. Yes; the port seems quiet and mysterious.

4 ▶ Critical Viewing

Possible response: The earth tones and dark shadings in the painting echo the rough, grim life faced by poor Chileans like the young boy in the story.

CUSTOMIZE INSTRUCTION FOR UNIVERSAL ACCESS

For Special Needs Students	For Gifted/Talented Students
Have students read p. 1088 again. Explain that the youth's hesitation before he refuses food probably indicates that he is indeed hungry. Ask students to discuss reasons a hungry person might turn down an offer of food. Guide students to recognize that the youth may be too proud or ashamed to accept the offer.	Ask students to discuss the cityscape depicted in the painting on pp. 1088–1089. Guide students with these questions: Is this area heavily populated? What sort of people would you find here? As they read, encourage students to sketch their own cityscapes based on Rojas's descriptions of the setting. Ask volunteers to share their sketches with the class.

❺ Vocabulary Development

Latin Suffix *-ity*

- Call students' attention to the word *timidity.* Explain that the Latin suffix *-ity* means "state, quality, or condition." The suffix *-ity* makes a noun when it is added to an adjective, such as the adjective *timid.*
- Have students suggest words that contain this suffix. List the suggestions on the board.
  Possible response: *Frigidity, stupidity, humidity,* and *civility all contain the suffix -ity.*
- Finally, direct students to reread the story, looking for words that can be replaced with a word containing the suffix *-ity.* Ask volunteers to read aloud their new sentences.

❻ Reading Strategy

Judging Characters' Actions

- Review with students the guidelines on p. 1087 for judging characters' actions. Remind students to base their judgments on specific criteria.
- Read the bracketed passage with the class. Tell students to pay special attention to the young man's feelings.
- Ask students the Reading Strategy question on p. 1090: Is the young man's decision to refuse the food wise? Explain your answer.
  Possible response: The decision is unwise because the young man has not eaten in three days.

Monitor Progress Have students discuss whether the young man's actions would be more or less wise if motivated by pride rather than timidity.

Reteach Explain that students' knowledge about pride, morality, and timidity are criteria by which they can judge the youth's actions. Use the Judging Characters' Actions transparency in **Literary Analysis and Reading Transparencies,** p. 100, to guide students as they judge.

"All right."

The sailor took his pipe out of his mouth, spat, and replacing it, looked away. The youth, ashamed that he had seemed to need charity, walked a little faster, as if afraid he might change his mind.

A moment later, a gaudy tramp with a long, blond beard and blue eyes, dressed in odd rags and oversized, torn shoes, passed before the sailor, who without greeting called to him:

"Are you hungry?"

He had not yet finished the phrase when the tramp looked with shining eyes at the package the sailor held in his hand and answered hurriedly:

"Yes, sir; I'm very much hungry!"

The sailor smiled. The package flew through the air and landed in the eager hands. The hungry fellow did not even say "thanks," but sat right down on the ground, opened the still-warm bundle, and happily rubbed his hands as he saw what it contained. A port loafer might not speak English well, but he would never forgive himself if he didn't know enough to ask food from someone who did speak it.

The youth who passed by first had stopped nearby, and had seen what happened.

He was hungry too. He had not eaten for exactly three days, three ❺ long days. And more from timidity and shame than from pride, he refused to wait by the gangways at mealtimes, hoping the generosity of the sailors would produce some package of left-overs and bits of meat. ❻ He could not do it, he would never be able to do it. And when, as just now, someone did offer him a handout, the boy refused it heroically, though he felt his hunger increase with the refusal.

He had been wandering for six days around the side-streets and docks of that port. An English vessel had left him there after bringing him from Punta Arenas,[2] where he had jumped a previous ship on which he had served as captain's mess boy. He had spent a month there helping an Austrian crabber and then had stowed away on the first ship bound north.

He was discovered the day after sailing, and put to work in the boiler room. At the first large port of call, he had been put off, and there he had remained, like a bale without a label, without an acquaintance, without a penny, and without a trade.

As long as the ship was in port, the boy managed to eat, but after that . . . The great city that rose up beyond the back streets with their taverns and cheap inns did not attract him; it seemed a place of slavery: stale, dark, without the grand sweep of the sea; among its high walls and narrow streets people lived and died bewildered by agonizing drudgery.

The boy was gripped by that fascination of the sea which molds the most peaceful and orderly lives as a strong arm a thin rod. Although

gaudy (gôd′ ē) *adj.* cheaply bright and showy

timidity (tə mid′ ə tē) *n.* quality of being shy and easily frightened

Reading Strategy
Judging Characters' Actions Is the young man's decision to refuse the food wise? Explain your answer.

drudgery (druj′ ər ē) *n.* hard, tiresome work

2. **Punta Arenas** (po͞on′ tä ä re′ näs) southernmost seaport in Chile.

ENRICHMENT: Geography Connection

The Chilean Coast

The setting for "The Glass of Milk" is a port city north of Punta Arenas in southern Chile. The city is not named, but it could be any one of the port cities in this area, including Puerto Natales, Puerto Aisén, Puerto Montt, and Puerto Varas. *Puerto* is Spanish for "port." Chile's coastline is 2,700 miles long, so it is not surprising that port cities serve as centers for industry. As a result of Chile's proximity to the Pacific Ocean, fishing and shipping play key roles in the country's economy. The ocean teems with life, including lobster, sardines, jack mackerel, and hundreds of varieties of mollusks.

Chileans catch more than 6 million tons of fish and shellfish each year, making the country a world leader in the fishing industry.

very young, he had already made several trips along the coast of South America on various ships, doing odd jobs and tasks, tasks and odd jobs which were almost useless on land.

After the ship left him, the boy walked and walked, hoping to chance upon something that would enable him to live somehow until he could get back to his home grounds; but he found nothing. The port was not very busy, and the few ships that had work would not take him on.

The docks were swarming with confirmed tramps: sailors on the beach, like himself, who had either jumped ship or were fleeing some crime; loafers given to idleness, who kept alive one knows not how, by begging or stealing, spending their days as if they were the beads of some grimy rosary,[3] waiting for who knows what extraordinary events, or not expecting anything; people of the strangest and most exotic races and places, and even some in whose existence one doesn't believe until one sees a living example.

7

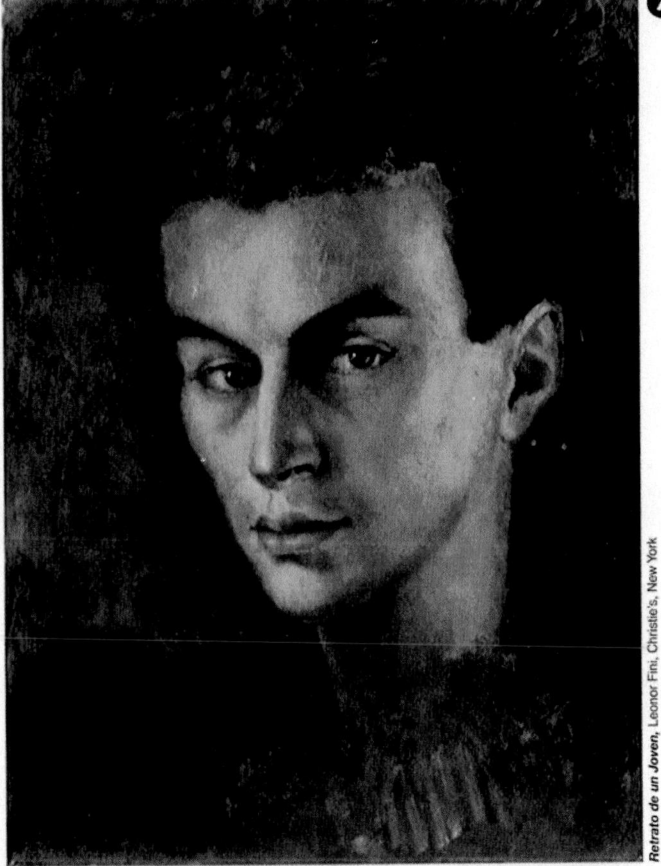

Retrato de un Joven, Leonor Fini, Christie's, New York

The following day, convinced that he could not hold out much longer, the youth decided to resort to any means to get some food.

Walking along, he found himself in front of a ship that had docked the night before, and was loading wheat. A line of men, heavy sacks on their shoulders, shuttled from the freight-cars, across the gangplank to the hatchways of the ship's hold where the stevedores[4] received the cargo.

He watched for a while, until he dared to speak to the foreman, offering his services. He was accepted, and enthusiastically he took his place in the long line of dock workers.

During the first period of the day he worked well; but later, he began to feel tired and dizzy; he swayed as he crossed the gangplank, the heavy load on his shoulder, on seeing at his feet the opening between

8 ▲ **Critical Viewing**

Does the boy depicted in this portrait seem like someone who would be too timid to accept an offer of food? **[Make a Judgment]**

9 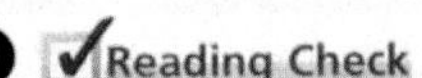

Reading Check

For how many days has the boy gone without food?

---

3. **rosary** (rō´ zər ē) *n.* string of beads used to keep count in saying prayers.
4. **stevedores** (stē´ və dôrz´) *n.* people employed at loading and unloading ships.

7 Background

Art

Retrato de un Joven (Portrait of a Youth), by Leonor Fini

Fini (1908–1996) was born in Buenos Aires, Argentina. Believing that the South American artistic community was less receptive to her work because she was a woman, she left her native land and traveled to Paris. There she was exposed to the works of Pablo Picasso, who became one of her main sources of inspiration. In 1936, Fini exhibited her paintings at a Surrealist show in New York and subsequently established herself as an internationally acclaimed artist. As is the case with this painting, her works typically have a realistic yet magical quality.

Use the following questions for discussion:

- What personal qualities does the young man in the painting seem to have?
  Possible response: The young man seems lonely, brooding, and suspicious of the world.
- How does Fini convey these qualities?
  Possible response: The dark background makes the youth seem solitary; the sharp angles of his face make him look fragile; and the shadows under his eyes and the line of his nose and jaw make him look suspicious yet vulnerable.

8 ▶ Critical Viewing

Possible response: The boy's young, smooth face and guarded eyes make him appear too timid to accept the offer; this youth looks too cunning to reject any such offer.

9 Reading Check

Answer: The boy has gone without food for three days.

CUSTOMIZE INSTRUCTION FOR UNIVERSAL ACCESS

For Special Needs Students	For Advanced Readers
To help students understand the seriousness of the youth's situation, ask them to identify basic human needs such as food, water, and shelter. Write the needs on the board. Then, explain to students that the youth is unable to meet most or all of these needs. Help students find clues in the text to support this statement.	Remind students that Rojas was heavily influenced by the modern American writer William Faulkner. Have students read a few Faulkner stories and then compare and contrast them with "The Glass of Milk." Ask them to summarize the writing styles of Rojas and Faulkner, noting what the two have in common.

⑩ Background

Art

Trabajadores, **by Hector Poleo**

Born in Caracas, Venezuela, Poleo (1918–1989) studied at the Academia de Bellas Artes through most of the 1930s. In 1938, he received a scholarship to study in Mexico City. When he returned to Venezuela, he quickly rose to prominence. In 1943, he won the John Boulton Prize at the Fourth National Salon of Venezuelan Art for his painting *The Three Commissaires.*

Poleo painted in a social realist style until the late 1940s when he became the first Venezuelan painter to experiment with Surrealism. His style soon grew simpler and less realistic.

In 1958, Poleo left Venezuela for Paris. *Trabajadores,* however, reflects the culture of his native land.

Use the following questions for discussion:

- How would you describe the spirit of the workers in this painting? Explain.
  Possible response: The workers do not seem happy, but they appear to have physical strength and confidence in their work habits.
- Why do you think the only figures visible in the painting are workers?
  Possible response: The painting portrays a part of the city in which most laborers live. The artist wanted to show that laborers live in a world different from that of people of higher social classes.

⑪ ▶Critical Viewing

Possible response: The figure on the far right best represents the boy in the story because he does not appear to be part of the group. He seems weaker and less confident than the other figures.

⑩

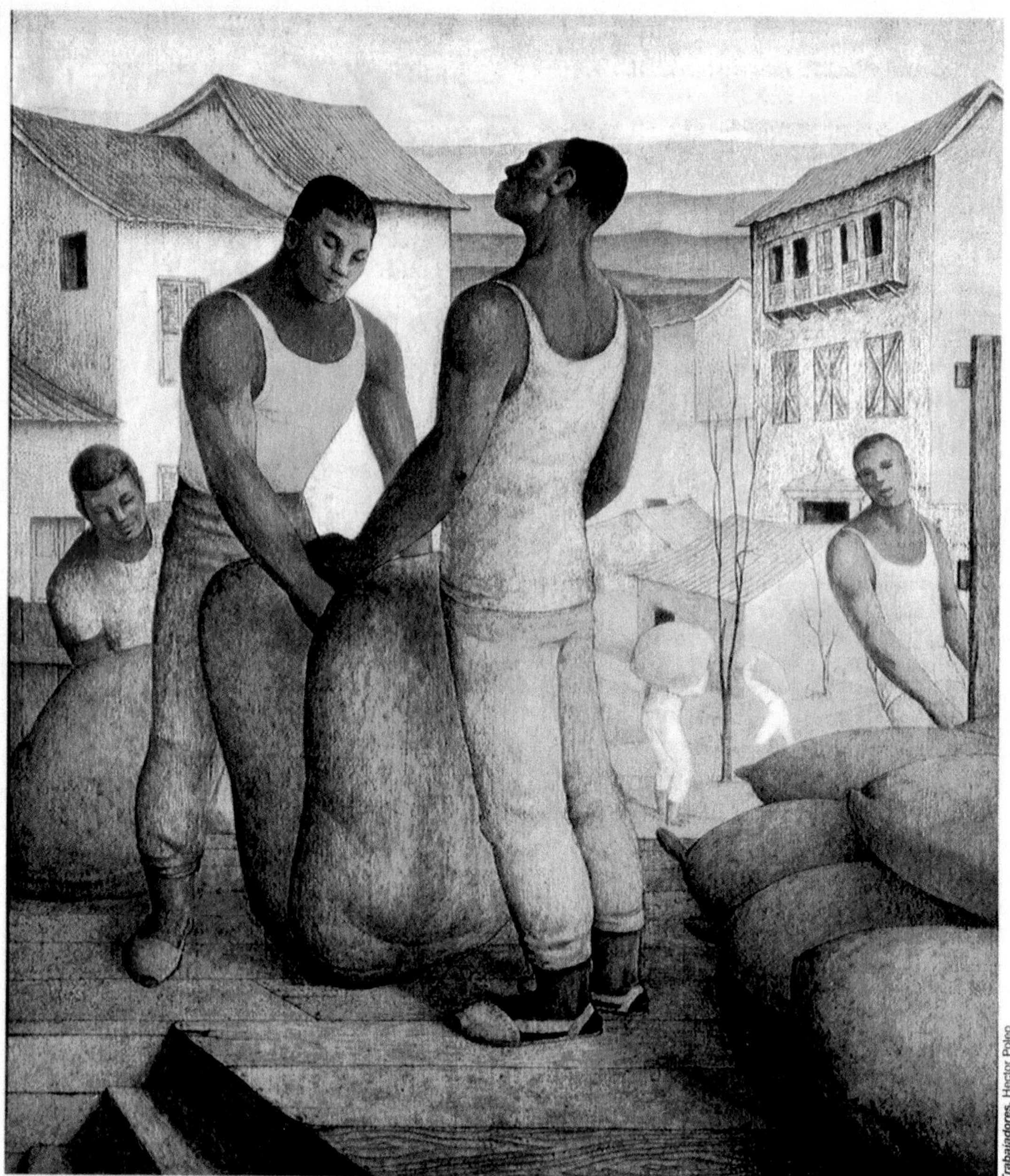

Trabajadores, Hector Poleo

⑪ ▲ **Critical Viewing** Which figure in this painting best represents the boy in the story? Explain your answer. **[Interpret]**

ENRICHMENT: Science Connection

Starvation

The young boy in "The Glass of Milk" is so hungry that he doubles over from a burning pain in his stomach. Even though the boy has not eaten for several days, it is unlikely that he is in immediate danger of starving to death. The early symptoms of starvation include rapid weight loss and sluggishness. A starving person's skin may turn pale and dry and even hang loosely. Some parts of a starving person's body may swell. Over time, a body deprived of food will begin to break down its own muscles and internal organs such as the liver, intestines, and heart. The mind of a starving person, however, can remain clear for a long time, even as the body falls apart.

Too much food can cause a starving person to go into shock or even die. Before eating solid foods, the person must first get used to drinking small amounts of sugared water and watered-down milk.

the side of the ship and the thick wall of the wharf, at the bottom of which the sea, stained with oil and littered with garbage, lapped quietly.

There was a brief pause at lunch time, and while some of the men went off to the nearby eating places, and others ate what they had brought, the boy stretched out on the ground to rest, hiding his hunger.

He finished the day's work feeling completely exhausted, covered with sweat, at the end of his rope. While the laborers were leaving, the boy sat on some sacks, watching for the foreman, and when the last man had gone, approached him; confused and stuttering, he asked, without explaining what was happening to him, if he could be paid immediately, or if it were possible to get an advance on his earnings.

The foreman answered that it was customary to pay at the end of the job, and that it would still be necessary to work the following day in order to finish loading the ship. One more day! On the other hand, they never paid a cent in advance.

"But," he said, "if you need it, I could lend you about forty cents . . . That's all I have."

The boy thanked him for his offer with an anguished smile, and left.

Then the boy was seized by acute despair. He was hungry, hungry, hungry! Hunger doubled him over, like a heavy, broad whiplash. He saw everything through a blue haze, and he staggered like a drunk when he walked. Nevertheless, he would not have been able to complain or to shout, for his suffering was deep and exhausting; it was not pain, but anguish, the end! It seemed to him that he was flattened out by a great weight.

Suddenly he felt his entrails on fire, and he stood still. He began to bend down, down, doubling over forcibly like a rod of steel, until he thought that he would drop. At that instant, as if a window opened
12 before him, he saw his home, the view from it, the faces of his mother, brothers and sisters, all that he wanted and loved appeared and disap-
13 peared before his eyes shut by fatigue. . . Then, little by little, the giddiness passed and he began to straighten up, while the burning subsided gradually. Finally, he straightened up, breathing deeply. One more hour and he would drop unconscious to the ground.

He quickened his step, as if fleeing another dizzy spell, and, as he walked, he made up his mind to eat anywhere, without paying, even if they shamed him, beat him, sent him to jail, anything; the main thing was to eat, eat, eat. A hundred times he mentally repeated the word: eat, eat, eat, until it lost its meaning, leaving his head feeling hot and empty.

He did not intend to run away; he would simply say to the owner, "Sir, I was hungry, hungry, hungry, and I can't pay . . . Do what you want."

He came to the outskirts of the city, and on one of the first streets he found a milk bar. It was a small, clean, and airy place, with little tables 14 with marble tops. Behind the counter stood a blonde lady in a very white apron.

Literary Analysis
Autobiographical Fiction
How do you think Rojas was able to describe the boy's discomfort with such detail and intensity?

anguished (aŋ′ gwisht) *adj.* showing worry, grief, or pain

acute (ə kyo͞ot′) *adj.* very serious; sharp; intense

entrails (en′ trālz) *n.* intestines; guts

✓Reading Check
What does the boy ask the foreman?

12 Literary Analysis
Autobiographical Fiction

- Review with students the Literary Analysis instruction on p. 1087. Remind students that autobiographical fiction is based partly on a writer's actual experiences.
- Remind students that Rojas had experienced poverty, hard labor, and the ports of Chile in his youth.
- Then, ask a volunteer to read aloud the bracketed passage. Call students' attention to the words and phrases describing the boy's emotions.
- Ask students the Literary Analysis question on p. 1093: How do you think Rojas was able to describe the boy's discomfort with such detail and intensity?
  Possible response: Rojas's own experience of poverty enabled him to recall and write about it in detail.

13 Reading Strategy
Judging Characters' Actions

- Reread aloud the bracketed passage. Place special emphasis on the descriptions of the boy's intense physical suffering.
- Then, ask students: Is the boy justified in his decision to do something illegal to obtain food? Why or why not?
  Possible response: He is not justified because he has turned down offers of food and money; he is justified because of his pain and willingness to accept the consequences of eating without paying.
- Discuss how students judged the boy's decision. Ask them to identify the specific criteria they used to make their judgments.

14 ✓Reading Check

Answer: The boy asks the foreman whether he can be paid immediately or receive an advance on his earnings.

CUSTOMIZE INSTRUCTION FOR UNIVERSAL ACCESS

For English Learners	For Gifted/Talented Students
Students may have difficulty understanding the words and figurative language used on p. 1093 to describe the youth's intense hunger. Encourage them to read these passages carefully, marking words or phrases that are unfamiliar or unclear. Then, have students work in pairs to find the meanings of these words and phrases. Encourage students to use context clues to decode the figurative language.	Have students reread the text on p. 1093. Encourage them to create their own artistic representations of the young boy's physical and mental anguish. Students may create drawings, paintings, or sculptures, or they may choose another medium for their creations. Then, have each student present his or her representation to the class, explaining how it illustrates the boy's condition.

15 Background

Rojas and the Literature of Social Protest

Social protest was an important trend in Latin American literature in the twentieth century. Even writers who were not considered part of the social protest movement showed its influence. Novelists such as Mexico's Rosario Castellanos and Carlos Fuentes, Colombia's Gabriel García Márquez, and Argentina's Ricardo Güiraldes have produced works that deal with social issues.

The trend was not limited to fiction, however; many Latin American poets were part of the social protest literary movement as well. César Vallejo of Peru and Pablo Neruda of Chile both spoke out in verse against the social conditions of their countries.

16 Reading Strategy

Judging Characters' Actions

- Before students read the bracketed passage, ask them to explain what the boy plans to do.
  Answer: The boy plans to order food, eat it, and then announce that he has no money.
- After students read the bracketed passage, ask them why the boy chooses the milk bar and waits outside for the old man to leave.
  Answer: The boy chooses the milk bar because it is on a relatively empty street with few passersby. The boy waits because he does not want to be humiliated.
- Ask students to consider the boy's behavior as they judge the action he plans to take.
  Possible response: The boy is nervous, a feeling that suggests that he is uneasy with his decision and wishes he did not have to go through with it. Some students may judge the boy more leniently because of this. Others may judge him more harshly because he has turned down charity.

He chose that place. There were few passersby. He could have eaten at one of the cheap grills near the wharves but they were always full of people who gambled and drank.

There was only one customer in the milk bar. He was a little old man with glasses, who sat reading, his nose stuck between the pages of a newspaper, motionless, as if glued to his chair. On the little table there was a half-empty glass of milk.

While he waited for him to leave, the boy walked up and down the sidewalk; he felt the burning sensation in his stomach returning little by little; and he waited five, ten, up to fifteen minutes. He grew tired, and stood to one side of the door, from where he cast glances like stones at the old man.

What the devil could he be reading with such attention? The boy even imagined the old man was his enemy, who knew his intentions and had decided to frustrate them. He felt like entering and saying something insulting that would force the old man to leave, a rude word or phrase that would show him **16** he had no right to sit there reading for an hour for so small a purchase.

Finally, the client finished what he was reading, or at least, interrupted it. He downed the rest of the milk in one gulp, rose slowly, paid, and walked toward the door. He went out. He was a stoop-shouldered old man, probably a carpenter or varnisher.

Once in the street, the old man put on his glasses, stuck his nose in the newspaper again, and walked slowly away, stopping every ten steps to read more closely.

The youth waited until he was some distance away, and then entered. For a moment the boy stood by the entrance, undecided, not knowing where to sit. Finally, he chose a table and walked toward it, but halfway there he changed his mind, walked backed, tripped over a chair, and finally installed himself in a corner.

The lady came, wiped the tabletop with a rag, and in a soft voice that had a trace of Castilian[5] accent, asked him:

"What will you have?"

"A glass of milk."

"Large?"

"Yes, large."

"Is that all?"

"Are there any biscuits?"

"No. Vanilla wafers."

"Well, vanilla wafers."

When the lady had turned away, he wiped his hands on his knees, rejoicing, as if he were cold and were about to drink something hot.

---

5. **Castilian** (kas til' yen) of Castile, a region in northern and central Spain.

Themes in World Literature

15 ***Rojas and the Literature of Social Protest***

During the twentieth century, many Latin American writers used literature as a means of addressing the problems facing their countries and as a vehicle for social protest. For example, writers have taken stands against repressive governments, against the exploitation of natural resources, and against the involvement of the United States in Latin American policy decisions. A number of writers have even gone beyond expressing their social and political concerns in their work and have become actively involved in politics. For example, the Peruvian novelist Mario Vargas Llosa emerged as one of the major political figures in his native country during the late 1980s.

During the early twentieth century, three Chilean writers devoted much time to addressing the dominant social concerns of their nation. These writers were Manuel Rojas, Joaquín Edwards Bello, and Eduardo Barrios. All three were widely regarded as champions of Chile's underprivileged classes. Yet, in actuality, these three writers were more interested in an unbiased representation of the realities of lower-class life than in advocating social solutions.

ENRICHMENT: Culture Connection

Milk Bars

The climax of "The Glass of Milk" unfolds in a Chilean milk bar—a café that serves vanilla wafers and fresh milk by the glass. Milk bars were not found only in South America; they have a long history in other parts of the world, too.

Milk bars were especially popular in Australia. The earliest Australian milk bar opened in Sydney in 1934. From Australia, the cafés spread to Great Britain, and by the 1940s, milk bars were everywhere in both countries. They were especially popular with young people who gathered at the neighborhood milk bar for ice cream, soft drinks, and, of course, milk. Jukeboxes and pinball machines made milk bars fun places for young people to spend their free time. Milk bars became less popular as fast-food restaurants spread across the globe. A few can still be found, however, in Great Britain and Australia.

The lady returned, and placed before him a large glass of milk, and a dish full of vanilla wafers; then she went back to her place behind the counter.

17 His first impulse was to drink the milk in one gulp and then eat the vanilla wafers; but he immediately changed his mind. He felt the woman's eyes watching him with curiosity and attention. He did not dare to look at her; he felt that if he did she would guess his situation and his shameful intentions, and he would have to get up and leave without touching what he had ordered.

Slowly, he took a vanilla wafer and moistening it in the milk, he took a bite; he took a sip of milk, and he felt the burning in his stomach diminishing, dying away. But he became aware of the reality of his desperate situation at once, and he felt something tight and hot well up inside, choking him. He realized that he was about to cry, to sob aloud, and although he knew that the lady was looking at him, he could neither hold back nor undo the burning knot of tears that grew tighter and tighter. He fought it, and as he fought he ate hurriedly, as if frightened, afraid that crying would keep him from eating. When he had finished the milk and the wafers, his eyes clouded and something hot rolled down his nose and into the glass. A terrible sob racked his whole body.

He held his head in his hands, and for a long time he cried, cried with rage, cried with shame, crying as he had never cried before.

18 He was hunched over crying when he felt a hand caress his tired head, and heard a woman's voice with a sweet Castilian accent say to him:

"Cry, son, cry . . ."

Again his eyes filled with tears and he cried as intensely as before, but this time, not with pain but with joy; he felt a great refreshing sensation spread inside him, extinguishing the hot something that had nearly strangled him. As he cried, it seemed to him that his life and feelings were cleansed like a glass under a stream of water, recovering the clearness and firmness of former days.

When the crying spell passed, he wiped his eyes and face with his handkerchief, feeling relieved. He raised his head and looked at the lady, but she was no longer looking at him, she was gazing out at the street, at a distant point in space, and her face seemed sad.

On the table before him there was another glass of milk and another dish heaped with vanilla wafers. He ate slowly, without thinking about anything, as if nothing had happened to him, as if he were at home and his mother were that woman who was standing behind the counter.

When he had finished, it had grown dark, and the place was lit by an electric light. He remained seated for a while, wondering what he would say to the lady when he left, without thinking of anything appropriate. 19

At last he got up and said simply,

"Thank you very much, ma'am; goodbye . . ."

Literary Analysis
Autobiographical Fiction and Point of View In what ways does the use of the third-person limited point of view heighten the tension when the boy first receives the food?

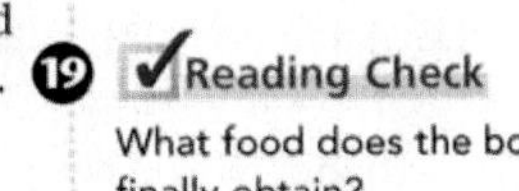

✓Reading Check
What food does the boy finally obtain?

17 Literary Analysis

Autobiographical Fiction and Point of View

- Remind students that a limited third-person narrator—the type Rojas uses in this story—presents the thoughts of a single character.
- Read aloud the bracketed passage, and then ask students to contrast the two paragraphs.
  Answer: The first paragraph describes the woman's actions; the second presents the boy's thoughts and feelings.
- Ask students the Literary Analysis question on p. 1095: In what ways does the use of the third-person limited point of view heighten the tension when the boy first receives the food?
  Answer: Like the boy, the reader does not know what the woman is thinking. The point of view lets the reader share the boy's anxiety.
- Encourage students to discuss how this scene would be different if it presented the woman's thoughts as well as, or instead of, the boy's thoughts.

18 Critical Thinking

Infer

- Have a volunteer read aloud the bracketed passage.
- Ask: On the basis of the woman's manner and comment, what inferences can you make about her?
  Possible response: The woman is kind, probably middle-aged because she calls the boy "son," and familiar with being a stranger because she speaks with an accent.

19 ✓Reading Check

Answer: The boy finally obtains two glasses of milk and two dishes of vanilla wafers.

CUSTOMIZE INSTRUCTION FOR UNIVERSAL ACCESS

For Special Needs Students	For Advanced Readers
Students may have difficulty following the main character's internal struggle on p. 1095. To increase understanding, have students read along with the recording on **Listening to Literature Audiocassettes** or **Audio CDs.** Then, encourage students to describe in their own words what happens in the milk bar.	Have students write a diary entry describing what happens in the milk bar. They may choose to write the entry from the point of view of the young boy or from the point of view of the waitress. After several students share their diary entries with the class, lead a discussion about how viewing the scene from different points of view affects the meaning or significance of the scene.

ASSESS

Answers for p. 1096

Review and Assess

1. Possible response: Most students will feel sympathy for the boy because of his plight. Some may say that he should have acted differently after getting the food.
2. **(a)** The bundle contains food. **(b)** The boy is too proud and timid to accept it. **(c)** The boy is ashamed; the tramp is not.
3. **(a)** The foreman offers to loan the boy forty cents. **(b)** Possible response: The boy is too proud to accept the loan—or too ashamed that he needs the money so badly.
4. **(a)** At first, the boy feels relief as his hunger subsides. Then, he feels rage toward his desperate situation. Finally, he begins to cry with shame. **(b)** Possible response: The boy feels overwhelmed by his situation.
5. **(a)** The waitress brings the boy more food. **(b)** The boy resolves to repay the woman. **(c)** The descriptions of the boy's grateful thoughts vanishing and events slipping into the past suggest that the boy will not keep his resolutions.
6. Possible response: Some students will say that the boy is not a better person because he forgets his hunger and the woman's kindness.

"Goodbye, son," she answered.

He went out. The wind blowing from the sea refreshed his face, still hot from crying. He walked about aimlessly for a while, then went down a street that led to the docks. It was a very beautiful night, and large stars gleamed in the summer sky.

He thought about the blonde lady who had treated him so generously, resolving to repay her, to reward her as she deserved, when he got some money. But these thoughts of gratitude vanished with the burning of his face, until not one remained, and the recent event receded and was lost in the recesses of his past life.

Suddenly, he surprised himself humming. He straightened up happily, strode on with assurance and determination.

He came to the edge of the sea, and walked back and forth with a spring in his step; he felt like a new man, as if his inner forces, previously scattered, had reassembled and united solidly.

Then he sat down on a pile of burlap sacks; fatigue, like a tingling sensation, climbed up his legs. He looked at the sea. The lights of the wharf and ships spread over the water in a reddish-gold ripple, trembling softly. He stretched out on his back, looking up at the sky for a long time. He did not feel like thinking, or singing, or talking. He just felt alive, that was all. Then he fell asleep with his face toward the sea.

Review and Assess

Thinking About the Selection

1. **Respond:** Do you feel sympathy for the boy? Why or why not?
2. **(a) Recall:** What is in the white bundle that the sailor offers, first to the boy and then to the tramp? **(b) Interpret:** Why does the boy refuse it? **(c) Compare and Contrast:** Based on their responses to the sailor, compare and contrast the boy and the tramp.
3. **(a) Recall:** What assistance does the foreman offer to the boy at the end of the day? **(b) Deduce:** Why does the youth refuse the foreman's help?
4. **(a) Interpret:** With what emotions does the boy react to his first bite of food? Explain your answer. **(b) Analyze:** Why do you think he reacts in this way?
5. **(a) Interpret:** How does the waitress respond to the boy's expression of emotion? **(b) Analyze Cause and Effect:** As a result of her behavior toward him, what does the boy resolve to do? **(c) Analyze:** Which details suggest that the boy will not keep these resolutions? Explain.
6. **Evaluate:** Is the boy a better person at the end of the story than he was at the beginning? Give evidence to support your opinion.

ASSESSMENT PRACTICE: Reading Comprehension

Identify Patterns of Organization (For more practice, see Test Preparation Workbook, p. 50.)

Many tests require students to identify patterns of organization within a written text. Use the following sample test item to help students understand this skill.

> He came to the outskirts of the city, and on one of the first streets he found a milk bar. It was a small, clean, and airy place, with little tables with marble tops. Behind the counter stood a blonde lady in a very white apron.

Which of the following best describes the pattern of organization found in this passage?

A cause and effect
B chronological
C specific to general
D general to specific

This passage does not present details in a cause-and-effect, chronological, or specific-to-general organization. Specific details follow a general description, so the correct answer is ***D***.

Review and Assess

Literary Analysis

Autobiographical Fiction

1. Rojas was known for writing **autobiographical fiction.** Based on this story, do you think that he went hungry as a young man? Explain your answer.
2. Would Rojas have been able to describe the milk bar so convincingly if he had not visited a place like it? Explain.
3. (a) What might motivate an author to write a story based on his or her own life? (b) What are some of the advantages and disadvantages of using one's own life as a creative source?

Connecting Literary Elements

4. In what ways does the use of the third-person limited **point of view** affect the kinds of details Rojas uses to convey the waitress's feelings toward the boy?
5. In what ways does the third-person limited point of view affect the choice of details in the scene between the foreman and the boy?
6. Select two scenes from this story. Then, use a chart like the one shown to explore the ways in which each scene would be different if Rojas had written it from the boy's first-person point of view or from the third-person omniscient point of view.

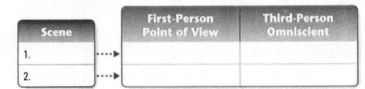

Scene	First-Person Point of View	Third-Person Omniscient
1.		
2.		

Reading Strategy

Judging Characters' Actions

7. (a) What do you think of the woman's behavior in the milk bar? (b) What criteria did you use to **judge** this **character's actions**?
8. How do you think the boy would justify his decision to obtain food by illegal means when he had already turned down the sailor's food and refused the foreman's loan? Explain your answer.

Extend Understanding

9. **Social Studies Connection:** In the United States, government agencies have taken some responsibility for assisting people who are hungry. Is this a proper role for government? Explain.

Quick Review

Autobiographical fiction is storytelling that is based upon actual people, events, and places from the author's life.

Point of view refers to the perspective from which a story is told. Most works of fiction use the first- or third-person point of view.

When you **judge characters' actions,** you evaluate their behavior in light of your personal values and experiences.

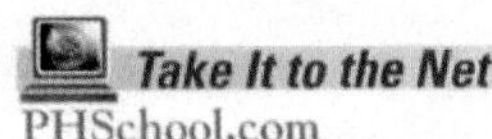

PHSchool.com

Take the interactive self-test online to check your understanding of this selection.

ENRICHMENT: Further Reading

Other Works by Manuel Rojas

We strongly encourage you to review any selection before assigning or recommending it to students.

Men of the South

Son of a Thief

Better Than Wine

Take It to the Net

Visit PHSchool.com for more information on Manuel Rojas.

Answers for p. 1097

Review and Assess

1. Possible response: Rojas might have gone hungry because of the story's vivid descriptions of hunger.
2. Possible response: The emotional resonance of the description may come only from personal experience.
3. **(a)** Possible response: An author may want to share his or her experiences. **(b)** An author's personal experiences may allow access to emotions that another author could not imagine. However, an author may be reluctant to embellish with fictional details.
4. The waitress's words and actions must convey her feelings.
5. The foreman is represented only by his words.
6. Possible response: **1. Scene:** Encounter with foreman; **First-Person:** The reader would learn more about the boy's shame and timidity; **Third-Person Omniscient:** The foreman's thoughts about the boy would be presented. **2. Scene:** Encounter at the milk bar; **First Person:** The boy's thoughts might be presented as interior monologue; **Third-Person Omniscient:** The waitress's thoughts about the boy would be presented.
7. **(a)** Possible response: The woman acts with compassion for the boy's suffering. **(b)** Possible response: Students' criteria should place a high value on kindness.
8. Possible response: The boy may say he turned down the offers before he was dangerously hungry.
9. Possible responses: Some students may say that people should take responsibility for themselves. Others will point out that some people need the government's help.

EXTEND

Answers for p. 1098

❶ Vocabulary Development

Word Analysis: Latin Suffix *-ity*

1. humanity: the condition of being human
2. purity: the state of being pure
3. generality: the condition of being general
4. curiosity: the condition of being curious

Spelling Strategy

1. budge
2. grudge

Fluency: Words in Context

Sample sentences:

1. *Gaudy* clothing attracts an audience's attention.
2. *Timidity* can overcome people when they meet celebrities.
3. Many consider cleaning gutters a form of *drudgery.*
4. Losing an election might force a candidate to give an *anguished* smile.
5. A person might express *acute* sadness by crying.
6. An injury to the *entrails* would be an injury to the abdomen.

❷ Grammar and Style

Practice

1. consequently
2. therefore
3. otherwise
4. finally
5. nevertheless

Writing Application

Sample sentences: The boy was very hungry; *however,* he was too timid to ask for food. He needed money; *consequently,* he took a job loading a ship. He worked all day; *then,* he asked the foreman for his pay. The foreman said the job wasn't finished; *besides,* he never gave advances. The boy was worried; *indeed,* he was worse off than before.

10TH GRADE For support in teaching the Grammar and Style Lesson to tenth graders, use **Writing and Grammar,** Platinum Level, Chapter 18, Section 2.

Integrate Language Skills

❶ Vocabulary Development Lesson

Word Analysis: Latin Suffix *-ity*

The suffix *-ity* means "state, quality, or condition." It is added to an adjective to form a noun. Hence, *timidity* means "the state or condition of being timid." Add the suffix *-ity* to each of the words below. Then, write a definition of each word.

1. human
2. pure
3. general
4. curious

Spelling Strategy

The *j* sound may be spelled with a g, as in *drudgery.* Write the correct spelling of the underlined word in each sentence.

1. The sailor did not <u>budje</u> from the railing.
2. The youth did not hold a <u>grudje.</u>

Fluency: Words in Context

Using the italicized word, write a one-sentence answer for each question below.

1. Why do many performers wear *gaudy* clothing?
2. Under what circumstances can people be overcome with *timidity?*
3. What task do many people consider a form of *drudgery?*
4. Under what circumstances might someone give an *anguished* smile?
5. How might a person express *acute* sadness?
6. Where would an injury to an animal's *entrails* be located?

❷ Grammar and Style Lesson

Conjunctive Adverbs

A **conjunctive adverb** is a word that joins only independent clauses—clauses that contain a subject and a verb and express a complete idea—not single words, phrases, or subordinate clauses. Conjunctive adverbs include the words *accordingly, also, besides, consequently, finally, however, indeed, moreover, nevertheless, then, otherwise,* and *therefore.*

Examples:

The lady returned, and placed before him a glass of milk; <u>then</u> she went back to her place behind the counter.

The boy refused the food; <u>consequently</u>, he felt his hunger increase.

Practice Complete each sentence below with a conjunctive adverb.

1. The boy had not eaten; ___?___, his stomach began to burn like fire.
2. He had no skills; ___?___, no one would hire him.
3. He needed to eat; ___?___, he could die.
4. He waited as long as he could; ___?___, he resolved to steal food.
5. The boy was broke; ___?___, he ordered food.

Writing Application Write five sentences about the boy in this story. Use a different conjunctive adverb in each sentence.

WG *Prentice Hall Writing and Grammar Connection: Diamond Level, Chapter 17, Section 4*

TEACHING RESOURCES

The following resources can be used to enrich or extend the instruction for pp. 1098–1099.

Vocabulary

- **Selection Support:** Build Vocabulary, p. 197
- **Vocabulary and Spelling Practice Book** (Use this booklet for skills instruction.) ■

Grammar

- **Selection Support:** Grammar and Style, p. 198
- **Writing and Grammar,** Diamond Level, p. 394
- **Daily Language Practice Transparencies** ■

Writing

- **Performance Assess. and Portfolio Mgmt.,** p. 16
- **Writing and Grammar,** Diamond Level, p. 82
- **Writing and Grammar iText CD-ROM**
- **Writing Models and Graphic Organizers on Transparencies,** pp. 103–106

Listening and Speaking

- **Performance Assess. and Portfolio Mgmt.,** p. 28

■ **BLOCK SCHEDULING:** Resources marked with this symbol provide varied instruction during 90-minute blocks.

3 Writing Lesson

Character Analysis

In Manuel Rojas's story, the boy's actions say a great deal about his personality, values, and sense of self. Write an essay in which you analyze the boy's character based on his actions.

Prewriting Reread the story, taking notes about the boy's decisions and actions. Identify the events that led the boy into his predicament, the reasons for his choices, and the ways in which he relates to other people.

Drafting Write an introduction in which you state your main idea. To build each paragraph that follows, state a supporting idea in one sentence, elaborate upon it in the next sentence or two, and add supporting details in the final sentence.

Revising Review your draft, highlighting the main ideas and underlining the supporting sentences in each paragraph. If sentences do not support the main idea, consider deleting or moving them.

Model: Revising to Create Unity

The boy was timid around other people. For example, even though he was starving, it took him a long time to work up his nerve to ask for work. ~~He did work very hard after he got the job.~~

Every sentence in a paragraph should support the main idea.

WG Prentice Hall Writing and Grammar Connection: Diamond Level, Chapter 5, Section 3

4 Extension Activities

Listening and Speaking With a partner, write and deliver to the class a retelling of the story from the waitress's point of view. Use these tips to prepare:

- Reread the story, looking for clues about the waitress's thoughts and feelings.
- Answer these questions: What is the waitress's life like? What does she think of the boy? What does she do after he leaves?

As you write, try to match the mood of Rojas's story. Then, present your work to the class. **[Group Activity]**

Research and Technology Use electronic and print resources to research how long a person can survive without food. Identify the effects of hunger, and examine how these effects build up as time passes. Using a computer program, create a **human hunger chart** in which you present your findings.

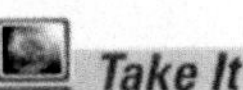 ***Take It to the Net*** PHSchool.com

Go online for an additional research activity using the Internet.

ASSESSMENT RESOURCES

The following resources can be used to assess students' knowledge and skills.

Selection Assessment

- **Formal Assessment,** pp. 176–178
- **Open-Book Tests,** pp. 148–150
- **Test Bank Software**

 ***Take It to the Net***

Visit PHSchool.com for self-tests on the selection.

Writing Rubric

- **Performance Assess. and Portfolio Mgmt.,** p. 16

Listening and Speaking Rubric

- **Performance Assess. and Portfolio Mgmt.,** p. 28

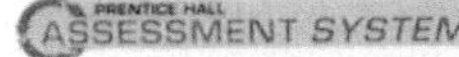

For additional diagnostics and remediation for skills covered in this grouping, use materials from the Prentice Hall Assessment System.

3 Writing Lesson

- Have students reread the story, focusing on the boy's actions. Tell them to note the motives behind the boy's actions and decisions.
- Have each student write a thesis statement about the boy's character. Each paragraph's main idea should support the thesis. Encourage students to use the Outline in **Writing Models and Graphic Organizers on Transparencies,** pp. 103–106, to organize their theses and main ideas.
- Use the Response to Literature rubric in **Performance Assessment and Portfolio Management,** p. 16, to evaluate students' work.

10TH GRADE For support in working through the Writing Lesson with tenth graders, use **Writing and Grammar,** Platinum Level, Chapter 5, Section 3.

4 Listening and Speaking

- Organize students into pairs; have them reread the story, focusing on the scene in the milk bar. Encourage students to use the questions on p. 1099 to find clues about the waitress's thoughts and feelings.
- Before pairs begin to write their retellings, tell them to choose a point of view for their retelling.
- Have pairs rehearse before presenting. Suggest that both partners participate.
- Use the Speaking: Delivering a Narrative Presentation rubric in **Performance Assessment and Portfolio Management,** p. 28, to evaluate students' retellings.

CUSTOMIZE INSTRUCTION For Universal Access

To address different learning styles, use the following activities suggested in the **Extension Activities** booklet, p. 50:

- For Verbal/Linguistic and Bodily/Kinesthetic Learners, use Activity 5.
- For Verbal/Linguistic and Logical/Mathematical Learners, use Activity 6.
- For Visual/Spatial Learners, use Activity 7.

Fear • The Prayer • Time • Green • Lightness

Lesson Objectives

1. **To analyze and respond to literary elements**
   - Literary Analysis: Imagery
   - Comparing Literary Works: Tone
2. **To read, comprehend, analyze, and critique a poem**
   - Reading Strategy: Restating for Understanding
   - Reading Check Questions
   - Review and Assess Questions
   - Assessment Practice (ATE)
3. **To develop word analysis skills, fluency, and systematic vocabulary**
   - Vocabulary Development Lesson: Latin Root *-prim-*
4. **To understand and apply written and oral language conventions**
   - Spelling Strategy
   - Grammar and Style Lesson: Direct Address
5. **To understand and apply appropriate writing and research strategies**
   - Writing Lesson: Interpretive Essay
   - Extension Activity: Color Chart
6. **To understand and apply listening and speaking strategies**
   - Extension Activity: Oral Interpretation

10TH GRADE TEACHING A TENTH-GRADE COURSE

The literature in this section can be taught as part of a rich, balanced world literature course for tenth-grade students. For a full outline of such a course, see pp. T47–T48 in Volume 1 of this Teacher's Edition.

STEP-BY-STEP TEACHING GUIDE	PACING GUIDE
PRETEACH	
Motivate Students and Provide Background	
Use the Motivation activity (ATE p. 1100)	5 min.
Read and discuss author and background features (SE pp. 1100, 1103, 1109; ATE p. 1100) [A]	5 min.
Introduce the Concepts	
Introduce the Literary Analysis and Reading Strategy concepts (SE/ATE p. 1101) [A]	15 min.
Pronounce the vocabulary words and read their definitions (SE p. 1101)	5 min.
TEACH	
Monitor Comprehension	
Informally monitor comprehension by circulating while students read [A]	25 min.
Monitor students' comprehension with the Reading Check note (SE/ATE pp. 1103, 1109)	as students read
Develop vocabulary with the Vocabulary notes (SE pp. 1103, 1105, 1106, 1110; ATE p. 1110)	as students read
Develop Understanding	
Develop students' understanding of imagery with the Literary Analysis annotations (SE pp. 1103, 1108; ATE pp. 1103, 1106, 1108, 1109) [A]	5 min.
Develop students' ability to restate for understanding, using the Reading Strategy annotations (SE pp. 1104, 1106; ATE pp. 1103, 1104, 1106)	5 min.
ASSESS	
Assess Mastery	
Assess students' mastery of the Reading Strategy and Literary Analysis concepts by having them answer the Review and Assess questions (SE/ATE p. 1111)	15 min.
Use one or more of the print, software, or transparecy Assessment Resources (ATE p. 1113) [A]	up to 45 min.
EXTEND	
Apply Understanding	
Have students complete the Vocabulary Development Lesson and the Grammar and Style Lesson (SE p. 1112)	20 min.
Apply students' ability to reorder paragraphs for coherence, using the Writing Lesson (SE/ATE p. 1113) [A]	45 min.
Apply students' understanding of the selections, using one or more of the Extension Activities (SE p. 1113)	20–90 min.

A ACCELERATED INSTRUCTION: Use the strategies and activities identified with an [A].

10TH GRADE TEACHING TENTH-GRADE STUDENTS For support in teaching tenth graders, see the Step-by-Step Teaching notes identified with this icon.

UNIVERSAL ACCESS
- ● = Below-Level Students
- ▲ = On-Level Students
- ■ = Above-Level Students

Time and Resource Manager

Reading Level: Easy, Average, Average, Average
Average Number of Instructional Days: 3

RESOURCES		
PRINT	**TRANSPARENCIES**	**TECHNOLOGY**
• **Beyond Literature,** Humanities Connection: Music and Art, p. 51 ▲ ■		
• **Selection Support Workbook:** ● ▲ ■ Literary Analysis, p. 204 Reading Strategy, p. 203 Build Vocabulary, p. 201	• **Literary Analysis and Reading Transparencies,** pp. 101 and 102 ● ▲ ■	
		• **Listening to Literature** ● ▲ ■ Audiocassettes Audio CDs
• **Literary Analysis for Enrichment,** p. 51 ■		
• **Formal Assessment:** Selection Test, pp. 179–181 ● ▲ ■ • **Open-Book Tests,** pp. 151–153 ● ▲ ■ • **Performance Assessment and Portfolio Management,** pp. 16, 31 ● ▲ ■ • PRENTICE HALL ASSESSMENT SYSTEM ● ▲ ■	• PRENTICE HALL ASSESSMENT SYSTEM ● ▲ ■ **Skills Practice Answers and Explanations on Transparencies**	• **Test Bank Software** ● ▲ ■
• **Selection Support Workbook:** ● ▲ ■ Grammar and Style, p. 202 • **Writing and Grammar,** Diamond Level ● ▲ ■ • **Extension Activities,** p. 51 ● ▲ ■	• **Daily Language Practice Transparencies** ● ▲ • **Writing Models and Graphic Organizers on Transparencies,** pp. 103–105 ● ▲ ■	• **Writing and Grammar iText CD-ROM** ● ▲ ■ ***Take It to the Net*** PHSchool.com

BLOCK SCHEDULING: Use one 90-minute class period to preteach the selection(s) and have students read them. Use a second 90-minute class period to assess students' mastery of skills and have them complete one of the Extension Activities.

PRETEACH

Step-by-Step Teaching Guide for pp. 1100–1101

Motivation

Present students with magazine pictures that might inspire the feelings suggested by these poems: a worried mother, which might suggest fear of the future; a funeral, to suggest abandonment and grief; and a beautiful woman in green, which could suggest longing. Encourage students to share their impressions of these pictures. Then, explain that the images in these poems evoke responses and make abstract ideas concrete. As they read the poems, invite students to look for ways in which imagery transforms abstract thoughts and feelings into tangible objects.

❶ Background

More About the Authors

Both of these poets are known for the melancholy nature of their work. Mistral became famous in South America for a group of three sonnets called the "Sonnets of Death." *Desolación*, the book that brought her international fame, deals primarily with despair, suffering, and death. Although Jiménez's poetry is not as dark as Mistral's, much of his work is characterized by a gentle sadness. This melancholy can be seen in both "Green" and "Lightness."

Geography Note

Use the map on this page to point out Mistral's home country, Chile. Although a great distance separates Chile and Jiménez's native Spain, the two countries are united by their official language—Spanish. The Spanish spoken in Chile and Spain is basically the same, with only a few minor differences in word usage and pronunciation.

Prepare to Read

❶ Fear ◆ The Prayer ◆ Time ◆ Green ◆ Lightness

Gabriela Mistral (1889–1957)

When Gabriela Mistral (gä′ brē ä′ lä mēs träl′) heard the news that she had won the Nobel Prize in Literature in 1945, she declared, "Perhaps it was because I was the candidate of the women and children." Ever since Mistral began writing poetry, women and children were her primary subjects. As an educator and diplomat, she devoted herself to improving their lives.

A Poet and Teacher Mistral's real name was Lucila Godoy Alcayaga (lo͞o sē′ lə gō doi′ al kī ä′ gə). At the age of fifteen, she began two of her careers—teacher and poet. Fearing that she might lose her teaching jobs because of the content of her poetry, Mistral published her work under pseudonyms. The name Gabriela Mistral came from the archangel Gabriel and the fierce mistral wind that blows over the south of France. It was under this name that Mistral became the first South American to win the Nobel Prize in Literature.

A Great Loss Mistral's fame spread to the United States in 1922 with the publication of her first book of poetry, *Desolación*. Mistral wrote *Desolación* shortly after the death of her fiancé. Many believe that his death became the driving force behind her creativity.

International Role The poet's literary fame and reputation as a champion of women and children drew the attention of politicians. In 1922, the Mexican minister of education invited Mistral to develop a program of education reform in his country. Mistral later became Chile's delegate to the Institute of Intellectual Cooperation, an organization that was part of the League of Nations—a precursor of today's United Nations. She also taught in the United States and served in many diplomatic posts. Mistral spent the last years of her life on Long Island in New York State.

Juan Ramón Jiménez (1881–1958)

Juan Ramón Jiménez is widely viewed as one of Spain's finest poets. Ironically, he spent much of his life in exile from his native land.

Becoming a Poet Jiménez was a law student at the University of Seville when he first published his poems in a magazine. These poems caught the attention of the celebrated Nicaraguan poet Ruben Darío, who was then living in the Spanish capital of Madrid. Soon, Jiménez moved to Madrid, where he became the editor of two literary magazines. In 1900, he published two volumes of poetry, though he later thought these so awful that he sought out and destroyed every copy he could. Within a few years, however, he had developed a lyrical power more to his liking. That skill is evident in poetry collections like *Pure Elegies* (1908) and in *Platero and I* (1914–1917), his popular prose poems about a man roaming the countryside with his donkey.

Love and Exile In 1912, Jiménez fell in love with Zenobia Camprubi, an American living in Madrid. When she returned to New York, he followed, and the two married. The couple returned to live in Spain until the 1930s, when Jiménez was asked to serve as the ambassador to the United States for Spain's democratic royalist government. After the fascists defeated the royalists in the Spanish Civil War (1936–1939), Jiménez refused to return home. Instead, he and Zenobia settled in Puerto Rico, where they lived out their remaining days. In 1956, Jiménez was awarded the Nobel Prize in Literature.

TEACHING RESOURCES

The following resources can be used to enrich or extend the instruction for pp. 1100–1101.

Background

Beyond Literature, p. 51 ■

Take It to the Net

Visit PHSchool.com for background on the authors.

Literary Analysis

Literary Analysis and Reading Transparencies, Imagery, p. 101 ■

Reading

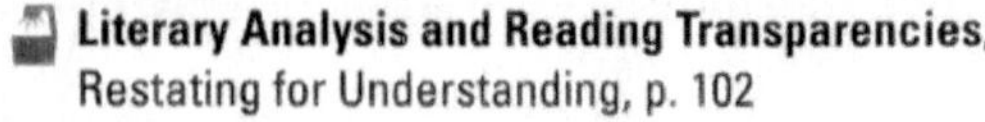

Literary Analysis and Reading Transparencies, Restating for Understanding, p. 102

Selection Support: Reading Strategy, p. 203;

■ **BLOCK SCHEDULING:** Resources marked with this symbol provide varied instruction during 90-minute blocks.

Preview

Connecting to the Literature

It has been said that great music is about love—whether it is love of a person, a place, an object, or life in general. These poems suggest that, in its essence, poetry also is about love.

❷ Literary Analysis

Imagery

Imagery is language that appeals to one or more of the five senses—sight, hearing, taste, smell, and touch. In literature, imagery conveys meaning and evokes emotion. For example, in "The Prayer," the speaker describes the man she loves with these images:

> my cup of freshness, honeycomb of my mouth, //
> lime of my bones, . . . / bird-trill to my ears . . .

Notice that these images appeal to the senses, convey different shades of meaning, and express emotions. As you read, use a chart like the one shown to identify the senses to which specific images appeal. Then, think about the meaning and emotions each image conveys.

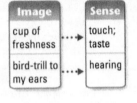

Image		Sense
cup of freshness	→	touch; taste
bird-trill to my ears	→	hearing

Comparing Literary Works

Tone is the speaker's attitude toward his or her audience or subject and can be described with the same words one uses to describe emotions, such as *humorous*, *sad*, *angry*, or *joyful*. For example, these lines from "Lightness" create a contemplative and joy-filled tone:

> My window-curtain, / in the majestic stillness and the silence /
> of the unruffled early morning, / moving softly to light breezes.

As you read these poems, compare each speaker's tone and identify the details that convey distinct attitudes.

❸ Reading Strategy

Restating for Understanding

Some poems contain passages that are especially challenging. To clarify the meaning of such passages, **restate** them in your own words. As you read these poems, pause whenever you are uncertain about the meaning of a line or passage and restate it for understanding.

Vocabulary Development

invokes (in vōks′) *v.* calls on (p. 1103)

anoint (ə noint′) *v.* to rub oil or ointment on (p. 1103)

sheaves (shēvz) *n.* bundles of cut stalks of grain (p. 1105)

cascade (kas kād′) *n.* small, steep waterfall (p. 1106)

primeval (prī mē′ vəl) *adj.* having to do with the earliest times (p. 1110)

impetus (im′ pə təs) *n.* driving force (p. 1110)

❷ Literary Analysis

Imagery

- Read aloud the definition of imagery on p. 1101. Illustrate the relationship between imagery and the senses by having students imagine an early morning walk along the beach. Invite them to use sensory language to describe the sights, sounds, tastes, smells, and sensations of the walk.
- Read the lines from "The Prayer" found on p. 1101. Explain that imagery conveys meaning and—especially in poetry—evokes emotions. Ask students what emotions the examples evoke.
- Encourage students to use the graphic organizer on p. 1101 to analyze the imagery in these poems. Have students expand the organizer by listing the emotions each image evokes.
- Revisit the descriptions students offered of the walk along the beach. Have students discuss the tone of each description and note the way word choice affects tone.

❸ Reading Strategy

Restating for Understanding

- Explain to students that a good first step in understanding difficult passages is to restate them in their own words.
- Use the Restating for Understanding transparency in **Literary Analysis and Reading Transparencies,** p. 101, to demonstrate this strategy.
- Encourage students to use this strategy whenever they encounter difficult passages.

Vocabulary Development

- Pronounce each vocabulary word for students, and read the definitions as a class. Have students identify any words with which they are already familiar.

CUSTOMIZE INSTRUCTION FOR UNIVERSAL ACCESS

For Less Proficient Readers	For English Learners	For Advanced Readers
Make the poems of Mistral and Jiménez more accessible by previewing with students the accompanying art. Encourage students to predict what the poems will be about on the basis of the thoughts and emotions evoked by the art. Help students grasp each poem's basic themes before they read.	Appreciation of imagery will depend on students' abilities to decode English words. Have students skim the poems and list unfamiliar words or phrases. Then, have students work in small groups and use dictionaries to find the meanings of the words and phrases on their lists.	Tell students that the poems in this grouping make heavy use of imagery. As students read, encourage them to keep a journal of their own thoughts and feelings about the poems' images.

E-Teach

Visit e-Teach at PHSchool.com for teachers' essays on how to teach, with questions and answers.

TEACH

Step-by-Step Teaching Guide for pp. 1102–1110

Teaching Tenth-Grade Students

10TH GRADE Although the emotional quality of these poems is very accessible, tenth-grade students may have difficulty with the vocabulary. Preteach the vocabulary words that appear on p. 1101.

1 About the Selection

In Mistral's poem "Fear," a mother reveals her deepest worries about what the future might hold for her daughter.

2 Background

Art

Woman and Child, by Pablo Picasso

Both highly imaginative and prolific, Picasso (1881–1973) contributed inestimably to the development of modern art in the twentieth century. Picasso was born in Málaga, Spain, and began painting seriously at the age of fourteen. A master of both realistic and abstract styles, he explored such human themes as love, war, and loneliness. His interpretations of these themes were sometimes tender and sometimes confrontational.

Use the following questions for discussion:

- Compare the feelings that the woman shows for the child in the painting and the poem.
  Possible response: Both women seem loving and protective.
- How do you think the child in the painting feels?
  Possible responses: The child feels content, comfortable, and safe.

3 ▶ Critical Viewing

Answer: The woman's eyes express concern. Her hand covers the child in a protective gesture.

1

Gabriela Mistral *translated by* Doris Dana

I don't want them to turn
my little girl into a swallow.
She would fly far away into the sky
and never fly again to my straw bed,
or she would nest in the eaves[1]
where I could not comb her hair.
I don't want them to turn
my little girl into a swallow.

I don't want them to make
my little girl a princess.
In tiny golden slippers
how could she play on the meadow?
And when night came, no longer
would she sleep at my side.
I don't want them to make
my little girl a princess.

And even less do I want them
one day to make her queen.
They would put her on a throne
where I could not go to see her.
And when nighttime came
I could never rock her . . .
I don't want them to make
my little girl a queen!

1. **eaves** (ēvz) *n.* lower edge(s) of a roof, usually projecting beyond the sides of a building.

2

Woman and Child, Pablo Picasso, Estate of Pablo Picasso/Artists Rights Society (ARS), New York. Museo Picasso, Barcelona, Spain. Scala

3 ▲ **Critical Viewing** Which details in this woman's expression and posture suggest a mother's concern for her child? Explain. **[Interpret]**

TEACHING RESOURCES

The following resources can be used to enrich or extend the instruction for pp. 1102–1110.

Literary Analysis

- **Selection Support:** Literary Analysis, p. 204

Reading

- **Selection Support:** Reading Strategy, p. 203; Build Vocabulary, p. 201
- **Selection SupportLiterary Analysis and Reading** Restating for Understanding, p. 102
- **Listening to Literature Audiocassettes**
- **Listening to Literature Audio CDs**

BLOCK SCHEDULING: Resources marked with this symbol provide varied instruction during 90-minute blocks.

❹ # The Prayer

Gabriela Mistral
translated by John A. Crowe

Background

When Gabriela Mistral was seventeen years old, she met Romelio Ureta, who became the love of her life. Unfortunately, the relationship ended with Ureta's early death, a loss from which Mistral never fully recovered. *Desolación* (1922), the collection in which "Fear" and "The Prayer" appear, reflects her intense sadness and despair over Ureta's death. It is her first great collection of poetry, one that brought her international fame.

❺
Thou knowest, Lord, with what flaming boldness,
my word <u>invokes</u> Thy help for strangers.
I come now to plead for one who was mine,
my cup of freshness, honeycomb of my mouth,

lime of my bones, sweet reason of life's journey,
bird-trill to my ears, girdle of my garment.
Even those who are no part of me are in my care.
Harden not Thine eyes if I plead with Thee for this one!

He was a good man, I say he was a man
whose heart was entirely open; a man
gentle in temper, frank as the light of day,
as filled with miracles as the spring of the year.

❻
Thou answerest harshly that he is unworthy of entreaty[1]
who did not <u>anoint</u> with prayer his fevered lips,
who went away that evening without waiting for Thy sign,
his temples shattered like fragile goblets.

1. **entreaty** (en trēt′ ē) *n.* earnest request.

Literary Analysis
Imagery and Tone What attitude toward her subject does the speaker express in the first stanza?

invokes (in vōks′) *v.* calls on

anoint (ə noint′) *v.* to rub oil or ointment on

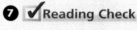

❼ ✔**Reading Check**
For whom does the speaker say she now comes "to plead"?

❹ About the Selection

The speaker of "The Prayer" pours out her intense grief over the untimely death of her beloved and asks for God's forgiveness.

❺ Literary Analysis

Imagery and Tone

- Make sure students understand that a poem's tone is the attitude of its speaker toward its subject.
- Read aloud the bracketed passage. Then, point out the images in the stanza's final line. Ask students what emotions the images evoke.
  Possible response: The images evoke the sweetness of love.
- Ask students the Literary Analysis question on p. 1103: What attitude toward her subject does the speaker express in the first stanza?
  Possible response: The speaker expresses an earnest plea on behalf of her beloved.

❻ Reading Strategy

Restating for Understanding

- Remind students that restating challenging passages in their own words can enhance their understanding of a work.
- Read aloud the bracketed stanza, and invite students to discuss its meaning. Focus the discussion by asking what students think happened to the speaker's beloved.
  Possible response: The speaker's beloved died suddenly or violently.
- Then, ask students to restate the stanza in their own words.
  Possible response: You angrily say that my beloved is not worth begging for because he did not pray when he was in trouble, did not wait for divine guidance, before dying a violent death.

❼ ✔Reading Check

Answer: The speaker says that she comes to plead "for one who was mine," her lost beloved.

CUSTOMIZE INSTRUCTION FOR UNIVERSAL ACCESS

For Special Needs Students	For English Learners	For Gifted/Talented Students
Students may find these poems difficult to understand, especially "The Prayer." Use **Listening to Literature Audiocassettes** or **Audio CDs** to enhance students' comprehension. Have students read along as they listen to the recordings.	Point out to students the words *Thou, Thy, Thine,* and *Thee* in the poem. Ask students to discuss why these particular words are capitalized. Guide students to understand that Mistral uses these pronouns to address God.	Challenge students to write poems of their own in which a speaker pleads on behalf of someone else. Ask student to use the formal language of "The Prayer" as a model for their poems.

8 Background

Art

The Revolution, by Manuel Rodríguez Lozano

Rodríguez Lozano (1896–1971) was born in Mexico City. He studied in Paris from 1914 to 1921 and was influenced by Picasso's purity of craftsmanship. The mysterious shrouded figures and somber colors in *The Revolution* are characteristic of his work, which often addresses themes of death, despair, and ecstasy.

Use the following question for discussion:

Do the colors and figures in the painting reflect the mood of the "The Prayer"? Explain.

Possible response: The mourning colors reflect the speaker's grief, and the supplicatory postures of the figures reflect the speaker's pleas to God.

9 ▶ Critical Viewing

Possible responses: The women's postures are physical representations of the speaker's grief.

10 Reading Strategy

Restating for Understanding

- Have a volunteer read aloud the bracketed passage. Discuss challenging words or phrases.
- Then, have students respond to the Reading Strategy item on p. 1104: Restate this stanza in your own words.

Possible response: You say he was mean? But, Lord, he knew how completely I loved him. You say he kept me from being happy? It does not matter. Lord, you know that I loved him!

▶ Monitor Progress Have students read and explain their restatement of the bracketed stanza.

▶ Reteach Use the Restating for Understanding transparency in **Literary Analysis and Reading Transparencies,** p. 101, to help students restate other stanzas in this poem.

8

The Revolution, Manuel Rodríguez Lozano, Museo Nacional de Arte Moderno, Mexico City

But I, my Lord, protest that I have touched,—
just like the spikenard[2] of his brow,—
his whole gentle and tormented heart:
and it was silky as a nascent[3] bud!

Thou sayest that he was cruel? Thou forgettest, Lord, that I loved him,
10 and that he knew my wounded heart was wholly his.
He troubled forever the waters of my gladness?
It does not matter! Thou knowest: I loved him, I loved him!

And to love (Thou knowest it well) is a bitter exercise;
a pressing of eyelids wet with tears,
a kissing-alive of hairshirt tresses,[4]
keeping, below them, the ecstatic eyes.

9 ▲ **Critical Viewing** Do you think these women are expressing the same emotions as the speaker in the poem? Explain. **[Interpret]**

Reading Strategy Restating for Understanding Restate this stanza in your own words.

2. **spikenard** (spik′ nərd) *n.* perennial North American plant with whitish flowers, purplish berries, and fragrant roots.
3. **nascent** (nas′ ənt) *adj.* coming into being.
4. **tresses** (tres′ əz) *n.* woman's or girl's hair.

ENRICHMENT: Biography Connection

The Death of Romelio Ureta

"The Prayer," along with many other poems by Gabriela Mistral, was inspired by the death of Mistral's great love, Romelio Ureta. Mistral met Ureta—a pale, dark-haired young man who worked for a railroad company—when she was just seventeen. Not much about their relationship is known for certain, yet Mistral described him as the love of her life.

Their love, however, soon came to a tragic end. To help a friend in dire financial straits, Ureta stole some money from the railroad company. He apparently planned to replace it but was unable to do so. Ureta was caught and charged with embezzlement. This crisis was more than Ureta could bear, and on November 25, 1909, he committed suicide. It is said that when his body was found, he had a card in his pocket inscribed with the name *Lucila Godoy*—Mistral's real name.

The piercing iron has a welcome chill,
when it opens, like sheaves of grain, the loving flesh.
And the cross (Thou rememberest, O King of the Jews!)
is softly borne, like a spray of roses.

Here I rest, Lord, my face bowed down
to the dust, talking with thee through the twilight,
through all the twilights that may stretch through life,
if Thou art long in telling me the word I await.

11 I shall weary Thine ears with prayers and sobs;
a timid greyhound, I shall lick Thy mantle's hem,
Thy loving eyes cannot escape me,
Thy foot avoid the hot rain of my tears.

Speak at last the word of pardon! It will scatter
in the wind the perfume of a hundred fragrant vials
as it empties; all waters will be dazzling;
the wilderness will blossom, the cobblestones will sparkle.

The dark eyes of wild beasts will moisten,
and the conscious mountain that Thou didst forge from stone
will weep through the white eyelids of its snowdrifts;
Thy whole earth will know that Thou hast forgiven!

sheaves (shēvz) *n.* bundles of cut stalks of grain

Review and Assess

Thinking About the Selections

1. **Respond:** Which poem did you find more moving? Why?
2. **(a) Recall:** In "Fear," what three things does the speaker say she does not want to happen? **(b) Infer:** What kind of life can you infer the speaker does not want for her child?
3. **(a) Interpret:** Who might "they" be in the poem? **(b) Connect:** In what ways does the title of the poem connect to the speaker's attitude toward "them"?
4. **(a) Recall:** In "The Prayer," for whom is the speaker of the poem pleading? **(b) Analyze:** What does the speaker want?
5. **(a) Interpret:** In stanza six, what two charges against the lost loved one does the speaker attribute to God? **(b) Generalize:** With what single argument does the speaker respond?
6. **(a) Interpret:** What does the speaker say will happen if God does as she asks? **(b) Draw Conclusions:** Why do you think the speaker believes the details noted in the final two stanzas will sway God? Explain.
7. **Make a Judgment:** How important do you think it is to be forgiven and to forgive? Explain your answer.

CUSTOMIZE INSTRUCTION FOR UNIVERSAL ACCESS

For Less Proficient Readers	For Advanced Readers
Point out to students the speaker's comparison of herself to a greyhound in line 38. Then, explain that this comparison is a metaphor, or a figure of speech in which one thing is spoken of as though it were something else. A metaphor suggests a comparison between the two things that are identified. Guide students as they review Mistral's poems, and help them identify other metaphors.	Tell students that writers throughout history have either written literature to a higher power or pondered humankind's relationship with that higher power. Invite students to seek other literary works addressed to or exploring the divine. Students may begin with the Psalms on pp. 73–76, the selections from the *Qur'an* on pp. 84–86, and the selections from the *Rig Veda* on pp. 164–166. Have each student write a brief analysis about the treatment of the divine in one or more of these selections.

11 Critical Thinking

Interpret

- Read aloud the bracketed passage. Discuss with students how the speaker describes herself as a "timid greyhound" at the foot of God, her master.
- Ask students how this image characterizes the speaker and further clarifies her meaning.

  Possible response: The image presents the speaker as tenacious, yet humble and servile. It conveys her intention to petition for God's pity

Answers for p. 1105

Review and Assess

1. Possible response: "The Prayer" may be more moving because of the intensity of the speaker's love and grief.
2. **(a)** The speaker does not want her daughter to be turned into a swallow, made a princess, or made a queen. **(b)** The speaker does not want a life of privilege, power, and isolation for her daughter.
3. **(a)** Possible response: "They" could refer to humankind or society. **(b)** The speaker has so many fears for her daughter that she cannot name all the sources of her fears.
4. **(a)** The speaker pleads on behalf of her deceased lover. **(b)** The speaker wants God to forgive her lover.
5. **(a)** The speaker believes that God charges the beloved with cruelty and with being the source of the speaker's unhappiness. **(b)** The speaker's argument is that she loved the beloved.
6. **(a)** The speaker says the world will be filled with beauty and emotion. **(b)** Possible response: The speaker knows that she can appeal to God's concern for beauty and peace.
7. Possible response: Forgiveness is important because people are imperfect, and forgiveness stimulates spiritual growth.

12 About the Selection

Although it is not as dark as "Fear" or "The Prayer," Gabriela Mistral's "Time" is equally evocative. Its speaker describes each stage of a day with vivid figurative language.

13 Reading Strategy

Restating for Understanding

- Read aloud the first stanza with the class. Ask students what this stanza describes.
  Answer: This stanza describes sunrise.
- Then, have a volunteer read aloud the first two lines of the second stanza. Ask students the Reading Strategy question on p. 1106: In your own words, what do the first two lines of the second stanza mean?
  Possible response: The speaker compares good and bad fortune to the rising and setting of the sun; the speaker knows that destiny cannot be controlled and so accepts it.

14 Literary Analysis

Imagery

- Have students read aloud the bracketed passage. Ask: To what does the speaker compare morning?
  Answer: The speaker compares morning to a leaping deer.
- Encourage students to visualize the leaping deer. Then, ask what thoughts and emotions the image evokes for them.
  Possible response: The deer is fast, energetic, and beautiful. The deer's leap may evoke the ease or happiness of an animal in its natural state.
- Guide students to recognize that the poem equates the energy and happiness of a leaping deer with the feelings the speaker has about morning.

12

Time

Gabriela Mistral *translated by* Doris Dana

DAYBREAK

My heart swells that the Universe
like a fiery cascade may enter.
The new day comes. Its coming
leaves me breathless.
13 I sing. Like a cavern brimming
I sing my new day.

For grace lost and recovered
I stand humble. Not giving. Receiving.
Until the Gorgon[1] night,
vanquished, flees.

MORNING

She has returned! She has returned!
Each morning the same and new.
Awaited every yesterday,
she must return this morning.

14

Mornings of empty hands
that promised and betrayed.
Behold this new morning unfold,
leap like a deer from the East,
awake, happy and new,
alert, eager and rich with deeds.

Brother, raise up your head
fallen to your breast. Receive her.
Be worthy of her who leaps up,
soars and darts like a halcyon,[2]
golden halcyon plunging earthward singing
Alleluia, alleluia, alleluia!

cascade (kas kād′) *n.* small, steep waterfall

Reading Strategy
Restating for Understanding In your own words, what do the first two lines of the second stanza mean?

1. **Gorgon** (gôr′ gən) any of three sisters with snakes for hair, so horrible that any beholder is turned to stone.
2. **halcyon** (hal′ sē ən) bird that, according to legend, nests on the sea and calms the waters.

ENRICHMENT: Science Connection

Deer and Gazelle

In "Time," the speaker compares morning to a deer and afternoon to a gazelle. These two animals may seem similar, but they are in fact quite different.

The species of deer found in most parts of the United States is the Virginia or white-tailed deer. These deer are about 3 feet tall at the shoulder and can weigh as much as 300 pounds. Deer have powerful legs that allow them to run and leap through the woods. Male deer have horns called antlers; sometimes males use their antlers to fight one another. For the speaker of "Time," the size and power of a deer evoke the bursting energy of the morning.

Gazelle, on the other hand, are native to Africa and Asia. Although they are similar in size to deer—and can be even larger—they are gentler animals. Both male and female have horns. Unlike deer antlers, gazelle horns are long, curved forward, and marked by dark rings. Gazelle are graceful animals, "silent and sweet" as the passing away of the afternoon the speaker of "Time" observes.

AFTERNOON

I feel my heart melt like wax
in this sweetness:
slow oil, not wine,
my veins,
I feel my life fleeting
silent and sweet as a gazelle.[3]

NIGHT

Mountain ranges dissolve,
cattle wander astray,
the sun returns to its forge,[4]
all the world slips away.

Orchard and garden are fading,
the farmhouse already immersed.
My mountains submerge their crests
and their living cry.

All creatures are sliding aslant
down toward forgetfulness and sleep.
You and I, also, my baby,
tumble down toward night's keep.

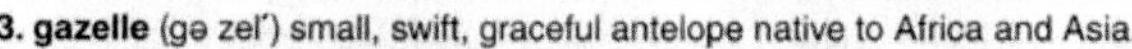

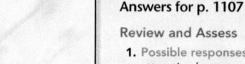

3. gazelle (gə zel′) small, swift, graceful antelope native to Africa and Asia.
4. forge (fôrj) furnace for heating metal.

Review and Assess

Thinking About the Selection

1. **Respond:** Based on these descriptions, which time of day do you find most attractive? Explain.
2. (a) **Recall:** Which parts of a day does Mistral describe? (b) **Classify:** At which times of day does the speaker seem to be exhilarated? Explain. (c) **Compare and Contrast:** At which times of day does the speaker seem more thoughtful? Explain.
3. (a) **Interpret:** Does this poem describe a particular day or one of many days? Explain. (b) **Generalize:** If you were to draw a picture of this poem, what geometric shape would it take? Explain.
4. (a) **Compare and Contrast:** Compare and contrast the depictions of night in the first section and in the final section of the poem. (b) **Generalize:** What does the speaker seem to feel about night?
5. (a) **Synthesize:** If this poem describes an entire human life, what stages of life might each section symbolize? Explain. (b) **Draw Conclusions:** Does this poem suggest a way in which one should live one's life? Explain.

Answers for p. 1107

Review and Assess

1. Possible responses: Daybreak is attractive because of dawn's special grace. Morning contains happiness and possibility. Afternoon brings overwhelming sweetness. Night is characterized by its gentle quiet.
2. **(a)** Mistral describes daybreak, morning, afternoon, and night. **(b)** The speaker is exhilarated at daybreak and in the morning, describing these time periods with passion, energy, and joy. **(c)** The speaker is more thoughtful in the afternoon and at night, while luxuriating in the slow disappearance of light and ponders the effect of the sun setting on the world.
3. **(a)** The poem describes one of many days because it avoids specifics. **(b)** Possible response: The visual representation might take the shape of a circle, representing the endless cycle of time.
4. **(a)** The depiction of night in the first section is frightening and dark, whereas its depiction in the final section is quiet and restful. **(b)** The speaker seems to welcome night as it arrives, as expressed in the final three stanzas, but grows to fear it by the end, as expressed in the second stanza.
5. **(a)** Daybreak, with its breathless arrival, represents birth; morning, with its boundless energy, represents youth; afternoon, with its quiet contentment and awareness of the passage of time, represents middle age; and night, with its fading images and description of sleep, represents old age and eventual death. **(b)** Possible response: The poem suggests that because each time of day has its own beauty, one should savor the particular pleasures of each stage of life.

CUSTOMIZE INSTRUCTION FOR UNIVERSAL ACCESS

For Special Needs Students	For English Learners	For Gifted/Talented Students
Preview each section of the poem before students read. Present each section's title, and then ask what emotions students associate with that time of day. Point out specific words and phrases that describe each time period.	Organize students into groups of four, and have each group present an oral reading of "Time." Have each student read one section. Coach students as they practice their readings.	Have students restate in their own words the basic meaning of each section of "Time." Then, encourage them to select a song to illustrate each of these sections. Have students write brief essays that explain their choices.

⑮ About the Selection

In this poem, the repitition of "green" emphasizes the power of color. The speaker's lingering passion is expressed by the color that shades his memory.

⑯ Literary Analysis

Imagery and Tone

- Read the poem aloud. Ask students to explain to what sense this poem appeals most strongly.
  Answer: The poem appeals most strongly to the sense of sight.
- Explain to students that tone—the speaker's attitude toward the subject—can be revealed by imagery.
- Invite a volunteer to read aloud the final two lines of the poem. Then, ask students the Literary Analysis question on p. 1108: What attitude toward the subject is suggested in the last two lines? Explain.
  Possible response: By saying that he will always leave a gate into his life open, it is apparent that the speaker still longs for the maiden.

⑰ Background

Art

Woman Under an Apple Tree,
by David Brayne

Best known for his watercolors, Brayne (b.1954) is from Great Britain. In the 1970s, he studied at the Nottingham School of Art and the Gloucestershire College of Art. His work is characterized by rich colors, like these in *Woman Under an Apple Tree.*

Use the following question for discussion:

How does the woman in the painting resemble the maiden of the poem? How is she different?
Possible response: Both women have strong connections to nature. The maiden has a mystical quality that the figure in the painting lacks.

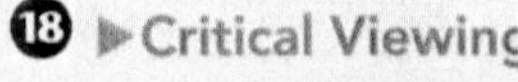

⑱ ▶ Critical Viewing

Answer: Although both the poem and painting make extensive use of the color green, the poem describes "the whole earth" as green.

⑮ Green

Juan Ramón Jiménez
translated by J. B. Trend

Green was the maiden, green, green!
Green her eyes were, green her hair.

The wild rose in her green wood
was neither red nor white, but green.

Through the green air she came.
(The whole earth turned green for her).

The shining gauze of her garment
was neither blue nor white, but green.

Over the green sea she came.
(And even the sky turned green then).

⑯ My life will always leave unlatched
a small green gate to let her in.

Literary Analysis
Imagery and Tone What attitude toward the subject is suggested in the last two lines? Explain.

⑰ ***Woman Under an Apple Tree,*** 1966, David Brayne, © The Grand Design, Leeds, England

⑱ ◀ **Critical Viewing**
In what ways are the uses of the color green in the poem and in the painting similar and different? **[Compare and Contrast]**

ENRICHMENT: Science Connection

Color

Color, a major element in the poetry of Juan Ramón Jiménez, is a complex phenomenon of light.

Light is actually a kind of electromagnetic vibration. Pure white light is made of vibrations with a certain wavelength. The full range or spectrum of color is contained within that wavelength. This means that white light can be split into all of the different colors. The human eye cannot see the spectrum within white light; however, our eyes can perceive the same colors through different means. For example, red, blue, and green are the primary colors of light. To our eyes, they can be combined to match any color in the spectrum.

Objects get their color from pigments that absorb some of the color in white light. These pigments come in combinations of red, yellow, and blue, called the *subtractive* primary colors because they subtract color from light. Green pigment, for example, absorbs the blue and red in light, so the eye perceives green.

19

Lightness

Juan Ramón Jiménez
translated by J. B. Trend

Background

Juan Ramón Jiménez was a poet for whom the visual world was extremely important. He was especially fond of color, which he found to be not merely decorative but full of emotion and meaning. Early in Jiménez's career, his poetry was dominated by green and yellow. However, as his style evolved, it became more formal and rigorous, matched by a change in his color palette to pure white. That evolution is evident in this poem.

My window-curtain,
in the majestic stillness and the silence
of the unruffled early morning,
moving softly to light breezes.

20 Oh, lovely moment
that makes the living brother to the dead,
one like another (there's no telling
which is the dead and which the living)
in the one great intensity of breathing!
. . . All the world must be dead now, or else all living still.

And those light breezes of the early morning
move the white, waving curtain
of my wide-open window . . .

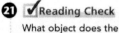

21 **Reading Check**
What object does the speaker observe in the early morning?

19 About the Selection

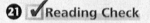

For the speaker of "Lightness," the light of the sun shining through a white curtain evokes the mysteries of the universe.

20 Literary Analysis

Imagery

- Point out that Jiménez's poetry is known for visual imagery. Then, read aloud the first stanza with the class. Ask students to explain what the speaker describes.
  Answer: The speaker describes a curtain in an open window, moving slightly in the gentle breeze of morning.
- Read aloud the second stanza with the class. Explain that the speaker is comparing the movement of the "dead" curtain to breathing.
- Ask students: In what way is the image of the curtain's movement like the process of breathing? Explain.
  Possible responses: Both the curtain's movement and breathing involve the movement of air. The speaker is watching the curtain so closely that its movement seems to match the speaker's breathing.

21 Reading Check

Answer: The speaker observes a curtain moving gently as a breeze blows through an open window.

CUSTOMIZE INSTRUCTION FOR UNIVERSAL ACCESS

For Less Proficient Readers	For Advanced Readers
Students may not recognize how every other stanza of "Lightness" is connected: Each stanza either focuses on the curtain or expresses the speaker's worldly contemplations. Have students restate in their own words the meaning of each stanza. Then, discuss the connections among the stanzas. Guide students to recognize that the curtain inspires complex thoughts for the speaker.	Students may be interested in researching the phenomenon that was so important to Jiménez—color. Start by pointing out that Jiménez's use of color shifted throughout his career. Call attention to the Background information on p. 1109, emphasizing the poet's move from green and yellow to white. Then, encourage interested students to research the scientific properties of color.

ASSESS

22 Vocabulary Development

Latin Root *-prim-*

- Call students' attention to the word *primeval,* and read its definition. Tell students that the Latin root *-prim-* means "first."
- Have students suggest other words that contain this root. List their suggestions on the board. Possible response: *Primary, primate, primitive,* and *primal* contain this root.
- Then, have students look up the meanings of the words on the board and write sentences in which they use each word correctly.

Answers for p. 1110

Review and Assess

1. Possible response: Some students will have had experiences similar to those described in "Green," when a romantic moment has stayed with them for a long time.
2. **(a)** The maiden's hair is green. **(b)** Possible response: The speaker is not describing a real person because the maiden is entirely green; however, she may be a real person as seen through the speaker's idealized memory.
3. **(a)** The speaker leaves open "a small green gate." **(b)** Possible response: The maiden is a memory the speaker treasures.
4. **(a)** The speaker observes a curtain. **(b)** Possible response: The curtain's movement mimics a person breathing.
5. **(a)** Jiménez gives a falling leaf, a sparkling drop, and a passing scent as examples. **(b)** Possible response: The curtain is similar in that it represents a simple, transient moment that inspires contemplation.
6. Possible response: Yes; green represents the eternal freshness of the speaker's memory, and white represents the purity of the speaker's contemplation.

        I think
this gentle movement of my curtain
is the life of the universe, all the breath
of the earth, all the strength
remaining with us
of earth's primeval impetus, the light sound
of its whirling, heavenly orbit.

        And the curtain's
moving now,
in the light breezes of the early morning,
all white . . .

        Oh, how full is the least thing
that fills the world, and fixes
the boundless contemplation
of such uncertainty: the leaf
that falls, the drop
that sparkles,
the scent that passes . . . !

        And the curtain
that's blue now and not white
—for it has been all night now
with me, to watch its swaying uncertainty—
is moving softly, still, in the light breeze.

primeval (pri mē′ vəl) *adj.* having to do with the earliest times

impetus (im′ pə təs) *n.* driving force

Review and Assess

Thinking About the Selections

1. **Respond:** Have you ever had an experience similar to those described in either of these poems? Explain.
2. **(a) Recall:** In "Green," what color is the maiden's hair? **(b) Interpret:** Is the speaker describing a real person? Explain.
3. **(a) Recall:** What does the speaker leave open for the maiden? **(b) Analyze:** Why do you think the speaker wants to let the maiden in?
4. **(a) Recall:** In "Lightness," what object does the speaker observe? **(b) Interpret:** Why does this object remind the speaker of something breathing?
5. **(a) Recall:** What examples does Jiménez give of the "least thing that fills the world"? **(b) Compare and Contrast:** How is the curtain like each of these examples?
6. **Make a Judgment:** Does Jiménez's symbolic use of color aid your understanding of these poems? Support your answer.

ASSESSMENT PRACTICE: Reading Comprehension

Identify Patterns of Organization (For more practice, see Test Preparation Workbook, p. 51.)

Many writing tests require students to identify patterns of organization. Use the following sample test item to help students practice this skill.

He was a good man, I say he was a man
whose heart was entirely open; a man
gentle in temper, frank as the light of day,
as filled with miracles as the spring of the year.

Which of the following best describes the organization of this stanza?

A general to specific
B chronological
C cause and effect
D specific to general

This stanza does not use a chronological, cause-and-effect, or specific-to-general organization. The main idea appears first and is supported by details. Therefore, the correct answer is *A*.

Review and Assess

Literary Analysis

Imagery

1. (a) In "Fear," in what ways does Mistral's **imagery** of a swallow provide a vivid sense of the mother's worries? (b) How are the images of the princess and queen both similar to and different from those of the swallow?
2. (a) In "The Prayer," identify one image that appeals to each of the five senses. (b) To which sense does the imagery in the poem appeal the most? Explain.
3. (a) What image does Jiménez use to describe the breathing of the universe in "Lightness"? (b) Create an outline of the poem that traces Jiménez's development of the meaning of this image.

Comparing Literary Works

4. (a) Which details in "Fear" and "Green" are reminiscent of fairy tales? (b) How is the **tone** of each poem similar and different?
5. (a) In what ways are the tones of "Lightness" and "Time" similar? (b) Which poem has more variation in tone? Why?

Reading Strategy

Restating for Understanding

6. **Restate** this passage from "The Prayer":
   Thou answerest harshly that he is unworthy of entreaty/
   who did not anoint with prayer his fevered lips, . . .
7. (a) Use a chart like the one shown to clarify two passages from "Lightness" that are unclear to you.

Passage	Restatement
1.	
2.	

   (b) Do you think this reading strategy is better suited to reading poetry or prose? Explain.

Extend Understanding

8. **Psychology Connection:** Do you think poems such as these can express more complex emotions than can other kinds of writing or art? Why or why not?

Quick Review

Imagery is language that appeals to one or more of the five senses.

Tone refers to the speaker's attitude toward his or her audience or subject.

To **restate for understanding** as you read, pause after challenging lines or passages and express them in your own words.

PHSchool.com

Take the interactive self-test online to check your understanding of these selections.

ENRICHMENT: Further Reading

Other Works by the Authors

We strongly encourage you to review any selection before assigning or recommending it to students.

Works by Gabriela Mistral

Desolación (Desolation)

Works by Juan Ramón Jiménez

Platero y Yo (Platero and I)

 ***Take It to the Net***

Visit PHSchool.com for more information on the authors.

Answers for p. 1111

Review and Assess

1. **(a)** The young bird's leaving the nest embodies the mother's fears. **(b)** The images are similar in that in each, a creature or person would be separated from its mother. The images are different in that birds' behavior is natural, but separating mothers and daughters, in certain roles, seems unnatural behavior for humans.
2. **(a)** Possible response: **Taste:** "honeycomb of my mouth"; **Hearing** "bird-trill to my ears"; **Touch** "silky as a nascent bud"; **Sight** "a timid greyhound"; and **Smell** "the perfume of a hundred fragrant vials." **(b)** Possible response: The poem appeals most to sight, because of the images of the beloved's death.
3. **(a)** Jiménez uses a white curtain. **(b)** Possible outline: I) White curtain moves in the wind. A) Movement equals breathing. B) Movement equals life of the universe. II) Curtain inspires contemplation. A) Small things make up the universe. B) Transient moments inspire thought. III) Curtain has turned blue with nightfall and continues to move.
4. **(a)** The princess, the queen, and the green maiden are reminiscent of fairy tales. **(b)** Possible response: Both poems convey love for a woman or a girl; however, in "Fear," love comes with worry whereas in "Green," love brings longing for the past.
5. **(a)** Possible response: The speakers exhibit a reverence for nature. **(b)** "Time" changes more in tone as the day is described.
6. Possible response: You say that my beloved does not deserve my prayers because he did not repent.
7. **(a)** Possible response: **Passage:** "all the strength / remaining with us / of earth's primeval impetus"; **Restatement:** The power that moves Earth exists in all of us; **Passage:** "Oh, how full is the least thing / that fills the world"; **Restatement:** Small things are important because they make up the whole world. **(b)** Possible response: Restatement is better suited to poetry because poetry's imagery can be challenging.

continued

continued from right column

8. Possible response: Poetry expresses complex emotions because its imagery can assume meaning, and its conciseness allows poets and readers to focus on complexities.

EXTEND

Answers for p. 1112

❶ Vocabulary Development

Word Analysis: Latin Root *-prim-*

1. primate
2. primary
3. primal

Spelling Strategy

1. invoking
2. chastised
3. abatement
4. debatable

Concept Development: Analogies

1. sheaves
2. impetus
3. primeval
4. anoint
5. cascade
6. invokes

❷ Grammar and Style

Practice

1. You forget, *Lord,* that I loved him. . . .
2. *My friend,* it was good to see you.
3. I assure you that I am well, *sister.*
4. Together, *my baby,* we tumble toward sleep.
5. I will do as you suggest, *sir.*

Writing Application

Possible response:

1. I'm not sure I agree, <u>Robert.</u>
2. <u>Mom,</u> can I go outside now?
3. I object, <u>your honor!</u>
4. <u>Melissa,</u> do you have the time?
5. You'll find, <u>my child,</u> that there is a great deal for you to learn.

10TH GRADE For support in teaching the Grammar and Style Lesson to tenth graders, use **Writing and Grammar,** Platinum Level, Chapter 28, Section 2.

Integrate Language Skills

❶ Vocabulary Development Lesson

Word Analysis: Latin Root *-prim-*

The Latin root *-prim-* means "first." Thus, *primeval* means "having to do with the earliest times." Complete the sentences that follow with the correct word from the list.

primary primal primate

1. The __?__ specialist studied gorillas.
2. The __?__ reason to sing is enjoyment.
3. In the dark woods, his __?__ fears kicked in.

Spelling Strategy

For words ending in silent *e*, drop the *e* before suffixes starting with vowels (*cascade* + *-ing* = *cascading*); keep the *e* for suffixes starting with consonants (*amuse* + *-ment* = *amusement*). Add the suffix shown to each word below.

1. invoke + *-ing*
2. chastise + *-ed*
3. abate + *-ment*
4. debate + *-able*

Concept Development: Analogies

An analogy is a comparison of the relationships between two different sets of ideas. Review the vocabulary list on page 1101. Then, complete each analogy that follows with the most appropriate word from the list.

invokes	cascade
anoint	primeval
sheaves	impetus

1. bales : hay :: __?__ : grain
2. __?__ : force :: impact : collision
3. __?__ : contemporary :: A : Z
4. speak : podium :: __?__ : altar
5. __?__ : waterfall :: pamphlet : book
6. __?__ : asks :: confesses : tells

❷ Grammar and Style Lesson

Direct Address

When the speaker in a literary work talks directly to someone or something, the form of speech is called **direct address.** Commas are used to separate the word or phrase of the direct address from the rest of the sentence, regardless of its position in the sentence.

Examples:

Middle: Here I rest, *Lord,* my face bowed down. . . .

Beginning: *Brother,* raise up your head. . . .

End: Do not forget me, *my love.*

Practice Identify the word or phrase of direct address in each sentence below. Add punctuation where needed.

1. You forget Lord that I loved him. . . .
2. My friend it was good to see you.
3. I assure you that I am well sister.
4. Together my baby we tumble toward sleep.
5. I will do as you suggest sir.

Writing Application Write five sentences using direct address. Underline the words of direct address and punctuate correctly.

WG *Prentice Hall Writing and Grammar Connection: Diamond Level, Chapter 27, Section 2*

TEACHING RESOURCES

The following resources can be used to enrich or extend the instruction for pp. 1112–1113.

Vocabulary

- **Selection Support:** Build Vocabulary, p. 201
- **Vocabulary and Spelling Practice Book** (Use this booklet for skills instruction.)

Grammar

- **Selection Support:** Grammar and Style, p. 202
- **Writing and Grammar,** Diamond Level, p. 694
- **Daily Language Practice Transparencies**

Writing

- **Performance Assess. and Portfolio Mgmt.,** p. 16
- **Writing and Grammar,** Diamond Level, p. 317
- **Writing and Grammar iText CD-ROM**
- **Writing Models and Graphic Organizers on Transparencies,** pp. 103–105

Listening and Speaking

- **Performance Assess. and Portfolio Mgmt.,** p. 31

❸ Writing Lesson

Interpretive Essay

In the citation for Gabriela Mistral's Nobel Prize in Literature, the Nobel committee described her work as "poems of love dedicated to death." In an essay, discuss what you think this phrase means and how it applies to one of Mistral's poems.

Prewriting Generate ideas by writing about the quotation for five minutes without stopping. After five minutes, review what you have written, circling ideas you want to develop further.

Drafting To organize your essay, state your main idea in one sentence. Then, list the ideas and details that support it. Elaborate upon each of these ideas in a paragraph. Organize the paragraphs in a logical order, and finish with a strong conclusion.

Revising As you review your essay, check that each paragraph flows logically into the next. Consider reordering paragraphs that seem out of place.

Model: Reordering Paragraphs for Coherence

The speaker admits that her lover was cruel, but then she says it doesn't matter because she loved him. That is reason enough to forgive him.

"The Prayer" is a poem about love and death. The speaker prays to God to forgive her dead lover. She offers God many reasons, but the strongest one is her love.

In an essay that is coherent, paragraphs flow in a logical order.

WG Prentice Hall Writing and Grammar Connection: Diamond Level, Chapter 14, Section 4

❹ Extension Activities

Listening and Speaking Choose the poem from this grouping that you like best. Then, prepare and deliver an **oral interpretation** of the poem. Use these tips to prepare:

- Vary the speed, rhythm, and pitch of your voice.
- Pause to emphasize ideas or add drama.
- Identify words and phrases that should be stressed.

As you deliver the poem for the class, use body language that expresses your feelings.

Research and Technology With a small group, use print and nonprint resources to research the symbolic meanings of colors. Select quotations from visual artists and writers and incorporate them into a **color chart.** Use the chart as the basis of a class discussion about the meaning of color in Jiménez's work. **[Group Activity]**

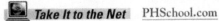

 ***Take It to the Net*** PHSchool.com

Go online for an additional research activity using the Internet.

ASSESSMENT RESOURCES

The following resources can be used to assess students' knowledge and skills.

Selection Assessment

Formal Assessment, pp. 179–181

Open-Book Tests, pp. 151–153

Test Bank Software

 ***Take It to the Net***

Visit PHSchool.com for self-tests on the selections.

Writing Rubric

Performance Assess. and Portfolio Mgmt., p. 16

Listening and Speaking Rubric

Performance Assess. and Portfolio Mgmt., p. 31

For additional diagnostics and remediation for skills covered in this grouping, use materials from the Prentice Hall Assessment System.

❸ Writing Lesson

- Have students complete the Prewriting activity on p. 1113. Then, have them work in pairs to choose main ideas for their essays.
- Encourage students to write outlines. Use the Outline organizer in **Writing Models and Graphic Organizers on Transparencies,** pp. 103–105, to model how ideas can be organized into an outline.
- Have students read aloud their drafts in small groups.
- Use the Response to Literature rubric in **Performance Assessment and Portfolio Management,** p. 16, to evaluate students' work.

10TH GRADE For support in working through the Writing Lesson with tenth graders, use **Writing and Grammar,** Platinum Level, Chapter 13, Section 4.

❹ Listening and Speaking

- Explain to students that an oral interpretation of a poem is more than a simple reading. Through their speed, rhythm, pitch, pauses, and emphases, students will convey the meaning of the poem.
- Encourage students to record themselves practicing their readings.
- Use the Speaking: Presenting an Oral Response to Literature rubric in **Performance Assessment and Portfolio Management,** p. 31, to evaluate students' oral interpretations.

CUSTOMIZE INSTRUCTION For Universal Access

To address different learning styles, use the following activities suggested in the **Extension Activities** booklet, p. 51:

- For Visual/Spatial Learners, use Activity 5.
- For Verbal/Linguistic Learners, use Activity 6.
- For Bodily/Kinesthetic and Musical/Rhythmic Learners, use Activity 7.

Under Reconstruction

Lesson Objectives

1. **To analyze and respond to literary elements**
   - Literary Analysis: Social Commentary
   - Connecting Literary Elements: Description
2. **To read, comprehend, analyze, and critique a short story**
   - Reading Strategy: Recognizing Cultural Details
   - Reading Check Questions
   - Review and Assess Questions
   - Assessment Practice (ATE)
3. **To develop word analysis skills, fluency, and systematic vocabulary**
   - Vocabulary Development Lesson: Latin Prefix *non-*
4. **To understand and apply written and oral language conventions**
   - Spelling Strategy
   - Grammar and Style Lesson: Gerunds
5. **To understand and apply appropriate writing and research strategies**
   - Writing Lesson: Character Sketch
   - Extension Activity: Slide Show Presentation
6. **To understand and apply listening and speaking strategies**
   - Extension Activity: Dialogue

10TH GRADE TEACHING A TENTH-GRADE COURSE

The literature in this section can be taught as part of a rich, balanced world literature course for tenth-grade students. For a full outline of such a course, see pp. T46–T48 in Volume 1 of this Teacher's Edition.

STEP-BY-STEP TEACHING GUIDE	PACING GUIDE
PRETEACH	
Motivate Students and Provide Background	
Use the Motivation activity (ATE p. 1114)	5 min.
Read and discuss author and background features (SE pp. 1114, 1117; ATE p. 1114) [A]	5 min.
Introduce the Concepts	
Introduce the Literary Analysis and Reading Strategy concepts (SE/ATE p. 1115) [A]	15 min.
Pronounce the vocabulary words and read their definitions (SE p. 1115)	5 min.
TEACH	
Monitor Comprehension	
Informally monitor comprehension by circulating while students read independently or in groups [A]	25 min.
Monitor students' comprehension with the Reading Check notes (SE/ATE pp. 1117, 1119, 1121)	as students read
Develop vocabulary with the Vocabulary notes (SE pp. 1117, 1119; ATE p. 1119)	as students read
Develop Understanding	
Develop students' understanding of social commentary with the Literary Analysis annotations (SE/ATE pp. 1118, 1121) [A]	5 min.
Develop students' ability to recognize cultural details, using the Reading Strategy annotations (SE/ATE pp. 1117, 1121)	5 min.
ASSESS	
Assess Mastery	
Assess students' mastery of the Reading Strategy and Literary Analysis concepts by having them answer the Review and Assess questions (SE/ATE p. 1123)	15 min.
Use one or more of the print or media Assessment Resources (ATE p. 1125) [A]	up to 45 min.
EXTEND	
Apply Understanding	
Have students complete the Vocabulary Development Lesson and the Grammar and Style Lesson (SE p. 1124)	20 min.
Apply students' ability to replace vague words with precise ones, using the Writing Lesson (SE/ATE p. 1125) [A]	45 min.
Apply students' understanding of the selections, using one or more of the Extension Activities (SE p. 1125)	20–90 min.

ACCELERATED INSTRUCTION: Use the strategies and activities identified with an [A].

10TH GRADE TEACHING TENTH-GRADE STUDENTS For support in teaching tenth graders, see the Step-by-Step Teaching notes identified with this icon.

UNIVERSAL ACCESS
- ● = Below-Level Students
- ▲ = On-Level Students
- ■ = Above-Level Students

Time and Resource Manager

Reading Level: Average
Average Number of Instructional Days: 3

RESOURCES		
PRINT	**TRANSPARENCIES**	**TECHNOLOGY**
• **Beyond Literature,** Community Connection: Automation, p. 52 ▲ ■		
• **Selection Support Workbook:** ● ▲ ■ Literary Analysis, p. 208 Reading Strategy, p. 207 Build Vocabulary, p. 205	• **Literary Analysis and Reading Transparencies,** pp. 103 and 104 ● ▲ ■	
		• **Listening to Literature** ● ▲ ■ Audiocassettes Audio CDs
• **Literary Analysis for Enrichment,** p. 52 ■		
• **Formal Assessment:** Selection Test, pp. 182–184 ● ▲ ■ • **Open-Book Tests,** pp. 154–156 ● ▲ ■ • **Performance Assessment and Portfolio Management,** pp. 19, 28 ● ▲ ■ • Prentice Hall Assessment System ● ▲ ■	• Prentice Hall Assessment System ● ▲ ■ **Skills Practice Answers and Explanations on Transparencies**	• **Test Bank Software** ● ▲ ■
• **Selection Support Workbook:** ● ▲ ■ Grammar and Style, p. 206 • **Writing and Grammar,** Diamond Level ● ▲ ■ • **Extension Activities,** p. 52 ● ▲ ■	• **Daily Language Practice Transparencies** ● ▲ • **Writing Models and Graphic Organizers on Transparencies,** pp. 13–16 ● ▲ ■	• **Writing and Grammar iText CD-ROM** ● ▲ ■ ***Take It to the Net*** PHSchool.com

BLOCK SCHEDULING: Use one 90-minute class period to preteach the selection(s) and have students read them. Use a second 90-minute class period to assess students' mastery of skills and have them complete one of the Extension Activities.

PRETEACH

Step-by-Step Teaching Guide for pp. 1114–1115

Motivation

Have students anticipate technological developments by describing what a typical day in the life of someone living fifty years from now might be like. Ask students what kinds of gadgets would be available for preparing breakfast and what kinds of transportation would take the person to work. Ask students to brainstorm aspects of everyday life from morning to night. Then, tell them that the story they are about to read addresses the consequences of technology and progress.

❶ Background

More About the Author

Many early twentieth-century Japanese fiction writers modeled their work after the French writer Emile Zola and the Naturalists. Following the example of their European predecessors, the Japanese Naturalists took a scientific approach to writing, rejecting personal experiences as subject matter for their work. Ōgai, on the other hand, openly opposed Naturalism. He believed that personal experiences should be one of the main sources of inspiration for a fiction writer and that the principles of science should not be applied.

Geography Note

Draw students' attention to the map on this page, and point out Japan. Remind students that in the late nineteenth century, Japan underwent sweeping changes and modernization. Within several decades, the nation transformed itself into a powerful industrialized state with a capitalist economy, a compulsory educational system, a formal constitution, and a good-sized national army and navy. In making this transformation, the Japanese abandoned many long-standing habits and traditions in favor of Western customs and practices.

Prepare to Read

❶ Under Reconstruction

Mori Ōgai (1862–1922)

When he was appointed to the post of surgeon general in 1907, Mori Ōgai (mō´ rē´ ō´ gä´ ē´) became the highest-ranking doctor in Japan. He held that position for nearly ten years. Yet, Ōgai is remembered far more for his contributions to literature than for his achievements as a doctor. Today, he is regarded not only as one of the leading writers of his time but also as one of the pioneers of modern Japanese literature.

Years in Germany Ōgai, whose father was also a doctor, earned his medical degree from Tokyo University. After enlisting in the Japanese imperial army, he was sent to Germany in 1884 to continue his studies in medicine.

During his four-year stay in Germany, Ōgai focused most of his studies in the areas of hygiene and bacteriology, which were then new frontiers in medicine. He excelled in his work and even published a paper documenting his research, in a German medical journal.

While in Germany, Ōgai also developed a passionate interest in both German literature and the German way of life. Many of his earliest literary works were translations of German poems and short stories. Ōgai wrote the first Japanese translations of works by Rainer Maria Rilke, August Strindberg, Henrik Ibsen, Gustave Flaubert, and many other great European writers. Perhaps his greatest accomplishment was the completion of the first Japanese translation of Johann Wolfgang von Goethe's *Faust* (1913). These works by European masters profoundly affected new generations of Japanese writers, thus helping to create modern Japanese literature.

Man of Many Talents A man of tremendous energy and intelligence, Ōgai quickly achieved success as both a writer and a doctor following his return to Japan. In his role as an army surgeon, he served in both the Sino-Japanese War (1895) and the Russo-Japanese War (1904–1905) before being promoted to the rank of surgeon general. As a writer, he became a literary celebrity in the 1890s when he published autobiographical works of fiction based on his experiences in Germany. His reputation as a writer continued to grow throughout the early part of the twentieth century with the publication of such well-known works as his novel *The Wild Goose* (1911–1913). During the final stage of his literary career, he wrote historical novels, stories, and biographies, which some readers and critics consider his finest works.

Lasting Influence In addition to his achievements as a fiction writer, Ōgai also made important contributions as a dramatist and a literary critic. As a dramatist, he not only wrote a number of Western-style plays but also strongly supported traditional Kabuki theater, a dramatic form dating back to the 1600s. As a critic, he played an important role in shaping the direction of Japanese poetry, drama, and fiction. Because of the wide scope of Ōgai's literary contributions, some contemporary critics consider him to be the most important Japanese literary figure of the entire twentieth century.

TEACHING RESOURCES

The following resources can be used to enrich or extend the instruction for pp. 1114–1115.

Background

Beyond Literature, p. 52

Take It to the Net

Visit PHSchool.com for background on the author.

Literary Analysis

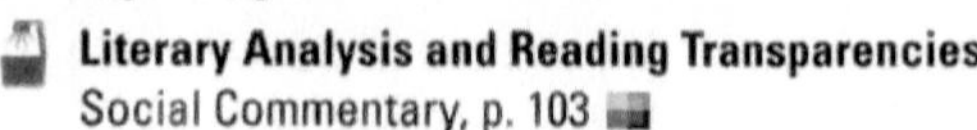

Literary Analysis and Reading Transparencies, Social Commentary, p. 103

Selection Support: Literary Analysis, p. 208

Reading

Literary Analysis and Reading Transparencies, Recognizing Cultural Details, p. 104

BLOCK SCHEDULING: Resources marked with this symbol provide varied instruction during 90-minute blocks.

Preview

Connecting to the Literature

Even though the end results may be beneficial, change can often be traumatic. This story focuses on a period of profound and unsettling change in the lives of not just one man but an entire nation.

❷ Literary Analysis

Social Commentary

Literary works often provide writers with a means of expressing their views about society. Such **social commentary** may simply be informative, offering insight into a society's values, customs, beliefs, or trends. For example, in these lines, Ōgai's narrator notices a departure from Japanese tradition:

> By the door was a pile of little cloths for wiping one's shoes and next to these a large Western doormat. . . . Apparently in this restaurant one was supposed to observe the Western custom and wear one's shoes indoors.

Social commentary may also be critical, exposing a society's hypocrisies, limitations, or failures. As you read, look for details that describe, explain, or criticize specific trends, customs, or values.

Connecting Literary Elements

Description is writing that presents details about the people, places, and things that populate a literary work. In works of fiction, descriptive writing usually includes

- sensory details—language that appeals to the five senses.
- details about characters' thoughts, appearance, and mannerisms.

Effective description can reveal more about the characters and setting than mere explanations provide. As you read, notice how Ōgai's use of description creates vivid pictures of the characters and their environment.

❸ Reading Strategy

Recognizing Cultural Details

Cultural details are those elements of daily life that signal how people in a specific place and time live, think, or worship. In this story, the author's use of cultural details shows a society in transition, suggesting that the story is about more than just a relationship between two people. As you read, use a chart like the one shown to record and interpret cultural details.

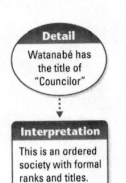

Detail
Watanabé has the title of "Councilor"

Interpretation

This is an ordered society with formal ranks and titles.

Vocabulary Development

oblique (ə blēk′) adj. inclined; slanted (p. 1117)

truncated (truŋ′ kāt əd) *adj.* cut short; with an angle cut off (p. 1117)

imposingly (im pō′ ziŋ lē) *adv.* making a strong, forceful impression (p. 1119)

nonchalantly (nän′ shə länt′ lē) *adv.* with a lack of concern (p. 1119)

Literary Analysis

Social Commentary

- Read aloud the Literary Analysis instruction on p. 1115. Explain to students that social commentary requires writers to consider the significance of cultural phenomena before offering opinions and making judgments about them.
- Ask students to list cultural trends, customs, or values. Then, lead a discussion in which students offer social commentary on any or all of these phenomena.
- For additional instruction on this concept, use the Social Commentary transparency in **Literary Analysis and Reading Transparencies,** p. 103.

❸ Reading Strategy

Recognizing Cultural Details

- Ask volunteers to read aloud the Reading Strategy instruction on p. 1115.
- Make sure students understand that literature often mirrors the culture that produces it. Tell students that cultural details can help a reader recognize the larger meaning of a literary work and understand more about the culture from which the work came.
- Explain the use of the graphic organizer on p. 1115. Encourage students to use this organizer as they read "Under Construction."

Vocabulary Development

- Pronounce each vocabulary word for students, and read the definitions as a class. Have students identify any words with which they are already familiar.

CUSTOMIZE INSTRUCTION FOR UNIVERSAL ACCESS

For Less Proficient Readers	For English Learners	For Advanced Readers
Ask students to talk to elderly family members, friends, or neighbors, asking how they feel about the cultural changes experienced during their lifetimes. Have students report their findings to the class.	Invite students to share their knowledge of the changes that took place in their native country in the late nineteenth and early twentieth centuries. Ask students to do research to supplement what they already know.	As students read "Under Reconstruction," have them gather information on Japanese culture and political history. Ask students to learn more about the events that led to Japan's modernization and admission of Western influence.

 ***e-Teach***

Visit e-Teach at PHSchool.com for teachers' essays on how to teach, with questions and answers.

TEACH

Step-by-Step Teaching Guide for pp. 1116–1122

Teaching Tenth-Grade Students

10TH GRADE Before students begin reading this selection, make sure they understand that when Japan began to trade with Western nations, Japanese culture changed.

❶ About the Selection

This selection highlights the societal and personal conflicts that can arise when different cultures interact. The story takes place in a hotel in Japan around the beginning of the twentieth century. A Japanese man and a German woman, who had once had a relationship in Germany, meet for dinner. The natural tension between them is compounded by the differences between German and Japanese social etiquette; as a result, their encounter turns out to be an unpleasant one.

❷ Background

Art

Ouda, by Takehiko Hironaga

Hironaga (b.1935) is a Japanese artist who specializes in traditional Japanese woodblock prints. His prints often depict rural villages and old country dwellings. In this print, for example, he portrays the Japanese village of Ouda.

Hironaga has used subtle shading to create a sense of depth in the work. The tiny figure helps create a sense of loneliness and isolation—feelings that are intensified by the dim, subdued colors he uses in the print.

Use the following question for discussion:

Which elements of the print contribute to its somber mood?
Answer: The gray sky and the absence of people contribute to the somber mood.

❸ ▶ Critical Viewing

Possible response: Traffic and commerce might replace the quaintness and quietness depicted in this print.

❶ Under Reconstruction

Mori Ōgai
translated by Ivan Morris

❷ 

❸ ▲ **Critical Viewing** In what ways might Western influences change this Japanese scene? **[Speculate]**

TEACHING RESOURCES

The following resources can be used to enrich or extend the instruction for pp. 1116–1122.

Literary Analysis

- **Selection Support:** Literary Analysis, p. 208
- **Literary Analysis and Reading Transparencies,** Social Commentary, p. 103 ■
- **Listening to Literature Audiocassettes** ■

Reading

- **Selection Support:** Reading Strategy, p. 207; Build Vocabulary, p. 205
- **Listening to Literature Audio CDs**

■ **BLOCK SCHEDULING:** Resources marked with this symbol provide varied instruction during 90-minute blocks.

Background

Today, Japan is one of the most highly developed countries in the world, with trade and technological links to all parts of the globe. In the mid-nineteenth century, however, it was an isolated society that still functioned under the feudal system, a decentralized form of government in which individual lords ruled over separate regions. Only with the visit of American naval officer Matthew C. Perry in 1853 and a change of government in the late 1860s did Japan open itself to contact and trade with the West. A period of rapid transformation and modernization followed. "Under Reconstruction" was written in 1910, while Japan was in the throes of these changes.

Ouda, Hironaga Takehiko, Courtesy of the Trustees of the British Museum

It had just stopped raining when Councilor Watanabé got off the tram in front of the Kabuki[1] playhouse. Carefully avoiding the puddles, he hurried through the Kobiki district in the direction of the Department of Communications. Surely that restaurant was somewhere around here, he thought as he strode along the canal; he remembered having noticed the signboard on one of these corners.

The streets were fairly empty. He passed a group of young men in Western clothes. They were talking noisily and looked as if they had all just left their office. Then a girl in a kimono[2] and a gaily-colored sash hurried by, almost bumping into him. She was probably a waitress from some local teahouse, he thought. A rickshaw[3] with its hood up passed him from behind.

Finally he caught sight of a small signboard with the inscription written horizontally in the Western style: *Seiyōken Hotel.* The front of the building facing the canal was covered with scaffolding. The side entrance was on a small street. There were two oblique flights of stairs outside the restaurant, forming a sort of truncated triangle. At the head of each staircase was a glass door; after hesitating a moment, Watanabé entered the one on the left on which were written the characters for *Entrance.*

Reading Strategy
Recognizing Cultural Details Which details in the first two paragraphs reveal some of the changes Japanese society is undergoing at the time of the story? Explain.

oblique (ə blēk′) *adj.* inclined; slanted

truncated (truŋ′ kāt əd) *adj.* cut short; with an angle cut off

1. **Kabuki** (kä bo͞o′ kē) *n.* a form of Japanese drama.
2. **kimono** (kə mō′ nō) *n.* traditional Japanese outer garment with short, wide sleeves and a sash.
3. **rickshaw** (rik′ shô′) *n.* small, two-wheeled carriage with a hood, pulled by one or two people.

5 

Reading Check
What business establishment does Councilor Watanabé enter?

4 Reading Strategy

Recognizing Cultural Details

- Review with students the Background on p. 1117. Ask students to summarize the changes that took place in Japan during the latter part of the nineteenth century.
  Answer: Contact with the West sparked a period of modernization and cultural transformation.
- Have students read the bracketed passage independently. Then, ask the Reading Strategy question on p. 1117: Which details in the first two paragraphs reveal some of the changes Japanese society is undergoing at the time of the story? Explain.
  Possible response: The tram, the group of noisy young men in Western clothes, and the unaccompanied girl in the kimono reflect the increasing Western influence and modernization of Japanese society.

5 Reading Check

Answer: Councilor Watanabé enters the Seiyōken Hotel.

CUSTOMIZE INSTRUCTION FOR UNIVERSAL ACCESS

For Special Needs Students	Less Proficient Readers	For Gifted/Talented Students
Review with students the vocabulary words and their side-column notes. Then, ask volunteers to read aloud the last paragraph on p. 1117, replacing the words *oblique* and *truncated* with *slanted* and *cut short.* Encourage students to use this strategy as they read.	Have students write journal entries in which they respond to these questions: In what ways do you think Japanese people in the late nineteenth century might have benefited from the rapid changes that were taking place? Why might some people have objected to these changes?	Have each student create a character from late nineteenth-century Japan and write a narrative from the character's perspective. Students' narratives should describe social and technological changes taking place and how those changes affect the characters' lives. Suggest that students conduct research to ensure that their narratives are historically accurate.

❻ Literary Analysis

Social Commentary and Description

- Remind students that social commentary offers insight into a society's values, customs, beliefs, or trends. Writers use descriptions—including sensory details and details about characters' thoughts, appearances, and mannerisms—to provide this insight.
- Read aloud the bracketed passage. Then, ask students: Which details in this passage reveal that the hotel is undergoing repairs? **Answer:** The sound of hammering and sawing, Watanabé's observation that the "place was under reconstruction," and the noise of the workmen reveal that the hotel is undergoing repairs.
- Then, ask the Literary Analysis question on p. 1118: In what ways might this description of the hotel under repair express the author's feelings about the state of Japanese society? **Possible response:** Like the hotel, Japanese society is undergoing a transformation. By describing the repair work at the hotel as loud and disruptive, Ōgai suggests that the cultural "reconstruction" sparked by Western influence and technological advances is disruptive to Japanese society.

Inside he found a wide passage. By the door was a pile of little cloths for wiping one's shoes and next to these a large Western doormat. Watanabé's shoes were muddy after the rain and he carefully cleaned them with both implements. Apparently in this restaurant one was supposed to observe the Western custom and wear one's shoes indoors.

There was no sign of life in the passage, but from the distance came a great sound of hammering and sawing. The place was under reconstruction, thought Watanabé.

He waited awhile, but as no one came to receive him, he walked to the end of the passage. Here he stopped, not knowing which way to turn. Suddenly he noticed a man with a napkin under his arm leaning against the wall a few yards away. He went up to him.

❻ "I telephoned yesterday for a reservation."

The man sprang to attention. "Oh yes, sir. A table for two, I believe? It's on the second floor. Would you mind coming with me, sir."

The waiter followed him up another flight of stairs. The man had known immediately who he was, thought Watanabé. Customers must be few and far between with the repairs underway. As he mounted the stairs, the clatter and banging of the workmen became almost deafening.

"Quite a lively place," said Watanabé, looking back at the waiter.

"Oh no, sir. The men go home at five o'clock. You won't be disturbed while you're dining, sir."

Literary Analysis
Social Commentary and Description In what ways might this description of the hotel under repair express the author's feelings about the state of Japanese society?

When they reached the top of the stairs, the waiter hurried past Watanabé and opened a door to the left. It was a large room overlooking the canal. It seemed rather big for just two people. Round each of the three small tables in the room were squeezed as many chairs as could possibly be fitted. Under the window was a huge sofa and next to it a potted vine about three feet high and a dwarfed plant with large hothouse grapes.

The waiter walked across the room and opened another door. "This is your dining room, sir." Watanabé followed him. The room was small—just right, in fact, for a couple. In the middle a table was elaborately set with two covers and a large basket of azaleas and rhododendrons.

With a certain feeling of satisfaction, Watanabé returned to the large room. The waiter withdrew and Watanabé again found himself alone. Abruptly the sound of hammering stopped. He looked at his watch: yes, it was exactly five o'clock. There was still half an hour till his appointment. Watanabé took a cigar from an open box on the table, pierced the end, and lit it.

Strangely enough, he did not have the slightest feeling of anticipation. It was as if it did not matter who was to join him in this room, as if he did not care in the slightest whose face it was that he would soon be seeing across that flower basket. He was surprised at his own coolness.

Puffing comfortably at his cigar, he walked over to the window and opened it. Directly below were stacked huge piles of timber. This was the main entrance. The water in the canal appeared completely stationary.

ENRICHMENT: History Connection

Commodore Matthew Perry

Commodore Matthew Perry (1794–1858)—best known for having opened Japanese ports to world trade—played a large part in the transformation of Japanese culture. In July 1853, Perry sailed the first U.S. Navy ships into Tokyo Bay. Shortly after his first meeting with the highest Japanese officials, Perry arranged a treaty with Japan, protecting American sailors and property in Japanese waters. Japan had had a previous history of hostility toward foreigners and had sealed itself off from all outside influence. Perry's diplomatic achievements not only made significant changes in American and European policy toward Japan, but also helped open Japan to the outside world.

On the other side he could see a row of wooden buildings. They looked like houses of assignation. Except for a woman with a child on her back, walking slowly back and forth outside one of the houses, there was no one in sight. At the far right, the massive redbrick structure of the Naval Museum imposingly blocked his view.

7 Watanabé sat down on the sofa and examined the room. The walls were decorated with an ill-assorted collection of pictures: nightingales on a plum tree, an illustration from a fairy tale, a hawk. The scrolls were small and narrow, and on the high walls they looked strangely short as if the bottom portions had been tucked under and concealed. Over the door was a large framed Buddhist text. And this is meant to be the land of art, thought Watanabé.

For a while he sat there smoking his cigar and simply enjoying a sensation of physical well-being. Then he heard the sound of voices in the passage and the door opened. It was she.

She wore a large Anne-Marie straw hat decorated with beads. Under her long gray coat he noticed a white embroidered batiste blouse. Her skirt was also gray. She carried a tiny umbrella with a tassel. Watanabé forced a smile to his face. Throwing his cigar in an ashtray, he got up from the sofa.

The German woman removed her veil and glanced back at the waiter, who had followed her into the room and who was now standing by the door. Then she turned her eyes to Watanabé. They were the large, brown eyes of a brunette. They were the eyes into which he had so often gazed in the past. Yet he did not remember those mauve shadows from their days in Berlin. . . .

"I'm sorry I kept you waiting," she said abruptly in German.

She transferred her umbrella to her left hand and stiffly extended the gloved fingers of her right hand. No doubt all this was for the benefit of the waiter, thought Watanabé as he courteously took the fingers in his hand.

"You can let me know when dinner is ready," he said, glancing at the door. The waiter bowed and left the room.

"How delightful to see you," he said in German.

9 The woman nonchalantly threw her umbrella on a chair and sat down on the sofa with a slight gasp of exhaustion. Putting her elbows on the table, she gazed silently at Watanabé. He drew up a chair next to the table and sat down.

"It's very quiet here, isn't it?" she said after a while.

"It's under reconstruction," said Watanabé. "They were making a terrible noise when I arrived."

"Oh, that explains it. The place does give one rather an unsettled feeling. Not that I'm a particularly calm sort of person at best."

Themes in World Literature

8 ***Japanese Literature: The Genius of Imitation***

While Japanese literature reflects Japanese culture, it is also strongly indebted to the literature of other countries. In the first few centuries A.D., Japanese lacked a written language. Influenced by Chinese thought, the Japanese adopted the Chinese writing system. Japanese literature then flowered with little outside influence until Admiral Perry, the American naval officer, arrived in 1853.

In the decades that followed, Japanese culture opened to the world, and Japanese writers discovered European literature. Japanese poets began writing in the language of everyday speech, and prose writers began exploring personal experiences in entirely new ways.

Today, Japan has one of the richest literary traditions in the world. By welcoming and transforming the influences of other cultures, Japanese writers have created a body of work that is a vital part of the world's literature while remaining distinctly Japanese.

imposingly (im pō′ ziŋ lē) *adv.* making a strong, forceful impression

nonchalantly (nän′ shə länt′ lē) *adv.* with a lack of concern

10 **✓Reading Check**

With whom does Councilor Watanabé have an appointment?

CUSTOMIZE INSTRUCTION FOR UNIVERSAL ACCESS

For Special Needs Students	For Gifted/Talented Students	For Advanced Readers
Have each student draw a simple diagram of the room as it is described in the story. Encourage students to sketch items in the room or use simple shapes with labels. Then, have students discuss why Watanabé would or would not want this room to represent his culture.	Have students draw the room and characters as they are described in the story. Students should focus not only on the room's décor, but also on the mood of the setting and the characters' behavior. Ask students to share their drawings with the class and explain their artistic choices.	Point out to students that Watanabé does not "have the slightest feeling of anticipation" before meeting his female friend. Have students write brief essays discussing what these details suggest about Watanabé, the woman, and the nature of their relationship.

7 Critical Thinking

Analyze

- After reading aloud the bracketed passage on p. 1119, call students' attention to the description of the artwork in the room.
- Ask students to discuss how this description reflects the condition of Japanese society during its transformation.
  Possible response: The description of the ill-matched and off-kilter art reflects the confusing merger of Western and Japanese cultures.

8 Background

Japanese Literature: The Genius of Imitation

Just as many Japanese writers were influenced by Western literature, a number of modern Western writers have been inspired by traditional Japanese literary forms and techniques. One of these writers was the American poet Ezra Pound, who founded the Imagist movement. Many Imagist poems bear a close resemblance to the Japanese verse forms of haiku and tanka, which generally evoke an emotional response through the presentation of a single image or a pair of contrasting images.

9 Vocabulary Development

Latin Prefix *non-*

- Call students' attention to the word *nonchalantly* on p. 1119, and read its definition.
- Tell students that *nonchalantly* contains the Latin prefix *non-*, which means "not."
- Then, have students use dictionaries to find other words that use the prefix *non-*.
  Possible response: The words *nonfiction, noninvasive,* and *nonstop* all use the prefix *non-*.

10 ✓Reading Check

Answer: Watanabé has an appointment with a German woman with whom he once had a relationship.

11 Background

Art

***Woman With a Black Hat*, by Kees van Dongen**

Van Dongen (1877–1968) was born in the Netherlands. After attending Rotterdam's Royal Academy of Fine Arts, twenty-year-old van Dongen moved to Paris.

Van Dongen met Henri Matisse and became involved in the Fauve movement. Fauve artists used very bright, unmixed colors. Van Dongen used this style to paint Parisian society, particularly portraits of women.

In this portrait, van Dongen's use of vivid green and bold black against a muted gray background makes the woman appear three-dimensional.

Use the following questions for a discussion:

- What is the mood of the woman in this painting?
  Possible response: The woman appears to be thoughtful.
- What details create this mood?
  Possible response: The stark gray background creates a feeling of isolation. The woman is neither smiling nor frowning, but simply gazing into the distance which suggests a pensive quality.

12 ▶Critical Viewing

Possible response: The German woman in the story and the woman in the picture wear large hats and have large dark eyes and brown hair.

"When did you arrive in Japan?"

"The day before yesterday. And then yesterday I happened to see you on the street."

"And why did you come?"

"Well, you see, I've been in Vladivostok[4] since the end of last year."

"I suppose you've been singing in that hotel there, whatever it's called."

"Yes."

"You obviously weren't alone. Were you with a company?"

"No, I wasn't with a company. But I wasn't alone either. . . . I was with a man. In fact you know him." She hesitated a moment. "I've been with Kosinsky."

"Oh, that Pole. So I suppose you're called Kosinskaya now."

"Don't be silly! It's simply that I sing and Kosinsky accompanies me."

"Are you sure that's all?"

"You mean, do we have a good time together? Well, I can't say it never happens."

"That's hardly surprising. I suppose he's in Tokyo with you?"

"Yes, we're both at the Aikokusan Hotel."

"But he lets you come out alone."

"My dear friend, I only let him accompany me in singing, you know." She used the word *begleiten.*[5] If he accompanied her on the piano, thought Watanabé, he accompanied her in other ways too.

"I told him that I'd seen you on the Ginza," she continued, "and he's very anxious to meet you."

"Allow me to deprive myself of that pleasure."

"Don't worry. He isn't short of money or anything."

12 ▼Critical Viewing Which qualities of the German woman in the story are captured in this portrait? **[Connect]**

***Woman With a Black Hat*, Kees van Dongen, © Scala**

4. **Vladivostok** (vlad´ i väs´ täk) seaport in southeastern Siberia, on the Sea of Japan.
5. ***begleiten*** (bə glī´ tən) German: accompany.

ENRICHMENT: Geography Connection

The Ginza

In the story, the German woman reveals that she saw Watanabé on the Ginza prior to their meeting at the hotel. For a long time, the Ginza has been the most glamorous shopping district in Tokyo and one of the best known in the world. It begins near the Imperial Palace, extending for close to two miles, and is crowded with shops. At night, the Ginza's bars and restaurants attract tourists from nearby hotels and theaters. The name *ginza* comes from the words *gin,* meaning "silver," and *za,* meaning "guild." This name comes from the silver mint that was established in the district by the Japanese government in 1612.

"No, but he probably will be before long if he stays here," said Watanabé with a smile. "And where do you plan to go next?"

"I'm going to America. Everyone tells me that Japan is hopeless, so I'm not going to count on getting work here."

"You're quite right. America is a good place to go after Russia. Japan is still backward. . . . It's still under reconstruction, you see."

"Good heavens! If you aren't careful, I'll tell them in America that a Japanese gentleman admitted his country was backward. In fact, I'll say it was a Japanese government official. You are a government official, aren't you?"

"Yes, I'm in the government."

"And behaving yourself very correctly, no doubt?"

"Frighteningly so! I've become a real *Fürst*,[6] you know. Tonight's the only exception."

"I'm very honored!" She slowly undid the buttons of her long gloves, took them off, and held out her right hand to Watanabé.

It was a beautiful, dazzlingly white hand. He clasped it firmly, amazed at its coldness. Without removing her hand from Watanabé's grasp, she looked steadily at him. Her large, brown eyes seemed with their dark shadows to have grown to twice their former size.

"Would you like me to kiss you?" she said.

13 Watanabé made a wry face. "We are in Japan," he said.

Without any warning, the door was flung open and the waiter appeared. "Dinner is served, sir."

"We are in Japan," repeated Watanabé. He got up and led the woman into the little dining room. The waiter suddenly turned on the glaring overhead lights.

The woman sat down opposite Watanabé and glanced round the room. "They've given us a *chambre séparée*,[7] she said laughing. "How exciting!" She straightened her back and looked directly at Watanabé as if to see how he would react.

"I'm sure it's quite by chance," he said calmly.

14 Three waiters were in constant attendance on the two of them. One poured sherry, the other served slices of melon, and the third bustled about ineffectually.

"The place is alive with waiters," said Watanabé.

"Yes, and they seem to be a clumsy lot," she said, squaring her elbows as she started on her melon. "They're just as bad at my hotel."

"I expect you and Kosinsky find they get in your way. Always barging in without knocking. . . ."

"You're wrong about all that, you know. Well, the melon is good anyway."

Literary Analysis
Social Commentary What is the effect of Watanabé's repeating the statement, "We are in Japan"?

Reading Strategy
Recognizing Cultural Details What does the bustling of the waiters tell you about Japanese culture?

15 **✔Reading Check**
What is the German woman's profession?

6. ***Fürst*** (fürst) German: Duke.
7. ***chambre séparée*** (shäṅ′ br′ sā pà rā′) French: separate room.

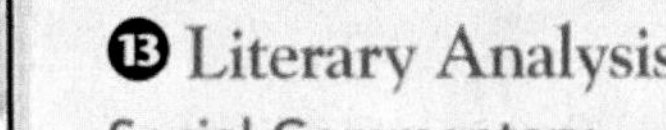

13 Literary Analysis
Social Commentary

- Review with students the Literary Analysis instruction on p. 1115. Remind them that dialogue, as well as other literary elements and techniques, can serve as vehicles for social commentary.
- Have students read the bracketed passage independently. Then, review the events leading up to this exchange. Remind students that prior to the passage, the woman asks Watanabé whether he would like her to kiss him.
- Then, ask students the Literary Analysis question on p. 1121: What is the effect of Watanabé's repeating the statement, "We are in Japan"?
Answer: By repeating this statement, Watanabé reinforces traditional Japanese behavior. Not only does he repeat the phrase to reprimand the woman, but he also seems to be trying to convince himself that traditional values still exist.

14 Reading Strategy
Recognizing Cultural Details

- Ask a volunteer to read aloud the bracketed passage. Then, ask students to define the word *bustling*.
Answer: *Bustling* means moving about quickly and causing a stir.
- Ask students the Reading Strategy question on p. 1121: What does the bustling of the waiters tell you about Japanese culture?
Answer: These waiters are not well trained and are unsure of what they should be doing. This reveals that at this point in Japan's transformation, the culture does not really understand the Western view of dining in a fine restaurant.

Monitor Progress As students continue reading, have them note other cultural details that show Japanese society in transition.

Reteach Guide students to use the graphic organizer on p. 1115 to interpret the cultural details about the waiters.

15 ✔Reading Check
Answer: The woman is a singer.

CUSTOMIZE INSTRUCTION FOR UNIVERSAL ACCESS

For Gifted/Talented Students	For Advanced Readers
Have students research Kabuki or Noh theater. Then, have students view one of the plays on videotape, if possible, and select a scene to act out. Provide students with time enough to prepare their scene and whatever props are essential. Then, have students perform the scene for the class, explaining unique elements of the particular type of drama they are presenting.	Organize students into small groups. Ask each group to brainstorm what it would be like if the United States were currently in the midst of a period of rapid transition, such as the one Japan experienced in the late nineteenth century. Have students address the following questions: What types of changes might this transition involve? By which cultures might American society be influenced and in what ways? How would the American public respond to these changes?

ASSESS

16 Critical Thinking

Speculate

- Before students read the bracketed passage, have them speculate about how the story will end. Possible response: Watanabé and the German woman will go their separate ways because they are unable to rekindle the relationship they once had.
- Then, have students read the bracketed passage and discuss whether their speculations were correct.

Answers for p. 1122

Review and Assess

1. Possible response: It would be exciting to see such changes; it may be sad to watch the town change so dramatically.
2. **(a)** Watanabé discovers a pile of small cloths and a Western doormat for wiping one's shoes. **(b)** This detail shows that Western influence is taking hold.
3. **(a)** As Watanabé arrives, workmen are remodeling the hotel. **(b)** Possible response: The construction at the hotel demonstrates that changes are permeating all aspects of Japanese society—buildings as well as customs.
4. **(a)** It appears that Watanabé and the German woman had a romantic relationship. **(b)** Possible response: The woman's eyes are "the eyes into which he had so often gazed in the past." Watanabé also seems somewhat jealous when he suspects that the woman is involved with someone else. Their uneasiness with one another indicates that they once were romantically involved.
5. **(a)** The German woman remembers sitting across from Watanabé at a restaurant. **(b)** Possible response: Now that Watanabé has returned to Japan, he adheres to Japanese customs, not Western ways.
6. Possible response: "Under Reconstruction" is a good title because it reflects the changes underway in Japanese culture.

"In America you'll be getting stacks of food to eat every morning as soon as you wake up."

The conversation drifted along lightly. Finally the waiters brought in fruit salad and poured champagne.

16 "Aren't you jealous—even a little?" the woman suddenly asked. All the time they had been eating and chatting away. She had remembered how they used to sit facing each other like this after the theater at the little restaurant above the Blühr Steps. Sometimes they had quarreled, but they had always made it up in the end. She had meant to sound as if she were joking; but despite herself, her voice was serious and she felt ashamed.

Watanabé lifted his champagne glass high above the flowers and said in a clear voice: "Kosinsky *soll leben!*" [8]

The woman silently raised her glass. There was a frozen smile on her face. Under the table her hand trembled uncontrollably.

It was still only half past eight when a solitary, black car drove slowly along the Ginza through an ocean of flickering lights. In the back sat a woman, her face hidden by a veil.

8. ***soll leben*** (zōl lā´ bən) German: shall live.

Review and Assess

Thinking About the Selection

1. **Respond:** How do you think you might feel if you saw your hometown undergoing changes like those taking place in the city in this story? Explain.
2. **(a) Recall:** What does Watanabé discover inside the door of the hotel? **(b) Generalize:** In what ways does this detail reflect larger issues in the society?
3. **(a) Recall:** What is happening at the hotel as Watanabé arrives? **(b) Analyze:** In what ways might the activity at the hotel symbolize larger trends in the society as a whole? Explain.
4. **(a) Infer:** What kind of relationship do you think Watanabé and the German woman shared in the past? **(b) Support:** Which details support your inference?
5. **(a) Distinguish:** What memory does the German woman have of her time with Watanabé in Germany? **(b) Analyze:** In what ways do you think Watanabé has changed now that he has returned to Japan?
6. **Assess:** Do you think "Under Reconstruction" is a good title for this story? Why or why not?

ASSESSMENT PRACTICE: Reading Comprehension

Notice Word Choice (For more practice, see Test Preparation Workbook, p. 52.)

Many tests require students to notice word choice in a reading passage. Use the following sample test item to give students practice with this skill.

Inside he found a wide passage. By the door was a pile of little cloths for wiping one's shoes and next to these a large Western doormat. Watanabé's shoes were muddy after the rain and he carefully cleaned them with both implements.

In this passage, the word implements means—

A toys.
B devices.
C shoes.
D restaurants.

A, C, and *D* do not make sense in the passage; *B* is the correct response.

Review and Assess

Literary Analysis

Social Commentary

1. (a) Which details about the sign announcing the Seiyoken Hotel does Watanabé observe? (b) In what ways might his observations, taken together, be an example of **social commentary**?
2. (a) With what statement does Watanabé sum up his study of the restaurant's decor? (b) How do you interpret this statement?
3. (a) How does the meeting between Watanabé and the German woman parallel the changes taking place in early twentieth-century Japan? (b) Is this story an example of social commentary or social criticism? Explain.

Connecting Literary Elements

4. Use a chart like the one shown to examine the **description** of the setting. Identify details describing both the exterior and interior of the hotel.

5. (a) Identify two details each that describe the German woman's appearance, her actions, and the qualities of her speech. (b) What impression of her personality does this description create? Explain.

Reading Strategy

Recognizing Cultural Details

6. (a) Identify four **cultural details** that Watanabé observes on his way to the hotel. (b) What do these details reveal about the nature of Japanese culture at this time?
7. What does the behavior of the waiters suggest about Japanese culture?

Extend Understanding

8. **Social Studies Connection:** Do you think technological advances, which make global communication easier, increase or decrease the need for awareness of cultural differences? Explain.

Quick Review

Social commentary is writing that describes, explains, or criticizes aspects of society or society as a whole.

Description is writing that provides details, often using sensory language, about the people, places, and things that populate a literary work.

To **recognize cultural details** as you read, notice the mention of objects, customs, religious practices, and other elements that paint a picture of life in a specific time and place.

PHSchool.com

Take the interactive self-test online to check your understanding of this selection.

ENRICHMENT: Further Reading

Other Works by Mori Ōgai

We strongly encourage you to review any selection before assigning or recommending it to students.

Historical Fiction of Mori Ōgai

The Incident at Sakai and Other Stories

The Wild Goose

Take It to the Net

Visit PHSchool.com for more information on Mori Ōgai.

Answers for p. 1123

Review and Assess

1. **(a)** Watanabé observes that the sign is small and written horizontally in the Western style. **(b)** These details might indicate Western culture's influence on Japanese society.
2. **(a)** Watanabé sums up the décor as an "ill-assorted collection of pictures." **(b)** Possible response: Watanabé finds the decor distasteful.
3. **(a)** The awkward meeting parallels Japan's awkwardness as it attempts to reconcile Japanese traditions with Western influence. **(b)** Possible response: The story is social commentary because it offers insight into traditional Japanese culture. The story can also be seen as social criticism because Ōgai exposes the difficulties of the Westernization of Japanese culture.
4. Details include the scaffolding on the building's exterior, the shoe cloths and large Western doormat, and the large room decorated with a hodgepodge of art.
5. **(a)** Possible response: The German woman wears a large hat and has dazzlingly white hands; she nonchalantly throws her umbrella on a chair and offers to kiss Watanabé; her speech is abrupt in the presence of the waiters and open when speaking only to Watanabé. **(b)** Possible response: These details reveal the woman as a product of Western culture.
6. **(a)** Watanabé notices the Kabuki playhouse, the Kobiki district, noisy young men in Western clothes, and a young woman wearing a kimono. **(b)** These details reveal that Japanese society is in flux.
7. The behavior of the waiters suggests that formal, Western-style dining in a restaurant differs from traditional Japanese dining.
8. Possible response: The rise of global communication may create a global culture, but the need for an awareness of cultural differences is still an important aspect of communication.

EXTEND

Answers for p. 1124

❶ Vocabulary Development Lesson

Word Analysis: Latin Prefix *non-*

1. b
2. a
3. c

Spelling Strategy

1. antique
2. critique
3. mystique

Fluency: True or False?

1. false; If a policeman looks at someone imposingly, he wants to assert his authority.
2. true; A window-shopper strolls through the mall without concern.
3. false; A truncated story is one that has been shortened.
4. true; A house with beams tilted obliquely would indicate that the house is not structurally sound.

❷ Grammar and Style

Practice

1. warning; object of the preposition
2. feeling; object of the preposition
3. hammering; object of the preposition
4. feeling; direct object
5. singing; object of the preposition

Writing Application

Sample response: Adopting Western practices became part of Japanese culture in the late nineteenth century. The result of changing their habits made some Japanese uneasy. The people's incorporating different practices brought new options to the culture.

10TH GRADE For support in teaching the Grammar and Style Lesson to tenth graders, use **Writing and Grammar**, Platinum Level, Chapter 20, Section 1.

Integrate Language Skills

❶ Vocabulary Development Lesson

Word Analysis: Latin Prefix *non-*

The adverb *nonchalantly* combines the prefix *non-*, which means "not," and the word part *calere*, which means "to be warm." Thus, a nonchalant person is cool or indifferent about something. Use the meanings of the roots in parentheses to match each word with its definition.

1. nondescript (describe)	a. without rival
2. nonpareil (equal)	b. lacking qualities
3. nonsense (logic)	c. without meaning

Spelling Strategy

In most words ending in *-que*, the long *e* sound preceding the *q* is spelled with an *i*. Use the clues on the left to finish the spelling of each incomplete word below.

1. old furnishings: ant________
2. summary of opinion: crit________
3. air of mystery: myst________

Fluency: True or False?

After reviewing the vocabulary list on page 1115, determine whether each of the following statements is true or false. Then, explain your answer.

1. If a policeman looks at someone *imposingly*, he wants the person to relax.
2. If a shopper *nonchalantly* strolls through the mall, he might be window-shopping.
3. If a story is *truncated*, it spins out at great length.
4. If the support beams of a house tilt at an *oblique* angle, the home is probably not safe for habitation.

❷ Grammar and Style Lesson

Gerunds

A **gerund** is a verb form that ends in *-ing* and acts like a noun. Gerunds can function as either subjects or objects in a sentence.

Subject: The clatter and banging of the workmen became almost deafening.

Object of Preposition: From the distance came a great sound of hammering and sawing.

Direct Object: Would you mind coming with me, sir?

Practice In each sentence below, identify the gerund and indicate its function.

1. With no warning, the door swung open.
2. With a feeling of satisfaction, he returned.
3. The sound of hammering stopped.
4. The place gives one an unsettled feeling.
5. I let him accompany me in singing.

Writing Application Write a paragraph describing what you learned about Japan in this story. Use and underline at least three gerunds.

WG Prentice Hall Writing and Grammar Connection: Diamond Level, Chapter 19, Section 2

TEACHING RESOURCES

The following resources can be used to enrich or extend the instruction for pp. 1124–1125.

Vocabulary

- **Selection Support:** Build Vocabulary, p. 205
- **Vocabulary and Spelling Practice Book** (Use this booklet for skills instruction.)

Grammar

- **Selection Support:** Grammar and Style, p. 206
- **Writing and Grammar,** Diamond Level, p. 446
- **Daily Language Practice Transparencies**

Writing

- **Performance Assess. and Portfolio Mgmt.,** p. 19
- **Writing and Grammar,** Diamond Level, p. 156
- **Writing and Grammar iText CD-ROM**
- **Writing Models and Graphic Organizers on Transparencies,** pp. 13–16

Listening and Speaking

- **Performance Assess. and Portfolio Mgmt.,** p. 28

BLOCK SCHEDULING: Resources marked with this symbol provide varied instruction during 90-minute blocks.

❸ Writing Lesson

Character Sketch

In "Under Reconstruction," some information is stated directly, while much is revealed indirectly. For example, Watanabé does not often make direct statements, yet the details he notices, his speech, and his actions reveal his feelings. Write a character sketch of Watanabé, basing your ideas on what he observes, says, and does.

Prewriting Reread the story, taking notes about Watanabé's observations, actions, and speech. Write a sentence summarizing these notes, which you will then refine into a thesis statement.

Drafting Write an introduction in which you state your thesis. Then, write a paragraph for each of your ideas, supporting each one with details from the story. Finish with a memorable conclusion.

Revising As you review your draft, highlight words and phrases that seem vague or imprecise. Consider replacing them with choices that are clearer and more specific.

Model: Revising to Replace Vague Words With Precise Ones

While in Japan, Watanabé is a very ~~nice~~ *cautious* man. He ~~goes~~ *hurries* to the ~~place~~ *hotel* early because he does not think it ~~okay~~ *proper* to be late.

Precise language makes writing more meaningful and informative.

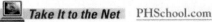

Prentice Hall Writing and Grammar Connection: Diamond Level, Chapter 8, Section 4

❹ Extension Activities

Listening and Speaking With a partner, write and perform the **dialogue** that might have occurred between Kosinsky and the German woman after her dinner with Watanabé. Use these tips to plan:

- Brainstorm for a list of questions or statements the two might say to each other.
- Role-play the encounter.

Write the dialogue. As you perform it for the class, use appropriate body language and eye contact. **[Group Activity]**

Research and Technology Japan is known for its distinctive design aesthetic. Use electronic and print resources to research examples of Japanese design, such as cars or ceramics. Use a computer program to create a **slide show presentation** that provides an overview of Japanese design.

Take It to the Net PHSchool.com

Go online for an additional research activity using the Internet.

❸ Writing Lesson

- Read the Writing Lesson instruction on p. 1125. Make sure students understand that a character sketch shows a character's personality and values.
- Use the Writing Lesson to guide students in developing their sketches. Students may draft their papers using the model in **Writing Models and Graphic Organizers on Transparencies,** pp.13–16, as a guide.
- Use the Description rubric in **Performance Assessment and Portfolio Management,** p. 19, to evaluate students' character sketches.

10TH GRADE For support in working through the Writing Lesson with tenth graders, use **Writing and Grammar,** Platinum Level, Chapter 6, Section 4.

❹ Listening and Speaking

- Explain to students that dialogue should show the characters' feelings.
- Adapt the Speaking: Delivering a Narrative Presentation rubric in **Performance Assessment and Portfolio Management,** p. 28, to evaluate students' dialogues.

CUSTOMIZE INSTRUCTION For Universal Access

To address different learning styles, use the following activities suggested in the **Extension Activities** booklet, p. 52:

- For Visual/Spatial and Bodily/Kinesthetic Learners, use Activity 5.
- For Verbal/Linguistic Learners, use Activity 6.
- For Logical/Mathematical Learners, use Activity 7.

ASSESSMENT RESOURCES

The following resources can be used to assess students' knowledge and skills.

Selection Assessment

- **Formal Assessment,** pp. 182–184
- **Open-Book Tests,** pp. 154–156
- **Test Bank Software**

Take It to the Net

Visit PHSchool.com for self-tests on the selection.

Writing Rubric

- **Performance Assess. and Portfolio Mgmt.,** p. 19

Listening and Speaking Rubric

- **Performance Assess. and Portfolio Mgmt.,** p. 28

For additional diagnostics and remediation for skills covered in this grouping, use materials from the Prentice Hall Assessment System.

My Old Home

Lesson Objectives

1. **To analyze and respond to literary elements**
   - Literary Analysis: Atmosphere
   - Connecting Literary Elements: Flashback
2. **To read, comprehend, analyze, and critique a short story**
   - Reading Strategy: Applying the Historical Context
   - Reading Check Questions
   - Review and Assess Questions
   - Assessment Practice (ATE)
3. **To develop word analysis skills, fluency, and systematic vocabulary**
   - Vocabulary Development Lesson: Latin Root *-dign-*
4. **To understand and apply written and oral language conventions**
   - Spelling Strategy
   - Grammar and Style Lesson: Correct Use of *than* and *then*
5. **To understand and apply appropriate writing and research strategies**
   - Writing Lesson: Comparison-and-Contrast Essay
   - Extension Activity: Visual Display
6. **To understand and apply listening and speaking strategies**
   - Extension Activity: Oral Report

10TH GRADE TEACHING A TENTH-GRADE COURSE
The literature in this section can be taught as part of a rich, balanced world literature course for tenth-grade students. For a full outline of such a course, see pp. T46–T48 in Volume I of this Teacher's Edition.

STEP-BY-STEP TEACHING GUIDE	PACING GUIDE
PRETEACH	
Motivate Students and Provide Background	
Use the Motivation activity (ATE p. 1126)	5 min.
Read and discuss author and background features (SE pp. 1126, 1128; ATE p. 1126) A	5 min.
Introduce the Concepts	
Introduce the Literary Analysis and Reading Strategy concepts (SE/ATE p. 1127) A	15 min.
Pronounce the vocabulary words and read their definitions (SE p. 1127)	5 min.
TEACH	
Monitor Comprehension	
Informally monitor comprehension by circulating while students read A	40 min.
Monitor students' comprehension with the Reading Check notes (SE/ATE pp. 1129, 1131, 1133, 1135)	as students read
Develop vocabulary with the Vocabulary notes (SE pp. 1128, 1130, 1131, 1132, 1133, 1135, 1136; ATE p. 1133)	as students read
Develop Understanding	
Develop students' understanding of atmosphere with the Literary Analysis annotations (SE/ATE pp. 1128, 1130, 1131, 1132) A	10 min.
Develop students' ability to apply the historical context, using the Reading Strategy annotations (SE/ATE pp. 1129, 1133, 1134, 1135) A	10 min.
ASSESS	
Assess Mastery	
Assess students' mastery of the Reading Strategy and Literary Analysis concepts by having them answer the Review and Assess questions (SE/ATE p. 1137)	15 min.
Use one or more of the print, software, or transparency or media Assessment Resources (ATE p. 1139) A	up to 45 min.
EXTEND	
Apply Understanding	
Have students complete the Vocabulary Development Lesson and the Grammar and Style Lesson (SE p. 1138) A	20 min.
Apply students' ability to revise to add transitions, using the Writing Lesson (SE/ATE p. 1139) A	45 min.
Apply students' understanding of the selection, using one or more of the Extension Activities (SE p. 1139)	20–90 min.

ACCELERATED INSTRUCTION:
Use the strategies and activities identified with an A.

10TH GRADE TEACHING TENTH-GRADE STUDENTS
For support in teaching tenth graders, see the Step-by-Step Teaching notes identified with the icons.

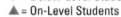

UNIVERSAL ACCESS
● = Below-Level Students
▲ = On-Level Students
■ = Above-Level Students

Time and Resource Manager

Reading Level: Average
Average Number of Instructional Days: 4

RESOURCES		
PRINT	**TRANSPARENCIES**	**TECHNOLOGY**
• **Beyond Literature,** Community Connection: Relocating, p. 53 ▲ ■		
• **Selection Support Workbook:** ● ▲ ■ Literary Analysis, p. 212 Reading Strategy, p. 211 Build Vocabulary, p. 209	• **Literary Analysis and Reading Transparencies,** pp. 105 and 106 ● ▲ ■	
• **Adapted Reader's Companion** ● • **Reader's Companion** ●		• **Listening to Literature** ● ▲ ■ Audiocassettes Audio CDs • **Reader's Companion Audio Program** ● • **Reader's Companion Adapted and English Learner's Version Audio Program** ● ▲
• **English Learner's Companion** ● ▲ • **Literary Analysis for Enrichment,** p. 53 ■		• **World Masterpieces iText CD-ROM**
• **Formal Assessment:** Selection Test, pp. 185–187 ● ▲ ■ • **Open-Book Tests,** pp. 157–159 ● ▲ ■ • **Performance Assessment and Portfolio Management,** pp. 15, 33 ● ▲ ■ • PRENTICE HALL ASSESSMENT SYSTEM ● ▲ ■	• PRENTICE HALL ASSESSMENT SYSTEM ● ▲ ■ **Skills Practice Answers and Explanations on Transparencies**	• **Test Bank Software** ● ▲ ■
• **Selection Support Workbook:** ● ▲ ■ Grammar and Style, p. 210 • **Writing and Grammar,** Diamond Level ● ▲ ■ • **Extension Activities,** p. 53 ● ▲ ■	• **Daily Language Practice Transparencies** ● ▲ • **Writing Models and Graphic Organizers on Transparencies,** pp. 95–98 ● ▲ ■	• **Writing and Grammar iText CD-ROM** ● ▲ ■ *Take It to the Net* PHSchool.com

BLOCK SCHEDULING: Use one 90-minute class period to preteach the selection(s) and have students read them. Use a second 90-minute class period to assess students' mastery of skills and have them complete one of the Extension Activities.

PRETEACH

Step-by-Step Teaching Guide for pp. 1126–1127

Motivation

Show students photographs of familiar places, taken in the past. Discuss how the places have changed. Invite students to share experiences or speculations related to visiting a place from earlier in their lives, such as an old neighborhood or a kindergarten class. How much of the difference reflects actual change, and how much reflects changes in the viewer's perspective? Tell students that these questions play an important role in this story about a man's return journey to the village where he was raised.

❶ Background

More About the Author

Lu Hsun spent part of his youth traveling abroad. He admitted that it was almost inevitable for him to search elsewhere for inspiration because he claimed that Chinese writers could not provide him with all he needed. He was most attentive to writers from Russia and Central Europe.

Geography Note

Draw students' attention to the map on this page, and identify China. Explain that throughout the late 1800s in China, a revolutionary movement aimed to overthrow the Chinese empire and establish a republic. Although the revolutionaries accomplished their goal, the new republican government turned out to be a failure.

Nearly a decade after the overthrow of the Chinese empire, Lu Hsun returned to his native town for the first time in twenty years. During this visit he realized that the upheaval had done nothing to improve people's lives.

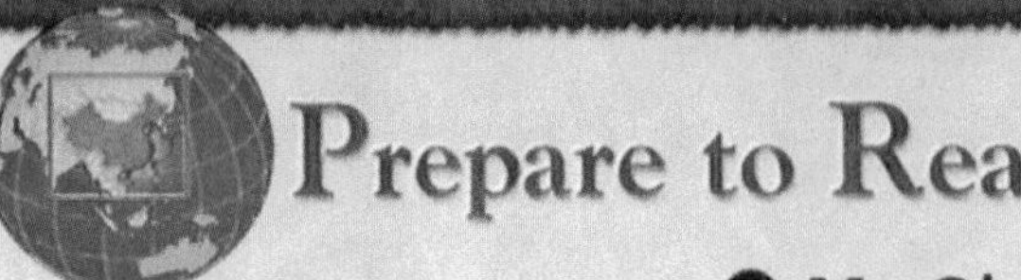

Prepare to Read

❶ My Old Home

Lu Hsun (1881–1936)

The most important event in Lu Hsun's (lo͞o shunz) life may have occurred in 1905 when he saw a film that showed a Chinese man, who had been accused of spying for the Russians, being executed by the Japanese during the Russo-Japanese War (1904–1905). For Lu Hsun, the meaning of this incident was all too clear—China, once the dominant force in the Far East, was now a backward, powerless country. China existed at the mercy not only of powerful Western nations but also of such emerging Asian powers as Japan. Although he had once been interested in medicine, Lu Hsun now believed that the real illness in Chinese society lay in the spirit of the people. He felt that literature, more than any other discipline, could provide the cure for the culture's apathy. He vowed to become a writer and to use his pen to help promote change in his country. He spent the rest of his life fulfilling this promise.

A Difficult Upbringing Lu Hsun was born into a wealthy family that stressed the ancient Chinese values of respect for education and learning. During his childhood, however, his family suffered severe financial setbacks that left them in poverty. Despite their financial problems, Lu Hsun attended a private school and later went to Japan to study medicine. However, after seeing the film of the Chinese man's execution, he abandoned the study of medicine to pursue his literary career.

The Foundations of a Writer To be a great writer, Lu Hsun understood that he needed to know more about the world and its literature. He learned to speak German and Russian, which enabled him to read original works by such writers as the Russians Nikolai Gogol and Anton Chekhov and the German Friedrich Nietzsche. He began publishing a journal called *New Life*, in which he included translations of stories by Western writers, along with articles encouraging the Chinese people to read the works of such influential Western thinkers as Nietzsche and Charles Darwin.

The New Culture Movement In 1918, Lu Hsun joined a rebellious circle of Chinese writers that came to be known as the New Culture Movement. Encouraged by the other members of this group, he wrote his first short story, "Diary of a Madman" (1918). The story is considered to be the first modern Chinese short story because it uses the real language of ordinary people rather than the scholarly language of most Chinese literature up to that time. Lu Hsun went on to become a prolific and successful writer, composing poems and essays as well as short stories. His most famous story, "The Story of Ah Q" (1921), is a satirical attack on contemporary Chinese society. His collection of stories *Old Stories Retold* (1935) also offers a darkly satirical portrait of Chinese society.

Support for the Revolution During the final years of his life, Lu Hsun's writing became increasingly political. Having witnessed the corruption and failure of China's republican government, Lu Hsun became convinced that a revolution was necessary. His work portrayed the plight of the poor and powerless and gave voice to rising revolutionary feeling. Because of his sympathy for the revolution, Lu Hsun's work has remained popular in contemporary China, even during periods when most literature was being suppressed by the government. Today, most scholars consider him to be the most important Chinese fiction writer of his time.

TEACHING RESOURCES

The following resources can be used to enrich or extend the instruction for pp. 1126–1127.

Background

Beyond Literature, p. 53

Take It to the Net

Visit PHSchool.com for background on the author.

Literary Analysis

Literary Analysis and Reading Transparencies, Atmosphere, p. 105 

Selection Support: Literary Analysis, p. 212

Reading

Literary Analysis and Reading Transparencies, Applying the Historical Context, p. 106

BLOCK SCHEDULING: Resources marked with this symbol provide varied instruction during 90-minute blocks.

Preview

Connecting to the Literature

Think what it might be like to return to a place from which you had moved. When the narrator of this story returns to his childhood village, his visit is full of both sadness and hope.

❷ Literary Analysis

Atmosphere

Emotions color perceptions. For example, when one is cheerful, the world looks quite different from the way it looks when one is dejected. In literature, this quality of reflected emotion is called **atmosphere**—the emotional nature of the world the author creates. Atmosphere arises from descriptions, especially those of the setting. As you read, use a chart like the one shown to interpret the atmosphere of this story.

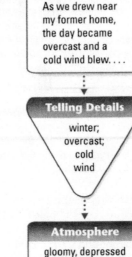

Excerpt
It was late winter. As we drew near my former home, the day became overcast and a cold wind blew. . . .

Telling Details
winter; overcast; cold wind

Atmosphere
gloomy, depressed

Connecting Literary Elements

A **flashback** is a section of a literary work that interrupts the present action of a story to relate an event from an earlier time. A flashback may take the form of a dream, a memory, a story, or an actual switch to a past time. Writers use flashbacks to provide background on events and characters in the present. In "My Old Home," Lu Hsun transitions evenly into a long flashback:

> At this point a strange picture suddenly flashed into my mind: a golden moon suspended in a deep blue sky . . .

As you read, identify the ways in which the flashback clarifies the narrator's perspective on the events he is experiencing in the present.

❸ Reading Strategy

Applying the Historical Context

In many literary works, the setting includes a **historical context** that shapes characters' attitudes and behavior. The historical context includes the elements of the setting, such as social attitudes, politics, and economics, that are particular to that place and time. As you read, apply the historical context to determine how the attitudes of the characters reflect the events and ideas of their day.

Vocabulary Development

somber (säm′ bər) *adj.* dark, gloomy; serious (p. 1128)

talisman (tal′ is mən) *n.* charm or token; lucky object (p. 1130)

stealthily (stel′ thə lē) *adv.* secretly (p. 1131)

ken (ken) *n.* range of understanding; comprehension (p. 1131)

contemptuously (kən temp′ cho͞o əs lē) *adv.* scornfully; disrespectfully (p. 1132)

indignantly (in dig′ nənt lē) *adv.* angrily (p. 1133)

gentry (jen′ trē) *n.* landowning families ranked just below the nobility (p. 1135)

dissipation (dis′ ə pā′ shən) *n.* wasteful or immoral behavior; overindulgence (p. 1136)

CUSTOMIZE INSTRUCTION FOR UNIVERSAL ACCESS

For Special Needs Students	For Less Proficient Readers	For English Learners
Have students read "My Old Home" in the **Adapted Reader's Companion.** This version provides basic-level instruction in an interactive format with questions and write-on lines. Completing the adapted version will prepare students to read the selection in the Student Edition.	Have students read the adapted version of the selection in the **Reader's Companion.** This version provides basic-level instruction in an interactive format with questions and write-on lines. After students finish the selection in **Reader's Companion,** have them complete the questions and activities in the Student Edition.	Have students read the adapted version of the selection in the **English Learner's Companion.** This version provides basic-level instruction in an interactive format with questions and write-on lines. Completing the adapted version will prepare students to read the selection in the Student Edition.

Atmosphere

- Ask students to describe the atmosphere, or mood, at school on the day before a big event such as the start of vacation. Point out that the atmosphere is something a visitor to the school could sense.
- Read aloud the Literary Analysis instruction. Make sure students understand that events and tone—the writer's attitude toward the subject, characters, or audience—can influence a work's atmosphere.
- Explain that atmosphere can help the reader understand the larger meaning or significance of a literary work.
- As students read, encourage them to use a graphic organizer like the one on p. 1127 to record details that reveal the atmosphere of the story.
- Read the Connecting Literary Elements instruction on p. 1127. Explain that a writer's use of flashback can also contribute to a work's atmosphere.

❸ Reading Strategy

Applying the Historical Context

- Ask students whether they have ever wondered why a historical figure acted as he or she did. Then, point out that historical context influences the choices people make.
- Explain that historical context also shapes what literary characters say and do; a character is bound to his or her time period.
- Have students use the Applying the Historical Context transparency in **Literary Analysis and Reading Transparencies,** p. 106, as students read "My Old Home."

Vocabulary Development

- Pronounce each vocabulary word for students, and read the definitions as a class. Have students identify any words with which they are already familiar.

E-Teach

Visit e-Teach at PHSchool.com for teachers' essays on how to teach, with questions and answers.

TEACH

Step-by-Step Teaching Guide for pp. 1128–1136

Teaching Tenth-Grade Students

10TH GRADE Ask students who have moved from one location to another to discuss the impact of the move on their relationships with friends and relatives.

1 About the Selection

Several years after the fall of the Chinese empire, the narrator of this story returns to the village of his youth. He discovers that the village and his childhood friend have changed dramatically, at least when compared with his memories. As students read, urge them to consider the narrator's adult perspective and the social changes that have taken place since the empire's fall.

2 Literary Analysis

Atmosphere

- After students read the bracketed passage, point out the word *somber*. Ask students to discuss the word's meaning and the emotions the word suggests.
  Answer: *Somber* means "dark," "gloomy," or "serious." This word suggests melancholy feelings.
- Then, ask the Literary Analysis question on p. 1128: In the first two paragraphs, which descriptive details suggest an atmosphere of gloom?
  Answer: The cold, the overcast sky, the frigid wind, the narrator's distance from home, and the desolate villages suggest an atmosphere of gloom.

3 ▶ Critical Viewing

Possible response: Warm colors and aggressive brush strokes give this landscape an intensity and vibrancy that the desolate villages in the story lack.

1 MY OLD HOME

Lu Hsun

translated by Yang Hsien-yi and Gladys Yang

Background

The Chinese Empire lasted for more than two thousand years, surviving wars, invasions, and rebellions. It produced some of the greatest cultural achievements in world history and fostered a deep respect for tradition. Yet, the society also suffered from sharp class distinctions, with an impoverished and uneducated majority who spent their lives in servitude to the rich.

From 1911 to 1912, a revolution replaced rule by an emperor with a republic. Unfortunately, the republic proved highly inefficient and weak. It was unable to centralize power effectively and factional fighting broke out, leading to widespread political instability. Poverty continued to plague the country, and many of the old social barriers remained in place. It is during this turbulent time in Chinese history that the events in this story unfold.

Braving the bitter cold, I traveled more than seven hundred miles back to the old home I had left over twenty years before.

2 It was late winter. As we drew near my former home the day became overcast and a cold wind blew into the cabin of our boat, while all one could see through the chinks in our bamboo awning were a few desolate villages, void of any sign of life, scattered far and near under the somber yellow sky. I could not help feeling depressed.

Ah! Surely this was not the old home I had remembered for the past twenty years?

The old home I remembered was not in the least like this. My old home was much better. But if you asked me to recall its peculiar charm or describe its beauties, I had no clear impression, no words to describe it. And now it seemed this was all there was to it. Then I rationalized the matter to myself, saying: Home was always like this, and although it has not improved, still it is not so depressing as I imagine: it is only my mood that has changed, because I am coming back to the country this time with no illusions.

This time I had come with the sole object of saying goodbye. The old house our clan had lived in for so many years had already been sold to another family, and was to change hands before the end of the year. I had to hurry there before New Year's Day to say goodbye forever to the

Literary Analysis
Atmosphere In the first two paragraphs, which descriptive details suggest an atmosphere of gloom?

somber (säm´ bər) *adj.* dark; gloomy; serious

3 **Critical Viewing ▶** Does the landscape depicted in this painting seem like one of the "desolate villages" the narrator observes? **[Interpret]**

TEACHING RESOURCES

The following resources can be used to enrich or extend the instruction for pp. 1128–1136.

Literary Analysis

- **Selection Support,** Literary Analysis, p. 212
- **Literary Analysis and Reading Transparencies,** Atmosphere, p. 105 ■

Reading

- **Selection Support:** Reading Strategy, p. 211; Build Vocabulary, p. 209 ■

- **Reader's Companion**
- **Adapted Reader's Companion**
- **English Learner's Companion**
- **Listening to Literature Audiocassettes**
- **Listening to Literature Audio CDs**

■ **BLOCK SCHEDULING:** Resources marked with this symbol provide varied instruction during 90-minute blocks.

familiar old house, and to move my family to another place where I was working, far from my old home town.

At dawn on the second day I reached the gateway of my home. Broken stems of withered grass on the roof, trembling in the wind, made very clear the reason why this old house could not avoid changing hands. Several branches of our clan had probably already moved away, so it was unusually quiet. By the time I reached the house my mother was already at the door to welcome me, and my eight-year-old nephew, Hung-erh, rushed out after her.

Though mother was delighted, she was also trying to hide a certain feeling of sadness. She told me to sit down and rest and have some tea, letting the removal wait for the time being. Hung-erh, who had never seen me before, stood watching me at a distance.

4 But finally we had to talk about the removal. I said that rooms had already been rented elsewhere, and I had bought a little furniture; in addition it would be necessary to sell all the furniture in the house in order to buy more things. Mother agreed, saying that the luggage was nearly all packed, and about half the furniture that could not easily be moved had already been sold. Only it was difficult to get people to pay up. 5

"You must rest for a day or two, and call on our relatives, and then we can go," said mother.

"Yes."

Reading Strategy Applying Historical Context Based on your knowledge of the political situation in China at the time, why might the family have had financial trouble?

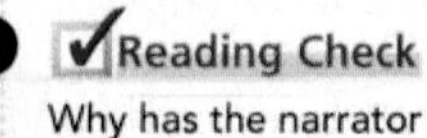

Why has the narrator returned home?

6

Landscape, Zhu Qizhan, Photo Courtesy of Joan Lebold Cohen

CUSTOMIZE INSTRUCTION FOR UNIVERSAL ACCESS

For English Learners	For Gifted/Talented Students	For Advanced Readers
Have students work with native English speakers to describe the places their families lived before settling where they are now. Have students also show their partners the locations on a map to help them develop map-reading skills in English.	Have students talk to older family members or friends who left their homes to move closer to family members. Have students ask their interview subjects to talk about why they moved, and then ask students to use the information they have learned to write a poem or a narrative.	Tell students that this story is a fictionalized account of the author's real-life return to his childhood village. Ask students to take notes as they read, speculating on which details are fictionalized and which are real. Then, have students discuss their notes and explain their speculations.

4 Reading Strategy
Applying Historical Context

- Have students reread the Background on p. 1128. Make sure they understand that "My Old Home" is set during a time of political and economic instability.
- Read aloud the bracketed passage. Then, ask students what detail indicates the family's financial problems.
  Answer: The family must sell what they have in order to buy things they need.
- Then, ask students the Reading Strategy question on p. 1129: Based on your knowledge of the political situation in China at the time, why might the family have had financial troubles?
  Possible response: The family has fallen victim to the widespread poverty brought on by political upheaval.

5 ✔Reading Check

Answer: The narrator has returned home to move his family to another place and to say goodbye.

6 Background
Art

Landscape, by Zhu Qizhan

Zhu Qizhan (1892–1996) was born in China and studied oil painting at the Shanghai College of Arts before becoming a teacher in 1913. He also studied Japanese and Western art, especially the works of Vincent van Gogh and Henri Matisse. Zhu Qizhan specialized in painting landscapes, flowers, and plants.

Use the following questions for discussion:

- How does this painting help illustrate the narrator's distance from his past?
  Possible response: The muddled composition suggests the narrator's unfamiliarity with the village he once knew. Like the narrator, a viewer can identify some elements in the scene (such as the structure in the right-hand corner), but the landscape as a whole is indistinct.
- How does the painting's composition convey the difficulty of traveling to the village?
  Possible response: The village is remote, sitting in a valley between high hills.

7 Literary Analysis

Atmosphere and Flashback

- Remind students that a flashback is a section of a literary work that interrupts the present action of a story to relate an event from an earlier time. Then, have a volunteer read aloud the bracketed passage.
- Ask students the first Literary Analysis question on p. 1130: Which clues in the text suggest that a flashback has begun?
  Answer: A strange picture flashing into the narrator's mind signals the beginning of the flashback.

Monitor Progress Have students compare the narrator's age and situation in the present action with the scenario in the flashback.
Possible response: In the present action of the story, the narrator is an adult at his old home, speaking with his aged mother about what must be done to prepare for the move. During the flashback, the narrator recalls a seaside scene, where a boy wearing a silver necklet confronts an animal in a watermelon patch.

Reteach If students are having difficulty recognizing flashbacks, direct their attention to the Connecting Literary Elements instruction on p. 1127. Make sure students understand the difference between present action of a story and flashback.

8 Literary Analysis

Atmosphere and Flashback

- Have students read the bracketed passage independently. Then, ask: What atmosphere does the narrator's attitude create?
  Possible response: The narrator's attitude toward Jun-tu creates an atmosphere of tenderness, innocence, and nostalgia.
- Ask students the second Literary Analysis question on p. 1130: What information does the flashback provide about the narrator's relationship with Jun-tu?
  Answer: The flashback reveals that the narrator was very likely Jun-tu's first friend.

"Then there is Jun-tu. Each time he comes here he always asks after you, and wants very much to see you again. I told him the probable date of your return home, and he may be coming any time."

7 At this point a strange picture suddenly flashed into my mind: a golden moon suspended in a deep blue sky and beneath it the seashore, planted as far as the eye could see with jade-green watermelons, while in their midst a boy of eleven or twelve, wearing a silver necklet and grasping a steel pitchfork in his hand, was thrusting with all his might at a *zha*[1] which dodged the blow and escaped between his legs.

Literary Analysis
Atmosphere and Flashback Which clues in the text suggest that a flashback has begun?

This boy was Jun-tu. When I first met him he was just over ten—that was thirty years ago, and at that time my father was still alive and the family well off, so I was really a spoiled child. That year it was our family's turn to take charge of a big ancestral sacrifice, which came round only once in thirty years, and hence was an important one. In the first month the ancestral images were presented and offerings made, and since the sacrificial vessels were very fine and there was such a crowd of worshippers, it was necessary to guard against theft. Our family had only one part-time laborer. (In our district we divide laborers into three classes: those who work all the year for one family are called full-timers; those who are hired by the day are called dailies; and those who farm their own land and only work for one family at New Year, during festivals or when rents are being collected are called part-timers.) And since there was so much to be done, he told my father that he would send for his son Jun-tu to look after the sacrificial vessels.

When my father gave his consent I was overjoyed, because I had long since heard of Jun-tu and knew that he was about my own age, born in the intercalary month,[2] and when his horoscope was told it was found that of the five elements[3] that of earth was lacking, so his father called him Jun-tu (Intercalary Earth). He could set traps and catch small birds.

Literary Analysis
Atmosphere and Flashback What information does the flashback provide about the narrator's relationship with Jun-tu?

8 I looked forward every day to New Year, for New Year would bring Jun-tu. At last, when the end of the year came, one day mother told me that Jun-tu had come, and I flew to see him. He was standing in the kitchen. He had a round, crimson face and wore a small felt cap on his head and a gleaming silver necklet round his neck, showing that his father doted on him and, fearing he might die, had made a pledge with the gods and buddhas,[4] using the necklet as a talisman. He was very shy, and I was the only person he was not afraid of. When there was no one else there, he would talk with me, so in a few hours we were fast friends.

talisman (tal' is mən) *n.* charm or token; lucky object

I don't know what we talked of then, but I remember that Jun-tu was in high spirits, saying that since he had come to town he had seen many new things.

1. ***zha*** (ja) badgerlike animal.
2. **intercalary month** Each year in the Chinese lunar calendar consists of 360 days, divided into twelve months of twenty-nine or thirty days. To compensate for the five additional days included in the traditional Western calendar, a thirteenth, or intercalary, month is added to the Chinese calendar every few years.
3. **the five elements** metal, water, fire, wood, and earth.
4. **buddhas** (bo͞o' dəz) In the Buddhist religion, buddhas are figures who embody divine wisdom and virtue.

ENRICHMENT: Science Connection

Calendars

The narrator says that Jun-tu was born in an intercalary month. The Chinese calendar is a lunar calendar, meaning that it follows the cycle of the moon as it completes its phases. This cycle is a fairly consistent 29 1/2 days. However, a year ends when the Earth completes its revolution around the Sun. The Chinese count that time period at 360 days, which does not result in an even number of months. That is why they must have the intercalary month. Other cultures that used a lunar month include the ancient Babylonians, the Romans, the ancient Greeks, and the ancient Hebrews. These calendars evolved into modern lunisolar calendars—the years are solar, and the months are lunar. This, again, requires an intercalary system of adjustments to make the months fit into the year.

The next day I wanted him to catch birds.

"Can't be done," he said. "It's only possible after a heavy snowfall. On our sands, after it snows, I sweep clear a patch of ground, prop up a big threshing basket with a short stick, and scatter husks of grain beneath. When the birds come there to eat, I tug a string tied to the stick, and the birds are caught in the basket. There are all kinds: wild pheasants, woodcocks, wood-pigeons, 'blue-backs.' . . ."

Accordingly I looked forward very eagerly to snow.

"Just now it is too cold," said Jun-tu another time, "but you must come to our place in summer. In the daytime we'll go to the seashore to look for shells, there are green ones and red ones, besides 'scare-devil' shells and 'buddha's hands.' In the evening when dad and I go to see to the watermelons, you shall come too."

"Is it to look out for thieves?"

"No. If passers-by are thirsty and pick a watermelon, folk down our way don't consider it as stealing. What we have to look out for are badgers, hedgehogs and *zha*. When under the moonlight you hear the crunching sound made by the *zha* when it bites the melons, then you take your pitchfork and creep stealthily over. . . ."

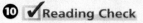

stealthily (stel' thə lē) *adv.* secretly

I had no idea then what this thing called *zha* was—and I am not much clearer now for that matter—but somehow I felt it was something

9 like a small dog, and very fierce.

"Don't they bite people?"

"You have a pitchfork. You go across, and when you see it you strike. It's a very cunning creature and will rush toward you and get away between your legs. Its fur is as slippery as oil. . . ."

Literary Analysis
Atmosphere and Flashback How would you describe the atmosphere created in this flashback? Explain your answer.

I had never known that all these strange things existed: at the seashore there were shells all colors of the rainbow; watermelons were exposed to such danger, yet all I had known of them before was that they were sold in the greengrocer's.

"On our shore, when the tide comes in, there are lots of jumping fish, each with two legs like a frog. . . ."

Jun-tu's mind was a treasure-house of such strange lore, all of it outside the ken of my former friends. They were ignorant of all these things and, while Jun-tu lived by the sea, they like me could see only the four corners of the sky above the high courtyard wall.

ken (ken) *n.* range of understanding; comprehension

Unfortunately, a month after New Year Jun-tu had to go home. I burst into tears and he took refuge in the kitchen, crying and refusing to come out, until finally his father carried him off. Later he sent me by his father a packet of shells and a few very beautiful feathers, and I sent him presents once or twice, but we never saw each other again.

Now that my mother mentioned him, this childhood memory sprang into life like a flash of lightning, and I seemed to see my beautiful old home. So I answered:

"Fine! And he—how is he?"

10 **✓Reading Check**
Which childhood friend does the narrator fondly recall?

9 Literary Analysis

Atmosphere and Flashback

- Have students take turns reading aloud the bracketed passage. Then, ask: How would a ten- or eleven-year-old child react to stories about unknown things from someone who lived far away? How does the narrator's description of Jun-tu reflect this reaction?
  Possible response: As a child, the narrator—like any child this age—responds with wonder and curiosity. Jun-tu's fascinating stories expose the narrator to a new realm of understanding and cause him to value Jun-tu more than his other friends.
- Point out to students that a story's present action and a flashback within a story can have entirely different atmospheres. Revisit the Literary Analysis question on p. 1128 and students' responses. Then, ask students the Literary Analysis question on p. 1131: How would you describe the atmosphere created in this flashback? Explain your answer.
  Possible response: The atmosphere is full of excitement and amazement. The narrator takes in all of Jun-tu's knowledge and lore, calling Jun-tu's mind "a treasure house."

10 ✓Reading Check

Answer: The narrator fondly recalls Jun-tu, the son of the family's part-time laborer.

CUSTOMIZE INSTRUCTION FOR UNIVERSAL ACCESS

For Special Needs Students	For Less Proficient Readers	For Advanced Readers
Have students recall people they know or have known who they believe have a great deal of knowledge. Lead students in a discussion about what they learned and how they felt about what they learned from these people.	Ask students to write journal entries about people they have known who have "treasure-house minds" like Jun-tu's. Have students write about whether their view of the people has changed over time and speculate whether the narrator's relationship with Jun-tu will change.	Have students reread p. 1131. Then, ask them to write brief essays discussing why Jun-tu's knowledge of birds and shells seems so important and so worthwhile to the narrator. Ask students to explain why the writer included this detail in the flashback.

11 Literary Analysis

Atmosphere and Flashback

- Have students describe the atmosphere of the part of the story that takes place in the present.
  Possible response: The atmosphere is one of sadness and frustration.
- Then, read aloud the bracketed passage. Ask students the Literary Analysis question on p. 1132: In what ways does the atmosphere of the flashback differ from the present? Explain.
  Possible response: The atmosphere of the flashback is much more joyful and optimistic than the present, which is characterized by melancholy and sadness.

12 ▶Critical Viewing

Possible response: The photograph resembles the narrator's family during affluent times because the family members are well dressed and wearing jewelry.

13 Background

Art

Postcard of Chinese Family, by Mark Rykoff

In Chinese society, the traditional family is patriarchal and patrilineal, meaning that the head of the family is male and that family membership is traced through male family members. A clan, such as the one the narrator refers to in "My Old Home," is a group of property-holding individuals who share a common surname.

Use the following questions for discussion:

- What elements of this photograph recall details in the story?
  Possible response: The necklaces recall Jun-tu wearing his silver necklet. The father is absent from this family photograph, just as the narrator's father is now absent.
- What is the atmosphere of this photograph? How does this atmosphere compare with both atmospheres created in the story?
  Possible response: The family members' serious expressions echo the somber atmosphere of the family's present situation. However, the family seems proud and worthy of admiration, qualities that match the atmosphere of the flashback.

"He? . . . He's not at all well off either," said mother. And then, looking out of the door: "Here come those people again. They say they want to buy our furniture; but actually they just want to see what they can pick up. I must go and watch them."

Mother stood up and went out. The voices of several women could be heard outside. I called Hung-erh to me and started talking to him, asking him whether he could write, and whether he would be glad to leave.

"Shall we be going by train?"

"Yes, we shall go by train."

"And boat?"

"We shall take a boat first."

11 "Oh! Like this! With such a long mustache!" A strange shrill voice suddenly rang out.

I looked up with a start, and saw a woman of about fifty with prominent cheekbones and thin lips. With her hands on her hips, not wearing a skirt but with her trousered legs apart, she stood in front of me just like the compass in a box of geometrical instruments.

I was flabbergasted.

"Don't you know me? Why, I have held you in my arms!"

I felt even more flabbergasted. Fortunately my mother came in just then and said:

"He has been away so long, you must excuse him for forgetting. You should remember," she said to me, "this is Mrs. Yang from across the road. . . . She has a beancurd shop."

Literary Analysis
Atmosphere and Flashback In what ways does the atmosphere of the flashback differ from the present? Explain.

12 **▼Critical Viewing** Do you think this photograph resembles the narrator's family during his affluent childhood or after they suffered financial hardship? Explain. **[Distinguish]**

13

Then, to be sure, I remembered. When I was a child there was a Mrs. Yang who used to sit nearly all day long in the beancurd shop across the road, and everybody used to call her Beancurd Beauty. She used to powder herself, and her cheekbones were not so prominent then nor her lips so thin; moreover she remained seated all the time, so that I had never noticed this resemblance to a compass. In those days people said that, thanks to her, that beancurd shop did very good business. But, probably on account of my age, she had made no impression on me, so that later I forgot her entirely. However, the Compass was extremely indignant and looked at me most contemptuously, just as one might look at a Frenchman who had never heard of Napoleon or an American who had never heard of Washington, and smiling sarcastically she said:

"You had forgotten? Naturally I am beneath your notice. . . ."

contemptuously (kən temp' cho͞o əs lē) *adv.* scornfully; disrespectfully

ENRICHMENT: Culinary Arts

Bean Curd

In "My Old Home," Mrs. Yang operates a successful bean curd shop. A common ingredient in Asian cooking, bean curd, also called *tofu*, is made from soybeans that have been soaked, pressed, and boiled. The resulting pulp and soy milk are separated, and coagulants are added to the milk to separate the curds from the whey. The milk is then poured into molds, and the whey is drained off, leaving custard-like cakes. These cakes are cut into squares and stored in water.

Fermented bean curd is popular in China. Unlike the Japanese variety, Chinese tofu has a more solid texture and a stronger flavor. Generally perceived to have a bland taste, tofu is extremely versatile and can be seasoned and used to create a variety of dishes. It is also rich in protein, calcium, potassium, and iron.

"Certainly not . . . I . . ." I answered nervously, getting to my feet.

"Then you listen to me, Master Hsun. You have grown rich, and they are too heavy to move, so you can't possibly want these old pieces of furniture anymore. You had better let me take them away. Poor people like us can do with them."

14 "I haven't grown rich. I must sell these in order to buy. . . ."

"Oh, come now, you have been made the intendant of a circuit,[5] how can you still say you're not rich? You have three concubines now, and whenever you go out it is in a big sedan-chair with eight bearers. Do you still say you're not rich? Hah! You can't hide anything from me."

Knowing there was nothing I could say, I remained silent.

"Come now, really, the more money people have the more miserly they get, and the more miserly they are the more money they get . . ."
15 remarked the Compass, turning indignantly away and walking slowly off, casually picking up a pair of mother's gloves and stuffing them into her pocket as she went out.

After this a number of relatives in the neighborhood came to call. In the intervals between entertaining them I did some packing, and so three or four days passed.

One very cold afternoon, I sat drinking tea after lunch when I was aware of someone coming in, and turned my head to see who it was. At the first glance I gave an involuntary start, hastily stood up and went over to welcome him.

The newcomer was Jun-tu. But although I knew at a glance that this was Jun-tu, it was not the Jun-tu I remembered. He had grown to twice his former size. His round face, once crimson, had become sallow and acquired deep lines and wrinkles; his eyes too had become like his father's, the rims swollen and red, a feature common to most peasants who work by the sea and are exposed all day to the wind from the ocean. He wore a shabby felt cap and just one very thin padded jacket, with the result that he was shivering from head to foot. He carried a paper package and a long pipe, nor was his hand the plump red hand I remembered, but coarse and clumsy and chapped, like the bark of a pine tree.

Delighted as I was, I did not know how to express myself, and could only say:

"Oh! Jun-tu—so it's you? . . ."

After this there were so many things I wanted to talk about, they should have poured out like a string of beads: woodcocks, jumping fish, shells, *zha*. . . . But I was tongue-tied, unable to put all I was thinking into words.

He stood there, mixed joy and sadness showing on his face. His lips moved, but not a sound did he utter. Finally, assuming a respectful attitude, he said clearly:

"Master! . . ."

5. **intendant of a circuit** an official position between the county and provincial levels.

Reading Strategy
Applying Historical Context In what ways do the Compass's remarks reflect the historical realities of the period?

indignantly (in dig′ nənt lē) *adv.* angrily

16  **Reading Check**

What level of status and wealth does the Compass believe the narrator has attained?

14 Reading Strategy

Applying Historical Context

- Review with students the historical context of this story by rereading the Background section on p. 1128. Remind students that historical context shapes the characters' attitudes and behaviors.
- Then, have a volunteer read aloud the bracketed passage. Ask students to compare the narrator's economic situation with that of the people who live in the village.
  Answer: The narrator has an official position that pays him well enough to help his family and grant him status symbols. Those who live in the village are poor.
- Ask students the Reading Strategy question on p. 1133: In what ways do the Compass's remarks reflect the historical realities of the period?
  Answer: The Compass's remarks show the difference between the social classes. Although the narrator does not see himself as wealthy, the Compass points out that the narrator has far more than the people in the village.

15 Vocabulary Development

Latin Root *-dign-*

- Draw students' attention to the word *indignantly* on p. 1133, and read its definition.
- Tell students that this word contains the Latin root *-dign-*, which means "worth" or "worthy." Therefore, *indignantly* means "showing anger at unworthy treatment."
- Have students use dictionaries to identify and list other words that use the root *-dign-*.
  Possible response: The words *indignant, dignify,* and *indignity* all use the root *-dign-*.
- Ask students to use each word in a sentence.

16 ✔Reading Check

Answer: The Compass believes that the narrator has attained a high level of status and wealth.

CUSTOMIZE INSTRUCTION FOR UNIVERSAL ACCESS

For Special Needs Students	For Less Proficient Readers	For Advanced Readers
Have students create a two-column chart entitled *Jun-tu.* In one column, have them list details about Jun-tu's appearance when he was a child. In the other column, have them list details about Jun-tu's adult appearance. Then, have students discuss the changes in Jun-tu and what might have caused them.	Have students make a two-column chart comparing Jun-tu and the narrator as adults. In the first column, have them list Jun-tu's situation and characteristics. In the other, have them list the narrator's situation and characteristics. Then, have students discuss how and why the characters' lives differ.	Have students compare the narrator's childhood view of Jun-tu with Jun-tu's adult reality. Have students speculate on the accuracy of the narrator's memory and how the narrator's maturity affects both his memory and his current observations.

17 Background

The Vernacular

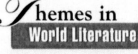

In addition to using the vernacular in dialogue, many writers use dialect, a form of a language spoken by people in a particular region or group. Dialects differ in pronunciation, grammar, and word choice. Writers often use dialect to make their characters seem realistic and to create local color.

18 Reading Strategy

Applying Historical Context

- Remind students that Jun-tu, as a laborer, occupies a different social class from the narrator's.
- Read aloud the bracketed passage. Then, ask students to discuss the social realities that Jun-tu failed to understand as a child that he now appreciates.
  Possible response: Jun-tu now understands that as a member of the labor class, he must contend with the realities of heavy taxation, unreliable income, and no government protection. He understands that the narrator occupies a higher social standing and views the bond he and the narrator shared as children as somewhat shameful.

I felt a shiver run through me; for I knew then what a lamentably thick wall had grown up between us. Yet I could not say anything.

He turned his head to call:

"Shui-sheng, bow to the master." Then he pulled forward a boy who had been hiding behind his back, and this was just the Jun-tu of twenty years before, only a little paler and thinner, and he had no silver necklet.

"This is my fifth," he said. "He's not used to company, so he's shy and awkward."

Mother came downstairs with Hung-erh, probably after hearing our voices.

"I got your letter some time ago, madam," said Jun-tu. "I was really so pleased to know the master was coming back. . . ."

"Now, why are you so polite? Weren't you playmates together in the past?" said mother gaily. "You had better still call him Brother Hsun as before."

18 "Oh, you are really too. . . . What bad manners that would be. I was a child then and didn't understand." As he was speaking Jun-tu motioned Shui-sheng to come and bow, but the child was shy, and stood stock-still behind his father.

"So he is Shui-sheng? Your fifth?" asked mother. "We are all strangers, you can't blame him for feeling shy. Hung-erh had better take him out to play."

When Hung-erh heard this he went over to Shui-sheng, and Shui-sheng went out with him, entirely at his ease. Mother asked Jun-tu to sit down, and after a little hesitation he did so; then leaning his long pipe against the table he handed over the paper package, saying:

"In winter there is nothing worth bringing; but these few beans we dried ourselves, if you will excuse the liberty, sir."

When I asked him how things were with him, he just shook his head.

"In a very bad way. Even my sixth can do a little work, but still we haven't enough to eat . . . and then there is no security . . . all sorts of people want money, there is no fixed rule . . . and the harvests are bad. You grow things, and when you take them to sell you always have to pay several taxes and lose money, while if you don't try to sell, the things may go bad. . . ."

He kept shaking his head; yet, although his face was lined with wrinkles, not one of them moved, just as if he were a stone statue. No doubt he felt intensely bitter, but could not express himself. After a pause he took up his pipe and began to smoke in silence.

From her chat with him, mother learned that he was busy at home and had to go back the next day; and since he had had no lunch, she told him to go to the kitchen and fry some rice for himself.

Themes in World Literature

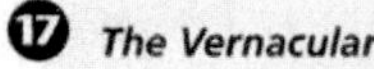

17 *The Vernacular*

A vibrant popular literature is only possible if the language in which books are written is familiar to the ordinary person. For example, if contemporary American writers restricted themselves to ancient Greek, it is unlikely that they would sell many books. The vernacular, or language of the common people, is critical for the flowering of popular literature.

Lu Hsun is considered the first modern Chinese writer because he used the vernacular and wrote about topics of concern to ordinary people. In Japan, Mori Ōgai (p. 1114) is credited with similar innovations.

Use of the vernacular in the West has a longer history. In the seventeenth century, Shakespeare combined the formal rhythms spoken by his heroes with the more casual language of his lower-class characters. In the nineteenth century, English Romantics used the ordinary diction of daily speech.

Today, one measure of the success of a literary work is that the dialogue sounds true-to-life. The wealth of contemporary literature worldwide is due, in large part, to the use of the vernacular.

ENRICHMENT: Culture Connection

Distinctions

Whether in a sharply divided class system such as that of early China or the more open system of modern America, all communities have groups within them. These groups may be defined by neighborhood, by ethnic heritage, by profession (such as all those who work for a major employer), by school, and so forth. Beyond these groups, people are also both producers and consumers of commercial goods. Of course, people move among many groups, as when a person who sells clothing decides to buy tires for his or her car.

In the historical context of this story, people are more clearly divided into consumers and service providers (or laborers). The story's narrator now faces the challenge of bridging the gap between himself, a consumer, and Jun-tu, a service provider.

19 After he had gone out, mother and I both shook our heads over his hard life: many children, famines, taxes, soldiers, bandits, officials and landed gentry, all had squeezed him as dry as a mummy. Mother said that we should offer him all the things we were not going to take away, letting him choose for himself.

That afternoon he picked out a number of things: two long tables, four chairs, an incense burner and candlesticks, and one balance. He also asked for all the ashes from the stove (in our part we cook over straw, and the ashes can be used to fertilize sandy soil), saying that when we left he would come to take them away by boat.

gentry (jen′ trē) *n.* landowning families ranked just below the nobility

That night we talked again, but not of anything serious; and the next morning he went away with Shui-sheng.

Reading Strategy
Applying Historical Context How have the political and economic realities of the time affected Jun-tu?

After another nine days it was time for us to leave. Jun-tu came in the morning. Shui-sheng did not come with him—he had just brought a little girl of five to watch the boat. We were very busy all day, and had no time to talk. We also had quite a number of visitors, some to see us off, some to fetch things, and some to do both. It was nearly evening when we left by boat, and by that time everything in the house, however old or shabby, large or small, fine or coarse, had been cleared away.

As we set off, in the dusk, the green mountains on either side of the river became deep blue, receding toward the stern of the boat.

Hung-erh and I, leaning against the cabin window, were looking out together at the indistinct scene outside, when suddenly he asked:

"Uncle, when shall we go back?"

"Go back? Do you mean that before you've left you want to go back?"

"Well, Shui-sheng has invited me to his home. . . ." He opened wide his black eyes in anxious thought.

Mother and I both felt rather sad, and so Jun-tu's name came up again. Mother said that ever since our family started packing up, Mrs. Yang from the beancurd shop had come over every day, and the day before in the ash-heap she had unearthed a dozen bowls and plates, which after some discussion she insisted must have been buried there by Jun-tu, so that when he came to remove the ashes he could take them home at the same time. After making this discovery Mrs. Yang was very pleased with herself, and flew off taking the dog-teaser with her. (The dog-teaser is used by poultry keepers in our parts. It is a wooden cage inside which food is put, so that hens can stretch their necks in to eat but dogs can only look on furiously.) And it was a marvel, considering the size of her feet, how fast she could run.

I was leaving the old house farther and farther behind, while the hills and rivers of my old home were also receding gradually ever farther in the distance. But I felt no regret. I only felt that all round me was an invisible high wall, cutting me off from my fellows, and this depressed me thoroughly. The vision of that small hero with the silver necklet among the watermelons had formerly been as clear as day, but now it suddenly blurred, adding to my depression.

Mother and Hung-erh fell asleep.

20 **✔ Reading Check**
What title of respect does Jun-tu use to address the narrator?

19 Reading Strategy
Applying Historical Context

- Ask a volunteer to describe Jun-tu's temperament as a child.
  Possible response: Jun-tu was shy, inquistive, and talkative with the narrator: he viewed himself as the narrator's equal.
- Then, ask students to read the bracketed passage independently. Have students describe Jun-tu's temperament in the present.
  Possible response: Jun-tu is deferential, defeated, and sad.
- Ask students the Reading Strategy question on p. 1135: How have the political and economic realities of the time affected Jun-tu?
  Answer: Jun-tu's lack of security and his inability to provide adequate food and other necessities for his family have destroyed the joy and confidence he had as a child.

20 ✔ Reading Check

Answer: Jun-tu refers to the narrator as "master."

CUSTOMIZE INSTRUCTION FOR UNIVERSAL ACCESS

For Gifted/Talented Students	For Advanced Readers
Organize students into small groups. Ask each group to create illustrations that depict the relationship between Jun-tu and the narrator both in the present and in the story's flashback. Encourage each group to use color, shading, and other techniques to capture the moods of each scene. After students have finished their illustrations, have each group present its work.	Have students consider the narrator's relationship with Jun-tu at present and during the flashback. Have students work in small groups to discuss the importance of the flashback to the theme of friendship. Remind them to specify the passages from the flashbacks that support the theme of friendship.

ASSESS

21 Critical Thinking

Draw Conclusions

- Have students read and paraphrase the bracketed passage. Then, ask students why the narrator uses the phrase "treadmill existence" to describe his own life and the word "stupefied" to describe Jun-tu.
Possible response: By referring to his life as a "treadmill existence," the narrator means that his life is monotonous. *Stupefied* means "made dull" or "stunned." The narrator uses this word to emphasize how suffering has worn down Jun-tu.
- Ask students what conclusions they can draw about the narrator's views of his nation's political evolution.
Possible response: The narrator acknowledges that despite the perception of class distinctions, the political situation has prevented members of any class from achieving or progressing.

Answers for p. 1136

Review and Assess

1. Possible response: Yes; the narrator's better fortune and his friendship require him to help Jun-tu. No; because he cannot change Jun-tu's life or status, the narrator can do nothing.
2. **(a)** The narrator finds his old house in disrepair. **(b)** The narrator's family no longer has money to maintain their house.
3. **(a)** As a child, the narrator admired Jun-tu and felt proud to be his friend. **(b)** As adults, the narrator's and Jun-tu's social positions prevent them from renewing their friendship. **(c)** Political and financial realities and sharp social distinctions have divided the two men.
4. **(a)** The narrator compares the worship of idols to hope. **(b)** The narrator wishes that the next generation will be free of social barriers.
5. Possible response: The story is better as a work of fiction because it makes a political issue more personal: however, the story is an effective document for political change because it may move people to action.

21 I lay down, listening to the water rippling beneath the boat, and knew that I was going my way. I thought: although there is such a barrier between Jun-tu and myself, the children still have much in common, for wasn't Hung-erh thinking of Shui-sheng just now? I hope they will not be like us, that they will not allow a barrier to grow up between them. But again I would not like them, because they want to be akin, all to have a treadmill existence like mine, nor to suffer like Jun-tu until they become stupefied,[6] nor yet, like others, to devote all their energies to dissipation. They should have a new life, a life we have never experienced.

dissipation (dis' ə pā' shən) *n.* wasteful or immoral behavior; overindulgence

The access of hope made me suddenly afraid. When Jun-tu asked for the incense burner and candlesticks I had laughed up my sleeve at him to think that he still worshiped idols and could not put them out of his mind. Yet what I now called hope was no more than an idol I created myself. The only difference was that what he desired was close at hand, while what I desired was less easily realized.

As I dozed, a stretch of jade-green seashore spread itself before my eyes, and above a round golden moon hung in a deep blue sky. I thought: hope cannot be said to exist, nor can it be said not to exist. It is just like roads across the earth. For actually the earth had no roads to begin with, but when many men pass one way, a road is made.

6. **stupefied** (sto͞o' pə fīd) *v.* stunned; made dull or lethargic.

Review and Assess

Thinking About the Selection

1. **Respond:** Do you think the narrator should have tried to help Jun-tu? Explain.
2. **(a) Recall:** In what state of repair does the narrator find his old house? **(b) Infer:** How have the family's circumstances changed since the narrator was a child? Explain.
3. **(a) Classify:** Describe the narrator's relationship with Jun-tu when they were children. **(b) Compare and Contrast:** As adults, how has their relationship changed? **(c) Analyze Cause and Effect:** What do you think is the main reason for this change? Explain.
4. **(a) Interpret:** At the end of the story, to what emotion does the narrator compare Jun-tu's worship of idols? **(b) Analyze:** In what ways does the narrator wish the next generation will be different from his own?
5. **Evaluate:** Do you think this story is more effective as a work of fiction or as a document advocating political change? Explain.

ASSESSMENT PRACTICE: Reading Comprehension

Notice Word Choice (For more practice, see Test Preparation Workbook, p. 53.)

Many standardized tests require students to answer questions about word choice. Use the following sample test item to help students practice this skill.

Then I rationalized the matter to myself, saying: Home was always like this, and although it has not improved, still it is not so depressing as I imagine.

In this passage, rationalized means—

A ignored.
B explained.
C imagined.
D saw.

Remind students to look for context clues to help them determine a word's meaning. *A*, C, and *D* do not make sense. *B* is the correct answer.

Review and Assess

Literary Analysis

Atmosphere

1. (a) How would you describe the **atmosphere** of this story? (b) Identify five details in the setting and action that create this atmosphere.
2. (a) How does the atmosphere created in the section describing the narrator's friendship with Jun-tu contrast with the atmosphere of the present time of the story? (b) What circumstances account for this difference?
3. (a) In what ways does this story suggest that the failure of Chinese society has damaged individuals? (b) How does the atmosphere of the story reinforce that message?

Connecting Literary Elements

4. (a) What prompts the narrator's **flashback** to his childhood friendship with Jun-tu? (b) How does the flashback help you understand the narrator's feelings when he meets the adult Jun-tu?
5. (a) What other techniques might the author have used to convey the information revealed in the flashback? (b) Why do you think the author used a flashback instead of another explanatory technique?

Reading Strategy

Applying the Historical Context

6. (a) Use a chart like this to **apply the historical context** to this story.

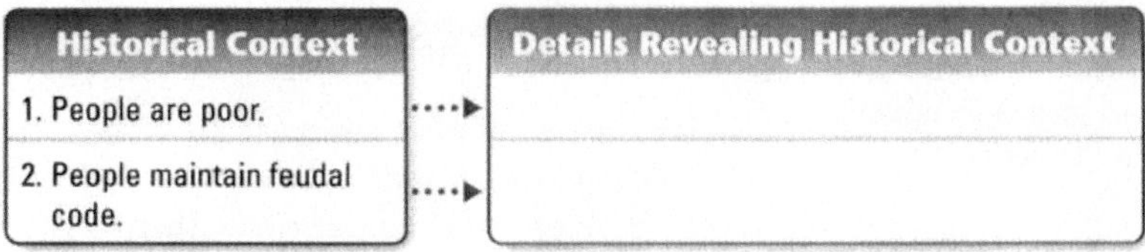

Historical Context	Details Revealing Historical Context
1. People are poor.	
2. People maintain feudal code.	

(b) Based on this story, how might the reading of fiction enhance one's understanding of history? Explain.

7. At the time of the story, China was experiencing overpopulation. How are Jun-tu's troubles indicative of this problem?

Extend Understanding

8. **Social Studies Connection:** Does American society suffer from any of the same problems that are evident in this story? Explain.

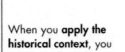

Quick Review

Atmosphere is the emotional quality of the world the author creates.

A **flashback** is a section of a literary work that interrupts the relating of events in the present to tell about an event from an earlier time.

When you **apply the historical context**, you determine how the circumstances and attitudes of the characters reflect the events and ideas of their day.

Take It to the Net

PHSchool.com

Take the interactive self-test online to check your understanding of this selection.

ENRICHMENT: Further Reading

Other Works by Lu Hsun

We strongly encourage you to review any selection before assigning or recommending it to students.

"Diary of a Madman"

Old Tales Retold

"The True Story of Ah Q"

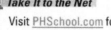

Take It to the Net

Visit PHSchool.com for more information on Lu Hsun.

Answers for p. 1137

Review and Assess

1. **(a)** The atmosphere is sad and depressing. **(b)** Details include the cold wind, the overcast sky, the desolate villages, the disrepair of the family home, and the destitution of the villagers.
2. **(a)** Unlike the atmosphere of the present, the atmosphere of the flashback is one of excitement, joy, and wonder. **(b)** When the narrator was young, he was affluent and unaware of the problems around him. As an adult, the narrator is less affluent and more aware of suffering, so the innocence of childhood is gone.
3. **(a)** Jun-tu, as a symbol of the spirit of the Chinese people, is shown as defeated by society and its hardships. We see him change from a vivacious young child to a miserable, wounded adult. **(b)** The juxtaposition of the story's two atmospheres demonstrates the drastic and devastating effects of the failure.
4. **(a)** The narrator's mother says that Jun-tu wants to see the narrator again. **(b)** Possible response: When the narrator sees Jun-tu as a defeated adult, the memory of Jun-tu's youth makes Jun-tu's transformation, and the narrator's resulting sadness, all the more poignant.
5. **(a)** The author could have started the story in the past, or dialogue could have revealed the past. **(b)** Possible response: Flashback allows the narrator to reflect on his past perceptions of Jun-tu and contrast them with his current feelings about his friend's situation.
6. **(a)** Possible responses: **Details Revealing Historical Context:** 1. People cannot pay for the furniture they have taken. 2. Jun-tu calls the narrator "master." **(b)** Fiction allows a reader to understand in a specific and personal way how historical events impact people's lives.

continued

continued from right column

7. It is difficult for Jun-tu to take care of his large family on his meager income.
8. Possible response: Even though American society does not have a formalized class system, it does have social distinctions and poverty.

EXTEND

Answers for p. 1138

❶ Vocabulary Development

Word Analysis: Latin Root *-dign-*

1. c 2. b 3. a

Spelling Strategy

1. plentiful
2. defiance
3. hastily
4. beautify

Fluency: Clarify Meaning

1. A somber sky often precedes a storm.
2. Someone might be indignant after he or she was insulted.
3. People treated contemptuously might react defensively.
4. The United States has no formal gentry, but there are wealthy families who wield power.
5. An animal might move stealthily when stalking prey.
6. A four-leaf clover might be considered a modern-day talisman.
7. One who lives a life of dissipation will never have anything because he or she wastes everything.
8. As space travel becomes more common, it will no longer lie outside the ken of most people, because in time, they will come to understand it.

❷ Grammar and Style

Practice

1. than
2. then
3. then
4. than
5. then

Writing Application

Sample response:

More *than* anything else, my home is a source of comfort. I clean my house on Monday, and *then* it stays tidy all week. Now I like my house more *than* I did when I first moved in. *Then* I was not sure I would like it more *than* my old apartment. I thought about it for a month, and *then* I was sure.

10TH GRADE For support in teaching the Grammar and Style Lesson to tenth graders, use **Writing and Grammar,** Platinum Level, Chapter 26, Section 2.

Integrate Language Skills

❶ Vocabulary Development Lesson

Word Analysis: Latin Root *-dign-*

The root of *indignant* is *-dign-*, which means "worth" or "worthy" in Latin. Therefore, *indignant* means "angry at being treated in an unworthy way." Match each word below with its definition.

1. dignified
2. dignity
3. dignitary

a. person of great worth
b. honor or respect
c. behaving with a strong sense of self-worth

Spelling Strategy

When a word ends in a consonant plus *y*, change the *y* to *i* before adding most suffixes: *stealthy* + *-ly* = *stealthily*. Add the suffix indicated to each of the words below.

1. plenty + *-ful*
2. defy + *-ance*
3. hasty + *-ly*
4. beauty + *-fy*

Fluency: Clarify Meaning

Answer each question below with a complete sentence, and then explain your reasoning.

1. When would you see a *somber* sky?
2. Why might someone become *indignant*?
3. If you speak *contemptuously*, how might people react?
4. Does the population of the United States include members of the *gentry*?
5. When might an animal move *stealthily*?
6. What object might be considered a modern-day *talisman*?
7. Why might someone who lives a life of *dissipation* have problems?
8. Will space travel remain outside the *ken* of most people?

❷ Grammar and Style Lesson

Commonly Confused Words: *than* and *then*

Than and *then* are two words that are often confused. The word *than* is a conjunction and is used in comparisons, while the word *then* is an adverb used to show time or sequence of events.

Than: I traveled more *than* seven hundred miles back to the old home I had left. *(comparison)*

Then: You hear the crunching sound, *then* you take your pitchfork and creep stealthily over. *(sequencing)*

Practice Identify the word that correctly completes each sentence below.

1. The narrator last saw his home more (than, then) twenty years ago.
2. Everyone was younger (than, then).
3. The narrator first travels by train and (than, then) boards a boat.
4. The house seems shabbier (than, then) it did when he was a child.
5. The narrator pauses briefly to look around; (than, then) he leaves his old house.

Writing Application Write five sentences about your home. Use either *than* or *then* in each sentence.

WG *Prentice Hall Writing and Grammar Connection: Diamond Level, Chapter 25, Section 2*

TEACHING RESOURCES

The following resources can be used to enrich or extend the instruction for pp. 1138–1139.

Vocabulary

- **Selection Support:** Build Vocabulary, p. 209
- **Vocabulary and Spelling Practice Book** (Use this booklet for skills instruction.)

Grammar

- **Selection Support:** Grammar and Style, p. 210
- **Writing and Grammar,** Diamond Level, p. 646
- **Daily Language Practice Transparencies**

Writing

- **Performance Assess. and Portfolio Mgmt.,** p. 15
- **Writing and Grammar,** Diamond Level, p. 168
- **Writing and Grammar iText CD-ROM**
- **Writing Models and Graphic Organizers on Transparencies,** pp. 95–98

Research and Technology

- **Performance Assess. and Portfolio Mgmt.,** p. 33

BLOCK SCHEDULING: Resources marked with this symbol provide varied instruction during 90-minute blocks

❸ Writing Lesson

Comparison-and-Contrast Essay

In "My Old Home," the narrator juxtaposes his memories of the past with the realities of the present. Following his example, write a comparison-and-contrast essay exploring the differences between the world of the narrator's childhood and that of his adulthood. Focus your essay by discussing one element, such as people, things, ideas, or emotions.

Prewriting Make a two-column chart in which you list the two things you are comparing and contrasting. Then, record specific details that reveal the similarities and differences between them.

Drafting In your introduction, state your topic and your main idea. In the body of your essay, present the details that support your ideas. Address each point of comparison and contrast thoroughly.

Revising Review your essay, making sure that your ideas flow logically. If the connections between ideas are unclear, add appropriate transitions.

Model: Revising to Add Transitions

The narrator saw a broken-down house with a damaged roof. *In contrast,* When he was a child, the house was well kept. *While it had once been full of relatives,* Only his mother and nephew lived there now.

Appropriate transitional words and phrases clarify the relationships between ideas.

WG Prentice Hall Writing and Grammar Connection: Diamond Level, Chapter 9, Sections 1–5

❹ Extension Activities

Listening and Speaking With a small group, research China's revolution of 1911–1912 and deliver an **oral report** on the subject. Use these tips to prepare:

- Organize the topic into categories, and assign independent research tasks.
- Choose a facilitator, and divide up responsibilities for the presentation.

As you prepare your report, create smooth transitions between topics and speakers. **[Group Activity]**

Research and Technology In this story, Jun-tu is born in the "intercalary" month. Using both electronic and print resources, research a calendar system created by another culture. Then, create a **visual display** that compares and contrasts the system you have researched with the one used in the West.

 ***Take It to the Net*** PHSchool.com

Go online for an additional research activity using the Internet.

ASSESSMENT RESOURCES

The following resources can be used to assess students' knowledge and skills.

Selection Assessment

- **Formal Assessment,** pp. 185–187
- **Open-Book Test,** pp. 157–159
- **Test Bank Software**

 ***Take It to the Net***

Visit PHSchool.com for self-tests on the selection.

Writing Rubric

- **Performance Assess. and Portfolio Mgmt.,** p. 15

Listening and Speaking Rubric

- **Performance Assess. and Portfolio Mgmt.,** p. 33

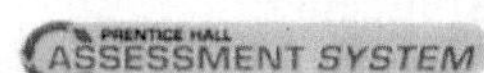

For additional diagnostics and remediation for skills covered in this grouping, use materials from the Prentice Hall Assessment System.

Lesson Support for p. 1139

❸ Writing Lesson

- Remind students that a comparison-and-contrast essay analyzes the similarities and differences between two or more things.
- Suggest that students skim the story to help them choose elements for their essays. Students should provide textual evidence to support their main ideas.
- Encourage students to use the Comparison-and-Contrast Organizer in **Writing Models and Graphic Organizers,** pp. 95–98, to help them organize their essays.
- Use the Exposition: Comparison-and-Contrast rubric in **Performance Assessment and Portfolio Management,** p.15, to evaluate students' essays.

10TH GRADE For support in working through the Writing Lesson with tenth graders, use **Writing and Grammer,** Platinum Level, Chapter 9, Section 1.

❹ Research and Technology

- Remind students that they will need to understand the way the alternate calendar works in order to create the visual display and explain it to the class.
- Have students present their visual displays to the class. Use the Listening and Speaking Progress Chart in **Performance Assessment and Portfolio Management,** p. 33, to evaluate students' work.

CUSTOMIZE INSTRUCTION
For Universal Access

To address different learning styles, use the following activities suggested in the **Extension Activities** booklet, p. 53:

- For Visual/Spatial Learners, use Activity 5.
- For Logical/Mathematical and Verbal/Linguistic Learners, use Activity 6.
- For Bodily/Kinesthetic Learners, use Activity 7.

The Artist

Lesson Objectives

1. **To analyze and respond to literary elements**
   - Literary Analysis: Conflict
   - Connecting Literary Elements: Round and Flat Characters
2. **To read, comprehend, analyze, and critique a poem**
   - Reading Strategy: Identifying Cause and Effect
   - Reading Check Questions
   - Review and Assess Questions
   - Assessment Practice (ATE)
3. **To develop word analysis skills, fluency, and systematic vocabulary**
   - Vocabulary Development Lesson: Greek Word Part *-logy*
4. **To understand and apply written and oral language conventions**
   - Spelling Strategy
   - Grammar and Style Lesson: Appositives and Appositive Phrases
5. **To understand and apply appropriate writing and research strategies**
   - Writing Lesson: Newspaper Editorial
   - Extension Activity: Group Report
6. **To understand and apply listening and speaking strategies**
   - Extension Activity: Themed Reading

10TH GRADE TEACHING A TENTH-GRADE COURSE

The literature in this section can be taught as part of a rich, balanced world literature course for tenth-grade students. For a full outline of such a course, see pp. T46–T48 in Volume 1 of this Teacher's Edition.

STEP-BY-STEP TEACHING GUIDE	PACING GUIDE
PRETEACH	
Motivate Students and Provide Background	
Use the Motivation activity (ATE p. 1140)	5 min.
Read and discuss author and background features (SE pp. 1140, 1142; ATE p. 1140) A	5 min.
Introduce the Concepts	
Introduce the Literary Analysis and Reading Strategy concepts (SE/ATE p. 1141) A	15 min.
Pronounce the vocabulary words and read their definitions (SE p. 1141)	5 min.
TEACH	
Monitor Comprehension	
Informally monitor comprehension by circulating while students read independently or in groups A	35 min.
Monitor students' comprehension with the Reading Check notes (SE/ATE pp. 1142, 1145, 1147)	as students read
Develop vocabulary with the Vocabulary notes (SE pp. 1142, 1144, 1146, 1147; ATE p. 1142)	as students read
Develop Understanding	
Develop students' understanding of conflict with the Literary Analysis annotations (SE/ATE p. 1145) A	10 min.
Develop students' ability to identify cause and effect, using the Reading Strategy annotations (SE/ATE p. 1148)	10 min.
ASSESS	
Assess Mastery	
Assess students' mastery of the Reading Strategy and Literary Analysis concepts by having them answer the Review and Assess questions (SE/ATE p. 1149)	15 min.
Use one or more of the print, software, or transparency Assessment Resources (ATE p. 1151) A	up to 45 min.
EXTEND	
Apply Understanding	
Have students complete the Vocabulary Development Lesson and the Grammar and Style Lesson (SE p. 1150) A	20 min.
Apply students' ability to address opposing viewpoints, using the Writing Lesson (SE/ATE p. 1151) A	45 min.
Apply students' understanding of the selections, using one or more of the Extension Activities (SE p. 1151)	20–90 min.

A ACCELERATED INSTRUCTION: Use the strategies and activities identified with an A.

UNIVERSAL ACCESS
- ● = Below-Level Students
- ▲ = On-Level Students
- ■ = Above-Level Students

10TH GRADE TEACHING TENTH-GRADE STUDENTS For support in teaching the selection(s) to tenth-grade students, see the step-by-step teaching notes identified with the icon shown here.

Time and Resource Manager

Reading Level: Average
Average Number of Instructional Days: 3

RESOURCES		
PRINT	**TRANSPARENCIES**	**TECHNOLOGY**
• **Beyond Literature,** Conflict Resolution, p. 54 ▲ ■		• **Interest Grabber Video,** Tape 2, Unit 8, Segment 8 ● ▲ ■
• **Selection Support Workbook:** ● ▲ ■ Literary Analysis, p. 216 Reading Strategy, p. 215 Build Vocabulary, p. 213	• **Literary Analysis and Reading Transparencies,** pp. 107 and 108 ● ▲ ■	
		• **Listening to Literature** ● ▲ ■ Audiocassettes Audio CDs
• **Literary Analysis for Enrichment,** p. 54 ■		
• **Formal Assessment:** Selection Test, pp. 188–190 ● ▲ ■ • **Open-Book Tests,** pp. 160–162 ● ▲ ■ • **Performance Assessment and Portfolio Management,** pp. 11, 33 ● ▲ ■ • Prentice Hall ASSESSMENT SYSTEM ● ▲ ■	Prentice Hall ASSESSMENT SYSTEM ● ▲ ■ **Skills Practice Answers and Explanations on Transparencies**	• **Test Bank Software** ● ▲ ■
• **Selection Support Workbook:** ● ▲ ■ Grammar and Style, p. 214 • **Writing and Grammar,** Diamond Level ● ▲ ■ • **Extension Activities,** p. 54 ● ▲ ■	• **Daily Language Practice Transparencies** ● ▲ • **Writing Models and Graphic Organizers on Transparencies,** pp. 103–106 ● ▲ ■	• **Writing and Grammar iText CD-ROM** ● ▲ ■ ***Take It to the Net*** PHSchool.com

PRETEACH

Step-by-Step Teaching Guide for pp. 1140–1141

Motivation

Tell students that, like the mother in the story they are about to read, some artists find commercial work distracting and unappealing. Ask students to name some jobs that combine the practical with the aesthetic in a way that is artistically satisfying and financially rewarding.

Interest Grabber Video

As an alternative, play "The Artist: The Indian Art of Rug-Making" on Tape 2 to engage student interest.

❶ Background

More About the Author

Tagore's striking appearance helped shape his image as a prophetic sage and teacher. He believed that children should be one with their natural surroundings and that they should be sensitive to the environmental balance of Earth. The school he founded in Bolpur in 1901 was called Santiniketan ("abode of peace"). Many of its classes were held under the campus trees. When the school expanded its program in 1922 to become Visva-Bharati University, the curriculum continued to emphasize Tagore's concern for social reform and for international unity.

Geography Note

Point out the map of India on this page. Tell students that India has a long artistic legacy. Among the most notable achievements of Indian art are the frescoes, or wall paintings, found in artificial caves near the village of Ajanta in western India. These caves were created by Buddhist monks during the period from the first century B.C. to the seventh century A.D. The vibrant and colorful paintings on the walls depict Buddhist themes.

Prepare to Read

❶ The Artist

Rabindranath Tagore (1861–1941)

In 1915, the Indian writer Rabindranath Tagore (rə bēn′ drə nät′ tä′ gôr) was knighted by the British government in recognition of his literary contributions. This was one of the British Empire's highest honors, yet four years later Tagore renounced his title. He did so to protest the Amritsar (əm rit′ sər) Massacre, in which British troops fired on a group of unarmed Indian protesters.

A Gifted Family Tagore was born in Bengal, which was then a province of British India. Tagore's family was highly accomplished. His father was a famous Hindu philosopher and religious reformer. Other members of Tagore's family distinguished themselves in art, music, and finance. A gifted child with a wide range of intellectual and artistic talents, Tagore began writing at the age of eight. He composed both poems and short stories, producing a series of books while he was still in his twenties. This highly productive period culminated with the publication of *Manasi* (mä nä′ sē), one of his finest collections of verse, in 1890.

A Witness to Suffering In 1891, Tagore moved to his father's estate in a rural section of Bengal, where he developed a deep awareness of the poverty and other hardships faced by so many of India's inhabitants. From that point on, his social concerns became the dominant focus of his life. Among the many contributions that he made to Indian society were his establishment of a university and a progressive, open-air school in western Bengal. He was also a vocal supporter of human rights and personal freedom, though he did not press for Indian independence from Britain.

A Prolific Writer Despite involvement in other activities, Tagore remained a productive writer throughout his life. Altogether he produced more than one thousand poems, two dozen plays, eight novels, and several collections of short stories.

Generally, Tagore's poems and stories are considered to be his strongest works. His poems are characterized by a quiet simplicity and dignity, and his short stories are noted for their irony, subtle humor, and social and philosophical themes. Among his most famous collections of poems and short stories are *The Golden Boat* (1893), *Late Harvest* (1896), *Dreams* (1896), *Song Offerings* (1910), and *Bunches of Tales* (1912).

Fame in the West With the publication of the English version of *Gitanjali: Song Offerings* in 1912, Tagore's reputation was firmly established in the West. In his introduction to the English translation, the great Irish poet William Butler Yeats commented, "These lyrics—which are in the original . . . full of subtlety of rhythm, untranslatable delicacies of color, of metrical invention—display in their thought a world I have dreamed of all my life long." The English translation of *Song Offerings*, along with his role in introducing Indian literature to the Western world, earned Tagore the Nobel Prize in Literature in 1913.

A Man of Many Talents Although it is not a well-known fact outside India, Tagore's artistic talents were by no means limited to writing. A gifted musician and composer, he wrote more than two thousand songs and helped create a new style of Indian music. In addition, he was also a talented painter, considered by many art critics to be the finest Indian artist of his time.

TEACHING RESOURCES

The following resources can be used to enrich or extend the instruction for pp. 1140–1141.

Motivation

Interest Grabber Video, Tape 2

Background

Beyond Literature, p. 54

Take It to the Net
Visit PHSchool.com for background on the author.

Literary Analysis

Literary Analysis and Reading Transparencies, Conflict, p. 107

Selection Support: Literary Analysis, p. 216

Reading

Literary Analysis and Reading Transparencies, Identifying Cause and Effect, p. 108

BLOCK SCHEDULING: Resources marked with this symbol provide varied instruction during 90-minute blocks.

Preview

Connecting to the Literature

The struggle between the pursuit of money and the pursuit of happiness is as ancient as civilization itself. In this story, that struggle becomes the dominant theme in the life of one family.

2 Literary Analysis

Conflict

Conflict, the struggle between opposing forces, is a key element of fiction because most plots develop from conflict. While there are many different types of literary conflict, they can be divided into two general categories:

- *Internal conflict* occurs within the mind of a character and involves a struggle with ideas, beliefs, attitudes, or emotions.
- *External conflict* takes place between a character and an outside force, such as another person, society, nature, fate, or God.

As you read, use a chart like the one shown to examine the conflicts in this story and to categorize them as either internal or external.

Conflicts	
External	Internal
1. Govinda's conflict with Satyabati	1.
2.	2.

Connecting Literary Elements

Characters are the people or animals who take part in the action of a literary work. Like a real person, **round characters** are complex and multifaceted, displaying both good and bad qualities. By contrast, **flat characters** are one-dimensional. As you read, analyze the characters and determine whether they are round and multifaceted or flat and one-dimensional.

3 Reading Strategy

Identifying Cause and Effect

A **cause** is an event, an action, or a feeling that produces a result. An **effect** is the result that is produced. Sometimes, words like *because, so,* and *therefore* signal causes and effects. However, fiction writers often develop events without presenting such obvious connections. As you read this story, identify the causes and effects of each character's feelings, thoughts, and actions.

Vocabulary Development

meager (mē´ gər) *adj.* thin; lean (p. 1142)

terminology (tʉr´ mə näl´ ə jē) *n.* terms used in a specific discipline (p. 1142)

frugality (fro͞o gal´ ə tē) *n.* thrift (p. 1144)

connotations (kän´ ə tā´ shənz) *n.* ideas suggested by a word that go beyond its concrete meaning (p. 1144)

equable (ek´ wə bəl) *adj.* steady; uniform (p. 1144)

squandered (skwän´ dərd) *v.* wasted (p. 1144)

disdain (dis dān´) *n.* strong dislike (p. 1146)

myriad (mir´ ē əd) *adj.* many; varied (p. 1147)

enumerating (ē no͞o´ mər āt´ iŋ) *v.* counting; listing (p. 1147)

CUSTOMIZE INSTRUCTION FOR UNIVERSAL ACCESS

For Less Proficient Readers	For English Learners	For Advanced Readers
Have students write journal entries about creative activities they enjoy. Have them include how they became interested in these activities, why they enjoy them, and how these activities might lead to careers in related fields.	Organize students into small groups, and then have them share their native cultures' views of art and the role of artists. Encourage students to discuss how these views differ from what they have observed in American society.	Have students research jobs that pay little but offer non-monetary benefits such as the opportunity to use one's creativity. Then, ask each student to interview someone who holds a job that fits such a description. Students can share their findings with the class.

2 Literary Analysis

Conflict

- Read aloud the Literary Analysis instruction on p. 1141. Then, tell students that conflict shapes most elements in a story: the characters, the setting, the theme, and particularly the point of view.
- Remind students that once they have identified a conflict, they should add it to a chart like the one shown on p. 1141 and then consider how this conflict shapes the characters' actions.
- If students have difficulty understanding the concept of conflict, use the Conflict transparency in **Literary Analysis and Reading Transparencies,** p. 107, to increase comprehension.

3 Reading Strategy

Identifying Cause and Effect

- On the board, write the following sentences: Jean hid Karl's study guide. If she could earn a better score on the test than he could, she would be first in the class.
- Ask students what Jean did. Then, ask them what caused Jean to take this particular action and what this action says about Jean's character. Answer: Jean hid Karl's study guide so she could earn a better score on the test. This action reveals Jean as a selfish and dishonest person.
- Point out to students that understanding the causes and effects of a character's behavior can uncover the deeper understanding of a literary work.

Vocabulary Development

- Pronounce each vocabulary word for students, and read the definitions as a class. Have students identify any words with which they are already familiar.

 **e-Teach**

Visit e-Teach at PHSchool.com for teachers' essays on how to teach, with questions and answers.

TEACH

Step-by-Step Teaching Guide for pp. 1142–1148

Teaching Tenth-Grade Students

10TH GRADE Have students discuss jobs they have had after school or in the summer. Ask them whether learning to make a living is as important as the academic training they receive in school. Why or why not? Ask students how academic and job training relate to one another.

1 About the Selection

In this selection, a widow who is under the care of her money-driven brother-in-law is ridiculed for her study of art. When her brother-in-law refuses to let her son draw, she must decide whether she wants her son to remain in such a materialistic environment.

2 Vocabulary Development

Greek Word Part *-logy*

- Call students' attention to the word *terminology* on p. 1142, and read the word aloud. Then, tell students that *terminology* contains the word part *-logy*, which means "the science, theory, or study of."
- Ask students to suggest other words containing *-logy*, and list the suggestions on the board. **Possible response:** The words *psychology, mythology, anthropology, sociology,* and *criminology* all contain the word part *-logy*.
- Then, have students look up the meanings of these words in a dictionary.

3 Reading Check

Answer: Govinda vowed to make money.

THE ARTIST 1

Rabindranath Tagore

translated by Mary Lago, Tarun Gupta, and Amiya Chakravarty

Background

Rabindranath Tagore is best known as a writer and painter, but he was also a teacher whose theories of education have had an international impact. For Tagore, creativity was the essence of both human beings and the natural world. He believed that traditional education, with its emphasis on uniformity and facts, encouraged children to ignore both their natural creativity and their connections to the world around them. To address this issue, Tagore established a school in Bengal in 1901. Classes were held outdoors. Each day began and ended with an artistic activity. This story reflects these same views about the importance of creativity in people's lives and provides an indictment of modern materialistic values.

Govinda came to Calcutta after graduation from high school in Mymensingh.[1] His widowed mother's savings were meager, but his own unwavering determination was his greatest resource. "I *will* make money," he vowed, "even if I have to give my whole life to it." In his terminology, wealth was always referred to as *pice*.[2] In other words he had in mind a very concrete image of something that could be seen, touched, and smelled; he was not greatly fascinated with fame, only with the very ordinary *pice*, eroded by circulation from market to market, from hand to hand, the tarnished *pice*, the *pice* that smells of copper, the original form of Kuvera,[3] who assumes the assorted guises of silver, gold, securities, and wills, and keeps men's minds in a turmoil.

After traveling many tortuous roads and getting muddied repeatedly in the process, Govinda had now arrived upon the solidly paved embankment of his wide and free-flowing stream of money. He was firmly seated in the manager's chair at the MacDougal Gunnysack Company. Everyone called him MacDulal.

When Govinda's lawyer-brother, Mukunda,[4] died, he left behind a wife, a four-year-old son, a house in Calcutta, and some cash savings.

meager (mē′ gər) *adj.* thin; lean

terminology (tʉr′ mə näl′ ə jē) *n.* terms used in a specific discipline

1. **Calcutta** (kal kut′ ə) . . . **Mymensingh** (mī′ mən siŋ′) Calcutta is a seaport in northeastern India; Mymensingh, now in Bangladesh, is about 190 miles northeast of Calcutta.
2. ***pice*** (pīs) Indian coin.
3. **Kuvera** (ko͞o ver′ ä) Hindu god of wealth, usually spelled Kubera.
4. **Mukunda** (mə ko͞on′ də).

3 **Reading Check**

After graduating from high school, what did Govinda vow?

TEACHING RESOURCES

The following resources can be used to enrich or extend the instruction for pp. 1142–1148.

Literary Analysis

- **Selection Support:** Literary Analysis, p. 216
- **Literary Analysis and Reading Transparencies,** Conflict, p. 107

Reading

- **Selection Support:** Reading Strategy, p. 215; Build Vocabulary, p. 213
- **Listening to Literature Audiocassettes**
- **Listening to Literature Audio CDs**

BLOCK SCHEDULING: Resources marked with this symbol provide varied instruction during 90-minute blocks.

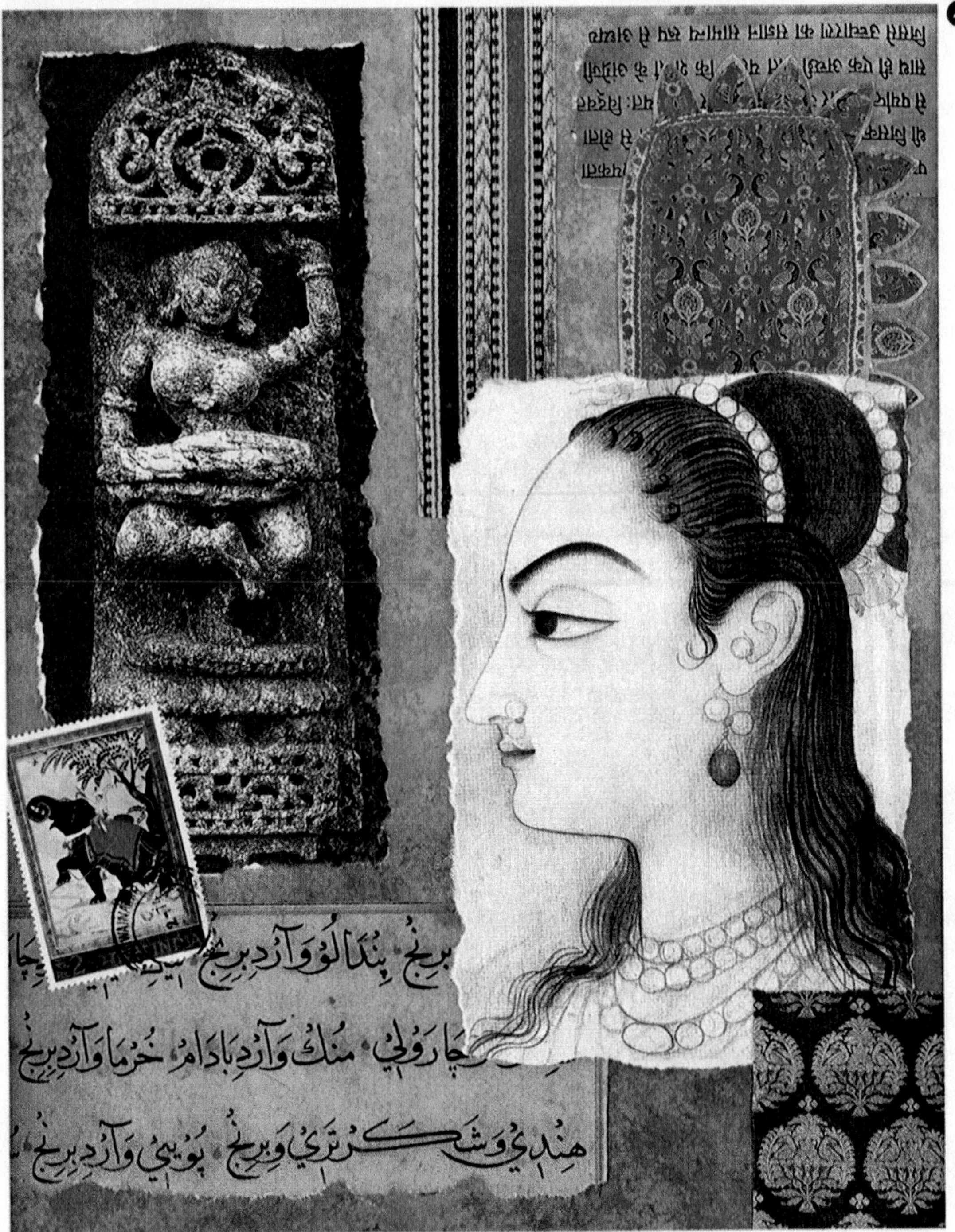

5 ▲ **Critical Viewing** This collage includes a postage stamp and an architectural detail. What do these images suggest about the role of art in daily Indian life? Explain. **[Draw Conclusions]**

4 Background

Art

Romantic India I, by Gerry Charm

Collage (from the French word meaning "pasting") is an artistic technique in which various decorative elements such as bits of fabric, found materials, printed items, and painting are assembled together on a canvas or other surface. This collage, created in 2000 by American artist Gerry Charm, combines several items and motifs from Indian culture to create a vibrant composition.

Use the following questions for discussion:

- Why might an artist choose to create a collage?
  Possible response: A collage allows an artist to combine different media in one composition. The variety of textures, colors, and motifs in a collage may appeal to an artist who feels limited by one medium.
- How does this collage capture feelings of both tradition and modernity?
  Possible response: The architectural detail and the portrait suggest traditional Indian culture. The postage stamp and the collage format itself are more modern.

5 ▶ Critical Viewing

Answer: The images of the postage stamp and the architectural detail suggest that Indian society views many aspects of everyday life—even the most mundane—as works of art.

CUSTOMIZE INSTRUCTION FOR UNIVERSAL ACCESS

For Special Needs Students	For Gifted/Talented Students
Lead a discussion in which students consider what the statement "I *will* make money, even if I have to give my whole life to it" tells the reader about Govinda. Make sure students understand the extent of Govinda's dedication to making money. Then, have students discuss the ways the desire to make money keeps some people's minds in turmoil.	As they read, have students note the character traits of Govinda and Satyabati. Then, have students use these traits to create collages to represent each character. Collages should incorporate pictures from magazines, computer clip art, drawings, and objects. Have students display their work in the classroom.

6 Background

Obsessions With Wealth

Leo Tolstoy's story "How Much Land Does a Man Need"—which appears in this text on p. 835—deals with a character's relationship with money. In this story, Tolstoy's protagonist Pahom struggles with his inability to be satisfied with what he has.

7 Background

A Simple Life

Just as Mukunda chooses to live a life unencumbered by materialism, so have some religious individuals such as Francis of Assisi. In certain traditions, the rejection of wealth and of the worship of money led to the vows of poverty taken by those who renounced the pursuit of affluence.

8 Critical Thinking

Apply

- Have a volunteer read aloud the bracketed passage on pp. 1144–1145. Then, ask students to describe what kind of person Mukunda was.
  Possible response: Mukunda was affectionate and tolerant, with little control or desire for control over his household. He defended Satyabati and her art. He was casual about money and enjoyed life.
- Have students explain why Mukunda made an ideal husband for Satyabati.
  Answer: Mukunda allowed Satyabati to do what she wished and supported her art without worrying about the expense. Mukunda also defended his wife's use of time and was interested in her drawings.

In addition to his property there was some debt; therefore, provision for his family's needs depended upon frugality. Thus his son, Chunilal,[5] was brought up in circumstances that were undistinguished in comparison with those of the neighbors.

Mukunda's will gave Govinda entire responsibility for this family. Ever since Chunilal was a baby, Govinda had bestowed spiritual initiation upon his nephew with the sacred words: "Make money."

The main obstacle to the boy's initiation was his mother, Satyabati.[6] She said nothing outright; her opposition showed in her behavior. Art had always been her hobby. There was no limit to her enthusiasm for creating all sorts of original and decorative things from flowers, fruits and leaves, even foodstuffs, from paper and cloth cutouts, from clay and flour, from berry juices and the juices of other fruits, from *jaba-* and *shiuli-*flower stems. This activity brought her considerable grief, because anything unessential or irrational has the character of flash floods in July: it has considerable mobility, but in relation to the utilitarian[7] concerns of life it is like a stalled ferry. Sometimes there were invitations to visit relatives; Satyabati forgot them and spent the time in her bedroom with the door shut, kneading a lump of clay. The relatives said, "She's terribly stuck-up." There was no satisfactory reply to this. Mukunda had known, even on the basis of his bookish knowledge, that value judgments can be made about art too. He had been thrilled by the noble connotations of the word "art," but he could not conceive of its having any connection with the work of his own wife.

This man's nature had been very equable. When his wife squandered time on unessential whims, he had smiled at it with affectionate delight. If anyone in the household made a slighting remark, he had protested immediately. There had been a singular self-contradiction in Mukunda's makeup; he had been an expert in the
7 practice of law, but it must be conceded that he had had no worldly wisdom with regard to his household affairs. Plenty of money had
8 passed through his hands, but since it had not preoccupied his thoughts, it had left his mind free. Nor could he have tyrannized over his dependents in order to get his own way. His living habits had been very simple; he had never made any unreasonable demands for the attention or services of his relatives.

Mukunda had immediately silenced anyone in the household who cast an aspersion[8] upon Satyabati's disinterest in housework. Now and

5. **Chunilal** (cho͞o′ nē lal)
6. **Satyabati** (sət′ yə bə′ tē)
7. **utilitarian** (yo͞o til ə ter′ ē ən) *adj.* stressing usefulness.
8. **aspersion** (ə spur′ zhən) *n.* damaging or disparaging remark.

Themes in World Literature

6 *Obsessions With Wealth*

Literature throughout the world expresses the uneasy relationship people have with money.

For Tagore, money is decidedly negative. Wealth and its pursuit is a distraction from the values of creativity and spirituality that really matter. In *The Canterbury Tales,* the English poet Geoffrey Chaucer adopted the biblical viewpoint that the love of money is the root of all evil.

Other writers treat the issue more gently. For example, Jane Austen, the English novelist, described characters who marry for love but gain fortune as a bonus. Likewise, Charles Dickens writes of characters who gain wealth without losing their virtue. For example, in his novel *Great Expectations,* a fortune comes to the kind, loyal, and industrious Pip. For Pip, riches are a blessing, not an evil.

frugality (fro͞o gal′ ə tē) *n.* thrift

connotations (kän′ ə tā′ shənz) *n.* ideas suggested by a word that go beyond its concrete meaning

equable (ek′ wə bəl) *adj.* steady; uniform

squandered (skwän′ dərd) *v.* wasted

ENRICHMENT: Literature Connection

Tagore's Success

W. B. Yeats introduced Tagore to the English-speaking world after grief forced the Indian poet into retirement from public life in 1907. Writing in 1912, the year before Tagore received the Nobel Prize, Yeats said that "he writes music for his words, and one understands at every moment that he is so abundant, so spontaneous, so daring in his passion, so full of surprise, because he is doing something which has never seemed strange, unnatural, or in need of defense."

then, on his way home from court, he would stop at Radhabazar to buy some paints, some colored silk and colored pencils, and stealthily[9] he would go and arrange them on the wooden chest in his wife's bedroom. Sometimes, picking up one of Satyabati's drawings, he would say, "Well, this one is certainly very beautiful." 9

One day he had held up a picture of a man, and since he had it upside down, he had decided that the legs must be a bird's head. He had said, "Satu, this should be framed—what a marvelous picture of a stork!" Mukunda had gotten a certain delight out of thinking of his wife's artwork as child's play, and the wife had taken a similar pleasure in her husband's judgment of art. Satyabati had known perfectly well that she could not hope for so much patience, so much indulgence, from any other family in Bengal.[10] No other family would have made way so lovingly for her overpowering devotion to art. So, whenever her husband had made extravagant remarks about her painting, Satyabati could scarcely restrain her tears.

Literary Analysis
Round and Flat Characters Would you describe Mukunda as a round or flat character? Explain.

One day Satyabati lost even this rare good fortune. Before his death her husband had realized one thing quite clearly: the responsibility for his debt-ridden property must be left in the hands of someone astute enough to skillfully steer even a leaky boat to the other shore. This is how Satyabati and her son came to be placed completely under Govinda's care. From the very first day Govinda made it plain to her that the *pice* was the first and foremost thing in life. There was such profound degradation in his advice that Satyabati would shrink with shame.

Literary Analysis
Conflict What is the nature of the conflict between Satyabati and Govinda?

Nevertheless, the worship of money continued in diverse forms in their daily life. If there had been some modesty about it, instead of such constant discussion, it wouldn't have been so bad. Satyabati knew in her heart that all of this lowered her son's standard of values, but there was nothing to do but endure it. Since those delicate emotions endowed with uncommon dignity are the most vulnerable, they are very easily hurt or ridiculed by rude or insensitive people. 11

✓Reading Check
To what activity is Satyabati devoted?

The study of art requires all sorts of supplies. Satyabati had received these for so long without even asking that she had felt no reticence[11] with regard to them. Amid the new circumstances in the family she felt terribly ashamed to charge all these unessential items to the housekeeping budget. So she would save money by economizing on her own food and have the supplies purchased and brought in secretly. Whatever work she did was done furtively,[12] behind closed

9. **stealthily** (stel′ thə lē) *adv.* secretly or slyly.
10. **Bengal** (ben gôl′) region in northeastern India.
11. **reticence** (ret′ ə səns) *n.* quality or state of being habitually silent or uncommunicative.
12. **furtively** (fur′ tiv lē) *adv.* slyly; secretively.

CUSTOMIZE INSTRUCTION FOR UNIVERSAL ACCESS

For English Learners	For Gifted/Talented Students	For Advanced Readers
Draw students' attention to the footnotes on this page and the corresponding words in the text. Then, have a volunteer read each note aloud. Answer any questions that students have about pronunciations or meanings.	Have students imagine a world without art or other creative works, a world in which only making money is important. Then, have students write a story or poem or create a piece of visual art expressing the nature of such a world and its effect on those who live in it.	Discuss the sacrifices some artists make before becoming commercially successful. Then, have students research the lives of other artists who have made similar sacrifices. Have students share their findings with the class.

9 Literary Analysis
Round and Flat Characters

- Remind students that a round character is complex and displays both bad and good characteristics; a flat character is one-dimensional and displays only one dominant trait.
- Have students reread the bracketed passage on pp. 1144–1145. Ask students the first Literary Analysis question on p. 1145: Would you describe Mukunda as a round or flat character? Explain.
  Possible response: Mukunda is a round character because he has both good and bad qualities. Although he cares for his wife and son, he is ignorant of household affairs and has not been careful with money.

10 Literary Analysis
Conflict

- Remind students that external conflict often takes place between characters.
- Ask students to describe Satyabati's character and Govinda's character.
  Possible response: Satyabati puts her devotion to art above the pursuit of money. Govinda believes that everyone in his household should share his goal of making money.
- Read aloud the bracketed passage. Ask students the second Literary Analysis question on p. 1145: What is the nature of the conflict between Satyabati and Govinda?
  Answer: The characters have different priorities: art for Satyabati and money for Govinda.

Monitor Progress Ask students to explain whether the conflict between Satyabati and Govinda is internal or external.
Answer: The conflict is primarily external, although each character struggles internally to reconcile his or her own values with those of the other character.

Reteach If students have difficulty identifying the conflict between Satyabati and Govinda, use the Conflict transparency in **Literary Analysis and Reading Transparencies,** p. 107, to provide additional support.

11 

Answer: Satyabati is devoted to creating art.

⓬ Background

Art

Two Gazelle, **from the** ***Babar Nama***

The *Babar Nama* is an illustrated book created by court painters to commemorate the rule of Babar from 1526 to 1530. Babar, a Turk descended from Genghis Khan, conquered Delhi in 1526, founding the Mogul Empire. The exploits of Babar were told as history and legend, illustrated with active figures.

Rulers of sixteenth-century India were interested in art for its aesthetics as well as its ability to create a sense of history and stability. Note the elegant lines, surface patterns, and decorative details of *Two Gazelle.*

Use the following question for discussion:

What feelings are evoked by *Two Gazelle*?

Possible response: The painting gives the viewer a feeling of peacefulness and abundance.

⓭ ▶Critical Viewing

Possible response: The painting—with its attention to detail and use of color—effectively captures Satyabati's and Chunilal's love of art.

⓬

doors. She was not afraid of a scolding, but the stares of insensitive observers embarrassed her.

Now Chuni was the only spectator and critic of her artistic activity. Gradually he became a participant. He began to feel its intoxication. The child's offense could not be concealed, since it overflowed the pages of his notebook onto the walls of the house. There were stains on his face, on his hands, on the cuffs of his shirt. Indra,[13] the king of the gods, does not spare even the soul of a little boy in the effort to tempt him away from the worship of money.

On the one hand the restraint increased, on the other hand the mother collaborated in the violations. Occasionally the head of the company would take his office manager, Govinda, along on business trips out of town. Then the mother and son would get together in unrestrained joy. This was the absolute extreme of childishness! They drew pictures of animals that God has yet to create. The likeness of the dog would get mixed up with that of the cat. It was difficult to distinguish between fish and fowl. There was no way to preserve all these creations; their traces had to be thoroughly obliterated before the head of the house returned. Only Brahma, the Creator, and Rudra, the Destroyer, witnessed the creative delight of these two persons; Vishnu,[14] the heavenly Preserver, never arrived.

Two Gazelle, From the Babar Nama, 1530, New Delhi National Museum, Borromeo

The compulsion for artistic creation ran strong in Satyabati's family. There was an older nephew, Rangalal, who rose overnight to fame as an artist. That is to say, the connoisseurs of the land roared with laughter at the unorthodoxy of his art. Since their stamp of imagination did not coincide with his, they had a violent scorn for his talent. But curiously enough, his reputation thrived upon disdain and flourished in this atmosphere of opposition and mockery. Those who imitated him most

⓭ ▲ **Critical Viewing**

Do you think this painting effectively captures Satyabati's and Chunilal's love of art? **[Evaluate]**

disdain (dis dān′) *n.* strong dislike

13. **Indra** (in′ drə) chief god of the early Hindu religion.
14. **Brahma** (brä′ mə) . . . **Rudra** (ro͞o′ drə) . . . **Vishnu** (vish′ no͞o) In the Hindu religion, Brahma is the creator of the universe, Rudra is the god of destruction and reproduction, and Vishnu is the god of preservation.

ENRICHMENT: Art Connection

Painting in Ancient India

India has a rich artistic tradition. In his book *The Wonder That Was India,* the historian A. L. Basham offers insights about the art of painting in ancient India.

> Painting was a very highly developed art in ancient India. Palaces and the homes of the rich were adorned with beautiful murals, and smaller paintings were made on prepared boards. Not only were there professional artists, but many men and women of the educated classes could ably handle a brush.
>
> Though now all in very bad condition, the surviving remains of ancient Indian painting are sufficient to show its achievement. They consist almost entirely of murals in certain of the cave temples.

took it upon themselves to prove that the man was a hoax as an artist, that there were obvious defects even in his technique.

This much-maligned artist came to his aunt's home one day, at a time when the office manager was absent. After persistent knocking and shoving at the door he finally got inside and found that there was nowhere to set foot on the floor. The cat was out of the bag.

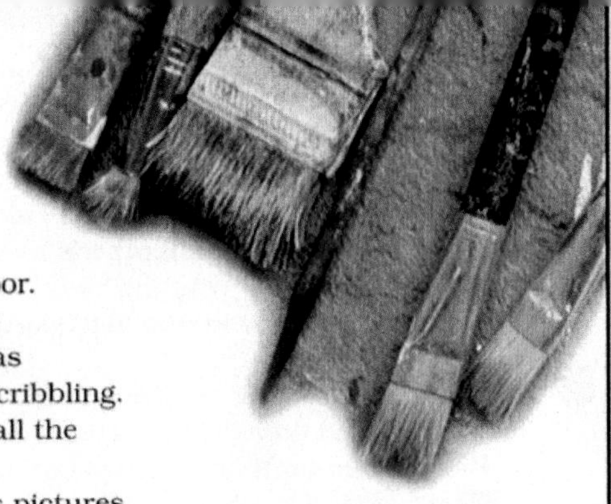

"It is obvious," said Rangalal, "that the image of creation has emerged anew from the soul of the artist; this is not random scribbling. He and that god who creates form are the same age. Get out all the drawings and show them to me."

14 Where should they get the drawings? That artist who draws pictures all over the sky in myriad colors, in light and shadow, calmly discards his mists and mirages. Their creations had gone the same way. With an oath Rangalal said to his aunt, "From now on, I'll come and get whatever you make."

myriad (mir′ ē əd) *adj.* many; varied

There came another day when the office manager had not returned. Since morning the sky had brooded in the shadows of July; it was raining. No one monitored the hands of the clock and no one wanted to know about them. Today Chuni began to draw a picture of a sailing boat while his mother was in the prayer room. The waves of the river looked like a flock of hungry seals just on the point of swallowing the boat. The clouds seemed to cheer them on and float their shawls overhead, but the seals were not conventional seals, and it would be no exaggeration to say of the clouds: "Light and mist merge in the watery waste." In the interests of truth it must be said that if boats were built like this one, insurance companies would never assume such risks. Thus the painting continued; the sky-artist drew fanciful pictures, and inside the room the wide-eyed boy did the same.

No one realized that the door was open. The office manager appeared. He roared in a thunderous voice, "What's going on?"

The boy's heart jumped and his face grew pale. Now Govinda perceived the real reason for Chunilal's examination errors in historical dates. Meanwhile the crime became all the more evident as Chunilal tried unsuccessfully to hide the drawing under his shirt. As Govinda snatched the picture away, the design he saw on it further astonished him. Errors in historical dates would be preferable to this. He tore the picture to pieces. Chunilal burst out crying.

From the prayer room Satyabati heard the boy's weeping, and she came running. Both Chunilal and the torn pieces of the picture were on the floor. Govinda went on enumerating the reasons for his nephew's failure in the history examination and suggesting dire remedies.

enumerating (ē no͞o′ mər āt′ iŋ) *v.* counting; listing

Satyabati had never said a word about Govinda's behavior toward them. She had quietly endured everything, remembering that this was the person on whom her husband had relied. Now her eyes were wet with tears, and shaking with anger, she said hoarsely, "Why did you tear up Chuni's picture?"

15 **✓Reading Check**

Who gradually becomes a participant in Satyabati's artistic activity?

14 Critical Thinking

Speculate

- Tell students to reas the bracketed passage.
- Ask students why Satyabati calmly discards her artwork. Prompt them to speculate on why a creator would do such a thing.
  Possible response: The value of art is in the process not the product.

15 ✓Reading Check

Answer: Chunilal gradually becomes a participant in Satyabati's artistic activity.

CUSTOMIZE INSTRUCTION FOR UNIVERSAL ACCESS

For Less Proficient Readers	For Advanced Readers
Lead a discussion in which students identify details about Govinda's personality. Then, have them discuss whether his outburst at Chunilal is predictable or inevitable. Have them explain their answers, using as many examples from the story as possible.	Have students research the rationale behind offering arts classes in school. Tell students to use the Internet to find research that supports the value of including art, drama, music, creative writing, and other artistic subjects in the curriculum. Then, have students present their findings to the class as visual presentations or oral reports.

ASSESS

16 Reading Strategy

Identifying Cause and Effect

- Remind students that a cause is an event, an action, or a feeling that produces an effect or result.
- Read aloud the bracketed passage. Then, ask students: What causes Satyabati to take Chunilal to her nephew's house?
  Answer: Govinda threatens to take Chunilal to boarding school.

Answers for p. 1148

Review and Assess

1. Possible response: Govinda's perspective is more realistic because without some financial support, Satyabati could not survive.
2. **(a)** Govinda is determined to obtain money. **(b)** Govinda regards Satyabati's art as a waste of time and money. **(c)** Mukunda, unlike Govinda, values art over money.
3. **(a)** The connoisseurs ridicule Rangalal's art. **(b)** The art is not appreciated by many. **(c)** Possible response: The author values art as an activity because the characters continue to make art despite others' negative reactions.
4. **(a)** Brahma, the creator of the universe, is the sky artist. **(b)** Tagore is suggesting that the creation of art is a spiritual activity.
5. **(a)** Govinda takes on the responsibility because his brother dies, leaving his wife and son without someone to take care of their finances. **(b)** Possible response: At the time of the story, Indian women did not handle their own affairs.
6. Possible response: Satyabati is wise to keep her son from becoming possessed by money; however, Chunilal may have difficulty supporting himself as an adult.

Govinda said, "Doesn't he have to study? What will become of him in the future?"

" Even if he becomes a beggar in the street," answered Satyabati, "he'll be better off in the future. But I hope he'll never be like you. May his pride in his God-given talent be more than your pride in *pices*. This is my blessing for him, a mother's blessing."

"I can't neglect my responsibility," said Govinda. "I will not tolerate this. Tomorrow I'll send him to a boarding school; otherwise, you'll ruin him."

16 The office manager returned to the office. The rain fell in torrents and the streets flowed with water.

Holding her son's hand, Satyabati said, "Let's go, dear."

Chuni said, "Go where, Mother?"

"Let's get out of this place."

The water was knee-deep at Rangalal's door. Satyabati came in with Chunilal. She said, "My dear boy, you take charge of him. Keep him from the worship of money."

Review and Assess

Thinking About the Selection

1. **Respond:** Which perspective of the world do you think is more realistic—Satyabati's or Govinda's? Explain.
2. **(a) Recall:** What did Govinda show an "unwavering determination" to obtain? **(b) Interpret:** How does he regard Satyabati's art? **(c) Compare and Contrast:** Compare and contrast Mukunda's attitude toward both money and art with Govinda's.
3. **(a) Recall:** How do "the connoisseurs of the land" regard Rangalal's art? **(b) Connect:** In what ways are Rangalal's art and that of Satyabati and Chunilal similar? **(c) Analyze:** Based on these descriptions, do you think the author values art more as a product or as an activity? Explain.
4. **(a) Interpret:** Who is the sky-artist? **(b) Analyze:** What is Tagore suggesting about the relationship between artistic expression and spirituality?
5. **(a) Interpret:** Why does Govinda take on the responsibility for Satyabati and Chunilal? **(b) Evaluate:** What does this arrangement suggest about Indian culture, particularly the roles of women, at the time of the story?
6. **Make a Judgment:** Do you think Satyabati's actions at the end of the story are wise? Explain.

ASSESSMENT PRACTICE: Reading Comprehension

Identify Patterns of Organization (For more practice, see Test Preparation Workbook, p. 54.)

Many tests require students to identify patterns of organization. Use this sample test item to give students practice with this skill.

After traveling many tortuous roads and getting muddied repeatedly in the process, Govinda had now arrived upon the solidly paved embankment of his wide and free-flowing stream of money. He was firmly seated in the manager's chair at the MacDougal Gunnysack Company.

Which of the following best describes the pattern of organization found in this passage?

A cause and effect
B specific to general
C chronological
D comparison and contrast

A and *B* are not applicable to this passage. *D* is not the best choice, as the passage is organized chronologically. *C* is the best choice.

Review and Assess

Literary Analysis

Conflict

1. (a) What values does Govinda try to instill in Chunilal? (b) In what ways do his values create an **external conflict** with Satyabati?
2. What **internal conflicts** does Satyabati experience as a result of her external conflict with Govinda?
3. (a) When does the conflict between Govinda and Satyabati reach its point of greatest intensity? (b) How is the conflict resolved?
4. Both Govinda and Satyabati embody specific values. (a) What values does each character represent? (b) Based on these values, what conflict in society as a whole does this story express? Explain.

Connecting Literary Elements

5. (a) When he was alive, how did Mukunda manage his work, his relationship with Satyabati, and his dealings with their relatives? (b) Is Mukunda a **flat** or a **round character**? Explain.
6. Both Govinda and Satyabati have obsessions. (a) Compare and contrast the effects these obsessions have on their lives. (b) Do you think either Govinda or Satyabati is a flat character? Explain.

Reading Strategy

Identifying Cause and Effect

7. (a) Use a chart like the one shown to **identify causes and effects** in this story, beginning with Mukunda's death.

Mukunda's Death		
Effect	Effect	Effect

(b) Choose one of these effects and describe how it, in turn, becomes the cause of another series of events.

8. (a) What is the cause of Satyabati's decision to practice her art in secret? (b) What effect does this secrecy have on her son?

Extend Understanding

9. **Cultural Connection:** How might this story be different if it were set in contemporary America? Explain your answer.

Quick Review

A **conflict** is a struggle between opposing forces. Conflicts can be internal or external.

Flat characters are one-dimensional, possessing a single dominant trait. Like real people, **round characters** are multidimensional, possessing many complex traits.

To **identify cause and effect**, note the circumstances that cause characters' actions and the effects their actions have on others.

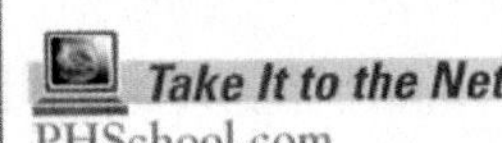

Take It to the Net

PHSchool.com

Take the interactive self-test online to check your understanding of this selection.

ENRICHMENT: Further Reading

Other Works by Rabindranath Tagore

We strongly encourage you to review any selection before assigning or recommending it to students.

The Hungry Stones and Other Stories

Glimpses of Bengal

The Home and the World

Take It to the Net

Visit PHSchool.com for more information on Rabindranath Tagore.

Answers for p. 1149

Review and Assess

1. **(a)** Govinda tries to persuade Chunilal that only money is important. **(b)** Satyabati believes that artistic expression is important, and she does not want her son cut off from art in order to pursue only money.
2. Satyabati's love of art conflicts with her reliance on Govinda to provide for her and Chunilal and causes her to question how to raise her son.
3. **(a)** The conflict is most intense when Govinda destroys Chunilal's artwork. **(b)** The conflict is resolved by Satyabati's taking her son to Rangalal.
4. **(a)** Govinda represents materialism. Satyabati represents artistic expression and spirituality. **(b)** The story expresses the conflict between materialism and art and spirituality.
5. **(a)** Mukunda was an expert lawyer who encouraged Satyabati, demanded little of others, and lived very simply. **(b)** Mukunda is a round character because despite his good characteristics, he was not careful with money.
6. **(a)** Govinda and Satyabati are both controlled by their passions. Govinda focuses on economic gain whereas Satyabati focuses on the joy and beauty of creation. **(b)** Govinda is a flat character because he is guided by a single obsession. He has no conflicting character traits.
7. **(a)** Possible response: Govinda's taking over the family, Satyabati's inability to pursue her art freely, and Govinda's attempt to control Chunilal are all effects of Mukunda's death. **(b)** Govinda's attempt to control Chunilal leads Satyabati to take Chunilal to Rangalal.
8. **(a)** Satyabati has been ridiculed for her art. **(b)** Chunilal begins to draw.
9. Possible response: In contemporary America, Satyabati would not be placed under the legal authority of her brother-in-law.

EXTEND

Answers for p. 1150

❶ Vocabulary Development

Word Analysis: Greek Word Part *-logy*

1. c
2. b
3. a

Spelling Strategy

1. certainly
2. claimed

Fluency: Words in Context

1. terminology
2. meager
3. disdain
4. squandered
5. equable
6. connotations
7. frugality
8. myriad

❷ Grammar and Style

Practice

1. Govinda, the villain, worshipped money.
2. He tried to influence his nephew Chunilal.
3. Satyabati, an artist, pursued her dream.
4. Rangalal, a painter, encouraged Satyabati.
5. Satyabati turned to her nephew, Rangalal, for help.

Writing Application

Possible response: Govinda, *a company manager*, values money, but his brother *Mukunda* did not. Satyabati, *Govinda's sister-in-law*, is an artist like her nephew *Rangalal*. Chunilal, *the son of Mukunda and Satyabati*, also loves art.

10TH GRADE For support in teaching the Grammar and Style Lesson to tenth graders, use **Writing and Grammar**, Platinum Level, Chapter 20, Section 1.

Integrate Language Skills

❶ Vocabulary Development Lesson

Word Analysis: Greek Word Part *-logy*

The Greek word part *-logy* means "the science, theory, or study of." Therefore, *terminology* means the "system of words used in a specific field." Match the word containing the word part *-logy* in the left column with its definition in the right column.

1. theology a. study of life
2. geology b. study of Earth's physical history
3. biology c. study of religion

Spelling Strategy

In words ending in a consonant preceded by two vowels, do not double the final consonant before adding a suffix: *disdain* + *-ed* = *disdained*. Add the indicated suffix to each of the words below.

1. certain + *-ly* 2. claim + *-ed*

Fluency: Words in Context

Review the vocabulary list on page 1141. Then, fill in the blanks in the paragraph with the appropriate words from the list.

The book was so successful, it created a whole new __?__. Kids used their __?__ funds to buy copies. While some adults looked on with __?__, believing that their kids had __?__ their money, others had more __?__ feelings. They felt that the book fostered good values and had no negative __?__. They encouraged __?__, but they also knew that their children would find a __?__ of products they wanted to buy.

❷ Grammar and Style Lesson

Appositives and Appositive Phrases

An **appositive** is a noun or pronoun placed near another noun or pronoun to provide additional information about it. When an appositive is accompanied by its own modifiers, it forms an **appositive phrase.**

If an appositive is essential to the meaning of a sentence, commas are not used. If an appositive can be omitted without affecting the meaning, it is set off with commas.

Nonessential: Indra, the king of the gods, does not spare even the soul of a little boy . . .

Essential: The story "The Artist" condemns materialism.

Practice Rewrite each sentence below, incorporating the information given as an appositive.

1. Govinda worshipped money. *(the villain)*
2. He tried to influence his nephew. *(Chunilal)*
3. Satyabati pursued her dream. *(an artist)*
4. Rangalal encouraged Satyabati. *(a painter)*
5. Satyabati turned to her nephew for help. *(Rangalal)*

Writing Application Write a paragraph in which you use an appositive or an appositive phrase to describe each character from "The Artist."

WG Prentice Hall Writing and Grammar Connection: Diamond Level, Chapter 19, Section 1

TEACHING RESOURCES

The following resources can be used to enrich or extend the instruction for pp. 1150–1151.

Vocabulary

- **Selection Support:** Build Vocabulary, p. 213
- **Vocabulary and Spelling Practice Book** (Use this book for skills instruction.)

Grammar

- **Selection Support:** Grammar and Style, p. 214
- **Writing and Grammar,** Diamond Level, p. 440
- **Daily Language Practice Transparencies**

Writing

- **Performance Assess. and Portfolio Mgmt.,** p. 11
- **Writing and Grammar,** Diamond Level, p. 140
- **Writing and Grammar iText CD-ROM**
- **Writing Models and Graphic Organizers on Transparencies,** pp. 103–106

Research and Technology

- **Performance Assess. and Portfolio Mgmt.,** p. 33

BLOCK SCHEDULING: Resources marked with this symbol provide varied instruction during 90-minute blocks.

❸ Writing Lesson

Newspaper Editorial

Newspaper editorials provide a public forum for citizens to express their opinions about pressing issues. As Satyabati, write an editorial in which you argue for a different emphasis in society's values.

Prewriting Reread the story, taking notes about the values that Satyabati holds dear. Identify experiences in her life that demonstrate the importance of these values. Note ways in which Govinda's worship of money is damaging to himself, his family, and society as a whole.

Drafting Write an introduction with a vivid anecdote or quotation. Then, clearly state Satyabati's thesis. As you build your body paragraphs, anticipate and address opposing viewpoints.

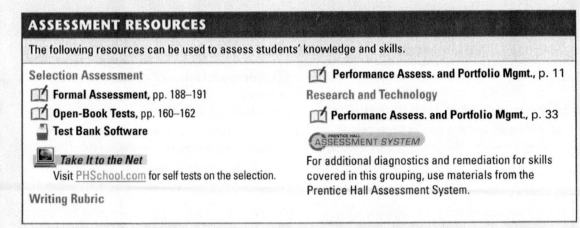

Model: Drafting to Address Opposing Viewpoints

Of course, we need a strong economy. We need people who can run businesses successfully. However, we also need creative people. Art does not detract from our financial success. Rather, it helps us be successful.

Anticipating and addressing opposing viewpoints strengthens an argument.

Revising Read your editorial to identify sections that could be more persuasive. Add or eliminate details to strengthen the overall impression.

Prentice Hall Writing and Grammar Connection: Diamond Level, Chapter 7, Section 7

❹ Extension Activities

Research and Technology In this story, Govinda assumes responsibility for his brother's family after the brother's death. With a small group, research and deliver a **group report** on the traditions and laws that dictate such after-death arrangements in India. Follow these tips to prepare:

- Use photographs, illustrations, or other visual aids.
- Organize the material so that ideas flow smoothly between speakers.

If necessary, do additional research to fill in gaps in your information. **[Group Activity]**

Listening and Speaking Find a collection of Tagore's poetry, and select two or three poems that share a similar theme. Write an introduction and conclusion, and deliver a **themed reading.** To prepare, read the poems aloud, stressing different words to emphasize meaning. Find an appropriate tone, and pace your delivery.

Take It to the Net PHSchool.com

Go online for an additional research activity using the Internet.

ASSESSMENT RESOURCES

The following resources can be used to assess students' knowledge and skills.

Selection Assessment

Formal Assessment, pp. 188–191

Open-Book Tests, pp. 160–162

Test Bank Software

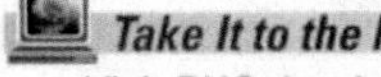
Take It to the Net

Visit PHSchool.com for self tests on the selection.

Writing Rubric

Performance Assess. and Portfolio Mgmt., p. 11

Research and Technology

Performanc Assess. and Portfolio Mgmt., p. 33

For additional diagnostics and remediation for skills covered in this grouping, use materials from the Prentice Hall Assessment System.

❸ Writing Lesson

- Read aloud the Writing Lesson instruction on p. 1151. Before students begin their editorials, ask them to brainstorm arguments on both sides of the issue.
- Use the Writing Lesson to guide students in developing their editorials. Encourage students to use specific details from the text to support their thesis statements.
- Students can use the Outline organizers in **Writing Models and Graphic Organizers on Transparencies,** pp. 103–106, to help them organize their editorials.
- Use the Persuasion: Persuasive Composition rubric in **Performance Assessment and Portfolio Management,** p. 11, to evaluate students' editorials.

10TH GRADE For support in working through the Writing Lesson with tenth graders, use **Writing and Grammar,** Platinum Level, Chapter 7, Section 7.

❹ Research and Technology

- After students read the Extension Activity instruction, organize them in small groups. Tell students to evaluate Internet sources to make sure that they are reliable.
- Have students present their reports to the class. Use the Listening and Speaking Progress Chart in **Performance Assessment and Portfolio Management,** p. 33, to evaluate students' reports.

CUSTOMIZE INSTRUCTION For Universal Access

To address different learning styles, use the following activities suggested in the **Extension Activities** booklet, p. 54:

- For Visual/Spatial Learners, use Activity 5.
- For Logical/Mathematical and Visual/Spatial Learners, use Activity 6.
- For Verbal/Linguistic and Logical/Mathematical Learners, use Activity 7.

Lesson Objectives

1. To write an essay comparing and contrasting the themes of uncertainty, alienation, and despair in the modern literature of two or more cultures
2. To use writing strategies to generate ideas, plan, organize, evaluate, and revise writing

Prewriting

- Point out that *uncertainty, alienation,* and *despair* are human emotions and conditions. As students review the literature in Unit 8, encourage them to find characters or speakers who embody or express these emotions.
- Remind students to choose works from two different cultures. Explain that in their essays, students will identify **(a)** how the literature from each culture treats a certain theme, such as alienation; and **(b)** how the two cultures' treatments of these literary themes are similar and different.
- Instruct students to use a chart like the one at the bottom of p. 1152 to narrow their search for two literary selections.
- After students have selected two works, they can collect textual evidence to support their choices.
- If students have trouble limiting their focus statements to one sentence, have them write short focus paragraphs. After they have written the paragraphs, have them condense each by generalizing or by combining sentences.

Writing About Literature

Compare and Contrast Literary Trends Across Cultures

The Modern Era, from 1890 to 1945, was a period remade by catastrophic wars, economic upheaval, and revolutionary discoveries in science and technology. Both the form and the content of the work of writers around the world reflected these turbulent times.

The literary movement known as Modernism focused on the themes of uncertainty, alienation, and despair. Write an essay that compares the treatment of these themes in selected works in this unit. Details of the assignment are outlined in the box at the right.

Assignment: Alienation Across Cultures

Write an essay comparing the themes of uncertainty, alienation, and despair in works of at least two of the cultures in this unit.

Criteria:

- Include a thesis statement that defines these themes and draws from your analysis of the literature.
- Support your thesis with detailed analyses of at least two works, each from a different culture.
- Cite evidence of each similarity and difference you explore.
- Approximate length: 1,500 words

Prewriting

Review the selections. Review the works in this unit, answering the following questions:

- Is the theme of alienation or despair stated or strongly implied in this work?
- In what ways does the writer develop this theme?
- Do formal aspects of this work—for example, the lack of exposition, transitions, and resolution or the use of free verse—reflect this theme?
- In what way does the writer's culture affect the treatment of the theme?

Read to Write

As you reread the texts, look for the theme in the setting, the plot, or the characters. In poetry, also look for the theme in symbols and in formal elements, such as the use of fragmented sentences.

Gather evidence. After you have chosen the works you will discuss in your paper, begin comparing and contrasting the selections by filling in a chart similar to the one below. Use your chart to begin sorting similarities and differences among the works by culture. Then, return to the works to select quotations and specific details of content or form to support your analysis.

Model: Charting to Compare and Contrast Treatments of Theme

Selection	How Work Demonstrates Theme	Cultural Tie
"Interior of the Rose"	mystery of a rose	rose common subject in poetry of Europe
"Everything Is Plundered"	acknowledges and rejects despair	destruction of homeland caused by war

Write three focus statements. Based on your review of the literature, write three focus statements. In the first, *define the themes* that you will explore in your essay. In the second, *explain the impact of the theme on form* (if any) in the works you have chosen. In the third, *explain the effect of culture on theme* in these works. Build the introduction for your essay around these three focus statements.

TEACHING RESOURCES

The following resources can be used to enrich or extend the instruction for pp. 1152–1153.

 **Writing and Grammar,** Diamond Level, Chapter 9, pp. 168–188

 **Performance Assess. and Portfolio Mgmt.,** p. 15

 **Writing Models and Graphic Organizers on Transparencies,** pp. 95–97

 **Writing and Grammar iText CD-ROM**

Students can use the following tools as they complete their comparison-and-contrast essays:

- Venn Diagram Organizer
- Customizable Outliner
- Language Variety Revising Tool

Drafting

Outline. Use information from your chart to make a working outline. In the major headings, list the similarities and differences you will discuss. In the subheadings, list the evidence from the literature.

Model: Making a Working Outline

I. World is strange, not set up in human terms
 A. "Interior of the Rose"
  1. Interior of the rose changes world
   a. ". . . a room enclosed in a dream"
 B. "Under Reconstruction"
  1. Construction work in hotel represents unsettledness of postwar life

Write to Learn Remember that your outline is only a guide. Include information that supports your arguments even if it doesn't fit neatly into your outline.

Refer to historical events. Be as specific as you can in describing historical events that shaped the writer's perspective and in explaining their significance.

Write to Explain Connect your thoughts clearly so that readers can follow your arguments. Do not leave out any logical steps. The more closely your readers can follow your thinking, the more persuasive your ideas will be.

Revising and Editing

Review content: Check for accuracy. Did the character wear a red jacket? Did the speaker say, "Oh, my aching heart" or "Oh, my breaking heart"? Absolute accuracy is essential if you want readers to take your ideas seriously. Check each reference in your paper for accuracy.

Review style: Vary sentence structure. Choose varied sentence structures to add variety to your writing.

Choppy: The love of nature is a universal theme in poetry. It is a theme that appears in all eras. But the tone of Rilke's "Interior of the Rose" is Modernist. The tone of pain and uncertainty in the poem shows this.

Varied: The love of nature is a universal theme in poetry, one that appears in all eras. But the tone of pain and uncertainty in Rilke's "Interior of the Rose" places the poem well within the Modernist camp.

Publishing and Presenting

Give a dramatic reading. Read excerpts for the class from two of the selections you discussed in your essay. Then, explain why you compared these selections.

WG *Writing and Grammar Connection: Diamond Level, Chapter 9*

CUSTOMIZE INSTRUCTION FOR UNIVERSAL ACCESS

For Less Proficient Writers	For English Learners	For Advanced Writers
Have students limit their subjects to two works of literature. Students can use Venn diagrams to compare and contrast the works they have selected. Provide students with the Comparison and Contrast Blackline Master in **Writing Models and Graphic Organizers on Transparencies,** pp. 95–97.	Encourage students to write about the works they found easiest to read and to understand. Before they begin writing, have students explain in their own words what each work is about and what theme(s) it explores.	In their essays, invite students to focus on a single literary element through which the writers of their chosen works express their themes. For example, students might compare the writers' use of character, setting, imagery, symbolism, or poetic form in two or more works.

Drafting

- As students create outlines, have them think of each work of literature as an illustration of the theme on which they are focusing.
- Remind students that historical events often shape cultural perspectives. Students can use quotations from historical research to support and explain the significance of literary themes.

Revising and Editing

- Ask students what message a job interviewee might send a potential employer if he or she arrived wearing a shirt that was buttoned into the wrong buttonholes.
  Possible response: The interviewee might send the message that he or she was disorganized and gave little attention to details.
- Next, point out that in many areas of life, small "inaccuracies" or oversights can have big consequences. Tell students that inaccurate writing can cause a writer to lose his or her reader's trust.
- Explain that varying sentence structure is an important part of revising and editing and that sentence variety makes writing more engaging. Write this sentence on the board: *Jack was tired and cold and wanted to go home.* Ask students to revise this sentence by relocating the adjectives.
  Answer: Tired and cold, Jack wanted to go home.
- Next, have students underline sentences in their drafts that begin with simple subjects. Challenge them to revise by reorganizing words or phrases in a sentence or by combining a sentence with one that comes before or after.

Publishing and Presenting

- Encourage students to select representative passages that express a work's style and theme.
- Suggest that students draw on the board or on a poster a Venn diagram showing one or two key points that they will compare and contrast in their essays.
- To support their analyses and diagrams, have students read aloud from passages that express the style or theme. Finally, invite audience members to identify other points of comparison or contrast.

Lesson Objectives

1. To prepare, write, and present a multimedia report
2. To use writing strategies to generate ideas, plan, organize, draft, evaluate, revise, and present a multimedia report

Model From Literature

The imagery in Federico García Lorca's "The Guitar" (pp. 1072–1073) might work well with audio and visual media. Ask students to imagine how a multimedia presentation could enhance Lorca's message.

Prewriting

- Explain to students that they need to select topics that support a strong exposition and for which different varieties of multimedia materials are available. After students narrow a list of topics, have them write a sentence for each that clarifies their topic.
- Tell students to read the Media Checklist. Ask whether they think the presentation described on the checklist will be engaging. Possible response: Because the presentation includes four of the five media listed in the checklist, it will probably be engaging.
- Encourage students to use a media checklist and to be discriminating as they review materials. Remind them to use resources that are reliable, informative, and interesting.
- Remind students to develop a strong thesis statement, using written and media components for support.
- Before students begin drafting, have them review the Rubric for Self-Assessment on p. 1157 so that they know what is expected of their reports.

Writing WORKSHOP

Exposition: Multimedia Report

In a **multimedia report,** a presenter shares information, enhancing narration and explanation with media, such as video images, slides, audiotape recordings, music, and art. In this workshop, you will plan, draft, and revise a multimedia report.

Assignment Criteria Your multimedia report should feature the following elements:

- Well-integrated, varied audio and visual features
- A clear and logical organization
- Innovative use of relevant media to convey key concepts
- Effective pacing of media with smooth transitions between elements to create a comprehensible whole
- An enticing introduction and memorable conclusion

To preview the criteria on which your multimedia report may be assessed, refer to the Rubric on page 1157.

Prewriting

Choose a topic. A good topic for a multimedia report is one that interests you and for which appropriate multimedia material is available. If no topic comes readily to mind, **browse** through magazines for inspiration. List possible topics, and then choose the one that offers the most possibilities for a multimedia presentation.

Create a media checklist. In a chart similar to the one shown here, list the various categories of media that you believe will be available for your topic. In the right-hand column, note your ideas about how to use the various media.

Media Checklist

☑ Music	Pachelbel *Canon in D*
☑ Videos	democracy flowchart
☑ Art	Rockwell's *Freedom of Speech* painting
☑ Photographs	various government images and symbols
☐ Computer Presentation	

Research the topic. As you research your topic, jot down ideas about creative ways to engage your audience. Consult your library for audio or video clips of interviews and for documentaries, music, and art resources. Search the Internet for similar resources. Consider using any medium that will help bring your topic to life.

Review for varied media. After your initial research, review the media you have located. If you find that most items fall into one category—for instance, still images—look for additional items to ensure that your report is rich in a variety of media, including sound clips, video, and still images.

Identify a thesis. Review your notes and materials. Develop a statement of the key ideas you intend to cover, and be guided by it as you draft.

TEACHING RESOURCES

The following resources can be used to enrich or extend the instruction for pp. 1154–1157.

- **Writing and Grammar,** Diamond Level, Chapter 12, pp. 246–268
- **Performance Assess. and Portfolio Mgmt.,** p. 32
- **Writing Models and Graphic Organizers on Transparencies,** pp. 103–105

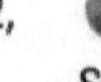
Writing and Grammar iText CD-ROM

Students can use the following tools as they complete their multimedia reports:

- Topic Bin
- Customizable Outliner
- Transition Words Revising Tool

Student Model

Before you begin drafting, read this student model and review the characteristics of an effective multimedia presentation.

Mark Sueyoshi
Palm Springs, California

The Government of the United States

Text	Audio and Video
[Cue AUDIO] There are three types of democracy. [Cue VIDEO]	AUDIO: Pachelbel *Canon in D* VIDEO CHART: A flowchart of democracy branching into different types, drawn out as the audience watches.
[Cue TRANSITION ZOOM] In democratic centralism, leaders (not elected by popular vote) decide what is best for the people. Examples of this form of democracy are the Soviet Union and China. [Cue SLIDES]	TRANSITION ZOOM: Zooms into Democratic Centralism rectangle. Democratic Centralism SLIDES: Rapid sequence showing flags or national symbols of USSR and China
[Cue VIDEO CHART, pause, then cue TRANSITION ZOOM] In direct democracy, each citizen participates directly in policy making. Governments that have used this form of democracy are ancient Greece and colonial New England. [Cue SLIDES]	TRANSITION ZOOM: Zooms into Direct Democracy rectangle. Direct Democracy SLIDES: Rapid sequence of images of ancient Athens, Norman Rockwell's *Freedom of Speech* painting of a New England town meeting, colonial Maryland
[Cue VIDEO CHART, pause, then cue TRANSITION ZOOM] And in representative democracy, citizens elect leaders to create policy. The United States maintains this form of government. [Cue SLIDES]	TRANSITION ZOOM: Zooms into Representative Democracy rectangle D.C. SLIDES: Rapid sequence of Washington images: Capitol Hill, White House, Lincoln Memorial
Direct democracy, appropriate for a town meeting, is not practical on a national level. [Cue VIDEO, AUDIO]	Busy People VIDEO: crowd scenes, such as city pedestrians at rush hour Crowd AUDIO: roar of a crowd
[Cue Timeline SLIDE] And so, for over 225 years the United States government has protected and served its citizens. [Cue VIDEO]	Timeline SLIDE: show major events in U.S. history Fireworks VIDEO: images of Fourth of July celebrations

Classical music establishes a formal tone appropriate to the subject.

Use of zoom technique adds motion and interest to charts on governments.

Mark provides clear directions to keep the flow of the presentation smooth.

Audiovisual elements provide a vivid and memorable conclusion.

Student Model

- Explain that the Student Model is a sample and that students' presentations may be longer.
- Call students' attention to the first call-out note. Point out that the bracketed cues in the Text column correspond to items in the Audio and Video column. Have students read the model silently. If possible, play a recording of Pachelbel's *Canon in D* while students read.
- As a class, discuss how the music influences the reading. Discuss how other musical selections might change the presentation's tone.
- Tell students to avoid dramatic special effects that distract from the main message and to make sure that any effects clarify and enhance the audience's understanding.
- Explain that a multimedia presentation, like an essay, should summarize and reinforce the thesis in the conclusion.

Real-World Connection

Multimedia presentations in the workplace: Explain that multimedia presentations are important tools in many businesses. For example, presentations are used for outlining goals and ideas, selling products and services, and training employees. Next, ask students whether they have encountered multimedia presentations at theme parks, museums, landmarks, or athletic stadiums. If so, have them discuss how these presentations influenced their experiences.

CUSTOMIZE INSTRUCTION FOR UNIVERSAL ACCESS

For Less Proficient Writers	For English Learners	For Advanced Writers
Students may find the research and selection process challenging. Guide them to select topics for which they are likely to find ample sources. Encourage them to write descriptions of the sources they locate. Students can then use these descriptions to narrow their choices and to organize their reports.	Students may encounter unfamiliar language in media sources, catalogues, labels, and technical instructions. Have students work in groups of mixed skill levels to complete their research and to organize their presentations. Encourage group members to help one another interpret unfamiliar terms and phrases.	Have students choose a controversial topic as the subject of their reports. Presentations should identify both sides of the issue, articulate the presenter's point of view, and attempt to persuade the audience to adopt the presenter's stance on the topic.

Drafting

- Explain that, like a written report, a multimedia report must be well organized. Review the Organize Your Report chart with the class.
- Ask students what parts of the chart they would include in an outline for a written report.
  Answer: An outline should include all three parts of the chart.
- After students outline their reports, have them draft their scripts, including a list of corresponding multimedia elements. (Students may want to refer to the Student Model on p. 1155.)
- Explain that a multimedia presentation must be choreographed and rehearsed. Allow students who have knowledge about different technologies to conduct in-class workshops for other students.

Revising

- Point out that the best way to revise a presentation is to practice delivering it and then revise as needed.
- Explain that presentations need to flow smoothly and logically. Have students read the Model on this page.
- Ask students why Mark decided not to repeat the Direct Democracy slides.
  Possible response: The slides of ancient Greece and colonial New England would confuse his audience and detract from the main idea that direct democracy is not practical at the national level.

(continued on page 1157)

Drafting

Outline your report. Create a broad working outline to organize your ideas in a logical fashion. The chart shown here outlines an effective sequence for a multimedia presentation.

Organize Your Report

Introduction: Present the topic and a thesis statement about it. Include a dramatic or vivid media element to win viewers' interest.
Body: Develop the thesis through exposition and examples, the text of which should be enhanced in places by other media.
Conclusion: Reiterate research that supports thesis.

Draft a script. Use your outline and notes to draft a script and plan your delivery. Write cues in your script to indicate what media to use and when to use them. Strive for a balance between the narrative, audio, and visual elements.

Prepare the equipment. Assemble all the equipment you will need for your presentation. Follow these suggestions for getting organized:

- Plan a logical arrangement of props and technology so you can reach each type of media easily.
- Cue pieces of equipment so you can run each with one touch at the appropriate moment in your script.
- Make sure everything is functioning properly.
- Work with an assistant if necessary.

Revising

Revise to clarify transitions and sequence. Make sure your report will flow smoothly when you present it to an audience.

1. Give a partner a copy of your script to follow as you present your report.
2. Ask your partner to place a check mark next to any points that were confusing, out of order, or that required transitions.
3. Rewrite as necessary to clarify sequence and connections among ideas. Eliminate awkward transitions.

Model: Revising to Improve Transitions

Direct democracy, appropriate for a town meeting, is not practical on a national level. ~~[Cue repeat of Direct Democracy SLIDES]~~ ∧ *[Cue Busy People VIDEO]*	~~Direct democracy SLIDES~~ ∧ *Busy People VIDEO: series of crowd scenes, such as city pedestrians at rush hour*

Mark deletes repetitive images and adds a more appropriate video to match his text.

USING TECHNOLOGY IN WRITING

Technology resources are useful for preparing and delivering multimedia presentations. If possible, provide students with access to audiocassette players, videocassette players and monitors, digital cameras and recorders, slide projectors, and compact disc players. Many computers are equipped with slide-show applications (such as Microsoft PowerPoint®). If students are not familiar with the equipment, arrange for audio visual tutorials or workshops.

Students can also use the organizing tools and revision checkers on the **Writing and Grammar iText CD-ROM.**

Revise to improve variety of media. Review your script for overuse of a particular form of media and revise for variety.

Without variety: Play audio of interview with actor.
Play audio of interview with artist.
Play audio of interview with musician.

With variety: Play video footage of actor in performance.
Play audio footage of interview with artist to accompany slides of work.
Play CD by musician.

The plans below show the multimedia element of part of a presentation. Compare the model and the nonmodel.

Nonmodel	Model
SLIDE: chart of representative democracy SLIDES: Washington, D.C., images SLIDE: picture of crowd of pedestrians	TRANSITION ZOOM: chart of representative democracy SLIDES: Washington, D.C., images VIDEO: crowd scenes, such as rush hour AUDIO: roar of a crowd

Publishing and Presenting

Present your report. Deliver your multimedia report to your class, following these guidelines:

- Practice to familiarize yourself with your script.
- Have a backup plan in case any piece of equipment fails.
- Speak at an appropriate pace and volume, and maintain eye contact.

WG *Writing and Grammar Connection: Diamond Level, Chapter 12*

Rubric for Self-Assessment

Evaluate your mutimedia report using the following criteria and rating scale:

Criteria	Rating Scale: Not very				Very
How varied are the media?	1	2	3	4	5
How well do media convey key ideas?	1	2	3	4	5
How well organized is the report?	1	2	3	4	5
How smooth are the transitions among media?	1	2	3	4	5
How effective is the pacing?	1	2	3	4	5

Revising (continued)

- Draw students' attention to the Without variety/With variety examples on this page.
- Then, ask students to compare the Nonmodel with the Model and determine which is more effective.
Answer: The Model is more effective because it uses a variety of media, including slides, video, audio, and a special effect: the transition zoom. The Nonmodel uses only slides.

Publishing and Presenting

- Suggest that students rehearse their reports at least five times before presenting them to the class.
- After students give their presentations to the class, challenge them to write short analyses of their experiences: What were the most useful things they learned? What were the most effective elements of their presentations? What aspects could they improve?

Assessment

- As a class, review the assessment criteria.
- Before students proceed with self-assessment, have them score the Student Model in class, using one or more of the rubric categories, to help them see how to apply the criteria. Then, direct students to use the rubric to assess their own presentations.
- An alternative rubric can be found on p. 32 of **Performance Assessment and Portfolio Management.**

TEST-TAKING TIP

Explain that few tests demand that students create exciting multimedia presentations, but many writing prompts require that they use techniques to persuade an audience. As in a multimedia presentation, students can write using specific strategies to capture an audience's attention. For example, if the audience is a group of gardeners, the writer can use nature imagery or gardening analogies to persuade the audience. Before students respond to prompts that require persuasive writing, they should ask themselves: Can I present information in a way that is engaging? What strategies can I use to achieve this?

Lesson Objectives

1. To analyze a media presentation
2. To determine the main idea and purpose of a media presentation
3. To evaluate the evidence used in a media presentation and to identify possible biases

Evaluate the Content

- Remind students that many television shows present information in a format that projects an image of objectivity while actually expressing a biased viewpoint.
- The next time students watch a television news show, tell them to identify the apparent main idea of a report and then determine whether an objective message is being conveyed.
- Explain that viewers should look for a balance of evidence. If a report acknowledges or explores only one perspective on an issue, then the report may not be objective.

Evaluate the Presentation

- Ask students how each of these images sends a different message: **(a)** a politician shaking hands with people in a crowd; or **(b)** a politician riding in a motorcade. Possible response: The first image suggests that the politician is in touch with constituents, and the second image suggests that the politician is remote.
- Encourage students to listen closely to word choices in media reports. For example, a reporter might use the word *mislead* rather than *lie*, or the word *situation* rather than *crisis* to influence the audience.
- Challenge students to discover whether the credentials of an "expert" are relevant to the issue at hand. For example, Dr. Jones might offer medical opinions, but he or she may actually hold a Ph.D. in history.

Listening and Speaking WORKSHOP

Analyze a Media Presentation

People are bombarded with information from various media sources daily. How can you wade through this deluge to evaluate the quality, thoroughness, and objectivity of the information that comes your way? The strategies on this page can help you **analyze media presentations**.

Evaluate the Content

News reports, documentaries, newsmagazines, editorials, and other types of media presentations have a specific purpose—to inform, to persuade, to entertain, or any combination of these. Consider the following points as you analyze news media presentations:

Identify the main idea. Like a headline in a newspaper, the first line of a broadcast report usually relates the most important idea of a news story. Pay careful attention to the type of story being reported and identify the viewpoint of the reporter.

Evaluate supporting evidence. Facts, statistics, quotations, and other evidence should give a sense of the diverse perspectives on an issue. Remember that so-called "objective" evidence can be used selectively to support a particular point of view.

Feedback Form for a Media Presentation

Rating System
+ = Excellent ✓ = Average – = Weak

Content
Topic of story ________
Main point ________

Supporting Evidence
Expert interviews (with whom? to what effect?)
____
Photographs/video (what is shown? to what effect?)
____
Language (slanted language? to what effect?)
____
What visual aids, if any, are used?
____

Production Values
Effects of set ________
Effects of graphics ________
Effects of music/sound effects ________
Behavior of anchors/reporters ________

Evaluate the Presentation

Following are some techniques that can be used to influence audience response:

- **Images** A photograph captures a moment in time, but an editor can choose among many photographs. The choice of a particular image can strongly influence an audience's feelings about a topic.
- **Slanted language** Commentators can present their views by means of explicit statements of opinion and subtle choices of words. Compare these sentences:

  The City Council approved the budget today. (objective)

  After avoiding the issues for a month, the City Council finally approved the budget today. (implies impatience)
- **"Experts"** Remember that the experts chosen to analyze news events have opinions. For example, an expert discussing a controversy in city policy may show bias by presenting the views of one side more sympathetically than the views of another. When you listen to an expert, consider that person's qualifications and motivations.

Activity: Analysis and Discussion Analyze a television news story using the Feedback Form above as a guide. Share your analysis in a class discussion.

CUSTOMIZE INSTRUCTION FOR UNIVERSAL ACCESS

For Less Proficient Writers	For English Learners	For Advanced Writers
Record a brief news report, and create an outline shell that lists the main topic of the report and provides columns for the students to record several images and their reactions to each one. It is a good idea to provide one example for students as a model. Play the news report two or three times.	Record a brief news report, and have students list the main topic of the report and provide examples of the images used. Encourage students to work as a group to record their reactions to each image in the report. Play the news report two or three times.	Have students analyze several news reports that cover a current event. Ask students to record the source of the news report, images used, and experts interviewed. Challenge them to compare and contrast the media reports and present their findings to the class.

Assessment WORKSHOP

Writer's Point of View

In the reading sections of some tests, you may be required to read a passage and interpret the writer's point of view. Use the following strategies to help you answer questions testing this skill:

- As you read, look for clues to the writer's attitude toward the subject.
- Remember that a writer can reveal his or her attitude in direct statements or indirectly through word choice or choice of details.
- The writer can reveal his or her attitude through tone. Ask yourself whether the tone of the passage is humorous, serious, or neutral.
- Look for changes in the writer's point of view.

Test-Taking Strategies

- As you read, ask yourself what other viewpoint the writer might have taken.
- Identify slanted language or loaded words that indicate the writer's feelings or opinions.

Sample Test Item

Directions: Read the passage, and then answer the question that follows.

To me, Mr. Smith exemplifies the quiet heroism that characterizes many of the men of his generation. When he learned of his fatal illness, he carried on with his life, going to the office every day that he was well enough. He celebrated the holidays with his family and enjoyed choosing the perfect gift for each family member. Mr. Smith died shortly after the first of the year on the day after his birthday. He died at home in the early evening—peacefully and with dignity, just as he had lived.

1. What is the writer's attitude toward Mr. Smith?
   - **A** amusement
   - **B** amazement
   - **C** annoyance
   - **D** admiration

Answer and Explanation

The correct answer is ***D***. From the first sentence, the writer clearly expresses admiration for Mr. Smith. At no point does the writer express a negative response, surprise, or humor, so responses ***A***, ***B***, and ***C*** are clearly incorrect.

Practice

Directions: Read the passage, and then answer the question that follows.

We all love wilderness areas, but did you know that Winnebago County already has 4,800 acres of wilderness? That's out of a county that has a total of only 53,000 acres! Fellow citizens, we will be going to the polls soon to vote on a referendum to add Parker's Bayou in perpetuity to the wilderness areas that remain undeveloped. Think twice, friends! Our county is having financial problems. Companies are leaving our area, in part because of a lack of land on which to build. Let's open Parker's Bayou to development. We could use more boating areas. We could use more industrial areas. We do not need more wilderness areas. Vote NO to additional wilderness acres on Tuesday.

1. Which statement best expresses the writer's point of view?
   - **A** Winnebago County already has enough wilderness areas.
   - **B** Winnebago County is a great place in which to live.
   - **C** Parker's Bayou is an unimportant part of Winnebago County.
   - **D** Winnebago County needs more wilderness areas.

Lesson Objective

To interpret a writer's point of view in a standardized test situation

Applying Reading Strategies

Explain that to interpret a writer's point of view, a reader must infer meaning from elements in the text. If students have trouble identifying a writer's tone as humorous, serious, or neutral, suggest that they first identify words or phrases that distinguish the tone as positive or negative.

Test-Taking Skills

- Have students read the passage for the Sample Test Item. Then, ask them to identify words and phrases that give hints about the writer's attitude.
- Next, have students read the Answer and Explanation. After students identify D as the correct answer, challenge them to revise the passage to support another answer choice.
- Have students read and respond to the Practice question.

Answer

The correct answer is A, as indicated by the last sentence in the passage. Answer *B* is incorrect because the passage does not evaluate Winnebago County's livability. Answer *C* is incorrect because the writer believes that Parker's Bayou is important to the future of Winnebago County, but not as a wilderness area. Answer *D* is incorrect because it expresses a point of view opposite that of the writer.

TEACHING RESOURCES

The following resources can be used to enrich or extend the instruction for p. 1159.

For additional diagnostics and remediation for skills covered in this grouping, use materials from the Prentice Hall Assessment System.

Unit Objectives

1. To read selections from world literature written during the period of 1946 to the present
2. To apply a variety of reading strategies, particularly those appropriate for reading fiction
3. To analyze literary elements
4. To use a variety of strategies to read unfamiliar words and to build vocabulary
5. To learn elements of grammar, usage, and style
6. To use recursive writing processes to write in a variety of forms
7. To develop listening and speaking skills
8. To express and support responses to various types of texts
9. To prepare, organize, and present literary interpretations

Meeting the Objectives

With each selection, you will find instructional materials through which students can meet these objectives. Further, you will find additional practice pages for reading strategies, literary analysis, vocabulary, and grammar in the **Selection Support: Skills Development Workbook** in your **Teaching Resources.**

Background

Art

Jazz le Cheval l'Écuyère et le Clown, by Henri Matisse

Henri Matisse was born in 1869 in Picardy, France. He did not begin to paint until 1890. In 1891, he left his job as a law clerk and became a professional artist. Matisse became well known in the Fauvist movement (artists who used a lot of color) and developed into perhaps the most significant twentieth century French painter. Matisse died in Nice, France, in 1954.

- How does Matisse use color in this painting to create interest?
  Possible response: Matisse's use of bright colors and strong contrasts make the figures leap from the canvas.

UNIT 9 The Contemporary World

Jazz le Cheval l'Écuyère et le Clown, Henri Matisse

UNIT FEATURES

Connections	Reading Informational Materials
Every unit contains a feature that connects literature to a related topic, such as art, science, or history. In this unit students will read **from Hiroshima, by John Hersey** on p. 1324. Use the information and questions on the Connections pages to help students enrich their understanding of the selections presented within the unit.	These selections will help students learn to analyze and evaluate informational texts, such as workplace documents, technical directions, and consumer materials. They will expose students to the organization and features unique to nonnarrative texts. In this unit, the focus is on Press Releases. **The Nobel Prize in Literature, Press Release,** is on p. 1280.

(1946–Present)

"Liberty is the possibility of doubting, the possibility of making a mistake, the possibility of searching and experimenting...."

— Ignazio Silone, from *The God That Failed*

Assessing Student Progress

Listed below are the tools that are available to measure the degree to which students meet the unit objectives.

Informal Assessment

The questions in the Review and Assess sections are a first level of response to the concepts and skills presented within the selections. Students' responses are a brief, informal measure of their grasp of the material. These responses can indicate where further instruction and practice are needed. Then, follow up with the practice pages in the **Selection Support: Skills Development Workbook.**

Formal Assessment

The **Formal Assessment** booklet contains Selection Tests and Unit Tests.

- Selection Tests measure comprehension and skills acquisition for each selection or group of selections.
- Each Unit Test provides students with thirty multiple-choice questions and five essay questions designed to assess students' knowledge of the literature and skills taught in the unit.

The **Open-Book Tests** ask students to demonstrate their ability to synthesize and communicate information from selections or groups of selections.

To assess students' writing, you will find rubrics and scoring models in the **Performance Assessment and Portfolio Management** booklet. In this booklet, you will also find scoring rubrics for listening and speaking activities.

Alternative Assessment

The **Extension Activities** booklet contains writing activities, listening and speaking activities, and research and technology activities that are appropriate for students with different ability levels. You may also use these activities as an alternative measurement of students' growth.

ASSESSMENT RESOURCES

The following resources can be used to assess students' knowledge and skills.

Selection Assessment

- **Selection Support:** Skills Development Workbook
- **Formal Assessment**
- **Open-Book Tests**
- **Performance Assessment and Portfolio Management**
- **Extension Activities**

Using the Timeline

The Timeline can serve a number of instructional purposes, as follows:

Getting an Overview

Use the Timeline to help students get a quick overview of themes and events of the period. This approach will benefit all students but may be especially helpful for Visual/Spatial Learners, English Learners, and Less Proficient Readers. (For strategies in using the Timeline as an overview, see the bottom of this page.)

Thinking Critically

Questions are provided on the facing page. Use these questions to have students review the events, discuss their significance, and examine the "so what" behind the "what happened."

Connecting to Selections

Have students refer to the Timeline when they begin to read individual selections. By consulting the Timeline regularly, they will gain a better sense of the period's chronology. In addition, they will appreciate world events that gave rise to these works of literature.

Projects

Students can use the Timeline as a launching pad for projects like these:

- **Author's Publication Timeline** Have students select one of the authors listed on the Timeline and research the books the author has written and their dates of publication, as well as any awards the author has received. Then, have each student create a timeline of that author's work, listing the titles and dates of publication, as well as the awards and dates of recognition.
- **Oral Report** Have students select one of the events on the Timeline and research what effect that event had on society and whether the event influenced subsequent literature. Then, have each student prepare an oral report and deliver it to the class. Students may wish to interview older relatives or friends who lived during that time for individual reactions to the event.

Timeline 1946–Present

1946 | 1956 | 1966

Political and Cultural Events

- **1947** The transistor is invented.
- **1947** India and Pakistan gain independence.
- **1948** UN approves the Universal Declaration of Human Rights.
- **1948** The state of Israel is born.
- **1949** Communists seize power in China.
- **1950–1953** The Korean War is fought.
- **1952** United States explodes first hydrogen bomb.
- **1953** Watson and Crick discover the chemical basis of DNA. ◄
- **1957** The Russian satellite *Sputnik* goes into orbit. ▼

- **1959** A communist revolution is successful in Cuba.
- **1962** The Cuban missile crisis occurs.
- **1968** Many nations sign the Nuclear Non-Proliferation Treaty.
- **1969** The United States lands a man on the moon. ▼
- **1970s** The feminist movement is active in Western countries.
- **1971** The first microprocessor chip is introduced in the United States.
- **1975** After 20 years, the Vietnam War ends.
- **1975** The communist regime in Cambodia begins killing millions of Cambodians.

Literary Events

- **1947** French author Albert Camus publishes his novel *The Plague.* ▼
- **1947** Italian author Primo Levi publishes *Survival in Auschwitz.*

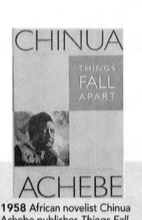

- **1958** African novelist Chinua Achebe publishes *Things Fall Apart.* ▲
- **1958** Romanian-born Elie Wiesel publishes his Holocaust novel *Night.*
- **1963** The Latin American "Boom" begins with the publication of Julio Cortázar's novel *Hopscotch.*
- **1966** German poet Nelly Sachs receives the Nobel Prize in Literature.
- **1967** Colombian Gabriel García Márquez publishes his novel *One Hundred Years of Solitude.*
- **1968** Japanese novelist Yasunari Kawabata wins the Nobel Prize in Literature.
- **1971** Pablo Neruda wins the Nobel Prize in Literature.
- **1973** Italian author Italo Calvino publishes *Invisible Cities.*

ENRICHMENT: Getting an Overview of the Period

Introduction	Key Events
To give students an overview of the period, have them indicate the span of dates in the title of the Timeline. Next, point out that the Timeline is divided into Political and Cultural Events (on the top) and Literary Events (on the bottom). Have students scan the Timeline, looking at both the Political and Cultural Events and the Literary Events. Finally, point out that the events in the Timeline often represent beginnings, turning points, and endings (for example the death of R. K. Narayan in 2001).	Have students name events that impact their lives. **Possible response:** Key events include the discovery of DNA and the advent of the personal computer. Ask students how modern events influence their world perspective differently than their parents or grandparents. **Possible response:** Technology has created a global community in contrast to the more isolated communities in which student's parents or grandparents may have been raised.

World Events

1976 | 1986 | 1996 | Present

- **1977** The first mass-produced personal computers appear in the United States. ◀
- **1980** From 1950 until this year, more than 50 new nations have emerged in Africa.
- **1981** The disease known as AIDS is first reported by United States investigators.
- **1982–1983** World music becomes a genre.
- **1980s** More than 50,000 nuclear weapons exist.
- **1980s** European nations form the European Union (EU).

- **1989** Chinese government suppresses student demonstration in Tiananmen Square. ▼
- **1990–1991** The United States and allies defeat Iraq in first Persian Gulf War.
- **1990s** Apartheid ends in South Africa. ▼
- **1991** Soviet Union collapses.
- **1994** About 500,000 civilians killed in Rwanda ethnic conflicts.

- **1997** The Kyoto Protocol is formulated to control global warming.
- **2000** The Internet, a worldwide computer network, thrives.
- **2001** On September 11, hijackers crash planes into the World Trade Center and the Pentagon.
- **2003** The United States defeats Iraq in the second Gulf War.

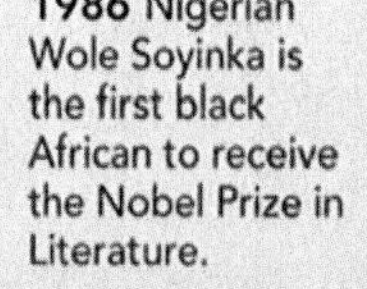

- **1982** Gabriel García Márquez wins the Nobel Prize in Literature.
- **1983** Indian novelist R. K. Narayan publishes *A Tiger for Malgudi.*
- **1983** Caribbean author Jamaica Kincaid publishes her first book, *At the Bottom of the River.*

- **1986** Nigerian Wole Soyinka is the first black African to receive the Nobel Prize in Literature.
- **1992** Caribbean writer Derek Walcott wins Nobel Prize in Literature.

- **1996** Jamaica Kincaid publishes *The Autobiography of My Mother.*
- **1998** Bei Dao publishes a book of poems entitled *Blue House.*
- **1999** Günter Grass receives the Nobel Prize in Literature.
- **2001** R. K. Narayan dies.
- **2001** Lebanese poet Vénus Khoury-Ghata publishes *Here There Was Once a Country.*

Analyzing the Timeline

1. **(a)** What scientific discovery occurred in 1953? **(b)** What does this discovery indicate about the emphasis on scientific research during this period? **[Deduce]**
   Possible response: **(a)** The DNA molecule was discovered. **(b)** Scientific research was focused on the basis of life.
2. **(a)** From 1950 to 1980, how many new nations emerged in Africa? **(b)** Judging from the Timeline, how did this emergence affect African writers? **[Infer]**
   Answer: **(a)** Over 50 new nations emerged in Africa during this time period. Possible response: **(b)** African writers began to receive worldwide recognition for their work.
3. **(a)** What two authors published books about the Holocaust? **(b)** What is the value of authors using their personal experiences as a basis for writing about world events? **[Evaluate]**
   Answer: **(a)** Primo Levi and Elie Wiesel wrote about the Holocaust. **(b)** Possible response: By using personal experience, authors provide readers with a more accurate view of what happened and help readers feel what the individuals experienced.
4. **(a)** What communication method was being used quite successfully in 2000? **(b)** What influence has this communication network had on the spread of information and the development of communication? **[Interpret]**
   Possible response: **(a)** The Internet had become a worldwide communication network. **(b)** Information can be passed almost instantaneously from one area to another throughout the world.
5. **(a)** What event took place on September 11, 2001? **(b)** How have the daily lives of Americans changed since this event? **[Apply]**
   Answer: **(a)** On September 11, 2001, hijackers crashed planes into the World Trade Center and the Pentagon. Possible response: **(b)** There have been changes in security, travel and tourism, and the economy.

continued

continued from right column

▶Critical Viewing

1. What does the illustration of the DNA molecule (1953) suggest about the molecule? **[Infer]**
   Possible response: It suggests that the molecule is complex and may have been difficult to isolate.
2. Compare and contrast the picture of *Sputnik* going into orbit (1957) with the picture of the man on the Moon (1969). **[Compare and Contrast]**
   Possible response: The picture of *Sputnik* is an artist's rendering, but the picture of man on the Moon is an actual photograph. The photo illustrates the progress of technology and space exploration since the time of *Sputnik*.
3. What conclusions can you draw about the Tiananmen Square demonstration (1989) on the basis of the picture provided? **[Draw Conclusions]**
   Possible response: The Chinese government used military tanks to overwhelm the student demonstration and the confrontation turned violent.

Literature of the Period

- In the excerpt from Derek Walcott's *Omeros* on p. 1198, students will read about the effects of colonialism.
- In Yehuda Amichai's poem "The Diameter of the Bomb," p. 1319, students will read about the effects of modern weaponry.
- Students will read about the human rights abuses that took place during the Holocaust in the memoirs of Primo Levi and Elie Wiesel, pp. 1260 and 1267.

▶Critical Viewing

Possible response: The photograph may remind students of viewing the Moon from Earth, that the Earth is only a tiny part of the Universe, or that there are still places to explore.

Background

Amnesty International

Amnesty International is an independent organization that helps put international pressure on governments that suppress human rights. The organization also strives to set free prisoners of conscience, ensure fair and prompt trials, and end torture and executions throughout the world. Amnesty International has approximately 750,000 members in over 150 countries.

The Contemporary World

(1946–PRESENT)

Historical Background

Perhaps the most important photograph of the postwar period is the picture of Earth from the moon. It shows a cloud-wrapped blue jewel of a planet, alone in the darkness of outer space. That jewel is ours. If we—the people of the world—do not learn how to cherish Earth and live in peace with one another, then our treasure will be lost. The history of the contemporary world reveals our failures and successes in this struggle.

The End of Colonialism and the Cold War In the postwar period, the colonial empires built by Western powers during the Age of Imperialism crumbled. In Asia and Africa, people demanded and won freedom. Between 1950 and 1980, more than 50 new nations arose in Africa alone. The new nations emerged into a world dominated and divided by the Cold War, a more than 40-year struggle between the United States and the Soviet Union. Each of these superpowers wanted new countries to adopt its ideology, or system of thought or belief—either capitalism or socialism.

Set up at the end of World War II as a forum for settling disputes, the United Nations (UN) played a vital role in decolonization. It has also tried to act as a peacekeeper and to provide valuable health, educational, and other services for the world's people.

Deadly Weapons Since the United States first exploded two atomic bombs in 1945, nations have been building nuclear weapons. The number of these weapons grew from 3 in 1945 to more than 50,000 in the 1980s. During the Cold War, efforts to curb the arms race had only limited success. Yet, in 1968, many nations signed the Nuclear Non-Proliferation Treaty (NPT), agreeing to halt the spread of nuclear weapons. In 1995, the treaty was renewed, but some nations still refused to sign.

Human Rights and Intervention In 1948, UN members approved the Universal Declaration of Human Rights, which proclaims that all people are entitled to basic freedoms. Nevertheless, human rights abuses, including torture and arbitrary arrest, continue to occur around the world. People have debated whether the world community should intervene to protect individual rights in a sovereign nation. The UN has a mixed record on intervention. In the 1990s, the UN sent peacekeepers to northern Iraq to protect the Kurds from persecution by the Iraqi government. The UN, however, was slow to move against Serbs who persecuted Muslims in Bosnia and did not intervene when Hutus massacred about one million Tutsis in Rwanda.

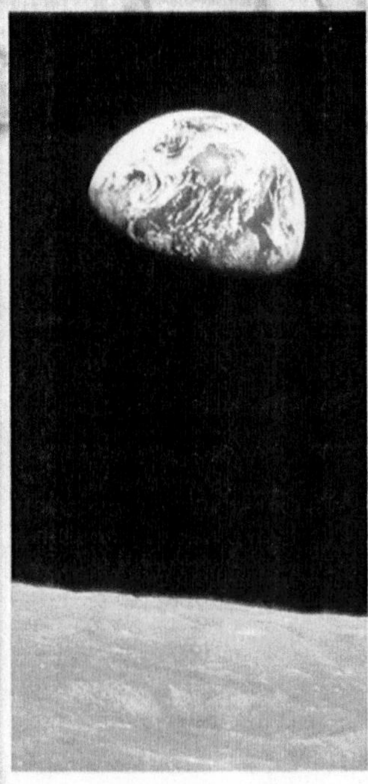

▲ **Critical Viewing** This photograph shows Earth as seen from the moon. What thoughts does it inspire in you? Explain. **[Respond]**

ENRICHMENT: History Connection

The End of Colonialism in Africa

In 1945, the only African nations not ruled by Europeans were Ethiopia and the Kingdom of Egypt. Among the European nations with colonies in Africa were France, Britain, Italy, Belgium, and Portugal. Some key dates in the movement toward African independence are as follows:

1954 Start of the Algerian war of independence

1956 Sudan, Tunisia, and Morocco gain independence

1957 Ghana becomes independent

1960 Seventeen African states are granted independence

1963 The Organization of African Unity is created

Terrorism: Deadly Politics Terrorism is the deliberate use of violence, especially against civilians, to achieve political results. Since the 1960s, incidents of terrorism have increased around the world. In 2001, an especially deadly incident occurred on United States soil when suicide bombers opposed to American policies in the Middle East crashed several hijacked airplanes into the World Trade Center in New York and the Pentagon in Washington, D.C., killing thousands.

The Global North and South The Cold War created an ideological split between the communist East and the capitalist West. Today, an economic gulf divides the world into two spheres—the relatively rich nations of the global North and the relatively poor nations of the global South. Nations of the North control much of the world's capital, trade, and technology. Yet, they depend increasingly on low-paid workers in developing states to provide manufactured goods as inexpensively as possible.

The Environment For both rich and poor nations, economic development has taken a heavy toll on the environment. In addition, over the last century, world temperatures have steadily increased. Scientists blame this global warming on the emission of gases into the upper atmosphere. Many warn that unless the world takes action, global warming will continue and cause great harm to the environment.

Old Ways and New In the Western world, industrialization and urbanization began during the Industrial Revolution. In the past fifty years, the rest of the world has experienced similar upheavals. Since 1945, people in the developing world have flocked to cities to find jobs and escape rural poverty. Many, settling in urban slums, have only changed the location of their poverty.

In recent times, religious revivals have swept many religions. Some religious reformers have been called fundamentalists because they stress what they see as the fundamental, or basic, values of their faiths. Many have sought political power to resist changes that they think undermine their beliefs.

▲ **Critical Viewing** In this photograph, three firemen raise the American flag at Ground Zero, where the World Trade Center had stood on September 11, 2001. What roles did firefighters, police officers, and emergency workers play during and after the terrorist attacks that took place on that day? **[Connect]**

Background

The Environment

Pollution poses a special problem in Eastern European nations that, now free from Soviet control, are struggling to establish market economies. Years of environmental neglect in these countries have taken a terrible toll. Water and soil have been contaminated by sewage, factory discharge, and toxic waste; and acid rain has damaged the forests in Central Europe's industrial belt.

▶Critical Viewing

Possible response: Emergency workers acted selflessly by rescuing victims of the attack and by trying to keep a sense of calm. In many cases these people gave up their lives trying to save those trapped in the burning buildings while others tirelessly searched for survivors.

CUSTOMIZE INSTRUCTION FOR UNIVERSAL ACCESS

For Less Proficient Readers	For English Learners	For Advanced Readers
As students read, have them focus on the end of the Cold War and the end of colonialism. Ask students how living with the threat of nuclear war or foreign control might affect the types of literature writers produce. Then, as they read, have students check to see whether their speculations are correct.	Students may have a difficult time understanding the terms *Cold War* and *colonialism*. Pair each student with a native English speaker, and have students work together to create a list of ways their lives would be different if they were living in a Cold War or colonial environment.	Ask students to use Internet or library resources to investigate one instance of colonialism in Africa or Asia. Have students make a list of the ways in which colonialism affected the people of the colony and how independence affected the people as they formed their new nation.

Background

DNA

In 1953, molecular biologists J. D. Watson and F. H. Crick discovered that DNA was composed of two strands coiled into a double helix configuration. DNA is found in the nucleus of the cell and is the chief material in chromosomes, the cells that control the heredity of living organisms.

Background

Space Exploration

On July 20, 1969, U.S. astronaut Neil Armstrong became the first man to step on the Moon. Edwin Aldrin, Jr., was the second man from the Apollo 11 lunar module, *Eagle*, to walk on the Moon's surface. The *Eagle* was on the Moon for nearly twenty-two hours.

Listening to Music

Play "African American Contemporary Music: 'Africa Home,' Universal Language," Track 13, on **Prentice Hall: Listening to Music: World Masterpieces.** This song honors Africa as the source of modern African-American musical traditions.

Women's Rights After 1945, women's movements brought changes to both the Western and the developing nations. The UN Charter supported "equal rights for men and women." By 1950, women had won the right to vote in many countries. In the industrialized world, more and more women worked outside the home; by the 1970s, the feminist movement sought equal rights for working women.

Science and Technology Since 1945, the computer has brought an information revolution. By 2000, a huge computer network, the Internet, linked individuals, governments, and businesses around the world, changing the way people learn, shop, and keep in touch with each other. (See Close-up on Culture, page 1170.)

In the field of medicine, vaccines helped prevent the spread of diseases. Recently, however, the spread of new deadly diseases, such as acquired immune deficiency syndrome (AIDS), has challenged researchers. In 1953, James Watson and Francis Crick analyzed the structure of DNA, the chemical underlying genetic inheritance. This discovery made possible the Human Genome Project (1990–present), whose goal is to locate every human gene and identify its chemical makeup.

The space age started in 1957 when the Soviet Union launched *Sputnik*, the first artificial satellite, into orbit. *Sputnik* set off a frantic "space race" between the superpowers. In 1969, the United States landed the first man on the moon. Since the Cold War ended, however, the United States and Russia have cooperated in joint space ventures.

Music in the Historical Context

The Growth of "World Music"

Portuguese fado, Brazilian samba, and Pakistani *qawwali* are diverse musical styles with something important in common. You can probably find all of them at a CD superstore under the category "world music." This grab bag of a genre includes traditional music from every corner of the globe, sometimes spiced with state-of-the-art technology or combined with current Western styles.

Almost every culture has been making music for countless years, but "world music," as such, is only about twenty years old. This genre was the brainchild of store owners and media executives in the United States and Britain who wanted to sell foreign music to Western consumers. Starting out as a marketing idea, it gained momentum with the establishment of a world music chart in 1990 and a world music Grammy Award in 1991.

Today, this category goes beyond CD ratings and sales. Like world literature, world music helps different cultures understand and appreciate one another.

So, if you want to learn about other cultures by adding new flavors to your musical diet, try feasting on Polynesian choirs, the epic songs of Baluchistan bards, or the calypsos of Costa Rica.

ENRICHMENT: Science Connection

The Discovery of DNA

Francis Crick, co-discoverer of DNA, made the following comments on his discovery:

> What, then, do Jim Watson and I deserve credit for? If we deserve any credit at all, it is for persistence and the willingness to discard ideas when they became untenable. One reviewer thought that we couldn't have been very clever because we went on so many false trails, but that is the way discoveries are usually made. Most attempts fail not because of lack of brains but because the investigator gets stuck in a cul-de-sac or gives up too soon. . . .
>
> However, I don't believe all this amounts to much. The major credit I think Jim and I deserve, considering how early we were in our research careers, is for selecting the right problem and sticking to it. . . .

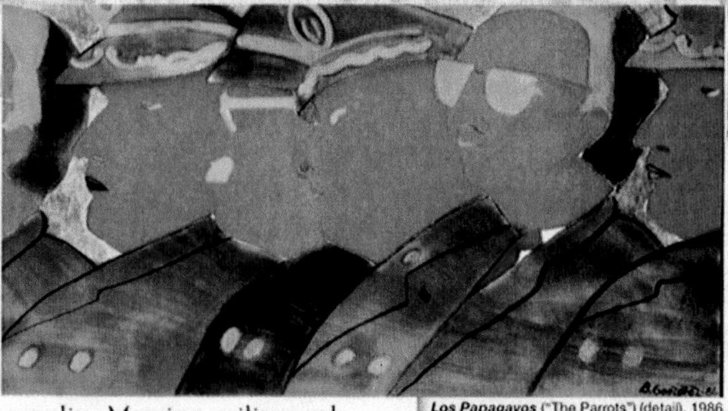

Los Papagayos ("The Parrots") (detail), 1986, Beatriz Gonzalez, Courtesy of the artist, Bogota, Colombia

Despite the importance of global issues and trends, not every region experienced the postwar period in the same way. The following summaries focus on specific areas.

Latin America Despite setbacks, Latin American nations have tried to sustain economic growth and overcome a legacy of poverty and social inequality. Marxism, military rule, and the Roman Catholic Church have been continuing influences in the region. The United States has also exerted a strong influence on Latin American politics. After the communist revolution in Cuba in 1959, the region became the focus of intense Cold War rivalries. Of the larger nations, Mexico enjoyed economic gains, but most of its people remained in poverty. As of 2003, Argentina was facing an economic crisis, and Brazil had just elected a leftist president.

Europe, West and East Many Western European nations joined with the United States in NATO (North Atlantic Treaty Organization), the alliance that opposed the Soviet Union during the Cold War. Protected by NATO's umbrella, Western Europe enjoyed strong economic growth. Many nations introduced the welfare state, although in the 1980s, economic slowdowns forced cuts in social programs. European nations formed the European Community (EC) in 1957 and the European Union (EU) in the 1980s and 1990s. In 1999, the EU launched a single currency called the euro.

Efforts to reform inefficiencies in government and the economy led to the collapse of the Soviet Union in 1991. After shaking off Soviet domination, nations of Eastern Europe faced economic challenges and ethnic conflicts. Many of them will join the EU. Yugoslavia, a Soviet ally, experienced a breakup into warring nations and ethnic groups, with NATO military pressure resolving crises in Bosnia and Kosovo.

The Middle East Nationalistic and religious struggles have made this region a trouble spot. Israel's declaration of statehood in 1948 represented a rebirth of the Jewish spirit after the Holocaust, the systematic destruction of Jews by the Nazis. Since 1948, however, Israelis and Arabs have engaged in a long struggle punctuated by several wars. In addition, the United States fought two wars against Iraq, in 1990–1991 and again in 2003, when it finally toppled the regime of Saddam Hussein. Both Islamic fundamentalism and pro-democratic movements are significant forces in this region.

Africa Leaders of new African nations set out to build strong central governments, achieve economic growth, and raise standards of living. They have faced a variety of obstacles, including economic dependency and political instability. After independence, a number of new nations experienced military or one-party rule. Many have since introduced multiparty democracy. African nations also experimented with different

▲ Critical Viewing
The Parrots, a painting by Beatriz Gonzalez, is a commentary on Latin American politics. Judging by the images and colors in this detail from the painting, what statement is the artist making? Explain. **[Interpret]**

ENRICHMENT: History Connection

The Partitioning of Palestine

In 1947, the United Nations passed a resolution partitioning Palestine into a Jewish state and a Palestinian Arab state. At that point, British troops withdrew from the region and fighting broke out between Zionists and Palestinian Arabs. Zionists won that battle, and after the State of Israel was proclaimed in 1948, this new state fought against its Arab neighbors. Repeated hostilities over the years led to the "Six-Day War" of 1967, in which Israel won a decisive victory over the Arabs. As a result of this war, Israel occupied portions of Syria, Egypt, and Jordan. Israel eventually negotiated a treaty with the Egyptians with the assistance of President Jimmy Carter and returned the Egyptian territories it had conquered. However, the area is still attempting to find a peaceful solution to the tensions between the Israelis and the Palestinians.

▶Critical Viewing

Possible response: The painting's images and bright colors suggest that the government officials are showy, but they are homogenous, not only in appearance but also in thought. Like the parrots in the title, the officials are engaged in imitation or unintelligent repetition rather than real leadership.

Background

Solidarity

Solidarity is an organization composed of approximately fifty Polish trade unions. In 1980, Lech Walesa became the leader of Poland's labor movement. Walesa's negotiations with the Polish government led to the government's recognition of Solidarity, which marked the first time labor unions had been recognized as independent from the Communist Party. In 1981, when government opposition to Solidarity grew, the Polish government suspended the organization's activities and arrested Walesa. He was released in 1982. That same year, the government officially outlawed Solidarity. Walesa continued to organize strikes and, in 1989, negotiated an agreement that made Solidarity legal again. In 1990, Lech Walesa was elected president of Poland.

Background

Art

Show students the Senufo Mask, on Transparency 19 in the **Fine Art Transparencies** booklet. Use the image to stimulate discussion about the importance of maintaining an artistic heritage in the face of political and social growth.

Background

Apartheid in South Africa

Apartheid was the system of racial segregation in the Republic of South Africa. Objections to the restrictions placed on black Afrikaners escalated to riots and deadly battles. In 1993, the Nobel Prize was awarded jointly to F. W. De Klerk, the prime minister of South Africa, and Nelson Mandela, an anti-apartheid activist and president of the African National Congress. They won the prize for working together to dismantle apartheid.

▶ Critical Viewing

Possible response: The photograph suggests that contemporary Africa is flourishing. Africans may face the dilemma of moving into the modern world without destroying their traditional and natural heritage.

Historical Background

Comprehension Check

1. What was the Cold War?
   Answer: The Cold War was a forty-year struggle between the United States and the Soviet Union.
2. How has the Internet affected the spread of information?
   Answer: The Internet has provided instantaneous worldwide communication between individuals, governments, and businesses.
3. What event triggered a conflict between Arabs and Israelis in the Middle East?
   Answer: Israel was declared a state in 1948.
4. What political trend in Africa led to many changes in government and economic growth?
   Answer: The end of colonialism led to the establishment of independent countries.
5. How did the Cold War affect Asia?
   Answer: The Cold War led to the Korean War, the Vietnam War, and the deaths of millions.

Critical Thinking

1. Why was the Cold War important politically throughout most of the world? **[Apply]**
   Answer: Because of the struggle between democracy and communism, conflicts arose in Asia, Europe, and Latin America.
2. Compare the changes in India and Pakistan since independence with the changes in Africa. **[Compare and Contrast]**
   Answer: India and Pakistan have faced rapid urbanization, population growth, and border conflicts. African nations have set out to build and grow strong economies and raise the standard of living.
3. Analyze the reasons for and the problems with the world community intervening in human rights abuses in a sovereign nation. **[Analyze]**

continued

▲ Critical Viewing This photograph was taken in Nairobi National Park, Kenya. What messages does it convey about a contemporary African nation? Explain. **[Interpret]**

economic systems, including socialism and mixed economies, which combine capitalism and central control. In the 1990s, after decades of conflict, South Africa abandoned its system of apartheid, or racial separation, and made a transition to democratic rule.

Asia After its defeat in World War II, Japan introduced democratic reforms and by the 1960s emerged as an economic superpower. Similarly, nations such as Taiwan, Singapore, and South Korea underwent rapid industrialization. In 1949, Mao Zedong led a communist takeover of power in China. Since Mao's death in 1976, communist leaders have attempted to modernize China economically. The violent suppression of student demonstrations in Tiananmen Square (1989), however, showed the regime's determination to keep individual freedoms in check.

Cold War tensions sparked devastating conflicts in Korea, Vietnam, and Cambodia. The Korean War (1950–1953) pitted North Korea and China against South Korea and United Nations forces led by the United States. In the Vietnam War (1955–1975), which was also fought in Cambodia and Laos, the United States failed to prevent communist North Vietnam from taking over South Vietnam. Cambodian communists who seized power after winning a civil war (1975) killed millions of Cambodians.

Since gaining independence in 1947, India and Pakistan have faced rapid urbanization, population growth, and border conflicts with one another. India has built on the legacy of British rule to create the world's largest democracy, although it is still troubled by conflicts between Muslims and Hindus. In Muslim Pakistan, the military has periodically seized power from corrupt civilian regimes, and Islamic parties have gained in recent elections.

continued from left column

Possible response: All people should have basic human rights and freedoms. However, a government has the right to establish its own laws.

ENRICHMENT: History Connection

Tiananmen Square

In April 1989, Beijing University students protested at Tiananmen Square in Beijing, China, against the government's lagging political reform and suppression of human rights. The "hardline" leaders, with the support of paramount leader Deng Kiaoping, feared the social unrest would pose dangers for China's future. On June 3, 1989, these leaders opted for military suppression of the demonstrators at Tiananmen Square; the crackdown resulted in hundreds of deaths.

Literature

No one knows which of today's works will become tomorrow's classics. (See the Point/Counterpoint feature, below.) What is sure, however, is that writers from many nations are producing exciting and challenging literature.

The Latin American "Boom" The postwar upsurge of literature in Latin America was so dramatic that it was called the "Boom." One of the leading figures of this "Boom" was Argentinian fiction writer Julio Cortázar (hōō′ lē′ ō kôr tə zär′). His experimental novel *Hopscotch* (1963) may be the work that first gained attention for Latin authors. Another landmark novel was *One Hundred Years of Solitude* (1967), by the Colombian Gabriel García Márquez (gäv rē el′ gär sē′ ä mär′ kəs). Poets Pablo Neruda (pä′ blō ne rōō′ də) of Chile and Octavio Paz (ôk tä′ vyô päs′) of Mexico also gained international reputations, and each won the Nobel Prize in Literature.

National and Literary Independence In the newly independent nations of Africa, Asia, and the Caribbean, political independence has gone hand in hand with literary accomplishment. It often seemed as if gifted writers from former British colonies were reconquering the colonizer's language, adding to it the richness of their own traditions.

Nigerians Wole Soyinka (wō′ lā shô yiŋ′ kə), a playwright and poet, and Chinua Achebe (chin′ wä′ ä chā′ bā), a fiction writer, have enhanced their works with African mythology and proverbs.

Point/Counterpoint

To Preserve or to Change the Literary Canon

Should contemporary multicultural writers be added to the literary canon, the authors accepted for serious study? Two scholars disagree.

Yes! "I'm a cultural historian, and I have been in education all my life. But I didn't know when I began reading for this book [on curriculum] that 'Western Civ' as a subject is as new as it is. The aura it has as the undying, indelible basis of American education is nonsense. . . . There is no final answer, I imagine, to . . . what the curriculum should be."

—Lawrence W. Levine, in *The Chronicle of Higher Education*

No! ". . . the Canon's true question remains: What shall the individual . . . read, this late in history? . . . When our English and other literature departments shrink to the dimensions of our current Classics departments . . . we will perhaps be able to return to the study of the inescapable, to Shakespeare and his few peers, who after all, invented all of us."

—Harold Bloom, *The Western Canon*

→← POINT/COUNTERPOINT

Point out that there has been much debate about which authors should be included in the literary canon. Some scholars believe that only those authors whose works are considered classics should be read and studied by American students. Others believe that there is no particular set of authors that should be the basis for education.

1. What do these two viewpoints have in common?
   Possible response: Both authors believe that books are important for education.
2. In what ways do these viewpoints differ?
   Possible response: Bloom believes that only a few authors have shaped our culture, particularly "Shakespeare and his few peers." Levine believes that there is no final answer as to what the basis for the American school curriculum should be.
3. Point out examples that could support either view.
   Possible response: Bloom's view is supported by the fact that people continue to enjoy Shakespeare and some of his peers. In addition, these works have retained their truth for human kind for hundreds of years, making them an excellent basis for the curriculum. On the other hand, multicultural texts reflect our diverse society, and including literature from other cultures will provide students with a broader understanding of the world.

Background

Exile

Exile has been a theme in literature for thousands of years. The Roman poet Ovid was forced into exile at Tomis, an outpost on the Black Sea. In the Middle Ages, Dante was banned from his native and beloved Florence. In our own times, many writers have been imprisoned or sent into exile for expressing their convictions. Czesław Miłosz went into exile, defecting from Poland. Like Alexander Solzhenitsyn, the Russian poet Joseph Brodsky was forced to live in exile.

The Indian writer R. K. Narayan painted a vivid, humorous portrait of everyday Indian life. Nobel Prize-winner Derek Walcott, from the Caribbean, has explored his complex relationship to the West Indies in elegant poetry. Fellow Caribbean author Jamaica Kincaid has written about family relationships and the colonial legacy in Antigua.

The Two Europes: Writers Without Illusions The West has produced such outstanding writers as Albert Camus (ka mo͞o′) of France, Günter Grass (go͞on′ tər gräs) of Germany, and Italo Calvino (ē tä′ lō käl vē′ nō) of Italy. These authors are familiar with the ravages of war and the temptations to escape into a material, unreflective existence in postwar society.

Worthy of special mention are Holocaust authors like poet Nelly Sachs and prose writers Primo Levi (prē′ mō lā′ vē) and Elie Wiesel (el′ ē wi zel′). These writers experienced the attempt of the Nazis to exterminate European Jewry and have borne witness to one of history's most terrifying episodes.

Writers from Eastern Europe contended with censorship and the disapproval of authoritarian governments. Their options were few. The Russian poet Yevgeny Yevtushenko (yev gen′ ē yev′ to͞o sheŋ′ kō) stayed and campaigned for more liberal policies. Another choice, with its own set of problems, was emigration and exile. The Polish poet Czesław Miłosz (ches′ wäf mē′ wōsh) went into exile, defecting to the West. Russia's Alexander Solzhenitsyn (sōl′ zhə nēt′ sin), however, was forced into exile.

Close-up on Culture

World Literature and the Internet

World literature, like so much else in today's culture, lives on the Internet. Here are a few ways to pursue foreign authors in the realms of cyberspace:

- **Authors or Works** To find a helpful site, key the name of an author or work into a search engine. The more famous the entry, the greater your chances of finding information. Bypass .com sites that often want to sell you something, and look for those sponsored by universities (.edu) or reputable organizations (.org).
- **Organizations** Two organizations whose sites have information on world literature are the Nobel Foundation and the Academy of American Poets. The Nobel site provides background on winners of the Nobel Prize in Literature. The Academy's site has information on many foreign poets, including Anna Akhmatova, C. P. Cavafy, Czesław Miłosz, and Octavio Paz.
- **Literary Databases** Many literary databases, like the one entitled Literary Resources at Rutgers University, are now available on the Internet. Under "Literary Resources—Other National Literatures," the Rutgers database has links to sites about authors from Australia, France, Germany, Italy, Japan, Russia, and other countries. For additional databases, key "literary databases" into a search engine.

ENRICHMENT: History Connection

The Vietnam War

Poet Nguyen Thi Vinh wrote about the war she witnessed in her homeland of Vietnam. Vietnam was temporarily divided into North Vietnam and South Vietnam by an international conference in Geneva (1954). Free elections were to be held in 1956 to reunite Vietnam. These elections, however, were never held, and in North Vietnam, Ho Chi Minh created a communist state. President Ngo Dinh Diem of South Vietnam sought aid from the United States for his anti-communist government. Throughout the 1960s, the United States gradually increased its assistance until, by 1968, it had sent in more than 500,000 soldiers. Mass protests in the United States called into question the aims of the war. After Richard Nixon was elected in 1969, American troops began to be withdrawn. Not until 1973, however, did the United States negotiate a cease-fire and withdraw most of its soldiers. The communists won the war in April 1975.

Embattled Writers Eastern Europe was not the only region where writers were censored and harassed. Nadine Gordimer, who is white, stayed in South Africa and attacked the policy of racial segregation and discrimination known as apartheid (ə pär′ tāt′). In China, Bei Dao (bā′ dou) wrote poetry and prose that inspired the student leaders of the Tiananmen Square demonstration. When that demonstration was suppressed, however, Bei Dao went into exile.

The Middle East, torn by political and religious conflict, has wounded its writers both literally and figuratively. In 1994, Nobel Prize-winning Egyptian novelist Naguib Mahfouz (nä′ hēb′ mä fūz′) was stabbed by an Islamic fundamentalist angered by Mahfouz's portrayal of God in a novel. The Turkish government imprisoned poet Nazim Hikmet (nä zəm′ hik met′) for years because of his leftist political beliefs. Both Palestinian Taha Muhammad Ali and Israeli poet Yehuda Amichai (yə hōō′ də ä′ mi khī) wrote of the pain brought by war.

Another witness to war is Vietnamese poet Nguyen Thi Vinh (nōō′ yin tī vin). She expresses in a few simple words the pain of the Vietnam War, which divided a country, families, and friends: "How can this happen to us / my friend / my foe?"

▼ Critical Viewing What links do you see between this painting by Picasso and Solzhenitsyn's concept of world literature as "the one great heart"? **[Connect]**

"The One Great Heart" World literature takes on a new meaning in an era when we can view Earth from the moon. Never before have all the cultures of the world talked to each other so directly and immediately. (See Close-up on Culture, page 1170.) Solzhenitsyn, noting this fact, has called world literature "the one great heart," and he looks to writers as a force for truth and justice.

Solzhenitsyn's vision is menaced in two different ways: by those who would censor or suppress books and by the forces of hunger, poverty, and illiteracy that make it difficult or impossible to read. These warnings aside, however, we should celebrate the achievements of contemporary authors. In few other eras have writers contended with such rapid changes or such breakdowns of traditional ways and truths. In no other era have they searched for identity and meaning with greater persistence or passion. Their spirited, playfully serious poems, essays, and novels are "the one great heart" of our time.

Round of Friendship . . ., Pablo Picasso

Background

Art

Round of Friendship. . ., by Pablo Picasso

The artist, Pablo Picasso, was born in Spain and was one of the most famous artists of the twentieth century. This painting shows people dancing around a central object.

- According to Solzhenitsyn's vision, what would the central object represent?
  Possible response: The central object would represent world literature.

▶Critical Viewing

Possible response: Picasso's painting shows a variety of people joined in celebration.

Literature of the Period

Comprehension Check

1. Which Latin American poets were awarded the Nobel Prize in Literature?
   Answer: Pablo Neruda of Chile and Octavio Paz of Mexico were awarded the Nobel Prize in Literature.
2. How has national independence influenced literature in the newly independent nations of Africa, Asia, and the Caribbean?
   Answer: Writers have enhanced their works with themes and traditions of their own nations.
3. What topics have European writers written about?
   Answer: The ravages of war, the Holocaust, materialism, and lack of freedom have been topics for European writers.
4. What elements threaten Alexander Solzhenitsyn's vision of world literature as "the one great heart?"
   Answer: Censorship, poverty, and illiteracy threaten Alexander Solzhenitsyn's vision.
5. What Middle East writers were affected by politics?
   Answer: Naguib Mahfouz, Nazim Hikmet, Taka Muhammad Ali, and Yehuda Amichai were affected by the politics of the area.

continued

continued from right column

Critical Thinking

1. Why do some writers who are punished for their writings choose to stay in their native countries rather than to go into exile? **[Speculate]**
   Possible response: The writers may want to fight the abuses in their countries by remaining there or stay because their country is their home.
2. Why is it important for writers to record the evils of war and protest against a lack of freedom of thought? **[Deduce]**
   Possible response: Those who have experienced the destruction and terrors of war and the Holocaust must record these terrors so that others can work to avoid future problems.
3. Why does Alexander Solzhenitsyn call world literature "the one great heart?" **[Infer]**
   Possible response: Solzhenitsyn views writers and their works as a force for truth and justice.

The Handsomest Drowned Man in the World · House Taken Over

Lesson Objectives

1. **To analyze and respond to literary elements**
   - Literary Analysis: Magical Realism
   - Comparing Literary Works: Archetypes
2. **To read, comprehend, analyze, and critique short stories**
   - Reading Strategy: Hypothesizing
   - Reading Check Questions
   - Review and Assess Questions
   - Assessment Practice (ATE)
3. **To develop word analysis skills, fluency, and systematic vocabulary**
   - Vocabulary Development Lesson: Latin Prefix *re-*
4. **To understand and apply written and oral language conventions**
   - Spelling Strategy
   - Grammar and Style Lesson: Punctuating Dialogue
5. **To understand and apply appropriate writing and research strategies**
   - Writing Lesson: Essay Tracing the Development of a Character
   - Extension Activity: Architectural Layout
6. **To understand and apply listening and speaking strategies**
   - Extension Activity: Interactive Story

TEACHING A TENTH-GRADE COURSE

The literature in this section can be taught as part of a rich, balanced world literature course for tenth-grade students. For a full outline of such a course, see pp. T46–T48 in Volume 1 of this Teacher's Edition.

STEP-BY-STEP TEACHING GUIDE	PACING GUIDE
PRETEACH	
Motivate Students and Provide Background	
Use the Motivation activity (ATE p. 1172)	5 min.
Read and discuss author and background features (SE pp. 1172, 1174, 1182; ATE p. 1172) A	5 min.
Introduce the Concepts	
Introduce the Literary Analysis and Reading Strategy concepts (SE/ATE p. 1173) A	15 min.
Pronounce the vocabulary words and read their definitions (SE p. 1173)	5 min.
TEACH	
Monitor Comprehension	
Informally monitor comprehension by circulating while students read independently or in groups A	50 min.
Monitor students' comprehension with the Reading Check notes (SE/ATE pp. 1175, 1177, 1179, 1182, 1185, 1187)	as students read
Develop vocabulary with the Vocabulary notes (SE pp. 1175, 1178, 1184, 1187; ATE p. 1184)	as students read
Develop Understanding	
Develop students' understanding of Magical Realism with the Literary Analysis annotations (SE/ATE pp. 1174, 1182, 1185, 1186; ATE p. 1179) A	10 min.
Develop students' ability to hypothesize, using the Reading Strategy annotations (SE/ATE pp. 1177, 1180)	10 min.
ASSESS	
Assess Mastery	
Assess students' mastery of the Reading Strategy and Literary Analysis concepts by having them answer the Review and Assess questions (SE/ATE p. 1189)	20 min.
Use one or more of the print, software, or transparency Assessment Resources (ATE p. 1191) A	up to 45 min.
EXTEND	
Apply Understanding	
Have students complete the Vocabulary Development Lesson and the Grammar and Style Lesson (SE p. 1190) A	20 min.
Apply students' ability to use transitions to clarify order of events, using the Writing Lesson (SE/ATE p. 1191) A	45 min.
Apply students' understanding of the selections, using one or more of the Extension Activities (SE p. 1191)	20–90 min.

ACCELERATED INSTRUCTION:
Use the strategies and activities identified with an A.

TEACHING TENTH-GRADE STUDENTS
For support in teaching the selection(s) to tenth-grade students,

UNIVERSAL ACCESS
● = Below-Level Students
▲ = On-Level Students
■ = Above-Level Students

Time and Resource Manager

Reading Level: Average, Average
Average Number of Instructional Days: 4

RESOURCES		
PRINT	**TRANSPARENCIES**	**TECHNOLOGY**
• **Beyond Literature,** Cross-Curricular Connection: Social Studies, p. 55 ▲ ■		• **Interest Grabber Video,** Tape 2, Unit 9, Segment 9 ● ▲ ■
• **Selection Support Workbook:** ● ▲ ■ Literary Analysis, p. 220 Reading Strategy, p. 219 Build Vocabulary, p. 217	• **Literary Analysis and Reading Transparencies,** pp. 109 and 110 ● ▲ ■	
• **Reader's Companion** ● • **Adapted Reader's Companion** ●		• **Listening to Literature** ● ▲ ■ Audiocassettes Audio CDs • **Reader's Companion Audio Program** ● • **Reader's Companion Adapted and English Learner's Version Audio Program** ● ▲
• **English Learner's Companion** • **Literary Analysis for Enrichment,** p. 55 ■		• **World Masterpieces iText CD-ROM** ● ▲ ■
• **Formal Assessment:** Selection Test, pp. 195–197 ● ▲ ■ • **Open-Book Tests,** pp. 163–165 ● ▲ ■ • **Performance Assessment and Portfolio Management,** pp. 16, 28 ● ▲ ■ • PRENTICE HALL ASSESSMENT SYSTEM ● ▲ ■	• PRENTICE HALL ASSESSMENT SYSTEM ● ▲ ■ **Skills Practice Answers and Explanations on Transparencies**	• **Test Bank Software** ● ▲ ■
• **Selection Support Workbook:** ● ▲ ■ Grammar and Style, p. 218 • **Writing and Grammar,** Diamond Level ● ▲ ■ • **Extension Activities,** p. 55 ● ▲ ■	• **Daily Language Practice Transparencies** ● ▲ • **Writing Models and Graphic Organizers on Transparencies,** pp. 103–105 ● ▲ ■	• **Writing and Grammar iText CD-ROM** ● ▲ ■ ***Take It to the Net*** PHSchool.com

BLOCK SCHEDULING: Use one 90-minute class period to preteach the selection(s) and have students read them. Use a second 90-minute class period to assess students' mastery of skills and have them complete one of the Extension Activities.

PREPEACH

Step-by-Step Teaching Guide for pp. 1172–1173

Motivation

Write this statement on the board: *Seeing is believing.* Have students write a paragraph or two in which they to agree or disagree with this statement. Use these questions to lead students in a discussion about the nature of reality: Have your perceptions ever misled you? Do important realities sometimes escape your perception? How do people react to the unknown, the mysterious, or the bizarre? What in human nature dictates these reactions?

Interest Grabber Video

As an alternative, play "'The Handsomest Drowned Man in the World': The Process of Mummification" on Tape 2 to engage student interest.

❶ Background

More About the Authors

All of García Márquez's fiction is set in the region of Aracataca, which is, in the words of critic Stephen Minta, a "tropical zone, a world of drama, movement, and light, of endless, and frequently oppressive, heat." The author was deeply influenced by his return to Aracataca in 1950 to sell his grandmother's house after she died. The loss of his childhood home inspired him to recreate in fiction the story of that house and community.

Cortázar maintained a boyish vitality even in his old age, and he was known for his skill in portraying adolescent characters. When asked about his sympathy for the young, he responded: "I am still very much a boy and am adolescent in many ways. In my life relationships, in my feelings, there is an adolescent element that prevails in me. In that sense, I think I am never going to get old."

Geography Note

Draw students' attention to the map on p. 1172. Point out that García Márquez and Cortázar have their roots in Colombia and Argentina.

Prepare to Read

❶ The Handsomest Drowned Man in the World ◆ House Taken Over

Gabriel García Márquez (b. 1928)

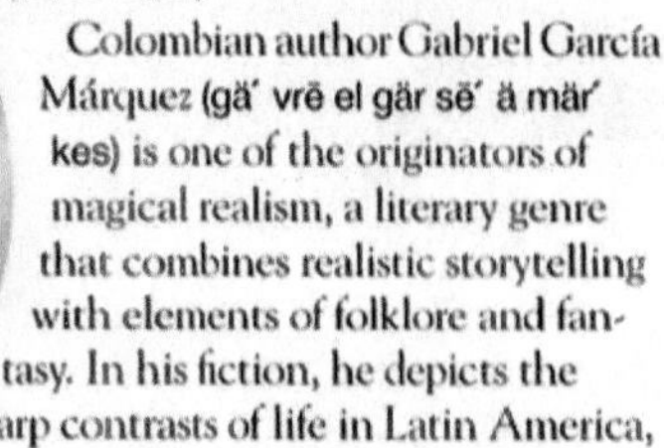

Colombian author Gabriel García Márquez (gä' vrē el gär sē' ä mär' kes) is one of the originators of magical realism, a literary genre that combines realistic storytelling with elements of folklore and fantasy. In his fiction, he depicts the sharp contrasts of life in Latin America, a continent known not only for its vibrant culture but also for terrible political violence.

Childhood Full of Stories García Márquez was born in Aracataca, a small village on Colombia's Caribbean coast. Because his parents were poor and struggling, García Márquez lived with his grandparents until he was eight years old. He loved listening to the mysterious fables recounted by his grandmother and the tales of military adventure narrated by his grandfather. Later, he adapted for his own work some of these stories he had heard as a child.

Worlds of Solitude In 1955, García Márquez published *Leaf Storm*, the collection of stories that introduced Macondo, a fictional town based on Aracataca. His later masterpiece, *One Hundred Years of Solitude* (1967), chronicles a century of life in Macondo. One of the finest examples of magical realism, the novel earned García Márquez the Nobel Prize in Literature in 1982.

Undoing Death "The Handsomest Drowned Man in the World" is typical of García Márquez's work in many ways. It marries real events with flights of fantasy. It also presents a dead person as the hero. While death is often lurking in García Márquez's work, the author's vision transforms it. Through the vitality of the story itself, the exuberance of its language, and the sheer power of imagination, death is undone.

Julio Cortázar (1914–1984)

Standing six feet tall, with long hair and a beard, the Argentinian Julio Cortázar (hōō' lē ō kôr tä' zər) was an imposing figure. He was also a towering presence as a writer, producing novels, short stories, and poetry and translating into Spanish the works of authors such as Edgar Allan Poe. He is best known, however, for his experimental fiction.

An International Sense of Identity Cortázar was born in Brussels, Belgium, to Argentinian parents. Although he returned to Argentina when he was a small boy, his sense of belonging to both Europe and Latin America was an important theme in his life.

In his early thirties, Cortázar landed a job as a translator for the United Nations and moved to Paris. While he had already begun writing the fiction that would make him famous, he did not publish it until 1951, when *Bestiary*, a collection of stories, appeared. *Cronopias and Famas* followed two years later. Experimental and playful, the volume opens with a selection entitled "The Instruction Manual," which provides detailed and wacky directions for such habitual actions as combing one's hair or descending a staircase.

Involving the Reader In 1963, Cortázar published his most remarkable novel, *Hopscotch*. Other experimental novels, including *62: A Model Kit* (1968) and *Last Round* (1969), also invite reader participation.

Cortázar once summarized his theory of fiction as follows: "The man of the future . . . will have to find the bases of a reality which is truly his and, at the same time, maintain the capacity of dreaming and playing . . . since it is through those doors that the Other, the fantastic dimension, and the unexpected will always slip. . . . " When you read "House Taken Over," you will step through one of "those doors."

TEACHING RESOURCES

The following resources can be used to enrich or extend the instruction for pp. 1172–1173.

Motivation

Interest Grabber Video, Tape 2

Background

Beyond Literature, p. 55

Take It to the Net

Visit PHSchool.com for background on the authors.

Literary Analysis

Literary Analysis and Reading Transparencies, Magical Realism, p. 109

Selection Support: Literary Analysis, p. 220

Reading

Literary Analysis and Reading Transparencies, Hypothesizing, p. 110

BLOCK SCHEDULING: Resources marked with this symbol provide varied instruction during 90-minute blocks.

Preview

Connecting to the Literature

Reality and dreams are not always opposites. Powerful dreams can have the force of real events, while real events can seem like the product of a dreamer's imagination. In these stories, dream and reality come together.

❷ Literary Analysis

Magical Realism

As its name suggests, **magical realism** combines realistic events with elements of myth, magic, and marvels of the natural world. Born out of the conflicts and beauty of Latin American culture, the style mixes reality and fantasy to create a rich sense of life's possibilities and limitations. For example, "The Handsomest Drowned Man in the World" begins with a grimly believable event: a dead body washes up on a beach. Soon, however, García Márquez's descriptions of the body give it mythic proportions:

> Not only was he the tallest, strongest, most virile, and best built man they had ever seen, but even though they were looking at him there was no room for him in their imagination.

As you read these stories, pay close attention to details. Think about which elements are realistic and which are strangely unreal.

Comparing Literary Works

Magical realist tales often use **archetypes**—universal symbols that evoke deep, even unconscious responses. For example, in "The Handsomest Drowned Man in the World," the archetype of the sea plays a critical role. As you read, identify other archetypes that García Márquez and Cortázar use, and compare the ways in which each adds to the mythic feeling of the stories.

❸ Reading Strategy

Hypothesizing

When you **hypothesize**, you make informed guesses or propose ideas based on clues in a text. Additional details in the text then prove your hypothesis true or false. As you read these stories, use a chart like the one shown to hypothesize.

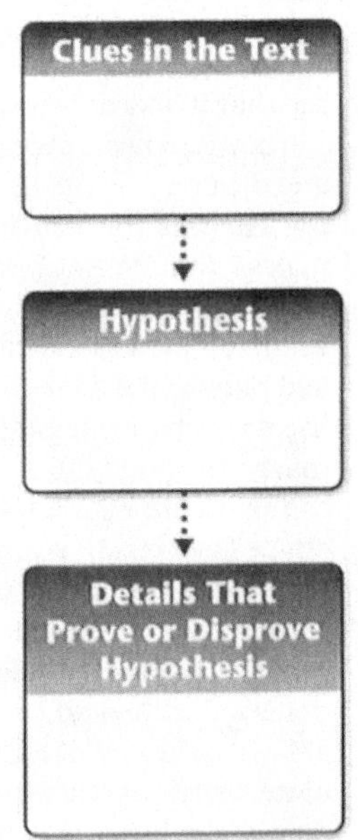

Vocabulary Development

bountiful (boun′ tə fəl) *adj.* generous; abundant (p. 1175)

labyrinths (lab′ ə rinths) *n.* structures with an intricate network of winding passages (p. 1175)

haggard (hag′ ərd) *adj.* wasted; worn; gaunt (p. 1175)

resistant (ri zis′ tənt) *adj.* strong; firm (p. 1178)

destitute (des′ tə to͞ot′) *adj.* completely poor (p. 1178)

replete (ri plēt′) *adj.* well-filled; stocked (p. 1184)

dexterity (deks ter′ ə tē) *n.* skillfulness in the use of one's hands (p. 1184)

brusquely (brusk′ lē) *adv.* in an abrupt manner (p. 1187)

❷ Literary Analysis

Magical Realism

- Make sure students understand that Magical Realism describes a combination of realistic and fantastic elements to express the possibilities and limitations of life.
- Invite students to share their memories of Santa Claus, the Easter Bunny, or the Tooth Fairy, for example. Help students understand that these myths combine elements of the real and magical.
- Ask a volunteer to read aloud the first paragraph of the story on p. 1174. Point out that the children easily synthesize elements of the real and the magical. In reality, a drowned man covered with sea debris washes onto the beach. The children use their imaginations to transform the bulge into an enemy ship and then into a whale.
- To help build student understanding of Magical Realism, use the Literary Analysis section of **Selection Support**, p. 220, for this selection.

❸ Reading Strategy

Hypothesizing

- Tell students that hypothesizing means proposing ideas based on clues they discover in a text.
- Ask students to use the graphic organizer on p. 1173 to form a hypothesis about the content of García Márquez's story on the basis of its title, subtitle, and first paragraph.
- Students can continue to use a graphic organizer like the one on p. 1173 to form and test other hypotheses as they read.

Vocabulary Development

- Pronounce each vocabulary word for students, and read the definitions as a class. Have students identify any words with which they are already familiar.

CUSTOMIZE INSTRUCTION FOR UNIVERSAL ACCESS

For Special Needs Students	For Less Proficient Readers	For English Learners
Have students read "The Handsomest Drowned Man in the World" in the **Adapted Reader's Companion.** This version provides basic-level instruction in an interactive format with questions and write-on lines. Completing the adapted version will prepare students to read the selection in the Student Edition.	Have students read the adapted version of the selection in the **Reader's Companion.** This version provides basic-level instruction in an interactive format with questions and write-on lines. After students finish the selection in the **Reader's Companion,** have them complete the questions and activities in the Student Edition.	Have students read the adapted version of the selection in the **English Learner's Companion.** This version provides basic-level instruction in an interactive format with questions and write-on lines. Completing the adapted version will prepare students to read the selection in the Student Edition.

E-Teach

Visit e-Teach at PHSchool.com for teachers' essays on how to teach, with questions and answers.

TEACH

Step-by-Step Teaching Guide for pp. 1174–1188

Teaching Tenth-Grade Students

10TH GRADE Tenth-grade students should find this story very accessible. Have them briefly note the sequence of events after they have finished reading. This technique will help prepare them to analyze the tale.

1 About the Selection

In this "tale for children," a drowned man washes up on the beach in a small fishing village. The body, shrouded in the mysteries of the sea, is that of a stranger. The women of the village are deeply affected by the drowned man's exceptional size and physical beauty. They name him Esteban and claim him as their own. At first, the men of the village see the drowned man as a bother, but they become affected by his presence as well. The villagers hold a grand funeral for the stranger, pledging to honor his memory.

2 Literary Analysis

Magical Realism

- Explain that García Márquez combines keen observation and fantastic elements in his fiction.
- Have students read the bracketed passage. Ask them to pay close attention to the details García Márquez describes.
- Ask students the Literary Analysis question on p. 1174: Which details in the description of the drowned man are so exaggerated that they seem unreal?
  Answer: The drowned man weighs "almost as much as a horse," "there was barely enough room for him in the house," and the reference to his "ability to keep on growing after death" are exaggerated details.

The Handsomest Drowned Man in the World

1

A Tale for Children

Gabriel García Márquez *translated by* **Gregory Rabassa**

Background

This story about an unlikely hero is set in a poor Colombian seaside village that closely resembles the author's home village of Aracataca. In this work and others, García Márquez re-creates and expands upon his grandmother's storytelling style. According to García Márquez, her memorable tales related "things that sounded supernatural and fantastic, but she told them with complete naturalness."

The first children who saw the dark and slinky bulge approaching through the sea let themselves think it was an enemy ship. Then they saw it had no flags or masts and they thought it was a whale. But when it washed up on the beach, they removed the clumps of seaweed, the jellyfish tentacles, and the remains of fish and flotsam, and only then did they see that it was a drowned man.

2 They had been playing with him all afternoon, burying him in the sand and digging him up again, when someone chanced to see them and spread the alarm in the village. The men who carried him to the nearest house noticed that he weighed more than any dead man they had ever known, almost as much as a horse, and they said to each other that maybe he'd been floating too long and the water had got into his bones. When they laid him on the floor they said he'd been taller than all other men because there was barely enough room for him in the house, but they thought that maybe the ability to keep on growing after death was part of the nature of certain drowned men. He had the smell of the sea about him and only his shape gave one to suppose that it was the corpse of a human being, because the skin was covered with a crust of mud and scales.

Literary Analysis
Magical Realism Which details in the description of the drowned man are so exaggerated that they seem unreal?

They did not even have to clean off his face to know that the dead man was a stranger. The village was made up of only twenty-odd wooden houses that had stone courtyards with no flowers and which were spread about on the end of a desertlike cape. There was so little land that mothers always went about with the fear that the wind would carry off their children and the few dead that the years had caused among them had to be

TEACHING RESOURCES

The following resources can be used to enrich or extend the instruction for pp. 1174–1188.

Literary Analysis

- **Selection Support:** Literary Analysis, p. 220
- **Literary Analysis and Reading Transparencies,** Magical Realism, p. 109 ■

Reading

- **Selection Support:** Reading Strategy, p. 219; Build Vocabulary, p. 217 ■

- **Reader's Companion**
- **Adapted Reader's Companion**
- **English Learner's Companion**
- **Listening to Literature Audiocassettes**
- **Listening to Literature Audio CDs**

■ **BLOCK SCHEDULING:** Resources marked with this symbol provide varied instruction during 90-minute blocks.

thrown off the cliffs. But the sea was calm and bountiful and all the men fit into seven boats. So when they found the drowned man they simply had to look at one another to see that they were all there.

That night they did not go out to work at sea. While the men went to find out if anyone was missing in neighboring villages, the women stayed behind to care for the drowned man. They took the mud off with grass swabs, they removed the underwater stones entangled in his hair, and they scraped the crust off with tools used for scaling fish. As they were doing that they noticed that the vegetation on him came from faraway oceans and deep water and that his clothes were in tatters, as if he had sailed through labyrinths of coral. They noticed too that he bore his death with pride, for he did not have the lonely look of other drowned men who came out of the sea or that haggard, needy look of men who drowned in rivers. But only when they finished cleaning him off did they become aware of the kind of man he was and it left them breathless. Not only was he the tallest, strongest, most virile, and best built man they had ever seen, but even though they were looking at him there was no room for him in their imagination.

They could not find a bed in the village large enough to lay him on nor was there a table solid enough to use for his wake. The tallest men's

bountiful (boun′ tə fəl) *adj.* generous; abundant

labyrinths (lab′ ə rinths) *n.* structures with an intricate network of winding passages

haggard (hag′ ərd) *adj.* wasted; worn; gaunt

3 **✓Reading Check**

Who first discovers the drowned man?

4

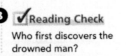

Waves, 1917, Christopher Nevinson, Phillips, The International Fine Art Auctioneers, UK

5 ▲ **Critical Viewing** Does this painting depict the sea as being "calm and bountiful," as it is described in the story? Why or why not? **[Evaluate]**

3 **✓Reading Check**

Answer: A group of village children first discover the drowned man.

4 Background

Art

Waves, by Christopher Nevinson

The English painter Christopher Nevinson (1889–1946) was the son of committed social activists. He began to study art in the early part of the twentieth century, spending the years 1909–1912 at the Slade School of Art in London. While in London, Nevinson discovered Futurism, a movement that influenced his early career. After finishing at Slade, he went to Paris, where he continued to study and explore modern art.

World War I was a critical juncture in Nevinson's life. After serving as an ambulance driver and hospital worker for over a year, he fell ill with rheumatic fever. Unable to serve, he began painting his wartime experiences. For some time, he created war paintings for Britain's War Propaganda Bureau, but he grew dissatisfied with this work. Although painted at the height of the war in 1917, *Waves* represents a departure from Nevinson's paintings of the machinery of destruction. After the war, he concentrated on painting cityscapes and, later, pastoral scenes.

Use the following question for discussion:

Do you think this painting is an appropriate illustration for this story? Why or why not?

Possible response: The painting is an appropriate illustration because it suggests the mystery of the ocean and thus parallels the mysterious origins of the drowned man.

5 ▶ **Critical Viewing**

Possible response: The gentle waves and the sense of the sea's vastness depict the sea as being "calm and bountiful."

CUSTOMIZE INSTRUCTION FOR UNIVERSAL ACCESS

For Less Proficient Readers	For English Learners	For Advanced Readers
Tell students that critics have described this story as "a Prometheus myth for Latin America." Help students locate and read a version of the Prometheus myth. Invite them to use a Venn diagram to compare and contrast the characters of Prometheus and Esteban.	Tell students that critics have described this story as "a Prometheus myth for Latin America." Help students locate and read an illustrated version of this myth. Invite students to compare and contrast the characters of Prometheus and Esteban. Have them use at least five adjectives for each character.	Tell students that critics have described this story as "a Prometheus myth for Latin America." Invite students to compare and contrast the characters of Prometheus and Esteban in analytical essays. Tell each student to write a thesis statement in which he or she agrees or disagrees with the critics' statement.

❻ Background

Art

Troubled Woman, by Egon Schiele

During his brief career, Schiele (1890–1918) became an important and controversial figure in his native Austria. Born outside Vienna, he began studying art in that city at the age of sixteen. The artist Gustav Klimt was an early friend and influence. Schiele's work began to move in different directions, however. Using distorted ink outlines, he began to produce unsettling paintings of contorted figures. His work was at the forefront of Austrian Expressionism. With roots in Germany, Austrian Expressionism as a movement emphasized personal expression through exaggeration and distortion.

Troubled Woman reflects Schiele's emphasis on awkward, uncomfortable figures. But the artist was also known for disturbing images of nudes. Many people were troubled by these paintings—so much so that in 1912, Schiele was arrested. Although he spent little time in prison, the experience was highly dispiriting. Within six years, he died of influenza.

Use the following questions for discussion:

- What elements in this painting suggest that the woman is troubled?
  Possible response: The pose in which the woman is depicted suggests that she is troubled. She crouches uncomfortably and holds her head in her hands. The splotchy color and angularity of her hands and feet add to the impression of trouble.
- What do you imagine is at the root of this woman's troubles? Why?
  Possible response: Her bowed head suggests mourning more than worry. The woman may be grieving over a significant loss.

❼ ▶ Critical Viewing

Possible response: The women of the village express enormous sympathy and sorrow for the drowned man, especially after they decide that his name is Esteban. However, the woman depicted in the painting expresses far more pain and anguish than do the women in the story.

❻

❼ ▲ **Critical Viewing** In what ways does this painting reflect the kinds of emotions expressed by the women caring for the drowned man? **[Connect]**

1176 ◆ *The Contemporary World*

ENRICHMENT: Literature Connection

Literature of the Fantastic

Fantasy is a key element of the Magical Realism of Gabriel García Márquez and Julio Cortázar. In literature of the fantastic, writers harness the power of fantasy to challenge, puzzle, discomfort, and entertain readers. Like dreams or daydreams, fantastic stories distort and expand our usual world. They open up passageways into mysterious places. One such story is Jorge Luis Borges's "The Secret Miracle," in which a man facing a firing squad is given a year to finish a play he is writing. The fantastic element of the tale is that the year takes place while the bullets are flying toward him! To everyone in the story, except the man, the year is just a split second.

According to the Argentine critic Alberto Manguel, "… fantastic literature deals with what can best be defined as the impossible seeping into the possible, what Wallace Stevens calls 'black water breaking into reality.'"

holiday pants would not fit him, nor the fattest ones' Sunday shirts, nor the shoes of the one with the biggest feet. Fascinated by his huge size and his beauty, the women then decided to make him some pants from a large piece of sail and a shirt from some bridal brabant[1] linen so that he could continue through his death with dignity. As they sewed, sitting in a circle and gazing at the corpse between stitches, it seemed to them that the wind had never been so steady nor the sea so restless as on that night and they supposed that the change had something to do with the dead man. They thought that if that magnificent man had lived in the village, his house would have had the widest doors, the highest ceiling, and the strongest floor, his bedstead would have been made from a midship frame held together by iron bolts, and his wife would have been the happiest woman. They thought that he would have had so much authority that he could have drawn fish out of the sea simply by calling
8 their names and that he would have put so much work into his land that springs would have burst forth from among the rocks so that he would have been able to plant flowers on the cliffs. They secretly compared him to their own men, thinking that for all their lives theirs were incapable of doing what he could do in one night, and they ended up dismissing them deep in their hearts as the weakest, meanest, and most useless creatures on earth. They were wandering through that maze of fantasy when the oldest woman, who as the oldest had looked upon the drowned man
9 with more compassion than passion, sighed:

"He has the face of someone called Esteban."

It was true. Most of them had only to take another look at him to see that he could not have any other name. The more stubborn among them, who were the youngest, still lived for a few hours with the illusion that when they put his clothes on and he lay among the flowers in patent leather shoes his name might be Lautaro. But it was a vain illusion. There had not been enough canvas, the poorly cut and worse sewn pants were too tight, and the hidden strength of his heart popped the buttons on his shirt. After midnight the whistling of the wind died down and the sea fell into its Wednesday drowsiness. The silence put an end to any last doubts: he was Esteban. The women who had dressed him, who had combed his hair, had cut his nails and shaved him were unable to hold back a shudder of pity when they had to resign themselves to his being dragged along the ground. It was then that they understood how unhappy he must have been with that huge body since it bothered him even after death. They could see him in life, condemned to going through doors sideways, cracking his head on crossbeams, remaining on his feet during visits, not

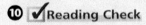

Reading Strategy
Hypothesizing In what ways do you think the arrival of the drowned man will affect life in this village? Explain.

10 **✓Reading Check**

What name do the village women give the drowned man?

1. **brabant** (brə bant´) region in Belgium and the Netherlands famous for its textile products.

CUSTOMIZE INSTRUCTION FOR UNIVERSAL ACCESS

For Special Needs Students	For English Learners
Help students note that none of the villagers has a name. The villagers are differentiated as children, men, and women. However, they give the drowned man a name, Esteban. Design a four-column name chart for students to complete. Label the columns as follows: *My Name, What My Family Says About My Name, What I Learned About My Name From Research,* and *What I Think About My Name.* Direct students to ask their family members for information about their names to help them complete their charts.	Help students note that none of the villagers has a name. They are differentiated as children, men, and women. Ironically, they have less individual identity than the dead man, whom they name Esteban. Help students understand that a name equates with an identity. Invite students to complete short writing assignments about their own names. Students may enjoy researching their names on the Internet as well as interviewing their parents about names. Invite volunteers to share their work with the class.

8 Reading Strategy

Hypothesizing

- Tell students that they can hypothesize about what will happen in a text by guessing on the basis of the details they have already read. Hypothesizing can help students evaluate and synthesize details in a text.
- Have students read the bracketed passage. Then, ask them the Reading Strategy question on p. 1177: In what ways do you think the arrival of the drowned man will affect life in this village? Explain.
  Possible response: The drowned man may prompt the women of the village to demand more from the men in their lives because they believe that the drowned man would have given them more than their husbands and fathers do.
- Have students write their hypotheses in a graphic organizer like the one on p. 1173. Tell them to look for details as they continue to read that either confirm or contradict their guesses.

9 Critical Thinking

Interpret

- Have students read the second bracketed passage. Through discussion, make sure they recognize that the name given to the drowned man, Esteban, is of great importance to the women of the village.
- Explain to students that *Esteban* translates as "Stephen" and that in the Bible, Stephen is the first Christian martyr.
- Ask: On the basis of this knowledge, why does García Márquez have the women identify the drowned man as Esteban?
  Possible response: García Márquez may use the name to suggest that the drowned man, too, is a kind of martyr and that his death will somehow benefit—even redeem—the village.
- Encourage students to keep this interpretation in mind as they continue to read the story.

10 ✓Reading Check

Answer: The women of the village name the drowned man Esteban.

⓫ Critical Thinking

Analyze

- Have students pause before they read p. 1178. Ask them to summarize the women's thoughts about the drowned man so far in the story.
  Answer: The women are at first impressed with the drowned man's size and good looks, so much so that they imagine him to be superior to their own husbands. This thinking begins to change when one of the older women names the drowned man Esteban.
- Have students read the bracketed passage. Tell them to pay close attention to the way in which the women characterize the drowned man now.
- Point out that although the women have previously expressed admiration for the drowned man, they now show irritation and then sympathy as he becomes like their own men. This transformation breeds a sense of ownership in the women. Ask students how this change in attitude is expressed.
  Answer: As they imagine the problems the drowned man's size might have caused him, the women give him words to speak. The drowned man comes to life as a believable, if large, person—at least in the minds of the women.
- Make sure students recognize that in this passage, the drowned man becomes more than just a waterlogged body or a cipher—he becomes a character with his own personality and voice.

⓬ ▶ Critical Viewing

Possible response: The coral in the photograph is intricate and mazelike, suggesting a sort of natural labyrinth.

knowing what to do with his soft, pink, sea lion hands while the lady of the house looked for her most resistant chair and begged him, frightened to death, sit here, Esteban, please, and he, leaning against the wall, smiling, don't bother, ma'am, I'm fine where I am, his heels raw and his back roasted from having done the same thing so many times whenever he paid a visit, don't bother, ma'am, I'm fine where I am, just to avoid the embarrassment of breaking up the chair, and never knowing perhaps that the ones who said don't go, Esteban, at least wait till the coffee's ready, were the ones who later on would whisper the big boob finally left, how nice, the handsome fool has gone. ⓫ That was what the women were thinking beside the body a little before dawn. Later, when they covered his face with a handkerchief so that the light would not bother him, he looked so forever dead, so defenseless, so much like their men that the first furrows of tears opened in their hearts. It was one of the younger ones who began the weeping. The others, coming to, went from sighs to wails, and the more they sobbed the more they felt like weeping, because the drowned man was becoming all the more Esteban for them, and so they wept so much, for he was the most destitute, most peaceful, and most obliging man on earth, poor Esteban. So when the men returned with the news that the drowned man was not from the neighboring villages either, the women felt an opening of jubilation in the midst of their tears.

"Praise the Lord," they sighed, "he's ours!"

resistant (ri zis′ tənt) *adj.* strong; firm

destitute (des′ tə to͞ot′) *adj.* completely poor

⓬ ▼ **Critical Viewing** In what ways does this undersea photograph support the narrator's description of "labyrinths" of coral? **[Support]**

ENRICHMENT: Literature Connection

Point of View and Perspective

Point of view is the vantage point from which a story is told. This story is told from an omniscient third-person point of view, meaning that the narrator remains outside the story but has access to the characters' thoughts.

This point of view itself does not change throughout the story. However, there are some surprising shifts in perspective within this point of view. For example, the dead man suddenly comes to life when the narrator gives him imagined dialogue to speak. This shift in perspective is all the more surprising because it takes place in mid-sentence, and Esteban's words are not placed in quotation marks. García Márquez may omit quotation marks from the dialogue to indicate that it is imagined rather than real.

13 The men thought the fuss was only womanish frivolity. Fatigued because of the difficult nighttime inquiries, all they wanted was to get rid of the bother of the newcomer once and for all before the sun grew strong on that arid, windless day. They improvised a litter with the remains of foremasts and gaffs,[2] tying it together with rigging[3] so that it would bear the weight of the body until they reached the cliffs. They wanted to tie the anchor from a cargo ship to him so that he would sink easily into the deepest waves, where fish are blind and divers die of nostalgia, and bad currents would not bring him back to shore, as had happened with other bodies. But the more they hurried, the more the women thought of ways to waste time. They walked about like startled hens, pecking with the sea charms on their breasts, some interfering on one side to put a scapular[4] of the good wind on the drowned man, some on the other side to put a wrist compass on him, and after a great deal of *get away from there, woman, stay out of the way, look, you almost made me fall on top of the dead man,* the men began to feel mistrust in their lives and started grumbling about why so many main-altar decorations for a stranger, because no matter how many nails and holy-water jars he had on him, the sharks would chew him all the same, but the women kept piling on their junk relics, running back and forth, stumbling, while they released in sighs what they did not in tears, so that the men finally exploded with *since when has there*

2. **gaffs** poles that are part of a ship's mast.
3. **rigging** ropes and other gear used to control the sails of a vessel.
4. **scapular** (skap′ yə lər) religious medal.

14 **✓Reading Check**

Why do the women cover the drowned man's face with a handkerchief?

13 Literary Analysis

Magical Realism

- Explain to students that realistic elements ground fantasy, and the fantastic elements reveal unimagined possibilities—unrecognized limitations—within real life.
- Have students read the bracketed passage on pp. 1179–1180. Then, ask them to identify the realistic and the fantastic elements in it.
  Answer: The materials the men use in the litter and their irritation at the women are realistic elements. The description of the deepest part of the sea is a fantastic element. The women's fantasy of the drowned man's life as Esteban is also present in this passage, but it is seen through the realistic lens of the men's annoyance.
- Ask students to describe how the fantastic elements in this passage affect its realism.
  Possible response: The fantastic elements reveal the limitations of the men's realistic and irritable view of their world, hinting at a possibility for transformation with the arrival of the drowned man that the men do not see.
- Encourage students to continue to pay attention to the interaction of realistic and fantastic elements in the remainder of the story, as well as to the differences between the behavior of the men and the women with regard to Esteban.

14 ✓Reading Check

Answer: The women cover the drowned man's face with a handkerchief "so that the light would not bother him."

CUSTOMIZE INSTRUCTION FOR UNIVERSAL ACCESS

For Less Proficient Readers	For English Learners	For Advanced Readers
Students may take special notice of the burial rituals undertaken by the people of the village on behalf of the drowned man. Encourage students to use the details in the story to draw illustrations of the preparations for Esteban's burial. Tell students to label each aspect of their drawings with quotations from the text.	Students may take special notice of the burial rituals undertaken on behalf of the drowned man by the people of the village. Encourage students to present information to the class about burial rituals undertaken in countries where they have lived or visited. Students might enjoy doing additional research on the Internet.	Students may take special notice of the burial rituals undertaken on behalf of the drowned man by the people of the village. Encourage students to research burial traditions in South American seaside villages. How much of García Márquez's description is realistic and how much is fantasy?

15 Background

García Márquez and William Faulkner

The importance of a fictional community can be seen on numerous levels in the works of both García Márquez and Faulkner. Consider their portrayals of the residents of their worlds. In "The Handsomest Drowned Man in the World," García Márquez does not distinguish among the different men and women of the village. The women, and then the men, speak and act together as a group. Similarly, in Faulkner's short story "A Rose for Emily," the people of the town of Jefferson not only act as one; they are, collectively, the narrator, speaking to the reader in the first-person plural.

16 Reading Strategy

Hypothesizing

- Reemphasize to students that hypothesizing must be based on the details in a text. A hypothesis is valuable only if the details in the text support it.
- Have students read the bracketed passage on pp. 1180–1181. Instruct them to pay close attention to the details.
- Ask students the Reading Strategy question on p. 1180: Do you think the village will remember Esteban after his funeral? Explain.
  Possible response: The villagers will remember Esteban long after the funeral because of the feeling of kinship that sweeps the village and because of the decision to bury Esteban at sea without an anchor, "so that he could come back if he wished."

ever been such a fuss over a drifting corpse, a drowned nobody, a piece of cold Wednesday meat. One of the women, mortified by so much lack of care, then removed the handkerchief from the dead man's face and the men were left breathless too.

He was Esteban. It was not necessary to repeat it for them to recognize him. If they had been told Sir Walter Raleigh,[5] even they might have been impressed with his gringo accent, the macaw on his shoulder, his cannibal-killing blunderbuss, but there could be only one Esteban in the world and there he was, stretched out like a sperm whale, shoeless, wearing the pants of an undersized child, and with those stony nails that had to be cut with a knife. They had only to take the handkerchief off his face to see that he was ashamed, that it was not his fault that he was so big or so heavy or so handsome, and if he had known that this was going to happen, he would have looked for a more discreet place to drown in, seriously, I even would have tied the anchor off a galleon around my neck and staggered off a cliff like someone who doesn't like things in order not to be upsetting people now with this Wednesday dead body, as you people say, in order not to be bothering anyone with this filthy piece of cold meat that doesn't have anything to do with me. There was so much truth in his manner that even the most mistrustful men, the ones who felt the bitterness of endless nights at sea fearing that their women would tire of dreaming about them and begin to dream of drowned men, even they and others who were harder still shuddered in the marrow of their bones at Esteban's sincerity.

That was how they came to hold the most splendid funeral they could conceive of for an abandoned drowned man. Some women who had gone to get flowers in the neighboring villages returned with other women who could not believe what they had been told, and those women went back for more flowers when they saw the dead man, and they brought more and more until there were so many flowers and so many people that it was hard to walk about. At the final moment it pained them to return him to the waters as an orphan and they chose a father and mother from among the best people, and aunts and uncles and cousins, so that through him all the inhabitants of the village became kinsmen. Some sailors who heard the weeping from a distance went off course and people heard of one who had himself tied to the mainmast, remembering ancient fables about sirens. While they fought for the privilege of carrying him on their shoulders along the steep escarpment[6] by the cliffs, men and women became aware for the first time of the desolation of their streets, the dryness of their courtyards, the narrowness of their dreams as they faced the splendor and beauty of their drowned man. They let him go without an anchor so that he could come back if he wished and whenever he wished, and they all held their breath for the fraction

of centuries the body took to fall into the abyss. They did not need to look at one another to realize that they were no longer all present, that

5. **Sir Walter Raleigh** English explorer (1552–1618) known for his charm and boldness; organized expeditions to North and South America.
6. **escarpment** (e skärp′ mənt) slope.

Themes in World Literature

15 *García Márquez and William Faulkner*

The fictional world of Gabriel García Márquez was strongly influenced by the American author William Faulkner, who wrote many stories and novels set in the imaginary Mississippi county of Yoknapatawpha (yŏk′ nə pə tô′ fə). Inspired by Faulkner's rich and intimate descriptions of Yoknapatawpha and its residents, García Márquez created his own fictional village of Macondo. He also decided that his earlier works had been "simply intellectual elaborations, nothing to do with my reality." To address this flaw, he changed his writing style, incorporating personal imagery, details, and knowledge.

While Macondo is clearly modeled on García Márquez's hometown of Aracataca, it is not merely the product of Márquez's observant eye. Rather, as a fictional setting, the town rests on a deep undercurrent of fantasy and magic, which frequently erupts. As it does, readers travel to a haunting landscape, where reality still holds sway but dream and imagination are equally powerful.

Reading Strategy
Hypothesizing Do you think the village will remember Esteban after his funeral? Explain.

ENRICHMENT: History Connection

The Death of Sir Walter Raleigh

Students may be puzzled by the reference to Sir Walter Raleigh on p. 1180. Why is this English explorer a figure of such significance that he would so impress the villagers in this story? When James I succeeded to the throne and became King of England in 1603, he regarded Raleigh as an enemy. The new king had Raleigh stripped of many of his privileges and possessions. Eventually, Raleigh was found guilty of treason.

However, in 1616, the aging explorer was released to make a voyage into Guiana in search of the fabled golden city of El Dorado. This would be his second such voyage—he had already hunted for the legendary city in 1595. Raleigh was warned not to interfere with any Spanish ships or possessions. During the course of the journey, however, one of his fellow explorers captured a Spanish town. This was a violation of Raleigh's order. On his return to England, he was executed. His boldness in South America cost him his life.

they would never be. But they also knew that everything would be different from then on, that their houses would have wider doors, higher ceilings, and stronger floors so that Esteban's memory could go everywhere without bumping into beams and so that no one in the future would dare whisper the big boob finally died, too bad, the handsome fool has finally died, because they were going to paint their house fronts gay colors to make Esteban's memory eternal and they were going to break their backs digging for springs among the stones and planting flowers on the cliffs so that in future years at dawn the passengers on great liners would awaken, suffocated by the smell of gardens on the high seas, and the captain would have to come down from the bridge in his dress uniform, with his astrolabe[7] his pole star, and his row of war medals and, pointing to the promontory of roses on the horizon, he would say in fourteen languages, look there, where the wind is so peaceful now that it's gone to sleep beneath the beds, over there, where the sun's so bright that the sunflowers don't know which way to turn, yes, over there, that's Esteban's village.

7. **astrolabe** (as´ trō lāb´) old-fashioned instrument used in navigating a ship.

Review and Assess

Thinking About the Selection

1. **Respond:** Which aspect of this story do you find most surprising? Explain.
2. **(a) Recall:** As the village men carry the drowned man from the beach, what do they observe about his size and weight?
   (b) Contrast: How does the drowned man's size contrast with the size of the village? **(c) Interpret:** What does this size relationship suggest about the importance of the drowned man?
3. **(a) Recall:** After the men bring the body to town, what do the women do with it? **(b) Analyze Cause and Effect:** As a result of their actions, what qualities do the women notice about the dead man?
4. **(a) Interpret:** With what emotions do the men first react to the women's fuss over the body? Explain. **(b) Analyze Cause and Effect:** What happens to change their minds? Explain.
5. **(a) Generalize:** In what ways does the town change as a result of its encounter with Esteban? **(b) Analyze:** What do these changes suggest about Esteban's symbolic value to the town?
6. **Evaluate:** Do you think that García Márquez intends his subtitle, "A Tale for Children," to be interpreted literally? Why or why not?
7. **Apply:** Philosophers have sometimes expressed the idea that the key to releasing human potential is to expand people's imagination. Explain how this story supports that notion.

CUSTOMIZE INSTRUCTION FOR UNIVERSAL ACCESS

For Gifted/Talented Students	For Advanced Readers
Tell students that anthropologists point out that many societies have initiation ceremonies by which a stranger is made one of the tribe. Help student groups select one world culture on which to focus research. Tell students to perform and narrate the initiation ceremony of their chosen culture for the class. We strongly recommend that you meet with each group during its planning phase to preview the classroom appropriateness of its material and to monitor the students' level of cultural respect.	Direct students to prepare a comparative chart in which they juxtapose quotations from this story to quotations from the works of literature to which they allude. Suggest that students investigate drowned men in Shakespeare's *The Tempest*; the gift of life or change in the myth of Prometheus; the name Stephen in the Bible; and a sailor tied to a mast in Homer's *Odyssey*. Help students understand that these references lend the weight of myth or legend to the story.

Answers for p. 1181

Review and Assess

1. Possible response: The most surprising aspect of the story is the normalcy with which the villagers treat the appearance of the drowned man. They even compare Esteban with other drowned men they have known.
2. **(a)** The men observe that the drowned man is larger and heavier than any other dead man they have carried. **(b)** Esteban is larger than life, whereas the village is remarkably small. **(c)** It suggests that the drowned man is very important.
3. **(a)** The women wash the drowned man, make him new clothes for his burial, and give him the name Esteban. **(b)** The women first notice the drowned man's size and good looks. After they name him, the women perceive his innocent, sincere, and piteous qualities.
4. **(a)** The men are irritated by the women's fuss, dismissing it as "womanish frivolity." **(b)** The men change their minds when one of the women reveals the drowned man's face. The men are awed by the same qualities the women have perceived in the drowned man.
5. **(a)** The villagers decide to build larger, more colorful houses and plant flowers to attract and accommodate those who are different from themselves. **(b)** Esteban brings a new dimension into the lives of the villagers, enlarging their hearts.
6. Possible response: The subtitle is not meant literally because the story is too complex for children. Rather, the subtitle is intended to suggest that adults need to work to retain the childlike quality of acceptance of that which is different. Remember that the first reaction of the village children to Esteban is to include him in their play without judgment.
7. Possible response: The change in attitude and style that comes to the villagers is a result of their imaginative ability to embrace Esteban's difference within their hearts, their minds, and the village itself.

⓱ About the Selection

In this eerie tale, a brother and sister living quietly in their ancestral home undergo a strange experience. Gradually, their house is "taken over" by forces or presences that remain entirely mysterious. These events—or are they entirely imagined?—lead to monumental change in the characters' previously monotonous lives.

⓲ Literary Analysis

Magical Realism and Archetypes

- Explain to students that Magical Realism often uses archetypes, or universal symbols, to evoke deep, and even unconscious, responses in readers.
- Have students read the bracketed passage. Suggest that, given the title of the story, the house may be a central archetype for Cortázar.
- Ask students the Literary Analysis question on p. 1182: Based on the first paragraph, what might a house represent for an individual? Possible response: A house can represent a family's history and memories, as the house in the story does for the narrator and his sister. A house is also a symbol of a family's identity.
- Encourage students to keep this level of symbolic meaning in mind as they read more about this house and its inhabitants.

Monitor Progress To evaluate students' understanding of archetypes, ask students to identify the symbolic meanings a house might have for a society rather than for individuals. Possible response: For a society, the house symbolizes the stability of the family, the strength of a community, the protection of the community's members, and the economic status of the community.

Reteach Tell students that archetypes can have social as well as individual meanings. Encourage them to consider both levels of meaning as they continue to read the story.

⓳ Reading Check

Answer: The narrator lives with his sister, Irene.

⓱

HOUSE TAKEN OVER

Julio Cortázar *translated by* Paul Blackburn

Background

Cortázar wrote this story while still in the grip of a frightening nightmare. Critic Evelyn Picon Garfield describes the story's origin, explaining that Cortázar "dreamt that he was alone in a house full of passageways when suddenly he heard a noise from the depths of the corridor. He had a sensation of nightmarish terror. After quickly closing the door and bolting it tight, for a few minutes he felt safe and thought that the nightmare would become a peaceful dream. All of a sudden the noise sounded on his side of the door. He woke up, and still in his pajamas, without taking time to brush his teeth or comb his hair, he sat down at the typewriter. In about an hour and a half 'House Taken Over' was written."

⓲ We liked the house because, apart from its being old and spacious (in a day when old houses go down for a profitable auction of their construction materials), it kept the memories of great-grandparents, our paternal grandfather, our parents and the whole of childhood.

Irene and I got used to staying in the house by ourselves, which was crazy, eight people could have lived in that place and not have gotten in each other's way. We rose at seven in the morning and got the cleaning done, and about eleven I left Irene to finish off whatever rooms and went to the kitchen. We lunched at noon precisely; then there was nothing left to do but a few dirty plates. It was pleasant to take lunch and commune with[1] the great hollow, silent house, and it was enough for us just to keep it clean. We ended up thinking, at times, that that was what had kept us from marrying. Irene turned down two suitors for no particular reason, and María Esther went and died on me before we could manage to get engaged. We were easing into our forties with the unvoiced concept that the quiet, simple marriage of sister and

Literary Analysis
Magical Realism and Archetypes Based on the first paragraph, what might a house represent for an individual?

⓳  Reading Check

With whom does the narrator live?

1. **commune** (kə myo͞on′) **with** be in close rapport or harmony with.

ENRICHMENT: Literature Connection

Ghosts and Ghost Stories, Conventional and Unconventional

"House Taken Over" is a kind of ghost story. However, it is far from a conventional ghost story. American writer Ambrose Bierce offers this definition of a ghost: "The outward and visible sign of an inward fear." This unconventional view of ghosts illuminates Cortázar's story. In Cortázar's fiction, routine and habit are seen as enemies. If characters do not rebel against these deadening influences, something extraordinary usually occurs to jar them out of their complacency. The brother and sister in this story fear giving up routine and habit. The "ghosts" who take over their house may be visible signs of this inward fear.

Another unusual view of ghosts is expressed in the Norwegian playwright Henrik Ibsen's *Ghosts:* "I'm inclined to think that we are all ghosts—every one of us," Ibsen wrote. "It's not just what we inherit from our mothers and fathers that haunts us. It's all kinds of old defunct theories, all sorts of old defunct beliefs, and things like that." Again, these are the kinds of ghosts that play a key role in "House Taken Over."

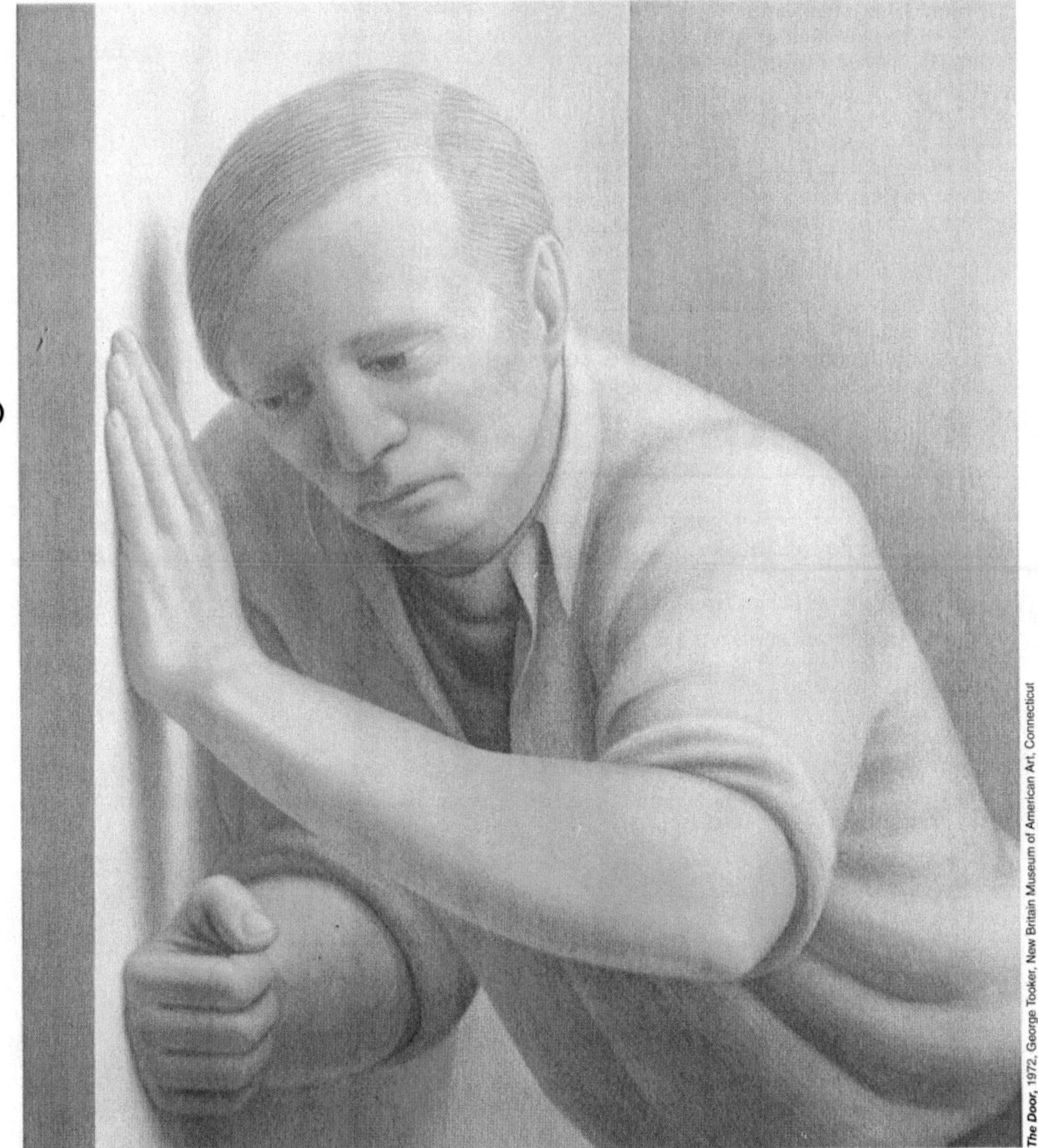

20

21 ▲ **Critical Viewing** Based on the title of the story and the man's posture and expression in this painting, what kinds of events do you think this story will include? **[Hypothesize]**

20 Background

Art

The Door, by George Tooker

The American painter George Tooker was born in Brooklyn, New York, in 1920. Even when he was a child, his goal was to be a painter, and he received lessons in painting. Later, he attended Phillips Academy in Andover, Massachusetts, and studied literature and art at Harvard University. Tooker continued his studies in New York City after his graduation. Here, he discovered egg tempera, a type of paint made of pigment, water, and egg yolk. The strange quality of the light in *The Door* comes from the egg tempera paint.

Tooker is best known for his paintings of scenes of American isolation. But images such as *The Door* have a strange enough quality that Tooker has been described as a Magical Realist. In 1960, he moved to Hartland, Vermont, where he still lives.

Use the following question for discussion:

Like the narrator in the story, the man in the painting seems to be trying to hold a door shut. What do you think is behind the door? Possible response: Intruders, evil spirits—or even the past—may be behind the door.

21 ▶Critical Viewing

Possible response: Something frightening will enter or attempt to enter part of the house, and the narrator will try to hold the door shut against the alarming presence.

CUSTOMIZE INSTRUCTION FOR UNIVERSAL ACCESS

For Special Needs Students	For Less Proficient Readers	For English Learners
Students may create a model of the house in the story. Help students read the descriptions of the house on pp. 1182–1186. Ask students to identify each detail of the house. Record these details on the board. Provide students with a variety of art supplies, and encourage them to draw a picture of the house or to build a model of it.	Keep students interested in what will happen by giving them hints of future events. Tell students to read the second paragraph. Ask them to use a graphic organizer like the one on p. 1173 to form a hypothesis about future events in the story and then read to confirm or refute their hypotheses.	Ask students to draw a simple two-column chart with the words *dexterous* and *sinister* at the top of each column. Then, have them use dictionaries to write synonyms under each word. Have the class take turns calling out a synonym, using it in a sentence, and explaining how it differs in meaning or connotation from the other words.

22 Vocabulary Development

Latin Prefix *re-*

- Call students' attention to the word *replete* and its definition. Tell students that the Latin prefix *re-* can mean "again" or "back."
- Have students suggest words that contain this prefix. List the suggestions on the board.
  Possible response: *Retell, recant,* and *review* all contain the Latin prefix *re-*.
- Next, have students look up the meanings of these words in a dictionary.
- Finally, direct students to write descriptions of their homes and to infuse the descriptions with elements of magic, making use of some of these vocabulary words.

23 Background

Art

La Nuit, **by René Magritte**

The Belgian painter René Magritte (1898–1967) was one of the best-known Surrealist painters. Surrealists tried to free painting from the restrictions of logic and consciousness and incorporate the magic of dreams in their work. Magritte's favorite technique for achieving this goal was to combine ordinary objects in unusual ways. He also depicted certain objects and figures in more than one painting so that they would come to have symbolic value. The man with the bowler hat in this painting, for instance, appears in a number of other Magritte paintings.

In *La Nuit* (*The Night*), on p. 1185, the man stands outside a warmly lit house, through which the sunset seems visible. Although neither the man, the hat, the house, nor the sunset is in itself unusual, their combination gives the work its eerie feeling. The man's apartness and isolation joins with the melancholy colors to add hints of loneliness.

Use the following question for discussion:

In this painting, how does Magritte use ordinary objects to create a fantastic image?
Possible response: Although Magritte's technique is realistic, his subject matter is not. This situation creates a strange conflict among the elements pictured and the way they relate to one another.

brother was the indispensable end to a line established in this house by our grandparents. We would die here someday, obscure and distant cousins would inherit the place, have it torn down, sell the bricks and get rich on the building plot; or more justly and better yet, we would topple it ourselves before it was too late.

Irene never bothered anyone. Once the morning housework was finished, she spent the rest of the day on the sofa in her bedroom, knitting. I couldn't tell you why she knitted so much; I think women knit when they discover that it's a fat excuse to do nothing at all. But Irene was not like that, she always knitted necessities, sweaters for winter, socks for me, handy morning robes and bedjackets for herself. Sometimes she would do a jacket, then unravel it the next moment because there was something that didn't please her; it was pleasant to see a pile of tangled wool in her knitting basket fighting a losing battle for a few hours to retain its shape. Saturdays I went downtown to buy wool; Irene had faith in my good taste, was pleased with the colors and never a skein[2] had to be returned. I took advantage of these trips to make the rounds of the bookstores, uselessly asking if they had anything new in French literature. Nothing worthwhile had arrived in Argentina since 1939.[3]

But it's the house I want to talk about, the house and Irene, I'm not very important. I wonder what Irene would have done without her knitting. One can reread a book, but once a pullover is finished you can't do it over again, it's some kind of disgrace. One day I found that
22 the drawer at the bottom of the chiffonier, replete with mothballs, was filled with shawls, white, green, lilac. Stacked amid a great smell of camphor—it was like a shop; I didn't have the nerve to ask her what she planned to do with them. We didn't have to earn our living, there was plenty coming in from the farms each month, even piling up. But Irene was only interested in the knitting and showed a wonderful dexterity, and for me the hours slipped away watching her, her hands like silver sea-urchins, needles flashing, and one or two knitting baskets on the floor, the balls of yarn jumping about. It was lovely.

replete (ri plēt´) *adj.* well-filled; stocked

dexterity (deks ter´ ə tē) *n.* skillfulness in the use of one's hands

How not to remember the layout of that house. The dining room, a living room with tapestries, the library and three large bedrooms in the section most recessed, the one that faced toward Rodríguez Peña.[4] Only a corridor with its massive oak door separated that part from the front wing, where there was a bath, the kitchen, our bedrooms and the hall. One entered the house through a vestibule with enameled tiles, and a wrought-iron grated door opened onto the living room. You had to come in through the vestibule and open the gate to go into the living room; the doors to our bedrooms were

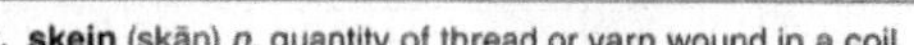

2. **skein** (skān) *n.* quantity of thread or yarn wound in a coil.
3. **Nothing . . . 1939** When World War II began in 1939, communications between Argentina and Europe were disrupted.
4. **Rodríguez Peña** (ro drē´ gəz pā´ nyə) fashionable street in Buenos Aires.

ENRICHMENT: Literature Connection

Symbolism in Julio Cortázar's Fiction

When an image repeats itself in a writer's work, readers may suspect that it has a symbolic meaning. Astute readers of "House Taken Over" will wonder about the significance of the house itself. In Cortázar's stories, a house is often invaded by unknown forces or strange creatures. For example, this pattern appears in the story "Cefalea," published together with "House Taken Over" in *Bestiary* (1951). The invaders in "Cefalea" are fantastic animals called "mancuspias." As they get loose from their cages and fill the house, their keepers are affected by a mysterious disease and eventually die. In addition, in the title story of *Bestiary,* a tiger prowls a house and threatens the family that lives there.

In each story, the being or creature that invades the house is linked to the suffering, thoughts, or desires of the characters. This connection has led some critics to believe that the house symbolizes the human mind beset by irrational forces.

La Nuit (Night), René Magritte, Private Collection/Herscovici/Art Resource, New York, NY

on either side of this, and opposite it was the corridor leading to the back section; going down the passage, one swung open the oak door beyond which was the other part of the house; or just before the door, one could turn to the left and go down a narrower passageway which led to the kitchen and the bath. When the door was open, you became aware of the size of the house; when it was closed, you had the impression of an apartment, like the ones they build today, with barely enough room to move around in. Irene and I always lived in this part of the house and hardly ever went beyond the oak door except to do the cleaning. Incredible how much dust collected on the furniture. It may be Buenos Aires[5] is a clean city, but she owes it to her population and nothing else. There's too much dust in the air, the slightest breeze and it's back on the marble console tops and in the diamond patterns of the tooled-leather desk set. It's a lot of work to get it off with a feather duster; the motes[6] rise and hang in the air, and settle again a minute later on the pianos and the furniture.

 **24 ▲ Critical Viewing**

Which details in this painting help convey a mood similar to that of the story? **[Connect]**

Literary Analysis

Magical Realism and Archetypes What universal human needs does the archetype of a house suggest?

26 ✓Reading Check

In which part of the house do Irene and the narrator spend most of their time?

5. **Buenos Aires** (bwā′ nəs er′ ēz) capital of Argentina.
6. **motes** specks of dust or other tiny particles.

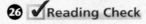

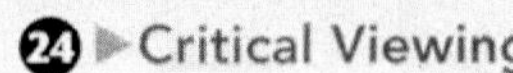

24 ▶ Critical Viewing

Possible response: The house—which is at once warmly inviting and mysterious—best reflects the mood of the story. The isolation and apparent ineffectuality of the man in the bowler hat parallels the story's narrator.

25 Literary Analysis

Magical Realism and Archetypes

- Point out that archetypes often appear in Magical Realist stories, where they can give enormous power to commonplace objects.
- Have students read the bracketed passage on pp. 1184–1185, paying close attention to the details the narrator emphasizes. Then, ask students the Literary Analysis question on p. 1185: What universal human needs does the archetype of a house suggest?
  Possible response: The archetype of the house suggests the universal human needs for shelter, comfort, and safeguarded family memories.
- Encourage students to discuss how Cortázar's use of the archetype of the house adds to the Magical Realist juxtaposition of realistic and fantastic elements.

26 ✓Reading Check

Answer: The narrator and his sister spend most of their time in the front wing of the house, which contains their bedrooms, the bathroom, and the kitchen.

CUSTOMIZE INSTRUCTION FOR UNIVERSAL ACCESS

For Gifted/Talented Students	For Advanced Readers
Tell students to write a story like Cortázar's in which fantastic elements invade a realistic scene. Suggest that students begin by choosing a setting. Then, have them decide on the element of fantasy they will introduce. Remind students to establish a realistic scene before they interject an element of fantasy. During revision, ask students to make sure that they have introduced the fantastic occurrence repeatedly, with greater emphasis each time. Also, tell them to ensure that they have not explained too much.	Tell students that many Latin American writers were influenced by the work of Edgar Allan Poe. Ask students to prepare a Venn diagram in which they compare and contrast "House Taken Over" with such works as "The Fall of the House of Usher," "The Tell-Tale Heart," or "The Black Cat." Remind students as they examine these works to view the house as a symbol of the human mind beset by outside forces. Invite students to share their discoveries with the class.

27 Literary Analysis

Magical Realism

- Ask students to identify realistic elements in the story so far. What makes these elements realistic?
  Answer: The house itself, the narrator and Irene, and their dull lives are realistic elements. The ordinariness of the elements is what makes them realistic.
- Have students read the bracketed passage. Then, ask them the Literary Analysis question on p. 1186: Which do you find more fantastic—the noises in the house or the narrator's reaction to them? Explain.
  Possible response: The narrator's reaction is more fantastic than the noises. He and his sister behave as if the source of the sound is known, even expected, and as if their strange course of action is entirely rational.

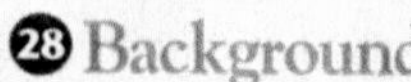

28 Background

Art

Still Life Reviving,
by Remedios Varo

The Spanish Surrealist painter Remedios Varo (1909–1963) is one of the few female artists of her generation to achieve recognition. Her work was greatly influenced by the founding artists of the Surrealist movement with whom she worked in Paris and Barcelona. The Spanish Civil War (1936–1939) caused her to flee her native country and settle in Mexico.

In *Still Life Reviving,* Varo uses the Surrealist technique of removing objects from their usual context. Orbiting like planets above the table, the pieces of fruit seem to take part in a magical, if miniature, solar system. Startling and modern as this painting is, however, it testifies to Varo's attention to detail. She paints with the care of an old master.

Use the following questions for discussion:

- A still life is a painting of fruit or other objects. Why do you think the painter called this work *Still Life Reviving?*
  Possible response: The title suggests that the objects in a traditional still life have lives of their own or that they are returning to life.

continued

I'll always have a clear memory of it because it happened so simply and without fuss. Irene was knitting in her bedroom, it was eight at night, and I suddenly decided to put the water up for *mate.*[7] I went down the corridor as far as the oak door, which was ajar, then turned into the hall toward the kitchen, when I heard something in the library or the dining room. The sound came through muted and indistinct, a chair being knocked over onto the carpet or the muffled buzzing of a
27 conversation. At the same time, or a second later, I heard it at the end of the passage which led from those two rooms toward the door. I hurled myself against the door before it was too late and shut it, leaned on it with the weight of my body; luckily, the key was on our side; moreover, I ran the great bolt into place, just to be safe.

I went down to the kitchen, heated the kettle, and when I got back with the tray of *mate,* I told Irene:

"I had to shut the door to the passage. They've taken over the back part."

She let her knitting fall and looked at me with her tired, serious eyes.

"You're sure?"

I nodded.

"In that case," she said, picking up her needles again, "we'll have to live on this side."

I sipped at the *mate* very carefully, but she took her time starting her work again. I remember it was a gray vest she was knitting. I liked that vest.

Literary Analysis
Magical Realism Which do you find more fantastic—the noises in the house or the narrator's reaction to them? Explain.

28

Still Life Reviving, Remedios Varos, Collection of Beatriz Varo de Cano, Valencia, Spain

The first few days were painful, since we'd both left so many things in the part that had been taken over. My collection of French literature, for example, was still in the library. Irene had left several folios of stationery and a pair of slippers that she used a lot in the winter. I missed my briar pipe, and Irene, I think, regretted the loss of an ancient bottle of Hesperidin.[8] It happened repeatedly (but only in the first few days) that we would close some drawer or cabinet and look at one another sadly.

"It's not here."

One thing more among the many lost on the other side of the house.

But there were advantages, too. The cleaning was so much simplified that, even when we got up late, nine-thirty for instance, by eleven we were sitting around with our arms folded. Irene got into the habit of coming to the kitchen with me to help get lunch. We thought about it and decided on this: while I prepared the lunch, Irene would cook up dishes that could be eaten cold in the evening. We were happy with the arrangement because it was

29 ▲ **Critical Viewing**
How is this painting similar to and different from your image of the mysterious happenings in this story? **[Compare and Contrast]**

7. ***mate*** (mä' tā') beverage made from the dried leaves of a South American evergreen tree.
8. **Hesperidin** (hes per' i din) vitamin that comes from the rind of green citrus fruits and is used for various medicinal purposes.

continued from left column

- How does this painting reflect the Magical Realism of "House Taken Over"?
  Possible response: The painting's combination of the ordinary—fruit, a table, a candle—and the fantasy of its miniature solar system reflect the Magical Realism in the story.

always such a bother to have to leave our bedrooms in the evening and start to cook. Now we made do with the table in Irene's room and platters of cold supper.

Since it left her more time for knitting, Irene was content. I was a little lost without my books, but so as not to inflict myself on my sister, I set about reordering papa's stamp collection; that killed some time. We amused ourselves sufficiently, each with his own thing, almost always getting together in Irene's bedroom, which was the more comfortable. Every once in a while, Irene might say:

"Look at this pattern I just figured out, doesn't it look like clover?"

After a bit it was I, pushing a small square of paper in front of her so that she could see the excellence of some stamp or another from Eupen-et-Malmédy.[9] We were fine, and little by little we stopped thinking. You can live without thinking.

31 (Whenever Irene talked in her sleep, I woke up immediately and stayed awake. I never could get used to this voice from a statue or a parrot, a voice that came out of the dreams, not from a throat. Irene said that in my sleep I flailed about enormously and shook the blankets off. We had the living room between us, but at night you could hear everything in the house. We heard each other breathing, coughing, could even feel each other reaching for the light switch when, as happened frequently, neither of us could fall asleep.

Aside from our nocturnal rumblings, everything was quiet in the house. During the day there were the household sounds, the metallic click of knitting needles, the rustle of stamp-album pages turning. The oak door was massive, I think I said that. In the kitchen or the bath, which adjoined the part that was taken over, we managed to talk loudly, or Irene sang lullabies. In a kitchen there's always too much noise, the plates and glasses, for there to be interruptions from other sounds. We seldom allowed ourselves silence there, but when we went back to our rooms or to the living room, then the house grew quiet, half-lit, we ended by stepping around more slowly so as not to disturb one another. I think it was because of this that I woke up irremediably[10] and at once when Irene began to talk in her sleep.)

Except for the consequences, it's nearly a matter of repeating the same scene over again. I was thirsty that night, and before we went to sleep, I told Irene that I was going to the kitchen for a glass of water. From the door of the bedroom (she was knitting) I heard the noise in the kitchen; if not the kitchen, then the bath, the passage off at that angle dulled the sound. Irene noticed how <u>brusquely</u> I had paused, and

9. **Eupen-et-Malmédy** (yōō pen′ ā mäl mā′ dē) districts in eastern Belgium.
10. **irremediably** (ir′ ri mē′ de ə blē) *adv.* in a way that cannot be helped or corrected.

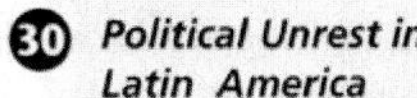

Themes in World Literature

30 ***Political Unrest in Latin America***

The histories of Latin American countries are filled with violent change and dramatic shifts in political ideology. In the twentieth century, many Latin American countries experienced *coups* (kōōz)—revolutions in which military leaders wrested power from civilian authorities and took control of the government. For example, from the mid-1940s through 1956, the dictator Juan Peron ruled Argentina. Intolerant of opposition, the government jailed critics and used violence to suppress dissension. In his Nobel Prize acceptance speech, Gabriel García Márquez described the plight of Latin America, saying that as of the early 1980s, hundreds of thousand of people throughout Latin America had simply disappeared or been killed for political reasons.

Because direct criticism of their governments was so dangerous, many Latin American writers resorted to indirect methods, such as the use of symbols and parables, to comment on the politics of their countries. As a result, many Latin American stories can be read on at least two levels. For example, while "House Taken Over" can be read as a mystery or a dreamlike ghost story, it can also be read as a parable about an aggressive new generation replacing an older, more placid one.

brusquely (brusk′ lē) *adv.* in an abrupt manner

32 ✓**Reading Check**

What does the narrator hear from the library or dining room?

CUSTOMIZE INSTRUCTION FOR UNIVERSAL ACCESS

For Less Proficient Readers	For Gifted/Talented Students	For Advanced Readers
Ask students to write a description of what they imagine the presence in the house to look like. Encourage students to use sensory details. Lead students in a discussion about why Cortázar chooses not to describe the presence in his story. Help students see that the unknown is generally more frightening than the known.	Tell students that the narrator makes an important thematic statement on p. 1187: "You can live without thinking." Challenge students to respond to the narrator's statement in any medium they choose—paint, clay, or language, for example. Tell students that their responses may include elements of the real or the magical.	Tell students that the narrator makes an important thematic statement on p. 1187: "You can live without thinking." Challenge students to put together a collection of responses to the narrator's statement from a variety of writers, artists, and thinkers. Encourage students to share their collection of responses with the class.

29 ▶ Critical Viewing

Possible response: Because the narrator seems to hear snippets of conversation, readers may envision a humanlike presence on the other side of the door, and the table in the painting resembles a table set for humans. However, the painting is less ominous and frightening than the presence in the story seems to be.

30 Background

Political Unrest in Latin America

Latin American political unrest has a long history. From the 1500s to the end of the 1700s, much of the region was under the control of European colonists—primarily the Spanish. In the 1800s, the people of Latin America overthrew their colonial rulers. By the 1830s, there were eighteen separate nations in the region, rather than one massive colony. But progress toward political stability was slow. As noted on p. 1187, the twentieth century was marked by revolutions and coups throughout Latin America.

García Márquez and Cortázar are not the only Latin American writers to address, directly or indirectly, the political crises of their region. Miguel Angel Asturias of Guatemala describes living under a dictatorship. Chilean poet Pablo Neruda, whose work appears on pp. 1196–1197, expresses anger at foreign influence in Latin America. Along with García Márquez, both Asturias and Neruda are Nobel laureates.

31 Critical Thinking

Make a Judgment

- Have students read the bracketed passage.
- Ask whether this passage offers evidence for or against the narrator's statement that "We were fine." Have students explain their responses.

  Possible response: The brother and sister are not "fine." The narrator's statement and inability to sleep show mental and emotional disorder.

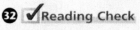

32 ✓ Reading Check

Answer: The narrator hears a sound so "indistinct" that it could be anything from a chair being knocked over to "the muffled buzzing of a conversation."

ASSESS

Answers for p. 1188

Review and Assess

1. **(a)** The narrator and his sister get up at seven, clean in the morning, and have lunch "at noon precisely." Irene knits in the afternoons. On Saturdays, the narrator goes to town for yarn and French books. **(b)** Possible response: The characters are well-to-do, quiet, and private. The narrator is well educated. They are orderly people who stick, dully, to their routines; they seem unimaginative and uninterested in other people.
2. **(a)** The narrator quickly closes and locks the massive oak door that separates the wings of the house, makes *mate*, and then informs his sister of what he has done. **(b)** The outward emotional reaction the narrator describes is so calm as to be almost nonexistent. His physical reaction, however—hurling himself at the door with all of his weight—reveals how frightened he is by the presence in the back of the house.
3. **(a)** Neither the narrator nor Irene sleeps well. He tosses and turns violently, and she begins to talk in her sleep. Often, they both give up and turn on their lights. **(b)** Despite their calm behavior when they are awake, they are both disturbed by the invasion of their home.
4. Possible response: Readers who favor the first interpretation may emphasize the social class of the narrator and his sister, pointing out that they are wealthy enough to live idly. Readers who lean toward the second interpretation may view the story from a psychological perspective, perhaps seeing the mysterious presence as an expression of suppressed energy. Especially perceptive readers may realize that the house might symbolize the mind itself.

came up beside me without a word. We stood listening to the noises, growing more and more sure that they were on our side of the oak door, if not the kitchen then the bath, or in the hall itself at the turn, almost next to us.

We didn't wait to look at one another. I took Irene's arm and forced her to run with me to the wrought-iron door, not waiting to look back. You could hear the noises, still muffled but louder, just behind us. I slammed the grating and we stopped in the vestibule. Now there was nothing to be heard.

"They've taken over our section," Irene said. The knitting had reeled off from her hands and the yarn ran back toward the door and disappeared under it. When she saw that the balls of yarn were on the other side, she dropped the knitting without looking at it.

"Did you have time to bring anything?" I asked hopelessly.

"No, nothing."

We had what we had on. I remembered fifteen thousand pesos[11] in the wardrobe in my bedroom. Too late now.

I still had my wrist watch on and saw that it was 11 P.M. I took Irene around the waist (I think she was crying) and that was how we went into the street. Before we left, I felt terrible; I locked the front door up tight and tossed the key down the sewer. It wouldn't do to have some poor devil decide to go in and rob the house, at that hour and with the house taken over.

---

11. **fifteen thousand pesos** large sum of money at that time, equivalent to over a thousand dollars.

Review and Assess

Thinking About the Selection

1. **(a) Recall:** What daily activities do the narrator and his sister engage in before the house is invaded? **(b) Draw Conclusions:** Based on their daily habits, what are these characters like? Explain.
2. **(a) Recall:** What does the narrator do when he hears the muffled sounds from the library or dining room? **(b) Compare and Contrast:** In what ways does the narrator's physical reaction differ from his outward emotional reaction to the invasion? Explain.
3. **(a) Recall:** After the intruders are in the house, what do the narrator and Irene do in their sleep? **(b) Infer:** What do the differences between their sleeping and waking lives suggest about their true reactions to the invasion of their house?
4. **Take a Position:** Some critics have suggested that the noises symbolize a social revolution overtaking the outdated lifestyle of this upper-class family. Others suggest that they represent the mysterious forces that can attack the mind. Which of these two interpretations do you favor? Why?

ASSESSMENT PRACTICE: Critical Reading

Analyzing an Author's Meaning and Style (For more practice, see Test Preparation Workbook, p. 55.)

Many standardized tests require students to read literary passages and identify the author's meaning or style.

Use this example from "The Handsomest Drowned Man in the World" to demonstrate:

> . . . they noticed that the vegetation on him came from faraway oceans and deep water and that his clothes were in tatters, as if he had sailed through labyrinths of coral.

Why does the author include that the vegetation came from faraway oceans and deep water?

A to emphasize the realism of the situation
B to appeal to readers interested in sea life
C to appeal to sensory perceptions
D to emphasize the foreignness of the body

D is supported by the detail about the vegetation and reflects the author's intent.

Review and Assess

Literary Analysis

Magical Realism

1. (a) For each story, use a chart like the one shown to identify realistic and fantastic details.

	Realistic Details	Fantastic Details
Characters		
Setting		
Events		

(b) Describe specific ways in which each story begins firmly rooted in the real and slowly develops a fantastic dimension. (c) Why do you think this structure is common in works of **magical realism**?

2. (a) In "The Handsomest Drowned Man in the World," how do the children's actions suggest that the world of the story is not quite the world of reality?
3. In "House Taken Over," how might the division of the house into a front and back section relate to the changing balance of reality and fantasy in the story?

Comparing Literary Works

4. (a) Which details in "The Handsomest Drowned Man in the World" present the **archetype** of the sea as the source of life? (b) Which details suggest the sea is a taker of life?
5. (a) In what ways does "House Taken Over," present the archetype of a shelter as a symbol for the individual? (b) In what ways does the house represent an entire family line?

Reading Strategy

Hypothesizing

6. (a) State one **hypothesis** you formed as you began to read "House Taken Over." (b) In what ways did the events of the story prove or disprove your hypothesis?
7. In what ways can hypothesizing increase your involvement in a work of literature? Explain.

Extend Understanding

8. **Psychology Connection:** Julio Cortázar believed that ". . . the fantastic dimension, and the unexpected" are important in both literature and life. Do you agree? Explain your answer.

Quick Review

Magical realism is a literary style that combines realistic events with elements of myth, magic, and other marvels of the natural world.

An **archetype** is a universal symbol that evokes deep, even unconscious responses.

When you **hypothesize,** you make informed guesses or propose ideas based on clues in a text. As you read further, use details to prove or disprove your hypothesis.

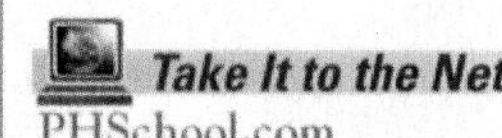

PHSchool.com

Take the interactive self-test online to check your understanding of these selections.

ENRICHMENT: Further Reading

Other Works by the Authors

We strongly encourage you to review any selection before assigning or recommending it to students.

Chronicle of a Death Foretold, García Márquez

The End of the Game and Other Stories, Cortázar

Take It to the Net

Visit PHSchool.com for more information about the authors.

Answers for p. 1189

Review and Assess

1. **(a)** Sample response: Márquez: **Realistic Details: Characters** grumbling of village men; emotionalism of village women; **Setting** small houses; **Events** drowned man washes up. **Fantastic Details: Characters** the villagers' reactions to Esteban's size and beauty; **Setting** the planned changes to the village; **Events** the elaborate funeral for a stranger. **(b)** Both stories begin with realistic characters in realistic settings. Fantastic elements enter the stories and drive their plots. **(c)** Possible response: This structure lulls readers into a sense of comfort before jarring their sense of reality.
2. It is not realistic that children would play with a dead body that washes up on the beach.
3. The back section of the house is where the noises originate. Eventually, the noises take over the rest of the house just as fantasy overtakes reality by the story's end.
4. **(a)** Possible response: The sea brings Esteban to the village, and his arrival stimulates a birth of cultural awareness. **(b)** Esteban is dead when the sea brings him to the village, and he remains dead when the villagers return him to the sea.
5. **(a)** Possible response: The narrator and his sister lead "sheltered" lives within the confines of their house. **(b)** The house "kept the memories" of the narrator's family.
6. **(a)** Possible response: A person will "invade" the house and come between the narrator and Irene. **(b)** This hypothesis is wrong because the invader is not human. The hypothesis is correct, because the characters' lives are disrupted.
7. Possible response: Hypothesizing makes readers analyze and evaluate details as they read.
8. Possible response: The fantastic and unexpected keep life interesting and vital, helping people avoid stagnation.

EXTEND

Answers for p. 1190

❶ Vocabulary Development

Word Analysis: Latin Prefix *re-*

1. reabsorb: to take in and make part of again
2. reoccurrence: a repeated appearance or happening
3. recurrent: returning from time to time
4. reanimate: to revive
5. reappraisal: a new evaluation
6. reconstruction: the action of building again

Spelling Strategy

1. heredity
2. society
3. scarcity
4. generosity

Concept Development: Synonyms or Antonyms?

1. synonyms
2. synonyms
3. antonyms
4. antonyms
5. antonyms
6. synonyms
7. antonyms
8. antonyms

❷ Grammar and Style

Practice

1. "Who is it?" asked the children.
2. "We must bury him," said the men.
3. "Don't go, Esteban," said the women.
4. "If they have come," said Irene, "we must leave at once."
5. I looked at my sister and said, "Yes."

Writing Application

Possible response:

"Well," I said, "here we are."

"Yes," said Irene, "here we are."

"Despite all the time and all that has happened," I said, "everything seems much the same as when we left."

"Yes," Irene agreed. "It's very odd, isn't it?"

"Yes," I said, "and no."

10TH GRADE For support in teaching the Grammar and Style Lesson to tenth graders, use **Writing and Grammar**, Platinum Level, Chapter 28, Section 4.

Integrate Language Skills

❶ Vocabulary Development Lesson

Word Analysis: Latin Prefix *re-*

The Latin prefix *re-* can mean "again" or "back." The word *replete*, which means "well filled," combines this prefix with the Latin root *-plete*, which means "filled." Add the prefix *re-* to each word below. Then, write a definition for each new word.

1. absorb
2. occurrence
3. current
4. animate
5. appraisal
6. construction

Spelling Strategy

The suffix *-ety* /*-ity* means "the state or quality of," but *-ity* is the more common variation in English. Add *-ety* or *-ity* to complete each word below.

1. hered_____
2. soci_____
3. scarc_____
4. generos_____

Concept Development: Synonyms or Antonyms?

Review the vocabulary words and definitions on page 1173, and notice the way the words are used in the context of each selection. Then, identify each of the following pairs of words as either synonyms (words with similar meanings) or antonyms (words with opposite meanings).

1. labyrinths, mazes
2. brusquely, abruptly
3. dexterity, clumsiness
4. replete, lacking
5. resistant, frail
6. haggard, exhausted
7. bountiful, scarce
8. destitute, prosperous

❷ Grammar and Style Lesson

Punctuating Dialogue

In "The Handsomest Drowned Man in the World," García Márquez includes dialogue without punctuation, allowing the story to shift seamlessly from the observations of the villagers to those of the dead man. However, in most pieces of writing, correct **punctuation of dialogue** is essential. To correctly punctuate dialogue, place quotation marks around the speaker's exact words. Locate periods and commas inside the quotation marks.

Examples:

"In that case," she said, picking up her needles again, "we'll have to live on this side."

"Did you have time to bring anything?" I asked hopelessly.

Practice Rewrite each item below, using correct punctuation.

1. Who is it asked the children
2. We must bury him said the men
3. Don't go, Esteban said the women
4. If they have come said Irene we must leave at once
5. I looked at my sister and said yes

Writing Application Suppose that the narrator of "House Taken Over" and his sister return to the house ten years later. Write a short dialogue that they share as they look over their old home. Punctuate each line of dialogue correctly.

WG Prentice Hall Writing and Grammar Connection: Diamond Level, Chapter 27, Section 4

TEACHING RESOURCES

The following resources can be used to enrich or extend the instruction for pp. 1190–1191.

Vocabulary

- **Selection Support** Vocabulary, p. 217
- **Vocabulary and Spelling Practice Book** (Use this booklet for skills instruction.) ■

Grammar

- **Selection Support:** Grammar and Style, p. 218
- **Writing and Grammar,** Diamond Level, p. 724
- **Daily Language Practice Transparencies** ■

Writing

- **Performance Assess. and Portfolio Mgmt.,** p. 16
- **Writing and Grammar,** Diamond Level, p. 202
- **Writing and Grammar iText CD-ROM** ■
- **Writing Models and Graphic Organizers on Transparencies,** pp. 103–105

Listening and Speaking

- **Performance Assess. and Portfolio Mgmt.,** p. 28

■ **BLOCK SCHEDULING:** Resources marked with this symbol provide varied instruction during 90-minute blocks.

❸ Writing Lesson

Essay Tracing the Development of a Character

In García Márquez's masterful story, the drowned man undergoes a surprising transformation from a less-than-human thing into a fully realized character. Write an essay in which you describe how the author achieves this unlikely feat of characterization.

Prewriting As you reread the story, collect details about the drowned man that appear in the beginning, middle, and end. Identify points at which the drowned man's character takes on new shades of personality and identity.

Drafting Write an introduction that describes the subject of the essay and includes a statement expressing your main idea. Then, in your body paragraphs, follow the chronology of the story to present your insights.

Model: Using Transitions to Clarify Order of Events

At the beginning of the story, the children treat the body as a toy. Then, the village men carry the body to town. There, the women clean and care for the body and make an amazing discovery—they realize that this is not a typical drowned man but a hero.

Transitions like *at the beginning* and *then* help readers follow the order of events.

Revising Reread your essay, making sure that you have clearly shown the development of the drowned man's character. Consider adding transitional words and phrases to clarify the logical flow of your ideas.

WG *Prentice Hall Writing and Grammar Connection: Diamond Level, Chapter 10, Section 3*

❹ Extension Activities

Listening and Speaking Storytellers often use ideas from their listeners when they spin stories. Julio Cortázar creates a similar feeling of audience participation in many of his written works. Follow those models by creating and delivering an **interactive story** of your own.

- Begin by describing characters, a setting, and a conflict.
- At key moments, pause and ask for suggestions from your audience.

Continue telling your story until the conflict is resolved. [Group Activity]

Research and Technology Use design software or paper and colored pencils to create a detailed **layout** of the house described in "House Taken Over." Show the location of rooms and furniture, and identify the locations where key story events occur. Choose a specific symbol to represent the mysterious forces that take over the house.

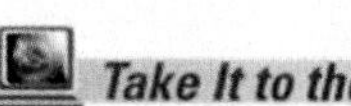
Take It to the Net PHSchool.com

Go online for an additional research activity using the Internet.

Lesson Support for p. 1191

❸ Writing Lesson

- Tell students that their essays should explain how García Márquez develops the title character of "The Handsomest Drowned Man in the World" from a waterlogged body into the fully realized character of Esteban.
- Tell students to examine the author's style choices—word choice, punctuation, juxtaposition of images, and sensory language—to determine how he creates this transformation.
- Model the chronological organizational strategy using the Outline transparency in **Writing Models and Graphic Organizers on Transparencies,** pp. 103–105.
- Use the Response to Literature rubric in **Performance Assessment and Portfolio Management,** p. 16, to evaluate students' work.

10TH GRADE For support in working through the Writing Lesson with tenth graders, use **Writing and Grammar,** Platinum Level, Chapter 10, Section 3.

❹ Listening and Speaking

- Tell students that their interactive stories should be stories told out loud that incorporate suggestions from the audience into the plot. If possible, show an episode of the television show *Whose Line Is It Anyway?* to model this activity.
- Explain to students that they should have key elements of the story—setting, major characters, conflict—planned in advance.
- Use the Delivering a Narrative Presentation rubric in **Performance Assessment and Portfolio Management,** p. 28, to evaluate students' work.

CUSTOMIZE INSTRUCTION
For Universal Access

To address different learning styles, use the following activities suggested in the **Extension Activities** booklet, p. 55:

- For Visual/Spatial Learners, use Activity 5.
- For Musical/Rhythmic Learners, use Activity 6.
- For Bodily/Kinesthetic Learners, use Activity 7.

ASSESSMENT RESOURCES

The following resources can be used to assess students' knowledge and skills.

Selection Assessment

- **Formal Assessment,** pp. 195–197
- **Open-Book Tests,** pp. 163–165
- **Test Bank Software**

Take It to the Net

Visit PHSchool.com for self-tests on the selections.

Writing Rubric

- **Performance Assess. and Portfolio Mgmt.,** p. 16

Listening and Speaking Rubric

- **Performance Assess. and Portfolio Mgmt.,** p. 28

For additional diagnostics and remediation for skills covered in this grouping, use materials from the Prentice Hall Assessment System.

BLOCK SCHEDULING: Resources marked with this symbol provide varied instruction during 90-minute blocks.

Fable · Concord · Sonnet 49 · Sonnet 71 · *from* Omeros

Lesson Objectives

1. **To analyze and respond to literary elements**
   - Literary Analysis: Surrealism
   - Comparing Literary Works: Personification
2. **To read, comprehend, analyze, and critique poetry**
   - Reading Strategy: Reading Verse for Meaning
   - Reading Check Questions
   - Review and Assess Questions
   - Assessment Practice (ATE)
3. **To develop word analysis skills, fluency, and systematic vocabulary**
   - Vocabulary Development Lesson: Latin Suffix *-al*
4. **To understand and apply written and oral language conventions**
   - Spelling Strategy
   - Grammar and Style Lesson: Correct Use of *between* and *among*
5. **To understand and apply appropriate writing and research strategies**
   - Writing Lesson: Letter to a Poet
   - Extension Activity: Anthology
6. **To understand and apply listening and speaking strategies**
   - Extension Activity: Contrasting Readings

STEP-BY-STEP TEACHING GUIDE	PACING GUIDE
PRETEACH	
Motivate Students and Provide Background	
Use the Motivation activity (ATE p. 1192)	5 min.
Read and discuss author and background features (SE pp. 1192, 1194, 1196, 1198; ATE p. 1192) [A]	5 min.
Introduce the Concepts	
Introduce the Literary Analysis and Reading Strategy concepts (SE/ATE p. 1193) [A]	15 min.
Pronounce the vocabulary words and read their definitions (SE p. 1193)	5 min.
TEACH	
Monitor Comprehension	
Informally monitor comprehension by circulating while students read independently [A]	35 min.
Monitor students' comprehension with the Reading Check notes (SE/ATE pp. 1198, 1201, 1203)	as students read
Develop vocabulary with the Vocabulary notes (SE pp. 1194, 1196, 1197; ATE p. 1196)	as students read
Develop Understanding	
Develop students' understanding of surrealism with the Literary Analysis annotations (SE pp. 1196, 1200, 1203; ATE 1196, 1200, 1201, 1203) [A]	10 min.
Develop students' ability to read verse for meaning by using the Reading Strategy annotations (SE/ATE pp. 1194, 1198)	10 min.
ASSESS	
Assess Mastery	
Assess students' mastery of the Reading Strategy and Literary Analysis concepts by having them answer the Review and Assess questions (SE/ATE p. 1205)	20 min.
Use one or more of the print, software, or transparency Assessment Resources (ATE p. 1207) [A]	up to 45 min.
EXTEND	
Apply Understanding	
Have students complete the Vocabulary Development Lesson and the Grammar and Style Lesson (SE p. 1206) [A]	20 min.
Apply students' ability to revise to create an appropriate tone, using the Writing Lesson (SE/ATE p. 1207) [A]	45 min.
Apply students' understanding of the selections, using one or more of the Extension Activities (SE p. 1207)	20–90 min.

[A] ACCELERATED INSTRUCTION: Use the strategies and activities identified with an [A].

10TH GRADE TEACHING TENTH-GRADE STUDENTS
For support in teaching tenth graders, see the Step-by-Step Teaching notes identified with this icon.

UNIVERSAL ACCESS
● = Below-Level Students
▲ = On-Level Students
■ = Above-Level Students

Time and Resource Manager

Reading Level: Challenging, Challenging, Challenging, Challenging, Challenging
Average Number of Instructional Days: 3

RESOURCES		
PRINT	**TRANSPARENCIES**	**TECHNOLOGY**
• **Beyond Literature,** Cultural Connection: Images of Childhood, p. 56 ▲ ■		
• **Selection Support Workbook:** ● ▲ ■ Literary Analysis, p. 224 Reading Strategy, p. 223 Build Vocabulary, p. 221	• **Literary Analysis and Reading Transparencies,** pp. 111 and 112 ● ▲ ■	
		• **Listening to Literature** ● ▲ ■ Audiocassettes Audio CDs
• **Literary Analysis for Enrichment,** p. 56 ■	• **Fine Art Transparencies,** Transparency 21 ● ▲ ■	
• **Formal Assessment:** Selection Test, pp. 198–200 ● ▲ ■ • **Open-Book Tests,** pp. 166–168 ● ▲ ■ • **Performance Assessment and Portfolio Management,** p. 18 ● ▲ ■ • PRENTICE HALL ASSESSMENT SYSTEM ● ▲ ■	• PRENTICE HALL ASSESSMENT SYSTEM ● ▲ ■ **Skills Practice Answers and Explanations on Transparencies**	• **Test Bank Software** ● ▲ ■
• **Selection Support Workbook:** ● ▲ ■ Grammar and Style, p. 222 • **Writing and Grammar,** Diamond Level ● ▲ ■ • **Extension Activities,** p. 56 ● ▲ ■	• **Daily Language Practice Transparencies** ● ▲ • **Writing Models and Graphic Organizers on Transparencies,** pp. 61–64 ● ▲ ■	• **Writing and Grammar iText CD-ROM** ● ▲ ■ ***Take It to the Net*** PHSchool.com

BLOCK SCHEDULING: Use one 90-minute class period to preteach the selection(s) and have students read them. Use a second 90-minute class period to assess students' mastery of skills and have them complete one of the Extension Activities.

Step-by-Step Teaching Guide for pp. 1192–1193

Motivation

Write these oxymorons on the board: *thunderous silence, tender hatred, sweet despair.* Tell students that these phrases are oxymorons, combinations of opposite or contradictory ideas. Have students explain what each of these phrases means. Then, tell them that poets use figures of speech to force the reader to think about the world differently.

❶ Background

More About the Authors

The Mexican poet Octavio Paz wrote, "The polar opposites that exist between Americans and Mexicans are epitomized in our attitudes toward change. To us the secret lies not in getting ahead but in managing to stay where we already are. . . . We instinctively relate the present to the past, whereas Americans relate it to the future."

After Pablo Neruda returned to Chile during the middle of the Spanish Civil War, he participated in Chilean politics and joined the Communist party. From 1948 to 1952, he left to escape persecution by Chile's right-wing government. Much of his later work is political; however, his poetry retains its irrational magic.

American poet James Dickey said of his friend Derek Walcott, "Here he is, a twentieth-century man . . . poised between . . . a lapsed colonial culture and the industrial North, between Africa and the West, between slavery and intellectualism, between the native Caribbean tongue and the English learned from books, between the black and white of his own body. . . ."

Geography Note

Draw students' attention to the map on this page. Point out that Paz and Neruda emerged from a Spanish American culture and write in Spanish. Walcott, on the other hand, grew up in the Caribbean, where English is the official language.

Prepare to Read

❶ Fable ◆ Concord ◆ Sonnet 49 ◆ Sonnet 71 ◆ *from* Omeros

Octavio Paz (1914–1998)

Mexican poet Octavio Paz (ok tāv´ yō päs) was born in a suburb of Mexico City. As a writer and diplomat, he spent time in Paris, Japan, India, and the United States. In each country, he discovered elements of art or culture that influenced his own work.

For example, his exposure to French Surrealism encouraged him to write imaginatively, without worrying about logical meaning. While the Mexican ambassador to India, he studied Indian religions and philosophies. These studies found their way into some of his poems, including "Blanco," which Paz arranged to mimic the sections of the sacred Indian diagram called a *mandala.*

Even though Paz embraced the cultures of other countries, he never compromised his Mexican identity. While he continued to write poetry, he also turned his attention to nonfiction examinations of Mexican culture. His book *The Labyrinth of Solitude* (1950) expresses these observations and has been hailed as a "Latin American classic."

Throughout the 1970s, Paz taught at Harvard University and other American colleges. He received the Nobel Prize in Literature in 1990.

Pablo Neruda (1904–1973)

The poet Pablo Neruda (pä´ blō ne rōō´ thä) drew inspiration from objects that most people barely notice: "It is well . . . to look closely at the world of objects at rest. Wheels that have crossed long, dusty distances with their mineral and vegetable burdens, sacks from coalbins, barrels and baskets . . . From them flow the contacts of the man with the earth. . . ."

Neruda was born in Parral, Chile, the son of a railway worker. When he was just twenty, his book *Twenty Love Poems and a Desperate Song* earned him recognition as one of his country's best poets. The Chilean government often sent promising writers abroad, and Neruda was assigned to various diplomatic positions. For the next twelve years, he traveled extensively, discovering artistic and cultural movements, including French Surrealism, that influenced his work.

In his later years, Neruda became increasingly involved in politics and expressed his opinions in his poems. Even his political opponents conceded his enormous talent. In 1971, Neruda received the Nobel Prize in Literature.

Derek Walcott (b. 1930)

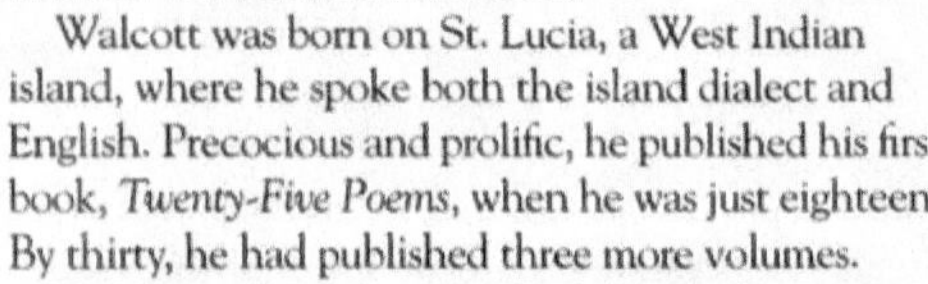

As a Caribbean islander, Derek Walcott has experienced a sense of cultural division: He owes allegiance to his own rich native traditions, which can be traced back to African sources, yet he is also drawn to Western traditions that hearken back to ancient Greece.

Walcott was born on St. Lucia, a West Indian island, where he spoke both the island dialect and English. Precocious and prolific, he published his first book, *Twenty-Five Poems,* when he was just eighteen. By thirty, he had published three more volumes.

Walcott is also a distinguished theater director and playwright. In his dramatic works, he explores his Caribbean roots more deeply than he does in his poetry. For example, one of Walcott's most famous plays, *Dream on Monkey Mountain,* is set in the back country of a Caribbean island. It portrays a world in which superstition and myth dominate.

Walcott divides his time between St. Lucia and the United States, where he teaches creative writing at Boston University. In 1992, Walcott received the Nobel Prize in Literature for his achievements as both poet and playwright.

TEACHING RESOURCES

The following resources can be used to enrich or extend the instruction for pp. 1192–1193.

Background

Beyond Literature, p. 56

Take It to the Net

Visit PHSchool.com for background on the authors.

Literary Analysis

Selection Support: Literary Analysis, p. 224

Literary Analysis and Reading Transparencies, Surrealism, p. 111 ■

Reading

Literary Analysis and Reading Transparencies, Reading Verse for Meaning, p. 112 ■

■ **BLOCK SCHEDULING:** Resources marked with this symbol provide varied instruction during 90-minute blocks.

Preview

Connecting to the Literature

Most of our daily activities emphasize logical thinking. However, these beautiful, surprising poems prove that the mind is far more mysterious and alive than our daily lives usually reveal.

❷ Literary Analysis

Surrealism

Surrealism, which means "beyond realism," is an artistic movement that emphasizes the irrational side of human nature. While Surrealists begin with familiar, everyday objects and experiences, they move quickly to the vivid, imaginative associations of the unconscious mind. Surrealists often rely on surprising juxtapositions, as these lines from Paz's "Fable" demonstrate:

Rain was a willow with unpinned hair
A tree grew in the palm of your hand . . .

Surrealist works can seem like dreams in which ordinary objects become extraordinary. As you read these poems, use a chart like the one shown to record common things that the poet's vision transforms.

Common Thing
↓
Surprising Description

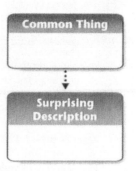

Comparing Literary Works

To emphasize the connections between the real and the imagined, Surrealists often use **personification,** a type of figurative language in which a nonhuman subject is given human traits. These poems are very different, but all use personification. For example, Neruda describes Tomorrow's "green footsteps," while Walcott refers to the "language's desire."

As you read, compare the ways in which each poet uses personification, and determine how it adds to the effect and meaning of each poem.

❸ Reading Strategy

Reading Verse for Meaning

When you **read verse for meaning,** focus on the sentences in poems, not the line breaks. Pause after commas and stop after periods. In poems in which punctuation has been omitted, imagine it there to guide your reading. Once you understand a poem's basic meaning, note the ways in which line breaks, stanza length, or omitted punctuation can emphasize certain ideas. Apply these techniques as you read these selections.

Vocabulary Development

prophesied (präf´ ə sīd) *v.* predicted (p. 1194)

divinations (div´ ə nā´ shənz) *n.* divine predictions (p. 1194)

nocturnal (näk tʉr´ nəl) *adj.* relating to or occurring during the night (p. 1196)

carnivorous (kär niv´ ə rəs) *adj.* meat-eating (p. 1197)

entwined (en twīnd´) *v.* twisted together (p. 1197)

CUSTOMIZE INSTRUCTION FOR UNIVERSAL ACCESS

For Less Proficient Readers	For English Learners	For Advanced Readers
Tell students to write about a strange dream. Then, tell them to circle all the important words in their entries and to copy these words onto separate pieces of paper. Instruct students to turn these pieces of paper upside down and arrange them as poems on their desks before turning them over to reveal Surrealistic poems.	Encourage students to use words and phrases from their first language along with English words and phrases when they complete the activity described for Less Proficient Readers. Lead students in a discussion about interesting word combinations that are not the result of the rational mind.	After students have completed their Surrealistic poems, tell them that they may add words if necessary but that they should not compromise the Surrealistic aspect of their poems by imposing rational meaning. Suggest that students research the works of Surrealist painters to serve as illustrations for their poems.

❷ Literary Analysis

Surrealism

- Tell students that Surrealism concerns itself with the mysterious, nighttime portion of the mind rather than the daylight self. Tell them also that this irrational side has its own emotional, imaginative logic that differs from rational thinking.
- Read aloud and discuss with students the characteristics of Surrealism. Invite them to create their own Surrealistic comparisons.
- Tell each student to exchange his or her Surrealistic comparison with another student. Instruct students to analyze their partners' comparisons using the graphic organizer on p. 1193. Invite student pairs to share their comparisons and analyses with the class.
- Advise students to use a graphic organizer like the one on p. 1193 to analyze Surrealistic comparisons as they read the poems.

❸ Reading Strategy

Reading Verse for Meaning

- Point out that punctuation serves the same purpose in poetry that it does in prose: to indicate breaks in thought.
- Orchestrate a student reading of "Sonnet 49" on p. 1196. Select eight volunteers to read the poem aloud for the class. Instruct students to change speakers each time they reach a colon, a period, or a semicolon. Remind students to pause briefly at each comma.
- Lead students in a discussion about how the change of voice at each punctuation mark helps emphasize the use of punctuation for meaning.

Vocabulary Development

- Pronounce each vocabulary word for students, and read the definitions as a class. Have students identify any words with which they are already familiar.

 **E-Teach**

Visit e-Teach at PHSchool.com for teachers' essays on how to teach, with questions and answers.

TEACH

Step-by-Step Teaching Guide for pp. 1194–1204

Teaching Tenth-Grade Students

10TH GRADE Ask tenth-grade students to recall fables they have read. They may mention the fables of Aesop or La Fontaine. Then, tell them that one of the poems they will be reading is called "Fable." Ask them to think about ways in which this poem resembles and differs from other fables.

❶ About the Selections

"Fable" can be interpreted as a description of childhood or of a mythological time that represents the childhood of civilization.

"Concord," based on the reversal of traditional meanings or perceptions, is fittingly dedicated to Carlos Fuentes. Fuentes is an influential Mexican writer and diplomat whose works are recognized for their experimental nature.

❷ Reading Strategy

Read Verse for Meaning

- Provide students with a copy of the poem "Fable." Then, ask them to insert punctuation marks.
- Ask students the Reading Strategy question on p. 1194: Where would you temporarily place punctuation marks to aid your understanding of this poem? Explain.
  Sample response: "Ages of fire and of air, Youth of water, From green to yellow, From yellow to red, From dream to watching, From desire to act."

  Explanation: A period has been inserted to indicate a complete thought. Commas have been inserted to indicate a series of phrases and to establish clarity.
- Ask: Why do you think Paz left the punctuation out of this poem?
  Possible response: The lack of punctuation imitates a dreaming state of mind.

❶ 

Octavio Paz

translated by Eliot Weinberger

Background

In his famous poem "Ode on a Grecian Urn," the British poet John Keats wrote that a great work of art can "tease us out of thought." The poetry of Octavio Paz does just that—inviting the reader into a new world where the imagination and the unconscious dominate. Instead of focusing on the rational and the realistic, Paz encourages readers to see the world with a deeper, more emotional logic, as these two poems demonstrate.

Ages of fire and of air
Youth of water
From green to yellow
From yellow to red
From dream to watching
From desire to act
It was only one step and you took it so lightly
Insects were living jewels
The heat rested by the side of the pond
Rain was a willow with unpinned hair
❷ A tree grew in the palm of your hand
And that tree laughed sang <u>prophesied</u>
Its <u>divinations</u> filled the air with wings
There were simple miracles called birds
Everything was for everyone
Everyone was everything
There was only one huge word with no back to it
A word like a sun
One day it broke into tiny pieces
They were the words of the language we now speak
Pieces that will never come together
Broken mirrors where the world sees itself shattered

Reading Strategy
Read Verse for Meaning Where would you temporarily place punctuation marks to aid your understanding of this poem? Explain.

prophesied (präf´ ə sīd) *v.* predicted

divinations (div ə nā´ shənz) *n.* divine predictions

TEACHING RESOURCES

The following resources can be used to enrich or extend the instruction for pp. 1194–1204.

Literary Analysis

- **Literary Analysis and Reading Transparencies,** Surrealism, p. 111

Reading

- **Selection Support:** Reading Strategy, p. 223; Build Vocabulary, p. 221 ■
- **Listening to Literature Audiocassettes**
- **Listening to Literature Audio CDs**

Extension

- **Fine Art Transparencies,** Art Transparency 21 (Explain that de Chirico was a precursor of the Surrealists, and discuss with students ways in which both Paz and de Chirico use strange juxtapositions to achieve their effects.) ■

■ **BLOCK SCHEDULING:** Resources marked with this symbol provide varied instruction during 90-minute blocks.

1 # Concord

Octavio Paz

translated by Eliot Weinberger

For Carlos Fuentes

Water above
Grove below
Wind on the roads

Quiet well
Bucket's black   Spring water

Water coming down to the trees
Sky rising to the lips

3

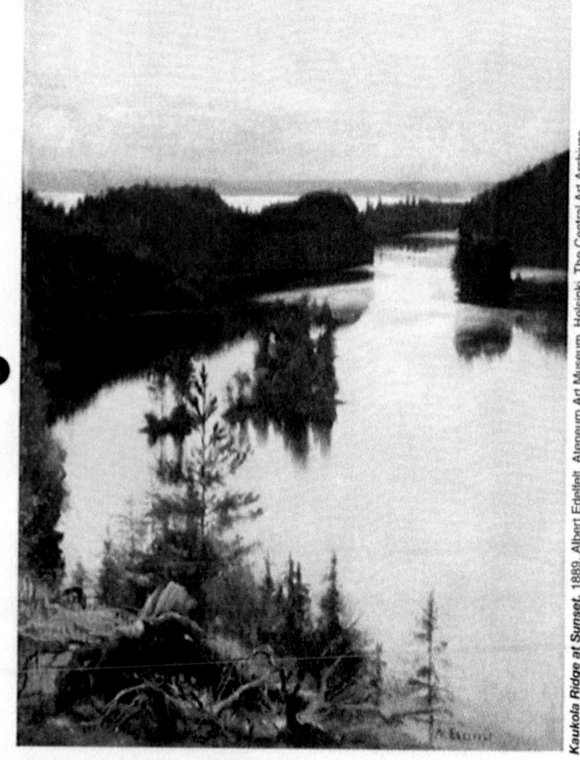

Kaukola Ridge at Sunset, 1889, Albert Edelfelt, Ateneum Art Museum, Helsinki, The Central Art Archives

4 ▲ **Critical Viewing**

Do you think this painting captures the spirit of this poem? Why or why not? **[Assess]**

Review and Assess

Thinking About the Selections

1. **Respond:** Which images, if any, in either poem remind you of something you have seen or felt before? Explain.
2. (a) **Recall:** In line 13 of "Fable," what does the speaker say "Everything" was for? (b) **Recall:** How does the speaker define "Everyone"? (c) **Deduce:** In what ways do the images in lines 6–12 provide examples of the generalizations in line 13?
3. (a) **Recall:** In line 16, what happens to the "one huge word" mentioned in line 14? (b) **Analyze Cause and Effect:** What is the result of this event, as described in the final four lines of the poem?
4. (a) **Recall:** In "Concord," identify two images in the first two lines. (b) **Infer:** In what ways do these images invert logic?
5. (a) **Recall:** What natural event is happening in the final two lines of the poem? (b) **Analyze:** How does Paz transform this everyday event into something extraordinary?

3 Background

Art

Kaukola Ridge at Sunset, by Albert Edelfelt

Albert Edelfelt (1854–1905) was a Finnish painter best known for his country scenes and for biblical scenes in contemporary settings.

Use the following question for discussion:

How does the perspective enhance the effect of the reflection?
Possible response: The perspective increases the span of the sky and the lake and even of the trees caught in the reflection.

4 ▶ Critical Viewing

Possible response: Yes; the reflections give the impression that water and sky are reversed.

Answers for p. 1195

Review and Assess

1. Possible response: In "Fable," the line "There were simple miracles called birds" may cause the reader to recall the innocence and wonder of childhood—a time in life when the aspects of nature are at once miraculous and accessible.
2. **(a)** The speaker says that "Everything was for everyone." **(b)** The speaker defines everyone as "everything." **(c)** Possible response: These images are part of both the material and immaterial world, which, according to the speaker, are interconnected.
3. **(a)** The word breaks into pieces. **(b)** Possible response: The one word that unifies the world splinters into many words that will never be reunited as a whole. The speakers of these partial words are aware that the world is broken but are powerless to remedy the situation.
4. **(a)** Possible response: One image is the water above; another is the grove below. **(b)** Normally, water is below, and groves grow above.
5. **(a)** It is raining. **(b)** Paz says that the sky is rising to the lips, something that is illogical, or surreal.

CUSTOMIZE INSTRUCTION FOR UNIVERSAL ACCESS

For Gifted/Talented Students	For Advanced Readers
Play a portion of Debussy's "Afternoon of a Faun" for students before they begin reading "Fable." Debussy's sinuous, hypnotic music may help prepare students for this poem about a mythological world or the world of childhood. Have students compare Debussy's "Afternoon of a Faun" with "Fable." It may profit students to have them work in groups. Suggest that students use a Venn diagram to assist them with the comparison. Invite students to share the results of their comparisons with the class.	Have students compare "Fable" with William Wordsworth's "Ode: Intimations of Immortality from Recollections of Early Childhood." Wordsworth's poem is explicitly about childhood, and Paz's lyric can be interpreted as a description of childhood or of a mythological time that represents the childhood of civilization. Students may benefit from working in groups. Suggest that students use Venn diagrams to assist them with their comparisons. Invite students to share the results of their comparisons with the class.

5 About the Selections

These two poems by Pablo Neruda are love poems. In many ways, this subject is ideally suited for a Surrealist poet. Surrealists typically juxtapose abstract ideas with wildly contrary images to suggest new meanings.

6 Background

Art

After Rain, by Roger Winter

Roger Winter describes himself as a photorealist because he begins with a photograph and then creates a painting. The painting does not duplicate the photograph but builds on it to create a unique moment in time and space.

Use the following question for discussion:

How does this painting resemble a photograph?
Possible response: Winter's realistic treatment of light makes the painting look like a photograph.

7 ▶ Critical Viewing

Possible response: Yes; the feathered clouds look like the wings of a large bird.

8 Literary Analysis

Surrealism and Personification

- Read aloud lines 9–10.
- Then, ask students the Literary Analysis question on p. 1196: In lines 9 and 10, which human qualities does Neruda give to the sky?
  Answer: The sky has the ability to lift the speaker's lover and carry him or her to the speaker's arms.

9 Vocabulary Development

Word Analysis: Latin Suffix *-al*

- Draw students' attention to the word *nocturnal,* and read its definition. Explain that the Latin suffix *-al* means "of," "like," or "suited for."
- Ask students to suggest and define other words with this suffix.
  Possible responses: *Paternal, anecdotal,* and *recreational* all feature the Latin suffix *-al.*

Sonnet 49 5

Pablo Neruda *translated by* Stephen Tapscott

After Rain, 1998, Roger Winter, Fischbach Gallery, New York 6

7 ◀ **Critical Viewing** The poet describes a sky with folded "wings." Does this painting create a similar image? Explain. **[Connect]**

Background

Neruda included these sonnets in his collection *One Hundred Love Sonnets,* written for his third wife, Matilde Urrutia, while he and Matilde were living in Isla Negra, a small Chilean fishing village. Images of the natural world, particularly the sea, fill these sonnets, which many critics consider to be among the greatest love poems ever written.

It's today: all of yesterday dropped away
among the fingers of the light and the sleeping eyes.
Tomorrow will come on its green footsteps;
no one can stop the river of the dawn.

No one can stop the river of your hands,
your eyes and their sleepiness, my dearest.
You are the trembling of time, which passes
between the vertical light and the darkening sky.

8 The sky folds its wings over you,
lifting you, carrying you to my arms
with its punctual, mysterious courtesy.

That's why I sing to the day and to the moon,
to the sea, to time, to all the planets,
9 to your daily voice, to your <u>nocturnal</u> skin.

Literary Analysis
Surrealism and Personification In lines 9 and 10, which human qualities does Neruda give to the sky?

nocturnal (näk tur´ nəl) *adj.* relating to or occurring during the night.

ENRICHMENT: Literature Connection

Pablo Neruda in His Own Words

In an interview, Neruda makes a distinction between two types of poets:

> I am not a theoretician, but I do see as one kind of poetry the poetry which is written in closed rooms. I'll give as an example Mallarmé, a very great French poet. I have sometimes seen photographs of his room; they were full of little beautiful objects—"abanicos"—fans. He used to write beautiful poems on fans. But his rooms were stuffy, all full of curtains, no air.
>
> He is a great poet of closed rooms and it seems that many of the New World poets follow this tradition: they don't open the windows and you not only have to open the window but come through the windows and live with rivers and animals and beasts....

5 # Sonnet 71

Pablo Neruda
translated by Stephen Tapscott

Love crosses its islands, from grief to grief,
it sets its roots, watered with tears,
and no one—no one—can escape the heart's progress
as it runs, silent and carnivorous.

You and I searched for a wide valley, for another planet
where the salt wouldn't touch your hair,
where sorrows couldn't grow because of anything I did,
where bread could live and not grow old.

A planet entwined with vistas and foliage,
a plain, a rock, hard and unoccupied:
we wanted to build a strong nest

with our own hands, without hurt or harm or speech,
but love was not like that: love was a lunatic city
with crowds of people blanching[1] on their porches.

carnivorous (kär niv′ ə rəs) *adj.* meat-eating

entwined (en twīnd′) *v.* twisted together

1. **blanching** (blanch′ iŋ) becoming pale; bleaching.

Review and Assess

Thinking About the Selections

1. **Respond:** Do you think these poems are more effective when read silently or aloud? Explain.
2. **(a) Recall:** In line 5 of "Sonnet 49," how does the speaker describe the loved one's hands? **(b) Infer:** Which other details in the poem suggest that love and the beloved are part of the natural world?
3. **(a) Recall:** What does the sky do in lines 9–11? **(b) Analyze:** In what ways does this image create a sense of the harmony between human beings and nature?
4. **(a) Recall:** In the first stanza of "Sonnet 71," what three things does love do? **(b) Analyze:** What is the speaker suggesting about the relationship between love and sadness?
5. **(a) Recall:** To what does the speaker compare love in the final image of the poem? **(b) Draw Conclusions:** In what ways is love different from the speaker's expectations?

Answers for p. 1197

Review and Assess

1. Possible response: The poems are more effective when read aloud because the reader gets a better sense of the rhythm, assonance, and alliteration—the musical qualities—of the poems.
2. **(a)** The speaker describes the hands as a river. **(b)** The speaker describes "fingers of the light," the "green footsteps," and the "river of the dawn" in the first stanza. In the second stanza, the beloved is "the trembling of time, which passes between the vertical light and the darkening sky." In the third stanza, the speaker says the sky "folds its wings" over the beloved, and in the final stanza, the speaker sings to the "day and to the moon, to the sea, to time, to all the planets" and refers to the beloved's "nocturnal skin."
3. **(a)** The sky "folds its wings" over the beloved and carries the beloved to the speaker's arms. **(b)** Possible response: This image shows how the sky, or nature, is integral to the human experience.
4. **(a)** Love "crosses its islands," "sets its roots," and "runs, silent and carnivorous." **(b)** The speaker suggests that sadness is inescapably part of loving someone.
5. **(a)** The speaker compares love to a lunatic city. **(b)** The speaker wants love to be safe and free from hurt or harm but finds that love is carnivorous.

CUSTOMIZE INSTRUCTION FOR UNIVERSAL ACCESS

For Special Needs Students	For English Learners
Play the recordings of Neruda's poems on **Listening to Literature Audiocassettes** or **CDs.** Pause after each stanza, and guide students in paraphrasing it. When they have worked through an entire poem, play it again for students, and have them read it aloud with the recording. Finally, help students summarize the entire poem. Work through the second poem in the same way.	If you have Spanish-speaking English learners, arrange for them to read the original Spanish version of these poems to the class. Verify that the students are literate in Spanish before suggesting this activity. Use the following questions to stimulate discussion, and encourage students to talk about the translation: How do the rhyme, alliteration, and assonance differ from the translation? How do the images and figures of speech differ? Does the translator faithfully convey the meaning of the poem?

⑩ About the Selection

The ghost of Walcott's father, the speaker as the poem begins, is referring to Castries, the capital of St. Lucia. This island was discovered for Europeans by Columbus in 1502. The British laid early claim to the island, but it was the French who built the first settlements. The British, however, persevered, fighting with the French for possession of the island through the seventeenth and eighteenth centuries. The British won firm control of the island in 1803. St. Lucia was a British colony until 1967, when it became self-governing, obtaining full independence in 1979.

⑪ Reading Strategy

Read Verse for Meaning

- Ask a volunteer to read aloud the bracketed passage. Then, ask another volunteer to read aloud line 12 through the first half of line 13.
- Ask students the Reading Strategy question on p. 1198: In what ways do the quotation marks help you understand what is happening in the poem?
  Answer: The quotation marks identify the lines as being spoken by someone other than the speaker of the poem.

Monitor Progress Ask: Where is the first pause in this poem? Where is the second pause?
Answer: The first pause comes at the end of line 2 at the semicolon. The second pause occurs at the end of line 4.

Reteach If students have difficulty with the verse form, write on the board the first four stanzas as a paragraph. Have a student read it aloud. Then, ask the class how it is different from the version in their books. Explain that if students have difficulty with a poem, they should imagine that it is prose and connect the lines, pausing only at punctuation marks.

⑫ Reading Check

Answer: The alleys of the speaker's hometown ended in a harbor.

from OMEROS

⑩ Chapter XIII

Derek Walcott

Background

Omeros is a book-length epic poem that describes the wanderings of a present-day Odysseus and the sufferings of others who are displaced and seeking home. The title of the poem is the Greek form of Homer's name. Walcott ties themes from Homer's ancient epics to his own experiences growing up on the Caribbean island of St. Lucia. In this excerpt, the ghost of Walcott's father describes his life on St. Lucia. He also gives his son a goal to strive for in his writing; that goal becomes one of the main themes of *Omeros*.

I

"I grew up where alleys ended in a harbor
and Infinity wasn't the name of our street;
where the town anarchist was the corner barber

with his own flagpole and revolving Speaker's seat.
There were rusted mirrors in which we would look back
on the world's events. There, toga'd[1] in a pinned sheet, ⑪

the curled hairs fell like commas. On their varnished rack,
The World's Great Classics read backwards in his mirrors
where he doubled as my chamberlain.[2] I was known

for quoting from them as he was for his scissors.
I bequeath you that clean sheet and an empty throne."
We'd arrived at that corner where the barber-pole

Reading Strategy
Read Verse for Meaning In what ways do the quotation marks help you understand what is happening in the poem?

⑫ **Reading Check**
Where does the speaker's father say the alleys of his hometown ended?

1. **toga'd** (tō′ ged) *v.* dressed like an ancient Roman, in a long, one-piece outer garment.
2. **chamberlain** (chām′ bər lin) *n.* personal attendant of a ruler or lord.

ENRICHMENT: Literature Connection

Homeric Influence on *Omeros*

In an essay in *The Art of Derek Walcott,* John Figueroa discusses the Homeric influence on *Omeros*:

> This poem is in no way written, as it were, over the template of the *Iliad* or the *Odyssey*. Helen (of St. Lucia) appears, and Hector and Achilles. And there is a fight over her mysterious beauty. But these St. Lucians also bear these names because of the tradition started in slavery of giving slaves such heroic names....
>
> The Homeric aspect, and context of meaning, in this poem is more in the sea and the struggles with it, in what men fight for in Homer and elsewhere, in the displacement and dislocation of people. . . .

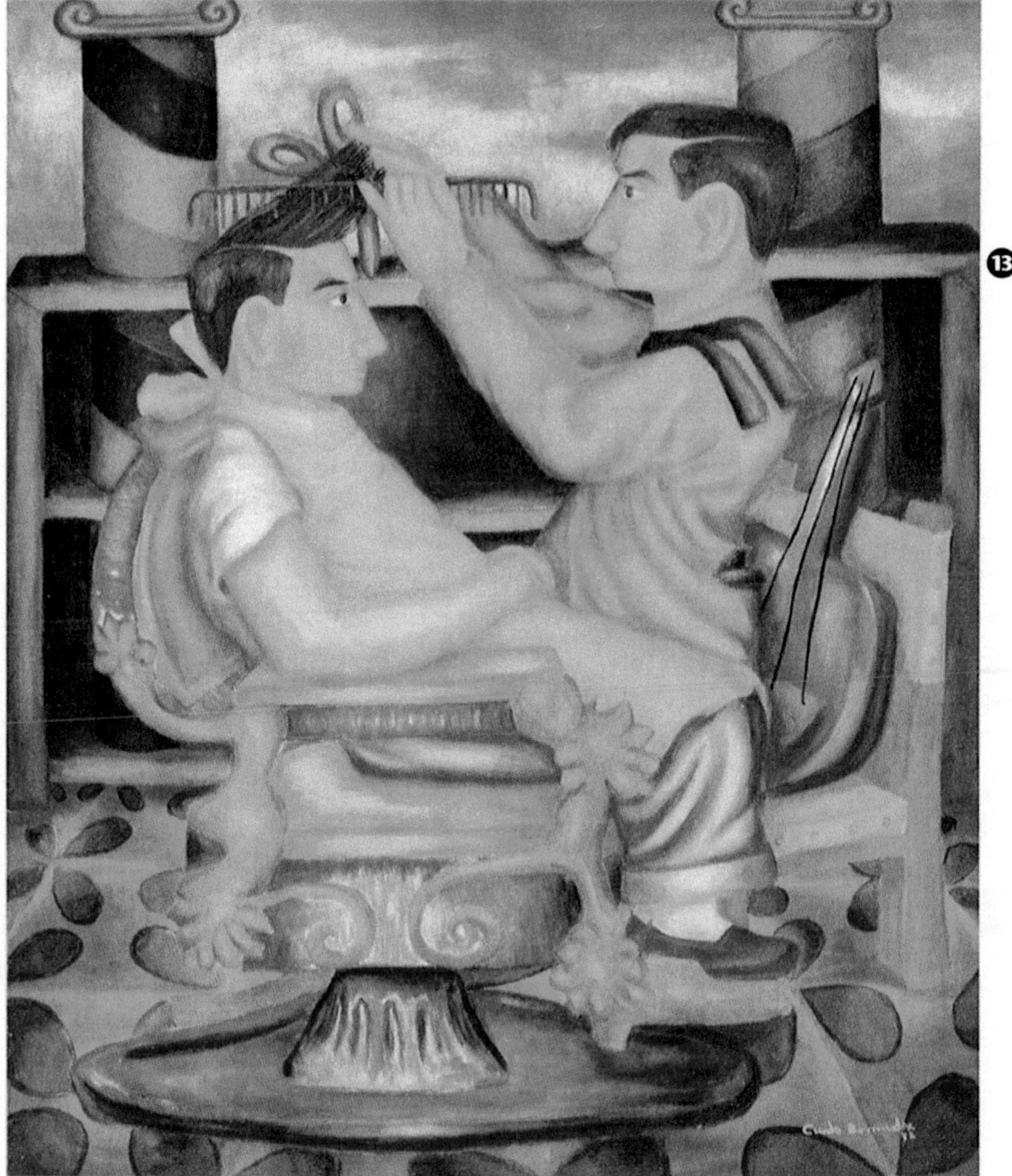

13

14 ▲ **Critical Viewing** Does the barber portrayed in this painting seem similar to the barber described in the poem? Why or why not? **[Compare and Contrast]**

13 Background

Art

Barber Shop, by Cundo Bermudez

Cuban American painter Cundo Bermudez was born in Havana, Cuba, in 1914. His Modernist work—such as this vibrant painting *Barber Shop*—demonstrates an intense love of color and form.

Use the following questions for discussion:

- Which details in this painting reflect the "classical" elements in the first section of Walcott's poem?
  Possible response: The client appears "toga'd in a pinned sheet;" the Doric columns in the background suggest a classical setting; and the ornate gold-adorned chair in which the client sits is thronelike and suggests antiquity.
- Why do you think Bermudez depicted the barber and the client as looking alike?
  Possible response: The barber provides the client with a "mirror-image," suggesting that the two men are in some ways identical.

14 ▶ Critical Viewing

Possible response: The barber in this painting seems younger, less experienced, and less distinguished than the barber in Walcott's poem.

CUSTOMIZE INSTRUCTION FOR UNIVERSAL ACCESS

For Gifted/Talented Students	For Advanced Readers
Tell students that writers are not the only ones who have been tempted to revise Homer. Filmmakers have taken their turn as well. Schedule for students a showing of the Coen brothers' *O Brother, Where Art Thou?* Direct students to compare and contrast the film with *Omeros.* Students might also enjoy looking at the work of painters such as Romare Bearden. Ask students to analyze how each of these artists incorporates his own interpretation of the *Odyssey* into his work.	Tell students that, like Derek Walcott, many other writers have been inspired by Homer's poem the *Odyssey.* Provide students with copies of other modern interpretations of the *Odyssey,* such as "Siren Song" by Margaret Atwood and "Ithaka" by Constantine Cavafy. Direct students to compare and contrast the work of Atwood and Cavafy with that of Walcott. Suggest that students use a Venn diagram to assist them with this comparison.

15 Literary Analysis

Surrealism and Personification

- Point out the comparison that is made between the color of the luxury liner, a mirage, and paper. Ask: How do these comparisons evoke a Surrealistic impression?
  Possible response: The comparisons suggest that two tangible objects—the liner and the paper—are not real; they are mirages.
- Explain to students that the magnificent liner symbolizes everything that Castries is not.
- Then, ask students the Literary Analysis question on p. 1200: Which word in line 36 gives human characteristics to the ocean liner? Explain.
  Answer: The word *preening* gives human qualities to the ocean liner. *Preening* means "priding oneself on some accomplishment," which is a human trait.

angled from the sidewalk, and the photographer,
who'd taken his portrait, and, as some think, his soul,
leant from a small window and scissored his own hair

in a mime, suggesting a trim was overdue
to my father, who laughed and said "Wait" with one hand.
Then the barber mimed a shave with his mouth askew,

and left the window to wait by his wooden door
framed with dead portraits, and he seemed to understand
something in the life opposite not seen before.

"The rock he lived on was nothing. Not a nation
or a people," my father said, and, in his eyes,
this was a curse. When he raged, his indignation

jabbed the air with his scissors, a swift catching flies,
as he pumped the throne serenely round to his view.
He gestured like Shylock: "Hath not a Jew eyes?"[3]

making his man a negative. An Adventist,
he's stuck on one glass that photograph of Garvey's
with the braided tricorne and gold-fringed epaulettes,

and that is his other Messiah.[4] His paradise
is a phantom Africa. Elephants. Trumpets.
And when I quote Shylock silver brims in his eyes.

II

"Walk me down to the wharf."
At the corner of Bridge
Street, we saw the liner as white as a mirage,
its hull bright as paper, preening with privilege.

"Measure the days you have left. Do just that labor
which marries your heart to your right hand: simplify
your life to one emblem, a sail leaving harbor

Literary Analysis
Surrealism and Personification Which word in line 36 gives human characteristics to the ocean liner? Explain.

3. **Shylock: "Hath . . . eyes?"** question asked by Shylock, a Jewish character in Shakespeare's *The Merchant of Venice*. Shylock's point is that a Jew does, of course, have eyes and is just as human as a Christian.
4. **an Adventist** (ad′ vent′ist) **. . . other Messiah** (mə sī′ ə) An Adventist is a member of a Christian sect that believes the world will soon come to an end. Marcus Garvey (1887–1940), an African American of Jamaican descent, believed that blacks around the world should unite and return to Africa. That is why some regard him as a messiah, or savior of his people.

ENRICHMENT: History Connection

The Slave Trade

The idea of returning to Africa is a key theme of *Omeros.* Just as Odysseus longs to return to his home on Ithaca, some black Caribbeans feel a longing for Africa—the continent from which they were brought as slaves to the Caribbean.

Beginning in about 1500, African rulers began selling African slaves to European ship captains who sailed along the coast of Africa. When the ships were full, the voyage, called the Middle Passage, began. Ships sailed to Brazil or an island in the Caribbean. When the ships arrived in Brazil or the Caribbean, the slaves were auctioned to buyers.

This stop lasted for about a year. During this time, the slaves either died from Western diseases or survived. Many North American slaves came from the Caribbean.

Caribbean slavery ended by action of the British Parliament on July 31, 1834. The British freeing of the Caribbean slaves can be attributed to moral protest and a shift in British interests from the West to the East.

and a sail coming in. All corruption will cry
to be taken aboard. Fame is that white liner
at the end of your street, a city to itself,

16

taller than the Fire Station, and much finer,
with its brass-ringed portholes, mounting shelf after shelf,
than anything Castries[5] could ever hope to build."

The immaculate hull insulted the tin roofs
beneath it, its pursers[6] were milk, even the bilge
bubbling from its stern in quietly muttering troughs

and its humming engines spewed expensive garbage
where boys balanced on logs or, riding old tires,
shouted up past the hull to tourists on the rails

17

to throw down coins, as cameras caught their black cries,
then jackknife or swan-dive—their somersaulting tails
like fishes flipped backwards—as the coins grew in size

in the wobbling depth; then, when they surfaced, fights
for possession, their heads butting like porpoises,
till, like a city leaving a city, the lights

blazed in its moving rooms, and the liner would glide
over its own phosphorus, and wash hit the wharves
long after stewards had set the service inside

the swaying chandeliered salons, and the black waves
settle down to their level. The stars would renew
their studded diagrams over Achille's canoe.[7]

From here, in his boyhood, he had seen women climb
like ants up a white flower-pot, baskets of coal
balanced on their torchoned[8] heads, without touching them,

up the black pyramids, each spine straight as a pole,
and with a strength that never altered its rhythm.
He spoke for those Helens[9] from an earlier time:

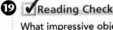

18 ▲ **Critical Viewing**
In what ways might a luxury liner like this one "insult" a small town? Explain. **[Connect]**

19 
Reading Check
What impressive object is visible at the corner of Bridge Street?

5. **Castries** (kas trēz′) capital of St. Lucia and Walcott's hometown.
6. **pursers** (purs′ ərz) *n.* ships' officers in charge of freight, tickets, and similar matters.
7. **Achille's** (ə shēlz′) **canoe** Achille, a fisherman, is one of the main characters in Walcott's *Omeros*, which is loosely based on the epics of the ancient Greek poet Homer (*Omeros* is Greek for Homer). Achille is named for Achilles (a kil′ ēz′), a hero whose exploits are described by Homer
8. **torchoned** (tôr′ shänd) *adj.* wrapped around with a cloth.
9. **Helens** Helen is one of the main characters in Homer's epic the *Iliad*. A beautiful Greek queen, she was kidnapped by a Trojan prince, and this deed provoked a war between the Greeks and the Trojans.

CUSTOMIZE INSTRUCTION FOR UNIVERSAL ACCESS

For English Learners	For Gifted/Talented Students
Bring to class photographs of the Aegean islands and a copy of *Palm Tree, Nassau* (1898) by Winslow Homer. Have students compare and contrast these scenes with Walcott's painting on p. 1202. Ask students why Walcott, as an island dweller, might be especially sympathetic to myths and stories from ancient Greece.	Students may enjoy dramatizing this excerpt from *Omeros*. Have volunteers read aloud the father's and the narrator's parts. Before students begin, ask them to read the poem silently, marking sections that call for specific emotions or particular emphasis. Remind them that they should follow the punctuation rather than the line breaks in order to make their reading sound as natural as possible.

16 Literary Analysis

Surrealism

- Read the bracketed passage aloud for students. Then, ask them to identify the Surrealistic image and the everyday image that are being compared.
  Answer: The Surrealistic image is the dreamlike ocean liner, and the everyday image is the town.
- Ask students: In what ways do the contrasts between the luxury liner and the town suggest that the ship's presence is dreamlike?
  Answer: The liner is described as "mounting shelf after shelf," suggesting almost endless height. The speaker also describes it as finer than anything the people of Castries could hope to build. Castries is the real world of the speaker. The liner, therefore, is something more than the real world. The hull is immaculate, something that seems impossible for a ship that sails across the ocean. The speaker does not say the pursers' uniforms are white like milk, but that the "pursers were milk," further confusing reality with a dreamlike state.

17 Critical Thinking

Draw Conclusions

- Have a volunteer read aloud the bracketed passage. Ask students to describe the image of the boys in the water and the tourists watching them from the rails. Ask: What can you conclude about the town from the description of the garbage and the boys diving? What details support this conclusion?
  Answer: The town is poor. The garbage is described as "expensive" in contrast to the boys who ride on old tires and beg for coins.
- What can you conclude about the attitude of the guests on the liner toward the town? Explain.
  Answer: They regard the boys as quaint and picturesque, taking souvenir pictures of them.

18 ▶ Critical Viewing

Possible response: The ostentatiousness of the liner insults by emphasizing the meager lifestyles of the townspeople.

19 

Reading Check

Answer: The white luxury liner is visible at the corner of Bridge Street.

20 Background

Art

St. Lucia—Looking at Rat Island, by Derek Walcott

In addition to his activities as a West Indian literary prodigy, Derek Walcott also pursued watercolor painting as a childhood pastime. The poet Derek Walcott is therefore also the painter Derek Walcott.

St. Lucia—Looking at Rat Island is typical of Walcott's paintings of his native island. In an interview, he describes St. Lucia as a place where "thick green hills boiled all day with their broad-leafed, volcanic vegetation" and as a "kind of prehistoric Eden." This painting portrays the effect of the scorching sun washing out the green of the palms and other colors of the landscape.

Use the following questions for discussion:

What is the mood of the figure in this painting? How does Walcott convey this mood?
Possible response: The figure's mood is introspective. The artist conveys this mood through the protective shade of the trees, the muted colors, and the pose of the figure.

21 ▶Critical Viewing

Possible response: The painting offers a calm and meditative perspective on the island, but the poem suggests colonial oppression.

20

St. Lucia—Looking at Rat Island, Derek Walcott, from the collection of Michael and Judy Chastanet

"Hell was built on those hills. In that country of coal
without fire, that inferno the same color
as their skins and shadows, every laboring soul

climbed with her hundredweight basket,[10] every load for
one copper penny, balanced erect on their necks
that were tight as the liner's hawsers[11] from the weight.

The carriers were women, not the fair, gentler sex.
Instead, they were darker and stronger, and their gait
was made beautiful by balance, in their ascending

the narrow wooden ramp built steeply to the hull
of a liner tall as a cloud, the unending
line crossing like ants without touching for the whole

day. That was one section of the wharf, opposite
your grandmother's house where I watched the silhouettes
of these women, while every hundredweight basket

21 ▲ Critical Viewing

Derek Walcott painted this watercolor of St. Lucia. Compare and contrast this view of the island with the descriptions in the poem. **[Compare and Contrast]**

---

10. **hundredweight basket** basket weighing one hundred pounds.
11. **hawsers** (hô′ zerz) *n.* large ropes used for towing or securing a ship.

ENRICHMENT: Literature Connection

Nobel Lecture

When accepting the Nobel Prize in Literature in 1992, Derek Walcott provided these insights into his process of composing poetry:

> Poetry, which is perfection's sweat but which must seem as fresh as the raindrops on a statue's brow, combines the natural and the marmoreal; it conjugates both tenses simultaneously: the past and the present, if the past is the sculpture and the present the beads of dew or rain on the forehead of the past. There is the buried language and there is the individual vocabulary, and the process of poetry is one of excavation and of self-discovery. Tonally the individual voice is a dialect; it shapes its own accent, its own vocabulary and melody in defiance of an imperial concept of language. . . . The dialects of my archipelago seem as fresh to me as those raindrops on the statue's forehead, not the sweat made from the classic exertion of frowning marble, but the condensations of a refreshing element, rain and salt.

was ticked by two tally clerks in their white pith-helmets,[12]
and the endless repetition as they climbed the
infernal anthracite hills[13] showed you hell, early."

III

22 "Along this coal-blackened wharf, what Time decided
to do with my treacherous body after this,"
he said, watching the women, "will stay in your head

as long as a question you have no right to ask,
only to doubt, not hate our infuriating
silence. I am only the shadow of that task

as much as their work, your pose of a question waiting,
as you crouch with a writing lamp over a desk,
remains in the darkness after the light has gone,

and whether night is palpable between dawn and dusk
is not for the living; so you mind your business,
which is life and work, like theirs, but I will say this:

O Thou, my Zero, is an impossible prayer,
utter extinction is still a doubtful conceit.
Though we pray to nothing, nothing cannot be there.[14]

Kneel to your load, then balance your staggering feet
and walk up that coal ladder as they do in time,
one bare foot after the next in ancestral rhyme.

23 Because Rhyme remains the parentheses of palms
shielding a candle's tongue, it is the language's
desire to enclose the loved world in its arms;

or heft a coal-basket; only by its stages
like those groaning women will you achieve that height
whose wooden planks in couplets lift your pages

higher than those hills of infernal anthracite.
There, like ants or angels, they see their native town,
unknown, raw, insignificant. They walk, you write;

Literary Analysis
Surrealism and Personification What human traits does the speaker attribute to Time?

Literary Analysis
Surrealism and Personification Which details in these lines personify language itself?

---

12. **two tally clerks . . . pith-helmets** The clerks who tallied, or counted, the baskets wore light, bell-shaped hats as protection from the sun.
13. **anthracite** (an′ thrə sīt′) **hills** mounds of hard coal.
14. **O Thou . . . conceit** (kən sēt′) **. . . be there** You cannot address a prayer to nothingness as if you were praying to God. The conceit, or idea, of nothingness probably does not correspond to anything real.

24 
Reading Check

How much money did the women receive for each load of coal?

22 Literary Analysis
Surrealism and Personification

- Ask students to paraphrase lines 76–81. Ask: What is surreal about this scene?
  Answer: The scene is surreal because it places a ghost on a blackened wharf, talking about Time as though it were a person, while simultaneously watching women of long ago carrying coal and lecturing his son about asking a question. This wild blending of images is dreamlike, or surreal.
- Ask students the first Literary Analysis question on p. 1203: What human traits does the speaker attribute to Time?
  Answer: The speaker credits Time with the ability to make decisions.

23 Literary Analysis
Surrealism and Personification

- Read aloud the bracketed passage. Ask students the second Literary Analysis question on p. 1203: Which details in these lines personify language itself?
  Answer: Language is personified when the speaker's father describes "language's desire to enclose the loved world in its arms; or heft a coal basket."
- Explain to students that Walcott employs an extended metaphor to compare the labor of the women with the labor of the poet. Tell students that the bracketed passage is the key thematic statement of Chapter XIII.

24 Reading Check

Answer: The women received "copper pittances," a barely sufficient allowance of money.

ASSESS

Answers for p. 1204

Review and Assess

1. Possible response: The women carrying the coal on their heads, climbing the ship like ants up a white flower pot is a striking image because a material object, the ship, is glorified, and the women are reduced to insects.
2. **(a)** The speaker says the ocean liner "insulted the tin roofs" of the town. **(b)** The ocean liner is large, white, and luxurious and emanates wealth; the town is small and poor. **(c)** Possible response: The townspeople might, on the one hand, welcome the liner with its wealthy tourists and, on the other hand, resent the wealth that is in such stark contrast to their own poverty.
3. **(a)** The father watched women carrying coal on their heads onto the ship. **(b)** The comparison suggests that these women embody regal beauty and power. **(c)** Possible response: The comparison is surprising because Helen is a Greek queen, and these women are poor peasants. However, the comparison is not surprising because all the women are beautiful captives: Helen has been kidnapped, and the women live under colonial oppression.
4. **(a)** Possible response: The following details compare the women's labor to writing poetry: "balance your staggering feet"; "like those groaning women will you achieve that height whose wooden planks in couplets lift your pages"; and "They walk, you write." **(b)** Possible response: In watching the women, the son was wounded by their unleashed power and beauty.
5. **(a)** The father advises the speaker to write as the women walk, in ancestral rhyme. **(b)** The rhythm is regular and balanced, and the three verses immediately following the "adore" contain end rhyme.

keep to that narrow causeway without looking down,
climbing in their footsteps, that slow, ancestral beat
of those used to climbing roads; your own work owes them

because the couplet of those multiplying feet
made your first rhymes. Look, they climb, and no one knows them;
they take their copper pittances, and your duty

from the time you watched them from your grandmother's house
as a child wounded by their power and beauty
is the chance you now have, to give those feet a voice."

We stood in the hot afternoon. My father took
his fob-watch[15] from its pocket, replaced it, then said,
lightly gripping my arm,
"He enjoys a good talk,

a serious trim, and I myself look ahead
to our appointment." He kissed me. I watched him walk
through a pillared balcony's alternating shade.

15. **fob-watch** (fäb′ wäch) watch carried in a small front pocket of a pair of trousers.

Review and Assess

Thinking About the Selection

1. **Respond:** Which images in this excerpt did you find most striking? Explain.
2. **(a) Recall:** In line 46, what does the speaker say the ocean liner does to the town? **(b) Compare and Contrast:** In what ways does the ocean liner differ from the town? **(c) Infer:** What mixed feelings do you think the townspeople might have for the ocean liner and its passengers? Explain.
3. **(a) Classify:** In his boyhood, what work did the father watch local women perform? **(b) Interpret:** When the father calls the women "Helens," he alludes to the Greek queen whose beauty helped spark the Trojan War. What does this comparison suggest about the women? **(c) Analyze:** In what ways is this comparison both surprising and not surprising?
4. **(a) Distinguish:** In lines 103–123, which details compare the women's labor to the art of writing poetry? **(b) Draw Conclusions:** According to the father, why is the son obligated to the women?
5. **(a) Infer:** What specific advice does the father give the son regarding the use of rhyme? **(b) Speculate:** What evidence does this excerpt provide that the son heeded the father's advice? Explain.

ASSESSMENT PRACTICE: Critical Reading

Analyzing an Author's Meaning and Style (For more practice, see Test Preparation Workbook, p. 51.)

Standardized tests often require students to answer questions about an author's meaning and style. Use the following sample test item to demonstrate.

Read this excerpt from "Sonnet 71" by Pablo Neruda.

Love crosses its islands, from grief to grief,
it sets its roots, watered with tears,
and no one—no one—can escape the
heart's progress
as it runs, silent and carnivorous.

Which literary technique is demonstrated in this passage?

A simile
B rhyme
C paradox
D personification

There is no evidence of *A, B,* or *C* in the passage. However, there is personification ("Love crosses"; the heart runs and is "silent and carnivorous"). *D* is the correct answer.

Review and Assess

Literary Analysis

Surrealism

1. Explain specific ways in which lines 8–14 of Paz's poem "Fable" contain two essential elements of **Surrealism**—surprising juxtapositions and extraordinary transformations of everyday objects.
2. Is Paz's poem "Concord" also an example of Surrealism? Explain.
3. (a) Which details in stanza two of Neruda's "Sonnet 71" could be classified as Surrealist? Explain. (b) Which details in the poem's final stanza could be considered Surrealist? Explain.
4. Using these poems as examples, describe specific ways in which Surrealist writers ground their fantastic visions in realistic details.

Comparing Literary Works

5. (a) Use a chart like the one shown to analyze examples of **personification** in these selections. (b) Which examples describe objects and which describe ideas?

Poem	Example	Human Trait	Emotional Effect

6. Based on these poems, explain how the use of personification to describe an abstraction, such as love, can help a reader perceive the author's ideas.
7. Using these poems as examples, why do you think Surrealist works often include examples of personification?

Reading Strategy

Reading Verse for Meaning

8. (a) When you **read** the excerpt from *Omeros* **for meaning,** where do you pause and where do you come to a full stop? (b) Explain how the three-line stanzas organize the speaker's ideas.
9. In lines 64–69 of the excerpt from *Omeros*, explain how the punctuation helps you understand what is happening in the poem.

Extend Understanding

10. **Mathematics Connection:** In what ways do you think scientists or mathematicians might make use of the kinds of whimsical thinking demonstrated by the Surrealists? Explain.

Quick Review

Surrealism is an artistic movement that emphasizes the irrational side of human nature. Surrealist works go beyond a realistic depiction of the world to portray the vivid, imaginative associations of the unconscious mind.

Personification is a type of figurative language in which a nonhuman subject is given human traits.

When you **read verse for meaning,** you first focus on the sentences rather than the line breaks of poems, using punctuation as a guide.

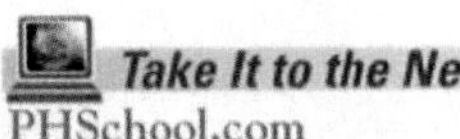

PHSchool.com

Take the interactive self-test online to check your understanding of these selections.

Answers for p. 1205

Review and Assess

1. Possible response: It is surprising to see rain compared to a willow with unpinned hair or a tree growing in the palm of a hand. The tree laughing and prophesying its divinations that turn into birds are extraordinary transformations of everyday objects.
2. Possible response: Yes; "Concord" is surrealistic because it reverses everyday images—water, a grove of trees, the wind, and sky—in unexpected ways.
3. **(a)** Possible responses: Searching for another planet where bread could live and not grow old is a surprising and unexpected transformation. **(b)** Comparing love to a lunatic city with blanching people is a surprising juxtaposition of ideas.
4. Possible response: In "Sonnet 49" for example, the poet describes the sky folding its wings around the beloved. Fast-moving clouds can resemble wings. It takes a leap of imagination to see the wings, but the image touches on reality before soaring into the unconscious.
5. **(a)** Sample response: **Poem:** "Fable"; **Example:** "tree laughed sang prophesied its divinations filled the air with wings"; **Human Trait:** The human traits are laughing, singing, and prophesying; **Emotional Effect:** The effect is one of organic hope. **(b)** The tree is an object.
6. Possible response: Personification concretizes an abstraction and thereby enables readers to understand.
7. Possible response: Readers can understand the odd juxtapositions of ideas better when they can identify with the idea through personification.
8. **(a)** The reader pauses briefly for the commas, longer for the semicolons, longer still for the colons, and stops for the end punctuation. **(b)** The three-line stanzas are similar to paragraphs; each basically contains one idea.
9. The first comma allows the reader to establish place; the second comma, time; and the

continued

continued from right column

third, action. Commas four through seven divide a series of descriptions. The period ends the thought.

10. Possible response: The whimsical thinking of the Surrealists might help scientists or mathematicians escape the bounds of conventional thinking and discover new ideas.

ENRICHMENT: Further Reading

Other Works by the Authors

We strongly encourage you to review any selections before assigning or recommending them to students.

The Labyrinth of Solitude, by Octavio Paz

100 Love Sonnets, by Pablo Neruda

Collected Poems 1948–1984, by Derek Walcott

Take It to the Net

Visit PHSchool.com for more information about the authors.

EXTEND

Answers for p. 1206

❶ Vocabulary Development

Word Analysis: Latin Suffix *-al*

1. of or like a father
2. of or like a story
3. suited for recreation
4. of or like a brother

Spelling Strategy

1. sign [silent]
2. ignorant [pronounced]
3. feigning [silent]
4. foreigner [silent]

Concept Development: Synonyms

1. c
2. b
3. c
4. c
5. a

❷ Grammar and Style

Practice

1. between
2. among
3. between
4. among
5. among

Writing Application

Possible response:

Among the poems in this grouping, "Sonnet 49" and "Sonnet 71" have the most in common. Both poems examine the joys and perils of love. "Sonnet 49" is optimistic, but *between* the two of them, "Sonnet 71" is more realistic.

10TH GRADE For support in teaching the Grammar and Style Lesson to tenth graders, use **Writing and Grammar,** Platinum Level, Chapter 26, Section 2.

Integrate Language Skills

❶ Vocabulary Development Lesson

Word Analysis: Latin Suffix *-al*

The Latin suffix *-al* means "of," "like," or "suited for." It combines with the root *-noctum-*, meaning "night," to form the adjective *nocturnal*, meaning "suited for or living at night." Use your knowledge of *-al* to define each adjective below.

1. paternal
2. anecdotal
3. recreational
4. fraternal

Spelling Strategy

The letter combination *gn* can be pronounced in two ways. In some words, both the *g* and the *n* are voiced *(signal)*. In many others, the *g* is silent *(gnarl)*. Complete the spelling of the words below. Then, identify those in which the *g* is silent.

1. si___
2. i___orant
3. fei___ing
4. forei___er

Concept Development: Synonyms

Review the vocabulary list on page 1193. Then, select the letter of the word that is closest in meaning to each of the numbered vocabulary words.

1. prophesied: (a) prejudged, (b) benefited, (c) forecasted
2. nocturnal: (a) annual, (b) nighttime, (c) periodic
3. carnivorous: (a) all-consuming, (b) hungry, (c) meat-eating
4. divinations: (a) separations, (b) constitutions, (c) predictions
5. entwined: (a) tangled, (b) complimentary, (c) compartmentalized

❷ Grammar and Style Lesson

Correct Use of *between* and *among*

Both of the prepositions *between* and *among* are used to show connections. *Between*, however, is used to show connections between two, and only two, things. *Among* always suggests connections among three or more things.

Examples:

You are the trembling of time, which passes between the vertical light and the darkening sky. *(connects no more than two things)*

. . . all of yesterday dropped away among the fingers of the light . . . *(connects three or more things)*

Practice Correctly complete each sentence below with *between* or *among*.

1. Some Surrealist poems create links __?__ the rational and the subconscious.
2. "Sonnet 49" appears __?__ ninety-nine other poems.
3. Walcott examines the conflict __?__ responsibility and obsession.
4. There are many similarities __?__ the visions of Paz, Neruda, and Walcott.
5. There are differences in interpretations __?__ the readers of any poem.

Writing Application Write a paragraph comparing and contrasting two poems in this grouping. Use *between* and *among* at least once each.

WG Prentice Hall Writing and Grammar Connection: Diamond Level, Chapter 25, Section 2

TEACHING RESOURCES

The following resources can be used to enrich or extend the instruction for pp. 1206–1207.

Vocabulary

- **Selection Support**: Build Vocabulary, p. 221
- **Vocabulary and Spelling Book** (Use this booklet for skills instruction.)

Grammar

- **Selection Support**, Grammar and Style, p. 222
- **Writing and Grammar,** Diamond Level, p. 646
- **Daily Language Practice Transparencies**

Writing

- **Performance Assess. and Portfolio Mgmt.,** p. 18
- **Writing and Grammar,** Diamond Level, p. 108
- **Writing and Grammar iText CD-ROM**
- **Writing Models and Graphic Organizers on Transparencies,** pp. 61–64

BLOCK SCHEDULING: Resources marked with this symbol provide varied instruction during 90-minute blocks.

❸ Writing Lesson

Letter to a Poet

Select the poem from this grouping that you like best and write a letter to the poet. In your letter, explain what you enjoyed about the poem and how it made you feel, and include any questions you would like to ask the poet.

Prewriting Select a poem and brainstorm for words and phrases that express the ways in which the poem affects you. Explore connections between the poem and your own life. Also, jot down any questions about the poem that you would like to ask the poet.

Drafting Begin by explaining your reason for writing. Then, discuss your personal impressions of the poem. End with your question.

Revising Review your letter, making sure that you have maintained a tone of appropriate respect. Highlight informal words or phrases and replace them with more formal alternatives.

Model: Revising to Create an Appropriate Tone

I ~~really got~~ [truly enjoyed reading] "Fable." ~~The part where the tree grew~~ [The image of the tree growing] out of someone's hand reminded me of a dream ~~of mine.~~ [I once had.] In ~~it~~ [my dream], my fingertips turned into roses.

A more formal tone shows an appropriate level of respect.

Prentice Hall Writing and Grammar Connection: Diamond Level, Chapter 6, Section 4

❹ Extension Activities

Listening and Speaking With a partner, select two of these poems that seem very different in subject, tone, or imagery and deliver **contrasting readings** for the class. Use these tips to prepare:

- Discuss how each poem should be read to clarify its meaning and tone for an audience.
- Select suitable sound effects or music.

As you deliver your readings, vary the volume and tone of your voice and use body language that enhances your presentation. **[Group Activity]**

Research and Technology Neruda's sonnets are part of a tradition of such poems. Use print and electronic sources to locate a variety of sonnets and create an **anthology.** Organize the sonnets by type or by theme. Write an introduction in which you define a sonnet and explain the process you used to make your selections. Choose appropriate illustrations for both the cover and the interior.

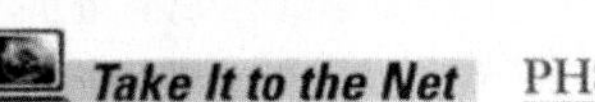
Take It to the Net PHSchool.com

Go online for an additional research activity using the Internet.

ASSESSMENT RESOURCES

The following resources can be used to assess students' knowledge and skills.

Selection Assessment

- **Formal Assessment,** pp. 198–200
- **Open-Book Tests,** pp. 166–168
- **Test Bank Software**

Take It to the Net

Visit PHSchool.com for self-tests on the selections.

Writing Rubric

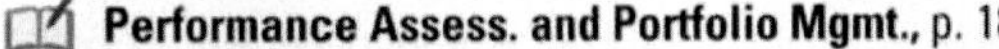
Performance Assess. and Portfolio Mgmt., p. 18

For additional diagnostics and remediation for skills covered in this grouping, use materials from the Prentice Hall Assessment System.

❸ Writing Lesson

- Encourage students to annotate a copy of the poem they choose with personal thoughts and connections as well as questions about the poem. Students can then refer to these notes when they begin drafting.
- Use the Writing Lesson to guide students in developing their letters. Review with students the proper format for a formal letter before they complete their final drafts. Use the Business Letter model on pp. 61–64 of **Writing Models and Graphic Organizers on Transparencies** as a guide.
- Use the Business Letter rubric on p. 18 of **Performance Assessment and Portfolio Management** to assess students' letters.

10TH GRADE For support in working through the Writing Lesson with tenth graders, use **Writing and Grammar,** Platinum Level, Chapter 15, Section 1.

❹ Listening and Speaking

- Suggest that students mark the lines on a copy of the poem so that they will remember which words and phrases to emphasize, when to speed up or slow down, and when to pause or stop and for how long.
- Urge students to practice reading their poems in front of a mirror so that they can observe and critique their body language and presence. They can also make audio recordings of their readings so that they can listen to them and work on their vocal presentations.

CUSTOMIZE INSTRUCTION For Universal Access

To address different learning styles, use the following activities suggested in the **Extension Activities** booklet, p. 56.

- For Visual/Spatial Learners, use Activity 5.
- For Intrapersonal Learners, use Activity 6.
- For Verbal/Linguistic Learners, use Activity 7.

Background

Solzhenitsyn's World Literature

The writings of Alexander Solzhenitsyn celebrate the concept of world literature, and depend on it in very concrete ways. Between the mid-1960s and late 1989, when the Soviet Union collapsed, Solzhenitsyn's works were banned in the Soviet Union and could be published only in foreign nations. The writer himself was eventually forced to leave the Soviet Union after being tried in 1974 for treason. As a resident of Switzerland, Solzhenitsyn was finally able to receive the Nobel Prize.

Background

Goethe's World Literature

"I am more and more convinced," Goethe said in 1827, "that poetry is the universal possession of mankind. . . . National literature is now a rather unmeaning term; the epoch of world literature is at hand. . . ." And indeed, Goethe's notion of *Weltliteratur* both recognized and helped catalyze a broadening cultural and literary perspective among people of the modern world. For Goethe, the sharing of literature among nations had both social and philosophical implications. He hoped, on the one hand, that it would further civilization by encouraging respect and understanding between different peoples; on the other hand, he believed it would help human beings accommodate the divisive polarities of reason and passion, heart and mind, and stability and change.

I, WITNESS

In the twentieth century, a new literature arose that gave voice to the victim and empowered the powerless.

In 1970, Alexander Solzhenitsyn, whose writing testified to the tyranny of the government of the Soviet Union, wrote a Nobel Prize acceptance speech called "The One Great Heart." The Soviet government would not allow Solzhenitsyn to travel to Sweden to deliver the speech, but it was published and widely read. In his speech, the author declared that "world literature is no longer an abstraction or a generalized concept invented by literary critics, but a common body and common spirit, a living, heartfelt unity reflecting the growing spiritual unity of mankind." More and more, Solzhenitsyn believed, readers and writers in even the most remote countries are connected to people around the globe. Where once there was sporadic communication, now there is dialogue and community.

New World Literature The concept of world literature is not new. In fact, the German writer Goethe used the phrase some 200 years ago. However, it was not until the twentieth century that two essential factors—decolonization and globalization—helped make the concept of world literature a reality. With decolonization, former colonies declared independence from colonial powers. For example, in 1947, India declared independence from Great Britain, becoming a self-governing country for the first time since 1757. As similar events took place around the globe, new forms of literature arose that emphasized the voices of former colonial subjects who had traditionally been ignored or silenced.

With globalization, new technologies such as television, the movies, the Internet, and rapid forms of travel have made the disparate cultures of the world increasingly accessible. The cultural cross-pollination that enriches our lives today allows new literary voices to spread far beyond their original geographical borders. For example, the Antiguan writer Jamaica Kincaid is lauded for her autobiographical novels about a girl growing up on a Caribbean island and leaving home for the United States. Vénus Khoury-Ghata, a Lebanese writer living in France, has achieved international recognition for her poems in French about her Arab heritage.

Witnesses to History Although the twentieth century ushered in a glorious parade of technological innovations, it also saw bloodshed on an unprecedented scale. Writers from all over the world have borne witness to these evils. During World War I, fighting forces routinely used machine guns, tanks, and chemical weapons. From the battlefields came the frank, anguished voices of young American and European poets turned soldiers, many of whom

ENRICHMENT: Sociology Connection

Globalization

Although technologies such as the Internet, satellite television, and rapid travel have exposed people to new cultures and ideas, some social scientists worry that globalization will yield not a richer world, but a flatter, more homogenous one—one in which most people think the same thoughts, eat the same foods, and wear the same clothes. Other experts dismiss as extreme the idea of a single world culture. They point to local experiences and customs that thrive despite the ubiquity of American fast food chains and media, claiming that the overwhelming majority of people do not belong to a disconnected global culture, as many have mistakenly asserted.

One thing sociologists do agree on, though, is that globalization is still in its early stages—and that no one can predict with certainty what the "global village" of the future will look like.

were killed in the conflict. Their work did not glorify the bloody battles, nor did it flinch from representing the human cost of the first truly modern war. Following World War II, European writers like Primo Levi, an Italian Jewish chemist who survived Auschwitz, and Paul Celan, a Romanian Jewish poet whose parents were deported and killed, documented the destruction of Europe's Jews at the hands of the Nazis.

Italian Landscape, Ben Shahn, © Estate of Ben Shahn/Licensed by VAGA, New York, NY

▲ **Critical Viewing**
How can literature help refugees like those depicted in this painting? **[Synthesize]**

Subjectivity and Truth Perhaps we look to writers to bear witness because they have the power to convey truths that fact can only suggest. Reading Chinua Achebe's short story "Marriage Is a Private Affair," we grasp the importance of tribal differences in rural Nigeria, not because they are explained to us but because we see what happens when a young man marries a woman his father refuses to accept. Through the poetry of Taha Muhammad Ali, who is Palestinian, and of Yehuda Amichai, who is an Israeli Jew, we begin to feel how deeply the conflict in the Middle East wounds the spirits of the people who live there.

In some of the most powerful twentieth-century literature, individual writers bear witness for those who can no longer speak. When we read Elie Wiesel's account of his father's death in a concentration camp and his own survival, we are reminded of the millions of people murdered by the Nazis who took their stories to the grave. Reading the Misty Poets, we think of the Chinese writers who have been imprisoned or killed for criticizing the Communist government.

Somewhere, Somebody Is Writing Because good writers tell the truth even when it is unwelcome, many of them are forced to write in secret or in exile. At this very moment, someone may be scribbling forbidden words that tell the truth of his or her experience. Some writers risk their lives again and again to share what they have witnessed. The words of writers like Vaclav Havel in Czechoslovakia and Leopold Sedar Senghor in Senegal carry such weight that the authors are chosen for political leadership, enabling them to embody the ideas they express. Wherever it is written, wherever it is read, world literature serves to remind us of our common humanity; in its pages, we hear the steady beat of "One Great Heart."

Background

The "War Poets"

The surge of poetry from the trenches of World War I was so substantial that its writers came to be regarded as a literary group unto themselves. Known as the "War Poets," these young men recorded in honest, jarring terms the horrors they witnessed and experienced. Among the most renowned of the War Poets are British writers Siegfried Sassoon and Wilfred Owen.

Background

Art

Italian Landscape, by Ben Shahn

American artist Ben Shahn (1898–1969) was born in Lithuania and immigrated to the United States in 1906. After working as a lithographer's apprentice as a young man, he attended several schools, including the National Academy of Design in New York. He was a successful painter, photographer, and graphic artist, using his work to comment on political and social issues.

Shahn's tempera-on-paper rendering of post-war destruction in *Italian Landscape* demonstrates his skill in capturing not only physical realities, but also emotional truths.

▶Critical Viewing

Possible response: Literature can help transform the unjust political and social systems by which refugees are victimized. Literature can also reassure refugees that their experiences are part of the broader human experience; it can teach them about the new culture in which they live; and it can comfort them and provide encouragement during difficult times.

Critical Thinking

1. How would you define the term "world literature"? **[Define]**
   Possible response: World literature is literature that is printed and read in cultures other than its original culture.
2. In your view, what are the functions of world literature? **[Apply]**
   Possible response: World literature functions to expose readers to new cultures and ideas, to

continued

continued from right column

give voice to those who are silenced or disenfranchised, to express universal human truths, to unite people, and to help transform the world.

A Walk to the Jetty *from* Annie John

Lesson Objectives

1. **To analyze and respond to literary elements**
   - Literary Analysis: Point of View
   - Connecting Literary Elements: Flashback
2. **To read, comprehend, analyze, and critique a novel**
   - Reading Strategy: Understanding Spatial Relationships
   - Reading Check Questions
   - Review and Assess Questions
   - Assessment Practice (ATE)
3. **To develop word analysis skills, fluency, and systematic vocabulary**
   - Vocabulary Development Lesson: Latin Root *-stup-*
4. **To understand and apply written and oral language conventions**
   - Spelling Strategy
   - Grammar and Style Lesson: Adjective Clauses
5. **To understand and apply appropriate writing and research strategies**
   - Writing Lesson: A Reminiscence
   - Extension Activity: Map of Annie's Walk
6. **To understand and apply listening and speaking strategies**
   - Extension Activity: Discussion

TEACHING A TENTH-GRADE COURSE

The literature in this section can be taught as part of a rich, balanced world literature course for tenth-grade students. For a full outline of such a course, see pp. T46–T48 in Volume I of this Teacher's Edition.

STEP-BY-STEP TEACHING GUIDE	PACING GUIDE
PRETEACH	
Motivate Students and Provide Background	
Use the Motivation activity (ATE p. 1210)	5 min.
Read and discuss author and background features (SE pp. 1210, 1212; ATE p. 1210) A	5 min.
Introduce the Concepts	
Introduce the Literary Analysis and Reading Strategy concepts (SE/ATE p. 1211) A	15 min.
Pronounce the vocabulary words and read their definitions (SE p. 1211)	5 min.
TEACH	
Monitor Comprehension	
Informally monitor comprehension by circulating while students read independently or in groups A	35 min.
Monitor students' comprehension with the Reading Check notes (SE/ATE pp. 1213, 1215, 1217)	as students read
Develop vocabulary with the Vocabulary notes (SE pp. 1213, 1217, 1218; ATE p. 1218)	as students read
Develop Understanding	
Develop students' understanding of point of view with the Literary Analysis annotations (SE/ATE pp. 1214, 1215) A	10 min.
Develop students' ability to understand spatial relationships, using the Reading Strategy annotations (SE/ATE pp. 1213, 1216)	10 min.
ASSESS	
Assess Mastery	
Assess students' mastery of the Reading Strategy and Literary Analysis concepts by having them answer the Review and Assess questions (SE/ATE p. 1219)	20 min.
Use one or more of the print, software, or transparency Assessment Resources (ATE p. 1221) A	up to 45 min.
EXTEND	
Apply Understanding	
Have students complete the Vocabulary Development Lesson and the Grammar and Style Lesson (SE/ATE p. 1220) A	20 min.
Apply students' ability to brainstorm for details, using the Writing Lesson (SE/ATE p. 1221) A	45 min.
Apply students' understanding of the selections, using one or more of the Extension Activities (SE p. 1221)	20–90 min.

A **ACCELERATED INSTRUCTION:**
Use the strategies and activities identified with an A.

TEACHING TENTH-GRADE STUDENTS
For support in teaching the selection(s) to tenth-grade students, see the Step-by-Step Teaching notes identified with the icon shown here.

UNIVERSAL ACCESS
● = Below-Level Students
▲ = On-Level Students
■ = Above-Level Students

Time and Resource Manager

Reading Level: Easy
Average Number of Instructional Days: 3

RESOURCES		
PRINT	**TRANSPARENCIES**	**TECHNOLOGY**
• **Beyond Literature,** Cross-Curricular Connection: Social Studies, p. 57 ▲ ■		
• **Selection Support Workbook:** ● ▲ ■ Literary Analysis, p. 228 Reading Strategy, p. 227 Build Vocabulary, p. 225	• **Literary Analysis and Reading Transparencies,** pp. 113 and 114 ● ▲ ■	
		• **Listening to Literature** ● ▲ ■ Audiocassettes Audio CDs
• **Literary Analysis for Enrichment,** p. 57 ■		
• **Formal Assessment:** Selection Test, pp. 201–203 ● ▲ ■ • **Open-Book Tests,** pp. 169–171 ● ▲ ■ • **Performance Assessment and Portfolio Management,** pp. 9, 27 ● ▲ ■ • PRENTICE HALL ASSESSMENT SYSTEM ● ▲ ■	• PRENTICE HALL ASSESSMENT SYSTEM ● ▲ ■ **Skills Practice Answers and Explanations on Transparencies**	• **Test Bank Software** ● ▲ ■
• **Selection Support Workbook:** ● ▲ ■ Grammar and Style, p. 226 • **Writing and Grammar,** Diamond Level ● ▲ ■ • **Extension Activities,** p. 57 ● ▲ ■	• **Daily Language Practice Transparencies** ● ▲	• **Writing and Grammar iText CD-ROM** ● ▲ ■ ***Take It to the Net*** PHSchool.com

BLOCK SCHEDULING: Use one 90-minute class period to preteach the selection(s) and have students read them. Use a second 90-minute class period to assess students' mastery of skills and have them complete one of the Extension Activities.

PRETEACH

Step-by-Step Teaching Guide for pp. 1210–1211

Motivation

Tell students that they will be reading a story about a dramatic event that establishes a young woman's independence in the adult world. Invite students to share some of the ways they have asserted their own identity and independence as they have grown toward adulthood.

❶ Background

More About the Author

Jamaica Kincaid first appeared in the pages of *The New Yorker* as a subject rather than a contributor. Her friend George W. S. Trow sometimes quoted her in the short nonfiction pieces about life in New York City that he wrote for the magazine. One day, Kincaid went to a West Indian carnival with Trow. Afterward, she wrote her impressions of the carnival and gave the notes to Trow. He passed them on to William Shawn, the legendary editor of *The New Yorker,* who published the notes without editing them at all. According to Kincaid, this appreciation of her writing changed her life forever. "When I saw it [the magazine piece], and it was just what I had put on paper, that is when I realized what my writing was. My writing was the thing that I thought. Not something else. Just what I thought."

Geography Note

Draw students' attention to the map on this page. Antigua won its independence from England in 1981. Until then, Antigua was a British colony, so many Antiguans have grown up speaking English, using British currency, and playing British games such as cricket.

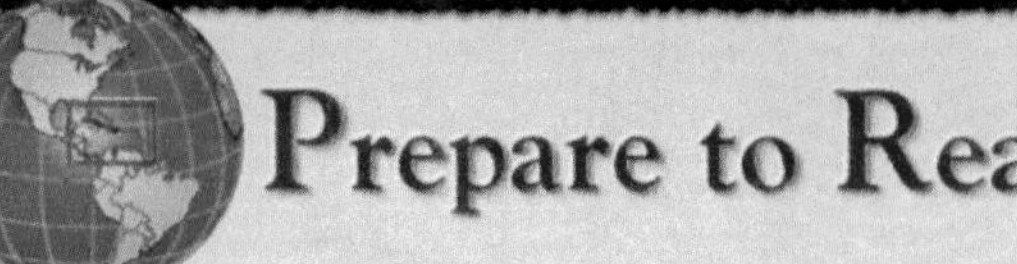

Prepare to Read

❶ A Walk to the Jetty *from* Annie John

Jamaica Kincaid (b. 1949)

"I've never really written about anyone except myself and my mother," says author Jamaica Kincaid. Drawn from her childhood experiences on the Caribbean island of Antigua, Kincaid's fiction explores the complex relationship between mother and daughter and the ways in which it changes, sometimes painfully, during a daughter's passage into adulthood.

Rural Childhood Jamaica Kincaid was born Elaine Potter Richardson on May 25, 1949, in St. John's, Antigua. Like most rural Antiguans, Kincaid grew up in a home without electricity or running water. Nonetheless, her early childhood was happy, primarily because of the deep connection she felt to her mother. That attachment changed, however, when Kincaid was nine years old and the first of her three younger brothers was born. The writer was devastated by this threat to a mother's love that she perceived as hers alone.

Salvation in Books Kincaid was highly intelligent, but her intellectual gifts went largely unrecognized by her teachers. Today, she attributes this oversight to the colonial system under which she grew up. At the time, Antigua was a British dependency. It became an independent nation in 1981. Racism and economic oppression ensured that expectations for young black women remained low. In the face of indifference both at home and at school, Kincaid retreated into the world of books, where she discovered a passion that was missing in other areas of her life. One of her favorite novels was Charlotte Brontë's *Jane Eyre.*

Struggle for Education By the time she was a teenager, Kincaid was determined to leave Antigua. At the age of sixteen, she secured a job as a nanny for a wealthy family living in a New York City suburb. From that position she moved on to a series of unskilled jobs and later to an unsuccessful attempt at getting a college degree. Despite educational and career setbacks, Kincaid made a number of connections in the New York City publishing world, and by the early 1970s she was publishing articles in several magazines for teens.

Hard-Won Success Eventually, Kincaid became a staff writer for *The New Yorker,* in which many of her stories first appeared. In 1983, she published *At the Bottom of the River,* a collection of short stories. While its imaginative metaphors seemed too obscure to some reviewers, others praised the book's lyrical prose and keen insights. Kincaid admits that the stories in the collection may be difficult to grasp; in writing them, she says she sometimes fell into a kind of hallucinatory state. Her later works demonstrate a more traditional narrative style.

Fictionalizing Her Life Kincaid's critically acclaimed novels *Annie John* (1985) and *Lucy* (1990) are both clearly autobiographical. *Annie John* relates the experiences of a young girl growing up on a Caribbean island. "A Walk to the Jetty," in which Annie leaves her childhood home—and, by inference, her childhood self—serves as the book's final scene. *Lucy* picks up the same story by relating the tale of a young Caribbean girl who travels to the United States to take a job caring for the children of a wealthy American couple. Both books are classic Jamaica Kincaid, rich in memories and charged with emotional intensity.

TEACHING RESOURCES

The following resources can be used to enrich or extend the instruction for pp. 1210–1211.

Background

Beyond Literature, p. 57

Take It to the Net

Visit PHSchool.com for background on the author.

Literary Analysis

Literary Analysis and Reading Transparencies, Point of View, p. 113

Writing Models and Graphic Organizers on Transparencies, pp. 79–81

Reading

Literary Analysis and Reading Transparencies, Understanding Spatial Relationships, p. 114

BLOCK SCHEDULING: Resources marked with this symbol provide varied instruction during 90-minute blocks.

Preview

Connecting to the Literature

If you have ever made a big change, such as moving across the country or even to another town, you will understand how the main character in this story feels. As Annie John prepares to leave her childhood home, she follows a road of bittersweet memories.

❷ Literary Analysis

Point of View

All works of fiction are related by a narrator who speaks from a distinct perspective, or **point of view.** Most stories are told from either a first-person or one of two types of third-person point of view. These are defined by the narrator's relationship to the action and by his or her knowledge of other characters' thoughts and feelings. This story is told from the first-person point of view, which has the following characteristics:

- The narrator is a character who is involved in the story.
- The narrator uses the pronouns "I," "we," "me," "our," and "us."

Point of view controls the information the reader receives. For example, the first-person point of view allows Annie John to share her thoughts and feelings, but it prevents other characters from doing the same. As you read, notice the ways in which the point of view shapes your understanding of the story.

Connecting Literary Elements

The first-person point of view lends itself to the use of **flashback**—a section of a literary work that relates an incident from the past. Flashbacks may take the form of dreams, memories, stories, or actual shifts in time. As you read, identify the details that spark Annie John's flashbacks, and notice the ways in which her memories suggest reasons for her decision to leave the island.

❸ Reading Strategy

Understanding Spatial Relationships

As Annie John walks to the jetty, landmarks along the way trigger her memories. In order to better appreciate Annie John's experience, it is helpful to **understand spatial relationships**—the arrangement of physical features within a setting. As you read, use a chart like the one shown to gain a clear picture of Annie John's walk.

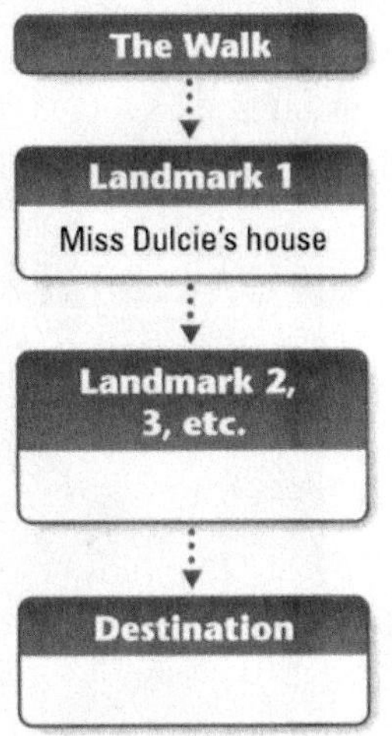

Vocabulary Development

jetty (jet' ē) *n.* wall or barrier built into a body of water to protect a harbor (p. 1213)

loomed (lo͞omd) *v.* appeared in a large or threatening form (p. 1213)

wharf (wôrf) *n.* structure built as a landing place for boats (p. 1217)

scorn (skôrn) *n.* contempt; open dislike or derision (p. 1217)

stupor (sto͞op' ər) *n.* mental dullness, as if drugged (p. 1218)

cue (kyo͞o) *n.* prompt or reminder (p. 1218)

❷ Literary Analysis

Point of View

- Remind students that the narrator, or person who tells a story, has a specific point of view, or perspective.
- On the board, rewrite the first five sentences of the selection in the third person. Suggest that students use a Venn diagram to compare and contrast the point of view of the original version with that of the new version.
- Recommend that students use the grid organizer on pp. 79–81 in **Writing Models and Graphic Organizers on Transparencies** to make a character chart. Students should list the names of the main characters across the top of the organizer. As they read, tell students to record what they learn about each character from the first-person narrator's point of view.

❸ Reading Strategy

Understanding Spatial Relationships

- Explain that settings are likely to affect characters in a work of literature. Remind students that a setting includes the arrangement of physical objects as well as time and geography.
- Tell students that creating charts or diagrams can help them envision a setting. Point out the graphic organizer on p. 1211 that begins to note the landmarks that Annie passes on her walk to the jetty.
- Have students complete a graphic organizer like this one as they read the selection.

Vocabulary Development

- Pronounce each vocabulary word for students, and read the definition as a class. Have students identify any words with which they are already familiar.

CUSTOMIZE INSTRUCTION FOR UNIVERSAL ACCESS

For Less Proficient Readers	For English Learners	For Advanced Readers
Encourage students to create a timeline of their lives. Ask them to include the significant events of the last sixteen to eighteen years. For each entry on the timeline, direct students to note a place that they associate with that event. Invite students to share their timelines with the class.	Use a discussion on reminiscences to call attention to the way words and phrases express the passage of time. Suggest that students use these words as they create a timeline for their lives. For each entry on the timeline, direct students to note a place they associate with that event.	Have students work in groups to research the island of Antigua—its history, geography, economy, and culture. Direct groups to create an annotated, visual timeline for the island. Suggest that students find someone who has visited Antigua or lived there and interview this person as an additional resource.

E-Teach

Visit e-Teach at PHSchool.com for teachers' essays on how to teach, with questions and answers.

TEACH

Step-by-Step Teaching Guide for pp. 1212–1218

Teaching Tenth-Grade Students

10TH GRADE Prepare tenth graders for the selection by having them draw maps of their neighborhoods and then asking them to annotate their maps with reminiscences.

❶ About the Selection

Fear, excitement, nostalgia, resentment, confusion—this autobiographical story captures all the emotions a young adult feels when taking the first steps toward independence. For Annie John, the emotions associated with leaving home are complicated by her conflicted relationship with her mother and her island home, as well as her need to rise above the low expectations for girls in her culture.

❷ Background

Art

Vista II, by Hughie Lee-Smith

Of his generation, Hughie Lee-Smith was considered one of the most important painters of African American subjects. Born in 1915 in Eustis, Florida, he studied in Cleveland, Ohio, and graduated from the Cleveland School of Art in 1938. He tried to include art in everything he did during his life and is known especially for drawing attention to social issues.

Use the following question for discussion:

What sensory details might Annie John describe if she were the girl in the painting?
Possible response: She might describe the smell of the water, the warmth of the sun, the coolness of the wind, and the sounds of the sea life around her.

❸ ▸Critical Viewing

Possible response: The woman in this picture seems to be waiting because she is not dressed for travel, and she does not have a bag or a suitcase with her.

❶ A Walk to the Jetty

from Annie John

Jamaica Kincaid

Background

At the beginning of *Annie John*, the novel from which "A Walk to the Jetty" is excerpted, Annie John is a happy ten-year-old. She loves both her parents, but she is especially close to her mother. However, when Annie is almost twelve, her mother's affections mysteriously sour. In front of Annie's father, "We were politeness and kindness and love and laughter." Alone, the enmity between the two deepens. When she is sixteen years old, Annie John decides to move to England. The final section of the novel, "A Walk to the Jetty" begins as she prepares to leave the island of her childhood.

❸ ▼**Critical Viewing** Does the woman in this painting seem to be departing, like the narrator in the story, or does she seem to be waiting? Explain. **[Make a Judgment]**

❷

Vista II, 1987, Hughie Lee-Smith, June Kelly Gallery

TEACHING RESOURCES

The following resources can be used to enrich or extend the instruction for pp. 1212–1218.

Literary Analysis

- **Selection Support:** Literary Analysis, p. 228
- **Literary Analysis and Reading Transparencies,** Point of View p. 113

Reading

- **Selection Support:** Reading Strategy, p. 227; Build Vocabulary, p. 225
- **Listening to Literature Audiocassettes** ■
- **Listening to Literature Audio CDs** ■

■ **BLOCK SCHEDULING:** Resources marked with this symbol provide varied instruction during 90-minute blocks.

My mother had arranged with a stevedore[1] to take my trunk to the jetty ahead of me. At ten o'clock on the dot, I was dressed, and we set off for the jetty. An hour after that, I would board a launch that would take me out to sea, where I then would board the ship. Starting out, as if for old time's sake and without giving it a thought, we lined up in the old way: I walking between my mother and my father. I loomed way above my father and could see the top of his head. We must have made a strange sight: a grown girl all dressed up in the middle of a morning, in the middle of the week, walking in step in the middle between her two parents, for people we didn't
4 know stared at us. It was all of half an hour's walk from our house to the jetty, but I was passing through most of the years of my life. We passed by the house where Miss Dulcie, the seamstress that I had been apprenticed to for a time, lived, and just as I was passing by, a wave of bad feeling for her came over me, because I suddenly remembered that the months I spent with her all she had me do was sweep the floor, which was always full of threads and pins and needles, and I never seemed to sweep it clean enough to please her. Then she would send me to the store to buy buttons or thread, though I was only allowed to do this if I was given a sample of the button or thread, and
5 then she would find fault even though they were an exact match of the samples she had given me. And all the while she said to me, "A girl like you will never learn to sew properly, you know." At the time, I don't suppose I minded it, because it was customary to treat the first-year apprentice with such scorn, but now I placed on the dustheap of my life Miss Dulcie and everything that I had had to do with her.

We were soon on the road that I had taken to school, to church, to Sunday school, to choir practice, to Brownie meetings, to Girl Guide meetings, to meet a friend. I was five years old when I first walked on this road unaccompanied by someone to hold my hand. My mother had placed three pennies in my little basket, which was a duplicate of her bigger basket, and sent me to the chemist's shop to buy a pennyworth of senna leaves, a pennyworth of eucalyptus leaves, and a pennyworth of camphor.[2] She then instructed me on what side of the road to walk, where to make a turn, where to cross, how to look carefully before I crossed, and if I met anyone that I knew to politely pass greetings and keep on my way. I was wearing a freshly ironed yellow dress that had printed on it scenes of acrobats flying through the air and swinging on a trapeze. I had just had a bath, and after it, instead of powdering me with my baby-smelling talcum powder, my mother had, as a special favor, let me use her own talcum powder, which smelled quite perfumy and came in a can that had painted on it people going out to dinner in nineteenth-century London and was called Mazie. How it pleased me to walk out the door and bend my head down to sniff at myself and see

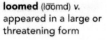

jetty (jet′ ē) *n.* wall or barrier built into a body of water to protect a harbor

loomed (lo͞omd) *v.* appeared in a large or threatening form

Reading Strategy
Understanding Spatial Relationships Where are Annie and her parents, and where are they headed?

6 ✔ **Reading Check**
Why is the narrator going to the jetty?

1. **stevedore** (stē′ və dôr) *n.* person whose job is the loading and unloading of ships.
2. **chemist's shop . . . camphor** (kam′ fər) *chemist's shop* is the British term for *pharmacy*; the items mentioned are small amounts of plant matter that are used in remedies.

CUSTOMIZE INSTRUCTION FOR UNIVERSAL ACCESS

For Less Proficient Readers	For English Learners
Check students' comprehension by having them summarize the events leading up to this point in the story. Then, encourage them to make predictions about how the story will end. Urge them to record their predictions and revise them as they proceed through the story.	Have students look at a variety of maps in an atlas or a social studies textbook and study the way the details are presented and how the map legend is constructed. Suggest that students take careful notes of the details of Annie's walk. Have students use their notes to create a map of Annie's neighborhood and the walk to the jetty. Students may enjoy using color or illustrations on their maps. Have students display their maps in the classroom.

4 Reading Strategy
Understanding Spatial Relationships

- To help students understand the spatial relationships in a story, explain the importance of identifying the beginning and end points of a journey.
- Ask students the Reading Strategy question on p. 1213: Where are Annie and her parents, and where are they headed?
  Answer: Starting at their house, they begin a half-hour walk to the jetty.
- Tell students to keep the beginning and ending points of the journey in mind as they read.

Monitor Progress Ask students to add the second landmark to the graphic organizers they began on p. 1211.

Reteach If students are having difficulty understanding spatial relationships, suggest that they use the **Selection Support** booklet, p. 227, for additional help.

5 Reading Strategy
Understanding Spatial Relationships

- Remind students that landmarks trigger Annie John's memories as she walks to the jetty.
- Help students recognize flashbacks by identifying word clues. Ask students how many flashbacks occur on p. 1213.
  Answer: Two flashbacks occur on p. 1213.
- Ask students to identify the word clues that signal these flashbacks.
  Answer: The words "remembered" and "I was five years old" are clues that a flashback is about to begin.

6 ✔ Reading Check

Answer: The narrator is going to the jetty to board a launch that will ferry her out to a ship.

7 Background

Art

San Antonio de Oriente, by José Antonio Velásquez

Latin American primitive painter José Antonio Velásquez (1906–1983) has lived all his life in the village of San Antonio de Oriente, Honduras.

Although he had no formal artistic training, the unaffected talent and ability of José Antonio Velásquez have earned him worldwide recognition as a notable Latin painter.

Use the following questions for discussion.

- Do you think you would like to live in this village? Why or why not? Possible response: Teenagers, noticing the lack of television antennas and satellite dishes as well as the laundry being dried on a line, may not be drawn to a village that is devoid of the technology on which they rely for entertainment and education.
- Why do you think the artist has chosen to remain in this village? Possible response: The artist may have chosen to remain here for the same reasons that American teenagers might choose not to. In addition, he might have close family in the village.

8 ▶Critical Viewing

Possible response: Like the narrator's home, this village appears serene. However, Annie's description emphasizes the bank and the library. In this painting, the artist draws attention to the church.

9 Literary Analysis

Point of View and Flashback

- Remind students that because this story is told by a first-person narrator, they get only one point of view.
- Ask students the Literary Analysis question on p. 1214: What information about Annie's relationship with her mother does this flashback provide? Possible response: Annie's relationship with her mother is unbalanced. The mother selflessly delivers carrot juice to Annie at school every day. Annie selfishly expresses no gratitude for this service.

that I smelled just like my mother. I went to the chemist's shop, and he had to come from behind the counter and bend down to hear what it was that I wanted to buy, my voice was so little and timid then. I went back just the way I had come, and when I walked into the yard and presented my basket with its three packages to my mother, her eyes filled with tears and she swooped me up and held me high in the air and said that I was wonderful and good and that there would never be anybody better. If I had just conquered Persia, she couldn't have been more proud of me.

San Antonio de Oriente, José Antonio Velásquez, Museum of Modern Art of Latin America 7

We passed by our church—the church in which I had been christened and received[3] and had sung in the junior choir. We passed by a house in which a girl I used to like and was sure I couldn't live without had lived. Once, when she had mumps, I went to visit her against my mother's wishes, and we sat on her bed and ate the cure of roasted, buttered sweet potatoes that had been placed on her swollen jaws, held there by a piece of white cloth. I don't know how, but my mother found out about it, and I don't know how, but she put an end to our friendship. Shortly after, the girl moved with her family across the sea to somewhere else. We passed the doll store, where I would go with my mother when I was little and point out the doll I wanted that year for Christmas. We passed the store where I bought the much-fought-over shoes I wore to church to be received in. We passed the bank. On my sixth birthday, I was given, among other things, the present of a sixpence.[4] My mother and I then went to this bank, and with the sixpence I opened my own savings account. I was given a little gray book with my name in big letters on it, and in the balance column it said "6d." Every Saturday morning after that, I was given a sixpence—later a shilling, and later a two-and-sixpence piece—and I would take it to the bank for deposit. I had never been allowed to withdraw even a farthing from my bank account until just a few weeks before I was to leave; then the whole account was closed out, and I received from the bank the sum of six pounds ten shillings and two and a half pence.

8 ▲ Critical Viewing How is this painting of a Caribbean village similar to and different from your image of the narrator's home in the story? Explain. **[Compare and Contrast]**

9 We passed the office of the doctor who told my mother three times that I did not need glasses, that if my eyes were feeling weak a glass of carrot juice a day would make them strong again. This happened when I was eight. And so every day at recess I would run to my school gate and meet my mother, who was waiting for me with a glass of juice from carrots she had just grated and then squeezed, and I would drink it and then run back to meet my chums. I knew there was nothing at all

Literary Analysis
Point of View and Flashback What information about Annie's relationship with her mother does this flashback provide?

3. **received** *v.* accepted into the congregation as a mature Christian.
4. **sixpence** *n.* monetary unit in the British commonwealth, worth six pennies (about 12 U.S. cents). A shilling is worth two sixpence, a two-and-sixpence is two and one-half shillings, two shillings and one sixpence or a pound is twenty shillings, and a farthing is a "fourthing": one fourth of a penny.

ENRICHMENT: History Connection

The Origin of a Strawberry

Until 1834, when slavery was abolished, the British brought African slaves to work on Antigua's sugar plantations. Most Antiguans, like Annie John and Jamaica Kincaid herself, are descendants of these African slaves.

Of her work, Jamaica Kincaid said, "I feel it's my duty to make everyone a little less happy. For instance, most of the nations that have serious gardening cultures also have, or have had, empires. You can't have this luxury of pleasure without somebody paying for it. This is nice to know. It's nice to know that when you sit down to enjoy a plate of strawberries, somebody got paid very little so that you could have your strawberries. It doesn't mean the strawberries will taste different, but it's nice to enjoy things less than we do. We enjoy things far too much, and it leads to incredible pain and suffering."

wrong with my eyes, but I had recently read a story in *The Schoolgirl's Own Annual* in which the heroine, a girl a few years older than I was then, cut such a figure to my mind with the way she was always adjusting her small, round, horn-rimmed glasses that I felt I must have a pair exactly like them. When it became clear that I didn't need glasses, I began to complain about the glare of the sun being too much for my eyes, and I walked around with my hands shielding them—especially in my mother's presence. My mother then bought for me a pair of sunglasses with the exact horn-rimmed frames I wanted, and how I enjoyed the gestures of blowing on the lenses, wiping them with the hem of my uniform, adjusting the glasses when they slipped down my nose, and just removing them from their case and putting them on. In three weeks, I grew tired of them and they found a nice resting place in a drawer, along with some other things that at one time or another I couldn't live without.

We passed the store that sold only grooming aids, all imported from England. This store had in it a large porcelain dog—white, with black spots all over and a red ribbon of satin tied around its neck. The dog sat in front of a white porcelain bowl that was always filled with fresh water, and it sat in such a way that it looked as if it had just taken a long drink. When I was a small child, I would ask my mother, if ever we
10 were near this store, to please take me to see the dog, and I would stand in front of it, bent over slightly, my hands resting on my knees, and stare at it and stare at it. I thought this dog more beautiful and more real than any actual dog I had ever seen or any actual dog I would ever see. I must have outgrown my interest in the dog, for when it disappeared I never asked what became of it. We passed the library, and if there was anything on this walk that I might have wept over leaving, this most surely would have been the thing. 11 My mother had been a member of the library long before I was born. And since she took me everywhere with her when I was quite little, when she went to the library she took me along there, too. I would sit in her lap very quietly as she read books that she did not want to take home with her. I could not read the words yet, but just the way they looked on the page was interesting to me. Once, a book she was reading had a large picture of a man in it, and when I asked her who he was she told me that he was Louis Pasteur[5] and that the book was about his life. It stuck in my mind, because she said it was because of him that she boiled my milk to purify it before I was allowed to drink it, that it was his idea, and that that was why the process was called pasteurization. One of the things I had put away in my mother's old trunk in which she kept all my childhood things was my library card. At that moment, I owed sevenpence in overdue fees.

Literary Analysis
Point of View In what ways does the first-person point of view allow the narrator to share specific private thoughts and feelings?

12 **✓Reading Check**
Which landmark from her childhood does the narrator almost weep over leaving?

5. **Louis Pasteur** (pas tʉr′) French chemist and bacteriologist (1822–1895) who developed pasteurization, the process for using heat to kill disease-causing bacteria in milk.

10 Literary Analysis

Point of View

- Remind students that a first-person narrator can share only his or her thoughts and feelings.
- Ask students the Literary Analysis question on p. 1215: In what ways does the first-person point of view allow the narrator to share specific private thoughts and feelings?
  Possible response: A first-person narrator is capable of relaying events and his or her thoughts and feelings about these events. Additionally, a first-person narrator can leap across time within a particular event to give the event depth. For example, when Annie narrates the story about the porcelain dog, she describes the setting, the dog, and her actions as well as her thoughts about the dog. She also leaps across time in the same narrative segment to comment on an older version of herself who did not notice the dog's disappearance.

11 Critical Thinking

Infer

- Read aloud the bracketed sentence.
- Ask students to infer why the library is such an important part of Annie's childhood.
  Possible response: It might have been important to Annie because it was important to her mother. Also, it might have been important because the books allowed the curious girl a wider view of the world outside her island home.

12 ✓Reading Check

Answer: Annie says that if there is anything on this walk that she might cry over leaving, it is the library.

CUSTOMIZE INSTRUCTION FOR UNIVERSAL ACCESS

For Gifted/Talented Students	For Advanced Readers
As Annie walks to the jetty, she passes community landmarks that remind her of her childhood. Every community has such landmarks. Ask students to consider the landmarks, such as buildings, parks, or monuments, in their own community. Then, have them consider "personal landmarks" similar to what Annie recalls in the story. Have each student write a description of his or her personal landmarks, explaining their importance.	Suggest that students read *The House on Mango Street* by Sandra Cisneros. Ask students to compare and contrast the setting and the characters in "A Walk to the Jetty" and *The House on Mango Street.* Suggest that students select some of the vignettes from *The House on Mango Street* and do oral readings for the class. Students can then share their insights about the similarities and differences between the two works.

13 Background

The Landscape and Climate of Antigua

A drought is a longer than average time with very little or no rainfall that persists long enough to cause crop damage, water supply shortages, and other serious problems. Even two or three weeks without rain can be damaging to an are a like Antigua that depends, in part, on crop production for its economy.

14 Reading Strategy

Understanding Spatial Relationships

- Remind students that a character's emotional state often mirrors the setting of the story.
- Ask students whether they have ever felt anxious during a storm or felt content while sitting beneath a tree on a warm day.
- Ask students the Reading Strategy question on p. 1216: What is the connection between Annie's physical location and her emotions? Possible response: Annie has an old fear of slipping between the boards of the jetty into the dark-green water. The emotions Annie associates with this setting are mirrored in her feelings about leaving home. She is suddenly frightened about exchanging the familiar people and surroundings of her childhood for the unknown.

As I passed by all these places, it was as if I were in a dream, for I didn't notice the people coming and going in and out of them, I didn't feel my feet touch ground, I didn't even feel my own body—I just saw these places as if they were hanging in the air, not having top or bottom, and as if I had gone in and out of them all in the same moment. The sun was bright; the sky was blue and just above my head. We then arrived at the jetty.

My heart now beat fast, and no matter how hard I tried, I couldn't keep my mouth from falling open and my nostrils from spreading to the ends of my face. My old fear of slipping between the boards of the jetty and falling into the dark-green water where the dark-green eels lived came over me. When my father's stomach started to go bad, the doctor had recommended a walk every evening right after he ate his dinner. Sometimes he would take me with him. When he took me with him, we usually went to the jetty, and there he would sit and talk to the night watchman about cricket[6] or some other thing that didn't interest me, because it was not personal; they didn't talk about their wives, or their children, or their parents, or about any of their likes and dislikes. They talked about things in such a strange way, and I didn't see what they found funny, but sometimes they made each other laugh so much that their guffaws would bound out to sea and send back an echo. I was always sorry when we got to the jetty and saw that the night watchman on duty was the one he enjoyed speaking to; it was like being locked up in a book filled with numbers and diagrams and what-ifs. For the thing about not being able to understand and enjoy what they were saying was I had nothing to take my mind off my fear of slipping in between the boards of the jetty.

Now, too, I had nothing to take my mind off what was happening to me. My mother and my father—I was leaving them forever. My home on an island—I was leaving it forever. What to make of everything? I felt a familiar hollow space inside. I felt I was being held down against my will. I felt I was burning up from head to toe. I felt that someone was tearing me up into little pieces and soon I would be able to see all the little pieces as they floated out into nothing in the deep blue sea. I didn't know whether to laugh or cry. I could see that it would be better not to think too clearly about any one thing. The launch was being made ready to take me, along with some other passengers, out to the ship that was anchored in the sea. My father paid our fares, and we joined a line of people waiting to board. My mother checked my bag to make sure that I had my passport, the money she had given me, and a sheet of paper placed between some pages in my Bible on which were

Literature in context — Humanities Connection

13 *The Landscape and Climate of Antigua*

White sand beaches, spectacular coral reefs, and an average temperature of 80 degrees make Antigua a popular vacation spot. There are 365 beaches on Antigua—one for each day of the year! The island is approximately 14 miles long and 11 miles wide, covering 108 square miles. With an average rainfall of only 40 inches per year, the island is one of the sunniest in the eastern Caribbean. While the steady supply of sunshine is a pleasure for tourists, the constant threat of drought can be devastating to the property and livelihoods of native Antiguans.

Reading Strategy Understanding Spatial Relationships What is the connection between Annie's physical location and her emotions?

6. **cricket** *n.* British game, similar to baseball but played with a flat bat and eleven players on each team.

ENRICHMENT: Linguistics Connection

British English

Students may be unfamiliar with such Britishisms as *chemist* (druggist or pharmacist) *cricket* (a game with some resemblance to baseball), and *sixpence* (a unit of money).

There are differences in pronunciation and vocabulary between British and American English. Viewing language as a process explains these differences. Three factors influence language development: inheritance, innovation, and isolation.

First, people acquire language from the society in which they are raised and from exposure to other languages. Second, new inventions and activities give rise to new words. Finally, geographical features like mountains or rivers separate people, so languages may develop differently.

written the names of the relatives—people I had not known existed—with whom I would live in England. Across from the jetty was a wharf, and some stevedores were loading and unloading barges. I don't know why seeing that struck me so, but suddenly a wave of strong feeling came over me, and my heart swelled with a great gladness as the words
15 "I shall never see this again" spilled out inside me. But then, just as quickly, my heart shriveled up and the words "I shall never see this again" stabbed at me. I don't know what stopped me from falling in a heap at my parents' feet.

When we were all on board, the launch headed out to sea. Away from the jetty, the water became the customary blue, and the launch left a wide path in it that looked like a road. I passed by sounds and smells that were so familiar that I had long ago stopped paying any attention to them. But now here they were, and the ever-present "I shall never see this again" bobbed up and down inside me. There was the sound of the sea-gull diving down into the water and coming up with something silverish in its mouth. There was the smell of the sea and the sight of small pieces of rubbish floating around in it. There were boats filled with fishermen coming in early. There was the sound of their voices as they shouted greetings to each other. There was the hot sun, there was the blue sea, there was the blue sky. Not very far away, there was the white sand of the shore, with the run-down houses all crowded in next to each other, for in some places only poor people lived near the shore. I was seated in the launch between my parents, and when I realized that I was gripping their hands tightly I glanced quickly to see if they were looking at me with scorn, for I felt sure that they must have known of
16 my never-see-this-again feelings. But instead my father kissed me on the forehead and my mother kissed me on the mouth, and they both gave over their hands to me, so that I could grip them as much as I wanted. I was on the verge of feeling that it had all been a mistake, but I remembered that I wasn't a child anymore, and that now when I made up my mind about something I had to see it through. At that moment, we came to the ship, and that was that.

The goodbyes had to be quick, the captain said. My mother introduced herself to him and then introduced me. She told him to keep an eye on me, for I had never gone this far away from home on my own. She gave him a letter to pass on to the captain of the next ship that I would board in Barbados.[7] They walked me to my cabin, a small space that I would share with someone else—a woman I did not know. I had never before slept in a room with someone I did not know. My father kissed me goodbye and told me to be good and to write home often. After he said this, he looked at me, then looked at the floor and swung his left foot, then looked at me again. I could see that he

7. **Barbados** (bär bā′ dōs) easternmost island in the West Indies, southeast of Antigua.

wharf (wôrf) *n.* structure built as a landing place for boats

scorn (skôrn) *n.* contempt; open dislike or derision

17 **Critical Viewing**
In what ways does this painting of a ship express the kinds of emotions the narrator experiences as she leaves her home? **[Connect]**

18 
Reading Check
What phrase is "ever present" in the narrator's mind?

15 Critical Thinking

Interpret

- Ask a volunteer to read aloud the bracketed passage.
- Then, ask students why the words "I shall never see this again" first cause Annie's heart to swell with gladness and then shrivel up?
  Possible response: Shxe has mixed emotions about leaving the people and places she knows. She longs for wider experience and opportunities, but she loves much of her past and fears her uncertain future.

16 Critical Thinking

Analyze

- Read aloud the second bracketed passage.
- Ask students how Annie's parents surprise her on the launch.
  Answer: Annie expects them to note her weakness, but instead they kiss her and offer their hands to her.
- Encourage students to explain what this scene suggests about Annie's relationship with her parents.
  Possible response: Annie discovers how much her parents love her and how much she depends on them.

17 Critical Viewing

Answer: The huge ship is overwhelming, and Annie feels overwhelmed by the idea of leaving home.

18 Reading Check

Answer: Annie keeps thinking, "I shall never see this again."

CUSTOMIZE INSTRUCTION FOR UNIVERSAL ACCESS

For Special Needs Students	For Gifted/Talented Students
Students might benefit from working with flash cards that stimulate them to experience flashbacks. Prepare flashcards with the following prompts: *When I was a baby,…, The first thing I remember is…, Before I started school,…,* and *Last summer, I…* Hold up a card, and encourage each student to share or describe in his or her journal a memory prompted by the card.	Students may enjoy thinking about how this story could be adapted into a play or movie format. Because so much of the "action" takes place inside the narrator's head, challenge students to think of ways they can *show* an audience what Annie is thinking and feeling. Ask students to rewrite this story as a play. Remind them to pay special attention to creating a setting and including physical details that will convey the emotions evoked in the story.

ASSESS

19 Vocabulary Development

The Latin Root *-stup-*

- Draw students' attention to the word *stupor,* and read its definition. Tell students that the word derives from the Latin root *-stup-*, meaning "stunned or amazed."
- Ask: How does understanding the root of the word *stupor* enhance your understanding of Annie's feelings about leaving?
  Possible response: The root *-stup-* means "stunned or amazed." Annie is literally on the border between childhood and adulthood. This passage generates in her a feeling of stunned amazement. She does not feel like the girl she used to be, and she has not yet become comfortable in the skin of the woman she will become.

Answers for p. 1218

Review and Assess

1. Possible response: Annie John is admirable for overcoming her fear and for seeking her own identity and independence.
2. **(a)** Possible response: Annie John passes Miss Dulcie's store, the library, the chemist's shop, and the church. **(b)** She relives formative events as she walks past the landmarks of her town.
3. **(a)** She experiences the old fear of slipping between the boards of the jetty, falling into the water, and being eaten by eels.
   (b) Possible response: Annie is afraid of losing herself in the unknown world she is about to enter.
4. **(a)** She compares the sound of the waves with the sound of liquid flowing from a vessel turned on its side. **(b)** Possible response: Annie is emptying herself of all her previous experiences and becoming an empty vessel ready for a new life and new experiences.
5. Possible response: Yes; although fate will play a role in Annie's future, her determination and curiosity should serve her well in her new life.

wanted to say something else, something that he had never said to me before, but then he just turned and walked away. My mother said, "Well," and then she threw her arms around me. Big tears streamed down her face, and it must have been that—for I could not bear to see my mother cry—which started me crying, too. She then tightened her arms around me and held me to her close, so that I felt that I couldn't breathe. With that, my tears dried up and I was suddenly on my guard. "What does she want now?" I said to myself. Still holding me close to her, she said, in a voice that raked across my skin, "It doesn't matter what you do or where you go, I'll always be your mother and this will always be your home."

19 I dragged myself away from her and backed off a little, and then I shook myself, as if to wake myself out of a stupor. We looked at each other for a long time with smiles on our faces, but I know the opposite of that was in my heart. As if responding to some invisible cue, we both said, at the very same moment, "Well." Then my mother turned around and walked out the cabin door. I stood there for I don't know how long, and then I remembered that it was customary to stand on deck and wave to your relatives who were returning to shore. From the deck, I could not see my father, but I could see my mother facing the ship, her eyes searching to pick me out. I removed from my bag a red cotton handkerchief that she had earlier given me for this purpose, and I waved it wildly in the air. Recognizing me immediately, she waved back just as wildly, and we continued to do this until she became just a dot in the matchbox-size launch swallowed up in the big blue sea.

stupor (sto͞op′ ər) *n.* mental dullness, as if drugged

cue (kyo͞o) *n.* prompt or reminder

I went back to my cabin and lay down on my berth. Everything trembled as if it had a spring at its very center. I could hear the small waves lap-lapping around the ship. They made an unexpected sound, as if a vessel filled with liquid had been placed on its side and now was slowly emptying out.

Review and Assess

Thinking About the Selection

1. **Respond:** Do you admire Annie John? Why or why not?
2. (a) **Recall:** Identify four places that Annie John passes.
   (b) **Interpret:** In what ways is Annie John walking through time as well as through space?
3. (a) **Recall:** As Annie John approaches the jetty, what old feeling does she experience? (b) **Analyze:** Why does she experience this feeling as she prepares to leave the island?
4. (a) **Recall:** In the story's final image, to what does Annie John compare the sound of the waves? (b) **Analyze:** In what ways does this image mirror her emotional state? Explain.
5. **Speculate:** Do you think Annie John will be successful in her new life? Why or why not?

ASSESSMENT PRACTICE: Critical Reading

Analyzing an Author's Meaning and Style (For more practice, see Test Preparation Workbook, p. 57.)

Use the following sample test item to demonstrate an author's meaning and style:

I went back to my cabin and lay down on my berth. Everything trembled as if it had a spring at its very center. I could hear the small waves lap-lapping around the ship. They made an unexpected sound, as if a vessel filled with liquid had been placed on its side and now was slowly emptying out.

Why does Kincaid choose to use the word *berth* instead of a synonym like *bunk?*

A *Berth* is a homophone for *birth.*
B The words *berth* and *back* create alliteration.
C Kincaid's writing style is extremely formal.
D Annie wants to sound like an adult.

A is the correct answer. There are many references to birth in the passage: Annie's body position, trembling, water, and emptying out.

Review and Assess

Literary Analysis

Point of View

1. Which elements of the text show that "A Walk to the Jetty" is narrated from the first-person **point of view**? Explain.
2. (a) Cite three passages in the text in which you learn something about Annie John's parents. (b) What do you learn? (c) In what specific ways does the first-person point of view limit information about characters other than the narrator?
3. Why might the first-person point of view generate more sympathy for the narrator than would another point of view?

Connecting Literary Elements

4. Each **flashback** in this excerpt is triggered as Annie John passes a familiar place. Use a chart like the one shown to analyze four of her flashbacks.

Place	Triggered Memory	What We Learn

5. What information do the flashbacks provide about Annie John's reasons for leaving home?

Reading Strategy

Understanding Spatial Relationships

6. (a) Describe the ways in which the **spatial relationships** between Annie John and her parents change as they begin their journey, travel on the launch, board the ship, and say goodbye. (b) In what ways do their spatial relationships express their emotional relationships?
7. In what ways does Annie John's physical journey relate to her emotional journey?

Extend Understanding

8. **Social Studies Connection:** While not a formal ceremony, Annie John's departure from home is a rite of passage—an event signifying that a child has become an adult. What rites of passage exist in American culture?

Quick Review

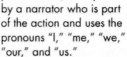

Point of view is the perspective from which a story is told. With a **first-person** point of view, a story is told by a narrator who is part of the action and uses the pronouns "I," "me," "we," "our," and "us."

A **flashback** is a section of a literary work that interrupts the sequence of events to relate an incident from the past.

To **understand spatial relationships** as you read, pay attention to details that describe the physical arrangements of elements in a setting.

PHSchool.com

Take the interactive self-test online to check your understanding of this selection.

ENRICHMENT: Further Reading

Other Works by Jamaica Kincaid

We strongly encourage you to review any selection before assigning or recommending it to students.

At the Bottom of the River

The Autobiography of My Mother

Take It to the Net

Visit PHSchool.com for more information about Jamaica Kincaid.

Answers for p. 1219

Review and Assess

1. Possible response: The narrator uses pronouns like "my," and "I."
2. **(a)** Possible response: The reader learns about Annie's parents in the following flashbacks: Annie's mother sending her to run errands, the passage about the carrot juice and the sunglasses, and the moment in which her father seems about to tell her something and then does not. **(b)** The first passage explains that Annie is happy to do things that make her mother happy. The second passage shows that when Annie really wants something, her mother makes sacrifices so that Annie can have it. The description of Annie saying goodbye to her father shows that they care deeply about each other, even if their feelings are unspoken. **(c)** Readers get no insight into Annie's parents' thoughts; they experience only Annie's interpretation of characters and events.
3. Possible response: Readers are more likely to sympathize with the character through whose eyes they see the events of the narrative.
4. Sample response: **Place:** shoe store; church **Triggered Memory:** fighting with her mother over shoes; her christening and the choir **What We Learn:** Sometimes Annie wins arguments with her mother; Annie has been raised as a Christian.
5. Possible response: They suggest that she feels limited by the people and circumstances of her childhood home.
6. **(a)** Annie begins her journey walking between her parents; when they reach the jetty, the physical arrangement changes so that she moves away from them. **(b)** Possible response: At first, the mother and father surround Annie, but in the end, she moves beyond their protection.
7. Possible response: Annie revisits her childhood as she walks past the physical landmarks; then, she leaves both the memories and the landmarks behind. Fittingly, on the ship, she feels empty.

continued

continued from right column

8. Possible response: A bar or bat mitzvah, getting a job, attending a prom, obtaining a driver's license, or graduating from school are American rites of passage.

EXTEND

Answers for p. 1220

1 Vocabulary Development

Word Analysis: Latin Root *-stup-*

1. b
2. c
3. a

Spelling Strategy

1. curiosity
2. occupant
3. vacuum
4. concur

Concept Development: Analogies

1. scorn
2. cue
3. jetty
4. stupor
5. loomed
6. wharf

2 Grammar and Style

Practice

1. "which reminded her of her mother"; modifies *store*
2. "whose chores involved sweeping"; modifies *Annie*
3. "that they had traveled many times before"; modifies *road*
4. "who often talked with her father"; modifies *watchman*
5. "that lapped against the boat"; modifies *waves*

Writing Application

Possible response:
Annie walked down the road that she used to get to church and school. Annie thought about the store that sold only imported grooming aids.

10TH GRADE For support in teaching the Grammar and Style Lesson to tenth graders, use **Writing and Grammar**, Platinum Level, Chapter 20, Section 2.

Integrate Language Skills

1 Vocabulary Development Lesson

Word Analysis: Latin Root *-stup-*

The word *stupor* contains the Latin root *-stup-*, which means "stunned or amazed." Use the meaning of this root to match each numbered word to its synonym.

1. stupefy
2. stupendous
3. stupefaction

a. bewilderment
b. numb
c. astonishing

Spelling Strategy

In most English words, when a *c* comes before the vowel *u*, it has a *k* sound, as in the word *cue*. In some words, the *c* before a *u* is doubled. Correctly complete the spelling of each word below with letters representing the *k* sound.

1. ___uriosity
2. o___upant
3. va___uum
4. con___ur

Concept Development: Analogies

Analogies present words in pairs to emphasize their relationships. Common links include synonym, antonym, degree of intensity, and part to whole. For each numbered item below, study the relationship presented in the first pair. Then, use the vocabulary words on page 1211 to complete word pairs that express the same relationship.

1. *Strength* is to *weakness* as __?__ is to *admiration*.
2. *Advice* is to *guidance* as __?__ is to *prompt*.
3. *Bumper* is to *automobile* as __?__ is to *harbor*.
4. *Frenzy* is to *calmness* as __?__ is to *lucidity*.
5. *Encouraged* is to *supported* as __?__ is to *threatened*.
6. *Hangar* is to *airplane* as __?__ is to *boat*.

2 Grammar and Style Lesson

Adjective Clauses

An **adjective clause** is a type of subordinate clause—one that contains a subject and a verb but cannot stand alone as a sentence. Adjective clauses modify nouns or pronouns and are introduced with relative pronouns, such as *who* or *whom*, *whose*, *which*, or *that*.

Example:

We were soon on the road that I(S) had taken(V) to school . . . (*modifies road*)

My mother had placed three pennies in my little basket, which(S) was(V) a duplicate of her bigger basket . . . (*modifies basket*)

Practice Identify the adjective clause and the word it modifies in each of the following sentences.

1. Annie walked past the store, which reminded her of her mother.
2. Miss Dulcie did not respect Annie, whose chores included sweeping.
3. The family walked down the road that they had traveled many times before.
4. Annie remembered the watchman who often talked with her father.
5. The waves that lapped against the boat made a sad sound.

Writing Application Write a paragraph to describe Annie's memories on the day she leaves home. Include one adjective clause in each sentence.

WG *Prentice Hall Writing and Grammar Connection: Diamond Level, Chapter 19, Section 3*

TEACHING RESOURCES

The following resources can be used to enrich or extend the instruction for pp. 1220–1221.

Vocabulary
- **Selection Support:** Build Vocabulary, p. 225
- **Vocabulary and Spelling Practice Book** (Use this booklet for skills instruction.)

Grammar
- **Selection Support:** Grammar and Style, p. 226
- **Writing and Grammar,** Diamond Level, p. 458 ■
- **Daily Language Practice Transparencies,** p. 459

Writing
- **Performance Assess. and Portfolio Mgmt.,** p. 37
- **Writing and Grammar,** Diamond Level, p. 54
- **Writing and Grammar iText CD-ROM**

Listening and Speaking
- **Performance Assess. and Portfolio Mgmt.,** p. 27

■ **BLOCK SCHEDULING:** Resources marked with this symbol provide varied instruction during 90-minute blocks.

❸ Writing Lesson

A Reminiscence

Imagine that you are walking through a familiar landscape, such as your neighborhood, a shopping mall, or your school. Write a reminiscence—a narrative that relates events from the past—in which memories are triggered by elements of the setting. You may write as yourself or as a fictional character.

Prewriting Brainstorm for memories and sensory details—elements that relate to the senses—by using a cluster diagram like the one shown. Try to identify larger themes or ideas that the memories capture.

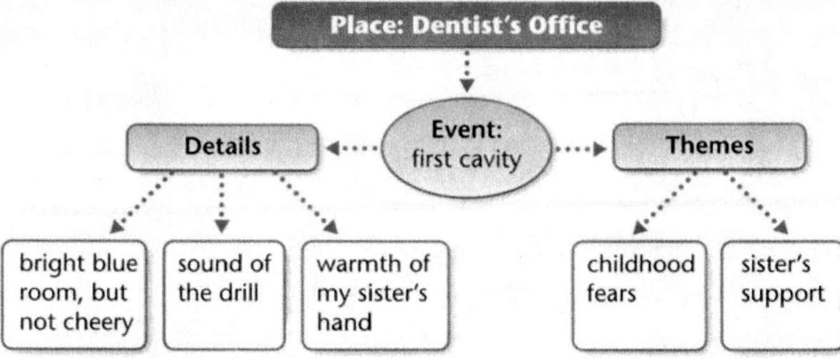

Drafting Begin by describing the purpose of your journey. Then, use the landscape itself to order the narrative. Describe each place you pass, and explain the memory it triggers.

Revising As you review your writing, make sure that you have used vivid sensory details. Consider adding details to enliven your reminiscence.

WG *Prentice Hall Writing and Grammar Connection: Diamond Level, Chapter 4, Section 2*

❹ Extension Activities

Listening and Speaking Conduct a **discussion** about the benefits and challenges of traveling or schooling abroad. Use these tips to prepare:

- Invite someone in your school to speak to your class about travel or education in another country.
- Generate a list of questions in advance.

You may wish to take notes about the discussion and write a report or interview for your school newspaper. **[Group Activity]**

Research and Technology Using details from the text, create a **map** showing Annie's walk to the jetty. Include landmarks, illustrations, and other references to help make your map a vivid representation of Kincaid's narrative. Include a key so that viewers can connect the illustrations with the related site on Annie's journey.

 ***Take It to the Net*** PHSchool.com

Go online for an additional research activity using the Internet.

ASSESSMENT RESOURCES

The following resources can be used to assess students' knowledge and skills.

Selection Assessment

- **Formal Assessment,** pp. 201–203
- **Open-Book Tests,** pp. 169–171
- **Test Bank Software**

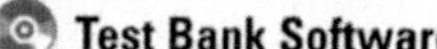

Take It to the Net

Visit PHSchool.com for self-tests on the selections.

Writing Rubric

- **Performance Assess. and Portfolio Mgmt.,** p. 9

Listening and Speaking Rubric

- **Performance Assess. and Portfolio Mgmt.,** p. 27

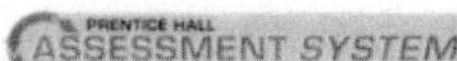

PRENTICE HALL ASSESSMENT SYSTEM

For additional diagnostics and remediation for skills covered in this grouping, use materials from the Prentice Hall Assessment System.

❸ Writing Lesson

- Students may need help extracting themes from their memories. Use the following key questions to help students make the leap from literal to thematic thinking: What did you learn from this event? Why are your memories of this event so vivid? Why do you remember this event when other memories have slipped away? Did this event change you in some way? Did this event affect your worldview in some way?
- After students have finished their essays, use the Narration: Autobiographical Narrative rubric in **Performance Assessment and Portfolio Management,** p. 9, to evaluate students' work.

10TH GRADE For support in working through the Writing Lesson with tenth graders, use **Writing and Grammar,** Platinum Level, Chapter 4, Section 2.

❹ Listening and Speaking

- Help students research the school system in the country where the guest speaker was educated or the country in which the speaker has traveled.
- Tell students to use their research to write informed and insightful questions for the speaker in advance.
- Use the Listening and Speaking: Interview Techniques rubric in **Performance Assessment and Portfolio Management,** p. 27, to assess students' performance.

CUSTOMIZE INSTRUCTION For Universal Access

To address different learning styles, use the following activities suggested in the **Extension Activities** booklet, p. 57.

- For Verbal/Linguistic and Interpersonal Learners, use Activity 5.
- For Logical/Mathematical and Verbal/Linguistic Learners, use Activity 6.
- For Visual/Spatial Learners, use Activity 7.

The Guest

Lesson Objectives

1. **To analyze and respond to literary elements**
   - Literary Analysis: Existentialism
   - Connecting Literary Elements: Setting and Theme
2. **To read, comprehend, analyze, and critique a short story**
   - Reading Strategy: Inferring Cultural Attitudes
   - Reading Check Questions
   - Review and Assess Questions
   - Assessment Practice (ATE)
3. **To develop word analysis skills, fluency, and systematic vocabulary**
   - Vocabulary Development Lesson: Anglo-Saxon Prefix *fore-*
4. **To understand and apply written and oral language conventions**
   - Spelling Strategy
   - Grammar and Style Lesson: Prepositional Phrases as Adjectives and Adverbs
5. **To understand and apply appropriate writing and research strategies**
   - Writing Lesson: Essay Evaluating Fiction as an Expression of Philosophy
   - Extension Activity: Timeline of Algerian History
6. **To understand and apply listening and speaking strategies**
   - Extension Activity: Performance of Story as a Play

STEP-BY-STEP TEACHING GUIDE	PACING GUIDE
PRETEACH	
Motivate Students and Provide Background	
Use the Motivation activity (ATE p. 1222)	5 min.
Read and discuss author and background features (SE pp.1222, 1225; ATE p. 1222) [A]	5 min.
Introduce the Concepts	
Introduce the Literary Analysis and Reading Strategy concepts (SE/ATE p. 1223) [A]	15 min.
Pronounce the vocabulary words and read their definitions (SE p. 1223)	5 min.
TEACH	
Monitor Comprehension	
Informally monitor comprehension by circulating while students read [A]	50 min.
Monitor students' comprehension with the Reading Check notes (SE/ATE pp. 1225, 1227, 1229, 1231, 1233, 1235, 1237)	as students read
Develop vocabulary with the Vocabulary notes (SE pp. 1225, 1226, 1227, 1229, 1231, 1234; ATE p. 1227)	as students read
Develop Understanding	
Develop students' understanding of Existentialism with the Literary Analysis annotations (SE/ATE pp. 1225, 1226, 1229, 1232, 1235, 1236) [A]	10 min.
Develop students' ability to infer cultural attitudes, using the Reading Strategy annotations (SE pp.1226, 1227, 1228, 1230, 1231, 1233, 1237; ATE pp. 1225, 1226, 1227, 1228, 1230, 1231, 1233, 1237) [A]	10 min.
ASSESS	
Assess Mastery	
Assess students' mastery of the Reading Strategy and Literary Analysis concepts by having them answer the Review and Assess questions (SE/ATE p. 1239)	20 min.
Use one or more of the print, software, or transparency Assessment Resources (ATE p. 1241) [A]	up to 45 min.
EXTEND	
Apply Understanding	
Have students complete the Vocabulary Development Lesson and the Grammar and Style Lesson (SE p. 1240) [A]	20 min.
Apply students' ability to compare fiction to philosophy, using the Writing Lesson (SE/ATE p. 1241) [A]	45 min.
Apply students' understanding of the selection, using one or more of the Extension Activities (SE p.1241)	20–90 min.

[A] ACCELERATED INSTRUCTION: Use the strategies and activities identified with an [A].

10TH GRADE TEACHING TENTH-GRADE STUDENTS For support in teaching tenth graders, see the Step-by-Step Teaching notes identified with this icon.

UNIVERSAL ACCESS
● = Below-Level Students
▲ = On-Level Students
■ = Above-Level Students

Time and Resource Manager

Reading Level: Challenging
Average Number of Instructional Days: 4

RESOURCES		
PRINT	**TRANSPARENCIES**	**TECHNOLOGY**
• **Beyond Literature,** Cross-Curricular Connection: Art, p. 58 ▲ ■		
• **Selection Support Workbook:** ● ▲ ■ Literary Analysis, p. 232 Reading Strategy, p. 231 Build Vocabulary, p. 229	• **Literary Analysis and Reading Transparencies,** pp. 115 and 116 ● ▲ ■	
		• **Listening to Literature** ● ▲ ■ Audiocassettes Audio CDs
• **Literary Analysis for Enrichment,** p. 58 ■		
• **Formal Assessment:** Selection Test, pp. 204–206 ● ▲ ■ • **Open-Book Tests,** pp. 172–174 ● ▲ ■ • **Performance Assessment and Portfolio Management,** pp. 15, 28 ● ▲ ■ • PRENTICE HALL ASSESSMENT SYSTEM ● ▲ ■	• PRENTICE HALL ASSESSMENT SYSTEM ● ▲ ■ **Skills Practice Answers and Explanations on Transparencies**	• **Test Bank Software** ● ▲ ■
• **Selection Support Workbook:** ● ▲ ■ Grammar and Style, p. 230 • **Writing and Grammar,** Diamond Level ● ▲ ■ • **Extension Activities,** p. 58 ● ▲ ■	• **Daily Language Practice Transparencies** ● ▲	• **Writing and Grammar iText CD-ROM** ● ▲ ■ ***Take It to the Net*** PHSchool.com

BLOCK SCHEDULING: Use one 90-minute class period to preteach the selection(s) and have students read them. Use a second 90-minute class period to assess students' mastery of skills and have them complete one of the Extension Activities.

PRETEACH

Step-by-Step Teaching Guide for pp. 1222–1223

Motivation

Ask students to imagine the following situation: You move to a new neighborhood just as simmering disagreement has split neighbors into two hostile sides. As tensions rise and arguments become increasingly bitter, even violent, you struggle to keep your distance. Soon, however, your neighbors begin to look at you suspiciously and wonder which side you are on.

Tell students that the main character in "The Guest" is in a position like this. He is caught up, not in a neighborhood dispute, but in the beginnings of a fierce war, and his life may depend on the choices he makes.

1 Background

More About the Author

During World War II, Albert Camus wrote unsigned editorials for a Parisian underground newspaper called *Combat*. Readers of these much-admired editorials did not know until after the liberation of Paris that their author was the man who wrote *The Stranger*. The following is an excerpt from an editorial Camus wrote as Allied and German troops fought in the streets of Paris:

> This huge Paris, all black and warm in the summer night, with a storm of bombers overhead and a storm of snipers in the streets, seems to us more brightly lighted than the City of Light the whole world used to envy us. It is bursting with all the fires of hope and suffering, it has the flame of lucid courage and all the glow, not only of liberation, but of tomorrow's liberty.

Geography Note

Draw students' attention to the map on this page. Point out the location of Algeria, Camus's birthplace, and tell students that the country contains large sections of the Sahara desert. Explain that in most of Algeria the heat of the sun is so intense that, during the middle of the day, people must wear clothes that cover most of their skin.

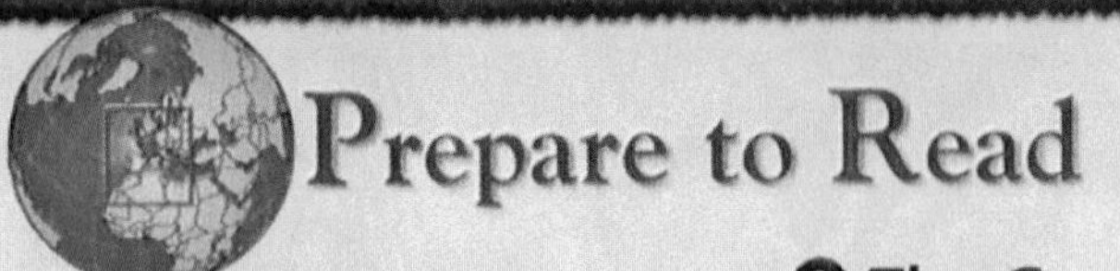

Prepare to Read

1 The Guest

Albert Camus (1913–1960)

When a now-famous Polish writer was an unknown student in Paris, he often wandered around the city at all hours. Late one night, he met a solitary man in a cheap café and the two shared a stimulating philosophical discussion. Only later, when he was home in bed, did he realize that he had been talking with the celebrated French author Albert Camus (ka mōō'). This remarkable anecdote illustrates several of Camus's most endearing qualities: his modesty, his searching intelligence, and his restless night-owl habits.

Early Hardship Camus was born in Mondovi, Algeria, to parents of European descent. His family was desperately poor and his mother was deaf. Camus's childhood became even more difficult when his father died in World War I.

Despite his poverty, Camus's intelligence shone; his teachers recognized his gifts and encouraged him in his studies. Although Camus had to work at odd jobs while attending the University of Algiers, he was an excellent scholar. In addition to his main studies in literature, he also helped found a small theater group that staged plays of interest to working-class people. Years later, when he wrote plays such as *Caligula* (1944), the drama of a Roman emperor who resembles modern dictators like Hitler and Mussolini, Camus drew on this early theatrical experience.

Tests of Integrity A man of strong moral principles, Camus sometimes suffered for his convictions. For instance, when he publicly criticized the French colonial government of Algiers, he was forced to leave the country. He emigrated to France, where he worked as an investigative reporter for a Parisian newspaper.

Camus's integrity was tested again when the Germans occupied France during World War II. At the risk of his life, Camus supported the French Resistance Movement by serving as the principal editor of *Combat*, an illegal newspaper. As an underground journalist, he won recognition for his independent views and the emphasis he placed on moral behavior.

First Important Works Despite the turmoil of World War II, Camus published two of his most influential works, the novel *The Stranger* (1942) and the essay "The Myth of Sisyphus" (1942), during the war years. The novel describes a man who realizes that conventional values are ultimately senseless and absurd—humans are uninvited guests in an indifferent universe. In 1947, Camus published another novel that deals with similar themes but in a more positive way. Set in the Algerian city of Oran, *The Plague* describes an epidemic that symbolizes both the German Occupation of France and all the other evils that beset humankind. In combating the plague, several of the characters learn the importance of honor and compassion.

Acknowledged as a major twentieth-century writer, Camus spent part of the late 1940s touring and lecturing in North and South America. On returning to Paris, he withdrew from public life and continued to produce essays and plays. In 1957, he received the Nobel Prize in Literature. Camus's death in an auto accident three years later cut short his brilliant career. However, in 1994, *The First Man*, a manuscript that had been found in the wreckage of his car, was published in France. English publication of the book followed in 1995. An autobiographical work-in-progress, the book reveals Camus in all his brilliance, modesty, and humanity.

TEACHING RESOURCES

The following resources can be used to enrich or extend the instruction for pp. 1222–1223.

Background

Beyond Literature, p. 58

Take It to the Net

Visit PHSchool.com for background on the author.

Literary Analysis

Literary Analysis and Reading Transparencies, Existentialism, p. 115

Selection Support: Literary Analysis, p. 232

Reading

Literary Analysis and Reading Transparencies, Inferring Cultural Attitudes, p. 116

BLOCK SCHEDULING: Resources marked with this symbol provide varied instruction during 90-minute blocks.

Preview

Connecting to the Literature

If you have ever resisted pressure to do something you felt was wrong, you will understand how the main character in this story feels. Caught between hostile parties as a revolution begins, Daru stands alone.

❷ Literary Analysis

Existentialism

Existentialism is a philosophy that teaches the importance of personal choice, not universal codes, in creating values. The various forms of Existentialism agree on these essential points:

- The universe is indifferent and can provide no answers.
- Our lives matter because of our own actions, not because we are part of a greater plan.
- The individual has total freedom to choose and to act.
- Human life is inherently valuable; freedom is an end in itself.

Although Camus did not accept the label of Existentialist, he is widely regarded as one of its foremost literary practitioners. As you read this story, look for details that suggest an Existentialist outlook.

Connecting Literary Elements

The **setting** of a story is the time and place of the action. In many stories, the setting is merely a context, like a painted backdrop on a stage. Sometimes, however, the setting adds meaning. For example, in "The Guest," the stark, windswept vistas reflect the **theme**—the story's central message. As you read, think about how the setting and theme are intertwined.

❸ Reading Strategy

Inferring Cultural Attitudes

Cultural attitudes are the customs, values, and beliefs that are held by people living in a distinct place and time. In most literary works, the author does not spell out these attitudes. Instead, he or she provides details, such as dialogue, actions, and descriptions, that allow readers to infer cultural attitudes. As you read, use a chart like the one shown to identify details and to infer the cultural attitudes they express.

Detail
Daru offers mint tea to the visitors.

↓

Cultural Attitude
Hospitality is important.

Vocabulary Development

plateau (pla tō′) *n.* elevated tract of relatively level land (p. 1225)

siege (sēj) *n.* the surrounding of a fortified place by an opposing force, such as an army (p. 1226)

foretaste (fôr′ tāst′) *n.* slight experience or hint of something that is still to come (p. 1227)

mobilized (mō′ bə līzd′) *v.* ready for action or battle (p. 1229)

denounce (dē nouns′) *v.* accuse publicly (p. 1231)

fraternized (frat′ ər nīzd′) *v.* associated in a brotherly way; socialized (p. 1234)

furtive (fur′ tiv) *adj.* done in a secret or sneaky way (p. 1234)

CUSTOMIZE INSTRUCTION FOR UNIVERSAL ACCESS

For Less Proficient Readers	For English Learners	For Advanced Readers
Guide students to explain in their own words the four essential points of Existentialism listed on p. 1223. Students can provide real-life examples of each point. Make sure students understand the importance of personal choice in the Existentialist philosophy.	Review with students each vocabulary word on p. 1223, and clarify pronunciations and definitions. Have students use the words in sentences that demonstrate understanding of each word's meaning.	Ask students to read Camus's essay "The Myth of Sisyphus," and then discuss the four essential points of Existentialism listed on p. 1223. Have students write essays in which they relate each of the four points to the situation of Sisyphus. Students can share their essays with the class.

❷ Literary Analysis

Existentialism

- Tell students that Existentialists recognize the absurdity of looking for meaning in an indifferent universe, yet they also believe that life is inherently valuable and that people are free to choose their own actions. Tell students that they will see evidence of the Existentialist viewpoint as they read this story.
- Read aloud the Literary Analysis instruction. Focus on the list of Existentialism's essential points. Remind students of the importance this philosophy places on individuals, not on larger constructs like society.
- As students read "The Guest," encourage them to consider how various elements of the story such as setting, plot, and characters present an Existentialist viewpoint.

❸ Reading Strategy

Inferring Cultural Attitudes

- Remind students that an inference is a logical assumption made by carefully considering evidence and one's previous experience.
- Tell students that readers find clues about the beliefs, values, and customs of characters by comparing them with other characters or by drawing on their own real-life experiences.
- Direct students' attention to the chart on p. 1223. Ask them to use a chart like this to record story details or descriptions that reveal cultural attitudes.
- Remind students that they will have to read between the lines to make inferences about cultural attitudes. Suggest that they try to assume a character's perspective in order to learn more about the culture of which the character is a part.

Vocabulary Development

- Pronounce each vocabulary word for students, and read the definitions as a class. Have students identify any words with which they are already familiar.

 **E-Teach**

Visit e-Teach at PHSchool.com for teachers' essays on how to teach, with questions and answers.

TEACH

Step-by-Step Teaching Guide for pp. 1224–1238

Teaching Tenth-Grade Students

10TH GRADE Ask students to jot down questions as they read. Questions should relate to the action, setting, and theme of the story. For example: Will the Arab try to hurt Daru? Will the Arab escape? In such an isolated place, can anyone help the Arab, hurt Daru, or help Daru? Is it better for Daru to do what the authorities expect or for him to try to help the Arab?

1 About the Selection

This short story resembles a parable on the futility of human action. In a time of growing conflict between French settlers and the colonized Algerians, a French schoolteacher named Daru struggles to act on his conscience in a time when brutality reigns and good intentions seem to count for very little.

2 Background

Art

Album de voyage: Spain, Morocco, Algeria, by Eugène Delacroix

The Romantic artists were interested in the natural world—in contrast to the sophisticated life of modern cities—and in the theme of a person's solitary position in the universe. Both of these concerns can be found in Camus's story. Encourage students to find these motifs in this painting.

Use the following question for discussion:

How would you describe the feelings this painting evokes?
Possible response: It evokes loneliness, peacefulness, and happiness in the midst of beauty, but it also evokes a sense of weariness during a long journey.

3 ▶Critical Viewing

Possible response: The vast landscape seems to hold no one but the man on horseback. An individual might feel alone in the vastness of the natural world.

1

The Guest

Albert Camus

translated by Justin O'Brien

2

Album de voyage: Spain, Morocco, Algeria, 1834, Eugène Delacroix, Musée Condé, Chantilly, France

3 ▲ **Critical Viewing** What details of this image capture the isolation of the setting Camus describes? **[Connect]**

TEACHING RESOURCES

The following resources can be used to enrich or extend the instruction for pp. 1224–1238.

Literary Analysis

- **Selection Support:** Literary Analysis, p. 232 ■
- **Literary Analysis and Reading Transparencies,** Existentialism, p. 115

Reading

- **Selection Support:** Reading Strategy, p. 231; Build Vocabulary, p. 229
- **Listening to Literature Audiocassettes** ■
- **Listening to Literature Audio CDs**

■ **BLOCK SCHEDULING:** Resources marked with this symbol provide varied instruction during 90-minute blocks.

Background ❹

In 1954, a war for independence began in the North African country of Algeria, which had been a colony of France since 1848. More than a century of colonialism had created a deeply divided society with a wealthy European elite, a small European working class, and a large Muslim majority that was mostly poor. The independence struggle began with terrorist attacks on police posts by a radical Muslim group, the National Liberation Front (FLN). As the revolt spread, the French military retaliated with severe reprisals. The early stages of the rebellion provide the historical context for this story.

The schoolmaster was watching the two men climb toward him. One was on horseback, the other on foot. They had not yet tackled the abrupt rise leading to the schoolhouse built on the hillside. They were toiling onward, making slow progress in the snow, among the stones, on the vast expanse of the high, deserted plateau. From time to time the horse stumbled. Without ❺ hearing anything yet, he could see the breath issuing from the horse's nostrils. One of the men, at least, knew the region. They were following the trail although it had disappeared days ago under a layer of dirty white snow. The schoolmaster calculated that it would take them half an hour to get onto the hill. It was cold; he went back into the school to get a sweater. ❻

Literary Analysis
Existentialism; Setting and Theme Why might this setting be appropriate in a story expressing Existentialist views?

plateau (pla tō′) *n.* elevated tract of relatively level land

❻ **✓Reading Check**
Why is the trail to the schoolhouse difficult for the men to follow?

❹ Reading Strategy

Inferring Cultural Attitudes

- Have a volunteer read aloud the Background information.
- Ask students to infer the cultural attitude the French may have held regarding the revolt in Algeria.
  Possible response: The French may have thought it was their right to preserve Algeria as it was because Algeria had been its colony for more than one hundred years.
- Then, have students infer what the attitude of the Muslim majority might have been.
  Possible response: The Muslims very likely wanted the French to leave Algeria because Muslim concerns were not being addressed.

❺ Literary Analysis

Existentialism; Setting and Theme

- Read aloud the bracketed passage. Ask students to describe the setting.
  Answer: The setting is a high, snow-covered and deserted plateau.
- Then, ask the Literary Analysis question on p. 1225: Why might this setting be appropriate in a story expressing Existentialist views?
  Possible response: The inhospitable landscape forces the characters to struggle to travel, feed themselves, and stay warm. This setting echoes the Existentialist view that the universe is indifferent and can provide no answers or meaning for human beings.

❻ ✓Reading Check

Answer: The trail is difficult to follow because it is covered with snow.

CUSTOMIZE INSTRUCTION FOR UNIVERSAL ACCESS

For Special Needs Students	For English Learners	For Gifted/Talented Students
Find and display several landscape photographs of the Algerian plateaus. Use these images to illustrate the paradox of plateaus being both high and flat. Then, have students use these images as a guide in creating sketches of the opening scene. Encourage students to share their work with the class.	Point out the word *plateau*. Guide students to use context clues, rather than the given definition, to determine its meaning. Point out that phrases and words such as "abrupt rise," "built on the hillside," "vast expanse," and "high" all convey that *plateau* means " elevated tract of relatively level land."	Ask students to translate Camus's descriptions of the setting into illustrations or maps of the terrain, making sure that they include the schoolhouse and its surroundings. Have students find photographs of the Algerian plateaus to ensure that their illustrations are accurate. Display artwork on a classroom bulletin board.

❼ Literary Analysis

Existentialism

- Have a volunteer read aloud the bracketed passage. Ask students to paraphrase its meaning.
Possible response: Daru is better off now than during the three-day snowstorm because he no longer has to stay in his room when he is not feeding the chickens or getting coal. He had received supplies shortly before the storm and expects another delivery in two days.
- Ask students the Literary Analysis question on p. 1226: In what ways does the description of Daru's circumstances during the blizzard reflect Existentialist ideas?
Possible response: Daru is alone and at the mercy of nature, which is indifferent to his plight. Still, he makes meaningful choices, such as feeding the chickens and burning coal to stay warm.

❽ Reading Strategy

Inferring Cultural Attitudes

- Have students read the bracketed passage on pp. 1226–1227 and then find phrases that apply to poverty and the land the poor population tries to cultivate and phrases that apply to Daru.
Possible response: Phrases that apply to poverty and the land include "ragged ghosts," "plateaus burned to a cinder," "earth shriveled up," "literally scorched," and "sheep had died." Phrases that apply to Daru include "satisfied with the little he had," "felt like a lord," "white-washed walls," "narrow couch," "unpainted shelves," "his well," and "weekly provision of water and food."
- Ask students the Reading Strategy question on p. 1226: What cultural attitudes toward wealth are suggested by this discussion of drought and poverty?
Possible response: Wealth is associated with a comfortable dwelling and a detachment from the difficulties of the terrain and weather. The administration trusts the wealthy to store and distribute their rations to the poor; the wealthy are expected to cooperate.

He crossed the empty, frigid classroom. On the blackboard the four rivers of France, drawn with four different colored chalks, had been flowing toward their estuaries for the past three days. Snow had suddenly fallen in mid-October after eight months of drought without the transition of rain, and the twenty pupils, more or less, who lived in the villages scattered over the plateau had stopped coming. With fair weather they would return. Daru now heated only the single room that was his lodging, adjoining the classroom and giving also onto the plateau to the east. Like the class windows, his window looked to the south too. On that side the school was a few kilometers[1] from the point where the plateau began to slope toward the south. In clear weather could be seen the purple mass of the mountain range where the gap opened onto the desert.

Somewhat warmed, Daru returned to the window from which he had first seen the two men. They were no longer visible. Hence they must have tackled the rise. The sky was not so dark, for the snow had stopped falling during the night. The morning had opened with a dirty light which had scarcely become brighter as the ceiling of clouds lifted. At two in the afternoon it seemed as if the day were merely beginning. But still this was better than those three days when the thick snow was falling amidst unbroken darkness with little gusts of wind that rattled the double door of the classroom. Then Daru had spent long hours in
7 his room, leaving it only to go to the shed and feed the chickens or get some coal. Fortunately the delivery truck from Tadjid,[2] the nearest village to the north, had brought his supplies two days before the blizzard. It would return in forty-eight hours.

Besides, he had enough to resist a siege, for the little room was cluttered with bags of wheat that the administration left as a stock to distribute to those of his pupils whose families had suffered from the drought. Actually they had all been victims because they were all poor. Every day Daru would distribute a ration to the children. They had missed it, he knew, during these bad days. Possibly one of the fathers or big brothers would come this afternoon and he could supply them with grain. It was just a matter of carrying them over to the next harvest. Now shiploads of wheat were arriving from France and the worst
8 was over. But it would be hard to forget that poverty, that army of ragged ghosts wandering in the sunlight, the plateaus burned to a cinder month after month, the earth shriveled up little by little, literally scorched, every stone bursting into dust under one's foot. The sheep had died then by thousands and even a few men, here and there, sometimes without anyone's knowing.

In contrast with such poverty, he who lived almost like a monk in his remote schoolhouse, nonetheless satisfied with the little he had and with the rough life, had felt like a lord with his white-washed walls, his

Literary Analysis
Existentialism In what ways does the description of Daru's circumstances during the blizzard reflect Existentialist ideas?

siege (sēj) *n.* the surrounding of a fortified place by an opposing force, such as an army

Reading Strategy
Inferring Cultural Attitudes What cultural attitudes toward wealth are suggested by this discussion of drought and poverty?

1. **kilometers** (kil′ ə mēt′ ərz) *n.* measures of distance, each of which is equal to 1,000 meters, or about five eighths of a mile.
2. **Tadjid** (tä jēd′)

narrow couch, his unpainted shelves, his well, and his weekly provision of water and food. And suddenly this snow, without warning, without
9 the foretaste of rain. This is the way the region was, cruel to live in, even without men—who didn't help matters either. But Daru had been born here. Everywhere else, he felt exiled.

He stepped out onto the terrace in front of the schoolhouse. The two men were now halfway up the slope. He recognized the horseman as Balducci, the old gendarme[3] he had known for a long time. Balducci was holding on the end of a rope an Arab who was walking behind him with hands bound and head lowered. The gendarme waved a greeting to which Daru did not reply, lost as he was in contemplation of the
10 Arab dressed in a faded blue jellaba,[4] his feet in sandals but covered with socks of heavy raw wool, his head surmounted by a narrow, short *chèche*.[5] They were approaching. Balducci was holding back his horse in order not to hurt the Arab, and the group was advancing slowly.

Within earshot, Balducci shouted: "One hour to do the three kilometers from El Ameur!"[6] Daru did not answer. Short and square in his thick sweater, he watched them climb. Not once had the Arab raised his head. "Hello," said Daru when they got up onto the terrace. "Come in and warm up." Balducci painfully got down from his horse without letting go the rope. From under his bristling mustache he smiled at the schoolmaster. His little dark eyes, deep-set under a tanned forehead,

foretaste (fôr' tāst') *n.* slight experience or hint of something that is still to come

Reading Strategy
Inferring Cultural Attitudes What can you infer about Daru based on his interest in the Arab's clothing?

11 **Reading Check**
Who are the two men who approach Daru's schoolhouse?

3. **gendarme** (zhän därm') *n.* French police officer.
4. **jellaba** (jə lä' bə) *n.* roomy, capelike outer garment worn in the Middle East.
5. ***chèche*** (shesh) *n.* cloth wrap worn as headware, common in rural Algeria.
6. **El Ameur** (el äm yoor')

12

Arab at the Door of His House, Eugène Delacroix, Rijksmuseum, Amsterdam

13 **Critical Viewing**
How is this dwelling similar to or different from your image of Daru's schoolhouse? **[Compare and Contrast]**

9 Vocabulary Development

Anglo-Saxon Prefix *fore-*

- Draw students' attention to the word *foretaste* on p. 1227. Tell students that the Anglo-Saxon prefix *fore-* means "before in time, place, order, or rank."
- Have students suggest other words with the prefix *fore-*.
  Answer: Words with the prefix *fore-* include *forearm, forebode,* and *forecast.*

10 Reading Strategy

Inferring Cultural Attitudes

- Read aloud the bracketed sentence, and ask students to use their own words to describe the Arab.
  Answer: The Arab is wearing a faded blue robe, heavy socks with sandals, and a head wrap.
- Ask students the Reading Strategy question on p. 1227: What can you infer about Daru based on his interest in the Arab's clothing?
  Answer: Daru is trying to figure out the relationship between the two men. The Arab's clothing indicates to Daru the man's social standing. Daru can also determine that the Arab is a native of the area, whereas the gendarme is not.

11 Reading Check

Answer: The two men are an old French police officer named Balducci and an unnamed Arab.

12 Background

Art

Arab at the Door of His House, by Eugène Delacroix

A major influence on Eugène Delacroix's work was an 1832 trip to North Africa. Like other Romantics, he found vitality in the natural world and the cultures of non-Europeans.

Use this question for discussion: Why would a painter from Paris in the 1830s paint this picture?
Possible response: He might have wanted to show his viewers an unusual, exotic scene.

13 Critical Viewing

Possible response: The dwelling is similar to Daru in that it is simple, spare, and modest.

CUSTOMIZE INSTRUCTION FOR UNIVERSAL ACCESS

For Special Needs Students	For English Learners
Have students use the Internet or library sources to research traditional clothing worn by people in North Africa. Have students create a list of reasons such garments might be better suited for life in North Africa than typical western clothes.	Draw students' attention to this passage on p. 1227: "But Daru had been born here. Everywhere else, he felt exiled." Explain the meaning of the word *exiled,* and ask students whether they have a similar attachment to their birthplaces or whether it is easy or difficult to live there. Ask volunteers to discuss the possible reasons for Daru's feelings toward Algeria, such as having family nearby or being part of the culture.

14 # Background

Art

The Ear of Grain (L'espiga de blat), by Joan Miró

Joan Miró is best known as one of the foremost Surrealist painters of the twentieth century. This work, not typical of his mature style, is one of a series of severe still life paintings done in 1922 and 1923. After this series, his style changed quite abruptly and no longer included realistic and recognizable objects.

This painting shows a lidded pitcher, a strainer, and an ear of grain. The background is a plain table with no cloth. All the objects are painted realistically, if somewhat two-dimensionally, and suggest a clean and simple way of life.

Use the following question for discussion:

In what way does this painting remind you of the life led by Daru? Answer: Daru's life, like the life suggested in the painting, is stark and simple with few luxuries.

15 ▶ Critical Viewing

Possible response: With its clean lines and careful rendering of details, the image conveys a feeling of simplicity. The table and the objects on it do not look worn out or poorly crafted, as they would if the painting conveyed a feeling of poverty.

16 # Reading Strategy

Inferring Cultural Attitudes

- Have a pair of students read aloud the bracketed passage, with each taking a role of one of the characters and using appropriate intonations to express the character's emotions.
- Ask the Reading Strategy question on p. 1228: Based on Daru's response to Balducci's instruction, what inference can you draw about his attitudes toward authority? Explain.
  Possible response: Daru apparently does not believe authority should be obeyed unquestioningly. He is compelled to question authority when told to do something that is not one of his duties or when he has an ethical argument against it.

and his mouth surrounded with wrinkles made him look attentive and studious. Daru took the bridle, led the horse to the shed, and came back to the two men, who were now waiting for him in the school. He led them into his room. "I am going to heat up the classroom," he said. "We'll be more comfortable there." When he entered the room again, Balducci was on the couch. He had undone the rope tying him to the Arab, who had squatted near the stove. His hands still bound, the *chèche* pushed back on his head, he was looking toward the window. At first Daru noticed only his huge lips, fat, smooth, almost Negroid; yet his nose was straight, his eyes were dark and full of fever. The *chèche* revealed an obstinate forehead and, under the weathered skin now rather discolored by the cold, the whole face had a restless and rebellious look that struck Daru when the Arab, turning his face toward him, looked him straight in the eyes. "Go into the other room," said the schoolmaster, "and I'll make you some mint tea." "Thanks," Balducci said. "What a chore! How I long for retirement." And addressing his prisoner in Arabic: "Come on, you." The Arab got up and, slowly, holding his bound wrists in front of him, went into the classroom.

14

The Ear of Grain (L'espiga de blat), 1922–1923, Joan Miró, © The Museum of Modern Art

15 ▲ Critical Viewing

Does this image convey a feeling of poverty, like that suffered by Daru's students, or merely a feeling of simplicity? Explain. **[Make a Judgment]**

With the tea, Daru brought a chair. But Balducci was already enthroned on the nearest pupil's desk and the Arab had squatted against the teacher's platform facing the stove, which stood between the desk and the window. When he held out the glass of tea to the prisoner, Daru hesitated at the sight of his bound hands. "He might perhaps be untied." "Sure," said Balducci. "That was for the trip." He started to get to his feet. But Daru, setting the glass on the floor, had knelt beside the Arab. Without saying anything, the Arab watched him with his feverish eyes. Once his hands were free, he rubbed his swollen wrists against each other, took the glass of tea, and sucked up the burning liquid in swift little sips.

"Good," said Daru. "And where are you headed?"

Balducci withdrew his mustache from the tea. "Here, son."

"Odd pupils! And you're spending the night?"

"No. I'm going back to El Ameur. And you will deliver this fellow to Tinguit.[7] He is expected at police headquarters."

16 Balducci was looking at Daru with a friendly little smile.

"What's this story?" asked the schoolmaster. "Are you pulling my leg?"

"No, son. Those are the orders."

"The orders? I'm not . . ." Daru hesitated, not wanting to hurt the old Corsican.[8] "I mean, that's not my job."

Reading Strategy
Inferring Cultural Attitudes
Based on Daru's response to Balducci's instruction, what inference can you draw about his attitudes toward authority? Explain.

7. **Tinguit** (tiŋ' wēt)
8. **Corsican** (kôr' si kən) native of Corsica, a Mediterranean island.

ENRICHMENT: Linguistics Connection

Arabic

Balducci speaks to the Arab prisoner in Arabic. This is a Semitic language spoken in most of the Arabian Peninsula and other parts of the Middle East and in North Africa. The language used in the *Qur'an* (the sacred book of Islam), it is used as the language of religion by all Muslims. Arabic sounds very different from English and other languages. It has many guttural sounds and some consonants that are pronounced by constricting the pharynx and raising the back of the tongue. There are three vowels (*a*, *i*, and *u*), each of which has a short and a long sound. A single consonant followed by a vowel begins every Arabic word, and long vowels are almost always followed by a single consonant. The language does not have any sound made by more than two consonants. All Arabic words have two parts: the root and the pattern of vowels used with the root. The root is usually three consonants, and the pattern of vowels determines the specific meaning of the root.

"What! What's the meaning of that? In wartime people do all kinds of jobs."

"Then I'll wait for the declaration of war!"

Balducci nodded.

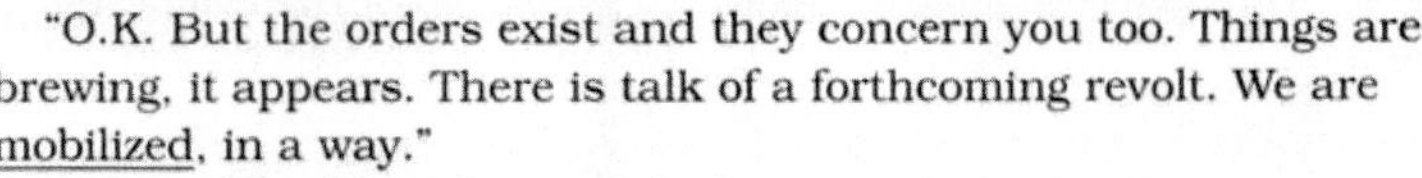

"O.K. But the orders exist and they concern you too. Things are
17 brewing, it appears. There is talk of a forthcoming revolt. We are
mobilized, in a way."

Daru still had his obstinate look.

"Listen, son," Balducci said. "I like you and you must understand. There's only a dozen of us at El Ameur to patrol throughout the whole territory of a small department[9] and I must get back in a hurry. I was told to hand this guy over to you and return without delay. He couldn't be kept there. His village was beginning to stir; they wanted to take him back. You must take him to Tinguit tomorrow before the day is over. Twenty kilometers shouldn't faze a husky fellow like you. After that, all will be over. You'll come back to your pupils and your comfortable life."

Behind the wall the horse could be heard snorting and pawing the earth. Daru was looking out the window. Decidedly, the weather was clearing and the light was increasing over the snowy plateau. When all the snow was melted, the sun would take over again and once more
18 would burn the fields of stone. For days, still, the unchanging sky would shed its dry light on the solitary expanse where nothing had any connection with man.

"After all," he said, turning around toward Balducci, "what did he do?" And, before the gendarme had opened his mouth, he asked: "Does he speak French?"

"No, not a word. We had been looking for him for a month, but they were hiding him. He killed his cousin."

"Is he against us?"

"I don't think so. But you can never be sure."

"Why did he kill?"

"A family squabble, I think. One owed the other grain, it seems. It's not at all clear. In short, he killed his cousin with a billhook.[10] You know, like a sheep, *kreezk!*"

Balducci made the gesture of drawing a blade across his throat and the Arab, his attention attracted, watched him with a sort of anxiety. Daru felt a sudden wrath against the man, against all men with their rotten spite, their tireless hates, their blood lust.

But the kettle was singing on the stove. He served Balducci more tea, hesitated, then served the Arab again, who, a second time, drank avidly. His raised arms made the jellaba fall open and the schoolmaster saw his thin, muscular chest.

"Thanks, kid," Balducci said. "And now, I'm off."

He got up and went toward the Arab, taking a small rope from his pocket.

9. department administrative district in France and certain other countries, similar to a state.
10. billhook tool with a carved or hooked blade, used for pruning or cutting.

Literary Analysis
Existentialism How does Balducci's statement that "the orders exist" represent a choice for Daru?

mobilized (mō' bə līzd') *v.* ready for action or battle

19 **✔Reading Check**
What crime has the Arab prisoner committed?

17 Literary Analysis

Existentialism

- Read aloud the bracketed passage. Point out to students that Balducci tries to convince Daru that he has no choice but to take the Arab to Tinguit the next day.
- Ask the Literary Analysis question on p. 1229: How does Balducci's statement that "the orders exist" represent a choice for Daru?
  Possible response: Balducci's orders are vague in that he does not tell Daru who expects him to take the Arab nor what will happen to him if he disobeys; Daru is able to choose what is meant by the word "exist" and then to act accordingly.

18 Critical Thinking

Infer

- Have students review the dialogue between Balducci and Daru, looking for clues about their relationship. Ask: Are these two men friendly with each other? Explain.
  Possible response: The men seem to be friendly. They talk in an informal manner, and Balducci calls Daru "son" and says "I like you."
- Ask students what they can infer about Daru and Balducci from this dialogue.
  Answer: Daru does not want to get involved; Balducci seems to think that Daru faces few difficulties because he says, "After that, all will be over. You'll come back to your pupils and your comfortable life."

19 ✔Reading Check

Answer: The Arab prisoner has killed his cousin.

CUSTOMIZE INSTRUCTION FOR UNIVERSAL ACCESS

For Less Proficient Readers	For English Learners	For Advanced Readers
Help students understand that the subtlety in the exchange between Balducci and Daru on p.1229 might be revealed in their dialogue and body language. Have students pantomime the way the characters would relate physically to each other during their conversation.	Direct students' attention to Daru's question on page 1228: "Are you pulling my leg?" Explain to students that this is an English idiom, an expression that is not to be taken literally. Tell them that to "pull someone's leg" is to get him or her to accept a ridiculous story as true. Have students brainstorm other English idioms.	Ask students to keep a log of the communications between Balducci and Daru and between Daru and the Arab. Have students track the information and feelings the characters convey to each other as well as the important failures of communication that occur. Then, have students write essays about how these failures are important to the story.

20 Background

Art

Album Afrique 1835–1845. Arab of Constantine, by Auguste Raffet

Auguste Raffet was an artist of the Romantic period who, although popular in his own time, is now much less known than his contemporaries Géricault and Delacroix. He was an expert in watercolors and in lithographs, which were used for book illustrations.

Like the Romantic artists, many scholars, writers, and musicians of the nineteenth century began to study non-Western and pre-industrial cultures around the world. Examples are the German folk stories collected by the Grimm brothers and the folk music used by composers in many countries.

Use the following question for discussion:

Why is it significant that the Arab in "The Guest," like the one in this painting, is wearing traditional clothing?
Possible response: He would be seen as a member of the traditional group in the colony and someone who has not joined the French settlers by adopting their style of dress.

21 ▶ Critical Viewing

Possible response: The prisoner probably wonders whether he should trust Daru and whether Daru trusts him; he is likely preoccupied with the thought of going to prison.

22 Reading Strategy

Inferring Cultural Attitudes

- After reading aloud the bracketed passage, have students compare Balducci's and Daru's attitudes about the importance of being armed.
  Possible response: They agree that it is important to have a weapon, but they disagree on the importance of keeping the weapon close at hand. Balducci thinks that Daru should keep his shotgun near his bed, but Daru says that he keeps it in the trunk because he has "nothing to fear."

continued

20

Album Afrique 1835–1845. Arab of Constantine, Auguste Raffet, Musée Condé, Chantilly, France

21 ◀ Critical Viewing
Imagine that this Arab is Balducci's prisoner. What might he be thinking? **[Speculate]**

"What are you doing?" Daru asked dryly.

Balducci, disconcerted, showed him the rope.

"Don't bother."

The old gendarme hesitated. "It's up to you. Of course, you are armed?"

"I have my shotgun."

"Where?"

"In the trunk."

"You ought to have it near your bed."

"Why? I have nothing to fear."

"You're crazy, son. If there's an uprising, no one is safe, we're all in the same boat."

22 "I'll defend myself. I'll have time to see them coming."

Balducci began to laugh, then suddenly the mustache covered the white teeth.

"You'll have time? O.K. That's just what I was saying. You have always been a little cracked. That's why I like you, my son was like that."

At the same time he took out his revolver and put it on the desk.

"Keep it; I don't need two weapons from here to El Ameur."

The revolver shone against the black paint of the table. When the gendarme turned toward him, the schoolmaster caught the smell of leather and horseflesh.

"Listen, Balducci," Daru said suddenly, "every bit of this disgusts me, and first of all your fellow here. But I won't hand him over. Fight, yes, if I have to. But not that."

The old gendarme stood in front of him and looked at him severely.

Reading Strategy
Inferring Cultural Attitudes
What does Balducci mean when he says, "we're all in the same boat"? Explain.

continued from left column

- Ask the Reading Strategy question on p. 1230: What does Balducci mean when he says, "we're all in the same boat"? Explain.
  Answer: Balducci means that all the non-Arabs in the area will be threatened by the native Arab population.

"You're being a fool," he said slowly. "I don't like it either. You don't get used to putting a rope on a man even after years of it, and you're even ashamed—yes, ashamed. But you can't let them have their way."

"I won't hand him over," Daru said again.

"It's an order, son, and I repeat it."

"That's right. Repeat to them what I've said to you: I won't hand him over."

Balducci made a visible effort to reflect. He looked at the Arab and at Daru. At last he decided.

23 "No, I won't tell them anything. If you want to drop us, go ahead; I'll not denounce you. I have an order to deliver the prisoner and I'm doing so. And now you'll just sign this paper for me."

"There's no need. I'll not deny that you left him with me."

"Don't be mean with me. I know you'll tell the truth. You're from hereabouts and you are a man. But you must sign, that's the rule."

Daru opened his drawer, took out a little square bottle of purple ink, the red wooden penholder with the "sergeant-major" pen he used for making models of penmanship, and signed. The gendarme carefully folded the paper and put it into his wallet. Then he moved toward the door.

"I'll see you off," Daru said.

"No," said Balducci. "There's no use being polite. You insulted me."

He looked at the Arab, motionless in the same spot, sniffed peevishly, and turned away toward the door. "Good-by, son," he said. The door shut behind him. Balducci appeared suddenly outside the window and then disappeared. His footsteps were muffled by the snow. The horse stirred on the other side of the wall and several chickens fluttered in fright. A moment later Balducci reappeared outside the window leading the horse by the bridle. He walked toward the little rise without turning around and disappeared from sight with the horse following him. A big stone could be heard bouncing down. Daru walked back toward the prisoner, who, without stirring, never took his eyes off him. "Wait," the schoolmaster said in Arabic and went toward the bedroom. As he was going through the door, he had a second thought, went to the desk, took the revolver, and stuck it in his pocket. Then, without looking back, he went into his room.

For some time he lay on his couch watching the sky gradually close over, listening to the silence. It was this silence that had seemed painful to him during the first days here, after the war. He had requested a post in the little town at the base of the foothills separating the upper plateaus from the desert. There, rocky walls, green and black to the north, pink and lavender to the south, marked the frontier of eternal summer. He had been named to a post farther north, on the plateau itself. In the beginning, the solitude and the silence had been hard for him on these wastelands peopled only by stones. Occasionally, furrows suggested cultivation, but they had been dug to uncover a certain kind 24 of stone good for building. The only plowing here was to harvest rocks. Elsewhere a thin layer of soil accumulated in the hollows would be

denounce (dē nouns′) *v.* accuse publicly

Reading Strategy
Inferring Cultural Attitudes What cultural attitudes are suggested by Balducci's statement, "I know you'll tell the truth. You're from hereabouts and you are a man"?

✓**Reading Check** What order does Daru refuse to follow?

23 Reading Strategy

Inferring Cultural Attitudes

- Call on a volunteer to read aloud the bracketed passage. Then, ask students to explain why Balducci wants Daru to sign the paper.
  Possible response: Balducci must prove to his superiors that he delivered the prisoner to Daru. This is the point at which his responsibility ends and Daru's begins.
- Ask students what the signing of the paper reveals about the culture of which Balducci and Daru are a part.
  Possible response: It reveals the culture to be literate and one that requires written proof in matters that in other cultures a person's word alone might suffice.
- Ask the Reading Strategy question on p. 1231: What cultural attitudes are suggested by Balducci's statement, "I know you'll tell the truth. You're from hereabouts and you are a man"?
  Possible response: The statement suggests that knowing where someone is from reveals something about his or her character; being male and from the area imply honesty.

Reteach If students have difficulty contributing to the discussion, review the use of the graphic organizer on p. 1223. Help students list details about Balducci and Daru that suggest cultural attitudes. For example:

- **Detail**
  Balducci says that he knows Daru will tell the truth because he is "from hereabouts."
- **Cultural Attitude**
  People within the French settlers' culture consider one another trustworthy.

24 ✓Reading Check

Answer: Daru refuses to follow the order to take the Arab on a twenty-kilometer journey to the prison.

CUSTOMIZE INSTRUCTION FOR UNIVERSAL ACCESS

For Advanced Readers

Have students use library and Internet sources to research the history of French colonialism in Algeria. They might concentrate on topics such as the following: Algeria before French annexation; use of French language and education in Algeria; relations between the French and Muslim populations; differences between French colonialism in Algeria and in other countries; the revolutionary conflict of the 1950s and 1960s; French influence in Algeria after independence.

When their research is complete, ask students to compare the conflict between Algerians and the French, leading to an independent Algeria, with the conflict between the Native Americans and American colonists in the 1770s.

Make sure students understand that one difference is that the Algerians were an indigenous population who opposed both the French government and the French-Algerian settlers, whereas the Native American population was unable to rebel successfully against either the English or the American colonists.

25 Literary Analysis

Existentialism; Setting and Theme

- Have a volunteer read aloud the bracketed passage. Then, ask this question: What is suggested by this description of the setting?
  Possible response: The harsh land supports a harsh way of life. Human life and society mean little in the face of the inhospitable immensity of the desert. This encourages Daru's pessimism in the face of apparently pointless human actions.
- Ask students the first Literary Analysis question on p. 1232: In what ways does the statement that "no one in this desert . . . mattered" reflect Existentialist thought?
  Possible response: The statement reflects the Existentialist view that the universe is indifferent to human life.

26 Literary Analysis

Existentialism

- Read aloud the bracketed passage. Ask students to speculate about why Daru puts the revolver in the desk drawer.
  Possible response: He realizes the incongruity of protecting himself from the hungry man with whom he will soon share a meal.
- Ask students the second Literary Analysis question on p. 1232: Which personal choices and values does Daru's replacing the revolver demonstrate? Explain.
  Possible response: When Daru replaces the revolver, he demonstrates that he has made his own decision regarding the Arab. It is clear that Daru does not intend to follow every bit of advice that Balducci has given him.

scraped out to enrich paltry village gardens. This is the way it was: bare rock covered three quarters of the region. Towns sprang up, flourished, then disappeared; men came by, loved one another or fought bitterly, then died. No one in this desert, neither he nor his guest, mattered. And yet, outside this desert neither of them, Daru knew, could have really lived.

When he got up, no noise came from the classroom. He was amazed at the unmixed joy he derived from the mere thought that the Arab might have fled and that he would be alone with no decision to make. But the prisoner was there. He had merely stretched out between the stove and the desk. With eyes open, he was staring at the ceiling. In that position, his thick lips were particularly noticeable, giving him a pouting look. "Come," said Daru. The Arab got up and followed him. In the bedroom, the schoolmaster pointed to a chair near the table under the window. The Arab sat down without taking his eyes off Daru.

"Are you hungry?"

"Yes," the prisoner said.

Daru set the table for two. He took flour and oil, shaped a cake in a frying-pan, and lighted the little stove that functioned on bottled gas. While the cake was cooking, he went out to the shed to get cheese, eggs, dates, and condensed milk. When the cake was done he set it on the window sill to cool, heated some condensed milk diluted with water, and beat up the eggs into an omelette. In one of his motions he knocked against the revolver stuck in his right pocket. He set the bowl down, went into the classroom, and put the revolver in his desk drawer. When he came back to the room, night was falling. He put on the light and served the Arab. "Eat," he said. The Arab took a piece of the cake, lifted it eagerly to his mouth, and stopped short.

"And you?" he asked.

"After you. I'll eat too."

The thick lips opened slightly. The Arab hesitated, then bit into the cake determinedly.

The meal over, the Arab looked at the schoolmaster. "Are you the judge?"

"No, I'm simply keeping you until tomorrow."

"Why do you eat with me?"

"I'm hungry."

The Arab fell silent. Daru got up and went out. He brought back a folding bed from the shed, set it up between the table and the stove, perpendicular to his own bed. From a large suitcase which, upright in a corner, served as a shelf for papers, he took two blankets and arranged them on the camp bed. Then he stopped, felt useless, and sat down on his bed. There was nothing more to do or to get ready. He had to look at this man. He looked at him, therefore, trying to imagine his face bursting with rage. He couldn't do so. He could see nothing but the dark yet shining eyes and the animal mouth.

"Why did you kill him?" he asked in a voice whose hostile tone surprised him.

The Arab looked away.

Literary Analysis
Existentialism; Setting and Theme In what ways does the statement that "no one in this desert . . . mattered" reflect Existentialist thought?

Literary Analysis
Existentialism Which personal choices and values does Daru's replacing the revolver demonstrate? Explain.

ENRICHMENT: Culinary Arts

Algerian Cuisine

The meal Daru serves the Arab is a simple but typical version of Algerian cuisine. French, Turkish, Arab, and Berber traditions are all found in the Algerian kitchen. Unleavened bread and couscous, a semolina-based pasta, are dietary staples, often served with a meat, chickpea and vegetable stew often highly spiced. Other common dishes include mutton, lamb, and poultry. Desserts often use native-grown figs, dates, almonds, and locally produced honey. Mint tea, which Daru offers to his guests, is a favorite drink in Algeria, as is strong, sweet, Turkish-style coffee.

27

Seated Arab, Eugène Delacroix, Réunion des Musées Nationaux

28 ◀ **Critical Viewing**
Is this man's clothing appropriate for the setting Camus describes? Why or why not? **[Assess]**

"He ran away. I ran after him."

He raised his eyes to Daru again and they were full of a sort of woeful interrogation. "Now what will they do to me?"

29 "Are you afraid?"

He stiffened, turning his eyes away.

"Are you sorry?"

The Arab stared at him openmouthed. Obviously he did not understand. Daru's annoyance was growing. At the same time he felt awkward and self-conscious with his big body wedged between the two beds.

"Lie down there," he said impatiently. "That's your bed."

The Arab didn't move. He called to Daru:

"Tell me!"

The schoolmaster looked at him.

"Is the gendarme coming back tomorrow?"

"I don't know."

"Are you coming with us?"

"I don't know. Why?"

The prisoner got up and stretched out on top of the blankets, his feet toward the window. The light from the electric bulb shone straight into his eyes and he closed them at once.

"Why?" Daru repeated, standing beside the bed.

The Arab opened his eyes under the blinding light and looked at him, trying not to blink.

"Come with us," he said.

In the middle of the night, Daru was still not asleep. He had gone to bed after undressing completely; he generally slept naked. But when he suddenly realized that he had nothing on, he hesitated. He felt vulnerable and the temptation came to him to put his clothes back on. Then he shrugged his shoulders; after all, he wasn't a child and, if need be,

Reading Strategy
Inferring Cultural Attitudes
Does the prisoner fail to grasp Daru's question ("Are you sorry?") because he holds different cultural attitudes, or is it simply a matter of his personality? Explain.

30  **Reading Check**
How does Daru feel at the thought his prisoner might have fled?

CUSTOMIZE INSTRUCTION FOR UNIVERSAL ACCESS

For Less Proficient Readers	For Gifted/Talented Students
Read aloud with students from "'Are you hungry?' " on p. 1232 to "'Come with us,' he said" on p. 1233. Help students focus on the actions that Daru performs—setting the table, cooking, putting the revolver away, putting on the light, serving the Arab, eating, talking, retrieving and setting up the folding bed, and so on—as well as the behavior of the Arab. Then, lead students in a discussion that compares the way Daru treats the Arab with the way Balducci treated him. Finally, discuss the reasons that the Arab asks Daru to travel with him and Balducci.	Have students reread the scene between Daru and the Arab, beginning with the second paragraph on p. 1232. Invite them to create works of art based on the scene. For example, they might create a musical composition appropriate for a dramatized version of the scene. Other possibilities include paintings, drawings, sculptures, or poems based on the scene. Encourage students to share their finished works with classmates.

27 Background

Art

Seated Arab, by Eugène Delacroix

In 1832, Delacroix (1798–1863) spent four months in North Africa, where he was inspired to paint images like this one. The man's simple clothing and meditative posture suggest quiet contemplation.

Use the following question for discussion:

What Existentialist attitude does the minimalist background of the painting suggest?
Possible response: The plain background emphasizes the man, not his surroundings.

28 ▶ Critical Viewing

Possible response: The man's clothing covers his body completely, protecting him from the harsh sun and whipping winds. Therefore, it is appropriate for the setting.

29 Reading Strategy

Inferring Cultural Attitudes

- Have a volunteer read aloud the bracketed passage. Then, ask students to describe the mood of the scene and the characters' interactions.
  Possible response: The mood is one of discomfort between the characters as they try to communicate. Daru asks the Arab a few questions to try to understand him, but the Arab seems wary and frightened.
- Ask the Reading Strategy question on p. 1233: Does the prisoner fail to grasp Daru's question ("Are you sorry?") because he holds different cultural attitudes, or is it simply a matter of his personality? Explain.
  Possible response: Perhaps it does not occur to the man that being sorry for a crime is relevant in Daru's culture. On the other hand, the man may simply be uncomfortable, taken aback by Daru's personal questions.

30 ✓ Reading Check

Answer: Daru feels glad at the thought that the Arab might have fled.

31 Background

The Existentialist Three: Camus, Sartre, and de Beauvoir

Jean Paul Sartre did not shy away from the label "Existentialist," as did other like-minded thinkers. He did, however, reject another label: that of Nobel Prize winner. In 1964, he refused to accept this prestigious award for work characterized by the Nobel organization as ". . . rich in ideas and filled with the spirit of freedom and the quest for truth, [which] has exerted a far-reaching influence on our age."

Simone de Beauvoir's contribution to the feminist movement in the middle of the twentieth century is as well known as her contribution to Existentialist thought. She and Sartre were at the center of the intellectual community of the Left Bank in Paris just after World War II.

32 Critical Thinking

Interpret

- Read with students the bracketed passage. Discuss Daru's mental state.
- Ask students why Daru is bothered by the man's presence.
  Possible response: Daru is bothered by the man's presence because he has grown accustomed to solitude; the man's presence reminds Daru of the community of friends he no longer has.
- Ask students to explain Daru's attitude toward the prisoner and toward the situation in which he finds himself.
  Possible response: Daru has mixed feelings toward the prisoner. He is angry that the prisoner has killed someone in what was probably a squabble over grain, yet he tries to establish a connection with the prisoner by treating him decently and asking him about his feelings. It is possible that Daru believes the prisoner should be judged by his own people rather than by the French colonials. Despite his anger toward the prisoner, he does not want to be the one to turn him over to the police.

he could break his adversary in two. From his bed he could observe him, lying on his back, still motionless with his eyes closed under the harsh light. When Daru turned out the light, the darkness seemed to coagulate all of a sudden. Little by little, the night came back to life in the window where the starless sky was stirring gently. The schoolmaster soon made out the body lying at his feet. The Arab still did not move, but his eyes seemed open. A faint wind was prowling around the schoolhouse. Perhaps it would drive away the clouds and the sun would reappear.

During the night the wind increased. The hens fluttered a little and then were silent. The Arab turned over on his side with his back to Daru, who thought he heard him moan. Then he listened for his guest's breathing, become heavier and more regular. He listened to that breath so close to him and mused without being able to go to sleep. In this room where he had been sleeping alone for a year, this presence bothered him. But it bothered him also by imposing on him a sort of brotherhood he knew well but refused to accept in the present circumstances. **32** Men who share the same rooms, soldiers or prisoners, develop a strange alliance as if, having cast off their armor with their clothing, they fraternized every evening, over and above their differences, in the ancient community of dream and fatigue. But Daru shook himself; he didn't like such musings, and it was essential to sleep.

A little later, however, when the Arab stirred slightly, the schoolmaster was still not asleep. When the prisoner made a second move, he stiffened, on the alert. The Arab was lifting himself slowly on his arms with almost the motion of a sleepwalker. Seated upright in bed, he waited motionless without turning his head toward Daru, as if he were listening attentively. Daru did not stir; it had just occurred to him that the revolver was still in the drawer of his desk. It was better to act at once. Yet he continued to observe the prisoner, who, with the same slithery motion, put his feet on the ground, waited again, then began to stand up slowly. Daru was about to call out to him when the Arab began to walk, in a quite natural but extraordinarily silent way. He was heading toward the door at the end of the room that opened into the shed. He lifted the latch with precaution and went out, pushing the door behind him but without shutting it. Daru had not stirred. "He is running away," he merely thought. "Good riddance!" Yet he listened attentively. The hens were not fluttering; the guest must be on the plateau. A faint sound of water reached him, and he didn't know what it was until the Arab again stood framed in the doorway, closed the door carefully, and came back to bed without a sound. Then Daru turned his back on him and fell asleep. Still later he seemed, from the depths of his sleep, to hear furtive steps around the schoolhouse. "I'm dreaming! I'm dreaming!" he repeated to himself. And he went on sleeping.

Themes in World Literature

31 ***The Existentialist Three: Camus, Sartre, and de Beauvoir***

When Albert Camus moved to France at the age of twenty-five, he entered a dynamic literary world in which other writers and philosophers were already exploring theories of individual freedom and morality. He became intimate friends with two of them: Jean-Paul Sartre (1905–1980) and Simone de Beauvoir (1908–1986). Together, they became leaders of the Existentialist movement, influencing French literature and philosophical thought through much of the twentieth century.

Sartre was the most prominent of the three. In books like *No Exit* (1946) and *Being and Nothingness* (1956), he popularized the Existentialist view of individual freedom, human dignity, and social responsibility.

De Beauvoir met Sartre in 1929, and they became lifelong companions. Today, she is best known as a pioneering feminist whose 1949 book, *The Second Sex*, influenced the changing roles of women.

fraternized (frat′ ər nīzd′) *v.* associated in a brotherly way; socialized

furtive (fur′ tiv) *adj.* done in a secret or sneaky way

ENRICHMENT: Linguistics Connection

The Word *Arab*

The character known as "the Arab" might be an Algerian Muslim. The word *Arab* was originally applied only to people from the Arabian region of Asia. It has also been used, as it is here, to refer to people who speak the Arabic language. Daru probably would not refer to the character as an "Algerian" because Daru, despite his French ancestry, is also Algerian.

When he awoke, the sky was clear; the loose window let in a cold, pure air. The Arab was asleep, hunched up under the blankets now, his mouth open, utterly relaxed. But when Daru shook him, he started dreadfully, staring at Daru with wild eyes as if he had never seen him and such a frightened expression that the schoolmaster stepped back. "Don't be afraid. It's me. You must eat." The Arab nodded his head and said yes. Calm had returned to his face, but his expression was vacant and listless.

The coffee was ready. They drank it seated together on the folding bed as they munched their pieces of the cake. Then Daru led the Arab under the shed and showed him the faucet where he washed. He went back into the room, folded the blankets and the bed, made his own bed and put the room in order. Then he went through the classroom and out onto the terrace. The sun was already rising in the blue sky; a soft, bright light was bathing the deserted plateau. On the ridge the snow was melting in spots. The stones were about to reappear. Crouched on the edge of the plateau, the schoolmaster looked at the deserted expanse. He thought of Balducci. He had hurt him, for he had sent him off in a way as if he didn't want to be associated with him. He could still hear the gendarme's farewell and, without knowing why, he felt
33 strangely empty and vulnerable. At that moment, from the other side of the schoolhouse, the prisoner coughed. Daru listened to him almost despite himself and then, furious, threw a pebble that whistled through the air before sinking into the snow. That man's stupid crime revolted him, but to hand him over was contrary to honor. Merely thinking of it made him smart with humiliation. And he cursed at one and the same time his own people who had sent him this Arab and the Arab too who had dared to kill and not managed to get away. Daru got up, walked in a circle on the terrace, waited motionless, and then went back into the schoolhouse.

The Arab, leaning over the cement floor of the shed, was washing his teeth with two fingers. Daru looked at him and said: "Come." He went back into the room ahead of the prisoner. He slipped a hunting-jacket on over his sweater and put on walking-shoes. Standing, he waited until the Arab had put on his *chèche* and sandals. They went into the classroom and the schoolmaster pointed to the exit, saying: "Go ahead." The fellow didn't budge. "I'm coming," said Daru. The Arab went out. Daru went back into the room and made a package of pieces of rusk,[11] dates, and sugar. In the classroom, before going out, he hesitated a second in front of his desk, then crossed the threshold and locked the door. "That's the way," he said. He started toward the east, followed by the prisoner. But, a short distance from the schoolhouse, he thought he heard a slight sound behind them. He retraced his steps and examined the surroundings of the house; there was no one there. The Arab watched him without seeming to understand. "Come on," said Daru.

11. **rusk** (rusk) *n.* sweet bread or cake, toasted or baked until crisp.

Literary Analysis
Existentialism; Setting and Theme In what ways does Daru's throwing the pebble into the desert reflect Existentialist views?

34 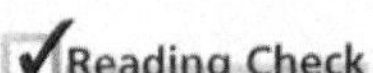
Reading Check
What does Daru hear "from the depths of his sleep"?

33 Literary Analysis
Existentialism; Setting and Theme

- Have a volunteer read aloud the bracketed passage. Then, ask students why Daru feels "empty and vulnerable" at this time.
  Possible response: Daru probably feels both the loss of his friend and the possibility of needing allies in case circumstances turn dangerous. He also feels alone in grappling with his decision about what to do with the Arab.
- Ask students the Literary Analysis question on p. 1235: In what ways does Daru's throwing the pebble into the desert reflect Existentialist views?
  Possible response: Daru expresses his anger by throwing the pebble, but nature answers with an indifferent response—it simply swallows up the pebble silently without even allowing it to reverberate.

34 Reading Check

Answer: Daru seems to hear furtive steps around the schoolhouse.

CUSTOMIZE INSTRUCTION FOR UNIVERSAL ACCESS

For Less Proficient Readers	For Advanced Readers
Discuss with students the two times Daru thinks he hears someone lurking around the schoolhouse (during the night "from the depths of his sleep," and the next morning when he and the prisoner are starting out). Ask students whether they think someone might really be there and if so, for what reason. Point out that Camus might have a dual purpose in including these incidents: to foreshadow coming events and to show that Daru is subject to fears based on his situation.	Suggest that students discuss this question before going on with the story: Should Daru be angrier with "his own people" who have given him the responsibility of dealing with the Arab or with the Arab for not escaping? Point out that this question presents Daru's basic problem: He deals with forces beyond his control, yet he must decide his best course of action under these circumstances.

35 Literary Analysis

Existentialism; Setting and Theme

- Read aloud the bracketed passage. Ask students to explain what is happening in the natural setting Camus describes.
  Answer: As the snow melts, puddles evaporate quickly in the morning sun, leaving the plateau dry. The occasional bird sings out suddenly.
- Ask students the Literary Analysis question on p. 1236: In what ways does the setting reflect both a change in Daru's mood and Existentialist ideas about personal freedom?
  Possible response: When Daru feels "a sort of rapture before the vast familiar expanse," he feels that he is not completely overwhelmed by his difficulties. Despite the dilemma he faces, he can feel joy at the beauty of nature, knowing that he does have a choice.

36 ▶Critical Viewing

Possible response: The man may be thinking about what he has done, wondering what his family and friends will do without him, and hoping that his punishment will be light.

---

35 They walked for an hour and rested beside a sharp peak of limestone. The snow was melting faster and faster and the sun was drinking up the puddles at once, rapidly cleaning the plateau, which gradually dried and vibrated like the air itself. When they resumed walking, the ground rang under their feet. From time to time a bird rent the space in front of them with a joyful cry. Daru breathed in deeply the fresh morning light. He felt a sort of rapture before the vast familiar expanse, now almost entirely yellow under its dome of blue sky. They walked an hour more, descending toward the south. They reached a level height made up of crumbly rocks. From there on, the plateau sloped down, eastward, toward a low plain where there were a few spindly trees and, to the south, toward outcroppings of rock that gave the landscape a chaotic look.

Daru surveyed the two directions. There was nothing but the sky on the horizon. Not a man could be seen. He turned toward the Arab, who was looking at him blankly. Daru held out the package to him. "Take it," he said. "There are dates, bread, and sugar. You can hold out for two days. Here are a thousand francs[12] too." The Arab took the package and the money but kept his full hands at chest level as if he didn't

Literary Analysis
Existentialism; Setting and Theme In what ways does the setting reflect both a change in Daru's mood and Existentialist ideas about personal freedom?

36 ▼ **Critical Viewing**
Imagine that this man is the prisoner, walking toward the police station. What might he be thinking as he turns himself in? **[Speculate]**

12. **a thousand francs** (fraŋks) *n.* at that time, monetary units of France and certain other countries, 1,000 francs being enough money for a few days' food and travel.

ENRICHMENT: Culture Connection

Algerian Culture

Algeria's two main ethnic groups are the Berbers and the Arabs. The Berbers, who have been in Algeria since at least 3000 B.C., generally live in rural villages, farming and herding. Traditional Berber households include an extended family. Each married couple has its own home, opening onto the family courtyard in the back. Family is so important to the Berbers that their village governments are based on it.

Arab culture became influential in Algeria in the A.D. 600s, when the Arabs began to conquer North Africa. Arab traditions are like Berber traditions in many ways. Both groups, for example, traditionally live with extended families. However, whereas Berbers tend to be farmers, some Arabs favor a nomadic lifestyle.

Over the centuries, Arabs and Berbers have had many conflicts. France's colonization of the area resulted in even more conflicts. Still, there have been long periods during which these different groups have lived peacefully and have learned from one another.

37 know what to do with what was being given him. "Now look," the schoolmaster said as he pointed in the direction of the east, "there's the way to Tinguit. You have a two-hour walk. At Tinguit you'll find the administration and the police. They are expecting you." The Arab looked toward the east, still holding the package and the money against his chest. Daru took his elbow and turned him rather roughly toward the south. At the foot of the height on which they stood could be seen a faint path. "That's the trail across the plateau. In a day's walk from here you'll find pasturelands and the first nomads. They'll take you in and shelter you according to their law." The Arab had now turned toward Daru and a sort of panic was visible in his expression. "Listen," he said. Daru shook his head: "No, be quiet. Now I'm leaving you." He turned his back on him, took two long steps in the direction of the school, looked hesitantly at the motionless Arab, and started off again. For a few minutes he heard nothing but his own step resounding on the cold ground and did not turn his head. A moment later, however, he turned around. The Arab was still there on the edge of the hill, his arms hanging now, and he was looking at the schoolmaster. Daru felt something rise in his throat. But he swore with impatience, waved vaguely, and started off again. He had already gone some distance when he again stopped and looked. There was no longer anyone on the hill.

Reading Strategy
Inferring Cultural Attitudes
Based on Daru's statement about the nomads, what can you infer about their cultural attitudes?

38 **✓Reading Check**
What items does Daru give the prisoner before he departs?

37 Reading Strategy

Inferring Cultural Attitudes

- Ask a volunteer to read aloud the bracketed passage. Then, ask this question: Why does Daru present a choice to the Arab, without stating directly that the Arab is getting a chance to escape?
  Possible response: Daru wants the Arab to make his own decision, free from outside influence.
- Ask students the Reading Strategy question on p. 1237: Based on Daru's statement about the nomads, what can you infer about their cultural attitudes?
  Possible response: Nomads believe it is important to help anyone who needs it, regardless of background or social class.

38 ✓Reading Check

Answer: Daru gives the prisoner a package that has enough dates, bread, and sugar to last two days. He also gives him a thousand francs.

ASSESS

Answers for p. 1238

Review and Assess

1. Possible response: Yes; Daru acted kindly toward the Arab and did not turn him in.
2. **(a)** Balducci and his Arab prisoner arrive at Daru's home. **(b)** Balducci is on a horse and an Arab with bound hands is walking behind him. **(c)** Possible response: Balducci is in charge and the Arab is powerless.
3. **(a)** Balducci demands that Daru deliver the prisoner to the police in Tinguit. **(b)** Possible response: Daru is thought to be on the side of the French and must take orders. **(c)** Possible response: Daru wants to remain neutral.
4. **(a)** The police believed that the villagers would not punish the Arab. **(b)** Possible response: The villagers will blame Daru for handing the Arab over to the authorities.
5. **(a)** Possible response: Daru is disgusted with the Arab for having killed a man and for not escaping. **(b)** No; Daru treats him as an equal.
6. **(a)** Daru gives the Arab the choice of turning himself in or escaping into the desert. **(b)** Possible response: Yes; Daru gave the man a choice. No; Daru should not turn a murderer loose on society.
7. Possible response: Daru would not have acted differently. If he turned the prisoner over to his Arab friends, he would risk the wrath of the French colonials; if he turned the prisoner over to the police, he would risk the wrath of the Arab's friends.

Daru hesitated. The sun was now rather high in the sky and was beginning to beat down on his head. The schoolmaster retraced his steps, at first somewhat uncertainly, then with decision. When he reached the little hill, he was bathed in sweat. He climbed it as fast as he could and stopped, out of breath, at the top. The rock-fields to the south stood out sharply against the blue sky, but on the plain to the east a steamy heat was already rising. And in that slight haze, Daru,
39 with heavy heart, made out the Arab walking slowly on the road to prison.

A little later, standing before the window of the classroom, the schoolmaster was watching the clear light bathing the whole surface of the plateau, but he hardly saw it. Behind him on the blackboard, among the winding French rivers, sprawled the clumsily chalked-up words he had just read: "You handed over our brother. You will pay for this." Daru looked at the sky, the plateau, and, beyond, the invisible lands stretching all the way to the sea. In this vast landscape he had loved so much, he was alone.

Review and Assess

Thinking About the Selection

1. **Respond:** Did you find the end of the story surprising? Why or why not?
2. **(a) Recall:** Who are the two men who arrive at Daru's home? **(b) Interpret:** As the men approach, what details in their appearance and behavior does Daru observe? **(c) Analyze:** What do these details suggest about the characters and status of the men?
3. **(a) Recall:** What demand does Balducci make of Daru with regard to the Arab prisoner? **(b) Infer:** Why is Daru expected to take orders delivered to him by Balducci? **(c) Analyze:** Why do you think Daru refuses to comply?
4. **(a) Recall:** Why did the police feel it necessary to remove the Arab prisoner from custody in his village? **(b) Draw Conclusions:** How does this situation emphasize the danger of Daru's position?
5. **(a) Infer:** What is Daru's opinion of the Arab? Support your answer. **(b) Interpret:** Do Daru's feelings about the Arab affect his treatment of the man? Explain.
6. **(a) Interpret:** How does Daru resolve his dilemma over the Arab? **(b) Make a Judgment:** Do you think this was a good resolution?
7. **Speculate:** Would Daru have acted differently if he had known the Arab's friends might seek revenge? Why or why not?

ASSESSMENT PRACTICE: Critical Reading

Analyzing an Author's Meaning and Style (For more practice, see Test Preparation Workbook, p. 58.)

What does Camus mean by having Daru struggle as he does only to find the following message on the blackboard?

"You handed over our brother. You will pay for this."

A In French colonies, anyone harboring criminals must pay their legal fees, whether they are guilty or innocent.

B One should always seek professional advice before making decisions that have social and political implications.

C Individuals must wrestle with their consciences in a world where conscience and good intentions matter little.

D Indecisiveness regarding right versus wrong is punishable even if one ultimately makes the right decision.

The correct answer is *C*. It explains an existential paradox: by making choices as if they mattered, one can create meaning in a world in which such choices are meaningless.

Review and Assess

Literary Analysis

Existentialism

1. Daru shows the Arab two paths and leaves him to make his own choice. In what ways does this decision reflect **Existentialist** ideas?
2. (a) How does Daru feel about the Arab's crime? (b) How does he treat the Arab? (c) What values do Daru's feelings and actions reflect? Explain.
3. What does the end of the story suggest about the difficulties of living one's life according to Existentialist principles? Explain.

Connecting Literary Elements

4. (a) Use a chart like the one shown to identify details about the

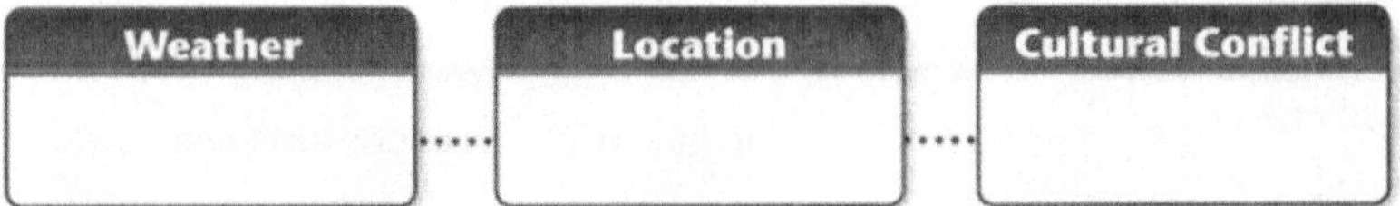

climate, the landscape, and the cultural conflict in this story. (b) Discuss the ways in which these details of the **setting** reflect ideas that are central to the story's meaning, or **theme.**

5. (a) Why do you think Daru feels that "outside this desert neither of them [Daru or the Arab] . . . could have really lived"? (b) In what ways does this statement contribute to the story's theme?
6. Who is the guest in this story—the Arab prisoner in Daru's house or Daru in Algeria? Explain.

Reading Strategy

Inferring Cultural Attitudes

7. Daru's blackboard shows the four rivers of France. **Infer cultural attitudes** by describing what this statement reveals about the mind-set of Europeans living in Algeria.
8. What cultural attitudes can you infer from the message the Arab's supporters leave on Daru's blackboard? Explain.

Extend Understanding

9. **Literature Connection:** Camus believed that he had a responsibility to serve humanity through his writing. In what ways do you think that literature can accomplish this goal?

Quick Review

Existentialism is a philosophy that emphasizes the value of personal choice in an indifferent world.

The **setting** is the time and the place in which a story occurs. The **theme** is the central message or insight about life that is communicated in a literary work.

To **infer cultural attitudes** when reading, look for clues about the values and customs of a group of people.

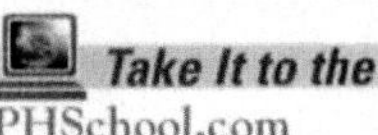
Take It to the Net

PHSchool.com

Take the interactive self-test online to check your understanding of this selection.

ENRICHMENT: Further Reading

Other Works by Albert Camus

We strongly encourage you to review any selection before assigning or recommending it to students.

The Stranger

The Plague

The First Man

Take It to the Net

Visit PHSchool.com for more information on Albert Camus.

Answers for p. 1239

Review and Assess

1. Possible response: Daru's decision gives the Arab the opportunity to choose his own action, just as Daru has had to do.
2. **(a)** Daru is disgusted and angry about the Arab's crime. **(b)** He treats the Arab as an equal. **(c)** Possible response: Daru's feelings and actions reflect his attitude that despite people's shortcomings they share a common humanity and should be treated with dignity and respect.
3. Possible response: Living one's life according to Existentialist principles is difficult because others may not understand one's choices and may, in fact, oppose them. No ultimate authority tells individuals what to do—they make their own decisions using only conscience as a guide.
4. **(a) Weather:** Extreme cold and heat; **Location:** Algeria; **Cultural Conflict:** The native population resents the French colonials. **(b)** Possible response: The details reflect the isolation that characters face as they make choices, take stands, and risk danger.
5. **(a)** Possible response: The Arab is a part of the native group in the desert, finding his identity there; Daru finds the desert well suited to his belief in the individual's acting autonomously. **(b)** Possible response: This statement emphasizes the dilemma both characters face. The Arab and Daru cannot escape their situations, nor can they look to others or to the universe for guidance.
6. Possible response: Each character can be seen as a guest. Although he serves as host to the Arab prisoner, Daru is a guest in Algeria. Even though he was born there, his ancestors are not among the native peoples of Algeria.
7. Possible response: This lesson implies that knowledge about France, the mother country, may be more valuable to the students' futures than knowledge about Algeria.
8. Possible response: The Arab's supporters believe that matters arising in their close-knit

continued

continued from right column

community should be kept there; the message also suggests that revenge is part of their culture.

9. Possible response: Literature can serve humanity by raising questions of ethics, conscience, and meaning, as Camus does in this story.

EXTEND

Answers for p. 1240

❶ Vocabulary Development

Word Analysis: Anglo-Saxon Prefix *fore-*

1. foreword: an introduction to a book
2. foresight: the act or power of looking ahead
3. forerunner: a warning or sign of something that is yet to arrive

Spelling Strategy

1. grief
2. brief
3. relieve
4. thief
5. achieve

Fluency: Sentence Completion

1. mobilized
2. plateau
3. foretaste
4. denounce
5. siege
6. fraternized
7. furtive

❷ Grammar and Style

Practice

1. along the trail, modifies *walked*, adverb phrase
2. with the jellaba, modifies *man*, adjective phrase
3. With quick movements, modifies *served*, adverb phrase
4. in a hurt tone, modifies *said*, adverb phrase
5. from the village, modifies *Arabs*, adjective phrase

Writing Application

Sample response: Daru's home is a single (room) *off his classroom* (adjective phrase). The (walls) *of the room* are white washed. (adjective phrase). Daru's room (is furnished) *in a simple manner* (adverb phrase).

10TH GRADE For support in teaching the Grammar and Style Lesson to tenth graders, use **Writing and Grammar,** Platinum Level, Chapter 20, Section 1.

Integrate Language Skills

❶ Vocabulary Development Lesson

Word Analysis: Anglo-Saxon Prefix *fore-*

The prefix *fore-*, as in *foretaste*, means "before in time, place, order, or rank." Add the prefix *fore-* to each of the words below. Then, write a definition for each new word.

1. word 2. sight 3. runner

Spelling Strategy

When *i* and *e* spell the long *e* sound, the letters usually appear as *ie*, as in *siege*. For each sentence below, write the correct spelling of the underlined word.

1. The Arab did not feel any greef.
2. Balducci stayed for a breef time.
3. Balducci wanted Daru to releeve him.
4. The Arab was not a theef.
5. Daru did not acheeve peace.

Fluency: Sentence Completion

Review the vocabulary list on page 1223. Then, complete the sentences below with words from the list.

1. As the battle neared, the village __?__ its forces.
2. The house overlooked a vast __?__.
3. The clash between Daru and the officer gave a __?__ of conflicts to come.
4. With little work, he had time for __?__.
5. The criminal feared that his friend would __?__ him.
6. He had enough food to survive a __?__.
7. He had never befriended his neighbor or __?__ with him.
8. Because he distrusted the prisoner, he kept a __?__ eye on him all night.

❷ Grammar and Style Lesson

Prepositional Phrases as Adjectives and Adverbs

A **prepositional phrase** is a group of words made up of a preposition and a noun or pronoun. When a prepositional phrase modifies a noun or pronoun, it is called an adjective phrase; when it modifies a verb, adjective, or adverb, it is called an adverb phrase.

Adverb: Snow had suddenly fallen . . . after eight months. (modifies *fallen*)

Adjective: It had disappeared under a layer of dirty white snow. (modifies *layer*)

Practice Identify the prepositional phrase in each sentence below, note the word it modifies, and state whether it is an adjective or adverb phrase.

1. The prisoner walked along the trail.
2. Daru studied the man with the jellaba.
3. With quick movements, Daru served tea.
4. Balducci said goodbye in a hurt tone.
5. The Arabs from the village were angry.

Writing Application Write a paragraph describing Daru's home. Identify adjective phrases and adverb phrases, circling the word each phrase modifies.

WG *Prentice Hall Writing and Grammar Connection: Diamond Level, Chapter 9, Section 1*

TEACHING RESOURCES

The following resources can be used to enrich or extend the instruction for pp. 1240–1241.

Vocabulary

- **Selection Support:** Build Vocabulary, p. 229 ■
- **Vocabulary and Spelling Practice Book** (Use this booklet for skills instruction.)

Grammar

- **Selection Support:** Grammar and Style, p. 230
- **Writing and Grammar,** Diamond Level, p. 440
- **Daily Language Practice Transparencies** ■

Writing

- **Performance Assess. and Portfolio Mgmt.,** p. 15
- **Writing and Grammar,** Diamond Level, p. 174
- **Writing and Grammar iText CD-ROM**

Listening and Speaking

- **Performance Assess. and Portfolio Mgmt.,** p. 28

■ **BLOCK SCHEDULING:** Resources marked with this symbol provide varied instruction during 90-minute blocks.

❸ Writing Lesson

Essay Evaluating Fiction as an Expression of Philosophy

Although Camus refused the label of Existentialist, his work has often been read as an expression of that philosophy. Write an essay in which you discuss the ways in which Daru's situation, thoughts, and actions in "The Guest" do or do not reflect an Existentialist stance.

Prewriting Scan the story for details describing Daru's circumstances, actions, thoughts, and statements. Use a chart like the one shown to analyze how each detail does or does not reflect Existentialist views.

Model: Using a Chart to Compare Fiction to Philosophy

Details		Existentialist Ideas
Daru's Situation: Daru is isolated and alone.	→	Human beings are alone in an indifferent universe.
Daru's Thoughts:	→	
Daru's Actions:	→	

Drafting Choose point-by-point or block organization for your essay. With the former, introduce each detail and discuss it in relationship to Existentialism. With the latter, discuss all the details that reflect Existentialist ideas. Then, discuss all of those that do not.

Revising As you reread your draft, underline your main ideas. If a paragraph lacks a clear main idea, add one or combine it with another paragraph. If a paragraph has more than one main idea, create two paragraphs.

WG Prentice Hall Writing and Grammar Connection: Diamond Level, Chapter 9, Section 2

❹ Extension Activities

Listening and Speaking With a small group, adapt and perform "The Guest" as a **play.** Use these tips to prepare:

- Reread the story, listing details about the characters.
- Write roles for the three characters, a narrator, and a director.
- Include stage directions.

Rehearse the play and then perform it for the class. **[Group Activity]**

Research and Technology Conduct research on the Internet to learn about the history of Algeria. Then, create a **timeline** that identifies important events and people. Include a notation identifying Camus's birth and the probable time during which the events in this story took place.

Take It to the Net PHSchool.com

Go online for an additional research activity using the Internet.

ASSESSMENT RESOURCES

The following resources can be used to assess students' knowledge and skills.

Selection Assessment

- **Formal Assessment,** pp. 204–206
- **Open-Book Tests,** pp. 172–174
- **Test Bank Software**

Take It to the Net

Visit PHSchool.com for self-tests on the selection.

Writing Rubric

- **Performance Assess. and Portfolio Mgmt.,** p. 15

Listening and Speaking Rubric

- **Performance Assess. and Portfolio Mgmt.,** p. 28

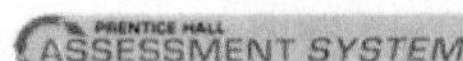

For additional diagnostics and remediation for skills covered in this grouping, use materials from the Prentice Hall Assessment System.

❸ Writing Lesson

- Tell students that in their evaluative essays, they will use evidence to support a view. In this case, they will evaluate whether Camus's story "The Guest" expresses an Existentialist attitude.
- Tell students that a good essay has an introduction that makes a strong statement of the writer's position. The introduction is followed by the body of the essay and a conclusion. Each part of the essay is connected to and supports the others.
- Point out that the body of the essay uses details to support the theme, or main point, of the essay. Tell students that using a chart is one way to organize their thoughts and keep the essay coherent.
- Adapt the Exposition: Comparison-and-Contrast Composition rubric in **Performance Assessment and Portfolio Management,** p. 15, to evaluate students' work.

10TH GRADE For support in working through the Writing Lesson with tenth graders, use **Writing and Grammar,** Platinum Level, Chapter 9, Section 2.

❹ Listening and Speaking

- Organize students into small groups, and have them follow the tips as they prepare their presentations.
- Allow time for students to rehearse before presenting their plays to the class.
- Use the Speaking: Delivering a Narrative Presentation rubric in **Performance Assessment and Portfolio Management,** p. 28, to evaluate students' work.

CUSTOMIZE INSTRUCTION
For Universal Access

To address different learning styles, use the following activities suggested in the **Extension Activities** booklet, p. 58:

- For Musical/Rhythmic Learners, use Activity 5.
- For Verbal/Linguistic Learners, use Activity 6.
- For Intrapersonal Learners, use Activity 7.

Folding Chairs • Food for Prophets • The Garden of Stubborn Cats

Lesson Objectives

1. **To analyze and respond to literary elements**
   - Literary Analysis: Symbolism
   - Comparing Literary Works: Theme
2. **To read, comprehend, analyze, and critique a poem**
   - Reading Strategy: Recognizing Symbols
   - Reading Check Questions
   - Review and Assess Questions
   - Assessment Practice (ATE)
3. **To develop word analysis skills, fluency, and systematic vocabulary**
   - Vocabulary Development Lesson: Latin Prefix *e-*
4. **To understand and apply written and oral language conventions**
   - Spelling Strategy
   - Grammar and Style Lesson: Usage: *lay* and *lie*
5. **To understand and apply appropriate writing and research strategies**
   - Writing Lesson: Location Scout's Report
   - Extension Activity: Visual Display
6. **To understand and apply listening and speaking strategies**
   - Extension Activity: Debate on Urban Development

STEP-BY-STEP TEACHING GUIDE	PACING GUIDE
PRETEACH	
Motivate Students and Provide Background	
Use the Motivation activity (ATE p. 1242)	5 min.
Read and discuss author and background features (SE pp. 1242, 1244, 1245, 1246; ATE p. 1242) A	5 min.
Introduce the Concepts	
Introduce the Literary Analysis and Reading Strategy concepts (SE/ATE p. 1243) A	15 min.
Pronounce the vocabulary words and read their definitions (SE p. 1243)	5 min.
TEACH	
Monitor Comprehension	
Informally monitor comprehension by circulating while students read independently or in groups A	45 min.
Monitor students' comprehension with the Reading Check notes (SE/ATE pp. 1247, 1249, 1251, 1253)	as students read
Develop vocabulary with the Vocabulary notes (SE pp. 1244, 1247, 1248; ATE p. 1244)	as students read
Develop Understanding	
Develop students' understanding of symbolism with the Literary Analysis annotations (SE/ATE pp. 1244, 1248, 1250, 1253) A	10 min.
Develop students' ability to recognize symbols, using the Reading Strategy annotations (SE/ATE pp. 1245, 1248, 1253)	10 min.
ASSESS	
Assess Mastery	
Assess students' mastery of the Reading Strategy and Literary Analysis concepts by having them answer the Review and Assess questions (SE/ATE p. 1255)	20 min.
Use one or more of the print, software, or transparency Assessment Resources (ATE p. 1257) A	up to 45 min.
EXTEND	
Apply Understanding	
Have students complete the Vocabulary Development Lesson and the Grammar and Style Lesson (SE p. 1256) A	20 min.
Apply students' ability to gather details, using the Writing Lesson (SE/ATE p. 1257) A	45 min.
Apply students' understanding of the selections, using one or more of the Extension Activities (SE p. 1257)	20–90 min.

ACCELERATED INSTRUCTION: Use the strategies and activities identified with an A.

10TH GRADE **TEACHING TENTH-GRADE STUDENTS** For support in teaching the selection(s) to tenth-grade students, see the Step-by-Step Teaching notes identified with the icon shown here.

UNIVERSAL ACCESS
● = Below-Level Students
▲ = On-Level Students
■ = Above-Level Students

Time and Resource Manager

Reading Level: Average, Average, Average
Average Number of Instructional Days: 3

RESOURCES		
PRINT	**TRANSPARENCIES**	**TECHNOLOGY**
• **Beyond Literature,** Community Connection: Considering Social Costs and Benefits of Technology, p. 59 ▲ ■		
• **Selection Support Workbook:** ● ▲ ■ Literary Analysis, p. 236 Reading Strategy, p. 235 Build Vocabulary, p. 233	• **Literary Analysis and Reading Transparencies,** pp. 117 and 118 ● ▲ ■	
		• **Listening to Literature** ● ▲ ■ Audiocassettes Audio CDs
• **Literary Analysis for Enrichment,** p. 59 ■		
• **Formal Assessment:** Selection Test, pp. 207–209 ● ▲ ■ • **Open-Book Tests,** pp. 175–177 ● ▲ ■ • **Performance Assessment and Portfolio Management,** pp. 19, 30 ● ▲ ■ • PRENTICE HALL ASSESSMENT SYSTEM ● ▲ ■	• PRENTICE HALL ASSESSMENT SYSTEM ● ▲ ■ **Skills Practice Answers and Explanations on Transparencies**	• **Test Bank Software** ● ▲ ■
• **Selection Support Workbook:** ● ▲ ■ Grammar and Style, p. 234 • **Writing and Grammar,** Diamond Level ● ▲ ■ • **Extension Activities,** p. 59 ● ▲ ■	• **Daily Language Practice Transparencies** ● ▲	• **Writing and Grammar iText CD-ROM** ● ▲ ■ ***Take It to the Net*** PHSchool.com

BLOCK SCHEDULING: Use one 90-minute class period to preteach the selection(s) and have students read them. Use a second 90-minute class period to assess students' mastery of skills and have them complete one of the Extension Activities.

PRETEACH

Step-by-Step Teaching Guide for pp. 1242–1243

Motivation

Ask students to describe a typical day in the life of someone living fifty years from now. What changes will result from technological developments? For example, what kinds of gadgets would be available for preparing breakfast, and what kind of transportation would the person take to work? Ask students to name other changes they expect to occur within the next fifty years, especially to the family structure. Then, tell them that the poems and story in this grouping explore the nature of change and the consequences of technology and urbanization.

1 Background

About the Authors

Although Günter Grass is more widely known as a novelist, his poetry has been well received. His early poetry exhibits a playfulness and exuberance that he later abandons in his examination of moral and political issues.

Neorealism was a major literary and cinematic movement in postwar Italy. Out of it came a number of filmmakers and first-rate writers, including Italo Calvino. Yet, even in Calvino's first Neorealistic novel, *The Path to the Nest of Spiders*, his fascination with fantasy was already present. Although Calvino was one of the best writers to come out of World War II Italy, his reputation was slow to grow outside that country. In time, however, he achieved international fame.

Geography Note

Draw students' attention to the map on this page. Explain that both Grass and Calvino grew up in Europe during World War II and were fundamentally affected by their experiences with that devastating conflict.

Prepare to Read

1 Folding Chairs ◆ Food for Prophets ◆ The Garden of Stubborn Cats

Günter Grass (b. 1927)

Günter Grass (gün′ tər gräs) survived the most problematic period in modern German history, the era of Adolf Hitler's dictatorship (1933–1945). Grass's experience of that nightmare period—and the lessons he drew from it—are at the heart of his writing and political activities. Today, Grass is viewed as the foremost voice of postwar German literature.

Facing Horror Grass was born in Danzig, now the Polish city of Gdansk (g′ dänsk′), where the first shots of World War II were fired. At sixteen, Grass was drafted. Later, he witnessed the horrors of the German concentration camp at Dachau, an experience that led him to reject Nazism.

Released from service in the spring of 1946, Grass pursued his interest in the arts. He apprenticed as a stonemason and then studied sculpting and graphics at the Düsseldorf Academy of Art. In the evenings, he worked as a jazz drummer.

A Triumph In 1954, after moving to Berlin, Grass married Anna Schwarz, a Swiss dancer. Anna encouraged Grass's writing, submitting some of his poems to a radio competition. Grass began publishing his poems, plays, and essays and started work on a novel. The result was his renowned work *The Tin Drum*, a survey of the Nazi era that mixes fairy tale, fantasy, and realism. The novel won Grass much praise and a number of literary prizes.

Facing the Future During the Cold War, when Germany was divided into two antagonistic countries, Grass organized meetings of writers from East Germany and West Germany and spoke out for peace. He has said that the one reliable ally literature has is the future, and both his writings and political activities reflect his faith in human possibility. In 1999, Grass's literary achievements earned him the Nobel Prize in Literature.

Italo Calvino (1923–1985)

The parents of Italo Calvino (ē′ täl ō kal vē′ nō′) were botanists, but although they had hoped he would become a scientist, Calvino said that he was "attracted to another kind of vegetation, that of the written word." Like a good botanist, Calvino spent time collecting "specimens": He edited a famous collection of Italian folk tales. It is his own novels and stories, however, that have earned him a reputation as one of Italy's most inventive writers.

Fighting Fascism Born in Cuba, Calvino grew up on the Italian Riviera at San Remo, where his father was curator of the botanical gardens. During World War II, Calvino fought in a partisan movement against Fascist control of Italy. His experience as a partisan was the basis for his first novel, *The Path to the Nest of Spiders* (1947). The war was also an inspiration for his short-story collections *Adam, One Afternoon, and Other Stories* (1949).

At the end of the war, Calvino studied literature in Turin. After graduating, he joined Einaudi, a publishing venture begun by Cesare Pavese, who shared literary and leftist political ideas with Calvino.

A New Vision While many postwar Italian writers worked within a harsh vision of society known as Neorealism, Calvino's work from the 1950s on is notable for its fairy-tale qualities. He believed that the pattern of the fable is the formula for all stories. Like heroes of fairy tales, lost in an enchanted wood, Calvino's characters face a mysterious, challenging environment. In Calvino's stories, however, a modern city often replaces an enchanted wood as the setting. Mixing imagination and humor with philosophy and science, Calvino has created true modern fairy tales.

TEACHING RESOURCES

The following resources can be used to enrich or extend the instruction for pp. 1242–1243.

Background

Beyond Literature, p. 59

Take It to the Net

Visit PHSchool.com for background about the authors.

Literary Anaylsis

Literary Analysis and Reading Transparencies, Symbolism, p. 117

Selection Support: Literary Analysis, p. 236

Reading

Literary Analysis and Reading Transparencies, Recognizing Symbols, p. 118

BLOCK SCHEDULING: Resources marked with this symbol provide varied instruction during 90-minute blocks.

Preview

Connecting to the Literature

The walls of a home hold warmth and memories in; they keep out rain and the feeling of being a stranger. These writers consider what it means to be "inside"—to feel at home—and whether even a city needs an "outside"—a place beyond human rules.

2 Literary Analysis

Symbolism

Symbolism is the use of concrete images that stand for abstract meanings. An image may be given symbolic meaning in a number of ways:

- The meaning may be evoked by emphasizing ordinary associations. For example, a folding chair is meant to be moved from place to place. In "Folding Chairs," Grass emphasizes this association. He employs images of folding chairs to symbolize the lack of a true home.
- Symbolic meaning may be evoked through the traditional associations of an image. For example, the locusts in "Food for Prophets" recall a biblical story: a plague of locusts sent as divine punishment.

As you read the selections, identify and interpret images used symbolically.

Comparing Literary Works

Symbolism is one device that writers use to express a theme. The **theme** of a work is the message it sends or the question it poses. In "Folding Chairs," Grass's title image symbolizes impermanence—the theme of the poem.

As you read, notice the ways the writers use symbols to probe themes.

3 Reading Strategy

Recognizing Symbols

To **recognize symbols,** look for characters, places, or objects that are

- emphasized by repeated appearances or vivid descriptions.
- rich in common associations that suggest a theme (for instance, Calvino's cats call up associations with nature's mysterious side).

Use a chart like the one shown to interpret symbols as you read.

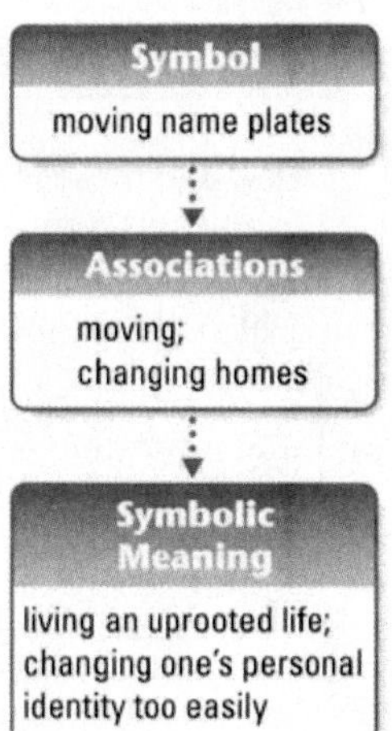

Vocabulary Development

emigrate (em´ i grāt´) *v.* leave one place to live in another (p. 1244)

laden (lād´ 'n) *adj.* carrying a heavy load (p. 1244)

environs (en vī´ rənz) *n.* surrounding area; vicinity (p. 1247)

convergent (kən vʉr´ jənt) *adj.* coming together at a point (p. 1248)

squalid (skwäl´ id) *adj.* foul, especially as the result of neglect; wretched (p. 1248)

altruistic (al´ troo is´ tik) *adj.* motivated by unselfish concern for the welfare of others (p. 1248)

CUSTOMIZE INSTRUCTION FOR UNIVERSAL ACCESS

For Less Proficient Readers	For English Learners	For Advanced Readers
Discuss the kinds of symbols students see every day in print or television advertising. Begin by discussing what the names of cars mean and what they symbolize. Challenge students to make their own lists of symbols using names of cars.	Symbols may vary from culture to culture. Review the symbols in the Symbolism transparency in **Literary Analysis and Reading Transparencies,** p. 117. Ask students whether these symbols are familiar and, if they are not, have students suggest symbols with similar meanings.	Have students work in pairs to create an original symbol, as Günter Grass does in "Folding Chairs." Encourage students to be creative and thoughtful in their choices. Review symbols such as the rose for youth and beauty or the moon for lunacy. Invite volunteers to explain their symbols to the class.

2 Literary Analysis

Symbolism

- Introduce students to symbolism—the use of a concrete object to stand for abstract meaning—and tell them that they will focus on the use of symbols in these selections.
- Read the Literary Analysis instruction aloud to students. Give some examples of familiar symbols, such as a red light for "stop" and a dove for "peace." Discuss with students how each symbol evokes abstract meaning.
- Explain that some symbols have several meanings. For example, rain can symbolize cleansing or death. Tell students to consider the context of an object that they find symbolic before making conclusions about its abstract meaning.

3 Reading Strategy

Recognizing Symbols

- Tell students that symbols help a writer convey ideas more fully by tapping into the reader's body of knowledge. For example, if readers link the image of a heart to the idea of love, authors can insert a heart into a story and suggest a role for love—all without expressly stating the link between the image and its meaning.
- Draw students' attention to the graphic organizer on p. 1243. Explain how identifying associations can help students understand the larger symbolic meanings of characters, places, or objects.
- Use the Recognizing Symbols transparency in **Literary Analysis and Reading Transparencies,** p. 118, to demonstrate for students how to recognize symbols.

Vocabulary Development

- Pronounce each vocabulary word for students, and read the definitions as a class. Have students identify any words with which they are already familiar.

E-Teach

Visit e-Teach at PHSchool.com for teachers' essays on how to teach, with questions and answers.

TEACH

Step-by-Step Teaching Guide for pp. 1244–1254

Teaching Tenth-Grade Students

10TH GRADE Have students memorize Grass's poetry to gain insights into it. Then, ask students to recite the poems aloud.

1 About the Selection

In this spare, but moving, poem, Günter Grass explores change as a consequence of modern society. He suggests that our fast-paced lives require adaptability. Here, folding chairs become symbols of impermanence.

2 Background

Art

***Chairs of Paris,* by André Kertész**

The Hungarian artist André Kertész (1894–1973) was a well-known pioneer of photography. Kertész often photographed familiar objects—such as the park chairs in this photograph—in unusual ways.

Use the following question for discussion:

Do you think Kertész's photograph expresses the same idea Grass does in this poem? Explain.
Possible response: Yes; both depict impermanence.

3 Literary Analysis

Symbolism

- Read lines 5–8 aloud, and discuss the uses of folding chairs.
- Ask the Literary Analysis question on p. 1244: What associations with folding chairs does Grass introduce in lines 5–8?
  Answer: Grass introduces associations with departure and emigration.

4 Vocabulary Development

Latin Prefix *e-*

- Call attention to the word *emigrate* and its definition. Tell students that the Latin prefix *e-* means "away from" or "out of."
- Ask students to suggest and define words beginning with the prefix *e-*.
  Possible response: Some words are *evict, efface, erase,* and *eject.*

Chairs of Paris, 1927, André Kertész

Folding Chairs

Günter Grass

translated by
Michael Hamburger

Background

During World War II, many Jews fled Nazi persecution in Germany, emigrating to other nations. The end of the war flooded Europe with an estimated 21 million refugees, including former prisoners of war. Millions left the devastated cities of Europe to search for a new life. In "Folding Chairs," Grass may be reflecting on this massive uprooting of Europeans.

How sad these changes are.
People unscrew the name plates from the doors,
take the saucepan of cabbage
and heat it up again, in a different place.

What sort of furniture is this
that advertises departure?
People take up their folding chairs
and emigrate.

Ships laden with homesickness and the urge to vomit
carry patented seating contraptions
and unpatented owners
to and fro.

Now on both sides of the great ocean
there are folding chairs;
how sad these changes are.

Literary Analysis
Symbolism What associations with folding chairs does Grass introduce in lines 5–8?

emigrate (em′ i grāt′) *v.* leave one place to live in another

laden (lād′ ′n) *adj.* carrying a heavy load

TEACHING RESOURCES

The following resources can be used to enrich or extend the instruction for pp. 1244–1254.

Literary Analysis

- **Selection Support:** Literary Analysis, p. 1236
- **Literary Analysis and Reading Transparencies,** Symbolism, p. 117

Reading

- **Selection Support:** Reading Strategy, p. 235; Build Vocabulary, p. 233 ■
- **Listening to Literature Audiocassettes**
- **Listening to Literature Audio CDs** ■

■ **BLOCK SCHEDULING:** Resources marked with this symbol provide varied instruction during 90-minute blocks.

5 # Food for Prophets

Günter Grass

translated by Anselm Hollo

Background

6 Grass adds authority and symbolic resonance to this poem by referring to two well-known biblical images. *Prophets* are religious leaders of Israel who are gifted with visions and healing powers. *Locusts* are grasshopperlike insects that emerge periodically in swarms, devastating crops.

When the locusts occupied our town,
7 | no milk came to the door, the dailies suffocated,
our jails were opened to release
all prophets.
They streamed through the streets,
3800 prophets,
talking and teaching without restriction,
and eating their fill of that gray
& jumpy mess
we called the plague.
So everything was fine and up to expectations.

Soon our milk came again; our papers reappeared;
and prophets filled our jails.

Reading Strategy
Recognizing Symbols Which two routines does Grass use to represent ordinary life?

Review and Assess

Thinking About the Selections

1. **Respond:** Do you agree that changing homes is sad? Explain.
2. **(a) Recall:** In line 6 of "Folding Chairs," what do folding chairs "advertise"? **(b) Analyze:** Why does the idea of portable furniture contradict some of our associations with home?
3. **Interpret:** In what sense are there now folding chairs "on both sides of the great ocean"?
4. **(a) Recall:** In "Food for Prophets," who is released from jail when the plague occurs? **(b) Hypothesize:** Why are these people released?
5. **(a) Recall:** Who is put in jail at the end of "Food for Prophets"? **(b) Draw Conclusions:** What contrast does the poem suggest between society in crisis and society in ordinary times?

CUSTOMIZE INSTRUCTION FOR UNIVERSAL ACCESS

For Less Proficient Readers	For English Learners	For Advanced Readers
Tell students that in biblical times, prophets were often the proponents of social change and were viewed as God's messengers. Have students write about a social change they would like to see occur. Invite volunteers to share their work with the class.	Use "Folding Chairs" to discuss the ideas of change and emigration. Ask students to write about a family member or friend who immigrated to another country and to describe some of the changes the person experienced. Invite volunteers to share their writing with the class.	Challenge students to consider the themes of change and impermanence in other works. Direct them to Catullus' poetry, p. 508, and de Ronsard's poetry, p. 678, both of which address these themes. Then, have students write journal entries about impermanence in their own lives and how they adapt to it.

5 About the Selection

In "Food for Prophets," Grass examines symbols from the Hebrew Bible. Locusts descend on a town, and the "prophets" are released from prison to preach freely.

6 Background

Locusts

Members of the grasshopper family, locusts migrate only occasionally. Following an enormous buildup of population, the locusts travel to feed on vegetation. Locust swarms are so dense that they actually blacken the sky. In the United States between 1874 and 1877, the Great Plains region was hit by locusts, wiping out billions of dollars worth of crops. A single swarm contained an estimated 124 billion insects.

7 Reading Strategy

Recognizing Symbols

- Read the bracketed line aloud. Explain that it was once common for milk to be delivered to homes each morning and that the "dailies" refers to newspapers left on people's doorsteps each day.
- Then, ask students the Reading Strategy question on p. 1245: Which two routines does Grass use to represent ordinary life?
Answer: Retrieving the milk and newspaper represent ordinary life.

Answers for p. 1245

Review and Assess

1. Possible response: Changing homes could be sad but also exciting.
2. **(a)** The chairs advertise departure. **(b)** Possible response: Home is a place of permanence, but folding chairs are temporary.
3. People emigrated from Europe while others came to Europe from other countries.
4. **(a)** Prophets are released. **(b)** Possible response: They are released as a result of the locust invasion, perhaps to remedy it.
5. **(a)** The prophets are put in jail. **(b)** Possible response: A society in crisis allows dissident views, but when order returns, such views are seen as dangerous.

Teaching Tenth-Grade Students

10TH GRADE Have students discuss their impressions of cats. What is the typical behavior of cats? Some students might share details peculiar to their own cats.

8 About the Selection

In this story, Marcovaldo, an Italian worker, becomes aware of cats and their pathways through a city. He discovers an old villa where the cats congregate and resist the efforts of construction workers to build a new structure. For Calvino, the cats symbolize nature's mysterious, persistent presence even in a busy city. They also symbolize nature's resistance to human aims and designs.

9 ▶ Critical Viewing

Possible response: The story will show that the cats' wildness lives side by side with architectural orderliness but is never changed by it.

10 Background

Urban Change

Point out to students that this description of urban change could easily apply to any Italian city because the country witnessed an amazing urban building boom after it recovered from World War II. For that reason, although the specific city described in the story is never named, it could easily be Turin, Calvino's adopted city.

8 The Garden of Stubborn Cats

Italo Calvino

translated by William Weaver

9 ▲ Critical Viewing On the basis of this image, predict how the story will contrast the wildness of cats with architectural orderliness. **[Predict]**

Background

10 The worldwide rebuilding that took place after World War II led to two parallel trends: modernization and urbanization. Bombed-out buildings were replaced using new technologies. In cities once dominated by stone buildings from the Middle Ages, concrete and steel office buildings bloomed. Advances in engineering led to higher and higher skyscrapers. At the same time, people flooded urban areas in search of employment. In this selection, Calvino looks at one side effect of this urban boom—the crowding out of wild spaces in which nature might lead its own life.

The city of cats and the city of men exist one inside the other, but they are not the same city. Few cats recall the time when there was no distinction: the streets and squares of men were also streets and squares of cats, and the lawns, courtyards, balconies, and fountains: you lived in a broad and various space. But for several generations now domestic felines have been prisoners of an uninhabitable city: the streets are uninterruptedly overrun by the mortal traffic of cat-crushing automobiles; in every square foot of terrain where once a garden extended or a vacant lot or the ruins of an old demolition, now condominiums loom up, welfare housing, brand-new skyscrapers; every entrance is crammed with parked cars; the courtyards, one by one, have been roofed by reinforced concrete and transformed into garages or movie houses or storerooms or workshops. And where a rolling plateau of low roofs once extended, copings, terraces, water tanks, balconies, skylights, corrugated-iron sheds, now one general

ENRICHMENT: Social Studies Connection

Urbanization

During times of widespread building, such as after World War II, there is intense pressure to allow development and urbanization. The situation in the story reflects the consequences of allowing developers to build wherever they wish, with no regard for the environmental impact of their construction. For example, after an area is developed commercially, more and more land surrounding that location has to accommodate the commercial center. The people who work in the office buildings and skyscrapers desire houses or apartments in which to live close to work. In turn, those people must have access to grocery and clothes shopping and recreational facilities. Ask students to discuss other ways in which urbanization places demands on the land and interferes with the natural habitat.

superstructure rises wherever structures can rise; the intermediate differences in height, between the low ground of the street and the supernal[1] heaven of the penthouses, disappear; the cat of a recent litter seeks in vain the itinerary[2] of its fathers, the point from which to make the soft leap from balustrade to cornice to drainpipe, or for the quick climb on the roof-tiles.

12 But in this vertical city, in this compressed city where all voids tend to fill up and every block of cement tends to mingle with other blocks of cement, a kind of counter-city opens, a negative city, that consists of empty slices between wall and wall, of the minimal distances ordained by the building regulations between two constructions, between the rear of one construction and the rear of the next; it is a city of cavities, wells, air conduits, driveways, inner yards, accesses to basements, like a network of dry canals on a planet of stucco and tar, and it is through this network, grazing the walls, that the ancient cat population still scurries.

On occasion, to pass the time, Marcovaldo would follow a cat. It was during the work-break, between noon and three, when all the personnel except Marcovaldo went home to eat, and he—who brought his lunch in his bag—laid his place among the packing-cases in the warehouse, chewed his snack, smoked a half-cigar, and wandered around, alone and idle, waiting for work to resume. In those hours, a cat that peeped in at a window was always welcome company, and a guide for new explorations. He had made friends with a tabby, well fed, a blue ribbon around its neck, surely living with some well-to-do family. This tabby shared with Marcovaldo the habit of an afternoon stroll right after lunch; and naturally a friendship sprang up.

Following his tabby friend, Marcovaldo had started looking at places as if through the round eyes of a cat and even if these places were the usual environs of his firm he saw them in a different light, as settings for cattish stories, with connections practicable only by light, velvety paws. Though from the outside the neighborhood seemed poor in cats, every day on his rounds Marcovaldo made the acquaintance of some new face, and a miau, a hiss, a stiffening of fur on an arched back was enough for him to sense ties and intrigues and rivalries among them. At those moments he thought he had already penetrated the secrecy of the felines' society: and then he felt himself scrutinized by pupils that became slits, under the surveillance of the antennae of taut whiskers,

1. **supernal** (sə purn′ əl) *adj.* celestial or divine.
2. **itinerary** (ī tin′ ər er′ ē) *n.* route.

11 

in context Design Connection

Traditional Architecture

Traditional architectural features are at risk in modern cities, although some survive. Calvino uses terms for a few such features:

- **balustrade** railing supported by small ornamental posts
- **belvedere** open, roofed gallery in an upper story, opening onto a view
- **capitals** tops of columns
- **copings** top layers of a stone or brick wall, sloped to carry off water
- **cornice** horizontal molding projecting from the top of a wall or building; overhanging part of a roof
- **transom** small window or shutter over a door or window

environs (en vī′ rənz) *n.* surrounding area; vicinity

13  Reading Check

What does Marcovaldo do on his lunchbreak?

11 Background

Traditional Architecture

Because many European cities are centuries old, often dating to Roman times, they incorporate architecture from many time periods. Much of the "traditional architecture" in these cities has classical roots, meaning that it either dates from classical Roman or Greek times or that it is inspired by these styles. Both original classical buildings and their later derivatives often incorporated architectural features such as the balustrade, capital, and transom.

Capitals, for example, were used in ancient Egyptian and Mesopotamian culture and then widely used by the Greeks. Transoms appeared frequently during the Renaissance, when windows were proportioned along classical dimensions, with a single transom division. This division allowed smaller parts of the window to be opened for air.

12 Critical Thinking

Analyze

- Read aloud the bracketed passage.
- Draw students' attention to the line in which Calvino describes the city as a "negative city." Ask: What does Calvino mean by "negative city"?
  Possible response: The "negative city" is characterized by empty spaces and cavities; it paradoxically exists through an absence of concrete structures.

13 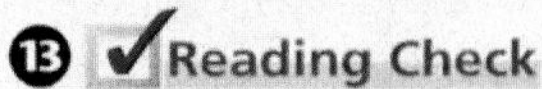

Answer: Marcovaldo follows a cat.

CUSTOMIZE INSTRUCTION FOR UNIVERSAL ACCESS

For Special Needs Students	For Less Proficient Readers	For English Learners
Encourage students to visualize the setting in the "city of men" to understand the story. Have students close their eyes as you read the opening paragraphs aloud. Point out details such as heavy traffic and apartment buildings and skyscrapers without grass or gardens.	Clarify the story's beginning for students. For example, explain that Marcovaldo has three hours off for lunch. Point out that in Italy, it is customary to take a long break at midday. Marcovaldo uses his time to follow a cat. Then, read aloud the last two paragraphs on p. 1247.	Explain sound words to students. For example, the words *miau* and *hiss* reflect sounds that the cats make. These sounds are made by cats everywhere but are described differently by speakers of different languages. Ask students how these words sound and are spelled in other languages they know.

14 Reading Strategy

Recognizing Symbols

- Tell students that references to elements from history or to common visual elements may be clues that the author is using a symbol.
- Remind students that these references draw upon the reader's existing associations. For example, describing a cat as a sphinx refers to ancient Egyptian sphinxes, which were part lion and part human. This reference suggests that the cats might possess human or mythical qualities.
- Read aloud the bracketed passage.
- Then, ask students the Reading Strategy question on p. 1248: What words in Calvino's description of the cats suggest that the animals have symbolic meaning?
  Answer: Calvino's use of *triangles* and *sphinxes*, and his use of the terms *realm, territories, ceremonies,* and *customs* suggest that the animals have symbolic meaning.
- Ask: How does using these shapes to describe the cats make them seem more symbolic than real?
  Answer: Because the cats are described as composites of shapes, they all seem to look alike. This similarity makes them seem to be symbolic cats rather than individual animals.

15 Literary Analysis

Symbolism

- Have students read the bracketed passage independently, paying particular attention to the descriptive language.
- Invite volunteers to paraphrase or summarize Calvino's description of the restaurant.
  Answer: Calvino describes the restaurant as elaborate, chaotic, and upside-down.
- Recall with students the context of postwar urbanization that provides the story's setting. Then, ask students the Literary Analysis question on p. 1248: Based on this description, what might the Biarritz Restaurant symbolize?
  Possible response: The restaurant might symbolize postwar Europe.

14 and all the cats around him sat impassive as sphinxes, the pink triangles of their noses convergent on the black triangles of their lips, and the only things that moved were the tips of the ears, with a vibrant jerk like radar. They reached the end of a narrow passage, between squalid blank walls; and, looking around, Marcovaldo saw that the cats that had led him this far had vanished, all of them together, no telling in which direction, even his tabby friend, and they had left him alone. Their realm had territories, ceremonies, customs that it was not yet granted to him to discover.

On the other hand, from the cat city there opened unsuspected peepholes onto the city of men: and one day the same tabby led him to discover the great Biarritz Restaurant.

15 Anyone wishing to see the Biarritz Restaurant had only to assume the posture of a cat, that is, proceed on all fours. Cat and man, in this fashion, walked around a kind of dome, at whose foot some low, rectangular little windows opened. Following the tabby's example, Marcovaldo looked down. They were transoms through which the luxurious hall received air and light. To the sound of gypsy violins, partridges and quails swirled by on silver dishes balanced by the white-gloved fingers of waiters in tailcoats. Or, more precisely, above the partridges and quails the dishes whirled, and above the dishes the white gloves, and poised on the waiters' patent-leather shoes, the gleaming parquet[3] floor, from which hung dwarf potted palms and tablecloths and crystal and buckets like bells with the champagne bottle for their clapper: everything was turned upside-down because Marcovaldo, for fear of being seen, wouldn't stick his head inside the window and confined himself to looking at the reversed reflection of the room in the tilted pane.

But it was not so much the windows of the dining-room as those of the kitchens that interested the cat: looking through the former you saw, distant and somehow transfigured, what in the kitchens presented itself—quite concrete and within paw's reach—as a plucked bird or a fresh fish. And it was toward the kitchens, in fact, that the tabby wanted to lead Marcovaldo, either through a gesture of altruistic friendship or else because it counted on the man's help for one of its raids. Marcovaldo, however, was reluctant to leave his belvedere over the main room: first as he was fascinated by the luxury of the place, and then because something down there had riveted his attention. To such an extent that, overcoming his fear of being seen, he kept peeking in, with his head in the transom.

In the midst of the room, directly under that pane, there was a little glass fish-tank, a kind of aquarium, where some fat trout were swimming. A special customer approached, a man with a shiny bald pate, black suit, black beard. An old waiter in tailcoat followed him, carrying a little net as if he were going to catch butterflies. The gentleman in black looked at the trout with a grave, intent air; then he raised one

convergent (kən vur′ jənt) *adj.* coming together at a point

Reading Strategy
Recognizing Symbols What words in Calvino's description of the cats suggest that the animals have symbolic meaning?

squalid (skwäl′ id) *adj.* foul, especially as the result of neglect; wretched

Literary Analysis
Symbolism Based on this description, what might the Biarritz Restaurant symbolize?

altruistic (al′ tro͞o is′ tik) *adj.* motivated by unselfish concern for the welfare of others

3. **parquet** (pär kā′) inlaid woodwork in geometric forms.

ENRICHMENT: Art Connection

Cats in Art

Italo Calvino's cats are among many that appear in the literary and visual arts. Because of their mysterious nature, their sensitivity to light and sound, and their skill as nighttime hunters, many cultures have credited cats with supernatural powers. The ancient Egyptians, for example, produced many statues of cats in honor of their cat-goddess, Bastet. Later, cats were associated with witches in European culture. Today, cats are sometimes depicted as cute, cuddly balls of fluff and sometimes as mysterious, predatory hunters.

One popular contemporary cat figure is *Garfield*, the cartoon cat created by Jim Davis. Although Davis has no cats himself—his wife is allergic—he has created an enormously beloved cat in Garfield. In fact, *Garfield* has become the most widely syndicated Sunday comic in the United States and has more than 220 million daily readers worldwide. In his images of Garfield, Davis presents a cat that has a strong, independent, dominating personality.

hand and with a slow, solemn gesture singled out a fish. The waiter dipped the net into the tank, pursued the appointed trout, captured it, headed for the kitchens, holding out in front of him, like a lance, the net in which the fish wriggled. The gentleman in black, solemn as a magistrate who has handed down a capital sentence, went to take his seat and wait for the return of the trout, sautéed "à la meunière."[4]

If I found a way to drop a line from up here and make one of those trout bite, Marcovaldo thought, I couldn't be accused of theft; at worst, of fishing in an unauthorized place. And ignoring the miaus that called him toward the kitchens, he went to collect his fishing tackle.

Nobody in the crowded dining-room of the Biarritz saw the long, fine line, armed with hook and bait, as it slowly dropped into the tank. The fish saw the bait, and flung themselves on it. In the fray one trout managed to bite the worm: and immediately it began to rise, rise, emerge from the water, a silvery flash, it darted up high, over the laid tables and the trolleys of hors d'oeuvres, over the blue flames of the crêpes Suzette,[5] until it vanished into the heavens of the transom.

16

Winter: Cat on a Cushion, Théophile-Alexandre Steinlen, The Metropolitan Museum of Art, New York

Marcovaldo had yanked the rod with the brisk snap of the expert fisherman, so the fish landed behind his back. The trout had barely touched the ground when the cat sprang. What little life the trout still had was lost between the tabby's teeth. Marcovaldo, who had abandoned his line at that moment to run and grab the fish, saw it snatched from under his nose, hook and all. He was quick to put one foot on the rod, but the snatch had been so strong that the rod was all the man had left, while the tabby ran off with the fish, pulling the line after it. Treacherous kitty! It had vanished.

But this time it wouldn't escape him: there was that long line trailing after him and showing the way he had taken. Though he had lost sight of the cat, Marcovaldo followed the end of the line: there it was, running along a wall; it climbed a parapet, wound through a doorway, was swallowed up by a basement . . . Marcovaldo, venturing into more and more cattish places, climbed roofs, straddled railings, always managed to catch a glimpse—perhaps only a second before it disappeared—of that moving trace that indicated the thief's path.

Now the line played out down a sidewalk, in the midst of the traffic, and Marcovaldo, running after it, almost managed to grab it. He flung himself down on his belly: there, he grabbed it! He managed to seize one end of the line before it slipped between the bars of a gate.

17 **▲ Critical Viewing**

Drawing on details in the painting, explain what it suggests about the nature of cats. **[Interpret]**

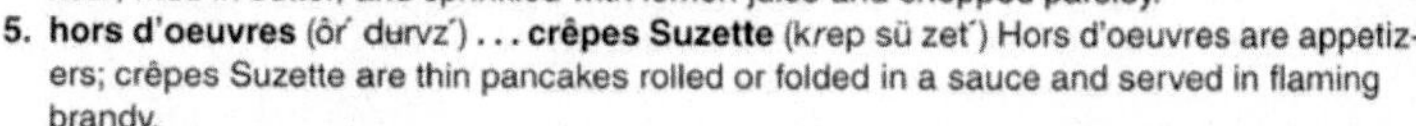

4. **sautéed "à la meunière"** (sō tād′ ä lä mə nyer′) describes fish prepared by being rolled in flour, fried in butter, and sprinkled with lemon juice and chopped parsley.
5. **hors d'oeuvres** (ôr′ durvz′) . . . **crêpes Suzette** (krep sü zet′) Hors d'oeuvres are appetizers; crêpes Suzette are thin pancakes rolled or folded in a sauce and served in flaming brandy.

18 **✔Reading Check**

How is Marcovaldo able to fish at the Biarritz Restaurant?

16 Background

Art

Winter: Cat on a Cushion, by Théophile-Alexandre Steinlen

Swiss-born Steinlen (1859–1923) came to France at the age of twenty. He made his career as a poster designer and political newspaper illustrator. Although many of his works carried important social commentary, Steinlen is best known for his images of cats. In this image, a cat lounges comfortably on a cushion, presumably to stay warm and cozy during the winter that the title references.

Use the following question for discussion:

How would you describe the expression on this cat's face?
Possible response: The cat stares inscrutably at viewers.

17 ▶Critical Viewing

Possible response: The painting suggests that cats like to keep warm and relax—this one is stretched out in comfort—and that they can be mysterious—this one gives away little with its expression.

18 ✔Reading Check

Answer: Marcovaldo is able to fish at the Biarritz because the restaurant has a holding tank from which patrons choose their fish for dinner. Marcovaldo lowers his line from the transom (in a window) into the tank.

CUSTOMIZE INSTRUCTION FOR UNIVERSAL ACCESS

For Less Proficient Readers	For English Learners	For Advanced Readers
Review the Reading Check question with students. Direct them to the final paragraph on p. 1248 and its continuation on p. 1249. Explain to students that it is common in an elegant Mediterranean restaurant for patrons to select their own seafood entrées from a tank before they are cooked.	Point out Marcovaldo's use of the word *theft* in describing his fishing activities. Clarify the situation for students—the fish are in a tank for patrons to view. Discuss with students whether they agree with Marcovaldo's reasoning that he cannot be accused of theft by hooking a trout from the tank.	Ask students whether they think the cat is being any more treacherous than Marcovaldo himself in stealing the fish. Challenge students to explain the criteria used in their moral reasoning. In other words, what, if anything, makes the theft acceptable or treacherous?

19 Literary Analysis

Symbolism and Theme

- Challenge students to identify the abstract ideas they think are symbolized by a garden and a city.
  Possible response: A garden symbolizes nature; a city symbolizes human activity.
- Have a volunteer read aloud the bracketed passage and describe the position of the garden and city.
  Answer: The city's skyscrapers rise all around the garden, which is in disrepair.
- Then, ask students the Literary Analysis question on p. 1250: What theme does the opposition between the garden and the modern city suggest?
  Answer: The opposition of the garden and the city suggests that the two are struggling against each other for supremacy and that the city, which surrounds the garden, is winning.

Reteach If students have difficulty answering the Literary Analysis question, review the instruction on theme found in the Comparing Literary Works section on p. 1243.

20 Critical Thinking

Speculate

- Have students read the bracketed passage.
- Then, ask: Whose yellow, skinny hands are depicted here?
  Answer: These hands are those of the villa's owner.
- Urge students to read p. 1251 to find out more about the Marchesa, who owns the villa.

Beyond a half-rusted gate and two bits of wall buried under climbing plants, there was a little rank[6] garden, with a small, abandoned-looking building at the far end of it. A carpet of dry leaves covered the path, and dry leaves lay everywhere under the boughs of the two plane-trees, forming actually some little mounds in the yard. A layer of leaves was yellowing in the green water of a pool. Enormous buildings rose all around, skyscrapers with thousands of windows, like so many eyes trained disapprovingly on that little square patch with two trees, a few tiles, and all those yellow leaves, surviving right in the middle of an area of great traffic.

And in this garden, perched on the capitals and balustrades, lying on the dry leaves of the flower-beds, climbing on the trunks of the trees or on the drainpipes, motionless on their four paws, their tails making a question-mark, seated to wash their faces, there were tiger cats, black cats, white cats, calico cats, tabbies, angoras, Persians, house cats and stray cats, perfumed cats and mangy cats. Marcovaldo realized he had finally reached the heart of the cats' realm, their secret island. And, in his emotion, he almost forgot his fish.

Literary Analysis
Symbolism and Theme What theme does the opposition between the garden and the modern city suggest?

It had remained, that fish, hanging by the line from the branch of a tree, out of reach of the cats' leaps; it must have dropped from its kidnapper's mouth at some clumsy movement, perhaps as it was defended from the others, or perhaps displayed as an extraordinary prize. The line had got tangled, and Marcovaldo, tug as he would, couldn't manage to yank it loose. A furious battle had meanwhile been joined among the cats, to reach that unreachable fish, or rather, to win the right to try and reach it. Each wanted to prevent the others from leaping: they hurled themselves on one another, they tangled in mid-air, they rolled around clutching each other, and finally a general war broke out in a whirl of dry, crackling leaves.

After many futile yanks, Marcovaldo now felt the line was free, but he took care not to pull it: the trout would have fallen right in the midst of that infuriated scrimmage of felines.

It was at this moment that, from the top of the walls of the gardens, a strange rain began to fall: fish-bones, heads, tails, even bits of lung and lights.[7] Immediately the cats' attention was distracted from the suspended trout and they flung themselves on the new delicacies. To Marcovaldo, this seemed the right moment to pull the line and regain his fish. But, before he had time to act, from a blind of the little villa, two yellow, skinny hands darted out: one was brandishing scissors; the other, a frying-pan. The hand with the scissors was raised above the trout, the hand with the frying-pan was thrust under it. The scissors cut the line, the trout fell into the pan; hands, scissors and pan withdrew, the blind closed: all in the space of a second. Marcovaldo was totally bewildered.

"Are you also a cat-lover?" A voice at his back made him turn round. He was surrounded by little old women, some of them ancient, wearing

6. **rank** (raŋk) *adj.* growing vigorously and coarsely.
7. **lights** term for animal organs used for catfood.

ENRICHMENT: Science Connection

Animal Shelters

Although many cats and dogs live on their own in both European and American cities, organizations are dedicated to matching these "wild" cats and dogs with owners or at least reducing their numbers. For example, the Society for the Prevention of Cruelty to Animals (SPCA) maintains animal shelters for abandoned pets, educates the public about pet ownership, and ensures the enforcement of laws protecting animals from cruel treatment. Other groups, such as the Feral Cat Coalition, focus on caring for cats like those described in Calvino's story. Statistics reveal a staggering number of feral cats because two breeding animals will breed exponentially, such that the offspring of the original pair could number 420,000 in just seven years. Many of these original breeders are the offspring of domestic cats or are abandoned domestic cats. Feral cats are often in ill health and suffer from lack of food and shelter. Although some can be matched with human companions, many are not suited for domestic life.

old-fashioned hats on their heads; others, younger, but with the look of spinsters; and all were carrying in their hands or their bags packages of left-over meat or fish, and some even had little pans of milk. "Will you help me throw this package over the fence, for those poor creatures?"

All the ladies, cat-lovers, gathered at this hour around the garden of dry leaves to take food to their protégés.[8]

"Can you tell me why they are all here, these cats?" Marcovaldo inquired.

"Where else could they go? This garden is all they have left! Cats come here from other neighborhoods, too, from miles and miles around . . ."

21

The Big White Cat, Gertrude Halsband, Private Collection

"And birds, as well," another lady added. "They're forced to live by the hundreds and hundreds on these few trees . . ."

"And the frogs, they're all in that pool, and at night they never stop croaking . . . You can hear them even on the eighth floor of the buildings around here."

"Who does this villa belong to anyway?" Marcovaldo asked. Now, outside the gate, there weren't just the cat-loving ladies but also other people: the man from the gas pump opposite, the apprentices from a mechanic's shop, the postman, the grocer, some passers-by. And none of them, men and women, had to be asked twice: all wanted to have their say, as always when a mysterious and controversial subject comes up.

"It belongs to a Marchesa.[9] She lives there, but you never see her . . ."

"She's been offered millions and millions, by developers, for this little patch of land, but she won't sell . . ."

"What would she do with millions, an old woman all alone in the world? She wants to hold on to her house, even if it's falling to pieces, rather than be forced to move . . ."

"It's the only undeveloped bit of land in the downtown area . . . Its value goes up every year . . . They've made her offers—"

"Offers! That's not all. Threats, intimidation, persecution . . . You don't know the half of it! Those contractors!"

"But she holds out. She's held out for years . . ."

"She's a saint. Without her, where would those poor animals go?"

"A lot she cares about the animals, the old miser! Have you ever seen her give them anything to eat?"

"How can she feed the cats when she doesn't have food for herself? She's the last descendant of a ruined family!"

8. **protégés** (prōt′ ə zhāz′) *n.* those guided and helped by another.
9. **Marchesa** (mär kā′ sə) title of an Italian noblewoman.

22 **Critical Viewing**

Contrast the way this cat fits in with a natural scene with the way cats fit in with the city in Calvino's story. **[Compare]**

Reading Check

What has become of Marcovaldo's trout?

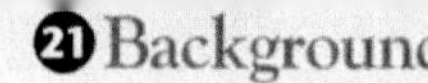

21 Background

Art

The Big White Cat, by Gertrude Halsband

In this painting, Gertrude Halsband (1917–1981) depicts a larger-than-life white cat. The cat appears as big as the trees yet sits atop the grass without crushing it. The cat's whiteness nearly fills the painting and further emphasizes the animal's size. Light touches in the stars and flowers accentuate the cat's whiteness.

Use the following question for discussion:

Does this cat look real? Why or why not?
Answer: No; in addition to the cat's exaggerated size, it is portrayed in an almost cartoon-like style. The fur is too smooth, and the features are too uniform for a real cat.

22 Critical Viewing

Answer: This large cat is surrounded by nature, perhaps even dominating nature in size. The cats in Calvino's story live in a small, wild parcel of nature surrounded by the city.

23 Critical Thinking

Analyze Causes and Effects

- Have two or three volunteers read aloud the bracketed passage.
- Ask: Why do the developers want the land?
  Answer: The developers want to build modern skyscrapers on the land, which is valuable because it is the last undeveloped space in the downtown area.
- Then ask: Why does the Marchesa refuse to sell it?
  Answer: The Marchesa wants to hold on to the land because she is old and does not want to give up her home.

24 Reading Check

Answer: The Marchesa has reached out from within the villa and cut the trout out of the tree for her frying pan.

CUSTOMIZE INSTRUCTION FOR UNIVERSAL ACCESS

For Special Needs Students	For Advanced Readers
Students may find the dialogue on pp. 1250–1251 easier to follow if they read along with an audio recording. Play the recording of the story from **Listening to Literature Audiocassettes** or **CDs.** Urge students to listen to the neighbor's argument about the fate of the Marchesa's land. Then, guide students in a discussion about which side of the argument they find more convincing.	This story reflects the consequences of allowing developers to build wherever they wish, with no regard for the environmental impact of their construction. In many cities today, urban planners balance a community's need for economic development with respect for the natural world. Have students research this topic and find examples of cities that have successfully balanced these two opposing forces. Ask students to use their research as the basis of an essay.

25 Critical Thinking

Draw Conclusions

- Read the bracketed passage aloud, conveying the attitudes of the speakers through tone and gesture.
- Ask: What opposing forces do the two groups of neighbors represent? What does each side want? Possible response: The two groups of neighbors represent the two opposing forces in the story: nature and urbanization. The neighbors who want to preserve the "little bit of green" represent the force of nature; the ones who would rather have a skyscraper represent the force of "progress."

26 ▶ Critical Viewing

Answer: This image emphasizes the wariness of cats.

"She hates cats! I've seen her chasing them and hitting them with an umbrella!"

"Because they were tearing up her flowerbeds!"

"What flowerbeds? I've never seen anything in this garden but a great crop of weeds!"

Marcovaldo realized that with regard to the old Marchesa opinions were sharply divided: some saw her as an angelic being, other as an egoist and a miser.

"It's the same with the birds; she never gives them a crumb!"

"She gives them hospitality. Isn't that plenty?"

"Like she gives the mosquitoes, you mean. They all come from here, from that pool. In the summertime the mosquitoes eat us alive, and it's all the fault of that Marchesa!"

"And the mice? This villa is a mine of mice. Under the dead leaves they have their burrows, and at night they come out . . ."

"As far as the mice go, the cats take care of them . . ."

"Oh, you and your cats! If we had to rely on them . . ."

"Why? Have you got something to say against cats?"

Here the discussion degenerated into a general quarrel.

25 "The authorities should do something: confiscate the villa!" one man cried.

"What gives them the right?" another protested.

"In a modern neighborhood like ours, a mouse-nest like this . . . it should be forbidden . . ."

"Why, I picked my apartment precisely because it overlooked this little bit of green . . ."

"Green, hell! Think of the fine skyscraper they could build here!"

Marcovaldo would have liked to add something of his own, but he couldn't get a word in. Finally, all in one breath, he exclaimed: "The Marchesa stole a trout from me!"

The unexpected news supplied fresh ammunition to the old woman's enemies, but her defenders exploited it as proof of the indigence[10] to which the unfortunate noblewoman was reduced. Both sides agreed that Marcovaldo should go and knock at her door to demand an explanation.

It wasn't clear whether the gate was locked or unlocked; in any case, it opened, after a push, with a mournful creak. Marcovaldo picked his way among the leaves and cats, climbed the steps to the porch, knocked hard at the entrance.

At a window (the very one where the frying-pan had appeared), the blind was raised slightly and in one corner a round, pale blue eye was seen, and a clump of hair dyed an undefinable color, and a dry skinny hand. A voice was heard, asking: "Who is it? Who's at the door?", the words accompanied by a cloud smelling of fried oil.

26 ▲ **Critical Viewing** Which characteristic of cats described in the story is emphasized by this image? **[Connect]**

10. **indigence** (in' di jəns) poverty.

ENRICHMENT: Culture Connection

Gender Roles

This story explores people's reactions to animals. In Italy, gender plays an important role in those reactions. Italy may have a more defined gender structure than does the United States, one that allows less flexibility in how men and women are regarded. But there is at least one exception to this general rule. In the United States, there is a widespread stereotype suggesting that men should prefer dogs as pets and women should prefer cats. In Italy, expressing affection toward domestic animals of all kinds is equally allowable to men and women. Point out to students that in "The Garden of the Stubborn Cats," it is a man whose affection for cats sets the story in motion, whereas it is a woman's dislike for cats that provides the story's primary conflict.

"It's me, Marchesa. The trout man," Marcovaldo explained. "I don't mean to trouble you. I only wanted to tell you, in case you didn't know, that the trout was stolen from me, by that cat, and I'm the one who caught it. In fact the line . . ."

"Those cats! It's always those cats . . ." the Marchesa said, from behind the shutter, with a shrill, somewhat nasal voice. "All my troubles come from the cats! Nobody knows what I go through! Prisoner night and day of those horrid beasts! And with all the refuse people throw over the walls to spite me!"

"But my trout . . ."

"Your trout! What am I supposed to know about your trout!" The Marchesa's voice became almost a scream, as if she wanted to drown out the sizzle of the oil in the pan, which came through the window along with the aroma of fried fish. "How can I make sense of anything, with all the stuff that rains into my house?"

"I understand, but did you take the trout or didn't you?"

"When I think of all the damage I suffer because of the cats! Ah, fine state of affairs! I'm not responsible for anything! I can't tell you what I've lost! Thanks to those cats, who've occupied house and garden for years! My life at the mercy of those animals! Go and find the owners! Make them pay damages! Damages? A whole life destroyed! A prisoner here, unable to move a step!"

"Excuse me for asking: but who's forcing you to stay?"

27 From the crack in the blind there appeared sometimes a round, pale blue eye, sometimes a mouth with two protruding teeth; for a moment the whole face was visible, and to Marcovaldo it seemed, bewilderingly, the face of a cat.

28 "They keep me prisoner, they do, those cats! Oh, I'd be glad to leave! What wouldn't I give for a little apartment all my own, in a nice clean modern building! But I can't go out . . . They follow me, they block my path, they trip me up!" The voice became a whisper, as if to confide a secret. "They're afraid I'll sell the lot . . . They won't leave me . . . won't allow me . . . When the builders come to offer me a contract, you should see them, those cats! They get in the way, pull out their claws; they even chased a lawyer off! Once I had the contract right here, I was about to sign it, and they dived in through the window, knocked over the inkwell, tore up all the pages . . ."

All of a sudden Marcovaldo remembered the time, the shipping department, the boss. He tiptoed off over the dried leaves, as the voice continued to come through the slats of the blind, enfolded in that cloud apparently from the oil of a frying-pan. "They even scratched me . . . I still have the scar . . . All alone here at the mercy of these demons . . ."

Winter came. A blossoming of white flakes decked the branches and capitals and the cats' tails. Under the snow, the dry leaves disolved into mush. The cats were rarely seen, the cat-lovers even less; the packages of fish-bones were consigned only to cats who came to the door. Nobody, for quite a while, had seen anything of the Marchesa. No smoke came now from the chimneypot of the villa. 29

Literary Analysis
Symbolism In what way does Marcovaldo's perception of the Marchesa as a cat add symbolic meaning to her character?

Reading Strategy
Recognizing Symbols Why does the relationship of the Marchesa to the cats suggest that she is a symbolic character?

✓Reading Check
According to the Marchesa, why do the cats interfere with her business?

27 Literary Analysis

Symbolism

- Read aloud the bracketed passage.
- Ask students to give the definition of a symbol.
  Answer: A symbol is a concrete image that stands for an abstract meaning.
- Point out that Marcovaldo describes the Marchesa as if she were something else—a cat.
- Then, ask students the Literary Analysis question on p. 1253: In what way does Marcovaldo's perception of the Marchesa as a cat add symbolic meaning to her character?
  Answer: Describing the Marchesa as a cat assigns to her all the associations readers of the story now have with cats.

28 Reading Strategy

Recognizing Symbols

- Have students read the bracketed text. Then, ask them to describe the relationship of the Marchesa to the cats.
  Answer: The Marchesa believes that she is a prisoner to the cats who control her life.
- Then, ask students the Reading Strategy question on p. 1253: Why does the relationship of the Marchesa to the cats suggest that she is a symbolic character?
  Answer: The Marchesa's relationship to the cats is not entirely realistic. She could have the cats removed. Because her feeling of being controlled is perceived rather than realistic, it is likely symbolic. The Marchesa symbolizes a loss of control.

Monitor Progress Have students identify the highly descriptive language the Marchesa uses, such as "But I can't go out ...They follow me, they block my path, they trip me up!" Explain that this description adds drama to the scene but also suggests that the cats have a larger-than-life, or symbolic, role.

29 ✓Reading Check

Answer: According to the Marchesa, the cats interfere with her business in order to keep her from selling the property in which they make their home.

CUSTOMIZE INSTRUCTION FOR UNIVERSAL ACCESS

Less Proficient Readers

Explain that "The Garden of Stubborn Cats" is a complex story in several ways. Dialogue may be hard to follow; the setting is complicated; and the sentences are often long. Clarification techniques can help students master the reading of complex texts such as this one. As students read a passage or selection for the first time, they may find that they have missed details or facts. In addition, they may have formulated questions that need to be answered. Rereading or reading ahead may be the best strategy to supply the missing information.

ASSESS

Answers for p. 1254

Review and Assess

1. Possible response: The cats, whose home is being gradually destroyed, and the Marchesa, who feels trapped in her situation are both sympathetic.
2. **(a)** The "negative city" consists of the in-between spaces that the cats inhabit. **(b)** Changes in the city have forced the cats to crowd into the Marchesa's garden.
3. **(a)** Marcovaldo follows a cat there because the cat has stolen his fish. **(b)** Possible response: The garden is unique in the city because it contains a low-roofed villa among skyscrapers; it is the only undeveloped land in the city; and it is filled with cats, birds, frogs, and other natural elements.
4. **(a)** Possible response: The Marchesa's hands, which are described before her character is introduced, and her voice, which is described from within the villa are mysterious. She never appears. **(b)** Possible response: The Marchesa belongs to the "city of cats" because she seems feral: she steals food and lives among the cats, at odds with them yet like them.
5. Possible response: Nature and progress are ever at odds. Calvino sees this struggle as unresolved.
6. Possible responses: Yes; some space should be allocated for unforeseen uses because a city houses life, and life cannot be controlled. No; all space should be planned for specific uses because preventing overcrowding and pollution requires good planning.

One snowy day, the garden was again full of cats, who had returned as if it were spring, and they were miauing as if on a moonlight night. The neighbors realized that something had happened: they went and knocked at the Marchesa's door. She didn't answer: she was dead.

In the spring, instead of the garden, there was a huge building site that a contractor had set up. The steam shovels dug down to great depths to make room for the foundations, cement poured into the iron armatures, a very high crane passed beams to the workmen who were making the scaffoldings. But how could they get on with their work? Cats walked along all the planks, they made bricks fall and upset buckets of mortar, they fought in the midst of the piles of sand. When you started to raise an armature, you found a cat perched on the top of it, hissing fiercely. More treacherous pusses climbed onto the masons' backs as if to purr, and there was no getting rid of them. And the birds continued making their nests in all the trestles, the cab of the crane looked like an aviary[11] . . . And you couldn't dip up a bucket of water that wasn't full of frogs, croaking and hopping . . .

11. **aviary** (ā′ vē er′ ē) large bird cage or building for housing many birds.

Review and Assess

Thinking About the Selection

1. **Respond:** With whom did you sympathize most—the Marchesa or the cats? Explain.
2. **(a) Recall:** What is the "negative city"? **(b) Infer:** How have changes in the city altered the way cats live?
3. **(a) Recall:** How does Marcovaldo find the secret garden of the cats? **(b) Analyze:** Cite three details from Calvino's descriptions that explain why this garden is unique in the city.
4. **(a) Analyze:** Identify two descriptive details that make the Marchesa seem mysterious. **(b) Draw Conclusions:** Does the Marchesa somehow belong to the "city of cats," or is she just a prisoner there? Explain.
5. **Make a Generalization:** Given what happens after the Marchesa's death, make a generalization about the two opposing forces in this story, and explain what Calvino suggests about their relationship.
6. **Make a Judgment:** Do you think that some spaces in a city should be used in unforeseen, improvised ways, or should all space be used only according to plan? Explain.

ASSESSMENT PRACTICE: Critical Reading

Analyzing an Author's Meaning and Style (For more practice, see Test Preparation Workbook, p. 59.)

Many standardized tests require students to analyze an author's meaning. Use the following sample test item to demonstrate:

The city of cats and the city of men exist one inside the other, but they are not the same city.

What is the author's meaning in this sentence?

A The cities share boundaries but hold different inhabitants.

B Cats and people should share the same city.

C The two cities have different boundaries that overlap.

D The city of cats has covered up the city of men.

Lead students to recognize that the correct answer is *A*. *B*, *C*, and *D* do not tell the author's meaning.

Review and Assess

Literary Analysis

Symbolism

1. (a) What is the **symbolism** of the folding chair in "Folding Chairs"? (b) Given the emigration of Europeans to America in the 1940s, explain how the final image expands on this symbolism.
2. (a) Explain what the locusts symbolize in "Food for Prophets." (b) Is the release of prophets from jail a solution to this problem? Explain.
3. (a) What is the relationship of the cats to the city in "The Garden of Stubborn Cats"? (b) Explain what symbolic meaning the final event of the story adds to the cats.

Comparing Literary Works

4. Starting from the symbols in which they are expressed, compare the **theme** of "Food for Prophets" with that of Calvino's story. Use a chart like the one shown to organize your ideas.

Image	Symbolism	Theme: What It Shows About Society
Locusts		
Cats		

5. Based on the problems with society that these selections address, list four characteristics of your ideal city. Explain how your ideal city would solve these problems.

Reading Strategy

Recognizing Symbols

6. In "Folding Chairs," what similarities among the images of name plates, cooking, and chairs help you **recognize** these images as **symbols**?
7. (a) Identify a symbol in Calvino's story. (b) Explain what clues helped you recognize the object or character as a symbol.

Extend Understanding

8. **Technology Connection:** (a) In what ways is the Internet a "folding chair," or a symbol of people's lack of a true home? (b) In what ways does the Internet create "gardens of cats," nurturing mystery or spontaneity? (c) Do you think the Internet is more isolating or nurturing? Explain.

Quick Review

Symbolism is the use of concrete images to stand for abstract meanings.

The **theme** of a literary work is the message it sends or the question it poses.

To **recognize symbols,** look for characters, places, or objects that appear repeatedly, are vividly described, have associations with a theme, or have a traditional symbolic meaning.

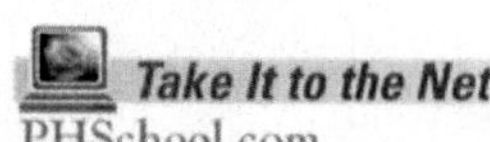
Take It to the Net

PHSchool.com

Take the interactive self-test online to check your understanding of these selections.

ENRICHMENT: Further Reading

Other Works by the Authors

We strongly encourage you to review any selection before assigning or recommending it to students.

Works by Günter Grass

The Tin Drum

Danzig Trilogy

Works by Italo Calvino

The Path to the Nest of Spiders

Italian Folktales

Take It to the Net

Visit PHSchool.com for more information on the authors.

Answers for p. 1255

Review and Assess

1. **(a)** The folding chair stands for the transitory nature of modern life. **(b)** Possible response: The final image suggests that emigrants continue moving and searching.
2. **(a)** The locusts in "Food for Prophets" represent disease or disaster. **(b)** Possible responses: Yes; the prophets may provide society with their wisdom, which could help solve social problems. No; the prophets will compound problems because there are no true prophets.
3. **(a)** Possible response: The cats' relationship to the city is adversarial. **(b)** The final event enhances the cats' symbolic role because the cats have become a symbol of nature's urge to halt human progress.
4. Possible response: **Image:** locusts; cats; **Symbolism:** society's disease; nature's force; **Themes:** Society repeats patterns; nature is at odds with human progress.
5. Possible response: Ideal city characteristics are a balance of nature and buildings, minimized traffic, space for all to live humanely, and sufficient planning to manage change. Students' responses should discuss solutions to the problems addressed in the selections.
6. The three images are all described in the context of moving them—unscrewing name plates, heating the pan in another kitchen, taking folding chairs to emigrate.
7. **(a)** Possible response: The Marchesa and the cats are symbols. **(b)** Possible response: The Marchesa is portrayed as catlike.
8. **(a)** Answer: The Internet has no real location. People can join it and leave it without committing to any one location. **(b)** Possible response: To achieve mystery, Internet users can mask their true identities or "homes." **(c)** Possible responses: The Internet is more isolating because it keeps people from face-to-face contact. The Internet is nurturing because it allows people to make connections they might otherwise not make.

EXTEND

Answers for p. 1256

❶ Vocabulary Development

Word Analysis: Latin Prefix *e-*

1. evacuate; move out of or make vacant
2. emission; a substance that comes out of an object, usually a machine
3. emerge; come out of hiding and into view
4. evaporate; move out of liquid form into vapor form

Fluency: Context

1. altruistic
2. convergent
3. emigrate
4. environs
5. squalid
6. laden

Spelling Strategy

1. independence
2. confidence
3. emergence

❷ Grammar and Style

Practice

1. laying
2. lie
3. laid
4. lays
5. lying

Writing Application

Sample sentences: When Marcovaldo arrived in the garden, cats were *lying* all around. He saw nature everywhere, from the leaves that *lay* all about the ground to the frogs in the pond. The Marchesa cut the fish from the tree and *laid* it on a plate. If only Marcovaldo had *laid* the fish on the plate back at the restaurant, he would have it now.

10TH GRADE For support in teaching the Grammar and Style Lesson to tenth graders, use **Writing and Grammar,** Platinum Level, Chapter 26, Section 2.

Integrate Language Skills

❶ Vocabulary Development Lesson

Word Analysis: Latin Prefix *e-*

The Latin prefix *e-* (a form of the prefix *ex-* used before certain consonants) means "away from" or "out of." The word *emigrate* means "to move away from one place to live in another."

Complete each of the sentences that follow with one of the words provided below. Then, write a definition of each word, incorporating the meaning of *e-*.

emerge emission evacuate evaporate

1. During World War II, many were forced by bombing raids to _____ their homes.
2. Some compared the _____ of toxic chemicals from the factory to a plague of locusts.
3. After a storm, the cats usually _____ from their hiding places.
4. The sun came out, and the puddles started to _____, disappearing by evening.

Fluency: Context

Review the vocabulary list on page 1243. Then, match each word listed to the correct clue below.

1. someone who volunteers for charities
2. describing three roads that meet
3. when people do this, they often become citizens of a new country
4. suburbs, in relation to cities
5. conditions in a run-down neighborhood
6. someone carrying two full grocery bags

Spelling Strategy

The suffix *-ence* is used to form a noun from an adjective that ends in *-ent*. For example, *convergent* becomes *convergence*.

Change each of these nouns to form an adjective. Use the suffix *-ence*.

independent confident emergent

❷ Grammar and Style Lesson

Usage: *lay* and *lie*

Lay means "to put or set something down" and is used with a direct object. Its principal parts are *lay*, *laying*, *laid*, and *laid*.

> DIR. OBJ.
> . . . he *laid* his place among the packing cases in the warehouse. . . .

Lie means "to rest" or "to recline" and is never used with a direct object. Its principal parts are *lie*, *lying*, *lay*, and *lain*.

> A carpet of dry leaves covered the path, and dry leaves *lay* everywhere under the boughs of the two plane-trees. . . .

Practice For each item below, choose the correct word.

1. After (lying, laying) the plate down, the waiter left the room.
2. The old woman went to (lie, lay) down.
3. The workers had (laid, lain) their tools on the ground by 5:00 P.M.
4. Marcovaldo (lies, lays) the fish down.
5. Cats were (lying, laying) everywhere.

Writing Application Using forms of *lay* twice and forms of *lie* twice, write four sentences describing Marcovaldo's visit to the cats' garden.

WG *Prentice Hall Writing and Grammar Connection: Diamond Level, Chapter 25, Section 2*

TEACHING RESOURCES

The following resources can be used to enrich or extend the instruction for pp. 1256–1257.

Vocabulary

- **Selection Support:** Build Vocabulary, p. 233
- **Vocabulary and Spelling Practice Book** (Use this booklet for skills instruction.)

Grammar

- **Selection Support:** Grammar and Style, p. 234
- **Writing and Grammar,** Diamond Level, p. 646
- **Daily Language Practice Transparencies** ■

Writing

- **Performance Assess. and Portfolio Mgmt.,** p. 19
- **Writing and Grammar,** Diamond Level, p. 102 ■
- **Writing and Grammar iText CD-ROM**

Listening and Speaking

- **Performance Assess. and Portfolio Mgmt.,** p. 30

■ **BLOCK SCHEDULING:** Resources marked with this symbol provide varied instruction during 90-minute blocks.

❸ Writing Lesson

Location Scout's Report

Imagine that shooting is about to begin for a film based on "The Garden of Stubborn Cats." As a location scout, write a description of a place you would recommend for filming a particular scene. To help the film director decide, include vivid descriptive details and a clear argument for using your location.

Prewriting Choose a scene from the story. Then, think of a place you know that corresponds to the setting of the scene. Use a cluster diagram like the one shown to collect details that describe your location and to show why it is appropriate.

Model: Gathering Details With a Cluster Diagram

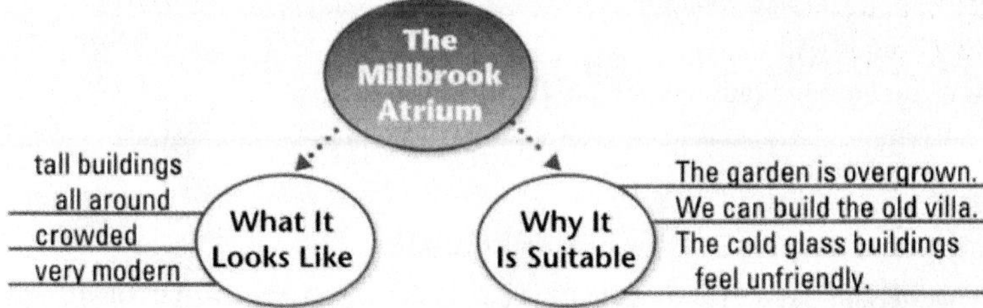

Drafting Make your chosen location come to life for the film's director by using exact details from your notes. Explain why the place is appropriate for the setting described in the story.

Revising Ask a partner to read your report and draw the scene you describe. If the sketch is inconsistent in parts with your location, add greater details to the corresponding parts of your report.

WG Prentice Hall Writing and Grammar Connection: Diamond Level, Chapter 6, Section 2

❹ Extension Activities

Listening and Speaking Divide a group into two teams, and hold a **debate** on this resolution: *We need to control urban development.* With teammates, develop the follow elements to support your position:

- logical arguments
- effective language
- illustrations from Grass's poems and Calvino's story

Hold your debate for the class. **[Group Activity]**

Research and Technology Develop a **visual display** that illustrates the characteristics and origins of several breeds of cats. Include breeds mentioned in "The Garden of Stubborn Cats." To make your chart both informative and easy to read, use annotations and symbols.

 ***Take It to the Net*** PHSchool.com

Go online for an additional research activity using the Internet.

ASSESSMENT RESOURCES

The following resources can be used to assess students' knowledge and skills.

Selection Assessment

- **Formal Assessment,** pp. 207–209
- **Open-Book Tests,** pp. 175–177
- **Test Bank Software**

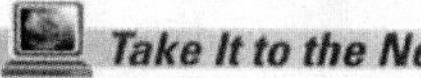 ***Take It to the Net***

Visit PHSchool.com for self-tests on the selections.

Writing Rubric

- **Performance Assess. and Portfolio Mgmt.,** p. 19

Listening and Speaking Rubric

- **Performance Assess. and Portfolio Mgmt.,** p. 30

PRENTICE HALL ASSESSMENT SYSTEM

For additional diagnostics and remediation for skills covered in this selection, use materials from the Prentice Hall Assessment System.

Lesson Support for p. 1257

❸ Writing Lesson

- Tell students that a scouting report is a place description that focuses on specific criteria.
- Tell students that an effective scouting report accomplishes three goals: it identifies the purpose of the report and names a specific place; it outlines the criteria for place selection, describes the place in detail, and evaluates the place against the criteria; it makes a recommendation.
- Introduce students to transition words such as *above, below, nearby,* and *opposite.* Model how to use these words to orient readers in space.
- Review the Writing Lesson model, and clarify how to link the visual description to the evaluative analysis.
- Use the Description rubric in **Performance Assessment and Portfolio Management,** p. 19, to evaluate students' reports.

10TH GRADE For support in working through the Writing Lesson with tenth graders, use **Writing and Grammar,** Platinum Level, Chapter 6, Section 2.

❹ Listening and Speaking

- Review the elements of debate, such as argument and rebuttal. Explain that debates should reflect effective persuasive speaking, with a solidly stated argument and clear supporting evidence.
- Suggest that students identify likely arguments for the opposing team's position. This will help them prepare a rebuttal.
- Encourage students to practice their debate arguments.
- Use the Speaking: Delivering a Persuasive Argument rubric in **Performance Assessment and Portfolio Management,** p. 30, to evaluate students' debates.

CUSTOMIZE INSTRUCTION For Universal Access

To address different learning styles, use the following activities suggested in the **Extension Activities** booklet, p. 59:

- For Visual/Spatial Learners, use Activity 5.
- For Interpersonal Learners, use Activity 6.
- For Logical/Mathematical Learners, use Activity 7.

from Survival in Auschwitz · *from* Night · When in early Summer . . .

Lesson Objectives

1. **To analyze and respond to literary elements**
   - Literary Analysis: Autobiography
   - Comparing Literary Works: Memoir
2. **To read, comprehend, analyze, and critique autobiography and poetry**
   - Reading Strategy: Connecting to Historical Context
   - Reading Check Questions
   - Review and Assess Questions
   - Assessment Practice (ATE)
3. **To develop word analysis skills, fluency, and systematic vocabulary**
   - Vocabulary Development Lesson: Latin Word Root *-port-*
4. **To understand and apply written and oral language conventions**
   - Spelling Strategy
   - Grammar and Style Lesson: Absolute Phrases
5. **To understand and apply appropriate writing and research strategies**
   - Writing Lesson: Persuasive Essay
   - Extension Activity: Multimedia Presentation
6. **To understand and apply listening and speaking strategies**
   - Extension Activity: Group Discussion

10TH GRADE TEACHING A TENTH-GRADE COURSE

The literature in this section can be taught as part of a rich, balanced world literature course for tenth-grade students. For a full outline of such a course, see pp. T46–T48 in Volume I of this Teacher's Edition.

STEP-BY-STEP TEACHING GUIDE	PACING GUIDE
PRETEACH	
Motivate Students and Provide Background	
Use the Motivation activity (ATE p. 1258)	5 min.
Read and discuss author and background features (SE pp. 1258, 1260, 1267; ATE p. 1258) A	5 min.
Introduce the Concepts	
Introduce the Literary Analysis and Reading Strategy concepts (SE/ATE p. 1259) A	15 min.
Pronounce the vocabulary words and read their definitions (SE p. 1259)	5 min.
TEACH	
Monitor Comprehension	
Informally monitor comprehension by circulating while students read independently or in groups A	50 min.
Monitor students' comprehension with the Reading Check notes (SE pp. 1265, 1267, 1269, 1271, 1273; ATE pp. 1261, 1265, 1267, 1269, 1271, 1273)	as students read
Develop vocabulary with the Vocabulary notes (SE pp. 1265, 1269, 1274; ATE p. 1274)	as students read
Develop Understanding	
Develop students' understanding of autobiography with the Literary Analysis annotations (SE/ATE pp. 1261, 1265, 1266, 1268, 1273) A	10 min.
Develop students' ability to connect to historical context by using the Reading Strategy annotations (SE pp. 1263, 1272; ATE pp. 1263, 1269, 1272) A	10 min.
ASSESS	
Assess Mastery	
Assess students' mastery of the Reading Strategy and Literary Analysis concepts by having them answer the Review and Assess questions (SE/ATE p. 1277)	20 min.
Use one or more of the print, software, or transparency Assessment Resources (ATE p. 1279) A	up to 45 min.
EXTEND	
Apply Understanding	
Have students complete the Vocabulary Development Lesson and the Grammar and Style Lesson (SE p. 1278) A	20 min.
Apply students' ability to revise for audience and purpose, using the Writing Lesson (SE/ATE p. 1279) A	45 min.
Apply students' understanding of the selections, using one or more of the Extension Activities (SE p. 1279)	20–90 min.

A ACCELERATED INSTRUCTION: Use the strategies and activities identified with an A.

10TH GRADE TEACHING TENTH-GRADE STUDENTS For support in teaching the selection(s) to tenth-grade students, see the Step-by-Step Teaching notes identified with the icon shown here.

UNIVERSAL ACCESS
● = Below-Level Students
▲ = On-Level Students
■ = Above-Level Students

Time and Resource Manager

Reading Level: Average, Average, Challenging
Average Number of Instructional Days: 5

RESOURCES		
PRINT	**TRANSPARENCIES**	**TECHNOLOGY**
• **Beyond Literature,** Humanities Connection: What Is Right? p. 60 ▲ ■		• **Interest Grabber Video,** Tape 2, Unit 9, Segment 10 ● ▲ ■
• **Selection Support Workbook:** ● ▲ ■ Literary Analysis, p. 240 Reading Strategy, p. 239 Build Vocabulary, p. 237	• **Literary Analysis and Reading Transparencies,** pp. 119 and 120 ● ▲ ■	
• **Reader's Companion** ● • **Adapted Reader's Companion** ●		• **Listening to Literature** ● ▲ ■ Audiocassettes Audio CDs • **Reader's Companion Audio Program** ● • **Reader's Companion Adapted and English Learner's Version Audio Program** ● ▲
• **English Learner's Companion** • **Literary Analysis for Enrichment,** p. 60 ■		• **World Masterpieces iText CD-ROM**
• **Formal Assessment:** Selection Test, pp. 210–212 ● ▲ ■ • **Open-Book Tests,** pp. 178–180 ● ▲ ■ • **Performance Assess. and Portfolio Mgmt.,** p. 11 ● ▲ ■ • PRENTICE HALL ASSESSMENT SYSTEM ● ▲ ■	• PRENTICE HALL ASSESSMENT SYSTEM ● ▲ ■ **Skills Practice Answers and Explanations on Transparencies**	• **Test Bank Software** ● ▲ ■
• **Selection Support Workbook:** ● ▲ ■ Grammar and Style, p. 238 • **Writing and Grammar,** Diamond Level ● ▲ ■ • **Extension Activities,** p. 60 ● ▲ ■	• **Daily Language Practice Transparencies** ● ▲ • **Writing Models and Graphic Organizers on Transparencies,** pp. 45–51 ● ▲ ■	• **Writing and Grammar iText CD-ROM** ● ▲ ■ *Take It to the Net* PHSchool.com

BLOCK SCHEDULING: Use one 90-minute class period to preteach the selection(s) and have students read them. Use a second 90-minute class period to assess students' mastery of skills and have them complete one of the Extension Activities.

PRETEACH

Step-by-Step Teaching Guide for pp. 1258–1259

Motivation

To acquaint students with the trauma of the Nazi concentration camps, assign a number to each seat in the classroom before class begins. When students arrive, begin addressing them by their seat numbers rather than their names. Be certain to maintain a somber classroom atmosphere during this exercise. After students are settled and the daily classroom start-up procedures are completed, lead students in a discussion about having their names replaced with numbers. Help students understand that removing a person's identity is a first step in dehumanization. Genocide is possible only after oppressors succeed in stripping victims of their humanity.

Interest Grabber Video

As an alternative, play "*Night:* Dachau: A Nazi Concentration Camp" on Tape 2.

❶ Background

More About the Authors

Primo Levi had little sense of his own Judaism growing up: "Religion did not count for much in my family." Yet, Judaism counted for an enormous amount as Nazism swept Europe. The Italian government enacted "racial laws" that placed heavy restrictions on Jews.

Unlike Levi, Elie Wiesel grew up in a devoutly religious family. Wiesel remains a man committed to Judaism. He wrote for a Yiddish newspaper and has authored books on the Holocaust and on the role of Jewish faith in the modern world.

Nelly Sachs grew up in a middle-class family and studied dance and music as well as literature. However, her comfortable life was obliterated by the Holocaust. During the war, she earned money translating Swedish poetry into German. Over the years, her own poetry brought her international recognition.

Geography Note

Draw students' attention to the map on p. 1258. Remind them that the enormous tragedy of the Holocaust was concentrated in this highlighted area of Europe.

Prepare to Read

❶ *from* Survival in Auschwitz ◆ *from* Night ◆ When in early summer . . .

Primo Levi (1919–1987)

Both a chemist and a writer, Primo Levi had more than one side. Yet his fate hinged on a single fact: He was Jewish. This fact alone was enough to send Levi, like millions of other Jews in the 1930s and 1940s, to a brutal concentration camp.

Captured When the Nazis occupied Italy in 1943, Levi, a native of Turin, joined a resistance group. In December, the Nazis captured the young chemist and deported him to the camp at Auschwitz, in Poland. Levi was freed when the Allies liberated the camp in 1944. He achieved fame when his early memoir of the experience, *Survival in Auschwitz* (1947), was republished in 1958.

Writer and Chemist Levi worked as a chemist until 1977, when he retired to write full time. In books such as *The Periodic Table* (1975), he explores science, literature, and history. In his last book, *The Drowned and the Saved* (1986), he returns to the Holocaust with a darker, less hopeful eye.

Elie Wiesel (b. 1928)

Convinced that he had survived the Holocaust in order to "bear witness" to its horrors, Elie Wiesel nonetheless waited a decade to relate his experiences. "I didn't want to use the wrong words," he recalls. Finally, in 1954, Wiesel published *Night*, his renowned memoir of the Holocaust.

A Family Broken Wiesel grew up in the small Romanian town of Sighet. As World War II raged, the Nazis shipped Sighet's Jews to Auschwitz. The family was split up. The sixteen-year-old Wiesel ended up with his father in Buchenwald, a concentration camp in Germany.

Remembering In 1944, American troops liberated the camp. Orphaned by the war, Wiesel went to France, where he began his career as a journalist and spokesperson against oppression. Over the decades, he has spoken out against apartheid in South Africa, "ethnic cleansing" in Bosnia, and other practices he found to resemble Nazism. For his humanitarian efforts, Wiesel was awarded the Nobel Peace Prize in 1986.

Nelly Sachs (1891–1970)

As a teenager in Berlin, Germany, Nelly Sachs wrote a letter to a favorite author, Sweden's Selma Lagerlöf. That fateful letter began a correspondence that eventually saved Sachs's life.

History Interrupts By the 1920s, Sachs, with Lagerlöf's encouragement, was publishing her poetry in a Berlin newspaper. She might have continued on to moderate literary success, but history intervened. The Nazis came to power in 1938, and Sachs, who was Jewish, watched as the world turned dark. In 1940, threat became reality: She learned that she was to be sent to a concentration camp.

A Friend Helps When Lagerlöf heard of her friend's danger, she lobbied Sweden's royalty for the permission Sachs and her mother needed to move to Sweden. The Swedish government issued visas to Sachs and her mother, and the two escaped Germany. Haunted by friends and relatives killed in the Holocaust, Sachs devoted much of her poetry to the event. Though she eventually became a Swedish citizen, she continued to write in German. In 1966, Sachs, like Selma Lagerlöf before her, was awarded the Nobel Prize in Literature.

TEACHING RESOURCES

The following resources can be used to enrich or extend the instruction for pp. 1258–1259.

Motivation

Interest Grabber Video, Tape 2

Background

Beyond Literature, p. 60

Take It to the Net

Visit PHSchool.com for background on the authors.

Literary Analysis

Literary Analysis and Reading Transparencies, Autobiography, p. 119

Selection Support: Literary Analysis, p. 240

Reading

Literary Analysis and Reading Transparencies, Connecting to Historical Context, p. 120

BLOCK SCHEDULING: Resources marked with this symbol provide varied instruction during 90-minute blocks.

Preview

Connecting to the Literature

Being somebody looks easy: "I'm somebody who jogs." "I'm somebody who likes rock music." Watch a former friend ignore you, though, and it's not hard to feel like a nobody. In the 1940s, a nation tried to turn these writers into nobodies. Their words speak for the nobody in all of us.

❷ Literary Analysis

Autobiography

An **autobiography** is a nonfiction work in which a person tells his or her own life story. An autobiography may be written for a number of reasons:

- Famous people may write autobiographies to satisfy readers' curiosity and to ensure accuracy about their lives.
- People who have shaped or witnessed historic events may write autobiographies to give insight into those events.

In their autobiographical writings, Primo Levi and Elie Wiesel give readers insight into the Holocaust. As you read, note ways in which the writers' purposes shape their autobiographies.

Comparing Literary Works

One form of autobiography is the **memoir,** a first-person account that focuses on one person or series of events in the writer's life, rather than telling the writer's full life story. Like many memoirs, Levi's and Wiesel's works offer an understanding of the meaning of events.

Use a chart like the one shown to compare the writers' insights.

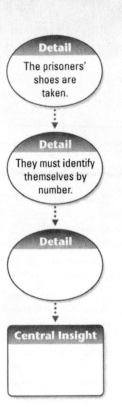

Detail
The prisoners' shoes are taken.

Detail
They must identify themselves by number.

Detail

Central Insight

❸ Reading Strategy

Connecting to Historical Context

Holocaust narratives offer universal truths, but they are also rooted in history. To understand these works fully, **connect to historical context,** linking the work to events of the time. For instance, to understand why Levi, an Italian, is a prisoner of the Germans, you need to know that the Nazis occupied Italy in 1943. As you read, connect the background information on pages 1258, 1260, and 1267 with events and images in the selections.

Vocabulary Development

sordid (sôr′ did) *adj.* filthy; depressingly wretched (p. 1265)

prophetic (prō fet′ ik) *adj.* giving a prediction of the future (p. 1265)

intuition (in′ to͞o ish′ ən) *n.* instinctive understanding (p. 1265)

affinity (ə fin′ i tē) *n.* close relationship; natural liking (p. 1265)

plaintive (plān′ tiv) *adj.* expressing sorrow; mournful (p. 1269)

beseeching (bē sēch′ iŋ) *adj.* asking for something earnestly (p. 1269)

liquidated (lik′ wi dāt′ id) *adj.* disposed of; ended; killed (p. 1274)

deportees (dē′ pôr tēz′) *n.* people ordered to leave a country (p. 1274)

CUSTOMIZE INSTRUCTION FOR UNIVERSAL ACCESS

For Special Needs Students	For Less Proficient Readers	For English Learners
Have students read the excerpt from *Survival in Auschwitz* in the **Adapted Reader's Companion.** This version provides basic-level instruction in an interactive format with questions and write-on lines. Completing the adapted version will prepare students to read the selection in the Student Edition.	Have students read the adapted version of the selection in the **Reader's Companion.** This version provides basic-level instruction in an interactive format with questions and write-on lines. After students finish the selection in the **Reader's Companion,** have them complete the questions and activities in the Student Edition.	Have students read the adapted version of the selection in the **English Learner's Companion.** This version provides basic-level instruction in an interactive format with questions and write-on lines. Completing the adapted version will prepare students to read the selection in the Student Edition.

❷ Literary Analysis

Autobiography

- Read aloud the Literary Analysis instruction. Make sure that students understand that in an autobiography, the author tells his or her own life story. Have students create quick timelines of the significant events in their lives, beginning with birth and ending with the present.
- After reading the Comparing Literary Works instruction, tell students to circle one memorable timeline event. Tell students that a memoir of this event would focus on specific details and would offer some insight into the event's significance.
- Tell students to use a graphic organizer like the one on p. 1259 to record three key details about the event they circled on their timelines.
- Then, help students complete their graphic organizers by adding central insights that the details suggest, given the vantage point of time and history.

❸ Reading Strategy

Connecting to Historical Context

- Ask a volunteer to read aloud the Reading Strategy instruction.
- Lead students in a discussion about the importance of historical context when reading memoirs. Tell students that memoirs like *Survival in Auschwitz* and *Night* present readers with in-depth, personal depictions of world-changing events. They offer universal truths, but they are also rooted in specific historical contexts.

Vocabulary Development

- Pronounce each vocabulary word for students, and read the definitions as a class. Have students identify any words with which they are already familiar.

 ***E-Teach***

Visit e-Teach at PHSchool.com for teachers' essays on how to teach, with questions and answers.

TEACH

Step-by-Step Teaching Guide for pp. 1260–1276

Teaching Tenth-Grade Students

10TH GRADE Tenth-grade students may find it difficult to comprehend the experiences described in these selections. Having their shoes and clothing taken away and being forced to wear issued clothing may be completely alien to students' experiences. Suggest correlations with which students can compare and contrast these experiences. For example, have them compare and contrast wearing prison clothing with wearing a uniform for sports teams or physical education. Lead students in a discussion about the purpose of dressing people uniformly. Help students understand that clothing is one way that human beings express their individuality. Uniformity suppresses this individuality.

❶ About the Selection

This harrowing selection depicts Primo Levi's arrival at Auschwitz, the notorious Nazi concentration camp. Arriving with a group of Italian Jews, Levi immediately recognizes Auschwitz as hell, the very bottom of human experience. Through interpreters, German SS officers mock the prisoners, order them to strip naked, and leave them standing and waiting for hours. The men are denied information about what is to happen to them and what is happening to their wives and daughters. Eventually, they are washed and shaved bare. They are issued prison clothing but forced to run naked through the cold before they can dress. Finally, Levi describes being tattooed with an identification number.

❷ ▶ Critical Viewing

Possible response: Some prisoners might imagine that the message communicates a sense of hope that they might be able to preserve themselves through work. However, Levi is highly perceptive, recognizing the true nature of what is happening while those around him attempt to deny it. A prisoner like Levi will probably note the irony of a sign about freedom placed above the gates of a prison.

from Survival in Auschwitz

Primo Levi
translated by Stuart Woolf

❶

Background

The Holocaust was the systematic persecution and murder of millions of Jews and others deemed unfit by Germany's Nazi party. The Nazis came to power in Germany in 1933. During World War II (1939–1945), Nazi forces rounded up Jews throughout German-occupied lands and shot them or shipped them to concentration camps. Here, the prisoners were worked or starved to death or killed, often by poison gas. In this excerpt, Primo Levi describes his arrival at the complex of three camps at Auschwitz, in Poland.

❷ ▲ **Critical Viewing**
Explain how a prisoner such as Levi might react to the sight of this sign, "Work Gives Freedom," over the gate of Auschwitz. **[Connect]**

On the Bottom

The journey did not last more than twenty minutes. Then the lorry[1] stopped, and we saw a large door, and above it a sign, brightly illuminated (its memory still strikes me in my dreams): *Arbeit Macht Frei,*[2] work gives freedom.

1. **lorry** (lor′ ē) *n.* British term for "truck."
2. ***Arbeit Macht Frei*** (ar′ bīt mäkt frī)

TEACHING RESOURCES

The following resources can be used to enrich or extend the instruction for pp. 1260–1276.

Literary Analysis
- **Selection Support:** Literary Analysis, p. 240
- **Literary Analysis and Reading Transparencies,** Autobiography, p. 119 ■

Reading
- **Selection Support:** Reading Strategy, p. 239; Build Vocabulary, p. 237 ■
- **Reader's Companion**
- **Adapted Reader's Companion**
- **English Learner's Companion**
- **Listening to Literature Audiocassettes**
- **Listening to Literature Audio CDs**

■ **BLOCK SCHEDULING:** Resources marked with this symbol provide varied instruction during 90-minute blocks.

We climb down, they make us enter an enormous empty room that is poorly heated. We have a terrible thirst. The weak gurgle of the water in the radiators makes us ferocious; we have had nothing to drink for four days. But there is also a tap—and above it a card which says that it is forbidden to drink as the water is dirty. Nonsense. It seems obvious that the card is a joke, "they" know that we are dying of thirst and they put us in a room, and there is a tap, and *Wassertrinken Verboten.*[3] I drink and I incite my companions to do likewise, but I have to spit it out, the water is tepid and sweetish, with the smell of a swamp.

3 This is hell. Today, in our times, hell must be like this. A huge, empty room: we are tired, standing on our feet, with a tap which drips while we cannot drink the water, and we wait for something which will certainly be terrible, and nothing happens and nothing continues to happen. What can one think about? One cannot think anymore, it is like being already dead. Someone sits down on the ground. The time passes drop by drop.

We are not dead. The door is opened and an SS[4] man enters, smoking. He looks at us slowly and asks, *"Wer kann Deutsch?"*[5] One of us whom I have never seen, named Flesch, moves forward; he will be our interpreter. This SS man makes a long calm speech; the interpreter translates. We have to form rows of five, with intervals of two yards between man and man; then we have to undress and make a bundle of the clothes in a special manner, the woolen garments on one side, all the rest on the other; we must take off our shoes but pay great attention that they are not stolen.

Stolen by whom? Why should our shoes be stolen? And what about our documents, the few things we have in our pockets, our watches? We all look at the interpreter, and the interpreter asks the German, and the German smokes and looks him through and through as if he were transparent, as if no one had spoken.

I had never seen old men naked. Mr. Bergmann wore a truss[6] and asked the interpreter if he should take it off, and the interpreter hesitated. But the German understood and spoke seriously to the interpreter pointing to someone. We saw the interpreter swallow and then he said: "The officer says, take off the truss, and you will be given that of Mr. Coen." One could see the words coming bitterly out of Flesch's mouth; this was the German manner of laughing.

3. ***Wassertrinken Verboten*** (väs´ ər trink´ 'n fer bōt´ 'n) German: "It is forbidden to drink the water."
4. **SS** abbreviation for the *Shutzstaffel* (shootz´ shtäf el), a quazi-military unit of the Nazi party, used as a secret police.
5. ***Wer kann Deutsch?*** (ver kän doich) German: "Who knows German?"
6. **truss** *n.* padded strap worn to support a hernia (an abdominal muscle rupture).

Literary Analysis
Autobiography Why does Levi tell some of his autobiography in the first-person plural (*we*)?

4 **▼ Critical Viewing**
What does this image of wedding rings taken from concentration camp prisoners suggest about the treatment Levi will receive? **[Interpret]**

5 **✓ Reading Check**
What happens to the prisoners' shoes after they are warned to guard them from theft?

CUSTOMIZE INSTRUCTION FOR UNIVERSAL ACCESS

For Special Needs Students	For Less Proficient Readers	For English Learners
Suggest to students that Levi measures time only by what he knows: here, the drip of the fetid water. Invite students to list the ways in which people mark time. Record their suggestions on the board. Lead students in a discussion about why people need or want to mark time.	Ask students to examine the author's use of quotation marks on p. 1261. Help students make a two-column chart. Tell students to record uses of quotation marks in the left-hand column. Then, tell students to record in the right-hand column their thoughts about why the author uses quotation marks in these instances.	Lead students in a discussion about why the Germans in the story speak only German but expect that some of the prisoners will speak both Italian and German. Ask students to discuss how language often becomes a vehicle for oppression.

3 Literary Analysis

Autobiography

- Explain that in an autobiography, the author relates, generally in the first-person, his or her own experiences. In *Survival in Auschwitz,* for example, Primo Levi presents his own experiences during the Holocaust and in the Nazi concentration camps.
- Have students read the bracketed passage independently. Ask them to point out anything unusual they notice about the way Levi narrates the events he describes.
  Answer: Levi primarily uses the first person plural (*we*) to narrate, rather than the first person singular (*I*).
- Ask students the Literary Analysis question on p. 1261: Why does Levi tell some of his autobiography in the first person plural (*we*)?
  Possible response: Levi is describing not only his own experiences but also historical events. The use of the first person plural conveys his understanding that what is happening to him is also happening to others. Additionally, because many Jews did not survive the Holocaust, Levi uses the first person plural to connect their untold stories with his own.
- Encourage students to note the points at which Levi's collective and individual stories converge and separate. Discuss why these convergences and separations occur at the points where they do.

4 ► Critical Viewing

Possible response: The huge pile of wedding rings shows the huge number of people upon whom the Nazi crimes were perpetrated and suggests that the Nazis will take everything—even the most personal of belongings—from their prisoners. The Nazis will attempt to strip Levi of his identity.

5 ✓ Reading Check

Answer: The prisoners are ordered to put all the shoes in one corner. From here, the shoes are swept out of the room in one big jumble.

❻ Background

Art

Concentration Camp Inmates, by Hellmut Bachrach-Barée

Although virtually no information about Hellmut Bachrach-Barée exists, the extraordinary emotional impact of *Concentration Camp Inmates* suggests that the artist witnessed what he depicts. The date of this work—February 1945, within a month of the liberation of Auschwitz—hints that the memory was fresh in the artist's mind.

Use the following question for discussion:

What elements of this painting suggest that the artist was in a concentration camp?
Possible response: The subjects' pain and hopelessness is so vivid that the artist must have had first-hand experience of the camps.

❼ ▶Critical Viewing

Possible response: The dull, drab colors and rough texture capture the grim experience of the prisoners as do the sorrowful facial expressions and hunched postures of the figures.

Now another German comes and tells us to put the shoes in a certain corner, and we put them there, because now it is all over and we feel outside this world and the only thing is to obey. Someone comes with a broom and sweeps away all the shoes, outside the door in a heap. He is crazy, he is mixing them all together, ninety-six pairs, they will be all mixed up. The outside door opens, a freezing wind enters and we are naked and cover ourselves up with our arms. The wind blows and slams the door; the German reopens it and stands watching with interest how we writhe[7] to hide from the wind, one behind the other. Then he leaves and closes it.

Now the second act begins. Four men with razors, soapbrushes and clippers burst in; they have trousers and jackets with stripes, with a number sewn on the front; perhaps they are the same sort as those others of this evening (this evening or yesterday evening?); but these are robust[8] and flourishing. We ask many questions but they catch hold of us and in a moment we find ourselves shaved and sheared. What comic faces we have without hair! The four speak a language which does not seem of this world. It is certainly not German, for I understand a little German.

Concentration Camp Inmates, February 1945, Pencil and watercolor on paper, Hellmut Bachrach-Barée, Gift of the artist. Courtesy of the Yad Vashem Art Museum, Jerusalem ❻

Finally another door is opened: here we are, locked in, naked, sheared and standing, with our feet in water—it is a shower-room. We are alone. Slowly the astonishment dissolves, and we speak, and everyone asks questions and no one answers. If we are naked in a shower-room, it means that we will have a shower. If we have a shower it is because they are not going to kill us yet. But why then do they keep us standing, and give us nothing to drink, while nobody explains anything, and we have no shoes or clothes, but we are all naked with our feet in the water, and we have been traveling five daysand cannot even sit down.

And our women?

Mr. Levi asks me if I think that our women are like us at this moment, and where they are, and if we will be able to see them again. I say yes, because he is married and has a daughter; certainly we will see them again. But by now my belief is that all this is a game to mock and

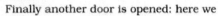

❼ ▲ **Critical Viewing** What details of style—color, texture, clarity, line—help this drawing of concentration camp prisoners convey a sad or even grim mood? Explain. **[Analyze]**

7. **writhe** (rīth) *v.* twist the body about, as in pain.
8. **robust** (rō bust′) *adj.* strong and healthy; full of vigor.

ENRICHMENT: History Connection

Terezin—"The Waiting Room for Hell"

The town of Terezin lies outside Prague, the capital of Czechoslovakia from 1918 to 1993. During the Holocaust, the Nazis used Terezin as a "model" concentration camp they could present to the world to hide the fact that they were systematically murdering the Jews of Europe. Jewish leaders and cultural figures were sent here. The shops were stocked with food, at least when Nazi cameras rolled to create propaganda films. The Red Cross was allowed to visit Terezin on one occasion. Even this international relief organization

But Terezin was not what it seemed. Although the Jews here were not treated as harshly as they were at such camps as Auschwitz, countless thousands died of hunger and disease. Large numbers of families and the elderly were sent to Terezin and then moved to other camps. Terezin became known as the "waiting room for hell."

sneer at us. Clearly they will kill us, whoever thinks he is going to live is mad, it means that he has swallowed the bait, but I have not; I have understood that it will soon all be over, perhaps in this same room, when they get bored of seeing us naked, dancing from foot to foot and trying every now and again to sit down on the floor. But there are two inches of cold water and we cannot sit down.

We walk up and down without sense, and we talk, everybody talks to everybody else, we make a great noise. The door opens, and a German enters; it is the officer of before. He speaks briefly, the interpreter translates. "The officer says you must be quiet, because this is not a rabbinical school."[9] One sees the words which are not his, the bad words, twist his mouth as they come out, as if he was spitting out a foul taste. We beg him to ask what we are waiting for, how long we will stay here,
8 about our women, everything; but he says no, that he does not want to ask. This Flesch, who is most unwilling to translate into Italian the hard cold German phrases and refuses to turn into German our questions because he knows that it is useless, is a German Jew of about fifty, who has a large scar on his face from a wound received fighting the Italians on the Piave.[10] He is a closed, taciturn[11] man, for whom I feel an instinctive respect as I feel that he has begun to suffer before us.

The German goes and we remain silent, although we are a little ashamed of our silence. It is still night and we wonder if the day will ever come. The door opens again, and someone else dressed in stripes comes in. He is different from the others, older, with glasses, a more civilized face, and much less robust. He speaks to us in Italian.

By now we are tired of being amazed. We seem to be watching some mad play, one of those plays in which the witches, the Holy Spirit and the devil appear. He speaks Italian badly, with a strong foreign accent. He makes a long speech, is very polite, and tries to reply to all our questions.

We are at Monowitz, near Auschwitz, in Upper Silesia, a region 9 inhabited by both Poles and Germans. This camp is a work-camp, in German one says *Arbeitslager*,[12] all

Reading Strategy
Connecting to Historical Context In what way do these difficulties over language reflect the actions and policies of the Nazis in Europe?

10 **▼ Critical Viewing**
Explain which aspect of Levi's experience the faceless figures in this image capture. **[Connect]**

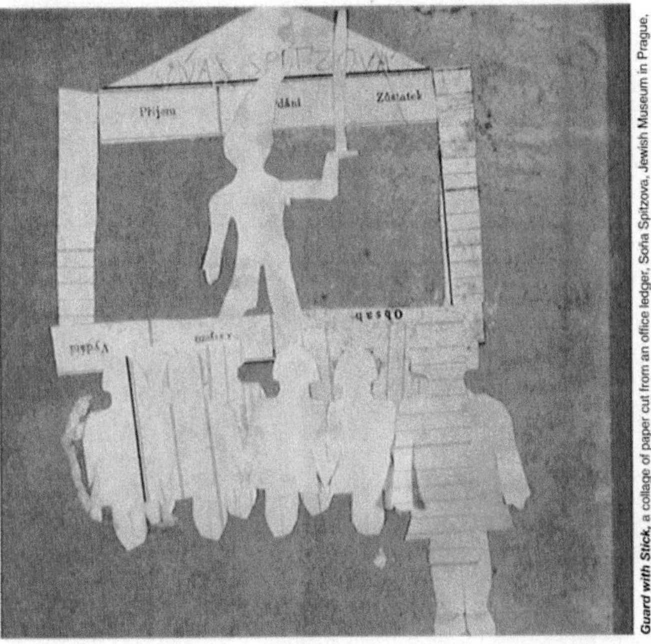

Guard with Stick, a collage of paper cut from an office ledger, Soňa Spitzova, Jewish Museum in Prague, Courtesy of the United States Holocaust Memorial Museum

9. **rabbinical school** school for the training of rabbis (scholars and teachers of Jewish law). The comment is a negative reference to the practice in such schools of orally disputing issues of law.
10. **Piave** (pyä´ vä) river in northeastern Italy, located between Padua and Venice.
11. **taciturn** (tas´ ə tʉrn´) *adj.* habitually silent; uncommunicative.
12. ***Arbeitslager*** (är´ bīts läg´ r)

CUSTOMIZE INSTRUCTION FOR UNIVERSAL ACCESS

For Less Proficient Readers	For Gifted/Talented Students
Invite students to bring photographs of themselves to class. Tell them that the photographs are for an art project, so they should bring photographs that they do not mind manipulating or color copies of favorite photographs. Provide students with scissors, and tell them to remove their hair from the photographs. Lead students in a discussion about how the lack of hair changes their appearances. Invite students to speculate about why the Nazis removed the hair of the Jews in the concentration camps.	The art on these pages may be especially moving for students. Encourage them to learn more about art created by victims and survivors of the Holocaust. Students should begin with the art reproduced in these selections. Then, students should work in groups to research work by other Holocaust artists. Have students put together presentations for the class, including reproductions of artwork and background on the artists. Students may also wish to connect Holocaust art to artwork produced during other wars and crises.

8 Reading Strategy

Connecting to Historical Context

- Have students read the bracketed passage independently.
- Ask students the Reading Strategy question on p. 1263: In what way do these difficulties over language reflect the actions and policies of the Nazis in Europe?

Possible response: Nazi policy dictated the murder of all European Jews. Oppression necessitates that the oppressors view the oppressed as less than human. The language difficulty reflects the Nazi belief that the Jews are not human and therefore not worthy, or capable, of being understood.

Reteach If students have difficulty connecting to the historical context of *Survival in Auschwitz*, use the Connecting to Historical Context transparency in **Literary Analysis and Reading Transparencies,** p.120.

9 Background

Art

Guard with Stick, by Soña Spitzova

Little is known about Soña Spitzova (1931–1944). In 1941, this young girl was imprisoned by the Nazis at Terezin. Here, Jewish artists such as Friedl Dicker were able to provide art lessons and materials to children like Spitzova. *Guard with Stick*, a paper collage, appears to be one of the art works Dicker made possible. Spitzova was sent to Auschwitz, where she died at the age of thirteen.

Use this question for discussion: What does the fact that Spitzova created this collage from an office ledger indicate about the regard for art in the concentration camps?

Possible response: The Germans did not value the art of the prisoners, so art supplies were not provided. Artists had to use available resources for their creations.

10 ▶Critical Viewing

Possible response: The faceless figures before the guard suggest the Jews who have been stripped of their identities. The facelessness of the guard may evoke the alien quality of the Nazi officer whose speech and behavior the Italian prisoners cannot understand.

11 Background

The Holocaust

There was a class of people in the camps designated as criminals. These prisoners probably included common criminals, who had a higher status than Jews. In Levi's account, however, the nature of the Hungarian doctor's crime is unclear.

12 Background

Art

Drawing for the Transportation Bas Relief, by Dee Clements

Colorado-based artist Dee Clements specializes in sculpture. He belongs to the National Sculptor's Guild and has created numerous public sculptures. Among these is the Desert Holocaust Memorial in Palm Desert, California, dedicated in 1995. The centerpiece of this memorial is a bronze sculpture of seven figures, European Jews whose lives were torn apart by the Holocaust. Also part of the memorial are eleven bas-reliefs—sculpted images that project outward from flat backgrounds—portraying various aspects of the great tragedy. Clements's *Drawing for the Transportation Bas Relief* depicts one of the trains the Nazis used to bring Jews from all over Europe to concentration camps such as Auschwitz.

Use the following questions for discussion:

- What does this image suggest about the nature of the Holocaust? Possible response: The train is a potent symbol of industry, suggesting that the mass murders of the Holocaust were carried out in an industrial, mechanical, and impersonal manner.
- Imagine a completed bas/relief of this image. How do you think the basrelief would affect you as a viewer? Possible response: The solidity and permanence of the basrelief might make the image even more powerful.

13 ▸ Critical Viewing

Possible response: The group of people, reaching almost as far as the eye can see, suggests that the human spirit is being crushed. These people are about to be packed together in the train's boxcars as if they were inhuman cargoand are about to undergo an experience that will be inhuman.

the prisoners (there are about ten thousand) work in a factory which produces a type of rubber called Buna, so that the camp itself is called Buna.

We will be given shoes and clothes—no, not our own—other shoes, other clothes, like his. We are naked now because we are waiting for the shower and the disinfection, which will take place immediately after the reveille, because one cannot enter the camp without being disinfected.

11 Certainly there will be work to do, everyone must work here. But there is work and work: he, for example, acts as doctor. He is a Hungarian doctor who studied in Italy and he is the dentist of the Lager.[13] He has been in the Lager for four and a half years (not in this one: Buna has only been open for a year and a half), but we can see that he is still quite well, not very thin. Why is he in the Lager? Is he Jewish like us? "No," he says simply, "I am a criminal."

We ask him many questions. He laughs, replies to some and not to others, and it is clear that he avoids certain subjects. He does not speak of the women: he says they are well, that we will see them again soon, but he does not say how or where. Instead he tells us other things, strange and crazy things, perhaps he too is playing with us. Perhaps he is mad—one goes mad in the Lager. He says that every Sunday there are concerts and football matches. He says that whoever boxes well can become cook. He says that whoever works well receives prize-coupons with which to buy tobacco and soap. He says that the water is really not drinkable, and that instead a coffee substitute is distributed every day, but generally nobody drinks it as the soup itself is sufficiently watery to quench thirst. We beg him to find us something to drink, but he says that he cannot, that he has come to see us secretly, against SS orders, as we still have to be disinfected, and that he must leave at once; he has come because he has a liking for Italians, and because, he says, he "has a little heart." We ask him if there are other Italians in the camp and he says there are some, a few, he does not know how many; and he at once changes the subject. Meanwhile a bell

13 ▼ Critical Viewing In what way does this image capture the "demolition of a man" discussed by Levi? **[Connect]**

13. **Lager** (läg' r) German: "camp."

12

Drawing for the Transportation Bas Relief, Dee Clements

ENRICHMENT: History Connection

The Holocaust in Italy

Italy had encouraged the Nazis' rise to power. But Italian dictator Benito Mussolini originally had little interest in persecuting Italy's Jews. In fact, the Italian Fascist party included a small number of Jewish members. Yet, as Germany and Italy drew closer together, Mussolini decided that Italy, too, needed to preserve its "racial purity." In November 1938, Italy's "racial laws" went into effect.

However, until the German invasion of 1943, Italian Jews such as Primo Levi were seldom deported to camps. Even after the German invasion, many Italians hid their Jewish neighbors or smuggled them to freedom. For this reason, about 85 percent of the 45,200 Italian Jews survived to the end of the war. Yet almost 7,000 were captured, loaded onto cattle cars, and sent to concentration camps. Primo Levi was one of the tiny minority who returned home to tell their stories.

rang and he immediately hurried off and left us stunned and disconcerted. Some feel refreshed but I do not. I still think that even this dentist, this incomprehensible person, wanted to amuse himself at our expense, and I do not want to believe a word of what he said.

At the sound of the bell, we can hear the still dark camp waking up. Unexpectedly the water gushes out boiling from the showers—five minutes of bliss; but immediately after, four men (perhaps they are the barbers) burst in yelling and shoving and drive us out, wet and steaming, into the adjoining room which is freezing; here other shouting people throw at us unrecognizable rags and thrust into our hands a pair of broken-down boots with wooden soles; we have no time to understand and we already find ourselves in the open, in the blue and icy snow of dawn, barefoot and naked, with all our clothing in our hands, with a hundred yards to run to the next hut. There we are finally allowed to get dressed.

When we finish, everyone remains in his own corner and we do not dare lift our eyes to look at one another. There is nowhere to look in a mirror, but our appearance stands in front of us, reflected in a hundred livid faces, in a hundred miserable and sordid puppets. We are transformed into the phantoms glimpsed yesterday evening.

sordid (sôr´ did) *adj.* filthy; depressingly wretched

Then for the first time we became aware that our language lacks words to express this offense, the demolition of a man. In a moment, with almost prophetic intuition, the reality was revealed to us: we had reached the bottom. It is not possible to sink lower than this; no human condition is more miserable than this, nor could it conceivably be so. Nothing belongs to us anymore; they have taken away our clothes, our shoes, even our hair; if we speak, they will not listen to us, and if they listen, they will not understand. They will even take away our name: and if we want to keep it, we will have to find in ourselves the strength to do so, to manage somehow so that behind the name something of us, of us as we were, still remains.

prophetic (prō fet´ ik) *adj.* giving a prediction of the future

intuition (in´ to͞o ish´ ən) *n.* instinctive understanding

14 We know that we will have difficulty in being understood, and this is as it should be. But consider what value, what meaning is enclosed even in the smallest of our daily habits, in the hundred possessions which even the poorest beggar owns: a handkerchief, an old letter, the photo of a cherished person. These things are part of us, almost like limbs of our body; nor is it conceivable that we can be deprived of them in our world, for we immediately find others to substitute the old ones, other objects which are ours in their personification and evocation of our memories.

Literary Analysis
Autobiography Identify one technique Levi uses to put "the demolition of a man" into words.

Imagine now a man who is deprived of everyone he loves, and at the same time of his house, his habits, his clothes, in short, of everything he possesses: he will be a hollow man, reduced to suffering and needs, forgetful of dignity and restraint, for he who loses all often easily loses himself. He will be a man whose life or death can be lightly decided with no sense of human affinity, in the most fortunate of cases, on the basis of a pure judgment of utility. It is in this way that one can understand

affinity (ə fin´ i tē) *n.* close relationship; natural liking

15 ✔ **Reading Check**
What does Levi say the prisoners are left with?

14 Literary Analysis

Autobiography

- Remind students that in an autobiography, an author tells his or her own life story and can offer personal insight into historical events.
- Have students read the first sentence in the bracketed passage, and call their attention to the phrase "the demolition of a man." Ask them to explain what Levi means by this.
  Possible response: The Nazis will destroy Levi and his comrades spiritually, emotionally, and physically.
- Suggest to students that for Levi, "the demolition of a man" is what the Nazis did to Jews beginning with their arrival at Auschwitz. It is a central focus of Levi's autobiography.
- Ask students the Literary Analysis question on p. 1265: Identify one technique Levi uses to put "the demolition of a man" into words.
  Possible response: Levi lists the things the Nazis have taken from the prisoners, including their clothes, their hair, the capacity to be understood, and their names; he describes the importance of "the smallest of [the individual's] daily habits" and possessions, all of which have been taken away; and he describes a person robbed of everything as "a hollow man" whom others will not consider human.
- Make sure that students recognize that in these paragraphs, Levi uses language, which he first denounces as lacking, to describe his experiences. Discuss the impact of this strategy on the reader.

15 ✔ Reading Check

Answer: Levi says that the prisoners are left with nothing at all.

CUSTOMIZE INSTRUCTION FOR UNIVERSAL ACCESS

For Less Proficient Readers	For Gifted/Talented Students	For Advanced Readers
Tell students that Levi recounts his nightmarish experience as a sequence of vivid details. Tell each student to choose one detail and answer the following questions about it: What is your response to this detail? Why do you think Levi included it? How does this detail contribute to the narrative as a whole?	Tell students that Levi's narrative shows how the Nazi treatment of prisoners was designed to strip individuals of their identities before putting them to death. Tell students to write personal essays about an experience that helped define their personal identities. Encourage students to share their essays with the class.	Remind students that irony is the discrepancy between appearance and reality, or between what is said and what is meant. Help students identify instances of irony in Levi's narrative. Tell students to write essays in which they analyze Levi's use of irony and how this irony contributes to the theme of the narrative.

⓰ Literary Analysis

Autobiography and Memoir

- Point out that *Survival in Auschwitz* is a memoir because it focuses on Levi's experiences during the Holocaust. Rather than telling his entire life story, he offers insight into this historical event.
- Have students read the bracketed passage. Then, ask the Reading Strategy question on p. 1266: By telling the reader about his number, what insight does Levi suggest? Explain.
Possible response: Levi suggests that the process of being numbered and tattooed is a "baptism" for death rather than for life.

Answers for p. 1266

Review and Assess

1. Possible response: This work could be recommended to anyone interested in the Holocaust. Anyone who believes that he or she is superior to any other group of human beings might benefit from reading Levi's narrative. It might force such readers to recognize the destruction of elitism and racism.
2. **(a)** Possible responses: The prisoners are deprived of water; their clothes are taken away; they are forced to stand and wait indefinitely while naked and cold; they are sheared; they are insulted by Nazi officers; and they are denied information. **(b)** Hell is the worst experience humanly imaginable. The treatment by the Nazis is worse than anything Levi has previously imagined. Therefore, the room with the water replaces any predetermined notions of hell, because the water, essential for life, is undrinkable.
3. **(a)** Flesch is a selective translator. He translates most, but not all, of the German words. **(b)** Possible response: Flesch is reluctant to be a conduit for oppression by inflicting the cruelty of the words and actions on his fellow prisoners.
4. **(a)** The prisoners are "renamed" when they are tattooed with numbers they must show to get food. **(b)** Levi describes the renaming as a baptism for death.

continued

the double sense of the term "extermination camp," and it is now clear what we seek to express with the phrase: "to lie on the bottom."

Häftling:[14] I have learnt that I am a Häftling. My number is 174517; we have been baptized, we will carry the tattoo on our left arm until we die.

⓰ The operation was slightly painful and extraordinarily rapid: they placed us all in a row, and one by one, according to the alphabetical order of our names, we filed past a skillful official, armed with a sort of pointed tool with a very short needle. It seems that this is the real, true initiation: only by "showing one's number" can one get bread and soup. Several days passed, and not a few cuffs and punches, before we became used to showing our number promptly enough not to disorder the daily operation of food-distribution; weeks and months were needed to learn its sound in the German language. And for many days, while the habits of freedom still led me to look for the time on my wristwatch, my new name ironically appeared instead, its number tattooed in bluish characters under the skin.

Literary Analysis
Autobiography and Memoir By telling the reader about his number, what insight does Levi suggest? Explain.

14. ***Häftling*** (heft' lin) German: "prisoner."

Review and Assess

Thinking About the Selection

1. **Respond:** To what audience would you recommend Levi's autobiography? Why?
2. **(a) Recall:** Describe three ways in which the prisoners are mistreated when they arrive at Auschwitz. **(b) Interpret:** What do you think Levi means when he writes "Today, in our times, hell must be like this"?
3. **(a) Recall:** Describe the way in which Flesch fulfills his role as translator. **(b) Infer:** Why is he reluctant to translate the German officer's comments into Italian?
4. **(a) Recall:** Explain the way in which the prisoners are "renamed" at the camp. **(b) Analyze:** What does Levi feel is the significance of this renaming?
5. **(a) Infer:** According to Levi, what makes up human identity? **(b) Draw Conclusions:** What does Levi suggest are the primary goals of the concentration camp?
6. **Draw Conclusions:** Referring to the Nazi treatment of the prisoners, Levi writes that "our language lacks words to express this offense, the demolition of a man." What does this remark imply about Levi's task of writing a memoir of this experience?

continued from left column

5. **(a)** Levi believes that family and home as well as many small things, like hair, clothes, minor possessions, and personal habits make up human identity. **(b)** Levi suggests that the concentration camp's goal is to strip away everything that makes up the human identities of its prisoners. Levi says a person robbed of identity is one "whose life or death can be lightly decided with no sense of human affinity."
6. Possible response: Levi acknowledges the inadequacy of words to convey the demolition of a man; yet, he writes his narrative anyway. Although language is a faulty tool, his act suggests that storytelling is the only means he has to rebuild a man.

17

from Night

Elie Wiesel

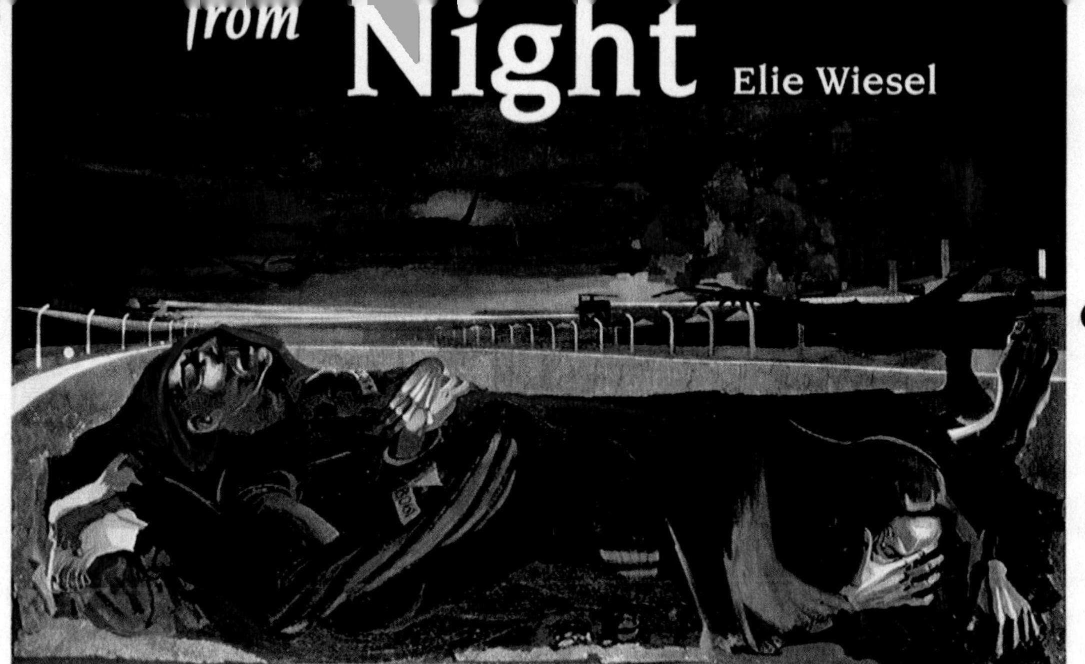

18

translated by Stella Rodway

Background

Toward the end of World War II (1939–1945), as the Allied armies fighting the Germans gained territory, German forces evacuated the inmates of the concentration camps in forced "death marches" and in "death trains." They hoped to send the prisoners deeper into Germany to prevent their liberation. In this excerpt from *Night,* Wiesel describes his experiences as a sixteen-year-old sent on such a journey with his father.

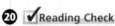

19 ▲ Critical Viewing
What does this painting suggest about the mood of Wiesel's memoir? **[Predict]**

That same evening, we reached our destination.

It was late at night. The guards came to unload us. The dead were abandoned in the train. Only those who could still stand were able to get out.

Meir Katz stayed in the train. The last day had been the most murderous. A hundred of us had got into the wagon. A dozen of us got out—among them, my father and I.

We had arrived at Buchenwald.[1]

20 ✓ Reading Check
What happened to many of Eliezer's fellow passengers?

1. **Buchenwald** (bo͝ok´ ′n wôld´) village in Germany that was the site of a Nazi concentration camp and extermination center.

CUSTOMIZE INSTRUCTION FOR UNIVERSAL ACCESS

For Less Proficient Readers	For English Learners	For Advanced Readers
Whereas Primo Levi's memoir is cerebral, Wiesel's *Night* is direct, with a great deal of dialogue. To help students appreciate the selection's rhythms, have them read along with **Listening to Literature Audiocassettes** or **Audio CDs**.	The language in *Night* should be accessible to students; use the selection to model the process of paraphrasing. Before students read, choose a few paragraphs and paraphrase them with students. Then, after students read, check their understanding by having them put selected passages into their own words.	Students may be interested in grappling with the moral issues in this selection. Begin by having them read "What Is Right?" in **Beyond Literature,** on p. 60. Then, ask students to note the moral dilemma Wiesel faces with his father's imminent death. Finally, have students prepare statements evaluating Wiesel's actions in the camp.

17 About the Selection

In his memoir *Night,* Eliezer (Elie) Wiesel describes his experiences during the Holocaust. This excerpt focuses on the Wiesels' last days in the camps. As the Nazis lose ground, he and his father are moved to the camp at Buchenwald. Here, his father weakens. Wiesel struggles with his own desire to survive—and his guilt—as he watches his father die. After his father is gone, the Nazis flee the camp. Soon, American tanks are at the gates.

18 Background

Art

To the Victims of Fascism,
by Hans Grundig

German painter Hans Grundig (1901–1958) and his wife, Lea, were both documentary artists who used their art to lead a campaign against the Nazis. During the war, Grundig was interned in a concentration camp.

In Grundig's *To the Victims of Fascism,* two corpses lie in the foreground of an enclosure fenced with barbed wire. Both wear the numbers of political prisoners, and one is also marked as a Jew. The color red, symbolizing blood, dominates the canvas.

Use the following questions for discussion:

- What feeling or mood does this painting convey? Explain.
  Possible response: The corpses left out in the open under a dark red sky evoke horror, shame, agony, and outrage.
- How does this painting convey the theme of the senselessness of human destruction?
  Possible response: The agonized appearance of the bodies and the apparent lack of dignity accorded to them convey this theme.

19 ▶ Critical Viewing

Possible response: The painting suggests that the mood will be grim and will confront the horrors of the concentration camp.

20 ✓ Reading Check

Answer: Nearly all of Eliezer's fellow passengers died on the train before reaching Buchenwald.

21 Critical Thinking

Infer

- Have students read the bracketed line. Then, ask them to consider the image of the teenage Eliezer holding his father's hand. Students may observe that this act may not be common in our society today.
- Ask students what inferences they can make about the relationship between Eliezer and his father from the image of the boy holding his father's hand.
  Possible response: Eliezer's experience in the camps has in some ways thwarted his rite of passage into adulthood; therefore, he clings, childlike, to his father, who is the last link with Eliezer's life before the camps.
- Tell students to bear this inference in mind as they read more about the complicated relationship between Eliezer and his father.

22 Literary Analysis

Autobiography

- Remind students that an autobiography is an author's telling of his or her life story.
- Explain to students that although it is very different in style from Primo Levi's *Survival in Auschwitz*, *Night* is also an autobiography that focuses on its author's experiences in the Nazi concentration camps.
- Point out that one of the key differences between Wiesel's and Levi's autobiographies is that Wiesel makes extensive use of dialogue.
- Have students read the bracketed passage on pp. 1268–1269 independently. Then, have them read it a second time, with different students taking turns reading the dialogue aloud.
- Ask students the Literary Analysis question on p. 1268: In what way does Wiesel's use of dialogue enrich his autobiography?
  Possible response: The suffering of Wiesel's father and the young Wiesel's frustration with his father are clearly conveyed through dialogue. The first-person narrator cannot relay his father's thoughts and feelings in any other way.

At the gate of the camp, SS[2] officers were waiting for us. They counted us. Then we were directed to the assembly place. Orders were given us through loudspeakers:

"Form fives!" "Form groups of a hundred!" "Five paces forward!"

21 I held onto my father's hand—the old, familiar fear: not to lose him.

Right next to us the high chimney of the crematory oven[3] rose up. It no longer made any impression on us. It scarcely attracted our attention.

An established inmate of Buchenwald told us that we should have a shower and then we could go into the blocks. The idea of having a hot bath fascinated me. My father was silent. He was breathing heavily beside me.

"Father," I said. "Only another moment more. Soon we can lie down—in a bed. You can rest. . . ."

He did not answer. I was so exhausted myself that his silence left me indifferent. My only wish was to take a bath as quickly as possible and lie down in a bed.

But it was not easy to reach the showers. Hundreds of prisoners were crowding there. The guards were unable to keep any order. They struck out right and left with no apparent result. Others, without the strength to push or even to stand up, had sat down in the snow. My father wanted to do the same. He groaned.

"I can't go on. . . . This is the end. . . . I'm going to die here. . . ."

He dragged me toward a hillock of snow from which emerged human shapes and ragged pieces of blanket.

"Leave me," he said to me. "I can't go on. . . . Have mercy on me. . . . I'll wait here until we can get into the baths. . . . You can come and find me."

I could have wept with rage. Having lived through so much, suffered so much, could I leave my father to die now? Now, when we could have a good hot bath and lie down?

"Father!" I screamed. "Father! Get up from here! Immediately! You're
22 killing yourself. . . ."

I seized him by the arm. He continued to groan.

"Don't shout, son. . . . Take pity on your old father. . . . Leave me to rest here. . . . Just for a bit, I'm so tired . . . at the end of my strength. . . ."

He had become like a child, weak, timid, vulnerable.

"Father," I said. "You can't stay here."

I showed him the corpses all around him; they too had wanted to rest here.

"I can see them, son. I can see them all right. Let them sleep. It's so long since they closed their eyes. . . . They are exhausted . . . exhausted. . . ."

His voice was tender.

I yelled against the wind:

Literary Analysis
Autobiography In what way does Wiesel's use of dialogue enrich his autobiography?

---

2. **SS** quasi-military unit of the Nazi party, used as a special police.
3. **crematory oven** large oven in which the corpses of Holocaust victims were burned. In some cases, victims were burned while still alive.

ENRICHMENT: History Connection

Life and Death in the Nazi Concentration Camps

The first concentration camps were established as early as 1933. By the time World War II had started, more than 20,000 people were imprisoned in the camps. The numbers grew tremendously over the next six years. Upon arrival at the camps, those who were not strong enough to work were gassed to death; their bodies were then burned in crematoriums. Those who could work were forced into slave labor and simply worked to death.

Countless prisoners died of starvation and disease and from the awful living conditions. Millions were gassed or shot. The Nazis often killed the sick. Nazi doctors performed medical experiments on the healthy. By the war's end—which was rapidly approaching in this excerpt from *Night*—the Nazis had killed about six million Jews—nearly two-thirds of Europe's entire Jewish population.

"They'll never wake again! Never! Don't you understand?"

For a long time this argument went on. I felt that I was not arguing with him, but with death itself, with the death that he had already chosen.

The sirens began to wail. An alert. The lights went out throughout the camp. The guards drove us toward the blocks. In a flash, there was no one left on the assembly place. We were only too glad not to have had to stay outside longer in the icy wind. We let ourselves sink down onto the planks. The beds were in several tiers. The cauldrons of soup at the entrance attracted no one. To sleep, that was all that mattered.

It was daytime when I awoke. And then I remembered that I had a father. Since the alert, I had followed the crowd without troubling about him. I had known that he was at the end, on the brink of death, and yet I had abandoned him.

I went to look for him.

23 But at the same moment this thought came into my mind: "Don't let me find him! If only I could get rid of this dead weight, so that I could use all my strength to struggle for my own survival, and only worry about myself." Immediately I felt ashamed of myself, ashamed forever.

I walked for hours without finding him. Then I came to the block where they were giving out black "coffee." The men were lining up and fighting.

A plaintive, beseeching voice caught me in the spine:

"Eliezer . . . my son . . . bring me . . . a drop of coffee. . . ."

I ran to him.

"Father! I've been looking for you for so long. . . . Where were you? Did you sleep? . . . How do you feel?"

24 He was burning with fever. Like a wild beast, I cleared a way for myself to the coffee cauldron. And I managed to carry back a cupful. I had a sip. The rest was for him. I can't forget the light of thankfulness in his eyes while he gulped it down—an animal gratitude. With those few gulps of hot water, I probably brought him more satisfaction than I had done during my whole childhood.

He was lying on a plank, livid,[4] his lips pale and dried up, shaken by tremors. I could not stay by him for long. Orders had been given to

4. **livid** (liv′ id) *adj.* here, bruised; grayish blue or pale.

25 **▲ Critical Viewing**

Does Wiesel's memoir suggest any possibility of understanding why a group of people reduced others to the condition of these inmates? Explain. **[Apply]**

plaintive (plān′ tiv) *adj.* expressing sorrow; mournful

beseeching (bē sēch′ iŋ) *adj.* asking for something earnestly

26 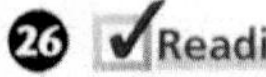

Reading Check

What problem with his father does Eliezer have to confront?

23 Reading Strategy

Connecting to Historical Context

- Have a volunteer read aloud the bracketed passage. Then, ask students whether they think Eliezer's thoughts and feelings about finding his father are selfish.
  Possible response: The reality of the concentration camp would probably make such thoughts unavoidable.
- Remind students of the unimaginable pressure on Eliezer and the difficulty of surviving in the camps. Read aloud the Enrichment note on p. 1268.
- Ask students whether, given the historical context, Eliezer's feelings are understandable.
  Possible response: Eliezer's conflicted feelings are understandable. His efforts to suppress his darkest thoughts are even heroic.

24 Critical Thinking

Analyze

- Ask students what comparison the author uses to describe his actions and his father's response in this passage.
  Answer: He compares himself to a wild beast in the way that he pushes himself through the crowd of men to get coffee for his father. He compares his father's thankfulness to animal gratitude.
- Then, ask students what the author's purpose is in making comparisons between human and animal behavior.
  Answer: The author wanted to show how dehumanized the prisoners had become. Humans had become like animals in their behavior—all actions focused on survival.

25 ▶ Critical Viewing

Possible response: Wiesel's memoir does not attempt to explains the *why* of the Holocaust. It explains how Jews were treated and how some survived.

26 Reading Check

Answer: Eliezer struggles—against his father's lack of will and his own survival instinct—to keep his father alive. Eliezer also struggles with his desire to be rid of the weight of caring for his father so that Eliezer can save himself.

CUSTOMIZE INSTRUCTION FOR UNIVERSAL ACCESS

For Special Needs Students	For Gifted/Talented Students
Students may have difficulty understanding the moral dilemma Eliezer faces as he deals with his father. Help students connect to Eliezer's situation by brainstorming times they have been at odds with their own parents or times they have faced a moral dilemma. Then, explain that his father's illness requires Eliezer to give up resources such as food and energy that are very limited in the camp. Eliezer recognizes that by giving these things up for his father, he is making his own survival more difficult.	In this section of Elie Wiesel's *Night,* Eliezer's father is a striking nonpresence. Near the end of the ordeal in the concentration camps, Eliezer's father seems reduced to little more than a "plaintive, beseeching voice." Ask students to create an artistic representation of Eliezer's father. Students may draw, paint, or sculpt. Regardless of medium, students' representations should capture the reduced state of Eliezer's father as well as the tension among life, death, duty, and survival.

27 Background

Art

***1943 A.D.*, by Ben Shahn**

Ben Shahn (1898–1969) did not witness the Holocaust firsthand. Nonetheless, he had a long history of addressing social issues in his work. His first solo exhibition was held in New York City in 1930. *The Passion of Sacco and Vanzetti*, scenes from the controversial murder trial of Italian-American anarchists painted between 1931 and 1932, made Shahn famous. He went on to create images of the Great Depression for the United States government.

1943 A.D. suggests the intense thoughtfulness characteristic of Shahn's work.

Use the following question for discussion:

What elements of this painting indicate that its subject is the Holocaust?

Possible response: The man in the foreground faces barbed wire, a piece of which appears to bind his forehead. His emaciated appearance and the laborers behind him also suggest the Holocaust. Finally, the title of the painting is the year the Holocaust was at its peak.

28 ▶Critical Viewing

Possible response: This prisoner may be struggling with moral conflicts as he tries to survive.

29 Critical Thinking

Infer

- Ask a volunteer to read the bracketed passage aloud.
- Then, ask students to explain what the author means when he says that his father spoke as if he were afraid he would not have time.

Answer: The father talks faster and faster because he is afraid he will die before he can tell his son where to find the gold and money.

clear the place for cleaning. Only the sick could stay.

We stayed outside for five hours. Soup was given out. As soon as we were allowed to go back to the blocks, I ran to my father.

"Have you had anything to eat?"

"No."

"Why not?"

"They didn't give us anything . . . they said that if we were ill we should die soon anyway and it would be a pity to waste the food. I can't go on any more. . . ."

I gave him what was left of my soup. But it was with a heavy heart. I felt that I was giving it up to him against my will. No better than Rabbi Eliahou's son[5] had I withstood the test.

He grew weaker day by day, his gaze veiled, his face the color of dead leaves. On the third day after our arrival at Buchenwald, everyone had to go to the showers. Even the sick, who had to go through last.

27 *1943 A.D.*, c.1943, Ben Shahn, Courtesy of the Syracuse University Art Collection. © Estate of Ben Shahn/Licensed by VAGA, New York, NY

28 ▲ **Critical Viewing** Given what you have read in Wiesel's memoir, explain what thoughts might preoccupy this prisoner. **[Apply]**

On the way back from the baths, we had to wait outside for a long time. They had not yet finished cleaning the blocks.

Seeing my father in the distance, I ran to meet him. He went by me like a ghost, passed me without stopping, without looking at me. I called to him. He did not come back. I ran after him:

"Father, where are you running to?"

He looked at me for a moment, and his gaze was distant, visionary; it was the face of someone else. A moment only and on he ran again.

Struck down with dysentery,[6] my father lay in his bunk, five other invalids with him. I sat by his side, watching him, not daring to believe that he could escape death again. Nevertheless, I did all I could to give him hope.

Suddenly, he raised himself on his bunk and put his feverish lips to my ear:

29 "Eliezer . . . I must tell you where to find the gold and the money I buried . . . in the cellar. . . . You know. . . ."

He began to talk faster and faster, as though he were afraid he would not have time to tell me. I tried to explain to him that this was not the

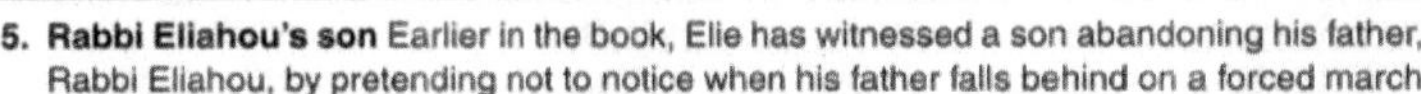

5. **Rabbi Eliahou's son** Earlier in the book, Elie has witnessed a son abandoning his father, Rabbi Eliahou, by pretending not to notice when his father falls behind on a forced march.
6. **dysentery** (dis′ ən ter′ ē) *n.* disease of the intestines.

ENRICHMENT: History Connection

The Holocaust's Other Victims

The elimination of the Jews of Europe was the goal of the Holocaust, and Jews were the main targets of the Nazi concentration camps. But they were not the only victims of the Nazis. Communists, Gypsies, and others whom the Nazi party believed did not exemplify German purity were imprisoned in concentration camps. Many suffered the same hideous treatment the Nazis meted out to their Jewish victims.

Many Jews have written remembrances of the atrocities they suffered during the Holocaust. But just as Jews were not the only victims, they have not been the only ones to bear witness. A great deal of powerful writing—for both adults and children—has come from the memoirs of non-Jews living in occupied Italy, Norway, Poland, Holland, and even within Germany itself. You may wish to recommend to students martyred Lutheran theologian Dietrich Bonhoeffer's *Letters and Papers from Prison*. Bonhoeffer wrote this work during his incarceration in a Nazi prison during the war.

end, that we would go back to the house together, but he would not listen to me. He could no longer listen to me. He was exhausted. A trickle of saliva, mingled with blood, was running from between his lips. He had closed his eyes. His breath was coming in gasps.

For a ration of bread, I managed to change beds with a prisoner in my father's bunk. In the afternoon the doctor came. I went and told him that my father was very ill.

"Bring him here!"

I explained that he could not stand up. But the doctor refused to listen to anything. Somehow, I brought my father to him. He stared at him, then questioned him in a clipped voice:

"What do you want?"

"My father's ill," I answered for him. "Dysentery . . ."

"Dysentery? That's not my business. I'm a surgeon. Go on! Make room for the others."

Protests did no good.

"I can't go on, son. . . . Take me back to my bunk. . . ."

I took him back and helped him to lie down. He was shivering.

"Try and sleep a bit, father. Try to go to sleep. . . ."

His breathing was labored, thick. He kept his eyes shut. Yet I was convinced that he could see everything, that now he could see the truth in all things.

Another doctor came to the block. But my father would not get up. He knew that it was useless.

31 Besides, this doctor had only come to finish off the sick. I could hear him shouting at them that they were lazy and just wanted to stay in bed. I felt like leaping at his throat, strangling him. But I no longer had the courage or the strength. I was riveted to my father's deathbed. My hands hurt, I was clenching them so hard. Oh, to strangle the doctor and the others! To burn the whole world! My father's murderers! But the cry stayed in my throat.

When I came back from the bread distribution, I found my father weeping like a child:

"Son, they keep hitting me!"

"Who?"

I thought he was delirious.

"Him, the Frenchman . . . and the Pole . . . they were hitting me."

Another wound to the heart, another hate, another reason for living lost.

"Eliezer . . . Eliezer . . . tell them not to hit me. . . . I haven't done anything . . . . Why do they keep hitting me?"

I began to abuse his neighbors. They laughed at me. I promised them bread, soup. They laughed. Then they got angry; they could not stand

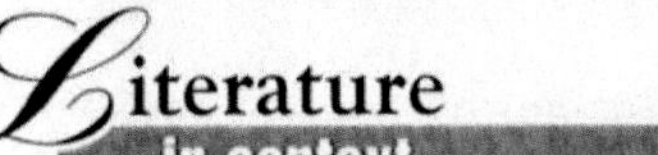

Literature in context Cultural Connection

30 ***Wiesel's Nobel Prize***

On December 10, 1986, Elie Wiesel was presented with the Nobel Prize for his contributions to world peace. The president of the Nobel Committee mentioned Wiesel's father in his introductory address. He said, "You were with your father when he passed away; it was the darkest hour of your life. And this is the most glorious. It is therefore fitting that your own son be with you as you receive the highest distinction humanity can bestow upon one of its own." In his memoir *All Rivers Run to the Sea*, Wiesel describes his response to the president's unexpected words: "I was shaken by the linking of my father and my son. I saw them standing together. My lips moved, but no sound came out. Tears filled my eyes, the tears I couldn't shed so long ago."

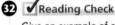

32  **Reading Check**

Give an example of a way in which Eliezer takes care of his father.

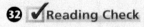

30 Background

Wiesel's Nobel Prize

Wiesel titled his Nobel acceptance speech "Keep Memory Alive." In it, he contemplated his own memories of the Holocaust, his childhood, and his father. "I remember:" he spoke. "It happened yesterday, or eternities ago. A young Jewish boy discovered the Kingdom of Night. I remember his bewilderment, I remember his anguish. It all happened so fast. The ghetto. The deportation. The sealed cattle car. The fiery altar upon which the history of our people and the future of mankind were meant to be sacrificed.

"I remember he asked his father: 'Can this be true? This is the twentieth century, not the Middle Ages. Who would allow such crimes to be committed? How could the world remain silent?'

"And now the boy is turning to me. 'Tell me,' he asks. 'What have you done with my future? What have you done with your life?'

"And I tell him that I have tried. That I have tried to keep memory alive, that I have tried to fight those who would forget. Because if we forget, we are guilty, we are accomplices."

31 Critical Thinking

Connect

- Have students pause before reading the bracketed passage. Ask them to describe Eliezer's feelings toward his father.
  Answer: Eliezer loves his father and has been willing to sacrifice dearly to try to save him. However, Eliezer has a desperate, guilty desire to be free of the burden of caring for his father.
- Have students read the bracketed passage independently. Ask them to connect the emotions Eliezer reveals with their previous impressions.
  Possible response: Eliezer's outpouring of rage illuminates the depth of his love for, and urge to protect, his father.

32 Reading Check

Possible responses: Eliezer shares his rations with his father, trades some of his bread to get a bunk near his father, and attempts to protect his father from the Nazis and the other prisoners.

CUSTOMIZE INSTRUCTION FOR UNIVERSAL ACCESS

For Less Proficient Readers	For Advanced Readers
Tell students that the night before the author and his family were rounded up by Nazi soldiers, they dug a dozen holes in the ground under the trees in their backyard. In the holes, the family buried what was left of their valuable possessions. The precious object that the author buried was the gold watch that had been given to him on his bar mitzvah. Ask students to share which of their possessions they might try to save in such a situation and why. Invite students to bring the objects (or photographs of the objects) to class.	Have students discuss why writers such as Elie Wiesel believe they must tell their experiences of the Holocaust. Share with students the excerpt from Wiesel's Nobel Peace Prize acceptance speech on ATE p. 1271. Ask students why Wiesel believes forgetting would make the world—even himself—share the guilt of the Nazis. Lead students to recognize that one of the goals of the Holocaust was to destroy the memory of life as well as life itself.

my father any longer, they said, because he was now unable to drag himself outside to relieve himself.

The following day he complained that they had taken his ration of bread.

"While you were asleep?"

"No. I wasn't asleep. They jumped on top of me. They snatched my bread . . . and they hit me . . . again. . . . I can't stand any more, son . . . a drop of water. . . ."

33 I knew that he must not drink. But he pleaded with me for so long that I gave in. Water was the worst poison he could have, but what else could I do for him? With water, without water, it would all be over soon anyway. . . .

"You, at least, have some mercy on me. . . ."

Have mercy on him! I, his only son!

A week went by like this.

"This is your father, isn't it?" asked the head of the block.

"Yes."

"He's very ill."

"The doctor won't do anything for him."

"The doctor *can't* do anything for him, now. And neither can you."

He put his great hairy hand on my shoulder and added:

"Listen to me, boy. Don't forget that you're in a concentration camp. Here, every man has to fight for himself and not think of anyone else. Even of his father. Here, there are no fathers, no brothers, no friends. Everyone lives and dies for himself alone. I'll give you a sound piece of advice—don't give your ration of bread and soup to your old father. There's nothing you can do for him. And you're killing yourself. Instead, you ought to be having his ration."

34 I listened to him without interrupting. He was right, I thought in the most secret region of my heart, but I dared not admit it. It's too late to save your old father, I said to myself. You ought to be having two rations of bread, two rations of soup. . . .

Only a fraction of a second, but I felt guilty. I ran to find a little soup to give my father. But he did not want it. All he wanted was water.

"Don't drink water . . . have some soup. . . ."

"I'm burning . . . why are you being so unkind to me, my son? Some water. . . ."

I brought him some water. Then I left the block for roll call. But I turned around and came back again. I lay down on the top bunk. Invalids were allowed to stay in the block. So I would be an invalid myself. I would not leave my father.

There was silence all round now, broken only by groans. In front of the block, the SS were giving orders. An officer passed by the beds. My father begged me:

"My son, some water. . . . I'm burning. . . . My stomach. . . ."

"Quiet, over there!" yelled the officer.

"Eliezer," went on my father, "some water. . . ."

Reading Strategy
Connecting to Historical Context Using facts about life in the concentration camps, explain why Wiesel was led to such dark thoughts.

33 Background

Science

Tell students that the author does not want to give his gravely ill father water because the water is most likely contaminated and one of the causes of his dysentery. On the other hand, people with dysentery can die from dehydration. Tell students that dysentery is transmitted through contaminated water and food and is commonly found in crowded, unsanitary conditions.

34 Reading Strategy

Connecting to Historical Context

- Ask students to explain what factual information they have learned about life in the concentration camps.
  Possible response: Life in the camps was brutal. Prisoners were stripped of their identities and denied basic necessities of life. Many found themselves reduced to the animal struggle to survive.
- Have students read the bracketed passage. Then, ask students to respond to the Reading Strategy item on p. 1272: Using facts about life in the concentration camps, explain why Wiesel was led to such dark thoughts.
  Possible response: Eliezer had long been deprived of adequate food and water and had faced the constant threat of violence and death at the hands of the Nazis.

Monitor Progress Ask students to explain how connecting the bracketed passage to its historical context enhances the power of the passage.
Possible response: The reality of life in the concentration camps makes Eliezer's rejection of his dark thoughts, and his guilt over thinking them at all, a powerful act of courage and human decency.

Reteach If students do not recognize the significance the historical context adds to this paragraph, have them reread the paragraph that precedes the bracketed passage. Then, explain that Eliezer rejects the head of the block's advice, choosing instead to be a son to his father.

ENRICHMENT: History Connection

The United States Holocaust Memorial Museum

Elie Wiesel headed the United States Holocaust Memorial Council from 1980 to 1986 and was instrumental in creating the United States Holocaust Memorial Museum. The museum opened in Washington, D.C., in April 1993, honoring victims, survivors, liberators, and rescuers. In his dedication speech, Wiesel stressed the importance of remembering those who died, saying, "Memory is not only a victory over time, it is also a triumph over injustice."

The officer came up to him and shouted at him to be quiet. But my father did not hear him. He went on calling me. The officer dealt him a violent blow on the head with his truncheon.

I did not move. I was afraid. My body was afraid of also receiving a blow.

Then my father made a rattling noise and it was my name: "Eliezer."

I could see that he was still breathing—spasmodically.[7]

I did not move.

When I got down after roll call, I could see his lips trembling as he murmured something. Bending over him, I stayed gazing at him for over an hour, engraving into myself the picture of his blood-stained face, his shattered skull.

Then I had to go to bed. I climbed into my bunk, above my father, who was still alive. It was January 28, 1945.

I awoke on January 29 at dawn. In my father's place lay another invalid. They must have taken him away before dawn and carried him to the crematory. He may still have been breathing.

35 There were no prayers at his grave. No candles were lit to his memory. His last word was my name. A summons, to which I did not respond.

I did not weep, and it pained me that I could not weep. But I had no more tears. And, in the depths of my being, in the recesses of my weakened conscience, could I have searched it, I might perhaps have found something like—free at last!

I had to stay at Buchenwald until April eleventh. I have nothing to say of my life during this period. It no longer mattered. After my father's death, nothing could touch me any more.

I was transferred to the children's block, where there were six hundred of us.

The front was drawing nearer.

I spent my days in a state of total idleness. And I had but one desire—to eat. I no longer thought of my father or of my mother.

7. **spasmodically** (spaz mäd' ik ə lē) *adv.* in spasms; intermittently; irregularly.

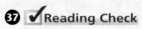

36 ▲ Critical Viewing

Explain what Wiesel's memoir adds to your reaction to this image of a young prisoner of Buchenwald. **[Respond]**

Literary Analysis

Autobiography and Memoir By focusing on his father, what basic human concerns does Wiesel dramatize?

37  **Reading Check**

What eventually happens to Eliezer's father?

35 Literary Analysis

Autobiography and Memoir

- Have students discuss Wiesel's depiction of his relationship with his father up to this point. Guide students to understand that Eliezer has struggled to remain loyal to his dying father, even when his loyalty threatens his own survival.
- Have students bear this in mind as they read the bracketed passage. Then, ask them the Literary Analysis question on p. 1273: By focusing on his father, what basic human concerns does Wiesel dramatize?
Possible response: Wiesel focuses on his father to dramatize the importance of family, even under such inhuman circumstances as the concentration camps. Wiesel also dramatizes his own struggle to remain human in an inhuman world.
- Point out to students that the style of Wiesel's memoir will change now that one of its central focuses—Eliezer's father—is gone.

36 ▶ Critical Viewing

Possible response: Wiesel's memoir has given readers a strong sense of what the boy in the photograph has endured and what he has yet to endure. It is also possible that the child may be waiting in line to be put to death. The young rarely survived the camps. If Eliezer had been this age, he may not have lived.

37 ✔ Reading Check

Answer: Eliezer's father is taken away during the night of January 28, 1945, presumably to the crematory. Wiesel speculates that he might have been barely alive when the guards took him.

CUSTOMIZE INSTRUCTION FOR UNIVERSAL ACCESS

For Special Needs Students	For English Learners	For Gifted/Talented Students
Although students should be able to follow the sequence of events Wiesel describes on pp. 1272–1273, they may have difficulty understanding his themes. Through discussion, lead students to understand that by caring for his father, Eliezer rejects the block head's advice: "Everyone lives and dies for himself alone."	The straightforward, accessible language of *Night* may offer students an ideal opportunity to practice speaking. Organize students into small groups. Within each group, have students take turns reading aloud, one or two paragraphs at a time. As groups read aloud, monitor student progress.	When his father finally dies, Eliezer is drastically changed: "nothing could touch me any more." Encourage students to write a story or poem that depicts this transformation. Tell students to describe what Eliezer is like before his father's death—and what he becomes.

From time to time I would dream of a drop of soup, of an extra ration of soup. . . .

On April fifth, the wheel of history turned.

It was late in the afternoon. We were standing in the block, waiting for an SS man to come and count us. He was late in coming. Such a delay was unknown till then in the history of Buchenwald. Something must have happened.

Two hours later the loudspeakers sent out an order from the head of the camp: all the Jews must come to the assembly place.

38 This was the end! Hitler was going to keep his promise.

The children in our block went toward the place. There was nothing else we could do. Gustav, the head of the block, made this clear to us with his truncheon. But on the way we met some prisoners who whispered to us:

"Go back to your block. The Germans are going to shoot you. Go back to your block, and don't move."

We went back to our block. We learned on the way that the camp resistance organization had decided not to abandon the Jews and was going to prevent their being liquidated.

As it was late and there was great upheaval—innumerable Jews had passed themselves off as non-Jews—the head of the camp decided that a general roll call would take place the following day. Everybody would have to be present.

The roll call took place. The head of the camp announced that Buchenwald was to be liquidated. 41 Ten blocks of deportees would be evacuated each day. From this moment, there would be no further distribution of bread and soup. And the evacuation began. Every day, several thousand prisoners went through the camp gate and never came back.

 39

liquidated (lik' wi dāt' id) *adj.* disposed of; ended; killed

deportees (dē' pôr tēz') *n.* people ordered to leave a country

40 ▼ **Critical Viewing**
What does Wiesel's account of daily life in Buchenwald add to your appreciation of the spirit of an inmate (see photograph) in drawing this portrait of another inmate? **[Interpret]**

38 Background

History

This "promise" refers to Hitler's "Final Solution" of killing all the Jews who lived in Germany and the lands Germany conquered during the war.

39 Background

Art

Portrait of an Unknown Prisoner, by Franciszek Jaz´wiecki

Jaz´wiecki (1900–1946) was born in Krakow, Poland. He studied graphic art at the Krakow Academy of Fine Arts. In 1940, he was arrested by the Nazis and he spent time in Auschwitz and in Buchenwald. All along, Jaz´wiecki (shown in the photograph at the bottom of the page) made portraits of fellow prisoners. Such art was not permitted by the Nazis, but Jaz´wiecki drew anyway. "I did not consider that drawing was forbidden and punished by death—it was not bravery," he wrote in his diary. "I simply disregarded the danger because to exist, to create, in one's own world, was irresistible."

Use the following question for discussion:

Do you think it was worth the risk of death to draw this portrait?
Possible response: To create, and thus to exist as a human being, is worth any risk. However, some viewers might be unable to imagine risking so much for art.

40 ▶ Critical Viewing

Possible response: Wiesel's account makes the viewer appreciate the courage to care enough about another person to draw his portrait. The drawing is evidence of the sustained humanity of the artist and subject.

41 Vocabulary Development

Latin Root *-port-*

- Call attention to the word *deportees* and its definition. Tell students that the Latin root *-port-* means "carry" or "move."
- Have students suggest words that contain this root. List suggestions on the board.
  Answer: *Import, portable,* and *transportation* feature *-port-*.
- Next, have students look up the meanings of these words.

ENRICHMENT: History Connection

The End of Elie Wiesel's War

Buchenwald, the concentration camp that Elie Wiesel describes in this section of *Night,* was located near the city of Weimar, Germany. More than 80,000 people were imprisoned there. Then, things changed: "On April fifth," Wiesel writes, "the wheel of history turned."

World War II was nearing its end in Europe. By April 1, Allied forces were in Germany. American troops were closing in on the Nazi's key industrial region, moving from the west. Weimar and Buchenwald were on the path to Berlin, the Nazi's capital.

The chaotic events Wiesel describes unfolded as Allied troops swept through Germany. The Nazi effort to evacuate the camp could have been stimulated only by the pressure of the imminent arrival of the Allies. American troops liberated the camp on April 11, according to Wiesel, after the Nazis had fled. By the end of that day, American forces were at the Elbe River. As April came to an end, Nazi resistance dwindled to virtually nothing. Hitler committed suicide on April 30. On May 8, 1945, the Nazis officially surrendered.

On April tenth, there were still about twenty thousand of us in the camp, including several hundred children. They decided to evacuate us all at once, right on until the evening. Afterward, they were going to blow up the camp.

So we were massed in the huge assembly square, in rows of five, waiting to see the gate open. Suddenly, the sirens began to wail. An alert! We went back to the blocks. It was too late to evacuate us that evening. The evacuation was postponed again to the following day.

We were tormented with hunger. We had eaten nothing for six days, except a bit of grass or some potato peelings found near the kitchens.

At ten o'clock in the morning the SS scattered through the camp, moving the last victims toward the assembly place.

Then the resistance movement decided to act. Armed men suddenly rose up everywhere. Bursts of firing. Grenades exploding. We children stayed flat on the ground in the block.

The battle did not last long. Toward noon everything was quiet again. The SS had fled and the resistance had taken charge of the running of the camp.

At about six o'clock in the evening, the first American tank stood at the gates of Buchenwald.

Review and Assess

Thinking About the Selection

1. **Respond:** Describe your reaction when sixteen-year-old Wiesel was liberated.
2. **(a) Recall:** In what ways does Wiesel change during his time in the camp? **(b) Analyze Cause and Effect:** What causes these changes?
3. **(a) Recall:** How does Wiesel respond to his father's illness? **(b) Compare and Contrast:** Contrast Wiesel's response with those of the doctor and his father's blockmates. **(c) Generalize:** What does this contrast show about basic human values in the camp?
4. **(a) Analyze:** While Wiesel's father is alive, what conflicting feelings does Wiesel experience? **(b) Infer:** Citing details, explain what Wiesel feels, in addition to sorrow, at his father's death.
5. **(a) Evaluate:** Do you think Wiesel's complicated feelings about his father show selfishness, or might anyone have experienced them? Explain.
6. **Extend:** Why might guilt be a common emotion experienced by the survivors of a tragedy? In your answer, draw on details from Wiesel's memoir.

Answers for p. 1275

Review and Assess

1. Possible response: Students may be torn between feelings of relief and lingering sorrow over the degree to which Eliezer's experiences have devastated his character.
2. **(a)** Although he clearly loves his father, Eliezer becomes hardened and unable to experience fully the grief of losing his father. **(b)** The dehumanizing conditions and daily brutality of the concentration camps cause these changes.
3. **(a)** Wiesel struggles to care for his father and, against all odds, to keep him from dying. **(b)** Eliezer is willing to risk his own survival for his father; others are not. The doctor and the blockmates see Eliezer's father as an annoyance to be eliminated. **(c)** The contrast shows that the camp is meant to destroy basic human values. Only through great struggle can inmates keep these values alive.
4. **(a)** Wiesel is torn between his desire to care for his father and his instinct to preserve his own life at all costs. **(b)** Wiesel feels free from having to care for and worry about his father. Wiesel thinks, "Free at last!" upon his father's death.
5. Possible response: Wiesel's feelings reveal a degree of selfishness. However, given the horrific conditions of the camps, Wiesel's complicated feelings are to be expected. Wiesel's effort to focus on caring for his father in such conditions is even heroic.
6. Possible response: Survivors of tragedies must deal with the fact that they have survived while many others—including those closest to them—have died. Survivors often wonder why they were spared when others were not.

CUSTOMIZE INSTRUCTION FOR UNIVERSAL ACCESS

For Special Needs Students	For Advanced Readers
Students may find Wiesel's depiction of the final days of the Buchenwald concentration camp confusing. Explain that the Nazis were losing the war at this point. Allied troops—in this case, Americans—were getting closer and closer to the camp. The Nazis did not want the camp to be discovered or its prisoners to be liberated. Have students read or reread pp. 1274–1275, pausing at key moments to review what has happened.	Encourage students to research the liberation of the concentration camps at the end of World War II. Students can begin by reading the rest of *Night*. Then, they should conduct research: When were the camps liberated and by which armies? How did people react when news of the Nazis' camps reached the rest of the world? What became of the prisoners? Have students share their findings with the class.

ASSESS

42 About the Selection

The speaker describes the beauty of early summer and the enchantment of dreams. However, the reverie is interrupted by memory. Children have been thrown to fiery deaths. How can the world go on, the speaker asks? Earth has not been discarded, and the sun and moon pretend they "have seen nothing."

Answers for p. 1276

Review and Assess

1. **Possible response:** The image of children "thrown like butterflies, / wings beating into the flames" may evoke powerful feelings of rage and sorrow.
2. **(a)** The speaker describes moonbeams and the blooming of lilies. **(b)** The opening lines suggest that the speaker is amazed by the beauty of nature and in awe of its mysteries.
3. **(a)** The voice accuses the world of playing games and "cheating time." **(b)** The children "thrown like butterflies" into fire—a reference to the Holocaust— should stop the world from its games. **(c) Possible response:** The memory of the Holocaust's horror interrupts the speaker's enchantment with the world, making it impossible to find pleasure in a world where such things have happened.
4. **Possible response:** The speaker might chastise poets who, after the Holocaust, write nature poems as if nothing has happened, calling them "witnesses who have seen nothing."

42

When in Early Summer

Nelly Sachs
translated by
Ruth and Matthew Mead

When in early summer the moon sends out secret signs,
the chalices of lilies scent of heaven,
some ear opens to listen
beneath the chirp of the cricket
to earth turning and the language of spirits set free.

But in dreams fish fly in the air
and a forest takes firm root in the floor of the room.

But in the midst of enchantment a voice speaks clearly and amazed:
World, how can you go on playing your games
and cheating time—
World, the little children were thrown like butterflies,
wings beating into the flames—

and your earth has not been thrown like a rotten apple
into the terror-roused abyss—

And sun and moon have gone on walking—
two cross-eyed witnesses who have seen nothing.

Review and Assess

Thinking About the Selection

1. **Respond:** Which image evoked your strongest response? Why?
2. **(a) Recall:** What natural events does the speaker describe in the first two lines? **(b) Interpret:** Describe the relationship between the poet and nature that is suggested by these opening lines.
3. **(a) Recall:** What does the "voice" accuse the world of doing in lines 9–10? **(b) Infer:** According to the voice, what event should prevent the world from doing these things? **(c) Interpret:** In what sense does the voice break the enchantment of the opening?
4. **Speculate:** What might Sachs's speaker say to a poet who, after the Holocaust, continued to write poetry about nature?

ASSESSMENT PRACTICE: Critical Reading

Analyzing an Author's Meaning and Style (For more practice, see Test Preparation Workbook, p. 60.)

Many standardized tests require students to read literary passages to identify the author's deepest meaning. Use the following sample test item to demonstrate.

> When we finish, everyone remains in his corner and we do not dare lift our eyes to look at one another. There is nowhere to look in a mirror, but our appearance stands in front of us, reflected in a hundred livid faces, in a hundred miserable and sordid puppets.

In the context of *Survival in Auschwitz,* what theme does the author imply in this passage?

A The prisoners are upset.
B The prisoners have lost their identities.
C The prisoners have been badly mistreated.
D The prisoners do not want to look at each other.

A, C, and *D* are all expressed by this passage, but they are not themes. The correct answer is *B.*

Review and Assess

Literary Analysis

Autobiography

1. (a) What might Levi's purpose be in writing an **autobiography**? Cite supporting details. (b) Identify one example of a way in which Levi draws the reader into events.
2. (a) What do you think Wiesel's purpose is in writing an **autobiography**? Cite supporting details. (b) Explain two ways in which Wiesel's report of his difficulties with his father helps readers understand concentration camp life.
3. Imagine that another writer has written an account of the lives of Levi and Wiesel. Identify two ways in which this account would differ from these autobiographies.

Comparing Literary Works

4. Compare and contrast the central insights of Levi's and Wiesel's **memoirs,** using a chart like the one shown.

	Events	Insights	Similarities/ Differences
Levi			
Wiesel			

5. (a) Explain Levi's insight into ways the concentration camp stripped people of words. (b) In Sachs's poem, what point is made about consequences of the Holocaust for poetry? (c) Using these insights, explain why it is difficult but important to put the Holocaust into words.

Reading Strategy

Connecting to Historical Context

6. Explain the way in which **historical context** adds to your understanding of the different nationalities of the people Levi first meets.
7. What historical facts help you understand the conclusion of the selection from *Night*? Explain.

Extend Understanding

8. **Social Studies Connection:** In today's world, what steps might people take to prevent governments from treating people in dehumanizing ways? Explain your answer.

Quick Review

An **autobiography** is a form of nonfiction in which a person tells his or her own life story.

A **memoir** is a first-person account that focuses on a person or series of events in the writer's life, offering insight into the person or the events.

To **connect works to their historical context,** link the details to the events and ideas of the writer's time.

Take It to the Net

PHSchool.com

Take the interactive self-test online to check your understanding of these selections.

Answers for p. 1277

Review and Assess

1. **(a)** Possible responses: Levi's purpose is to make clear the impact of the camps on the human psyche. Such details as the steps taken by the Nazis to prepare the prisoners and Levi's description of the effect of these preparations on individual humanity emphasize this purpose. **(b)** Possible response: Levi draws the reader into events by allowing the reader to experience the same unsettling confusion as the prisoners.
2. **(a)** Possible responses: Wiesel's purpose in writing an autobiography is to bear witness to the Holocaust: to illustrate how the camps made the prisoners mistreat and abandon one another. Eliezer's efforts to help his father and his descriptions of the abuses prisoners endured from one another support this purpose. **(b)** Possible response: Wiesel's difficulties with his father convey the daily struggle between life and death and how the camps destroyed human sentiment.
3. Possible response: The author of the two biographies would not be able to convey the inner thoughts and emotions of Levi and Wiesel. The biographies would also lack some of the eyewitness accounts.
4. Possible responses: **Levi: Events:** New prisoners at Auschwitz are stripped of clothing, hair, and names; **Insights:** The prisoners lose their identities in the process; **Similarities/ Differences:** Levi and Wiesel both focus on the loss of identity; however, Levi ties identity to small things. **Wiesel: Events:** In the last days at Buchenwald, Wiesel loses his father; **Insights:** Without his father, Wiesel loses his humanity; **Similarities/ Differences:** Wiesel and Levi both focus on the loss of humanity, but Wiesel struggles much longer to prevent this loss.
5. **(a)** Possible responses: Levi believes that the abuse of the concentration camps was so profound that language cannot describe it. Also, the Germans do not speak Italian, so the pris-

continued

continued from right column

oners are stripped of their ability to communicate with their captors. **(b)** Sachs's speaker believes that after the Holocaust, poetry can no longer embrace the beauty of the world. **(c)** It is important to find language to describe the Holocaust to prevent the world from acting as though nothing had happened.

6. From every nation the Nazis occupied, they deported Jews.
7. The Allies liberated the concentration camps, as the Nazis fled in defeat. This situation helps explain the chaos at the conclusion of *Night*.
8. Possible response: Powerful nations or international organizations can prevent other nations from oppressing or dehumanizing their citizens.

EXTEND

Answers for p. 1278

❶ Vocabulary Development

Word Analysis: Latin Root *-port-*

1. An *importer* carries items into one country or region from another.
2. Something that is *portable* can be carried or moved easily.
3. A person's *deportment* is the manner in which that person carries himself or herself.

Spelling Strategy

1. liquidation
2. indecision
3. succession

Concept Development: Antonyms

1. b	5. a
2. b	6. a
3. c	7. b
4. a	8. c

❷ Grammar and Style

Practice

1. its number tattooed in bluish characters under the skin
2. none
3. his lips [being] pale and dried up
4. none
5. wings beating into the flames

Writing Application

Possible response: The Nazis fled the concentration camp, *the officers stopping for nothing*. The prisoners waited throughout the day. The Americans arrived that evening, *tanks bearing the promise of food and shelter*.

10TH GRADE For support in teaching the Grammar and Style Lesson to tenth graders, use **Writing and Grammar,** Platinum Level, Chapter 20, Section 1.

Integrate Language Skills

❶ Vocabulary Development Lesson

Word Analysis: Latin Root *-port-*

The Latin root *-port-* means "carry" or "move." The word *deportees* means "people who are moved away," or expelled from a country. Explain what *-port-* adds to the meaning of these words:

1. importer 2. portable 3. deportment

Spelling Strategy

The *-tion* ending, found in *intuition*, makes the *shun* sound. The ending *-sion* is generally pronounced *zhun*, as in *diversion*. The ending *-ssion*, pronounced *shun*, is common with base words that end in *-ss*—for example, *possess, possession*. Complete each word with the correct ending: *-tion*, *-sion*, or *-ssion*.

1. liquida____ 2. indeci____ 3. succe____

Concept Development: Antonyms

In each item, choose the antonym, or word opposite in meaning, of the first word.

1. affinity: (a) similarity, (b) hatred, (c) friendliness
2. deportees: (a) teachers, (b) immigrants, (c) promises
3. intuition: (a) payment, (b) thoughtfulness, (c) incomprehension
4. liquidated: (a) made, (b) destroyed, (c) ate
5. prophetic: (a) commemorative, (b) intelligent, (c) strong
6. beseeching: (a) answering, (b) asking, (c) wondering
7. sordid: (a) ugly, (b) clean, (c) jumbled
8. plaintive: (a) old, (b) fancy, (c) cheerful

❷ Grammar and Style Lesson

Absolute Phrases

An **absolute phrase,** or nominative absolute, consists of a noun or a pronoun modified by a participle or a participial phrase. Unlike a participial phrase, an absolute phrase does not modify a subject or an object elsewhere in the sentence. It has no grammatical relationship to the rest of the sentence. Study this example from *Night*, noting how the phrase adds descriptive detail in few words.

Absolute Phrase: My father grew weaker day by day, *his gaze veiled.* (NOUN: gaze; PART.: veiled)

Participial (Not Absolute) Phrase: Having lived through so much, . . . could I leave my father to die now?

Practice Identify the absolute phrase in each item, or write *none* if the item lacks such a phrase.

1. . . . my new name ironically appeared instead, its number tattooed in bluish characters under the skin.
2. Imagine now a man who is deprived of everyone he loves. . . .
3. He was lying on a plank, livid, his lips [being] pale and dried up. . . .
4. Seeing my father in the distance, I ran to meet him.
5. . . . the little children were thrown like butterflies, / wings beating into the flames. . . .

Writing Application Use two absolute phrases in a description of Wiesel's liberation.

WG *Prentice Hall Writing and Grammar Connection: Diamond Level, Chapter 19, Section 2*

TEACHING RESOURCES

The following resources can be used to enrich or extend the instruction for pp. 1278–1279.

Vocabulary

- **Selection Support:** Build Vocabulary, p. 237
- **Vocabulary and Spelling Practice Book** (Use this booklet for skills instruction.) ■

Grammar

- **Selection Support:** Grammar and Style, p. 238
- **Writing and Grammar,** Diamond Level, p. 446
- **Daily Language Practice Transparencies** ■

Writing

- **Performance Assess. and Portfolio Mgmt.,** p. 11
- **Writing and Grammar,** Diamond Level, p. 133
- **Writing and Grammar iText CD-ROM**
- **Writing Models and Graphic Organizers on Transparencies,** pp. 45–51

■ **BLOCK SCHEDULING:** Resources marked with this symbol provide varied instruction during 90-minute blocks.

❸ Writing Lesson

Persuasive Essay

Imagine that your school is planning a curriculum unit to teach students about the Holocaust. Write an essay supporting the inclusion in the unit of Levi's or Wiesel's memoir or Sachs' poem. In your essay, explain your choice, using reasons suited to your audience—the teachers at your school.

Prewriting First, choose the selection you will propose. You might choose a work on the basis of its emotional impact or its strong historical insight. Then, list at least three reasons that this selection should be included in a unit about the Holocaust.

Drafting Begin your draft with a clear statement of your opinion. Then, provide supporting arguments in a logical order. Use strong, direct language that will reinforce your points.

Revising Review your essay to ensure that you have included details and used language appropriate to your audience and purpose. Replace words that are weak or that might not be suitable. Add details that your audience will find persuasive.

Model: Revising for Audience and Purpose

Finally, ~~I thought~~ what Levi says about identity is ~~cool.~~ *profound.* He shows how important respect for the identity of others is. *In addition to learning history, students reading the memoir will reflect on basic values.*

WG Prentice Hall Writing and Grammar Connection: Diamond Level, Chapter 7, Section 4

❹ Extension Activities

Research and Technology Using the Web site for the United States Holocaust Memorial Museum in Washington, D.C., research Holocaust memorials around the world. Then, create a **multimedia presentation,** using a slide-show program. Compare the following aspects of each memorial:

- main purpose, including commemoration or documentation, and any specific focus
- distinctive features, including art, architecture, exhibits, and archives

Give your presentation to the class.

Listening and Speaking Hold a **group discussion** in which you compare Wiesel's and Levi's memoirs. For instance, you might compare their use of certain types of sentences for effect, as well as their themes. In your discussion, listen actively to build on the contributions of others. **[Group Activity]**

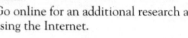

Take It to the Net PHSchool.com

Go online for an additional research activity using the Internet.

ASSESSMENT RESOURCES

The following resources can be used to assess students' knowledge and skills.

Selection Assessment

- **Formal Assessment,** pp. 210–212
- **Open-Book Tests,** pp. 178–180
- **Test Bank Software**

Take It to the Net

Visit PHSchool.com for self-tests on the selections.

Writing Rubric

- **Performance Assess. and Portfolio Mgmt.,** p. 11

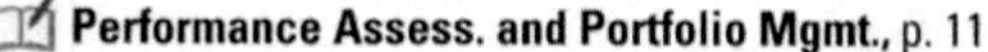

For additional diagnostics and remediation for skills covered in this grouping, use materials from the Prentice Hall Assessment System.

❸ Writing Lesson

- Remind students that their arguments should be aimed at the audience—in this case, the teachers who will decide what to include in the Holocaust unit. Help students brainstorm a list of criteria teachers might consider when developing curriculum.
- After they have chosen the selections about which they will write, tell students to develop at least three reasons for including their choice in the unit.
- Use the Writing Lesson to guide students in developing their essays. Encourage students to use the Persuasive Essay model in **Writing Models and Graphic Organizers on Transparencies,** pp. 45–51, as a guide.
- Use the Persuasion: Persuasive Composition rubric in **Performance Assessment and Portfolio Management,** p. 11, to evaluate students' work.

10TH GRADE For support in working through the Writing Lesson with tenth graders, use **Writing and Grammar,** Platinum Level, Chapter 7, Section 4.

❹ Research and Technology

- Tell students that their multimedia presentations should combine images of Holocaust memorials around the world with explanations and descriptions of each one.
- Monitor students as they research memorials. To avoid anti-Semitic Web sites, make sure that students conduct their searches from the official website of the United States Holocaust Memorial Museum.

CUSTOMIZE INSTRUCTION For Universal Access

To address different learning styles, use the following activities suggested in the **Extension Activities** booklet, p. 60:

- For Musical/Rhythmic Learners, use Activity 5.
- For Visual/Spatial Learners, use Activity 6.
- For Verbal/Linguistic and Bodily/Kinesthetic Learners, use Activity 7.

Lesson Objectives

1. To distinguish between fact and opinion in press releases
2. To recognize language that signals facts or opinions
3. To understand the intention and importance of information included in press releases

About Press Releases

- After students read the "About Press Releases" instruction, discuss whether they have ever read or seen a press release, such as the school board's announcement of a new program or a new staff member. Explain that they may have seen excerpts of press releases included in news stories on television or in newspapers or magazines.
- Ask students how press releases are typically presented.
  Answer: Press releases may be presented in writing, to a news reporter for example, or verbally at a press conference.
- Discuss how understanding the goal of a press release could help the audience evaluate the press release's information. Point out that distinguishing facts from opinions is a key skill in such an evaluation.
- Have students preview the press release and the corresponding call-out notes.

Reading Strategy

Distinguishing Fact From Opinion

- After students read the Reading Strategy instruction, ask volunteers to read aloud each bulleted item in the chart. On the board, summarize the information.
- Ask students to give additional examples of facts and opinions to verify their understanding of the definitions in the chart.
  Possible response: Michael Jordan accumulated 32,292 points during his basketball career. Michael Jordan's athletic ability is unparalled by any current player in the N.B.A.

continued

READING INFORMATIONAL MATERIALS

Press Releases

About Press Releases

A **press release** is a brief document circulated to news agencies that announces or responds to an event or a trend. By distributing a press release, individuals or organizations encourage the news media to report on the event or viewpoint discussed in the release.

Press releases are often written not simply to inform reporters, but to influence the way in which a news story is presented. In fact, journalists are invited to reprint material in a press release as part of an article. A responsible reporter will always attribute words from a press release to the organization or individual in whose name the release is issued.

Reading Strategy

Distinguishing Fact From Opinion

In using press releases, journalists must carefully **distinguish between fact and opinion**—between statements that can be verified and statements that express a viewpoint on the facts. Like a responsible journalist, you should distinguish facts from opinions when reading a press release or other public statement.

As you read the press release on pages 1281 and 1282, **distinguish between facts and opinions** by using the information in the chart below.

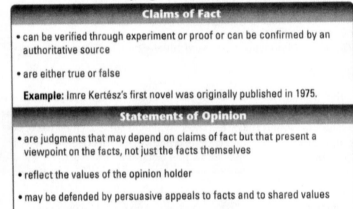

Identifying Facts and Opinions

Claims of Fact
• can be verified through experiment or proof or can be confirmed by an authoritative source
• are either true or false
Example: Imre Kertész's first novel was originally published in 1975.
Statements of Opinion
• are judgments that may depend on claims of fact but that present a viewpoint on the facts, not just the facts themselves
• reflect the values of the opinion holder
• may be defended by persuasive appeals to facts and to shared values
Example: Kertész ". . . inspires a singular freedom of thought."

continued from left column

- Discuss why readers need to be able to recognize facts and opinions. Explain that opinions in a press release are an attempt to influence readers' views.
- Suggest that readers keep the Identifying Facts and Opinions chart at hand as they read the press release on pp. 1281–1282.

Who Is Imre Kertész?

Born in Budapest, Hungary, Imre Kertész was a teenager in 1944, a time when Hungary was collaborating with Germany's Nazi government to confine Jews to ghettos, confiscate their property, and deport them to concentration camps such as Auschwitz and Buchenwald. Kertész's experiences in Auschwitz pervade his writing. Two of his novels that have been translated into English are *Fateless* and *Kaddish for a Child not Born*. Like the great philosophers and writers mentioned in this press release, Kertész's works deal with fundamental issues related to life, death, and human existence.

The Swedish Academy
PRESS RELEASE
10 October 2002

SVENSKA AKADEMIEN

The Nobel Prize in Literature 2002
Recipient: Imre Kertész

The Nobel Prize in Literature for 2002 is awarded to the Hungarian writer Imre Kertész

> "for writing that upholds the fragile experience of the individual against the barbaric arbitrariness of history."

In his writing Imre Kertész explores the possibility of continuing to live and think as an individual in an era in which the subjection of human beings to social forces has become increasingly complete. His works return unremittingly to the decisive experience of his life: the period spent in Auschwitz, to which he was taken as a teenage boy during the Nazi persecution of Hungary's Jews. For him, Auschwitz is not an exceptional occurrence that, like an alien body, subsists outside the normal history of Western Europe. It is the ultimate truth about human degradation in modern existence.

Key biographical facts describing experiences that shaped Kertész's life and work appear near the beginning of the article.

Kertész's first novel, *Sorstalanság*, 1975 (*Fateless*, 1992), deals with the young Köves, who is arrested and taken to a concentration camp but conforms and survives. The novel uses the alienating device of taking the reality of the camp completely for granted, an everyday existence like any other, admittedly with conditions that are thankless, but not without moments of happiness. Köves regards events as a child would, without completely understanding them and without finding them unnatural or disquieting. He lacks our ready-made answers.

The Nobel Prize in Literature 2002 Recipient: Imre Kertész

- Have a volunteer read aloud the background information at the top of the page. Explain that this is not part of the actual press release.
- Direct students' attention to the press release letterhead. Ask students who issued the information and when it was issued.
  Answer: The Swedish Academy issued the information on October 10, 2002.
- Point out the quotation that appears within the first sentence. Explain that this quotation reflects the actual language used in the award. Stress that a quotation may include an opinion, as this one does, or it may include facts.
- Have students read the first page of the press release and the first call-out note. Then, ask students why important biographical facts might be placed at the beginning of a press release.
  Answer: Press releases often include key facts, such as biographical facts, at the beginning in order to emphasize information. These facts also provide background for additional information found later in the press release.
- Point out the first sentence of the final paragraph on p. 1281. Ask students whether this sentence contains facts or opinions, and have them explain their answers.
  Answer: This sentence contains facts, such as the name and date of publication of Kertész's first novel, and a brief synopsis of the novel's content. This information can all be verified through research or by reading the book.

CUSTOMIZE INSTRUCTION FOR UNIVERSAL ACCESS

For Special Needs Students	For Less Proficient Readers	For English Learners
Have students work in pairs to record facts from the press release. Provide and review a list of likely types of facts, such as titles and dates of publication, biographical facts, and summaries of written works. Then, have students reread the press release to identify opinions.	Have students work in pairs to rewrite the press release in simpler language. Suggest that students look for the main subject and verb in each sentence and then arrange the sentence in a subject-verb sequence. Students can use dictionaries to find definitions to help them rewrite the press release.	Clarify for students that Kertész wrote in Hungarian. His name and the titles of his books include letters not used in the English language. Point out the English translations of titles in parentheses. Students can use English-Hungarian dictionaries at the library or on the Internet for help with pronunciations.

The Nobel Prize in Literature 2002 Recipient: Imre Kertész

- Have students read the remainder of the press release and the call-out notes that accompany it.
- Review with students any difficult or unfamiliar words or phrases. Provide students with dictionaries, and guide them as they find definitions for these words and phrases.
- Then, ask a volunteer to read the highlighted text at the top of the page and the call-out note that accompanies it. Explain that writers of press releases often include opinion sentences in the hope that journalists will quote the opinion.
- After students read the second call-out note on the page, discuss why repetition might be useful in a press release. Explain that in addition to making it easier for journalists to quote from the material, repetition also emphasizes key facts or opinions to encourage readers to remember them.
- Remind students that they should consider why each piece of information is included in a press release. For example, the opinion offered in the final paragraph may be included to help bring together a particular journalist's views about Kertész. As students read the final call-out note at the bottom of the page, point out that opinions written in a press release can be used by writers for book reviews, for example.

Sentences like this one include an opinion of Kertész's novel. A journalist may then adapt such subjective material to describe Kertész's work to readers.

The shocking credibility of the description derives perhaps from this very absence of any element of the moral indignation or metaphysical protest that the subject cries out for. The reader is confronted not only with the cruelty of the atrocities but just as much with the thoughtlessness that characterized their execution. Both perpetrators and victims were preoccupied with insistent practical problems; the major questions did not exist. Kertész's message is that *to live is to conform*. The capacity of the captives to come to terms with Auschwitz is one outcome of the same principle that finds expression in everyday human coexistence.

In thinking like this, the author concurs with a philosophical tradition in which life and human spirit are enemies. In *Kaddis a meg nem született gyermekért*, 1990 (*Kaddish for a Child not Born*, 1997), Kertész presents a consistently negative picture of childhood and from this pre-history derives the paradoxical feeling of being at home in the concentration camp. He completes his implacable existential analysis by depicting love as the highest stage of conformism, total capitulation to the desire to exist at any cost. For Kertész the spiritual dimension of man lies in his inability to adapt to life. Individual experience seems useless as soon as it is considered in the light of the needs and interests of the human collective.

In his collection of fragments, *Gályanapló* ("*Galley Diary*"), 1992, Kertész demonstrates his full intellectual scope. "Theoretical justifications are merely constructions," he writes, but nevertheless he conducts an untiring dialogue with the great tradition of cultural criticism – Pascal, Goethe, Schopenhauer, Nietzsche, Kafka, Camus, Beckett, Bernhard. In essence, Imre Kertész is a minority consisting of one individual. He regards his kinship with the concept of a Jew as a definition inflicted on him by the enemy. But through its consequences this arbitrary categorization has nevertheless been his initiation into the deepest knowledge of humanity and the age in which he lives.

The publication dates for each novel are facts that appear earlier in the press release, but the press release repeats the dates here to make it easier for an editor to take this paragraph exactly as it is and incorporate it into a news article.

The novels that succeeded *Sorstalanság*, 1975 (*Fateless*, 1992), *A kudarc* ("*Fiasco*"), 1988, and *Kaddis a meg nem született gyermekért*, 1990 (*Kaddish for a Child not Born*, 1997), can almost be characterized as comments and additions to the first and decisive work. This provides the theme of *A kudarc*. While he waits for an expected refusal of his real novel, the one about Auschwitz, the aging author spends his days writing a contemporary novel in the style of Kafka, a claustrophobic description of socialist Eastern Europe. In the end, he is informed that his previous book will, in spite of everything, be published, but all he can feel is emptiness. On display in the literary marketplace, his personality is transformed into an object, his secrets into banalities.

This opinion of Kertész's style might provide a writer with an apt quotation for a review or book jacket blurb.

The refusal to compromise in Kertész's stance can be perceived clearly in his style, which is reminiscent of a thickset hawthorn hedge, dense and thorny for unsuspecting visitors. But he relieves his readers of the burden of compulsory emotions and inspires a singular freedom of thought.

Check Your Comprehension

1. What is Kertész's country of origin?
2. What harrowing experience marked his teenage years?
3. According to the press release, what is distinctive about the way in which Kertész presents a similar experience in his first novel, *Fateless*?

Applying the Reading Strategy

Distinguishing Fact From Opinion

4. Cite an example of a fact in the press release.
5. (a) Cite an example of a statement of opinion in the press release.
(b) Explain which values or tastes this statement reflects. Record your responses in a chart like the one shown.

Statement of Opinion	
Statement: ______	
☐ Does statement express a judgment of taste or value? ☐ Is statement open to being proved as fact? ☐ Does statement explain facts?	**Values** What does the statement assume is good or valuable?

Activity

Writing a News Article

Using this press release and additional research, write a newspaper article on the award of the 2002 Nobel Prize in Literature to Imre Kertész. Your news article should include an informative headline and address the questions *Who? What? When? Where?* and *Why?* As you work, follow these guidelines for responsible journalism:

- Confirm claims in one source by checking them against another source.
- Avoid reporting opinions as if they were facts.
- Attribute quotations to a source.

Comparing Informational Materials

Press Releases and Book Reviews

Book reviews, which appear in magazines and newpapers, usually provide a brief summary of the book along with the reviewer's evaluation of it. Consider the ways in which this press release about Kertész would be similar to or different from a book review of one of his novels.

Write a brief essay explaining the similarities and differences between this press release and a book review. Discuss which details from the press release might appear in a book review and what new details might be added. Also, discuss any differences in format.

Answers for p. 1283

Check Your Comprehension

1. Kertész's country of origin is Hungary.
2. During his teenage years, Kertész was imprisoned in the Nazi concentration camp at Auschwitz.
3. The press release suggests that Kertész's first novel is distinctive because it presents the ordeal of Auschwitz without moral indignation but rather as a common human experience.

Applying the Reading Strategy

4. Possible response: An example of a fact in the press release is, "The Nobel Prize in Literature for 2002 is awarded to the Hungarian writer Imre Kertész. . . ."
5. **(a)** Possible response: An example of opinion in the press release is "The refusal to compromise in Kertész's stance can be perceived clearly in his style, which is reminiscent of a thickset hawthorn hedge, dense and thorny for unsuspecting visitors." **(b)** Possible response: A checkmark should appear in the box next to the first question only. **Values:** The statement assumes that a refusal to compromise is good or valuable.

Activity

Students should include in their articles pertinent facts about Kertész and the Nobel Prize. They should also include information from another source about the Nobel Prize. Students must properly indicate quotations with quotation marks and clear source attributions.

Comparing Informational Materials

Students may note that book reviews highlight opinions and that viewers expect to read a writer's opinion in a review. Press releases are presented primarily as conveyors of fact, although they may have embedded opinions. The same information might be presented in both formats, but a book review would be more direct in presenting its opinions.

A Song on the End of the World • The End and the Beginning

Lesson Objectives

1. **To analyze and respond to literary elements**
   - Literary Analysis: Irony
   - Comparing Literary Works: History as a Theme
2. **To read, comprehend, analyze, and critique a poem**
   - Reading Strategy: Evaluating the Writer's Statement of Philosophy
   - Reading Check Questions
   - Review and Assess Questions
   - Assessment Practice (ATE)
3. **To develop word analysis skills, fluency, and systematic vocabulary**
   - Vocabulary Development Lesson: Related Words: *glaze* and *glimmering*
4. **To understand and apply written and oral language conventions**
   - Spelling Strategy
   - Grammar and Style Lesson: Indefinite and Demonstrative Pronouns
5. **To understand and apply appropriate writing and research strategies**
   - Writing Lesson: Narrative About a Quiet Hero
   - Extension Activity: Maps of Poland
6. **To understand and apply listening and speaking strategies**
   - Extension Activity: Multimedia Poetry Reading

STEP-BY-STEP TEACHING GUIDE	PACING GUIDE
PRETEACH	
Motivate Students and Provide Background	
Use the Motivation activity (ATE p. 1284)	5 min.
Read and discuss author and background features (SE pp. 1284, 1286; ATE p. 1284) A	5 min.
Introduce the Concepts	
Introduce the Literary Analysis and Reading Strategy concepts (SE/ATE p. 1285) A	15 min.
Pronounce the vocabulary words and read their definitions (SE p. 1285)	5 min.
TEACH	
Monitor Comprehension	
Informally monitor comprehension by circulating while students read independently or in groups A	20 min.
Develop vocabulary with the Vocabulary notes (SE pp. 1286, 1287, 1288, 1290; ATE p. 1286)	as students read
Develop Understanding	
Develop students' understanding of irony with the Literary Analysis annotations (SE/ATE pp. 1286, 1290) A	5 min.
Develop students' ability to evaluate the writer's statement of philosophy, using the Reading Strategy annotations (SE/ATE pp. 1287, 1288) A	5 min.
ASSESS	
Assess Mastery	
Assess students' mastery of the Reading Strategy and Literary Analysis concepts by having them answer the Review and Assess questions (SE/ATE p. 1291)	15 min.
Use one or more of the print, software, or transparency Assessment Resources (ATE p. 1293) A	up to 45 min.
EXTEND	
Apply Understanding	
Have students complete the Vocabulary Development Lesson and the Grammar and Style Lesson (SE p. 1292) A	20 min.
Apply students' ability to list relevant details, using the Writing Lesson (SE/ATE p. 1293) A	45 min.
Apply students' understanding of the selections, using one or more of the Extension Activities (SE p. 1293)	20–90 min.

A **ACCELERATED INSTRUCTION:** Use the strategies and activities identified with an A.

TEACHING TENTH-GRADE STUDENTS For support in teaching the selection(s) to tenth-grade students, see the Step-by-Step Teaching notes identified with the icons shown here.

UNIVERSAL ACCESS
● = Below-Level Students
▲ = On-Level Students
■ = Above-Level Students

Time and Resource Manager

Reading Level: Average, Average
Average Number of Instructional Days: 2

RESOURCES		
PRINT	**TRANSPARENCIES**	**TECHNOLOGY**
• **Beyond Literature,** Cross-Curricular Connection: History, p. 61 ▲ ■		• **Interest Grabber Video,** Tape 2, Unit 9, Segment 11 ● ▲ ■
• **Selection Support Workbook:** ● ▲ ■ Literary Analysis, p. 244 Reading Strategy, p. 243 Build Vocabulary, p. 241	• **Literary Analysis and Reading Transparencies,** pp. 121 and 122 ● ▲ ■	
		• **Listening to Literature** ● ▲ ■ Audiocassettes Audio CDs
• **Literary Analysis for Enrichment,** p. 61 ■		
• **Formal Assessment:** Selection Test, pp. 213–215 ● ▲ ■ • **Open-Book Tests,** pp. 181–183 ● ▲ ■ • **Performance Assessment and Portfolio Management,** p. 14 ● ▲ ■ • PRENTICE HALL ASSESSMENT SYSTEM ● ▲ ■	• PRENTICE HALL ASSESSMENT SYSTEM ● ▲ ■ **Skills Practice Answers and Explanations on Transparencies**	• **Test Bank Software** ● ▲ ■
• **Selection Support Workbook:** ● ▲ ■ Grammar and Style, p. 242 • **Writing and Grammar,** Diamond Level ● ▲ ■ • **Extension Activities,** p. 61 ● ▲ ■	• **Daily Language Practice Transparencies** ● ▲ • **Writing Models and Graphic Organizers on Transparencies,** pp. 83–85 ● ▲ ■	• **Writing and Grammar iText CD-ROM** ● ▲ ■ ***Take It to the Net*** PHSchool.com

BLOCK SCHEDULING: Use one 90-minute class period to preteach the selection(s) and have students read them. Use a second 90-minute class period to assess students' mastery of skills and have them complete one of the Extension Activities.

PRETEACH

Step-by-Step Teaching Guide for pp. 1284–1285

Motivation

Ask students to recall books, movies, or news stories in which people faced crisis situations. Have students describe those situations, and the people's reactions, in vivid detail. Then, explain to students that they may be surprised by the way these poets describe desperate situations.

Interest Grabber Video

As an alternative, play "'A Song on the End of the World': Student Response" on Tape 2 to engage student interest.

❶ Background

More About the Authors

When Czesław Miłosz was a young man, he admired his uncle, Oscar Miłosz, who had sold his family's estate and become a well-known poet in Paris. A reader of many languages, Oscar Miłosz became a role model for his nephew.

Wisława Szymborska has said, "No questions are of such significance as those that are naive." Her poetry asks direct questions about the meaning of life and death. Upon granting her the 1996 Nobel Prize for Literature, the Swedish Academy called her the "Mozart of poetry."

Geography Note

Draw students' attention to the map on this page. Explain that both poets have played important roles in Polish culture. Both Miłosz and Szymborska show appreciation for the history of a nation that has many times faced the kinds of crises described in these poems.

Prepare to Read

❶ A Song on the End of the World ◆ The End and the Beginning

Czesław Miłosz (b. 1911)

Poet, essayist, and novelist Czeslaw Miłosz (chez′ wäf mē′ wōsh) has lived as many lives as the legendary cat. From a young writer haunted by "gloomy visions" to a diplomat in Washington, D.C., to a university professor in California, Miłosz is widely known today as a distinguished Nobel Prize winner.

Born in the Lithuanian city of Wilno (also known as Vilna), young Miłosz decided to study law. Hitler had just seized control in Germany, and Miłosz rejected the Nazi glorification of the state. Communism seemed like an antidote, yet Miłosz questioned the rigidity of its doctrines. His early poetry captures the violence-haunted atmosphere of the 1930s.

Defiance and Resignation After World War II broke out, Miłosz moved to Warsaw, Poland, where he participated in underground publishing activities carried on in defiance of the Nazi occupiers. After the war, when the Communist U.S.S.R. dominated Poland, Miłosz served as a diplomat for Poland in Washington, D.C. Miłosz was not a hard-line Communist; he hoped for reform. In 1951, though, he gave up hopes of working for change from within and broke with the Communist government. Moving first to France, he later became a professor of literature at the University of California at Berkeley.

Leading by Example Although he says he is uncomfortable in the role of moral leader, Miłosz's independence of mind has been widely admired by younger generations of Poles. His poems have carried a great deal of moral authority in Poland. In 1980, his international stature was confirmed when he received the Nobel Prize in Literature.

Wisława Szymborska (b. 1923)

For Wisława Szymborska (vis wa′ va shim boor′ ska), inspiration begins when a poet says "I don't know." Her work centers around the rediscovery of astonishment. "[I]n the language of poetry," she said in her 1996 Nobel Prize acceptance speech, "where every word is weighed, nothing is usual or normal. Not a single stone or a single cloud above it."

Born in the small town of Bnin, Poland (now a part of Kórnik), Szymborska moved in 1931 to Krakow, where she still lives today. In 1945, her first published poem appeared in a daily newspaper. In 1953, she became the poetry editor at a literary magazine.

Privacy and Politics Unlike her fellow Pole Miłosz, Szymborska has led much of her life out of the public eye. Still, politics left an inevitable mark on her work.

In the early 1950s, Szymborska wrote in the government-permitted style of the time. A relaxation of government regulations allowed her to publish in her own voice, but in the 1980s, the government again cracked down on dissent. During that time, Szymborska contributed to underground and exile periodicals. The triumph of Poland's Solidarity movement in 1989 brought an end to strict government oversight of culture.

A Distinguished Honor Szymborska has published more than sixteen collections of poetry, as well as a collection of essays. She has refused to give readings, however, out of her dislike for publicity. When told she had won the 1996 Nobel Prize in Literature, Szymborska said it felt as if the world "came crashing down on me." Although she valued the honor, she told Miłosz at the time, "I am a private person."

TEACHING RESOURCES

The following resources can be used to enrich or extend the instruction for pp. 1284–1285.

Motivation

Interest Grabber Video, Tape 2

Background

Beyond Literature, p. 61 ■

Take It to the Net

Visit PHSchool.com for background on the authors.

Literary Analysis

Literary Analysis and Reading Transparencies, Irony, p. 121

Reading

Literary Analysis and Reading Transparencies, Evaluating the Writer's Statement of Philosophy, p. 122

Selection Support: Reading Strategy, p. 243 ■

■ **BLOCK SCHEDULING:** Resources marked with this symbol provide varied instruction during 90-minute blocks.

Preview

Connecting to the Literature

If you have ever rediscovered your first-grade class picture or revisited a long-forgotten childhood playground, then you know that, as these poets show, time is measured by how much we forget more than by what we remember.

❷ Literary Analysis

Irony

Irony occurs when writers create a contrast between what is stated and what is meant or between what is expected to happen and what actually happens. Irony can take the following forms:

- **Situational irony** is an opposition between events and expectations. In his poem, Miłosz insists that the day the world ends will be like any other, although we expect it to be more dramatic.
- **Verbal irony** is a clash between the words used for a thing and its reality. Szymborska writes "After every war / someone has to tidy up," ironically understating the damage caused by war.

As you read, note the poets' use of verbal and situational irony.

Comparing Literary Works

These poets use irony to challenge our ideas of history. They take **history as a theme,** looking for a meaning or a pattern in historical events.

- Miłosz's irony makes us reconsider just what an ordinary day is.
- Szymborska's irony suggests that progress means forgetting, not learning from, the past.

As you read, compare the lessons about history in these poems. Consider whether history appears as a cycle that repeats itself or as a straight line.

❸ Reading Strategy

Evaluating the Writer's Statement of Philosophy

To **evaluate a writer's philosophy,** first identify the writer's view of life. Begin by analyzing patterns in the work, such as similarities in details that point to a common meaning. Then, decide whether the writer's view is supported by your own ideas and experiences.

As you read, evaluate each poet's philosophy, using a chart like this one.

Details
"A Song on the End of the World"
"A bee circles clover . . ."
"A fisherman mends a glimmering net."

↓

Meanings They Suggest
Ordinary events seem extraordinary on the day the world ends.

↓

Philosophy
Ordinary life is precious; we just forget how precious.

↓

Evaluation

Vocabulary Development

glimmering (glimʹ ər iŋ) *v.* flickering; giving a faint, unsteady light (p. 1286)

prophet (präfʹ ət) *n.* inspired person who speaks great truths or foretells the future (p. 1287)

shards (shärdz) *n.* sharp fragments (p. 1288)

glaze (glāz) *v.* fit glass to a window; cover with a shiny finish (p. 1288)

gawking (gôkʹ iŋ) *v.* staring foolishly; gaping (p. 1290)

CUSTOMIZE INSTRUCTION FOR UNIVERSAL ACCESS

For Less Proficient Readers	For English Learners	For Advanced Readers
Have students complete charts that include these headings: *Events, Expectations, Words,* and *Reality.* For example: Events—"Happy porpoises jump in the sea"; Expectations—animals should suspect the end of the world; Words—"someone has to tidy up"; Reality—lives and cities have been destroyed by war.	To help students understand irony, have them work with partners to determine the subtle meanings of difficult words. For example, the word *glimmering* on p. 1286 may include the suggestion of a light flickering out. This image suggests the flickering of the world's light, or the end of the world.	Tell students that irony is often easier to recognize when works are read aloud, as it invites a change in tone of voice. Have students work in pairs, reading the two poems aloud. Listening partners should work to identify the ironic moments so that both partners can utilize an appropriate tone of voice for these lines.

❷ Literary Analysis

Irony

- Read with students the Literary Analysis instruction, and ask students to give examples of situational and verbal irony. Prompt them with a real-life example of situational irony, such as the many people who survived the September 11, 2001, World Trade Center attacks because they were late to work that day. Typically, being late causes problems rather than prevents them.
- As students read, urge them to relate to the situations in these poems by visualizing the many scenes of war that play out daily in the current news. Discuss the irony in the contrast between our distant image of war and its reality.
- Use the Irony transparency in **Literary Analysis and Reading Transparencies,** p. 121, for additional practice in recognizing irony.

❸ Reading Strategy

Evaluating the Writer's Statement of Philosophy

- After reading aloud the Reading Strategy instruction, remind students that a philosophy is a way of looking at the world. People often filter their descriptions or experiences through a central philosophy, for example, that "all people are essentially good."
- As they read each poem, have students look for recurring images or descriptions that suggest the writer's view of life.
- Review the graphic organizer on p. 1285, read aloud each box, and discuss each entry. As a class, agree on an entry for the "Evaluation" cell, such as "This makes sense to me because . . ." or "I agree because . . ."

Vocabulary Development

- Pronounce each vocabulary word for students, and read the definitions as a class. Have students identify any words with which they are already familiar.

 ***E-Teach***

Visit e-Teach at PHSchool.com for teachers' essays on how to teach, with questions and answers.

TEACH

Step-by-Step Teaching Guide for pp. 1286–1290

Teaching Tenth-Grade Students

10TH GRADE Help students imagine the situations to which these poems respond. Inspire their historical imaginations by locating and reading excerpts from Emanuel Ringelblum's *Notes from the Warsaw Ghetto.*

❶ About the Selection

This poem contrasts the everyday experiences of people and animals amidst war and devastation in the Warsaw Ghetto. Milosz makes the powerful argument that continuing with everyday tasks despite war's horrors reflects heroism.

❷ Literary Analysis

Irony

- Have a volunteer read aloud the bracketed stanzas. Ask students what they would expect the world to be like on the day it ends.
  Possible response: The world might be full of portentous signs of disaster, such as those described in biblical accounts.
- Then, ask students to respond to the Literary Analysis item on p. 1286: Explain why the details in these two stanzas are ironic, given the situation.
  Answer: Given that the world is ending, one would expect more unpleasant events to be occurring, not the ordinary, everyday events described in these stanzas.

❸ Vocabulary Development

Related Words: *glaze* and *glimmering*

- Point out the word *glimmering* on this page and the word *glaze* on p. 1288. Read the definitions for both words.
- Tell students that both words come from a root meaning "to shine or to glow." Ask students how this meaning is reflected in the word *glimmer.*
  Possible response: Something that glimmers appears to shine.

❶ A Song on the End of the World

Czesław Miłosz *translated by* **Anthony Miłosz**

Background

Written in 1944, this poem reflects historical events: A world *did* come to an end in the Polish capital of Warsaw during World War II. In 1939, Nazi Germany and the Soviet Union invaded Poland and divided the country between them. In the summer of 1944, as the Polish resistance movement rebelled against Nazi rule, Warsaw was nearly leveled.

Miłosz thought it unlikely that he would survive the war, but he found wisdom in the advice of Martin Luther, a leader of the Protestant movement for religious reform: "[W]hen asked what he would do if he knew tomorrow was going to be the end of the world, he said, 'I would plant apple trees.'"

The calm conviction of Miłosz's poem reflects this insight into the value of the ordinary. It also reflects Poland's long history as the target of invasion and occupation, a history that also echoes in Szymborska's poem "The End and the Beginning."

On the day the world ends
A bee circles a clover,
A fisherman mends a <u>glimmering</u> net. ❸
Happy porpoises jump in the sea,
By the rainspout young sparrows are playing
And the snake is gold-skinned as it should always be.

❷ On the day the world ends
Women walk through the fields under their umbrellas,
A drunkard grows sleepy at the edge of a lawn,
Vegetable peddlers shout in the street
And a yellow-sailed boat comes nearer the island,
The voice of a violin lasts in the air
And leads into a starry night.

glimmering (glim′ ər iŋ) *v.* flickering; giving a faint, unsteady light

Literary Analysis
Irony Explain why the details in these two stanzas are ironic, given the situation.

TEACHING RESOURCES

The following resources can be used to enrich or extend the instruction for pp. 1286–1290.

Literary Analysis

- **Selection Support:** Literary Analysis, p. 244 ■
- **Literary Analysis and Reading Transparencies,** Irony, p. 121

Reading

- **Selection Support:** Reading Strategy, p. 243; Build Vocabulary, p. 241
- **Listening to Literature Audiocassettes**
- **Listening to Literature Audio CDs** ■

■ **BLOCK SCHEDULING:** Resources marked with this symbol provide varied instruction during 90-minute blocks.

And those who expected lightning and thunder
Are disappointed.
And those who expected signs and archangels' trumps[1]
❹ Do not believe it is happening now.
As long as the sun and the moon are above,
As long as the bumblebee visits a rose,
As long as rosy infants are born
No one believes it is happening now.

Only a white-haired old man, who would be a prophet
Yet is not a prophet, for he's much too busy,
Repeats while he binds his tomatoes:
There will be no other end of the world,
There will be no other end of the world.

Warsaw, 1944

Reading Strategy
Evaluating the Writer's Statement of Philosophy What do these lines suggest about the writer's view of how we ordinarily live?

prophet (präf' ət) *n.* inspired person who speaks great truths or foretells the future

1. **trumps** *n.* trumpets.

Review and Assess

Thinking About the Selection

1. **Respond:** Are you disturbed or comforted by Miłosz's poem? Explain.
2. **(a) Recall:** With what phrase do the first two stanzas begin? **(b) Compare:** What do the details that follow each phrase have in common? **(c) Analyze:** What is surprising about them?
3. **(a) Recall:** In the third stanza, what does the speaker say that some people are expecting? **(b) Infer:** What traditional views about the end of the world do these expectations reflect? **(c) Draw Conclusions:** Why do these people not believe that the world is ending?
4. **(a) Infer:** Why do you think the old man binds tomatoes if he believes the world is ending? **(b) Interpret:** What is the meaning of the poem's last line? **(c) Analyze:** What is the effect of repeating this line?
5. **(a) Generalize:** In what sense might one appreciate every day as if it were the last day? **(b) Draw Conclusions:** What point does the poet make about the value of ordinary things?
6. **(a) Compare:** What do the speaker and the white-haired "prophet" have in common? **(b) Evaluate:** Prophets are said to foresee fateful events, such as the end of the world. In what sense does the writer of this poem play the role of a prophet?

CUSTOMIZE INSTRUCTION FOR UNIVERSAL ACCESS

For English Learners	For Gifted/Talented Students	For Advanced Readers
The crisis in Miłosz's poem may be unfamiliar, depending on students' backgrounds. If appropriate, ask students to tell about the experience of their people in World War II. Then, explain that many European cities were bombed during the war, ghettos such as the Warsaw Ghetto isolated Jews and others in terrible conditions.	Stress that Miłosz's poem looks at a time of crisis for Poland. Note that Miłosz wrote several poems during this period. Have students analyze some of these works. Direct students to Miłosz's *Selected Poems,* published by Ecco Press. Ask students to relate the poems to "A Song on the End of the World."	Challenge students to locate and read The Book of Revelations in the Bible. Point out that this text describes a crisis for the entire world, for human existence. Read portions aloud to demonstrate the apocalyptic tone and imagery in the selection. Students can then contrast this tone and imagery with that of Miłosz's poem.

❹ Reading Strategy

Evaluating the Writer's Statement of Philosophy

- Read the bracketed stanza aloud, and ask students to paraphrase it. Possible response: People who expect the end of the world to be heralded by fanfare and drama will be fooled by everyday activities that continue as the world ends.
- Then, ask students the Reading Strategy question on p. 1287: What do these lines suggest about the writer's view of how we ordinarily live? Answer: The writer believes that we live by doing everyday tasks and experiencing everyday events. We assume that if these tasks and events continue, all is well.

Answers for p. 1287

Review and Assess

1. Possible response: The idea that a cataclysmic event could arrive so unexpectedly might disturb some readers.
2. **(a)** The stanzas begin with "On the day the world ends." **(b)** The details describe peaceful and ordinary occurrences. **(c)** It is surprising that normal events occur on a disastrous day.
3. **(a)** Some people are expecting lightning, thunder, and archangels' trumpets. **(b)** The signs reflect a biblical view of the world's ending. **(c)** These people have not seen the signs they expect, and everyday events continue to occur.
4. **(a)** Possible response: The act reflects that the man is continuing with life in the face of danger. **(b)** Possible response: The line means, "Appearances to the contrary, the world is really ending." **(c)** Repetition stresses the meaning of the final line.
5. **(a)** Possible response: One might appreciate ordinary events. **(b)** Possible response: Ordinary things are especially valuable in troubled times.
6. **(a)** Possible response: Both believe in continuing on in the face of disaster. **(b)** Possible response: He describes events and behaviors at the end of the world.

5 About the Selection

In this moving and prosaic poem, Wisława Szymborska describes the everyday tasks people must accomplish to repair their world after war. As windows are replaced and bridges rebuilt, the speaker acknowledges that the crisis passes. Time moves forward, and those who do not remember the crisis begin to outnumber those who lived it, demonstrating the relentlessness of time and progress.

6 ▶ Critical Viewing

Possible response: The woman in the painting does not represent the "someone" in the poem. The "someone" from the poem has a more indomitable spirit that keeps trying to repair the destruction, whereas the woman in the painting seems overwhelmed and despairing of accomplishing repairs.

7 Reading Strategy

Evaluating the Writer's Statement of Philosophy

- After students silently read the bracketed stanzas, invite them to define "sound bites" and "photo opportunities."
  Answer: Sound bites are small snippets of a speech that create a particular image of a person or situation. Photo opportunities are apparently spontaneous situations that lend themselves to photographs.
- Ask students the Reading Strategy question on p. 1288: What view of modern life does the speaker express in these lines?
  Answer: The speaker suggests that modern life reflects an interest in the superficial.

▶ **Reteach** If students have difficulty answering the Reading Strategy question, point out that "all the cameras have gone to other wars," presumably because media interest in any one war lasts only until there is a newer, more horrible war to photograph. Help students understand the clue that this detail offers about the writer's philosophy.

5 The End and the Beginning

Wisława Szymborska

***translated by* Stanislaw Baranczak and Clare Cavanaugh**

After every war
someone has to tidy up.
Things won't pick
themselves up, after all.

Someone has to shove
the rubble to the roadsides
so the carts loaded with corpses
can get by.

Someone has to trudge
through sludge and ashes,
through the sofa springs,
the shards of glass,
the bloody rags.

Someone has to lug the post
to prop the wall,
someone has to glaze the window,
set the door in its frame.

7 No sound bites, no photo opportunities,
and it takes years.
All the cameras have gone
to other wars.

The bridges need to be rebuilt,
the railroad stations, too.
8 Shirtsleeves will be rolled
to shreds.

shards (shärdz) *n.* sharp fragments

glaze (gläz) *v.* fit glass to a window; cover with a shiny finish

6 **Critical Viewing** ▶ Might this woman represent the "someone" in the poem, or does that "someone" have a different spirit? Explain. **[Connect]**

Reading Strategy
Evaluating the Writer's Statement of Philosophy What view of modern life does the speaker express in these lines?

ENRICHMENT: History Connection

War in Poland

Poland has many times faced the wartime destruction both Miłosz and Szymborska describe. In particular, during World War II, Poland saw terrible devastation. German Nazis invaded on September 1, 1939, and quickly took over. Within two weeks, Germany had made a deal with the Soviet Union—which had invaded from the east—to divide the occupied lands.

The Nazis hated Christian Poles as much as they despised the Jews, whom they did not regard as Polish citizens even though Jews had lived in Poland for a thousand years. All Poles were subject to brutal treatment. They could be rounded up at a moment's notice for dangerous work details, or they could be tortured and killed at the Nazis' whim.

The Polish Resistance movement mounted its own rebellion against Nazi rule in the summer of 1944. In the course of this uprising, which ultimately failed, Warsaw was nearly leveled.

Aftermath, 1945, Karl Hofer, Hamburg Kunsthalle, Hamburg, Germany

❽ Critical Thinking

Analyze

- Ask a volunteer to read aloud the bracketed sentence on p. 1288.
- Then, have students explain the meaning of the sentence.
  Possible response: Those participating in the rebuilding will roll up their shirtsleeves in preparation to work. The sleeves will be rolled up so many times during the course of the work that they will become tattered and torn.
- In what way does this image reflect the emotions of those rebuilding?
  Possible response: The work is so demanding and relentless that those rebuilding feel emotionally shredded.

❾ Background

Art

Aftermath, by Karl Hofer

Karl Hofer (1878–1955) knew of Nazi discrimination and destruction firsthand. Hofer was both figuratively cast out by the Nazis for what they called his "degenerative art" and physically cast out when they ransacked his art studio. Many of Hofer's works reflect despair and emotional isolation, as does this image of an old woman surrounded by debris.

Use the following question for discussion:

How does this painting capture the emotions that rebuilding after war might bring?
Possible response: The woman's posture and expression reflect the overwhelming feelings of sorrow and helplessness of those faced with rebuilding. In addition, the dark colors and angular figures create a feeling of confinement.

CUSTOMIZE INSTRUCTION FOR UNIVERSAL ACCESS

For Special Needs Students	For English Learners
In order to discern the alliteration in the poem, students may benefit from hearing the poem read aloud. Refer them to the **Listening to Literature Audiocassettes** or **CDs.** Encourage students to listen to the recording several times. Then, present examples of alliteration, such as "the rubble to the roadsides" or "the carts loaded with corpses." Discuss how the repeated sounds create an almost chantlike effect that suggests the numbness a war survivor might feel.	Review multiple meanings in the poem's details so that students can better appreciate the text. For example, the word *springs* refers to the coils inside the sofa, not to the time of year, and the word *bites* refers to small selections of sound, not to the bites a person takes of food. Have students refer to dictionaries to search for multiple meanings of these and other words.

ASSESS

(10) Literary Analysis

Irony and History as a Theme

- Have students read the bracketed stanzas.
- Then, ask students the Literary Analysis question on p. 1290: According to the speaker, what pattern does history follow after a war?
  Possible response: In time, people who lived through the war die, and succeeding generations grow up knowing less and less about it.

Answers for p. 1290

Review and Assess

1. Possible response: Some readers will say that their views have changed because Szymborska emphasizes the importance of recognizing and understanding history.
2. **(a)** A war has taken place before the poem begins. **(b)** The aftermath requires survivors to rebuild both physical and emotional structures. **(c)** People forget about the war as those who know little or nothing of the war outnumber those who do, as referenced in the lines "Those who knew/what this was all about/ must make way for those/who know little."
3. **(a)** The word "someone" indicates who must do the work. **(b)** The speaker is referring to any individual who takes up the tasks of repair. **(c)** Possible response: The word suggests the nameless many who historically have taken up the task of rebuilding.
4. **(a)** The "others" are busy and find the war memories boring. **(b)** The attitude of the "others" encourages poeple to forget or to ignore the causes and effects of war.
5. Possible response: The end of the poem may suggest healing, as people move beyond war's damage; however, it also suggests that forgetting about war's causes and effects will allow it to recur. Therefore, the conclusion represents a superficial healing and conceals danger.

Someone, broom in hand,
still remembers how it was.
Someone else listens, nodding
his unshattered head.
But others are bound to be bustling nearby
who'll find all that
a little boring.

(10) From time to time someone still must
dig up a rusted argument
from underneath a bush
and haul it off to the dump.

Those who knew
what this was all about
must make way for those
who know little.
And less than that.
And at last nothing less than nothing.

Someone has to lie there
in the grass that covers up
the causes and effects
with a cornstalk in his teeth,
gawking at clouds.

Literary Analysis
Irony and History as a Theme According to the speaker, what pattern does history follow after a war?

gawking (gôk′ iŋ) v. staring foolishly; gaping

Review and Assess

Thinking About the Selection

1. **Respond:** Does this poem cause you to rethink your own feelings about history, or does it leave them unchanged? Explain.
2. **(a) Recall:** What event has taken place before the poem begins? **(b) Generalize:** Identify what kinds of tasks the aftermath of this event requires. **(c) Interpret:** What is the ultimate result of this work? Cite details to support your answer.
3. **(a) Recall:** What repeated word indicates who must do this work? **(b) Infer:** To whom is the speaker referring? **(c) Interpret:** What does the use of this word indicate about the reason that people do the work and, eventually, forget the event?
4. **(a) Interpret:** What is the attitude of the "others" in line 30? **(b) Connect:** In what way does the attitude of the "others" allow "someone" to just lie in the grass?
5. **Make a Judgment:** Does the conclusion of the poem represent a healing of society or does it conceal a danger? Explain.

ASSESSMENT PRACTICE: Writing Skills

Strategy (For more practice, see Test Preparation Workbook, p. 61.)

Many standardized tests require students to recognize various writing strategies. Use the following sample test item to demonstrate this skill.

The destruction of Warsaw during World War II certainly explains why Miłosz was thinking about the world's end. However, the reaction to these events expressed in the poem is at first puzzling. Miłosz evokes a peaceful, almost lyrical world, ending with a description of a man binding tomatoes.

Which of the following would be the best addition to the end of this paragraph?

A Miłosz's writing is very powerful.
B The tomato captures the readers' attention.
C This quality of the poem invites serious thought.
D The old man in Miłosz's poem is heroic.

C is the correct answer. Miłosz wants readers to think differently about the world's end.

Review and Assess

Literary Analysis

Irony

1. (a) Identify an example of **verbal irony** in lines 22–26 of "A Song on the End of the World." (b) Explain what the irony in your example involves.
2. In what way is the central idea of the poem—that the day the world ends will be an ordinary day—an example of **situational irony**?
3. (a) Explain one verbal irony in the first stanza of "The End and the Beginning." (b) Explain the irony in the last stanza. (c) In what way does the irony in the first and last stanzas relate to the poem's title?
4. Explain the way in which each poem might be different if its message were stated directly, without irony.

Comparing Literary Works

5. (a) Compare **history as a theme** in each poem, using a chart like the one shown.

Events Described	"Final" Event	Pattern of History	Optimistic/ Pessimistic

(b) In your opinion, which poem presents the more optimistic view? Explain.

6. (a) In what sense does the speaker in each poem remember something that others forget or ignore? (b) What role in history does each poem suggest that poets have? Explain.

Reading Strategy

Evaluating the Writer's Statement of Philosophy

7. (a) What **philosophical statement** does Miłosz make about the value of an ordinary day? Give details from the poem in support. (b) What philosophical statement does Szymborska make about our ability to learn from the past? Support your answer with details.
8. With which philosophy do you agree? Explain.

Extend Understanding

9. **Social Studies Connection:** In the early twentieth century, many believed progress was making the world a better place. How do these late-twentieth-century poems challenge that idea?

Quick Review

Irony occurs when writers create a contrast between appearance or expectation and reality. **Situational irony** involves an opposition between expectations and actual events. **Verbal irony** is a clash between the words used for a thing and its reality.

When writers take **history as a theme,** they look for a meaning or a general pattern in events, such as a repeating cycle.

To **evaluate the writer's statement of philosophy,** decide whether your own experiences and ideas support the view of life suggested by the work.

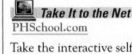

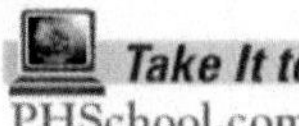
Take It to the Net
PHSchool.com

Take the interactive self-test online to check your understanding of these selections.

ENRICHMENT: Further Reading

Other Works by the Authors

We strongly encourage you to review any selection before assigning or recommending it to students.

Native Realm, by Czesław Miłosz

View with a Grain of Sand, by Wisława Szymborska

Take It to the Net

Visit PHSchool.com for more information on the authors.

Answers for p. 1291

Review and Assess

1. **(a)** In these lines, the man is described both as a "white-haired old man" and a "prophet." **(b)** Miłosz seems at once to ridicule and revere the man.
2. The poem plays on the difference between the drama that one would expect to accompany the end of the world and the ordinary events that are occurring on that day.
3. **(a)** Szymborska understates the damage caused by war by writing "After every war/someone has to tidy up." **(b)** Someone who forgets the war lies on grass that covers up the causes and effects of that war. **(c)** In both the first and last stanzas, the speaker includes an end and a beginning. History is cyclical; the end of the war and its results will be the beginning of the next one.
4. Possible response: Without irony, the poems might have an angrier tone.
5. **(a) Events Described:** war; **"Final" Event:** the end of the world; the end of the war; **Pattern of History:** everyday events continue amidst horror; everyday events in time cover up horror; **Optimistic/Pessimistic:** optimistic; pessimistic **(b)** Possible response: The Miłosz poem is more optimistic because it shows the persistence of the human spirit in the face of disaster.
6. **(a)** The speaker in Miłosz's poem recognizes signs of the end of the world that others ignore. The speaker in Szymborska's poem remembers the war that others forget. **(b)** Possible response: A poet's role is to remember and record history.
7. **(a)** Miłosz states that an ordinary day is valuable. For example, he describes the prophet who is busy with his tomatoes in the face of the world's end. **(b)** Szymborska's poem suggests that time goes on despite the horrors of war and limits one's ability to learn from the past. An example is the boredom felt by those who come after the war.
8. Possible response: Miłosz's philosophy is appealing because

continued

continued from right column

people must go on living their daily lives, regardless of what happens in the world.

9. Possible response: These poems suggest that technology has created devastating weapons and war machines that allow people to inflict great damage on one another.

EXTEND

Answers for p. 1292

❶ Vocabulary Development

Related Words: *glaze* and *glimmering*

1. A glimpse is a quick look at something or a flicker of light.
2. Gold is a shiny metal.
3. If an object glints, it shines in the light.

Spelling Strategy

1. short
2. long
3. long

Concept Development: Analogies

1. prophet
2. glaze
3. glimmering
4. shards
5. gawking

❷ Grammar and Style

Practice

1. No one, I
2. Someone, I
3. others, I; that, D
4. Those, D; this, D; those, D
5. that, D

Writing Application

Sample sentences: *No one* (I) who survived the terrorist attack of September 11, 2001, will ever forget that day. An event like *that* (D) can haunt *someone* (I) forever. *Those* (D) who perished will never be forgotten.

10TH GRADE For support in teaching the Grammar and Style Lesson to tenth graders, use **Writing and Grammar,** Platinum Level, Chapter 16, Section 2.

Integrate Language Skills

❶ Vocabulary Development Lesson

Related Words: *glaze* and *glimmering*

Glaze and *glimmering* are related to the Indo-European root *ghel*, meaning "to shine or to glow." To *glaze* is to fit glass, a shiny substance, to a window. A *glimmering* is a faint shining. Explain how the root meaning "to shine" adds to the meaning of each of these related words:

1. glimpse 2. gold 3. glint

Spelling Strategy

If a word is spelled with a doubled consonant preceded by a single vowel, the vowel sound is short. *Glimmering* has a short *i* sound. In contrast, if a single consonant appears between two vowels, the first vowel sound is often long. *Glaze* has a long *a* sound. Explain whether the boldface vowel in each of these words is short or long.

1. dapper 2. vacate 3. potential

Concept Development: Analogies

For each item below, study the relationship presented in the first pair. Then, complete the analogies by using the vocabulary words on page 1285 to build word pairs expressing the same relationship.

1. *Storyteller* is to *tale* as ___?___ is to *prediction*.
2. *Upholster* is to *cloth* as ___?___ is to *glass*.
3. *Drizzling* is to *rain* as ___?___ is to *light*.
4. *Rocks* are to *stones* as ___?___ are to *fragments*.
5. *Yelling* is to *whispering* as ___?___ is to *peeking*.

❷ Grammar and Style Lesson

Indefinite and Demonstrative Pronouns

An **indefinite pronoun** is used to refer to persons, places, or things without specifying which one. Indefinite pronouns include such words as *each*, *everything*, and *someone*. A **demonstrative pronoun** is used to point out a specific person, place, or thing. These pronouns include *this*, *that*, *these*, and *those*.

Indefinite: Someone has to shove / the rubble to the roadsides. . . .

Demonstrative: . . . those who expected thunder and lightning . . .

Practice For each item, identify the indefinite or demonstrative pronouns, and label each *I* or *D*.

1. No one believes it is happening now.
2. Someone, broom in hand, / still remembers how it was.
3. But others are bound to be bustling nearby / who'll find all that / a little boring.
4. Those who knew / what this was all about / must make way for those / who know little.
5. And less than that.

Writing Application Write four sentences about an event from history, using at least one indefinite and one demonstrative pronoun.

Prentice Hall Writing and Grammar Connection: Diamond Level, Chapter 17, Section 1

TEACHING RESOURCES

The following resources can be used to enrich or extend the instruction for pp. 1292–1293.

Vocabulary

- **Selection Support:** Build Vocabulary, p. 241
- **Vocabulary and Spelling Practice Book** (Use this booklet for skills instruction.)

Grammar

- **Selection Support:** Grammar and Style, p. 242
- **Writing and Grammar,** Diamond Level, p. 368
- **Daily Language Practice Transparencies**

Writing

- **Performance Assess. and Portfolio Mgmt.,** p. 14
- **Writing and Grammar,** Diamond Level, p. 102
- **Writing and Grammar iText CD-ROM**
- **Writing Models and Graphic Organizers on Transparencies,** pp. 83–85

BLOCK SCHEDULING: Resources marked with this symbol provide varied instruction during 90-minute blocks.

❸ Writing Lesson

Narrative About a Quiet Hero

The old man in Miłosz's poem shows heroic devotion to ordinary pursuits in the midst of danger. Write an account of a person, real or fictional, with such a devotion, showing why he or she deserves your admiration.

Prewriting Begin by listing details that describe the dangerous situation and the way in which your subject managed to keep a sense of quiet dignity. Circle those that are most vivid or significant.

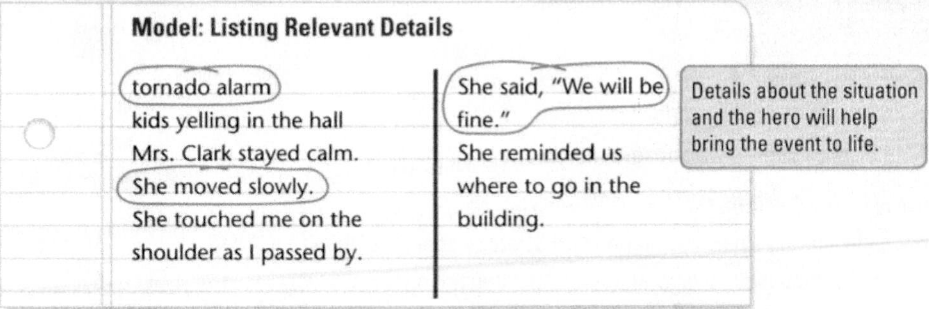

Model: Listing Relevant Details
tornado alarm
kids yelling in the hall
Mrs. Clark stayed calm.
She moved slowly.
She touched me on the shoulder as I passed by.
She said, "We will be fine."
She reminded us where to go in the building.
Details about the situation and the hero will help bring the event to life.

Drafting As you draft, remember that understatement is often more effective than exaggeration. Choose precise verbs and adjectives to *show* the quiet heroism of your character, rather than announcing it.

Revising As you revise your account, add specific details that will help the reader imagine the scene.

WG Prentice Hall Writing and Grammar Connection: Diamond Level, Chapter 6, Section 2

❹ Extension Activities

Listening and Speaking With a partner, present a **multimedia reading** of one of the poems. Accompany your reading with appropriate audiovisuals, such as music or slides. Use these tips to prepare:

- Select musical and visual qualities of the poem to emphasize, such as repetition.
- Practice the timing of your presentation before you perform it for the class.

After your presentation, ask audience members to evaluate the effectiveness of each of its elements. **[Group Activity]**

Research and Technology In their poems, Miłosz and Szymborska respond to Poland's difficult history. Create a **map or set of maps** showing Poland's shifting boundaries over time. Clearly indicate which nations have ruled Poland, as well as the birthplace or main city of residence of each poet.

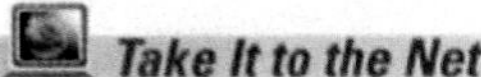
Take It to the Net PHSchool.com

Go online for an additional research activity using the Internet.

- For Musical/Rhythmic Learners, use Activity 7.

ASSESSMENT RESOURCES

The following resources can be used to assess students' knowledge and skills.

Selection Assessment

- **Formal Assessment,** pp. 213–215
- **Open-Book Tests,** pp. 181–183
- **Test Bank Software**

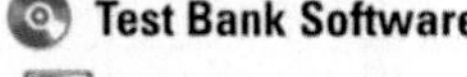
Take It to the Net

Visit PHSchool.com for self-tests on the selections.

Writing Rubric

- **Performance Assess. and Portfolio Mgmt.,** p. 14

For additional diagnostics and remediation for skills covered in this grouping, use materials from the Prentice Hall Assessment System.

❸ Writing Lesson

- Narratives usually recount a specific event or events and how the central figures respond to the events. This narrative should focus on how the central figure responds to danger.
- Explain that an effective narrative should begin by introducing the central figure and situation. Writers often do this by using dialogue or by describing the central figure in action. The narrative should then develop toward its crisis or climax. In this case, the crisis could be the presentation of danger.
- In selecting the central figure for their narratives, students should review fictional characters from recent reading or focus on real characters from personal experience or news stories.
- Use the Writing Lesson to guide students as they write their narratives. Then, refer students to the Story Map organizer in **Writing Models and Graphic Organizers on Transparencies,** pp. 83–85, as a planning tool.
- Use the Narration: Short Story rubric in **Performance Assessment and Portfolio Management,** p. 14, to evaluate students' work.

10TH GRADE For support in working through the Writing Lesson with tenth graders, use **Writing and Grammar,** Platinum Level, Chapter 6, Section 2.

❹ Research and Technology

- Clarify the difference between using one map and using a set of maps. If using one map, students will need multiple layers or colors. If using a set of maps, students can show each time period separately.
- Discuss likely information sources with students, such as historical atlases and Internet sites that focus on Polish history.

CUSTOMIZE INSTRUCTION For Universal Access

To address different learning styles, use the following activities suggested in the **Extension Activities** booklet, p. 61:

- For Interpersonal Learners, use Activity 5.
- For Visual/Spatial Learners, use Activity 6.

Freedom to Breathe • *from* Nobel Lecture • Visit

Lesson Objectives

1. **To analyze and respond to literary elements**
   - Literary Analysis: Speaker
   - Comparing Literary Works: Changes in the Speaker's Role
2. **To read, comprehend, analyze, and critique a speech, a prose poem, and a poem**
   - Reading Strategy: Inferring the Speaker's Attitude
   - Reading Check Questions
   - Review and Assess Questions
   - Assessment Practice (ATE)
3. **To develop word analysis skills, fluency, and systematic vocabulary**
   - Vocabulary Development Lesson: Usage: Forms of *reciprocity*
4. **To understand and apply written and oral language conventions**
   - Spelling Strategy
   - Grammar and Style Lesson: Using Dashes
5. **To understand and apply appropriate writing and research strategies**
   - Writing Lesson: Persuasive Speech
   - Research and Technology: Annotated List
6. **To understand and apply listening and speaking strategies**
   - Extension Activity: Oral Description

10TH GRADE TEACHING A TENTH-GRADE COURSE

The literature in this section can be taught as part of a rich, balanced world literature course for tenth-grade students. For a full outline of such a course, see pp. T46–T48 in Volume 1 of this Teacher's Edition.

STEP-BY-STEP TEACHING GUIDE	PACING GUIDE
PRETEACH	
Motivate Students and Provide Background	
Use the Motivation activity (ATE p. 1294)	5 min.
Read and discuss author and background features (SE pp. 1294, 1296; ATE p. 1294) A	5 min.
Introduce the Concepts	
Introduce the Literary Analysis and Reading Strategy concepts (SE/ATE p. 1295) A	15 min.
Pronounce the vocabulary words and read their definitions (SE p. 1295)	5 min.
TEACH	
Monitor Comprehension	
Informally monitor comprehension by circulating while students read independently or in groups A	35 min.
Monitor students' comprehension with the Reading Check notes (SE/ATE pp. 1297, 1299, 1301)	as students read
Develop vocabulary with the Vocabulary notes (SE pp. 1296, 1297, 1298, 1299, 1302; ATE p. 1297)	as students read
Develop Understanding	
Develop students' understanding of speaker with the Literary Analysis annotations (SE/ATE pp. 1296, 1299) A	5 min.
Develop students' ability to infer the speaker's attitude by using the Reading Strategy annotations (SE/ATE p. 1302) A	5 min.
ASSESS	
Assess Mastery	
Assess students' mastery of the Reading Strategy and Literary Analysis concepts by having them answer the Review and Assess questions (SE/ATE p. 1303)	20 min.
Use one or more of the print, software, or transparency Assessment Resources (ATE p. 1305) A	up to 45 min.
EXTEND	
Apply Understanding	
Have students complete the Vocabulary Development Lesson and the Grammar and Style Lesson (SE p. 1304) A	20 min.
Apply students' ability to choose effective persuasive language by using the Writing Lesson (SE/ATE p. 1305) A	45 min.
Apply students' understanding of the selections, using one or more of the Extension Activities (SE p. 1305)	20–90 min.

ACCELERATED INSTRUCTION: Use the strategies and activities identified with an A.

10TH GRADE TEACHING TENTH-GRADE STUDENTS For support in teaching the selection(s) to tenth-grade students, see the Step-by-Step Teaching notes identified with the icon shown here.

UNIVERSAL ACCESS
- ● = Below-Level Students
- ▲ = On-Level Students
- ■ = Above-Level Students

Time and Resource Manager

Reading Level: Average, Average, Challenging
Average Number of Instructional Days: 3

RESOURCES			
	PRINT	**TRANSPARENCIES**	**TECHNOLOGY**
	• **Beyond Literature,** Humanities Connection: Art, p. 62 ▲ ■		
	• **Selection Support Workbook:** ● ▲ ■ Literary Analysis, p. 248 Reading Strategy, p. 247 Build Vocabulary, p. 245	• **Literary Analysis and Reading Transparencies,** pp. 123 and 124 ● ▲ ■	
			• **Listening to Literature** ● ▲ ■ Audiocassettes Audio CDs
	• **Literary Analysis for Enrichment,** p. 62 ■		
	• **Formal Assessment:** Selection Test, pp. 216–218 ● ▲ ■ • **Open-Book Tests,** pp. 184–186 ● ▲ ■ • **Performance Assessment and Portfolio Management,** p. 11 ● ▲ ■ • PRENTICE HALL ASSESSMENT SYSTEM ● ▲ ■	• PRENTICE HALL ASSESSMENT SYSTEM ● ▲ ■ **Skills Practice Answers and Explanations on Transparencies**	• **Test Bank Software** ● ▲ ■
	• **Selection Support Workbook:** ● ▲ ■ Grammar and Style, p. 246 • **Writing and Grammar,** Diamond Level ● ▲ ■ • **Extension Activities,** p. 62 ● ▲ ■	• **Daily Language Practice Transparencies** ● ▲ • **Writing Models and Graphic Organizers on Transparencies,** pp. 45–51 ● ▲ ■	• **Writing and Grammar iText CD-ROM** ● ▲ ■ *Take It to the Net* PHSchool.com

BLOCK SCHEDULING: Use one 90-minute class period to preteach the selection(s) and have students read them. Use a second 90-minute class period to assess students' mastery of skills and have them complete one of the Extension Activities.

PRETEACH

Step-by-Step Teaching Guide for pp. 1294–1295

Motivation

Ask students to imagine that they have suddenly been stricken with amnesia. They can still speak and function, but they have no memories of the past. Discuss with them how they would be different people. Lead them to see that remembering the past—both the good and the bad—is an essential part of self-understanding. Tell them that the two authors they are about to read show the importance of memory and reflection on the past.

❶ Background

More About the Authors

During World War II, Solzhenitsyn served in the Red Army where he rose to the rank of artillery captain and was decorated for bravery. After completing his eight-year prison sentence, he was exiled to Kazakhstan. His citizenship was restored in 1956, three years after Soviet leader Josef Stalin's death.

Yevtushenko grew up in the open spaces of central Asia, a region not unlike western Colorado. Ironically, this most Russian of writers was not Russian by birth. His mother came from Latvia. His father's family was Ukranian and had been exiled to Siberia by the czar in the 1800s. As a member of the Congress of People's Deputies, he supported what he calls "revolution from below"—a reform of Soviet society directed by the Soviet people.

Geography Note

Draw students' attention to the map on this page. Tell them that the former Soviet Union was the world's largest nation. It consisted of fifteen republics, comprised more than one hundred nationalities, covered 8,650,000 square miles, and had the longest coastline of any nation.

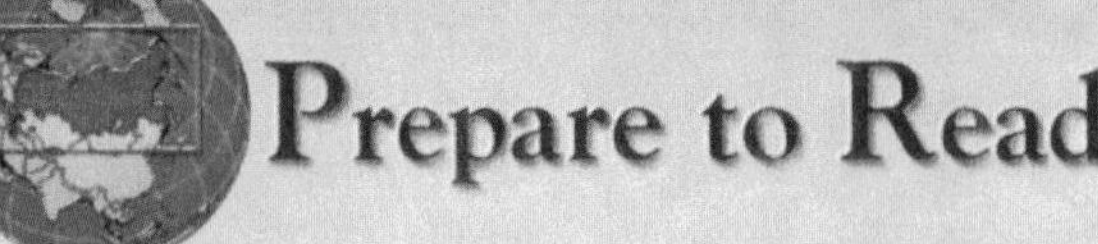

Prepare to Read

❶ Freedom to Breathe ◆ *from* Nobel Lecture ◆ Visit

Alexander Solzhenitsyn (b. 1918)

Alexander Solzhenitsyn (sōl' zhə nēt' sin) spent years in Soviet prison camps. There, he resolved to survive as a witness to oppression. His unsparing accounts of the camps are among the most important documents of the twentieth century.

Early Imprisonment Born in Kislovodsk, a city in southern Russia, Solzhenitsyn served in the Soviet army during World War II. While a soldier, he was convicted of treason—he had written letters critical of Josef Stalin, the Soviet leader. Solzhenitsyn found himself in a windswept camp in central Asia, where prisoners did backbreaking work on a meager diet.

Released in 1953, Solzhenitsyn eventually wrote a novel about life in the camps, *One Day in the Life of Ivan Denisovich* (1962). Although the government encouraged this novel's publication, the political tide soon shifted. After 1963, the government banned further publication of Solzhenitsyn's books.

Exile Officially rejected in Russia, Solzhenitsyn began to publish his novels in the West. The faster his prestige grew abroad, the worse his fortunes were at home. When he was awarded the Nobel Prize in Literature in 1970, Solzhenitsyn would not travel to accept it, fearing that the Soviet government would not let him return. Finally, in 1973, Solzhenitsyn published the first volume of *The Gulag Archipelago, 1918–1956*, a chronicle of the prison camps. Within months, he was deported by the Soviet government.

Solzhenitsyn eventually settled in the United States, where he continues to speak out on behalf of freedom. His life and work bear witness to the power of words—a power mighty enough to upset a nation.

Yevgeny Yevtushenko (b. 1933)

Perhaps the best introduction to Russian poet Yevgeny Yevtushenko (yev gen' ē yev' to͞o shen' kō) is one of his recordings. Yevtushenko is a remarkable performer, his voice fit to calm a child or storm a barricade. He has not been afraid to raise this voice against injustice.

The Celebrity Poet Born in 1933 in Zima Junction, along the Trans-Siberian Railroad, Yevtushenko published his first book, *Prospectors of the Future* (1952), while he was still in college. Over the next nine years, his poems and his public readings made him a celebrity in the Soviet Union, as popular as any movie star in the West. Yevtushenko did not merely read his poems: He acted them, lived them—lowering his voice to a whisper, then breaking out in a mighty roar, all the while gesturing dramatically.

Breaking Silence In 1961, Yevtushenko's fame became international with the poem "Babi Yar." It was at Babi Yar, near Kiev, that German troops murdered 34,000 Jews during two days in 1941. In his poem, Yevtushenko boldly referred to Russian anti-Semitism, a forbidden subject in Soviet Russia. The editor of the Russian *Literary Gazette* agonized over the poem, knowing that printing it could cost him his job. As the magazine's presses began to roll, and after consulting with his wife, he decided to take the risk. The poem's passionate attack on prejudice won Yevtushenko admirers in the West.

Elected in 1989 to the Congress of People's Deputies, Yevtushenko supported Mikhail Gorbachev's *perestroika*, or restructuring of Soviet society. His most recent work is *Don't Die Before You're Dead* (1993), a novel concerning life after the dismantling of the Soviet Union.

TEACHING RESOURCES

The following resources can be used to enrich or extend the instruction for pp. 1294–1295.

Background

Beyond Literature, p. 62

Take It to the Net

Visit PHSchool.com for background on the authors.

Literary Analysis

Literary Analysis and Reading Transparencies, Speaker, p. 123 ■

Selection Support: Literary Analysis, p. 248

Reading

Literary Analysis and Reading Transparencies, Inferring the Speaker's Attitude, p.124 ■

■ **BLOCK SCHEDULING:** Resources marked with this symbol provide varied instruction during 90-minute blocks.

Preview

Connecting to the Literature

Perhaps you have awakened early on a spring morning and, in the unfamiliar stillness, found the person you have always been. Perhaps you felt then how far a day might carry you—how large the future is. Literature, as these writers show, is also a moment to rediscover freedom and the future.

❷ Literary Analysis

Speaker

The **speaker** of a work is the character who "says" its words, or the voice of the work. There are various types of speaker. A speaker may be

- a distinctive fictional character.
- a character bearing a close resemblance to the writer.
- a writer's representation of himself or herself.
- a generalized, impersonal voice, as in a factual essay.

In Yevtushenko's poem "Visit," the speaker has an intimate, personal voice and uses details from the poet's experience. In this poem, the speaker is the poet's representation of himself. Solzhenitsyn himself is the speaker in his Nobel Lecture, yet he carefully crafts a particular public voice for himself. As you read, note the qualities of the speaker in each work.

Comparing Literary Works

As each of these works develops, the speaker takes on a new role, ensuring a dramatic conclusion. In Solzhenitsyn's Nobel Lecture, for example, the speaker turns from his role as award recipient to a role as spokesperson for truth. In Yevtushenko's poem, the speaker shifts from one who remembers the past to one who is confronted by it. As you read, compare the speakers' changes, noting ways in which they add drama to the works.

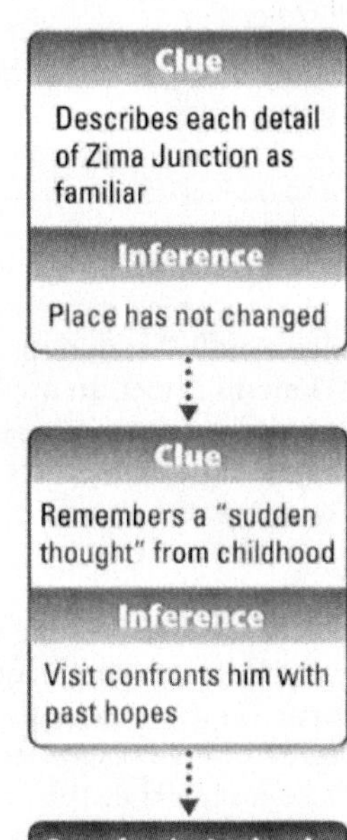

Clue
Describes each detail of Zima Junction as familiar
Inference
Place has not changed
Clue
Remembers a "sudden thought" from childhood
Inference
Visit confronts him with past hopes
Speaker's Attitude
The speaker realizes how much he has changed.

❸ Reading Strategy

Inferring the Speaker's Attitude

To fully understand a work, use the details to **infer the speaker's attitude,** determining the speaker's views of ideas and events. Use a chart like the one shown to list and interpret clues to the speaker's attitude.

Vocabulary Development

glistens (glis´ ənz) *v.* shines or sparkles with reflected light (p. 1296)

reciprocity (res´ ə präs´ ə tē) *n.* mutual exchange (p. 1297)

assimilate (ə sim´ ə lāt´) *v.* absorb; incorporate into a greater body (p. 1298)

inexorably (in eks´ ə rə blē) *adv.* relentlessly (p. 1299)

oratory (ôr´ ə tôr´ ē) *n.* skillful public speaking (p. 1299)

fungus (fuŋ´ gəs) *n.* mildew; any of a group of plants lacking leaves and roots (p. 1302)

clenched (klencht) *adj.* gripped firmly or tightly (p. 1302)

❷ Literary Analysis

Speaker

- On the board, list works from other units, and ask students to identify the speakers or narrators: for example, "How Much Land Does a Man Need?" (a distinctive fictional character); from *Annie John* (a character bearing a close resemblance to the writer); from *History of the Peloponnesian War* (a generalized, impersonal voice).
- Remind students that the speaker is not necessarily the writer. In some cases, the speaker and the writer may be one and the same, but they are often different.
- Give students extra practice using the Speaker transparency in **Literary Analysis and Reading Transparencies,** p. 123.

❸ Reading Strategy

Inferring the Speaker's Attitude

- Remind students that an inference is a conclusion made from hints and implications in a text.
- Direct students to use the graphic organizer on p. 1295 as they read the selections. Explain that identifying detailed clues from a text allows readers to make conclusions about the speaker's thoughts and, in turn, his or her attitude. Understanding a speaker's attitude can lead to more accurate interpretations of a text.

Vocabulary Development

- Pronounce each vocabulary word for students, and read the definitions as a class. Have students identify any words with which they are familiar.

CUSTOMIZE INSTRUCTION FOR UNIVERSAL ACCESS

For Less Proficient Readers	For English Learners	For Advanced Readers
Students may find these works difficult because of their abstract concepts and challenging language. Have students work in small groups with one or two advanced students to read and discuss the essays. Have them work on defining the ideas of "freedom," "world literature," and "memory."	In the spirit of Solzhenitsyn's Nobel address, have English learners share with the class the great writers and works of their countries. Encourage them to present in both English and their first languages.	Suggest to students that they read an excerpt from Elie Wiesel's *Night* or parts of Solzhenitsyn's novel *One Day in the Life of Ivan Denisovich* and then give a brief report to the class. Have students explain how these works fulfill their authors' purpose to keep memory alive or expose lies.

 ***E-Teach***

Visit e-Teach at PHSchool.com for teachers' essays on how to teach, with questions and answers.

TEACH

Step-by-Step Teaching Guide for pp. 1296–1302

Teaching Tenth-Grade Students

10TH GRADE These essays and poems may be difficult for tenth-grade students. Read sections aloud, periodically stopping to clarify points and ask questions.

❶ About the Selection

In the essay "Freedom to Breathe," Solzhenitsyn reflects on how imprisonment altered his appreciation of the simple act of breathing.

❷ Critical Thinking

Infer

- Have students read the last two paragraphs on p. 1296.
- Ask students what they can infer about the speaker from this passage.
  Possible response: The speaker's prison confinement has stripped away a focus on material values and distractions and replaced them with an appreciation for the simple pleasures of nature and of life. The speaker's return to elemental pleasures gives him hope for humanity.
- Then, ask: Do you think most people in the United States would have the same experience while standing under an apple tree? Explain why or why not.
  Possible response: Most Americans would probably appreciate the beauty of the experience to a lesser degree because they often take their freedom for granted.

❸ Literary Analysis

Speaker and Dramatic Conclusion

- Remind students that setting is often an integral part of a literary work.
- Read aloud the bracketed passage. Then, ask the Literary Analysis question on p. 1296: Why is it surprising to learn these details about the setting at the conclusion?
  Possible response: It is surprising because the reader has been led to believe that the setting is pastoral when, in reality, it is urban.

❶ Freedom to Breathe

Alexander Solzhenitsyn
translated by Michael Glenny

Background

In this brief essay and in his Nobel Lecture, Alexander Solzhenitsyn argues for the power of freedom and of truth. During the Soviet period in Russia, freedom of speech was curtailed. Writers could publish legally only with the approval of the state. Dissenting opinions and alternative literature circulated secretly, as typewritten manuscript, in a literary underground. Solzhenitsyn himself was exiled for his dissent. Clearly, the Soviet government would have agreed with Solzhenitsyn's assessment—freedom is our truth, and truth is dangerous to an oppressive government.

A shower fell in the night and now dark clouds drift across the sky, occasionally sprinkling a fine film of rain.

I stand under an apple tree in blossom and I breathe. Not only the apple tree but the grass round it glistens with moisture; words cannot describe the sweet fragrance that pervades the air. I inhale as deeply as I can, and the aroma invades my whole being; I breathe with my eyes open, I breathe with my eyes closed—I cannot say which gives me the greater pleasure.

This, I believe, is the single most precious freedom that prison takes away from us: the freedom to breathe freely, as I now can. No food on earth, no wine, not even a woman's kiss is sweeter to me than this air steeped in the fragrance of flowers, of moisture and freshness. ❸

❷ No matter that this is only a tiny garden, hemmed in by five-story houses like cages in a zoo. I cease to hear the motorcycles backfiring, radios whining, the burble of loudspeakers. As long as there is fresh air to breathe under an apple tree after a shower, we may survive a little longer.

glistens (glis′ enz) *v.* shines or sparkles with reflected light

Literary Analysis
Speaker and Dramatic Conclusion Why is it surprising to learn these details about the setting at the conclusion?

TEACHING RESOURCES

The following resources can be used to enrich or extend the instruction for pp. 1296–1302.

Literary Analysis

- **Selection Support:** Literary Analysis, p. 248
- **Literary Analysis and Reading Transparencies,** Speaker, p. 123 ■

Reading

- **Selection Support:** Reading Strategy, p. 247; Build Vocabulary, p. 245
- **Listening to Literature Audiocassettes** ■
- **Listening to Literature CDs**

■ **BLOCK SCHEDULING:** Resources marked with this symbol provide varied instruction during 90-minute blocks.

4 # from *Nobel Lecture*

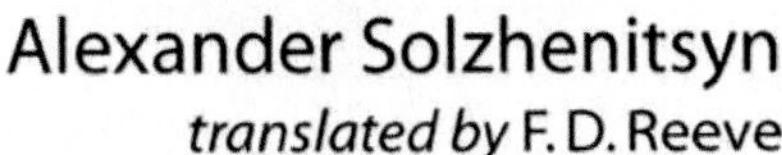

Alexander Solzhenitsyn

translated by F. D. Reeve

5 I am, however, encouraged by a keen sense of WORLD LITERATURE as the one great heart that beats for the cares and misfortunes of our world, even though each corner sees and experiences them in a different way.

In past times, also, besides age-old national literatures there existed a concept of world literature as the link between the summits of national literatures and as the aggregate[1] of reciprocal literary influences. But there was a time lag: readers and writers came to know foreign writers only belatedly, sometimes centuries later, so that mutual influences were delayed and the network of national literary high points was visible not to contemporaries but to later generations.

Today, between writers of one country and the readers and writers of
6 another, there is an almost instantaneous reciprocity, as I myself know. My books, unpublished, alas, in my own country, despite hasty and often bad translations have quickly found a responsive world readership. Critical analysis of them has been undertaken by such leading
7 Western writers as Heinrich Böll.[2] During all these recent years, when both my work and my freedom did not collapse, when against the laws of gravity they held on seemingly in thin air, seemingly ON NOTHING, on the invisible, mute surface tension of sympathetic people, with warm gratitude I learned, to my complete surprise, of the support of the world's writing fraternity. On my fiftieth birthday I was astounded to receive greetings from well-known European writers. No pressure put on me now passed unnoticed. During the dangerous weeks when I was 8

reciprocity (res´ ə präs´ ə tē) *n.* mutual exchange

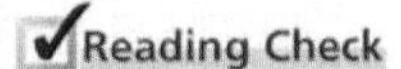

Reading Check

According to Solzhenitsyn, what is the main difference between world literature in the past and in the present?

1. **aggregate** (ag´ rə git) *n.* group of things gathered together and considered as a whole.
2. **Heinrich Böll** (hin´ riH böl) German novelist (1917–1985) and winner of the Nobel Prize in Literature.

4 About the Selection

Solzhenitsyn reflects on the importance of literature that bears witness—writers whose voices override lies and readers who respond to and align with the writers. He celebrates unity in the writing community—solidarity that he describes as "one great heart."

5 Critical Thinking

Interpret

- Ask students what Solzhenitsyn means by saying that world literature is "one great heart." Possible response: People from all over the world can share experiences and gain understanding of one another through literature.
- Then, ask: How can literature's "great heart" help authors build an international network? Possible response: Authors around the globe can respond to one another's themes and ideas.

6 Vocabulary Development

- Call students' attention to the word *reciprocity,* and read its definition. Tell students that several English words are forms of *reciprocity,* meaning "mutual exchange."
- Invite students to suggest other forms of the word. Possible response: Students may suggest *reciprocate, or reciprocal.*
- Ask students why this word is particularly appropriate here. Possible response: Solzhenitsyn believes in writing as a process in which readers and writers exchange beliefs.

7 Background

Literature

Böll expressed controversial views. He wrote on the horrors of war, criticized government and religious institutions, and denounced nuclear weapons and human rights violations.

8 Reading Check

Answer: In times past, world literature was disseminated slowly. Today, it can be known to writers and readers almost instantly.

CUSTOMIZE INSTRUCTION FOR UNIVERSAL ACCESS

For Gifted/Talented Sudents	For Advanced Readers
Tell students that in describing Solzhenitsyn's book *The Oak and the Calf,* one reviewer has written, "As literature, it carries his unique eloquence. As memoir, it is a revealing expression of his personality and prejudices. As a document, . . . it provides additional testimony to the obtuse, cruel, and mediocre regime that rules from the Kremlin." Have students reread *Nobel Lecture* to find examples of each element: talent for literature, personality and prejudices, and testimony.	Have students compare this excerpt from Solzhenitsyn's Nobel address with those given by Ernest Hemingway in 1954 and Chilean writer Pablo Neruda in 1971. Both were published in book form and should be available in a library. Ask students to compare both the content and the styles of the three speeches. It might help students to use a triple Venn diagram for this comparison. Invite students to share their results with the class.

9 Background

Stalinism

Stalin accused of treason those who did not agree with his policies. Between seven and fifteen million Soviets were imprisoned in labor camps, which Stalin used to bolster the economy.

Solzhenitsyn's books, the first of which was published in 1962, have had a powerful effect on Soviet readers. A sample of these responses appears in Michael Scammell's biography of Solzhenitsyn, published in 1984: "My face was smothered in tears. I didn't wipe them away or feel ashamed, because all this . . . was mine, intimately mine, mine for every day of the fifteen years I spent in the camps." Another wrote, "Thank you, dear friend, comrade, and brother! . . . You have already left your name in the history of Soviet literature, and nothing can wipe it away."

Still another said, "For me and others like me your story was the last hope that justice still exists somewhere, that it has not vanished or died out."

10 Critical Thinking

Draw Conclusions

- Read aloud the bracketed passage. Then, ask:
- Why is it important that one country's literature be read by people from other countries?
  Possible response: Literature can inform people of problems occurring around the world. It can also reveal people's common interests and beliefs, helping them solve problems together.
- Have students explain what Solzhenitsyn means by saying that literature is a "sensitive and responsive" tool for unifying mankind?
  Possible response: Literature brings together East and West, helping people of diverse cultures understand and care about one another.

being expelled from the Writers' Union,[3] THE PROTECTIVE WALL put forward by prominent writers of the world saved me from worse persecution, and Norwegian writers and artists hospitably prepared shelter for me in the event that I was exiled from my country. Finally, my being nominated for a Nobel Prize was originated not in the land where I live and write but by François Mauriac[4] and his colleagues. Afterward, national writers' organizations expressed unanimous support for me.

As I have understood it and experienced it myself, world literature is no longer an abstraction or a generalized concept invented by literary critics, but a common body and common spirit, a living, heartfelt unity reflecting the growing spiritual unity of mankind. State borders still turn crimson, heated red-hot by electric fences and machine-gun fire; some ministries of internal affairs still suppose that literature is "an internal affair" of the countries under their jurisdiction; and newspaper headlines still herald, "They have no right to interfere in our internal affairs!" Meanwhile, no such thing as INTERNAL AFFAIRS remains on our crowded Earth. Mankind's salvation lies exclusively in everyone's making everything his business, in the people of the East being anything but indifferent to what is thought in the West, and in the people of the West being anything but indifferent to what happens in the East. Literature, one of the most sensitive and responsive tools of human
10 existence, has been the first to pick up, adopt, and assimilate this sense of the growing unity of mankind. I therefore confidently turn to the world literature of the present, to hundreds of friends whom I have not met face to face and perhaps never will see.

Bust of Soviet leader V. I. Lenin.

My friends! Let us try to be helpful, if we are worth anything. In our own countries, torn by differences among parties, movements, castes, and groups, who for ages past has been not the dividing but the uniting force? This, essentially, is the position of writers, spokesmen of a national language, of the chief tie binding the nation, the very soil which the people inhabit, and, in fortunate circumstances, the nation's spirit too.

I think that world literature has the power in these frightening times to help mankind see itself accurately despite what is advocated by partisans[5] and by parties. It has the power to transmit the condensed experience of one region to another, so that different scales of values

3. **Writers' Union** official Soviet writers' organization. In addition to being expelled from this union, Solzhenitsyn was forbidden to live in Moscow.
4. **François Mauriac** (frän swá´ mô´ rē ak´) French novelist and essayist (1885–1970).
5. **partisans** (pärt´ i zənz) *n.* emotional supporters of a party or viewpoint.

Literature in context — History Connection

9 *Stalinism*

During Josef Stalin's rule of the Union of Soviet Socialist Republics, Solzhenitsyn, like millions of other Russians, was confined to a prison camp. Through these camps and his extensive secret police, Stalin (1879–1953) turned the U.S.S.R. into a totalitarian state.

The U.S.S.R. was formed in the Russian Revolution of 1917, when Russia's common people had overthrown the czar (monarch). Soon, democratic ideals gave way to the oppressive realities of Communist party rule. Stalin, who by 1929 had come to dominate the party, pushed the U.S.S.R. to develop its industries. He collectivized agriculture, combining the small farms of peasants into large government-controlled farms. In the 1930s, millions who refused to join these collective farms were sent to prison camps, while dissenters were imprisoned or shot. As many as 20 million people may have been killed in Stalin's persecutions of the 1930s.

assimilate (ə sim´ ə lāt´) *v.* absorb; incorporate into a greater body

ENRICHMENT: Literature Connection

Forbidden Literature

The oral tradition has always been especially important in the Soviet Union. During the Stalinist purge of "undesirables" and the ban on publishing particular writers' works, banned or forbidden poetry was committed to memory and whispered by one person to another throughout the Soviet Union. Nadezda Mandel'shtam, for example, memorized Osip Mandel'shtam's poetry. After his death and after the ban was lifted, she wrote down her husband's poems and published many of them.

While Solzhenitsyn was in the labor camp, he wrote poetry by memorizing it. Later, when he was exiled, he wrote prose in secret. He says that "During all the years until 1961, not only was I convinced that I should never see a single line of mine in print in my lifetime, but, also, I scarcely dared allow any of my close acquaintances to read anything I had written because I feared that this would become known."

are combined, and so that one people accurately and concisely knows the true history of another with a power of recognition and acute awareness as if it had lived through that history itself—and could thus be spared repeating old mistakes. At the same time, perhaps we ourselves may succeed in developing our own WORLD-WIDE VIEW, like any man, with the center of the eye seeing what is nearby but the periphery[6] of vision taking in what is happening in the rest of the world. We will make correlations[7] and maintain world-wide standards.

11 Who, if not writers, are to condemn their own unsuccessful governments (in some states this is the easiest way to make a living; everyone who is not too lazy does it) as well as society itself, whether for its cowardly humiliation or for its self-satisfied weakness, or the lightheaded escapades of the young, or the youthful pirates brandishing knives?

We will be told: What can literature do against the pitiless onslaught of naked violence? Let us not forget that violence does not and cannot flourish by itself; it is inevitably intertwined with LYING. Between them there is the closest, the most profound and natural bond: nothing screens violence except lies, and the only way lies can hold out is by violence. Whoever has once announced violence as his METHOD must inexorably choose lying as his PRINCIPLE. At birth, violence behaves openly and even proudly. But as soon as it becomes stronger and firmly established, it senses the thinning of the air around it and cannot go on without befogging itself in lies, coating itself with lying's sugary oratory. It does not always or necessarily go straight for the gullet; usually it demands of its victims only allegiance to the lie, only complicity in the lie.

The simple act of an ordinary courageous man is not to take part, not to support lies! Let *that* come into the world and even reign over it, but not through me. Writers and artists can do more: they can VANQUISH LIES! In the struggle against lies, art has always won and always will. Conspicuously, incontestably for everyone. Lies can stand up against much in the world, but not against art.

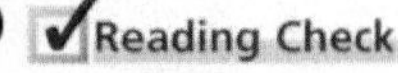

Once lies have been dispelled, the repulsive nakedness of violence will be exposed—and hollow violence will collapse.

That, my friends, is why I think we can help the world in its red-hot hour: not by the nay-saying of having no armaments, not by abandoning oneself to the carefree life, but by going into battle! 13

6. **periphery** (pə rif´ ər ē) surrounding area; boundary; perimeter.
7. **correlations** (kôr´ ə lā´ shənz) analysis of relationships or connections.

Literary Analysis
Speaker In addition to the role of award recipient, what other role does Solzhenitsyn assume through this speech?

inexorably (in eks´ ə rə blē) *adv.* relentlessly

oratory (ôr´ ə tôr´ ē) *n.* skillful public speaking

12 **▼ Critical Viewing**
What do stamps such as the ones on these pages suggest about the role of modern communications in creating a world literature? **[Draw a Conclusion]**

✓ Reading Check
Identify one reason that, according to Solzhenitsyn, writers have the power to serve justice.

11 Literary Analysis
Speaker

- Have students reread Solzhenitsyn's biography on p. 1294. Ask them how he describes the Soviet government in his writings.
  Answer: Solzhenitsyn wrote letters critical of Stalin and accounts of Stalin's oppressive labor camps.
- Why would Solzhenitsyn have the moral authority to call on writers to "condemn their own unsuccessful governments"?
  Possible response: Solzhenitsyn himself "condemned" Stalinism and suffered for his beliefs.
- Ask students the Literary Analysis question on p. 1299: In addition to the role of award recipient, what other role does Solzhenitsyn assume through this speech?
  Possible response: Solzhenitsyn serves as a model of what writers can accomplish if they continue to speak the truth and resist governments that are unfair or repressive.

▶ Monitor Progress Ask students to describe Solzhenitsyn's view of a writer's role.
Possible response: Solzhenitsyn views the writer as a social or political activist.

▶ Reteach If students have difficulty with the Literary Analysis skill, use the **Literary Analysis and Reading Transparencies** booklet, p. 123, to model this skill.

12 ▶ Critical Viewing

Possible response: The images of these stamps illustrate that countries around the world proudly display their great writers on postage stamps. The stamps are placed on letters that will travel the globe and spread information about literatures of the world.

13 ✓ Reading Check

Answer: Writers can vanquish lies in literature, conspicuously serving justice.

CUSTOMIZE INSTRUCTION FOR UNIVERSAL ACCESS

For Less Proficient Readers	For Gifted/Talented Students
Play appropriate audio selections from **World Masterpieces Listening to Literature** for students. Tell students that listening to the story on tape may enhance their comprehension or help them appreciate the urgency of Solzhenitsyn's message. After students listen to the reading, have them reread the text on p. 1299 and work in groups to summarize key points.	Play appropriate audio selections from **World Masterpieces Listening to Literature** so that students can listen to the text on p. 1299. Then, ask students to write a short story that portrays an "ordinary courageous man," or woman, like the one Solzhenitsyn mentions. Have them describe a situation in which it would be easier to ignore events or a lie than to act. Students' stories should illustrate simple, ordinary situations in which telling the truth about a lie might create positive change.

Answers for p. 1300

Review and Assess

1. Possible response: Yes; reading works from other cultures broadens one's perspective and promotes understanding and growth by forcing the reader to evaluate circumstances from other perspectives.
2. **(a)** The writer describes light rain on a dark night. **(b)** The setting is calm and peaceful. **(c)** Possible response: The description of the chaotic surroundings allows readers to become aware of the freedom that breathing represents.
3. **(a)** Prison takes away the ability to breathe freely. **(b)** The speaker says that the ability to breathe freely is more important than food, wine, or a kiss.
4. Possible response: Yes; without a sense of freedom, people are prevented from learning, creating, and interacting honestly.
5. **(a)** Prominent writers were prepared to harbor Solzhenitsyn if exiled from the Soviet Union, and they nominated him for the Nobel Prize. **(b)** Possible response: Solzhenitsyn believes that it is the responsibility of writers to "vanquish lies." He has done so with his own writing.
6. **(a)** Possible response: A nation's literature illuminates a country's common values as well as its controversies, both of which unite people. **(b)** Possible response: World literature is the lifeblood of humanity.
7. Possible response: Yes; literature combats violence by exposing it to people. Visibility is crucial to reform.
8. Possible response: The political situations in countries such as Iraq under Saddam Hussein serve as examples of governmental oppression of free speech. Solzhenitsyn might say that freedom is preserved at the cost of suffering.

In Russian, proverbs about TRUTH are favorites. They persistently express the considerable, bitter, grim experience of the people, often astonishingly:

ONE WORD OF TRUTH OUTWEIGHS THE WORLD.

On such a seemingly fantastic violation of the law of the conservation of mass and energy[8] are based both my own activities and my appeal to the writers of the whole world.

8. **the law of the conservation of mass and energy** law of physics stating that in any physical or chemical change, the sum of mass and energy must remain constant: Energy and matter are not created by nature from nothing.

Review and Assess

Thinking About the Selections

1. **Respond:** Have you found that your own readings in world literature have broadened your understanding of the world? Explain.
2. **(a) Recall:** In the first paragraph of "Freedom to Breathe," what details does the writer use to set the scene? **(b) Interpret:** Describe the mood of this setting. **(c) Evaluate:** Does the description of the surrounding area help you appreciate the speaker's delight? Explain.
3. **(a) Recall:** What fundamental freedom does prison take away, according to "Freedom to Breathe"? **(b) Compare:** With what does the speaker contrast this freedom?
4. **Evaluate:** Do you agree that "freedom to breathe" is a basic necessity? Explain.
5. **(a) Recall:** Name two ways in which, according to Solzhenitsyn's Nobel Lecture, European writers showed support for Solzhenitsyn. **(b) Connect:** How does Solzhenitsyn's own career exemplify his idea of a modern world literature?
6. **(a) Infer:** Why does Solzhenitsyn say in his Nobel Lecture that a nation's literature is a "uniting force"? **(b) Interpret:** In what sense does he call world literature "the one great heart"?
7. **Evaluate:** Is Solzhenitsyn's claim about the power of literature to contest violence valid? Explain.
8. **Apply:** Give a modern instance in which people are discouraged from speaking their minds, and explain what Solzhenitsyn might say about this situation.

ENRICHMENT: Literature Connection

Russian Writers and Social Reform

Russia has a long tradition of viewing the writer as someone who searches for the truth and speaks out against social injustice. Poets and novelists have played a highly influential part in Russian life.

Alexander Pushkin began the tradition of the writer as public spokesman in the early nineteenth century by speaking out against the mistreatment of the Russian poor. His example inspired the novelist Leo Tolstoy to take even stronger action later in the century.

In Tolstoy's day, most work in Russia was done by peasants who were desperately poor, and most of the wealth was held by a few rich families. Believing this situation to be immoral, Tolstoy, a wealthy man, gave everything he owned away, even the copyrights of his highly successful books. He lived simply and took a leading role in social reform or, as the Russians call it, "community action."

⓮ # *Visit*

Yevgeny Yevtushenko
translated by
Robin Milner-Gulland
and Peter Levi, S.J.

⓯

Going to Zima Junction,[1] quiet place.
Watching out for it in the distance
with the window of the carriage wide open,
familiar houses, ornamental carving.
The jump down from the train before it stops,
crunching along on the warm slag;[2]
the linesman working with a hose
cursing and swearing in the stifling heat.
The ducks in midstream with their heads buried,
the perches where the poultry crow at dawn,
along the sidings ornamental stars
of white and colored bricks set in the wall.
Walking along the dusty paving-boards,
passing the clock that sits on the town hall,
hearing behind the fence of the old market
rustle of oats and clink of weights and measures:
and there the painted wooden fruit-baskets,
the cranberries wet on the low counters,
and the bright yellow butter-balls afloat
in basins made of flower-painted china.
Same cranny where the birds are still nesting,
and, most familiar, the faded gate.
And the house is exactly the same size,
the log fence still mended with boards,
the same broom leaning upon the stove,

 **✔Reading Check**

What is the speaker's likely connection to the place he describes?

1. **Zima** (zē′ mə) **Junction** town in the Asian part of Russia (formerly part of the Soviet Union), just west of Lake Baikal and north of Mongolia.
2. **slag** (slag) refuse separated from a metal in the process of smelting.

⓮ About the Selection

"Visit" describes Yevtushenko's return home from Moscow to Zima Junction in Central Asia in the summer of 1953. That year was a pivotal one in Soviet history: Stalin had died that spring, after twenty-four years of tyrannical rule, and the nation looked forward to what might lie ahead with a mixture of hope and concern.

⓯ Background

Yevgeny Yevtushenko wrote and directed a film about his World War II experiences in his hometown of Zima Junction. He called the film *Kindergarten* because, he said, the war was a "classroom" in which his generation first learned about life's difficulties.

⓰ ✔Reading Check

Answer: The speaker knows the place well and seems fond of it. The speaker probably grew up there.

CUSTOMIZE INSTRUCTION FOR UNIVERSAL ACCESS

Special Needs Students	For English Learners	For Advanced Students
Have students create a word web for "Visit." In the center, have students write *Zima Junction* and on the web's rays, list areas des-cribed in the poem: town hall, market, speaker's house, river, and woods. Ask students to record the details that describe the speaker's hometown.	Point out that a sudden change in chronology occurs in line 29. Explain that up to this point, the speaker is describing the return home. At line 29, the speaker begins to remember events that happened when the speaker was younger. Ask students to make a timeline of the poem's events.	Tell students that the idea of returning home is a durable theme in world literature. Have students read *The Epic of Gilgamesh* or "My Old Home" by Lu Hsun. Direct students to write an analytical essay in which they discuss the treatment of this theme in two or more works.

ASSESS

17 Reading Strategy

Inferring the Speaker's Attitude

- Ask students what role memory plays when they return to a special place they have not seen in some time.
  Possible response: Memory can allow one to revisit a special time, and it can measure how a place or a person has changed.
- Have students describe the mood of the poem during the description of the boys playing in the river.
  Possible response: The mood is one of happy recollection.
- Have students reread the poem. Then, ask the Reading Strategy question on p. 1302: Confronted by this concluding memory, what questions might the speaker ask about his present life?
  Possible response: The speaker might ask himself how he is different from the boy he sees in his memory; how his present life reflects this boy; and how he can reconcile the boy and the man.

Answers for p. 1302

Review and Assess

1. Possible response: Readers may enjoy visiting places that hold happy memories but may shy away from places that hold troubling memories.
2. **(a)** The speaker describes walking from the train station, past the town hall, and through the marketplace. **(b)** When the speaker reaches the house (line 29), the poem shifts into memories of the past. The ellipses and the next line indicate a flashback.
3. Possible response: The speaker's past seems to have been a time of innocence. As the speaker reflects on the past, he sees how little he achieved as a boy and how much he can accomplish in the future.
4. Possible response: Memories of events ten years in the past may evoke the same reaction in the reader as they do in the author—nostalgia, regret, and hope.

the same tinned mushrooms on the window-sill,
the crack in the stairs is not different,
darkening deeply down, feeding fungus. . . .
Some nut or bolt or other I'd picked up
just as I always picked something up
was clenched happily in my hand
and dropped again as I went hurrying
down to the river and the river-mist,
and wandering sometimes in the woods
by a path choked in a tangle of tall weeds
in search of some deep-colored country flower,
and working with the freckled ferry girl,
heaving the glossy hawser hand by hand.
Trying the quality of "old honey"
where the beehives rear up above the pond,
rocking along slow-motion in the cart,
slow rhythms of the whip's lazy flicking.
17 Wandering through the cranberry patches
with a casual crowd of idle lads,
and fishing beneath bridges with the noise
of trains thundering above your head,
joking, throwing your shirt off in the grass,
and diving in high from the river-bank,
with one sudden thought, how little I
have done in life, how much I can do.

fungus (fuŋ′ gəs) *n.* mildew; any of a group of plants lacking leaves and roots

clenched (klencht) *v.* gripped firmly or tightly

Reading Strategy
Inferring the Speaker's Attitude Confronted by this concluding memory, what questions might the speaker ask about his present life?

Review and Assess

Thinking About the Selection

1. **Respond:** Do you like revisiting places where you once spent a great deal of time? Why or why not?
2. **(a) Recall:** Identify three scenes described by the speaker as he moves through the town toward his old home. **(b) Infer:** At what point does the poem shift from the speaker's present visit to his memories of the past? Explain your response.
3. **Interpret:** In what sense do the speaker's memories of the past lead him to confront his present and his future?
4. **Relate:** Imagine that, ten years from now, you are remembering today, as the adult speaker remembers his childhood. What reactions might you have?

ASSESSMENT PRACTICE: Writing Skills

Style (For more practice, see Test Preparation Workbook, p. 62.)

Style questions on standardized tests often focus on understanding the author's purpose on the basis of his or her effective use of language. Read this paragraph from p. 1299:

> "Once lies have been dispelled, the repulsive nakedness of violence will be exposed—and hollow violence will collapse."

Why does Solzhenitsyn isolate this sentence as a stand-alone paragraph?

A to emphasize the word *nakedness*
B to describe Russian politics
C to describe how lies function
D to draw attention to an idea

A, B, and *C* do not reflect the stylistic purpose of the paragraph. ***D*** is the correct answer. a one-sentence paragraph amidst longer paragraphs stands out.

Review and Assess

Literary Analysis

Speaker

1. (a) For each of the three works, identify statements in the following categories: personal details, public facts, generalizations, and exclamations. (b) Characterize each **speaker,** explaining whether he speaks in a personal voice, a public voice, or a mixed voice.
2. (a) Identify two ways in which Solzhenitsyn's Nobel Lecture links general themes to personal experience. (b) Why does this link add authority to the speaker's general points?
3. In "Visit," what contrast does the speaker suggest between his present and his past? Explain your answer, citing details.

Comparing Literary Works

4. (a) Compare the dramatic endings created by the call to action in the Nobel Lecture and the turn from *I* to *we* in "Freedom to Breathe." (b) In what way do these endings extend the speakers' preceding points?
5. Compare the shift in the speaker's role in "Freedom to Breathe" and in "Visit," analyzing details with a chart like the one shown.

Speaker's Role		Meaning of Events	
Beginning	End	Beginning	End

Reading Strategy

Inferring the Speaker's Attitude

6. What is the **speaker's attitude** toward city life in "Freedom to Breathe"? Give details in support.
7. What is Solzhenitsyn's attitude toward literature in his Nobel Lecture? Identify two details supporting your answer.
8. From images and direct statements in Yevtushenko's "Visit," what can you infer about the speaker's attitude toward his visit?

Extend Understanding

9. **Science Connection:** Explain why Solzhenitsyn thinks literature "violates" the law of the conservation of mass and energy.

Quick Review

The **speaker** is the character or voice that "says" the words of a literary work. A change in the speaker's role or purpose in a work can add drama.

To **infer the speaker's attitude,** look for details that suggest how a speaker views his or her subject.

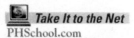

Take It to the Net

PHSchool.com

Take the interactive self-test online to check your understanding of these selections.

ENRICHMENT: Further Reading

Other Works by the Authors

We strongly encourage you to review any selection before assigning or recommending it to students.

Works by Alexander Solzhenitsyn

The First Circle; Warning to the West

Works by Yevgeny Yevtushenko

Don't Die Before You're Dead; Early Poems

Take It to the Net

Visit PHSchool.com for more information on the authors.

Answers for p. 1303

Review and Assess

1. Possible response: **Personal: Freedom;** I stand under the apple tree and I breathe. **Nobel;** I was astounded to receive greetings. . . **Visit;** I went hurrying down to the river. **Public: Freedom;** a small garden **Nobel;** Critical Analysis . . . by Heinrich Böll. **Visit;** And the house . . . fungus. **Generalization: Freedom;** As long as there is fresh . . . longer. **Nobel;** first paragraph **Visit** how little I have done in life **Exclamation: Nobel;** words in small capital letters, My friends! **Visit;** How I can do. **(b) Freedom;** mixed voice **Nobel;** public voice; **Visit;** personal voice.
2. **(a)** Possible response: The speaker links world literature to Böll's critique and protection of European authors. **(b)** The links provide examples and validate the authors' experiences.
3. Possible response: The simplicity of the past ("idle lads") is juxtaposed with the difficulties ("cursing and swearing") of adulthood.
4. **(a)** All people must work against lies and violence. **(b)** Literature can improve the human condition.
5. Sample for **Freedom: Speaker's Role Beginning** enjoy nature **End** reflects on survival **Meaning: Beginning:** prisoner returns to freedom **End** freedom means survival **Visit: Speaker's Role Beginning** describes hometown **End** demonstrates self-awareness **Meaning: Beginning** life changes yet remains the same **End** self-awareness motivates change.
6. Possible response: The speaker describes city life with :houses like cages in a zoo," "motorcycles backfiring,""radios whining," and the "burble of loudspeakers" as a minor distraction that does not interfere with what the speaker finds most important – freedom.
7. Literature teaches humanity "to see itself accurately," and writers can "vanquish lies."
8. His attitude is regret mixed with hope.
9. Truth weighs more than the Earth.

EXTEND

Answers for p. 1304

❶ Vocabulary Development

Usage: Forms of *reciprocity*

1. b
2. c
3. a

Spelling Strategy

1. stimulus
2. campus
3. adventurous

Concept Development: Synonyms

1. b
2. b
3. a
4. c
5. a
6. c
7. b

❷ Grammar and Style

Practice

1. Solzhenitsyn—whose life was saved by his readers—writes of the power of literature.
2. The speaker—and this is the strange part—is actually in a small inner-city garden.
3. Scenes at the railroad station, scenes along the road—each is as familiar as the next.
4. The speaker remembers discovering that he had a future—but now he is that future!
5. Three Russian writers—Pushkin, Pasternak, and Solzhenitsyn—have all believed in the writer's role as social critic.

Writing Application

Possible response:

The garden—tiny though it is—provides peace and comfort to the neighborhood. People of all ages—from babies to grandparents—love to sit near the cool fountain. The garden changes the atmosphere of the entire neighborhood. Such green spaces are a model for other communities—and even other nations—that want to promote peace.

10TH GRADE For support in teaching the Grammar and Style Lesson to tenth graders, use **Writing and Grammar,** Platinum Level, Chapter 28, Section 5.

Integrate Language Skills

❶ Vocabulary Development Lesson

Usage: Forms of *reciprocity*

The noun *reciprocity*, meaning "mutual exchange," has adjective, adverb, and verb forms. Complete each item with a form of *reciprocity*.

a. reciprocally **b.** reciprocal **c.** reciprocate

1. Pen pals have a __?__ arrangement.
2. Although he could not __?__, he appreciated the support of other writers.
3. Just as others supported his rights, he acts __?__ to support the rights of others.

Spelling Strategy

In some nouns derived from Latin, such as *fungus*, the final sound *us* is spelled *us*. In an adjective, this final sound is usually spelled *ous*. For each word below, add the correct ending.

1. stimul__ 2. camp__ 3. adventur__

Concept Development: Synonyms

Review the vocabulary list on page 1295. Then, for each numbered vocabulary word listed below, select the letter of its synonym, the word closest to it in meaning.

1. assimilate: (a) calculate, (b) absorb, (c) compare
2. glistens: (a) glides, (b) shines, (c) speaks
3. oratory: (a) eloquence, (b) radiance, (c) benevolence
4. clenched: (a) kissed, (b) soaked, (c) gripped
5. inexorably: (a) inevitably, (b) endlessly, (c) bluntly
6. fungus: (a) rash, (b) shrub, (c) mildew
7. reciprocity: (a) suburb, (b) exchange, (c) cookery

❷ Grammar and Style Lesson

Using Dashes

A **dash** (—) indicates a longer, more emphatic pause than a comma does. A dash usually signals an interruption in the sequence of ideas and may be used to indicate an abrupt shift of focus, a dramatic exclamation, or a break from listing details to generalizing about them. Review this sentence from "Freedom to Breathe":

> . . . I breathe with my eyes open, I breathe with my eyes closed—I cannot say which gives me the greater pleasure.

Writers can use dashes to set up distinctive rhythms in their writing, achieving the feeling of a living voice that wanders off or bursts into digressions, exclamations, and explanations.

Practice Insert dashes where necessary in the following sentences.

1. Solzhenitsyn whose life was saved by his readers writes of the power of literature.
2. The speaker and this is the strange part is actually in a small inner-city garden.
3. Scenes at the railroad station, scenes along the road each is as familiar as the next.
4. The speaker remembers discovering that he had a future but now he *is* that future!
5. Three Russian writers Pushkin, Pasternak, and Solzhenitsyn have all believed in the writer's role as social critic.

Writing Application Write a brief description of a garden, using dashes correctly in three sentences.

WG Prentice Hall Writing and Grammar Connection: Diamond Level, Chapter 27, Section 5

TEACHING RESOURCES

The following resources can be used to enrich or extend the instruction for pp. 1304–1305.

Vocabulary

- **Selection Support:** Build Vocabulary, p. 245
- **Vocabulary and Spelling Practice Book** (Use this booklet for skills instruction.)

Grammar

- **Selection Support:** Grammar and Style, p. 246
- **Writing and Grammar,** Diamond Level, p. 736
- **Daily Language Transparencies**

Writing

- **Performance Assess. and Portfolio Mgmt.,** p. 11
- **Writing and Grammar,** Diamond Level, p. 132
- **Writing and Grammar iText CD-ROM**
- **Writing Models and Graphic Organizers on Transparencies,** pp. 45–51

BLOCK SCHEDULING: Resources marked with this symbol provide varied instruction during 90-minute blocks.

❸ Writing Lesson

Persuasive Speech

The written word may seem without force, but in his Nobel Lecture, Solzhenitsyn argues that the word can conquer violence. Write a persuasive speech in which you support or refute Solzhenitsyn's view of the power of words and truth. To persuade your readers, use precise and powerful language.

Prewriting Reread the Nobel Lecture, jotting down each important point Solzhenitsyn makes. Write a one-sentence summary of his idea of truth, and decide whether or not you agree with it. Then, list reasons, examples, and other details to support your position.

Drafting Begin your essay with a statement of your position. As you draft, make sure you use charged, precise words to add persuasive force.

Model: Choose Effective Persuasive Language

A man of (profound moral authority,) Solzhenitsyn uses (compelling) examples from his personal experience to support his claims.

Charged words and phrases, such as *profound moral authority* and *compelling,* add persuasive force.

Revising Review your speech. Identify any weak or unclear wording, and replace it with stronger phrasing.

WG Prentice Hall Writing and Grammar Connection: Diamond Level, Chapter 7, Section 3

❹ Extension Activities

Listening and Speaking Using "Freedom to Breathe" or "Visit" as a model, present an **oral description** of the sights and smells of one of your favorite places. Use these tips to prepare:

- Before you write, brainstorm for vivid imagery appealing to the five senses.
- As you practice, pay special attention to your tempo, speaking slowly enough to be understood, but not dragging.
- Give a dress rehearsal for a small audience.

Present your description to the class.

Research and Technology Solzhenitsyn is a famous Nobel Prize winner. Working in a small group, compile an **annotated list** of Nobel Prize winners in literature. For each writer, include a capsule biography and a brief description of his or her works. Post your list in the classroom. **[Group Activity]**

Take It to the Net PHSchool.com

Go online for an additional research activity using the Internet.

Lesson Support for p. 1305

❸ Writing Lesson

- Encourage students to reread Solzhenitsyn's *Nobel Lecture,* making sure that they clearly understand his argument that literature can overcome violence.
- Review the definition of a persuasive speech. Discuss with students how strong, specific language convinces readers that an author's opinion is sound.
- Refer students to Writing Process Model 7: Persuasive Essay in **Writing Models and Graphic Organizers on Transparencies,** pp. 45–51, to help them plan their persuasive essays.
- Use the Persuasion: Persuasive Composition rubric on p. 11 of **Performance Assessment and Portfolio Management** to assess students' work.

10TH GRADE For support in working through the Writing Lesson with tenth graders, use **Writing and Grammar,** Platinum Level, Chapter 7, Section 3.

❹ Research and Technology

- Encourage English learners to research Nobel Prize winners from countries where they or their families have lived. Suggest that students read excerpts from the Nobel Prize winners' speeches aloud to the class.
- Encourage students to include Internet links in their annotated lists. The links will allow class members to read more about Nobel winners whom they want to research individually.

CUSTOMIZE INSTRUCTION For Universal Access

To address different learning styles, use the following activities suggested in the **Extension Activities** booklet, p. 62.

- For Musical/Rhythmic and Interpersonal Learners, use Activity 5.
- For Visual/Spatial Learners, use Activity 6.
- For Verbal/Linguistic Learners, use Activity 7.

ASSESSMENT RESOURCES

The following resources can be used to assess students' knowledge and skills.

Selection Assessment

- **Formal Assessment,** pp. 216–218
- **Open-Book Tests,** pp. 184–186
- **Test Bank Software**

Take It to the Net

Visit PHSchool.com for self-tests on the selections.

Writing Rubric

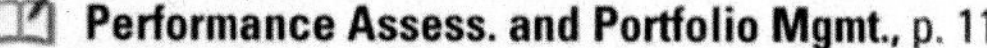

Performance Assess. and Portfolio Mgmt., p. 11

For additional diagnostics and remediation for skills covered in this grouping, use materials from the Prentice Hall Assessment System.

BLOCK SCHEDULING: Resources marked with this symbol provide varied instruction during 90-minute blocks.

Half a Day

Lesson Objectives

1. **To analyze and respond to literary elements**
   - Literary Analysis: Surrealism
   - Connecting Literary Elements: Theme
2. **To read, comprehend, analyze, and critique a short story**
   - Reading Strategy: Determining the Author's Purpose
   - Reading Check Questions
   - Review and Assess Questions
   - Assessment Practice (ATE)
3. **To develop word analysis skills, fluency, and systematic vocabulary**
   - Vocabulary Development Lesson: Connotations: Words for Crowds
4. **To understand and apply written and oral language conventions**
   - Spelling Strategy
   - Grammar and Style Lesson: Agreement in Inverted Sentences
5. **To understand and apply appropriate writing and research strategies**
   - Writing Lesson: Surrealistic Descriptive Essay
   - Extension Activity: Multimedia Presentation
6. **To understand and apply listening and speaking strategies**
   - Extension Activity: Discussion Panel

10TH GRADE TEACHING A TENTH-GRADE COURSE

The literature in this section can be taught as part of a rich, balanced world literature course for tenth-grade students. For a full outline of such a course, see pp. T46–T48 in Volume 1 of this Teacher's Edition.

STEP-BY-STEP TEACHING GUIDE	PACING GUIDE
PRETEACH	
Motivate Students and Provide Background	
Use the Motivation activity (ATE p. 1306)	5 min.
Read and discuss author and background features (SE pp. 1306, 1309; ATE p. 1306) A	5 min.
Introduce the Concepts	
Introduce the Literary Analysis and Reading Strategy concepts (SE/ATE p. 1307) A	15 min.
Pronounce the vocabulary words and read their definitions (SE p. 1307)	5 min.
TEACH	
Monitor Comprehension	
Informally monitor comprehension by circulating while students read independently or in groups A	25 min.
Monitor students' comprehension with the Reading Check notes (SE/ATE pp. 1309, 1311)	as students read
Develop vocabulary with the Vocabulary notes (SE pp. 1309, 1310, 1311, 1312; ATE p. 1311)	as students read
Develop Understanding	
Develop students' understanding of Surrealism with the Literary Analysis annotations (SE/ATE p. 1309) A	5 min.
Develop students' ability to determine the author's purpose by using the Reading Strategy annotations (SE p. 1312; ATE p. 1311, 1312) A	5 min.
ASSESS	
Assess Mastery	
Assess students' mastery of the Reading Strategy and Literary Analysis concepts by having them answer the Review and Assess questions (SE/ATE p. 1313)	15 min.
Use one or more of the print, software, or transparency Assessment Resources (ATE p. 1315) A.	up to 45 min.
EXTEND	
Apply Understanding	
Have students complete the Vocabulary Development Lesson and the Grammar and Style Lesson (SE p. 1314) A	20 min.
Apply students' ability to add descriptive detail, using the Writing Lesson (SE/ATE p. 1315) A	45 min.
Apply students' understanding of the selections, using one or more of the Extension Activities (SE p. 1315)	20–90 min.

ACCELERATED INSTRUCTION:
Use the strategies and activities identified with an A.

10TH GRADE TEACHING TENTH-GRADE STUDENTS
For support in teaching the selection to tenth-grade students, see the Step-by-Step Teaching notes identified with the icon shown here.

UNIVERSAL ACCESS
● = Below-Level Students
▲ = On-Level Students
■ = Above-Level Students

Time and Resource Manager

Reading Level: Average
Average Number of Instructional Days: 3

RESOURCES		
PRINT	**TRANSPARENCIES**	**TECHNOLOGY**
• **Beyond Literature,** Cultural Connection: Education p. 63 ▲ ■		• **Interest Grabber Video,** Tape 2, Unit 9, Segment 12 ● ▲ ■
• **Selection Support Workbook:** ● ▲ ■ Literary Analysis, p. 252 Reading Strategy, p. 251 Build Vocabulary, p. 249	• **Literary Analysis and Reading Transparencies,** pp. 125 and 126 ● ▲ ■	
• **Reader's Companion** ● • **Adapted Reader's Companion** ●		• **Listening to Literature** ● ▲ ■ Audiocassettes Audio CDs • **Reader's Companion Audio Program** ● • **Reader's Companion Adapted and English Learner's Version Audio Program** ● ▲
• **English Learner's Companion** ● ▲ • **Literary Analysis for Enrichment,** p. 63 ■		• **World Masterpieces iText CD-ROM**
• **Formal Assessment:** Selection Test, pp. 219–221 ● ▲ ■ • **Open-Book Tests,** pp. 187–189 ● ▲ ■ • **Performance Assess. and Portfolio Mgmt.,** pp. 19, 25 ● ▲ ■ • PRENTICE HALL ASSESSMENT SYSTEM ● ▲ ■	• PRENTICE HALL ASSESSMENT SYSTEM ● ▲ ■ **Skills Practice Answers and Explanations on Transparencies**	• **Test Bank Software** ● ▲ ■
• **Selection Support Workbook:** ● ▲ ■ Grammar and Style, p. 250 • **Writing and Grammar,** Diamond Level ● ▲ ■ • **Extension Activities,** p. 63 ● ▲ ■	• **Daily Language Practice Transparencies** ● ▲	• **Writing and Grammar iText CD-ROM** ● ▲ ■ *Take It to the Net* PHSchool.com

BLOCK SCHEDULING: Use one 90-minute class period to preteach the selection(s) and have students read them. Use a second 90-minute class period to assess students' mastery of skills and have them complete one of the Extension Activities.

PRETEACH

Step-by-Step Teaching Guide for pp. 1306–1307

Motivation

Play for students a recording of the Joni Mitchell song "The Circle Game." Have students listen several times, writing down phrases and images from the song that catch their attention. Then, ask them to summarize its message. (Time passes quickly, and people grow older before they know it.) Conclude by telling them that the story they are about to read has a similar message, although it is presented in a different way and comes from a different culture.

Interest Grabber Video

As an alternative, play "'Half a Day': Egyptian Schools Today" on Tape 2 to engage student interest.

❶ Background

More About the Author

Mahfouz's novels have been considered the "Baedeker guide" to Gamaliya, the Cairo neighborhood where Mahfouz grew up. His vivid depiction of the alleys, houses, palaces, mosques, and people is one of the most outstanding characteristics of his work. He captures the soul of Egypt as he describes the Egyptian family, which is at the core of the country. In his description of the Egyptian family, he draws heavily on autobiography; like one of his characters, Mahfouz was the youngest son of a merchant family.

Geography Note

Draw students' attention to the map on this page. Tell students that many of Mahfouz's stories are set in Cairo, the capital of Egypt and the largest city on the African continent. Cairo, which means "the victorious" in Arabic, has stood on the banks of the Nile for more than one thousand years. Although Cairo is located in the foothills of the Arabian Desert, irrigation from the Nile gives the city lush vegetation.

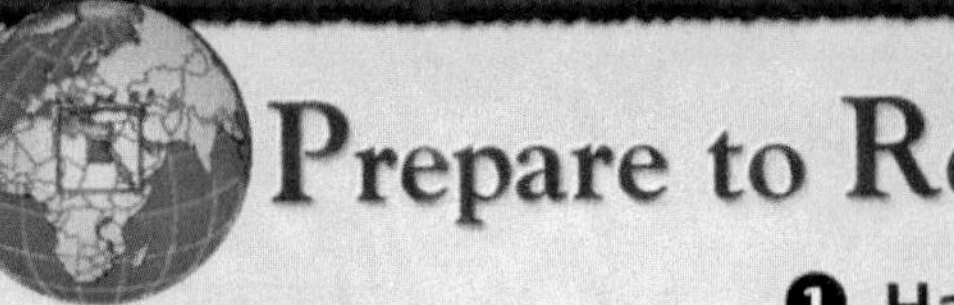

Prepare to Read

❶ Half a Day

Naguib Mahfouz (b. 1911)

A writer may become so closely associated with a place that the two seem inseparable. Charles Dickens seems to have created Victorian England just for his novels; the American Dust Bowl itself seems to speak through John Steinbeck's works. Novelist Naguib Mahfouz (nä' heb' mä fo͞oz') has just such a special relationship with Egypt. For his vivid depictions of twentieth-century Cairo, the Egyptian capital, Western literary critics have compared him to Dickens and to Honoré de Balzac, the great chronicler of French life. Strangely, the very country for which Mahfouz is a voice forced him to find new, indirect ways to speak his mind.

Dangerous Times Mahfouz was born in 1911 in an old quarter of Cairo. In 1930, he entered the University of Cairo, where he studied philosophy. Throughout his undergraduate career, he contributed essays on philosophical subjects to various magazines. Although his readings in literature were slim, classes at the University of Cairo were in English and French, and Mahfouz's access to those languages increased the scope of his reading. Among his favorite authors were Tolstoy, Chekhov, Kafka, and Ibsen.

Mahfouz began his career as a novelist in a politically dangerous, repressive period. In 1930, Ismail Sidki, the new prime minister, had suspended Egypt's 1923 constitution. Once in power, Sidki brutally crushed any attempt to question his authority. Two of Mahfouz's main influences, the writers Taha Hussein and Abbas al-Akkad, were persecuted during this time: Hussein was accused of heresy, and al-Akkad was imprisoned.

Telling the Truth The harsh treatment of Hussein, al-Akkad, and others made Mahfouz realize the futility of direct criticism of the government. He turned instead to narrative. During World War II, he wrote three historical novels set in ancient Egypt.

Mixing history with symbolism, Mahfouz's tales of tyrannical rule and foreign occupation had strong contemporary implications. At the time Mahfouz was writing, Egypt was ruled by a despot, dominated by an aristocracy of foreign (largely Turkish) origins, and occupied by British troops. Yet because the novels were not "about" the present, telling instead of ancient history, Mahfouz escaped censorship. In the end, these novels express a tragic vision that extends beyond their specific political implications.

Master of Many Styles Mahfouz wrote prolifically through the 1940s, withdrew from writing for much of the 1950s, and returned to literature in the 1960s. During his career, he has experimented widely with style. Some of his short stories of the 1960s are surrealistic. Later novels, such as *Arabian Nights and Days* (1982), have an open-ended structure reminiscent of traditional Arabic narratives.

Mahfouz is perhaps most celebrated, though, for mastering the novel, a Western genre, and making it relevant to Egyptian life. He also modernized the literary language of the Arab tradition. By shaping classical Arabic into a vehicle of popular speech, he created an authoritative voice in which to tell of the lives of ordinary Egyptians.

The Master Honored In 1988, Mahfouz won the Nobel Prize. The award, he remarked, made way for a new international recognition of Arab literature: "Egypt and the Arab world also get the Nobel Prize with me. . . . [I]n the future, literate people will look for Arab literature, and Arab literature deserves that recognition." Now almost deaf and partially blind, Mahfouz claims to live only to write; he has said, "If the urge should ever leave me, I want that day to be my last."

TEACHING RESOURCES

The following resources can be used to enrich or extend the instruction for pp. 1306–1307.

Motivation

Interest Grabber Video, Tape 2

Background

Beyond Literature, p. 63

Take It to the Net

Visit PHSchool.com for background on the author.

Literary Analysis

Literary Analysis and Reading Transparencies, Surrealism, p. 125

Selection Support: Literary Analysis, p. 252

Reading

Literary Analysis and Reading Transparencies, Determining the Author's Purpose, p. 126

BLOCK SCHEDULING: Resources marked with this symbol provide varied instruction during 90-minute blocks.

Preview

Connecting to the Literature

"If you take out the trash every day, then we'll talk about getting a dog." Sometimes, life seems like one big detour. But what if all of life really *is* a detour, and we can never get to what we wanted in the first place? In this story, Mahfouz plays a trick with time to confront us with this question.

❷ Literary Analysis

Surrealism

Surrealism, meaning "beyond realism," refers to works that use realism to create a dreamlike world. Surrealist works generally portray people and objects in realistic detail. By connecting realistic elements in strange ways, though, surrealistic works break rules of logic and sequence. In this passage from "Half a Day," for example, realistic details create a dreamlike situation—in one day, the world has changed:

> I proceeded a few steps, then came to a startled halt. . . . Where was the street lined with gardens? Where had it disappeared to?

As you read, use a chart like this one to note realistic elements and the ways they become dreamlike.

Realistic Details
Surrealistic Connections

Connecting Literary Elements

By causing confusion and surprise, Mahfouz's surrealism pushes the reader to see life from a shocking new angle. In this way, Mahfouz uses surrealism to convey his **theme,** or message about life. As you read, note ways in which your reactions to events help you better appreciate the theme.

❸ Reading Strategy

Determining the Author's Purpose

To **determine the author's purpose** in writing, think about the effect the work is meant to have on readers. For example, in "Half a Day," Mahfouz includes details that make readers think about the way life works. His purpose is to convey an insight into life. To fully understand Mahfouz's purpose, connect his choice of details to possible insights as you read.

Vocabulary Development

unmarred (un märd′) *adj.* unspoiled; unimpaired (p. 1309)

intimacy (in′ tə mə sē) *n.* familiarity; warmth (p. 1309)

intricate (in′ tri kit) *adj.* complicated; elaborate (p. 1310)

presumed (prē zōōmd′) *v.* expected; supposed (p. 1310)

throngs (thrôŋz) *n.* crowds (p. 1311)

hordes (hôrdz) *n.* large moving crowds; wandering tribes (p. 1311)

hastened (hās′ ənd) *v.* hurried; moved swiftly (p. 1312)

❷ Literary Analysis

Surrealism

- Tell students that as they read, they will encounter details that may not seem to make sense in the story's context. Discuss how the narrative of a surrealistic story does not follow a logical pattern.
- Model the use of the chart on p. 1307, and direct each student to complete a similar chart as he or she reads the story.
- Give students extra practice identifying surrealistic elements by using the Surrealism transparency in **Literary Analysis and Reading Transparencies,** p. 125.

❸ Reading Strategy

Determining the Author's Purpose

- Ask students whether they have ever read a story or seen a program that made them feel confused about what was going on. Have them discuss why an author might want to throw readers off guard and leave them wondering about events.
- Remind students that the surrealism of Mahfouz's story is designed to keep readers guessing what is real and what is not.
- Ask students to discuss whether things in life must always make sense and whether there are always good reasons for the way things in life happen.

Vocabulary Development

- Pronounce each vocabulary word for students, and read the definitions as a class. Have students identify any words with which they are familiar.

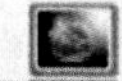

E-Teach

Visit e-Teach at PHSchool.com for teachers' essays on how to teach, with questions and answers.

CUSTOMIZE INSTRUCTION FOR UNIVERSAL ACCESS

For Special Needs Students	For Less Proficient Readers	For English Learners
Have students read "Half a Day" in the **Adapted Reader's Companion.** This version provides basic-level instruction in an interactive format with questions and write-on lines. Completing the adapted version will prepare students to read the selection in the Student Edition.	Have students read the adapted version of the selection in the **Reader's Companion.** This version provides basic-level instruction in an interactive format with questions and write-on lines. After students finish the selection in the **Reader's Companion,** have them complete the questions and activities in the Student Edition.	Have students read the adapted version of the selection in the **English Learner's Companion.** This version provides basic-level instruction in an interactive format with questions and write-on lines. Completing the adapted version will prepare students to read the selection in the Student Edition.

TEACH

Step-by-Step Teaching Guide for pp. 1308–1312

Teaching Tenth-Grade Students

10TH GRADE Ask tenth-grade students to write a one-page journal entry about a time when they started school—either for the first time or at a new school. Have them explain the significance of beginning school and their feelings about the event.

❶ About the Selection

A young Egyptian boy fearfully begins his first day of school, gradually overcomes his fears, and learns to enjoy the resources and opportunities school offers. As if by magic, time passes, the boy is grown, and the world he returns to at the end of "half a day" is very different from the one he woke up to that morning.

❶ # Half a Day

Naguib Mahfouz

translated by Denys Johnson-Davies

TEACHING RESOURCES

The following resources can be used to enrich or extend the instruction for pp. 1308–1312.

Literary Analysis

- **Selection Support:** Literary Analysis, p. 252
- **Literary Analysis and Reading Transparencies,** Surrealism, p. 125

Reading

- **Selection Support:** Reading Strategy, p. 251; Build Vocabulary, p. 249

- **Reader's Companion**
- **Adapted Reader's Companion**
- **English Learner's Companion**
- **Listening to Literature Audiocassettes** ■
- **Listening to Literature Audio CDs** ■

■ **BLOCK SCHEDULING:** Resources marked with this symbol provide varied instruction during 90-minute blocks.

Background

"Half a Day" is set in Cairo, the capital of Egypt and the city in which Naguib Mahfouz grew up. Cairo itself embodies the mysteries of time that Mahfouz explores in the story. Ancient and modern exist there side by side. Along the skyline, contemporary hotels rub shoulders with the ancient pyramids. Narrow, twisting streets where camels, horses, and pedestrians once jostled are now choked with vehicular traffic. Modern Western influences are visible in people's clothing and in the fast-food restaurants, alongside traditional garb and open-air markets. As you read Mahfouz's story, you will encounter hints of the changes that brought the modern world to ancient Cairo.

I proceeded alongside my father, clutching his right hand, running to keep up with the long strides he was taking. All my clothes were new: the black shoes, the green school uniform, and the red tarboosh.[1] My delight in my new clothes, however, was not altogether unmarred, for this was no feast day but the day on which I was to be cast into school for the first time.

My mother stood at the window watching our progress, and I would turn toward her from time to time, as though appealing for help. We walked along a street lined with gardens; on both sides were extensive fields planted with crops, prickly pears, henna trees, and a few date palms.

"Why school?" I challenged my father openly. "I shall never do anything to annoy you."

"I'm not punishing you," he said, laughing. "School's not a punishment. It's the factory that makes useful men out of boys. Don't you want to be like your father and brothers?"

2 I was not convinced. I did not believe there was really any good to be had in tearing me away from the intimacy of my home and throwing me into this building that stood at the end of the road like some huge, high-walled fortress, exceedingly stern and grim.

When we arrived at the gate we could see the courtyard, vast and crammed full of boys and girls. "Go in by yourself," said my father, "and join them. Put a smile on your face and be a good example to others."

I hesitated and clung to his hand, but he gently pushed me from him. "Be a man," he said. "Today you truly begin life. You will find me waiting for you when it's time to leave."

I took a few steps, then stopped and looked but saw nothing. Then the faces of boys and girls came into view. I did not know a single one of them, and none of them knew me. I felt I was a stranger who had lost his way. But glances of curiosity were directed toward me, and one boy approached and asked, "Who brought you?"

1. **tarboosh** (tär bo͞osh′) *n.* brimless cap of felt or other cloth shaped like a truncated cone.

unmarred (un märd′) *adj.* unspoiled; unimpaired

Literary Analysis
Surrealism What ordinary details give the opening descriptions a realistic quality?

intimacy (in′ tə mə sē) *n.* familiarity; warmth

3 **Critical Viewing**
What does this photograph suggest about contrasts between ancient and modern in the setting of the story? **[Connect]**

4 **Reading Check**
Why is the day an important one for the boy?

2 Literary Analysis

Surrealism

- Ask students what small children might think or worry about on their first day of school.
  Possible answer: They might be concerned about their clothing and school supplies, leaving home for the first time, the appearance of the classroom, the demeanor of their classmates, and the attitude of the teacher.
- Read aloud the bracketed passage. Then, ask the Literary Analysis question on p. 1309: What ordinary details give the opening descriptions a realistic quality?
  Answer: The boy's new clothes, the different types of trees lining the street, the mother standing at the window, the boy's exchange with his father, the boy's hesitation on entering the courtyard, and the other students' curiosity give the opening scene a realistic quality.

3 Critical Viewing

Answer: The photograph suggests that the ancient and the modern will clash or that time will alternate between them. Because the modern features are in the foreground, readers may expect them to dominate.

4 Reading Check

Answer: The day is important for the boy because he is starting school.

CUSTOMIZE INSTRUCTION FOR UNIVERSAL ACCESS

For Special Needs Students	For English Learners	For Gifted/Talented Students
Help students follow both the story's literal and surreal narrative by mapping the events in the text. Invite students to use the story map organizer, from **Writing Models and Graphic Organizers on Transparencies,** pp. 83–85.	Ask students to share anecdotes and reminiscences, either their own or those of relatives, of school days in another country or culture. Have them explain how schooling and attitudes toward education compare with those of this country.	Ask students to depict the passing of time in artistic works of their own creation. These artistic responses can be in the form of paintings, drawings, sculptures, musical compositions, poems or stories, dances, videos, or any other media.

5 Critical Thinking

Interpret

- Review with students the relationship that the narrator appears to have with his father.
- Draw students' attention to the two bracketed lines, and read them aloud.
- Ask students what they think the effect of the boy's statement might be on the narrator.
  Possible response: It might serve as his introduction to the real world, where people die and other people's experiences differ greatly from the ones he has had; it might also be the narrator's first experience of sharing feelings with another person, an experience which could lead to friendship.

6 Background

Surrealism in Art

Surrealism in art and literature was popular in Europe between World War I and World War II. The "anti-art" of Surrealism was a reaction against the European "rationalism" in culture and politics. André Breton's *Manifesto* described Surrealism as "the real process of thought...free from any control by the reason and of any aesthetic or moral preoccupation." Surrealist paintings could be designed to shock viewers. For example, one work by René Magritte illustrated a table setting with a slice of ham on a plate—and a human eye looking out from the ham.

7 Background

Art

The Persistence of Memory, by Salvador Dalí

Salvador Dalí's *The Persistence of Memory* includes a representative image of the coast of Catalonia, Spain, his home. The drooping watches, however, are part of a Surrealist landscape. The timepieces droop like soft cheese; indeed, Dalí called the image "the camembert of time."

Use this question for discussion:

What does the shape of the watches in the picture imply about the passage of time?
Possible response: The drooping watches imply that time has lost its meaning.

5 "My father," I whispered.

"My father's dead," he said quite simply.

I did not know what to say. The gate was closed, letting out a pitiable screech. Some of the children burst into tears. The bell rang. A lady came along, followed by a group of men. The men began sorting us into ranks. We were formed into an <u>intricate</u> pattern in the great courtyard surrounded on three sides by high buildings of several floors; from each floor we were overlooked by a long balcony roofed in wood.

"This is your new home," said the woman. "Here too there are mothers and fathers. Here there is everything that is enjoyable and beneficial to knowledge and religion. Dry your tears and face life joyfully."

We submitted to the facts, and this submission brought a sort of contentment. Living beings were drawn to other living beings, and from the first moments my heart made friends with such boys as were to be my friends and fell in love with such girls as I was to be in love with, so that it seemed my misgivings had had no basis. I had never imagined school would have this rich variety. We played all sorts of different games: swings, the vaulting horse, ball games. In the music room we chanted our first songs. We also had our first introduction to language. We saw a globe of the Earth, which revolved and showed the various continents and countries. We started learning the numbers. The story of the Creator of the universe was read to us, we were told of His present world and of His Hereafter, and we heard examples of what He said. We ate delicious food, took a little nap, and woke up to go on with friendship and love, play and learning.

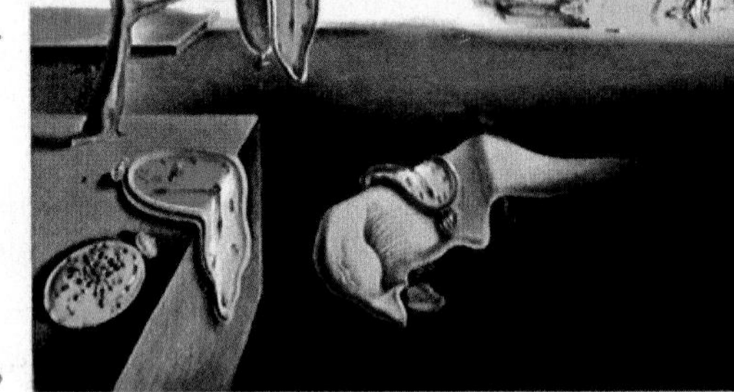

The Persistence of Memory, Salvador Dalí, 1931, The Museum of Modern Art / Artists Rights Society (ARS), New York

7

As our path revealed itself to us, however, we did not find it as totally sweet and unclouded as we had <u>presumed.</u> Dust-laden winds and unexpected accidents came about suddenly, so we had to be watchful, at the ready, and very patient. It was not all a matter of playing and fooling around. Rivalries could bring about pain and hatred or give rise to fighting. And while the lady would sometimes smile, she would often scowl and scold. Even more frequently she would resort to physical punishment.

In addition, the time for changing one's mind was over and gone and there was no question of ever returning to the paradise of home. Nothing lay ahead of us but exertion, struggle, and perseverance. Those who

Literature in context — Humanities Connection 6

Surrealism in Art

Surrealism is a movement in art and literature that favors mysterious, dreamlike imagery and rejects convention and reason. The French writer André Breton first described the movement's goals in his *Manifesto of Surrealism* (1924). He and other surrealists aimed to give the unconscious mind a voice through art. Their ideas of the unconscious were influenced by the writings of the psychoanalyst Sigmund Freud, whose work Breton had read and whom he had met in 1921. One method the Surrealists used was automatic writing, a technique similar to Freud's free association.

Surrealist painters included Salvador Dali, Max Ernst, René Magritte, and Joan Miró. In more recent times, Surrealism has influenced Latin American writers such as Julio Cortázar.

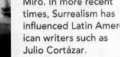

intricate (in′ tri kit) *adj.* complicated; elaborate

presumed (prē zo͞omd′) *v.* expected; supposed

ENRICHMENT: Geography Connection

The Land of the Pharaohs

Egypt, the homeland of Naguib Mahfouz, is one of the oldest civilizations in the world. As early as 3000 B.C., the land of Egypt was a united kingdom, ruled by an absolute monarch called a pharaoh.

Today, Egypt is a country balanced between ancient ways and modern ideas that sometimes come into conflict. About 95 percent of Egyptians are Muslims, some of whom do not agree with the ongoing modernization and liberalization of the country's institutions. Egyptian president Anwar Sadat, a Nobel Prize winner like Mahfouz, was murdered in 1981 by Islamic militants who disagreed with his departure from religious orthodoxy.

In area, Egypt is about the size of Texas and New Mexico combined. The population of Egypt is about 66 million people, about half of whom live in the Cairo area and along the fertile Nile Valley. The mighty Aswan Dam, which supplies irrigation water to over a million acres, was completed in 1971. One of Egypt's most important industries is clothing and textiles.

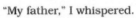

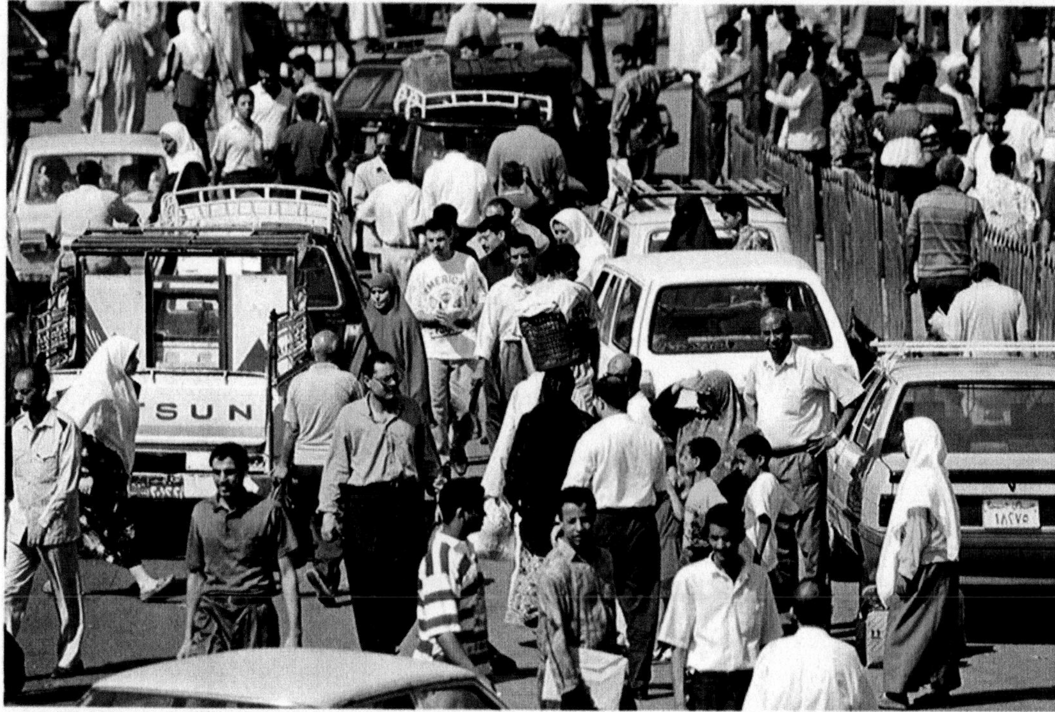

were able took advantage of the opportunities for success and happiness that presented themselves amid the worries.

The bell rang announcing the passing of the day and the end of
9 work. The throngs of children rushed toward the gate, which was opened again. I bade farewell to friends and sweethearts and passed through the gate. I peered around but found no trace of my father, who had promised to be there. I stepped aside to wait. When I had waited for a long time without avail, I decided to return home on my own. After I had taken a few steps, a middle-aged man passed by, and I realized at once that I knew him. He came toward me, smiling, and shook me by the hand, saying, "It's a long time since we last met—how are you?"

With a nod of my head, I agreed with him and in turn asked, "And you, how are you?"

"As you can see, not all that good, the Almighty be praised!"

Again he shook me by the hand and went off. I proceeded a few steps, then came to a startled halt. . . . Where was the street lined with gardens? Where had it disappeared to? When did all these vehicles
10 invade it? And when did all these hordes of humanity come to rest upon its surface? How did these hills of refuse come to cover its sides? And where were the fields that bordered it? High buildings had taken over, the street surged with children, and disturbing noises shook the air. At various points stood conjurers showing off their tricks and making snakes appear from baskets. Then there was a band announcing

8 ▲ **Critical Viewing**

Explain which part of the story this image illustrates—the world before or the world after the narrator's day at school. **[Connect]**

throngs (thrôŋz) *n.* crowds

hordes (hôrdz) *n.* large moving crowds; wandering tribes

11 ✔ **Reading Check**

What is the reason for the narrator's confusion?

CUSTOMIZE INSTRUCTION FOR UNIVERSAL ACCESS

For Less Proficient Readers	For English Learners
Give students more practice with the concept of Surrealism by having them identify surrealistic and realistic details in a number of Surrealist paintings. Have them keep lists of each type of detail as they view several pieces of art. When their lists are complete, ask students to share them with the class.	Ask students to list several words for the same basic concept that differ in connotation in the same way as the words for *crowd* do. To help students get started, ask them to think of or find in a thesaurus synonyms with slightly different meanings for the following words: *shout, run* (verb), *work* (noun), *friend, sad, complicated,* and *smart.*

8 ▶ **Critical Viewing**

Answer: The image illustrates the world after the narrator's day at school. The world has changed and become crowded and modern.

9 Vocabulary Development

Connotations: Words for Crowds

- Remind students that words with similar meanings can have different connotations, or associations.
- Point out the word *throngs* in the bracketed line, and read its definition. Have students suggest other words that mean "crowd."
  Possible responses: Words that mean "crowd" include *group, clique, gang, team, multitude, mob,* and *party.*
- Ask students to use each word for "crowd" in a sentence and discuss its connotation. Have students identify whether each word's connotation is positive or negative.

10 Reading Strategy

Determining the Author's Purpose

- Have students read aloud the bracketed passage.
- Ask students: Which details in these paragraphs suggest that Mahfouz's purpose is to play tricks with time?
  Possible response: The narrator's father never comes, probably because time has passed and he has died. When the narrator knows and greets a middle-aged person, he is probably middle-aged himself

▶ **Monitor Progress** Ask students to discuss what insight into life Mahfouz is offering.

▶ **Reteach** Use the Determining the Author's Purpose transparency in **Literary Analysis and Reading Transparencies,** p. 126, for additional support.

11 ✔ **Reading Check**

Answer: The narrator is confused because the world has changed while he was in school. He does not realize how quickly time has passed.

the opening of a circus, with clowns and weight lifters walking in front. A line of trucks carrying central security troops crawled majestically by. The siren of a fire engine shrieked, and it was not clear how the vehicle would cleave its way to reach the blazing fire. A battle raged between a taxi driver and his passenger, while the passenger's wife called out for help and no one answered. . . . I was in a daze. My head spun. I almost went crazy. How could all this have happened in half a day, between early morning and sunset? I would find the answer at home with my father. But where was my home? I could see only tall buildings and hordes of people. I hastened on to the crossroads between the gardens and Abu Khoda. I had to cross Abu Khoda to reach my house, but the stream of cars would not let up. The fire engine's siren was shrieking at full pitch as it moved at a snail's pace, and I said to myself, "Let the fire take its pleasure in what it consumes." Extremely irritated, I wondered when I would be able to cross. I stood there a long time, until the young lad employed at the ironing shop on the corner

12 came up to me. He stretched out his arm and said gallantly, "Grandpa, let me take you across."

hastened (hās´ ənd) *v.* hurried; moved swiftly

Reading Strategy
Determining the Author's Purpose What does the final sentence suggest about the writer's purpose?

Review and Assess

Thinking About the Selection

1. **Respond:** At the story's conclusion, did you feel sympathy for the narrator? Why or why not?
2. **(a) Recall:** Where does the father take the narrator?
   (b) Interpret: How does the narrator feel as he faces this change?
3. **(a) Recall:** What does the narrator learn from the first boy with whom he speaks? **(b) Infer:** What is the effect of the boy's statement on the narrator? **(c) Connect:** In what sense does this statement point to the end of the story?
4. **(a) Recall:** What discovery does the narrator make in the paragraph beginning, "As our path revealed itself . . . "? **(b) Interpret:** What view of people's paths through life underlies this passage?
5. **(a) Recall:** After the bell rings and the narrator goes outside the gates, whom does he meet? **(b) Hypothesize:** Who might this person be? Explain your answer.
6. **(a) Analyze:** What has happened to the narrator by the end of the story? Give two details in support of your answer.
   (b) Draw Conclusions: What does the story suggest about people's ability to make a home for themselves in the world?
7. **Make a Judgment:** Explain whether you think adulthood can be fulfilling or whether you agree with Mahfouz's suggestion that adulthood cannot replace the lost paradise of childhood.

ASSESS

12 Reading Strategy

Determining the Author's Purpose

- Ask students whether the story has offered any explanations for the changes the narrator sees.
  Possible response: The story has not offered explanations.
- Ask the Reading Strategy question on p. 1312: What does the final sentence suggest about the writer's purpose?
  Possible response: The writer wants to convey that life is so brief that in what seems like only "half a day" people pass from youth to old age.

Answers for p. 1312

Review and Assess

1. Possible response: Yes; the narrator cannot comprehend the world around him.
2. **(a)** The father takes the narrator to school. **(b)** He is hesitant but gains confidence as he greets the children.
3. **(a)** The narrator learns that the boy's father has died. **(b)** The narrator does not know what to say. **(c)** At the end, the narrator's father never arrives.
4. **(a)** The narrator and his classmates find that they can be hurt both physically and emotionally. **(b)** The passage indicates that pain and change are certainties.
5. **(a)** The narrator meets a middle-aged man he knows. **(b)** The person might be a friend of the narrator. The narrator doesn't recognize him at first because the friend and the narrator have aged.
6. **(a)** The narrator has aged. He does not recognize the modern world around him, and a young man calls him "Grandpa." **(b)** Possible response: People can become accustomed to one view of themselves and not realize that change and aging are inevitable.
7. Possible response: Both can be fulfilling. Childhood may seem easier because children have few responsibilities. Yet adulthood might offer direction, satisfaction, and understanding.

ASSESSMENT PRACTICE: Writing Skills

Organization (For more practice, see Test Preparation Workbook, p. 63.)

To give students practice in organization, use the following test item.

(1) When he won the Nobel Prize, Mahfouz became known in the West. (2) *The Cairo Trilogy* was published in 1956–1957. (3) However, *The Cairo Trilogy* was not available in translation for many years. (4) Because his fiction is now widely available, readers in the West can understand why Mahfouz is considered the finest modern writer in the Arabic language. (5) Mahfouz published his first novel more than fifty years ago.

Choose the sequence of sentence numbers that makes the structure most logical.

A 2, 3, 1, 5, 4 **C** 1, 2, 3, 4, 5
B 1, 2, 3, 5, 4 **D** 5, 1, 2, 3, 4

The best organization for this information is chronological. ***D*** is the correct answer.

Review and Assess

Literary Analysis

Surrealism

1. (a) What everyday event does "Half a Day" explore? (b) At what point in the story do events turn **surreal**? Explain.
2. (a) Identify two dreamlike details, descriptions, or events in the story. (b) For each example, explain the way in which an ordinary, realistic context adds to its dreamlike quality.
3. Is the ending of the story realistic, surreal, or both? Explain your answer.

Connecting Literary Elements

4. Explain in what way the following passage reflects the story's **theme:** "[T]he time for changing one's mind was over and gone and there was no question of ever returning to the paradise of home." (b) What insight about life is expressed in the narrator's final attempt to return home?
5. Do you think the surprise ending of the story helps a reader grasp the story's insight into time? Explain why or why not.

Reading Strategy

Determining the Author's Purpose

6. How does the story's title, repeated in the last paragraph, help you determine the **author's purpose**?
7. Use a chart like the one below to list three details that serve as clues to the author's purpose. For each, explain what the detail indicates about that purpose.

Detail	What It Shows About the Author's Purpose

Extend Understanding

8. **Cultural Connection:** What lesson does the story suggest about modern times, when new technology may change the world dramatically during one person's lifetime?

Quick Review

Surrealism is the use of realistic elements to create a dreamlike effect, often by breaking the rules of logic or sequence.

The **theme** of a work is its central message about life.

To **determine the author's purpose,** think about the effect the work, including its use of details, is meant to have on readers.

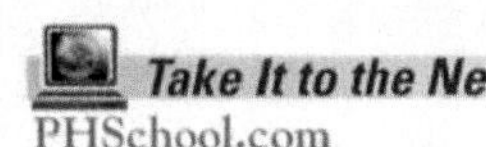

Take It to the Net

PHSchool.com

Take the interactive self-test online to check your understanding of this selection.

ENRICHMENT: Further Reading

Other Works by Naguib Mahfouz

We strongly encourage you to review any selection before assigning or recommending it to students.

The Cairo Trilogy: Palace Walk, Palace of Desire, Sugar Street

Children of the Alley

Echoes of an Autobiography

Miramar

Take It to the Net

Visit PHSchool.com for more information about Naguib Mahfouz.

Answers for p. 1313

Review and Assess

1. **(a)** "Half a Day" explores a boy's first day of school. **(b)** The events turn surreal when the boy leaves school and finds that the world has changed.
2. **(a)** Possible response: One event is the rush of people leaving school while the narrator waits for his father. Another event is his attempt to walk home through a street that has been transformed. **(b)** Possible response: The scenario of the boy waiting for his father is realistic, but the boy's transformation into an old man adds a dreamlike quality. The realistic act of walking home after school emphasizes the dreamlike quality of the narrator not recognizing what was once familiar.
3. Both; the ending is surreal because the narrator has aged without realizing it. It is realistic because it depicts a young person helping an elderly man.
4. **(a)** The passage reflects the story's theme that life passes quickly, and the "paradise of home" cannot be recaptured. **(b)** Possible response: People cannot return to the homes or the times of their youth.
5. Possible response: Yes; the surprise ending emphasizes the writer's theme about the passage of time.
6. Possible response: The title emphasizes the passage of time. A half day is brief, but it cannot be regained when lost.
7. Possible responses: **Detail:** The narrator meets a child whose father is dead. **Shows:** The boy faces mortality. **Detail:** The boy's father does not appear. **Shows:** The boy's youth has passed and his father is gone. **Detail:** Young man calls narrator "Grandpa." **Shows:** The narrator has become old in an astonishingly short time.
8. Possible response: New technology introduces change and removes familiar touchstones.

EXTEND

Answers for p. 1314

❶ Vocabulary Development

Connotations: Words for Crowds

1. *Masses* connotes a large number of average people.
2. *Throngs* connotes an uncomfortable, crowded group.
3. *Swarms* connotes people congregating and moving as a group of bees might.

Spelling Strategy

1. occurred
2. benefited
3. repelled

Fluency: Words in Context

1. Yes; an *unmarred* piece would not be damaged and would cost more than a marred piece.
2. No; one would feel comfortable.
3. No: an *intricate* dance step might be difficult to learn.
4. No; a person *presumed* innocent should not be found guilty or be punished.
5. No; a desert island would likely be uninhabited.
6. Feeding *hordes* would require large amounts of food.
7. No; one would not wait long for a person who hurried to one's side.

❷ Grammar and Style

Practice

1. There were many moments . . .
2. Here were a few students . . .
3. correct
4. There was the boy's father . . .
5. From the street come loud noises.

Writing Application

Possible response:

There is usually a great deal of activity in my neighborhood. People stop to visit with neighbors. On the sidewalk are parents pushing baby strollers.

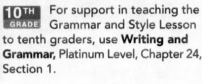

10TH GRADE For support in teaching the Grammar and Style Lesson to tenth graders, use **Writing and Grammar,** Platinum Level, Chapter 24, Section 1.

Integrate Language Skills

❶ Vocabulary Development Lesson

Connotations: Words for Crowds

The word *throngs* is one of several words meaning "crowds." Each of these words has different connotations, or associations. For example, *horde* has negative associations, suggesting a destructive crowd, whereas *assembly* has positive ones, suggesting an orderly decision-making group. Identify the connotations of each of the following "crowd" words.

1. masses 2. throngs 3. swarms

Spelling Strategy

When adding the suffix *-ed* to a word ending "consonant + vowel + consonant," double the final consonant only if the last syllable is stressed. For example, *re fer´* + *-ed* becomes *referred*. If the last syllable is not stressed, make no change. For example, *has´ ten* + *-ed* becomes *hastened*. Copy the following words, adding the suffix *-ed* to each.

1. occur 2. benefit 3. repel

Fluency: Words in Context

Use your knowledge of the italicized words to answer the following questions:

1. Is an *unmarred* piece of furniture likely to cost more than a marred piece? Explain.
2. Would you feel "on guard" in an atmosphere of *intimacy*? Why or why not?
3. Is an *intricate* dance step easy to learn? Explain.
4. If someone is *presumed* to be innocent, should he or she be punished? Explain.
5. Would you be likely to see *throngs* on a desert island? Why or why not?
6. If *hordes* are coming to dinner, how much food will you have to make? Explain.
7. If a person *hastened* to your side, would you have to wait a long time? Explain.

❷ Grammar and Style Lesson

Agreement in Inverted Sentences

In an **inverted sentence,** the subject follows the verb. As in any sentence, the subject and verb must agree. Common examples are sentences beginning with *here* or *there*, such as this model from "Half a Day":

Example: . . . there was (V) a band (S) announcing the opening of a circus . . .

Writers may choose to invert sentences to create emphasis or vary the rhythm of their prose. When Mahfouz writes, "At various points stood conjurers . . .", he creates a small build-up to the word *conjurers*, adding a sense of surprise.

Practice Rewrite each sentence below to correct errors in subject-verb agreement. For any sentence without an error, write *correct*.

1. There was many moments when the boy enjoyed school.
2. Here was a few students he had not met yet.
3. There were lessons in geography and science.
4. There were the boy's father, outside the school.
5. From the street comes loud noises.

Writing Application Write a paragraph about your neighborhood. Include at least two inverted sentences. Check that subjects and verbs agree.

WG Prentice Hall Writing and Grammar Connection: Diamond Level, Chapter 23, Section 1

TEACHING RESOURCES

The following resources can be used to enrich or extend the instruction for pp. 1314–1315.

Vocabulary

- **Selection Support:** Build Vocabulary, p. 249
- **Vocabulary and Spelling Practice Book** (Use this booklet for skills instruction.)

Grammar

- **Selection Support:** Grammar and Style, p. 250
- **Writing and Grammar,** Diamond Level, p. 586
- **Daily Language Transparencies** ■

Writing

- **Performance Assess. and Portfolio Mgmt.**, p. 19
- **Writing and Grammar,** Diamond Level, p. 109
- **Writing and Grammar iText CD-ROM** ■

■ **BLOCK SCHEDULING:** Resources marked with this symbol provide varied instruction during 90-minute blocks.

❸ Writing Lesson

Surrealistic Descriptive Essay

In "Half a Day," Mahfouz writes about ordinary life using the logic of a dream. Using this surrealistic logic, write a description of an object or event. Make sure to provide enough precise details to support your surrealistic effects.

Prewriting Once you have a topic, make a T-chart, listing realistic details on the left and surrealistic connections between them on the right.

Drafting As you draft, focus on providing complete, vividly realistic descriptions to support your surrealistic flights of fantasy.

Revising Reread your description. Mark passages in which your descriptions are vague. Consider adding specific details to those passages.

Model: Revising to Add Descriptive Detail

freckled *,bending its neck with a queen's grace,*
The ^ giraffe ^ unclipped its long nose and left it
piercing
hanging on the tree. The modest tree shed three ^
musical notes, bringing the night to peer out from
crystal
the cracks in its ^ mountain. Soon, the world was
plunged into gloom.

Adding vivid, descriptive details supports the surrealistic logic of this description.

WG *Prentice Hall Writing and Grammar Connection: Diamond Level, Chapter 6, Section 4*

❹ Extension Activities

Listening and Speaking Mahfouz's story suggests that change makes it impossible to reach what one wants. Form a **discussion panel** with classmates to talk about the effects of change.

- Have one member moderate, ensuring that all have a fair chance to contribute.
- Appoint a notetaker.
- Listen actively to other panelists' ideas, responding with questions for clarification.

Post a summary of your discussion in class. **[Group Activity]**

Research and Technology Prepare and present a **multimedia presentation** on the culture of Egypt, Mahfouz's homeland, including daily life, religion, and the arts, using photographs, videos, maps, and music. Familiarize yourself beforehand with the equipment you will use, and test it to make sure it works properly.

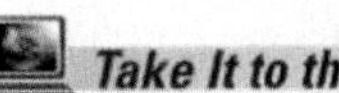
Take It to the Net PHSchool.com

Go online for an additional research activity using the Internet.

ASSESSMENT RESOURCES

The following resources can be used to assess students' knowledge and skills.

Selection Assessment

- **Formal Assessment,** pp. 219–221
- **Open-Book Tests,** pp. 187–189
- **Test Bank Software**

Take It to the Net

Visit PHSchool.com for self-tests on the selections.

Writing Rubric

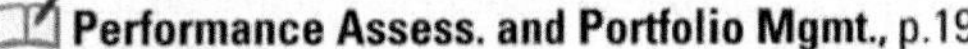
Performance Assess. and Portfolio Mgmt., p.19

For additional diagnostics and remediation for skills covered in this grouping, use materials from the Prentice Hall Assessment System.

Lesson Support for p. 1315

❸ Writing Lesson

- Tell students that their surrealistic descriptive essays will leave behind the logic and reason of the everyday world and will make impossible, magical connections unimaginable in real life.
- Tell students that they can choose a topic by asking themselves questions beginning with "What if," such as "What if trees could talk?" or "What if you could start a day over again?"
- Use the Description rubric in **Performance Assessment and Portfolio Management,** p. 19, to evaluate students' work.

10TH GRADE For support in working through the Writing Lesson with tenth graders, use **Writing and Grammar,** Platinum Level, Chapter 6, Section 4.

❹ Research and Technology

- Organize the class into small groups for the presentations, and make sure that all of the listed elements of Egyptian culture are covered by at least one group.
- Discuss potential research sources, such as Web sites for online encyclopedias, as well as the Egyptian Museum in Cairo and the Bibliotheca Alexandrina.
- Invite students to present their reports to the class as part of a celebration of Egyptian history and culture.
- Use the Analyzing a Media Presentation rubric in **Performance Assessment and Portfolio Management,** p. 25, to assess student presentations.

CUSTOMIZE INSTRUCTION
For Universal Access

To address different learning styles, use the following activities suggested in the **Extension Activities** booklet, p. 63.

- For Verbal/Linguistic Learners, use Activity 5.
- For Visual/Spatial Learners, use Activity 6.
- For Musical/Rhythmic and Interpersonal Learners, use Activity 7.

Pride • The Diameter of the Bomb • From the Book of Esther I Filtered the Sediment

Lesson Objectives

1. **To analyze and respond to literary elements**
   - Literary Analysis: Imagery
   - Comparing Literary Works: Figurative Language
2. **To read, comprehend, analyze, and critique poetry**
   - Reading Strategy: Evaluating a Writer's Message
   - Reading Check Questions
   - Review and Assess Questions
   - Assessment Practice (ATE)
3. **To develop word analysis skills, fluency, and systematic vocabulary**
   - Vocabulary Development Lesson: Latin Word Origins: *vulgar*
4. **To understand and apply written and oral language conventions**
   - Spelling Strategy
   - Grammar and Style Lesson: Elliptical Clauses
5. **To understand and apply appropriate writing and research strategies**
   - Writing Lesson: Poem With a Strong Central Image
   - Extension Activity: Multimedia Presentation
6. **To understand and apply listening and speaking strategies**
   - Extension Activity: Oral Interpretation

STEP-BY-STEP TEACHING GUIDE	PACING GUIDE
PRETEACH	
Motivate Students and Provide Background	
Use the Motivation activity (ATE p. 1316)	5 min.
Read and discuss author and background features (SE pp. 1316, 1318; ATE p. 1316) A	5 min.
Introduce the Concepts	
Introduce the Literary Analysis and Reading Strategy concepts (SE/ATE p. 1317) A	15 min.
Pronounce the vocabulary words and read their definitions (SE p. 1317)	5 min.
TEACH	
Monitor Comprehension	
Informally monitor comprehension by circulating while students read independently or in groups A	25 min.
Develop vocabulary with the Vocabulary notes (SE pp. 1318, 1319, 1320; ATE p. 1320)	as students read
Develop Understanding	
Develop students' understanding of imagery with the Literary Analysis annotations (SE/ATE pp. 1318, 1319) A	5 min.
Develop students' ability to evaluate a writer's message by using the Reading Strategy annotations (SE/ATE p. 1320)	5 min.
ASSESS	
Assess Mastery	
Assess students' mastery of the Reading Strategy and Literary Analysis concepts by having them answer the Review and Assess questions (SE/ATE p. 1321)	15 min.
Use one or more of the print, software, or transparency Assessment Resources (ATE p. 1323) A	up to 45 min.
EXTEND	
Apply Understanding	
Have students complete the Vocabulary Development Lesson and the Grammar and Style Lesson (SE p. 1322) A	20 min.
Apply students' ability to revise to strengthen a central image by using the Writing Lesson (SE/ATE p. 1323) A	45 min.
Apply students' understanding of the selections, using one or more of the Extension Activities (SE p. 1323)	20–90 min.

A ACCELERATED INSTRUCTION: Use the strategies and activities identified with an A.

10TH GRADE TEACHING TENTH-GRADE STUDENTS
For support in teaching the selection(s) to tenth-grade students, see the Step-by-Step Teaching notes identified with the icon shown here.

UNIVERSAL ACCESS
● = Below-Level Students
▲ = On-Level Students
■ = Above-Level Students

Time and Resource Manager

Reading Level: Average, Challenging, Average
Average Number of Instructional Days: 3

RESOURCES		
PRINT	**TRANSPARENCIES**	**TECHNOLOGY**
• **Beyond Literature,** Cross-Curricular Connection: Science, p. 64 ▲ ■		
• **Selection Support Workbook:** ● ▲ ■ Literary Analysis, p. 256 Reading Strategy, p. 255 Build Vocabulary, p. 253	• **Literary Analysis and Reading Transparencies,** pp. 127 and 128 ● ▲ ■	
		• **Listening to Literature** ● ▲ ■ Audiocassettes Audio CDs
• **Literary Analysis for Enrichment,** p. 64 ■		
• **Formal Assessment:** Selection Test, pp. 222–224 ● ▲ ■ • **Open-Book Tests,** pp. 190–192 ● ▲ ■ • **Performance Assessment and Portfolio Management,** pp. 16, 31 ● ▲ ■ • PRENTICE HALL ASSESSMENT SYSTEM ● ▲ ■	• PRENTICE HALL ASSESSMENT SYSTEM ● ▲ ■ **Skills Practice Answers and Explanations on Transparencies**	• **Test Bank Software** ● ▲ ■
• **Selection Support Workbook:** ● ▲ ■ Grammar and Style, p. 254 • **Writing and Grammar,** Diamond Level ● ▲ ■ • **Extension Activities,** p. 64 ● ▲ ■	• **Daily Language Practice Transparencies** ● ▲ • **Writing Models and Graphic Organizers on Transparencies,** pp. 75–77 ● ▲ ■	• **Writing and Grammar iText CD-ROM** ● ▲ ■ *Take It to the Net* PHSchool.com

BLOCK SCHEDULING: Use one 90-minute class period to preteach the selection(s) and have students read them. Use a second 90-minute class period to assess students' mastery of skills and have them complete one of the Extension Activities.

PRETEACH

Step-by-Step Teaching Guide for pp. 1316–1317

Motivation

Display pictures with bold headlines from newspapers and magazines, depicting the effects of life-changing events, such as natural disasters, accidents, or violence. Then, guide students to recognize that disturbing or painful events can be turning points for those who experience or witness them. Such events may have so deep an emotional impact on people that they are changed forever. Suggest that students keep the emotional power of the images in mind as they read.

❶ Background

More About the Authors

Ravikovitch is known for her translations of children's literature—including Mary Poppins and Cinderella—as well as the works of William Butler Yeats, Edgar Allan Poe, and T. S. Eliot. She has been awarded the Bialik Prize for literature and received the 1990 Israel Prize, Israel's highest honor.

Amichai's poems are extremely popular in Israel. Each of his books of poems sells about 15,000 copies. This may not sound like a large number until the relative proportions are calculated. There are only three million readers of Hebrew in Israel, which means that one out of every 200 of these readers buys his books. If Israel were the size of the United States and had 36 million readers, each of Amichai's books would sell 180,000 copies!

Geography Note

Draw students' attention to the map on this page. Tell students that Israel developed from the desire for a Jewish homeland. The State of Israel came into being in 1948 and has been plagued by tension and war with its neighbors.

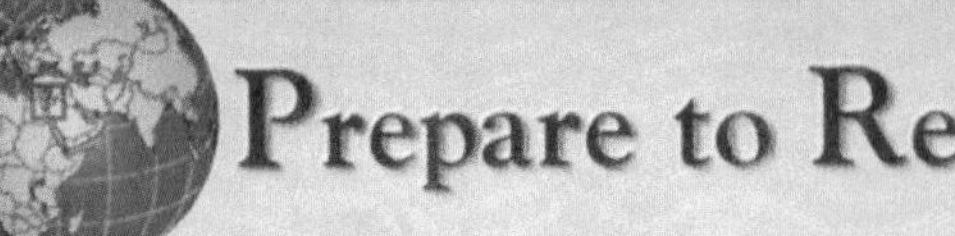

Prepare to Read

❶ Pride ◆ The Diameter of the Bomb ◆ From the Book of Esther I Filtered the Sediment

Dahlia Ravikovitch (b. 1936)

"Can't you write about me without me?" poet Dahlia Ravikovitch once asked an interviewer. Painfully shy, Ravikovitch has always shunned the limelight. Yet her poems are filled with intense feeling, fusing emotional revelation with images of history, religion, and mythology. Ravikovitch is probably Israel's most prominent female poet.

A Traumatic Childhood Ravikovitch was born in Ramat Gan, a suburb of Tel Aviv, twelve years before Israel became a nation. When she was six, her father was killed in a hit-and-run accident, and she moved with the rest of her family to an Israeli communal farm, or kibbutz. Her father's death left a lifelong scar, but it also made her deeply sympathetic to the suffering of others. "Because I know what it is like to be hurt," she explains, "I try not to hurt anyone."

Turning Pain to Poetry Poetry became the means by which Ravikovitch expressed her deepest feelings. Drawing on the Bible as well as the English literature she had studied in college, she published her first full volume of poetry in 1959. Two collections, *A Dress of Fire* (1978) and *The Window* (1998), have been translated into English.

Working for Peace Ravikovitch's compassion also marks her involvement in the Israeli peace movement. Israel has an uneasy, sometimes violent, relationship with the Palestinian inhabitants of the region. In 1997, when uprisings drove many Israelis away from Palestinian areas, the sixty-year-old Ravikovitch continued to visit the city of Hebron, bringing chocolates and cheer to a ten-year-old Palestinian boy she had met there.

Yehuda Amichai (1924–2000)

In modern Israel, the language of the streets and shops is Hebrew, the ancient language of the Bible. As the Israeli poet Yehuda Amichai observes, "Every word we use carries in and of itself connotations from the Bible. . . . Every word reverberates through the halls of Jewish history." Amichai's genius lay in his ear for both the traditional and modern resonances of the language.

Rebellion and Loss Amichai was born in Germany. Before the outbreak of World War II, however, his Orthodox Jewish family emigrated to Palestine, the region in which Israel was later (1948) to be established. Eventually, the family settled in Jerusalem. The young Amichai rebelled against his father's strict religious practices, yet his great love for his father survived the conflict.

Apprenticeships As a young man, Amichai served in World War II and in Israel's War of Independence. An early collection of short stories is based in part on his wartime experiences. During this period, he began reading the English poets W. H. Auden and T. S. Eliot. Both poets, especially Auden, inspired him to use colloquial language in his work.

Speaking for Others Amichai published his first collection of poems in 1955, but it was with his second book of poetry, *Two Hopes Away* (1958), that Amichai was embraced as the spokesperson for his generation, capturing its disillusionment. In this book, Amichai introduced what one critic called the characteristic themes of his subsequent work: "love, war, the passage of time, his relationship with his father, his father's death, and his own undefined guilt."

TEACHING RESOURCES

The following resources can be used to enrich or extend the instruction for pp. 1316–1317.

Background

Beyond Literature, p. 64

Take It to the Net

Visit PHSchool.com for background on the authors.

Literary Analysis

Literary Analysis and Reading Transparencies, Imagery, p. 127 ■

Selection Support: Literary Analysis, p. 256

Reading

Literary Analysis and Reading Transparencies, Evaluating a Writer's Message, p. 128 ■

■ **BLOCK SCHEDULING:** Resources marked with this symbol provide varied instruction during 90-minute blocks.

Preview

Connecting to the Literature

"What would I do if I had total control?" Most people have a quick answer—they would win every time. These poems ask a trickier question: "What happens when we want to control life—but find we can't?"

❷ Literary Analysis

Imagery

Imagery is descriptive language that re-creates sensory experience. An **image** is a specific word picture created using such language. For example, "Pride" contains powerful images of movement and rest:

> And so the moss flourishes, the seaweed / whips around, / the sea pushes through and rolls back—/ the rocks seem motionless.

A **sustained image** is one that is extended over a number of lines. As you read, note the effects of both brief and sustained images.

Comparing Literary Works

Poets often use imagery to develop **figurative language,** or language that is not meant to be taken literally. Figures of speech include

- **metaphor,** in which one thing is spoken of as if it were another kind of thing
- **simile,** in which one thing is compared to another using *like* or *as*
- **personification,** in which a nonhuman subject is given human characteristics.

For example, in "From the Book of Esther . . . ," the poet speaks of numbing oneself to the pains and joys of life as "filtering sediment." In this metaphor, a habit of mind is described as if it were a physical act. As you read, compare the poets' uses of figurative language to probe life.

❸ Reading Strategy

Evaluating a Writer's Message

To **evaluate a writer's message,** identify the work's main insight. Then, consider whether the insight makes sense and whether it is well supported. For example, in "The Diameter of the Bomb," Amichai's message concerns the effects of a single act. He supports his message with a vivid, sustained image. As you read, use a chart like this one to evaluate the writers' messages.

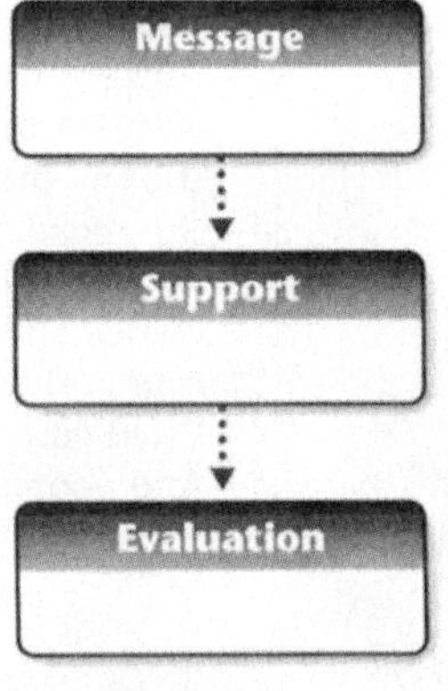

Vocabulary Development

flourishes (flʉr′ ish ez) *v.* thrives; grows vigorously (p. 1318)

considerably (kən sid′ er ə blē) *adv.* to a great degree (p. 1319)

solitary (säl′ ə ter′ ē) *adj.* lone; single; sole (p. 1319)

sediment (sed′ ə mənt) *n.* waste material that settles to the bottom of a liquid (p. 1320)

vulgar (vul′ gər) *adj.* coarse; common (p. 1320)

CUSTOMIZE INSTRUCTION FOR UNIVERSAL ACCESS

For Less Proficient Readers	For English Learners	For Advanced Readers
To ensure literal comprehension, review the "story" of each poem. Pair less proficient readers with more proficient partners. Have the partners read each poem and then use their own words to tell each other what happens in each selection and what imagery the poets use.	Use Amichai's and Ravikovitch's works as the starting point for a discussion of figurative language. Then, have each student find a sustained image or metaphor in a poem from his or her culture. Ask students to translate these poems for the class and explain the sustained figure of speech.	Have students make a chart noting the various kinds of imagery and figurative language—similes, metaphors, or personification—that appear in these poems. Then, ask students to compare and contrast the imagery used by the two poets by considering content, grammar, diction, and tone. Discuss the results as a class.

❷ Literary Analysis

Imagery

- Explain to students that using imagery is the same as using descriptive or figurative language to create word pictures for readers. These word pictures employ language that appeals to the senses of sight, hearing, touch, taste, and smell to help readers imagine and experience, to some extent, the image.
- Have groups of students choose an item and describe it. Challenge each group to see how many sensory details they can generate for each item.
- Give students extra practice with this Literary Analysis Strategy by using the Imagery transparency in **Literary Analysis and Reading Transparencies,** p. 127.

❸ Reading Strategy

Evaluating a Writer's Message

- Remind students that strong, powerful images can be convincing support for a writer's insight.
- During their initial reading of the poems, have students use a graphic organizer like the one on p. 1317 to jot down notes about the poems' messages and supporting details. Instruct students to fill in the graphic organizer's "Evaluation" box by using these notes to assess how effectively each poem's message is conveyed.

Vocabulary Development

- Pronounce each vocabulary word for students, and read the definitions as a class. Have students identify any words with which they are already familiar.

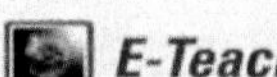

E-Teach

Visit e-Teach at PHSchool.com for teachers' essays on how to teach, with questions and answers.

TEACH

Step-by-Step Teaching Guide for pp. 1318–1320

Teaching Tenth-Grade Students

10TH GRADE Write Robert Frost's fourteen-line poem "The Silken Tent" on the board, and read it aloud. Go over the poem in detail with students, pointing out the sustained comparison between the woman and the tent. Explain that, like Frost, both Amichai and Ravikovitch use sustained images and figures of speech.

❶ About the Selections

Rich in imagery, "Pride" addresses a fateful moment for people.

"The Diameter of the Bomb" alludes to a terrorist attack that killed four people and wounded eleven.

❷ Literary Analysis

Imagery and Figurative Language

- Have students read aloud the first eight lines of "Pride."
- Then, have students respond to the Literary Analysis item on p. 1318: Identify two words or phrases that personify the rocks, giving them human qualities.
  Possible response: The rocks "lie on their backs"; they seem "peaceful" and "don't move."

Monitor Progress Ask students to infer how the rocks in this poem are like people.
Possible response: With people, as with rocks, a crack that starts small can become a complete break under pressure.

Reteach If students have difficulty with the Literary Analysis strategy, suggest that they use p. 256 in the **Selection Support** workbook for help.

❶ Pride

Dahlia Ravikovitch
translated by Chana Bloch *and* Ariel Bloch

Background

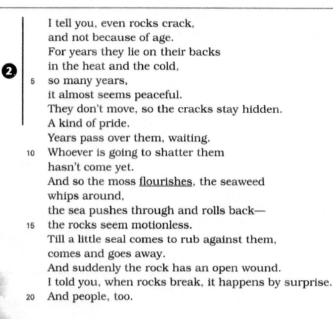

Before the onset of World War II, Jews had begun to return to Palestine, the Jewish homeland in biblical times. Violence flared up between the Arab inhabitants of Palestine and the new immigrants. In 1948, the United Nations divided Palestine, creating the state of Israel for Jewish settlers, who now included refugees from the Holocaust. Palestinians and their Arab allies were outraged, and the region was plunged into a series of wars and uprisings. The work of these poets suggests that, exposed day after day to threats and horrors, people in the region face a kind of moral weariness.

❷
I tell you, even rocks crack,
and not because of age.
For years they lie on their backs
in the heat and the cold,
so many years,
it almost seems peaceful.
They don't move, so the cracks stay hidden.
A kind of pride.
Years pass over them, waiting.
Whoever is going to shatter them
hasn't come yet.
And so the moss flourishes, the seaweed
whips around,
the sea pushes through and rolls back—
the rocks seem motionless.
Till a little seal comes to rub against them,
comes and goes away.
And suddenly the rock has an open wound.
I told you, when rocks break, it happens by surprise.
And people, too.

Literary Analysis
Imagery and Figurative Language Identify two words or phrases that personify the rocks, giving them human qualities.

flourishes (flur' ish ez) *v.* thrives; grows vigorously

TEACHING RESOURCES

The following resources can be used to enrich or extend the instruction for pp. 1318–1320.

Literary Analysis

- **Selection Support:** Literary Analysis, p. 256
- **Literary Analysis and Reading Transparencies,** Imagery, p. 127 ■

Reading

- **Selection Support:** Reading Strategy, p. 255; Build Vocabulary, p. 253
- **Listening to Literature Audiocassettes** ■
- **Listening to Literature CDs**

■ **BLOCK SCHEDULING:** Resources marked with this symbol provide varied instruction during 90-minute blocks.

❸

The Diameter of the Bomb

Yehuda Amichai

translated by Chana Bloch

❹

The diameter of the bomb was thirty centimeters
and the diameter of its effective range about seven meters,
with four dead and eleven wounded.
And around these, in a larger circle
of pain and time, two hospitals are scattered
and one graveyard. But the young woman
who was buried in the city she came from,
at a distance of more than a hundred kilometers,
enlarges the circle <u>considerably</u>,
and the <u>solitary</u> man mourning her death
at the distant shores of a country far across the sea
includes the entire world in the circle.
And I won't even mention the crying of orphans
that reaches up to the throne of God and
beyond, making
a circle with no end and no God.

Literary Analysis
Imagery How does the visual image of the circle change in lines 1–6?

considerably (kən sid′ ər ə blē) *adv.* to a great degree

solitary (säl′ ə ter′ ē) *adj.* lone; single; sole

Review and Assess

Thinking About the Selections

1. **Respond:** In each poem, what most surprised you? Explain.
2. **(a) Recall:** What happens to the rocks at the end of "Pride"? **(b) Analyze Cause and Effect:** Compare the apparent cause of this event with its deeper causes.
3. **(a) Interpret:** What does the expansion of the circle in the poem suggest about human suffering? **(b) Draw Conclusions:** What lesson about justice does the poem suggest?

CUSTOMIZE INSTRUCTION FOR UNIVERSAL ACCESS

For Special Needs Students	For Gifted/Talented Students	For Advanced Readers
Before students read "Pride," provide them with pictures of glaciers or other images in which wind, water, sand, or abrasion have worn away rock. Tell students that erosion is a literal physical process but also a metaphor for difficulty and stress. Read and discuss the poem with students.	If there is a Hebrew speaker in your school or community, invite him or her to read the Hebrew versions of these poems to the class. Encourage students to ask questions about the ways in which the original poems differ from and resemble the translations.	Provide students with a copy of "The Diameter of the Bomb" translated by Ted Hughes. Ask volunteers to read both versions aloud according to the punctuation, not the line breaks. List differences on the board, taking time to summarize the varying messages behind each difference.

❸ About the Translation

Compare the Bloch/Mitchell translation of "The Diameter of the Bomb" (see the SE page) with that of Ted Hughes:

The diameter of the bomb was/ thirty centimeters/and the diameter of its effective/range—about seven meters./And in it four dead and eleven/wounded./And around them in a greater circle/of pain and time are scattered/two hospitals and one cemetery./But the young woman who was/buried where she came from/over a hundred kilometers away/enlarges the circle greatly./ And the lone man who weeps over/ her death/in a far corner of a distant country/includes the whole world in the/circle./And I won't speak at all about the crying of orphans/that reaches to the seat of God/and from there onward, making/the circle without end and without/God.

Consider these contrasts:

- The Hughes version has eighteen lines; the Bloch version has sixteen. (The poem in Hebrew is sixteen lines long.)
- Hughes's lines sound more clipped than those of Bloch. Overall, Hughes's version is less "eloquent" than Blochs translation.

❹ Literary Analysis

Imagery

- Tell students that concentric circles share a common center. Draw several concentric circles on the board.
- Ask the Literary Analysis question on p. 1319: How does the visual image of the circle change in lines 1–6?
  Answer: The circle grows larger as details are added.

Answers for p. 1319

Review and Assess

1. Possible response: The last line of "Pride" surprises readers by stating that humans break like rocks. The last line of "The Diameter of the Bomb" surprises readers by showing how far one act of violence reaches.
2. **(a)** The rocks suddenly break. **(b)** The rocks break because they have not been able to change.
3. **(a)** Human suffering is shared. **(b)** The poem suggests that there is no justice and "no God."

ASSESS

❺ Vocabulary Development

Latin Word Origins: *vulgar*

- Draw students' attention to the word *vulgar* and its definitions.
- Ask students which definition fits best in the context of the poem.
  Answer: "Common" joy makes the most sense in the poem.

❻ Critical Thinking

Interpret

- Tell students to analyze the nature of the "peace" the poet has gained.
- Ask: Does the word *peace* have its usual positive connotations in this context?
  Possible response: In this context, *peace* is synonymous with spiritual death.

❼ Reading Strategy

Evaluating a Writer's Message

- Discuss with students how those who allow themselves to feel great joy may also feel great pain.
- Then, ask students the Reading Strategy question on p. 1320: What do these lines suggest about the speaker's reason for living a life "censored and pasted and limited and in peace"?
  Answer: The speaker is tired of sadness and has drained all emotion from life to avoid pain.

Answers for p. 1320

Review and Assess

1. **Possible response:** The poem's hopelessness makes it difficult to empathize with the speaker's weariness.
2. **(a)** The speaker filters vulgar joy, pain, and the search for love. **(b)** The "sediment" includes human experience. The sanitized "new Bible" will be emotionally sterile, granting the speaker emotional freedom.
3. **(a)** The "great weariness" leads him or her to lie. **(b)** The phrases "another woman," "already died," and "before her time" indicate that the friend died an untimely death.
4. **Possible response:** Without joy and pain, life will mean little.

From the Book of Esther I Filtered the Sediment

Yehuda Amichai
translated by Chana Bloch

❺ From the Book of Esther I filtered the sediment
of vulgar joy, and from the Book of Jeremiah
the howl of pain in the guts. And from
the Song of Songs the endless
search for love, and from Genesis the dreams
and Cain, and from Ecclesiastes
the despair, and from the Book of Job: Job.
And with what was left, I pasted myself a new Bible.
❻ Now I live censored and pasted and limited and in peace.

A woman asked me last night on the dark street
how another woman was
❼ who'd already died. Before her time—and not
in anyone else's time either.
Out of a great weariness I answered,
"She's fine, she's fine."

sediment (sed′ ə mənt) *n.* waste material that settles to the bottom of a liquid

vulgar (vul′ gər) *adj.* coarse; common

Reading Strategy
Evaluating a Writer's Message What do these lines suggest about the speaker's reason for living a life "censored and pasted and limited and in peace"?

Review and Assess

Thinking About the Selection

1. **Respond:** How did you react to the speaker's "weariness"?
2. **(a) Recall:** List three examples of the "sediment" that the speaker filters from the Bible. **(b) Connect:** Explain the connection between the "sediment" the speaker removes and the type of life mapped out in his "new Bible."
3. **(a) Analyze:** What does the speaker's "great weariness" lead him to do in the last line? **(b) Infer:** What is the probable source of his attitude? Cite details to support your answer.
4. **Apply:** What advice might you offer someone in the speaker's position?

ASSESSMENT PRACTICE: Writing Skills

Style (For more practice, see Test Preparation Workbook, p. 64.)

Style questions on standardized tests focus on the writer's point of view and effective use of language. Use the following passage and question to help students assess their understanding of style.

And so the moss flourishes, the seaweed
whips around,
the sea pushes through and rolls back—
the rocks seem motionless.

The author's description of the rocks in the sea relies mostly on the reader's sense of—

A touch. **C** taste.
B sound. **D** smell.

The poet does not use language in the passage that appeals to the reader's sense of taste, sound, or smell, so answers *B, C,* and *D* are not correct. The writer's use of words like *whips* and *pushes* appeals to the reader's sense of touch, so *A* is the correct answer.

Review and Assess

Literary Analysis

Imagery

1. (a) Identify three **images** in "Pride," explaining to which sense each one appeals. (b) Explain the connection between each image and the "pride" to which the title refers.
2. (a) What **sustained image** is central to "The Diameter of the Bomb"? (b) Using a chart like this one, explain how the development of this image moves from a specific event to a general idea.

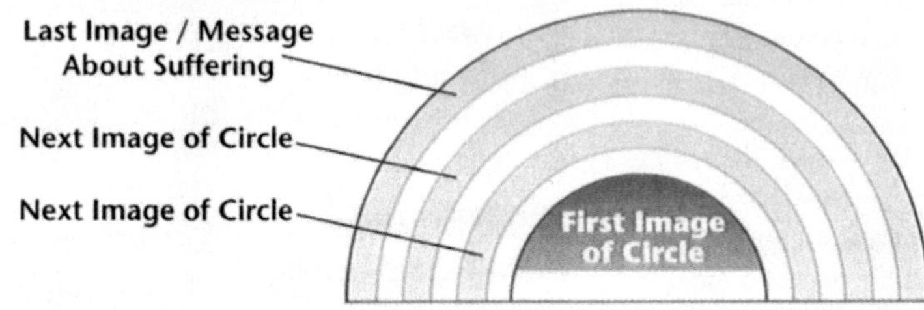

3. (a) How is the image of "sediment" in "From the Book of Esther . . ." contradicted by the experiences it symbolizes? (b) In using this image, what attitude does the speaker reveal? Explain.

Comparing Literary Works

4. Identify the types of **figurative language** used in "Pride" and "The Diameter of the Bomb."
5. Compare the image of the circle in "The Diameter of the Bomb" with the image of sediment in "From the Book of Esther . . . ."
(a) Which image expands the reader's vision of the world? Explain.
(b) Which gives more insight into the poem's speaker? Explain.

Reading Strategy

Evaluating a Writer's Message

6. (a) Identify the **writer's message** in each of the three poems.
(b) For each one, identify the way in which the poet supports it (makes it understandable and compelling).
7. In your judgment, which message is best supported? Explain.

Extend Understanding

8. **Math Connection:** (a) Using the terms *circumference* and *diameter*, describe the last circle in Amichai's poem. (b) Do you think such a circle can be defined using a mathematical equation? Explain.

Quick Review

Imagery is descriptive language that re-creates sensory experience. An **image** is a specific word picture created using such language. A **sustained image** is an image that extends over several lines or throughout an entire work.

Figurative language is language that is not meant to be taken literally. Figures of speech include: **metaphor, simile,** and **personification.**

To **evaluate a writer's message,** identify the work's main insight and consider whether it is well supported.

Take It to the Net
PHSchool.com

Take the interactive self-test online to check your understanding of these selections.

ENRICHMENT: Further Reading

Other Works by the Authors

We strongly encourage you to review any selection before assigning or recommending it to students.

Half an Hour Before the Monsoon, Ravikovitch

Not of This Time, Not of This Place, Amichai

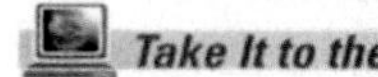
Take It to the Net

Visit PHSchool.com for more information about the authors.

Answers for p. 1321

Review and Assess

1. **(a)** Possible response: Sight: rocks lying on their backs; Touch: the seal rubbing against the rocks; the rocks in the heat and cold. **(b)** Sample response: The description of rocks exposed to the elements shows how people are exposed to the "weathering" of emotions.
2. **(a)** The sustained image of concentric circles is central to the poem. **(b)** First Image: bomb leaves four dead and eleven wounded; Second Image: two hospitals and a graveyard; Third Image: a woman buried in a distant city; Fourth Image: a man in a foreign country mourning the woman's death; Last Image: crying orphans; Message: Violence continues unmitigated.
3. **(a)** The image of "sediment" is a negative one, like an impurity that must be cleansed. However, the "sediment" represents positive, human emotions. **(b)** By using the negative image of "sediment," the speaker demonstrates emotional distance.
4. In "Pride," the poet uses personification. In "The Diameter of the Bomb," the poet uses a metaphor.
5. **(a)** Possible response: The circle in "The Diameter of the Bomb" expands the readers' vision of the world by starting in one central spot and expanding outward. **(b)** Possible response: The sediment in "From the Book of Esther. . ." gives more insight into the poem's speaker by showing the speaker's damaged, restricted emotional range.
6. **(a)** Sample response: The message of "The Diameter of the Bomb" is that one act of violence spreads pain worldwide. **(b)** Sample response: "The Diameter of the Bomb" supports the message by providing an ever-widening map of suffering.
7. Possible response: The message of "The Diameter of the Bomb" is best supported because it takes readers through layers of pain and suffering.

continued

continued from right column

8. **(a)** The diameter of Amichai's poem connects the center of the bomb to the throne of God. The last circle of Amichai's poem has the largest circumference, expanding to include the entire universe. **(b)** Possible response: The circle could be defined using an equation that defines infinity.

EXTEND

Answers for p. 1322

❶ Vocabulary Development

Latin Word Origins: *vulgar*

1. Priests in the Middle Ages spoke Latin, but farmers used vulgar languages.
2. A feast is a vulgar affair; it invites unchecked gluttony.
3. Only a vulgar person would yawn loudly throughout a performance.

Concept Development: Synonyms and Antonyms

1. antonyms
2. antonyms
3. synonyms
4. synonyms
5. antonyms

Spelling Strategy

1. comfortably
2. miserably
3. agreeably

❷ Grammar and Style

Practice

1. and [they crack] not because of age
2. and from the Book of Jeremiah [I filtered] the howl of pain in the guts.
3. Ravikovitch's [are] more concrete.
4. Ravikovitch [writes] with a large heart
5. great art [is born] of great suffering

Writing Application

Possible response:

People respond to suffering in different ways. Some people show their grief, *others not*. Some people view emotional display as a sign of weakness, *others of hysteria*.

10TH GRADE For support in teaching the Grammar and Style Lesson to tenth graders, use **Writing and Grammar,** Platinum Level, Chapter 20, Section 2.

Integrate Language Skills

❶ Vocabulary Development Lesson

Latin Word Origins: *vulgar*

The word *vulgar*, meaning "common" or "coarse," is related to the Latin word *vulgus*, meaning "the common people" or "the public." Historically, *vulgar* also came to refer to the spoken language of a country (as opposed to Latin, used by the church and in government). Today, *vulgar* is often used to mean "improper." The original meaning of the root *-vulg-* can be detected, though, in words such as *divulge*, meaning "to make public."

For each item below, write a sentence that includes the word *vulgar*.

1. the language spoken by medieval farmers
2. a common pleasure, such as sharing a meal
3. an audience member who sniffs, yawns, and stretches loudly throughout a performance

Concept Development: Synonyms and Antonyms

Synonyms are words that are the same or nearly the same in meaning. Antonyms are opposites. Identify each synonym or antonym pair below.

1. flourishes / withers
2. considerably / slightly
3. solitary / sole
4. sediment / residue
5. vulgar / courtly

Spelling Strategy

When adding the suffix *-ly* to a word ending in a consonant + *le*, drop the *le*. Add *-ly* to each of the following words.

1. comfortable 2. miserable 3. agreeable

❷ Grammar and Style Lesson

Elliptical Clauses

Elliptical comes from the word *ellipsis*, meaning "omission." In an **elliptical clause,** some words are left out, but the clause is understood as if they were present. Review the following example:

Elliptical Clause: The diameter of the bomb was thirty centimeters / and the diameter of its effective range [. . .] about seven meters, . . . (*was* is understood)

Practice For each item below, write the elliptical clauses and the understood words.

1. "I tell you, even rocks crack, / and not because of age."
2. "From the Book of Esther I filtered the sediment / of vulgar joy, and from the Book of Jeremiah / the howl of pain in the guts."
3. Amichai's images are more abstract; Ravikovitch's, more concrete.
4. Amichai writes with a keen eye; Ravikovitch, with a large heart.
5. They might agree on this idea: Art is born of suffering; great art, of great suffering.

Writing Application Write a paragraph about people's responses to misfortune. Include two sentences with elliptical clauses.

WG *Prentice Hall Writing and Grammar Connection: Diamond Level, Chapter 22, Section 2*

TEACHING RESOURCES

The following resources can be used to enrich or extend the instruction for pp. 1322–1323.

Vocabulary

- **Selection Support:** Build Vocabulary, p. 253
- **Vocabulary and Spelling Practice Book** (Use this booklet for skills instruction.)

Grammar

- **Selection Support:** Grammar and Style, p. 254
- **Writing and Grammar,** Diamond Level, p. 574
- **Daily Language Practice Transparencies** ■

Writing

- **Performance Assess. and Portfolio Mgmt.,** p. 16
- **Writing and Grammar,** Diamond Level, p. 108
- **Writing and Grammar iText CD-ROM** ■
- **Writing Models and Graphic Organizers on Transparencies,** pp. 75–77

Listening and Speaking

- **Performance Assess. and Portfolio Mgmt.,** p. 31

■ **BLOCK SCHEDULING:** Resources marked with this symbol provide varied instruction during 90-minute blocks.

❸ Writing Lesson

Poem With a Strong Central Image

Following the examples of Ravikovitch and Amichai, write a poem with a strong central image that conveys a message about life. For the best effect, make sure that your poem is focused, with each detail supporting your central image.

Prewriting Select a topic, such as *kindness*, and write several sentences about it. Use these sentences to develop a message for your poem. Next, list images that will help convey this message. Circle the strongest one.

Drafting As you draft, keep your central image and message in mind. Bring the image to life by using words that appeal to the senses.

Revising Underline in one color those details in your poem that develop the central image. Use another color to underline details that distract from it. Consider eliminating distracting details and elaborating on those that strengthen the central image.

Model: Revising to Strengthen Your Central Image

A smile, a word of kindness, a needed hug—
a seed, planted in the soil of someone's day
it holds a waiting flower,
unfurling it sunward,
~~leaving its mark~~ after you have gone.

Eliminating distracting details and providing additional support help clarify the central image.

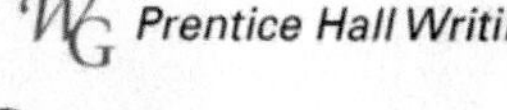

Prentice Hall Writing and Grammar Connection: Diamond Level, Chapter 6, Section 4

❹ Extension Activities

Listening and Speaking The speaker in "From the Book of Esther . . ." has a sharp, ironic understanding of his own "weariness." Give an **oral interpretation** of the poem, using these tips:

- Jot down notes on the speaker's attitude toward life.
- Identify the reaction to that attitude—does the speaker feel self-contempt? Resignation?
- Experiment with various tones of voice and pacing to convey the speaker's personality.

Present your interpretation to the class.

Research and Technology The rocks in "Pride" lie along the ocean shore. In a group, produce a **multimedia presentation** on seaside geology. Divide tasks and conduct research on the following subtopics: Types of Rocks, Rock Formation, and Erosion. Use visuals to present your information to the class. **[Group Activity]**

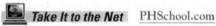

Take It to the Net PHSchool.com

Go online for an additional research activity using the Internet.

ASSESSMENT RESOURCES

The following resources can be used to assess students' knowledge and skills.

Selection Assessment

- **Formal Assessment,** pp. 222–224
- **Open-Book Tests,** pp. 190–192
- **Test Bank Software**

Take It to the Net

Visit PHSchool.com for self-tests on the selections.

Writing Rubric

- **Performance Assess. and Portfolio Mgmt.,** p. 16

Listening and Speaking

- **Performance Assess. Rubric and Portfolio Mgmt.,** p. 31

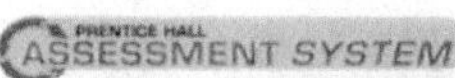

For additional diagnostics and remediation for skills covered in this grouping, use materials from the Prentice Hall Assessment System.

Lesson Support for p. 1323

❸ Writing Lesson

- Point out to students that their successful completion of a poem using imagery depends on their choice of subject matter. Tell students that they will need to select a central image that can represent a larger idea or theme.
- Have students use a chart such as the Herringbone Organizer in **Writing Models and Graphic Organizers on Transparencies,** pp. 75–77, to help organize information about their central image.
- Use the Response to Literature Rubric, p. 16, in **Performance Assessment and Portfolio Management** to evaluate students' work.

10TH GRADE For support in working through the Writing Lesson with tenth graders, use **Writing and Grammar,** Platinum Level, Chapter 6, Section 4.

❹ Listening and Speaking

- Have students paraphrase each line (in its entirety) for a listener as part of the preparation process. Any line that they cannot paraphrase—or that the listener fails to comprehend—indicates a passage that needs further study.
- Use the Presenting an Oral Response to Literature Rubric, p. 31, in **Performance Assessment and Portfolio Management** to evaluate students' work.

CUSTOMIZE INSTRUCTION For Universal Access

To address different learning styles, use the following activities suggested in the **Extension Activities** booklet, p. 64.

- For Visual/Spatial Learners, use Activity 5.
- For Mathematical/Logical and Verbal/Linguistic Learners, use Activity 6.
- For Interpersonal Learners, use Activity 7.

Lesson Objectives

1. To understand the connection between past and present descriptions of war's devastation
2. To understand how different genres, such as poetry and nonfiction, reflect writers' experiences of and attitudes toward war

Connections

War everywhere and in every time creates havoc in people's lives. Individuals are killed, injured, left to grieve, and made homeless. Through poetry or nonfiction journalism, war descriptions bring these vivid images alive in reader's minds. Have students reread Yehuda Amichai's "The Diameter of the Bomb" on p. 1319 after they have read the excerpt from John Hersey's *Hiroshima*. Discuss how the results of these two wars are similar and different, and how the authors' reactions to war overlap or differ.

In the Shadows of Destruction

- Explain that John Hersey's reporting recorded a turning point in the history of modern warfare. After nearly six years of fighting, American President Harry Truman chose to use new technology with the hope of bringing an end to World War II. An atomic bomb was dropped on Hiroshima, killing tens of thousands of people. A second bomb was dropped on Nagasaki.
- Point out that both Amichai's poem and Hersey's account focus on how bombs affect individual people rather than descriptions of buildings or military activities.
- Discuss how details narrow the focus of both of these accounts, giving the reader more accessibility to the characters. For example, Amichai describes the size of the bomb, and Hersey describes the daily activities of survivors.

CONNECTIONS

Literature Past and Present

In the Shadows of Destruction

from *Hiroshima*

JOHN HERSEY

In Yehuda Amichai's poem "The Diameter of the Bomb" (p. 1319), the circle of devastation that is described extends physically and metaphorically in all directions and for eternal distances. Modern and contemporary literature has all too often had occasion to address issues related to war, bombing, and destruction, as well as their dramatic effect on the everyday lives of individuals.

The Ultimate Weapon John Hersey's account of the dropping of the atomic bomb on Hiroshima in 1945 provides a deceptively calm and objective account of horror. In this excerpt from *Hiroshima*, the specific details of Miss Toshiko Sasaki's normal morning activities form the story of a step-by-step journey toward disaster. In this nonfiction account, as in the fiction, poetry, and other nonfiction in this unit, similar mundane details serve as reminders that ordinary lives can become extraordinary in an instant and that those directly affected by violence and tragedy are—up to that moment—just like everyone else.

ENRICHMENT: History Connection

Hiroshima and Nagasaki

Familiarize students with the geography and history of the Japanese cities of Hiroshima and Nagasaki. Explain that Japan, as a chain of islands, can be attacked only by air or by sea. Its western neighbors are North and South Korea, Russia, and China. The four main islands of Japan are Hokkaido, Honshu, Shikoku, and Kyushu.

Hiroshima is a port city on the southwest coast of Honshu. Nagasaki is a port city on the west coast of Kyushu. During World War II, both of these cities had military installations and a certain amount of industry. The cities were mostly destroyed by the bombs but were reconstructed in the 1950s. Today, both house important tourist sites and monuments that attract antiwar and antinuclear supporters from around the world.

At exactly fifteen minutes past eight in the morning, on August 6, 1945, Japanese time, at the moment when the atomic bomb flashed above Hiroshima, Miss Toshiko Sasaki, a clerk in the personnel department of the East Asia Tin Works, had just sat down at her place in the plant office and was turning her head to speak to the girl at the next desk. At that same moment, Dr. Masakazu Fujii was settling down cross-legged to read the Osaka *Asahi* on the porch of his private hospital, overhanging one of the seven deltaic rivers which divide Hiroshima; Mrs. Hatsuyo Nakamura, a tailor's widow, stood by the window of her kitchen, watching a neighbor tearing down his house because it lay in the path of an air-raid-defense fire lane; . . . and the Reverend Mr. Kiyoshi Tanimoto, pastor of the Hiroshima Methodist Church, paused at the door of a rich man's house in Koi, the city's western suburb, and prepared to unload a handcart full of things he had evacuated from town in fear of the massive B-29 raid which everyone expected Hiroshima to suffer. A hundred thousand people were killed by the atomic bomb, and these [four] were among the survivors. They still wonder why they lived when so many others died. Each of them counts many small items of chance or volition—a step taken in time, a decision to go indoors, catching one streetcar instead of the next—that spared him. And now each knows that in the act of survival he lived a dozen lives and saw more death than he ever thought he would see. At the time, none of them knew anything. . . .

▲ Critical Viewing There are no people shown in this photograph—nor in many others depicting the devastation wrought by the Hiroshima bomb. Does the lack of humanity lessen or intensify the power of the image? Explain. **[Assess]**

evacuated (ē vak´ yo͞o āt´ əd) *v.* made empty; withdrawn

volition (vō lish´ ən) *n.* act of using the will

▶Critical Viewing
Possible response: The impact of the image is greater without people because the bomb appears to have erased all signs of life.

In the Shadows of Destruction

- Ask a volunteer to read aloud the last five sentences on p. 1325.
- Explain that Hersey chooses to tell the story of the dropping of the bomb through the lives of four survivors. Ask students why they think Hersey chose these four survivors as his focus.
  Possible response: These survivors were chosen for their ordinariness. By describing typical people living in Hiroshima at the time of the bombing, Hersey makes the point that the victims of the bomb were helpless civilians.
- Point out that Hersey notes that small acts and decisions made the difference between life and death for the survivors. Ask students what they can infer about war from these details.
  Possible response: The details of everyday life for the survivors suggest the arbitrariness and senselessness of war.

CUSTOMIZE INSTRUCTION FOR UNIVERSAL ACCESS

For Less Proficient Readers	For English Learners	For Advanced Readers
Explain that *Hiroshima* is a work of nonfiction that discusses actual events. Help students track the events in the excerpt by creating a chart with these headings: *Person, Description, Before the Bomb, After the Bomb.* Encourage volunteers to share and discuss their charts with the class.	Clarify the chronology of the excerpt by explaining that the excerpt from *Hiroshima* begins with the actions of four people and then jumps back to before the bomb struck. Ask students to make a timeline of events on the board.	Stress that this excerpt from *Hiroshima* describes actual events in a way that affects readers' emotions. Challenge students to look for details and literary devices that move the account beyond a typical news article and into the realm of literature. Have students write a paragraph showing how Hersey achieves his emotional impact.

In the Shadows of Destruction

- After students independently read the text on p. 1326, point out that Hersey includes a number of mundane details about Miss Sasaki's morning.
- Ask students the following question: Knowing that the bomb is about to fall, how do these mundane details affect your response to the article?
  Possible response: These details help readers relate to Miss Sasaki as a fellow human being and make the coming disaster seem much more tragic and painful.

▶Critical Viewing

Possible response: The remains of the sacred tree convey the physical and emotional devastation of the blast quite effectively. The gnarled remnants of the tree, as well as the bricks and debris scattered about the tree illustrate the physical damage in the area. The fact that the decimated tree is a sacred one helps underscore the emotional pain that the people of Hiroshima must have felt.

Miss Toshiko Sasaki, the East Asia Tin Works clerk, . . . got up at three o'clock in the morning on the day the bomb fell. There was extra housework to do. Her eleven-month-old brother, Akio, had come down the day before with a serious stomach upset; her mother had taken him to the Tamura Pediatric Hospital and was staying there with him. Miss Sasaki, who was about twenty, had to cook breakfast for her father, a brother, a sister, and herself, and—since the hospital, because of the war, was unable to provide food—to prepare a whole day's meals for her mother and the baby, in time for her father, who worked in a factory making rubber earplugs for artillery crews, to take the food by on his way to the plant. When she had finished

▼Critical Viewing How effectively do these remains of the sacred tree of a Hiroshima temple convey the physical and emotional devastation of the blast? Explain. **[Evaluate]**

ENRICHMENT: Science Connection

The Manhattan Project

In 1939, Albert Einstein wrote to President Roosevelt, warning him that the Germans were trying to build a nuclear weapon. Roosevelt put the Army's chief engineer in charge of developing an American bomb first. A number of Nobel Prize-winning physicists, along with several university laboratories, were involved in the Manhattan Project, the program that developed the first atomic bomb. The top-secret undertaking took seven years, employed over 120,000 people, and cost more than two billion dollars.

The main laboratory, in Los Alamos, New Mexico, was run by physicist J. Robert Oppenheimer. There, scientists worked out the problems of maintaining the nuclear chain reaction necessary for a sustained explosion. Complexes in Tennessee and Washington state provided the unstable forms of uranium and plutonium that would power the bomb.

and had cleaned and put away the cooking things, it was nearly seven. The family lived in Koi, and she had a forty-five-minute trip to the tin works, in the section of town called Kannonmachi. She was in charge of the personnel records in the factory. She left Koi at seven, and as soon as she reached the plant, she went with some of the other girls from the personnel department to the factory auditorium. A prominent local Navy man, a former employee, had committed suicide the day before by throwing himself under a train—a death considered honorable enough to warrant a memorial service, which was to be held at the tin works at ten o'clock that morning. In the large hall, Miss Sasaki and the others made suitable preparations for the meeting. This work took about twenty minutes.

Miss Sasaki went back to her office and sat down at her desk. She was quite far from the windows, which were off to her left, and behind her were a couple of tall bookcases containing all the books of the factory library, which the personnel department had organized. She settled herself at her desk, put some things in a drawer, and shifted papers. She thought that before she began to make entries in her lists of new employees, discharges, and departures for the Army, she would chat for a moment with the girl at her right. Just as she turned her head away from the windows, the room was filled with a blinding light. She was paralyzed by fear, fixed still in her chair for a long moment (the plant was 1,600 yards from the center).

Everything fell, and Miss Sasaki lost consciousness. The ceiling dropped suddenly and the wooden floor above collapsed in splinters and the people up there came down and the roof above them gave way; but principally and first of all, the bookcases right behind her swooped forward and the contents threw her down, with her left leg horribly twisted and breaking underneath her. There, in the tin factory, in the first moment of the atomic age, a human being was crushed by books.

John Hersey

(1914–1993)

Born in China to American parents and raised there until age ten, John Hersey returned repeatedly to East Asia during his long career as a war correspondent, novelist, and essayist. During the 1940s, Hersey traveled to China and Japan as a correspondent for *The New Yorker* and *Time* magazines. He also used these visits to gather material for his most famous and acclaimed book, *Hiroshima*. This remarkable report of the devastation caused by the atomic bomb first appeared in *The New Yorker*, when Wallace Shawn, the editor at that time, made the unprecedented decision to bump all of the magazine's other editorial content to publish Hersey's work as a four-part article.

Connecting Literature Past and Present

1. (a) In what way are the everyday details that Hersey provides about Miss Toshiko Sasaki's life similar to those provided in Amichai's poem "The Diameter of the Bomb"? (b) How do they differ?
2. Which has a stronger impact on you—the poetic account of a terrorist's bomb or this nonfiction account of a wartime bombing? Explain.
3. In what other literary works that you have read have tiny, ordinary decisions made the difference between life and death? Explain.

CUSTOMIZE INSTRUCTION FOR UNIVERSAL ACCESS

For Special Needs Students	For Gifted/Talented Students
Focus students' attention on the emotional reactions Hersey's work achieves. Clarify that because the work was written as a nonfiction news article, it features real people with real experiences. Read several passages aloud, directing students' attention to phrases and descriptions that might be especially moving or disturbing. Invite students to share their own feelings about war with the class aloud or on paper.	Remind students of how Hersey uses details to evoke emotion. Students can depict the emotions of the survivors by writing and performing a dramatic reading. Have each student choose a character from the selection. Then, they can write a story from their chosen character's point of view, as if he or she is speaking to an audience. Students should describe the events of the characters' daily lives before and after the bomb dropped. Each student can perform his or her dramatic reading for the class.

In the Shadows of Destruction

- After students read the last paragraph on p. 1327, draw their attention to the bookcases that fell on Miss Sasaki.
- Ask students the following question: What might the bookcases and the books they hold represent? Possible response: Hersey is calling attention to a great irony. In the atomic age, the knowledge embodied in books can be used not only to help and enlighten people but also to destroy them.

Background

John Hersey

Tell students that the ability to report on the progress of World War II fighting from virtually any location around the world via print, radio, and film allowed journalists such as John Hersey to bring the horrors of war home to many people in a way that previously had not been possible. In addition, rapid reporting allowed Hersey to discuss the moral implications of this and other current political and historical events. For example, in 1945, he won a Pulitzer Prize for his novel *A Bell for Adano*, in which an American major discovers the human dignity of the villagers who were his enemies in World War II.

Answers

Connecting Literature Past and Present

1. **(a)** Both Hersey and Amichai provide everyday details about the impact of a bomb on a young woman. **(b)** Hersey's account names the woman and gives details of her day before the bomb hits. Amichai does not name the woman and focuses on her experience (death) after the bomb hits.
2. Possible response: The nonfiction account has a stronger impact because it includes more detail, names the people, and is a true story.
3. Possible response: In his account *Night*, Elie Wiesel's many ordinary and extraordinary decisions, such as his decision about whether to share his food with his father, make the difference between life and death.

Twigs • My mother would lose herself ... • She used to throw her old crockery ... • On Living

Lesson Objectives

1. **To analyze and respond to literary elements**
   - Literary Analysis: Free Verse
   - Comparing Literary Works: Theme: The Extraordinary in the Ordinary
2. **To read, comprehend, analyze, and critique poetry**
   - Reading Strategy: Listening
   - Reading Check Questions
   - Review and Assess Questions
   - Assessment Practice (ATE)
3. **To develop word analysis skills, fluency, and systematic vocabulary**
   - Vocabulary Development Lesson: Latin Prefixes *con-* and *contra-*
4. **To understand and apply written and oral language conventions**
   - Spelling Strategy
   - Grammar and Style Lesson: Linking Verbs and Subject Complements
5. **To understand and apply appropriate writing and research strategies**
   - Writing Lesson: Comparison-and-Contrast Essay
   - Extension Activity: Letter to the World
6. **To understand and apply listening and speaking strategies**
   - Extension Activity: Illustrated Reading

10TH GRADE TEACHING A TENTH-GRADE COURSE

The literature in this section can be taught as part of a rich, balanced world literature course for tenth-grade students. For a full outline of such a course, see pp. T46–T48 in Volume I of this Teacher's Edition.

STEP-BY-STEP TEACHING GUIDE	PACING GUIDE
PRETEACH	
Motivate Students and Provide Background	
Use the Motivation activity (ATE p. 1328)	5 min.
Read and discuss author and background features (SE pp. 1328, 1330, 1332, 1334; ATE p. 1328) [A]	5 min.
Introduce the Concepts	
Introduce the Literary Analysis and Reading Strategy concepts (SE/ATE p. 1329) [A]	15 min.
Pronounce the vocabulary words and read their definitions (SE p. 1329)	5 min.
TEACH	
Monitor Comprehension	
Informally monitor comprehension by circulating while students read independently or in groups [A]	25 min.
Monitor students' comprehension with the Reading Check note (SE/ATE p. 1335)	as students read
Develop vocabulary with the Vocabulary notes (SE pp. 1330, 1331, 1332, 1333; ATE p. 1330)	as students read
Develop Understanding	
Develop students' understanding of free verse with the Literary Analysis annotations (SE/ATE pp. 1330, 1333, 1335) [A]	5 min.
Develop students' ability to listen to sounds in poetry, using the Reading Strategy annotations (SE/ATE pp. 1332, 1336) [A]	5 min.
ASSESS	
Assess Mastery	
Assess students' mastery of the Reading Strategy and Literary Analysis concepts by having them answer the Review and Assess questions (SE/ATE p. 1337)	15 min.
Use one or more of the print, software, or transparency Assessment Resources (ATE p. 1339) [A]	up to 45 min.
EXTEND	
Apply Understanding	
Have students complete the Vocabulary Development Lesson and the Grammar and Style Lesson (SE p. 1338) [A]	20 min.
Apply students' ability to use questions to gather details, using the Writing Lesson (SE/ATE p. 1339) [A]	45 min.
Apply students' understanding of the selections, using one or more of the Extension Activities (SE p. 1339)	20–90 min.

[A] ACCELERATED INSTRUCTION: Use the strategies and activities identified with an [A].

10TH GRADE TEACHING TENTH-GRADE STUDENTS For support in teaching the selection(s) to tenth-grade students, see the Step-by-Step Teaching notes identified with the icon shown here.

UNIVERSAL ACCESS
- ● = Below-Level Students
- ▲ = On-Level Students
- ■ = Above-Level Students

Time and Resource Manager

Reading Level: Average, Challenging, Challenging, Average
Average Number of Instructional Days: 3

RESOURCES		
PRINT	**TRANSPARENCIES**	**TECHNOLOGY**
• **Beyond Literature,** Cross-Curricular Connection: Geography, p. 65 ▲ ■		
• **Selection Support Workbook:** ● ▲ ■ Literary Analysis, p. 260 Reading Strategy, p. 259 Build Vocabulary, p. 257	• **Literary Analysis and Reading Transparencies,** pp. 129 and 130 ● ▲ ■	
		• **Listening to Literature** ● ▲ ■ Audiocassettes Audio CDs
• **Literary Analysis for Enrichment,** p. 65 ■	• **Fine Art Transparencies,** Art Transparency 25 ● ▲ ■	
• **Formal Assessment:** Selection Test, pp. 225–227 ● ▲ ■ • **Open-Book Tests,** pp. 193–195 ● ▲ ■ • **Performance Assessment and Portfolio Management,** pp. 15, 31 ● ▲ ■ • PRENTICE HALL ASSESSMENT SYSTEM ● ▲ ■	• PRENTICE HALL ASSESSMENT SYSTEM ● ▲ ■ **Skills Practice Answers and Explanations on Transparencies**	• **Test Bank Software** ● ▲ ■
• **Selection Support Workbook:** ● ▲ ■ Grammar and Style, p. 258 • **Writing and Grammar,** Diamond Level ● ▲ ■ • **Extension Activities,** p. 65 ● ▲ ■	• **Daily Language Practice Transparencies** ● ▲ • **Writing Models and Graphic Organizers on Transparencies,** pp. 95–97 ● ▲ ■	• **Writing and Grammar iText CD-ROM** ● ▲ ■ ***Take It to the Net*** PHSchool.com

BLOCK SCHEDULING: Use one 90-minute class period to preteach the selection(s) and have students read them. Use a second 90-minute class period to assess students' mastery of skills and have them complete one of the Extension Activities.

PRETEACH

Step-by-Step Teaching Guide for pp. 1328–1329

Motivation

Invite students to imagine that they suddenly have been forced to leave their homes to live in another country. Then, ask them to list ordinary events, people, or objects they might miss. To guide students in creating their lists, explain that sometimes the things most important to a person may seem small and unremarkable to someone else: the taste of certain foods or the sight of someone sweeping a floor.

❶ Background

More About the Authors

Taha Muhammad Ali has lived through Arab-Israeli conflicts since his village was destroyed in 1948. His poetry, constructed of short lines with differing rhythms and filled with everyday village imagery, depicts the color and violence of his besieged land.

Both Arabic and French culture infuse the work of Lebanese poet and novelist Vénus Khoury-Ghata. Her subject matter is often based on childhood experiences in her mother's Lebanese village.

Nazlm Hikmet combines elements of Turkish folk and classical poetry as well as Western and Eastern traditions in his poems, which realistically address universal humanist and political themes. His poetry and plays, initially censored in Turkey, were published and widely read there after his death.

Geography Note

Draw students' attention to the map on this page. Point out that Turkey was once part of the Ottoman Empire, which lasted for 600 years and encompassed territories from southeast Europe to North Africa and included the Arabian Peninsula.

Prepare to Read

Twigs ◆ My mother would lose herself . . . ◆ ❶ She used to throw her old crockery . . . ◆ On Living

Taha Muhammad Ali (b. 1931)

Galilee, the native land of Taha Muhammad Ali (ta′ Ha moo Ham′ id a lē′), is a bit of history come to life. According to the Bible, Jesus grew up and preached in the region. Now a part of Israel, the land also bears the scars where history has been violently erased. Saffuriya, the small Galilean village in which Ali was born, was largely destroyed in the first Arab-Israeli war of 1948.

Escape Ali and his family escaped the destruction of their village by fleeing to Lebanon. A year later, Ali crossed back into Israel and resettled in the city of Nazareth, also in Galilee.

Memory It is perhaps ironic that, although part of his past had been destroyed, Ali turned to the work of memory. By day, he operated a souvenir shop in the old quarter of Nazareth, selling items to tourists who wanted to remember the city. At night, Ali educated himself in classical Arabic poetry. Eventually, he began writing poems himself. Today, Ali is among the foremost contemporary Palestinian poets.

Nazlm Hikmet (1902–1963)

As an old empire crumbled, Nazlm Hikmet (nä zəm′ hik met′) turned to a radical vision of the future. The son of a Turkish diplomat, Hikmet was born in Salonika, Greece. The collapse of Turkey's Ottoman Empire at the end of World War I prompted Hikmet to join the cause of Turkish nationalism. Later, he traveled to the Soviet Union, where he studied radical political theory.

Dangerous Rebellions Hikmet returned home to fight injustice, publishing essays, plays, and poetry. A rebel in more than politics, Hikmet wrote free verse in defiance of literary conventions. The authoritarian Turkish government prosecuted him for his political views, and he served years in prison.

Prison and Exile In 1938, Hikmet was accused of inciting a military revolt—soldiers had been found reading his poetry. Imprisoned again, he was not released until 1950. A year later, further persecution forced him to flee Turkey by motorboat in a storm. Hikmet spent the rest of his life in exile. Today, he is considered modern Turkey's greatest poet.

Vénus Khoury-Ghata (b. 1937)

Vénus Khoury-Ghata (vā no͞os′ khour′ ē gha′ ta) has lived up to her first name, taken from the Roman goddess of love and beauty—she was honored as Miss Beirut in 1959! Today, however, this accomplished poet is better remembered for the literary awards she has won, such as the prestigious Prix Apollinaire.

Becoming Inspired Khoury-Ghata was born in Lebanon when that nation was still under French rule. She grew up in Beirut, the capital, but spent summers in her mother's village, the hometown of renowned poet Kahlil Gibran. Stories about Gibran brought out Khoury-Ghata's interest in poetry. She began writing poems in French.

Becoming Famous One day, a Beirut neighbor who was also a poet read her poems. Impressed, he took them to a small publisher, who put out a volume of Khoury-Ghata's verse. A French scholar visiting Beirut brought the book to a larger publisher. Eventually, Khoury-Ghata and her husband, a French scientist, moved to Paris. There, she began winning prizes for her poetry. She has also published more than a dozen novels.

TEACHING RESOURCES

The following resources can be used to enrich or extend the instruction for pp. 1328–1329.

Background

Beyond Literature, p. 65

Take It to the Net

Visit PHSchool.com for background on the authors.

Literary Analysis

Literary Analysis and Reading Transparencies, Free Verse, p. 129 ■

Selection Support: Literary Analysis, p. 260

Reading

Literary Analysis and Reading Transparencies, Listening, p. 130 ■

■ **BLOCK SCHEDULING:** Resources marked with this symbol provide varied instruction during 90-minute blocks.

Preview

Connecting to the Literature

The beating sun, the thud of waves—a shocking rush of cold water . . . Afterward, riding home, you realize how dazzling the day was—just when it is over. These poets look at loss to show how dazzling life itself is.

2 Literary Analysis

Free Verse

Free verse is poetry not unified by a regular, rhythmical pattern, or meter. To unify their poems, free-verse writers use other strategies, including these:

- creating a lively voice using conversational speech
- writing in fragments, each of which, like a saying or a riddle, combines ideas and images to provoke thought
- weaving together vivid images using dreamlike associations

Note the techniques these free-verse poets use to unify their work.

Comparing Literary Works

One source of unity in a free-verse poem is a **theme,** or central message. These three poems share a theme: The ordinary routines, pleasures, and needs of life are actually the most extraordinary—they are immeasurably valuable. In "Twigs," for example, the poet muses that

it has taken me / all of sixty years / to understand / that water
is the finest drink, / and bread the most delicious food, . . .

As you read, use a chart like this one to compare ways in which the poets develop the theme of the extraordinary in the ordinary.

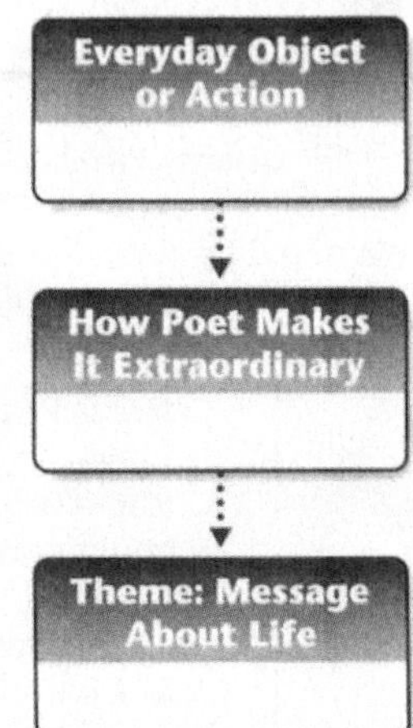

3 Reading Strategy

Listening

To appreciate a poem, **listen** to the music the poet (or translator) has created with words. Read the poem aloud, listening for the following:

- rhythms of the lines, whether soothing or rousing, lazy or busy
- echoes, such as repeated phrases or repeated consonant sounds
- contrasts in sound, such as between long and short vowels
- texture of words, such as the "crunchiness" of *crunchy*

Vocabulary Development

consolation (kän′ sə lā′ shən) *n.* comfort; something that eases disappointment or sadness (p. 1330)

brevity (brev′ ə tē) *n.* briefness (p. 1330)

putrefy (pyo͞o′ trə fī′) *v.* rot (p. 1331)

foundering (foun′ dər iŋ) *n.* stumbling; sinking; becoming stuck (p. 1332)

self-abnegation (self ab′ nə gā′ shən) *n.* self-denial; lack of consideration for oneself or one's own interests (p. 1332)

contrary (kän′ trer′ ē) *adj.* unfavorable; opposing (p. 1333)

dubious (do͞o′ bē əs) *adj.* doubtful; uncertain; suspect (p. 1333)

2 Literary Analysis

Free Verse

- Tell students that as they read, they will focus on free verse—poetry that lacks a regular rhythmic pattern.
- Model the use of the graphic organizer on the student page, and direct students to use a similar organizer as they read the poems to understand how ordinary objects become special.
- Use the Free Verse transparency in **Literary Analysis and Reading Transparencies,** p. 129, to demonstrate how poets create works using irregular meter.

3 Reading Strategy

Listening

- Play samples of different types of music for students, stopping after each piece to ask students to describe the mental images created by the music. Tell students that the effect of a poem comes not just from the literal meaning of its words but also from rhythms, echoes, contrasts, and word textures.
- As students read these selections, ask them to identify examples of rhythm, echo, contrast, and word texture.
- If students need extra practice in listening for music in poetry, use the Listening transparency in **Literary Analysis and Reading Transparencies,** p. 130.

Vocabulary Development

- Pronounce each vocabulary word for students, and read the definitions as a class. Have students identify any words with which they are already familiar.

CUSTOMIZE INSTRUCTION FOR UNIVERSAL ACCESS

For Less Proficient Readers	For English Learners	For Advanced Readers
Before students read, have them skim the poems to find the periods that mark the end of a thought. This process will help them look for closure beyond the end of each line. Then, pair students and have them take turns reading each stanza aloud to each other, paying close attention to all the punctuation marks.	To help students understand difficult vocabulary and complicated poetic images, do a preliminary reading of the poems with them, defining and pronouncing unfamiliar words. Then, invite them to listen to the selections on the **Listening to Literature Audiocassettes** or **Listening to Literature CDs.**	Invite students to write about Ali's reference to Shakespeare's *King Lear* in his poem "Twigs." Students should also speculate about why this English play appeals to this contemporary Palestinian poet. Help students consider universal themes in both works.

E-Teach

Visit e-Teach at PHSchool.com for teachers' essays on how to teach, with questions and answers.

TEACH

Step-by-Step Teaching Guide for pp. 1330–1336

Teaching Tenth-Grade Students

10TH GRADE Tell students that the poems in this grouping have been inspired by the loss of loved ones and home, either through political upheaval or through the process of growing up and becoming assimilated into another culture.

1 About the Selection

In "Twigs," the speaker reflects on how quickly life on Earth passes and discusses learning to appreciate simple things and fundamental values.

2 Literary Analysis

Free Verse

- Explain that *scansion* is the process of analyzing a poem's metrical pattern.
- Have students scan the first three lines. Ask whether the meter is regular or irregular.
  Answer: The scansion is: nEIther MUsic/ FAME nor WEALTH/ NOT EVen POeTRY itSELF. The meter is irregular.
- Ask students to respond to the Literary Analysis item on p. 1320: Identify two characteristics of this stanza that show that the poem is in free verse.
  Answer: The poem's meter and rhyme are not regular, and the poem uses riddlelike fragments to refer to *King Lear*.

3 Vocabulary Development

Word Analysis: Latin Prefixes *con-* and *contra-*

- Invite a volunteer to read aloud the definition of *consolation*.
- Then, have students link their knowledge of the Latin prefix *con-* to the definition. Encourage them to consult a dictionary if needed.
  Answer: *Consolation* means "being comforted." The prefix *con-*, which means "with" or "together," is combined with the root *solari*, which means "solace."

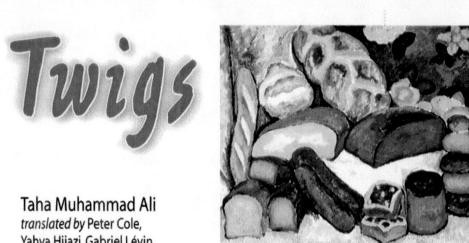

1

Twigs

Taha Muhammad Ali
translated by Peter Cole, Yahya Hijazi, Gabriel Lévin

Background

Although Taha Muhammad Ali's Galilean hometown of Saffuriya was destroyed in the Arab-Israeli war of 1948, the language of that village—a spoken dialect of Arabic—is very much alive in Ali's poems. Ali is known for using both spoken Arabic and traditional literary Arabic (a descendant of the language of the Qur'an) in his works. This synthesis makes his poems at once intensely personal and powerfully universal.

2

Neither music
fame nor wealth,
not even poetry itself,
could provide consolation
for life's brevity,
or the fact that *King Lear*
is a mere eighty pages long, and comes to an end,
and for the thought that one might suffer greatly
on account of a rebellious child.

*

My love for you
is what's magnificent,
but I, you, and the others,
most likely,
are ordinary people.

*

My poem
goes beyond poetry
because you
exist
beyond the realm of women.

Literary Analysis
Free Verse Identify two characteristics of this stanza that show that the poem is in free verse.

consolation (kän′ sə lā′ shən) *n.* comfort; something that eases disappointment or sadness

brevity (brev′ ə tē) *n.* briefness

TEACHING RESOURCES

The following resources can be used to enrich or extend the instruction for pp. 1330–1336.

Literary Analysis

- **Selection Support:** Literary Analysis, p. 260
- **Writing Models and Graphic Organizers on Transparencies,** pp. 75–77

Reading

- **Selection Support:** Reading Strategy, p. 259; Build Vocabulary, p. 257

- **Listening to Literature Audiocassettes**
- **Listening to Literature CDs**

Extension

- **Fine Art Transparencies,** Art Transparency 25 (Have students compare ways in which both Robert Rauschenberg in this assemblage and the poets in these groupings make use of fragments or "snapshots" of life.)

BLOCK SCHEDULING: Resources marked with this symbol provide varied instruction during 90-minute blocks.

*

And so
it has taken me
all of sixty years
to understand
that water is the finest drink,
and bread the most delicious food,
and that art is worthless
unless it plants
a measure of splendor in people's hearts.

*

After we die,
and the weary heart
has lowered its final eyelid
on all that we've done,
and on all that we've longed for,
on all that we've dreamt of,
all we've desired
or felt,
hate will be
the first thing
to putrefy
within us.

1989–1991

putrefy (pyōō´ trə fī´) v. rot

Review and Assess

Thinking About the Selection

1. **Respond:** Do you find this poem comforting? Why or why not?
2. **(a) Recall:** Name the three facts in the first stanza that make the speaker inconsolable. **(b) Connect:** What do these three facts have in common?
3. **(a) Recall:** In the second stanza, what is called "magnificent" and what "ordinary"? **(b) Interpret:** In what sense does what is magnificent go beyond the ordinary, yet stay within it? **(c) Connect:** Given this magnificence in ordinary life, explain why the person addressed in this stanza exists "beyond the realm of women."
4. **(a) Interpret:** Restate the messages of the fourth and fifth stanzas in your own words. **(b) Draw Conclusions:** In what sense are these stanzas answers to the first stanza?
5. **Connect:** Explain the sense in which each stanza is like a "twig" growing from a larger, common branch.

Themes in World Literature

4 *Writers in Exile*

Ali, Khoury-Ghata, and Hikmet all have lived through exile in one form or another. For some writers, exile is voluntary. In other cases, like Hikmet's, the exiled writer has been forced to leave a politically troubled nation where honest, critical writing is dangerous. Among these prominent writers-in-exile are:

- ancient Latin poet Ovid (43 B.C.–A.D. 17?), who offended the Roman emperor Augustus and was sent to live in a fishing village by the Black Sea, far from his beloved Rome. (For more on Ovid, see page 514.)
- contemporary Russian novelist Alexander Solzhenitsyn (b. 1918), who was deported from the U.S.S.R. in 1973 after publishing *The Gulag Archipelago*, his history of Soviet forced labor camps. He now lives in the United States. (For more on Solzhenitsyn, see page 1294.)
- contemporary African poet Abena Busia (b. 1953). Busia followed her father, one of Ghana's first modern leaders, into exile when his government was overturned. Today, she lives, writes, and teaches in New Jersey.

CUSTOMIZE INSTRUCTION FOR UNIVERSAL ACCESS

For English Learners	For Gifted/Talented Students
Students may be unfamiliar with William Shakespeare's play *King Lear*. Discuss the story line with them, helping them see why the play continues to be read, staged, and enjoyed hundreds of years after it was written. Explain to students the tension between King Lear and his three daughters, showing how "a rebellious child" opens a rift that leads to tragedy both in Lear's kingdom and in his family. Ask students to share stories from their own cultures that are beloved and read by generation after generation.	Ask students to describe the types of love that are presented in the poem: love of life, love of a story, love of a child, love of a woman. Ask students whether the poem makes distinctions about which of these types of love is the most important. Have students create visual representations, in any medium they choose, of the kind of unconditional love that can plant "splendor" in people's hearts and how the things that people love can change as they grow older.

4 Background

Writers in Exile

Abena Busia, according to her own account, was exiled twice: once as a child (1959–1966) and once as a young woman (1972–1978). In the first instance, her father was the leader of the opposition, and in the second instance, the ousted prime minister. In her book *Testimonies of Exile*, Abena Busia explores the theme of alienation in a series of fifty-six poems. She examines the ramifications of alienation from one's homeland, noting that alienation transcends geographical borders and infiltrates one's sense of history, culture, and self.

Answers for p. 1331

Review and Assess

1. Possible response: The poem is comforting because it offers the hope of wisdom and peace.
2. **(a)** Life is brief; *King Lear* is only eighty pages long; and a rebellious child causes suffering. **(b)** They share the idea of loss: through death, the end of a story, and estrangement from a child.
3. **(a)** The speaker's love for a woman is "magnificent." People are "ordinary." **(b)** "Ordinary" people are limited by their humanity. They surpass this limitation when they love others. **(c)** The poet's feelings for the woman elevate her from the ordinary to the world of people and things made extraordinary by love.
4. **(a)** Fourth stanza: Age brings appreciation for life's ordinary elements. Fifth stanza: Hate does not have the power to endure. **(b)** Stanzas 4 and 5 render the poet's concerns in stanza 1 meaningless.
5. The common branch is loss, or the human condition. Each twig or stanza represents a stage in the speaker's growing ability to cope with loss, from the first inconsolable reaction to its inevitability and then to mature understanding of the power of love.

5 About the Selection

In "My mother would lose herself . . .," the author paints a portrait of her mother absorbed in the intensity and fervor of her sweeping. The speaker gives the mother an all-encompassing power, conjuring up the "wind" as she completes her tasks.

6 Reading Strategy

Listening

- Discuss with students how the texture of words such as *puffing* and *battling* can mimic the actions of the speaker's mother.
- Then, draw students' attention to the Reading Strategy item on p. 1332: Find a phrase in lines 1–4 with a distinctive sound texture and describe that texture.
  Possible response: The phrase "lose herself in puffing movements of her broom" contrasts smooth vowels with sharp consonants. The sustained, gliding "oo" sound in *lose, movements,* and *broom* contrasts with the quicker *p* and *f* sounds in *puffing.*

Monitor Progress Ask students to find other examples of distinctive sound textures in the first stanza of the poem.
Possible response: In the phrase "the dampness she called crumbled water swamp," the smooth, sustained sound of *s* in *dampness* and *she* contrasts with the sharp, abrupt sounds of *c, d,* and *t* in *crumbled water.*

Reteach If students have difficulty with the Reading Strategy, use the **Selection Support** booklet, p. 259, to help them practice the strategy.

7 Critical Thinking

Interpret

- Invite a volunteer to read aloud the bracketed passage.
- Ask students what the speaker thinks of her mother's sweeping.
  Possible response: The speaker admires her mother's determination and absorption in her task. Her mother's sweeping seems larger than life, or as powerful as the wind.

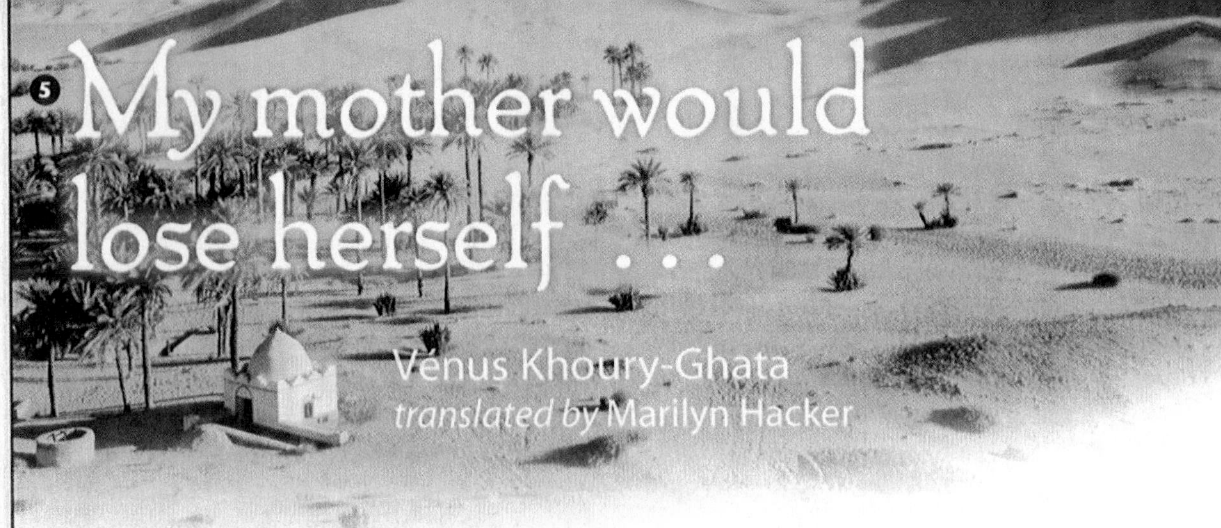

5 My mother would lose herself . . .

Vénus Khoury-Ghata
translated by Marilyn Hacker

Background

In summers as a child, Vénus Khoury-Ghata would visit her mother's village, a joyful escape from city life. There, she read the works of the village's most famous son, poet Kahlil Gibran, and watched the mountain women go about their daily chores with steady industry. Her memories of these visits have sustained her as an adult. The grown-up Khoury-Ghata realized one day that despite her material wealth, her life was lacking in joy. She says, "I had to produce something, and live the way my mother had lived. . . . After seven hours of writing I'm glad to do some ironing." These poems by Khoury-Ghata will introduce you both to her mother and to her magical memories of summers in a beloved village.

6

My mother would lose herself in the puffing movements of her
 broom
battling the sand which she called desert
the dampness she called crumbled water
swamp

7

remote from the world her sweeper's hands
exhumed invisible corpses
pursued the least <u>foundering</u> of the wind
the slightest stain of darkness
she swept with so much <u>self-abnegation</u>
and burst out laughing in the worst storm
for fear of appearing ill-tempered

Mother you were so modest
you took no credit for the wind which blew just for your arms as
 they swept.

Reading Strategy
Listening Find a phrase in lines 1–4 with a distinctive sound texture and describe that texture.

foundering (foun′ dər iŋ) *n.* stumbling; sinking; becoming stuck

self-abnegation (self ăb′ nə gā′ shən) *n.* self-denial; lack of consideration for oneself or one's own interests

ENRICHMENT: Literature Connection

A Double Life

Vénus Khoury-Ghata is a Lebanese poet who has lived in France for many years and writes in French. In an Afterword to her book of poetry *She Says*, Khoury-Ghata explains what it is like to live with two languages:

> I'm a bigamist. I lead a double life under cover of writing. One day I'll write a book revealing the life I lead in the light of day with the French language and my clandestine life with Arabic. I move from the first, rigorous, meticulous, to the second: ample, generous in its leaps and gambols. . . .
>
> Why, I've asked myself for years, do I stubbornly insist on telling my country's story in a language not its own? The answer is simple: living in Lebanon, I wouldn't have written books; I would have had children and cooked. The need to tell about Lebanon has come with distance. I needed to reinvent it as it was, divided, wounded, to give myself the illusion of sharing the daily terrors of my compatriots.

8 # She used to throw her old crockery . . .

Vénus Khoury-Ghata *translated by* Marilyn Hacker

She used to throw her old crockery at the moon
9 which mends chipped plates
darns wedding sheets
and sorts lamplight-yellowed snapshots by degrees of sadness

The whole universe shared my mother's household chores
contrary winds blew into her bureau drawers
bargained between her shutters
and swept towards town the dream-crumbs she nibbled in her sleep

Negligent mother
clouds of a dubious whiteness dried out on your clothesline
provoking the nightingales' sarcasm and saddening the sun
you reported them missing to the police when the wind carried them out of the valley
called the wind a thief of sheets and cattle
then withdrew your complaint when the clouds came home to you,
fog kneeling on your doorstep.

Literary Analysis
Free Verse In what way do lines 2–4 echo one another?

contrary (kän′ trer′ ē) *adj.* unfavorable; opposing

dubious (do͞o′ bē əs) *adj.* doubtful; uncertain; suspect

Review and Assess

Thinking About the Selections

1. **Respond:** Would you like to meet the poet's mother? Explain.
2. **(a) Recall:** In line 1 of "My mother would lose herself . . . ," what does the poet say her mother would do? **(b) Infer:** What does this phrase suggest about the mother's personality?
3. **(a) Interpret:** Explain why the images in the second stanza make her sweeping seem like a serious task. **(b) Connect:** In what sense do the last two lines of the poem turn around the idea that the mother disappears into her sweeping?
4. **(a) Recall:** What does the universe do in the second stanza of "She used to throw her old crockery . . . "? **(b) Interpret:** How does this image capture a child's idea of his or her mother?
5. **Connect:** Explain the way in which the concluding image of fog builds on the notion of the mother's relation to the world.

CUSTOMIZE INSTRUCTION FOR UNIVERSAL ACCESS

For Less Proficient Readers	For Gifted/Talented Students
Lead students in a group discussion about their own mothers. Encourage students to share anecdotes that illustrate the essence of their mothers. Also, invite students to discuss the difference between the way they viewed their mothers ten years ago and the way they do now. Encourage students to write about their mothers after the discussion. Invite students to share their writing with the class.	Ask students to create poems in which they capture the essence of their own mothers. Tell students to combine reality with whimsy in much the same way that Khoury-Ghata does in her poems. Then, have students present their poems to the class, explaining their choice of language, style, and imagery. Suggest that students give these poems as gifts to their mothers.

8 About the Selection

In "She used to throw her old crockery . . . ," the poet captures the energy and spirit of a passionate, industrious woman. The poem celebrates the mother, who seems at once to command and to be victim to the powerful, changeable forces of nature.

9 Literary Analysis

Free Verse

- Read aloud the first stanza.
- Discuss with students how the line breaks affect their reading of the poem.
- Then, ask students the Literary Analysis question on p. 1333: In what way do lines 2–4 echo one another?
  Possible response: The three lines have a parallel grammatical construction.

Answers for p. 1333

Review and Assess

1. Possible response: Yes; she sounds passionate and amusing.
2. **(a)** The poet's mother would lose herself in the puffing movements of her broom. **(b)** The mother is focused and energetic.
3. **(a)** The task seems serious because the "whole universe" participates. The inclusion of the wind's resistance adds gravity to ordinary work. **(b)** In the last two lines, the mother and the wind become separate.
4. **(a)** The universe shares the chores with the mother.
   (b) Possible response: The image shows the power that children attribute to their parents' actions.
5. Possible response: The image suggests that the mother has the power to reach out into the world, find her lost "clouds," and return them to their proper places.

❿ About the Selection

In "On Living," the poet emphasizes the importance of living life with intensity, even with ferocity. To live "as if we will never die," says the author, people must take nothing for granted, must love with their whole being, and must always keep in mind that the great gift of life will someday end.

⓫ Background

Literature

Nazlm Hikmet is often compared with the nineteenth-century American poet Walt Whitman. Thematically and stylistically, both poets shared an idealism and a freshness that earned them many followers. Both flouted traditional poetic conventions in favor of free verse and colloquial language. Both celebrated the self for its own sake while never forgetting the self as a national citizen and, more broadly, as a member of the human race.

Unlike Whitman, however, Hikmet was persecuted and exiled because of his political vision. Whereas Whitman expressed his young nation's collective optimism, Hikmet criticized an ancient, repressive government and suffered greatly for doing so.

❿ On Living

Nazım Hikmet

translated by Randy Blasing *and* Mutlu Konuk

Background

Nazım Hikmet was one of Turkey's greatest modern poets. His commitment to a grand political vision, his influence on later poets, and his expansive style are comparable to those of the nineteenth-century American poet ⓫ Walt Whitman. His poems, including the one that appears here, are at once personal and public. They speak of the poet's self while speaking simultaneously of his beloved country and of the wider world.

ENRICHMENT: History Connection

From Ottoman Empire to the Republic of Turkey

The Ottoman Empire was founded by a Turkish tribal chieftain in the fourteenth century. The Empire began its slow decline beginning in the second half of the sixteenth century because its weak central government eventually resulted in lost territory and power. By 1853, Czar Nicholas I of Russia observed that the Empire could not endure much longer, saying, "We have on our hands a sick man, a very sick man."

Divergent European interests, especially those of Great Britain and Russia, supported the existence of the ailing Ottoman Empire until after World War I, during which it was allied with Germany. Defeat in this war and anger at postwar settlements, however, strengthened already fervent feelings of Turkish nationalism growing in the country.

Nationalists, under the leadership of Mustafa Kemal, formed their own government in Ankara, Turkey, effectively dissolving what remained of the Ottoman Empire.

I

Living is no laughing matter:
you must live with great seriousness
like a squirrel, for example—
I mean without looking for something beyond and above living,
I mean living must be your whole occupation.
Living is no laughing matter:
you must take it seriously,
12 so much so and to such a degree
that, for example, your hands tied behind your back,
your back to the wall,
or else in a laboratory
in your white coat and safety glasses,
you can die for people—
even for people whose faces you've never seen,
even though you know living
is the most real, the most beautiful thing.
I mean, you must take living so seriously
that even at seventy, for example, you'll plant olive trees—
and not for your children, either,
but because although you fear death you don't believe it,
because living, I mean, weighs heavier.

II

Let's say we're seriously ill, need surgery—
which is to say we might not get up
from the white table.
Even though it's impossible not to feel sad
about going a little too soon,
we'll still laugh at the jokes being told,
we'll look out the window to see if it's raining,
or still wait anxiously
for the latest newscast . . .
Let's say we're at the front—
for something worth fighting for, say.
There, in the first offensive, on that very day,
13 we might fall on our face, dead.
We'll know this with a curious anger,
but we'll still worry ourselves to death
about the outcome of the war, which could last years.
Let's say we're in prison
and close to fifty,
and we have eighteen more years, say,
before the iron doors will open.
We'll still live with the outside,
with its people and animals, struggle and wind—
I mean with the outside beyond the walls.
I mean, however and wherever we are,
we must live as if we will never die.

Literary Analysis
Free Verse Identify two phrases that make the poem sound conversational.

14 ✓**Reading Check**
According to the speaker, what might one do in old age, showing that one takes life "seriously"?

12 Critical Thinking

Interpret

- Have students read the bracketed passage independently.
- Ask them what the poet means when he says we must live "with great seriousness like a squirrel." Possible response: The whole focus of a squirrel's existence is the act of living. The squirrel does not look for meaning or existence beyond life.
- Then, ask students how the two situations in lines 5–16 are examples of living and dying seriously. Possible response: In the first situation, the poet describes being restrained and threatened with death, possibly by firing squad. In the second situation, a person is doing potentially dangerous experiments in a laboratory. In both instances, one must be willing to sacrifice one's own life for the benefit of life as a whole.

13 Literary Analysis

Free Verse

- Invite a pair of students to read aloud lines 22–46 to each other. Have them sit casually at a table and take turns reading the text, making their tone as conversational as possible.
- After this activity, read aloud the Literary Analysis item on p. 1335: Identify two phrases that make the poem sound conversational. Answer: "Let's say" and "I mean" are two conversational phrases in this section of the poem.

14 ✓Reading Check

In old age, one might plant olive trees.

CUSTOMIZE INSTRUCTION FOR UNIVERSAL ACCESS

For Special Needs Students	For Less Proficient Readers
Students may find the poem's long sentences difficult to follow. Point out the different types of punctuation used in the poem: colons, dashes, commas, and ellipses. Encourage students to pause when they come to these different types of punctuation. Tell students that they can then review the ideas that have been presented. In addition, have students read along with the **Listening to Literature Audiocassette** or **CD**.	Help students follow the "advice" the poem conveys on taking life seriously. Have them use the herringbone graphic organizer on pp. 75–77 of **Writing Models and Graphic Organizers on Transparencies** to help organize the speaker's arguments and images. When students have completed the herringbone organizer, have them talk through the "story" of the poem in their own words.

ASSESS

15 Reading Strategy

Listening

- Read aloud line 50.
- Ask the Reading Strategy item on p. 1336: Describe the contrasting vowel sounds in line 50.
  Possible response: The long vowel sounds in the words *mote* and *blue* contrast with the short vowel sounds in *gilded* and *velvet*.

Answers for p. 1336

Review and Assess

1. Possible response: The poet discusses a difficult topic in direct language.
2. **(a)** Serious living includes dying for a cause, taking risks to advance science, and planting trees. **(b)** Possible response: All are selfless actions.
3. **(a)** The three situations are a seriously ill person, a person injured in war, and a person in prison. **(b)** Possible response: Each person remains interested in the world although death is imminent.
4. Possible response: The nearness of death emphasizes that life is precious and should be experienced.
5. **(a)** The first two stanzas are about life; the last is about death. **(b)** Possible response: The last stanza supports the earlier ones in that "life is serious" and everything perishes, even the earth. The generalized message is that loving the world is the only way to say "I have lived."
6. Possible response: The conversational vocabulary is consistent with the seriousness of the message because it must be understood by everyone, not only academics.
7. **(a)** Possible response: A relative entered into what was her final illness. **(b)** Possible response: In this circumstance, as in those described by Hikmet, family members helped one another selflessly.

III

This earth will grow cold,
a star among stars
and one of the smallest,
a gilded mote on blue velvet—
I mean *this*, our great earth.
This earth will grow cold one day,
not like a block of ice
or a dead cloud even
but like an empty walnut it will roll along
in pitch-black space . . .
You must grieve for this right now
—you have to feel this sorrow now—
for the world must be loved this much
if you're going to say "I lived". . .

February 1948

Reading Strategy
Listening Describe the contrasting vowel sounds in line 50.

Review and Assess

Thinking About the Selection

1. **Respond:** What do you like or dislike about the poet's style? Explain.
2. **(a) Recall:** In the first stanza, what are the three examples of a person living "seriously"? **(b) Analyze:** What do the three examples have in common?
3. **(a) Recall:** What three situations are described in the second stanza? **(b) Connect:** How does each support the idea in line 45 that "we must live as if we will never die"?
4. **Generalize:** In the poem, what does the nearness of death emphasize about life?
5. **(a) Compare and Contrast:** Describe the main difference between the last stanza and the first two. **(b) Connect:** Discuss a way in which this stanza supports the message of the previous two, as well as a way in which it makes that message more general.
6. **Evaluate:** Do you think the poet's use of phrases such as "I mean" and "Let's say" helps convey the seriousness of his subject? Explain.
7. **(a) Apply:** Describe an event or a circumstance you have encountered in literature, film, or your own life in which life appeared in all its "seriousness." **(b) Compare:** Compare this circumstance to a situation described by Hikmet.

ASSESSMENT PRACTICE: Reading Comprehension

Using Context Clues to Determine Meanings (For more practice, see Test Preparation Workbook, p. 1.)

Many tests require students to use context clues to determine the meanings of unfamiliar words. Use the following example to show students how to use context clues to determine the meaning of a word.

Let's say we're at the front—
for something worth fighting for, say.
There, in the first offensive, on that very day,
We might fall on our face, dead.

In this passage, offensive means—

A impolite
B attack
C surrender
D warning

The context clues "for something worth fighting for" and "We might fall on our face, dead," indicate war or conflict. *A* is an adjective. *C* and *D* do not fit the context. *B* correctly fits the context clue of a fight or war.

Review and Assess

Literary Analysis

Free Verse

1. (a) In the **free-verse** poem "Twigs," in what way do the irregular line lengths in the first stanza match the pacing of the speaker's ideas?
2. (a) Identify four references to wind or air in "My mother would lose herself. . . ." (b) In what way is the last reference different from the first? (c) Explain how this pattern of imagery helps the reader see the mother as her child sees her—at the center of the world.
3. (a) In "She used to throw her old crockery . . . ," identify two images in which the poet weaves the natural world into her mother's housekeeping. (b) Explain how the last stanza turns this relationship between nature and mother into a small drama.
4. (a) Identify two repeated phrases in "On Living" that give it a conversational tone. (b) Why is this tone suited to a poem about the "seriousness" of even the small things in life?

Comparing Literary Works

5. Compare the speaker's **theme** in "Twigs" with the discoveries about life in one of the other poems.
6. Explain the way in which death helps Hikmet see the extraordinary value of the ordinary, whereas Khoury-Ghata finds this value in memories of her vanished childhood.

Reading Strategy

Listening

7. Using a chart like the one shown, examine sound devices in each of the four poems. In the first column, quote an example of a sound device and identify it (repetition, rhythm, or contrast). In the second column, explain which idea or image this device emphasizes.

Sound Device	Idea or Image Emphasized

Extend Understanding

8. **Cultural Connection:** Identify three ways individuals or groups in the United States may show respect for the beauty of everyday life.

Quick Review

Free verse is poetry that is not unified by a regular, rhythmical pattern. Writers of free verse may unify their poems by writing a series of thought-provoking fragments, by following the dream logic of images, or by creating a lively, conversational voice.

A **theme** is a central message or insight revealed by a literary work.

To **listen** to a work of poetry, notice the rhythm of its lines, repeated words or sounds, contrasting sounds, and the texture of words.

Take It to the Net

PHSchool.com

Take the interactive self-test online to check your understanding of these selections.

Answers for p. 1337

Review and Assess

1. Possible response: The varied line lengths reflect the way in which the speaker gathers thoughts and makes connections.
2. **(a)** The references to air are "puffing movements," "foundering of the wind," "worst storm," and "the wind which blew just for your arms." **(b)** The mother's sweeping has grown from small "puffing movements" to a powerful wind. **(c)** The imagery transforms the ordinary act of sweeping into the extraordinary act of harnessing the wind. The imagery credits the mother with being a force of nature.
3. **(a)** The natural world is woven into the mother's housekeeping when winds blow into bureau drawers and the sun is saddened by her imperfect "clouds." **(b)** The last stanza creates a drama when the mother reports to the police that the wind has stolen her "clouds." Mother and nature appear as equal forces in this clash.
4. **(a)** The phrases are "Let's say" and "I mean." **(b)** The tone is suited to a poem about life's seriousness because it makes the message accessible for all.
5. Possible response: "Twigs" uses the ordinary objects of "music," "wealth," "water," and "bread," to reinforce the theme that nothing in life is consolation for its loss. Similarly, "On Living" presents us with objects such as "the white table," "latest newscast,""iron doors," and "dead cloud," to describe junctures at which life could be lost.
6. In Hikmet's poem, each ordinary act in relation to death becomes life-affirming and "serious." The smallest events seem poignant and wondrous. Through her recollections, Khoury-Ghata invests her mother's actions with power and magic.
7. Possible response: **"Twigs": Sound Device:** "On all that we've done, and on all . . . on all . . . all (repetition); **Idea or Image:** the entirety of life; **"My mother": Sound Device:** " . . . she swept with so much self-abnegation" (alliteration); **Idea or Image:** playfulness; **"She**

continued

continued from right column

used to throw": Sound Device: "called the wind a thief of sheets and cattle" (rhythm); **Idea or Image:** the mother's displeasure; **"On Living": Sound Device:** Living is no laughing matter" (repetition); **Idea or Image:** Life must be lived seriously.

8. Possible response: People might show respect by planting neighborhood gardens, by disposing of trash, or by visiting the elderly.

ENRICHMENT: Further Reading

Other Works by the Authors

We strongly encourage you to review any selection before assigning or recommending it to students.

Never Mind: Twenty Poems And A Story, Ali

She Says: Bilingual Edition, Khoury-Ghata

Human Landscapes from My Country, Hikmet

Take It to the Net

Visit PHSchool.com for more information about the authors.

EXTEND

Answers for p. 1338

❶ Vocabulary Development

Word Analysis: Latin Prefixes con- and contra-

1. flowing together
2. to say the opposite
3. to make by bringing different elements together
4. goods whose import or export is against the law
5. to be in touch with

Fluency: Words in Context

Possible response:

1. The flowers provided consolation for the losers.
2. The party was so enjoyable that we were sorry for its brevity.
3. The vegetables began to putrefy after three weeks.
4. The foundering team lost the football game by twenty points.
5. Because of her self-abnegation, she gets little credit for her work.
6. The suspect claimed innocence, but evidence proved the contrary.
7. The possibility of sun tomorrow is dubious because of the clouds overhead.

Spelling Strategy

1. opposition
2. composition
3. declaration

❷ Grammar and Style

Practice

1. are ordinary people
2. none
3. is no laughing matter
4. none
5. it's impossible not to feel sad

Writing Application

Possible response:

The native grass is a waving lake. Its surface never seems still.

On the prairie, I become part of a never-ending story. I feel alive.

10TH GRADE For support in teaching the Grammar and Style Lesson to tenth graders, use **Writing and Grammar,** Platinum Level, Chapter 16, Section 3.

Integrate Language Skills

❶ Vocabulary Development Lesson

Word Analysis: Latin Prefixes *con-* and *contra-*

The prefix *con-* means "with" or "together." The prefix appears in the word *consolation,* which refers to a thing that "brings a person together with" comfort.

Do not confuse *con-* with the prefix *contra-,* meaning "against." This prefix appears in the word *contrary,* meaning "opposing or against something else."

With the help of a dictionary, define each of these words, using *with, together, against,* or *opposite* in each definition.

1. confluence
2. contradict
3. concoct
4. contraband
5. contact

Fluency: Words in Context

To practice using the vocabulary words listed on page 1329, write one sentence on each of the following topics, using the word given.

1. sad event (*consolation*)
2. party (*brevity*)
3. vegetable (*putrefy*)
4. football game (*foundering*)
5. injustice (*self-abnegation*)
6. evidence (*contrary*)
7. weather (*dubious*)

Spelling Strategy

When adding a suffix to a verb ending in *e,* the *e* is usually dropped or changed to another vowel. For example, *console* becomes *consolation.* Add the suffix *-tion* to each of these words:

1. oppose 2. compose 3. declare

❷ Grammar and Style Lesson

Linking Verbs and Subject Complements

A **linking verb**—such as *be, become, seem,* or *feel*—expresses a state of being. To determine whether a verb is a linking verb, replace it with a form of *be.* If the sentence still makes sense, then usually the verb is a linking verb.

A **subject complement** is the noun, pronoun, adjective, or clause that follows a linking verb and identifies or describes the subject of the sentence.

Examples: My love for you / is (LV) what's magnificent, (SUBJ. COMP.) . . .

This earth will grow (LV) cold (SUBJ. COMP.) one day, . . .

Practice Copy each item below. Double-underline any linking verbs and single-underline any subject complements. Write *none* if there are none.

1. . . . but I, you, and the others, / most likely, / are ordinary people.
2. . . . you took no credit for the wind. . . .
3. Living is no laughing matter: . . .
4. . . . living . . . weighs heavier.
5. . . . it's impossible not to feel sad. . . .

Writing Application Write a four-line poem describing a person or an object. Use a linking verb and a subject complement in each line.

WG ***Prentice Hall Writing and Grammar Connection: Diamond Level, Chapter 18, Section 3***

TEACHING RESOURCES

The following resources can be used to enrich or extend the instruction for pp. 1338–1339.

Vocabulary

- **Selection Support:** Build Vocabulary, p. 257
- **Vocabulary and Spelling Practice Book** (Use this booklet for skills instruction.)

Grammar

- **Selection Support:** Grammar and Style, p. 258
- **Writing and Grammar,** Diamond Level, p. 426
- **Daily Language Practice Transparencies** ■

Writing

- **Performance Assess. and Portfolio Mgmt.,** p. 15
- **Writing and Grammar,** Diamond Level, p. 174
- **Writing and Grammar iText CD-ROM** ■
- **Writing Models and Graphic Organizers on Transparencies,** pp. 95–97

Listening and Speaking

- **Performance Assess. and Portfolio Mgmt.,** p 31

■ **BLOCK SCHEDULING:** Resources marked with this symbol provide varied instruction during 90-minute blocks.

❸ Writing Lesson

Comparison-and-Contrast Essay

In "Twigs" and "On Living," Ali and Hikmet offer powerful messages about life. Write an essay in which you compare and contrast the two poems. For each point in your essay, quote relevant, supporting passages from the poems.

Prewriting Reread the poems, gathering details that will support your comparison. Begin by listing questions that will help you focus your search.

Model: Answering Questions to Gather Details

- What is each poet saying about life's ending?
  Ali: Life is too short; "not even poetry itself, / could provide consolation for life's brevity, . . ."
- In what ways are the poets' voices similar?

Answering questions such as these makes reviewing the poems and organizing a comparison a more efficient, focused task.

Drafting As you draft, answer the questions you identified in your prewriting. Follow a logical order, focusing on the questions that you find most important.

Revising Reread your essay, marking each comparision you have made, and check to make sure you have quoted sufficient support from the poems.

WG *Prentice Hall Writing and Grammar Connection: Diamond Level, Chapter 9, Section 2*

❹ Extension Activities

Listening and Speaking With a partner, conduct research to find paintings or photographs that echo the situation, events, mood, or images of Vénus Khoury-Ghata's poems. Choose a series of strong images, and then incorporate them into an **illustrated reading** of the poems. Use these tips:

- Consider various presentation methods, such as projecting slides or hanging posters.
- Practice the timing of your reading, coordinating the display of images with the text.
- Present your reading to the class. Afterward, explain your choices of images.

[Group Activity]

Research and Technology Even in the contemporary world, a writer's attempts to tell the truth or express an opinion can lead to a prison sentence, or worse. Conduct research on another writer who, like Hikmet, has been imprisoned or exiled for his or her work. Compose a persuasive **letter to the world,** arguing that the author's rights be restored. Use stirring language and the specific details you find in researching the case.

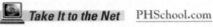

PHSchool.com

Go online for an additional research activity using the Internet.

ASSESSMENT RESOURCES

The following resources can be used to assess students' knowledge and skills.

Selection Assessment

- **Formal Assessment,** pp. 225–227
- **Open-Book Tests,** pp. 193–195
- **Test Bank Software**

Visit PHSchool.com for self-tests on the selections.

Writing Rubric

- **Performance Assess. and Portfolio Mgmt.,** p. 15

Listening and Speaking Rubric

- **Performance Assess. and Portfolio Mgmt.,** p. 31

For additional diagnostics and remediation for skills covered in this grouping, use materials from the Prentice Hall Assessment System.

❸ Writing Lesson

- Lead a class brainstorming session to supplement the list of questions in the Model on p. 1339. Record student questions on the board. Make sure students understand that the quotations they gather from each poem should answer the questions they use to formulate their essays.
- Students may want to record their notes in the Comparison-and-Contrast Organizer, pp. 95–97, of **Writing Models and Graphic Organizers on Transparencies.**
- Use the Comparison-and-Contrast Essay rubric, p. 15, of **Performance Assessment and Portfolio Management** to evaluate students' work.

10TH GRADE For support in working through the Writing Lesson with tenth graders, use **Writing and Grammar,** Platinum Level, Chapter 9, Section 2.

❹ Listening and Speaking

- Encourage partners to divide their work equally so that each partner is responsible for both research and presentation tasks.
- Suggest that two pairs of partners practice together to give one another hints on expressive reading styles, correlation of reading and images, and feedback on which images are most effective.
- Adapt the Speaking: Presenting an Oral Response to Literature rubric in **Portfolio Assessment and Portfolio Management,** p. 31, to assess students' readings.

CUSTOMIZE INSTRUCTION
For Universal Access

To address different learning styles, use the following activities suggested in the **Extension Activities** booklet, p. 65:

- For Verbal/Linguistic and Musical/Rhythmic Learners, use Activity 5.
- For Visual/Spatial Learners, use Activity 6.
- For Logical/Mathematical Learners, use Activity 7.

Prayer to Masks • Season

Lesson Objectives

1. **To analyze and respond to literary elements**
   - Literary Analysis: Rhetorical Devices
   - Comparing Literary Works: Using Rhetorical Devices
2. **To read, comprehend, analyze, and critique a poem**
   - Reading Strategy: Applying Literary Background Information
   - Reading Check Questions
   - Review and Assess Questions
   - Assessment Practice (ATE)
3. **To develop word analysis skills, fluency, and systematic vocabulary**
   - Vocabulary Development Lesson: Greek Suffix *-ism*
4. **To understand and apply written and oral language conventions**
   - Spelling Strategy
   - Grammar and Style Lesson: Correct Use of *who* and *whom*
5. **To understand and apply appropriate writing and research strategies**
   - Writing Lesson: Descriptive Essay
   - Extension Activity: Annotated Bibliography
6. **To understand and apply listening and speaking strategies**
   - Extension Activity: Debate on Consequences of Colonialism

STEP-BY-STEP TEACHING GUIDE	PACING GUIDE
PRETEACH	
Motivate Students and Provide Background	
Use the Motivation activity (ATE p. 1340)	5 min.
Read and discuss author and background features (SE pp. 1340, 1342; ATE p. 1340) [A]	5 min.
Introduce the Concepts	
Introduce the Literary Analysis and Reading Strategy concepts (SE/ATE p. 1341) [A]	15 min.
Pronounce the vocabulary words and read their definitions (SE p. 1341)	5 min.
TEACH	
Monitor Comprehension	
Informally monitor comprehension by circulating while students read independently or in groups [A]	25 min.
Develop vocabulary with the Vocabulary notes (SE pp. 1342, 1343, 1344; ATE p. 1343)	as students read
Develop Understanding	
Develop students' understanding of rhetorical devices with the Literary Analysis annotations (SE/ATE pp. 1342, 1344) [A]	5 min.
Develop students' ability to apply literary background information, using the Reading Strategy annotations (SE/ATE p. 1343)	5 min.
ASSESS	
Assess Mastery	
Assess students' mastery of the Reading Strategy and Literary Analysis concepts by having them answer the Review and Assess questions (SE/ATE p. 1345)	15 min.
Use one or more of the print, software, or transparency Assessment Resources (ATE p. 1347) [A]	up to 45 min.
EXTEND	
Apply Understanding	
Have students complete the Vocabulary Development Lesson and the Grammar and Style Lesson (SE p. 1346) [A]	20 min.
Apply students' ability to develop a list of descriptive details, using the Writing Lesson (SE/ATE p. 1347) [A]	45 min.
Apply students' understanding of the selections, using one or more of the Extension Activities (SE p. 1347)	20–90 min.

[A] **ACCELERATED INSTRUCTION:**
Use the strategies and activities identified with an [A].

UNIVERSAL ACCESS
● = Below-Level Students
▲ = On-Level Students
■ = Above-Level Students

TEACHING TENTH-GRADE STUDENTS
For support in teaching the selection(s) to tenth-grade students, see the Step-by-Step Teaching notes identified with the icon shown here.

Time and Resource Manager

Reading Level: Challenging, Challenging
Average Number of Instructional Days: 2

RESOURCES		
PRINT	**TRANSPARENCIES**	**TECHNOLOGY**
• **Beyond Literature,** Career Connection: Anthropology, p. 66 ▲ ■		
• **Selection Support Workbook:** ● ▲ ■ Literary Analysis, p. 264 Reading Strategy, p. 263 Build Vocabulary, p. 261	• **Literary Analysis and Reading Transparencies,** pp. 131 and 132 ● ▲ ■	
		• **Listening to Literature** ● ▲ ■ Audiocassettes Audio CDs
• **Literary Analysis for Enrichment,** p. 66 ■	• **Fine Art Transparencies,** Art Transparency 19 ● ▲ ■	
• **Formal Assessment:** Selection Test, pp. 228–230 ● ▲ ■ • **Open-Book Tests,** pp. 196–198 ● ▲ ■ • **Performance Assessment and Portfolio Management,** p. 19 ● ▲ ■ • PRENTICE HALL ASSESSMENT SYSTEM ● ▲ ■	• PRENTICE HALL ASSESSMENT SYSTEM ● ▲ ■ **Skills Practice Answers and Explanations on Transparencies**	• **Test Bank Software** ● ▲ ■
• **Selection Support Workbook:** ● ▲ ■ Grammar and Style, p. 262 • **Writing and Grammar,** Diamond Level ● ▲ ■ • **Extension Activities,** p. 66 ● ▲ ■	• **Daily Language Practice Transparencies** ● ▲ • **Writing Models and Graphic Organizers on Transparencies,** pp. 103–105 ● ▲ ■	• **Writing and Grammar iText CD-ROM** ● ▲ ■ *Take It to the Net* PHSchool.com

BLOCK SCHEDULING: Use one 90-minute class period to preteach the selection(s) and have students read them. Use a second 90-minute class period to assess students' mastery of skills and have them complete one of the Extension Activities.

PRETEACH

Step-by-Step Teaching Guide for pp. 1340–1341

Motivation

Tell students that in the poem "Prayer to Masks," the speaker addresses various carved masks that represent the speaker's ancestors. Ask students what kinds of things a person might want to ask or tell his or her ancestors. Encourage them to continue thinking about this question as they read Senghor's poem.

Before students read "Season," have them discuss common images of and associations with autumn. Have students discuss what is paradoxical about the season being both a time of death for plants and a time of harvest for plants.

❶ Background

More About the Authors

Senghor began promoting African poetry during his days as a student in Paris. During the 1930s, he helped publish a literary magazine called *The Black Student.* In 1948, Senghor edited the *Anthology of New Negro and Malagasy Poetry in French.* This groundbreaking collection, featuring an introduction by the influential French writer Jean-Paul Sartre, won a wide audience for the poets of Negritude.

One of the most striking aspects of Soyinka's literary career is his wide range of creative activities. In addition to writing poetry, prose, criticism, and drama, Soyinka is a noted producer, director, and stage actor. Soyinka has staged many of his own plays and plays written by others. His productions have been presented in Africa, Europe, and North America.

Geography Note

Draw students' attention to the map on this page. Point out that Senegal and Nigeria are located on Africa's western coast. Explain to students that both nations experienced colonial rule: Senegal by the Dutch, the British, and the French; Nigeria by the British.

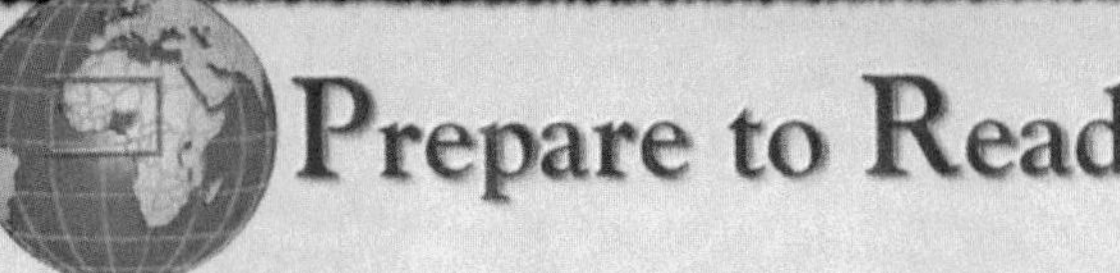

Prepare to Read

❶ Prayer to Masks ◆ Season

Léopold Sédar Senghor (1906–2001)

Poets are often thought to live dreamy, impractical lives, but Léopold Sédar Senghor (lā ô pōld′ sā dàr′ sän gôr′) is a clear exception. One of the greatest African poets writing in French, he also served as president of the West African nation of Senegal from its independence in 1960 until his retirement at the end of 1980.

Studying Abroad Senghor was born in the small village of Joal on the coast of Senegal, a predominantly Muslim country. In 1928, he traveled to France and studied literature at the Sorbonne, France's equivalent to Harvard.

Returning to the Past During his student years, Senghor and other young black writers launched the Negritude Movement, aimed at promoting traditional African cultural values in literature. At the same time, Senghor strongly believed that black literature in French was possible and that by writing in French, he could reach a large audience. He looked to the success of Harlem Renaissance writers such as Langston Hughes, who wedded African consciousness with English literary forms.

Traditions United After graduating from the Sorbonne, Senghor taught in France until World War II, when he joined the French army. In 1940, he was captured by the Germans and held prisoner for two years. During this decade, Senghor wrote his first two books of poetry, *Chants d'ombre* (1945; *Shadow Songs*) and *Hosties noires* (1948; *Black Hosts*). In 1948, Senghor also published a groundbreaking anthology of Caribbean and African poetry. He was elected in 1983 to the Académie Française, the first black member since this prestigious literary institution's founding in 1635.

Wole Soyinka (b. 1934)

Travel sometimes helps people rediscover the value of what they have left behind. Wole Soyinka (wō′ lā shô yin′ kə), perhaps Nigeria's finest contemporary dramatist, studied and worked in England for a time. When he returned to Nigeria in 1960, he was ready to begin a literary campaign in celebration of traditional African culture.

Mining His Heritage Soyinka belongs to the Yoruba people of Nigeria. He has long argued for the value of traditional African culture in solving the problems of post-colonial Africa. Many of his plays, including *The Swamp Dwellers* (performed 1958), depict the conflict between Yoruba and European values. Yoruba proverbs, dance, and music feature prominently in his plays.

Trouble at Home In 1966, a group of northern Nigerians seized power and divided Nigeria into twelve states. The eastern region rebelled, forming the Republic of Biafra. Civil war followed, causing widespread famine and destruction. The war ended in 1970 with the surrender of Biafra.

Speaking Up In 1967, Soyinka was imprisoned because of his outspoken criticism of the impending civil war. He recorded his two-year prison experience in *Poems from Prison* (1969) and in a memoir, *The Man Died* (1972). Many of his later plays, including *A Play of Giants* (1984), are satires decrying the succession of military regimes that have ruled Nigeria.

Soyinka is truly an African writer, one whose work is immersed both in traditional West African culture and in contemporary West African politics. In 1986, he became the first African to receive the Nobel Prize in Literature.

TEACHING RESOURCES

The following resources can be used to enrich or extend the instruction for pp. 1340–1341.

Background

Beyond Literature, p. 66

Take It to the Net

Visit PHSchool.com for background on the authors.

Literary Analysis

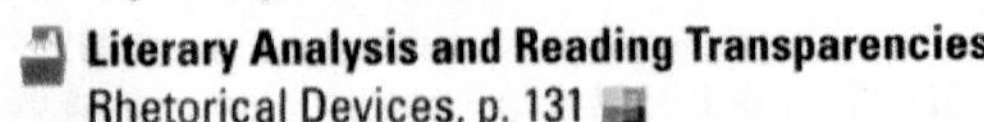

Literary Analysis and Reading Transparencies, Rhetorical Devices, p. 131 ▪

Selection Support: Literary Analysis, p. 264

Reading

Literary Analysis and Reading Transparencies, Applying Literary Background Information, p. 132 ▪

▪ **BLOCK SCHEDULING:** Resources marked with this symbol provide varied instruction during 90-minute blocks.

Preview

Connecting to the Literature

You can call a rainy Saturday a drag. Or you can call it an opportunity—your chance to bake a cake, say. What you call a thing can affect how you see it. These poets call the past and future of Africa by hopeful new names.

❷ Literary Analysis

Rhetorical Devices

Poets, like persuasive speakers, use rhetorical devices, patterns of words and ideas that create emphasis. Rhetorical devices include the following:

- **repetition,** the repeating of words or sentence patterns
- **elaboration,** the addition of details that extend a key idea
- **paradox,** a self-contradictory idea that reveals a deeper truth

Soyinka uses all three of these devices in the opening lines of "Season":

Rust is ripeness, rust, / and the wilted corn-plume

He repeats the word *rust*, emphasizing the decline of plants in autumn. He elaborates by joining "wilted corn-plume" to "rust." In addition, he uses a paradox, setting decay equal to ripeness to suggest that an ending is a beginning. As you read, note the use and impact of rhetorical devices.

Comparing Literary Works

Poets and other writers may use rhetorical devices so they can freshly imagine a situation. For instance, Senghor confronts a situation in which African culture seems secondary to European culture. Throughout "A Prayer to Masks," he uses rhetorical devices to affirm the central importance of African culture. As you read, compare the situations confronted by the speakers and the writers' uses of rhetorical devices.

❸ Reading Strategy

Applying Literary Background Information

To **apply literary background information,** use biographical and historical information to help you interpret details in a writer's work. Review the information in the author biographies on page 1340 and in the Background note on page 1342. As you read, apply the information in these features to the poems, using a chart like the one shown.

Detail in Work
The speaker's face is an "image" of traditional African masks.
Literary Background
Senghor, educated in Europe, founded the Negritude Movement, promoting black culture.
Interpretation
Senghor asserts his African identity—his resemblance to the masks—over his European education.

Vocabulary Development

despotism (des′ pət iz′ əm) *n.* tyranny; system of government in which the ruler has absolute power (p. 1342)

pitiable (pit′ ē ə bəl) *adj.* inspiring pity (may be used scornfully) (p. 1342)

immobile (i mō′ bəl) *adj.* not moving; unchanging (p. 1343)

laden (lād′ ′n) *adj.* loaded (p. 1344)

❷ Literary Analysis

Rhetorical Devices

- Read aloud the Literary Analysis instruction. Tell students that writers use rhetorical devices to present their ideas in original, interesting ways.
- Explain to students that rhetorical devices can challenge readers to look at a familiar subject in a new or more complicated way.
- Read lines 5–9 on p. 1342 with students and discuss the effect of the poem's repetition ("You guard," "You purify," "You have"). Then, have students write four lines of poetry using a rhetorical device.
- If students need more practice with this skill, use the Rhetorical Devices transparency in **Literary Analysis and Reading Transparencies,** p. 131.

❸ Reading Strategy

Applying Literary Background Information

- Tell students that reviewing information in their textbooks about the authors, African history, and African culture will prepare them for interpreting and understanding the selections in this grouping.
- Explain the use of the graphic organizer on p. 1341. Encourage students to use a chart like the one on p. 1341 to connect relevant background information about the author to the text.
- To provide students with additional support in using this strategy, use the Applying Literary Background Information transparency in **Literary Analysis and Reading Transparencies,** p. 132.

Vocabulary Development

- Pronounce each vocabulary word for students, and read the definitions as a class. Have students identify any words with which they are familiar.

CUSTOMIZE INSTRUCTION FOR UNIVERSAL ACCESS

For Less Proficient Readers	For English Learners	For Advanced Readers
These poems may present difficulty because of their sentence length, complicated syntax, and complex language. Help students work through each poem line by line describing in their own words the action and other developments. Discuss students' interpretations of the lines.	Guide students to use context clues to help determine the meanings of unfamiliar words such as *ancestor, eternity, sacrifice, garment, spliced, slivers,* and *wreathe.* Have students use a two-column chart to record these words and the context clues that aid them in determining their definitions.	The writers in this section have used literature to explore their cultural heritage. Have students compile an anthology of poetry and other writings that explore pride in one's culture, race, or family background. Then, ask students to present their anthologies to the class, explaining why they chose the selections they did.

 **E-Teach**

Visit e-Teach at PHSchool.com for teachers' essays on how to teach, with questions and answers.

TEACH

Step-by-Step Teaching Guide for pp. 1342–1344

Teaching Tenth-Grade Students

10TH GRADE Lead a discussion on other works students have read that reveal unique features of a particular culture or region. Ask students to suggest aspects of a culture that are best conveyed through literature.

❶ About the Selection

In "Prayer to Masks," the speaker addresses ancestral masks that are specifically African, but that evoke a respect for tradition that is universal. The speaker asks the masks to help show the world the value of African culture.

❷ Background

Art

Masks from the Ivory Coast

The bottom mask, produced by the Baoulé people, features loops of hair characteristic of Baoulé design. This mask was probably used in ritual dances before the hunt. The top mask, carved by people of the Ivory Coast, is used in ritual dancing. It represents an ancestral spirit.

Use the following question for discussion.

What do the horns on the Baoulé mask suggest?

Answer: The horns suggest that the wearer of the mask represents a horned animal.

❸ Literary Analysis

Rhetorical Devices

- Remind students that a paradox is a self-contradictory idea that reveals a deeper truth.
- Read aloud the bracketed passage. Then, ask students the Literary Analysis question on p. 1342: Why is it a paradox for the speaker to refer to his face as an "image" of the mask?
  Answer: The speaker refers to himself as a representation of an original, a creation of the masks, when in fact, the masks are representations and creations.

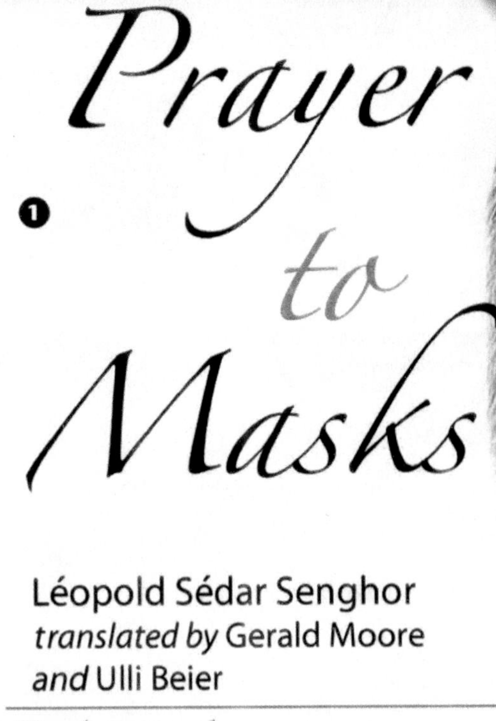

❶ Prayer to Masks

Léopold Sédar Senghor
translated by Gerald Moore
and Ulli Beier

Background

Begun by Léopold Sédar Senghor and other French-speaking black students in Paris in 1932, the Negritude Movement was originally a response to the French government policy toward native cultures. In their colonies, the French tried to assimilate, or absorb, Africans into French culture. Negritude was a bold assertion that African culture was as valuable as French culture. As it spread, the Negritude Movement helped revitalize pride in African cultural identity among blacks worldwide.

Black mask, red mask, you black and white masks,
Rectangular masks through whom the spirit breathes,
I greet you in silence!
And you too, my lionheaded ancestor.
You guard this place, that is closed to any feminine laughter, to
any mortal smile.
You purify the air of eternity, here where I breathe the air of my
fathers.
❸ Masks of markless faces, free from dimples and wrinkles,
You have composed this image, this my face that bends over the
altar of white paper.
In the name of your image, listen to me!
❹ Now while the Africa of despotism is dying—it is the agony of a
pitiable princess

Literary Analysis
Rhetorical Devices
Why is it a paradox for the speaker to refer to his face as an "image" of the mask?

despotism (des´ pət iz´ əm) *n.* tyranny; system of government in which the ruler has absolute power

pitiable (pit´ ē ə bəl) *adj.* inspiring pity (may be used scornfully)

TEACHING RESOURCES

The following resources can be used to enrich or extend the instruction for pp. 1342–1344.

Literary Analysis

- **Literary Analysis and Reading Transparencies,** Rhetorical Devices, p. 131 ■

Reading

- **Selection Support:** Reading Strategy, p. 263; Build Vocabulary, p. 261
- **Listening to Literature Audiocassettes** ■
- **Listening to Literature CDs**

Extension

- **Fine Art Transparencies,** Art Transparency 19
  (Have students characterize this mask from the Côte d'Ivoire and explain how viewing it changes or enriches their understanding of the masks in Senghor's poem.)

■ **BLOCK SCHEDULING:** Resources marked with this symbol provide varied instruction during 90-minute blocks.

Like that of Europe to whom she is connected through the navel[1]—
Now fix your immobile eyes upon your children who have been
called
And who sacrifice their lives like the poor man his last garment
So that hereafter we may cry "here" at the rebirth of the world
being the leaven[2] that the white flour needs.
For who else would teach rhythm to the world that has died of
machines and cannons?
For who else should ejaculate the cry of joy, that arouses the dead
and the wise in a new dawn?
Say, who else could return the memory of life to men with a
torn hope?
❺ They call us cotton heads, and coffee men, and oily men,
They call us men of death.
But we are the men of the dance whose feet only gain power when
they beat the hard soil.

immobile (i mō′ bəl) *adj.* not moving; unchanging

Reading Strategy
Applying Literary Background Information In lines 18–19, who are "they"?

1. **navel** (nā′ vəl) *n.* scar marking the place where the umbilical cord, which supplies oxygen and nutrients from the mother, attached the baby to its mother while in the womb.
2. **leaven** (lev′ ən) *n.* small piece of fermenting dough that is added to a larger batch of dough to make it rise.

Review and Assess

Thinking About the Selection

1. **Respond:** If you, like the speaker of "Masks," were to address a symbol of your ancestors, what might you say?
2. **(a) Recall:** Name three things that the speaker calls on in the opening of the poem. **(b) Interpret:** What is the mood of the place where these things are located? Give details in support.
3. **(a) Recall:** In line 8, over what does the speaker bend? **(b) Hypothesize:** Where might he be writing? Explain.
4. **(a) Recall:** According to the speaker, what is the relationship between the masks and the speaker's own face? **(b) Interpret:** What does this relationship suggest about his connection to the values and traditions of his ancestors? Explain.
5. **(a) Analyze:** Explain the difference between the first part of the poem and lines 9–14. **(b) Interpret:** What event does the speaker call on the masks to witness?
6. **(a) Infer:** According to the speaker, what values might African culture teach Europeans? Support your answer with details from the poem. **(b) Draw Conclusions:** Explain the sort of "rebirth of the world" that the speaker envisions.
7. **Apply:** What values do you think American culture has adapted from African culture?

CUSTOMIZE INSTRUCTION FOR UNIVERSAL ACCESS

For Special Needs Students	For Gifted/Talented Students
Clarify for students a few examples of metaphorical language, such as the "altar of white paper" (line 8) and "white flour" (line 14). Then, explain that the use of such figures of speech is one way for a poet to suggest several meanings at the same time. Point out the contrast of the white paper and the speaker's black skin. Then, ask students to discuss why this contrast is both appropriate and powerful in a poem about European influence in Africa.	Ask each student to create his or her own ancestral mask, either as a drawing or as a three-dimensional model. Remind students that their masks should represent those beliefs and traditions valued by their ancestors, such as parents or grandparents. Before students begin, have them brainstorm a list of beliefs and traditions and images or symbols that convey those beliefs and traditions. Have each student present and explain his or her mask to the class.

❹ Vocabulary Development

Greek Suffix *-ism*

- Have a volunteer read aloud the bracketed passage on p. 1342. Explain that *despotism* contains the Greek suffix *-ism,* which often means "the doctrine, belief, or practice of."
- Have students suggest other words that contain *-ism.* Possible responses: *Chauvinism, elitism,* and *racism* all feature *-ism.*

❺ Reading Strategy

Applying Literary Background Information

- Read aloud the bracketed passage.
- Then, ask students the Reading Strategy question on p. 1343: In lines 18–19, who are "they"? Answer: "They" are the French.

Answers for p. 1343

Review and Assess

1. Possible response: We honor the sacrifices of our ancestors who, like windmills, stood tall on the prairie.
2. **(a)** The speaker calls on black, red, black and white, rectangular, and lionheaded masks. **(b)** The place is solemn, as evidenced by the line "closed to any feminine laughter, to any mortal smile."
3. **(a)** The speaker bends over a sheet of white paper. **(b)** The speaker may be writing in a museum that displays works.
4. **(a)** The masks formed the speaker's own face. **(b)** The speaker's values have been shaped by his ancestors.
5. **(a)** At first, the speaker greets ancestors and describes their importance. In lines 9–14, the speaker describes the consequences of colonialism. **(b)** The speaker calls on the masks to witness the sacrifices of their children who are struggling to bring a "rebirth" to Africa.
6. **(a)** African culture can teach Europeans about rhythm, joy, and hope (lines 15–17). **(b)** The rebirth involves a return to ancestral values and repair of damage inflicted by Western cultures.
7. Possible response: American culture has adapted the value of taking pride in cultural heritage.

ASSESS

6 About the Selection

In "Season," the speaker describes the events during the time in which corn is ripening. Images of decay, such as wilted tassels and a fungus called "rust," seemingly contradict the bounty of the corn harvest.

7 Literary Analysis

Rhetorical Devices

- Read aloud the bracketed passage. Then, ask students the Literary Analysis question on p. 1344: In what way does the speaker elaborate on the description of the swallows?
  Answer: The speaker calls the swallows "winged streaks of light," their flight "a dance of feathered arrows."

Reteach Review elaboration by using the Rhetorical Devices transparency in **Literary Analysis and Reading Transparencies,** p. 131.

Answers for p. 1344

Review and Assess

1. Possible response: Fall means harvest and cooler temperatures.
2. **(a)** The rust and wilted corn-plume indicate ripeness. **(b)** Decay, indicated by the rust and the corn's wilted tassels, happens at the same time that the corn ripens.
3. **(a)** The pollen symbolizes mating time for swallows. **(b)** While the birds begin their own reproductive cycle, the corn ripens.
4. **(a)** The speaker describes the swallows as "feathered arrows" and as "winged streaks of light." **(b)** These images are ones of speed and light. The images in the second stanza indicate anticipation and darkness.
5. **(a) Joining:** "weave a dance" and "thread corn-stalks" **Cutting:** "Spliced phrases," "corn-leaves pierce," and "slivers." **(b)** Unlike the actions described in the first stanza, the garnerers "draw long shadows," "wreathe dry thatch," and watch the "laden stalks."
6. (a) The literal "promise of the rust" is the promise of bountiful harvest. (b) A society should maintain hope even in times of crisis.

6 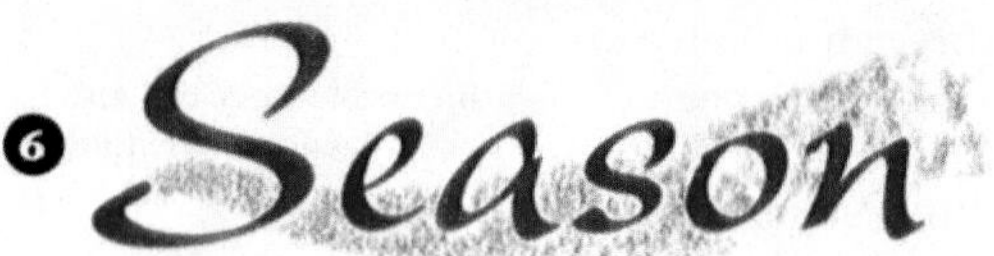

Season

Wole Soyinka

Rust is ripeness, rust,
And the wilted corn-plume;
Pollen is mating-time when swallows
Weave a dance
Of feathered arrows
Thread corn-stalks in winged
Streaks of light. And, we loved to hear
Spliced phrases of the wind, to hear
Rasps[1] in the field, where corn-leaves
Pierce like bamboo slivers.

Now, garnerers[2] we
Awaiting rust on tassels, draw
Long shadows from the dusk, wreathe
Dry thatch in wood-smoke. Laden stalks
Ride the germ's[3] decay—we await
The promise of the rust.

Literary Analysis
Rhetorical Devices In what way does the speaker elaborate on the description of the swallows?

laden (lād′ ′n) *adj.* loaded

1. **rasps** (rasps) *n.* rough, grating tones (usually a verb).
2. **garnerers** (gär′ nər ərz) *n.* harvesters; gatherers.
3. **germ's** *n.* here, of a seed or bud.

Review and Assess

Thinking About the Selection

1. **Respond:** Describe your own associations with fall.
2. **(a) Recall:** Identify two signs of ripeness in the poem. **(b) Intepret:** In what way does harvest time combine decay and ripeness?
3. **(a) Recall:** What "time" does pollen symbolize? **(b) Infer:** What is the relationship between this season and the time of ripeness?
4. **(a) Recall:** Identify two images used to describe the flight of sparrows. **(b) Compare:** In what way do these images contrast with the images of shadows and smoke in the second stanza?
5. **(a) Classify:** Divide the images in lines 3–10 between those that involve joining together and those that involve cutting. **(b) Compare:** Contrast these activities with those in the second stanza.
6. **(a) Infer:** What is the literal "promise of the rust" for which the harvesters wait? **(b) Connect:** In what larger sense might a society look for hope in a time of "rust"?

ASSESSMENT PRACTICE: Reading Comprehension

Using Context Clues to Determine Meanings (For more practice, see Test Preparation Workbook, p. 2.)

Many tests require students to use context clues to determine the meanings of unfamiliar words. Use the following sample test item to demonstrate how to use this skill.

The Negritude Movement was originally intended as a response to French government policy toward native cultures. In their colonies, the French tried to assimilate native cultures into French culture.

In this passage, the word assimilate means—

A support.
B ridicule.
C absorb.
D destroy.

Answers *A, B,* and *D* do not make sense within the context of the passage. The word *into* is a context clue that reveals that during assimilation, native cultures would become part of or be absorbed into French culture. Therefore, *C* is the correct answer.

Review and Assess

Literary Analysis

Rhetorical Devices

1. (a) Identify two uses of the **rhetorical device** of word **repetition** in "Prayer to Masks." (b) Identify one instance in which a sentence pattern is repeated. (c) Explain what effect each instance of repetition has on the impact of the poem.
2. (a) Find an instance of **elaboration** in "Prayer to Masks." (b) Explain why the poem might have lacked energy if the poet had not added details to his main idea.
3. Interpret the **paradox** in the last two lines of "Season," explaining why the idea seems like a self-contradiction but actually expresses a truth.

Comparing Literary Works

4. Using a chart like the one shown, compare the ways in which each of the two poems imaginatively transforms a situation or problem.

Poem	Old Situation	New Interpretation	Rhetorical Devices Used

5. Compare the poets' attitudes toward the past and the future, given their present situation.

Reading Strategy

Applying Literary Background Information

6. Use your knowledge of the Negritude Movement to interpret two ideas or images in "Prayer to Masks."
7. Explain why "Season" might be read as a comment on Nigeria's history—from its independence from Britain in 1960, to its civil war in 1967, to the periods of dictatorship that followed. In your answer, give details from the poem.

Extend Understanding

8. **Psychology Connection:** Give an example from your own experience of a mask—a role or an image—with which people identify.

Quick Review

Rhetorical devices, patterns of words and ideas that create emphasis, include the following: **repetition,** the repeating of sentence patterns as well as of individual words; **elaboration,** the addition of details that extend a key idea; and **paradox,** a self-contradictory idea that reveals a deeper truth.

To **apply literary background information,** use biographical and historical information to help you interpret details in a writer's work.

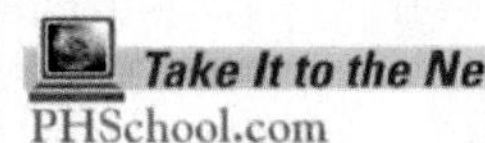

Take It to the Net

PHSchool.com

Take the interactive self-test online to check your understanding of these selections.

Review and Assess

1. **(a)** In the first two lines, the word "mask(s)" is used four times. In lines 15–17, "(for) who else" is repeated. **(b)** "They call us" is repeated in lines 18–19. **(c)** Each instance of repetition emphasizes, the speaker's point.
2. **(a)** In lines 15–17, the speaker elaborates on the cultural qualities that Africa can contribute to the world. **(b)** Without details about African culture, the poem might have been a dry political analysis.
3. The paradox is the simultaneous image of bounty and decay.
4. **Poem:** "Prayer to Masks"; **Old Situation:** viewing traditional masks; **New Interpretation:** asking masks to witness the importance of African culture; **Rhetorical Devices:** repetition, elaboration. **Poem:** "Season"; **Old Situation:** ripening corn indicated by rust; **New Interpretation:** decay and bounty are bound together; **Rhetorical Devices:** paradox, elaboration.
5. Possible response: Both poems see hope for the future; however, "Prayer to Masks" details difficulties in Africa's past in a way that "Season" does not.
6. Possible response: Africans are called "the leaven that the white flour needs." Members of the Negritude Movement might consider "white flour" to be European literature; African authors might add their values—leaven—to European literature. The poem also celebrates Africans as the only people who can bring about a rebirth of the world; this reaffirms the Movement's goal to revitalize pride in African culture.
7. Possible response: "Season" might be said to comment on Nigeria's independence from Britain in its image of swallows, the "winged / Streaks of light" that fly freely. The periods of civil war and dictatorship could be intimated in the "Long shadows from the dusk" and "woodsmoke." Waiting for the "promise of the rust" could represent the speaker's hope for a more stable government.

continued

continued from right column

8. Possible response: Many people assume identities from professional roles—for example, an outgoing salesperson or an introspective scientist. Some people assume identities from family roles—for example, a responsible older sister or a fun-loving younger brother.

ENRICHMENT: Further Reading

Other Works by the Authors

We strongly encourage you to review any selection before assigning or recommending it to students.

Nocturnes by Léopold Sédar Senghor

The Swamp Dwellers by Wole Soyinka

Take It to the Net

Visit PHSchool.com for more information about the authors.

EXTEND

Answers for p. 1346

❶ Vocabulary Development

Word Analysis: Greek suffix *-ism*

1. *Minimalism* is the practice of using the smallest amount of an item to achieve the desired effect.
2. *Pacifism* is the doctrine of rejecting all forms of war and violence.
3. *Feminism* is the belief in the rights of women.
4. *Athleticism* is the practice of athletic exercise.
5. *Pietism* is the belief in strict religious practice.

Concept Development: Synonyms

1. c
2. d
3. a
4. b

Spelling Strategy

1. amplifier
2. defiant
3. verifiable

❷ Grammar and Style

Practice

1. whom
2. who
3. who
4. whom
5. who

Writing Application

Sample poem:

Our great-grandmothers.
Women who raised large families with very little means.
Who instilled in their families courage, pride, and a fierce love of home.
Your children, whom you healed with soup, tears, and very little medicine, and
Your granddaughters, whom you taught by your example,
Thank you.

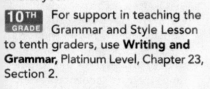

10TH GRADE For support in teaching the Grammar and Style Lesson to tenth graders, use **Writing and Grammar,** Platinum Level, Chapter 23, Section 2.

Integrate Language Skills

❶ Vocabulary Development Lesson

Word Analysis: Greek suffix *-ism*

The Greek suffix *-ism* often means "the doctrine, belief, or practice of." The word *despotism* means "the practice of absolute rule." In Senghor's poem, the word refers specifically to the absolute power of European powers over regions of Africa during the colonial period.

Using the meaning of the suffix, define each of the following words. Check your definitions using a dictionary.

1. minimalism
2. pacifism
3. feminism
4. athleticism
5. pietism

Concept Development: Synonyms

For each of the numbered vocabulary words below, write the letter of the correct synonym, or word closest to it in meaning.

1. despotism
2. pitiable
3. immobile
4. laden

a. paralyzed
b. burdened
c. dictatorship
d. helpless

Spelling Strategy

When a word ends in a consonant and a *y*, change the *y* to *i* before adding most suffixes. For example, *pity* becomes *pitiable*. Add the suffix in parentheses to each of the following words.

1. amplify *(-er)* **2.** defy *(-ant)* **3.** verify *(-able)*

❷ Grammar and Style Lesson

Correct Use of *who* and *whom*

The correct use of *who* and *whom* helps a poet refer clearly to people or groups of people. **Who,** like *he* or *she*, is used as a subject or a subject complement. **Whom,** like *him* or *her*, is used as an object or an object of a preposition. Study these examples:

Subject: Now fix your immobile eyes upon your children who have been called / And who sacrifice their lives. . . . [*Who* is the subject of the verbs *have been called* and *sacrifice*.]

Object: Rectangular masks through whom the spirit breathes, / I greet you in silence! [*Whom* is the object of the preposition *through*.]

Practice Identify which word, *who* or *whom*, correctly completes each sentence below.

1. The Africans (who, whom) Europeans educated were caught between cultures.
2. The Europeans (who, whom) educated them rarely valued African culture.
3. The writers (who, whom) formed the Negritude Movement celebrated black culture.
4. Some were inspired by Langston Hughes, for (who, whom) both European and African traditions were important.
5. For a writer such as Soyinka, (who, whom) speaks out for both tradition and reform, the future is as important as the past.

Writing Application Write a poem about the past, using both *who* and *whom* correctly twice.

WG *Prentice Hall Writing and Grammar Connection: Diamond Level, Chapter 22, Section 2*

TEACHING RESOURCES

The following resources can be used to enrich or extend the instruction for pp. 1346–1347.

Vocabulary

- **Selection Support:** Build Vocabulary, p. 261
- **Vocabulary and Spelling Practice Book** (Use this booklet for skills instruction.)

Grammar

- **Selection Support:** Grammar and Style, p. 262
- **Writing and Grammar,** Diamond Level, p. 574
- **Daily Language Practice Transparencies**

Writing

- **Performance Assess. and Portfolio Mgmt.,** p. 19
- **Writing and Grammar,** Diamond Level, p. 102
- **Writing and Grammar iText CD-ROM**

Listening and Speaking

- **Writing Models and Graphic Organizers on Transparencies,** pp. 103–105

BLOCK SCHEDULING: Resources marked with this symbol provide varied instruction during 90-minute blocks.

❸ Writing Lesson

Descriptive Essay

As "Prayer to Masks" suggests, masks have important symbolic value in African culture, as they do in many other societies around the world. Conduct research on the use of masks in several cultures. Then, write an essay describing one of the masks you have studied. In your essay, include enough specific details to help readers visualize the mask and imagine the feelings that it projects.

Prewriting Begin by listing details about the mask, using a chart like the one shown.

Model: Listing Details by Category

Expression	Colors	Materials	Textures	Used for . . .

Drafting In your first paragraph, use a striking detail to introduce the mask and identify its culture of origin. As you draft the body of your essay, include descriptive details from among those you listed in your prewriting.

Revising Reread your essay, circling any passages that seem vague or general. Consider adding descriptive details to strengthen these passages.

WG Prentice Hall Writing and Grammar Connection: Diamond Level, Chapter 6, Section 2

❹ Extension Activities

Listening and Speaking Divide a group into two sides, and hold a **debate** on this issue: Did European colonialism in Africa have more negative or more positive consequences? To prepare, research specific historical examples of European colonies in Africa. Choose evidence that supports your persuasive purpose. In your arguments, include persuasive devices of these types:

- appeals to logic, such as cause-and-effect arguments
- appeals to ethics, such as arguments about fairness and morality
- charged language appealing to emotions

Hold your debate before the class. **[Group Activity]**

Research and Technology Conduct research on the Negritude Movement, the authors associated with it, and the works that it fostered. Note the influence of the movement in the United States and in the Caribbean, as well as in Africa. Then, compile an **annotated bibliography** of works influenced by the movement. For each work you list, include publication information, a brief description of the work, and a summary of its significance to the movement.

Go online for an additional research activity using the Internet.

ASSESSMENT RESOURCES

The following resources can be used to assess students' knowledge and skills.

Selection Assessment

- **Formal Assessment,** pp. 228–230
- **Open-Book Tests,** pp. 196–198
- **Test Bank Software**

Take It to the Net

Visit PHSchool.com for self-tests on the selections.

Writing Rubric

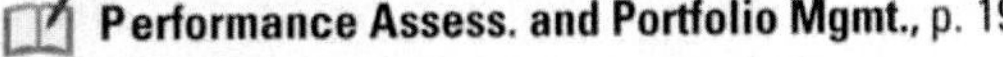

For additional diagnostics and remediation for skills covered in this grouping, use materials from the Prentice Hall Assessment System.

❸ Writing Lesson

- Remind students that their essays, in order to be effective, must create vivid pictures of masks from around the world. Tell students that using sensory language, including adjectives and adverbs, will allow them to present descriptions of complicated and beautiful masks.
- Discuss with students the resources they can use for their assignments, including anthropological studies and online references.
- Use the Writing Lesson to guide students in developing their essays. When students have finished their essays, use the Description rubric in **Performance Assessment and Portfolio Management,** p. 19, to evaluate students' work.

10TH GRADE For support in working through the Writing Lesson with tenth graders, use **Writing and Grammar,** Platinum Level, Chapter 6, Section 2.

❹ Listening and Speaking

- Remind students that a debate is a formal public-speaking situation in which participants prepare and present arguments on opposing sides of a question, stated as a proposition.
- After students complete their research, encourage them to use the Outline organizer in **Writing Models and Graphic Organizers on Transparencies,** pp. 103–105, to help them record their main arguments and supporting evidence.

CUSTOMIZE INSTRUCTION For Universal Access

To address different learning styles, use the following activities suggested in the **Extension Activities** booklet, p. 66.

- For Visual/Spatial Learners, use Activity 5.
- For Musical/Rhythmic and Bodily/Kinesthetic Learners, use Activity 6.
- For Intrapersonal and Verbal/Linguistic Learners, use Activity 7.

Comrades • Marriage Is a Private Affair

Lesson Objectives

1. **To analyze and respond to literary elements**
   - Literary Analysis: Atmosphere
   - Comparing Literary Works: Cultural Tensions
2. **To read, comprehend, analyze, and critique a short story**
   - Reading Strategy: Identifying With a Character
   - Reading Check Questions
   - Review and Assess Questions
   - Assessment Practice (ATE)
3. **To develop word analysis skills, fluency, and systematic vocabulary**
   - Vocabulary Development Lesson: Greek Prefix *eu-*
4. **To understand and apply written and oral language conventions**
   - Spelling Strategy
   - Grammar and Style Lesson: Noun Clauses
5. **To understand and apply appropriate writing and research strategies**
   - Writing Lesson: Manual on How to Change a Story's Atmosphere
   - Extension Activity: Five-Minute Research Presentation
6. **To understand and apply listening and speaking strategies**
   - Extension Activity: Dramatization

10TH GRADE TEACHING A TENTH-GRADE COURSE

The literature in this section can be taught as part of a rich, balanced world literature course for tenth grade students. For a full outline of such a course, see pp. T46–T48 in Volume 1 of this Teacher's Edition.

STEP-BY-STEP TEACHING GUIDE	PACING GUIDE
PRETEACH	
Motivate Students and Provide Background	
Use the Motivation activity (ATE p. 1348)	5 min.
Read and discuss author and background features (SE pp. 1348, 1350, 1355; ATE p. 1348) A	5 min.
Introduce the Concepts	
Introduce the Literary Analysis and Reading Strategy concepts (SE/ATE p. 1349) A	15 min.
Pronounce the vocabulary words and read their definitions (SE p. 1349)	5 min.
TEACH	
Monitor Comprehension	
Informally monitor comprehension by circulating while students read A	40 min.
Monitor students' comprehension with the Reading Check notes (SE/ATE pp. 1351, 1353, 1355, 1357, 1359)	as students read
Develop vocabulary with the Vocabulary notes (SE pp. 1351, 1352, 1354, 1356, 1357, 1359, 1360; ATE p. 1353)	as students read
Develop Understanding	
Develop students' understanding of atmosphere with the Literary Analysis annotations (SE/ATE pp. 1350, 1352, 1357, 1358, 1359, 1360) A	10 min.
Develop students' ability to identify with a character, using the Reading Strategy annotations (SE/ATE pp. 1350, 1351, 1353, 1356, 1359)	10 min.
ASSESS	
Assess Mastery	
Assess students' mastery of the Reading Strategy and Literary Analysis concepts by having them answer the Review and Assess questions (SE/ATE p. 1361)	20 min.
Use one or more of the print, software, or transparency Assessment Resources (ATE p. 1363) A	up to 45 min.
EXTEND	
Apply Understanding	
Have students complete the Vocabulary Development Lesson and the Grammar and Style Lesson (SE p. 1362) A	20 min.
Apply students' ability to introduce examples, using the Writing Lesson (SE/ATE p. 1363) A	45 min.
Apply students' understanding of the selections, using one or more of the Extension Activities (SE p. 1363)	20–90 min.

ACCELERATED INSTRUCTION: Use the strategies and activities identified with an A.

10TH GRADE TEACHING TENTH-GRADE STUDENTS For support in teaching tenth graders, see the Step-by-Step Teaching notes identified with this icon.

UNIVERSAL ACCESS
- ● = Below-Level Students
- ▲ = On-Level Students
- ■ = Above-Level Students

Time and Resource Manager

Reading Level: Average
Average Number of Instructional Days: 4

RESOURCES		
PRINT	**TRANSPARENCIES**	**TECHNOLOGY**
• **Beyond Literature,** Workplace Connection, p. 67 ▲ ■		• **Interest Grabber Video,** Tape 2, Unit 9, Segment 13 ● ▲ ■
• **Selection Support Workbook:** ● ▲ ■ Literary Analysis, p. 268 Reading Strategy, p. 267 Build Vocabulary, p. 265	• **Literary Analysis and Reading Transparencies,** pp. 133 and 134 ● ▲ ■	
		• **Listening to Literature** ● ▲ ■ Audiocassettes Audio CDs
• **Literary Analysis for Enrichment,** p. 67 ■		
• **Formal Assessment:** Selection Test, pp. 231–233 ● ▲ ■ • **Open-Book Tests,** pp. 199–201 ● ▲ ■ • **Performance Assess. and Portfolio Mgmt.,** pp. 10, 33 ● ▲ ■ • PRENTICE HALL ASSESSMENT SYSTEM ● ▲ ■	• PRENTICE HALL ASSESSMENT SYSTEM ● ▲ ■ **Skills Practice Answers and Explanations on Transparencies**	• **Test Bank Software** ● ▲ ■
• **Selection Support Workbook:** ● ▲ ■ Grammar and Style, p. 266 • **Writing and Grammar,** Diamond Level ● ▲ ■ • **Extension Activities,** p. 67 ● ▲ ■	• **Daily Language Practice Transparencies** ● ▲	• **Writing and Grammar iText CD-ROM** ● ▲ ■ ***Take It to the Net*** PHSchool.com

BLOCK SCHEDULING: Use one 90-minute class period to preteach the selection(s) and have students read them. Use a second 90-minute class period to assess students' mastery of skills and have them complete one of the Extension Activities.

PRETEACH

Step-by-Step Teaching Guide for pp. 1348–1349

Motivation

Tell students that the two selections in this grouping provide a look at Africa during a time in which strong traditional values were giving way to new ideas of freedom and justice. Ask students to discuss a time in their lives when an established way of doing things changed.

Interest Grabber Video

As an alternative, play "'Comrades': Apartheid in South Africa" on Tape 2 to engage student interest.

❶ Background

More About the Authors

South African writer Nadine Gordimer once described herself as "not a politically minded person by nature." She said, "I don't suppose if I had lived elsewhere, my writing would have reflected politics much, if at all." Nonetheless, her novels and story collections do reflect politics, like an unforgiving mirror held up to South African society; the images have sometimes been so ugly that three of her books were banned by the South African government.

In addition to directing a radio station and serving as a diplomat in Nigerian politics, Chinua Achebe has worked as a teacher. Today, he earns his living as an instructor in Nigeria and the United States, teaching courses at such universities as Northwestern and the City University of New York.

Geography Note

Draw students' attention to the map on this page. Point out that the Federal Republic of Nigeria is today the most populous African nation and one of the most diverse. The Republic of South Africa is larger than Nigeria, but its location at the tip of the African continent isolates it from other countries.

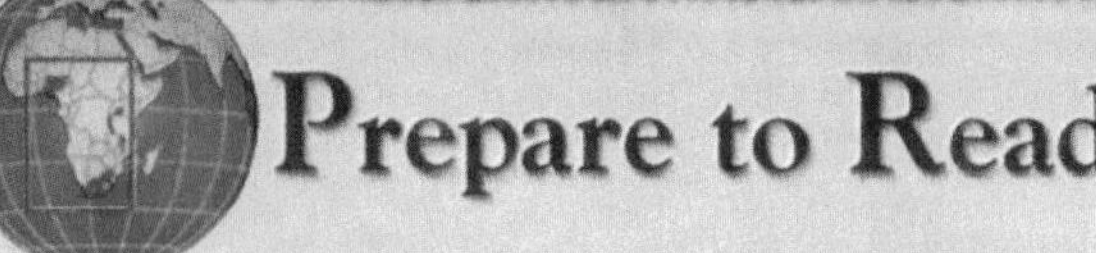

Prepare to Read

❶ Comrades ◆ Marriage Is a Private Affair

Nadine Gordimer (b. 1923)

Most of Nadine Gordimer's fiction is set in her native country of South Africa. During the years of apartheid—South Africa's official policy of racial segregation that ended in 1990—Gordimer wrote passionately in favor of racial justice. In her fiction, she demonstrates how institutionalized racism damages everyone in a society. It harms the oppressed by denying their rights to health, education, economic security, and political determination; it harms the oppressors by distorting their deepest human feelings.

Early Bloomer Born in Springs, South Africa, Gordimer grew up in a profoundly segregated society. Like most other white middle-class children in South Africa at the time, she attended private, all-white schools and lived in all-white neighborhoods. Her mother believed her daughter had a delicate constitution and often kept her home. As a result, Gordimer turned to writing to occupy herself. Her literary gifts bore fruit, and by the time she was fifteen years old, Gordimer was publishing regularly. As she grew older and became more aware of her country's problems, she applied her talents to describing the damage suffered by all South Africans under apartheid.

International Stardom Today, Gordimer is one of the most successful writers in the world. Her many literary works include *The Soft Voice of the Serpent* (1952), *Not for Publication* (1965), *The Conservationist* (1974), *The Essential Gesture: Writing, Politics, and Place* (1988), *Jump and Other Stories* (1991), and *The House Gun* (1998). In 1991, Gordimer added the Nobel Prize in Literature to her long list of honors.

Chinua Achebe (b. 1930)

During the Nigerian civil war, which lasted from 1967 to 1970, Chinua Achebe (chin wä′ ə cheb′ ā) survived the bombing of his house by fleeing for his life, leaving behind an unpublished manuscript. When Achebe eventually returned home, he found one remaining copy, which someone had managed to save. This manuscript—*How the Leopard Got His Claws*, Achebe's parable about Nigeria—was published in 1972.

Living in Two Worlds Achebe was born in the Ibo village of Ogibi, Nigeria. His parents named him Albert, after Prince Albert, the husband of England's Queen Victoria. As a university student, Achebe later abandoned his English name in favor of Chinua, his Ibo name. The duality reflected in Achebe's names permeates his work, which describes the effects of Western customs and values on traditional African society.

Writing in English One legacy of British colonialism in Nigeria is the widespread use of English in education and government. As an educated Nigerian, Achebe writes in English, but he uses Ibo parables, words, and attitudes to convey a distinctly Nigerian sensibility. His keen ear and satiric sensibility have made him one of the most highly esteemed African writers in English.

A Landmark Work Achebe's signature work, the novel *Things Fall Apart*, was published to international acclaim in 1958. Many critics consider the book to be the first major work of fiction to emerge from Africa. Both a critical and popular success, the novel has been translated into more than fifty languages and has exerted a major influence on other African writers.

TEACHING RESOURCES

The following resources can be used to enrich or extend the instruction for pp. 1348–1349.

Motivation

Interest Grabber Video, Tape 2

Background

Beyond Literature, p. 67

Take It to the Net

Visit PHSchool.com for background on the authors.

Literary Analysis

Literary Analysis and Reading Transparencies, Atmosphere, p. 133

Selection Support: Literary Analysis, p. 268

Reading

Literary Analysis and Reading Transparencies, Identifying With a Character, p. 134

BLOCK SCHEDULING: Resources marked with this symbol provide varied instruction during 90-minute blocks.

Preview

Connecting to the Literature

Most people who have known only peace and comfort develop a view of reality quite different from that of those who have known war and suffering. In these selections, characters struggle to bridge their differences.

2 Literary Analysis

Atmosphere

In literature, **atmosphere** refers to the emotional quality of the world the author creates. Atmosphere arises from descriptive details, setting, or plot and often mirrors the emotions of the characters themselves. In "Marriage Is a Private Affair," for example, descriptions of the weather reflect the pain and confusion in an old man's heart:

> He leaned against a window and looked out. The sky was overcast with heavy black clouds and a high wind began to blow. . . .

As you read these stories, look for descriptive details that reflect the characters' emotions and create distinctive atmospheres.

Comparing Literary Works

Both of these selections explore the ways in which intense cultural tensions can distort the kind feelings and good intentions of well-meaning people. As you read, identify the cultural tensions each story examines. Then, compare the ways in which both stories show that the damage caused by such tensions can be private and subtle but still devastating.

3 Reading Strategy

Identifying With a Character

You may better appreciate each of these stories if you **identify with a character** who appears in the work. To do so, imagine yourself in the character's situation. Think about what you would do and feel. As you read, use a chart like the one shown to explore similarities between yourself and a key character.

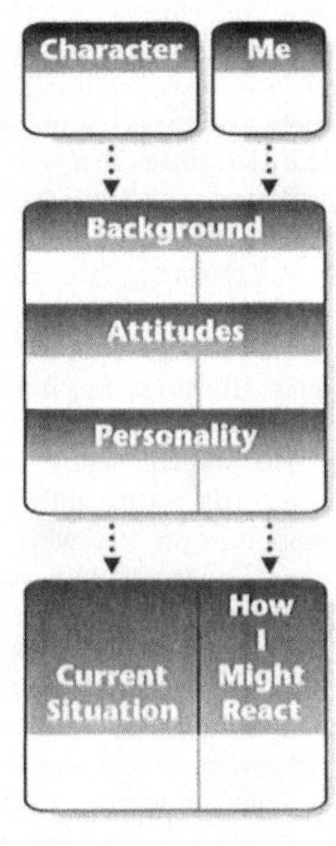

Vocabulary Development

assent (ə sent′) *n.* expression of agreement (p. 1351)

euphemisms (yo͞o′ fə miz′ əmz) *n.* words or phrases that are less expressive or direct but considered less distasteful or offensive than others (p. 1353)

furtively (fur′ tiv lē) *adv.* in a sneaky manner, as if to hinder observation (p. 1354)

revelation (rev′ ə lā′ shən) *n.* striking disclosure of something (p. 1354)

disposed (di spōzd′) *adj.* inclined; tending toward (p. 1356)

vehemently (vē′ ə mənt lē) *adv.* forcefully; intensely (p. 1357)

deference (def′ ər əns) *n.* submission to the desires or opinions of another; courteous respect (p. 1359)

perfunctorily (pər fuŋk′ tôr i lē) *adv.* indifferently; with little interest or care (p. 1360)

CUSTOMIZE INSTRUCTION FOR UNIVERSAL ACCESS

For Less Proficient Readers	For English Learners	For Advanced Readers
Students may have difficulty with Gordimer's unusual punctuation of dialogue and her mixing of external and internal dialogue. Read several paragraphs aloud, modeling through your intonation how the dashes function as quotation marks. Then, have students take turns reading paragraphs aloud to one another.	Point out that Gordimer usually uses dashes (—) to set off dialogue and that she does not always identify the speaker. Review some of the dialogue with students, and then have them work with an English-speaking partner to read the story.	Explain to students that Gordimer's story shifts almost imperceptibly between dialogue and action and the character's thoughts or memories. Using dashes blurs the demarcation between external and internal communication. Have students contrast Mrs. Telford's words with her thoughts and memories.

2 Literary Analysis

Atmosphere

- Read aloud the Literary Analysis instruction. Explain that the term *atmosphere* in the context of literature (and film) often communicates to the reader or audience one or more characters' emotional patterns.
- Have students reread the example from "Marriage Is a Private Affair." Then, point out that writers evoke a story's atmosphere not only through setting or character but also through language. Ask students to identify the words in the example that reinforce the atmosphere of pain and confusion.
Possible responses: The words *overcast*, *heavy*, *black*, *clouds*, and *wind* create this atmosphere.
- Use the Atmosphere transparency in **Literary Analysis and Reading Transparencies,** p. 133, to demonstrate how students can identify the atmosphere of a literary work.
- Read aloud the Comparing Literary Works instruction. Explain to students that cultural tensions can contribute to a work's atmosphere. Encourage students to consider how cultural tensions create or contribute to each selection's atmosphere.

3 Reading Strategy

Identifying With a Character

- Encourage students to analyze each character in the selections to assess his or her situation. Students may use a graphic organizer like the one on p. 1349 to facilitate this process.
- Point out that an analysis and assessment of a character will help students see how complex well-written characters can be—just as real people are complex.

Vocabulary Development

- Pronounce each vocabulary word for students, and read the definition as a class. Have students identify any words with which they are already familiar.

 ***E-Teach***

Visit e-Teach at PHSchool.com for teacher's essays on how to teach, with questions and answers.

TEACH

Step-by-Step Teaching Guide for pp. 1350–1360

Teaching Tenth-Grade Students

10TH GRADE Read aloud the Background information on p. 1350. Then, draw students' attention to the image on p. 1351. Point out that this photograph shows a protest against discrimination in South Africa. Ask students to discuss how these citizens of South Africa might feel.

1 About the Selection

In "Comrades," a white, middle-class woman activist engaged in the struggle against apartheid finds herself confronted with the reality of the lives of young black men who live under that system of injustice.

2 Literary Analysis

Atmosphere

- Remind students that atmosphere is the emotional quality of a work. Then, read aloud the bracketed passage.
- Ask students the Literary Analysis question on p. 1350: In the first paragraph, which descriptive details contribute to an atmosphere of tension?
  Answer: Opposites (the "city street" and the "enclave of learning"; the "tended flowerbeds" and the "guards and dogs"; the "people to be educated" and the "committee"; the "white and black activists"; and the "leftists secular and Christian") create a sense of tension.

3 Reading Strategy

Identifying With a Character

- After students have read the bracketed passage, have them discuss how both Mrs. Telford and the boys feel during this initial encounter.
- Ask students the Reading Strategy question on p. 1350: Can you identify with Mrs. Telford's mixed feelings as she agrees to take the youths to town? Why or why not?
  Possible response: Students may identify with how Mrs. Telford is torn between doing the right thing (giving the youths a ride) and her desire to get home.

1 

Comrades

Nadine Gordimer

Background

From 1948 until 1990, the country of South Africa operated under the apartheid system—the government policy that called for strict racial segregation and political and economic discrimination against nonwhites. Many South Africans, both white and black, fought against the apartheid system. While much of the dissent was political and peaceful, the tensions sometimes boiled over into violence. It is against this backdrop of painful political and cultural divisions that this story takes place.

2 As Mrs. Hattie Telford pressed the electronic gadget that deactivates the alarm device in her car a group of youngsters came up behind her. Black. But no need to be afraid; this was not a city street. This was a non-racial enclave of learning, a place where tended flowerbeds and trees bearing botanical identification plates civilized the wild reminder of campus guards and dogs. The youngsters, like her, were part of the crowd loosening into dispersion after a university conference on People's Education. They were the people to be educated; she was one of the committee of white and black activists (convenient generic for revolutionaries, leftists secular and Christian, fellow-travelers and liberals) up on the platform.

—Comrade . . . — She was settling in the driver's seat when one so slight and slim he seemed a figure in profile came up to her window. He drew courage from the friendly lift of the woman's eyebrows above blue eyes, the tilt of her freckled white face: —Comrade, are you going to town?—

3 No, she was going in the opposite direction, home . . . but quickly, in the spirit of the hall where these young people had been somewhere, somehow present with her (ah no, she with them) stamping and singing Freedom songs, she would take them to the bus station their spokesman named. —Climb aboard!—

The others got in the back, the spokesman beside her. She saw the nervous white of his eyes as he glanced at and away from her. She searched for talk to set them at ease. Questions, of course. Older people always start with questioning young ones. Did they come from Soweto?

They came from Harrismith, Phoneng Location.

Literary Analysis
Atmosphere In the first paragraph, which descriptive details contribute to an atmosphere of tension?

Reading Strategy
Identifying With a Character Can you identify with Mrs. Telford's mixed feelings as she agrees to take the boys to town? Why or why not?

TEACHING RESOURCES

The following resources can be used to enrich or extend the instruction for pp. 1350–1360.

Literary Analysis	Reading
Selection Support: Literary Analysis, p. 268 **Literary Analysis and Reading Transparencies,** Atmosphere, p. 133	**Selection Support:** Reading Strategy, p. 267; Build Vocabulary, p. 265 ■ **Listening to Literature Audiocassettes** **Listening to Literature Audio CDs** ■

■ **BLOCK SCHEDULING:** Resources marked with this symbol provide varied instruction during 90-minute blocks.

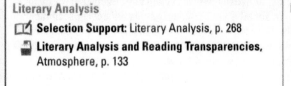

She made the calculation: about two hundred kilometers distant. How did they get here? Who told them about the conference?

—We are Youth Congress in Phoneng.—

A delegation. They had come by bus; one of the groups and stragglers who kept arriving long after the conference had started. They had missed, then, the free lunch?

4 At the back, no one seemed even to be breathing. The spokesman must have had some silent communication with them, some obligation to speak for them created by the journey or by other shared experience in the mysterious bonds of the young—these young. —We are hungry.— And from the back seats was drawn an assent like the suction of air in a compressing silence.

She was silent in response, for the beat of a breath or two. These large gatherings both excited and left her overexposed, open and vulnerable to the rub and twitch of the mass shuffling across rows of seats and loping up the aisles, babies' fudge-brown soft legs waving as their napkins are changed on mothers' laps, little girls with plaited loops on their heads listening like old crones, heavy women swaying to chants, men with fierce, unreadably black faces breaking into harmony tender and deep as they sing to God for his protection of Umkhonto weSizwe,

Reading Strategy
Identifying With a Character What do you think the boys are feeling as they sit in the back of Mrs. Telford's car?

assent (ə sent') *n.* expression of agreement

5 **✓Reading Check**

What gathering have Mrs. Telford and the group of boys just attended?

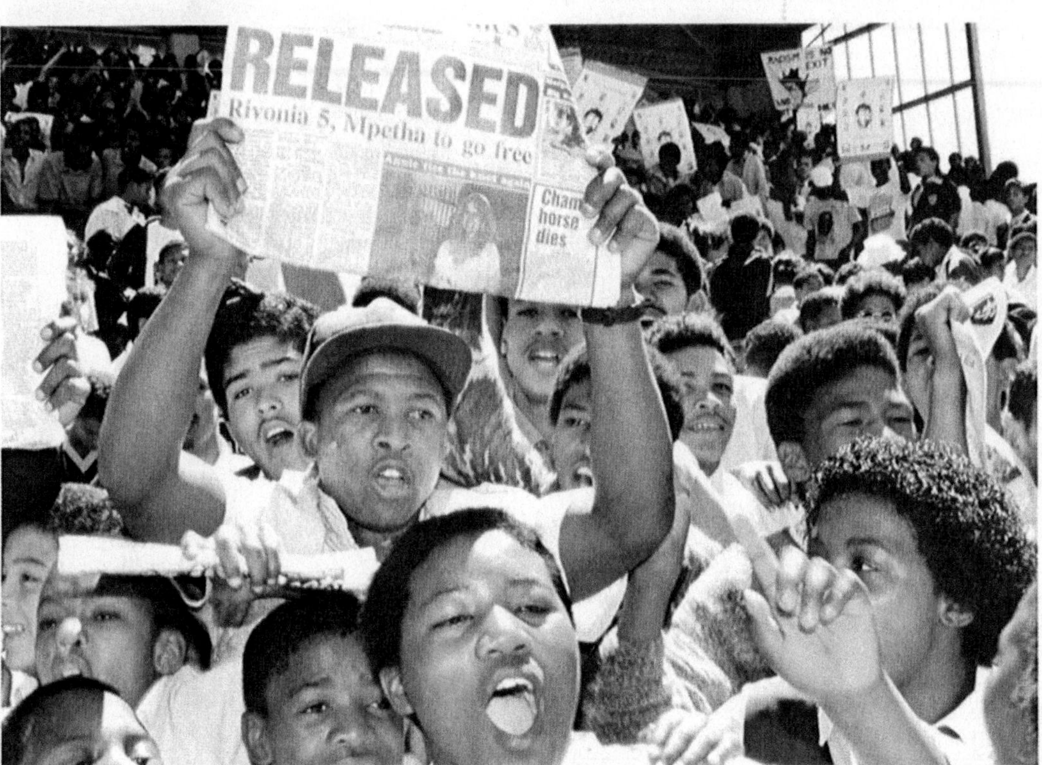

6 ▲ **Critical Viewing** In what ways do you think this scene of an anti-apartheid demonstration might resemble the event attended by Mrs. Telford and the students? Explain. **[Connect]**

4 Reading Strategy

Identifying With a Character

- Have a volunteer read aloud the bracketed passage.
- Ask students the Reading Strategy question on p. 1351: What do you think the boys are feeling as they sit in the back of Mrs. Telford's car?
  Possible response: The boys are probably feeling nervous or uncomfortable riding in a car with a white woman.

▶ **Monitor Progress** Ask students to discuss how they know what the boys are feeling. Remind them that in order to identify with a character, the reader must imagine himself or herself in the character's situation.
Possible response: Evidence from the text—such as the description of the group collectively holding its breath and the "silent communication"—and personal experiences with discomfort help readers infer what the boys' are feeling.

▶ **Reteach** Point out to students that the boys may feel uncomfortable with Mrs. Telford not only because of their difference in race but also because of their difference in age. Ask students to discuss experiences when they felt a "generational gap" or a moment of awkwardness caused by a difference in age.

5 ✓Reading Check

Answer: Mrs. Telford and the boys have just attended a university conference on People's Education.

6 ▶Critical Viewing

Answer: This scene and the conference have the same spirit—in both, people share the goal of abolishing apartheid.

CUSTOMIZE INSTRUCTION FOR UNIVERSAL ACCESS

For Special Needs Students	For Gifted/Talented Students
Guide students to use Venn diagrams to compare and contrast the life of Mrs. Telford with the lives of the young men. On the board, draw a Venn diagram, labeling one circle *Mrs. Telford* and the other *The Young Men.* Reserve the intersecting area for similarities between the characters. Guide students as they read to record details in the appropriate area of the diagram.	Have students locate photographs of demonstrations from the era of the American civil rights movement. Have them compare and contrast those photographs with the one on p. 1351. Then, lead a class discussion in which students present their photographs and comment on how the demonstrations are similar and different.

7 Critical Thinking

Analyze

- Have a volunteer read aloud the bracketed passage. Then, ask students to explain the "historical slight" to which the text alludes. Answer: Historically, the back door served as the servants' entrance and the entrance for all blacks regardless of their employment. Mrs. Telford recognizes that many would misconstrue the act of bringing the boys in through the back as a "slight" or an insult.
- Ask students: Why does Mrs. Telford, despite her understanding of the social implications of using the back entrance, bring the boys in through the back door? Answer: Mrs. Telford usually enters her house through the back door and she knows that the boys will not misconstrue this act.

8 Background

Art

This South African sculpture of a leopard and cub probably was carved from Mukwa wood, also known as African teak. This wood, prized for its attractive wide grain and warm range of colors, is considered by many one of the best furniture woods in existence.

Use the following question for discussion.

- How does the inclusion of this piece contribute to the story? Possible responses: The carving helps readers visualize Mrs. Telford's carving, despite the differences between them. Also, the sculpture emphasizes the importance of maintaining South African culture.

9 Literary Analysis

Atmosphere

- Have students read the bracketed passage independently.
- Ask students the Literary Analysis question on p. 1352: Which details contribute to an atmosphere of tension or suspense in Mrs. Telford's house? Explain. Possible response: The obvious class differences between Mrs. Telford and the boys, the boys' silence and extreme hunger, and Mrs. Telford's self-conscious chatter all create tension.

as people on both sides have always, everywhere, claimed divine protection for their soldiers, their wars. At the end of a day like this she wanted a drink, she wanted the depraved luxury of solitude and quiet in which she would be restored (enriched, oh yes! by the day) to the familiar limits of her own being.

Hungry. Not for iced whiskey and feet up. It seemed she had scarcely hesitated: —Look. I live nearby, come back to my house and have something to eat. Then I'll run you into town.—

—That will be very nice. We can be glad for that.— And at the back the tight vacuum relaxed.

8

They followed her in through the gate, shrinking away from the dog—she assured them he was harmless but he was large, with a fancy collar by which she held him. She trooped them in through

7 the kitchen because that was the way she always entered her house, something she would not have done if they had been adult, her black friends whose sophistication might lead them to believe the choice of entrance was an unthinking historical slight. As she was going to feed them, she took them not into her living-room with its sofas and flowers but into her dining-room, so that they could sit at table right away. It was a room in confident taste that could afford to be spare: bare floorboards, matching golden wooden ceiling, antique brass chandelier, reed blinds instead of stuffy curtains. An African wooden sculpture represented a lion marvelously released from its matrix in the grain of a Mukwa tree-trunk. She pulled up the chairs and left the four young men while she went back to the kitchen to make coffee and see what there was in the refrigerator for sandwiches. They had greeted the maid, in the language she and they shared, on their way through the kitchen, but when the maid and the lady of the house had finished preparing cold meat and bread, and the coffee was ready, she suddenly did not want them to see that the maid waited on her. She herself carried the heavy tray into the dining-room.

9

They are sitting round the table, silent, and there is no impression that they stopped an undertone exchange when they heard her approaching. She doles out plates, cups. They stare at the food but their eyes seem focused on something she can't see; something that overwhelms. She urges them—Just cold meat, I'm afraid, but there's chutney[1] if you like it . . . milk everybody? . . . is the coffee too strong, I have a heavy hand, I know. Would anyone like to add some hot water?—

They eat. When she tries to talk to one of the others, he says *Ekskuus?* And she realizes he doesn't understand English, of the white man's languages knows perhaps only a little of that of the Afrikaners in the rural town he comes from. Another gives his name, as if in some delicate acknowledgement of the food. —I'm Shadrack Nsutsha.— She repeats the surname to get it right. But he does not speak again. There

Literary Analysis
Atmosphere Which details contribute to an atmosphere of tension or suspense in Mrs. Telford's house? Explain.

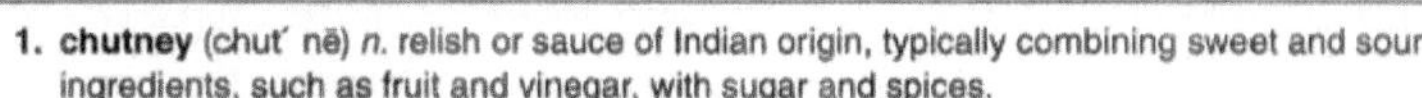

1. **chutney** (chut′ nē) *n.* relish or sauce of Indian origin, typically combining sweet and sour ingredients, such as fruit and vinegar, with sugar and spices.

ENRICHMENT: Political Science Connection

African National Congress

The African National Congress (ANC) is the oldest political body in South Africa. Founded in 1912 and originally named the South African Native National Congress, the organization's goal was to maintain voting rights for blacks and persons of mixed race. In the 1940s, young ANC leaders such as Nelson Mandela began to use boycotts, marches, and nonviolent protests to gain equal treatment. In 1948, when apartheid—the system of racial separation and discrimination—became official South African policy, ANC membership grew rapidly. In 1960, the ANC was outlawed, following a demonstration in which police shot hundreds of demonstrators. Without political recourse, the ANC turned to guerrilla tactics.

The government ban against the ANC was lifted in 1990, and the ANC agreed to stop its guerrilla activities. Nelson Mandela headed negotiations with the South African government for an elected government that included people of all races. In 1994, the ANC swept elections, making Mandela president.

is an urgent exchange of eye-language, and the spokesman holds out the emptied sugar-bowl to her. —Please.— She hurries to the kitchen and brings it back refilled. They need carbohydrate, they are hungry, they are young, they need it, they burn it up. She is distressed at the inadequacy of the meal and then notices the fruit bowl, her big copper
10 fruit bowl, filled with apples and bananas and perhaps there is a peach or two under the grape leaves with which she likes to complete an edible still life. —Have some fruit. Help yourselves.—

They are stacking their plates and cups, not knowing what they are expected to do with them in this room which is a room where apparently people only eat, do not cook, do not sleep. While they finish the bananas and apples (Shadrack Nsutsha had seen the single peach and quickly got there first) she talks to the spokesman, whose name she has asked for: Dumile. —Are you still at school, Dumile?— Of course he is not at school—*they* are not at school; youngsters their age have not been at school for several years, they are the children growing into young men and women for whom school is a battleground, a place of boycotts and demonstrations, the literacy of political rhetoric, the education of revolt against having to live the life their parents live. They have pompous titles of responsibility beyond childhood: he is chairman of his branch of the Youth Congress, he was expelled two years ago—for leading a boycott? Throwing stones at the police? Maybe burning the school down? He calls it all—quietly, abstractly, doesn't know many
11 ordinary, concrete words but knows these euphemisms— "political activity." No school for two years? No. —So what have you been able to do with yourself, all that time?—

She isn't giving him a chance to eat his apple. He swallows a large bite, shaking his head on its thin, little-boy neck. —I was inside. Detained from this June for six months.—

She looks round the others. —And you?—

Shadrack seems to nod slightly. The other two look at her. She should know, she should have known, it's a common enough answer from youths like them, their color. They're not going to be saying they've been selected for the 1st Eleven at cricket or that they're off on a student tour to Europe in the school holidays.

The spokesman, Dumile, tells her he wants to study by correspondence, "get his matric" that he was preparing for two years ago; two years ago when he was still a child, when he didn't have the hair that is now appearing on his face, making him a man, taking away the childhood. In the hesitations, the silences of the table, where there is nervously spilt coffee among plates of banana skins, there grows the certainty that he will never get the papers filled in for the correspondence college, he will never get the two years back. She looks at them all and cannot believe what she knows: that, they, suddenly here in her house, will carry the AK-47s[2] they only sing about, now, miming death as they sing. They will have a career of wiring explosives to the under- 12

2. **AK-47s** military assault rifles.

Reading Strategy
Identifying With a Character With whom do you identify more strongly—the students or Mrs. Telford? Explain.

euphemisms (yo͞o′ fə miz′ əmz) *n.* words or phrases that are less expressive or direct but considered less distasteful or offensive than others

✓Reading Check
For how long have the boys not attended school?

CUSTOMIZE INSTRUCTION FOR UNIVERSAL ACCESS

For Less Proficient Readers	For English Learners	For Advanced Readers
The narrator says that "political activity" is a euphemism for violence. Have students suggest other euphemisms. Then, lead a discussion in which students consider the purpose euphemisms serve and the advantages and disadvantages of using such word.	Ask students to share and discuss euphemisms that exist in their native languages. Invite students to say these euphemisms in their native languages, translate them literally, and explain the purpose they serve. Then, as a class identify and discuss similar euphemisms in English.	Have students use the Internet or library resources to conduct research on euphemisms used during military engagements or periods of political upheaval. Some examples include *peacekeeper missiles, collateral damage, relocation centers,* and *ethnic cleansing.* Ask students to explain their findings to the class.

10 Reading Strategy

Identifying With a Character

- Review with students the Reading Strategy instruction on p. 1349. Remind them that a reader must use his or her imagination and experience to understand a situation and to appreciate what a character must be feeling.
- Then, read aloud the bracketed passage on pp. 1352–1353. Ask students what this passage tells the reader about the experiences of the young men.
  Possible response: The young men live—without much sustenance—in one-room houses in which all residents eat, cook, and sleep.
- Ask students the Reading Strategy question on p. 1353: With whom do you identify more strongly—the students or Mrs. Telford? Explain.
  Possible responses: Some readers may identify with Mrs. Telford because they have no experience living in dire poverty. Others may relate to the youths, having lived in such a house or having experienced a situation in which they did not know what was expected of them or in which they experienced a communication breakdown.

11 Vocabulary Development

Greek Prefix *eu-*

- Draw students' attention to the word *euphemisms,* and read its definition.
- Tell students that *euphemisms* contains the Greek prefix *eu-,* which means "good" or "well." Then, have students discuss how the meaning of this prefix relates to the word *euphemisms.*
  Answer: A euphemism is a "good" way of conveying information that would otherwise be considered unpleasant or crass.
- Have students suggest other words that use the prefix *eu-,* and discuss how the meaning of the prefix relates to the meaning of each word.
  Possible responses: *Euphoria, eugenic,* and *euphony* all feature *eu-.*

12 ✓Reading Check

Answer: The boys have not attended school for two years.

Answers for p. 1354

Review and Assess

1. Possible responses: Readers may have hoped for an ending in which the boys are not revealed to be future killers. Others may have hoped that Mrs. Telford would offer to help the boys finish school.
2. **(a)** The university conference on People's Education has just ended. **(b)** Mrs. Telford was on the committee of activists who sat on the stage. The students attended the conference. **(c)** Mrs. Telford's participation suggests that she is active in the movement against apartheid.
3. **(a)** The boy draws courage from Mrs. Telford's friendly uplifted eyebrows and tilted face. **(b)** Mrs. Telford's expression suggests that she is open, friendly, and approachable. **(c)** The student is black, and it is illegal for the races to mix under apartheid.
4. **(a)** The boys are hungry, and Mrs. Telford intends to feed them. **(b)** The boys' physical hunger might represent the spiritual depravity induced by apartheid.
5. **(a)** The wooden floors and ceilings, the antique chandelier, and carved wooden statue suggest Mrs. Telford's affluence. **(b)** Mrs. Telford lives in a safe, comfortable environment; the students live in a violent, unstable environment. **(c)** Mrs. Telford lives alone in a house with many rooms and has plenty of food on hand. The students probably live with many people in one room and must struggle to survive. She enjoys freedom of movement and association and the right to vote; the students do not.
6. **(a)** They were expelled for participating in "political activity." **(b)** Mrs. Telford realizes that education is not in the boys' future but that violence and death certainly are. **(c)** Possible response: Violence is all that the boys know, and so their future immersion in it is inevitable but not justified.
7. Possible response: Political struggles often bring together people of different backgrounds and beliefs because they share ideals.

sides of vehicles, they will go away and come back through the bush to dig holes not to plant trees to shade home, but to plant land-mines. She can see they have been terribly harmed but cannot believe they could harm. They are wiping their fruit-sticky hands furtively palm against palm.

She breaks the silence; says something, anything.

—How d'you like my lion? Isn't he beautiful? He's made by a Zimbabwean artist, I think the name's Dube.—

But the foolish interruption becomes revelation. Dumile, in his gaze—distant, lingering, speechless this time—reveals what has overwhelmed them. In this room, the space, the expensive antique chandelier, the consciously simple choice of reed blinds, the carved lion: all are on the same level of impact, phenomena undifferentiated, undecipherable. Only the food that fed their hunger was real.

furtively (fur′ tiv lē) *adv.* in a sneaky manner, as if to hinder observation

revelation (rev′ ə lā′ shən) *n.* striking disclosure of something

Review and Assess

Thinking About the Selection

1. **Respond:** As you read the story, what outcome did you hope for?
2. **(a) Recall:** When the students approach Mrs. Telford, what event has just ended? **(b) Distinguish:** What different roles did Mrs. Telford and the students play at the event? **(c) Infer:** What does her participation in the event reveal about Mrs. Telford's politics?
3. **(a) Recall:** When the student first approaches Mrs. Telford in her car, which details in her appearance give him courage? **(b) Generalize:** What do these details suggest about her character? Explain. **(c) Analyze:** Why do you think the student needs courage to speak with Mrs. Telford?
4. **(a) Recall:** Why does Mrs. Telford take the students to her house instead of to town? **(b) Interpret:** What emotion or idea might the students' physical hunger represent? Explain.
5. **(a) Classify:** Which details in the description of Mrs. Telford's home suggest her affluence? **(b) Infer:** In what ways does Mrs. Telford's home stand in sharp contrast to the environment in which the students live? **(c) Support:** Which details in the text support your answer? Explain.
6. **(a) Deduce:** Why do the boys no longer attend school? **(b) Infer:** What realization does Mrs. Telford have about the students' futures? **(c) Take a Position:** Do you think the harm the boys have suffered justifies any harm they will do in the future? Explain.
7. **Synthesize:** Why might shared political struggles involve groups with otherwise very different backgrounds and beliefs?

ENRICHMENT: Literature Connection

The Work of Nadine Gordimer

By the time Nadine Gordimer's first collection of stories was published in 1949, she had become actively opposed to the government's policy of apartheid. Beginning with *The Lying Days* (1953), her ten novels are powerful indictments of a legal system that enabled a white minority to control and oppress the country's black majority.

In her complex tales of human relationships under apartheid, everyone suffers—blacks, whites, men, women, parents, and children. No one is exempt.

13 Marriage Is a Private Affair

Chinua Achebe

Background

The main characters in this story belong to two different Nigerian ethnic groups, the Ibo (ē′ bō′) (also called the Igbo) and the Ibibio (ib′ ə bē′ ō′). The Ibo are the largest ethnic group in southeastern Nigeria and one of the largest in the nation. During Britain's colonial rule of Nigeria, many Ibo were educated in British missionary schools, and today most of the Ibo population is Christian. The Ibo strongly supported the independence of southeastern Nigeria during the civil war of 1967–1970, and as a result, they earned the resentment of powerful Nigerian ethnic groups in the north. The Ibibio, also of southeastern Nigeria, are a smaller but nevertheless powerful group. Conflict between traditional Ibo values and those of modern life are at the center of this story.

"Have you written to your dad yet?" asked Nene[1] one afternoon as she sat with Nnaemeka[2] in her room at 16 Kasanga Street, Lagos.[3]

"No. I've been thinking about it. I think it's better to tell him when I get home on leave!"

14 "But why? Your leave is such a long way off yet—six whole weeks. He should be let into our happiness now."

Nnaemeka was silent for a while, and then began very slowly as if he groped for his words: "I wish I were sure it would be happiness to him."

"Of course it must," replied Nene, a little surprised. "Why shouldn't it?"

"You have lived in Lagos all your life, and you know very little about people in remote parts of the country."

1. **Nene** (nā′ nā′)
2. **Nnaemeka** ('n nē′ mə kə)
3. **Lagos** (lā′ gäs′) former capital city of Nigeria.

15 ✓ **Reading Check**

What has Nnaemaka been thinking about doing?

Teaching Tenth-Grade Students

10TH GRADE Ask students to consider both the positive and negative effects of breaking a tradition, such as not visiting family members during a holiday or choosing to follow a different religion. Encourage students as they read the selection to look for the positive and negative effects of breaking tradition.

13 About the Selection

Chinua Achebe's story "Marriage Is a Private Affair" is about clashes between cultures and generations. It focuses on the rift between a father and a son after the son announces his engagement to a woman from a different tribe. The father sees the son's move as a betrayal. The son sees the father as stubborn and too influenced by tradition. Achebe's tale reflects the upheaval Nigerians endured in the twentieth century as they moved into a more modern, Westernized, and secular world.

14 Critical Thinking

Speculate

- Remind students that when a reader speculates, he or she uses evidence to theorize about the actions within a literary work.
- Have a volunteer read aloud the bracketed passage. Then, have students speculate about the conflicts that will fuel this story. Students should support their speculations with evidence from the text.
  Possible responses: The conflict between Nnaemeka and his father will be central to this story. This conflict is made evident by Nnaemeka's reluctance to contact his father. The exchange between Nnaemeka and Nene sets up a conflict of beliefs that the story may also explore.

15 ✓ Reading Check

Answer: Nnaemeka has been thinking about writing to his father.

CUSTOMIZE INSTRUCTION FOR UNIVERSAL ACCESS

For Special Needs Students	For Less Proficient Readers	For Advanced Readers
Before students read the selection, preview the vocabulary and footnotes by pronouncing the words and reading the definitions or explanations. Then, have student pairs skim the text to identify other words and phrases with which they are unfamiliar.	Students may have difficulty grounding themselves within the story. Establish context by explaining that the "happiness" to which Nene refers is her engagement to Nnaemeka. Students should understand that Nnaemeka's father, an Ibo, will disapprove of his son's marriage to an Ibibio.	The clash of modern and traditional lifestyles and Christian and traditional faiths is a prominent theme of Achebe's novel *Things Fall Apart.* Have students read the novel, looking for parallels between its characters and the characters in "Marriage Is a Private Affair."

16 Reading Strategy

Identifying With a Character

- Remind students that readers cannot identify with a character, until they understand the character's motives and actions.
- Read aloud the bracketed passage. Then, ask students to describe the action each character wants to take and the motives behind these actions.
  Answer: Nene is happy about her impending marriage to Nnaemeka; consequently, she wants Nnaemeka to tell his father the news of their engagement. She probably thinks that Nnaemeka's father has a right to know about the marriage. Nnaemeka, fearing his father's disapproval, does not want to share the news.
- Ask students the Reading Strategy question on p. 1356: With which character do you identify most—the one who wants to share the news or the one who fears doing so?
  Possible responses: Readers may identify with Nene's happiness and her desire to share the news. Others may identify with Nnaemeka's desire to avoid confrontation.

17 Critical Thinking

Infer

- Ask a volunteer to read aloud the bracketed passage. Remind students that this letter reveals the father's own words and ideas about his son's marriage.
- Ask students: On the basis of this letter, what can you infer about Nnaemeka's father? What is he like? What does he value?
  Possible response: Nnaemeka's father is a Christian who believes in the tradition of arranged marriage. He believes that a wife should have little or no education and proper religious training.

18 ▶ Critical Viewing

Possible response: The painting, with its presentation in two parts, captures the separation between Nnaemeka and his father and between tradition and modern life. The figures in each box look similar but not harmonious.

---

16 "That's what you always say. But I don't believe anybody will be so unlike other people that they will be unhappy when their sons are engaged to marry."

"Yes. They are most unhappy if the engagement is not arranged by them. In our case it's worse—you are not even an Ibo."

This was said so seriously and so bluntly that Nene could not find speech immediately. In the cosmopolitan atmosphere of the city it had always seemed to her something of a joke that a person's tribe could determine whom he married.

At last she said, "You don't really mean that he will object to your marrying me simply on that account? I had always thought you Ibos were kindly disposed to other people."

"So we are. But when it comes to marriage, well, it's not quite so simple. And this," he added, "is not peculiar to the Ibos. If your father were alive and lived in the heart of Ibibio-land he would be exactly like my father."

"I don't know. But anyway, as your father is so fond of you, I'm sure he will forgive you soon enough. Come on then, be a good boy and send him a nice lovely letter . . ."

"It would not be wise to break the news to him by writing. A letter will bring it upon him with a shock. I'm quite sure about that."

"All right, honey, suit yourself. You know your father."

As Nnaemeka walked home that evening he turned over in his mind the different ways of overcoming his father's opposition, especially now that he had gone and found a girl for him. He had thought of showing his letter to Nene but decided on second thoughts not to, at least for the moment. He read it again when he got home and couldn't help smiling to himself. He remembered Ugoye[4] quite well, an Amazon[5] of a girl who used to beat up all the boys, himself included, on the way to the stream, a complete dunce at school.

17 *I have found a girl who will suit you admirably—Ugoye Nweke,[6] the eldest daughter of our neighbor, Jacob Nweke. She has a proper Christian upbringing. When she stopped schooling some years ago her father (a man of sound judgment) sent her to live in the house of a pastor where she has received all the training a wife could need. Her Sunday School teacher has told me that she reads her Bible very fluently. I hope we shall begin negotiations when you come home in December.*

On the second evening of his return from Lagos Nnaemeka sat with his father under a cassia tree. This was the old man's retreat where he went to read his Bible when the parching December sun had set and a fresh, reviving wind blew on the leaves.

"Father," began Nnaemeka suddenly, "I have come to ask forgiveness."

"Forgiveness? For what, my son?" he asked in amazement.

"It's about this marriage question."

Reading Strategy
Identifying With a Character With which character do you identify most—the one who wants to share the news or the one who fears doing so?

disposed (di spōzd') *adj.* inclined; tending toward

18 **Critical Viewing ▶** Do you think this painting captures the characters and mood of this story? Why or why not? **[Generalize]**

4. **Ugoye** (yōō gō' yə)
5. **Amazon** (am' ə zän) large, strong, masculine woman. In Greek mythology, the Amazons were a race of female warriors.
6. **Nweke** ('n wā' kā)

ENRICHMENT: History Connection

Nigeria

Nigeria, the setting for "Marriage Is a Private Affair," has had a long history. In the late 1800's, the British annexed lands in west Africa, eventually setting up the colony of Nigeria. Local rulers resisted British domination, and in 1960, Nigeria finally achieved independence.

Religious, economic, and ethnic divisions flared after independence. The Ibo in the southeast felt that the Muslim Huasa-Fulani of the north dominated Nigeria. The Ibo seceded from Nigeria, setting up the independent Republic of Biafra. A brutal civil war followed, and in 1970, a defeated Biafra rejoined Nigeria.

19 "Which marriage question?"

"I can't—we must—I mean it is impossible for me to marry Nweke's daughter."

"Impossible? Why?" asked his father.

"I don't love her."

"Nobody said you did. Why should you?" he asked.

"Marriage today is different . . ."

"Look here, my son," interrupted his father, "nothing is different. What one looks for in a wife are a good character and a Christian background."

Nnaemeka saw there was no hope along the present line of argument.

"Moreover," he said, "I am engaged to marry another girl who has all of Ugoye's good qualities, and who . . ."

His father did not believe his ears. "What did you say?" he asked slowly and disconcertingly.

"She is a good Christian," his son went on, "and a teacher in a Girls' School in Lagos."

"Teacher, did you say? If you consider that a qualification for a good wife I should like to point out to you, Emeka, that no Christian woman should teach. St. Paul in his letter to the Corinthians[7] says that women should keep silence." He rose slowly from his seat and paced forwards and backwards. This was his pet subject, and he condemned vehemently those church leaders who encouraged women to teach in their **20**

Literary Analysis
Atmosphere What atmosphere do Nnaemeka's disturbed emotions create?

vehemently (vē′ ə mənt lē) *adv.* forcefully; intensely

20 ✔Reading Check
What arrangement has Nnaemeka's father made for his son's marriage?

7. **St. Paul . . . Corinthians** reference to the Bible's New Testament (1 Corinthians 14:34), in which Paul writes, "Let your women keep silent in the churches."

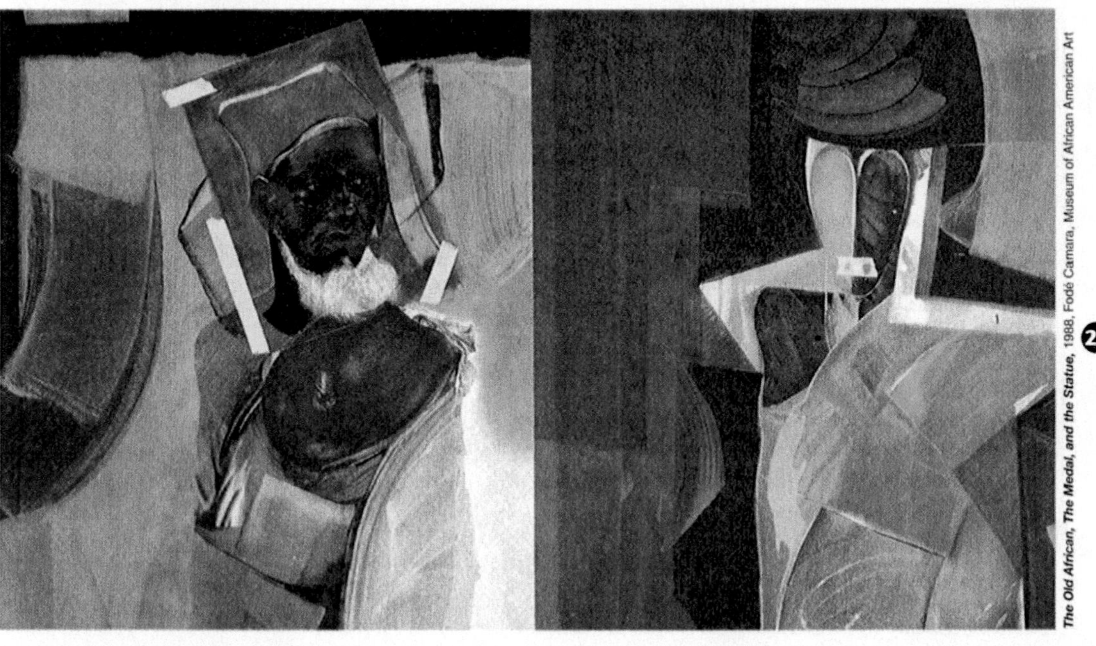

The Old African, The Medal, and the Statue, 1988, Fodé Camara, Museum of African American Art **21**

19 Literary Analysis
Atmosphere

- Review with students the Literary Analysis instruction on p. 1349. Make sure students understand that the emotions of the characters tinge the overall atmosphere of a work.
- Ask a volunteer to read aloud the bracketed passage on pp. 1356–1357. Then, have students cite examples from the passage that reveal Nnaemeka's unease.
  Answer: Uncertain of how to approach his father, Nnaemeka stammers, "I can't—we must—I mean it is impossible for me to marry Nweke's daughter." It is clear that Nnaemeka is reluctant and uncomfortable.
- Ask students the Literary Analysis question on p. 1357: What atmosphere do Nnaemeka's disturbed emotions create?
  Answer: Nnaemeka's emotions create an atmosphere of tension and conflict.

20 ✔Reading Check

Answer: Nnaemeka's father has planned to start negotiations for his son to marry the daughter of a neighbor.

21 Background
Art

The Old African, The Medal, and the Statue, by Fodé Camara

Contemporary artist Fodé Camara, a native of Dakar, Sénégal, studied at the Institut National des Arts du Sénégal and in Paris at the École Nationale Supérieure des Arts Décoratifs. His bright, abstract paintings provide an expressive insight into the issues of colonialism and colonial identity.

Use the following question for discussion.

What adjectives describe the figure on the left side of the painting?
Possible response: The figure looks serious, pondering, confused, and focused.

CUSTOMIZE INSTRUCTION FOR UNIVERSAL ACCESS

For Special Needs Students	For Advanced Readers
As students read the story, explain that its events take place over the course of eight years. Guide students to create a four-box flowchart with the headings *As the Story Begins, A Few Weeks Later* (p. 1358), *Six Months Later* (p. 1359), and *Eight Years Later* (p. 1359). Have students use the organizer to record notable events for each time period. Then, after students have finished reading the entire story, lead a class discussion in which they consider why the story's resolution takes as long as it does.	Tell students that Achebe once said, "Stories are not just meant to make people smile . . . our life depends on them." Encourage students to keep this quotation in mind as they read "Marriage Is a Private Affair" and to take notes on specific examples in the text that support or refute this assertion. Then, have students use their notes to write brief essays in which they discuss the relevance of this quotation to the story. Encourage volunteers to share their work with the class.

22 Background

Arranged Marriages

The custom of arranged marriages is practiced to some degree in the United States today, most often within small communities of immigrants from countries such as India or Iraq, where arranged marriage is an established tradition. Although many Americans consider an arranged marriage an infringement on personal choice, cultures for which this practice is a custom defend it for its focus on family and roots in traditional culture.

23 Literary Analysis

Atmosphere

- After students have read the bracketed passage, ask: What is the atmosphere of this passage? What words and phrases in the passage create this atmosphere?
  Answer: Words and phrases such as *deeply affected*, *grief*, and *less optimistic* create an atmosphere of sorrow and loss.
- Ask students the Literary Analysis question on p. 1358: In what ways does this paragraph intensify the sense of Nnaemeka's isolation?
  Answer: In this paragraph, it becomes clear that the men believe that Nnaemeka will be the first and only Ibo man to marry outside his cultural group. Therefore, Nnaemeka faces the rejection of not only his father but also his entire culture.

Reteach If students have difficulty answering the Literary Analysis question, use the Atmosphere transparency in **Literary Analysis and Reading Transparencies,** p. 133, to review the importance of identifying the emotional quality of a work.

schools. After he had spent his emotion on a long homily[8] he at last came back to his son's engagement, in a seemingly milder tone.

"Whose daughter is she, anyway?"

"She is Nene Atang."

"What!" All the mildness was gone again. "Did you say Neneataga, what does that mean?"

"Nene Atang from Calabar.[9] She is the only girl I can marry." This was a very rash reply and Nnaemeka expected the storm to burst. But it did not. His father merely walked away into his room. This was most unexpected and perplexed Nnaemeka. His father's silence was infinitely more menacing than a flood of threatening speech. That night the old man did not eat.

When he sent for Nnaemeka a day later he applied all possible ways of dissuasion. But the young man's heart was hardened, and his father eventually gave him up as lost.

"I owe it to you, my son, as a duty to show you what is right and what is wrong. Whoever put this idea into your head might as well have cut your throat. It is Satan's work." He waved his son away.

"You will change your mind, Father, when you know Nene."

"I shall never see her," was the reply. From that night the father scarcely spoke to his son. He did not, however, cease hoping that he would realize how serious was the danger he was heading for. Day and night he put him in his prayers.

Nnaemeka, for his own part, was very deeply affected by his father's grief. But he kept hoping that it would pass away. If it had occurred to him that never in the history of his people had a man married a woman who spoke a different tongue, he might have
23 been less optimistic. "It has never been heard," was the verdict of an old man speaking a few weeks later. In that short sentence he spoke for all of his people. This man had come with others to commiserate with Okeke[10] when news went round about his son's behavior. By that time the son had gone back to Lagos.

"It has never been heard," said the old man again with a sad shake of his head.

"What did Our Lord say?" asked another gentleman. "Sons shall rise against their Fathers; it is there in the Holy Book."

"It is the beginning of the end," said another.

The discussion thus tending to become theological, Madubogwu, a highly practical man, brought it down once more to the ordinary level.

"Have you thought of consulting a native doctor about your son?" he asked Nnaemeka's father.

"He isn't sick," was the reply.

"What is he then? The boy's mind is diseased and only a good

8. **homily** (häm´ ə lē) *n.* religious speech.
9. **Calabar** (kal´ ə bär) seaport in southeast Nigeria.
10. **Okeke** (o kā´ kā)

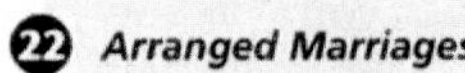

Themes in World Literature

22 ***Arranged Marriages***

Until the twentieth century, arranged marriages were common in almost all cultures of the world. It is no surprise, then, that this nuptial custom has been both chronicled and critiqued by countless writers throughout history. The author of the Old Testament book of Genesis, for example, describes the arranged marriage between Isaac, son of Abraham, and Rebekah. Two millennia later, Shakespeare treats the same theme—but far less objectively—in his tragedy *Romeo and Juliet* (1595). More recently, writers from India and other parts of Asia have tackled this difficult subject, most notably Chitra Divakaruni in her collection of short stories *Arranged Marriages* (1995). The theme also appears in Yasunari Kawabata's short story "The Jay" (p. 1382).

Literary Analysis

Atmosphere In what ways does this paragraph intensify the sense of Nnaemeka's isolation?

ENRICHMENT: Linguistics Connection

Writing in English

Although Achebe writes in English, he recognizes the pitfalls of doing so. In an article in *Nigeria* magazine (June 1964), Achebe discussed some of the problems he faced in using English.

> For an African, writing in English is not without its serious setbacks. He often finds himself describing situations or modes of thought which have no direct equivalent in the English way of life. Caught in that situation he can do one of two things. He can try and contain what he wants to say within the limits of conventional English or he can try to push back those limits to accommodate his ideas. The first method produces competent, uninspired and rather flat work. The second method can produce something new and valuable to the English language as well as to the material he is trying to put over.

24 herbalist can bring him back to his right senses. The medicine he requires is *Amalile*, the same that women apply with success to recapture their husbands' straying affection."

"Madubogwu is right," said another gentleman. "This thing calls for medicine."

"I shall not call in a native doctor." Nnaemeka's father was known to be obstinately ahead of his more superstitious neighbors in these matters. "I will not be another Mrs. Ochuba. If my son wants to kill himself let him do it with his own hands. It is not for me to help him."

"But it was her fault," said Madubogwu. "She ought to have gone to an honest herbalist. She was a clever woman, nevertheless."

"She was a wicked murderess," said Jonathan who rarely argued with his neighbors because, he often said, they were incapable of reasoning. "The medicine was prepared for her husband, it was his name they called in its preparation and I am sure it would have been perfectly beneficial to him. It was wicked to put it into the herbalist's food, and say you were only trying it out."

Literary Analysis
Atmosphere How does the discussion between the old men show that Nnaemeka's conflict with his father is part of a much larger societal conflict?

Six months later, Nnaemeka was showing his young wife a short letter from his father:

It amazes me that you could be so unfeeling as to send me your wedding picture. I would have sent it back. But on further thought I decided just to cut off your wife and send it back to you because I have nothing to do with her. How I wish that I had nothing to do with you either.

25 When Nene read through this letter and looked at the mutilated picture her eyes filled with tears, and she began to sob.

"Don't cry, my darling," said her husband. "He is essentially good-natured and will one day look more kindly on our marriage." But years passed and that one day did not come.

Reading Strategy
Identifying With a Character Can you identify with Nene's reaction to the letter and photograph? Explain.

For eight years, Okeke would have nothing to do with his son, Nnaemeka. Only three times (when Nnaemeka asked to come home and spend his leave) did he write to him.

"I can't have you in my house," he replied on one occasion. "It can be of no interest to me where or how you spend your leave—or your life, for that matter."

The prejudice against Nnaemeka's marriage was not confined to his little village. In Lagos, especially among his people who worked there, it showed itself in a different way. Their women, when they met at their village meeting, were not hostile to Nene. Rather, they paid her such excessive deference as to make her feel she was not one of them. But as time went on, Nene gradually broke through some of this prejudice and even began to make friends among them. Slowly and grudgingly they began to admit that she kept her home much better than most of them. 26

deference (def′ ər əns) *n.* submission to the desires or opinions of another; courteous respect

✓Reading Check
For how long does Okeke avoid all contact with his son?

The story eventually got to the little village in the heart of the Ibo country that Nnaemeka and his young wife were a most happy couple. But his father was one of the few people who knew nothing about this.

24 Literary Analysis
Atmosphere

- After students have read the bracketed passage independently, ask them to identify words that describe the atmosphere, or mood, in the village when the old men meet to talk.
  Possible response: The atmosphere is somber as the men consider the cultural ramifications of Nnaemeka's marriage, but it is also a little comical as the men hyperbolize and speculate on Nnaemeka's "sickness."
- Ask students the Literary Analysis question on p. 1359: How does the discussion among the old men show that Nnaemeka's conflict with his father is part of a larger societal conflict?
  Answer: It is clear from the men's discussion that not only tribal but also religious conflicts—between ancient paganism, Christianity, and modern secularism—exist in the community.

25 Reading Strategy
Identifying With a Character

- Read aloud the bracketed sentence. Then, ask students the Reading Strategy question on p. 1359: Can you identify with Nene's reaction to the letter and photograph? Explain.
  Possible responses: Some readers may identify with Nene's frustration at being prejudged by Okeke.

26 ✓Reading Check

Answer: Okeke avoids contact with Nnaemeka for eight years.

CUSTOMIZE INSTRUCTION FOR UNIVERSAL ACCESS

For English Learners	For Gifted/Talented Students
Organize students into small groups, and have them discuss marriage traditions in their native cultures. Before students begin, you might list on the board terms related to Western wedding traditions, such as *bride, groom, cake, minister, priest, judge,* and *rabbi.* Ask students to draw comparisons among Western traditions and their native cultures' traditions. Then, have students consider how these approaches to marriage compare with the way marriage is presented in Achebe's story.	Organize students into groups of four, and have them improvise a scene in which they role-play a discussion among Okeke, Nnaemeka, Nene, and a mediator. Three of the students should review the story to prepare for their roles as characters. The fourth student should prepare to ask questions and make suggestions to the characters for ways to resolve their differences. Encourage students to perform their improvisations for the class.

ASSESS

27 Literary Analysis

Atmosphere

- Have a volunteer read aloud the bracketed passage. Then, ask students to consider the atmosphere of the story prior to this letter.
  Possible response: The atmosphere of the story up to this point has been one of sorrow and hopelessness.
- Then, ask students the Literary Analysis question on p. 1360: In what ways does Nene's letter change the story's atmosphere?
  Answer: The atmosphere becomes hopeful as Nene's letter melts Okeke's resolve to continue to shun his son and daughter-in-law.

Answers for p. 1360

Review and Assess

1. Possible responses: Some readers may want to shame Okeke for wasting eight years of his life by being angry at his son. Others may want to commend Okeke for sticking to his principles.
2. **(a)** A suitable wife should be a good Christian and poorly educated. She should also be an Ibo. **(b)** Nnaemeka chooses Nene because she is a good person, well educated, a respected teacher, and a good Christian. Also, he loves her. **(c)** By making Nene so sympathetic and likeable, it is clear that the author favors Nnaemeka's criteria.
3. **(a)** Reading the letter from Nene triggers the father's emotional trauma. **(b)** Possible response: The father, overcome with remorse, will reconcile with his son and meet his grandsons as soon as possible.
4. Possible responses: Readers may say that choosing a mate is a very personal decision and that the opinions of others should play no role. Others may suggest that it is important to consider the opinions of friends and relatives because their experience—and resulting advice—may prove useful.

He always displayed so much temper whenever his son's name was mentioned that everyone avoided it in his presence. By a tremendous effort of will he had succeeded in pushing his son to the back of his mind. The strain had nearly killed him but he had persevered, and won.

Then one day he received a letter from Nene, and in spite of himself he began to glance through it perfunctorily until all of a sudden the expression on his face changed and he began to read more carefully.

perfunctorily (pər fuŋk′ tôr i lē) *adv.* indifferently; with little interest or care

27 *. . . Our two sons, from the day they learnt that they have a grandfather, have insisted on being taken to him. I find it impossible to tell them that you will not see them. I implore you to allow Nnaemeka to bring them home for a short time during his leave next month. I shall remain here in Lagos . . .*

Literary Analysis
Atmosphere In what ways does Nene's letter change the story's atmosphere?

The old man at once felt the resolution he had built up over so many years falling in. He was telling himself that he must not give in. He tried to steel his heart against all emotional appeals. It was a re-enactment of that other struggle. He leaned against a window and looked out. The sky was overcast with heavy black clouds and a high wind began to blow filling the air with dust and dry leaves. It was one of those rare occasions when even Nature takes a hand in a human fight. Very soon it began to rain, the first rain in the year. It came down in large sharp drops and was accompanied by the lightning and thunder which mark a change of season. Okeke was trying hard not to think of his two grandsons. But he knew he was now fighting a losing battle. He tried to hum a favorite hymn but the pattering of large rain drops on the roof broke up the tune. His mind immediately returned to the children. How could he shut his door against them? By a curious mental process he imagined them standing, sad and forsaken, under the harsh angry weather—shut out from his house.

That night he hardly slept, from remorse—and a vague fear that he might die without making it up to them.

Review and Assess

Thinking About the Selection

1. **Respond:** What would you like to say to Nnaemeka's father at the end of the story? Explain.
2. **(a) Recall:** What criteria does Nnaemeka's father use to judge the suitability of a wife? **(b) Infer:** What criteria has Nnaemeka used to choose Nene? **(c) Evaluate:** Does the author seem to favor one set of criteria over the other? Explain.
3. **(a) Analyze Cause and Effect:** Which event triggers the father's emotional trauma at the end of the story? **(b) Predict:** Based on the story's final scene, what do you think the father will do?
4. **Take a Position:** Should marriage be an entirely private affair or should the opinions of friends and relatives play a role? Explain.

ASSESSMENT PRACTICE: Reading Comprehension

Using Context Clues to Determine Meanings (For more practice, see Test Preparation Workbook, p. 3.)

The reading sections of many tests require students to use context clues to determine the appropriate meaning of a word in a given passage. Use the following sample test item to demonstrate.

> These large gatherings both excited and left her overexposed, open and vulnerable to the rub and twitch of the mass shuffling across rows of seats and loping up the aisles. . . .

In this passage, the word vulnerable most nearly means—

A impolite.
B sensitive.
C respected.
D strong.

Answers *A, C,* and *D* do not make sense within the context of the sentence. Two words—*overexposed* and *open*—suggest a sensitivity to being hurt and act as clues to the meaning of *vulnerable*. *B* is the correct answer.

Review and Assess

Literary Analysis

Atmosphere

1. (a) How would you describe the **atmosphere** in the opening paragraph of "Comrades"? (b) Use a chart like the one shown to identify descriptive details that contribute to this atmosphere.

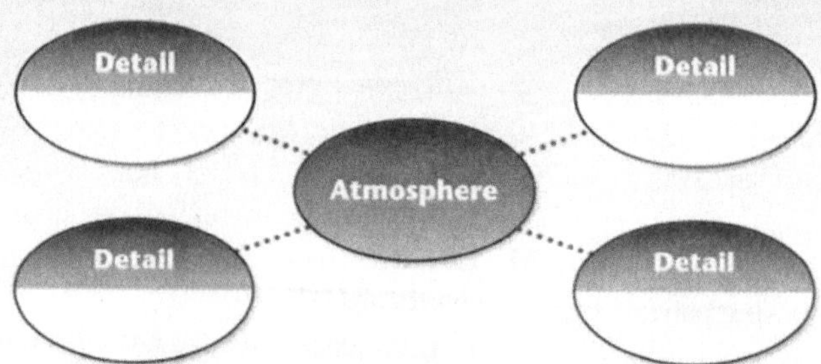

2. (a) After Mrs. Telford carries the tray into the dining room, how does the story's verb tense change? (b) What is the effect of this change on the story's atmosphere?
3. (a) In "Marriage Is a Private Affair," which details contribute to the story's atmosphere of intense but restrained emotion? Explain. (b) At what point does the atmosphere change, and why?

Comparing Literary Works

4. Which specific cultural pressures or tensions are at work in each of these stories?
5. (a) In what ways do both Mrs. Telford and Nnaemeka's father try to behave honorably? (b) Do they succeed? Why or why not?
6. What does each story say about the cruelties of prejudice? Explain.

Reading Strategy

Identifying With a Character

7. With which character or situation in each story do you most strongly **identify**? Explain.
8. At which point in each story would you have felt or acted differently than the character did? Explain.

Extend Understanding

9. **Career Connection:** Mediators are professionals who help people settle disputes peacefully. If you were a mediator, what advice would you give to Nnaemeka and his father?

Quick Review

Atmosphere is the emotional quality of the world the author creates in a work of literature.

To **identify with a character** as you read, imagine yourself in the place of a character and try to experience events through his or her eyes.

Take It to the Net

PHSchool.com

Take the interactive self-test online to check your understanding of these selections.

Answers for p. 1361

Review and Assess

1. **(a)** The atmosphere is tense. **(b)** Possible response: Mrs. Telford is aware that the young men are approaching her from behind; Mrs. Telford has just unlocked her car, making her vulnerable; Mrs. Telford is aware that the young men are black; Mrs. Telford has to remind herself that she is not in the city and probably not in danger.
2. **(a)** The verb tense changes from past tense to present tense. **(b)** The change in tense makes the scene at the table seem as if it were happening at the present moment, creating a paradoxical atmosphere of immediacy and suspense.
3. **(a)** The use of letters to communicate, Nnaemeka's aversion to talking to his father, and Okeke's refusal to talk about his son all indicate restrained emotion. **(b)** The atmosphere changes immediately after Okeke reads the letter from Nene. When he learns about his grandsons, Okeke's anger and prejudices are washed away.
4. In "Comrades," Mrs. Telford feels pressure to be friendly and open toward the young men. In "Marriage Is a Private Affair," Nnaemeka resists pressure from his father and his culture. His refusal to follow tradition causes tension between him and his father.
5. **(a)** Mrs. Telford tries to behave honorably by giving the young men a ride and by inviting them in for lunch. Nnaemeka's father tries to behave honorably by adhering to his cultural traditions. **(b)** Mrs. Telford feeds the young men, but she has no way of connecting with them. Nnaemeka's father succeeds for eight years in upholding his tradition, but denying love to a son in favor of a tradition based on prejudice has no honor.
6. In "Comrades," the young men have suffered as a result of prejudice. In "Marriage Is a Private Affair," Okeke's prejudice costs him a relationship with his son's family.
7. Possible response: Readers may identify with the young characters

continued

continued from right column

because the characters are breaking traditions that they feel do not work.

8. Possible response: Readers may suggest that they would not disown a son because he chose to marry a member of another ethnic group.
9. Possible response: A mediator should make both characters aware of the gains and losses inherent in any decision. A mediator might also suggest the need for a concession from each character.

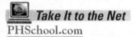

ENRICHMENT: Further Reading

Other Works by Nadine Gordimer and Chinua Achebe

We strongly encourage you to review any selection before assigning or recommending it to students.

Nadine Gordimer
The Conservationist

Chinua Achebe
Things Fall Apart

Take It to the Net

Visit PHSchool.com for more information about the authors.

EXTEND

Answers for p. 1362

❶ Vocabulary Development

Word Analysis: Greek Prefix *eu-*

1. eulogy: a speech that speaks well of someone
2. euphonious: sweet sounding or melodious

Spelling Strategy

1. apostrophe
2. megaphone
3. sorrowful
4. graphite

Fluency: Words in Context

1. Yes; those inclined to eat fish would try salmon.
2. Yes; one should show a queen courteous respect.
3. No; Lee would need to give the materials more attention.
4. Yes; you will be busy completing those tasks that you agreed to do.
5. No; a phone call conducted in a sneaky manner would be difficult to hear.
6. No; Mike will not play a game he intensely dislikes.
7. Yes; the disclosure of a password would make access easier.
8. Yes; such indirect phrases would not offend.

❷ Grammar and Style

Practice

1. what was in the refrigerator; direct object
2. how nicely she kept her home; direct object
3. what she knows; direct object
4. that the letter would change his feelings; direct object
5. why she was upset; direct object

Writing Application

Possible response: Nnaemeka knew *that his father would be upset by* the *news of his marriage to Nene.* Later, Nene wrote in a letter *that her sons wanted to meet their grandfather.*

10TH GRADE For support in teaching the Grammar and Style Lesson to tenth graders, use **Writing and Grammar,** Platinum Level, Chapter 20, Section 2.

Integrate Language Skills

❶ Vocabulary Development Lesson

Word Analysis: Greek Prefix *eu-*

The prefix *eu-* means "good" or "well." Use the clues in parentheses and your knowledge of the meaning of the prefix *eu-* to write a definition of both words below.

1. eulogy (*-logy* = word or speech)
2. euphonious (*-phonious* = sounding)

Spelling Strategy

In many English words of Greek origin, *ph* is used to spell the *f* sound, as in *euphemism, telephone*, and *graph*. For each of the following pairs, choose the correct spelling.

1. apostrofe/apostrophe
2. megafone/megaphone
3. sorrowful/sorrowphul
4. grafite/graphite

Fluency: Words in Context

Answer *yes* or *no* to each question below. Explain each response.

1. If you are *disposed* to eating fish, would you try salmon?
2. Is *deference* proper when meeting a queen?
3. If Lee studies *perfunctorily*, can she expect to earn an A?
4. If you *assent* to more, will you be busier?
5. Could a phone call made *furtively* be easily overheard?
6. If Mike *vehemently* dislikes soccer, will he choose to play the game?
7. Would the *revelation* of a password help you gain access to something?
8. Could you use *euphemisms* to avoid disturbing someone?

❷ Grammar and Style Lesson

Noun Clauses

A subordinate clause is a group of words with a subject and a verb that cannot stand by itself as a complete sentence. A **noun clause** is a subordinate clause that functions as a noun. It can serve as the subject of a verb, a direct object, or the object of a preposition. Noun clauses are often introduced by the words *that, what, which, how*, and *why*.

Subject: "What one looks for in a wife are a good character and a Christian background."

Direct Object: They're not going to be saying . . . that they're off on a student tour in Europe.

Practice For each item below, identify the noun clause and explain its function in the sentence.

1. She went to the kitchen to see what was in the refrigerator.
2. The women saw how nicely she kept her home.
3. She cannot believe what she knows.
4. She did not know that the letter would change his feelings.
5. He understood why she was upset.

Writing Application Write a summary of the events in one of these stories. Include at least two noun clauses.

WG Prentice Hall Writing and Grammar Connection: Diamond Level, Chapter 19, Section 3

TEACHING RESOURCES

The following resources can be used to enrich or extend the instruction for pp. 1362–1363.

Vocabulary

- **Selection Support:** Build Vocabulary, p. 265
- **Vocabulary and Spelling Practice Book** (Use this booklet for skills instruction.)

Grammar

- **Selection Support:** Grammar and Style, p. 266
- **Writing and Grammar,** Diamond Level, p. 458
- **Daily Language Practice Transparencies**

Writing

- **Performance Assess. and Portfolio Mgmt.,** p. 10
- **Writing and Grammar,** Diamond Level, p. 102
- **Writing and Grammar iText CD-ROM**

Listening and Speaking

- **Performance Assess. and Portfolio Mgmt.,** p. 33

BLOCK SCHEDULING: Resources marked with this symbol provide varied instruction during 90-minute blocks.

❸ Writing Lesson

Manual on How to Change a Story's Atmosphere

Gordimer uses precise descriptive details to create an intense and vivid atmosphere in "Comrades." Using her story as an example, write a manual for young authors on how to create various types of atmosphere in a story.

Prewriting Reread "Comrades" and list details Gordimer uses to create a tense atmosphere. Then, brainstorm for other types of atmosphere that a story might create and the kinds of details that would be effective.

Drafting Explain the concept of atmosphere. Follow with three sections, each of which describes how to create a different type of atmosphere and provides examples. Introduce each example.

Model: Drafting to Introduce Example Text

For example, notice how altered details change the atmosphere from one of tension to one of friendliness:
Original Text: The others got in the back, the spokesman beside her. She saw the nervous white of his eyes.
New Text: The others tumbled into the back, the spokesman beside her. She saw weary gratitude in his eyes as he sent her a silent *thanks.*

A clear introduction to an example clarifies its purpose.

Revising As you review your work, make sure that your examples clearly evoke the types of atmospheres you specify. Consider altering details as needed to create the desired effect.

WG *Prentice Hall Writing and Grammar Connection: Diamond Level, Chapter 6, Section 2*

❹ Extension Activities

Listening and Speaking With a small group, write and perform a **dramatization** of a scene from "Comrades." Use these tips to prepare:

- As a group, choose a scene to dramatize.
- Review the scene, noting details that suggest characters' posture and attitudes.
- Write the dramatization in script form.

Use both dialogue and body language to re-create the story's tension. **[Group Activity]**

Research and Technology Conduct research on the nation of Nigeria. Focus your research by organizing it into the following categories: geography; population; economy; art and culture; and history. Share your findings in a five-minute **presentation** for the class.

Take It to the Net PHSchool.com

Go online for an additional research activity using the Internet.

ASSESSMENT RESOURCES

The following resources can be used to assess students' knowledge and skills.

Selection Assessment

Formal Assessment, pp. 231–233

Open-Book Tests, pp. 199–201

Test Bank Software

Take It to the Net

Visit PHSchool.com for self-tests on the selections.

Writing Rubric

Performance Assess. and Portfolio Mgmt., p. 10

Listening and Speaking Rubric

Performance Assess. and Portfolio Mgmt., p. 33

For additional diagnostics and remediation for skills covered in this grouping, use materials from the Prentice Hall Assessment System.

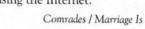

❸ Writing Lesson

- Remind students that a manual should give directions in a logical, step-by-step fashion. Each set of instructions should be followed by clear examples.
- If students have difficulty brainstorming types of atmosphere, get them started by listing moods and atmospheres such as joyful, mysterious, and sorrowful.
- Then, use the Writing Lesson to guide students in developing their manuals. Use the Technical Manual rubric in **Performance Assessment and Portfolio Management,** p. 10, to evaluate students' work.

10TH GRADE For support in working through the Writing Lesson with tenth graders, use **Writing and Grammar,** Platinum Level, Chapter 6, Section 2.

❹ Listening and Speaking

- Organize students into groups of three or four. Consider assigning sequential scenes to the groups so that they can recreate the narrative of the story.
- Remind students as they review their scenes to consider dialogue separately from action. Suggest that students act out the scenes without spoken dialogue in order to hone their body language.
- Allow students time to rehearse their scenes before performing for the class. Use the Listening and Speaking Progress Chart in **Performance Assessment and Portfolio Management,** p. 33, to evaluate students' dramatizations.

CUSTOMIZE INSTRUCTION
For Universal Access

To address different learning styles, use the following activities suggested in the **Extension Activities** booklet, p. 67:

- For Visual/Spatial Learners, use Activity 5.
- For Musical/Rhythmic Learners, use Activity 6.
- For Verbal/Linguistic Learners, use Activity 7.

An Astrologer's Day • By Any Other Name

Lesson Objectives

1. **To analyze and respond to literary elements**
   - Literary Analysis: Plot
   - Comparing Literary Works: Issues of Identity
2. **To read, comprehend, analyze, and critique a short story and a memoir**
   - Reading Strategy: Recognizing Ironic Details
   - Reading Check Questions
   - Review and Assess Questions
   - Assessment Practice (ATE)
3. **To develop word analysis skills, fluency, and systematic vocabulary**
   - Vocabulary Development Lesson: Latin Root *-cant-*
4. **To understand and apply written and oral language conventions**
   - Spelling Strategy
   - Grammar and Style Lesson: Correct Use of Adjectives and Adverbs
5. **To understand and apply appropriate writing and research strategies**
   - Writing Lesson: Personal Essay With a Surprise Ending
   - Extension Activity: Multimedia Presentation
6. **To understand and apply listening and speaking strategies**
   - Extension Activity: Oral Report on Names

TEACHING A TENTH-GRADE COURSE

The literature in this section can be taught as part of a rich, balanced world literature course for tenth-grade students. For a full outline of such a course, see pp. T46–T48 in Volume I of this Teacher's Edition.

STEP-BY-STEP TEACHING GUIDE	PACING GUIDE
PRETEACH	
Motivate Students and Provide Background	
Use the Motivation activity (ATE p. 1364)	5 min.
Read and discuss author and background features (SE pp. 1364, 1366, 1371; ATE p. 1364) [A]	5 min.
Introduce the Concepts	
Introduce the Literary Analysis and Reading Strategy concepts (SE/ATE p. 1365) [A]	15 min.
Pronounce the vocabulary words and read their definitions (SE p. 1365)	5 min.
TEACH	
Monitor Comprehension	
Informally monitor comprehension by circulating while students read independently [A]	40 min.
Monitor students' comprehension with the Reading Check notes (SE/ATE pp. 1367, 1369, 1371, 1373, 1375)	as students read
Develop vocabulary with the Vocabulary notes (SE pp. 1366, 1368, 1369, 1372, 1374; ATE p. 1369)	as students read
Develop Understanding	
Develop students' understanding of plot structure with the Literary Analysis annotations (SE pp. 1369, 1371, 1372, 1374; ATE pp. 1368, 1369, 1371, 1372, 1374, 1375) [A]	10 min.
Develop students' ability to recognize ironic details, using the Reading Strategy annotations (SE pp. 1366, 1367, 1370, 1373; ATE pp. 1366, 1367, 1370, 1373, 1375)	10 min.
ASSESS	
Assess Mastery	
Assess students' mastery of the Reading Strategy and Literary Analysis concepts by having them answer the Review and Assess questions (SE/ATE p. 1377)	20 min.
Use one or more of the print, software, or transparency Assessment Resources (ATE p. 1379) [A]	up to 45 min.
EXTEND	
Apply Understanding	
Have students complete the Vocabulary Development Lesson and the Grammar and Style Lesson (SE p. 1378) [A]	20 min.
Apply students' ability to revise to retain a surprise ending, using the Writing Lesson (SE/ATE p. 1379) [A]	45 min.
Apply students' understanding of the selections, using one or more of the Extension Activities (SE p. 1379)	20–90 min.

[A] ACCELERATED INSTRUCTION: Use the strategies and activities identified with an [A].

10TH GRADE TEACHING TENTH-GRADE STUDENTS For support in teaching tenth graders, see the Step-by-Step Teaching notes identified with this icon.

UNIVERSAL ACCESS

● = Below-Level Students
▲ = On-Level Students
■ = Above-Level Students

Time and Resource Manager

Reading Level: Average, Average
Average Number of Instructional Days: 3

RESOURCES		
PRINT	**TRANSPARENCIES**	**TECHNOLOGY**
• **Beyond Literature,** Cross-Curricular Connection: Social Studies, p. 68 ▲ ■		
• **Selection Support Workbook:** ● ▲ ■ Literary Analysis, p. 272 Reading Strategy, p. 271 Build Vocabulary, p. 269	• **Literary Analysis and Reading Transparencies,** pp. 135 and 136 ● ▲ ■	
		• **Listening to Literature** ● ▲ ■ Audiocassettes Audio CDs
• **Literary Analysis for Enrichment,** p. 68 ■		
• **Formal Assessment:** Selection Test, pp. 234–236 ● ▲ ■ • **Open-Book Tests,** pp. 202–204 ● ▲ ■ • **Performance Assessment and Portfolio Management,** pp. 9, 32 ● ▲ ■ • PRENTICE HALL ASSESSMENT SYSTEM ● ▲ ■	• PRENTICE HALL ASSESSMENT SYSTEM ● ▲ ■ **Skills Practice Answers and Explanations on Transparencies**	• **Test Bank Software** ● ▲ ■
• **Selection Support Workbook:** ● ▲ ■ Grammar and Style, p. 270 • **Writing and Grammar,** Diamond Level ● ▲ ■ • **Extension Activities,** p. 68 ● ▲ ■	• **Daily Language Practice Transparencies** ● ▲ • **Writing Models and Graphic Organizers on Transparencies,** pp. 83–85 ● ▲ ■	• **Writing and Grammar iText CD-ROM** ● ▲ ■ ***Take It to the Net*** PHSchool.com

BLOCK SCHEDULING: Use one 90-minute class period to preteach the selection(s) and have students read them. Use a second 90-minute class period to assess students' mastery of skills and have them complete one of the Extension Activities.

PRETEACH

Step-by-Step Teaching Guide for pp. 1364–1365

Motivation

Invite students to make a list of the people they see every day—family members, friends, and neighbors. Perhaps some of these people are colorful characters who stand out because of their ideas or behavior. Suggest that as students read the stories, they think about whether the characters remind them of people in their own lives. Ask students to consider the qualities that make the characters memorable or interesting.

❶ Background

More About the Authors

English novelist Graham Greene, who, like Narayan, was born under the astrological sign of Libra, once joked that astrology played a part in Narayan's attempts to get his first fiction published. Greene received a manuscript of Narayan's first novel, *Swami and Friends*, from a mutual friend. He ignored the manuscript for many weeks. When he finally did read it, he realized that it deserved to be published. Greene did not know that he was Narayan's last hope; the manuscript had been rejected by numerous other publishers. Later, Greene, aware of Narayan's belief in astrology, suggested facetiously that their shared birth signs had brought the two writers together.

Santha Rama Rau has spent much of her life traveling far from India. Rama Rau's novels and nonfiction reflect her travel experiences in the United States, Asia, Russia, and Africa and are known for their autobiographical detail, their accurate depiction of varied peoples and customs, and their portrayal of the conflict between Western and Indian culture.

Geography Note

Draw students' attention to the map on this page, and point out India. Tell students that Narayan and Rama Rau were both born in Madras, on the southeastern coast of India on the Bay of Bengal. During the years of British rule, Madras was the administrative capital of southern India.

Prepare to Read

❶ An Astrologer's Day ◆ By Any Other Name

R. K. Narayan (1906–2001)

Indian writer R. K. Narayan once said, "If one pauses to think, one realizes that there is little one could say about one's self." Others, however, have much to say about Narayan. For instance, critic John Upside called Narayan "the foremost Indian writer of fiction in English." English novelist Graham Greene said, "It was Mr. Narayan with his *Swami and Friends* who first brought India . . . alive to me." Throughout his career, Narayan's work met with critical acclaim and was translated into every European language as well as Hebrew.

A Grandmother's Influence Narayan was born in Madras, India, on October 10, 1906. His father traveled frequently for his work, and his mother was frail. As a result, Narayan was raised by his grandmother and an uncle. After school, Narayan's grandmother recited stories and poetry in Tamil, an Indian language. She also received numerous visitors—local people seeking advice on marriages, treatment for scorpion bites, or horoscope readings. These colorful characters became the subjects of Narayan's early fiction.

First Success After graduating from college, Narayan worked as a teacher, but he soon devoted himself entirely to writing. His first major effort, the novel *Swami and Friends*, became an international success. In the novel, Narayan created the fictional setting of Malgudi, which was based on the town of Mysore. Like William Faulkner's Yoknapatawpha (yŏk' nə pə tô' fə) County or Gabriel García Márquez's Macondo, Malgudi is a literary microcosm—a little world that represents both the local concerns of Indians and the universal concerns of people everywhere.

Narayan was one of the finest writers to depict India from an insider's perspective. He chose his characters from the middle class—street vendors, holy men, students, teachers—and wrote about them with wit and sympathy. His work demonstrates the valiant struggle to harmonize ancient traditions with the confusions of contemporary life.

Santha Rama Rau (b. 1923)

Born to an affluent family in Madras, India, Santha Rama Rau has traveled the world and lived far from her homeland for many years. However, she never forgot her Indian roots, which infuse her work with color and wisdom.

Daughter of India Rama Rau's father was a prominent diplomat and her mother, a noted social reformer. Born when India was still a British colony, Rama Rau was sent to school in England and graduated in 1939 from the St. Paul's School for Girls in London. Two years later, she enrolled at Wellesley College in the United States. In between, she made a trip back to India that became the basis of her first nonfiction book, *Home to India*. Published in 1945, the book became an international bestseller.

Resettling in America When India won independence in 1947, Rama Rau's father was appointed as his nation's first ambassador to Japan. While traveling with her father to Tokyo, Rama Rau met her first husband, an American. The couple settled in New York City, where she published nonfiction and novels and also adapted E. M. Forster's novel *A Passage to India* into a Broadway play.

A Writing Philosophy Rama Rau was once asked for her advice on writing. "Really, in the end," she explained, "the only thing that can make you a writer is the person that you are, the intensity of your feeling, the honesty of your vision, the unsentimental acknowledgement of the endless interest of the life around and within you."

TEACHING RESOURCES

The following resources can be used to enrich or extend the instruction for pp. 1364–1365.

Background

Beyond Literature, p. 68

Take It to the Net

Visit PHSchool.com for background on the authors.

Literary Analysis

Literary Analysis and Reading Transparencies, Plot, p. 135

Selection Support: Literary Analysis, p. 272

Reading

Literary Analysis and Reading Transparencies, Recognizing Ironic Details, p. 136

BLOCK SCHEDULING: Resources marked with this symbol provide varied instruction during 90-minute blocks.

Preview

Connecting to the Literature

One's name and history are basic to one's sense of self. Imagine, then, what it would feel like to simply be assigned a new name or to have to abandon one's past. That is the experience of the characters in these selections.

❷ Literary Analysis

Plot

Plot is the sequence of events in a literary work. Most plots involve characters and a conflict and follow a specific pattern:

- ***Exposition:*** The basic situation is introduced.
- ***Inciting Incident:*** The conflict is revealed.
- ***Development:*** The conflict increases in intensity.
- ***Climax:*** The conflict reaches its highest point.
- ***Falling Action:*** Events that occur after the climax are described.
- ***Resolution:*** The story ends with details that reveal insight.

In these selections, both the falling action and the resolution provide new information. As you read, identify the climax in each selection. Then, notice the surprising information you learn as each selection concludes.

Comparing Literary Works

In both Narayan's short story and Rama Rau's memoir, the main characters experience an identity crisis. As you read, determine what each story suggests about the extent to which one's identity can truly be altered.

❸ Reading Strategy

Recognizing Ironic Details

Verbal irony involves a contrast between what is stated and what is meant. *Situational irony* involves a contrast between what is expected and what actually happens. As you read, use a chart like the one shown to **recognize ironic details.** Note details that create expectations in your mind. Then, decide whether your expectations are fulfilled.

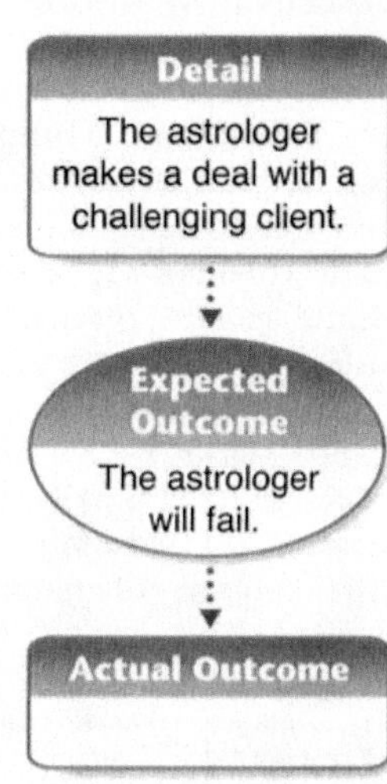
Detail
The astrologer makes a deal with a challenging client.
Expected Outcome
The astrologer will fail.
Actual Outcome

Vocabulary Development

prophetic (prō fet′ ik) *adj.* having to do with predicting the future (p. 1366)

ancestral (an ses′ trəl) *adj.* relating to the people from whom one is descended (p. 1368)

paraphernalia (par′ ə fər nāl′ yə) *n.* articles of equipment (p. 1368)

incantations (in′ kan tā′ shənz) *n.* chants sung as part of a ritual (p. 1369)

provincial (prō vin′ shəl) *adj.* lacking in sophistication (p. 1372)

insular (in′ sə lər) *adj.* having a narrow viewpoint (p. 1372)

wizened (wiz′ ənd) *adj.* dried up and wrinkled due to age (p. 1374)

❷ Literary Analysis

Plot

- Read aloud the Literary Analysis instruction on p. 1365.
- Students may benefit from seeing a visual, like the plot chart that appears on p. 1377. On the board, draw a similar chart. Challenge students to identify places on the chart in which the plot elements listed on p. 1365 fit.
- Then, help students become familiar with the plot chart by having them review the plot of a favorite movie or book and enter the plot events along the diagram.
- Suggest that as students read, they create their own plot charts to record events from the stories.
- If students need additional support identifying the parts of a plot, use the Plot transparency in **Literary Analysis and Reading Transparencies,** p. 135.

❸ Reading Strategy

Recognizing Ironic Details

- Students may benefit from a review of the concept of irony.
- Have students read the definitions of verbal and situational irony on p. 1365. Then, ask them for examples of verbal irony that they have heard or used recently.
- Explain the use of the graphic organizer on p. 1365. Have students use the organizer as they read Narayan's story.

Vocabulary Development

- Pronounce each vocabulary word for students, and read the definition as a class. Have students identify any words with which they are already familiar.

CUSTOMIZE INSTRUCTION FOR UNIVERSAL ACCESS

For Less Proficient Readers	For English Learners	For Advanced Readers
Have students use the Story Map organizer in **Writing Models and Graphic Organizers on Transparencies,** pp. 83–85, as they read the stories. Have students create a story map for each selection and record events. Review students' story maps to ensure understanding of the plot elements of each story.	Use the discussion of plot as an opportunity to review words that indicate sequence. Have students work alone or in pairs to generate a list of words and phrases that indicate a sequence of events. Encourage students to use the words and phrases as they track the plots of the selections in this grouping.	Have students read at least two more of Narayan's stories individually. Then, have them form small groups and discuss the stories they read. What plot parallels, if any, exist between the stories they read and "An Astrologer's Day"? Suggest that students compile notes about each element of the plot pattern for each story.

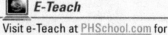

E-Teach

Visit e-Teach at PHSchool.com for teachers' essays on how to teach, with questions and answers.

TEACH

Step-by-Step Teaching Guide for pp. 1366–1376

Teaching Tenth-Grade Students

10TH GRADE Initiate a discussion about astrology by asking which students believe in it and which do not. Encourage students who are knowledgeable about the subject to share their views about astrology as a "science" or a "superstition."

1 About the Selection

The story "An Astrologer's Day" focuses on a fateful encounter between an Indian astrologer and one of his customers. Neither man is who he appears to be—both have secrets. In this story, Narayan explores the ironies of seeking the truth from our fellow human beings.

2 Reading Strategy

Recognizing Ironic Details

- Read aloud the bracketed passage. Then, tell students that the narrator wants the reader to know that the astrologer is an impostor.
- Ask students which details in the first paragraph reveal the narrator's ironic attitude toward the astrologer's equipment.
  Possible response: The narrator describes the astrologer's equipment as "professional" but goes on to detail the mundane, almost childish nature of the items. The narrator provides other details that on the surface create a mystical portrait of the astrologer but then undercuts the portrait with words such as "simple," "abnormal," and "half-wit's."
- Ask students the Reading Strategy question on p. 1366: In what ways do the details about the astrologer's appearance provide the reader with information that his clients do not have?
  Answer: The narrator, in presenting these details, makes sure the reader understands that the astrologer is not what he appears to be.

1 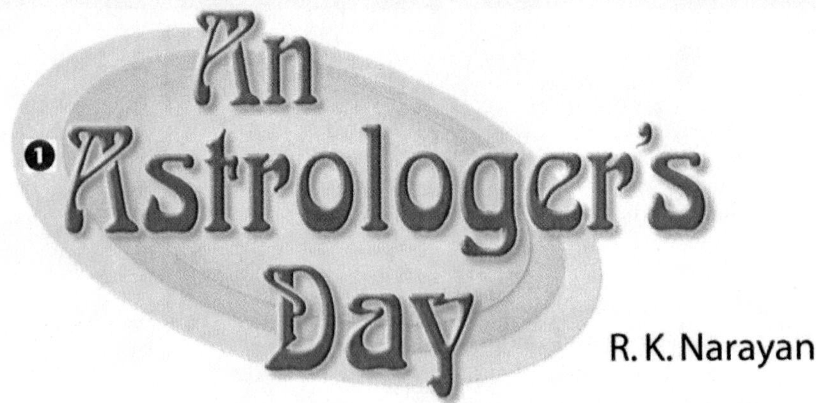

R. K. Narayan

Background

The English word *astrology* combines the Greek word *astro-*, which means "star or other heavenly body," with the Greek suffix *-logy*, which means "the study of." Hence, astrology is the study of the ways in which heavenly bodies, such as the sun, moon, stars, and planets, affect life on Earth. Some people believe that the stars and planets exert influences that affect individuals and can reveal the future. However, unlike astronomy, which is a hard science, astrology is considered by many people to be a body of superstitions and the arena of frauds. In this selection, the astrologer may or may not be one such fraud.

Punctually at midday he opened his bag and spread out his professional equipment, which consisted of a dozen cowrie shells,[1] a square piece of cloth with obscure mystic charts on it, a notebook, and a bundle of palmyra writing. His forehead was resplendent with sacred ash and vermilion,[2] and his eyes sparkled with a sharp abnormal gleam which was really an outcome of a continual searching look for customers, but which his simple clients took to be a prophetic light and felt
2 comforted. The power of his eyes was considerably enhanced by their position—placed as they were between the painted forehead and the dark whiskers which streamed down his cheeks: even a half-wit's eyes would sparkle in such a setting. To crown the effect he wound a saffron-colored turban around his head. This color scheme never failed. People were attracted to him as bees are attracted to cosmos or dahlia stalks. He sat under the boughs of a spreading tamarind tree which flanked a path running through the town hall park. It was a remarkable place in many ways: a surging crowd was always moving up and down this narrow road morning till night. A variety of trades

Reading Strategy
Recognizing Ironic Details In what ways do the details about the astrologer's appearance provide the reader with information that his clients do not have?

prophetic (prō fet′ ik) *adj.* having to do with predicting the future

1. **cowrie** (kou′ rē) **shells** brightly colored, glossy seashells.
2. **sacred ash and vermilion** religious marking originally used only by Brahmins, the highest caste in Indian society.

TEACHING RESOURCES

The following resources can be used to enrich or extend the instruction for pp. 1366–1376.

Literary Analysis
- **Selection Support:** Literary Analysis, p. 272
- **Literary Analysis and Reading Transparencies,** Plot, p. 135

Reading
- **Selection Support:** Reading Strategy, p. 271; Build Vocabulary, p. 269
- **Listening to Literature Audiocassettes**
- **Listening to Literature Audio CDs**

BLOCK SCHEDULING: Resources marked with this symbol provide varied instruction during 90-minute blocks.

and occupations was represented all along its way: medicine sellers, sellers of stolen hardware and junk, magicians, and, above all, an auctioneer of cheap cloth, who created enough din all day to attract the whole town. Next to him in vociferousness came a vendor of fried groundnut, who gave his ware a fancy name each day, calling it "Bombay Ice Cream" one day, and on the next "Delhi Almond," and on the third "Raja's Delicacy," and so on and so forth, and people flocked to him. A considerable portion of this crowd dallied before the astrologer too. The astrologer transacted his business by the light of a flare which crackled and smoked up above the groundnut heap nearby. Half the enchantment of the place was due to the fact that it did not have the benefit of municipal lighting. The place was lit up by shop lights. One or two had hissing gaslights, some had naked flares stuck on poles, some were lit up by old cycle lamps, and one or two, like the astrologer's, managed without lights of their own. It was a bewildering crisscross of light rays and moving shadows. This suited the astrologer very well, for the simple reason that he had not in the least intended to be an astrologer when he began life; and he knew no more of what was going to happen to others than he knew what was going to happen to himself next minute. He was as much a stranger to the stars as were his innocent customers. Yet he said things which pleased and astonished everyone: that was more a matter of study, practice, and shrewd guesswork. All the same, it was as much an honest man's labor as any other, and he deserved the wages he carried home at the end of a day.

3 (margin marker beside bracketed passage)

Reading Strategy
Recognizing Ironic Details In what ways is the information about the astrologer's true abilities ironic?

4 **✓Reading Check**
Where does the astrologer conduct his business?

5 ▲ **Critical Viewing** In what ways is the market shown in this photograph both similar to and different from the site where the astrologer does business? **[Compare and Contrast]**

3 Reading Strategy

Recognizing Ironic Details

- Ask students: What skills or knowledge do you expect an astrologer to have?
  Possible response: An astrologer should have knowledge of the stars and the zodiac.
- Have a volunteer read aloud the bracketed passage. Remind students that situational irony involves a contrast between what is expected and what actually happens.
- Then, ask students the Reading Strategy question on p. 1367: In what ways is the information about the astrologer's true abilities ironic?
  Answer: Because one expects an astrologer to be knowledgeable about the stars and their patterns, it is ironic that Narayan's astrologer does not have this knowledge. The astrologer is successful because he can read people, not the stars.

4 ✓Reading Check

Answer: The astrologer conducts his business under a tamarind tree in an open air market in the town hall park.

5 ▶Critical Viewing

Possible response: The scene in the photograph, like the scene in the story, is a busy and crowded open air market. The streets are lined with sellers and their goods. The scene in the photograph is a daytime scene; however, the scene in the story takes place after dark.

CUSTOMIZE INSTRUCTION FOR UNIVERSAL ACCESS

For Special Needs Students	For Advanced Readers
Because the paragraphs in this selection are long, students may have trouble perceiving the irony of the details and events in the story. Organize students into pairs, and guide each pair to create a two-column chart with the headings *What do the people in the story see or know?* and *What does the narrator see or know?* After reading half a page or so, students should stop and try to answer the questions in order to see the difference between what is stated and what is meant.	Ask students to work in small groups to discuss examples of other stories, books, movies, or television programs that use irony. Invite students to explain the ironies of their examples and to compare them with the ironic details and events in this story. Then, ask students to discuss how irony contributes to the impact and significance of a story. Finally, ask students how "An Astrologer's Day" measures up to their favorite ironic stories.

6 Critical Thinking

Make a Judgment

- After reading aloud the bracketed passage, ask students what techniques the astrologer uses to get to know his customers.
  Answer: The astrologer listens to his customers speak for ten minutes thereby providing him with enough information before he speaks.
- Then, ask students: Who is more responsible for the deception taking place? Is the astrologer taking advantage of his clients, or are his clients suffering the consequences of their gullibility?
  Possible response: The astrologer and his clients are equally responsible for the deception taking place. The astrologer is masking his keen knowledge of human nature as astrology. The clients are encouraging this charade by naively investing in it.

7 ▶Critical Viewing

Possible response: The photograph may help readers visualize some of the details of the astrologer's appearance, including his paraphernalia.

8 Literary Analysis

Plot

- Review with students the Literary Analysis instruction on p. 1365. Remind students that an inciting incident reveals a conflict within the narrative.
- Have students read the bracketed passage independently. Then, ask them what conflict is revealed in this passage.
  Answer: A customer confronts the astrologer and calls his skill into question. The astrologer cannot rely on his usual techniques.
- Then, ask students how the narrator signals to the reader that this interaction between the astrologer and a client will be different from past interactions.
  Possible response: By describing the darkness and the way the customer blocks out the weird green light, the narrator establishes this encounter as unusual. The client, not the astrologer, becomes the source of mystery.

He had left his village without any previous thought or plan. If he had continued there he would have carried on the work of his forefathers—namely, tilling the land, living, marrying, and ripening in his cornfield and ancestral home. But that was not to be. He had to leave home without telling anyone, and he could not rest till he left it behind a couple of hundred miles. To a villager it is a great deal, as if an ocean flowed between.

ancestral (an ses´ trəl) *adj.* relating to the people from whom one is descended

6 He had a working analysis of mankind's troubles: marriage, money, and the tangles of human ties. Long practice had sharpened his perception. Within five minutes he understood what was wrong. He charged three paise[3] per question, never opened his mouth till the other had spoken for at least ten minutes, which provided him enough stuff for a dozen answers and advices. When he told the person before him, gazing at his palm, "In many ways you are not getting the fullest results for your efforts," nine out of ten were disposed to agree with him. Or he questioned: "Is there any woman in your family, maybe even a distant relative, who is not well disposed towards you?" Or he gave an analysis of character: "Most of your troubles are due to your nature. How can you be otherwise with Saturn where he is? You have an impetuous[4] nature and a rough exterior." This endeared him to their hearts immediately, for even the mildest of us loves to think that he has a forbidding exterior.

paraphernalia (par´ ə fər nāl´ yə) *n.* articles of equipment

7 ▼Critical Viewing In what way does this photograph affect your mental picture of the characters in this story? **[Connect]**

The nuts vendor blew out his flare and rose to go home. This was a signal for the astrologer to bundle up too, since it left him in darkness except for a little shaft of green light which strayed in from somewhere and touched the ground before him. He picked up his cowrie shells and paraphernalia and was putting them back into his bag when the green shaft of light was blotted out; he looked up and saw a man standing before him. He sensed a possible client and said, "You look so careworn. It will do you good to sit down for a while and chat with me." The
8 other grumbled some reply vaguely. The astrologer pressed his invitation; whereupon the other thrust his palm under his nose, saying, "You call yourself an astrologer?" The astrologer felt challenged and said, tilting the other's palm towards the green shaft of light, "Yours is a nature . . ." "Oh, stop that," the other said. "Tell me something worthwhile. . . ."

Our friend felt piqued.[5] "I charge only three paise per question, and what you get ought to be good enough for your money. . . ." At this the other withdrew his arm, took out an anna, and flung it out to him, saying, "I have some questions to ask. If I prove you are bluffing, you must return that anna to me with interest."

"If you find my answers satisfactory, will you give me five rupees?"

"No."

3. **paise** (pī´ se), *plural of* **paisa** (pī´ sä´) monetary unit of India or Pakistan, equal to one hundredth of a rupee.
4. **impetuous** (im pech´ o͞o əs) *adj.* rash; impulsive.
5. **piqued** (pēkt) *adj.* displeased; resentful.

ENRICHMENT: History Connection

Astrology Across the Ages

Astrology, once widely considered a science, is the ancient technique of predicting events by observing the planets and stars. The practice has undergone numerous modifications during its passage through many world cultures.

Mesopotamians believed that the gods communicated with humans through signs or omens in the sky. Prognosticators called *barus* studied the night skies for omens that suggested what the gods were thinking or feeling. The barus "read" the omens and then advised their rulers how to act accordingly.

Indian astrology was directly influenced by the Mesopotamians. Around the fifth century B.C., Indian scholars gained access to ancient astrological texts. The old ideas were tailored to fit certain aspects of Indian society and religious belief. Over the centuries, the astrological beliefs of other cultures, such as Arabic and Persian, influenced Indian astrology, too, making it a very complicated system.

"Or will you give me eight annas?"

"All right, provided you give me twice as much if you are wrong," said the stranger. This pact was accepted after a little further argument. The astrologer sent up a prayer to heaven as the other lit a cheroot. The astrologer caught a glimpse of his face by the match light. There was a pause as cars hooted on the road, jutka[6] drivers swore at their horses, and the babble of the crowd agitated the semidarkness of the park. The other sat down, sucking his cheroot, puffing out, sat there ruthlessly.
9 The astrologer felt very uncomfortable. "Here, take your anna back. I am not used to such challenges. It is late for me today. . . ." He made preparations to bundle up. The other held his wrist and said, "You can't get out of it now. You dragged me in while I was passing." The astrologer shivered in his grip; and his voice shook and became faint. "Leave me today. I will speak to you tomorrow." The other thrust his palm in his face and said, "Challenge is challenge. Go on." The astrologer proceeded with his throat drying up, "There is a woman . . ."

"Stop," said the other. "I don't want all that. Shall I succeed in my present search or not? Answer this and go. Otherwise I will not let
10 you go till you disgorge all your coins." The astrologer muttered a few incantations and replied, "All right. I will speak. But will you give me a rupee if what I say is convincing? Otherwise I will not open my mouth, and you may do what you like." After a good deal of haggling the other agreed. The astrologer said, "You were left for dead. Am I right?"

"Ah, tell me more."

"A knife has passed through you once?" said the astrologer.

"Good fellow!" He bared his chest to show the scar. "What else?"

"And then you were pushed into a well nearby in the field. You were left for dead."

"I should have been dead if some passerby had not chanced to peep into the well," exclaimed the other, overwhelmed by enthusiasm. "When shall I get at him?" he asked, clenching his fist.

"In the next world," answered the astrologer. "He died four months ago in a far-off town. You will never see any more of him." The other groaned on hearing it. The astrologer proceeded:

"Guru Nayak—"

"You know my name!" the other said, taken aback.

"As I know all other things. Guru Nayak, listen carefully to what I have to say. Your village is two days' journey due north of this town. Take the next train and begone. I see once again great danger to your life if you go from home." He took out a pinch of sacred ash and held it to him. "Rub it on your forehead and go home. Never travel southward again, and you will live to be a hundred."

"Why should I leave home again?" the other said reflectively. "I was only going away now and then to look for him and to choke out his life if I met him." He shook his head regretfully. "He has escaped my hands.

Literary Analysis
Plot Which details intensify the conflict the astrologer is experiencing? Explain.

incantations (in' kan tā' shənz) *n.* chants sung as part of a ritual

11 **✓Reading Check**

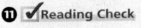

What single question does the client want the astrologer to answer?

6. **jutka** (jut' kə) Hindi word for a one-horse vehicle, hired out as a taxi.

9 Literary Analysis

Plot

- After students have read the bracketed passage, ask them to identify the conflict the astrologer is experiencing. Remind students that conflict is a struggle between opposing forces that can be manifested either internally or externally.
  Answer: The astrologer is struggling against the client's aggression and against the realization that the client is not "typical." The astrologer is conflicted because he cannot rely on his old bag of tricks—he cannot appeal to the client's emotions in order to deceive him.
- Then, ask students the Literary Analysis question on p. 1369: Which details intensify the conflict the astrologer is experiencing? Explain.
  Answer: The details that intensify the conflict include the client's confidence—he is cynical, not mystified. The client's persistent demeanor is foreign to the astrologer and pushes the astrologer beyond his comfort zone.

10 Vocabulary Development

Latin root *-cant-*

- Read aloud the word *incantations* and its definition on p. 1369. Explain that this word contains the Latin root *-cant-*, which means "sing" or "chant."
- Ask students to use dictionaries to find other words that include the root *-cant-*.
  Possible response: *Canticle* and *cantabile* also contain the Latin root *-cant-*.
- Make sure students understand that the root *-cant-* has different origins than the contraction *can't*.

11 ✓Reading Check

Answer: The client wants the answer to the question "Shall I succeed in my present search or not?"

CUSTOMIZE INSTRUCTION FOR UNIVERSAL ACCESS

For Gifted/Talented Students

As students read p. 1369, they may easily imagine the scene in cinematic form. Organize students into pairs, and ask them to create a screenplay for this scene. Then, have students create storyboards with hand-drawn pictures that illustrate the camera shots in their screenplays. Encourage students to look at books on writing screenplays to get a sense of terminology and format. When they have finished, allow them to read from their screenplays and to display their storyboards for the class. During their presentations, students should offer a statement of artistic intent, explaining why they have chosen to present the scene in a particular way.

I hope at least he died as he deserved." "Yes," said the astrologer. "He was crushed under a lorry." The other looked gratified to hear it.

The place was deserted by the time the astrologer picked up his articles and put them into his bag. The green shaft was also gone, leaving the place in darkness and silence. The stranger had gone off into the night, after giving the astrologer a handful of coins.

It was nearly midnight when the astrologer reached home. His wife was waiting for him at the door and demanded an explanation. He flung the coins at her and said, "Count them. One man gave all that."

"Twelve and a half annas," she said, counting. She was overjoyed. "I can buy some jaggery[7] and coconut tomorrow. The child has been asking for sweets for so many days now. I will prepare some nice stuff for her."

12 "The swine has cheated me! He promised me a rupee," said the astrologer. She looked up at him. "You look worried. What is wrong?"

"Nothing."

After dinner, sitting on the pyol,[8] he told her, "Do you know a great load is gone from me today? I thought I had the blood of a man on my hands all these years. That was the reason why I ran away from home, settled here, and married you. He is alive."

She gasped. "You tried to kill!"

"Yes, in our village, when I was a silly youngster. We drank, gambled, and quarreled badly one day—why think of it now? Time to sleep," he said, yawning, and stretched himself on the pyol.

7. **jaggery** (jag′ ər ē) *n.* dark, crude sugar from the sap of certain palm trees.
8. **pyol** (pī′ əl) collection of material on which a person can sit or sleep.

Reading Strategy
Recognizing Ironic Details Is the astrologer's statement about being cheated ironic? Explain.

Review and Assess

Thinking About the Selection

1. **Respond:** Do you find the astrologer amusing? Why or why not?
2. **(a) Recall:** Does the astrologer actually read the stars or predict the future? **(b) Summarize:** What methods does he use to tell people's fortunes? **(c) Evaluate:** Do you agree with the narrator that the astrologer performs "an honest man's labor"? Explain.
3. **(a) Recall:** What is the last piece of advice that the astrologer gives Nayak? **(b) Deduce:** What is the astrologer's true motive in giving Nayak this advice? **(c) Make a Judgment:** Do you think the astrologer acts ethically? Explain.
4. **(a) Speculate:** What might the astrologer have told Nayak if he had not recognized him? **(b) Evaluate:** Would Nayak have been satisfied with such a message? Explain.
5. **Take a Position:** Do you think justice is served in the case of the astrologer and Nayak? Why or why not?

12 Reading Strategy

Recognizing Ironic Details

- Remind students that irony is a difference between appearance and reality, expectation and result, or meaning and intention.
- Read aloud the bracketed passage. Ask students the Reading Strategy question on p. 1370: Is the astrologer's statement about being cheated ironic? Explain.
Answer: The astrologer's claim that he has been cheated is ironic because the astrologer cheats the customer by pretending to divine information the astrologer already knows about the customer. Also, the astrologer cheats the customer out of his revenge—killing the astrologer.

Answers for p. 1370

Review and Assess

1. **Possible responses:** Yes; the astrologer is amusing because he is quick-witted and lucky. No; the astrologer make his living dishonestly.
2. **(a)** No; the astrologer does not read the stars or predict the future. **(b)** He reads people's appearances and waits for them to tell him information he can use to fabricate predictions. **(c) Possible response:** The astrologer works hard at duping his customers.
3. **(a)** The astrologer tells Nayak to go home and never travel south again. **(b)** The astrologer's true motive is to prevent another encounter with Nayak. **(c) Possible response:** The astrologer is certainly not honest; he acts out of self-preservation.
4. **(a)** The astrologer might have told Nayak the same vague and generic things he tells other customers. **(b)** Nayak would not have been satisfied. That is why he bargained for the answer to his question.
5. **Possible responses:** No; justice is not served because the astrologer has not paid for the crime of attacking Nayak. Yes; justice does not need to be served because the astrologer did not kill Nayak but relieved him of his burden of anger.

ENRICHMENT: Film Connection

Bollywood

Part of Narayan's appeal as a writer is his depiction of Indian life in art. The desire for stories that reflect Indian life is also what drives the Indian film industry.

Since the 1930s, the industry, called Bollywood (Hollywood plus Bombay equals Bollywood), has been producing hundreds of movies a year. Bollywood movies are usually three or more hours long and tell melodramatic stories with convoluted plots often based on Indian mythology.

Indian viewers flock to Bollywood movies for the chance to watch familiar stories in which beautiful movie stars sing and dance and perform fight scenes in traditional costumes. The movies are celebrated in India in part because they reflect the values of Indian culture, but also because they provide millions of viewers with an escape from daily life.

By Any Other Name

Santha Rama Rau

Background

India was under direct British control from about 1860 until 1947, when it became an independent country. During that time, the British set up a school system geared mostly to middle- and upper-class Indian students. The goals of this system were to instill British beliefs and values into Indian youth and to train students for jobs in government and various other professions. It was expected that these students would champion British policies among the rest of the population, an approach that was largely successful. Remnants of the British education system remain in India today.

14 At the Anglo-Indian day school in Zorinabad to which my sister and I were sent when she was eight and I was five and a half, they changed our names. On the first day of school, a hot, windless morning of a north Indian September, we stood in the headmistress's[1] study and she said, "Now you're the *new* girls. What are your names?"

My sister answered for us. "I am Premila, and she"—nodding in my direction—"is Santha."

The headmistress had been in India, I suppose, fifteen years or so, but she still smiled her helpless inability to cope with Indian names. Her rimless half-glasses glittered, and the precarious bun on the top of her head trembled as she shook her head. "Oh, my dears, those are much too hard for me. Suppose we give you pretty English names. Wouldn't that be more jolly? Let's see, now—Pamela for you, I think." She shrugged in a baffled way at my sister. "That's as close as I can get. And for *you*," she said to me, "how about Cynthia? Isn't that nice?"

My sister was always less easily intimidated than I was, and while she kept a stubborn silence, I said, "Thank you," in a very tiny voice. 15

Literary Analysis

Plot In what ways does the first sentence establish the conflict as relating to an identity crisis?

 **Reading Check**

What new names does the headmistress give to Premila and Santha?

1. **headmistress** woman in charge of a school; principal, especially of a private school.

Teaching Tenth-Grade Students

10TH GRADE Start a discussion with tenth-grade students about the importance of names. Ask volunteers to share the history or background of their own names, or the nicknames they have chosen for themselves. Have students talk about the intentions behind name-giving. For example, parents often mean to honor someone when they name their children after that person. Students should understand the difference between choosing a name for oneself and being given a name.

13 About the Selection

"By Any Other Name" is an autobiographical narrative based on an incident in the author's life as a child in India. The story explores, through a young girl's eyes, the effects of racism in colonial India on two school girls, the author and her older sister. Attending a British school for the first time, the sisters are given new British names by an insensitive schoolmistress. The girls learn new customs and make friends at the school, but when the narrator's sister is accused of cheating because she is Indian, the desire to assimilate diminishes.

14 Literary Analysis

Plot

- Read aloud the bracketed passage.
- Then, ask students the Literary Analysis question on p. 1371: In what ways does the first sentence establish the conflict as relating to an identity crisis?
  Answer: On their first day of school, the narrator and her sister have their names changed. It is clear from the narrator's tone that this change is made without the girls' permission.

15 Reading Check

Answer: Premila is renamed Pamela, and Santha is renamed Cynthia.

CUSTOMIZE INSTRUCTION FOR UNIVERSAL ACCESS

For English Learners	For Advanced Readers
Students may identify with the attempts of Santha and her sister to fit in at their new school. Have volunteers share their experiences with fitting in. Ask students to consider the following questions: Was it easy or difficult to fit into this new situation? Did you have to change your behavior or appearance to fit in? What are some of the advantages to fitting in? What are some of the disadvantages? Students may feel more comfortable discussing their experiences in small groups.	Ask students to begin a K-W-L chart, identifying what they already know about India and what they want to know. After students finish reading the story, have them complete the chart by identifying what they have learned. Then, ask them to consider whether the story confirmed or changed their ideas about India. Ask them what they still would like to know about life in colonial India. Encourage them to research their topics and to give short oral presentations based on their findings.

16 Background

Indian Clothing

India is a large and diverse country, and the clothing of its people varies accordingly. Many Indians, particularly those who live in the large cities, wear modern Western clothing such as blue jeans and business suits. Traditional clothing is often worn in smaller towns and rural regions. Saris are not the only traditional form of dress worn by women. In the northwest, in Punjab, women wear saris only on special occasions. They prefer pajama-like trousers and long shirts for regular wear. Farther south, in Rajasthan, women wear long flowing skirts and blouses.

17 Critical Thinking

Analyze

- Ask a volunteer to read aloud the bracketed passage.
- Ask students to explain the mother's analogy.
- Possible response: The mother suggests that narrow-mindedness is a trait inherent in the British. She uses the analogy of the dog's tail to emphasize the futility in trying to change the British attitude.

18 Literary Analysis

Plot

- Remind students that conflict is a crucial part of plot.
- Read aloud the bracketed passage. Then, ask students the Literary Analysis question on p. 1372: In what ways does the little girl's clothing and jewelry exemplify the conflict Premila and Santha are experiencing?
  Answer: The girl's dress is western, but her jewelry and kohl-rimmed eyes are Indian. She physically represents a fusion of East and West, the fusion with which both Premila and Santha are struggling.

We had been sent to that school because my father, among his responsibilities as an officer of the civil service, had a tour of duty to perform in the villages around that steamy little provincial town, where he had his headquarters at that time. He used to make his shorter inspection tours on horseback, and a week before, in the stale heat of a typically postmonsoon day[2] we had waved goodbye to him and a little procession—an assistant, a secretary, two bearers,[3] and the man to look after the bedding rolls and luggage. They rode away through our large garden, still bright green from the rains, and we turned back into the twilight of the house and the sound of fans whispering in every room.

17 Up to then, my mother had refused to send Premila to school in the British-run establishments of that time, because, she used to say, "you can bury a dog's tail for seven years and it still comes out curly, and you can take a Britisher away from his home for a lifetime and he still remains insular." The examinations and degrees from entirely Indian schools were not, in those days, considered valid. In my case, the question had never come up, and probably never would have come up if Mother's extraordinary good health had not broken down. For the first time in my life, she was not able to continue the lessons she had been giving us every morning. So our Hindi books were put away, the stories of the Lord Krishna[4] as a little boy were left in mid-air, and we were sent to the Anglo-Indian school.

That first day at school is still, when I think of it, a remarkable one. At that age, if one's name is changed, one develops a curious form of dual personality. I remember having a certain detached and disbelieving concern in the actions of "Cynthia," but certainly no responsibility. Accordingly, I followed the thin, erect back of the headmistress down the veranda to my classroom feeling, at most, a passing interest in what was going to happen to me in this strange, new atmosphere of School.

The building was Indian in design, with wide verandas opening onto a central courtyard, but Indian verandas are usually whitewashed, with stone floors. These, in the tradition of British schools, were painted dark brown and had matting on the floors. It gave a feeling of extra intensity to the heat.

I suppose there were about a dozen Indian children in the school—which contained perhaps forty children in all—and four of them were in my class. They were all sitting at the back of the room, and I went to join them. 18 I sat next to a small, solemn girl who didn't smile at me. She had long, glossy-black braids and wore a cotton dress, but she still kept on her Indian jewelry—a gold chain around her neck, thin gold bracelets, and tiny ruby studs in her ears. Like most Indian children, she had a rim of black kohl[5] around her eyes. The cotton dress should

2. **postmonsoon day** day that follows a heavy rainfall.
3. **bearers** porters; people who carry luggage.
4. **Lord Krishna** incarnation of Vishnu, one of the three most important gods in Hinduism.
5. **kohl** (kōl) *n.* cosmetic eyeliner worn by women in some parts of Asia. It is applied with the fingers, rather than a pencil or a brush.

Literature in context Cultural Connection

16 ***Indian Clothing***

Many Indian women and girls wear a sari (sä′rē), a long piece of brightly colored cloth wrapped over a blouse around the body. One end of the sari forms an ankle-length skirt, and the other is draped over the shoulder or sometimes the head. Saris woven into colorful patterns have been worn by Indian women for many centuries. Saris are sometimes made of silk, but cotton is more common.

provincial (prō vin′ shəl) *adj.* lacking in sophistication

insular (in′ sə lər) *adj.* having a narrow viewpoint

Literary Analysis
Plot In what ways does the little girl's clothing and jewelry exemplify the conflict Premila and Santha are experiencing?

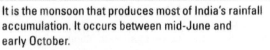

ENRICHMENT: Science Connection

Monsoon Season

India is a large country, but almost every region relies on substantial annual rainfall. India's climate, however, tends to alternate between wet and dry. Monsoons are responsible for this weather pattern. Monsoon systems bring wind and rain or dry air to the Indian peninsula.

There are two types of monsoons. The southwest monsoon brings moisture from the Indian Ocean across the continent, causing heavy rain and flooding. It is the monsoon that produces most of India's rainfall accumulation. It occurs between mid-June and early October.

The retreating monsoon is almost the complete opposite of the southwest monsoon. From November to February, it pulls dry air from Asia to the Indian Ocean, bringing little or no rain.

have looked strange, but all I could think of was that I should ask my mother if I couldn't wear a dress to school, too, instead of my Indian clothes.

19 I can't remember too much about the proceedings in class that day, except for the beginning. The teacher pointed to me and asked me to stand up. "Now, dear, tell the class your name."

I said nothing.

"Come along," she said, frowning slightly. "What's your name, dear?"

"I don't know," I said, finally.

The English children in the front of the class—there were about eight or ten of them—giggled and twisted around in their chairs to look at me. I sat down quickly and opened my eyes very wide, hoping in that way to dry them off. The little girl with the braids put out her hand and very lightly touched my arm. She still didn't smile.

Most of that morning I was rather bored. I looked briefly at the children's drawings pinned to the wall, and then concentrated on a lizard clinging to the ledge of the high, barred window behind the teacher's head. Occasionally it would shoot out its long yellow tongue for a fly, and then it would rest, with its eyes closed and its belly palpitating, as though it were swallowing several times quickly. The lessons were mostly concerned with reading and writing and simple numbers—things that my mother had already taught me—and I paid very little attention. The teacher wrote on the easel blackboard words like "bat" and "cat," which seemed babyish to me; only "apple" was new and incomprehensible.

When it was time for the lunch recess, I followed the girl with braids out onto the veranda. There the children from the other classes were assembled. I saw Premila at once and ran over to her, as she had charge of our lunchbox. The children were all opening packages and sitting down to eat sandwiches. Premila and I were the only ones who
20 had Indian food—thin wheat chapatties,[6] some vegetable curry, and a bottle of buttermilk. Premila thrust half of it into my hand and whispered fiercely that I should go and sit with my class, because that was what the others seemed to be doing.

The enormous black eyes of the little Indian girl from my class looked at my food longingly, so I offered her some. But she only shook her head and plowed her way solemnly through her sandwiches.

I was very sleepy after lunch, because at home we always took a siesta.[7] It was usually a pleasant time of day, with the bedroom darkened against the harsh afternoon sun, the drifting off into sleep with the sound of Mother's voice reading a story in one's mind, and, finally, the shrill, fussy voice of the ayah[8] waking one for tea.

At school, we rested for a short time on low, folding cots on the veranda, and then we were expected to play games. During the hot part

6. **chapatties** (chə pät′ ēz) *n.* round, flat, unleavened breads baked in a dry skillet; a staple of Indian cuisine.
7. **siesta** (sē es′ tə) *n.* afternoon nap or rest.
8. **ayah** (ä′ yə) *n.* nursemaid or lady's maid.

Reading Strategy
Recognizing Ironic Details What is ironic about Santha's answer to the question of what her name is?

21 
Reading Check

Why are Premila and Santha sent to the British-run school?

19 Reading Strategy

Recognizing Ironic Details

- Make sure students understand that irony exists when there is a contrast between what is expected and what actually happens.
- Read aloud the bracketed passage. Then, ask students the Reading Strategy question on p. 1373: What is ironic about Santha's answer to the question of what her name is?
  Answer: It is ironic that Santha now has two names but chooses to divulge neither.

▶ **Monitor Progress** Ask: Why is Santha's response to the teacher surprising?
Answer: The reader expects Santha to offer one of her names—either the real one or the new one—not entirely refuse to provide a name.

▶ **Reteach** If students have difficulty answering the Reading Strategy question suggest that they use the graphic organizer on p. 1365 to recognize the irony in Santha's response.

20 Critical Thinking

Infer

- After reading aloud the bracketed passage, point out to students that this is the first time readers have seen Premila since she was given her new name that morning. Ask: On the basis of Premila's actions and tone of voice, what can you infer about the experiences she has had during the morning?
  Answer: During the morning, Premila has probably observed the other students, noting how one can fit in. These observations have allowed her to recognize that certain things—such as eating traditional Indian food and not sitting with the class—may prevent the sisters from fitting in.

21 ✓Reading Check

Answer: The sisters are sent to school because their mother has become too ill to teach them.

CUSTOMIZE INSTRUCTION FOR UNIVERSAL ACCESS

For Less Proficient Readers	For Gifted/Talented Students
To help students anchor the narrator's whereabouts in each scene, draw on the board a two-column chart with the headings *Present* and *Past.* Guide students to fill in the chart with events from pp. 1372 and 1373.	Draw students' attention to the first paragraph on p. 1372. Then, point out that although the narrator is recalling an incident many years in the past, she relates her experiences with a keen eye for vivid visual and tactile details. Have students make a list of the details that they find most striking in this passage. Then, give them time to create a drawing or collage that represents those details. Students may choose to include text from the story in their artwork.

22 Literary Analysis

Plot

- Review with students the different elements of plot listed on p. 1365: Exposition, Inciting Incident, Development, Climax, Falling Action, and Resolution.
- Then, have a volunteer read aloud the bracketed passage. Ask: Of which plot element are the events in this passage an example?
  Answer: The events in this passage serve as development.
- Ask students the Literary Analysis question on p. 1374: Why does Premila want to take sandwiches to school?
  Answer: Although Premila says she thinks sandwiches will be more convenient for her sister, she really wants sandwiches because the other students eat them for lunch.

of the afternoon we played indoors, and after the shadows had begun to lengthen and the slight breeze of the evening had come up we moved outside to the wide courtyard.

I had never really grasped the system of competitive games. At home, whenever we played tag or guessing games, I was always allowed to "win"—"because," Mother used to tell Premila, "she is the youngest, and we have to allow for that." I had often heard her say it, and it seemed quite reasonable to me, but the result was that I had no clear idea of what "winning" meant.

When we played twos-and-threes that afternoon at school, in accordance with my training, I let one of the small English boys catch me, but was naturally rather puzzled when the other children did not return the courtesy. I ran about for what seemed like hours without ever catching anyone, until it was time for school to close. Much later I learned that my attitude was called "not being a good sport," and I stopped allowing myself to be caught, but it was not for years that I really learned the spirit of the thing.

When I saw our car come up to the school gate, I broke away from my classmates and rushed toward it yelling, "Ayah! Ayah!" It seemed like an eternity since I had seen her that morning—a wizened, affectionate figure in her white cotton sari, giving me dozens of urgent and useless instructions on how to be a good girl at school. Premila followed more sedately, and she told me on the way home never to do that again in front of the other children.

wizened (wiz′ ənd) *adj.* dried up and wrinkled due to age

When we got home we went straight to Mother's high, white room to have tea with her, and I immediately climbed onto the bed and bounced gently up and down on the springs. Mother asked how we had liked our first day in school. I was so pleased to be home and to have left that peculiar Cynthia behind that I had nothing whatever to say about school, except to ask what "apple" meant. But Premila told Mother about the classes, and added that in her class they had weekly tests to
22 see if they had learned their lessons well.

I asked, "What's a test?"

Premila said, "You're too small to have them. You won't have them in your class for donkey's years." She had learned the expression that day and was using it for the first time. We all laughed enormously at her wit. She also told Mother, in an aside, that we should take sandwiches to school the next day. Not, she said, that *she* minded. But they would be simpler for me to handle.

Literary Analysis
Plot Why does Premila want to take sandwiches to school?

That whole lovely evening I didn't think about school at all. I sprinted barefoot across the lawns with my favorite playmate, the cook's son, to the stream at the end of the garden. We quarreled in our usual way, waded in the tepid water under the lime trees, and waited for the night to bring out the smell of the jasmine. I listened with fascination to his stories of ghosts and demons, until I was too frightened to cross the garden alone in the semidarkness. The ayah found me, shouted at the cook's son, scolded me, hurried me in to supper—it was an entirely usual, wonderful evening.

ENRICHMENT: Culture Connection

India's Caste System

India's caste system is similar to the class system of the West. The difference is that the Western class system is based primarily on wealth. In India's caste system, which is thousands of years old, one's caste is based on the level of society into which one is born, and it cannot be changed.

According to the traditional system, there are four castes: the Brahmans, the Kshatriyas, the Vaishyas, and the Shudras. Brahmans, members of the most honored caste, serve as priests and scholars. Kshatriyas are soldiers; Vaishyas are members of the merchant class; and the Shudras comprise the peasant or working class. Some Indians belong to a fifth group, the Panchamas, which is not truly a caste because its members are considered impure. This last group was once called the untouchables.

Traditionally, people are expected not only to do work according to their castes but also to marry within their castes and follow strict rules about diet and hygiene.

It was a week later, the day of Premila's first test, that our lives changed rather abruptly. I was sitting at the back of my class, in my usual inattentive way, only half listening to the teacher. I had started a rather guarded friendship with the girl with the braids, whose name turned out to be Nalini (Nancy, in school). The three other Indian children were already fast friends. Even at that age it was apparent to all of us that friendship with the English or Anglo-
23 Indian children was out of the question. Occasionally, during the class, my new friend and I would draw pictures and show them to each other secretly.

The door opened sharply and Premila marched in. At first, the teacher smiled at her in a kindly and encouraging way and said, "Now, you're little Cynthia's sister?"

Premila didn't even look at her. She stood with her feet planted firmly apart and her shoulders rigid, and addressed herself directly to me. "Get up," she said. "We're going home."

I didn't know what had happened, but I was aware that it was a crisis of some sort. I rose obediently and started to walk toward my sister.

"Bring your pencils and your notebook," she said.

I went back for them, and together we left the room. The teacher
25 started to say something just as Premila closed the door, but we didn't wait to hear what it was.

In complete silence we left the school grounds and started to walk home. Then I asked Premila what the matter was. All she would say was "We're going home for good."

It was a very tiring walk for a child of five and a half, and I dragged along behind Premila with my pencils growing sticky in my hand. I can still remember looking at the dusty hedges, and the tangles of thorns in the ditches by the side of the road, smelling the faint fragrance from the eucalyptus trees and wondering whether we would ever reach home. Occasionally a horse-drawn tonga[9] passed us, and the women, in their pink or green silks, stared at Premila and me trudging along on the side of the road. A few coolies[10] and a line of women carrying baskets of vegetables on their heads smiled at us. But it was nearing the hottest time of day, and the road was almost deserted. I walked more and more slowly, and shouted to Premila, from time to time, "Wait for me!" with increasing peevishness. She spoke to me only once, and that was to tell me to carry my notebook on my head, because of the sun.

24 ▲ Critical Viewing

Does this photograph of a street in Bombay, India, seem like the "little provincial town" Rama Rau describes in this memoir? Explain. **[Evaluate]**

26 

Reading Check

Why does the narrator fail to grasp the idea of competition?

9. **tonga** (täŋ´ gə) *n.* two-wheeled, horse-drawn carriage.
10. **coolies** (ko͞o´ lēz) *n.* unskilled laborers who work for low wages.

23 Reading Strategy

Recognizing Ironic Details

- Remind students that situational irony involves a contrast between what is expected and what actually happens.
- Have students read the bracketed passage independently. Then, ask students to discuss the situational irony that unfolds on p. 1375.
  Answer: Just as Santha is learning to make friends and fit in at school, her sister, who seemed to fit in immediately, declares that she will not stay at the school.
- Have students offer predictions as to why Premila has changed her mind. What do they think has happened? Compile a list of students' suggestions, and revisit the list after they have finished reading the story.

24 ▶ Critical Viewing

Possible response: No; the photograph shows a busy and crowded city, not a small provincial town.

25 Literary Analysis

Plot

- Remind students that the climax of a story occurs when the conflict reaches its highest point. Have students reread p. 1375 and identify the climax of the story.
  Answer: The scene in which the girls leave the classroom is the story's climax.
- Then, use a plot chart like the one shown on p. 1377 to record the events leading up to the climax. Have students identify inciting incidents, exposition, and developments.

26 ✔ Reading Check

Answer: The narrator does not understand competition because as the younger child she has never had to compete. She has always been allowed to win.

CUSTOMIZE INSTRUCTION FOR UNIVERSAL ACCESS

For Less Proficient Readers	For Advanced Readers
Students may benefit from working in small groups to retell the events of the narrative in their own words. Allow students to meet to discuss their notes or Story Maps. Students may either take turns retelling the story in its entirety or retell the story round-robin style, with each person telling one incident or detail from the plot in sequence. Students should take time to double-check that they have the events in the correct order.	Challenge students to write short essays comparing the lives and works of R. K. Narayan and Santha Rama Rau. In particular, ask students to consider how the two writers treat ordinary people and events in the narratives in this grouping. Students may wish to research more about the authors' lives as well as read professional criticism and reviews the writers have received. Encourage students to read their essays to the class or to post or publish them on a class bulletin board, in a school newspaper, or on a school Web site.

ASSESS

Answers for p. 1376

Review and Assess

1. Possible responses: Premila's actions are surprising because she seemed to be fitting in at the new school very well.
2. **(a)** The girls were sent to the British school because their mother became too ill to teach them at home. **(b)** The girls' mother believes that the British are narrow-minded and prejudiced. **(c)** The mother's concern foreshadows the girls' renaming and the teacher's expectation that the Indian students will cheat on tests.
3. **(a)** Premila tells Santha to sit with her class. **(b)** Premila is concerned with fitting in. **(c)** Premila becomes aware of certain prejudices that she will never overcome by "fitting in."
4. **(a)** The narrator happily put away her memory and understanding of what happened to her and her sister at the British school. **(b)** She is able to dismiss the experience because it was assigned to her "British" alter-ego, Cynthia.
5. **(a)** Possible response: The Indian students may develop the attitude that they are inferior to their British classmates. They may also resent the British students who receive better treatment. **(b)** Possible response: Because Premila was the one who was insulted, she may remember the event more clearly and painfully than her sister.
6. Possible response: The story warns against insularity and prejudice and suggests that those of different cultures should attempt to understand and accept one another.

When we got to our house the ayah was just taking a tray of lunch into Mother's room. She immediately started a long, worried questioning about what are you children doing back here at this hour of the day.

Mother looked very startled and very concerned, and asked Premila what had happened.

Premila said, "We had our test today, and She made me and the other Indians sit at the back of the room, with a desk between each one."

Mother said, "Why was that, darling?"

"She said it was because Indians cheat," Premila added. "So I don't think we should go back to that school."

Mother looked very distant, and was silent a long time. At last she said, "Of course not, darling." She sounded displeased.

We all shared the curry she was having for lunch, and afterward I was sent off to the beautifully familiar bedroom for my siesta. I could hear Mother and Premila talking through the open door.

Mother said, "Do you suppose she understood all that?"

Premila said, "I shouldn't think so. She's a baby."

Mother said, "Well, I hope it won't bother her."

Of course, they were both wrong. I understood it perfectly, and I remember it all very clearly. But I put it happily away, because it had all happened to a girl called Cynthia, and I never was really particularly interested in her.

Review and Assess

Thinking About the Selection

1. **Respond:** Do you find Premila's actions surprising? Explain.
2. **(a) Recall:** Why were the two girls sent to the British school? **(b) Interpret:** What explanation does the girls' mother give for not wanting to send them there? **(c) Infer:** In what ways does her statement foreshadow, or hint at, what the school will be like?
3. **(a) Recall:** What does Premila tell Santha to do at lunch recess? **(b) Interpret:** What concerns or fears does her statement reveal? **(c) Analyze Cause and Effect:** In what ways does the test change her feelings?
4. **(a) Recall:** At the end of the story, what does the narrator say she put "happily away"? **(b) Analyze:** Why is she able to dismiss the experience so easily?
5. **(a) Speculate:** What attitudes toward both themselves and the British might the Indian children who remain at the school develop? **(b) Make a Judgment:** Do you think their experience will have long-term effects on Premila or on Santha? Explain.
6. **Generalize:** What does this story suggest about the ways in which people of different cultures should relate to each other?

ASSESSMENT PRACTICE: Reading Comprehension

Using Context Clues to Determine Meaning (For more practice, see Test Preparation Workbook, p. 4.)

The reading sections of many tests require students to use context clues to identify the appropriate meaning of a word in a given passage. Use the following sample test item to demonstrate.

The building was Indian in design, with wide verandas opening onto a central courtyard, but Indian verandas are usually whitewashed, with stone floors.

In this passage, verandas means—

A storerooms
B flowers
C windows
D porches

Storerooms would not be wide or open, so *A* is not the correct answer. Flowers and windows would not be whitewashed, so *B* and *C* are not correct answers. *D*, porches, is the correct answer.

Review and Assess

Literary Analysis

Plot

1. Use a chart like the one shown to analyze the **plot** of "An Astrologer's Day." (a) Which events lead to the *climax?* (b) What is the *conflict?* (c) Which events form the *falling action?*

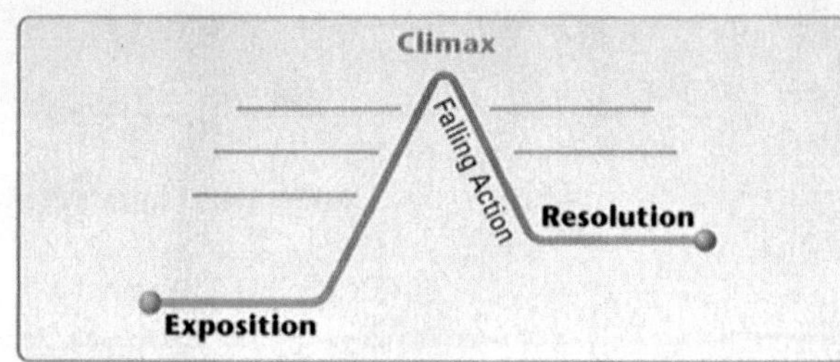

2. Why is the information about the astrologer that is revealed in the falling action important for a complete understanding of the story?
3. (a) In "By Any Other Name," which events build up to the climax? (b) Summarize Rama Rau's reaction to events as she describes it in the *resolution.*

Comparing Literary Works

4. (a) In "An Astrologer's Day," what measures does the astrologer take to conceal his identity? (b) What are his motives?
5. In "By Any Other Name," does the headmistress give the girls new identities simply because she cannot pronounce their names? Explain.
6. What statement about personal identity might both the astrologer and Premila offer?

Reading Strategy

Recognizing Ironic Details

7. Which details in the resolution of "An Astrologer's Day" are examples of situational **irony** because they contradict your expectations?
8. (a) In "By Any Other Name," identify three details that demonstrate *verbal irony.* (b) How is the narrator's reaction to her experience at the British school an example of *situational irony?* Explain.

Extend Understanding

9. **History Connection:** In what ways might an imperial power like England leave its mark on former colonies or dependencies?

Quick Review

Plot is the sequence of events in a literary work. Most plots follow a specific pattern in which a conflict is introduced, built to a climax, and followed by falling action and a resolution.

To **recognize ironic details,** note descriptions, dialogue, and other details that create expectations in your mind. As you read further, use other details to determine whether or not your expectations are fulfilled.

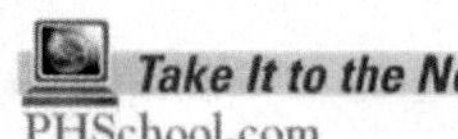

PHSchool.com

Take the interactive self-test online to check your understanding of these selections.

ENRICHMENT: Further Reading

Other Works by the Authors

We strongly encourage you to review any selection before assigning or recommending it to students.

Works by R. K. Narayan

The Painter of Signs

Swami and Friends

Works by Santha Rama Rau

Remember the House

The Adventuress: A Novel

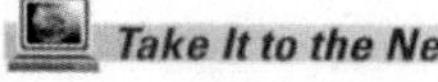

Visit PHSchool.com for more information on the authors.

Answers for p. 1377

Review and Assess

1. **(a)** The arrival of the customer, the haggling over price, and the astrologer's predictions lead to the climax. **(b)** The astrologer wants to make money and to save himself. **(c)** The falling actions include the customer's departure and the astrologer's confession to his wife.
2. The information is important because it is not clear how the astrologer knows about the client.
3. **(a)** The girls' renaming, Santha's making friends and learning games, Premila's telling her mother about school, and Santha's playing at home lead to the climax. **(b)** Rama Rau's younger self understood everything that happened, but she was able to forget about it because she believed it had happened to "Cynthia."
4. **(a)** The astrologer is in costume, with his face covered in paint and whiskers, and he works in the dim light of the marketplace. **(b)** His motives are to make himself seem mysterious and to conceal his identity.
5. The headmistress says that she cannot cope with Indian names, but the author suggests that racism is the cause.
6. Both the astrologer and Premila might say that identity reflects culture and family.
7. The astrologer gives the Nayak an accurate prediction; the customer cheats the astrologer; and the astrologer complains that the payment is too little.
8. **(a)** Santha tells her class that she does not know her name; Premila tells her mother to pack sandwiches, and Premila says she does not think that Santha understood what happened. **(b)** The narrator's reaction is ironic because she says that she forgot about the experience; yet, she writes about it in great detail.
9. Possible response: An imperial power like England leaves its language, its form of government, and its prejudices on its former colonies or dependencies

EXTEND

Answers for p. 1378

❶ Vocabulary Development

Word Analysis: Latin Root *-cant-*

1. b
2. a
3. c

Spelling Strategy

1. polar
2. globular
3. molecular
4. spectacular

Concept Development: Synonyms

1. b
2. a
3. a
4. c
5. a
6. b
7. a

❷ Grammar and Style

Practice

1. The astrologer felt anxious when he recognized the man.
2. He was lucky to have escaped him for such an extraordinarily long time.
3. He did well in describing the man's life because he knew him.
4. Premila and Santha felt bad about changing their names.
5. The headmistress spoke gently, but her words stung.

Writing Application

Possible response:

Changing my name would feel *strange*. I have a name that is *common*. But my mother would react *terribly* if I suddenly told her that I had changed my name from Mary to Ursula, which is *somewhat unusual*. She *lovingly* chose my name to honor her *best* friend.

10TH GRADE For support in teaching the Grammar and Style Lesson to tenth graders, use **Writing and Grammar,** Platinum Level, Chapter 25, Section 1; Chapter 16, Section 3.

Integrate Language Skills

❶ Vocabulary Development Lesson

Word Analysis: Latin Root *-cant-*

The Latin root *-cant-*, which appears in the word *incantations*, means "sing" or "chant." Use this information to match each word on the left with its definition on the right.

1. cantor	a. division of a long poem
2. canto	b. singer of religious music
3. cantata	c. song or hymn

Spelling Strategy

The *r* sound at the end of many adjectives is spelled *ar*, as in the word *insular*. Write the adjective ending in *ar* that is related to each noun below.

1. pole
2. globule
3. molecule
4. spectacle

Concept Development: Synonyms

For each numbered word below, choose the letter of the word that is its synonym.

1. paraphernalia: (a) garbage, (b) equipment, (c) whistle
2. incantations: (a) chants, (b) books, (c) injections
3. insular: (a) isolated, (b) trendy, (c) waterlogged
4. prophetic: (a) ignored, (b) ancient, (c) predictive
5. wizened: (a) decrepit, (b) angry, (c) foolish
6. provincial: (a) old, (b) unsophisticated, (c) evil
7. ancestral: (a) familial, (b) wealthy, (c) stolen

❷ Grammar and Style Lesson

Correct Use of Adjectives and Adverbs

An **adjective** modifies a noun or pronoun. Always use an adjective after a linking verb (*is*, *are*, *seems*, and *feels*) if the modifier describes the subject. An **adverb** modifies a verb, an adjective, or another adverb. Always use an adverb to modify an action verb.

Adjective after a linking verb:

S LV ADJ
His forehead was resplendent with sacred ash. . . .

Adverb after an action verb:

S V ADV
I sat down quickly. . . .

Practice Rewrite each sentence below, correcting errors in adjective and adverb use.

1. The astrologer felt anxiously when he recognized the man.
2. He was lucky to have escaped him for such an extraordinary long time.
3. He did good in describing the man's life because he knew him.
4. Premila and Santha felt badly about changing their names.
5. The headmistress spoke gentle but her words stung.

Writing Application Write a paragraph describing how you would feel about changing your name. Correctly use at least three adjectives and three adverbs.

WG Prentice Hall Writing and Grammar Connection: Diamond Level, Chapter 24, Section 1; Chapter 17, Section 2

TEACHING RESOURCES

The following resources can be used to enrich or extend the instruction for pp. 1378–1379.

Vocabulary

- **Selection Support:** Build Vocabulary, p. 269
- **Vocabulary and Spelling Practice Book** (Use this booklet for skills instruction.)

Grammar

- **Selection Support:** Grammar and Style, p. 270
- **Writing and Grammar,** Diamond Level, pp. 622, 379
- **Daily Language Practice Transparencies** ■

Writing

- **Performance Assess. and Portfolio Mgmt.,** p. 9
- **Writing and Grammar,** Diamond Level, p. 84
- **Writing and Grammar iText CD-ROM**
- **Writing Models and Graphic Organizers on Transparencies,** pp. 83–85 ■

Listening and Speaking

- **Performance Assess. and Portfolio Mgmt.,** p. 32

■ **BLOCK SCHEDULING:** Resources marked with this symbol provide varied instruction during 90-minute blocks.

❸ Writing Lesson

Personal Essay With a Surprise Ending

In "An Astrologer's Day," R. K. Narayan reveals information at the end of the story that changes our understanding of the characters and events. Write a personal essay that tells a story and offers readers a similar surprise ending.

Prewriting Choose an experience that centers on an interesting problem. Brainstorm for details about the people, setting, and events. Then, list the details in chronological order.

Drafting Begin with an introduction that states the problem. As you tell the story, use your list of details to bring it to life. By the end of the story, show how the problem was resolved in a surprising way.

Revising As you review your essay, make sure that you have not presented telltale details too early. Remove or revise your hints if they disclose too much information, spoiling the surprise.

Model: Revising to Avoid Revealing a Surprise Ending

Although her five brothers usually showed up, cousin Jill never came to our family reunions. ~~This year, she thought she might make it.~~ When my cousins arrived, I was sort of surprised that the guys were toting a floral suitcase. . . .

The omission of certain details preserves the surprise of the ending.

WG Prentice Hall Writing and Grammar Connection: Diamond Level, Chapter 5, Section 4

❹ Extension Activities

Listening and Speaking Conduct research on the most common names in several countries, including India. Create and deliver an **oral report on names** for your class. Use these tips to prepare:

- Create an introduction that will grab listeners' attention.
- Use photographs, maps, and other visual aids to spark interest.

As you speak, help your listeners follow the flow of information by creating smooth transitions between sections of the report.

Research and Technology With a small group, prepare a **multimedia presentation** about R. K. Narayan's life and works. Use the Internet and other sources to locate pictures of Narayan and the places he wrote about. Then, combine them into a video or slide show. Select passages from his works and Indian music to accompany the images. **[Group Activity]**

Take It to the Net PHSchool.com

Go online for an additional research activity using the Internet.

ASSESSMENT RESOURCES

The following resources can be used to assess students' knowledge and skills.

Selection Assessment

- **Formal Assessment,** pp. 234–236
- **Open-Book Tests,** pp. 202–204
- **Test Bank Software**

Take It to the Net

Visit PHSchool.com for self-tests on the selections.

Writing Rubric

- **Performance Assess. and Portfolio Mgmt.,** p. 9

Listening and Speaking Rubric

- **Performance Assess. and Portfolio Mgmt.,** p. 32

For additional diagnostics and remediation for skills covered in this grouping, use materials from the Prentice Hall Assessment System.

❸ Writing Lesson

- Remind students that events in a personal essay are usually presented in chronological order, although some may be presented through flashback.
- Have students use the Story Map organizer in **Writing Models and Graphic Organizers on Transparencies,** pp. 83–85, to plot their essays.
- After they have completed a first draft, students should check to make sure that their narratives have the five plot parts mentioned on p. 1365.
- Use the Narration: Autobiographical Narrative rubric in **Performance Assessment and Portfolio Management,** p. 9, to evaluate students' essays.

10TH GRADE For support in working through the Writing Lesson with tenth graders, use **Writing and Grammar,** Platinum Level, Chapter 5, Section 4.

❹ Listening and Speaking

- Remind students that a good oral report has a structure. It should have a clear introduction, at least three solid examples, and a conclusion.
- Use the Speaking: Multimedia Presentation rubric in **Performance Assessment and Portfolio Management,** p. 32, to evaluate students' reports.

CUSTOMIZE INSTRUCTION For Universal Access

To address different learning styles, use the following activities suggested in the **Extension Activities** booklet, p. 68:

- For Visual/Spatial Learners, use Activities 5, 6, and 7.
- For Verbal/Linguistic Learners, use Activity 6.
- For Logical/Mathematical Learners, use Activity 7.

The Jay

Lesson Objectives

1. **To analyze and respond to literary elements**
   - Literary Analysis: Thematic Imagery
   - Connecting Literary Elements: Mood
2. **To read, comprehend, analyze, and critique a short story**
   - Reading Strategy: Judging Characters' Actions
   - Reading Check Questions
   - Review and Assess Questions
   - Assessment Practice (ATE)
3. **To develop word analysis skills, fluency, and systematic vocabulary**
   - Vocabulary Development Lesson: Latin Root *-spec-*
4. **To understand and apply written and oral language conventions**
   - Spelling Strategy
   - Grammar and Style Lesson: Subjunctive Mood
5. **To understand and apply appropriate writing and research strategies**
   - Writing Lesson: Proposal for a Program for the Elderly
   - Extension Activity: Science Report about Birds
6. **To understand and apply listening and speaking strategies**
   - Extension Activity: Oral Report on Japan

 **TEACHING A TENTH-GRADE COURSE**

The literature in this section can be taught as part of a rich, balanced world literature course for tenth-grade students. For a full outline of such a course, see pp. T46–T48 in Volume 1 of this Teacher's Edition.

STEP-BY-STEP TEACHING GUIDE	PACING GUIDE
PRETEACH	
Motivate Students and Provide Background	
Use the Motivation activity (ATE p. 1380)	5 min.
Read and discuss author and background features (SE pp. 1380, 1382; ATE p. 1380) [A]	5 min.
Introduce the Concepts	
Introduce the Literary Analysis and Reading Strategy concepts (SE/ATE p. 1381) [A]	15 min.
Pronounce the vocabulary words and read their definitions (SE p. 1381)	5 min.
TEACH	
Monitor Comprehension	
Informally monitor comprehension by circulating while students read independently or in groups [A]	20 min.
Monitor students' comprehension with the Reading Check notes (SE/ATE pp. 1383, 1385)	as students read
Develop vocabulary with the Vocabulary notes (SE pp. 1383, 1385, 1386; ATE p. 1385)	as students read
Develop Understanding	
Develop students' understanding of thematic imagery with the Literary Analysis annotations (SE/ATE pp. 1383, 1386) [A]	5 min.
Develop students' ability to judge characters' actions by using the Reading Strategy annotations (SE/ATE pp. 1382, 1385)	5 min.
ASSESS	
Assess Mastery	
Assess students' mastery of the Reading Strategy and Literary Analysis concepts by having them answer the Review and Assess questions (SE/ATE p. 1387)	15 min.
Use one or more of the print, software, or transparency Assessment Resources (ATE p. 1389) [A]	up to 45 min.
EXTEND	
Apply Understanding	
Have students complete the Vocabulary Development Lesson and the Grammar and Style Lesson (SE p. 1388) [A]	20 min.
Apply students' ability to outline, using the Writing Lesson (SE/ATE p. 1389) [A]	45 min.
Apply students' understanding of the selection, using one or more of the Extension Activities (SE p. 1389)	20–90 min.

[A] **ACCELERATED INSTRUCTION:** Use the strategies and activities identified with an [A].

 **TEACHING TENTH-GRADE STUDENTS** For support in teaching tenth-grade students, see the Step-by-Step Teaching notes identified with the icon shown here.

UNIVERSAL ACCESS

● = Below-Level Students

▲ = On-Level Students

■ = Above-Level Students

Time and Resource Manager

Reading Level: Average
Average Number of Instructional Days: 3

RESOURCES		
PRINT	**TRANSPARENCIES**	**TECHNOLOGY**
• **Beyond Literature,** Cultural Connection: Beliefs That Shape Japanese Character, p. 69 ▲ ■		
• **Selection Support Workbook:** ● ▲ ■ Literary Analysis, p. 276 Reading Strategy, p. 275 Build Vocabulary, p. 273	• **Literary Analysis and Reading Transparencies,** pp. 137 and 138 ● ▲ ■	
		• **Listening to Literature** ● ▲ ■ Audiocassettes Audio CDs
• **Literary Analysis for Enrichment,** p. 69 ■		
• **Formal Assessment:** Selection Test, pp. 237–239 ● ▲ ■ • **Open-Book Tests,** pp. 205–207 ● ▲ ■ • **Performance Assess. and Portfolio Mgmt.,** pp. 22, 32 ● ▲ ■ • PRENTICE HALL ASSESSMENT SYSTEM ● ▲ ■	• PRENTICE HALL ASSESSMENT SYSTEM ● ▲ ■ **Skills Practice Answers and Explanations on Transparencies**	• **Test Bank Software** ● ▲ ■
• **Selection Support Workbook:** ● ▲ ■ Grammar and Style, p. 274 • **Writing and Grammar,** Diamond Level ● ▲ ■ • **Extension Activities,** p. 69 ● ▲ ■	• **Daily Language Practice Transparencies** ● ▲ • **Writing Models and Graphic Organizers on Transparencies,** pp. 103–105 ● ▲ ■	• **Writing and Grammar iText CD-ROM** ● ▲ ■ ***Take It to the Net*** PHSchool.com

BLOCK SCHEDULING: Use one 90-minute class period to preteach the selection(s) and have students read them. Use a second 90-minute class period to assess students' mastery of skills and have them complete one of the Extension Activities.

PRETEACH

Step-by-Step Teaching Guide for pp. 1380–1381

Motivation

Call on students' prior knowledge by asking them to name a family object or pattern that has taken on a meaning over the years, one that cannot ever be completely expressed in words, such as a keepsake handed down by a grandparent or a special way of celebrating a holiday. Lead students in a discussion about how such things can be used as thematic images in telling a story about their families.

❶ Background

More About the Author

Kawabata and his close friend, the writer Riichi Yokomitsu, founded a journal called *Bungei Jidai* (*The Artistic Age*). The journal became an influential advocate for Neosensualism, a new literary movement that called for close attention to sensory detail. Both writers were additionally influenced by modernist French literature that began to appear after World War I. This influence is revealed through Kawabata's abrupt transitions, startling imagery that mixes incongruous details, and juxtaposition of beautiful and ugly elements. These are qualities, however, that also occur in earlier Japanese literature, and it is to these models that Kawabata was increasingly drawn in his later years. His work is still greatly admired for its lyricism, its intuitive structure, and its remarkable and diverse portraits of women.

Geography Note

Draw students' attention to the map on this page, and point out that Japan consists of four main islands: Hokkaido, Honshu, Shikoku, and Kyushu. Kawabata was born on the largest island, Honshu, in the city of Osaka. Honshu, which features Mount Fuji (Japan's largest mountain) and Lake Biwa (Japan's largest lake), is considered the Japanese mainland.

Prepare to Read

❶ The Jay

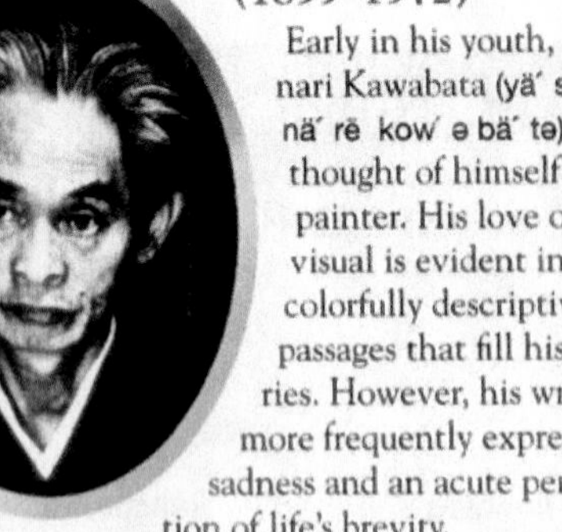

Yasunari Kawabata (1899–1972)

Early in his youth, Yasunari Kawabata (yä′ sōō nä′ rē kow′ ə bä′ tə) thought of himself as a painter. His love of the visual is evident in the colorfully descriptive passages that fill his stories. However, his writing more frequently expresses sadness and an acute perception of life's brevity.

Early Sorrows Many critics see Kawabata's pensive fiction as a reflection of a very difficult childhood. By the time he was sixteen years old, Kawabata was entirely alone in the world. His father had died when the writer was only two years old, and his mother died the following year. Kawabata lived with his grandfather until the elder's death nine years later. After his grandfather's death, Kawabata attended the elite First High School in Tokyo and Tokyo Imperial University, where he studied Japanese literature.

A Young Writer's Diary Although it was not published for years, Kawabata's first important work was *Diary of a Sixteen-Year-Old.* According to the author, he composed the diary in 1914, during twelve days in May. He stopped writing in the diary a week before his grandfather died. The memories of his grandfather's last days often recur in Kawabata's fiction, but the *Diary* has the most evocative passages. Some scholars question the *Diary*'s authenticity, arguing that it was probably written in 1925, the year it was published. But Kawabata insists that he found the manuscript on student composition paper in an uncle's warehouse. He said, "The strangest thing was that I had not the least recollection of the events described in the diary. . . . I confronted honest emotions of a forgotten past. But the grandfather I had described was uglier than the grandfather of my memory. For ten years my mind had been constantly cleansing my grandfather's image."

First Successes Kawabata's first published story, "A View of the Yasukuni Festival," attracted favorable attention. It was an auspicious beginning for his career because it impressed several important figures in the Japanese literary world. As a result of these contacts, Kawabata started work on a literary magazine, *Bungei Shunju*. He also met the novelist Riichi Yokomitsu, who became a close friend and influenced Kawabata's writing for the rest of his career. Yokomitsu and Kawabata eventually became the two major Japanese novelists of the era.

Encouraging Free Speech For years, Kawabata led an extremely private life, but in 1933 he began to participate more actively in the literary world. He joined the staff of magazines, and he was appointed to the Literary Discussion Group, an organization that tried to foster cooperation between writers and the repressive Japanese government. While Kawabata willingly cooperated with the government's strictures, he continued to publish articles in which he argued for free speech and encouraged a spirit of rebellion against social conventions. In his words, "Without rebellion against conventional morality there can be no pure literature." Kawabata proved that point with his own work, including the novel *Snow Country* (1937), which many critics consider his masterpiece.

In later life, Kawabata's influence on Japanese literature was fully recognized. He won numerous awards and served as one of the judges of Japan's most prestigious literary prize. His starring role in Japanese literature was confirmed in 1968 when he became the first Japanese writer to win the Nobel Prize in Literature.

TEACHING RESOURCES

The following resources can be used to enrich or extend the instruction for pp. 1380–1381.

Background

Beyond Literature, p. 69

Take It to the Net

Visit PHSchool.com for background on the author.

Literary Analysis

Literary Analysis and Reading Transparencies, Thematic Imagery, p. 137

Selection Support: Literary Analysis, p. 276

Reading

Literary Analysis and Reading Transparencies, Judging Characters' Actions, p. 138

BLOCK SCHEDULING: Resources marked with this symbol provide varied instruction during 90-minute blocks.

Preview

Connecting to the Literature

Sometimes, even in company, we can feel more alone than when we are by ourselves. That is the plight of the young woman in this story, who holds quiet but deeply felt emotions.

❷ Literary Analysis

Thematic Imagery

Images are word pictures created through language that appeals to one or more of the five senses. Imagery provides concrete representations of ideas or emotions. For example, in "The Jay," imagery of a distraught mother bird and her lost nestling reflects the story's human drama of a young woman separated from both her real mother and her stepmother:

> The jay flew to the chestnut, skimmed the ground, and flew back again, calling out all the while.
>
> Would the nestling still be near, that the mother was so reluctant to leave?

When imagery in a work extends beyond a single moment and connects to the central message, it is called **thematic imagery.** As you read, consider ways in which the imagery of the birds suggests larger, thematic concepts.

Connecting Literary Elements

Imagery is one tool a writer can use to create **mood**—the feeling that a literary work evokes in a reader. A mood of fragility and isolation pervades much of "The Jay." As you read, notice how the mood is connected to the descriptions of the birds, and identify the point at which the mood abruptly shifts.

❸ Reading Strategy

Judging Characters' Actions

The characters in this story are caught in a complicated family web, which has caused them to react in different ways. When you **judge characters' actions,** you measure a character's behavior against certain criteria, such as your personal experiences, values, and understanding of human nature. As you read, use a chart like the one shown to identify each character's thoughts and feelings and the actions he or she takes. Then, form a judgment about each character.

Vocabulary Development

reluctant (ri luk′ tənt) *adj.* showing hesitation; unwilling (p. 1383)

deficiency (dē fish′ ən sē) *n.* shortage of a necessary substance (p. 1383)

extravagant (ek strav′ ə gənt) *adj.* excessive; spending much more than is necessary (p. 1383)

prospective (prō spek′ tiv) *adj.* likely to be or to become in the future (p. 1385)

forlornly (fôr lôrn′ lē) *adv.* in a sad or lonely manner because of isolation or desertion (p. 1386)

❷ Literary Analysis

Thematic Imagery

- Remind students that the theme of a work is its central idea, concern, or purpose. Thematic imagery can give a concrete shape to this idea, concern, or purpose.
- Lead students in a discussion about how an author might use the image of a bridge to express connection.
- Use the Thematic Imagery transparency in **Literary Analysis and Reading Transparencies,** p. 137, to help students identify and understand examples of thematic imagery.

❸ Reading Strategy

Judging Characters' Actions

- Point out that readers form opinions about characters on the basis of the characters' thoughts, feelings, and actions as well as their own values and experiences.
- Help students understand how to judge a character's actions by modeling the use of the graphic organizer on p. 1381. Suggest a value such as "Children and parents should respect one another's feelings" for the "My Criteria for Judging" box. Then, have students suggest an action and complete the organizer by drawing a conclusion about, or judging, the action according to the criteria chosen.
- As they read the story, encourage students to use a graphic organizer like the one on p. 1381 to evaluate Yoshiko's thoughts and feelings.

Vocabulary Development

- Pronounce each vocabulary word for students, and read the definitions as a class. Have students identify any words with which they are familiar.

CUSTOMIZE INSTRUCTION FOR UNIVERSAL ACCESS

For Less Proficient Readers	For English Learners	For Advanced Readers
Remind students that the mood and images of "The Jay" are as important as the story's plot and action. Ask students to record any images that seem unclear as they read the story. Then, discuss these images with the class when students have finished reading.	Have students write about or describe orally a time when they had to care for someone or something that needed their help. Ask students to write about the associations this type of situation brings to mind. Tell students to draw from imagination if they have never had such an experience.	Have students discuss their own experiences with films and stories that include thematic imagery. Many students, for example, may have read Mark Twain's *The Adventures of Huckleberry Finn,* in which the Mississippi River runs through the story as a thematic image.

 ***E-Teach***

Visit e-Teach at PHSchool.com for teachers' essays on how to teach, with questions and answers.

TEACH

Step-by-Step Teaching Guide for pp. 1382–1386

Teaching Tenth-Grade Students

10TH GRADE Provide students with information about jays, the birds seen and heard in Kawabata's story. Explain that the jays are known for having loud, harsh calls. The Latin name of the Eurasian jay is *Garrulus glandarius;* the Latin word *garrulus* means "chattering." The English word *garrulous* describes a person who talks a great deal.

❶ About the Selection

In "The Jay," Kawabata connects an image of a fragile, injured bird with the characters in his story. Each character is somehow alienated or hurt, like the injured bird. Fear, loneliness, pain—qualities Kawabata indirectly associates with the injured bird—surface in each of the characters. The bird's need for parental nourishment is also an important need for the characters.

❷ Reading Strategy

Judging Characters' Actions

- Read aloud the bracketed passage. Then, have students explain the difference in how the grandmother and the brother respond to the jay.
  Answer: The jay's raucous call annoys the brother. The grandmother reacts with more sympathy, explaining that the bird is upset because she has lost her nestling.
- Remind students that judging characters' actions involves evaluating their actions against one's own experiences and values.
- Ask students the Reading Strategy question on p. 1382: What judgments can you make about the brother and the grandmother based on their differing reactions to the jay? Explain.
  Possible response: The brother is young and impatient. The grandmother is wise and, though blind, knows how to interpret information around her.

The Jay ❶

Yasunari Kawabata

translated by Edward Seidensticker

Background

From the mid-1800s until the end of World War II, arranged marriages were common in Japanese society. Marital partners were chosen by one's parents, sometimes with the help of relatives or other close associates. When arranging marriages, matchmakers evaluated the social standing of the prospective spouse's family and his or her financial circumstances. Usually, the bride and groom were at least introduced before the wedding day, but they had no chance to get to know each other, and their feelings were secondary to issues of status and wealth. In this story, Yoshiko's father's failed first marriage has shaped the lives of all the characters.

The jay was noisy from dawn.

It seemed to have flown from a lower branch of the pine tree as Yoshiko was opening the shutters and then come back again. They could hear its wings from the breakfast table.

"What a racket," said her brother, starting to get up.

❷ "Leave it alone," said her grandmother. "I think the little one must have fallen from the nest yesterday. I could still hear the mother last night after dark. I suppose she couldn't find it. And isn't that nice, here she is back again this morning."

"Are you sure?" asked Yoshiko.

Save for a liver attack some ten years before, her grandmother had never been ill, but she had suffered from cataracts[1] ever since she was

Reading Strategy
Judging Characters' Actions What judgments can you make about the brother and the grandmother based on their differing reactions to the jay? Explain.

1. **cataracts** (kat' ə rakts') eye disease in which the lens or its capsule becomes opaque, causing partial or total blindness.

TEACHING RESOURCES

The following resources can be used to enrich or extend the instruction for pp. 1382–1386.

Literary Analysis

- **Selection Support:** Literary Analysis, p. 276 ■
- **Literary Analysis and Reading Transparencies,** Thematic Imagery, p. 137

Reading

- **Selection Support:** Reading Strategy, p. 275; Build Vocabulary, p. 273 ■
- **Listening to Literature Audiocassettes** ■
- **Listening to Literature CDs**

■ **BLOCK SCHEDULING:** Resources marked with this symbol provide varied instruction during 90-minute blocks.

very young. Now she could barely see, and with the left eye only. She had to be handed her food. She could grope her way around the house, but she never went out alone into the garden.

3 She would sometimes stand or sit at the glass door and gaze at her fingers, spread out in the sunlight. Her whole life seemed to be concentrated in the gaze.

Yoshiko would be afraid of her. She would want to call from behind, and then she would slip away.

Yoshiko was filled with admiration that her blind grandmother could talk about the jay as if she had seen it.

When she went out to do the breakfast dishes, the jay was calling from the roof next door.

There were a chestnut and several persimmons in the back yard. She could see against them that a gentle rain was falling, so gentle that she could not make it out except against the dark background.

The jay flew to the chestnut, skimmed the ground, and flew back again, calling out all the while.

Would the nestling still be near, that the mother was so reluctant to leave?

Yoshiko went to her room. She must be ready by noon.

Her mother and father would be bringing her fiancé's mother.

As she sat down before the mirror she glanced at the white dots on her fingernails. They were said to be a sign that someone would come with gifts, but she had read in a newspaper that they really showed a deficiency in vitamin C or something of the sort. She was pleased with her face when she had finished making herself up. She thought her eyebrows and lips rather charming. She liked the set of her kimono.[2]

She had thought she would wait for her mother to help her, and then she was glad that she had dressed by herself.

4 Her father and mother, actually her stepmother, did not live with them.

Her father had divorced her mother when Yoshiko was four and her brother two. It was said that her mother had been gaudy and extravagant, but Yoshiko suspected that there had been deeper causes.

Her father had said nothing when her brother had found a picture of their mother and shown it to him. He had frowned and torn the picture to pieces.

When Yoshiko was thirteen her new mother came into the house. Later Yoshiko was to think it rather remarkable of her father to have waited almost ten years. Her new mother was a kind woman and they lived a quiet, happy life.

When her brother entered high school and went to live in a dormitory, it was plain to all of them that his attitude toward his stepmother was changing.

"I've seen Mother," he said to Yoshiko. "She is married and living in Azabu.[3] She is very beautiful. She was glad to see me."

2. **kimono** (kə mō´ nō) *n.* robe with wide sleeves and a sash, part of the traditional costume of Japanese men and women.
3. **Azabu** (ä´ zä´ bo͞o´) street in Tokyo.

Literary Analysis
Thematic Imagery and Mood What mood does this description of the grandmother create? Explain.

reluctant (ri luk´ tənt) *adj.* showing hesitation; unwilling

deficiency (dē fish´ ən sē) *n.* shortage of a necessary substance

Literary Analysis
Thematic Imagery In what ways does Yoshiko's situation mirror that of the lost nestling?

extravagant (ek strav´ ə gənt) *adj.* excessive; spending much more than is necessary

5 **✔ Reading Check**
Why is the jay making a racket?

CUSTOMIZE INSTRUCTION FOR UNIVERSAL ACCESS

For Gifted/Talented Students

Tell students that at the time Yasunari Kawabata and Riichi Yokomitsu founded their movement of Neosensualism, most established Japanese writers were using their literary works to call for political reform. In contrast, these two writers named their movement Neosensualism because they were convinced that the major function of literature was artistic and not propagandistic. They put a great emphasis on writing that appealed to the senses in and for themselves; they believed that sensory detail did not have to carry hidden messages to justify its existence.

Have students use the Internet or other library resources to research Neosensualism and then write stories or poems that reflect this movement's aesthetic. Before they begin, students may find it beneficial to read other works by Kawabata or Yokomitsu. Encourage students to present to the class their final stories or poems, discussing the elements of Neosensualism they used in their work.

3 Literary Analysis

Thematic Imagery and Mood

- Point out to students that imagery and mood are often linked—a writer can use specific images to evoke particular emotions.
- Ask students the first Literary Analysis question on p. 1383: What mood does this description of the grandmother create? Explain.
Possible response: The description of the grandmother's blindness, her awareness despite this blindness, and Yoshiko's fear create a mood of anxiety or tension.

4 Literary Analysis

Thematic Imagery

- Have students read the bracketed passage independently.
- Then, ask them to summarize what has happened to Yoshiko's parents.
Answer: Yoshiko's parents are divorced. Despite his happy remarriage to another woman, Yoshiko's father remains angry with his ex-wife.
- Ask students the second Literary Analysis question on p. 1383: In what ways does Yoshiko's situation mirror that of the lost nestling?
Possible response: Yoshiko is separated from her own mother, just as the nestling is separated from its mother. Yoshiko seems to feel frightened and alone, like a motherless nestling.

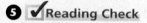

Monitor Progress Suggest that students create a Venn diagram in which they compare and contrast Yoshiko with the nestling.

Reteach Review the Literary Analysis instruction on p. 1381. Make sure students understand that the birds in the story are functioning as thematic images. The dynamic between the birds mirrors the dynamic among Yoshiko, her real mother, and her stepmother.

5 ✔ Reading Check

Answer: The jay is making noise because she is searching for her nestling, which fell from the nest a day earlier.

❻ Background

Art

Yuki, **by Kotondo**

Kotondo (1900–1976), whose real name was Saitô Akira, was born in Tokyo. His adoptive father was an artist who taught him printmaking and billboard design. Kotondo designed about twenty-one prints in the genre called *bijin-ga,* or "pictures of beautiful women." His *bijin-ga* prints present women in thoughtful, nostalgic poses.

Use the following question for discussion:

What is the mood of this picture?
Possible response: The mood is both contemplative and vibrant. The woman's expression suggests pensiveness; the bright colors suggest vigor.

❼ ▶Critical Viewing

Possible response: The woman in the image looks reserved and rather pensive. She is a young woman who, like Yoshiko, may be thinking about how her life will change as she becomes an adult. The woman is similar to Yoshiko in that she seems to be thoughtful and worried.

❽ Critical Thinking

Analyze Cause and Effect

- Have students read aloud the bracketed passage beginning on p. 1383 and continuing on p. 1385.
- Then ask: Why does Yoshiko cry when her brother describes seeing their mother?
  Possible response: Yoshiko may miss their mother more than her brother does but may feel that, unlike him, she lacked the courage to defy their father by visiting her. She also knows that her brother's defiance will enrage their father, and she is frightened of the family conflict that may follow.

❻

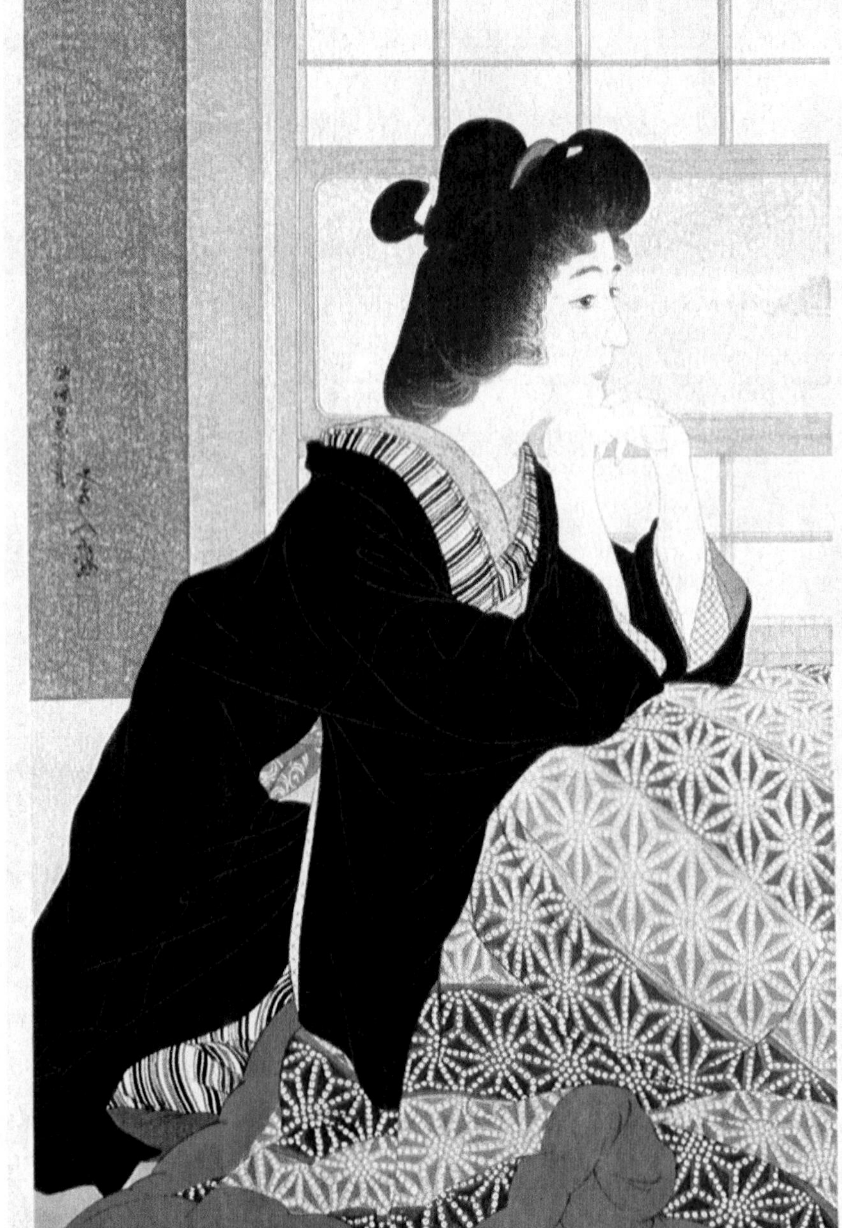

Yuki, 1929, Kotondo, Courtesy Ronin Gallery, New York

❼ ▲ **Critical Viewing** Do you think this painting of a Japanese woman captures Yoshiko's character and circumstances? Why or why not? **[Assess]**

ENRICHMENT: Art Connection

Tradition in Artistic Discipline

Kawabata believed strongly in the importance of tradition in artistic discipline, as he explained in the following excerpt from his *Complete Works:*

> It is part of the discipline of the different arts of Japan, as well as a guidepost to the spirit, for a man to make his way in the footsteps of his predecessors, journeying a hundred times to the famous places and old sites, but not to waste time traipsing over unknown mountains and rivers … The utensils used by the men of the past have been considered treasures and they have also produced new beauty. Disciples who have attempted while still immature to display their individuality have been disowned. The custom of maintaining strict control over the transmission of the arts had its origins in the national character (kunigara) of Japan.

8 Yoshiko was too startled to answer. She was sure that she had turned white, and she was trembling.

Her stepmother came in from the next room.

"It's all right. There's nothing wrong at all with his seeing his own mother. It's only natural. I knew it would happen. It doesn't bother me at all."

Her stepmother seemed drained of strength, and so tiny that Yoshiko felt somehow protective.

Her brother got up and went out. Yoshiko wanted to slap him.

"You are not to say anything, Yoshiko," said her stepmother softly. "It would only make things worse."

Yoshiko was in tears.

Her father brought her brother home from the dormitory. She thought that would be the end of the matter; and then her father and stepmother moved away.

She was frightened. She felt that she had had the full force of—a man's anger, perhaps, or vengefulness? She wondered if she and her brother had something of the same thing in them. She had felt certain, as he had left the room, that her brother had inherited that terrible masculine something.

Yet she felt too that she knew her father's loneliness those ten years he had waited to take a new wife.

10 She was startled when her father came with talk of a prospective bridegroom.

11 "You have had a hard time of it, Yoshiko, and I am sorry. I have told his mother that I want you to have the girlhood you never had."

There were tears in Yoshiko's eyes.

With Yoshiko married, there would be no one to take care of her grandmother and brother, and so it was decided that they would live with her father and stepmother. The decision was what touched Yoshiko most. Because of what her father had been through she had been frightened of marriage, but now that it was coming it did not seem so frightening after all.

She went to her grandmother when she had finished dressing.

"Can you see the red, Grandmother?"

"I can see that there is something red." She pulled Yoshiko to her and looked intently at her kimono and obi.[4] "I have forgotten what you look like, Yoshiko. How nice if I could see you again."

Embarrassed, Yoshiko put her hand to her grandmother's head.

She went out into the garden. She wanted to run and meet her father and stepmother. She opened a hand, but the rain was scarcely enough to wet it. Lifting her skirts she looked through the shrubs and bamboo, and found the nestling jay in the grass under the *hagi*.[5]

She stole up to it. Head pulled in, it was a tight little ball. It seemed without strength and she had no trouble taking it. She looked around but could not find the mother.

4. **obi** (ō´ bē) *n.* broad sash with a bow in the back, worn with a kimono.
5. ***hagi*** (hä´ gē´) Japanese name for the bush-clover plant.

9 ***Linked Verse***

Some critics feel that the structure of Kawabata's stories resembles a poetic form known as linked verse. In linked verse, brief moments are strung together in a meandering, seemingly irrational way. This stringing together of fleeting feelings and brief snippets of dialogue works to convey a strong sense of the characters' emotional states, their memories and desires, and their conections to the natural world. Thus, while stories like "The Jay" may be devoid of heavy plotting, they create moments of intense meaning.

prospective (prō spek´ tiv) *adj.* likely to be or to become in the future

Reading Strategy
Judging Characters' Actions Do you think Yoshiko's father has arranged her marriage out of anger, kindness, or another emotion? Explain.

12 ✔**Reading Check**

Whom does the brother go to visit?

9 Background

Linked Verse

The genre of linked verse, or *renga*, developed in medieval Japan. In this type of verse, multiple authors could contribute to a single poem. *Renga* originated among the noble classes but soon became popular with common people as well.

10 Vocabulary Development

The Latin Root *-spec-*

- Draw students' attention to the word *prospective*, and read its definition. Then, tell students that the word contains the Latin root *-spec-*, which means "see" or "look."
- Ask students how the meaning of this word relates to the meaning of the root *-spec-*.
  Answer: *Prospective* has to do with looking forward or planning into the future.
- Then, have students list other words that use the root *-spec-*, and discuss how this root contributes to the meaning of each word.
  Possible response: *Speculate, spectator, spectacle,* and *respect* contain the Latin root *-spec-*.

11 Reading Strategy

Judging Characters' Actions

- Remind students that arranged marriages were common in Japanese tradition.
- Then, ask students the Reading Strategy question on p. 1385: Do you think Yoshiko's father has arranged her marriage out of anger, kindness, or another emotion? Explain.
  Possible response: Yoshiko's father has arranged her marriage out of kindness. For many years, she has cared for her grandmother and brother. By moving from her grandmother's house, her father thinks, Yoshiko can enjoy being young, without having to bear so many responsibilities.

12 ✔Reading Check

Answer: The brother goes to visit his birth mother.

CUSTOMIZE INSTRUCTION FOR UNIVERSAL ACCESS

For Special Needs Students	For Less Proficient Readers	For English Learners
Point out to students that at the time of the story, and sometimes even today, it was customary for parents to arrange marriages for their children without the young couple having met. Lead a discussion in which students consider how this knowledge affects their understanding of Yoshiko's tears on p. 1385.	Students may have difficulty understanding situations that are not clearly explained or have no transitions. Have students draw a family tree of Yoshiko's family—including her mother and stepmother—and record details that explain the mother's actions and Yoshiko's feelings about them.	Point out to students the complexity of emotions that readers glimpse indirectly in the scene on p. 1385. Ask students to discuss why, in spite of the stepmother's understanding, Yoshiko feels protective of her and why the stepmother herself seems so drained of strength.

ASSESS

13 Background
Modern Details

Many early traditional Japanese stories are very similar to "The Jay" in the way they use images to reveal character. The clues that this is a modern story, however, can be seen in details that have only recently been part of Japanese life: divorce, the glass door, concern about a vitamin deficiency, and a power line.

14 Literary Analysis
Thematic Imagery and Mood

- Remind students that the birds, as thematic images, function to reveal the story's larger, central message.
- Ask the Literary Analysis question on p. 1386: In what ways does the bird's response to its mother change the mood of the story? Explain.
  Possible response: The story's mood changes from one of anxiety and loneliness to one of hope.

Answers for p. 1386

1. Possible response: Yes; Yoshiko saves the jay, and she looks forward to seeing her father and stepmother.
2. **(a)** Yoshiko's grandmother has cataracts and is almost blind. **(b)** The grandmother cannot see her grandchildren, and she needs help with her daily tasks. **(c)** No; her other senses are highly developed, and she has a keen understanding of her surroundings.
3. **(a)** Yoshiko's father tears up the picture. **(b)** The father has negative feelings about his first wife.
4. **(a)** The brother visits his birth mother. **(b)** The brother hurts his stepmother's feelings, and their relationship becomes strained.
5. **(a)** When Yoshiko moves into a new home with her husband, she will not be able to care for her brother and grandmother. **(b)** Because she has spent much of her time caring for her grandmother and brother, Yoshiko has had little time to herself.
6. Possible response: Yoshiko may seek to avoid conflict because her parents' divorce made her own life difficult.

She ran to the house.

"I've found it, Grandmother. It seems very weak."

"Really? You must give it water."

Her grandmother was very calm.

She brought a cup of water and put its beak in, and it drank most prettily, swelling its small throat.

"Kikikikiki." It quickly revived.

13 Hearing, the mother jay called from a power line.

"Kikiki." The nestling struggled in Yoshiko's hand.

"How very nice," said her grandmother. "You must give it back."

Yoshiko went into the garden. The mother jay left the power line and sat watching Yoshiko from the cherry tree.

Raising her hand to show the nestling, Yoshiko put it on the ground.

She watched from inside the glass door. The nestling called forlornly up. The mother came nearer and then was at the lower branches of the pine tree just above. The nestling flapped its wings as if it were about to take flight, and fell forward, calling out to its mother.

14 Very cautious, the mother still did not alight.

Then, in a swoop, it was beside the nestling, whose joy was boundless. The head shook, the outstretched wings were trembling, it was like a spoiled child. The mother seemed to be feeding it.

Yoshiko wished that her father and stepmother would hurry. She wanted them to see.

Literary Analysis
Thematic Imagery and Mood In what ways does the bird's response to its mother change the mood of the story? Explain.

forlornly (fôr lôrn' lē) *adv.* in a sad or lonely manner because of isolation or desertion

Review and Assess

Thinking About the Selection

1. **Respond:** Were you satisfied with the ending of this story? Why or why not?
2. **(a) Recall:** From what physical ailment does Yoshiko's grandmother suffer? **(b) Interpret:** In what ways does the grandmother's physical ailment isolate her? **(c) Analyze:** Is the grandmother completely isolated because of her ailment? Why or why not?
3. **(a) Recall:** With what action does Yoshiko's father respond when the brother shows him a picture of the mother? **(b) Infer:** What do the father's actions suggest about his feelings?
4. **(a) Recall:** Whom does the brother visit while he is living in the school dormitory? **(b) Analyze Cause and Effect:** What are some of the results of this visit?
5. **(a) Deduce:** Why will the grandmother and brother live with the father and stepmother after Yoshiko marries? **(b) Draw Conclusions:** What does this suggest about Yoshiko's life up to this point? Explain.
6. **Speculate:** After her marriage, how do you think Yoshiko will react if there is conflict with her husband? Explain.

ASSESSMENT PRACTICE: Reading Comprehension

Vocabulary (For more practice, see Test Preparation Workbook, p. 5.)

Many tests require students to determine the meaning of vocabulary words by their context. Use the following sample test item to give students practice at this skill.

When Yoshiko was thirteen her new mother came into the house. Later Yoshiko was to think it rather remarkable of her father to have waited almost ten years. Her new mother was a kind woman and they lived a quiet, happy life.

In this passage, the word remarkable means—

A humorous.
B extraordinary.
C untraditional.
D insensitive.

The word *remarkable* means "uncommon or extraordinary." Answers *A, C,* and *D* do not reflect this meaning. Therefore, the correct answer is *B*.

Review and Assess

Literary Analysis

Thematic Imagery

1. (a) Describe the plight of the mother bird and nestling in this story. (b) In what specific ways do descriptions of the birds serve as **thematic imagery** that mirrors the situation of the human family?
2. (a) How does the brother react to the birds? (b) What do his reactions suggest about his relationship with his family?
3. At the end of the story, why do you think Yoshiko wants her father and stepmother to see the birds?

Connecting Literary Elements

4. (a) How would you define the **mood** of this story? Explain. (b) Use a chart like the one shown to identify details that contribute to this mood.

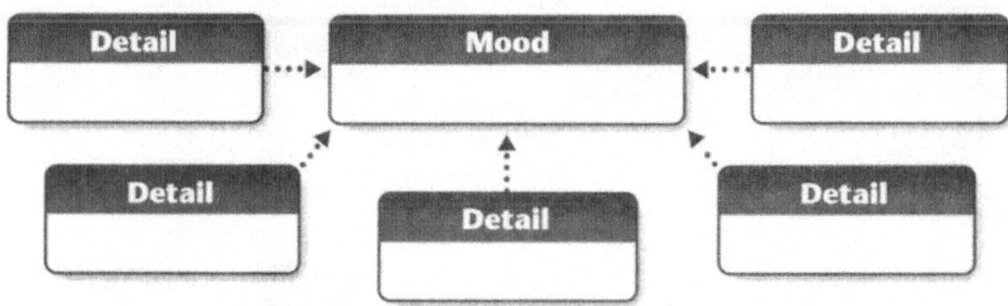

5. (a) At what point does the mood of the story change? (b) Which details convey this change?

Reading Strategy

Judging Characters' Actions

6. (a) Express your **judgment** of Yoshiko, her brother, her father, her stepmother, and her grandmother in one sentence each. (b) Explain the criteria you used to make each judgment.
7. Based on her experiences with her father, does Yoshiko's fear of a "terrible masculine something" seem realistic? Explain.

Extend Understanding

8. **Humanities Connection:** (a) What does this story suggest about the nature of relationships between young people and their elders in Japanese society? (b) How do such relationships compare to those in American culture?

Quick Review

Images are word pictures created through language that appeals to the senses. **Thematic imagery** repeats throughout a literary work and helps express its theme, or central message.

Mood is the feeling that a literary work evokes in a reader.

To **judge characters' actions,** evaluate their behavior against a set of criteria, such as your personal experience, values, and understanding of human nature.

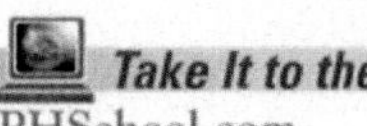
Take It to the Net

PHSchool.com

Take the interactive self-test online to check your understanding of this selection.

Answers for p. 1387

Review and Assess

1. **(a)** A jay nestling has fallen from its nest before it has learned to fly, and its mother calls as she looks for it. **(b)** Like the baby bird, Yoshiko is separated from her family. Her mother has left because of divorce, and she is emotionally estranged from her father.
2. **(a)** The brother is annoyed by the mother bird's calling. **(b)** The brother's reactions suggest that he is distant from his family and has little patience with them.
3. Possible response: Yoshiko wants her father and stepmother to see how happy the nestling and its mother are after being reunited.
4. **(a)** The mood of the story is one of melancholy and yearning. **(b) Mood:** yearning and melancholy; **Detail:** Yoshiko's grandmother gazes silently at her fingers; **Detail:** Yoshiko turns white and trembles when she hears about her birth mother; **Detail:** Yoshiko's stepmother looks tiny and drained after hearing about Yoshiko's mother; **Detail:** Yoshiko has tears in her eyes when her father tells her about her marriage; **Detail:** Yoshiko looks for the nestling and restores it to its mother.
5. **(a)** The mood of the story changes when Yoshiko takes action and finds the nestling. **(b)** Details that convey a change in mood include the baby jay's revival, the mother bird's joy, the mother bird bringing food to the baby, and Yoshiko's own interest in seeing her father and stepmother again.
6. Possible responses: **(a)** Yoshiko is initially fearful and timid. Yoshiko's brother is impatient and inconsiderate. Yoshiko's father cannot communicate well with his children. Yoshiko's stepmother treats her stepchildren with consideration. Yoshiko's grandmother is quietly courageous. **(b)** Possible response: Readers may say that they used their own experiences, values, and understanding of human nature to evaluate each character.
7. Yoshiko's fear seems realistic. The story demonstrates how her

continued

continued from right column

father's anger is hurtful and drives her family apart.

8. Possible response: **(a)** The story suggests that young people long for their elders' love, guidance, and approval. It also suggests that children take care of elderly parents and grandparents. **(b)** In American culture, young people often long for independence more than guidance and approval from their parents.

ENRICHMENT: Further Reading

Other Works by Yasunari Kawabata

We strongly encourage you to review any selection before assigning or recommending it to students.

House of the Sleeping Beauties and Other Stories

Snow Country

Thousand Cranes

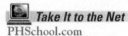

Take It to the Net

Visit PHSchool.com for more information about Yasunari Kawabata.

EXTEND

Answers for p. 1388

❶ Vocabulary Development

Word Analysis: Latin Root *-spec-*

1. introspective: looking inward or contemplating one's own thoughts
2. retrospective: looking at the past

Spelling Strategy

1. conscience
2. omniscient
3. ceiling
4. deceive

Concept Development: Antonyms

1. b
2. a
3. a
4. c
5. b

❷ Grammar and Style

Practice

1. could choose
2. should arrive
3. would stop
4. could be
5. should leave

Writing Application

Possible response: If I could tell you about my friend Emma you surely would laugh. If you could imagine the world's wittiest tenth grader, you would get the idea. If you should see me doubled over laughing, it could be from something Emma said.

10TH GRADE For support in teaching the Grammar and Style Lesson to tenth graders, use **Writing and Grammar,** Platinum Level, Chapter 22, Section 1.

Integrate Language Skills

❶ Vocabulary Development Lesson

Word Analysis: Latin Root *-spec-*

The word *prospective* combines the prefix *pro-* ("before" or "forward") with the root *-spec-* ("see" or "look"). Thus, *prospective* means "foreseen, or expected." Use your knowledge of the root *-spec-* and the definitions of the prefixes given in parentheses to define each word below.

1. introspective (*intro* = into; inside)
2. retrospective (*retro* = backward)

Spelling Strategy

When the *sh* or *ch* sound is spelled *c*, it may be followed by *ie*, as in the word *deficiency*, but not by *ei*. Complete the following words with *ie* or *ei*.

1. consc __ nce
2. omnisc __ nt
3. c __ ling
4. dec __ ve

Concept Development: Antonyms

Review the vocabulary words listed on page 1381 and notice their use in the selection. Then, for each numbered word below, select the letter of the word that is its antonym, or word of opposite meaning.

1. prospective: **(a)** visible, **(b)** previous, **(c)** hopeful
2. reluctant: **(a)** enthusiastic, **(b)** uncertain, **(c)** recent
3. deficiency: **(a)** surplus, **(b)** lack, **(c)** sorrow
4. forlornly: **(a)** uselessly, **(b)** quickly, **(c)** happily
5. extravagant: **(a)** large, **(b)** frugal, **(c)** calm

❷ Grammar and Style Lesson

Subjunctive Mood

The **subjunctive mood** is any verb form indicating possibility, supposition, or desire. *Could, would,* or *should* are sometimes used to help a verb express the subjunctive mood.

Examples:

They were said to be a sign that someone would come with gifts. . . . *(possibility)*

She thought that would be the end of the matter. . . . *(supposition)*

She would want to call from behind, and then she would slip away. *(desire)*

Practice Replace the underlined words in each item below with a subjunctive verb form, using the word indicated in parentheses.

1. If Yoshiko were to choose anything she wanted, it would be harmony. *(could)*
2. If he were to arrive late, he would call and let her know. *(should)*
3. Yoshiko knew her brother might relax if her father were to stop criticizing him. *(would)*
4. Her sadness might decrease if he were able to be more loving. *(could)*
5. If their father were to leave, she knew her brother would suffer. *(should)*

Writing Application Write a paragraph about your friends. Include at least three examples of the subjunctive mood using *could, would,* or *should.*

WG Prentice Hall Writing and Grammar Connection: Diamond Level, Chapter 21, Section 3

TEACHING RESOURCES

The following resources can be used to enrich or extend the instruction for pp. 1388–1389.

Vocabulary

- **Selection Support:** Build Vocabulary, p. 273
- **Vocabulary and Spelling Practice Book** (Use this booklet for skills instruction.)

Grammar

- **Selection Support:** Grammar and Style, p. 274
- **Writing and Grammar,** Diamond Level, p. 548
- **Daily Language Transparencies** ■

Writing

- **Performance Assess. and Portfolio Mgmt.,** p. 22
- **Writing and Grammar,** Diamond Level, p. 240
- **Writing and Grammar iText CD-ROM** ■
- **Writing Models and Graphic Organizers on Transparencies,** pp. 103–105

■ **BLOCK SCHEDULING:** Resources marked with this symbol provide varied instruction during 90-minute blocks.

❸ Writing Lesson

Proposal for a Program for the Elderly

Elderly people such as the grandmother in "The Jay" often benefit from community programs designed to make their days more interesting. Write a proposal explaining how such a program could be set up and administered. Use the grandmother in this story as a case study, or model, to defend your ideas.

Prewriting Write an outline that organizes the sections of your proposal. Include notes about the supporting information that you will use in each section.

Model: Outlining for Organization and Clarity

III. Activities (support: quotation from national study on aging)
- **A. Creative Activities**
  - **1.** Writing (support: Self-expression can be vital.)
  - **2.** Crafts, such as quilt-making
- **B. Physical Activities**
  - **1.** Dance
  - **2.** Outdoor sports; walking

Notes about supporting information make an outline even more effective.

Drafting Begin with an introduction that states your purpose and asserts the importance of this program. As you follow your outline, use details from the story to support your ideas.

Revising Review your proposal, making sure that you have organized your ideas logically. Consider reordering sections to create a better flow.

WG *Prentice Hall Writing and Grammar Connection: Diamond Level, Chapter 11, Connected Assignment*

❹ Extension Activities

Listening and Speaking Prepare an **oral report** on the literary history of Japan. Use both print and electronic sources, including the Internet, to gather information. Follow these tips as you prepare:

- Organize your material in chronological order.
- Summarize the lives of important writers and the plots of key works.

As you deliver your presentation, use effective body language and speak with enthusiasm.

Research and Technology With a small group, prepare a **science report** about birds. Consider the various types of bird nests, as well as migration instincts and patterns. Augment your report with illustrations, recordings, charts, and diagrams, and then present it to the class. **[Group Activity]**

 ***Take It to the Net*** PHSchool.com

Go online for an additional research activity using the Internet.

ASSESSMENT RESOURCES

The following resources can be used to assess students' knowledge and skills.

Selection Assessment

- **Formal Assessment,** pp. 237–239
- **Open-Book Tests,** pp. 205–207
- **Test Bank Software**

Take It to the Net

Visit PHSchool.com for self-tests on the selection.

Writing Rubric

- **Performance Assess. and Portfolio Mgmt.,** p. 22

Research and Technology Rubric

- **Performance Assess. and Portfolio Mgmt.,** p. 32

For additional diagnostics and remediation for skills covered in this grouping, use materials from the Prentice Hall Assessment System.

❸ Writing Lesson

- Tell students that a proposal defines a particular course of action. For a proposal to be effective, it must demonstrate that it would benefit the individuals affected and would be worth the time and effort needed to put it into action.
- Students can use the Outline organizer in **Writing Models and Graphic Organizers on Transparencies,** pp. 103–105, to help them complete their outlines.
- After students have finished their proposals, use the Exposition: Problem-Solution Essay rubric in **Performance Assessment and Portfolio Management,** p. 22, to evaluate students' work.

10TH GRADE For support in working through the Writing Lesson with tenth graders, use **Writing and Grammar,** Platinum Level, Chapter 11, Connected Assignment.

❹ Research and Technology

- Encourage students to interview members of local bird-watching organizations to get firsthand information about watching jays and members of the jay family.
- Have students research their topics thoroughly before the interview so that their questions are focused.
- Use the Speaking: Multimedia Presentation rubric in **Performance Assessment and Portfolio Management,** p. 32, to assess students' presentations.

CUSTOMIZE INSTRUCTION
For Universal Access

To address different learning styles, use the following activities suggested in the **Extension Activities** booklet, p. 69.

- For Visual/Spatial Learners, use Activity 5.
- For Musical/Rhythmic Learners, use Activity 6.
- For Logical/Mathematical Learners, use Activity 7.

Thoughts of Hanoi • All • Also All • Assembly Line

Lesson Objectives

1. **To analyze and respond to literary elements**
   - Literary Analysis: Political Poetry
   - Comparing Literary Works: Responses to Suffering
2. **To read, comprehend, analyze, and critique a poem**
   - Reading Strategy: Connecting to Historical Context
   - Reading Check Questions
   - Review and Assess Questions
   - Assessment Practice (ATE)
3. **To develop word analysis skills, fluency, and systematic vocabulary**
   - Vocabulary Development Lesson: Latin Root *-temp-*
4. **To understand and apply written and oral language conventions**
   - Spelling Strategy
   - Grammar and Style Lesson: Parallelism
5. **To understand and apply appropriate writing and research strategies**
   - Writing Lesson: Literary Analysis
   - Extension Activity: Multimedia Report
6. **To understand and apply listening and speaking strategies**
   - Extension Activity: Dialogue

10TH GRADE TEACHING A TENTH-GRADE COURSE

The literature in this section can be taught as part of a rich, balanced world literature course for tenth-grade students. For a full outline of such a course, see pp. T46–T48 in Volume I of this Teacher's Edition.

STEP-BY-STEP TEACHING GUIDE	PACING GUIDE
PRETEACH	
Motivate Students and Provide Background	
Use the Motivation activity (ATE p. 1390)	5 min.
Read and discuss author and background features (SE: pp. 1390, 1393, 1396; ATE: pp. 1390, 1396) [A]	5 min.
Introduce the Concepts	
Introduce the Literary Analysis and Reading Strategy concepts (SE/ATE p. 1391) [A]	15 min.
Pronounce the vocabulary words and read their definitions (SE p. 1391)	5 min.
TEACH	
Monitor Comprehension	
Informally monitor comprehension by circulating while students read independently or in groups [A]	25 min.
Monitor students' comprehension with the Reading Check note (SE/ATE p. 1393)	as students read
Develop vocabulary with the Vocabulary notes (SE pp. 1394, 1395, 1396, 1397, 1398; ATE p. 1398)	as students read
Develop Understanding	
Develop students' understanding of political poetry with the Literary Analysis annotations (SE/ATE pp. 1395, 1396, 1397) [A]	5 min.
Develop students' ability to connect literature to its historical context by using the Reading Strategy annotations (SE/ATE pp. 1393, 1398) [A]	5 min.
ASSESS	
Assess Mastery	
Assess students' mastery of the Reading Strategy and Literary Analysis concepts by having them answer the Review and Assess questions (SE/ATE p. 1399)	15 min.
Use one or more of the print, software, or transparency Assessment Resources (ATE p. 1401) [A]	up to 45 min.
EXTEND	
Apply Understanding	
Have students complete the Vocabulary Development Lesson and the Grammar and Style Lesson (SE p. 1400) [A]	20 min.
Apply students' ability to combine sentences for variety, using the Writing Lesson (SE/ATE p. 1401) [A]	45 min.
Apply students' understanding of the selections, using one or more of the Extension Activities (SE p. 1401)	20–90 min.

[A] ACCELERATED INSTRUCTION: Use the strategies and activities identified with an [A].

10TH GRADE TEACHING TENTH-GRADE STUDENTS For support in teaching tenth-graders, see the Step-by-Step Teaching notes identified with this icon.

UNIVERSAL ACCESS
● = Below-Level Students
▲ = On-Level Students
■ = Above-Level Students

Time and Resource Manager

Reading Level: Average, Challenging, Easy, Average
Average Number of Instructional Days: 3

RESOURCES		
PRINT	**TRANSPARENCIES**	**TECHNOLOGY**
• **Beyond Literature,** Cross-Curricular Connection: Geography, p. 70 ▲ ■		• **Interest Grabber Video,** Tape 2, Unit 9, Segment 14 ● ▲ ■
• **Selection Support Workbook:** ● ▲ ■ Literary Analysis, p. 280 Reading Strategy, p. 279 Build Vocabulary, p. 277	• **Literary Analysis and Reading Transparencies,** pp. 139 and 140 ● ▲ ■	
		• **Listening to Literature** ● ▲ ■ Audiocassettes Audio CDs
• **Literary Analysis for Enrichment,** p. 70 ■		
• **Formal Assessment:** Selection Test, pp. 240–242 ● ▲ ■ • **Open-Book Tests,** pp. 208–210 ● ▲ ■ • **Performance Assessment and Portfolio Management,** pp. 16, 33 ● ▲ ■ • Prentice Hall Assessment System ● ▲ ■	• Prentice Hall Assessment System ● ▲ ■ **Skills Practice Answers and Explanations on Transparencies**	• **Test Bank Software** ● ▲ ■
• **Selection Support Workbook:** ● ▲ ■ Grammar and Style, p. 278 • **Writing and Grammar,** Diamond Level ● ▲ ■ • **Extension Activities,** p. 70 ● ▲ ■	• **Daily Language Practice Transparencies** ● ▲ • **Writing Models and Graphic Organizers on Transparencies,** pp.53–59	• **Writing and Grammar iText CD-ROM** ● ▲ ■ ***Take It to the Net*** PHSchool.com

BLOCK SCHEDULING: Use one 90-minute class period to preteach the selection(s) and have students read them. Use a second 90-minute class period to assess students' mastery of skills and have them complete one of the Extension Activities.

PRETEACH

Step-by-Step Teaching Guide for pp. 1390–1391

Motivation

Discuss with students what they know about the United States Civil War. Then, tell them that Nguyen Thi Vinh describes a civil war in Vietnam that split families and forced brothers to fight brothers. To draw students into the selections from China, tell them about the 1989 Tiananmen Square massacre, in which students in Beijing protested government tactics. In response, the Chinese government shot hundreds of young people. With the class, compare and contrast civil wars and protest movements students have heard of, such as the civil rights movement in the United States and the anti-apartheid movement in South Africa.

Interest Grabber Video

As an alternative, play "'Thoughts of Hanoi': The Roots of the Vietnam War" on Tape 2 to engage student interest.

❶ Background

More About the Authors

Until 1975, Nguyen Thi Vinh served as editor-in-chief of the journal *New Wind* and director of the magazine *The East*. She is a well-educated poet writing in an accessible style and about accessible subjects.

Bei Dao's family was from the region of Shanghai and the lower Chang River valley, which was both a center of traditional Chinese civilization and a region under the influence of the West. Bei Dao draws on Chinese and Western traditions in his work.

Shu Ting is the pen name of Gong Peiyu. In 1981 and 1983, she received China's National Poetry Award.

Geography Note

Draw students' attention to the map on this page, and point out China and Vietnam. The Vietnamese literary tradition grew from Chinese influences. Thus, early Vietnamese poetry often reflected Confucian beliefs and was considered an exercise for rulers and scholars.

Prepare to Read

❶ Thoughts of Hanoi ◆ All ◆ Also All ◆ Assembly Line

Nguyen Thi Vinh (b. 1924)

Nguyen Thi Vinh (nōō' yin tĭ vin) was born in Ha Dong Province in the Red River Delta of North Vietnam. She is a novelist, poet, and editor, but most of all she is a writer of short stories. Her first and most famous work is the novel *Two Sisters*, published in 1953. She is also the author of six other books of fiction, as well as a collection of poetry.

In 1954, the country of Vietnam was divided into two independent countries: communist North Vietnam and democratic South Vietnam. Prior to the installation of the communist government in the North, nearly one million North Vietnamese fled south. Among these was Nguyen Thi Vinh. In 1975, North Vietnam defeated South Vietnam and invaded Saigon, the country's capital. Up until that moment, Nguyen had been a prominent member of the Saigon community of writers. After the fall of Saigon, she remained in Vietnam but refused to play any public role. In 1983, Nguyen joined her family in Norway, thus becoming a refugee once again.

Bei Dao (b. 1949)

Bei Dao (bā dou) was born just two months before China's communists founded the People's Republic. He attended one of China's best schools and seemed destined for a position in the communist bureaucracy. Instead, in 1965, he became a member of the Red Guard, the quasi-military group that enforced the Cultural Revolution. At first, this movement sought to revitalize revolutionary fervor, but it soon degenerated into wholesale persecution of artists, teachers, and intellectuals.

Disillusioned, Bei Dao turned to poetry. Bold, questioning, and vivid, his poems express a deep dissatisfaction with Chinese society. Eventually, he became associated with a like-minded group of writers called the Misty Poets.

When a new wave of discontent swept China in 1976, Bei Dao's poem "Answer" became a rallying cry for change. In 1978, students set up large bulletin boards in public spaces, where they posted dissident writings. This unusual form of publication became known as the Democracy Wall Movement, and it brought Bei Dao's work to a wide audience.

During the Tiananmen Square massacre in 1989, Bei Dao was traveling abroad. The period of repression that followed the massacre prevented his return home. Today, he lives and works in the West, separated from his wife and daughter, who remain in China.

Shu Ting (b. 1952)

Shu Ting (shōō tiŋ) was born in Jinjiang County of Fujian Province. Still in middle school during China's Cultural Revolution, she was forced to leave her home, abandon her education, and go to live in a small, impoverished peasant village. When she returned to Fujian in 1973, she worked on construction sites and in factories. In spite of these experiences, she began writing poetry and, while still in her twenties, gained nationwide fame as a poet. Shu Ting became associated with the Misty Poets when her work appeared in the underground literary magazine *Today*. Shu Ting still lives in China, in the seaport city of Xiamen.

TEACHING RESOURCES

The following resources can be used to enrich or extend the instruction for pp. 1390–1391.

Motivation

Interest Grabber Video, Tape 2

Background

Beyond Literature, p. 70

Take It to the Net

Visit PHSchool.com for background on the authors.

Literary Analysis

Literary Analysis and Reading Transparencies, Political Poetry, p. 139

Selection Support: Literary Analysis, p. 280

Reading

Literary Analysis and Reading Transparencies, Connecting to Historical Context, p. 140

BLOCK SCHEDULING: Resources marked with this symbol provide varied instruction during 90-minute blocks.

Preview

Connecting to the Literature

If you are like most American students, you had no direct experience of political violence before September 11, 2001. Think of what life must be like for people who face the ravages of war daily, whose right to free speech is stifled. The authors of these poems offer some insights.

❷ Literary Analysis

Political Poetry

Political poetry connects the realm of private emotion to the political or social arena. While political poems often tell stories and express personal feelings, they are written in reaction to political events or as commentary about a political situation. For example, in "Thoughts of Hanoi," the speaker expresses the personal pain caused by the Vietnam War:

> Brother, I am afraid
> that one day I'll be with the March-North Army
> meeting you on your way to the South.
> I might be the one to shoot you then. . . .

As you read these poems, think about how each one examines the effects of political events or conditions on the private lives of individuals.

Comparing Literary Works

People respond to the suffering caused by war or repression in different ways. Some become hopeless, while others hold on to a belief in the human spirit. As you read these poems, compare each speaker's attitude toward both the sufferings of the present and the promise of the future.

❸ Reading Strategy

Connecting to Historical Context

Political poems will carry deeper meaning for you if you **connect to the historical context** that they reflect. Use a chart like the one shown to list details from each poem that pertain to the historical situation from which it arose. Then, form an overall sense of the writer's message. Use the poets' biographies and the background notes to help you as you read.

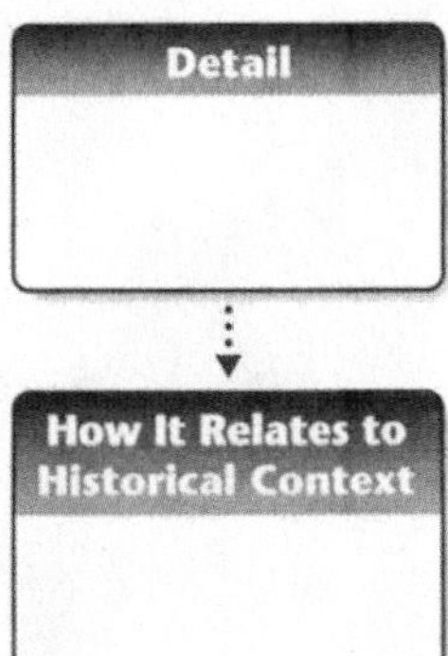

Vocabulary Development

jubilant (jo͞o′ bə lənt) *adj.* extremely happy; exultant (p. 1394)

obsolete (äb′ sə lēt′) *adj.* out of date; out of use (p. 1395)

lamentation (lam′ ən tā′ shən) *n.* outward expression of grief; weeping or wailing (p. 1396)

heralds (her′ əldz) *v.* announces; introduces (p. 1396)

reverberates (ri vʉr′ bə rātz′) *v.* echoes; sounds again (p. 1396)

chasm (kaz′ əm) *n.* deep crack in Earth's surface (p. 1397)

monotony (mə nät′ ′n ē) *n.* tedious sameness (p. 1398)

tempo (tem′ pō) *n.* rate of speed; pace (p. 1398)

CUSTOMIZE INSTRUCTION FOR UNIVERSAL ACCESS

For Less Proficient Readers	For English Learners	For Advanced Readers
Preview with students the vocabulary and footnotes in each selection. Take time to clarify pronunciations and definitions, answering any questions that students may have. Also, make sure that students understand the political context in which each poem was written.	Ask native Vietnamese and Chinese students (or students who know these languages) to read the poems in this grouping in their original languages. Bring in copies of the original poems written in Vietnamese and Chinese, and ask students to explain to the class what the characters mean.	Tell students that war and political intrigue create fateful moments for people in cultures everywhere, despite differences in specific situations. Ask students to identify some examples of these situations from current news events and to discuss the types of decisions and emotions people might face in such fateful moments.

❷ Literary Analysis

Political Poetry

- After reading aloud the Literary Analysis instruction, remind students that political poetry often protests injustice or oppression. Explain that political poetry may protest specific government policies, such as the oppression of free speech, or more general cultural injustices, such as racism or sexism.
- Tell students that political speech is dangerous in some countries. Students may find the political criticism within poems such as "All" indirect, because the poems use images and allusions instead of direct speech.
- Use the Political Poetry transparency in **Literary Analysis and Reading Transparencies,** p. 139, to demonstrate how poems can record and analyze citizens' objections to unfair political conditions.

❸ Reading Strategy

Connecting to Historical Context

- Have a volunteer read aloud the Reading Strategy instruction. Explain that knowing historical context can help a reader understand the thoughts, feelings, and images presented in a work.
- Present students with these lines from "Thoughts of Hanoi": "Brother, I am afraid / that one day I'll be with the March-North Army / meeting you on your way to the South."
- Set the historical context for these lines by explaining that the poem refers to Vietnam's division into democratic South Vietnam and communist North Vietnam.
- Then, explain the use of the graphic organizer on p. 1391. Encourage students to use a similar chart to make connections between a poem's details and the historical situation from which they arose.

Vocabulary Development

- Pronounce each vocabulary word for students, and read the definitions as a class. Have students identify any words with which they are familiar.

E-Teach

Visit e-Teach at PHSchool.com for teachers' essays on how to teach, with questions and answers.

TEACH

Step-by-Step Teaching Guide for pp. 1392–1398

Teaching Tenth-Grade Students

10TH GRADE Ask students to discuss which of the visual images in "Thoughts of Hanoi" is most memorable, vivid, and realistic. Lead students to see why an image is memorable or vivid so that they can apply this knowledge in their own writing.

❶ About the Selection

"Thoughts of Hanoi" examines the conflicted feelings of having a peacetime friend become a wartime enemy. In this poem, a speaker who has fled North Vietnam asks about beloved places in Hanoi. The speaker, now a resident of South Vietnam, fears that he or she will have to face this friend as an enemy.

❷ Background

Art

Morning Rain, by Bich Nguyet

With its intense use of color and aggressive brush strokes, this oil-on-canvas painting by Vietnamese artist Bich Nguyet (.1956) creates a bold yet quaint image of figures caught in a downpour.

Use the following questions to stimulate discussion.

How would you describe the mood of this painting? What details or techniques create this mood?
Possible response: The mood of this painting is melancholy. The varying hues of blue and obscured background create this mood.

❸ ▶Critical Viewing

Possible response: Yes; the scene might recall a happy memory for the speaker. The speaker fondly remembers ordinary events in Hanoi before the war.

❶ THOUGHTS OF HANOI

Nguyen Thi Vinh

translated by Nguyen Ngoc Bich *with* Burton Raffel *and* W. S. Merwin

❷

Morning Rain, 2001, Bich Nguyet, Courtesy of Galeria La Vong Ltd.

❸ ▲ **Critical Viewing** Does this scene of people in the morning rain seem like a memory for which the speaker of this poem might yearn? Why or why not? **[Connect]**

TEACHING RESOURCES

The following resources can be used to enrich or extend the instruction for pp. 1392–1398.

Literary Analysis

- **Selection Support:** Literary Analysis, p. 280
- **Literary Analysis and Reading Transparencies,** Political Poetry, p. 139 ■

Reading

- **Selection Support:** Reading Strategy, p. 279; Build Vocabulary, p. 277
- **Listening to Literature Audiocassettes** ■
- **Listening to Literature CDs**

■ **BLOCK SCHEDULING:** Resources marked with this symbol provide varied instruction during 90-minute blocks.

Background

Vietnam was a colony of France until 1954, when the French suffered a major defeat at the hands of Vietnamese insurgent leader Ho Chi Minh. A cease-fire agreement divided the country into communist North Vietnam and democratic South Vietnam, with Ho ruling the North from Hanoi. The cease-fire called for elections to determine the fate of the country, but they were never held. Ho Chi Minh's troops, the Viet Cong, who were supported by Russia and China, battled the South Vietnamese government and its American backers. In the war that ensued, members of the same family sometimes fought on different sides. It was in this climate that Nguyen Thi Vinh wrote "Thoughts of Hanoi," her personal lyric about the Vietnam War from the perspective of a North Vietnamese living in the South.

The night is deep and chill
as in early autumn. Pitchblack,
it thickens after each lightning flash.
I dream of Hanoi:
Co-ngu[1] Road
ten years of separation
the way back sliced by a frontier of hatred.
❹ I want to bury the past
to burn the future
still I yearn
still I fear
those endless nights
waiting for dawn.

❺
Brother,
how is Hang Dao[2] now?
How is Ngoc Son[3] temple?
Do the trains still run
each day from Hanoi
to the neighboring towns?
To Bac-ninh, Cam-giang, Yen-bai,[4]
the small villages, islands
of brown thatch in a lush green sea?

The girls
    bright eyes
        ruddy cheeks
    four-piece dresses

Reading Strategy
Connecting to Historical Context What "past" do you think the speaker wishes to "bury"?

❻ **✔Reading Check**

For how many years has the speaker been away from Hanoi?

1. **Co-ngu** (cô go͞o)
2. **Hang Dao** (häŋ dou)
3. **Ngoc Son** (nōk sōn)
4. **Bac-ninh** (bäk nin), **Cam-giang** (käm gyäŋ), **Yen-bai** (ēŋ bī)

❹ Reading Strategy

Connecting to Historical Context

- Explain that Nyugen's reference in line 6 to "ten years of separation" (the separation between North Vietnam and South Vietnam) indicates that this poem was written in the early 1970s.
- Have students read the bracketed line independently. Then, ask the Reading Strategy question on p. 1393: What "past" do you think the speaker wishes to "bury"?
  Possible response: The speaker wants to bury Vietnam's internal conflict.

Monitor Progress Ask students to explain the speaker's situation in the first stanza.
Answer: Because of political upheaval, the speaker cannot return to Hanoi. The speaker questions whether the things he or she loved about the city still exist.

Reteach Use the Connecting to Historical Context transparency in **Literary Analysis and Reading Transparencies,** p. 140, to help students understand the connection between historical context and a work's larger meaning.

❺ Critical Thinking

Infer

- Read aloud the bracketed passage. Then, ask students to make an inference about the poem's speaker.
  Answer: The speaker is a Vietnamese person familiar with Hanoi. Because of the war, the speaker can no longer return to this familiar city and its people.
- Ask students: To whom does the speaker direct questions? Why does the speaker call the person "Brother"?
  Answer: The person addressed is someone living in North Vietnam. The person is called "Brother" because the two are from the same place or are related either literally or symbolically.

❻ ✔Reading Check

Answer: The speaker has been away from Hanoi for ten years.

CUSTOMIZE INSTRUCTION FOR UNIVERSAL ACCESS

For English Learners	For Gifted/Talented Students	For Advanced Readers
Explain to students that poetry should be read according to its punctuation rather than its line breaks. Model this strategy by reading aloud the first stanza of "Thoughts of Hanoi." Invite volunteers to read aloud additional lines, and work with students to correct their pacing.	Challenge students to retell "Thoughts of Hanoi" in prose by reshaping the images and ideas into a short paragraph or story. Encourage volunteers to share their prose versions with the class. Then, lead a discussion in which students compare and contrast the poetry and prose forms.	Ask students to research one of the places mentioned on p. 1393, such as Hanoi, Co-ngu Road, Hang Dao, Ngoc Son temple, Bac-ninh, Cam-giang, or Yen-bai. Encourage students to discover how these places were affected by the Vietnam War and report their findings to the class as a news broadcast.

7 Background

Art

Peacefulness, by Tran Nguyen Dan

Hanoi painter Tran Nguyen Dan (.1941) specializes in woodcuts depicting traditional Vietnamese scenes, such as festivals and temples. A graduate of the Hanoi College of Industrial Fine Arts, Tran Nguyen Dan has won numerous awards and has work exhibited in the Fine Arts Museum of Vietnam and the Asia-Pacific Museum of Poland.

Use the following questions for discussion:

- What elements of the poem does this woodcut illustrate?
  Answer: The woodcut captures the tranquillity and beauty described in the poem. It also captures the sense of safety that the speaker describes prior to the war.
- What elements of the woodcut create a feeling of peace?
  Possible response: The muted colors, harmonious figures, and sense of symmetry all create a feeling of peace.

8 ▶ Critical Viewing

Possible response: The painting depicts serenity before the war.

9 Critical Thinking

Analyze

- Ask a volunteer to read aloud the bracketed passage. Then, point out to students that in this passage, the speaker refers to several generations. Have students identify the words and phrases that indicate these generations.
  Answer: The speaker refers to "children," "village graybeards," and "grandmothers."
- Ask students why the speaker includes these references.
  Possible response: These references reinforce the feeling of community in Hanoi and the image the speaker has created. The speaker suggests that all—young and old—have been affected by the war.

7

Peacefulness, Tran Nguyen Dan, Indochina Arts Project

8 ◀ **Critical Viewing** What image of Vietnamese society does this painting convey? **[Interpret]**

raven-bill scarves
sowing harvesting
spinning weaving
all year round,
the boys
plowing
transplanting
in the fields
in their shops
running across
the meadow at evening
to fly kites
and sing alternating songs.

9

Stainless blue sky,
jubilant voices of children
stumbling through the alphabet,
village graybeards strolling to the temple,
grandmothers basking in twilight sun,
chewing betel leaves
while the children run—

jubilant (jo͞o′ bə lənt) *adj.* extremely happy; exultant

ENRICHMENT: Geography Connection

Hanoi

Originally called Long Bien, Hanoi was founded in the sixth century and briefly served as the country's capital. It became the capital again in the eleventh century. In 1883, the French renamed the city Hanoi and fourteen years later, made it the seat of the French Indochinese government.

When Vietnam was divided in 1954, Hanoi became the capital of North Vietnam. From 1965 to 1972, Hanoi was the target of frequent bombings that wiped out most of the city's factories and resources. Although most of Hanoi was destroyed, the Vietnamese rebuilt the city, and it again became the capital when the country was reunited in 1976.

Located in the north on the Red River, Hanoi is the country's cultural center. It has been the hub of the country for decades, with rail connections to Saigon.

Before the war, Saigon was the capital of South Vietnam. Now a major industrial port of the Socialist Republic of Vietnam, Saigon was renamed Ho Chi Minh City in 1976.

Brother,
how is all that now?
Or is it obsolete?
Are you like me,
reliving the past,
imagining the future?
Do you count me as a friend
10 or am I the enemy in your eyes?
Brother, I am afraid
that one day I'll be with the March-North Army
meeting you on your way to the South.
I might be the one to shoot you then
or you me
but please
not with hatred.

For don't you remember how it was,
you and I in school together,
plotting our lives together?
Those roots go deep!

Brother, we are men,
conscious of more
than material needs.
How can this happen to us
my friend
my foe?

obsolete (äb′ sə lēt′) *adj.* out of date; out of use

Literary Analysis
Political Poetry What truth about the people fighting the Vietnam War does this stanza express?

Review and Assess

Thinking About the Selection

1. **Respond:** Which images do you find the most vivid? Explain.
2. **(a) Recall:** In the first three lines, which details describe the night in which the speaker is dreaming? **(b) Generalize:** How would you describe the mood the speaker establishes in these lines?
3. **(a) Recall:** By what boundary does the speaker say the "way back" is sliced? **(b) Interpret:** Is this a physical boundary, an emotional boundary, or both? Explain.
4. **(a) Interpret:** Which experiences has the speaker shared with the "Brother"? Explain. **(b) Infer:** What emotional bond do these experiences suggest? **(c) Analyze:** How has that bond been tested by war?
5. **Take a Position:** While all war is terrible, do you think that civil war, like the one in Vietnam, is especially devastating? Why or why not?

10 Literary Analysis

Political Poetry

- Have a volunteer read aloud the bracketed passage. Then, ask: How does Nguyen focus on the individual in this passage?
Possible response: The question format suggests a personal exchange between the speaker and the "Brother." The use of "me" and "I" emphasizes individual identity.
- Ask students the Literary Analysis question on p. 1395: What truth about the people fighting the Vietnam War does this stanza express?
Answer: Friends, neighbors, and family members often fought on opposing sides. Despite political differences, these people continued to care about one another.

Answers for p. 1395

Review and Assess

1. Possible response: The image of two friends, or brothers, marching toward one another in battle depicts the personal anguish of war.
2. **(a)** The "night is deep and chill"; the season is autumn. Lightning strikes in a "pitchblack" sky. **(b)** Possible response: The speaker establishes a foreboding mood.
3. **(a)** The "way back" is sliced "by a frontier of hatred." **(b)** Both; the geographical boundary reflects the ideological differences within Vietnam.
4. **(a)** The two attended school and planned their lives together. **(b)** The two shared childhood experiences and have the emotional bond of siblings. **(c)** The war calls into question whether they are personal friends or political enemies.
5. Possible response: Yes; instead of uniting against a common enemy, friends and families may become political enemies.

CUSTOMIZE INSTRUCTION FOR UNIVERSAL ACCESS

For Less Proficient Readers	For Advanced Readers
Read aloud the last two stanzas of the poem as students follow along. Help students identify the four complete sentences that make up these stanzas by pointing out that the author asks two questions, makes one exclamation, and makes one statement. Remind students that political poetry connects the realm of private emotion to the political or social arena. On the board, write the four sentences, and ask students to consider what emotion is behind each.	Tell students that Vietnamese literature is continually being translated from French and Vietnamese into English. Challenge them to read other Vietnamese selections. Then, ask students to share in oral presentations their readings and their discoveries about Vietnam and Vietnamese culture.

⓫ About the Selections

In "All," Bei Dao criticizes a repressive Chinese regime for taking away its citizens' hope and joy.

Shu Ting counters Bei Dao in "Also All." Her poem argues that China's people will succeed. It defends the power of hope and the promise of tomorrow.

⓬ Background

Gu Cheng

Gu Cheng was the youngest of the so-called Misty Poets. Because his father, Gu Gong, was a prominent poet, his family was forced to leave Beijing during the Cultural Revolution in the late 1960s. When Gu Cheng returned there in 1974, he earned his living as a carpenter and wrote poetry in his spare time.

Five years later, his first poems appeared in print, and he subsequently became one of the most respected poets writing in Chinese. In the years before his death, he lived in New Zealand; however, in 1992, he gave a series of readings in the United States.

⓭ Literary Analysis

Political Poetry

- Tell students that at the time the poem was written, China was ruled by a totalitarian government. The Communist party wielded absolute control over all aspects of Chinese citizens' lives and suppressed political and cultural expression.
- Discuss with students how, in a country where private feelings are suspect, the expression of personal feelings in poetry could be viewed as a political act.
- Have students read the bracketed line. Then, ask the Literary Analysis question on p. 1396: Within the context of a repressive government, why might "every speech" be a "repetition"?
  Possible response: If people are not allowed to express their feelings or to disagree with government policy, every speech might praise the government and thus sound like a repetition of the same speech.

⓫ 

All

Bei Dao *translated by* Donald Finkel *and* Xueliang Chen

Background

⓬ In 1980, a Chinese poet named Gu Cheng published a poem that depicted two children in bright colors emerging from a world of gray. At that time, Chinese life was very regimented: People's jobs and even their style of dress were dictated by the state. Gu Cheng's poem seemed to criticize the dull grayness of that life and of the kind of literature the state prescribed: realistic, supportive of communism, and not subjective or personal. When a state literary critic attacked Gu Cheng's poem as "misty," Gu Cheng and some of his fellow poets adopted the term as a badge of honor, calling themselves the Misty Poets. Bei Dao and Shu Ting are two of the best known of the Misty Poets.

All is fated,
all cloudy,

all an endless beginning,
all a search for what vanishes,

all joys grave,
all griefs tearless,

⓭ | every speech a repetition,
every meeting a first encounter,

all love buried in the heart,
all history prisoned in a dream,

all hope hedged with doubt,
all faith drowned in lamentation.

Every explosion heralds an instant of stillness,
every death reverberates forever.

Literary Analysis
Political Poetry Within the context of a repressive government, why might "every speech" be a "repetition"?

lamentation (lam ən tā′ shən) *n.* outward expression of grief; weeping or wailing

heralds (her′ əldz) *v.* announces; introduces

reverberates (ri vur′ bə rāts′) *v.* echoes; sounds again

ENRICHMENT: Literature Connection

The Misty Poets

The Misty Poets, including Bei Dao and Shu Ting, took as their model neither traditional Chinese poetry nor the "gray" literature of communism. Instead, they patterned their work after Western poets like Baudelaire and Sylvia Plath, writers known for their surprising images and highly personal emotions.

In the late 1980s, people in China challenged totalitarian rule and demanded a say in their government, as they had in 1976. The new poets fueled these yearnings—even though, to a North American reader, some of their poems may not seem openly political. Living in a society that places a high value on conformity, the Misty Poets continued to find a way to express their individuality through vivid images that convey raw emotions. The inclusion of these elements alone would be enough to place the poets in conflict with their country's rulers; however, they continue to challenge—directly or indirectly—the communist bureaucracy.

Also All

In Answer to Bei Dao's "All"

Shu Ting *translated by* Donald Finkel *and* Jinsheng Yi

Not all trees are felled by storms.
Not every seed finds barren soil.
Not all the wings of dream are broken,
nor is all affection doomed
to wither in a desolate heart.

No, not all is as you say.

Not all flames consume themselves,
shedding no light on other lives.
14 Not all stars announce the night
and never dawn. Not every song
will drift past every ear and heart.

No, not all is as you say.

Not every cry for help is silenced,
nor every loss beyond recall.
Not every chasm spells disaster.
Not only the weak will be brought to their knees,
nor every soul be trodden under.

It won't all end in tears and blood.
Today is heavy with tomorrow—
the future was planted yesterday.
15 Hope is a burden all of us shoulder
though we might stumble under the load.

Literary Analysis
Political Poetry Which people in Chinese society might the speaker be describing as "flames"? Explain.

chasm (kaz´ əm) *n.* deep crack in Earth's surface

Review and Assess

Thinking About the Selections

1. **(a) Recall:** In lines 5–6 of "All," which adjective describes "joys"? **(b) Recall:** Which adjective describes "griefs"? **(c) Analyze:** What is the speaker saying about the kinds of emotions that are possible in a repressive society? Explain.
2. **(a) Recall:** According to the subtitle of "Also All," to whom and to what is the speaker responding in this poem? **(b) Generalize:** Which repeated line suggests the poet's motivation for writing this poem?
3. **Make a Judgment:** Do you think "Also All" can be read independently of "All" and still carry the same meaning? Why or why not?

14 Literary Analysis

Political Poetry

- Read aloud the bracketed passage. Ask: How would flames that do not "consume themselves" burn?
  Possible response: These flames would burn continuously and illuminate the surrounding areas.
- Make sure that students understand that the image of the flame is a metaphor for certain kinds of people. Ask: What kind of person would shed light "on other lives"?
  Possible response: Someone whose behavior is inspiring would shed light on other lives.
- Ask students the Literary Analysis question on p. 1397: Which people in Chinese society might the speaker be describing as "flames"? Explain.
  Possible response: "Flames" might be student leaders, protestors, or even poets who inspire action.

15 Critical Thinking

Compare and Contrast

- Have students read independently the last four lines of "All" on p. 1396. Then, have them read the second bracketed passage on p. 1397.
- Have students compare and contrast the messages in the two passages.
  Answer: Bei Dao says that life is hopeless; Shu Ting says that everyone must have hope for the sake of the future.

Answers for p. 1397

Review and Assess

1. **(a)** The adjective "grave" describes "joys." **(b)** The adjective "tearless" describes "griefs." **(c)** The speaker says that even ordinary emotions are distorted in a repressive society.
2. **(a)** The speaker is responding to Bei Dao's poem "All." **(b)** The line "No, not all is as you say" suggests Shu Ting's motivation.
3. Possible responses: Yes; "Also All" could stand alone because the negatives can be seen as poetic devices rather than refutations. On the other hand; Shu Ting's vision requires the contrast of Bei Dao's bleak hopelessness.

CUSTOMIZE INSTRUCTION FOR UNIVERSAL ACCESS

For Special Needs Students	For Gifted/Talented Students
On the board, draw a two-column chart, labeling one column *Resignation* and one *Hope*. Have students choose a line from "All" that shows resignation, such as "all cloudy" and explain what the line means. Record comments in the first column. Then, have students choose a line from "Also All" that offers hope, such as "Not all the wings of dream are broken" and explain what the line means. Record comments in the second column.	Have students work in pairs to act out an exchange between Bei Dao and Shu Ting in which the poets explain their reasons for writing "All" and "Also All" and their reasons for presenting images of discouragement and hope. Encourage students to base their statements on what they have learned about this historical period so that they can speak knowledgeably about Chinese politics and political poetry of the time. Then, ask volunteers to present short "debates" between the two authors.

ASSESS

16 About the Selection

In "Assembly Line," factory workers march home after the night shift. The poem shows the bleakness of factory work and the way in which it strips workers of humanity.

17 Reading Strategy

Connecting to Historical Context

- Have students read the bracketed passage independently. Then, have students describe assembly lines and suggest images associated with them.
  Possible response: Assembly lines require workers to perform the same task in repetition. Assembly lines evoke images of monotony, boredom, drudgery, and conformity.
- Ask the Reading Strategy question on p. 1398: What does the first stanza suggest about the lives of Chinese citizens at this time?
  Answer: Chinese citizens work long hours at dehumanizing jobs that dull the senses.

18 Vocabulary Development

Latin Root *-temp-*

- Point out the word *tempo* and its definition. Tell students that *tempo* contains the Latin root *-temp-*, which is based on the Latin word meaning "time."
- Have students use dictionaries to find other words with the root *-temp*.
  Possible responses: *Temporary, contemporary, temper,* and *temperance* all feature this root.

Answers for p. 1398

Review and Assess

1. Possible response: Students may picture factory images or a foreboding night.
2. **(a)** The speaker notices stars and trees. **(b)** The speaker sees the trees and stars positioned as if on assembly lines. Adjectives that could apply to assembly lines and workers describe the stars and trees.
3. **(a)** Possible response: The speaker's fate is "manufactured" because it is controlled by the assembly line. **(b)** The speaker's humanity has been lost because the speaker thinks of himself or herself as a part of a machine.

16 Assembly Line

Shu Ting ***translated by*** **Carolyn Kizer**

In time's assembly line
Night presses against night.
We come off the factory night-shift
In line as we march towards home.
17 Over our heads in a row
The assembly line of stars
Stretches across the sky.
Beside us, little trees
Stand numb in assembly lines.

The stars must be exhausted
After thousands of years
Of journeys which never change.
The little trees are all sick,
Choked on smog and monotony,
Stripped of their color and shape.
It's not hard to feel for them;
18 We share the same tempo and rhythm.

Yes, I'm numb to my own existence
As if, like the trees and stars
—perhaps just out of habit
—perhaps just out of sorrow,
I'm unable to show concern
For my own manufactured fate.

Reading Strategy
Connecting to Historical Context What does the first stanza suggest about the lives of Chinese citizens at this time?

monotony (mə nät′ 'n ē) *n.* tedious sameness

tempo (tem′ pō) *n.* rate of speed; pace

Review and Assess

Thinking About the Selection

1. **Respond:** Describe the mental picture you formed while reading this poem.
2. **(a) Recall:** In lines 6–9, what natural objects does the speaker notice? **(b) Analyze:** How are the speaker and the natural objects alike?
3. **(a) Analyze:** Why is the speaker's fate "manufactured"? **(b) Analyze Cause and Effect:** What is the speaker saying about the ways in which an "assembly line" existence harms the human spirit?

ASSESSMENT PRACTICE: Reading Comprehension

Using Context Clues to Determine Meanings (For more practice, see Test Preparation Workbook, p. 6.)

Use the following sample test item to demonstrate how to use context clues to determine word meanings.

Although the Misty Poets are alike in their struggle to bring democracy to China, the poets express these ideas quite differently. In fact, Shu Ting's poem "Also All" provides a direct rebuttal of Bei Dao's "All."

In this passage, rebuttal means

A confirmation **C** defense
B refutation **D** explanation

The context clues *although* and *quite differently* indicate that "All" and "Also All" are poems with contradictory messages. A *confirmation* is an affirmation; a *defense* is an argument in support of something; and an *explanation* makes something understandable. Therefore, *B* is the best choice because a *rebuttal* is a refutation.

Review and Assess

Literary Analysis

Political Poetry

1. (a) Use a chart like the one shown to identify personal and political details in each poem. (b) Which poem speaks to a specific political event most directly? Explain.

	Thoughts of Hanoi	All	Also All	Assembly Line
Personal details				
Political details				

2. (a) How does each of these examples of **political poetry** express the speaker's powerlessness in the face of terrible circumstances? (b) How do these examples suggest the power of a single voice?

Comparing Literary Works

3. In lines 10–11 of "Thoughts of Hanoi," the speaker describes both yearning and fear. Which emotion is stronger in the poem? Explain.
4. (a) Cite images in "Also All" that present a balance between hope and destruction. (b) How are the emotions of yearning and fear that Nguyen expresses also expressed in the poems by Shu Ting? (c) Does Bei Dao convey a similar mix of emotions? Explain.

Reading Strategy

Connecting to Historical Context

5. What information in the poet's biography or the background helps you **connect to the historical context** of "Thoughts of Hanoi"? Explain.
6. Choose a single line from "All" or "Also All" that you think best expresses the historical context of China's repressive rule. Explain your choice.

Extend Understanding

7. **Social Studies Connection:** In what ways do you think works of literature can affect political or social change? Explain.

Quick Review

Political poetry is verse that is written in response to or as commentary about political events or circumstances.

To **connect to the historical context** as you read, decide how details in the poem reflect the specific circumstances of the political climate in which they were written.

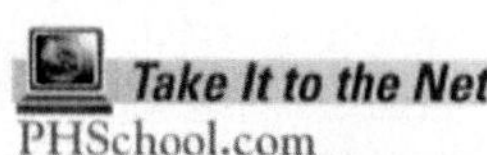

PHSchool.com

Take the interactive self-test online to check your understanding of these selections.

ENRICHMENT: Further Reading

Other Works by the Authors

We strongly encourage you to review any selection before assigning or recommending it to students.

Works by Nguyen Thi Vinh

Birthmark *A Poor Hamlet*

Works by Bei Dao

Old Snow *Unlock* *Waves*

Works by Shu Ting

Selected Poems

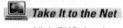

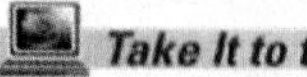

Visit PHSchool.com for more information about the authors.

Answers for p. 1399

Review and Assess

1. **(a)** Possible response: **Thoughts: Personal:** going to school with "Brother"; **Political:** separation of North and South Vietnam; **All: Personal:** hopelessness; **Political:** oppressive government; **Also All: Personal:** hope; **Political:** activists working against the regime; **Assembly Line: Personal:** dehumanization of workers; **Political:** communist regime's control over citizens **(b)** "Thoughts of Hanoi" directly addresses the civil war in Vietnam.
2. **(a)** "Thoughts of Hanoi" describes how the speaker may face a friend in war. "All" describes how a repressive government regulates the display of private emotions. "Also All" says that everyone bears the burden of hope. "Assembly Line" illustrates how people lose their humanity when they are treated like machines. **(b)** All voice discontent with political situations and call for change.
3. Yearning is stronger. The speaker spends most of the poem yearning for things and people.
4. **(a)** Images include "trees . . . felled by storms," "seed finds barren soil," "wings of dream," and "affection doomed." **(b)** Possible response: In "Also All," Shu Ting yearns when she refers to not "every loss beyond recall." In "Assembly Line," she expresses fear of dehumanization. **(c)** Bei Dao's poem argues that "all" hope and faith are beyond recovery.
5. Possible response: Like the poem's speaker, Nguyen was forced to leave North Vietnam and live in South Vietnam.
6. Possible response: The line "every speech a repetition" best expresses the historical context of China's repression. Every speech could be only a "repetition" of accepted policies.
7. Possible response: Literature encourages citizens to see that others share their dissatisfaction and calls them to action.

EXTEND

nswers for p. 1400

Vocabulary Development

ord Analysis: Latin Root -temp-

1. c
2. a
3. b

pelling Strategy

1. chemistry
2. chaotic

oncept Development: ynonyms or Antonyms?

1. antonyms
2. synonyms
3. antonyms
4. antonyms
5. synonyms
6. synonyms
7. antonyms
8. antonyms

2 Grammar and Style

ractice

1. still I yearn / still I fear /; parallel construction and repetition of words
2. —perhaps just out of habit / —perhaps just out of sorrow; parallel construction and repetition of words
3. village greybeards strolling . . . / grandmothers basking . . .; parallel construction of clauses with parallel use of participles
4. all love buried in the heart, / all history prisoned in a dream; parallel construction
5. Choked on smog and monotony, / Stripped of their color and shape; parallel construction with participle phrases

Writing Application

Possible response:
We remember our country united and free, then:
We pause and smile.
We pause and weep.

10TH GRADE For support in teaching the Grammar and Style Lesson to tenth graders, use **Writing and Grammar,** Platinum Level, Chapter 7, Section 4.

Integrate Language Skills

1 Vocabulary Development Lesson

Word Analysis: Latin Root *-temp-*

Some time-related words in English contain the root *-temp-*, which is based on the Latin word *tempus*, meaning *time*. Thus, *tempo* refers to a rate of speed. Use your knowledge of the root to match each word below with its definition.

1. temporal
2. temporize
3. extemporaneous

a. delay; evade
b. done without preparation
c. worldly

Spelling Strategy

In many words of Greek origin that begin with a *k* sound, the sound is spelled *ch*, as in *chasm*. Complete the spelling of the words in each sentence below.

1. She took courses in __emistry.
2. His life was busy and __aotic.

Concept Development: Synonyms or Antonyms?

Review the vocabulary list on page 1391 and notice the way each word is used in the context of the selections. Then, determine whether the words in each pair below are synonyms (words with similar meanings) or antonyms (words with opposite meanings).

1. monotony/excitement
2. heralds/greets
3. chasm/mountaintop
4. jubilant/distressed
5. reverberates/echoes
6. tempo/pace
7. obsolete/new
8. lamentations/rejoicings

2 Grammar and Style Lesson

Parallelism

Parallelism is the repeated expression of similar ideas in a similar grammatical form—words, phrases, clauses, or whole sentences. Parallelism is used to emphasize equal relationships between ideas and to create a smooth, musical flow of language.

Examples:

Not every cry for help is silenced,
nor every loss beyond recall. (parallel repetition of similar words)

the boys / plowing / transplanting / in the fields (parallel use of participles)

Practice Identify and explain the uses of parallelism in each item below.

1. still I yearn / still I fear /
2. —perhaps just out of habit / —perhaps just out of sorrow,
3. village greybeards strolling . . . / grandmothers basking . . .
4. all love buried in the heart, / all history prisoned in a dream,
5. Choked on smog and monotony, / Stripped of their color and shape.

Writing Application Write a few lines of poetry. Include at least two examples of parallelism.

WG *Prentice Hall Writing and Grammar Connection: Diamond Level, Chapter 20, Section 6*

TEACHING RESOURCES

The following resources can be used to enrich or extend the instruction for pp. 1400–1401.

Vocabulary

- **Selection Support:** Build Vocabulary, p. 277
- **Vocabulary and Spelling Practice Book** (Use this booklet for skills instruction.)

Grammar

- **Selection Support:** Grammar and Style, p. 278
- **Writing and Grammar,** Diamond Level, p. 505
- **Daily Language Practice Transparencies**

Writing

- **Performance Assess. and Portfolio Mgmt.**, p. 16
- **Writing and Grammar,** Diamond Level, p. 488
- **Writing Models and Graphic Organizers on Transparencies,** pp. 53–59

Listening and Speaking

- **Performance Assess. and Portfolio Mgmt.**, p. 33

BLOCK SCHEDULING: Resources marked with this symbol provide varied instruction during 90-minute blocks.

❸ Writing Lesson

Literary Analysis

Write a literary analysis of one of the poems in this group. In your literary analysis, explore how elements of the poem work together to support its overall theme.

Prewriting Choose a poem and reread it carefully. As you read, jot down details that seem especially important or powerful. Identify ways in which the details combine to express a single message, or theme.

Drafting Begin with an introduction stating your thesis—a brief statement summarizing the poem's overall effect or theme and the elements that contribute to it. In the body of the paper, support your thesis with specific details from the poem.

Revising As you reread your work, double-check the structure of your sentences. If you have too many short, choppy sentences, combine them to achieve variety.

Model: Revising Sentences to Create Variety and Interest

In "Thoughts of Hanoi," ^Nguyen uses images like a series of frames in a film ~~in "Thoughts of Hanoi." She does this~~ to re-create a sense of the ^*untroubled* life of the past. ~~That life was untroubled.~~

Combining short, repetitive sentences creates a more interesting flow.

Prentice Hall Writing and Grammar Connection: Diamond Level, Chapter 20, Section 3

❹ Extension Activities

Listening and Speaking With a partner, prepare a **dialogue** that might have occurred between the speaker in "Thoughts of Hanoi" and her friend after the war. Use these tips to prepare:

- Make a list of questions the two might ask each other and their likely responses.
- Decide whether the two will rediscover their friendship or will remain hostile.

Practice until your dialogue sounds natural and spontaneous. Then, present it to the class.

Research and Technology With a small group, prepare a **multimedia report** on the events that occurred at Tiananmen Square in 1989. Use books, magazines, and the Internet to gather information about government leaders, leaders of the democracy movement, and the Democracy Wall. **[Group Activity]**

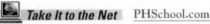

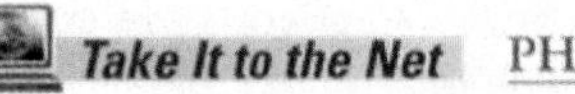
PHSchool.com

Go online for an additional research activity using the Internet.

ASSESSMENT RESOURCES

The following resources can be used to assess students' knowledge and skills.

Selection Assessment

Formal Assessment, pp. 240–242

Open-Book Tests, pp. 208–210

Test Bank Software

Take It to the Net

Visit PHSchool.com for self-tests on the selections.

Writing Rubric

Performance Assess. and Portfolio Mgmt., p. 16

Listening and Speaking Rubric

Performance Assess. and Portfolio Mgmt., p. 33

For additional diagnostics and remediation for skills covered in this grouping, use materials from the Prentice Hall Assessment System.

Lesson Support for p. 1401

❸ Writing Lesson

- Remind students that in a literary analysis, a writer takes a critical look at important elements in a work. The writer then explains how the work uses those elements and how they work together to convey the message.
- Use the Writing Lesson to guide students as they create their analyses. Refer students to Writing Process Model 8: Interpreting a Work of Literature in **Writing Models and Graphic Organizers on Transparencies,** pp. 53–59, to help them plan their analyses.
- Use the Response to Literature rubric in **Performance Assessment and Portfolio Management,** p. 16, to assess students' work.

10TH GRADE For support in working through the Writing Lesson with tenth graders, use **Writing and Grammar,** Platinum Level, Chapter 13, Section 1.

❹ Listening and Speaking

- Remind students to consider the political positions held by the speaker and his or her friend.
- Encourage students to research North and South Vietnam to provide details for their dialogues and settings. They may want to consult maps to include local landmarks or find information about the two countries' leaders and ideologies.
- Allow students time to rehearse and perform their dialogues for the class. Use the Listening and Speaking Progress Chart in **Performance Assessment and Portfolio Management,** p. 33, to evaluate students' dialogues.

CUSTOMIZE INSTRUCTION For Universal Access

To address different learning styles, use the following activities suggested in the **Extension Activities** booklet, p. 70.

- For Verbal/Linguistic and Musical/Rythmic Learners, use Activity 5.
- For Visual/Spatial Learners, use Activity 6.
- For Bodily/Kinesthetic Learners, use Activity 7.

Lesson Objectives

1. To write a comparison-and-contrast essay on literary themes across cultures
2. To review literary works for thematic relevance
3. To use concise and efficient language in evaluating literary works
4. To use writing strategies to generate ideas, plan, organize, evaluate, and revise writing

Prewriting

- Have a volunteer read aloud the boxed Assignment. Clarify that students are to write about two selections from two cultures, for a total of four selections.
- Organize students into teams or small groups to review the unit selections. Write the selection titles on the board, and invite teams or groups to share their views on how each selection addresses the relationship between society and the individual. Encourage students to choose selections that speak strongly about this relationship.
- Ask students to consider their familiarity with various cultures when making a final choice. Students may want to write about cultures with which they have personal experience.
- Review the Model Chart at the bottom of the page, and discuss its use.
- Emphasize the importance of developing a working thesis statement before beginning to draft. It is critical to plan for effective writing, even if the thesis statement needs to be modified as students revise.

Writing About Literature

Compare and Contrast Literary Themes Across Cultures

For many writers, the world wars, totalitarian states, and consumer economy of our era mark the failure of society to give meaningful form to life. The individual seems left on his or her own to make sense of the world, as in Camus's "The Guest." Yet the global scale of current events emphasizes the interconnections among lives. In this spirit, some writers chart the ways individual lives are shaped by the history of a group, as Derek Walcott does in *Omeros*. Camus, Walcott, and others share a general insight: The place where individual and society meet is haunted by unsettled—and unsettling—questions.

Write an essay in which you compare this theme across cultures. Refer to the box at right for details of the assignment.

Assignment: Who Am I? The Individual Across Cultures

Write an analytical essay that compares the theme of the individual in society in works from two of the following cultures included in this unit: the Americas, Western Europe, Eastern Europe, the Middle East, Africa, and Asia.

Criteria:

- Include a thesis statement drawn from your analysis of the literature of the two cultures.
- Support your thesis with detailed comparisons and contrasts of at least two selections from each culture.
- Cite several examples from each work.
- Approximate length: 1,500 words

Prewriting

Choose selections. Review the selections to identify those with themes that relate to the individual's place in society. Choose at least two works from two cultures for your analysis. Ask questions such as the following to help guide your search:

- What does this selection suggest about the relationship between society and the individual?
- How is this theme revealed: through the plot, setting, characterization, language, or a combination of elements?
- In what ways is the relationship between individual and society in this selection like or unlike their relationship in other works?

Drawing on your notes, fill out a chart like the one shown. Then, review the chart and choose four or more selections, at least two from each of two cultures. To ensure that your essay will be interesting and rich in detail, choose works that show striking similarities or contrasts.

Read to Write

As you reread the texts, analyze the tone. Tone, the author's attitude toward the subject and the reader, can help you understand the theme of a work.

Model: Charting to Compare and Contrast Themes

Selection	Theme	Evidence of Theme
"The Handsomest Drowned Man in the World"	Individuals perceive and imagine together, collectively.	Women agree the drowned man's name is Esteban.

Write a working thesis. After you have decided which aspects of the theme appear in the works you have chosen, write a working thesis. Introduce the selections you will compare and contrast and the specific ways they present the individual in society.

TEACHING RESOURCES

The following resources can be used to enrich or extend the instruction for pp. 1402–1403.

- **Writing and Grammar,** Diamond Level, Chapter 9, pp. 168–188
- **Performance Assess. and Portfolio Mgmt.,** p. 16
- **Writing Models and Graphic Organizers on Transparencies,** pp. 53–59

 **Writing and Grammar iText CD-ROM**

Students can use the following tools as they complete their comparison-and-contrast essays:

- List Organizer
- Customizable Outliner
- Unity and Coherence Revising Tool

Drafting

Prepare an outline. Make an outline to help you organize your essay. Each main heading preceded by a Roman numeral should stand for an important idea that you plan to explore in its own paragraph. Under each subheading, list supporting examples.

Model: Using a Working Outline

I. Writers of the Americas emphasize family and heritage
  A. "Handsomest Drowned Man in the World"
    1. Groups of men and women think alike
    2. Village agrees on what to do with drowned man
  B. "House Taken Over"
    1. Brother and sister live in family house

Refer to history. To strengthen your arguments, support them with references to historical events or cultural movements. Explain, where appropriate, the effect of historical circumstances on the works.

Revising and Editing

Review content: Reformulate points for accuracy. Reread your draft. Circle each sentence in which you state a main point. Then, review your circled points. For each, consider whether it accurately sums up an insight to which your paper leads. Rewrite as necessary to ensure that you have used just the right terms to explain your ideas.

Review style: Delete unnecessary words. Make sure that you have communicated your ideas in the simplest, most straightforward way possible. Take out any unnecessary words that you may have used.

Wordy: Very obviously, the title of the story gives a strong hint about its nature and tone. From the very first sentence, the reader knows that the story will not be completely realistic and will probably include elements of fantasy.

Revised: The title gives a strong hint about the tone of the story. From the first sentence, the reader knows that the story will include elements of fantasy.

Publishing and Presenting

Have a discussion. Gather with classmates who wrote about the same selections you did. Compare group members' interpretations of the literature.

WG Writing and Grammar Connection: Diamond Level, Chapter 9

Write to Learn
As you write your first draft, you may notice that some examples from the selections do not adequately support your ideas. Look back at the selections to make sure you have chosen the details or quotations that best illustrate the theme of the individual in society.

Write to Explain
Use parallel construction to make your comparisons and contrasts as clear as possible to readers.

Drafting

- Review sources of cultural information, such as background notes in the student text and classroom or Internet resources. Remind students to support any references to historical events or cultural movements with accurate information.
- Point out how the working outline model addresses each selection under its own heading. Have students find examples in the text to support the model, such as ways in which families or gender groups live.
- Students should list page references in their outlines so that they will be able to find text examples more easily as they draft.

Revising and Editing

- Have students compare their drafts with their outlines. They should confirm that they have included each main point and item of supporting evidence. Then, have students exchange papers with partners to determine whether their analytic arguments are convincing.
- Stress the importance of the style review. Point out that many writers make the mistake of favoring length over conciseness. More is not necessarily better. Work through the provided models, identifying unnecessary words. Have a volunteer read aloud the Revised example. Point out that it conveys the point concisely and effectively.

Publishing and Presenting

As an alternative, create groups in which all the selections are represented. Students can then share ideas about how each selection addresses the issue of the relationship between individuals and societies.

CUSTOMIZE INSTRUCTION FOR UNIVERSAL ACCESS

For Less Proficient Writers	For English Learners	For Advanced Writers
To help students make comparisons and contrasts, review comparative and superlative transition words and adjectives. Explain that words and phrases such as *similarly, also, on the other hand,* and *instead* can help show comparison and contrast. Words such as *more* and *most* can help create degrees of description.	Invite students to share knowledge from their native cultures about the relationship between society and the individual. In particular, if students share cultural origins with writers from the unit selections, ask them to share that knowledge with the class as a whole.	Encourage students to include significant historical and cultural references in their essays. Students may do this through research. Remind students that it is not enough to provide only background, however. Students must clearly link the historical events or cultural movements to their essays' themes.

Writing WORKSHOP

Workplace Writing: Job Portfolio

A **job portfolio** consists of the materials a candidate submits to a potential employer. Core elements are the **résumé,** a summary of qualifications and experience, and a cover letter that introduces the job seeker. Other materials may include references and writing or other work samples. In this workshop, you will write an effective résumé.

Assignment Criteria Your résumé should include the following elements:

- Prominently displayed name, address, and contact information
- Summaries of work history, education, and related experience tailored for the job under consideration
- Consistent style and precise language, including active verbs
- Easy-to-follow, consistent résumé format

To preview the criteria on which your résumé may be assessed, refer to the Rubric for Self-Assessment on page 1407.

Prewriting

List information. List all of your work experience. Include exact dates of employment, employers' names and addresses, and your duties. Also note relevant extracurricular, volunteer, and educational experiences, as well as any special skills, such as word processing.

Type of Job:
working with or supervising children
–summer camp
–crafts and activities
Experience to Emphasize:
camp counselor assistant
mother's helper
Skills to Emphasize:
sports
arts and crafts experience
Other Accomplishments:
baby-sitting certification
teen character award

Choose a place to which to apply. Determine the type of job you wish to obtain, and apply to suitable employers. To conduct a thorough, well-informed job search, follow these steps:

- Consult library resources, visit employment agencies, and speak with guidance counselors, friends, and family to familiarize yourself with various types of jobs.
- Review print or Web guides to local businesses, and list employers of interest to you.
- Consult job listings at your school, at an employment agency, and in the Help Wanted section of the newspaper.

Match your experience to the job. Determine which of your experiences will be of most interest for a given application. Emphasize those experiences in your cover letter and résumé. For example, a store advertising for help with displays might want to see evidence of creativity. A store looking for a cashier might be more interested in mathematical skills.

Lesson Objectives

1. To create a job portfolio, including a résumé
2. To use writing strategies to generate ideas, plan, organize, evaluate, and revise writing

Model from Literature

The short story "An Astrologer's Day", pp. 1366–1370, describes one character's experiences during a day on the job. The descriptions students include in their job portfolios will be less detailed than those in the story but will present readers with a picture of the writer's experience.

Prewriting

- Have students share what criteria they might look for when searching for a job. For example, a job applicant may want to know how much experience is required, whether the job has flexible hours, or whether he or she could work with children or work outdoors. Tell students that it is as important to think about a job's environment—for example, large office or small shop—as it is to consider the job's actual tasks. Choosing a job that fits with one's interests and strengths increases an applicant's chances of being hired.
- Have students brainstorm a list of Internet job search resources. For example, students might identify local companies through a city's Web site and then visit the companies' Web sites for additional information. Also, help students identify people-based resources, such as family friends or businesses.
- Encourage students to list their work experience creatively. For example, if a student has regularly prepared family meals, this represents important experience. It has taught the student to plan, organize, and execute in a position of responsibility. Employers generally recognize that high school students have had limited paid job experience.
- Encourage students to review the Self-Assessment Rubric on p. 1407 so that they will know what is expected of their job portfolios.

TEACHING RESOURCES

The following resources can be used to enrich or extend the instruction for pp. 1404–1407.

Writing and Grammar, Diamond Level, Chapter 16, pp. 348–357

Performance Assess. and Portfolio Mgmt., p. 18

Writing Models and Graphic Organizers on Transparencies, pp. 61–64

Writing and Grammar iText CD-ROM

Students can use the following tools as they complete their job portfolios:

- Listing Organizer
- Character Trait Word Bin
- Editing Tool
- Vague Adjectives Tool

Student Model

Before you begin drafting your résumé, read this student model and review the characteristics of an effective résumé.

Megan Mary Mahoney
1234 Anystreet
Hickory, NC 28601
(888) 555-5555
e-mail@e-mail.com

Name and contact information are placed prominently at the top of the page and set in a larger font size.

OBJECTIVE
To obtain a position as a camp counselor in order to work with children

EDUCATION

Megan uses clear headings to label her education, work, and other relevant experiences.

August 2001 to Present — **St. Stephen High School,** Hickory, NC
Expected graduation date: June 2005. Honor student.
Special courses: Journalism; Advanced Placement English
Extracurricular activities: Beta Club, yearbook staff, varsity tennis, JV soccer, and JV basketball

WORK EXPERIENCE

Summer 2002 and 2003 — **Counselor's Assistant**
Camp Joy, Hickory, NC
Helped campers with arts, sports, games, and social interaction at this nonprofit camp for underprivileged children.

Megan provides specific details about experiences related to her objective.

2002 to Present — **Part-time Mother's Helper**
Sue Smith, Hickory, NC
Assist mother of severely handicapped daughter. Help with feeding and medications and watch over the child when the mother does errands.

2000 to Present — **Baby Sitter**
Hickory, NC
Care for several different children; regular duties include feeding, bathing, playing games, and reading bedtime stories.

SKILLS

- Sports: tennis, soccer, basketball, volleyball
- Arts and crafts, piano
- Computer skills: word processing, Internet research

SPECIAL ACHIEVEMENTS

- Received Baby-Sitting Certification at Frye Regional Hospital in December 2001. Was trained in basic first aid and baby-sitting.
- Received the Teen Character Award from the local YMCA in May 2001. Nominated for this award by teachers.

Bullets and boldface headings make Megan's information clear and easy to follow. Headings, dates, and bulleted items are aligned consistently.

CUSTOMIZE INSTRUCTION FOR UNIVERSAL ACCESS

For Less Proficient Writers	For English Learners	For Advanced Writers
Have students review their work and life experience in time order. They may use the Timeline Tool on the **Writing and Grammar iText CD-ROM** as an aid. Have students think back to each school year and ask: What responsibilities did I have? What skills did I learn? In which activities did I participate?	Stress that accuracy and consistency in a résumé are far more important than elaborate language. Students should feel comfortable using simple language, provided they ensure that it is used correctly. Verb tenses must be consistent; punctuation must be correct; and spelling must be accurate.	Encourage students to use powerful and descriptive verbs and adverbs to describe their experiences. For example, Megan might have added the word *Sole* before her Baby Sitter description. This would highlight the responsibility that she had for the children. Students should choose specific verbs for their résumés.

Student Model

- Explain that the Student Model is a sample and that students' own résumés may be shorter or longer. Note that as a rule, résumés should not exceed two pages. At this point in their working lives, students' résumés should be only one page.
- Point out to students that the Student Model uses layout to enhance readability. For example, Megan positioned her name prominently at the top of the page and used labels for education, work experience, skills, and special achievements. Megan did not use special typefaces, italics, or underlining. This allows employers to easily scan the document into a computer.
- Point out the shorthand format of a résumé. Megan began her sentences with a verb rather than with a first-person pronoun. Students should take care, however, to keep their verb tense consistent within an entry.
- Emphasize that the goal of a résumé is to present experience pertinent to a particular job. This may mean writing different versions of a résumé, such as a version that highlights experience with children or another that focuses on work with computers.
- Review the bulleted items at the bottom of Megan's résumé. Students can list skills here that paint an overall picture. This helps employers gain a sense of the applicant's potential, especially when the applicant is a high school student with limited work experience.

Real-World Connection

Job portfolios in the real world: Students will almost certainly need to create a job portfolio at least once in their lives. Both paying and volunteer positions usually require the presentation of work experience. Often the portfolio is the first introduction a potential employer has to the applicant. It must be effective, or the applicant may never get the chance to present himself or herself in person.

Drafting

- Explain that there are many correct styles for résumés. The critical point is that any résumé must be consistent within its own style. Inconsistency will distract the reader from the résumé's content and weaken the portfolio.
- Remind students to use the Résumé Conventions checklist as they draft. No matter which format they use, the résumé should contain all of the features listed.
- Stress again the importance of accuracy in a résumé. Remind students to work slowly and carefully, checking their text repeatedly.

Revising

- Point out that proofreading may be the most important step in writing a résumé. First impressions are vital in a job search, and mistakes are difficult to undo after the résumé has been delivered.
- Encourage students to review the language in their résumés. They should ask: Is the language precise? Is it vivid? Does it portray experiences effectively? Is it varied, using different verbs and adjectives? Is it concise enough to fit on one page?

Drafting

Select a style. Choose a résumé style, and apply the style consistently as you draft your résumé. For example, you may choose to use either sentences or phrases in the descriptions of your job history, or to mix the two in each entry. Select one of these styles, and use it consistently.

- **Whole sentences:** Responsibilities included routing copy, running errands, and assisting reporters.
- **Phrases:** Routed copy; ran errands; assisted reporters

Select a format. Résumés can follow several possible formats. The model on page 1405 shows one format. The key to an effective format is an easy-to-follow organization. No matter what format you choose, follow it consistently. Always include these features:

- Name, address, phone number, e-mail address, and other contact information, displayed prominently at the top of the document
- List of work and other applicable experiences and accomplishments, beginning with the most recent
- Names and addresses of employers in boldface or otherwise set off
- Dates of terms of employment with each employer
- Brief description of responsibilities for each job listing

Follow résumé language conventions. Do not use the pronoun *I*. Write, for example, "Took responsibility for" or "Responsible for" instead of "I took responsibility for."

Résumé Conventions

- ☐ **Heading** includes the candidate's name, address, and contact information.
- ☐ **Objective** or **Summary** provides a brief statement about the candidate and his or her professional goals.
- ☐ **Experience** lists details of work and other relevant history.
- ☐ **Education** provides a history of the candidate's schooling and other training.
- ☐ **Skills** section notes special abilities, such as computer training or fluency in a foreign language.
- ☐ **Honors/Activities/Memberships** is a flexible category that includes applicable activities that do not fit into other sections of the résumé.

Revising

Revise for consistency. Make sure you have followed a consistent organizational strategy, as well as format and style. Mark any inconsistencies as you scan your résumé.

1. Make sure the entries are aligned consistently.
2. Make sure the headings are boldfaced and capitalized.
3. Make sure all the information in a section is organized following the same pattern.

Correct any inconsistencies that you note.

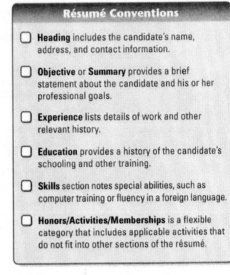

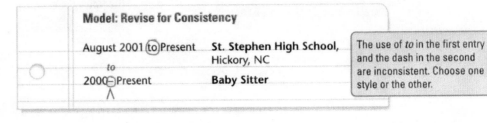

Model: Revise for Consistency

August 2001 to Present	**St. Stephen High School,** Hickory, NC
2000 – Present (*to*)	**Baby Sitter**

The use of *to* in the first entry and the dash in the second are inconsistent. Choose one style or the other.

Using Technology in Writing

Some word processing programs offer résumé templates that students may find useful. If these programs are not available, students can use auto-format features such as bulleted lists and hanging indents to create a layout such as in the Student Model. Remind students to use these features carefully because auto-formatting can contain hidden settings. Students can modify these settings under "AutoCorrect" or other similar features in the Tools menu of many programs. Encourage students to choose a simple, readable typeface, such as Times or Helvetica, but to experiment with variations in type size and the use of boldface to highlight important features. Students should use the "Best" quality feature when printing.

Students can also use the organizing tools and revision checkers on the **Writing and Grammar iText CD-ROM.**

Revise language. Avoid vague words and passive verbs.

Vague: Was assigned work on brochures

Specific: Researched and wrote copy for four-color brochures for advertising agency

Compare the model and the nonmodel. Ask yourself: Why is the model more effective?

Nonmodel	Model
Employed by a mother of a severely handicapped child.	Assist mother of severely handicapped daughter. Help with feeding and medications and watch over the child when the mother does errands.

Publishing and Presenting

Put together a job portfolio. To accompany your résumé and complete your job portfolio, write a cover letter. Include the following elements:

- A brief, pertinent statement about yourself
- An expression of your interest in the job
- An overview of your qualifications for the job
- Contact information
- Thanks for consideration of your résumé

Follow standard business-letter format for your cover letter. Proofread your draft carefully to ensure that the final copy is free of errors.

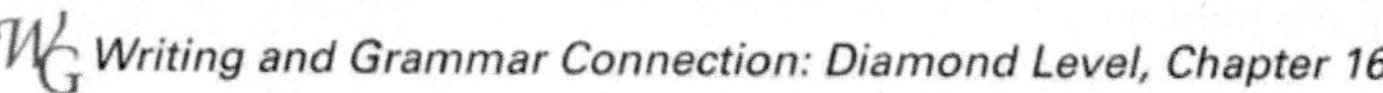

Writing and Grammar Connection: Diamond Level, Chapter 16

Rubric for Self-Assessment

Evaluate your résumé using the following criteria and rating scale:

Criteria	Rating Scale: Not very				Very
How visible are the name, address, and contact information?	1	2	3	4	5
How well does the résumé describe qualifications and experiences?	1	2	3	4	5
How consistent is the format?	1	2	3	4	5
How precise and active is the language?	1	2	3	4	5
How clear is the organization?	1	2	3	4	5

Publishing and Presenting

- Show students a variety of résumés. You might find these on the Internet or in a book on the topic. Point out that résumés should be printed on high-quality, neutral-color paper. Direct students to stationery stores for appropriate paper.
- Review the features of a business letter, and have students include a specific follow-up proposal, such as a plan to call the employer in a week's time.

Assessment

- Encourage students to read the assessment criteria before finalizing their résumés. Make sure that they understand how each of the criteria is reflected in the Student Model.
- Agree as a class on an acceptable score, such as at least two 4s and no score less than a 3. This will give students a benchmark for acceptability.
- An alternative rubric can be found on p. 18 of **Performance Assessment and Portfolio Management.**

TEST-TAKING TIP

Tell students that because résumés require such careful proofreading, standardized tests might include them in proofreading items. When presented with such questions, students should remember résumé conventions such as the use of phrases that are punctuated as sentences and the importance of consistency in format. Students should then quickly review the résumé example to identify its chosen format before looking for any deviations or errors.

Lesson Objectives

1. To prepare and deliver a multimedia presentation
2. To effectively use technology to support the presentation's goals
3. To deliver a well-documented presentation with confidence

Prepare Your Content

- Review with students the features and tools of a multimedia presentation. Make sure that they understand the function of each component. List this information on the board.
- Discuss the items in the bulleted list. Invite students to share examples of different media from effective presentations they have viewed. Prompt students by recalling such presentations at museums or libraries.
- Remind students to vary the media in their presentations where possible. Audience members will respond to different types of media, so a presentation that smoothly incorporates both visual and auditory media can reach more people effectively. Students should take care, however, not to present competing media simultaneously.

Prepare Your Delivery

- Students should practice their presentations several times, preferably with an audience and in a room similar to that of the actual presentation. This will enable students to become familiar with lighting, distances, and sound conditions.
- Give students the opportunity to examine the available audiovisual equipment. Offer a demonstration, or invite an experienced student or teacher to model equipment use.
- Remind students that they may want—or need, in the event of technology failure—to deliver parts of the presentation live. Students should therefore have note cards prepared for a speech and should practice delivering that speech.

Listening and Speaking WORKSHOP

Multimedia Presentation

Many presentations can be enhanced through the use of sounds and visuals. When you give a **multimedia presentation,** you might use an overhead projector, a slide projector, a video or audio player, a computer, or another electronic device. The following strategies will help you develop and deliver an effective multimedia presentation.

Prepare Your Content

The suggestions below will help you develop your multimedia presentation:

- Outline your presentation, and decide which parts can be effectively presented through, or with the support of, visual or sound media.
- Choose media that suit your topic. For example, if your topic is American life during World War II, you might play popular music of the time as background.
- Use audio or visual support throughout your presentation, not just at the beginning or at the end.

Prepare Your Delivery

Multimedia presentations can be wonderful experiences for presenter and audience alike—but only if all the technology functions as intended. These tips may help you prepare to use audio and visual technology in your presentation:

- Rehearse your presentation with the multimedia equipment you will use. Become familiar with the equipment, and learn how to make volume, focus, and other adjustments to it.
- Before the presentation, double-check the equipment to make sure that all of it is functioning properly.
- Make sure visuals will be seen and the audio portion will be heard by the entire audience.
- Have a backup plan, in case the equipment fails. For example, you might have on hand photocopies of charts and graphs to pass out to the audience in case the overhead projector fails.

Feedback Form for Oral Response to Literature

Rating System
+ = Excellent ✓ = Average – = Weak

Content
Match of media and topic ______
Media enhance topic ______
Media used at appropriate points ______

Delivery
Smoothness of presentation ______
Ability to adjust equipment ______
Ability to work around glitches in equipment ______

Activity: Presentation and Feedback Prepare a multimedia presentation in which you explain how to make or do something at which you excel. Practice your presentation with a partner, using the Feedback Form shown to evaluate your content and delivery. Use the evaluation to help you polish your presentation, and then deliver it to the class.

CUSTOMIZE INSTRUCTION FOR UNIVERSAL ACCESS

For Special Needs Students	For English Learners
Offer students additional time to practice with the multimedia equipment. If possible, arrange for one-on-one direction from a knowledgeable guide. Explain that multimedia presentations need not be complex in order to be effective. In fact, the choice of media allows students to draw on their strengths and minimize any weaknesses. Work with students to identify those strengths and weaknesses, and then brainstorm which media will fit closely with these.	Stress the opportunity that multimedia presentations offer. Much of the spoken component can be prerecorded in an environment where the student does not feel the pressure of an audience. Further, the visual and audio components offer students an opportunity to extend creativity without concern about language. Ask students to present elements of their presentations in their native language if it is appropriate to the topic.

Assessment WORKSHOP

Analyzing an Author's Meaning

In the reading sections of some tests, you may be required to read a passage and interpret the author's ideas or opinions.

- Identify the main idea and supporting details of the passage.
- Select the correct answers to questions about the passage, based on your own knowledge and the information in the passage.
- Eliminate answer choices that are unrelated to information in the passage.

Test-Taking Strategies

- To interpret parts a passage, restate the ideas in your own words.
- Read all the words in a passage carefully. Even small details may give clues to correct answers.

Sample Test Question

Directions: Read the passage, and then answer the question that follows.

America is experiencing an epidemic of obesity. Assign much of the blame to our frenetic lifestyles. We are too busy to prepare and eat home-cooked meals very often, and besides, fast food is delicious. Also, have you taken a good look at portion sizes lately? They are enormous! Hamburgers, which used to weigh 4 ounces, now weigh 8, 12, or even 16 ounces. Popcorn sold in movie theaters, which used to come in small bags or dainty boxes, is now served in huge vats—and with "free" refills. This trend is probably good for the fast-food and movie-theaters profits, but it's wreaking havoc on Americans' waistlines and health.

1. With which statement would the writer of the passage clearly agree?

A We need to make fast food more tasty.

B We need to eat less fast food.

C We need to close down fast-food restaurants.

D We need to install gyms in fast-food restaurants.

Answer and Explanation

The correct answer is *B*. The writer believes people should eat less fast food. The writer does not discuss either option ***C*** or ***D***, and ***A*** is contradicted in the passage.

Practice

Directions: Read the following, and then complete the item that follows.

The mayor's plan to drain the swamp behind the Mayville town park is a sound one, but you may be surprised to learn the strongest reason for it. You might think at first of the mosquitoes that breed in the swamp. It is true that draining the swamp will help greatly, but pesticides could be used to eliminate mosquito larvae instead. You might think of the town's need for land on which to build a new school. The town has recently acquired three properties through tax foreclosures, however, any one of which would be suitable for a school.

The truth is that our town has hit hard times. A project such as draining the swamp, financed in part by state grants, is just what Mayville's unemployed need to find temporary work until there is a full economic recovery.

1. The author's main point is that

A the mosquitoes should be killed.

B Mayville has hit hard times.

C the swamp should be drained to give Mayville's unemployed work.

D the swamp should be drained for many reasons.

TEACHING RESOURCES

The following resources can be used to enrich or extend the instruction for p. 1409.

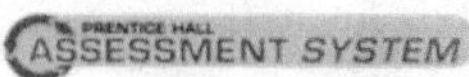

For additional diagnostics and remediation for skills covered in this grouping, use materials from the Prentice Hall Assessment System.

Lesson Objectives

To analyze an author's meaning in standardized-test situations

Applying Reading Strategies

Remind students that main ideas are the most important ideas in a passage. They are often found in the first or last few sentences of a passage. Students should ask themselves: What is the author trying to say? The answer to this question is probably the main idea and a clue to the author's meaning.

Test-Taking Skills

- Have students read the Sample Test Question. Then, ask them to identify the topic and the main idea of the passage.
  Answer: The passage topic is the rising level of obesity in America, and the main idea is that fast-paced lifestyles and fast foods contribute to this problem.
- Invite volunteers to identify clues in the text that support the main idea.
  Possible response: Clues such as "too busy," "have you taken a good look at portion sizes," or "Popcorn sold in movie theaters ... is now served in huge vats ..." support the main idea.
- Have students test each answer choice against the passage content. They should notice that *D* can be ruled out because it contains information not included in the passage. *A* can be ruled out because the passage states that fast food is delicious. *B* and *C* are more difficult to analyze because *C* could happen as a result of *B*. However, the author does not actually discuss fast-food restaurants being closed down, so *C* should be eliminated. *B* is the correct answer.
- Have students read and respond to the Practice item.

Answer

The correct answer is C. Although the author presents and agrees with three reasons for draining the swamp, the main idea of the passage is to learn the *strongest* reason for draining the swamp.

Resources

Handbooks

Indexes

Suggestions for Sustained Reading

Following are some suggestions for longer works that will give you the opportunity to experience the fun of sustained reading. Each of the suggestions further explores one of the time periods, themes, or literary movements in this book. Many of the titles are included in the **Prentice Hall Library,** featuring the **Penguin Literature Library**.

You may want to consult your teacher before choosing one of these longer works.

Unit One

The Bible's Greatest Stories

Paul Roche, *translator and reteller, Signet Classic, 2001*

The stories of Noah and the flood and of Ruth's loyalty to Naomi are only two of the many classic Bible tales related in this comprehensive collection. In this publication, translator and reteller Paul Roche includes maps of Palestine and the Greco-Roman world to help readers place major events that occur in the stories. Introductory material links related tales while, at the same time, making them accessible to today's readers. All the themes of great literature can be found in these stories: love, honor, war, pride, celebration, and death. These themes emerge in dramatic episodes—such as the birth of Moses or the story of Joseph's coat of many colors—gathered from such biblical books as Genesis, the four Gospels, and Acts of the Apostles.

Tales of Ancient Egypt

Selected and retold by Roger Lancelyn Green, *Puffin Classic, 1996*

Ancient Egypt is a land of fables. In *Tales of Ancient Egypt,* Roger Lancelyn Green retells twenty of these stories. Some are as close to us as our own childhoods—"The Girl with the Red-Rose Slippers," for instance, is the earliest version of the Cinderella story. Others, such as the story of how the goddess Isis tricked the god Ra, give glimpses of faraway ancient beliefs—beliefs in the power of names and in a person's immortal double. Discovered carved in temple walls or written on papyrus scrolls, some of these tales explain why a particular monument was built. Others tell of life's fundamentals—of love, of the desire to be remembered, of the struggle for justice. In these tales, readers will encounter some familiar themes; they may also rediscover the strange scent of mystery that makes tales from the past so fascinating.

The Epic of Gilgamesh

Anonymous, *translated by N. K. Sandars, Penguin Classic, 1960*

If sampling a portion of this work has given you an appetite for more, treat yourself to the complete book.

Related British Literature: Early Irish Myths and Sagas

Anonymous, *translated by Jeffrey Gantz, Penguin Classic, 1982*

The Celtic people who told the stirring tales in this book lived at about the same time as the ancient Mesopotamians, Egyptians, and Hebrews.

Related American Literature: The Conquest of New Spain

Bernal Díaz del Castillo, *translated by J. M. Cohen, Penguin Classic, 1963*

The author provides a vivid firsthand account of how the Spaniard Hernán Cortés conquered the Aztecs, one of the ancient peoples of Mexico.

Unit Two

A Tiger for Malgudi

R. K. Narayan, *Penguin Classic, 1994*

This novel by one of India's most celebrated authors features an unusual first-person narrator: a tiger. Set in the fictional South-Indian territory of Malgudi, *A Tiger for Malgudi* traces the life of a tiger named Raja from his days as a cub in the jungle to his misery as a circus animal to his eventual happiness in the care of a kind master. As the old tiger—now living in a zoo—reflects on his life and his experiences, readers gain a glimpse into Indian culture and even learn some Hindu philosophy. Raja also points out how absurd some human behaviors can seem when viewed through the eyes of a wild animal.

The Penguin Gandhi Reader

Mohandas K. Gandhi, *Penguin, 1995*

Gandhi was one of the most important political leaders of the twentieth century. His method of uncompromising yet peaceful protest helped gain India's freedom from British rule and inspired the world. This reader presents many of Gandhi's most important writings. The book is divided into eight sections, focusing on the following themes that occupied Gandhi's work and life: his

To the Teacher:

Because great literature reflects all of life's realities, classroom discussions of literature can raise sensitive or controversial issues. Before you recommend literature to your students, consider the values and sensitivities of the community in which you teach as well as the sophistication of your students. Preview any literature before recommending it to your students. The notes below offer guidance on specific titles.

Unit 1

The Bible's Greatest Stories
Paul Roche, translator and reteller

Sensitive Issues: These tales include depictions of violence, portray subjugated women and peoples, and refer to rape and incest. To prepare students to read these tales, discuss their setting and didactic purpose.

Tales of Ancient Egypt
Selected and retold by Roger Lancelyn Green

Sensitive Issues: These tales include brief depictions of violence and magic, as well as references to drunkenness and to wine and beer. Religiously ordained marriages between brother and sister gods or rulers are also mentioned.

The Epic of Gilgamesh
Anonymous, translated by N. K. Sandars

Sensitive Issues: Battle scenes are graphically described, and, in one case, men attempt to appease Gilgamesh by "giving" him a woman.

Related British Literature:
Early Irish Myths and Sagas
Anonymous, translated by Jeffrey Gantz

These myths and sagas include graphic descriptions of violence. They also include references to sexual relations, intimate body parts, pregnancy, incest, and drunkenness, as well as to the magic of druids.

Related American Literature:
The Conquest of New Spain
Bernal Díaz del Castillo, translated by J. M. Cohen

Sensitive Issues: This classic record of cultural encounter includes accounts of human sacrifice and

continued

continued from right column

ritual cannibalism, as well as violence, torture, slavery, and prejudice. To prepare students to understand these elements, discuss the historical and cultural context.

Unit 2

A Tiger for Malgudi
R. K. Narayan

Sensitive Issues: The story's narrator, a tiger, kills animals and, in one case, a human. The book also makes references to smoking, guns, cruelty to animals, and drinking. A major character leaves his wife and children.

The Penguin Gandhi Reader
Mohandas K. Gandhi

Sensitive Issues: Gandhi expresses a belief in the "intrinsic superiority of India to the West." He also comments on gambling, the use of alcohol and tobacco, and the subjugation of women.

Unit 2 *(continued)*

The Ramayana
R. K. Narayan, editor and reteller

Sensitive Issues: The *Ramayana* contains sexual references and several scenes of graphic violence, as well as references to suicide. To prepare students, discuss ways in which epics map a culture's experience from the depths to the heights.

Related British Literature:
Kim
Rudyard Kipling

Sensitive Issues: This panoramic novel of India under British rule includes occasional stereotyping generalizations about Asian peoples, as well as references to magic and prostitution. There are allusions to drink, drugs, and intoxication, and a hill woman attempts, unsuccessfully, to seduce Kim.

Related American Literature:
Why We Can't Wait
Martin Luther King, Jr.

Sensitive Issues: This work raises questions of racial oppression and historical responsibility that should be discussed with sensitivity. To prepare students, discuss the history of the civil rights movement.

Unit 3

Treason by the Book
Jonathan D. Spence

Sensitive Issues: This compelling narrative history contains references to torture, execution, drinking, abuse of women, and philosophies of racial or ethnic purity.

The Narrow Road to the Deep North
Matsuo Bashō, translated by Nobuyuki Yuasa

Sensitive Issues: Among the stories is the mention of "concubines" in a room next door. To prepare students to read, discuss Zen Buddhism and its didactic use of parables.

The Analects
Confucius, translated by Arthur Waley

Sensitive Issues: This founding work of one of the world's great schools of thought refers to Confucius' birth as the result of an "illicit union."

Related British Literature:
Across the Nightingale Floor
Lian Hearn

Sensitive Issues: Set in a world of

continued

continued from left column

feudal warlords, this text includes descriptions of violence and references to the occult.

Related American Literature:
The Joy Luck Club
Amy Tan

Sensitive Issues: This novel describes the hardships of war, including death and the abandonment of children. Tan also refers to divorce.

Unit 4

The Three Theban Plays
Sophocles, translated by Robert Fagles

Sensitive Issues: Sophocles' great tragedies tell of incest and suicide. They include references to torture as well as expressions of sexist attitudes. The introduction to *Oedipus the King* quotes Sigmund Freud on the Oedipus Complex. To prepare students to read the plays, discuss the way tragedy traces the boundaries of our common experience through extreme events and actions.

Unit Two (continued)

criticism of modern culture and rejection of materialism; the principles of *swaraj* (independence, or self-rule) and *swadeshi* (responsibility to one's immediate community); the doctrine of nonviolence; his participation in mass protest movements; his opinions about the role of women; his arguments against the Indian caste system; his thoughts on economic and social systems; his belief in religious tolerance; his commitment to a united India; and his struggle for Indian independence.

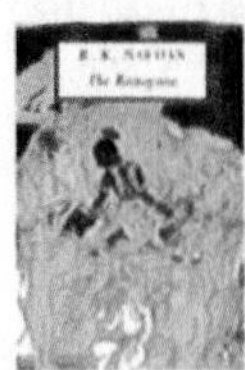

The Ramayana
R. K. Narayan, editor and reteller, *Penguin Classic, 1972*

If sampling a portion of this work has given you an appetite for more, treat yourself to the complete book.

Related British Literature:
Kim
Rudyard Kipling, *Penguin Classic, 1987*

This novel by a Nobel Prize-winning British author tells how a young boy learns the deadly game of espionage in nineteenth-century India.

Related American Literature:
Why We Can't Wait
Martin Luther King, Jr., *Signet Classic, 2000*

Dr. King describes his use of nonviolent action, a principle he learned from the life and writings of Indian leader Mohandas K. Gandhi.

Unit Three

Treason by the Book
Jonathan D. Spence, *Penguin, 2002*

Part history and part mystery, *Treason by the Book* details a plot to overthrow Yongzheng, the Manchu emperor of China. This true story begins in 1728 when a treasonous letter addressed to the emperor is passed to one of the emperor's generals. After reading the letter, Yongzheng launches a massive investigation to find its author. When the guilty party is identified, Yongzheng does something quite unexpected. Inspired by Confucian ideas about leading by example, the emperor decides to engage in a public written dialogue with the letter's author in order to disprove his accusations and stem the tide of rebellion. *Treason by the Book* is a study not only of imperial power but also of the power of the written word.

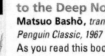

The Narrow Road to the Deep North
Matsuo Bashō, *translated by Nobuyuki Yuasa, Penguin Classic, 1967*

As you read this book, you will be traveling through seventeenth-century Japan with an adventurous and sensitive companion, the poet Matsuo Bashō. He is more concerned with the spiritual benefits of his journey than he is with material comforts. Being poor, he cannot pay much for lodgings, but he is always ready to "pay" with a poem for the beauty he sees. For example, on finding a famous ruined castle, he sits on his hat, weeps, and writes, "A thicket of summer grass / Is all that remains / Of the dreams and ambitions / Of ancient warriors." Share sights and insights with this poet who, three hundred years before the highway adventures of America's beatniks, knew how to travel with an empty wallet and a full spirit.

The Analects
Confucius, *translated by Arthur Waley, Penguin Classic, 1979*

If sampling a portion of this work has given you an appetite for more, treat yourself to the complete book.

Related British Literature:
Across the Nightingale Floor
Lian Hearn, *Riverhead, 2003*

This novel by a British author tells about an orphan boy and his magical destiny in medieval Japan.

Related American Literature:
The Joy Luck Club
Amy Tan, *Putnam, 1989*

In her celebrated first novel, Amy Tan weaves together the stories of Chinese Americans living in San Francisco.

Unit Four

The Three Theban Plays
Sophocles, *translated by Robert Fagles, Penguin Classic, 1984*

This collection contains Sophocles' three tragedies about the royal house of Thebes. In addition to *Oedipus the King*, which appears in Unit 4 of *Prentice Hall World Masterpieces*, the collection includes the plays *Oedipus at Colonus* and *Antigone*. *Oedipus at Colonus* focuses on the end of Oedipus' life, following his downfall in *Oedipus the*

King. In *Antigone*, Oedipus is gone, but his legacy remains. His daughter, Antigone, refuses to compromise her ideals and submit to the orders of Creon, the new king of Thebes. Like her father, Antigone is strong-willed, and like him, she meets a tragic fate. These three plays are considered to be not only the greatest works by Sophocles but also the finest examples of Greek tragedy. They are ably translated by Robert Fagles, who also translated Homer's *Iliad* and *Odyssey*.

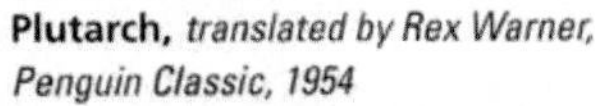

The Fall of the Roman Republic (Six Lives)

Plutarch, *translated by Rex Warner, Penguin Classic, 1954*

The Roman historian Plutarch was especially interested in the biographies of great men and the moral lessons that could be drawn from them. In this volume, he narrates the lives of six prominent Romans involved in the violence leading to the fall of the Roman republic: Marius, Sulla, Crassus, Pompey, Caesar, and Cicero. Plutarch had a flair for capturing vivid details. That is why Shakespeare relied so heavily on *Plutarch's Lives* while writing plays like *Julius Caesar*. Note, for example, how dramatically Plutarch describes the assassination of Julius Caesar: "when he [Caesar] saw that Brutus had drawn his dagger, he covered his head with his toga and sank down to the ground." Opening this book is like pulling aside the curtains of a stage and viewing the most dramatic events of Roman history.

The Iliad

Homer, *translated by Robert Fagles, Penguin Classic, 1991*

If sampling a portion of this work has given you an appetite for more, treat yourself to the complete book.

The Aeneid

Virgil, *translated by Patric Dickinson, Signet Classic, 2002*

If sampling a portion of this work has given you an appetite for more, treat yourself to the complete book.

Related British Literature: The Extraordinary Voyage of Pytheas the Greek

Barry Cunliffe

A British archaeologist tells the true story of a Greek who, more than 2,000 years ago, made a dangerous sea voyage all the way to Iceland.

Related American Literature: The Federalist Papers

Alexander Hamilton et al., *Penguin Classic, 1987*

Looking to the classical world as their model, three of America's greatest founding fathers set forth the principles of government that still guide us today.

Unit Five

The Divine Comedy: Paradiso

Dante Alighieri, *translated by Mark Musa, Penguin Classic, 1986*

The *Paradiso* is the last of the three volumes that form *The Divine Comedy*, Dante's allegory of his journey through the afterlife. In the *Inferno*, Dante travels through Hell under the guidance of the Roman poet Virgil. In the *Purgatorio*, Dante and Virgil ascend the Mount of Purgatory. At the mountain's summit, Virgil departs, and Beatrice, a woman Dante had loved before her death, becomes his guide. The *Paradiso* begins as Dante soars into Heaven with Beatrice. Like Hell and Purgatory, Dante's Heaven has its own geography and order. The lowest level is the Moon, followed by Mercury, Venus, the Sun, Mars, Jupiter, Saturn, the Stars, and the *Primum Mobile*—the source of all time and motion. The highest level is the Empyrean, the dwelling place of God. Dante ascends to the Empyrean, where he gazes upon the radiance of God, is overwhelmed, and later cannot remember what he saw.

Egil's Saga

Snorri Sturluson, *translated by Hermann Pálsson and Paul Edwards, Penguin Classic, 1977*

Composed in the thirteenth century by a master storyteller, this tale is set in tenth-century Iceland, Norway, and England. Egil, the hero of the book, is a formidable man, even by the standards of his dangerous Viking world. A brooding outsider, he has the courage to defy kings and to battle with the crazed warriors known as berserkers. Yet behind his impressive appearance—"wide forehead, bushy eyebrows . . . great broad beard . . . far above normal height but well-proportioned . . . bald . . ."—is an equally impressive mind. Egil is loyal and intelligent, a poet who can lament the death of his son in eloquent verse. When this fierce and complex man dies shortly before Iceland is converted to Christianity, his death seems to mark the passing of an era.

The Fall of the Roman Republic (Six Lives)

Plutarch, translated by Rex Warner

Sensitive Issues: Throughout these classic biographies, a source for Shakespeare and later writers, Plutarch describes battle and death. The text also refers to sexual relationships, including incest and homosexuality, and to suicide. There are suggestions of anti-Semitic attitudes. To prepare students to read this work, discuss Roman attitudes toward war and the state.

The Iliad

Homer, translated by Robert Fagles

Sensitive Issues: Homer describes his heroes' lives with even-handed realism, from their noble self-sacrifice to child-like sulks and the brutal acts that arise in warfare. To prepare students to the read the work, discuss the direct nature of epic style.

The Aeneid

Virgil, translated by Patric Dickinson

Sensitive Issues: Violence, occasionally graphic, is depicted throughout Virgil's *Aeneid*. There are also occasional references to suicide, rape, and drinking, as well as a reference to Romans as "the master-race." To prepare students to read this work, discuss Virgil's use of Homeric models and the relationship of the work to the ideology of the Roman Empire.

Related British Literature:
The Extraordinary Voyage of Pytheas the Greek

Barry Cunliffe

Sensitive Issues: Most issues arise in the context of anthropological discussions of the peoples that Pytheas probably encountered on his journey. These issues include a reference to wife-sharing among male family members, cannibalism, and the consumption of beer and wine.

Related American Literature:
The Federalist Papers

Alexander Hamilton, John Jay, and James Madison

Sensitive Issues: The framers of the Constitution did not include African Americans, Native Americans, or women in their concept of self government. To prepare students to read this work, discuss the subsequent evolution of American democracy.

continued

continued from right column

Unit 5

The Divine Comedy: Paradiso

Dante Alighieri, translated by Mark Musa

Sensitive Issues: On his visionary pilgrimage, Dante repeats an anti-Semitic belief, common in his day, that the Jews were responsible for the crucifixion of Jesus. In addition, there is a mention of the rape of the Sabine women, as well as references to suicide. To prepare students to read Dante's epic, discuss the medieval Christian traditions in which it is rooted.

Egil's Saga

Snorri Sturluson, translated by Hermann Pálsson and Paul Edwards

Sensitive Issues: Because this Norse tale grows out of a male-oriented, warrior culture, there are frequent depictions of violence and drunkenness, allusions to slavery and the mistreatment of women, and, in one instance, frank and direct language regarding one character's diminished sexual powers. To prepare students, discuss the values of warrior cultures.

Unit Five (continued)

The Nibelungenlied

Anonymous, *translated by A. T. Hatto, Penguin Classic, 1965*

If sampling a portion of this work has given you an appetite for more, treat yourself to the complete book.

The Song of Roland

Anonymous, *translated by Glyn S. Burgess, Penguin Classic, 1990*

If sampling a portion of this work has given you an appetite for more, treat yourself to the complete book.

Related British Literature:

The Canterbury Tales

Geoffrey Chaucer, *translated by Nevill Coghill, Penguin Classic, 2003*

In this array of storytellers and their rhymed stories, a great poet portrays the many-sided life of medieval England.

Related American Literature:

A Connecticut Yankee in King Arthur's Court

Mark Twain, *Signet Classic, 1963*

Making a fictional journey backward in time, America's greatest humorist casts a satirical but affectionate eye on the doings of King Arthur's court.

Unit Six

The Prince

Niccolò Machiavelli, *translated by George Bull, Penguin Classic, 2003*

In *The Prince,* a book about statecraft, Italian Renaissance author Machiavelli stresses the degree to which his views of political morality differ from those of previous writers. Where other theorists discuss how rulers ought to act, Machiavelli says that he deals with how rulers do act. Where others say that public deeds should reflect private morality, Machiavelli insists that personal morality has no place in politics. Rulers do not survive by their goodness but by their strength, cunning, and ability. Machiavelli's success can be measured by the enduring appeal of his work and by the continued use of his name as an adjective to denote craftiness and deceit: *Machiavellian.*

Tartuffe and Other Plays

Jean-Baptiste Molière, *translated by Donald M. Frame, Signet Classic, 1960*

In Molière's comedy *Tartuffe,* religiously devout but gullible Orgon opens his home to a stranger—Tartuffe—who poses as a pious, generous humanitarian. Unbeknownst to Orgon, however, Tartuffe is a con artist and hypocrite, a trickster who is both the creator and victim of schemes and lies that draw Orgon's seventeenth-century household into riotous chaos. Along with *Tartuffe,* this edition includes additional Molière comedies such as *The Ridiculous Précieuses* and *School for Husbands.* In general, these plays feature such character types as the hypocrite, the misanthrope, and the hypochondriac, all of whom serve to expose the absurdities of the playwright's society.

Candide

François Voltaire, *translated by John Butt, Penguin Classic, 1950*

If sampling a portion of this work has given you an appetite for more, treat yourself to the complete book.

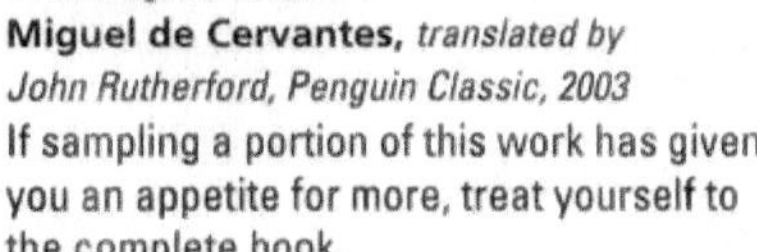

Don Quixote

Miguel de Cervantes, *translated by John Rutherford, Penguin Classic, 2003*

If sampling a portion of this work has given you an appetite for more, treat yourself to the complete book.

Related British Literature:

The Tempest

William Shakespeare, *Pearson Prentice Hall, 2000*

In his final play, England's greatest author says farewell to the theater and explores Renaissance ideas concerning savagery and civilization.

Related American Literature:

The Falcon

John Tanner, *Penguin, 2003*

The author was captured as a boy by Ojibwa Indians, and his autobiography is the fascinating story of the encounter between white and Indian cultures.

Unit 5 *(continued)*

The Nibelungenlied
Anonymous, translated by A. T. Hatto

Sensitive Issues: This epic includes descriptions of the hero Siegfried's physical coercion and sexual conquest of Brunhild and references to lovemaking, couched in mild, nonexplicit language. Kriemhild's ultimate revenge for Siegfried's death leads to numerous bloody acts.

The Song of Roland
translated by Glyn S. Burgess

Sensitive Issues: This epic poem includes scenes of bloody violence and death. In addition, the poem depicts non-Christians negatively. To prepare students, discuss with them the world view of medieval Europe.

Related British Literature:

The Canterbury Tales
Geoffrey Chaucer, translated by Nevill Coghill

Sensitive Issues: Chaucer satirizes the society of his day; no community—religious or lay—is left untargeted. In addition, these tales contain murder and other violence, rape, family betrayals, and clergy who break their vows.

Related American Literature:

A Connecticut Yankee in King Arthur's Court
Mark Twain

Sensitive Issues: This novel contains strong criticism of organized religion in general and the Roman Catholic Church in particular.

Unit 6

The Prince
Niccolò Machiavelli, translated by George Bull

Sensitive Issues: None

Tartuffe and Other Plays
Jean-Baptiste Molière, translated by Donald M. Frame

Sensitive Issues: Molière's play attacks the abuse of religious piety by a confidence man. To prepare students to read, discuss the use of satire to expose hypocrisy.

Candide
Voltaire, translated by John Butt

Sensitive Issues: This great satire of human philosophy and foibles contains lighthearted references to violence, sexual acts, drunkenness, and slavery and refers to numerous cultures as primitive or barbarous.

continued

continued from left column

Don Quixote
Miguel de Cervantes, translated by John Rutherford

Sensitive Issues: Sensitive issues include ethnic labels, references to sexual acts, and the poor treatment of women.

Related British Literature:

The Tempest
William Shakespeare

Sensitive Issues: Possible sensitive issues include occasional bawdiness and references to drinking. The drunkard Trinculo introduces the monster Caliban to wine.

Related American Literature:

The Falcon
John Tanner

Sensitive Issues: The writer's difficult and dangerous life includes the constant threat of hunger and violence. Polygamy, magical totems, and the brutal treatment of women, children, and animals are part of the book's cultural landscape.

Related American Literature:
Galileo's Daughter
Dava Sobel, *Penguin, 2000*
In this biography of a great scientist's daughter, American author Dava Sobel explores religion, science, and family relations during the Renaissance.

Unit Seven

The Hunchback of Notre Dame

Victor Hugo, *translated by Walter J. Cobb, Signet Classic, 2001*

This novel is set in medieval Paris in the shadow of the majestic Notre-Dame cathedral. Its main characters are Quasimodo, an orphaned hunchback who serves as the cathedral bell-ringer; Claude Frollo, the priest who has adopted Quasimodo; and Esmerelda, the gypsy dancer to whom Frollo is desperately attracted. The story, which begins with Quasimodo being shamefully crowned the Pope of Fools by the Parisian mob, is a tragic tale of love, loyalty, and betrayal. It is filled with unforgettable images, such as the description of a mob's assault on Notre-Dame as "a layer of living monsters crawling over the stone monsters of the façade." The story also vividly conveys two of Hugo's most important Romantic beliefs—the essential value of the outcast or outsider and the close relationship between beauty and ugliness.

Diary of a Madman and Other Stories

Nikolai Gogol, *translated by Ronald Wilks, Penguin Classic, 1973*

Trudging through the mists of nineteenth-century St. Petersburg, mumbling to themselves as they go, the harried nobodies of Nikolai Gogol's stories reflect the new sorrow of the modern world—the life of the anonymous. Gogol's faceless clerks and petty bureaucrats battle their own insignificance. His genius is to make their struggle against erasure both deeply sad and outrageously funny. "The Nose" is the grotesque tale of a man who must pursue through the city his own nose, grown into a haughty official. In "The Overcoat," a poor clerk is broken and dies after he is robbed of his expensive new overcoat. In "The Diary of a Madman," an obscure bureaucrat descends into comical madness, but his delusion rescues him from insignificance—he realizes that he is the king of Spain! In these absurd yet moving tales, society's forgettable "little people" become literature's unforgettable characters.

Faust, Part One
Faust, Part Two

Johann Wolfgang von Goethe, *translated by Philip Wayne, Penguin Classic, 1950 and 1960*

If sampling a portion of this work has given you an appetite for more, treat yourself to the complete book.

Related British Literature:
Wuthering Heights
Emily Brontë, *Pearson Prentice Hall, 2000*
Set in the wild moors of northern England, this Romantic novel tells about the love between Catherine Earnshaw and the mysterious outsider Heathcliff.

Related American Literature:
The Science Fiction of Edgar Allan Poe
Edgar Allan Poe, *Penguin Classic, 1976*
These tales of time travel, hypnotism, and electromagnetism reveal that Poe was not only the inventor of the detective story, but also a pioneer of science fiction.

Unit Eight

Siddhartha

Herman Hesse, *translated by Joachim Neugroschel, Penguin Classic, 2002*

Set in India during the sixth century B.C., this novel tells the tale of the handsome and gifted Siddhartha, whose search for wisdom shapes his life. With his friend Govinda, Siddhartha joins a band of ascetics, called *samanas*, who live in poverty and spend their days in meditation. After they pass several years with the samanas, word of a great teacher—the Buddha—reaches Siddhartha and Govinda. The friends go in search of the Buddha. When they find him, Govinda chooses to follow the Buddha, but Siddhartha departs. Alone, Siddhartha discovers the beauty of the world. He settles in a town, becomes involved with a woman, and works in business. Over the course of many years, he gains wealth, but his success soon turns to decadence. Finally, he abandons his town life and resumes his search for wisdom. Read this book to learn whether he finally discovers the truth he has sought.

Related American Literature:
Galileo's Daughter
Dava Sobel

Sensitive Issues: This book makes frequent references to religious rituals and includes references to conflicts between science and religion. Galileo's illegitimate children are also discussed. To prepare students to read this work, discuss the cultural context of Galileo's thought.

Unit 7

The Hunchback of Notre Dame
Victor Hugo, translated by Walter J. Cobb

Sensitive Issues: Hugo's novel is a triumph of melodrama and of the romanticization of history. It includes accusations of witchcraft, defamation of gypsies, suicide, murder, physical torture, and inhumane treatment of the mentally ill.

Diary of a Madman and Other Stories
Nikolai Gogol, translated by Ronald Wilks

Sensitive Issues: These tales include a few remarks reflecting anti-Semitism, and the brutalization of Jews by soldiers is referred to once. Incidental references are made to liquor, drunkenness, tobacco, card-playing, and gambling. Mild expletives and references to the Devil appear; the clerk in "The Overcoat" reappears as a ghost.

Faust, Parts One and Two
Johann Wolfgang von Goethe, translated by Philip Wayne

Sensitive Issues: Faust's deep questions about life lead him to bargain with the devil; this work refers frequently to Hell and damnation and includes derogatory comments about Christians. Violent events are depicted, and there is some insensitive labeling of people with disabilities.

Related British Literature:
Wuthering Heights
Emily Brontë

Sensitive Issues: Heathcliff's behavior is at times violent, and the fact that he is adopted contributes to his uncertain status. This work includes references to ghosts and to the digging up of Catherine's coffin. To prepare students to read this work, discuss the ways groups depict the Outsider, noting the Romantic sympathy with the role.

continued

continued from right column

Related American Literature:
The Science Fiction of Edgar Allan Poe
Edgar Allan Poe

Sensitive Issues: Poe is a master of horror and speculative fiction, and his stories contain gruesome scenes, as well as philosophical discussions about death and God. Other sensitive issues include references to mesmerism, suicide, and controlled substances. To prepare students, discuss reasons writers and readers are attracted to the "unimaginable"— the horrible, grotesque, or degraded.

Unit 8

Siddhartha
Herman Hesse, translated by Joachim Neugroschel

Sensitive Issues: Siddhartha's quest poses the problem of freedom from earthly desire, and references to sexuality feature significantly. There are also references to gambling and to pregnancy out of wedlock, and Siddhartha meets a courtesan. He briefly contemplates suicide. To prepare students to read this work, discuss Buddhist concepts of the wheel of life.

Unit 8 *(continued)*

Cyrano de Bergerac
Edmond Rostand, translated by Lowell Bair

Sensitive Issues: Rostand's famous cavalier and his fellows live high, and the play includes card playing, drinking, and drunkenness. The discussion of Cyrano's ugliness—his nose is enormous—should be handled with sensitivity.

The Transformation and Other Stories
Franz Kafka, translated by Malcolm Pasley

Sensitive Issues: Some stories contain minor references to drinking, smoking, and sexual encounters. Other tales, however, describe scenes of death or dying in graphic or emotionally wrenching detail.

Related British Literature:
A Portrait of the Artist as a Young Man
James Joyce

Sensitive Issues: Joyce's account of the formative experiences of an artist includes references to gambling, the consumption of alcohol, and promiscuity, and a description of the maltreatment of a child.

Related American Literature:
My Antonía
Willa Cather

Sensitive Issues: Cather's exploration of character among the pioneers of the West features racial attitudes, evinced in remarks about "foreigners," racial epithets, and stereotyping. Under the stress of pioneer life, Antonía's father commits suicide.

Unit 9

Things Fall Apart
Chinua Achebe

Sensitive Issues: Achebe's novel of the conflict in Nigeria between European and African cultures features polygamy, war-time violence, alcohol, and overt sexual references.

One Day in the Life of Ivan Denisovich
Alexander Solzhenitsyn, translated by Ralph Parker

Sensitive Issues: Solzhenitsyn graphically portrays life at a Soviet labor camp in the 1950s, including the inhumane, unsanitary conditions there. The prisoners frequently mention tobacco and smoking, one of the few pleasures they have.

continued

Unit Eight (continued)

Cyrano de Bergerac
Edmond Rostand, *translated by Lowell Bair, Signet Classic, 2003*

This verse drama in five acts, performed in 1897 and published the following year, is set in seventeenth-century Paris. The action revolves around the noble, swashbuckling Cyrano, who, despite his many gifts, feels that no woman can ever love him because he has an enormous nose. Secretly in love with the lovely Roxane, Cyrano agrees to help his inarticulate rival, Christian, win her heart by allowing him to present as his own Cyrano's love poems, speeches, and letters. Cyrano's dramatic and beautifully written protestations of love included in letters from the battlefield reinforce Roxane's love for Christian and contribute to a romantic irony that continues to fascinate critics and audiences alike.

The Transformation and Other Stories
Franz Kafka, *translated by Malcolm Pasley, Penguin Classic, 1995*

If sampling a portion of this work has given you an appetite for more, treat yourself to the complete book.

Related British Literature:
A Portrait of the Artist as a Young Man
James Joyce, *Signet Classic, 1991*

In a novel closely based on his own life, Joyce describes a young man's coming of age in Catholic Ireland and his rebellion against conventional social values.

Related American Literature:
My Ántonia
Willa Cather, *Pearson Prentice Hall, 2000*

Drawing from her girlhood experiences on a Nebraska ranch, Cather tells the fictional story of a young woman growing up on the prairie in the late 1800s.

Unit Nine

Things Fall Apart
Chinua Achebe, *Anchor Books, 1959*

Set in Umofia, a small Ibo village in Nigeria, this novel explores the destructive effects of European values on African culture. The story centers on Okonkwo, one of the most honored men of his village. Okonkwo is wealthy, industrious, and brave, but he also has a violent temper and is overly concerned about his status. When he accidentally kills a member of his tribe, he is sent into exile for seven years. During Okonkwo's exile, a Christian missionary arrives in Umofia and converts many of the Ibo. This development is set within the context of an escalating British presence, which includes a new government and the threat of vast military might. Under these pressures, traditional Ibo society simply collapses. When Okonkwo returns to Umofia, he tries to fight the British presence, a decision that leads to disastrous consequences.

One Day in the Life of Ivan Denisovich
Alexander Solzhenitsyn, *translated by Ralph Parker, Signet Classic, 1998*

This powerful work of fiction exposes the brutality and inhumanity of the former Soviet Union's political oppression. Set in a Siberian forced-labor prison camp, the novel details the events of an ordinary day in January 1951 as seen through the eyes of a political prisoner, Ivan Denisovich Shukhov. The prisoner, wrongfully convicted of treason during World War II and sentenced to ten years in the labor camp, manages to maintain his humanity and dignity despite the camp's relentless dehumanization. His strength and his determination to survive are moving tributes to the human spirit.

Night
Elie Wiesel, *translated by Stella Rodway, Pearson Prentice Hall, 2000*

If sampling a portion of this work has given you an appetite for more, treat yourself to the complete book.

Related British Literature:
Lord of the Flies
William Golding, *Perigee, 1987*

This novel about British schoolboys stranded on an island is both an adventure story and a parable about the nature of evil.

Related American Literature:
Something to Declare
Julia Alvarez, *Plume, 1999*

In this collection of amusing and insightful essays, Alvarez discusses her life as a Dominican immigrant in America and her struggles to become a writer.

continued from left column

Night
Elie Wiesel, translated by Stella Rodway

Sensitive Issues: Night, a Holocaust memoir in the form of a novel, deals with intrinsically disturbing subjects—the Holocaust and life in Nazi concentration camps. Suffering, death, and the moral degradation of inmates pervade the work.

Related British Literature:
Lord of the Flies
William Golding

Sensitive Issues: Golding's allegory for the forces of barbarity in human nature involves violence. Sexual imagery is used when the "beast"—a central symbol—is slaughtered.

Related American Literature:
Something to Declare
Julia Alvarez

Sensitive Issues: This work includes accounts of racial and gender stereotyping. It also refers to the use of illegal substances.

abases (ā bās′ əz) *v.* lowers, brings down
abhor (ab hôr′) *v.* feel disgust for; hate
accolade (ak′ ə lād′) *n.* anything done as a sign of praise or respect
accordance (ə kôrd′ 'ns) *n.* agreement
accrue (ə kro͞o′) *v.* come to as an advantage or a right
acute (ə kyo͞ot′) *adj.* sharp; intense
adjured (a joord′) *v.* ordered solemnly
adroit (ə droit′) *adj.* skillful
affably (af′ ə blē) *adv.* in a friendly manner
affidavit (af′ ə dā′ vit) *n.* legal document containing sworn testimony
affinity (ə fin′ i tē) *n.* natural liking
affliction (ə flik′ shən) *n.* something that causes pain or distress
altruistic (al′ tro͞o is′ tik) *adj.* selfless
ancestral (an ses′ trəl) *adj.* relating to the people from whom one is descended
anguish (aŋ′ gwish) *n.* great suffering
anguished (aŋ′ gwisht) *adj.* showing worry, grief, or pain
anoint (ə noint′) *v.* rub oil or ointment on
anticipate (an tis′ ə pāt) *v.* expect
antiquity (an tik′ wə tē) *n.* early history
appropriate (ə prō′ prē āt′) *v.* take for one's own use
assent (ə sent′) *n.* expression of agreement
assertions (ə sur′ shənz) *n.* claims
assimilate (ə sim′ ə lāt′) *v.* absorb; incorporate into a greater body
avail (ə vāl′) *n.* benefit; use
avenged (ə venjd′) *v.* took revenge on behalf of
avenger (ə venj′ er) *n.* one who takes revenge
awe (ô) *n.* feelings of fear and wonder
babel (bab′ əl) *n.* confusion of voices
bangle (baŋ′g'l) *n.* decorative bracelet
bashful (bash′ fəl) *adj.* shy
beneficent (be nef′ ə sənt) *adj.* kind; helpful
benevolent (bə nev′ ə lənt) *adj.* charitable
bereft (bē reft′) *adj.* deprived or robbed
beseeching (bē sēch′ iŋ) *adj.* pleading
bewildered (bi wil′ dərd) *adj.* puzzled; confused
bias (bī′ əs) *n.* prejudice; partiality
bland (bland) *adj.* mild
blaspheming (blas fēm′ iŋ) *adj.* irreverent
blasphemous (blas′ fə məs) *adj.* showing disrespect toward God or religious teachings
blight (blīt) *n.* destructive disease
bountiful (boun′ tə fəl) *adj.* abundant
brandished (bran′ dishd) *v.* waved or shook in a threatening manner
brazen (brā′ zən) *adj.* literally, of brass; shamelessly bold
brevity (brev′ ə tē) *n.* briefness
brusquely (brusk′ lē) *adv.* abruptly
buffeted (buf′ it id) *v.* struck sharply
calamity (kə lam′ ə tē) *n.* deep trouble
calculating (kal′ kyo͞o lāt iŋ) *adj.* shrewd
candor (kan′ dər) *n.* open honesty
caricature (kar′ i kə chər) *n.* imitation that is so distorted or inferior as to seem ridiculous
carnivorous (kär niv′ ə rəs) *adj.* meat-eating
cascade (kas kād′) *n.* small, steep waterfall
chasm (kaz′ əm) *n.* deep crack in Earth's surface
chastised (chas′ tīzd) *v.* punished
chastisements (chas′ tiz mənts) *n.* punishments
chide (chīd) *v.* scold
clemency (klem′ ən sē) *n.* mercy
clenched (klencht) *adj.* gripped firmly
commiserate (kə miz′ ər āt) *v.* share grief
compassionate (kəm pash′ ən it) *adj.* feeling or showing sympathy or pity
comprised (kəm prīzd′) *v.* included; consisted of
conflagration (kän′ flə grā′ shən) *n.* large, destructive fire
congealed (kən jēld′) *v.* thickened; solidified
conjectures (kən jek′ chərz) *n.* guesses
connoisseur (kän′ ə sur′) *n.* person with expert judgment and taste
connotations (kän′ ə tā′ shənz) *n.* ideas associated with a word
considerably (kən sid′ er ə blē) *adv.* to a great degree
consolation (kän′ sə lā′ shən) *n.* comfort; something that eases sadness
consonant (kän′ sə nənt) *adj.* in agreement
constitution (kän stə to͞o′ shən) *n.* structure or make-up of a person or thing
consult (kən sult′) *v.* seek advice from
consummation (kän′ sə mā′ shən) *n.* state of supreme perfection
contemplation (kän′ təm plā′ shən) *n.* thoughtful inspection or study
contemptuously (kən temp′ cho͞o əs lē) *adv.* scornfully; disrespectfully
contention (kən ten′ shən) *n.* quarreling
contraband (kän′ trə band′) *n.* unlawful or forbidden goods
contrary (kän′ trer′ ē) *adj.* opposing
convalescent (kän′ və les′ 'nt) *n.* person who is recovering health after illness
convergent (kən vur′ jənt) *adj.* coming together at a point
corrupt (kə rupt′) *adj.* spoiled by sin or dishonesty; rotten
countenance (koun′ tə nəns) *n.* the look on a person's face
courtly (kôrt′ lē) *adj.* dignified; polite
covenant (kuv′ ə nənt) *n.* serious, binding agreement
crone (krōn) *n.* very old woman
cue (kyo͞o) *n.* prompt or reminder
culmination (kul′ mə nā′ shən) *n.* climax
debacle (di bäk′ əl) *n.* overwhelming failure or defeat
deference (def′ ər əns) *n.* respectful submission to the desires or opinions of another
deficiency (dē fish′ ən sē) *n.* shortage
degree (di grē′) *n.* step; stage; level
demarcation (dē′ mär kā′ shən) *n.* boundary
denounce (dē nouns′) *v.* accuse publicly
deportees (dē′ pôr tēz′) *n.* people forced by official order to leave a country
desecrating (des′ i krāt′ iŋ) *v.* treating as not sacred
despicable (dəs′ pi kə bəl) *adj.* deserving to be despised; contemptible
despond (di spänd′) *v.* lose
despondent (di spän′ dənt) *adj.* hopeless
despotism (des′ pət iz′ əm) *n.* system of government in which the ruler has absolute power
destitute (des′ tə to͞ot′) *adj.* extremely poor
dexterity (deks ter′ ə tē) *n.* skillfulness in the use of one's hands
diabolical (dī ə bäl′ ik əl) *adj.* wicked
discord (dis′ kôrd) *n.* dissension; conflict
discrimination (dis krim′ ə nā′ shən) *n.* show of partiality or prejudice
disdain (dis dān′) *n.* strong dislike
dispatch (di spach′) *v.* kill
dispel (di spel′) *v.* cause to vanish
dispersed (di spurst′) *adj.* scattered
disposed (di spōzd′) *adj.* tending toward
disreputable (dis rep′ yoo tə bəl) *adj.* not fit to be seen or approved
dissipation (dis′ ə pā′ shən) *n.* wasteful or immoral behavior; overindulgence
distinguishing (di stiŋ′ gwish iŋ) *adj.* serving to mark as separate or different
divergent (də vur′ jənt) *adj.* differing from each other
divinations (div′ ə nā′ shənz) *n.* divine predictions
dominion (də min′ yən) *n.* area of rule
dregs (dregz) *n.* last, most undesirable parts
drudgery (druj′ ər ē) *n.* hard, tiresome work
dubious (do͞o′ bē əs) *adj.* doubtful; suspect
duped (do͞opt) *v.* tricked; fooled
earnest (ur′ nist) *adj.* serious; not joking

ecstasy (ek´ stə sē) *n.* great joy

eddies (ed´ ēz) *n.* waters moving in circles against the main current

elated (ē lāt´ əd) *adj.* extremely happy; joyful

elixir (ē liks´ ir) *n.* magical potion that cures all ailments

eloquence (el´ ə kwəns) *n.* skillful speech

emigrate (em´ i grāt´) *v.* leave one place to live in another

endeavor (en dev´ ər) *n.* earnest attempt at achievement

endowed (en doud´) *v.* provided with

enmity (en´ mə tē) *n.* state of being enemies; antagonism; hostility

enraptured (en rap´ chərd) *adj.* completely delighted; spellbound

entrails (en´ trālz) *n.* intestines; guts

entwined (en twīnd´) *v.* twisted together

entwines (en twīnz´) *v.* twists together

enumerating (ē no͞o´ mər āt´ iŋ) *v.* counting; listing

environs (en vī ´ rənz) *n.* surrounding area

envoys (än´ voiz) *n.* messengers

epidemic (ep´ ə dem´ ik) *n.* rapidly and widely spreading disease

equable (ek´ wə bəl) *adj.* steady; uniform

esteemed (e stēmd´) *v.* valued; respected

estranged (e strānjd´) *adj.* isolated and unfriendly; alienated

euphemisms (yo͞o´ fə miz´ əmz) *n.* words or phrases that are less expressive or direct but are considered less offensive than others

evasions (i vā´ shənz) *n.* attempts to avoid duties or questions

exalted (ig zôlt´ əd) *adj.* lifted high because of dignity or honor

excruciating (eks kro͞o´ shē āt´ iŋ) *adj.* causing intense mental or bodily pain

exhorting (eg zôrt´ iŋ) *v.* urging

exhumed (eks hyo͞omd´) *v.* brought up from a grave; brought to light

expanse (ek spans´) *n.* very large open area

extirpate (ek´ stər pāt´) *v.* exterminate

extortions (eks tôr´ shənz) *n.* acts of obtaining money or something else through threats, violence, or misuse of authority

extravagant (ek strav´ ə gənt) *adj.* excessive; spending more than is needed

exuded (ig zo͞od´ id) *v.* discharged a liquid through the skin

exulting (eg zult´ iŋ) *v.* rejoicing

exults (eg zults´) *v.* rejoices greatly

fathom (fa*th*´ əm) *v.* probe the depths of; understand

fathomless (fa*th*´ əm les) *adj.* immeasurably deep

feigning (fān´ iŋ) *adj.* pretending

fervent (fʉr´ vənt) *adj.* intensely devoted

fervor (fʉr´ vər) *n.* strong feeling; zeal

fettered (fet´ ərd) *v.* shackled; chained

fetters (fet´ ərz) *n.* shackles; chains

flittering (flit´ ər iŋ) *adj.* flapping the wings rapidly; fluttering

flounders (floun´ dərz) *v.* struggles to move

flourish (flʉr´ ish) *n.* fanfare, as of trumpets

flourishes (flʉr´ ish ez) *v.* thrives

foretaste (fôr´ tāst´) *n.* slight experience or hint of something that is still to come

forlornly (fôr lôrn´ lē) *adv.* in a sad or lonely manner because of isolation or desertion

foundering (foun´ dər iŋ) *n.* stumbling; sinking; becoming stuck

fraternized (frat´ ər nīzd´) *v.* associated in a brotherly way; socialized

frivolous (friv´ ə ləs) *adj.* silly and light-minded; not sensible

frugality (fro͞o gal´ ə tē) *n.* thrift

frugally (fro͞o´ gə lē) *adv.* thriftily

fungus (fuŋ´ gəs) *n.* mildew; any of a group of plants lacking leaves and roots, including mushrooms, mold, and so on

furtive (fʉr´ tiv) *adj.* done in a sneaky way

furtively (fʉr´ tiv lē) *adv.* in a sneaky manner, as if to hinder observation

gaudy (gôd´ ē) *adj.* tastelessly showy

gaunt (gônt) *adj.* thin and bony; haggard

gawking (gôk´ iŋ) *v.* staring foolishly; gaping

gentry (jen´ trē) *n.* landowning families ranked just below the nobility

glaze (glāz) *v.* fit glass to a window; cover with a shiny finish

glean (glēn) *v.* collect grain left by reapers

glimmering (glim´ ər iŋ) *v.* flickering; giving a faint, unsteady light

glistens (glis´ ənz) *v.* shines or sparkles with reflected light

grafter (graft´ ər) *n.* someone who takes advantage of his or her position to gain money or property dishonestly

gratify (grat´ i fī´) *v.* please

grotesque (grō tesk´) *adj.* strangely distorted

guile (gīl) *n.* trickery

gyration (jī rā´ shən) *n.* circular motion

haggard ((hag´ ərd) *adj.* wasted; worn

harrowed (har´ ōd) *v.* distressed

harrowing (har´ ō iŋ) *adj.* frightening

hastened (hās´ ənd) *v.* hurried

hazards (haz´ ərdz) *n.* dangers

heralds (her´ əldz) *v.* announces; introduces

homage (häm´ ij) *n.* act of reverence

hordes (hôrdz) *n.* large moving crowds; tribes

hypocrite (hip´ ə krit) *n.* someone who pretends to be virtuous

illustrious (i lus´ trē əs) *adj.* outstanding

imminent (im´ ə nənt) *adj.* about to happen

immobile (i mō´ bəl) *adj.* not moving

immolation (im´ ə lā´ shən) *n.* offering or killing made as a sacrifice

immortality (im´ môr tal´ i tē) *n.* unending existence

imperceptibly (im´ pər sep´ tə blē) *adv.* without being noticed

imperishable (im per´ ish ə bəl) *adj.* indestructible

impertinence (im pʉrt´ ′n əns) *n.* insolence

impervious (im pʉr´ vē əs) *adj.* not affected by, or unable to be damaged

impetus (im´ pə təs) *n.* driving force

implore (im plôr´) *v.* beg

importunity (im´ pôr to͞on´ i tē) *n.* persistence

imposingly (im pō´ ziŋ lē) *adv.* making a strong, forceful impression

impracticable (im prak´ ti kə bəl) *adj.* not capable of being put into practice

impudence (im´ pyo͞o dəns) *n.* boldness

impulsive (im pul´ siv) *adj.* sudden and unthinking

incantation (in´ kan tā´ shən) *n.* chant

incantations (in´ kan tā´ shənz) *n.* chants sung as part of a ritual

incensed (in senst´) *adj.* very angry

incongruous (in käŋ´ gro͞o əs) *adj.* inconsistent; not fitting a situation

incredulous (in krej´ o͞o ləs) *adj.* disbelieving; doubtful; skeptical

incurred (in kʉrd´) *v.* brought about through one's own actions

indefinitely (in def´ ə nit lē) *adv.* without a specified limit

indictment (in dīt´ mənt) *n.* formal accusation

indignantly (in dig´ nənt lē) *adv.* in a way showing righteous anger or scorn

indiscreet (in di skrēt´) *adj.* unwise or not careful

induced (in do͞ost´) *v.* persuaded; caused

inexorably (in eks´ ə rə blē´) *adv.* without a chance of being stopped

infamous (in´ fə məs) *adj.* disgraceful

infatuation (in fach´ o͞o ā´ shən) *n.* foolish or shallow feelings of affection

infirmity (in fʉr´ mə tē) *n.* weakness; illness

ingenuity (in´ jə no͞o´ ə tē) *n.* inventiveness

innuendo (in´ yo͞o en´ dō) *n.* indirect remark or gesture that hints at something

insatiableness (in sā´ shə bəl nəs) *n.* the quality of being impossible to fill

insular (in´ sə lər) *adj.* having a narrow viewpoint

intimacy (in´ tə mə sē) *n.* familiarity; warmth

intolerable (in täl´ ər ə bəl) *adj.* unbearable

intrepid (in trep´ id) *adj.* brave; fearless

intricate (in´ tri kit) *adj.* complicated

intuition (in´ to͞o ish´ ən) *n.* instinctive understanding

inverted (in vʉrt´ id) *adj.* upside down

invoke (in vōk´) *v.* summon; cause to appear

invoked (in vōkt´) *v.* called on for help

invokes (in vōks´) *v.* calls on

iridescent (ir´ ə des´ ənt) *adj.* showing rainbowlike shifts in color

jetty (jet´ ē) *n.* wall or barrier built into a body of water to protect a harbor

jubilant (jo͞o´ bə lənt) *adj.* extremely happy

ken (ken) *n.* range of understanding

labyrinths (lab´ ə rinths) *n.* structures with an intricate network of winding passages

laden (lād´ 'n) *adj.* carrying a heavy load

lamentation (lam´ ən tā´ shən) *n.* outward expression of grief; weeping; wailing

lamented (lə men´ tid) *v.* felt sorrow for

languishing (laŋ´ gwish iŋ) *v.* becoming weak

leaden (led´ 'n) *adj.* depressed; dispirited

liquidated (lik´ wi dāt´ id) *adj.* disposed of; ended; killed

loathsome (lōth´ səm) *adj.* detestable

loomed (lo͞omd) *v.* appeared in a large or threatening form

lucid (lo͞o´ sid) *adj.* clear; apparent

lustrous (lus´ trəs) *adj.* shining

malice (mal´ is) *n.* ill will; spite

malicious (mə lish´ əs) *adj.* intending harm

malignant (mə lig´ nənt) *adj.* very harmful

manifestations (man´ ə fes tā´ shənz) *n.* material forms

manifested (man´ ə fest´ id) *v.* proved or revealed

manifold (man´ ə fōld´) *adj.* many; various

marshals (mär´ shəlz) *v.* commands

meager (mē´ gər) *adj.* thin; lean

mediocre (mē´ dē ō´ kər) *adj.* inferior

mitigated (mit´ ə gāt´ id) *v.* eased

mobilized (mō´ bə lizd) *v.* prepared for action or battle

monotone (män´ ə tōn´) *n.* sound or song that repeats a single note

monotonously (mə nät´ 'n əs lē) *adv.* going on and on without variation

monotony (mə nät´ 'n ē) *n.* tedious sameness

morose (mə rōs´) *adj.* gloomy

munificence (myo͞o nif´ ə səns) *n.* great generosity

murmur (mʉr´ mər) *n.* low, indistinct, continuous sound

mutely (myo͞ot´ lē) *adv.* silently; without the capacity to speak

myriad (mir´ ē əd) *adj.* many; varied

myriads (mir´ ē ədz) *n.* great numbers of persons or things

naturalistic (nach´ ər ə lis´ tik) *adj.* faithful to nature, or in imitation of what is natural

navigated (nav´ i gāt´ əd) *v.* piloted; steered a boat

nimble (nim´ bəl) *adj.* able to move quickly and lightly; agile

nocturnal (näk tʉr´ nəl) *adj.* relating to or occurring during the night

nonchalantly (nän´ shə länt´ lē) *adv.* in a casually indifferent manner

notions (nō´ shənz) *n.* ideas

oblique (ə blēk´) *adj.* not straightforward

obsequiously (əb sē´ kwē əs lē) *adv.* in a manner that shows a willingness to serve

obsessed (əb sest´) *adj.* greatly preoccupied

obsolete (äb´ sə lēt´) *adj.* no longer useful

obstinacy (äb´ stə nə sē) *n.* stubbornness

obstinate (äb´ stə nət) *adj.* stubborn

ominous (äm´ ə nəs) *adj.* hinting at bad things to come

omnipotent (äm nip´ ə tənt) *adj.* having unlimited power or authority

opaque (ō pāk´) *adj.* not shining; dull

oratory (ôr´ ə tôr´ ē) *n.* public speaking

painstakingly (pānz´ tāk iŋ lē) *adv.* using great diligence or care

pallid (pal´ id) *adj.* pale

palpable (pal´ pə bəl) *adj.* able to be touched, felt, or handled

paraphernalia (par´ ə fər nāl´ yə) *n.* articles of equipment

paternal (pə tʉr´ nəl) *adj.* like a father

pathos (pā´ thäs´) *n.* quality in something that evokes pity or compassion

perfunctorily (pər fuŋk´ tôr i lē) *adv.* indifferently; with little interest or care

perilous (per´ ə ləs) *adj.* dangerous

perjured (pʉr´ jərd) *adj.* purposely false

pervades (pər vādz´) *v.* spreads throughout

pestilence (pes´ tə ləns) *n.* plague

piety (pī´ ə tē) *n.* devotion to religious duties

pillaging (pil´ ij iŋ) *v.* plundering; looting

pitiable (pit´ ē ə bəl) *adj.* inspiring or deserving of pity (may be used scornfully)

placidly (plas´ id lē) *adv.* calmly

plaintive (plān´ tiv) *adj.* expressing sorrow

plateau (pla tō´) *n.* elevated tract of relatively level land

plight (plīt) *n.* sad or difficult situation

plunder (plun´ dər) *v.* rob by force in warfare

plundered (plun ´dərd) *adj.* stripped of possessions

poised (poizd) *adj.* balanced and steady, as though suspended

pomp (pämp) *n.* ceremonial splendor

portents (pôr´ tents) *n.* signs that suggest what is about to occur

posterity (päs ter´ ə tē) *n.* future generations of people

precepts (prē´ septs) *n.* rules of conduct

precipitous (prē sip´ ə təs) *adj.* steep like a precipice; sheer

presumed (prē zo͞omd´) *v.* supposed

primal (prī´ məl) *adj.* original; fundamental

primeval (prī mē´ vəl) *adj.* having to do with the earliest times

pristine (pris´ tēn´) *adj.* unspoiled

proclaim (prō klām´) *v.* declare

proclaiming (prō klām´ iŋ) *v.* declaring

prodigal (präd´ i gəl) *n.* person who spends money wastefully

prodigy (präd´ ə jē) *n.* person of very great ability

proffering (präf´ ər iŋ) *v.* offering

profusion (prə fyo͞o´ zhən) *n.* abundance

prone (prōn) *adj.* lying face downward

prophecy (präf´ ə sē) *n.* prediction

prophesied (präf´ ə sīd) *v.* predicted

prophet (präf´ ət) *n.* inspired person who speaks great truths or foretells the future

prophetic (prō fet´ ik) *adj.* having to do with predicting the future; giving a prediction

proprieties (prə prī´ ə tēz) *n.* conformities with what is fitting, suitable, or proper

prospective (prō spek´ tiv) *adj.* likely to be or to become in the future

prostrate (präs´ trāt) *adj.* lying face downward

protracted (prō trakt´ id) *adj.* extended

provincial (prō vin´ shəl) *adj.* lacking in sophistication

prowess (prou´ is) *n.* ability

putrefy (pyo͞o´ trə fī´) *v.* rot; decompose

putrid (pyo͞o´ trid) *adj.* rotten; stinking

rank (raŋk) *adj.* foul; odorous

reapers (rē´ pərz) *n.* those who gather a crop by cutting

rebuked (ri byo͞okt´) *v.* scolded sharply

reciprocity (res´ ə präs´ ə tē) *n.* mutual exchange

recompense (rek´ əm pens´) *n.* payment of what is owed; reward

rectify (rek´ tə fī) *v.* right

redeem (ri dēm´) *v.* buy back; fulfill a promise

reluctant (ri luk´ tənt) *adj.* showing hesitation; unwilling

renown (ri noun´) *n.* fame

repentance (ri pen´ təns) *n.* sorrow for wrongdoing; remorse

replete (ri plēt´) *adj.* well-filled; stocked

reposes (ri´ pōz´ əz) *v.* puts to rest

reprimand (rep´ rə mand´) *v.* chastise; blame

reprobate (rep´ rə bāt) *n.* scoundrel

resistant (ri zis´ tənt) *adj.* strong; firm

resolutely (rez´ ə lo͞ot´ lē) *adv.* in a determined way; without hesitation

resplendent (ri splen´ dənt) *adj.* brightly shining; dazzling

retorted (ri tôrt´ id) *v.* replied, especially in a sharp or challenging way

retribution (re´ trə byo͞o´ shən) *n.* punishment; revenge

revelation (rev´ ə lā´ shən) *n.* striking disclosure of something

reverberates (ri vʉr´ bə rātz´) *v.* echoes; sounds again

reverence (rev´ rəns) *v.* show great respect

ritual (rich´ o͞o əl) *n.* observance of prescribed rules

sacrosanct (sak′ rō saŋkt′) *adj.* sacred
sated (sāt′ id) *v.* completely satisfied
scorn (skôrn) *n.* contempt; open dislike or derision; *v.* reject
scruples (skro͞o′ pəlz) *n.* feelings of doubt over what is ethical
scurry (skur′ ē) *v.* run hastily; scamper
sediment (sed′ ə mənt) *n.* waste material that settles to the bottom of a liquid
self-abnegation (self ab′ ne gā′ shən) *n.* self-denial; lack of consideration for oneself or one's own interests
sensual (sen′ sho͞o əl) *adj.* pleasing to the senses
sequence (sē′ kwəns) *n.* order; succession
serene (sə rēn′) *adj.* clear; calm; peaceful
serenity (sə ren′ ə tē) *n.* peace; tranquillity
serpentine (sur′ pən tēn′) *adj.* snakelike
shards (shärdz) *n.* sharp fragments
sheaves (shēvz) *n.* bundles of cut stalks of grain
shrewdest (shro͞od′ est) *adj.* most cunning or clever
shroud (shroud) *n.* cloth sometimes used to wrap a corpse for burial
siege (sēj) *n.* the surrounding of a fortified place by an opposing force, such as an army
sinister (sin′ is tər) *adj.* wicked
skulks (skulks) *v.* lurks in a cowardly way
sleek (slēk) *adj.* smooth; glossy
sojourn (sō′ jurn) *n.* visit
solitary (säl′ ə ter′ ē) *adj.* lone; single; sole
solitude (säl′ ə to͞od′) *n.* seclusion; isolation
somber (säm′ bər) *adj.* dark; gloomy; serious
sordid (sôr′ did) *adj.* filthy; depressingly wretched
sovereign (säv′ rən) *adj.* chief, superior; highest; *n.* monarch or ruler
spendthrift (spend′ thrift′) *n.* person who spends money carelessly
squalid (skwäl′ id) *adj.* foul, especially as the result of neglect; wretched
squandered (skwän′ dərd) *v.* wasted
squandering (skwän′ dər iŋ) *v.* spending money wastefully
steadfast (sted′ fast′) *adj.* firm; not changing
stealthily (stel′ thə lē) *adv.* secretly
stems (stemz) *v.* stops or dams up (as a river)
stinted (stint′ id) *v.* limited to a certain quantity
stoically (stō′ iklē) *adv.* done with indifference to pain or pleasure
strains (strānz) *n.* passages of music; tunes
stupor (sto͞op′ ər) *n.* mental dullness
submerges (səb murj′ əz) *v.* covers over
submissive (sub mis′ iv) *adj.* yielding; giving in without resistance
subordinate (sə bôr′ də nit) *adj.* inferior; ranking under or below
subsided (səb sīd′ ed) *v.* settled; lessened
succor (suk′ ər) *n.* aid; relief
suffuses (sə fyo͞o′ zəz) *v.* overspreads; fills with a glow
summit (sum′ it) *n.* highest point
sumptuous (sump′ cho͞o əs) *adj.* lavish
superimposed (so͞o′ pər im pōzd′) *v.* placed on top of something else
supple (sup′ əl) *adj.* easily bent; flexible
sustained (sə stānd′) *v.* maintained; supported
taciturn (tas′ ə turn) *adj.* not given to talking; almost always silent
tactless (takt′ lis) *adj.* unskilled in dealing with people
talisman (tal′ is mən) *n.* charm or token; lucky object
tangible (tan′ jə bəl) *adj.* definite; objective
tardily (tär′ də lē) *adv.* late
teemed (tēmd) *v.* was full of; swarmed
tempest (tem′ pist) *n.* storm
tempo ((tem′ pō) *n.* rate of speed; pace
tenacity (tə nas′ ə tē) *n.* persistence
tenuous (ten′ yo͞o əs) *adj.* slender or fine, as a fiber
terminal (tur′ mə nəl) *adj.* fatal; ending in death
terminology (tur′mə näl′ ə jē) *n.* terms used in a specific discipline
throngs (thrôŋz) *n.* crowds
thwarted (thwôrt′ əd) *v.* hindered
timidity (tə mid′ ə tē) *n.* quality of being shy and easily frightened
tremulous (trem′ yo͞o ləs) *adj.* quivering; shaking; trembling
troop (tro͞op) *v.* march in a group
truncated (truŋ′ kāt əd) *adj.* cut short; with an angle cut off
tumult (to͞o′ mult′) *n.* commotion; confusion
unfettered (un fet′ ərd) *adj.* unrestrained
unhampered (un ham′ pərd) *adv.* freely; without interference
unmarred (un märd′) *adj.* unspoiled
unrestrained (un ri strānd′) *v.* not checked or controlled
vassal (vas′ əl) *n.* person who holds land under the feudal system, pledging loyalty to an overlord
vehemently (vē′ ə mənt lē) *adv.* intensely
veiled (vāld) *v.* covered or masked
vitality (vī tal′ ə tē) *n.* energy; life force
vivacity (vī vas′ ə tē) *n.* liveliness
void (void) *n.* empty space; total emptiness
vulgar (vul′ gər) *adj.* coarse; common
ward (wôrd) *v.* turn aside (something threatening)
well-being (wel bē′ iŋ) *n.* the state of being well; health, happiness, or prosperity
wharf (wôrf) *n.* structure built as a landing place for boats
whetted (wet′ id) *adj.* sharpened
wiles (wīlz) *n.* sly tricks
wizened (wiz′ ənd) *adj.* dried up and wrinkled due to age
writhes (rīthz) *v.* twists and turns the body, as in agony
zeal (zēl) *n.* ardor; fervor

LITERARY TERMS HANDBOOK

ALLEGORY An *allegory* is a literary work with two or more levels of meaning—a literal level and one or more symbolic levels. The events, settings, objects, or characters in an allegory—the literal level—stand for ideas or qualities, such as goodness, tyranny, salvation, and so on. Dante's *Divine Comedy* (p. 613) is an allegory written in the Middle Ages, when allegorical writing was common. Many works can be read allegorically as well as literally, requiring a reader's effort to match every element at the literal level with a corresponding element at the symbolic level. Allegories are also written in the form of parables.

See also Fable *and* Parable.

ALLITERATION *Alliteration* is the repetition of initial consonant sounds in accented syllables. Derek Walcott uses alliteration in these lines from "Omeros" (p. 1203):

> . . . higher than those hills / of infernal anthracite.

Especially in poetry, alliteration is used to emphasize and to link words, as well as to create musical sounds.

ALLUSION An *allusion* is a reference to a well-known person, place, event, literary work, or work of art. Writers often make allusions to the Bible, classical Greek and Roman myths, plays by Shakespeare, historical events, and other material with which they expect their readers to be familiar. Canto V of the *Inferno* by Dante (p. 629) contains an allusion to the story of Lancelot.

AMBIGUITY *Ambiguity* is the effect created when words suggest and support two or more divergent interpretations. Ambiguity may be used in literature to express experiences or truths that are complex or even contradictory.

See also Irony.

ANALOGY An *analogy* is an extended comparison of relationships. It is based on the idea or insight that the relationship between one pair of things is like the relationship between another pair. Unlike a metaphor, another form of comparison, an analogy involves an explicit comparison, often using the word *like* or *as*.

See also Metaphor *and* Simile.

ANAPEST *See* Meter.

ARCHETYPAL LITERARY ELEMENTS *Archetypal literary elements* are patterns in literature found around the world. For instance, the occurrence of events in threes is an archetypal element of fairy tales. *The Epic of Gilgamesh* (p. 15) presents an archetypal battle between the forces of good and the forces of evil. Certain character types, such as mysterious guides, are also archetypal elements of traditional stories. According to some critics, these elements express in symbolic form truths about the human mind.

ASSONANCE *Assonance* is the repetition of vowel sounds in stressed syllables containing dissimilar consonant sounds.

See also Consonance.

BALLAD A *ballad* is a song that tells a story, often about adventure or romance, or a poem imitating such a song. Most ballads are divided into four- or six-line stanzas, are rhymed, use simple language, and depict dramatic action. Many ballads employ a repeated refrain. Some use incremental repetition, in which the refrain is varied slightly each time it appears.

BLANK VERSE *Blank verse* is unrhymed poetry usually written in iambic pentameter (*see* Meter). Occasional variations in rhythm are introduced in blank verse to create emphasis, variety, and naturalness of sound. Because blank verse sounds much like ordinary spoken English, it is often used in drama, as by Shakespeare, and in poetry.

See also Meter.

CARPE DIEM A Latin phrase, *carpe diem* means "seize the day" or "make the most of passing time." Many great literary works have been written with the *carpe diem* theme.

CHARACTER A person (though not necessarily a human being) who takes part in the action of a literary work is known as a character. Characters can be classified in different ways. A character who plays an important role is called a *major character*. A character who does not is called a *minor character*. A character who plays the central role in a story is called the *protagonist*. A character who opposes the *protagonist* is called the *antagonist*. A *round character* has many aspects to his or her personality. A *flat character* is defined by only a few qualities. A character who changes is called *dynamic*; a character who does not change is called *static*.

See also Characterization *and* Motivation.

CHARACTERIZATION *Characterization* is the act of creating and developing a character. A writer uses *direct characterization* when he or she describes a character's traits explicitly. Writers also use *indirect characterization*. A character's traits can be revealed indirectly in what he or she says, thinks, or does; in a description of his or her appearance; or in the statements, thoughts, or actions of other characters.

See also Character *and* Motivation.

CHOKA A traditional Japanese verse form, *choka* are poems that consist of alternating lines of five and seven syllables, with an additional seven-syllable line at the end. There is no limit to the number of lines in a choka. Choka frequently end with one or more *envoys* consisting of five lines of five, seven, five, seven, and seven syllables. Generally, the envoys elaborate or summarize the theme of the main poem.

CLIMAX The *climax* is the high point of interest or suspense in a literary work. Often, the climax is also the crisis in the plot, the point at which the protagonist changes his or her understanding or situation. Sometimes, the climax coincides with the *resolution*, the point at which the central conflict is ended.

See also Plot.

COMEDY A *comedy* is a literary work, especially a play, that has a happy ending. A comedy often shows ordinary characters in conflict with their society. Types of comedy include *romantic comedy*, which involves problems between lovers, and the *comedy of manners*, which satirically challenges the social customs of a sophisticated society. Comedy is often contrasted with tragedy, in which the protagonist meets an unfortunate end.

See also Drama *and* Tragedy.

CONCEIT A *conceit* is an unusual and surprising comparison between two very different things. This special kind of metaphor or complicated analogy is often the basis for a whole poem. *Petrarchan conceits* make extravagant claims about the beloved's beauty or the speaker's suffering, with comparisons to divine beings, powerful natural forces, and objects that contain a given quality in the highest degree. See Petrarch's "Laura" (p. 675) for an example.

See also Metaphor.

CONFLICT A *conflict* is a struggle between opposing forces. Sometimes, this struggle is internal, or within a character. At other times, the struggle is external, or between the character and some outside force. The outside force may be another character, nature, or some element of society, such as a custom or a political institution. Often, the conflict in a work combines several of these possibilities.

See also Plot.

CONNOTATION *Connotation* refers to the associations that a word calls to mind in addition to its dictionary meaning. For example, the words *home* and *domicile* have the same dictionary meaning. However, the first has positive connotations of warmth and security, whereas the second does not.

See also Denotation.

CONSONANCE *Consonance* is the repetition of final consonant sounds in stressed syllables containing dissimilar vowel sounds. Following are some examples of consonance: *black/block; slip/slop; creak/croak; feat/fit; slick/slack.* When each word in the pair is used at the end of a line, the effect is one form of *slant rhyme.*

See also Assonance.

COUPLET A *couplet* is a pair of rhyming lines written in the same meter. A *heroic couplet* is a rhymed pair of iambic pentameter lines. In a *closed couplet*, the meaning and grammar are completed within the two lines.

See also Sonnet.

DACTYL *See* Meter.

DENOTATION *Denotation* is the objective meaning of a word—that to which the word refers, independent of other associations that the word calls to mind. Dictionaries list the denotative meanings of words.

See also Connotation.

DIALECT *Dialect* is the form of a language spoken by people in a particular region or group. Dialects differ from one another in grammar, vocabulary, and pronunciation.

DIALOGUE *Dialogue* is a conversation between characters. Writers use dialogue to reveal character, to present events, to add variety to narratives, and to interest readers. Dialogue in a story is usually set off by quotation marks and paragraphing. Dialogue in a play script generally follows the name of the speaker.

DIARY A *diary* is a personal record of daily events, usually written in prose. Most diaries are not written for publication; sometimes, however, interesting diaries or diaries written by influential people are published.

DICTION *Diction* is a writer's word choice. It can be a major determinant of the writer's style. Diction can be described as formal or informal, abstract or concrete, plain or ornate, ordinary or technical.

See also Style.

DIMETER *See* Meter.

DRAMA A *drama* is a story written to be performed by actors. It may consist of one or more large sections, called acts, which are made up of any number of smaller sections, called scenes.

Drama originated in the religious rituals and symbolic reenactments of primitive peoples. The ancient Greeks, who developed drama into a sophisticated art form, created such dramatic forms as tragedy and comedy.

Oedipus the King (p. 426) is a definitive example of Greek tragedy. The classical dramas of the Greeks and the Romans faded away as the Roman empire declined.

Drama revived in Europe during the Middle Ages. The Renaissance produced a number of great dramatists, most notably England's William Shakespeare. Molière's *Tartuffe* is a comedy of manners, a form of drama popular in the seventeenth century. Goethe's tragic *Faust* (p. 768) represents a peak of nineteenth-century Romanticism. Henrik Ibsen's

A Doll House (p. 864) began a trend toward realistic prose drama and away from drama in verse form. Most of the great plays of the twentieth century are written in prose.

Among the many forms of drama from non-Western cultures are the Nō plays of Japan, such as Zeami's *The Deserted Crone.*

See also Comedy *and* Tragedy.

DRAMATIC MONOLOGUE A *dramatic monologue* is a poem in which an imaginary character speaks to a silent listener. During the monologue, the speaker reveals his or her personality, usually at a moment of crisis.

ELEGY An *elegy* is a solemn and formal lyric poem about death. It may mourn a particular person or reflect on a serious or tragic theme, such as the passing of youth or beauty.

See also Lyric Poem.

END-STOPPED LINE An *end-stopped line* is a line of poetry concluding with a break in the meter and in the meaning. This pause at the end of a line is often punctuated by a period, comma, dash, or semicolon.

See also Run-on Line.

EPIC An *epic* is a long narrative poem about the adventures of gods or of a hero. A *folk epic* is one that was composed orally and passed from storyteller to storyteller. The ancient Greek epics attributed to Homer—the *Iliad* (p. 326) and the *Odyssey*—are folk epics. The *Aeneid* (p. 492), by the Roman poet Virgil, and *The Divine Comedy* (p. 613), by the Italian poet Dante Alighieri, are examples of literary epics from the Classical and Medieval periods, respectively. An epic presents an encyclopedic portrait of the culture in which it was produced.

Epic conventions are traditional characteristics of epic poems, including an opening statement of the theme; an appeal for supernatural help in telling the story (an invocation); a beginning *in medias res* (Latin: "in the middle of things"); catalogs of people and things; accounts of past events; and descriptive phrases.

EPIGRAM An *epigram* is a brief statement in prose or in verse. The concluding couplet in a sonnet may be epigrammatic. An essay may be written in an epigrammatic style.

EPIPHANY *Epiphany* is a term introduced by James Joyce to describe a moment of insight in which a character recognizes a truth. In Colette's "The Bracelet" (p. 1046), the main character's epiphany comes at the end of the story when she realizes she cannot recapture her past.

EPITAPH An *epitaph* is an inscription written on a tomb or burial place. In literature, epitaphs include serious or humorous lines written as if intended for such use. Catullus' "I Crossed Many Lands and a Lot of Ocean" (p. 509) is an example from classical literature.

ESSAY An *essay* is a short nonfiction work about a particular subject. Essays are of many types but may be classified by tone or style as formal or informal. An essay is often classed by its main purpose as descriptive, narrative, expository, argumentative, or persuasive.

EXTENDED METAPHOR *See* Metaphor.

FABLE A *fable* is a brief story, usually with animal characters, that teaches a lesson or moral. The earliest known fables are those attributed to Aesop, a Greek writer of the sixth century B.C. Jean de La Fontaine continued this tradition during the Age of Rationalism with such fables as "The Fox and the Crow" (p. 720) and "The Oak and the Reed" (p. 723).

See also Allegory *and* Parable.

FICTION *Fiction* is prose writing about imaginary characters and events. Some writers of fiction base their stories on real events, whereas others rely solely on their imaginations.

See also Narration *and* Prose.

FIGURATIVE LANGUAGE *Figurative language* is writing or speech not meant to be interpreted literally. Poets and other writers use figurative language to paint vivid word pictures, to make their writing emotionally intense and concentrated, and to state their ideas in new and unusual ways.

Figurative language is classified into various *figures of speech,* including hyperbole, irony, metaphor, metonymy, oxymoron, paradox, personification, simile, and synecdoche.

See also the entries for individual figures of speech.

FOLKLORE The stories, legends, myths, ballads, riddles, sayings, and other traditional works produced orally by a culture are known as *folklore.* Folklore influences written literature in many ways. "The Fisherman and the Jinnee," from *The Thousand and One Nights* (p. 92), is an example of folklore.

FOOT *See* Meter.

FREE VERSE *Free verse* is poetry not written in a regular, rhythmical pattern, or meter. Instead of having metrical feet and lines, free verse has a rhythm that suits its meaning and that uses the sounds of spoken language in lines of different lengths. Free verse has been widely used in twentieth-century poetry. An example is this stanza from Nguyen Thi Vinh's "Thoughts of Hanoi" (p. 1392):

> Brother, we are men,
> conscious of more
> than material needs.
> How can this happen to us
> my friend
> my foe?

GOTHIC *Gothic* is a term used to describe literary works that make extensive use of primitive, medieval, wild, mysterious, or natural elements.

HEPTAMETER *See* Meter.

HEXAMETER *See* Meter.

HYPERBOLE *Hyperbole* is a deliberate exaggeration or overstatement. In *Candide* (p. 732), Voltaire turns a philosophical idea into this figure of speech:

> Pangloss taught metaphysico-theologo-cosmolonigology. He proved admirably that there is no effect without a cause and that in this best of all possible worlds, My Lord the Baron's castle was the best of castles and his wife the best of all possible Baronesses.

Hyperbole may be used for heightened seriousness or for comic effect.

See also Figurative Language.

IAMBIC PENTAMETER *See* Meter.

IMAGE An *image* is a word or phrase that appeals to one or more of the senses—sight, hearing, touch, taste, or smell. In a famous essay on *Hamlet,* T. S. Eliot explained how a group of images can be used as an "objective correlative." By this phrase, Eliot meant that a complex emotional state can be suggested by images that are carefully chosen to evoke this state.

See also Imagery.

IMAGERY *Imagery* is the descriptive language used in literature to re-create sensory experiences. Imagery enriches writing by making it more vivid, setting a tone, suggesting emotions, and guiding readers' reactions. The following lines from Boris Pasternak's "The Weeping Orchard" (p. 1032) show how a poet can use imagery to appeal to several senses in describing the aftermath of a storm:

> Silence. No breath of leaf, nothing
>   in the dark but this weird
> gulping, and flapping of slippers,
>   and sighs, broken by tears.

IRONY *Irony* is the general name given to literary techniques that involve surprising, interesting, or amusing contradictions. In *verbal irony,* words are used to suggest the opposite of their usual meaning. In *dramatic irony,* there is a contradiction between what a character thinks and what the reader or audience knows to be true. In *irony of situation,* an event occurs that directly contradicts expectations.

LEGEND A *legend* is a widely told story about the past that may or may not be based in fact. A legend often reflects a people's identity or cultural values, generally with more historical truth than that in a myth. *The Epic of Gilgamesh* (p. 15) from Sumeria and the *Shah-nama* from Persia are both based in part on legends. In Europe, the well-known German legend of Johann Faust inspired novels and plays, including Goethe's *Faust* (p. 768).

See also Fable *and* Myth.

LYRIC POEM A *lyric poem* is a poem expressing the observations and feelings of a single speaker. Unlike a narrative poem, it presents an experience or a single effect, but it does not tell a full story. Early Greeks defined a lyric poem as that which was expressed by a single voice accompanied by a lyre. The poems of Archilochus, Callinus, Sappho (p. 376), and Pindar (p. 380) are lyric. Although they are no longer designed to be sung to the accompaniment of a lyre, lyric poems retain a melodic quality that results from the rhythmic patterns of rhymed or unrhymed verse. Modern forms of lyric poems include the elegy, the ode, and the sonnet.

METAPHOR A *metaphor* is a figure of speech in which one thing is spoken of as though it were something else, as in "death, that long sleep." Through this identification of dissimilar things, a comparison is suggested or implied. Octavio Paz uses the following metaphor in his poem "Fable" (p. 1194): "Insects were living jewels." The metaphor suggests the similarities between insects and precious stones.

An *extended metaphor* is developed at length and involves several points of comparison. A mixed metaphor occurs when two metaphors are jumbled together, as in "The thorns of life rained down on him."

A *dead metaphor* is one that has been so overused that its original metaphorical impact has been lost. Examples of dead metaphors include "the foot of the bed" and "toe the line."

See also Figurative Language.

METER *Meter* is the rhythmical pattern of a poem. This pattern is determined by the number and types of stresses, or beats, in each line. To describe the meter of a poem, you must scan its lines. Scanning involves marking the stressed and unstressed syllables, as follows in this excerpt from "Carpe Diem" by Horace (p. 510):

> Bĕ wíse! | Drĭnk frée, | ănd ín | sŏ shórt | ă spáce
> Dŏ nót | prŏtrác | tĕd hópes | ŏf lífe | ĕmbráce:
> Whĭlst wé | ăre tálk | ĭng, én | vĭous tíme | dŏth slíde;
> Thĭs dáy's | thĭne ówn; | thĕ néxt | măy bé | dĕníed.

As you can see, each stressed syllable is marked with a slanted line (´) and each unstressed syllable with a horseshoe symbol (˘). The stresses are then divided by vertical lines into groups called feet. The following types of feet are common in English poetry:

1. *Iamb:* a foot with one unstressed syllable followed by one stressed syllable, as in the word *afraid*
2. *Trochee:* a foot with one stressed syllable followed by one unstressed syllable, as in the word *heather*

3. *Anapest:* a foot with two unstressed syllables followed by one stressed syllable, as in the word *disembark*
4. *Dactyl:* a foot with one stressed syllable followed by two unstressed syllables, as in the word *solitude*
5. *Spondee:* a foot with two stressed syllables, as in the word *workday*
6. *Pyrrhic:* a foot with two unstressed syllables, as in the last foot of the word *unspeak | ably*
7. *Amphibrach:* a foot with an unstressed syllable, one stressed syllable, and another unstressed syllable, as in the word *another*
8. *Amphimacer:* a foot with a stressed syllable, one unstressed syllable, and another stressed syllable, as in *up and down*

A line of poetry is described as *iambic, trochaic, anapestic,* or *dactylic* according to the kind of foot that appears most often in the line. Lines are also described in terms of the number of feet that occur in them, as follows:

1. *Monometer:* verse written in one-foot lines
2. *Dimeter:* verse written in two-foot lines
3. *Trimeter:* verse written in three-foot lines
4. *Tetrameter:* verse written in four-foot lines
5. *Pentameter:* verse written in five-foot lines
6. *Hexameter:* verse written in six-foot lines
7. *Heptameter:* verse written in seven-foot lines

A complete description of the meter of a line tells both how many feet there are in the line and what kind of foot is most common. Thus, the translated stanza from Horace's ode quoted at the beginning of this entry would be described as being made up of iambic pentameter lines with the occasional use of an anapest or a trochee for variety. Poetry that does not have a regular meter is called *free verse*.

See also Free Verse.

METONYMY *Metonymy* is a figure of speech that substitutes something closely related for the thing actually meant. For example, in Genesis (p. 44), it is said, "By the sweat of your brow / Shall you get bread to eat." Here the word *sweat* represents hard labor.

See also Figurative Language.

MOCK EPIC A *mock epic* is a poem about a trivial matter written in the style of a serious epic. The incongruity of style and subject matter produces comic effects.

MODERNISM *Modernism* describes an international movement in the arts during the early twentieth century. Modernists rejected old forms and experimented with the new. Literary Modernists used images as symbols. They presented human experiences in fragments, rather than as a coherent whole, which led to new experiments in the forms of poetry and fiction.

MONOLOGUE A *monologue* is a speech or performance given entirely by one person or by one character.

See also Dramatic Monologue *and* Soliloquy.

MOOD *Mood,* or atmosphere, is the feeling created in the reader by a literary work or passage. Mood may be suggested by the writer's choice of words, by events in the work, or by the physical setting. Julio Cortázar's "House Taken Over" (p. 1182) begins with a description of the narrator's life that sets a mood of comfort and routine. He later introduces an element of unknown danger that contrasts with and finally overcomes the pleasant mood at the beginning.

See also Setting *and* Tone.

MOTIVATION *Motivation* is a reason that explains or partially explains a character's thoughts, feelings, actions, or speech. Characters may be motivated by their physical needs; by their wants, wishes, desires, or dreams; or by their beliefs, values, and ideals. Effective characterization involves creating motivations that make characters seem believable.

MYTH A *myth* is a fictional tale, originally with religious significance, that explains the actions of gods or heroes, the causes of natural phenomena, or both. Allusions to characters and motifs from Greek, Roman, Norse, and Celtic myths are common in English literature. In addition, mythological stories are often retold or adapted.

See also Fable *and* Legend.

NARRATION *Narration* is writing that tells a story. The act of telling a story is also called narration. The *narrative,* or story, is told by a character or speaker called the *narrator.* Biographies, autobiographies, journals, reports, novels, short stories, plays, narrative poems, anecdotes, fables, parables, myths, legends, folk tales, ballads, and epic poems are all narratives, or types of narration.

See also Point of View.

NARRATIVE POEM A *narrative poem* is a poem that tells a story in verse. Three traditional types of narrative poems are ballads, epics, and metrical romances. The *Shah-nama,* the *Iliad* (p. 326), the *Aeneid* (p. 492), and the *Song of Roland* (p. 556) are epic narrative poems. Poets who have written narrative poems include Alexander Pushkin, Victor Hugo, and Wole Soyinka.

NATURALISM *Naturalism* was a literary movement among writers at the end of the nineteenth century and during the early decades of the twentieth century. The Naturalists depicted life in its grimmer details and viewed people as hopeless victims of natural laws.

See also Realism.

NEOCLASSICISM *Neoclassicism* was a literary movement of the late seventeenth and the eighteenth centuries in which writers turned to classical Greek and Roman literary models. Like the ancients, many Neoclassical writers dealt with themes related to proper human conduct. The most popular literary forms of the day—essays, letters, early novels, epigrams, parodies, and satires—reflected this emphasis.

See also Romanticism.

NOVEL A *novel* is an extended work of fiction that often has a complicated plot, many major and minor characters, a unifying theme, and several settings. Novels can be grouped in many ways, based on the historical periods in which they are written (such as Victorian), on the subjects and themes that they treat (such as Gothic or regional), on the techniques used in them (such as stream of consciousness), or on their part in literary movements (such as in Naturalism or Realism). A *novella* is not as long as a novel but is longer than a short story.

OBJECTIVE CORRELATIVE *See* Image.

OCTAVE *See* Stanza.

ODE An *ode* is a long, formal lyric poem with a serious theme. It may have a traditional structure with stanzas grouped in threes, called the *strophe*, the *antistrophe*, and the *epode*. Odes often honor people, commemorate events, or respond to natural scenes. The ancient Greek poet Pindar is famous for odes such as "Olympia 11" (p. 380), praising victorious athletes.

See also Lyric Poem.

ONOMATOPOEIA *Onomatopoeia* is the use of words that imitate sounds. Examples of such words are *buzz, hiss, murmur,* and *rustle.* In the line ". . . to hear / Rasps in the field," from Wole Soyinka's "Season" (p. 1344), *Rasps* is onomatopoeic. Onomatopoeia creates musical effects and reinforces meaning.

ORAL TRADITION *Oral tradition* is the body of songs, stories, and poems preserved by being passed from generation to generation by word of mouth. Folk epics, ballads, myths, legends, folk tales, folk songs, proverbs, and nursery rhymes are all products of the oral tradition.

See also Ballad, Folklore, Legend, *and* Myth.

OXYMORON An *oxymoron* is a figure of speech that fuses two contradictory ideas, such as "freezing fire" or "happy grief," thus suggesting a paradox in just a few words.

See also Figurative Language *and* Paradox.

PARABLE A *parable* is a short, simple story from which a moral or religious lesson can be drawn. The most famous parables are those in the New Testament. Leo Tolstoy's "How Much Land Does a Man Need?" (p. 835) echoes a biblical parable.

PARADOX A *paradox* is a statement that seems to be contradictory but that actually presents a truth. Wole Soyinka's "Season" (p. 1344) presents this paradox, "Rust is ripeness, rust / And the wilted-corn plume. . . ." Because rust is often associated with metallic corrosion, the statement seems contradictory. However, in the context of the color of harvested crops, the statement makes sense. Because a paradox is surprising or even shocking, it draws the reader's attention to what is being said.

See also Figurative Language *and* Oxymoron.

PARODY A *parody* is a humorous imitation of another work or of a type of work.

PASTORAL *Pastoral* refers to literary works that deal with the pleasures of a simple rural life or with escape to a simpler place and time. The tradition of pastoral literature began in ancient Greece with the poetic idylls of Theocritus. The Roman poet Virgil also wrote a famous collection of pastoral poems, the *Eclogues*.

PENTAMETER *See* Meter.

PERSONA *Persona* means, literally, "a mask." A persona is a fictional self created by an author—a self through whom the narrative of a poem or story is told.

See also Speaker.

PERSONIFICATION *Personification* is a figure of speech in which a nonhuman subject is given human characteristics. Effective personification of things or ideas makes their qualities seem unified, like the characteristics of a person, and their relationship with the reader seem closer.

See also Figurative Language *and* Metaphor.

PLOT *Plot* is the sequence of events in a literary work. The two primary elements of any plot are characters and a conflict. Most plots can be analyzed into many or all of the following parts:

1. The *exposition* introduces the setting, the characters, and the basic situation.
2. The *inciting incident* introduces the central conflict.
3. During the *development*, the conflict runs its course and usually intensifies.
4. At the *climax*, the conflict reaches a high point of interest or suspense.
5. The *denouement* ties up loose ends that remain after the climax of the conflict.
6. At the *resolution*, the story is resolved and an insight is revealed.

There are many variations on the standard plot structure. Some stories begin *in medias res* ("in the middle of things"), after the inciting incident has already occurred. In some stories, the expository material appears toward the middle, in flashbacks. In many stories, there is no denouement. Occasionally, the conflict is left unresolved.

POETRY *Poetry* is one of the three major types, or genres, of literature, the others being prose and drama. Poetry defies simple definition because there is no single characteristic that is found in all poems and not found in all nonpoems.

Often, poems are divided into lines and stanzas. Poems such as sonnets, odes, villanelles, and sestinas are governed by rules regarding the number of lines, the number and placement of stressed syllables in each line, and the rhyme scheme. In the case of villanelles and sestinas, the repetition of words at the ends of lines or of entire lines is required. However, some poems are written in free verse. Most poems make use of highly concise, musical, and emotionally charged language. Many also use imagery, figurative language, and devices of sound like rhyme.

Types of poetry include *narrative poetry* (ballads, epics, and metrical romances); *dramatic poetry* (dramatic monologues and dramatic dialogues); *lyrics* (sonnets, odes, elegies, and love poems); and *concrete poetry* (a poem presented on the page in a shape that suggests its subject).

POINT OF VIEW The perspective, or vantage point, from which a story is told is its *point of view.* If a character within the story narrates, then it is told from the *first-person point of view.* If a voice from outside the story tells it, then the story is told from the *third-person point of view.* If the knowledge of the storyteller is limited to the internal states of one character, then the storyteller has a *limited point of view.* If the storyteller's knowledge extends to the internal states of all the characters, then the storyteller has an *omniscient point of view.*

PROSE *Prose* is the ordinary form of written language and one of the three major types of literature. Most writing that is not poetry, drama, or song is considered prose. Prose occurs in two major forms: fiction and nonfiction.

PROTAGONIST The *protagonist* is the main character in a literary work. In R. K. Narayan's "An Astrologer's Day" (p. 1366), the protagonist is the astrologer.

PYRRHIC *See* Meter.

QUATRAIN *See* Stanza.

REALISM *Realism* is the presentation in art of details from actual life. During the last part of the nineteenth century and the first part of the twentieth, Realism enjoyed considerable popularity among writers in the English-speaking world. Novels often dealt with grim social realities and presented realistic portrayals of the psychological states of characters.

See also Symbolism.

REFRAIN A *refrain* is a regularly repeated line or group of lines in a poem or song.

See also Ballad.

REGIONALISM *Regionalism* is the tendency to confine one's writing to the presentation of the distinct culture of an area, including its speech, customs, and history.

RHYME *Rhyme* is the repetition of sounds at the ends of words. *End rhyme* occurs when rhyming words appear at the ends of lines. *Internal rhyme* occurs when rhyming words fall within a line. *Exact rhyme* is the use of identical rhyming sounds, as in *love* and *dove. Approximate,* or *slant, rhyme* is the use of sounds that are similar but not identical, as in *prove* and *glove.*

RHYME SCHEME *Rhyme scheme* is the regular pattern of rhyming words in a poem or stanza. To indicate a rhyme scheme, assign a different letter to each final sound in the poem or stanza. The following lines from Morris Bishop's translation of Petrarch's "Laura" (p. 675) have been marked.

She used to let her golden hair fly free *a*
  For the wind to toy and tangle and molest; *b*
  Her eyes were brighter than the radiant west. *b*
  (Seldom they shine so now.) I used to see *a*
  Pity look out of those deep eyes on me. *a*

RHYTHM *See* Meter.

ROMANCE A *romance* is a story that presents remote or imaginative incidents rather than ordinary, realistic experience. The term *romance* was originally used to refer to medieval tales of the deeds and loves of noble knights and ladies. From the eighteenth century on, the term *romance* has been used to describe sentimental novels about love.

ROMANTICISM *Romanticism* was a literary and artistic movement of the eighteenth and nineteenth centuries. In reaction to Neoclassicism, the Romantics emphasized imagination, fancy, freedom, emotion, wildness, the beauty of the untamed natural world, the rights of the individual, the nobility of the common man, and the attractiveness of pastoral life. Important figures in the Romantic Movement include Johann Wolfgang von Goethe, Victor Hugo, and Heinrich Heine.

RUN-ON LINE A *run-on line* is a line that does not contain a pause or a stop at the end. The flow of words carries the reader to the following line. A poet may use run-on lines to avoid creating a sing-song effect, in which each line is separated from the next by a pause.

See also End-Stopped Line.

SATIRE *Satire* is writing that ridicules or holds up to contempt the faults of individuals or groups. Although a satire is often humorous, its purpose is not simply to make readers laugh but also to correct the flaws and shortcomings that it points out.

SCANSION *Scansion* is the process of analyzing the metrical pattern of a poem.

See also Meter.

SESTET *See* Stanza.

SETTING The *setting* is the time and place of the action of a literary work. A setting can provide a backdrop for the action. It can be the force that the protagonist struggles against and thus the source of the central conflict. It can also be used to create an atmosphere. In many works, the setting symbolizes a point that the author wishes to emphasize. In Albert Camus's short story "The Guest" (p. 1225), the setting is a lonely desert plateau in an Arab country occupied by France. Fearing an Arab insurrection, and unable to spare anyone for a long trip, the local French police ask a schoolteacher to take an Arab suspect to the authorities. Such a situation would only arise in an isolated colonial area. The setting also adds a grim atmosphere and conveys a theme—human freedom. In the following scene, a character must choose between two directions:

> They reached a level height made up of crumbly rocks. From there on, the plateau sloped down, eastward, toward a low plain where there were a few spindly trees and, to the south, toward outcroppings of rock that gave the landscape a chaotic look.
>
> Daru surveyed the two directions. There was nothing but the sky on the horizon. Not a man could be seen.

See also Mood *and* Symbol.

SHORT STORY A *short story* is a brief work of fiction. The short story resembles the longer novel, but it generally has a simpler plot and setting. In addition, a short story tends to reveal a character at a crucial moment, rather than to develop a character through many incidents.

SIMILE A *simile* is a figure of speech that compares two apparently dissimilar things using *like* or *as*. Many similes appear in the *Iliad* (p. 326), including the following:

> And swift Achilles kept on coursing Hector, nonstop
> as a hound in the mountains starts a fawn from its lair,
> hunting him down the gorges, down the narrow glens.

By comparing apparently dissimilar things, the writer of a simile surprises the reader into an appreciation of the hidden similarities of the things being compared.

See also Figurative Language.

SOLILOQUY A *soliloquy* is a long speech in a play or in a prose work made by a character who is alone and thus reveals private thoughts and feelings to the audience or reader.

See also Monologue.

SONNET A sonnet is a fourteen-line lyric poem with a single theme. Sonnets are usually written in iambic pentameter. The *Petrarchan*, or *Italian, sonnet* is divided into two parts, an eight-line octave and a six-line sestet. The octave rhymes *abba abba*, while the sestet generally rhymes *cde cde* or uses some combination of *cd* rhymes. The octave raises a question, states a problem, or presents a brief narrative, and the sestet answers the question, solves the problem, or comments on the narrative.

The *Shakespearean*, or *English, sonnet* has three four-line quatrains plus a concluding two-line couplet. The rhyme scheme of such a sonnet is usually *abab cdcd efef gg*. Each of the three quatrains usually explores a different variation of the main theme. Then, the couplet presents a summarizing or concluding statement.

See also Lyric Poem *and* Sonnet Sequence.

SONNET SEQUENCE A *sonnet sequence* is a series or group of sonnets, most often written to or about a beloved. Although each sonnet can stand alone as a separate poem, the sequence lets the poet trace the development of a relationship or examine different aspects of a single subject.

See also Sonnet.

SPEAKER The *speaker* is the imaginary voice assumed by the writer of a poem; the character who "says" the poem. This character is often not identified by name but may be identified otherwise. For instance, in the opening line of an ancient Egyptian poem (p. 37), the lovelorn speaker's desire for attention is made clear in the opening:

> I think I'll go home and lie very still,
> feigning terminal illness

Recognizing the speaker and thinking about his or her characteristics are often central to interpreting a lyric poem.

See also Persona *and* Point of View.

SPONDEE *See* Meter.

STANZA A *stanza* is a group of lines in a poem, which is seen as a unit. Many poems are divided into stanzas that are separated by spaces. Stanzas often function like paragraphs in prose. Each stanza states and develops one main idea.

Stanzas are commonly named according to the number of lines found in them, as follows:

1. *Couplet:* a two-line stanza
2. *Tercet:* a three-line stanza
3. *Quatrain:* a four-line stanza
4. *Cinquain:* a five-line stanza
5. *Sestet:* a six-line stanza
6. *Heptastich:* a seven-line stanza

7. *Octave:* an eight-line stanza

See also Sonnet.

STYLE *Style* is a writer's typical way of writing. Determinants of a writer's style include formality, use of figurative language, use of rhythm, typical grammatical patterns, typical sentence lengths, and typical methods of organization. For example, Yehuda Amichai's colloquial style in a poem such as "From the Book of Esther I Filtered the Sediment" (p. 1320), is an innovation in Hebrew literature.

See also Diction.

SURREALISM *Surrealism* is a movement in art and literature that emphasizes the irrational side of human nature. It focuses on the imaginary world of dreams and the unconscious mind. Originating in France following World War I, Surrealism was a protest against the so-called Rationalism that led the world into catastrophic war. Surrealism can be found in Latin American poems such as Octavio Paz's "Fable" (p. 1194).

SYMBOL A *symbol* is a sign, word, phrase, image, or other object that stands for or represents something else. Thus, a flag can symbolize a country, a spoken word can symbolize an object, a fine car can symbolize wealth, and so on. In literary criticism, a distinction is often made between traditional or conventional symbols—those that are part of our general cultural inheritance—and *personal symbols*—those that are created by particular authors for use in particular works.

Conventional symbolism is often based on elements of nature. For example, youth is often symbolized by greenery or springtime, middle age by summer, and old age by autumn or winter. Conventional symbols are also borrowed from religion and politics. For example, a cross may be a symbol of Christianity, or the color red may be a symbol of Marxist ideology.

SYMBOLISM *Symbolism* was a literary movement of nineteenth-century France. The Symbolist writers reacted against Realism and stressed the importance of emotional states, especially by means of symbols corresponding to these states. The Symbolists were also concerned with using sound to achieve emotional effects. Arthur Rimbaud and Paul Verlaine are among the best-known Symbolist poets. Many twentieth-century writers around the world were influenced by the Symbolist movement.

See also Realism.

SYNECDOCHE *Synecdoche* is a figure of speech in which a part of something is used to stand for the whole. For example, one might speak of "hands" to refer to the crew of a ship, "wheels" to refer to a car, or "the law" to refer to the whole criminal justice system.

See also Figurative Language.

TANKA *Tanka* is a form of Japanese poetry consisting of five lines of five, seven, five, seven, and seven syllables. Tanka is the most prevalent verse form in traditional Japanese literature. Tanka often tell a brief story or express a single feeling or thought.

TETRAMETER *See* Meter.

THEME *Theme* is the central idea, concern, or purpose in a literary work. In an essay, the theme might be directly stated in what is known as a thesis statement. In a serious literary work, the theme is usually expressed indirectly rather than directly. A light work, one written strictly for entertainment, may not have a theme.

TONE *Tone* is the writer's attitude toward the readers and toward the subject. It may be formal or informal, friendly or distant, personal or pompous. The tone of Gabriela Mistral's poem "Fear" (p. 1102) is, not surprisingly, fearful.

See also Mood.

TRADITION In literary study and practice, a *tradition* is a past body of work, developed over the course of history. A literary tradition may be unified by form (the tradition of the sonnet), by language (literature in Spanish), or by nationality (Japanese literature). A tradition develops through the acknowledgment of works, forms, and styles as classic. Writers participate in a tradition if only by following conventions about the suitable forms and subjects for literature. They make conscious use of the tradition when they use references, stories, or forms from old literature to give authority to their work.

TRAGEDY *Tragedy* is a type of drama or literature that shows the downfall or destruction of a noble or outstanding person, traditionally one who possesses a character weakness called a *tragic flaw*. The *tragic hero* is caught up in a sequence of events that inevitably results in disaster. Because the protagonist is neither a wicked villain nor an innocent victim, the audience reacts with mixed emotions—both pity and fear, according to the Greek philosopher Aristotle, who defined tragedy in the *Poetics*. The outcome of a tragedy, in which the protagonist is isolated from society, contrasts with the happy resolution of a comedy, in which the protagonist makes peace with society. Sophocles' *Oedipus the King* (p. 426) is a Greek tragedy.

See also Comedy *and* Drama.

TRIMETER *See* Meter.

TROCHEE *See* Meter.

Summary of Grammar

Nouns A **noun** names a person, place, or thing. A **common noun**, such as *country*, names any one of a class of people, places, or things. A **proper noun**, such as *Great Britain*, names a specific person, place, or thing.

Pronouns Pronouns are words that stand for nouns or for words that take the place of nouns. **Personal pronouns** refer to the person speaking; the person spoken to; or the person, place, or thing spoken about.

	Singular	*Plural*
First Person	I, me, my, mine	we, us, our, ours
Second Person	you, your, yours	you, your, yours
Third Person	he, him, his, she, her, hers, it, its	they, them, their, theirs

A **reflexive pronoun** ends in *-self* or *-selves* and names the person or thing receiving an action when that person or thing is the same as the one performing the action.

An **intensive pronoun** also ends in *-self* or *-selves*. It adds emphasis to a noun or pronoun.

> ". . . I should like to take breakfast with you this morning, together with my companion here, but you must not put *yourself* to any trouble." (reflexive) (Boccaccio, p. 691)

Demonstrative pronouns—such as *this, that, these,* and *those*—single out specific people, places, or things.

A **relative pronoun** begins a subordinate clause and connects it to another idea in the sentence.

> "Did you imagine I should not observe the crafty scheme *that* stole upon me. . .?" (Sophocles, p. 462)

Interrogative pronouns are used to begin questions.

> "*Who* sent you to us?" (Sophocles, p. 462)

Indefinite pronouns refer to people, places, or things, often without specifying which ones.

> *One* ate whatever one could get. (Maupassant, p. 828)

Verbs A **verb** is a word or group of words that express an action, a condition, or the fact that something exists, while indicating the time of the action, condition, or fact. An **action verb** tells what action someone or something is performing. An action verb is **transitive** if it directs action toward someone or something named in the same sentence.

> On his airy perch among the branches
> Master Crow *was holding* cheese in his beak.
> (La Fontaine, p. 720)

An action verb is **intransitive** if it does not direct action toward something or someone named in the same sentence.

> No smoke *came* now from the chimney pot of the villa. (Calvino, p. 1253)

A **linking verb** expresses the subject's condition by connecting the subject with another word.

> She *felt* restless. . . . (Colette, p. 1049)

Helping verbs are verbs added to another verb to make a single verb phrase. They indicate the time at which an action takes place or whether it actually happens, could happen, or should happen.

> "It *can be stopped* right away." (Kafka, p. 1012)

Adjectives An **adjective** is a word used to describe what is named by a noun or pronoun or to give a noun or pronoun a more specific meaning. Adjectives answer these questions:

> What kind? *purple* hat, *happy* face
> Which one? *this* bowl, *those* cameras
> How many? *three* cars, *several* dishes
> How much? *less* attention, *enough* food

The **articles** *the, a,* and *an* are adjectives. *An* is used before a word beginning with a vowel sound. *This, that, these,* and *those* are used as **demonstrative adjectives** when they appear directly before a noun.

A noun may sometimes be used as an adjective:

> *language* lesson　　*chemistry* book

Adverbs An **adverb** is a word that modifies a verb, an adjective, or another adverb. Adverbs answer the questions *where, when, how,* or *to what extent.*

> She will answer *soon.* (modifies verb *will answer*)
> I was *extremely* sad. (modifies adjective *sad*)
> You called *more* often than I. (modifies adverb *often*)

Prepositions A preposition is a word that relates a noun or pronoun that appears with it to another word in the sentence. It can indicate relations of time, place, causality, responsibility, and motivation. Prepositions are almost always followed by nouns or pronouns.

around the fire	*for* us
in sight	*till* sunrise

Conjunctions A conjunction is used to connect other words or groups of words.

Coordinating conjunctions connect similar kinds or groups of words:

bread *and* wine	brief *but* powerful

Correlative conjunctions are used in pairs to connect similar words or groups of words:

both Luis *and* Rosa	*neither* you *nor* I

Subordinating conjunctions indicate the connection between two ideas by placing one below the other in rank or importance:

> *When* the man's speech returned once more, he told him of his adventure. (Marie de France, p. 602)

Interjections An **interjection** is a word or phrase that expresses feeling or emotion and functions independently of a sentence.

> "*Oh*, what an awful awakening!" (Ibsen, p. 935)

Sentences A **sentence** is a group of words with a subject and predicate, expressing a complete thought. A sentence fragment is a group of words that does not express a complete thought. Sentence fragments should be avoided in writing, unless used for effect, as in realistic dialogue.

Phrases A **phrase** is a group of words without a subject and verb that functions as one part of speech. A **prepositional phrase** includes a preposition and a noun or pronoun.

before dawn	*as a result of* the rain

An **adjective phrase** is a prepositional phrase that modifies a noun or pronoun.

> The likeness *of the dog* would get mixed up with that *of the cat.* (Tagore, p. 1146)

An **adverb phrase** is a prepositional phrase that modifies a verb, an adjective, or an adverb.

> From every side men ran *to the succor of the dame.* (Marie de France, p. 601)

An **appositive phrase** is a noun or pronoun with modifiers, placed next to a noun or pronoun to add information and details.

> And Icarus, *[Daedalus'] son,* stood by and watched him, . . . (Ovid, p. 517)

A **participial phrase** is a participle that is modified by an adjective or adverb phrase or that has a complement (a group of words that completes the participle's meaning). The entire phrase acts as an adjective.

> Her stepmother seemed *drained of strength.* . . . (Kawabata, p. 1385)

A **gerund** is a noun formed from the present participle of a verb (ending in *-ing*). A **gerund phrase** is a gerund with modifiers or a complement (words that complete its meaning), all acting together as a noun.

> "This *getting up so early,*" he thought, "makes anyone a complete idiot." (Kafka, p. 979)

An **infinitive phrase** is an infinitive with modifiers, complements (words completing its meaning), or a subject, all acting together as a single part of speech. (In the example, the second infinitive phrase is part of the complement of the first.)

> And he felt it his duty *to explain* to his traveling companions that the poor woman was *to be* pitied. . . . (Pirandello, p. 1056)

Clauses A **clause** is a group of words with its own subject and verb. An **independent clause** can stand by itself as a complete sentence. A **subordinate clause** cannot stand by itself as a complete sentence.

An **adjective clause** is a subordinate clause that modifies a noun or pronoun by telling *what kind* or *which one.*

> The more stubborn among them, *who were the youngest,* still lived for a few hours with the illusion that . . . his name might be Lautaro. (García Márquez, p. 1177)

Subordinate adverb clauses modify verbs, adjectives, adverbs, or verbals by telling *where, when, in what way, to what extent, under what condition,* or *why.*

> The room fell silent, and all eyes were on him,
> As Father Aeneas from his high couch began . . .
> (Virgil, p. 493)

Subordinate noun clauses act as nouns.

> . . . she thanked them in tears for the dismissal, as if for *the greatest favor that had ever been done to her in this house.* . . . (Kafka, p. 996)

Summary of Capitalization and Punctuation

Capitalization

Capitalize the first word in sentences, interjections, and complete questions. Also, capitalize the first word in a quotation if the quotation is a complete sentence.

> Finally, all in one breath, he exclaimed: "The Marchesa stole a trout from me!" (Calvino, p. 1252)

Capitalize all proper nouns and adjectives.

> Trinidadian Thames River

Capitalize titles showing family relationships when they refer to a specific person unless they are preceded by a possessive noun or pronoun.

> Uncle Oscar Mangan's sister

Capitalize the first word and all other key words in the titles of books, periodicals, poems, stories, plays, songs, and other works of art.

> *Faust* "Two Friends"

Punctuation

End Marks Use a **period** to end a declarative sentence, an imperative sentence, an indirect question, and most abbreviations.

> Irene never bothered anyone. . . .
> I wonder what Irene would have done without her knitting. (Cortázar, p. 1184)

Use a **question mark** to end an interrogative sentence.

> "A knife has passed through you once?" said the astrologer.
> "Good fellow!" He bared his chest to show the scar. "What else?" (Narayan, p. 1369)

Use an **exclamation mark** after an exclamatory sentence, a forceful imperative sentence, or an interjection expressing strong emotion.

> "Oh, you and your cats!" (Calvino, p. 1252)

Commas Use a **comma** before the conjunction to separate two independent clauses in a compound sentence.

> The youth began his journey from
> the castle, and the daytime whole
> he did not meet one living soul. . . .
> (Chrétien de Troyes, p. 584)

Use commas to separate three or more words, phrases, or clauses in a series.

> . . . he opened his bag and spread out his professional equipment, which consisted of a dozen cowrie shells, a square piece of cloth with obscure mystic charts on it, a notebook, and a bundle of palmyra writing. (Narayan, p. 1366)

Use commas to separate adjectives unless they must stay in a specific order.

> Her new mother was a kind woman and they lived a quiet, happy life. (Kawabata, p. 1383)

Use a comma after an introductory word, phrase, or clause.

> As soon as Pakhom and his family reached their new abode, he applied for admission into the council of a large village. (Tolstoy, p. 840)

Use commas to set off nonessential expressions.

> Sasha Uskov, the young man of twenty-five who was the cause of all the commotion, had arrived some time before. . . . (Chekhov, p. 851)

Use commas with places, dates, and titles.

> Cairo, Egypt
>
> September 1, 1939
>
> Reginald Farrars, M. P.

Use commas after items in addresses, after the salutation in a personal letter, after the closing in all letters, and in numbers of more than three digits.

> Paris, France
>
> Dear Randolph,
>
> Yours faithfully,
>
> 9,744

Use a comma to indicate words left out of parallel clauses, to set off a direct quotation, and to prevent a sentence from being misunderstood.

> In Rimbaud's poetry, I admire the music; in Pasternak's, the deep emotion.
>
> "In that case," she said, picking up her needles again, "we'll have to live on this side." (Cortázar, p. 1186)

Semicolons Use a **semicolon** to join independent clauses that are not already joined by a conjunction.

> She fastened it on her wrist, and shook it, throwing off blue sparks under the electric candles; a hundred tiny rainbows, blazing with color, danced on the white tablecloth. (Colette, p. 1046)

Use semicolons to avoid confusion when independent clauses or items in a series already contain commas.

> I enjoy reading ancient authors: Homer, for the action; Catullus, for his bluntness; and Plato, for his ideas.

Colons Use a **colon** before a list of items following an independent clause.

> When the greatest of French poetry is discussed, the following names are certain to be mentioned: Charles Baudelaire, Arthur Rimbaud, Paul Valéry, and Victor Hugo.

Use a colon to introduce a formal or lengthy quotation.

> Finally M. Sauvage pulled himself together: "Come on! On our way! But let's go carefully." (Maupassant, p. 831)

Use a colon to introduce an independent clause that summarizes or explains the sentence before it.

> One empty bier is decorated and carried in the procession: this is for the missing, whose bodies could not be recovered. (Thucydides, p. 386)

Quotation Marks A **direct quotation** represents a person's exact speech or thoughts and is enclosed within quotation marks.

> "We are in Japan," repeated Watanabé. (Ōgai, p. 1121)

An **indirect quotation** reports only the general meaning of what a person said or thought and does not require quotation marks.

> A woman asked me last night on the dark street
> how another woman was
> who'd already died. . . . (Amichai, p. 1320)

Always place a comma or a period inside the final quotation mark.

> Out of a great weariness I answered,
> "She's fine, she's fine." (Amichai, p. 1320)

Always place a question mark or an exclamation mark inside the final quotation mark if the end mark is part of the quotation; if it is not part of the quotation, place it outside the final quotation mark.

> "Why school?" I challenged my father openly. (Mahfouz, p. 1309)

Use single quotation marks for a quotation within a quotation.

> Pointing out clues about character in dialogue, the teacher told her students, "We can infer that Margaret Atwood's mother did not approve of swearing by the fact that she substitutes 'blankety-blank' for stronger language."

Italicize the titles of long written works, movies, television and radio shows, lengthy works of music, paintings, and sculpture. Also, italicize foreign words not yet accepted into English and words you wish to stress.

If you are writing by hand or working in some other format that does not allow you to italicize text, underline such titles and words.

Oedipus the King	60 Minutes
Guernica	déjà vu

Use quotation marks around the titles of short written works, episodes in a series, songs, and titles of works mentioned as parts of collections.

> "An Astrologer's Day" "Boswell Meets Johnson"

Parentheses Use **parentheses** to set off asides and explanations only when the material is not essential or when it consists of one or more sentences.

> And to love (Thou knowest it well) is a bitter exercise. . . . (Mistral, p. 1104)

Hyphens Use a **hyphen** with certain numbers, after certain prefixes, with two or more words used as one word, with a compound modifier, and within a word when a combination of letters might otherwise be confusing.

twenty-nine	re-create
pre-Romantic	brother-in-law

Apostrophe Add an **apostrophe** and an *s* to show the possessive case of most singular nouns and of plural nouns that do not end in *-s* or *-es.*

Rilke's poems	the mice's whiskers

Add an apostrophe to show the possessive case of plural nouns ending in *-s* and *-es.*

the girls' songs	the Ortizes' car

Use an apostrophe in a contraction to indicate the position of the missing letter or letters.

> That's all I'd have to try with my boss; I'd be fired on the spot. (Kafka, p. 979)

Use an apostrophe and an *-s* to write the plurals of numbers, symbols, letters, and words used to name themselves.

5's and 20's	no *if's* or *but's*
five *a's*	

Glossary of Common Usage

among, between

Among is generally used with three or more items. *Between* is generally used with only two items.

> *Among* Ibsen's characters, my favorite has always been Nora in *A Doll House.*

> The main character is at first torn *between* social conventions and her own moral principles.

amount, number

Amount refers to quantity or a unit, whereas *number* refers to individual items that can be counted. *Amount* generally appears with a singular noun, and *number* appears with a plural noun.

> The *amount* of attention that great writers have paid to the Faust legend is remarkable.

> A considerable *number* of important writers have been fascinated by the legend of Joan of Arc.

as, because, like, as to

To avoid confusion, use *because* rather than *as* when you want to indicate cause and effect.

> *Because* he felt he had fulfilled himself as a poet, Arthur Rimbaud set down his pen and pursued a life of adventure.

Do not use the preposition *like* to introduce a clause that requires the conjunction *as.*

> *As* we might expect from the verse of Baudelaire, the tone of "Invitation to the Voyage" is sultry and musical.

The use of *as to* for *about* is awkward and should be avoided.

bad, badly

Use the predicate adjective *bad* after linking verbs such as *feel, look,* and *seem.* Use *badly* when an adverb is required.

> In "The Handsomest Drowned Man in the World," the men of the village feel *bad* that the women are attracted to a stranger.

> At the end of *A Doll House,* Nora chooses to leave her husband, realizing just how *badly* she'd been affected by seven years in a loveless marriage.

because of, due to

Use *due to* if it can logically replace the phrase *caused by.* In introductory phrases, however, *because of* is better usage than *due to.*

> The resurgence of interest in Ibsen's *A Doll House* in recent decades may be *due to* its feminist themes.

> *Because of* the expansion of the reading public, writers during the eighteenth century became less dependent on wealthy patrons for support.

compare, contrast

The verb *compare* can involve both similarities and differences. The verb *contrast* always involves differences. Use *to* or *with* after *compare.* Use *with* after *contrast.*

> Harvey's report *compared* the bohemian lifestyle of Baudelaire *to* that of Rimbaud, noting parallels in their writing styles as well.

> The Greeks *contrasted* inner vision *with* physical vision; thus, the legend that Homer was a blind bard indicates how highly they esteemed introspection.

continual, continuous

Continual means "occurring again and again in succession (but with pauses or breaks)," whereas *continuous* means "occurring without interruption."

> In the poem "Invitation to the Voyage," Baudelaire's *continual* use of a two-line refrain creates a feeling of the rolling ocean waves.

> Though critics assert that Pablo Neruda spent many painstaking hours shaping his verse, the exuberant voice of the speaker in "Ode to My Socks" suggests that he may have written this poem in a single *continuous* burst of inspiration.

different from, different than

The preferred usage is *different from.*

> Colette's third marriage was very *different from* her previous ones simply because it brought her great happiness and satisfaction.

farther, further

Use *farther* when you refer to distance. Use *further* when you mean "to a greater degree" or "additional."

> Discontented with his new life in Paris, the young French poet Rimbaud traveled *farther* east to quench his thirst for adventure.

> In Ibsen's *A Doll House,* Nora realizes that staying in her unhappy marriage will only bring *further* psychological abuse.

fewer, less

Use *fewer* for things that can be counted. Use *less* for amounts or quantities that cannot be counted.

> When asked to compare the two versions of the Faust legend they had read, *fewer* students preferred Christopher Marlowe's version. Most found it to be *less* dramatic than Goethe's.

just, only

Only should appear directly before the word it modifies. *Just,* used as an adverb meaning "no more than," also belongs directly before the word it modifies.

> The form of the villanelle allows a poet to use *just* two rhymes.

> Poet Arthur Rimbaud was *only* fifteen years old when he was first published.

lay, lie

Lay is a transitive verb meaning "to set or put something down." Its principal parts are *lay, laying, laid, laid.*

Lie is an intransitive verb meaning "to recline." Its principal parts are *lie, lying, lay, lain.*

> In Shakespeare's *The Tempest,* Prospero has the power to *lay* strange curses and spells on his enemies.

> According to Blaise Pascal, an individual *lies* somewhere in the midst of a paradoxical universe, unable to comprehend the extremes of nature.

plurals that do not end in *-s*

The plurals of certain nouns from Greek and Latin are formed as they were in their original language. Words such as *data, criteria, media,* and *phenomena* are plural and should be treated as such. Each has its own distinctive singular form: *datum, criterion, medium, phenomenon.*

> Are the electronic *media* of the twentieth century contributing to the death of literature?

raise, rise

Raise is a transitive verb that usually takes a direct object. *Rise* is intransitive and never takes a direct object.

> In "On an Autumn Evening in the Mountains," poet Wang Wei *raises* an allegorical question about mortality.

> As the poets in Dante's *Inferno* pass the Gates of Hell, they hear the anguished cries of the opportunists *rise* within.

that, which, who

Use the relative pronoun *that* to refer to things. Use *which* only for things and *who* only for people. Use *that* when introducing a subordinate clause that singles out a particular thing or person.

> The Ibsen play that I most enjoy is *A Doll House.*

Which is usually used to introduce a subordinate clause that is not essential to identifying the thing or person in question:

> World War II, *which* disrupted Colette's personal life, did not affect her literary output.

Who can be used to introduce either essential or nonessential subordinate clauses:

> Derek Walcott, *who* is deeply admired by many critics, won the Nobel Prize in Literature.

when, where

Do not directly follow a linking verb with *when* or *where.* Also, be careful not to use *where* when your context requires *that.*

> Evaluation is ~~when you make~~ *the process of making* a judgment about the quality or value of something.

> Colin read ~~where~~ *that* even though he was a physician, Anton Chekhov was plagued by poor health.

who, whom

Remember to use *who* only as a subject in clauses and sentences and *whom* only as an object.

> Goethe, *who* spent more than sixty years writing his masterpiece, first encountered the Faust story in a puppet show at a country fair.

> Alexander Pushkin, *whom* critics perceive as a man of plain words, wove magical tales with his simple dialogue.

INTERNET RESEARCH HANDBOOK

Introduction to the Internet

The Internet is a series of networks that are interconnected all over the world. The Internet allows users to have almost unlimited access to information stored on the networks. Dr. Berners-Lee, a physicist, created the Internet in the 1980s by writing a small computer program that allowed pages to be linked together using key words. The Internet was mostly text-based until 1992, when a computer program called the NCSA Mosaic (National Center for Supercomputing Applications) was created at the University of Illinois. This program was the first Web browser. The development of Web browsers greatly eased the ability of the user to navigate through all the pages stored on the Web. Very soon, the appearance of the Web was altered as well. More appealing visuals were added, and sound was implemented. This change made the Web more user-friendly and more appealing to the general public.

Using the Internet for Research

Key-Word Search

Before you begin a search, you should identify your specific topic. To make searching easier, narrow your subject to a key word or a group of key words. These are your search terms, and they should be as specific as possible. For example, if you are looking for the latest concert dates for your favorite musical group, you might use the band's name as a key word. However, if you were to enter the name of the group in the query box of the search engine, you might be presented with thousands of links to information about the group that is unrelated to what you want to know. You might locate such information as band member biographies, the group's history, fan reviews of concerts, and hundreds of sites with related names containing information that is irrelevant to your search. Because you used such a broad key word, you might need to navigate through all that information before you could find a link or subheading for concert dates. In contrast, if you were to type in "Duplex Arena and [band name]," you would have a better chance of locating pages that contain this information.

How to Narrow Your Search

If you have a large group of key words and still do not know which ones to use, write out a list of all the words you are considering. Once you have completed the list, scrutinize it. Then, delete the words that are least important to your search, and highlight those that are most important.

These **key search connectors** can help you fine-tune your search:

AND: Narrows a search by retrieving documents that include both terms. For example: *baseball* AND *playoffs*

OR: Broadens a search by retrieving documents including any of the terms. For example: *playoffs* OR *championships*

NOT: Narrows a search by excluding documents containing certain words. For example: *baseball* NOT *history of*

Tips for an Effective Search

1. Remember that search engines can be case-sensitive. If your first attempt at searching fails, check your search terms for misspellings and try again.
2. If you are entering a group of key words, present them in order from the most important to the least important key word.
3. Avoid opening the link to every single page in your results list. Search engines present pages in descending order of relevancy. The most useful pages will be located at the top of the list. However, read the description of each link before you open the page.
4. Some search engines provide helpful tips for specializing your search. Take the opportunity to learn more about effective searching.

Other Ways to Search

Using Online Reference Sites How you search should be tailored to what you are hoping to find. If you are looking for data and facts, use reference sites before you jump onto a simple search engine. For example, you can find reference sites to provide definitions of words, statistics about almost any subject, biographies, maps, and concise information on many topics. Here are some useful online reference sites:

Online libraries

Online periodicals

Almanacs

Encyclopedias

You can find these sources using subject searches.

Conducting Subject Searches As you prepare to go online, consider your subject and the best way to find information to suit your needs. If you are looking for general information on a topic and you want your search results to be extensive, consider the subject search indexes on most search engines. These indexes, in the form of category and subject lists, often appear on the first page of a search engine. When you click a specific highlighted word, you will be presented with a new screen containing subcategories of the topic you chose.

Evaluating the Reliability of Internet Resources

Just as you would evaluate the quality, bias, and validity of any other research material you locate, check the source of information you find online. Compare these two sites containing information about the poet and writer Langston Hughes:

Site A is a personal Web site constructed by a college student. It contains no bibliographic information or links to sites that he used. Included on the site are several poems by Langston Hughes and a student essay about the poet's use of symbolism. It has not been updated in more than six months.

Site B is a Web site constructed and maintained by the English Department of a major university. Information on Hughes is presented in a scholarly format, with a bibliography and credits for the writer. The site includes links to other sites and indicates new features that are added weekly.

For your own research, consider the information you find on Site B to be more reliable and accurate than that on Site A. Because it is maintained by experts in their field who are held accountable for their work, the university site will be a better research tool than the student-generated one.

Tips for Evaluating Internet Sources

1. Consider who constructed and who now maintains the Web page. Determine whether this author is a reputable source. Often, the URL endings indicate a source.
   - Sites ending in *.edu* are maintained by educational institutions.
   - Sites ending in *.gov* are maintained by government agencies (federal, state, or local).
   - Sites ending in *.org* are normally maintained by nonprofit organizations and agencies.
   - Sites ending in *.com* are commercially or personally maintained.
2. Skim the official and trademarked Web pages first. It is safe to assume that the information you draw from Web pages of reputable institutions, online encyclopedias, online versions of major daily newspapers, or government-owned sites produce information as reliable as the material you would find in print. In contrast, unbranded sites or those generated by individuals tend to borrow information from other sources without providing documentation. As information travels from one source to another, it could have been muddled, misinterpreted, edited, or revised.
3. You can still find valuable information in the less "official" sites. Check for the writer's credentials, and then consider these factors:
   - Do not be misled by official-looking graphics or presentations.
   - Make sure that the information is updated enough to suit your needs. Many Web pages will indicate how recently they have been updated.
   - If the information is borrowed, notice whether you can trace it back to its original source.

Respecting Copyrighted Material

Because the Internet is a relatively new and quickly growing medium, issues of copyright and ownership arise almost daily. As laws begin to govern the use and reuse of material posted online, they may change the way that people can access or reprint material.

Text, photographs, music, and fine art printed online may not be reproduced without acknowledged permission of the copyright owner.

CITING SOURCES

In research writing, cite your sources. In the body of your paper, provide a footnote, an endnote, or an internal citation, identifying the sources of facts, opinions, or quotations. At the end of your paper, provide a bibliography or a works-cited list, a list of all the sources you cite. Follow an established format, such as Modern Library Association (MLA) Style.

Works-Cited List (MLA Style)

A works-cited list must contain accurate information sufficient to enable a reader to locate each source you cite. The basic components of an entry are as follows:

- Name of the author, editor, translator, or group responsible for the work
- Title
- Place and date of publication
- Publisher

For print materials, the information required for a citation generally appears on the copyright and title pages of a work. For the format of works-cited list entries, consult the examples at right and in the chart on page R29.

Internal Citations (MLA Style)

An internal citation briefly identifies the source from which you have taken a specific quotation, factual claim, or opinion. It refers the reader to one of the entries on your works-cited list. An internal citation has the following features:

- It appears in parentheses.
- It identifies the source by the last name of the author, editor, or translator.
- It gives a page reference, identifying the page of the source on which the information cited can be found.

Punctuation An internal citation generally falls outside a closing quotation mark but within the final punctuation of a clause or sentence. For a long quotation set off from the rest of your text, place the citation at the end of the excerpt without any punctuation following.

Special Cases

- If the author is an organization, use the organization's name, in a shortened version if necessary.
- If you cite more than one work by the same author, add the title or a shortened version of the title.

Sample Works-Cited Lists

Carwardine, Mark, Erich Hoyt, R. Ewan Fordyce, and Peter Gill. *The Nature Company Guides: Whales, Dolphins, and Porpoises.* New York: Time-Life Books, 1998.

Whales in Danger. "Discovering Whales." 18 Oct. 1999. <http://whales.magna.com.au/DISCOVER>

Neruda, Pablo. "Ode to Spring." *Odes to Opposites.* Trans. Ken Krabbenhoft. Ed. and illus. Ferris Cook. Boston: Little, Brown and Company, 1995.

The Saga of the Volsungs. Trans. Jesse L. Byock. London: Penguin Books, 1990.

List an anonymous work by title.

List both the title of the work and the title of the collection in which it is found.

Sample Internal Citations

It makes sense that baleen whales such as the blue whale, the bowhead whale, the humpback whale, and the sei whale (to name just a few) grow to immense sizes (Carwardine, Hoyt, and Fordyce 19–21). The blue whale has grooves running from under its chin to partway along the length of its underbelly. As in some other whales, these grooves expand and allow even more food and water to be taken in (Ellis 18–21).

Authors' last names

Page numbers where information can be found

MLA Style for Listing Sources

Book with one author	Pyles, Thomas. *The Origins and Development of the English Language.* 2nd ed. New York: Harcourt Brace Jovanovich, Inc., 1971.
Book with two or three authors	McCrum, Robert, William Cran, and Robert MacNeil. *The Story of English.* New York: Penguin Books, 1987.
Book with an editor	Truth, Sojourner. *Narrative of Sojourner Truth.* Ed. Margaret Washington. New York: Vintage Books, 1993.
Book with more than three authors or editors	Donald, Robert B., et al. *Writing Clear Essays.* Upper Saddle River, NJ: Prentice-Hall, Inc., 1996.
Single work from an anthology	Hawthorne, Nathaniel. "Young Goodman Brown." *Literature: An Introduction to Reading and Writing.* Ed. Edgar V. Roberts and Henry E. Jacobs. Upper Saddle River, NJ: Prentice-Hall, Inc., 1998. 376–385. [Indicate pages for the entire selection.]
Introduction in a published edition	Washington, Margaret. Introduction. *Narrative of Sojourner Truth.* By Sojourner Truth. New York: Vintage Books, 1993, pp. v–xi.
Signed article in a weekly magazine	Wallace, Charles. "A Vodacious Deal." *Time,* 14 Feb. 2000: 63.
Signed article in a monthly magazine	Gustaitis, Joseph. "The Sticky History of Chewing Gum." *American History,* Oct. 1998: 30–38.
Unsigned editorial or story	"Selective Silence." Editorial. *Wall Street Journal,* 11 Feb. 2000: A14. [If the editorial or story is signed, begin with the author's name.]
Signed pamphlet	[Treat the pamphlet as though it were a book.]
Pamphlet with no author, publisher, or date	*Are You at Risk of Heart Attack?* n.p. n.d. [n.p. n.d. indicates that there is no known publisher or date]
Filmstrips, slide programs, and videotapes	*The Diary of Anne Frank.* Dir. George Stevens. Perf. Millie Perkins, Shelley Winters, Joseph Schildkraut, Lou Jacobi, and Richard Beymer. Twentieth Century Fox, 1959.
Radio or television program transcript	"The First Immortal Generation." *Ockham's Razor.* Host Robyn Williams. Guest Damien Broderick. National Public Radio. 23 May 1999. Transcript.
Internet	*National Association of Chewing Gum Manufacturers.* 19 Dec. 1999 <http://www.nacgm.org/consumer/funfacts.html> [Indicate the date you accessed the information. Content and addresses at Web sites change frequently.]
Newspaper	Thurow, Roger. "South Africans Who Fought for Sanctions Now Scrap for Investors." *Wall Street Journal,* 11 Feb. 2000: A1+ [For a multipage article, write only the first page number on which it appears, followed by a plus sign.]
Personal interview	Smith, Jane. Personal interview. 10 Feb. 2000.
CD (with multiple publishers)	Simms, James, ed. *Romeo and Juliet.* By William Shakespeare. CD-ROM. Oxford: Attica Cybernetics Ltd.; London: BBC Education; London: HarperCollins Publishers, 1995.
Signed article from an encyclopedia	Askeland, Donald R. (1991). "Welding." *World Book Encyclopedia.* 1991 ed.

COLLEGE APPLICATION ESSAYS

If you are applying for admission to a college, you will probably need to submit an essay as part of your application. This essay is your introduction to a college applications committee. It will help committee members get a sense of you as a person and as a student. Review the chart at right for general strategies, and then follow the guidelines below to ensure that your college application essay does the best job presenting you.

Strategies for Writing an Effective College Application Essay

- **Choose the right topic.** If you have a choice of essay topics, choose the one that interests you.
- **Organize.** Use a strong organization that carries the reader from introduction to conclusion.
- **Begin with a bang.** Open with an introduction that has a good chance of sparking the reader's interest.
- **Elaborate.** Be sure to explain why the experiences you discuss are important to you or what you learned from them.
- **Show style.** Bring life to your essay through vivid descriptions, precise word choice, and sophisticated sentence structure, such as parallelism. Consider including dialogue where appropriate.
- **Close with a clincher.** Write a conclusion that effectively sums up your ideas.
- **Do a clean job.** Proofread your essay carefully to ensure that it is error-free.

Selecting a Topic

Read the essay question on the application form with care. Mark key criteria and direction words such as *describe* and *explain.* After you have written a first draft, check to make sure you have met all of the requirements of the question. Your essay has a better chance of succeeding if it meets the requirements exactly.

General Questions About You

The essay question on a college application may be as general as "Describe a significant experience or event in your life and explain its consequences for you." To choose the right topic for such a question, think of an event or experience that truly is meaningful to you—a camping trip, a volunteer event, a family reunion. Test the subject by drafting a letter about it to a good friend or relative. If you find that your enthusiasm for the subject grows as you write, and if your discussion reveals something about your growth or your outlook on life, the topic may be the right one for your essay.

Directed Questions

The essay question on an application may be more directed than a simple "tell us about yourself." For instance, you may be asked to select three figures from history you would like to meet and to explain your choices.

In such cases, do not give an answer just because you think it will please reviewers. Instead, consult your own interests and instincts. Your most convincing writing will come from genuine interest in the subject. You might discover the best topic by jotting down a diary entry or a letter to a friend in which you discuss possible subjects.

Style

Though an essay is a chance to tell something about yourself, it is also a formal document addressed to strangers. Use a formal to semiformal style. Avoid incomplete sentences and slang unless you are using them for clear stylistic effect. Use words with precision, selecting one or two accurate words for what you mean, rather than piling up words in the hope that one of them will hit the mark.

Format

Most applications limit the length of essays. Do not exceed the allowed space or number of words. Your college application essay should be neatly typed or printed, using adequate margins. Proofread your final draft carefully. If you submit a separate copy of the essay (rather than writing on the application form), number the pages and include your name and contact information on each page.

Reusing Your Essay

Most students apply to a number of different colleges in order to ensure their admission to a school for the next semester. Once you have written a strong essay for one application, you should consider adapting it for others.

Do not submit a single essay to several schools blindly. Always read the application essay question carefully to ensure that the essay you submit fulfills all of its requirements.

By writing **criticism**—writing that analyzes literature—readers share their responses to a written work. Criticism is also a way for a reader to deepen his or her own understanding and appreciation of the work and to help others deepen theirs.

The information in this handbook will guide you through the process of writing criticism. In addition, it will help you refine your critical perceptions to ensure that you are ready to produce work at the college level.

Understanding Criticism

There are a few different types of criticism. Each can enhance understanding and deepen appreciation of literature in a distinctive way. All types share similar functions.

The Types of Criticism

Analysis Students are frequently asked to analyze, or break into parts and examine, a passage or a work. When you write an analysis, you must support your ideas with references to the text, as in this example:

> **Conclusion:** In "Heat," the poet H.D. creates an enduring image of heat. There is no deeper meaning here; her task is to commemorate physical experience in words.
>
> **Support:** The poem's imagery gives heat solidity and depth. In the first stanza, the speaker asks the wind to "cut apart the heat" and, in the third stanza, to "plow through it," as if heat were a thick substance like earth.

Biographical Criticism Biographical criticism uses information about a writer's life to shed light on his or her work, as in this passage by Kenneth Silverman:

> Much of [Poe's] later writing, despite its variety of forms and styles, places and characters, is driven by the question of whether the dead remain dead. . . . [C]hildren who lose a parent at an early age, as Edgar lost Eliza Poe [his mother], invest more feeling in and magnify the parent's image. . . . The young child . . . cannot comprehend the finality of death. . . .

Historical Criticism Historical criticism traces connections between an author's work and the events, circumstances, or ideas that shaped the writer's historical era. For example, Jean H. Hagstrum analyzes William Blake's character of Urizen by showing how the character symbolizes the Enlightenment ideas of the scientist Isaac Newton and the philosopher John Locke.

> Urizen is also an active force. Dividing, partitioning, dropping the plummet line, applying Newton's compasses to the world, he creates abstract mathematical forms. Like Locke, he shrinks the senses, narrows the perceptions, binds man to the natural fact.

The Functions of Criticism

In each of the previous examples of criticism, you can find evidence of the following critical functions:

Making Connections All criticism makes connections between two or more things. For instance, the analysis of H.D.'s poetry connects different parts of a poem (the images of heat being cut or parted by a plow).

Making Distinctions Criticism must make distinctions as well as connections. In the analysis of "Heat," the critic distinguishes between two possible purposes for poetry: first, to create an enduring image and, second, to present a deeper meaning.

Achieving Insight By making connections and distinctions, criticism achieves insight. The analysis of H.D.'s poem reaches the insight that the poem stands on its own as a work of beauty apart from any deeper meaning.

Making a Judgment Assessing the value of a work is an important function of criticism. A critic may assess a work by comparing it with other works and by using a standard such as enjoyment, insight, or beauty.

"Placing" the Work Critics guide readers not by telling them *what* to think but by giving them *terms in which to think.* In the passage quoted above, Hagstrum helps us "place" Urizen. We cannot respond to Urizen, she reminds us, as if he were an individual like Macbeth or Holden Caufield. Instead, we respond to him best by perceiving him as a historical force—the pursuit of reason—personified. The terms on which we appreciate and understand each of these characters are different.

Writing Criticism

Like all solid writing, a work of criticism presents a thesis (a central idea) and supports it with arguments and evidence. Follow the strategies below to develop a critical thesis and gather support for it.

Formulate a Working Thesis

Once you have chosen a work or works on which to write, formulate a working thesis. First, ask yourself questions like these:

- What strikes you most about the work or the writer that your paper will address? What puzzles you most?
- In what ways is the work unlike others you have read?
- What makes the techniques used by the writer so well suited to (or so poorly chosen for) conveying the theme of the work?

Jot down notes answering your questions. Then, reread passages that illustrate your answers, jotting down notes about what each passage contributes to the work. Review your notes, and write a sentence that draws a conclusion about the work.

If your thesis concerns . . .	look for support in the form of . . .
Character	• dialogue • character's actions • writer's descriptions of the character • other characters' reactions to the character
Theme	• fate of characters • patterns and contrasts of imagery, character, or events • mood • writer's attitude toward the action
Style	• memorable descriptions, observations • passages that "sound like" the writer • examples of rhetorical devices, such as exaggeration and irony
Historical Context	• references to historical events and personalities • evidence of social or political pressures on characters • socially significant contrasts between characters (for example, between the rich and the poor)
Literary Influences	• writer's chosen form or genre • passages that "sound like" another writer • events or situations that resemble those in other works • evidence of an outlook similar to that of another writer

Gather Support

Taking Notes From the Work Once you have a working thesis, take notes on passages in the work that confirm it. To aid your search for support, consider the type of support suited to your thesis, as in the chart.

Conducting Additional Research If you are writing biographical or historical criticism, you will need to consult sources on the writer's life and era. Even if you are writing a close analysis of a poem, you should consider consulting the works of critics to benefit from their insights and understanding.

Take Notes

Consider recording notes from the works you are analyzing, as well as from any critical works you consult, on a set of note cards. A good set of note cards enables you to recall details accurately, to organize your ideas effectively, and to see connections between ideas.

One Card, One Idea If you use note cards while researching, record each key passage, theme, critical opinion, or fact on a separate note card. A good note card includes a brief quotation or summary of an idea and a record of the source, including the page number, in which you found the information. When copying a sentence from a work, use quotation marks and check to make sure you have copied it correctly.

Coding Sources Keep a working bibliography, a list of all works you consult, as you conduct research. Assign a code, such as a letter, to each work on the list. For each note you take, include the code for the source.

Coding Cards Organize your note cards by labeling each with the subtopic it concerns.

Present Support Appropriately

As you draft, consider how much support you need for each point and the form that support should take. You can provide support in the following forms:

- **Summaries** are short accounts in your own words of important elements of the work, such as events, a character's traits, or the writer's ideas. They are appropriate for background information.
- **Paraphrases** are restatements of passages from a work in your own words. They are appropriate for background and for information incidental to your main point.
- **Quotations of key passages** are direct transcriptions of the writer's words, enclosed in quotation marks or, if longer than three lines, set as indented text. If a passage is crucial to your thesis, you should quote it directly and at whatever length is necessary.

Stage of the Writing Process	The Developing Thesis Statement
Prewriting: A student rereads Sartre's story "The Wall" to find passages that support her thesis.	**First formulation:** "In his short story 'The Wall,' Sartre illustrates the belief that human life is ruled by inescapable fate."
Drafting: As the student summarizes the story's ending, she is struck by the fact that the narrator's final act has exactly the opposite effect from what he intended. She revises her thesis statement.	**Second formulation:** "In his short story 'The Wall,' Sartre demonstrates the power of fate by showing how the effects of a person's actions can completely contradict the person's intentions."
Revising: As the student rereads her first draft, she grows dissatisfied with her explanation of the story's ending. Why does the writer spend so much time showing the narrator's resignation to fate, only to have fate strike unexpectedly? She reworks her paper to support a new thesis statement.	**Final formulation:** "In his short story 'The Wall,' Sartre shows that 'fate' is a myth: However hard we try to resign ourselves to fate, we can never eliminate our responsibility for our own actions."

Quotations of multiple examples are required to support claims about general features of a work, such as a claim about the writer's ironic style or use of cartoonlike characters.

Revise Ideas as You Draft

When writing criticism, do not be afraid to revise your early ideas based on what you learn as you research or write further. As you draft, allow the insights—or the difficulties—that emerge to guide you back to the writer's works or other sources for clarification or support. What you discover may lead you to modify your thesis.

The chart above presents an example of the way this circular process can work.

Do's and Don'ts of Academic Writing

Avoid gender and cultural bias. Certain terms and usages reflect the bias of past generations. To eliminate bias in any academic work you do, edit with the following rules in mind:

- **Pronoun usage** When referring to an unspecified individual in a case in which his or her gender is irrelevant, use forms of the pronoun phrase *he or she*. Example: "A lawyer is trained to use his or her mind."
- **"Culture-centric" terms** Replace terms that reflect a bias toward one culture with more generally accepted synonyms. For instance, replace terms such as *primitive* (used for hunting-gathering peoples), *the Orient* (used to refer to Asia), and *Indians* (used for Native Americans), all of which suggest a view of the world centered in Western European culture.

Avoid plagiarism. Presenting someone else's ideas, research, or exact words as your own is plagiarism, the equivalent of stealing or fraud. Laws protect the rights of writers and researchers in cases of commercial plagiarism. Academic standards protect their rights in cases of academic plagiarism.

To avoid plagiarism, follow these practices:

- Read from several sources.
- Synthesize what you learn.
- Let the ideas of experts help you draw your own conclusions.
- Always credit your sources properly when using someone else's ideas to support your view.

By following these guidelines, you will also push yourself to think independently.

Forming Your Critical Vocabulary

To enhance your critical perceptions—the connections you find and the distinctions you make—improve your critical vocabulary. The following glossary shows contrasting pairs of critical terms. Some of these pairs define a spectrum along which you can place a work; others define simple opposites.

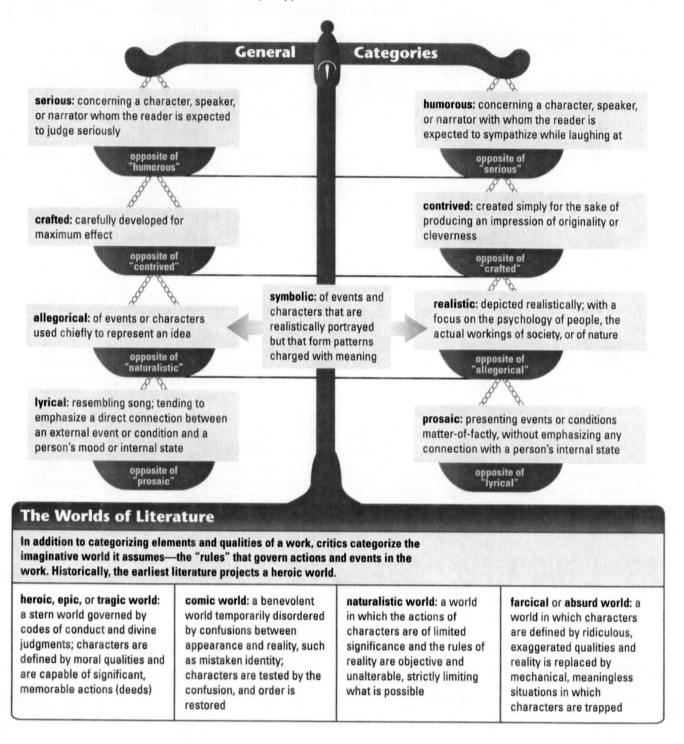

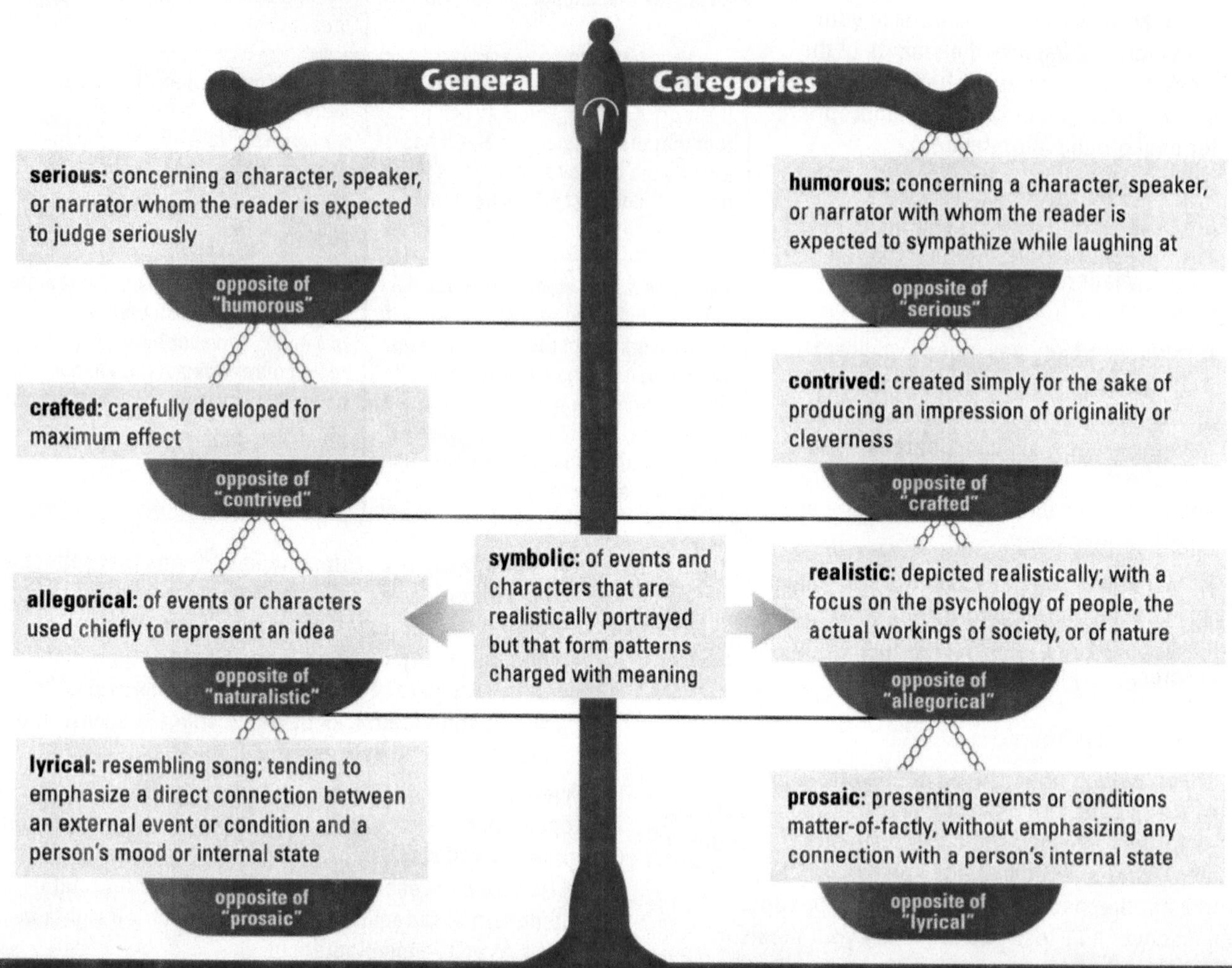

General Categories
serious: concerning a character, speaker, or narrator whom the reader is expected to judge seriously
opposite of "humorous"
humorous: concerning a character, speaker, or narrator with whom the reader is expected to sympathize while laughing at
opposite of "serious"
crafted: carefully developed for maximum effect
opposite of "contrived"
contrived: created simply for the sake of producing an impression of originality or cleverness
opposite of "crafted"
allegorical: of events or characters used chiefly to represent an idea
opposite of "naturalistic"
symbolic: of events and characters that are realistically portrayed but that form patterns charged with meaning
realistic: depicted realistically; with a focus on the psychology of people, the actual workings of society, or of nature
opposite of "allegorical"
lyrical: resembling song; tending to emphasize a direct connection between an external event or condition and a person's mood or internal state
opposite of "prosaic"
prosaic: presenting events or conditions matter-of-factly, without emphasizing any connection with a person's internal state
opposite of "lyrical"

The Worlds of Literature

In addition to categorizing elements and qualities of a work, critics categorize the imaginative world it assumes—the "rules" that govern actions and events in the work. Historically, the earliest literature projects a heroic world.

heroic, epic, or **tragic world:** a stern world governed by codes of conduct and divine judgments; characters are defined by moral qualities and are capable of significant, memorable actions (deeds)	**comic world:** a benevolent world temporarily disordered by confusions between appearance and reality, such as mistaken identity; characters are tested by the confusion, and order is restored	**naturalistic world:** a world in which the actions of characters are of limited significance and the rules of reality are objective and unalterable, strictly limiting what is possible	**farcical** or **absurd world:** a world in which characters are defined by ridiculous, exaggerated qualities and reality is replaced by mechanical, meaningless situations in which characters are trapped

Character

the people, animals, or other beings who perform or receive the action of a story	
flat: marked by one dominant characteristic	**rounded:** having a complex set of characteristics
static: unchanging	**dynamic:** developing and growing
self-aware: acting with an understanding of his or her own motives and the consequences of his or her actions	**blind** or **fated:** acting with no understanding of his or her own motives or of the consequences of his or her actions

Plot

the narrated sequence of events in a work; the storyline, usually divided into an exposition (in which situation and characters are introduced), the rising action, the climax (or moment of greatest tension), the falling action, and the resolution	
simple: telling of a single stream of events; each event affects the same set of characters	**complex:** telling of a number of streams of events, each involving a different set of characters (sets of characters may overlap)
dramatic: events unfold to build a maximum of tension or suspense, leading to a resolution	**episodic:** a series of loosely connected events occur, without building to a single, central climax or resolution
plot as driver: the question of "what happens next?" is intended to be the reader's primary interest in the work	**plot as vehicle:** the plot serves primarily to express a theme, display a character, or link together descriptions

Imagery

language used to suggest sensory experience, especially sensory experience linked by association to emotions and ideas	
original: unique to the writer; distinctive	**conventional:** expected; patterned after previous work
sensual: devoted to re-creating sensory experience	**metaphysical:** devoted to expressing abstract ideas or complicated analogies
effusive: pouring out; piled up	**patterned:** structured; controlled

Style

the distinctive features of a writer's choice of words and imagery, sentence length and structure, rhythm, and so on	
elaborate: characterized by complex detail	**direct:** simple; to the point
sincere: attempting to convey ideas without drawing attention to the style of their presentation	**parodic:** drawing attention to style in order to mock a style that other writers use seriously
straightforward: attempting to convey ideas directly	**ironic:** conveying ideas or attitudes by stating their opposites
conversational: resembling the style in which one friend might address another	**oracular:** suggesting that the writer is pronouncing deep truths without any particular concern that he or she be understood

Index of Authors and Titles

Page numbers in *italics* refer to biographical or background information. Some works have unknown authors, so the culture and literature type are given instead (e.g., Arabic prose).

Index of Skills (Numbers in **boldface** indicate definitions. Nonboldface numbers indicate examples.)

Literary Analysis

Reading Strategies

Grammar and Style

Vocabulary

Critical Thinking and Viewing

Writing Applications

Writing Strategies

Listening and Speaking

Research and Technology

Index of Features

ACKNOWLEDGMENTS

Grateful acknowledgment is made to the following for copyrighted material:

Ruth Harwood Cline and The University of Georgia Press "The Grail" by Chrétien de Troyes from *Perceval or The Story of the Grail,* translated by Ruth Harwood Cline. Copyright © 1983 by Ruth Harwood Cline. Reprinted by permission of The University of Georgia Press.

Toby Cole, Actors & Authors Agency "War" from *The Medals and Other Stories* by Luigi Pirandello. © E.P. Dutton, NY, 1932, 1967. Reprinted by permission of Toby Cole, Agent for the Pirandello Estate. All rights reserved. For performance rights in all media apply to Toby Cole, Agent for the Pirandello Estate, 295 Derby Street, #225, Berkeley, CA 94705.

Copper Canyon Press c/o The Permissions Company "Form, Shadow, Spirit" by T'ao Ch'ien, translated by David Hinton, from *Selected Poems of T'ao Ch'ien.* Copyright © 1993 by David Hinton. Reprinted with permission of Copper Canyon Press, P.O. Box 271, Port Townsend, WA 98368-0271, c/o The Permissions Company, High Bridge, New Jersey.

Darhansoff, Verrill, Feldman Literary Agents "I Am Not One of Those Who Left the Land" and "Everything Is Plundered" by Anna Akhmatova, translated by Stanley Kunitz, from *Poems of Akhmatova* by Stanley Kunitz with Max Hayward. Copyright © 1967, 1968, 1972, 1973 by Stanley Kunitz and Max Hayward. All rights reserved. Reprinted courtesy of Darhansoff Verrill Feldman Literary Agents.

Joan Daves Agency/Writer's House, Inc. c/o The Permissions Company "Fear" and "Time" by Gabriela Mistral, translated by Doris Dana, from *Selected Poems of Gabriela Mistral: A Bilingual Translation* (Baltimore: The Johns Hopkins University Press, 1971). Copyright © 1961, 1964, 1970, 1971 by Doris Dana. Reprinted with the permission of Joan Daves Agency/Writer's House, Inc., New York, on behalf of the proprietors; c/o The Permissions Company, High Bridge, New Jersey.

Doubleday, a division of Random House, Inc. "Marriage Is a Private Affair" from *Girls at War and Other Stories* by Chinua Achebe, copyright © 1972, 1973 by Chinua Achebe. "Half a Day" from *The Time and the Place and Other Stories* by Naguib Mahfouz, translated by Denys Johnson-Davies. Copyright © 1991 by the American University in Cairo Press. "Clouds come from time to time . . ." and "The sun's way . . ." two haikus by Matsuo Bashō from *An Introduction to Haiku* by Harold G. Henderson, copyright © 1958 by Harold G. Henderson. Used by permission of Doubleday, a division of Random House, Inc.

Dutton Signet, a division of Penguin Group (USA), Inc. "A Doll House" from *The Complete Major Prose Plays of Henrik Ibsen,* translated by Rolf Fjelde, copyright © 1965, 1970, 1978 by Rolf Fjelde. Used by permission of Dutton Signet, a division of Penguin Group (USA), Inc.

Everyman's Library "The Lay of the Werewolf" by Marie de France, translated by Eugene Mason, from *Lays of Marie de France and Other French Legends.* By permission of Everyman's Library.

Faber and Faber Limited "Folding Chairs" from *Selected Poems* by Günter Grass, translated by Michael Hamburger. Reprinted by permission of the publisher, Faber and Faber Ltd.

Farrar, Straus & Giroux, Inc. "When in early summer" by Nelly Sachs, translated by Ruth and Matthew Mead, from *The Seeker and Other Poems.* Copyright © 1970 by Farrar, Straus & Giroux, Inc. "Chapter XIII" from *Omeros* by Derek Walcott. Copyright © 1990 by Derek Walcott. "Freedom to Breathe" by Alexander Solzhenitsyn, translated by Michael Glenny, from *Alexander Solzhenitsyn: Stories and Prose Poems.* Translation copyright © 1970, 1971 by Michael Glenny. "The Grownup" by Rainer Maria Rilke, translated by Randall Jarrell, from *An Anthology of German Poetry from Hoderine to Rilke in English Translation.* "Comrades" from *Jump and Other Stories* by Nadine Gordimer. Copyright © 1991 by Felix Licensing B.V. All rights reserved. "A Walk to the Jetty" from *Annie John* by Jamaica Kincaid. © 1985 by Jamaica Kincaid. "Also All" and "Assembly Line" by Shu Ting, translated by Donald Finkel and Jinsheng Yi; "All" by Bei Dao, translated by Donald Finkel and Xueliang Chen, from *A Splintered Mirror, Chinese Poetry from the Democracy.* Translation copyright © 1991 by Donald Finkel. Excerpt from *Nobel Lecture* by Alexander Solzhenitsyn, translated by F. D. Reeve. Copyright © 1972 by the Nobel Foundation. Translation copyright © 1972 by Farrar, Straus & Giroux. "The Bracelet" from *The Collected Stories of Colette* by Colette. Translation copyright © 1957, 1966, 1983 by Farrar, Straus & Giroux, Inc. "from *The Expiation*: Russia 1812" by Victor Hugo, translated by Robert Lowell, from *Imitations.* Copyright © 1958, 1959, 1960, 1961 by Robert Lowell.

The Estate of Angel Flores c/o The Permissions Company Paul Valery, "Palm," translated by Kate Flores, and "The Friendly Wood," translated by Vernon Watkins; Arthur Rimbaud, "Ophelia," translated by Daisy Alden, from Angel Flores, ed., *An Anthology of French Poetry from Nerval to Valery in English Translation with French Originals* (New York: Anchor Books, 1958). Copyright © 1958 and renewed 1986 by Angel Flores. Rainer Maria Rilke, "Interior of the Rose," translated by Kate Flores, from *An Anthology of German Poetry from Holderlin to Rilke in English Translation with German Originals* (New York: Anchor Books, 1960). Copyright © 1960 and renewed 1988 by Angel Flores. Reprinted with permission of the Estate of Angel Flores, c/o The Permissions Company, High Bridge, New Jersey.

Foreign Languages Press "My Old Home" by Lu Hsun, translated by Yang Hsien-Yi and Gladys Young, from *Selected Stories of Lu Hsun.* Published and copyrighted by Foreign Languages Press, Bejing, China, 1960. Reprinted by permission.

David R. Godine, Publisher, Inc. "The Albatross" from *Les Fleurs du Mal* by Charles Baudelaire, translated from the French by Richard Howard, illustrations by Michael Mazur. Copyright © 1982 by Charles Baudelaire. Reprinted by permission of David R. Godine, Publisher, Inc.

Grove/Atlantic, Inc. "I Built My House Near Where Others Dwell" by T'ao Ch'ien, translated by William Acker, from *Anthology of Chinese Literature: From early times to the fourteenth century.* Copyright © 1965 by Grove Press, Inc. "The Soul With Boundaries" by Fernando Pessoa, translated by Richard Zenith, from *Fernando Pessoa & Co.: Selected Poems,* translation copyright © 1998 by Richard Zenith.

Harcourt, Inc. "Invitation to the Voyage" ("L'Invitation au Voyage") by Charles Baudelaire, from *Things of this World,* English translation, copyright © 1956 and renewed 1984 by Richard Wilbur. "The End and the Beginning" from *View with a Grain of Sand,* copyright © 1993 by Wisława Szymborska, English translation by Stanislaw Baranczak and Clare Cavanagh, copyright © 1995 by Harcourt, Inc. "The Garden of Stubborn Cats" from *Marcovaldo or the Seasons in the City* by Italo Calvino, copyright © 1963 by Giulio Einaudi editore, s.p.a., Torino, English translation by William Weaver, copyright © 1983 by Harcourt, Inc., and Martin Secker & Warburg, Ltd. Reprinted by permission of the publisher, Harcourt, Inc. This material may not be reproduced in any form or by any means without prior written permission of the publisher.

HarperCollins Publishers, Ltd. "By Any Other Name" from *Gifts of Passage* by Santha Rama Rau. Copyright © 1951 by Santha Rama Rau. Copyright renewed © 1979 by Santha Rama Rau. "By Any Other Name" originally appeared in *The New Yorker.* "The Handsomest Drowned Man in the World," from *Leaf Storm and Other Stories* by Gabriel Garcia Marquez. Copyright © 1971 by Gabriel Garcia Marquez. "A Song on the End of the World," from *The Collected Poems, 1931–1987* by Czesław Miłosz and translated by Robert Hass. Copyright © 1988 by Czesław Miłosz Royalties, Inc. Reprinted by permission of HarperCollins Publishers, Inc. "The Manner of Kings" by Sa'di, translated by Edward Rehatsek from *The Gulistan, or Rose Garden, of Sa'di.*

Hill and Wang, an imprint of Farrar, Straus & Giroux, Inc. From *Night* by Elie Wiesel, translated by Stella Rodway. Copyright © 1960 by MacGibbon & Kee; originally published in French by Les Editions de Minuit, copyright © 1958.

Hispanic Society of America "The Guitar" by Federico Garcia Lorca, from *Translations from Hispanic Poets.* Copyright © 1938 by The Hispanic Society of America. Reprinted with the permission of The Hispanic Society of America.

Barbara Hogenson Agency, Inc. "The Tiger Who Would Be King" by James Thurber, from *Further Fables for Our Time.* Copyright © 1956 by James Thurber. Copyright © renewed 1984 by Rosemary A. Thurber. Reprinted by arrangement with Rosemary A. Thurber and The Barbara Hogensen Agency, Inc.

Grateful acknowledgment is made to the following for copyrighted material:

Dutton Signet, an imprint of New American Library, a division of Penguin Putnam, Inc. Excerpt from "Foreword," from *Henrik Ibsen: Four Major Plays, Volume I* translated by Rolf Fjelde. Published by Dutton Signet, an imprint of New American Library, a division of Penguin Putnam, Inc. Copyright © by Rolf Fjelde, 1965, 1992. Note on the revised edition copyright © Rolf Fjelde, 1992. All rights reserved.

continued

Anselm Hollo "Food For Prophets" by Günter Grass, translated by Anselm Hollo, from *Modern European Poetry: French, German, Greek, Italian, Russian, Spanish.* Translation copyright Anselm Hollo 1966, 2003. Reprinted by permission of the translator.

Houghton Mifflin Company "Sent to Li Po as a Gift" by Tu Fu, translated by Florence Ayscough and Amy Lowell, from *Fir-Flower Tablets: Poems translated from the Chinese.* Published in 1921 by Houghton Mifflin Company, Boston, Mass. Copyright © 1921 by Florence Ayscough and Amy Lowell. Reprinted by Permission.

Ibis Editions "Twigs" by Taha Mahammad Ali, from *Never Mind: Twenty Poems and a Story*, translated by Peter Cole, Yahya Hijazi, and Gabriel Levin. Copyright © 2000 by Peter Cole, Yahya Hijazi, and Gabriel Levin. All rights reserved. Reprinted by permission of Peter Cole, Ibis Editions, P.O. Box 8074, Jerusalem, Israel, Telephone: 972-2-627-7035.

Indiana University Press "The Story of Daedalus and Icarus" by Ovid from *Ovid: Metamorphoses*, translated by Rolfe Humphries. Copyright © 1955 by Indiana University Press. Reprinted by permission of Indiana University Press.

International African Institute "African Proverbs: Liberia: The Jabo: 'The one who listens . . .', 'Children are the wisdom . . .', 'Daring talk . . .', 'One who cannot pick up an ant . . .', 'The butterfly that flies among . . .', 'A man's ways are good . . .'," from *Jabo Proverbs from Liberia: Maxims in the Life of Native Tribe.* Published for the International Institute of African Languages & Cultures by Oxford University Press, London: Humphrey Milford, 1936. By permission of the International African Institute.

The Estate of Alta Jablow "African Proverbs: Nigeria: The Yoruba: 'One does not set. . .'," from *Yes and No: The Intimate Folklore of Africa: Dilemma Tales, Proverbs and Stories of Love, and Adult Riddles* by Alta Jablow. Copyright © 1961 by Alta Jablow.

Melanie Jackson Agency, L.L.C. "Season," from *Idanre and Other Poems* by Wole Soyinka. Copyright © 1967, 1995 Wole Soyinka. All rights reserved. Reprinted by permission of Melanie Jackson Agency, L.L.C.

The Jewish Publication Society "Genesis 1–3: The Creation and the Fall," "Genesis 6–9: The Story of the Flood," "Book of Ruth" "Psalm 8," "Psalm 19," "Psalm 23," and "Psalm 137," reprinted from *Tanakh: A New Translation of the Holy Scriptures According to the Hebrew Text.* Copyright © 1985, by the Jewish Publication Society. Reprinted by permission.

John Johnson Ltd. "I have visited again" by Alexander Pushkin, translation © 1982 by D. M. Thomas, from *The Bronze Horseman: Selected Poems of Alexander Pushkin*, The Viking Press, New York, 1982. Reprinted by permission.

Alfred A. Knopf, Inc, a division of Random House, Inc. "The Guest," from *Exile and the Kingdom* by Albert Camus, translated by Justin O'Brien, copyright © 1957, 1958 by Alfred A. Knopf, Inc. a division of Random House, Inc. *Hiroshima* by John Hersey, copyright © 1946 and renewed 1974 by John Hersey. Used by permission of Alfred A. Knopf, Inc. a division of Random House, Inc.

L. R. Lind "Laura," "The White Doe," and "Spring" from *Canzoniere* by Francesco Petrarch, translated by Morris Bishop, reprinted by permission of L.R. Lind, Editor, from *Lyric Poetry of the Italian Renaissance*, copyright 1954. Used by permission.

Marian S. MacIntyre "Caesar" by Paul Valery, translated by C. F. MacIntyre, from *War and The Poet: An Anthology of Poetry Expressing Man's Attitudes to War From Ancient Times to The Present.*

Macmillan, Oxford, a division of Macmillan Publishers Ltd. Christopher Marlowe,*The Tragical History of Doctor Faustus.* Text of 1604, with Introduction and Notes by William Modlen (London: Macmillan & Co., repr. 1966), reproduced by permission of Macmillan, Oxford, a division of Macmillan Publishers, Ltd.

The Modern Library, an imprint of Random House, Inc. Chapter I and Chapter II from *Candide; And Philosophical Letters* by Voltaire, translated by Richard Aldington, copyright © 1928, 1956, 1984 by Random House, Inc. Used by permission of Modern Library, a division of Random House, Inc.

Jonathan Musere "African Proverbs: Uganda: The Bagada: 'A small deed out of friendship . . .,' 'Two people can keep the words a secret . . .,' 'One who loves you, warns you . . .,' 'The one who is hopeful . . .,' 'The one who has not made the journey . . .,' 'The one who travels is the one who sees things . . .,' 'Words are easy, but friendship is difficult . . .,' and 'Where there are no dogs . . .' " from *African Proverbs and Proverbial Names* by Jonathan Musere. Copyright © 1999 by Ariko Publications. Reprinted by permission.

Museum of Science, Boston From "The Quest for Immortality" brochure. Materials courtesy of the Museum of Science, Boston.

New Directions Publishing Corporation "Jade Flower Palace" by Tu Fu, translated by Kenneth Rexroth, from *One Hundred Poems from the Chinese*, copyright © 1971 by Kenneth Rexroth. "The River-Merchant's Wife: A Letter" by Ezra Pound, from *Personae*, copyright © 1926 by Ezra Pound. "Absent Soul" (from *Lament for Ignacio Sanchez Mejias*) by Federico Garcia Lorca, translated by Stephen Spender and J.K. Gili, from *The Selected Poems of Federico Garcia Lorca*, copyright © 1955 by New Directions Publishing Corp. "Concord" by Octavio Paz, translated by Eliot Weinberger, from *Collected Poems: 1957–1987*, copyright © 1986 by Octavio Paz and Eliot Weinberger. "Fable" by Octavio Paz, translated by Muriel Rukeyser, from *Early Poems of Octavio Paz*, copyright © 1973 by Octavio Paz and Muriel Rukeyser. Reprinted by permission of New Directions Publishing Corp.

Northwestern University Press and Helen F. Pratt, Inc. Literary Agency Pasternak, Boris. "The Weeping Orchard," from *My Sister – Life.* Translated by Mark Rudman with Bohdan Boychuk. Evanston: Northwestern University Press, 1992, p.13. Copyright © 1983 by Mark Rudman. First published in 1983 by Ardis. Northwestern University Press edition 1992. All rights reserved. Reprinted by permission by Northwestern University Press.

New York Times Co. "Leonardo: The Eye, the Hand, the Mind" by Holland Cotter, from *The New York Times*, January 24, 2003. Copyright © 2003 by the New York Times Co. Reprinted by permission.

Harold Ober Associates, Incorporated "Marriage Is a Private Affair," from *Girls at War and Other Stories* by Chinua Achebe, copyright © 1972, 1973 by Chinua Achebe. Reprinted by permission of Harold Ober Associates, Incorporated.

Oberlin College Press "She used to throw away her old crockery" and "My mother would lose herself" by Vénus Khoury-Ghata, translated by Marilyn Hacker, from *Here There Was Once a Country*, copyright © 2001 by Oberlin College. Reprinted by Oberlin College Press.

Oxford University Press, Inc. and David Higham Associates Ltd. "The First Part of the Tragedy: Night" and "Prologue in Heaven" from *Faust* by Johann Wolfgang von Goethe, translated by Louis MacNeice, copyright © 1951, 1954 by Federick Louis MacNeice; renewed 1979 by Hedi MacNeice. Used by permission of Oxford University Press, Inc.

The Clarendon Press, an imprint of Oxford University Press "African Proverbs: Tanzania and Kenya: The Masai: 'We begin by being foolish . . .,' 'Do not repair another man's fence . . .', 'Nobody can say . . .', 'It is better to be poor . . .', 'Baboons do not go far . . .', 'The hyena said . . .', 'The zebra cannot do away . . .'," from *The Masai: Their Language and Folklore* by A. C. Hollis. Published in 1905 by The Clarendon Press.

Oxford University Press, UK and Columbia University Press "The Cat Who Lived in the Palace," "Things That Arouse a Fond Memory of the Past," and "I Remember a Clear Morning" from *The Pillow Book of Sei Shōnagon* by Sei Shōnagon, translated and edited by Ivan Morris. Copyright © Ivan Morris 1967.

Pantheon Books, a division of Random House, Inc. "House Taken Over," from *End of the Game and Other Stories* by Julio Cortazar, translated by Paul Blackburn, copyright © 1963, 1967 by Random House, Inc. Used by permission of Pantheon Books, a division of Random House, Inc.

Pearson Education, Inc. publishing as Pearson Prentice Hall "What Is an Insect?" from *Prentice Hall Biology* by Kenneth R. Miller, Ph.D., and Joseph Levine, Ph.D. © 2002 Pearson Education, Inc., publishing as Pearson Prentice Hall. Used by permission.

Pearson Education Ltd. "Childhood" and "The Lion's Awakening" from *Sundiata: An Epic of Old Mali* by D. T. Niane, translated by G.D. Pickett. Copyright © Présence Africaine, 1960 (original French version: *Soundjata, ou L'Epopée Mandingue*). © 1965 Longman Group Ltd. (English). Reprinted by permission of Pearson Education Limited.

Penguin Books Ltd., London "The Burning of Rome," from *The Annals of Imperial Rome* by Tacitus, translated by Michael Grant (Penguin Classics 1956, Sixth revised edition 1989), copyright © Michael Grant Publications

Acknowledgments continued

Graywolf Press
Excerpt from "Afterword," by Venus Khoury-Ghata from *She Says* translated by Marilyn Hacker. Copyright © 1999, 2000, 2003 by Venus Khoury-Ghata (French). Translation and Introduction copyright © 2003 by Marilyn Hacker. Published by Graywolf Press, 2402 University Avenue, Suite 203, Saint Paul, Minnesota, 55114. All rights reserved. *continued*

Ltd., 1969. "The Fisherman and the Jinnee," from *Tales from the Thousand and One Nights*, translated by N. J. Dawood (Penguin Classics 1954, Revised edition 1973), translation copyright © N. J. Dawood, 1954, 1973. "Creation Hymn" and "Night," from *The Rig Veda, An Anthology*, translated by Wendy Doniger O'Flaherty (Penguin Classics, 1981). Copyright © Wendy Doniger O'Flaherty, 1981. "Visit" by Yevgeny Yevtushenko from *Yevtushenko: Selected Poems*, translated by Robin Milner-Gulla and Peter Levi, S.J. (Penguin Books, 1962), copyright © Robin Milner-Gulla and Peter Levi, 1962. "The Qur'an" from *The Koran*, translated by N. J. Dawood (Penguin Classics, 1956, Fifth revised edition 1990). Copyright © N. J. Dawood, 1956, 1959, 1966, 1968, 1974, 1990. "Prayer to Masks" by Léopold Sédar Senghor, translated by Gerald Moore and Ulli Beier, from *The Penguin Book of Modern African Poetry*, edited by Gerald Moore and Ulli Beier, first published as *Modern Poetry from Africa*, 1963 (Penguin Books, 1984). Copyright © Gerald Moore and Ulli Beier, 1963, 1968, 1984. "Federigo's Falcon" (originally titled "Ninth Story") from *The Decameron* by Giovanni Boccaccio, translated by G.H. McWilliam (Penguin Classics, 1972, Second Edition, 1995). Copyright © G.H. McWilliam, 1972, 1995. "Pericles' Funeral Oration" by Thucydides from *History of the Peloponnesian Wars*, translated by Rex Warner (Penguin Classics, 1954). Translation copyright © Rex Warner, 1954. "Prologue," "The Battle with Humbaba," "The Death of Enkidu," "The Story of The Flood," and "The Return," from *The Epic of Gilgamesh*, translated by N. K. Sanders (Penguin Classics 1960, Third Edition 1972). Copyright © N. K. Sanders, 1960, 1964, 1972. "I, III, IX & XLIII," from *Tao Te Ching: The Book of Meaning and Life* by Lao Tzu, translated into English by Richard Wilhelm, translated into German by H. G. Ostwald (Arkana, 1989), copyright © Eugen Diederichs Verlad GmbH & Co, Koln, 1985. English translation copyright © Routeledge & Kegan Paul, 1985. "How Siegfried Was Slain" from *The Nibelungenlied*, translated by A. T. Hatto (Penguin Classics, 1965, revised edition 1969), copyright © A. T. Hatto, 1965, 1969. Tanka: "Was it that I went to sleep . . . ," 5 lines by Ono Komachi; Tanka: "When I went to visit . . . ," 5 lines by Ki Tsurayuki; Tanka: "One cannot ask loneliness . . . ," 4 lines by Priest Jakuren; Haiku: "The cuckoo . . . ," "Seven sights were veiled . . . ," and "Summer grasses . . . ," 9 lines by Matsuo Bashō; Haiku: "A World of Dew . . ." "Far-off mountain peaks . . . ," "With Bland Serenity . . . ," and "Beautiful, seen through holes . . . ," 12 lines by Yosa Buson; Haiku: "Spring Rain: Telling a tale as they go . . . ," "Soaking on the roof . . . ," "A man lives here . . . ," and "In our sedan . . . ," 12 lines by Yosa Buson, from *The Penguin Book of Japanese Verse*, translated by Geoffrey Bownas and Anthony Thwaite (Penguin Books 1964, Revised edition 1998). Translation copyright © Geoffrey Bownas and Anthony Thwaite, 1964, 1998. Reproduced by permission of Penguin Books Ltd.

The Sheep Meadow Press "Pride" by Dahlia Ravikovitch, from *A Dress of Fire*, translated by Chana Bloch, The Sheep Meadow Press, Riverdale-on-Hudson. Reprinted by permission.

Persea Books, Inc. "On Living," from *Poems of Nazım Hikmet*, translated by Randy Blasing and Mutlu Konuk. Translation copyright © 1994, 2002 by Randy Blasing and Mutlu Konuk. Reprinted by permission of Persea Books, Inc. (New York).

Peter Pauper Press, Inc. "African Proverbs: Nigeria: The Yoruba: 'A wise man who knows proverbs . . .,' 'The day on which one starts out . . .,' 'He who is being carried does not realize . . .,' 'Time destroys all things.' and 'Little is better than nothing.'" "African Proverbs: Tanzania and Kenya: The Masai: 'Do not say the first thing . . .,' and 'A man who has once been tossed by a buffalo . . .'" "African Proverbs: Ghana: The Ashanti: 'Rain beats a leopard skin . . .,' 'If you are in hiding . . .,' 'One falsehood . . .,' and 'No one tests the depth of a river . . . '" from *African Proverbs*, compiled by Charlotte and Wolfe Leslau. Copyright © 1962, Peter Pauper Press. Reprinted by permission.

Princeton University Press "Ithaka" by C. P. Cavafy, from *C. P. Cavafy: Selected Poems*, translated by Edmund Keeley and Philip Sherrard. Copyright © 1972 by Edmund Keeley and Philip Sherrard. Reprinted by permission of Princeton University Press.

Random House, Inc. "Book II: How They Took the City" from *The Aeneid* by Virgil, translated by Robert Fitzgerald, copyright © 1980, 1982, 1983 by Robert Fitzgerald. Used by permission of Random House, Inc.

Rosalie Torres-Rioseco "The Glass of Milk" by Manuel Rojas, translated by Zoila Nelken, from *Short Stories of Latin America*, edited by Arturo Torres-Rioseco, translated by Zoila Nelken and Rosalie Torres-Rioseco. Copyright 1963 by Las Americas Publishing Company. Reprinted by permission of Rosalie Torres-Rioseco.

Rupert Crew Limited on behalf of Steve and Megumi Biddle "The Origins of Origami" by Steve and Megumi Biddle from *Origami: Inspired by Japanese Prints*. Copyright © 1998 by The Metropolitan Museum of Art. Introduction, instructions, diagrams and models © 1998 by Steve and Megumi Biddle. All rights reserved. Reprinted by permission.

Carl Sesar "My Woman Says There's Nobody She'd Rather Marry," "I Crossed Many Lands and a Lot of Ocean," and "I Hate Her and I Love Her" by Gaius Valerius Catullus from *Selected Poems of Catullus*, translated by Carl Sesar. Copyright © 1974, 2001 by Carl Sesar. Reprinted by permission of the translator, Carl Sesar.

Edward Seidensticker "The Jay" by Yasunari Kawabata, translated by Edward Seidensticker, from *Contemporary Japanese Literature, An Anthology of Fiction, Film, and Other Writing Since 1945*, edited by Howard Hibbett. Copyright © 1977. Reprinted by permission of the translator, Edward Seidensticker.

Simon & Schuster Adult Publishing Group "The Wooden People," reprinted with permission of Simon & Schuster Adult Publishing Group from *Popol Vuh: The Definitive Edition of the Mayan Book of the Dawn of Life and the Glories of Gods and Kings*, translated by Dennis Tedlock. Copyright © Dennis Tedlock, 1985, 1996.

William Jay Smith "The Sleeper in the Valley" by Arthur Rimbaud, translated by William Jay Smith, from *Collected Translations: Italian, French, Spanish, Portuguese*, New Rivers Press, 1985, copyright © 1967 by William Jay Smith. Reprinted by permission.

Elyse Sommer "CurtainUp Guest Review: A Doll's House," copyright April 1997, Elyse Sommer, *CurtainUp*. *CurtainUp.com* is a 7-year-old online theater magazine: *www.curtainup.com*. Reproduced by permission of Elyse Sommer.

David Spencer "A Doll's House by Henrik Ibsen, a new version by Frank McGuinness," reviewed by David Spencer, from *www.aislesay.com*. Reprinted by permission of the author, David Spencer.

Story Line Press "Autumn Song" by Paul Verlaine, translated by Louis Simpson, from *Modern Poets of France, A Bilingual Anthology*. Copyright © 1997, 1998 by Louis Simpson. Reprinted by permission of the translator and Story Line Press.

The Swedish Academy "Imre Kertesz: Recipient of the Nobel Prize in Literature, 2002," by The Swedish Academy.

Tufts University, Perseus Project, Classics Department "from The Perseus Digital Library (*http://www.perseus.tufts.edu/Olympics/*)," reproduced by kind permission of Tufts University, Perseus Project.

Charles E. Tuttle Co, Inc. of Boston, Massachussetts and Tokyo, Japan "Zen Parables: 'A Parable,' 'The Taste of Banzo's Sword,' and 'Publishing the Sutras,'" from *Zen Flesh, Zen Bones: A Collection of Zen & Pre-Zen Writings*, compiled by Paul Reps. Reprinted by permission.

UNESCO Publishing "Under Reconstruction" by Mori Ōgai, translated by Ivan Morris, from *Modern Japanese Stories: An Anthology*, edited by Ivan Morris. Copyright © 1962 for the English translation by UNESCO Publishing. UNESCO Collection of Representative Works—Japanese Series. Reproduced by permission of UNESCO.

The University of California Press "He is More Than a Hero" and "You Know the Place: Then" by Sappho from *Sappho: A New Translation*, translated by Mary Barnard. Copyright © 1958, by The Regents of the University of California. "Lightness" and "Green" by Juan Ramon Jimenez, from *Juan Ramon Jimenez: Fifty Spanish Poems*, translated by J. B. Trend. "The Diameter of the Bomb" and "From The Book of Esther I Filtered the Sediment" by Yehuda Amichai, from *The Selected Poetry of Yehuda Amichai*, translated by Chana Boch and Stephen Mitchell. English translation copyright © 1986 by Chana Boch and Stephen Mitchell. Reprinted by permission.

The University of Chicago Press "Olympia 11" by Pindar, from *The Odes of Pindar, Second Edition*, translated by Richmond Lattimore. Copyright © 1947, 1976 by The University of Chicago Press. "He Is More Than a Hero" by Sappho, from *Greek Lyrics*, translated by Richmond Lattimore. Copyright © 1949 and 1955 by Richmond Lattimore. "Numskull and the Rabbit" from *The Panchatantra*, translated by Arthur W. Ryder. Copyright © 1925 by The University of Chicago. Copyright renewed 1953 by Mary E. Ryder and Winifred Ryder. "Oedipus the King" by Sophocles, D. Grene, translator, from *The Complete Greek Tragedies: Oedipus the King, Oedipus at Colonus, Antigone,*

Acknowledgments continued

HarperCollins Publishers, Ltd.
From *Yehuda Amichai: Time* (originally titled "20") translated from the Hebrew by the author with Ted Hughes. Published by Oxford University Press, 1979. Copyright © Yehuda Amichai, 1979. All rights reserved. Reprinted by permission of HarperCollins Publishers, Ltd.

continued

Volume II, D. Grene and Richmond Lattimore, editors, pp. 11–76. Copyright © 1942 by The University of Chicago. All rights reserved. Reprinted by permission of The University of Chicago Press.

University of Texas Press "Sonnet 49" (p. 105) and "Sonnet 71" (p. 151) from *100 Love Sonnets: Cien Sonetos de Amor*, by Pablo Neruda, translated by Stephen Tapscott. Copyright © Pablo Neruda 1959 and Fundacion Pablo Neruda, Copyright © 1986 by the University Texas Press. By permission of the University of Texas Press.

University of Texas Press "The voice of the swallow, flittering, calls to me" and "I think I'll go home and lie very still," from *Love Songs of the New Kingdom*, translated from the Ancient Egyptian by John L. Foster, illustrated with hieroglyphs drawn by John L. Foster, Copyright © 1969, 1970, 1971, 1972, 1973, 1974 by John L. Foster. By permission of the University of Texas Press.

Vedanta Society of Southern California "The Yoga of Knowledge" from *The Song of God: Bhagavad-Gita*, translated by Swami Prabhavananda and Christopher Isherwood. Copyright © 1944, 1951 by The Vedanta Society of Southern California. Reprinted by permission.

Viking Penguin, a division of Penguin Group (USA) Inc. "from Book 1: The Quarrel (originally titled "from Book 1: The Rage of Achilles")," "from Book 6: The Meeting of Hector and Andromache (originally titled "from Book 6: Hector Returns to Troy")," "from Book 24: Achilleus and Priam," "from Book 22: The Death of Hector," from *The Iliad* by Homer, translated by Robert Fagles, copyright © 1990 by Robert Fagles. "The Fox and the Crow," copyright © 1952 by Marianne Moore, renewed © 1980 by Lawrence E. Brinn and Louise Crane, Executors of the Estate, "The Oak and the Reed," from *The Fables of La Fontaine*, translated by Marianne Moore, copyright © 1952, 1953, 1954, © 1964 by Marianne Moore, renewed © 1980, 1981, 1982 by Lawrence Brinn and Louise Crane, Executors of the Estate. "On the Bottom" from *If This Is a Man (Survival in Auschwitz)* by Primo Levi, translated by Stuart Woolf, copyright © 1959 by Orion Press, Inc., © 1958 by Giulio Einaudi editore, s.p.a. "The Ingenious Gentleman Don Quixote de la Mancha" from *Don Quixote* by Miguel de Cervantes Saavedra, translated by Samuel Putnam, copyright © 1949 by The Viking Press, Inc. "Rama and Ravana in the Battle" from *The Ramayana* by R.K. Narayan, copyright © 1972 by R. K. Narayan. Used by permission of Viking Penguin, a division of Penguin Group (USA), Inc.

Visva-Bharati Publishing Department, Visva Bharati University "The Artist" by Rabindranath Tagore, from *The Housewarming and Other Selected Writings*, translated by Amiya Chakravarty, Mary Lago, and Tarun Gupta. Copyright © 1965 Amiya Chakravarty. All rights reserved. Used by permission.

W. W. Norton & Company, Inc. From *The Song of Roland*, translated by Frederick Goldin. Copyright © 1978 by W.W. Norton & Company, Inc. Cantos I, III, V, and XXXIV from the *Divine Comedy: Inferno* by Dante Alighieri, translated by John Ciardi. Copyright © 1954, 1957, 1959, 1960, 1965, 1967, 1970 by the Ciardi Family Publishing Trust. This selection may not be reproduced, stored in a retrieval system or transmitted in any form or by any means without prior written permission of the publisher. Used by permission of W.W. Norton & Company, Inc.

The Arthur Waley Estate "from *The Book of Songs:* 34" and "from *The Book of Songs:* 24," from *Translations from the Chinese*, and "from *The Analects of Confucius*," translated by Arthur Waley, George Allen & Unwin, Ltd. London. All rights reserved. Reprinted by permission of the Arthur Waley Estate.

Wallace Literary Agency, Inc. "An Astrologer's Day" by R. K. Narayan, from *The Grandmother's Tale*. Copyright © 1994 by R. K. Narayan. Ecco Press, Hopewell, NJ. Used by permission of the Wallace Literary Agency, Inc. "Sibi," from *The Mahabharata* by R. K. Narayan, from *Gods, Demons, and Others*. Copyright © 1964 by R. K. Narayan. Used by permission of the Wallace Literary Agency.

Washington Post Writers Group "A Lot of Baggage for Nora to Carry: After a History of Misinterpretation, Ibsen's Leave-Taking Heroine Finally Gets Her Due" by Lloyd Rose from *The Washington Post*, April 20, 1997. Copyright © 1997, The Washington Post. Reprinted with permission.

Gwendoline Mary Watkins "Comme on voit sur la branche . . ." ("Roses") by Pierre Ronsard, translated by Vernon Watkins. Reprinted by permission.

Witswaterarand University Press "African Proverbs: South Africa: The Zulu: 'You cannot chase two gazelles,' 'The one offended never forgets,' 'There is no river,' 'No dew ever competed,' 'It never dawns in the same way,' 'Look as you fell a tree,' 'Do not speak of rhinoceros,' 'Eyes do not see all,' 'There is no foot,' 'What has happened before,' 'Almost is not eaten,'" from *Zulu Proverbs*, edited by C. L. Sibusiso Nyembezi, M.A. Copyright 1954 Witswaterarand University Press. All rights reserved. Reprinted by permission.

The Wylie Agency, Inc. for The Estate of Italo Calvino "The Garden of Stubborn Cats" from *Marcovaldo or the Seasons in the City* by Italo Calvino, translated by William Weaver. Copyright © 1983, The Estate of Italo Calvino, reprinted by permission of the Wylie Agency, Inc.

Yale University Press "The most beautiful youth who ever happened," translated by William Kelly Simpson, from *The Literature of Ancient Egypt: An Anthology of Stories, Instructions, and Poetry*, edited, with an introduction by William Kelly Simpson, with translations by R.O. Faulkner, Edward F. Wente, Jr. and William Kelly Simpson. Copyright © 1972 by Yale University. "To Helene" by Pierre de Ronsard, from *Lyrics of the French Renaissance: Marot, Du Bellay, Ronsard*, translated by Norman R. Shapiro. Copyright © 2002 by Yale University. "The voice of the wild goose," translated by William Kelly Simpson, from *The Literature of Ancient Egypt: An Anthology of Stories, Instructions, and Poetry*, edited by William Kelly Simpson. Copyright © 1972 by Yale University. All rights reserved. This book may not be reproduced in whole or in part, in any form (except by reviewers for the public press) without written permission from the publishers. Reprinted by permission.

The Estate of Avrahm Yarmolinsky "The Drowsy Garden" by Boris Pasternak, translated by Avrahm Yarmolinsky, from *Two Centuries of Russian Verse: An Anthology from Lomonosov to Voznesensky*.

Note: Every effort has been made to locate the copyright owner of material reprinted in this book. Omissions brought to our attention will be corrected in subsequent editions.

Acknowledgments continued

Penguin Press, a division of Penguin Books Ltd., London Approximately 4 lines from "The Ballad of Ch'ang-Kan (The Sailor's Wife)," by Li Po from *Li Po And Tu Fu: Poems Selected And Translated* translated by Arthur Cooper (Penguin Classics, 1973). Copyright © Arthur Cooper, 1973. All rights reserved. Reprinted by permission of Penguin Press, a division of Penguin Books Ltd., London.

continued

CREDITS

Cover and Title Page *Charles Bridge and the Hradcany Castle in Prague*, 1935, Oskar Kokoschka, National Gallery, Prague, Czech Republic, © 2003 Artists Rights Society (ARS), New York / Pro Litteris, Zurich; **vi–vii** *The Creation of Adam* (detail), Michelangelo, Scala/Art Resource, New York; **viii** © Matthias Kulka/CORBIS; **ix** CORBIS; **xi** *Achilles Deciding to Resume Fighting Upon the Death of Patroclus*, 1620, Dirck van Baburen/Bridgeman Art Library, London/New York; **xii** Araldo de Luca/CORBIS; **xiii (l.)** The Granger Collection, New York; **xiii (r.)** Geoff Dann/© Dorling Kindersley; **xiv** © Dorling Kindersley; **xvi** *Cornfield at Ewell*, William Holman Hunt, Art Resource; **xvii** *Three Graces* (detail), Botticelli, Giraudon/Art Resource, New York; **xviii** © Linda Bartlett/Photo Researchers, Inc.; **xx** Christie's Images/CORBIS; **1** *Walking Lion in Relief* (detail), 605–562 B.C., Mesopotamia, Babylonian mosaic, The Metropolitan Museum of Art, Fletcher Fund, 1931, © Copyright 1973/84 by The Metropolitan Museum of Art; **2 (m.l.)** Head of an Acadion Ruler, Nineveh, 2300–2200 B.C., Baghdad Museum, Scala/Art Resource, New York; **2 (m.r.)** Boltin Picture Library; **2 (t.)** Araldo de Luca/CORBIS; **2 (b.l.)** Founders Society purchase, General Membership Fund/Bridgeman Art Library, London/New York; **2 (b.r.)** The Palma Collection/Getty Images; **3 (m.)** Art Resource, New York; **3 (t.)** The Art Archive/Ethnic Jewellery Exhibition Milan/Dagli Orti; **3 (b.)** Senegalese glass painting used on Sundiata, from the collection of Professor Donal Cruise-O'Brien, Courtesy of Longman International Education; **4** Babylonian globe, c. 5000 B.C., The British Museum, Bridgeman/Art Resource, New York; **6** Page from the *Book of the Dead*, c. 1100 B.C., Egyptian, The British Museum, Photo by Michael Holford; **7** Stone/Getty Images; **8** Mary Evans/Edwin Wallace; **9** Bojan Brecelj/CORBIS; **11** *The Simurgh Brings Zal to Sam*, Leaf from *Shah-nameh* by Ferdowsi, 14th century, The Metropolitan Museum of Art, Rogers Fund, 1969, © Copyright by The Metropolitan Museum of Art; **12** Photo: Herve Lewandowski. Louvre, Paris, France/Art Resource, NY; **14** Photo: Herve Lewandowski. Louvre, Paris, France/Art Resource, NY; **16–17** Yann Arthus-Bertrand/CORBIS; **18** Scala/Art Resource, NY; **19** Kabul Museum, Afghanistan/Bridgeman Art Library, London/New York; **22** Front of lyre from tomb of Queen Pu-abi, Early Dynastic period, c. 2685–2290 B.C., British Museum, London; **24–25** Erich Lessing/Art Resource, NY; **26–27** Academy of Natural Sciences of Philadelphia/CORBIS; **32&34** Archivo Iconografico, S.A./CORBIS; **36** Peter Willi/Bridgeman Art Library, London/New York; **37** Archivo Iconografico, S.A./CORBIS; **44** *The Creation of Adam*, Michelangelo, Scala/Art Resource, New York; **46–47** *The Creation of Adam*, Michelangelo, Scala/Art Resource, New York; **48** Scala/Art Resource, NY; **50** Bettmann/CORBIS; **53** Corel Professional Photos CD-ROM™; **54** *Noah's Ark*, Aaron Douglas, Fisk University Fine Art Galleries, Nashville, Tennessee; **60** Harvey Lloyd/Getty Images; **61** Dick S. Ramsay Fund, The Brooklyn Museum; **62** Werner Forman Archive, Liverpool Museum, Liverpool/Art Resource, NY; **66** Corel Professional Photos CD-ROM™; **68** Historical Picture Archive/CORBIS; **71** The Jewish Museum , NY/Art Resource, NY; **73** *Il Buon Pastore (The Good Shepherd)*, Early Christian, 4th century, Vatican Museum, Scala/Art Resource, New York; **75** David Composing the Psalms, Illustrated by Paris Psalter, 10th century, Photo Bibliothèque Nationale, Paris; **81** The Granger Collection, New York; **84** CORBIS; **85** Courtesy of the Freer Gallery of Art, Smithsonian Institution, Washington, D.C.; **90** *Scheherazade and King Shahriyar* (detail), Anton Pieck. Illustration from *Stories of the Arabian Nights*. Retold by Naomi Lewis. Illus. © 1984 by B.V. Elsevier. Uitgeversmaatschappij, Amsterdam. Photo by Rex Joseph.; **92** Nick Koudis/Getty Images; **95** Illustration from *Arabian Nights*, for the story "The Fisherman and the Genie," Edmund Dulac, NY, Scribner's & Sons: 1907, Photo courtesy of the New York Public Library, Astor, Lenox and Tilden Foundations.; **96** Monique le Luhandre/© Dorling Kindersley; **100–101** Christie's Images/CORBIS; **106 (t.)** Bettmann/CORBIS; **106 (b.)** New York Public Library (Rare Book Division or Print Collection. Miriam and Ira D. Wallach Division of Art, Prints and Photographs); Astor, Lenox and Tilden Foundations; **106 (m.)** The Art Archive/Dagle Orti (A); **109** *Rubáiyát of Omar Khayyám*, Edmund Dulac, Photo by John Lei/Omni-Photo Communications, Inc.; **110** Photo by John Lei/Omni-Photo Communications, Inc.; **113** National Gallery Collection; By kind permission of the Trustees of the National Gallery, London/CORBIS; **115** The Art Archive/Biblioteca Nazionale Marciana Venice/Dagli Orti; **117** *Concourse of the Birds*, c. 1600, Habib Allah, The Metropolitan Museum of Art, Fletcher Fund, 1963. (63.210.11). Photograph © 1982 The Metropolitan Museum of Art; **122** Heine Schneebeli/Bridgeman Art Library, London/New York; **124** Werner Forman/Art Resource, NY; **127** Pearson Education/PH School Division; **128** Cover of *Sundiata: Lion King of Mali*, David Wisniewski; **131** © Michael Melford; **133** Monique le Luhandre/© Dorling Kindersley; **139** The Art Archive/Egyptian Museum, Cairo/Dagli Orti; **144** Getty Images; **150–151** *Krishna's Magic Flute*, Unknown artist, Kangra Valley, c. 18th–19th century. New York Public Library, Astor, Lenox and Tilden Foundations.; **152 (t.l.)** The Granger Collection, New York; **152 (t.m.)** B.P.S. Walia/© Dorling Kindersley; **152 (t.r.)** Buddha Standing, bronze, 1st half of 7th century, The Metropolitan Museum of Art, Purchase, Bequest of Florance Waterbury, 1969, © Copyright by The Metropolitan Museum of Art; **152 (b.l.)** Bridgeman Art Library, London/New York; **152 (b.r.)** Attic Red Figure Nolan Amphora: *Hephaestus Making Armor for Achilles*, The Dutuit painter, Francis Bartlett Fund, Courtesy, Museum of Fine Arts, Boston; **153 (t.l.)** Scala/Art Resource, New York; **153 (t.r.)** Christies Images—All rights reserved.; **153 (b.)** Werner Forman/Art Resource, NY; **157 (l.)** David Buffington/Getty Images; **157 (r.)** Art Resource, NY; **158** *Zero*, 1980–1996, Robert Indiana, Morgan Art Foundation Limited/Art Resource, NY, © Copyright ARS, NY; **159** *Rama and Lakshman Confer with the Animal Armies*, from the *Adventures of Rama*, Courtesy of the Freer Gallery of Art, Smithsonian Institution, Washington, D.C., fol. 194v, full view; **160** Dinodia/Omni-Photo Communications, Inc.; **162** Ann and Bury Peerless Picture Library/Bridgeman Art Library, London/New York; **164–165** © Matthias Kulka/CORBIS; **166** © Otto Rogge/CORBIS; **171** The Granger Collection, New York; **172** *Krishna on a Swing*, Scala/Art Resource, NY; **174** Indra, engraved by Marlet et Cie, The Stapleton Collection/Bridgeman Art Library, London/New York; **176** *Vishnu and Lakshmi Riding on Garuda*, Ann & Bury Peerless Picture Library/Bridgeman Art Library, London/New York; **179** *A Hawk*, Indian Mughal, 18th-century miniature, Victoria and Albert Museum, Photo by Michael Holford; **180** *King Sibi's Sacrifice to the God Indra*, Gandharan Art, c. 2nd century, Courtesy of the Trustees of the British Museum; **182** © Art Resource, New York; **184** *Arjuna and Krishna in the Chariot Between the Two Armies*, Illustration from *Bhagavad-Gita*, Photo by Lynn Saville; **187** © Werner Forman/Art Resource, NY; **193** Corel Professional Photos CD-ROM™; **194** Ingo Jezierski/Getty Images; **195** *Rama and Lakshmana shooting arrows at the demon Ravana*. gouache on paper. Dehle of Jaipur school. 19th century, © Victoria & Albert Museum, London/Art Resource, NY; **196** Lyndsay Hebberd/CORBIS; **198** Kangra Valley Painting, New York Public Library; **201** *A Lion at Rest*, The Metropolitan Museum of Art, The Alice and Nasli Heeramaneck Collection, Gift of Alice Heeramaneck, 1985. (1985.221); **203** Monique le Luhandre/© Dorling Kindersley; **212** Royalty-Free/CORBIS; **213** Bettmann/CORBIS; **216** © Dorling Kindersley; **226–227** Katsusika Hokusai (1760–1849). *The Great Wave of Kanagawa*, from *36 Views of Mount Fuji*. Private Collection. Art Resource, NY; **228 (t.l.)** Pearson Education EMG Education Management Group; **228 (t.r.)** Mary Evans Picture Library; **228 (b.)** Pawel Kumelowski/Omni-Photo Communications, Inc.; **229 (t.r.)** *First Landing at Kurihama*, July 14, 1853, Gessan Ogata, Courtesy of United States Naval Academy Museum; **229 (t.l.)** © Will and Deni McIntyre/Photo Researchers, Inc.; **229 (b.)** Reuters NewMedia Inc./CORBIS; **231** Dallas and John Heaton/CORBIS; **232** Tokyo National Museum; **233** Pearson Education Corporate Digital Archive; **234** *The Poet Li Po Admiring a Waterfall*, Hokusai, Honolulu Academy of Arts, Gift of James A. Michener; **237** Asian Art & Archaeology, Inc./CORBIS; **238 (l.)** Foto Marburg/Art Resource, NY; **238 (r.)** The Granger Collection, New York; **241** *Poet on a Mountain Top*, Shen Chou, The Nelson-Atkins Museum of Art, Kansas City, Missouri; **242** *Old Trees by Cold Waterfall*, 1470–1559, Wen Zhengming, The Los Angeles County Museum of Art, Ernest Larsen Blancok Memorial Fund.; **248** The Granger Collection, New York; **249** *Benjamin Franklin* (detail), c. 1790, Pierre Michel Alix, National Portrait Gallery, Smithsonian Institution, Washington, D.C./Art Resource, New York; **250 (t.)** New York Public Library; **250 (b.l.)** *T'ao Ch'ien*, Collection of the National Palace Museum, Taipei, Taiwan, Republic of China; **250 (b.r.)** New York Public Library Picture Collection; **255** *A Myriad of Trees on Strange Peaks*, Yen Wen-Kuei (Northern Sung Dynasty), The Granger Collection, New York; **257** *River and Mountains in Autumn Color*, 1120–1182, Zhao Boju, Imperial Palace Museum, Beijing, China; **259** *River Village in a Rainstorm*, Hanging scroll, ink and slight color on silk, 169.2 x 103.5 cm, Lü Wenying, Chinese, active c. 1490–1507, © The Cleveland Museum of Art, John L. Severance Fund, 70.76; **260** Eyewire/Getty Images; **261** *Conversation in Autumn*, Hanging scroll, ink and color on paper, 1732, 115.3 x 39.7 cm, Hua Yen, Chinese, 1682–c. 1762, Qing Dynasty, © The Cleveland Museum of Art, John L. Severance Fund, 54.263; **262** Corel Professional Photos CD-ROM™; **266 (t.l.)** *Kino Tsurayuki*, Heibonsha/Pacific Press Service; **266 (m.l.)** *Onono-komachi*, Heibonsha/Pacific Press Service; **266 (b.l.)** *Jakuren Houshi*, Heibonsha/Pacific Press Service; **266 (t.r.)** *Bashō*, The Granger Collection, New York; **266 (m.r.)** *Yosa Buson*, Heibonsha/Pacific Press Service; **266 (b.r.)** *Kobayashi Issa*, Heibonsha/Pacific Press Service; **268** *Snow at Senso-ji Temple in Asakusa*, Victoria and Albert Museum, London/Art Resource, NY; **270** *The Monkey Bridge in Koshu Province*, 1841, Hiroshige Hitsu, Christie's, New York; **271** *Sudden Shower on Ohashi Bridge*, Hiroshige, Art Resource, New York; **272** Artville/Getty Images; **276** *Sei Shōnagon*, Heibonsha/Pacific Press Service; **279** *Triptych of Snow, Moon, and Flower* (Center Panel), c.1780's, Shunsho, Museum of Art, Tami, Japan; **281** *Sei Shōnagon*, Heibonsha/Pacific Press Service; **286** *The Celebrated Beauty of the Teahouse, Kagiya, at Kasamori Shrine*, Suzuki Harunobu, 18th century, The Metropolitan Museum of Art, the Henry L. Phillips Collection, Bequest of Henry L. Phillips, 1940, © Copyright by The Metropolitan Museum of Art; **288** *Large Enso*, hanging scroll, Torei Enji, Gitter-Yelen Art Center; **290** CORBIS; **291** Monique le Luhandre/© Dorling Kindersley; **297 (t.)** Instructions, diagram and models © 1998 by Steve and Megumi Biddle. Models photograph by Les Morsillo. Photograph © 1998 The Metropolitan Museum; **297 (b.)** Instructions, diagram and models © 1998 by Steve and Megumi Biddle. Models photograph by Les Morsillo. Photograph © 1998 The Metropolitan Museum; **298** Instructions, diagram and models © 1998 by Steve and Megumi Biddle. Models

Acknowledgments continued

Note: Every effort has been made to locate the copyright owner of material reprinted in this book. Omissions brought to our attention will be corrected in subsequent editions.

photograph by Les Morsillo. Photograph © 1998 The Metropolitan Museum; **299 (t.)** Instructions, diagram and models © 1998 by Steve and Megumi Biddle. Models photograph by Les Morsillo. Photograph © 1998 The Metropolitan Museum; **304** CORBIS; **310–311** *Aeneas at Delos*, Claude Lorrain, © National Gallery Collection; By kind permission of the Trustees of the National Gallery, London/CORBIS; **312 (t.)** Getty Images; **312 (m.)** Mimmo Jodice/CORBIS; **312 (b.l.)** Ann & Bury Peerless Picture Library/Bridgeman Art Library, London/New York; **312 (b.r.)** Seattle Art Museum/CORBIS; **313 (t.l.)** Roman Mosaic: Gladiator with Leopard, Galleria Borghese, Scala/Art Resource, New York; **313 (t.r.)** Bettmann/CORBIS; **313 (b.)** Michael S. Yamashita/CORBIS; **316** *The Apollo Belvedere*, Roman marble copy probably of Greek original of late 4th (or 1st) century BC, Vatican Museums, Rome, Scala/Art Resource, New York; **317** Erich Lessing/Art Resource, NY; **318** Richard Quataert/Folio, Inc.; **319** *Circe Meanwhile Had Gone Her Ways . . .* , 1924, From *The Odyssey* by Homer, William Russell Flint, Collection of the New York Public Library; Astor, Lenox and Tilden Foundations; **320** The Art Archive/Biblioteca Braidense Milan/Dagli Orti; **321** The Art Archive/Dagli Orti; **322** Bettmann/CORBIS; **325** Mimmo Jodice/CORBIS; **327** Historical Picture Archive/CORBIS; **328** Kimbell Art Museum/CORBIS; **331** Hirmer Verlag Munchen; **332** *Minerva restrains Achilles from killing Agamemnon*, GiambattistaTiepolo, Scala/Art Resource, New York; **334** Liz McAulay/© Dorling Kindersley; **339** *Hector Taking Leave of Andromache*, Angelica Kauffmann, Tate Gallery, London/Art Resource, New York; **341** *Odysseus' Mission to Achilles*, Cleophrades Painter, 485–475 B.C., Staatliche Antikensammlungen und Glyptothek, Munich; **346** Francis G. Mayer/CORBIS; **348** Araldo de Luca/CORBIS; **353** *Achilles defeating Hector*, Peter Paul Rubens, Musée des Beaux-Arts, Giraudon/Art Resource, New York; **354** *Achilles Deciding to Resume Fighting Upon the Death of Patroclus*, 1620, Dirck van Baburen/Bridgeman Art Library, London/New York; **357** *Andromache and Astyanax*, 1789, Richard Cosway, Courtesy of the Trustees of Sir John Soane's Museum, London/Bridgeman Art Library, London/New York; **359** "Achilles," detail from the fresco "Thetis consoling Achilles," Giovanni Battista Tiepolo, Scala/Art Resource, New York; **363** The Granger Collection, New York; **364** Nationalmuseet, Copenhagen, Denmark/Bridgeman Art Library, London/New York; **369** *Andromache mourning Hector*, Jacques Louis Pushkin, Peter Willi/Bridgeman Art Library, London/New York; **398** CORBIS; **399** Courtesy of the Library of Congress; **422** The Metropolitan Museum of Art, NY, Hewitt Fund, 1911, Rogers Fund, 1921, Munsey Fund, 1936, and Anonymous Gift, 1951 (11.185); **424** Archivo Iconografico/CORBIS; **426** Two Sphinxes Surmounted by Two Lions, 450 B.C., Egyptian, Gable end from a relief from a tomb at Xanthos, The British Museum, London/Bridgeman/Art Resource, New York; **428–429** ImageState/Pictor Images; **430** Fotopic/Omni-Photo Communications, Inc.; **433** Roman Mosaic: Theatre masks, Capitoline Museum, Rome, Scala/Art Resource, New York; **436** The Art Museum, Princeton University, Museum purchase, Caroline G. Mather Fund. Photographer: Bruce White; **437** © AFP/CORBIS Sygma; **439** Jeffrey M. Spielman/The Image Bank; **441** Archivo Iconografico, S.A./CORBIS; **442–443** Robbie Jack/CORBIS; **446** The Art Museum, Princeton University, Museum purchase, Caroline G. Mather Fund. Photographer: Bruce White; **450** © Pizzoli Alberto/CORBIS Sygma; **453 (t.)** Bettmann/CORBIS; **453 (b.)** Michael Nicholson/CORBIS; **461** Two Sphinxes Surmounted by Two Lions, 450 B.C., Egyptian, Gable end from a relief from a tomb at Xanthos, The British Museum, London/Bridgeman/Art Resource, New York; **462** ImageState/Pictor Images; **464–465** © AFP/CORBIS Sygma; **466** © AFP/CORBIS Sygma; **468** Robbie Jack/CORBIS; **471** Monique le Luhandre/© Dorling Kindersley; **472–473** Robbie Jack/CORBIS; **478–479** Robbie Jack/CORBIS; **536** Omni-Photo Communications, Inc.; **542–543** Corel Professional Photos CD-ROM™; **544 (t.l.)** Courtesy of the Trustees of British Library; **544 (t.r.)** Werner Forman/Art Resource, NY; **544 (b.)** Index Stock Photography, Inc.; **545 (t.)** Mary Evans Picture Library; **545 (m.)** Philip Gatward/© Dorling Kindersley; **545 (b.)** The Granger Collection, New York; **546** Franz-Marc Frei/CORBIS; **547** Geoff Dann/© Dorling Kindersley; **548** *The Crowning of Charlemagne and Other Scenes from His Life*, V. de Beauvais, 15th century, Réunion des Musées Nationaux/Art Resource, New York, Musée Condé, Chantilly, France; **550 (t.)** Giraudon/Art Resource, NY; **550 (b.)** Omni-Photo Communications, Inc.; **551** Geoff Dann/© Dorling Kindersley; **552** The Art Achive/University Library Heidelberg/Dagli Orti; **553** The Granger Collection, New York; **554** *Death of Roland*, Vincent de Beauvais, Giraudon/Art Resource, NY; **556** © Dorling Kindersley; **557** Giraudon/Art Resource, NY; **559** The Granger Collection, New York; **560** © Hulton/Archive Photos; **562** Geoff Dann/© Dorling Kindersley; **563** *Death of Roland*, Vincent de Beauvais, Giraudon/Art Resource, NY; **564** Geoff Dann/© Dorling Kindersley; **566–567** The Granger Collection, New York; **568** Simone End/© Dorling Kindersley; **569** Kenneth Lilly/© Dorling Kindersley; **570** *Siegfried's Death*, Staatsbibliothek Preussischer Kulturbesitz, Berlin; Photo Bildarchiv Preussischer Kulturbesitz; **573** *The Burial of Siegfried*, Richard Jack, City of New York Art Gallery/SuperStock; **579** Shane L. Amaya, *www.rolandcomic.com*; **580** Shane L. Amaya, *www.rolandcomic.com*; **582** English Greenwich, Field and tournament armor for man, 1527, Made in the royal workshops at Greenwich, steel and gold, G. 73 in. (185.5 cm); Wt. 80 lb, 4 oz. (36.7 kg): The Metropolitan Museum of Art, Purchase, William H. Riggs Gift and Rogers Fund, 1919. (19.131.1-2). Photograph © 1987 The Metropolitan Museum of Art; **584** Courtesy of Joyce Patti/Morgan Gaynin, Inc.; **586** Martin Weigan /SuperStock; **588** Monique le Luhandre/© Dorling Kindersley; **589** Bayerische Staatsbibliothek Munchen; **590** *The Damsel of Sanct Grael*, 1857, Dante Gabriel Rossetti, Tate Gallery, London/Art Resource, NY; **593** *Perceval at Amfortas*, wall painting from the "Parsifal saga," Ferdinand Piloty, The Younger, AKG London; **595** Art Resource, NY; **596** © Dorling Kindersley; **597** *Werewolf Attacking a Man*, German woodcut, 15th cenutry, The Granger Collection, New York; **598** Diantha York-Ripley/SuperStock; **599** Jim Stamates/Getty Images; **600** Giraudon/Art Resource, NY; **607** *Sir Galahad*, George Frederick Watts, Trustees of the National Museums & Galleries on Merseyside/Bridgeman Art Library, London/New York; **608** The Granger Collection, New York; **609** Alfred Lord Tennyson (detail), c. 1840, S. Laurence, by courtesy of the National Portrait Gallery, London; **610** *Dante*, Andrea del Castagno, Firenze, Santa Apollonia, Scala/Art Resource, New York; **612** *The Forest, Inferno I*, 1862, Gustave Doré, New York Public Library Special Collections, *L'Enfer de Dante Alighieri avec dessins de Gustave Doré*, 1862; **614** University of Texas at Austin; **615 (t.)** University of Texas at Austin; **615 (b.)** University of Texas at Austin; **616** The Granger Collection, New York; **619** University of Texas at Austin; **623** Monique le Luhandre/© Dorling Kindersley; **624** The Granger Collection, New York; **630** The Granger Collection, New York; **632** The Granger Collection, New York; **635** *Paolo and Francesca*, 1855, Dante Gabriel Rossetti, Tate Gallery, London/Art Resource, NY; **638** Mary Evans Picture Library; **640** *Judecca—Lucifer, Inferno XXXIV*, 1862, Gustave Doré, New York Public Library Special Collections, *L'Enfer de Dante Alighieri avec dessins de Gustave Doré*, 1862; **642** Monique le Luhandre/© Dorling Kindersley; **643** *Poets emerge from Hell*, Inferno XXXIV, 139, Gustave Doré, 1862, New York Public Library Special Collections, *L'Enfer de Dante Alighieri avec dessins de Gustave Doré*, 1862; **648** John Heseltine/© Dorling Kindersley; **652** John Henley/CORBIS; **660–661** *The School of Athens*, Raphael, Scala/Art Resource, NY; **662 (t.)** Scala/Art Resource, NY; **662 (m.l.)** Bettmann/CORBIS; **662 (b.)** Philip Blenkinsop/© Dorling Kindersley; **662 (m.r.)** Boltin Picture Library; **663 (t.l.)** NASA; **663 (t.r.)** *Night of August 4, 1789*, or "Patriotic Delirium," Bibliothèque Nationale, Paris, Giraudon/Art Resource, New York; **663 (b.l.)** Réunion des Musées Nationaux/Art Resource, NY; **663 (b.r.)** *View of the Imperial Bank and Environs*, Giraudon/Art Resource, New York; **665** *Mona Lisa*. Oil on wood (1503 and 1506) 77 x 53 cm., Leonardo da Vinci (1452–1519), Louvre, Dep. des Peintures, Paris, France. Photograph by Erich Lessing; **666** The Granger Collection, New York; **668** Florence Museo delle Scienze/AKG London; **669** *Lorenzo il Magnifico*, G. Vasari, Scala/Art Resource, New York; **670** Nicolo Orsi Battaglini/Art Resource, NY; **671** The Granger Collection, New York; **672 (l.)** *Petrarch*, Alinari/Art Resource, New York; **672 (r.)** *Portrait of Ronsard*, Anonymous artist, early 17th century, Giraudon/Art Resource, New York; **674** *Three Graces* (detail), Botticelli, Giraudon/Art Resource, New York; **676** D. Robert & Lorri Franz/CORBIS; **676** Monique le Luhandre/© Dorling Kindersley; **677** Corel Professional Photos CD-ROM™; **679** Cameraphoto Arte, Venice/Art Resource, NY; **680** Corel Professional Photos CD-ROM™; **685 (t.)** The Granger Collection, New York; **685 (b.)** *William Shakespeare* (detail), attributed to John Taylor, by courtesy of the National Portrait Gallery, London; **686** Giovanni Boccaccio, Scala/Art Resource, New York; **688** © Dorling Kindersley; **689** *Robert Cheseman*, Hans Holbein the Younger, Scala/Art Resource, New York; **690** Réunion des Musées Nationaux/Art Resource, NY; **692** The Granger Collection, New York; **693** Monique le Luhandre/© Dorling Kindersley; **698** Miguel de Cervantes, The Granger Collection, New York; **701** *Don Quixote*, Honoré Daumier, Scala/Art Resource, NY; **702** The Palma Collection/Getty Images; **705** *Don Quixote Preparing His Armor;* scene from the novel by Cervantes, Zacarias Velazquez Gonzalez, Caylus Anticuario, Madrid, Spain/Bridgeman Art Library, London/New York; **706** *Dulcinea Del Toboso* from Cervantes, *Don Quixote*, 1839, Charles Robert Leslie, Art Resource, NY; **709** *Don Quixote and Sancho Panza Riding Clavileno*, Zacarias Velazquez Gonzalez, Caylus Anticuario, Madrid, Spain/Bridgeman Art Library, London/New York; **710** Monique le Luhandre/© Dorling Kindersley; **712 (t.)** The Granger Collection, New York; **712 (b.)** *Niccolo Macchiavelli*, Florence Uffizi, Art Resource, New York; **713** *Don Quixote and the Windmill*, Francisco J. Torrome (fl. 1890–1908), Bonhams, London/Bridgeman Art Library, London/New York; **713 (t.)** Bettmann/CORBIS; **713 (b.)** The Granger Collection, New York; **718** Jean de La Fontaine, The Bettmann Archive; **721** Private Collection/Bridgeman Art Library, London/New York; **722** Alan Kearney/Getty Images; **730** *Voltaire in 1718*, 18th- century French school after N. de Largilliere, Paris, Musée Carnavalet, Giraudon, Erich Lessing/Art Resource, New York; **733** Bibliothèque Nationale, Paris, France/Bridgeman Art Library, London/New York; **735** Josef Beck/Getty Images—Taxi; **741** *A Rider on a Rearing Horse in a Profile View*, Leonardo da Vinci, Fitzwilliam Museum, University of Cambridge; **743** *Head of the Virgin in Three-Quarter View Facing to the Right*, Black and colored chalks on paper, Leonardo da Vinci, The Metropolitan Museum of Art, Harris Brisbane Dick Fund, 1951. (51.90) Photograph © 1992 The Metropolitan Museum of Art; **748** David Young-Wolff/PhotoEdit; **754–755** *Terrace at Sainte-Adresse*, Claude Oscar Monet, The Metropolitan Museum of Art, Purchased with special contributions and purchase funds given or bequeathed by friends of the Museum, 1967, © Copyright by The Metropolitan Museum of Art; **756 (t.l.)** *Napoleon Bonaparte as First Consul*, Jean Auguste Dominque Ingres, Musée des Beaux-Arts, Liège, Belgium, Scala/Art

Resource, New York; **756 (t.m.)** Photofest; **756 (t.r.)** *The Stone Breakers*, Gustave Courbet/SuperStock; **756 (b.l.)** Joseph Sohm; Visions of American/CORBIS; **756 (b.r.)** *Fuji from Noge in Yokohama*, Musashi, Ando Hiroshige, The Newark Museum, John Cotton Dana Collection/Art Resource, NY; **757 (t.)** Private Collection/Bridgeman Art Library, London/New York; **757 (m.)** *A Berber of Southern Tunis*, c. 1898, Harry Hamilton Johnston, Private Collection/Bridgeman Art Library, London/New York; **757 (b.)** The Granger Collection, New York; **760** Erich Lessing/Art Resource, NY; **761** Burstein Collection/CORBIS; **762** *The Wanderer Over the Sea of Clouds*, 1818, by Caspar-David Friedrich (1774–1840), Kunsthalle, Hamburg/Bridgeman Art Library, London/New York; **763** Ludwig van Beethoven, portrait by Joseph Karl Stieler, 1820. Beethoven-Haus, Bonn; **765** *On the Bank of the Seine, Bennecourt*, 1868, Claude Monet, Potter Palmer Collection, 1922.427, reproduction, The Art Institute of Chicago. All Rights Reserved; **766** *Johann Wolfgang von Goethe*, J. K. Stieler, The Granger Collection, New York; **768–769** © Thomas Wiewandt/Photo Researchers, Inc.; **771** *Mephistopheles*, 1863, Eugène Delacroix, Giraudon/Art Resource, New York; **774** The Granger Collection, New York; **777** The Granger Collection, New York; **779** Monique le Luhandre/© Dorling Kindersley; **781** *Dunstanburgh Castle in a Thunderstorm*, Thomas Girtin, Ashmolean Museum, Oxford, UK/Bridgeman Art Library, London/New York; **782** *Vanitas*, Edwaert Collier, Johnny van Haeften Gallery, London, UK/Bridgeman Art Library, London/New York; **788** Corel Professional Photos CD-ROM™; **791** *Mephistopheles Appears Before Faust*, Eugène Delacroix, Reproduced by the permission of the Trustees of the Wallace Collection; **792–793** Corel Professional Photos CD-ROM™; **793** The Granger Collection, New York; **794 (l.)** *Alexander Pushkin*, Orest Kiprensky, The Granger Collection, New York; **794 (r.)** © Bettmann/CORBIS; **797** *Lake Scene in France*, oil on canvas, Josephine Bowes, The Bowes Museum, Barnard Castle, County Durham, UK/Bridgeman Art Library, London/New York; **799** Uwe Schmid/CORBIS; **800** © Gregory G. Dimijian/Photo Researchers, Inc.; **804** Bettmann/CORBIS; **806** *Campaign of France*, 1814, Ernest Meissonier, Giraudon/Art Resource, New York; **807** The Granger Collection, New York; **812 (t.)** © Bettmann/CORBIS; **812 (m.)** The Granger Collection, New York; **812 (b.)** The Granger Collection, New York; **815** *Erminia in the Rough Sea*, 1869, National Trust Photographic Library/John Hammond/Bridgeman Art Library, London/New York; **816** Kenneth Lilly/© Dorling Kindersley; **817** The Granger Collection, New York; **818** *Ophelia*, John Everett Millais, Tate Gallery, London/Art Resource, New York; **820** The Granger Collection, New York; **826 (t.)** Corbis-Bettmann; **826 (m.)** Getty Images Inc./Hulton Archive Photos; **826 (b.)** L. N. Tolstoi, I. E. Repin, Sovfoto/Eastfoto; **829** *Les Maisons Cabassud à la Ville d'Avray*, Camille Corot, The Louvre, Paris, Scala/Art Resource, New York; **831** Stephen Oliver/© Dorling Kindersley; **832** The Granger Collection, New York; **836** Vladmir Stozharov, *The Village of Andreikovo* (detail), 1958, The Tretyakov Gallery, Moscow; **839** Dallas and John Heaton/CORBIS; **840–841** *Cornfield at Ewell*, William Holman Hunt, Art Resource; **842** Frank Greenway/© Dorling Kindersley; **845** Monique le Luhandre/© Dorling Kindersley; **846–847** © David Brookover/Photonica; **850–851** *The Library at Windsor Castle*, Joseph Nash, National Trust Photographic Library/John Hammond/Bridgeman Art Library, London/New York; **853** *Ball at the Moulin de la Galette*, 1876, Pierre Auguste Renoir, Collection of Mr. and Mrs. John Hay Whitney, New York, USA/Bridgeman Art Library, London/New York; **854** *E. Duranty*, 1879, Edgar Degas, Glasgow Museums: The Burrell Collection; **857** Corel Professional Photos CD-ROM™; **862** *Henrik Ibsen*, George T. Tobin, The Granger Collection, New York; **864** Private Collection/Bridgeman Art Library, London/New York; **866** Paramount Pictures. The Kobal Collection, New York; **868** *A Lark*, Archibald Thorburn, John Spike Fine Watercolours, London, UK/Bridgeman Art Library, London/New York; **871** Artville/Getty Images; **873** © Dorling Kindersley; **875** Paramount Pictures. The Kobal Collection, New York; **877** Artville/Getty Images; **878–879** Paramount Pictures. The Kobal Collection, New York; **880** Dave King/© Dorling Kindersley; **883** Paramount Pictures. The Kobal Collection, New York; **886** Artville/Getty Images; **890** © Hulton/Archive Photos; **897** Private Collection/Bridgeman Art Library, London/New York; **899** *Lady with a Fur Muff*, Theodore Bruckner, Whitford & Hughes, London, UK/Bridgeman Art Library, London/New York; **902** Paramount Pictures. The Kobal Collection, New York; **905** Steve Cole/Getty Images; **908** Owaki-Kulla/CORBIS; **910** © Dorling Kindersley; **912–913** Paramount Pictures. The Kobal Collection, New York; **915** Artville/Getty Images; **918** Dave King/© Dorling Kindersley; **923** Private Collection/Bridgeman Art Library, London/New York; **925** Paramount Pictures. The Kobal Collection, New York; **927** Paramount Pictures. The Kobal Collection, New York; **928** Owaki-Kulla/CORBIS; **931** Paramount Pictures. The Kobal Collection, New York; **934** Paramount Pictures. The Kobal Collection, New York; **936** *A Lark*, Archibald Thorburn, John Spike Fine Watercolours, London, UK/Bridgeman Art Library, London/New York; **941** Private Collection/Bridgeman Art Library, London/New York; **942** © National Gallery Collection; By kind permission of the Trustees of the National Gallery, London/CORBIS; **949 (l.)** John Heseltine/CORBIS; **949 (m.)** Wolfgang Kaehler/CORBIS; **949 (r.)** Wolfgang Kaehler/CORBIS; **952** Robbie Jack/CORBIS; **958** Bob Daemmrich/The Image Works; **964–965** Pablo Picasso, *Guernica*, 1937, oil on canvas. 11'5 1/2 x 25'5 3/4. © 2004 Estate of Pablo Picasso/Artists Rights Society (ARS), New York / Art Resource, NY; **966 (t.)** Ewing Galloway/Index Stock Photography, Inc.; **966 (m.l.)** Bettmann/CORBIS; **966 (m.r.)** "Shattering a German Charge," from "The Literary Digest," Culver Pictures, Inc.; **966 (b.)** The Granger Collection, New York; **967 (t.l.)** The Granger Collection, New York; **967 (t.m.)** Bettmann/CORBIS; **967 (t.r.)** Getty Images; **967 (b.)** Photofest; **968** © Science VU/National Laboratory of Medicine/Visuals Unlimited; **969 (t.)** Davis Factor/CORBIS; **969 (b.)** *Les Demoiselles d'Avignon*, 1907, Pablo Picasso, The Museum of Modern Art. Acquired through the Lillie P. Bliss Bequest/Art Resource, NY; **970 (inset)** Bettmann/CORBIS; **970** Heinrich Hoffmann/TIMEPIX; **971** *View of Terezin*, paper collage, Hanus Weinberg, State Jewish Museum, Prague; **973** The Art Archive/Conservatoire Prague/Dagli Orti; **975** *La condition humaine (The Human Condition)*, 1933, René Magritte, Copyright 1997 Board of Trustees, National Gallery of Art, Washington, Gift of the Collectors Committee, 1933. © 1998 C. Herscovici, Brussels/Artists Rights Society (ARS), New York; **976** The Granger Collection, New York; **978–979** Steve Gorton/© Dorling Kindersley; **980** Pictor/ImageState; **982** *Walking Man*, bronze statue 150 x 60 x 133 cm, Rick Amor, Niagara Galleries; **983** Steve Gorton/© Dorling Kindersley; **984** Getty Images; **984** Steve Gorton/© Dorling Kindersley; **987** Martha Swope Photography; **988** Dorling Kindersley; **990** Steve Gorton/© Dorling Kindersley; **992** Steve Gorton/© Dorling Kindersley; **993** Verlag Klaus Wagenbach; **994** Steve Gorton/© Dorling Kindersley; **995** Monique le Luhandre/© Dorling Kindersley; **996** Martha Swope Photography; **999** Steve Gorton/© Dorling Kindersley; **1000** © Dorling Kindersley; **1003** Susan Watkins, *Lady in Yellow (Eleanor Reeves)*, ca. 1905. Oil on canvas, 44 1/2 x 35 1/2 inches. Chrysler Museum of Art, Norfolk, VA, Bequest of Goldsborough Serpell 46.76.137; **1006** USDA Photo; **1007** Steve Gorton/© Dorling Kindersley; **1008 (t.l.)** *Anna Akhmatova*, N. I. Altman, The Granger Collection, New York; **1008 (t.r.)** The Granger Collection, New York; **1008 (b.l.)** Cornell Capa/Magnum Photos, Inc.; **1008 (b.r.)** The Granger Collection, New York; **1008** Steve Gorton/© Dorling Kindersley; **1010** Gjon Mili/Time-Pix; **1010** Munch, Edvard (1863–1944), *Starry Night*, 1923–1924. Oil on canvas, 120.5cm x 100cm. © Erich Lessing/ARS/Art Resource, NY. © 2003 The Munch Museum/The Munch-Ellingsen Group/ Artists Rights Society (ARS), New York/ ADAGP, Paris.; **1011** *Starting Over, Western Russia*, Petr Ossorsky, 1941–45, Tretyakov Gallery; **1012–1013** Richard Berenholtz/CORBIS; **1013** Monique le Luhandre/© Dorling Kindersley; **1014** *Inger on the Beach*, Edvard Munch, Rasmus Meyers Samlinger; **1014** Steve Gorton/© Dorling Kindersley; **1017** Museum of Czech Literature, Prague; **1019** Verlag Klaus Wagenbach; **1025** Frank Greenaway/© Dorling Kindersley; **1035** Corel Professional Photos CD-ROM™; **1037** Art Wolfe/Photo Researchers, Inc.; **1038** Monique le Luhandre/© Dorling Kindersley; **1039** Burstein Collection/CORBIS; **1044** Henri Manuel/CORBIS; **1047** *Madame Mayden*, Amedeo Modigliani/SuperStock; **1048** © Sotheby's/CORBIS SYGMA; **1049** Artville/Getty Images; **1054** *Luigi Pirandello*, Primo Conti, Giraudon/Art Resource, New York; **1057** *A Star Shell*, exh. 1916, Christopher R.W. Nevinson, © Tate Gallery, London/Art Resource, NY; **1058** *Italian Soldiers*, Karl Fahringer, Heeresgeschichtliches Museum, Vienna, Austria; **1064** Royalty-Free/CORBIS; **1067** *The Hailstorm*, Thomas Hart Benton, Joslyn Art Museum, Omaha, Nebraska, Gift of James A. Douglas Foundation; **1068** H. Armstrong Roberts/CORBIS; **1069** Bettmann/CORBIS; **1070 (t.)** The Granger Collection, New York; **1070 (b.)** The Granger Collection, New York; **1070 (m.)** Ferdinando Scianna/Magnum Photos; **1072** *The Old Guitarist*, 1903, Pablo Picasso, Spanish, 1881–1973, oil on panel 122.9 x 82.6 cm, Helen Birch Bartlett Memorial Collection, 1926.253, photograph courtesy of The Art Institute of Chicago, Estate of Pablo Picasso/Artists Rights Society (ARS), New York; **1074–1075** © Linda Bartlett/Photo Researchers, Inc.; **1078** © Stephen Krasemann/Photo Researchers, Inc.; **1084 (t.)** AFP/CORBIS; **1084 (b.)** AFP/CORBIS; **1085** AP/Wide World Photos/Pressens Bild/Henrik Montgomery/pool; **1086** Editorial Sudamericana S.A.; **1088–1089** *Puerto de Villefranche*, Joaquim Torres-Garcia, Christie's, New York; **1091** *Retrato de un Joven*, Leonor Fini, Christie's, New York; **1092** *Trabajadores*, Hector Poleo/Christie's Images; **1094** Monique le Luhandre/© Dorling Kindersley; **1095** David Murray/© Dorling Kindersley; **1100 (l.)** Corbis-Bettmann; **1100 (r.)** AP/Wide World Photos; **1102** *Woman and Child*, Pablo Picasso, Estate of Pablo Pi-casso/Artists RIghts Society (ARS), New York. Museo Picasso, Barcelona, Spain. Scala/Art Resource, NY; **1104** *The Revolution*, Manuel Rodriguez Lozano, Museo Nacional de Arte Moderno, Mexico City, Photo Laurie Platt Winfrey; **1106 (t.)** Getty Images; **1106 (b.)** Getty Images; **1107** Getty Images; **1108** *Woman Under an Apple Tree*, 1966, David Brayne, © The Grand Design, Leeds, England/SuperStock; **1109** Brian David Stevens/Photonica; **1114** Ohgai Mori/Pacific Press Service; **1116** *Ouda*, Hironaga Takehiko, Courtesy of the Trustees of the British Museum, Photo: John Lei/Omni-Photo Communications.; **1118** Neil Fletcher/© Dorling Kindersley; **1119** Monique le Luhandre/© Dorling Kindersley; **1120** *Woman With a Black Hat*, Kees van Dongen, © Scala/Art Resource, NY; **1121** Liz McAulay/© Dorling Kindersley; **1126** China Photo Service/Eastfoto; **1129** *Landscape*, Zhu Qizhan, Photo Courtesy of Joan Lebold Cohen; **1131** © Dorling Kindersley; **1132** © Rykoff Collection/CORBIS; **1133** © Deborah Davis/PhotoEdit; **1134** Monique le Luhandre/© Dorling Kindersley; **1135** © Seattle Art Museum/CORBIS; **1140** The Granger Collection, New York; **1143** © Gerry Charm/SuperStock; **1144** Monique le Luhandre/© Dorling Kindersley; **1145** © Carmen J. Redondo/CORBIS; **1146** *Two Gazelles*, from the

Babar Nama, 1530, New Delhi National Museum, Borromeo/Art Resource, New York; **1147** © Danny Lehman/CORBIS; **1154** CORBIS; **1160–1161** *Jazz Le Cheval L'Ecuyère Et Le Clown*, Henri Matisse/Bridgeman Art Library, London/New York; **1162 (t.)** © Getty Images, Inc.—Hulton Archive Photos; **1162 (m.l.)** Division of Computer Research and Technology, National Institute of Health/Science Photo Library/Photo Researchers, Inc.; **1162 (m.r.)** NASA; **1162 (m.m.)** From THINGS FALL APART (JACKET COVER) by Chinua Achebe. Copyright. Used by permission of Doubleday, a division of Bantam Doubleday Dell Publishing Group, Inc.; **1162 (b.)** © Bettmann/CORBIS; **1163 (t.l.)** © Dorling Kindersley; **1163 (t.r.)** AP/Wide World Photos; **1163 (b.)** AP/Wide World Photos; **1164** NASA; **1165** © 2001 *The Record* (Bergen County, NJ), Thomas E. Franklin, Staff Photographer; **1166 (t.)** Shanachie Entertainment Corp.; **1166 (b.)** Published by SBK Songs, France; Design by In Like Flynn; **1167** *Los Papagayos* ("The Parrots"), 1986, Beatriz Gonzalez, Courtesy of the artist, Bogota, Colombia. Photo by Julio Cesar Florez; **1168** Joseph Van Os/Getty Images; **1170** Herrmann/Starke/CORBIS; **1171** *Round of Friendship Dedicated to the Virgin of . . .*, Pablo Picasso/SuperStock; **1172 (l.)** Susan Meiselas/Magnum Photos, Inc.; **1172 (r.)** Susan Meiselas/Magnum Photos, Inc.; **1174** CORBIS; **1175** *Waves*, 1917, Christopher Nevinson, Phillips, The International Fine Art Auctioneers, UK/Bridgeman Art Library, London/New York; **1176** Geoffrey Clements/CORBIS; **1177** Getty Images; **1178–1179** Hiroshi Takano/Omni-Photo Communications, Inc.; **1180** Monique le Luhandre/© Dorling Kindersley; **1183** *The Door*, 1972, George Tooker, From the collection of the New Britain Museum of American Art, Connecticut. Gift of Olga H. Knoepke; **1184** Getty Images; **1185** *La Nuit*, René Magritte, Art Resource, NY; **1186** *Still Life Reviving*, Remedios Varos, Collection of Beatriz Varo de Cano, Valencia, Spain. Photo courtesy of Walter Gruen; **1187** Monique le Luhandre/© Dorling Kindersley; **1192 (t.)** Thomas Victor; **1192 (m.)** Eugene Richards/Magnum Photos, Inc.; **1192 (b.)** Sergio Larrain/Magnum Photos, Inc.; **1195** Albert Edelfelt, *Kaukola Ridge at Sunset*, 1889, Ateneum Art Museum, Helsinki, The Central Art Archives/Matti Janas; **1196** *After Rain*, 1998, Roger Winter, Fischbach Gallery, New York; **1201** © Getty Images, Inc.—Hulton/Archive Photos; **1202** *St. Lucia—Looking at Rat Island*, Watercolor by Derek Walcott, from the collection of Michael and Judy Chastanet; **1209** Burstein Collection/CORBIS; **1210** Sigrid Estrada; **1212** *Vista II*, 1987, Hughie Lee-Smith, June Kelly Gallery; **1213** C Squared Studios/Getty Images; **1214** *San Antonio de Oriente*, Museum of Modern Art of Latin America; **1215** © Dorling Kindersley; **1217** Daniel Mackie/Digital Vision, Ltd.; **1222** © Bettmann/CORBIS; **1224–1225** Eugène Delacroix, *Album de voyage: Spain, Morocco, Algeria*, 1834, Chantilly. Musée Condé, Chantilly, France. Giraudon/Art Resource, NY.; **1227** *Arab at the Door of His House*, Eugène Delacroix, Rijksmuseum, Amsterdam; **1228** *The Ear of Grain* (L'espiga de blat), 1922–1923, Joan Miro, © The Museum of Modern Art/Licensed by Scala/Art Resource, NY; **1230** Auguste Raffet, *Album Afrique* 1835–1845. Arab of Constantine. Musée Conde, Chantilly, France. Giraudon/Art Resource, NY.; **1233** *Seated Arab*, Eugène Delacroix, Réunion des Musées Nationaux/Art Resource, NY; **1234** Monique le Luhandre/© Dorling Kindersley; **1236–1237** © Sylvain Grandadam/Photo Researchers, Inc.; **1294 (l.)** Sovfoto/Eastfoto; **1294 (r.)** AP/Wide World Photos/Ron Frehm; **1298** Horace Bristol/CORBIS; **1301** Wolfgang Kaehler/CORBIS; **1306** Barry Iverson/TIMEPIX; **1310** Salvador Dali, *The Persistance of Memory*, 1931, oil on canvas, 9 1/2 x 13 in. © The Museum of Modern Art/Licensed by Scala/Art Resource, NY. Given anonymously. © 2002 Kingdom of Spain, Gala-Salvador Dale Foundation/Artists Rights Society (ARS), New York; **1311** Thomas Hartwell/CORBIS; **1316 (l.)** Inge Morath/Magnum Photos, Inc.; **1316 (r.)** Dina Gona; **1318** G. R. Roberts/Omni-Photo Communications, Inc.; **1319** *Thrust*, 1959, Adolph Gottlieb, The Metropolitan Museum of Art, George A. Hearn Fund, 1959, Photography by Malcolm Varon, © Copyright by The Metropolitan Museum of Art; **1324** FPG International Corp.; **1325** Courtesy National Archives; **1326** FPG International Corp.; **1327** AP/Wide World Photos; **1328 (t.)** photography by Nina Subin; **1328 (m.)** Bassouls Sophie/CORBIS Sygma; **1328 (b.)** AP/Wide World Photos; **1330** *Still Life with Loaves of Bread*, Ilya Ivanovich Mashkov, State Russian Museum, St. Petersburg, Russia/Bridgeman Art Library, London/New York; **1331** Monique le Luhandre/© Dorling Kindersley; **1332** Robert Everts/Getty Images; **1333** Robert Everts/Getty Images; **1334** Owen Franken/CORBIS; **1340 (l.)** Peter Jordan/Liaison Agency; **1340 (r.)** Alan Mothner/AP/Wide World Photos; **1342** Marc and Evelyn Bernheim/Woodfin Camp & Associates; **1344** John Pemberton, III, Amherst College; **1348 (l.)** Thomas Victor; **1348 (r.)** AP/Wide World Photos; **1351** Ulli Michel/CORBIS; **1352** Heini Schneebeli/Bridgeman Art Library, London/New York; **1357** *The Old African, The Medal, and the Statue*, 1988, Fodé Camara, Museum of African American Art, Collection: Abourahim Agne; **1358** Monique le Luhandre/© Dorling Kindersley; **1364 (l.)** AP/Wide World Photos; **1364 (r.)** Allan Grant/TIMEPIX; **1367** V. Muthuraman/SuperStock; **1368** Susan McCartney/Photo Researchers, Inc.; **1371** The Granger Collection, New York; **1372** Craig Lovell/CORBIS; **1375** © Hulton/Archive Photos; **1380** The Granger Collection, New York; **1382** SuperStock; **1384** *Yuki*, 1929, Kotondo, Courtesy Ronin Gallery, New York; **1385** Monique le Luhandre/© Dorling Kindersley; **1390 (l.)** Dorothy Alexander; **1390 (r.)** Dorothy Alexander; **1392** *Morning Rain*, 2001, oil on canvas, Bich Nguyet, Courtesy of Galeria La Vong Ltd.; **1394** *Peacefulness*, Tran Nguyen Dan, Indochina Arts Project; **1396–1397** Royalty-Free/CORBIS; **1404** CORBIS

Staff Credits

The people who made up the ***Prentice Hall Literature—World Masterpieces*** team—representing design services, editorial, editorial services, manufacturing and inventory planning, market research, marketing services, education technology, planning and budgeting, product planning, production services, project office, publishing processes, and rights and permissions—are listed below. Bold type denotes the core team members.

Rosalyn Arcilla, Justin Belinski, Betsy Bostwick, Kerry Lyn Buckley, **Louise B. Capuano, Irene Ehrmann,** Philip Fried, Maggie Fritz, **Elaine Goldman,** Monduane Harris, Catherine Johnson, **Kate Krimsky,** Carol Lavis, David Liston, **Mary Luthi,** Gregory Lynch, **George Lychock,** Kerrie A. Miller, **Melissa Shustyk,** Annette Simmons, **Rita M. Sullivan, Cynthia Summers,** Elizabeth Torjussen, Doug Utigard, **Jeff Zoda**

Additional Credits

Greg Abrom, Ernest Albanese, Diane Alimena, Michele Angelucci, Penny Baker, Evonne Burgess, Rui Camarinha, John Carle, Jaime L. Cohen, Jason Cuoco, Richard Foster, Phillip Gagler, Joe Galka, Kathy Gavilanes, Michael Ginsberg, Allen Gold, Beth Hyslip, Vicki A. Kane, William McAllister, Michael McLaughlin, Art Mkrtchyan, Meg Montgomery, Kenneth J. Myett, Kim Ortell, Ray Parenteau, Dorothy Preston, Bruce Rolff, Carolyn C. Sapontzis, Mildred Schulte, Enrique Sevilla, Michele Stevens, Debi Taffet

Prentice Hall gratefully acknowledges the following teachers who provided the student models that are published in this book.

Cina Adams, Gaye Ingram, Catherine Linn, Janet Matthews, Sarah Oakes, Dr. Joy Pohl, Cathy Robbs